The Elder Scrolls V

SKYRIM

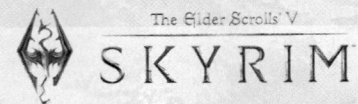

SONG OF THE DRAGONBORN

(Chorus)
Dovahkiin, Dovahkiin, naal ok zin los vahriin,
Wah dein vokul mahfaeraak ahst vaal!
Ahrk fin norok paal graan fod nust hon zindro zaan,
Dovahkiin, fah hin kogaan mu draal!

    (Chorus)
    Dragonborn, Dragonborn, by his honor is sworn,
    To keep evil forever at bay!
    And the fiercest foes rout when they hear triumph's shout,
    Dragonborn, for your blessing we pray!

Huzrah nu, kul do od, wah aan bok lingrah vod,
Ahrk fin tey, boziik fun, do fin gein!
Wo lost fron wah ney dov, ahrk fin reyliik do jul,
Voth aan suleyk wah ronit faal krein!

    Hearken now, sons of snow, to an age, long ago,
    And the tale, boldly told, of the one!
    Who was kin to both wyrm, and the races of man,
    With a power to rival the sun!

Ahrk fin zul, rok drey kod, nau tol morokei frod,
Rul lot Taazokaan motaad voth kein!
Sahrot Thu'um, med aan tuz, vey zeim hokoron pah,
Ol fin Dovahkiin komeyt ok rein!

    And the voice, he did wield, on that glorious field,
    When great Tamriel shuddered with war!
    Mighty Thu'um, like a blade, cut through enemies all,
    As the Dragonborn issued his roar!

(Chorus)
Dovahkiin, Dovahkiin, naal ok zin los vahriin,
Wah dein vokul mahfaeraak ahst vaal!
Ahrk fin norok paal graan fod nust hon zindro zaan,
Dovahkiin, fah hin kogaan mu draal!

    (Chorus)
    Dragonborn, Dragonborn, by his honor is sworn,
    To keep evil forever at bay!
    And the fiercest foes rout when they hear triumph's shout,
    Dragonborn, for your blessing we pray!

Ahrk fin Kel lost prodah, do ved viing ko fin krah,
Tol fod zeymah win kein meyz fundein!
Alduin, feyn do jun, kruziik vokun staadnau,
Voth aan bahlok wah diivon fin lein!

    And the Scrolls have foretold, of black wings in the cold,
    That when brothers wage war come unfurled!
    Alduin, Bane of Kings, ancient shadow unbound,
    With a hunger to swallow the world!

Nuz aan sul, fent alok, fod fin vul dovah nok,
Fen kos nahlot mahfaeraak ahrk ruz!
Paaz Keizaal fen kos stin nol bein Alduin jot,
Dovahkiin kos fin saviik do muz!

    But a day, shall arise, when the dark dragon's lies,
    Will be silenced forever and then!
    Fair Skyrim will be free from foul Alduin's maw,
    Dragonborn be the savior of men!

(Chorus)
Dovahkiin, Dovahkiin, naal ok zin los vahriin,
Wah dein vokul mahfaeraak ahst vaal!
Ahrk fin norok paal graan fodnust vok zin dro zaan,
Dovahkiin, fah hin kogaan mu draal!

    (Chorus)
    Dragonborn, Dragonborn, by his honor is sworn,
    To keep evil forever at bay!
    And the fiercest foes rout when they hear triumph's shout,
    Dragonborn, for your blessing we pray!

WELCOME TO SKYRIM

The Character Creation section of the Training Chapter has been designed to give you tactical advice in the same order as you make decisions while adventuring across the wilds of Skyrim. To begin with, we reveal the benefits of choosing a particular Race. Then all 18 of the Skills – and the Perks associated with each of them – are thoroughly explored, so you know what each Skill does, how you increase it, and what Perks to select based on your playing style. Finally, we present a host of Character Archetypes; exceptional explorers tailored to a specific role; renowned heroes that use the very best combinations of Skills and equipment to suit a particular play-style.

 TIP Please read through the Instruction Manual that you received with your game, and familiarize yourself with the tenets of this adventure. This training pre-supposes you have already read and digested this information.

 # SELECTING A RACE

PART I: THE RACES OF SKYRIM

As you begin your adventure across Skyrim, the historic Elder Scrolls mantra – "you are what you play" – still rings true: Although statistically, an Orc Wizard or a High Elven Thief may not be the optimal character choices based on starting Skill bonuses and racial powers, this doesn't matter in the long run: Choose the race that most appeals to you, and don't worry about statistics and abilities.

You can overcome low starting Skill values just by using the Skills you wish to become more proficient in; such minor deficiencies are easily overcome. No Races have any intrinsic shortfalls that will prevent you from becoming the type of hero you want to be.

However, there are certain advantages to picking a particular race. For those adventurers that wish to maximize every single advantage, it is useful to know which Favored Skills each race begins with bonuses to, and understanding the unique Racial Powers they possess that can aid you when choosing a particular style of play.

In short, this section reveals which Races are best suited to a particular style of adventuring, whether favoring melee weapons, magic, stealth, or some combination of these styles.

 ## Racial Skill Advantages

The following table shows the starting Skill statistics for each Race. The higher the number (over the base level of 15), the better. Values of 20 indicate this is a Favored Skill of the race. Values of 25 indicate this is a Primary Skill of the race.

 NOTE For example, if you were to choose a Khajiit character, you'd receive a +5 bonus to your One-Handed, Archery, Lockpicking, Pickpocket, and Alchemy; and a +10 to your Sneak Skill.

Notes on Gender: There are no differences between the males and females of a particular race; they share exactly the same set of starting skill values, spells, powers, and abilities. In short, you are free to create the character that most appeals to you without penalty.

RACE	SMITHING	HEAVY ARMOR	BLOCK	TWO-HANDED	ONE-HANDED	ARCHERY	LIGHT ARMOR	SNEAK	LOCKPICKING	PICKPOCKET	SPEECH	ALCHEMY	ILLUSION	CONJURATION	DESTRUCTION	RESTORATION	ALTERATION	ENCHANTING
Argonian	15	15	15	15	15	15	20	20	25	20	15	15	15	15	15	20	20	15
Breton	15	15	15	15	15	15	15	15	15	15	20	20	20	25	15	20	20	15
Dark Elf	15	15	15	15	15	15	20	20	15	15	15	20	20	15	25	15	20	15
High Elf	15	15	15	15	15	15	15	15	15	15	15	15	25	20	20	20	20	20
Imperial	15	20	20	15	20	15	15	15	15	15	15	15	15	15	15	25	15	20
Khajiit	15	15	15	15	20	20	15	25	20	20	15	20	15	15	15	15	15	15
Nord	20	15	20	25	20	20	20	15	15	15	20	15	15	15	15	15	15	15
Orc	20	25	20	20	20	15	15	15	15	15	15	15	15	15	15	15	15	20
Redguard	20	15	15	15	25	15	15	15	15	15	15	15	15	15	15	15	20	15
Wood Elf	15	15	15	15	15	25	20	20	20	20	15	20	15	15	15	15	15	15

Starting Spells, Racial Powers, and Abilities

In addition to a slight boost to the base value of certain Skills, each Race has its own set of starting Spells; Racial Powers that offer a unique bonus such as the ability to regenerate or absorb Magicka; and innate Racial Abilities, such a resistance to Frost damage. A tactical overview of each Race follows.

> **NOTE** **Racial Commentary:** The Race you choose will have an effect on the greetings and passing comments the citizens of Skyrim make when you speak to them, or pass by them.
>
> **Races and Gameplay:** Very rarely, your race may also a small effect on gameplay. For example:
>
> When infiltrating the Thalmor Embassy dressed in the robes of that High Elf faction, High Elves (and, to a lesser extent, other Elves) will find it easier to sneak around undetected than members of the other races.
>
> Orcs are welcome in Skyrim's Orc Strongholds, while members of other races must first prove themselves worthy.
>
> The tone and color of some dialogue choices may change depending on your race and the situation.
>
> If your Race has a noticeable effect on an interaction, that will be noted when relevant. But this isn't something to be concerned about: nothing is closed to you because of your race; indeed, you may be surprised by a positive benefit when you least expect it!

Argonians

Favored Skills: +10 Lockpicking, +5 Pickpocket, Sneak, Light Armor, Alteration, Restoration
Starting Spells: Flames, Healing
Racial Power: Histskin: You regenerate health 10x faster for 60 seconds
Racial Abilities: 50% Disease Resistance, Underwater Breathing
Ideal Play Style: Thief (Defensive)

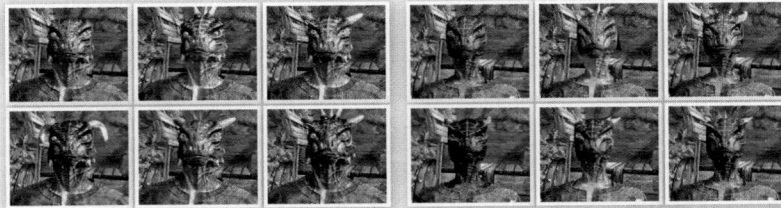
A Male Argonian   A Female Argonian

Little is known, and less is understood, about the reptilian denizens of Black Marsh. Years of defending their borders have made the Argonians experts in guerilla warfare, and their natural abilities make them equally at home in water and on land. They are well suited for the treacherous swamps of their homeland, and have developed natural immunity to the diseases that have doomed many would-be explorers into the region.

> **TIP** Histskin is a fantastic ability for any character, capable of quickly bringing you back from the brink of death. Even better, as a Power, it allows you to keep attacking while it does its work — no concentration required.
>
> Resist Disease reduces the chance that you'll contract a disease from an animal or trap; it doesn't affect the severity of any diseases you might already have. Diseases are rarely a significant threat in Skyrim, although they can be debilitating if you let them pile up. Visit a shrine periodically, and you shouldn't have any trouble.
>
> Underwater Breathing means you'll never have to worry about drowning damage. Diving is rarely required, but this ability may allow you to claim the occasional sunken treasure or explore shipwrecks more easily.

Breton

Favored Skills: +10 Conjuration, +5 Illusion, Restoration, Speech, Alchemy, Alteration
Starting Spells: Flames, Healing, Conjure Familiar
Racial Power: Dragonskin: You absorb 50% of the Magicka from incoming spells for 60 seconds
Racial Abilities: 25% Magic Resistance
Ideal Play Style: Mage (Defensive)

A Male Breton   A Female Breton

Bretons feel an inborn, instinctive bond with the mercurial forces of magic and the supernatural. Many great sorcerers have come from the home province of High Rock, and in addition to their quick and perceptive grasp of spellcraft, enchantment, and alchemy, even the humblest of Bretons can boast a resistance to spells.

> **TIP** Bretons are fantastic at taking on other mages; both Dragonskin and Magic Resistance support this theme, and are strong abilities even in the late game.
>
> Magic Resistance significantly increases your survivability against enemy casters, while Dragonskin is great at keeping your Magicka up, helping you maintain the Ward spells that are your first line of defense.

Dark Elf

Favored Skills: +10 Destruction, +5 Alteration, Illusion, Sneak, Light Armor, Alchemy

Starting Spells: Flames, Sparks, Healing

Racial Power: Ancestor's Wrath: Creates a Flame Cloak that does 10 damage to nearby foes for 60 seconds.

Racial Abilities: 50% Fire Resistance

Ideal Play Style: Nightblade (Mage/Thief)

A Male Dark Elf   A Female Dark Elf

In the Empire, "Dark Elves" is the common usage, but in their Morrowind homeland, they call themselves the "Dunmer". The dark-skinned, red-eyed Dunmer combine powerful intellect with strong and agile physiques, producing superior warriors and sorcerers. On the battlefield, Dark Elves are noted for their skilled and balanced integration of swordsmen, marksmen, and war wizards.

> **TIP** Ancestor's Wrath is a weaker version of the Adept-level Destruction spell Flame Cloak. While good at early levels—where you're likely to be in melee a lot—it's less valuable once you can cast the spell on your own. It's also less useful if you plan to play a ranged character, such as an archer or pure mage.
>
> Fire Resistance is helpful against Flame Atronachs, fire-wielding casters, and fire-breathing dragons. No one enemy type uses fire spells, so it's hard to predict when exactly this ability will come into play—it's not really something you can use strategically.

High Elf

Favored Skills: +10 Illusion, +5 Alteration, Conjuration, Destruction, Restoration, Enchanting

Starting Spells: Flames, Fury, Healing

Racial Power: Highborn: For 60 seconds, you regenerate 25% of your maximum Magicka each second

Racial Abilities: Highborn Magicka (+50 Magicka)

Ideal Play Style: Mage (Offensive)

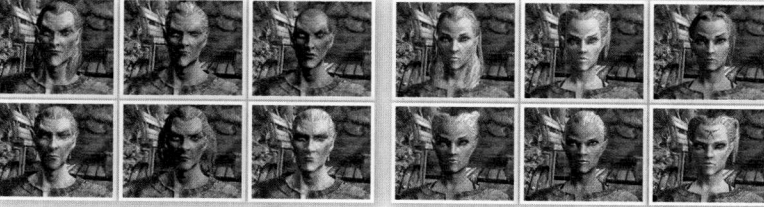

A Male High Elf   A Female High Elf

The High Elves, or Altmer, are the proud, tall, golden-skinned peoples of Summerset Isle. The common tongue of the Empire, Tamrielic, is based on their speech and writing, and most of the Empire's arts, crafts, and sciences are derived from High Elven traditions. High Elves are the driving force behind the rising Aldmeri Dominion, and their agents, the Thalmor, are bitterly resented by the Nords of Skyrim.

> **TIP** Highborn will rapidly refill your Magicka, allowing you to continue casting when you need it most. Extremely strong at any level, this Power is a mage's lifeline.
>
> Highborn Magicka is like getting five free levels. It's a powerful head start for any mage—you may never need to fall back on your melee skills.

Imperial

Favored Skills: +10 Restoration, +5 Destruction, Enchanting, One-Handed, Block, Heavy Armor

Starting Spells: Flames, Healing

Racial Power: Voice of the Emperor: Calms nearby people for 60 seconds

Racial Abilities: Imperial Luck (Adds a small amount of gold to most containers)

Ideal Play Style: Battlemage (Mage/Warrior)

A Male Imperial   A Female Imperial

Natives of the civilized, cosmopolitan province of Cyrodiil, Imperials are well-educated and well-spoken. Though physically less imposing than the other races, Imperials have proven to be shrewd diplomats and traders, and these traits, along with their remarkable skill and training as light infantry, have allowed them to rule an empire spanning the continent for centuries.

> **TIP** Voice of the Emperor is a weaker version of the Expert-level Illusion spell Pacify, with the effect centered on your position. This can be powerful if you're surrounded by a mob of enemies, but it's less useful against smaller groups or ranged foes.
>
> Imperial Luck adds a few extra coins to most of the chests you find. While this bonus is small (10 or less), it adds up over time. But there are plenty of other ways to make money in Skyrim.

 Khajiit

Favored Skills: +10 Sneak, +5 Lockpicking, Pickpocket, Alchemy, One-Handed, Archery
Starting Spells: Flames, Healing
Racial Power: Night Eye: Improved night vision for 60 seconds
Racial Abilities: Claws (4x Unarmed Damage)
Ideal Play Style: Thief (Offensive)

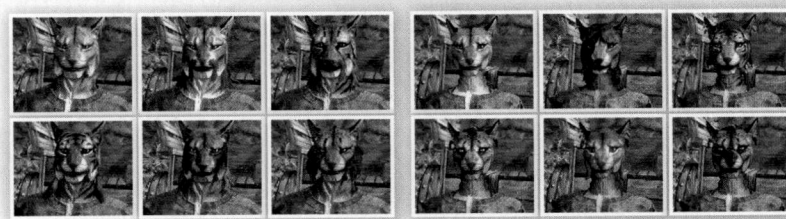

A Male Khajiit   A Female Khajiit

Khajiit hail from the province of Elsweyr, and can vary in appearance from nearly Elven to the cathay-raht "jaguar men" to the great Senche-Tiger. The most common breed, the suthay-raht, is intelligent, quick, and agile. Many Khajiit disdain weapons in favor of their natural claws. They make excellent thieves due to their natural agility and deft hands.

 TIP Night Eye gives you night vision, allowing you to see clearly in dark environments without the need for a light source that might expose your presence. Occasionally useful—but there's usually enough light in dungeons that you can get by without it. Unlike most powers, Night Eye can be used multiple times a day without restriction.

Claws give you an overwhelming advantage in unarmed combat and brawls. Coupled with the Heavy Armor perk Fists of Steel or appropriate gear, this ability can help unarmed combat remain viable for longer than you might expect. But remember that unarmed combat isn't a skill, doesn't give you skill uses, and won't help you level up. Most of the time, it only comes into play in the occasional brawl. But if you're a dedicated role-player who really wants to box your way through Skyrim, well, this is the ability for you.

 Nord

Favored Skills: +10 Two-Handed, +5 One-Handed, Block, Smithing, Speech, Light Armor
Starting Spells: Flames, Healing
Racial Power: Battle Cry: All nearby foes flee for 30 seconds
Racial Abilities: 50% Frost Resistance
Ideal Play Style: Warrior (Offensive)

A Male Nord   A Female Nord

The natives of Skyrim are a tall and fair-haired people, aggressive and fearless in war, industrious and enterprising in trade and exploration. Strong, willful, and hardy, Nords are famous for their resistance to cold, even magical frost. Violence is an accepted and time-honored part of Nordic culture; Nords face battle with an ecstatic ferocity that shocks and appalls their enemies.

TIP Battle Cry is a weaker version of the Master-level Illusion spell Hysteria. Good against a swarm of weak foes, it buys you a few seconds to recover, reposition, or run before the fight resumes. Useful in the right situation, though it rarely helps you win a fight outright.

Frost Resistance is good against Frost Atronachs, frost-wielding wizards, and frost dragons. But it's at its best in Skyrim's many tombs and crypts, where the undead Draugr wield frost spells almost exclusively.

Orc

Favored Skills: +10 Heavy Armor, +5 Smithing, One-Handed, Two-Handed, Block, Enchanting
Starting Spells: Flames, Healing
Racial Power: Berserk: For 60 seconds, you take half damage, and inflict double damage in melee combat.
Racial Abilities: None
Ideal Play Style: Warrior (Defensive)

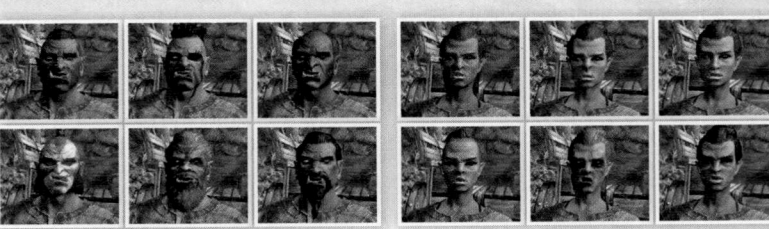

A Male Orc   A Female Orc

These sophisticated barbarians of the Wrothgarian and Dragontail Mountains are noted for their unshakeable courage in war and their unflinching endurance of hardships. In the past, Orcs have been widely feared and hated by the other nations and races of Tamriel, but they have slowly won acceptance in the Empire. Orcish armorers are prized for their craftsmanship, and Orc warriors in heavy armor are among the finest front-line troops in the Empire.

TIP Berserk is the Orcs' only racial ability, but it's worth it—for a minute's time, you become an unstoppable force of destruction. Great in any combat situation, from fending off a swarm of smaller enemies to taking on a powerful dragon, it's strong at any level.

The Elder Scrolls V
SKYRIM

Redguard

Favored Skills: +10 One-Handed, +5 Archery, Block, Smithing, Destruction, Alteration
Starting Spells: Flames, Healing
Racial Power: Adrenaline Rush: You regenerate Stamina 10x faster for 60 seconds
Racial Abilities: 50% Poison Resistance
Ideal Play Style: Spellsword (Warrior/Mage), Dual-Wielding

A Male Redguard   *A Female Redguard*

The most naturally talented warriors in Tamriel, the dark-skinned, wiry-haired Redguards of Hammerfell seem born to battle, though their pride and fierce independence of spirit makes them more suitable as scouts, skirmishers, or free-ranging heroes and adventurers than as rank-and-file soldiers. Redguards are uniquely versatile combatants, capable of switching between bow, sword, spell, or shield at will and adapting their tactics to the battle at hand.

TIP Adrenaline Rush is the Stamina version of Histskin or Highborn. Although less broadly useful than Health or Magicka regen, it will allow you to keep up your power attacks in a protracted battle — or sprint away if the need arises.

Poison Resistance is helpful against the few enemies that use poison — Forsworn, Falmer, Chaurus, and Spiders — and the rare poison gas trap. Not as broadly useful as most other abilities.

Wood Elf

Favored Skills: +10 Archery, +5 Sneak, Lockpicking, Pickpocket, Light Armor, Alchemy
Starting Spells: Flames, Healing
Racial Power: Command Animal: Target animal becomes your ally for 60 seconds.
Racial Abilities: 50% Disease and Poison Resistance
Ideal Play Style: Thief (Archer)

A Male Wood Elf   *A Female Wood Elf*

The clanfolk of the Western Valenwood forests. In the Empire, they are called "Wood Elves," but call themselves the Bosmer, or the 'Tree-Sap' people. Wood Elves are nimble and quick in body and wit. Their curious natures and natural agility make them good scouts, agents, and thieves, and there are no finer archers in all of Tamriel.

TIP Command Animal is a powerful, single-target version of the Animal Allegiance Shout. Its main restriction is that, well, it only works on animals. Good outdoors, or in animal dens and caves, but not in most dungeons.

Poison and Disease Resistance is a combined version of the Argonian's Disease Resistance and Redguard's Poison Resistance abilities. Like them, it can be useful in some situations, but it just isn't a factor most of the time.

SKILLS AND PERKS

This section is arguably the most important in terms of character development. It details every Skill and Perk in the game, and offers advice on what Perks to take based on your play style. Remember: You are what you play. You can develop any Skill you want, at any time; don't ever feel 'locked in' to a specific path just because you've focused on it in the past.

SKILLS OVERVIEW

Skill Effects

There are 18 Skills in Skyrim, divided into three major sets: Combat, Magic, and Stealth. As each Skill increases, its primary effect improves; you also gain access to Perks in that Skill that can grant you powerful new abilities or bonuses.

What does each Skill do? Their primary effects are listed below:

COMBAT SKILLS: THE PATH OF MIGHT

✓	SKILL NAME	PRIMARY EFFECT(S)
	Smithing	Improves the value and properties of items you improve.
	Heavy Armor	Reduces the damage you take while wearing heavy armor.
	Block	Reduces the damage you take and the amount you stagger when blocking attacks.
	Two-Handed	Increases the damage you inflict with two-handed weapons.
	One-Handed	Increases the damage you inflict with one-handed weapons.
	Archery	Increases the damage you inflict with bows.

STEALTH SKILLS: THE PATH OF SHADOW

✔	SKILL NAME	PRIMARY EFFECT(S)
☐	Light Armor	Reduces the damage you take while wearing light armor.
☐	Sneak	Improves your ability to avoid detection while sneaking.
☐	Lockpicking	Increases your ability to pick a lock successfully. Specifically, this skill increases the arc at which the pick succeeds, and reduces the chance that a pick will break.
☐	Pickpocket	Increases the chance that you can successfully pickpocket an item.
☐	Speech	Improves the prices you receive when buying or selling items, and improves your success at (Persuade), (Bribe), and (Intimidate) dialogue challenges.
☐	Alchemy	Improves the potency of potions and poisons you craft.

MAGIC SKILLS: THE PATH OF SORCERY

✔	SKILL NAME	PRIMARY EFFECT(S)
☐	Illusion	Reduces the cost of Illusion spells.
☐	Conjuration	Reduces the cost of Conjuration spells.
☐	Destruction	Reduces the cost of Destruction spells.
☐	Restoration	Reduces the cost of Restoration spells.
☐	Alteration	Reduces the cost of Alteration spells.
☐	Enchanting	Improves the potency of items you enchant.

▷ Improving Skills: Skill Use

In *The Elder Scrolls*, you are what you play. In Skyrim, your skill growth and level progression are determined by Skill Uses, a system that tracks the actions you perform and increases your skills accordingly. You don't have to understand how this works — just play the way you want to play, and you'll get better at it. But if you're the kind of adventurer who wants to know everything you can to maximize your potential, read on.

What are Skill Uses?

Each of the 18 Skills is "watching" for particular events to occur in the game. When one of those events occurs, the Skill gains points based on the magnitude of the event. What magnitude actually means varies by event, and is explained in more detail below.

When the number of points in a Skill passes a threshold, the skill increases. These thresholds are ever-increasing, so raising a Skill from 40 to 41 takes more uses, and/or higher-magnitude uses, than raising that same Skill from 20 to 21.

Each time a Skill increases, it also contributes points towards your character's next Level. The number of points depends on the level of the Skill that increased, so raising a skill from a skill from 40 to 41 will take you further towards your next level than raising a Skill from 20 to 21.

It's important to remember two key rules:

Your Skills only improve if you use them effectively. For example:

◇ Just swinging your sword around doesn't improve your One-Handed Skill. However, hitting someone with it does.

◇ Just summoning an Atronach over and over again doesn't improve your Conjuration Skill. But using the Atronach in combat does.

◇ Just talking to everyone you meet doesn't improve your Speech Skill. You have to actually buy and sell items and pass dialogue challenges.

Your skills generally improve faster if you use them in more challenging situations. For example:

◇ Your Archery skill improves faster if you use more powerful bows that do more damage.

◇ Your Illusion skill improves faster if you cast more difficult spells.

◇ Your Lockpicking skill improves faster if you unlock harder chests.

▷ Improving Skills: Training

During your journey, you will occasionally meet someone who has dedicated their lives to mastering a particular Skill. These are extremely talented individuals, and speaking to them allows you to request Training from them in the Skill they specialize in. Most will be happy to oblige you... for a price.

Each Trainer has a degree of competence, known by the titles of Journeyman, Expert, and Master:

Journeyman Trainers can improve your Skill to a maximum of 50.

Expert Trainers can improve your Skill to a maximum of 75.

Master Trainers can improve your Skill to a maximum of 90.

Even the most proficient Trainers in Skyrim cannot train you past 90. You'll have to earn your way to 100!

The cost to train in a skill is based on your current skill level – the skill of the trainer has no effect. However, the Expert and Master Trainers are often are members of a faction, and will only train you if you're a member in good standing. Joining a faction is usually easy, so if you want access to a particular trainer (or set of trainers), it's worth doing early even if you don't plan to pursue that faction's quests right away.

When working with a trainer, you will receive one skill increase each time you train. This can be repeated a maximum of five times with any combination of trainers before you have to level up. You can then return to any Trainer and pay for up to five more Skill points. If you gain a level while training, go level up, then speak to the Trainer again if you want to train some more.

An Example: Maximizing your Training

Runil is happy to teach you his knowledge of the arts of Conjuration. For a price.

You wish to improve your Conjuration Skill (which is 20), so you visit Runil – the Journeyman Trainer – at the graveyard in Falkreath. He offers to train you for 250 gold. Train with him, and you exchange the gold for one Skill Point. You can train with him four more times this level, at a slightly higher cost each time. When you're done, your Skill is now 25, and you've spent a total of 1350 gold. You must now Level up before you can pay to train again. You could have received the same training from Phinis Gestor (College of Winterhold) or Falion (in Morthal), or any combination of the three of them, but you could never have trained your skill above 25.

If you're focused on (let's not use the term "obsessed") with increasing your favorite Skills, be sure visit their Trainers often, ideally just after you level up. For best results, train and then use the skill to help increase it as quickly as possible. Remember that you can visit a variety of Trainers to increase multiple Skills!

Some Trainers can also be Followers, and a few of them are even candidates for marriage!

The Trainers of Skyrim

Combat Skills: The Path of Might

Smithing

Journeyman Trainer: Ghorza of Markarth.

Expert Trainer: Balimund of Riften.

Master Trainer: Eorlund Gray-Mane of Whiterun.

Heavy Armor

Journeyman Trainer: Hermir Strongheart of Windhelm.

Expert Trainer: Gharol of Dushnikh Yal, in The Reach.

Master Trainer: Farkas of The Companions, in Whiterun.

Block

There is no Journeyman Trainer for this Skill.

Expert Trainer: Njade Stonearm of The Companions, in Whiterun.

Master Trainer: Larak of Mor Khazgur, in The Reach.

Two-Handed

There is no Journeyman Trainer for this Skill.

Expert Trainer: Torbjorn Shatter-Shield of Windhelm.

Master Trainer: Vilkas, of The Companions, in Whiterun.

One-Handed

Journeyman Trainer: Amren of Whiterun.

Expert Trainer: Athis of The Companions in Whiterun.

Master Trainer: Burguk, of Dushnikh Yal in The Reach.

Archery

Journeyman Trainer: Faendal, of Riverwood.

Expert Trainer: Aela the Huntress, of The Companions in Whiterun.

Master Trainer: Niruin, of The Thieves Guild, in Riften.

Stealth Skills: The Path of Shadow

Light Armor

Journeyman Trainer: Scouts-Many-Marshes of Windhelm.

Expert Trainer: Grelka of Riften.

Master Trainer: Nazir, of The Dark Brotherhood.

Sneak

Journeyman Trainer: Khayla, of the Khajiit Caravans.

Expert Trainer: Garvey, of Markarth.

Master Trainer: Delven Mallory, of The Thieves Guild, in Riften.

Lockpicking

There is no Journeyman Trainer for this Skill.

Expert Trainer: Majhad of the Khajiit Caravans.

Master Trainer: Vex, of The Thieves Guild, in Riften.

Pickpocket

Journeyman Trainer: Ahkari, of the Khajiit Caravans.

Expert Trainer: Silda the Unseen, of Windhelm.

Master Trainer: Vipir, of The Thieves Guild, of Riften.

Speech

Journeyman Trainer #1: Dro'marash of the Khajiit Caravans.

Journeyman Trainer #2: Revyn Sadri of Windhelm.

Expert Trainer: Ogmund the Skald, of Markarth.

Master Trainer: Geraud Gemaine, of The Bards College in Solitude.

Alchemy

Journeyman Trainer: Lami of Morthal.

Expert Trainer: Arcadia, of Whiterun.

Master Trainer: Babette, of The Dark Brotherhood.

Magic Skills: The Path of Sorcery

Illusion

There is no Journeyman Trainer for this Skill.

Expert Trainer: Atub, of Largashbur in The Rift.

Master Trainer: Drevis Neloren, of the College of Winterhold.

Conjuration

Journeyman Trainer: Runil of Falkreath.

Expert Trainer: Phinis Gestor, of the College of Winterhold.

Master Trainer: Falion of Morthal.

Destruction

Journeyman Trainer: Wuunferth the Unliving, of Windhelm.

Expert Trainer: Sybille Stentor of Solitude.

Master Trainer: Faralda, of the College of Winterhold.

Restoration

Expert Trainer: Keeper Carcette, in the Hall of the Vigilant.

Expert Trainer: Colette Marence, of the College of Winterhold.

Master Trainer: Danica Pure-Spring, of Whiterun.

Alteration

Journeyman Trainer: Melaran, of Solitude.

Expert Trainer: Dravynea, of Kynesgrove, in Eastmarch.

Master Trainer: Tolfdir, of the College of Winterhold.

Enchanting

There is no Journeyman Trainer for this Skill.

Expert Trainer: Sergius Turrianus, of the College of Winterhold.

Master Trainer: Hamal, or Markarth.

Skill Trainers are also referenced when they relate to Quests or specific Atlas locations later in this guide.

IMPROVING SKILLS: SKILL BOOKS

The Doors of Oblivion (Conjuration), one of five copies known to exist.

Scattered throughout Skyrim are a number of rare Skill Books, each associated with a particular Skill. The first time you read each book, the associated Skill increases by one. There are five different named books for each Skill (90 different book titles), so a diligent collector can potentially increase each Skill by five points.

It's worth noting that there are multiple copies of each book in the world (usually 3-5). However, you only gain a Skill point the first time you read a book – rereading that book, or any of its copies, has no further effect.

For example: Those interested in the Sneak Skill should look for the following books: Three Thieves (four copies), 2920, Last Seed, v8 (four copies), Sacred Witness (four copies), Legend of Krately House (three copies), and The Red Kitchen Reader (five copies). This means there is a total of 20 Sneak Skill Books, and five points you can add to your Sneak from reading the first copy you encounter of each tome.

IMPROVING SKILLS: AUGMENTATIONS

An Amulet of Dibella, which adds +15 to your Speech.

There are a variety of other ways to temporarily boost your Skills (or their primary effects):

Equip enchanted items that increases that Skill.

Drink a potion that boosts the Skill.

Acquire a Shrine Blessing or other temporary bonus to the Skill.

For example: Say you have a Speech of 40, but want to get better prices for a collection of loot you're about to sell. You could look for ways to permanently increase your skill, like completing dialogue challenges, training, or reading skill books. You can also equip an Amulet of Dibella (+15 Speech), pray at a Shrine of Dibella (+10% Better Prices), give a beggar a gold piece to receive The Gift of Charity (+10 Speech), and quaff a Potion of Glibness (+20 Speech). Then head over to your merchant of choice and wring out every last gold coin you can.

⬡ General Advice on Improving Skills

When improving your Skills, heed the following advice:

In general, it's better to increase your Skills and level up naturally, rather than trying to find ways to exploit the game. In fact, it may make your adventure harder, since you'll lack the gear and tactics needed to survive higher-level combat.

There is no fixed "maximum level" (i.e., Level 50) for you to attain. However, if you were to raise all of your Skills to 100, this would – eventually – take you to around Level 80. As you're only able to choose one perk each time you level up, and there are well over 200 Skill-based perks, don't fixate on obtaining every single one, as that's impossible. Instead, focus on improving the Skills you're most interested in, and ignore perks you won't take advantage of, even if they're in a Skill you use constantly.

Statistically, it's better to save Skill Books for higher levels, when the amount of effort or the cost of training needed to increase a skill rises dramatically. However, this tends to be difficult to do in practice, since you automatically read a book when picking it up, and won't know in advance that it's a skill book. Unless you're intent on raising every Skill to 100, it's best not to worry about this.

If you're most of the way to your next level and just need one or two more skill increases, here are some options:

Training: If you have the gold, Training is always a good option. If you're short on gold, try Training in a Skill you haven't used as much, as it will be less expensive (although it also won't count as much toward your next level).

Do you have any Skill Books you haven't read?

Are there any Ingredients you haven't sampled? Especially at low Skill levels, your Alchemy skill rises quickly just by eating common ingredients and learning their first effect.

Do you have a lot of ingredients? You may be able to make some potions. Give Alchemy a try!

Do you have any ingots or smithing supplies? You might be able to forge or improve something. Try your hand at Smithing.

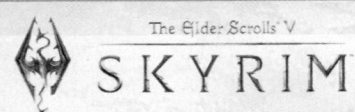

SKILL CONSTELLATIONS

This vast section of knowledge explores the entirety of the Skill Constellations. These are color-coded for Combat Skills: The Path of Might (red), Stealth Skills: The Path of Shadow (green), and Magic Skills: The Path of Sorcery (blue).

There are three general categories of perks that deserve special mention:

Skill Improvement Perks: Many constellations offer a perk that simply makes you better at that Skill's primary effect (examples include Agile Defender for Light Armor, Juggernaut for Heavy Armor, Stealth for Sneak, as well as others). Choosing these perks is akin to receiving a huge number of Skill increases for that Skill all at once. These perks may not be as "flashy" or instantly gratifying as some of the other perks, but they are always a strong, effective choice.

Magic Rank Perks: The five schools of magic each have a series of "rank" perks (Novice, Apprentice, Adept, Expert, and Master) that dramatically decrease the cost of spells from that School. These perks are absolutely critical to your ability to use magic effectively, and should be a top priority for any serious Mage.

Tiered Perks: Some perks can be selected multiple times for increased effect. These bonuses do not stack. For example, Heavy Armor's Juggernaut 1 Perk increases your armor rating by 20%, while Juggernaut 2 increases your armor rating by 40%. After taking Juggernaut 2, you will have a bonus of 40%, not 60%.

> **NOTE** ★ = This highlights some of the best some of the best or most interesting perks in a particular Skill Constellation.

COMBAT SKILLS: THE PATH OF MIGHT

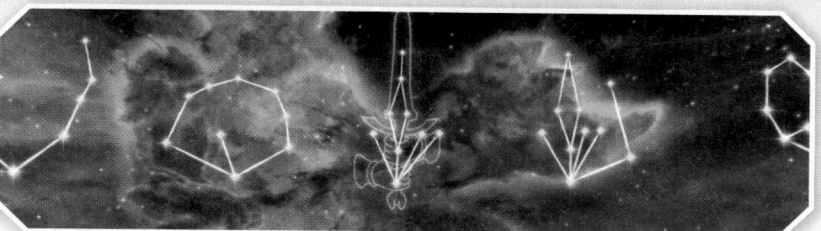

Total Perks for all Combat Skills: 91

◈ Smithing

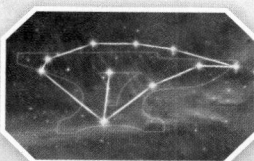

Constellation: Path of Might
Available Perks: 10

Smithing is the art of creating and improving weapons and armor. Smithing workstations include the Blacksmith Forge, Grindstone (for Weapons), and Workbench (for Armor). Any improvements made at any of these stations count towards your Smithing skill, with the amount of increase based on the value of the item you craft or improve. To increase this skill as quickly as possible, forge your own items and then improve them. You can make Hide and Iron items without taking any perks. You can improve any item without taking any perks. However, you need perks to create any advanced items, such as Dwarven or Ebony weapons and armor.

Mining, Smelting, and Tanning provide raw materials for Smithing, although they do not count towards this skill. Smithing synergizes well with Enchanting, since it guarantees you a ready supply of items to enchant. For more information on all of these activities, see the Crafting section on page 41.

The main choice presented by your Smithing Perks is obvious: are you interested in making and improving Light Armor, like Elven, Scale, Glass, and Dragonscale, or Heavy Armor, like Steel, Dwarven, Orcish, Ebony, Daedric, and Dragonplate? Focus on the side of the constellation that appeals most to you.

1. STEEL SMITHING
Can create Steel armor and weapons at forges, and improve them twice as much.
Requires: Smithing 20

2. ARCANE BLACKSMITH ★
You can improve magical weapons and armor.
Requires: Smithing 60

One of the most useful Smithing Perks, especially if you plan to focus on Enchanting as well. If your Enchanting skill is low, you can improve a piece of gear with a powerful enchantment but a weak armor rating to keep it viable for longer, or to make an already great item even better. If you're a master artisan, you can make your own gear from scratch, enchant it, temper it, and then either use it or sell it for a considerable profit.

3. ELVEN SMITHING
Can create Elven armor and weapons at forges, and improve them twice as much.
Requires: Smithing 40, Steel Smithing

4. ADVANCED ARMORS
Can create Scaled and Steel Plate armor at forges, and improve them twice as much.
Requires: Smithing 50, Elven Smithing

5. GLASS SMITHING
Can create Glass armor and weapons at forges, and improve them twice as much.
Requires: Smithing 70, Advanced Armors

6. DWARVEN SMITHING ★
Can create Dwarven armor and weapons at forges, and improve them twice as much.
Requires: Smithing 30, Steel Smithing

Once you begin exploring Dwarven Ruins, you'll discover tons of scrap metal that can be smelted down into ingots. This is a great source of free, convenient crafting materials for your Smithing practice. Taking this perk allows you to make better (and thus more valuable) Dwarven items from these ingots, which improves your Smithing skill even more quickly, and allows you to turn a nice profit, too.

7. ORCISH SMITHING
Can create Orcish armor and weapons at forges, and improve them twice as much.
Requires: Smithing 50, Dwarven Smithing

8. EBONY SMITHING
Can create Ebony armor and weapons at forges, and improve them twice as much.
Requires: Smithing 80, Orcish Smithing

9. DAEDRIC SMITHING
Can create Daedric armor and weapons at forges, and improve them twice as much.
Requires: Smithing 90, Ebony Smithing

Daedric weapons and armor are not available in shops, so the only way to get them is to find or make them.

10. DRAGON ARMOR
Can create Dragon armor at forges, and improve them twice as much.
Requires: Smithing 100, Glass Smithing OR Daedric Smithing

Dragonplate and Dragonscale armors are not available in shops, so the only way to get them is to find or make them.

Heavy Armor

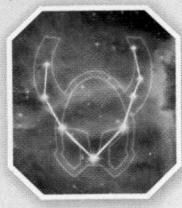

Heavy Armor allows you to make more effective use of Iron, Steel, Dwarven, Orcish, Ebony, Dragonplate, and Daedric armors. Heavy Armor offers excellent protection, though its weight will slow you down and reduce the amount of gear you can carry. High-end sets of Heavy Armor are especially rare, so you may

Constellation: Path of Might
Available Perks: 12

wish to consider Smithing so you can craft your own when the time comes.

Your Heavy Armor skill increases when you take damage while wearing heavy armor, based on the damage of the incoming blow. If you're wearing more than one kind of armor, the incoming damage is divided up among the pieces before being used to calculate skill uses. So, the more Heavy Armor you're wearing, the more damage will be assigned to it, and the faster this Skill will increase.

The Heavy Armor constellation has two main themes: the left arc focuses on unusual perks, or those useful in specific situations, while the right arc emphasizes statistically-powerful perks for heavy armor purists.

1-5. JUGGERNAUT (5 RANKS) ★

Rank 1: Increases the armor rating of your Heavy Armor by 20%.
Requires: None
Rank 2: Increases the armor rating of your Heavy Armor by 40%.

Requires: Heavy Armor 20, Juggernaut 1
Rank 3: Increases the armor rating of your Heavy Armor by 60%.
Requires: Heavy Armor 40, Juggernaut 2
Rank 4: Increases the armor rating of your Heavy Armor by 80%.
Requires: Heavy Armor 60, Juggernaut 3
Rank 5: Increases the armor rating of your Heavy Armor by 100%.
Requires: Heavy Armor 80, Juggernaut 4

6. FISTS OF STEEL

Unarmed attacks with heavy armor gauntlets do their armor base rating in extra damage.
Requires: Heavy Armor 30, Juggernaut 1

Although unarmed combat doesn't increase any of your Skills, it can still be a viable option, especially for Khajiits (whose Claws racial ability also improves unarmed attacks). This perk also makes Brawls dramatically easier.

7. WELL FITTED ★

25% Armor bonus if wearing all Heavy Armor : head, chest, hands, feet.
Requires: Heavy Armor 30, Juggernaut 1

This bonus stacks with Juggernaut and Matching Set; a must-have for anyone serious about using Heavy Armor.

8. CUSHIONED

Half damage from falling if wearing all Heavy Armor: head, chest, hands, feet.
Requires: Heavy Armor 50, Fists of Steel

Worth considering if you enjoy climbing mountains and scampering up rocks, and don't want to worry about fall damage.

9. TOWER OF STRENGTH

50% less stagger when wearing only Heavy Armor.
Requires: Heavy Armor 50, Well-Fitted

10. CONDITIONING

Heavy Armor weighs nothing and doesn't slow you down when worn.
Requires: Heavy Armor 70, Cushioned

Conditioning reduces the weight of heavy armor you're wearing (it doesn't affect the weight of armor in your inventory), and eliminates the speed penalty for wearing heavy armor. If that appeals to you, but you aren't excited about having to take Fists of Steel and Cushioned to reach this perk, try out the Steed Stone ability (from one of the Standing Stones) instead: it has almost the same effect, and won't cost you any perks.

11. MATCHING SET

Additional 25% Armor bonus if wearing a matched set of Heavy Armor.
Requires: Heavy Armor 70, Tower of Strength

This bonus stacks with Juggernaut and Well Fitted. It's challenging to acquire a complete set of the high-end Heavy Armors (unless you're specializing in Smithing), so make sure you have a matching set before taking this perk.

12. REFLECT BLOWS

10% chance to reflect melee damage back to the enemy while wearing all Heavy Armor: head, chest, hands, feet.
Requires: Heavy Armor 100, Matching Set

Block

Block is the art of deflecting an enemy's blows with your shield or weapon. Your Block skill reduces the damage you take and the amount you stagger when you block an attack. Your skill increases when you successfully block damage (based on the damage of the blow before it was blocked), or when you successfully bash an enemy with a weapon or shield.

Constellation: Path of Might
Available Perks: 13

Note that parries with One- or Two-handed weapons are also improved by your Block Skill and many Block Perks– you don't have to be using a shield to benefit from this skill. But remember that if you have a second weapon or spell equipped in your left hand, you can't block at all.

In the Block constellation, the left arc offers shield-specific damage reduction perks, while the right arc focuses on bash and power bash perks that work with both shield and weapon blocks.

1-5. SHIELD WALL (5 RANKS)

Rank 1: Blocking is 20% more effective.
Requires: None
Rank 2: Blocking is 25% more effective.
Requires: Block 20, Shield Wall 1
Rank 3: Blocking is 30% more effective.
Requires: Block 40, Shield Wall 2
Rank 4: Blocking is 35% more effective.
Requires: Block 60, Shield Wall 3
Rank 5: Blocking is 40% more effective.
Requires: Block 80, Shield Wall 4

6. DEFLECT ARROWS

When blocking with a shield, arrows that hit the shield do no damage.
Requires: Block 30, Shield Wall 1

This perk greatly reduces the damage you take while rushing archers, but it's much less effective once you've engaged the enemy, since your shield may not be in the right place at the right time.

7. POWER BASH

Able to do a power bash.
Requires: Block 30, Shield Wall 1

This perk unlocks a new Power Bash move that sends enemies flying. This is a great addition to your arsenal, especially if you're employing a weapon-and-shield combat style.

8. QUICK REFLEXES

Time slows down if you are blocking during an enemy's power attack
Requires: Block 30, Shield Wall 1

Quick Reflexes gives you a chance to react and dodge or (better yet) respond with a bash to counter the attack.

9. DEADLY BASH

Bashing does five times more damage.
Requires: Block 50, Power Bash

While this sounds powerful, bashes don't do much damage to start with. The damage bonus certainly doesn't hurt, but it's still much faster to kill enemies with your weapon than with your shield.

10. ELEMENTAL PROTECTION ★

Blocking with a shield reduces incoming fire, frost, and shock damage by 50%.
Requires: Block 50, Deflect Arrows

This perk is especially powerful when fighting mages. Combine with the Breton's Magic Resistance or the Alteration Magic Resistance Perks for almost impenetrable defense, allowing you to shrug off enemy spells with ease!

11. BLOCK RUNNER

Able to move faster with a shield raised.
Requires: Block 70, Elemental Protection

Block Runner helps you close the distance with a ranged mage or archer, and allows you to cover more ground when making a Shield Charge.

12. DISARMING BASH ★

Chance to disarm when power bashing.
Requires: Block 70, Deadly Bash

Disarming Bash gives you a chance to knock away an enemy's equipped weapon if he is in the middle of executing a power attack. While many enemies have backup weapons (often daggers), they're significantly less powerful, so you can usually crush a disarmed foe with ease. This is a great perk, at least until you learn the Disarm Shout, which does this more reliably. Consult the Shouts section to find out how to acquire this; you may wish to ignore this perk if the Shout becomes more useful to you.

13. SHIELD CHARGE

Sprinting with a shield raised knocks down most targets.
Requires: Block 100, Block Runner OR Disarming Bash

Shield Charge is great at forcing your way out of a mob of enemies if you get surrounded, or buying a few moments to recover in the middle of a difficult battle.

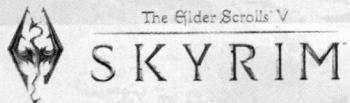

Two-Handed

Constellation: Path of Might
Available Perks: 19

The Two-Handed Skill governs the use of large weapons such as greatswords, battle axes, and warhammers. Those trained in this skill deliver more lethal and powerful blows. To improve this skill, damage enemies with a two-handed weapon. The skill improves based on the amount of damage you do (minus any enchantments), not the number of swings you take, so you get the same increase regardless of how many hits it takes to fell your foe.

A number of perks in the Two-Handed constellation improve a specific type of two-handed weapon. If you generally use the best weapon you can find (no matter what type it is), it's wiser to invest your perks elsewhere: better to have a bonus you can rely on than one you only see occasionally.

1-5. BARBARIAN (5 RANKS) ★

Rank 1: Two-Handed weapons do 20% more damage.
Requires: None
Rank 2: Two-Handed weapons do 40% more damage.
Requires: Two-Handed 20, Barbarian 1
Rank 3: Two-Handed weapons do 60% more damage.
Requires: Two-Handed 40, Barbarian 2
Rank 4: Two-Handed weapons do 80% more damage.
Requires: Two-Handed 60, Barbarian 3
Rank 5: Two-Handed weapons do twice as much damage.
Requires: Two-Handed 80, Barbarian 4

This perk provides a massive +20% bonus to your two-handed weapon damage with each rank. This is a huge boost; make this perk your top priority whenever your skill level permits.

6. CHAMPION'S STANCE ★

Power attacks with two-handed weapons cost 25% less stamina.
Requires: Two-Handed 20, Barbarian 1

In effect, this perk allows you to power attack more often. Two-handed weapons excel at devastating power attacks, so this is a solid choice.

7-9. DEEP WOUNDS (3 RANKS)

Rank 1: Attacks with greatswords have a 10% chance of doing critical damage.
Requires: Two-Handed 30, Barbarian 1
Rank 2: Attacks with greatswords have a 15% chance of doing even more critical damage.
Requires: Two-Handed 60, Deep Wounds 1
Rank 3: Attacks with greatswords have a 20% chance of doing even more critical damage.
Requires: Two-Handed 90, Deep Wounds 2

When a weapon scores a critical hit, it deals 50% more damage, more for ranks 2 and 3. Statistically, this perk works out to a 5% boost in your average damage over time at Rank 1, and a 15% boost by Rank 3. That's not nothing, but Barbarian is still better.

10-12. LIMBSPLITTER (3 RANKS)

Rank 1: Attacks with battle axes cause extra bleeding damage.
Requires: Two-Handed 30
Rank 2: Attacks with battle axes cause more bleeding damage.
Requires: Two-Handed 60, Limbsplitter 1
Rank 3: Attacks with battle axes cause even more bleeding damage.
Requires: Two-Handed 90, Limbsplitter 2

The exact amount of bleeding damage depends on the axe, but in general, this perk causes each hit to do 1-3 points of damage each second for 3-6 seconds, with the higher ranks pushing higher into that range, making this roughly equivalent to a short-lived lingering poison.

13-15. SKULLCRUSHER (3 RANKS)

Rank 1: Attacks with warhammers ignore 25% of armor.
Requires: Two-Handed 30

Rank 2: Attacks with warhammers ignore 50% of armor.
Requires: Two-Handed 60, Skullcrusher 1
Rank 3: Attacks with warhammers ignore 75% of armor.
Requires: Two-Handed 90, Skullcrusher 2

This perk has no effect against unarmored enemies, but it can make it significantly easier to take down a heavily armored foe, such as many bosses.

16. DEVASTATING BLOW

Standing power attacks do 25% bonus damage with a chance to decapitate your enemies.
Requires: Two-Handed 50, Champion's Stance

This is a strong, reliable damage bonus. The decapitation adds a grotesquely satisfying visual touch, but only applies if your attack already killed the enemy (this perk doesn't give you a chance of an instant kill).

17. GREAT CRITICAL CHARGE

Can do a two-handed power attack while sprinting that does double critical damage.
Requires: Two-Handed 50, Champion's Stance

Less powerful than it might appear, the "double critical damage" bonus only applies if you land a critical hit in the first place, and (more importantly) you have to remember to use it for it to be effective. Take this if you find yourself making "berserker rushes" on your own anyway.

18. SWEEP

Sideways power attacks with two-handed weapons hit all targets in front of you.
Requires: Two-Handed 70, Devastating Blow OR Great Critical Charge

Great at clearing out swaths of enemies in a single blow.

19. WARMASTER

Backwards power attacks have a 25% chance to paralyze the target.
Requires: Two-Handed 100, Sweep

One-Handed

Constellation: Path of Might
Available Perks: 21

The One-Handed Skill governs the use of weapons like the sword, war axe, mace, and dagger. Those trained in this skill deliver more deadly blows. To improve this skill, you must damage enemies with a one-handed weapon. The skill improves based on the amount of damage you do (minus any enchantments), not the number of swings you take, so while it might take ten hits to kill a bandit with a dagger, you would get the same skill increase for killing him in three with a mace.

A number of perks in the One-Handed constellation improve a specific type of one-handed weapon. If you generally use the best weapon you can find (no matter what type it is), it's wiser to invest your perks elsewhere: better to have a bonus you can rely on than one you only see occasionally.

1-5. ARMSMAN (5 RANKS) ★

Rank 1: One-Handed weapons do 20% more damage.
Requires: None
Rank 2: One-Handed weapons do 40% more damage.
Requires: One-Handed 20, Armsman 1
Rank 3: One-Handed weapons do 60% more damage.
Requires: One-Handed 40, Armsman 2
Rank 4: One-Handed weapons do 80% more damage.
Requires: One-Handed 60, Armsman 3
Rank 5: One-Handed weapons do twice as much damage.
Requires: One-Handed 80, Armsman 4

This perk provides a massive +20% bonus to your one-handed weapon damage with each rank. This is a huge boost; make this perk your top priority whenever your skill level permits.

6. FIGHTING STANCE ★

Power attacks with one-handed weapons cost 25% less stamina.
Requires: One-Handed 20, Armsman 1

By conserving your stamina, this perk allows you to power attack or bash more often. A solid choice, especially if you dual-wield one-handed weapons, as this bonus works well with the Dual Flurry and Dual Savagery Perks.

7-9. BLADESMAN (3 RANKS)

Rank 1: Attacks with swords have a 10% chance of doing critical damage.
Requires: One-Handed 30, Armsman 1
Rank 2: Attacks with swords have a 15% chance of doing more critical damage.
Requires: One-Handed 60, Bladesman 1
Rank 3: Attacks with swords have a 20% chance of doing even more critical damage.
Requires: One-Handed 90, Bladesman 2

When a weapon scores a critical hit, it deals 50% more damage, more for ranks 2 and 3. Statistically, this perk works out to a 5% boost in your average damage over time at Rank 1, and a 15% boost by Rank 3. That's not nothing, but Armsman is still better.

10-12. BONE BREAKER (3 RANKS)

Rank 1: Attacks with maces ignore 25% of armor.
Requires: One-Handed 30, Armsman 1
Rank 2: Attacks with maces ignore 50% of armor.
Requires: One-Handed 60, Bone Breaker 1
Rank 3: Attacks with maces ignore 75% of armor.
Requires: One-Handed 90, Bone Breaker 2

This perk has no effect against unarmored enemies, but it can make it significantly easier to take down a heavily armored foe, such as many bosses.

13-15. HACK AND SLASH (3 RANKS)

Rank 1: Attacks with war axes cause extra bleeding damage
Requires: One-Handed 30, Armsman 1
Rank 2: Attacks with war axes cause more bleeding damage
Requires: One-Handed 60, Hack and Slash 1
Rank 3: Attacks with war axes cause even more bleeding damage
Requires: One-Handed 90, Hack and Slash 2

The exact amount of bleeding damage depends on the axe, but in general, this perk causes each hit to do 1-3 points of damage each second for 3-6 seconds, with the higher ranks pushing higher into that range, making this roughly equivalent to a short-lived lingering poison.

16-17. DUAL FLURRY (2 RANKS)

Rank 1: Dual wielding attacks are 20% faster.
Requires: One-Handed 30, Armsman 1
Rank 2: Dual wielding attacks are 35% faster.
Requires: One-Handed 50, Dual Flurry 1

18. CRITICAL CHARGE

Can do a one-handed power attack while sprinting that does double critical damage.
Requires: One-Handed 50, Fighting Stance

This perk still requires that you land a critical hit in the first place in order to receive the damage bonus. Worth taking if you find yourself making berserker rushes on your own, if you've taken the Bladesman Perks, or if you're dual-wielding (since you've got a better chance of getting a critical hit with at least one weapon).

19. SAVAGE STRIKE

Standing power attacks do 25% bonus damage with a chance to decapitate your enemies.
Requires: One-Handed 50, Fighting Stance

This is a strong, reliable damage bonus, though the decapitation only applies if you've already killed the enemy. But standing over the headless corpse of your kill is a satisfying way to temper your bloodlust!

20. DUAL SAVAGERY ★

Duel wielding power attacks do 50% more damage.
Requires: One-Handed 70, Dual Flurry 1

A great pick if you're focused on dual wielding, this is stronger than Savage Strike or Critical Charge, and stacks with both of them, making your power attacks incredibly deadly.

21. PARALYZING STRIKE

Your backwards power attack has a 25% chance to paralyze the target.
Requires: One-Handed 100, Savage Strike OR Critical Charge

Paralyzing Strike is a powerful ability... if you remember to use it. When it works, you can inflict massive damage (and often kill your foes outright) before they can get back on their feet. But... how often do you use backward power attacks?

Archery

Constellation: Path of Might
Available Perks: 16

Archery represents the skill and training needed to wield a bow effectively in combat. The greater your skill, the more deadly your shots. Your Archery skill improves when you damage enemies with a bow and arrows, with the amount of increase based on the damage that you do (minus any enchantments). Of course, only shots that hit their mark will count.

1-5. OVERDRAW (5 RANKS) ★

Rank 1: Bows do 20% more damage.
Requires: None
Rank 2: Bows do 40% more damage.
Requires: Archery 20, Overdraw 1
Rank 3: Bows do 60% more damage.
Requires: Archery 40, Overdraw 2
Rank 4: Bows do 80% more damage.
Requires: Archery 60, Overdraw 3
Rank 5: Bows do twice as much damage.
Requires: Archery 80, Overdraw 4

This perk provides a massive +20% bonus to your bow damage with each rank. This is a huge boost; make this perk your top priority whenever your skill level permits.

6-8. CRITICAL SHOT (3 RANKS)

Rank 1: 10% chance of a critical hit that does extra damage.
Requires: Archery 30, Overdraw 1
Rank 2: 15% chance of a critical hit that does 25% more critical damage.
Requires: Archery 60, Critical Shot 1
Rank 3: 20% chance of a critical hit that does 50% more critical damage.
Requires: Archery 90, Critical Shot 2

When a weapon scores a critical hit, it deals 50% more damage. Statistically, this perk works out to a 5% boost in your average damage over time at Rank 1, and a 15% boost by Rank 3. That's not nothing, but Overdraw is still better.

9. EAGLE EYE ★

Pressing Block while aiming will zoom in your view.
Requires: Archery 30, Overdraw 1

This perk allows you to snipe enemies more accurately from a greater distance. This is a great choice for stealth archers: Since you may only get one shot, make it count!

10-11. STEADY HAND (2 RANKS)

Rank 1: Zooming in with a bow slows time by 25%
Requires: Archery 40, Eagle Eye
Rank 2: Zooming in with a bow slows time by 50%
Requires: Archery 60, Steady Hand 1

This perk is useful for minimizing the chance that your target will move while you line up a stealth shot, or for making sure an important shot hits its mark. It's especially effective against dragons in the air; you'll still have to lead your shot a little (that is, aim at where you think the creature will be when the arrow arrives, not where it is when you fire), but this improves your odds of hitting them significantly.

12. HUNTER'S DISCIPLINE

Recover twice as many arrows from dead bodies.
Requires: Archery 50, Critical Shot 1

A fine choice if you find yourself running out of arrows frequently, or use a lot of high-end arrows. If you mainly use basic Iron or Steel Arrows, take something else; they're so cheap and so common that recovering more of them just isn't worth the perk.

13. POWER SHOT ★

Arrows stagger all but the largest opponents 50% of the time.
Requires: Archery 50, Eagle Eye

Power Shot is surprisingly powerful: In the time it takes an enemy to stagger and recover, you may be able to fire off another shot or two. The stagger will also interrupt an enemy's charge or block, briefly giving you a clear opening. Or when all else fails, take that second or two to put some space between you and your opponent.

14. RANGER

Able to move faster with a drawn bow.
Requires: Archery 60, Hunter's Dicipline

15. QUICK SHOT

Can draw a bow 30% faster.
Requires: Archery 70, Power Shot

16. BULLSEYE

15% chance of paralyzing the target for 10 seconds.
Requires: Archery 100, Quick Shot OR Ranger

Bullseye gives you a chance to paralyze opponents with each shot. This is fantastic at medium and short ranges, where it can take an enemy out of a fight and allows you to finish them off quickly. It's somewhat less effective at long range, since enemies fall over when paralyzed, making it more difficult (or impossible) to hit them again from that distance.

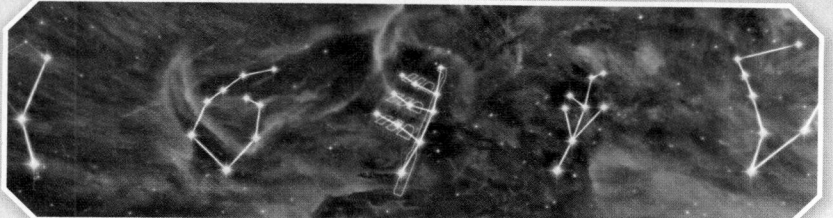

Total Perks for all Stealth Skills: 74

Light Armor

Constellation: Path of Shadow
Available Perks: 10

Light Armor allows you to make more effective use of Hide, Leather, Elven, Glass, and Dragonscale armor. Light Armor offers a good balance between weight, protection, and mobility, and is recommended for stealthy characters or those with other forms of protection (such as a good shield or the occasional ward) to supplement their defenses.

Your Light Armor skill increases when you take damage while wearing light armor, based on the damage of the incoming blow. If you're wearing more than one kind of armor, the incoming damage is divided up among the pieces before being used to calculate skill uses, so wearing more light armor will allow this skill to develop faster.

1-5. AGILE DEFENDER (5 RANKS) ★

Rank 1: Increase armor rating for Light armor by 20%.
Requires: None
Rank 2: Increases the armor rating of your Light Armor by 40%.
Requires: Light Armor 20, Agile Defender 1
Rank 3: Increases the armor rating of your Light Armor by 60%.
Requires: Light Armor 40, Agile Defender 2
Rank 4: Increases the armor rating of your Light Armor by 80%.
Requires: Light Armor 60, Agile Defender 3
Rank 5: Increases the armor rating of your Light Armor by 100%.
Requires: Light Armor 80, Agile Defender 4

6. CUSTOM FIT ★

25% armor bonus if wearing all Light Armor: head, chest, hands, feet.
Requires: Light Armor 30, Agile Defender 1
This bonus stacks with Agile Defender and Matching Set; a must-have for anyone serious about using Light Armor.

7. UNHINDERED

Light Armor weighs nothing and doesn't slow you down when worn.
Requires: Light Armor 50, Custom Fit
This perk reduces the weight of the light armor you're wearing (it doesn't affect the weight of armor in your inventory), and eliminates its movement penalty. If you're not sure whether this perk is for you, try out the Steed Stone ability (from one of the Standing Stones) first: it has almost the same effect, and won't cost you a perk.

8. WIND WALKER

Stamina regenerates 50% faster in all Light Armor: head, chest, hands, feet.
Requires: Light Armor 60, Unhindered

9. MATCHING SET

Additional 25% Armor bonus if wearing a matched set of Light Armor
Requires: Light Armor 70, Custom Fit
This bonus stacks with Agile Defender and Custom Fit. Make sure you have a matching set before taking this perk, though.

10. DEFT MOVEMENT

10% chance of avoiding all damage from a melee attack while wearing all Light Armor: head, chest, hands, feet.
Requires: Light Armor 100, Wind Walker OR Matching Set
This perk gives you a 10% chance of avoiding all damage from a hit when wearing a full set of light armor. It's a noticeable but unreliable bonus: if you're lucky, it might spare you from a lethal blow… or it may not.

Sneak

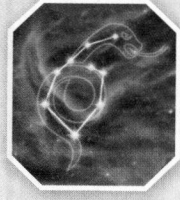

Constellation: Path of Shadow
Available Perks: 13

Sneak is the art of moving unseen and unheard. This skill improves when you sneak past someone, or perform a successful sneak attack. You don't get credit for sneaking in an empty hallway, or for just standing around– you must be sneaking (crouched) near someone who can detect you. Avoiding detection is also critical: the moment you are spotted, your sneak attempt has failed, and you can no longer perform a sneak attack (until you hide again).

1-5. STEALTH (5 RANKS) ★

Rank 1: You are 20% harder to detect when sneaking.
Requires: None
Rank 2: You are 25% harder to detect when sneaking.
Requires: Sneak 20, Stealth 1
Rank 3: You are 30% harder to detect when sneaking.
Requires: Sneak 40, Stealth 2
Rank 4: You are 35% harder to detect when sneaking.
Requires: Sneak 60, Stealth 3
Rank 5: You are 40% harder to detect when sneaking.
Requires: Sneak 80, Stealth 4

This perk makes it dramatically easier to sneak past enemies unnoticed. The first rank in this skill (+20%) is absolutely critical to being able to sneak effectively. Subsequent ranks have diminishing returns, but are still a good choice if you're focused on stealth and find yourself being detected too quickly. Even if Stealth isn't your focus, it's worth taking the basic Stealth Perk just in case you someday need to sneak out of a dangerous situation.

6. BACKSTAB

Sneak attacks with one-handed weapons now do six times damage.
Requires: Sneak 30, Stealth 1
Backstab doubles your sneak attack damage (to 6x normal). If you're skilled enough to reliably sneak up behind enemies, this can make one-hit kills a real possibility, especially on weaker foes.

7. MUFFLED MOVEMENT

Noise from armor is reduced by 50%.
Requires: Sneak 30, Stealth 1
This perk is good at low levels, but is much less useful later on, when it's eclipsed by Silence, Muffle-enchanted equipment, or the Muffle spell (Illusion Skill), all of which silence your movement entirely.

8. DEADLY AIM ★

Sneak attacks with bows now do three times damage.
Requires: Sneak 40, Backstab

Deadly Aim increases the sneak attack damage done by bows (from 2x to 3x). The extra damage is noticeable, though not as dramatic as Backstab's bonus.

9. LIGHT FOOT

You won't trigger pressure plates.
Requires: Sneak 40, Muffled Movement
This perk presents an interesting dilemma. It has advantages: you'll no longer have to worry about almost half the traps you encounter. But enemies and your Followers can still set them off, which generally gives you less warning than you might otherwise have had. Also, you can no longer deliberately use traps to kill enemies, which limits your options and takes some of the fun out of them. So think carefully before taking this perk, or just be cautious and avoid pressure plates in the first place.

10. ASSASSIN'S BLADE

Sneak attacks with daggers now do a total of fifteen times normal damage.
Requires: Sneak 50, Deadly Aim
This perk affects only daggers, but it does make them significantly more effective at sneak attacks. With this perk, daggers do about twice the sneak attack damage of a full-sized weapon like a sword or mace. That's a solid improvement, and a good reason to choose daggers, at least for your first blow.

11. SILENT ROLL

Sprinting while sneaking executes a silent forward roll.

Requires: Sneak 50, Light Foot

Silent Roll allows you to quickly dodge behind cover while sneaking, although the drain on your Stamina prevents you from using it to roll long distances.

12. SILENCE

Walking and running does not affect detection.

Requires: Sneak 70, Silent Roll

This perk gives you a permanent Muffle effect. However, since you can receive the same effect from a spell or piece of enchanted armor, consider whether it's really worth spending one of your perk selections on.

13. SHADOW WARRIOR

Crouching stops combat for a moment and forces distant opponents to search for a target.

Requires: Sneak 100, Silence

Shadow Warrior can give you a chance to recover or make a hasty getaway if your stealth attempt goes terribly wrong. It's most effective if you can put some distance between yourself and your foes; if you use it right in front of an enemy, they'll spot you again almost immediately.

Lockpicking

Constellation: Path of Shadow
Available Perks: 11

Lockpicking allows you to open locked doors and containers faster, more easily, and with fewer broken lockpicks. This skill increases when you pick the lock on a door, container, or trap trigger hinge, based on the difficulty of the lock. It also increases (slightly) if you break a pick, so if you try picking a difficult lock and fail, it isn't a total loss.

The Novice, Apprentice, Adept, Expert, and Master Locks Perks decrease the difficulty of picking locks of the corresponding level. This helps save on lockpicks (and frustration), but depending on your Lockpicking skill and your own personal skill at Lockpicking, you may not find them necessary.

Note that the fabled Skeleton Key gives you the high-end Unbreakable Perk while you possess it, though you must surrender the Skeleton Key as a part of the Thieves' Guild questline. While you have it, take the opportunity to unlock any Expert or Master locks you wish and quickly level your Lockpicking skill.

1. NOVICE LOCKS

Novice locks are much easier to pick.

Requires: None

2. APPRENTICE LOCKS

Apprentice locks are much easier to pick.

Requires: Lockpicking 25, Novice Locks

3. QUICK HANDS

Able to pick locks without being noticed.

Requires: Lockpicking 40, Apprentice Locks

Quick Hands allows you to pick locks without a Crime being detected. This is sometimes useful for breaking into homes and containers without attracting too much attention… although trespass and theft will still be noticed.

4. WAX KEY

Automatically gives you a copy of a picked lock's key if it has one.

Requires: Lockpicking 50, Quick Hands

In essence, this perk allows you to automatically reopen most doors you've picked in the past. This may be useful if you find a couple of wealthy houses you can rob repeatedly (after their treasures have been replaced), or if you find yourself back in a Dungeon you've been to before.

5. ADEPT LOCKS

Adept locks are much easier to pick.

Requires: Lockpicking 50, Apprentice Locks

6. GOLDEN TOUCH ★

Find more gold in chests.

Requires: Lockpicking 60, Adept Locks

Golden Touch adds a fair amount of gold to most chests (up to +100 gold pieces per chest). This stacks with the Imperial Luck racial ability, though it's significantly better.

7. TREASURE HUNTER ★

50% greater chance of finding special treasure.

Requires: Lockpicking 70, Golden Touch

This perk significantly increases your chance of finding special loot in some chests, especially large chests. What kind of loot? It could be literally anything, from an Iron Sword on up to a Dragonplate Cuirass. This is always a gamble, but it occasionally gives you something that's far better than anything you can get through any normal means. Are you feeling lucky?

8. EXPERT LOCKS

Expert locks are much easier to pick.

Requires: Lockpicking 75, Adept Locks

9. LOCKSMITH

Pick starts close to the lock opening position.

Requires: Lockpicking 80, Expert Locks

10. UNBREAKABLE

Lockpicks never break.

Requires: Lockpicking 100, Locksmith

With this perk – and enough patience – you can eventually pick the lock on any chest with a single pick. Take this, and you won't need the Master Locks Perk.

11. MASTER LOCKS

Master Locks are much easier to pick.

Requires: Lockpicking 100, Expert Locks

Pickpocket

Constellation: Path of Shadow
Available Perks: 12

Pickpocket is the stealthy art of lifting gold and other valuables from an unsuspecting target. This skill increases whenever you successfully steal an item, based on the value of the item. Fail to pickpocket something, and you don't receive credit for the attempt.

Of course, that's probably the least of your worries at that point…!

The highest-level Pickpocket Perks, Misdirection and Perfect Touch, allow you to steal equipped weapons and armor off of a creature. An excellent trick for a stealthy assassin, there are few more satisfying ways to take down a difficult foe than to strip them down to their underwear before stabbing them in the back…

1-5. LIGHT FINGERS (5 RANKS)

Rank 1: Pickpocketing bonus of 20%. Item weight and value reduce pickpocketing odds.

Requires: None

Rank 2: Pickpocketing bonus of 40%. Item weight and value reduce pickpocketing odds.

Requires: Pickpocket 20, Light Fingers 1

Rank 3: Pickpocketing bonus of 60%. Item weight and value reduce pickpocketing odds.

Requires: Pickpocket 40, Light Fingers 2

Rank 4: Pickpocketing bonus of 80%. Item weight and value reduce pickpocketing odds.

Requires: Pickpocket 60, Light Fingers 3

Rank 5: Pickpocketing bonus of 100%. Item weight and value reduce pickpocketing odds.

Requires: Pickpocket 80, Light Fingers 4

6. NIGHT THIEF

+25% chance to pickpocket if the target is asleep.

Requires: Pickpocket 20

Night Thief makes pickpocketing a sleeping character much easier. Find out where your target sleeps, hide nearby, wait for nightfall, and then rob them at your leisure. Stacks with Light Fingers.

7. CUTPURSE

Pickpocketing gold is 50% easier.

Requires: Pickpocket 40, Night Thief

8. POISONED

Silently harm enemies by placing poisons in their pockets.

Requires: Pickpocket 40, Night Thief

This is a good way of sapping an enemy's strength, and can kill many civilians outright. This is a great tactic for some Dark Brotherhood assassinations.

9. EXTRA POCKETS ★

Carrying capacity is increased by 100 points.

Requires: Pickpocket 50, Night Thief

Increases your Max Carry weight by 100. This great for any character, especially if you've been neglecting your stamina when leveling up.

10. KEYMASTER

Pickpocketing keys always works.

Requires: Pickpocket 60, Cutpurse

Gold and items are great, but keys can be even better once you have access to a good Fence– go rob a well-to-do character's house while they're out, and the haul will often be worth far more than what they were carrying. If you need someone to fence your stolen goods, join the Thieves' Guild, or take the Speech skill's Fence perk.

11. MISDIRECTION

Can pickpocket equipped weapons.

Requires: Pickpocket 70, Cutpurse

12. PERFECT TOUCH

Can pickpocket equipped items.

Requires: Pickpocket 100, Misdirection

Speech

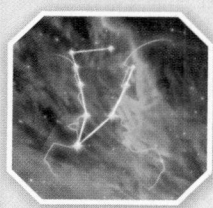

Speech allows you to haggle, bribe, persuade, and intimidate others to do as you ask. The higher your Speech skill, the better the prices you get when buying or selling items, and the greater your odds of success at dialogue challenges. Your Speech skill doesn't require any special effort to raise: it increases naturally when you sell items to a merchant (based on the value of the item), or when you succeed at a Persuade or Intimidate challenge (based on its difficulty).

Constellation: Path of Shadow
Available Perks: 13

1-5. HAGGLING (5 RANKS) ★

Rank 1: Buying and selling prices are 10% better.
Requires: None
Rank 2: Buying and selling prices are 15% better.
Requires: Speech 20, Haggling 1
Rank 3: Buying and selling prices are 20% better.
Requires: Speech 40, Haggling 2
Rank 4: Buying and selling prices are 25% better.
Requires: Speech 60, Haggling 3
Rank 5: Buying and selling prices are 30% better.
Requires: Speech 80, Haggling 4

Haggling significantly improves the prices you get in shops, though with diminishing returns after the first rank. Even if you don't plan to focus on Speech, it's worth picking up the first rank of this perk.

6. ALLURE
10% better prices with the opposite sex.
Requires: Speech 30, Haggling 1

Allure allows you to get slightly better prices from some merchants. While this can add up over time, make sure to take advantage of it by finding merchants of the correct gender. Stacks with Haggling.

7. BRIBERY
Can bribe guards to ignore crimes.
Requires: Speech 30, Haggling 1

This perk allows you to bribe guards to overlook non-violent crimes. The crime doesn't go away, they just don't arrest you right now. If you're already a member of the Thieves' Guild, you can do this for free, so there's no need to spend a Perk on it. This is also unimportant if you're a law-abiding citizen of Skyrim.

8. MERCHANT ★
Can sell any type of item to any kind of merchant.
Requires: Speech 50, Allure

The Merchant Perk makes the process of selling off your loot significantly faster, since you no longer need to visit multiple vendors to sell everything.

9. PERSUASION
Persuasion attempts are 30% easier.
Requires: Speech 50, Bribery

This perk increases your effective Speech score for the purpose of Persuade challenges. This is rarely necessary, although it can help if you find yourself struggling with them.

10. INTIMIDATION
Intimidation is twice as successful.
Requires: Speech 70, Persuasion

Like Persuasion, this Perk increases your effective Speech score for the purpose of Intimidate challenges. Also like Persuasion, it's rarely necessary, and there's no real reason to take both this and Persuasion, unless you have a strong roleplaying preference.

11. INVESTOR
Can invest 500 gold with a shopkeeper to increase his available gold permanently.
Requires: Speech 70, Merchant

Permanently increases the amount of gold that merchants have to trade with you. Coupled with the Merchant Perk, this makes it even easier to sell your loot to one just convenient merchant, reducing your downtime between quests.

12. FENCE
Can barter stolen goods with any merchant you have invested in.
Requires: Speech 90, Investor

If you're already a member of the Thieves' Guild, you may not need another Fence, although this will make it more convenient to sell stolen items as it increases the number of Fences you have access to.

13. MASTER TRADER
Every merchant in the world gains 1,000 gold for bartering.
Requires: Speech 100, Fence

Alchemy

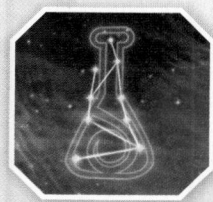

Alchemy allows you to create potent potions and deadly poisons. Their effects are determined by the ingredients you use, but their potency is based on your Alchemy skill. Your skill increases when you discover a new ingredient effect or successfully craft a potion (based on the value of the potion). It also increases slightly if you attempt to craft a potion but fail– while you may lose the ingredients, the experiment isn't a complete loss.

Constellation: Path of Shadow
Available Perks: 15

The Crafting section, beginning on page 41, has extensive details about the Alchemy system, including a full list of ingredients and their effects.

1-5. ALCHEMIST (5 RANKS) ★

Rank 1: Potions and poisons you make are 20% stronger.
Requires: None
Rank 2: Potions and poisons you make are 40% stronger.
Requires: Alchemy 20, Alchemist 1
Rank 3: Potions and poisons you make are 60% stronger.
Requires: Alchemy 40, Alchemist 2
Rank 4: Potions and poisons you make are 80% stronger.
Requires: Alchemy 60, Alchemist 3
Rank 5: Potions and poisons you make are twice as strong.
Requires: Alchemy 80, Alchemist 4

6. PHYSICIAN
Potions you mix that restore Health, Magicka, or Stamina are 25% more powerful.
Requires: Alchemy 20, Alchemist 1

Physician stacks with the Alchemist perks to make significantly more powerful restorative potions.

7. BENEFACTOR
Potions you mix with beneficial effects have an additional 25% greater magnitude.
Requires: Alchemy 30, Physician 1

Benefactor stacks with both the Alchemist and Physician perks, but improves a broader range of potions than Physician.

8. POISONER
Poisons you mix are 25% more effective.
Requires: Alchemy 30, Physician 1

9-11. EXPERIMENTER (3 RANKS)
Rank 1: Eating an ingredient reveals first two effects.
Requires: Alchemy 50, Benefactor
Rank 2: Eating an ingredient reveals first three effects.
Requires: Alchemy 70, Experimenter 1
Rank 3: Eating an ingredient reveals all its effects.
Requires: Alchemy 90, Experimenter 2

The Experimenter Perks allow you to learn more effects just by eating ingredients. If mixing and matching ingredients isn't something you're interested in, this can help you learn effects faster… but remember that there's a complete table of Ingredient effects in the Inventory section, and you don't need to learn an Ingredient's effects (in the game) in order to use it in a potion or poison.

12. CONCENTRATED POISON
Poisons applied to weapons last for twice as many hits.
Requires: Alchemy 60, Poisoner

Since poisons normally only last for one hit, Concentrated Poison effectively doubles the strength of all your Poisons. It's definitely worth taking if you use poisons frequently.

13. GREEN THUMB ★
Two ingredients are gathered from plants.
Requires: Alchemy 70, Concentrated Poison

This perk effectively doubles the plant ingredients you have at your disposal. More ingredients means more opportunities to craft potions and poisons, which helps your Alchemy skill increase even faster. Unless you buy all your ingredients from shops, this is worth taking this as soon as possible.

14. SNAKEBLOOD
+50% Poison Resistance
Requires: Alchemy 80, Experimenter 1 OR Concentrated Poison

Increases your resistance to poison, which is helpful when fighting Falmer, Chaurus, or Frostbite Spiders. This stacks with any racial abilities you may have.

15. PURITY
All negative effects are removed from created potions, and all positive effects are removed from created poisons.
Requires: Alchemy 100, Snakeblood

Purity "cleans up" your Alchemy results, if they need it. You may be better off just finding a better combination of ingredients to achieve the effect you want, though.

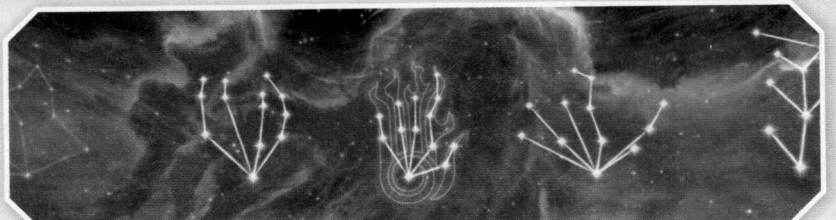

Total Perks for all Magic Skills: 86

Illusion

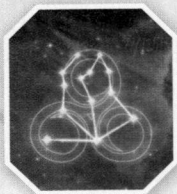

Constellation: Path of Magic
Available Perks: 13

Illusion Magic manipulates the minds of those around you, sending them into a frenzy or compelling them to flee in terror. Illusion also offers a number of useful spells for a stealthy character, such as Invisibility and Muffle. Your Illusion skill increases when you cast a useful Illusion spell on a valid target. For example, you don't get credit for casting Fear on a character that's immune to the spell, or Invisibility when no one is around to see you.

Many Illusion Perks are designed to help you overcome the major limitation of Illusion magic: the level restrictions on who your spells can affect. See the Spell List for the individual level restrictions on each spell, and the Bestiary for a guide to identifying enemies by level.

1. NOVICE ILLUSION ★
Cast Novice level Illusion spells for half magicka.
Requires: None

2. ANIMAGE
Illusion spells now work on higher level animals.
Requires: Illusion 20, Novice Illusion
Illusion spells now affect animals up to 8 levels higher than the spell's usual limit. Stacks with all other perks.

3. ILLUSION DUAL CASTING ★
Dual casting an Illusion spell overcharges the effects into an even more powerful version.
Requires: Illusion 20, Novice Illusion

Dualcasting more than doubles the duration of your Illusion spells, and allows them to affect targets twice as high as the spell's level cap would normally permit. This dramatically increases the effectiveness of all Illusion spells, especially until you begin taking other Perks in this school to raise those level restrictions. It also works well for the stealth-focused spells (Invisibility, Muffle), which could give you away if they wear off too early.

4. APPRENTICE ILLUSION ★
Cast Apprentice level Illusion spells for half magicka.
Requires: Illusion 25, Novice Illusion

5. HYPNOTIC GAZE
Calm spells now work on higher level opponents. Cumulative with Kindred Mage and Animage.
Requires: Illusion 30, Novice Illusion
Calm spells now affect enemies up to 8 levels higher than the spell's usual limit. Stacks with all other perks.

6. KINDRED MAGE
All Illusion spells work on higher level people.
Requires: Illusion 40, Animage
Illusion spells now affect people up to 10 levels higher than the spell's usual limit. Stacks with all other perks.

7. ADEPT ILLUSION ★
Cast Adept level Illusion spells for half magicka.
Requires: Illusion 50, Apprentice Illusion

8. ASPECT OF TERROR
Fear spells work on higher level opponents. Cumulative with Kindred Mage and Animage.
Requires: Illusion 50, Hypnotic Gaze
Fear spells now affect enemies up to 10 levels higher than the spell's usual limit. Stacks with all other perks.

9. QUIET CASTING
All spells you cast from any school of magic are silent to others.
Requires: Illusion 50, Kindred Mage
A great choice for any stealth-focused character dabbling in magic, or any mage interested in stealth. With this Perk, you can cast spells like Fear or Frenzy while remaining hidden, or recast Invisibility if it wears off unexpectedly.

10. RAGE
Frenzy spells work on higher level opponents. Cumulative with Kindred Mage and Animage.
Requires: Illusion 70, Aspect of Terror
Frenzy spells now affect enemies up to 12 levels higher than the spell's usual limit. Stacks with all other perks.

11. EXPERT ILLUSION ★
Cast Expert level Illusion spells for half magicka.
Requires: Illusion 75, Adept Illusion

12. MASTER OF THE MIND ★
Illusion spells work on undead, daedra and automations.
Requires: Illusion 90, Rage OR Quiet Casting

13. MASTER ILLUSION
Cast Master level Illusion spells for half magicka.
Requires: Illusion 100, Expert Illusion

Conjuration

Constellation: Path of Magic
Available Perks: 16

Conjuration Spells allow you to raise the dead, summon creatures from Oblivion, draw powerful Bound Weapons from thin air, and trap the souls of your defeated foes. Your Conjuration skill increases when you cast a Conjuration spell and use it effectively, such as sending your summoned creature into battle, doing damage with a bound weapon, or successfully trapping a soul.

1. NOVICE CONJURATION ★
Cast Novice level Conjuration spells for half magicka.
Requires: None

2. MYSTIC BINDING
Bound weapons do more damage.
Requires: Conjuration 20, Novice Conjuration

Improves the damage of bound weapons by 50%. If you use them, that's a noticeable improvement.

3. CONJURATION DUAL CASTING
Dual casting a Conjuration spell overcharges the spell, allowing it to last longer.
Requires: Conjuration 20, Novice Conjuration

Dualcasting increases the duration of your Conjuration spells, not their strength. This is useful if you raise undead frequently– you'll get more use from your zombies before they turn to ash– but it's less effective if you primarily conjure creatures, since you can always conjure them again if the battle is taking a long time to conclude.

4. APPRENTICE CONJURATION ★
Cast Apprentice level Conjuration spells for half magicka.
Requires: Conjuration 25, Novice Conjuration

5-6. SUMMONER (2 RANKS)
Rank 1: Can summon atronachs or raise undead twice as far away.
Requires: Conjuration 30, Novice Conjuration
Rank 2: Can summon atronachs or raise undead three times as far away.
Requires: Conjuration 70, Summoner 1

This perk allows you to summon Atronachs or raise undead at a distance. This tends to be less useful in the tight confines of many dungeons, but works very well outdoors, where you can "throw" an Atronach well out ahead of you and let it wreak havoc on your enemies before you even get close (or remain in cover and let your minion fight for you).

7. SOUL STEALER
Bound weapons cast Soul Trap on targets.
Requires: Conjuration 30, Mystic Binding

Casts Soul Trap on targets hit with your bound weapons. If you're interested in Enchanting and keep a ready supply of empty soul gems on hand, this is a great combination. But make sure you have a gem appropriate to the creature you're killing; don't trap that Skeever soul in your Grand Soul Gem. Check the Enchanting section for more information on Soul Gems.

8. ATROMANCY
Double duration for conjured Atronachs.
Requires: Conjuration 40, Summoner 1
Again, the duration of your conjured creatures is rarely an issue, since you can just resummon them if necessary.

9. NECROMANCY

Greater duration for reanimated undead.
Requires: Conjuration 40, Novice Conjuration

Since undead disintegrate when your spell wears off, Necromancy significantly increases the effectiveness of these spells. For best results, take Conjuration Dual Casting and dualcast your spell for an even longer duration!

10. ADEPT CONJURATION ★

Cast Adept level Conjuration spells for half magicka.
Requires: Conjuration 50, Apprentice Conjuration

11. OBLIVION BINDING

Bound weapons will banish summoned creatures and turn raised ones.
Requires: Conjuration 50, Soul Stealer

Oblivion Binding works like a powerful Turn Undead or Expel Daedra spell. It's a good alternative to the single-target versions of those spells, since it works repeatedly and without any Magicka cost.

12. DARK SOULS

Reanimated undead have 100 points more health.
Requires: Conjuration 70, Necromancy

Increases the health of your undead, allowing you to squeeze more "life" out of them before they collapse.

13. EXPERT CONJURATION ★

Cast Expert level Conjuration spells for half magicka.
Requires: Conjuration 75, Adept Conjuration

14. ELEMENTAL POTENCY ★

Conjured Atronachs are 50% more powerful.
Requires: Conjuration 80, Atromancy

Elemental Potency makes all Atronachs, including the top-tier Elemental Thralls, dramatically more powerful without increasing their casting cost.

15. MASTER CONJURATION ★

Cast Master level Conjuration spells for half magicka.
Requires: Conjuration 100, Expert Conjuration

16. TWIN SOULS ★

You can have two atronachs or reanimated zombies.
Requires: Conjuration 100, Dark Souls OR Elemental Potency

Twin Souls allows you to have two summoned or reanimated creatures (or one of each) active at once. Add a Follower to your adventuring party, and few enemies will even be able to get close to you!

Destruction

Constellation: Path of Magic
Available Perks: 17

Destruction Magic harnesses the elemental forces of fire, frost, and shock to obliterate your foes. This skill improves when you damage enemies with Destruction spells, based on the amount of damage you do. You get the same increase for killing a Frost Troll with one Fire Storm as for killing it with ten Lightning Bolts, and no increase at all if the spell misses its target.

In addition to its listed damage, each element has its own innate effect: Flame spells set your enemies on fire (doing damage over time), Frost spells slow your foes and sap their stamina, and Shock spells drain their magicka.

1. NOVICE DESTRUCTION ★

Cast Novice level Destruction spells for half magicka.
Requires: None

2. DESTRUCTION DUAL CASTING ★

Dual casting a Destruction spell overcharges the effects into an even more powerful version.
Requires: Destruction 20, Novice Destruction

Dualcasting more than doubles the damage of your Destruction spells. This is a great choice, especially at early levels, where inflicting that extra damage with Flames or Frostbite often means the difference between life and death.

3. APPRENTICE DESTRUCTION ★

Cast Apprentice level Destruction spells for half magicka.
Requires: Destruction 25, Novice Destruction

4-5. AUGMENTED FLAMES (2 RANKS)

Rank 1: Fire spells do 25% more damage.
Requires: Destruction 30, Novice Destruction
Rank 2: Fire spells do 50% more damage.
Requires: Destruction 60, Augmented Flames 1

6-7. AUGMENTED FROST (2 RANKS)

Rank 1: Frost spells do 25% more damage.
Requires: Destruction 30, Novice Destruction
Rank 2: Frost spells do 50% more damage.
Requires: Destruction 60, Augmented Frost 1

8-9. AUGMENTED SHOCK (2 RANKS)

Rank 1: Shock spells do 25% more damage.
Requires: Destruction 30, Novice Destruction
Rank 2: Shock spells do 50% more damage.
Requires: Destruction 60, Augmented Shock 1

10. IMPACT

Most destruction spells will stagger an opponent when dual cast.
Requires: Destruction 40, Destruction Dual Casting

Impact adds a stagger effect to most dualcast spells. Flames, Frostbite, and Sparks are not included in this set, so you can't stagger enemies at will, but this can still be a powerful effect, allowing you to slow an enemy who's trying to close with you, or giving you a chance to run if you find yourself overwhelmed.

11. RUNE MASTER

Can place runes five times farther away.
Requires: Destruction 40, Apprentice Destruction

Rune Spells allow you to create traps that enemies can trigger. The Rune Master Perk allows you to place them dramatically farther away, making it much easier to throw them into an enemy's path or place them near an existing trap (to create a "killing zone") without being detected.

12. ADEPT DESTRUCTION ★

Cast Adept level Destruction spells for half magicka.
Requires: Destruction 50, Apprentice Destruction

13. INTENSE FLAMES

Fire damage causes targets to flee if their health is below 20%.
Requires: Destruction 50, Augmented Flames 1

Sure, by the time this perk takes effect, your enemy was almost dead anyway– but watching a flaming foe run screaming off the edge of a cliff is just priceless.

14. DEEP FREEZE

Frost damage paralyzes targets if their health is below 20%.
Requires: Destruction 60, Augmented Frost 1

Deep Freeze paralyzes enemies near death, allowing you to kill them with impunity or turn your attention to more pressing threats. It often prevents a foe from completing their last attack (or two), which may be a lifesaver if your health is also low.

15. DISINTEGRATE

Shock damage disintegrates targets if their health is below 15%.
Requires: Destruction 70, Augmented Shock 1

Disintegrate effectively increases your damage output, instantly killing an enemy whenever your shock spells reduce their health below 15%. For pure efficiency, this is the best of the three low-health perks.

16. EXPERT DESTRUCTION ★

Cast Expert level Destruction spells for half magicka.
Requires: Destruction 75, Adept Destruction

17. MASTER DESTRUCTION ★

Cast Master level Destruction spells for half magicka.
Requires: Destruction 100, Expert Destruction

Restoration

Constellation: Path of Magic
Available Perks: 13

Restoration spells shape life energy, allowing you to heal yourself and your companions, drive back the undead, and create protective wards. Your Restoration skill increases when you use these spells effectively: to heal damage, turn undead, or shield yourself in combat. It does not increase if you heal someone who is already at full health, or cast a Turn Undead spell when no undead are around.

1. NOVICE RESTORATION ★
Cast Novice level Restoration spells for half magicka.
Requires: None

2. REGENERATION ★
Healing spells cure 50% more.
Requires: Restoration 20, Novice Restoration

Regeneration makes all healing spells more effective. It has a low skill requirement, and is definitely worth taking early, when the concentration spell Healing may be your only restorative spell. Those few extra points of health a second can make all the difference during a particularly dangerous battle.

3. RESTORATION DUAL CASTING
Dual casting a Restoration spell overcharges the effects into an even more powerful version.
Requires: Restoration 20, Novice Restoration

Dualcasting doubles the effectiveness of some Restoration spells (Healing, Wards) and the duration of others (Turn Undead). But except in the most dire of circumstances, you're far more likely to want a weapon in your other hand than a second Restoration spell.

4. APPRENTICE RESTORATION ★
Cast Apprentice level Restoration spells for half magicka.
Requires: Restoration 25, Novice Restoration

5-6. RECOVERY (2 RANKS) ★
Rank 1: Magicka regenerates 25% faster.
Requires: Restoration 30, Novice Restoration
Rank 2: Magicka regenerates 50% faster.
Requires: Restoration 60, Recovery 1

A fantastic perk for any mage– after all, who can resist having more Magicka? It's also a fine choice for non-mages who still want to use magic occasionally, as it helps make up for the Magicka regeneration they miss out on by not wearing mage robes.

7. RESPITE ★
Healing spells also restore Stamina.
Requires: Restoration 40, Novice Restoration

Respite is ideal for warriors, but less effective for a pure mage, since you may not use Stamina except when sprinting away.

8. ADEPT RESTORATION ★
Cast Adept level Restoration spells for half magicka.
Requires: Restoration 50, Apprentice Restoration

9. WARD ABSORB
Wards recharge your magicka when hit with spells.
Requires: Restoration 60, Novice Restoration

This perk allows your Wards to absorb 25% of the Magicka from incoming spells. This is handy if you use Wards extensively, as the additional Magicka helps to offset their cost and allows you to maintain them for longer.

10. NECROMAGE
All spells are more effective against undead.
Requires: Restoration 70, Regeneration

Necromage improves all of your spells, not just Turn Undead spells. Spells with a duration last 50% longer; spells with a magnitude are 25% stronger. So your Destruction spells now do 25% more damage to undead.

11. EXPERT RESTORATION ★
Cast Expert level Restoration spells for half magicka.
Requires: Restoration 75, Adept Restoration

12. AVOID DEATH
Once a day, heals 250 points automatically if you fall below 10% health.
Requires: Restoration 90

Effectively an "extra life", Avoid Death is a free, passive power that automatically activates to restore your health when you need it most. The Restoration skill requirement is steep, but if you can meet it, it's well worth your time.

13. MASTER RESTORATION ★
Cast Master level Restoration spells for half magicka.
Requires: Restoration 100, Expert Restoration

Alteration

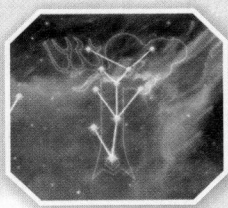

Constellation: Path of Magic
Available Perks: 14

Alteration spells manipulate the physical world and its natural properties. This school includes some of the best defensive spells available (the 'Flesh' spells), as well as a wide range of utility spells like Waterbreathing, Telekenesis, and Paralysis.

Your Alteration skill increases when you cast a useful Alteration spell on a valid target. For example, you don't get credit for casting Oakflesh but never entering combat, casting Waterbreathing but never entering the water, or Detect Life if no one is around.

1. NOVICE ALTERATION ★
Cast Novice level Alteration spells for half magicka.
Requires: None

2. ALTERATION DUAL CASTING
Dual casting an Alteration spell overcharges the effects into an even more powerful version.
Requires: Alteration 20, Novice Alteration

Dualcasting doubles the duration of most Alteration spells. Especially at early levels, this primarily affects the "Flesh" line of spells, so make sure you're using them frequently enough and really need that extra time before taking this Perk.

3. APPRENTICE ALTERATION ★
Cast Apprentice level Alteration spells for half magicka.
Requires: Alteration 25, Novice Alteration

4-6. MAGE ARMOR (3 RANKS) ★
Rank 1: Protection spells like Stoneflesh are twice as strong if not wearing armor.
Requires: Alteration 30, Apprentice Alteration
Rank 2: Protection spells like Stoneflesh are 2.5 times as strong if not wearing armor.
Requires: Alteration 50, Apprentice Alteration
Rank 3: Protection spells like Stoneflesh are three times as strong if not wearing armor.
Requires: Alteration 70, Apprentice Alteration

The Mage Armor perks significantly increases the effectiveness of "Flesh" line of spells if you're not wearing any armor. If you're willing to commit to these spells as your primary means of defense, these perks are incredibly useful. But be sure you're willing to accept the "no armor" restriction before you invest in them.

7-9. MAGIC RESISTANCE (3 RANKS) ★
Rank 1: Blocks 10% of a spell's effects.
Requires: Alteration 30, Apprentice Alteration
Rank 2: Blocks 20% of a spell's effects.
Requires: Alteration 50, Apprentice Alteration
Rank 3: Blocks 30% of a spell's effects.
Requires: Alteration 70, Apprentice Alteration

These perks are a great way of boosting your defense against magic, either instead of, or in addition to, the Restoration line of Ward spells. This is a solid choice for any caster, and is especially good for Bretons, as it stacks with their racial magic resistance.

10. ADEPT ALTERATION ★
Cast Adept level Alteration spells for half magicka.
Requires: Alteration 50, Apprentice Alteration

11. STABILITY
Alteration spells have greater duration.
Requires: Alteration 70, Adept Alteration

Stability increases the duration of all Alteration spells by 50%. At this point in the Alteration tree, you may have begun to experiment with spells like Paralysis, where the longer duration can definitely make a difference. If you plan to use it extensively, or need even longer-lasting "Flesh" spells, it's worth taking Stability (and possibly Alteration Dual Casting as well) to get the most from each cast.

12. EXPERT ALTERATION ★
Cast Expert level Alteration spells for half magicka.
Requires: Alteration 75, Adept Alteration

13. ATRONACH
Absorb 30% of the magicka of any spells that hit you.
Requires: Alteration 100, Expert Alteration

This perk is worthwhile if you still find yourself running low on Magicka at high levels.

14. MASTER ALTERATION ★
Cast Master level Alteration spells for half magicka.
Requires: Alteration 100, Expert Alteration

Enchanting

Enchanting allows you to enchant your own magic arms and armor. Your Enchanting Skill increases whenever you enchant or disenchant an item (based on the value of the enchantment), and when you recharge an enchanted item.

Constellation: Path of Magic
Available Perks: 13

While initially more difficult to level than Smithing or Alchemy, Enchanting is especially powerful in allowing you to maximize your potential with the right combination of enchantments. If you plan to explore Enchanting later in your adventure, it's worth disenchanting the magic items you find early on to build up your Enchanting skill and learn a wide variety of effects. You may also want to develop your Smithing skill to ensure you have a ready supply of weapons and armor to work with. See the Crafting section, beginning on page 41, for more details.

1-5. ENCHANTER (5 RANKS) ★
Rank 1: New enchantments are 20% stronger.
Requires: None
Rank 2: New enchantments are 40% stronger.
Requires: Enchanting 20, Enchanter 1
Rank 3: New enchantments are 60% stronger.
Requires: Enchanting 40, Enchanter 2
Rank 4: New enchantments are 80% stronger.
Requires: Enchanting 60, Enchanter 3
Rank 5: New enchantments are 100% stronger.
Requires: Enchanting 80, Enchanter 4

The Enchanter perks increase the strength of your Enchantments across the board, making weapons use fewer charges per hit, and armor enchantments more powerful. At +20% per rank, it's almost as effective as the other Enchanting Perks, and much more broadly useful. Take ranks in this whenever your skill level permits.

6. SOUL SQUEEZER
Soul gems provide 250 extra energy for recharging items.
Requires: Enchanting 20, Enchanter 1

7. FIRE ENCHANTER
Fire enchantments on weapons and armor are 25% stronger.
Requires: Enchanting 30, Enchanter 1

The Fire, Frost, and Storm Enchanter perks enhance enchantments of their element. While these effects appear on both weapons and armor, they're most important on weapons, and as you only need one weapon at a time, you may want to take the Fire Enchanter perk early and save the other two for later.

8. FROST ENCHANTER
Frost enchantments on weapons and armor are 25% stronger.
Requires: Enchanting 40, Fire Enchanter

9. SOUL SIPHON
Death blows to creatures, but not people, trap 5% of the victim's soul, recharging the weapon.
Requires: Enchanting 40, Soul Squeezer

10. INSIGHTFUL ENCHANTER
Skill enchantments on armor are 25% stronger.
Requires: Enchanting 50, Enchanter 1

11. STORM ENCHANTER
Shock enchantments on weapons and armor are 25% stronger.
Requires: Enchanting 50, Frost Enchanter

12. CORPUS ENCHANTER
Health, magicka, and stamina enchantments on armor are 25% stronger.
Requires: Enchanting 70, Insightful Enchanter

13. EXTRA EFFECT ★
Can put two enchantments on the same item.
Requires: Enchanting 100, Storm Enchanter OR Corpus Enchanter

Extra Effect allows you to apply two enchantments to any item. Double-enchant everything you have, and you'll notice a tremendous leap in your power level!

CHARACTER ARCHETYPES

OVERVIEW

The following sample characters are a rogues' gallery of battle-hardened adventurers, with races, skills, perks, and equipment chosen to maximize their effectiveness. They have titles like "Battlemage," "Berserker," or "Assassin," but these labels only describe their specialties; they don't appear in game. This is because you can literally create any type of character you wish, focus on any combination of Skills and Perks, carry and wield any weapon or spell – and choose any type of reaction to enemies and citizens of this world. But if this infinite flexibility leaves you feeling a little overwhelmed, the following Archetypes are a good place to start.

While these Archetypes have been tuned to perform well at their specific style of play, you should feel free to adapt them to suit your particular skills or interests. They are here to aid you in understanding how the choices you make can affect your character, and guide you in developing an effective style of play. Remember to cross-reference the following information with the section on Skills, Perks, Items, and Followers for more information.

Character Archetype Legend

Title: The style of play the character primarily exhibits.

Race: The character's race; picked to accentuate the style of play.

Gender: This has no effect on the character, aside from occasional citizen reactions.

Statistic Focus: How to distribute the Health, Magicka, and Stamina bonuses you receive when leveling up.

Primary Skills: Two key skills that govern the character's style of play; these should be raised as quickly as possible.

Secondary Skills: Two other skills important to the character that should be developed heavily.

Stone Ability: Which of the Stones of Power you should visit to receive an ability from.

Essential Perks: The Perks most critical to the character's development; you should always purchase these as they become available. Once Essential Perks are purchased, consider buying other Perks from your Primary Skills, and then your Secondary Skills.

Weapons: The type of combat this character is best suited to (such as melee, spells, bow and arrows).

Armor: The type of outfits and/or armor you should seek out (or Craft).

Follower: A Follower or Hireling that compliments this style of play.

Archetype Advice: Useful tips and plans for progression as you explore Skyrim.

The Warrior

Race: Nord
Gender: Male
Statistic Focus: Health 60% / Stamina 40%
Primary Skills: One-Handed, Block
Secondary Skills: Light Armor, Archery
Stone Ability: Warrior Stone
Essential Perks:

Armsman
Fighting Stance
Power Bash
Disarming Bash
Elemental Protection
Agile Defender

Weapons: One-Handed Weapon and Shield; Bow and Arrows for backup.

Armor: Light Armor; with your Shield for defense, Heavy Armor will just weigh you down.

Follower: You can command the attention of your foes in melee combat, so take a ranged Follower to maximize your damage potential. Marcurio and Jenassa are both good choices.

ARCHETYPE ADVICE:

As a Nord, you start with bonuses to your most critical Skills, and Racial abilities that help you thrive in the thick of combat.

Before each combat, quickly take stock of the area and decide where you want the fight to take place; give yourself enough room to maneuver, but don't let your enemies surround you. Your shield is useless against attacks from behind.

Stand your ground and let the enemy come to you. Use your bow to fire off a few shots from range before switching back to a weapon and shield for melee combat (switch using Favorites).

Hold the attention of your foes. If enemies begin to target your Follower, take them down quickly so your Follower can return to their own attacks.

Don't hesitate to fall back if you feel like you're getting overwhelmed, or if enemies begin to flank you. A doorway or narrow hall won't leave you much room to maneuver, but it will ensure you only have to address one enemy at a time.

If you do find yourself surrounded, invoke your Battle Cry Power to scatter your foes and give yourself a few seconds to recover and reposition.

Master the rhythm of combat, and learn how to use your attack, power attack, and shield bash for greatest effect.

One-Handed Perks like Armsman and Fighting Stance improve your damage output, but don't forget to take Block Perks as well: Power Bash, Disarming Bash, and Elemental Protection are all critical to taking full advantage of your shield's potential.

If you can block attacks effectively, you won't take much damage, making Light Armor an efficient choice that allows you to remain mobile in combat. If you find yourself struggling, you can always switch to Heavy Armor instead.

While you may not take many Perks in Archery, it's always a good idea to keep a bow on hand for pulling enemies or taking out a lone sniper.

The Warrior Stone is a solid choice, helping three of your four major skills increase more quickly.

The Mage

Race: High Elf
Gender: Female
Statistic Focus: Magicka 80% / Health 20%
Primary Skills: Destruction, Conjuration
Secondary Skills: Illusion, Restoration
Stone Ability: Mage Stone
Essential Perks:

Spellcasting Rank Perks
Destruction Dual Casting
Augmented Flames, Frost, or Shock
Summoner
Elemental Potency
Illusion Dual Casting

Weapons: Spells

Armor: Mage Robes. Always take the highest Magicka Regeneration rate robe you can find. Then look for more gear that increases your regeneration, adds to your total Magicka, or decreases the cost of your spells.

Follower: Keep a heavily-armored warrior at your side to hold foes at bay. Vorstag and Lydia are both good choices, especially early on.

ARCHETYPE ADVICE:

As a High Elf Wizard, you'll have the highest starting Magicka of any race, and can maintain that advantage by focusing on Magicka bonuses as you level.

When even that's not enough, call on your Highborn Racial power to sustain your casting in even the longest battles. Highborn is your lifeline; make sure it's your active Power (and a Favorite) unless you need to use something else, and switch back to it when you're done.

Prepare for each battle by summoning a creature, then start the fight with your best Destruction spell from range.

In combat, expect to spend most of your time casting Destruction and Restoration spells.

Learn what each type of Destruction spell is best at and how to use them effectively.

Take advantage of the spells' secondary effects; spray a room with flames to set your foes on fire, or hit a foe with ice from a distance to slow them down, allowing you to keep casting as they struggle to advance.

When not dualcasting, keep a ward in hand to deflect blows and shield yourself from enemy spells.

This is a powerful but fragile character; while you have plenty of Magicka to cast devastating spells, your health is low and your defenses are weak, putting you in serious risk if attacked directly.

Let your Follower and summoned creatures distract enemies and soak up damage while you focus on taking out each foe in turn. If your summoned creature is destroyed, resummon it immediately.

Keep a close eye on your Health and cast Healing or Fast Healing when needed, or drink a potion (remember you can tag Potions as Favorites).

If an enemy closes to melee range, check their health and quickly decide whether to keep your Ward up and maintain your attack, or escalate by Dualcasting Destruction (for a quick takedown), Fear (to send them running), or Calm (so you can escape).

When in doubt, remember that your robes are lighter than your enemies' armor. Sprint to make a clean getaway, or tactically retreat to put some distance between yourself and your foes so you have time to finish one more spell.

Because of your low health and ever-increasing need for Magicka, you'll use potions at a faster rate than most other characters. For this reason, consider taking up Alchemy to supplement what you find in dungeons and save your gold.

As with all mages, buy Spell Tomes! This should always be your top shopping priority. Join the College of Winterhold early for convenient access to all the best spell vendors.

The Mage Stone is a solid choice for this character, allowing you to quickly increase your Skills and master a wide range of spells across all diciplines.

The Elder Scrolls V
SKYRIM

▷ The Archer

Race: Wood Elf

Gender: Male

Statistic Focus: Health 80% / Stamina 20%

Primary Skills: Archery, Sneak

Secondary Skills: Light Armor, Block

Stone Ability: Thief Stone

Essential Perks:

Overdraw
Eagle Eye
Power Shot
Quick Shot
Stealth
Deadly Aim

Weapons: Bow and Arrows; the best you can afford. Ideally, find a bow with a fire, frost, or shock enchantment for even more damage. Keep a One-Handed weapon for backup.

Armor: Light Armor, for protection without sacrificing speed and stealth.

Follower: For an aggressive choice, take Jenassa or Faendal. For a sturdier companion, try a warrior like Vorstag or Argis.

ARCHETYPE ADVICE:

As a Wood Elf, you excel at stealth archery, with bonuses in all your critical skills.

If you spot an enemy, drop into a stealth crouch immediately, then creep closer and start the battle with a sneak attack for maximum damage.

Use your bow exclusively to raise your Archery skill as quickly as possible. When rushed by an enemy, bash them with your bow, then back up and keep firing.

Every single Archery Perk is worthwhile for the stealth archer; the real choice is not what perks to take, but when to take them.

Always take Overdraw whenever your skill allows it. A 20% damage bonus per shot is just too good to pass up.

Want more help lining up your shots? Take Eagle Eye and Steady Hand.

Need to increase your damage output? Grab Deadly Aim and Power Shot.

Don't neglect your Sneak skill, either. Practice sneaking up on even low-level enemies, or your skill may not be high enough to help you when it really matters.

Take Light Armor to gain some protection without sacrificing your ability to Sneak effectively. It also won't hamper your mobility as much, allowing you to dodge or back away as you continue to fire at an especially persistent foe.

Block is a good choice for another skill. While you can't take advantage of its Shield-specific perks, Power Bash and Disarming Bash work just as well with a bow, and give you an opening to make one last shot at point-blank range.

Stat bonuses are less important for your character than most, since many of your foes will never make it to melee range. A high Health never hurts, but take a little Stamina as well to ensure you can bash when you really need to.

When assaulting an outdoor Camp or Redoubt, find a nearby predator and use Command Animal on them. If your first shot isn't quite enough to take out the sentries, your new pet wolf or bear will probably do the job; or at least keep them at bay.

The Thief Stone is a good match for the Sniper, helping your Sneak and Light Armor skills keep pace with your Archery and ensuring they remain effective.

▷ The Berserker

Race: Orc

Gender: Male

Statistic Focus: Health 50% / Stamina 50%

Primary Skills: Two-Handed, Heavy Armor

Secondary Skills: Smithing, Block

Stone Ability: Lord Stone

Essential Perks:

Barbarian
Champion's Stance
Juggernaut
Well-Fitted
Tower of Strength
Power Bash

Weapons: Two-Handed Weapon, the strongest you can find.

Armor: Heavy Armor, for added defense.

Follower: Find a melee Follower who can wade into combat at your side: Stenvar is an aggressive choice, while Belrand offers more versatility. When fighting in the wilderness, take along an animal companion as well; both Vigilance and Meeko will help distract your foes.

ARCHETYPE ADVICE:

As an Orc, you have solid skill bonuses and use of the deadly Berserk Power.

Charge into combat and hit hard. Your attacks may be slow, but they connect with devastating force, staggering foes and dealing massive damage.

Power Attacks are critical to using Two-Handed Weapons effectively, so boost your Stamina and take Perks that improve them, especially Champion's Stance.

Your greatest risk is wading into the thick of combat and becoming surrounded. Keep a Follower and/or animal companion with you to divide your enemies' focus and keep their numbers manageable.

If you do find yourself surrounded, invoke your Berserk power to increase your damage resistance and gain the damage bonus you need to carve a path through your foes.

This is not a traditional berserker: Instead of hides and war paint, outfit your warrior in a full suit of heavy armor to offset the lack of a protective shield or spell. With the right Heavy Armor Perks, you can shrug off even the most powerful blows.

The Lord Stone improves your defenses even further, allowing you to endure whatever your adversaries can throw at you.

Remember that parrying an attack with your weapon counts as a block. While the shield-based perks in the Block constellation won't be of use to you, you can still take advantage of perks like Power Bash or Disarming Bash.

Since your combat style relies exclusively on your weapons and armor, Smithing makes a great supporting skill, allowing you to forge and improve your own gear.

⚔ The Spellsword

Race: Dark Elf

Gender: Female

Statistic Focus: Health 40% / Magicka 30% / Stamina 30%

Primary Skills: One-Handed, Destruction

Secondary Skills: Light Armor, Illusion

Stone Ability: Lover Stone

Essential Perks:

 Armsman
 Fighting Stance
 Destruction Rank Perks
 Augmented Flames, Frost, or Shock
 Impact
 Agile Defender

Weapons: One-Handed Weapon and Spell

Armor: Light Armor for speed and mobility. For best results, look for enchanted armor that increases your maximum Magicka or Magicka regeneration rate.

Follower: If you want a friend to absorb damage, find a warrior like Lydia or Vorstag. For a more ranged support, take Jenassa or Marcurio.

ARCHETYPE ADVICE:

As a Dark Elf, you may have to work a little harder to increase your One-Handed Skill (which doesn't start with a bonus), but your other Skills are an excellent fit.

A Spellsword is all about flexibility, switching between weapons and spells as the situation demands, aggressively creating and exploiting enemy weaknesses.

Use Destruction spells to soften up foes from a distance before they can close to melee range. Hit weaker enemies with fire spells to quickly cut down their health, use frost on stronger foes to slow their approach, and target mages with shock spells.

In melee combat, your best defense is a good offense.

Early on, spray Flames or Sparks with one hand while you hack away with your weapon; you'll be surprised at how quickly your enemies fall.

As time goes on, staggering foes becomes increasingly important. Take Fighting Stance (which allows you to Power Attack more frequently) and Impact (to allow your spells to stagger enemies as well).

Use your Ancestor's Wrath Racial Power to inflict even more damage in close combat. At later levels, Destruction's line of Cloak spells is more powerful, but Ancestor's Wrath may still be useful if you need to conserve Magicka.

Although most of your attention will be on offense, learn a Ward spell for better protection when fighting Mages, or a "Flesh" spell (Oakflesh, Ironflesh, etc.) for an armor boost against hard-hitting warriors. Both will supplement your defenses without slowing you down.

Try to balance your One-Handed and Destruction skills. If either falls too far behind, you may not be able to rely on it when you need it most.

Don't neglect Light Armor Perks, either. Without a shield or the ability to block, you're reliant on your armor and spells for protection.

Illusion spells like Fear and Frenzy are helpful at disrupting large groups of foes, allowing you to concentrate on each enemy in turn without becoming overwhelmed.

Since your skills are so wide-ranging, the Lovers Stone is a good choice to help all of them advance quickly. If you notice any of them starting to fall behind, switch to a more specific stone (Warrior, Mage, or Thief) to balance them out again.

⚔ The Necromancer

Race: Breton

Gender: Male

Statistic Focus: Magicka 70% / Health 30%

Primary Skills: Conjuration, Illusion

Secondary Skills: Alteration, Restoration

Stone Ability: Ritual Stone

Essential Perks:

 Spellcasting Rank Perks
 Conjuration Dual Casting
 Necromancy
 Dark Souls
 Mystic Binding
 Mage Armor

Weapons: Spells, Bound Weapons

Armor: Mage Robes. Always take the highest Magicka Regeneration rate robe you can find. Then look for more gear that increases your regeneration, adds to your total Magicka, or decreases the cost of your spells.

Follower: Bring a tough, high-damage Follower to create corpses you can resurrect. Stenvar or Ahtar are good choices.

ARCHETYPE ADVICE:

As a Breton, you have strong skill bonuses and a fantastic resistance to magic.

Prepare for each fight by casting your best Flesh spell (Oakflesh, Ironflesh, etc.). Early on, this is expensive – you may want to wait a few seconds to let your Magicka recover – but it becomes less of an issue as your Magicka improves.

Necromancy has one major drawback: you need fresh corpses to resurrect. When you approach a combat, quickly size up your options and decide how to proceed:

If there are any dead bodies lying around, exploit them! Raise the corpse, and your new zombie will charge in ahead of you.

Against a group of foes, try an Illusion spell like Frenzy. One enemy may well kill another, giving you fresh zombie material.

Or conjure a bound weapon and attack. Work with your follower to quickly take down the first enemy, resurrect them, and then take on the remaining foes with your new ally.

With only your Flesh spells to protect you, you're susceptible to damage in melee combat. If an enemy rushes you, use Illusion spells like Fear or Calm to stop their attack and escape, or conjure a Bound Weapon to quickly cut them down.

When confronting mages, call on your Dragonskin Power to absorb their spells as Magicka and use it to power your own spells. For even more resilience, cast a Ward– combined with your innate magic resistance, this can make you almost invulnerable.

If a battle is taking a long time to conclude, rush out into the center of the battlefield and invoke the Ritual Stone's Power to raise all the surrounding dead at once, creating a zombie army to quickly overrun your opposition!

When combat has ended, your work has not– resurrect one final zombie before moving on. You never know what lurks around the next corner.

As with all mages, buy Spell Tomes! This should always be your top shopping priority. Join the College of Winterhold early for convenient access to all the finest spell vendors.

The Assassin

Race: Khajiit

Gender: Female

Statistic Focus: Health 60% / Magicka 20% / Stamina 20%

Primary Skills: Sneak, One-Handed

Secondary Skills: Alchemy, Pickpocket

Stone Ability: Shadow Stone

Essential Perks:

Stealth

Backstab

Assassin's Blade

Armsman

Dual Flurry

Dual Savagery

Weapons: Dual One-Handed Weapons (move to daggers once you take Assassin's Blade). Keep a bow on hand for situations where no good stealth route is available, and for misdirecting foes.

Armor: Light Armor, for protection without sacrificing speed and stealth.

Follower: None. Or take a warrior such as Iona or Vorstag, but have them wait at a distance in case you need the backup. Stealth is tricky enough without having to worry about a Follower.

ARCHETYPE ADVICE:

As a Khajiit, you start with the Sneak and One-Handed skills needed to be an effective assassin, and bonuses to your Archery, Alchemy, and Lockpicking skills for support.

For you, every encounter is a puzzle waiting to be solved. If you spot an enemy, drop into stealthy crouch immediately, then look for a way to sneak up behind them for a lethal back-stab.

When assaulting an exterior camp or ruin, you may have better luck at night, when the cover of darkness provides better concealment. Weather matters, too: a stormy night offers better concealment than a clear one.

In dungeons, look for alternate paths and ways to get the drop on your foes.

In Crypts and Catacombs, your high Sneak skill may allow you to slip past the Draugr without disturbing their rest. But don't hesitate to lash out with a preemptive attack; few things are more satisfying than ambushing a foe before they can ambush you.

Sneak is your most critical skill. At early levels, it may be difficult to sneak up on an enemy without being spotted, but keep practicing! You'll be amazed at how well you can avoid detection once your skill is high enough.

As an Assassin, you need a fast, powerful offense to cut down your foes before they can retaliate. Take Perks in One-Handed and Sneak to increase your damage output as much as possible.

Alchemy is a great supporting skill; poisons make every strike count, while potions can restore your health and shore up your otherwise-fragile defenses. Don't forget to add both Potions and Poisons to your Favorites.

Pickpocket is also worth exploring. With your high Sneak skill, you should have little trouble concealing yourself from townsfolk (which improves your odds of success). At low levels, you can pilfer items for a little extra gold or the occasional enchanted treasure. But the real reward comes at higher levels, where you can steal the weapons and armor off your foes before stabbing them in the back.

Use your racial Night Eye Power whenever you want better visibility. This is ideal for a stealthy character; it is free, unrestricted, and absolutely silent.

The Shadow Stone's Power gives you free use of Invisibility once per day. Even if you learn the Invisibility spell, this can still be useful, giving you a chance to disengage with foes and make your escape, or set up another sneak attack.

The Battlemage

Race: Imperial

Gender: Male

Statistic Focus: Magicka 60% / Health 40%

Primary Skills: Destruction, Restoration

Secondary Skills: Illusion, Heavy Armor

Stone Ability: Apprentice Stone

Essential Perks:

Spellcasting Rank Perks

Illusion Dual Casting

Destruction Dual Casting

Augmented Flames, Frost, or Shock

Recovery

Juggernaut

Weapons: Spells, supplemented by staffs or a one-handed weapon as needed.

Armor: Heavy Armor, ideally enchanted to increase your Magicka or Magicka Regen.

Follower: As a spellcaster that can stand up to melee combat, almost any Follower can complement your skills. Belrand or Stenvar are both good choices for a more aggressive melee companion.

ARCHETYPE ADVICE:

As an Imperial, you have the right mixture of magic and martial skills needed to succeed as a Battlemage.

Long a respected profession in Tamriel, the Battlemage combines the mage's power and versatility with a warrior's durability. Though magic is your primary focus, you can endure the rigors of melee combat if needed.

As a Battlemage, you can choose your own approach to any combat situation:

Use Destruction spells to blast foes from a distance, or pull them in, where you can switch to a Dualcast spell to finish them off.

Use Restoration spells to sustain yourself or strengthen your allies.

Use wards to protect yourself from Mages, while countering their elemental magic with your own.

Use Illusion spells to weaken and disrupt groups of foes at range.

Dabble in Conjuration to summon allies or raise the dead, or try Alteration for an even stronger defense in melee.

Without the benefit of enchanted robes, your Magicka will regenerate far more slowly than a pure Mage's, severely restricting your spellcasting. You have options here, too:

Take more Magicka bonuses when leveling up to increase your maximum Magicka.

Invest in (or make) armor and items that fortify your Magicka or Magicka regeneration.

Take Restoration's line of Recovery perks, which increase your regeneration rate.

Draw on the Apprentice Stone's power to increase your Magicka regeneration rate, and offset the lower magic resistance with other items or wards.

Keep staffs, scrolls, or a melee weapon as back-up, just in case.

Destruction is your primary means of damaging your foes. Take new ranks in Destruction as they become available, as well as any other Perks you can use increase your damage output.

Restoration provides you with magical wards to supplement your armor, and healing spells to sustain yourself and your allies.

Illusion spells allow you to disrupt larger groups of foes, and to fortify your companions in battle.

Heavy Armor is what sets a Battlemage apart from any other wizard. While the Juggernaut perks are important, you will probably need to put spellcasting rank Perks ahead of the other Heavy Armor perks.

If you find yourself surrounded, don't forget to use your Voice of the Emperor ability to pacify nearby foes, giving you time to make a tactical retreat.

You might also consider a different race: A Breton Battlemage can take the Apprentice Stone with less of a penalty due to their innate magic resistance, while a High Elf Battlemage will have a higher starting Magicka and the benefit of their racial Highborn ability.

 The Weaponmaster

Race: Redguard
Gender: Female
Statistic Focus: Health 60% / Stamina 40%
Primary Skills: One-Handed, Heavy Armor
Secondary Skills: Archery, Enchanting
Stone Ability: Steed Stone
Essential Perks:
   Armsman
   Fighting Stance
   Dual Flurry
   Dual Savagery
   Juggernaut
   Well Fitted

Weapons: Two One-Handed Weapons (Dual-Wielding), Bow and Arrows for backup.

Armor: Heavy Armor for maximum defense.

Follower: You can hold your own in melee combat, so bring a ranged follower like Marcurio or Illia for ranged support.

ARCHETYPE ADVICE:

As a Redguard, your One-Handed skill bonus is magnified by a dual-wielding combat style, making you a whirlwind of destruction in close combat.

Choose how to address each battle.

In some cases, you may be better off rushing your foes to engage them as quickly as possible, before they can ready their defenses.

At other times, you may want to find a defensible position (such as a doorway or higher ground) and let your enemies come to you. Use a bow to draw your foes to you, then switch back to your weapons as your foes close in.

Attack relentlessly. One-Handed Perks like Dual Flurry allows you to strike more quickly, while Dual Savagery improves the strength of your Dual Power Attack.

Since you can't block while wielding two weapons, take Heavy Armor for the extra defense; you'll appreciate the additional resilience in combat.

Enchanting is especially effective for a dual-wielding warrior, since you can apply a different enchantment to each weapon; or double up for a stronger effect. You may also want to consider Smithing to forge and improve your own weapons and armor.

Early on, the Steed Stone is a great choice for offsetting the weight and movement penalties of Heavy Armor. If you decide to take Heavy Armor's Conditioning Perk, switch to the Lord or Lady Stones for more active combat bonuses.

Don't forget about your Adrenaline Rush Power, which can rapidly refill your Stamina during an extended battle, allowing you to sustain a flurry of power attacks.

 The Rogue

Race: Argonian
Gender: Female
Statistic Focus: Health 40% / Magicka 40% / Stamina 20%
Primary Skills: Sneak, Illusion
Secondary Skills: Archery, One-Handed
Stone Ability: Serpent Stone
Essential Perks:
   Stealth
   Illusion Rank Perks
   Illusion Dual Casting
   Quiet Casting
   Overdraw
   Armsman

Weapons: Spells, Bow and Arrows, One-Handed Weapon for backup.

Armor: Light Armor, ideally with enchantments to improve your Magicka or Magicka Regen.

Follower: Seek out a stealthy archer like Jenassa or Faendal.

ARCHETYPE ADVICE:

As an Argonian, your natural abilities skills provide a solid foundation for a stealthy character, though your magic skills will take a little more time to build up.

The Rogue is a hybrid mage-thief. Less narrowly focused than most of the other archetypes, it offers a great deal of versatility, and is a fun choice if you enjoy toying with your enemies instead of assaulting them directly.

When you spot a foe, drop into a stealthy crouch and creep closer to assess the situation. You have a range of options at your disposal:

Cast Invisibility and Muffle and sneak past your foes undetected.

Cast Frenzy or Fear to disrupt and disorient them.

Fire a well-placed arrow to catch a foe's attention and lure them into a trap.

Snipe a foe from range, starting combat with a devastating sneak attack.

Creep closer and backstab for maximum damage.

Once combat begins, don't hesitate to attack with bow or blade. If you want to take on a foe directly, draw a second weapon to deal even more damage.

If you feel yourself getting overwhelmed, pull out an ace:

Cast Fear to send your enemies running, then pelt them with arrows as they flee.

Cast Calm to stop combat for a moment, giving yourself time to quaff a potion or make a tactical retreat.

Call on the Serpent Stone's Power to paralyze a foe and take them out of the fight completely. This gives you time to heal, deal with other enemies, or slaughter the now-helpless foe at your leisure.

Your Histskin Power is an amazing racial ability, capable of pulling you back from the brink of death. Give it a few seconds to do its work, then wade back into the thick of combat.

With such a wide array of tactics at your disposal, you can find a solution to any challenge. Focus on the core improvement perks for each skill (Stealth, Illusion Ranks, Armsman, and Overdraw) to make sure each tactic remains viable, then branch out depending on what seems most useful to you.

If you have any perks left over, explore Lockpicking or Pickpocket to take advantage of your racial skill bonuses and complete your stealthy arsenal.

 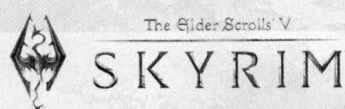

TRAINING PART 2:
COMBAT, DEVELOPMENT, AND CRAFTING

This section explores the vast array of actions and activities you can perform in Skyrim. Advice is given on how to improve your character as you level up, crucial tactical details on all facets of combat and exploration (includeing Shouts) are provided, and Crafting systems are explained in detail.

CHARACTER ADVANCEMENT

Leveling Advice

Tactically Level Up during a particularly frightening combat, as shown.

As your skills increase, you gradually make progress towards gaining a level. There are several aspects of this process worth taking a closer look at:

Improve what you use: The Skills you use will improve naturally as you use them. There is no need to go out of your way to improve a skill you never plan to use; this doesn't level your character any faster, and won't make your character any stronger or more effective.

Use what you improve: When selecting perks, be sure you're ready to take full advantage of them. For example, don't purchase Adept-level Magic Perks until you have Adept-level spells to cast. Don't take Enchanting Perks unless you're planning on Enchanting something in the immediate future.

Patience and Perks: If you aren't sure which perk to choose when you Level up, or find yourself a few Skill points away from a perk you really want, it is usually better to save the choice for later. This gives you more flexibility and allows you to change your mind. Remember, once you select a perk, you can't take it back!

Tactical Leveling: Leveling up fully restores your Health, Magicka, and Stamina. This can literally save your life if you find yourself bereft of potions during a difficult battle. For example, if you gain a level while exploring a dungeon, you may want to wait and level up during the final (or most difficult) fight. Conversely, there's no point in hoarding Levels; once you begin leveling up, you must claim all of the levels you've earned.

COMBAT IMPROVEMENT

By now, you should have skills that aid you in dispatching enemies through melee, ranged, or magical attacks. This section offers advice on maximizing your combat potential no matter how you decide to fight your foes.

General Advice

Don't overlook your Shout or Powers; they can win the fight for you!

As you set off to explore the realm, you may be overwhelmed with the choices you can make. But remember this following sage advice, and you'll thrive in the wilds of Skyrim!

Conserve your Resources: Your three statistics – Health, Magicka, and Stamina – are all resources you need to conserve. If you sprint into battle (using Stamina), recast your spells right before heading into battle (Magicka), or push on after a difficult battle without pausing to recover your Health, you're at a disadvantage. Stop and wait for a moment (optionally swigging down a potion) to ensure all three stats have recovered fully before you continue.

Remember your Shouts and Powers: While most of your attention will be on the weapons, spells, or shield in your hands, remember that you have a third option at your disposal. Shouts and Powers are among your most devestating abilities: they don't cost anything to use, and they can dramatically turn the tide of battle in your favor. Make sure to Favorite them, and always know which one you have equipped. Then call on them whenever you need a some additional offensive firepower.

Consumable Consumption: Do you find yourself struggling against a particularly troublesome set of foes? Then stop, rummage around in your inventory, and see if you have an item that might help. This could be a healing or fortifying potion, a poison for your weapon, or a Scroll with a powerful magic effect. Don't hoard scrolls; use them!

Active Effects: It's easy to forget about the Brain Rot you contracted a few hours ago, or not to notice when a blessing or buff has worn off. Check the Active Effects list in the Magic menu every so often to ensure you know what is ailing or enhancing you.

The Favorites Menu: Discussed later in this chapter, the Favorites Menu not only allows you to quickly switch between weapons and spells, but opening it also pauses time without blocking your view, giving you time to consider your next move.

Save Early. Save Often! Although the game saves your progress automatically, it's always prudent to make a save before trying something dangerous, like running down a hallway lined with swinging blades or investigating that ominous-looking tomb.

Tuning in the Difficulty: The System > Settings > Gameplay menu allows you to change the game's difficulty at any time – even during combat – which you should try if you're really struggling, or you're having too easy a time. Adjust this to suit your preferences.

Melee Combat

To maximize your potential in melee combat, choose a weapon you like, learn its rhythm, improve the associated perks, and try to find (or forge) the most potent version of it that you can. If you have problems effectively bringing down foes, be sure you know how to respond to and counter their attacks.

Choose your weapon: Early in your adventure, try out a variety of weapons and combat styles and see what works best for you. Do you prefer one or two-handed weapons? If you enjoy wielding a one-handed weapon, do you want a shield, spell, or another weapon in your free hand? Then figure out whether daggers (fast, lowest damage), swords, axes, or maces (slow, highest damage) are your favorite. By learning what you're most comfortable wielding, you can choose the perks that compliment that style.

The Rhythm of Combat: Once you've settled on a weapon or combat style, practice your tactics. Remember that you and your opponent have a regular Attack, a Power Attack (holding the attack button down for a slower but more damaging strike), Block (raising your shield or weapon to deflect an enemy blow), and Bash (hitting your foe with a shield or the flat of a weapon). Try to get a feel for how long it takes you to perform these actions with your chosen weapon, and how long it takes for your enemies to do the same. As your sense of timing improves, you can better decide whether to attack or defend during a fight, and choose your tactics more strategically.

Observe and Counter: Combat involves more than just attacking. You can take down enemies faster and more effectively by observing their actions and choosing the appropriate counter.

Block if your enemy uses a regular attack.

Bash if your enemy uses a Power Attack to quickly interrupt and stagger them.

Power Attack if your enemy is blocking to break their block and stagger them.

Attack swiftly if your enemy is staggered to cut them down.

Wearing a Cloak: The Destruction line of Cloak Spells (Flame, Frost, and Lightning) are ideal if you plan to engage in close combat – even if you're primarily a warrior with little interest in magic – as they allow you to damage enemies with both your weapons and the cloak's magical effects, without requiring much attention (or Magicka expenditure). Cloak Spells also don't damage your Followers, so there's no need to worry in close quarters.

Ranged Combat

A Dragon Attack: If you only focus on melee combat, your options against Dragons are limited.

Whether you're an accomplished archer or learning how to fire an arrow for the first time, it's always worth keeping ranged combat in mind.

The Backup Bow: It always pays to keep a bow and some arrows on hand, even if you don't plan on specializing in it. You never know when you might encounter a dragon or need to soften up a particularly difficult foe from range.

Arrow Gathering: Be sure to grab arrows at every opportunity. Since they have no weight, there's no reason not to take and keep every arrow you can find. There's nothing more frustrating than running out of arrows in the middle of a dungeon, especially if you're focused on Archery.

Remember to Bash: Don't forget that you can Bash with your Bow. This usually gives you enough time to fire off one more shot, or to sprint away while your enemy recovers so you can line up and fire again.

Perks of Power: Archery Perks have a significant effect on your ranged combat repertoire, giving you the ability to zoom in, slow time, and stagger enemies after a successful hit. Just relying on Archery can be a very satisfying way to play; and also makes hunting certain skittish animals, such as Elk and Deer, a lot easier.

Ranged Combat Only: Rarely, you may encounter a foe that can't be reached by melee weapons. On these occasions, a bow and arrow is imperative, unless you have a ranged spell.

Combat Tactics

Get the Gear: Be sure you're searching for the correct gear. If you plan to focus on Archery, Dual-Wielding, or another aggressive combat style, then offense is your best defense: Look for enchanted weapons and armor that increase your damage-dealing potential. It is often worth wearing a "weaker" piece of armor if it carries an enchantment that helps your damage output.

Prepare Poisons: Poisons are a great way of quickly increasing your damage potential. Keeping some poisons on hand (via Favorites) is an excellent way to deal with mages using Wards, or heavily-armored warriors: Even if your weapon doesn't strike for maximum damage, the poison will.

Speed and Sidestepping: Use speed to your advantage. When wearing Light Armor or Robes, you're more agile than most of your opponents. This allows you to sidestep their Power Attacks (and then counter), or to sprint away if you need some space to recover and regroup.

Staggering Attempts: A staggered enemy is much easier to cut down with a flurry of attacks. Power Attack and Bashes stagger most foes, but look for other effects that can achieve this too, such as the Unrelenting Force Shout.

Magic-based Combat

The dead rise again: There's something satisfying about raising recently-slain enemies to attack their own!

The five schools of magic offer a wide range of offensive and defensive spells to help crush your foes, shield yourself, or augment other combat styles.

The blended approach: In Skyrim, you don't have to be a "pure" mage to enjoy spellcasting. Any warrior can benefit from a conjured ally, healing spell, or elemental cloak, and thieves can especially appreciate the benefits of Invisibility. Even if you don't plan to focus on magic, look for spells that can enhance your combat style.

Spell-casting Rank Perks: Each school of magic has a series of "Rank" Perks (Novice, Apprentice, Adept, Expert, and Master) that dramatically decrease the cost of Spells from that school. These Perks are critical to your ability to use Spells from that school effectively, and should be a top priority for any serious mage.

Offensive Spells

Know your Area of Effect: Many spells damage anything in a wide area. While you can't be hurt by your own spells, your Followers can be, so use them with care to avoid any

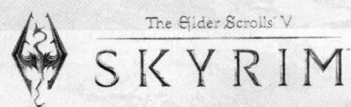

unintended consequences. On the other hand, if your only Follower is a summoned Atronach, use spells that match their element at will, since they're immune to them.

Set your own Traps: Rune Traps allow you to turn the environment to your advantage. Set one in a narrow space enemies will have to run through, or drop one in a hall you can retreat past if a combat goes poorly. In a pinch, you can also cast them directly at an enemy, although your other spells are much more cost-effective.

Raising the Walls: Though initially somewhat weak, Wall spells become dramatically more powerful at higher levels. Cast them at the feet of a waking Draugr to kill them before they can finish standing up, or back down a hall as you cast a wall out in front of you; as any enemies that advance will blindly race through your death zone.

Conjuring up companions: Be sure to summon a creature or raise a zombie before heading into any major battle. When summoning a creature, pick the one that's best for your situation; do you need the ranged offense of a Flame Atronach, or the melee toughness of a Frost Atronach? When raising a zombie from those you've recently slain, pick someone you haven't looted already; even zombies are more powerful when well-armed and armored.

Defensive Spells

Know your defenses: Both the Restoration line of Ward spells and the Alteration line of Flesh spells offer defensive options for spellcasters. Wards require concentration (tying up a hand) and have a per-second cost, but are more effective against Spells. Flesh spells have a higher initial cost, but don't require concentration. Use Wards when fighting mages, Flesh spells against melee foes, or both in large or mixed combats where you need the extra protection.

Be ready with Healing: There are a variety of healing spells to choose from; some heal a large amount of Health at once, others heal over time at a reduced cost. Most heal only you, but some can heal your Followers as well. Learn a variety of these spells (and flag each of them as Favorites) to be prepared for any situation.

Learn spells for specific situations: Delving into a Draugr Crypt? Then pick up a Turn Undead or Detect Dead spell. Exploring a shipwreck? Then grab Waterbreathing to make your diving stress-free. Whatever your need, you can probably find a spell to make your exploration easier or more entertaining.

Stealth-based Combat

A stab in the dark (and the back): Stealthy adventurers seek to slay any foe with a swift attack their enemies never see coming.

For those who lurk in the shadows, hoping to sneak past their enemies (or a watchful guard) undetected, or waiting for an opportunity to leap out and assassinate their hapless foes, you'd do well to heed the following advice:

Gain the right perspective: It's dramatically easier to Sneak using third-person view, since you can see patrolling enemies more easily than in first-person.

Stay Hidden: Line of sight is by far the biggest factor in determining whether an enemy can see you. Stay hidden behind walls or cover to remain out of sight. And it goes without saying that using Stealth Mode (crouching) is imperative.

Seek magical aid: Invisibility and Muffle conceal you from your enemies' sight and hearing, making it much easier to sneak by unnoticed. Learn these spells, collect Invisibility potions, and look for Muffle-enchanted gear to improve your chances of a successful stealth experience. Then give the same augmentations to your Followers. Otherwise, lurk alone.

Draw out your foes: Enemies leave their posts to investigate sounds, such as an arrow impact. Place your shot carefully, and you can draw them out into the open, giving you a chance to perform a Sneak attack, fire a second arrow (this one into the enemy himself), or slip by undetected.

Lure foes into traps! For an even more devious twist, shoot an arrow near a trap, and the enemy that goes to investigate may blunder into it and set it off. Combine this with a well-placed Rune Trap spell to create your own kill zones!

> **NOTE** **Finishing Moves:** Spectacular and usually gruesome, every melee weapon you carry has a finishing flourish you can inflict on an enemy at the end of a fight. Although there's no guarantee of executing one, your best bet for seeing one is to perform a Power Attack on the last enemy in a battle. Most importantly, there is no tactical advantage to performing one either (they don't inflict more damage, for example). But they are viscerally more satisfying!

Choosing Favorites

The Favorites System means less time spent rummaging through your inventory and more time spent in battle. It allows you to rapidly swap between your preferred weapons, spells, and outfits more easily, and to quickly ready a power, potion, or scroll when the need arises. Because it takes the hassle out of managing your inventory, it also helps you fight more effectively: you won't hesitate to change your gear when you can do so in a matter of seconds.

> **TIP** The Favorites menu also allows you to hotkey the items you use most frequently. Console players can press Left or Right to to tag an item; PC players can press a number (1-8). Then press that button in game to use or switch to that item instantly!

Here is some additional advice on selecting the most effective Favorites:

Melee combat: Make sure to keep your weapon (or weapons) of choice in your Favorites menu. If you use a one-handed weapon, tag a shield as well. If you have enchanted weapons that you only use occasionally (such as weapons with Soul Trap or Paralyze enchantments), those are good choices as well.

Ranged combat: Always keep a bow in your Favorites list– even mages may need to fall back on it when battling dragons. If you're primarily focused on Archery, you may want to Favorite specific types of arrows as well– your weakest for dispatching standard enemies, and your best for dragons or a particularly dangerous boss.

Spellcasting: Make sure to tag your favorite offensive and defensive spells, including your best Healing spell. Warriors should tag a Cloak spell to make sure they remember to cast it; Thieves should tag Invisibility and Muffle, and Mages should tag all the key elements of their arsenal.

Shouts and Powers: Don't forget to add Shouts and Powers to your Favorites list! Your Racial Power and Standing Stone Power are both essential. Also make sure to tag the Shouts you use most frequently.

Armor and Outfits: Depending on your play style, you may find it helpful to Favorite armor or sets of clothing as well. Thieves in particular may find it useful to Favorite a set of armor or clothing to use when sneaking– and another to switch back to if you're discovered!

Items: Tag a set of healing potions as a Favorite so you can quickly swig them in combat without frantically fiddling with the Inventory during a fraught battle. Warriors may want to do the same with stamina potions, and Mages with magicka potions.

Activities: Don't forget to Favorite items depending on your current activity. If you're exploring a dungeon, you may want to Favorite a torch or staff for light. When hunting for a hidden treasure, Favorite the treasure map for quick reference.

The Nords have long practiced a unique, spiritual form of magic known as "The Way of the Voice". Nords consider themselves to be the children of the sky, and the breath and the voice of a Nord is his vital essence. Through the use of the Voice, this power can be articulated into a thu'um, or shout. Shouts can be used to sharpen blades, strike enemies at a distance, or command time itself to stand still. Masters of the Voice are known as Tongues, and their power is legendary. The most powerful Tongues cannot speak without causing destruction, and must remain gagged at all times, communicating through sign language and the scribing of runes.

> **NOTE** The Words of Power used in Shouts are actual words from the ancient language of the Dragons-- for example, the Kyne's Peace Shout invokes the Words for 'Kyne' 'Peace' 'Trust'. You will learn these Words in context from ancient inscriptions found on Word Walls throughout Skyrim. To learn more about the meaning behind these words, and to read translated versions of the inscriptions, see The Language of Dragons, beginning on page 645.

The Rule of Thu'um

A Shout is the utterance of one or more Words of Power in order to achieve a specific magical effect. Each Shout has a unique effect, such as summoning or commanding a creature, striking foes with a blast of force to stun or disarm them, or calling down a powerful lightning storm. These should be seen as powerful special abilities and used frequently; as the Dragonborn, you have an incredible gift that few heroes have ever possessed!

There are some important general points to remember regarding Shouts:

Each Shout consists of three Words of Power.

You will learn the vast majority of these Words by absorbing them, one at a time, from Word Walls found throughout Skyrim. A few Shouts are also taught to you during the Main Quest, mostly by the Greybeards of High Hrothgar. You always collect Words of Power in the order of the three-word final phrase, so it doesn't matter which Word Wall you visit first.

After you learn a Word, you must unlock it, which requires a Dragon Soul. You can only obtain Dragon Souls by slaying dragons. Since the return of the dragons only begins in earnest after Main Quest: Dragon Rising, you must complete that quest in order to begin unlocking Words and using Shouts.

You need one Dragon Soul for each Word you want to unlock. You can begin using a Shout after learning and unlocking only its first Word, but each additional Word allows you to invoke a more powerful version of the Shout.

Do you know all three Words for five Shouts? Then you'll need to slay and absorb the souls of fifteen dragons to fully unlock them all. That's a tall order, so consider carefully which Shouts you really need, and spend your Dragon Souls wisely. For example, the Aura Whisper Shout (which tracks the movement of a foe) is great for an assassin, but is less useful for a berserker who simply charges into the fray.

Shouts can be added to your Favorites, making switching between them (and employing them for different situations) quick and easy.

Each Shout has up to three levels, corresponding to the Words of Power you've unlocked:

Level 1: Tap the button. One word. Exhale. This is the weakest Shout, but takes the shortest amount of time to recharge.

Level 2: Briefly hold, then release the button. Two words. Inhale, then exhale. This is the mid-level shout.

Level 3: Hold the button. Three words. Inhale, inhale, then exhale. This is the highest level shout, and the most powerful, but takes the longest to recharge.

The longer you hold the Shout button, the more powerful the shout. When you bellow a Shout, you drain your Thu'um (Shouting power), which slowly rebuilds across your compass. When the compass changes from a pulsing blue back to its regular grey, you can Shout again.

> **TIP** If you don't have (or haven't unlocked) all three Words, holding the button uses the strongest shout you've unlocked.

A Shout Example: Frost Breath

You begin by learning "Fo" (Frost), the first Word of this Shout, from a Word Wall. After scouring the lands for the second syllable "Krah" (Cold), and third syllable "Diin" (Freeze), you spend three Dragon Souls to unlock all three Words. You can now use the weak, average, or strong version of this Shout.

Weak Shout: Bellow "Fo!" by tapping the Shout button.

Medium Shout: Bellow "Fo, Krah!" by briefly holding the Shout button, then releasing it.

Strong Shout: Bellow "Fo, Krah, Diin!" by holding the Shout button.

Words to Live By

Some Word Walls are set in Skyrim's exterior, such as this Wall at Shearpoint.

But most Word Walls are hidden in long-forgotten Dungeons, such as the Wall in Labyrinthian.

This section lists all of the available Shouts. Each Shout's name is followed by its three Words, the locations where you can learn them, any Quests related to those locations, and some notes and tips on using each Shout. A complete table of Shouts with detailed statistics appears at the end of this section.

Animal Allegiance
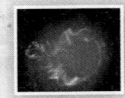
Words of Power: Raan (Animal) – Mir (Allegiance) – Tah (Pack)
Word Wall Locations:
Angarvunde (The Rift): Dungeon Quest: Medresi Dran and the Wandering Dead
Ancient's Ascent (Falkreath Hold): This is a Dragon Lair.
Ysgramor's Tomb (Winterhold Hold): The Companions Quest: Glory of the Dead.
Description: A Shout for help from the beasts of the wild, who come to fight in your defense.
Notes: This Shout 'charms' all nearby animals, who fight for you for a short time. You can attack them without breaking this effect, so it's easy to kill them before the Shout wears off. Note that this Shout does not affect summoned creatures (like Familiars), or creatures already under the control of someone else (like animals controlled by Spriggans).

Aura Whisper

Words of Power: Laas (Life) – Yah (Seek) – Nir (Hunt)
Word Wall Locations:
Northwind Summit (The Rift): This is a Dragon Lair.
Valthume (The Reach): Dungeon Quest: Evil in Waiting. This is a dragon priest's lair.
Volunruud (The Pale): Dark Brotherhood Quest: The Silence Has Been Broken; Dungeon Quest: Silenced Tongues

 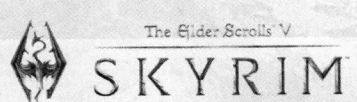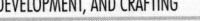

Description: Your Voice is not a Shout, but a whisper, revealing the life forces of any and all.

Notes: For a short time, this Shout allows you to see an aura around all living or undead creatures, even through walls. The Shout is silent, so it won't create a sound that would cause enemies to detect you. Great for thieves, archers, and assassins!

Become Ethereal

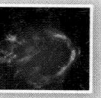

Words of Power: Feim (Fade) – Zii (Spirit) – Gron (Bind)

Word Wall Locations:

Ironbind Barrow (Winterhold Hold)

Lost Valley Redoubt (The Reach)

Ustengrav (Hjaalmarch): Main Quest: The Horn of Jurgen Windcaller

Description: The Thu'um reaches out to the Void, changing your form to one that cannot harm, or be harmed.

Notes: While Ethereal, you are invulnerable, can't attack or cast spells, and recover magicka and stamina. This Shout gives you a few seconds to safely retreat or reposition yourself during a difficult battle. You can also use it to bypass most traps without fear of taking damage.

Call Dragon

Words of Power: Od (Snow) – Ah (Hunter) – Viing (Wing)

Word Wall Locations:

None. You learn this Shout during Main Quest: The Fallen.

Description: Odahviing! Hear my Voice and come forth. I summon you in my time of need.

Notes: This Shout summons the dragon Odahviing to battle during Main Quest: The Fallen. After you complete the Main Quest, you can summon Odahviing to aid you (in most exterior areas). Note that this Shout has no effect unless all three words are used.

Call of Valor

Words of Power: Hun (Hero) – Kaal (Champion) – Zoor (Legend)

Word Wall Locations:

None. You learn this Shout at the end of the Main Quest.

Description: The valiant of Sovngarde hear your Voice, and journey beyond space and time to lend their aid.

Notes: Each level of this Shout summons a different hero from Sovngarde, each with unique equipment and abilities. Choose the one that best meets your needs for the current battle. "Hun" summons Gormlaith Golden-Hilt, who wields a bow, sword, shield, and a few Shouts. "Hun, Kaal" summons Felldir the Old, who wields a greatsword and has a number of damaging Shouts. "Hun, Kaal, Zoor" summons Hakon One-Eye, who wields a battleaxe and uses melee Shouts.

Clear Skies

Words of Power: Lok (Sky) – Vah (Spring) – Koor (Summer)

Word Wall Locations:

None. You learn this shout from the Greybeards during Main Quest: The Throat of the World.

Description: Skyrim itself yields before the Thu'um, as you clear away fog and inclement weather.

Notes: This not only clears the weather and disperses fog, it also dispels poison gas traps.

Disarm

Words of Power: Zun (Weapon) – Haal (Hand) – Viik (Defeat)

Word Wall Locations:

Eldersblood Peak (Hjaalmarch): This is a Dragon Lair.

Silverdrift Lair (The Pale)

Snow Veil Sanctum (Winterhold Hold): Thieves Guild Quest: Speaking With Silence

Description: Shout defies steel, as you rip the weapon from an opponent's grasp.

Notes: This Shout only affects enemies up to a specific level, with higher levels of the Shout allowing you to disarm higher-level foes. Refer to the chart at the end of this section for details. Note that some enemies cannot be disarmed.

Dismaying Shout

Words of Power: Faas (Fear) – Ru (Run) – Maar (Terror)

Word Wall Locations:

Dead Crone Rock (The Reach): Daedric Quest: Pieces of the Past

Labyrinthian (Hjaalmarch): In Shalidor's Maze

Lost Tongue Overlook (The Rift): This is a Dragon Lair.

Description: And the weak shall fear the Thu'um, and flee in terror.

Notes: This Shout only affects enemies up to a specific level, with higher levels of the Shout allowing you to affect higher-level foes. See to the chart at the end of this section for details.

Dragonrend

Words of Power: Joor (Mortal) – Zah (Finite) – Frul (Temporary)

Word Wall Locations:

None. You learn this shout during Main Quest: Alduin's Bane.

Description: Your Voice lashes out at a dragon's very soul, forcing the beast to land.

Notes: This Shout is extremely useful for fighting Alduin or other dragons if you prefer to face them in melee combat.

Elemental Fury

Words of Power: Su (Air) – Grah (Battle) – Dun (Grace)

Word Wall Locations:

Dragontooth Crater (The Reach): This is a Dragon Lair.

Kilkreath Ruins (Haafingar): Daedric Quest: The Break of Dawn

Shriekwind Bastion (Falkreath Hold)

Description: The Thu'um imbues your arms with the speed of wind, allowing for faster weapon strikes.

Notes: This Shout only lasts a short time, but increases your damage output by 30-70%. Time it well, and you can do some serious damage.

Fire Breath

Words of Power: Yol (Fire) – Toor (Inferno) – Shul (Sun)

Word Wall Locations:

Dustman's Cairn (Whiterun Hold): The Companions Quest: Proving Honor

Sunderstone Gorge (Falkreath Hold)

Throat of the World (Whiterun Hold): Main Quest: The Throat of the World.

Description: Inhale air, exhale flame, and behold the Thu'um as inferno.

Notes: Fire Breath does high damage in a quick burst and sets enemies on fire. Great against foes already susceptible to fire damage (such as Vampires or Frost Atronachs).

Frost Breath

Words of Power: Fo (Frost) – Krah (Cold) – Diin (Freeze)

Word Wall Locations:

Bonestrewn Crest (Eastmarch): This is a Dragon Lair.

Folgunthur (Hjaalmarch): Side Quest: Forbidden Legend

Skyborn Altar (Hjaalmarch): This is a Dragon Lair.

Description: Your breath is winter, you Thu'um a blizzard.

Notes: Frost Breath does about the same damage over time as Fire Breath, but slows your enemies instead of setting them on fire. If your foes are more susceptible to Frost than Flame (such as Fire Atronachs), or you can take advantage of the slowing effect, this is a good choice.

Ice Form

Words of Power: Iiz (Ice) – Slen (Flesh) – Nus (Statue)

Word Wall Locations:

Frostmere Crypt (The Pale): Dungeon Quest: The Pale Lady

Mount Anthor (Winterhold Hold): This is a Dragon Lair.

Saarthal (Winterhold Hold): College of Winterhold Quest: Under Saarthal; Side Quest: Forbidden Legend

Description: Your Thu'um freezes an opponent solid.

Notes: This Shout takes the form of a wave of frost that freezes your enemies solid. Foes struck by this Shout are encased in ice and effectively paralyzed, and take frost damage over time. If an enemy encased in ice is struck by an attack, the ice shatters, allowing them to recover. Use this Shout to take one or more foes out of the fight temporarily, or to buy yourself a few free attacks before they can recover.

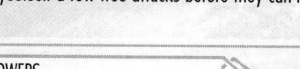
 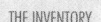

Kyne's Peace

Words of Power: Kaan (Kyne) – Drem (Peace) – Ov (Trust)

Word Wall Locations:

Ragnvald (The Reach): This is a Dragon Priest's lair.

Rannveig's Fast (Whiterun Hold)

Shroud Hearth Barrow (The Rift): Dungeon Quest: Wilhelm's Scream

Description: The Voice soothes wild beasts, who lose their desire to fight of flee.

Notes: This Shout only affects Wild Animals, with the radius and duriation of the Shout increasing at higher levels. This allows you to navigate animal dens without fighting, or to pacify a pack of animals before picking them off one by one.

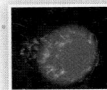

Marked for Death

Words of Power: Krii (Kill) – Lun (Leech) – Aus (Suffer)

Word Wall Locations:

Autumnwatch Tower (The Rift): This is a Dragon Lair.

Dark Brotherhood Sanctuary (Falkreath Hold)

Forsaken Cave (The Pale): Side Quest: The White Phial

Description: Speak, and let your Voice herald doom, as an opponent's armor and lifeforce are weakened.

Notes: This Shout saps your foes' armor and causes damage over time, allowing you to kill them more quickly. Good to use on bosses.

Slow Time

Words of Power: Tiid (Time) – Klo (Sand) – Ul (Eternity)

Word Wall Locations:

Hag's End (The Reach): Dark Brotherhood Radiant Quest: The Feeble Fortune

Korvanjund (The Pale): Civil War Quest: The Jagged Crown

Labyrinthian (Hjaalmarch): College of Winterhold Quest: The Staff of Magnus; this is a Dragon Priest's lair.

Description: Shout at time, and command it to obey, as the world around you stands still.

Notes: This Shout buys you extra time, which you can use for any purpose: to rush in and assault a helpless enemy, to line up a perfect sniper shot, or to easily outrun any foe. Incredibly useful!

Storm Call

Words of Power: Strun (Storm) – Bah (Wrath) – Qo (Lightning)

Word Wall Locations:

Forelhost (The Rift): This is a Dragon Priest's lair.

High Gate Ruins (The Pale): This is a Dragon Priest's lair.

Skuldafn (Other Realm): Main Quest: The World-Eater's Eyrie. This is a Dragon Priest's lair.

Description: A Shout to the skies, a cry to the clouds, that awakens the destructive force of Skyrim's lightning.

Notes: Summons a thunderstorm with powerful lightning that lashes out at anything and anyone. Only works outdoors. It's fantastic against dragons, but be careful– the lightning can and will kill civilians and your followers.

Throw Voice

Words of Power: Zul (Voice) – Mey (Fool) – Gut (Far)

Word Wall Locations:

Shearpoint (The Pale): This is a Dragon Lair and a Dragon Priest lair.

Description: The Thu'um is heard, but its source unknown, fooling those into seeking it out.

Notes: This Shout produces no sound at your location, instead throwing your voice to the target. Enemies will detect the sound and investigate, allowing you to lure them away from their posts or into traps or other hazards. This is immensely useful when sneaking. Throw Voice is unique in that its Word Wall teaches you all three Words of the Shout.

Unrelenting Force

Words of Power: Fus (Force) – Ro (Balance) – Dah (Push)

Word Wall Locations:

Bleak Falls Barrow (Falkreath Hold): Main Quest: Bleak Falls Barrow; Side Quest: The Golden Claw

High Hrothgar (Whiterun Hold): Main Quest: The Way of the Voice. You learn both the second and third Words from the Greybeards.

Description: Your Voice is raw power, pushing aside anything – or anyone – who stands in your path.

Notes: This Shout staggers enemies or sends them flying, and does some light damage. Aim carefully to push your foes into traps, or follow up with a swift melee or ranged attack to take advantage of the stagger.

Whirlwind Sprint

Words of Power: Wuld (Whirlwind) – Nah (Fury) – Kest (Tempest)

Word Wall Locations:

Dead Men's Respite (Hjaalmarch): The Bards' College Quest: Tending the Flames

High Hrothgar (Whiterun Hold): Main Quest: The Way of the Voice. Learned from the Greybeards.

Volskygge (Haafingar): This is a Dragon Priest's lair.

Description: The Thu'um rushes forward, carrying you in its wake with the speed of a tempest.

Notes: This surge forwards is useful reaching otherwise-inaccessible ledges or platforms.

The Shouting Table

The following table provides a summary of all the Shouts and their effects:

SHOUTS				
✓ SHOUT NAME	WORD	REBUILD TIME	DESCRIPTION	QUEST / SPECIAL RESTRICTIONS
Animal Allegiance	Raan	50	Command Animal, Small Radius, Max Lv20, 30s	
	Mir	60	Command Animal, Medium Radius, Max Lv20, 45s	
	Tah	70	Command Animal, Large Radius, Max Lv20, 60s	
Aura Whisper	Laas	30	Detect Life & Undead, 10s	
	Yah	40	Detect Life & Undead, 20s	
	Nir	50	Detect Life & Undead, 30s	
Become Ethereal	Feim	20	Ethereal, 8s	
	Zii	30	Ethereal, 13s	
	Gron	40	Ethereal, 18s	
Call Dragon	Od	5	–No effect–	Learned during Main Quest: The Fallen
	Ah	5	–No effect–	Learned during Main Quest: The Fallen
	Viing	300	Summons Odahviing	Learned during Main Quest: The Fallen
Call of Valor	Hun	180	Summons Gormlaith, 1m	Learned during Main Quest: Epilogue
	Kaal	180	Summons Felldir, 1m	Learned during Main Quest: Epilogue
	Zoor	180	Summons Hakon, 1m	Learned during Main Quest: Epilogue
Clear Skies	Lok	5	Clear Skies, 25s	Learned during Main Quest: The Throat of the World
	Vah	10	Clear Skies, 40s	Learned during Main Quest: The Throat of the World
	Koor	15	Clear Skies, 60s	Learned during Main Quest: The Throat of the World
Disarm	Zun	30	Disarm, Max Lv12	
	Haal	35	Disarm, Max Lv20	
	Viik	40	Disarm, Max Lv30	
Dismay	Faas	40	Fear, Max Lv7	
	Ru	45	Fear, Max Lv15	
	Maar	50	Fear, Max Lv24	

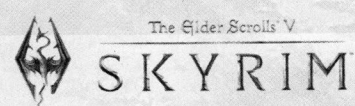

✓	SHOUT NAME	WORD	REBUILD TIME	DESCRIPTION	QUEST / SPECIAL RESTRICTIONS
☐	Dragonrend	Joor	10	Force Dragons to land; 15s	Learned during Main Quest: Alduin's Bane
☐		Zah	12	Force Dragons to land; 18s	Learned during Main Quest: Alduin's Bane
☐		Frul	15	Force Dragons to land; 22s	Learned during Main Quest: Alduin's Bane
☐	Elemental Fury	Su	30	Increase Attack Speed (1.3x), 15s	
☐		Grah	40	Increase Attack Speed (1.5x), 15s	
☐		Dun	50	Increase Attack Speed (1.7x), 15s	
☐	Fire Breath	Yol	30	Fire Breath; 50 Fire Damage	
☐		Toor	50	Fire Breath; 70 Fire Damage	
☐		Shul	100	Fire Breath; 90 Fire Damage	
☐	Frost Breath	Fo	30	Frost Breath, Frost Damage 10/s for 5s, Slow	
☐		Krah	50	Frost Breath, Frost Damage 14/s for 5s, Slow	
☐		Diin	100	Frost Breath, Frost Damage 18/s for 5s, Slow	
☐	Ice Form	Iiz	60	Ice Form Paralyze, Frost Damage 2/s, 15s	
☐		Slen	90	Ice Form Paralyze, Frost Damage 2/s, 30s	
☐		Nus	120	Ice Form Paralyze, Frost Damage 2/s, 60s	
☐	Kyne's Peace	Kaan	40	Calm Animal, Small Area, Max Lv20, 60s	
☐		Drem	50	Calm Animal, Medium Area, Max Lv20, 120s	

✓	SHOUT NAME	WORD	REBUILD TIME	DESCRIPTION	QUEST / SPECIAL RESTRICTIONS
☐		Ov	60	Calm Animal, Large Radius, Max Lv20, 180s	
☐	Marked for Death	Krii	20	-25 Armor, Damage Health 1/s, 60s	
☐		Lun	30	-50 Armor, Damage Health 2/s, 60s	
☐		Aus	40	-75 Armor, Damage Health 3/s, 60s	
☐	Slow Time	Tiid	30	Slow Time (70%), 8s	
☐		Klo	45	Slow Time (80%), 12s	
☐		Ul	60	Slow Time (90%), 16s	
☐	Storm Call	Strun	300	Call Storm, 60s	
☐		Bah	480	Call Storm, 120s	
☐		Qo	600	Call Storm, 180s	
☐	Throw Voice	Zul	30	Throw Voice	
☐		Mey	15	Throw Voice	
☐		Gut	5	Throw Voice	
☐	Unrelenting Force	Fus	15	Unrelenting Force (Weak), 2 Damage	Learned in Bleak Falls Barrow.
☐		Ro	20	Unrelenting Force (Med), 5 Damage	Learned during Main Quest: The Way of the Voice
☐		Dah	45	Unrelenting Force (Strong), 10 Damage	Learned during Main Quest: The Way of the Voice
☐	Whirlwind Sprint	Wuld	20	Whirlwind Sprint (Short)	
☐		Nah	25	Whirlwind Sprint (Med)	
☐		Kest	35	Whirlwind Sprint (Long)	

▷ Other Powers and Abilities

Powers

As Dragonborn, Shouts are your most numerous type of Power, but there are a number of other powers and abilities that you can acquire during your time in Skyrim. These include:

Racial Powers, as described in this Chapter.

Standing Stone Powers, as described in this Chapter.

Vampire Powers, as described in this Chapter.

Werewolf Powers, as described in this Chapter.

Nightingale Powers, as described at the end of the Thieves Guild Questline, on page 220.

A Dark Brotherhood Power, your reward for Dark Brotherhood Quest: Bound Until Death, as described on page 241.

Abilities

Most special abilities are offered as rewards for quests, or for performing specific actions. They typically appear in your Active Effects list. Note that some are presented explicitly (with dialogue and/or on-screen text), while others may not be. A few are not visible to you at all, so learn when you can obtain them, and how long they last.

PERMANENT ABILITIES (PERKS)

✓	NAME	DESCRIPTION	ASSOCIATED QUEST
☐	Agent of Dibella	+10% melee damage to the opposite sex.	Temple Quest: The Heart of Dibella
☐	Agent of Mara	+15% Resist Magic	Temple Quest: The Book of Love
☐	Ancient Knowledge	+25% Armor if wearing all Dwarven armor. Your Smithing skill increases 15% faster.	Side Quest: Unfathomable Depths
☐	Archmage's Authority	Better prices from members of the College (50% Enthir, 10% Others)	College of Winterhold Quest: The Eye of Magnus
☐	Assassin's Aegis	+25% Armor if wearing all Dark Brotherhood Armor	Dark Brotherhood Quest: Sanctuary
☐	Dragon Infusion	You take 25% less Melee Damage from Dragons	Blades Quest: Dragon Research
☐	Eternal Spirit	While Ethereal, you recover health 25% faster.	Greybeards Quest: Meditations on the Words of Power
☐	Force Without Effort	You stagger 25% less, and foes stagger 25% more.	Greybeards Quest: Meditations on the Words of Power
☐	Gift of the Gab	Your Speech skill increases 15% faster.	Bards College Quest: Tending the Flames
☐	Nightingale's Aegis	+25% Armor if wearing all Nightingale Armor	Thieves Guild Quest: Trinity Restored
☐	Prowler's Profit	Chance of finding additional gems in chests.	Thieves Guild Quest: No Stone Unturned
☐	Sailor's Repose	Healing Spells restore 10% more health.	Dungeon Quest: What Lies Beneath
☐	Sinderion's Serendipity	When you make a potion, you have a 25% chance of creating a second, duplicate potion.	Side Quest: A Return to Your Roots
☐	The Fire Within	Your Fire Breath Shout deals 25% more damage.	Greybeards Quest: Meditations on the Words of Power

TEMPORARY ABILITIES (BUFFS)

✓	NAME	DESCRIPTION	ASSOCIATED ACTIVITY
	Voice of the Sky	Animals will neither attack nor flee from you; lasts 1 day	Complete the Pilgrimage of The Seven Thousand Steps (Secondary Location [6.X])
	The Gift of Charity	+10 Speech; lasts 1 hour	Give a coin to any beggar.
	Dragonslayer's Blessing	+10% Critical Hit Chance vs. Dragons; lasts 5 days	Blades Quest: Dragonslayer's Blessing
	Rested	All skills improve 5% faster; lasts 8 hours.	Sleep in any bed.
	Well Rested	All skills improve 10% faster; lasts 8 hours.	Sleep in a bed you own or rent.
	Lover's Comfort	All skills improve 15% faster; lasts 8 hours.	Sleep in the same location as your spouse.

DISEASES

▷ Catching a Disease: Dirty Vermin!

Clawed by a Hagraven? Then you may have Brain Rot!

Adventuring is dangerous, especially when battling diseased foes. Every time one of these enemies strike you, there is a chance that you may contract the disease they carry. If you have a resistance to disease (thanks to your race or equipment), this chance is lessened, but under most circumstances, the chance of catching something is around 5-10% per wound you suffer. The following table lists the possible diseases, their effects, and how you can contract them.

✓	NAME	EFFECT	CONTRACTED FROM
	Ataxia	Lockpicking & Pickpocket 25% harder	Traps, Skeevers
	Bone Break Fever	-25 Stamina	Traps, Bears
	Brain Rot	-25 Magicka	Traps, Hagravens
	Dragonslayer's Blessing	+10% Critical Hit Chance vs. Dragons	Blades Quest: Dragonslayer's Blessing Lasts for five days.
	Rattles	Stamina recovers 50% slower	Traps, Chaurus
	Rockjoint	25% less effective with melee weapons	Traps, Wolves, Foxes
	Sanguinare Vampiris	-25 Health, progresses to Vampirism	Vampires
	Witbane	Magicka recovers 50% slower	Traps, Sabrecats

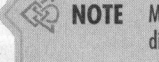 **NOTE** Most Traps have a small chance of infecting you with a random disease.

Curing a Disease: By Potion

Drinking a Cure Disease Potion is the fastest and easiest way to rid you of your pox. You can buy these potions in many shops, find them in the wild, or make them yourself.

Curing Disease: The Shrines of Skyrim

The Temple of the Eight Divines in Solitude. Only Talos -- outlawed by the Thalmor -- is not worshipped here.

Most people in Skyrim follow the religion of the Divines. Shrines to the Divines can be found throughout the land, in cities, settlements, and in the wilderness. Their locations are detailed throughout the Atlas.

Praying at a Shrine cures any diseases you may have, and confers a unique blessing that lasts eight hours. Only one blessing can be active at a time; praying at a different Shrine will remove any prior blessings.

> **CAUTION** The worship of Talos is a major factor in the Civil War that currently rages across Skyrim. His worship has been outlawed in areas controlled by the Empire, though Shrines to Talos may will still appear in Stormcloak strongholds. If the Stormcloaks are victorious, Shrines to Talos will return to the cities of Skyrim.

Akatosh: Cure all diseases, +10% Magicka Regeneration Rate

Arkay: Cure all diseases, +25 Health

Dibella: Cure all diseases, +10 Speechcraft

Julianos: Cure all diseases, +25 Magicka

Kynareth: Cure all diseases, +25 Stamina

Mara: Cure all diseases, +10% Healing Effects

Stendarr: Cure all diseases, +10% Blocking Effectiveness

Talos: Cure all diseases, +20% Shout Recovery

Zenithar: Cure all diseases, 10% Better Prices (Bartering)

> **NOTE** There are other Shrines (such as the Shrine of Azura and the Shrine of Boethiah), but these aren't related to the Nine Divines; only to Daedric Quests.

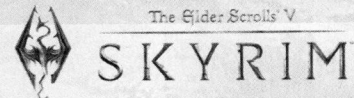

Curing Disease: Other Means

The Vigilants of Stendarr are a relatively new religious order. Zealous followers of the god of justice and mercy, they seek to wipe out abominations like Vampires and Werewolves, and to purge the land of Daedra Worship. If you encounter them in one of their strongholds (like the Hall of the Vigilant [3.09] or Stendarr's Beacon [9.46]), or elsewhere in the wilderness, you can ask them to cure your diseases.

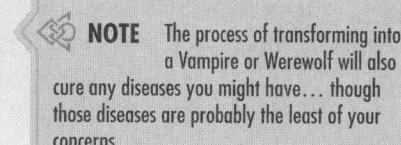

NOTE The process of transforming into a Vampire or Werewolf will also cure any diseases you might have... though those diseases are probably the least of your concerns....

 LYCANTHROPY

Contracting Lycanthropy

A ferocious Werewolf, a powerful and sinewy predator.

Werewolves are lycanthropes: Men and women who can transform into powerful wolf-like creatures. Some see this as a blessing, a way of drawing on the strength and ferocity of their inner beast. Some see it as a curse, a twisting of their wills and nature. And for some, it is simply a way of life.

Lycanthropy can only be contracted as part of the blood ritual that occurs during The Companions Quest: The Silver Hand. Your first transformation is particularly violent, causing you to prowl the streets of Whiterun as the inhabitants of the city flee for their lives. Soon you black out, and from this point on, you are able more fully in control of your animal nature.

Beast Form

When you become a werewolf, you acquire a new Power known as Beast Form. This allows you to transform into a werewolf once per day. Once transformed, you remain as a werewolf for 2.5 minutes of real time. You can extend this time by approaching a corpse and activating it to feed on it. This restores 50 points of Health, and gives you another 30 seconds of time as a werewolf.

◊ Advantages of Beast Form include:

Your maximum health increases by 100 points, but does not regenerate. Your maximum stamina also increases by 100.

You have a faster sprint speed (faster even than horses can run!).

Wolves will treat you as an ally, and won't attack you.

Any Crimes you commit as a werewolf don't count against your "normal" self, with one caveat (below).

◊ But there are some disadvantages as well:

You can't loot any corpses you slay.

You can't pick up or use any items you find. Since this includes keys, you may find your progress blocked in some dungeons.

You can't equip or use any of your normal weapons, spells, items, equipment, Shouts, or Powers. You can't even open the Inventory Menu. Your large, hulking form may have trouble fitting through some narrow passages.

You can't speak with anyone, even your own Companions breatheren.

Citizens of Skyrim are rightly terrified of you; some of them flee, while the battle-hardened, brave, or foolish stand their ground and attack you.

If anyone sees you transform to or from a beast, the transformation is considered a major Crime. Consult the Crime and Punishment section on page 39.

 TIP If you want to return to human form at any time, simply wait (or use the Wait system), and you'll transform back automatically.

Powers

As a werewolf, you gain an impressive array of combat-related bonuses:

Increased Melee Damage: When in Beast Form, you attack with your claws. For every swipe that connects, you inflict 20 points of damage on a foe. This increases at higher Levels:

Base:	20
Level 11-15:	+5
Level 16-20:	+15
Level 21-25:	+25
Level 26-30:	+30
Level 31-35:	+35
Level 36-40:	+40
Level 41-45:	+50
Level 45 and over:	+60

Immunity to Disease: You are completely immune to all diseases in both normal and Beast Form. Among other things, this protects you from Sanguinare Vampiris (the Vampire Disease), allowing you to fight Vampires without having to worry about contracting the condition yourself.

As an additional bonus, when you first become a werewolf, any diseases you had at the time will be cured. This includes both Sanguinare Vampiris and full-blown Vampirism. You can't be both a werewolf and a vampire at the same time.

Increased Dexterity: In Beast Form, you can sprint on all-fours at an impressively fast pace, and jump a lot further than normal.

Restless Blood: As a Werewolf, you can never receive a bonus for being Rested.

Werewolf Powers: While in Beast Form, you can call upon a special set of Werewolf-exclusive Powers, called Howls. You can use these as often as you like while your transformation lasts. Your default howl strikes fear (literally) into the hearts of men. However, by completing The Companions Radiant Quest: Totems of Hircine, you can acquire Totems that allow you to exchange this Howl for a different Power. You can change Howls as often as you like, though only one can be active at a time. Check page 168 for more information.

Initial Howl: Fear grips nearby foes up to Lv25; lasts 30 seconds.

Totem Howl: Detect Life in a large radius around your location; lasts 60 seconds.

Totem Howl: Summon two wolves to fight at your side.

Ring of Hircine: During Daedric Quest: Ill Met By Moonlight (page 301), you are given the cursed Ring of Hircine. While the curse has no effect on most humans, if worn by a Lycanthrope, it can cause you to randomly shift into your Beast Form! It is wise to complete this Quest or risk revealing your beast form at an inopportune moment! The curse is lifted at the end of the Quest.

The Ring of Hircine (whether cursed or not) allows you to assume Beast Form one additional time per day.

Living as a Werewolf

You are fortunate that your Shield-Brothers and Sisters in the Companions are there to help you come to terms with your new beast form, and that this strain of Lycanthropy is not affected by the waxing and waning of the moons. Therefore, it is quite possible to take full advantage of the powers of the wolf for the remainder of your adventure. Call upon your Beast Form when the speed and strength of the wolf are to your benefit, or when facing a multitude of weaker foes.

Curing Lycanthropy

At the end of the Companions Questline, a Radiant Quest: Purity becomes available (see page 168) for those adventurers who wish to rid themselves of the beast within. As a part of that quest, you must cut off the head of a Glenmoril Witch, bringing it into the depths of the Tomb of Ysgramor, draw the spirit of the wolf from your body, and defeat it. Once the ritual is complete, your cure is permanent, and you cannot contract lycanthropy again.

Werewolf Powers

The following chart lists all of the available Werewolf Powers.

✔	NAME	DESCRIPTION	ONCE PER DAY?	NOTES AND RESTRICTIONS
☐	Beast Form	Transform into werewolf form	Yes	Part of Compaions Quest: The Silver Hand
☐	Ring of Hircine	Transform into werewolf form	Yes	The Ring of Hircine only works if you are already a werewolf, granting you one additional transformation per day. Reward for Daedric Quest: Ill Met by Moonlight
☐	Howl of Rage	Fear nearby foes up to Lv25, 30s	No	Beast Form only; default Howl.
☐	Scent of Blood	Detect Life in a large area, 60s	No	Beast Form only; replaces Howl of Rage; available after Companions Radiant Quest: Totems of Hircine
☐	Howl of the Pack	Summon two wolves to fight at your side	No	Beast Form only; replaces Howl of Rage; available after Companions Radiant Quest: Totems of Hircine

VAMPIRISM

◈ Contracting Vampirism

A hated Vampire, attacking with Drain Life.

Facing those that feed on the blood of the living presents a number of perils. In addition to their terrifying visage, zombified Thralls, and skill at both melee and magical combat, Vampires have a unique Drain Life ability. Not only can this rapidly sap your health while restoring theirs, each time it strikes you, have a ten percent chance of contracting the disease *Sanguinare Vampiris*, a disease that will eventually cause you to join their ranks.

After any battle with Vampires, check your Active Effects list. If you see Sanguinare Vampiris, quickly drink a Cure Disease potion or make haste to a Shrine for healing. As the diseases runs its course, you'll receive a message at twilight that reads "you feel a strange thirst as the sun sets," and a second notification the following dawn; "You feel weaker as the sun rises." After three days of this, the disease takes over completely, and you transform into a Vampire!

Stages of Vampirism

Becoming a vampire changes your appearance.

As a Vampire, you must feed on human blood! Vampirism has four distinct stages, based on how long it has been since you last fed. The more time has elapsed, the more severe the advantages and disadvantages of this condition become. In order to survive as a Vampire, it is worth knowing exactly what these benefits and drawbacks are:

Advantages

◇ **Immune to Disease:** You are completely immune to disease. Any diseases you had upon becoming a vampire are instantly cured.

◇ **Immune to Poison:** You are completely immune to all forms of poison.

◇ **Champion of the Night:** Illusion spells that you cast are 25% more powerful.

◇ **Nightstalker's Footsteps:** You are 25% harder to detect while Sneaking.

◇ **Resist Frost:** The stage of your Vampirism adds to your Frost Resistance:

Stage 1 Vampirism: Resist Frost 25%.
Stage 2 Vampirism: Resist Frost 50%.
Stage 3 Vampirism: Resist Frost 75%.
Stage 4 Vampirism: Resist Frost 100%.

Disadvantages

◇ **Hatred:** Stages 1, 2, 3 Vampirism: Citizens of Skyrim and guards will not recognize you as a Vampire, but may (25% of the time) remark that you're looking distinctly "pale" or "hungry."

◇ **Hatred:** Stage 4 Vampirism: All citizens and guards within a settlement will recognize exactly what you are, and attack you on sight.

◇ **Weakness to Sunlight:** When outdoors between the hours of 5am and 7pm, your Health, Magicka, and Stamina will not regenerate. Their maximum values are also reduced:

Stage 1 Vampirism: Health, Magicka, and Stamina are reduced by 15 points.
Stage 2 Vampirism: Health, Magicka, and Stamina are reduced by 30 points.
Stage 3 Vampirism: Health, Magicka, and Stamina are reduced by 45 points.
Stage 4 Vampirism: Health, Magicka, and Stamina are reduced by 60 points.

◇ **Weakness to Fire:** The stage of your Vampirism also gives you a Weakness to Fire:

Stage 1 Vampirism: Weakness to Fire 25%.
Stage 2 Vampirism: Weakness to Fire 50%.
Stage 3 Vampirism: Weakness to Fire 75%.
Stage 4 Vampirism: Weakness to Fire 100%.

Powers

As your Vampirism progresses, you gain an increasingly powerful set of additional abilities:

◇ **Stage 1 Vampirism:**

Vampire's Sight: For one minute, you can see better in dark environments. This Power can be used as often as you like and has no cost.

Vampiric Drain: A special Destruction spell, Vampiric Drain absorbs 2 Health per second from your target.

Vampire's Servant: Once per day, you can reanimate a dead creature to fight for you for 60 seconds. Only works on creatures of level 6 or less.

◇ **Stage 2 Vampirism:**

All powers from Stage 1, plus:

Vampire's Seduction: Creatures and people up to level 8 won't fight or flee for 30s.

Vampiric Drain: Increases to 3 Health drained per second.

Vampire's Servant: Now affects creatures of level 13 or less.

◇ **Stage 3 Vampirism:**

All powers from Stages 1 and 2, plus:

Vampiric Drain: Increases to 4 Health drained per second.

Vampire's Servant: Now affects creatures of level 21 or less.

◇ **Stage 4 Vampirism:**

All powers from Stages 1, 2, and 3, plus:

Embrace of Shadows: Once per day, you can invoke this power to gain Vampire's Sight and Invisibility for 3 minutes.

Vampiric Drain: Increases to 5 Health drained per second.

Vampire's Servant: Now affects creatures of level 30 or less.

Maintaining Vampirism: Feeding

As a Vampire, the only way you can continue to function in normal society is to feed. Feasting on the blood of the living can be tricky: you must find a sleeping human (citizens and guards tend to be the easiest, though a sleeping soldier, bandit, or warlock will work as well), then activate them to feed on their blood. Doing so reverts your disease back to Stage 1.

Life as a Vampire

Aside from the panic and hostility you spread as a Stage 4 Vampire, the main problems you encounter are your weaknesses to sunlight and fire. Minimize these risks here by exploring subterranean catacombs and dungeons during the daytime, and prowl the countryside at night.

You may also want to draw on the power of the Lady Stone (see Standing Stones, page 59), which helps to offset the the lack of normal Health or Stamina regeneration during daylight.

If you plan to let your disease progress, trading will become difficult. Learn to craft your own potions and equipment, and try to become as self-sufficient as possible. When you must interact with others, slip into a remote settlement to feed, then continue on to the nearest city to trade before your disease advances once more.

As a Vampire, you receive a number of bonuses that improve your stealth abilities, making Vampirism a blessing for Thieves, Archers, and Assassins. You will also find it significantly easier to explore Falmer Hives (since you're immune to the poisons that they, their Chaurus, and their Spiders use), Nordic Ruins (since the Draugr use Frost Magic almost exclusively), and Vampire Lairs (since you no longer need fear contracting the disease). You also have a dramatic advantage when fighting frost-breathing dragons, though a corresponding weakness to fire-breathing dragons. Keep some potions of Fire Resistance on hand, just in case!

Curing Vampirism

There are but two ways to cure yourself of this affliction.

As mentioned previously, you can contract Lycanthropy. The blood ritual that transforms you into a werewolf will cure any diseases you have, even full-blown Vampirism. Of course, you now have other, more hairy problems to contend with....

Or, you can visit a mage named Falion in Morthal, the Hold Capital of Hjaalmarch, and complete Side Quest: Rising at Dawn. Consult page 367 for more information.

 NOTE Vampirism can be caught more than once.

CRIME AND PUNISHMENT

While exploring the Nine Holds of Skyrim, there are bound to be points in your adventure where you commit a Crime and have a Bounty placed on your head. Whether this is a petty theft from a citizen of Markarth or an all-out assault on the city guard of Riften, it is prudent to learn the laws that govern Crime and Punishment... and how you can bend them to your advantage!

◈ Criminal Activities and Holds

Perhaps the most important lesson to learn is that each of the Nine Holds keeps their own record of crimes and bounties. You may be wanted in Haafingar Hold, but your bounty doesn't transfer to neighboring Hjaalmarch, where you may still be considered a model citizen.

Your actions are only considered criminal if they affect a non-hostile character or their property. Defending yourself is never a crime. So feel free to fight back if:

You were attacked first, and the attack was unprovoked.
You have agreed to a duel or brawl during a conversation.
You're attacking an enemy, regardless of who attacked first.

Usual Crimes

The following evidence indicates the usual categories of crimes that you're likely to commit, and what Bounty this places on your head:

✓	CRIME	BOUNTY
	Trespassing; entering an area that is off-limits. Depending on the level of security, you will often be warned and given a chance to leave peacefully before the crime is triggered.	5 gold
	Pickpocketing a guard or civilian and being spotted. Just looking at their inventory is not a crime; you have to actually take something.	25 gold
	Theft; swiping an item marked "Steal".	Half the item's value
	Theft; stealing a Horse. You acquire this bounty each time you mount the stolen horse.	50 (each time)
	Assault; attacking a guard or civilian with your fists, weapon, or spells.	40
	Murder; killing a guard or civilian.	1,000
	Escaping from Jail after being imprisoned.	100

Unusual Crimes

The following list includes the more... *unspeakable* ways you can incur a Bounty:

✓	CRIME	BOUNTY
	(Vampirism): Feeding on the blood of a guard or civilian and being spotted.	40
	(Vampirism): Once you reach Stage 4 and become a full-fledged Vampire, all guards and civilians will be hostile to you. Fighting back against them is considered a Crime, and Bounty accumulates as normal.	
	(Lycanthropy): Transforming to or from Beast Form in sight of a guard or civilian.	1,000
	(Lycanthropy): While in Werewolf form, all guards and civilians will be hostile. However, fighting back against them is not considered a Crime (since they don't recognize you), and Bounty will not accumulate.	
	(Cannibalism): Eating a corpse while wearing the Ring of Namira is considered assault.	40

NOTE For more information on these special cases, consult the section on Vampirism (page 38), Lycanthropy (page 37), and Daedric Quest: The Taste of Death (page 312).

Witnesses and Retaliation

Crimes are only a problem if you're seen committing them. The Bounties you receive are noticed by witnesses, and depending upon the situation, you may wish to "silence" anyone who saw your less-than lawful activities. For example, if you assault a citizen of Riften (+40 Bounty), and then kill them before they can report the assault (+1,000 Bounty), as long as nobody is around to witness the murder, your Bounty will be cleared. Naturally, attempts to increase and then remove your Bounty can fail spectacularly; if you're spotted attempting to kill a guard by three other guards, expect them to respond with lethal force!

If you allow too much time to pass, the witnesses will report the crime, and killing them will no longer reduce your Bounty. So act quickly if you plan to take out the witnesses.

With this in mind, retaliating for a crime is worth doing only when as few people as possible are watching you (and ideally, none). It is easier to try this within buildings where you can easily see onlookers. If your Crime is non-violent (i.e. Stealing), try entering without being noticed or at night, when people are likely to be sleeping.

Guard Actions and Reactions

Reactions: When a guard sees you commit a crime, or hears a call for help from a witness, they attempt the following:

- ◊ For Minor Crimes, such as Pickpocketing, Theft, or Trespassing, they attempt to arrest you.
- ◊ For Major Crimes, such as Assault or Murder, they attack you. If you yield (sheathe your weapon), they will attempt to arrest you.
- ◊ For Severe Crimes, such as Escaping from Jail, Vampirism, or Lycanthropy, they simply attack.

Your Actions: If a guard attempts to arrest you, and you successfully avoid the initial arrest (by sprinting to an exit gate or hiding in a building for example), you can attempt the following:

- ◊ With a low Bounty (less than 3000 gold), you can wait a day or so for the situation to calm down, then return to the scene of the crime and turn yourself in. You're then arrested.
- ◊ With a high bounty (more than 3000 gold), you should avoid civilization altogether. Wander in the wilderness for a few days, and a bounty collector will eventually approach you and offer to pay off your debt to society. Don't wait for him, just keep moving.

Preventing Prison Time

The way you interact with Guards greatly affects the price you have to pay for your crimes. Once in dialogue, your options are as follows. You can:

1. **Pay a fine** equal to your Bounty, if you have the gold. Any stolen items are confiscated, and you are moved to the jail exit.

2. **Agree to go to Jail**, where you can serve your time, or attempt to escape. See below for more details on your options once in jail.

3. **Resist arrest**, if you wish to battle your way out of the location. This is also what happens if you try to back out of dialogue with any guard.

4. **Bribe the guard.** This option is only available if you aren't currently trespassing, and one of the following conditions holds:
   - ◊ You have committed only minor Crimes, and have the Speech Skill's Bribery Perk.
   - ◊ You are a member of the Thieves Guild
   - ◊ You haven't bribed or persuaded another guard in the past 24 hours.

   If you pay the bribe, it stops the current pursuit, and you're able to keep any stolen items. However, your Bounty is still in effect, and if you speak to the same (or any other) guard again, you'll turn yourself in, and the guard will attempt to arrest you.

5. **Persuade the Guard.** If you have a Speech Skill of 75 or higher, you're not currently trespassing, you've only committed minor crimes, and you haven't bribed or persuaded another guard in the past 24 hours, you can convince the guard to overlook your crimes. The option only appears once all of these conditions have been met.

   Persuasion works just like a Bribe: It stops the current pursuit, and you're able to keep any stolen items. However, your Bounty is still in effect, and if you speak to the same (or any other) guard again, you'll turn yourself in, and the guard will attempt to arrest you.

   However, you don't have to pay for a persuasion, making it a cheaper option if you can meet the skill requirement.

6. **Pay off the Guard**, if you're a member of the Thieves Guild and you've completed the City Influence Quest for the Hold that you've committed the crime in.

   There are four City Influence Quests (detailed on page 225), for Solitude (Haafingar), Markarth (The Reach), Whiterun (Whiterun Hold), and Windhelm (Eastmarch).

   The Thieves Guild is based in Riften (The Rift), so you only need to be inducted into the guild (during Thieves Guild Quest: Loud and Clear), in order to pay off the guards there.

   The other four Holds do not have City Influence Quests, so this option is not available in Morthal (Hjaalmarch), Dawnstar (The Pale), Winterhold (Winterhold Hold), or Falkreath (Falkreath Hold).

   The price to pay off the guard is always half your current Bounty. This removes the entire bounty and allows you to keep any stolen items in your posession, so it's always the best option if you can afford it.

7. **Invoke Thane's Privilege.** This is only available if you're the Thane of a particular Hold.

   You can be a Thane of any or all of the Holds provided you've completed the appropriate Thane Task, detailed on page 404.

   If your Bounty is less than 2,000, you can remind the guards of your social standing to convince them to overlook your deeds. This only works once per Hold, so save it for some pretty devious activities!

8. **Civil War:** As the Civil War rages on, Holds will fall to either the Imperial or Stormcloak factions.

   If your faction takes control of a Hold, any Bounty you may have accrued in that Hold is wiped out due to the change in government. Time this correctly, you can get up to all kinds of mayhem, flee a Hold just before your side takes control of its capital, and then return after your misdemeanors are forgotten! Information on the Civil War begins on page 261.

   Incidentally, you can also become a Thane of the newly-installed Jarl, giving you an additional use of the Thane's Privilege claim, if you're so inclined.

Serving Prison Time

A loose wall results in a lucky escape from certain prisons.

But for those caught in Markarth, no one escapes Cidhna Mine....

 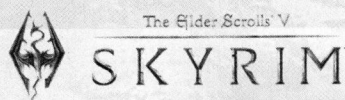

If you choose (willingly or otherwise) to be taken to jail, your entire inventory and stolen items are confiscated, and moved to the jail's Belongings Chest and Evidence Chest, respectively. You are then placed in a cell with a single Lockpick in your inventory. At this point, you can:

1. **Serve out your sentence:**

Interact with the bed in your cell, and serve your time.

In Markarth's Cidhna Mine, you must interact with the pickaxe instead to serve your time.

Serving your sentence wipes out any progress towards your next Skill increase in a number of randomly-chosen Skills. The number of Skills that are penalized is determined by your Bounty. For example, a petty crime like stealing a single potion might reset only one skill, while a murder or two will likely reset all of them!

Note that you only lose progress towards your next skill increase– your skills don't actually decline, and you don't lose any progress towards the next level from skills that have already increased. So this sentence is relatively light, especially at low levels.

After serving your sentence, you are moved to the jail's entrance, and your inventory is returned. Any items you've stolen remain inside the jail's Evidence Chest. Naturally, you can re-enter the jail and steal them back, if you want (and you're competent enough).

2. **Or, you can try to escape.** Your prospects vary depending on where you're imprisoned:

Solitude (Haafingar), Whiterun (Whiterun Hold), and Riften (The Rift) have large jails with several guards. While you can always pick the lock on your cell door and sneak out if you're up to the challenge, the cells in each of these cities also have secret escape routes that you can use to sneak out undetected, as long as you're careful. This only works once for each jail (the next time you're imprisoned in that Hold, the guards have sealed the escape route). Don't forget to grab your items from the jail's Belongings Chest on your way out, which you can usually reach via a convenient hole in the wall from the escape passage.

Morthal (Hjaalmarch), Dawnstar (The Pale), and Falkreath (Falkreath Hold) have rudimentary jails. Pick the lock and fend off a single jailer to make your escape. But do this quickly before reinforcements arrive, and don't forget to reclaim your items on your way out!

Winterhold (Winterhold Hold) has a jail known as The Chill, which is well away from the settlement, among the icebergs of the Sea of Ghosts. As befits the city home to the College of Winterhold, The Chill features Frost Atronach "jailors". Force your way past them, then swim across the freezing waters and ice floes to reach dry land and complete your escape. Your inventory is not confiscated in this jail, so don't worry about looking for a Belongings Chest.

Windhelm's jail is rather basic, but it has two attentive jailors, and the Belongings and Evidence Chests are upstairs in one corner of the City Guard Barracks. Try to escape here, and expect to have a real fight on your hands.

Markarth's jail is Cidhna Mine. No one escapes Cidhna Mine....

Crime and the Guilds

All of the above rules apply to every Hold in Skyrim, with the exception of locations owned and operated by the major Guilds. The Companions of Whiterun, the Mages of the College of Winterhold, the Thieves Guild of Riften, and the Dark Brotherhood have all developed very particular ways of dealing with crime among their own members. For example, the Dark Brotherhood only cares about assaults you inflict upon other members, and imposes a fixed fine for such actions. Consult their appropriate Quests later in this book for all the information.

> During the course of your adventure, you may find that your Guild actually encourages (if not downright orders) you to commit crimes. Therefore, it's worth remembering the tactics above before trying such anti-social activities.   **CAUTION**

 # CRAFTING

When not delving into crumbling ruins in search of treasure, there are a number of other Skills any would-be Adventurer should explore. This section reveals just how rewarding the Skills of Alchemy, Enchanting, Smithing, and the lesser crafting activities can be.

 ## ALCHEMY

> **NOTE** For advice on which Alchemy Perks to take, and general information on improving your Alchemy Skill, consult the Skills and Perks section, back on page 9.

▶ Alchemic Experimentation: An Overview

With an Alchemy Lab, combinations of ingredients become great elixirs or potent poisons.

Alchemy is the craft of combining ingredients to create beneficial potions or debilitating poisons. The key to mastering this art is experimentation: When you Smith or Enchant an item, you already know what the end result of what the crafting process is going to be; the recipes or combinations of materials are clearly laid out in advance. Not so with Alchemy; you often have no idea what you're making, and discovering a powerful new potion or effect is a thrill unto itself.

In short: The process of Alchemy involves **foraging for ingredients**, **learning their effects**, and then **experimenting by combining them with other ingredients** to make **potions and poisons**.

▶ Foraging for Ingredients
The Foraging Process

Living off the land is more than just farming crops: Scour Skyrim for ingredients.

The realm of Skyrim is filled with dozens of unique ingredients. Ingredients can be categorized into three major groups: Ingredients that are grown (such as flowers, mushrooms, and crops); Ingredients that are alive (such as dragonflies or butterflies); and Ingredients taken from an enemy's corpse (such as Falmer Ears, Hagraven Feathers, or Troll Fat). All of these are stored in the Ingredients menu in your Inventory.

TIP If you plan to focus on your Alchemy Skill, scour the world collecting everything you see: Pick flowers, catch insects, hunt, and go fishing (that is, grab fish while swimming, rather than casting a line). Steal any ingredients you see lying around in buildings, if you can get away with it-- potions made with stolen ingredients are not treated as stolen. The more (and wider variety) of Ingredients you have, the quicker your skills will advance.

If Foraging isn't something you want to do, you can always purchase your ingredients from Merchants. The best selections can be found in Alchemist shops, located in all the major cities. However, this makes Alchemy a much more expensive prospect.

Learning Ingredient Effects

Once you've collected one or more Ingredients, you can study it in your Inventory. Notice that under its weight and value, there are four effects – the ingredient's alchemic properties – which are all initially "unknown". Your ongoing task is to learn what all four of these effects are. Until you do, your initial attempts at crafting Potions can be a little hit-or-miss.

Ingredient Digestion: The easiest way to learn the properties of an ingredient is to eat it! This always reveals the first effect, and depending on your Alchemy Perks, it may reveal more. The advantage of eating ingredients is that you always receive the first property; it always works. The downside is that for rare items, you'll have to consume the item for no directly beneficial effect.

Experimental Potions: Or, you can learn an Ingredient's properties by attempting to craft a potion with the ingredient. Constant use of a particular ingredient will gradually allow you to learn its effects and discover good combinations with other ingredients.

Crib-Sheets: Or, you can consult this guide, which helpfully lists the four alchemic properties for every Ingredient in Skyrim.

An Example:
Giant's Toe

After wiping out a camp of Giants, you salvage three Giant Toes from their corpses.

You eat one, and learn that its first effect is 'Damage Stamina'. Easy!

A little later, you return to an Alchemy Lab and try combining it with Bone Meal, another ingredient that has the "Damage Stamina" effect. It works, creating a Damage Stamina Poison, but since you already knew both ingredients had that effect, you don't learn anything new.

You then decide to be a little more adventurous, and try combining it with Wheat, an ingredient you know nothing about. Success! Both the Giant Toe and Wheat have two effects in common– "Fortify Health" (the second effect on both ingredients) and "Damage Stamina Regen" (the third effect on Wheat, and the fourth on Giant Toe). You learn the four new effects, and acquire an interesting potion that fortifies your health at the cost of reducing your stamina regen.

⬡ Crafting Potions

In order to craft potions, you must use an Alchemy Lab. If you plan to focus on Alchemy, you'll want to find an Alchemy Lab that you can access quickly, and return to it frequently. Near the start of your adventure, one good location is the Alchemy Lab inside the Sleeping Giant Inn in Riverwood. Later on, you may want to purchase a house (see page 404) for convenient access to your own Alchemy Lab, and plenty of storage space for ingredients.

Selecting Ingredients: Step up to the Alchemy Lab, pick two distinct ingredients (you cannot combine two identical ingredients), and mix them together. You can optionally add a third ingredient if you wish (and want to further experiment).

Experimental Potions: If you don't know any effects that the ingredients share, the Alchemy Lab will caution you that the result is a "Potion of Unknown Effect", but you can still try it.

When you combine Ingredients, the Alchemy Lab checks the complete list of the two (or three) ingredients' effects. If none of those effects match, the crafting fails. If there is one or more match, it succeeds.

Failure: If there were no matches, you receive nothing and use up the ingredients, but still receive a small Alchemy Skill improvement. The Alchemy Lab remembers that the combination failed and grays it out, indicating you don't need to try it again.

Success: If there was a match, the resulting potion or poison has all of the effects that matched, in a much more potent form than simply eating one of the ingredients would have given you. Most of the time, you receive an item with only one effect, but you may end up with two, three, or even four matches.

Potion, or Poison? The resulting mixture is classified as a Potion if its primary effect is beneficial, or a Poison if its primary effect is harmful. You can have Potions with lesser negative effects and Poisons with lesser positive effects, although these aren't usually worth making more than once during experimentation. The Purity Perk allows you to remove these side effects from your mixtures, creating wholly positive potions and negative poisons.

Effect Reference: The Alchemy Lab menu handles all the bookkeeping for you– it knows which ingredients you have, which effects you've learned, and which combinations you've tried before without success. Based on this information, it even recommends ingredients that you know you can combine to produce a specific result, like 'Restore Health'. While these recommendations are great for quickly creating just the potion you need, don't forget to experiment to continue learning new effects.

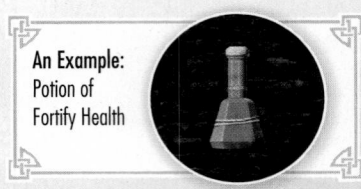

An Example:
Potion of
Fortify Health

After collecting a Blue Mountain Flower (Restore Health, Fortify Conjuration, **Fortify Health**, Damage Magicka Regen), and a Glowing Mushroom (Damage Stamina, **Fortify Health**, Fortify Carry Weight, Damage Stamina Regen), you can combine them to create a **Fortify Health Potion**.

⬡ Advanced Alchemy

Alchemy Skill and Potion Creation

Your Alchemy Skill improves the effectiveness of the potions and poisons you craft:

◇ If an effect has only a magnitude (i.e., Restore 50 Health), your Skill increases it.
◇ If an effect has only a duration (i.e., Invisibility for 30 seconds), your Skill extends it.
◇ If an effect has both a magnitude and a duration, only one of the two values will increase, never both. For Potions and Poisons that affect regeneration rate, the duration increases; for everything else, the magnitude increases.

In addition to your raw skill, the perks in the Alchemy Tree dramatically increase the effectiveness of potions you craft. Because of the number of factors that can affect the potency of these potions, exact statistics are not listed in this guide. Consult the exact values in the Alchemy Lab to see what you can create given your current skill and perks.

Your Alchemy skill increases when:

◇ You learn a new effect for an ingredient.
◇ You successfully craft a potion.
◇ You attempt to craft a potion, but fail (a very small increase).

Three-Ingredient Potions

Potions with three ingredients are more likely succeed (with 12 effects between them, there's a greater chance of at least one match). However, they are also more likely to produce results with multiple effects... which may or may not be a good thing. You might end up with an excellent potion that has three or even four positive effects– or one that has a bizarre mix of positive and negative properties. These can still helpful when trying to learn ingredient effects as quickly as possible, but you may not be able to get much use out of the resulting potion.

After collecting a Giant's Toe (**Damage Stamina**, **Fortify Health**, Fortify Carry Weight, Damage Stamina Regen), some Hanging Moss (Damage Magicka, **Fortify Health**, Damage Magicka Regen, **Fortify One-handed**), and a Rock Warbler Egg (Restore Health, **Fortify One-handed**, **Damage Stamina**, Weakness to Magic) you combine these together to create a Potion. The resulting potion has all three effects that matched: it will Fortify Health, Fortify One-Handed, and Damage Stamina.

An Example: Potion of Fortify Health, Fortify One-Handed, and Damage Stamina

Alchemic Recipes and Combinations

Novice Recipes

If you're just starting out on your adventure, here are a few good recipes to try:

✓	POTION EFFECT	INGREDIENT #1	INGREDIENT #2†
	HEALTH POTIONS		
	Restore Health	Blue Mountain Flower	Butterfly Wing
	Fortify Health	Giant's Toe	Hanging Moss
	Regenerate Health	Juniper Berries	Nordic Barnacle
	MAGICKA POTIONS		
	Restore Magicka	Creep Cluster	Red Mountain Flower
	Fortify Magicka	Red Mountain Flower	Tundra Cotton
	Regenerate Magicka	Garlic	Salt Pile
	STAMINA POTIONS		
	Restore Stamina	Pine Thrush Egg	Purple Mountain Flower
	Fortify Stamina	Garlic	Lavender
	Regenerate Stamina	Bee	Mora Tapinella
	RESISTANCE POTIONS		
	Resist Fire	Fly Amanita	Snowberries
	Resist Frost	Snowberries	Thistle Branch
	Resist Shock	Glowdust	Snowberries
	UTILITY POTIONS		
	Invisibility	Chaurus Eggs	Nirnroot
	Waterbreathing	Chicken's Egg	Nordic Barnacle
	POISONS		
	Damage Health (Weak)	Falmer Ear	Imp Stool
	Damage Health (Strong)	Falmer Ear	River Betty
	Damage Magicka	Butterfly Wing	Hanging Moss
	Paralysis	Canis Root	Imp Stool

Advanced Recipes

At higher levels, once you have a wider range of ingredients at your disposal, you can begin to construct potions with more and more complex effects. Here are just a few examples:

✓	POTION EFFECT	INGREDIENT #1	INGREDIENT #2	INGREDIENT #3†
	TWO-EFFECT POTIONS			
	Restore Health and Fortify Health	Blue Mountain Flower	Wheat	None
	Invisibility and Regen Health	Luna Moth Wing	Vampire Dust	None
	Paralysis and Damage Health	Canis Root	Imp Stool	River Betty
	THREE-EFFECT POTIONS			
	Fortify Heavy Armor, Fortify Block, Resist Frost	Briar Heart	Slaughterfish Scales	Thistle Branch
	Fortify One-handed, Fortify Sneak, Fortify Light Armor	Beehive Husk	Hawk Feathers	Rock Warbler Egg
	Fortify Magicka, Fortify Destruction, Restore Magicka	Briar Heart	Ectoplasm	Glowdust
	Regen Magicka, Fortify Magicka, Restore Magicka	Briar Heart	Jazbay Grapes	Moon Sugar
	FOUR-EFFECT POTIONS			
	Regen Magicka, Resist Frost, Resist Fire, Restore Magicka	Fire Salts	Moon Sugar	Snowberries
	Invisibility, Regen Health, Fortify Light Armor, Cure Disease	Hawk Feathers	Luna Moth Wing	Vampire Dust

 NOTE († The order in which you mix the ingredients doesn't matter).

Please see the Inventory Chapter for tables listing all of the available ingredients and their properties (weight, value, effects). In addition, three sample locations are given where each ingredient can be found (usually in abundance). There is also an Alchemy Effects List, which reveals every effect of an ingredient, and which ingredients have these effects.

ENCHANTING

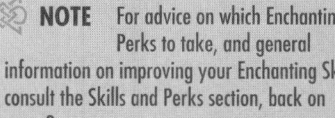 **NOTE** For advice on which Enchanting Perks to take, and general information on improving your Enchanting Skill, consult the Skills and Perks section, back on page 9.

Arcane Enchanting: An Overview

With an Arcane Enchanter, items are both ruined and reborn as new and more powerful objects.

Enchanting requires you to make short-term sacrifices for long-term rewards. The important (and sometimes difficult) choices you make throughout this process determine what items you can create, and how powerful they will be.

In short: Enchanting is the art of **imbuing an item** with **magical enchantments** powered by **soul energy**. However, this is done at the expense of other enchanted items.

To enchant an item, you need:

◊ **An Enchantment.** Before you can imbue an item with an enchantment, you must first learn that enchantment by disenchanting an item with the same base effect.

◊ **A filled Soul Gem.** While you can find filled Soul Gems in the world, you can also create them by using an empty Soul Gem and the Soul Trap spell (Conjuration) or a weapon enchanted with the Soul Trap enchantment.

◊ **An unenchanted item.** These are easy to find, though you may wish to Smith your own in order to have a ready supply of items to enchant.

◊ **The Arcane Enchanter:** To enchant an item, you will also need to use an Arcane Enchanter. If you plan to focus on Enchanting, locate an Arcane Enchanter you can return to quickly and easily, and make a point of visiting it often. Two locations close to your starting point of Helgen are Anise's Cabin across the river from Riverwood, and Farengar's study in Whiterun's palace of Dragonsreach. Later on, you may want to purchase a house with an Arcane Enchanter (see page 404).

Disenchanting Items

The only way to learn new enchantments is to disenchant an existing enchanted item. The disenchanting process destroys the original item, and teaches you the item's base enchantment—that is, its fundamental ability (e.g., 'Fortify Health'), not its specific value ('Fortify Health 50'). Once you learn an enchantment, you can apply it to as many other items as you wish.

Early on, disenchanting may be a difficult, even painful decision— enchanted items are both useful and extremely valuable, while the enchantment you learn does nothing in and of itself. You should definitely make use of enchanted items you find, rather than rushing to disenchant them all. But when you outgrow an item, or find something you aren't interested in, consider disenchanting it instead of selling it— you're making an investment in your future.

It is important to remember that you learn only the base (or general) enchantment, and not the specific enchantment that appears on the item. Because of this, disenchanting a more valuable item doesn't give you a better enchantment, as these examples show:

An Item Example: Boots with Fortify Sneak

Dragonscale Boots of Peerless Sneaking (Value 2,614).

Hide Boots of Minor Sneaking (Value 797).

Both of these items, when disenchanted (and destroyed) teach you the Fortify Sneak base enchantment.

A Weapon Example: Weapons with Absorb Health

Daedric Warhammer of the Vampire (Value 5,236).

Dwarven Dagger of Absorption (Value 324).

Both of these weapons, when disenchanted, grant you the Absorb Health base enchantment.

The conclusion? That – to start with, at least – it is better to destroy a low value item rather than a high value one, especially if you want to use or sell the higher-value item.

However, there is one advantage to disenchanting more expensive items: disenchanting helps increase your Enchanting Skill, and your skill will increase faster when you disenchant a high-value item than when you disenchant a lower-value one.

If you plan to focus on Enchanting, disenchant enchanted items early and often, as soon as they're no longer of use to you, to quickly build your repertoire of effects. If you're coming to Enchanting at a later level (20+), you may want to disenchant higher-valued items to help your skill advance more quickly. You can only learn each base enchantment once, so don't expect to disenchant your way to 100.

> **NOTE** Don't worry about disenchanting Quest or Unique Items; they don't even show up in the Enchanting menu!

Soul Gems

Acquiring Soul Gems

A collection of Soul Gems, just ready to be gathered up and filled.

You can acquire Soul Gems in a number of ways:

Purchasing Filled Soul Gems: You can buy filled soul gems from merchants directly. However, this is an extremely expensive proposition, as a filled gem is three to four times more expensive than a comparable empty one.

Purchasing Empty Soul Gems: If you need to buy a Soul Gem, you're better off purchasing an empty one and filling it yourself. Although this takes a little more work, the savings can help you break even (or even turn a profit) on the item you enchant.

Finding Soul Gems: An even better option is to find (or steal) the Soul Gems you need:

Any Dwarven City, Warlock Den, Vampire Lair, or Nordic Ruin will usually have Soul Gems lying around. Enemies in these areas (especially Dwarven Automatons) often carry Soul Gems as well.

There are a number of areas in the College of Winterhold where you can simply take Soul Gems for free.

Or you can steal them from other mages, such as the Court Wizards or the mages of the College.

Filling Soul Gems

A successful Soul Trap captures a wild animal's essence for your arcane antics.

In order to trap a creature's soul in an empty Soul Gem, you will need either:

The Soul Trap Spell: Cast this spell on a creature and kill it before the spell wears off to snare its soul. If you plan to focus on Enchanting, make sure to purchase this spell from Farengar, the Court Wizard of Whiterun, as soon as possible.

A Soul Trap Enchantment: If casting Soul Trap becomes a nuisance, look for a weapon with the Soul Trap enchantment imbued in it. Then all you need to do is slay the creature using the weapon to capture its soul. You can obviously enchant a weapon for this purpose, as well as finding one.

TIP — When filling a Soul Gem, there are some key points to remember:

◇ Most Soul Gems only hold the souls of creatures, and not humans (or humanoid races).

◇ They only hold souls up to a specific level. To Soul Trap a stronger creature, you need a larger Soul Gem.

◇ After slaying a Soul Trapped creature, their soul is automatically absorbed by the smallest possible empty Soul Gem in your inventory (so you don't need to pick or equip one).

◇ Warning! If you don't have a Soul Gem of the correct size, the soul is captured by the next largest Soul Gem. Although this works, you lose some of that Soul Gem's potential value.

◇ Warning! If you don't have any empty Soul Gems, or Soul Gems large enough to hold the creature's soul, the soul is lost.

◇ Conclusion: Heed these warnings and carry multiple Soul Gems of each size, and check frequently to make sure you know what you're carrying, or you risk wasting a valuable or rare Soul Gem!

◇ Black Soul Gems are rare, but also available. These can hold any human soul, regardless of level.

◇ Undead (Draugr, Skeletons), Daedra, and Dwarven Automatons (Dwarven Spheres, Centurions) don't have souls, and can't be Soul Trapped.

◇ Conjured Atronachs, raised zombies, and Dwarven Automatons (Dwarven Spheres, Centurions) don't have souls and can't be Soul Trapped.

CAUTION — Petty Soul Gems are almost worthless for Enchanting— you'll rarely receive bonuses of more than a point or two. Save them for recharging your weapons, and plan to use at least a Lesser Soul Gem.

NOTE — Need to know exactly what Soul Gem to use on a particular creature? Then cross-reference the level of creature the Soul Gem can hold (in the Soul Gems chart of The Inventory Chapter, on page 86), with the level of the creature in this guide's Bestiary (page 101). Then you'll know which type of Soul Gem is correct for your purposes.

Unenchanted Items

This selection of weaponry looks good enough to try your enchanting on.

Unenchanted weapons and armor can obtained in one of three ways:

By Purchasing Them: This is obviously the fastest and most straightforward option, as most Merchants have a wide variety of unenchanted items for sale. However, if you hope to turn a profit with your Enchanting, you'll need a high Speech Skill (in order to barter the prices down), or the merchant's cut (both when you buy the original item, and then sell the enchanted version of it back to them) will leave you with a loss, not a profit.

By Finding Them: This is a much better plan. Simply grab them while on your travels.

By Smithing Them: True artisans should consider smithing their own weapons and armor (on a Forge), enchanting them, improving them (on a Grindstone or Workbench), and then selling them for incredible profits. If you're not motivated by money, Smithing also allows you to create and enchant exactly the item you want.

Enchanting

Enchanting a Weapon

The tell tale glow of an enchanted weapon, made stronger by a professional imbuer!

Now that your preparations are complete, journey to any Arcane Enchanter with the items you wish to enchant in your inventory. Select the weapon and the Soul Gem first, and then pick the enchantment. This is important, because the type of Soul Gem you use has a huge impact on the next decision you must make: how strong to make the enchantment. Remember, Enchanting is all about choices!

Enchanted Weapons and Charges

All Enchanted Weapons have charges. These represent the amount of soul energy that remains within the weapon. When all of an item's charges are expended, the weapon's enchantment ceases to function (and it essentially becomes a "normal" or unenchanted weapon) until you recharge it.

Think of this as a formula: Charge Capacity ÷ Enchantment Cost = Charges.

Charge Capacity: The item's capacity is determined by the strength of the soul used during the enchanting process. For example, a Grand Soul Gem containing a Grand Soul has a greater capacity than a Petty Soul Gem containing a Petty Soul. Note that capacity is determined by the soul, not the gem– a Grand Soul Gem containing a Petty Soul is no better than a Petty Soul Gem with that soul.

Enchantment Cost: The item's Enchantment Cost depends on three factors:

Inherent Strength. Some enchantments are simply more powerful (and thus more expensive) than others.

Selected Strength. When you select a weapon enchantment, you can use the slider to choose how powerful to make the enchantment. The stronger you make it, the higher the cost, and the fewer total uses you can get from the item.

Your Enchanting Skill. The higher your skill, the lower the cost, and the more total uses you can get from the item.

The soul and your Enchanting Skill also determine the maximum strength of the enchantment you can apply to the item.

The right balance: This choice is entirely up to you– experiment and see what works best for your play style. If you keep a large supply of Soul Gems on hand, recharging a weapon frequently may not be much of an issue. If you don't, or keep forgetting to recharge your weapon, a weaker but longer-lasting enchantment may work out better.

Recharging Weapons

To recharge an enchanted weapon, you need a partially or completely-depleted weapon and a filled Soul Gem. Select the weapon in your inventory, pick Recharge, and then select the Soul Gem you want to use.

TIP — Recharging an enchanted weapon gives you a small boost to your Enchanting skill, and is a great way to use up those Petty Soul Gems.

NOTE — A weapon's maximum charge is fixed when it is created. You can't use the recharging process to give it more charges than it originally had; any excess charges (from a Soul Gem with more charges than the one you used during the initial Enchantment, for example) are lost.

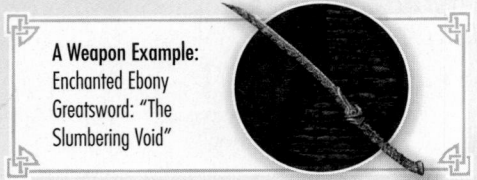

A Weapon Example:
Enchanted Ebony
Greatsword: "The
Slumbering Void"

After constructing an Ebony Greatsword on the Forge (Damage 22, Weight 22, Value 1,440), you take it to an Arcane Enchanter. You pick a Grand Soul Gem and the Absorb Health Enchantment. With an Enchanting skill of 55 and several perks in Enchanting, you have a range of strengths to choose from, from [Absorb Health 1, 800 Charges] to [Absorb Health 13, 47 Charges]. You select the strongest version of the effect, rename the item, and craft it. You now posess "The Slumbering Void" (Damage 22, Weight 22, Value 2,304, Absorb 13 points of health.).

> **NOTE** Remember, your version of "The Slumbering Void" may have different statistics, as it changes depending on your skills.

Enchanting Armor

Crafting a set of armor and enchanting it gives you the very best in outfits.

To enchant a piece of armor, visit an Arcane Enchanter with the items in your inventory. Always choose the armor piece first, then the enchantment, and then the soul gem.

Enchantment Restrictions: Not all Armor Enchantments can be applied to all pieces of armor. Sometimes, these restrictions are logical: Muffle (quiet movement) can only be placed on boots. Waterbreathing can be placed on Helmets, but never boots. But other restrictions are more complex and less obvious. Fortunately, the armor enchantment chart in The Inventory chapter has all the details.

Enchanted Armor Strength: Once you've selected a piece of armor and an enchantment you want to apply to it, you still need to choose a Soul Gem. Unlike Enchanted Weapons, Enchanted Armor does not have charges: the armor grants you a constant bonus as long as you wear it. Instead, the soul's capacity, in combination with your Enchanting Skill, determines the strength of the enchantment you can create. In effect, your skill allows you to squeeze more power from a given Soul Gem.

> **TIP** Remember, all numeric bonuses from Enchantments "stack", meaning you can increase any stat you wish by (for example) enchanting a helmet and armor with the same Enchantment. This only applies to Enchantments with numeric values; you can't (for example) have a Waterbreathing Enchantment on two pieces of equipment and expect any additional benefit.

An Armor Example:
Enchanted Daedric
Armor: "Azura's Wall"

After constructing a suit of Daedric Armor on the Forge (Armor 49, Weight 50, Value 3200), you take it across to an Arcane Enchanter and pick the Fortify Healing Rate Enchantment. You then need to select a Soul Gem. With an Enchanting skill of 55 and several perks in Enchanting, a Common Soul Gem will give you [+5% Healing Rate], a Greater Soul Gem [+11%], and a Grand Soul Gem [+17%]. You select the Grand Soul Gem, rename the item, and craft it. You now posess "Azura's Wall" (Armor 49, Weight 50, Value 3842, Health regenerates 17% faster.)

General Advice

> **TIP** If you want to make money with Enchanting, find or make most of the components yourself. Otherwise, the merchant's mark-up on the item and Soul Gem will wipe out the additional value you create by adding the enchantment.

Your character level and the item you are enchanting have no effect on the strength of the enchantment. You can infuse the same enchantment into an Iron Helm as into a Daedric Helm.

All Armor Enchantments stack, so a Cuirass and Gauntlets that both increase your Heavy Armor skill by +10% will together give you a bonus of +20%. Stacking is especially powerful with Elemental Resistance Enchantments (to Fire, Frost, or Shock): keep a few items on hand and equip them as appropriate if a dragon attacks. Note that there is a limit to this-- at most, you can have an 85% Resistance to Magic, Fire, Frost, or Shock damage. Beyond that point, any further bonuses are wasted.

If you wield two weapons, don't forget to enchant them with complimentary enchantments! Two Fire, Frost, or Shock damage enchantments are great for causing maximum damage, or combine Absorb Health and Absorb Stamina enchantments to sustain you in a long battle.

You can't make your own enchanted Staffs, Scrolls, or Spell Tomes.

Disenchant junk. If you don't need the gold, it pays to disenchant any cheap enchanted items you find so you can take advantage of their effects later on. If an enchanted item has outlived its usefulness and been drained of charges, instead of recharging it, you may want to disenchant it, learn its effect, and apply that effect to another item instead.

Get Soul Trap. The Soul Trap spell is critical to Enchanting, and worth picking up as soon as possible if you plan to focus on this skill. Provided you have the Soul Gems, Soul Trap everything you can so you have filled gems to power and recharge your items.

Combine both Smithing and Enchanting to get the maximum benefit from both skills, crafting and enchanting incredibly powerful weapons and armor to enhance your style of play.

> **NOTE** The Inventory Chapter has tables listing the Base Enchantments for weapons and armor you disenchant, Enchantment Modifiers (the Enchantments that appear on items you find in the world), all the different kinds of Soul Gems, and the levels of the creature they can hold.

SMITHING

NOTE For advice on which Smithing Perks to take, and general information on improving your Smithing Skill, consult the Skills and Perks section, back on page 9.

Forging Ahead: An Overview

A noble Nord profession, a trade of gruff artisans occurring across the realm.

Smithing is the art of creating and improving weapons and armor, accomplished through a series of progressive improvements. Smithing is straightforward, fast, and reliable. Unlike Alchemy and Enchanting, there are no complicated choices or arcane experiments to perform: You know precisely what is needed to construct or improve an item, and what the end result of your sweat and toil will be.

In short: Smithing involves **Forging** and **progressively Improving Items**.

TIP There are a number of secondary crafting activities that you may want explore if you plan to focus on Smithing, as they produce many of the raw materials required for this craft. These activities are not required (you can buy everything you need from other smiths), and do not improve your Smithing skill, but they are the cheapest way to obtain raw materials (outside of stealing them). For more information on Mining, Smelting, and Tanning, see page 52.

Forging

The Forging Process

The Blacksmith's Forge: Mold raw materials into fabled weapons and armor.

The first step in Smithing is to locate a Blacksmith's Forge or Anvil, where the process of making new weapons and armor first begins. When you interact with a Forge, a complete list of the items you can create, and the components you need to make them, is shown. This list expands dramatically as you take perks in your Smithing Skill. If you have the necessary materials, simply choose the item you wish to craft, and it is hammered out on the Forge. Simple!

NOTE Your Smithing Skill improves each time you craft an item using the Forge (although it may not increase by a full point). However, remember that your Skill has no direct effect on the items you create: an Iron Sword is an Iron Sword, whether it was made by a novice Blacksmith in Riften or Eorlund Gray-Mane on the Skyforge itself!

As your adventure begins, your Smithing Skill is low, meaning you can only work with a few kinds of basic materials, such as Iron, Hide, and Leather. However, as your Smithing Skill increases, and you begin to choose perks in the Smithing constellation, you gradually unlock the ability to Forge more and more varieties of materials into weapons and armor. At the highest levels, this includes the fabled Daedric, Dragonplate, and Dragonscale gear!

Approach the Blacksmith's Forge with 4 Iron Ingots and 3 Leather Strips in your inventory. Activate the Forge, select the Iron Warhammer from the Iron category, and craft it. Your materials are consumed by the forging process, and you receive a shiny new Iron Warhammer.

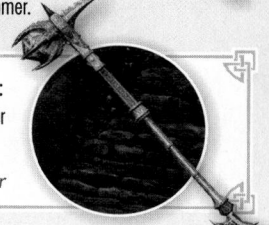

A Novice Example: Iron Warhammer

An Iron Warhammer

Once your Smithing Skill reaches 90, and you've taken the Daedric Smithing Perk, approach the Blacksmith's Forge with 5 Ebony Ingots, 3 Leather Strips, and a Daedra Heart in your inventory. Activate the Forge, select the Daedric Warhammer from the Daedric category, and craft it. Your materials are consumed, and you receive this wicked-looking warhammer.

A Master Example: Daedric Warhammer

A Daedric Warhammer

Forging Materials

Forging usually requires components like metal ingots, leather, and leather strips. However, the highest-quality items may also require more or expensive materials, such as quicksilver, dragon scales, or daeda hearts. Knowing what is needed to forge your next level of gear is imperative so you can keep an eye out for it on your travels.

Purchasing Materials: The easiest way to acquire materials is simply to purchase them. In towns (such as Riverwood), you'll almost always find a Blacksmith working the Forge. These craftsmen and women typically have ingots, ore, leather, and leather strips for sale. As your level increases, Smiths begin to carry higher-level materials too. However, you will always have to search for the rarest of components.

The Purist Smithy: The purist won't settle for purchasing materials when they're free for the taking in the wild! Instead, they seek out mines (or ore veins dotted throughout the wilderness), to mine your own ore with a trusty Pickaxe, and use the Smelter to smelt your own ingots. Hunt wild animals, gather their pelts and use Tanning Racks to turn their hides into the leather and leather strips you require. You're free to live off the land; not fill some blacksmith's sweaty pockets!

In short: Purchasing materials is far faster and easier. Finding your own materials takes time, but allows you to turn a better profit.

The Economics of Forging

Unless you're aggressively focusing your Smithing Skill, you can often find or purchase gear of a particular type before you're able to forge it yourself. Forging is still great for completing a set of armor (for example, hammering out a Dwarven Helmet to go with your Dwarven Armor), so you can quality for the Matching Set (Heavy Armor Perk) or Custom Fit (Light Armor Perk) bonuses.

The very best weapons and armor (Ebony, Daedric, Dragonscale, and Dragonplate) can never be bought in shops, so you must either find them in dungeons or forge them yourself. Smithing really pays off here– while it's still challenging to forge a complete set of Daedric or Dragonplate gear, it's far easier than scrounging through dungeon after dungeon in the hope of finding just the right piece to complete a set. Smithing is also excellent for creating non-enchanted items you're planning to enchant later using your Enchanting Skill.

While you can make money by forging your own items and then selling them, you need to be careful in how you go about it. Purchasing materials from a merchant, taking them to a Forge to create an item, and then returning to sell the item back to the merchant may help you improve your Smithing Skill, but financially, it's always a losing proposition. If you want to use Smithing to make money, it's always better to gather materials from the wild, although that can become a time-consuming process.

If you decide to focus on Smithing, you'll occasionally find you require certain materials before they're commonly available from merchants. Once again, this is when foraging in the wilderness, or swinging a pickaxe at an ore vein is your best option. Check the Mining section on page 52 for locations where rare ores can be found.

Check the Mining section on page 52 for locations where rare ores can be found.

> **NOTE** All Blacksmith Forges allow you to forge of the same weapons and armor; there's no difference between them. With one exception. After completing The Companions Quest: Glory of the Dead, you can craft a unique set of Nord Hero weapons at Eorlund Gray-Mane's Skyforge in Whiterun.

Improving Items

The Grindstone: Sharpen a blade to improve its damage and value.

The Workbench: Temper armor into defensive and wearable works of art.

Contrary to what you might believe, the heart of Smithing lies not in crafting items, but in improving them. As with Forging, these improvements are simple, and result in equally straightforward bonuses to your attack (weapons) and defense (armor) that can significantly improve your combat effectiveness. As you might expect, arms and armor improved in this way also commands a premium when sold to merchants.

> **TIP** A Master Blacksmith can improve plain Steel Armor to make it almost as strong as Dragonplate. And if he's improving Dragonplate? The results are even more spectacular!

The Grindstone: You improve weapons by sharpening them at a Grindstone.

The Workbench: You improve armor by tempering it at a Workbench.

When interacting with either of these crafting stations, you are given a complete list of the items you have (whether they were found, bought, stolen, or made by you) that can be improved, along with the materials you need to improve each of them. Improving a weapon or piece of armor always requires one piece of that item's primary material; so sharpening an Iron Sword requires one Iron Ingot, while tempering a Dragonscale Cuirass requires one Dragon Scale. The clue is in the name!

In exchange for using this material, you receive a bonus to your weapon's damage, or armor's defense rating based on your Smithing Skill and Perks. As your Smithing Skill improves, you're able to return to a Grindstone or Workbench and improve the same item again (at the cost of one material each time), to increase that bonus still further, if you wish.

Rules to remember

Bonuses are Not Cumulative: Having sharpened an Iron Sword with a Smithing Skill of 25 (using an Iron Ingot), you return to the Grindstone with a Smithing Skill of 50 (and expend another Iron Ingot) to receive a better bonus. However, if you'd waited and brought the sword to the Grindstone for the first time at Skill 50, the bonus would be the same.

Bonuses stack with Enchantments: However, if you're a skilled craftsman in the arts of Smithing and Enchanting, you can Forge an item, then both Improve and Enchant it for maximum damage. Note that you need the Arcane Blacksmith Perk in order to improve enchanted weapons and armor, so if you don't have it, make sure to sharpen or temper the item before you enchant it! Otherwise, the order doesn't matter.

Nomenclature: When you improve an item, it receives a modifier that indicates the amount of improvement you've made to the weapon. This modifier is based on your Smithing Skill and Perks. After you've improved an item, you can only improve it again once your Smithing Skill and Perks will allow you to raise it to the next modifier rank. For example:

If you have a Smithing Skill of 39 and the Steel Smithing Perk, and improve a Steel Sword at a Grindstone, the sword will receive the 'Superior' modifier and a [+3] damage bonus.

Return with a Smithing Skill of 40, and your skill has reached the next threshold, allowing you to improve the sword again. This gives it the 'Exquisite' modifier and a better bonus, [+5].

If you come back with a Smithing Skill of 55, your skill has not yet reached the next threshold, so you can't improve that sword again. If you have a different Steel Sword you want to improve, it will also receive the 'Exquisite' modifier and a [+5] bonus.

> **CAUTION** There are no perks that improve iron weapons; only weapons of other metal types.

Approach a Grindstone with an Iron Warhammer and an Iron Ingot in your inventory. Interact with the Grindstone, select the Iron Warhammer, and hit Craft. With a Smithing Skill of 42, the Iron Warhammer (Superior) receives +3 Damage and its value increases by +20 (25%).

A Novice Example: Improving the Iron Warhammer

The Iron Warhammer (Superior)

Bring a Daedric Warhammer and an Ebony Ingot to the grindstone and improve it. With a Smithing Skill of 100 and the Daedric Smithing Perk, the Daedric Warhammer (Legendary) receives +11 Damage and its value doubles, increasing by 4000. Given that the ingot costs a mere 150 gold, that's a 3,850 gold profit!

A Master Example: Improving a Daedric Warhammer

The Daedric Warhammer (Legendary)

The Economics of Improvements

Improving the items you find (as well as those you forge) is simple, quick, and relatively inexpensive, making this an excellent way to both increase your Smithing Skill and earn some extra gold. Simply collect weapons and armor throughout your travels, then improve them before selling them for a profit.

At lower levels, this yields dividends, as you're constantly using your Skill, and may even make your money back (especially if you mine, smelt, or tan your own materials). At higher levels, with good Smithing (and Speech Skills for bartering), you can easily rake in hundreds or even thousands of additional gold for each haul of loot.

General Advice

Improve and Sharpen everything. As discussed above, this is one of the fastest and easiest ways to make money, especially later in the game, with high Smithing and Speech skills.

Stop Overpaying for Materials. Smithing can be an expensive hobby if you have to buy all your components from local merchants. If you're tired of paying a premium on leather or ingots, and you have some time to spare, make them yourself!

Delve into Dwarven Ruins. One of the easiest ways to level your Smithing Skill is to clear out a Dwarven Ruin, then go back and make a second trip to haul out all of the scrap metal you can carry. Smelt it down into Dwarven Metal Ingots, and you'll have more materials than you know what do to with.

Save those Daedra Hearts. Daedra Hearts are among the rarest ingredients, but they're essential for forging Daedric Weapons and Armor. If you find any early in your adventure, save them until you're ready for them. Otherwise, you'll have to make them yourself with an equally rare ingredient (in College of Winterhold Radiant Quest: The Atronach Forge) or track down the one merchant who sells them (Enthir, also at the College of Winterhold) and pay an outrageous premium.

Smithing Recipes

> **NOTE** The following table lists the recipes for forging each weapon and piece of armor. Since the Tempering recipes are straightforward (always one item of the primary material), they aren't necessary to show.

SMITHING IMPROVEMENT MODIFIERS

✓	NAME	SKILL (WITH PERKS)	✓	NAME	SKILL (WITH PERKS)
	Fine	0-19		Flawless	60-79
	Superior	20-39		Epic	80-99
	Exquisite	40-59		Legendary	100

✓	INGREDIENTS	NAME	DMG/AMR	WEIGHT	VALUE
	HIDE				
	3 Leather Strips, 4 Leather	Hide Armor	20	5	50
	2 Leather Strips, 2 Leather	Hide Boots	5	1	10
	2 Leather Strips, 1 Leather	Hide Bracers	5	1	10
	1 Leather Strips, 2 Leather	Hide Helmet	10	2	25
	2 Leather Strips, 4 Leather	Hide Shield	15	4	25
	IRON				
	3 Leather Strips, 5 Iron Ingot, Corundum Ingot	Banded Iron Armor	28	35	200
	1 Leather Strips, 4 Iron Ingot, Corundum Ingot	Banded Iron Shield	22	12	100
	3 Leather Strips, 5 Iron Ingot	Iron Armor	25	30	125
	2 Leather Strips, 4 Iron Ingot	Iron Battleaxe	16	20	55
	2 Leather Strips, 3 Iron Ingot	Iron Boots	10	6	25
	1 Leather Strips, 1 Iron Ingot	Iron Dagger	4	2	10
	2 Leather Strips, 2 Iron Ingot	Iron Gauntlets	10	5	25
	2 Leather Strips, 4 Iron Ingot	Iron Greatsword	15	16	50
	2 Leather Strips, 3 Iron Ingot	Iron Helmet	15	5	60
	2 Leather Strips, 3 Iron Ingot	Iron Mace	9	13	35
	1 Leather Strips, 4 Iron Ingot	Iron Shield	20	12	60
	1 Leather Strips, 2 Iron Ingot	Iron Sword	7	9	25
	2 Leather Strips, 2 Iron Ingot	Iron War Axe	8	11	30
	3 Leather Strips, 4 Iron Ingot	Iron Warhammer	18	24	60
	STUDDED				
	3 Leather Strips, 4 Leather, 1 Iron Ingot	Studded Armor	23	6	75
	IMPERIAL				
	3 Leather Strips, 2 Leather, 4 Steel Ingot	Imperial Armor	25	35	100
	2 Leather Strips, 1 Leather, 2 Steel Ingot	Imperial Boots	10	8	20
	2 Leather Strips, 1 Leather, 2 Steel Ingot	Imperial Bracers	10	4	15
	1 Leather Strips, 1 Leather, 2 Steel Ingot	Imperial Helmet	15	5	50
	2 Leather Strips, 4 Steel Ingot	Imperial Shield	20	12	50

✓	INGREDIENTS	NAME	DMG/AMR	WEIGHT	VALUE
	STEEL				
	3 Leather Strips, 2 Leather, 3 Steel Ingot, 2 Corundum Ingot	Scaled Armor	32	6	350
	2 Leather Strips, 1 Leather, 2 Steel Ingot, 1 Corundum Ingot	Scaled Boots	9	2	70
	2 Leather Strips, 1 Leather, 1 Steel Ingot, 1 Corundum Ingot	Scaled Bracers	9	2	70
	1 Leather Strips, 1 Leather, 2 Steel Ingot	Scaled Helmet	14	2	175
	3 Leather Strips, 4 Steel Ingot, 1 Iron Ingot	Steel Armor	31	35	275
	2 Leather Strips, 4 Steel Ingot, 1 Iron Ingot	Steel Battleaxe	18	21	100
	2 Leather Strips, 3 Steel Ingot, 1 Iron Ingot	Steel Cuffed Boots	12	8	55
	1 Leather Strips, 1 Steel Ingot, 1 Iron Ingot	Steel Dagger	5	2.5	18
	3 Leather Strips, 4 Steel Ingot, 2 Iron Ingot	Steel Greatsword	17	17	90
	2 Leather Strips, 2 Steel Ingot, 1 Iron Ingot	Steel Helmet	17	5	125
	2 Leather Strips, 2 Steel Ingot, 1 Iron Ingot	Steel Horned Helmet	17	5	125
	2 Leather Strips, 2 Steel Ingot, 1 Iron Ingot	Steel Imperial Gauntlets	12	4	55
	1 Leather Strips, 3 Steel Ingot, 1 Iron Ingot	Steel Mace	10	14	65
	2 Leather Strips, 2 Steel Ingot, 1 Iron Ingot	Steel Nordic Gauntlets	12	4	55
	3 Leather Strips, 3 Steel Ingot, 1 Iron Ingot, 1 Corundum Ingot	Steel Plate Armor	40	38	625
	2 Leather Strips, 2 Steel Ingot, 1 Iron Ingot, 1 Corundum Ingot	Steel Plate Boots	14	9	125
	2 Leather Strips, 2 Steel Ingot, 1 Iron Ingot, 1 Corundum Ingot	Steel Plate Gauntlets	14	6	125
	2 Leather Strips, 2 Steel Ingot, 1 Iron Ingot, 1 Corundum Ingot	Steel Plate Helmet	19	6	300
	1 Leather Strips, 3 Steel Ingot, 1 Iron Ingot	Steel Shield	24	12	150
	2 Leather Strips, 3 Steel Ingot, 1 Iron Ingot	Steel Shin Boots	12	8	55
	1 Leather Strips, 2 Steel Ingot, 1 Iron Ingot	Steel Sword	8	10	45
	2 Leather Strips, 2 Steel Ingot, 1 Iron Ingot	Steel War Axe	9	12	55
	3 Leather Strips, 4 Steel Ingot, 1 Iron Ingot	Steel Warhammer	20	25	110
	LEATHER				
	3 Leather Strips, 4 Leather	Leather Armor	26	6	125
	2 Leather Strips, 2 Leather	Leather Boots	7	2	25
	2 Leather Strips, 1 Leather	Leather Bracers	7	2	25

☑	INGREDIENTS	NAME	DMG/AMR	WEIGHT	VALUE
	1 Leather Strips, 2 Leather	Leather Helmet	12	2	60

DWARVEN

☑	INGREDIENTS	NAME	DMG/AMR	WEIGHT	VALUE
	3 Leather Strips, 3 Dwarven Metal Ingot, 1 Iron Ingot, 1 Steel Ingot	Dwarven Armor	34	45	400
	2 Leather Strips, 2 Dwarven Metal Ingot, 1 Iron Ingot, 2 Steel Ingot	Dwarven Battleaxe	20	23	300
	2 Leather Strips, 1 Dwarven Metal Ingot, 1 Iron Ingot, 1 Steel Ingot	Dwarven Boots	13	10	85
	2 Dwarven Metal Ingot, 1 Iron Ingot	Dwarven Bow	12	10	270
	1 Leather Strips, 1 Dwarven Metal Ingot, 1 Iron Ingot, 1 Steel Ingot	Dwarven Dagger	7	3.5	55
	2 Leather Strips, 1 Dwarven Metal Ingot, 1 Iron Ingot, 1 Steel Ingot	Dwarven Gauntlets	13	8	85
	3 Leather Strips, 2 Dwarven Metal Ingot, 2 Iron Ingot, 2 Steel Ingot	Dwarven Greatsword	19	19	270
	2 Leather Strips, 2 Dwarven Metal Ingot, 1 Iron Ingot, 1 Steel Ingot	Dwarven Helmet	18	12	200
	1 Leather Strips, 2 Dwarven Metal Ingot, 1 Iron Ingot, 1 Steel Ingot	Dwarven Mace	12	16	190
	1 Leather Strips, 2 Dwarven Metal Ingot, 1 Iron Ingot, 1 Steel Ingot	Dwarven Shield	26	12	225
	1 Leather Strips, 1 Dwarven Metal Ingot, 1 Iron Ingot, 1 Steel Ingot	Dwarven Sword	10	12	135
	2 Leather Strips, 1 Dwarven Metal Ingot, 1 Iron Ingot, 1 Steel Ingot	Dwarven War Axe	11	14	165
	3 Leather Strips, 2 Dwarven Metal Ingot, 1 Iron Ingot, 2 Steel Ingot	Dwarven Warhammer	22	27	325

ELVEN

☑	INGREDIENTS	NAME	DMG/AMR	WEIGHT	VALUE
	3 Leather Strips, 1 Leather, 4 Refined Moonstone, 1 Iron Ingot	Elven Armor	29	4	225
	2 Leather Strips, 2 Refined Moonstone, 2 Iron Ingot, 1 Quicksilver Ingot	Elven Battleaxe	21	24	520
	2 Leather Strips, 1 Leather, 2 Refined Moonstone, 1 Iron Ingot	Elven Boots	8	1	45
	2 Refined Moonstone, 1 Quicksilver Ingot	Elven Bow	13	12	470
	1 Leather Strips, 1 Refined Moonstone, 1 Iron Ingot, 1 Quicksilver Ingot	Elven Dagger	8	4	95
	2 Leather Strips, 1 Leather, 1 Refined Moonstone, 1 Iron Ingot	Elven Gauntlets	8	1	45
	3 Leather Strips, 4 Refined Moonstone, 1 Iron Ingot, 1 Quicksilver Ingot	Elven Gilded Armor	35	4	550
	3 Leather Strips, 2 Refined Moonstone, 2 Iron Ingot, 1 Quicksilver Ingot	Elven Greatsword	20	20	470
	1 Leather Strips, 1 Leather, 2 Refined Moonstone, 1 Iron Ingot	Elven Helmet	13	1	110
	1 Leather Strips, 2 Refined Moonstone, 1 Iron Ingot, 1 Quicksilver Ingot	Elven Mace	13	17	330
	2 Leather Strips, 4 Refined Moonstone, 1 Iron Ingot	Elven Shield	21	4	115
	1 Leather Strips, 1 Refined Moonstone, 1 Iron Ingot, 1 Quicksilver Ingot	Elven Sword	11	13	235
	2 Leather Strips, 1 Refined Moonstone, 1 Iron Ingot, 1 Quicksilver Ingot	Elven War Axe	12	15	280
	3 Leather Strips, 2 Refined Moonstone, 2 Iron Ingot, 1 Quicksilver Ingot	Elven Warhammer	23	28	565

ORCISH

☑	INGREDIENTS	NAME	DMG/AMR	WEIGHT	VALUE
	3 Leather Strips, 4 Orichalcum Ingot, 1 Iron Ingot	Orcish Armor	40	35	1000
	2 Leather Strips, 4 Orichalcum Ingot, 1 Iron Ingot	Orcish Battleaxe	19	25	165
	2 Leather Strips, 3 Orichalcum Ingot, 1 Iron Ingot	Orcish Boots	15	7	200
	2 Orichalcum Ingot, 1 Iron Ingot	Orcish Bow	10	9	150
	1 Leather Strips, 1 Orichalcum Ingot, 1 Iron Ingot	Orcish Dagger	6	3	30
	2 Leather Strips, 2 Orichalcum Ingot, 1 Iron Ingot	Orcish Gauntlets	15	7	200
	3 Leather Strips, 4 Orichalcum Ingot, 2 Iron Ingot	Orcish Greatsword	18	18	75
	2 Leather Strips, 2 Orichalcum Ingot, 1 Iron Ingot	Orcish Helmet	20	8	500
	1 Leather Strips, 3 Orichalcum Ingot, 1 Iron Ingot	Orcish Mace	11	15	105
	2 Leather Strips, 3 Orichalcum Ingot, 1 Iron Ingot	Orcish Shield	30	14	500
	1 Leather Strips, 2 Orichalcum Ingot, 1 Iron Ingot	Orcish Sword	9	11	75
	2 Leather Strips, 2 Orichalcum Ingot, 1 Iron Ingot	Orcish War Axe	10	13	90
	3 Leather Strips, 4 Orichalcum Ingot, 1 Iron Ingot	Orcish Warhammer	21	26	180

EBONY

☑	INGREDIENTS	NAME	DMG/AMR	WEIGHT	VALUE
	3 Leather Strips, 5 Ebony Ingot	Ebony Armor	43	38	1500
	2 Leather Strips, 5 Ebony Ingot	Ebony Battleaxe	23	26	1585
	2 Leather Strips, 3 Ebony Ingot	Ebony Boots	16	7	275
	3 Ebony Ingot	Ebony Bow	17	16	1440
	1 Leather Strips, 1 Ebony Ingot	Ebony Dagger	10	5	290
	2 Leather Strips, 2 Ebony Ingot	Ebony Gauntlets	16	7	275
	3 Leather Strips, 5 Ebony Ingot	Ebony Greatsword	22	22	1440
	2 Leather Strips, 3 Ebony Ingot	Ebony Helmet	21	10	750
	1 Leather Strips, 3 Ebony Ingot	Ebony Mace	16	19	1000
	1 Leather Strips, 4 Ebony Ingot	Ebony Shield	32	14	750
	1 Leather Strips, 2 Ebony Ingot	Ebony Sword	13	15	720
	2 Leather Strips, 2 Ebony Ingot	Ebony War Axe	15	17	865
	3 Leather Strips, 5 Ebony Ingot	Ebony Warhammer	25	30	1725

GLASS

☑	INGREDIENTS	NAME	DMG/AMR	WEIGHT	VALUE
	3 Leather Strips, 1 Leather, 4 Refined Malachite, 2 Refined Moonstone	Glass Armor	38	7	900
	2 Leather Strips, 2 Refined Malachite, 2 Refined Moonstone	Glass Arrow	18	0	6
	2 Leather Strips, 1 Leather, 2 Refined Malachite, 1 Refined Moonstone	Glass Battleaxe	22	25	900
	2 Refined Malachite, 1 Refined Moonstone	Glass Boots	11	2	190
	1 Leather Strips, 1 Refined Malachite, 1 Refined Moonstone	Glass Bow	15	14	820
	2 Leather Strips, 1 Leather, 1 Refined Malachite, 1 Refined Moonstone	Glass Dagger	9	4.5	165
	3 Leather Strips, 2 Refined Malachite, 2 Refined Moonstone	Glass Gauntlets	11	2	190
	1 Leather Strips, 1 Leather, 2 Refined Malachite, 1 Refined Moonstone	Glass Greatsword	21	22	820
	3 Leather Strips, 2 Refined Malachite, 1 Refined Moonstone	Glass Helmet	16	2	450
	1 Leather Strips, 2 Refined Malachite, 1 Refined Moonstone	Glass Mace	14	18	575

✓	INGREDIENTS	NAME	DMG/AMR	WEIGHT	VALUE
☐	2 Leather Strips, 4 Refined Malachite, 1 Refined Moonstone	Glass Shield	27	6	450
☐	1 Leather Strips, 1 Refined Malachite, 1 Refined Moonstone	Glass Sword	12	14	410
☐	2 Leather Strips, 1 Refined Malachite, 1 Refined Moonstone	Glass War Axe	13	16	490
☐	3 Leather Strips, 3 Refined Malachite, 2 Refined Moonstone	Glass Warhammer	24	29	985

DRAGON

✓	INGREDIENTS	NAME	DMG/AMR	WEIGHT	VALUE
☐	3 Leather Strips, 3 Dragon Scales, 2 Dragon Bone	Dragonplate Armor	46	40	2125
☐	2 Leather Strips, 3 Dragon Scales, 1 Dragon Bone	Dragonplate Boots	17	8	425
☐	2 Leather Strips, 2 Dragon Scales, 1 Dragon Bone	Dragonplate Gauntlets	17	8	425
☐	2 Leather Strips, 2 Dragon Scales, 1 Dragon Bone	Dragonplate Helmet	22	8	1050
☐	1 Leather Strips, 3 Dragon Scales, 1 Dragon Bone	Dragonplate Shield	34	15	1050
☐	3 Leather Strips, 1 Leather, 4 Dragon Scales, 2 Iron Ingot	Dragonscale Armor	41	10	1500
☐	2 Leather Strips, 1 Leather, 2 Dragon Scales, 1 Iron Ingot	Dragonscale Boots	12	3	300
☐	2 Leather Strips, 1 Leather, 2 Dragon Scales, 1 Iron Ingot	Dragonscale Gauntlets	12	3	300
☐	1 Leather Strips, 1 Leather, 2 Dragon Scales, 1 Iron Ingot	Dragonscale Helmet	17	4	750
☐	2 Leather Strips, 4 Dragon Scales, 2 Iron Ingot	Dragonscale Shield	29	6	750

DAEDRIC

✓	INGREDIENTS	NAME	DMG/AMR	WEIGHT	VALUE
☐	3 Leather Strips, 5 Ebony Ingot, 1 Daedra Heart	Daedric Armor	49	50	3200
☐	2 Leather Strips, 5 Ebony Ingot, 1 Daedra Heart	Daedric Battleaxe	25	27	2750
☐	2 Leather Strips, 3 Ebony Ingot, 1 Daedra Heart	Daedric Boots	18	10	625
☐	3 Ebony Ingot, 1 Daedra Heart	Daedric Bow	19	18	2500
☐	1 Leather Strips, 1 Ebony Ingot, 1 Daedra Heart	Daedric Dagger	11	6	500
☐	2 Leather Strips, 2 Ebony Ingot, 1 Daedra Heart	Daedric Gauntlets	18	6	625
☐	3 Leather Strips, 5 Ebony Ingot, 1 Daedra Heart	Daedric Greatsword	24	23	2500
☐	2 Leather Strips, 3 Ebony Ingot, 1 Daedra Heart	Daedric Helmet	23	15	1600
☐	1 Leather Strips, 3 Ebony Ingot, 1 Daedra Heart	Daedric Mace	16	20	1750
☐	1 Leather Strips, 4 Ebony Ingot, 1 Daedra Heart	Daedric Shield	36	15	1600

✓	INGREDIENTS	NAME	DMG/AMR	WEIGHT	VALUE
☐	1 Leather Strips, 2 Ebony Ingot, 1 Daedra Heart	Daedric Sword	14	16	1250
☐	2 Leather Strips, 2 Ebony Ingot, 1 Daedra Heart	Daedric War Axe	15	18	1500
☐	3 Leather Strips, 5 Ebony Ingot, 1 Daedra Heart	Daedric Warhammer	27	31	4000

JEWELRY

✓	INGREDIENTS	NAME	DMG/AMR	WEIGHT	VALUE
☐	1 Flawless Diamond, 1 Gold Ingot	Gold Diamond Necklace	0	0.5	1200
☐	1 Diamond, 1 Gold Ingot	Gold Diamond Ring	0	0.25	900
☐	1 Emerald, 1 Gold Ingot	Gold Emerald Ring	0	0.25	700
☐	2 Flawless Amethyst, 1 Gold Ingot	Gold Jeweled Necklace	0	0.5	485
☐	1 Gold Ingot	Gold Necklace	0	0.5	120
☐	1 Gold Ingot	2 Gold Ring	0	0.25	75
☐	1 Flawless Ruby, 1 Gold Ingot	Gold Ruby Necklace	0	0.5	550
☐	1 Sapphire, 1 Gold Ingot	Gold Sapphire Ring	0	0.25	500
☐	1 Amethyst, 1 Silver Ingot	Silver Amethyst Ring	0	0.25	180
☐	1 Flawless Emerald, 1 Silver Ingot	Silver Emerald Necklace	0	0.5	830
☐	1 Garnet, 1 Silver Ingot	Silver Garnet Ring	0	0.25	160
☐	1 Flawless Garnet, 1 Silver Ingot	Silver Jeweled Necklace	0	0.5	380
☐	1 Silver Ingot	Silver Necklace	0	0.5	60
☐	1 Silver Ingot	2 Silver Ring	0	0.25	30
☐	1 Ruby, 1 Silver Ingot	Silver Ruby Ring	0	0.25	260
☐	1 Flawless Sapphire, 1 Silver Ingot	Silver Sapphire Necklace	0	0.5	580

DRAUGR (SKYFORGE ONLY, AFTER GLORY OF THE DEAD)

✓	INGREDIENTS	NAME	DMG/AMR	WEIGHT	VALUE
☐	3 Leather Strips, 3 Steel Ingot, 1 Ancient Nord Battle Axe	Nord Hero Battle Axe	32	20	239
☐	3 Leather Strips, 3 Steel Ingot, 1 Ancient Nord Greatsword	Nord Hero Greatsword	30	16	199
☐	2 Leather Strips, 2 Steel Ingot, 1 Ancient Sword	Nord Hero Sword	30	9	107
☐	2 Leather Strips, 2 Steel Ingot, 1 Ancient Nord War Axe	Nord Hero War Axe	32	11	131

OTHER CRAFTING ACTIVITIES

 Cooking

 NOTE Cooking meats, soups, and stews does not increase any skill.

Throw the meat, plants, and other ingredients (often mead-related) into a pot. Stir and stave off the hunger pangs.

Cooking allows you to transform meat, vegetables, and other ingredients into better-tasting, higher-quality food. Cooking is a rudimentary method of living off the land, and is far surpassed by Alchemy (which is a skill, and creates Potions that are much more potent).

Cooking requires a Cooking Pot or Cooking Spit, which can easily be found in every town and village across Skyrim – almost every house has one by the fireplace. You can also find them in other inhabited locations like forts or bandit camps.

Interact with a Cooking Pot (or Cooking Spit) to bring up the Cooking Menu, which lists the food you can cook. All of the Cooking Recipes are readily available at any Cooking Pot or Spit, as long as you have the ingredients for them. If you're missing ingredients, the recipe is still shown, but grayed out.

Most of the food you can cook isn't all that helpful, typically restoring 5-10 points of Health or Stamina– less than you'd receive from even the cheapest of Potions. Moreover, the ingredients are often the same price or more expensive than the resulting food, and can often be put to better use in Alchemy instead.

However, for a new adventurer embarking on their travels across the realm and scrabbling to get by, cooked food is a way to recover a little health in a pinch. For those that wish to live as the Nords do, killing their own meats, harvesting their own vegetables, and cooking the resulting ingredients into a somewhat murky-looking stew; this is an authentic way to satiate hunger and fatigue. But for everyone else, Alchemy is a better bet, as it helps to advance your level and makes significantly better restorative items…

…with one delicious exception: The Elsweyr Fondue is excellent.

A Cooking Example: The Elsweyr Fondue

Approach a Cooking Pot to learn the recipe for Elsweyr Fondue. It requires:

Moon Sugar, an extremely rare ingredient. Your best bet is to buy this from one of the travelling Khajiit Caravans.

An Eidar Cheese Wheel. This is the full wheel of moldy white cheese– the sliced and wedge versions of the cheese won't do. You can't buy a full wheel in any shop, so keep an eye out for it when exploring towns, settlements, and other inhabited locations.

Ale, found in most inhabited locations and sold in almost any inn or tavern.

After gathering all three components, return to a Cooking Pot, activate it, and create the amazing Elsweyr Fondue (Fortify Magicka 100, +25% Magicka Regeneration, lasts 12 minutes). This is by far the best non-Alchemic consumable you can craft.

Cooking Recipes

The following table shows every single Recipe you can make, including the ingredients and the effects of the food once mixed together.

✓	INGREDIENTS	PRODUCES	WEIGHT	VALUE	EFFECT
	Cabbage, Red Apple, Salt Pile	Apple Cabbage Stew	0.5	8	Restore Health 10, Restore Stamina 15
	Carrot, Garlic, Raw Beef, Salt Pile	Beef Stew	0.5	8	Fortify Stamina 25/12m, Regenerate Stamina 2/12m
	Cabbage, Leek, Potato, Salt Pile	Cabbage Potato Soup	0.5	5	Restore Health 10, Restore Stamina 10
	Cabbage	Cabbage Soup	0.5	5	Restore Health 10, Restore Stamina 10
	Raw Beef, Salt Pile	Cooked Beef	0.5	5	Restore Health 10
	Ale, Eidar Cheese Wheel, Moon Sugar	Elsweyr Fondue	0.5	5	Fortify Magicka 100/12m, Regenerate Magicka 25%/12m
	Chicken Breast, Salt Pile	Grilled Chicken Breast	0.2	4	Restore Health 5
	Horker Meat, Salt Pile	Horker Loaf	1	4	Restore Health 10
	Garlic, Horker Meat, Lavender, Tomato	Horker Stew	0.5	8	Restore Health 15, Restore Stamina 15, Regenerate Health 1/12m
	Horse Meat, Salt Pile	Horse Haunch	2	4	Restore Health 10
	Leg of Goat, Salt Pile	Leg of Goat Roast	1	4	Restore Health 10
	Mammoth Snout, Salt Pile	Mammoth Steak	2	8	Restore Health 10
	Pheasant Breast, Salt Pile	Pheasant Roast	0.2	4	Restore Health 5
	Raw Rabbit Leg, Salt Pile	Rabbit Haunch	0.1	3	Restore Health 5

✓	INGREDIENTS	PRODUCES	WEIGHT	VALUE	EFFECT
	Salmon Meat, Salt Pile	Salmon Steak	0.1	4	Restore Health 5
	Garlic, Leek, Tomato, Salt Pile	Tomato Soup	0.5	5	Restore Health 10, Restore Stamina 10
	Cabbage, Leek, Potato, Tomato	Vegetable Soup	0.5	5	Regenerate Health 1/12m, Regenerate Stamina 1/12m
	Venison, Salt Pile	Venison Chop	2	5	Restore Health 5
	Leek, Potato, Salt Pile, Venison	Venison Stew	0.5	8	Restore Stamina 15, Regenerate Health 1/12m, Regenerate Stamina 1/12m

Mining

> **NOTE** Mining minerals and gems does not increase any skill.

Assaulting an ore vein with dual-wielded pickaxes is the quickest (and craziest) way to mine.

Throughout Skyrim, there are a variety of natural mineral deposits, concentrated in ore veins. Extracting minerals and gems from these veins can make you a small amount of gold, but more importantly, it helps you gather raw materials for Smithing (which can save you a huge amount of money if you aim to craft your own items). In order to extract the ore, you first need a Pickaxe. You can purchase one from almost any Blacksmith or General Store Merchant, or find them (for free) in any mine.

To mine ore, approach an ore vein with a Pickaxe in your inventory and interact with it. Typically, a vein produces around three pieces of ore before becoming depleted. Along with each piece of ore, you also have a 10 percent chance of extracting a (random) gemstone.

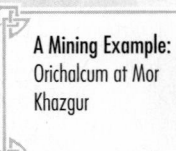

Malachite Ore; among the rarest in Skyrim.

> **TIP** **Ore attack!** Instead of activating an ore vein and waiting for your character to mine the ore, you can also attack the ore with a Pickaxe instead, which mines it at a slightly faster rate. Dual-wield Pickaxes for even faster ore removal, if you really must.

Once mined, Ore can be sold for a (generally small) amount of gold, or Smelted down to make ingots (a slightly better way to earn money from your digging).

> **TIP** Have you exhausted all the veins in a mine? Then wait about a month, and the veins will reset and can be mined again.

A Mining Example: Orichalcum at Mor Khazgur

After becoming Blood-Kin with the Orcs of Mor Khazgur, enter the mine above their longhouse and pick up a Pickaxe from the table. Approach an Orichalcum Ore Vein and activate it. After a few seconds, you'll mine three pieces of Orichalcum Ore (each Weight 1, Value 20). Then use the Smelter just outside of the mine to smelt two pieces of Ore into an Orichalcum Ingot (Weight 1, Value 45).

Where to Mine?

You can look for minerals in the wilderness of Skyrim's windswept Holds, though the best and most reliable sources can be found inside the realm's many mines.

A few general plans if you plan to delve into mining:

◇ **Keep a pickaxe handy.** You never know where you might run into some valuable ore, whether out in the wilds or in the depths of a dungeon.

◇ **Look for Mines.** Many settlements have mines, which give you easy access to a specific type of ore. When you befriend the Orc Strongholds, you also get access to their rich Orichalcum and Ebony mines.

◇ **Plan your return trip.** Every in-game month or so, ore veins that have been depleted will replenish. Check back occasionally to strip them of their new ore.

The Holds of Skyrim

If you're scouring the landscape, here are some general tips for finding ore deposits:

Falkreath Hold (near Helgen and Riverwood) has a slightly higher concentration of Iron Ore veins than usual.

The central tundra of Whiterun Hold is a good place to look for Corundum ore.

More valuable ores (Gold, Silver, Moonstone, Oricalchum, and Quicksilver) are most often found in more extreme environments, such as deep in the mountains or along the northern coast.

The Mines of Skyrim

The following tables list the mines of Skyrim and the ores they produce. The first table is listed by mineral type, the second by location. Note that the settlements of Dawnstar and Karthwasten each have two mines.

ORE DISTRIBUTION

✓	MINERAL	NUMBER OF MINES	LOCATIONS
	Iron	6	Iron-Breaker Mine (Dawnstar), Left Hand Mine (Markarth), Redbelly Mine (Shor's Stone), Rockwallow Mine (Stonehills)", Whistling Mine
	Orichalcum	3	Dushnik Mine (Dushnik Yal), Bilegulch Mine, Mor Khazgur
	Silver	3	Cidna Mine (Markarth), Fenn's Gulch Mine (Karthwasten), Sanuarach Mine (Karthwasten)
	Corundum	2	Darkwater Crossing
	Ebony	1	Gloombound Mine
	Gold	1	Kolskeggr Mine
	Moonstone	1	Soljund's Sinkhole
	Malachite	1	Steamscorch Mine (Kynesgrove)
	Quicksilver	1	Quicksilver Mine (Dawnstar)

MINE PRODUCTION

✓	NAME OF MINE AND LOCATION	ORE PRODUCED
	Darkwater Crossing (Goldenrock Mine)	Corundum
	Dawnstar (Iron-Breaker Mine)	Iron
	Dawnstar (Quicksilver Mine)	Quicksilver
	Dushnikh Yal (Dushnikh Mine)	Orichalcum
	Gloombound Mine	Ebony
	Karthwasten (Fenn's Gulch Mine)	Silver
	Karthwasten (Sanuarach Mine)	Silver
	Kolskeggr Mine	Gold
	Kynesgrove (Steamscorch Mine)	Malachite
	Bilegulch Mine	Orichalcum
	Markarth (Cidna Mine)	Silver

✓	NAME OF MINE AND LOCATION	ORE PRODUCED
	Markarth (Left Hand Mine)	Iron
	Mor Khazgur	Orichalcum
	Shor's Stone (Redbelly Mine)	Iron
	Soljund's Sinkhole	Moonstone
	Stonehills (Rockwallow Mine)	Iron
	Whistling Mine	Iron

Smelting

Approach the domed Smelter, withstand the great heat, and transform your Ore into ingots.

You can purchase Ore from most blacksmiths, or mine it yourself if money is a concern. But what do you do with the Ore?

Raw Ore isn't useful on its own, and doesn't sell for many gold pieces. However, if you bring your Ore to a Smelter, you can smelt the ore into metal ingots, which you can then sell for more gold pieces, or use to Smith your own weapons and armor.

An Ebony Ingot; smelted from two clumps of Ebony Ore.

TIP Make sure you Mine and Smelt the minerals you're proficient in making items with!

Also, scour Dwarven Ruins in search of scrap metal. You can find a lot of loose metal lying around, and even more in the remains of Dwarven Automatons (such as Dwarven Spheres) once you've reduced them to scrap. Dwarven scrap can be smelted down into Dwarven Metal Ingots. This may cause Calcelmo, the Dwarven researcher in Markarth, a slight case of conniptions, but it increases their value significantly. Pick up everything you can carry and haul it back to town. You can forge weapons and armor with the ingots to rapidly improve your Smithing skill, or sell it to recoup the cost of other materials.

NOTE Ingots can be found in your Misc Inventory menu.

Smelting Recipes

The following table lists all of the available Smelting Recipes, and the type of Ingots produced by each. All of these recipes are available to you immediately; you just need the Ore or scrap metal required for them.

✓	INGREDIENTS	PRODUCES	WEIGHT	VALUE
	2 Corundum Ore	Corundum Ingot	1	40
	Large Decorative Dwemer Strut	Dwarven Metal Ingot (2)	1	30
	Small Dwemer Plate Metal	Dwarven Metal Ingot (3)	1	30
	Bent Dwemer Scrap Metal	Dwarven Metal Ingot (3)	1	30
	Large Dwemer Strut	Dwarven Metal Ingot (3)	1	30
	Large Dwemer Plate Metal	Dwarven Metal Ingot (3)	1	30
	Solid Dwemer Metal	Dwarven Metal Ingot (5)	1	30
	2 Ebony Ore	Ebony Ingot	1	150
	2 Gold Ore	Gold Ingot	1	100
	1 Iron Ore	Iron Ingot	1	7
	2 Orichalcum Ore	Orichalcum Ingot	1	45
	2 Quicksilver Ore	Quicksilver Ingot	1	60
	2 Malachite Ore	Refined Malachite	1	100
	2 Moonstone Ore	Refined Moonstone	1	75
	2 Silver Ore	Silver Ingot	1	50
	2 Iron Ore	Steel Ingot	1	20

Tanning

> **NOTE** Tanning animal hides into leather and leather strips does not increase any skill.

Approach a Tanning Rack, and transform a wild animal hide into leather or leather strips.

Tanning is a simple process; it allows you to transform animal hides into leather or leather strips. These can then be sold or used in your own Smithing. Larger pelts produce more leather... but are often more valuable as pelts, rather then broken down into their leather components. Therefore, it is wise to think twice before tanning everything you've skinned!

> **TIP** Keep an eye on value. Depending on your Speech skill, you may be better off selling a valuable pelt and then buying leather from a merchant, rather than tanning that same pelt into leather.

Tanning Recipes
The following table lists all of the available Tanning Recipes. All of these recipes are available to you immediately; you just need the hides for them.

✓	INGREDIENTS	PRODUCES	WEIGHT	VALUE
	Leather	Leather Strips (4)	0.1	10
	2 Goat Hide	Leather	2	10
	Fox Pelt	Leather	2	10
	Snow Fox Pelt	Leather	2	10

✓	INGREDIENTS	PRODUCES	WEIGHT	VALUE
	Wolf Pelt	Leather	2	10
	Ice Wolf Pelt	Leather	2	10
	Deer Hide	Leather (2)	2	10
	Cow Hide	Leather (3)	2	10
	Horse Hide	Leather (3)	2	10
	Bear Pelt	Leather (4)	2	10
	Cave Bear Pelt	Leather (4)	2	10
	Sabre Cat Pelt	Leather (4)	2	10
	Sabre Cat Snow Pelt	Leather (4)	2	10
	Snow Bear Pelt	Leather (4)	2	10

Wood Chopping

> **NOTE** This manual labor does not increase any skill.

Swing a Woodcutter's Axe, cleaving a small log in twain. Now repeat until you've had enough.

There are a number of Wood Chopping Blocks throughout Skyrim, which allow you to execute this most simple of all Crafting exercises: chopping wood. For this, you need a Woodcutter's Axe, which can be purchased from almost any General Store Merchant, or found (for free) at any lumber mill. Simply approach the Wood Chopping Block, interact with it, and you begin chopping. For each chop, two pieces of firewood are added to your Misc Inventory. When you're finished, sell the Firewood to any lumber foreman for 5 gold per piece of wood. You won't get a better deal from any merchant.

> **NOTE** Chopping Firewood is a slow and methodical way to earn a tiny amount of gold. While it is something you can do eke out the last few coins you need for a piece of armor, it's mostly just a little way of interacting with the world. You can also load lumber logs onto the wooden conveyor belt at lumber mills and watch as they're sliced with a vertical saw. This manual labor is free, just something to pass the time.

Lumber Mill Locations
If you're determined to sell your firewood for the best possible prices, do so at the following locations, where you can speak to (and obtain payment from) the lumber mill owner or operator. Note that not all of these Lumber Mills have a Wood Chopping Block.

✓	LUMBER MILL	LOCATION (HOLD)
	Dragon Bridge	Haafingar
	Solitude Sawmill	Haafingar
	Morthal	Hjaalmarch
	Anga's Mill	The Pale
	Riverwood	Whiterun

✓	LUMBER MILL	LOCATION (HOLD)
	Mixwater Mill	Eastmarch
	Falkreath	Falkreath
	Half-moon Mill	Falkreath
	Helgen	Falkreath
	Heartwood Mill	The Rift

The Elder Scrolls V
S K Y R I M

TRAINING PART 3: ADVENTURING ACROSS SKYRIM

This section looks at the broader aspects of adventuring in Skyrim. There's information on how Skyrim is segmented, so you can grasp how big it really is, and where you are within the realm. The different types of map locations are explained, so you know what kinds of enemies and challenges await you. Finally, there are a range of tips on mapping, what expect when exploring Dungeons, who there is to speak to in Skyrim and why, and lastly what Services, Areas of Interest, and Collectibles you should look for.

THE HOLDS OF SKYRIM

Skyrim is divided into nine separate Holds: Haafingar, Hjaalmarch, The Pale, Winterhold Hold, The Reach, Whiterun Hold, Eastmarch, Falkreath Hold, and The Rift. Each of these Holds has a distinct atmosphere to it, from the Autumnal Forest of The Rift, to the Tundra Plains of Whiterun Hold, to the ragged and rugged Northern Coast of The Pale. The borders of these Holds can't be seen on your World Map, but they are present on this guide's maps. Wherever possible, cartographers have used rivers, roads, and treacherous mountains to separate Holds, so it's easier to find a location in this guide.

Each Hold has a Capital City: Solitude, Morthal, Dawnstar, Winterhold, Markarth, Whiterun, Windhelm, Falkreath, and Riften. These are the nine shields (crests) that you can see on your World Map. While most Holds contain smaller towns and settlements as well, the Capital is always the most important and highly-populated location within the Hold, and also among the safest places to be (unless it's under siege during the Civil War, of course...).

Habitations

A city, town, or dwelling populated with citizens that are almost always neutral, if not civil and friendly towards you.

Windhelm, Capital of Eastmarch

Habitations range in size from a small group of Khajiit Caravaneers to the rugged majesty of Solitude, the sprawling capital of Haafingar Hold. Here, you're likely to find citizens in need of help (or at least a favor or two), rumors and scuttlebutt, tasks to accomplish, Quests to start, and interactions that test your social skills more than your skill at arms. The major types of Habitations are listed in this guide's Atlas.

Dungeons

A location populated with hostile people or creatures that typically attack you on sight.

High Gate Ruins, in The Pale

A "Dungeon" is a place where exploration and combat can be had. It is an all-encompassing term for a location with few (usually no) friendly faces; a place where you must face wild animals, brigands, or worse. When you fully explore a dungeon, you usually leave with a reward that makes the harrowing trek worth your time and sanity. Dungeons vary widely in size, from small caves to massive, multi-storied ruins. Most have a high-level foe you most defeat (known colloquially as a "boss"), and some even have their own small Quests. Others are woven into the larger Quests that dominate your adventure.

When you clear a dungeon (that is, explore it and defeat all of the major foes within), your map typically marks it as "cleared". Some locations cannot be cleared, and others can be cleared only under special circumstances.

Most dungeons will repopulate over time. This can happen in as little as a week for a location you left midway through, and may not happen for a month or more (if ever) for a dungeon you have cleared. Note that your map will not indicate when a location has repopulated (once cleared, always cleared), so be careful– you may find enemies where you least expect them.

Other Locations

There are also a large number of minor locations and encounters not flagged on your in-game World Map (though all of them are listed on this guide's map). These are Secondary Locations; usually small shrines, lost treasure chests, tiny campsites, dragon burial mounds, or other odd occurrences that you can stumble upon. There are also World Encounters, small events that occur randomly. This could be anything from a fox chasing some chickens, to a challenge from an Orc, to a Khajiit with a penchant for being economical with the truth....

> **NOTE** All of these locations are noted on this guide's maps, and are detailed in the Atlas. Although this guide's map is exhaustive, there are a number of scattered cases, satchels, and other loot hidden throughout this realm that are not shown. However, as there are much easier places to find identical items, these have not been flagged.

Mapping and Movement

> **NOTE** The realm of Skyrim is vast and foreboding, and at times almost overwhelming-- there are over 350 Primary Locations to discover! Although you can go where you want, do what you want, and see what you want, it is worth considering the following plans to explore a location more logically:

Plan 1: The Base Camp: Use a location you've cleared out, or a location you know is safe (such as Riverwood) as a base camp until you're familiar with your surroundings. Learn how far a new location is from this "safe" place.

Plan 2: The Landmarks: Look for landmarks when you travel. No matter where you are in Skyrim, you should be able to spin around slowly in a circle and spot two familiar landmarks to get your bearings. This is easiest in some Holds (such as Whiterun, with its capital and the towering Throat of the World mountain), and more difficult in others (such as craggy The Reach). However, once you know the locations around a big landmark, you can investigate other locations close to it without becoming lost. Also use smaller landmarks (such as roadside shrines, bridges, or signposts) to remember where you've been.

Plan 3: Roads and Paths: You may be tempted to charge off into the wilderness, and this is perfectly fine. But to efficiently discover everything in the area of a Hold you're exploring, it is worth using the network of roads (cobblestones, with signposts) and pathways (tracks, goat trails, and even foot-tracked snow). These almost always lead you close or directly to a Primary Location. Follow the roads to make a circular trek around a Hold, then return and methodically search areas off this beaten track.

Plan 4: Your Destination Marker: If you select an empty spot on the world map, you can place your own Destination Marker there. This is extremely useful when used in conjunction with this guide's Atlas, as there are close to 200 Secondary Locations, which don't show up on your World Map! Simply gauge where a Secondary Location is by comparing the World Map to the Guide Map, place the marker, and head there.

Plan 5: Use the Atlas: This guide has a sizable section revealing every single location in Skyrim. Reference the locations and maps in that giant chapter to help you on your way.

DUNGEON EXPLORATION

◆ Finding Your Way

Whether you're assaulting a ruined fortress filled with bandits or stealthily creeping through some long-forgotten crypt, Dungeons are at the heart of your adventuring experience. Although they may appear confusing at first glance, the winding tunnels and twisting corridors generally lead you to a final chamber, where you must defeat a powerful foe to claim your reward. In Skyrim, many dungeons also have a secret exit or shortcut– a hidden passage, barred door, elevated tunnel, or dwarven elevator that leads back to the entrance. This allows you to exit a dungeon without having to traipse all the way back (although that's possible if you want to).

Lighting Your Way

Carrying a torch or employing a staff or spell to light your way makes the frightening darkness of dungeons a little less intimidating. Be sure to have a light source tagged as a Favorite so you can quickly switch between it and your combat weapons as needed.

Khajiit and Vampires can call on their Nighteye Power to see in the dark without a light source, allowing them to more easily slip through the darkness undetected.

The positions of lanterns, torches, and braziers inside dungeons is also worth noting, as they are almost always visual cues that coax you in the correct direction. If you're lost, look for these light sources to guide you on your way.

◆ Dungeon Puzzles

● MINOR SPOILERS

Many dungeons were sealed for a reason– they contain the dormant (and often undead) remains of a once-powerful entity. To protect these tombs from grave-robbers and brigands, the ancient Nords concocted a number of puzzles to flummox and foil the unwary. The same is true, but on a far grander scale, inside Dwarven Ruins. Here is what you can expect:

Switches, Levers, Chains, and Handles

If you're stuck in a chamber, look for any of these devices to open the doors, gates, and portcullises that prevent your progress. Chains are usually the most difficult to spot, hanging on a gloomy wall. Sometimes, these must be triggered in a specific order to open the path forward.

Nordic Puzzle Door

A series of concentric metal rings are embedded in an impenetrable door, each embossed with three animal glyphs. Explore the dungeon to find the Dragon Claw associated with the door– a precious artifact that holds the key to this puzzle. In your inventory, inspect the palm of the claw to find the solution to the door. Line up the three animals glyphs in the correct order, then activate the central 'keyhole' with the Dragon Claw to unlock the door.

Nordic Puzzle Pillars and Petroglyphs

Many chambers require you to rotate two or more stone pillars to face the correct direction in order to open a path forward. These pillars have been inscribed with a set of animal petroglyphs on them, which correspond to another set of glyphs somewhere in the surrounding chamber. Match the two sets of animal carvings to solve the puzzle.

Rotating Walls

Stone walls controlled by a hidden mechanism can rotate to open or close paths in a dungeon. When you encounter them, look for a set of Nordic Puzzle Pillars, or a lever, chain, or switch you can use to open the way forward.

Dwarven Puzzles

Long ago, the ancient Dwarves constructed immense clockwork mechanisms and complex steamworks. The ruins of this long-lost race still yield a variety of intricate and unique puzzles, from trying to stop the flow of poisonous gas into a chamber, to carefully aligning a system of mirrors in an Oculory, to inserting an other-worldly key into a strange slot. In some cases, you may need to find the "key" object beforehand, or your progress will be limited at best.

Other Puzzles

There are occasionally other puzzles that are more complicated, requiring a Shout or other technique to solve. These are duly noted.

 TIP   Every single Puzzle has a solution; check the Atlas location of the Dungeon in question, or the Quest you've embarked on, for more details.

Traps and Triggers

Dungeon exploration would be nowhere near as terrifying without the tension of possibly stumbling over a tripwire and being pin-cushioned by a dozen rusty darts! Throughout your adventure, expect to run into, step on, or trigger any of 25 different traps, using one or more of four different trigger mechanisms. The following chart lists every major type of Trap and Trigger, along with advice on how best to avoid them.

Note that most traps have a small chance of infecting you with a random disease. It might be worth keeping around a cure disease potion just in case...

The infamous Oil Lamp Trap: Turn the burn on your enemies, if you're quick and clever!

TRAP	DAMAGE	THREAT LEVEL	MOST COMMON IN...	TIPS
Bear Trap	Average	Nuisance	Bandit Camps, Outdoors	Watch where you step! Bear Traps are often hidden in the bushes or under low grass, ready to snap if you aren't careful. You can often lure enemies into stepping on them. Interacting with the trap will also allow you to close or open them.
Battering Ram Trap	High	High	Nordic Ruins	Talk about a headache! Battering Ram traps cover a long arc, and at higher levels, can kill you or your foes in a single hit. Look out for the triggers that set them off, and keep an eye on the ceiling for them. Lure enemies into them to take them out in one shot.
Bone Alarm Trap	None	Nuisance	Bandit Camps, Forsworn Redoubts	Bone Alarm traps don't do any damage, but alert enemies to your presence. If you aren't sneaking anyway, they won't make much difference. If you are, watch your step and try to avoid them if you can. Shooting them with a bow will draw unaware enemies to them, allowing you to set up an ambush.
Dart Trap	Average	Average	Nordic Ruins, Dwarven Ruins	The most common kind of trap, dart traps are also among the most avoidable. Even if you trigger them by accident, you can often just jump out of the way to minimize the damage you take. They deal a small amount of poison damage.
Dwarven Ballista Trap	High	Low	Dwarven Ruins	Dwarven Ballistas shoot a large bolt that explodes on impact, doing massive damage to anything in the blast radius. Functional ballistas are extremely rare, and often something you can turn to your advantage– look for a valve or lever you can use to turn the trap on your enemies.
Dwarven Fire Pillar Trap	Average	Average	Dwarven Ruins	Initially resembling a pressure plate, Dwarven Fire Pillars rise from the ground and rotate, spewing gouts of flame. Spotting these traps in advance is key to avoiding them.
Dwarven Piston Trap	None	Nuisance	Dwarven Ruins	Dwarven Pistons shove anything in front of them away. They don't do any damage, but they hit hard, and have a habit of pushing you (or your enemies) into something nasty.
Dwarven Thresher	Average	High	Dwarven Ruins	Dwarven Threshers are a pair of whirling blades that rise from the floor, sometimes remaining in place and sometimes moving along a track built into the ground. Often appearing in narrow corridors, they are highly dangerous, capable of killing you, your followers, or your enemies with a few solid hits. If you see one, get out of the way!
Explosive Gas Trap	Average	Low	Nordic Ruins, Caves	See that ripple in the air? It might be a cloud of flammable, explosive gas. Put away your torch, keep your Flames spell in check, and you shouldn't have any problems with them. Explosive Gas is extremely rare.
Flail Trap	High	Average	Bandit Camps	Also fairly rare, Flail traps tend to be located on the ceiling, ready to drop a large, spiked sphere into your head. If you see it coming, back away– once the trap has come to a full and complete stop, it's harmless.
Flamethrower Trap	Average	Average	Any Dungeon	Often built into the mouths of Nordic dragon statues or set into pressure plates, flamethrower traps are a threat most adventurers will see from time to time. Because their flame travels in a narrow, focused beam, your best bet is to quickly step out of the way and let the trap subside.
Magic Caster Trap	Varies	Varies	Any Dungeon	Magic Casters consist of a runed pedestal powered by a Soul Gem. When triggered, the Soul Gem casts a preset spell, which could be anything from Flames to Ice Storm. If you can't avoid the trap altogether, you can disarm it by removing the Soul Gem– taking it directly works, but you can also hit it with an arrow from a safe distance, or grab it with Telekenesis.
Mammoth Skull Trap	High	Low	Any Dungeon	When triggered, this huge mammoth skull swings forward on its support ropes, slamming into anything in front of it with lethal force. This trap tends to be easy to spot– you can't exactly overlook a giant mammoth skull– so it's rarely much of a threat to you, though you can lure your enemies into it.
Oil Lamp Trap	Low	Low	Nordic Ruins	The oil lamp itself isn't usually a problem. It's the pool of oil that often sits under the lamp that you should keep an eye on, and lure your enemies into if possible. Then hit or shoot down the lamp to set the oil ablaze. They are often triggered by tripwires, but shooting or attacking them will also cause the lamp to drop.
Oil Pool Trap	Average	Low	Any Dungeon	Oil Pools are easily turned against your foes– just lure them into the oil and light it with any fire source. Oil Lamp traps are often conveniently nearby, but lacking one of those a Flames Spell, or Fire Atronach will work just as well.
Poison Gas Trap	Average	Average	Dwarven Ruins	Poison Gas does steady damage over time if you stand in it. When you find a patch of poison gas, look around for a way to turn it off. Failing that, make a run for it, using a Healing spell or potions to keep your health up. The Clear Skies Shout can also be used to dissipate the gas.
Rockfall Trap	Average	Average	Bandit Camps, Nordic Ruins, Mines, Caves	Rockfall traps are fairly rare, but the sheer number of rocks they contain can make them a threat if you're standing in the wrong place. If you see one, your best bet is to get out of the way.
Rune Trap	Average	High	Any Dungeon	Rune Traps look much like the Fire, Frost, and Shock Runes that you can place with the Destruction spells of the same name. And like those spells, these traps pack a quite a punch, exploding automatically if you get close enough. Your best bet is to lure an enemy to run across them and set them off. Failing that, you can shoot them with a spell to set them off, but keep your distance.
Spear Trap	Average	High	Any Dungeon	A single spear trap is no threat... but spear traps tend to come in groups of five or more, lashing out unexpectedly from the floor or walls. Your best bet is to look for the ports from which they emerge and try to avoid setting them off in the first place.
Swinging Blade Trap	Average	Average	Nordic Ruins	Blade traps often appear in sets in long, narrow hallways. They're usually easy enough for you to dodge, although enemies (and your followers) have a harder time, making them a great kill zone. When you're ready to go through, tell your follower to stay behind, time your run carefully, and look for a lever on the far side to disable them.
Swinging Wall Trap	High	High	Any Dungeon	Swinging wall traps are fast, lethal, and sometimes hard to distinguish from other wood or metal beams in a dungeon. If you notice a freestanding beam that doesn't quite reach the ceiling, be careful. And try to snare an enemy with it if possible– few things are as satisfying as watching them get hurled into the wall by this trap.
Hinge Trigger	None	Varies	Any Dungeon	Find a suspicious-looking chest or door? Then look for this little metal hinge and wire on the side. Carefully activate it, and you can pick its lock to safely disable it before opening the object it was attached to. You can also hit it with an attack from a distance to break it and set off the trap in (relative) safety.
Pressure Pedestal	None	Varies	Nordic Ruins	If you see a flat-topped pedestal with a tantilizing item on it, be careful– it could be a pressure pedestal trap. If the pedestal isn't weighted down, a trap will be set off. Grab the item from a distance (Telekenesis is great for this), or drop something else on the pedestal to keep it weighed down. Or just grab the item and run for it.
Pressure Plate	None	Varies	Any Dungeon	By far the most common trap-triggering mechanism, Pressure Plates can be found in almost any dungeon– just look for suspicious raised stones and avoid them. Or take the Sneak skill's Light Foot perk to avoid setting these off altogether.
Tripwire	None	Varies	Any Dungeon	See a low-lying white wire? That's a tripwire. Leap over it or skirt around it to avoid setting it off. Or edge forward very carefully to see what happens when it breaks. You can also interact with the tripwire to disarm it. Tripwire-triggered traps only fire once.

NOTE Throughout the Quest and Atlas Chapters, Traps are mentioned when they are a major obstacle, or block your path to finishing an Objective or location walkthrough. However, due to their sheer number, Traps are not tracked in this guide.

Dragon Mounds

Dotted across the fells and forests, the plains and snowlines of Skyrim are strange circular mounds, surrounded by a scattering of standing stones. These are actually ancient dragon burial mounds; the final resting place of these creatures when they were slain centuries ago. But now, the Dragons are back! Alduin the World-Eater, a terror out of the most ancient legends, has returned to Skyrim, and over the course of the Main Quest, he opens these mounds and resurrects the dragons within, calling them forth to wreak havoc once more!

How Dragon Mounds Open

There are 22 Dragon Mounds scattered throughout the nine Holds of Skyrim. When you encounter one (all are listed in the Atlas, and marked on the Hold maps), it will be in one of four states. Over the course of the Main Quest, these mounds gradually open, releasing the dragons trapped within.

State I: Dormant

Each Dragon Mound opens in response to a specific objective in the Main Quest. Before that point, the Dragon Mound is dormant. The ground is covered, and the site could easily be mistaken for an ancient Nordic burial mound, as the two are quite similar.

State II: Deserted

As the Main Quest develops, you may find some mounds that have been opened, but have no dragon nearby. That is, Alduin has visited this site, resurrected a dragon from the mound, and both creatures have flown away. There is little for you to do here. But look around carefully–you may well spot the dragon at a nearby Dragon Lair!

State III: Awakened

As the Main Quest goes on, you will find more and more mounds in this state. Alduin has visited the site, resurrected the dragon from the mound, and flown away. Meanwhile, the reborn dragon remains here, gathering its strength and waiting for a chance to strike. Slay the beast and claim its soul to unlock your power as Dragonborn!

State IV: Resurrection

And in a few cases, if you stumble across just the right mound at just the right time, you may encounter Alduin himself! If you watch, Alduin will resurrect the dragon before your eyes, then fly off to his next destination. Attack, and Alduin roars into the skies, mocking you, before making his escape (he cannot be harmed). Meanwhile, the resurrected dragon will turn and attack! If you miss this opportunity, the mound will change to State III, with the newly-resurrected dragon remaining near its mound until you arrive to challenge it.

Dragon Mound Stages Chart

The following chart lists (by Hold) all of the Dragon Mounds, when they are opened, and what state the mound will be in when it opens.

✓	NAME OF DRAGON MOUND	HOLD LOCATION	STATE	DRAGON?	MAIN QUEST NOTES
☐	[2.C] Dragon Mound: Karth River Forest	Hjaalmarch	II	No	Opens during Act II: Diplomatic Immunity
☐	[2.G] Dragon Mound: Robber's Gorge Bluffs	Hjaalmarch	III	Yes	Opens during Act II: Diplomatic Immunity
☐	[2.P] Dragon Mound: Labyrinthian Peaks	Hjaalmarch	II	No	Opens during Act II: Elder Knowledge
☐	[3.D] Dragon Mound: Sea Shore Foothills	The Pale	III	Yes	Opens during Act II: Elder Knowledge
☐	[3.M] Dragon Mound: Shimmermist Hills	The Pale	III	Yes	Opens during Act II: Elder Knowledge

✓	NAME OF DRAGON MOUND	HOLD LOCATION	STATE	DRAGON?	MAIN QUEST NOTES
☐	[3.Q] Dragon Mound: Yorgrim Resurrection	The Pale	IV	Yes	Opens during Act II: Elder Knowledge. Visit this location before Act II: Alduin's Bane is complete in order to witness the resurrection!
☐	[5.B] Dragon Mound: Reachwater Pass	The Reach	III	Yes	Opens during Act II: Elder Knowledge
☐	[5.I] Dragon Mound: Ragnvald Vale	The Reach	III	Yes	Opens during Act II: Elder Knowledge
☐	[5.T] Dragon Mound: Karthspire Bluffs	The Reach	III	Yes	Opens during Act II: Alduin's Wall
☐	[6.B] Dragon Mound: Rorikstead Resurrection	Whiterun Hold	IV	Yes	Opens during Act II: Alduin's Wall. Visit this location before Act II: Elder Knowledge begins in order to witness the resurrection!
☐	[6.K] Dragon Mound: Great Henge Resurrection	Whiterun Hold	IV	Yes	Opens during Act II: Diplomatic Immunity. Visit this location before Act II: Alduin's Wall begins in order to witness the resurrection!
☐	[6.O] Dragon Mound: Lone Mountain	Whiterun Hold	III	Yes	Opens during Act II: Alduin's Wall
☐	[7.H] Dragon Mound: Kynesgrove Resurrection	Eastmarch	IV	Yes	Opens during Act I: A Blade in the Dark. You will visit this location during Main Quest: A Blade in the Dark, witness the resurrection, and kill resurrected dragon.
☐	[7.L] Dragon Mound: Bonestrewn Crest	Eastmarch	II	No	Opens during Act I: Dragon Rising
☐	[7.N] Dragon Mound: Witchmist Grove	Eastmarch	II	No	Opens during Act I: The Way of the Voice
☐	[7.T] Dragon Mound: Mzulft Foothills	Eastmarch	II	No	Opens during Act I: Dragon Rising
☐	[8.A] Dragon Mound: Bilegulch Ridge	Falkreath Hold	II	No	Opens during Act II: Alduin's Wall
☐	[8.L] Dragon Mound: Evergreen Woods	Falkreath Hold	III	Yes	Opens during Act II: Alduin's Wall
☐	[8.AI] Dragon Mound: Bloodlet Peaks	Falkreath Hold	II	No	Opens during Act II: Alduin's Wall
☐	[9.F] Dragon Mound: Autumnwatch Woods	The Rift	II	No	Opens during Act II: Diplomatic Immunity
☐	[9.M] Dragon Mound: Autumnshade Woods	The Rift	II	No	Opens during Act I: Bleak Falls Barrow
☐	[9.Q] Dragon Mound: Lost Tongue Pass	The Rift	II	No	Opens during Act II: Diplomatic Immunity

TIP Want to face a dragon, or see Alduin before he flies away? Then simply complete your current Main Quest, consult this chart, and head off to find any mounds that have triggered.

Standing Stones

Throughout the wilderness of Skyrim, you can find thirteen of these ancient and powerful standing stones. Etched into each is the sign of one of the major constellations known throughout Tamriel. Touch the Stone, and you can choose to receive its blessing. You'll focus the stone, and a bolt of pure magic arcs to the heavens. This blessing is now permanent, until you visit a different Stone and receive its blessing, which supersedes the previous one. You may only have one blessing at a time. Standing Stones can be divided into two major sets: 4 Skill Improvement Stones, and 9 Other Stones.

Skill Improvement Stones

 *The Warrior Stone: Located at The Guardian Stones (Falkreath Hold). Combat skills increase 20% faster.*

 *The Mage Stone: Located at The Guardian Stones (Falkreath Hold). Magic skills improve 20% faster.*

 *The Thief Stone: Located at The Guardian Stones (Falkreath Hold). Stealth skills increase 20% faster.*

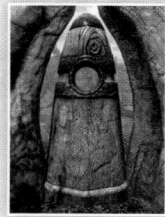 *The Lover Stone: Located in The Reach. All skills improve 15% faster.*

Four Standing Stones – Warrior, Thief, Mage, and Lover – increase the rate at which your Skills improve. The choice to use or not to use these stones is more important than you may think.

Accept one of these Stones' Blessings if:

You crave high-level spells and perks, and want access to them as quickly as possible.

You want to trek through high-level Dungeons (such as Dwarven Ruins and Dragon Priest crypts) as soon as you can.

You're trying to maintain a second set of skills that you don't use as often: For example, your primary focus might be as a warrior, with a secondary interest in stealth. You may want to take the Thief Stone just to help your stealth-based skills keep pace.

You want to quickly increase a skill or set of skills that you haven't used before, or that you've neglected: For example, if you decide to add Restoration Spells to your Warrior's repertoire, or want to pick up some Illusion Magic to complement your Thief's skills, the Mage Stone will help you master them more quickly.

Resist these Stones' Blessings (and choose one of the other stones) if:

You want to make your adventure as long and rewarding as possible, and want to see and do everything you possibly can in Skyrim. Your adventure is most entertaining when you're below Level 50. Impatience isn't rewarded....

You're more interested in experimenting with the dramatic and varied effects that the other Stones can have on your style of play, rather than accepting these 'hidden' bonuses.

NOTE A few points to remember:

The Warrior, The Mage, and The Thief Stones provide bonuses to skill growth in their respective skills, while the Lovers Stone provides a slightly smaller bonus to skill growth in all skills. This is great if you like to try a little of everything, or have a character that draws heavily on skills across multiple disciplines.

Don't expect to crush your foes just because your skills increase more quickly. In fact, these Stones may make your adventure slightly more difficult, since you'll have less time per level to find and upgrade your equipment and master advanced combat tactics.

Don't feel 'locked in' to any particular Stone blessing. If you want to try out one of the others, you can always change back later-- just fast-travel back to your Stone of choice and touch it again. It's that simple.

Other Stones

 *The Apprentice Stone: Located in Hjaalmarch Hold. Recover Magicka twice as fast; twice as vulnerable to magic.*

This Stone offers a slightly risky option for Mages who find themselves running out of Magicka too frequently, or for Battlemages who don't want to sacrifice the protection of their armor for the Magicka Regeneration bonuses of mage robes. The weakness to Magicka is a real liability – especially in Warlock or Vampire dungeons, where almost all of your foes cast spells – but it can be offset by having a summoned creature or Follower to help soak up the damage. For Bretons, this weakness is also offset by your racial Magic Resistance, making it much more palatable.

 *The Atronach Stone: Located in Eastmarch Hold. 50 extra points of magicka, 50% absorb spells, -50% magicka regen.*

This gives you the benefits of two of the best racial abilities – the High Elves' Highborn Magicka and the Breton's Dragonskin (as a constant effect) – with the huge drawback of halved magicka regen. You can easily offset or overcome this drawback by equipping mage robes or other items that increase your magicka regeneration rate.

 *The Lady Stone: Located in Falkreath Hold. Regenerate Health and Stamina 25% faster.*

This is a solid, effective choice for offensive Warriors. The bonus isn't spectacular, but it will give you more staying power in combat. It's also an excellent choice for Vampires, as it can offset your Health and Stamina regeneration penalties while in sunlight.

The Lord Stone: Located in The Pale. 50 points of damage resistance, 25% magic resistance.

This grants you two excellent resistance bonuses in one! The damage resistance bonus is the equivalent of 50 points of armor, which is like giving your robed mage a Daedric Cuirass (and makes an already well-armored warrior even more resilient)! The magic resistance bonus is also solid, cutting spell damage by a quarter. Overall, this is a good choice for any character who wants to shore up their defenses.

The Ritual Stone: Located in Whiterun Hold. Raises all dead around you to fight for you.

Arguably the most entertaining, as well as one of the most useful blessings, the Ritual Stone grants you a Power that raises all the dead around you – from the mightiest Draugr Deathlord to the lowliest Chicken – and causes them to fight for you. Useful in a wide range of situations, this Power really shines in the large-scale battles at the end of many dungeons, where you can find yourself quickly raising 5-10 corpses to take on their former allies!

The Serpent Stone: Located in Winterhold Hold. Paralyze the target for 5 seconds, and do 25 points of damage.

Paralyze is a useful ability to have on hand, allowing you to quickly score multiple hits on a foe before they can recover, take one enemy out of the fight so you can deal with others, or simply buy yourself a few seconds to retreat and regroup. It's especially useful when fighting individual, high-level foes. However, you can achieve the same effect with a spell or poison, so this Power may be less useful at higher levels once you have other options at your disposal.

The Shadow Stone: Located in The Rift. Invisibility for 60 seconds.

This Power is exceptionally useful for a stealthy character– it can be invoked instantly, silently, with no Illusion Skill or casting time required. You can achieve the same effect with a spell – and you definitely want that spell – but even after obtaining it, the Shadow Stone's Power can still be useful to keep around as a back-up.

The Steed Stone: Located in Haafingar Hold. Carry weight +100, no movement penalty from armor.

Although this blessing doesn't bring you the instant gratification or protection of those that help you in combat, it is worth considering the Steed Stone's ability if you rely on Heavy Armor: you'll appreciate the extra mobility and Carry Weight it affords you. It's also worth trying this ability before taking the Conditioned (Heavy Armor) or Unhindered (Light Armor) Perks– you may even want to take it instead of those perks, and select another perk instead.

The Tower Stone: Located in Winterhold Hold. Unlock any Expert level lock (or lower) once per day.

If you constantly find yourself out of Lockpicks, or simply don't enjoy Lockpicking, the Tower Stone's Power will help you open one locked door or treasure chest per day. For everyone else, there are more useful abilities to choose from.

 NOTE Standing Stones are all Primary Locations, and their locations are shown throughout the Atlas of this guide.

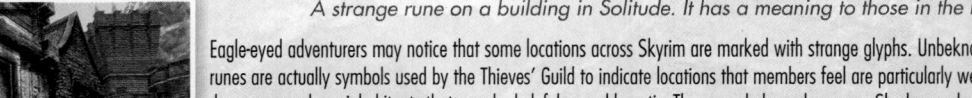

SHADOWMARKS

A strange rune on a building in Solitude. It has a meaning to those in the know.

Eagle-eyed adventurers may notice that some locations across Skyrim are marked with strange glyphs. Unbeknownst to most, these runes are actually symbols used by the Thieves' Guild to indicate locations that members feel are particularly wealthy targets, safe, dangerous, or have inhabitants that may be helpful or problematic. These symbols are known as Shadowmarks. In order to learn more about Shadowmarks, search the Thieves Guild for a book written by Delvin Mallory called Shadowmarks, which lists all of the markings that the Thieves Guild uses. For more information on Shadowmarks, see page 222.

BOOKS

Voracious readers will be pleased to learn that a wealth of knowledge can be found in dozens of different books. These fall into one of five general categories:

Skill Books

The Doors of Oblivion (Conjuration), one of only five copies of this rare book.

When read, these books increase one of your skills by a single point. There are five different Skill Books books associated with each skill (meaning 90 different book titles), but multiple copies of each book (usually 3-5 each), bringing the total number of Skill Books to well over 400. However, you only receive a skill increase the first time you read any particular title– rereading that book, or any of its copies, has no further effect. This means you can only use Skill Books to increase each skill by a maximum of five points.

For example: Those interested in the Sneak Skill should look for the following books: Three Thieves (four copies), 2920, Last Seed, v8 (four copies), Sacred Witness (four copies), Legend of Krately House (three copies), and The Red Kitchen Reader (five copies). This means there is a total of 20 Sneak Skill Books, and five points you can add to your Sneak from reading the first copy you encounter of each tome.

Spell Tomes

Spell Tome: Ice Storm (Destruction), which can be found in the world or purchased from select vendors.

Spell Tomes are books of magic with the sigil of their school embossed on the front cover. When you read them, the book is consumed, and you instantly learn the spell it contained. If you later find another copy of the same Spell Tome, sell it, as it isn't of any use to you anymore. Spell Tomes can be purchased from a few select vendors, the Court Wizards in each of the Major Hold Capitals, and the mages of the College of Winterhold. You can also find Spell Tomes randomly in dungeons.

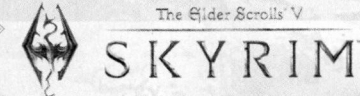

Functional Books

Lost Legends of Skyrim hints at an ancient mystery.

Functional Books describe actual locations, legends, or mysteries to be discovered in the wilds of Skyrim. When read, they add locations to your World Map, and might trigger a Quest or Objective related to the contents of the book. There are four of these types of books, each with several copies. Once you've read one copy, you never need to read another copy of the same book, as the information is identical.

Common Books

The Lusty Argonian Maid, v2, one of only three copies of this scandalous work.

There are wide variety of other books in Skyrim. They provide stories, histories, advice on battle, fiction, and many other types of reading material to add a little flavor to your adventure. Many of these books provide interesting asides to locations you visit. However, none of these books grant you any kind of bonus; they are simply there to be read. Across Skyrim, there are 215 different books to read (or collect, if you like). Some are quite common, while others are rare and valuable.

Notes and Journals

A Note from Falk Firebeard of Solitude, delivered by courier during Side Quest: The Wolf Queen Awakened.

In addition to books, there are a wide variety of notes and journals used throughout your adventure to convey shorter or more personal messages, from the important to the trivial. Some are given or found during Quests, while others can be picked up in houses and dungeons. Quest notes are listed in the appropriate Quests, while most other notes simply aren't important enough to be tracked in this guide. But they're all worth a read, if you have the time.

 NOTE Sample locations of every Functional and Common book are shown in the Inventory Chapter (page 70). The two easiest locations to find every type of the Skill Book are also presented in the Appendices, as well as across the Atlas.

IMPROVING YOUR STANDING IN SKYRIM

Quests

Quests are a series of related objectives that make up a single mission or story. These range from the simple to the epic, and a large amount of this guide is spent detailing every single one of them! In game, the Quest Journal tracks all of your current and former quests, while the General Stats page keeps a count of how many quests you've completed. Remember that there are dozens of Miscellaneous Objectives, Favor Quests, and World Encounters and Interactions to discover as well. Every single Quest is documented later in this guide.

 TIP The Quest Target Marker is exceptionally useful, and you should always keep the target for your current quest(s) turned on. Remember to set your Quest or Objective 'Active' first, then highlight the quest and press 'Show on Map' to display the World Map centered on the location you need to reach. The Marker will also appear on your compass to guide you.

Favors and Friendship

When visiting a city, town, or settlement, take a moment to speak with everyone you meet. In addition to learning more about the area, they often have a Favor or other task they could use your help with. Complete it, and they react to you much more favorably.

Keep this up among folks in the same settlement, and you'll soon hear the guards mention your pleasant reputation. Consult the Miscellaneous Objectives and Favor Quest chapters, beginning on page 392, for a list of the huge number of favors you can perform.

Making friends has a number of useful benefits:

◊ Your friends will often be willing to help you in return.

◊ They will occasionally give you gifts.

◊ They may allow you to take items from their house, shop, or market stall without paying for them (you'll notice that many items are no longer marked 'steal'– help yourself!).

◊ They're willing to put you up for the night– when in their home, you are no longer trespassing, and you can sleep in any bed they own. An unscrupulous 'friend' could take advantage of this hospitality to rob them blind...

◊ Some may even be willing to join you on your adventure if you ask! Consult the Followers list later in this section for details.

 NOTE Completing Favors for the inhabitants of a Hold also wins you the attention of the Jarl. Complete the Jarl's Quest or Favors, and you will be granted the title of Thane. Thanes are granted the services of a Housecarl (see Followers, page 62), and receive more lenient treatment for crimes they commit (see Crime, page 39). You can become the Thane of any or all of the Nine Holds.

Houses

Buying a House

When the time comes to establish yourself as more than just a wandering dragon-slayer, you can put down roots in any (or all) of Skyrim's Major Capitals by purchasing a House. You can't just saunter into town with a hefty bag of gold and demand a dwelling, though: you must first win the trust of the Jarl. Speak to them and complete the Quests or Favors they assign until you earn their friendship and permission to buy a house in the city. For more details on what you need to do, see the appropriate Thane Task in the Favors section (see page 404).

> Remember, the Civil War affects who controls each of the five major cities. If your faction takes control of a city, you can be sure the newly-installed Jarl will reward your efforts, and may give you permission to purchase a house immediately! **CAUTION**

With the Jarl's approval, you can now approach the Steward (who is usually nearby) and ask about purchasing a home. The price is displayed (and is non-negotiable). Pay the Steward, and you receive the key to the dwelling.

Decorating Your Property

Once you've purchased a house, you can leave it in its current (usually sparse and cobwebbed) state, or speak to the Steward again to begin decorating it. Each house comes with a

Home Decorating Guide that describes the options available to you, so you can make an informed decision about which furnishings to purchase. In addition to purely cosmetic items like chairs or cupboards, decorations also include useful items like crafting stations, weapon racks, mannequins, and bookshelves. Simply return to the Steward, buy the decorations you want, and when you return to your house, they have been installed.

Benefits of Home Ownership

Owning a house gives you a variety of useful benefits:

◊ It gives you a convenient base of operations in the city, with a number of easily accessible crafting stations and a bed you own (for the Well Rested or Lover's Comfort bonuses – see page 36).

◊ You can store any weapons, armor, crafting materials, or other items you have in your house, safe in the knowledge that they will always be there when you return.

◊ You can prominently display the weapons, artifacts, and items that you've collected on a variety of weapon racks, weapon plaques, mannequins, and bookshelves.

◊ If you've been named Thane of the Hold, you can find your Housecarl in your house, ready to join you at a moment's notice.

◊ If you're married (see Side Quest: The Bonds of Matrimony, page 336), you can also ask your spouse to move in with you, instead of meeting them in the inn or bedding down in their (often rudimentary) place!

Available Properties

Proudspire Manor, Solitude (Haafingar Hold)

Price: 25,000 gold
Jarl: Jarl Elisif the Fair
Steward: Falk Firebeard
Available Decorations:
  Bedroom (2000)
  Living Room (2000)
  Alchemy Laboratory (2500)
  Enchanting Laboratory (2500)
  Patio Decorations (500)
  Kitchen (1500)
Total Cost: 36,000 gold

Vlindrel Hall, Markarth (The Reach)

Price: 8,000 gold
Jarl: Jarl Igmund or Jarl Thongvor Silverfish
Steward: Raerek or Reburrus Quintilius
Available Decorations:
  Bedroom (800)
  Living Room (900)
  Alchemy Laboratory (1000)
  Enchanting Laboratory (1000)
  Entrance Hall (500)
Total Cost: 12,200 gold

Breezehome, Whiterun (Whiterun Hold)

Price: 5,000 gold
Jarl: Jarl Balgruuf the Greater or Jarl Vignar the Revered
Steward: Proventus Avenicci or Brill
Available Decorations:
  Alchemy Laboratory (500)
  Bedroom (300)
  Loft (200)
  Dining Room (250)
Total Cost: 6,250 gold

Hjerim, Windhelm (Eastmarch)

Price: 12,000 gold
Jarl: Jarl Ulfric Stormcloak or Jarl Brunwulf Free-Winter
Steward: Jorleif or Captain Lonely-Gale
Available Decorations:
  Kitchen (1000)
  Bedroom (1000)
  Living Room (1500)
  Alchemy Laboratory (1500)
  Enchanting Laboratory (1500)
  Armory (2000)
  Clean up that murderer's mess (500)
Total Cost: 21,000 gold

> **NOTE** To purchase Hjerim, you must complete the first part of Side Quest: Blood on the Ice.

Honeyside, Riften (The Rift)

Price: 8,000 gold
Jarl: Jarl Laila Lawgiver or Jarl Maven Black-Briar
Steward: Anuriel or Hemming Black-Briar
Available Decorations:
  Bedroom (600)
  Kitchen (500)
  Alchemy Laboratory (1000)
  Enchanting Laboratory (1000)
  Garden (800)
  Porch (400)
Total Cost: 12,200 gold pieces

> **NOTE** The precise location of every house you can buy is indicated in the Atlas. Pictures and the exact method of purchasing each House is detailed in the Thane's Tasks, part of the Favors section of the Quests chapter, on page 404.

FOLLOWERS

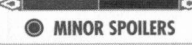
● MINOR SPOILERS

Throughout the realm, there are those that stand ready to join you in your adventure, and are prepared to lay down their lives in your service. These selfless companions are broadly known as Followers. Followers may join you for any number of reasons, whether because you've hired their services, helped them in the past, or are simply taking on a charge that they have an interest in. Some join you only for the duration of a specific quest, while others will follow you indefinitely. This section explores these and other details about your Followers.

> **NOTE** Typically, you can only have only one human Follower and one animal (dog) Follower at a time, although additional Followers may join you temporarily for a quest that they have an interest in.

 ## General Traits

Your Follower normally acts as a shadow, bodyguard, item repository, and friend.

When a Follower has agreed to join you on your adventure, there are a number of advantages they bring, and help you can expect from them.

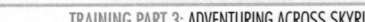

Equipment: Your Followers will always equip the best weapons, armor, and items they have available, and try to use staffs and other items effectively. They take their own skills and proficiencies into account when making these decisions, so all else being equal, expect Jenassa (an archer) to prefer a bow to a two-handed sword, and light armor to heavy plate.

Skills: All Followers have a specific set of favored skills (listed below), which improve as their level increases. Unlike your character, Followers do not become better at the skills they use– no matter how you try to force Marcurio (a mage) to be a greatsword-wielding warrior, he'll always be better with magic. Make sure to select a follower whose skill set meets your needs.

Levels: Most Followers automatically level up when you do, so there's no need to worry about a Follower 'falling behind' if you go off and adventure on your own, or want to work with someone else for a while.

Tactics: Followers will try to follow your lead whenever possible:

When you Sneak, they will Sneak as well, and stop when you do. Don't expect them to take cover on their own, though– if you want them to hide in a particular location, order them to move to it.

When you draw or sheathe your weapons, so will they.

When attacked, they will use their best weapons, spells, and tactics to defend both themselves and you.

Catching Up: If you travel on horseback (or with the great loping strides of a werewolf), you may find that your Followers have a tendency to fall behind. Don't worry about losing them– there are several ways you can help them catch up.

Just Wait (using the Wait System), and they'll use the time to catch up.

Load in to any new space, and they'll be right behind you.

Fast-travel anywhere, and they'll arrive next to you.

Heading Home: If you dismiss a follower, they will return home and take up their original routine. Most followers will rejoin you if you ask, though you may need to pay for the services of Hirelings again if too much time has passed.

Death and Dying: When a Follower's health is exhausted, they will collapse. Heal them, or finish the combat and wait for their health to regenerate, and they will recover, none the worse for wear.

> Be careful, though-- if you inflict lethal damage on a Follower, either directly (say, by hitting them with an errant attack) or indirectly (from the blast of a fireball), they will die. Permanently. **CAUTION**

At Your Command

You can also issue a orders to your Followers. To issue an order, either speak to them or enter Command Mode (target them, then press and hold the Activate button until the cursor changes). The available orders are:

Wait/Follow: If you want to explore an area on your own or try a stealthy approach, use the Wait command to tell your Follower to stop shadowing you. Once you're done, return to your Follower and tell them to accompany you again. Note there are some situations and locations where Followers can't accompany you (such as to jail, if you're arrested). If you leave a Follower at a location and don't return, they eventually return home.

Do Something: You can order your Follower to do something specific, which can be helpful in all kinds of situations. Move your target crosshairs onto something you want your Follower to use, take, steal, or attack, then press Activate to give the order.

Trade Items: This allows you to exchange items between your inventory and your follower's. Some notes:

All Followers start with some basic equipment. You can't take these items from them.

You can, however, give your Followers better gear, such as items that you've improved, enchanted, or think your Follower might be more adept at using. If they judge the item is better than what they currently have, they'll equip it immediately.

You can have your Follower carry their share of the treasure, effectively turning them into a "pack mule". This roughly doubles the amount of loot you can carry, which is handy if you're trying to gather as much as you can from a dungeon before returning to town and selling it off. Note that your Followers do have a maximum carry weight (not shown), so there is a limit to what they can carry as well.

Part Ways: If this relationship just isn't working out, you can tell your follower that you no longer need their services. They'll head home, and you can then acquire a different follower or set off on your own.

Other Notes and Tips

> **TIP** When choosing a Follower, make sure to pick one that complements your style of play. If you're adept at sneaking and silent ranged takedowns with a bow, find someone with similar prowess. If you're a robed mage, seek the company of a powerful warrior to hold your foes at bay. Experiment around with the available Followers until you find one you enjoy adventuring with. Then add a dog!

It's almost always a good idea to bring a Follower along; they can distract foes, soak up damage on your behalf, and help you to take down enemies more quickly. However, there are two cases to be wary of:

If you plan to take a stealthy approach to your next mission, Followers can be more of a hindrance than a help. Even with a well-outfitted stealthy follower, they can't use cover and concealment as effectively as you can. When stealth is essential, you may want to go it alone.

If you're a Mage with a lot of area-of-effect spells, the collateral damage can be lethal to your Followers. Control your casting carefully, or leave your Follower at home and take up Conjuration instead-- Atronachs are immune to spells of their element, and Zombies are, well, dead anyway.

> **NOTE** Many Followers are also Trainers. Bring them with you, and you will be able to train whenever you like, so long as you have the funds.

You can also be romantically tied to many Followers. Consult Side Quest: The Bonds of Matrimony (page 336) for more details.

Types of Followers

The following lists identify all of the characters who can become your Followers. For each Follower, this this section identifies their primary combat style (e.g., Warrior) and their favored skills. Any prerequisites for obtaining them are also noted.

In general, Followers can be classified into five major categories:

Hirelings. Mercenaries who will accompany you if you hire them.

Housecarls. If you are named Thane of a Major Hold, the Jarl will appoint a Housecarl as your bodyguard.

Guildmates. If you join one of the major guilds, you may be able to ask your fellow guild members to follow you.

Quest or Dungeon Followers. These characters will follow you once you complete their quest or dungeon.

Favor Followers. Friends you have completed Favors for may join you if you ask.

Animal Companions. Loyal dogs who will fight at your side in combat.

> **TIP** To find the exact location of every Follower, simply look up the settlement mentioned in their description in the Atlas later in the guide.

Hirelings

Hirelings are mercenaries for hire, each with their own unique combat style. To purchase their services, you must pay a flat fee of 500 gold pieces. Dismiss them, they may charge you that fee again.

Notes: You must complete Miscellaneous Objective: Erik the Slayer before you can hire Erik.

Belrand, in Solitude (Haafingar).

Spellsword: One-Handed, Light Armor, Destruction, Restoration

Vorstag, in Markarth (The Reach).

Warrior: One-Handed, Heavy Armor, Archery, Block

Jenassa, in Whiterun (Whiterun Hold).

Archer: Archery, Light Armor, One-Handed, Block, Sneak

Stenvar, in Windhelm (Eastmarch).

Knight: Two-Handed, Heavy Armor, Archery, Block

Marcurio, in Riften (The Rift).

Mage: Destruction, Restoration, Alteration, Conjuration, Sneak

Erik the Slayer, in Rorikstead (Whiterun Hold).

Barbarian: Two-Handed, Light Armor, Archery, Block

Housecarls

Housecarls are bodyguards sworn to your service as Thane. For advice on becoming the Thane of one or more Holds, consult page 404.

Jordis the Sword-Maiden, Housecarl of Solitude (Haafingar)

Housecarl: One-Handed, Heavy Armor, Archery, Block

Argis the Bulwark, Housecarl of Markarth (The Reach)

Housecarl: One-Handed, Heavy Armor, Archery, Block

Lydia, Housecarl of Whiterun (Whiterun Hold)

Housecarl: One-Handed, Heavy Armor, Archery, Block

Calder, Housecarl of Windhelm (Windhelm Hold)

Housecarl: One-Handed, Heavy Armor, Archery, Block

Iona, Housecarl of Riften (The Rift)

Housecarl: One-Handed, Heavy Armor, Archery, Block

The Companions

This ancient and renowned order of warriors is headquartered in Whiterun. Companions have an extremely close bond, referring to each other as Shield-Siblings. Once you complete their questline, they become available as Followers. Visit Jorrvaskr in Whiterun to find them.

Aela the Huntress

Archer: Archery, Light Armor, Sneak, Speech, One-Handed

Notes: Expert Trainer: Archery

Athis

Warrior: One-Handed, Block, Archery, Light Armor

Notes: Expert Trainer: One-Handed

Farkas

Warrior: One-Handed, Heavy Armor, Smithing, Speech

Notes: Master Trainer: Heavy Armor

Njada Stonearm

Warrior: One-Handed, Block, Speech

Notes: Expert Trainer: Block

Ria

Warrior: One-Handed, Heavy Armor, Archery, Block

Torvar

Warrior: One-Handed, Heavy Armor, Archery, Block

Vilkas

Knight: Two-Handed, Heavy Armor, Archery, Block

Notes: Master Trainer: Two-Handed

The College of Winterhold

Your fellow students at the College of Winterhold will join you once you are a member of the College and complete their specific College of Winterhold Radiant Quest.

Onmund

Sorcerer: Destruction, Illusion, One-Handed, Heavy Armor

J'Zargo

Sorcerer: Destruction, Illusion, One-Handed, Heavy Armor

Brelyna Maryon

Mage: Alteration, Illusion, Conjuration, Sneak

Dark Brotherhood Assassins

After completing the Dark Brotherhood Questline, a number of new initiates, and a strange jester are available to aid and abet you in your adventures. You'll find them at the Dawnstar Sanctuary in The Pale Hold.

Dark Brotherhood Initiate (Male and Female)

Assassin: Sneak, One-Handed, Archery, Light Armor

Cicero, the Fool of Hearts, Jester and Keeper of the Night Mother.

Assassin: Sneak, One-Handed, Archery, Light Armor

Quest-Related Followers

The following citizens of Skyrim are willing to join you after you've finished the Quest they are involved in (providing they survive the Quest as well). Consult each Quest for more information.

Adelaisa Vendicci. Side Quest: Rise in the East.

Townsperson: Alchemy, Enchanting, Smithing, Speech

Aranea. Daedric Quest: The Black Star.

Mage: Destruction, Restoration, Conjuration, Alteration

Eola. Daedric Quest: The Taste of Death.

Nightblade: Destruction, One-Handed, Alteration, Sneak

Erandur. Daedric Quest: Waking Nightmare.

Healer: Restoration, Conjuration, Speech, Alchemy

Lob. Daedric Quest: The Cursed Tribe

Archer: Archery, Light Armor, One-Handed, Block, Sneak

Ogol. Daedric Quest: The Cursed Tribe

Warrior: One-Handed, Heavy Armor, Archery, Sneak

Ugor. Daedric Quest: The Cursed Tribe

Archer: Archery, Light Armor, One-Handed, Block, Sneak

Dungeon-Related Followers

The following denizens of the Dungeons of Skyrim are available to help your cause once you clear the Dungeon you find them in. Providing they survive. Consult the Dungeon Quests 377 for more information.

Illia. Darklight Tower (The Rift)

Mage: Destruction, Restoration, Conjuration, Alteration

Golldir. Hillgrund's Tomb (Whiterun Hold)

Warrior: One-Handed, Heavy Armor, Archery, Block

Favor Followers

The following inhabitants of Skyrim agree to join you once you've befriended them by completing a Task or Favor that they set for you. Consult Favors (on page 399) for more information.

Ahtar the Jailor, in Solitude's Castle Dour (Haafingar).

Knight: Two-Handed, Heavy Armor, Archery, Block

Benor, the guard lieutenant of Morthal (Hjaalmarch).

Knight: Two-Handed, Heavy Armor, Archery, Block

Cosnach, the drunkard in Markarth (The Reach).

Warrior: One-Handed, Heavy Armor, Archery, Block

Borgakh, the daughter of Bagrak, in Mor Khazgur (The Reach).

Warrior: One-Handed, Heavy Armor, Archery, Sneak

Ghorbash, the brother of the Orc Chief of Dushnikh Yal (The Reach).

Archer: Archery, Light Armor, One-Handed, Block, Sneak

Uthgerd the Unbroken, the brawling warrior of Whiterun (Whiterun Hold).

Warrior: One-Handed, Heavy Armor, Archery, Block

Sven, the minstrel and lumberjack of Riverwood (Whiterun Hold).

Townsperson: Alchemy, Enchanting, Smithing, Archery

Faendal, the hunter and lumberjack of Riverwood (Whiterun Hold)

Archer: Archery, Light Armor, One-Handed, Sneak

Notes: Journeyman Trainer: Archery

Roggi Knot-Beard, the Nord miner of Kynesgrove (Eastmarch).

Townsperson: Alchemy, Enchanting, Smithing, One-Handed

Derkeethus, the kidnapped fisherman, held in Darkwater Pass (Eastmarch).

Archer: Archery, Light Armor, One-Handed, Block, Sneak

Annekke Crag-Jumper, the adventuress of Darkwater Crossing (Eastmarch).

Archer: Archery, Light Armor, One-Handed, Block, Sneak

Mjoll the Lioness, adventuress, in Riften (The Rift).

Knight: Two-Handed, Heavy Armor, Archery, Block

Kharjo, the bodyguard for Ahkari's Caravan (Khajiit Caravans).

Warrior: One-Handed, Heavy Armor, Archery, Block

Animal Companions

Two-legged Followers aren't the only ones you can bring with you on adventures. Four-legged friends are also an option. The following Dogs (who can follow, stay, and attack, but can't carry items) are possible companions.

Vigilance, a War Dog you can purchase from Banning at Markarth Stables for 500 gold (The Reach).

Meeko, a Dog you find in the wilderness close to Meeko's Shack, in Hjaalmarch.

Stray Dog; a dog you can meet in a random World Encounter (Corpses in the Aftermath of a Dragon Attack or Dog Fending Off A Pair of Wolves; see page 409).

Horses

The ultimate steed of Skyrim: Shadowmere.

Horses can be purchased and used by adventurers to speed travel between far-flung destinations. There are a number of different ways in which you can acquire a horse:

Buying a Horse:

You can purchase a Horse at the stables adjacent to each of the five Major Hold Capitals– the four Minor Hold Capitals (Morthal, Dawnstar, Winterhold, and Falkreath) do not have stables.

Each stable sells a particular type of horse. The price of each horse, regardless of its type, is 1,000 gold pieces. This price is fixed, and isn't affected by your Speech Skill, Speech Perks, or other effects (such as a Potion of Haggling). Horses are all identical in terms of speed, health, and performance; the only difference is their coloration.

Available Horses

✓	HORSE TYPE	HOLD NAME	LOCATION OF PURCHASE	PRICE
	Black	Whiterun Hold	Whiterun Stables	1000
	Brown	Eastmarch	Windhelm Stables	1000
	Grey	The Reach	Riften Stables	1000
	Paint	The Reach	Markarth Stables	1000
	Palomino	Haafingar	Katla's Farm (Solitude)	1000
	Frost	The Rift	Special	N/A
	Shadowmere	Falkreath	Special	N/A

Owning a Horse

Horses that you've paid for are considered to be owned by you. Horses you own are always saddled, and have your name added to their title (for example, "Prisoner's Horse"). This helps you differentiate between your horse and any others that may be around– just look for the name and saddle.

You can own all five types of horses, providing you have the gold to pay for each of them. If you own more than one horse, the horse you've most recently ridden travels with you if you decide to fast-travel to a location. All of your other horses return to the stables where they were purchased, and wait for you there (you can return and use them whenever you wish).

Borrowing or Stealing a Horse

You can steal horses from a number of different locations. The best places to look are the stables where you can purchase a steed, any Military Camp or Military Fort, and from Wor Encounters. To steal a horse, simply walk up to it and mount it. Stealing a Horse adds 50 to your bounty for that Hold. Dismounting from a stolen steed, and then mounting it again counts as a separate theft, adding 50 more gold to your bounty. Horse rustling can get expensive fast.

Occasionally, you can "borrow" an unowned horse (one not marked 'Steal') from a Location, World Encounter, or Military Fort. Unowned horses behave in the same manner as stolen horses, except that riding them isn't a crime, and your bounty won't increase.

Using a Horse

It is important to learn what you and your steed are capable of:

Horses can move at a canter (run) and gallop (sprint) speed equal to your very best run and sprint speeds while on foot. However, horses aren't weighed down by your armor, and they likely have more stamina than you do, making them a faster way to travel overall. Plus, you get to conserve your stamina, so you won't be worn out if you find yourself ambushed by brigands on the road.

Horses can charge through or leap over low or small obstacles (essentially anything you could jump across when on foot). Larger obstacles can't be jumped, so avoid them or move around them.

The Elder Scrolls V
SKYRIM

Horses are by nature unaggressive, and although able to attack, they generally flee from combat once you dismount.

Your Followers can't ride horses. If you ride off on horseback, your Follower will run after you, but is likely to fall behind. When you approach your destination, you may want to stop and use the Wait command, which will give them a chance to catch up.

Controlling a Horse

When riding a horse, it's important to note the following controls:

While riding a horse, the camera is locked into a third-person view, and the View-switch button centers the camera behind you instead.

The Activate button allows you to dismount. You must dismount in order to activate objects or speak to others.

The Jump button causes your horse to rear dramatically. You can't jump while on horseback.

The Sprint button allows you to gallop.

While mounted, you can't fight (attack with weapons, cast spells, Shout, or use any Powers). Should you be attacked, quickly decide whether to fight or flee. If you decide to fight, dismount, slay your foes, mount up again, and continue on your way. Or take advantage of the horse's speed and stamina to barrel through your foes and gallop away– you can outrun most human adversaries if given enough time and space.

Fast-Traveling and Horses

If you own one or more horses, the horse you most recently rode will fast-travel with you. This is handy if you've lost your horse after a fight, or emerged from a dungeon in a different location– simply fast-travel somewhere nearby, and your horse will be standing next to you.

If you're riding a stolen or borrowed horse, your horse will only fast-travel with you if you're riding it when you trigger the fast-travel. Otherwise, you'll leave it behind.

Horses won't accompany you into cities, dungeons, or other interiors. If you fast-travel to a city, your horse will be left at the stables just outside.

The Death of a Horse

While riding a horse, most of the damage from falls and enemy attacks will absorbed by your horse. When a horse is reduced to 10% of its health or less, it drops you and tries to flee. If your horse takes lethal damage, it will die.

If you own a horse and it expires, a new horse of the same type will become available for purchase at the same stables as previously indicated. The same cannot be said for Frost or Shadowmere; when they expire it is usually permanent.

Unique Horses: Frost and Shadowmere

There are two unique horses you may wish to seek out.

Frost: As part of Side Quest: Promises to Keep (see page 363), you're tasked with stealing Frost from the Black-Briar Lodge in The Rift. At the end of this Quest, you have the option to betray the man who sent you on that mission, Louis Letrush, and keep Frost for yourself. If you

do, you gain legal ownership of Frost. Aside from the fact this didn't cost you any gold, Frost is a normal horse in every other respect.

Shadowmere: At the start of Dark Brotherhood Quest: The Cure for Madness (see page 244), Astrid – the leader of the Dark Brotherhood – summons Shadowmere, a powerful steed. From this point forward, you have ownership of Shadowmere. Aside from the fact this didn't cost you any gold, Shadowmere has other advantages too:

He has twice the stamina and almost three times the health of a normal horse.

When injured, his health regenerates rapidly, making him extremely difficult for foes to kill.

He is much more aggressive than a normal horse, fighting with you instead of fleeing from danger.

With glowing eyes, a unique saddle, and a jet black mane, Shadowmere is the ultimate steed of Skyrim!

▶ Carriages

Travel between Hold Capitals in some style and comfort.

If you can't afford a horse of your own, Carriages are another good way to speed your travel around Skyrim. Outside each of the five Major Hold Capitals (generally near the stables), you can find a horse-cart hitched up and ready to go. Speak to the driver to learn that he offers a carriage service, and will gladly ferry you to any of Skyrim's capitals for a nominal fee.

20 Gold for a ride to the Major Hold Capitals: Solitude, Markarth, Whiterun, Windhelm, or Riften.

50 Gold for a ride to the Minor Hold Capitals: Morthal, Dawnstar, Winterhold, or Falkreath Pay the fee, then head around back and activate the Carriage to climb aboard. The driver will mention a piece of lore as you set off. A moment later, you'll find yourself at your destination.

> **TIP** Is this a good deal? It depends on your personal playstyle. If you'd rather walk or ride from one location to another, you may find the journey as rewarding as the destination, with dozens of locations to explore and challenges to face along the way. If you simply want to reach your goal as quickly as possible, a Carriage Ride will take you to the nearest city in record time. Spend 300 gold, and you can quickly unlock all of the capital cities, allowing you to fast-travel to them whenever you wish.

SERVICES, COLLECTIBLES, AND ITEMS OF INTEREST

 **MINOR SPOILERS**

In this final section of the Training Chapter, we briefly highlight the services, merchants, collectibles, and objects of interest that you can discover on your adventure. Those marked with a "*" are tracked in the Atlas. Those marked with a "†" have a table in the Appendix that shows every location or instance of them in the game, or in the case of Skill Books, the two easiest locations to find in the game. Those marked with a "‡" have a chart or table elsewhere in this guide that shows all of their locations or instances.

If there's something that you're looking for that isn't listed here or in a specific location in this guide's Inventory, Bestiary, Atlas, or Appendices, it probably occurs randomly in the world, and is thus impossible to track.

▶ Achievements/Trophies

If you want to obtain all the different Achievements (PC and Xbox 360) or Trophies (Playstation 3) that Skyrim has to offer, consult the Appendices at the end of this guide. It lists all of them, and provides advice on how to obtain each. You are wise to consult this chart now, so you know how to unlock each of these rewards ahead of time.

Services and Traders

Apothecary *†

Number Available: 12

A shop where Alchemy Ingredients and Potions are sold. Apothecaries can be found in most towns and cities, and typically display a sign such as the one shown here.

Innkeeper/Bartender *†

Number Available: 15/5

The proprietors of Inns and Taverns sell food and drink, and rent rooms where weary travellers can sleep for the night. They are also a great source of local rumors, which often lead to Quests and Objectives.

Blacksmith/Fletcher *†

Number Available: 33/3

In medium or large settlements, you can often find a Smithy, which typically includes a number of Smithing and crafting stations, often manned by a smith who sells weapons and armor. Most display a sign like the one shown here.

Caravan * ‡

Number Available: 3

Three Khajiit Caravans travel the roads of Skyrim, selling their wares and trading with anyone they meet. The routes they take are listed in the Atlas.

Follower/Hireling *‡

Number Available: 47

A person who may be willing to join you on your adventure, lending sword or spell to your cause. Hirelings charge a fee for their services. Consult the information earlier in the Training, on page 62.

Stables/Carriage Drivers *

Number Available: 5/5

A location, always close to a Hold Capital, where Horses can be purchased (or stolen). You can usually find a Carriage nearby as well; pay the carriage driver a nominal fee for a ride to any of Skyrim's other major cities. These are Primary Locations in the Atlas.

Trader (Vendor) *†

Number Available: 53

These merchants sell a variety of general goods, pawned items, and the like. Fences for stolen items are also included in this category, although not all vendors are fences (and none will serve as fences right away).

Fence: 10
Food Vendor: 9
General Goods Vendor: 19
"Special" Vendor: 3
Spell Vendor: 12

Trainer *‡

Number Available: 50

A skilled individual (who may also be a Follower or Trader) who can help you improve a particular skill. Consult the information earlier in the Training, on page 11.

Crafting Stations

NOTE Due to the large number of crafting stations, only one or two examples of each type of crafting station are listed for each Hold. However, individual locations within the Atlas that have stations are noted.

Alchemy Lab *

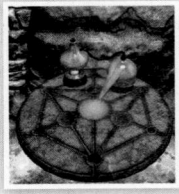

A table-sized laboratory where you can mix Ingredients into potions and poisons by using your Alchemy Skill.

Arcane Enchanter *

A table-sized piece of furniture where you can enchant or disenchant magical items using your Enchanting Skill.

Anvil or Blacksmith Forge *

The tools of a Blacksmith, a Forge or Anvil allow you to forge metal, leather, and more esoteric materials into weapons, armor, and jewelry by using your Smithing Skill.

Cooking Pot and Spit

A spit, stew-pot, or other implement where meats and ingredients can be cooked. There are a huge number of these; one in almost every house.

Grindstone *

A foot-driven stone wheel that allows you to sharpen and improve weapons by using your Smithing Skill.

Smelter *

A furnace that allows you to Smelt Ore (and some Dwarven materials) into Ingots for Smithing or selling.

Tanning Rack *

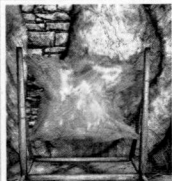

A wooden rack that allows you to dry pelts and tan them into leather (or leather strips) for Smithing or selling.

Wood Chopping Block

An old tree stump where you can split logs into firewood. They can be found in almost any lumber camp or settlement.

Workbench *

A sturdy bench that allows you to temper and improve armor by using your Smithing Skill.

Collectibles

Captured Critter * ‡

Number Available: 5

An insect caught in a glass jar. Find these as part of Side Quest: Captured Critters*.

Crimson Nirnroot *‡

Number Available: 30+

Related Character: Avrusa Sarethi (Sarenthi Farm in The Rift)

A special red variant of the odd, chiming plant, found only in the underground realm of Blackreach. Collect these as part of Side Quest: A Return to your Roots.

Dragon Priest Mask * ‡

Number Available: 10

An ancient ceremonial mask, infused with great power and borne by a formidable Dragon Priest. Find these as part of Side Quest: Masks of the Dragon Priests.

Books ‡

A wide range of Spell Tomes, Functional Books, and Common Books can be found throughout the world. Consult The Inventory for more information, as well as earlier in this chapter.

Skill Book *† ‡

Each of these books increases a specific Skill by a single point when first read. There are five distinct books for each Skill, for a total of 90 titles and 90 Skill Increases that you can earn (though there are multiple copies of each book). Two copies (the easiest to find) of each book are listed in the Appendices, although each Atlas location with a skill book is also flagged.

Treasure Map * ‡

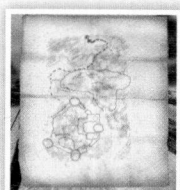

Number Available: 12

These pieces of parchment have a visual map drawn on them, revealing the location of a hidden treasure. Consult Side Quest: The Great Skyrim Treasure Hunt for details.

Unique Weapon *†‡

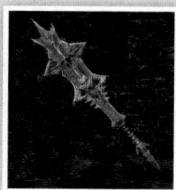

Number Available: 80

These items are separated into Unique Weapons found in Dungeons, those found or given to you as part of a Quest, and Daedric Artifacts. Details about all of these weapons can be found in The Inventory Chapter on page 75.

Unique Armor or Item *†‡

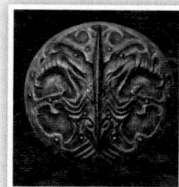

Number Available: 112

These items are separated into Unique Armor and Outfits found in Dungeons, those found or given to you as part of a Quest, and Daedric Artifacts. Details about all of these items can be found in the Inventory chapter on page 77.

Unusual Gem *‡

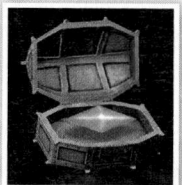

Number Available: 24 (plus Crown)

Related Character: Vex (Thieves Guild in Riften)

Occasionally, you may stumble across one of these Unusual Gems, which are actually stones from the legendary Crown of Barenziah. Consult Thieves Guild Radiant Quest: No Stone Unturned.

Items of Interest

Standing Stones *‡

Number Available: 13

These standing stones can be activated to receive a powerful blessing. Standing Stones are Primary Locations in the Atlas, and are described earlier in this guide on page 59.

Shrines *†

Number Available: 69

Activate a Shrine to one of the Nine Divines to receive a blessing. The locations of these shrines are listed in the Atlas as well as the Appendices.

Civil War Maps *

These maps show the current state of the Civil War that rages across Skyrim. Activate the flags on the map to add each location to your World Map. These are flagged in the Atlas only, as each is identical.

Word Walls *‡

Number Available: 42

These ancient stone walls are (usually) inscribed with one of three Words of Power from a specific Shout. Approach them and absorb their Word, then unlock it with a Dragon Soul to increase the power of your Thu'um. Consult the Atlas or page 32 for locations.

Dragon Mounds *‡

Number Available: 22

These ancient burial mounds mark the spot where the dragons of old were slain. Now, the dragons are being resurrected, and the Mounds are opening, one by one. Dragon Mounds are Secondary Locations in the Atlas, and are described earlier in this Training Chapter, on page 58.

Watch the skies!

SPELLS, WEAPONS, ARMOR AND ITEMS

Behold the charts and tables of Skyrim! The following pages deluge you with information on the thousands of spells, weapons, armor sets, and items that you can acquire during your adventure. If you're interested in the properties of an item you haven't found yet, want to compare it to another item, or simply want to see everything that is possible to find, you'll find the information here.

There are a few general rules you should be aware of before digging in:

As described in the skills section of Training (see page 9), many skills, perks, and enchantments affect the damage you do with weapons, the protection you receive from armor, and the cost of your spells. To account for this, the game automatically calculates those effects and applies them to the spells and items you see in game. The values listed below are the base values for the item in question: you will rarely, if ever, see these exact numbers because of the impact of your skills. But this list is still an effective way of comparing two items to gauge the relative differences between them.

Some items, especially unique weapons and armor, are marked as being Leveled. This means that the actual item you receive in game will be dependent on your level, and may have better statistics and stronger versions of the enchantments listed here.

Some enchantments and effects are said to Stack with others. This means that the benefits of those effects are cumulative; they combine to give you a stronger result.

◈ Table I: Spells

Spells are an essential tool for many characters, from Arch-mages who have mastered the intricacies of all five Schools of Magic to those that merely dabble in sorcery to suit their needs, such as a Thief who relies on Invisibility, or a Warrior who invokes a healing spell to cure his wounds. This section lists all of the spells available to you. You will find or buy most of these in the form of Spell Tomes, although you may be taught a few of them directly.

Spell List Notes

Only spells that can be used by your character are included on this list. It does not include Powers, such as a Vampire's Embrace of Shadows or a Werewolf's Beast Form, or enemy spells or spell-like effects that you can't acquire.

All Destruction Spells have secondary effects based on their element, regardless of whether those effects are listed in the spell description.

All Fire spells can light enemies on fire, causing your foes to take additional damage for several seconds. This makes fire spells especially effective against foes with high health.

All Frost spells do Stamina damage equal to their Health damage, and slow targets by 50% for several seconds (the exact duration varies by spell). This makes them especially effective against berserkers and other foes who rely on power attacks, shield bashes, and other tactics that depend on stamina.

All Shock spells do Magicka damage equal to half their Health damage (except where otherwise noted). This makes them ideal for crippling enemy mages.

Spell List Key

Spell Name: The name of the spell as it appears in your Magic Menu.

Level: The level of the spell (Novice - Master). Unique or quest-based spells in each School of Magic are included in a 'Special' category at the bottom of the list.

Standard Cost: The cost of the spell after taking the relevant spell level perk, with the minimum skill required to do so. So Novice Spells are displayed at Skill 15, Apprentice at 25, etc. This is the most useful number, as it provides the most realistic basis for cost comparison among spells.

Base Cost: The cost of the spell at skill level 15, with no perks.

Skill 100 Cost: The cost of the spell at skill level 100, after taking all of the spell level perks. This is provided for comparison so you can see how the costs diminish as you become more proficient.

Description: The description of the spell as it appears in your Magic Menu.

Notes and Restrictions: Lists any quests or other significant limiting factors that govern when you can acquire the spell. Also provides clarifications on how the spell works, and tips on using it effectively.

✔	SPELL NAME	LEVEL	STANDARD COST	BASE COST	SKILL 100 COST	DESCRIPTION	NOTES AND RESTRICTIONS
						ALTERATION	
☐	Candlelight	Novice	9	18	6	Creates a hovering light that lasts for 60s.	
☐	Oakflesh	Novice	45	91	30	Improves the caster's armor rating by 40 points for 60s.	
☐	Magelight	Apprentice	35	74	25	Ball of light that lasts 60s and sticks where it strikes.	
☐	Stoneflesh	Apprentice	81	171	57	Improves the caster's armor rating by 60 points for 60s.	

✓	SPELL NAME	LEVEL	STANDARD COST	BASE COST	SKILL 100 COST	DESCRIPTION	NOTES AND RESTRICTIONS
☐	Detect Life	Adept	37/s	88/s	29/s	Nearby living creatures, but not undead, machines, or daedra, can be seen through walls.	Excellent in stealth situations for keeping track of patrolling guards. The color of the glow indicates whether the creature is hostile towards you.
☐	Ironflesh	Adept	98	235	79	Improves the caster's armor rating by 80 points for 60s.	
☐	Telekenesis	Adept	63/s	149/s	50/s	Can pull an object to you from a distance. Add it to your inventory or throw it.	Great for pulling items off pressure plates from a safe distance, or rearranging items (say, in your house).
☐	Waterbreathing	Adept	82	196	66	Can breathe water for 60s.	Watch for the glow around your body to fade, indicating that the spell has worn off. When it does, you have the equivalent of a full breath (as if you'd just surfaced) before you begin to drown.
☐	Detect Dead	Expert	49/s	130/s	43/s	Nearby dead can be seen through walls.	This spell detects undead and corpses. Great for spotting Draugr lurking in dark catacombs.
☐	Ebonyflesh	Expert	113	300	101	Improves the caster's armor rating by 100 points for 60s.	
☐	Paralyze	Expert	149	396	133	Targets that fail to resist are paralyzed for 10s.	Paralyzed creatures near a ledge will often fall to their deaths.
☐	Dragonhide	Master	248	738	248	Caster ignores 80% of all physical damage for 30s.	Reward for College of Winterhold Radiant Quest: Alteration Ritual Spell.
☐	Mass Paralysis	Master	278	826	278	All targets in the area that fail to resist are paralyzed for 15s.	Sold by Tolfdir, after completing College of Winterhold Radiant Quest: Alteration Ritual Spell.
☐	Equilibrium	Special - Novice	0	0	0	Converts 25 points of health into magicka per second. Caster can be killed by this effect.	Can only be found in Labyrinthian Chasm, during College of Winterhold Quest: The Staff of Magnus, in a side chamber. A risky spell, but it is a fast, low-cost way to recover a lot of Magicka in a hurry.
☐	Transmute	Special - Adept	37	88	29	Transmute one piece of unrefined Iron Ore to Silver, or Silver Ore to Gold, if the caster is carrying any.	This spell is sometimes sold by Enthir, though you can also find copies in Halted Stream Camp, Ansilvund Burial Chamber, and Knifepoint Ridge Mine. Cast this spell twice to transform a piece of Iron Ore (2 gold) to Gold Ore (50 gold). Profit!

CONJURATION

✓	SPELL NAME	LEVEL	STANDARD COST	BASE COST	SKILL 100 COST	DESCRIPTION	NOTES AND RESTRICTIONS
☐	Bound Sword	Novice	41	82	27	Creates a magic sword for 120s. Sheathe it to dispel.	Dualcasting this spell does not give you dual bound swords. If that's what you want, cast the spell seperately in each hand.
☐	Conjure Familiar	Novice	47	94	31	Summons a Familiar for 60s wherever the caster is pointing.	
☐	Raise Zombie	Novice	45	90	30	Reanimate a weak dead body to fight for you for 60s.	Works on creatures up to Lv6.
☐	Bound Battleaxe	Apprentice	70	149	50	Creates a magic battle axe for 120s. Sheathe it to dispel.	
☐	Conjure Flame Atronach	Apprentice	62	132	44	Summons a Flame Atronach for 60s wherever the caster is pointing.	Flame Atronachs do good ranged damage, but are fairly weak in melee.
☐	Reanimate Corpse	Apprentice	60	127	42	Reanimate a more powerful dead body to fight for you for 60s.	Works on creatures up to Lv13.
☐	Soul Trap	Apprentice	44	94	31	If a target dies within 60s, fills a soul gem.	This spell always places the soul into the smallest soul gem that can hold it. But keep an eye on your soul gem inventory– you don't want to waste a Grand Soul Gem on a Skeever's soul. Remember that human souls can only be captured in Black Soul Gems.
☐	Banish Daedra	Adept	72	173	58	Weaker summoned daedra are sent back to Oblivion.	Only works on conjured daedra (not on 'permanent' ones, like those in some Warlock dungeons). Works on Daedra up to Lv15 (Familiars and Flame Atronachs). In addition to its stated effect, this spell will also stagger any Daedra it hits, making it useful in buying you some space against even higher-level foes.
☐	Bound Bow	Adept	76	183	61	Creates a magic bow for 120s. Sheathe it to dispel.	In addition to the bow, this spell also creates bound arrows that last for the life of the bow.
☐	Conjure Frost Atronach	Adept	79	189	63	Summons a Frost Atronach for 60s wherever the caster is pointing.	Frost Atronachs do good melee damage and have high health, but lack a ranged attack.
☐	Revenant	Adept	68	162	54	Reanimate a powerful dead body to fight for you for 60s.	Works on creatures up to Lv21.
☐	Command Daedra	Expert	80	214	72	Powerful summoned and raised creatures are put under your control.	Only works on conjured daedra (not on 'permanent' ones, like those in many Warlock dungeons). Works on Daedra up to Lv20 (Frost Atronachs and lower).
☐	Conjure Dremora Lord	Expert	118	316	106	Summons a Dremora Lord for 60s.	Dremora Lords are powerful melee combatants with a number of fire spells at their disposal.
☐	Conjure Storm Atronach	Expert	107	284	95	Summons a Storm Atronach for 60s wherever the caster is pointing.	Storm Atronachs are powerful ranged combatants.
☐	Dread Zombie	Expert	100	266	89	Reanimate a very powerful dead body to fight for you for 60s.	Works on creatures up to Lv30.
☐	Expel Daedra	Expert	71	190	64	Powerful summoned daedra creatures are sent back to Oblivion.	Only works on conjured daedra (not on 'permanent' ones, like those in many Warlock dungeons). Works on Daedra up to Lv20 (Frost Atronachs and lower). Staggers any Daedra it hits.
☐	Dead Thrall	Master	296	881	296	Reanimate a dead body permanently to fight for you. Only works on people.	Works on creatures up to Lv40.
☐	Flame Thrall	Master	267	793	267	Summons a Flame Atronach permanently.	Reward for College of Winterhold Radiant Quest: Conjuration Ritual Spell. Thralls are stronger versions of the standard atronachs. After casting this spell, consider resting or waiting to recover your magicka.
☐	Frost Thrall	Master	326	969	326	Summons a Frost Atronach permanently.	Sold by Phinis, after completing College of Winterhold Radiant Quest: Conjuration Ritual Spell.
☐	Storm Thrall	Master	356	1057	356	Summons a Storm Atronach permanently.	Sold by Phinis, after completing College of Winterhold Radiant Quest: Conjuration Ritual Spell.
☐	Flaming Familiar	Special - Apprentice	24	50	17	Summons a Flaming Familiar which will charge into battle and explode.	Reward for Dungeon Quest: A Scroll for Anska. The Flaming Familiar will behave like a standard Familiar for a few seconds, then explode for 40 points of damage.
☐	Summon Arniel's Shade	Special - Apprentice	0	0	0	Summons the Shade of Arniel Gane for 60s wherever the caster is pointing.	Reward for College of Winterhold Radiant Quest: Arniel's Endeavor. Arniel's Shade is physically weak, but a powerful spellcaster.
☐	Summon Unbound Dremora	Special - Novice	88	176	59	Summons an unbound Dremora.	Quest spell for College of Winterhold Radiant Quest: Conjuration Ritual Spell. Summons an Unbound Dremora in a specific location for the quest. Otherwise, no effect.

DESTRUCTION

✓	SPELL NAME	LEVEL	STANDARD COST	BASE COST	SKILL 100 COST	DESCRIPTION	NOTES AND RESTRICTIONS
☐	Flames	Novice	6/s	13/s	4/s	A gout of fire that does 8 points per second. Targets on fire take extra damage.	Targets on fire take more damage because they're burning; the spell doesn't do bonus damage if they're burning.

✓	SPELL NAME	LEVEL	STANDARD COST	BASE COST	SKILL 100 COST	DESCRIPTION	NOTES AND RESTRICTIONS
☐	Frostbite	Novice	7/s	14/s	4/s	A blast of cold that does 8 points of damage per second to Health and Stamina.	
☐	Sparks	Novice	8/s	16/s	5/s	Lightning that does 8 points of shock damage to Health and Magicka per second.	
☐	Fire Rune	Apprentice	98	207	69	Cast on a nearby surface, it explodes for 50 points of fire damage when enemies come near.	Runes last indefinately, but you can only place one at a time. For best results, place them in a corridor the enemy will have to use, then pull them towards you. In a pinch, you can also cast a rune directly under an enemy to trigger the explosion immediately, although that's less efficient than your other spells.
☐	Firebolt	Apprentice	17	36	12	A blast of fire that does 25 points of damage. Targets on fire take extra damage.	
☐	Frost Rune	Apprentice	122	258	87	Cast on a nearby surface, it explodes for 50 points of frost damage when enemies come near.	
☐	Ice Spike	Apprentice	25	42	14	A spike of ice that does 25 points of frost damage to Health and Stamina.	
☐	Lightning Bolt	Apprentice	21	45	15	A bolt of lightning that does 25 points of shock damage to Health and half that to Magicka.	
☐	Lightning Rune	Apprentice	134	284	95	Cast on a nearby surface, it explodes for 50 points of shock damage when enemies come near.	
☐	Chain Lightning	Adept	57	137	46	Lightning bolt that does 40 points of shock damage to Health and half to Magicka, then leaps to a new target.	
☐	Fireball	Adept	40	117	39	A fiery explosion for 40 points of damage in a 15 foot radius. Targets on fire take extra damage.	
☐	Flame Cloak	Adept	107	254	85	For 60s, opponents in melee range take 8 points of fire damage per second. Targets on fire take extra damage.	Cloak spells are great if you expect to be in melee frequently, or prefer short-range spells (Flames, Wall of Flames, etc.), as they significantly increase your damage output.
☐	Frost Cloak	Adept	117	278	93	For 60s, opponents in melee range take 8 points of frost damage and Stamina damage per second.	
☐	Ice Storm	Adept	53	127	42	A freezing whirlwind that does 40 points of frost damage per second to Health and Stamina.	
☐	Lightning Cloak	Adept	137	326	110	For 60s, nearby opponents take 8 points of shock damage and half magicka damage.	
☐	Icy Spear	Expert	106	282	95	A spear of ice that does 60 points of frost damage to Health and Stamina.	
☐	Incinerate	Expert	98	262	88	A blast of fire that does 60 points of damage. Targets on fire take extra damage.	
☐	Thunderbolt	Expert	113	302	101	A Thunderbolt that does 60 points of shock damage to Health and half that to Magicka.	
☐	Wall of Flames	Expert	39/s	104/s	35/s	Sprayed on the ground, it creates a wall of fire that does 50 points of fire damage per second.	
☐	Wall of Frost	Expert	45/s	121/s	40/s	Sprayed on the ground, it creates a wall of frost that does 50 points of frost damage per second.	
☐	Wall of Storms	Expert	48/s	128/s	43/s	Sprayed on the ground, it creates a wall of lightning that does 50 points of shock damage per second.	
☐	Blizzard	Master	328	975	328	Targets take 20 points of frost damage for 10s, plus Stamina damage.	Sold by Faralda, after completing College of Winterhold Radiant Quest: Destruction Ritual Spell. Damages everything in a large radius around the caster for 10s.
☐	Fire Storm	Master	423	1257	423	A 100 point firey explosion centered on the caster. Does more damage to closer targets.	Reward for College of Winterhold Radiant Quest: Destruction Ritual Spell. Does extra damage to things closer to the caster.
☐	Lightning Storm	Master	41/s	122/s	41/s	Target takes 75 points of shock damage per second to Health, and half that to Magicka.	Sold by Faralda, after completing College of Winterhold Radiant Quest: Destruction Ritual Spell. Not an area-of-effect spell, Lightning Storm is a single concentrated bolt that does massive damage and disintegrates targets.
☐	Arniel's Convection	Special - Novice	1	1	1	Burns the target 1 points per second. Targets on fire take extra damage.	Quest spell for College of Winterhold Radiant Quest: Arniel's Endeavor. Heats Dwarven Convectors for the quest. Otherwise, not especially useful.
☐	Vampiric Drain	Special - Novice	Varies	Varies	Varies	Absorb health from the target.	A spell unique to Vampires, Vampiric Drain both damages your foes and restores your own health.

ILLUSION

✓	SPELL NAME	LEVEL	STANDARD COST	BASE COST	SKILL 100 COST	DESCRIPTION	NOTES AND RESTRICTIONS
☐	Courage	Novice	17	35	11	Target won't flee for 60s and gets some extra health and stamina.	Best used to strengthen a follower. In a pinch, you can also use it as a cheap way to stop weak enemies from fleeing.
☐	Clairvoyance	Novice	11/s	22/s	7/s	Shows the path to the current goal.	Clairvoyance isn't a spell you'll need very often, but it can be a real help if you get lost in a dungeon.
☐	Fury	Novice	29	59	20	Creatures and people up to Lv6 will attack anything nearby for 30s.	Targets a single foe. Best cast at range, since they'll attack anyone nearby indiscriminately, including you.
☐	Calm	Apprentice	61	129	43	Creatures and people up to Lv9 won't fight for 30s.	Targets a single foe.
☐	Fear	Apprentice	64	135	45	Creatures and people up to Lv9 flee from combat for 30s.	Targets a single foe.
☐	Muffle	Apprentice	60	127	42	You move more quietly for 180s.	Silences your movement. Important for stealthy characters, or anyone who wants to try sneaking around while wearing armor.
☐	Frenzy	Adept	77	184	62	Creatures and people up to Lv14 will attack anyone nearby for 60s.	Targets a single foe.
☐	Rally	Adept	42	100	33	Targets won't flee for 60s and get extra health and stamina.	Targets a single foe.
☐	Invisibility	Expert	111	295	99	Caster is invisible for 30s. Activating an object or attacking will break the spell.	Another important spell for stealthy characters. Combined with Muffle, you should be able to sneak by most foes without too much difficulty.
☐	Pacify	Expert	96	256	86	Creatures and people up to Lv20 won't fight for 60s.	Affects all foes in a small area.

The Elder Scrolls V
SKYRIM

☑	SPELL NAME	LEVEL	STANDARD COST	BASE COST	SKILL 100 COST	DESCRIPTION	NOTES AND RESTRICTIONS
☐	Rout	Expert	104	278	93	Creatures and people up to level 20 flee from combat for 30s.	Affects all foes in a small area.
☐	Call to Arms	Master	194	577	194	Targets have improved combat skills, health, and stamina for 10m.	Sold by Drevis, after completing College of Winterhold Radiant Quest: Illusion Ritual Spell. Affects all allies in a large area.
☐	Harmony	Master	312	927	312	Creatures and people up to Lv25 nearby won't fight for 60s.	Sold by Drevis, after completing College of Winterhold Radiant Quest: Illusion Ritual Spell. Affects all foes in a large area.
☐	Hysteria	Master	257	763	257	Creatures and people up to Lv25 flee from combat for 60s.	Sold by Drevis, after completing College of Winterhold Radiant Quest: Illusion Ritual Spell. Affects all foes in a large area.
☐	Mayhem	Master	294	873	294	Creatures and people up to Lv25 will attack anyone nearby for 60s.	Reward for College of Winterhold Radiant Quest: Illusion Ritual Spell. Affects all foes in a large area.
☐	Vision of the Tenth Eye	Special - Novice	0	0	0	See what others cannot.	Quest spell for College of Winterhold Radiant Quest: Illusion Ritual Spell. Reveals the location of the four Master Illusion Texts needed for the quest; otherwise useless.
☐	Vision of the Tenth Eye	Special - Novice	0	0	0	See what others cannot.	Reveals the location of the four Master Illusion Texts in Illusion Ritual Spell. Otherwise useless. Mage's Guild Radiant Quest: Illusion Ritual Spell.
	RESTORATION						
☐	Healing	Novice	5/s	11/s	3/s	Heals the caster 10 points per second.	If someone is attacking you, Healing rarely heals enough to keep you from dying. Back away and let a follower or summoned creature step in to buy you some time.
☐	Lesser Ward	Novice	15/s	30/s	10/s	Increases armor rating by 40 points and negates up to 40 points of spell damage or effects.	A Ward's armor bonus stacks with the Alteration line of 'flesh' spells for an even stronger defense. Wards are far more effective against spells, although they tie up a hand and cost more to maintain.
☐	Fast Healing	Apprentice	30	65	21	Heals the caster 50 points.	Direct healing spells are less efficient than heal-over-time spells, but they're faster, and may be fast enough to pull you back from the brink of death in a close battle.
☐	Healing Hands	Apprentice	10/s	22/s	7/s	Heals the target 10 points per second, but not undead, atronachs, or machines.	
☐	Steadfast Ward	Apprentice	24/s	51/s	17/s	Increases armor rating by 60 points and negates up to 60 points of spell damage or effects.	
☐	Turn Lesser Undead	Apprentice	35	74	24	Undead up to Lv6 flee for 30s.	Targets a single foe.
☐	Close Wounds	Adept	46	111	37	Heals the caster 100 points.	
☐	Greater Ward	Adept	32/s	76/s	25/s	Increases armor rating by 80 points and negates up to 80 points of spell damage or effects.	
☐	Heal Other	Adept	29	71	24	Heals the target 75 points, but not undead, atronachs, or machines.	
☐	Repel Lesser Undead	Adept	42	101	34	All affected undead up to level 8 flee for 30s.	Affects all undead in the arc of fire.
☐	Turn Undead	Adept	62	148	50	Undead up to Lv13 flee for 30s.	Targets a single foe.
☐	Circle of Protection	Expert	56	151	50	Undead up to Lv30 entering the circle will flee.	Creates a warding circle around the location where the spell is cast.
☐	Grand Healing	Expert	84	224	75	Heals everyone close to the caster 200 points.	Does not heal Daedra, Automatons, or Undead. But it can heal other enemies, so use this carefully.
☐	Repel Undead	Expert	117	311	105	All affected undead up to Lv16 flee for 30s.	Affects all undead in the arc of fire.
☐	Turn Greater Undead	Expert	88	235	79	Undead up to Lv21 flee for 30s.	Targets a single foe.
☐	Bane of the Undead	Master	293	871	293	Sets undead up to Lv30 on fire and makes them flee for 30s.	Reward for College of Winterhold Radiant Quest: Restoration Ritual Spell. Affects all nearby undead in a large area.
☐	Guardian Circle	Master	212	632	212	Undead up to Lv35 entering the circle will flee. Caster heals 20 health per second inside it.	Sold by Colette, after completing College of Winterhold Radiant Quest: Restoration Ritual Spell. Creates a warding circle around the location where the spell is cast.

Table II: General Data

Weapon Base Properties

This section lists the relative speed and stagger chance for each type of weapon, allowing you to choose the one best suited to your needs.

Standard Weapon, Heavy Armor, and Light Armor Progression

This section lists the standard weapon and armor materials in order of increasing value and damage/armor rating.

For each material, the table identifies the level at which it normally begins to appear.

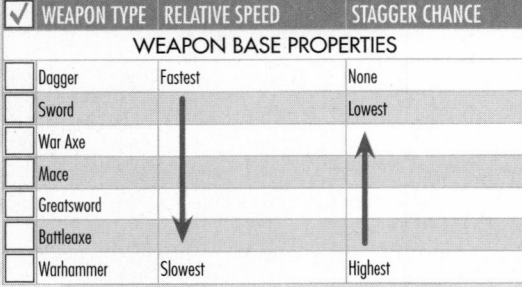

◇ You can obtain items earlier than the indicated level in a variety of ways, such as aggressively increasing your Smithing skill, discovering an exceptional item in a treasure chest, or clearing a dungeon well above your current level.

◇ Non-enchanted items show up at lower levels than their enchanted versions. Typically, enchanted items show up ~1-5 levels after the stated 'Commonly Available' level.

For each material, the level of the enchantments typically found on it are also listed. This is always a range, corresponding to the 'Enchantment Level' column in the Derived Enchantments Table. So, for example:

◇ Orcish Swords can be found with Ench Level 2-4 enchantments. So you might find an Orcish Sword of Flames (Fire Damage Ench Level 4), but never an Orcish Sword of the Inferno (Fire Damage Ench Level 6).

◇ Dragonscale Boots can be found with level 4-6 enchantments. So you might find a Dragonscale Boots of the Ox (Carry Weight Ench Level 5), but never a Dragonscale Boots of Lifting (Carry Weight Ench Level 1).

This range does not restrict the kinds of items you can enchant. So while you're never given an Orcish Sword of the Inferno, you could enchant an Orcish Sword with a comparable fire enchantment if you really wanted to.

WEAPON TYPE	RELATIVE SPEED	STAGGER CHANCE
WEAPON BASE PROPERTIES		
Dagger	Fastest	None
Sword		Lowest
War Axe		
Mace		
Greatsword		
Battleaxe		
Warhammer	Slowest	Highest

MATERIAL	COMMONLY AVAILABLE	ENCHANTMENT LEVELS
STANDARD WEAPON PROGRESSION		
Iron	Lv 1	1-3
Steel	Lv 2	1-3
Orcish	Lv 6	2-4
Dwarven	Lv 12	2-4
Elven	Lv 19	3-5
Glass	Lv 27	3-5
Ebony	Lv 36	4-6
Daedric	Lv 46	4-6

MATERIAL	COMMONLY AVAILABLE	ENCHANTMENT LEVELS
STANDARD HEAVY ARMOR PROGRESSION		
Iron	Lv 1	1-3
Steel	Lv 6	1-3
Dwarven	Lv 12	2-4
Steel Plate	Lv 18	2-4
Orcish	Lv 25	3-5
Ebony	Lv 32	3-5
Dragonplate	Lv 40	4-6
Daedric	Lv 48	4-6

MATERIAL	COMMONLY AVAILABLE	ENCHANTMENT LEVELS
STANDARD LIGHT ARMOR PROGRESSION		
Hide	Lv 1	1-3
Leather	Lv 6	1-3
Elven	Lv 12	2-4
Scaled	Lv 27	2-4
Glass	Lv 36	3-5
Dragonscale	Lv 48	4-6

Table III: Weapons

This section lists all of the weapons in the game and their properties.

The critical damage of all weapons is always equal to half their base damage, rounded down.

Weapons marked "Uses [Material] enchant list" have the same enchantment levels as an item of the indicated material type.

Enchanted weapons will have a higher value than shown here. The additional value added by the enchantment depends on the type and strength of the enchantment.

Weapons marked "Leveled" have several different leveled variants; you will always receive the one most appropriate to your level. Higher-level versions may have better statistics and stronger enchantments than the example listed here.

All weapons with the exception of Unique Weapons (of any type) can be found in a variety of locations throughout the world. Unique Weapons are tracked in the Atlas Chapter (page 414) and Appendices of this guide. Note that unique items typically can't be disenchanted unless their enchantment is one of the base enchantments.

☑ NAME	DAMAGE	WEIGHT	VALUE
STANDARD ONE-HANDED WEAPONS			
Iron Dagger	4	2	10
Iron Mace	9	13	35
Iron Sword	7	9	25
Iron War Axe	8	11	30
Steel Dagger	5	2.5	18
Steel Mace	10	14	65
Steel Sword	8	10	45
Steel War Axe	9	12	55
Orcish Dagger	6	3	30
Orcish Mace	11	15	105
Orcish Sword	9	11	75
Orcish War Axe	10	13	90
Dwarven Dagger	7	3.5	55
Dwarven Mace	12	16	190
Dwarven Sword	10	12	135
Dwarven War Axe	11	14	165
Elven Dagger	8	4	95
Elven Mace	13	17	330
Elven Sword	11	13	235
Elven War Axe	12	15	280
Glass Dagger	9	4.5	165
Glass Mace	14	18	575
Glass Sword	12	14	410
Glass War Axe	13	16	490
Ebony Dagger	10	5	290
Ebony Mace	16	19	1000
Ebony Sword	13	15	720
Ebony War Axe	15	17	865
Daedric Dagger	11	6	500
Daedric Mace	16	20	1750
Daedric Sword	14	16	1250
Daedric War Axe	15	18	1500

☑ NAME	DAMAGE	WEIGHT	VALUE
STANDARD TWO-HANDED WEAPONS			
Iron Battleaxe	16	20	55
Iron Greatsword	15	16	50
Iron Warhammer	18	24	60
Steel Battleaxe	18	21	100
Steel Greatsword	17	17	90
Steel Warhammer	20	25	110
Orcish Battleaxe	19	25	165
Orcish Greatsword	18	18	75
Orcish Warhammer	21	26	180
Dwarven Battleaxe	20	23	300
Dwarven Greatsword	19	19	270
Dwarven Warhammer	22	27	325
Elven Battleaxe	21	24	520
Elven Greatsword	20	20	470
Elven Warhammer	23	28	565
Glass Battleaxe	22	25	900
Glass Greatsword	21	22	820
Glass Warhammer	24	29	985
Ebony Battleaxe	23	26	1585
Ebony Greatsword	22	22	1440
Ebony Warhammer	25	30	1725
Daedric Battleaxe	25	27	2750
Daedric Greatsword	24	23	2500
Daedric Warhammer	27	31	4000
STANDARD BOWS			
Long Bow	6	5	30
Hunting Bow	7	7	50
Note: Uses Iron enchant list.			
Orcish Bow	10	9	150
Dwarven Bow	12	10	270
Elven Bow	13	12	470
Glass Bow	15	14	820
Ebony Bow	17	16	1440
Daedric Bow	19	18	2500

☑ NAME	DAMAGE	WEIGHT	VALUE
ARROWS			
Iron Arrow	8	0	1
Steel Arrow	10	0	2
Orcish Arrow	12	0	3
Dwarven Arrow	14	0	4
Elven Arrow	16	0	5
Glass Arrow	18	0	6
Ebony Arrow	20	0	7
Daedric Arrow	24	0	8
SKYFORGE WEAPONS			
Skyforge Steel Battleaxe*	23	23	150
Skyforge Steel Dagger*	8	2.5	25
Skyforge Steel Greatsword*	19	17	140
Skyforge Steel Sword*	10	10	70
Skyforge Steel War Axe*	14	12	80
*Note: Sold only at Skyforge.			
Nord Hero Battle Axe*	18	22	28
Nord Hero Bow*	8	12	45
Nord Hero Greatsword*	17	18	35
Nord Hero Sword*	8	12	13
Nord Hero War Axe*	9	14	15
Nord Hero Arrow*	24	0	5
*Note: Can forge at Skyforge after Glory of the Dead.			
ENEMY / FACTION-SPECIFIC WEAPONS			
Ancient Nord Battle Axe*	18	22	28
Ancient Nord Greatsword*	17	18	35
Ancient Nord Sword*	8	12	13
Ancient Nord War Axe*	9	14	15
Ancient Nord Bow*	8	12	45
Honed Ancient Nord Battle Axe*	21	25	50

☑ NAME	DAMAGE	WEIGHT	VALUE
Honed Ancient Nord Greatsword*	20	21	63
Honed Ancient Nord Sword*	11	15	23
Honed Ancient Nord War Axe*	12	16	27
Supple Ancient Nord Bow*	14	18	235
*Note: Uses Iron enchant list.			
Ancient Nord Arrow	10	0	1
Dragon Priest Dagger	6	5	9
Falmer Bow	12	15	135
Falmer Sword	10	18	67
Falmer War Axe	11	21	82
Falmer Supple Bow	15	20	410
Falmer Arrow	7	0	1
Honed Falmer Sword	12	18	205
Honed Falmer War Axe	13	21	245
Forsworn Axe	14	14	81
Forsworn Bow	8	9	95
Forsworn Sword	8	12	5
Forsworn Arrow	7	0	1
Silver Greatsword	17	12	160
Silver Sword	8	7	100
Imperial Bow*	9	8	90
Imperial Sword*	8	10	23
*Note: Uses Iron enchant list.			
OTHER WEAPONS & TOOLS			
Blades Sword	11	10	300
Pickaxe	5	10	5
Note: Required to mine ore.			
Scimitar	11	10	5
Woodcutter's Axe	5	10	5
Note: Required to chop wood.			

STAFFS

✓	NAME	DAMAGE	WEIGHT	VALUE	ENCHANTMENT	NOTES
	Forsworn Staff	0	8	183	Flames	
	Grand Staff of Charming	0	8	1393	Calm	
	Grand Staff of Repulsion	0	8	1289	Repel Undead	
	Grand Staff of Turning	0	8	1520	Turn Greater Undead	
	Minor Staff of Turning	0	8	556	Turn Lesser Undead	
	Staff of Banishing	0	8	926	Banish Daedra	
	Staff of Chain Lightning	0	8	1494	Chain Lightning	
	Staff of Calm	0	8	1153	Calm	
	Staff of Courage	0	8	79	Courage	
	Staff of Daedric Command	0	8	2307	Command Daedra	
	Staff of Dread Zombies	0	8	1248	Dread Zombie	
	Staff of Expulsion	0	8	2092	Expel Daedra	
	Staff of Fear	0	8	2443	Fear	
	Staff of Fireballs	0	8	1309	Fireball	
	Staff of Firebolts	0	8	456	Firebolt	
	Staff of Flames	0	8	183	Flames	
	Staff of Frenzy	0	8	1149	Frenzy	
	Staff of Frostbite	0	8	198	Frostbite	
	Staff of Fury	0	8	803	Fury	
	Staff of Ice Spikes	0	8	511	Ice Spike	
	Staff of Ice Storms	0	8	1401	Ice Storm	
	Staff of Inspiration	0	8	317	Rally	
	Staff of Lightning Bolts	0	8	538	Lightning Bolt	
	Staff of Magelight	0	8	239	Magelight	
	Staff of Mending	0	8	613	Heal Other	
	Staff of Paralysis	0	8	3965	Paralyze	
	Staff of Reanimation	0	8	949	Reanimate Corpse	
	Staff of Repulsion	0	8	675	Repel Lesser Undead	
	Staff of Revenants	0	8	824	Revenant	
	Staff of Soul Trapping	0	8	986	Soul Trap	
	Staff of Sparks	0	8	218	Sparks	
	Staff of the Familiar	0	8	926	Conjure Familiar	
	Staff of the Flame Atronach	0	8	727	Conjure Flame Atronach	
	Staff of the Flame Wall	0	8	1310	Wall of Flames	
	Staff of the Frost Atronach	0	8	1106	Conjure Frost Atronach	
	Staff of the Frost Wall	0	8	1468	Wall of Frost	
	Staff of the Healing Hand	0	8	198	Healing Hands	
	Staff of the Storm Atronach	0	8	1656	Conjure Storm Atronach	
	Staff of the Storm Wall	0	8	1531	Wall of Storms	
	Staff of Turning	0	8	1036	Turn Undead	
	Staff of Vanquishment	0	8	1807	Rout	
	Staff of Zombies	0	8	449	Raise Zombie	

UNIQUE WEAPONS - DUNGEONS

✓	NAME	DAMAGE	WEIGHT	VALUE	ENCHANTMENT	NOTES
	Aegisbane	18	24	135	Frost Damage 5	
	Angi's Bow	7	7	50		
	Bloodthorn	5	2.5	183	Soul Trap	
	Bolar's Oathblade	11	10	1014	Damage Stamina 25, Fear	
	Borvir's Dagger	8	4	18		
	Bow of the Hunt	10	7	434	+20 Damage to Animals	
	Ceremonial Axe	9	14	5		
	Ceremonial Sword	8	12	5		
	Dragon Priest Staff	0	8	1570	Wall of Flames	
	Dragon Priest Staff	0	8	1431	Wall of Storms	
	Drainblood Battleaxe	21	5	266	Absorb Health 15	
	Drainheart Sword	11	3	73	Absorb Stamina 15	
	Drainspell Bow	14	6	458	Absorb Magicka 15	
	Eduj	11	9	300	Frost Damage 10	
	Eye of Melka	0	8	1234	Fireball	
	Froki's Bow	6	5	307	Damage Stamina 10	
	Gadnor's Staff of Charming	0	8	803	Fury	
	Gauldur Blackblade	8	12	234	Absorb Health	Leveled
	Gauldur Blackbow	14	18	750	Absorb Magicka	Leveled
	Ghostblade	8	1	300	+3 Damage (Ignores Armor)	
	Halldir's Staff	0	8	1874	Calm & Soul Trap	
	Hevnoraak's Staff	0	8	1791	Wall of Storms	
	Lunar Iron Mace	9	13	99	Bonus Fire Damage at Night	Leveled
	Lunar Iron Sword	7	9	89	Bonus Fire Damage at Night	Leveled
	Lunar Iron War Axe	8	11	94	Bonus Fire Damage at Night	Leveled
	Lunar Steel Mace	10	14	129	Bonus Fire Damage at Night	Leveled
	Lunar Steel Sword	8	10	69	Bonus Fire Damage at Night	Leveled
	Lunar Steel War Axe	9	12	119	Bonus Fire Damage at Night	Leveled
	Notched Pickaxe	5	10	303	Fortify Smithing 5, Shock Damage 5	Can be used to mine ore.
	Okin	12	11	320	Frost Damage 10	
	Poacher's Axe	5	10	31	+3 Damage to Animals	
	Red Eagle's Bane	11	15	345	Burn Undead, Turn Undead	
	Red Eagle's Fury	8	12	97	Fire Damage 5	
	Rundi's Dagger	5	2.5	18		
	Spider Control Rod	1	8	153	Place Spider Beacon	
	Staff of Hag's Wrath	0	8	1310	Wall of Flames	
	Staff of Jyrik Gauldurson	0	8	594	Lightning Bolt	
	Steel Battleaxe of Fiery Souls	18	21	320	Soul Trap, Fire Damage 10	
	The Longhammer	21	18	90	Faster swings	
	The Pale Blade	8	12	169	Frost Damage, Fear	Leveled
	The Woodsman's Friend	17	20	28		
	Trollsbane	20	25	121	Fire Damage 15 to Trolls	
	Windshear	11	10	40	Knockdown on Bash 60%	

UNIQUE WEAPONS - QUEST REWARDS

✓	NAME	DAMAGE	WEIGHT	VALUE	ENCHANTMENT	NOTES
	Blade of Woe	12	7	880	Absorb Health 10	
	Chillrend	10	11	552	Frost Damage, Paralyze	Leveled
	Dragonbane	10	10	789	Shock Damage, Bonus Damage to Dragons	Leveled
	Firiniel's End	13	12	785	Frost Damage 20	
	Keening	8	4	13	Absorb Health, Magicka, Stamina 10	
	Nightingale Blade	10	11	426	Absorb Health, Absorb Stamina	Leveled
	Nightingale Bow	12	9	493	Frost Damage, Shock Damage	Leveled
	Shiv	5	2	5		
	Staff of Magnus	0	8	1468	Absorb Magicka, then Health	
	The Rueful Axe	22	10	1183	Damage Stamina 20	
	Valdr's Lucky Dagger	5	2.5	15	25% Critical Hit Chance	
	Wuuthrad	25	25	2000	1.2x Damage to Elves	

The Elder Scrolls V SKYRIM

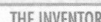

✓	NAME	DAMAGE	WEIGHT	VALUE	ENCHANTMENT	NOTES
	UNIQUE WEAPONS - QUEST ITEMS					
	Alessandra's Dagger	5	1	10		
	Amren's Family Sword	7	9	25		
	Balgruuf's Greatsword	17	17	200		
	Blade of Sacrifice	10	4	144		
	Broken Staff	17	10	5		
	Dravin's Bow	8	7	50		
	Ghorbash's Ancestral Axe	8	11	30		
	Grimsever	12	14	727	Frost Damage 15	
	Headsman's Axe	17	11	15		

✓	NAME	DAMAGE	WEIGHT	VALUE	ENCHANTMENT	NOTES
	Hjalti's Sword	8	12	13		
	Kahvozein's Fang	6	5	9		
	Nettlebane	6	10	5		
	Queen Freydis's Sword	8	10	45		
	Rusty Mace	7	13	5		
	Shagrol's Warhammer	21	26	200		
	Staff of Arcane Authority	0	8	2443	Fear	
	Staff of Tandil	0	8	2530	Mass Calm	
	Steel Sword	8	10	23		

▷ Table IV: Armor

This section lists all of the armor, robes, and other clothing available to you, and their properties.

Armor and Clothing marked "Uses [Material] enchant list" has the same enchantment levels as an item of the indicated material type.

Circlets, Rings, and Necklaces may appear with armor enchantments of any level.

Enchanted armor will have a higher value than shown here. The additional value added by the enchantment depends on the type and strength of the enchantment.

Armor and Clothing marked "Leveled" has several different leveled variants; you will always receive the one most appropriate to your level. Higher-level versions may have better statistics and stronger enchantments than the example listed here.

All shields are listed as being 'Heavy Armor'. However, they don't count as Heavy Armor for the purposes of skills or perks. For example:

◇ Your Heavy Armor skill doesn't make you any better with a shield.

◇ If you have perks that only work if you're wearing a full set of light armor or no armor, holding a shield doesn't count against you.

Clothing often comes in a variety of appearances that aren't distinguished by name (there are at least a half-dozen 'boots', for example). So a representative item from each set has been listed here. Be aware that an item's appearance and properties may vary slightly between instances of these items.

All Armor and Clothing, with the exception of Unique Armor (of any type) can be found in a variety of locations throughout the world. Unique Armor and Outfits are tracked in the Atlas Chapter (page 414) and Appendices of this guide.

✓	NAME	ARMOR	WEIGHT	VALUE	TYPE
	STANDARD HEAVY ARMOR SETS				
	Iron Armor	25	30	125	Heavy
	Iron Boots	10	6	25	Heavy
	Iron Gauntlets	10	5	25	Heavy
	Iron Helmet	15	5	60	Heavy
	Iron Shield	20	12	60	Heavy
	Steel Armor	31	35	275	Heavy
	Steel Cuffed Boots	12	8	55	Heavy
	Steel Shin Boots	12	8	55	Heavy
	Steel Nordic Gauntlets	12	4	55	Heavy
	Steel Imperial Gauntlets	12	4	55	Heavy
	Steel Helmet	17	5	125	Heavy
	Steel Horned Helmet	17	5	125	Heavy
	Steel Shield	24	12	150	Heavy
	Dwarven Armor	34	45	400	Heavy
	Dwarven Boots	13	10	85	Heavy
	Dwarven Gauntlets	13	8	85	Heavy
	Dwarven Helmet	18	12	200	Heavy
	Dwarven Shield	26	12	225	Heavy
	Steel Plate Armor	40	38	625	Heavy
	Steel Plate Boots	14	9	125	Heavy

✓	NAME	ARMOR	WEIGHT	VALUE	TYPE
	Steel Plate Gauntlets	14	6	125	Heavy
	Steel Plate Helmet	19	6	300	Heavy
	Steel Plate Shield	28	14	325	Heavy
	Orcish Armor	40	35	1000	Heavy
	Orcish Boots	15	7	200	Heavy
	Orcish Gauntlets	15	7	200	Heavy
	Orcish Helmet	20	8	500	Heavy
	Orcish Shield	30	14	500	Heavy
	Ebony Armor	43	38	1500	Heavy
	Ebony Boots	16	7	275	Heavy
	Ebony Gauntlets	16	7	275	Heavy
	Ebony Helmet	21	10	750	Heavy
	Ebony Shield	32	14	750	Heavy
	Dragonplate Armor	46	40	2125	Heavy
	Dragonplate Boots	17	8	425	Heavy
	Dragonplate Gauntlets	17	8	425	Heavy
	Dragonplate Helmet	22	8	1050	Heavy
	Dragonplate Shield	34	15	1050	Heavy
	Daedric Armor	49	50	3200	Heavy
	Daedric Boots	18	10	625	Heavy
	Daedric Gauntlets	18	6	625	Heavy

✓	NAME	ARMOR	WEIGHT	VALUE	TYPE
	Daedric Helmet	23	15	1600	Heavy
	Daedric Shield	36	15	1600	Heavy
	STANDARD LIGHT ARMOR SETS				
	Hide Armor	20	5	50	Light
	Hide Boots	5	1	10	Light
	Hide Bracers	5	1	10	Light
	Hide Helmet	10	2	25	Light
	Hide Shield	15	4	25	Light
	Leather Armor	26	6	125	Light
	Leather Boots	7	2	25	Light
	Leather Bracers	7	2	25	Light
	Leather Helmet	12	2	60	Light
	Elven Armor	29	4	225	Light
	Elven Boots	8	1	45	Light
	Elven Gauntlets	8	1	45	Light
	Elven Helmet	13	1	110	Light
	Elven Shield	21	4	115	Light
	Scaled Armor	32	6	350	Light
	Scaled Horn Armor	32	6	350	Light
	Scaled Boots	9	2	70	Light
	Scaled Bracers	9	2	70	Light

✓	NAME	ARMOR	WEIGHT	VALUE	TYPE
☐	Scaled Helmet	14	2	175	Light
☐	Glass Armor	38	7	900	Light
☐	Glass Boots	11	2	190	Light
☐	Glass Gauntlets	11	2	190	Light
☐	Glass Helmet	16	2	450	Light
☐	Glass Shield	27	6	450	Light
☐	Dragonscale Armor	41	10	1500	Light
☐	Dragonscale Boots	12	3	300	Light
☐	Dragonscale Gauntlets	12	3	300	Light
☐	Dragonscale Helmet	17	4	750	Light
☐	Dragonscale Shield	29	6	750	Light

STANDARD ARMOR PIECES

These pieces are not part of a complete set, but use enchantments from the standard list.

✓	NAME	ARMOR	WEIGHT	VALUE	TYPE
☐	Banded Iron Armor	28	35	200	Heavy

Note: Uses Iron enchant list.

✓	NAME	ARMOR	WEIGHT	VALUE	TYPE
☐	Banded Iron Shield	22	12	100	Heavy

Note: Uses Iron enchant list.

✓	NAME	ARMOR	WEIGHT	VALUE	TYPE
☐	Studded Armor	23	6	75	Light

Note: Uses Leather enchant list.

✓	NAME	ARMOR	WEIGHT	VALUE	TYPE
☐	Elven Gilded Armor	35	4	550	Light

Note: Uses Glass enchant list.

SOLDIER AND GUARD ARMOR

✓	NAME	ARMOR	WEIGHT	VALUE	TYPE
☐	Imperial Light Armor*	23	6	75	Light
☐	Imperial Light Boots*	6	2	15	Light
☐	Imperial Light Bracers*	6	1	15	Light
☐	Imperial Light Helmet*	11	2	35	Light
☐	Imperial Light Shield*	19	4	40	Light
☐	Studded Imperial Armor*	23	6	125	Light

*Note: Uses Leather enchant list.

✓	NAME	ARMOR	WEIGHT	VALUE	TYPE
☐	Imperial Armor*	25	35	100	Heavy
☐	Imperial Boots*	10	8	20	Heavy
☐	Imperial Bracers*	10	4	15	Heavy
☐	Imperial Helmet*	15	5	50	Heavy

*Note: Uses Steel enchant list.

✓	NAME	ARMOR	WEIGHT	VALUE	TYPE
☐	Imperial Helmet	18	5	30	Heavy
☐	Imperial Officer's Helmet	17	4	30	Heavy
☐	Imperial Shield	20	12	50	Heavy
☐	Stormcloak Cuirass	21	8	25	Light
☐	Stormcloak Helmet	10	2	12	Light
☐	Fur Boots	5	2	5	Light
☐	Fur Gauntlets	5	2	5	Light
☐	Stormcloak Officer Armor	27	8	35	Light
☐	Stormcloak Officer Boots	7	2	7	Light
☐	Stormcloak Officer Bracers	7	2	7	Light
☐	Stormcloak Officer Helmet	12	2	15	Light
☐	Eastmarch Guard Helmet	12	2	12	Light
☐	Falkreath Guard's Armor	23	6	75	Light
☐	Falkreath Guard's Helmet	11	2	35	Light
☐	Falkreath Guard's Shield	17	3	40	Heavy
☐	Hjaalmarch Guard's Armor	23	6	75	Light
☐	Hjaalmarch Guard's Helmet	11	2	35	Light
☐	Hjaalmarch Guard's Shield	17	3	40	Heavy
☐	Markarth Guard's Armor	23	6	75	Light

✓	NAME	ARMOR	WEIGHT	VALUE	TYPE
☐	Markarth Guard's Helmet	11	2	35	Light
☐	Markarth Guard's Shield	17	3	40	Heavy
☐	Pale Guard's Armor	23	6	75	Light
☐	Pale Guard's Helmet	11	2	35	Light
☐	Pale Guard's Shield	17	3	40	Heavy
☐	Riften Guard's Armor	23	6	75	Light
☐	Riften Guard's Helmet	11	2	35	Light
☐	Riften Guard's Shield	17	3	40	Heavy
☐	Solitude Guard's Armor	23	6	75	Light
☐	Solitude Guard's Helmet	11	2	35	Light
☐	Solitude Guard's Shield	17	3	40	Heavy
☐	Whiterun Guard's Armor	23	6	75	Light
☐	Whiterun Guard's Helmet	11	2	35	Light
☐	Whiterun Guard's Shield	17	3	40	Heavy
☐	Windhelm Guard's Shield	17	3	40	Heavy
☐	Winterhold Guard's Armor	23	6	75	Light
☐	Winterhold Guard's Helmet	11	2	35	Light
☐	Winterhold Guard's Shield	17	3	40	Heavy

ENEMY / FACTION-SPECIFIC ARMOR

✓	NAME	ARMOR	WEIGHT	VALUE	TYPE
☐	Ancient Nord Armor	25	28	125	Heavy
☐	Ancient Nord Boots	10	5	25	Heavy
☐	Ancient Nord Gauntlets	10	4	25	Heavy
☐	Ancient Nord Helmet	15	4	60	Heavy
☐	Blades Armor	44	45	400	Heavy
☐	Blades Boots	13	10	85	Heavy
☐	Blades Gauntlets	13	8	85	Heavy
☐	Blades Helmet	18	12	200	Heavy
☐	Blades Shield	26	12	225	Heavy
☐	Falmer Armor	31	20	275	Heavy
☐	Falmer Boots	12	4	55	Heavy
☐	Falmer Gauntlets	12	4	55	Heavy
☐	Falmer Helmet	10	5	25	Heavy
☐	Falmer Shield	28	15	10	Heavy
☐	Forsworn Armor	26	6	100	Light
☐	Forsworn Boots	7	2	20	Light
☐	Forsworn Gauntlets	7	2	20	Light
☐	Forsworn Headdress	12	2	50	Light
☐	Fur Armor	23	6	50	Light
☐	Fur Bracers	6	1	10	Light
☐	Fur Helmet	11	1	23	Light
☐	Fur Shoes	6	2	4	Light
☐	Penitus Oculatus Armor	23	6	75	Light
☐	Penitus Oculatus Boots	6	1	15	Light
☐	Penitus Oculatus Bracers	6	1	15	Light
☐	Penitus Oculatus Helmet	11	1	35	Light
☐	Thalmor Boots	5	1	10	
☐	Thalmor Gloves	5	1	10	
☐	Thalmor Hood	5	1	10	
☐	Thalmor Robes*	0	4	410	
☐	Hooded Thalmor Robes*	20	5	410	

*Note: Destruction spells cost 12% less to cast.

✓	NAME	ARMOR	WEIGHT	VALUE	TYPE
☐	Elven Light Armor	26	4	125	Light

✓	NAME	ARMOR	WEIGHT	VALUE	TYPE
☐	Elven Light Boots	7	1	25	Light
☐	Elven Light Gauntlets	7	1	25	Light
☐	Elven Light Helmet	12	1	60	Light
☐	Wolf Armor	31	20	55	Heavy
☐	Wolf Boots	12	4	11	Heavy
☐	Wolf Gauntlets	12	4	11	Heavy
☐	Wolf Helmet	17	4	125	Heavy
☐	Vaermina Robes	8	5	10	

STANDARD ROBES & HOODS

Some robes come in several visual styles that do not affect their names or other properties.

✓	NAME	ARMOR	WEIGHT	VALUE	TYPE
☐	Black Robes	0	1	5	
☐	Blue Robes	0	1	5	
☐	College Robes	0	1	10	
☐	Hooded Black Robes	0	1	5	
☐	Hooded Blue Robes	0	1	5	
☐	Mantled College Robes	0	1	5	
☐	Black Mage Robes*	0	1	153	
☐	Hooded Black Mage Robes*	0	1	55	
☐	Necromancer Robes*	0	1	55	
☐	Hooded Necromancer Robes*	0	1	55	

*Note: +50% Magicka Regen.

✓	NAME	ARMOR	WEIGHT	VALUE	TYPE
☐	Robes	0	1	5	

Note: Uses Warlock Robes enchant list.

✓	NAME	ARMOR	WEIGHT	VALUE	TYPE
☐	Novice Robes	0	1	153	

Note: +50% Magicka Regen; additionally uses College Robes enchant list.

✓	NAME	ARMOR	WEIGHT	VALUE	TYPE
☐	Apprentice Robes	0	1	539	

Note: +75% Magicka Regen; additionally uses College Robes enchant list.

✓	NAME	ARMOR	WEIGHT	VALUE	TYPE
☐	Adept Robes	0	1	977	

Note: +100% Magicka Regen; additionally uses College Robes enchant list.

✓	NAME	ARMOR	WEIGHT	VALUE	TYPE
☐	Expert Robes	0	1	1517	

Note: +125% Magicka Regen; additionally uses College Robes enchant list.

✓	NAME	ARMOR	WEIGHT	VALUE	TYPE
☐	Master Robes	0	1	2298	

Note: +150% Magicka Regen; additionally uses College Robes enchant list.

✓	NAME	ARMOR	WEIGHT	VALUE	TYPE
☐	Novice Hood	0	1	305	

Note: +30 Magicka

✓	NAME	ARMOR	WEIGHT	VALUE	TYPE
☐	Apprentice Hood	0	1	415	

Note: +40 Magicka

✓	NAME	ARMOR	WEIGHT	VALUE	TYPE
☐	Adept Hood	0	1	528	

Note: +50 Magicka

JEWELRY - CIRCLETS

✓	NAME	ARMOR	WEIGHT	VALUE	TYPE
☐	Copper and Onyx Circlet	0	2	50	
☐	Copper and Moonstone Circlet	0	2	100	
☐	Copper and Ruby Circlet	0	2	150	
☐	Copper and Sapphire Circlet	0	2	200	
☐	Silver and Moonstone Circlet	0	2	250	
☐	Jade and Sapphire Circlet	0	2	300	
☐	Jade and Emerald Circlet	0	2	350	
☐	Silver and Sapphire Circlet	0	2	400	
☐	Gold and Ruby Circlet	0	2	450	

NAME	ARMOR	WEIGHT	VALUE	TYPE
Gold and Emerald Circlet	0	2	500	
JEWELRY - RINGS				
Silver Ring	0	0.25	30	
Gold Ring	0	0.25	75	
Silver Garnet Ring	0	0.25	160	
Silver Amethyst Ring	0	0.25	180	
Silver Ruby Ring	0	0.25	260	

NAME	ARMOR	WEIGHT	VALUE	TYPE
Gold Sapphire Ring	0	0.25	500	
Gold Emerald Ring	0	0.25	700	
Gold Diamond Ring	0	0.25	900	
JEWELRY - NECKLACES & AMULETS				
Silver Necklace	0	0.5	60	
Gold Necklace	0	0.5	120	
Silver Jeweled Necklace	0	0.5	380	

NAME	ARMOR	WEIGHT	VALUE	TYPE
Gold Jeweled Necklace	0	0.5	485	
Gold Ruby Necklace	0	0.5	550	
Silver Sapphire Necklace	0	0.5	580	
Silver Emerald Necklace	0	0.5	830	
Gold Diamond Necklace	0	0.5	1200	
Ancient Nord Amulet	0	1	100	

NAME	ARMOR	WEIGHT	VALUE	TYPE	ENCHANTMENT
JEWELRY - DIVINES AMULETS					
Amulet of Akatosh	0	1	89		+25% Magicka Regen
Amulet of Arkay	0	1	114		+10 Health
Amulet of Dibella	0	1	118		+15 Speechcraft
Amulet of Julianos	0	1	108		+10 Magicka
Amulet of Kynareth	0	1	96		+10 Stamina
Amulet of Mara	0	1	316		Restoration spells cost 10% less to cast.
Amulet of Stendarr	0	1	196		Shields block 10% more damage.
Amulet of Talos	0	1	25		Time between Shouts reduced by 20%.
Amulet of Zenithar	0	1	511		Prices are 10% better.
UNIQUE ARMOR - DUNGEON REWARDS					
Ancient Helmet of the Unburned	15	4	841	Heavy	Resist Fire 40%
Diadem of the Savant	7	4	1201	Light	All spells cost 5% less to cast.
Fjola's Wedding Band	0	0.3	150		
Gloves of the Pugilist	5	2	194	Light	+10 Unarmed damage
Helm of Yngol	21	8	565	Heavy	Resist Frost 30%
Ironhand Gauntlets	12	4	444	Heavy	Improve Two-Handed 15%
Kyne's Token	0	1	325		Improve Archery 5%, Damage from Animals -10%
Movarth's Boots	5	1	792	Light	Improve Sneaking 15
Predator's Grace	5	1	117	Light	Muffle, Stamina Regenerates Faster
Targe of the Blooded	20	8	300	Heavy	Bashes do 3 Bleeding Damage / 5s.
UNIQUE ARMOR - DRAGON PRIEST MASKS					
Hevnoraak	23	9	891	Heavy	+40 Heavy Armor
Konahrik	24	7	3200	Heavy	Heal wearer and damage enemies when health is low. Chance to summon a Dragon Priest
Krosis	21	5	1615	Light	Improve Lockpicking 20%, Archery 20%, Alchemy 20%
Morokei	5	4	637	Light	+100% Magicka Regen
Nahkriin	23	9	2173	Heavy	+50 Magicka; Improve Destruction 20%, Restoration 20%
Otar	23	9	1521	Heavy	Resist Fire 30%, Resist Frost 30%, Resist Shock 30%
Rahgot	23	9	962	Heavy	+70 Stamina
Vokun	23	9	2182	Heavy	Improve Conjuration 20%, Illusion 20%, Alteration 20%
Volsung	23	9	4611	Light	+20 Carry Weight, Improve Prices 20%, Waterbreathing
Wooden Mask	2	2	40	Light	Timeshift the Labyrinthian Sanctuary
UNIQUE ARMOR - QUEST REWARDS					
Amulet of Articulation	2	1	1067	Light	Improve Speech, Persuade checks always succeed
Note: Leveled					
Ancient Shrouded Armor	33	5	617	Light	Resist Poison 100%
Ancient Shrouded Boots	12	0.5	355	Light	Muffle

NAME	ARMOR	WEIGHT	VALUE	TYPE	ENCHANTMENT
Ancient Shrouded Cowl	15	1	1199	Light	Improve Archery 35%
Ancient Shrouded Gloves	12	1	175	Light	Double One-Handed sneak attack damage
Archmage's Robes	0	1	2409		All spells cost 15% less to cast
Armor of the Old Gods	24	3	611	Light	Destruction spells cost 15% less to cast
Asgeir's Wedding Band	0	0.3	100		
Boots	0	1	603		Resist Shock 40%
Boots of the Old Gods	7	1.5	1104	Light	Improve Sneak 20%
Cicero's Boots	0	0.5	355		Muffle
Cicero's Clothes	0	1	1946		Improve One-Handed 20%, Improve Prices 20%
Cicero's Gloves	0	0.5	175		Double One-Handed sneak attack damage
Cicero's Hat	0	0.5	2168		Improve Sneak 35%
Gauldur Amulet Fragment (Folgunthur)	0	0.5	816		+30 Health
Gauldur Amulet Fragment (Geirmund's Hall)	0	0.5	753		+30 Stamina
Gauldur Amulet Fragment (Saarthal)	0	0.5	795		+30 Magicka
Gauntlets of the Old Gods	8	0.5	592	Light	Improve Archery 20%
Guild Master's Armor	38	10	1779	Light	+50 Carry Weight
Guild Master's Boots	11	2	649	Light	Improve Pickpocket 35%
Guild Master's Gloves	11	2	599	Light	Improve Lockpick 35%
Guild Master's Hood	16	3	1252	Light	Improve Speech 20%
Helm of Winterhold	17	5	125	Heavy	
Helmet of the Old Gods	12	1	345	Light	+30 Magicka
Jester's Boots	0	1	305		Muffle
Jester's Clothes	0	1	1163		Improve One-Handed 12%, Improve Prices 12%
Jester's Gloves	0	0.5	125		Double One-Handed sneak attack damage
Jester's Hat	0	0.5	1806		Improve Sneak 30%
Jeweled Amulet	0	0.5	1000		
Linwe's Armor	31	8	368	Light	+15 Stamina
Linwe's Boots	11	2	837	Light	Improve Sneak 15%
Linwe's Gloves	11	2	483	Light	Improve One-Handed 15%
Linwe's Hood	16	2	563	Light	Improve Archery 15%
Mage's Circlet	0	2	509		Improve Magicka
Note: Leveled					
Muiri's Ring	0	0.3	434		Improve Alchemy 15%
Note: Bonus reward for Dark Brotherhood Quest Sentenced to Death.					
Necromancer Amulet	0	0.5	2635		+50 Magicka, Improve Conjuration 25%, -75% Health and Stamina Regen
Nightingale Armor*	34	12	1249	Light	+ Stamina, Resist Frost
Nightingale Boots*	10	2	295	Light	Muffle
Nightingale Gloves*	10	2	819	Light	Improve Lockpick, Improve One-Handed

☑	NAME	ARMOR	WEIGHT	VALUE	TYPE	ENCHANTMENT
	Nightingale Hood*	15	2	804	Light	Imrove Illusion
*Note: Leveled						
	Nightweaver's Band	0	0.3	1131		Improve Sneak 10%, Destruction 10%
	Savos Aren's Amulet	0	1	818		+50 Magicka
	Shield of Solitude	26	12	555	Heavy	Resist Magic, Improve Block
Note: Leveled						
	Shield of Ysgramor	30	12	1715	Heavy	+20 Health, Resist Magic 20%
	Shrouded Armor	29	7	373	Light	Resist Poison 50%
	Shrouded Boots	8	2	305	Light	Muffle
	Shrouded Cowl	13	2	677	Light	Improve Archery 20%
	Shrouded Cowl Maskless	13	2	677	Light	Improve Archery 20%
	Shrouded Gloves	8	2	125	Light	Backstab does double damage
	Shrouded Hand Wraps	0	0.5	50	Light	Double One-Handed sneak attack damage
	Shrouded Hood	0	0.5	1485	Light	Improve Sneak 25%
	Shrouded Robes	0	0.5	711	Light	Improve Destruction 15%
	Shrouded Shoes	0	0.5	150	Light	Muffle
	Silver-Blood Family Ring	0	0.3	772		Improve Smithing 20%
	The Bond of Matrimony	0	0.3	496		Improve Restoration 10%
	The Gauldur Amulet	0	0	1864		+30 Health, +30 Magicka, +30 Stamina
	Thieves Guild Armor	29	7	665	Light	+20 Carry Weight
	Thieves Guild Armor (Improved)	30	6	1299	Light	+35 Carry Weight
	Thieves Guild Boots	9	1.5	241	Light	Improve Pickpocket 15%
	Thieves Guild Boots (Improved)	10	1	479	Light	Improve Pickpocket 25%
	Thieves Guild Gloves	9	1	222	Light	Improve Lockpick 15%
	Thieves Guild Gloves (Improved)	10	1	445	Light	Improve Lockpick 25%
	Thieves Guild Hood	13	1.5	551	Light	Improve Prices 10%
	Thieves Guild Hood (Improved)	15	1	967	Light	Improve Prices 15%
	Tumblerbane Gloves	7	2	325	Light	Improve Lockpick 20%
	Vittoria's Wedding Band	0	0.3	100		
	Worn Shrouded Armor	20	6	80	Light	
	Worn Shrouded Boots	3	2	45	Light	

☑	NAME	ARMOR	WEIGHT	VALUE	TYPE	ENCHANTMENT
	Worn Shrouded Cowl	8	2	50	Light	
	Worn Shrouded Gloves	4	2	50	Light	Backstab does double damage
UNIQUE ARMOR - QUEST ITEMS						
	Andurs' Amulet of Arkay	0	1	294		+10 Health
	Calcelmo's Ring	0	0.3	20		
	Charmed Necklace	0	0.5	790		+25 Carry Weight
	Cursed Ring of Hircine	0	0.3	50		Random werewolf transformations.
Note: No effect except on werewolves.						
	Enchanted Ring	0	0.3	207		+20 Health
	Execution Hood	0	0.5	5		
	Fjotli's Silver Locket	0	0.5	30		
	Focusing Gloves	0	0	0		
	Hrolfdir's Shield	24	12	60	Heavy	
	Ilas-Tei's Ring	0	0.3	40		
	Jagged Crown	23	9	5000	Heavy	
	Leather Hood	0	1	10		
	Madesi's Silver Ring	0	0.3	10		
	Moon Amulet	0	0.5	250		
	Noster's Helmet	11	2	35	Light	
	Ogmund's Amulet of Talos	0	1	25		Time between Shouts reduced by 20%
	Party Boots	0	0	25		
	Party Clothes	0	1	25		
	Raerek's Inscribed Amulet of Talos	0	1	205		Time between Shouts reduced by 20%
	Reyda's Necklace	0	0.5	30		
	Ring of Pure Mixtures	0	0.3	337		Improve Alchemy 12%
	Roggi's Ancestral Shield	20	12	60	Heavy	
	Saarthal Amulet	0	0.8	184		Spells cost 3% less to cast.
	Shahvee's Amulet of Zenithar	0	1	691		Improve Prices 10%
	Strange Amulet	0	0	1000		
	The Forgemaster's Fingers	10	5	394	Heavy	Improve Smithing 15%
	Viola's Gold Ring	0	0.3	75		
	Yisra's Necklace	0	0.5	50		

☑	NAME	ARMOR	WEIGHT	VALUE	TYPE
CLOTHES - STANDARD OUTFITS					
Common clothes worn by people throughout Skyrim. Most outfits have several visual styles, but similar or identical names.					
	Arm Bandages	0	0.5	1	
	Belted Tunic	0	1	2	
	Blacksmith's Apron	0	1	8	
	Boots	0	1	3	
	Brown Robes	0	1	5	
	Child's Clothes	0	1	4	
	Clothes	0	1	5	
	College Boots	8	0	0	Light
	Cowl	0	1	1	
	Cuffed Boots	0	1	25	
	Embellished Robes	2	3	100	
	Embroidered Garment	0	1	100	

☑	NAME	ARMOR	WEIGHT	VALUE	TYPE
	Fine Armguards	7	0.5	25	Light
	Fine Boots	0	0	20	
	Fine Clothes	0	1	50	
	Fine Hat	0	0.5	25	
	Fine Raiment	0	1	100	
	Footwraps	0	1	1	
	Fur-lined Boots	0	1	25	
	Fur-Trimmed Cloak	0	1	100	
	Gilded Wristguards	7	0.5	21	Light
	Gloves	0	0.5	1	
	Green Robes	0	1	5	
	Grey Robes	0	1	5	
	Hammerfell Garb	0	1	5	
	Hat	0	0.5	1	
	Head bandages	5	0	0	

☑	NAME	ARMOR	WEIGHT	VALUE	TYPE
	Hooded Brown Robes	0	1	5	
	Hooded Green Robes	0	1	5	
	Hooded Grey Robes	0	1	5	
	Hooded Monk Robes	0	1	5	
	Hooded Necromancer Robes	0	1	5	
	Hooded Red Robes	0	1	5	
	Mage Hood	0	1	1	
	Mantled College Robes	0	1	5	
	Miner's Clothes	0	1	2	
	Monk Robes	0	1	5	
	Necromancer Robes	0	1	5	
	Noble Clothes	2	3	100	
	Pleated Shoes	0	1	25	
	Radiant Raiment Fine Clothes	0	1	55	
	Ragged Boots	0	1	1	

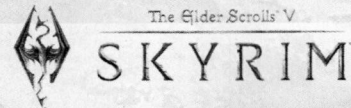

The Elder Scrolls V
SKYRIM

✓	NAME	ARMOR	WEIGHT	VALUE	TYPE
☐	Ragged Cap	0	0.5	1	
☐	Ragged Robes	1	1	1	
☐	Ragged Trousers	0	1	1	
☐	Red Robes	0	1	5	
☐	Redguard Boots	0	1	3	
☐	Refined Tunic	2	3	100	
☐	Roughspun Tunic	0	1	1	
☐	Shoes	1	0	2	
☐	Chef's Tunic	0	1	8	

✓	NAME	ARMOR	WEIGHT	VALUE	TYPE
☐	Chef's Hat	0	0.5	1	
☐	Mourner's Hat	0	0.5	1	
☐	Mourner's Clothes	0	1	2	
☐	Alik'r Hood	0	0.5	2	

QUEST / UNIQUE OUTFITS

Unique outfits worn by important characters or during special events.

✓	NAME	ARMOR	WEIGHT	VALUE	TYPE
☐	Emperor's Robes	0	1	100	
☐	Mythic Dawn Boots	0	1	15	
☐	Mythic Dawn Gloves	0	1	25	
☐	Mythic Dawn Robes	0	2	25	

✓	NAME	ARMOR	WEIGHT	VALUE	TYPE
☐	Mythic Dawn Robes	0	2	25	
☐	Ulfric's Clothes	0	1	100	
☐	Ulfric's Boots	0	1	25	
☐	Ulfric's Bracers	5	0.5	25	Light
☐	Wedding Dress	0	1	50	
☐	Wedding Sandals	0	1	20	
☐	Wedding Wreath	0	0.5	10	
☐	General Tullius' Armor	31	18	65	Heavy

CRAFTING: ALCHEMY

▶ Table V: Ingredients

This table lists all the available ingredients and their properties (weight, value, effects). In addition, three sample locations are shown where the ingredients can be found (usually in abundance, although this varies as some ingredients are only encountered as a single item rather than in clusters).

✓	INGREDIENT NAME	WEIGHT	VALUE	EFFECT 1	EFFECT 2	EFFECT 3	EFFECT 4	LOCATION A (AMOUNT IF APPLICABLE)	LOCATION B (AMOUNT IF APPLICABLE)	LOCATION C (AMOUNT IF APPLICABLE)	NOTES
☐	Abecean Longfin	0.5	15	Weakness to Frost	Fortify Sneak	Weakness to Poison	Fortify Restoration	[9.00] Riften (Plankside)	[7.00] Windhelm (Docks)	[–]	Catch these fish randomly in lakes, rivers, and the ocean.
☐	Bear Claws	0.1	2	Restore Stamina	Fortify Health	Fortify One-handed	Damage Magicka Regen	[9.33] Fallowstone Cave	[8.05] Moss Mother Cavern	Pine Forest Exterior (hunt the animal)	Found on bear corpses. Check the Atlas for locations that have bears or predators.
☐	Bee	0.1	3	Restore Stamina	Ravage Stamina	Regenerate Stamina	Weakness to Shock	[9.10] Honeystrand Cave	[9.29] Goldenglow Estate	[–]	Commonly found near beehives, which are plentiful here.
☐	Beehive Husk	1	5	Resist Poison	Fortify Light Armor	Fortify Sneak	Fortify Destruction	[9.10] Honeystrand Cave	[9.29] Goldenglow Estate	[–]	Commonly found near beehives, which are plentiful here.
☐	Bleeding Crown	0.3	10	Weakness to Fire	Fortify Block	Weakness to Poison	Resist Magic	[1.10] Pinemoon Cave (45)	[2.02] Chillwind Depths (34)	[9.04] Geirmund's Hall (34)	Plentiful in these caves.
☐	Blisterwort	0.2	12	Damage Stamina	Frenzy	Restore Health	Fortify Smithing	[2.02] Chillwind Depths (59)	[8.21] Halldir's Cairn (9)	[9.34] Lost Prospect Mine (9)	Plentiful in these caves.
☐	Blue Butterfly Wing	0.1	2	Damage Stamina	Fortify Conjuration	Damage Magicka Regen	Fortify Enchanting	[7.00] Windhelm (Wuunferth's Quarters)	[8.10] Evergreen Grove	Pine Forest Exterior	Catch butterflies from midair to pluck their wings.
☐	Blue Dartwing	0.1	1	Resist Shock	Fortify Pickpocket	Restore Health	Fear	[6.01] Lund's Hut (3)	[7.21] Steamcrag Camp	Any wilderness.	These blue dragonflies are common in the wilderness, especially around shallow ponds.
☐	Blue Mountain Flower	0.1	2	Restore Health	Fortify Conjuration	Fortify Health	Damage Magicka Regen	[1.00] Solitude (7)	[9.00] Riften (7)	Any wilderness.	Plentiful around these Capitals.
☐	Bone Meal	0.5	5	Damage Stamina	Resist Fire	Fortify Conjuration	Ravage Stamina	[8.18] Bleak Falls Barrow	[5.42] Valthume (4)	Any Draugr Dungeon	Found on Skeletons and Draugr. Check the Atlas for references to this creature.
☐	Briar Heart	0.5	20	Restore Magicka	Fortify Block	Paralysis	Fortify Magicka	[5.44] Lost Valley Redoubt	[5.26] Red Eagle Redoubt	[5.18] Broken Tower Redoubt	Found on Forsworn Briar-Hearts, the leaders of most Forsworn Redoubts. Check the Atlas for locations.
☐	Butterfly Wing	0.1	3	Restore Health	Fortify Barter	Lingering Damage Stamina	Damage Magicka	[3.06] Nightcaller Temple (4)	[1.20] Shadowgreen Cavern	Pine Forest Exterior	Catch butterflies from midair to pluck their wings.
☐	Canis Root	0.1	5	Damage Stamina	Fortify One-handed	Fortify Marksman	Paralysis	[2.08] Swamp ground southeast of Folgunthur (9)	[2.K] Summoning Stones (close by) (5)	[2.00] Morthal (5)	Usually grows in frozen coast or marshland.
☐	Charred Skeever Hide	0.5	1	Restore Stamina	Cure Disease	Resist Poison	Restore Health	[3.10] Fort Dunstad (2)	[6.08] Sleeping Tree Camp (2)	[3.07] Red Road Pass (2)	Usually roasting on bonfires. This cannot be cooked.

✓	INGREDIENT NAME	WEIGHT	VALUE	EFFECT 1	EFFECT 2	EFFECT 3	EFFECT 4	LOCATION A (AMOUNT IF APPLICABLE)	LOCATION B (AMOUNT IF APPLICABLE)	LOCATION C (AMOUNT IF APPLICABLE)	NOTES
☐	Chaurus Eggs	0.2	10	Weakness to Poison	Fortify Stamina	Damage Magicka	Invisibility	[4.06] Frostflow Lighthouse (Abyss) (200+)	[2.02] Chillwind Depths (150+)	[9.23] Tolvald's Cave (100+)	Found on this enemy, as well as across these Caves.
☐	Chicken's Egg	0.5	2	Resist Magic	Damage Magicka Regen	Waterbreathing	Lingering Damage Stamina	[5.20] Salvius Farm (3)	[7.15] Mixwater Mill (3)	[8.11] Half-Moon Mill (2)	Usually found in Chicken Nests.
☐	Creep Cluster	0.2	1	Restore Magicka	Damage Stamina Regen	Fortify Carry Weight	Weakness to Magic	[7.20] Bonestrewn Crest (7)	[7.05] Kynesgrove (close by) (6)	[7.17] Cronvangr Cave (6)	Mainly found in Eastmarch Hold.
☐	Crimson Nirnroot	0.2	10	Damage Health	Damage Stamina	Invisibility	Resist Magic	[10.02] Blackreach (44)	[-]	[-]	Only found in Blackreach. See Blackreach map for more information.
☐	Cyrodilic Spadetail	0.25	15	Damage Stamina	Fortify Restoration	Fear	Ravage Health	[9.00] Riften (Plankside)	[7.00] Windhelm (Docks)	[-]	Catch these fish randomly in lakes, rivers, and the ocean.
☐	Daedra Heart	0.5	250	Restore Health	Damage Stamina Regen	Damage Magicka	Fear	[3.06] Nightcaller Temple (2)	Daedric Quests: The Black Star or Pieces of the Past	College of Winterhold Radiant Quest: The Atronach Forge	Found on Dremora. Cannot be obtained from summoned Dremora. Check the Atlas for references to this creature.
☐	Deathbell	0.1	4	Damage Health	Ravage Stamina	Slow	Weakness to Poison	[2.23] Labyrinthian (Shalidor's Maze) (5)	[2.08] Folgunthur (5+)	[1.00] Solitude (inside Bards' College) (5)	Usually grows in frozen coast or marshland.
☐	Dragon's Tongue	0.1	5	Resist Fire	Fortify Barter	Fortify Illusion	Fortify Two-handed	[7.20] Bonestrewn Crest (15+)	[7.05] Kynesgrove (7)	[7.30] Eldergleam Sanctuary (5+)	A plant that looks like a dragon's tongue, not actually the tongue of a dragon! Usually found in Eastmarch.
☐	Dwarven Oil	0.25	15	Weakness to Magic	Fortify Illusion	Regenerate Magicka	Restore Magicka	[2.18] Mzinchaleft (8)	[3.31] Irkngthand (2)	[4.13] Alftand (1)	Found on many Dwarven Automatons. Otherwise, very rare.
☐	Ectoplasm	0.1	25	Restore Magicka	Fortify Destruction	Fortify Magicka	Damage Health	[6.09] Rannveig's Fast	[4.00] College of Winterhold (5)	[4.02] Yngvild	Found on Ghosts. Check the Atlas for references to this creature.
☐	Elves Ear	0.1	10	Restore Magicka	Fortify Marksman	Weakness to Frost	Resist Fire	[1.00] Riften (Bee and Barb) (7)	[6.00] Whiterun (Dragonsreach) (9)	[9.35] Black-Briar Lodge (7)	Dried Elves Ear can be found in most dwellings.
☐	Eye of Sabre Cat	0.1	2	Restore Stamina	Ravage Health	Damage Magicka	Restore Health	[5.29] Karthspire Camp (2)	Pine Forest Exterior (hunt the animal)	Snowy mountains (hunt the animal)	Found on Sabre Cats, regardless of pelt type. Check the Atlas for references to this creature.
☐	Falmer Ear	0.2	10	Damage Health	Frenzy	Resist Poison	Fortify Lockpicking	[4.13] Alftand (7)	[4.00] College of Winterhold (3+)	Any Dwarven Dungeon.	Found on Falmer. Check the Atlas for references to this creature.
☐	Fire Salts	0.25	50	Weakness to Frost	Resist Fire	Restore Magicka	Regenerate Magicka	[8.02] Sunderstone Gorge (3)	[3.06] Nightcaller Temple (3)	[4.20] Septimus Signus' Outpost	Found on Flame Atronachs, but cannot be obtained from summoned Atronachs. Check the Atlas for references to this creature.
☐	Fly Amanita	0.1	2	Resist Fire	Fortify Two-handed	Frenzy	Regenerate Stamina	[1.10] Pinemoon Cave (60+)	[9.04] Geirmund's Hall (40+)	[2.02] Chillwind Depths (30+)	Plentiful in these caves.
☐	Frost Mirriam	0.1	1	Resist Frost	Fortify Sneak	Ravage Magicka	Damage Stamina Regen	[9.35] Black-Briar Lodge (5)	[9.00] Riften (Temple of Mara) (4)	[5.00] Markarth (Vindrell Hall) (3)	Many buildings in Riften contain Dried Frost Mirriam.
☐	Frost Salts	0.25	100	Weakness to Fire	Resist Frost	Restore Magicka	Fortify Conjuration	[9.00] Riften (Mistveil Keep and Honeyside) (5)	[4.00] College of Winterhold (4+)	[5.09] Harmugstahl	Found on Frost Atronachs, but cannot be obtained from summoned Atronachs. Check the Atlas for references to this creature.
☐	Garlic	0.25	1	Resist Poison	Fortify Stamina	Regenerate Magicka	Regenerate Health	[1.24] East Empire Warehouse (9)	[1.00] Solitude (Vittoria Vici's House_ (8)	[3.10] Fort Dunstad (7)	Usually found in many dwellings.
☐	Giant Lichen	0.25	5	Weakness to Shock	Ravage Health	Weakness to Poison	Restore Magicka	[2.10] Fort Snowhawk (marsh exterior) (14)	[2.21] Kjenstag Ruins (west of location) (9)	[2.16] Ustengrav (8)	Mostly found outside.
☐	Giant's Toe	1	20	Damage Stamina	Fortify Health	Fortify Carry Weight	Damage Stamina Regen	[2.07] Talking Stone Camp	[6.08] Sleeping Tree Camp	[8.17] Secunda's Kiss	Found on Giants. Check the Atlas for references to this creature.
☐	Glow Dust	0.5	20	Damage Magicka	Damage Magicka Regen	Fortify Destruction	Resist Shock	[3.11] Shrine of Mehrunes Dagon (3)	[7.00] Windhelm (Palace of the Kings) (3)	[3.08] Frostmere Crypt	Found on Wispmothers. Check the Atlas for references.
☐	Glowing Mushroom	0.2	5	Resist Shock	Fortify Destruction	Fortify Smithing	Fortify Health	[9.23] Tolvald's Cave (250+)	[4.06] Frostflow Lighthouse (90+)	[1.06] Lost Echo Cave (57)	Plentiful in these caves.
☐	Grass Pod	0.1	1	Resist Poison	Ravage Magicka	Fortify Alteration	Restore Magicka	[10.04] Japhet's Folly	[3.00] Dawnstar (coastal plain to the northwest)	Northern coastline	Plentiful along the marshy northern coastline.
☐	Hagraven Claw	0.25	20	Resist Magic	Lingering Damage Magicka	Fortify Enchanting	Fortify Barter	[5.03] Hag's End	[5.36] Dead Crone Rock	[8.03] Glenmoril Coven	Found on Hagravens. Check the Atlas for references to this creature.
☐	Hagraven Feathers	0.1	20	Damage Magicka	Fortify Conjuration	Frenzy	Weakness to Shock	[5.03] Hag's End	[5.36] Dead Crone Rock	[8.03] Glenmoril Coven	Found on Hagravens. Check the Atlas for references to this creature.
☐	Hanging Moss	0.25	1	Damage Magicka	Fortify Health	Damage Magicka Regen	Fortify One-handed	[1.00] Solitude (Hall of the Dead) (60+)	[6.12] Dustman's Cairn (45+)	[8.02] Sunderstone Gorge (22+)	Usually found clinging to stone buildings, and the rocky outcrops across The Reach.

The Elder Scrolls V
SKYRIM

	INGREDIENT NAME	WEIGHT	VALUE	EFFECT 1	EFFECT 2	EFFECT 3	EFFECT 4	LOCATION A (AMOUNT IF APPLICABLE)	LOCATION B (AMOUNT IF APPLICABLE)	LOCATION C (AMOUNT IF APPLICABLE)	NOTES
☑											
☐	Hawk Beak	0.25	15	Restore Stamina	Resist Frost	Fortify Carry Weight	Resist Shock	[1.00] Solitude (Exterior, Docks)	[8.12] Bloated Man's Grotto	Any Silver Hand Location	Shoot hawks from the sky to claim this ingredient from them, or from Silver Hand Members during The Companions Quests.
☐	Hawk Feathers	0.1	15	Cure Disease	Fortify Light Armor	Fortify One-handed	Fortify Sneak	[1.00] Solitude (Exterior, Docks)	[8.12] Bloated Man's Grotto	Any Silver Hand Location	Shoot hawks from the sky to claim this ingredient from them, or from Silver Hand Members during The Companions Quests.
☐	Histcarp	0.25	6	Restore Stamina	Fortify Magicka	Damage Stamina Regen	Waterbreathing	[9.00] Riften (Plankside)	[7.00] Windhelm (Docks)	[–]	Catch these fish randomly in lakes, rivers, and the ocean.
☐	Honeycomb	1	5	Restore Stamina	Fortify Block	Fortify Light Armor	Ravage Stamina	[9.10] Honeystrand Cave	[9.29] Goldenglow Estate	[–]	Commonly found near beehives, which are plentiful here.
☐	Human Flesh	0.25	1	Damage Health	Paralysis	Restore Magicka	Fortify Sneak	[4.13] Aftand (3)	[9.23] Tolvald's Cave (3)	[5.41] Reachcliff Cave (2)	Very rare.
☐	Human Heart	1	0	Damage Health	Damage Magicka	Damage Magicka Regen	Frenzy	[5.44] Lost Valley Redoubt (1)	[8.02] Sunderstone Gorge (1)	[8.13] North Brittle Shin Pass (1)	Very rare, usually found in Dungeons.
☐	Ice Wraith Teeth	0.25	30	Weakness to Frost	Fortify Heavy Armor	Invisibility	Weakness to Fire	[4.00] College of Winterhold (5)	[6.00] Whiterun (Jorrvasker) (5)	[3.00] Dawnstar (The White Hall) (4)	Found on Ice Wraiths. Check the Atlas for references to this creature.
☐	Imp Stool	0.3	0	Damage Health	Lingering Damage Health	Paralysis	Restore Health	[2.02] Chillwind Depths (50+)	[8.21] Halldir's Cairn (20+)	[6.26] White River Watch (19)	Plentiful in these caves.
☐	Jarrin Root	0.5	10	Damage Health	Damage Magicka	Damage Stamina	Damage Magicka Regen	Dark Brotherhood Quest: To Kill an Empire	[–]	[–]	Unique Ingredient: The only Jarrin Root in Skyrim is given to you by Astrid during Dark Brotherhood Quest: To Kill an Empire. You can use it for the quest, but don't have to. Eating it will kill you instantly. It makes by far the strongest poisons of any ingredient.
☐	Jazbay Grapes	0.2	1	Weakness to Magic	Fortify Magicka	Regenerate Magicka	Ravage Health	[7.Q] Mistwatch Folly (8)	[8.33] South Skybound Watch (Interior) (8)	[7.32] The Atronach Stone (5)	Mainly found in Eastmarch Hold.
☐	Juniper Berries	0.1	1	Weakness to Fire	Fortify Marksman	Regenerate Health	Damage Stamina Regen	[5.00] Markarth (exterior and Cidhna Mines) (15+)	[5.Z] Shrine of Dibella: Bridge at Old Hroldan (8)	[5.X] Reachwind Burial Mound (8)	Mainly found in The Reach.
☐	Large Antlers	0.1	2	Restore Stamina	Fortify Stamina	Slow	Damage Stamina Regen	Pine Forest Exterior (hunt the animal)	The Rift (hunt the animal)	Tundra Plains (hunt the animal)	Found on Elk. Check the Atlas for references to this creature.
☐	Lavender	0.1	1	Resist Magic	Fortify Stamina	Ravage Magicka	Fortify Conjuration	[6.00] Whiterun (Temple of Kynareth, Wind District, and Dragonsreach) (40+)	[5.12] Cliffside Retreat (east of location) (8)	[5.28] Rebel's Cairn (5)	Grows across the Tundra plains of Whiterun Hold.
☐	Luna Moth Wing	0.1	5	Damage Magicka	Fortify Light Armor	Regenerate Health	Invisibility	[3.06] Nightcaller Temple (5)	[1.20] Shadowgreen Cavern	[6.08] Sleeping Tree Camp	Catch butterflies from midair to pluck their wings. Pale-winged Luna Moths can be found most easily at night.
☐	Moon Sugar	0.25	50	Weakness to Fire	Resist Frost	Restore Magicka	Regenerate Magicka	[9.00] Riften (Warehouse) (6)	[7.37] Cragslane Cavern (2)	[8.02] Sunderstone Gorge (1)	Sold by Khajiit Caravans. Otherwise, very rare.
☐	Mora Tapinella	0.25	4	Restore Magicka	Lingering Damage Health	Regenerate Stamina	Fortify Illusion	[3.08] Frostmere Crypt (4+)	"[2.H] Swamp Pond Massacre (ground to the north) (3)"	[2.03] Robber's Gorge (Exterior) (3)	This species of mushroom grows on dead tree stumps, mainly outside across pine forests.
☐	Mudcrab Chitin	0.25	2	Restore Stamina	Cure Disease	Resist Poison	Resist Fire	[6.27] Riverwood (river banks)	[6.H] King of the Mudcrabs	The banks of most rivers and lakes.	Found on Mudcrabs. Check the Atlas for references to this creature.
☐	Namira's Rot	0.25	0	Damage Magicka	Fortify Lockpicking	Fear	Regenerate Health	[2.02] Chillwind Depths (60)	[8.21] Halldir's Cairn (18+)	[5.11] Liar's Retreat (10)	Reasonably plentiful in these caves.
☐	Nightshade	0.1	8	Damage Health	Damage Magicka Regen	Lingering Damage Stamina	Fortify Destruction	[2.23] Labyrinthian (10+)	[8.00] Falkreath (10+)	[1.00] Solitude (Arch) (7)	Reasonably plentiful in these areas. Grows outside (mainly in pine forests) and inside some dungeons.
☐	Nirnroot	0.2	10	Damage Health	Damage Stamina	Invisibility	Resist Magic	[9.06] Sarethi Camp (8)	[8.K] Alchemist's Camp: Evergreen Woods (3)	[3.00] Dawnstar (coast) (3)	Aside from Sarethi's Farm, these are found along river banks.
☐	Nordic Barnacle	0.2	5	Damage Magicka	Waterbreathing	Regenerate Health	Fortify Pickpocket	[1.07] Orphan's Tear (19)	[4.01] Hela's Folly (19)	[2.05] Crabber's Shanty (coast nearby)	Usually found on shipwrecks, or along the coast.
☐	Orange Dartwing	0.1	1	Restore Stamina	Ravage Magicka	Fortify Pickpocket	Lingering Damage Health	[1.00] Solitude (Hall of the Dead) (6)	[3.27] Forsaken Cave (5)	Any wilderness.	These orange dragonflies are common in the wilderness, especially around shallow ponds.
☐	Pearl	0.1	2	Restore Stamina	Fortify Block	Restore Magicka	Resist Shock	[9.04] Geirmund's Hall (3)	[4.13] Alftand (1)	[–]	Easier to purchase from Apothecary traders. Otherwise very rare.

✓	INGREDIENT NAME	WEIGHT	VALUE	EFFECT 1	EFFECT 2	EFFECT 3	EFFECT 4	LOCATION A (AMOUNT IF APPLICABLE)	LOCATION B (AMOUNT IF APPLICABLE)	LOCATION C (AMOUNT IF APPLICABLE)	NOTES
☐	Pine Thrush Egg	0.5	2	Restore Stamina	Fortify Lockpicking	Weakness to Poison	Resist Shock	[9.25] Shor's Stone (Sylgja's House) (6)	[6.02] Rorikstead (Lemkil's House) (5)	[9.18] Avanchnzel (exterior)	Look for birds' nests with these mottled brown eggs, mainly in forested areas.
☐	Powdered Mammoth Tusk	0.1	2	Restore Stamina	Fortify Sneak	Weakness to Fire	Fear	[2.07] Talking Stone Camp	[6.08] Sleeping Tree Camp	[8.17] Secunda's Kiss	Found on a Mammoth. Check the Atlas for references to this creature.
☐	Purple Mountain Flower	0.1	2	Restore Stamina	Fortify Sneak	Lingering Damage Magicka	Resist Frost	[1.17] Dragon Bridge (11)	[5.13] Dragon Bridge Overlook (7)	Any wilderness.	Plentiful around these areas.
☐	Red Mountain Flower	0.1	2	Restore Magicka	Ravage Magicka	Fortify Magicka	Damage Health	[6.00] Whiterun (10)	[1.20] Shadowgreen Cavern (10)	Any wilderness.	Plentiful around the Capital of Whiterun and within the spacious Shadowgreen Cavern.
☐	River Betty	0.25	15	Damage Health	Fortify Alteration	Slow	Fortify Carry Weight	[9.00] Riften (Plankside)	[7.00] Windhelm (Docks)	[–]	Catch these fish randomly in lakes, rivers, and the ocean.
☐	Rock Warbler Egg	0.5	2	Restore Health	Fortify One-handed	Damage Stamina	Weakness to Magic	[5.00] Markarth (Warrens) (3)	[5.42] Valthume (rocks east of entrance)	[5.20] Salvius Farm (nearby ridges)	Look for birds' nests with these large, green eggs, mainly in the Reach.
☐	Sabre Cat Tooth	0.1	2	Restore Stamina	Fortify Heavy Armor	Fortify Smithing	Weakness to Poison	[6.10] Drelas' Cottage (2)	Pine Forest Exterior (hunt the animal)	Snowy mountains (hunt the animal)	Found on a Sabre Cat. Check the Atlas for references to this creature.
☐	Salt Pile	0.2	2	Weakness to Magic	Fortify Restoration	Slow	Regenerate Magicka	[4.00] College of Winterhold (Midden) (7)	[6.29] Fellglow Keep (5)	[3.10] Fort Dunstad (5)	Most merchants carry this.
☐	Scaly Pholiota	0.25	4	Weakness to Magic	Fortify Illusion	Regenerate Stamina	Fortify Carry Weight	[9.B] Wood Cutter's Camp: Lake Geir (3)	[9.L] Altar in the Woods: Autumnshade (3)	[9.37] Darklight Tower (north, closer to the lake) (3)	Usually found on or near fallen trees or stumps.
☐	Silverside Perch	0.25	15	Restore Stamina	Damage Stamina Regen	Ravage Health	Resist Frost	[9.00] Riften (Plankside)	[7.00] Windhelm (Docks)	[–]	Catch these fish randomly in lakes, rivers, and the ocean.
☐	Skeever Tail	0.2	3	Damage Stamina Regen	Ravage Health	Damage Health	Fortify Light Armor	[3.10] Fort Dunstad (8)	[3.06] Nightcaller Temple (4)	[5.11] Liar's Retreat (4)	Found on Skeevers. Check the Atlas for references to this creature.
☐	Slaughterfish Egg	0.2	3	Resist Poison	Fortify Pickpocket	Lingering Damage Health	Fortify Stamina	[3.A] Horker Standing Stones (15)	[3.02] Wreck Of The Brinehammer (ocean) (10)	[9.45] Forelhost (7+)	Usually found close to water, or Slaughterfish.
☐	Slaughterfish Scales	0.1	3	Resist Frost	Lingering Damage Health	Fortify Heavy Armor	Fortify Block	[8.03] Glenmoril Coven (6)	[9.23] Tolvald's Cave (4)	Any lake in Skyrim where Slaughterfish dwell.	Found on Slaughterfish. Check the Atlas for references to this creature.
☐	Small Antlers	0.1	2	Weakness to Poison	Fortify Restoration	Lingering Damage Stamina	Damage Health	Pine Forest Exterior (hunt the animal)	The Rift (hunt the animal)	Tundra Plains (hunt the animal)	Found on Deer. Check the Atlas for references to this creature.
☐	Small Pearl	0.1	2	Restore Stamina	Fortify One-handed	Fortify Restoration	Resist Frost	[9.04] Geirmund's Hall (3)	[4.13] Alftand (1)	[–]	Easier to purchase from Apothecary traders. Otherwise very rare.
☐	Snowberries	0.1	4	Resist Fire	Fortify Enchanting	Resist Frost	Resist Shock	[4.07] Driftshade Refuge (25)	[7.10] Traitor's Post (12)	[4.00] College of Winterhold (11)	Find these outside, where snow is on the ground.
☐	Spider Egg	0.2	5	Damage Stamina	Damage Magicka Regen	Fortify Lockpicking	Fortify Marksman	[4.15] Ironbind Barrow (11)	[5.09] Harmugstah (8)	[6.00] Whiterun (Jorrvaskr) (7)	Found on some Frostbite Spiders, or close by their lairs. Check the Atlas for references to this creature.
☐	Spriggan Sap	0.2	15	Damage Magicka Regen	Fortify Enchanting	Fortify Smithing	Fortify Alteration	[8.05] Moss Mother Cavern	[1.20] Shadowgreen Cavern	[4.00] College of Winterhold (2)	Found on Spriggans. Check the Atlas for references to this creature.
☐	Swamp Fungal Pod	0.25	5	Resist Shock	Lingering Damage Magicka	Paralysis	Restore Health	[2.19] Movarth's Lair (Exterior) (10)	[2.00] Morthal (swamp to the northwest and west) (15+)	[–]	Mainly found in the wet ground of Hjaalmarch Hold.
☐	Taproot	0.5	15	Weakness to Magic	Fortify Illusion	Regenerate Magicka	Restore Magicka	[8.05] Moss Mother Cavern	[1.20] Shadowgreen Cavern	[1.11] Clearpine Pond	Found on Spriggans. Check the Atlas for references to this creature.
☐	Thistle Branch	0.1	1	Resist Frost	Ravage Stamina	Resist Poison	Fortify Heavy Armor	[1.00] Solitude (Arch and Blue Palace)	[1.17] Dragon Bridge (7)	[6.27] Riverwood (7)	Mainly found in scrubland and around settlements.
☐	Torchbug Thorax	0.1	1	Restore Stamina	Lingering Damage Magicka	Weakness to Magic	Fortify Stamina	[4.00] College of Winterhold (10+)	[3.27] Forsaken Cave (5+)	[3.00] Dawnstar (The White Hall) (3)	Look for these glowing insects at dusk or night, across the wilderness (but not at altitude).
☐	Troll Fat	1	15	Resist Poison	Fortify Two-handed	Frenzy	Damage Health	[1.24] East Empire Warehouse (15+)	[6.30] Graywinter Watch	Animal Dens across the wilderness.	Found on Trolls. Check the Atlas for references to this creature.
☐	Tundra Cotton	0.1	1	Resist Magic	Fortify Magicka	Fortify Block	Fortify Barter	[1.00] Solitude (Buildings in The Avenues District)	[6.14] Redoran's Retreat (13)	[8.12] Bloated Man's Grotto (10)	Found growing outside, at low altitudes.

The Elder Scrolls V
SKYRIM

	INGREDIENT NAME	WEIGHT	VALUE	EFFECT 1	EFFECT 2	EFFECT 3	EFFECT 4	LOCATION A (AMOUNT IF APPLICABLE)	LOCATION B (AMOUNT IF APPLICABLE)	LOCATION C (AMOUNT IF APPLICABLE)	NOTES
☐	Vampire Dust	0.2	25	Invisibility	Restore Magicka	Regenerate Health	Cure Disease	[8.25] North Shriekwind Bastion	[6.07] Broken Fang Cave	Any Court Wizard's Quarters, or your house's Alchemy Lab.	Found on Vampires. Check the Atlas for references to this creature.
☐	Void Salts	0.2	125	Weakness to Shock	Resist Magic	Damage Health	Fortify Magicka	[1.00] Solitude (Proudspire Manor Alchemy Lab) (4)	[9.00] Riften (Honeyside Alchemy Lab) (3)	[4.00] College of Winterhold (Archmage's Quarters)	Found on Storm Atronachs, but cannot be obtained from summoned Atronachs. Check the Atlas for references to this creature.
☐	Wheat	0.1	5	Restore Health	Fortify Health	Damage Stamina Regen	Lingering Damage Magicka	[1.23] Katla's Farm	[6.02] Rorikshead	[6.24] Battle-Born Farm	Check the larger towns (such as Rorikshead), or consult Favor (Activity): Harvesting Crops†.
☐	White Cap	0.3	0	Weakness to Frost	Fortify Heavy Armor	Restore Magicka	Ravage Magicka	[2.02] Chillwind Depths (40+)	[8.21] Halldir's Cairn (20+)	[6.26] White River Watch (15+)	Plentiful in these locations.
☐	Wisp Wrappings	0.1	2	Restore Stamina	Fortify Destruction	Fortify Carry Weight	Resist Magic	[3.08] Frostmere Crypt	[2.23] Labyrinthian	[5.J] Dwarven Ruins: Lair of the Wispmother	Found on Wispmothers. Check the Atlas for references.

◈ Table VI: Alchemy Effects List

This list that reveals every Alchemic Effect, and which ingredients have those effects.

	EFFECT NAME	INGREDIENTS WITH THIS EFFECT
☐	Cure Disease	Charred Skeever Hide, Hawk Feathers, Mudcrab Chitin, Vampire Dust
☐	Damage Health	Crimson Nirnroot, Deathbell, Ectoplasm, Falmer Ear, Human Flesh, Human Heart, Imp Stool, Jarrin Root, Mora Tapinella, Nightshade, Nirnroot, Orange Dartwing, Red Mountain Flower, River Betty, Skeever Tail, Slaughterfish Egg, Slaughterfish Scales, Small Antlers, Troll Fat, Void Salts
☐	Damage Magicka	Bear Claws, Blue Butterfly Wing, Blue Mountain Flower, Butterfly Wing, Chaurus Eggs, Chicken's Egg, Daedra Heart, Eye of Sabre Cat, Glow Dust, Hagraven Claw, Hagraven Feathers, Hanging Moss, Human Heart, Jarrin Root, Luna Moth Wing, Namira's Rot, Nightshade, Nordic Barnacle, Purple Mountain Flower, Spider Egg, Spriggan Sap, Swamp Fungal Pod, Torchbug Thorax, Wheat
☐	Damage Magicka Regen	Bear Claws, Blue Butterfly Wing, Blue Mountain Flower, Chicken's Egg, Glow Dust, Hanging Moss, Human Heart, Jarrin Root, Nightshade, Spider Egg, Spriggan Sap
☐	Damage Stamina	Blisterwort, Blue Butterfly Wing, Bone Meal, Butterfly Wing, Canis Root, Chicken's Egg, Creep Cluster, Crimson Nirnroot, Cyrodilic Spadetail, Daedra Heart, Frost Mirriam, Giant's Toe, Histcarp, Jarrin Root, Juniper Berries, Large Antlers, Nightshade, Nirnroot, Rock Warbler Egg, Silverside Perch, Skeever Tail, Small Antlers, Spider Egg, Wheat
☐	Damage Stamina Regen	Creep Cluster, Daedra Heart, Frost Mirriam, Giant's Toe, Histcarp, Juniper Berries, Large Antlers, Silverside Perch, Skeever Tail, Wheat
☐	Fear	Blue Dartwing, Cyrodilic Spadetail, Daedra Heart, Namira's Rot, Powdered Mammoth Tusk
☐	Fortify Alteration	Grass Pod, River Betty, Spriggan Sap
☐	Fortify Barter	Butterfly Wing, Dragon's Tongue, Hagraven Claw, Tundra Cotton
☐	Fortify Block	Bleeding Crown, Briar Heart, Honeycomb, Pearl, Slaughterfish Scales, Tundra Cotton
☐	Fortify Carry Weight	Creep Cluster, Giant's Toe, Hawk Beak, River Betty, Scaly Pholiota, Wisp Wrappings
☐	Fortify Conjuration	Blue Butterfly Wing, Blue Mountain Flower, Bone Meal, Frost Salts, Hagraven Feathers, Lavender
☐	Fortify Destruction	Beehive Husk, Ectoplasm, Glow Dust, Glowing Mushroom, Nightshade, Wisp Wrappings
☐	Fortify Enchanting	Blue Butterfly Wing, Hagraven Claw, Snowberries, Spriggan Sap

	EFFECT NAME	INGREDIENTS WITH THIS EFFECT
☐	Fortify Health	Bear Claws, Blue Mountain Flower, Giant's Toe, Glowing Mushroom, Hanging Moss, Wheat
☐	Fortify Heavy Armor	Ice Wraith Teeth, Sabre Cat Tooth, Slaughterfish Scales, Thistle Branch, White Cap
☐	Fortify Illusion	Dragon's Tongue, Dwarven Oil, Mora Tapinella, Scaly Pholiota, Taproot
☐	Fortify Light Armor	Beehive Husk, Hawk Feathers, Honeycomb, Luna Moth Wing, Skeever Tail
☐	Fortify Lockpicking	Falmer Ear, Namira's Rot, Pine Thrush Egg, Spider Egg
☐	Fortify Magicka	Briar Heart, Ectoplasm, Histcarp, Jazbay Grapes, Red Mountain Flower, Tundra Cotton, Void Salts
☐	Fortify Marksman	Canis Root, Elves Ear, Juniper Berries, Spider Egg
☐	Fortify One-handed	Bear Claws, Canis Root, Hanging Moss, Hawk Feathers, Rock Warbler Egg, Small Pearl
☐	Fortify Pickpocket	Blue Dartwing, Nordic Barnacle Orange Dartwing, Slaughterfish Egg
☐	Fortify Restoration	Abecean Longfin, Cyrodilic Spadetail, Salt Pile, Small Antlers, Small Pearl
☐	Fortify Smithing	Blisterwort, Glowing Mushroom, Sabre Cat Tooth, Spriggan Sap
☐	Fortify Sneak	Abecean Longfin, Beehive Husk, Frost Mirriam, Hawk Feathers, Human Flesh, Powdered Mammoth Tusk, Purple Mountain Flower
☐	Fortify Stamina	Chaurus Eggs, Garlic, Large Antlers, Lavender, Slaughterfish Egg, Torchbug Thorax
☐	Fortify Two-handed	Dragon's Tongue, Fly Amanita, Troll Fat
☐	Frenzy	Blisterwort, Falmer Ear, Fly Amanita, Hagraven Feathers, Human Heart, Troll Fat
☐	Invisibility	Chaurus Eggs, Crimson Nirnroot, Ice Wraith Teeth, Luna Moth Wing, Nirnroot, Vampire Dust
☐	Lingering Damage Health	Imp Stool, Mora Tapinella, Orange Dartwing, Slaughterfish Egg, Slaughterfish Scales
☐	Lingering Damage Magicka	Hagraven Claw, Purple Mountain Flower, Swamp Fungal Pod, Torchbug Thorax, Wheat

✓	EFFECT NAME	INGREDIENTS WITH THIS EFFECT
☐	Lingering Damage Stamina	Butterfly Wing, Chicken's Egg, Nightshade, Small Antlers
☐	Paralysis	Briar Heart, Canis Root, Human Flesh, Imp Stool, Swamp Fungal Pod
☐	Ravage Health	Cyrodilic Spadetail, Eye of Sabre Cat, Giant Lichen, Jazbay Grapes, Silverside Perch, Skeever Tail
☐	Ravage Magicka	Frost Mirriam, Grass Pod, Lavender, Orange Dartwing, Red Mountain Flower, White Cap
☐	Ravage Stamina	Bee, Bone Meal, Deathbell, Honeycomb, Thistle Branch
☐	Regenerate Health	Garlic, Juniper Berries, Luna Moth Wing, Namira's Rot, Nordic Barnacle, Vampire Dust
☐	Regenerate Magicka	Dwarven Oil, Fire Salts, Garlic, Jazbay Grapes, Moon Sugar, Salt Pile, Taproot
☐	Regenerate Stamina	Bee, Fly Amanita, Mora Tapinella, Scaly Pholiota
☐	Resist Fire	Bone Meal, Dragon's Tongue, Elves Ear, Fire Salts, Fly Amanita, Mudcrab Chitin, Snowberries
☐	Resist Frost	Frost Mirriam, Frost Salts, Hawk Beak, Moon Sugar, Purple Mountain Flower, Silverside Perch, Slaughterfish Scales, Small Pearl, Snowberries, Thistle Branch
☐	Resist Magic	Bleeding Crown, Chicken's Egg, Crimson Nirnroot, Hagraven Claw, Lavender, Nirnroot, Tundra Cotton, Void Salts, Wisp Wrappings
☐	Resist Poison	Beehive Husk, Charred Skeever Hide, Falmer Ear, Garlic, Grass Pod, Mudcrab Chitin, Slaughterfish Egg, Thistle Branch, Troll Fat

✓	EFFECT NAME	INGREDIENTS WITH THIS EFFECT
☐	Resist Shock	Blue Dartwing, Glow Dust, Glowing Mushroom, Hawk Beak, Pearl, Pine Thrush Egg, Snowberries, Swamp Fungal Pod
☐	Restore Health	Blisterwort, Blue Dartwing, Blue Mountain Flower, Butterfly Wing, Charred Skeever Hide, Daedra Heart, Eye of Sabre Cat, Imp Stool, Rock Warbler Egg, Swamp Fungal Pod, Wheat
☐	Restore Magicka	Briar Heart, Creep Cluster, Dwarven Oil, Ectoplasm, Elves Ear, Fire Salts, Frost Salts, Giant Lichen, Grass Pod, Human Flesh, Moon Sugar, Mora Tapinella, Pearl, Red Mountain Flower, Taproot, Vampire Dust, White Cap
☐	Restore Stamina	Bear Claws, Bee, Charred Skeever Hide, Eye of Sabre Cat, Hawk Beak, Histcarp, Honeycomb, Large Antlers, Mudcrab Chitin, Orange Dartwing, Pearl, Pine Thrush Egg, Powdered Mammoth Tusk, Purple Mountain Flower, Sabre Cat Tooth, Silverside Perch, Small Pearl, Torchbug Thorax, Wisp Wrappings
☐	Slow	Deathbell, Large Antlers, River Betty, Salt Pile
☐	Waterbreathing	Chicken's Egg, Histcarp, Nordic Barnacle
☐	Weakness to Fire	Bleeding Crown, Frost Salts, Ice Wraith Teeth, Juniper Berries, Moon Sugar, Powdered Mammoth Tusk
☐	Weakness to Frost	Abecean Longfin, Elves Ear, Fire Salts, Ice Wraith Teeth, White Cap
☐	Weakness to Magic	Creep Cluster, Dwarven Oil, Jazbay Grapes, Rock Warbler Egg, Salt Pile, Scaly Pholiota, Taproot, Torchbug Thorax
☐	Weakness to Poison	Abecean Longfin, Bleeding Crown, Chaurus Eggs, Deathbell, Giant Lichen, Pine Thrush Egg, Sabre Cat Tooth, Small Antlers
☐	Weakness to Shock	Bee, Giant Lichen, Hagraven Feathers, Void Salts

CRAFTING: ENCHANTMENTS

▷ Table VII: Soul Gems

A list of soul gems and their properties. Note that the Filled Soul Gems listed here are the 'standard' filled soul gems you can find in the world. If you Soul Trap a weaker creature into a larger gem, the resulting value will be reduced.

✓	NAME	WEIGHT	VALUE	CAPACITY	NOTES
☐	Petty Soul Gem	0.1	10	250	Can hold creature souls below Lv4.
☐	Lesser Soul Gem	0.2	25	500	Can hold creature souls below Lv16.
☐	Common Soul Gem	0.3	50	1000	Can hold creature souls below Lv28.
☐	Greater Soul Gem	0.4	100	2000	Can hold creature souls below Lv38.
☐	Grand Soul Gem	0.5	200	3000	Can hold any creature soul.
☐	Black Soul Gem	1	500	3000	Can hold any human soul.
☐	Petty Soul Gem (Filled)	0.1	40	250	Holds a petty soul.
☐	Lesser Soul Gem (Filled)	0.2	80	500	Holds a lesser soul.
☐	Common Soul Gem (Filled)	0.3	150	1000	Holds a common soul.
☐	Greater Soul Gem (Filled)	0.4	350	2000	Holds a greater soul.
☐	Grand Soul Gem (Filled)	0.5	500	3000	Holds a grand soul.
☐	Black Soul Gem (Filled)	1	1200	3000	Holds a human soul.

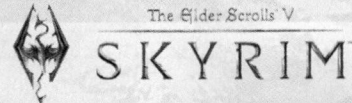

The Elder Scrolls V
SKYRIM™

Table VIII: Base Enchantments

The two tables below list all of the base weapon and armor enchantments.

When Disenchanting an item, you always learn its Base Enchantment.

◊ So disenchanting a Daedric Mace of the Inferno teaches you 'Fire Damage'.

◊ But disenchanting an Iron Sword of Embers also teaches you 'Fire Damage'. Despite the cheaper item, you learn the same effect.

When Enchanting an item:

◊ You can apply any weapon enchantment to any weapon.

◊ You can apply armor enchantments only to a subset of armor pieces, as shown below.

Examples:

You can enchant any weapon with Fire Damage, from a dagger to a warhammer.

You can apply Waterbreathing to any Helm, Ring, or Necklace.

You can put Muffle on any pair of Boots, but only on Boots.

BASE ENCHANTMENT	EFFECT
WEAPON BASE ENCHANTMENTS	
Absorb Health	Absorb # Health.
Absorb Magicka	Absorb # Magicka.
Absorb Stamina	Absorb # Stamina.
Banish	Banishes summoned daedra below level #.
Fear	Creatures below level # flee for 30s.
Fire Damage	+# fire damage.

BASE ENCHANTMENT	EFFECT
Frost Damage	+# frost damage.
Magicka Damage	+# magicka damage.
Paralyze	Paralyzes creatures below level #.
Shock Damage	+# shock damage.
Soul Trap	Soul traps creatures that die within # seconds.
Stamina Damage	+# magicka damage.
Turn Undead	Undead below level # flee for 30s.

MODIFIER	BASE ENCHANTMENT	HEAD	CHEST	HANDS	FEET	SHIELD	RING	NECKLACE
STANDARD ARMOR ENCHANTMENTS								
Fortify Alchemy	Potions and poisons you craft are #% stronger.	X		X			X	X
Fortify Alteration	Alteration spells cost #% less to cast.	X	X				X	X
Fortify Archery	Increases bow damage by #%.	X		X			X	X
Fortify Block	When blocking, you block #% more damage.			X		X	X	X
Fortify Carry Weight	+# Carry Weight			X	X		X	X
Fortify Conjuration	Conjuration spells cost #% less to cast.	X	X				X	X
Fortify Destruction	Destruction spells cost #% less to cast.	X	X				X	X
Fortify Healing Rate	Increases your health regeneration rate by #%.		X				X	X
Fortify Health	+# Health		X			X	X	X
Fortify Heavy Armor	Increases your Heavy Armor skill by #.		X	X			X	X
Fortify Illusion	Illusion spells cost #% less to cast.	X	X				X	X
Fortify Light Armor	Increases your Light Armor skill by #.		X	X			X	X
Fortify Lockpicking	Locks are #% easier to pick.	X		X			X	X
Fortify Magicka	+# Magicka	X		X			X	X
Fortify Magicka Rate	Increases your magicka regeneration rate by #%.	X	X				X	
Fortify One-Handed	Increases one-handed weapon damage by #%.			X	X		X	X

MODIFIER	BASE ENCHANTMENT	HEAD	CHEST	HANDS	FEET	SHIELD	RING	NECKLACE
Fortify Pickpocket	Pickpocketing items is #% easier.			X	X		X	X
Fortify Restoration	Restoration spells cost #% less to cast.	X	X				X	X
Fortify Smithing	Weapons and armor improvements are #% stronger.		X	X			X	X
Fortify Sneak	Sneaking is #% easier.			X	X		X	X
Fortify Speech	Prices you get are #% better.							X
Fortify Stamina	+# Stamina		X		X		X	X
Fortify Stamina Rate	Increases your stamina regeneration rate by #%.		X		X			X
Fortify Two-Handed	Increases two-handed weapon damage by #%.			X	X		X	X
Muffle	You move silently when sneaking.				X			
Resist Disease	+#% Disease Resistance		X			X	X	X
Resist Fire	+#% Fire Resistance				X	X	X	X
Resist Frost	+#% Frost Resistance				X	X	X	X
Resist Magic	+#% Magic Resistance (all forms of magic)					X	X	X
Resist Poison	+#% Poison Resistance		X			X	X	X
Resist Shock	+#% Shock Resistance				X	X	X	X
Waterbreathing	You do not drown when swimming.	X					X	X

Table IX: Derived Enchantments

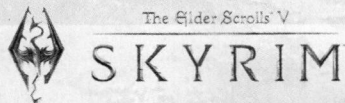

This table lists all of the Enchantments that can appear on items you find in the world.

Derived Enchantments Key

Modifier: The item suffix (or, occasionally, prefix) that identifies the enchantment.

Base Enchantment: The enchantment that you learn if you disenchant the item. Cross-reference this with the Base Enchantments Table for a complete description of the enchantment.

Ench Level: The level of this particular enchantment. Cross-reference this with the General Data Table to identify which material types this enchantment can appear on.

Magnitude: The "strength" of this particular enchantment, which might be expressed as a percentage, duration, level, or raw modifier. Plug this into the "#" in the base enchantment's description.

Not every possible combination of weapon, material, and enchantment permitted under this system exists in Skyrim... but the vast majority do.

For Example: You find an Elven Mace of Enervating. Looking it up on this table, you find that its Base Enchantment is "Magicka Damage", and its magnitude is "50". Cross-referencing this with the Base Enchantments Table tells you that it does "+50 Magicka Damage".

Note that the College of Winterhold Robes work a little differently:

There are five basic robes: Novice, Apprentice, Adept, Expert, Master. Each of these robes has a specific Fortify Magicka Rate enchantment on it, as listed on the Armor page.

In addition to that enchantment, these robes may also have an additional enchantment related to one of the five schools of magic. The modifier is just the name of the school, since the magnitude is determined by the type of robe. So, for example, you can find:

Novice Robes of Conjuration [+50% Magicka Regen; 12% Conjuration]

Apprentice Robes of Conjuration [+75% Magicka Regen; 15% Conjuration]

Apprentice Robes of Destruction [+75% Magicka Regen; 15% Destruction]

☑ MODIFIER	BASE ENCHANTMENT	ENCH LEVEL	MAGNITUDE
STANDARD WEAPON ENCHANTMENT MODIFIERS			
of Absorption	Absorb Health	2	5
of Consuming	Absorb Health	3	10
of Devouring	Absorb Health	4	15
of Leeching	Absorb Health	5	20
of the Vampire	Absorb Health	6	25
of Siphoning	Absorb Magicka	2	10
of Harrowing	Absorb Magicka	3	15
of Winnowing	Absorb Magicka	4	20
of Evoking	Absorb Magicka	5	25
of the Sorcerer	Absorb Magicka	6	30
of Gleaning	Absorb Stamina	2	10
of Reaping	Absorb Stamina	3	15
of Harvesting	Absorb Stamina	4	20
of Garnering	Absorb Stamina	5	25
of Subsuming	Absorb Stamina	6	30
of Banishing	Banish	4	Lv12
of Expelling	Banish	5	Lv20
of Annihilating	Banish	6	Lv36
of Dismay	Fear	1	Lv5
of Cowardice	Fear	2	Lv7
of Fear	Fear	3	Lv10
of Despair	Fear	4	Lv13
of Dread	Fear	5	Lv16

☑ MODIFIER	BASE ENCHANTMENT	ENCH LEVEL	MAGNITUDE
of Terror	Fear	6	Lv20
of Embers	Fire Damage	1	5
of Burning	Fire Damage	2	10
of Scorching	Fire Damage	3	15
of Fire / Flames	Fire Damage	4	20
of the Blaze	Fire Damage	5	25
of the Inferno	Fire Damage	6	30
of Cold / Chills	Frost Damage	1	5
of Frost	Frost Damage	2	10
of Ice	Frost Damage	3	15
of Freezing	Frost Damage	4	20
of Blizzards	Frost Damage	5	25
of Winter	Frost Damage	6	30
of Sapping	Magicka Damage	1	10
of Draining	Magicka Damage	2	20
of Diminishing	Magicka Damage	3	30
of Depleting	Magicka Damage	4	40
of Enervating	Magicka Damage	5	50
of Nullifying	Magicka Damage	6	60
of Stunning	Paralyze	4	2s
of Immobilizing	Paralyze	5	4s
of Petrifying	Paralyze	6	6s
of Sparks	Shock Damage	1	5
of Arcing	Shock Damage	2	10
of Shocks	Shock Damage	3	15
of Thunderbolts	Shock Damage	4	20

☑ MODIFIER	BASE ENCHANTMENT	ENCH LEVEL	MAGNITUDE
of Lightning	Shock Damage	5	25
of Storms	Shock Damage	6	30
of Souls	Soul Trap	1	3s
of Soul Snares	Soul Trap	2	5s
of Binding	Soul Trap	3	7s
of Animus	Soul Trap	4	10s
of Malediction	Soul Trap	5	15s
of Damnation	Soul Trap	6	20s
of Fatigue	Stamina Damage	1	5
of Weariness	Stamina Damage	2	10
of Torpor	Stamina Damage	3	15
of Debilitation	Stamina Damage	4	20
of Lethargy	Stamina Damage	5	25
of Exhaustion	Stamina Damage	6	30
Blessed	Turn Undead	1	Lv3
Sanctified	Turn Undead	2	Lv7
Reverent	Turn Undead	3	Lv13
Hallowed	Turn Undead	4	Lv21
Virtuous	Turn Undead	5	Lv30
Holy	Turn Undead	6	Lv40
STANDARD ARMOR ENCHANTMENTS			
of Minor Alchemy	Fortify Alchemy	1	12%
of Alchemy	Fortify Alchemy	2	15%
of Major Alchemy	Fortify Alchemy	3	17%
of Eminent Alchemy	Fortify Alchemy	4	20%

☑ MODIFIER	BASE ENCHANTMENT	ENCH LEVEL	MAGNITUDE
of Extreme Alchemy	Fortify Alchemy	5	22%
of Peerless Alchemy	Fortify Alchemy	6	25%
of Minor Alteration	Fortify Alteration	1	12%
of Alteration	Fortify Alteration	2	15%
of Major Alteration	Fortify Alteration	3	17%
of Eminent Alteration	Fortify Alteration	4	20%
of Extreme Alteration	Fortify Alteration	5	22%
of Peerless Alteration	Fortify Alteration	6	25%
of Minor Blocking	Fortify Block	1	15%
of Blocking	Fortify Block	2	20%
of Major Blocking	Fortify Block	3	25%
of Eminent Blocking	Fortify Block	4	30%
of Extreme Blocking	Fortify Block	5	35%
of Peerless Blocking	Fortify Block	6	40%
of Lifting	Fortify Carry Weight	1	+25
of Hauling	Fortify Carry Weight	2	+30
of Strength	Fortify Carry Weight	3	+35
of Brawn	Fortify Carry Weight	4	+40
of the Ox	Fortify Carry Weight	5	+45
of the Mammoth	Fortify Carry Weight	6	+50
of Minor Conjuring / Conjuration	Fortify Conjuration	1	12%
of Conjuring / Conjuration	Fortify Conjuration	2	15%
of Major Conjuring / Conjuration	Fortify Conjuration	3	17%
of Eminent Conjuring / Conjuration	Fortify Conjuration	4	20%
of Extreme Conjuring / Conjuration	Fortify Conjuration	5	22%
of Peerless Conjuring / Conjuration	Fortify Conjuration	6	25%
of Minor Destruction	Fortify Destruction	1	12%
of Destruction	Fortify Destruction	2	15%
of Major Destruction	Fortify Destruction	3	17%
of Eminent Destruction	Fortify Destruction	4	20%
of Extreme Destruction	Fortify Destruction	5	22%
of Peerless Destruction	Fortify Destruction	6	25%
of Remedy	Fortify Healing Rate	3	20%
of Mending	Fortify Healing Rate	4	30%
of Regeneration	Fortify Healing Rate	5	40%
of Revival	Fortify Healing Rate	6	50%
of Minor Health	Fortify Health	1	+20
of Health	Fortify Health	2	+30
of Major Health	Fortify Health	3	+40
of Eminent Health	Fortify Health	4	+50
of Extreme Health	Fortify Health	5	+60

☑ MODIFIER	BASE ENCHANTMENT	ENCH LEVEL	MAGNITUDE
of Peerless Health	Fortify Health	6	+70
of the Minor Knight	Fortify Heavy Armor	1	12
of the Knight	Fortify Heavy Armor	2	15
of the Major Knight	Fortify Heavy Armor	3	17
of the Eminent Knight	Fortify Heavy Armor	4	20
of the Extreme Knight	Fortify Heavy Armor	5	22
of the Peerless Knight	Fortify Heavy Armor	6	25
of Minor Illusion	Fortify Illusion	1	12%
of Illusion	Fortify Illusion	2	15%
of Major Illusion	Fortify Illusion	3	17%
of Eminent Illusion	Fortify Illusion	4	20%
of Extreme Illusion	Fortify Illusion	5	22%
of Peerless Illusion	Fortify Illusion	6	25%
of the Minor Squire	Fortify Light Armor	1	12
of the Squire	Fortify Light Armor	2	15
of the Major Squire	Fortify Light Armor	3	17
of the Eminent Squire	Fortify Light Armor	4	20
of the Extreme Squire	Fortify Light Armor	5	22
of the Peerless Squire	Fortify Light Armor	6	25
of Minor Lockpicking	Fortify Lockpicking	1	15%
of Lockpicking	Fortify Lockpicking	2	20%
of Major Lockpicking	Fortify Lockpicking	3	25%
of Eminent Lockpicking	Fortify Lockpicking	4	30%
of Extreme Lockpicking	Fortify Lockpicking	5	35%
of Peerless Lockpicking	Fortify Lockpicking	6	40%
of Magicka	Fortify Magicka	1	+20
of Magicka	Fortify Magicka	2	+30
of Major Magicka	Fortify Magicka	3	+40
of Eminent Magicka	Fortify Magicka	4	+50
of Extreme Magicka	Fortify Magicka	5	+60
of Peerless Magicka	Fortify Magicka	6	+70
of Recharging	Fortify Magicka Rate	3	40%
of Replenishing	Fortify Magicka Rate	4	60%
of Resurgence	Fortify Magicka Rate	5	80%
of Recovery	Fortify Magicka Rate	6	100%
of Minor Archery	Fortify Archery	1	15%
of Archery	Fortify Archery	2	20%
of Major Archery	Fortify Archery	3	25%
of Eminent Archery	Fortify Archery	4	30%
of Extreme Archery	Fortify Archery	5	35%
of Peerless Archery	Fortify Archery	6	40%
of Minor Wielding	Fortify One-Handed	1	15%
of Wielding	Fortify One-Handed	2	20%

☑ MODIFIER	BASE ENCHANTMENT	ENCH LEVEL	MAGNITUDE
of Major Wielding	Fortify One-Handed	3	25%
of Eminent Wielding	Fortify One-Handed	4	30%
of Extreme Wielding	Fortify One-Handed	5	35%
of Peerless Wielding	Fortify One-Handed	6	40%
of Minor Deft Hands	Fortify Pickpocket	1	15%
of Deft Hands	Fortify Pickpocket	2	20%
of Major Deft Hands	Fortify Pickpocket	3	25%
of Eminent Deft Hands	Fortify Pickpocket	4	30%
of Extreme Deft Hands	Fortify Pickpocket	5	35%
of Peerless Deft Hands	Fortify Pickpocket	6	40%
of Minor Restoration	Fortify Restoration	1	12%
of Restoration	Fortify Restoration	2	15%
of Major Restoration	Fortify Restoration	3	17%
of Eminent Restoration	Fortify Restoration	4	20%
of Extreme Restoration	Fortify Restoration	5	22%
of Peerless Restoration	Fortify Restoration	6	25%
of Minor Smithing	Fortify Smithing	1	12%
of Smithing	Fortify Smithing	2	15%
of Major Smithing	Fortify Smithing	3	17%
of Eminent Smithing	Fortify Smithing	4	20%
of Extreme Smithing	Fortify Smithing	5	22%
of Peerless Smithing	Fortify Smithing	6	25%
of Minor Sneaking	Fortify Sneak	1	15%
of Sneaking	Fortify Sneak	2	20%
of Major Sneaking	Fortify Sneak	3	25%
of Eminent Sneaking	Fortify Sneak	4	30%
of ExtremeSneaking	Fortify Sneak	5	35%
of Peerless Sneaking	Fortify Sneak	6	40%
of Minor Haggling	Fortify Speech	1	12%
of Haggling	Fortify Speech	2	15%
of Major Haggling	Fortify Speech	3	17%
of Eminent Haggling	Fortify Speech	4	20%
of Extreme Haggling	Fortify Speech	5	22%
of Peerless Haggling	Fortify Speech	6	25%
of Minor Stamina	Fortify Stamina	1	+20
of Stamina	Fortify Stamina	2	+30
of Major Stamina	Fortify Stamina	3	+40
of Eminent Stamina	Fortify Stamina	4	+50
of Extreme Stamina	Fortify Stamina	5	+60
of Peerless Stamina	Fortify Stamina	6	+70

✔	MODIFIER	BASE ENCHANTMENT	ENCH LEVEL	MAGNITUDE
	of Recuperation	Fortify Stamina Rate	3	20%
	of Rejuvenation	Fortify Stamina Rate	4	30%
	of Invigoration	Fortify Stamina Rate	5	40%
	of Renewal	Fortify Stamina Rate	6	50%
	of Minor Sure Grip	Fortify Two-Handed	1	15%
	of Sure Grip	Fortify Two-Handed	2	20%
	of Major Sure Grip	Fortify Two-Handed	3	25%
	of Eminent Sure Grip	Fortify Two-Handed	4	30%
	of Extreme Striking	Fortify Two-Handed	5	35%
	of Peerless Sure Grip	Fortify Two-Handed	6	40%
	of Muffling	Muffle	3 & 4	–
	of Disease Resistance	Resist Disease	[Neck Only]	50%
	of Disease Immunity	Resist Disease	[Neck Only]	100%
	of Resist Fire	Resist Fire	1	15%
	of Waning Fire	Resist Fire	2	30%
	of Dwindling Fire / Flames	Resist Fire	3	40%
	of Fire / Flame Suppression	Resist Fire	4	50%
	of Fire Abatement	Resist Fire	5	60%
	of the Firewalker	Resist Fire	6	70%
	of Resist Frost	Resist Frost	1	15%
	of Waning Frost	Resist Frost	2	30%
	of Dwindling Frost	Resist Frost	3	40%
	of Frost Suppression	Resist Frost	4	50%
	of Frost Abatement	Resist Frost	5	60%
	of Warmth	Resist Frost	6	70%
	of Resist Magic	Resist Magic	1	10%
	of Waning Magic	Resist Magic	2	12%
	of Dwindling Magic	Resist Magic	3	15%
	of Magic Suppression	Resist Magic	4	17%
	of Magic Abatement	Resist Magic	5	20%
	of Nullification	Resist Magic	6	22%
	of Poison Resistance	Resist Poison	[Neck Only]	50%
	of Poison Immunity	Resist Poison	[Neck Only]	100%
	of Resist Shock	Resist Shock	1	15%
	of Waning Shock	Resist Shock	2	30%
	of Dwindling Shock	Resist Shock	3	40%
	of Shock Suppression	Resist Shock	4	50%

✔	MODIFIER	BASE ENCHANTMENT	ENCH LEVEL	MAGNITUDE
	of Shock Abatement	Resist Shock	5	60%
	of Grounding	Resist Shock	6	70%
	of Waterbreathing	Waterbreathing	3 & 4	–

WARLOCK ROBE ENCHANTMENTS

All Warlock Robes have an additional [Fortify Magicka Rate 50%] enchantment that can't be learned by disenchanting the robe. The only robes you can learn that enchantment from are the [Fortify Magicka Rate] ones below, which have their stated rate instead of this default.

✔	MODIFIER	BASE ENCHANTMENT		MAGNITUDE
	of Minor Alteration	Fortify Alteration		12%
	of Alteration	Fortify Alteration		15%
	of Major Alteration	Fortify Alteration		17%
	of Eminent Alteration	Fortify Alteration		20%
	of Extreme Alteration	Fortify Alteration		22%
	of Peerless Alteration	Fortify Alteration		25%
	of Minor Conjuration	Fortify Conjuration		12%
	of Conjuration	Fortify Conjuration		15%
	of Major Conjuration	Fortify Conjuration		17%
	of Eminent Conjuration	Fortify Conjuration		20%
	of Extreme Conjuration	Fortify Conjuration		22%
	of Peerless Conjuration	Fortify Conjuration		25%
	of Minor Destruction	Fortify Destruction		12%
	of Destruction	Fortify Destruction		15%
	of Major Destruction	Fortify Destruction		17%
	of Eminent Destruction	Fortify Destruction		20%
	of Extreme Destruction	Fortify Destruction		22%
	of Peerless Destruction	Fortify Destruction		25%
	of Minor Illusion	Fortify Illusion		12%
	of Illusion	Fortify Illusion		15%
	of Major Illusion	Fortify Illusion		17%
	of Eminent Illusion	Fortify Illusion		20%
	of Extreme Illusion	Fortify Illusion		22%
	of Peerless Illusion	Fortify Illusion		25%
	of Minor Restoration	Fortify Restoration		12%
	of Restoration	Fortify Restoration		15%
	of Major Restoration	Fortify Restoration		17%
	of Eminent Restoration	Fortify Restoration		20%
	of Extreme Restoration	Fortify Restoration		22%
	of Peerless Restoration	Fortify Restoration		25%

✔	MODIFIER	BASE ENCHANTMENT	ENCH LEVEL	MAGNITUDE
	of Quickening	Fortify Magicka Rate		75%
	of Recharging	Fortify Magicka Rate		100%
	of Replenishing	Fortify Magicka Rate		125%
	of Resurgence	Fortify Magicka Rate		150%

COLLEGE OF WINTERHOLD ROBE ENCHANTMENTS

✔	MODIFIER	BASE ENCHANTMENT	ENCH LEVEL	MAGNITUDE
	[Novice Robes] of Alteration	Fortify Alteration		12%
	[Apprentice Robes] of Alteration	Fortify Alteration		15%
	[Adept Robes] of Alteration	Fortify Alteration		17%
	[Expert Robes] of Alteration	Fortify Alteration		20%
	[Master Robes] of Alteration	Fortify Alteration		22%
	[Novice Robes] of Conjuration	Fortify Conjuration		12%
	[Apprentice Robes] of Conjuration	Fortify Conjuration		15%
	[Adept Robes] of Conjuration	Fortify Conjuration		17%
	[Expert Robes] of Conjuration	Fortify Conjuration		20%
	[Master Robes] of Conjuration	Fortify Conjuration		22%
	[Novice Robes] of Destruction	Fortify Destruction		12%
	[Apprentice Robes] of Destruction	Fortify Destruction		15%
	[Adept Robes] of Destruction	Fortify Destruction		17%
	[Expert Robes] of Destruction	Fortify Destruction		20%
	[Master Robes] of Destruction	Fortify Destruction		22%
	[Novice Robes] of Illusion	Fortify Illusion		12%
	[Apprentice Robes] of Illusion	Fortify Illusion		15%
	[Adept Robes] of Illusion	Fortify Illusion		17%
	[Expert Robes] of Illusion	Fortify Illusion		20%
	[Master Robes] of Illusion	Fortify Illusion		22%
	[Novice Robes] of Restoration	Fortify Restoration		12%
	[Apprentice Robes] of Restoration	Fortify Restoration		15%
	[Adept Robes] of Restoration	Fortify Restoration		17%
	[Expert Robes] of Restoration	Fortify Restoration		20%
	[Master Robes] of Restoration	Fortify Restoration		22%

 NOTE For Smithing Recipes, consult the Training Section on Smithing, beginning on page 47.

The Elder Scrolls V
SKYRIM

OTHER ITEMS

▷ Table X: Daedric Artifacts

A list all of the Daedric Artifacts and their abilities. Daedric Artifacts can only be obtained by completing the relevant Daedric Quest. See the Daedric Quests chapter or the Atlas for more details.

☑	NAME	ITEM TYPE	DAMAGE	WEIGHT	VALUE	ENCHANTMENT	NOTES
						DAEDRIC ARTIFACTS - WEAPONS	
	Dawnbreaker	Sword	12	10	740	+10 Fire Damage; Casts Bane of the Undead on killing an undead	
	Ebony Blade	Sword	13	10	2000	Absorb Health 10-30.	
	Mace of Molag Bal	Mace	16	18	1257	25 Magicka Damage, 25 Stamina Damage, Soul Trap	Begins at 10, increases to 30 as you kill 10 friends.
	Mehrunes' Razor	Dagger	11	3	860	1% Instant Kill	
	Sanguine Rose	Staff	0	10	2087	Summons a Dremora for 60s.	
	Skull of Corruption	Staff	0	10	1680	20 Damage, or 50 if powered with dreams from sleeping people	A Dremora Lord.
	Volendrung	Warhammer	25	26	1843	Absorb Stamina 50	
	Wabbajack	Staff	0	10	1565	Change target creature into another random creature	
						DAEDRIC ARTIFACTS - ARMOR	
	Ebony Mail	Armor	45	28	5000	Muffle while sneaking, Poison Cloak when in combat	
	Ring of Hircine	Ring	0	0.3	400	+1 Werewolf Transform / Day	Must already be a werewolf to use this.
	Ring of Namira	Ring	0	0.3	870	+50 Stamina. Feeding from NPC corpses raises Health by 50 and Health Regen by 50% for 4 hours	
	Savior's Hide	Armor	26	6	2679	Resist Magic 15%, Resist Poison 50%	
	Spellbreaker	Shield	38	12	277	Automatic Strength-50 spell ward while blocking	
						DAEDRIC ARTIFACTS - OTHER ITEMS	
	Azura's Star	Soul Gem		0	1000	Reusable Grand Soul Gem	
	Oghma Infinium	Book		1	2500	Once only, +5 Skill Increases to your choice of Combat, Magic, or Stealth skills.	Black Soul Gems store human souls.
	Skeleton Key	Lockpick		0.5	0	Unbreakable Lockpick	
	The Black Star	Soul Gem		0	1000	Reusable Black Soul Gem	

▷ Table XI: Books

A list of all the books in the game, including Skill Books, Functional Books, and Common Books. Sample locations of every Common and Functional book are listed here; sample locations for Skill Books are listed in the Appendices, as well as across the Atlas.

☑	NAME	WEIGHT	VALUE	ASSOCIATED SKILL
	SKILL BOOKS			
	The Armorer's Challenge	1	70	Smithing
	Last Scabbard of Akrash	1	70	Smithing
	Light Armor Forging	1	70	Smithing
	Cherim's Heart	1	70	Smithing
	Heavy Armor Forging	1	70	Smithing
	Death Blow of Abernanit	1	50	Block

☑	NAME	WEIGHT	VALUE	ASSOCIATED SKILL
	The Mirror	1	50	Block
	A Dance in Fire, v2	1	50	Block
	Warrior	1	50	Block
	Battle of Red Mountain	1	50	Block
	Hallgerd's Tale	1	70	Heavy Armor
	2920, MidYear, v6	1	70	Heavy Armor
	Chimarvamidium	1	70	Heavy Armor

☑	NAME	WEIGHT	VALUE	ASSOCIATED SKILL
	Orsinium and the Orcs	1	70	Heavy Armor
	The Knights of the Nine	1	70	Heavy Armor
	The Rear Guard	1	50	Light Armor
	Ice and Chitin	1	50	Light Armor
	Jornibret's Last Dance	1	50	Light Armor
	The Refugees	1	50	Light Armor
	Rislav The Righteous	1	50	Light Armor

✓	NAME	WEIGHT	VALUE	ASSOCIATED SKILL
	The Importance of Where	1	50	One-Handed
	2920, Morning Star, v1	1	50	One-Handed
	Fire and Darkness	1	50	One-Handed
	Night Falls on Sentinel	1	50	One-Handed
	Mace Etiquette	1	50	One-Handed
	Words and Philosophy	1	50	Two-Handed
	The Legendary Sancre Tor	1	50	Two-Handed
	King	1	50	Two-Handed
	Song Of Hrormir	1	50	Two-Handed
	Battle of Sancre Tor	1	50	Two-Handed
	Enchanter's Primer	1	50	Enchanting
	A Tragedy in Black	1	50	Enchanting
	Twin Secrets	1	50	Enchanting
	Catalogue of Weapon Enchantments	1	50	Enchanting
	Catalogue of Armor Enchantments	1	50	Enchanting
	Daughter of the Niben	1	60	Alteration
	Breathing Water	1	60	Alteration
	Sithis	1	60	Alteration
	Reality & Other Falsehoods	1	60	Alteration
	The Lunar Lorkhan	1	60	Alteration
	The Doors of Oblivion	1	50	Conjuration
	Liminal Bridges	1	50	Conjuration
	2920, Hearth Fire, v9	1	50	Conjuration
	2920, Frostfall, v10	1	50	Conjuration

✓	NAME	WEIGHT	VALUE	ASSOCIATED SKILL
	The Warrior's Charge	1	50	Conjuration
	Horrors of Castle Xyr	1	55	Destruction
	Response to Bero's Speech	1	55	Destruction
	A Hypothetical Treachery	1	55	Destruction
	The Art of War Magic	1	55	Destruction
	Mystery of Talara, v3	1	55	Destruction
	Incident at Necrom	1	60	Illusion
	2920, Sun's Dawn, v2	1	60	Illusion
	The Black Arts On Trial	1	60	Illusion
	Before the Ages of Man	1	60	Illusion
	Mystery of Talara, Part 4	1	60	Illusion
	Withershins	1	55	Restoration
	Racial Phylogeny	1	55	Restoration
	The Exodus	1	55	Restoration
	2920, Rain's Hand, v4	1	55	Restoration
	Mystery of Talara, v 2	1	55	Restoration
	A Game at Dinner	1	55	Alchemy
	Mannimarco, King of Worms	1	55	Alchemy
	Song of the Alchemists	1	55	Alchemy
	De Rerum Dirennis	1	55	Alchemy
	Herbalist's Guide to Skyrim	1	55	Alchemy
	The Locked Room	1	75	Lockpicking
	The Wolf Queen, v1	1	75	Lockpicking
	Proper Lock Design	1	75	Lockpicking

✓	NAME	WEIGHT	VALUE	ASSOCIATED SKILL
	Advances in Lockpicking	1	75	Lockpicking
	Surfeit of Thieves	1	75	Lockpicking
	The Gold Ribbon of Merit	1	65	Archery
	The Marksmanship Lesson	1	65	Archery
	Vernaccus and Bourlor	1	65	Archery
	Father Of The Niben	1	65	Archery
	The Black Arrow, v2	1	65	Archery
	Purloined Shadows	1	60	Pickpocket
	Thief	1	60	Pickpocket
	Aevar Stone-Singer	1	60	Pickpocket
	Beggar	1	60	Pickpocket
	Wulfmare's Guide to Better Thieving	1	60	Pickpocket
	Three Thieves	1	75	Sneak
	2920, Last Seed, v8	1	75	Sneak
	Sacred Witness	1	75	Sneak
	Legend of Krately House	1	75	Sneak
	The Red Kitchen Reader	1	75	Sneak
	A Dance in Fire, v6	1	60	Speech
	A Dance in Fire, v7	1	60	Speech
	2920, Second Seed, v5	1	60	Speech
	The Buying Game	1	60	Speech
	Biography of the Wolf Queen	1	60	Speech

✓	NAME	WEIGHT	VALUE	SAMPLE LOCATION	APPROX NUMBER ACROSS SKYRIM
	FUNCTIONAL BOOKS				
	An Explorer's Guide to Skyrim	1	8	[1.00] Solitude (The Bards' College)	16
	Adds Map Markers to several Stones of Fate.				
	The Legend of Red Eagle	1	5	[1.00] Solitude (The Bards' College)	38
	Starts Dungeon Quest: The Legend of Red Eagle.				
	Lost Legends	1	11	[1.00] Solitude (The Bards' College)	24
	Starts Side Quest: Forbidden Legend.				
	Boethiah's Proving	1	25	[4.20] Sepitmus Signus's Outpost	4
	Starts Daedric Quest: Boethiah's Calling. Only appears after you reach Level 32.				
	COMMON BOOKS				
	16 Accords of Madness, v. VI	1	25	[3.06] Nightcaller Temple	1
	2920, Evening Star, v12	1	11	[1.00] Solitude (Angeline's Aromatics)	3
	2920, First Seed, v3	1	11	[7.00] Windhelm (Palace of the Kings)	3
	2920, Sun's Dusk, v11	1	11	[1.00] Solitude (Angeline's Aromatics)	3
	2920, Sun's Height, v7	1	3	[9.16] Treva's Watch	2
	A Children's Anuad	1	6	[1.00] Solitude (The Bards' College)	21
	A Dance in Fire, v1	1	3	[1.00] Solitude (The Bards' College)	16
	A Dance in Fire, v3	1	3	[1.00] Solitude (The Bards' College)	5
	A Dance in Fire, v4	1	4	[1.00] Solitude (The Bards' College)	14
	A Dance in Fire, v5	1	30	[9.00] Riften (Mistveil Keep)	1
	A Dream of Sovngarde	1	8	[1.00] Solitude (The Bards' College)	15
	A Gentleman's Guide to Whiterun	1	3	[1.00] Solitude (The Bards' College)	21
	A Kiss, Sweet Mother	1	6	[1.00] Solitude (The Bards' College)	20
	A Minor Maze	1	8	[1.00] Solitude (The Bards' College)	14

✓	NAME	WEIGHT	VALUE	SAMPLE LOCATION	APPROX NUMBER ACROSS SKYRIM
	Aedra and Daedra	1	5	[1.00] Solitude (The Bards' College)	29
	Ahzirr Traajijazeri	1	4	[7.00] Windhelm (Palace of the Kings)	2
	Alduin is Real	1	8	[1.00] Solitude (The Bards' College)	17
	Amongst the Draugr	1	14	[1.00] Solitude (The Winking Skeever)	1
	Ancestors and the Dunmer	1	8	[1.00] Solitude (Angeline's Aromatics)	24
	Antecedants of Dwemer Law	1	5	[1.00] Solitude (The Bards' College)	40
	Arcana Restored	1	25	[4.00] College of Winterhold (Arcanaeum)	2
	Argonian Account, Book 1	1	2	[1.00] Solitude (The Bards' College)	17
	Argonian Account, Book 2	1	12	[1.00] Solitude (Temple of the Divines)	3
	Argonian Account, Book 3	1	3	[1.00] Solitude (The Bards' College)	21
	Argonian Account, Book 4	1	12	[4.07] Driftshade Refuge	2
	Azura and the Box	1	10	[4.00] College of Winterhold (Hall of Attainment)	6
	Beggar Prince	1	5	[1.00] Solitude (The Bards' College)	45
	Biography of Barenziah, v1	1	3	[1.00] Solitude (The Bards' College)	44
	Biography of Barenziah, v2	1	3	[1.00] Solitude (The Bards' College)	40
	Biography of Barenziah, v3	1	3	[1.00] Solitude (The Bards' College)	49
	Brief History of the Empire, v1	1	2	[1.00] Solitude (The Bards' College)	56
	Brief History of the Empire, v2	1	2	[1.00] Solitude (The Bards' College)	57
	Brief History of the Empire, v3	1	2	[1.00] Solitude (The Bards' College)	48
	Brief History of the Empire, v4	1	2	[1.00] Solitude (The Bards' College)	46
	Brothers of Darkness	1	30	[1.28] Katariah (Dark Brotherhood Quest: Hail Sithis!)	1
	Cats of Skyrim	1	7	[4.00] College of Winterhold (Arcanaeum)	15
	Chance's Folly	1	6	[4.00] College of Winterhold (Arcanaeum)	34

✓	NAME	WEIGHT	VALUE	SAMPLE LOCATION	APPROX NUMBER ACROSS SKYRIM
☐	Charwich-Koniinge Letters, v1	1	13	[1.00] Solitude (The Bards' College)	3
☐	Charwich-Koniinge Letters, v3	1	13	[1.00] Solitude (Vittoria Vici's House)	1
☐	Charwich-Koniinge, v2	1	13	[4.07] Driftshade Refuge	1
☐	Chaurus Pie: A Recipe	1	11	[5.00] Markarth (Endon's House)	1
☐	Children of the Sky	1	25	[9.00] Riften (Ratway Warrens: Esbern's Hideout)	2
☐	Chimarvamidium	1	20	[4.20] Septimus Signus's Outpost	4
☐	Chronicles of Nchuleft	1	30	[5.00] Markarth (Dwemer Museum)	1
☐	Cleansing of the Fane	1	20	[Random Dungeon] (College of Winterhold Radiant Quest: Valuable Book Procurement)	1
☐	Darkest Darkness	1	5	[1.00] Solitude (The Bards' College)	47
☐	Death of a Wanderer	1	12	[1.00] Solitude (Castle Dour, Thalmor Headquarters)	1
☐	Dragon Language: Myth no More	1	14	[5.31] Sky Haven Temple	1
☐	Dunmer of Skyrim	1	7	[1.00] Solitude (The Bards' College)	16
☐	Dwarves, v1	1	10	[5.00] Markarth (Dwemer Museum Bookshelf)	6
☐	Dwarves, v2	1	10	[5.00] Markarth (Dwemer Museum Bookshelf)	5
☐	Dwarves, v3	1	10	[5.00] Markarth (Arnleif and Sons)	2
☐	Dwemer History and Culture	1	13	[1.00] Solitude (Castle Dour)	9
☐	Dwemer Inquiries Vol I	1	6	[5.00] Markarth (Dwemer Museum Bookshelf)	19
☐	Dwemer Inquiries Vol II	1	6	[1.00] Solitude (The Bards' College)	16
☐	Dwemer Inquiries Vol III	1	6	[5.00] Markarth (Dwemer Museum Bookshelf)	21
☐	Effects of the Elder Scrolls	1	25	[4.00] College of Winterhold (Arcanaeum)	3
☐	Fall from Glory	1	8	[4.00] College of Winterhold (Arcanaeum)	20
☐	Fall of the Snow Prince	1	11	[1.00] Solitude (Radiant Raiment)	2
☐	Feyfolken I	1	12	[1.00] Solitude (The Bards' College)	2
☐	Feyfolken II	1	12	[1.00] Solitude (The Bards' College)	3
☐	Feyfolken III	1	12	[4.00] Winterhold (Jarl's Longhouse)	2
☐	Final Lesson	1	14	[5.34] Old Hroldan Inn	1
☐	Five Songs of King Wulfharth	1	30	[7.00] Windhelm (Palace of the Kings)	1
☐	Flight from the Thalmor	1	13	[5.31] Sky Haven Temple	2
☐	Forge, Hammer and Anvil	1	14	[4.07] Driftshade Refuge	1
☐	Fragment: On Artaeum	1	20	[6.29] Fellglow Keep (College of Winterhold Quest: Hitting the Books)	1
☐	Frontier, Conquest	1	5	[1.00] Solitude (The Bards' College)	29
☐	Galerion The Mystic	1	6	[1.00] Solitude (The Bards' College)	34
☐	Ghosts in the Storm	1	13	[8.00] Falkreath (Jarl's Longhouse)	2
☐	Glories and Laments	1	25	[1.28] Katariah (Dark Brotherhood Quest: Hail Sithis!)	1
☐	Gods and Worship	1	5	[1.00] Solitude (The Bards' College)	31
☐	Great Harbingers	1	13	[6.00] Whiterun (Jorrvaskr)	1
☐	Hanging Gardens	1	30	[9.36] Largashbur	2
☐	Harvesting Frostbite Spider Venom	1	7	[1.00] Solitude (The Bards' College)	14
☐	Herbane's Bestiary: Automatons	1	14	[4.00] College of Winterhold (Arcanaeum)	2
☐	Herbane's Bestiary: Hagravens	1	6	[1.00] Solitude (The Bards' College)	18
☐	Herbane's Bestiary: Ice Wraiths	1	7	[1.00] Solitude (The Bards' College)	16
☐	Horker Attacks	1	4	[1.00] Solitude (The Bards' College)	19
☐	Immortal Blood	1	4	[1.00] Solitude (The Bards' College)	18
☐	Imperial Report on Saarthal	1	13	[4.00] College of Winterhold (Arcanaeum)	3
☐	Invocation of Azura	1	20	[1.00] Solitude (The Bards' College)	1
☐	Killing - Before You're Killed	1	3	[1.00] Solitude (The Bards' College)	20
☐	Kolb & the Dragon	1	2	[1.00] Solitude (The Bards' College)	18
☐	Last King of the Ayleids	1	25	[6.29] Fellglow Keep (College of Winterhold Quest: Hitting the Books)	1

✓	NAME	WEIGHT	VALUE	SAMPLE LOCATION	APPROX NUMBER ACROSS SKYRIM
☐	Life of Uriel Septim VII	1	5	[1.00] Solitude (The Bards' College)	47
☐	Lycanthropic Legends of Skyrim	1	20	[6.00] Whiterun (Jorrvaskr)	1
☐	Magic from the Sky	1	12	[9.02] Shroud Hearth Barrow	3
☐	Mixed Unit Tactics	1	5	[1.00] Solitude (The Bards' College)	48
☐	Mysterious Akavir	1	5	[4.00] College of Winterhold (Arcanaeum)	30
☐	Mystery of Talara, v 1	1	3	[1.00] Solitude (The Bards' College)	17
☐	Mystery of Talara, v5	1	11	[1.00] Solitude (The Bards' College)	2
☐	Myths of Sheogorath	1	2	[1.00] Solitude (The Bards' College)	31
☐	Nerevar Moon and Star	1	30	[5.00] Markarth (Dwemer Museum)	1
☐	N'Gasta! Kvata! Kvakis!	1	20	[1.00] Solitude (The Bards' College)	1
☐	Nightingales: Fact or Fiction?	1	3	[4.00] College of Winterhold (Arcanaeum)	10
☐	Nords Arise!	1	4	[1.00] Solitude (The Bards' College)	19
☐	Nords of Skyrim	1	6	[1.00] Solitude (The Bards' College)	16
☐	Ode To The Tundrastriders	1	8	[1.00] Solitude (The Bards' College)	13
☐	Of Crossed Daggers	1	5	[1.00] Solitude (The Bards' College)	17
☐	Of Fjori and Holgeir	1	6	[1.00] Solitude (The Bards' College)	16
☐	Olaf and the Dragon	1	2	[1.00] Solitude (The Bards' College)	19
☐	On Oblivion	1	10	[1.00] Solitude (The Bards' College)	4
☐	On Stepping Lightly	1	12	[1.00] Solitude (The Bards' College)	1
☐	On the Great Collapse	1	12	[5.00] Markarth (Dwemer Museum Bookshelf)	6
☐	Palla, volume 1	1	3	[1.00] Solitude (Castle Dour Dungeons)	6
☐	Palla, volume 2	1	10	[9.00] Riften (Elgrim's Elixirs)	1
☐	Pension of the Ancestor Moth	1	8	[1.00] Solitude (The Bards' College)	15
☐	Physicalities of Werewolves	1	14	[8.11] Half-Moon Mill	2
☐	Pirate King of the Abecean	1	6	[1.00] Solitude (The Bards' College)	19
☐	Remanada	1	20	[5.31] Sky Haven Temple	3
☐	Report: Disaster at Ionith	1	3	[1.00] Solitude (The Bards' College)	25
☐	Rising Threat, Vol. I	1	6	[1.00] Solitude (The Bards' College)	13
☐	Rising Threat, Vol. II	1	6	[1.00] Solitude (The Bards' College)	14
☐	Rising Threat, Vol. III	1	6	[1.00] Solitude (The Bards' College)	16
☐	Rising Threat, Vol. IV	1	6	[1.00] Solitude (The Bards' College)	14
☐	Ruins of Kemel-Ze	1	7	[6.00] Whiterun (Jorrvaskr)	22
☐	Scourge of the Gray Quarter	1	8	[1.00] Solitude (The Bards' College)	16
☐	Shadowmarks	1	30	[9.00] Riften (The Ratway Cistern)	4
☐	Shezarr and the Divines	1	11	[1.00] Solitude (The Winking Skeever)	3
☐	Short History of Morrowind	1	15	[1.00] Solitude (The Blue Palace)	4
☐	Song of the Askelde Men	1	5	[1.00] Solitude (The Bards' College)	16
☐	Songs of Skyrim	1	10	[7.05] Kynesgrove (Braidwood Inn)	1
☐	Songs of Skyrim: Revised	1	14	[6.21] Pelagia Farm	1
☐	Songs of the Return, Vol 19	1	6	[1.00] Solitude (The Bards' College)	18
☐	Songs of the Return, Vol 2	1	6	[1.00] Solitude (The Bards' College)	21
☐	Songs of the Return, vol 24	1	30	[6.00] Whiterun (Jorrvaskr)	1
☐	Songs of the Return, Vol 56	1	6	[1.00] Solitude (The Bards' College)	20
☐	Songs of the Return, Vol 7	1	6	[1.00] Solitude (The Bards' College)	17
☐	Souls, Black and White	1	20	[4.00] College of Winterhold (Hall of Attainment)	1
☐	Sovngarde: A Reexamination	1	12	[9.00] Riften (Riften Jail)	2
☐	Spirit of Nirn	1	6	[1.00] Solitude (The Bards' College)	33
☐	Spirit of the Daedra	1	25	[6.02] Rorikshead (Rorik's Manor)	1
☐	The "Madmen" of the Reach	1	7	[1.00] Solitude (The Bards' College)	18
☐	The Adabal-a	1	25	[1.28] Katariah (Dark Brotherhood Quest: Hail Sithis!)	2
☐	The Alduin/Akatosh Dichotomy	1	8	[1.00] Solitude (The Bards' College)	12

	NAME	WEIGHT	VALUE	SAMPLE LOCATION	APPROX NUMBER ACROSS SKYRIM
☐	The Amulet of Kings	1	6	[1.00] Solitude (The Bards' College)	22
☐	The Apprentice's Assistant	1	12	[8.00] Falkreath (Corpslight Farm)	2
☐	The Arcturian Heresy	1	6	[1.00] Solitude (The Bards' College)	22
☐	The Bear of Markarth	1	8	[1.00] Solitude (The Bards' College)	17
☐	The Black Arrow, v1	1	2	[1.00] Solitude (The Bards' College)	9
☐	The Book of Daedra	1	5	[1.00] Solitude (The Bards' College)	42
☐	The Book of the Dragonborn	1	12	[4.00] College of Winterhold (Arcanaeum)	4
☐	The Cabin in the Woods	1	8	[1.00] Solitude (The Bards' College)	13
☐	The Cake and The Diamond	1	5	[1.00] Solitude (The Bards' College)	47
☐	The City of Stone	1	4	[1.00] Solitude (The Bards' College)	24
☐	The Code of Malacath	1	2	[1.00] Solitude (The Bards' College)	23
☐	The Dowry	1	11	[9.00] Riften (Mistveil Keep)	1
☐	The Dragon Break	1	14	[9.00] Riften (Ratway Warrens: Esbern's Hideout)	2
☐	The Dragon War	1	12	[9.00] Riften (Ratway Warrens: Esbern's Hideout)	3
☐	The Falmer: A Study	1	11	[4.00] College of Winterhold (Arcanaeum)	3
☐	The Firmament	1	5	[1.00] Solitude (The Bards' College)	54
☐	The Firsthold Revolt	1	7	[1.00] Solitude (The Bards' College)	32
☐	The Great War	1	6	[1.00] Solitude (The Bards' College)	15
☐	The Holds of Skyrim	1	3	[1.00] Solitude (The Bards' College)	19
☐	The Hope of the Redoran	1	5	[1.00] Solitude (The Bards' College)	31
☐	The Legendary Scourge	1	30	[Random Dungeon] (College of Winterhold Radiant Quest: Valuable Book Procurement)	1
☐	The Lusty Argonian Maid, v1	1	14	[9.00] Riften (Haelga's Bunkhouse)	4
☐	The Lusty Argonian Maid, v2	1	14	[9.00] Riften (Haelga's Bunkhouse)	3
☐	The Madness of Pelagius	1	12	[6.00] Whiterun (Dragonsreach Jarl's Quarters)	1
☐	The Monomyth	1	8	[1.00] Solitude (The Bards' College)	13
☐	The Night Mother's Truth	1	25	[8.00] Falkreath (Jarl's Longhouse)	2
☐	The Oblivion Crisis	1	6	[1.00] Solitude (The Bards' College)	17
☐	The Old Ways	1	30	[4.19] Fort Kastav	1
☐	The Pig Children	1	20	[1.00] Solitude (The Bards' College)	1
☐	The Ransom of Zarek	1	2	[1.00] Solitude (The Bards' College)	14
☐	The Real Barenziah, v1	1	5	[1.00] Solitude (The Bards' College)	21
☐	The Real Barenziah, v2	1	5	[1.00] Solitude (The Bards' College)	41
☐	The Real Barenziah, v3	1	5	[1.00] Solitude (The Bards' College)	37
☐	The Real Barenziah, v4	1	5	[1.00] Solitude (The Bards' College)	37
☐	The Real Barenziah, v5	1	5	[6.00] Whiterun (Jorrvaskr)	25
☐	The Red Book of Riddles	1	30	[3.25] Nightgate Inn (Carried by Fultheim)	1
☐	The Rise and Fall of the Blades	1	11	[4.00] College of Winterhold (Arcanaeum)	5
☐	The Seed	1	10	[1.00] Solitude (The Bards' College)	3
☐	The Song of Pelinal, v1	1	5	[9.00] Riften (Temple of Mara)	15

	NAME	WEIGHT	VALUE	SAMPLE LOCATION	APPROX NUMBER ACROSS SKYRIM
☐	The Song of Pelinal, v2	1	5	[1.00] Solitude (The Bards' College)	18
☐	The Song of Pelinal, v3	1	5	[1.00] Solitude (The Bards' College)	15
☐	The Song of Pelinal, v4	1	5	[1.00] Solitude (The Bards' College)	14
☐	The Song of Pelinal, v5	1	5	[1.00] Solitude (The Bards' College)	18
☐	The Song of Pelinal, v6	1	5	[1.00] Solitude (The Bards' College)	12
☐	The Song of Pelinal, v7	1	5	[1.00] Solitude (The Bards' College)	11
☐	The Song of Pelinal, v8	1	5	[1.00] Solitude (The Bards' College)	12
☐	The Tale of Dro'Zira	1	11	[8.00] Falkreath (Dengeir's House)	2
☐	The Talos Mistake	1	7	[1.00] Solitude (The Blue Palace)	18
☐	The Third Door	1	11	[5.00] Markarth (Vlindrell Hall)	1
☐	The Third Era Timeline	1	8	[1.00] Solitude (The Bards' College)	16
☐	The True Nature of Orcs	1	20	[5.38] Dushnikh Yal	4
☐	The Waters of Oblivion	1	30	[Random Dungeon] (College of Winterhold Radiant Quest: Valuable Book Procurement)	1
☐	The Wild Elves	1	25	[1.00] Solitude (The Bards' College)	1
☐	The Windhelm Letters	1	7	[1.00] Solitude (The Bards' College)	15
☐	The Wispmother	1	8	[4.00] College of Winterhold (Arcanaeum)	15
☐	The Wolf Queen, v2	1	4	[1.00] Solitude (The Bards' College)	22
☐	The Wolf Queen, v3	1	4	[1.00] Solitude (The Bards' College)	27
☐	The Wolf Queen, v4	1	4	[1.00] Solitude (The Bards' College)	17
☐	The Wolf Queen, v5	1	4	[1.00] Solitude (The Bards' College)	21
☐	The Wolf Queen, v6	1	30	[6.00] Whiterun (Dragonsreach)	2
☐	The Wolf Queen, v7	1	4	[1.00] Solitude (The Bards' College)	19
☐	The Wolf Queen, v8	1	12	[1.00] Solitude (Proudspire Manor)	2
☐	The Woodcutter's Wife	1	8	[1.00] Solitude (The Bards' College)	14
☐	There Be Dragons	1	11	[6.27] Riverwood (Sleeping Giant Inn)	1
☐	Thief of Virtue	1	5	[1.00] Solitude (The Bards' College)	42
☐	Treatise on Ayleidic Cities	1	25	[3.00] Dawnstar (The White Hall)	1
☐	Trials of St. Alessia	1	5	[1.00] Solitude (The Bards' College)	13
☐	Troll Slaying	1	8	[1.00] Solitude (The Bards' College)	15
☐	Uncommon Taste	1	3	[1.00] Solitude (The Bards' College)	28
☐	Varieties of Daedra	1	11	[3.06] Nightcaller Temple (Daedric Quest: Waking Nightmare)	2
☐	Vernaccus and Bourlor	1	6	[1.00] Solitude (The Bards' College)	19
☐	Wabbajack	1	7	[1.00] Solitude (The Bards' College)	15
☐	Walking the World, Vol XI	1	8	[1.00] Solitude (The Bards' College)	15
☐	War of the First Council	1	25	[5.00] Markarth (Dwemer Museum)	1
☐	Watcher of Stones	1	8	[1.00] Solitude (The Bards' College)	16
☐	Words of Clan Mother Ahnissi	1	14	[4.00] Winterhold (The Frozen Hearth)	1
☐	Wraith's Wedding Dowry	1	10	[1.25] Brinewater Grotto	2
☐	Yellow Book of Riddles	1	3	[1.00] Solitude (The Bards' College)	31
☐	Yngol and the Sea-Ghosts	1	5	[1.00] Solitude (The Bards' College)	37

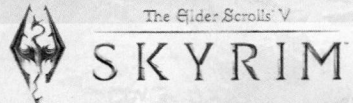

The Elder Scrolls V

SKYRIM

PRIMA OFFICIAL GAME GUIDE   WWW.PRIMAGAMES.COM

Table XII: Spell Tomes

A list of spell tomes. Cross-reference this list with the Spell Table (on page 70) to identify any restrictions.

✓	NAME	WEIGHT	VALUE	TEACHES SPELL
	SPELL TOMES			
☐	Spell Tome: Bane of the Undead	1	1200	Bane of the Undead
☐	Spell Tome: Banish Daedra	1	346	Banish Daedra
☐	Spell Tome: Blizzard	1	1350	Blizzard
☐	Spell Tome: Bound Battleaxe	1	99	Bound Battleaxe
☐	Spell Tome: Bound Bow	1	335	Bound Bow
☐	Spell Tome: Bound Sword	1	49	Bound Sword
☐	Spell Tome: Call To Arms	1	1150	Call to Arms
☐	Spell Tome: Calm	1	91	Calm
☐	Spell Tome: Candlelight	1	44	Candlelight
☐	Spell Tome: Chain Lightning	1	390	Chain Lightning
☐	Spell Tome: Circle Of Protection	1	650	Circle of Protection
☐	Spell Tome: Clairvoyance	1	50	Clairvoyance
☐	Spell Tome: Close Wounds	1	360	Close Wounds
☐	Spell Tome: Command Daedra	1	660	Command Daedra
☐	Spell Tome: Conjure Dremora Lord	1	730	Conjure Dremora Lord
☐	Spell Tome: Conjure Familiar	1	49	Conjure Familiar
☐	Spell Tome: Conjure Flame Atronach	1	99	Conjure Flame Atronach
☐	Spell Tome: Conjure Frost Atronach	1	347	Conjure Frost Atronach
☐	Spell Tome: Conjure Storm Atronach	1	690	Conjure Storm Atronach
☐	Spell Tome: Courage	1	46	Courage
☐	Spell Tome: Dead Thrall	1	1270	Dead Thrall
☐	Spell Tome: Detect Life	1	332	Detect Life
☐	Spell Tome: Detect Undead	1	600	Detect Dead
☐	Spell Tome: Dragonhide	1	1389	Dragonhide
☐	Spell Tome: Dread Zombie	1	630	Dread Zombie
☐	Spell Tome: Ebonyflesh	1	650	Ebonyflesh
☐	Spell Tome: Expel Daedra	1	620	Expel Daedra
☐	Spell Tome: Fast Healing	1	94	Fast Healing

✓	NAME	WEIGHT	VALUE	TEACHES SPELL
☐	Spell Tome: Fear	1	80	Fear
☐	Spell Tome: Fire Rune	1	90	Fire Rune
☐	Spell Tome: Fire Storm	1	1290	Fire Storm
☐	Spell Tome: Fireball	1	345	Fireball
☐	Spell Tome: Firebolt	1	96	Firebolt
☐	Spell Tome: Flame Cloak	1	325	Flame Cloak
☐	Spell Tome: Flame Thrall	1	1260	Flame Thrall
☐	Spell Tome: Flames	1	50	Flames
☐	Spell Tome: Frenzy	1	330	Frenzy
☐	Spell Tome: Frost Cloak	1	340	Frost Cloak
☐	Spell Tome: Frost Rune	1	92	Frost Rune
☐	Spell Tome: Frost Thrall	1	1300	Frost Thrall
☐	Spell Tome: Frostbite	1	47	Frostbite
☐	Spell Tome: Fury	1	43	Fury
☐	Spell Tome: Grand Healing	1	680	Grand Healing
☐	Spell Tome: Greater Ward	1	341	Greater Ward
☐	Spell Tome: Guardian Circle	1	1220	Guardian Circle
☐	Spell Tome: Harmony	1	1220	Harmony
☐	Spell Tome: Heal Other	1	300	Heal Other
☐	Spell Tome: Healing	1	50	Healing
☐	Spell Tome: Healing Hands	1	89	Healing Hands
☐	Spell Tome: Hysteria	1	1240	Hysteria
☐	Spell Tome: Ice Spike	1	96	Ice Spike
☐	Spell Tome: Ice Storm	1	360	Ice Storm
☐	Spell Tome: Icy Spear	1	725	Icy Spear
☐	Spell Tome: Incinerate	1	710	Incinerate
☐	Spell Tome: Invisibility	1	625	Invisibility
☐	Spell Tome: Ironflesh	1	341	Ironflesh
☐	Spell Tome: Lesser Ward	1	45	Lesser Ward
☐	Spell Tome: Lightning Bolt	1	95	Lightning Bolt
☐	Spell Tome: Lightning Cloak	1	355	Lightning Cloak
☐	Spell Tome: Lightning Rune	1	93	Lightning Rune
☐	Spell Tome: Lightning Storm	1	1400	Lightning Storm

✓	NAME	WEIGHT	VALUE	TEACHES SPELL
☐	Spell Tome: Magelight	1	87	Magelight
☐	Spell Tome: Mass Paralysis	1	1280	Mass Paralysis
☐	Spell Tome: Mayhem	1	1250	Mayhem
☐	Spell Tome: Muffle	1	88	Muffle
☐	Spell Tome: Oakflesh	1	44	Oakflesh
☐	Spell Tome: Pacify	1	610	Pacify
☐	Spell Tome: Paralyze	1	685	Paralyze
☐	Spell Tome: Raise Zombie	1	49	Raise Zombie
☐	Spell Tome: Rally	1	300	Rally
☐	Spell Tome: Reanimate Corpse	1	99	Reanimate Corpse
☐	Spell Tome: Repel Lesser Undead	1	333	Repel Lesser Undead
☐	Spell Tome: Repel Undead	1	655	Repel Undead
☐	Spell Tome: Revenant	1	340	Revenant
☐	Spell Tome: Rout	1	653	Rout
☐	Spell Tome: Soul Trap	1	100	Soul Trap
☐	Spell Tome: Sparks	1	46	Sparks
☐	Spell Tome: Steadfast Ward	1	92	Steadfast Ward
☐	Spell Tome: Stoneflesh	1	95	Stoneflesh
☐	Spell Tome: Storm Thrall	1	1350	Storm Thrall
☐	Spell Tome: Telekinesis	1	326	Telekinesis
☐	Spell Tome: Thunderbolt	1	750	Thunderbolt
☐	Spell Tome: Transmute Mineral Ore	1	900	Transmute
☐	Spell Tome: Turn Greater Undead	1	664	Turn Greater Undead
☐	Spell Tome: Turn Lesser Undead	1	89	Turn Lesser Undead
☐	Spell Tome: Turn Undead	1	323	Turn Undead
☐	Spell Tome: Wall of Flames	1	680	Wall of Flames
☐	Spell Tome: Wall of Frost	1	700	Wall of Frost
☐	Spell Tome: Wall of Storms	1	725	Wall of Storms
☐	Spell Tome: Waterbreathing	1	340	Waterbreathing

Table XIII: Potions

A list of all the standard potions and poisons in the realm, including usable potions acquired as part of a quest (like Vaermina's Torpor). Non-usable potions (for example, potions you are asked to deliver to someone) are listed on a table in the Other Items section.

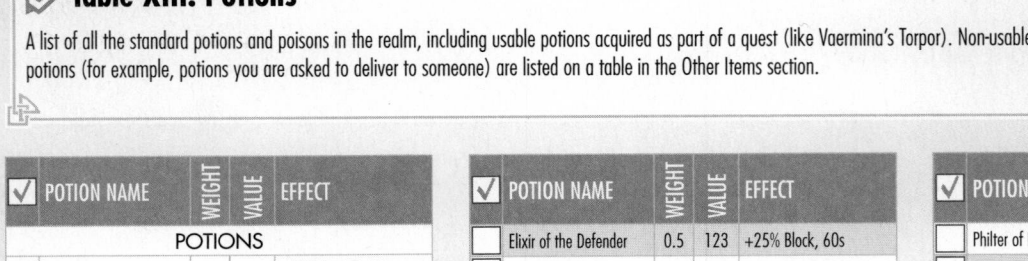

✓	POTION NAME	WEIGHT	VALUE	EFFECT
	POTIONS			
	Ice Wraith Essence	0.5	96	+20% Frost Resistance, 60s
	Potion of Cure Disease	0.5	79	Cures all active diseases.
	Cure Poison	0.5	31	Cures all active poisons.
	Potion of Strength	0.5	170	+20 Carry Weight, 5m
	Draught of Strength	0.5	266	+30 Carry Weight, 5m
	Solution of Strength	0.5	365	+40 Carry Weight, 5m
	Philter of Strength	0.5	467	+50 Carry Weight, 5m
	Elixir of Strength	0.5	571	+60 Carry Weight, 5m
	Potion of Regeneration	0.5	311	+50% Health Regen, 5m
	Draught of Regeneration	0.5	380	+60% Health Regen, 5m
	Solution of Regeneration	0.5	451	+70% Health Regen, 5m
	Philter of Regeneration	0.5	522	+80% Health Regen, 5m
	Elixir of Regeneration	0.5	668	+100% Health Regen, 5m
	Potion of Health	0.5	67	+20 Max Health, 60s
	Draught of Health	0.5	145	+40 Max Health, 60s
	Solution of Health	0.5	226	+60 Max Health, 60s
	Philter of Health	0.5	311	+80 Max Health, 60s
	Elixir of Health	0.5	398	+100 Max Health, 60s
	Potion of Extra Magicka	0.5	58	+20 Max Magicka, 60s
	Draught of Extra Magicka	0.5	124	+40 Max Magicka, 60s
	Solution of Extra Magicka	0.5	194	+60 Max Magicka, 60s
	Philter of Extra Magicka	0.5	266	+80 Max Magicka, 60s
	Elixir of Extra Magicka	0.5	341	+100 Max Magicka, 60s
	Potion of Lasting Potency	0.5	311	+50% Magicka Regen, 5m
	Draught of Lasting Potency	0.5	380	+60% Magicka Regen, 5m
	Solution of Lasting Potency	0.5	451	+70% Magicka Regen, 5m
	Philter of Lasting Potency	0.5	522	+80% Magicka Regen, 5m
	Elixir of Lasting Potency	0.5	668	+100% Magicka Regen, 5m
	Potion of Alteration	0.5	49	+25% Alteration, 60s
	Draught of Alteration	0.5	106	+50% Alteration, 60s
	Philter of Alteration	0.5	165	+75% Alteration, 60s
	Elixir of Alteration	0.5	227	+100% Alteration, 60s
	Potion of Haggling	0.5	84	+10% Better Prices, 30s
	Draught of Haggling	0.5	131	+15% Better Prices, 30s
	Philter of Haggling	0.5	180	+25% Better Prices, 30s
	Elixir of Haggling	0.5	230	+30% Better Prices, 30s
	Potion of the Defender	0.5	45	+10% Block, 60s
	Draught of the Defender	0.5	70	+15% Block, 60s
	Philter of the Defender	0.5	96	+20% Block, 60s

✓	POTION NAME	WEIGHT	VALUE	EFFECT
	Elixir of the Defender	0.5	123	+25% Block, 60s
	Conjurer's Potion	0.5	61	+25% Conjuration, 60s
	Conjurer's Draught	0.5	132	+50% Conjuration, 60s
	Conjurer's Philter	0.5	207	+75% Conjuration, 60s
	Conjurer's Elixir	0.5	284	+100% Conjuration, 60s
	Potion of Destruction	0.5	96	+20% Destruction, 60s
	Draught of Destruction	0.5	151	+30% Destruction, 60s
	Philter of Destruction	0.5	207	+40% Destruction, 60s
	Elixir of Destruction	0.5	265	+50% Destruction, 60s
	Enchanter's Potion	0.5	54	+10% Enchanting, 60s
	Enchanter's Draught	0.5	84	+15% Enchanting, 60s
	Enchanter's Philter	0.5	116	+20% Enchanting, 60s
	Enchanter's Elixir	0.5	148	+25% Enchanting, 60s
	Potion of the Knight	0.5	45	+10 Heavy Armor, 60s
	Draught of the Knight	0.5	70	+15 Heavy Armor, 60s
	Philter of the Knight	0.5	96	+20 Heavy Armor, 60s
	Elixir of the Knight	0.5	123	+25 Heavy Armor, 60s
	Potion of Illusion	0.5	99	+25% Illusion, 60s
	Draught of Illusion	0.5	212	+50% Illusion, 60s
	Philter of Illusion	0.5	331	+75% Illusion, 60s
	Elixir of Illusion	0.5	455	+100% Illusion, 60s
	Skirmisher's Potion	0.5	45	+10 Light Armor, 60s
	Skirmisher's Draught	0.5	70	+15 Light Armor, 60s
	Skirmisher's Philter	0.5	96	+20 Light Armor, 60s
	Skirmisher's Elixir	0.5	123	+25 Light Armor, 60s
	Potion of Lockpicking	0.5	45	+20% Lockpicking, 30s
	Draught of Lockpicking	0.5	70	+30% Lockpicking, 30s
	Philter of Lockpicking	0.5	96	+40% Lockpicking, 30s
	Elixir of Lockpicking	0.5	123	+50% Lockpicking, 30s
	Potion of True Shot	0.5	96	+20% Bow Damage, 60s
	Draught of True Shot	0.5	151	+30% Bow Damage, 60s
	Philter of True Shot	0.5	207	+40% Bow Damage, 60s
	Elixir of True Shot	0.5	265	+50% Bow Damage, 60s
	Potion of the Warrior	0.5	96	+20% One-Handed Damage, 60s
	Draught of the Warrior	0.5	151	+30% One-Handed Damage, 60s
	Philter of the Warrior	0.5	207	+40% One-Handed Damage, 60s
	Elixir of the Warrior	0.5	265	+50% One-Handed Damage, 60s
	Potion of Glibness	0.5	96	+20 Speech, 60s
	Draught of Glibness	0.5	151	+30 Speech, 60s
	Philter of Glibness	0.5	207	+40 Speech, 60s
	Elixir of Glibness	0.5	265	+50 Speech, 60s
	Potion of Pickpocketing	0.5	96	+20% Pickpocket, 60s
	Draught of Pickpocketing	0.5	151	+30% Pickpocket, 60s

✓	POTION NAME	WEIGHT	VALUE	EFFECT
	Philter of Pickpocketing	0.5	207	+40% Pickpocket, 60s
	Elixir of Pickpocketing	0.5	265	+50% Pickpocket, 60s
	Potion of the Healer	0.5	96	+20% Restoration, 60s
	Draught of the Healer	0.5	151	+30% Restoration, 60s
	Philter of the Healer	0.5	207	+40% Restoration, 60s
	Elixir of the Healer	0.5	265	+50% Restoration, 60s
	Blacksmith's Potion	0.5	67	+20% Smithing, 30s
	Blacksmith's Draught	0.5	105	+30% Smithing, 30s
	Blacksmith's Philter	0.5	145	+40% Smithing, 30s
	Blacksmith's Elixir	0.5	185	+50% Smithing, 30s
	Potion of Light Feet	0.5	45	+10% Sneak, 60s
	Draught of Light Feet	0.5	70	+15% Sneak, 60s
	Philter of Light Feet	0.5	96	+20% Sneak, 60s
	Elixir of Light Feet	0.5	123	+25% Sneak, 60s
	Potion of the Berserker	0.5	96	+20% Two-Handed Damage, 60s
	Draught of the Berserker	0.5	151	+30% Two-Handed Damage, 60s
	Philter of the Berserker	0.5	207	+40% Two-Handed Damage, 60s
	Elixir of the Berserker	0.5	265	+50% Two-Handed Damage, 60s
	Potion of Enhanced Stamina	0.5	341	+20 Max Stamina, 5m
	Draught of Enhanced Stamina	0.5	731	+40 Max Stamina, 5m
	Solution of Enhanced Stamina	0.5	1142	+60 Max Stamina, 5m
	Philter of Enhanced Stamina	0.5	1568	+80 Max Stamina, 5m
	Elixir of Enhanced Stamina	0.5	341	+100 Max Stamina, 5m
	Potion of Vigor	0.5	311	+50% Stamina Regen, 5m
	Draught of Vigor	0.5	380	+60% Stamina Regen, 5m
	Solution of Vigor	0.5	451	+70% Stamina Regen, 5m
	Philter of Vigor	0.5	522	+80% Stamina Regen, 5m
	Elixir of Vigor	0.5	668	+100% Stamina Regen, 5m
	Potion of Brief Invisibility	0.5	214	Invisibility 20s
	Potion of Extended Invisibility	0.5	334	Invisibility 30s
	Potion of Enduring Invisibility	0.5	459	Invisibility 40s
	Potion of Prolonged Invisibility	0.5	587	Invisibility 50s
	Elixir of Fire Resistance	0.5	265	+50% Fire Resistance
	Potion of Fire Resistance	0.5	96	+20% Fire Resistance
	Draught of Fire Resistance	0.5	151	+30% Fire Resistance

POTION NAME	WEIGHT	VALUE	EFFECT
Philter of Fire Resistance	0.5	207	+40% Fire Resistance
Elixir of Resistance Cold	0.5	265	+50% Frost Resistance
Potion of Resistance Cold	0.5	96	+20% Frost Resistance
Draught of Resistance Cold	0.5	151	+30% Frost Resistance
Philter of Resistance Cold	0.5	207	+40% Frost Resistance
Elixir of Magic Resistance	0.5	247	+25% Magic Resistance
Potion of Magic Resistance	0.5	90	+10% Magic Resistance
Draught of Magic Resistance	0.5	141	+15% Magic Resistance
Philter of Magic Resistance	0.5	193	+20% Magic Resistance
Elixir of Shock Resistance	0.5	265	+50% Shock Resistance
Potion of Shock Resistance	0.5	96	+20% Shock Resistance
Draught of Shock Resistance	0.5	151	+30% Shock Resistance
Philter of Shock Resistance	0.5	207	+40% Shock Resistance
Potion of Minor Healing	0.5	17	Restore Health 25
Potion of Healing	0.5	36	Restore Health 50
Potion of Plentiful Healing	0.5	57	Restore Health 75
Potion of Vigorous Healing	0.5	79	Restore Health 100
Potion of Extreme Healing	0.5	123	Restore Health 150
Potion of Ultimate Healing	0.5	251	Restore Health Full
Potion of Minor Magicka	0.5	20	Restore Magicka 25
Potion of Magicka	0.5	44	Restore Magicka 50
Potion of Plentiful Magicka	0.5	69	Restore Magicka 75
Potion of Vigorous Magicka	0.5	95	Restore Magicka 100
Potion of Extreme Magicka	0.5	148	Restore Magicka 150
Potion of Ultimate Magicka	0.5	150	Restore Magicka Full
Potion of Minor Stamina	0.5	20	Restore Stamina 25
Potion of Stamina	0.5	44	Restore Stamina 50
Potion of Plentiful Stamina	0.5	69	Restore Stamina 75
Potion of Vigorous Stamina	0.5	95	Restore Stamina 100
Potion of Extreme Stamina	0.5	148	Restore Stamina 150
Potion of Ultimate Stamina	0.5	150	Restore Stamina Full

POISONS

POTION NAME	WEIGHT	VALUE	EFFECT
Weak Poison	0.5	58	Damage Health 15
Poison	0.5	103	Damage Health 25
Potent Poison	0.5	149	Damage Health 35
Virulent Poison	0.5	221	Damage Health 50
Deadly Poison	0.5	296	Damage Health 65
Weak Lingering Poison	0.5	12	Damage Health 1/s, 10s
Lingering Poison	0.5	18	Damage Health 1/s, 15s
Potent Lingering Poison	0.5	40	Damage Health 2/s, 15s
Malign Lingering Poison	0.5	55	Damage Health 2/s, 20s
Deadly Lingering Poison	0.5	86	Damage Health 3/s, 20s

POTION NAME	WEIGHT	VALUE	EFFECT
Weak Magicka Poison	0.5	92	Damage Magicka 30
Magicka Poison	0.5	162	Damage Magicka 50
Potent Magicka Poison	0.5	235	Damage Magicka 70
Malign Magicka Poison	0.5	348	Damage Magicka 100
Deadly Magicka Poison	0.5	465	Damage Magicka 130
Lingering Magicka Poison	0.5	10	Damage Magicka 1/s, 10s
Enduring Magicka Poison	0.5	15	Damage Magicka 1/s, 15s
Lasting Magicka Poison	0.5	33	Damage Magicka 2/s, 15s
Persisting Magicka Poison	0.5	45	Damage Magicka 2/s, 20s
Unceasing Magicka Poison	0.5	71	Damage Magicka 3/s, 20s
Weak Recovery Poison	0.5	79	-100% Magicka Regen, 10s
Magicka Recovery Poison	0.5	169	-100% Magicka Regen, 20s
Potent Recovery Poison	0.5	265	-100% Magicka Regen, 30s
Malign Recovery Poison	0.5	414	-100% Magicka Regen, 45s
Deadly Recovery Poison	0.5	568	-100% Magicka Regen, 60s
Weak Stamina Poison	0.5	75	Damaga Stamina 30
Stamina Poison	0.5	133	Damage Stamina 50
Potent Stamina Poison	0.5	192	Damage Stamina 70
Virulent Stamina Poison	0.5	285	Damage Stamina 100
Deadly Stamina Poison	0.5	380	Damage Stamina 130
Lingering Stamina Poison	0.5	6	Damage Stamina 1/s, 30s
Enduring Stamina Poison	0.5	12	Damage Stamina 2/s, 30s
Lasting Stamina Poison	0.5	20	Damage Stamina 3/s, 30s
Persisting Stamina Poison	0.5	27	Damage Stamina 4/s, 30s
Unceasing Stamina Poison	0.5	35	Damage Stamina 5/s, 30s
Weak Vigor Poison	0.5	74	-100% Stamina Regen, 15s
Vigor Poison	0.5	159	-100% Stamina Regen, 30s
Potent Vigor Poison	0.5	248	-100% Stamina Regen, 45s
Malign Vigor Poison	0.5	341	-100% Stamina Regen, 60s
Weak Fear Poison	0.5	98	Fear (up to Lv5), 30s
Fear Poison	0.5	164	Fear (up to Lv8), 30s
Potent Fear Poison	0.5	281	Fear (up to Lv13), 30s
Virulent Fear Poison	0.5	402	Fear (up to Lv18), 30s
Deadly Fear Poison	0.5	526	Fear (up to Lv23), 30s
Weak Frenzy Poison	0.5	88	Frenzy (up to Lv5), 10s
Frenzy Poison	0.5	147	Frenzy (up to Lv8), 10s
Potent Frenzy Poison	0.5	252	Frenzy (up to Lv13), 10s
Virulent Frenzy Poison	0.5	360	Frenzy (up to Lv18), 10s
Deadly Frenzy Poison	0.5	472	Frenzy (up to Lv23), 10s
Weak Paralysis Poison	0.5	132	Paralysis, 3s
Paralysis Poison	0.5	233	Paralysis, 5s
Potent Paralysis Poison	0.5	337	Paralysis, 7s
Virulent Paralysis Poison	0.5	500	Paralysis, 10s
Deadly Paralysis Poison	0.5	781	Paralysis, 15s

POTION NAME	WEIGHT	VALUE	EFFECT
Weak Aversion to Fire	0.5	116	-40% Fire Resistance, 30s
Aversion to Fire	0.5	164	-55% Fire Resistance, 30s
Potent Aversion to Fire	0.5	215	-70% Fire Resistance, 30s
Malign Aversion to Fire	0.5	266	-85% Fire Resistance, 30s
Deadly Aversion to Fire	0.5	318	-100% Fire Resistance, 30s
Weak Aversion to Frost	0.5	96	-40% Frost Resistance, 30s
Aversion to Frost	0.5	137	-55% Frost Resistance, 30s
Potent Aversion to Frost	0.5	179	-70% Frost Resistance, 30s
Malign Aversion to Frost	0.5	221	-85% Frost Resistance, 30s
Deadly Aversion to Frost	0.5	265	-100% Frost Resistance, 30s
Weak Aversion to Magic	0.5	193	-40% Magic Resistance, 30s
Aversion to Magic	0.5	274	-55% Magic Resistance, 30s
Potent Aversion to Magic	0.5	358	-70% Magic Resistance, 30s
Malign Aversion to Magic	0.5	443	-85% Magic Resistance, 30s
Deadly Aversion to Magic	0.5	530	-100% Magic Resistance, 30s
Weak Aversion to Shock	0.5	135	-40% Shock Resistance, 30s
Aversion to Shock	0.5	192	-55% Shock Resistance, 30s
Potent Aversion to Shock	0.5	250	-70% Shock Resistance, 30s
Malign Aversion to Shock	0.5	310	-85% Shock Resistance, 30s
Deadly Aversion to Shock	0.5	371	-100% Shock Resistance, 30s
Frostbite Venom	0.5	21	Damage Health 5/s, Damage Magicka 5/s, 4s

THIEVES' GUILD COMPOUND POTIONS

POTION NAME	WEIGHT	VALUE	EFFECT
Potion of Conflict	0.5	115	+10 Light Armor, +15% One-Handed Damage, 60s
Draught of Conflict	0.5	166	+15 Light Armor, +20% One-Handed Damage, 60s
Philter of Conflict	0.5	219	+20 Light Armor, +25% One-Handed Damage, 60s
Elixir of Conflict	0.5	330	+30 Light Armor, +35% One-Handed Damage, 60s
Grand Elixir of Conflict	0.5	443	+40 Light Armor, +45% One-Handed Damage, 60s
Prime Elixir of Conflict	0.5	559	+50 Light Armor, +55% One-Handed Damage, 60s
Potion of Escape	0.5	351	Invisibility 30s, Restore Health 25
Draught of Escape	0.5	495	Invisibility 40s, Restore Health 50
Philter of Escape	0.5	580	Invisibility 45s, Restore Health 75
Elixir of Escape	0.5	666	Invisibility 50s, Restore Health 100
Grand Elixir of Escape	0.5	753	Invisibility 55s, Restore Health 125

POTION NAME	WEIGHT	VALUE	EFFECT
Prime Elixir of Escape	0.5	840	Invisibility 60s, Restore Health 150
Potion of Keenshot	0.5	74	+15% Bow Damage, +5% Stamina Regen, 60s
Draught of Keenshot	0.5	102	+20% Bow Damage, +7% Stamina Regen, 60s
Philter of Keenshot	0.5	131	+25% Bow Damage, +9% Stamina Regen, 60s
Elixir of Keenshot	0.5	161	+30% Bow Damage, +11% Stamina Regen, 60s
Grand Elixir of Keenshot	0.5	191	+35% Bow Damage, +13% Stamina Regen, 60s
Prime Elixir of Keenshot	0.5	221	+40% Bow Damage, +15% Stamina Regen, 60s
Potion of Larceny	0.5	140	+15% Lockpicking, +15% Pickpocket

POTION NAME	WEIGHT	VALUE	EFFECT
Draught of Larceny	0.5	192	+20% Lockpicking, +20% Pickpocket
Philter of Larceny	0.5	246	+25% Lockpicking, +25% Pickpocket
Elixir of Larceny	0.5	302	+30% Lockpicking, +30% Pickpocket
Grand Elixir of Larceny	0.5	358	+35% Lockpicking, +35% Pickpocket
Prime Elixir of Larceny	0.5	414	+40% Lockpicking, +40% Pickpocket
Potion of Plunder	0.5	511	+20 Carry Weight, +20 Max Stamina, 5m
Draught of Plunder	0.5	799	+30 Carry Weight, +30 Max Stamina, 5m
Philter of Plunder	0.5	1096	+40 Carry Weight, +40 Max Stamina, 5m
Elixir of Plunder	0.5	1402	+50 Carry Weight, +50 Max Stamina, 5m
Grand Elixir of Plunder	0.5	1713	+60 Carry Weight, +60 Max Stamina, 5m
Prime Elixir of Plunder	0.5	2029	+70 Carry Weight, +70 Max Stamina, 5m

POTION NAME	WEIGHT	VALUE	EFFECT
QUEST POTIONS			
Lotus Extract	0.5	86	Damage Health 6/s, 10s
Ice Wraith Bane	0.5	221	Damage Health 50
Nightshade Extract	0.5	12	Damage Health 1, 10s
Sleeping Tree Sap	0.5	100	+100 Max Health, Slow 25%, 45s
Esbern's Potion	0.5	250	Dragons do 25% less damage.
Vaermina's Torpor	0.5	0	Enter the dreams of those around you.
The White Phial (Full)	0.5	341	Varies by effect.
Philter of the Phantom	0.5	50	Look like a ghost for 30s.
Falmer Blood Elixir	0.5	1	Restore Health 1
Velvet LeChance	0.5	5	Restore Stamina 25
White-Gold Tower	0.5	5	Restore Stamina 25
Cliff Racer	0.5	5	Restore Stamina 25

▣ Table XIV: Other Items

This section lists all of the other major items you can find in Skyrim.

NAME	WEIGHT	VALUE	EFFECT
SCROLLS			
While these scrolls are the most common, you may occasionally find a scroll that casts a lesser spell.			
Scroll of Bane of the Undead	0.5	500	Bane of the Undead
Scroll of Blizzard	0.5	500	Blizzard
Scroll of Call to Arms	0.5	500	Call to Arms
Scroll of Dead Thrall	0.5	500	Dead Thrall
Scroll of Dragonhide	0.5	250	Dragonhide
Scroll of Fire Storm	0.5	500	Fire Storm
Scroll of Flame Thrall	0.5	500	Flame Thrall
Scroll of Frost Thrall	0.5	500	Frost Thrall
Scroll of Guardian Circle	0.5	250	Guardian Circle
Scroll of Harmony	0.5	500	Harmony
Scroll of Hysteria	0.5	500	Hysteria
Scroll of Mass Paralysis	0.5	500	Mass Paralysis

NAME	WEIGHT	VALUE	EFFECT
Scroll of Mayhem	0.5	500	Mayhem
Scroll of Storm Thrall	0.5	500	Storm Thrall
Shalidor's Insights: Alteration*	0.5	50	For 2m, Alteration spells cost 50% less and last 100% longer.
Shalidor's Insights: Conjuration*	0.5	50	For 2m, Conjuration spells cost 50% less and last 100% longer.
Shalidor's Insights: Destruction*	0.5	50	For 2m, Destruction spells cost 50% less and last 100% longer.
Shalidor's Insights: Illusion*	0.5	50	For 2m, Illusion spells cost 50% less and last 100% longer.
Shalidor's Insights: Magicka*	0.5	50	For 2m, +100 Magicka and +100% Magicka Regeneration.
Shalidor's Insights: Restoration*	0.5	50	For 2m, Restoration spells cost 50% less and last 100% longer.

*Note: Reward for College of Winterhold quest Shalidor's Insight.

NAME	WEIGHT	VALUE	EFFECT
J'zargo's Flame Cloak Scroll	0.5	100	Flame Cloak, explodes near undead.

Note: Quest item for College of Winterhold quest J'zargo's Experiment.

NAME	WEIGHT	VALUE
INGOTS		
Iron Ingot	1	7
Steel Ingot	1	20
Dwarven Metal Ingot	1	30
Corundum Ingot	1	40
Orichalcum Ingot	1	45
Silver Ingot	1	50
Quicksilver Ingot	1	60
Refined Moonstone	1	75
Gold Ingot	1	100
Refined Malachite	1	100
Ebony Ingot	1	150

NAME	WEIGHT	VALUE
ORE		
Iron Ore	1	2
Corundum Ore	1	20
Orichalcum Ore	1	20
Quicksilver Ore	1	25
Silver Ore	1	25
Malachite Ore	1	30
Moonstone Ore	1	30
Gold Ore	1	50
Ebony Ore	1	60

NAME	WEIGHT	VALUE
GEMS		
Garnet	0.1	100
Amethyst	0.1	120
Flawless Garnet	0.1	150
Flawless Amethyst	0.1	180
Ruby	0.1	200
Flawless Ruby	0.1	350
Sapphire	0.1	400
Flawless Sapphire	0.1	500
Emerald	0.1	600
Flawless Emerald	0.1	750
Diamond	0.1	800
Flawless Diamond	0.1	1000

NAME	WEIGHT	VALUE
LEATHER & HIDES		
Leather	2	10
Leather Strips	0.1	3
Goat Hide	1	5

NAME	WEIGHT	VALUE
Fox Pelt	0.5	5
Snow Fox Pelt	0.5	7
Wolf Pelt	1	10
Ice Wolf Pelt	1	15

NAME	WEIGHT	VALUE
Deer Hide	2	10
Cow Hide	2	10
Horse Hide	2	15
Bear Pelt	3	50

NAME	WEIGHT	VALUE
Cave Bear Pelt	3	60
Sabre Cat Pelt	2	25
Sabre Cat Snow Pelt	2	40
Snow Bear Pelt	3	75

NAME	WEIGHT	VALUE	EFFECT
FOOD			
Alto Wine	0.5	12	Restore Stamina 15
Apple Cabbage Stew	0.5	8	Restore Health 10, Restore Stamina 15
Apple Pie	0.5	5	Restore Health 10
Baked Potatoes	0.1	2	Restore Health 5
Beef Stew	0.5	8	+25 Max Stamina/12m, Regenerate Stamina 2/s for 12m
Black-Briar Mead	0.2	25	Restore Stamina 20
Black-Briar Reserve	0.5	100	Restore Stamina 30
Boiled Creme Treat	0.5	4	Restore Health 10
Bread	0.2	2	Restore Health 2
Bread	0.2	2	Restore Health 2
Cabbage	0.25	2	Restore Health 1
Cabbage Potato Soup	0.5	5	Restore Health 10, Restore Stamina 10
Cabbage Soup	0.5	5	Restore Health 10, Restore Stamina 10
Carrot	0.1	1	Restore Health 1
Charred Skeever Meat	0.2	4	Restore Health 2
Chicken Breast	0.2	3	Restore Health 2
Clam Meat	0.1	1	Restore Health 1
Cooked Beef	0.5	5	Restore Health 10
Dog Meat	0.2	3	Restore Health 2
Eidar Cheese Wedge	0.25	5	Restore Health 1
Eidar Cheese Wheel	2	13	Restore Health 15
Elsweyr Fondue	0.5	5	+100 Max Magicka/12m, +25% Magicka Regen/12m

NAME	WEIGHT	VALUE	EFFECT
Goat Cheese Wedge	0.25	4	Restore Health 1
Goat Cheese Wheel	2	10	Restore Health 15
Gourd	0.2	1	Restore Health 1
Green Apple	0.1	3	Restore Health 2
Grilled Chicken Breast	0.2	5	Restore Health 5
Grilled Leeks	0.1	2	Restore Health 6
Homecooked Meal	5	1	+25% Health, Magicka, and Stamina Regen/10m
Honey	0.1	2	Restore Health 2
Honey Nut Treat	0.1	2	Restore Health 5
Honningbrew Mead	0.5	20	Restore Stamina 20
Horker Loaf	1	4	Restore Health 10
Horker Meat	1	3	Restore Health 1
Horker Stew	0.5	8	Restore Health 15, Restore Stamina 15, Regenerate Health 1/s /12m
Horse Haunch	2	4	Restore Health 10
Horse Meat	2	3	Restore Health 2
Leek	0.1	1	Restore Health 1
Leg of Goat	1	3	Restore Health 2
Leg of Goat Roast	1	4	Restore Health 10
Long Taffy Treat	0.1	3	Restore Health 10
Mammoth Cheese Bowl	0.5	3	Restore Health 10
Mammoth Snout	3	6	Restore Health 5
Mammoth Steak	2	8	Restore Health 10
Nord Mead	0.5	5	Restore Stamina 15

NAME	WEIGHT	VALUE	EFFECT
Pheasant Breast	0.2	3	Restore Health 2
Pheasant Roast	0.2	4	Restore Health 5
Potato	0.1	1	Restore Health 1
Rabbit Haunch	0.1	3	Restore Health 5
Raw Beef	0.2	4	Restore Health 2
Raw Rabbit Leg	0.1	2	Restore Health 2
Red Apple	0.1	3	Restore Health 2
Salmon Meat	0.1	3	Restore Health 2
Salmon Steak	0.1	4	Restore Health 5
Seared Slaughterfish	0.1	5	Restore Health 5
Sliced Eidar Cheese	2	10	Restore Health 15
Sliced Goat Cheese	2	8	Restore Health 15
Spiced Wine	0.5	7	Restore Stamina 25
Sweet Roll	0.1	2	Restore Health 5
Tomato	0.1	4	Restore Health 1
Tomato Soup	0.5	5	Restore Health 10, Restore Stamina 10
Vegetable Soup	0.5	5	Regenerate Health 1/12m, Regenerate Stamina 1/12m
Venison	2	4	Restore Health 2
Venison Chop	2	5	Restore Health 5
Venison Stew	0.5	8	Restore Stamina 15, Regenerate Health 1/12m, Regenerate Stamina 1/12m
Wine	0.5	7	Restore Stamina 15

ZONE #	CLOSEST LOCATION	NAME	GLYPH SEQUENCE	VALUE
DRAGON CLAWS				
[10.05]	Skuldafn	Diamond Claw	Fox, Moth, Dragon	1000
[2.04]	Dead Men's Respite	Ruby Dragon Claw	Wolf, Hawk, Wolf	400
[2.08]	Folgunthur	Ivory Dragon Claw	Hawk, Hawk, Dragon	200
[3.22]	Korvanjund	Ebony Claw	Fox, Moth, Dragon	800
[4.30]	Yngol Barrow	Coral Dragon Claw	Snake, Wolf, Moth	150
[5.39]	Reachwater Rock	Emerald Dragon Claw	Bear, Whale, Snake	600
[5.42]	Valthume	Iron Claw	Dragon, Hawk, Wolf	75
[8.18]	Bleak Falls Barrow	Golden Claw	Bear, Moth, Owl	100

ZONE #	CLOSEST LOCATION	NAME	GLYPH SEQUENCE	VALUE
[9.01]	Ivarstead	Sapphire Dragon Claw	Moth, Owl, Wolf	500
[9.45]	Forelhost	Glass Claw	Fox, Owl, Snake	700
CAPTURED CRITTERS				
[3.19]	Duskglow Crevice	Moth in a Jar	1	1
[4.06]	Frostflow Lighthouse	Torchbug in a Jar	1	1
[5.38]	Dushnikh Yal	Dragonfly in a Jar	1	1
[9.09]	Alchemist's Shack	Butterfly in a Jar	1	1
[9.29]	Goldenglow Estate	Bee in a Jar	1	1

NAME	WEIGHT	VALUE
CLUTTER		
Many items have variants with different weights and values than those listed below.		
Basket	0.5	1
Bellows	1	1
Bent Dwemer Scrap Metal	2	15

NAME	WEIGHT	VALUE
Bloody Rags	1	1
Bowl	0.5	5
Broken Iron Mace Handle	5	5
Broken Iron Mace Head	8	5
Broken Iron Sword Blade	6	5

NAME	WEIGHT	VALUE
Broken Iron Sword Handle	3	5
Broken Iron War Axe Handle	5	5
Broken Iron War Axe Head	6	5
Broken Steel Battle Axe Handle	9	10

NAME	WEIGHT	VALUE
Broken Steel Battle Axe Head	12	10
Broken Steel Greatsword Blade	10	10
Broken Steel Greatsword Handle	7	10

NAME	WEIGHT	VALUE
Broken Steel Sword Blade	6	10
Broken Steel Sword Handle	4	10
Broken Steel Warhammer Handle	10	10
Broken Steel Warhammer Head	15	10
Broom	1	1
Bucket	0.5	1
Burned Book	2	0
Candlestick	1	25
Candlestick	1	25
Cast Iron Pot	6	8
Charcoal	0.5	2
Chaurus Chitin	4	50
Clothes Iron	3	7
Cup	0.5	5
Dragon Bone	15	500
Dragon Scales	10	250
Drum	4	10
Dwemer Cup	0.5	6
Dwemer Dish	0.5	8
Dwemer Gear	2	15
Dwemer Gyro	2	15
Dwemer Lever	2	15
Dwemer Pan	0.5	8
Dwemer Pan	3	10
Dwemer Plate	1	8
Dwemer Scrap Metal	2	15
Embalming Tool	0.5	3
Empty Wine Bottle	0.5	1
Firewood	5	5
Flagon	0.5	1
Flower Basket	1	5
Flute	2	25
Goblet	0.5	5
Hammer	3	1
Horker Tusk	1	15
Imperial War Horn	5	70
Inkwell	0.3	1
Jug	2	10
Kettle	2	4
Knife	0.5	6
Lantern	2	1
Large Decorative Dwemer Strut	15	10
Large Dwemer Plate Metal	2	15
Large Dwemer Strut	20	15
Linen Wrap	3	2
Lockpick	0	2
Lute	4	25
Mammoth Tusk	5	150
Nord War Horn	5	70
Pitchfork	4	1
Pitchfork	4	1
Plate	0.5	1

NAME	WEIGHT	VALUE
Platter	0.5	5
Pot	3	5
Quill	0.5	1
Roll of Paper	1	4
Ruined Book	2	5
Ruined Book	2	5
Saw	2	3
Shovel	4	3
Skull	2	5
Small Dwemer Lever	2	15
Small Dwemer Plate Metal	2	15
Solid Dwemer Metal	25	25
Soul Gem Fragment	0.1	5
Spigot	2	1
Spoon	0.5	6
Tankard	0.5	1
Tongs	1	1
Troll Skull	3.5	5
Wooden Bowl	0.5	1
Wooden Ladle	0.5	1
Wooden Plate	0.5	1
Fork	0.5	3

QUEST ITEMS

NAME	WEIGHT	VALUE
Argonian Ale	0.5	5
Glenmoril Witch Head	4	0
Fragments of Wuuthrad	0	0
Silver Hand Stratagem	0	0
Werewolf Totem	0.5	1
Imperial Documents	0	0
StormCloak Documents	0	0
Broken Azura's Star	0.5	0
Malyn's Black Soul Gem	0.5	0
Attunement Sphere	0	0
Blank Lexicon	0	0
Runed Lexicon	0	0
Elder Scroll	0	20
Essence Extractor	1	0
Sinding's Skin	4	0
Shards of Mehrunes' Razor	6	0
Hilt of Mehrunes' Razor	2	0
Pommel Stone of Mehrunes' Razor	2	0
Scabbard of Mehrunes' Razor	3	0
Strange crystal	1	10
Meridia's Beacon	0.5	0
Wedding Ring	0.5	0
Pelagius' Hip Bone	1	250
The Dancer's Flute	2	3
Aretino Family Heirloom	0.5	100
Jeweled Pendant	0.5	200
Jeweled Amulet	0.5	100
Sealed Letter	0.5	100
Olava's Token	0.5	100

NAME	WEIGHT	VALUE
Jarrin Root	0.5	100
Heart of Winter	0.5	100
Torture Tools	2	15
Empty Skooma Bottle	0.5	0
Habd's Remains	1	0
Balwen's Ornamental Ring	3	0
Katarina's Ornamental Ring	3	0
Pithi's Ornamental Ring	3	0
Treoy's Ornamental Ring	3	0
Saerek's Skull Key	0.3	100
Torsten's Skull Key	0.3	100
Iron Claw	0.5	75
Opaque Vessel	0	0
Strange Gem	0.5	0
Ancient Traveler's Skull	5	0
Dwemer Bowl	2	20
Centurion Dynamo Core	4	131
Dwemer Cog	10	5
Ysgramor's Soup Spoon	0.5	3
Spiced Beef	0.5	4
Stros M'Kai Rum	0.5	12
Sapphire Dragon Claw	0.5	500
Klimmek's Supplies	0	0
Mark of Dibella	0.5	0
Wylandriah's Spoon	0	0
Quicksilver Ore	1	25
Black-Briar Mead Keg	20	0
Sylgja's Satchel	0	0
Verner's Satchel	0	0
Burial Urn	1	0
Firebrand Wine	0.5	137
Kordir's Skooma	0.5	20
Dragon's Breath Mead	0.5	5
Quill of Gemination	0.1	150
Sealed Scroll	0.5	0
Stallion's Potion	0.5	341
Focusing Crystal	1	10
Torc of Labyrinthian	1	10
Tolfdir's Alembic	2	0
Petty Soul Gem	0.5	0
Warped Soul Gem	0.5	0
Dragon Heartscales	10	250
Mead with Juniper Berry	0.5	5
Dragonstone	25	0
Horn of Jurgen Windcaller	4	0
Map of Dragon Burials	0	0
Colovian Brandy	0.5	100
Lexicon	0	0
Potema's Skull	0	0
Briar Heart	1	0
Mammoth Tusk Powder	0.5	0
Nurelion's Mixture	5	15
Unmelting Snow	1	0

NAME	WEIGHT	VALUE
The White Phial (Empty)	0.5	0
Cracked White Phial	0.5	0
Golden Claw	0.5	100
Michaela's Flagon	0.5	1
Jessica's Wine	0.5	12
Sigil Stone	0	0
Skooma	0.5	20
Torygg's War Horn	5	0
Package for Grelka	2	0
Package for Verner	2	0
Dibella Statue	2	100
Statue of Dibella	3	100
Eldergleam Sap	1	0
Eldergleam Sapling	1	0
Honey Jar	1	0
Pest Poison	0.5	0
Firebrand Wine Case	6	0
Calcelmo's Stone Rubbing	0.5	0
Mercer's Plans	0.5	0
Skeleton Key	0.5	0
Coinpurse	0	0
Crown of Barenziah	0	0
Barenziahs Crown	0	0
Unusual Gem	0.5	200
Satchel of Moon Sugar	0	0
Queen Bee Statue	0	0
Honningbrew Decanter	0	0
East Empire Shipping Map	0	0
Model Ship	0	0
Dwemer Puzzle Cube	0	0
Bust of the Gray Fox	0	0
Right Eye of the Falmer	5	2500
Left Eye of the Falmer	5	2500
Jeweled Candlestick	0	0
Ornate Drinking Horn	0	0
Jeweled Flagon	0	0
Jeweled Goblet	0	0
Golden Urn	0	0
Jeweled Pitcher	0	0
Golden Ship Model	0	0
Silver Candlestick	1	75
Curious Silver Mold	1	250
Balmora Blue	0.5	67
Cyrodilic Brandy	0.5	150
Double-Distilled Skooma	0.5	44
Gildergreen Sapling	8	0
Fragment of Wuuthrad	2	0
Pantea's Flute	2	25
Rjorn's Drum	4	10
Finn's Lute	4	25

The Elder Scrolls V
SKYRIM

PRIMA OFFICIAL GAME GUIDE — WWW.PRIMAGAMES.COM

THE BESTIARY OF SKYRIM

● MINOR SPOILERS

The wild and untamed lands of Skyrim are teeming with adversaries, from the wretched to the powerful, and the monstrous to the meek. This chapter presents them alphabetized by type, so you can identify the foes you're about to engage in battle. This allows you to identify weaknesses that you can exploit, bolster your defenses against the spells and abilities your enemies will use, and know what kind of loot to expect. Heed the following notes before exploring the Bestiary in detail.

BESTIARY ADVICE

▷ Enemies

Enemies that are members of one the ten races that you can choose from have all the benefits of their race (which you can read about at the start of the Training Chapter) in addition to any statistics indicated in the Bestiary below.

For example: a High Elf Warlock has a higher Magicka than indicated due to their Highborn Magicka racial ability. A Breton Warlock will be more resistant to spells because of their Magic Resistance ability. A Nord Warlock will shrug off frost spells (Frost Resistance), while a Dark Elf Warlock will be more resistant to fire (Fire Resistance).

As your level increases, the difficulty of the enemies you encounter will typically increase in stages. This is most visible when you read the name of your adversaries, which usually indicates their level. For example, a 'Novice Necromancer' (Level 1) is noticeably weaker than an 'Apprentice Necromancer' (Level 6) or a 'Master Necromancer' (Level 36).

A few characters (such as your followers) work differently: their level will gradually increase as your level does, though possibly at a slower rate.

Ordinary Citizens of Skyrim and unique enemies for particular Quests are not listed in this section. The vast majority of unique enemies borrow their statistics from a related creature that is on the chart, perhaps with a slight change to their weapons, armor, or spells.

For example, all of the Civil War Military Camps have a commander with a unique name. However, these are simply named versions of the "Imperial Legate" or "Stormcloak Commander" characters in the Bestiary.

▷ Items and Spells

Italics indicate that an item carried by an enemy is leveled. The higher your level, the higher the quality of the item the creature may have (though lower-quality items will still continue to appear).

(Parenthesis) indicate that an item may or may not be present; there is a random chance per creature.

A / Slash indicates that one of the items will be present, while the others will not.

[Brackets] indicate that the version of the item carried by the creature cannot be looted from their body. For example, most Draugr armor can't be taken from Draugr corpses.

Many creatures are also listed as having some kind of general Loot Items (for example, Draugr Loot). These are typically random collections of small items (food, ingredients, etc.) that the entity may be carrying; they may have none, one, or several of these items on them when killed. For each creature type, a brief summary of the kinds of items they're likely to be carrying is provided.

▷ Afflicted

The Afflicted of Peryite have a damaging Vile Vapor ability in addition to their normal attacks.

THE BESTIARY CHART LEGEND

COLUMN	NOTES
Name	Name of the creature as it appears on-screen when you encounter it.
Subtype	*Not* visible in game, this field provides a title or description to help to help identify the creature if the name isn't sufficient on its own.
Lv	Level of the creature. This roughly suggests the level at which you should be able to reasonably defeat it. Depending on your particular mix of Skills and Perks, your actual experience may vary.*
Health	The creature's base Health.
Magicka	The creature's base Magicka.
Stamina	The creature's base Stamina.
Weapons	The weapon(s) the creature possesses.
Armor	The armor the creature wears.
Items	Any loose items the creature carries.
Spells	The creature's list of spells or spell-like special abilities.
Notes	Any special properties, such as elemental weaknesses or resistances that may affect how you choose to fight the creature.

NOTE * If a Level number is starred (for example, "30*"), this creature is one that levels with you: As your level and statistics increase, so will its level and statistics. The values in the table represent the creature's stats for the indicated level, which is often the creature's lowest possible level.

NOTE A Note on Ghosts

All ghosts use the statistics, spells, and abilities of their original forms (often Bandits or Draugr). They disintegrate into Ectoplasm when killed.

AFFLICTED — ARCHERS

NAME	SUBTYPE	LV	HEALTH	MAGICKA	STAMINA	WEAPONS	ARMOR	ITEMS	SPELLS
Afflicted	Archer	1	30	25	70	Bow, Arrows	Clothes, Gloves, Hat, Boots	(Lockpick), (Gold)	Vile Vapor
Afflicted	Archer	5	74	25	86	Bow, Arrows, Iron Dagger	Clothes, Gloves, Hat, Boots	(Lockpick), (Gold)	Vile Vapor
Afflicted	Archer	9	118	25	102	Bow, Arrows, Steel Dagger	Clothes, Gloves, Hat, Boots	(Lockpick), (Gold)	Vile Vapor
Afflicted	Archer	14	173	25	122	Bow, Arrows, Steel Dagger	Clothes, Gloves, Hat, Boots	(Lockpick), (Gold)	Vile Vapor
Afflicted	Archer	19	228	25	142	Bow, Arrows, Steel Dagger	Clothes, Gloves, Hat, Boots	(Lockpick), (Gold)	Vile Vapor
Afflicted	Archer	24	283	25	162	Bow, Arrows, Steel Dagger	Clothes, Gloves, Hat, Boots	(Lockpick), (Gold)	Vile Vapor

Afflicted

AFFLICTED – GUARDIANS

NAME	SUBTYPE	LV	HEALTH	MAGICKA	STAMINA	WEAPONS	ARMOR	ITEMS	SPELLS
Afflicted	Guardian	1	30	25	70	1H Weapon	(Heavy Cuirass / Light Cuirass / Clothes), Heavy Gauntlets, Heavy Boots, Heavy Helmet, Heavy Shield	(Lockpick), (Gold)	Vile Vapor
Afflicted	Guardian	5	94	25	86	1H Weapon	(Heavy Cuirass / Light Cuirass / Clothes), Heavy Gauntlets, Heavy Boots, Heavy Helmet, Heavy Shield	(Lockpick), (Gold)	Vile Vapor
Afflicted	Guardian	9	118	25	102	1H Weapon	(Heavy Cuirass / Light Cuirass / Clothes), Heavy Gauntlets, Heavy Boots, Heavy Helmet, Heavy Shield	(Lockpick), (Gold)	Vile Vapor
Afflicted	Guardian	14	173	25	122	1H Weapon	(Heavy Cuirass / Light Cuirass / Clothes), Heavy Gauntlets, Heavy Boots, Heavy Helmet, Heavy Shield	(Lockpick), (Gold)	Vile Vapor
Afflicted	Guardian	19	228	25	142	1H Weapon	(Heavy Cuirass / Light Cuirass / Clothes), Heavy Gauntlets, Heavy Boots, Heavy Helmet, Heavy Shield	(Lockpick), (Gold)	Vile Vapor
Afflicted	Guardian	24	283	25	162	1H Weapon	(Heavy Cuirass / Light Cuirass / Clothes), Heavy Gauntlets, Heavy Boots, Heavy Helmet, Heavy Shield	(Lockpick), (Gold)	Vile Vapor

AFFLICTED – MAGES

NAME	SUBTYPE	LV	HEALTH	MAGICKA	STAMINA	WEAPONS	ARMOR	ITEMS	SPELLS
Afflicted	Mage	1	30	100	70	Iron Dagger	Mage Robes, Boots	(Lockpick), (Gold)	(Frostbite / Flames / Sparks), Healing, Oakflesh, Lesser Ward, Vile Vapor
Afflicted	Mage	5	66	124	70	Iron Dagger	Mage Robes, Boots	(Lockpick), (Gold)	(Frostbite / Flames / Sparks), Healing, Oakflesh, Lesser Ward, Vile Vapor
Afflicted	Mage	9	102	123	70	Steel Dagger	Mage Robes, Boots	(Lockpick), (Gold)	(Ice Spike / Firebolt / Lightning Bolt), Fast Healing, Stoneflesh, Steadfast Ward, Vile Vapor
Afflicted	Mage	14	147	153	70	Dwarven Dagger, Iron Dagger	Mage Robes, Boots	(Lockpick), (Gold)	(Ice Spike / Firebolt / Lightning Bolt), Fast Healing, Stoneflesh, Steadfast Ward, Vile Vapor
Afflicted	Mage	19	192	183	70	Dwarven Dagger, Iron Dagger	Mage Robes, Boots	(Lockpick), (Gold)	(Ice Spike / Firebolt / Lightning Bolt), Fast Healing, Stoneflesh, Steadfast Ward, Vile Vapor

AFFLICTED – WARRIORS

NAME	SUBTYPE	LV	HEALTH	MAGICKA	STAMINA	WEAPONS	ARMOR	ITEMS	SPELLS
Afflicted	Warrior	1	30	25	70	1H Weapon	(Light Cuirass / Heavy Cuirass / Clothes), Light Boots, Light Gauntlets, (Light Helmet), (Light Shield)	(Lockpick), (Gold)	Vile Vapor
Afflicted	Warrior	5	94	25	86	1H Weapon	(Light Cuirass / Heavy Cuirass / Clothes), Light Boots, Light Gauntlets, (Light Helmet), (Light Shield)	(Lockpick), (Gold)	Vile Vapor
Afflicted	Warrior	9	118	25	102	1H Weapon	(Light Cuirass / Heavy Cuirass / Clothes), Light Boots, Light Gauntlets, (Light Helmet), (Light Shield)	(Lockpick), (Gold)	Vile Vapor
Afflicted	Warrior	14	173	25	122	1H Weapon	(Light Cuirass / Heavy Cuirass / Clothes), Light Boots, Light Gauntlets, (Light Helmet), (Light Shield)	(Lockpick), (Gold)	Vile Vapor
Afflicted	Warrior	19	228	25	142	1H Weapon, Orcish Dagger	(Light Cuirass / Heavy Cuirass / Clothes), Light Boots, Light Gauntlets, (Light Helmet), (Light Shield)	(Lockpick), (Gold)	Vile Vapor
Afflicted	Warrior	24	283	25	162	1H Weapon, Orcish Dagger	(Light Cuirass / Heavy Cuirass / Clothes), Light Boots, Light Gauntlets, (Light Helmet), (Light Shield)	(Lockpick), (Gold)	Vile Vapor

◈ Alik'r

ALIK'R – ARCHERS

NAME	SUBTYPE	LV	HEALTH	MAGICKA	STAMINA	WEAPONS	ARMOR	ITEMS	SPELLS
Alik'r Warrior	Archer	1	40	25	25	Bow, Arrows, Iron Dagger	Hammerfell Garb, Redguard Hood, Redguard Boots	Gold, (Lockpick)	
Alik'r Warrior	Archer	6	85	25	45	Bow, Arrows, Iron Dagger	Hammerfell Garb, Redguard Hood, Redguard Boots	Gold, (Lockpick)	
Alik'r Warrior	Archer	14	173	25	77	Bow, Arrows, Steel Dagger	Hammerfell Garb, Redguard Hood, Redguard Boots	Gold, (Lockpick)	
Alik'r Warrior	Archer	24	283	25	117	Bow, Arrows, Steel Dagger	Hammerfell Garb, Redguard Hood, Redguard Boots	Gold, (Lockpick)	
Alik'r Warrior	Archer	34	393	25	157	Bow, Arrows, Steel Dagger	Hammerfell Garb, Redguard Hood, Redguard Boots	Gold, (Lockpick)	
Alik'r Warrior	Archer	44	503	25	197	Bow, Arrows, Steel Dagger	Hammerfell Garb, Redguard Hood, Redguard Boots	Gold, (Lockpick)	

Alik'r (Berserker)

ALIK'R – BERSERKERS

NAME	SUBTYPE	LV	HEALTH	MAGICKA	STAMINA	WEAPONS	ARMOR	ITEMS	SPELLS
Alik'r Warrior	Berserker	1	40	25	25	Iron Dagger	Hammerfell Garb, Redguard Hood, Redguard Boots	Gold, (Lockpick)	
Alik'r Warrior	Berserker	6	85	25	45	Iron Dagger	Hammerfell Garb, Redguard Hood, Redguard Boots	Gold, (Lockpick)	
Alik'r Warrior	Berserker	14	173	25	77	Steel Dagger	Hammerfell Garb, Redguard Hood, Redguard Boots	Gold, (Lockpick)	
Alik'r Warrior	Berserker	24	283	25	117	Steel Dagger	Hammerfell Garb, Redguard Hood, Redguard Boots	Gold, (Lockpick)	
Alik'r Warrior	Berserker	34	393	25	157	Orcish Dagger	Hammerfell Garb, Redguard Hood, Redguard Boots	Gold, (Lockpick)	
Alik'r Warrior	Berserker	44	503	25	197	Orcish Dagger	Hammerfell Garb, Redguard Hood, Redguard Boots	Gold, (Lockpick)	

Alik'r (Mage)

ALIK'R – MAGES

NAME	SUBTYPE	LV	HEALTH	MAGICKA	STAMINA	WEAPONS	ARMOR	ITEMS	SPELLS
Alik'r Warrior	Mage	1	40	25	25	Iron Dagger	Hammerfell Garb, Redguard Hood, Redguard Boots	Gold, (Lockpick)	(Frostbite, Flames, Shock), Healing, Lesser Ward
Alik'r Warrior	Mage	6	75	55	25	Iron Dagger	Hammerfell Garb, Redguard Hood, Redguard Boots	Gold, (Lockpick)	(Frostbite, Flames, Shock), Healing, Lesser Ward
Alik'r Warrior	Mage	14	147	103	25	Iron Dagger	Hammerfell Garb, Redguard Hood, Redguard Boots	Gold, (Lockpick)	(Ice Spike / Firebolt / Lightning Bolt), Fast Healing, Steadfast Ward
Alik'r Warrior	Mage	24	237	163	25	Iron Dagger	Hammerfell Garb, Redguard Hood, Redguard Boots	Gold, (Lockpick)	(Ice Spike / Firebolt / Lightning Bolt), Fast Healing, Steadfast Ward
Alik'r Warrior	Mage	34	327	223	25	Iron Dagger	Hammerfell Garb, Redguard Hood, Redguard Boots	Gold, (Lockpick)	(Ice Spike / Firebolt / Lightning Bolt), Fast Healing, Steadfast Ward
Alik'r Warrior	Mage	44	417	283	25	Iron Dagger	Hammerfell Garb, Redguard Hood, Redguard Boots	Gold, (Lockpick)	(Ice Spike / Firebolt / Lightning Bolt), Fast Healing, Steadfast Ward

ALIK'R – WARRIORS

NAME	SUBTYPE	LV	HEALTH	MAGICKA	STAMINA	WEAPONS	ARMOR	ITEMS	SPELLS
Alik'r Warrior	Warrior	1	40	25	25	Scimitar, Iron Dagger	Hammerfell Garb, Redguard Hood, Redguard Boots	Gold, (Lockpick)	
Alik'r Warrior	Warrior	6	85	25	45	Scimitar, Iron Dagger	Hammerfell Garb, Redguard Hood, Redguard Boots	Gold, (Lockpick)	
Alik'r Warrior	Warrior	14	173	25	77	Scimitar, Steel Dagger	Hammerfell Garb, Redguard Hood, Redguard Boots	Gold, (Lockpick)	
Alik'r Warrior	Warrior	24	283	25	117	Scimitar, Steel Dagger	Hammerfell Garb, Redguard Hood, Redguard Boots	Gold, (Lockpick)	
Alik'r Warrior	Warrior	34	393	25	157	Scimitar, Orcish Dagger	Hammerfell Garb, Redguard Hood, Redguard Boots	Gold, (Lockpick)	
Alik'r Warrior	Warrior	44	503	25	197	Scimitar, Orcish Dagger	Hammerfell Garb, Redguard Hood, Redguard Boots	Gold, (Lockpick)	

Alik'r (Warrior)

◈ Animals

This list includes wild and domesticated animals that appear in only one or two forms. Minor Treasure includes a tiny chance of: A few gold, a gem, or a ring.

DOMESTICATED ANIMALS

NAME	SUBTYPE	LV	HEALTH	MAGICKA	STAMINA	WEAPONS	ARMOR	ITEMS	SPELLS	NOTES
Chicken		1	5	0	25	2 Dmg		Chicken Breast		
Dog		2	21	0	24	8 Dmg		Dog Meat, (Minor Treasure)		
Cow		3	87	0	33	10 Dmg		Raw Beef, Cow Hide, (Minor Treasure)		
Goat		3	22	0	8	7 Dmg		Goat Hide, Leg of Goat, (Minor Treasure)		Resist Frost 50%

Domesticated Animal (Dog)

WILD PREDATORS

NAME	SUBTYPE	LV	HEALTH	MAGICKA	STAMINA	WEAPONS	ARMOR	ITEMS	SPELLS	NOTES
Skeever		1	15	0	15	5 Dmg		Skeever Tail, (Minor Treasure)		
Wolf		2	22	0	205	5 Dmg		Wolf Pelt, (Minor Treasure)		
Ice Wolf		6	137	0	255	20 Dmg		Ice Wolf Pelt, (Minor Treasure)		Resist Frost 50%
Sabre Cat		6	150	0	225	35 Dmg		Sabre Cat Pelt, (Sabre Cat Eyeball / Sabre Cat Tooth), (Minor Treasure)		
Sabre Cat, Snowy		11	275	0	300	45 Dmg		Sabre Cat Snow Pelt, (Sabre Cat Eyeball / Sabre Cat Tooth), (Minor Treasure)		Resist Frost 50%
Bear		12	260	0	225	35 Dmg		Bear Pelt, Bear Claws, (Minor Treasure)		
Bear, Cave		16	450	0	425	30 Dmg		Bear Pelt, Bear Claws, (Minor Treasure)		
Bear, Snow		20	550	0	400	45 Dmg		Bear Pelt, Bear Claws, (Minor Treasure)		Resist Frost 50%
Mudcrab		1	5	0	25	5 Dmg		Mudcrab Chitin, (Minor Treasure)		Waterbreathing
Mudcrab	Large	2	35	0	30	20 Dmg		Mudcrab Chitin, (Minor Treasure)		Waterbreathing
Mudcrab	Giant	3	55	0	35	25 Dmg		2 Mudcrab Chitin, (Minor Treasure)		Waterbreathing
Slaughterfish		1	35	0	25	5 Dmg		Slaughterfish Scales, (Minor Treasure)		Waterbreathing
Horker		3	175	0	185	15 Dmg		Horker Meat, Horker Tusk, (Minor Treasure)		
Ice Wraiths		9	193	50	227	40 Dmg + Frost 7/s for 3s		Ice Wraith Teeth, Ice Wraith Essence		Immune to Frost, Weak to Fire 25%, Waterwalking

Wild Predator (Snow Bear)

WILD PREY

NAME	SUBTYPE	LV	HEALTH	MAGICKA	STAMINA	WEAPONS	ARMOR	ITEMS	SPELLS	NOTES
Deer		1	50	0	25	5 Dmg		Venison, Deer Hide, (Minor Treasure)		
Elk	Male	1	50	0	25	5 Dmg		Venison, Deer Hide, (Minor Treasure)		
Elk	Female	1	50	0	25	5 Dmg		Venison, Deer Hide, (Minor Treasure)		
Goat	Wild	1	25	0	25	7 Dmg		Goat Hide, Leg of Goat, (Minor Treasure)		Resist Frost 50%
Hare		1	5	0	25	2 Dmg		Raw Rabbit Leg		
Fox		2	22	0	25	5 Dmg		Fox Pelt		
Snow Fox		2	22	0	25	5 Dmg		Snow Fox Pelt		Resist Frost 50%
Mammoth		38	931	0	424	65 Dmg		Mammoth Meat, Mammoth Tusk, (Minor Treasure)		Resist Frost 33%

Domesticated Animal (Chicken)

Wild Predator (Ice Wolf)

Wild Predator (Sabre Cat)

Wild Prey (Elk)

⚔ Bandits

Bandits are among the most common threats in Skyrim, and include members of every race.

BANDIT ARCHERS

NAME	SUBTYPE	LV	HEALTH	MAGICKA	STAMINA	WEAPONS	ARMOR	ITEMS	SPELLS	NOTES
Bandit	Archer	1	35	25	70	Bow, Arrows, Dagger	Light Cuirass, Light Boots, (Light Gauntlets)	(Gold)		
Bandit Outlaw	Archer	5	109	25	86	Bow, Arrows, Dagger	Light Cuirass, Light Boots, (Light Gauntlets)	(Gold)		
Bandit Thug	Archer	9	238	25	107	Bow, Arrows, Dagger	Light Cuirass, Light Boots, (Light Gauntlets)	(Gold)		
Bandit Highwayman	Archer	14	318	25	122	Bow, Arrows, Dagger	Light Cuirass, Light Boots, (Light Gauntlets)	(Gold)		
Bandit Plunderer	Archer	19	398	25	172	Bow, Arrows, Dagger	Light Cuirass, Light Boots, (Light Gauntlets)	Gold, (Lockpick)		
Bandit Marauder	Archer	25	489	25	246	Bow, Arrows, Dagger	Light Cuirass, Light Boots, (Light Gauntlets)	Gold, (Lockpick)		

Bandit (Berserker)

BANDIT BERSERKERS

NAME	SUBTYPE	LV	HEALTH	MAGICKA	STAMINA	WEAPONS	ARMOR	ITEMS	SPELLS	NOTES
Bandit	Berserker	1	35	25	70	2H Weapon	Light Cuirass, Light Boots, (Light Gauntlets)	(Gold), (Lockpick)		
Bandit Outlaw	Berserker	5	109	25	86	2H Weapon	Light Cuirass, Light Boots, (Light Gauntlets)	(Gold), (Lockpick)		
Bandit Thug	Berserker	9	238	25	107	2H Weapon	Light Cuirass, Light Boots, (Light Gauntlets)	(Gold), (Lockpick)		
Bandit Highwayman	Berserker	14	318	25	122	2H Weapon	Light Cuirass, Light Boots, (Light Gauntlets)	(Gold), (Lockpick)		
Bandit Plunderer	Berserker	19	398	25	172	2H Weapon, Orcish Dagger	Light Cuirass, Light Boots, (Light Gauntlets)	Gold		
Bandit Marauder	Berserker	25	489	25	246	2H Weapon, Orcish Dagger	Light Cuirass, Light Boots, (Light Gauntlets)	Gold		

Bandit (Warrior)

BANDIT GUARDIANS

NAME	SUBTYPE	LV	HEALTH	MAGICKA	STAMINA	WEAPONS	ARMOR	ITEMS	SPELLS	NOTES
Bandit	Guardian	1	35	25	70	1H Weapon	Heavy Cuirass, Heavy Boots, (Heavy Gauntlets), Heavy Helmet, Shield	(Gold), (Lockpick)		
Bandit Outlaw	Guardian	5	109	25	86	1H Weapon	Heavy Cuirass, Heavy Boots, (Heavy Gauntlets), Heavy Helmet, Shield	(Gold), (Lockpick)		
Bandit Thug	Guardian	9	238	25	107	1H Weapon	Heavy Cuirass, Heavy Boots, (Heavy Gauntlets), Heavy Helmet, Shield	(Gold), (Lockpick)		
Bandit Highwayman	Guardian	14	318	25	122	1H Weapon	Heavy Cuirass, Heavy Boots, (Heavy Gauntlets), Heavy Helmet, Shield	(Gold), (Lockpick)		
Bandit Plunderer	Guardian	19	398	25	172	1H Weapon, Orcish Dagger	Heavy Cuirass, Heavy Boots, (Heavy Gauntlets), Heavy Helmet, Shield	Gold		
Bandit Marauder	Guardian	25	489	25	246	1H Weapon, Orcish Dagger	Heavy Cuirass, Heavy Boots, (Heavy Gauntlets), Heavy Helmet, Shield	Gold		

BANDIT WARRIORS — 1H

NAME	SUBTYPE	LV	HEALTH	MAGICKA	STAMINA	WEAPONS	ARMOR	ITEMS	SPELLS	NOTES
Bandit	1H Warrior	1	35	25	70	1H Weapon	Light Cuirass, Light Boots, (Light Gauntlets), (Shield)	(Gold)		
Bandit Outlaw	1H Warrior	5	109	25	86	1H Weapon	Light Cuirass, Light Boots, (Light Gauntlets), (Shield)	(Gold)		
Bandit Thug	1H Warrior	9	238	25	107	1H Weapon	Light Cuirass, Light Boots, (Light Gauntlets), (Shield)	(Gold)		
Bandit Highwayman	1H Warrior	14	318	25	122	1H Weapon	Light Cuirass, Light Boots, (Light Gauntlets), (Shield)	(Gold)		
Bandit Plunderer	1H Warrior	19	398	25	172	1H Weapon	Light Cuirass, Light Boots, (Light Gauntlets), (Shield)	Gold		
Bandit Marauder	1H Warrior	25	489	25	246	1H Weapon	Light Cuirass, Light Boots, (Light Gauntlets), (Shield)	Gold		

Bandit (Wizard)

BANDIT WARRIORS — 2H

NAME	SUBTYPE	LV	HEALTH	MAGICKA	STAMINA	WEAPONS	ARMOR	ITEMS	SPELLS	NOTES
Bandit	2H Warrior	1	35	25	70	2H Weapon	Light Cuirass, Light Boots, (Light Gauntlets)	(Gold), (Lockpick)		
Bandit Outlaw	2H Warrior	5	109	25	86	2H Weapon	Light Cuirass, Light Boots, (Light Gauntlets)	(Gold), (Lockpick)		
Bandit Thug	2H Warrior	9	238	25	107	2H Weapon	Light Cuirass, Light Boots, (Light Gauntlets)	(Gold), (Lockpick)		
Bandit Highwayman	2H Warrior	14	318	25	122	2H Weapon	Light Cuirass, Light Boots, (Light Gauntlets)	(Gold), (Lockpick)		
Bandit Plunderer	2H Warrior	19	398	25	172	2H Weapon, Orcish Dagger	Light Cuirass, Light Boots, (Light Gauntlets)	Gold, (Lockpick)		
Bandit Marauder	2H Warrior	25	489	25	246	2H Weapon, Orcish Dagger	Light Cuirass, Light Boots, (Light Gauntlets)	Gold, (Lockpick)		

Bandit (Warrior)

BANDIT WIZARDS

NAME	SUBTYPE	LV	HEALTH	MAGICKA	STAMINA	WEAPONS	ARMOR	ITEMS	SPELLS	NOTES
Bandit	Wizard	1	35	100	50	Iron Dagger	Fur Armor, Boots	(Gold)	Healing, (Frostbite / Flames / Sparks), Oakflesh, Lesser Ward	
Bandit Outlaw	Wizard	5	101	124	70	Iron Dagger	Fur Armor, Boots	(Gold)	Healing, (Frostbite / Flames / Sparks), Oakflesh, Lesser Ward	
Bandit Thug	Wizard	9	222	173	75	Steel Dagger	Fur Armor, Boots	(Gold)	Fast Healing, Stoneflesh, (Ice Spike, Firebolt, Lightning Bolt), Steadfast Ward	
Bandit Highwayman	Wizard	14	292	153	70	Dagger	Fur Armor, Boots	(Gold)	Fast Healing, Stoneflesh, (Ice Spike, Firebolt, Lightning Bolt), Steadfast Ward	
Bandit Plunderer	Wizard	19	362	183	70	Dagger	Fur Armor, Boots	Gold, (Lockpick)	Fast Healing, Stoneflesh, (Ice Storm / Fireball / Chain Lightning), (Ice Spike, Firebolt, Lightning Bolt), Steadfast Ward	
Bandit Marauder	Wizard	25	441	294	150	Dagger	Fur Armor, Boots	Gold, (Lockpick)	Close Wounds, Fast Healing, Ironflesh, (Ice Storm / Fireball / Chain Lightning), (Ice Spike, Firebolt, Lightning Bolt), Steadfast Ward	

BANDIT CHIEFS – 1H

NAME	SUBTYPE	LV	HEALTH	MAGICKA	STAMINA	WEAPONS	ARMOR	ITEMS	SPELLS	NOTES
Bandit Chief	1H Warrior	6	155	25	95	1H Weapon, Steel Dagger	Heavy Cuirass, Heavy Boots, (Heavy Gauntlets), Heavy Helmet, Shield	Gold		
Bandit Chief	1H Warrior	10	224	25	126	1H Weapon, Steel Dagger	Heavy Cuirass, Heavy Boots, (Heavy Gauntlets), Heavy Helmet, Shield	Gold		
Bandit Chief	1H Warrior	16	315	25	160	1H Weapon, Orcish Dagger	Heavy Cuirass, Heavy Boots, (Heavy Gauntlets), Heavy Helmet, Shield	Gold		
Bandit Chief	1H Warrior	21	395	25	195	1H Weapon, Elven Dagger	Heavy Cuirass, Heavy Boots, (Heavy Gauntlets), Heavy Helmet, Shield	Gold		
Bandit Chief	1H Warrior	28	497	25	258	1H Weapon, Elven Dagger	Heavy Cuirass, Heavy Boots, (Heavy Gauntlets), (Heavy Helmet), Shield	Gold		

Bandit (Bandit Chief)

BANDIT CHIEFS – 2H

NAME	SUBTYPE	LV	HEALTH	MAGICKA	STAMINA	WEAPONS	ARMOR	ITEMS	SPELLS	NOTES
Bandit Chief	1H Warrior	6	155	25	95	2H Weapon, Steel Dagger	Heavy Cuirass, Heavy Boots, (Heavy Gauntlets), Heavy Helmet, (Shield)	Gold		
Bandit Chief	1H Warrior	10	224	25	126	2H Weapon, Steel Dagger	Heavy Cuirass, Heavy Boots, (Heavy Gauntlets), Heavy Helmet, (Shield)	Gold		
Bandit Chief	1H Warrior	16	315	25	160	2H Weapon, Orcish Dagger	Heavy Cuirass, Heavy Boots, (Heavy Gauntlets), Heavy Helmet, (Shield)	Gold		
Bandit Chief	1H Warrior	21	395	25	195	2H Weapon, Elven Dagger	Heavy Cuirass, Heavy Boots, (Heavy Gauntlets), Heavy Helmet, (Shield)	Gold		
Bandit Chief	1H Warrior	28	497	25	258	2H Weapon, Elven Dagger	Heavy Cuirass, Heavy Boots, (Heavy Gauntlets), Heavy Helmet, (Shield)	Gold		

Bandit (Bandit Chief)

▷ Chaurus

The insectoid Chaurus often fight alongside their Falmer masters. Be sure to improve your resistance to poison with potions or enchantments when you face them. Minor Treasure includes a tiny chance of: A few gold, a gem, or a ring.

CHAURUS

NAME	SUBTYPE	LV	HEALTH	MAGICKA	STAMINA	WEAPONS	ARMOR	ITEMS	SPELLS	NOTES
Chaurus		12	253	0	137	20 Dmg + Poison 5/s for 5s		Chaurus Chitin, (Chaurus Eggs), (Minor Treasure)	Poison Spit Attack	Resist Poison 50%
Chaurus Reaper		20	371	0	214	55 Dmg + Poison 7/s for 7s		Chaurus Chitin, (Chaurus Eggs), (Minor Treasure)	Poison Spit Attack	Resist Poison 50%

Chaurus

▷ Daedra

Daedra include all manner of creatures native to Oblivion, from the elemental Atronachs to the powerful Dremora. All of the Daedra in this list will be affected by Daedra-banishing spells and effects (Banish Daedra, Expel Daedra, etc.). Don't bother using Illusion spells against Daedra, but do take advantage of the Atronachs' elemental weaknesses — obviously, fire spells are best against Frost Atronachs, and frost spells against Flame Atronachs.

Note that Atronachs summoned by the common conjuration spells are generally weaker than those bound in more permanent ways (such as the ones you often find in Warlock dungeons). You can claim Daedra Hearts from the bodies of slain Dremora; these are one of the rarest ingredients in the game, and essential for smithing Daedric items.

Daedra (Dremora Lord)

DAEDRA

NAME	SUBTYPE	LV	HEALTH	MAGICKA	STAMINA	WEAPONS	ARMOR	ITEMS	SPELLS	NOTES
Familiar	Conjured	2	32	0	205	5 Dmg				
Flame Atronach	Conjured	5	111	174	50	5 Dmg + 10 Fire			Firebolt	Immune to Fire, Weak to Frost 33%, Flame Cloak, Waterwalking, Death Explosion (Flame)
Flame Atronach		5	111	174	50	5 Dmg + 10 Fire		Flame Salts	Firebolt	Immune to Fire, Weak to Frost 33%, Flame Cloak, Waterwalking, Death Explosion (Flame)
Frost Atronach	Conjured	16	300	25	125	20 Dmg + 25 Frost				Immune to Frost, Weak to Fire 33%, Frost Cloak, Waterbreathing, Death Explosion (Frost)
Frost Atronach		16	400	25	250	20 Dmg + 25 Frost		Frost Salts		Immune to Frost, Weak to Fire 33%, Frost Cloak, Waterbreathing, Death Explosion (Frost)
Storm Atronach	Conjured	30	241	197	147	30 Dmg + 20 Shock			Chain Lightning, Lightning Bolt	Immune to Shock, Shock Cloak, Waterwalking, Death Explosion (Shock)
Storm Atronach		30	441	197	247	30 Dmg + 20 Shock		Void Salts	Chain Lightning, Lightning Bolt	Immune to Shock, Shock Cloak, Waterwalking, Death Explosion (Shock)

DAEDRA (CONTINUED)

NAME	SUBTYPE	LV	HEALTH	MAGICKA	STAMINA	WEAPONS	ARMOR	ITEMS	SPELLS	NOTES
Dremora		25*	289	25	121	Sword, Iron Dagger	[Dremora Armor]	Daedra Heart	Conjure Flame Atronach, Fire Storm, Wall of Flames	
Dremora Lord	Conjured	30	491	247	197	[Daedric Mace of the Inferno]	[Dremora Armor]		Firebolt, Flame Cloak, Incinerate, Steadfast Ward	
Dremora		25*	289	25	121	Sword, Iron Dagger	[Dremora Armor]	Daedra Heart	Conjure Flame Atronach, Fire Storm, Wall of Flames	
Dremora Churl		6	92	183	50	(1H/2H Weapon), Iron Dagger	[Dremora Robes]	Daedra Heart	Fast Healing, Flames, Oakflesh, Lesser Ward	
Dremora Caitiff		12	142	223	50	(1H/2H Weapon), Iron Dagger	[Dremora Robes]	Daedra Heart	Fast Healing, Firebolt, Stoneflesh, Lesser Ward	
Dremora Kynval		19	200	270	50	(1H/2H Weapon), Iron Dagger	[Dremora Robes]	Daedra Heart	Close Wounds, Fireball, Firebolt, Flame Cloak, Stoneflesh, Steadfast Ward	
Dremora Kynreeve		27	267	323	50	(1H/2H Weapon), Iron Dagger	[Dremora Robes]	Daedra Heart	Close Wounds, Fireball, Firebolt, Flame Cloak, Ironflesh, Steadfast Ward	
Dremora Markynaz		36	342	383	50	(1H/2H Weapon), Iron Dagger	[Dremora Robes]	Daedra Heart	Close Wounds, Fireball, Flame Cloak, Incinerate, Ironflesh, Steadfast Ward	
Dremora Valkynaz		46	425	450	50	(1H/2H Weapon), Iron Dagger	[Dremora Robes]	Daedra Heart	Close Wounds, Fireball, Flame Cloak, Incinerate, Ironflesh, Steadfast Ward	

Dragons

Dragons are among the most formidable enemies, with vast reserves of health. Stay on the move when fighting a dragon—patience and ranged attacks are best. Dragon Loot includes a chance of: Dragon Bones, Dragon Scales, Gold, Gems, Weapons, or Armor; Dragons usually have several of these items. If you intend to smith Dragon armor, make sure to save a couple dozen Dragon Scales, or a few Dragon Bones.

Blood Dragon

Ancient Dragon

DRAGONS

NAME	SUBTYPE	LV	HEALTH	MAGICKA	STAMINA	WEAPONS	ARMOR	ITEMS	SPELLS	NOTES
Dragon	Brown, Fire	10	905	150	130	Bite, 37 Dmg		(Dragon Loot), Dragon Bone, Dragon Scales	Fire Breath Shout, Fireball Shout	Resist Fire 50%, Weak to Frost 25%
Dragon	Brown, Frost	10	905	150	130	Bite, 37 Dmg		(Dragon Loot), Dragon Bone, Dragon Scales	Frost Breath Shout, Ice Storm Shout	Resist Frost 50%, Weak to Fire 25%
Blood Dragon	Green, Fire	20	1421	150	164	Bite, 75 Dmg		(Dragon Loot), Dragon Bone, Dragon Scales	Fire Breath Shout, Fireball Shout, Unrelenting Force Shout	Resist Fire 50%, Weak to Frost 25%
Blood Dragon	Green, Frost	20	1421	150	164	Bite, 75 Dmg		(Dragon Loot), Dragon Bone, Dragon Scales	Frost Breath Shout, Ice Storm Shout	Resist Frost 50%, Weak to Fire 25%
Frost Dragon	White, Frost	30	1860	150	197	Bite, 150 Dmg		(Dragon Loot), Dragon Bone, Dragon Scales	Frost Breath Shout, Ice Storm Shout, Unrelenting Force Shout	Resist Frost 50%, Weak to Fire 25%
Elder Dragon	Bronze, Fire	40	2255	150	230	Bite, 225 Dmg		(Dragon Loot), Dragon Bone, Dragon Scales	Fire Breath Shout, Fireball Shout, Unrelenting Force Shout	Resist Fire 50%, Weak to Frost 25%
Elder Dragon	Bronze, Frost	40	2255	150	230	Bite, 225 Dmg		(Dragon Loot), Dragon Bone, Dragon Scales	Frost Breath Shout, Ice Storm Shout, Unrelenting Force Shout	Resist Frost 50%, Weak to Fire 25%
Ancient Dragon	Red/Black, Fire	50	3071	150	264	Bite, 300 Dmg		(Dragon Loot), Dragon Bone, Dragon Scales	Fire Breath Shout, Fireball Shout, Unrelenting Force Shout	Resist Fire 50%, Weak to Frost 25%
Ancient Dragon	Red/Black, Frost	50	3071	150	264	Bite, 300 Dmg		(Dragon Loot), Dragon Bone, Dragon Scales	Frost Breath Shout, Ice Storm Shout, Unrelenting Force Shout	Resist Frost 50%, Weak to Fire 25%

ALDUIN

NAME	SUBTYPE	LV	HEALTH	MAGICKA	STAMINA	WEAPONS	ARMOR	ITEMS	SPELLS	NOTES
Alduin	Alduin's Bane	20*	2471	50	114	Bite, 75 Dmg			Meteor Storm Shout, Unrelenting Force Shout, Fire Breath Shout, Frost Breath Shout, Fireball Shout, Ice Storm Shout	Resist Fire 50%, Weak to Frost 25%. This is Alduin as he appears during Main Quest: Alduin's Bane. Alduin is invulnerable unless weakened by the Dragonrend Shout.
Alduin	Dragonslayer	20*	2671	50	114	Bite, 75 Dmg			Meteor Storm Shout, Unrelenting Force Shout, Fire Breath Shout, Frost Breath Shout, Fireball Shout, Ice Storm Shout	Resist Fire 50%, Weak to Frost 25%. This is Alduin as he appears during Main Quest: Dragonslayer. Alduin is invulnerable unless weakened by the Dragonrend Shout.
Alduin	Dragonslayer	40*	2905	50	180	Bite, 75 Dmg				See above; this just illustrates his stats at a different level.
Alduin	Dragonslayer	60*	3138	50	247	Bite, 75 Dmg				See above; this just illustrates his stats at a different level.

Draugr

Draugr are among the most common foes in Skyrim's many crypts and catacombs. Fire is your best weapon against them. High-level Draugr, like Dragon Priests and Deathlords, are especially deadly foes—don't go toe-to-toe with Deathlords unless your damage rating is exceptionally high. Draugr Loot includes a chance of jewelry, gems, soul gems, ingots, or potions. Note that you can't loot their armor (would you really want it?).

Draugr (Draugr Wight)

Draugr (Draugr Deathlord)

Draugr (Dragon Priest)

DRAUGR ARCHERS

NAME	SUBTYPE	LV	HEALTH	MAGICKA	STAMINA	WEAPONS	ARMOR	ITEMS	SPELLS	NOTES
Draugr	Archer	1	50	0	80	Ancient Nord Bow, Ancient Nord Arrows, Ancient Nord War Axe	[Draugr Armor]	Draugr Loot		Immune to Poison, Resist Frost 50%
Restless Draugr	Archer	6	175	0	205	Ancient Nord Bow, Ancient Nord Arrows, Ancient Nord War Axe	[Draugr Armor]	Draugr Loot		Immune to Poison, Resist Frost 50%
Draugr Wight	Archer	13	400	0	340	Ancient Nord Bow, Ancient Nord Arrows, Ancient Nord War Axe	[Draugr Armor]	Draugr Loot		Immune to Poison, Resist Frost 50%
Draugr Scourge	Archer	21	900	0	480	Ancient Nord Bow, Ancient Nord Arrows, Ancient Nord War Axe	[Draugr Armor]	Draugr Loot	Unrelenting Force Shout	Immune to Poison, Resist Frost 50%
Draugr Deathlord	Archer	30	1000	10	575	Ancient Nord Bow, Orcish Arrows, Ancient Nord War Axe	[Draugr Armor]	Draugr Loot	Frost Cloak, Disarm Shout, Unrelenting Force Shout	Immune to Poison, Resist Frost 50%
Draugr Deathlord	Archer	40	1300	10	625	Ebony Bow, Ebony Arrows, Ancient Nord War Axe	[Draugr Armor]	Draugr Loot	Frost Cloak, Disarm Shout, Unrelenting Force Shout	Immune to Poison, Resist Frost 50%

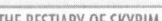

DRAUGR WARRIORS – 1H

NAME	SUBTYPE	LV	HEALTH	MAGICKA	STAMINA	WEAPONS	ARMOR	ITEMS	SPELLS	NOTES
Draugr	1H Warrior	1	50	0	80	1H Ancient Nord Weapon	[Draugr Armor], (Iron Shield)	Draugr Loot		Immune to Poison, Resist Frost 50%
Restless Draugr	1H Warrior	6	150	0	204	1H Ancient Nord Weapon	[Draugr Armor], (Iron Shield)	Draugr Loot		Immune to Poison, Resist Frost 50%
Draugr Wight	1H Warrior	13	320	0	340	1H Ancient Nord Weapon	[Draugr Armor], (Iron Shield)	Draugr Loot		Immune to Poison, Resist Frost 50%
Draugr Scourge	1H Warrior	21	700	0	480	1H Ancient Nord Weapon	[Draugr Armor], (Iron Shield)	Draugr Loot	Unrelenting Force Shout	Immune to Poison, Resist Frost 50%
Draugr Deathlord	1H Warrior	30	1000	10	575	1H Ebony Weapon	[Draugr Armor], (Iron Shield)	Draugr Loot	Frost Cloak, Disarm Shout, Unrelenting Force Shout	Immune to Poison, Resist Frost 50%
Draugr Deathlord	1H Warrior	30	1000	10	575	1H Ebony Weapon	[Draugr Armor], (Ebony Shield)	Draugr Loot	Frost Cloak, Disarm Shout, Unrelenting Force Shout	Immune to Poison, Resist Frost 50%

DRAUGR WARRIORS – 2H

NAME	SUBTYPE	LV	HEALTH	MAGICKA	STAMINA	WEAPONS	ARMOR	ITEMS	SPELLS	NOTES
Draugr	2H Warrior	1	50	0	80	2H Ancient Nord Weapon	[Draugr Armor]	Draugr Loot		Immune to Poison, Resist Frost 50%
Restless Draugr	2H Warrior	6	150	0	204	2H Ancient Nord Weapon	[Draugr Armor]	Draugr Loot		Immune to Poison, Resist Frost 50%
Draugr Wight	2H Warrior	13	320	0	340	2H Ancient Nord Weapon	[Draugr Armor]	Draugr Loot		Immune to Poison, Resist Frost 50%
Draugr Scourge	2H Warrior	21	700	0	480	2H Ancient Nord Weapon	[Draugr Armor]	Draugr Loot	Unrelenting Force Shout	Immune to Poison, Resist Frost 50%
Draugr Deathlord	2H Warrior	30	1000	10	575	2H Ancient Nord Weapon	[Draugr Armor]	Draugr Loot	Frost Cloak, Disarm Shout, Unrelenting Force Shout	Immune to Poison, Resist Frost 50%
Draugr Deathlord	2H Warrior	30	1000	10	575	2H Ebony Weapon	[Draugr Armor]	Draugr Loot	Frost Cloak, Disarm Shout, Unrelenting Force Shout	Immune to Poison, Resist Frost 50%

DRAUGR WARLOCKS

NAME	SUBTYPE	LV	HEALTH	MAGICKA	STAMINA	WEAPONS	ARMOR	ITEMS	SPELLS	NOTES
Restless Draugr	2H Warrior	6	150	50	180	1H Ancient Nord Weapon	[Draugr Armor]	Draugr Loot	Frostbite	Immune to Poison, Resist Frost 50%
Draugr Wight	2H Warrior	13	490	100	280	1H Ancient Nord Weapon	[Draugr Armor]	Draugr Loot	Frostbite, Ice Spike	Immune to Poison, Resist Frost 50%
Draugr Scourge	2H Warrior	21	700	160	380	1H Ancient Nord Weapon	[Draugr Armor]	Draugr Loot	Conjure Frost Atronach, Frostbite, Ice Spike	Immune to Poison, Resist Frost 50%

DRAUGR OVERLORDS

NAME	SUBTYPE	LV	HEALTH	MAGICKA	STAMINA	WEAPONS	ARMOR	ITEMS	SPELLS	NOTES
Draugr Overlord		7	210	0	260	1H/2H Enchanted Ancient Nord Weapon	[Draugr Armor], (Iron Shield)	Draugr Loot	Unrelenting Force Shout	Immune to Poison, Resist Frost 50%
Draugr Wight Overlord		15	490	0	450	1H/2H Enchanted Ancient Nord Weapon	[Draugr Armor], (Iron Shield)	Draugr Loot	Disarm Shout, Unrelenting Force Shout	Immune to Poison, Resist Frost 50%
Draugr Scourge Lord		24	880	0	595	1H/2H Enchanted Ancient Nord Weapon	[Draugr Armor], (Iron Shield)	Draugr Loot	Disarm Shout, Unrelenting Force Shout, Frost Breath Shout	Immune to Poison, Resist Frost 50%
Draugr Death Overlord		34	1290	10	645	1H/2H Enchanted Ancient Nord Weapon	[Draugr Armor], (Iron Shield)	Draugr Loot	Frost Cloak, Disarm Shout, Unrelenting Force Shout, Frost Breath Shout	Immune to Poison, Resist Frost 50%
Draugr Death Overlord		45	1400	10	700	1H/2H Ebony Weapon	[Draugr Armor], (Iron Shield)	Draugr Loot	Frost Cloak, Disarm Shout, Unrelenting Force Shout, Frost Breath Shout	Immune to Poison, Resist Frost 50%

DRAGON PRIESTS

NAME	SUBTYPE	LV	HEALTH	MAGICKA	STAMINA	WEAPONS	ARMOR	ITEMS	SPELLS	NOTES
Dragon Priest	Fire	50	1490	545	0		[Dragon Priest Robes]	Bone Meal, Gold	Greater Ward, Conjure Flame Atronach, Fireball, Ebonyflesh, Command Daedra, Incinerate	Immune to Poison
Dragon Priest	Frost	50	1490	545	0		[Dragon Priest Robes]	Bone Meal, Gold	Ice Storm, Greater Ward, Conjure Frost Atronach, Command Daedra, Ebonyflesh, Icy Spear	Immune to Poison
Dragon Priest	Shock	50	1490	545	0		[Dragon Priest Robes]	Bone Meal, Gold	Greater Ward, Conjure Storm Atronach, Chain Lightning, Thunderbolt, Command Daedra, Ebonyflesh	Immune to Poison

▷ Dwarven Automatons

Dwarven Automatons are the mechanical constructs left behind by the Dwarves who once inhabited Skyrim. As constructs, Automatons are immune to poison, Illusion spells, and Frost spells, and Soul Trap. Dwarven Loot includes a chance of: arrows, scrap metal, oil, ore, gems, or soul gems. Spheres give more (and more valuable) loot than Spiders, and Centurions more than Spheres.

DWARVEN SPIDERS

NAME	SUBTYPE	LV	HEALTH	MAGICKA	STAMINA	WEAPONS	ARMOR	ITEMS	SPELLS	NOTES
Dwarven Spider Worker		12	125	3	120	11 Dmg		Dwarven Loot	Electrical Shock	Immune to Poison, Immune to Frost, Resist Magic 25%
Dwarven Spider		16	175	3	160	15 Dmg		Dwarven Loot	Electrical Shock	Explode on death (shock damage). Immune to Poison, Immune to Frost, Resist Magic 25%
Dwarven Spider Guardian		22	225	3	200	22 Dmg		Dwarven Loot	Electrical Shock	Explode on death (shock damage). Immune to Poison, Immune to Frost, Resist Magic 25%

Dwarven Automatons (Centurion)

DWARVEN SPHERES

NAME	SUBTYPE	LV	HEALTH	MAGICKA	STAMINA	WEAPONS	ARMOR	ITEMS	SPELLS	NOTES
Dwarven Sphere		16	315	0	170	55 Dmg		Dwarven Loot		Immune to Poison, Immune to Frost, Resist Magic 25%
Dwarven Sphere Guardian		24	453	0	262	55 Dmg		Dwarven Loot		Immune to Poison, Immune to Frost, Resist Magic 25%
Dwarven Sphere Master		30	619	0	301	82 Dmg		Dwarven Loot		Immune to Poison, Immune to Frost, Resist Magic 25%

DWARVEN CENTURION

NAME	SUBTYPE	LV	HEALTH	MAGICKA	STAMINA	WEAPONS	ARMOR	ITEMS	SPELLS	NOTES
Dwarven Centurion		24	653	15	292	75 Dmg		Dwarven Loot	Steam Breath	Immune to Poison, Immune to Frost, Resist Magic 25%
Dwarven Centurion Guardian		30	819	15	416	100 Dmg		Dwarven Loot	Steam Breath	Immune to Poison, Immune to Frost, Resist Magic 25%
Dwarven Centurion Master		36	1000	15	540	112 Dmg		Dwarven Loot	Steam Breath	Immune to Poison, Immune to Frost, Resist Magic 25%

Falmer

Falmer inhabit the deep caves and dwarven ruins of Skyrim, often accompanied by pet Chaurus or Spiders. Most poison their weapons for added damage. Since Falmer are blind, you can use light spells and torches without being detected. They have excellent hearing, though, so keep your distance and move slowly if you plan a stealthy approach. Falmer Loot includes a chance of: Falmer Ears, Poisons, or Gold.

Falmer (Shadowmaster)

FALMER ARCHER

NAME	SUBTYPE	LV	HEALTH	MAGICKA	STAMINA	WEAPONS	ARMOR	ITEMS	SPELLS	NOTES
Falmer	Archer	9	180	177	163	Falmer Bow, Falmer Sword, Falmer Arrows, (Arrows)		Falmer Loot, Gold		5 Poison Damage / 3s on hit.
Falmer Skulker	Archer	15	290	247	198	Falmer Bow, Falmer Arrows, (Arrows)		Falmer Loot, Gold		6 Poison Damage / 3s on hit.
Falmer Gloomlurker	Archer	22	410	220	210	Falmer Bow, Falmer Arrows, (Arrows)	Falmer Helmet	Falmer Loot, Gold		7 Poison Damage / 3s on hit.
Falmer Nightprowler	Archer	30	550	197	300	Falmer Bow, Falmer Arrows, (Arrows)	Falmer Helmet	Falmer Loot, Gold		9 Poison Damage / 3s on hit.
Falmer Shadowmaster	Archer	38	700	273	362	Falmer Bow, Falmer Arrows, (Arrows)	Falmer Helmet	Falmer Loot, Gold		12 Poison Damage / 3s on hit.

FALMER SHAMAN

NAME	SUBTYPE	LV	HEALTH	MAGICKA	STAMINA	WEAPONS	ARMOR	ITEMS	SPELLS	NOTES
Falmer	Shaman	5	133	120	157			Falmer Loot, Gold	Bound Sword, Fast Healing, Ice Spike, Oakflesh, Sparks, Lesser Ward	
Falmer Skulker	Shaman	8	183	185	187			Falmer Loot, Gold	Bound Sword, Frostbite, Lightning Bolt, Stoneflesh, Steadfast Ward	
Falmer Gloomlurker	Shaman	14	258	265	197			Falmer Loot, Gold	Bound Sword, Fast Healing, Frostbite, Ice Spike	Lightning Cloak, Steadfast Ward
Falmer Nightprowler	Shaman	19	350	340	230			Falmer Loot, Gold	Bound Sword, Fast Healing, Ice Spike, Sparks, Stoneflesh, Steadfast Ward	
Falmer Shadowmaster	Shaman	25	400	420	240			Falmer Loot, Gold	Bound Sword, Fast Healing, Frost Cloak, Ironflesh, Lightning Bolt, Steadfast Ward	

FALMER SPELLSWORDS

NAME	SUBTYPE	LV	HEALTH	MAGICKA	STAMINA	WEAPONS	ARMOR	ITEMS	SPELLS	NOTES
Falmer	Spellsword	9	180	177	163	1H Falmer Weapon		Falmer Loot, Gold	Frostbite, Healing	5 Poison Damage / 3s on hit.
Falmer Skulker	Spellsword	15	290	247	198	1H Falmer Weapon		Falmer Loot, Gold	Healing, Ice Spike, Sparks	6 Poison Damage / 3s on hit.
Falmer Gloomlurker	Spellsword	22	410	220	210	1H Falmer Weapon	Falmer Helmet	Falmer Loot, Gold	Frostbite, Frost Cloak, Healing, Lightning Bolt	7 Poison Damage / 3s on hit.
Falmer Nightprowler	Spellsword	30	550	197	300	1H Falmer Weapon	Falmer Helmet	Falmer Loot, Gold	Chain Lightning, Healing, Ice Spike, Sparks	9 Poison Damage / 3s on hit.
Falmer Shadowmaster	Spellsword	38	700	273	362	1H Falmer Weapon	Falmer Helmet	Falmer Loot, Gold	Chain Lightning, Healing, Ice Spike, Wall of Frost	12 Poison Damage / 3s on hit.

FALMER WARRIORS

NAME	SUBTYPE	LV	HEALTH	MAGICKA	STAMINA	WEAPONS	ARMOR	ITEMS	SPELLS	NOTES
Falmer	Warrior	9	180	177	163	1H Falmer Weapon	Falmer Shield	Falmer Loot, Gold		5 Poison Damage / 3s on hit.
Falmer Skulker	Warrior	15	290	247	198	1H Falmer Weapon	Falmer Shield	Falmer Loot, (Retore Health Potion), Gold		6 Poison Damage / 3s on hit.
Falmer Gloomlurker	Warrior	22	410	220	210	1H Falmer Weapon	Falmer Helmet, Falmer Shield	Falmer Loot, (Retore Health Potion), Gold		7 Poison Damage / 3s on hit.
Falmer Nightprowler	Warrior	30	550	197	300	1H Falmer Weapon	Falmer Helmet, Falmer Shield	Falmer Loot, (Retore Health Potion), Gold		9 Poison Damage / 3s on hit.
Falmer Shadowmaster	Warrior	38	700	273	362	1H Falmer Weapon	Falmer Helmet, Falmer Shield	Falmer Loot, Restore Health Potion, Gold		12 Poison Damage / 3s on hit.

FALMER BOSS – SPELLSWORD

NAME	SUBTYPE	LV	HEALTH	MAGICKA	STAMINA	WEAPONS	ARMOR	ITEMS	SPELLS	NOTES
Falmer Skulker	Spellsword	18	370	257	203	1H Falmer Weapon		Falmer Loot, Gold	Healing, Ice Spike, Sparks	6 Poison Damage / 3s on hit.
Falmer Gloomlurker	Spellsword	26	500	283	242	1H Falmer Weapon	Falmer Helmet	Falmer Loot, Gold	Frostbite, Frost Cloak, Healing, Lightning Bolt	7 Poison Damage / 3s on hit.
Falmer Nightprowler	Spellsword	35	640	313	307	1H Falmer Weapon	Falmer Helmet	Falmer Loot, Gold	Chain Lightning, Healing, Ice Spike, Sparks	9 Poison Damage / 3s on hit.
Falmer Shadowmaster	Spellsword	44	830	403	272	1H Falmer Weapon	Falmer Helmet	Falmer Loot, Gold	Chain Lightning, Healing, Ice Spike, Wall of Frost	12 Poison Damage / 3s on hit.

FALMER BOSS – WARRIOR

NAME	SUBTYPE	LV	HEALTH	MAGICKA	STAMINA	WEAPONS	ARMOR	ITEMS	SPELLS	NOTES
Falmer Skulker	Spellsword	18	370	182	228	1H Falmer Weapon	Falmer Shield	Falmer Loot, Gold	Healing	6 Poison Damage / 3s on hit.
Falmer Gloomlurker	Spellsword	26	500	233	242	1H Falmer Weapon	Falmer Helmet, Falmer Shield	Falmer Loot, Gold	Healing	7 Poison Damage / 3s on hit.
Falmer Nightprowler	Spellsword	35	640	213	357	1H Falmer Weapon	Falmer Helmet, Falmer Shield	Falmer Loot, Gold	Healing	9 Poison Damage / 3s on hit.
Falmer Shadowmaster	Spellsword	44	830	293	372	1H Falmer Weapon	Falmer Helmet, Falmer Shield	Falmer Loot, Gold	Healing	12 Poison Damage / 3s on hit.

◗ Forsworn

The tribal natives of the Reach, Forsworn revere Hagravens and fight to drive invaders from their lands. Forsworn Wizard Loot includes a chance of ingredients, potions, soul gems, or a forsworn weapon.

FORSWORN ARCHER

Forsworn (Berserker)

NAME	SUBTYPE	LV	HEALTH	MAGICKA	STAMINA	WEAPONS	ARMOR	ITEMS	SPELLS	NOTES
Forsworn	Archer	1	50	50	50	Forsworn Bow, Forsworn Arrows, Dagger	Forsworn Cuirass, Forsworn Boots, (Forsworn Helmet), (Forsworn Gauntlets)	(Gold)	Healing	
Forsworn Forager	Archer	6	95	60	70	Forsworn Bow, Forsworn Arrows, Dagger	Forsworn Cuirass, Forsworn Boots, (Forsworn Helmet), (Forsworn Gauntlets)	(Gold)	Healing	
Forsworn Looter	Archer	14	192	76	152	Forsworn Bow, Forsworn Arrows, Dagger	Forsworn Cuirass, Forsworn Boots, (Forsworn Helmet), (Forsworn Gauntlets)	(Gold)	Fast Healing	
Forsworn Pillager	Archer	24	357	96	192	Forsworn Bow, Forsworn Arrows, Dagger	Forsworn Cuirass, Forsworn Boots, (Forsworn Helmet), (Forsworn Gauntlets)	(Gold)	Fast Healing	
Forsworn Ravager	Archer	34	447	116	182	Forsworn Bow, Forsworn Arrows, Dagger	Forsworn Cuirass, Forsworn Boots, (Forsworn Helmet), (Forsworn Gauntlets)	(Gold)	Fast Healing	
Forsworn Warlord	Archer	46	455	140	230	Forsworn Bow, Forsworn Arrows, Dagger	Forsworn Cuirass, Forsworn Boots, (Forsworn Helmet), (Forsworn Gauntlets)	(Gold)	Close Wounds	

FORSWORN BERSERKERS

NAME	SUBTYPE	LV	HEALTH	MAGICKA	STAMINA	WEAPONS	ARMOR	ITEMS	SPELLS	NOTES
Forsworn	Berserker	1	50	50	50	2x (Forsworn Axe / Forsworn Sword)	Forsworn Cuirass, Forsworn Boots, (Forsworn Helmet), (Forsworn Gauntlets)	(Gold)		
Forsworn Forager	Berserker	6	95	70	85	2x (Forsworn Axe / Forsworn Sword)	Forsworn Cuirass, Forsworn Boots, (Forsworn Helmet), (Forsworn Gauntlets)	(Gold)		
Forsworn Looter	Berserker	14	192	102	126	2x (Forsworn Axe / Forsworn Sword)	Forsworn Cuirass, Forsworn Boots, (Forsworn Helmet), (Forsworn Gauntlets)	(Gold)		
Forsworn Pillager	Berserker	24	357	142	146	2x (Forsworn Axe / Forsworn Sword)	Forsworn Cuirass, Forsworn Boots, (Forsworn Helmet), (Forsworn Gauntlets)	(Gold)		
Forsworn Ravager	Berserker	34	447	182	116	2x (Forsworn Axe / Forsworn Sword)	Forsworn Cuirass, Forsworn Boots, (Forsworn Helmet), (Forsworn Gauntlets)	(Gold)		
Forsworn Warlord	Berserker	46	455	230	140	2x (Forsworn Axe / Forsworn Sword)	Forsworn Cuirass, Forsworn Boots, (Forsworn Helmet), (Forsworn Gauntlets)	(Gold)		

FORSWORN SHAMAN

Forsworn (Shaman)

NAME	SUBTYPE	LV	HEALTH	MAGICKA	STAMINA	WEAPONS	ARMOR	ITEMS	SPELLS	NOTES
Forsworn	Shaman	1	50	100	50	Dagger	Forsworn Cuirass, Forsworn Boots, (Forsworn Helmet), (Forsworn Gauntlets)	Forsworn Wizard Loot	Flames, Healing, Lesser Ward	
Forsworn Forager	Shaman	6	95	130	50	Dagger	Forsworn Cuirass, Forsworn Boots, (Forsworn Helmet), (Forsworn Gauntlets)	Forsworn Wizard Loot	Conjure Flame Atronach, Flames, Healing, Lesser Ward	
Forsworn Looter	Shaman	14	192	178	50	Dagger	Forsworn Cuirass, Forsworn Boots, (Forsworn Helmet), (Forsworn Gauntlets)	Forsworn Wizard Loot	Conjure Flame Atronach, Firebolt, Flames, Healing, Lesser Ward	
Forsworn Pillager	Shaman	24	357	288	50	Dagger	Forsworn Cuirass, Forsworn Boots, (Forsworn Helmet), (Forsworn Gauntlets)	Forsworn Wizard Loot	Conjure Frost Atronach, Fast Healing, Ice Spike, Ice Storm, Stoneflesh, Steadfast Ward	
Forsworn Ravager	Shaman	34	447	248	50	Dagger	Forsworn Cuirass, Forsworn Boots, (Forsworn Helmet), (Forsworn Gauntlets)	Forsworn Wizard Loot	Conjure Frost Atronach, Frost Cloak, Ice Spike, Ice Storm, Icy Spear, Stoneflesh, Steadfast Ward	
Forsworn Warlord	Shaman	46	455	320	50	Dagger	Forsworn Cuirass, Forsworn Boots, (Forsworn Helmet), (Forsworn Gauntlets)	Forsworn Wizard Loot	Chain Lightning, Close Wounds, Conjure Storm Atronach, Expel Daedra, Ironflesh, Lightning Bolt, Lightning Cloak, Thunderbolt, Greater Ward	

FORSWORN BOSS – BERSERKER

Forsworn (Briarheart)

NAME	SUBTYPE	LV	HEALTH	MAGICKA	STAMINA	WEAPONS	ARMOR	ITEMS	SPELLS	NOTES
Forsworn Briarheart	Warrior	7	104	74	112	2x 1H Forsworn Weapon	[Briarheart Armor], Forsworn Boots, Forsworn Helmet	(Gold), Briarheart		
Forsworn Briarheart	Warrior	16	235	110	130	2x 1H Forsworn Weapon	[Briarheart Armor], Forsworn Boots, Forsworn Helmet	(Gold), Briarheart		
Forsworn Briarheart	Warrior	27	434	154	152	2x 1H Forsworn Weapon	[Briarheart Armor], Forsworn Boots, Forsworn Helmet	(Gold), Briarheart		
Forsworn Briarheart	Warrior	38	533	198	174	2x 1H Forsworn Weapon	[Briarheart Armor], Forsworn Boots, Forsworn Helmet	(Gold), Briarheart		
Forsworn Briarheart	Warrior	51	623	350	195	2x 1H Forsworn Weapon	[Briarheart Armor], Forsworn Boots, Forsworn Helmet	(Gold), Briarheart		

FORSWORN BOSS — SHAMAN

NAME	SUBTYPE	LV	HEALTH	MAGICKA	STAMINA	WEAPONS	ARMOR	ITEMS	SPELLS	NOTES
Forsworn Briarheart	Shaman	7	104	86	50	Dagger	[Briarheart Armor], Forsworn Boots, Forsworn Helmet	Forsworn Wizard Loot, Briarheart	Conjure Flame Atronach, Flames, Healing, Lesser Ward	
Forsworn Briarheart	Shaman	16	235	110	50	Dagger	[Briarheart Armor], Forsworn Boots, Forsworn Helmet	Forsworn Wizard Loot, Briarheart	Conjure Flame Atronach, Firebolt, Flames, Healing, Lesser Ward	
Forsworn Briarheart	Shaman	27	434	306	50	Dagger	[Briarheart Armor], Forsworn Boots, Forsworn Helmet	Forsworn Wizard Loot, Briarheart	Conjure Frost Atronach, Fast Healing, Ice Spike, Ice Storm, Stoneflesh, Steadfast Ward	
Forsworn Briarheart	Shaman	38	533	272	50	Dagger	[Briarheart Armor], Forsworn Boots, Forsworn Helmet	Forsworn Wizard Loot, Briarheart	Conjure Frost Atronach, Frost Cloak, Ice Spike, Ice Storm, Icy Spear, Stoneflesh, Steadfast Ward	
Forsworn Briarheart	Shaman	51	620	350	50	Dagger	[Briarheart Armor], Forsworn Boots, Forsworn Helmet	Forsworn Wizard Loot, Briarheart	Chain Lightning, Close Wounds, Conjure Storm Atronach, Expel Daedra, Ironflesh, Lightning Bolt, Lightning Cloak, Thunderbolt, Greater Ward	

▷ Frostbite Spiders

Frostbite Spiders are giant arachnids often found in Skyrim's caves and ruins. They have a dangerous poison spit attack, though their bite is just as poisonous—try to keep your distance and focus on ranged attacks. Despite their name, they are not actually resistant to frost. The white variety of spiders is somewhat tougher than the red variety for each size category. Minor Treasure includes a tiny chance of: A few gold, a gem, or a ring.

CHAURUS

NAME	SUBTYPE	LV	HEALTH	MAGICKA	STAMINA	WEAPONS	ARMOR	ITEMS	SPELLS	NOTES
Frostbite Spider	Small, Red	1	15	0	25	5 Dmg + Poison 3/s for 3s		Frostbite Venom, (Minor Treasure)	Poison Spit Attack	
Frostbite Spider	Small, White	3	35	0	35	5 Dmg + Poison 3/s for 3s		Frostbite Venom, (Minor Treasure)	Poison Spit Attack	
Frostbite Spider	Large, Red	6	150	0	200	15 Dmg + Poison 5/s for 3s		Frostbite Venom, (Minor Treasure)	Poison Spit Attack	
Frostbite Spider	Large, White	8	220	0	235	15 Dmg + Poison 5/s for 3s		Frostbite Venom, (Minor Treasure)	Poison Spit Attack	
Giant Frostbite Spider	Giant, Red	14	380	0	315	45 Dmg + Poison 10/s for 3s		2x Frostbite Venom, (Minor Treasure)	Poison Spit Attack	
Giant Frostbite Spider	Giant, White	17	510	0	430	45 Dmg + Poison 10/s for 3s		2x Frostbite Venom, (Minor Treasure)	Poison Spit Attack	

Frostbite Spider

▷ Giants

The nomadic Giants shepherd their mammoth herds across the Tundra of central Skyrim. They are generally peaceful if left alone. If you decide to fight them, don't let them get within melee range—they are deceptively fast, so don't get caught in the open. Giant Loot typically includes several of: Giant Toes, Giant Weapons, Giant Armor, Gold, Gems, Soul Gems, and Animal Parts.

GIANT

NAME	SUBTYPE	LV	HEALTH	MAGICKA	STAMINA	WEAPONS	ARMOR	ITEMS	SPELLS	NOTES
Giant		32	591	0	374	[Giant Club] 60 Dmg		Giant Toe, (Giant Loot)	Giant Stomp	Resist Magic 33%

Giant

▷ Hagravens

Witches who surrender their humanity become Hagravens, creatures of corruption and decay revered by the Forsworn of the Reach. Before fighting them, do what you can to bolster your fire resistance. Warriors should close to melee range rather than try to take them on at a distance.

HAGRAVENS

NAME	SUBTYPE	LV	HEALTH	MAGICKA	STAMINA	WEAPONS	ARMOR	ITEMS	SPELLS	NOTES
Hagraven		20	471	314	50			Hagraven Feathers	Close Wounds, Fast Healing, Fireball, Firebolt	

Hagraven

▷ Horses

HORSES

NAME	SUBTYPE	LV	HEALTH	MAGICKA	STAMINA	WEAPONS	ARMOR	ITEMS	SPELLS	NOTES
Horse	Black	4	289	0	106			Horse Meat, Horse Hide, (Minor Treasure)		
Horse	Paint	4	289	0	106			Horse Meat, Horse Hide, (Minor Treasure)		
Horse	Brown	4	289	0	106			Horse Meat, Horse Hide, (Minor Treasure)		
Horse	Grey	4	289	0	106			Horse Meat, Horse Hide, (Minor Treasure)		
Horse	Palomino	4	289	0	106			Horse Meat, Horse Hide, (Minor Treasure)		
Frost	Palomino	4	289	0	106			Horse Meat, Horse Hide, (Minor Treasure)		
Shadowmere	Black	50	887	0	198			Horse Meat, Horse Hide, (Minor Treasure)		Regenerates Health, Aggressive

Horse (Brown)

The Elder Scrolls V

SKYRIM

▶ Hunters

Skyrim's vast forests are home to any number of hunters, who prefer the wilderness to life in the cities. Orcs in particular often take up this nomadic lifestyle. Most are glad to barter with a passing adventurer.

Hunter

HUNTERS

NAME	SUBTYPE	LV	HEALTH	MAGICKA	STAMINA	WEAPONS	ARMOR	ITEMS	SPELLS	NOTES
Hunter		5*	79	25	41	Bow, Arrows, Dagger	Hide Cuirass, Gloves, (Hat), Clothes	(Meat), (Animal Parts), (Gold)		
Orc Hunter		1	30	25	70	Bow, Arrows, Dagger	Light Cuirass, Light Boots, (Gauntlets)	(Lockpick), (Meat), (Animal Parts), (Gold)		

▶ Penitus Oculatus

After the fall of the Blades, the Penitus Oculatus were created to serve as the Emperor's personal security force. They have an outpost in Dragon Bridge.

Penitus Oculatus

PENITUS OCULATUS ARCHERS

NAME	SUBTYPE	LV	HEALTH	MAGICKA	STAMINA	WEAPONS	ARMOR	ITEMS	SPELLS	NOTES
Penitus Oculatus Agent	Battlemage	1	50	50	50	Imperial Bow, Arrows, Iron Dagger	Penitus Oculatus Armor, Penitus Oculatus Boots, Penitus Oculatus Bracers	Gold		
Penitus Oculatus Agent	Battlemage	4	85	60	60	Imperial Bow, Arrows, Iron Dagger	Penitus Oculatus Armor, Penitus Oculatus Boots, Penitus Oculatus Bracers	Gold		
Penitus Oculatus Agent	Battlemage	8	128	73	74	Imperial Bow, Arrows, Iron Dagger	Penitus Oculatus Armor, Penitus Oculatus Boots, Penitus Oculatus Bracers	Gold		
Penitus Oculatus Agent	Battlemage	13	180	90	90	Imperial Bow, Arrows, Iron Dagger	Penitus Oculatus Armor, Penitus Oculatus Boots, Penitus Oculatus Bracers	Gold		
Penitus Oculatus Agent	Battlemage	18	231	107	107	Imperial Bow, Arrows, Iron Dagger	Penitus Oculatus Armor, Penitus Oculatus Boots, Penitus Oculatus Bracers	Gold		
Penitus Oculatus Agent	Battlemage	23	283	123	124	Imperial Bow, Arrows, Iron Dagger	Penitus Oculatus Armor, Penitus Oculatus Boots, Penitus Oculatus Bracers	Gold		

PENITUS OCULATUS BATTLEMAGES

NAME	SUBTYPE	LV	HEALTH	MAGICKA	STAMINA	WEAPONS	ARMOR	ITEMS	SPELLS	NOTES
Penitus Oculatus Agent	Battlemage	1	50	50	50	2x Imperial Sword	Penitus Oculatus Armor, Penitus Oculatus Boots, Penitus Oculatus Bracers, Penitus Oculatus Helmet		Fast Healing, (Flames/Sparks), Lesser Ward	
Penitus Oculatus Agent	Battlemage	4	85	60	60	2x Imperial Sword	Penitus Oculatus Armor, Penitus Oculatus Boots, Penitus Oculatus Bracers, Penitus Oculatus Helmet		Fast Healing, (Firebolt/Lightning Bolt), Lesser Ward	
Penitus Oculatus Agent	Battlemage	8	128	73	74	2x Imperial Sword	Penitus Oculatus Armor, Penitus Oculatus Boots, Penitus Oculatus Bracers, Penitus Oculatus Helmet		Fast Healing, (Firebolt/Lightning Bolt), Lesser Ward	
Penitus Oculatus Agent	Battlemage	13	180	90	90	2x Imperial Sword	Penitus Oculatus Armor, Penitus Oculatus Boots, Penitus Oculatus Bracers, Penitus Oculatus Helmet		Fast Healing, (Firebolt/Lightning Bolt), Lesser Ward	
Penitus Oculatus Agent	Battlemage	18	231	107	107	2x Imperial Sword	Penitus Oculatus Armor, Penitus Oculatus Boots, Penitus Oculatus Bracers, Penitus Oculatus Helmet		Fast Healing, (Fireball/Chain Lightning), Lesser Ward	
Penitus Oculatus Agent	Battlemage	23	283	123	124	2x Imperial Sword	Penitus Oculatus Armor, Penitus Oculatus Boots, Penitus Oculatus Bracers, Penitus Oculatus Helmet		Fast Healing, (Fireball/Chain Lightning), Lesser Ward	

PENITUS OCULATUS WARRIORS

NAME	SUBTYPE	LV	HEALTH	MAGICKA	STAMINA	WEAPONS	ARMOR	ITEMS	SPELLS	NOTES
Penitus Oculatus Agent	Battlemage	1	50	50	50	Imperial Sword, Imperial Shield	Penitus Oculatus Armor, Penitus Oculatus Boots, Penitus Oculatus Bracers, Penitus Oculatus Helmet	Gold		
Penitus Oculatus Agent	Battlemage	4	85	60	60	Imperial Sword, Imperial Shield	Penitus Oculatus Armor, Penitus Oculatus Boots, Penitus Oculatus Bracers, Penitus Oculatus Helmet	Gold		
Penitus Oculatus Agent	Battlemage	8	128	73	74	Imperial Sword, Imperial Shield	Penitus Oculatus Armor, Penitus Oculatus Boots, Penitus Oculatus Bracers, Penitus Oculatus Helmet	Gold		
Penitus Oculatus Agent	Battlemage	13	180	90	90	Imperial Sword, Imperial Shield	Penitus Oculatus Armor, Penitus Oculatus Boots, Penitus Oculatus Bracers, Penitus Oculatus Helmet	Gold		
Penitus Oculatus Agent	Battlemage	18	231	107	107	Imperial Sword, Imperial Shield	Penitus Oculatus Armor, Penitus Oculatus Boots, Penitus Oculatus Bracers, Penitus Oculatus Helmet	Gold		
Penitus Oculatus Agent	Battlemage	23	283	123	124	Imperial Sword, Imperial Shield	Penitus Oculatus Armor, Penitus Oculatus Boots, Penitus Oculatus Bracers, Penitus Oculatus Helmet	Gold		

▶ Sailor

Solitude, Dawnstar, and Windhelm are all important Imperial ports, and many sailors from those cities crew the ships that ply the waters along the Sea of Ghosts.

Sailor

SAILOR

NAME	SUBTYPE	LV	HEALTH	MAGICKA	STAMINA	WEAPONS	ARMOR	ITEMS	SPELLS	NOTES
Sailor		1	10	25	25	Dagger	Clothes	(Gold)		

Skeletons

Though weaker than Draugr, Skeletons can still be dangerous in large numbers. They are frequently seen in the company of necromancers.

SKELETONS

NAME	SUBTYPE	LV	HEALTH	MAGICKA	STAMINA	WEAPONS	ARMOR	ITEMS	SPELLS	NOTES
Skeleton	1H Warrior	1	20	0	80	1H Ancient Nord Weapon, (Shield)		Draugr Loot, Bone Meal		
Skeleton	2H Warrior	1	20	0	80	2H Ancient Nord Weapon		Bone Meal		
Skeleton	Archer	1	20	0	80	Ancient Nord Bow, Ancient Nord Arrows		Draugr Loot, Bone Meal		
Skeleton	Robed	1	20	0	80	Ancient Nord Sword	[Warlock Hood]	Draugr Loot, Bone Meal, (Spellbook), Soul Gem		

Skeleton

Soldiers & Guards

Each of Skyrim's Nine Holds maintains its own standing force of guards, who owe their loyalty to the Jarl. As the Civil War rages between the Imperial Legion and the Stormcloaks, their soldiers will take posession of the military camps, forts, towns, and cities of Skyrim, replacing some of the local guards.

HOLD GUARDS

NAME	SUBTYPE	LV	HEALTH	MAGICKA	STAMINA	WEAPONS	ARMOR	ITEMS	SPELLS	NOTES
[Hold] Guard		20*	252	50	183	(Imperial/Stormcloak Weapon)	[Hold] Armor, [Hold] Shield, Boots, Helmet	(Torch), (Food), (Drink), (Amulet), (Gold)		Guards use the weapons of the faction their Hold is loyal to.

*Soldiers & Guard
(Hold Guard)*

IMPERIAL LEGION

NAME	SUBTYPE	LV	HEALTH	MAGICKA	STAMINA	WEAPONS	ARMOR	ITEMS	SPELLS	NOTES
Imperial Soldier	Guard	20*	252	50	183	Imperial Sword, Imperial Bow, Steel Arrows, Steel Dagger	Imperial Light Cuirass, Imperial Light Boots, Imperial Light Gauntlets, Imperial Light Helmet	(Torch), (Food), (Drink), (Amulet), (Gold)		
Imperial Soldier	Fort / Siege	5*	74	50	71	Imperial Sword, Imperial Bow, Steel Arrows, Steel Dagger	Imperial Light Cuirass, Imperial Light Boots, Imperial Light Gauntlets, Imperial Light Helmet	(Torch), (Food), (Drink), (Amulet), (Gold)		
Fort Commander		5*	74	50	71	Imperial Sword, Imperial Bow, Steel Arrows, Steel Dagger	Imperial Light Cuirass, Imperial Light Boots, Imperial Light Gauntlets, Imperial Light Helmet	(Torch), (Food), (Drink), (Amulet), (Gold)		
Imperial Legate		5*	74	50	71	Imperial Sword, Imperial Bow, Steel Arrows, Steel Dagger	Imperial Heavy Cuirass, Imperial Heavy Boots, Imperial Heavy Gauntlets			
Imperial General		5*	74	50	71	Imperial Sword, Imperial Bow, Steel Arrows, Steel Dagger	Imperial Heavy Cuirass, Imperial Heavy Boots, Imperial Heavy Gauntlets, Imperial Light Shield	(Torch), (Food), (Drink), (Amulet), (Gold)		

STORMCLOAKS

NAME	SUBTYPE	LV	HEALTH	MAGICKA	STAMINA	WEAPONS	ARMOR	ITEMS	SPELLS	NOTES
Stormcloak Soldier	Guard	20*	252	50	183	(1H Weapon & Shield / 2H Weapon), Hunting Bow, Arrows	Stormcloak Cuirass, Fur Boots, Fur Gauntlets, Stormcloak Helmet	(Torch), (Food), (Drink), (Amulet), (Gold)		
Stormcloak Soldier	Fort / Siege	5*	74	50	71	(1H Weapon & Shield / 2H Weapon), Hunting Bow, Arrows	Stormcloak Cuirass, Fur Boots, Fur Gauntlets, Stormcloak Helmet	(Torch), (Food), (Drink), (Amulet), (Gold)		
Fort Commander		5*	74	50	71	(1H Weapon & Shield / 2H Weapon), Hunting Bow, Arrows	Stormcloak Cuirass, Fur Boots, Fur Gauntlets, Stormcloak Helmet	(Torch), (Food), (Drink), (Amulet), (Gold)		
Stormcloak Commander		5*	74	50	71	(1H Weapon & Shield / 2H Weapon), Hunting Bow, Steel Arrows, Steel Dagger	Stormcloak Officer Cuirass, Stormcloak Officer Boots, Stormcloak Officer Gauntlets			
Stormcloak General		5*	74	50	71	(1H Weapon & Shield / 2H Weapon), Hunting Bow, Arrows	Stormcloak Officer Cuirass, Stormcloak Officer Boots, Stormcloak Officer Gauntlets, Stormcloak Officer Helmet, Steel Shield	(Torch), (Food), (Drink), (Amulet), (Gold)		

Spriggan

Spriggans are spirits of the forest, often dwelling in secluded groves and grottos. They are frequently accompanied by bears, wolves, and sabre cats that will fight to protect them. They are just as tough in melee as with ranged attacks. Use fire against them whenever possible.

SPRIGGAN

NAME	SUBTYPE	LV	HEALTH	MAGICKA	STAMINA	WEAPONS	ARMOR	ITEMS	SPELLS	NOTES
Spriggan		8	195	150	85			Taproot	Leaf Blast, Call Creatures, Heal	Weak to Fire 33%
Spriggan Matron		18	445	250	135			Taproot	Leaf Blast, Call Creatures, Heal	Weak to Fire 33%

Spriggan

⏻ Thalmor

The Thalmor are the agents of the elven Aldmeri Dominion, charged with overseeing the implementation of the White-Gold Concordat, the peace treaty between the Dominion and the Empire. Most view them as spies, or worse. Thalmor Loot includes a chance of gems, food, or drink. Thalmor Wizard Loot includes a chance of gems, soul gems, potions, or ingredients.

THALMOR ARCHER

NAME	SUBTYPE	LV	HEALTH	MAGICKA	STAMINA	WEAPONS	ARMOR	ITEMS	SPELLS	NOTES
Thalmor Soldier	Archer	4	127	56	62	Bow, Arrows, Dagger	Cuirass, Boots, Helmet, Gauntlets	Thalmor Loot	Bound Sword, Fast Healing	
Thalmor Soldier	Archer	12	249	72	94	Bow, Arrows, Dagger	Cuirass, Boots, Helmet, Gauntlets	Thalmor Loot	Bound Sword, Fast Healing	
Thalmor Soldier	Archer	20	371	88	126	Bow, Arrows, Dagger	Cuirass, Boots, Helmet, Gauntlets	Thalmor Loot	Bound Sword, Fast Healing	
Thalmor Soldier	Archer	28	493	104	158	Bow, Arrows, Dagger	Cuirass, Boots, Helmet, Gauntlets	Thalmor Loot	Bound Sword, Fast Healing	
Thalmor Soldier	Archer	36	565	120	190	Bow, Arrows, Dagger	Cuirass, Boots, Helmet, Gauntlets	Thalmor Loot	Bound Sword, Fast Healing	

Thalmor (Guardian)

THALMOR GUARDIAN

NAME	SUBTYPE	LV	HEALTH	MAGICKA	STAMINA	WEAPONS	ARMOR	ITEMS	SPELLS	NOTES
Thalmor Soldier	Guardian	4	127	56	62	1H Weapon, Dagger	Cuirass, Boots, Helmet, Gauntlets, Shield			
Thalmor Soldier	Guardian	12	249	72	94	1H Weapon, Dagger	Cuirass, Boots, Helmet, Gauntlets, Shield			
Thalmor Soldier	Guardian	20	371	88	126	1H Weapon, Dagger	Cuirass, Boots, Helmet, Gauntlets, Shield			
Thalmor Soldier	Guardian	28	493	104	158	1H Weapon, Dagger	Cuirass, Boots, Helmet, Gauntlets, Shield			
Thalmor Soldier	Guardian	36	565	120	190	1H Weapon, Dagger	Cuirass, Boots, Helmet, Gauntlets, Shield			

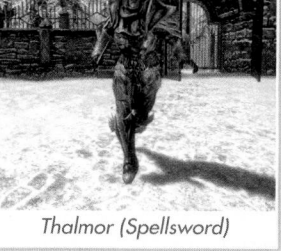

Thalmor (Spellsword)

THALMOR SPELLSWORD

NAME	SUBTYPE	LV	HEALTH	MAGICKA	STAMINA	WEAPONS	ARMOR	ITEMS	SPELLS	NOTES
Thalmor Soldier	Spellsword	4	127	56	62	1H Weapon, Dagger	Cuirass, Boots, Helmet, Gauntlets		Flames, Fast Healing	
Thalmor Soldier	Spellsword	12	249	72	94	1H Weapon, Dagger	Cuirass, Boots, Helmet, Gauntlets		Flames, Fast Healing	
Thalmor Soldier	Spellsword	20	371	88	126	1H Weapon, Dagger	Cuirass, Boots, Helmet, Gauntlets		Flames, Fast Healing	
Thalmor Soldier	Spellsword	28	493	104	158	1H Weapon, Dagger	Cuirass, Boots, Helmet, Gauntlets		Flames, Fast Healing	
Thalmor Soldier	Spellsword	36	565	120	190	1H Weapon, Dagger	Cuirass, Boots, Helmet, Gauntlets		Flames, Fast Healing	

Thalmor (Warrior)

THALMOR WARRIOR

NAME	SUBTYPE	LV	HEALTH	MAGICKA	STAMINA	WEAPONS	ARMOR	ITEMS	SPELLS	NOTES
Thalmor Soldier	Warrior	4	127	56	62	1H Weapon	Cuirass, Boots, Helmet, Gauntlets, (Shield)		Bound Sword	
Thalmor Soldier	Warrior	12	249	72	94	1H Weapon	Cuirass, Boots, Helmet, Gauntlets, (Shield)		Bound Sword	
Thalmor Soldier	Warrior	20	371	88	126	1H Weapon	Cuirass, Boots, Helmet, Gauntlets, (Shield)		Bound Sword	
Thalmor Soldier	Warrior	28	493	104	158	1H Weapon	Cuirass, Boots, Helmet, Gauntlets, (Shield)		Bound Sword	
Thalmor Soldier	Warrior	36	565	120	190	1H Weapon	Cuirass, Boots, Helmet, Gauntlets, (Shield)		Bound Sword	

Thalmor (Wizard)

THALMOR WIZARD

NAME	SUBTYPE	LV	HEALTH	MAGICKA	STAMINA	WEAPONS	ARMOR	ITEMS	SPELLS	NOTES
Thalmor Wizard		4	127	118	50	Dagger	Thalmor Robes, Thalmor Boots, Thalmor Gloves, Thalmor Hood	Thalmor Wizard Loot	Flames, Frostbite, Healing, Oakflesh, Sparks, Lesser Ward	
Thalmor Wizard		12	249	166	50	Dagger	Thalmor Robes, Thalmor Boots, Thalmor Gloves, Thalmor Hood	Thalmor Wizard Loot	Conjure Flame Atronach, Fast Healing, Firebolt, Lightning Bolt, Oakflesh, Lesser Ward	
Thalmor Wizard		20	371	239	50	Dagger	Thalmor Robes, Thalmor Boots, Thalmor Gloves, Thalmor Hood	Thalmor Wizard Loot	Banish Daedra, Chain Lightning, Conjure Flame Atronach, Fast Healing, Fireball, Lightning Bolt, Oakflesh, Steadfast Ward	
Thalmor Wizard		28	493	312	50	Dagger	Thalmor Robes, Thalmor Boots, Thalmor Gloves, Thalmor Hood	Thalmor Wizard Loot	Chain Lightning, Conjure Flame Atronach, Fast Healing, Fireball, Lightning Bolt, Incinerate, Stoneflesh, Thunderbolt, Turn Lesser Undead, Steadfast Ward	
Thalmor Wizard		36	565	385	50	Dagger	Thalmor Robes, Thalmor Boots, Thalmor Gloves, Thalmor Hood	Thalmor Wizard Loot	Banish Daedra, Chain Lightning, Close Wounds, Conjure Storm Atronach, Expel Daedra, Fast Healing, Incinerate, Stoneflesh, Thunderbolt, Turn Undead, Steadfast Ward	
Thalmor Wizard		44	637	458	50	Dagger	Thalmor Robes, Thalmor Boots, Thalmor Gloves, Thalmor Hood	Thalmor Wizard Loot	Banish Daedra, Chain Lightning, Close Wounds, Conjure Storm Atronach, Expel Daedra, Fast Healing, Incinerate, Ironflesh, Thunderbolt, Turn Undead, Steadfast Ward	

THALMOR WIZARD – BOSS

NAME	SUBTYPE	LV	HEALTH	MAGICKA	STAMINA	WEAPONS	ARMOR	ITEMS	SPELLS	NOTES
Thalmor Wizard	Boss	14	317	228	50	Dagger	Thalmor Robes, Thalmor Boots, Thalmor Gloves, Thalmor Hood	Thalmor Wizard Loot	Conjure Flame Atronach, Fast Healing, Firebolt, Lightning Bolt, Oakflesh, Lesser Ward	
Thalmor Wizard	Boss	23	448	282	50	Dagger	Thalmor Robes, Thalmor Boots, Thalmor Gloves, Thalmor Hood	Thalmor Wizard Loot	Banish Daedra, Chain Lightning, Conjure Flame Atronach, Fast Healing, Fireball, Lightning Bolt, Oakflesh, Steadfast Ward	
Thalmor Wizard	Boss	32	579	386	50	Dagger	Thalmor Robes, Thalmor Boots, Thalmor Gloves, Thalmor Hood	Thalmor Wizard Loot	Chain Lightning, Conjure Storm Atronach, Fast Healing, Incinerate, Stoneflesh, Thunderbolt, Turn Lesser Undead, Steadfast Ward	
Thalmor Wizard	Boss	40	651	434	50	Dagger	Thalmor Robes, Thalmor Boots, Thalmor Gloves, Thalmor Hood	Thalmor Wizard Loot	Banish Daedra, Chain Lightning, Close Wounds, Conjure Storm Atronach, Expel Daedra, Fast Healing, Incinerate, Stoneflesh, Thunderbolt, Turn Undead, Steadfast Ward	
Thalmor Wizard	Boss	50	791	544	50	Dagger	Thalmor Robes, Thalmor Boots, Thalmor Gloves, Thalmor Hood	Thalmor Wizard Loot	Banish Daedra, Chain Lightning, Close Wounds, Conjure Storm Atronach, Expel Daedra, Fast Healing, Incinerate, Ironflesh, Thunderbolt, Turn Undead, Steadfast Ward	

Trolls

Trolls are among the most feared of Skyrim's predators. They regenerate health, so attack aggressively — it's worth taking some punishment to keep the attacks up. Trolls are notably weak to fire. Minor Treasure includes a tiny chance of: A few gold, a gem, or a ring.

TROLLS

NAME	SUBTYPE	LV	HEALTH	MAGICKA	STAMINA	WEAPONS	ARMOR	ITEMS	SPELLS	NOTES
Troll		14	280	0	340	35 Dmg		Troll Fat, (Minor Treasure)		Regenerate Health, Weak to Fire 50%
Frost Troll		22	460	0	480	65 Dmg		Troll Fat, (Minor Treasure)		Regenerate Health, Weak to Fire 50%

Troll (Frost Troll)

Vampires

Vampirism begins as a disease, Sanguinare Vampiris, but quickly progresses to something much worse if left untreated. Vampires tend to congregate in clans, and their fearsome reputation is well deserved. It's worth spending those scrolls and potions you've been hording to defeat higher-level vampires. You can't let the fight drag on because their primary attack heals them while hurting you. Vampire Loot includes a chance of: Lockpicks, Potions, Jewelry, Gems, Gold, Books, or Staffs.

Vampire

VAMPIRES

NAME	SUBTYPE	LV	HEALTH	MAGICKA	STAMINA	WEAPONS	ARMOR	ITEMS	SPELLS	NOTES
Vampire Fledgling		1	35	75	50	(1H Sword / 1H Axe)	(Mage Robes / Armor), Boots	Vampire Loot, (Gold)	Vampire Drain Life, Invisibility, Raise Zombie	50% Resist Frost, 50% Weak to Fire, Damage from Sunlight
Vampire		6	120	120	90	(1H Sword / 1H Axe)	(Mage Robes / Armor), Boots	Vampire Loot, (Gold)	Vampire Drain Life, Invisibility, Raise Zombie	50% Resist Frost, 50% Weak to Fire, Damage from Sunlight
Blooded Vampire		12	224	169	112	(1H Sword / 1H Axe)	(Mage Robes / Armor), Boots	Vampire Loot, (Gold)	Vampire Drain Life, Invisibility, Raise Zombie	50% Resist Frost, 50% Weak to Fire, Damage from Sunlight, +5 Unarmed Damage
Vampire Mistwalker		20	331	226	148	(1H Sword / 1H Axe)	(Mage Robes / Armor), Boots	Vampire Loot, (Gold)	Vampire Drain Life, Invisibility, Reanimate Corpse, Ice Spike	50% Resist Frost, 50% Weak to Fire, Damage from Sunlight, +7 Unarmed Damage
Vampire Nightstalker		28	413	283	179	(1H Sword / 1H Axe)	(Mage Robes / Armor), Boots	Vampire Loot, (Gold)	Vampire Drain Life, Invisibility, Ice Spike, Lightning Bolt, Reanimate Corpse	50% Resist Frost, 50% Weak to Fire, Damage from Sunlight, +10 Unarmed Damage
Ancient Vampire		38	583	348	224	(1H Sword / 1H Axe)	(Mage Robes / Armor), Boots	Vampire Loot, (Gold)	Vampire Drain Life, Invisibility, Ice Spike, Lightning, Revenant	50% Resist Frost, 50% Weak to Fire, Damage from Sunlight, +15 Unarmed Damage
Volkihar Vampire		48	823	413	294	(1H Sword / 1H Axe)	(Mage Robes / Armor), Boots	Vampire Loot, (Gold)	Vampire Drain Life, Invisibility, Chain Lightning, Ice Storm, Revenant	50% Resist Frost, 50% Weak to Fire, Damage from Sunlight, +20 Unarmed Damage

MASTER VAMPIRES

NAME	SUBTYPE	LV	HEALTH	MAGICKA	STAMINA	WEAPONS	ARMOR	ITEMS	SPELLS	NOTES
Master Vampire		14	252	177	126	(1H Sword / 1H Axe)	(Mage Robes / Armor), Boots	Vampire Loot, (Gold)	Vampire Drain Life, Invisibility, Raise Zombie	50% Resist Frost, 50% Weak to Fire, Damage from Sunlight, +5 Unarmed Damage
Master Vampire		23	378	238	169	(1H Sword / 1H Axe)	(Mage Robes / Armor), Boots	Vampire Loot, (Gold)	Vampire Drain Life, Invisibility, Reanimate Corpse, Ice Spike	50% Resist Frost, 50% Weak to Fire, Damage from Sunlight, +7 Unarmed Damage
Master Vampire		31	500	310	210	(1H Sword / 1H Axe)	(Mage Robes / Armor), Boots	Vampire Loot, (Gold)	Vampire Drain Life, Invisibility, Ice Spike, Lightning Bolt, Reanimate Corpse	50% Resist Frost, 50% Weak to Fire, Damage from Sunlight, +10 Unarmed Damage
Master Vampire		42	669	414	257	(1H Sword / 1H Axe)	(Mage Robes / Armor), Boots	Vampire Loot, (Gold)	Vampire Drain Life, Invisibility, Ice Spike, Lightning, Revenant	50% Resist Frost, 50% Weak to Fire, Damage from Sunlight, +15 Unarmed Damage
Volkihar Master Vampire		53	968	458	354	(1H Sword / 1H Axe)	(Mage Robes / Armor), Boots	Vampire Loot, (Gold)	Vampire Drain Life, Invisibility, Chain Lightning, Ice Storm, Revenant	50% Resist Frost, 50% Weak to Fire, Damage from Sunlight, +20 Unarmed Damage

The Elder Scrolls V

SKYRIM

Vigilants of Stendarr

The Vigilants of Stendarr are priests in the service of Stendarr, the Divine of Mercy. They will gladly lend their aid to a hero who fits their ideals of virtue. But werewolves, vampires, and daedra worshippers have reason to fear their wrath.

VIGILANTS OF STENDARR

NAME	SUBTYPE	LV	HEALTH	MAGICKA	STAMINA	WEAPONS	ARMOR	ITEMS	SPELLS	NOTES
Vigilant of Stendarr		5	90	57	63	Mace, Torch	Steel Boots, Steel Gauntlets, Mage Robes, Mage Hood, Amulet of Stendarr	Potions, Books	Healing, Oakflesh, Lesser Ward	
Vigilant of Stendarr		9	130	63	77	Mace, Torch	Steel Boots, Steel Gauntlets, Mage Robes, Mage Hood, Amulet of Stendarr	Potions, Books	Healing, Oakflesh, Lesser Ward	
Vigilant of Stendarr		14	180	72	93	Mace, Torch	Steel Boots, Steel Gauntlets, Mage Robes, Mage Hood, Amulet of Stendarr	Potions, Books	Healing, Oakflesh, Lesser Ward	
Vigilant of Stendarr		19	230	80	110	Mace, Torch	Steel Boots, Steel Gauntlets, Mage Robes, Mage Hood, Amulet of Stendarr	Potions, Books	Healing, Oakflesh, Lesser Ward	
Vigilant of Stendarr		25	290	90	130	Mace, Torch	Steel Boots, Steel Gauntlets, Mage Robes, Mage Hood, Amulet of Stendarr	Potions, Books	Healing, Oakflesh, Lesser Ward	

Vigilant of Stendarr

Warlocks

Warlocks is a catchall term for the mages, wizards, conjurers, and necromancers that you may face on your journey. Warlocks encountered as bosses have more magicka than their non-boss counterparts, and are more likely to carry a staff. Warlock Loot includes a chance of: soul gems, potions, recipes, and alchemy ingredients.

FIRE MAGES

NAME	SUBTYPE	LV	HEALTH	MAGICKA	STAMINA	WEAPONS	ARMOR	ITEMS	SPELLS	NOTES
Novice Fire Mage		1	50	100	25	Dagger, (Staff)	Mage Robes, Boots	(Warlock Loot)	Flames, Lesser Ward	
Apprentice Fire Mage		6	142	158	25	Dagger, (Staff)	Mage Robes, Boots	(Warlock Loot)	Firebolt, Flames, Healing, Oakflesh, Lesser Ward	
Fire Mage Adept		12	192	198	25	Dagger, (Staff)	Mage Robes, Boots	(Warlock Loot)	Fast Healing, Firebolt, Flames, Stoneflesh, Steadfast Ward	
Fire Mage		19	275	270	25	Dagger, (Staff)	Mage Robes, Boots	(Warlock Loot)	Fast Healing, Fireball, Firebolt, Flame Cloak, Stoneflesh, Steadfast Ward	
Fire Wizard		27	367	323	25	Dagger, (Staff)	Mage Robes, Boots	(Warlock Loot)	Close Wounds, Fast Healing, Fireball, Firebolt, Flame Cloak, Ironflesh, Steadfast Ward	
Pyromancer		36	467	383	25	Dagger, (Staff of Fireballs)	Mage Robes, Boots	(Warlock Loot)	Close Wounds, Fireball, Flame Cloak, Grand Healing, Incinerate, Ironflesh, Greater Ward	
Arch Pyromancer		46	575	500	50	Dagger, (Staff of Fireballs)	Mage Robes, Boots	(Warlock Loot)	Close Wounds, Fireball, Flame Cloak, Grand Healing, Incinerate, Ironflesh, Greater Ward	

Warlock (Arch Necromancer)

ICE MAGES

NAME	SUBTYPE	LV	HEALTH	MAGICKA	STAMINA	WEAPONS	ARMOR	ITEMS	SPELLS	NOTES
Novice Ice Mage		1	50	100	25	Dagger, (Staff)	Mage Robes, Boots	(Warlock Loot)	Frostbite, Lesser Ward	
Apprentice Ice Mage		6	142	158	25	Dagger, (Staff)	Mage Robes, Boots	(Warlock Loot)	Frostbite, Healing, Ice Spike, Oakflesh, Lesser Ward	
Ice Mage Adept		12	192	198	25	Dagger, (Staff)	Mage Robes, Boots	(Warlock Loot)	Fast Healing, Frostbite, Ice Spike, Stoneflesh, Steadfast Ward	
Ice Mage		19	275	270	25	Dagger, (Staff)	Mage Robes, Boots	(Warlock Loot)	Fast Healing, Frost Cloak, Ice Spike, Ice Storm, Stoneflesh, Steadfast Ward	
Ice Wizard		27	367	323	25	Dagger, (Staff)	Mage Robes, Boots	(Warlock Loot)	Close Wounds, Fast Healing, Frost Cloak, Ice Spike, Ice Storm, Ironflesh, Steadfast Ward	
Cryomancer		36	467	383	25	Dagger, (Staff of Ice Storm)	Mage Robes, Boots	(Warlock Loot)	Close Wounds, Frost Cloak, Grand Healing, Ice Storm, Icy Spear, Ironflesh, Greater Ward	
Arch Cryomancer		46	575	500	50	Dagger, (Staff of Ice Storm)	Mage Robes, Boots	(Warlock Loot)	Close Wounds, Frost Cloak, Grand Healing, Ice Storm, Icy Spear, Ironflesh, Greater Ward	

STORM MAGES

NAME	SUBTYPE	LV	HEALTH	MAGICKA	STAMINA	WEAPONS	ARMOR	ITEMS	SPELLS	NOTES
Novice Storm Mage		1	50	100	25	Dagger, (Staff)	Mage Robes, Boots	(Warlock Loot)	Sparks, Lesser Ward	
Apprentice Storm Mage		6	142	158	25	Dagger, (Staff)	Mage Robes, Boots	(Warlock Loot)	Fast Healing, Lightning Bolt, Oakflesh, Sparks, Lesser Ward	
Storm Mage Adept		12	192	198	25	Dagger, (Staff)	Mage Robes, Boots	(Warlock Loot)	Fast Healing, Lightning Bolt, Sparks, Stoneflesh, Steadfast Ward	
Storm Mage		19	275	270	25	Dagger, (Staff)	Mage Robes, Boots	(Warlock Loot)	Chain Lightning, Fast Healing, Lightning Bolt, Lightning Cloak, Stoneflesh, Steadfast Ward	
Storm Wizard		27	367	323	25	Dagger, (Staff)	Mage Robes, Boots	(Warlock Loot)	Chain Lightning, Close Wounds, Fast Healing, Ironflesh, Lightning Bolt, Lightning Cloak, Steadfast Ward	
Electromancer		36	467	383	25	Dagger, (Staff of Chain Lightning)	Mage Robes, Boots	(Warlock Loot)	Chain Lightning, Close Wounds, Grand Healing, Ironflesh, Lightning Cloak, Thunderbolt, Greater Ward	
Arch Electromancer		46	575	500	50	Dagger, (Staff of Chain Lightning)	Mage Robes, Boots	(Warlock Loot)	Chain Lightning, Close Wounds, Grand Healing, Ironflesh, Lightning Cloak, Thunderbolt, Greater Ward	

CONJURERS

NAME	SUBTYPE	LV	HEALTH	MAGICKA	STAMINA	WEAPONS	ARMOR	ITEMS	SPELLS	NOTES
Novice Conjurer		1	50	100	25	Dagger, (Staff)	Mage Robes, Boots	(Warlock Loot)	Conjure Familiar, Flames, Oakflesh, Lesser Ward	
Apprentice Conjurer		6	142	158	25	Dagger, (Staff)	Mage Robes, Boots	(Warlock Loot)	Conjure Flame Atronach, Fast Healing, Flames, Oakflesh, Lesser Ward	
Conjurer Adept		12	192	198	25	Dagger, (Staff)	Mage Robes, Boots	(Warlock Loot)	Conjure Flame Atronach, Fast Healing, Firebolt, Flames, Stoneflesh, Steadfast Ward	
Conjurer		19	275	270	25	Dagger, (Staff)	Mage Robes, Boots	(Warlock Loot)	Banish Daedra, Close Wounds, Conjure Frost Atronach, Fast Healing, Frostbite, Ice Spike, Stoneflesh, Steadfast Ward	
Ascendant Conjurer		27	367	323	25	Dagger, (Staff)	Mage Robes, Boots	(Warlock Loot)	Close Wounds, Command Daedra, Conjure Storm Atronach, Expel Daedra, Fast Healing, Ice Spike, Ice Storm, Stoneflesh, Steadfast Ward	
Master Conjurer		36	467	383	25	Dagger, (Staff)	Mage Robes, Boots	(Warlock Loot)	Chain Lightning, Close Wounds, Command Daedra, Conjure Storm Atronach, Expel Daedra, Ironflesh, Thunderbolt, Greater Ward	
Arch Conjurer		46	575	500	50	Dagger, (Staff)	Mage Robes, Boots	(Warlock Loot)	Chain Lightning, Close Wounds, Command Daedra, Conjure Storm Atronach, Expel Daedra, Ironflesh, Thunderbolt, Greater Ward	

NECROMANCERS

NAME	SUBTYPE	LV	HEALTH	MAGICKA	STAMINA	WEAPONS	ARMOR	ITEMS	SPELLS	NOTES
Novice Necromancer		1	50	100	25	Dagger	Necromancer Robes, Necromancer Boots	(Warlock Loot)	Frostbite, Raise Zombie, Lesser Ward	
Apprentice Necromaner		6	142	158	25	Dagger, (Soul Gems)	Necromancer Robes, Necromancer Boots	(Warlock Loot)	Fast Healing, Frostbite, Ice Spike, Oakflesh, Raise Zombie, Lesser Ward	
Necromancer Adept		12	192	198	25	Dagger, (Soul Gems)	Necromancer Robes, Necromancer Boots	(Warlock Loot)	Fast Healing, Frostbite, Ice Spike, Reanimate Corpse, Stoneflesh, Steadfast Ward	
Necromage		19	275	270	25	Dagger, (Soul Gems)	Necromancer Robes, Necromancer Boots	(Warlock Loot)	Fast Healing, Ice Spike, Reanimate Corpse, Revenant, Stoneflesh, Turn Undead, Steadfast Ward	
Ascendant Necromancer		27	367	323	25	Dagger, (Soul Gems)	Necromancer Robes, Necromancer Boots	(Warlock Loot)	Close Wounds, Dread Zombie, Fast Healing, Ice Spike, Ice Storm, Ironflesh, Revenant, Turn Undead, Steadfast Ward	
Master Necromancer		36	467	383	25	Dagger, (Staff), (Soul Gems)	Necromancer Robes, Necromancer Boots	(Warlock Loot)	Close Wounds, Dread Zombie, Grand Healing, Ice Spike, Ice Storm, Ironflesh, Revenant, Turn Greater Undead, Greater Ward	
Arch Necromancer		46	575	500	50	Dagger, (Staff), (Soul Gems)	Necromancer Robes, Necromancer Boots	(Warlock Loot)	Close Wounds, Dread Zombie, Grand Healing, Ice Spike, Ice Storm, Ironflesh, Revenant, Turn Greater Undead, Greater Ward	

▷ Wisps

Wispmothers are always found with a group of Wisps (typically 3). While the Wisps live, each grants the Wispmother a bonus to her Health, Magicka, or Stamina. Make sure to kill the Wisps before attacking the Wispmother directly; she is much weaker without them. When her health is low, the Wispmother will conjure two illusory Shades as a distraction.

NAME	SUBTYPE	LV	HEALTH	MAGICKA	STAMINA	WEAPONS	ARMOR	ITEMS	SPELLS	NOTES
Wisp		1	50	50	50				Energy Sap	Waterwalking
Shade		5	36	224	50				Frostbite	Waterwalking
Wispmother		28	600	300	50			Glowdust, Wisp Wrappings	Ice Volley, Conjure Shades	Speed Burst, Regeneration, Waterwalking

Wisp (Wispmother)

▷ Witches

Witches are female sorcerers training to become Hagravens, and often serve under them.

NAME	SUBTYPE	LV	HEALTH	MAGICKA	STAMINA	WEAPONS	ARMOR	ITEMS	SPELLS	NOTES
Witch	Fire	4	75	70	25	Dagger	Mage Robes, Boots		Firebolt, Flames, Oakflesh, Lesser Ward	
Witch	Frost	4	75	70	25	Dagger	Mage Robes, Boots		Frostbite, Ice Spike, Oakflesh, Lesser Ward	
Witch	Shock	4	75	70	25	Dagger	Mage Robes, Boots		Lightning Bolt, Sparks, Oakflesh, Lesser Ward	
Hag	Fire	8	109	96	25	Dagger	Mage Robes, Boots		Flames, Firebolt, Stoneflesh, Steadfast Ward	
Hag	Frost	8	109	96	25	Dagger	Mage Robes, Boots		Frostbite, Ice Spike, Stoneflesh, Steadfast Ward	
Hag	Shock	8	109	96	25	Dagger	Mage Robes, Boots		Lightning Bolt, Sparks, Stoneflesh, Steadfast Ward	

Witch

The Elder Scrolls V

SKYRIM

MAIN QUEST

OVERVIEW

The Main Quest begins the moment you start your adventure. Over the course of three acts, these quests involve some of the most important and wide-ranging events in Skyrim. Once you escape the town of Helgen, you are free to continue or ignore the Main Quest whenever you wish. However, it is recommended that you complete most of the first act sooner rather than later, as you're rewarded with several important powers (including Shouts) that can make your other adventures less fraught and more entertaining. Remember that you can completely finish the Main Quest and then return to tackle any other quests (or just explore) without penalty.

NOTE   **Cross-Referencing:** Do you want to see maps and learn more about the traps, non-quest-related items, collectibles, crafting areas, and other important rooms of note in every location during these quests? Then cross-reference the location you travel to with the information on that location contained in this guide's Atlas.

NOTE   The main quest also involves a number of Skyrim's other factions. For more information, consult their Quest listings. For information on Hadvar, Ralof, General Tullius, and Ulfric Stormcloak, consult the Civil War Quest Introduction.

AVAILABLE QUESTS

There are a total of 20 different Main Quests in three acts. Each quest leads directly into the next, as shown in the following table:

✔	QUEST NAME	PREREQUISITES
	ACT I	
	Main Quest: Unbound	None
	Main Quest: Before the Storm	Complete Main Quest: Unbound
	Main Quest: Bleak Falls Barrow	Complete Main Quest: Before the Storm
	Main Quest: Dragon Rising	Complete Main Quest: Bleak Falls Barrow
	Main Quest: The Way of the Voice	Complete Main Quest: Dragon Rising
	Main Quest: The Horn of Jurgen Windcaller	Complete Main Quest: The Way of the Voice
	Main Quest: A Blade in the Dark	Complete Main Quest: The Horn of Jurgen Windcaller

✔	QUEST NAME	PREREQUISITES
	ACT II	
	Main Quest: Diplomatic Immunity	Complete Main Quest: A Blade in the Dark
	Main Quest: A Cornered Rat	Complete Main Quest: Diplomatic Immunity
	Main Quest: Alduin's Wall	Complete Main Quest: A Cornered Rat
	Main Quest: The Throat of the World	Complete Main Quest: Alduin's Wall
	Main Quest: Elder Knowledge	Complete Main Quest: The Throat of the World
	Main Quest: Alduin's Bane	Complete Main Quest: Elder Knowledge

✔	QUEST NAME	PREREQUISITES
	ACT III	
	Main Quest: The Fallen	Complete Main Quest: Alduin's Bane
	Main Quest: Paarthurnax†	Complete Main Quest: Alduin's Bane
	Main Quest: Season Unending‡	Complete Main Quest: Alduin's Bane
	Main Quest: The World-Eater's Eyrie	Complete Main Quest: The Fallen
	Main Quest: Sovngarde	Complete Main Quest: The World-Eater's Eyrie
	Main Quest: Dragonslayer	Complete Main Quest: Sovngarde
	Main Quest: Epilogue	Complete Main Quest: Dragonslayer

NOTE   † This quest is optional and can be completed at any point after Alduin's Bane, even after the Main Quest is over.

‡ This quest occurs only if the Civil War still rages across Skyrim. See its description for more details.

The Greybeards and the Blades have their own Faction Radiant Quests. Consult the section marked "Other Factions: Quests" on page 322 for more information.

 # MAIN QUEST: ACT I

UNBOUND

INTERSECTING QUESTS: Main Quest: Before the Storm

LOCATIONS: Helgen

CHARACTERS: Alduin, Elenwen, General Tullius, Gunjar, Gunnar, Hadvar, Haming, Imperial Captain, Imperial Soldier, Ingrid, Lokir, Matlara, Priestess of Arkay, Ralof, Stormcloak Soldier, Thalmor Soldier, Torolf, Torturer, Torturer's Assistant, Ulfric Stormcloak, Vilod

ENEMIES: Cave Bear, Frostbite Spider, Imperial Soldier, Stormcloak Soldier, Torturer, Torturer's Assistant

◊ **OBJECTIVES:** Make your way to the Keep, Enter the Keep with Hadvar or Ralof, Escape Helgen, Find some equipment, Loot Gunjar's body, (Optional) Search the barrel for potions, (Optional) Attempt to pick the lock to the cage

Bound for the Block

The clattering of hooves against cobblestone and the sway of the prison cart wakes you. Ralof, a Stormcloak rebel, wastes no time in talking to you. You're joined on this condemned wagon by a horse rustler named Lokir who hails from a town called Rorikstead and a large, imposing man who is bound and gagged. After Lokir addresses the man without proper respect, Ralof tells him to watch his tongue: he's speaking to Ulfric Stormcloak, the true High King of Skyrim and leader of the Stormcloak Rebellion against the Empire!

The convoy continues toward the gates of Helgen, a fortified hamlet in Falkreath Hold. You pass by General Tullius, leader of the Imperial forces in Skyrim, and his Thalmor advisors. Ralof looks around the settlement, remembering his youthful indiscretions. You pass a boy named Haming, who wants to watch the soldiers parading in his town. His father quickly herds him back indoors. The wagon stops. This is the end of the line. The prisoners disembark, and their names are recorded. Lokir attempts to flee but is cut down by Imperial archers. An Imperial Soldier named Hadvar beckons you forward and asks for your name.

> **NOTE** At this point, you should create the precise character you wish to adventure as. You need only choose your character's race, gender, and distinguishing features (from the size of your nose to the scars on your face). The only choice that affects your adventure is your race, as each race has specific strengths and powers. Consult the Training section of this guide on page 4 for more insight. For the purposes of this guide, a Male Nord named Dovahkiin was created.

Hadvar turns to his superior and asks her what to do with you, as you're not on the list of captured rebels. The Imperial Captain tells Hadvar to ignore the list; you're going to the block. You step forward, where General Tullius has a rather one-sided discussion with Ulfric Stormcloak, interrupted only by a strange guttural sound in the distance. A Priestess of Arkay attempts to bless the rebels before they're put to death, mentioning the "Eight Divines" (Thalmor law prohibits the worship of the Nordic god Talos, Tiber Septim; this infuriates the Stormcloaks). After the headsman swings his axe, the first rebel is beheaded, and you're summoned to the block just as another bellow echoes through the mountains. Resting your head on the block, the headsman raises his axe...and a gigantic black creature arcs through the skies, landing heavily on Helgen's central tower and unleashing a Thu'um (or Shout) that scatters everyone, both rebel and Imperial alike!

◊ **OBJECTIVE:** Make your way to the Keep

The World-Eater Returns

Amid the chaos, Ralof yells for you to follow him. Oblige him (as you're still bound, and dashing about in a panic doesn't further your cause). Follow Ralof as he reconvenes with Ulfric Stormcloak inside the Keep and beckons you to follow him up the steps. As you reach the Keep's second landing, a section of exterior wall comes crashing down, and the

black dragon roasts the area with fire before flying out of view. Ralof tells you to leap across to the ruins of the town's inn. Jump across, landing in the upstairs area, then head down to ground level.

The streets are filled with fire, wreckage, and panicked citizens. Hadvar is removing the boy Haming from danger, before recommending you follow him to (relative) safety. Shadow Hadvar as you both weave through the ruins of Helgen, briefly pausing to watch hapless Imperial forces trying to bring down the dragon. You can't help or search corpses, as your hands are still tied. Eventually, Hadvar brings you to the main Keep, where you both run into Ralof. After a short but tense standoff, they run to separate doors of the Keep and shout for you to head inside with them.

◊ **OBJECTIVE:** Enter the Keep with Hadvar or Ralof

> **NOTE**   This quest splits into two parallel paths at this point. The general route out of Helgen through the Keep is the same, but your allies and enemies will be different. The person you join with here affects who you journey with in the next quest and sets you up with an alliance for the Civil War Quests to come. However, you can still switch sides after this quest, so it doesn't matter who you escape with.

◊ **OBJECTIVE:** Escape Helgen

Battle Through the Keep

Path A: Helping Hadvar

Follow Hadvar into Helgen's Keep, where he removes your bindings and recommends you search the barracks for any weapons and items you can find. Step over to the Warden's Chest, which has what you need.

◊ **OBJECTIVE:** Find some equipment

- ➤ **Imperial Light Armor**
- ➤ **Iron Sword**
- ➤ **Imperial Light Boots**
- ➤ **Helgen Keep Key**

After searching the room (there's a weapon on the weapon rack by the wall and more items in one of the other chests), Hadvar opens the wooden grating, allowing you to continue down a corridor to a second pull chain and grating. Equip your new weapons and armor, and then slaughter the Stormcloak Soldiers in the room beyond. When they are both dead, you can ransack their bodies for items and different equipment. Unlock the gate to the west and proceed.

Path B: Rendezvous with Ralof

Follow Ralof into Helgen's Keep, where he encounters the remains of his comrade, Gunjar. After wishing him a quick journey to Sovngarde, he cuts your bonds and instructs you to take Gunjar's gear.

◊ **OBJECTIVE:** Loot Gunjar's body

➤ **Iron War Axe**   ➤ **Stormcloak Cuirass**   ➤ **Fur Boots**

After inspecting both exits (which are locked), Ralof notices some incoming Imperials and crouches down ready to ambush them. Equip your new weapons and armor, and then slaughter the Imperial Captain and Soldier. When they are both dead, you can ransack their corpses for items and different equipment. You'll find the Helgen Keep Key on the Captain's body. Unlock the gate to the west and proceed.

➤ **Helgen Keep Key**

> **TIP** **Character Development:** During either Path A or Path B, you should be learning all of the following:
>
> How to loot corpses, learning what to take and leave behind and seeing which items give you the best stat increases. The small triangle next to items in your inventory signifies that they are better than the ones you currently have equipped.
>
> How to equip weapons and armor, as well as any spells or powers you may have because of your race.
>
> What it feels like to wield a weapon, a spell, a weapon and shield, or two weapons. Or, take the two-handed weapon one of your enemies was carrying and use it. These help to increase different skills, which you can start doing right now!
>
> How to ready and sheathe your weapon(s), perform regular and power attacks, and block (either with a weapon or a shield).
>
> You can set your Favorites to a combination of weapons and powers that you enjoy, and then a second set to switch between.
>
> You can switch between first- and third-person views to see which you prefer.

Merged Path: Helgen Escape

Follow your ally through the gate and down the steps. The dragon causes the roof to collapse, forcing you left and into a storage room. Two enemies (of the opposing faction) are in this chamber. Bring them both down, helping your ally as much or as little as you wish. He recommends you look around the room for potions; you'll need them!

 ◊ **OBJECTIVE:** (Optional) Search the barrel for potions

You can search for whatever you wish. However, simply look in the barrel indicated, collect the potions, and meet up again with your ally.

➤ **Potions**

Head back out into the main corridor (on the other side of the roof collapse), and follow your friend down into the torture chamber. The Torturer and his assistant (both Imperials) are fighting Stormcloaks in here. After the commotion is over, grab the items from the knapsack on the table, read or take the *Book of the Dragonborn*, and steal a dagger and any other weapons from the chamber. Your ally notices that one of the torturer's cages houses the corpse of a mage and suggests you pry open the lock. You're given lockpicks for this purpose. Open the lock (Novice), and take the mage's clothing and your first Spell Tome. Then head out of the chamber.

➤ **The Book of the Dragonborn**   ➤ **Novice Hood**
➤ **Lockpick (12)**   ➤ **Novice Robes**
➤ **Loose gear**   ➤ **Spell Tome:** Sparks

> **TIP** **Character Development:** At this point, you should be:
>
> Swapping, dropping, and equipping weapons that you find interesting.
>
> Opening the two other cells to further improve your Lockpicking skill.
>
> Reading both books and learning the Sparks spell from the Tome. Now equip this spell in one of your hands if you want to try it out.
>
> Donning the mage's Novice Hood and Robes if their enchantment suits you better than your previous outfit.

Wind your way past the prison cells and down the steps, and be ready to combat enemies in the two-level lower dungeon. You can leave your ally to soak up most of the damage or wade in yourself. There are some particular methods of tackling the foes in here:

The terrain is narrow, meaning movement is restricted. So watch your step, as well as the foes armed with bows.

Quickly take down a foe and grab a bow and some arrows. Use those on the enemy, ideally from range and the upper level.

If you have a fire-based spell (because of your race), you can set fire to the pool of oil on the opposite side, burning some foes.

Or you can use Sparks and weaken enemies with electrical damage from a distance.

Follow your ally out of the lower dungeon to a bridge that he lowers using the lever (or you can do this if you're impatient). After crossing the bridge, a giant slab of stone crushes the structure, stopping you from backtracking. However, you can drop through the wreckage and follow the path down the rushing subterranean stream. Follow the flow of water past a skeleton (take its coin purse) and down into a cobweb-filled cave. It is here that you're set upon by around six Frostbite Spiders. Use ranged attacks to weaken them, followed by melee strikes to finish them; this is the best way to battle them. Leave your ally to attack his own arachnids, or team up and make quick work of them.

After crossing a small natural bridge, your ally crouches and indicates the presence of a bear just ahead. He suggests two ways to get past her: sneaking so as not to disturb her, or hitting her with an arrow from the bow he gives you. The choice is yours. You can:

Crouch (which means you're sneaking) and quietly head left (southeast) down the cave into a tunnel, avoiding the bear completely.

Equip the bow (you may wish to have already set up a melee weapon or weapon and spell in your Favorites to quickly swap to), fire up to three shots before she reaches you, and then finish her off with your ally's help.

Use the weapons or spells you prefer to take down the bear. You may want to invoke your racial power in this fight, if it helps. Wood Elves, in particular, can use Command Animal to simply turn the bear into an ally and walk right by.

Or simply sprint past the bear and down the tunnel as quickly as possible.

➤ **Long Bow**   ➤ **Iron Arrow (12)**

Quest Conclusion

After the bear encounter, the cave narrows to a winding tunnel, with light streaming from the far end. This is the way out! Main Quest: Before the Storm begins immediately.

PREREQUISITES: Character Generation, Complete Main Quest: Unbound
INTERSECTING QUESTS: Main Quest: Unbound, Main Quest: Bleak Falls Barrow, Side Quest: The Golden Claw
LOCATIONS:, Helgen, Riverwood, Alvor and Sigrid's House, Hod and Gerdur's House, Whiterun, Dragonsreach
CHARACTERS: Alvor, Dorthe, Frodnar, Gerdur, Hadvar, Hilde, Hod, Irileth, Jarl Balgruuf the Greater of Whiterun, Proventus Avenicci, Ralof, Sigrid, Sven
ENEMIES: Rabbit, Wolf
◊ **OBJECTIVES:** Talk to Alvor in Riverwood, Talk to Gerdur in Riverwood, Talk to the Jarl of Whiterun

▶ A Wander Down to Riverwood

You emerge into the bright light of Falkreath Hold, north of the still-shouldering ruin of Helgen. You and your companion watch as the dragon responsible for disrupting your execution flies away to the north.

This is Hadvar. You will follow him if you befriended this Imperial soldier while escaping Helgen.

This is Ralof. You will follow him if you befriended this Stormcloak operative while escaping Helgen.

Speak to him so the objective updates. At this point, you can:

◊ Follow him down the hillside, which is advisable if you want to complete this quest.

◊ Head off alone, ignoring him: To continue this quest, simply meet up with Hadvar's or Ralof's contact in Riverwood, or journey to Whiterun and speak to the Jarl there.

Civil War: The lands of Skyrim are engaged in a fierce Civil War between the Imperials and Stormcloaks. In fact, if you decide to begin the long and bloody routing of the faction you oppose, consult the Civil War Quests elsewhere in this guide. The Civil War can affect some of the Main Quest after this quest, but only if you've made decisions during the Civil War Quests. Such variations are flagged throughout the Main Quest. If applicable, they give you ample time to side with your Faction if you wish.

 ◊ **OBJECTIVE:** Talk to Alvor in Riverwood

 ◊ **OBJECTIVE:** Talk to Gerdur in Riverwood
♦ **TARGET:** Your friend's contact, in the town of Riverwood

Follow your friend down the hillside. He points out the ominous ruins on the river's opposite side: Bleak Falls Barrow. Continue to the edge of the White River, which flows from Lake Ilinalta to the west. Your friend is talking about the current situation regarding your chosen Faction when a couple of wolves interrupt him. Join in the attack, or watch your friend defeat them. Then follow the path along the riverbank and into Riverwood, which is on the edge of Whiterun Hold.

TIP **Roaming Around:** Investigate any nearby Primary Locations on your way to Riverwood. Either before or after you reach Riverwood, be sure to inspect the Guardian Stones and perhaps fight off a few bandits inside Embershard Mine. You can also spot salmon leaping the rapids, try the bow and shoot a rabbit or two, and pick any wildflowers or other ingredients growing nearby. Consult the guide's Atlas Chapter (beginning on page 414) to see every nearby location, and what each contains.

NOTE **Compass:** Nearby Primary Locations are black on your compass. After you discover them, they change to white. Once you "clear" them, this is flagged on your world map. Remember that "cleared" doesn't mean "ransacked"; you can leave the treasures inside a dungeon, and your map will still mark it as cleared.

Imperials: Alvor and Sigrid

Enter Riverwood, where Hadvar beckons you to meet his uncle. Head to the blacksmith's, where Uncle Alvor is hammering away in his forge. He seems confused and troubled by his nephew's appearance and is convinced to head inside his house to talk. Sigrid (Alvor's wife) will prepare some vittles; it looks like you could use some sustenance.

Head inside Alvor and Sigrid's House. Hadvar tells of his assignment to General Tullius's guard and the dragon attack in Helgen. Alvor accuses Hadvar of being drunk, saying the dragons were wiped out long ago. Hadvar finishes the story, telling Alvor that he owes his life to you. Hadvar wishes to leave for Solitude, but you both need food and a place to stay. Alvor offers you a gift, while his daughter Dorthe watches silently. You can take any or all of the items offered. Then Alvor turns to you: Riverwood needs your help. Jarl Balgruuf of Whiterun needs to know if there's a dragon on the loose, as Riverwood is defenseless against it. Soldiers must be sent here. Your Quest Objective updates, along with your map, and you can ask Alvor, Sigrid, or anyone else further questions before you leave.

➤ **Gift**

Stormcloaks: Gerdur and Hod

Enter Riverood, where Ralof walks around the left (northern) side of the Blacksmith's to meet his sister. Sven and his mother, Hilde, can be heard arguing about the dragon she saw. Ralof shouts a greeting to his sister Gerdur, who is delighted to see him.

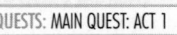

She seems concerned, especially after learning that Ulfric Stormcloak had been captured. She is convinced to move to a quieter area away from eavesdroppers. She yells for her husband, Hod.

By the river, Hod and Gerdur (and later, Gerdur's son Frodnar) listens to Ralof as he recalls the ambush by the Imperials outside Darkwater Crossing. It was as if they knew the Stormcloaks were there. After narrowly escaping the headsman's block, and after a mistrial for Ulfric, a dragon appeared over Helgen and inadvertently saved them! Now you both need food and a place to say. Gerdur offers you a key to her home, and a gift. Then she tells you that Riverwood is defenseless, and Jarl Balgruuf of Whiterun needs to know if there's a dragon on the loose. While Ralof and his relatives head back to Gerdur's home, you can follow them or set off. Your Quest Objective updates, along with your map. You may also ask Gerdur, Hod, or anyone else further questions before you leave.

➤ Key to Gerdur's House   ➤ Gift

TIP Although you may choose one gift, it is advisable to take everything: The items you don't need you can sell at the Riverwood Trader across the thoroughfare. At the very least, take the Potions of Minor Healing; they are most useful.

NOTE **Talk Is Cheap:** You are encouraged to speak to any of the townsfolk. Some have problems or tasks you can solve (known as Favors). Some offer a background to this realm. A few may embroil you in local politics. Others won't even give you the time of day. All of these conversations are optional.

Sleep Is Cheaper: You are fortunate that your friend's relatives have a place in Riverwood that you can return to. Sleep in a bed to refresh you, until you find other accommodation. Fast-Travel back to Riverwood to relieve your fatigue, aches, and pains.

Crafting Makes You Money: Alvor has a forge and other blacksmithing tools. Or try out the Alchemy Lab in the Sleeping Giant Inn just up the road.

Quest Objectives: The Quest menu lists the active quests and the related objectives, and it keeps track of miscellaneous objectives, or more minor tasks you can optionally try. To prevent confusion, use the Toggle Active feature in the Quest menu, and select only the quests you're interested in. Also, you can click over to the Objectives submenu and use the Show on Map feature so you know exactly where you're going.

Intersecting Quest: These are quests that take place in the main location you're currently in or will be visiting. We list them in this guide so you don't have to backtrack much. In this particular case, Side Quest: The Golden Claw is available if you visit the Riverwood Trader and speak to Lucan or Camilla Valerius. You can do this before or after the start of the next Main Quest: Bleak Falls Barrow.

▶ The Fortress-City of Whiterun

◊ **OBJECTIVE:** Talk to the Jarl of Whiterun
♦ **TARGET:** Jarl Balgruuf, inside Dragonsreach, in Whiterun

You must now make your way to Whiterun, the capital to the north. The optimal route is to cross the bridge as you exit Riverwood, follow the path with the waterfall rapids to your right (east), and begin a hill descent. You may have a World Encounter on the way down. Take the left (west) path at the two bridges, on the opposite side of the stream to Chillfurrow Farm, and pass the Honningbrew Meadery. You may hear the sounds of combat coming from the outskirts of Pelagia Farm; a giant has lumbered into this area, and a group of fighters called The Companions is fighting it.

 NOTE You can help the fighters out and begin The Companions Quests if you wish.

Make your way past the Whiterun Stables and then up the hill, over the drawbridge, and to the main Whiterun gate. As you approach, a guard stops you; the city is closed with the news of the dragons spreading faster than you can travel. You can:

◊ Tell the guard that Riverwood calls for the Jarl's aid. This is the optimal plan, and only available with this quest active.

◊ (Persuade) Or you can tell the guard you have news from Helgen about the dragon attack.

◊ (Bribe) Or bribe the guard with a portion of your collected gold.

◊ (Intimidate) Or order the guard to stand aside.

Once you're inside the walls of Whiterun, there is much to do and see. Don't worry about roaming this city, entering buildings, and interacting with the locals. But once you decide to complete this quest, head north, up to the hilltop that the city sits on, past the Gildergreen Tree (part of the Kynareth Temple), and the Shrine to Talos. Climb the stone steps to discover Dragonsreach, home of the Jarl.

Walk toward the huge central fire on either side of the banquet tables. The inhabitants of Dragonsreach are a little on edge. As you step forward, you are met by Irileth, Jarl Balgruuf's Housecarl. Explain to her that you're here to see the Jarl; you can be as forthright or secretive with the information, depending on how annoyed you wish Irileth to be. After a stare-down, the Jarl requests your presence. Speak to him about the dragon that destroyed Helgen.

 Begin to tell the Jarl your tale; your responses result in the same course of action (assuming you don't go mad and launch into an attack inside Dragonsreach):

 If you mention Alvor, Jarl Balgruuf notes that he's a reliable, solid fellow and not prone to flights of fancy.

 If you mention Gerdur, Jarl Balgruuf says that she's a pillar of the community and not prone to flights of fancy.

This gives more credence to your story. You can give the Jarl as many personal details as you wish in the course of his questioning and your story. After a discussion in which Irileth wisely asks for troops to be sent to Riverwood immediately, Proventus Avenicci (the Jarl's steward) warns that the Jarl of Falkreath may see this as provocation.

CAUTION The Jarl of Whiterun and his court can be attacked but not killed. It is unwise to shed their blood, as you're likely to be overwhelmed. If you employ violence, accidental or otherwise, return here after three 3 (or more) days to recommence talks.

Quest Conclusion

After Avenicci slinks off to tend to other duties, Jarl Balgruuf thanks you for your initiative and gives you a small token of his esteem, based on whichever Armor Skill (Light or Heavy) is higher.

➤ **Leveled Armor**

Postquest Activities

Main Quest: Bleak Falls Barrow begins immediately.

BLEAK FALLS BARROW

PREREQUISITES: Complete Main Quest: Before the Storm
INTERSECTING QUESTS: Main Quest: Before the Storm, Main Quest: Dragon Rising, Side Quest: The Golden Claw
LOCATIONS: Bleak Falls Barrow, Bleak Falls Temple, Bleak Falls Sanctum, Riverwood, Sleeping Giant Inn, Whiterun, Dragonsreach
CHARACTERS: Camilla Valerius, Delphine, Farengar Secret-Fire, Jarl Balgruuf the Greater of Whiterun, Lucan Valerius
ENEMIES: Arvel the Swift, Bandits, Draugr, Frostbite Spider, Frost Troll, Skeever
◊ **OBJECTIVES:** Talk to Farengar , Retrieve the Dragonstone, Deliver the Dragonstone to Farengar

▶ Reliable Sources

◊ **OBJECTIVE:** Talk to Farengar

At the end of your conversation with Jarl Balgruuf the Greater, he asks you to consult with his court wizard, Farengar Secret-Fire. Follow the Jarl into Farengar's study, where the Jarl introduces you. Farengar has a job for you almost immediately: to delve into a dangerous ruin in search of an ancient stone tablet. Ask for further information, and Farengar explains you're to look for something called a "Dragonstone," a tablet said to contain a map of the dragon burial sites across Skyrim. Farengar believes the stone is interred in the main chamber of Bleak Falls Barrow, and he has "reliable sources" that have confirmed as much. Before you leave, you can speak to Farengar about a variety of topics to gain a deeper understanding of his role in the Jarl's court.

NOTE If you've already explored Bleak Falls Barrow and found the Dragonstone, you can simply inform Farengar and hand it over, shortening this quest considerably. Skip to the "Quest Conclusion" section for your next actions.

◊ **OBJECTIVE:** Retrieve the Dragonstone
♦ **TARGET:** Dragonstone, on Draugr Lord, inside Bleak Falls Barrow

NOTE **Traveling Options:** At this point, you have three possible options to reach Riverwood, which is the closest place to Bleak Falls Barrow that you've already visited. You can:

◊ Trek there on foot. This takes longer, but you receive more experience from any encounters along the way.

◊ Head down to the Whiterun Stables and purchase a horse. This is faster, and occurs in "real time," but horses are pricey.

◊ Or bring up your world map and Fast-Travel back to Riverwood. The last option avoids combat but also any encounters.

Taking a carriage from Whiterun Stables is not an option, as these trips only take you to Hold Capitals.

TIP **Intersecting Quest:** Bleak Falls Barrow is the main location for Side Quest: The Golden Claw. You actually begin this quest, too, once you enter the Barrow. For more information, consult the "Side Quest: The Golden Claw" section later in this guide; begin at the Riverwood Trader and speak to the proprietors, Lucan and his sister Camilla Valerius.

▶ Unreliable Bandits

Head up the mountain path north of Riverwood, passing the Riverwood Folly (where bandits roam). At the summit, the Nord tomb appears through the blizzard. Expect more bandit activity in this area. Locate the arched carved door leading into Bleak Falls Temple.

Inside the first chamber, you hear two bandits around a campfire talking about a Dark Elf heading farther into the Barrow. End their conversation swiftly before venturing down the stairs.

Pass through the spiderwebs and the burial urns, and around the dead Skeever. Engage another bandit on your way to a ceremonial entrance room. A portcullis blocks your path, and the lever nearby is currently inactive. In the alcoves to the left are a trio of three-sided pillars. Approach the first; they can be activated. Each side has a different animal carving: the Hawk, Whale, and Snake.

Puzzle Solution: Rotate the pillars so a Snake, Snake, and Whale face out. The carved Nord heads above the portcullis (and the fallen middle one) hold the answer in their maws.

NOTE (Sneak) If you're remaining unseen as you move through this Barrow, you can follow the third bandit into the ceremonial entrance room and activate the lever on the ground. He succumbs to the dart trap immediately.

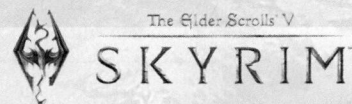

Descend the spiral steps beyond, battling a few Skeevers on your way down. As the thick spider silk begins to cover the walls, you hear a voice up ahead and to your left. Cut through the doorway covered in webbing, and enter the lair of a Giant Frostbite Spider. Attack the arachnid before venturing toward the trussed-up Dark Elf—one of the bandits from the raiding party you slaughtered previously. This is Arvel the Swift, who is carrying a Golden Claw, which is pertinent to both this quest and the Side Quest. He quickly tells you he knows how it fits into the door in the Hall of Stories. The bandit is babbling. But he needs cutting down first. Oblige him.

After a couple of weapon swipes (or magical blasts), Arvel's sticky prison gives way. He immediately flees, laughing that he won't be sharing his treasure with the likes of you. This is correct, but that's due to his imminent departure from this realm. This can be by your hands—a quick arrow or two in the back or other ranged attack—or by the denizens that lurk deeper in this crypt.

> It isn't wise to rush after Arvel; you'll soon catch up with him, and it is better to be prepared rather than rush headlong into an unknown chamber. **CAUTION**

▷ Knee-Deep in the Nordic Dead

Follow Arvel, passing through the crypt entrance and down into the catacombs. The Swift soon meets the dead, as Arvel falls under a flurry of Draugr attacks. The Nord undead now turn their attention to you. Battle them back or run north toward the open spiked gate and pressure plate. Keep to the extreme left, and you can activate the swinging gate trap without being hit. Use it as a skewering device against the Draugr; then search Arvel. Among his belongings are the Golden Claw and the Dark Elf's journal. Read it for more clues on this Barrow's secret.

➤ **Golden Claw**   ➤ **Arvel's Journal**

Continue downward, battling Draugr and searching corpses, both resting and animated, as you go. At the swinging blades, sprint forward the moment the closest blade swings past you. Brandish your weaponry but don't be overzealous with fire in the passageway with puddles; this is actually oil leaking from a hanging lamp, and the corridor erupts if flames touch the ground. Use this as a trap against your bony foes.

Eventually, you climb steps into a tall chamber with a waterfall, and another Draugr. The Barrow's secret lies past a portcullis above the rushing stream. Locate the chain next to the portcullis and activate it before splashing down the stream and into a larger cavern with an opening at the far end. Head to a natural bridge below the waterfall, or stand atop the waterfall and fire down on the enemy below (this is either a Draugr or a Frost Troll). By the bridge, optionally scavenge on the curved path below. Then follow the path into the illuminated entrance to Bleak Falls Sanctum.

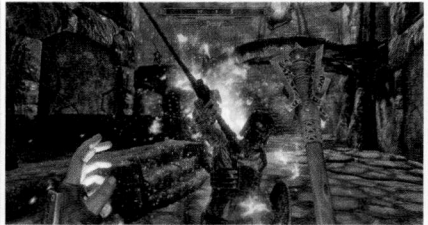

Open the Sanctum doors, and weave your way to a bladed corridor. Coax the Draugr beyond into this trap before dashing through it, into the Great Chamber. Expect attacks from Draugr bowmen on the bridge above and melee strikes

from the ground. Remember you can drop oil lamps and burn these foes as you head over the bridge and to the Iron Door leading into the long Hall of Stories and to a Nordic Puzzle Door.

Puzzle Solution: The door consists of three "rings" that rotate when you activate them. Each of them has three animals plated into the structure, and you unlock the central keyhole by using the Golden Claw itself. This puzzle is inaccessible without it. The puzzle solution is actually on the palm of the Golden Claw; rotate it in your inventory to see the three circular petroglyph carvings on the Claw's palm. Move the rings so the Bear, Moth, and Owl appear on the outer, middle, and inner rings, respectively. Then insert the Golden Claw into the keyhole.

▷ Guardian of the Dragonstone

This reveals the Barrow's secret at last: a ceremonial burial grotto with waterfalls surrounding the long-forgotten chamber. Move to the carved stone center, and check the chest and scavenge what you need; then inspect the Word Wall, where you're granted a Word of Power! However, this stirs a toughened Draugr from his rest, and you must defend yourself from this final Barrow guardian. After the fight, inspect the corpse of the Draugr; he is carrying the Dragonstone you seek! Grab this before taking the staircase on the chamber's left side, activating the handle to raise a secret stone slab door out in an upper Barrow alcove, and then exit out into Skyrim.

➤ **Word of Power:** Unrelenting Force   ➤ **Dragonstone**

> ◊ **OBJECTIVE:** Deliver the Dragonstone to Farengar
> ♦ **TARGET:** Farengar Secret-Fire, Dragonsreach, in Whiterun

> **TIP** **The Golden Claw:** Remember you still have it! If you want to complete the Side Quest, too, return it to Lucan in the Riverwood Trader first. He rewards you with a large sum of gold (the amount you receive depends on your level).

> **NOTE** Shouts are made up of Words of Power, and the one you've absorbed from the Word Wall may be your first. If you open the Magic Menu, you'll see that you can't use or equip it until you've absorbed a Dragon Soul from a dragon you've killed. Be patient—that will happen soon enough.

TIP **Equipping for Adventure:** At this point, it is worth learning how to strengthen your resolve, spend your gold, or barter your unwanted equipment. You can:

◊ Visit Riverwood and purchase or barter at the Riverwood Trader. Locate Alvor the Blacksmith for all your smithing needs. Visit the Sleeping Giant Inn and locate the Alchemy Lab Lab to craft some potions.

◊ Visit Whiterun and peruse the market area, which has various stalls, shops, and a Blacksmith. Farengar Secret-Fire also has a handy Enchanting Workbench and sells spells.

Quest Conclusion

Return to Dragonsreach (the quickest way is to Fast-Travel directly to it), and immediately consult with Farengar. If this is the second time you've visited him, he is joined in his study by a mysterious hooded figure named Delphine—possibly the "reliable source" he referred to earlier. He is talking about the cross-referencing of texts that mention dragons. Finally, Farengar turns to you, impressed that you didn't die in the Barrow. As you hand over the Dragonstone, he says that you're a cut above the usual brutes the Jarl sends his way. Speak to the Jarl for your reward, which occurs during the initial conversations of the next quest.

NOTE If you already had the Dragonstone prior to this quest and visited Farengar only once, Delphine isn't here. Don't worry—you'll meet her soon enough!

Postquest Activities

Main Quest: Dragon Rising begins immediately.

PREREQUISITES: Complete Main Quest: Bleak Falls Barrow

INTERSECTING QUESTS: Main Quest: Bleak Falls Barrow, Main Quest: The Way of the Voice

LOCATIONS: Western Watchtower, Whiterun, Dragonsreach

CHARACTERS: Farengar, Hrongar, Irileth, Jarl Balgruuf the Greater, Proventus Avenicci, Whiterun Guard

ENEMY: Mirmulnir ("Loyal Mortal Hunter")

◊ **OBJECTIVES:** Talk to Jarl Balgruuf, Meet Irileth near the Western Watchtower, Kill the dragon, Investigate the dragon, Report back to Jarl Balgruuf, (Optional) Use your new Shout power

All Along the Watchtower

◊ **OBJECTIVE:** Talk to Jarl Balgruuf

As you finish your conversation about the Dragonstone with Farengar, Irileth interrupts you with some troubling news: A dragon has been sighted nearby! Farengar seems positively giddy, while Irileth seems unsure if they could stop an attack on Whiterun. Locate the Jarl, who is questioning the Whiterun Guard who reported seeing the beast. Jarl Balgruuf orders Irileth to bolster the Western Watchtower with more men, a plan Irileth is already undertaking. Then the Jarl turns to you, seeking your help once again. Your experience at Helgen means you're most experienced in dealing with dragons. As a token of his esteem, he's instructed Avenicci that you're permitted to purchase property in Whiterun. Assuming you're alive and have enough gold! You're also gifted something from the Jarl's personal armory:

➤ **Leveled Armor**

◊ **OBJECTIVE:** Meet Irileth near the Western Watchtower

NOTE **Property Purchasing:** Locate Avenicci (he's usually within the walls of Dragonsreach, and within whispering distance of the Jarl), ideally after you return from your dragon slaying. A house is quite expensive—5,000 gold pieces—so be sure to have enough funds. Consult the Thane Tasks for further information.

TIP **Weaponry Purchasing:** At this point, consider purchasing additional supplies, especially Healing potions (if you aren't using Healing spells), and utilizing your "Favorites" to set up both long- and melee-range offense.

As the Jarl prevents Farengar from viewing the dragon, exit Dragonsreach. If you stride through Whiterun with Irileth, she gathers some Whiterun Guards and explains the situation. Or you can leave Whiterun. Follow the stone path that winds between the tundra plains, heading for the lone tower in the middle distance. As you get close, step up to Irileth who is hiding behind a rocky outcrop. If Irileth is behind you, you can either wait for her (and the soldiers) to arrive, or investigate the Watchtower on your own.

NOTE In fact, you can skip talking to the Jarl entirely. As soon as Irileth interrupts Farengar, you can go directly to the Watchtower and trigger the dragon attack after approaching the survivor. Irileth will arrive with troops as the battle begins.

If she's with you, Irileth notes that the Western Watchtower looks to have been ferociously attacked. The small fires and rubble confirm this assertion. She believes the dragon is still skulking nearby and orders you to spread out and look for survivors.

A closer inspection supports Irileth's summation; the place has been struck and lives lost. Move into the tower. As you enter, a fearful Whiterun Guard yells that the beast is still out there and has already taken two guards named Hroki and Tor when they tried to flee! Moments later, a bone-shaking roar announces the return of the dragon!

◊ **OBJECTIVE:** Kill the dragon

▷ Dragonborn Rising

There's little time to watch the giant lizard circling overhead; you must try to kill the creature as proficiently as possible.

Dragon Slaying: Switch to whatever long-range offensive weaponry you have, ideally ranged magic or a bow and arrow.

You are fortunate that Irileth and a few Whiterun Guards are attempting to strike the dragon, too, thus keeping it from predominantly attacking you. Irileth's magic is strong, so aid her by attacking from an opposite direction. Split up so there are fewer of you to fry at once!

If you're using a bow and arrow, remember to aim (and slow time, if you have the perk) for a better chance to hit.

This dragon breathes fire, so consuming potions or casting magic that lessens fire-based damage (see The Inventory Chapter on page 70) is a good idea.

When the dragon drops to a hover, it is usually preparing a gout of fiery breath. Take as many ranged shots as you deem safe, and then rush under or around the creature. Fire again as the dragon flies off.

When the dragon lands, attack from the sides; ranged attacks are still just as strong, but melee attacks are now possible, as long as you try cutting down the dragon between breath attacks or from the side.

If worse comes to worst, flee into the tower and use some Health potions. You can also attack from the tower's top or use the stairs to head down, out of the dragon's breath attacks.

◊ **OBJECTIVE:** Investigate the dragon

Approach the dead dragon. As you get close, it begins to burn! Fortunately, this isn't harmful; in fact, the crackling flesh merges into the ethereal soul of the dragon, and a maelstrom of energy and light whirls around you. You're actively absorbing the soul of Mirmulnir! Once the light subsides, search the dragon for some valuables. Now approach Irileth. The normally stoic Dark Elf is showing a little emotion after this battle.

➤ **Dragon Soul Absorbed**

◊ **OBJECTIVE:** Report back to Jarl Balgruuf
◊ **OBJECTIVE:** (Optional) Use your new Shout power

> With a keen eye, it appears the dragon that attacked Helgen **CAUTION** is not the one you just fought. This means that more than one dragon has returned—a bigger problem than first thought!

Access your Magic menu, scroll down to Shouts, and equip the Unrelenting Force Shout. You have the Dragon Soul necessary to conjure this Shout, so try it out. It isn't wise to do this on your allies (although they won't attack back), so try staggering a nearby enemy or just yelling at the tundra itself. Your Shout then recharges; note the Compass gradually fills from blue to bright white before becoming a normal white color. With Irileth taking command at the Watchtower, you should leave for Jarl Balgruuf's at once.

Quest Conclusion

Return to Dragonsreach and approach the Jarl, who has recently been joined by his equally imposing brother, Hrongar. Explain to the Jarl that you're actually "Dragonborn" and that you absorbed some of the dragon's power when it was slain. Jarl Balgruuf is shocked; it appears that the Masters of the Way of the Voice—known colloquially as the Greybeards—were not only correct in their predictions, but also are actively summoning you. Your reward? A trek to meet them!

Postquest Activities

Continue the conversation with Jarl Balgruuf as Main Quest: The Way of the Voice begins.

THE WAY OF THE VOICE

PREREQUISITES: Complete Main Quest: Dragon Rising

INTERSECTING QUESTS: Main Quest: Dragon Rising, Main Quest: The Horn of Jurgen Windcaller

LOCATIONS: High Hrothgar, Ivarstead, High Hrothgar Courtyard, Whiterun, Dragonsreach

CHARACTERS: Hrongar, Jarl Balgruuf the Greater, Lydia, Master Arngeir, Master Borri, Master Einarth, Master Wulfgar, Proventus Avenicci

ENEMIES: Bandit, Frost Troll, Sabre Cat, Wolf

◊ **OBJECTIVES:** Speak to the Greybeards, Demonstrate your "Unrelenting Force" Shout, Speak to Arngeir, Learn the Word of Power from Einarth, Demonstrate your "Unrelenting Force" Shout (3), Learn the Word of Power from Borri, Demonstrate your "Whirlwind Sprint" Shout, Speak to Arngeir for further training

Arise, Thane of Whiterun

◊ **OBJECTIVE:** Speak to the Greybeards

Continue to speak with Jarl Balgruuf about the Greybeards. He informs you that these venerable monks live in secluded isolation high on the slopes of the Throat of the World (the largest mountain in Skyrim). They have the ability to focus your vital essence into a Thu'um, or Shout, and they give you the location of their monastery in High Hrothgar — atop a 7,000-step climb! After a verbal altercation between Hrongar and Proventus Avenicci over Nordic sacred traditions, Jarl Balgruuf grants you the greatest honor within his power: You are named Thane of Whiterun. You also receive a weapon from the Jarl's armory and a Housecarl of your own.

➤ **Axe of Whiterun** ➤ **Follower:** Lydia (Housecarl)

> **NOTE Followers:** Lydia may be your first Follower. You may take her with you on your trek or journey there alone. Lydia remains in Dragonsreach until you instruct her to accompany you on any adventure. Although you have an adept bodyguard, your Follower requires armor and weaponry. For more information on Followers, consult page 62.
>
> **Becoming Thane:** This is an accomplishment to be proud of. Your new title means you're treated with the utmost respect by the guards and many inhabitants of the city of which you're Thane. You can also purchase property in the city. For more information, consult page 404.
>
> If you ignored this meeting with the Jarl and trekked to High Hrothgar first, the Jarl will be here to reward you when you return. However, you do not witness the tension between Hrongar and Proventus Avenicci.

Journeying to Ivarstead

The route to High Hrothgar involves a lengthy, spiraling journey clockwise around the base of the throat of the World. the first stop along this path is at the base of the 7,000 steps, in the town of Ivarstead. exit Whiterun and trek east, passing the Honningbrew Meadery. Cross the stone bridge over the White River, and follow the marked signpost to ivarstead. Continue along this stone path past a few encounters with wolves to a fork in the paths. At this point, you can choose one of two recommended routes to Ivarstead: the long and winding road or the short and steep trail.

The Long and Winding Road

You may continue along the marked path, ignoring the track up to the Giants of Guldun Rock. Prepare to pay a toll (or fight) at the bandit-infested Valtheim Towers. Then descend past the waterfall, along the same path past some drystone walls and the stone trilithon at the base of a stepped side path indicating the entrance to Hillgrund's Tomb. Cross the bridge

over Darkwater River and journey south (and southeast), right past Fort Amol. Head over another bridge close to a waterfall and continue along the stone path. Beware of more animal encounters, including a Sabre Cat or two! Head over another bridge, next to an even-more impressive waterfall, and trek east up a hill, where the stone path deteriorates.

The path soon turns southwest, up a long, steep slope, past Snapleg Cave. Continue southwest, ignoring the bridge. Head into birch woodland where Sarethi Farm is located. Expect elk, deer, a hunter's tent or two, and a view of Lake Geir from the bridge over the Treva River. Continue farther into the forest as the path winds west, past a junction and more drystone walls. Then turn right (northwest) at the small stone ruins near Honeystrand Cave. You finally reach Ivarstead after crossing another stone bridge.

The Short and Steep Trail

Or you can try this shortcut. Follow the path around to the right (east) just after you pass White River Watch, and come up to The Ritual Stone on your left. Cut south close to the Whiterun stormcloak camp, and up through the snowy foothills of the mountain, up an unmarked goat trail. Be sure you're traveling southeast up a steep embankment and into the snow. This levels out eventually, after you make several zigzags up very steep terrain above the snow line. Pass a few goats as the trail levels out and then quickly descends, joining a more recognizable trail. Head southeast and over the brow of the hill and past a copse of birch trees to the rushing rapids of Darkwater River. Cross the river, listening for the strange chime of a Nimroot growing around the corpses of a Troll's victims at Darkwater Overhang. Fight or flee from the Troll, then trek up the left side of the roaring waterfalls and into Ivarstead.

> Climbing directly up the mountain's side to reach High Hrothgar quickly results in you becoming stuck or falling to your death. **CAUTION**

> **TIP Making Inroads:** At this point, you should have learned that taking a long road to an important objective (in this case, Ivarstead) isn't a journey wasted, as you uncover several Primary Locations along the way. You can explore these immediately or at your leisure. You should also learn that using the paths, trails, and rivers is the best way to understand and remember where you are in the rugged lands of Skyrim.
>
> **Road Markings:** Both signposts and markers (the collections of stacked flat stones, sometimes with a primitive flag attached to them) are visual notes that indicate a nearby area of interest. Look for them.

7,000 Steps Above Ivarstead

Ivarstead is a slightly depressing place. The inhabitants are leaving for the greener (or at least, less snowy) pastures of Riften. You can stay and chat with the locals (mainly about their troubles or the supplies they need to send up to the Greybeards), or listen to them talk about the path up to High Hrothgar; they don't think the 7,000 steps are safe. You'll find out soon enough!

Your pilgrimage begins at the other side of the stone bridge. Almost immediately, you spot a small shrine. Inspect it more closely, and you'll see an Etched Tablet carved into the shrine arch. Read the emblem for the first of ten verses detailing the history of dragons and man.

PRIMA OFFICIAL GAME GUIDE   WWW.PRIMAGAMES.COM

Follow the winding path: At the second shrine, you may find a hunter named Barknar praying. He tells you to watch for wolves. You're now at the edge of the snow level. Continue up the precarious path: Expect a couple of wolf attacks along the way. The third shrine is nestled on a small snowy plateau. Follow the path down and up two sets of snowbound steps; remain on the side of the mountain, as the drop is precipitous. The fourth shrine is near some stab stones and a small copse of fir trees. You may find another traveler at this shrine, a pilgrim named Karita.

Use the marker stones as you wander up, into a granite gully. A Frost Troll is likely to be guarding this area, leaping down to maul you. Retaliate or run. The fifth shrine is just beyond the Frost Troll ambush. The blizzard is worsening; trek north down the snow steps, passing a few windswept trees to the sixth shrine, in front of a stone marker. Continue north and locate the seventh shrine jutting out to the west, on a precarious promontory. If you could see it, you'd be looking out across southern Eastmarch. Turn north, and look for the eighth shrine in front of a rocky outcrop, to your left (northwest).

The ninth shrine is below a stone statue to Talos. You'll see this as you round the bend in the path and come across the High Hrothgar monastery. As you close in on the final set of steps (did you count 7,000?), the final shrine is set off to the right (southeast) side, by the entrance stairs. Climb the entrance steps, grab any supplies and offerings at the base of the stairs, and then ascend the left set of stairs to enter High Hrothgar.

▶ Something to Shout About

The monastery is adorned with carvings from ancient times and banners bearing the strange symbols of the dragon language. An old monk in a long robe steps forward; this is Arngeir, the leader of the Greybeards. He knows who you are. Speak with him, and he asks for a taste of your voice. Oblige him.

◇ **OBJECTIVE:** Demonstrate your "Unrelenting Force" Shout
◇ **OBJECTIVE:** Speak to Arngeir
♦ **TARGET:** Arngeir, inside High Hrothgar

Select the Unrelenting Force Shout from your Magic menu, and bellow at or near Arngeir. The other Greybeards, Borri, Einarth, and Wulfgar come to watch. Your fate is confirmed; speak with him again, and he welcomes you to the monastery. Master Arngeir speaks for the Greybeards and asks why you have come. Answer any way you wish (questions lead to more information on the monastery and the Greybeards' existence). When you are ready, tell Arngeir that you're "ready to learn." Arngeir wishes to train you so you're better able to execute a Thu'um, or Shout.

◇ **OBJECTIVE:** Learn the Word of Power from Einarth

Master Arngeir explains that all Shouts are made up of three Words of Power. As you master each Word, your Shout becomes progressively stronger. Currently, you have only learned *Fus* (or

"Force"), the first Word of your Unrelenting Force Shout. Master Einarth now teaches you *Ro* (or "Balance"), the second Word. This allows you to focus your Thu'um more sharply. Einarth Shouts into the hallowed stone of the monastery. Step onto the dragon runes that glow from the Shout, and absorb this second word.

▶ **Word of Power:** Balance, Unrelenting Force

Your learning impresses Arngeir, but he warns you that to unlock its meaning, you must constantly practice. As part of your initiation, Master Einarth allows you to tap into his understanding of Ro. Einarth glows with an orange light, imparting his knowledge onto you, in the same way you absorb the soul of a dragon. Now comes the real test: to see how quickly you've mastered the entire Shout!

◇ **OBJECTIVE:** Demonstrate your Unrelenting Force Shout (3x)

The monks have three targets for you to bellow your Shout toward. As the first ghostly monk figure is conjured, execute your Shout. The trick to this Shout's strength is the length of time that you hold the Shout button down. Continuously hold the button until the Shout is omitted. Tap the button if you wish to lessen the stagger you inflict upon your foes (or in this case, your ghostly Greybeard). After you complete three Shouts to Arngeir's satisfaction, he congratulates you and motions for you to follow Master Borri into the courtyard.

 TIP Play around with the length of time you hold the button down before releasing it to strengthen or weaken your Shout, so you know how long to attempt this ability.

◇ **OBJECTIVE:** Learn the Word of Power from Borri

Follow Master Borri to the door to High Hrothgar Courtyard and step outside, stopping next to Borri, who is ready to teach you a new Shout—the *Wuld* (or "Whirlwind"). Stand over the snow that Borri has projected the Shout into, and absorb the Shout. Then approach Borri and he glows, gifting you his knowledge of the Word.

NOTE The Word of Power that Borri teaches you may be different if (during the course of your adventures) you've found a Word Wall and absorbed one or two of the other parts of the phrase for the Whirlwind Sprint Shout. If you have all three Words of Power, this Shout (like all others) is much more potent. Check the Appendices (page 632) for a list of locations where all Shouts can be found.

▶ **Word of Power:** Whirlwind, Whirlwind Sprint

◇ **OBJECTIVE:** Demonstrate your "Whirlwind Sprint" Shout

Master Borri walks toward an iron gate. Before following him, enter the Magic > Shouts menu to change your Shout to Whirlwind Sprint (you don't want to bellow Unrelenting Force at the gate!). Stand between the two stone columns facing the gate, with Master Wulfgar in view. He demonstrates the Whirlwind Sprint, rushing at an amazing speed through the gate before it closes. Now it is your turn: The moment the gate opens, execute the Shout and rush forward, aiming for the single stone column by the cliff edge. You should easily pass through before the gate closes. If you don't, try again.

◊ **OBJECTIVE:** Speak to Arngeir for further training

Quest Conclusion

Master Arngeir is astonished at your quick mastery of a new Thu'um. He tells you that the gods gave you this gift for a reason, but it is up to you to figure out how best to utilize it. For now, though, you are ready for the final part of your trial: Retrieve the Horn of Jurgen Windcaller, the founder of the Greybeards. Arngeir tells you that the horn is in Windcaller's tomb in the ancient fane (temple) of Ustengrav. If you remain true to the Way of the Voice, you will return.

Postquest Activities

Continue to ask Arngeir questions if you wish. Main Quest: The Horn of Jurgen Windcaller has already begun!

THE HORN OF JURGEN WINDCALLER

PREREQUISITES: Complete Main Quest: The Way of the Voice, 10 gold pieces
INTERSECTING QUESTS: Main Quest: The Way of the Voice, Main Quest: The Horn of Jurgen Windcaller
LOCATIONS: High Hrothgar, High Hrothgar Courtyard, Riverwood, Sleeping Giant Inn, Ustengrav, Ustengrav Depths
CHARACTERS: Delphine, Master Arngeir, Master Borri, Master Einarth, Master Wulfgar, Orgnar
ENEMIES: Bandit, Bandit Thrall, Conjurer, Draugr, Fire Mage, Frostbite Spider, Necromancer, Skeleton
◊ **OBJECTIVES:** Retrieve the horn, Meet with whoever took the horn, Return the horn to Arngeir, Learn the Word of Power from Wulfgar, Receive the Greybeards' greeting

Underground in Ustengrav

◊ **OBJECTIVE:** Retrieve the horn
♦ **TARGET:** Horn of Jurgen Windcaller, inside Ustengrav

Once Arngeir gives you this quest, you may ask him about the Greybeards, why dragons are returning, who Jurgen Windcaller is, and other conversation topics. Turn to your world map and locate Ustengrav on the eastern edge of the great marsh, northeast of Morthal in Hjaalmarch Hold. Your first task is to descend from High Hrothgar.

> **TIP** Your descent can be done on foot or by horse (if you came on a steed), but a much quicker plan is to halve the distance between here at Ustengrav and Fast-Travel to Whiterun, the Western Watchtower, or any location closest to the temple tomb. Don't forget to use your new Whirlwind Sprint Shout to cover distances more swiftly than before!

When you finally reach Ustengrav, you may find a small campfire and lean-to by the circular barrow entrance. Expect a confrontation with bandits and a necromancer. Then descend the barrow steps and open the door to Ustengrav.

Heading down the wide steps, into the gloom of the ancient temple, you stumble upon a group of mages and conjurers picking clean the remains of a thwarted bandit attack. You can slink by using Sneak or engage the magicians in combat.

> **TIP** The Bandit Thralls are being controlled by a necromancer—kill him, and the thralls die too.

Locate the opening in the northeast wall of the temple entrance, and follow the trail of lanterns down the steps. This soon becomes a trail of mage corpses, as you watch a group of Draugr demolish the wizards and make a run at you. Cut down the Draugr, or use whatever cunning magic or sneaking you wish, before continuing into the first burial crypt. Scavenge whatever you wish, then head east and turn south, down a passage lit by candles.

There are steps down to your right (west), leading to a small crypt. Grab the items and yank the pull-chain. A section of wall rumbles open, leading you down a cramped tunnel to a secret dead-end chamber and a treasure chest. Retrace your steps. Enter the great hall, with a stone bridge ahead of and above you. Fend off the Draugr that clamber out of their vertical tombs. Then climb the interior stairwell, and cross the bridge you just passed under. Locate the iron door and enter the Ustengrav Depths.

Head down the winding tunnel until it opens into a gigantic, multilevel grotto. It is immense enough to have trees, a waterfall, and a Word Wall! Continue down the tree-root ledge and tunnel, heading south and then east. You appear on a bridge overlooking an ancient banqueting hall. Follow the steps down, eliminating Draugr as you go. To the east are the remains of a food-preparation area running parallel to the hall. Head south, up more stairs, and cross a second bridge to exit the hall.

The tunnel to the southwest widens into an entrance room with a middle pillar. To the left is a double portcullis (open it with two wall handles; one is farther along the southwest wall) behind which is a small room with treasure. Take this and optionally shoot the lamp down onto the oil below to burn any Draugr that come to investigate you. Head west through a gap in the wall. Here, there are steps up to a small preparation alcove, and more importantly, an earthen and rock corridor that leads into the gigantic grotto.

Follow the collapsed bridge down to the massive pillars under the chamber, where parts of an ancient fire trap still burn and skeletons roam. Cut down all the bony fiends in this two-floor area, inspect the throne area (with another skeleton to slaughter),

and then run northeast around the perimeter wall ledge, down to the rocky base of the grotto. Moments later, you learn a word from the Become Ethereal Shout. Afterward, you fight with a Draugr over a treasure chest behind the waterfall. Before you leave, try your Whirlwind Sprint Shout and traverse the collapsed bridges in this area, leading to a small chamber you can loot.

➤ **Word of Power:** Become Ethereal

The Tomb Raider

Backtrack to the throne area where you fought the skeletons, and look to your east. Cross the large natural bridge that spans the grotto, to a second two-floor underchamber on the eastern side. First, clear out the skeletons from the balcony above, and then inspect a set of three strange stones back on the lower underchamber area.

Puzzle Solution: If you stand close to each one of the three stones, they pulse with an eerie, magical glow. This has the added effect of opening one of three portcullises in the tunnel to the east. However, after a second or two, the light switches off, blocking your path. This is the only way the portcullises open. If you get through one or two of them, you must turn back; all three must be raised for you to continue. The trick here is to line yourself up on the western side of the stones, as shown in the preceding picture with the stones between you and the portcullises. Then execute a Whirlwind Sprint Shout, followed by another to make sure you dash past the stones and the opening portcullises immediately.

Continue east, jumping to the natural rock on either side of the circular floor tiles, as they blast gouts of fire when you stand on them. This can prove handy when you reach the raised section of floor in the room of alcoves—a pack of Frostbite Spiders descends from the ceiling to attack. Optionally back up so the spiders scuttle onto the floor tiles and are burned along with your own attacks. Exit by hacking the cobwebs from the doorway to the east. Then open the wooden door.

Pull the chain to raise the portcullis that leads into the final resting place of Jurgen Windcaller. As you step forward, four dragon statue heads rumble up from the water. Continue across the bridge over the flooded lower floor and approach the ornate tomb. The horn should be still clutched by the carved arm of Jurgen in his sarcophagus...but it isn't! Instead, there's a small piece of paper. Take and read it. The damned thief who took the horn has left you a note; it requests that you rent the attic room at the Sleeping Giant Inn in Riverwood, and it is signed "A friend."

➤ **Mysterious Note**

◊ **OBJECTIVE FAILED:** Retrieve the horn
◊ **OBJECTIVE:** Meet with whoever took the horn
♦ **TARGET:** "A friend" inside Sleeping Giant Inn, in Riverwood

This may be the first time that you've failed an objective. This is mandatory; you cannot succeed at this particular objective at the moment. **CAUTION**

A Mysterious Stranger

You'd think "a friend" wouldn't want you risking your life in a Draugr dungeon! Stifle any indignant rage you may be experiencing, and console yourself with any treasure you find through the wooden door behind the sarcophagus. There is an exit tunnel in the left (north) wall, offering a shortcut to an iron door, and a lever that lowers a section of stone wall, allowing you to step into the initial crypt, up into the temple entrance, and out of Ustengrav.

Fast-Travel (or trek back) to Riverwood, and follow the instructions of the Mysterious Note. Locate the Sleeping Giant Inn, enter, and locate Delphine, who owns the place with her slightly dense friend Orgnar. Step up to Delphine and ask to rent the attic room for 10 gold.

After the money changes hands, she tells you the Sleeping Giant doesn't have an attic room, but you can take the room on the left. Enter the room, and after a few moments, Delphine joins you. Apparently you're the Dragonborn she's been hearing so much about. As a way of a peace offering, she hands you the horn that you seek.

➤ **Horn of Jurgen Windcaller**

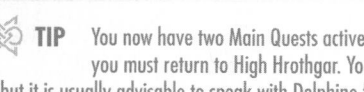

◊ **MAIN QUEST:** A Blade in the Dark begins
◊ **OBJECTIVE:** Return the horn to Arngeir
♦ **TARGET:** Master Arngeir, in High Hrothgar

🔍 **TIP** You now have two Main Quests active. In order to finish this one, you must return to High Hrothgar. You can attempt this at any time, but it is usually advisable to speak with Delphine first (the initial part of the next Main Quest). Once you leave the Sleeping Giant, trek (or Fast-Travel) back to High Hrothgar.

Quest Conclusion

Enter High Hrothgar, and head through the monastery until you spot Arngeir. He already knows you have returned with the Horn of Jurgen Windcaller and remarks that the time has come for the Greybeards to recognize you formally as Dragonborn.

◊ **OBJECTIVE:** Learn the Word of Power from Wulfgar
♦ **TARGET:** Master Wulfgar, in High Hrothgar

Return to the central chamber inside High Hrothgar as the Greybeards assemble. Master Wulfgar approaches the center of the floor and bellows the word *Dah* ("Push") into the granite. Step onto the glowing runes and absorb the Word of Power. You can now utilize the Shout Unrelenting Force with maximum potency! Absorb the learning from Wulfgar as well.

➤ **Word of Power:** Push, Unrelenting Force

◊ **OBJECTIVE:** Receive the Greybeards' greeting

Remain in the center of the room. The Greybeards stand at each point of the diamond paving, and Arngeir greets you with a ferocious chant in dragon tongue. You withstand the blast, which pleases and impresses Arngeir. You've tasted the Voice of the Greybeards and passed through unscathed. High Hrothgar is now open to you!

Postquest Activities

There are two tasks you can attempt with the Greybeards from this point on. Look up the Other Faction Quests on page 322. Also remember that Main Quest: A Blade in the Dark is already under way!

Return to Ustengrav and activate Jurgen Windcaller's tomb. The horn returns to its rightful resting place, and you receive a bonus Dragon Soul.

➤ **Dragon Soul**

A BLADE IN THE DARK

PREREQUISITES: Complete Main Quest: The Horn of Jurgen Windcaller
INTERSECTING QUESTS: Main Quest: The Horn of Jurgen Windcaller, Main Quest: Diplomatic Immunity
LOCATIONS: Kynesgrove, Kynesgrove Dragon Mound, Riverwood, Sleeping Giant Inn
CHARACTERS: Delphine, Iddra, Orgnar
ENEMIES: Alduin ("World Eater"), Sahloknir ("Phantom Sky Hunter")
◊ **OBJECTIVES:** Talk to Delphine, Locate the dragon burial site, Kill the dragon Sahloknir, Talk to Delphine

 MINOR SPOILERS

▷ Grave Concerns

◊ **OBJECTIVE:** Talk to Delphine
♦ **TARGET:** Delphine, the Sleeping Giant Inn, in Riverwood

Once Delphine has given you the Horn of Jurgen Windcaller, she requests that you follow her. Oblige her, walking across the inn to the bedroom opposite, where Delphine opens a cabinet and pushes the fake back, revealing a secret set of cellar steps. This leads to a war room of sorts, complete with a map of Skyrim on a central table and various potions and items you can take. Delphine mentions the Dragonborn, and through conversation choices (answer as you wish), you realize Delphine was the one who took the horn (she was Farengar Secret-Fire's "reliable source" back in Dragonsreach who found the location of the Dragonstone). She knows that Thalmor spies are everywhere, so she took precautions to arrange this meeting.

Delphine is part of a group that has been searching for someone like you—a Dragonborn—for a very long time. Delphine needs to know if you can devour a dragon's soul, as you'll have a chance to prove it soon enough. She also holds a low opinion of the Greybeards. Finally, she reveals the reasons for her agitation: She's discovered that dragons aren't just coming back—they're coming back to life! It seems that the dragons weren't banished; they were extinguished from this land, and now something is bringing them back from the dead. Using a pattern she discovered on the Dragonstone you found, Delphine has deciphered the location where she believes the next dragon will rise from the dead, and she needs you to help her stop it. The location is Kynesgrove in Eastmarch.

◊ **OBJECTIVE:** Locate the dragon burial site
♦ **TARGET:** Dragon mound above Kynesgrove

 TIP After speaking with Delphine, you should head to High Hrothgar once you emerge from the Sleeping Giant Inn so you complete the previous Main Quest as quickly as possible.

Use the annotated map bearing all of the dragon burial sites as the basis for tracking and killing all the dragons that may return to Skyrim.

Once you tell Delphine that you're ready, she dons her leathers, informs Orgnar that she's traveling, and sets off on the long walk to Kynesgrove. This settlement is in the northern part of Eastmarch Hold, just southwest of Windhelm. To reach there, you can do the following:

Take the journey on foot. You can either keep up with Delphine or you can fight your way alone. Stay on the roads, prepare for world encounters, and discover as many Primary Locations along the way as possible (that you can return to and explore later). Remember to also use your Whirlwind Sprint for a faster pace.

Or, if you've already made some discoveries in the area in and around Kynesgrove (by visiting Windhelm, for example), you may wish to Fast-Travel to the nearest unlocked location and then travel to Kynesgrove.

Or, you can take a horse for a slightly faster journey.

When you reach Kynesgrove, Delphine should be ahead of you (if she isn't, wait for her). She senses something is wrong; this is soon proven correct when Iddra (a resident of the hamlet) runs over, shouting that a dragon attacking at the top of the hill! Delphine starts sprinting.

▷ A Terrible Resurrection

Delphine slows to an incredulous stumble as a huge black dragon with piercing red eyes hovers above a dragon mound at the top of the hill. It bellows a guttural roar in dragon tongue. The dragon mound where Alduin concentrated his Shout begins

to swirl with a strange energy, not unlike the ethereal material you've absorbed during previous dragon confrontations. The next moment, the mound bursts open, and a huge skeletal dragon begins to emerge from deathly slumber. The dragons speak quickly to each other, before Alduin turns, mocks your claim to be "dovahkiin," and departs the area as quickly as he arrives.

 TIP You may interrupt this resurrection and attack the newly returned dragon as quickly as you wish.

◊ **OBJECTIVE:** Kill the dragon Sahloknir

The skeletal Sahloknir clambers out of his grave and is resurrected by Alduin's powerful magic. Before Sahloknir's skin can gather around his bones and he regains his powers, race in with your most impressive melee implements and deliver a series of attacks to weaken the dragon's health.

 TIP Remember! Attacking a skeletal dragon before it grows flesh and wings to fly is a much easier battle: Get in early and quickly with your weapons.

Delphine fires arrows, then rushes in with melee attacks when the dragon lands; you should demonstrate your offensive powers too. Follow the same set of tactics laid out during Main Quest: Dragon Rising, when you faced Mirmulnir the "Loyal Mortal Hunter." One overriding plan is to ensure that Sahloknir's life is as short as possible!

When Sahloknir has been reduced back into a pile of bones, the beast splits apart into hundreds of scaly shards, and you absorb another Dragon Soul. Search the dragon, and then head over to Delphine for her promised revelations.

➤ **Dragon Soul absorbed**

◊ **OBJECTIVE:** Talk to Delphine

Quest Conclusion

Delphine lives up to her promise and answers any questions you have. Most importantly, she reveals herself to be one of the last members of the Blades. Long ago, the Blades were dragonslayers, serving the Dragonborn, the greatest dragonslayer. For 200 years, the Blades have been searching for a purpose. Now that purpose is clear. You may mention that you've seen Alduin before; he rampaged through Helgen and prevented your execution. Delphine finds this interesting but is annoyed that she's still blundering around in the dark.

Your next move is to find out who is controlling these dragons, and the Thalmor—the faction that rules the Aldmeri Dominion—are the best lead. Even if they aren't involved, they'll know who is. Delphine believes that there are no worse enemy to humankind than the Thalmor. She also has some ideas for getting you into the Thalmor Embassy, but she needs time to plan. You receive her secret Key and are told to meet her back in Riverwood.

➤ **Delphine's Secret Door Key**

Postquest Activities

Delphine's Secret Door Key opens the cabinet in her room in the Sleeping Giant Inn. Return to Riverwood when you wish to begin Main Quest: Diplomatic Immunity. Act I now concludes.

MAIN QUEST: ACT II

DIPLOMATIC IMMUNITY

PREREQUISITES: Complete Main Quest: A Blade in the Dark

INTERSECTING QUESTS: Main Quest: A Blade in the Dark, Civil War Quest: Message to Whiterun, Dark Brotherhood Quest: Bound Until Death, Thieves Guild Quest: Dampened Spirits, Miscellaneous Objective: Malborn's Long Shadow*

LOCATIONS: Riverwood, Sleeping Giant Inn, Solitude, Winking Skeever, Thalmor Embassy, Reeking Cave, Thalmor Embassy, Elenwen's Solar, Dungeon

CHARACTERS: Brelas, Delphine, Erikur, Etienne Rarnis, General Tullius, Illdi, Malborn, Jarl Balgruuf, Jarl Elisif the Fair, Jarl Idgrod Ravencrone, Jarl Igmund, Jarl Siddgeir, Maven Black-Briar, Ondolemar, Orthus Endario, Proventus Avenicci, Razelan, Tsavani, Vittoria Vici

ENEMIES: Elenwen, Frost Troll, Gissur, Rulindil, Thalmor Guard, Thalmor Soldier, Thalmor Wizard

◊ **OBJECTIVES:** Meet Delphine in Riverwood, Meet Malborn in Solitude, Give Malborn the equipment, Meet Delphine at the stables, Create a distraction and get away from the party, (Optional) Retrieve your gear, Search for information about the dragons returning, Escape the Thalmor Embassy, Talk to Delphine, Recover your equipment

 NOTE ✱ Quest names marked with this symbol do not appear in your Quest Menu list, although objectives may.

The Thinking Schemer

◊ **OBJECTIVE:** Meet Delphine in Riverwood
♦ **TARGET:** The Sleeping Giant Inn, in Riverwood

When you are ready to continue prying into the secretive and powerful Thalmor faction, return to Riverwood and seek out Delphine in her usual resting spot—the cellar of the Sleeping Giant Inn. She has crafted a plan to infiltrate you into the Thalmor Embassy, mainly because you're unknown to their organization, while Delphine would stand out like a Stormcloak in Solitude. She tells you that the Thalmor ambassador, Elenwen, is renowned for throwing parties where the rich and connected hobnob with the Thalmor. Once you infiltrate the Embassy, you'll excuse yourself from the glad-handing and attempt to find any of Elenwen's secret files. Delphine has a contact—a Wood Elf named Malborn—inside the Embassy who can help but who doesn't want any exposure. You're to meet him at the Winking Skeever. You can bombard Delphine with several questions about the contact, how you'll get into the party, and other matters if you wish.

◊ **OBJECTIVE:** Meet Malborn in Solitude
◊ **OBJECTIVE:** Give Malborn the equipment
♦ **TARGET:** Malborn, inside the Winking Skeever, in Solitude

Journey to Solitude, and locate the Winking Skeever tavern, close to the main gates. Step inside and find the shifty-looking character, Malborn. Tell him that a mutual friend sent you, and he says that he can smuggle some equipment into the Embassy that you can pick up once you're inside, just in case you need a weapon or two if you're accidentally discovered or if the plan becomes problematic. He tells you to hand over what you can't live without, and he'll have it ready to grab once you're inside.

⚑ **TIP** **What to Bring:** Follow Malborn's advice, and bring items that aid your sneaking, such as a dagger you can inflict sneak attacks with; items that soften your footfalls; and potions or augmentations that can keep you healthy (or full of Stamina or Magicka) during combat.

If you stink at sneaking, simply load Malborn up with your favorite weapons, some potions, and a full suit of armor. You can hand over anything you wish to him.

After you hand over your preferred equipment to Malborn, he tells you that he'll seek you out at the party, and says to meet up with Delphine, who has some appropriate attire and an invitation to the event.

◊ **OBJECTIVE:** Meet Delphine at the stables
♦ **TARGET:** Delphine, at Katla's Farm

Travel to Katla's Farm, halfway up the hill on which Solitude sits. As the Thalmor Guards will notice an adventuring type who's armed to the teeth, Delphine gives you more suitable attire for socializing with the noblemen of Skyrim. She also hands you an Invitation to Elenwen's Reception and says that she'll keep the rest of your gear safe until you return. When you're inside, you'll have only what Malborn smuggled in and whatever there is to hand in the Embassy. Don the outfit that Delphine gave you; remove any gauntlets, helmets, or shields you're carrying (although amulets and rings are fine to wear). Delphine gives you a quick once-over and asks if you're ready to take the carriage to the Thalmor Embassy. Agree when you wish to continue. The remaining equipment is now removed.

➤ **Party Clothes**   ➤ **Invitation to Elenwen's Reception**
➤ **Party Boots**

You disembark from the carriage in the snowy courtyard within the walls of the Thalmor Embassy compound. As you're heading toward the steps and a Thalmor Guard, you hear a man murmuring behind you. Optionally turn and listen to Razelan, who's late for the party and in a slightly rambunctious mood. He's certain there's not enough drinking going on in the world today. Politely leave him, and amble over to talk with the Thalmor Guard and show him your invitation. You have other conversation options, but you can't proceed until the invitation is shown. Head up the steps, past the guard and into the Embassy.

Be warned! From this moment until the end of this quest, you cannot Fast-Travel. You also cannot draw or use weapons until you've left the party with Malborn. **CAUTION**

⚑ **TIP** You may explore the grounds of the Embassy (with some deft sneaking), but it's not practical, nor necessary—there's ample opportunity to move around the grounds in a few moments.

◊ **OBJECTIVE:** Create a distraction and get away from the party
♦ **TARGET:** Various, then Malborn, at the Thalmor Embassy

Scene, Not Heard

Elenwen greets you as you enter. Make small talk for a few moments (your conversation topics range from asking for a drink to other pleasantries), and before Elenwen's suspicions are raised by any strange or mistaken answers you give her, Malborn calls her from the bar counter, saying that he's run out of the Alto Wine. You now know where Malborn is stationed and can quickly slip away from Elenwen as she says she'll catch up to you later and greets Razelan. Mingle in the main chamber. Here, you'll bump into several important dignitaries from across Skyrim:

Erikur, the conniving, greedy, and vain owner of the lumber mill in Solitude.

General Tullius, the right hand of the Emperor in charge of Skyrim's Imperials.

Jarl Balgruuf, the key Imperial ally and Nord leader of Whiterun.

Jarl Elisif the Fair, the naive and patriotic new Jarl of Solitude.

Jarl Idgrod Ravencrone, the odd, hunched crone and leader of Morthal.

Jarl Igmund, the leader of Markarth and staunch supporter of the Imperials.

Jarl Siddgeir, the self-assured, entitled bully of a leader of Falkreath.

Maven Black-Briar, the shrewd family matriarch and meadery owner in Riften.

Ondolemar, the haughty Thalmor liasion to the Imperial Justicars in Markath.

Orthus Endario, who runs the East Empire Company's office in Windhelm.

Proventus Avenicci, the political and inept steward for the Jarl of Whiterun.

Vittoria Vici, the owner of the East Empire Company and cousin of the Emperor.

Brelas, a respectful and self-effacing Embassy servant who works the other bar.

Illdi, the hired bard, offering timid and underwhelming performances.

> **NOTE** Depending on who you've killed or how the Civil War is progressing, the partygoers may change from the ones shown in the preceding list. Here's who to expect:
>
> A guest will not be here if you've killed them, or if they are hostile to you for any reason.
>
> None of the guests are here if you've been openly hostile to them previously and are not on friendly terms.
>
> The Imperial Jarls won't make an appearance if their Hold Cities have been captured by the Stormcloaks.
>
> Vittoria Vici will not be here if Dark Brotherhood Quest: Bound Until Death is active.
>
> Maven Black-Briar will not be here if Thieves Guild Quest: Dampened Spirits is active.
>
> General Tullius isn't here if Civil War Quest: Message to Whiterun hasn't been completed. He is also missing if a city siege is under way.
>
> Proventus Avenicci and Jarl Balgruuf will not be here if Civil War Quest: Message to Whiterun is active or if has been completed.

With the party already under way, you have a few different options to try when attempting a disturbance:

Razing a Ruckus

The loudmouthed fellow you met outside is usually sitting down, away from the mingling. Strike up a conversation with the reprobate, and he'll ask for a drink. Return to Malborn or head over to Brelas and order a drink; then return to Razelan and hand the drink over. He thanks you for it; you then ask if he can cause a distraction. Sure enough, he wanders into the throng and commences a ruckus. Head to Malborn quickly!

➤ **Colovian Brandy**

A Fractious Favor

You may spot a good friend among the assembled guests. Possible friendships include Vittoria Vici, Maven Black-Briar, Ondolemar, or any of the Jarls, depending on your previous interactions with them. Begin a quiet chat with one of them and ask if they would cause a small disturbance. When they agree, back away toward Malborn, and watch your friend cause a scene with Razelan, despite the drunkard's innocence. Head to Malborn quickly!

> **TIP** You'll know if you're friendly with a guest, as you'll be able to ask them to do something for you when you speak with them. If you're reading this prior to the quest commencing, refer to the Favor Quests on page 399 for information about how to win Favor with these guests. Some of your "friends" may require a Speech-based Persuasion to agree to cause a distraction:
>
> These friends will act without Persuasion: Jarl Idgrod Ravencrone, Maven Black-Briar, Jarl Balgruuf, or Orthus Endario.
>
> These friends will act once you Persuade them: Jarl Igmund, Jarl Elisif, Jarl Siddgeir, or Ondolemar.
>
> Vittoria Vici is never a friend but can be Persuaded to cause a distraction.
>
> Ondolemar is furious with your actions after you Persuade him and becomes your enemy after this quest.

You Can't Get the Staff These Days

Speak to Erikur at the party, and you'll see that he has his eye on Brelas, one of the waitstaff. Speak to Erikur and offer to talk to Brelas to see whether she's interested in a clandestine rendezvous with Erikur. Brelas, being of high morals (and taste), declines the offer. Return to Erikur and tell him:

(Lie) That she's interested, or

That she isn't interested at all.

Either response makes Erikur accost Brelas, causing a distraction and allowing you to head to Malborn, and quickly!

During any of these distractions, Malborn heads to the door leading into the kitchens and waits for you to approach. He'll then open the door and close it behind you.

> ◊ **OBJECTIVE:** (Optional) Retrieve your gear
> ♦ **TARGET:** Chest, in the Thalmor Embassy larder
> ◊ **OBJECTIVE:** Search for information about the dragons returning
> ♦ **TARGET 1:** Small chests (2), Thalmor Embassy, Elenwen's Solar and Dungeon
> ♦ **TARGET 2:** Etienne Rarnis, Thalmor Embassy, Dungeon

Embassy Evidence

Enter the kitchens, now that no one saw you slip away. While Malborn preoccupies Tsavani the cook, open the next door on the left side of the kitchen and enter the larder. The wooden chest on the left has the equipment you gave Malborn back at the Winking Skeever. Take the exit door opposite the chest and begin a clandestine sweep of the Embassy chambers.

➤ Smuggled Equipment

In reality, the sweep doesn't have to be that sneaky, as long as you're prepared for a fight with the well-armed Thalmor Soldiers patrolling the building. From the first corridor, face south, and check the room to your left (east), into a long hallway with two Thalmor Guards. You may engage them in combat, or stay out of sight (behind the doorway, or via a spell or sneaking) and wait for them to leave so you can sneak past them, or shut the door and easily sneak by. Use the small storage room or the room divider to hide behind, if necessary.

THALMOR THEATRICS

(Sneak) Locate the room on your right as you begin this infiltration. It contains a spare set of Thalmor Robes. Donning these robes allows you to sneak around the Embassy buildings a little more easily. Guards now attack only if they see your face and you're close enough (within around ten feet) to draw their suspicions. Just how easily spotted you are depends on your race:

Beast races, such as Orcs, Khajiit, or Argonians are easily spotted by guards.

Human races, such as Nords, Bretons, or Redguard, have a slightly easier time.

Wood and Dark Elves have a better chance at passing through without drawing suspicion.

High Elves are almost able to wander the Embassy with impunity!

➤ Thalmor Robes

From the long hallway, you can head east and open the door to the exterior courtyard (western side). Or you can maneuver around the bar, up the stairs to the upper floor, and creep past (or bludgeon) the guard patrolling this area. To your right (east) is a corridor leading to a dining area (with wine, poisons, and potions to pilfer). To the left (west) is a bedroom, which is on your right (north) and an office to the left (south), which also has a door leading to the exterior courtyard (eastern side). Pick either of the exits and head outside.

 NOTE From this point on, you have a choice regarding how you find the information the objective has requested:

Plan 1: You can search the solar and the dungeon for written materials from the Thalmor. This allows you to leave without interacting with the prisoner.

Plan 2: You can move through the solar, down to the dungeon, and then free Etienne Rarnis. This is the prisoner a Thalmor spy named Gissur picked up. He has been viciously tortured by a Thalmor named Rulindil. He then escapes with you.

Plan 3: Or you can execute both plans, as the following section reveals:

Creep through the snow, along the perimeter of the Thalmor Embassy grounds, taking care not to be seen by the patrolling guards (or rush in and attack them if you don't believe in the element of surprise). Either perimeter path allows you access into the snow-laden garden, and the door into Elenwen's Solar. Enter that door as soon as you can.

(Sneak) If you're disguised or sneaking, there's usually a Thalmor Mage guarding this door.

(High Elf) If you're a High Elf and wearing Thalmor Robes, you can actually trick the guard into leaving his post with a quick conversation!

When you enter the solar, you hear a Thalmor called Rulindil (one of the spymasters responsible for receiving and utilizing clandestine chatter) talking to one of his spies, a weasely man named Gissur. They mention an interrogation room below. Beware of a patrolling guard here as you move quietly to the bar and storage room (if you're hiding), or into the withdrawing room that has multiple exits.

Upstairs are two bedrooms and a small storage area. Aside from a variety of expensive items (that aren't critical to your quest), there's nothing to take up here. Instead, remain on the ground floor and sneak (or rush) into the northwest office, next to Rulindil's study. There are books to check out, and a small chest holds some evidence: a Dragon Investigation document (which notes a prisoner in the cellar dungeon who is the key to unlocking the dragon phenomenon), the Interrogation Chamber Key, and two dossiers — one on Delphine and the other on Ulfric Stormcloak. It all makes for some very interesting reading. If you're just considering the prisoner, you can also head west and challenge Rulindil in his study. You can spring into an attack or try to pickpocket Rulindil (which is difficult) for the Interrogation Chamber Key.

- ➤ **Interrogation Chamber Key (2)**
- ➤ **Dragon Investigation:** Current Status
- ➤ **Thalmor Dossier:** Delphine
- ➤ **Thalmor Dossier:** Ulfric Stormcloak

There are two staircases leading down; both lead to a similar-looking door to the Embassy Dungeon (which can also be picked [Expert]). You can head through either door, but the stairs and door to the northeast place you on a balcony where you can see a single guard patrolling.

If you entered this area via Elenwen's Study (the one farthest from Rulindil), then you can sneak down here and watch Rulindil descend the steps from his office and begin a rather unpleasant interrogation. Otherwise, he is likely to have attacked you, or been killed already, along with his spy, Gissur.

Fewer guards make it easier to sneak down the steps, move past the rack, and execute the guard with a sneak attack. Before you investigate that moaning, check the small chest by the table with the rolls of paper on it; there's another dossier, this one on a gentleman named Esbern. Now read all the materials you've gathered (the Dragon Investigation and all three dossiers) to complete your objective.

- ➤ **Thalmor Dossier:** Esbern

You may talk to the prisoner moaning in the first cell (and Brelas if you used her as a party distraction). The prisoner's name is Etienne Rarnis, and if you speak to him, he reveals that he may have mentioned the location of a man named Esbern who may shed some light on the resurrected dragons returning to Skyrim. The Thalmor are certainly interested in him. As you release the prisoner, two Thalmor Soldiers and Malborn appear, so fight off the Thalmor if they attack. Take down any guards and search them for the Trap Door Key (there are two available); otherwise you won't be able to escape.

➤ Trap Door Key (2)

◊ **OBJECTIVE:** Escape the Thalmor Embassy
♦ **TARGET:** Reeking Cave exit

Drop through the trapdoor—with Malborn, Etienne, and Brelas by your side if they are alive and freed—and enter the Reeking Cave (so named because of the stench of the Frost Troll who lives here who slaughters travelers and brings them back here to consume). You can attack the troll before dropping down so he can't strike you back. Watch out; Etienne or Brelas can die fighting or fleeing from this creature. The cave itself is small; locate the exit, where Malborn, Etienne, and Brelas all flee. You don't need to follow them.

◊ **OBJECTIVE:** Talk to Delphine
◊ **OBJECTIVE:** Recover your equipment
♦ **TARGET:** Sleeping Giant Inn, in Riverwood

Quest Conclusion

Delphine is waiting for you in the secret cellar downstairs in the Sleeping Giant Inn. Return here and locate the large chest on the left (north) wall to obtain all the equipment you gave her before visiting the Embassy. Delphine wants to know if you've found out anything useful. Mention that the Thalmor are looking for someone named Esbern. Delphine seems to instantly know who this "crazy old man" is. She reveals Esbern is a Blade archivist who is an expert on the ancient dragonlore of the Blades. From your earned knowledge, it seems Esbern is hiding out somewhere in the city of Riften. Perhaps a well-connected man named Brynjolf can help. To get him to trust you, ask him to remember the 30th of Frostfall.

Postquest Activities

Time is racing; you must now hunt down Esbern, convince him to help your cause, and hope the Thalmor don't get there first! Main Quest: A Cornered Rat begins now. If you visit Windhelm, and Malborn is still alive, you can find him inside the Gnisis Corner Club and begin Miscellaneous Objective: Malborn's Long Shadow.

  A CORNERED RAT

PREREQUISITES: Complete Main Quest: Diplomatic Immunity
INTERSECTING QUESTS: Main Quest: Diplomatic Immunity, Main Quest: Alduin's Wall, Thieves Guild Quest: A Chance Arrangement
LOCATIONS: Riften, The Bee and Barb, The Ragged Flagon, The Ratway, The Ratway Vaults, The Ratway Warrens, Riftweald Manor, Riverwood, Sleeping Giant Inn
CHARACTERS: Brand-Shei, Brynjolf, Delphine , Esbern , Keerava, Madesi, Riften Guard, Salvianus, Vekel the Man
ENEMIES: Drahff, Gissur, Hefid the Deaf, Hewnon
Black-Skeever, Knjakr, Shavari, Skeever, Thalmor Soldier, Thalmor Wizard
◊ **OBJECTIVES:** Talk to Brynjolf, Search the Ratway for Esbern's hideout , Find Esbern in the Ratway Warrens, Talk to Esbern

◈ A Den of Iniquity

◊ **OBJECTIVE:** Talk to Brynjolf
♦ **TARGET:** Brynjolf, in Riften

Delphine instructs you to meet with her contact, a member of the Thieves Guild named Brynjolf. However, before you go, ask her about your birthright. You can also ask why the Blades are on the run. Turns out it's because the Thalmor were systematically hunting them down thanks to the White-Gold Concordat, which was signed with the Empire. It ended the war but gave the Thalmor free rein to stomp out the worship of Talos. You may also ask about the Thalmor, the arrogant and extreme rulers of the Aldmeri Dominion, or what used to be the Imperial provinces of Summerset Isle and Valenwood. When you've heard enough, leave the Sleeping Giant Inn and travel to Riften.

 TIP Remember the equipment you just gathered from where Delphine deposited it? If you need to equip any of it or arrange your Favorites, do this right now.

When you arrive at either of the city's gates for the first time, a guard halts you and attempts to shake you down for a "visitor's tax." You can:

(Persuade) Realize this for what it is.

(Gold) Realize this for what it is but pay up (the amount varies, depending on how poor you are)

(Intimidate) Threaten that you kill thieves

Any of these options (if successful) allows the guard to open the door. Butchering the guard also gets you into Riften, after dramatically increasing your bounty and forcing you to spend time in the jail.

Brynjolf

You meet a mysterious character in the Grand Plaza (during daylight hours) or inside the Bee and Barb the first time you look around the Grand Plaza in Riften.

First-time Thief: If you're meeting Brynjolf for the first time, and if you have some general skills in concealment or silent stealth or you've dealt with the guard at the Riften gate without resorting to violence, a man named Brynjolf strikes up a conversation with you. He may have an errand for you to perform to test your skills and may reward you with gold. Thieves Guild Quest: A Chance Arrangement must now be completed before Brynjolf releases the knowledge of where Esbern is hiding out.

(Persuade) Or you can use your verbal charms to reveal the location of Esbern, without playing Brynjolf's little game. If so, you can skip A Chance Arrangement.

Guild Member: If you're meeting Brynjolf and you've already proved yourself skilled by completing Thieves Guild Quest: A Chance Arrangement, Brynjolf is happy to point you in the direction of where Esbern is hiding out, once you ask him about these matters.

> **TIP** You don't have to play along with Brynjolf's schemes, though.
>
> (Persuade) You can speak to Keerava inside the Bee and Barb to learn about the Ragged Flagon, which gets you partway there.
>
> Or you can skip ahead to 'The Ratway Hidey-hole' and just follow the directions straight to Esbern.

▶ Interlude: A Chance Arrangement

He tells you to pilfer a silver ring from a stall owned by Madesi in the marketplace while he creates a distraction. Place it in the pocket of a Dark Elf vendor named Brand-Shei. If you're caught, you're on your own, but if you succeed, he'll have some better-paying schemes. If you've met Brynjolf during the evening or night, he'll be waiting between eight in the morning and eight in the evening for you. If you met Brynjolf at night, wait until daylight and meet up again.

> ◊ **A CHANCE ARRANGEMENT OBJECTIVE:** Meet Brynjolf during daytime
> ♦ **TARGET:** Brynjolf, Grand Plaza in Riften
> ◊ **A CHANCE ARRANGEMENT OBJECTIVE:** Steal Madesi's Ring
> ♦ **TARGET:** Madesi's stand, Grand Plaza in Riften

Brynjolf is waiting for you by his own plaza stand, where he's about to hawk his "amazing" Falmerblood Elixir. Naturally, this patter is designed to draw a crowd (including Madesi and Brand-Shei), allowing you to quickly move around the plaza's perimeter via the stone wall and crouch behind Madesi's stall.

(Lockpick [Novice]) Produce your lockpicks, and unlock the sliding door under the stall counter. Quickly rummage around inside Madesi's strongbox. You can happily help yourself to any of the items here, but the valuable you're concerned with is the Silver Ring. Steal it quickly, before any of the city guards spot you.

> You must attempt to pick this lock only after any city guards **CAUTION** pass you, and you're hidden from view while sneaking.

➤ **Madesi's Silver Ring**

> ◊ **A CHANCE ARRANGEMENT OBJECTIVE:** Plant Madesi's Ring
> ♦ **TARGET:** Brand-Shei, Grand Plaza in Riften

Creep around so the assembled beggars and storekeepers don't see you, and position yourself behind Brand-Shei.

(Sneak) You must now "reverse-pickpocket" the Dark Elf. This involves pickpocketing, choosing your own Apparel menu, selecting Madesi's Silver Ring, and giving it to Brand-Shei to finish the technique. Remember, no one must see you attempt this!

If you're successful, Brand-Shei is mistaken for a thief and hauled away to Riften prison. Your paths may cross again in the future....

> ◊ **A CHANCE ARRANGEMENT OBJECTIVE:** Speak to Brynjolf
> ♦ **TARGET:** Brynjolf, Grand Plaza in Riften

> If you're arrested, or you leave Riften and wait more than **CAUTION** half a day to complete Brynjolf's Objective, or you murder someone during his distraction, Thieves Guild Quest: A Chance Arrangement still completes. However, this is no reward, and Brynjolf isn't pleased with your inadequacies. This is not the way to impress a future mentor!

Speak to Brynjolf after the ring-plant misdirection, and he congratulates (and rewards) you. You receive no monetary gain if you failed. Then he mentions his organization has been having some bad luck but mentions that there's more money to earn if you can handle it. Reply that you can, and Brynjolf recommends you meet him at the Ragged Flagon tavern, deep inside Riften's subterranean Ratway. He also points you in the direction of Esbern when you ask him; he's down in the Ratway.

➤ **100 gold pieces**

> ◊ **OBJECTIVE:** Search the Ratway for Esbern's hideout
> ♦ **TARGET:** Ragged Flagon, inside the Ratway, in Riften

> **TIP** This is an optimal time to strike up a friendship with other members of the Thieves Guild and perhaps begin a series of quests with them. Consult the Thieves Guild Quests starting on page 196 for all the pertinent information.

▶ The Ratway Hidey-hole

Open the barred gate by the water's edge and go into the sewers that run the length and breadth of Riften. Down the first tunnel, you may stumble across two equally odious characters: Drahff and Hewnon Black-Skeever. They attempt to mug you for all your equipment. You can:

(Persuade) Try to let Drahff know that you've killed dozens like him.

Any other option results in violence. This doesn't impact your standing in Riften and is the recommended choice.

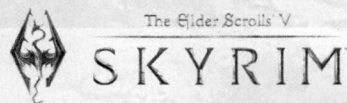

Now continue through this small maze of interlocking sewage tunnels. Watch for hanging oil traps, and a bear trap along the way. If your Lockpick skill is high enough, there's a chamber to check out, but your main purpose is finding the Ragged Flagon.

The tavern is unique, being constructed on and above a sewage conduit chamber. When you spot Brynjolf, he is talking with the barkeep (Vekel the Man), speaking about Brynjolf's predicament with his "organization." Speak to Vekel the Man, or seek out another Thieves Guild member named Dirge and ask either of them if they've seen "an old guy, hiding out" somewhere in Riften. Both Vekel's and Dirge's minds are cloudy, so you may need to clear them by:

(Persuade) Appealing to his sense of urgency and telling your contact that Esbern's life is in danger.

(Gold) Appealing to his sense of greed and offering gold so he remembers.

(Brawl) Appealing to his boisterous side and proving your might with a bare-knuckle fight. No weapons, or this suddenly gets a lot less friendly!

When one of these choices succeeds, Vekel or Dirge tells you that Esbern is holed up in the Ratway Warrens and hardly ever leaves the place.

If you're already a full-fledged member of the Thieves Guild, which requires you to have Thieves Guild Quest: Loud and Clear active and to have been awarded your thief's clothing, Vekel and Dirge also point you in the direction of the Ratway Warrens.

◊ **OBJECTIVE:** Find Esbern in the Ratway Warrens
♦ **TARGET:** Esbern, inside the Ratway, in Riften

CROSSING THE THALMOR: GISSUR'S REVENGE

Dispatching Gissur back at the Embassy prevents him from shadowing your movements.

If you left Spymaster Rulindil's spy Gissur alive during the previous quest, you may spot him in the Ragged Flagon. You can slay him or leave him alone. If you speak with either Dirge or Vekel, Gissur eavesdrops and sneaks out of the Ragged Flagon, into the Ratway. If you (carefully) follow him, you can eavesdrop as he tells the Thalmor troops where you are. You may wish to attack at any time, or:

You can remain hidden, as the Thalmor enter the Ragged Flagon, confront Dirge or Vekel, and are given a menacing brush-off by the Thieves Guild.

Or, you can reveal yourself (accidentally or otherwise) and turn the Ragged Flagon into a slaughterhouse. Leave no Thalmor alive!

CROSSING THE THALMOR: SHAVARI THE ASSASSIN

The Thalmor are hiring proficient assassins to track and kill you.

Unbeknownst to you, once you escaped the Thalmor Embassy, Elenwen placed a bounty on your head, which attracted the attention of a Khajiit assassin named Shavari. As soon as you enter the Ragged Flagon or the Ratway Vaults, she enters the Ratway after you. Be quick if you spot an unknown Khajiit in these parts; slay her before she can fulfill her task. Inspect her corpse for a note from "E" that proves the Thalmor plot against you.

➤ **Shavari's Note**

▶ Remembering the 30th of Frostfall

If you were directed into the Ratway Warrens or even stumbled here on your own, the Thalmor are already prowling this maze of connecting corridors around a central hub room (which you've just entered).

However, if Dirge or Vekel directed you to the Warrens, you are forewarned about the Thalmor ambush, allowing you to expect any attacks and even trying to ambush the guards and gain the upper hand. Either way, unless your sneaking ability is exceptional, expect to fight around four of these enemies throughout your navigation of the Warrens.

From either entrance into the Warrens, there are two possible routes:

The first is to navigate around the interconnected corridors and chambers, sneaking past or fighting Thalmor enemies and a few Skeever along the way. This is the long route, but it allows you to remain hidden, or at least clear the Warrens of foes for the moment.

Or, you can appear on the upper balcony of the multifloored central hub room, which is well lit and has a cart and hay bale at the base of it. Drop to the open gate on the eastern side of the bottom floor. The entrance to the Ratway Vaults is just south of this point, at the bottom of the Warrens.

Open the wooden door and enter the Ratway Vaults. The Thalmor haven't found this area yet, and it is rarely trafficked. One of the reasons may be the lunatics who populate the chambers here. Beware of Hefid the Deaf, and Knjakr the mad chef, as both of them get violent when they spot you. You'll also have to contend with a brain-addled man named Salvianus, who talks to himself. But you're actually here to locate the well-locked door on the upper balcony of the hub chamber, in the southwest corner.

Sidle up to the door and activate it, and you'll hear an old man shouting for you to go away. Persist, and the door's shutter slides open and a pair of eyes peer out. They are attached to a man who claims to not know who Esbern is.

No amount of persuasion or pleading gets the man to unlock the door. Use the quote Delphine told you to tell the man: "remember the 30th of Frostfall." Only then does the man reveal himself to be Esbern and unlock the door.

If you haven't spoken to Delphine after escaping the Thalmor Embassy, you can inform Esbern that you're Dragonborn, which is enough to pique his interest.

◇ **OBJECTIVE:** Talk to Esbern

Quest Conclusion

Once you're inside Esbern's hidey-hole, he asks how Delphine is after all these years, regarding the situation as "hopeless." He tells you that Alduin has returned, just as the prophecy said. Esbern believes it to be the end of the world. In fact, the only glimmer of hope would be if a Dragonborn returned....

Postquest Activities

During the conversation, Main Quest: Alduin's Wall begins immediately.

ALDUIN'S WALL

PREREQUISITES: Complete Main Quest: A Cornered Rat
INTERSECTING QUESTS: Main Quest: A Cornered Rat, Main Quest: The Throat of the World
LOCATIONS: Karthspire, Riften, The Ragged Flagon, The Ratway, The Ratway Warrens, Riverwood, Sleeping Giant Inn, Sky Haven Temple, Alduin's Wall
CHARACTERS: Delphine, Esbern, Orgnar
ENEMIES: Forsworn, Thalmor Soldier, Thalmor Wizard
◇ **OBJECTIVES:** Escort Esbern to Riverwood, Talk to Esbern, Gain entrance to Sky Haven Temple, Learn the secret of Alduin's Wall

 MINOR SPOILERS

History and Prophecy

◇ **OBJECTIVE:** Escort Esbern to Riverwood
◆ **TARGET:** The Sleeping Giant Inn, in Riverwood

Now that Brynjolf and the Thieves Guild have helped you locate the slightly deranged Esbern, it is your job to chaperone him to Riverwood. Ask him if he knows the way out of here, and he sets off running. Follow him out of his hidey-hole or request that he follow you. Head down the stairs in the sewer junction chamber. As you both enter the sewer passages, Thalmor agents begin to appear. Defeat them. Combat continues as you push up the stairs and into the Ratway Warrens. Let Esbern fight the Thalmor Soldiers that may appear; Esbern is a powerful wizard and can handle himself in a fight.

Head west, through the open gate in the hub room and into the connecting sewer tunnel. Go north past the tree routes and up the stairs by the dining chamber. Next, travel around to the south, above the hub room. Cross the middle balcony of the hub room, and go to the upper balcony overlooking this same hub room chamber. Head west into the Ragged Flagon. From here, head west, into the Ratway mead-tasting room; then turn right (north) and use the wall lever to lower the wooden bridge if you haven't done this already. From here, you're one winding corridor away from exiting into Riften. At this point, you can Fast-Travel or trek back to Riverwood and the Sleeping Giant Inn.

⟡ **TIP** Esbern simply crouches when overwhelmed by enemy attacks and then rises again. Don't worry about him being killed.

◇ **OBJECTIVE:** Talk to Esbern

Inform Delphine that you've found Esbern, and she's most thankful, taking you both down into her secret cellar. Esbern reveals a particularly important historical location: Sky Haven Temple, constructed around one of the main Akaviri military camps in the Reach, during the conquest of Skyrim. He also places a book on the table. Read it at your leisure for some history.

➤ **Annals of the Dragonguard**

Delphine isn't impressed until Esbern informs you both that the Sky Haven Temple is where Alduin's Wall was built to set in stone all their accumulated dragonlore. But the location of the wall, one of the wonders of the ancient world, was lost. Fortunately, Esbern knows where it is and why the three of you should journey there: The ancient Blades recorded both history and prophecy on Aduin's Wall. With any luck, it may reveal how to defeat Alduin himself.

◇ **OBJECTIVE:** Gain entrance to Sky Haven Temple

Forsworn and Forsaken

Delphine knows that Esbern's description fits an area of Skyrim called Karthspire, in the Karth River Canyon. She asks whether you should all travel there together or whether you should meet them at the Sky Haven Temple entrance. The choice is yours. You can:

- Fast-Travel to the nearest location closest to the temple, and then walk there. Or Fast-Travel to the temple entrance itself, if you've already discovered it.

- Travel the path along Falkreath Hold, which involves fending off any enemies along the way and fighting as a trio. This takes longer but allows you to raise levels and watch your teammates' considerable fighting talents. Neither of them can die from enemy attacks, so you can back them up in combat if that's your style.

- Take the same, lengthy route on your own or on horseback. You won't need to wait around, but you have no backup during any fights.

- Catch a carriage from Whiterun to Markarth, and then approach on foot from the west, as Delphine recommends.

After the meeting, Delphine says her last good-byes to Orgnar the barkeep and leaves the Sleeping Giant Inn for good.

The Forsworn—primitive tribesmen fighting to drive the Nords out of this western hold—are active in this area. They are formidable warriors and mages, especially in groups as large as those you find at the Karthspire exterior. Depending on your play style and whether you're traveling alone or with Delphine and Esbern, expect a protracted and furious battle across the sprawling wooden and stone battlements as you cross the platforms spanning the Karth River. After some fine sneaking or impressive combat, seek the inky-black cave entrance and enter Karthspire interior.

> **TIP** If you lose Delphine and Esbern during the journey to the Sky Haven Temple, they appear when you enter the Karthspire interior. If you told them to go ahead, they will be waiting on the road close to the entrance, near the Karthspire Forsworn Camp (unless you reach there first).

Fighting continues inside Karthspire as you head through a Forsworn camp and into a narrow ascension chamber, with stone buttresses and temple columns carved by the early Akaviri. There is an entrance high above you to the west, but it is currently impassable. There is a trick to releasing the two raised bridges that cross the width of the chamber. Move up to the three tricornered small pillars atop the dirt ramp.

Puzzle Solution: The square tile in the middle of each column is significant; study the hieroglyph in each one. One looks like an eye with a pair of horns above it. One looks like a ceremonial bowl with stylized fire. The third looks like two dragon heads facing each other and an arrow pointing down. This is the symbol of the Dragonborn. Activate the pillars so the "Dragonborn" tile is shown and the line atop each pillar points east to west. The bridge to your left (south) lowers with a rumble.

Cross the bridge and wait for Esbern to give his opinion on the tiled floor in the connecting chamber. Expect a fiery death if you step on the incorrect pressure plate. But there is a method to this madness:

Puzzle Solution: Look for the plates that have the "Dragonborn" hieroglyph on them. Step only on those plates to wind your way across the floor, before you finally reach a carved dragon head and a lever. Pull the lever, and the second crossing lowers. This has the added bonus of switching off the pressure-plate trap.

Allegory and Mythic Symbolism

Head north across the two lowered bridges and into the Sky Haven Temple entrance, a large and remarkably well-preserved chamber. Esbern strides toward a big stone head at the far (west) end. Speak to Esbern about the entrance. He studies the circular floor carvings, murmuring something about them being a "blood seal." The mechanism needs blood to activate: your blood. The ancient Blades revered Reman Cyrodiil, and the whole place appears to be a shrine to him. Esbern explains the historical significance of this site. Listen for as long as you wish, but when you are ready, stand in the center of the circular floor carving and activate the blood seal. You cut your palm, dripping blood into the floor seal, and Reman Cyrodiil's giant carved head lifts open.

◊ **OBJECTIVE:** Learn the secret of Alduin's Wall

Quest Conclusion

You may wish to run on ahead or witness Esbern's excited discovery of Akaviri bas-reliefs. But the main chamber holds the real prize. While Delphine waits impatiently, Esbern explores the entirety of Alduin's Wall, which dominates this chamber. In the middle of the wall, Esbern discovers that the ancient Nords used a Shout to defeat Alduin. Delphine asks if you know of such a Shout. Answer that the Greybeards might know. Delphine responds with a few choice words about the Greybeards; she believes they shrank from their responsibilities and destiny. She recommends you head off to see them while she remains; Esbern is likely to be here a while.

> "When misrule takes its place at the eight corners of the world,
> When the Brass Tower walks and Time is reshaped,
> When the thrice-blessed fail and the Red Tower trembles,
> When the Dragonborn Ruler loses his throne, and the White Tower falls,
> When the Snow Tower lies sundered, kingless, bleeding,
> The World-Eater wakes, and the Wheel turns upon the Last Dragonborn."

Postquest Activities

Esbern continues to inspect Alduin's Wall as Main Quest: The Throat of the World begins. In addition, you can start to befriend Delphine and Esbern inside the Sky Haven Temple and complete the four Blades Factions Quests, earning you Followers, items, dragons to kill, and blessings from Esbern. Consult that Chapter for details.

THE THROAT OF THE WORLD

PREREQUISITES: Complete Main Quest: Alduin's Wall

INTERSECTING QUESTS: Main Quest: Alduin's Wall, Main Quest: Elder Knowledge Favorites, Main Quest: Paarthurnax

LOCATIONS: High Hrothgar, High Hrothgar Courtyard, Sky Haven Temple, Throat of the World

CHARACTERS: Delphine, Esbern, Master Arngeir, Master Einarth, Paarthurnax

ENEMIES: Ice Wraith, Troll

◊ **OBJECTIVES:** Talk to Arngeir, Learn the Clear Skies Shout, Use the Clear Skies Shout to open the path, Talk to Paarthurnax, Learn the Word of Power from Paarthurnax, Use your Fire Breath Shout on Paarthurnax, Talk to Paarthurnax

⦿ MINOR SPOILERS

Sky Above, Voice Within

◇ **OBJECTIVE:** Talk to Arngeir
◆ **TARGET:** Master Arngeir, High Hrothgar

While Esbern inspects the third panel of Alduin's Wall (and offers his opinion of it if you wish to listen), you should exit Sky Haven Temple. Head up and north, and exit through any of the "dragon arrow" doors to an outside ruin offering excellent views over the Reach.

You have a long trek back toward Whiterun, and then must navigate the 7,000 steps again to High Hrothgar. You should Fast-Travel if you're feeling impatient. Seek out Master Arngeir, and inform him that you need to learn the Shout that was used to defeat Alduin. The Greybeard is angered by your request, blaming the meddling Blades for their reckless arrogance. Arngeir ends the conversation (no matter what you say) by admonishing you for straying from the path of wisdom.

Master Einarth murmurs something to Arngeir in dragon tongue, and Arngeir calls for you to stop. He apologizes for his outburst and informs you that the Shout is called "Dragonrend." It is unknown, even to the Greybeards of High Hrothgar, as it is deemed evil. Only the master of the Greybeards—Paarthurnax—can answer your questions. You are beckoned into the courtyard and are taught another Shout that will open the way to Paarthurnax.

◇ **OBJECTIVE:** Learn the Clear Skies Shout
◆ **TARGET:** Master Arngeir, High Hrothgar Courtyard

Follow Arngeir toward the ceremonial fire pit on the raised area of the courtyard, where he bellows three glowing, runic words into the carved stone on the ground below. Step onto and absorb each of them, so your Clear Skies Shout is the strongest it can be. Then absorb the knowledge from the glowing Master Arngeir. You learn Lok ("Sky"), Vah ("Spring"), and Koor ("Summer"). Then enter your Magic > Shout Inventory menu, and select this Shout.

➤ **Word of Power:** Sky, Clear Skies
➤ **Word of Power:** Spring, Clear Skies
➤ **Word of Power:** Summer, Clear Skies

◇ **OBJECTIVE:** Use the Clear Skies Shout to open the path
◆ **TARGET:** The mountain fog, atop the High Hrothgar steps

Clearing the Throat

With the Shout selected, turn and depart from High Hrothgar, heading up the steps from the fire pit to the southeast. You are greeted by a perimeter arch, through which is an impenetrable fog. Execute the Clear Skies Shout and the fog dissipates for a few seconds before blanketing the mountain again. This gives you a clear view of the path to the mountaintop.

◇ **OBJECTIVE:** Talk to Paarthurnax
◆ **TARGET:** Paarthurnax, the Throat of the World summit

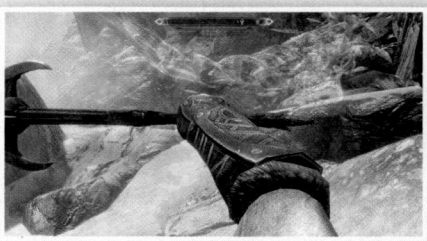

Continue up the path until you reach the edge of the fog bank. If the fog returns, then Shout again. As you progress up the zigzagging path, look out for the marker stones and the flags affixed to them. The pace is slow, but you eventually emerge above the fog bank and discover the Throat of the World—the summit of the largest mountain in Skyrim.

> **CAUTION** Don't wander around blindly in the gray mist; this is dangerous. Lingering in the fog can drain your Stamina, and you'll have to contend with Ice Wraiths and possibly a troll along the way.

A deep booming voice echoes around the giant rocks and snowbanks atop the mountain. Paarthurnax greets you. Speak to this giant white dragon, who asks why you intrude upon his meditation. Explain that you need to learn the Dragonrend Shout. He responds that patience is required and that formalities must be observed. Paarthurnax lands on the ground nearby and encourages you to hear his Thu'um and respond—if you are truly Dovahkiin! He opens his maw and scorches a nearby rock in a great gout of fire!

◇ **OBJECTIVE:** Learn the Word of Power from Paarthurnax

The rock soon glows with a runic Word of Power. Take this as the gift it is intended to be, and absorb another new Word of the Fire Breath Shout. You then absorb Paarthurnax's knowledge of the Word...except the beast is still alive and doesn't need slaying.

➤ **Word of Power:** Fire Breath

◇ **OBJECTIVE:** Use your Fire Breath Shout on Paarthurnax

Paarthurnax now wishes you to greet him, not as a mortal but as a dovah ("dragon"). Select the Fire Breath Shout from your inventory, and yell it directly into the dragon, bathing him in your fiery blast. Paarthurnax doesn't become hostile; this is the ceremonial greeting he was expecting.

> **CAUTION** Of course, don't follow this up with actual combat, or Paarthurnax actually becomes hostile, and you can't kill him now.

◇ **OBJECTIVE:** Talk to Paarthurnax

Watcher at the Time-Wound

Paarthurnax is happy to make your acquaintance and asks what you wish of him. When you repeat your request to learn the Dragonrend Shout, Paarthurnax has been expecting this. After further conversation, the great dragon says that even he does not know the Thu'um that you seek. After another question, he asks why you want to learn the Shout. Reply with any answer you wish, but do tell him you need to stop Alduin. Paarthurnax describes his elder brother as "troublesome." This hermit soon asks you why he lives up here.

The Elder Scrolls V
SKYRIM

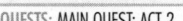

Your answers won't be correct, so he tells you he meditates at this spot, as it was where Alduin was defeated by the ancient Tongues. But even the Dragonrend Shout wasn't enough; they had to employ the Kel—or Elder Scroll—to create a Tiid-Ahraan, or Time-Wound, and cast him adrift on the currents of Time. If you ask, he explains what an Elder Scroll is and reveals he has been waiting: For thousands of years, until Alduin began to emerge from Time. This is important to your cause. If you found an Elder Scroll at this exact location, you might be able to cast yourself back to the other end of the time break—and learn Dragonrend from those who created it!

Quest Conclusion

You're left with one overwhelming question...

Postquest Activities

...which is answered during Main Quest: Elder Knowledge!

 ## ELDER KNOWLEDGE

PREREQUISITES: Complete Main Quest: The Throat of the World

INTERSECTING QUESTS: Main Quest: The Throat of the World, Main Quest: Alduin's Bane, Main Quest: Paarthurnax, Daedric Quest: Discerning the Transmundane, Other Faction Quests (The Greybeards Quests): Word Wall Revelations*, Other Faction Quests (The Greybeards Quests): Meditations on Words of Power*, College of Winterhold Quest: First Lessons

LOCATIONS: Alftand, Alftand Animonculory, Alftand Cathedral, Alftand Glacial Ruins, Alftand Ruined Tower, Blackreach, College of Winterhold, Hall of the Elements, The Arcanaeum, High Hrothgar, High Hrothgar Courtyard, Septimus Signus's Outpost, Sky Haven Temple, Throat of the World, Tower of Mzark, Oculory

CHARACTERS: Esbern, Faralda, Master Arngeir, Paarthurnax, Septimus Signus, Urag gro-Shub

ENEMIES: Dwarven Centurion, Dwarven Sphere, Dwarven Spider, Falmer, Frostbite Spider, Horker, Ice Wolf, J'darr, Skeever, Wolf

◊ **OBJECTIVES:** Learn the location of the Elder Scroll, (Optional) Talk to Esbern, OR (Optional) Talk to Arngeir, Objective: Recover the Elder Scroll

> **NOTE** * Quest names marked with this symbol do not appear in your Quest Menu list, although objectives may.

Higher Learning

◊ **OBJECTIVE:** Learn the location of the Elder Scroll

♦ **TARGET:** College of Winterhold

◊ **OBJECTIVE:** (Optional) Talk to Esbern

♦ **TARGET:** Esbern, at the Sky Haven Temple

◊ **OBJECTIVE:** OR (Optional) Talk to Arngeir

♦ **TARGET:** Master Arngeir, at High Hrothgar

Finish your conversation with Paarthurnax by asking him to impart all the information about the Elder Scroll that he can. According to him, when you return with the Scroll, you shall meet Hakon, Gormlaith, and Felldir—the first mortals to whom Paarthurnax taught the Thu'um and who led the rebellion against Alduin. Complete your talk with Paarthurnax, and then leave to locate the Elder Scroll, if you haven't found it yet. There are two optional clues that point you in the correct direction.

> **NOTE** Do you already have the Elder Scroll in your possession? This is possible, if you've completed Daedric Quest: Discerning the Transmundane. If so, you can skip this quest and begin Main Quest: Alduin's Bane.

> **NOTE** Remember that, you can still return to him to meditate on Words of Power. Consult Other Factions Quests (The Greybeards Quests): Meditations on Words of Power for more details. This quest becomes available once you complete Main Quest: The Horn of Jurgen Windcaller.

Talking to Esbern: To learn more about your Elder Scroll search, you may wish to return to the Sky Haven Temple. Esbern is usually standing outside, atop the mountain the temple is dug into, gazing over the Reach. Approach the temple pavilion and speak to him. He recommends you visit the College of Winterhold. Your map updates.

Talking to Arngeir: To learn more about your Elder Scroll search, you can visit High Hrothgar and speak with Master Arngeir. The Greybeards do not concern themselves with the Scrolls, but such blasphemies have always been the stock-in-trade of the mages of Winterhold. He suggests you try their College. Your map updates.

> **NOTE** At this point, you can speak to Arngeir and learn the locations of additional Words of Power. Consult Other Factions Quests (The Greybeards Quests): Word Wall Revelations for more details.

Insane Ruminations

Begin your journey to the city of Winterhold. The College is linked to it by a bridge. At the bridge's near end, a High Elf wizard guards the entrance. She stops you, warning that it's not safe to cross the bridge and that you will be denied entrance to the city. She will become hostile if you take a swing at her. Although she has some complaints about the College, which you can ask her about, you really just want to enter the College. Ask if this is possible, and she asks why. Choose the answer that best suits your demeanor. She requires that you take a test to show you're at least competent in the use of magic. You can:

Walk right in without dealing with Faralda, if you're already a member of the College of Winterhold and started that line of Side Quests.

(Persuade) Tell her that you both know you'll be successful.

Agree to take the test. When the test begins, Faralda requests you aim a spell at the seal on the ground near to her.

Ask if she would grant entry to the Dragonborn. Faralda asks if you really have the Voice. Show her any Shout you have.

Spell Casting: Bring up your Magic menu and choose the spell Faralda has requested. She can choose Firebolt, Magelight, Fury, Conjure Flame Atronach, or Healing Hands, depending on your available spells and knowledge of particular magic styles. Aim at the seal and cast the spell. After a successful casting, Faralda tells you to find Mirabelle Ervine inside the College.

Dragon Shouting: Bring up your Shout inventory, choose any Shout (a good choice is Fire Breath), aim it at the seal, and bellow. After you strike the seal, Faralda tells you that there is much you both can learn from each other and that you'd be a superb addition to the College.

You can now ask Faralda more questions about Mirabelle and the College, or even receive training in the arts of Destruction Magic. College of Winterhold Quest: First Lessons is now active, and you are told to report to Mirabelle Ervine. However, this objective is not required or part of the Main Quest. Cross the bridge, enter the College's exterior courtyard, open the grand doors, and enter the Hall of the Elements. Immediately make a right (east) turn and enter the Arcanaeum.

> **CAUTION** Be extremely careful where you wave your fingers! Don't aim (accidentally or otherwise) at Faralda or choose a spell (or Shout) that has a large area of effect. If you cast a wider flame-based attack, you risk setting Faralda on fire, effectively ending your tryout as an apprentice mage!

> **TIP** Do you want to mingle with other mages? Then consult the College of Winterhold Quests for further information on the denizens of this epicenter of magic in Skyrim. This is also a great time to start their quests, if you haven't done so already.

Look for the Orc Mage named Urag gro-Shub, who runs the Arcanaeum. Although you can ask to assist him in College business (which allows you to accomplish several College-related tasks unrelated to this quest) and can ask about the Arcanaeum library, you're here to ask him about the Elder Scroll. Urag isn't too happy with you offhandedly asking about such a powerful artifact. You may listen to an overview of the Scrolls before asking if there's an Elder Scroll you could use. Urag laughs at this question; he wouldn't show the likes of you, even if he obtained one. Ask if he at least has any information on them. He agrees to locate a couple of arcane tomes that may have some clues. But mostly they contain lies leavened with rumors.

Urag gro-Shub locates and places two tomes on the nearby desk: *Effects of the Elder Scrolls* and *Ruminations on the Elder Scrolls*. After reading both books (which you may keep or leave on the desk), you find that the Ruminations tome is the work of a madman. Daedric Quest: Discerning the Transmundane now begins.

➤ *Effects of the Elder Scrolls*   ➤ *Ruminations on the Elder Scrolls*

◊ **DAEDRIC QUEST OBJECTIVE:** Ask Urag about the insane book

Return to Urag and let him know that the Ruminations book is incomprehensible. He doesn't seem surprised; after all, this book was the work of Septimus Signus. Although Signus is the world's master of the nature of Elder Scrolls, Urag tells you he's "been gone for a long while." You suspect he means both mentally and physically. He currently resides north of the College in the treacherous Ice Fields.

◊ **DAEDRIC QUEST OBJECTIVE:** Find Septimus Signus
♦ **TARGET:** Septimus Signus's Outpost

The Hermit of Hermaeus Mora

The giant chunks of ice floating off the Northern Coast are your next destination. Exit the College and run down to the frigid coastal waters. Hop across any floating ice that you can, navigating your way north. Expect to slice into a few Horkers along the way,

and you may encounter wolves and Ice Wolves.

Septimus Signus's Outpost is cut into one of the hill-sized icebergs, close to a moored rowing boat. Climb down the ladder and the slope to reach a lone mage in a chamber of ice. He appears to be guarding some kind of Dwemer box about the size of a house.

Asking Septimus about the Elder Scrolls results in a torrent of knowledge. Ask where the Scroll is, and after receiving moderately useless information, ask once more (either pleasantly or with a more threatening tone). Septimus agrees to tell you, but in return, you must venture into Blackreach, a strange underground Dwemer city that lies below Alftand.

Ask about getting into Blackreach. Septimus keeps up his riddle-based prattling and hands you two items: The first is an odd-edged lexicon, used by the Dwemer for inscribing. The second is an Attunement Sphere, which apparently "sings" when you near an important Dwemer door. Once these are in your grasp, your Main Quest updates. Stay and speak further with Septimus if your sanity can stand it.

➤ **Attunement Sphere**   ➤ **Blank Lexicon**

◊ **DAEDRIC QUEST OBJECTIVE:** Transcribe the Lexicon
♦ **TARGET:** Tower of Mzark
◊ **OBJECTIVE:** Recover the Elder Scroll
♦ **TARGET:** Tower of Mzark

Trek to the Tower

> **TIP** You must have the Attunement Sphere on your person in order to continue; otherwise, you cannot access the route necessary to reach the Elder Scroll. The following location is one of a few entrances to a giant underground city called Blackreach. This is the optimal path, but there are others. Consult the Atlas to see all the ways to enter this subterranean citadel and the Tower of Mzark.

Alftand is located on the glacial mountains southwest of Winterhold. Your trek there is usually interrupted by wild animal attacks. The exterior of Alftand is a series of dotted structures, both Dwarven and Nordic in nature. Below the glaciers is the Alftand Ruined Tower, which offers a dangerous route to the glacier's top. A much better way is to stay outside to reach the two windswept huts, an inaccessible Dwarven tower, and a precarious platform that winds down and around the rooftops, on the side of the glacier. Head down the planked bridges until you reach the entrance to the Alftand Glacial Ruins. This is the way to go.

Wind through the glacial tunnels that have been mined out and left in a real mess, with debris and cooking equipment strewn about, and the signs of fighting everywhere you look. Follow the tunnel down until you reach the beginnings of the Dwarven architecture, a stone tunnel that ends in a connecting room with a stone table, and a large barred doorway to the north. This can only be unlocked from the other side.

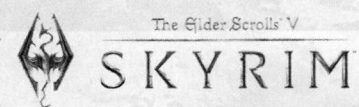

On the nearby table you'll find Research Notes. Whoever wrote it thought he saw a strange human figure on the other side of the barred doorway.

➤ Research Notes

At this point, the passage west heads up a ramp and down the other side, into another glacial intrusion. Watch for attacks from a Dwarven Spider as you go. A Skooma-addled Khajiit is shouting about being trapped here and attacks if he sees you. Drop him, and continue down into the start of the main Dwarven ruins. The ceilings tower above you as you reach a cog and piston room with a raised center and two Dwarven Spheres appearing from their wall holes to attack. Continue north to a vent chamber with a locked gate (Novice) leading to a few scraps of treasure. Head through the gold door and up to a Dwarven Spider—infested passage stretching south. This leads to a locked (Apprentice) gold door with items to steal behind it, and a main path around to the east, which brings you back into the cog and piston room. This time, you're above the raised center. Navigate the pistons (jump over them, or you risk being pushed off by them) in a counterclockwise route to the short corridor and door to the Alftand Animonculory.

> **TIP** There are many trinkets of Dwemer origin to pick up (and sell once you leave). Among the vendors across Skyrim, a wizard named Calcelmo in Markarth's Understone Keep is most interested in these items and gives a good price, although you can sell them to any merchant or vendor who wants them.

Move through the green-tinged corridor to an opening on your left (east). This leads to a large pipeworks corridor. Avoid two Dwarven Spheres by staying on the low ground, and head through the gap in the gold fencing to the left of the stone steps. Otherwise, head up the steps, over the pipes, and up the ramp with the central slit. Walk on the slit so you don't trigger a blade trap by stepping on the pressure plates. At the barred doorway, use the lever on your right to lower the bars. The lever behind the bars raises them, which isn't necessary unless you're being pursued and want to halt your attackers. Step out into the grand Animonculory shaft—a long vertical drop you need to descend without falling. Remove any Dwarven Spider threats, and head down the sloping stone walkway to an arched entrance platform. The gold door here (Apprentice) just leads to a dead end and more treasure.

Peer over the edge of the stone platform facing into the shaft. The walkway below has crumbled, forcing you to drop onto the jutting gold pipe and then the rubble platform. There is a walkway to the west, heading up to a precarious ledge, a Dwarven Spider battle, and a piston that can push you over the edge. The way forward and downward is to the northeast. Look for the lantern and falling water, as the sloping walkway is hidden.

As you descend, something horrific shuffles out of the shadows: an eyeless figure, thought to be myth. These are Falmer, the degenerate remnants of the original Elven inhabitants of Skyrim! Dispatch four of them as you follow the winding platform down. Take care not to lose your footing and fall to your death. Next, face the jet of fire blasting the entrance to a gold door. Dart through or around, and enter a Falmer nest.

Falmer appear from their huts, forcing you to fight or sneak by. Follow the passage down to a second set of Falmer in a boiler chamber. Watch for those rattling, hanging bones if you're sneaking, as these startle the Falmer into finding you. Head down the steps, watching for Skeever attacks, and look for a gold door on the southeast wall. This is the way onward, but you may wish to turn to the northwest, open a gate, and enter an ancient Dwarven Elevator. Pull the lever and you ascend to the Alftand Glacial Ruins.

Step around the rubble and to the barred doorway where you found the Research Notes. Pull a wall lever here, so the bars retract. This allows you to easily navigate up and down the Animonculory if you explore here in the future. For now, use the elevator to head back down, and open the gold door in the southeast wall. This leads down the sloping walkway to the shaft's bottom, where you encounter another Falmer attack and face a Frostbite Spider. From here, you have only one set of corridor steps and a claw trap (move around the trip wire) before you enter the Alftand Cathedral.

Battle a Falmer and navigate some floor trigger plates to reach a gold door that leads out into the main cathedral chamber—a massive echoing cavern with a central structure and a doorway barred with spears. Check the area for Falmer and the steps to your left (south) before heading to a gold lever above the entrance from which you came. This raises the spears, enabling you to enter the cathedral platform, where a giant steam-powered mechanical monster roars into life. This Dwarven Centurion is a frightening form, but you should defeat it, as it carries a handy key.

➤ Key to Alftand Lift

Climb to the gate (southwest) at the platform's top, open it, and then listen to the arguments of two thieves, Sulla and Umana. You must slay them, as there's no reasoning with them. Now open the gate beyond the strange Dwarven Mechanism. This leads up to the top of the Alftand glacier, and a tower you couldn't access when you first reached here. Open the gate from the inside using the wall lever (so you can access the cathedral directly from the surface during future adventures); then travel back down to the cathedral. Approach the Dwarven Mechanism now, and insert the Attunement Sphere Septimus gave you. The floor parts, revealing stairs down to a hidden gold door and an entrance into the mysterious undercity of Blackreach.

> **NOTE** Take a moment to adjust to the vastness of this cavern. Aside from firing a Dwarven crossbow using an adjacent lever and investigating the small stone building to the southwest (Sinderion's Field Laboratory, where you can start collecting Crimson Nirnroot and begin Side Quest: A Return to Your Roots), there is a sprawling area to adventure through. Consult the Atlas for information on the entire area; this walkthrough points you directly to the exit necessary to reach the Elder Scroll.

Exiting Blackreach using the appropriate Dwarven Elevator involves a romp west. First, though, you may wish to head southeast, to a golden button encased on a Dwarven head pedestal. Press it, and the elevator behind lights up, allowing you to ascend and exit back outside. Open the gate, allowing you to enter from the Great Lift of Alftand (a new tower entrance northeast of Nightgate Inn). Return to Blackreach and find the cobblestone path heading roughly west. Follow it past ancient structures and towering luminescent fungi. Continue with a giant lake and cascading waterfalls to your left (south), heading over a stone bridge. Go west and turn left (south) to reach a colossal elevator that allows you to ascend into the Tower of Mzark, your destination.

Oculory Operation

Venture along a corridor with a burst steam pipe and small camping area, and through gold doors into a gigantic, circular Aedrome chamber. The chamber is dominated by a huge sphere. This appears to be some kind of massive Oculory, with a variety of focusing lenses and other golden machinery attached. Head to the cluster of controls on the platform above the Oculory. The controls are comprised of five cylindrical devices: a Lexicon Receptacle and four positioning buttons embedded in pedestals. There is a certain way to use these devices to produce something hidden in one of the lenses.

Puzzle solution: Activate the Lexicon Receptacle, so the Blank Lexicon rests on top of it. The two pedestals to the Receptacle's right—the only ones currently active—open and close the Oculory lenses. Press the taller of the two pedestals (right of the middle one with the lens chart on it) three or four times, until the pedestal with the blue button to the left of the middle one starts to glow. Move to this new pedestal (at this point, the Blank Lexicon may be glowing blue). The two pedestals to the left of the Receptacle—the taller of which is now active—control the ceiling lens array. Press the button of the taller, left pedestal twice, until the button on the far left, smaller pedestal begins to glow. Now press that button, and a large set of lens crystals descends from the ceiling and stops. The main crystal rotates and splits apart to reveal a tubelike carrying device.

Quest Conclusion

Drop down from the balcony controls and approach the open lens crystal. Take the Elder Scroll from its elaborate compartment. Then exit using the door under the Lexicon Receptacle. This leads to one final Dwarven Elevator, which allows you to open the gate from the Tower of Mzark, step out into the exterior, and add another possible entrance to Blackreach, if you decide to return.

➤ **Elder Scroll**

Postquest Activities

As soon as you take the Elder Scroll, Main Quest: Alduin's Bane begins. In addition, you are able to return to the giant underground city of Blackreach and can continue Daedric Quest: Discerning the Transmundane from this point on. Consult that quest for further information.

  **ALDUIN'S BANE**

 MAJOR SPOILERS

PREREQUISITES: Complete Main Quest: Elder Knowledge

INTERSECTING QUESTS: Main Quest: Elder Knowledge, Main Quest: The Fallen, Main Quest: Paarthurnax, Other Faction Quests (The Greybeards Quests): Meditations on Words of Power*, Other Faction Quests (The Greybeards Quests): Words of Power*, College of Winterhold Quest: First Lessons

LOCATIONS: Throat of the World, Tower of Mzark, Oculory

CHARACTERS: Felldir, Gormlaith, Hakon, Paarthurnax

ENEMIES: Alduin

◊ **OBJECTIVES:** Read the Elder Scroll at the Time-Wound , Learn the Dragonrend Shout from the Nord heroes, Defeat Alduin

---

NOTE ✳ Quest names marked with this symbol do not appear in your Quest Menu list, although objectives may.

A Blast from the Past

◊ **OBJECTIVE:** Read the Elder Scroll at the Time-Wound
♦ **TARGET:** Throat of the World (mountain summit)

CAUTION
Be sure you use the correct elevator to leave the Tower of Mzark. The one you access via the corridor under the balcony controls returns you to Skyrim's surface, whereas the one located on the lower part of the Oculory, accessed down the stone ramp and short corridor, leaves you exploring the terrifying Blackreach, which is only necessary during Daedric Quest: Discerning the Transmundane!

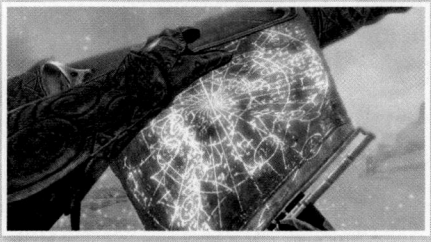

Once you've taken the Elder Scroll from the Oculory inside the Tower of Mzark, simply return to the Dwarven Elevator and head outside. Once you're back on Skyrim's surface, you can travel (by your preferred means) to the Throat of the World, where Paarthurnax is perched on his rock, watching you intently. Move near the Time-Wound, which glows brighter as you advance upon it, and read the Elder Scroll from your inventory.

◊ **OBJECTIVE:** Learn the Dragonrend Shout from the Nord heroes
♦ **TARGET:** Hakon, Gormlaith, and Felldir, through the Elder Scroll

Your vision pitches back into the past, thousands of years ago, when the Nord heroes of old first fought Alduin and his dragon brethren. But Gormlaith, Hakon, and Felldir are seen as if you could reach out and touch them. You cannot move while watching this memory play out. You watch as Gormlaith and Hakon deliver a series of killing blows to a dragon, with Hakon worrying that Alduin may not appear and fall into the trap they have set for him. Felldir has seen none of his kin stand against Alduin, not Galthor, Sorri, or Birkir. Gormlaith replies that they did not have Dragonrend. But as Alduin cannot be slain like a lesser dragon, Felldir has brought something to even the odds—an Elder Scroll!

The giant black dragon soon descends on the trio of Nord warriors. As planned, the three heroes bellow out Joor ("Mortal"), Zah ("Finite"), Frul ("Temporary")! At the same moment in present time, you absorb the knowledge of this Shout yourself. Alduin is confused, and sees fear for the first time. While Gormlaith is torn and tossed about by an enraged Alduin, Hakon yells to Felldir to use the Elder Scroll. After Felldir yells the incantation, Alduin is consumed by a massive ball of energy, sucked into the Elder Scroll, and is banished from the world of Skyrim... of the past. But what of the present?

- ➤ **Word of Power:** Mortal, Dragonrend
- ➤ **Word of Power:** Finite, Dragonrend
- ➤ **Word of Power:** Temporary, Dragonrend

◇ **OBJECTIVE:** Defeat Alduin
♦ **TARGET:** Alduin, Throat of the World

Rending the World-Eater Asunder

Something black and jagged arcs through the blizzard. Alduin has seen your attempts at reading the Elder Scroll but arrives too late to prevent you from learning the Shout that may be his downfall. Paarthurnax attempts to intercept Alduin's attack but is cut down and lands heavily near you. He tells you to use the Dragonrend Shout if you can.

Dragon Slaying: Immediately select Dragonrend from the Shouts, and target the Thu'um directly at Alduin as he flies down to a hover, swoops past, or lands.

Try to lengthen the attack of the Shout (by holding down the Shout button). When he lands heavily, utilize your favored attack (which can be a second or third Shout as well as your magic and ranged or melee weapons).

If Alduin takes to the skies, use Dragonrend again; it is the only guaranteed way of dropping him back down to earth.

 **Warning!** Alduin is completely invincible except when he's affected by Dragonrend! **CAUTION**

Continue combat, which is the most difficult that you've likely faced, and make use of any Health, Magicka, or Stamina potions that you've acquired for this battle.

Quest Conclusion
The battle ends only after you've depleted Alduin's health, or he's savaged you to death; there is no respite. Kill or be killed!

Postquest Activities
Once you've dealt a final blow to Alduin, Main Quest: The Fallen begins.

MAIN QUEST: ACT III

THE FALLEN

PREREQUISITES: Complete Main Quest: Alduin's Bane
INTERSECTING QUESTS: Main Quest: The Fallen, Main Quest: Paarthurnax, Other Faction Quests (The Greybeards Quests): Word Wall Revelations*, Other Faction Quests (The Greybeards Quests): Meditations on Words of Power*
LOCATIONS: Whiterun, Dragonsreach
CHARACTERS: Esbern, General Tullius, Jarl Balgruuf the Greater, Jarl Vignar the Revered, Master Arngeir, Paarthurnax, Ulfric Stormcloak
ENEMIES: Alduin, Odahviing
◇ **OBJECTIVES:** Talk to Paarthurnax, OR Talk to Arngeir, OR Talk to Esbern, Talk to the Jarl of Whiterun, Learn Shout to call Odahviing, Prepare trap for Odahviing, Call Odahviing to Dragonsreach, Defeat and trap Odahviing, Interrogate Odahviing

 NOTE ✱ Quest names marked with this symbol do not appear in your Quest Menu list, although objectives may.

Part 1: Expert Mediation

◇ **OBJECTIVE:** Talk to Paarthurnax
♦ **TARGET:** Throat of the World
◇ **OBJECTIVE:** OR Talk to Arngeir
♦ **TARGET:** High Hrothgar
◇ **OBJECTIVE:** OR Talk to Esbern
♦ **TARGET:** Sky Haven Temple

Alduin collapses to the ground after you deal him a particularly impressive blow. But the arch-dragon isn't some common serpent; he is firstborn of Akatosh! He cannot be slain here, even by you. He takes to the skies, and even your Dragonrend cannot stop him. He seems weakened; he's down but not out. Now you must seek the guidance of your chosen ally. You have three to choose from:

1. Paarthurnax

If you are favoring the kinship of the Greybeards over the Blades, you may seek council with Paarthurnax. Mention that you need to find out where Alduin went, and the dragon ponders this. Perhaps an ally of his could be convinced to betray him. Paarthurnax mentions that the palace in Whiterun — Dragonsreach — was originally built to house a captive dovah (dragon). It would be a fine place to trap an Alduin ally. You mention that the Jarl might need some convincing (as the quest updates). Then Paarthurnax tells you the story of how the place came to be named Dragonsreach.

2. Arngeir

You may visit Master Arngeir, who heard the Dragonrend Shout from High Hrothgar. Arngeir tells you that Alduin can travel to Sovngarde to devour the souls of the dead, but no one knows how this is achieved. You reply that one of his dragon allies might reveal this. But there is one possibility: Dragonsreach, which was originally built to hold a captive dragon. This did indeed occur in the time of Olaf One-Eye, thousands of years ago. You might be able to trap a dragon there, once you have the Jarl's cooperation.

3. Esbern

Or you can return to Esbern at the Sky Temple pavilion outside, and he asks what happened. He believes Alduin returned to Sovngarde to feed on the souls of the dead, and if you don't find him soon, he'll return stronger than ever. When you mention that his dragon allies might know where the portal to Sovngarde is, Esbern agrees and asks you about Dragonsreach. Apparently it was built to hold a captive dragon, back before the Akaviri crusaders cleansed Skyrim of dragons. You could trap a dragon there, but getting the Jarl to use his palace as a dragon trap might be impossible.

> ◇ **OBJECTIVE:** Talk to the Jarl of Whiterun
> ♦ **TARGET:** The Jarl of Whiterun, in Dragonsreach, in Whiterun

> **NOTE** Esbern has another problem if you speak with him. He's discovered who the Greybeards' leader really is — a dragon responsible for many atrocities during the ancient Dragon War. On behalf of the Blades, he demands that Paarthurnax die for these crimes. Furthermore, Esbern's oath as a Blade prevents him from offering you aid or comfort until this dragon is slain.

> **NOTE** Main Quest: Paarthurnax begins officially at this point. Consult Main Quest: Paarthurnax for further information. It can also occur if you speak to Delphine. You must complete this quest to access help at the Sky Haven Temple from the Blades; otherwise Delphine and Esbern will speak but offer no assistance to you, which takes the form of the four Other Factions Quests involving the Blades.

Return to Whiterun and visit Dragonsreach within its walls. Approach the Jarl, who is usually sitting under Numinex's skull. Numinex is the dragon that Jarl Olaf One-Eye brought back to Whiterun. Request that the Jarl help you, as you require a trap to snare a dragon in the Jarl's palace. The Jarl's responses, and even the Jarl himself differs, depending on how the Civil War is progressing:

 Jarl Balgruuf the Greater is the Jarl if the Imperials still have this Hold during the Civil War or if you haven't decided to start the Civil War.

If the Stormcloaks have one Hold left or have been completely wiped out, and the Imperials (to which Jarl Balgruuf has pledged loyalty) have emerged victorious in the Civil War, the Jarl begrudgingly agrees to let you try out your insane dragon-trapping plan. You can skip Main Quest: Season Unending (which occurs in the middle of this quest), and continue your plan on the Dragonsreach balcony. Main Quest: The Fallen (Part 2) begins.

If the Stormcloaks have more than one Hold left during the Civil War, or you haven't started any of the Civil War Quests yet, the Jarl has more pressing matters than your lunatic schemes: Quest Conclusion Part 1 begins.

Jarl Vignar the Revered is the Jarl if you've attacked Whiterun and driven out the forces loyal to Jarl Balgruuf and the Imperials and slaughtered those who defended the city.

If the Imperials have one Hold left or have been completely obliterated from the Holds' major cities, and the Stormcloaks (who have installed this newly appointed Jarl) are victorious in the Civil War, the Jarl reluctantly agrees to let you perform your dragon-snaring act. You can skip Main Quest: Season Unending (which occurs in the middle of this quest), and continue the plan on the Dragonsreach balcony. Main Quest: The Fallen (Part 2) begins.

If the Imperials have more than one Hold left during the Civil War, but the Civil War is under way and Whiterun has fallen to the Stormcloaks, the Jarl has problems with the ongoing Civil War conflict. Quest Conclusion Part 1 begins.

Quest Conclusion Part 1

The Jarl has no time (or additional men) to spare to trap a dragon. Explain that this is the only way to find Alduin. The Jarl says he wants to help, but he requires your aid first. Ulfric Stormcloak and General Tullius are both waiting for the Jarl to make the wrong move, and the Jarl's enemies won't sit idly by while a dragon slaughters the Jarl's forces. The Jarl cannot weaken the city while the threat of enemy attacks is looming. That threat would have to be nullified, even temporarily, for the Jarl to agree to your plan. For this to happen, both sides must agree to a truce, but the Jarl feels the bitterness runs too deep.

But all is not lost. The Greybeards might be willing to hold a peace council, and then perhaps Ulfric and Tullius will listen. You're told to negotiate a peace deal, and so begins Main Quest: Season Unending.

> ◇ **MAIN QUEST:** Season Unending
> ◇ **OBJECTIVE:** Get Greybeards' help in negotiating a truce
> ♦ **TARGET:** Master Arngeir, in High Hrothgar

▷ Part 2: Epic Entanglement

> ◇ **OBJECTIVE:** Learn Shout to call Odahviing
> ♦ **TARGET:** Esbern, in the Sky Haven Temple
> ♦ **TARGET:** OR Paarthurnax, at the Throat of the World

Once you have convinced the Jarl to aid you, you still need a way to lure a dragon into your trap. You have a choice of teachers:

Esbern: who has been busy in the Sky Haven Temple library. It appears that the ancient Blades recorded many of the names of the dragons they slew. By cross-referencing the burial-site map that Delphine created from the Dragonstone, Esbern has identified one of Alduin's raised dragons.

Paarthurnax: whose arcane knowledge and commanding expertise of Shouts enables him to easily inform you of the Shout that you seek.

Because the names of dragons are always three Words of Power (Shouts), the dragon will hear and come to you when his name is bellowed. Your teacher has the name of Od-Ah-Viing ("Winged Snow Hunter"), and you learn the Shout to call Odahviing.

➤ **Word of Power:** Snow, Call Dragon

➤ **Word of Power:** Hunter, Call Dragon

➤ **Word of Power:** Wing, Call Dragon

> **NOTE** Delphine, if she's with Esbern, now has a bone to pick with you. She assures you that the Blades won't be nearly as accommodating if you don't slay Paarthurnax up at the Throat of the World. This is another hint to start Main Quest: Paarthurnax. Once again, it is purely optional. Consult that quest for more information.

> ◇ **OBJECTIVE:** Prepare trap for Odahviing
> ♦ **TARGET:** Jarl of Whiterun, in Dragonsreach

Now that you've learned the Call Dragon Shout, you can try it out anywhere. Odahviing appears in the skies, but he's too far away to bring down using Dragonrend. As there's no way to capture Odahviing until you reach Dragonsreach, return to Whiterun and speak with the Jarl. He is ready, so inform him you're prepared to catch a dragon. Follow the Jarl up the steps to the side of his throne and out the doors to the northeast.

◊ **OBJECTIVE:** Call Odahviing to Dragonsreach
♦ **TARGET:** Battlements, atop Dragonsreach

You emerge on the large stone battlements, which have a dragon-sized porch area. Move to the crenellations at the structure's northeast edge, where the Jarl tells you to call; his men are ready. Execute the Call Dragon Shout and wait a few moments. The ominous sound of leathery wings echoes across the tundra.

◊ **OBJECTIVE:** Defeat and trap Odahviing

The mighty red beast soars up and attacks the battlements. At this point, you must bring Odahviing down and spring the trap:

Dragon Trapping: It is important to note that you're trapping — and not killing — Odahviing. Attacking with ranged spells or arrows usually annoys Odahviing enough for him to swoop and land on the battlements.

An easier plan is to yell the Dragonrend Shout at Odahviing. This hampers his flying and makes him drop onto the battlements without having to lengthen this already-difficult battle.

When he drops onto Dragonsreach, Odahviing advances on his wings, furious at being forced to land. Back up (to the southwest) so Odahviing enters the giant hallway and passes between the two huge chains attached to the giant stocks contraption. When the dragon moves forward, the stocks slam down, trapping Odahviing!

◊ **OBJECTIVE:** Interrogate Odahviing

> Remember, you're interrogating, not killing, Odahviing. You cannot dispatch him, so concentrate on trapping him. **CAUTION**

Odahviing feels humiliated and is perhaps a little impressed by your trapping talents. Ask where Alduin is hiding (and then ask again), and Odahviing reveals Alduin has traveled to Sovngarde to regain his strength. The door to Sovngarde is located at Skuldafn, one of his ancient fanes (temples) high in the eastern mountains. After answering your questions, Odahviing asks to be freed. Answer that he must serve you. Odahviing initially refuses but remembers one important detail he forgot to mention...

Quest Conclusion Part 2

It seems that Skuldafn can be entered only by flying. Odahviing offers to fly you there, but only after you free him. This conundrum is concluded at the start of the next quest.

Postquest Activities

Once you're pondering how to reach Skuldafn and setting Odahviing free, Main Quest: The World-Eater's Eyrie begins.

PAARTHURNAX

PREREQUISITES: Complete Main Quest: Alduin's Bane
INTERSECTING QUESTS: Main Quest: Alduin's Bane, Other Faction Quests (The Greybeards Quests): Word Wall Revelations* ,
   Other Faction Quests (The Greybeards Quests): Meditations on Words of Power*, College of Winterhold Quest: First Lessons
LOCATIONS: Riverwood, Sleeping Giant Inn, Sky Haven Temple, Throat of the World
CHARACTERS: Delphine, Esbern, Master Arngeir
ENEMIES: Paarthurnax
◊ **OBJECTIVES:** Kill Paarthurnax, Talk to Delphine or Esbern

 ● MINOR SPOILERS

> **NOTE** * Quest names marked with this symbol do not appear in your Quest Menu list, although objectives may.

▶ Slaying the Summit's Hermit

◊ **OBJECTIVE:** Kill Paarthurnax
♦ **TARGET:** Throat of the World (mountain summit)

Your alliance with the Blades sits uneasily upon a knife edge. They refuse to help you (which basically means you cannot access their Other Faction Quests) until you've defeated the monster at the Throat of the World. Reasoning with them that Paarthurnax

has changed his ways and now embodies peace and meditation falls on deaf ears. They simply want you to remove Paarthurnax, as they perceive him to be partly responsible for the many deaths of their ancestral clan members.

> Remember! This quest is completely optional. You will lose standing with the Greybeards if you complete this task, so it is time to pick a side. **CAUTION**

> **NOTE** Killing Paarthurnax does not affect the future Main Quests; you will still be able to complete your task of killing Paarthurnax's brother, Alduin, without any complications.

Return to the Throat of the World (or remain here after the end of Main Quest: Alduin's Bane) and approach Paarthurnax. Kill him using your favorite weaponry. One method is to launch Fire Breath (the Shout he actually taught you) into him until he starts to flinch and takes to the skies. Then wound and bring him down to the ground with Dragonrend. Finish with your other attacks, using a bow, magic, or melee weapons. Gather the gold and bones from Paarthurnax's corpse, but only after absorbing his soul.

➤ **Dragon's Soul**

◇ **OBJECTIVE:** Talk to Delphine or Esbern
♦ **TARGET:** Riverwood or Sky Haven Temple

Quest Conclusion

Return to Delphine or to Esbern. Depending on when you killed Paarthurnax or who gave you this quest, expect a similar response from either of them: They are extremely happy; the ancient evil is avenged, and the shades of many Blades salute you this day!

Return to Master Arngeir, and the greeting is slightly colder. You are lucky the Greybeards are men of peace, as you've tested their philosophy beyond the breaking point. You've thrown your lot in with a cabal of Akaviri barbarians. You are no longer welcome in High Hrothgar.

TIP To gain the most knowledge and help from both the Greybeards and the Blades, complete both of the Other Factions Greybeards Quests to your satisfaction, and then complete this quest. After that, you have limited contact with the Greybeards but are on excellent terms with the Blades. You can complete the four different (and some repeatable) Other Factions Blade Quests afterward.

Postquest Activities

Your other Main Quests continue as normal. Contact with the Greybeards is now kept to a minimum; they want nothing more to do with the likes of you. The Blades welcome you into their fold. You may begin any of their Other Faction Quests after speaking to Esbern or Delphine.

SEASON UNENDING

PREREQUISITES: Partial Complete Main Quest: The Fallen
INTERSECTING QUESTS: Main Quest: The Fallen, Main Quest: Paarthurnax, Other Faction Quests (The Greybeards Quests): Word Wall Revelations*, Other Faction Quests (The Greybeards Quests): Meditations on Words of Power*
LOCATIONS: High Hrothgar, Solitude, Castle Dour, Whiterun, Dragonsreach, Windhelm, Palace of the Kings

CHARACTERS: Delphine, Elenwen, Esbern, Galmar Stone-Fist, General Tullius, Jarl Balgruuf the Greater, Jarl Elisif the Fair, Jarl Vignar the Revered , Legate Rikke, Master Arngeir, Ulfric Stormcloak
ENEMIES: None
◇ **OBJECTIVES:** Get Greybeards' help in negotiating a truce, Talk to Arngeir, Talk to General Tullius, Talk to Ulfric Stormcloak, Talk to Arngeir, Take your seat, Negotiate a truce

NOTE * Quest names marked with this symbol do not appear in your Quest Menu list, although objectives may.

NOTE Season Unending only occurs if the Civil War still rages across Skyrim; consult the previous quest for more details. In order to convince General Tullius and Jarl Ulfric to attend, you may need to finish your current Civil War quest. Once both have agreed to attend the council, the Civil War effectively comes to a halt, and you cannot obtain any more Civil War Quests until you finish the Main Quest.

▷ A Modicum of Civility

◇ **OBJECTIVE:** Get Greybeards' help in negotiating a truce
◇ **OBJECTIVE:** Talk to Arngeir
♦ **TARGET:** Master Arngeir, in High Hrothgar

Return to High Hrothgar and seek out Master Arngeir. Initially, he talks about the difficulties in capturing a dragon. Inform him that you're actually here to get his help stopping the Civil War. Arngeir reluctantly agrees to this and requests that you journey to Ulfric Stormcloak and General Tullius, and tell them that the Greybeards wish to speak to them. You may approach the leader of the Stormcloaks and the Imperials in either order.

◇ **OBJECTIVE:** Talk to General Tullius
♦ **TARGET:** Castle Dour, in Solitude
◇ **OBJECTIVE:** Talk to Ulfric Stormcloak
♦ **TARGET:** Palace of the Kings, in Windhelm

Tullius, tell him that Ulfric has already agreed (if this is the case) agrees to the treaty.

General Tullius: Plot a path and trek to Solitude. Enter the walled city. Progress to the entrance to Castle Dour, where the high-ranking Imperials command the ongoing war efforts. Approach General Tullius. He has a different greeting depending on how the Civil War is progressing and whose side you've chosen, but he certainly remembers you from Helgen. Speak to the general again if he fobs you off and tell him you have a message from the Greybeards — they are convening a peace council at High Hrothgar. You can attempt to persuade him or convince him with answers that you choose: Eventually he

Ulfric Stormcloak: Figure out a favored route and journey to Windhelm. Step inside the walled city. Move to the entrance to the Palace of the Kings, where the Stormcloak chieftains plan their ongoing raids. Approach Ulfric Stormcloak. His opinion on you differs, depending on how the Civil War is progressing and the side you've chosen, but he can't forget his time at Helgen. Inform him of the message from the Greybeards, that they have requested a peace council at High Hrothgar. You can try persuading Ulfric, letting him know Tullius has already agreed (if this has happened), or bring him around with answers of your choosing. Finally, he agrees to the sit-down treaty meeting.

OBJECTIVE: Talk to Arngeir

TARGET: Master Arngeir, in High Hrothgar

▷ War and Peace

Journey back to High Hrothgar and locate Master Arngeir. As you arrive, Delphine and Esbern are having a heated discussion with the Greybeards, demanding to be part of the meeting. If you've completed Main Quest: Paarthurnax, the conversation is slightly different, depending on how you've dealt with the dragon. The conversation ends, Arngeir expresses further concerns to you—especially that this place was built and dedicated to peace—before all parties are requested to take their seats for the council.

OBJECTIVE: Take your seat

Enter the grand hall in High Hrothgar, and take your seat opposite the entrance. The various members of the factions attending this meeting are as follows:

 Legate Rikke, a loyal and disciplined second-in-command and a true believer in the rightness of the Imperial cause.

 Jarl Elisif the Fair, the figurehead of Solitude who defers to Tullius.

 General Tullius, the leader of the Imperial forces in Skyrim. He is practical but impatient and unimaginative.

 Jarl Balgruuf the Greater, of Whiterun. A strong, noble, and valiant leader, he attends if he still rules his city.

Elenwen, a steely, determined, and ruthless head of the Thalmor observers. She sits near the Imperials, but her machinations are more complex.

Arngeir, Delphine, and Esbern sit in the adjacent chairs, opposite you. Their alliances are disparate but well known to you.

 Ulfric Stormcloak, the fiery and charismatic Jarl of Windhelm, is attempting to win Skyrim's independence.

 Galmar Stone-Fist is Ulfric's grizzled, hard-bitten, and fearless housecarl. Importantly, he is also completely loyal.

 Jarl Vignar of Whiterun, if the Civil War has progressed and the Stormcloaks have Whiterun under their control.

OBJECTIVE: Negotiate a truce

Opening Remarks

The negotiations now begin. Due to the variations that your previous choices have already had on this peace process, there are several variations and discussions. But it is vitally important for your own machinations that you understand what you should be seeking to accomplish from this:

Failure is not an option

The good news is, unless you start brandishing a weapon and slashing dignitaries, there is no way to "fail" in this meeting. But you must tailor the agreements to your personal wishes. Here's how this all breaks down:

Every time you're asked your opinion, you need to favor a faction, either the Imperials or the Stormcloaks. Logically, you should side with the faction you are helping (or wanting to help) in the Civil War; strongly agree with all their statements.

Or, you can favor the opposing faction. This is counterintuitive, as it will only anger your allies and (if you're interested in the Civil War) will force you to retake any Holds you gave away thanks to your terrible negotiations.

You can favor one faction a little or a lot. Read the answers you're about to give to determine what are strongly or weakly favored responses.

Or, you can favor neither side if the Civil War doesn't interest you, the Civil War Quests haven't started yet, or you wish to simply be impartial. This has no real effects on the faction you may be leaning toward.

▷ Negotiations Begin: Whose Side Are You On?

Hold Importance

First, you should understand how the Holds of Skyrim are broken down, in terms of "type," for this meeting. The following table shows which Holds are strongholds (the base of operations for a faction), which are major Holds (important), and which are minor Holds (less important):

✓	NAME OF HOLD	CAPITAL CITY	HOLD TYPE
	Haarfingar	Solitude	Stronghold: Imperials
	Hjaalmarch	Morthal	Minor
	The Pale	Dawnstar	Minor
	Winterhold	Winterhold	Minor
	The Reach	Markarth	Major
	Whiterun	Whiterun	Major
	Eastmarch	Windhelm	Stronghold: Stormcloaks
	Falkreath	Falkreath	Minor
	The Rift	Riften	Major

Negotiation 1: Elenwen

As soon as the negotiations begin, Ulfric raises objections about Elenwen even being involved in this council. Tullius or Ulfric asks you what your thoughts are:

 To agree with Ulfric and kick out this unwanted entity

 To disagree with Ulfric and keep Elenwen in the meeting

Negotiation 2: Markarth or Riften

The next item to discuss is giving up a major Hold. If you take the Stormcloak side, General Tullius will demand that Riften be turned over to the Empire. Otherwise, Ulfric will demand Markarth be surrendered to the Stormcloaks. The opposing faction's reaction depends on the state of the Civil War:

The faction that controls Markarth or Riften asks you what you think is a fair trade for the city. Your answer is always one of two choices:

◇ An exchange of a major Hold the opposition has

◇ An exchange of a minor Hold the opposition has

The council goes along with whatever choice you make. Bear in mind that the side that controls Markarth or Riften will be unhappy if it is bargained for a minor Hold!

Negotiation 3: The Archivist Speaks

At this point, one of the factions threatens to leave the bargaining table. This is always the faction that is most unhappy at the moment (the one you have favored the least). Esbern restores order with an impassioned speech about the greater danger, and both sides grudgingly agree to continue.

Negotiation 4: Concessions

It is now time for the faction that you've favored less (and thus "losing" the negotiations) to ask for additional concessions.

For each demand, you can choose whether to agree to the concession. This continues until the side demanding a concession from you receives it or they run out of concessions to ask for (which requires you to refuse all their demands).

 TIP This is an excellent opportunity to really stick it to the side you aren't allied with! Remember that any changes you agree to (such as a hold changing hands) from here on will affect any Civil War Quests that are currently active.

Quest Conclusion

The council now concludes. If you've favored the enemy over your initial allies, you will be scolded by your allies. The quest then concludes.

Postquest Activities

At this point, Main Quest: The Fallen begins. Consult Part 2 of this quest (shown previously) for more information.

THE WORLD-EATER'S EYRIE

PREREQUISITES: Complete Main Quest: The Fallen

INTERSECTING QUESTS: Main Quest: The Fallen, Main Quest: Sovngarde, Main Quest: Paarthurnax, Other Faction Quests (The Greybeards Quests): Word Wall Revelations* , Other Faction Quests (The Greybeards Quests): Meditations on Words of Power*, Side Quest: Masks of the Dragon Priests*

LOCATIONS: Skuldafn, Skuldafn North Tower, Skuldafn South Tower , Skuldafn Temple, Whiterun, Dragonsreach

CHARACTERS: Jarl Balgruuf the Greater, Jarl Vignar the Revered, Odahviing ("Winged Snow Hunter"), Whiterun Guard

ENEMIES: Dragon, Draugr, Frostbite Spider, Nahkriin the Dragon Priest

◊ **OBJECTIVES:** Set Odahviing free, Talk to Odahviing, Reach Alduin's portal to Sovngarde, Enter Sovngarde

◉ MINOR SPOILERS

NOTE ✷ Quest names marked with this symbol do not appear in your Quest Menu list, although objectives may.

Eastward, to the Afterlife

◊ **OBJECTIVE:** Set Odahviing free
♦ **TARGET:** Odanviing, Dragonsreach in Whiterun

Although you're right to be suspicious, the only way to reach Skuldafn is to agree to free Odahviing, on the condition that he transport you there. You may also witness Irileth's and Farengar Secret-Fire's reactions and questioning of the dragon. Then climb the steps to the side of the hall where Odahviing is waiting. Instruct the guard to open the trap. The guard isn't too happy, so confirm these are your wishes. If you don't wish to wait, you may activate the pull-chain yourself.

◊ **OBJECTIVE:** Talk to Odahviing

When you return to the dragon, he turns and lumbers to the parapet and waits for your arrival. Odahviing is awaiting your command. When you are ready (and fully equipped for this final adventure), tell Odahviing you're ready to be taken to Skuldafn. You clamber aboard the dragon and set off for a flight across the eastern mountains.

◊ **OBJECTIVE:** Reach Alduin's portal to Sovngarde
♦ **TARGET:** Exterior portal, the roof of Skuldafn Temple

Odahviing deposits you on the edge of the Skuldafn fane (temple) and departs; this is as far as he can take you. Bring up your map; you're on the eastern side of the Velothi Mountains, out of the Skyrim realm. Edge through the first

of two giant stone arches and cross the bridge. You're likely to be set upon by a dragon at this point, but it may depart the area before you can take it down (or utilize Dragonrend). Don't overstretch yourself fighting it if it flees (or use Dragonrend if you want it to flee). After passing through the second archway on the bridge's opposite side, there are other foes to concern yourself with.

The first of these are Draugr that clatter down the stone steps as you intercept (or sneak past) them. Continue south, into a cracked courtyard with temple outbuildings to investigate. But first, the dragon returns to try and finish you. As with your other dragon battles, employ the tactics already learned: down the beast with Dragonrend, and then dispatch it with your favorite killing implements or augmentations. You absorb the Dragon Soul after you slay the creature. There is little time to rest; another dragon attacks only moments later. Deal with it in a similar fashion. Should you wish to flee, the only areas suitable are the side temples, filled with Draugr. Absorb another Dragon Soul before continuing your Draugr dispatching.

➤ **Dragon Soul (2)**

Take a moment to survey the scenery: This sprawling fane is comprised of a South Temple Tower, a north temple tower, and a main temple interior, which is the likely location to head to when looking for Alduin's Portal. Before you climb the main stone stairs, split by a torch and a stone column, inspect the Skuldafn South Tower. Inside is a spiral staircase and a small chamber with items to gather. A second chamber is atop the stairs and has a chest and a few other items. Expect at least six Draugrs as you battle through this tower. Two upper exits allow you to safely check the main temple and the courtyard from which you just came.

Head back down to the courtyard. Move east up either of the two stone staircases and under either arch to a small open folly with a treasure chest at the top. Next, head north, under another arch, before beginning a pitched battle (or a sneaking maneuver) against the remains of the Nord dead. The Draugr continue to appear as you encroach up the main stairs toward the main temple sanctum. When you're fighting up the stairs, beware of Draugr perched atop the temple's roof, as they can strike you with ranged fire. Fight back using your own projectile attacks, or move to the door so the rooftop foes can't aim at you.

Before entering the main temple, you can optionally turn around and head south, down the eastern platform overlooking the ruined outer buildings you just navigated, to the entrance of Skuldafn North Tower. This provides more Draugr for you to defeat. Take the spiral staircase to an upper chamber and exterior balcony. The balcony leads back to an otherwise-inaccessible interior corridor with a treasure chest to raid. After you emerge back on the eastern platform, investigate the exterior steps to the southwest, which leads to an altar and a battle with a particularly powerful Draugr. Open the treasure chest on the altar, then use the aqueduct bridge and head north. Finally you reach and open the door to Skuldafn Temple.

Prelude to the Maelstrom

You are greeted by ancient Nordic architecture and a central ceremonial buttress with an embalming table to your right. Venture down either corridor (the right has a chest to open, while the left as a floor trigger and a dart trap). Engage the Draugr guarding the connecting passages ahead of you, surrounding a second embalming table. Ascend either set of steps to an upper chamber, where the vertical Draugr coffin lids fly open, and out spills more emaciated bags of bones for you to thwart. After eliminating the Draugr, you'll notice the two archways ahead are blocked by portcullises. Investigate the pillars and lever to continue your progress.

Puzzle Solution Part 1: A lever raises the portcullises, but it is currently not attached to the mechanism. In the upper chamber, there are three pillars with carved animal petroglyphs on them. Investigate the two outer pillars first. On the outside of the ceremonial arch structure they are sitting under is a second carving, which is resting in the mouth of a stone head. Move the pillar on the western side so the Whale glyph is facing the chamber's western side (in the same direction as the carving above the pillar). Move the pillar on the eastern side so the Snake glyph is facing the chamber's eastern side. The mechanism is now attached.

Puzzle Solution Part 2: Before you move the middle pillar, peer at the two portcullises. Above each is a stone head, and in the mouth of each head is another glyph, partially obscured by the stone crossbeam. The left (northwest) mouth has a Snake. The right (northeast) has a Hawk. Now rotate the middle pillar so the Snake or the Hawk faces the lever pedestal. Then pull the lever, and the portcullis corresponding to the Snake or Hawk opens. You can have only one portcullis open at a time.

Take the steps through the left portcullis up to a hallway (as the right one leads to a blocked area and small chest), and drop to the altar and embalming table below. Fight through cobwebs and Frostbite Spiders, and climb some stairs (some cobwebbed alcoves reveal a hidden chest or some egg sacs). Locate an iron double door leading to a second puzzle chamber. Clear the chamber of Draugr and ransack any treasure chests before you concentrate on the animal petroglyphs.

Puzzle Solution: Begin on the ground floor. Head east, and walk around the room until you spot a carved head with a Snake petroglyph in its mouth. Return to the pillar facing the double doors you entered, and turn it so the Snake faces the doors (west). Ascend to the bridge area above. Locate the second carved head with a Hawk in its mouth. Match that so the Hawk is facing the same direction (outward or to the north) in the alcove underneath this head.

Turn around (to the north), and match the Whale on the pedestal in the opposite alcove, with the final head above it. Then pull the lever on the pedestal. This lowers the bridge, allowing you to exit.

Follow the corridor around to another embalming room with steps up to a gallery and a bridge to cross into the next chamber. Demolish Draugr along the way. Beware of the spiral steps; there's a pressure plate directly in front of you that releases darts and an oil lamp that falls onto flammable oil. Gather any items before climbing the steps, bring down more Draugr in the connecting chamber with the blocked portcullis exit, and then enter the antechamber with a chest and a lever pedestal to raise the portcullis. Now follow the wide ceremonial corridor up, watching for oil-lamp traps. Continue toward a Nordic Puzzle Door, guarded by a high-ranking Draugr. Fight this fiend until he collapses; his corpse holds the Diamond Claw, the key to exiting this place.

➤ **Diamond Claw**

Puzzle Solution: Approach the Nordic Puzzle Door, but first inspect the palm of the Diamond Claw you just picked up. The three symbols etched into the palm are Wolf, Moth, and Dragon. These correspond to the animal symbols on the door's outer, middle, and inner rings, respectively.

The door rumbles down, allowing you to step into a huge main crypt. The place is silent compared to the Draugr infestations you've beaten back previously. Approach the Word Wall at the crypt's far end and absorb another—and extremely potent—Word of Power. Then depart the temple interior, optionally checking an embalming chamber to the side, before opening the double wooden doors to the temple exterior.

➤ **Word of Power:** Storm Call

You appear on the roof of the temple you've just navigated. Deliver some killing blows to any remaining Draugr you failed to cull while on the lower ground. Although there's some side battlements to investigate, there's little to find. Instead, locate the stone steps and the jet of molten fire roaring into the skies.

◊ **OBJECTIVE:** Enter Sovngarde

Two large dragons flank you, sitting atop carved columns to your left and right. In the courtyard's center are steps where a Dragon Priest is attempting to close the portal using dragon tongue incantations. The priest's name is Nahkriin, and he carries a staff that opens the maw he's just closed (although it is possible to kill him before this chant is completed). Engage Nahkriin in battle, but beware of his electrical prowess; use the arches and stairs as cover if you need to, and watch for the dragons that intermittently swoop in to attack. Fight back with Dragonrend, and slay each dragon before turning your attention to the priest. Fight him until all that remains is a pile of dust. Aside from some sizable gold, you receive Nahkriin's Mask (useful for Side Quest: Masks of the Dragon Priests*) and the Dragon Priest Staff.

➤ **Dragon Soul (2)**   ➤ **Dragon Priest Staff**   ➤ **Nahkriin**

Quest Conclusion

Ascend the ceremonial steps. Activate the Dragon Seal at the top of the steps, and you jam the staff's shaft into the seal's center. A great gout of fire blasts forth from a whirling vortex—a gateway to the Aetherius realm, where Alduin cheats death and feeds off the souls of heroes past. Step down into the light and into Sovngarde!

Postquest Activities

After you step into this writhing gateway, Main Quest: Sovngarde begins. Before you enter, know that you can never explore Skuldafn again. If there are items you wish to collect, do so before entering the gateway.

  **SOVNGARDE**

PREREQUISITES: Complete Main Quest: The World-Eater's Eyrie

INTERSECTING QUESTS: Main Quest: The World-Eater's Eyrie, Main Quest: Dragonslayer

LOCATIONS: Sovngarde, Hall of Valor, Shadowed Vale, Whalebone Bridge

CHARACTERS: Erlendr the Quick, Felldir, Gormlaith Golden-Hilt, Hakon, Hunroor the Agile, Jurgen Windcaller ("The Calm"), Olaf One-Eye, Stormcloak Soldier, Tsun, Ulfgar the Unending, Ysgramor, and many others.

ENEMIES: Alduin

◊ **OBJECTIVES:** Find out how to defeat Alduin, Gain admittance to the Hall of Valor, Talk to the heroes of Sovngarde

⬤ **MAJOR SPOILERS**

▶ Terror in the Shadowed Vale

◊ **OBJECTIVE:** Find out how to defeat Alduin

♦ **TARGET:** Lost soul, in the Shadowed Vale

You have crossed the threshold of the living and entered the afterlife, the realm of Aetherius. Alduin's presence is powerful here; indeed, you can see the dragon in the distance, below the red glow of the eternal sunset. Follow the pathway down (north), passing between the mammoth tusks and the monolithic cowled statues and into the valley of mists—the Shadowed Vale.

The mists—created by Alduin—begin to thicken, impeding your path and vision. Use the Clear Skies Shout to clear the fog back for a few moments. Look at the winding path through the misty valley, which is interspersed with runic stones and blue torchlight that indicates the main route to take. Soon you make out a figure, a Stormcloak Soldier, lost and terrified. He pleads with you to turn back. The fellow splutters out a riddle: "vain is all courage against the peril that guards the way." You surmise he's talking about Alduin.

He tells the tale of his own demise but is even more terrified of Alduin, whose hunger is insatiable. The dragon hunts the lost souls snared within this shadowed valley, feasts upon them to regain his power, and returns to Tamriel. The soldier pleads with you to take him to Shor's Hall, where the heroes of old await their eternity in safety from Alduin's hunt. Answer him in any way you wish. Perhaps you might seek some help inside this Hall of Valor?

◊ **OBJECTIVE:** Gain admittance to the Hall of Valor

♦ **TARGET:** Tsun, in Sovngarde

Execute the Clear Skies Shout once more to spot the Hall of Valor silhouetted against the gloomy skies in the distance to the north. Venture farther into the valley, and the path splits, continuing around both sides of a central rock outcrop. You can climb the steps cut into the outcrop. Watch Alduin as he swoops about in the middle distance, plucking souls lost in the fog and devouring them. Atop this central outcrop, above the fog, you can also view the entrance to the Hall of Valor, a gigantic whale skeleton that spans a bottomless chasm void.

▶ Seeking Valor

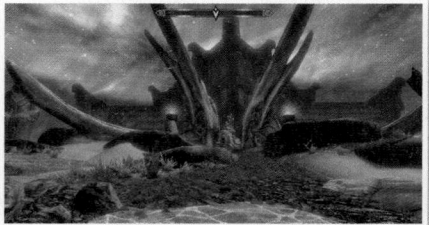

Return to the path below. No matter which path to the whalebone bridge that you take, expect to encounter two or three lost souls caught forever in the fog. Expect both Stormcloaks and Imperials here, along with those you may have dispatched during your adventure. Along the left-hand path, you can also meet High King Torygg, whose death at the hands of Ulfric Stormcloak plunged Skyrim into civil war. All fear the World-Eater. Emerge from Shadowed Vale and approach the steps leading to the whalebone bridge, where a mighty figure stands before you.

Approach Tsun. If you've studied your Tamriel history, you'll know he is a hero of ancient times, the brother of Stendarr, shield-thane to Shor, and a warrior of supreme quality. To Nords, he is revered as the greatest warrior who ever lived. As you approach, he asks what brings you to Sovngarde. You can:

> Ignore him and attempt to cross the bridge without his permission. It takes but a moment for Tsun to catch you in this maneuver, and lightning is summoned from the skies. It strikes you repeatedly, forcing you to stop, die, or leap from the bridge and to your death.

> Speak to Tsun. When you ask, he tells you that he judges those fit to join the fellowship of honor inside the Hall of Valor. After further posturing, inform Tsun that you seek to enter the Hall and that you have a right of birth; you are Dragonborn.

Tsun greets you with a series of verses. This warrior poetry is filled with illuminating, rugged beauty. You receive a separate response if you've achieved any (or all) of the following:

◇ Become the leader of the Companions.

◇ Become the head of the College of Winterhold.

◇ Achieved the status as the head of the Dark Brotherhood.

◇ Achieved the status as the leader of the Thieves Guild.

Tsun agrees to let you into the Hall, but only after you pass the warrior's test. Tsun unsheathes his two-handed battle-ax and advances upon you!

This battle need not be difficult. You may utilize any of the Shouts that you've learned that damage foes in combat (Fire Breath is a good choice). Back these ranged attacks with your favored offensive weaponry. Once you wound Tsun enough, he halts the attack, judges that you fought well, and steps aside, allowing you to cross the Whalebone Bridge. Don't fall off the bridge as you cross!

◇ **OBJECTIVE:** Talk to the heroes of Sovngarde
◆ **TARGETS:** Gormlaith Golden-Hilt, Felldir, and Hakon, in the Hall of Valor

The giant doors to the Hall of Valor appear before you. Push one open and enter the grand hall. Heroes from Tamriel's recent and distant past walk this Hall, which is dominated by mead and meat: A banquet, including a huge spit-roast is underway, and Shor's subjects make merry, awaiting his summons to the last battle. You are greeted by the mighty warrior who adapted Nordic writing from the elves, Ysgramor. This revered ancestor of the Companions tells you that three warriors stand ready, awaiting your word to loose their fury upon the perilous foe. Their names are Gormlaith the Fearless, Hakon the Valiant, and Felldir the Old. You may remember them as the Nordic warriors you saw in your Elder Scrolls vision. Seek them out among the other heroes of Sovngarde.

The following heroic fighters from yore are among the honored guests in the Hall of Valor:

Erlendr the Quick, a friend of Ulfgar, who was turned into a stone pillar by a mage named Grimkell.

Jurgen Windcaller ("The Calm"), the founder of the Way of the Voice. The Greybeards honor him.

Hunroor the Agile, a companion of Ulfgar, who was turned into a stone pillar by a mage called Grimkell.

Ulfgar the Unending, a Nord barbarian who has finally found his way home, along with his brethren.

Olaf One-Eye, a first-era king who helped capture a mighty dragon named Numinex and housed him in Dragonsreach.

Quest Conclusion

When you're done wandering among the heroes, locate the three Nordic warriors who defeated Alduin the first time around: Gormlaith Golden-Hilt, Hakon One-Eye, and Felldir the Old. Gormlaith is raring to seal Alduin's doom, but hold council before the battle begins. They agree that Alduin's mist is more than a snare; it is his shield and cloak. With the four voices of the heroes and Dragonborn joined in unison, the mist can be removed and Alduin brought to battle. The World-Eater fears you, Dragonborn!

Postquest Activities

Once the Nordic heroes agree to fight Alduin, Main Quest: Dragonslayer begins.

DRAGONSLAYER

PREREQUISITES: Complete Main Quest: Sovngarde

MAJOR SPOILERS

INTERSECTING QUESTS: Main Quest: Sovngarde, Main Quest: Epilogue

LOCATIONS: Sovngarde, Hall of Valor, Shadowed Vale, Whalebone Bridge

CHARACTERS: Gormlaith Golden-Hilt, Hakon One-Eye, and Felldir the Old

ENEMIES: Alduin

◇ **OBJECTIVES:** Help the heroes of Sovngarde dispel Alduin's mist, Defeat Alduin

▶ "I've Waited an Eternity for This Day"

◇ **OBJECTIVE:** Help the heroes of Sovngarde dispel Alduin's mist
◆ **TARGET:** Nordic heroes, Shadowed Vale, in Sovngarde

Leave the Hall of Valor and cross the Whalebone Bridge to the edge of the Shadowed Vale, where your Nordic brethren are gathered. They are eager to slay Alduin for a second time, while the World-Eater roars away in this mist. When the three heroes have assembled, use your Clear Skies Shout to blow away the nearby mist — your allies will join you. Alduin bellows back with a Shout of his own, and the mist descends once again. Continue your Shouts until Alduin's might is broken.

> **TIP** Have all your favorite weapons, spells, and Shouts set up so you can switch between them quickly, depending on how combat goes.

◇ **OBJECTIVE:** Defeat Alduin

With the mists permanently dispelled, Alduin's massive, jagged form swoops down into the vale. He begins to launch a barrage of fire attacks at you, the Nords, and any of the lost souls that have been freed from their permanent fog. The time has come to finish Alduin forever!

Dragon Slaying: Alduin is a lot less mobile when he's writhing in agony and having to land after a Dragonrend attack strikes him. Make this your earliest priority, and dodge any attacks he launches from his mouth.

Utilizing the Dragonrend is imperative; Alduin is invulnerable unless he's writhing and descending to the ground or unless he's on the ground after being affected by Dragonrend. If he isn't bathed in the blue light from this attack, he's impervious to your weapons.

Stand close to your fellow fighters so you can vary the attacks and so you don't face Alduin on your own. If your coordinated attacks come from different directions, Alduin won't focus all his attention on you. Meanwhile, you have the luxury of striking only him.

You need only one Dragonrend to down Alduin; you can switch to another Shout (such as Fire Breath) and attack with that and with your favored weapons. Use any that you've employed successfully against dragons in the past. But remember to attempt this only when Dragonrend is still affecting him.

Quest Conclusion

After you strike the killing blow, Alduin writhes in agony and his soul begins to dissipate....

Postquest Activities

After you strike the killing blow, Main Quest: Epilogue begins.

EPILOGUE

PREREQUISITES: Complete Main Quest: Dragonslayer

INTERSECTING QUESTS: Main Quest: Dragonslayer, Main Quest: Paarthurnax

LOCATIONS: High Hrothgar, Sky Haven Temple, Sovngarde, Hall of Valor, Shadowed Vale, Whalebone Bridge, Throat of the World

CHARACTERS: Delphine, Esbern, Felldir, Gormlaith Golden-Hilt, Hakon, Master Arngeir, Odahviing, Paarthurnax, Tsun

ENEMIES: Alduin

◊ **OBJECTIVES:** Speak to Tsun to return to Skyrim

● MAJOR SPOILERS

⬓ Banishment: Ziil gro dovah ulse!

> **NOTE** Once you complete Main Quest: Dragonslayer, this quest automatically begins.

> ◊ **OBJECTIVE:** Speak to Tsun to return to Skyrim
> ♦ **TARGET:** Tsun, Whalebone Bridge, in Sovngarde

Alduin thrashes on the ground as his soul leaves his corporeal form. With a final, thunderous spasm, Alduin is torn apart; not even his skeleton remains in this afterlife. Tsun is the first to congratulate you on your mighty deed; you have cleansed Sovngarde of Alduin's evil snare. They will sing of this battle in the Hall of Valor! You may speak to any of the heroes who helped you in battle. When you're ready to leave, only Tsun can transport you from this place. Tsun summons Shor's Might and returns you to the Throat of the World. First, though, he grants you a Shout, one that brings a hero from Sovngarde to your side in your hour of need.

➤ **Word of Power:** Hero, Call of Valor

➤ **Word of Power:** Champion, Call of Valor

➤ **Word of Power:** Legend, Call of Valor

Quest Conclusion

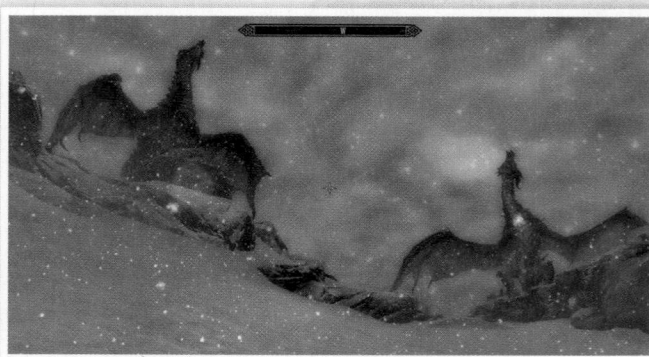

You return to the Throat of the World, with a full complement of dragons perched on the mountaintop at your arrival. The two recognizable beasts are Odahviing and Paarthurnax (if he is still alive). These beasts roar in a death chant for their fallen god—their leader, Alduin, and then take to the skies. Should you attack, they depart without fighting back. Paarthurnax greets you, impressed by your feats. Then he, too, flies away, leaving only Odahviing. Speak with him, and he informs you that he is now in your service.

> **NOTE** The Call Dragon Shout now summons him to do your bidding.

Return to High Hrothgar and speak with Master Arngeir. Inform him of your actions; he believes Alduin may yet rise again, but that is for the gods to decide.

If you return to Sky Haven Temple, Delphine asks whether you have good news. But there's still the matter of Paarthurnax, if he lives. The Blades are grateful but are certainly more appreciative if Alduin's brother is also slain.

Postquest Activities

Once you return to the Throat of the World, you can continue exploring Skyrim and finish any other quests.

OVERVIEW

Optimal Quest Start

You can start the Companions Quests when you arrive at Whiterun for the first time, or at any point thereafter. Warriors may wish to join sooner rather than later for access to a wide range of combat skill trainers.

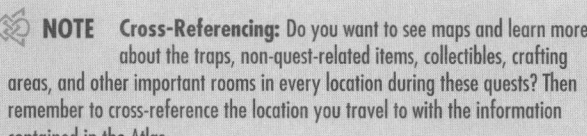

NOTE **Cross-Referencing:** Do you want to see maps and learn more about the traps, non-quest-related items, collectibles, crafting areas, and other important rooms in every location during these quests? Then remember to cross-reference the location you travel to with the information contained in the Atlas.

Sanctuary: Jorrvaskr, in Whiterun

Jorrvaskr exterior, as seen from the Whiterun Plaza.

Jorrvaskr interior, during a drinking session.

The Companions' sanctuary is the Nordic longhouse adjacent to Dragonsreach, on the upper end of Whiterun. This is an ancient and honored mead hall where generations of Companions have met. According to local legend, Jorrvaskr is actually the oldest building in all of Whiterun. It existed alone on the mountain while the city was built up around it over the centuries. It features a main dining area, below which are the living quarters for the whelps and for the Circle and Harbinger.

Outside, there is a training area, and close by is the Skyforge, where the Companions' weapons are formed. The forge itself is large, ancient, and built outside on a mountain, close to the sky. Below the Skyforge is a ceremonial area known as the Underforge, which is out of bounds except on rare occasions.

Important Characters

Founder: Ysgramor

Ysgramor was born in Atmora, the ancestral land for all humans. He and two of his sons were the only survivors of the Night of Tears, when the elves attacked Saarthal and killed all the other inhabitants. Ysgramor retreated to Atmora, rallied an army of Five Hundred Companions, and led them to vanquish the elves and drive them out of Skyrim.

Harbinger: Kodlak Whitemane

For 20 years now, Kodlak has commanded the Companions, balancing his tactical skill, ferocity in combat, and commanding presence. But those days are drawing to a close. A year ago, Kodlak contracted the rot and his condition has rapidly diminished. He has become weak in body, and his frustration shows. He's taken to locking himself behind closed doors, poring over old documents, desperate to cure himself of lycanthropy.

The Circle: Aela the Huntress

Aela is the latest in a long family of women in the Companions. Her mother was a member, as was her grandmother and every woman in her family for generations. Aela claims that her line runs back to Hrotti Blackblade, one of the original Five Hundred Companions. Aela was not raised in the Companions like Vilkas and Farkas were, but it has been a fixture in her life from a very early age.

➤ **Trainer (Archery: Expert):** Aela the Huntress

The Circle: Farkas

Farkas and his twin brother, Vilkas, were both raised in the Companions by a man named Jergen, who rescued them from a circle of necromancers. Farkas is a bit cavalier with his Beast Form and a bit loose with his tongue, even to his superiors. This is not a big deal in the Companions, but he shows more disrespect to the older members than others do. Farkas is also...a bit slow.

➤ **Trainer (Heavy Armor: Master):** Farkas

The Circle: Vilkas

Vilkas and his twin brother, Farkas, were raised in Jorrvaskr—a place not accustomed to the sight of children. Only Tilma the Haggard offered them anything in the way of comfort. Several years ago, Jergen was killed in a battle with brigands near Dawnstar. Vilkas serves as the Master at Arms and is in charge of training younger members in weapon combat. He is hard on his students but is an excellent teacher.

➤ **Trainer (Two-Handed: Master):** Vilkas

The Circle: Skjor the Scarred

Skjor's early life was one common among the Companions. He fought in the Great War and returned to Skyrim after the Empire's defeat. He earned a reputation as being a sword for hire and was eventually recruited by the Companions. Skjor has always seen his role as the steady and loyal friend to those in power. He has few ambitions of his own, beyond supporting and standing by those to whom he has sworn loyalty. There is no one in the Companions with a greater sense of duty and honor.

Member: Athis

Adept in one-handed weaponry, Athis is a Dark Elf who keeps quiet most of the time. He is civil and loyal, but never at the forefront of any battles.

➤ **Trainer (One-Handed:** Expert): Athis

Member: Njada Stonearm

An impressive brawler and expert at blocking, but with an unpleasant attitude and uncaring disposition, Njada has few friends, which is just how she likes it.

➤ **Trainer (Block: Expert):** Njada Stonearm

Member: Ria

Ria is the youngest of the whelp recruits and is determined to fight and die alongside her Shield-Brothers. She is especially in awe of Aela the Huntress.

Member: Torvar

Torvar is a recent whelp and isn't taking well to the intensive training. He grows ever weary and anxious; the thought of dying in battle terrifies him.

Member: Vignar the Revered

Vignar the Revered was once a general and commander in the Legion during the Great War. He led brave warriors for nearly 30 years. That was a long time, though, and now Vignar lives a life of peace and relative quiet. He holds a place of honor among the Companions, and the group welcomes his council.

Housekeeper: Tilma the Haggard

Tilma the Haggard has been the single servant of Jorrvaskr for as long as anyone can remember. The Companions joke that they built the mead hall around her. To an outsider, it may seem as if Tilma is little more than a slave. But she is definitely there by choice and is committed to her duties and the warriors of Jorrvaskr.

Blacksmith: Eorlund Gray-Mane

Eorlund Gray-Mane is the patriarch of Clan Gray-Mane, one of the oldest, most respected families in Whiterun. Eorlund is widely known to be the best blacksmith in all of Skyrim. Although not a Companion himself, his wares have become the stuff of legend and are especially prized by the Companions. Eorlund is very old (and has a brilliant mane of long gray hair), but his long hours working the Skyforge have kept him incredibly fit.

➤ **Trainer (Smithing: Master):** Eorlund Gray-Mane

> **TIP** **Forging Ahead:** Once you complete Companions Quest: Glory of the Dead, the Skyforge can forge a unique set of Nord Hero weapons. Skyforge steel weaponry is slightly better than normal steel.

> **NOTE** **Intimate Companionship:** Farkas, Vilkas, Aela, Athis, Ria, Njada, and Torvar are all able to be married once Companions Quest: Glory of the Dead is over. Consult Temple Side Quest: The Bonds of Matrimony (page 336) for more details.

▶ Training

The main members of this guild of fighters are extremely talented in a particular skill. Speak to each of them and increase the chosen skill by a point, to a maximum of five points before you level up. If you have enough gold, you can complete this numerous times:

✓	SKILL	RANK	TRAINER
	Archery	Expert	Aela the Huntress
	Block	Expert	Njada Stonearm
	Heavy Armor	Master	Farkas
	One-Handed	Expert	Athis
	Smithing	Master	Eorlund Gray-Mane
	Two-Handed	Master	Vilkas

▶ Available Quests

There are a total of 19 quests available with the Companions. Six of these are Critical Path Quests, and 13 are Radiant Quests.

Critical Path Quests

Simply referred to as "quests," these are the main quests you attempt with the Companions. All but the first quest have one or more prerequisites, as shown in the following table:

✓	QUEST NAME	PREREQUISITES
	Companions Quest: Take Up Arms	None
	Companions Quest: Proving Honor	Complete Companions Quest: Take Up Arms, and one or more Radiant Quests.
	Companions Quest: The Silver Hand	Complete Companions Quest: Proving Honor, and one or more Radiant Quests.
	Companions Quest: Blood's Honor	Complete Companions Quest: The Silver Hand, and three or more Radiant Quests.
	Companions Quest: Purity of Revenge	Complete Companions Quest: Blood's Honor.
	Companions Quest: Glory of the Dead	Complete Companions Quest: Purity of Revenge.

Radiant Quests

These are usually smaller quests that require you to complete a task for a particular Companion. The Initial Wave Radiant Quests are available first, and remain available after the critical path quests are complete. The Second Wave quests are next; you must complete two to begin Companions Quest: Blood's Honor. The Final Wave quests only become available after all of the critical path quests are complete.

In each case, the objectives of a Radiant Quest are usually random. They are listed in more detail after the Critical Path Quests, but consult the following table to learn the prerequisites required to begin every Radiant Quest:

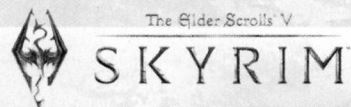

The Elder Scrolls V

SKYRIM

CHRONOLOGY	QUEST GIVER	RADIANT QUEST NAME	PREREQUISITES
Initial Wave	Aela	Animal Extermination (I)	Once the Companions Quest: Take Up Arms has been completed.
Initial Wave	Aela	Animal Extermination (II)	Once the Companions Quest: Take Up Arms has been completed.
Initial Wave	Farkas	Hired Muscle	Once the Companions Quest: Take Up Arms has been completed.
Initial Wave	Farkas	Trouble in Skyrim	Once the Companions Quest: Take Up Arms has been completed.
Initial Wave	Skjor or Vilkas	Family Heirloom	Once the Companions Quest: Take Up Arms has been completed.
Initial Wave	Skjor or Vilkas	Escaped Criminal	Once the Companions Quest: Take Up Arms has been completed.
Initial Wave	Skjor or Vilkas	Rescue Mission	Once the Companions Quest: Take Up Arms has been completed.
Second Wave	Aela	Striking the Heart	Once the Companions Quest: The Silver Hand has been completed but before Blood's Honor begins.
Second Wave	Aela	Stealing Plans	Once the Companions Quest: The Silver Hand has been completed but before Blood's Honor begins.
Second Wave	Aela	Retrieval	Once the Companions Quest: The Silver Hand has been completed but before Blood's Honor begins.
Final Wave	Aela	Totems of Hircine	Once the Companions Quest: Glory of the Dead has been completed.
Final Wave	Farkas or Vilkas	Purity	Once the Companions Quest: Glory of the Dead has been completed.
Final Wave	Farkas or Vilkas	Dragon Seekers	Once both the Companions Quest: Glory of the Dead and Main Quest: A Blade in the Dark have been completed.

TAKE UP ARMS

PREREQUISITES: None

INTERSECTING QUESTS: Companions Quest: Proving Honor, Companions Radiant Quests

LOCATIONS: Pelagia Farm, Whiterun, Jorrvaskr, Living Quarters, Skyforge

CHARACTERS: Aela the Huntress, Athis, Eorlund Gray-Mane, Farkas, Kodlak Whitemane, Njada Stonearm, Ria, Skjor, Vilkas

ENEMIES: Giant

◊ **OBJECTIVES:** Speak to Kodlak Whitemane, Train with Vilkas, Give Vilkas's sword to Eorlund, Bring Aela her shield, Follow Farkas to your quarters

▶ Training the Whelp

You hear the sounds of a pitched battle across the plains, close to Pelagia Farm, within the outskirts of Whiterun. Come closer to the fight, and you'll witness two warriors attempting to topple a giant who was trespassing too far into the farmland. You may watch or join the fracas. After the giant is killed (you can search him without penalty), you may speak with Aela the Huntress, Ria, or Farkas, the warriors who slew the giant. They explain who the Companions are and how you may join their Guild: Head to Jorrvaskr if you're worth anything in a fight.

Enter the city of Whiterun and climb the streets until you reach the steps leading up to Jorrvaskr, the Companions' longhouse. When you step inside, you'll likely see a training fight in progress, with two recruits (Athis and Njada Stonearm) brawling. The other Companions watching the melee offer words of encouragement. The sparring is overseen by an intimidating, one-eyed man named Skjor. Speak to him when you wish to proceed with important knowledge about this Guild. He explains the Companions are known by many names,

and not all of them complimentary. The battle switches to fists, and Njada Stonearm lives up to her last name, finishing her opponent and ending the fight.

You may speak with her and listen to her rude replies. But when you ask her (or other Companions) who is in charge, she mentions someone named Kodlak Whitemane, who is the Harbinger; this is the closest to a leader this rabble have and to whom they pledge their loyalty. Once you learn about Kodlak, this quest officially commences.

◊ **OBJECTIVE:** Speak to Kodlak Whitemane

Head to the longhouse's south end, down the stairs, and open the doors to the Living Quarters. Head along the main lower-floor corridor to reach Kodlak. He is usually speaking with Vilkas, who still hears the call of the blood, which Kodlak calls "a burden to bear." They finish speaking and look at you: There is a stranger in their hall.

You can ask Kodlak who the Companions are, why he joined them, where they stand on the Civil War, and, most importantly for this quest, if you can join them. Although Vilkas voices his disapproval, Kodlak says that Jorrvaskr has some empty beds for those with a fire burning in their hearts. He then asks how you are in battle. You may answer how you wish; it results in Kodlak requesting that Vilkas take you outside to see how you handle yourself.

◊ **OBJECTIVE:** Train with Vilkas

Exit Jorrvaskr and head into the courtyard to the structure's rear. Vilkas instructs you to take a few swings at him. Oblige by unsheathing your favored melee weapon and striking Vilkas, who expertly blocks with his shield. Stop your attacks when instructed (or you'll soon learn why crossing the Companions isn't a good idea). Vilkas seems to think you have an inkling of promise, but you're still considered a whelp to them. In the meantime, you have some orders to take care of: Vilkas wants you to take his sword up to Eorlund Gray-Mane, who is waiting to sharpen it.

➤ **Skyforge Steel Sword**

◊ **OBJECTIVE:** Give Vilkas's sword to Eorlund
♦ **TARGET:** Skyforge, in Whiterun

Take the sword (optionally testing it out in an unrelated adventure or two), and bring it up the steps hewn into the rocky outcrop to the north of Jorrvaskr. You reach the Skyforge, an impressively large forge where Eorlund Gray-Mane works the steel. Inform Eorlund of your errand. Depending on your answers, Eorlund tells you to remember that nobody rules anyone in the Companions, so subservient attitudes aren't necessary. They haven't had any leaders since Ysgramor. Eorlund isn't a Companion, but he's an expert in working the Skyforge, which produces the best steel in all of Skyrim. Before you go, Eorlund has a request: He wants you to take a shield to Aela the Huntress. Seeing the irony of this request is optional.

➤ **Steel Shield**

◊ **OBJECTIVE:** Bring Aela her shield
♦ **TARGET:** Aela the Huntress, in Jorrvaskr in Whiterun

Return to Jorrvaskr, and search the hall or the Living Quarters for Aela the Huntress, who is usually speaking with Skjor. Tell her you have her shield, and she gratefully receives it. She learns who you are and of your fight with Vilkas. She asks how you'd handle yourself in a real fight with him. Answer how you wish, although she won't like it if you threaten violence to a Shield-Brother. She tells you to speak to Farkas, who arrives at the end of this conversation.

◊ **OBJECTIVE:** Follow Farkas to your quarters

Quest Conclusion

Farkas seems pleasant enough; in fact, he's glad of the company. He takes you down the main hall of the Living Quarters, to the dormitory you'll be sharing. You can pick any bed that isn't being slept in. The quest concludes.

Postquest Activities

Farkas ends the conversation, asking whether you might help with a problem they are having. You may speak to him or ignore him and seek out employment from another Companion: And so begins your Faction Radiant Quests (consult the quest name that appears after agreeing to the task, and cross-reference it with the Radiant Quest in this chapter). You'll need to complete at least one of these before Companions Quest: Proving Honor begins.

PROVING HONOR

PREREQUISITES: Complete the Companions Quest: Take up Arms, Complete one Faction Radiant Quest
INTERSECTING QUESTS: The Companions Quest: Take up Arms, The Companions Quest: Proving Honor , The Companions Quest: Brotherhood, The Companions Quest: The Silver Hand, The Companions Radiant Quests
LOCATIONS: Dustman's Cairn, Whiterun, Jorrvaskr
CHARACTERS: Farkas, Skjor
ENEMIES: Draugr, Frostbite Spider, Giant Frostbite Spider, Silver Hand, Skeever
◊ **OBJECTIVES:** Talk to Skjor, Speak to Farkas, Retrieve the fragment, Return to Jorrvaskr

⊙ MINOR SPOILERS

▶ Trial of the Cohort

◊ **OBJECTIVE:** Talk to Skjor

The Companions have witnessed your previous work ethic, and once you revisit Whiterun, enter Jorrvaskr, and search out Skjor, you are greeted more warmly. He has a more interesting task for you to help with. It appears a scholar visited the Companions a week ago, explaining where they could find another fragment of Ysgramor's Blade. Seeking out the fragment is considered a trial; do well, and you can consider yourself a member of the Companions. Farkas is your Shield-Sibling for this adventure.

◊ **OBJECTIVE:** Speak to Farkas

Farkas is usually within Jorrvaskr and is ready to retrieve the fragment when you are. You may speak also to Farkas about personal matters if you wish.

◊ **OBJECTIVE:** Retrieve the fragment
♦ **TARGET:** Fragment of Ysgramor's Blade, inside Dustman's Cairn

Ysgramor's Blessing

After a trek through the wilderness with Farkas, navigate northwest of Whiterun and up to Dustman's Cairn. Drop below the standing stones. Arm yourself and begin to navigate through these catacombs, and listen for Farkas's advice. Take any treasure as you descend past the loose burial stones. Continue deeper into a ceremonial hub chamber with multiple archways and a couple of thrones.

The way forward is blocked. The only area of interest is an archway with a raised portcullis, which leads to a small alcove with a lever. Activate it, and the portcullis drops, trapping you inside but raising the portcullis of a nearby archway. Farkas looks in and tells you he'll find the release, but as he does, he is surrounded by the members of the Silver Hand! Severely outnumbered, Farkas backs up before letting out a guttural growl and transforming into a massive werewolf that slaughters the Silver Hand where they cower! After freeing you, speak to Farkas, who explains his metamorphosis (known colloquially as his Beast Form)is a blessing bestowed upon some of the Companions.

Press on through the archway Farkas just opened. You face multiple Draugr and Silver Hand as you descend into this elongated crypt. Beware of occasional dart traps (watch for pressure stones beneath your feet that trigger them), and continue the slaughtering up until you reach the large crypt chamber with a locked iron door at the eastern end. Check the burial urns nearby for a key that opens this door.

➤ **Dustman's Cairn Key**

Quickly deal with the Skeever problem once you're through the door, passing interconnecting chambers and stone passageways. A battle against a Giant Frostbite Spider occurs soon afterward. Continue through another bank of crypts, until you reach the major tomb room, where a Draugr Wight is buried. Strange chanting draws you to the area behind the raised tomb; this is a Word Wall, and a Word of Power is drummed into your subconscious! With the chant fresh in your memory, inspect the raised tomb and take the fragment lying on top of it (along with any other spoils you wish).

➤ **Word of Power:** Fire Breath   ➤ **Fragment of Ysgramor's Blade**

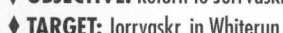

◊ **OBJECTIVE:** Return to Jorrvaskr
♦ **TARGET:** Jorrvaskr, in Whiterun

If you check your map (or the map provided in the Atlas), you'll spot an exit corridor off to the side of this tomb room, behind the raised stone alcove. Alas, when you attempt to breach it, the burial stones will not shift, but the Draugr begin to attack. Drop into the main chamber, where a protracted battle with at least 20 Draugr (including a dreaded high-ranking Draugr that clambers out of the raised tomb) takes place. Keep moving, retreat to safety if you need to, and don't leave Farkas to fend for himself! A final Draugr crashes through the burial stone, allowing access up a tight side tunnel. At the tunnel's end is a lever, which opens a secret rock door leading back to the cairn's entrance.

Quest Conclusion: Brotherhood

From here, it is a simple matter of returning to Jorrvaskr and seeking out Skjor, who gladly takes the fragment of Ysgramor's Blade from you. Vilkas is also waiting, having heard how well you did as a Shield-Sibling. The Companions are assembled in the rear courtyard. They are concluding a circle of judgment, and Kodlak informs you that you are now a member of the Companions. You are welcomed into the fold, but you still need to prove yourself.

Postquest Activities
Speak to Aela, Farkas, Skjor, or Vilkas, and tell them you're looking for work to begin any other Faction Radiant Quests.

THE SILVER HAND

PREREQUISITES: Complete the Companions Quest: Proving Honor, Complete one Faction Radiant Quest
INTERSECTING QUESTS: The Companions Quest: Proving Honor, The Companions Radiant Quests
LOCATIONS: Gallows Rock, Whiterun, Jorrvaskr, Skyforge, Underforge
CHARACTERS: Aela the Huntress, Farkas, Skjor, Werewolf
ENEMIES: Krev the Skinner, Silver Hand, Skeever
◊ **OBJECTIVES:** Talk to Skjor, Meet with Skjor at night, Enter the Underforge, Participate in the blood ritual, Talk to Aela, Kill the werewolf hunters, Talk to Aela

◉ **MINOR SPOILERS**

Forging the Lycanthrope

◊ **OBJECTIVE:** Talk to Skjor

After completing the Companions Quest: Proving Honor, Skjor has spent enough time judging your worthiness to become one of the Companions. When you find Skjor, he says he has something a little different planned for your next task and requests you meet him at the entrance to the Underforge after nightfall.

◊ **OBJECTIVE:** Meet with Skjor at night
◊ **OBJECTIVE:** Enter the Underforge
♦ **TARGET:** Underforge, in Whiterun

Once the sun has set (any time between 06:00 p.m. and 08:00 a.m.), head around the left (north) side of Jorrvaskr building and meet with Skjor by a massive protrusion of stone, below the Skyforge. Skjor explains this is the most ancient part of Whiterun and that the Underforge taps a vein of magic older than men or elves. Skjor beckons for you to open the rock wall that shifts apart, allowing entrance into the Underforge.

Skjor enters the Underforge with you. Aela the Huntress has taken a lupine form and is waiting around the Sacred Font. Skjor explains the ceremony you will undertake is to be done in secret, as Kodlak is busy trying to throw away the gift the Companions have been granted; he thinks it a curse rather than a blessing. Now join in the shared blood of the wolf and activate the Sacred Font.

◊ **OBJECTIVE:** Participate in the blood ritual

You experience a tremendous change in your body structure. Your vision is much improved. Your speed is like that of the wolf. Your social standing with the locals is possibly not worth testing out at the moment. Soon, your eyes close and everything turns to black.

◊ **OBJECTIVE:** Talk to Aela
♦ **TARGET:** Aela the Huntress, on the moors outside Gallows Rock

> **TIP** As a werewolf, any crime you commit will not count against you, as your identity is not known. However, everyone (except for the Companions) is hostile and will fight or flee from you. If you kill anyone, they remain dead (so don't slay a merchant accidentally!). You can howl and sprint places on all fours for an even quicker dash. You may turn into a werewolf once per day.

Clawing the Silver Hand

You wake up on the moors, clad in little more than your modesty. Aela the Huntress is with you and explains that your transformation was not easy but successful. To celebrate becoming part of the Companions, you are to slaughter a pack of werewolf hunters known as the Silver Hand, who are camped nearby. But first, ask Aela any questions about your "condition" that you wish. Then place your armor and clothing back on, and arm up for the assault.

◊ **OBJECTIVE:** Kill the werewolf hunters
♦ **TARGET:** Silver Hand clan, in Gallows Rock

Charge or prowl around the exterior battlements of the Gallows Rock fortification before slaying the two Silver Hand guarding the entrance. Then step inside. Judging by the spear bars on the doorway, the Silver Hand must have locked the place down once Skjor charged in. Activate the lever and head down the stairs. Make sure Aela accompanies you, as she's helpful in combat as a Shield-Sibling. Continue through this complex of stone corridors, removing Skeever vermin and Silver Hand as you go.

> **TIP** Remember you can use your Beast Form during this quest. Access it via your Magic menu.

Many of your brethren lie dead in the cells; release any who are alive so they can savage their captors. Then push down the stairs, into a stone hall with skinned pelt hangings. Battle through and down the stairs to the circular chamber with the columns. This is the lair of Krev the Skinner, the Silver Hand leader in these parts. He is flanked by two lackeys. Muster your combat potential and savagely dispatch them all. Then ransack the chamber (and optionally, the entire area) for loot.

◊ **OBJECTIVE:** Talk to Aela

Quest Conclusion

There are no rewards here, only sadness. Alas, Aela has seen the body of Skjor. He is dead; he should not have come here without a Shield-Brother. Skjor will be avenged. The plot to kill all of those responsible for this outrage begins now!

Postquest Activities

You must now complete two additional Radiant Quests for Aela (and her only) to begin The Companions Quest: Blood's Honor.

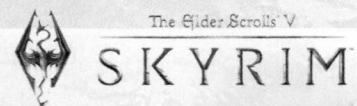

PREREQUISITES: Complete the Companions Quest: The Silver Hand, Complete two Companions Radiant Quests

INTERSECTING QUESTS: The Companions Quest: The Silver Hand, The Companions Quest: Purity of Revenge, The Companions Radiant Quests

LOCATIONS: Glenmoril Coven, Whiterun, Jorrvaskr, Jorrvaskr Living Quarters

CHARACTERS: Aela the Huntress, Kodlak Whitemane, Vilkas

ENEMIES: Frostbite Spider, Glenmoril Witch, Silver Hand, Skeever

◊ **OBJECTIVES:** Collect a Glenmoril Witch's head, (Optional) Wipe out the Glenmoril Witches, Return to Kodlak

◉ MAJOR SPOILERS

Hircine's Curse

After completing the Companions Quest: Proving Honor and then tending to other business, visit Kodlak, who is usually down in his Living Quarters in Jorrvaskr. Sit next to him and begin to talk. After telling him what you've been up to, Kodlak asks if you've heard the story of how the Companions became werewolves. The Order of the Companions is almost 5,000 years old, but the beastblood has only "troubled" them for a few hundred. One of Kodlak's predecessors made a bargain with the witches of Glenmoril Coven; if the Companions were to hunt in the name of their lord, Hircine, they would be granted great power. But there was deception!

Although in wolf form the Companions are powerful, the disease of lycanthropy seeps into the spirit, and upon death, werewolves are claimed by Hircine for his Hunting Grounds. For some, the eternal chase and capture is a boon, but for a true Nord like Kodlak, it is a curse, for he wishes Sovngarde to be his spirit home. Rather than resigning himself to a wolf's death, Kodlak has spent his twilight years trying to find a cure. The answer lies in the same magic that the witches used to ensnare the Companions. You are to go to their coven and strike down all witches. Return with their heads—the seat of their abilities.

◊ **OBJECTIVE:** Collect a Glenmoril Witch's head
◊ **OBJECTIVE:** (Optional) Wipe out the Glenmoril Witches
♦ **TARGET:** Glenmoril Witch, in Glenmoril Coven

Trek across the tundra plains and southwest, into the mountains, keeping below the snow line. The trappings of witchcraft hang from the gnarled trees at the Coven's entrance. Enter the Coven, which is formed around a central hub cavern, where a Glenmoril Witch awaits. Strike her with sneak, ranged, or melee attacks. Beware of her frost spells and her familiar. Continue combat until one of you falls—be sure it's the crone! Then inspect the withered corpse and collect the head (as well as any Hagraven Feathers you may need for crafting).

➤ **Glenmoril Witch Head**

◊ **OBJECTIVE:** Return to Kodlak

At this point, you are prompted to return to Kodlak. Before you return (which is a critical part of this quest), you can also hunt down the four other Glenmoril Witches who inhabit this coven.

 TIP If you're having trouble locating any of the witches' chambers, carefully inspect the hub chamber (where the first witch was), as some connecting tunnels can be hard to spot.

Journey back to Whiterun, and head toward Jorrvaskr. Judging from the onlookers, Aela's drawn weapon, and the slaughtered Silver Hand at her feet, the longhouse was the scene of a vicious Silver Hand attack while you were away. Enter Jorrvaskr and speak with Vilkas. He has some sorrowful news; Kodlak was killed during the fighting.

Quest Conclusion

The Silver Hand made off with all the fragments of Wuuthrad that you had collected. Vilkas vows that you and he will bring the battle to their chief camp. Kodlak will be avenged.

Postquest Activities

The Companions Quest: Purity of Revenge begins immediately. There are now no Radiant Quests available, due to the recent Silver Hand attack. Although you may think the Witch Heads aren't of use, they become important during Companions Quest: Glory of the Dead and afterward.

PREREQUISITES: Complete the Companions Quest: Blood's Honor
INTERSECTING QUESTS: The Companions Quest: Blood's Honor, The Companions Quest: Glory of the Dead, The Companions Radiant Quests
LOCATIONS: Driftshade Refuge, Driftshade Cellar, Whiterun , Jorrvaskr
CHARACTERS: Vilkas, Werewolf
ENEMIES: Silver Hand
◊ **OBJECTIVES:** Retrieve the fragments of Wuuthrad, (Optional) Wipe out the Silver Hand, Return to Jorrvaskr

▷ Severing the Silver Hand

◊ **OBJECTIVE:** Retrieve the fragments of Wuuthrad
◊ **OBJECTIVE:** (Optional) Wipe out the Silver Hand
♦ **TARGET:** Wuuthrad fragments, inside Driftshade Refuge

Vilkas wishes to immediately depart for the Silver Hand stronghold of Driftshade Refuge and accompanies you as your Shield-Brother. Purchase any equipment if necessary, and then journey north into the Mountains of Winterhold, to the southeast of Dawnstar.

Combat begins immediately. Sneaking is inadvisable for a Companion, especially one with an optional objective to fulfill and a recently slain advisor. Dispatch the foes guarding the entrance to the Refuge. Kill the one on the roof with ranged weapons, or sneak up the steps to the rear of the entrance.

Descend the stone-stepped corridor and into a lower shrine room, with moss-covered pillars and Silver Hand to cut down with speed and ferociousness. Make a systematic sweep of every chamber via the connecting corridors, culling foes as you go. Leave no one alive, lest you mock the death of the beloved Kodlak! Eventually, you reach a chamber with vertical spears blocking an entrance. Activate the lever just to the right of the spears, and they retract, allowing you into Driftshade Cellar.

Fight your way past the stacked wood and barrels, watching for the pressure plate lest you receive a swinging gate trap in the face—a fate you can attempt for any foes if you wish. Venture farther into the cellar, and split open the Silver Hand guarding a large distillery tank of mead. Exit via a hole in the stone wall and into a snow tunnel. You appear in a small cavern complete with holding cells. Release any werewolves still alive (they are locals afflicted with lycanthropy, rather than Companions). The snow tunnel connects back into the cellar.

Pass the remains of a werewolf and shred the foes in the torture room. Enter the remains of the cellar's grand hall, now full of collapsed masonry. After more Silver Hand slaughtering, head south, up the steps and back into the refuge area. Enter the small dungeon room, then turn left and bound up the stairs. The remaining Silver Hand are in this chamber. Kill them all. Your optional objective should complete at this point. Then inspect the table on the elevated dining area, where all the fragments of Ysgramor's Blade can be found...again. Take them before resting for a moment with Vilkas, who seems to have finally realized your prowess as a fighter.

➤ **Fragments of Wuuthrad**

◊ **OBJECTIVE:** Return to Jorrvaskr

Quest Conclusion

Head south out of Driftshade Refuge, back outside, and then to Whiterun and your longhouse home. As you near Jorrvaskr, Vilkas remarks that your brethren should have finished preparing the funeral of Kodlak by now.

Postquest Activities

The Companions Quest: Glory of the Dead begins immediately. There are now no Radiant Quests available, due to the preparations for Kodlak's departure.

PREREQUISITES: Complete the Companions Quest: Purity of Revenge
INTERSECTING QUESTS: The Companions Quest: Purity of Revenge, The Companions Radiant Quests
LOCATIONS: Whiterun, Jorrvaskr, Jorrvaskr Living Quarters, Skyforge, Underforge, Ysgramor's Tomb
CHARACTERS: Aela the Huntress, Danica Pure-Spring, Eorlund Gray-Mane, Farkas, Jarl of Whiterun, Kodlak Whitemane, Vilkas

 MAJOR SPOILERS

continued on next page

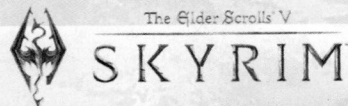

ENEMIES: Companion Ghost, Frostbite Spider, Kodlak's Wolf Spirit, Skeever
◊ **OBJECTIVES:** Attend Kodlak's funeral, Retrieve Kodlak's fragment, Give the final fragment to Eorlund, Meet the Circle, Go to Ysgramor's Tomb with the Circle, Return Wuuthrad to Ysgramor, Get to the burial chamber, Speak to Kodlak, Put witch head into fire, Defeat the wolf spirit, Speak to Kodlak

⏵ Out of the Strong Comes Forth Steel

◊ **OBJECTIVE:** Attend Kodlak's funeral
♦ **TARGET:** Skyforge, north of Jorrvaskr, in Whiterun

Upon your return to Jorrvaskr, there is no one inside the building; they are all at the Skyforge, where Eorlund has prepared the pyre for Kodlak's funeral. The Companions are there, along with some of Whiterun's population, including the Jarl and the priestess Danica Pure-Spring. Aela steps forward to join Eorlund and Vilkas in a simple, strong-hearted eulogy. Aela lights the pyre, and Kodlak's body is set ablaze. With his spirit departed, she requests that the members of the Circle should withdraw to the Underforge to grieve together. Before you leave with them, Eorlund asks whether you have the Fragments of Wuuthrad; he needs to prepare them for mounting back in Jorrvaskr. There is a final piece of the Wuuthrad that Kodlak always kept close. Eorlund requests that you go to Kodlak's chambers and bring the piece back for him.

◊ **OBJECTIVE:** Retrieve Kodlak's fragment
♦ **TARGET:** Living Quarters, in Jorrvaskr in Whiterun

Enter Jorrvaskr and descend into the Living Quarters. Head north, past the chair where you and Kodlak sat and talked. His bedroom is to the right (east). Check the bedside table and grab the two items within. One is the fragment Eorlund mentioned, and the other is Kodlak's Journal. You may optionally read it. Kodlak's wishes for your role within the Companions are detailed in it.

⏵ **Fragment of Ysgramor's Blade**   ⏵ **Kodlak's Journal**

◊ **OBJECTIVE:** Give the final fragment to Eorlund

Return to Eorlund, who is usually at the Skyforge, and hand over the fragment. He thanks you and says the Companions are waiting for you inside the Underforge.

◊ **OBJECTIVE:** Meet the Circle
♦ **TARGET:** Underforge, in Whiterun

Open the loose rock wall below the Skyforge and enter the place where you were once baptized into the moon-born. Vilkas and Aela are having a heated discussion over Kodlak's final wishes. Although Aela is at one with her Beast Form,

Vilkas knows that Kodlak wished to meet Ysgramor and know the glories of Sovngarde and the Hall of Valor. The curse of lycanthropy took that from him. Aela relents, understanding that Kodlak's wishes are to be respected.

Vilkas then tells you of the Tomb of Ysgramor, where the souls of Harbingers past heed the call of northern steel. But the tomb cannot be entered because Ysgramor's Blade is in pieces. Eorlund informs them that tools are meant to be broken...and repaired! This is the first time that all pieces of the Blade have been returned together, and the flames of Kodlak fuel the rebirth of Wuuthrad! Eorlund hands you the blade, which is now in one piece, and the Circle of Companions set off to enter the tomb and help cast Kodlak off into the Nordic realm of the afterlife.

⏵ **Wuuthrad**

◊ **OBJECTIVE:** Go to Ysgramor's Tomb with the Circle
♦ **TARGET:** Entrance to Ysgramor's Tomb

TIP Wuuthrad the Elf-Slayer is a powerful two-handed weapon that does 20% more damage to elven foes. It is a suitable reward for someone who has brought honor to the Companions.

⏵ Taming the Wolf

Northwest of Winterhold, in the ice fields of the Sea of Ghosts, lies the Nordic cairn indicating the entrance to Ysgramor's Tomb. Climb over the lip of the cairn and open the iron door that leads into the tomb interior. Your Shield-Siblings are already inspecting the weaponless statue at the tomb's entrance plinth. Vilkas says this is the resting place of Ysgramor and his most trusted generals, and you should be cautious. Then Vilkas reveals that he won't be accompanying you on this final mission; his mind is too fogged and his heart grieved. He then instructs you to grant Ysgramor's statue its rightful blade.

◊ **OBJECTIVE:** Return Wuuthrad to Ysgramor

Approach the statue of Ysgramor and place the Wuuthrad in the statue's grip. The tomb entrance behind (north of) the statue slides open. You, Farkas, and Aela the Huntress will now meet Ysgramor's guardians and fight your way to the resting place of Ysgramor.

◊ **OBJECTIVE:** Get to the burial chamber

Brush aside the cobwebs and investigate the tunnel beyond, which turns west and ends at a double door with an alcove on either side. From each alcove, a Companion Ghost appears, ready to test your mettle. Slay them as if they were enemies; you are proving yourself to them in battle, and there is no greater honor. Open the double doors and enter the entrance hall, where three more ghosts appear to thwart you. Tackle them, checking on your Shield-Siblings in case they need your support.

Head south, down another level, and into the hall of crypts. Return several more Companion Ghosts to Sovngarde as they emerge from their vertical tombs, then head south, hacking at the entrance filled with cobwebs. Farkas parts company with you at this point. The cobwebs lead to two connected chambers filled with Frostbite Spiders (expect at least one to be Giant). Dispatch them all before activating the chain by the portcullis to the south. Venture into the main tomb. At least six more Companion Ghosts appear to stop you between here and the corridor and the steps up to an iron door.

Open the door to reach a long hall with a pedestal at its far end. Atop the pedestal is a handle. Pull it to open the portcullis in the sunken corridor on your left (north). Head down into a giant ceremonial chamber, with the skull of a mammoth dominating the central embalming table. At least four more Companion Ghosts appear. Stick your bladed weapon into their ethereal forms. When the fight is over, you may climb the final steps, open the double doors, and enter Ysgramor's burial chamber.

◊ **OBJECTIVE:** Speak to Kodlak

And So Slain the Beast Inside

Stride over to meet the spirit of Kodlak, who (along with his fellow Harbingers from history) have been warming themselves in this chamber and trying to evade Hircine. Although you can see only Kodlak's spirit, he assures you his predecessors are with you, in this most sacred of chambers. Tell Kodlak that Vilkas mentioned a cure was still possible, and Kodlak instructs you to take one of the witches' heads and throw it into the blue fire. It will release their magic—for him at least.

◊ **OBJECTIVE:** Put witch head into fire
◊ **OBJECTIVE:** Defeat the wolf spirit

Approach the Flame of the Harbinger and drop a witch's head into it. The moment the blue flames begin to devour the head and the witch's magical grip loosens, Kodlak's Wolf Spirit appears. You must destroy it in combat.

◊ **OBJECTIVE:** Speak to Kodlak

Quest Conclusion

Return to Kodlak's spirit and tell him you killed his beast spirit. He thanks you for this gift, one tainted by sadness that the other Harbingers remain trapped by Hircine. Perhaps a battle for their souls could be waged from Sovngarde. For today, however, you must triumph in your victory and lead the Companions to further glory!

Postquest Activities

Locate any treasure chests you wish to plunder. Pull the chain and exit via the raised area on the chamber's eastern side. Head up the spiral stairs to a second chain that removes a section of rock wall. Return to the entrance chamber where Ysgramor's statue is standing. You may now return to Jorrvaskr at your leisure. Although your critical Companions Quests are over, there are now three additional Radiant Quests available (along with the initial ones). You enjoy the companionship of your Shield-Brothers and Sisters as you return, victorious, as Harbinger!

➤ **Word of Power:** Animal Allegiance

◈ **TIP** You may wish to take Wuuthrad from Ysgramor's statue before you leave, and use this weapon.

◈ **TIP** **Forging Ahead:** The Skyforge, burning with Kodlak's Spirit, can now forge a unique set of Nord Hero weapons if you have the skill to craft them.

◈ **NOTE** **Intimate Companionship:** Farkas, Vilkas, Aela, Athis, Ria, Njada, and Torvar are all able to be married once Companions Quest: Glory of the Dead is over. Consult Temple Side Quest: The Bonds of Matrimony (page 336) for more details.

THE COMPANIONS RADIANT QUESTS

The following 13 Radiant Quests occur between (and after) the critical Companions Quests and typically offer you a random task to accomplish. These tasks are available in three different "waves," depending on how far you are in the critical Companions Quests. For a complete list of how to unlock each Radiant Quest, consult the Introduction to the Companions Quests, at the start of this chapter.

INITIAL WAVE: ANIMAL EXTERMINATION (I)

Quest giver: Aela

Speak to Aela and request some work. It seems that someone has a problem with a wild animal loose in their dwelling and has requested a Companion to help eradicate the menace. Aela orders you to locate the animal and kill it quickly.

◊ **OBJECTIVE:** Kill the [random animal]
◆ **TARGET:** Random animal, random location

Journey to the dwelling where the reported animal intrusion occurred. Draw your preferred weapon as you enter; the animal usually strikes once you're inside the premises. Cut down the animal, obtaining its pelt if you wish.

◊ **OBJECTIVE:** Return to Aela

Quest Conclusion

Return to Jorrvaskr, and seek out Aela. Inform her of the quick and noble death you've given the creature. You're given some coin for your troubles.

➤ **Gold pieces (leveled)**

Postquest Activities

You may now speak to another Companion and begin another Radiant Quest (or access the critical Companions Quest if you haven't already).

INITIAL WAVE: ANIMAL EXTERMINATION (II)

Quest giver: Aela

Speak to Aela and request some work. It seems that there is an animal den located close to a group of friends of the Companions, and periodically, the animals attack them. Aela orders you to eradicate the threat; you are to find all the animals within the den and dispatch them.

◇ **OBJECTIVE:** Clear out the [random animal den]
♦ **TARGET:** Random animal den, random location

Trek to the animal den indicated on your world map, and draw your weapons. Investigate all areas of this location. Whenever you encounter an animal, kill it. Continue with your animal slaughter (obtaining pelts if you wish, and if applicable) until the quest updates.

◇ **OBJECTIVE:** Return to Aela

Quest Conclusion

Return to Jorrvaskr and seek out Aela. Inform her that you've dealt with the animals within the den. You're given some coin for your troubles.

➤ **Gold pieces (leveled)**

Postquest Activities

You may now speak to another Companion and begin another Radiant Quest (or access the critical Companions Quest if you haven't already).

INITIAL WAVE: HIRED MUSCLE

Quest giver: Farkas

Tell Farkas that you're looking for work. As it happens, he has received a letter requesting some "muscle." Farkas doesn't know what the fight is about, and it isn't the Companions' business anyway, but he needs you to head to the place of the altercation and scare the ruffian into submission. This is to be a roughing up, not a killing!

◇ **OBJECTIVE:** Intimidate a [random troublemaker] in a [random location]
♦ **TARGET:** Random target, random location

(Brawl) Journey to the location where the troublemaker is causing a fuss. Journey to the location where the troublemaker is causing a fuss. Step up to the annoyance. Step up to the annoyance, and explain that you're here to resolve a dispute. Then pummel them in a brawl until they collapse to the ground. Do not kill them, as this reduces your reward.

◇ **OBJECTIVE:** Return to Farkas

Quest Conclusion

Return to Jorrvaskr and seek out Farkas. Inform him of your success at pummeling some sense into the troublemaker. You're given some coin for your troubles.

➤ **Gold pieces (leveled)**

Postquest Activities

You may now speak to another Companion and begin another Radiant Quest (or access the critical Companions Quest if you haven't already).

INITIAL WAVE: TROUBLE IN SKYRIM

Quest giver: Farkas

Tell Farkas you're looking for work. Fortunately, he has a job that requires your immediate attention. Farkas has received word that a group of aggressors are causing a disturbance and must be dealt with using your combat mettle. He needs you to journey to the place where the problem has arisen and slay those responsible. This is to be a killing; take no prisoners!

◇ **OBJECTIVE:** Kill the leader of a [random location]
♦ **TARGET:** Random target, random location

Travel to the place indicated on your world map where a group of enemies is causing problems for one of the Companions' clients. Locate the leader. Proceed to slay this enemy as swiftly as possible. You can dispatch anyone who attempts to stop you, although you need kill only the leader for this quest to complete. This is a simple slaying mission.

◇ **OBJECTIVE:** Return to Farkas

Quest Conclusion

Return to Jorrvaskr and seek out Farkas. Inform him of your success at massacring those who sought to upset the Companions' clients. You're given some coin for your heroics.

➤ **Gold pieces (leveled)**

Postquest Activities

You may now speak to another Companion and begin another Radiant Quest (or access the critical Companions Quest if you haven't already).

INITIAL WAVE: FAMILY HEIRLOOM

Quest giver: Skjor   Quest giver: Vilkas

Speak with either Skjor or Vilkas, and they inform you that they have work that involves locating and retrieving a valuable family heirloom, lost to a high-ranking family or other well-connected faction that the Companions are friendly with. You are to find the heirloom, said to be hidden somewhere in a Primary Location in Skyrim, and bring it back to the quest giver.

◊ **OBJECTIVE:** Retrieve the [valuable heirloom] from a [random location]
♦ **TARGET:** Random item, random location

Journey to the random location, and utilize your sneaking or combat abilities on any entity blocking your path, both before and after you enter the interior of the place, which is usually a castle, keep, or dungeon. Creep or carve your way to the location flagged on your local map, and pry the item away from the enemies; it is usually hidden in a chest. Finding the item is your only task; no bloodshed need occur, although it is encouraged!

◊ **OBJECTIVE:** Return to Skjor or Vilkas

Quest Conclusion

Return to Jorrvaskr, and seek out Skjor or Vilkas to inform him that you've located the heirloom. Hand it over. You're given gold pieces for your time.

➤ **Gold pieces (leveled)**

Postquest Activities

You may now speak to another Companion and begin another Radiant Quest (or access the critical Companions Quest if you haven't already).

INITIAL WAVE: ESCAPED CRIMINAL

Quest giver: Skjor   Quest giver: Vilkas

Speak with either Skjor or Vilkas, and he informs you that a wanted fugitive is fleeing from authorities, who are able to pay for the killing of the criminal. You are to locate this ne'er-do-well, face him in combat, and make sure he dies.

◊ **OBJECTIVE:** Kill the [random criminal]
♦ **TARGET:** Random criminal, random location

Set off to the location indicated on your world map, with the express intention of slaying this criminal. As the troublemaker may be flanked by foes who normally reside in this location, prepare for attacks throughout the criminal's hideout. When you finally reach the criminal in question, there's no pleading and no stalling, just a quick and justified death.

◊ **OBJECTIVE:** Return to Skjor or Vilkas

Quest Conclusion

Return to Jorrvaskr and seek out Skjor or Vilkas. Inform him that the criminal has been brought to justice—Companion justice—and he is satisfied with your progress. You receive a cut of the reward.

➤ **Gold pieces (leveled)**

Postquest Activities

You may now speak to another Companion and begin another Radiant Quest (or access the critical Companions Quest if you haven't already).

INITIAL WAVE: RESCUE MISSION

Quest giver: Skjor   Quest giver: Vilkas

Speak with either Skjor or Vilkas, and he lets you know that a member of an important family or organization with ties to the Companions has been kidnapped. Those responsible have taken the victim to a hiding place. You are to find the victim and return him to the location from which they were kidnapped. Obviously, the victim's health is of paramount importance.

◊ **OBJECTIVE:** Rescue a [random victim] from a [random location]
♦ **TARGET:** Random victim, random location

Journey to the location where the enemies took the victim. Begin to battle your way toward the victim's location. The target is usually close to any enemy leader or imprisoned in a cell or a cage. Unlock them if necessary, using Lockpick, searching any nearby foes you've slain for a key, or finding a lever to release the victim from their prison.

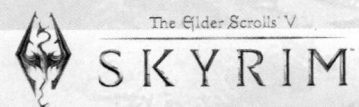

◊ **OBJECTIVE:** Return the [random victim] to [where they were kidnapped from]

♦ **TARGET:** Random victim, random location

With the victim found and released, they become a Follower, and you must emerge from your current location with them in tow. Once you reach the surface, having protected the target throughout the rest of the escape, Fast-Travel to the safe location indicated or the nearest already-discovered location and walk the rest of the way, defending the victim from any further attacks.

◊ **OBJECTIVE:** Return to Skjor or Vilkas

Quest Conclusion

Return to Jorrvaskr and seek out Skjor or Vilkas to inform him you recovered the kidnapping victim alive and chaperoned them back to a safe place. Your quest-giver is pleased with this outcome, and you receive some of the reward.

➤ **Gold pieces (leveled)**

Postquest Activities

You may now speak to another Companion and begin another Radiant Quest (or access the critical Companions Quest if you haven't already).

SECOND WAVE: STRIKING THE HEART

Quest giver: Aela the Huntress

Speak with Aela and ask what her targets are. She mentions a group of Silver Hand, holed up in a fortification. You're to assault this location and slaughter the Silver Hand leader inside.

◊ **OBJECTIVE:** Assassinate the Silver Hand leader

♦ **TARGET:** Silver Hand leader, [random location]

Journey to the settlement Aela has indicated and begin a systematic slaughter of the Silver Hand foes within, along with any indigenous foes that attack. This battle culminates in a confrontation with the Silver Hand lieutenant. Cut the fiend down with a final offensive flourish. The location of the Silver Hand leader is important; you may not need to scour the entire fortification to find him. As always, utilize your local map to learn where the leader is holed up and to learn any shortcuts to his location. But it is just as satisfying to plow through the leader's troops first!

◊ **OBJECTIVE:** Return to Aela

Quest Conclusion

With the blood of the Silver Hand leader still coating your melee weapon, head back to Jorrvaskr, inside Whiterun, and let Aela know of your victory. You receive no reward; just your vengeance satiated.

Postquest Activities

If this was your first Second Wave quest, Aela will present your next target. If you have now completed two of these quests, Companions Quest: Blood's Honor will begin.

SECOND WAVE: STEALING PLANS

Quest giver: Aela the Huntress

Speak with Aela and ask whether she has additional work for you. She's heard rumors of a Silver Hand camp, with a set of plans somewhere inside that could contain information helpful to the Companions; for example, it could enable a Silver Hand lieutenant to be tracked and killed. You're tasked with obtaining the plans.

◊ **OBJECTIVE:** Steal the plans from a [random Silver Hand camp]

Locate the Silver Hand camp specified by Aela (these are usually keeps, caves, or other fortifications known to house bandits), and cut a swathe through the defending enemies inside (or attempt a sneaky infiltration). The plans are usually resting on or under a table or other furniture, rather than inside a chest. Look carefully for the Stratagem, then depart with it.

➤ **Silver Hand Stratagem**

◊ **OBJECTIVE:** Return to Aela

♦ **TARGET:** Aela the Huntress, Jorrvaskr, Whiterun

Quest Conclusion

Return to Jorrvaskr, inside Whiterun, and inform Aela that you've been successful. Aside from furthering this quest line and a verbal congratulations from Aela, there are no rewards.

Postquest Activities

If this was your first Second Wave quest, Aela will present your next target. If you have now completed two of these quests, Companions Quest: Blood's Honor will begin.

SECOND WAVE: RETRIEVAL

Quest giver: Aela the Huntress

Speak with Aela and ask what her targets are. She mentions a fragment of the Wuuthrad, hidden somewhere in Skyrim.

 OBJECTIVE: Retrieve the fragment of Wuuthrad
 TARGET: Fragment of Ysgramor's Blade, in a [random location]

Journey to the location Aela has indicated, and slay the Silver Hand forces inside, along with any foes lurking at this locale. The fragments of the blade are usually inside a treasure chest or on a piece of furniture. It is almost always

in the same chamber where you found the leader of the Silver Hand. Retrieve the fragments immediately.

➤ **Fragment of Ysgramor's Blade**

 OBJECTIVE: Return to Aela
 TARGET: Aela the Huntress, Jorrvaskr, Whiterun

Quest Conclusion

With the Fragment of Ysgramor's Blade in your possession, journey back to Jorrvaskr, inside Whiterun, and inform Aela that you've been successful. Aside from furthering this quest line and receiving a verbal congratulations from Aela, there are no rewards.

Postquest Activities

If this was your first Second Wave quest, Aela will present your next target. If you have now completed two of these quests, Companions Quest: Blood's Honor will begin.

FINAL WAVE: TOTEMS OF HIRCINE

Quest giver: Aela the Huntress

Speak with Aela and ask what additional work there is to achieve. She mentions a powerful object — a Totem of Hircine — that could channel the power of the Companions' Beast Forms in a new direction. Aela instructs you to head to a particular location to find it.

 OBJECTIVE: Retrieve the Totem of Hircine
 TARGET: Totem of Hircine, in a [random location]

Journey to the location Aela has indicated (with Aela as your Shield-Sister), and slay the foes lurking around. The Totem is located inside a treasure chest or on a piece of furniture in the chamber farthest away from the location's entrance. Battle to this point and take the Totem.

➤ **Totem of Hircine**

 OBJECTIVE: Take the Totem to the Underforge
 TARGET: Underforge, Whiterun

Quest Conclusion

With the Totem of Hircine in your possession, journey back to Jorrvaskr, inside Whiterun, and head to the Underforge. Place the Totem on this stand. The Totem allows you to change your Werewolf Power. Repeat this quest for more Totems.

➤ **Totem of the Hunt (Detect Life)**
➤ **Totem of Brotherhood (Summon Spirit Wolves)**

Postquest Activities

You may now speak to another Companion and begin another Radiant Quest.

FINAL WAVE: PURITY

Quest giver: Farkas   Quest giver: Vilkas

Talk to Farkas or Vilkas. They are worried that when they pass from this realm, they, too, will share the same fate that befell Kodlak — trapped in a purgatory and desperately avoiding Hircine's Hunting Grounds. The quest giver wants the curse of lycanthropy to be purged from his spirit and asks for your help in acquiring the necessary ingredients to make this possible.

OBJECTIVE: Collect a Glenmoril Witch Head
TARGET: Glenmoril Witch Head, Glenmoril Coven

There are two options at this point: If you have already culled the Glenmoril Coven of all five witches, you should have a spare Witch Head in your inventory. If you don't, you should journey to the Glenmoril Coven, sever another Witch Head, and return to Farkas's or Vilkas's location.

➤ **Glenmoril Witch Head**

OBJECTIVE: Cleanse [the quest giver] of beastblood

Only one location has the necessary magic to thwart the power of Hircine, and that is Ysgramor's Tomb. Follow the route set out in the Companions Quest: Glory of the Dead (with the quest giver as your Shield-Brother) until you reach the chamber with

the Flame of the Harbinger. At this point, you have two objectives to complete:

◊ **OBJECTIVE:** Collect a Glenmoril Witch Head
◊ **OBJECTIVE:** Kill [the quest giver's] wolf spirit

Quest Conclusion

Place one of the Witch Heads into the flickering blue flame, and then defeat the wolf spirit that leaves the body. Once this combat is over, Farkas or Vilkas is effectively "cured" of lycanthropy.

You can also drop a head into the flames and cure yourself. But be warned: Once cured, you lose your Beast Form ability forever.

Postquest Activities

You may now speak to another Companion and begin another Radiant Quest.

◄ FINAL WAVE: DRAGON SEEKERS ►

Quest giver: Farkas   Quest giver: Vilkas

Either Farkas or Vilkas tells you that a dragon is terrorizing a nearby Hold. The exact details are scarce, but this would be a fine and victorious combat victory and would help keep the denizens of Skyrim safe. You are given instructions on where this dragon's lair may be.

◊ **OBJECTIVE:** Kill the dragon at [a random dragon's lair]

Walk the path to the dragon's location (with the quest giver as your Shield-Brother), and begin combat with this monstrous beast. Depending on how far through the Main Quest you are, the Shouts you have learned can very much help in this epic confrontation. Defeat the dragon and claim its soul for your own.

> **TIP**   If you require more information on how to defeat the dragon, consult the tactics listed in Main Quest: Dragon Rising or Main Quest: A Blade in the Dark. If you've learned the Dragonrend Shout (after completing Main Quest: Alduin's Bane), fighting with melee weapons suddenly becomes a whole lot easier.

➤ **Dragon Soul**

◊ **OBJECTIVE:** Talk to [the quest giver]

Quest Conclusion

Farkas or Vilkas are impressed by your dragon-slaying abilities. You are truly the Harbinger of the Companions!

Postquest Activities

You may now speak to another Companion and begin another Radiant Quest.

OVERVIEW

Optimal Quest Start

The College of Winterhold Quests begin when you arrive at the College for the first time. They give you access to trainers and vendors that considerably increase your magical abilities and skills. You can join the College whenever you like, although Magic-focused characters may want to join sooner rather than later to gain access to this ready source of spells. Most other characters will come to the College much later, as part of Main Quest: Elder Knowledge.

> **NOTE** **Cross-Referencing:** Do you want to see maps and learn more about the traps, non-quest-related items, collectibles, crafting areas, and other important rooms of note in every location during these quests? Then cross-reference the location you travel to with the information on that location contained in this guide's Atlas.

Sanctuary: College of Winterhold

The College of Winterhold, perched on its pillar of rock.

Inside the College, where mages perfect their magic.

The threadbare Hold City of Winterhold has seen most of its population driven away. The center of life in these parts nowadays is the College of Winterhold. Once a prominent, influential location in Skyrim, Winterhold has fallen on hard times but is still a haven for mages in Skyrim, a safe refuge from distrustful Nords. Largely self-sufficient, the College of Winterhold is quite content to be isolated from the rest of the province, although a more peaceful coexistence with the outside world is always preferred.

The College of Winterhold is situated on a cliff overlooking the Sea of Ghosts. Over the years, the cliff has fallen into the sea, taking nearly all of the original city with it. Only a few buildings remain, though somehow the College of Winterhold has largely been untouched by the damage. It now resides on a free-standing crag of rock and ice. Inside, the College is split into three distinctive towers: Halls of Countenance and Attainment where apprentices and senior mages reside; the Hall of the Elements, where the Arch-Mage resides, gatherings are held, and the Arcanaeum (the College's great library) is kept. Below the College lies the Midden, a warren of icy tunnels where the remnants of long-forgotten experiments reside.

Important Characters

Arch-Mage: Savos Aren

Savos has been the Arch-Mage of the College for a very long time and tried to assure the people that the College was not responsible for the Great Collapse. He took threats seriously after the White-Gold Concordat and helped secure the grounds of the College. Through it all, he's managed to maintain his good demeanor and his faith in humanity. He has little concern for public perception these days, believing that if the mages of the College keep to themselves, no one will bother them. As such, he has every intention of staying out of the Civil War and the Thalmor's rise to power.

Thalmor Advisor: Ancano

A Thalmor agent currently residing at the College of Winterhold, acting in an "advisory" position, Ancano's patronizing tone and haughtiness have made this High Elf into a hated figure. Feeling he has no one to answer to, Ancano is using his time at the College to find out any secrets he can and relay them to his masters back at the Embassy in Haafingar. He isn't winning any popularity awards in the College.

Master-Wizard: Mirabelle Ervine

Mirabelle may be second-in-command, but she's the one who really runs the College. The day-to-day operations are under her jurisdiction, which doesn't make her popular, but she knows someone has to do the job. Mirabelle is frustrated that the College is seen as a black mark, that magic in general is shunned, and takes very seriously any allegations of wrongdoing leveled at the College or its members. She has no use for either the Psijics or the Thalmor — they're all just getting in the way and giving the College a bad reputation.

Wizard: Sergius Turrianus

Well aware of the contempt Nirya and Faralda have for one another, Sergius takes time from his duties as Enchanting instructor to instigate conflict between the two women, in the hopes that Faralda will turn to him for comfort. While he's sure this is going to backfire on him eventually, he's going to enjoy it while he can.

➤ **Trainer (Enchanting: Expert):** Sergius Turrianus

Wizard: Drevis Neloren

Drevis is a strange duck. Quite versed in Illusion, he's well liked by the apprentices but has little presence outside his class. His colleagues barely seem to acknowledge him; he floats through the day leaving little mark on anything. If they were paying attention, one might question whether he's really there at all....Drevis has a habit of wandering into the Arcanaeum and talking Urag gro-Shub's ear off, largely because Urag can't get away.

➤ **Vendor:** Illusion spells

➤ **Trainer (Illusion: Master):** Drevis Neloren

Wizard: Faralda

Faralda has her eye on Mirabelle Ervine's position, a stepping stone on her way to being Arch-Mage. Recently she's noticed that Nirya seems to have her sights set on the same position, and the two have developed a bitter rivalry over it. Rumors of sabotaged experiments and undermined research provide plenty of gossip for the other mages. When upset over something Nirya has done, Faralda goes running to Sergius Turrianus, who is in fact playing up both sides of this conflict to get close to Faralda.

➤ **Vendor:** Destruction spells

➤ **Trainer (Destruction:** Expert): Faralda

Wizard: Phinis Gestor

Phinis has little concern for the affairs of mortals. He's a wizard who conjures creatures from the Beyond—what else matters? Phinis is also interested in Necromancy and takes solace in the notion that the College is one of the few places he can get away with honing his art without being stoned to death in the process. He regularly relies on Enthir to procure some of the more sensitive items his conjurations require, but only interacts socially with Arniel Gane, the one person in the College who doesn't seem nervous when speaking to him.

➤ **Vendor:** Conjuration spells

➤ **Trainer (Conjuration:** Expert): Phinis Gestor

Scholar: Arniel Gane

Arniel is a small, frail little man who's never been entirely comfortable in his own skin. He feels weak and helpless, and while turning to magic has alleviated some of that, he wants to take it a step further. His ultimate (and very secret) goal is to research dwarven artifacts and figure out why the civilization disappeared. To that end, he occasionally procures the services of Enthir for some controversial items.

Scholar: Colette Marence

Colette is the Restoration teacher at the College and is well aware that she's been labeled as a peace-loving star-gazing Spriggan-hugger. Having made repeated attempts to break out of that role and finding that everyone treated her even worse when she no longer fit the image they'd created for her, she's finally given in and accepted that no one will ever see her differently.

➤ **Vendor:** Restoration spells

➤ **Trainer (Restoration: Expert):** Colette Marence

Scholar: Enthir

Enthir is the "man who knows how to obtain materials" in the College. While the College has very flexible rules on what's acceptable research and what's not, there are some reagents and spell components that just can't be acquired through legal means. Enthir, working with Birna in Winterhold, is the elf who takes care of that. He also becomes a Fence in Winterhold during the Thieves Guild Quests.

➤ **Fence (Thieves Guild)**

Scholar: Nirya

Nirya is supremely confident of her abilities and is far more interested in jostling for a leadership position than improving her skills. As Faralda seems to be the only other mage to share these ambitions, she's decided to take her down. Sergius provides insight as to how to go about doing this, and while Nirya has a sense that he may be using her, she can't imagine what his motivation is and so she doesn't worry about it.

Wizard: Tolfdir

Tolfdir is old. Very old. And while it's easy for the others to write him off as a doddering old fool, he is actually one of the few real masters of Alteration magic. He loves his work, offering to give new apprentices their first taste of the College, and is always available to help if it's needed and if it doesn't involve too much physical activity. Despite his elderly nature, those with perceptive qualities know to treat him as the venerable mentor and advisor that his years have taught him to be.

➤ **Vendor:** Alteration spells

➤ **Trainer (Alteration: Master):** Tolfdir

Lorekeeper: Urag gro-Shub

Urag's never been a "normal" Orc, preferring books and spells to blades and war paint. He put on a good show for as long as he could, then quietly snuck off to the College of Winterhold when he had the chance. While he's very good at what he does and loves it, he's still somewhat conflicted by how contrary this is to what's perceived as typical Orc behavior. As such, he feels it necessary to attempt to maintain a gruff, serious exterior. He's actually developed a close relationship with Savos Aren and with Drevis Neloren (against his better judgment), largely because Drevis seems oblivious at Urag's attempts to drive him away.

➤ **Vendor:** Books

Apprentice: Brelyna Maryon

Brelyna comes from a line of Telvanni wizards, well known for their proficiency. However, she is struggling with magic and has opted to study at the College, out of sight of her friends and relatives. Her plan is to get over whatever problem she's having and then return to Solstheim to finish her studies—and do so as quickly as possible.

➤ **Follower:** Brelyna Maryon

Apprentice: J'Zargo

Encouraged by his peers to seek greater magical knowledge, he's traveled to Skyrim to learn what the Nords have to offer about magic. J'Zargo is not intimidated to be the only of his kind at the College; rather, he takes this as a sign that he's an exceptional mage. He believes himself superior to his fellow apprentices and thinks the only reason he hasn't already been made a scholar (or higher) is protocol.

➤ **Follower:** J'Zargo

Apprentice: Onmund

As a Nord, Onmund's natural magical ability was seriously frowned upon by his family. Coming from a difficult childhood as a result, he's happy to finally be someplace where everyone is more like him. Unfortunately, no one seems quite as happy as he is, which he finds to be very puzzling. His frequent attempts to make friends and engage in social activities often fall flat, but this has not dampened his enthusiasm.

➤ **Follower:** Onmund

Augur of Dunlain

Formerly a mage from Dunlain in High Rock, Augur was working on some unapproved experiments in the Midden and wound up fused to the magical energies that flow through the College. Now incorporeal, he has sequestered himself in a locked room in the Midden but keeps tabs on everything going on in the College.

Psijic Monk: Quaranir

Quaranir is a member of the Psijic Order, a group that teaches a philosophy called the Elder Way, peaceful meditation to reach a higher state of consciousness and manipulation of the living world. These monks have been known to guide particularly adept mages, and Quaranir believes that his guidance is needed now.

▶ Training and other Notes

In addition to a warm bed and like-minded brethren, some of the members of this College of mages are extremely talented in a particular skill. Speak to each of them and increase the chosen skill by a point, to a maximum of five points before you level up. If you have enough gold, you can complete this numerous times:

✓	SKILL	RANK	TRAINER
	Alteration	Master	Tolfdir
	Conjuration	Expert	Phinis Gestor
	Destruction	Master	Faralda
	Illusion	Master	Drevis Neloren
	Restoration	Expert	Colette Marence
	Enchanting	Expert	Sergius Turrianus

Followers and Marriage

Any of the three Apprentices—Brelyna, Onmund, and J'Zargo—can become Followers once you complete their Faction Radiant Quests. In addition, Onmund and Brelyna are candidates for marriage. Consult Side Quest: The Bonds of Matrimony for more details on the nuptials.

Magic Robes

Scour the College for a series of different-colored variations of College Robes; these are the finest premade enchanted robes you can obtain and are rarely found as loot. You can find them from merchants and randomly lying around in chests, wardrobes, or other containers.

▶ Available Quests

There are 29 different quests available with the College of Winterhold. Eight of these are Critical Path Quests; 21 are Radiant Quests.

Critical Path Quests

Simply referred to as "quests," these are the main quests you attempt. All but the first quest have one or more prerequisites, as shown in the following table:

✓	QUEST NAME	PREREQUISITES
	College of Winterhold Quest: First Lessons	None
	College of Winterhold Quest: Under Saarthal	Complete College of Winterhold Quest: First Lessons
	College of Winterhold Quest: Hitting the Books	Complete College of Winterhold Quest: Under Saarthal
	College of Winterhold Quest: Good Intentions	Complete College of Winterhold Quest: Hitting the Books
	College of Winterhold Quest: Revealing the Unseen	Complete College of Winterhold Quest: Good Intentions
	College of Winterhold Quest: Containment	Complete College of Winterhold Quest: Revealing the Unseen
	College of Winterhold Quest: The Staff of Magnus	Complete College of Winterhold Quest: Containment
	College of Winterhold Quest: The Eye of Magnus	Complete College of Winterhold Quest: The Staff of Magnus

Radiant Quests

Also known as "Faction Radiant Quests," these are usually smaller quests that require you to complete an objective for a particular person. New quests of this nature appear as you progress through the Critical Path Quests. In most cases, the objectives of a Radiant Quest are randomized. They are listed in more detail after the Critical Path Quests, but for the prerequisites required to begin every Radiant Quest, consult the following table:

✓	QUEST NAME	QUEST GIVER	PREREQUISITES
	Radiant Quest: Rejoining the College	N/A	Complete College of Winterhold Quest: First Lessons, violence against a member
	Radiant Quest: Tolfdir's Alembic*	Tolfdir	Complete College of Winterhold Quest: First Lessons
	Radiant Quest: Out of Balance*	Drevis Neloren	Complete College of Winterhold Quest: First Lessons
	Radiant Quest: An Enchanted Journey*	Sergius Turrianus	Complete College of Winterhold Quest: First Lessons
	Radiant Quest: Restocking Soul Gems*	Sergius Turrianus	Complete College of Winterhold Quest: First Lessons
	Radiant Quest: Valuable Book Procurement*	Urag gro-Shub	Complete College of Winterhold Quest: First Lessons
	Radiant Quest: Shalidor's Insights	Urag gro-Shub	Complete College of Winterhold Quest: First Lessons
	Radiant Quest: The Atronach Forge*	N/A	Complete College of Winterhold Quest: First Lessons; Ritual Spell Quests: Conjuration Ritual Spell to unlock the forge's full potential.
	Radiant Quest: Forgotten Names*	N/A	Complete College of Winterhold Quest: First Lessons
	Radiant Quest: Aftershock	Tolfdir	Complete College of Winterhold Quest: The Eye of Magnus
	Radiant Quest: Rogue Wizard	Tolfdir	Complete College of Winterhold Quest: The Eye of Magnus
	Arniel's Endeavors: Arniel's Endeavor (Part 1)	Arniel Gane	Complete College of Winterhold: Under Saarthal
	Arniel's Endeavors: Arniel's Endeavor (Part 2)	Arniel Gane	Complete College of Arniel's Endeavors: Arniel's Endeavor (Part 1)
	Arniel's Endeavors: Arniel's Endeavor (Part 3)	Arniel Gane	Complete College of Arniel's Endeavors: Arniel's Endeavor (Part 2), and College of Winterhold Quest: The Eye of Magnus
	Arniel's Endeavors: Arniel's Endeavor (Part 4)	Arniel Gane	Complete College of Arniel's Endeavors: Arniel's Endeavor (Part 3) and College of Winterhold Quest: The Eye of Magnus
	Apprentice Radiant Quest: Brelyna's Practice	Brelyna Maryon	Complete College of Winterhold: Under Saarthal
	Apprentice Radiant Quest: J'Zargo's Experiment	J'Zargo	Complete College of Winterhold: Under Saarthal

	QUEST NAME	QUEST GIVER	PREREQUISITES
	Apprentice Radiant Quest: Onmund's Request	Onmund	Complete College of Winterhold: Under Saarthal
	Ritual Spell Quests: Destruction Ritual Spell	Faralda	Destruction Skill of 90
	Ritual Spell Quests: Illusion Ritual Spell	Drevis Neloren	Illusion Skill of 90
	Ritual Spell Quests: Conjuration Ritual Spell	Phinis Gestor	Conjuration Skill of 90
	Ritual Spell Quests: Restoration Ritual Spell	Colette Marence	Restoration Skill of 90
	Ritual Spell Quests: Alteration Ritual Spell	Tolfdir	Alteration Skill of 90

NOTE ✳ Indicates the quest name does not appear in your Quest menu; check the "Miscellaneous" area for objectives that may appear.

FIRST LESSONS

PREREQUISITES: None
INTERSECTING QUESTS: The College of Winterhold Quest: Under Saarthal, Main Quest: Elder Knowledge
LOCATIONS: College of Winterhold, Hall of Attainment, Hall of Countenance, Hall of the Elements, Winterhold
CHARACTERS: Brelyna Maryon, Faralda, J'Zargo, Mirabelle Ervine, Onmund, Tolfdir
ENEMIES: None
◊ **OBJECTIVES:** Visit the College of Winterhold, Cast a [chosen] spell, Report to Mirabelle Ervine, Tour the College of Winterhold, Listen to Tolfdir

A Cold to a Warm Reception

During your adventuring, you soon learn of a great college to the north, adjacent to the Hold City of Winterhold. You can speak to various folk across Skyrim and receive the following objective. Denizens include:

Innkeepers or barkeeps in each of the Hold's inns or taverns

Court wizards in the Jarl's service in each Hold City, where available

Ambarys Rendar in Windhelm

Corpulus Vinius in Solitude

Dagur in Winterhold

Dravynea in Kynesgrove

Elda in Windhelm

Faida in Dragon Bridge

Frabbi in Markarth

Hadring in Nightgate Inn

Haelga in Riften

Hulda in Whiterun

Iddra in Kynesgrove

Jonna in Morthal

Keerava in Riften

Kleppr in Markarth

Madena in Dawnstar

Melaran in Solitude

Mralki in Rorikstead

Orgnar in Riverwood

Skuli in Old Hroldan Inn

Sybille Stentor in Solitude

Valga Vinicia in Falkreath

Vilod in Helgen

Wilhelm in Ivarstead

Wylandriah in Riften

◊ **OBJECTIVE:** Visit the College of Winterhold

Alternatively, you can simply journey to Winterhold and approach the bridge spanning from the city to the College.

At the near end of the bridge that links Winterhold to the College, a High Elf wizard guards the entrance. She stops you (and warns you to stop if you ignore her or try to gain entry into the sealed College without her approval). Although she has some complaints about the College (which you can ask her about), your real reason for being here is

to enter the College. Ask if this is possible, and she asks why. Choose the answer that best suits you. She requires that you take a test to show you're at least possibly competent in the use of magic. You can:

(Persuasion) Attempt to gain entry without completing her unnecessary test.

Agree to take the test. When the test begins, Faralda requests you aim a spell at the seal on the ground near her.

◊ **OBJECTIVE:** Cast a [chosen] spell
♦ **TARGET:** Marker stone, College of Winterhold entrance

Ask if she would grant entry to the Dragonborn. Faralda asks if you really have the Voice. Show her using your Fire Breath (or any other) Shout.

Spell-casting: Bring up your Magic menu and choose the spell Faralda has requested. She can choose Firebolt, Magelight, Fury, Conjure Flame Atronach, or Healing Hands, depending on your available spells and knowledge of particular Magic styles. Aim at the seal, and cast the spell. After your successful casting, Faralda tells you to find Mirabelle Ervine inside the College.

TIP If you don't have any spells, Faralda offers to sell you one for 30 gold pieces. This is a great way to obtain an Apprentice-level spell for a cheap price!

CAUTION Be extremely careful where you're waving your fingers! Don't aim at Faralda or choose a spell (or Shout) that has a large area of effect. If you cast a wider flame-based attack, you risk setting Faralda on fire, effectively ending your tryout as an apprentice mage!

Dragon Shouting: Bring up your Shout inventory, choose any Shout (a good choice is Fire Breath), and bellow. After you strike the seal, Faralda walks over and tells you that there is much you both can learn from each other and that you'd be a superb addition to the College.

You can now ask Faralda more questions about Mirabelle and the College, and you can even receive training in the arts of Destruction magic. College of Winterhold Quest: First Lessons is now active, and you are told to report to Mirabelle Ervine.

NOTE The entire tour of the College is optional; you can ignore it and run straight into the Hall of the Elements and find Tolfdir.

The Makings of a Mage

Walk across the bridge to the impressive stone edifice, a fortress both highly defensible and remote enough for its students to concentrate on their studies. Head into the outer exterior courtyard, and meet with Mirabelle Ervine. She greets you and hands you the garb of a mage (which you can wear if you wish). She then begins a tour of the College, and you are most definitely encouraged to follow her.

➤ **Apprentice Hood of Magicka**   ➤ **Boots**

➤ **Apprentice Robes of Destruction**

◊ **OBJECTIVE:** Tour the College of Winterhold

Mirabelle explains that the Hall of the Elements is the primary location for lectures, practice sessions, and meetings. She also points out that the Arch-Mage's quarters are adjacent but are strictly off-limits to students. Follow Mirabelle to the living quarters. She talks about recent problems the College has been having with Nords. Newest members stay in the Hall of Countenance, where students may be working on spell-casting or experiments. Mirabelle then takes you to the Hall of the Elements.

She tells you that your teacher is likely to be Tolfdir, who is probably already addressing the new Apprentices. She encourages you to report any problems to a senior member before handing you off to Tolfdir.

➤ **College of Winterhold:** Bed

◊ **OBJECTIVE:** Listen to Tolfdir

♦ **TARGET:** Tolfdir, in the Hall of the Elements

Find Tolfdir, who tells you that the lesson has just started. Mingle with the other students —Brelyna Maryon, J'Zargo, and Onmund—and heed Tolfdir's advice, although a few of the apprentices are more keen on mage dueling than on hearing a verbal lesson. Tolfdir advises them against impulsive behavior and seeks your thoughts. You may answer with an unsure, practical, or safety-based response. Soon enough, Tolfdir agrees to a practical lesson in the art of Wards.

Wards are protective spells that block magic. Tolfdir has made sure no one within the Hall of the Elements will be hurt and then turns to you and asks if you know a Ward spell. You can answer with one of these options:

You don't have a Ward spell; Tolfdir immediately teaches you Lesser Ward.

You have a Ward spell but don't know how to use it. Tolfdir then explains how they work.

You have a Ward spell and know how to use it. Tolfdir begins a practical demonstration, which eventually happens no matter which answer you choose.

➤ **Spell:** Lesser Ward

Select a Ward spell from your list and activate it. Tolfdir throws a fire-based spell at you, which you absorb. Once you complete this, Tolfdir seems more confident in the newcomers' abilities and says that he will be leaving soon and taking the Apprentices to Saathal, a Draugr tomb and the site of an ongoing excavation by the College of Winterhold. He expects you to meet him there in a few hours. The lesson now ends.

Quest Conclusion

You are now a member of the College and are free to roam the College of Winterhold.

Postquest Activities

The College of Winterhold Quest: Under Saarthal begins immediately. You can also begin to complete Faction Radiant Quests for the College's many mages.

 **UNDER SAARTHAL**

PREREQUISITES: Complete the College of Winterhold Quest: First Lessons

INTERSECTING QUESTS: The College of Winterhold Quest: First Lessons, The College of Winterhold Quest: Hitting the Books, Side Quest: Forbidden Legend

LOCATIONS: College of Winterhold, Hall of Countenance, Hall of the Elements, Saarthal, Saarthal Excavation

CHARACTERS: Arniel Gane, Brelyna Maryon, J'Zargo, Onmund, Nerien, Savos Aren, Tolfdir

ENEMIES: Draugr, Jyrik Gauldurson

◊ **OBJECTIVES:** Meet Tolfdir outside Saarthal, Follow Tolfdir, Find Arniel Gane, Search for magical artifacts (4), Use the Saarthal Amulet to escape the trap, Follow Tolfdir, Tell Tolfdir about the vision, Follow Tolfdir, Find the danger within Saarthal, Talk to the Arch-Mage

⊙ MINOR SPOILERS

A New Vision for Saarthal

This quest begins immediately after you complete the College of Winterhold Quest: First Lessons. Completing this is also part of Side Quest: Forbidden Legend. Check that quest for more information.

◊ **OBJECTIVE:** Meet Tolfdir outside Saarthal

Tolfdir has already made preparations to take his Apprentices (including you) to Saarthal — the remains of an ancient Nordic burial site of great importance and unknown depths and the site of an ongoing excavation by the College. Saarthal is southwest of Winterhold, in a treacherous part of the mountains where wolves like to roam. If you reach the entrance first, wait for the others; they may have been held up by an unexpected encounter. You may converse with any or all of them, but let Tolfdir know when you're ready to begin the exploration. Find out more about the site by asking him, too. Then follow him into the Saarthal Excavation.

◊ **OBJECTIVE:** Follow Tolfdir

 NOTE The Saarthal Excavation door is firmly sealed and opened only during this quest.

Tolfdir descends the rickety steps into the entrance chamber, explaining that Saarthal was one of the earliest Nord settlements in Skyrim, and the largest. It was sacked during the infamous Night of Tears, but little else is known about what happened to the settlement. After some further instruction, ask Tolfdir what he needs, and he asks you to help Arniel Gane catalog some finds and locate enchanted items.

◊ **OBJECTIVE:** Find Arniel Gane

Follow the path of lanterns along the passages and into a multifloored chamber with wooden scaffolding. Drop from the bridge, and find Arniel Gane in a side corridor. He instructs you to look around the chambers to his north and to be careful.

◊ **OBJECTIVE:** Search for magical artifacts (4)

The intersecting passages north of Arniel Gane aren't dangerous, but the enchanted items dotted around here may be difficult to spot. Make slow, deliberate sweeps of each area until you find the items in question. Once you have the first three easy-to-spot items, head to this strange, torch-lit carved arch with the Saarthal Amulet on it. Grab it, and you immediately hear strange, scraping sounds. You triggered a spear trap. Tolfdir appears to see if you're all right. Explain what happened, and he suggests using it in some way.

➤ Enchanted Ring (3)   ➤ Saarthal Amulet

◊ **OBJECTIVE:** Use the Saarthal Amulet to escape the trap
◊ **OBJECTIVE:** Follow Tolfdir

Select the Saarthal Amulet from your inventory and wear it. Tolfdir remarks that the wall from which you took the amulet may be susceptible to your magic. Launch a Firebolt (or other target-based spell) at the carved wall section, and it shatters back into an unexplored passage.

The spear trap recedes. Instead of rushing through, wait for Tolfdir to approach, and follow him into the rocky tunnel. As Tolfdir plods ahead, he wonders why this place was sealed off. You both step into a small mausoleum chamber, where Tolfdir tells you to be on your guard.

▷ The Saarthal Discovery

A moment later, an apparition named Nerien appears in a startling vision. He is unknown to you, and you appear to be the only one who is communicating with him. He mutters a warning that the events you've set in motion cannot be undone. But judgment on you will be based on your forthcoming actions and how you deal with the dangers ahead. The Psijic Order believes in you. You alone have the ability to prevent disaster. Take great care, and know that the Order is watching....

◊ **OBJECTIVE:** Tell Tolfdir about the vision
◊ **OBJECTIVE:** Follow Tolfdir

Immediately inform Tolfdir about your vision, and the message. Tolfdir thinks this is all very odd, as the Psijics have no connection to these ruins, and no one has seen their order in a long time. He suspects the coffins embedded around this room are connected to deeper chambers. His excavation techniques are quickly abandoned as a Draugr breaks through from the other side. After dispatching the Draugr, follow Tolfdir into another newly discovered passage beyond.

Pull the lever at the bottom of the passage to open the portcullis. This leads into a grand, circular chamber with a bridge crossing a chasm. Fortunately, grating prevents you from plummeting to your death. Around the chamber are coffin alcoves. The Draugr start to stir. Back Tolfdir up as you bring your magic (or other attacks) to bear on the advancing undead. Once you down the Draugr, Tolfdir begins inspecting the chamber in greater detail and wishes to remain here. You're tasked with finding out what terrible dangers the Psijic Order mentioned in your vision. On your own...

◊ **OBJECTIVE:** Find the danger within Saarthal

▷ Awakening the Scourge of Skyrim

Head north, removing the spear bars and portcullis from the iron door by activating a lever on both sides of the door. Step into Saarthal itself, and work your way through a grand burial crypt. You awaken the Draugr, so expect them to step out of their wall coffins as you progress. Head up the wooden steps, inspect the raised sarcophagus near the iron door, and pass through into a sloping stone burial tunnel. Watch for traps of a flame and dart-based nature. Then enter the crypt corridor of carvings.

At this corridor's far end is a barred archway with a lever on a pedestal. Activate the lever, and you're struck by darts. Along the sides of the corridor are a total of six pillars, each with a trio of animal petroglyphs carved into them.

Puzzle solution: The trick here is to notice a smaller carving above each pillar. Make sure that the pillar below matches this smaller carving. Along the north wall from left to right, adjust the pillars so the following animal forms are facing out: Whale, Snake, and Hawk. Along the south wall from left to right: Hawk, Hawk, and Whale.

Inside the two-level ceremony room beyond, you encounter a power Draugr close to the wooden side steps. Battle it, then take the upper door exit past the treasure chest. Avoid the runic traps and reach a second puzzle passage. Expect a dart trap if you pull the lever before correctly positioning the four carved pillars.

Puzzle solution: The four correct positions are displayed in the large carved mouths on each side of the passage and behind each movable pillar. On the west wall from left right: Hawk and Whale. On the east wall from left to right: Snake and Whale. Each pillar makes

 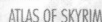

several other pillars move too. This causes no end of adjustment problems if you don't know how many pillars move during each activation (look at the nearby picture, which has each pillar numbered):

Pillar 1 (Whale): Activate it to move all four pillars.

Pillar 2 (Snake): Activate it to move pillars 2, 3, and 4.

Pillar 3 (Hawk): Activate it to move pillars 3 and 4.

Pillar 4 (Whale): Activate it and only it moves.

The solution is deceptively simple: Turn the pillar that rotates the most number of pillars first, and continue activating pillars that rotate consecutively fewer pillars until the puzzle is solved. That way you affect fewer pillars as you go. Face the portcullis archway (to the south):

Activate pillar 1 to show the Whale.

Activate pillar 2 to show the Snake.

Activate pillar 3 to show the Hawk.

Activate pillar 4 to show the Whale.

Watch for more runic and dart traps as Tolfdir catches up with you. He finds all of this fascinating. You can ask him further questions about the Psijic Order and then continue exploring. Open the iron door and enter the chamber of Jyrik Gauldurson. Tolfdir is transfixed by a massive ten-foot glowing orb, floating in a bubble of writhing magic, at the room's opposite end. It is pulsing and made of some strange, unknown material. Tolfdir averts his gaze when a ferocious-looking Draugr rises from his eternal throne chair; you're about to face Jyrik Gauldurson. This most evil of Nords was sealed down here to prevent his reanimation. Not anymore!

Jyrik Gauldurson is coursing with evil magic, and for the first ten seconds of the battle, he is utterly impervious to any attacks. Use this time to step behind cover, or let any summoned creatures or Followers bear the brunt of his attacks. Eventually, Tolfdir realizes that all your combined offensive capabilities aren't having an effect, so he turns to the

Eye and focuses his attacks on the crackling globe. A few seconds later, he yells that Jyrik is vulnerable. Attack!

To further complicate matters, Jyrik is bathed in an elemental shield that cycles through the different elements; he is impervious to attacks from the same element. So, if he's bathed in fire, then any Flame-based spells have no effect on him. Use attacks from any other element instead. If you have only one type of elemental magic (i.e., only Fire), wait a few seconds until Jyric's shielding changes elements and then strike!

> **TIP** Jyrik is extremely vulnerable to frost damage when he's on fire, and when encased in a frost shield, he's very vulnerable to fire. Use this to your advantage!

◊ **OBJECTIVE:** Talk to the Arch-Mage

Quest Conclusion

With Jyrik Gauldurson gurgling his last curse, turn your attention to the giant orb. Tolfdir agrees that the Arch-Mage at the College of Winterhold should be informed immediately. Use the iron door behind the orb to exit the chamber, which leads to a fern-filled grotto and an ancient Word Wall. Absorb the power before you return to the excavation site, releasing the portcullis exit with a wall handle, and leave Saarthal.

➤ **Gauldur Amulet Fragment**   ➤ **Writ of Sealing**

➤ **Word of Power:** Ice Storm   ➤ **Staff of Jyrik Gauldurson**

> **TIP** Be sure to take the Gauldur Amulet Fragment, as it imbues you with +30 Magicka! Read the Writ of Sealing, and you begin Side Quest: Forbidden Legend. It seems there are two other Gauldurson brothers to face elsewhere in Skyrim! Consult Side Quest: Forbidden Legend quest (on page 342) for more information.

Return to the College and seek out Savos Aren, either in the Hall of Countenance or Hall of the Elements. You may ask him about the Psijic Order, but you're here to speak to him about the Saarthal discovery. Savos Aren is taken aback by your findings and believes more research is needed while he journeys to Saarthal to inspect the orb. You are rewarded for your efforts.

➤ **Staff of Magelight**

Postquest Activities

The College of Winterhold Quest: Hitting the Books begins immediately. You can now speak to each of Tolfdir's three students and Arniel, and engage in some more Radiant Quests from this point on.

HITTING THE BOOKS

PREREQUISITES: Complete the College of Winterhold Quest: Under Saarthal

INTERSECTING QUESTS: The College of Winterhold Quest: Under Saarthal, The College of Winterhold Quest: Good Intentions, The College of Winterhold Faction Radiant Quests

LOCATIONS: College of Winterhold, Arcanaeum, Hall of Countenance, Hall of the Elements, Fellglow Keep, Fellglow Keep Dungeons, Fellglow Keep Ritual Chamber

CHARACTERS: Orthorn, Savos Aren, Urag gro-Shub

ENEMIES: Atronach, The Caller, Conjurer, Fire Mage, Frost Atronach, Frostbite Spider, Ice Mage, Necromancer, Skeleton, Storm Atronach, Storm Mage, Vampire, Wolf

◊ **OBJECTIVES:** Speak with Urag gro-Shub, Find the stolen books (3), (Optional) Free Orthorn, Return the books

▶ Tardy Bookkeeping

This quest begins immediately after you complete the College of Winterhold Quest: Under Saarthal.

◊ **OBJECTIVE:** Speak with Urag gro-Shub

♦ **TARGET:** Urag gro-Shub, in the Arcanaeum

  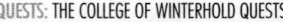

The former student Orthorn is one of the captured souls inside a cell. You can speak with him. He appears remorseful and pleads with you to release him; he'll lead you straight to the books you seek. Pull the middle lever to free him, or you can kill him, tell him his services aren't needed, or ask him to accompany you.

Arch-Mage Savos Aren will form a plan for dealing with the large undulating orb you found in the depths of Saarthal. In the meantime, locate the Arcanaeum off the Hall of the Elements. Seek out Urag gro-Shub the Lorekeeper in his library. There are several questions you can ask him, and you can help him find special books (aside from this quest). But to further this quest, tell him you need to learn about the orb that was found in Saarthal. Urag has no information on the matter.

However, he is aware of some missing texts, taken from the library by a student and never returned. One of these may have some knowledge to impart. The student's name was Orthorn. If you ask about him, Urag tells you the books were stolen so Orthorn could ingratiate himself with a group of warlocks who left the College long ago over a "difference of opinion." You may ask more about where Urag believes Orthorn is holed up—a place called Fellglow Keep.

> ◊ **OBJECTIVE:** Find the stolen books (3)
> ♦ **TARGET:** Ritual Chamber, inside Fellglow Keep

Before you leave the Arcanaeum, Ancano the Thalmor adviser appears. He's showing considerable interest in what was found at Saarthal and asks about it. Answer him however you wish. Many mages feel he's not to be trusted.

Assault on the Warlocks

Fellglow Keep is east of Whiterun, on the edge of the Tundra just below the snow line. This crumbling fortification has a group of Fire and Ice Mages watching from the remains of a beacon and the ramparts. The Keep's front door is locked, so follow your quest target to the stone spiral steps in the foundations of the west tower. As there's an Atronach close to the top of the stairs, combat is favored over sneaking.

Make your way through the ankle-deep flooded chambers, and engage the first warlock and his two "pet" spiders in the chamber with the crumbling support pillar. Watch for dart traps as you exit via the upper passage and head through a small maze of passages into the dungeon chamber with cells.

Once you've defeated the jailer, you can unlock the cells or just pull the levers on the wall nearby to release the captive vampires, who rush forward into the next room to attack the warlocks there. Join the melee or sneak past it; then head down a cobwebbed corridor to a second circular prison chamber. Levers in the middle unlock the cells around the perimeter.

> ⚖ **TIP** If you don't attack the vampires, they won't attack you. If they manage to kill the warlocks in the next room (with or without your help), they'll flee the dungeon. It's not really worth the trouble to kill them—as prisoners, they don't have any loot worth taking.

As you enter the prison chamber, the warlock on the room's far side spots you and rushes for the levers. If he reaches them, he'll release the two wolves in the far cell, which makes combat here more difficult. Rush him or take him out with an arrow to the head before that can happen.

> ◊ **OBJECTIVE:** (Optional) Free Orthorn

> ➤ **Follower:** Orthorn (temporary)

Whether Orthorn is backing you up or not, descend past the root cellar and tackle the mages practicing their magical attacks in the firing range. Then continue up into the undercroft, where two necromancers set upon you and beckon skeletons from the coffins on either side of the chamber. The door at the end of this crypt allows further access into the Keep area.

Expect a fierce battle if you aggressively attack the mages in the ruined chapel. Don't forget to grab the Conjuration skill book from the podium before moving on into the dining room and great hall where further combat can commence. Storm Mages and other warlocks attempt to thwart your progress.

After climbing the stairs in the great hall, loot the workroom on the right, then take the eastern exit up to a circular library. From there you find a corridor with a giant boulder in it and the entrance to the Keep tower. Climb the candlelit staircase, loot the shelves at the top, and enter the Ritual Chamber.

> ⚖ **TIP** The shelves before the Ritual Chamber have several extremely useful items, such as Fire Resist potions, Ice Spike Scrolls, and Health potions. Gather them all, as you'll need them for the battle to come, especially at low levels.

> ➤ **Shelving Loot**

Silencing the Caller

Speak to the Caller, who is most put out that you've disrupted her plans during your Keep infiltration. If Orthorn has made it this far, you can arrange a trade—she gives you the books, and you give her Orthorn (who, naturally, is less than pleased with this arrangement). Carefully collect the books and leave the way you came. There's no need to trek back through the dungeons; collect the front door key from any of the mages on the upper level, then leave through the double doors in the great hall.

Otherwise, you have no choice but to fight. The Caller summons one or two Atronachs (the type and number depend on your level) and attacks. When she takes damage, she uses a unique spell to teleport away, often shifting one of her summoned Atronachs into her previous position.

At low levels, the Atronachs are especially dangerous. Take them out quickly, and the Caller's teleporting can actually work in your favor: When she warps away, it buys you a few seconds to heal and regroup.

At higher levels, you may find yourself facing two Frost Atronachs or (if you're particularly unlucky) Storm Atronachs! At this point, the Caller is the easier target. Ignore the Atronachs as best you can and focus all your offensive fire on her to bring her down.

When the Caller finally falls, search her corpse for a key, and scour the chamber for the three missing tomes. Then unlock the door in the northwest wall, scavenging any treasure from the room beyond before using the trapdoor that leads back down to the barred door in the great hall and an exit outside. If alive, Orthorn thanks you but will not follow you.

➤ **Fellglow Ritual Chamber Key**
➤ **Fragment:** On Artaeum
➤ **Night of Tears**
➤ **The Last King of the Ayleids**

◊ **OBJECTIVE:** Return the books
♦ **TARGET:** Urag gro-Shub, in the Arcanaeum

Quest Conclusion

Back at the College of Winterhold, locate Urag gro-Shub (who is usually in the Arcanaeum) and hand over the books. Urag reminisces about the tomes and surmises that there is much to learn from them that may help your cause. This will take some time, however. For now, you are rewarded with a small library of books, all of which increase magic skills once you read them. Do that now!

 TIP Once you've acquired the skill increases from the books, return to Urag and sell the books back to him for some considerable coin. This is doubly rewarding!

➤ **Withershins**
➤ **Daughter of the Niben**
➤ **The Doors of Oblivion**
➤ **Enchanter's Primer**
➤ **Horrors of Castle Xyr**
➤ **Incident at Necrom**

Postquest Activities

The College of Winterhold Quest: Good Intentions begins immediately.

 **GOOD INTENTIONS**

 MINOR SPOILERS

PREREQUISITES: Complete the College of Winterhold Quest: Hitting the Books
INTERSECTING QUESTS: The College of Winterhold Quest: Hitting the Books, The College of Winterhold Quest: Revealing the Unseen, The College of Winterhold Faction Radiant Quests
LOCATIONS: College of Winterhold, Arcanaeum, Arch-Mage's Quarters, Hall of Countenance, Hall of the Elements, Midden, The Midden Dark
CHARACTERS: Ancano, Arch-Mage Savos Aren, Arniel Gane, Augur of Dunlain, Colette Marence, Enthir, Faralda, Mirabelle Ervine, Nirya, Phinis Gestor, Quaranir, Tolfdin, Urag gro-Shub
ENEMIES: Draugr, Flame Atronach
◊ **OBJECTIVES:** Speak with Tolfdir , Listen to Tolfdir, Follow Ancano, Find the Augur of Dunlain, Report to Savos Aren

▶ Witnessing the Eye of Magnus

This quest begins immediately after you complete the College of Winterhold Quest: Hitting the Books.

◊ **OBJECTIVE:** Speak with Tolfdir
♦ **TARGET:** Tolfdir, in the College of Winterhold

Tolfdir has returned from Saarthal and with the help of the Arch-Mage has moved the giant floating orb of crackling energy into the Hall of the Elements. Tolfdir is nearby. You can ask him if he has any lower-priority tasks for you to complete (beginning any of the College's additional quests), be sure to tell him that Urag suggested you come see him and that you found a book entitled Night of Tears. He tells you he'll have to read it, but he's having difficulty tearing himself away from the beauty of the orb, which some people have called the Eye of Magnus. If you'll permit him (and you should), he wishes to make a few observations.

◊ **OBJECTIVE:** Listen to Tolfdir

He observes that the markings are quite unlike anything seen before; not even Falmer runes are a match. The object is also radiating Magicka, and this has caused the Arch-Mage to fully commit to researching the orb. Tolfdir is about to continue, when he is interrupted by Ancano, a gaunt High Elf with a highfalutin attitude that riles Tolfdir. He reluctantly agrees to let you leave with Ancano, who has important information to impart.

◊ **OBJECTIVE:** Follow Ancano

Ancano says that someone from the Psijic Order has appeared at the College and is asking for you by name. Ask Ancano for further information if you wish. Then follow him out of the Hall of the Elements and into the Arch-Mage's Quarters. You have little time to speak with Savos Aren or Ancano; the cowled figure wearing the same robes as the initial mage you saw in your vision pauses time and introduces himself as Quaranir. Time is fleeting, so he is quick to impart that the Order has had little success in contacting you previously and that this is probably because of the Eye of Magnus.

According to Quaranir, the longer the Eye remains in the College, the more dangerous the situation becomes. They expect dire consequences if the Eye isn't banished, but the future is obscure, and the Psijic Order is unsure how you must act. Seeking out the Augur of Dunlain is the next logical step. Moments later, there is a flash of light, and time resumes as normal.

◊ **OBJECTIVE:** Find the Augur of Dunlain
♦ **TARGET:** Augur of Dunlain, in the Midden, below the College

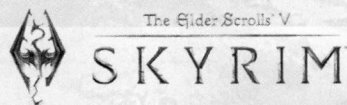
The Elder Scrolls V
SKYRIM

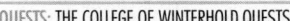

Forgotten Experiments

Ancano is furious at the Psijic Order's interruption and vows to get to the bottom of this matter. Begin searching out the mages within the College and asking them about the Augur of Dunlain (if you don't wish to immediately journey to his location). No one is aware of the stoppage of time except you. Here's what the main inhabitants of the College know (or reveal) about the Augur:

Ancano is rather cagey, professing to know nothing about the Augur.

Savos Aren is rather annoyed that Tolfdir has been telling stories again, and he hopes you'll instruct the old fellow to knock it off.

Colette Marence relates a tragic story of an experiment gone horribly wrong; the ghost of the unfortunate College member is said to still roam the halls.

Urag gro-Shub has little to say on the subject.

Mirabelle Ervine says that the Augur is nothing that need concern you and remains tight-lipped about whatever was going on.

(Persuade) Mirabelle can be persuaded to reveal the location of the Augur if you speak with her.

Arniel, Enthir, and the other Apprentices say they don't know anything, but suggest you speak to Tolfdir about it.

Nirya is more concerned with her animosity with Faralda. Other mages in the Hall of Countenance and around the College are professing to know nothing about the Augur.

Hidden in the Midden

The most trustworthy of your close colleagues has the information you require. Ask Tolfdir about the Augur of Dunlain, and he tells you it has been years since he's spoken with him. The Augur is down in the Midden. Now seek either of the entrances and descend into the Midden. The icy and dank dungeons known as the Midden are beneath the College. It consists of a series of passages and stairs. The remains of innumerable experiments are scattered about and long forgotten. Unhappy Draugr and Atronachs roam these gloomy corridors, so expect a few fights along the way.

As you cross an icy bridge, you begin to hear the voice of the Augur, echoing through the tunnels. He tells you there is nothing for you here and that your perseverance will only lead to disappointment. The sealed door to the Augur's chamber is locked. Try it, and your persistence is rewarded; the Augur lets you into his grim oubliette. Speak to this maelstrom of writhing oddness and flame, who believes events are too late to change. You also find out that you aren't the only one who's visited the Augur recently. A Thalmor named Ancano has been here too. Thinking that Ancano was simply here to strengthen his own hand, the Augur neglected to tell him that the Eye of Magnus is extremely dangerous, and a staff of great power is required to mitigate this threat. Find the Staff of Magnus at the earliest opportunity.

◊ **OBJECTIVE:** Report to Savos Aren
♦ **TARGET:** Arch-Mage Savos Aren, in his quarters or Hall of the Elements

Quest Conclusion

Return to Savos Aren, who is probably gazing at the Eye of Magnus. Tell him you have important information. He initially scoffs at your request to find the Staff of Magnus, but after you mention who gave you this information, his tune changes. He is impressed with your initiative and wants someone to follow up on locating the staff. He means you. He remembers Mirabelle Ervine mentioning something about the staff, but that was a while ago. Receive the Arch-Mage's gratitude:

➤ **Mage's Circlet**

Postquest Activities

The College of Winterhold Quest: Revealing the Unseen begins immediately. Shorter additional quests are also available.

REVEALING THE UNSEEN

PREREQUISITES: Complete the College of Winterhold Quest: Good Intentions
INTERSECTING QUESTS: The College of Winterhold Quest: Good Intentions, The College of Winterhold Quest: Containment, The College of Winterhold Faction Radiant Quests

 MINOR SPOILERS

LOCATIONS: College of Winterhold, Hall of the Elements, Mzulft, Mzulft Aedrome, Mzulft Boilery, Oculory
CHARACTERS: Ancano, Arch-Mage Savos Aren, Gavros Plinius, Mirabelle Ervine, Paratus Decimius, Quaranir, Synod Researcher
ENEMIES: Chaurus, Dwarven Sphere, Dwarven Spider, Falmer, Gloomlurker
◊ **OBJECTIVES:** Speak with Mirabelle Ervine, Find the ruins of Mzulft, Search for Synod researchers, Reach the Oculory, Find the Focusing Crystal, Return the Crystal to Paratus, Follow Paratus, Place the Crystal into the Oculory, Focus the Oculory, Talk to Paratus, Report to Savos Aren

Secrets of the Synod

This quest begins immediately after you complete the College of Winterhold Quest: Good Intentions.

◊ **OBJECTIVE:** Speak with Mirabelle Ervine
♦ **TARGET:** Mirabelle Ervine, in the College of Winterhold

Arch-Mage Savos Aren has requested that you speak to Mirabelle Ervine, who may have some knowledge regarding the Staff of Magnus. You may find her wandering the Hall of the Elements or in the exterior courtyard within the College. Ask her about the staff, and after a few roundabout conversations, Mirabelle recalls that some Imperials from the Synod were interested in it and came to the College to question them. Leaving empty-handed, it appears they had a secondary plan: to head toward the sprawling dwarven ruins of Mzulft, which apparently has a derelict observatory that would somehow help locate the staff.

◊ **OBJECTIVE:** Find the ruins of Mzulft

In the foothills by the edge of the mountains that carve through Eastmarch Hold, south and a little east of Windhelm, you come across ancient carved stone columns and archway entrances and a spectacular stone-and-pipework facade with steam still hissing from the hillside. Enter the huge golden door and step inside.

◊ **OBJECTIVE:** Search for Synod researchers
♦ **TARGET:** Gavros Plinius, inside Mzulft

Slumped to the right of the second interior door is an Imperial named Gavros Plinius. He was ambushed while attempting to reach the Oculory, where another member of the Synod, Paratus, is holed up. Before collapsing, he murmurs something about a crystal being stolen. Search his robes for a couple of important items: a key so you can enter Mzulft and a Research Log. Reading the log allows you to understand who exactly was here (an attendant on behalf of the First Adjunct Oronrel) and what he was doing (delivering a new Focusing Crystal to the Oculory). Unfortunately, the crystal that is mentioned is nowhere to be found. Now use the key to open the second door.

➤ **Mzulft Key**   ➤ **Research Log**

◊ **OBJECTIVE:** Reach the Oculory
♦ **TARGET:** Mzulft Aedrome

Onward and Upward

Enter this dwarven labyrinth, heading along the corridor and checking the body of a Synod Researcher. As you reach a connecting corridor of belching steam pipes, tough mechanical Dwarven Spiders attack you. These pester you as you continue up the linked corridors. Soon you're met by more Dwarven Spiders and a huge gold door. Head through into a more natural cavern, but with elements of dwarven architecture still visible. In a natural rock cavern, engage your first Chaurus. Use the wooden scaffold to escape it during this war of attrition. Your third and fourth dead Synod Researchers are found here, at the foot and the top of the ramped scaffold.

Beware of a trip wire releasing a pile of rocks as you move through into a second, much taller cavern with a mammoth skeleton, more Chaurus, and an arched granite entrance. Enter another ramped corridor and expect Dwarven Spheres to elongate and attack at the top. Then continue up, pausing to dispatch Dwarven Spiders along a mechanical corridor. Head past a sunken chamber with stone steps until you reach a pipe-pillar room, where you tackle more dwarven creations. Your internal mountain climb continues, past the corpses of a dead Falmer or two, and finally to the gold doors leading into the Mzulft Boilery.

⟨ **TIP** You may wish to sprint (or sneak) past the enemies in these corridors, if they are proving too difficult to defeat.

Gaining Focus

The upper chambers inside the Boilery are less tall and have had periodic rockfalls in the past, where ferns now grow. Falmer roam these halls. Dispatch them. Continue into a hub room with cage doors. Go through the open doors to the east, across a raised platform, and through a gap in the wall, caused by Falmer tunneling. This continues past a chest; expect further Chaurus and Falmer incursions. As the tunnels take on a more eerie glow caused by fungus, battle (or sneak past) a small Falmer camp, and ascend farther up into another broken wall. Step back into the dwarven-built chambers.

The ceilings are higher and the chambers more impressive as you reach a huge gallery with a sunken central area. Falmer are swarming about in this location. Search any chests you wish, but be sure to head up the steps in the west wall and into one last corridor. The doors at this corridor's end lead to the Mzulft Aedrome.

The Aedrome is comprised of three giant chambers connected by corridors of ornate pillars and snaking pipes (the locked door [Master] to the north ends abruptly with a Falmer chest). The central chamber has numerous Falmer, but one is especially important: a boss that carries a Focusing Crystal. Pry it from its corpse (or pickpocket it if you're being extremely stealthy), and then head east, passing the plinth with dwarven metal resting on it, into a dead-end chamber dotted with Falmer corpses and a powerful automaton. There is an important chest here; it contains the key that will open the important chambers on this level. This brings up the following two quest objectives:

◊ **OBJECTIVE:** Find the Focusing Crystal
♦ **TARGET:** Falmer Boss, Mzulft Aedrome
◊ **OBJECTIVE:** Return the Crystal to Paratus
♦ **TARGET:** Paratus Decimius, Mzulft Aedrome

➤ **Focusing Crystal**   ➤ **Mzulft Observatory Key**

Oculory Jocularity

Paratus Decimius is behind a closed door up the western corridor ramp, accessed via the key. He is expecting Gavros (the Synod Researcher you found dead at the entrance) and is displeased by your presence. Inform him you have the Crystal, and Paratus strolls along the corridor leading to a giant Dwarven Armillary.

◊ **OBJECTIVE:** Follow Paratus

Paratus isn't sure what the dwarves called this huge focusing globe, but from the Synod's research, the machinery appears to have been made to collect starlight, for an as-yet-unknown purpose. Paratus replaced one of the elements with his crystal, after months of perfecting it. Using the Focusing Crystal will allow the Synod's research to continue. And you're the one who has to activate the giant, tumbling machinery!

◊ **OBJECTIVE:** Place the Crystal into the Oculory

After you follow Paratus into the Armillary chamber (and optionally speak to him about related matters), you are instructed to approach the Oculory, the giant series of lenses atop the Armillary. Activate the Dwarven Armillary.

The Elder Scrolls V

SKYRIM

◊ **OBJECTIVE:** Focus the Oculory

Gaze around the curved observatory chamber, and you'll notice a series of circular blue focusing mirrors on the ceiling panels around you. Directly above the center of the Oculory are three focusing lenses. A stream of bright light bounces off them, onto the ceiling. Some of the blue focusing mirrors are lit with starlight, as is the main circular mirror in the center of the ceiling. Head up either ramp and look to the stone table, upon which is a number of valuable items:

➤ **Antecedents of Dwemer Law**   ➤ **Dwemer Inquiries Vol. II**
➤ **Dwemer Cog** (3)   ➤ **Dwemer Inquiries Vol. III**
➤ **Dwemer History and Culture**   ➤ **Spell Tome:** Flames
➤ **Dwemer Inquiries Vol. I**   ➤ **Spell Tome:** Frostbite

Puzzle Solution: You may read all the tomes, but the ones you must memorize (if you haven't already) are the Flames and Frostbite spells. However, any ranged fire and frost spells you already use are just as effective. Brandish both spells, one in each hand, and stand underneath or within range of the lenses. Now accurately shoot both fire and ice projectiles at the lens until the beam of light each one has captured hits the middle of each of the horizontal panels with the blue mirrors in them.

 TIP Make sure the three light beams are each hitting the center of a separate panel.

Now move the blue mirrors. Each of the dwarven pedestals atop the ramp rotate one of the three horizontal ceiling panels. The trick is to press the button on each pedestal so the panels shift sideways until one of the blue mirrors lines up with the light beam. The beam then ricochets off and up to the ceiling mirror. When all three light beams hit the ceiling, you know the Oculory is focused properly.

◊ **OBJECTIVE:** Talk to Paratus

As a map of the northern part of Tamriel is projected onto the wall underneath the buttons, Paratus is initially excited to watch the results of his months of work. However, this is tempered slightly as the results come in: Something is creating a huge amount of interference, something at Winterhold. You can speak to Paratus (and be as honest or as cagey as you like), but he is highly suspicious of the mages. He angrily wants to know what you did and thinks you have something at your College. Whether you tell him about the Eye of Magnus or not, steer the conversation to the Staff of Magnus's location. Paratus finally reveals its location: Labyrinthian! Now leave before Paratus gets any more testy.

◊ **OBJECTIVE:** Report to Savos Aren
◆ **TARGET:** Arch-Mage Savos Aren, College of Winterhold

Quaranir appears from a side corridor to tell you that trying times are ahead. It is imperative that you return to your College immediately. You must take swift action and show what you're capable of. He believes you will prevail. Now exit through the pair of doors Quaranir was standing behind (the latter of which you unlock with the Mzulft Observatory Key), and step outside into the inclement weather. Unless you fancy a precarious descent, Fast-Travel back to the College.

Quest Conclusion

Arch-Mage Savos Aren is in a vexed state when you return, and this situation is about to take a turn for the explosive. Ancano—the erstwhile conspirator and now a full-fledged traitor—has magically barricaded himself in the Hall of the Elements, with the Eye of Magnus! The Arch-Mage, having little time to talk about your quest to find the Staff of Magnus, is embroiled in a battle to break through Ancano's magical barrier and confront him. As Aren closes, there is a huge flash and an explosion. Everything fades to white. Your reward is escaping with your life (and with the spells and books you uncovered during your exploration)!

Postquest Activities

Through the smoke and dust, you find Mirabelle Ervine lying on the ground. The College of Winterhold Quest: Containment begins immediately. There are shorter, additional Radiant Quests to complete, too.

 **CONTAINMENT**

PREREQUISITES: Complete the College of Winterhold Quest: Revealing the Unseen
INTERSECTING QUESTS: The College of Winterhold Quest: Revealing the Unseen, The College of Winterhold Quest: The Staff of Magnus, The College of Winterhold Faction Radiant Quests

 ● **MAJOR SPOILERS**

LOCATIONS: College of Winterhold, Hall of the Elements, Winterhold
CHARACTERS: Arch-Mage Savos Aren, Arniel Gane, Faralda, Mirabelle Ervine, Tolfdir
ENEMIES: Ancano, Magic Anomaly
◊ **OBJECTIVES:** Find the Arch-Mage, Protect the town of Winterhold, Defeat the creatures infesting Winterhold (10), Report to Mirabelle Ervine

▶ A Plague on Winterhold

This quest begins immediately after you complete the College of Winterhold Quest: Revealing the Unseen.

◊ **OBJECTIVE:** Find the Arch-Mage
◆ **TARGET:** Exterior courtyard, in the College of Winterhold

Mirabelle Ervine rouses you from the battle-scarred Hall of the Elements, where strange magics are emanating from the Eye of Magnus. Ancano remains with the Eye, protected by bonded magic too strong to pierce. Mirabelle's most pressing concern is finding the Arch-Mage, who was knocked away by the explosion. Rendezvous in the exterior courtyard, where a crowd is forming around the crumpled form of Savos Aren. Tolfdir confirms the shocking news; Savos Aren has succumbed to the wounds he suffered during the battle with Ancano. But the time for mourning will come later; Winterhold is being overrun with entities summoned by the Eye!

◇ **OBJECTIVE:** Protect the town of Winterhold
♦ **TARGET:** The bridge to Winterhold

The danger present in Winterhold is threatening the entire town. A plague of odd, wisplike balls of terror are attacking the townsfolk! Although optional, it's worth stopping on the bridge to tell Faralda of the situation. Ask her to help; she gladly brings her considerable magic to bear on the enemy and manages to coax Arniel Gane into the fight as well. The three of you should help even the odds once you cross the bridge into Winterhold.

◇ **OBJECTIVE:** Defeat the creatures infesting Winterhold (10)
♦ **TARGET:** The streets of Winterhold

The ten Magic Anomalies are easily spotted and quickly removed. Ranged magic is a good choice, but pinpoint spells that don't hit the townsfolk who are under Anomalies attack work best; you don't want collateral damage killing off the very people you're here to protect! You may wish to rush over to any groups of these magical entities and leave Faralda and Arniel to deal with them; this allows you to coax as many of them away from the townsfolk as possible. If Faralda is here when the ten magical foes are dead, she shouts that she'll stay here and check for any more incursions. Pick up any Soul Gems that the Magic Anomalies dropped when they were dispatched.

Although the chance is small, the attacking Anomalies may kill one or more of Winterhold's townsfolk, and it may not be possible to save them. This may affect other quests, so exhaust your talking options with the inhabitants of the town prior to their infestation problem.

CAUTION ⇨

◇ **OBJECTIVE:** Report to Mirabelle Ervine
♦ **TARGET:** Mirabelle Ervine, the College of Winterhold

Quest Conclusion

Return to the College and seek out Mirabelle Ervine, letting her know that Winterhold is safe for now. She wishes she could say the same for the College. While she attempts to keep the Eye of Magnus contained with her fellow mages, you are to locate the Staff of Magnus once and for all. Mention that you're off to Labyrinthian, and Mirabelle is taken aback: The Arch-Mage gave her an item from this place and told her she'd know what to do with it. She hands the following items over to you and tells you to leave. Quickly.

➤ **Torc of Labyrinthian**   ➤ **Savos Aren's Amulet**

Postquest Activities

The College of Winterhold Quest: The Staff of Magnus begins immediately. The Amulet is great to wear, as it boosts Magicka regeneration.

THE STAFF OF MAGNUS

PREREQUISITES: Complete the College of Winterhold Quest: Containment
INTERSECTING QUESTS: The College of Winterhold Quest: Containment, The College of Winterhold Quest: The Eye of Magnus, The College of Winterhold Faction Radiant Quests, Side Quest: Masks of the Dragon Priests*
LOCATIONS: College of Winterhold, Hall of the Elements, Labyrinthian, Labyrinthian Chasm, Labyrinthian Thoroughfare, Labyrinthian, Tribune
CHARACTERS: Atmah (Ghost), Elvali Veren (Ghost), Girduin (Ghost), Hafnar Ice-Fist (Ghost), Mirabelle Ervine, Savos Aren (Ghost), Takes-in-Light (Ghost), Tolfdir
ENEMIES: Dragon Priest Morokei, Draugr, Estormo, Frost Troll, Skeletal Dragon, Skeleton, Troll, Wisp, Wispmother, Wizard Thrall
◇ **OBJECTIVES:** Entrance to Labyrinthian, Find the Staff of Magnus, Return to Tolfdir

⦿ MAJOR SPOILERS

NOTE ✳ Quest names marked with this symbol do not appear in your Quest menu list, although objectives may.

▷ Getting Lost in Labyrinthian

This quest begins immediately after you complete the College of Winterhold Quest: Containment. Be sure you have the Torc of Labyrinthian (given to you by Mirabelle Ervine at the end of College of Winterhold Quest: Containment).

◇ **OBJECTIVE:** Enter Labyrinthian
♦ **TARGET:** Entrance to Labyrinthian, Hjaalmarch Hold

Mirabelle and Tolfdir have retreated back, unable to halt the tide of magic sweeping across the College. The Staff of Magnus is needed, and now! Trek west—the mountain crags to the south and east of Morthal is where the vast and sprawling remains of this ancient Nordic city are located. Enter the surface courtyards from the mountains above, or the forest below, using the stairs and the dried aqueducts.

Ignore the Lost Valkygg area to the east as well as the ceremonial buildings, steps, and statuary; focus on the Frost Trolls and the giant low arch of the Labyrinthian entrance. Look for the strange, glowing figures standing beneath the giant overhang. The spirit of Savos Aren is here. You can't speak to him or to the other ghosts standing in front of Labyrinthian's entrance — Girduin, Hafnar Ice-Fist, Atmah, Elvali Veren, and Takes-in-Light. This appears to be a recording from a time before Savos Aren became the Arch-Mage, an imprint from the past. The party is wondering about entering the place. Once they disappear, move to the Ceremonial Door and activate it. You automatically remove the Torc of Labyrinthian and slot it into the door. The entrance rumbles apart.

Chilled to the Bone

Walk forward from the entrance, and Savos Aren's spectral party appears once again, hoping to find enchanted weapons and lost spell books. After they depart again, open the double doors and activate the lever to raise the portcullis. This allows you into a tremendously epic main chamber. The rattling of old bones announces the animation of a group of skeletons guarding this huge temple hall. There are bowmen in the distance, and a massive Skeletal Dragon rises from the earth and attempts to thwart you! Dodge the incoming attacks, concentrating on the Skeletal Dragon (and any skeleton you're close enough to strike), and prepare for a lengthy battle.

 TIP The massive stone columns in this chamber are most helpful; take cover and recharge behind them.

This Skeletal Dragon was summoned by dark magic within this place and doesn't have a soul to steal. Continue east, down the tunnel to an Etched Tablet, where Savos Aren's specters appear again, confused after losing one of their own. They vow to continue on, and so should you. The Tablet has a suitably troubling verse to dissuade tomb robbers. Now head down and open the doors to Labyrinthian Chasm.

◊ **OBJECTIVE:** Find the Staff of Magnus
♦ **TARGET:** Staff of Magnus, carried by Dragon Priest Morokei

Pass the nightshade plant and gnarled tree, and check the left, caved-in tunnel for trinkets; then take the right tunnel to continue. As you reach a door sealed by ice to your right (west), you hear a strange voice rasping the tongue of dragons. Draugr appear. Dispatch any that trouble you before checking the arched alcove, where a pedestal holds a Spell Tome. Pick up Flames if you haven't learned it already, and read the book at once. Equip Flames as an offensive spell, and blast the door sealed by ice. When it slides open, step through into a precarious path of descent.

➤ **Spell Tome:** Flames

Carnage in the Chasm

The voice echoes this chamber again, and Draugr begin to stir. Avoid or fight these bony fiends while navigating the narrow cliff path down to a junction. A side passage to the south leads to steps, several Draugr, and a tunnel collapse that prevents progress. However, in a side chamber, you find the remains of a conjurer, a Spell Tome (which you should learn immediately), an Alchemy Lab, and an Arcane Enchanter. This is your last opportunity to utilize these crafting facilities before unearthing the deeper secrets of Labyrinthian! Now return to the path of descent, face west, and continue down the bridges across the chasm. The voice in the dark now speaks to you in your native tongue and seems to be growing impatient.

➤ **Spell Tome:** Equilibrium

You may head to the bottom of the chasm, where a Nirnroot grows and a fast-flowing underground stream coaxes you toward an Iron Door. Or you can exit via the tunnel above, cross the remains of a bridge, and head into a great hall of alcoves. Expect Draugr foes as you head down the steps, out into a rocky fissure, and reach the fast-flowing stream from this direction. The voice mentions the return of Aren as you open the door to Labyrinthian Thoroughfare.

Thoroughfare Fights

There are two routes to choose from, and both take you through some waiting skeletons. One has a gate (Novice) to unlock and a stream to follow to an exit above an open archway. The other way requires less lockpicking and more combat. Follow the running water into the pens, where you may encounter a troll or two. Ahead are three grated windows you cannot budge. Instead, tackle the troll and use the side passage to exit the pens. The voice in the dark mocks you. In the main thoroughfare, you have more skeletons to disassemble. The voice calls again, noting you're not Aren but were sent in his place.

Head west across a bridge, to a side cave where trolls and treasure can be found. Then move north, cutting down more skeletons. You also encounter the turquoise glow of wisps as you reach a series of small standing stones and a flaming basin. You can face the Wispmother or flee from it on the raised end of the thoroughfare. Cross the wooden bridge to the northeast. The voice in the dark mocks your power. The door at the bridge's far side is sealed with fire. Utilize an ice-based spell (such as Frostbite) to open it.

Open the gate to the north and stumble upon the spectral party, now down to four members. They have grave concerns, but Savos Aren urges them to push on. You're unable to access the spiral steps they were standing by, as they are blocked. Instead, dispatch the skeletons at the end of the cylindrical sewage corridor and pick one of two routes heading down:

The Watery Fall: Stand on the trapdoor by the waterfall and open it, aiming to land on the series of crossbeams so you don't suffer falling damage. A troll is usually attacking a Draugr. You can wait for them to damage each other and drop in to finish the straggler, or wait on a crossbeam and launch ranged attacks on them both. The exit from this circular room is through the archway to the west, ending in an Iron Door.

The Side Chambers: Or you can walk over the trapdoor and head through the opening to the east. Follow the tunnel as it dries up and ends at a balcony guarded by Draugr. Drop to the adjacent earthen floor and open the wooden door to the west. The dark and narrow corridor leads down to the circular room where the troll and Draugr are fighting. Use the same western archway to exit to the Iron Door.

Prelude to a Dragon Priest

The tunnel is riddled with tree roots and the long-dead remains of Nordic warriors. As you reach an open double door to your right (west), expect more Draugr attacks. Before you head down the connecting passage, take the Spell Tome on the pedestal if you haven't learned Steadfast Ward yet. Now head into the corridor, watching for crackling electrical attacks from Soul Gem Pedestal traps and Floor Runes. Take the Soul Gems from the pedestals to deactivate them, or use the Steadfast Ward to shield yourself. Head up the tower steps to an outside ramp.

You encounter more Draugr if you inspect the chest at the top. Otherwise, locate the tunnel to the west.

➤ **Spell Tome:** Steadfast Ward

Pass the locked gate (or optionally open it to find some impressive loot) and head through the small torture dungeon and the double doors. Expect vicious combat with a high-ranking Draugr, sitting on his throne and guarding a Word Wall. Absorb another Word of Power and optionally use it in the columned hall to the west. Several Draugr and skeletons roam here, so use the columns to dodge them and seek cover if necessary. Then meet up with the ghostly Savos Aren and his two remaining followers. They stare at a door: This is it, they say!

➤ **Word of Power:** Slow Time

CAUTION
Although your progress is encouraging with a newly learned Word of Power, it is also tempered by the strange voice of a powerful Dragon Priest echoing in your ears. This foe speaks in the language of dragons and then in your native tongue, initially believing you to be Savos Aren. Each time you hear him, he completely drains you of all your Magicka! Depending on your augmentations and equipment, your Magicka can return slowly or quickly; either way, this leaves you at a disadvantage for a few seconds. When you hear the voice, seek an empty area and wait, or switch to nonmagical attacks.

Within Your Clutches

Fling the doors open, and enter the ceremonial chamber where Morokei has been sealed in an impenetrable magic ward by two Wizard Thralls.

Dragon Priest Slaying: There is a beam supporting Morokei's barrier, and the barrier gives the Dragon Priest invulnerability to your attacks. Interrupt the thralls from their ritual by striking or killing them (either one or both) to break the beam. Once the barrier falls, Morokei becomes vulnerable and attacks you. Retaliate, using the chamber's topography to hide, dodge, or face the fearsome foe out in the open using your favored offensive weaponry.

TIP When you deal the final blow to the Dragon Priest, be sure to inspect his crumpled form: He carries the Staff of Magnus! You can also pry off his mask, which is extremely important when completing Side Quest: Masks of the Dragon Priests.* Consult that quest on page 375 for more details.

➤ **Staff of Magnus** ➤ **Morokei**

◊ **OBJECTIVE:** Return to Tolfdir
♦ **TARGET:** Tolfdir, College of Winterhold

Exit from the ceremonial chamber via the eastern doors. After a final encounter with the ghost of Savos Aren, who sealed Morokei, you can continue up the stairs, opening the portcullis using the wall lever. As you step through, a Thalmor agent named Estormo appears and informs you that Ancano was correct; you are a threat. He wants the staff and wants you dead! So begins another battle. Muster your remaining magic and deal a death blow to Estormo before navigating your way out of one final crypt, up the southern steps, and outside. You are back at labyrinthian's sprawling exterior. Avoid or face the Frost Trolls and head back to the College.

Quest Conclusion

Back at the College, the surviving members have pulled back to the bridge from Winterhold. Sadly, when you ask Tolfdir where Mirabelle is, he tells you she didn't make it; she died to save the others. Tolfdir is now in charge, but none of the College members can come close to countering the magic at Ancano's disposal. Agree to face Ancano with the Staff of Magnus in hand. There may be a way to stop him yet!

Postquest Activities

The College of Winterhold Quest: The Eye of Magnus begins immediately.

THE EYE OF MAGNUS

PREREQUISITES: Complete the College of Winterhold Quest: The Staff of Magnus
INTERSECTING QUESTS: The College of Winterhold Quest: The Eye of Magnus, The College of Winterhold Faction Radiant Quests
LOCATIONS: College of Winterhold, Hall of the Elements
CHARACTERS: Gelebros, Quaranir, Tandil, Tolfdir
ENEMIES: Ancano
◊ **OBJECTIVES:** Use the Staff of Magnus to enter the College of Winterhold, Reach the Hall of the Elements, Defeat Ancano, Talk to Tolfdir, Speak with Quaranir

MAJOR SPOILERS

Into the Eye of the Maelstrom

This quest begins immediately after you complete the College of Winterhold Quest: The Staff of Magnus.

◊ **OBJECTIVE:** Use the Staff of Magnus to enter the College of Winterhold
◊ **OBJECTIVE:** Reach the Hall of the Elements

Approach the College of Winterhold, now caught in an increasingly unstable maelstrom of magic. Equip the Staff of Magnus, and use it to force your way across the courtyard and into the Hall of the Elements. Ancano is waiting within the mass of crackling and ethereal discharge. Face Ancano and attack the Eye of Magnus and the Thalmor traitor directly.

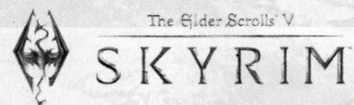

◊ OBJECTIVE: Defeat Ancano

Upon arriving at the Hall of the Elements, Ancano is well aware of your presence. The mad elf spots you and Tolfdir, taunting you and crowing that he's so far beyond your pitiful attempts at magic that you cannot even touch him. Unfortunately, this is true, as you both find out when Tolfdir's aimed fireball dissipates harmlessly. The old mage has just enough time to tell you to bring out the Staff of Magnus and use it on the Eye before an enraged Ancano strikes him—and anyone else (such as Followers) in your vicinity—with a Mass Paralysis spell, leaving you standing alone. Ancano decides to finish you himself, opening the Eye of Magnus and tapping into its full and incredible power.

Defeating Ancano: While Ancano opens the Eye, he's still invincible. Wait until the Eye is fully open. When this occurs, a casting from your Staff of Magnus absorbs its energy, and the Eye begins to close. Now is the time to thwart Ancano! Strike often and hard, because eventually the Eye reopens and Ancano becomes invincible again. When the Eye is pried open a second time, several Magic Anomalies are also let loose. Although you must deal with them, their presence has the potential to be very useful, as the Soul Gems they drop can recharge the staff if it is out of charge.

Use the chamber's topography to your advantage, keeping your distance from Ancano, which gives you more time to maneuver around his spells. If possible, stand behind one of the chamber's many pillars, or the Eye itself, blocking the full force of Ancano's attacks. Your own summoned creatures can also provide temporary distractions.

Switching between Favorites and utilizing your different weapon combinations is imperative, too. However, equip the Staff of Magnus in one hand to remove Ancano's invulnerability and power up a spell in your other hand, readying it for the moment you can hit Ancano. Then immediately switch to spells in both hands to deal the maximum amount of damage before the Eye reopens. Keep this up, and you may rid the College of this enormous anomaly!

▷ The Nick of Time

◊ OBJECTIVE: Talk to Tolfdir
◊ OBJECTIVE: Speak with Quaranir

With the hated High Elf now dispatched for good, you can return to Tolfdir. He is thankful you have stopped Ancano but has no idea how to dispel the gathering crescendo of power that the Eye of Magnus is magnifying. Fortunately, Quaranir has appeared just in the nick of time. Speak to him, and although he is as cryptic as ever, he tells you that the Psijic Order always believed in you, and your actions have proved that you are ready to lead the College of Winterhold. Now that the Eye has grown unstable, it may not only destroy the College, but also the entire world! Ancano's actions proved that this world is not ready for such power; Quaranir prepares to secure the Eye. The Psijic Order will maintain the Eye for now, and he summons his brethren, Gelebros and Tandil, to perform a binding ritual. The monks and the Eye soon disappear from this world.

Quest Conclusion

Now that you have been appointed as the new Arch-Mage, return to Tolfdir and speak with him.

Postquest Activities

You should now complete as many outstanding additional Faction Radiant Quests as you wish, including a couple of newly available ones. Tolfdir presents you with the key to the Arch-Mage's Quarters and your own robe and hood. You also receive a 10 percent discount when purchasing from College vendors.

- ➤ **Key to Arch-Mage's Quarters**
- ➤ **Arch-Mage's Hood**
- ➤ **Arch-Mage's Robe**

THE COLLEGE RADIANT QUESTS

The following Radiant Quests occur throughout (and between) the critical College of Winterhold Quests and offer you a (sometimes random) task to accomplish. These objectives become available based on two factors: where you are in the critical College Quests and your skill in the five Schools of Magic. For a complete list of how to unlock each Radiant Quest, consult the Introduction to the College of Winterhold Quests, at the start of this chapter.

 NOTE Task names marked with an asterisk (*) do not appear in your Quest menu list, although objectives may.

REJOINING THE COLLEGE

If you commit a minor crime, such as accidentally striking a College member or pickpocketing them, you're usually let off with a warning. However, if you commit a serious crime, such as assaulting or murdering one of the College members, all of them become hostile and will attack you. At this point, you can:

Continue on the killing spree, which doesn't result in much else besides dead bodies and fewer places to sell or train.

Yield by sheathing your weapons, or flee the College, wait three days, and return. Don't expect the College members to be hostile, but they won't be friendly toward you either.

If you speak to Tolfdir, he is concerned but a little more understanding. However, he requires a sum of gold be paid to the College before you can rejoin. Pay up, and you become firm friends again. Refuse, and expect to be ostracized until you pay the fine. You must pay 250 gold for your first offense, 500 gold for the second, and 1,000 gold for every subsequent offense.

TOLFDIR'S ALEMBIC*

NOTE This Radiant Quest becomes available as soon as you join the College. You can complete it once per day. It is always given to you by Tolfdir.

Start a conversation with Tolfdir, and tell him that he looks like he could use a hand. He sheepishly admits to misplacing his Alembic, an alchemic still (two vessels connected by a tube). He's hoping you might find it, as it has sentimental value for him. If you see it, will you bring it back to him?

Visit the Hall of Countenance and search the following locations to find the Alembic:

Top floor, in the chamber directly across from the stairs, on top of a barrel.

In the chamber with the Arcane Enchanter, under a display case.

Ground floor, in the room with the large cask, on top of a crate.

➤ **Tolfdir's Alembic**

Quest Conclusion

When you have the Alembic, return to Tolfdir and tell him you found what he was looking for. He thanks you for your help and rewards you.

➤ **30 gold pieces**   ➤ **Filled Soul Gem (random)**

Postquest Activities

You may now speak to Tolfdir or another mage and begin another Radiant Quest. You can repeat this quest once a day.

OUT OF BALANCE*

> **NOTE** This Radiant Quest becomes available as soon as you join the College. It is repeatable, but once you complete it, you must wait two or three days for it to become available again. It is always given to you by Drevis Neloren and always randomly.

Talk to Drevis Neloren, and he's initially astonished that you can see him; his illusion spell still needs a little tinkering. If you ask about College business that you can help with, he tells you that the various points of focus for magic energies around the College have become polluted. Agree to help with their cleansing, and he hands you a special pair of enchanted gloves that allow you to delve into these focal points. He warns you of possible "consequences" that this cleansing may have on you, and urges caution.

➤ **Mystic Tuning Gloves**

> ◊ **OBJECTIVE:** Cleanse the focal points for magical energies around the College.

The Mystic Focal Points—pillars of light with a strange glow—were visible to you previously but are easy to spot now you're attuned to them. There is one in the courtyard's center, one in the middle of the Hall of Attainment, and one in the middle of the Hall of Countenance. Beware of a random and sometimes beneficial or slightly harmful discharge as you purify these points. These are completely random and range from items to damage-causing effects.

> ◊ **OBJECTIVE:** Return to Drevis Neloren

Quest Conclusion

Once you cleanse the three focal points, return to Drevis Neloren, who is already feeling the difference you've made. He congratulates you and removes the gloves from your person.

Postquest Activities

You may now speak to another mage and begin another Radiant Quest.

AN ENCHANTED JOURNEY*

> **NOTE** This Radiant Quest becomes available as soon as you join the College. You can repeat it multiple times. It is always given to you by Sergius and always randomly.

Speak to Sergius the Enchanter to check whether there's College business you can be part of. Sergius earns a steady income enchanting weapons for local residents of Skyrim, who aren't happy about mages inhabiting their lands but seem to have no qualms utilizing their services.

Sergius has already set up an interested party, but it falls to you to take the item back to Sergius for enchanting.

> ◊ **OBJECTIVE:** Go to [the indicated random person] in [a random location] and pick up the item

Head over to the person indicated when your objective updated (the objective is in your Miscellaneous list). They are usually in one of the nine major Hold cities. Talk to them, asking about the item they want enchanted. The person hands it over to you.

➤ **A [random item] for enchanting**

> ◊ **OBJECTIVE:** Return the item to Sergius Turrianus

Quest Conclusion

Back at the College of Winterhold, Sergius takes the item from you. He'll get around to that enchanting when he's good and ready. He hands over some coins for your troubles.

➤ **100 to 200 gold pieces**

Postquest Activities

You may now speak to him again or to another mage and begin another Radiant Quest.

RESTOCKING SOUL GEMS*

> **NOTE** This Radiant Quest becomes available as soon as you join the College. You can repeat it multiple times. It is always given to you by Sergius and always randomly.

Speak to Sergius the Enchanter, and ask if there is any College business you can assist with. Sergius tells you he's running low on Soul Gems and requires you to retrieve some more for him. He'll pay you when you collect the ones he specifies.

◊ **OBJECTIVE***: Collect [a random number] of [a random type of] Soul Gems

Quest Conclusion

The type (Lesser, Common, Greater, etc.) and number are random. Sergius won't be interested in your collecting antics until you have the exact number (or more) of the Soul Gems he has specified. Then return and give them over. He's relatively pleased and rewards you.

➤ **Gold pieces**

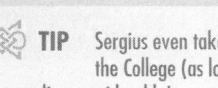 **TIP** Sergius even takes Soul Gems you find lining the shelves across the College (as long as you aren't stealing them), reducing your traveling considerably!

Postquest Activities

You may now speak to him again or to another mage, and begin another Radiant Quest. The gold pieces you are awarded are 120 percent of the value of the gems you delivered, making this worth your time.

VALUABLE BOOK PROCUREMENT*

 **NOTE** This Radiant Quest becomes available as soon as you join the College. You can repeat it multiple times. It is always given to you by Urag gro-Shub. It is separate from Radiant Quest: Shalidor's Insights.

Talk with Urag gro-Shub in the College's Arcanaeum, and ask whether there's any College business you can help him with. He's always wanting more books for the library and pays for those collected from more dangerous areas. Agree to this work, and Urag updates your map and objective with the last known location of a particularly important tome.

◊ **OBJECTIVE:** Find the copy of [a random book]
♦ **TARGET:** [A random book] in [a random location]

Quest Conclusion

Journey to the location indicated on your in-game world map, which can be any dungeon or fortification that has a large treasure chest within its walls. Battle through the enemies until you reach the book's location: a large treasure chest.

➤ **[A random book]**

◊ **OBJECTIVE:** Return the book to Urag gro-Shub

Take the book, head back to the Arcanaeum, and tell Urag you have the book he was looking for. He is pleased with your progress and offers a reward for your troubles.

➤ **Gold pieces**

Postquest Activities

You may now speak to him again or to another mage and begin another Radiant Quest. The gold pieces you are awarded are 120 percent of the value of the books you delivered. Continue this indefinitely, as you wish.

SHALIDOR'S INSIGHTS

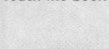 **NOTE** This Radiant Quest becomes available as soon as you join the College. It is repeatable, but once you complete it, you must wait two or three days for it to become available again. It is always given to you by Urag gro-Shub and is separate from Radiant Quest: Valuable Book Procurement.*

Speak to Urag gro-Shub in the College's Arcanaeum. During the conversation, ask him if there are any special books he's looking for. He mentions Shalidor, a powerful mage from the First Era. His writings are scattered across Skyrim, and only Urag can translate them. He's heard whispers that more of his work has turned up, and he wants you to find it.

◊ **OBJECTIVE:** Find Shalidor's writings
♦ **TARGET:** Shalidor's Insights, in [a random location]

Quest Conclusion

Head to the location indicated on your in-game world map, which can be any dungeon or fortification with a large treasure chest. Battle through the denizens there until you reach the book's location: inside a large treasure chest.

➤ **Shalidor's Insights**

◊ **OBJECTIVE:** Talk to Urag gro-Shub

Take the book, head back to the Arcanaeum, and give the book over. Then return after 48 hours, which gives Urag enough time to translate the script within the tome. As a reward, he (randomly) gives you three of any of the following scrolls or increases one of your magic skills:

➤ **Shalidor's Insights:** Alteration (3) or
➤ **Shalidor's Insights:** Conjuration (3) or
➤ **Shalidor's Insights:** Destruction (3) or
➤ **Shalidor's Insights:** Illusion (3) or
➤ **Shalidor's Insights:** Restoration (3) or
➤ **Shalidor's Insights:** Magicka (3)
➤ **+1 to Alteration, Conjuration, Destruction, Illusion, or Restoration skill**

 **NOTE** The Alteration, Conjuration, Destruction, Illusion, and Restoration scrolls halve the Magicka cost of spells of that specific skill and double their duration. This lasts two minutes. The Magicka scroll fortifies Magicka by 100 and doubles regeneration for two minutes.

Postquest Activities

You may now speak to Urag gro-Shub again or to another mage and begin another Radiant Quest.

TOLFDIR'S ALEMBIC ◊ OUT OF BALANCE ◊ AN ENCHANTED JOURNEY ◊ RESTOCKING SOUL GEMS ◊ VALUABLE BOOK PROCUREMENT ◊ SHALIDOR'S INSIGHTS   187

TRAINING   THE INVENTORY   THE BESTIARY   ◆ QUESTS   ATLAS OF SKYRIM   APPENDICES AND INDEX

While exploring the forgotten catacombs beneath Winterhold College, you'll probably stumble upon a large dais in a chamber seemingly reserved for conjuration...and possibly darker arts! This is the Atronach forge, an arcane device capable of converting mundane items into various relics from beyond Oblivion. A nearby book provides details on the forge and on a few basic recipes for conjuring Atronachs at the forge. However, the real power of the forge lies in its ability to turn several mundane items into something much more potent and arcane.

Beware! These aren't the subservient Atronachs you'll control with a typical Conjuration spell; they attack on sight.

CAUTION

➤ **Book:** The Atronach Forge

NOTE Once you meet the Augur during the College of Winterhold Quests, additional recipes can be found while exploring Skyrim, especially when battling magic-using enemies. Loot containers or corpses to find more of them. Or simply read on!

Basic Recipes: To create an arcane item, place the required mundane items for a specific recipe into the golden offering box and activate the nearby pull bar. The forge combines and consumes the items for the first complete recipe it finds. The created item (or creature) then appears on the dais.

Daedric Recipes—Hail Sigil!: After completing the Conjuration Ritual Spell Quest, you're awarded with a Sigil Stone. That item can upgrade the Atronach forge, and with the Sigil Stone in place, more powerful Daedric items can be crafted! These recipes are also found as rare loot but appear only after you receive the Sigil Stone.

BASIC RECIPES

✓	ARCANE ITEM (TO BE CREATED)	MUNDANE ITEM 1	MUNDANE ITEM 2	MUNDANE ITEM 3	MUNDANE ITEM 4
	Atronach, Flame	Fire Salts	Gem Ruby		
	Atronach, Frost	Frost Salts	Gem Sapphire		
	Atronach, Storm	Void Salts	Gem Amethyst		
	Conjurer's Elixir	Empty Bottle	Ectoplasm	Soul Gem (any)	
	Fire Salts	Salt	Gem Ruby	Soul Gem (any)	
	Frost Salts	Salt	Gem Sapphire	Soul Gem (any)	
	Void Salts	Salt	Gem Amethyst	Soul Gem (any)	
	Scroll: Flame Atronach	Fire Salts	Charcoal	Paper Roll	
	Scroll: Frost Atronach	Frost Salts	Charcoal	Paper Roll	
	Scroll: Storm Atronach	Void Salts	Charcoal	Paper Roll	
	Staff: Flame Atronach	Fire Salts	Great/Grand/Black Soul Gem	Broom	Corundum Ingot/Ore
	Staff: Frost Atronach	Frost Salts	Great/Grand/Black Soul Gem	Broom	Moonstone Ingot/Ore
	Staff: Storm Atronach	Void Salts	Great/Grand/Black Soul Gem	Broom	Orichalum Ingot/Ore
	Tome: Flame Atronach	Fire Salts	Ruined Book	Dragon's Tongue	Bear Pelt
	Tome: Frost Atronach	Frost Salts	Ruined Book	Frost Mirriam	Ice Wolf Pelt
	Tome: Storm Atronach	Void Salts	Ruined Book	Deathbell	Mammoth Tusk
	Tome: Soul Trap	Salt	Ruined Book	Soul Gem (any)	Torchbug Thorax

DAEDRIC RECIPES

✓	ARCANE ITEM (TO BE CREATED)	MUNDANE ITEM 1	MUNDANE ITEM 2	MUNDANE ITEM 3	MUNDANE ITEM 4
	Daedric Boots	Ebony Boots	Daedra Heart	Black Soul Gem	Centurion Core
	Daedric Cuirass	Ebony Cuirass	Daedra Heart	Black Soul Gem	Centurion Core

DAEDRIC RECIPES (CONT.)

✓	ARCANE ITEM (TO BE CREATED)	MUNDANE ITEM 1	MUNDANE ITEM 2	MUNDANE ITEM 3	MUNDANE ITEM 4
	Daedric Gauntlets	Ebony Gauntlets	Daedra Heart	Black Soul Gem	Centurion Core
	Daedric Helmet	Ebony Helmet	Daedra Heart	Black Soul Gem	Centurion Core
	Daedric Shield	Ebony Shield	Daedra Heart	Black Soul Gem	Centurion Core
	Daedric Battleaxe	Ebony Battleaxe	Daedra Heart	Black Soul Gem	Centurion Core
	Daedric Bow	Ebony Bow	Daedra Heart	Black Soul Gem	Centurion Core
	Daedric Dagger	Ebony Dagger	Daedra Heart	Black Soul Gem	Centurion Core
	Daedric Greatsword	Ebony Greatsword	Daedra Heart	Black Soul Gem	Centurion Core
	Daedric Mace	Ebony Mace	Daedra Heart	Black Soul Gem	Centurion Core
	Daedric Sword	Ebony Sword	Daedra Heart	Black Soul Gem	Centurion Core
	Daedric War Axe	Ebony War Axe	Daedra Heart	Black Soul Gem	Centurion Core
	Daedric Warhammer	Ebony Warhammer	Daedra Heart	Black Soul Gem	Centurion Core
	Daedric Armor (Random and Enchanted)	Ebony Ingot	Daedra Heart	Void Salts	Filled Soul Gem (Greater/Grand/Black)
	Daedric Weapon (Random and Enchanted)	Ebony Ingot	Daedra Heart	Silver Sword	Filled Soul Gem (Greater/Grand/Black)
	Daedra Heart	Human Heart	Black Soul Gem		
	Dremora	Daedra Heart	Raw Meat**	Raw Meat**	Human Skull

NOTE ** Raw Meat is any raw meat found on a dead dog, goat, horker, horse, or mammoth.

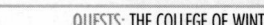

Venture into the deepest reaches of the Midden Dark and find the bizarre remnants of magical experiments gone awry. Among those is a relic in the shape of a Daedric Gauntlet emblazoned with the Sigil of Oblivion. Nearby is a key and journal that once belonged to a mage who was investigating the disappearance of four students.

➤ **Book (relating to Daedric Relic)**　　➤ **Key to Arcanaeum Chest**

Read the book to learn that there was little trace of the missing students, but four mysterious ringlike relics were recovered from the gauntlet and locked away in the Arcanaeum, where they still remain. Try to avoid being noticed as you reclaim these from an Investigation Chest on the north wall of the library.

(Pickpocket) Or, simply pick the lock and steal the rings; if you're expedient, you can attempt this before entering the Midden.

➤ **Ceremonial Rings (4)**

Return to the Midden Dark with the ceremonial rings, and attempt to match each ring to its corresponding finger. There's no penalty for guessing incorrectly. Pithiken's ring belongs on the little finger, Balwen's fits the ring finger, Treoy's ring belongs on the middle finger, and Katarina's fits the index finger. When all four rings are fitted, the fingers of the relic curl shut, and a disoriented Dremora is summoned into the chamber with you! This is Velehk Sain, who the students unwittingly permitted into the world. He's since made himself a legendary pirate of the Abecean Sea and will offer a share of his booty if you'll release him. Otherwise, prepare yourself to tangle with an ethereal foe from beyond!

If you release the Dremora, a treasure map appears in your inventory. The treasure is magically concealed and only reveals when the map comes within its range. You can find this stash to the west of Winterhold College, at the foot of a shelf below a large Talos shrine. Look for it on a small, coastal island just offshore.

➤ **Velehk's Treasure Map**　　➤ **Velehk's Stash**

 NOTE This Radiant Quest becomes available once you complete College of Winterhold Quest: The Eye of Magnus. You can repeat it multiple times. It is always given to you by Tolfdir.

Once the events of the Eye of the Magnus have subsided, converse with Tolfdir. He informs you there have been reports of some kind of magical anomaly appearing in Skyrim. He fears this may be a side effect of Ancano's meddling with the Eye of Magnus and requests that you find out what is going on. He also recommends bringing along the Staff of Magnus.

◊ **OBJECTIVE:** Close the rupture
♦ **TARGET:** Rupture, in [a random location]

Journey to the outdoor location with the perceived rift (which can be anywhere on Skyrim's exterior surface, in any Hold), and battle any entities you see prowling the area close by. Brandish your Staff of Magnus,

and destroy the three Magic Anomalies surrounding the rupture. This seals it away and restores what passes for normality around these parts.

◊ **OBJECTIVE:** Talk to Tolfidr

Quest Conclusion

Return to the College of Winterhold and speak with Tolfdir, confirming that the rupture was there, and you dealt with it. You are not rewarded if the rift occurred in Winterhold Hold, as this was part of the College's problem and needed to be covered up before the already-angry population got any more furious with mages. If the rift occurred in any other Hold, you're given the following:

➤ **300 to 500 gold pieces**

Postquest Activities

You may now speak to Tolfdir again or to another mage and begin another Radiant Quest.

 NOTE This Radiant Quest becomes available once you complete College of Winterhold Quest: The Eye of Magnus. You can repeat it multiple times. It is always given to you by Tolfdir.

When the events of the Eye of the Magnus have quieted down, converse with Tolfdir. The venerable mage says that he has received word of a troublesome mage who is hell-bent on wrecking havoc in the realm. The sorcerer in question is formidable and may have felt the effects of the Eye closing.

◊ **OBJECTIVE:** Deal with the rogue wizard
♦ **TARGET:** Rogue wizard, in [a random location]

Head to the dungeon or building where the enemy mage was last sighted, and battle your way to a confrontation. The Insane College Wizard is usually powerful and may have strong allies to defeat, too. The wizard is always wearing the College's robes. He is hardly a good role model for the organization, considering its ongoing struggles for acceptance in Nordic Skyrim. Finish the foe off, grabbing any nearby loot that is dropped or on the corpse.

◊ **OBJECTIVE:** Talk to Tolfidr

Quest Conclusion

Return to the College of Winterhold and speak with Tolfdir, letting him know you have defeated this appalling advertisement for the College. Your only reward is thanks from the College.

Postquest Activities

You may now speak to Tolfdir again or to another mage and begin another Radiant Quest.

These four Radiant Quests are available from Arniel, a reclusive and timid experimenter within the College.

▷ Arniel's Endeavor (Part 1)

> **NOTE** This Radiant Quest becomes available after you complete College of Winterhold: Under Saarthal. It is given to you only by Arniel, and you can complete it only once.

Locate Arniel Gane and ask if there's any College business you can assist him with. There's nothing officially, the nervous mage tells you, but he does mention a "project" that he's been working on. He refuses to divulge any information about it, but he requires you to bring him 10 Dwemer Cogs. He needs to examine them.

> ◊ **OBJECTIVE:** Bring Arniel Gane Dwemer Cogs (10)

The Dwemer Cogs in question are golden, and many are scattered throughout the Dwarven Ruins and dungeons of Skyrim. Check every stone table, chest, and dwarven machinery for possible cogs to gather. Be patient, as this takes some time. You may wish to combine your searching with other quests (such as Main Quest: Elder Knowledge).

> **TIP** Another option is to visit Understone Keep in Marthal, search the ruins of Nchuand-Zel, and then sneak into Calcelmo's Museum (or get his permission to visit) and steal any cogs you haven't found—or grab all ten from there. There's obvious hostility consequences if you're caught trying to enter the museum, though.

> ➤ **Dwemer Cog (10)**

> ◊ **OBJECTIVE:** Deliver the Dwemer Cogs to Arniel Gane

Quest Conclusion

He is most pleased and rewards you with some gold.

> ➤ **[Leveled] gold pieces**

Postquest Activities

Arniel continues his research, but it is three entire days before it produces results.

▷ Arniel's Endeavor (Part 2)

> **NOTE** This Radiant Quest becomes available after you complete Arniel's Endeavor (Part 1) and wait three days. It is given to you only by Arniel and can be completed only once.

After you hand over the Dwemer Cogs Arniel had requested, he thanks you, and you can ask if he requires further assistance. He needs more help with his project, but this involves a fellow wizard. Enthir is refusing to follow through on a trade regarding an important item Arniel needs for his work. He hopes you'll talk to Enthir on his behalf.

> ◊ **OBJECTIVE:** Speak to Enthir

When you find Enthir and ask about the item, he tells you Arniel misinformed you; he was going to sell the item to Arniel but decided against it. You can have the item, but Enthir needs you to find a staff one of Enthir's "friends" (likely himself) wishes to acquire. The staff is in the hands of unfriendly folks. If you bring Enthir the staff, he'll consider it payment for Arniel's item.

> ◊ **OBJECTIVE:** Acquire the Staff
> ♦ **TARGET:** Staff of Tandil, in [a random dungeon]

Set off to the dungeon or fortification Enthir specified (on your world map), and battle a hardy foe for the staff, which is usually on his or her corpse.

> ➤ **Staff of Tandil**

> ◊ **OBJECTIVE:** Deliver the staff to Enthir

Quest Conclusion

Return to the College and hand over the staff you obtained. Enthir honors his end of the deal and gives you a gem Arniel was after. Find Arniel, speak to him to give over the Soul Gem Enthir just handed you, and he thanks you profusely.

> ➤ **Warped Soul Gem**

Postquest Activities

Arniel continues his research, but it may be a while before it produces results. Complete the indicated quests to begin the third part.

▷ Arniel's Endeavor (Part 3)

> **NOTE** This Radiant Quest becomes available after you complete Arniel's Endeavor (Part 2) and after the College of Winterhold Quest: The Eye of Magnus ends. You can complete it only once, and it is given to you only by Arniel.

In the aftermath of the battle for the College of Winterhold, Arniel has been beavering away on his secret project. Ask how the project is coming along, and the news isn't good. He's destroyed a prototype and explains that the Dwemer technology he's tinkering with was put together by a race of beings that mastered magic in a way that is inconceivable to current mages. He's trying to re-create the circumstances of the failure to see what he can learn. While the Dwemer tapped power from the Heart of Lorkhan (a dead god), Arniel is making do with a Warped Soul Gem. But the Gem needs to be purified in a Dwarven Convector, which Arniel constructed and recently destroyed.

If you're willing to help, the Convector machines that exist deep within the dwarven ruins could be used to heat the Gem. Arniel even teaches you the spell to heat a Convector to the correct temperature. You are to find a Dwarven Convector, place the Warped Soul Gem inside, and heat it for at least three seconds. Approximately three Convectors will be needed, so this is a quest that requires much trekking.

> ➤ **Warped Soul Gem**   ➤ **Spell:** Arniel's Convection

 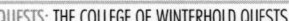

◊ **OBJECTIVE:** Place the Warped Soul Gem into a Convector

♦ **TARGET:** Dwarven Convector, [in a random location]

Your journey into Dwarven Ruins begins now! Follow your Quest Targets and fight or sneak through the indicated locations until you reach a Convector. Convectors can be found in the following locations:

Inside the first interior location of Mzulft

Inside a small dungeon located near the main entrance to Mzulft

Out in the wilderness southwest of Shor's Stone

Outside the entrance to Bthalft

Outdoors near Deep Folk Crossing

Along the river, northeast of Druadach Redoubt

You find each Convector easily, as it has a quest target on your compass. When you finally arrive at the Convector, access it and store the Warped Soul Gem in the Convector. Remember to store it first! Your objective updates:

◊ **OBJECTIVE:** Heat the Convector

◊ **OBJECTIVE:** Retrieve the Soul Gem

Now equip Arniel's Convection spell and blast the Convector for three seconds to heat it up. The Soul Gem becomes superheated, while its extremities remain oddly cold to the touch. Take the Soul Gem from the Convector and begin a lengthy trek to the next Convector scattered around Skyrim; it will be pinpointed on your world map. When you've superheated the Warped Soul Gem in three separate Convectors, the Gem finally becomes potent enough to be used in whatever clandestine experiment Arniel is conducting.

◊ **OBJECTIVE:** Return to Arniel Gane

Quest Conclusion

Return to Arniel's location, and hand over the Warped Soul Gem. The single-minded tinkerer thanks you for your help. Perhaps you'll see his actual experiment at some point?

Postquest Activities

Arniel continues his research, but it may be a while before it produces results.

▶ Arniel's Endeavor (Part 4)

> **NOTE** This Radiant Quest becomes available after you complete Arniel's Endeavor (Part 3) and the College of Winterhold Quest: The Eye of Magnus ends. You can complete it only once, and it is given to you only by Arniel.

Wait 30 hours and speak to Arniel once again. Although he's been having success using your Warped Soul Gem, he still requires an incredibly important piece of this puzzle (which you still haven't seen yet), and that pesky Enthir is failing to uphold an agreement to deliver the item. Arniel asks you to sort this problem out.

◊ **OBJECTIVE:** Talk to Enthir

Enthir is usually in the College or the Hold City of Winterhold. When you quiz him about the package Arniel wants, he appears a little exasperated, explaining that he doesn't need

money—Arniel overpaid for the item—but the courier never arrived from Morrowind. He has little idea where the courier is but knows the package is likely to be with the courier.

◊ **OBJECTIVE:** Find the courier

♦ **TARGET:** Courier, in [a random dungeon]

Journey to the location indicated on your world map, and begin a systematic search of the area until you find the Courier, who's looking a little worse for wear. Fortunately, whatever killed him ignored the package he was seeking to deliver. Remove a strange-looking dwarven dagger named Keening.

➤ **Keening**

◊ **OBJECTIVE:** Deliver the package to Arniel

> **TIP** You can try out the dagger against foes if you wish.

Head back to Arniel's location at the College. Inform him you have the dagger that he wanted. He is both excited and worried; it seems the courier company didn't even wrap the item correctly!

> **NOTE** Arniel is right to be worried: Keening is a blade made infamous during the adventures of a champion of Morrowind. At the time, this weapon was an immensely powerful and dangerous artifact that could kill the wielder if used without the proper equipment. This explains why Arniel is concerned about the state it has arrived in and why he didn't inform Enthir of the true value of this fabled artifact!

◊ **OBJECTIVE:** Observe Arniel's experiment

Quest Conclusion

Ask Arniel if he has everything he needs, and he excitedly exclaims that he does. Keening was one of the great tools of the dwarves and a nearly priceless artifact. It was used to tap into the Heart of Lorkahn. With this dagger, Arniel can test his theories regarding why the dwarves disappeared. This grand experiment was to re-create those events and thus unravel the mystery. Arniel begins the experiment. Watch as nothing continues to happen, until Arniel applies some considerable pressure, loses his temper, and then blinks out of existence completely!

Postquest Activities

Arniel has disappeared! He leaves Keening behind. Keep it as a memento (it absorbs Health, Magicka, and Stamina). Who knows if he'll ever be seen again? Well, actually you do; you are granted a new spell. Try this out and see who arrives and what he has to say....

➤ **Spell:** Summon Arniel's Shade

APPRENTICE RADIANT QUESTS

These three Radiant Quests are available from the Apprentices you trained with under Mage Tolfdir.

BRELYNA'S PRACTICE

 NOTE This Apprentice Radiant Quest becomes available after you complete the College of Winterhold Quest: Under Saarthal. You can complete it only once, and it is given to you only by Brelyna.

After a couple of chats with Brelyna, she asks if you have a moment to help her with something. Agree, and she says the reason she's here is to become a better mage, just like the rest of you. But she needs a willing volunteer she can cast practice spells on. Apparently, they aren't dangerous. You can refuse, agree, or ask what's in it for you, and she begrudgingly offers you an amulet if you'll help.

Stand still in front of her, and Brelyna releases a spell that turns everything green. Her reassurances that this wasn't supposed to happen aren't reassuring. Wait until the spell's effects wear off and you can

see properly again. Then return to Brelyna. Agree to more aural punishment, as she tries a "variation" on the first spell. You transform into a cow. Then you appear as a horse and a dog. Finally, you return to normal. She isn't convinced this has worked any better and suggests it's probably better to stop.

Quest Conclusion
After those spell failures, Brelyna is thankful that you helped her test out her spells and offers to help you on your travels.

➤ **Follower:** Brelyna   ➤ **Enchanted Necklace (random)**

J'ZARGO'S EXPERIMENT

 NOTE This Apprentice Radiant Quest becomes available after you complete the College of Winterhold Quest: Under Saarthal. You can complete it only once, and it is given to you only by J'Zargo.

After a few conversations with J'Zargo, he asks if you could possibly help him. Ask what he needs, and he tells you he's been working hard learning new spells but has little time to test them. If he gives you scrolls with a spell he's inscribed, you're to use them and report back with the results. Agree, and J'Zargo tells you about the excellent variation on a Flame Cloak spell, with special potency against the undead. He hands them over.

➤ **J'Zargo's Flame Cloak Scroll (10)**

◇ **OBJECTIVE:** Test J'Zargo's Flame Cloak spell on the undead (3)
♦ **TARGET:** Draugr, in [any Draugr-infested location]

Journey to any Nordic crypt where the Draugr are restless. You can do this while other, more crucial quests are in progress. When you conjure the Flame Cloak, you're submerged in writhing fire, which promptly explodes, causing damage to everything living and undead in a six-foot radius from you. Try coaxing three Draugr close to you so you

need cast this only once. If you run out of scrolls without burning three Draugr, you can ask J'Zargo for more.

 TIP Using the scrolls is a lot faster if you select them as "Favorites" and quickly flick between a scroll and your usual weaponry. Also use items or spells to reduce your fire damage (or have a healing spell close at hand). Remember that this is has most of the properties of a Flame Cloak spell, except it explodes when you near undead (and only undead).

The damage inflicted on you by this Flame Cloak can be severe. It isn't wise to employ it when multiple Draugr are near!	**CAUTION** 

◇ **OBJECTIVE:** Test Speak to J'Zargo

Quest Conclusion
After that burning sensation, J'Zargo apologizes. He is grateful that you helped him test out his spell and offers to help you on your adventures.

➤ **Follower:** J'Zargo

ONMUND'S REQUEST

NOTE This Apprentice Radiant Quest becomes available after you complete the College of Winterhold Quest: Under Saarthal. You can complete it only once, and it is given to you only by Onmund.

After a couple of conversations with Onmund, he asks you for help regarding a private matter. When you ask what is wrong, he tells you he's entered into an "agreement" with Enthir. Onmund has mistakenly traded an amulet that belongs to his family, and he regrets parting with it. He hopes you can talk to him and get it back. Ask him more questions about the amulet if you wish before heading off to find Enthir.

◊ **OBJECTIVE:** Speak with Enthir

Head to Enthir's room in the Hall of Attainment, or elsewhere in the College if he's wandering, and tell him that he has something of Onmund's, who wants it back. Enthir scoffs and tells you his trades are firm and final. Apparently, there's nothing more to be said. You can:

(Persuade) Tell him it's in everyone's best interest if he returns the amulet.

Or ask him if there's something you can do to change his mind.

Enthir isn't interested in you buying the amulet, and the persuasion is difficult (but not impossible). Usually, you're left with a task Enthir wishes you to complete: He tells you a story about someone (him) who traded some valuables for a staff. Afterward, that someone (Enthir) realized the staff might be misused. This would make that person (him) look bad. So he wants the staff back and fails to see any irony in this task. Agree to this.

◊ **OBJECTIVE:** Find the staff for Enthir
♦ **TARGET:** Grand Staff of Charming, in [a random location]

The staff is located randomly, somewhere in one of Skyrim's dungeons or crypts. Find it on your world map, enter the location, and fight your way to the staff, which is always in a large treasure chest.

➤ **Grand Staff of Charming**

◊ **OBJECTIVE:** Deliver the staff to Enthir

Quest Conclusion

Return to Enthir and make the swap.

➤ **Onmund's Amulet**

◊ **OBJECTIVE:** Deliver the amulet to Onmund

Now find Onmund and return the amulet to him. He thanks you and now values you as a true friend. He offers to help you on your travels.

➤ **Follower: Onmund**

RITUAL SPELL RADIANT QUESTS

 DESTRUCTION RITUAL SPELL

PREREQUISITES: Destruction Skill of 90
INTERSECTING QUESTS: None

NOTE This Ritual Spell Quest becomes available as soon as your Destruction skill reaches 90. It is always given to you by Faralda.

Talk to Faralda inside the College, and ask her if there's anything else to be learned regarding Destruction magic. But of course there is a fabled tome known as the *Power of the Elements*, which Faralda hands to you. It is imbued with power, but most of the magical text inscribed on it is missing. Faralda wishes you to travel to various locations within Skyrim to finish imbuing the tome to increase its potency. Return with the completed book.

➤ **Power of the Elements**

◊ **OBJECTIVE:** Complete the book *Powers of the Elements*
♦ **TARGET:** Windward Ruins, North Skybound Watch, Four Skulls

Power Convergence: When you examine the book, a vague description points you to a source of power for this tome: Windward Ruins. Journey there and locate the pedestal. Place the book on it and begin your imbuing by casting any flame-based

spell at the book. Instead of burning, there's a small explosion. Pick the book up, and there is additional writing. Study this and the tome points you toward North Skybound Watch. Find the pedestal here and place the book on it once more; this time, cast any frost-based spell. After another explosion and more writing appearing, your journey points you to Four Skulls. Find the final pedestal here, and cast any shock-based magic at it. When you pick the book up this time, its secrets are revealed:

➤ **Power of the Elements (completed)**    ➤ **Spell: Fire Storm**

◊ **OBJECTIVE:** Return to Faralda

Quest Conclusion

Return to Faralda and show her the Power of the Elements. She is pleased with both your abilities and the Destruction spells she can study and learn.

Postquest Activities

Along with the Fire Storm spell, Faralda now has the following spells for sale, should you wish to buy any:

➤ **Spell: Blizzard**    ➤ **Spell: Lightning Storm**

 ILLUSION RITUAL SPELL

PREREQUISITES: Illusion Skill of 90
INTERSECTING QUESTS: None

NOTE This Ritual Spell Quest becomes available as soon as your Illusion skill reaches 90. It is always given to you by Drevis Neloren.

Talk to Drevis Neloren inside the College, and ask him if there's anything else to be learned regarding Illusion magic. Indeed there is; there are several books that Urag isn't even aware of, hidden tomes completely invisible to the naked eye, that are scattered around the College. They contain information that, when read together, may unlock some as-yet-unknown Illusion spells. You are granted a spell that enhances your vision—the only possible method of finding these books. Return with the books. Ask further questions if you need to.

➤ **Spell:** Vision of the Tenth Eye

◊ **OBJECTIVE:** Bring the Four Master Illusion Texts to Drevis Neloren
♦ **TARGET:** Master Illusion Texts, within College of Winterhold

Focusing the Tenth Eye: Begin a careful search of the entire College of Winterhold. There are four texts to find, and they are reasonably easier to spot if you're being thorough, checking on top of barrels, below benches, on tables, or bookshelves. It also helps to know where each of the texts

resides: There is book in the Arcanaeum, one in the Hall of Countenance, one in the Hall of Attainment, and one in the Midden. Search each area thoroughly.

➤ **Master Illusion Text (4)**

◊ **OBJECTIVE:** Bring the Four Master Illusion Texts to Drevis Neloren

Quest Conclusion

Return to Drevis Neloren and reveal the four Master Illusion Texts in your possession. He is impressed and immediately awards you with a spell:

➤ **Spell Tome:** Hysteria

Postquest Activities

Along with the Hysteria spell, Drevis Neloren now has the following spells for sale, should you wish to buy any:

➤ **Spell:** Call to Arms   ➤ **Spell:** Harmony   ➤ **Spell:** Mayhem

CONJURATION RITUAL SPELL

PREREQUISITES: Conjuration Skill of 90   **INTERSECTING QUESTS:** Radiant Quest: The Atronach Forge*

NOTE This Ritual Spell Quest becomes available as soon as your Conjuration skill reaches 90. It is always given to you by Phinis Gestor. Completing this allows you to create more powerful items as you upgrade the Atronach forge.

Speak to Phinis Gestor inside the College, and ask him if there's anything else to be learned regarding Conjuration magic. Indeed there is: powerful spells that can more closely and permanently bind creatures to your will. One of the riskiest involves summoning and commanding an Unbound Dremora. Phinis agrees to teach you the summoning spell, but it will work only in a properly prepared location. When you summon the Dremora, you must order it to deliver you a Sigil Stone from an Oblivion gate. Return with the stone, and Phinis will inscribe the spells you've yet to learn. Ask further questions if you need to.

➤ **Summon Unbound Dremora**

◊ **OBJECTIVE:** Summon and subdue an Unbound Dremora
♦ **TARGET:** Unbound Dremora, top of the Hall of Attainment, College of Winterhold

Binding the Unbound: Once you're on the roof of the Hall of Attainment, approach the area Phinis has prepared and attempt the spell. When the Dremora appears, it is extremely angry at your impertinence and refuses to yield to you. Quickly change your weapons to those you favor when fighting foes, and battle the Dremora. Dispatch it, banishing it back to Oblivion. Rest if you need to and summon the Dremora again. Seething with rage, it again refuses to yield. Kill it so it is banished once more.

When you summon the Dremora for a third time, its demeanor is somewhat subdued. Speak to it, commanding it to bend to your will. Summon it one more time. On this fourth occasion, it grudgingly obliges your wishes: Order it to retrieve the Sigil Stone. It disappears and returns with the Sigil Stone.

➤ **Sigil Stone**

◊ **OBJECTIVE:** Return to Phinis Gestor

Quest Conclusion

Return to Phinis and present him with the Sigil Stone. He is pleased with both your abilities and the Conjuration spells he can release. In return, he hands you back the Sigil Stone and teaches you a new spell.

➤ **Spell:** Flame Thrall

Postquest Activities

Along with the Flame Thrall spell, Phinis now has the following spells for sale, should you wish to buy any:

➤ **Spell:** Dead Thrall   ➤ **Spell:** Storm Thrall
➤ **Spell:** Frost Thrall

In addition, you can plug the Sigil Stone into the Atronach forge in the Midden. Otherwise, this is a very pretty paperweight.

PREREQUISITES: Restoration Skill of 90
INTERSECTING QUESTS: None

> **NOTE** This Ritual Spell Quest becomes available as soon as your Restoration skill reaches 90 and after you meet the Augur during College of Winterhold Quest: Good Intentions. It is always given to you by Colette Marence.

Talk to Colette Marence inside the College, and question her about what else there is to learn about Restoration magic. She's comforted that you've not dismissed this art, unlike the other College members. It seems you are ready to speak with the Augur, who was especially gifted when it came to Restoration magic. He's very particular about who he shares his knowledge with. You need his approval first.

◊ **OBJECTIVE:** Gain the Augur's approval
♦ **TARGET:** Augur of Dunlain, in the Midden, in the College of Winterhold

Journey into the Midden under the College, and seek out the Augur of Dunlain's circular chamber. This sage already knew you were coming to seek something and that he has it. He asks if you are prepared. Answer how you wish, and the Augur explains that you're about to be tested not on your belongings, scrolls, or potions, but on what lies within. Are you ready to step into the light? Confirm you are with the Augur.

The Augur conjures a portal, and you must step through it. At that very moment, you are stripped of all your equipment, including melee weapons, potions, armor, and any clothing. The door to the Augur's chamber is sealed. The only protection you have are your Restoration spells. Use these to survive as a ghost appears in this chamber. After the first ghost appears, a second one manifests after ten seconds, and then a third appears after ten more seconds. All are invincible to any other attacks. After ten more seconds, all the ghosts disappear.

Quest Conclusion

The Augur appears after a few moments and is impressed by your learning of magic. He returns all of your equipment and rewards you with the following spell:

➤ **Spell Tome:** Bane of the Undead

Postquest Activities

Colette now has the following spell for sale, should you wish to purchase it:

➤ **Spell:** Guardian Circle

PREREQUISITES: Alteration Skill of 90
INTERSECTING QUESTS: None

> **NOTE** This Ritual Spell Quest becomes available as soon as your Alteration skill reaches 90. It is always given to you by Tolfdir.

Speak to Tolfdir inside the College, and ask if there's anything more you can learn about Alteration magic. As it happens, Tolfdir has been working on an improvement on the Ebonyflesh spell and has hit a snag. He requires dragon scales for his incantations, as he uses their essence, but they lack potency. From ancient records, he's discovered references to dragon "Heartscales." In addition, there are stories of a dagger called "Kavohzein's Fang," which is sharp enough to carve these scales off a dragon. You are to retrieve the dagger, use it to carve off a few Heartscales from a dragon's corpse, and return the scales to him.

◊ **OBJECTIVE:** Use Kavohzein's Fang to collect Heartscales
♦ **TARGET:** Kavohzein's Fang, inside [a Dragon Priest's dungeon]

Finding the Fang: The dagger is randomly located in one of the large dungeon crypts and guarded by a fearsome Dragon Priest. Battle through the dungeon, slay the Dragon Priest, and locate the treasure chest close to its corpse. The chest contains Kavohzein's Fang. The following table shows the possible locations to try:

✓	DRAGON PRIEST	LOCATION	INTERSECTING QUEST
	Rahgot	Forelhost	Dungeon Quest: Siege on the Dragon Cult
	Vokun	High Gate Ruins	Dungeon Quest: A Scroll for Anska
	Morokei	Labyrinthian	College of Winterhold Quest: The Staff of Magnus
	Krosis	Kilkreath Ruins	None
	Otar	Ragnvald	Dungeon Quest: Sarcophagus of Ragnvald*
	Nahkriin	Skuldafn	Main Quest: The World Eater's Eyrie
	Hevnoraak	Valthume	Dungeon Quest: Evil in Waiting
	Volsung	Volskygge	None

➤ **Kavohzein's Fang**

> **NOTE** For more information on Dragon Priests, consult Side Quest: Masks of the Dragon Priests.*

Scavenging the Scales: Now that you have the dagger, you need to find a dragon. If you haven't completed Main Quest: Dragon Rising, do so now. Otherwise:

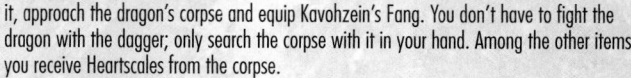

Battle a dragon with any and all offensive weaponry you have. After you kill it, approach the dragon's corpse and equip Kavohzein's Fang. You don't have to fight the dragon with the dagger; only search the corpse with it in your hand. Among the other items, you receive Heartscales from the corpse.

Or, simply return to any dragon you've previously killed, and search the corpse. This is a much quicker and easier option!

➤ **Heartscales**

◊ **OBJECTIVE:** Return to Tolfdir

Quest Conclusion

Meet Tolfdir again, and inform him that you have the dragon Heartscales that he requires. He is most excited about this and crafts a brand-new spell.

➤ **Spell:** Dragonskin

Postquest Activities

Along with the Dragonskin spell, Tolfdir now has the following spell for sale, should you wish to purchase it:

➤ **Spell:** Mass Paralysis

THIEVES GUILD QUESTS

OVERVIEW

▷ Optimal Quest Start

The Thieves Guild Quests begin when you arrive at Riften for the first time. You can join the Guild whenever you like, although Stealth-focused characters may want to join sooner rather than later to gain access to this ready source of missions and trainers. Most of the other characters will encounter the Guild much later, as part of Main Quest: A Cornered Rat.

> **NOTE** **Cross-Referencing:** Do you want to see maps and learn more about the traps, non-quest-related items, collectibles, crafting areas, and other important rooms of note in every location during these quests? Then cross-reference the location you travel to with the information on that location contained in this guide's Atlas.

▷ Sanctuary: The Ragged Flagon, under Riften

The Ratway's main entrance, under the marketplace.

The Ragged Flagon, a hub of thievery and camaraderie.

The Ratway is the underbelly of Riften, both literally and figuratively. It is a cross-section of old avenues, buildings, and catacombs buried beneath the shifting surface of the city. After navigating these treacherous tunnels, fending off beggars, muggers, and Skeevers, you reach the Ragged Flagon, where mead and machinations run wild. The Ragged Flagon is retrofitted into the Cistern located beneath the well in the center of Riften's marketplace; it's the market beneath the market. This is the central part of the Ratway, and offers access into the Warrens (where only the most deranged of madfolk dwell) and the inner chambers of the Cistern.

The Cistern, where the senior Guild members reside.

Currently hidden in the woodland south of Riften, away from those who aren't blessed by Nocturnal herself, Nightingale Hall is the source of power and residence for the Nightingales, a strange and secretive subsect of the Thieves Guild. No one knows quite what these powerful individuals are up to, but many scholars have speculated that Nightingales carry out the wishes of Nocturnal.

▷ Important Characters

Patron: Nocturnal

Nocturnal, the Mistress of Shadows, is the daedric lord of twilight and shadow and the patron of thieves and gamblers, and influences luck throughout the realm. Her passiveness in the affairs of man only deepen her mystery. On the occasions where she deals directly with mortals, such as in the case of the Nightingales, she usually refers to everything in almost businesslike terms, calling oaths "transactions" and making "deals" with her followers.

Guild Master: Mercer Frey

Mercer grew up with Delvin Mallory in the Guild but climbed the ladder a little faster and was able to attain his rank in the Guild through manipulation and skill. He is the current head of the Thieves Guild of Skyrim. Frey is very clever, and even though he is a bit older, he is certainly not weak, maintaining a calm veneer and never appearing troubled or agitated.

Guild Second: Brynjolf

Brynjolf is a go-between, passing Mercer Frey's rulings down to the newer recruits, whom he mentors and is fiercely proud of. He is extremely loyal to the Thieves Guild and has a reputation for being a problem solver, especially within Riften, where he maintains an excellent rapport with those who cooperate with them. When not in the Guild itself, he is often at the Ragged Flagon or the marketplace topside, scoping out possibilities for new recruits.

Former Guild Second (Outcast): Karliah

Karliah, a female Dunmer, was exiled from Riften after being accused of murdering Gallus. Her exile was self-imposed, under duress. She has been keeping an ear open for the right opportunity to arise and repay certain Guild members for their treachery. At first glance, Karliah is very cold and withdrawn. She isn't used to much company, keeping herself in isolation. But those who warm to her will find Karliah to be quite cunning and agile.

Former Guild Master (Deceased): Gallus Desidenius

Gallus was Mercer Frey's predecessor as Guild Master for the Thieves Guild in Skyrim. He was also a member of the Nightingale Trinity along with Karliah. Gallus was killed under suspicious circumstances.

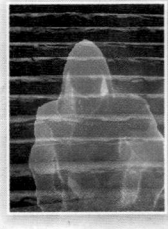

Guild Third: Delvin Mallory

Delvin grew up in Riften's Honorhall Orphanage. He was taken in by Gallus, but Delvin accidentally killed a man while on a robbery. Gallus arranged to have Delvin stay with the Dark Brotherhood, and he remained in hiding in their sanctuary for a year. While there, Delvin gained a new respect for the shadowy organization. After the death was long forgotten, Delvin Mallory returned to Riften, and the embrace of the Thieves Guild, but never forgot his friends in the Dark Brotherhood (and his lover, Astrid).

➤ **Additional Jobs Giver**
➤ **Fence**
➤ **Trainer (Stealth: Master):** Delvin Mallory

Guild Third: Vex

One of the newer members of the Thieves Guild, Vex is quiet and rarely shares in the normal camaraderie of her fellow guildmates. Since she refuses to give her real name and based on her actions, others began to call her "Vex." She is an exceptional thief and is well aware that her behavior alienates her. And she likes it that way. Of all the Guild members, she is the best combatant (save for Mercer Frey). Accosting her in the Ragged Flagon was the last mistake several of its non-Guild denizens ever made.

➤ **Additional Jobs Giver**
➤ **Trainer (Lockpicking: Master):** Vex

Guild Matron: Maven Black-Briar

A powerful businesswoman, Maven is virtually unapproachable and elitist. Maven's wealth, power, and influence in Riften make her an important asset to the Thieves Guild. She holds the actual pulse of Riften within her crushing grasp; nothing gets done without her say-so. She's well connected within the Empire and Skyrim alike. Anyone who crosses her usually ends up dead or in prison—even her son, Sibbi Black-Briar.

Guild Member: Etienne Rarnis

Defiant, tough, but ultimately broken by the Thalmor, Etienne was responsible for revealing the location of Esbern's hideout during Main Quest: Diplomatic Immunity. He seeks revenge on the man that caused his arrest; a ne'er-do-well spy named Gissur.

Guild Member: Dirge

Dirge is a hulking behemoth of an Imperial who serves as the bouncer and general crowd control for the Ragged Flagon. Dirge earned his nickname because his voice is the last thing people hear before they die. He has been good friends with Vekel the Man for years.

Guild Member: Vipir the Fleet

Vipir earned his name from the speed at which he can run and outmaneuver armored opponents. He plays to his strength and is most adept at pickpocketing and snatch-and-grab robberies. Of all the Thieves Guild members, Vipir is the most down-to-earth. He rarely acts condescendingly and is never overly rude or brash, but he can still handle himself when backed into a corner. He's quite approachable and excellent for learning what's new around the Guild.

➤ **Trainer (Pickpocket: Master):** Vipir the Fleet

Guild Member: Niruin

Niruin wandered into the Ragged Flagon with a well-worn travel cloak and a huge sack of coin that he "gifted" to Mercer Frey. He grew up in Valenwood as the son of a very wealthy Wood Elf Lord but very quickly grew tired of the pomp and circumstance that was expected of him. Thinking himself quite cavalier, he raided his father's treasury and joined the Guild but possesses very little aptitude for actual theft. The only thing that has kept Niruin in the Guild's good graces is his gift of gab.

➤ **Trainer (Archery: Master):** Niruin

Guild Member: Sapphire

Sapphire (the name she goes by within the Guild) left the Dark Brotherhood several years ago to satisfy her lust for wealth. Joining the Thieves Guild, she instantly became a natural at larceny, specializing in lifting the valuable (and favored) gemstones bearing her name. Sapphire is extraordinarily withdrawn, spending her time day training, always honing her skills with both the bow and the blade.

Guild Member: Cynric Endell

Cynric is an older member of the Thieves Guild, joining shortly after Brynjolf and Delvin Mallory. He's quiet, reserved, and generally not as boisterous as the rest of his fellow Guild members, but once in conversation, his extreme cynicism surfaces. His specialty is break-ins, which he executes with his superior lockpicking abilities. He's never been a problem for the Guild but tends to shy away from leadership, explaining why Vex surpassed him as a Guild Third.

Guild Member: Thrynn

Thrynn ran with a group of bandits for years until they forced him to slaughter a farming village full of women and children. He couldn't take that way of life anymore. He wandered Skyrim and bumped into Brynjolf in Riften. Despite his attitude, Brynjolf saw Thrynn's potential with a blade and allowed him to join. Thrynn has little experience as a stealthy thief. However, when the Guild needs a troubleshooter and brute force is necessary, Thrynn is generally the first one selected to carry out the assignment.

Guild Member: Rune

As a child, Rune was rescued from a sinking ship in the Sea of Ghosts. He was taken in by a fisherman who discovered a small stone covered in unidentifiable runes. It took Rune several weeks to recover, only to discover that he couldn't remember who he was. Shown the mysterious stone, Rune vowed someday to discover his identity. He lived a happy childhood with the fisherman. When he reached the age of 16, Rune set out on adventure and met Brynjolf.

Guild Member: Garthar

Appearing in the Guild with an attitude problem but ready to help out and make a bit of money, Garthar considers himself a problem-solver. When something needs to get done and heads need to be knocked together, he's the person others call upon. Even though he has a large frame and looks like quite the brute, Garthar is actually rather smart and is quite adept at stealth, lockpicking, and pickpocketing; he is quite a unique asset for the Thieves Guild.

> **NOTE** Garthar appears once your Thieves Guild growth reaches Stage 3‡.

NOTE ‡ For more information on the "Stages" of the Thieves Guild, refer to the section City Influence Quests: Ultimate Rewards on page 230.

Guild Member: Ravyn Imyan

Ravyn was a member of the Morag Tong (Morrowind's assassin's guild and bitter rivals of the Dark Brotherhood) and left it when the Red Mountain erupted and the great evacuation of Morrowind occurred. He is in the Guild biding his time until the Tong one day re-forms.

NOTE Ravyn Imyan appears once your Thieves Guild growth reaches Stage 4‡.

Guild Vendor: Vekel the Man

A sly Nord who owns and operates the Ragged Flagon tavern, Vekel was once a resident of the Honorhall Orphanage and continually got into trouble for concocting strange and powerful alcoholic drinks that kept his fellow orphans in a near continual stupor. He eventually ran away and saved enough from his burgeoning pickpocketing career to afford the tavern. He is loved and respected by his fellow thieves, partly because of his confidence, but also because of his amazing skills as a brewer.

➤ **Vendor (Bartender)**

Guild Vendor: Syndus

Syndus has strung bows for as long as he could remember. He has spent most of his life plying his trade in various places all over Tamriel, until finally settling in Solitude. After the city fell back under the Thieves Guild's influence, Syndus decided to apply his knowledge of the ranged weapons for the darker side of the law and made contact with the Guild hoping to strike up a relationship.

➤ **Vendor (Fletcher)**

 NOTE Syndus appears once your Thieves Guild growth reaches Stage 1‡.

Guild Vendor: Herluin Lothaire

Herluin is young but is a very sharp apothecary with unique skills who can aid the Thieves Guild through his unusual concoctions. He is always preoccupied, a bit off into space when being spoken to, but that shouldn't be mistaken for absentmindedness.

➤ **Vendor (Apothecary)**

 NOTE Herluin Lothaire appears once your Thieves Guild growth reaches Stage 2‡.

Guild Vendor: Arnskar Ember-Master

Arnskar's imposing appearance and boisterous Nordic temperament masks a shrewd and cheery man with an impressive skill at the forge.

➤ **Vendor (Blacksmith)**

 NOTE Arnskar Ember-Master appears once your Thieves Guild growth reaches Stage 3‡.

Guild Vendor: Vanryth Gatharian

Vanryth is the Guild's light armor vendor. He's dismissive and a bit rude but is an expert craftsman when it comes to armor and armor repair.

➤ **Vendor (Light Armor)**

 NOTE Vanryth Gatharian appears once your Thieves Guild growth reaches Stage 4‡.

Guild Fence (Riften): Tonilia

Tonilia is a fetching Redguard who is the Thieves Guild's main fence. She's pretty, sure of herself, and quite cocky at times.

➤ **Fence**

 NOTE Tonilia appears immediately but becomes a Fence after you complete Thieves Guild Quest: Loud and Clear.

Guild Fence (Solitude): Gulum-Ei

Gulum-Ei has long been a contact for the Thieves Guild in the East Empire Company but has become quite greedy and rarely pays the proper respects to the Guild any longer. He's greedy and has set up an entire smuggling operation of his own in Brinewater Grotto.

➤ **Fence (Solitude)**

 NOTE Gulum-Ei becomes a Fence if he survives Thieves Guild Quest: Scoundrel's Folly.

Guild Fence (Whiterun): Mallus Maccius

Mallus left Cyrodiil many years ago to seek his fortunes in Skyrim. All he got for his trouble was an empty coin purse and a menial job at the Honningbrew Meadery. The owner, Sabjorn, saw an opportunity to exploit Mallus when he walked through the door to the meadery that first day, a way to place poor Mallus in debt and make him work it off very slowly over time. Mallus fell in with Maven Black-Briar, and together they hatched a plan to take Sabjorn out of the picture.

➤ **Fence (Whiterun)**

 NOTE Mallus Maccius becomes a Fence if he survives Thieves Guild Quest: Dampened Spirits.

Guild Fence (Winterhold): Enthir

Enthir is the "man who knows how to get things" in the College. While the College has very flexible rules on what's acceptable research and what's not, there are some reagents and spell components they don't acquire through exactly legal means. Enthir, working with Birna in Winterhold, is the mage who takes care of that. He fancies himself a ladies' man and believes that Birna helps him because she's in love with him. Enthir and Gallus were good friends for a very long time (Gallus always fancied himself as somewhat of a scholar).

➤ **Fence (Winterhold)**

 NOTE Enthir becomes a Fence once you complete Thieves Guild Quest: Hard Answers.

Guild Fence (Windhelm): Niranye

A beautiful High Elf who runs a stall in the Stone Quarter, many attribute her fortune to membership in the Thieves Guild, so they keep a wide berth. In actuality, Niranye is the Fence for the Summerset Shadows Thieves Guild. Linwe is the leader, and they maintain a small headquarters of about a dozen Altmer thieves in Uttering Hills Cave.

➤ **Fence (Windhelm)**

 NOTE Niranye becomes a Fence if she survives (and once you complete) City Influence Quest: Summerset Shadows.

Guild Fence (Markarth): Endon

Endon is a silversmith in Markarth, like his forefathers and mothers before him. He is proud of the long cosmopolitan tradition in Markarth (unlike most of the rest of Skyrim), which is not widely known, and he deplores the sad state that the feuding of the Nords and Reachmen (known as the Forsworn) has brought the city. Endon works out of his small but tidy house in Dryside. His wife, Kerah, works with him, and also sells their jewelry in the market during the day. His daughter Adara is his apprentice.

➤ **Fence (Markarth)**

 NOTE Endon becomes a Fence if he survives (and once you complete) City Influence Quest: Silver Lining.

Guild Fence (Caravan): Ri'saad

Ri'saad is the patriarch of Skyrim's Khajiit Caravans. A skilled merchant and gifted leader, he has organized a small syndicate of independent merchant caravans that travel the roads and cities of Skyrim.

Guild Fence (Caravan): Atahba

Ri'saad's first wife is a shrewd businesswoman in her own right. She's with Ri'saad mostly because he's the shrewdest Khajiit in Skyrim and had more money than anyone else she knew, but she's also grown to love him over the years. She refuses to talk about her past.

➤ **Fence (Caravan)**

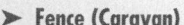 **NOTE** Ri'saad and Atahba become a Fence once your Thieves Guild growth reaches Stage 3‡ and you complete Quest: Moon Sugar Rush*.

Guild Fence (Caravan): Ma'jhad

Ma'jahd is a bodyguard in Ma'dran's caravan, which travels the roads between Windhelm and Solitude. He is a seasoned safecracker, and is always willing to train customers in the fine art of Lockpicking.

➤ **Fence (Caravan)**
➤ **Trainer (Lockpicking: Expert): Ma'jhad**

NOTE Ma'jhad becomes a Fence once your Thieves Guild growth reaches Stage 3‡ and you complete Quest: Moon Sugar Rush*.

Guild Fence (Caravan): Zaynabi

Struck by wanderlust, Zaynabi has traveled far and wide. She's seen her fair share of troubles, but nothing seems to phase her go-lucky attitude. She has become quite the archer. She occasionally freelances out her scouting services and offers her services as a bowyer and fletcher.

➤ **Fence (Caravan)**

 NOTE Zaynabi becomes a Fence once your Thieves Guild growth reaches Stage 3‡ and you complete Quest: Moon Sugar Rush*.

The following table details the names, occupations, and quest prerequisites (or Stage that the Thieves Guild needs to be at) for allies of the Thieves Guild to arrive at the Ragged Flagon or Cistern or to set up in a Hold City:

✔	NAME OF NEW GUILD MEMBER (AND LOCATION)	OCCUPATION	PREREQUISITE
	Tonilia	Fence	Thieves Guild Quest: Loud and Clear
	Gulum-Ei (in Solitude)	Fence	Thieves Guild Quest: Scoundrel's Folly
	Mallus Maccius (in Whiterun)	Fence	Thieves Guild Quest: Dampened Spirits
	Enthir (Winterhold)	Fence	Thieves Guild Quest: Hard Answers
	Niranye (Windhelm)	Fence	City Influence Quest: Summerset Shadows
	Endon (Markarth)	Fence	City Influence Quest: Silver Lining
	Syndus	Vendor (Fletcher)	Stage 1
	Herluin Lothaire	Vendor (Apothecary)	Stage 2

✔	NAME OF NEW GUILD MEMBER (AND LOCATION)	OCCUPATION	PREREQUISITE
	Arnskar Ember-Master	Vendor (Blacksmith)	Stage 3
	Atahba (Caravan)	Fence	Stage 3
	Garthar	Member	Stage 3
	Ma'jhad (Caravan)	Fence	Stage 3
	Ri'saad (Caravan)	Fence	Stage 3
	Zaynabi (Caravan)	Fence	Stage 3
	Ravyn Imyan	Member	Stage 4
	Vanryth Gatharian	Vendor (Light Armor)	Stage 4

In addition to a warm bed and companionship, the main members of this guild of thieves and their associates are extremely talented in particular skills.

✔	SKILL	RANK	TRAINER
	Archery	Master	Niruin
	Pickpocket	Master	Vipir the Fleet
	Lockpicking	Master	Vex

✔	SKILL	RANK	TRAINER
	Lockpicking	Expert	Ma'jhad
	Sneak	Master	Delvin Mallory

 Guild Chests

In addition to your kinsmen and an influx of like-minded ne'er-do-wells joining the Guild as news spreads of its power and influence, there are other advantages of being a Thieves Guild member. In the Cistern, there are a group of "Guild Chests" that you can loot: They contain useful items such as lockpicks, potions, and gold. But the real advantage is that you can use the chests to store your items, without fear of them being lost. Use this as a dumping ground for extra equipment you wish to sell, craft, or otherwise dispose of.

Mercer's Bookcases

The shelving behind Mercer's desk in the Cistern slowly fills with trophies relevant to your exploits and with any Larceny Targets you may recover and sell to Delvin. As you finish the Additional Jobs that Vex and Delvin give you, trophies of recovered items begin to fill the shelves too:

Jeweled Candlesticks appear after you complete five jobs.

An Ornate Drinking Horn appears after you complete 15 jobs.

A Golden Ship Model appears after you complete 25 jobs.

A Golden Urn appears after you complete 35 jobs.

A Jeweled Goblet appears after you complete 45 jobs.

A Jeweled Pitcher appears after you complete 55 jobs.

A Jeweled Flagon appears after you complete 75 jobs.

A safe appears along the back wall, next to the bookcases, after you complete 125 jobs. It contains gems, gold, and some very useful customized Thief potions!

If you complete Thieves Guild Radiant Quest: No Stone Unturned, the Crown will appear on the bust and pedestal behind the desk, between the bookshelves.

If you complete Thieves Guild Quest: Darkness Returns, a Shrine of Nocturnal appears in the Cistern. This is the same as the other temple shrines scattered across Skyrim, which cure diseases. This bestows a Sneak Blessing.

If you become the Guild Master, a tribute chest appears in front of the desk in the Cistern. It contains gold and gems and is periodically restocked.

The Guild has four visible Stages of growth. As the Stages progress, you will witness more opulent furnishings; additional boxes, barrels, and banners; and the occasional new Guild member. A new vendor appears in the Ragged Flagon in an empty niche, one per Stage.

Alas, no one in the Thieves Guild is the marrying type.

There are 29 different quests available within the Thieves Guild. Twelve of these are Critical Path Quests, while 17 are Radiant Quests or Additional Objectives.

Critical Path Quests

Simply referred to as "quests," these are the main quests you attempt. All but the first quest require one or more prerequisites, as shown in the following table:

✓	QUEST NAME	PREREQUISITES
	Thieves Guild Quest: A Chance Arrangement	None
	Thieves Guild Quest: Taking Care of Business	Complete Thieves Guild Quest: A Chance Arrangement
	Thieves Guild Quest: Loud and Clear	Complete Thieves Guild Quest: Taking Care of Business
	Thieves Guild Quest: Meet the Family*	Complete Thieves Guild Quest: Loud and Clear
	Thieves Guild Quest: Dampened Spirits	Complete Thieves Guild Quest: Loud and Clear
	Thieves Guild Quest: Scoundrel's Folly	Complete Thieves Guild Quest: Dampened Spirits

✓	QUEST NAME	PREREQUISITES
	Thieves Guild Quest: Speaking with Silence	Complete Thieves Guild Quest: Scoundrel's Folly
	Thieves Guild Quest: Hard Answers	Complete Thieves Guild Quest: Speaking with Silence
	Thieves Guild Quest: The Pursuit	Complete Thieves Guild Quest: Hard Answers
	Thieves Guild Quest: Trinity Restored	Complete Thieves Guild Quest: The Pursuit
	Thieves Guild Quest: Blindsighted	Complete Trinity Restored
	Thieves Guild Quest: Darkness Returns	Complete Blindsighted

Radiant Quests

These are usually smaller quests and are split into three subsections. There are "Radiant Quests," which you can opt to attempt and are grouped together as they affect your relationships with the Guild. There are additional objectives that you can complete to strengthen the ties the Thieves Guild have across Skyrim. Finally, there are City Influence Quests (culminating in you becoming the Guild Leader), which complete your Guild domination across this realm, as merchants and new thieves flock to your sewer.

In some cases, the Additional Objectives are randomized. The prerequisites required to begin every Radiant Quest is in the following table:

✓	QUEST NAME	PREREQUISITES
	Radiant Quest: No Stone Unturned	None
	Radiant Quest: Reparations‡	Complete Thieves Guild Quest: Taking Care of Business
	Radiant Quest: Moon Sugar Rush*	Complete Thieves Guild Quest: Meet the Family
	Radiant Quest: Armor Exchange*	Complete Thieves Guild Quest: Scoundrel's Folly
	Radiant Quest: The Litany of Larceny*	Complete Thieves Guild Quest: Meet the Family (and finding a Larceny Target in a subsequent quest)

✓	QUEST NAME	PREREQUISITES
	Additional Job: The Numbers Job	Complete Thieves Guild Quest: Meet the Family
	Additional Job: The Fishing Job	Complete Thieves Guild Quest: Meet the Family
	Additional Job: The Bedlam Job	Complete Thieves Guild Quest: Meet the Family
	Additional Job: The Burglary Job	Complete Thieves Guild Quest: Meet the Family
	Additional Job: The Shill Job	Complete Thieves Guild Quest: Meet the Family
	Additional Job: The Sweep Job	Complete Thieves Guild Quest: Meet the Family
	Additional Job: The Heist Job	Complete Thieves Guild Quest: Meet the Family
	City Influence Quest: Silver Lining	Complete Thieves Guild Quest: Meet the Family and 5 Additional Jobs in Markarth
	City Influence Quest: The Dainty Sload	Complete Thieves Guild Quest: Meet the Family and 5 Additional Jobs in Solitude
	City Influence Quest: Imitation Amnesty	Complete Thieves Guild Quest: Meet the Family and 5 Additional Jobs in Whiterun
	City Influence Quest: Summerset Shadows	Complete Thieves Guild Quest: Meet the Family and 5 Additional Jobs in Windhelm
	Leadership Quest: Under New Management	Complete Thieves Guild Quest: Darkness Returns and all four City Influence Quests

NOTE ‡ Indicates you must have been kicked out of the Guild to begin this Radiant Quest.

NOTE ✱ = Indicates the quest name does not appear in your Quest menu; check the "Miscellaneous" area for objectives that may appear.

PREREQUISITES: None

INTERSECTING QUESTS: Main Quest: A Cornered Rat, Thieves Guild Quest: Taking Care of Business, Thieves Guild Quest: No Stone Unturned

LOCATIONS: Riften, The Bee and Barb, Marketplace

CHARACTERS: Brand-Shei, Brynjolf, Madesi,

ENEMIES: None

◊ **OBJECTIVES:** Meet Brynjolf during daytime, Steal Madesi's Ring, Plant Madesi's Ring, Speak to Brynjolf

Sizing up Your Mark

The first time you visit the Bee and Barb or look around the marketplace in Riften, a man named Brynjolf strikes up a conversation with you. He has an errand he wants your help with, and will reward you with gold.

He tells you to pilfer a silver ring from Madesi's stall in the marketplace while he creates a distraction. You are then to place it in the pocket of a Dark Elf vendor named Brand-Shei. If you're caught, you're on your own; if you succeed, Brynjolf will have some better-paying schemes. If you've met Brynjolf during the evening or night, he'll be waiting between eight in the morning and eight in the evening for you. If you met Brynjolf during the night, wait until daylight and meet up again.

◊ **OBJECTIVE:** Meet Brynjolf during daytime
♦ **TARGET:** Brynjolf, marketplace in Riften
◊ **OBJECTIVE:** Steal Madesi's Ring
♦ **TARGET:** Madesi's stand, marketplace in Riften

Making Your Mark

Brynjolf is waiting for you by his plaza stand, where he's about to hawk his "amazing" Falmerblood Elixir. Naturally, this patter is designed to draw a crowd (including Madesi and Brand-Shei), allowing you to quickly move around the plaza's perimeter stone wall and crouch behind Madesi's stall.

(Lockpick [Novice]) Produce your lockpicks and unlock the sliding door under the stall counter; then unlock Madesi's strongbox and quickly rummage around inside. You can help yourself to any of the items here, but the valuable you're concerned with is Madesi's Silver Ring. Steal it quickly, before any of the city guards spot you. Attempt this Lockpick only after any city guards pass you by, and you're hidden from view while sneaking.

 **Madesi's Silver Ring**

◊ **OBJECTIVE:** Plant Madesi's Ring
♦ **TARGET:** Brand-Shei, marketplace in Riften

Creep around so you're unseen by most of the assembled beggars and storekeepers, and position yourself behind Brand-Shei.

(Sneak and Pickpocket) You must now "reverse-pickpocket" the Dark Elf. This involves Pickpocketing, choosing your own Apparel menu, selecting Madesi's Silver Ring, and giving it to Brand-Shei to finish the technique, without being seen by anyone. As this is likely your first attempt at such an action, you have a slight boost to your Pickpocket skill, but don't expect this to happen again!

If you're successful, Brand-Shei is mistaken for a thief and hauled away to Riften prison. Your paths may cross again in the future....

◊ **OBJECTIVE:** Speak to Brynjolf
♦ **TARGET:** Brynjolf, marketplace in Riften

CAUTION If you're arrested, you leave Riften, wait more than half a day to complete Brynjolf's objective, or you murder someone during his distraction. Thieves Guild Quest: A Chance Arrangement still completes. However, there is no reward, and Brynjolf isn't pleased with your inadequacy. This is not the way to impress a future mentor!

Quest Conclusion

Speak to Brynjolf after the misdirection goes down, and he congratulates (and rewards) you if the plan was a success. You receive no monetary gain if you failed. Then he mentions his organization has been having a run of bad luck, but quickly mentions that there's more money to earn if you can handle it. Reply that you can, and Brynjolf recommends you meet him at the Ragged Flagon tavern, deep inside Riften's subterranean Ratway.

➤ **100 gold pieces**

Postquest Activities

Thieves Guild Quest: Taking Care of Business is now active. After this quest concludes, stay for a moment and watch the guard arrest Brand-Shei. He's hauled off toward Mistveil Keep and spends a week there before being released back into Riften. Visit him during this time if you like, but he doesn't have much to say to the likes of you!

If you encountered a man named Maul close to Riften's north gate, you have another chance to get to know the Thieves Guild, but only if you're carrying an Unusual Gem you may have found scattered around Skyrim. Consult Thieves Guild Quest: No Stone Unturned for more information. Maul points you toward Brynjolf if you're not yet a member of the Thieves Guild.

TAKING CARE OF BUSINESS

PREREQUISITES: Complete Thieves Guild Quest: A Chance Arrangement
INTERSECTING QUESTS: Thieves Guild Quest: Loud and Clear
LOCATIONS: Riften, The Bee and Barb, Haelga's Bunkhouse, Pawned Prawn, Ragged Flagon, Ratway
CHARACTERS: Bersi Honey-Hand, Brynjolf, Haelga, Keerava, Talen-Jei, Vekel the Man,
ENEMIES: Drahff, Hewnon Black-Skeever
◊ **OBJECTIVES:** Locate Brynjolf at the Ragged Flagon, Collect Keerava's debt, Collect Bersi Honey-Hand's debt, Collect Haelga's debt, (Optional) Use Talen-Jei to get to Keerava, (Optional) Smash Bersi's prized Dwarven Urn, (Optional) Steal Haelga's Statue of Dibella, Return to Brynjolf

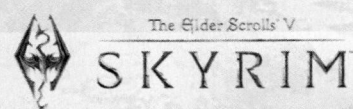

To the Tavern

◊ **OBJECTIVE:** Locate Brynjolf at the Ragged Flagon

♦ **TARGET:** Ragged Flagon, in the Ratway in Riften

Begin with this objective already active. Search for the entrance to the Ratway, which is under the Grand Plaza by the water's edge, on the town's south side. Once you're through the iron gate, prepare to stumble across a couple of inept thugs looking for a victim to mug. You can sneak by them if you wait until Drahff patrols the Ratway entrance and Hewnon has his back to you.

Now continue through this small maze of interlocking sewage tunnels. Watch for a hanging oil trap and a bear trap along the way. If your Lockpick skill is high enough, there's a chamber to check out, but your main purpose is finding the Ragged Flagon.

The tavern has a unique floorplan, being constructed within the space below Riften's central well. When you spot Brynjolf, he is conversing with the barkeep, Vekel the Man, about Brynjolf's predicament with his "organization." Speak to Brynjolf, and he asks if you'd be interested in handling a few deadbeats for him. Do a good job, and Brynjolf predicts a permanent place in his guild. Ask how to collect the dues owed, and Brynjolf recommends anything short of killing them.

◊ **OBJECTIVE:** Collect Keerava's debt

♦ **TARGET:** Keerava, in the Bee and Barb in Riften

◊ **OBJECTIVE:** Collect Bersi Honey-Hand's debt

♦ **TARGET:** Bersi Honey-Hand, in the Pawned Prawn, in Riften

◊ **OBJECTIVE:** Collect Haelga's debt

♦ **TARGET:** Haelga, in Haelga's Bunkhouse in Riften

(Optional) Remain in the Ragged Flagon for a moment and quiz Brynjolf on each of the targets to gain more information. You learn about Keerava's lover Talen-Jei, Bersi's love of dwarven pottery, and Haelga's devotion to the goddess Dibella. Be sure your quest updates with the following:

◊ **OBJECTIVE:** (Optional) Use Talen-Jei to get to Keerava

◊ **OBJECTIVE:** (Optional) Smash Bersi's prized Dwarven Urn

◊ **OBJECTIVE:** (Optional) Steal Haelga's Statue of Dibella

Shopkeeper Shakedowns

Return to the surface, ensuring you activate the lever in the Ratway that lowers the bridge, enabling a fast exit. Now visit each of the three shopkeepers on Brynjolf's list, while remembering the following:

1. You can approach any of the three shopkeepers in any order. Apply the information you've learned...

2. You may impose your unarmed prowess against them but can do so only the first time you talk to your target. Be sure you begin this from a conversation, or you'll have the whole town against you!

3. Once two of the three shopkeepers have paid up, the third has heard of your intimidation and hands over their payment without any fuss.

4. You must collect all three payments before returning to Brynjolf to complete the quest. Brynjolf is essentially expecting 300 gold. If you spend some of the payments the shopkeepers gave you (dropping your total below 300), Brynjolf won't be satisfied until you bring the entire amount. No skimming!

Keerava's Comeuppance

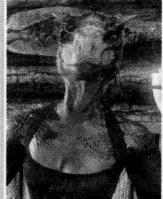

Enter the Bee and Barb, and venture toward Keerava. You may:

(Brawl) Speak to her before pummeling her with your fists. Once she's knocked down, she pays up.

Or tell her you've finished wasting your time talking to her. Then seek out Talen-Jei.

Talen-Jei is usually inside the tavern, close to his lover. Converse with him and tell him to talk some sense into Keerava. He lets you in on the location of Keerava's family. This is something you can use to your advantage. Return to her and threaten to visit "that farm in Morrowind." Her bravery falters. She begs you not to hurt her family and then pays up.

➤ **100 gold pieces**

Bersi's Reimbursement

Enter the Pawned Prawn and locate Bersi Honey-Hand at the counter. You can:

(Brawl) Tell him to shut his mouth, and beat him down with your fists until he pays his dues.

Or tell him you've had enough of this banter and look around the room for something to break.

Behind you is a rather fine example of dwarven pottery. Produce your favored smashing implement and strike the urn until it shatters. Ignore the yells from Bersi and his wife. When the pottery is in pieces, return to Bersi and ask if he wants anything else broken. This does the trick, and he hands over the gold he owes.

➤ **100 gold pieces**

Haelga's Hostage

Step into Haelga's Bunkhouse and find the proprietor. You're able to:

(Brawl) Tell her that she'll have to pay in more than just coin, and beat her into agreement.

Or inform her that the Guild has run out of patience with her. Gaze around the interior for something to steal.

On the wall near the door is a small shrine dedicated to the goddess of women, Dibella. Steal the Statue of Dibella, then return to Haelga and threaten to drop it down a well. Soon the monies owed appears in your hands.

➤ **100 gold pieces**

Quest Conclusion

Find Brynjolf back in the Ragged Flagon. He's impressed you managed to both acquire the gold and keep it "clean"—not resorting to bloodshed. In return for your services, he gives you a cut of the gold you've collected and offers you the following:

➤ **One Poison** [random]
➤ **One Healing potion** [random and leveled]
➤ **Fortify Stealth Skill potion** [random and leveled]

◇ **OBJECTIVE:** Return to Brynjolf
♦ **TARGET:** Ragged Flagon, in the Ratway in Riften

TIP **The Ripper of Riften:** Remember all that talk about keeping the targets alive? Well, you can completely disregard that and murder any or all of the targets! Aside from forfeiting the potion rewards, you receive a severe dressing-down from Brynjolf, who takes exception to your actions. But the quest still completes.

Brynjolf recognizes the telltale signs of a practiced thief in you and thinks you'll fit in with the rest of the team. After telling you not to worry about the rough patch the Guild has been in, Brynjolf offers to show you what the Thieves Guild is all about.

Postquest Activities

Thieves Guild Quest: Loud and Clear is now active.

LOUD AND CLEAR

PREREQUISITES: Complete Thieves Guild Quest: Taking Care of Business
INTERSECTING QUESTS: Thieves Guild Quest: Additional Jobs, Thieves Guild Quest: Larceny Targets, Thieves Guild Quest: Dampened Spirits
LOCATIONS: Goldenglow Estate, Goldenglow Estate Basement, Goldenglow Estate Second Floor, Riften, Ragged Flagon, Cistern, Ratway
CHARACTERS: Brynjolf, Delvin Mallory, Maven Black-Briar, Mercer Frey, Tonilia, Vex,
ENEMIES: Aringoth, Mercenaries, Skeevers
◇ **OBJECTIVES:** Follow Brynjolf, Listen to Mercer Frey, Talk to Brynjolf, Burn three beehives, Clear out Aringoth's safe, (Optional) Speak to Vex about, Goldenglow Estate, Meet the Family: Learn more about the Thieves Guild from Vex, Meet the Family: Learn more about the Thieves Guild from Delvin, Meet the Family: Retrieve your Thieves Guild Armor from Tonilia, (Optional) Enter Goldenglow using the sewer, (Optional) Obtain the key to Aringoth's safe, Return to Brynjolf

▶ Do as You're Told, and Keep Your Blade Clean

◇ **OBJECTIVE:** Follow Brynjolf
♦ **TARGET:** Ragged Flagon, in the Ratway in Riften

You begin this quest with the previous objective already active. Follow Brynjolf into the Ragged Flagon's Cistern. The time has come to meet the rest of his team, including the leader of this small operation—Mercer Frey.

◇ **OBJECTIVE:** Listen to Mercer Frey
◇ **OBJECTIVE:** Talk to Brynjolf
♦ **TARGET:** Mercer Frey and Brynjolf, in the Cistern in Riften

Mercer Frey is initially suspicious of you and tells you that acting like a maverick will result in a docking of your pay. You may be with thieves, but there is a code to uphold. Once you agree, Mercer Frey has a job for you, one that Brynjolf is worried may be much too difficult. It involves infiltrating Goldenglow Estate, just outside of town; even one of Mercer's own found this job too dangerous. The farm's proprietor is no longer honoring his bargain with the Guild; you must go there to teach him a lesson. Brynjolf suggests you speak to more of the Guild members to gain a better perspective of both your task and the Guild in general.

◇ **OBJECTIVE:** Burn three beehives
◇ **OBJECTIVE:** Clear out Aringoth's safe
♦ **TARGET:** Beehives, Goldenglow Estate

Ask Brynjolf about the Goldenglow job. The farm is owned by some smart-mouthed Wood Elf named Aringoth. Honey production is a valuable commodity on the farm, so setting fire to some

of the hives there is your first instruction. Then clear out the safe inside the main house. You can't set the whole place ablaze, though, as an important client with ties to Goldenglow Estate would be furious. Ask for more information, and Brynjolf mentions the estate is guarded by mercenaries; the entire island is fortified, and Brynjolf recommends you find out more from Vex, who already scouted the area and narrowly missed being killed.

◇ **OBJECTIVE:** (Optional) Speak to Vex about Goldenglow Estate
◇ **OBJECTIVE:** Meet the Family: Learn more about the Thieves Guild from Vex
◇ **OBJECTIVE:** Meet the Family: Learn more about the Thieves Guild from Delvin
◇ **OBJECTIVE:** Meet the Family: Retrieve your Thieves Guild Armor from Tonilia
♦ **TARGET:** Ragged Flagon, in the Ratway in Riften

Back in the Ragged Flagon, seek out Vex, who sees the recent Guild problems as a run of bad luck. You can speak to her about some extra work: This starts the Thieves Guild Quest: Additional Jobs (consult this quest for more information). You can also pay her to train you in Lockpicking if you have the coin. Lastly, if you ask her about Goldenglow, she mentions a sewer access point running under the estate, which could be a more clandestine way of entering the premises.

◇ **OBJECTIVE:** (Optional) Enter Goldenglow using the sewer
♦ **TARGET:** Goldenglow Estate

A few years ago, the Ragged Flagon was as busy as an Imperial City, but speak to Delvin Mallory and he firmly believes a curse was responsible for the Guild's downfall. Speak to him, and he offers you the chance to earn more coin: This starts the Thieves Guild Quest: Additional Jobs (consult this quest for more information). He can also train you in the art of Sneaking, provided you have the gold to pay him.

Speak with Tonilia, who gives a "warts and all" review of this little Guild—you're only as good as the gold you're bringing in. She buys and sells, but on this one occasion, she has something for free; you're given your Thieves Guild attire. You can now begin your first major infiltration!

- ➤ Thieves Guild Boots (Fortify Pickpocket)
- ➤ Thieves Guild Armor (Fortify Carry)
- ➤ Thieves Guild Gloves (Fortify Lockpicking)
- ➤ Thieves Guild Hood (Fortify Speech)

Compare the statistical increases of this attire to your normal apparel and see which you favor; the magical bonuses offered by the Thieves Guild clothing makes them extremely useful.

Goldenglow Estate: Reconnoiter

The Goldenglow Estate consists of three connected islands in the middle of a lake. How you choose to access this location influences how dangerous this task becomes. Bear in mind any or all of the following plans before you set foot on Aringoth's property.

To enter the property, you can:

Slay the gate guard at the main gates and search his corpse for the key to the main gates. Use this to unlock the main gates for an easier way onto the island.

Fire on the mercenaries from a distance and take down any you can before setting foot on the islands.

Swim around to the jetty behind the main building, and sneak up to the house from this point.

Locate the sewer entrance on the northwest side as Vex described. Drop down and follow it to the back entrance of the estate house.

There are other helpful methods of completing this task. You can:

Infiltrate the estate under cover of darkness; this makes you less likely to be spotted by the mercenary guards.

Complete the beehive destruction first, as this lures more mercenaries out of the estate house, helping your main infiltration.

Throw caution to the wind and wade into the establishment. Although not normally tolerated, killing any mercenaries. This isn't a problem.

(Sneak) You may also utilize Sneak throughout this task, creeping around to either estate entrance and moving through the house, launching Sneak attacks on enemies you cannot pass before hiding and continuing on. There is a locked rear entrance to the estate building just near the exit from the sewers. It's a difficult lock but a great way to slip inside unseen.

Beehive Burn

Set the bees ablaze, but don't snuff out all the hives. Do this at any time, but coaxing more mercenaries out of the house before you enter the dwelling means you can fight them in an open area and at distance, which is easier. Burn the hives before or after alerting the mercenaries. You can:

Use a ranged fire attack (such as a fireball or arrow fired from a flame-enchanted bow).

Use a melee-range fire attack (such as a torch).

Continue with this ransacking until three of the hives are alight. Ignore the other hives or face a dock in your reward and an annoyed Brynjolf if you set more than three ablaze.

Sneak to the Safe

> ◊ **OBJECTIVE:** (Optional) Obtain the key to Aringoth's safe
> ♦ **TARGET:** Aringoth, Goldenglow Estate

No matter which route (or entrance) you took to infiltrate the estate house, once inside, an additional objective becomes available: As Aringoth's safe is tricky to unlock, you may wish to seek out Aringoth and take both of his keys. If you want them, head up to the second floor and search for the Wood Elf. You may be able to avoid further bloodshed. You can:

(Persuade) Try a little light threatening to make him hand over the key.

(Fight) Or use violent bloodshed, a normally frowned-upon plan but one sanctioned for this task.

(Sneak) You may also be able to sneak up to his room and pickpocket the key from him.

- ➤ **Goldenglow Cellar Key**
- ➤ **Goldenglow Safe Key**

QUEST: LARCENY TARGET

Aside from helping yourself to any valuables you find throughout your estate infiltration, keep a lookout for your first Larceny Target: The Queen Bee Statue is found on a bedside table upstairs in Aringoth's bedroom. Sell it to Delvin or keep it if you wish. Consult the Thieves Guild Quest: Larceny Targets for further information.

- ➤ **Queen Bee Statue**

If you don't want the hassle of confronting Aringoth for the keys, head to the gate door that leads to the cellar. You can:

(Lockpick [Novice]) Unlock it using your skills.

Or utilize the Goldenglow Cellar Key.

After navigating down more steps and encountering additional mercenaries, you finally locate the safe. You can:

(Lockpick [Expert]) Utilize your talents and open the safe.

Or use the Goldenglow Safe Key, which you pried from Aringoth.

Inside the safe is the Goldenglow Bill of Sale and some gold. Take everything!

- ➤ **Goldenglow Bill of Sale**

> ◊ **OBJECTIVE:** Return to Brynjolf
> ♦ **TARGET:** Ragged Flagon, in the Ratway in Riften

Quest Conclusion

Locate Brynjolf in the Ragged Flagon and hand the Bill of Sale over to him. Assuming you burned the correct number of beehives, he rewards you with gold for your troubles. The Bill of Sale is of particular interest, as it reveals that the estate was purchased by an unidentified buyer who seems to be aligning against the Thieves Guild! The note has a strange dagger symbol on it, but no one is certain what it means. Maven Black-Briar will be furious now that she's been cut out of a deal. Brynjolf rewards you and then tells you it is time to meet the real power behind the Guild.

- ➤ **Leveled gold pieces**

Postquest Activities: Meet the Family

Thieves Guild Quest: Dampened Spirits is now active. After your induction into the Thieves Guild, you are requested to speak to Vex and Delvin Mallory about Thieves Guild Quest: Additional Jobs.

 NOTE ✳ Quest names marked with this symbol do not appear in your Quest Menu list, although objectives may.

Now that Mercer Frey has fully inducted you into the Thieves Guild, there are now several benefits of having close ties to this organization, which are available to you from this point on:

◊ The Caches hidden in Riften are now available. Consult the City Influence Quests: Ultimate Rewards table on page 231 to learn more about these.

◊ The hidden Hall of the Dead Mausoleum entrance for the Thieves Guild is now accessible from the graveyard. Press the button on the face of the mausoleum. The entire slab slides into the wall, leading to some steps to a hatch and into the Cistern. This means you need not traverse the Ratway any longer and can Fast-Travel directly to this location, as it becomes a map marker!

◊ You can now bribe and pay off Guards in The Rift, giving you more options for dealing with any bounties you may acquire. See the Crime and Punishment section on page 39 for details.

◊ You are now part of the Thieves Guild faction! Everything contained within the Cistern (including Guild chests, books, and anything else you may have wanted to steal) can now be looted!

DAMPENED SPIRITS

PREREQUISITES: Complete Thieves Guild Quest: Loud and Clear

INTERSECTING QUESTS: Thieves Guild Quest: Additional Jobs, Thieves Guild Quest: Larceny Targets, Thieves Guild Quest: Scoundrel's Folly

LOCATIONS: Honningbrew Meadery, Honningbrew Basement, Honningbrew Boilery, Riften, The Bee and Barb, Black-Briar Manor, Cistern, Ratway, The Ragged Flagon, Whiterun, The Bannered Mare

CHARACTERS: Brynjolf, Commander Caius (if Imperials hold Whiterun), Mallus Maccius, Maven Black-Briar, Sabjorn, Sinmir (if Stormcloaks hold Whiterun)

ENEMIES: Frostbite Spider, Hamelyn, Venomfang Skeever,

◊ **OBJECTIVES:** Speak to Maven Black-Briar, Speak to Mallus Maccius, Speak to Sabjorn, Poison the Nest, Poison the Honningbrew Vat, Return to Sabjorn, Attend the tasting ceremony, Speak to Mallus Maccius, Identify Sabjorn's silent partner, Return to Maven Black-Briar, Return to Brynjolf

▷ A Plan Is Brewing

◊ **OBJECTIVE:** Speak to Maven Black-Briar
◆ **TARGET:** Black-Briar Manor or the Bee and Barb in Riften

You begin this quest with the previous objective already active. Leave the Ragged Flagon and find Maven. You can be as flippant or sycophantic as you like in your responses to this ale baroness; she still has a particular role for you to undertake once you agree to it. This involves her only real competition in Skyrim: the Honningbrew Meadery located close to Whiterun. With the mead production of the Goldenglow Farm being interrupted, this has a knock-on effect with her production too. Her rival, a Nord named Sabjorn who owns the Honningbrew Meadery, cannot be allowed to up his production and cut into her profits. You're to head to Whiterun and seek out Mallus Maccius, Sabjorn's disgruntled assistant (and unofficial contact for Maven), and hatch a plan to bring Sabjorn down. Maven is also keen to learn who backed Sabjorn financially.

◊ **OBJECTIVE:** Speak to Mallus Maccius
◆ **TARGET:** The Bannered Mare in Whiterun

Enter Whiterun and the Bannered Mare, before locating the weasel-like Mallus Maccius. He has already formulated a plan to bring Sabjorn down: The Honningbrew Meadery has a well-known Skeever infestation (partly because he told the townsfolk about it). The vermin are interfering with Sabjorn's latest batch of "Honningbrew Reserve," which is being readied for Whiterun's Captain of the Guard. A tasting ceremony cannot be held until the meadery is cleared of Skeevers. This is where you come in. You're to pose as a helper, ready to poison the rodents, but you'll also sabotage the brewing vats too.

◊ **OBJECTIVE:** Speak to Sabjorn
◆ **TARGET:** Honningbrew Meadery

This upcoming plan is one of infiltration, not violence: Do not target Sabjorn or Mallus in battle. **CAUTION**

 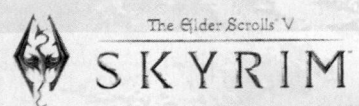

Sabjorn's Subjugation

You can ask Mallus further questions to gain more understanding of the situation if you wish. Then travel a short distance to the meadery and enter the main building. Sabjorn is just inside, worried about his Skeever problem and annoyed that his no-good assistant Mallus isn't around to help. After agreeing to help, you can:

(Persuade) Request payment in advance.

(Intimidate) Threaten him to obtain a payment in advance.

Agree to receive the payment once the job is done. This isn't the most prudent of options.

If you're successful in your Persuasion or Intimidation, Sabjorn agrees to pay you half your reward (500 gold pieces) now.

➤ **Honningbrew Meadery Key**   ➤ **500 gold pieces**

➤ **Pest Poison**

◊ **OBJECTIVE:** Poison the Nest
◊ **OBJECTIVE:** Poison the Honningbrew Vat
♦ **TARGET:** Nest and vat, inside Honningbrew Meadery

Head into the barrel storage room and venture into Honningbrew Basement. The door is only accessible once Sabjorn gives you the key. Watch for bear traps and a Venomfang Skeever scurrying out of a small fissure at the cellar's far (south) end. The fissure opens up into underground warrens. Bring down any Venomfang Skeevers and a small family of Frostbite Spiders as you continue south. Locate the mound of straw and the chest. Poison this nest.

During this frenzied clearing, you should begin to uncover the source of the Venomfang Skeever infestation: It didn't begin by accident but rather is the result of a series of macabre experiments undertaken by a mad mage named Hamelyn. He had constructed a makeshift laboratory at the nest site, where he has been creating these fiends. If you slay him, you can read his journal, which speaks of his exile from Winterhold and his strange notion of being a "parent" to his army of Skeever. However, to defeat him, you'll need to attack with cunning, as he's tough. Check any nearby chests for some particularly satisfying loot.

Continue farther into the warrens and up into a second cellar. Open the door in the eastern wall leading into the Honningbrew Boilery. Step up to the Honningbrew Reserve vat and poison it. You need poison only one vat. Then leave via the door leading outside.

◊ **OBJECTIVE:** Return to Sabjorn

Back in the meadery tasting room, inform Sabjorn that the job is finished, and claim the rest (or all) of your reward. Alas, Sabjorn isn't prepared to pay you until after the tasting ceremony.

◊ **OBJECTIVE:** Attend the tasting ceremony
♦ **TARGET:** Honningbrew Meadery

Step back and watch the Captain of the Guards — Commander Caius (if Whiterun is under Imperial rule) or Commander Sinmir (if Whiterun is under Stormcloak control during the Civil War) — as he impatiently asks for a flagon of Sabjorn's latest reserve. After Sabjorn proudly plonks it down, the Commander drinks from the poisoned reserve and certainly finds the taste not to his liking. He escorts a bewildered Sabjorn out of the building, with the intention of imprisoning him in Whiterun's Dragonsreach prison for almost poisoning him, and temporarily puts Mallus in charge of the meadery!

⟨⟩ **TIP**   Success or not, you don't receive any additional payment from Sabjorn. Remember to shake him down earlier for half the proposed payment!

◊ **OBJECTIVE:** Speak to Mallus Maccius
♦ **TARGET:** Honningbrew Meadery

Keeping the Mead Flowing

Find Mallus Maccius skulking around the meadery. He can't believe how well the plan went. Tell him you need to look at Sabjorn's books. He hands you a key and tells you to look upstairs, in Sabjorn's desk:

➤ **Sabjorn's Dresser Key**

◊ **OBJECTIVE:** Identify Sabjorn's silent partner
♦ **TARGET:** Sabjorn's dresser, inside Honningbrew Meadery

After speaking to Mallus about future operations for this meadery (it is now effectively in Black-Briar hands), head upstairs from the barrel storage room and use the Honningbrew Meadery Key to open the bedroom door (which is otherwise [Adept] level to unlock). Now open the dresser with Sabjorn's Dresser Key. There's a Promissory Note inside.

➤ **Promissory Note**

◊ **OBJECTIVE:** Return to Maven Black-Briar
♦ **TARGET:** Black-Briar Manor or the Bee and Barb, in Riften

QUEST: LARCENY TARGET

You'd do well to unlock the door (Hard) inside Sabjorn's bedroom just after obtaining the Promissory Note. There's a Honningbrew Decanter on the table inside the room. Take the Decanter and hand it to Delvin Mallory for a cash reward. Consult the Thieves Guild Quest: Larceny Targets for further information.

➤ **Honningbrew Decanter**

Quest Conclusion

Head back to Riften and seek out Maven, handing over the Promissory Note when she asks. The strange marking (a dagger symbol) you saw on the Goldenglow Estate deed is also on this note. Maven wants you to bring this information to the Thieves Guild immediately. Then you're given your payment.

➤ **Leveled Enchanted Weapon**

◇ **OBJECTIVE:** Return to Brynjolf
♦ **TARGET:** The Ragged Flagon, inside the Ratway in Riften

Locate Brynjolf (either in the Ragged Flagon or the adjacent Cistern). He already knows about the fate of Sabjorn; in fact, he thinks this is a good example of how the Thieves Guild's system works. But there is something else; the strange symbol is beyond coincidence. Brynjolf believes someone is trying to drive a wedge between Maven and the Guild. A furious Mercer believes he's figured out how to reveal this new thorn in the Guild's side and wants to meet you right away.

Postquest Activities

Thieves Guild Quest: Scoundrel's Folly is now active. Optionally speak to Vex and Delvin Mallory and continue Thieves Guild Quest: Additional Jobs. Optionally visit Mallus at the Honningbrew Meadery; he is now the bartender and a Fence, allowing you to sell him stolen goods. The first time you return to the meadery, all of the external signs have been changed to "Black-Briar" and all the Honningbrew Mead is gone, replaced by Black-Briar Mead. Maven works with a swiftness that matches her machinations and cunning!

➤ **Mallus:** Fence

SCOUNDREL'S FOLLY

PREREQUISITES: Complete Thieves Guild Quest: Dampened Spirits

INTERSECTING QUESTS: Thieves Guild Quest: Additional Jobs, Thieves Guild Quest: Larceny Targets, Thieves Guild Quest: Speaking With Silence

LOCATIONS: East Empire Company, East Empire Company Warehouse, Brinewater Grotto, Riften, Cistern, Ratway, The Ragged Flagon, Solitude, Blue Palace, The Winking Skeever

CHARACTERS: Brynjolf, Delvin Mallory, Gulum-Ei, Mercer Frey, Tonilia

ENEMIES: Bandit, East Empire Dockworker, East Empire Warden, Horker

◇ **OBJECTIVES:** Speak to Mercer Frey, (Optional) Speak to Brynjolf, Speak to Gulum-Ei, Steal case of Firebrand Wine, Get information from Gulum-Ei, Shadow Gulum-Ei, Confront Gulum-Ei, Return to Mercer Frey, Speak to Tonilia about exchanging a piece of armor, Find an Alternative Source of Information

◉ MINOR SPOILERS

▶ An Argonian with Answers

◇ **OBJECTIVE:** Speak to Mercer Frey
♦ **TARGET:** Cistern or the Ragged Flagon, in the Ratway in Riften

You commence this quest with the previous objective already active. Speak to Mercer, who reckons the entity responsible for weakening the Thieves Guild is certainly cunning and shares similar methods to his own! But the Promissory Note refers to a name that Mercer knows as a nom de plume of an Argonian named Gulum-Ei. He's the Guild's inside man at the East Empire Company and needs to be shaken down regarding his role in this nefarious plot.

◇ **OBJECTIVE:** (Optional) Speak to Brynjolf
♦ **TARGET:** Cistern or the Ragged Flagon, in the Ratway in Riften
◇ **OBJECTIVE:** Speak to Gulum-Ei
♦ **TARGET:** Gulum-Ei, in Solitude

Find Brynjolf, who seems surprised that an Argonian as hapless as Gulum-Ei could be involved in such schemes. Gulum-Ei is an adept scammer but lacks the brains to devise a plan to weaken the Guild. Still, this lizard is stubborn. You'll likely need to buy him off or follow him to see what he's up to. But you must keep him alive; killing someone as valuable to the Guild as Gulum-Ei is not an option. Before you leave, you can learn more about the East Empire Company and the Argonian by further conversation.

Track Gulum-Ei down to a location within the walls of Solitude. His usual haunt is the Winking Skeever tavern (indeed, he remains here once this quest concludes, providing he survives to the end of this quest). Gulum-Ei seems overly dismissive, denying involvement with the Goldenglow Estate; he says he only deals in goods. But when you use the "code name" of Gajul-Lei (that was in the Promissory Note), he softens a bit but can't remember every detail. Jog his memory by:

(Persuade) Asking him to identify the buyer, after which the Guild will forget his involvement.

(Bribe) Asking him what it would take to identify the buyer.

(Intimidate) Threatening to kill him.

If the first or third plans are successful (or when you return the Firebrand Wine Case, below), Gulum-Ei reveals that he was approached by a woman who wanted him to act as a broker for the Goldenglow Estate purchase. The only other information he gives is she was quite angry at Mercer Frey but never mentioned why. But for the bribe, the lizard is after something more than gold: a case of Firebrand Wine. (Gulum-Ei is really not being helpful here. He's sidestepping the truth and showing his true colors as a scam artist. You will ultimately have no choice but to follow him and see if he's up to something.)

The Elder Scrolls V
SKYRIM

> **TIP** You may wish to choose bribery over other techniques, as Gulum-Ei rewards you with Soul Gems if you retrieve the wine, and these are always helpful to have!

◊ **OBJECTIVE:** Steal case of Firebrand Wine
◊ **OBJECTIVE:** Get information from Gulum-Ei
♦ **TARGET:** Blue Palace, in Solitude

BRIBERY: FINDING THE FIREBRAND WIRE

If you choose bribery when speaking to Gulum-Ei, he requests a case of Firebrand Wine that he knows is kept in the Blue Palace. Travel there (it is still within the walls of Solitude), and head to Elisif's room to pick up the case. The quest updates, and you should return to him. Hand over the case and receive a reward for your troubles.

➤ **Firebrand Wine Case**   ➤ **Leveled Soul Gem (3)**

Gulum-Ei finally reveals that he was approached by a woman who wanted to use Gulum-Ei as a broker for "something big": the Goldenglow Farm deeds. He didn't ask too many questions, but the woman did seem angry and directed much of the anger toward Mercer Frey. You won't get anything more from Gulum-Ei, and as you're under strict instructions not to spill any Argonian blood, there's only one other pertinent action to take: follow him.

◊ **OBJECTIVE:** Shadow Gulum-Ei

Down on the Docks

With the conversation over, Gulum-Ei leaves for the East Empire Company. Follow him at a safe distance. If he notices you following, he'll wave you off and ask you to stop, but this will not hinder his progress toward the warehouse. Instead, keep farther back or dive into cover and remain at a greater distance as he continues down onto the docks, onto the main waterside jetty, past the warehouse store, and into the warehouse itself. This is where your proper shadowing begins.

Once inside the warehouse, continue to sneak, keeping your distance. If Gulum-Ei spots you and yells for help, engage any East Empire Wardens who react violently to your trespassing. Just past the guard station, you can walk up a log leaning against the shelves, and gain some height. This provides a good view of the warehouse and keeps you out of the guards' path. You can also swim across, but be careful nobody sees you when you emerge on the warehouse's other side.

Whether you're keeping this shadowing clandestine (without combat) or carnage-filled (after Gulum-Ei raises the alarm), the Argonian continues to the same place and seems to disappear into the storage bays. Depending on whether you've been spotted, he runs frantically or strolls into the water underneath the large barrel and stairs along the north side of the gigantic warehouse cavern. Be careful when he walks close to the large door at the front of the warehouse, as he changes the ledger and doubles back shortly, making you easy to spot if you take this opportunity to move.

Gulum-Ei now heads up a ramp and enters the Brinewater Grotto. Before you follow him inside, visit the foreman's office and obtain the East Empire Shipping Map.

◊ **OBJECTIVE:** Confront Gulum-Ei
♦ **TARGET:** Gulum-Ei, in Brinewater Gully

> **TIP** The art of shadowing occurs once Gulum-Ei enters the East Empire Warehouse. The wardens inside are hostile when they see you. They are not Solitude Guards, so you won't increase your Crime in Haafingar Hold. However, it is far better to sneak through here without being detected.

QUEST: LARCENY TARGET

Inside the East Empire Company Warehouse is a dock overseer's hut, on the higher ground in the northwest corner. Climb up to it and take what you wish to steal, but make sure one of these items is the East Empire Shipping Map. Remember to return it to Delvin Mallory for a cash reward.

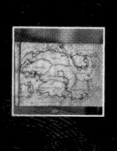

➤ **East Empire Shipping Map**

Gulum-Ei's Grotto Confession

Inside the grotto, be ever mindful of the trip-wire traps at your feet, unless you want a mace to the face. Expect to face bandits in this location, which continues along an underground river to a storage area and a Horker pen.

Witnessing your dogged determination, Gulum-Ei suddenly becomes a lot more forthcoming with information, claiming he was approached by a Dunmer named "Karliah" who murdered someone named Gallus and was headed to "where the end began." He hands over the Bill of Sale as further proof, and a goodwill gesture. This exhausts your interrogation tactics. Remember to keep Gulum-Ei alive afterwards!

➤ **Goldenglow Bill of Sale.**

> **TIP** Killing Gulum-Ei is both unwise and foolish, as he becomes a Fence for the Thieves Guild from this point on. You'll find him based out of the Winking Skeever in Solitude.

◊ **OBJECTIVE:** Return to Mercer Frey
♦ **TARGET:** Cistern or the Ragged Flagon, in the Ratway in Riften

Depart for Riften. Once you're back in the Cistern, reveal your information to Mercer Frey. Frey's demeanor changes for the first time; he seems shocked and stammers when you mention Karliah's name. Mercer tells you Karliah is a murderess, killing Mercer's former colleague Gallus in cold blood. Then she vanished...until now! Mercer is sure she's back to kill him, as the only remaining Guild member from the old days. Mercer knows she must be at Snow Veil Sanctum, and you must venture there to kill her before she disappears again. Now ready yourself by obtaining some additional armor as a reward.

◊ **OBJECTIVE:** Speak to Tonilia about exchanging a piece of armor
♦ **TARGET:** Tonilia, at the Ragged Flagon, in the Ratway in Riften

An Early Argonian Ending

Was Gulum-Ei slain during this quest before he revealed any information about Karliah? Then the objectives change. "Shadow Gulum-Ei" or "Confront Gulum-Ei" now fail.

◊ **OBJECTIVE:** Find an Alternative Source of Information

You must journey via the route that Gulum-Ei takes to a chest located in Brinewater Grotto. Inside is a note.

➤ **Note:** Gulum-Ei's Confession

The note is written by Gulum-Ei to his brother. It, too, reveals the name of Karliah, her murder of Gallus, and the fact that she's after Mercer Frey, heading to "where the end began." You are now instructed to return to Brynjolf. As expected, killing Gulum-Ei results in a severely negative reaction from both Brynjolf and Mercer, and you won't be able to exchange any of your armor. Follow instructions, won't you!

Quest Conclusion

This is purely optional: Visit Tonilia and choose which section of Guild clothing you wish to trade for the new (and improved) section. You receive an enhanced version of *only one* of the following:

➤ **Thieves Guild Boots** (Improve Pickpocket 25%)

➤ **Thieves Guild Armor** (+35 Carry Weight)

➤ **Thieves Guild Gloves** (Improve Lockpick 25%)

➤ **Thieves Guild Hood** (Improve Prices 15%)

Postquest Activities

Thieves Guild Quest: Speaking with Silence is now active. Continue Thieves Guild Quest: Additional Jobs; it is in your best interest to increase the Guild's influence over many Holds in Skyrim.

SPEAKING WITH SILENCE

PREREQUISITES: Complete Thieves Guild Quest: Scoundrel's Folly

INTERSECTING QUESTS: Thieves Guild Quest: Additional Jobs, Thieves Guild Quest: Larceny Targets, Thieves Guild Quest: Hard Answers

LOCATIONS: Riften, Cistern, Ratway, The Ragged Flagon, Snow Veil Sanctum, Snow Veil Catacombs

CHARACTERS: Karliah, Mercer Frey

ENEMIES: Draugr

◊ **OBJECTIVES:** Meet Mercer Frey outside Snow Veil Sanctum, Enter Snow Veil Sanctum, Find Karliah, Speak to Karliah

● MAJOR SPOILERS

▶ A Crypt of Snares and Traps

◊ **OBJECTIVE:** Meet Mercer Frey outside Snow Veil Sanctum
◊ **OBJECTIVE:** Enter Snow Veil Sanctum
◆ **TARGET:** Mercer Frey, outside Snow Veil Sanctum

You commence this quest with the previous objective already active. Travel to the icy Tundra and locate Mercer standing outside the cairn entrance to the Sanctum. He wants you to lead him into the underground catacombs. Before you head inside, speak to Mercer to gain more information about how Gallus died, about Karliah, and about other matters that are informative but not critical to this quest. After you drop into the circular depression, wait for Mercer to open the door into the Snow Veil Catacombs.

◊ **OBJECTIVE:** Find Karliah
◆ **TARGET:** Karliah, in Snow Veil Sanctum

Ready your favored offensive equipment or magic, and venture into the vast connecting crypts filled with burial urns and intermittent Draugr attacks. Be constantly on the lookout for traps, such as the swinging gate just to the right of the first portcullis chain in the first coffin chamber. As the Draugr dislodge from the wall, you may also rely on Mercer to follow up with his own (exceptional) strikes; he appears to be supremely adept at bladed combat.

Deeper into this dungeon, beware of bear traps, a hanging oil lamp with which to burn Draugr (but hopefully not yourself), and a trip wire to trigger further Draugr incursions. Watch for the rattling bone chimes; brushing against them summons more Draugr. When you reach the upper caged stone paths, you're close to entering the actual Sanctum.

QUEST: LARCENY TARGET

Just before the corridor to the upper caged stone paths, there's a large open chamber with several Draugr to fight and a low central platform with two coffins on it. Head south, up the wooden steps. Follow the corridor south and around to the north, to an upper balcony and pedestal. Your Larceny Target is either resting on the pedestal or has fallen off it. Remember to return it to Delvin Mallory for a cash reward.

➤ **Ship Model**

▶ A Silent Shout

The Sanctum's crypts are taller and the Draugr more restless than ever. Beware of bone trip wires that summon more corpses, although this keeps Mercer's weapons bloody. Progress deeper still, opening the portcullis that knocks over a cluster of jars, and fight your way to the double Iron Door, where a more mighty Draugr rises from his slumber. Strike him and his cohorts down before approaching a Word Wall on the opposite side of the raised burial crypt and learning a new Word of Power.

➤ **Word of Power:** Disarm

With the Word of Power ringing in your ears, venture down a final corridor that leads to one of the infamous Nordic Puzzle Doors. Avoid the bear traps and let Mercer approach the puzzle.

Puzzle Solution: Mercer figures that Karliah has probably taken the necessary Key Claw and that the door has a specific weak spot only Mercer can exploit. He opens the door without your help or the need for puzzle-solving.

The two of you arrive in the central burial chamber where Karliah supposedly murdered Gallus. It takes a moment before you realize you've been poisoned.

Song of the Nightingales

An arrow arcs through the black crypt. Your vision blurs and you black out. You awaken on the ground. You cannot move, and you're still smarting from the poison-laced missile. Stepping out of the darkness, Karliah notches another arrow, approaches Mercer, and the two begin a startling exchange.

Revelations Abound: The conversation turns Mercer's story on its head; Gallus was actually slain by Mercer Frey, but he blamed Karliah for it, causing her exile from the Thieves Guild. Karliah also mentions a mysterious group known as the "Nightingales," alluding that both Mercer and Karliah were part of it. Although you're expecting combat, Karliah places a potion to her lips and sips, slipping back into the shadows without firing. She seems to know she's no match for Mercer. After a few choice words (and blades) leveled at you, Mercer seems satisfied that he's finished you off. Your vision turns to black once again.

◊ **OBJECTIVE:** Speak to Karliah
♦ **TARGET:** Karliah, outside Snow Veil Sanctum

You awaken in a wobbly state outside Snow Veil Sanctum, looking straight at Karliah. She explains that aside from saving your life and dragging you from the catacombs, she requires your help in tracking down Mercer. The traitor must be brought before the Guild to answer for his crimes: He must be hunted like she was. She was at the Sanctum for two reasons. The first was to capture Mercer using her special paralyzing poison arrow. However, she elected to use it on you instead, foiling the first half of her mission but saving your life in the process. The other reason she visited Snow Veil Sanctum was to locate a journal penned by Gallus, the third Nightingale. She believes this book may contain information you both could bring to the Guild as proof of Mercer's foul deeds. But the journal is written in an unrecognizable language. You must journey to Winterhold and find Enthir, a good friend of Gallus, who may be able to decipher it.

Quest Conclusion

You are given the journal to take to Enthir, and you receive four doses of a random Leveled Poison. It appears Karliah's attributes extend to that of alchemist too.

➤ **Gallus's Encoded Journal**   ➤ **Leveled Poison [random] (4)**

Postquest Activities

After some optional additional questions about Gallus's and Karliah's movements, Thieves Guild Quest: Hard Answers is now available to start. In addition, the Thieves Guild's reach should extend to the main Holds in Skyrim as you progress through Thieves Guild Quest: Additional Jobs.

 **HARD ANSWERS**

 MINOR SPOILERS

PREREQUISITES: Complete Thieves Guild Quest: Speaking with Silence
INTERSECTING QUESTS: Temple Quest: The Book of Love, Miscellaneous Objective: Calcelmo's Ring*, Miscellaneous Objective: Neutralizing Nimhe*, Thieves Guild Quest: Additional Jobs, Thieves Guild Quest: Larceny Targets, Thieves Guild Quest: The Pursuit
LOCATIONS: Markarth, Understone Keep, Calcelmo's Laboratory, Calcelmo's Tower, Dwemer Museum, Markarth Wizards' Balcony, Winterhold, The Frozen Hearth
CHARACTERS: Aicantar, Calcelmo, Enthir, Karliah
ENEMIES: Captain Aquilius, Markarth City Guard, Wizard's Guard
◊ **OBJECTIVES:** Speak with Enthir, Speak with Calcelmo, Gain entry to Calcelmo's Museum, (Optional) Obtain the key to Calcelmo's Museum, Obtain Calcelmo's Falmer Translating Guide, Duplicate the writing on Calcelmo's Stone, Return to Enthir, Speak to Enthir, Speak to Karliah

Calcelmo's Secrets

◊ **OBJECTIVE:** Speak with Enthir
♦ **TARGET:** The Frozen Hearth, in Winterhold

You commence this quest with the objective already active. Trudge up to Winterhold, where you can find Enthir in the cellar of the Frozen Hearth Inn (usually he wanders the College of Winterhold). After you speak with him, he reveals Gallus's Journal to be written in Ancient Falmer, a long-dead language of the Snow Elves. Even he won't be able to translate this, but he believes that Calcelmo, the court wizard of Markarth, may have the materials needed for the translation. But he warns you that Calcelmo guards his research fiercely, and getting the information won't be easy. You can also ask Enthir about Gallus, what the Falmer actually were, and other related questions before stepping out into the cold.

◊ **OBJECTIVE:** Speak with Calcelmo
♦ **TARGET:** Understone Keep, in Markarth

Make your way west toward the canyon city of Markarth. Once through the front gates, scale the stone steps to reach Understone Keep, the site of major excavation work. You'll find Calcelmo to the left (west), checking over artifacts and the progression of the dig inside a gigantic Dwemer entrance chamber. Alas, Calcelmo is extremely overworked and uncooperative (even if you helped him during Temple Quest: The Book of Love). He says your idea to view his work on the Falmer tongue is "preposterous," and he won't allow anyone to view it before it is completed. You can:

(Persuade) Inform him you're a great admirer of his work. With a high enough Persuade, Calcelmo allows you access to the Museum part of his quarters but still keeps the Laboratory off-limits. You also receive a key to the Museum, which is reasonably handy for this quest but still means you must break into the Laboratory.

(Bribe) Ask what it'll cost to change his mind. He isn't interested in personal wealth, so this option leads you nowhere.

(Intimidate) Threaten him. He isn't interested in your threats, so this fails as well.

Calcelmo also remembers if you've helped him before but points out he's already given you access to the Museum. Alas, none of these options allow you access to Calcelmo's research, which is likely to be ready in several more years. You need another plan. The only way you're getting into that laboratory is by clandestine sneaking, lockpicking, out-and-out brutality, or a mixture of these.

Trespasser in the Keep (Part 1)

> ◊ OBJECTIVE: Gain entry to Calcelmo's Museum
> ◊ OBJECTIVE: (Optional) Obtain the key to Calcelmo's Museum
> ♦ TARGET: Understone Keep, in Markarth

If you've helped Calcelmo in the past, you may already have access to his Museum (both Temple Quest: The Book of Love and Miscellaneous Objective: Neutralizing Nimhe* award you the key and his permission to enter the Museum). If not, you can do either of those quests now. Having legitimate access to the Museum will make the next part of this quest much easier, especially if you have a low Sneak skill.

Alternately, you can steal a key. Your quest target points you to one on the low plinth nearby, hidden among Calcelmo's artifacts. Both Calcelmo and the guard near the Museum entrance (at the top of the stairs in the keep's entry chamber) have keys you can pickpocket.

Or you can simply pick the Adept Lock on the Museum door and slip in while the guard's back is turned.

➤ **Dwemer Museum Key**

> ◊ OBJECTIVE: Obtain Calcelmo's Falmer Translating Guide
> ♦ TARGET: Calcelmo's Tower, inside Understone Keep in Markarth

As you enter the Museum, creep forward to overhear a conversation between two of the guards. This eavesdropping gives you a preview of your objectives to come; it sounds as if Calcelmo has called in every one of his favors to populate and secure the upper level using his own private expedition team. As Calcelmo's overriding plan is to ensure

his research is protected, your tasks just got a lot tougher. From the Museum, you have three options:

Plan A: Walk on through with nonchalance. If Calcelmo gave you the key and permission to visit the Museum, the guards have already been informed and won't ask any questions. Provided you don't try to steal anything, you can head through, take in the sights, and then continue through the western door to the second level. This is both straightforward, safe, and direct.

Plan B: Blind, ugly violence. Despite all the valuables, Calcelmo's Museum is protected by just three city guards. Depending on your level, you may be able to take them out with melee strikes or (preferably) with some well-placed arrows, allowing you to loot the room at your leisure. When you're done here, continue to the western door. Note that these are Markarth Guards, so you'll pick up a hefty Bounty (3,000+ in Crime Gold) for their murders.

Plan C: Stealth. The museum is large, well lit, open, and patrolled by three guards, so expect a significant challenge here. All the usual tips on Sneaking still apply—use anything you have to increase your Sneak; use spells, potions, abilities, or items that give you Invisibility or Muffle, and take off those heavy boots. Then, when you're ready, carefully take the following path:

1. From the entryway, observe the guard on the north side. When he passes by, carefully sneak along behind him and crouch behind the spider display in the room's northeastern corner.

2. When the northern guard steps into the room's center, carefully head west. This time, watch the guard in the center. When he faces back south, duck into the northern hallway.

3. Wait for the northern guard to begin another loop, then creep west. When the center guard turns away again, carefully sneak into the western hallway (ducking behind the pillar if necessary on the way).

If you've chosen Plan A or B, it's worth spending some time in the Museum. There are more lockpicking opportunities in this room than anywhere else in Skyrim, making this a fantastic place to improve your skills. Also, the loot here is exceptional (provided you don't get caught). The two side rooms off the main chamber are also worth exploring.

Your ultimate target is the door at the Museum's west end. This leads to Calcelmo's Laboratory. You can:

Unlock the door with the Museum Key, which you may already have, or you can pickpocket/loot from any of the guards in this room.

(Lockpick [Adept]) Or pick the lock on the door if you don't.

Trespasser in the Keep (Part 2)

> **NOTE** Much of this section of Understone Keep is accessible only during this quest, so it is worth fully exploring this entire area.

Enter the Laboratory and note the scene between Aicantar and the soldier up ahead. You're not facing city guards any longer. Calcelmo's men have orders to kill intruders on sight and will call for reinforcements if they spot you. Your permission from Calcelmo doesn't extend to this floor of the Keep, so you'll have to sneak or fight your way through.

Initial Two Chambers

There are two guards in this first area. One already patrols the second room to the west; the other enters after a minute or two through the previously sealed eastern door, once Aicantar has finished with him. You can:

Try to sneak by. This is all but impossible without Invisibility, as the western guard keeps a close eye on the exit.

Fight them head-on. They're tough, and they'll call for reinforcements if they spot you—one guard who enters from the far eastern door.

Take them out with the traps in this space. You have plenty of options to choose from: The first room has a large pool of flammable oil and a row of dart traps. The second room has a wall trap, a set of threshers, and a ballista in the hallway littered with rubble.

But by far the most unusual (and entertaining) option is just to your left as you enter the first room. On the table in this small chamber is a unique item: Aicantar's Spider Control Rod and a journal that explains it. When you take the Rod, a Dwemer Spider drops in, ready to help you take on the guards.

➤ **Spider Control Rod**   ➤ **Aicantar's Lab Journal**

The door on the western end of the second room is locked (unless you triggered the reinforcements). You can:

(Lockpicking [Adept]) Pick the lock.

Or unlock the door with one of the Laboratory Keys. All of the Wizards' Guards carry a key, or you can find one in Calcelmo's bedroom on the north side of the second chamber.

➤ **Calcelmo's Laboratory Key (2)**   ➤ **Dwemer Museum Key**

The Steam Hall

Two guards patrol the steam hall and comment on one of the traps there as you approach. As before, you can try to sneak by them (which is extremely difficult) or fight them and their reinforcements (with or without the help of the Dwarven Spider).

A better option is to continue past them and take the ramp to the lower level, where the hallway is blocked by clouds of noxious steam. Sneak through here, out of sight of the guards, stopping on the pressure plates as necessary to turn off the gas and allow your health to recover. If the spider is following you, direct it onto the pressure plate to keep the gas off, allowing you to walk through.

Back on the upper level, the valve at the hall's far end will turn on the thresher traps, easily wiping out the guards. Loot them and the treasure in the side rooms before continuing on.

The Statue Room

The next chamber, decorated with two Dwarven Sphere statues, is relatively easy to sneak through. Just wait until the guard by the eastern door leaves his post. Or, as always, you can fight your way through.

Aicantar's chamber offers one final set of options. Once again, sneaking here is difficult: Aicantar keeps close watch on the exit. You can certainly fight him, the guard, and a pair of reinforcements (optionally with your spider). But a better option is to sneak into the control booth on the walkway and turn the valve.

Chaos breaks out below. All the traps in the room turn on, and Aicantar and the guard panic, yelling for everyone to flee the Laboratory. They and any surviving guards in the Laboratory make a break for the Museum. They may not get far, as Aicantar's robes have a nasty tendency to get caught in the thresher....

QUEST: LARCENY TARGET

Before you struggle out of the Laboratory, check the alcove on your right, which has a Dwemer Puzzle Box on display. Snag it now, as you won't be returning this way. Hand it to Delvin Mallory for a cash reward. Consult the Thieves Guild Quest: Larceny Targets for further information.

➤ **Dwemer Puzzle Cube**

Continue out onto the Markarth wizards' balcony.

▶ There's the Rub

After marveling at the impressive vista, clamber up the steps and enter Calcelmo's Tower. On this room's upper level, you can see an ornate stone covered in hieroglyphics: there appear to be verses written in Ancient Falmer and Dwemer. This looks to be the guide to translating Gallus's Journal! However, getting it back may pose a challenge....

Continue up the stairs on the left (east) and enter Calcelmo's private office, packed with artifacts and rubbings. A door from the office leads out to the stone. But interacting with it won't get you far: The stone is much too heavy to lift.

◊ **OBJECTIVE:** Duplicate the writing on Calcelmo's Stone
♦ **TARGET:** Calcelmo's Tower, in Understone Keep in Markarth

---

Puzzle Solution: Sift through the valuables and check the main table. Calcelmo has been making some rubbings on paper, and these are scattered everywhere. Take a roll of paper and some charcoal from a side table. Return to Calcelmo's Stone and make a rubbing of the text there. (It's possible to find the roll of paper and charcoal in the world prior to this quest, but it isn't necessary; there's plenty of it around.)

➤ **Roll of Paper**   ➤ **Calcelmo's Stone Rubbing**
➤ **Charcoal**

◊ **OBJECTIVE:** Return to Enthir
♦ **TARGET:** The Frozen Hearth in Winterhold

▶ Nocturnal's Quisling

Now for the small matter of an escape plan. Mere moments after you make the rubbing, the doors to the tower open and a group of soldiers enter, led by Captain Aquilius of the Wizards' Guard. They are joined by Aicantar (if he's still alive). After a brief argument, they spread out to scour the tower.

You can try to fight or run past them. With an excellent Sneak skill, you may even be able to get out undetected: drop onto the platform to the west and head up the stairs. At the gap, leap onto the narrow metal catwalk and race for the door.

Out on the balcony, you have a choice: You can try to backtrack through the Laboratory, Museum, and Keep, but between the Wizards' Guards and the city guard, you've probably made some enemies by now. Your quest target suggests a better option: On the balcony's east side, some of the stonework has fallen away, exposing a narrow stone path. Follow it, leap into the waterfall at the end, and make your getaway. Fast-Travel back to Winterhold at your earliest convenience.

Back inside the Frozen Hearth, hand the stone rubbing to Enthir and tell him it should help with the translation. Karliah will be here when you arrive with the rubbing. As Enthir pores over the rubbing and Gallus's Journal, he reveals the disturbing truth: Gallus suspected Mercer's wavering allegiance to the Thieves Guild for months; this included a vast expenditure on a lavish lifestyle of gold and trinkets. Mercer was apparently paying for this by removing valuables from the Guild's treasure vaults without anyone's knowledge! There is also talk of Mercer desecrating something known as the Twilight Sepulcher, which disgusts Karliah.

◊ **OBJECTIVE:** Speak to Enthir

◊ **OBJECTIVE:** Speak to Karliah

◆ **TARGET:** The Frozen Hearth, in Winterhold

Quest Conclusion

Speak to Enthir again, and he urges you to help Karliah and reveal the traitor to your brethren. He also thanks you for your help and tells you that if you're ever in this area again, he can fence any goods you may have gathered via slightly nefarious means.

➤ **Gallus's Translated Journal (Item)**

➤ **Vendor (Fence):** Enthir

Locate Karliah nearby, who tells you the Twilight Sepulcher is the sacred temple to Nocturnal, the patron of thieves and gamblers. Defiling the sacred ground he swore to protect, Mercer is now revealed as an insidious fiend. But getting the rest of the Guild on your side may require more than simple guile. For your part, Karliah rewards you with Gallus's old weapon.

➤ **Nightingale Blade**

Postquest Activities

The Nightingale Blade is a leveled weapon, with an Absorb Health and Drain Stamina enchantment on it. After some optional additional questions, Thieves Guild Quest: The Pursuit commences. Build up influence in more cities by continuing Thieves Guild Quest: Additional Jobs. You may want to return to Markarth, especially if you've slain the museum guards, and brush up on your Lockpicking before cleaning the place out, as there's a wealth of loot to pick over.

THE PURSUIT

PREREQUISITES: Complete Thieves Guild Quest: Hard Answers

INTERSECTING QUESTS: Thieves Guild Quest: Additional Jobs, Thieves Guild Quest: Larceny Targets, Thieves Guild Quest: Trinity Restored

LOCATIONS: Lake Honrich, Riften, The Bee and Barb, Black-Briar Manor, Mercer's House, The Ratway, Cistern, The Ragged Flagon, The Ratway Sewers, Riftweald Manor

CHARACTERS: Brynjolf, Delvin Mallory, Karliah, Maven Black-Briar, Vex

ENEMIES: Bandit, Mjoll the Lioness, Thug, Vald

◊ **OBJECTIVES:** Meet Karliah at the Ragged Flagon, Follow Karliah, Speak to Brynjolf, Infiltrate Mercer's House, (Optional) Shoot the mechanism to lower the ramp, (Optional) Speak to Vex about Vald, Miscellaneous Objective: (Optional) Talk to Maven about Vald's debt, Miscellaneous Objective: Locate the Quill of Gemination under Lake Honrich, Miscellaneous Objective: Bring the Quill of Gemination to Maven, Discover evidence of Mercer's location, Speak to Brynjolf

● **MAJOR SPOILERS**

NOTE The quests listed as "Miscellaneous Objective" do not appear within "The Pursuit" quest but are here in case you wish to perform this optional plan.

➤ A Perfect Heist

◊ **OBJECTIVE:** Meet Karliah at the Ragged Flagon

◊ **OBJECTIVE:** Follow Karliah

◆ **TARGET:** Inside the Ratway, in Riften

This quest begins with the first objective already in play. Return to the familiar grounds of the Thieves Guild, and you'll find your usual entrance point by the Hall of the Dead Mausoleum is locked. You must navigate the sights (and smells) of the Ratway, down to the Ragged Flagon, where you'll meet Karliah. She has Gallus's translated journal ready to show the Guild members who require convincing. Agree to back her up and move into the Cistern. As expected, Brynjolf (flanked by Vex and Delvin Mallory) draws his blade and sharply asks why you're here with "a murderer." Armed with proof of Mercer's betrayal, Karliah hands over Gallus's Journal.

◊ **OBJECTIVE:** Speak to Brynjolf

Brynjolf cannot believe Mercer has been stealing from the Guild, so he orders Delvin to open the vault. The gold, the jewels...they're all gone! It takes two keys to unlock the vault. Delvin, Brynjolf, and Mercer are the only ones who carry such keys, so how did Mercer break into the vault alone? The answer is a mystery (even though Karliah quietly has

her suspicions). Although vindicated, Karliah is just as angered by this as the rest of the Guild, except perhaps for the seething Vex, who vows to kill Mercer immediately. Brynjolf's cooler head prevails, and he orders Vex and Delvin to guard the Ragged Flagon. Then he turns to you and asks what you've learned from Karliah.

Explain that Mercer killed Gallus, that the three of them were Nightingales, and that Karliah was behind Goldenglow and Honningbrew (a cunning plan to try and make Mercer look weak in front of Maven Black-Briar). Then Brynjolf has an important task for you: Break into Mercer's Riften house—Riftweald Manor—and gather any information that may indicate where the traitor has gone. Before you leave Brynjolf, ask him what is the best way into Riftweald Manor. You receive information about a "watchdog" and an exterior ramp with a mechanism to lower it, which could aid in your escape. Then ask about the "watchdog" named Vald. Brynjolf indicates Vex may have more information to provide. These grant you two optional objectives.

◊ **OBJECTIVE:** Infiltrate Mercer's House

◊ **OBJECTIVE:** (Optional) Shoot the mechanism to lower the ramp

◊ **OBJECTIVE:** (Optional) Speak to Vex about Vald

◆ **TARGET:** Riftweald Manor, in Riften

Locate Vex in the Cistern or Ragged Flagon, and ask her about Vald. She tells you he's only interested in gold, so buying him off is a possibility. But even Vald might not betray Mercer Frey (as he wouldn't live long enough to spend his bribe). Instead, Vex suggests you speak to Maven Black-Briar about erasing Vald's debt. Or you could run him through with your blade... Vex doesn't care either way.

◊ **OBJECTIVE:** (Optional) Talk to Maven about Vald's debt

◆ **TARGET:** Maven Black-Briar, in Riften

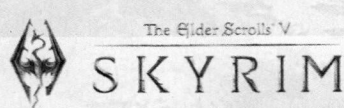

OPTIONAL: ERASING VALD'S DEBT

Locate Maven Black-Briar in the Bee and Barb, the marketplace, or Black-Briar Manor. Tell her you'd like to remove Vald's debt. Maven isn't receptive to this; she tells you she commissioned a unique Quill, and Vald was hired to ensure it reached her safely. Because of his blundering, it ended up at the bottom of Lake Honrich, and she's very keen to have it retrieved. She'll call the debt satisfied if you'll fish it out. You can also ask her about the properties of this fabled Quill and how it ended up in the lake. Finally, Maven can also give you vague directions to the Quill's location if you ask if she has ideas where to look for it: underwater, and close to one of the small islands in the lake.

◊ **OBJECTIVE:** Locate the Quill of Gemination under Lake Honrich
♦ **TARGET:** Beneath a small island, in Lake Honrich

The sunken rowboat's location isn't on your world or local maps, so consult the adjacent picture. The "current location" shows the exact spot where the rowboat sank, south of a small island and halfway between Riften (to the east) and Goldenglow Farm (to the west). The murky water makes finding this extremely tricky, but it isn't that far down. When you find the half-embedded boat, search for Vald's Strongbox [Average], and use your Lockpick skill to open it. Grab the gold and the Quill, and swim back to Riften.

➤ **Quill of Gemination**

◊ **OBJECTIVE:** Bring the Quill of Gemination to Maven

Find Maven and hand over the Quill. She gives you a document absolving Vald of his debt, but she doesn't want to ever see him in Riften again. Rejoin the main part of this quest.

➤ **Vald's Debt**

 **NOTE** If you wish, you can keep this Quill, complete this quest, and then sell it for around 150 gold pieces.

▶ Ransacking Riftweald Manor

Whether or not you went swimming for a Quill, you should figure out how best to enter Mercer Frey's abode. All of the ground-level doors are barred from the inside and are never accessible. The only way in is the door off the balcony.

Head to the rear gate and speak to Vald. He is immune to Bribery or Intimidation, and ignores you unless you present him with Vald's debt document. He agrees to flee the area, unlocks the (otherwise impassable) side gate, and gives you the key to Mercer's house.

A successful Persuade will trick him into leaving you to guard the house, and he'll present you with the key to the house. He'll then walk away from the house and you are free to bring down the ramp.

(Lockpick [Expert]) Or, you can lockpick the rear gate. You need to deal with Vald, but remember that killing him in cold blood doesn't win over the local guards and increases your Bounty. The moment you enter the backyard in this manner, Vald will become hostile and attack.

For those less inclined to lockpick: Vald's patrol causes him to pause with his back to the gate. It's possible to pick his pocket and grab the key right off of him, but you may still have to deal with him if he detects you once you pop the lock and enter the yard!

➤ **Mercer's House Key**

 NOTE This key unlocks the upper rear entrance to Mercer's House and both the side and rear gates.

Time for a spot of precision archery: Aim your arrow at the mechanism just below and to the left of the upper balcony, and fire. This releases the ramp, allowing you a much more stealthy way into the residence, instead of through the front door. Climb the ramp, and use the house key to unlock the otherwise-difficult-to-open door (Lockpick [Expert]).

◊ **OBJECTIVE:** Discover evidence of Mercer's location
♦ **TARGET:** Mercer's House, in Riften

Head through Mercer's House, electing to sneak by or slaughter any bandits guarding the location. Progress downstairs and find the room with the bench table and single chair. Adjacent to the barred door is a suspicious cabinet. Open it and activate the false back panel. Step into a secret room with stairs leading down into a subterranean cellar; this is part of the sewer system linking to the Ratway. Head through, watching for dart, fire, and swinging traps, and open the door into Mercer's hidden office. Gather some gold and his plans. Before you leave, attempt to open the display case (Master), which houses Mercer's exceptional frost sword!

➤ **Mercer's Plans**   ➤ **Chillrend**

QUEST: LARCENY TARGET

While you're rummaging around in Mercer's private office, snag that expensive-looking bust up onto the bookshelf. Consult the Thieves Guild Quest: Larceny Targets for further information.

➤ **Bust of the Gray Fox**

◊ **OBJECTIVE:** Speak to Brynjolf
♦ **TARGET:** The Ragged Flagon or Cistern, in the Ratway

Either retrace your steps back to the surface or (better yet) head into the Ratway Sewers, which offer you a quick route back to the Ragged Flagon.

Quest Conclusion

Return to Brynjolf, who hasn't had any luck in tracking Mercer down. But after you produce the plans, these reveal that Mercer is intent on taking the Eyes of the Falmer, a heist Gallus had been planning for years. The only course of action is clear: to pursue this cur into an ancient Falmer dungeon and intercept him before he can take this invaluable item! Aside from Chillrend, there are no other rewards, only a summoning to meet Karliah at once.

Postquest Activities

Thieves Guild Quest: Trinity Restored now commences.

PREREQUISITES: Complete Thieves Guild Quest: The Pursuit

INTERSECTING QUESTS: Thieves Guild Quest: Additional Jobs, Thieves Guild Quest: Larceny Targets, Thieves Guild Quest: Blindsighted

LOCATIONS: Nightingale Hall , Twilight Sepulcher , Riften, The Ragged Flagon, Cistern, The Ratway

CHARACTERS: Brynjolf, Karliah

◊ **OBJECTIVES:** Listen to Karliah, Meet Karliah at the Standing Stone, Follow Karliah, Activate the Armor Stone, Equip the Nightingale Armor, Follow Karliah, Stand on vacant floor glyph, Speak to Karliah, Speak to Brynjolf

⊙ **MAJOR SPOILERS**

▷ An Audience with Lady Nocturnal

◊ **OBJECTIVE:** Listen to Karliah
♦ **TARGET:** Inside the Ratway, in Riften

This quest begins with the first objective already under way. Although Karliah is a Nightingale, it falls to the current acting leader of the Thieves Guild to order the murder of Mercer. Brynjolf has no qualms about this, but Karliah points out that great care must be taken; after all, Mercer is a Nightingale, and an agent of Nocturnal. She suggests meeting Mercer on equal footing. Just outside Riften is a clearing and an old standing stone. She cryptically asks that you meet there.

◊ **OBJECTIVE:** Meet Karliah at the Standing Stone
♦ **TARGET:** Nightingale Hall, just southwest of Riften

Take the southwest exit from Riften and walk the path until you see the large petroglyph stone among the silver birch trees. Both Brynjolf and Karliah are waiting for you. Karliah explains this is the headquarters of the Nightingales, and you're here to seek an edge in the forthcoming fight with Mercer. You may ask her further questions, but she says she'll tell you more once you're inside Nightingale Hall. Follow her inside. A secret door in the face of the rocky cliff will open, revealing a door into Nightingale Hall.

◊ **OBJECTIVE:** Follow Karliah

Step through the still air of the entrance tunnel. Brynjolf can't believe this place existed but doesn't know why he's here. Karliah reveals you are the first of the uninitiated to set foot in here in over a century. You are to accompany Karliah to the armory to don the armor of a Nightingale and begin the oath. Your roles should now become increasingly clear.

◊ **OBJECTIVE:** Activate the Armor Stone
◊ **OBJECTIVE:** Equip the Nightingale Armor

Cross the bridge, and through the archway are plinths with the same petroglyph carvings—that of the Nightingale and dark moon. Activate the Armor Stone, and the armor will be added to your inventory. Then go into your apparel and equip the armor to continue.

➤ **Nightingale Armor**
➤ **Nightingale Boots**
➤ **Nightingale Gloves**
➤ **Nightingale Hood**

◊ **OBJECTIVE:** Follow Karliah
◊ **OBJECTIVE:** Stand on vacant floor glyph

▷ Nocturnal at Our Backs

Stride toward the entrance to the Welkinsight Chamber, where Karliah explains the steps to becoming a Nightingale. After some hesitation on Brynjolf's part, follow the procession forward as the gate opens, and stand on the ancient circle glyph inscribed into the ground. Karliah performs the oath, and a dialogue with Lady Nocturnal begins. (Her voice emanates from a ball of energy. She doesn't appear in person at this point.)

◊ **OBJECTIVE:** Speak to Karliah
◊ **OBJECTIVE:** Speak to Brynjolf

Once the ceremony is over, Karliah reveals the last secret of the Nightingales: Their purpose is to guard not only the Twilight Sepulcher, but also the secret kept within—the Skeleton Key of Nocturnal. Mercer stole this key, which opens any lock (indeed, the artifact allowed him to bypass the otherwise-sealed locks on the Guild's vault doors), and the powers of the key may have imbued him with powers beyond normal reckoning.

 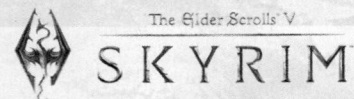

Quest Conclusion

Brynjolf tells you that due to the circumstances that have befallen the Thieves Guild, there is no one qualified to lead the forces except for you.

At this point, if you've completed all of the City Influence Quests, Brynjolf indicates that after this whole sorry affair is over, you are to become Guild Master.

At this point, if you haven't completed all of the City Influence Quests, Brynjolf says that as soon as Delvin tells him the Guild has regained a foothold in Skyrim, you are to become Guild Master.

Postquest Activities

Thieves Guild Quest: Blindsighted begins now!

 BLINDSIGHTED

PREREQUISITES: Complete Thieves Guild Quest: Trinity Restored

INTERSECTING QUESTS: Thieves Guild Quest: Additional Jobs, Thieves Guild Quest: Larceny Targets, Thieves Guild Quest: Trinity Restored

⬤ MAJOR SPOILERS

LOCATIONS: Bronze Water Cave, Irkngthand, Irkngthand Arcanex, Irkngthand Grand Cavern, Irkngthand Sanctuary, Irkngthand Slave Pens

CHARACTERS: Brynjolf, Karliah

ENEMIES: Bandit, Chaurus, Dwarven Centurion, Dwarven Sphere, Dwarven Spider, Falmer, Frostbite Spider, Mercer Frey

◊ **OBJECTIVES:** Travel to Irkngthand, Speak to Karliah, Locate Mercer Frey, Slay Mercer Frey, Retrieve the Skeleton Key, Escape from Irkngthand, Speak to Karliah

▶ Infiltration of Irkngthand

◊ **OBJECTIVE:** Travel to Irkngthand
♦ **TARGET:** Entrance to Irkngthand Arcanex

This quest begins with the first objective already under way. Head to Irkngthand, in the mountains above Lake Yorgrim. The exterior is a sprawling jumble of fallen dwarven ruins, a sealed gate, and a complement of bandits you must sneak past or slay. Ignore the gate with the bars and instead head right (west), under the fallen columns, and to the stone steps near some bear traps. Step onto the upper ledge next to the dwarven exterior, and head southeast. Follow the ledge to a corridor in the right wall, watching for the spear trap as you exit. Find the rickety wooden steps and follow this precarious path across the domed rooftops and over two wood bridges to the upper entrance of the main structure, Irkngthand Arcanex. Another option is to locate a lever along the path that drops the gate, allowing an easier access in and out.

◊ **OBJECTIVE:** Speak to Karliah
♦ **TARGET:** Entrance to Irkngthand Grand Cavern

Step into the golden gloom. Pass the bloodstained camp, moving southwest into a ceremonial pool chamber with more strewn dwarven machinery. A sphere springs to life here. Head into a chamber of faint green mist, and quickly avoid the numerous fire pillars, following the path among the rubble to the southeast gate. Once through the gate, locate the Dwarven Elevator and ride it down to the Grand Cavern. You meet Karliah and Brynjolf down the steps. Mention the bandits Mercer slew, and commence your hunt for Mercer Frey.

◊ **OBJECTIVE:** Locate Mercer Frey
♦ **TARGET:** Irkngthand Sanctuary

Moving around to the large balcony overlooking the last chamber in this area, Karliah spots Mercer Frey skulking close to the exit. You can't directly access this lower stepped chamber, so head through the door and along the winding corridors to a giant chamber of dwarven ruins. Cut down the Falmer that inhabit these parts before moving west along the ledge. There's a locked (Master) cage where an ancient ballista can be fired on foes down below. Head to a ledge with a lever. There is a second lever on the room's opposite side. Brynjolf mentions that these levers hold the key to your progress:

Puzzle Solution: Both the levers must be pulled to lower the bars that block your passage. Each lever is on either side of the raised area. If you aren't quick enough, the levers reset, so remove the enemy threats first. Then pull the lever farthest from the exit, and quickly rush to the opposite side and pull the other. This gives you the most amount of time to reach the exit. Both lamps by the door should be lit for you to proceed.

Now descend to the earthen floor, fighting Falmer and Dwarven Spheres, and head through the exit you created.

 TIP You can run off on your own if you wish; Karliah and Brynjolf will join you in a subsequent section of this place. If you get too far from them, they will attempt to catch up.

The subsequent chamber is in an even more dilapidated state. Climb atop the rubble and rooftops, fighting Falmer as you go. Head west to the stone ramps and up to the gold door. Beyond is a small study area and a gate to the southeast. Although Mercer has already ransacked this area, he neglected to grab a couple of Detect Life Scrolls strewn in this room; grab them, as they are useful later during your battle with him.

➤ **Scroll:** Detect Life (3)

Enter the gate, and your route opens up into a massive grand cavern. This is actually the location you saw from the balcony, which is in this chamber. Now you can battle through the Falmer to the opposite side, optionally challenging a Dwarven Centurion to fight if you wish or jumping off the small bridge and pressing the button on the console to release the Centurion on the hapless Falmer. Climb the stone ramp and run across the ledge to reach the upper Falmer camp. Exit into the Irkngthand Slave Pens.

Brynjolf notices the stench in these parts; you're going to be encountering several Falmer and their nasty pets, the Chaurus. First, though, destroy a Dwarven Spider or two, pass a locked gate (Apprentice), and head down the steps into a Dwarven Torture Chamber with bone chimes that alert the Falmer of your movements. If you sneak up on them, you can use the lever on the overlook to unleash a dwarven thresher trap on the Falmer below.

Journey down the corridor, turning right (south) into a Falmer camp. Slaughter (or sneak) your way east and south, opening the Chaurus pens to reach a chamber of pipes. Take the low road or high ledge to the drop-down at the eastern end, which leads to your ultimate destination: the Irkngthand Sanctuary. Or you can sneak across the dwarven pipes that run along the ceiling in one area, allowing you to cross most of this large expanse undetected.

No Mercy: Into the Frey!

A giant Falmer statue greets you from the opposite side of this huge Sanctuary chamber. Mercer has set about defiling it already, and Falmer blood has been spilled. Although Karliah and Brynjolf attempt silence, Mercer Frey finishes prying out the statue's massive eyes, notices you all, and casts a shock-wave-type spell that disrupts and destabilizes the massive chamber. The pipes in the ceiling burst, and water floods the chamber to about ankle depth. There's an immediate rumbling as you tumble down from the ledge, which splits apart, leaving your brethren stranded. You must face Mercer Frey alone! He speaks to you from your fallen position. You can speak to Frey about Nocturnal and the key, but there's only one way this ends: with one of you at the end of a blade!

◇ **OBJECTIVE:** Slay Mercer Frey

Target: Mercer Frey. Mercer is a vicious swordsman. He is nimble and dextrous and can turn himself invisible. Even before you fight him, he uses one of his stolen Nightingale powers to Frenzy Brynjolf, who turns on Karliah, effectively keeping them from helping you in this battle. This causes no end of problems, especially as the chamber you're on is getting wetter and is very steep. There are steps around the statue, and you can cross the statue's lap.

Mercer Frey may be invisible for most of the fight, but keep an eye on the water, as it will ripple when Mercer runs through it.

If you grabbed the Detect Life Scrolls or have a spell of the same name, now would be an exceptionally good time to use it!

Strike Mercer with your Nightingale Blade. This drains him and leaves a shimmering trail from him, even when he's invisible. Use that to your advantage. Keep moving so he can't sneak up on you, and keep your back to a wall so he can't hit you from behind.

Mercer's form is shimmering and isn't completely invisible; strike out quickly when you see this shape. If you're attacking at melee range, remember you can still block and then counterattack immediately. This helps when fighting blind. Spells with ongoing effects also help, such as Flames, which coat Mercer in fire, allowing you to see him more clearly.

After the shadows take him, search Mercer Frey quickly. Among his belongings, you can claim the two Eyes of the Falmer and the Skeleton Key Karliah spoke of. Now is the time to make good your escape!

◇ **OBJECTIVE:** Retrieve the Skeleton Key
◇ **OBJECTIVE:** Escape from Irkngthand
◆ **TARGET:** Bronze Water Cave

➤ **Eye of the Falmer (2)**   ➤ **Skeleton Key**

QUEST: LARCENY TARGET

Make sure to bring these enormous gems to Delvin. Consult Thieves Guild Quest: Larceny Targets for more information.

The statue chamber becomes increasingly unstable, with torrents of water cascading down from an increasing number of holes in the ceiling. Karliah yells that there must be a way out, and yet the water still rises. Stay calm, and after snagging your final Larceny Target, turn and face the chamber's southeastern side, just above the head of the Falmer Statue. Right before the cavern completely fills with water, a cluster of rocks dislodge, revealing a tunnel opening—but only if you have the power of the Skeleton Key, so be sure to grab it off Mercer's corpse. Don't waste any more time; scramble up into the tunnel and escape!

◇ **OBJECTIVE:** Speak to Karliah

Quest Conclusion

You emerge into the Bronze Water Cave, on the shore of Lake Yorgrim. Brynjolf has matters to attend to, but Karliah speaks with you for a few moments, realizing her 25-year exile is over and presenting you with a token of her esteem. Now it is time to return the Skeleton Key to its rightful place, by traversing the Pilgrim's Path in the Twilight Sepulcher. This is a journey you'll be taking alone.

➤ **Nightingale Bow**

Postquest Activities

This is a leveled bow that deals Frost and Shock damage and slows the target slightly. Thieves Guild Quest: Darkness Returns begins now!

> **TIP** From the point you obtain the Skeleton Key to the end of the next quest, you have an unbreakable Lockpick! This means you can try your hand to any lock for as long as you like with no fear of snapping a pick! You may wish to unlock some particularly troublesome locks across Skyrim before continuing!

  **DARKNESS RETURNS**

PREREQUISITES: Complete Thieves Guild Quest: Blindsighted
INTERSECTING QUESTS: Thieves Guild Quest: Additional Jobs, Thieves Guild Quest: Larceny Targets, Thieves Guild Quest: Under New Management
LOCATIONS: Twilight Sepulcher, Ebonmere, Twilight Sepulcher Inner Sanctum
CHARACTERS: Gallus, Karliah, Nocturnal
ENEMIES: Nightingale Sentinel
◇ **OBJECTIVES:** Enter the Twilight Sepulcher, Speak to the Nightingale Sentinel, Follow the Pilgrim's Path, (Optional) Retrieve Nystrom's Journal, Return the Skeleton Key to the Ebonmere, Listen to Nocturnal, Speak to Karliah, Choose Nightingale Role

⬤ **MAJOR SPOILERS**

A Dark Journey: Pilgrim's Path

◊ **OBJECTIVE:** Enter the Twilight Sepulcher
◊ **OBJECTIVE:** Speak to the Nightingale Sentinel

This quest begins with the first objective already under way. Journey to the mountains to the west of Falkreath, and find the entrance to the Twilight Sepulcher, close to a rushing mountain stream. Open the ornate Iron Door, and step into this sacred site. The large entrance cavern is dominated by an arched entrance ahead (south) of you. Waiting for you at the steps below the entrance is a ghostly figure. Speak to the last of the Nightingale Sentinels, who blames himself for this predicament after allowing Mercer Frey to lure him to his fate and steal the Skeleton Key.

You recognize this entity to be Gallus, although this spirit hasn't gone by that name in a long time. Explain you have the key. Continue the conversation, mentioning Karliah is still alive and telling him the key has been returned. Alas, Gallus cannot help you, as this place holds the Ebonmere—a conduit to Nocturnal's realm of Evergloam. When Mercer removed the key, it closed the conduit, weakening the guardians of this place and causing them to forget their true purpose. To rectify this situation, you must take the Pilgrim's Path.

◊ **OBJECTIVE:** Follow the Pilgrim's Path
♦ **TARGET:** Entrance to Evergloam, in Twilight Sepulcher Inner Sanctum

You can ask Gallus more questions about what is wrong with the other Sentinels, how the Ebonmere affects you, and what you'll face along Pilgrim's Path. For this question, the spirit recommends you read the journal of a long-dead adventurer who had hoped to take the Path.

◊ **OBJECTIVE:** (Optional) Retrieve Nystrom's Journal

Nystrom's skeletal remains lie in this chamber, to the east. Search him and check out his weapon, but the real prize is the journal on his corpse.

➤ **Nystrom's Journal**

THE FIVE TESTS OF PILGRIM'S PATH

The journal mentions five tests, giving obtuse advice on each of them:

1. "Shadows of their former selves, sentinels of the dark. They wander ever more and deal swift death to defilers."
2. "Above all they stand, vigilance everlasting. Beholden to the murk yet contentious of the glow."
3. "Offer what She desires most, but reject the material. For her greatest want is that which cannot be seen, felt or carried."
4. "Direct and yet indirect. The path to salvation a route cunning with fortune betraying the foolish."
5. "The journey is complete, the Empress's embrace awaits the fallen. Hesitate not if you wish to gift her your eternal devotion."

Puzzle Solution: The five clues refer to the following sections of your forthcoming quest:

1. This refers to the Sentinels guarding this place.

2. This refers to the chamber with the areas of light and darkness and the archers that fire upon you, and that the light is damaging.

3. This refers to the offering room with the basin; Nocturnal desires darkness more than anything else, so the basin is a red herring; extinguish all of the braziers to create darkness.

4. This refers to the long gauntlet of traps in the narrow passage that can be bypassed by picking the lock and avoiding it.

5. This refers to the shaft with no exit.

Party of the First Part: Sentinels

Head up the stairs, weaving your way past a sealed grating and down through an Iron Door, into a candlelit crypt. Nightingale Sentinels are poised here to repel intruders and cannot be reasoned with. Slay those you encounter, pausing only to sift through any books in the upper library. Next, squeeze past the central pedestal, past a floor trigger in the next corridor, and head west to an Iron Door.

Party of the Second Part: Shadows

> **CAUTION**
> Beware! This chamber of shadows can burn you to a crisp in moments. You may wish to save your game before proceeding!

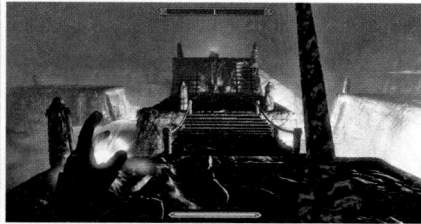

Enter a chamber of shadows. Urns glow with inhuman light. Stone plateaus and a weaving path coax you forward. Then the burning starts! You begin to lose health at an alarming rate as you walk through this collection of cursed passages and platforms.

Puzzle Solution: Walk into the lit areas, and your health plummets. The darker the areas, the less your health diminishes. As you enter, run west (and slightly north, to the right) and climb atop the first platform, dodging any dart traps you trigger. Wait up here to regain your health. Turn southwest and rush *behind* the next structure, and use the wooden steps to climb up after a sharp left (east) turn. Next, rush over the wooden bridge, stepping to the right to avoid more darts. Run up the wooden steps, past the cauldron of light, to the dark edge of the ledge. Regain your health and look southwest. Drop down, running south up the dark middle of the steps to the exit door.

Party of the Third Part: Struck

Walk through the crypt to a pedestal of Nocturnal with a dead bandit at the foot of it. The two ornate wall torches are each hiding the pull chain; yank this to reveal a false wall that rumbles open. Weave through the corridor, heading west, to a group of swinging axes blocking your path. Look left to see a locked door. Pick the lock (Lockpick [Master]) and you can bypass all the traps and head straight to the fourth part). Or, watch for a floor trigger that launches darts. Sprint between them to the Iron Door, avoiding another floor trigger that skewers you with spears by the door. Wait as the door opens and a battering ram swings at you. Step to the right to avoid it, and run under it as it repositions. You can enter the Inner

Sanctum from here, or optionally investigate a ghostly banquet hall with items to scavenge and two more Sentinels to dispatch.

Party of the Fourth Part: Skeleton

Amble through a candlelit hallway with a faint purple mist in the air. This leads to a nasty drop down a circular well. At the bottom are the skeletal remains of Anders, an adventurer. Read his message if you wish, before realizing you're well and truly stuck down this well.

Puzzle solution: After a few moments of sweating, you produce the Skeleton Key automatically; the arcane device seems to "know" what you want to unlock and allows you to pass through the floor and into the Ebonmere chamber.

➤ **Anders's Message**

Party of the Fifth Part: Summoning

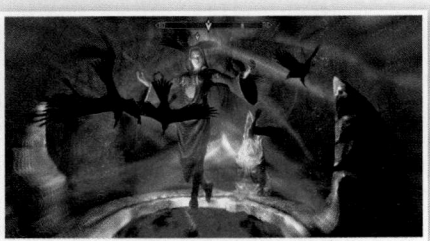

After producing the Skeleton Key and dropping the down the well and into the entrance to Evergloam, you have but one choice: Return the Skeleton Key to the Ebonmere.

◊ **OBJECTIVE:** Return the Skeleton Key to the Ebonmere
◊ **OBJECTIVE:** Listen to Nocturnal
◊ **OBJECTIVE:** Speak to Karliah

A circle of impossibly deep blue vapors congeals around the Ebonmere, a three-pronged portal to Evergloam. A flock of black nightingales departs, announcing the arrival of Nocturnal. She notes that a champion has returned the Skeleton Key to the Sepulcher and the Ebonmere is restored. You shall have your trinkets of reward and must drink deeply from the Ebonmere to become an Agent of Nocturnal! It seems this Skeleton Key unlocks more than just doors; it also reveals inner potential.

Once you choose the power, you can now freely and quickly leave the temple. This ends the Thieves Guild critical path quests.

Quest Conclusion

You have done well in the eyes of Nocturnal. Karliah has also appeared. She is visited by the spirit of Gallus one final time; his tormented imprisonment has been lifted, and he leaves his love to walk with the shadows. Speak with Karliah, and she gives you more information about the circles at the base of the Ebonmere. These imbue you with powers befitting a Nightingale Agent. The symbol is of the waxing and waning moon. You can return here once every 24 hours to change your ability, and one day you may be forced back to defend this place; this is your pact with Nocturnal. For now, though, there are pockets brimming with coin and coffers ripe for the picking all across Skyrim!

◊ **OBJECTIVE:** Choose Nightingale Role

➤ **Agent of Shadow:** For two minutes, you are invisible when sneaking. Note that attacking or activating something makes you appear, just as with standard invisibility. You simply need to begin to sneak again, and the invisibility will instantly reactivate. This is a power, so you can use it only once per day.

➤ **Agent of Subterfuge:** You can cast a massive Fury spell that can Frenzy any target regardless of its level. This is a power, so you can use it only once per day.

➤ **Agent of Strife:** You can cast a huge blast of energy that damages the health of the target for 100 points and grants this same health to you. This is a power, so you can use it only once per day.

Postquest Activities

Karliah makes Nightingale Hall her home, and you can visit her there. Activate the portal to reach the Sepulcher's entrance hall, and head back to finish any remaining additional jobs. This allows you to finally assume the leadership of the Thieves Guild. But your Critical Path Quests are now over.

 # THIEVES GUILD RADIANT QUESTS

The following 18 Radiant Quests, Additional Jobs, and City Influence Quests occur throughout (and between) the critical Thieves Guild Quests and offer you a different task to accomplish, usually with a sizable reward. Additional Jobs can be completed multiple times. These are available depending on how far along through the critical quests you are. For a complete list of how to unlock each quest, consult the Introduction to the Thieves Guild Quests, at the start of this chapter.

  ## NO STONE UNTURNED

PREREQUISITES: None
INTERSECTING QUESTS: Dark Brotherhood Quest: With Friends Like These… , Dark Brotherhood Quest: Destroy the Dark Brotherhood!, Main Quest: Diplomatic Immunity, Thieves Guild City Influence Quest: Silver Lining
◊ **OBJECTIVES:** Objective: Bring the Unusual Gem to an appraiser of stolen goods, Objective: Bring the Unusual Gem to Vex in the Thieves Guild, Objective: Recover the Stones of Barenziah (24), Objective: Recover the Crown of Barenziah, Objective: Return to Vex

▷ A Crowning Achievement

During your adventures, you may stumble upon an odd-looking but possibly extremely valuable gemstone. This particular valuable stands out from the rest and is called an "Unusual Gem." Any other precious stone is irrelevant to this quest. Once you take (or steal) the gem, the quest begins and one of two objectives appear. The first occurs if you haven't yet joined the Thieves Guild.

➤ **Unusual Gem**

◊ **OBJECTIVE:** Bring the Unusual Gem to an appraiser of stolen goods
◊ **OBJECTIVE:** Bring the Unusual Gem to Vex in the Thieves Guild

NOTE If you haven't met any Thieves Guild members yet, journey to Riften's Stables and enter via the northern gate. A lout named Maul (the brother of Guild member Dirge) accosts you as you enter Riften. You can speak with him, using Persuasion, Bribing, or Brawling to test his mettle. Then ask about the Unusual Gem you have, and you're directed toward Vex (although he doesn't mention her by name until you're a full member of the Thieves Guild). If Maul has died or you've angered him to the point that you're not on speaking terms, you must simply stumble upon Vex.

Once you know to speak with Vex, meet her at the Ragged Flagon in Riften. Ask her if the Unusual Gem you found is worth anything, and she tells you the gem is a Stone of Barenziah. Although it isn't worth anything in its current state, it is one of 24 prized gems pried off Barenziah's ceremonial crown. Many have attempted to collect all the gems but have failed. Until now! She will pay for a full set of gems and asks you to talk to her again once you've found all 24.

 OBJECTIVE: Recover the Stones of Barenziah (24)

NOTE Any Unusual Gems (including any you've already found) are called "Stones of Barenziah."

You must now begin to collect the remaining Stones of Barenziah. There are 24 total, minus any you've already found (which must be a minimum of one to trigger this quest). Consult the following table for guidance regarding every Stone's location:

✓	NUMBER	ZONE #	LOCATION	DESCRIPTION	PREREQUISITE
	[1/24]	[1.00]	Solitude (Proudspire Manor)	In the master bedroom of Proudspire Manor	Proudspire Manor purchased
✗	[2/24]	[1.00]	Solitude (Blue Palace)	On a shelf in Jarl Elisif the Fair's quarters.	None
	[3/24]	[1.21]	Thalmor Embassy	In Elenwen's Solar in the Thalmor Embassy, in one of the bedrooms.	During or after Main Quest: Diplomatic Immunity
	[4/24]	[1.27]	Dainty Sload	On a small table in the Captain's Quarters of the Dainty Sload, moored near Solitude.	None
	[5/24]	[4.00]	College of Winterhold	On a shelf in the Arch-Mage's Quarters.	None
	[6/24]	[4.02]	Yngvild	In the Throne Room area of Yngvild, in the chamber behind the throne.	None
	[7/24]	[4.05]	Hob's Fall Cave	In the necromancers' sleeping area.	None
	[8/24]	[5.00]	Markarth (Treasury House)	On a nightstand next to the bed in the master bedroom.	None
	[9/24]	[5.00]	Markarth (Understone Keep)	On a table in a locked side room of the Dwemer Museum.	None
	[10/24]	[5.36]	Dead Crone Rock	On a makeshift altar at Dead Crone Rock.	None
	[11/24]	[6.00]	Whiterun (Jorrvaskr)	In Kodlak Whitemane's bedroom.	None
	[12/24]	[6.00]	Whiterun (Hall of the Dead)	In one of the wall crypts at the foot of a skeleton.	None
	[13/24]	[6.00]	Whiterun (Dragonsreach)	In the Jarl's bedroom area of the Jarl's Quarters.	None
	[14/24]	[6.09]	Rannveig's Fast	On a table near the watery prison within Rannveig's Fast.	None
	[15/24]	[6.29]	Fellglow Keep	On a counter in the workroom at the top of the front foyer.	None
	[16/24]	[7.00]	Windhelm (House of Clan Shatter-Shield)	In a bedroom of the Shatter-Shield home.	None
	[17/24]	[7.00]	Windhelm (Palace of the Kings)	On a table in Wuunferth the Unliving's quarters.	None
	[18/24]	[7.36]	Stony Creek Cave	In the Bandit Wizard's cavern in Stony Creek Cave.	None
	[19/24]	[7.38]	Ansilvund	Near Fjori's ghost in the burial chambers of Ansilvund.	None
	[20/24]	[8.02]	Sunderstone Gorge	On the altar in front of the Word Wall.	None
	[21/24]	[8.22]	Dark Brotherhood Sanctuary	On the dresser in Astrid's room.	During or after Dark Brotherhood Quest: With Friends Like These... OR Dark Brotherhood Quest: Destroy the Dark Brotherhood!
	[22/24]	[8.28]	Pinewatch	In a locked treasure room in the Pinewatch Bandit Sanctuary.	None
	[23/24]	[9.00]	Riften (Mistveil Keep)	In the Jarl's Chambers in Mistveil Keep, on the bedside table.	None
	[24/24]	[9.35]	Riften (Black-Briar Lodge)	In the upstairs master bedroom of Black-Briar Lodge.	None

After you collect all 24 Stones of Barenziah, return to Vex, and she lets you in on a little secret: She knows the location of the Crown of Barenziah, and she'll pay handsomely if you bring it back. Naturally, this involves a long and dangerous trek through Tolvald's Cave, to the southwest of Riften. This place is infested with wild animals and worse—Falmer and their horrific pets, the Chaurus. Battle through this maze of caves to Tolvald's Crossing, moving to a large, dead-end chamber. There's a refuse pile at the end of the path that winds to the right, just after the waterfall. Sort through the pile for the crown.

➤ **Crown of Barenziah**

Quest Conclusion

Back at the Ragged Flagon, tell Vex you've found the Crown of Barenziah. She's suitably impressed and rewards you with the Prowler's Profit perk, which vastly increases the chances of finding gems while scavenging dungeons. You can then sell these for substantial sums of gold. The completed crown with gems is in the Guild behind Mercer's desk once you complete the quest.

➤ **Perk:** Prowler's Profit

REPARATIONS

If you commit a minor crime, such as accidentally striking a Guild member or pickpocketing them, you're usually let off with a warning (if you're caught). However, if you commit a serious crime, such as assaulting or murdering a Thieves Guild member, all of them become hostile and will attack you. At this point, you can:

Continue on the killing spree, which doesn't result in much else besides dead bodies and fewer places to sell or train. Note that Vex, Delvin, Brynjolf, and Mercer are essential, so surviving in this state is going to be exceedingly difficult!

Yield by sheathing your weapons, or flee the Ragged Flagon, wait three days, and return. Expect the Guild to be unfriendly but not hostile toward you.

Speak to Vex. She requires the princely sum of 1,000 gold pieces paid to the Guild as reparations. Pay up, and you become firm friends again. Refuse, and expect to be ostracized until you pay the fine. This halts all quest progress, including Additional Quests and City Influence Quests. Until reparations are made, you are all alone.

SHADOWMARKS*

> **NOTE** ✳ Quest names marked with this symbol do not appear in your Quest Menu list, although objectives may.

Eagle-eyed members of the Thieves Guild may notice certain locations across Skyrim are marked with strange little pictorial signs. These inscriptions, which are unknown markings to outsiders, are actually a cryptolect that the Guild uses to flag locations that members feel are particularly safe or dangerous or that have entities that may be helpful or problematic. The symbols are known as Shadowmarks.

To learn more about Shadowmarks, search the Thieves Guild premises for a particularly well-researched book called *Shadowmarks*, written by Delvin Mallory. It contains all the markings the Thieves Guild uses.

➤ **Shadowmarks**

GLOSSARY OF SHADOWMARKS

The following Shadowmarks appear throughout the realm of Skyrim. Here's what they mean:

✓		SHADOWMARK	DESCRIPTION
☐	◇	"The Guild"	This place is as safe as the Flagon's Cistern. Someone from the Guild is nearby for certain.
☐	△	"Safe"	A safe way around an obstacle, such as a hallway without traps or a house already cleared out. Head the way it is pointing to be safe.
☐	▽	"Danger"	Head the other way or take your life in your hands. Danger lurks beyond this point!
☐	⊕	"Escape Route"	If you find yourself in jail, look for this marking and find an escape route nearby.
☐	◈	"Protected"	Don't go here when thieving; the people at this location are under the Guild's protection and should never be robbed or assaulted.
☐	⬧	"Fence"	This should become your favorite landmark; expect to sell your hard-earned stolen goods here at a fair price.
☐	◇	"Thieves' Cache"	Find this on a chest or barrel; expect a gift. Membership has its privileges.
☐	⬚	"Loot"	There's something near here worth stealing.
☐	⬭	"Empty"	Pass over this place, as there's nothing of note inside.

These markings can reveal (for example) who they consider a Fence, so if you're prowling a new town, you can learn where friends, foes, thieving opportunities, and like-minded souls reside. This can also help during certain Jobs so you know what's likely to be inside a house before you enter it; every one of the five largest Hold Cities (Solitude, Markarth, Whiterun, Windhelm, and Riften) has these markings to find. Also note that Guild Cache barrels are clearly emblazoned with the Thieves Cache Shadowmark, making them easier to spot for eagle-eyed thieves exploring the five largest capitals.

When you speak with Tonilla after being inducted into the Guild, she tells you that she has something for you to do. The Guild is lacking a reliable way to transport merchandise across Skyrim. Tonilia reckons the shrewd Khajiit caravaneers might want a cut of the profits for selling (and fencing) for the Guild. Their leader, Ri'saad, should make a deal if you present him with the satchel of Moon Sugar she gives you.

➤ **Satchel of Moon Sugar**

◊ **OBJECTIVE:** Deliver Moon Sugar to Ri'saad

Take this unrefined narcotic to Ri'saad, and tell him you bring an offer from the Thieves Guild. Hand over the Moon Sugar, and he's swayed into an agreement. From this point on, any Khajiit Caravan you meet across Skyrim will be happy to purchase your stolen goods for a fair sum. Ask him further questions and barter with him if you wish.

◊ **OBJECTIVE:** Return to Tonilia

Head back to the Ragged Flagon, inform Tonilia of your success, and she gives you some gold for your troubles. Much more importantly, you can sell stolen property to the following Fences, in each of the Caravans!

➤ **Leveled gold pieces**
➤ **Fence (Caravan):** Atahba
➤ **Fence (Caravan):** Majhad
➤ **Fence (Caravan):** Zaynabi
➤ **Fence (Caravan):** Ri'saad

ARMOR EXCHANGE*

Once you successfully complete Thieves Guild Quest: Scoundrel's Folly, Brynjolf mentions that Tonilia has a special piece of armor that you can exchange. When you speak to her, she offers to exchange one of your four pieces of Thieves Armor for a piece that's more enhanced. Choose from the hood, cuirass, gloves, or boots. You can choose only one and can't go back on your choice. The quest then concludes.

➤ **Thieves Guild Armor (+35 Carry Weight)**
➤ **Thieves Guild Boots (Improve Pickpocket 25%)**
➤ **Thieves Guild Gloves (Improve Lockpick 25%)**
➤ **Thieves Guild Hood (Improve Prices 15%)**

LARCENY TARGETS*

Throughout almost all of the Thieves Guild Critical Path Quests, you'll find a valuable item to steal, with the express intention of making a little money from it. The exact location of each Larceny Target is detailed in each specific quest. Return and speak to Delvin about cashing in your stolen goods for gold. The following table lists all available Larceny Targets and the quests they appear in:

Queen Bee Statue | Honningbrew Decanter | East Empire Shipping Map | Model Ship | Dwemer Puzzle Cube | Bust of the Gray Fox | Eye of the Falmer (Second Gem)

✓	LARCENY TARGET	THIEVES GUILD QUEST	LOCATION	DESCRIPTION
	Queen Bee Statue	Loud and Clear	Goldenglow Estate second floor	On a bedside table upstairs in Aringoth's bedroom
	Honningbrew Decanter	Dampened Spirits	Honningbrew Meadery	Locked upstairs office belonging to Sabjorn
	East Empire Shipping Map	Scoundrel's Folly	East Empire Trading Company Warehouse	In the dock overseer's hut, northwest corner
	Model Ship	Speaking with Silence	Snow Veil Sanctum	Fallen from a pedestal, deep in the dungeon
	Dwemer Puzzle Cube	Hard Answers	Calcelmo's Laboratory	In an alcove, near Calcelmo's assistant Aicantar
	Bust of the Gray Fox	The Pursuit	Mercer's House	In Mercer Frey's cellar office, in his house in Riften
	Eye of the Falmer (Second Gem)	Blindsighted	Irkngthand Sanctuary	Taken from Mercer Frey's corpse.

TIP Did you miss one of these trinkets? Then return to the location and snag it; all should still be there. Also look for sold Larceny Targets to appear as trophies on one of the bookcases behind Mercer's desk in the Cistern and for the bust of the Gray Fox on the desk.

➤ **150 to 300 gold pieces (per item)**

ADDITIONAL JOBS

PREREQUISITES: Complete Thieves Guild Quest: Taking Care of Business

AN OVERVIEW

Ready for some extra work? Once Brynjolf instructs you to speak with Vex and Delvin Mallory about additional work they may have for you (after you complete Thieves Guild Quest: Taking Care of Business and you "officially" join the Guild), immediately chat with either of your new brethren. Aside from offering you training in Lockpicking (Vex) and Sneaking (Delvin), ask them to explain the jobs they have to offer you, and then begin any you wish. You can have one Additional Job from each of them active at any given time. The Guild frowns on you quitting jobs you may be finding too difficult, but this is possible too. When you successfully finish a certain number (and variety) of Additional Jobs, Part 3: City Influence Quests become accessible (see below).

➤ **Leveled gold pieces**

✓	JOB GIVER	TYPE OF JOB	✓	JOB GIVER	TYPE OF JOB
	Delvin Mallory	The Numbers Job		Vex	The Shill Job
	Delvin Mallory	The Fishing Job		Vex	The Sweep Job
	Delvin Mallory	The Bedlam Job		Vex	The Heist Job
	Vex	The Burglary Job			

> **NOTE** The following gives general information on all seven types of jobs and provides a particular example of each. You can continue to choose jobs for as long as you like; there's no upper limit.

> **CAUTION** Be warned! Killing witnesses or the owners of any object you are pilfering is against the Thieves Guild code and fails the active job. Thieves steal valuables, not lives! Even worse, once the job fails, there is no gold reward, and the job does not count toward unlocking the City Influence Quests!

 **DELVIN'S ADDITIONAL JOBS**

The Numbers Job

> ◊ **OBJECTIVE:** Make changes in the ledger at [business name] in a Hold City
> ◊ **OBJECTIVE:** Return to Delvin

Delvin is concerned with skimming a little off the top: To this end, he requires you to visit a store somewhere in the realm and make some subtle changes to the ledger. Enter the establishment, find the ledger, and fix it. You only need to complete the ledger changes without being spotted, although some ledgers are in the same room as a vendor, meaning you need to enter at night or use Sneak abilities.

The Fishing Job

> ◊ **OBJECTIVE:** Retrieve [item] from [mark] in [Hold City].
> ◊ **OBJECTIVE:** Return the valuable to Delvin.

Delvin has numerous jobs to test one of the oldest and most important skills that a thief must possess: a penchant for pickpocketing! Move to the location indicated and observe the person. Check the route they take and be patient; then quickly crouch and follow them. Swipe the valuable before they can react or even know it's gone! Augmentations both magical and skillful help here.

The Bedlam Job

> ◊ **OBJECTIVE:** Steal [a set amount of] gold in goods, from a Hold city
> ◊ **OBJECTIVE:** Return the valuables to Delvin

Delvin's third job involves surreptitiously entering a city and emptying it of a set number of valuables up to a value in gold pieces that Delvin has determined. The trick here is to know where in the city you can pillage (everywhere within the local map but not adjacent locations such as the Blue Palace in Solitude or Understone Keep in Markarth) and to take items only while you're hidden; therefore, crouch and check every time, just before you make the snatch. If you are seen taking an object, it doesn't count toward the total, so make sure you are completely hidden. Basically, keep stealing until the quest triggers that you're done!

> **TIP** The best locations to pilfer from are stores, marketplaces, and private residences. The Dwemer Museum in Markarth does not count. Any additional stolen goods can be sold to Tonilia, as this is the one job where you're allowed to keep the items at the end!

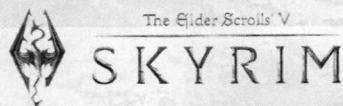

The Burglary Job

◊ **OBJECTIVE:** Retrieve [an item] from [a wealthy home] somewhere in a Hold city
◊ **OBJECTIVE:** Return the valuable to Vex

Vex requires you to break into a location (usually the residence of a high-ranking or wealthy person) and steal a valuable object that the Thieves Guild can sell. This almost always requires you to wait until any residents of the location have left or to utilize your Sneak and Lockpick talents to unlock one of the location's doors, steal the valuable, and leave quickly.

The Shill Job

◊ **OBJECTIVE:** Plant [evidence] in [a wealthy home] somewhere in a Hold City
◊ **OBJECTIVE:** Return to Vex

Vex wants you to take a stolen item acquired by the Guild and place it inside the home of a high-ranking person, in order to implicate them in a crime. Aside from taking the usual precautions when entering and exiting the building (ensuring no one sees you inside or out), you must locate a chest or other object that holds items and place the stolen item in it. Remember; only place the specific item you're carrying!

The Sweep Job

◊ **OBJECTIVE:** Clear [a wealthy home], somewhere in a Hold City, of [valuables]
◊ **OBJECTIVE:** Return the valuables to Vex

Vex orders you to head to a location the Guild has staked out and believes has numerous high-quality items. You must enter the premises unseen. Once inside, you are to clear the house of a specific number of valuables (and optionally, anything else you can get away with, although this isn't necessary for this quest). Then return to Vex without arousing suspicion at any time.

The Heist Job

◊ **OBJECTIVE:** Steal [an item] from [a store] in a Hold City
◊ **OBJECTIVE:** Return [the item] to Vex

The last type of job Vex has is similar to burglary but with an important difference: You're taking a valuable item from a store rather than a private residence. As there's usually someone in a store and in a storeroom where a strongbox usually holds the valuable item, proficient sneaking, usually at nighttime, is the only way to avoid angering the locals and increasing your Bounty (which can occur but is not recommended).

 TIP Common sense should prevail when you're trying to complete jobs without being caught:

Burglarize stores when they are closed so the vendors don't see you.

Stake out private residences and watch when the inhabitants leave; when the house is empty, pick the lock and steal without the possibility of discovery.

The more risk you take by attempting crimes with vendors or residents gazing at you, the harder you're making it for yourself.

There's no reason to rush; spend time staking places out and learning where the targets are, and come back later to attempt the deed.

 # CITY INFLUENCE QUESTS

 GROWING THE GUILD AND GAINING INFLUENCE

An Overview

As you become continuously successful with your jobs, you can inquire during conversations with Delvin Mallory or Vex about the reasons for these jobs and how they help the Guild. The reasons are simple: Years ago, the Guild had a foothold in every major city in Skyrim—folks wouldn't dare lifting an apple without checking with the Guild first—but as the Guild collapsed, they lost Fences, influential contacts, and, most importantly, respect. With your help, the Guild can be taken seriously and start to take the cities back again.

Thanks to Maven Black-Briar, you have some pull in Riften, but if you're caught in a nefarious act in Whiterun or another Skyrim city, you should expect an extended jail stay. But once you complete a unique job for an influential and powerful individual within each prominent city, you can expect a much more lenient attitude. However, these city leaders won't approach the Guild until numerous smaller "jobs" have been completed—the tasks you're undertaking already.

To activate the following City Influence Quests (one per city), you must complete a total of 5 Additional Jobs within that city. After you successfully finish 5 Additional Jobs in a particular city, contact Delvin Mallory inside the Ragged Flagon and begin one or more of the following jobs. Continue to complete Additional Jobs until you successfully finish 5 or more in every city.

Obviously, with the random nature of the jobs, you may have to complete more than 10 before receiving a job for a city you haven't finished all the necessary jobs in yet. The cities that the Thieves Guild wishes to gain influence in are:

✓	NAME OF CITY	ADDITIONAL JOBS COMPLETED?	AVAILABLE QUEST
	Markarth	5	Silver Lining
	Solitude	5	The Dainty Sload
	Whiterun	5	Imitation Amnesty
	Windhelm	5	Summerset Shadows
	Riften	0	None†

NOTE † Additional Jobs are available but no additional quest is available. You can perform jobs there, but they don't contribute to the City Influence Quests.

The rewards you receive for spreading the Thieves Guild's influence across Skyrim are detailed after the following four City Influence Quests.

  SILVER LINING

PREREQUISITES: Complete Thieves Guild Quests: Additional Jobs in Markarth (5)
INTERSECTING QUESTS: All further Thieves Guild Quests
LOCATIONS: Pinewatch, Pinewatch Bandit's Sanctuary, Riften, Ratway, Cistern, The Ragged Flagon
CHARACTERS: Adora, Delvin Mallory, Endon, Rhorlak
ENEMIES: Bandit, Rigel Strong-Arm
◊ **OBJECTIVES:** Speak to Endon the Silversmith, Enter Pinewatch, Recover Endon's Silver Mold, Return to Endon

Molding Endon's Alliance

◊ **OBJECTIVE:** Speak to Endon the Silversmith
♦ **TARGET:** Endon, in Markarth

After you complete 5 (or more) successful Additional Jobs in Markarth, Delvin Mallory receives word that one of the finest Silversmiths in all of Skyrim, a man named Endon, has ordered a special mold from far-off Valenwood but it never arrived at his shop. Meet Endon (and his daughter, Adora) and tell him Delvin sent you. He informs you that bandits were most likely to blame. As Markarth's other resources are stretched thin, he has requested that the Thieves Guild handle this. Endon promises both his loyalty and some of his wealth in exchange for returning the invaluable mold.

◊ **OBJECTIVE:** Enter Pinewatch

Journey to the remote farmhouse known as Pinewatch in the middle of the pine forest, and pick the lock of the door (Average). Step inside, and your objective updates.

◊ **OBJECTIVE:** Recover Endon's Silver Mold
♦ **TARGET:** Inside the Pinewatch Bandit's Sanctuary, in Pinewatch

The lone farmhouse is deceptively small. Head to the cellar and locate (or wake up) Rhorlak. To progress further, try one of the following:

Choose to kill him. Search the cellar, find the note on the table and read it, and locate the secret trigger button.

(Bribe) Offer to loosen his tongue with money. He mentions a secret trigger button in the cellar wall.

Or simply ignore Rhorlak (the cheapest, nonviolent option) and simply find the button in the wall, with or without reading the note.

Or find the note tacked onto the wall with a dagger, by the door to the wilderness.

Across from the cellar fireplace is a suspiciously empty shelving cabinet. Check to the right of it for a button, above a basket. Press it. The cabinet swings out, revealing a tunnel behind it.

➤ **Note to Rhorlak**

Cross the wooden bridges and through the roughly hewn connecting tunnels, as Pinewatch's underground maze opens up before you. Bandits are guarding this area, so approach each chamber with your armaments at the ready. Continue past a large collection of barrels, down the craggy path, and fight more bandits to reach a door leading to the Pinewatch Bandit's Sanctuary.

In the first Sanctuary chamber, use the stacked barrels as cover when fighting off (or sneaking past) another group of bandits. Look for the opening in the upper western wall. Go past the cage room and up the stone steps to a wooden door and a small crypt room. The dead Draugr inform you that bandits are farther inside these catacombs; travel into the makeshift camp where you'll encounter more fighting. Head into the chamber with the hanging bone chimes; brush into them if you wish to alert Rigel Strong-Arm, the leader of this motley crew. Search (or pickpocket) her for the necessary keys to enter all additional chambers.

➤ **Pinewatch Key**   ➤ **Pinewatch Treasure Room Key**

At the next wooden door, pick the lock (Very Hard) or use the Pinewatch Treasure Room Key. Just beyond is an iron door leading across a precarious pair of wooden beams with dart traps on either side. Sprint across, open another wooden door, and watch for two trigger stones in the floor; they both release traps—swinging blades and a battering ram, respectively—as you progress to the main crypt. You're greeted with a mace trap to the face, so take a step back and duck into the chamber. Sitting in the despoiled sarcophagus is the unique item you've been tasked to find. Take it, any coin, and the Silver Candlestick (which you can fence back at the Ragged Flagon). The treasure chest is worth prying open, too!

 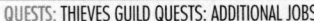

 Endon's Silver Mold ➤ Silver Candlestick

◊ **OBJECTIVE:** Return to Endon
♦ **TARGET:** Endon, in Markarth

⟨⟨ **TIP** Pinewatch is not locked prior to this quest, and you can actually obtain the Silver Mold at any time, carrying it with you throughout your adventures until this quest begins. In this event, you can immediately give the item to Endon when you first meet him, completing the quest almost immediately.

Quest Conclusion

Open the door with the bar on it, which is a shortcut back to the cellar and out into Skyrim. Travel back to Markarth, and speak with Endon. He takes the mold and is now an influential ally in Markarth and a Fence in the city if you wish to sell stolen goods.

➤ **Fence:** Endon ➤ **Leveled Enchanted Light Armor**

THE DAINTY SLOAD

PREREQUISITES: Complete Thieves Guild Quests: Additional Jobs in Solitude (5)

INTERSECTING QUESTS: All further Thieves Guild Quests

LOCATIONS: The Dainty Sload, East Empire Company Warehouse, Red Wave, Riften, Ratway, Cistern, The Ragged Flagon, Solitude, Blue Palace, Erikur's House

CHARACTERS: Delvin Mallory, Erikur, Sabine Nytte

ENEMIES: First Mate, Sailor

◊ **OBJECTIVES:** Speak to Erikur, Acquire Balmora Blue, Plant the Balmora Blue, Return to Erikur

▷ Erikur's Devious Delivery

◊ **OBJECTIVE:** Speak to Erikur
♦ **TARGET:** Erikur, in Solitude

 After completing 5 (or more) Additional Jobs in Solitude, Delvin Mallory informs you about a matter regarding Erikur, a businessman in Solitude. Find this Thane in the Blue Palace or near his impressive home. Whether it is by hook or by crook, as long as his business affairs flourish, Erikur is not afraid to get a little dirty. Recently, Captain Volf of the cargo ship *The Dainty Sload* has defaulted on a trade agreement he had with the Thane. The details of the agreement aren't clear, but whatever happened, Erikur stands to lose quite a bit of money. This, and the Captain's stubbornness, have made Erikur decide to contact the Thieves Guild for assistance on the matter.

The Guild has worked with Erikur before, and matters usually ended mutually beneficial for both parties. Trying to resolve the matters through legal channels would prove difficult, as the Captain of the vessel has covered his bases. To this end, Erikur has requested that you plant a substance known as "Balmora Blue" aboard the ship, framing the Captain as a smuggler. You'll find the source of the contraband close to a second vessel, the *Red Wave*, moored in the harbor below Solitude.

◊ **OBJECTIVE:** Acquire Balmora Blue
♦ **TARGET:** Sabine Nytte, on the *Red Wave*, East Empire Company Warehouse

 Your contact is a deckhand named Sabine Nytte. Travel to the East Empire Company Warehouse, and look for a large ship moored off the jetty outside the East Empire store. Board the ship and speak to Sabine (she'll always be up on deck during this quest). She has the merchandise you require, but it's going to cost you! You can:

(1,500 gold) Pay Sabine a large amount of gold and receive the Balmora Blue immediately.

Ask if there's another way to earn it. There isn't.

(Pickpocket) Oh, but there is! Carefully pick her pockets and obtain the key.

Protest at the price. Sabine isn't budging, and she isn't stupid. She isn't carrying the contraband for you to steal!

(Sneak, Pickpocket) Or, you can find a second key on Sabine, pickpocket it, and then head into the bowels of the *Red Wave* to a safe. Inside the safe is a note pinpointing the location of the Balmora Blue Chest. Execute this plan if you've annoyed Sabine to the point of her refusing to speak to you or if you prefer a stealthy route to reach this objective.

Or you can ignore Sabine completely and use this guide to pinpoint the hidden footlocker, swim down, and save yourself some coin!

Once you pay the money, Sabine hands you a key and explains where the stash is located: underwater, and close by.

➤ **Sabine's Footlocker Key** ➤ **Sabine's Red Wave Key**

Sabine's contraband is sealed inside a footlocker below the jetty adjacent to the *Red Wave*. Dive down and locate the chest, using either Lockpick (Hard) or your key to open it.

➤ **Balmora Blue**

◊ **OBJECTIVE:** Plant the Balmora Blue
♦ **TARGET:** Captain's Chest, below deck aboard the *Dainty Sload*

 Journey to the *Dainty Sload* and attempt to sneak aboard, or utilize your magic to enter the hold. The sailors stationed here will attack on sight. Sprint past the sailors as you head counterclockwise through the ship's interior to the hold stairs. Or simply use Invisibility and Pacify. Once inside the hold, cross to the opposite side, pass the first mate, and drop the Balmora Blue into the Captain's Chest after you first unlock it (Average).

◊ **OBJECTIVE:** Return to Erikur
♦ **TARGET:** Erikur, in Solitude

Quest Conclusion

When you return to Erikur to announce your success, he has already heard about it. He gives you something for your troubles and is now happy to reopen any doors the Guild needs in the city of Solitude. You receive the following from him:

➤ **Spell Tome (Leveled)**

IMITATION AMNESTY

PREREQUISITES: Complete Thieves Guild Quests: Additional Jobs in Whiterun (5)
INTERSECTING QUESTS: All further Thieves Guild Quests
LOCATIONS: Riften, Ratway, Cistern, The Ragged Flagon, Whiterun, Dragonsreach, Dragonsreach Jarl's Quarters
CHARACTERS: Irileth, Olfrid Battle-Born
ENEMIES: None
◊ **OBJECTIVES:** Speak to Olfrid Battle-Born, Steal the letter incriminating Arn, Forge the prison registry, Return to Olfrid Battle-Born

▷ Letter of Intent

◊ **OBJECTIVE:** Speak to Olfrid Battle-Born
♦ **TARGET:** Olfrid Battle-Born, in Whiterun

After finishing 5 (or more) successful Additional Jobs in Whiterun, Delvin Mallory receives an urgent missive from Olfrid Battle-Born, a wealthy Nord residing in Whiterun. It appears that Arn, an old friend of Olfrid, was incarcerated inside Whiterun's prison for a serious crime he committed in Solitude, a crime that will result in his execution. Fortunately, the Whiterun authorities are not aware of his friend's identity; he was arrested on the simple charge of drunken and lewd behavior. The problem is that the authorities in Solitude recently dispatched a letter to the Jarl of Whiterun, outlining criminals for whom they are searching. If the Jarl reads the letter and makes the connection with Olfrid's friend, he'll be sent to his death. Olfrid proposes that you infiltrate the Jarl's private quarters in Whiterun and steal the letter. While you're at it, you might as well make a change in the prison logbook with his friend's identity written inside.

◊ **OBJECTIVE:** Steal the letter incriminating Arn
♦ **TARGET:** Bedroom, in the Dragonsreach Jarl's Quarters
◊ **OBJECTIVE:** Forge the prison registry
♦ **TARGET:** Study, in the Dragonsreach Jarl's Quarters

Such a brazen act of trespass won't be tolerated by the leaders of Whiterun, so be sure you're carrying the proper cloaking attire or magical accoutrements to make your infiltration successful. After some additional conversation with Olfrid to pinpoint the letter's location (and other, optional information), head into the imposing Dragonsreach.

Once inside, if you're simply wandering around in full view of the guards, Irileth usually stops you. Simply mention that you want to see the Jarl, and you're given a very temporary reprieve. If the guards or other dwellers turn hostile, do not engage them in battle, as killing those you seek to win the influence of is a terrible idea.

Head northwest from the great hall's entrance stairs. Go down the side steps and into the Dragonsreach Jarl's Quarters. The prison registry is on a table in the corner of a bedroom on the other side.

Continue through the Jarl's personal chambers, heading in a roughly southwest direction until you open the doors into the Jarl's study. On the table is a letter from Solitude. Grab that, and then flee the area, ideally without being spotted or murdering anyone.

➤ **Letter from Solitude**

◊ **OBJECTIVE:** Return to Olfrid Battle-Born
♦ **TARGET:** Olfrid Battle-Born, in Whiterun

> **CAUTION** You're taking your life into your own hands thinking you'll better the sheer number of guards and tough folks roaming these parts; it is better to remain with weapons sheathed, and exit without combat.

Quest Conclusion

Scour the streets of Whiterun for Olfrid Battle-Born, who may be wandering about or hanging inside a dwelling. Although he keeps quiet about Arn, he's happy to receive the letter and tells you to let Delvin know the Guild will be "quite pleased" with what Olfrid can do to influence the powers that run this city. You are also given the an Enchanted Ring.

➤ **Enchanted Ring (Leveled)**

PREREQUISITES: Complete Thieves Guild Quests: Additional Jobs in Windhelm (5)
INTERSECTING QUESTS: All further Thieves Guild Quests
LOCATIONS: Riften, Ratway, Cistern, The Ragged Flagon, Uttering Hills Caves, Windhelm, House of Clan Cruel-Sea
CHARACTERS: Fjotli, Niranye, Torsten Cruel-Sea
ENEMIES: Linwe, Summerset Shadow
◊ **OBJECTIVES:** Speak to Torsten Cruel-Sea , Speak to Niranye, (Optional) Discover leverage to sway Niranye, Travel to Uttering Hills Cave, Recover Fjolti's Silver Locket, (Optional) Destroy the Summerset Shadow's Banner, Return to Torsten Cruel-Sea

Snuffing out a Rival Sect

◊ **OBJECTIVE:** Speak to Torsten Cruel-Sea
♦ **TARGET:** Torsten Cruel-Sea, in Windhelm

After wrapping up 5 (or more) successful Additional Jobs in Windhelm, Delvin Mallory has information from a wealthy merchant farmer named Torsten Cruel-Sea, who resides in Windhelm. Travel to Windhelm and find the merchant in the area near the House of Clan Cruel-Sea. Torsten has been lamenting the murder of his jewelry adorned daughter Fjotli, whose body was left without a sentimental Silver Locket. Through detective work, the potential culprit has been tracked down, an Altmer (High Elf) named Niranye. Strangely, Torsten's sources say Niranye is part of a rival Thieves Guild, which Delvin Mallory has denied his part in to Torsten. You are to hunt down this locket—a Cruel-Sea family heirloom—and he suggests searching Niranye's house first.

You now have two possible locations to search: the market stall in the southwest corner of Windhelm where Niranye plies her wares (usually during the daytime) or her house in the southeast corner of town.

◊ **OBJECTIVE:** Speak to Niranye
♦ **TARGET:** Niranye, in Windhelm

Niranye herself: Whether you meet her in her house or within the walls of Windhelm, Niranye tries to pretend she's still shocked by Fjotli's death, until you tell her to drop the act. You can:

(Persuade) Comment on her awful acting abilities.

(Intimidate) Threaten a similar ending to Fjotli's.

Or just kill her for wasting your time, which yields the note to Uttering Hills Cave.

If you're unable to intimidate or persuade her, you can simply respond "My mistake." This opens the following objective:

◊ **(OPTIONAL) OBJECTIVE:** Discover leverage to sway Niranye

In the safe in her hidden basement is a note you can use as leverage. Show it to Niranye after she's clammed up, and she'll start to talk, clearing the objective. Unless there are no other witnesses, the third option (to kill her) may be problematic. If you use verbal sparring, Niranye speaks about a small group of Altmer thieves who call themselves the "Summerset Shadows" and have a base inside the Uttering Hills Caves. She warns you about the craziness of their leader, Linwe, who is infamous for robbing the dead of their valuables.

➤ **Second Letter from Linwe**   ➤ **Niranye's House Key**

◊ **OBJECTIVE:** Travel to Uttering Hills Cave
◊ **OBJECTIVE:** Recover Fjolti's Silver Locket
♦ **TARGET:** Linwe, inside Uttering Hills Cave

Journey across the snow-laden ground toward the Uttering Hills Cave, and prepare for a violent welcome from two Summerset Shadow guards close to the campfire and the entrance embedded into the mountain. Once you're inside, the objective updates and you must find the locket. Head through the snowy tunnel, passing or attacking additional Summerset Shadow thieves, until you reach a circular stone tower staircase. Head down a connecting corridor at the tower's base and into the Shadows' sanctum. There's a banner in the largest of the rooms, where the thieves gather to eat.

◊ **OBJECTIVE:** (Optional) Destroy the Summerset Shadows' Banner

Before you investigate any further, light the burner underneath the banner until it begins to burn; snuffing out any trace of a rival Thieves Guild should be of utmost importance! Locate Linwe, the pretender thief master himself, in an adjacent room. The very fact that he's wearing the garb of a Thief should be cause enough to cut him down! Defeat this charlatan and claim the following from his corpse:

➤ **Fjotli's Silver Locket**
➤ **Linwe's Armor**
➤ **Linwe's Boots**
➤ **Linwe's Gauntlets**
➤ **Linwe's Helmet**

◊ **OBJECTIVE:** Return to Torsten Cruel-Sea
♦ **TARGET:** Torsten Cruel-Sea, in Windhelm

Quest Conclusion

Return to Windhelm and find Torsten Cruel-Sea. Return the locket, and Torsten is most pleased, even a little envious of your adventuring life. But he makes sure you know that he is a trusted ally in this city. He isn't the only one; Niranye becomes a helpful Fence in this city, assuming you didn't kill her.

 **Vendor (Fence):** Niranye

 **Leveled gold pieces**

 **Enchanted Jewelry (Amulet, Ring, or Necklace; Leveled; if you burned the banner)**

CITY INFLUENCE QUESTS: ULTIMATE REWARDS

Stages of Influence

Building the Thieves Guild's influence across Skyrim is the key to continued success and wealth. The can be measured, based in stages. The following table shows how each of the stages are triggered:

✓	STAGE NUMBER	CITY INFLUENCE QUESTS COMPLETED (OUT OF 4)
	Stage 0	None: Only Riften is influenced
	Stage 1	Riften + one City Influence Quest
	Stage 2	Riften + two City Influence Quests
	Stage 3	Riften + three City Influence Quests
	Stage 4‡	Riften + all four City Influence Quests

NOTE ‡ This is one prerequisite to becoming Thieves Guild Master.

Reward 1: Additional Visitors and Vendors

As your influence grows, additional visitors appear (they offer little more than conversation), and vendors take up residence in the niches across from the Ragged Flagon, plying a variety of special or themed wares. Be sure to inspect, barter, and purchase from them. The following table shows who turns up, and when.

✓	STAGE NUMBER	VISITOR	VENDOR
	Stage 1	None	Syndus; Wood Elf Fletcher
	Stage 2	None	Arnskar Ember-Master; Nord Blacksmith
	Stage 3	Garthar	Herluin Lothaire; Breton Apothecary
	Stage 4	Ravyn Imyan	Vanryth Gatharian; Dark Elf Light Armorsmith

Reward 2: Guild Fence Gold

As you should be aware, Tonila—and every other Fence you bring into the cause—fences any items you may have "appropriated" from across Skyrim, as most other merchants don't touch stolen goods. The amount of available gold they offer for items you wish to fence increased depending on your City Influence stage, as shown:

✓	STAGE NUMBER	AVAILABLE GOLD
	Stage 0	1,000 gold pieces
	Stage 1	1,500 gold pieces
	Stage 2	2,250 gold pieces
	Stage 3	3,000 gold pieces
	Stage 4	4,000 gold pieces

Reward 3: Crime Amnesty

When you enter one of the Holds that has a completed City Influence Quest—The Rift (Riften), The Reach (Markarth), Haafingar (Solitude), Whiterun (Whiterun), and Eastmarch (Windhelm)—and a guard from one of those cities attempts to arrest you for a crime you've caused, you have two additional options:

1. You can pay the guard to overlook the crime this once. This won't work on violent crimes (murder), but it's a great way to prevent getting arrested for theft when you have a bag full of stolen loot you'd hate to lose. This only works on a given guard once per day. Also note that the bounty on your head remains in place; nothing is cleared. Therefore, if you reengage another guard in dialogue, they might just try and arrest you again.

2. If your pockets are brimming with gold, you can immediately pay off your bounty for that Hold, regardless of the crime. This will also allow the guard to overlook the crime. The amount of gold required to pay off the crime is equal to half your bounty.

The advantage to either option above is twofold:

1. You aren't moved to the Keep (unless you were trespassing—then you are still moved to the Keep) as if you were released from jail.

2. Best of all, none of your stolen loot is confiscated. Normally, when you're arrested, all stolen loot is completely stripped, never to return. In these instances, the thief can avoid that inconvenience!

Reward 4: Guild Growth

For every stage that the Thieves Guild attains, it visibly changes: You should start to notice more containers that can be looted, more expensive and lavish furnishings, and of course, the arrival of the aforementioned vendors. Their "shops" now appear in the Ragged Flagon area, in one of the wall niches across from the bar.

Reward 5: Thief Caches

When you complete a City Influence Quest, "Thief Caches" appear in that Hold's Capital City. These are wooden barrels emblazoned with the "Thieves' Cache" Shadowmark. Each city has three such barrels hidden somewhere within the city walls. The chart below reveals their locations:

SOLITUDE THIEF CACHES		
✓	CACHE	LOCATION
	1	Amid the barrels to the right of the entrance to Erikur's house.
	2	Behind Vittoria Vici's House, tucked into an alcove.
	3	At the end of the alley between the Winking Skeever and Angeline's Aromatics, behind the pine shrubs.

MARKARTH THIEF CACHES		
✓	CACHE	LOCATION
	1	Where the water from Ghorza Gra-Bagol's Blacksmith shop cascades into the river, half submerged.
	2	In a plain, covered walkway in the city's northwest corner; follow the walkway west from Nepos's front door.
	3	On the landing, just outside Vlindrel Hall.

WHITERUN THIEF CACHES

✓	CACHE	LOCATION
	1	Behind Carlotta Valentia's house
	2	South of House Gray-Mane in the corner of the city's wall (next to the gate connecting the Plains to the Wind Districts)
	3	Tucked up against the rear exterior wall of the Bannered Mane.

WINDHELM THIEF CACHES

✓	CACHE	LOCATION
	1	In the small courtyard on the side of Niranye's house.
	2	Right next to the door to Sadri's used wares.
	3	Tucked at the end of a tiny alley to the left of Hjerim's entrance

RIFTEN THIEF CACHES

✓	CACHE	LOCATION
	1	On the lower walkway along the canal, almost directly across from Valindor's house.
	2	In a corner on the balcony walkway overlooking the training grounds at Mistveil Keep.
	3	In the garden area of Honeyside, against the city wall.

These caches are occasionally restocked, so they are well worth checking out: A cache always contains a random number of lockpicks and arrows and may contain the following (randomly, and leveled):

Potions

Gems

Enchanted Weapon, Light Armor, or Bow

LEADERSHIP QUEST: UNDER NEW MANAGEMENT

PREREQUISITES: Complete Thieves Guild Quests: Additional Jobs in all Holds (20), Complete Thieves Guild Quests: City Influence Quests in all Holds (4), Complete Thieves Guild Quest: Darkness Returns

◊ **OBJECTIVES:** Speak to Brynjolf about becoming the Guild Master, Proceed to the center of Cistern, Become Guild Master for the Thieves Guild, Speak to Brynjolf about being Guild Master, Retrieve your Guild Leader Armor from Tonilia

 ● MINOR SPOILERS

◈ A Real Honor Among Thieves

This is likely to be the final quest during your time at the Thieves Guild, as the prerequisites are lengthy: You need to have finished all of the Additional Jobs necessary to trigger the four City Influence Quests and have completed those quests too. In addition, you must have finished all of the Critical Path Quests and finished Thieves Guild Quest: Darkness Returns.

◊ **OBJECTIVE:** Speak to Brynjolf about becoming the Guild Master

Move into the Cistern and converse with your old friend and mentor. Brynjolf is in the training area, and he tells you that the time has come for you to lead this merry band of ne'er-do-wells based on your continuous hard work and impressive performances. He wishes you to head to the Cistern so the ceremony can begin.

◊ **OBJECTIVE:** Proceed to the center of Cistern
◊ **OBJECTIVE:** Become Guild Master for the Thieves Guild
◊ **OBJECTIVE:** Speak to Brynjolf about being Guild Master

You receive a full welcome from all of the main Thieves Guild members (except Mercer Frey of course), including Maven Black-Briar. The ceremony begins, and your virtues are extolled, with Delvin, Vex, and Karliah all agreeing that you'd make an excellent leader. With the new honor bestowed upon you, speak to Brynjolf again. After further congratulations, he hands over a couple of prized possessions, as tradition dictates. Then he recommends you speak to Tonilia, who has a special gift for you.

➤ **Amulet of Articulation**   ➤ **Tribute Chest Key**

> **NOTE** The Amulet of Articulation has two functions: First, it has a Speech enchantment, ranging from 5 to 25 percent (leveled to when you receive it). Second, when you wear the Amulet, your Persuade will succeed almost every time, regardless of difficulty. Although there are a few select Persuade Checks that won't work, these are few and far between. However, the vast majority of the time, you can persuade anyone to do your bidding, including guards when talking your way out of nonviolent crimes!

◊ **OBJECTIVE:** Retrieve your Guild Leader Armor from Tonilia

Quest Conclusion

Your status-raising ceremony concludes with a full set of Guild Leader Armor. Take these from Tonilia and wear them as you wish. The Tribute Chest contains gold and gems (leveled). Keep checking it, as it is sometimes replenished. At this point, some of your crew may refer to you as "boss."

➤ **Guild Leader Armor**   ➤ **Guild Leader Gloves**
➤ **Guild Leader Boots**   ➤ **Guild Leader Hood**

THE DARK BROTHERHOOD QUESTS

OVERVIEW

Interaction with the Dark Brotherhood is never explicitly felt. You may hear rumors about the Brotherhood and may even encounter an assassin who has in their possession a mysterious contract to kill you. But to experience as much of the Dark Brotherhood as you can, begin your investigations by locating the broken cart with the odd little jester, close to the Loreius Farm, on the road north of Whiterun.

▷ Dark Brotherhood Sanctuary

The Black Door, approached from the fetid pond.

Sanctuary interior, inside the grotto area.

The Dark Brotherhood Sanctuary is located off the road, in an eerie area of woodland within the southern Pine Forest of Falkreath Hold. The Black Door is not visible to travelers; only those inquisitive enough to venture off the beaten path will see it. The Black Door guards the Dark Brotherhood sanctuary and is magically sealed from intruders. It asks visitors for a passphrase, which they must already know in order to enter.

The initial area houses Astrid's study and bedroom and a secret door (that will open later). Down the main stairs is the grotto cavern, containing Arnbjorn's forge, an area for combat practice, and a waterfall pool with a Word Wall where you'll learn an impressive Shout called Marked for Death.

Farther into the linked cave tunnels are the various bedrooms of the Dark Brotherhood Family, a dining chamber, and a laboratory that connects back to the grotto. In addition, Cicero's room and a chapel — home to a strange little man and an odd sarcophagus — are also available to explore.

➤ **Word of Power:** Marked for Death

▷ Important Characters

The Night Mother

Existing in the physical realm as an emaciated corpse drained and half-mummified, resting inside an iron sarcophagus, the Night Mother was brought to Skyrim by her keeper, Cicero. During the Dark Brotherhood's prime, the Listener had the honored ability to hear her frightening voice as fragmented snippets. She receives the call of the Black Sacrament, and disperses the information to her "Children."

Leader: Astrid

Astrid is the loving and caring leader of the Skyrim Sanctuary. She is very open about her feelings, and she will be loyal to the Dark Brotherhood until her dying breath. Astrid is married to Arnbjorn, and the two have as healthy a relationship as two Dark Brotherhood assassins can. She is the primary quest-giver.

Assassin: Festus Krex

Krex is old, cranky, and completely unsociable. He is also the one member of the Sanctuary who prefers to use spells over cold steel. Impressively unapproachable, the rest of the Dark Brotherhood accept him as an especially touchy member of the Family and do their best to shrug off his curmudgeonly nature. He does keep an ear to the ground about interesting happenings across Skyrim, which he very occasionally shares.

Assassin: Nazir

Nazir is a Redguard who wields a giant scimitar. He is older than many of the other assassins and serves as a father figure to them. He is noble, humorous, and tactical in his thinking and actions. He always ponders decisions before making them. He is also extremely talented in the Light Armor skill, and hands out minor contracts when the Black Sacrament has been completed somewhere in Skyrim. Check with Nazir for these side contracts when Astrid doesn't have anything available.

➤ **Trainer (Light Armor):** Nazir

Assassin: Gabriella

Gabriella is a quiet, mysterious member of the Dark Brotherhood, who much prefers the company of her pet Frostbite Spider. After you complete a contract to kill Gaius Maro (and complete the bonus objective), you receive a token from Gabriella to have your fortune read by her dear friend Olava in Whiterun.

Assassin: Babette

A happy and accommodating ten-year-old girl and an obviously respected member, Babette is also obsessed with Alchemy, which she will sell to you, along with many other useful items. She seems wise well beyond her years, due to the fact she is actually a nearly two-hundred-year-old vampire. She is extremely adept at Alchemy magic.

➤ **Trainer (Alchemy):** Babette
➤ **Vendor (Potions):** Babette

Keeper: Cicero

Cicero, the "Fool of Hearts," is a psychotic, singsong speaking, knife-wielding jester. He is also the Keeper of the Night Mother and arrives at the Sanctuary with her body. Overly paranoid, he constantly speaks with "Mother" and furiously protects her. If he ever hears of a threat to the Brotherhood, he acts quickly and impulsively.

Shadowscale: Veezara

Veezara is a Shadowscale, an Argonian born under the sign of the Shadow. For years he served the king of High Marsh. When he was honorably released from service, he wandered Tamriel and eventually made his way to the Sanctuary in Skyrim. He is friendly and somewhat quiet, but extremely skilled.

Assassin and Blacksmith: Arnbjorn

Arnbjorn is a boisterous Nordic barbarian and husband to Astrid, who's been the only one to tame him—since he also happens to be a werewolf. His loyalty to her is unwavering and unquestioning. He was once a Companion, but his barbaric ways and eagerness for killing made it an uneasy association. After wandering the paths of Skyrim, he found this shadowy organization a much better fit for him. He sometimes works the forge inside the Sanctuary.

➤ **Blacksmith:** Arnbjorn

Familiar: Lis

More of a pet than a familiar, Gabriella's Frostbite Spider, Lis, is a permanent resident and unofficial mascot of the Dark Brotherhood Sanctuary. Don't confuse this with a wild spider; it is friendly to members, and it would be a shame if someone slew it out of spite or perverse amusement...especially as all the other Dark Brotherhood members turn hostile if you're foolish enough to slay such a fine and furry beast!

Assassination Effects

Before you enter the world of clandestine murder, check the targets you are terminating. Some of them may have other quest-related objectives that change or disappear completely after you assassinate them. Although this never prevents you from completing essential quests, checking the Atlas and the Index prior to taking a victim down is worthwhile.

Skills to Learn

Entering buildings, finding a target, quietly slaying them, and leaving without raising the alarm (or even being seen) requires proficiency in the following skills, which you should think about improving through training and constant use:

One-Handed: for daggers and stealth attacks

Archery: for removing foes from long range without causing a ruckus

Light Armor: so you can sneak and still take damage

Sneak: arguably the most important skill if you're taking a clandestine approach to assassinations

Lockpicking: helpful when trespassing in a locked a building

Illusion spells: such as Invisibility to help you sneak, and Fear or Pacify for an easier getaway

Alchemy: for creating poisons to tip your weapons with

Occasional other spells: such as Detect Life when you're looking for foes, friends, or targets

The Assassination Itself

> **TIP** The following are some overall tactics that are worth thinking about employing:
>
> **The basic kill:** Find the target. Produce your preferred melee weapon. Hit the target with it until he or she expires. Then fight or flee out of the location (if you're spotted), and damn the consequences!
>
> **The ranged kill:** If you prefer longer-ranged magic or bows, utilize them when attacking the target. If you can fire from cover and without being seen (crouch to check), so much the better.
>
> **The stealth kill:** Increase your Sneak using augmentations to decrease your visibility, attack in the dead of night and from behind, and then merge back into the shadows if you're spotted.
>
> **The poison kill:** When culling your target, you obviously want to complete the task as quickly as possible, so coat your assassination weapon in poison so your target dies with one swipe.

TRAINING

In addition to a comfy bed and like-minded attitudes, the main members of this assassin guild are dazzlingly proficient in a particular skill. Speak to each of them, and increase the chosen skill by a point. If you have the gold, you can complete this numerous times:

✓	SKILL	RANK	TRAINER
	Light Armor	Master	Nazir
	Alchemy	Master	Babette

AVAILABLE QUESTS AND TASKS

There are 37 different quests available with the Dark Brotherhood. Thirteen of these are Critical Path Quests (plus an additional introductory quest involving Cicero). Twelve are Side Contract Quests. The remaining 11 are additional quests.

Critical Path Quests

Simply referred to as "quests," these are the main missions you attempt for the Dark Brotherhood. All but the first quest have one or more prerequisites, as shown in the following table:

✓	QUEST NAME	PREREQUISITES
	Dark Brotherhood Quest: Delayed Burial	None
	Dark Brotherhood Quest: Innocence Lost	None
	Dark Brotherhood Quest: With Friends Like These...	Complete Dark Brotherhood Quest: Innocence Lost

✓	QUEST NAME	PREREQUISITES
☐	Dark Brotherhood Quest: Sanctuary	Complete Dark Brotherhood Quest: With Friends Like These...
☐	Dark Brotherhood Quest: Sentenced to Death	Complete Dark Brotherhood Quest: Sanctuary
☐	Dark Brotherhood Quest: Whispers in the Dark	Complete Dark Brotherhood Quest: Sentenced to Death
☐	Dark Brotherhood Quest: The Silence Has Been Broken	Complete Dark Brotherhood Quest: Whispers in the Dark
☐	Dark Brotherhood Quest: Bound Until Death	Complete Dark Brotherhood Quest: The Silence Has Been Broken
☐	Dark Brotherhood Quest: Breaching Security	Complete Dark Brotherhood Quest: Bound Until Death

✓	QUEST NAME	PREREQUISITES
☐	Dark Brotherhood Quest: The Cure for Madness	Complete Dark Brotherhood Quest: Breaching Security
☐	Dark Brotherhood Quest: Recipe for Disaster	Complete Dark Brotherhood Quest: The Cure for Madness
☐	Dark Brotherhood Quest: To Kill an Empire	Complete Dark Brotherhood Quest: Recipe for Disaster
☐	Dark Brotherhood Quest: Death Incarnate	Complete Dark Brotherhood Quest: To Kill an Empire
☐	Dark Brotherhood Quest: Hail Sithis!	Complete Dark Brotherhood Quest: Death Incarnate

Side Contract Quests

Referred to as "Side Contracts," these are assassinations you complete for Nazir, in six parts. Sometimes you are given two or more targets and sometimes only one. Here's how you access them:

✓	QUEST NAME	PREREQUISITES
☐	Side Contract: Kill Narfi	Complete Dark Brotherhood Quest: Sanctuary. Unavailable during Dark Brotherhood Quest: Death Incarnate.
☐	Side Contract: Kill Ennodius Papius	Complete Dark Brotherhood Quest: Sanctuary. Unavailable during Dark Brotherhood Quest: Death Incarnate.
☐	Side Contract: Kill Beitild	Complete Dark Brotherhood Quest: Sanctuary. Unavailable during Dark Brotherhood Quest: Death Incarnate.
☐	Side Contract: Kill Hern	Complete first three Side Contracts. Available during Dark Brotherhood Quest: Whispers in the Dark. Unavailable during Dark Brotherhood Quest: Death Incarnate.
☐	Side Contract: Kill Lurbuk	Complete first three Side Contracts. Available during Dark Brotherhood Quest: Whispers in the Dark. Unavailable during Dark Brotherhood Quest: Death Incarnate.
☐	Side Contract: Kill Deekus	Complete first five Side Contracts. Available during Dark Brotherhood Quest: The Silence Has Been Broken. Unavailable during Dark Brotherhood Quest: Death Incarnate.

✓	QUEST NAME	PREREQUISITES
☐	Side Contract: Kill Ma'randru-jo	Complete first five Side Contracts. Available during Dark Brotherhood Quest: The Silence Has Been Broken. Unavailable during Dark Brotherhood Quest: Death Incarnate.
☐	Side Contract: Kill Anoriath	Complete first five Side Contracts. Available during Dark Brotherhood Quest: The Silence Has Been Broken. Unavailable during Dark Brotherhood Quest: Death Incarnate.
☐	Side Contract: Kill Agnis	Complete the eight previous Side Contracts. Available after completion of Dark Brotherhood Quest: The Silence Has Been Broken. Unavailable during Dark Brotherhood Quest: Death Incarnate.
☐	Side Contract: Kill Maluril	Complete the nine previous Side Contracts. Unavailable during Dark Brotherhood Quest: Death Incarnate.
☐	Side Contract: Kill Helvard	Complete the nine previous Side Contracts. Unavailable during Dark Brotherhood Quest: Death Incarnate.
☐	Side Contract: Kill Safia	Complete all previous Side Contracts. Unavailable during Dark Brotherhood Quest: Death Incarnate.

Radiant Quests

Any other objectives or jobs with the Dark Brotherhood are listed here. A few of them have random targets, items, or other interactions. They are listed in more detail after the Critical Path Quests, but for the prerequisites required to begin every additional quest, consult the following table:

✓	RADIANT QUESTS	PREREQUISITES
☐	Destroy the Dark Brotherhood!	Complete Dark Brotherhood Quest: Innocence Lost, and kill Astrid
☐	Honor Thy Family	Complete Dark Brotherhood Quest: With Friends Like These...
☐	The Feeble Fortune*	Complete Dark Brotherhood Quest: Breaching Security, and earn the bonus
☐	Where You Hang Your Enemy's Head...	Complete Dark Brotherhood Quest: Hail Sithis!
☐	Welcome to the Brotherhood†	Complete Dark Brotherhood Quest: Hail Sithis!
☐	Cicero's Return*	Complete Dark Brotherhood Quest: Hail Sithis!

✓	RADIANT QUESTS	PREREQUISITES
☐	The Dark Brotherhood Forever!	Complete Dark Brotherhood Quest: Hail Sithis!
☐	The Torturer's Treasure: Part I*	Complete Radiant Quest: Where You Hang Your Enemy's Head...
☐	The Torturer's Treasure: Part II*	Complete Radiant Quest: Where You Hang Your Enemy's Head...
☐	The Torturer's Treasure: Part III*	Complete Radiant Quest: Where You Hang Your Enemy's Head...
☐	The Torturer's Treasure: Part IV*	Complete Radiant Quest: Where You Hang Your Enemy's Head...

 NOTE ***** = Indicates the quest name does not appear in your menu; check the "Miscellaneous" area for objectives that may appear.

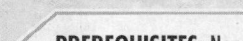 **DELAYED BURIAL**

PREREQUISITES: None
INTERSECTING QUESTS: Dark Brotherhood Quest: Innocence Lost
LOCATIONS: Loreius Farm
CHARACTERS: Cicero, Curwe, Roadside Guard, Vantus Loreius
ENEMIES: None
◊ **OBJECTIVES:** Convince Loreius to fix the wheel, Convince Loreius OR report Cicero, Talk to Cicero, OR talk to Loreius

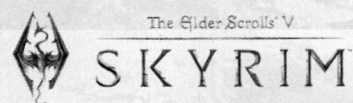

> **TIP** It is recommended you complete this quest before beginning Dark Brotherhood Quest: With Friends Like These... and joining the Dark Brotherhood, as Cicero has some additional words for you, depending on your actions during this quest. You may also gain additional flavor depending on your actions here.

Surely You Jest

The road north of Whiterun is sometimes treacherous. Should you follow this path north from the city or visit Shimmermist Cave and journey due northwest from that location, you encounter a strange little man dressed as a jester, standing by a horse-drawn cart. Inspect the cart, and you'll see one of its wheels has detached from the axle. On the cart is a hefty-looking wooden crate.

The jester is named Cicero. He seems to be a little crazy but does need some help. He says the crate contains the body of his dear, departed mother. They were on their way from Cyrodiil to her new resting place, but the wheel on the cart broke. Although the farmer nearby must have proper tools to repair the cart, he refuses to, likely because of Cicero's strange demeanor and dress. Cicero asks you to speak with Vantus Loreius the farmer on his behalf. There's coin in it for you, too.

> ◊ **OBJECTIVE:** Convince Loreius to fix the wheel
> ♦ **TARGET:** Vantus Loreius, in Loreius Farm

Head roughly west toward the Loreius Farm and locate the farmer and his wife, Curwe. Speak with Vantus Loreius and explain Cicero's predicament. Loreius is extremely suspicious of Cicero, from his outfit to the contents of the crate he insists

is his mother, and he doesn't want to be caught up in anything. You can steer the conversation toward siding with Loreius or talking him into helping Cicero. As the conversation progresses, you realize you have two choices: convincing Loreius or reporting Cicero.

> ◊ **OBJECTIVE:** Convince Loreius OR report Cicero
> ♦ **TARGET:** Vantus Loreius, OR Roadside Guard

Convincing Loreius: Vantus Loreius is easily convinced that his suspicions are unfounded and that Cicero is simply an unfortunate character in need of his wheelwright prowess. Be sure Loreius agrees to this, and then return to Cicero to tell him the good news.

Reporting Cicero: If Loreius has convinced you that Cicero is a suspicious character, head back down to the road and locate the Roadside Guard patrolling close by. Speak to the guard and make up any tall tale that is detrimental to Cicero's character. The guard promptly strides off to arrest Cicero, and you can return to Loreius to celebrate framing a weird (but possibly innocent) man.

> ◊ **OBJECTIVE:** Talk to Cicero, OR Talk to Loreius

Quest Conclusion

You receive gold as a reward no matter who you side with.

➤ **50 gold pieces**

Postquest Activities

If you side with Loreius and inform the guard, once you join the Dark Brotherhood and return to see Vantus Loreius and his wife again, you'll find them murdered on their farm. The culprit is unknown, although you have your suspicions....

INNOCENCE LOST

PREREQUISITES: None
INTERSECTING QUESTS: Dark Brotherhood Quest: With Friends Like These...
LOCATIONS: Riften, Honorhall Orphanage, Windhelm, Aretino Residence
CHARACTERS: Aventus Aretino, Constance Michel, Francois Beaufort, Grimvar Cruel-Sea, Hroar, Idesa Sadri, Runa Fair-Shield, Samuel
ENEMIES: Grelod the Kind
◊ **OBJECTIVES:** Talk to Aventus Aretino, Kill Grelod the Kind, Tell Aventus Aretino that Grelod is dead

The Black Sacrament Enacted

Begin this quest in a number of different ways:

1. You can hear a rumor that mentions a boy named Aventus Aretino if you visit any of the inns or taverns across Skyrim. The nearest to your starting location in Helgen is the Sleeping Giant Inn in Riverwood. The one closest to this quest is Candlehearth Hall in Windhelm. Keep asking about rumors until Aventus's name is mentioned; then follow up on this information.

2. Or, you can visit the Honorhall Orphanage in Riften. Enter the premises and watch as Grelod the Kind doesn't live up to her name. Once the harridan has ordered her children to bed, speak with any of the "guttersnipes." Francois Beaufort, Samuel, Runa Fair-Shield, or Hroar all point you in the direction of the escaped orphan, Aventus Aretino, and his location in Windhelm.

3. Or, if you're already in Windhelm, the first city guard you speak to mentions something about the ritual going on in a building inside this settlement. If you're close to the Aretino Residence, you can witness a conversation between Grimvar Cruel-Sea and Idesa Sadri; speak to them about this "cursed" child who some have heard reciting the "Black Sacrament." As the house is close by, you can easily check whether these stories hold weight.

◊ **OBJECTIVE:** Talk to Aventus Aretino
♦ **TARGET:** Aretino Residence, in Windhelm

▷ The Sadist Headmistress Redacted

It appears the rumors are true; Aventus Aretino, a recently orphaned child, has fled from Riften and headed back to his family home.

(Lockpick [Novice]) The only way into the dwelling is to pick the lock. Once inside, you find Aventus in a trancelike state, reciting the Black Sacrament—the means by which those wishing revenge are said to contact the Dark Brotherhood. Aventus isn't concerned that you've found him out; in fact, he's thrilled that a Dark Brotherhood assassin has come to arrange a murder! Even if this wasn't your intention, Aventus doesn't listen; he wants the cruel and sadistic headmistress of the Honorhall Orphanage dead, mainly to save the other children from her violence and so her more compassionate subordinate, Constance Michel, can take over.

◊ **OBJECTIVE:** Kill Grelod the Kind
♦ **TARGET:** Honorhall Orphanage, in Riften

Travel to the Honorhall Orphanage and speak with Grelod the Kind. You may reveal as little or as much of your plan as you want. Immediately afterward, you must kill her for her crimes against children.

◊ **OBJECTIVE:** Tell Aventus Aretino that Grelod is dead
♦ **TARGET:** Aretino Residence, in Windhelm

Beware that once you murder Grelod the Kind, your bounty level in this Hold is raised significantly if anyone witnessed this dark deed. **CAUTION**

(Sneak) Just like any murder you commit as part of the Dark Brotherhood, slaying your target while remaining stealthy is preferred so nobody witnesses the crime. With Grelod, this can involve waiting until she's sleeping. However, Grelod will scream when she dies, alerting the children and Constance, and everyone becomes suspicious of you, even if your Bounty hasn't increased in the Rift.

Quest Conclusion

Travel back to Aventus and inform him that the assassination is complete. He is thrilled and rewards you with a fancy family trinket. It appears this quest is over.

➤ **Aretino Family Heirloom**

Postquest Activities

An odd occurrence gives you pause. Once you leave Windhelm and enter any other city in Skyrim, a courier approaches you (assuming you don't run past him). He was told to deliver a message. Examine the black handprint and the words inside that state simply, "We know." The commencement of Dark Brotherhood Quest: With Friends Like These... will follow.

 TIP You don't have to wait for a courier to appear for the next quest to commence: Simply find a bed to sleep in (outside Windhelm) and have your dreams interrupted by an assassin named Astrid.

WITH FRIENDS LIKE THESE...

PREREQUISITES: Complete Dark Brotherhood Quest: Innocence Lost
INTERSECTING QUESTS: Dark Brotherhood Quest: Innocence Lost, Dark Brotherhood Quest: Sanctuary
LOCATIONS: Abandoned Shack, Dark Brotherhood Sanctuary
CHARACTERS: Alea Quintus, Astrid, Fultheim the Fearless, Nazir, Vasha
ENEMIES: None
◊ **OBJECTIVES:** Kill one of the captives, Enter the Dark Brotherhood Sanctuary

A Waking Nightmare

This quest begins once you complete Dark Brotherhood Quest: Innocence Lost.

The Dark Brotherhood has their eye on you. You cannot flee from their gaze, a fact that becomes increasingly obvious the next time you decide to sleep. Instead of waking up where you were, you appear inside a strange shack in the northern reaches of Skyrim. Your only option is to converse with a mysterious veiled figure in black.

The woman introduces herself as Astrid, representative for the Dark Brotherhood. Although you've demonstrated an aptitude for deathcraft and would be an asset to the Brotherhood, you've created a problem. The person you slew— Grelod the Kind—was one of the Brotherhood's legitimate targets. Therefore, you owe the Dark Brotherhood a kill.

Astrid tells you there are three bound captives in this shack. One of them has a contract on their life. You're tasked with figuring out which one and then slaying them. Only after the bloodshed will Astrid give you the necessary key to unlock the Abandoned Shack, allowing you to leave.

◊ **OBJECTIVE:** Kill one of the captives
♦ **TARGET:** Any captive in Abandoned Shack

CAUTION
As soon as Astrid finishes her speech, you can attack and kill her, obtaining the Shack Key and fleeing the scene; however, you won't be able to continue any further down this line of quests. This begins a new task: Dark Brotherhood Quest: Destroy the Dark Brotherhood! Consult page 255 for more information.

(Intimidate; Persuade) With each captive, you have a possible Intimidate or Persuade check you can make. Then make your choice and kill the captive you think is guilty:

Captive 1: Fultheim the Fearless. This giant Nord warrior becomes more of a sniveling coward the more you question him.

Captive 2: Alea Quintus. This mother of six children has certain anger issues. She'd kill you with her bare hands if given the chance.

Captive 3: Vasha: A Khajiit crime lord who utilizes both threats and negotiation in order to win his release.

Guilt. Innocence. Right. Wrong. Irrelevant?

Spoiler Alert: Return to Astrid after killing the captive, and she's impressed by your deductions. But the guilt of the victim you chose wasn't important—after all, each captive was innocent. It was the loyalty and unquestioning nature of your kill that has repaid your debt. You are free to leave. But why part ways? Astrid officially extends an invitation to join her family and gives you a passphrase to use to enter the Dark Brotherhood's Sanctuary.

➤ **Abandoned Shack Key**

◊ **OBJECTIVE:** Enter the Dark Brotherhood Sanctuary

Quest Conclusion

Journey south to the Pine Forest and locate the door marked with the skull. When prompted, reply with, "Silence, my brother." The door unlocks, allowing you under the road and into the Sanctuary. Astrid welcomes you as part of the Family and hands you the Shrouded Armor. She is preparing a target for you, as well as the arrival of the Night Mother, but for now Nazir has some side missions to undertake for fun and profit. Head deeper into the Sanctuary and meet your new brethren. You can listen in on a conversation where the Family members share some of their exploits.

➤ **Shrouded Armor** ➤ **Shrouded Gloves**
➤ **Shrouded Boots** ➤ **Shrouded Helmet**

Postquest Activities

Dark Brotherhood Quest: Sanctuary begins immediately.

 TIP **Shrouded Armor:** This is arguably the ultimate attire for an assassin, as it has enchantments that boost those murderous skills you'll be using. There's some ancient Shrouded Armor (which is even more impressive) available in Hag's End, but you'll have to complete more missions for this organization before you can attempt to find it. See Dark Brotherhood Quest: The Feeble Fortune* on page 257 for more information.

 NOTE * Quest names marked with this symbol do not appear in your Quest Menu list.

SANCTUARY

PREREQUISITES: Complete Dark Brotherhood Quest: With Friends Like These...
INTERSECTING QUESTS: Dark Brotherhood Quest: With Friends Like These..., Dark Brotherhood Quest: Side Contract: Kill Narfi, Dark Brotherhood Quest: Side Contract: Kill Ennodius Papius, Dark Brotherhood Quest: Side Contract: Kill Beitild, Dark Brotherhood Quest: Sentenced to Death
LOCATIONS: Dark Brotherhood Sanctuary
CHARACTERS: Arnbjorn , Astrid, Babette, Cicero , Festus Krex, Gabriella , Nazir , The Night Mother, Veezara
ENEMIES: None
◊ **OBJECTIVES:** Speak with Nazir, Receive the first set of contracts from Nazir

Your Brotherhood Brethren

This quest begins once you complete Dark Brotherhood Quest: With Friends Like These....

◊ **OBJECTIVE:** Speak with Nazir

Heed Astrid's instructions, and venture deeper into the Dark Brotherhood's Sanctuary, where Nazir and the rest of the Brotherhood are talking about their clandestine activities with an air of mirth. You can speak to the other members, but your only critical contact is Nazir.

This man has some side contracts you may be interested in fulfilling. Nazir is also a Trainer and can teach you how to be more effective when wearing Light Armor.

➤ **Trainer (Light Armor):** Nazir

◊ **OBJECTIVE:** Receive the first set of contracts from Nazir

MEETING THE BROTHERHOOD

In addition to Astrid and Nazir, you can converse with (and inquire about) other Brotherhood members—Arnbjorn, Babette, Cicero, Festus Krex, Gabriella, Nazir, the Night Mother, and Veezara—who offer you advice on any future quest related to this faction (speak to each between Dark Brotherhood Quests). For more information on these Dark Brotherhood members, check the "Overview" section at the start of this chapter.

 NOTE At this point, the Dark Brotherhood Quest: Side Contracts also begin. They are given by Nazir. Consult the "Dark Brotherhood Radiant Quests" and "Dark Brotherhood Quest: Side Contracts" sections of this chapter. These detail every contract and how to obtain them.

Quest Conclusion

After completing one or more of Nazir's side contracts, when you return to the Dark Brotherhood Sanctuary and move into the grotto area, there's a flurry of activity as Cicero has arrived with his mother; check the next quest for all of the details.

After speaking with Astrid, head to Nazir if you're collecting payment for any of the first three contracts.

Postquest Activities

You usually return to Nazir once Dark Brotherhood Quest: Sentenced to Death has already begun.

 SENTENCED TO DEATH

PREREQUISITES: Complete Dark Brotherhood Quest: Sanctuary
INTERSECTING QUESTS: Dark Brotherhood Quest: Sanctuary, Dark Brotherhood Quest: Whispers in the Dark
LOCATIONS: Dark Brotherhood Sanctuary , Markarth, The Hag's Cure, Raldbthar, Raldbthar Consortium, Windhelm, The White Phial, Blacksmith Quarters
CHARACTERS: Arnbjorn, Astrid, Babette, Cicero, Festus Krex, Gabriella, Muiri, Nazir, The Night Mother, Veezara
ENEMIES: Alain Dufont , Bandits, Nilsine Shatter-Shield
◊ **OBJECTIVES:** Talk to Muiri, Kill Alain Dufont, (Optional) Kill Nilsine Shatter-Shield, Talk to Muiri, Report back to Astrid

▶ Clowning Around

This quest begins once you complete Dark Brotherhood Quest: Sanctuary.

After returning from your first side contract (or later), it appears the Dark Brotherhood are welcoming a new visitor. Cicero and his oversized coffin have arrived; you'll find them in the grotto. Cicero is engaged in a slightly tense conversation with Arnbjorn. Astrid isn't overly fond of the jester but still welcomes him into the fold, along with his cargo. Ask Astrid about a contract, and she gives you instructions. An Apothecary's Apprentice over in Markarth has completed the Black Sacrament. Find her and follow her wishes. You can ask Astrid about the Night Mother (the corpse Cicero has hauled in with him), advice on the contracts, and other rules to follow if you desire.

◊ **OBJECTIVE:** Talk to Muiri
♦ **TARGET:** The Hag's Cure, in Markarth

CAUTION

Cicero is a psychotic, knife-wielding jester. He is also the Keeper of the Night Mother. He is grateful if you helped convince Vantus Loreius to fix his wagon during Dark Brotherhood Quest: Delayed Burial but is most put out if you didn't. You can ask him about himself, the Night Mother, and a variety of other topics, but you may wish to watch this fellow; he could be unpredictable.

▶ The Hag's Helper

Journey to Markarth and seek out Muiri, who may be hanging around inside the Silver-Blood Inn, walking nearby, or heading toward the Hag's Cure apothecary shop (or already inside). Tell her that you've come, and she speaks conspiratorially about her problem: While visiting the wealthy Shatter-Shield family in Windhelm—who were old and dear friends and recently lost their daughter to a murderer—Muiri went to the local tavern to drown her sorrows; there she

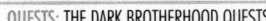

fell in love with a dashing stranger named Alain Dufont. What Muiri didn't know at the time was that Alain was actually using her so he could infiltrate the family and rob them blind. Alain, who turned out to be a local bandit leader, made off with an impressive haul.

The Shatter-Shields blame Muiri, and the family matriarch (who once viewed Muiri as another daughter) now wants nothing more to do with her. So, not only has Muiri been betrayed by the man she thought loved her, but she's also been disowned by the Shatter-Shields. What does Muiri want? Revenge. Twice over! She wants you to travel to where Alain and his bandits are holed up and kill the thieving liar. But she also offers you an optional objective: to kill Nilsine Shatter-Shield. With both of her real daughters now dead, family matriarch Tova will surely accept Muiri once more as her surrogate daughter. Or so her addled mind believes. Before you go, Muiri offers you some doses of a particularly potent poison, which you can use on your targets if you wish.

➤ **Lotus Extract (2)**

◊ **OBJECTIVE:** Kill Alain Dufont
♦ **TARGET:** Alain Dufont, in Raldbthar
◊ **OBJECTIVE:** (Optional) Kill Nilsine Shatter-Shield
♦ **TARGET:** Nilsine Shatter-Shield, in Windhelm

> **NOTE** The following two assassinations may occur in whichever order you wish.

Contract: Alain Dufont

Plod through the snow until you reach the spectacular carved dwarven stronghold. If you aren't being particularly sneaky (and you don't need to be), prepare for bandit attacks as you ascend the outer stairs. Deal with these light threats and open the door leading to Raldbthar Consortium.

Enter the Consortium level. Cut down the bandits you see as you navigate the fire trap and head down the sloping corridor to a giant chamber of crumbling columns. Alain Dufont's bandit clan are having a conference. A single arrow dipped in Lotus Extract is a professional method of taking Alain out, or you can wade in with your favored offensive spells

or melee weapons. Don't forget to poison your weapon before it strikes Alain to drop him in a single strike. Afterward, take his unique weapon, Aegisbane, before you depart. This weapon is the stolen family symbol of Clan Shatter-Shield. You can:

Continue to explore this stronghold (consult the Atlas starting on page 414 for more details)
Journey back to Muiri
Or continue your assassinations by tackling the optional target, Nilsine Shatter-Shield.

➤ **Unique Weapon:** Aegisbane

 Nilsine Shatter-Shield (Optional)

Set off to Windhelm and search out the location of Nilsine, who is usually in the market area between the White Phial and the Blacksmith Quarters. You can speak to her about the recent death of her twin sister, but that isn't the reason you're here. You're here to kill her (ideally after coating your blade or arrow with a dose of Lotus Extract). If you're spotted, it is usually better to flee than be overwhelmed by the city guard.

> **TIP** **In the Shadows:** It is safer to wait until nightfall and follow Nilsine to a secluded location, such as her home or an area en route to her house with no other onlookers, before completing the despicable deed.

◊ **OBJECTIVE:** Talk to Muiri
♦ **TARGET:** The Hag's Cure, in Markarth

Quest Conclusion

Trek back to Markarth and explain to Muiri who you've killed. She is pleased with the demise of Alain Dufont and is ecstatic if you also carried out her optional wishes. She rewards you accordingly:

➤ **50 gold pieces (Alain Dufont)**
➤ **Muiri's Ring (Nilsine Shatter-Shield)**

◊ **OBJECTIVE:** Report back to Astrid
♦ **TARGET:** Dark Brotherhood Sanctuary

Postquest Activities

Return to the Dark Brotherhood Sanctuary and locate Astrid. She is happy that you finished your contract, but she needs your help with a matter of a more personal nature. Although she may be paranoid, you're sure that jester is part of it! Dark Brotherhood Quest: Whispers in the Dark now begins.

WHISPERS IN THE DARK

PREREQUISITES: Complete Dark Brotherhood Quest: Sentenced to Death
INTERSECTING QUESTS: Dark Brotherhood Quest: Sentenced to Death, Dark Brotherhood Quest: Side Contract: Kill Hern,
  Dark Brotherhood Quest: Side Contract: Kill Lurbuk, Dark Brotherhood Quest: The Silence Has Been Broken
LOCATIONS: Dark Brotherhood Sanctuary
CHARACTERS: Astrid, Cicero, Nazir, Night Mother
ENEMIES: None
◊ **OBJECTIVES:** Hide in the Night Mother's coffin, Talk to Cicero, Talk to Astrid, Receive a side contract from Nazir

 ● MINOR SPOILERS

▷ Listen to Your Mother

This quest begins once you complete Dark Brotherhood Quest: Sentenced to Death.

Back at the Dark Brotherhood Sanctuary, Astrid tells you about a personal matter she's worried about: It seems Cicero is acting erratically, locking himself inside the chamber where the Night Mother is stored, and she hears whispering voices. She fears a conspiracy, but who is he talking to? Feel free to ask more questions after you agree to eavesdrop from the most secure location in the room: inside the Night Mother's coffin!

◊ **OBJECTIVE:** Hide in the Night Mother's coffin
♦ **TARGET:** Dark Brotherhood Sanctuary

The coffin is now out of its carrying crate and is installed just behind the circular stained-glass window. Unlock it and step inside; there's just enough room between you and the Night Mother's remains. With the doors shut behind you, you can hear Cicero engaged in conversation with the corpse. There's no conspiracy talk here, just one-sided chatter from the jester about keeping the Night Mother safe and finding the "Listener." Then something odd happens; the face of the Night Mother begins to glow, and a voice appears inside your head! She informs you that "you're the one," and the coffin doors swing open.

◊ **OBJECTIVE:** Talk to Cicero
◊ **OBJECTIVE:** Talk to Astrid

MEETING THE BROTHERHOOD

The Night Mother

In the physical realm, the Night Mother exists as a mummified corpse, resting inside a large sarcophagus. Her Keeper, Cicero, brought her here. She exists as a voice inside your head; at first it's just fragmented snippets, but later you receive more structured communications.

"Defiler!" Cicero stops short of an all-out attack but is alarmed at your subterfuge. However, as you relate what the Night Mother has told you, the jester's anger dissipates and is replaced with excitement that he's found "the Listener." After you convince Cicero, Astrid enters the chamber, wanting to know what the commotion is about. You relay the events and the Night Mother's request that you speak with someone named Amaund Motierre in Volunruud. Astrid needs time to think about this possible contract from a long-dead matriarch and instructs you to attempt other work in the meantime.

◊ **OBJECTIVE:** Receive a side contract from Nazir

 NOTE You can visit Amaund in Volunruud before speaking to Astrid, and receive the items you need to hand over to her, but you must speak with Astrid eventually (during the next Quest).

You may tell Nazir about the recent occurrences, but be sure to ask about some additional work. You must finish the previous three side contracts before receiving information on two more targets for you to swiftly dispatch: a fearsome vampire named Hern and a bard called Lurbuk. Tackle either target in any order you wish.

 NOTE Consult the "Dark Brotherhood Radiant Quests" and "Dark Brotherhood Quest: Side Contracts" sections of this chapter. These detail every contract and how to obtain them.

Quest Conclusion

Return to the Dark Brotherhood Sanctuary. After a conversation with Astrid (detailed in the next quest), locate Nazir to collect any additional payments for side contracts you've finished. You may wish to finish any outstanding assassinations at this point, too.

Postquest Activities

You usually return to Nazir once Dark Brotherhood Quest: The Silence Has Been Broken begins.

⚜ THE SILENCE HAS BEEN BROKEN ⚜

PREREQUISITES: Complete Dark Brotherhood Quest: Whispers in the Dark
INTERSECTING QUESTS: Dark Brotherhood Quest: Whispers in the Dark, Dark Brotherhood Quest: Bound Until Death
LOCATIONS: Dark Brotherhood Sanctuary, Riften, Ratway, The Ragged Flagon, Volunruud
CHARACTERS: Amaund Motierre, Astrid, Delvin Mallory, Nazir, Rexus
ENEMIES: Draugr
◊ **OBJECTIVES:** Speak with Amaund Motierre, Talk to Rexus, Deliver the letter and amulet to Astrid, Show the amulet to Delvin Mallory, Report back to Astrid

▷ Dark Machinations

This quest begins once you complete Dark Brotherhood Quest: Whispers in the Dark and the two side contracts, and after you speak with Astrid.

The next time you visit the Dark Brotherhood Sanctuary, Astrid stops you to talk. Although she isn't sure what's happening with you and the voices inside your head, she feels it would be beneficial for you to complete the liaison with the contact the Night Mother mentioned to you. You're to set off for Volunruud, a crypt to the northeast, at your earliest convenience. Afterward, conclude any business you may have with your side contracts by visiting Nazir. Talk to the Brotherhood members about this quest if you wish, and then set off.

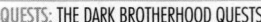

◊ **OBJECTIVE:** Speak with Amaund Motierre
◊ **OBJECTIVE:** Talk to Rexus
♦ **TARGET:** Inside Volunruud

Travel to the earthen mound with the entrance over the embankment guarded by standing stones, and ready your weapon for a small altercation with Draugr warriors. Although there are many rooms and tunnels throughout this complex, you need only reach the bottom of the first set of stairs, turn left, and walk southwest to a small antechamber with Draugr corpses among the ferns. In the room beyond is Amaund Motierre and his bodyguard, Rexus. Motierre's revelations are astonishing; he wishes to hire the Dark Brotherhood to remove several people, culminating with an assassination of the Emperor of Tamriel! He ends his diatribe by motioning to Rexus, who strides forward to hand over the following items:

➤ **Sealed Letter**   ➤ **Jeweled Amulet**

◊ **OBJECTIVE:** Deliver the letter and amulet to Astrid
♦ **TARGET:** Dark Brotherhood Sanctuary

Motierre explains the Amulet can be used for purchasing necessities for the forthcoming contracts, and the Sealed Letter is an agreement with the Dark Brotherhood; both are for Astrid. Optionally investigate further into Volunruud, then exit and return to Astrid. She's understandably incredulous. Show her the items, and she begins to believe. Surely the Night Mother wouldn't misdirect the Brotherhood....

For the moment, Astrid will take the letter, while you journey to Riften and locate a fence and friend of the Brotherhood called Delvin Mallory, who should be able to appraise the Amulet. He's a trusted ally and is holed up in the underbelly of the town.

◊ **OBJECTIVE:** Show the amulet to Delvin Mallory
♦ **TARGET:** The Ragged Flagon, inside the Ratway in Riften

On the Fence

Trek to Riften and find the entrance to the Ratway, by the water's edge underneath the Scorched Hammer. Navigate the maze of sewer tunnels until you find the door into the Ragged Flagon, and then tell Delvin Mallory that the Dark Brotherhood requires his services. He asks how Astrid is, and then you hand over the Jeweled Amulet (via conversation rather than inventory access). Mallory inspects the Amulet and identifies it as belonging to the Emperor's Elder Council. Although worried about who the Brotherhood had to murder to obtain it, when you ask him to purchase it, he eagerly hands over a letter of credit to cover any expenses Astrid requires.

➤ **Letter of Credit**

> 🔹 **NOTE**   You may already be familiar with Delvin Mallory if you're engaged in the Thieves Guild Faction Quests. He has some additional dialogue if you're partway through those missions.

◊ **OBJECTIVE:** Report back to Astrid
♦ **TARGET:** The Dark Brotherhood Sanctuary

Quest Rewards

Back in the Sanctuary, once you explain the credit Delvin Mallory just opened, your only reward from Astrid are the beginnings of Amaund Motierre's most devious of plans, which are now being put into action: She hopes you have something fancy to wear; you're going to a wedding....

> 🔹 **NOTE**   Astrid reprimands you at this point if you broke the seal to read the letter, which contains a list of forthcoming targets, but this doesn't have a lasting effect on your relationship.

Postquest Activities

Dark Brotherhood Quest: Bound Until Death begins immediately. In addition, more side contracts are now available from Nazir.

BOUND UNTIL DEATH

PREREQUISITES: Complete Dark Brotherhood Quest: The Silence Has Been Broken
INTERSECTING QUESTS: Dark Brotherhood Quest: The Silence Has Been Broken, Dark Brotherhood Quest: Breaching Security
LOCATIONS: Dark Brotherhood Sanctuary, Solitude, Temple of the Divines
CHARACTERS: Alexia Vici, Asgeir Snow-Shod, Astrid, Babette, Gabriella, Jarl Elisif the Fair, Kayd, Lodi, Noster Eagle-Eye, Nura Snow-Shod, Pantea Ateia, Veezara, Vivienne Onis, Vuwulf Snow-Shod
ENEMIES: Vittoria Vici
◊ **OBJECTIVES:** Kill Vittoria Vici, Report back to Astrid

⬤ **MINOR SPOILERS**

A Marriage of Inconvenience

This quest begins once you complete Dark Brotherhood Quest: The Silence Has Been Broken.

Upon completion of your previous Dark Brotherhood Quest, a rendezvous with Astrid reveals more about the first of Amaund Motierre's list of targets: Vittoria Vici, an Imperial with pro-Empire sentiments. She is set to be married to her Nord fiancé, Asgeir Snow-Shod, who has strong ties to the Stormcloaks. Although invited, the Emperor respectfully declined. But no matter; his family will be directly affected, for Vittoria Vici is the Emperor's first cousin. The current animosity in the region means that the assassination of the Emperor's cousin will force him into involvement in the Civil War.

◊ **OBJECTIVE:** Kill Vittoria Vici
♦ **TARGET:** Vittoria Vici, Temple of the Divines, in Solitude

> **TIP** Converse with Astrid, Babette, and Gabriella. Astrid insists that this assassination must be a daring public display, messy and loud. There is no hiding in the shadows on this occasion! Babette and Gabriella mention two different ways you can slay Vittoria. Consult the next section for more information.

Divines Retribution

Locate the imposing rock fortress of Solitude and enter the city. Pass through the outer bailey of market shops and houses and into the large inner courtyard to the northeast, which is adjacent to the Temple of the Divines. Step through either archway, and you'll see the ceremony reception is already under way. You can chat with any number of guests: Noster Eagle-Eye, Vivienne Onis, Vuwulf Snow-Shod, Kayd, Alexia Vici, Nura Snow-Shod, Jarl Elisif the Fair, Pantea Ateia, and Lodi.

You may even wish to give your regards to the bride and groom for flavor and fun.

> **TIP** Consult the map of Solitude in the Atlas (pg. 418), and trace a route back to an exit. Run back there once or twice before you make the kill so you know exactly where to escape.

With the ceremony under way, you have numerous methods of removing Vittoria Vici:

Fire from afar: Take to the battlements via the stone steps in the adjacent courtyard, working your way up and around to the crenellations above the temple and then striking Vittoria with a well-aimed arrow or magical attack (dip an arrow in Lotus Extract to ensure a one-hit kill). This allows you to escape more easily.

Babette's advice: She mentions an old statue that rests rather precariously over the balcony where Vittoria will be giving her speech. Take one of the side doors or the crenellations to the statue and push it off so it lands on Vittoria's head.

Gabriella's advice: She tells you of a small parapet (accessed via a side door near the reception courtyard) directly across from the balcony where the speech will be given. She's already left a present: arrows and a special enchanted bow named Firiniel's End. Locate the parapet, and use this bow instead of your own.

A more messy death: Of course, you can run her through with your pointy weapon, bludgeon her to death with a warhammer, or attack her from close quarters. This has few advantages other than seeing your victim die in close proximity to you.

> **TIP** Remember to time your killing so that Vittoria collapses during her speech, where the assembled throng is at its most attentive: There's a bonus in it for you.

➤ **Firiniel's End**

◊ **OBJECTIVE:** Report back to Astrid
♦ **TARGET:** Dark Brotherhood Sanctuary

As you might expect, your bounty in Haafingar has risen considerably. Expect all guards to be hostile as you flee Solitude. **CAUTION**

Escaping Solitude

Now that the marriage is over and the reception ruined, you must make good your escape. Along the way, you may run into Veezara, who Astrid has sent to keep an eye on you. He tells you to run while he holds off the enemy. Oblige him rather than sticking around to face overwhelming odds; Veezara can take care of himself. Rush to an exit, flee the city, and continue into the countryside until you aren't chased anymore. Fast-Travel (or trek) back to the Dark Brotherhood Sanctuary.

Quest Conclusion

Rendezvous with Astrid, and once you confirm the bride's demise, Astrid seems quite excited at the path you've trodden and rewards you with an impressive spell. If you killed Vittoria as she addressed the crowd, you are given additional gold pieces. Then Astrid requests you go speak to Gabriella; she has some information on your next quest.

➤ **Summon Spectral Assassin (Power)**
➤ **Gold pieces (bonus)**

Postquest Activities

Dark Brotherhood Quest: Breaching Security begins immediately.

> **TIP** **A Ghost of LaChance:** The Spectral Assassin you're now able to conjure from the afterlife is none other than Lucien LaChance, the Dark Brotherhood speaker from Oblivion! Not only will he fight by your side (summon him once per day), but also you can converse with him. He'll offer advice on your current quest or the location you're visiting. Be sure to meet this legend!

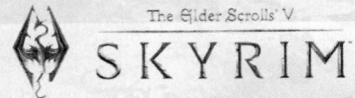

PREREQUISITES: Complete Dark Brotherhood Quest: Bound Until Death

INTERSECTING QUESTS: Dark Brotherhood Quest: Bound Until Death, Dark Brotherhood Quest: The Cure for Madness

LOCATIONS: Dark Brotherhood Sanctuary, Dragon Bridge, Penitus Oculatus Outpost, Markarth, Guard Tower, Understone Keep, Riften, Mistveil Keep, Solitude, Castle Dour, Emperor's Tower, Windhelm, Bloodworks, Palace of the Kings, Whiterun, The Bannered Mare, Dragonsreach

CHARACTERS: Astrid, Cicero, Gabriella

ENEMIES: Gaius Maro

◊ **OBJECTIVES:** Speak with Gabriella, Kill Gaius Maro, (Optional) Steal Gaius Maro's travel schedule, Plant the Incriminating Letter on Gaius Maro's body, Report back to Gabriella

▶ Eyes on the Penitus Oculatus

This quest begins once you complete Dark Brotherhood Quest: Bound Until Death.

◊ OBJECTIVE: Speak with Gabriella

After your talk with Astrid, she recommends you speak with Gabriella, who was also working on the details of the next contract while you were away. Optionally pass by Veezara (who you can speak with regarding his help during the escape from Solitude); then converse with Gabriella, who tells you your next target, a man named Gaius Maro — apparently an agent of the Emperor's security force known as the Penitus Oculatus. Gaius's superior officer (and father) — Commander Maro — has given his son instructions to check the security of every major settlement in Skyrim, in preparation for the Emperor's visit.

Your task is to implicate him in a plot to kill the Emperor by dispatching him and planting an incriminating letter on his corpse. This should distract Commander Maro and make the Penitus Oculatus think the only threat to the Emperor has been quashed. Gaius Maro is also the only man who knows the identity of the "Gourmet," a famous chef scheduled to cook for the Emperor at a private dinner. Gabriella also reveals the possibility of a travel schedule, allowing you to kill Gaius while he is away from the garrison town of Dragon Bridge and earn a bonus. Speak to her for a little more information.

▶ Incriminating Letter

◊ **OBJECTIVE:** Kill Gaius Maro
◊ **OBJECTIVE:** (Optional) Steal Gaius Maro's travel schedule
♦ **TARGET:** Gaius Maro, in Dragon Bridge (or various locations)

> **NOTE** At this point, there are two plans to try. The first is easier but does not net you a bonus. The second is longer, requires some waiting, and could take multiple days to accomplish, but it is more rewarding. In either plan, you must travel to Dragon Bridge. Note that the "quest target" on your in-game compass and map appears differently depending on your actions: If you steal the travel schedule, you can see where Gaius Maro is, wherever you are. If you haven't, his quest target marker appears only when you're in his general vicinity.

Plan A: Death at Dragon Bridge

When you reach the spectacular carved bridge over the Karth River, stop and survey the settlement. If you journeyed here from the Dark Brotherhood Sanctuary, Gaius Maro is usually on the main thoroughfare, talking with his father, Commander Maro, and then his "love," Faida. He then sets off on foot. Simply plant an arrow or melee strike into him, poison-tipped or not. Then promptly flee the scene. You don't need the travel schedule if you aren't interested in the bonus.

Plan B: The Stalking Assassin

Your first task is to try locating the travel schedule, which is on a table inside the Penitus Oculatus Outpost. You can sneak in there; the guards will say you are in the wrong place but won't attack you. Be sure to read and take the schedule so you can refer to it during your stalking of Maro.

➤ Gaius Maro's Schedule

THE SCHEDULE OF GAIUS MAROS

Snagging the schedule allows you to plan an assassination based on the day of the week and your other active quests. Use the list below to see the general time and location of Gaius Maro:

DAY OF THE WEEK	LOCATION	BUILDING NAME
Morndas	Solitude	The Emperor's Tower
Morndas evening	Solitude	Castle Dour (food and sleep)
Tirdas	Windhelm	The Palace of the Kings
Tirdas evening	Windhelm	Barracks (food and sleep)
Middas	Riften	Mistveil Keep
Turdas	Whiterun	Dragonsreach
Turdas evening	Whiterun	The Bannered Mare (food and sleep)
Fredas	Markarth	Understone Keep
Fredas evening	Markarth	Guard Tower (food and sleep)
Loredas and Sundas	Riften	The Bee and Barb

> **TIP** When you rest or sleep, the Rest menu displays the exact day, time, and date. Figure out when to strike based off this information. For the exact locations of each structure within a city, consult this guide's Atlas (pg. 414).

With the schedule in hand, you can now time your arrival at any of the major cities in Skyrim to coincide with Gaius's visit. You may, for example, wish to complete other quests or business, or simply wait (or sleep) until the appropriate day and time. When you finally wish to face Gaius, there are a few matters to bear in mind:

To gain the bonus, do not kill Gaius Maro in Dragon Bridge or on the road as he travels between cities.

The various assassination techniques listed when you started the side contracts during Dark Brotherhood Quest: Sanctuary apply here, too. Check that section for possible execution plans.

Find the unlocked chamber where Gaius is, and then murder him while he sleeps. This is one reason why nighttime assassinations are recommended.

Or, use simple combat followed by placing the letter and then fleeing from authorities.

Finally, you can head to Dragon Bridge and follow him at a discreet distance as he walks to a Hold City. To be sure of claiming your bonus, wait until he enters the city to kill him. You may be able to kill him just outside the gates… but if he runs, you'll lose credit for the bonus.

◇ **OBJECTIVE:** Plant the Incriminating Letter on Gaius Maro's body

No matter where Gaius finally rests, be sure you stop to place on his body the Incriminating Letter that Gabriella gave you.

◇ **OBJECTIVE:** Report back to Gabriella
◆ **TARGET:** Gabriella, in Dark Brotherhood Sanctuary

Quest Conclusion

Gabriella is anxiously awaiting your return. She already knows you did the deed and quickly rewards you accordingly. Then she immediately informs you of a more pressing matter. There has been an "incident" involving Cicero. Astrid will explain.

➤ **100 gold pieces**

◇ **DARK BROTHERHOOD QUEST:** The Feeble Fortune* begins (Bonus)

 NOTE * Quest names marked with this symbol do not appear in your Quest Menu list, although objectives may.

Postquest Activities

Dark Brotherhood Quest: The Cure for Madness begins immediately. Remember to consult with Olava the Feeble in Whiterun and listen to your fortune; this quest information is on page 257.

 THE CURE FOR MADNESS

PREREQUISITES: Complete Dark Brotherhood Quest: Breaching Security
INTERSECTING QUESTS: Dark Brotherhood Quest: Breaching Security, Dark Brotherhood Quest: Side Contract: Kill Deekus, Dark Brotherhood Quest: Side Contract: Kill Ma'randru-jo, Dark Brotherhood Quest: Side Contract: Kill Anoriath, Dark Brotherhood Quest: Side Contract: Kill Agnis, Dark Brotherhood Quest: Side Contract: Kill Maluril, Dark Brotherhood Quest: Side Contract: Kill Helvard, Dark Brotherhood Quest: Side Contract: Kill Safia, Dark Brotherhood Quest: Recipe for Disaster
LOCATIONS: Dark Brotherhood Sanctuary, Dawnstar Sanctuary
CHARACTERS: Arnbjorn, Astrid, Festus Krex, Gabriella, Nazir, Shadowmere, Veezara
ENEMIES: Cicero, Sanctuary Guardian, Udefrykte
◇ **OBJECTIVES:** Talk to Astrid, Search Cicero's Room, Talk to Astrid, Behold Shadowmere, Locate Arnbjorn, Talk to Arnbjorn, Enter the Dawnstar Sanctuary, Kill Cicero , Kill Cicero or leave the Sanctuary, Report back to Astrid

⬤ MINOR SPOILERS

 The Savagery of Cicero

This quest begins once you complete Dark Brotherhood Quest: Breaching Security.

◇ **OBJECTIVE:** Talk to Astrid

Inside the main grotto chamber of the Sanctuary, the Dark Brotherhood are gathered around Veezara, who was bleeding from a deep wound. Speak to Astrid, and she reveals that Cicero has gone mad. She says the maniac didn't like some remarks Astrid had made regarding the Night Mother and attempted to kill her. Veezara stopped him but was wounded. Cicero fled into the forest. Arnbjorn gave chase and hasn't been seen since. Astrid is worried for her husband's safety. She is also calling on you to kill Cicero for this treachery! She suggests you find evidence in Cicero's chamber.

 NOTE Although this may not seem like the most opportune time to start some side contracts, all the remaining targets are now available. There are three active targets, followed by one, then another two, and then the final assassination. Advice on these seven tasks are listed after Cicero has been dealt with, in the "Dark Brotherhood Quest: Side Contracts" section.

◇ **OBJECTIVE:** Search Cicero's Room

Search the Sanctuary until you find Cicero's chamber and the Journal on top of the barrel. Pick up the Journal to read about Cicero's exploits upon his arrival in Skyrim and his knowledge of another, older Sanctuary near Dawnstar. The book also has the passphrase to enter the Sanctuary and some evidence of what (and who) resides inside. Also revealed is Cicero's distaste for Astrid and her "new ways."

➤ **Cicero's Journal, Final Volume**

◇ **OBJECTIVE:** Talk to Astrid

Return to Astrid, and she orders you to the Dawnstar Sanctuary as quickly as possible; in fact, she has secured a steed named Shadowmere to quicken your progress to your destination if you wish.

◊ **OBJECTIVE:** Behold Shadowmere
♦ **TARGET:** Fetid pond, outside Dawnstar Sanctuary
◊ **OBJECTIVE:** Locate Arnbjorn
◊ **OBJECTIVE:** Talk to Arnbjorn
♦ **TARGET:** Dawnstar Sanctuary

Race, by foot, horse, or Fast-Travel to Dawnstar, to the Black Door cut into the beachside cliffs. Just outside you'll find the crumpled form of Arnbjorn. It seems the jester is a deft hand with his "butter knife," as Arnbjorn calls it, indicating the nasty wound. Arnbjorn reckons he wounded Cicero, too, judging by the trail of blood the fool left behind as he entered the Dawnstar Sanctuary. Arnbjorn would have followed but couldn't open the Black Door. Convince Arnbjorn to return to Astrid, while you follow the blood.

Puzzle Solution: At the Black Door, when it asks, "What is life's greatest illusion?" answer "Innocence, by Brother." You'll know this if you read Cicero's Journal.

◊ **OBJECTIVE:** Enter the Dawnstar Sanctuary
◊ **OBJECTIVE:** Kill Cicero

A Fool's Errand

Head down the stairs, and you can hear Cicero deeper in the maze of connecting chambers, saying that Astrid has "sent the best" to defeat him. He is hurt; notice the intermittent puddles and drops of blood on the floor and walls. Follow the trail to Cicero. Draw your weapons as you move through the rooms; there are Sanctuary Guardians to kill as you continue deeper down. Note the gold haul you usually find in their remains. Then ready yourself for the traps:

Spear Trapped Bridge:
Approach this bridge carefully; three spears shoot out from the right. You should also strike the hanging oil lamps either side of the bridge to lessen the severity of a trap in the oil room directly below.

Oil Room: Set fire to the oil on the floor before you enter this room, or the oil lamps on either side of the bridge drop and roast you alive. Deal with the Sanctuary Guardians from a distance, coaxing them into frying in the room.

Bear Traps: Pass through the broken circular window into the ice tunnels, but watch yourself by the dead goat; there are bear traps to maneuver over or around.

Udefrykte: The beast Cicero wrote about in his journal waits for you inside the ice tunnels. Slay this demented troll with a mixture of ranged attacks, swipes, and dodges around the narrow cave with the chest in it.

Sanctuary Crypt: Retract the vertical spears by using the pull chain. Head down the stairs and face more Sanctuary Guardians as Cicero asks whether you'll let bygones by bygones. Then climb the stairs opposite, lift the door bar so you can easily exit the Sanctuary after facing Cicero, then open the door to the torture room.

Keeper of the Old Ways

Flanked by two dead skeletons, Cicero awaits your fury. You can immediately attack or remain silent and let Cicero explain himself; after all, you are the Listener. While lacking in clarity, Cicero tells you Astrid is a "pretender" who had no right to "blaspheme" the Night Mother; he was simply compelled through his sense of duty as the Keeper. Or this could be the rambling nonsense of a Fool of Hearts. You have a choice to make: kill him or leave the Sanctuary.

◊ **OBJECTIVE:** Kill Cicero, or leave the Sanctuary

Choose to slay this battle-hardened fool, who isn't quite as wounded as he may have let on; you have a real fight on your hands! Or, follow Cicero's advice and leave the Sanctuary, lifting the door bar and exiting quickly via the central chamber. As you step out onto the beach, your quest updates.

◊ **OBJECTIVE:** Report back to Astrid

Quest Conclusion

Back at the first Sanctuary, Astrid is anxious about the news of Cicero's demise. You let her know the jester is dead, either telling her the truth (if you killed him) or lying (if you left him alone). Leave Cicero alive, and an additional quest, Cicero's Return, can occur at the end of this series of quests. For now, there are other matters to attend to and important fellows to murder. Consult with Festus Krex for further details.

Postquest Activities

Dark Brotherhood Quest: Recipe for Disaster begins immediately. Your remaining side contracts are also available, and it is wise to attempt as many of these as you wish as early as possible.

PREREQUISITES: Complete Dark Brotherhood Quest: The Cure for Madness

INTERSECTING QUESTS: Dark Brotherhood Quest: The Cure for Madness, Dark Brotherhood Side Contract Quests, Dark Brotherhood Quest: To Kill an Empire, Side Quest: No One Escapes Cidhna Mine, Thane of the Reach

LOCATIONS: Dark Brotherhood Sanctuary, Markarth, Understone Keep, Nightgate Inn, Nightgate Inn Cellar

CHARACTERS: Astrid, Festus Krex

ENEMIES: Anton Virane, Balagog gro-Nolob, Markarth Guard

◊ **OBJECTIVES:** Report to Festus Krex, Question Anton Virane, Kill Anton Virane, Kill Balagog gro-Nolob, (Optional) Drag Balagog's body to a hiding place, Report back to Festus Krex

⬦ Carving the Cook

This quest begins once you complete Dark Brotherhood Quest: The Cure for Madness.

> ◊ **OBJECTIVE:** Report to Festus Krex

Astrid mentions there is one more target for you before the strike against the Emperor; she asks if you've heard of the "Gourmet," a chef and author of a realm-famous cookbook. The Gourmet is scheduled to cook for the Emperor. But not after you kill him, steal his Writ of Passage, and assume his role of master chef. Follow Astrid's advice and talk to Festus Krex for further details. When you visit Krex deeper in the Sanctuary, he tells you the mission is slightly more tricky than a simple slice-and-dice; the Dark Brotherhood don't actually know who the Gourmet is.

Krex then shows you a cookbook signed by the Gourmet; it is signed to a man named Anton Virane, who has been tracked to the keep in Markarth. Virane is the cook there. You are to find Virane, have him tell you who and where the Gourmet really is, and then tie up any "loose ends": You'll be assassinating two cooks for this task. After you kill the Gourmet, Krex hopes that you'll hide the body so any authorities take longer to reveal the Gourmet's identity and what you've done. You can ask any additional questions you wish (more about the Gourmet, the cookbook, or the Gourmet's location in Skyrim) before departing.

➤ **Uncommon Taste—Signed**

> ◊ **OBJECTIVE:** Question Anton Virane
> ♦ **TARGET:** Anton Virane, Understone Keep, in Markarth

> **NOTE** Technically, you can head to the Gourmet's hiding place right away and kill him. However, when you return to Festus Krex, he still requires you to assassinate Anton Virane, so attempting this in order is recommended.

 Travel to Markarth, enter the canyon city, and scale the precarious stone steps to the Understone Keep. Head west, between the two guards, and turn left before you reach the stairs to the Jarl's chamber. Enter the kitchens to the south, where Anton Virane and his two helpers are located. When you speak with Anton (you must pry information from him before the murder), he insists he's a Breton; he's been previously accused of being a Reachman—and with the Forsworn activity in this Hold, this isn't the highest of compliments. But no matter; you're here to ask Anton who and where the Gourmet is.

After initially refusing to divulge this information, Anton changes his tune after you intimidate him and he realizes who you work for. He reveals the Gourmet is an Orc named Balagog gro-Nolob, who is staying at the Nightgate Inn. Then Anton nervously asks that you let him go. You can lie and tell him he's safe, or begin the execution right away. The only reason to lie is if you aren't quite prepared to assassinate Anton or if you want to mess with him.

> ◊ **OBJECTIVE:** Kill Anton Virane

Draw your blade and plunge it into Anton. Don't stop until he's dead. Do this only after he imparts the necessary information. You may use any weapon you wish (including magic or Shouts), and from your previous assassination experience, you should be aware that this attack is going to cause you problems within Markarth's walls. You can get around this by completing one of the following:

Kill Anton and then flee the city. Keep going until you outrun the guards. However, your bounty will still be high, and Markarth's guards will remember you if you return.

Become Thane of Markarth by completing the Thane Quest at this Capital City (detailed later in this guide). After the murder, you can explain to the guard who you are, and they let you off with a warning.

Elect to pay off your debts or give yourself up, since killing every guard in Markarth is impossible.

Or, you can rely on your trusted Sneak, attacking from behind or waiting and attacking him while he sleeps or when he's on his own.

> **NOTE** For further details on committing murder in a Hold City, consult the Crime and Punishment section of this guide (pg.39).

> ◊ **OBJECTIVE:** Kill Balagog gro-Nolob
> ♦ **TARGET:** Balagog gro-Nolob, Nightgate Inn Cellar

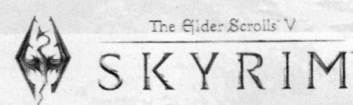

Needs More Assault

Offering pristine views of Yorgrim Lake to the west of Windhelm, Nightgate Inn is a perfect spot for a reclusive chef to write his books. Or for an assassin to commit murder. Journey to this out-of-the-way spot and search the side of the building for a trapdoor. Open it and drop into the Nightgate Inn Cellar. Balagog gro-Nolob is usually sitting in the bedroom down here, close to the mead barrels.

Frighten him with a flourish of prose or cut him down without conversation. Whatever you choose, your fight ends with Balagog gro-Nolob dying on the stone cellar floor. With no one else about, this murder is far easier to commit than that of Anton Virane. Pocket the Writ of Passage when you search his corpse. Balagog also goes outside and stands by the lake, so you can kill him outside as well. Do that, and the hiding place for the body is the lake.

➤ Gourmet's Writ of Passage

◇ **OBJECTIVE:** (Optional) Drag Balagog's body to a hiding place
◆ **TARGET:** Hiding place, Nightgate Inn Cellar

Hiding the corpse is an optional but recommended objective to complete, as it is straightforward and nets you a bonus at the end of this quest. Simply grab the corpse and move it to any of the indicated target spots in the cellar: behind a mead barrel or in an alcove. Your objective updates after you place it in a correct spot, of which there are plenty.

◇ **OBJECTIVE:** Report back to Festus Krex
◆ **TARGET:** Festus Krex, Dark Brotherhood Sanctuary

Quest Conclusion

Return to Festus Krex at the Dark Brotherhood Sanctuary, and inform him the deed has been done. Depending on your actions, he is impressed by your competence (if you killed both cooks and hid Balagog's corpse), and a little less so if Balagog's body is still lying where you killed him. Festus offers you a reward: gold for completing the quest, and the bonus of a ring if you hid the corpse. Then he suggests you see Astrid to commence the final stage of this grand and glorious operation.

➤ **300 gold pieces**   ➤ **Nightweaver's Band (Bonus only)**

Postquest Activities

Dark Brotherhood Quest: To Kill an Empire begins immediately. Your remaining side contracts are also available.

TO KILL AN EMPIRE

PREREQUISITES: Complete Dark Brotherhood Quest: Recipe for Disaster
INTERSECTING QUESTS: Dark Brotherhood Quest: Recipe for Disaster, Dark Brotherhood Side Contract Quests, Dark Brotherhood Quest: Death Incarnate, Thane of Haafingar
LOCATIONS: Dark Brotherhood Sanctuary, Solitude, Castle Dour, Castle Dour, Emperor's Tower
CHARACTERS: Astrid, Festus Krex, Gianna, Nobleman
ENEMIES: Commander Maro, Emperor Titus Mede II, Penitus Oculatus Agent, Solitude Guard
◇ **OBJECTIVES:** Report to Astrid, Report to Commander Maro, Report to Gianna, Report to Gianna while wearing a chef's hat, Make the Potage le Magnifique, Follow Gianna to the dining room, Kill the Emperor, Escape the Tower!, Return to the Sanctuary

◉ MAJOR SPOILERS

The Last Supper

This quest begins once you complete Dark Brotherhood Quest: Recipe for Disaster.

◇ **OBJECTIVE:** Report to Astrid

⟡ **TIP** Don't forget to wear the Nightweaver's Band if you acquired it during the previous quest!

Astrid realizes what you've accomplished and prepares you for the honor of assassinating the Emperor. You're to head to Castle Dour in Solitude and present the Gourmet's Writ of Passage to the officer in charge, Commander Maro. Astrid then tells you that you're going to prepare a special meal for the Emperor, with an extra ingredient that she hands you. Before you depart, you can ask for more details on Jarrin Root and other information. (Astrid tells you one taste of Jarrin Root is deadly, and she means it. Go to your inventory and eat it, and you'll drop dead.)

➤ Jarrin Root

◇ **OBJECTIVE:** Report to Commander Maro
◆ **TARGET:** Castle Dour courtyard, in Solitude

Journey to Solitude and locate the sprawling Castle Dour atop the hill. Step into the large courtyard and find Commander Maro waiting by the tower entrance. He certainly isn't going to let anyone in with the Emperor staying. There's no need to use violence or sneaking; instead, speak to Maro and show him the Gourmet's Writ of Passage. Maro reads the missive and is promptly most apologetic, realizing you're the "Gourmet." He allows you into the Emperor's Tower and requests you meet the castle chef, Gianna. Outside you can also eavesdrop on a conversation between two Penitus Oculatus Agents, talking about Commander Maro and his state of mind, now that his son is not only dead, but also apparently a traitor.

◇ **OBJECTIVE:** Report to Gianna
◆ **TARGET:** Castle Dour kitchens, in Solitude

This Soup Is to Die For

Enter the tower. Head left (east) and then right along (south) the corridor to reach the kitchens. Gianna is busily preparing the banquet feast and mistakes you for a delivery person. She is extremely apologetic when you reveal that you are the "Gourmet"! She requests that you don the proper attire; you can't very well cook without a chef's hat.

> ◊ **OBJECTIVE:** Report to Gianna while wearing a chef's hat

The shelves with the hanging garlic to your left (east) have a selection of chef's hats you can wear. Take one, and then replace your current headgear with it. Then speak to Gianna again. She would be honored to prepare your signature dish, the *Potage le Magnifique*, to your exacting specifications. Gianna now asks you for a series of ingredients you can add to the base broth.

➤ Chef's Hat

> ◊ **OBJECTIVE:** Make the Potage le Magnifique

Begin to choose the ingredients. You can:

Answer with expected ingredients, such as carrots, a splash of mead, Nirnroot, or diced Horker meat.

Answer with more "esoteric" ingredients, such as a sweetroll, Vampire Dust, a Giant Toe, or a septim.

Or remain silent and let Gianna figure out what she would add, as a "test" for her.

You can add as many expected or odd ingredients as you wish. When she asks whether the soup is done, tell her there is one final ingredient and hand over the Jarrin Root. Although she's unsure, your "special ingredient" makes it into the broth. She takes the soup in a stew pot to the dining room.

> **TIP** You may elect not to poison the soup and plan a (usually) more violent method of slaying the Emperor, once the soup is served.

> ◊ **OBJECTIVE:** Follow Gianna to the dining room

Follow Gianna across the throne room, up the stairs, and along to the dining room, where you can hear Emperor Titus Mede II talking to three noble guests and taking a rather blasé attitude toward the murder of his cousin, Vittoria Vici. After Gianna takes a deep breath and prepares to present the Potage, you have this opportunity to strike.

> ◊ **OBJECTIVE:** Kill the Emperor

The Emperor prepares to have the first taste of the Potage le Magnifique, takes a few slurps, comments on its deliciousness, and then keels over dead. The same effect can be achieved if you quickly attack him. Either way, your bounty suddenly skyrockets, the Penitus Oculatus Agent yells for some help, and general pandemonium breaks out. If you've poisoned the Potage, when the Emperor dies, one of the Penitus Oculatus Agents yells that you and the cook have done the dirty deed, and poor Gianna is also attacked in the confusion. Fortunately, this can serve as a distraction while you escape.

> ◊ **OBJECTIVE:** Escape the Tower!
> ♦ **TARGET:** Tower battlements, above Solitude

Dupe le Magnifique

In the midst of the commotion, dodge any of the guests milling about and disappear out of the entrance to the south, which is only a few steps away. You appear on the Tower battlements, where a cluster of guards and a greeting from Commander Maro stops you.

Instead of fury, Maro greets you with a contemptible glee. It appears you've killed a decoy of the Emperor; a member of your "Family" tipped off Maro about the operation! You were traded for the Dark Brotherhood's continued well-being, but Maro has grown tired of this little operation and now vows to butcher all of your clan—starting with you.

> ◊ **OBJECTIVE:** Return to the Sanctuary
> ♦ **TARGET:** Dark Brotherhood Sanctuary

To flee Solitude, you can simply dash past the Penitus Oculatus on the stairs, and then quickly descend the tower's spiral stairs to the ground level (don't exit into Solitude itself, unless you're trying to hide and blend in with the population, or you're using a spell or Sneak to obscure yourself). Continue down the stairs until you reach a lower exit out into Skyrim and the harbor under the gigantic stone arch.

Quest Conclusion

The Brotherhood Sanctuary has disappeared from your world map, making a direct Fast-Travel impossible. Instead, Fast-Travel to Falkreath and head along the road until you spot Penitus Oculatus carts on the road. Or, sneak through the backwoods for a stealthier approach. This quest concludes as you approach the hidden entrance. You hear the sounds of fighting, and Imperials swarm the area. Has the Sanctuary been compromised?

> **NOTE** Remember that the Penitus Oculatus is a separate and distinct faction from the Imperial Legion. Your dealings with the Penitus Oculatus will not harm your standing with the Legion if you're siding with them during the Civil War.

Postquest Activities

Dark Brotherhood Quest: Death Incarnate begins immediately.

  **DEATH INCARNATE**

PREREQUISITES: Complete Dark Brotherhood Quest: To Kill an Empire
INTERSECTING QUESTS: Dark Brotherhood Quest: To Kill an Empire, Dark Brotherhood Quest: Hail Sithis!
LOCATIONS: Dark Brotherhood Sanctuary

 ● **MAJOR SPOILERS**

continued on next page

CHARACTERS: Babette, Nazir, The Night Mother
ENEMIES: Arcturus, Penitus Oculatus Agent
◊ **OBJECTIVES:** Enter the Sanctuary, Search for survivors, Kill Nazir's attacker!, Speak with Nazir, Escape the Sanctuary, Embrace the Night Mother, Talk to Astrid, Kill Astrid, (Optional) Retrieve the Blade of Woe, Return to the Night Mother

▷ The Brotherhood Burns

This quest begins once you complete Dark Brotherhood Quest: To Kill an Empire.

◊ **OBJECTIVE:** Enter the Sanctuary

Commander Maro's men have found your secret sanctuary and are currently ransacking it. This terrible sight becomes all-too real as you enter the road close by the Sanctuary entrance, where at least four Penitus Oculatus Agents are milling about. You can:

Engage them in furious and brutal combat, slaying them all where they stand for desecrating your home.

(Sneak) Or, you can sneak to the Sanctuary entrance without being spotted, ignoring the enemy so you can save your fury for the foes inside the Sanctuary. Head for the Black Door and quickly enter your home.

◊ **OBJECTIVE:** Search for survivors

There is a thick sheen to the air. Force (or sneak) your way down to where you usually meet Astrid. Here, you'll face two Penitus Oculatus Agents. If you're silent, you can overhear them talking about the spreading fire inside the Sanctuary and how an agent named Arcturus led some men deeper into the Sanctuary. Kill the foes quickly, and watch out when you're using fire-based attacks; the area is awash in spilled oil. The only way is down, into the flaming grotto, with more fighting against agents. You'll see the last moments of Arnbjorn's life; now in werewolf form, he tears into two agents before being felled by arrows. There is nothing you can do to save him. Quickly locate the dining hall, where Nazir (the only remaining Dark Brotherhood member you've found alive so far) is battling with more agents.

◊ **OBJECTIVE:** Kill Nazir's attacker!
◊ **OBJECTIVE:** Speak with Nazir

Arcturus, one of Maro's henchmen, is attempting to murder Nazir, so bound over to Nazir's location and help him dispatch this Imperial swine. Show no mercy! Next, kill any other agents who are near to either of you; then quickly stop to tell Nazir about the setup. Nazir had already figured this out. There's little time for chitchatting; you need to flee the Sanctuary before you're roasted alive!

◊ **OBJECTIVE:** Escape the Sanctuary
◊ **OBJECTIVE:** Embrace the Night Mother

Follow Nazir to the southeast, into the connecting corridor above the stained-glass window. Amid the turmoil and flames, the Night Mother calls to you. She tells you to embrace her, as she is your only salvation. Cut down any foes on your way to opening the iron door to the south, and enter the Night Mother's chamber. Open her sarcophagus, step inside, and fall asleep. The Night Mother causes her coffin to fall through the window. You survive in the coffin, and that gives Nazir a way out. It appears Nazir and Babette are maneuvering the coffin into an upright position. Just before the doors open, the Night Mother tells you to speak with Astrid, here in the Sanctuary.

◊ **OBJECTIVE:** Talk to Astrid

▷ The Dread Lord Beckons

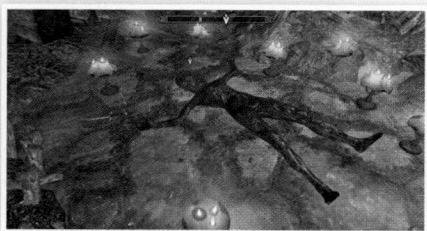

As you step out of the coffin, Nazir tells you to slow down. You can reply in whatever way you wish, but moments later, you should move out of the grotto and up the stone stairs to the south, past the charred remains of the entrance chamber. Turn right (west) and head north, where Astrid is waiting. Or more accurately, burned beyond recognition, surrounded by a flickering candle configuration used in the Black Sacrament. Astrid is almost unrecognizable but has much to say, and only moments left to say it. She betrayed you to the Penitus Oculatus, in return for their promise to spare the Dark Brotherhood.

You may react with seething rage, pity, or silence. Astrid knows what she has done was an unforgiveable mistake, and the Dread Lord Sithis shall judge her accordingly. She also knows that there is still a chance, that you could rebuild the Dark Brotherhood and start over again. She enacted a Black Sacrament and prayed for a contract. You lead this family now. Her Blade of Woe is yours, to see through the transfer of power, which is achieved by killing her.

◊ **OBJECTIVE:** Kill Astrid
◊ **OBJECTIVE:** (Optional) Retrieve the Blade of Woe
◊ **OBJECTIVE:** Return to the Night Mother

Quest Conclusion

Step over to Astrid's ruined form and swiftly end her life. Although she wishes you to take the Blade of Woe, it isn't necessary to kill her with it (but the weapon is well worth using from this point on). Once Astrid has found redemption in the Void, return to the Night Mother's sarcophagus. Your rebuilding of the Dark Brotherhood begins now.

➤ **Blade of Woe**

Postquest Activities

Dark Brotherhood Quest: Hail Sithis! begins immediately. Alas, all the members of the Dark Brotherhood, save for Babette and Nazir, perished in the battle.

 HAIL SITHIS!

PREREQUISITES: Complete Dark Brotherhood Quest: Death Incarnate
INTERSECTING QUESTS: Dark Brotherhood Quest: Death Incarnate, Dark Brotherhood Quest: Where You Hang Your Enemy's Head...
LOCATIONS: Dark Brotherhood Sanctuary, East Empire Company Warehouse, Katariah, Volunruud , Whiterun, Bannered Mare
CHARACTERS: Amaund Motierre, Babette, Nazir, The Night Mother
ENEMIES: Captain Avidius, Commander Maro, Emperor Titus Mede II, Lieutenant Salvarus, Penitus Oculatus Agent, Sailor, Solitude Guard
◊ **OBJECTIVES:** Talk to Nazir, Talk to Amaund Motierre, Board the Katariah, (Optional) Kill Commander Maro, Kill the Emperor!, Report to Amaund Motierre, Retrieve the payment, (Optional) Kill Amaund Motierre, Report to Nazir

 ● MAJOR SPOILERS

Death to the Emperor

This quest begins once you complete Dark Brotherhood Quest: Death Incarnate.

◊ **OBJECTIVE:** Talk to Nazir

Only Nazir and Babette remain, as you come to grips with your Family's slaughter. Babette will follow Nazir's lead, so speak with him; he dejectedly believes this is the end for the Dark Brotherhood. But tell him the Night Mother has spoken to you again, and the original contract must be carried out. You're to speak with Amaund Motierre, and the true Emperor must be assassinated. While you muster a second attempt at regicide, Nazir recommends moving the Dark Brotherhood's Sanctuary to the one near Dawnstar, where you followed Cicero. You'll meet Nazir there afterward, ideally with a barrel full of gold.

◊ **OBJECTIVE:** Talk to Amaund Motierre
♦ **TARGET:** Amaund Motierre, Bannered Mare, in Whiterun

Amaund Motierre has taken up residence in the Bannered Mare, over in Whiterun. Travel there, and open the door to the room at the rear of the tavern. He's more than a little startled at your arrival, considering the news about the sacking of the Sanctuary. He babbles about having nothing to do with the violence to your Family and still wants the Emperor dead. You are here to honor your contract, so ask him where the Emperor is. Amaund tells you he's aboard his ship, the *Katariah*, now moored in the Solitude inlet. Upon your return after a successful assassination, Amaund will reveal the location of the dead drop that holds your payment. Ask him additional questions (about security and getting aboard the ship) if you wish. Demanding to know where Commander Maro is nets you an optional objective.

◊ **OBJECTIVE:** Board the *Katariah*
♦ **TARGET:** *Katariah* ship, Solitude inlet
◊ **OBJECTIVE:** (Optional) Kill Commander Maro
♦ **TARGET:** Wharf of Solitude docks, near East Empire Company Warehouse

(Optional) Additional Executions I

NOTE You may optionally kill Commander Maro at any point before the end of this quest, ideally before or after you assassinate the real Emperor.

Travel to Solitude's docks, close to the East Empire Company Warehouse, and search the wharf for the Commander. There's no time or point in talking; simply approach and kill him with a charge, sneak attack, long-range magic, or bow fire. Expect the nearby Solitude Guards to try and stop you. Fleeing the scene is usually the best option if you're spotted; the alternatives are to give up and go to jail or raise your bounty in this Hold considerably.

Bringing Down an Empire

Travel to Solitude's inlet, under the giant arch that the city rests upon, and locate the impressive galleon moored in the waters here. Swim alongside the vessel, dipping down underwater as you search for the anchor chain. Grab this, and haul yourself aboard the *Katariah*. You actually load *into* the cargo hold; don't climb the chain to the deck.

◊ **OBJECTIVE:** Kill the Emperor!
♦ **TARGET:** Emperor Titus Mede II, Emperor's Quarters, on the *Katariah*

TIP The *Katariah* is anchored in the Solitude inlet when this quest began and remains here for the rest of your adventure. You may wish to give the ship a thorough search for valuable items. Consult the Atlas for the important areas to check.

You clamber into the hold of the *Katariah*, and your quest updates. At this point, your usual infiltration plans commence. You may explore this ship using magical augmentations that make you harder to see or the enemies less alert. You can also sneak (see below) or simply wade through and clobber anyone who gets it your way.

You don't need to return to this ship, so inspect every chamber for items you may wish to claim. Work your way south along the lower deck, into the large central dining galley. Climb the steps and expect more enemies as you reach the jail area. You're attacking both sailors and Penitus Oculatus Agents. This floor also has a small armory and dormitories; additional foes and items can be found here.

Your first critical foe to face is Captain Avidius, who is usually in his cabin by the storeroom and ladder. Kill (or pickpocket) them, and secure the Katariah Master Key from his corpse; this makes navigating the locked doors much more straightforward. Otherwise, you'll need extremely impressive Lockpick abilities.

➤ **Katariah Master Key**

The ladder up to the deck isn't necessary; instead, move north to the gold door that was locked previously (Expert), and open it — either with your Lockpick ability or the Key. Repel the foes in this dormitory area, and sneak past or destroy Lieutenant Salvarus, who is stationed behind the gold door at the northern end of this floor. Climb up the nearby steps, and you're a room away from meeting the Emperor. The real one this time!

> **TIP Sneaking to the Emperor's Quarters:** From the initial room, follow the sailor as he meets his friend and wanders into the galley. When they enter, wait for another sailor to exit from the barracks at the hall's end, and head into the galley as well. Now wait for the guard to move away from the bar, and then sneak around to the chamber's right side. The bard with the flute moves out of the way, allowing a clear path to the stairs. At the top of the stairs, pick the locked door (Expert). You don't have to deal with the captain or the two soldiers in the central room!

> **TIP Further Fighting:** If you're in the mood for more combat, use the ladder up to the trapdoor near Captain Avidius's cabin, or the gold door opposite the door to the Emperor's Quarters. Exit out onto the *Katariah*'s exterior deck. Here, you can slice into the Emperor's agents if you wish. This is one option as an escape route, too. If you want to avoid fighting the captain, you can sneak across the deck. It's much harder (try it at night), but you can go this way if you want to.

Approach the door to the Emperor's Quarters (Master). This requires an impressive Lockpick or the use of the Katariah Master Key. (If you didn't get it from the captain, Lieutenant Salvarus downstairs has another.) Step forward, and the Emperor greets you: Not with a blade or a string of curses but with a well-mannered speech. He knew Commander Maro to be a fool; one cannot stop the Dark Brotherhood!

You can:

Execute the Emperor immediately.

Or speak with him and give him a moment to say a few words before you run him through. He asks for a favor. Not as part of a Black Sacrament, but as an old man's dying wish. There is one who set this assassination forth, and the Emperor wants him punished for his treachery. You are to kill that person. You need not commit to this deed. Now the Emperor turns and waits for death. Oblige him.

➤ **Emperor's Robes**

➤ **Katariah Master Key**

> ◇ **OBJECTIVE:** Report to Amaund Motierre
> ♦ **TARGET:** Amaund Motierre, Bannered Mare, in Whiterun

Ransack the Emperor's Quarters for any books or other items you wish; the Emperor's chest in his bedroom has some good loot. Leave via the door in the northeast wall that leads to an exterior balcony, allowing you to dive into the waters and swim to safety, or backtrack and enter the deck, if you want more fighting. Whatever your route, travel back to Whiterun, enter the Bannered Mare once again. Speak with Amaund, and inform him that Titus Mede II lies dead. Amaund has just heard this information himself and is extremely pleased: As you shall be; there is a considerable payment inside an urn, in the chamber where you first met, back in Volunruud. Amaund wants you to leave now and never cross paths with him again.

> ◇ **OBJECTIVE:** Retrieve the payment
> ♦ **TARGET:** Urn, in Volunruud
> ◇ **OBJECTIVE:** (Optional) Kill Amaund Motierre

(Optional) Additional Executions II

If you wish to kill Amaund and honor the Emperor's wishes, you can tell him there's just one more matter to clear up and then tell him you're doing a favor for an honorable man. Or, you can choose to answer him differently (or remain silent) and attack him anyway! Turn your blade into him and dispatch this aloof traitor (grab his pocketful of gems). Your bounty in Whiterun skyrockets, so expect Guards to confront you moments after the murder.

Quest Conclusion

Amaund Motierre lived up to his part of the bargain; travel to Volunruud, dismantle any skeletal foes that greet you, and search the initial room where you met previously. Inside the urn is a considerable sum of gold!

➤ **20,000 gold pieces**

> ◇ **OBJECTIVE:** Report to Nazir
> ♦ **TARGET:** Nazir, Dawnstar Sanctuary

Now journey to the Darkstar Sanctuary and approach the Black Door. The door opens, allowing you down into the main chamber with the smashed circular window and large fireplace. Nazir is waiting for word on the Emperor. Inform him that you've done the deed, and tell him how much gold you were paid as a reward. You can be truthful or lie (it doesn't matter). Nazir recommends you go to Riften and search out a man named Delvin Mallory, someone Astrid already had you visit previously. This time, though, the "obtainer of goods" will refit this Sanctuary, using the money you earned, and make a true home for this Family once again.

Postquest Activities

Dark Brotherhood Quest: Where You Hang Your Enemy's Head... begins immediately, along with additional quests.

The following 12 Side Contract Quests occur throughout the critical Dark Brotherhood Quests, and offer you several targets to assassinate. Some are accessible earlier than others, and all have a limited window of opportunity. For a complete list of how to unlock each Side Contract Quest, consult the Introduction to the Dark Brotherhood Quests, at the start of this chapter.

Side Contracts: Overview

The contracts Nazir gives you are the first in a long line of assassinations you can (and should) elect to attempt in the name of the Dark Brotherhood. Each requires you to seek out the targets, kill them, and then report back to Nazir (either in between or after completing any other quests). Although each assassination takes place in a different locale, the overall tactics detailed in the introduction to these quests on page 233 are worth employing.

> **TIP** Consult the section called Crime and Punishment on page 39 for a complete overview of how crimes, bounty, and assassinations work.

SIDE CONTRACTS: PART 1

Contract: Narfi

◊ **OBJECTIVE:** Kill Narfi
♦ **TARGET:** Narfi, in Ivarstead

Narfi is a beggar with unpaid debts. When you reach Ivarstead, cross by the rapids (or sneak around via the base of the mountain on the river's opposite side), and deliver a swift death to this unfortunate soul. You're out in the open and easily spotted, so be careful (or fleet of foot).

Contract: Ennodius Papius

◊ **OBJECTIVE:** Kill Ennodius Papius
♦ **TARGET:** Ennodius Papius, at Anga's Mill

Ennodius is usually found outside the settlement of Anga's Mill, near or inside a small tent close to the stream. You may converse with the paranoid layabout or simply end his life. Then check his corpse and possessions for items of interest, and depart.

Contract: Beitild

◊ **OBJECTIVE:** Kill Beitild
♦ **TARGET:** Beitild, in Dawnstar

Beitild is in Darkstar, either inside her house or on the thoroughfare. The guards don't take kindly to a massacre on their doorstep, so be careful (or run quickly afterward). Slay Beitild and take her house key; ransack the residence if you wish (mainly for the gold), and then leave.

➤ **Key to Beitild's House**

Quest Conclusions

◊ **OBJECTIVE:** Report back to Nazir

When you return to the Dark Brotherhood Sanctuary, move into the grotto area. Find Nazir to collect your payment for the first three contracts. Nazir is often in the banquet hall but could be anywhere in the Sanctuary.

➤ **Leveled gold (Narfi)**
➤ **Leveled gold (Ennodius Papius)**
➤ **Leveled gold (Beitild)**

Postquest Activities

You usually return to Nazir once Dark Brotherhood Quest: Mourning Never Comes begins.

▶ Contract: Hern

◊ **OBJECTIVE:** Kill Hern
♦ **TARGET:** Hern, at Half-Moon Mill

Journey to Half-Moon Mill and scout the small cluster of buildings for one with the vampire Hern in or outside it. Then deliver a quick and killing blow (ideally using any remaining Lotus Extract) for a one-strike death. Beware of Hern's vampire wife, Hert, as she fights to the death, too. Optionally ransack the Mill afterward.

> **TIP** Attacking during the day is helpful, as vampires are more powerful at night. Try to slay at least one of these bloodsuckers while they sleep, which usually requires sneaking rather than mayhem! For more information on vampirism (including a possible cure), consult the information on page 38 of the Training section of this guide.

▶ Contract: Lurbuk

◊ **OBJECTIVE:** Kill Lurbuk
♦ **TARGET:** Lurbuk, in Morthal

Set off toward the town of Morthal, on the edge of the Karth River delta. Investigate the buildings until you reach the Moorside Inn, a known location where Lurbuk has sung before. When you find him, you can optionally request a "song of fear and death" before you run him through with an implement of your choosing.

Quest Conclusions

◊ **OBJECTIVE:** Report back to Nazir

Return to the Dark Brotherhood Sanctuary and locate Nazir. Collect your additional payments for side contracts four and five.

➤ Leveled gold (Hern) ➤ Leveled gold (Lurbuk)

Postquest Activities

You usually return to Nazir after Dark Brotherhood Quest: The Silence Has Been Broken begins.

▶ Contract: Deekus

◊ **OBJECTIVE:** Kill Deekus
♦ **TARGET:** Deekus, by Hela's Folly

Deekus left his old life and spends his time eking out an existence at a small camp with scattered stolen trinkets, close to the shipwreck Hela's Folly (which is near Yngvild), and braving the frigid waters of the Northern Coast. There isn't anyone near to hear Deekus's screams; this is an easy kill. Loot both the possessions, and the contents of Hela's Folly afterward, if you wish.

▶ Contract: Ma'randru-jo

◊ **OBJECTIVE:** Kill Ma'randru-jo
♦ **TARGET:** Ma'randru-jo, near Solitude

This Khajiit is a member of Ri'saad's caravan, so the two are friends and will react accordingly if you attack. Ma'randru-jo is always found traveling with the caravan itself. Expect nearby friends of Ma'randru-jo to defend him when you pounce; longer-range assassinations are safe in this case.

▶ Contract: Anoriath

◊ **OBJECTIVE:** Kill Anoriath
♦ **TARGET:** Anoriath, in Whiterun

◊ **OBJECTIVE:** Report back to Nazir

Anoriath and his brother Elrindir, have made a successful archery business in Whiterun, and they have a market store selling fresh venison. He's likely to be either hanging out at the Drunken Huntsman or selling at the marketplace close to the Bannered Mare. Although it may be fitting to kill him using your bow, melee strikes or other takedowns work, too. Beware of combat in cities; prepare to run once your bounty rises!

Nazir's Rewards

Once you have fulfilled these three side contracts, return to Nazir and receive your payment. Then ask about any other contracts, and Nazir tells you about Agnis, your next kill.

➤ **Leveled gold (Deekus)**
➤ **Leveled gold (Ma'randru-jo)**
➤ **Leveled gold (Anoriath)**

SIDE CONTRACTS: PART 4

▷ Contract: Agnis

◊ **OBJECTIVE:** Kill Agnis
♦ **TARGET:** Agnis, in Fort Greymoor

Set off for Fort Greymoor and assault this stronghold, which is initially teeming with bandits. Although sneaking is an option, your hunt usually degenerates into combat pretty quickly. Slay the bandits (or other enemies, should this location have been taken over) as you progress through the prison until you reach Agnis the cleaning servant, who is easily cut down.

TIP If you are ensconced in the ongoing turmoil of the Civil War Quests, this fortification is a key location. Instead of bandits, there are soldiers of the faction that controls Whiterun Hold (which starts in Imperial hands). If you're on the same side as the soldiers, you need not fight them, making this task a lot easier!

◊ **OBJECTIVE:** Report back to Nazir

Nazir's Rewards

Agnis is a single side contract; you must return to Nazir and inform him of your success before he offers you the next two contracts. Don't forget to train in Light Armor with him, if you have the coin.

➤ **Leveled gold (Agnis)**

SIDE CONTRACTS: PART 5

▷ Contract: Maluril

◊ **OBJECTIVE:** Kill Maluril
♦ **TARGET:** Maluril, in Mzinchaleft

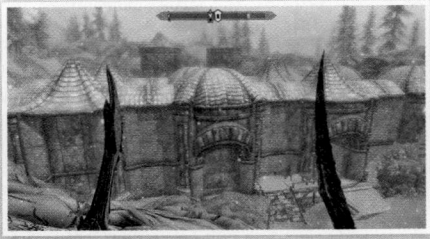

Prepare for a dungeon crawl and set off for the ancient and spectacular Mzinchaleft, introducing the assorted bandits to your style of combat and entering the giant underground structure. Battle down to a locked door and a guard outside. Search the guard for a key if you're having trouble opening the door.

(Lockpick [Average]) Use your prowess to open it, confront Maluril as he pours over Dwemer artifacts, and kill the wizard.

▷ Contract: Helvard

◊ **OBJECTIVE:** Kill Helvard
♦ **TARGET:** Helvard, in Falkreath

Helvard is the Housecarl in the service of the Jarl of Falkreath. He is either striding about town or planning actions inside the Jarl's Longhouse with Siddgeir. Helvard doesn't feel Siddgeir is up to the task, which is probably why you're here. It may be wise to coat your blade in poison, as Helvard's quick death means you can flee without slaughtering the high-ranking town officials. Unless you want to.

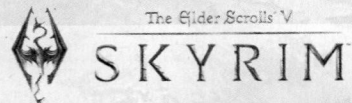

TIP The Jarl cannot be killed, and the only way to survive this with your integrity (and equipment) intact is to complete the assassination. And then run!

◇ **OBJECTIVE:** Report back to Nazir

Nazir's Rewards

Back at the Dark Brotherhood Sanctuary, Nazir is rapidly running out of targets for you to cull. But he has one last assassination, that of a formidable pirate known as Safia.

➤ Leveled gold (Maluril)

➤ Leveled gold (Helvard)

SIDE CONTRACTS: PART 6

▷ Contract: Safia

◇ **OBJECTIVE:** Kill Safia

♦ **TARGET:** Safia, moored near the East Empire Company Warehouse

Journey to the East Empire Company Warehouse and look for the Red Wave, a pirate ship docked on the main jetty.

(Lockpick [Novice]) Pick the lock and enter the vessel after boarding it. Safia is in the hold at the ship's bottom. She seems to have predicted your arrival (if you speak with her) and prepares for a fight, with intermittent fleeing. Cut her down!

➤ Leveled weapon

◇ **OBJECTIVE:** Report back to Nazir

Quest Rewards

With the cutthroat defeated, you may return to Nazir and receive the final payment for your last side contract.

➤ Leveled gold (Safia)

Postquest Activities

This concludes Nazir's business for now, although once Dark Brotherhood Quest: Hail Sithis! has been completed, you may receive further work...just not from Nazir.

DESTROY THE DARK BROTHERHOOD!

PREREQUISITES: Commencement of Dark Brotherhood Quest: With Friends Like These...

INTERSECTING QUESTS: Dark Brotherhood Quest: With Friends Like These...

LOCATIONS: Abandoned Shack, Dark Brotherhood Sanctuary, Dragon Bridge, Penitus Oculatus Outpost

CHARACTERS: Alea Quintus, Commander Maro, Fultheim the Fearless, Vasha

ENEMIES: Arnbjorn, Astrid, Festus Krex, Gabriella, Lis, Nazir, Veezara

◇ **OBJECTIVES:** Report Astrid's death to a guard, Speak with Commander Maro, Kill everyone in the Sanctuary!, Report back to Commander Maro

▷ Fail, Sithis!

NOTE This quest begins only after you start Dark Brotherhood Quest: With Friends Like These...

Completing this quest will make any remaining Dark Brotherhood Quests inaccessible to you. **CAUTION**

When Astrid first captures you and forces you to kill one of the three hostages in the Abandoned Shack, she notes that "someone isn't leaving here alive." That "someone" doesn't need to be pleading for their life with a bag on their head. Instead of spilling innocent blood, you can turn and attack Astrid. She is very strong, so ensure you get as many attacks in as possible before she drops from her perch and begins attacking you. When Astrid drops dead, gurgling "well done" as she falls, search her for the items listed here. Before you leave, you have the option to untie the three prisoners.

➤ Abandoned Shack Key ➤ Blade of Woe

◇ **OBJECTIVE:** Report Astrid's death to a guard

♦ **TARGET:** Any Guard

Step out of the Abandoned Shack, situate yourself after your kidnap, and then decide where to journey to find a guard. One easy example is to head to Solitude and speak to any guard there. Or, if you don't want to travel, simply go to Dragon Bridge. Inform a guard that you killed the leader of the Dark Brotherhood, and they are stunned. You're told to report this action to Commander Maro immediately.

SIDE CONTRACTS PART 3, 4, 5, 6 ◇ DESTROY THE DARK BROTHERHOOD!

255

TRAINING   THE INVENTORY   THE BESTIARY   ◇ QUESTS   ATLAS OF SKYRIM   APPENDICES AND INDEX

◇ **OBJECTIVE:** Speak with Commander Maro
◆ **TARGET:** Command Maro, inside the Penitus Oculatus Outpost, in Dragon Bridge

Journey to the Imperial settlement of Dragon Bridge and find the straw-roofed dwelling with Imperial banners out front, used as a Penitus Oculatus Outpost. Once inside, speak to Commander Maro, who is ecstatic at this turn of events and realizes it's time to strike against the Dark Brotherhood. He wants you to pay them a visit. Use the passphrase "Silence, my brother," and murder every assassin in that hole! Return to Maro afterward and expect considerable compensation.

◇ **OBJECTIVE:** Kill everyone in the Sanctuary!
◆ **TARGET:** All assassins, Dark Brotherhood Sanctuary

► Mass Murder in the Sanctuary

Journey to the Dark Brotherhood Sanctuary in Falkreath, and step up to the Black Door. Answer the question "What is the music of life?" with the passphrase you just learned from Maro. If Maro hasn't told you the passphrase yet, this isn't available as an answer. Head down the steps into the Sanctuary, and begin the first of a series of fraught battles with each member of the Dark Brotherhood (Babette does not fight and is nowhere to be found). They instantly recognize you as an intruder and begin to attack.

CAUTION
These toughened assassins are specialized fighters, and you won't just cut through them. Running through the Sanctuary is like signing your own death warrant. If you beckon more than one attacker at a time, you'll run into a large amount of trouble. Face them one at a time!

You meet the Dark Brotherhood in the following order:

Arnbjorn is in his chamber, prior to entering the grotto. He carries an enchanted warhammer and attacks with the ferocity of a wolf man.

Veezara is in the main grotto area and wields two weapons with amazing dexterity. He is a force to be reckoned with and should be approached with caution.

Gabriella (and Lis the spider) are in the laboratory area. Both are formidable foes. At this point, you can backtrack to the previously explored areas for a breather, if necessary.

Nazir carries a scimitar and isn't afraid to stick it between your ribs. He's holed up in the dining room chamber, which can be difficult to maneuver through.

Festus is the final member of the Dark Brotherhood to fall to your might. He guards the Chapel and has several nasty spells he doesn't mind casting on you.

Eventually, when the last assassin falls or between combat altercations, you may search the dead Brotherhood and ransack their hideout for more Shrouded outfits, weapons, and other common items.

► **Potions (various)**   ► **Leveled Armor and Outfits**
► **Enchanted and Leveled Weapons**

CAUTION
You can't waltz into the Sanctuary and carve up the Dark Brotherhood once you finish Dark Brotherhood Quest: With Friends Like These... The Dark Brotherhood simply murder you if you try an assassination within the ranks.

TIP
Is this wanton carnage too much for you? Then you can flee the Sanctuary, only to return and finish the job at your leisure.

◇ **OBJECTIVE:** Report back to Commander Maro

Quest Conclusion

Head back to Dragon Bridge and inform Commander Maro of your penchant for assassination. He congratulates you on striking a blow against the Dark Brotherhood, which they aren't likely to recover from. Accept your blood money.

► **3,000 gold pieces**

Postquest Activities

All the remaining Dark Brotherhood Quests are now inaccessible to you.

WHERE YOU HANG YOUR ENEMY'S HEAD...

PREREQUISITES: Complete Dark Brotherhood Quest: Hail Sithis!
INTERSECTING QUESTS: Dark Brotherhood Quest: Hail Sithis!
LOCATIONS: Dawnstar Sanctuary, Riften , The Ratway, The Ragged Flagon
CHARACTERS: Babette , Cicero , Delvin Mallory , Nazir
ENEMIES: None
◇ **OBJECTIVE:** Employ Delvin Mallory's services

► That's Your Home

This quest begins once you complete Dark Brotherhood Quest: Hail Sithis!

◇ **OBJECTIVE:** Employ Delvin Mallory's services

Nazir says that you can use the large haul of gold you received from your previous quest to modify the Dawnstar Sanctuary. If you spend the funds on this place rather than on yourself and your inventory, set off to Riften and follow the Ratway to the Ragged Flagon, where the Thieves Guild members reside.

NOTE You may run into Cicero as you exit the Dawnstar Sanctuary for the first time after Nazir and Babette move there. Consult the Dark Brotherhood Radiant Quests: Cicero's Return for more details.

 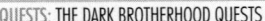

Find Delvin and ask if he can repair and refit the Dawnstar Sanctuary. He says it will cost you, but he can help. Spruce up the place with any of the possible repairs:

IMPROVEMENT	DESCRIPTION	COST
New Banners	The black hand of the Dark Brotherhood now adorns many a wall.	1,000 gold pieces
Poisoner's Nook	An Alchemy Lab, complete with potions and special plants (that regrow and can be used in poisons) is installed near the tiny plant allotment upstairs.	5,000 gold pieces
Torture Chamber	Four prisoners hang here, shackled and ready to reveal the locations of their hidden caches.	5,000 gold pieces
Secret Entrance	Travel to and from the rocky ground above the sanctuary. The exterior entrance is next to the Dawnstar Fast-Travel marker, which makes it even easier to get in and out of the Sanctuary.	5,000 gold pieces
Master Bedroom	In addition to a place to hang your weapons and sleep, you gain some special items fit for a Listener.	3,000 gold pieces
	Total:	19,000 gold pieces

Quest Conclusion

The next time you return to the Dawnstar Sanctuary, any improvements will be made, which you can inspect.

Postquest Activities

Your critical quests are now over. As the leader of the Dark Brotherhood, there are Radiant Quests to complete from this point and an old friend to possibly meet up with....

 # DARK BROTHER RADIANT QUESTS

In addition to the Dark Brotherhood Contract Quests, the following jobs or quests occur throughout (and between) the critical Dark Brotherhood Quests and offer you a variety of objectives to accomplish. Some are accessible earlier than others. For a complete list of how each additional quest is unlocked, consult the Introduction to the Dark Brotherhood Quests at the start of this chapter.

> **NOTE** Task names marked with an asterisk (*) do not appear in your Quest menu list, although objectives may.

  ## HONOR THY FAMILY

Have you slighted a member of the Dark Brotherhood Family? They aren't concerned with you stealing anything from the Sanctuary, but they draw the line at violence. This objective triggers if you strike (accidentally or otherwise) any Family member once and then sheath your weapon. This is important; continue to brandish your weapon, and the whole Family turns hostile! After you calm down, you are instructed to speak with Nazir and pay the fine imposed for your behavior. Return with 500 gold pieces, and you may continue working with the Dark Brotherhood.

  ## THE FEEBLE FORTUNE*

PREREQUISITES: Complete Dark Brotherhood Quest: Breaching Security (with bonus)

INTERSECTING QUESTS: Dark Brotherhood Quest: Breaching Security, Dark Brotherhood Quest: The Cure for Madness

LOCATIONS: Dark Brotherhood Sanctuary, Deepwood Redoubt, Deepwood Vale, Hag's End, Whiterun, Olava the Feeble's House

CHARACTERS: Dark Brotherhood Assassin, Gabriella, Olava the Feeble

ENEMIES: Forsworn, Frostbite Spider, Hagraven, Witch

◊ **OBJECTIVES:** Receive a reading from Olava the Feeble, Locate the assassin of old

▷ A Token Gesture

Assuming you've killed Gaius Maro by following Gabriella's instructions to the letter and securing the bonus, when you speak to her at the Dark Brotherhood Sanctuary, she hands you a token, mentions a fortune-teller named Olava, and suggests you visit her for a reading. She quickly tells you about the problems that occur at the start of Dark Brotherhood Quest: The Cure for Madness. When you have a spare moment, head to see Olava.

◊ **OBJECTIVE:** Receive a reading from Olava the Feeble
♦ **TARGET:** Olava the Feeble's House, in Whiterun

DESTROY THE DARK BROTHERHOOD! ◊ WHERE YOU HANG YOUR ENEMY'S HEAD... ◊ RADIANT QUESTS ◊ HONOR THY FAMILY ◊ THE FEEBLE FORTUNE

257

TRANING · THE INVENTORY · THE BESTIARY · QUESTS · ATLAS OF SKYRIM · APPENDICES AND INDEX

Journey to Whiterun and locate Olava the Feeble's House, off the main path in the southern part of the city. Tell her you have a token for her, and she shakes off her bad mood, realizes you're a friend of Gabriella's, and agrees to give you a reading. She sees a Sanctuary but with snow and lit by the star of dawn. There are other shadowy figures she spies in the ether, and before you are Family, she sees a great spillage of blood. But before that, she sees a ruin ripe for the plunder—Deepwood Redoubt. Through there is a place named Hag's End, where an assassin of old bequeaths his ancient earthly possessions to you!

> ◊ **OBJECTIVE:** Locate the assassin of old
> ♦ **TARGET:** Dark Brotherhood Assassin (dead), behind rock panel inside Hag's End

▷ Danger at Deepwood

Trek to the mountains west of Dragon Bridge, using any path to the north of Hag's End. The path disappears, forcing you to hike to the perimeter, which is flanked by a few large snow-capped stones. Head up the stairs and find the illuminated iron door in the southeast overhang dug into the mountains. There's a campfire to your left and an altar to your right. Forsworn instantly attack if they spot you. The iron door leads to Deepwood Redoubt's interior.

Pass a few tomb corpses and head through a gate and up some stairs, watching out for a dart trap (check the floor and step over the trigger plate). Turn left (southeast) and begin fighting through more Forsworn. There are bowmen on the bridge, so head right, through an old Nord crypt entrance (watching for swinging axes, which you can switch off using the lever at the end) and into a ruined embalming room. There is an iron door here and three Rune Traps. The iron door is locked (Expert); unlock it using your Lockpick skill or the key you find on the corpse of the Forsworn you must fight in the adjacent bedroom.

> **TIP** For such Rune Traps, try to avoid them or try to trigger them by coaxing an enemy onto them, dragging a body onto them, or summoning a creature onto them. In this example, the Forsworn in the bedroom is an excellent victim to lure onto the runes.

> ➤ **Deepwood Redoubt Key**

Once through the door, check the floor for a trigger plate to avoid getting hit by a wall trap, open the iron door, and cross the bridge you saw earlier. Head northeast. Move up the stairs to a larger iron door. This brings you into Deepwood Vale.

This hidden vale is a large, multileveled entrance to Hag's End. You'll probably face around ten Forsworn on the various balconies, turrets, and upper ledges as you progress. You may systematically check everywhere while fighting through these foes, race for the entrance to Hag's End, or take a more long-range approach, sneaking along the sides and firing your bow from range. There are wooden steps below a slightly sunken arch; use those, climb up the arch span instead, or use the stone steps farther south. Deal with the Forsworn boss on the upper level, then continue up and locate the iron door leading into Hag's End.

> **TIP** A frontal assault is highly dangerous, and the main entrance is a death trap. You're likely to be mobbed by four or five Forsworn, but this is an option for those with a thirst for blood (and health potions).

Heading right, picking the lock of the lower door on the right tower, and sneaking in from the side allows you to sneak (or dash) to the stairs. Combat is safer on this side of the vale.

Heading left, hop across the cliffs around the left tower and enter from this side. Although you must fight across the whole camp, the way the enemies meet you means you're in less danger than running up the middle with a sword and a death wish.

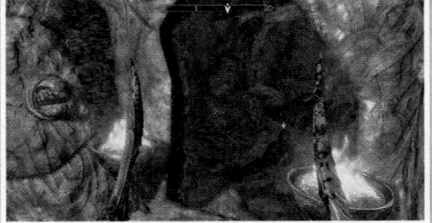

Open the double doors to the northeast and enter a witches' banqueting hall. To continue, dispatch three witches and a Hagraven. When you damage or pass the Hagraven, she will teleport away; you'll have to fight her again later. Open the door at the hall's opposite end; this leads to a dead-end room with more ice traps.

Look right (southeast) and climb the stairs, watching out for a trigger plate that launches a battering ram from the left. Disarm the hinge trigger to open the chest on the shelf in this area. Turn right (southwest), and battle your way through two more witches and the Hagraven in the alcove throne room. Ignore the raised bridge for the moment, and check for a handle on the wall behind the throne. Pull that, and a section of wall opens, revealing a hidden alcove. This is where the slain Dark Brotherhood Assassin lies. Take whatever treasure you wish from the corpse and nearby chest. The assassin's outfit is of particular interest.

> ➤ **Ancient Shrouded Armor**   ➤ **Ancient Shrouded Gloves**
> ➤ **Ancient Shrouded Boots**   ➤ **Ancient Shrouded Helmet**

> You can't simply wander to this secret rock panel and use the handle to open it. The handle doesn't appear until Olava has read your fortune. **CAUTION**

> **NOTE** At this point, you can finish your exploration of Hag's End or retrace your steps.

Assuming you wish to complete your investigation of Hag's End, use the lever next to the bridge to lower it. Cross and fight a witch, then ascend more stairs to a junction with a gate (Master) leading to a treasure chest and fire trap. Open this using the Hag's End Key, located on the mantel in the Hagraven's bedroom (in this hall) or on the Hagraven once you kill her.

On your right (northeast) is a handle. Pull it, and three portcullises open. Wait for the spear traps to recede before moving into a circular chamber with spilled oil. Treat the Hagraven and two witches to a burning (there's an oil lamp in the dragon statue's teeth), before yanking the chain attached to the statue, opening another portcullis, and exiting up into a grand hall, where the Nordic voices call you to a Word Wall!

> ➤ **Word of Power:** Slow Time

Conclusion

With a new Shout learned, open the door to Deepwood Vale. You emerge on a high ledge overlooking the exterior area. Your final Hagraven battle occurs here; watch for her "pets" — Skeevers, Frostbite Spiders, or even Trolls — that you must tackle before you can cut the old crone down. Inspect the Hagraven, as she carries the Hag's End Key,

which can open the gate you saw earlier. Also check the sacrificed witch on the altar; here you'll find the impressive Bloodthorn dagger. Then face the waterfall, drop to the Hag's End entrance, and retrace your steps back into the wilds of Skyrim.

> **TIP** Wait! From the upper platform atop Hag's End, look for a little valley from which the waterfalls descend. Employ a Whirlwind Sprint Shout to reach this valley, and locate the chest with a pair of Unique boots.

> ➤ **Hag's End Key**   ➤ **Predator's Grace Boots**
> ➤ **Bloodthorn**

WELCOME TO THE BROTHERHOOD*

> **NOTE** This objective becomes available as soon as Dark Brotherhood Quest: Hail Sithis! concludes.

When you return to the Dawnstar Sanctuary, ideally after refurbishment, Nazir has managed to attract two Dark Brotherhood Initiates. You can select either of them to accompany you on your adventures; it would be an honor for them to serve the Listener. Further Initiates arrive if any are slain during the course of a more hectic exploration.

> ➤ **Follower:** Dark Brotherhood Initiate

CICERO'S RETURN*

> **NOTE** Previously, you've had at least two opportunities to fight Cicero, most prominently during Dark Brotherhood Quest: Delayed Burial and The Cure for Madness. If you didn't defeat him during the latter quest, this is active.

If you kept Cicero alive (even if that meant lying to Astrid), he usually gives you a startling greeting outside Dawnstar Sanctuary the first time you leave the premises. After one more jest, Cicero says he's here to serve the Night Mother.

From this point on, you'll find him inside the Sanctuary, where you can ignore or speak to him. You may keep him alive for the hilarity, or you may bring him on an adventure. Whether he returns from that adventure, of course, depends on what you equip him with and how helpful you are during a combat situation....

> ➤ **Follower:** Cicero

> **NOTE** Cicero has a particular prowess at melee fighting. You can give him orders, and he comments when you visit certain locations and sings songs to himself.

THE DARK BROTHERHOOD FOREVER!

> ◇ **OBJECTIVES:** Approach the Night Mother, Speak with the contact, Kill the target

> ◇ **OBJECTIVE:** Speak with the contact
> ♦ **TARGET:** Random person. Random location.

▷ Murder for Mother

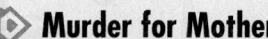

> ◇ **OBJECTIVE:** Approach the Night Mother

When you reach the newly claimed Dawnstar Sanctuary, the Night Mother tells you to approach her. Do as she asks, and she informs you that somewhere in Skyrim, the Black Sacrament has been completed, and someone wishes to pay the Dark Brotherhood for their services. You are to meet them and gain further information on that target.

Travel to the location where the contact wishes to speak to you. They quickly hand over a payment, along with instructions on how to find their target and kill them. This is a simple assassination, and one that pays.

> ➤ **Leveled gold pieces**

> ◇ **OBJECTIVE:** Kill the target
> ♦ **TARGET:** Random person. Random location.

The contacts and targets are randomly chosen from the following lists (they won't be the same each time):

Contacts

A nervous patron at Candlehearth Hall in Windhelm

A wary outlaw at the Bee and Barb in Riften

corrupt agent at the Penitus Oculatus Outpost in Dragon Bridge

scheming servant at the Keep in Markarth

A desperate gambler at the Barracks in Windhelm

blasphemous priest at the Temple of Kynareth in Whiterun

dishonored skald at the Bards College in Solitude

An indolent farmer at the Vilemyr Inn in Ivarstead

An grief-stricken chef at the Windpeak Inn, here in Dawnstar

An unemployed laborer at the Frostfruit Inn in Rorikstead

Targets

visiting noble at Dragonsreach in Whiterun

A big laborer at Katla's Farm

An itinerant lumberjack in Morthal, at the logging camp

A reckless mage in the Frozen Hearth Inn in Winterhold.

A seasoned hunter, just outside Falkreath

A poor fishwife, on the Riften Docks

grim shieldmaiden walking the streets of Markarth

A traveling dignitary in Solitude

A coldhearted gravedigger, who tends to work in the Hall of the Dead in Windhelm

A beautiful barbarian, in Ivarstead

Conclusion

Approach your target, who is usually within the walls of a city or other highly populated location, and quickly dispatch them. To deal with any guards or others who see you, use the same techniques you did in previous Dark Brotherhood missions.

Postquest Activities

Once the target is dead, this objective automatically starts again. Return to the Night Mother and locate your next contact.

THE TORTURER'S TREASURE: PARTS I, II, III, IV*

Visit your newly constructed torture chamber, and you'll discover that Nazir has clamped four torture victims to the stone walls. If you speak to one of them, they give a variety of angry or frightened answers. Continue talking to the victim, and they eventually let you know of a hidden stash of treasure. Leave your victim to hang, and progress to your next victim, repeating this process until all four victims have revealed where each of their caches lie.

◊ **MISCELLANEOUS:** Take the hidden treasure

> **TIP** There are four treasure stashes, so it's better to interrogate all four victims and collect each of the four stashes once, rather than interrogating one at a time. This treasure is accessible only after this is active.

Conclusion

> **NOTE** Consult your Miscellaneous Quest menu and flag all four objectives so they are shown on the map. Then journey to each of them and uncover a Hollowed-Out Rock or Hollowed-Out Tree Stump at the specified location. Search this and pry out a sizable cache of gold, usually between 1,000 to 2,000 gold pieces per stash. This typically pays for the torture chamber's construction and leaves you with an extra 1,000 to 1,200 gold pieces after all four caches are cleared.

➤ **1,000 to 2,000 gold pieces (4)**

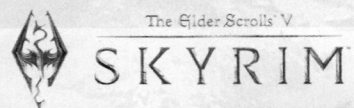

The Civil War Quests automatically begin the moment you meet your ally during the escape from Helgen. From this point, you begin to make important choices with ramifications across Skyrim. You may choose to side with either the Imperial Legion or the Stormcloak Rebellion and complete quests for your chosen faction. Main Quests: The Fallen and Season Unending are affected by your actions within the Civil War; consult those quests for more information.

▶ Picking a Side

Choosing a side can be done quickly or delayed until the very last moment. You can work with the person you escaped Helgen with — either Hadvar (Imperials) or Ralof (Stormcloaks). However, you haven't officially picked a side until you've visited the stronghold of your chosen faction and sworn an oath to the Imperials (in Solitude) or Stormcloaks (in Windhelm).

There is a last-minute change you can make after that: At the very end of Civil War Quest: The Jagged Crown, you can decide to bring the Crown itself to the enemy leader. At this point, there is no turning back!

> **NOTE Cross-Referencing:** Do you want to see maps and learn more about the traps, non-quest-related items, collectibles, crafting areas, and other important rooms of note in every location during these quests? Then cross-reference the location you travel to with the information on that location contained in this guide's Atlas.

CIVIL WAR MAP

Province of Skyrim
4E 182 Nataly Dravarol, Cartographer

◆ Imperial Territory

1 FORT HRAGGSTAD	5 MORTHAL	9 FORT SUNGARD	13 FALKREATH
2 SOLITUDE	6 KARTHWASTEN	10 FORT GREYMOOR	14 HELGEN
3 DRAGON BRIDGE	7 MARKARTH	11 WHITERUN	15 FORT NEUGRAD
4 FORT SNOWHAWK	8 RORIKSTEAD	12 RIVERWOOD	

Stormcloak Territory

16 WINTERHOLD	21 FORT AMOL
17 DAWNSTAR	22 IVARSTEAD
18 FORT DUNSTAD	23 SHOR'S STONE
19 FORT KASTAV	24 FORT GREENWALL
20 WINDHELM	25 RIFTEN

MAP LEGEND

> This shows the important tactical locations of Skyrim and who controls them at the start of the Civil War.

Imperial Headquarters: Castle Dour, in Solitude

Castle Dour, on approach from Solitude interior.

A strategic planning.

Solitude is the capital of Skyrim (and Haafingar Hold) and is the one, true cosmopolitan city of Skyrim. Dominating the city's northern district is Castle Dour. Thick-walled and imposing, it protected its inhabitants from invaders. As the city grew, walls were added to surround the other, newer buildings. During a long period of peace, a palace was built for the Jarl. Castle Dour was converted into the Imperial Garrison, and the Jarl moved to the Blue Palace in the south of the city.

Important Characters: Imperial Legion

General Tullius

Tullius is a no-nonsense military man, impatient with politicians and compromise. He believes the best solution is to crush the rebellion ruthlessly. Although historically competent, his recent tactics have inflamed the tensions after he allowed the Thalmor to begin enforcing the terms of the hated White-Gold Concordat. He is practical and dedicated, but he lacks imagination and is impatient.

Legate Rikke

Rikke is widely respected by the Skyrim legions she commands and is strictly loyal to Tullius's orders even when she disagrees with them. Although from Nordic stock, she is a true believer in the rightness of the Imperial cause. She is both loyal and disciplined.

Hadvar

A loyal, brave, and enthusiastic Imperial soldier who befriends you during the escape from Helgen. He is related to Alvor the Blacksmith, in Riverwood.

Available Quests

There are a total of 12 different Critical Path Quests available during the Civil War if you side with the Imperials. One of these is an Overview Quest—the Reunification of Skyrim. All but the first quest have one or more prerequisites, as shown in the following table:

✔	QUEST NAME	PREREQUISITES
	Civil War Quest: Joining the Legion	None
	Civil War Quest: The Jagged Crown	Complete Civil War Quest: Joining the Legion
	Civil War Quest: Message to Whiterun	Complete Civil War Quest: The Jagged Crown
	Civil War Quest: Defense of Whiterun	Complete Civil War Quest: Message to Whiterun
	Civil War Quest: Reunification of Skyrim†	Complete Civil War Quest: Message to Whiterun
	Civil War Quest: A False Front	Complete Civil War Quest: Defense of Whiterun
	Civil War Quest: The Battle for Fort Dunstad	Complete Civil War Quest: A False Front
	Civil War Quest: Compelling Tribute	Complete Civil War Quest: The Battle for Fort Dunstad
	Civil War Quest: The Battle for Fort Greenwall	Complete Civil War Quest: Compelling Tribute
	Civil War Quest: Rescue from Fort Kastav	Complete Civil War Quest: The Battle for Fort Greenwall
	Civil War Quest: The Battle for Fort Amol	Complete Civil War Quest: Rescue from Fort Kastav
	Civil War Quest: Battle for Windhelm	Complete Civil War Quest: The Battle for Fort Amol

NOTE † = Civil War Quest: Reunification of Skyrim is an Overview Quest that continues until the end of Civil War Quest: Battle for Windhelm.

 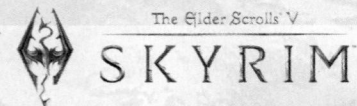

Stormcloak Sanctuary: Palace of the Kings, in Windhelm

Palace of the Kings, on approach from Windhelm interior.

The war room, during tactical planning.

Windhelm sits on the northern bank of the White River and is an imposing sight. The Palace of the Kings (also known historically as the Palace of Ysgramor) is an ancient stone fortress and the city's main keep. These days, the palace serves as the headquarters of the Stormcloaks, under the leadership of Jarl Ulfric Stormcloak, who sits upon the ancient Throne of Ysgramor. And so the Palace of the Kings is, as such, the center of the pro-Nord war effort in the Civil War.

Important Characters: Stormcloak Rebellion

Jarl Ulfric Stormcloak

Ulfric fought in the Imperial Legions during the Great War against the Aldmeri Dominion. Disillusioned over the Markarth incident, he founded the Stormcloaks as an underground group centered around now-proscribed worship of Talos. After killing the High King of Skyrim in the throne room of Solitude after declaring him a lackey of the Empire, he was arrested in surprisingly swift time, possibly aided by Thalmor agents. Only recently has he escaped the chopping block at Helgen. He is fiery and impetuous and a born leader, but he lacks the cool head of a strategist.

Galmar Stone-Fist

Galmar may be old, but he is still hale. A very experienced Nord warrior, he is also Ulfric's right-hand man and Housecarl. He served Ulfric's father and is more concerned with winning the war than the politics behind it. He is Ulfric's most trusted ally and acts as his field commander. He is a firm believer in the old ways of Talos, and distrusts High Elves. A grizzled bear of a man, he is imposing and gruff, but fair.

Ralof

A loyal, brave, and enthusiastic Stormcloak soldier who befriends you during the escape from Helgen. He is related to Gerdur the lumber mill owner, in Riverwood.

Available Quests

There are a total of 12 different Critical Path Quests available during the Civil War if you side with the Stormcloaks. One of these is an Overview Quest—the Liberation of Skyrim. All but the first quest have one or more prerequisites, as shown in the following table:

	QUEST NAME	PREREQUISITES
	Civil War Quest: Joining the Stormcloaks	None
	Civil War Quest: The Jagged Crown	Complete Civil War Quest: Joining the Stormcloaks
	Civil War Quest: Message to Whiterun	Complete Civil War Quest: The Jagged Crown
	Civil War Quest: Battle for Whiterun	Complete Civil War Quest: Message to Whiterun
	Civil War Quest: Liberation of Skyrim†	Complete Civil War Quest: Battle for Whiterun
	Civil War Quest: Rescue from Fort Neugrad	Complete Civil War Quest: Battle for Whiterun
	Civil War Quest: Compelling Tribute	Complete Civil War Quest: Rescue from Fort Neugrad
	Civil War Quest: The Battle for Fort Sungard	Complete Civil War Quest: Compelling Tribute
	Civil War Quest: A False Front	Complete Civil War Quest: The Battle for Fort Sungard
	Civil War Quest: The Battle for Fort Snowhawk	Complete Civil War Quest: A False Front
	Civil War Quest: The Battle for Fort Hraggstad	Complete Civil War Quest: The Battle for Fort Snowhawk
	Civil War Quest: Battle for Solitude	Complete Civil War Quest: The Battle for Fort Hraggstad

> **NOTE** † = Civil War Quest: Liberation of Skyrim is an Overview Quest that continues until the end of Civil War Quest: Battle for Solitude.

Reconnaissance: Preliminary Planning

Halt! Before beginning a Civil War Quest that involves attacking a fortification, you may wish to employ some smart reconnaissance, visiting the any fort you'll be assaulting later in the Civil War and inspecting the exterior battlements, learning where the stairs and upper crenellations are. However, remember the following advice and caveats:

◇ Once you've accepted the quest that sends you to a Hold, a reconnaissance is too late; enemy soldiers attack if you approach the fort. However, if you arrive before you receive the particular quest to assault the fort, you can walk around. The soldiers will call you out as a trespasser, but they probably won't attack you on sight. For best results, sneak.

◇ You can visit any or all of the forts before the Civil War starts. This will give you a chance to inspect them and collect some loot from the enemies (usually warlocks or bandits) who occupy them before the soldiers move in.

◇ Finally, the "real" attack on the fortification doesn't start until the specific quest is running. If you arrived here earlier and tried to take out the garrison all by yourself, the enemy will be back up to full strength when the proper attack begins.

> **CAUTION**
> There is one matter to be careful of: If you've been here before, you'll have a map marker to the fort. If you Fast-Travel there, the soldiers usually spot you immediately, and the battle starts early, and without your side backing you up! Therefore, it is always better to Fast-Travel to an adjacent location and meet up with your men first.

> **NOTE** As always, study the Atlas section for each location.

Attacking Forts: A Fighting Chance

Whenever you're outside a fortified structure, attempting to get in, raze the place, and cut down the enemy guards inside, there are a few general strategies you should employ:

◇ Your main goal is to lead and support your soldiers. While you can attack from another entrance, you risk getting overwhelmed. You're likely better off if you stay with your men unless you're trying to achieve some tactical goal.

◇ Don't head into an interior part of the structure. Stay with your allies and give yourself room to maneuver.

◇ There's usually more than one entrance. Check the exterior walls for gaps, fallen sections you can leap over, or other debris for infiltration purposes.

◇ Move carefully and deliberately. If you get out too far ahead of your troops, the enemy may surround you.

◇ You have two basic choices: you can move through the fort and fight soldiers as you go, or find and secure one position and let the enemy come to you.

◇ Most entrances to strongholds are bolstered by barricades. Destroy these with magic or melee weapons if you want your allies to storm the area.

◇ Need a rest? Then back away and administer magic or potions before returning into the fray.

◇ Gain height. It is always advantageous to gain the highest ground, whether it is a turret or battlements section.

◇ Use any walls as cover, and attack foes grouped together with area-of-effect weapons. However, these same area-of-effect weapons can damage your own forces. Be very aware of who you're fighting!

◇ Stormcloaks are clad in dark blue. Those folks in red? Imperials! Make sure you know which side you're on!

◇ You can fight with long-range arrows or magic, or rush in with a melee or a combination of both. As long as you're killing foes, you aren't penalized for the way you're dispatching them.

◇ (Melee) Keep an eye out for archers on the walls. If you see one of your men fighting the enemy, help them—the enemy can't block both of your attacks at once.

◇ (Ranged) Find a good sniping spot, somewhere you can maximize your damage and have good sight lines. Ideally, shadow some of your soldiers so if your position is attacked, they can deal with the enemy while you back away and continue to strike from range.

Your mission is complete when the enemy garrison is all but wiped out. A few stragglers may remain, but these are optional kills.

CIVIL WAR QUESTS: IMPERIAL

 ### JOINING THE LEGION

PREREQUISITES: None

INTERSECTING QUESTS: None

LOCATIONS: Fort Hraggstad, Fort Hraggstad Prison, Helgen (Location), Solitude, Castle Dour

CHARACTERS: Beirand, General Tullius, Hadvar, Legate Rikke

ENEMIES: Bandit, Bandit Chief

◇ **OBJECTIVES:** Miscellaneous: Join the Imperial Legion, Clear out Fort Hraggstad, Report to Legate Rikke, Take the oath, Miscellaneous: Get Imperial gear from Beirand

The Elder Scrolls V
SKYRIM

Before the Undying Loyalty, Unwavering Obedience

> **NOTE** The following quest assumes you pick a side in the Civil War and stick with them. Consult the introduction to these quests to see when you can switch sides (the last possible moment is at the end of Civil War Quest: The Jagged Crown). If you side with the Stormcloak Rebellion, consult the Civil War Quest: Joining the Stormcloaks, on page 279. Although the Civil War rages on, it only affects your adventure if you let it by completing this series of quests.

After escaping from underneath the battlements of the burning town of Helgen, and watching the dragon responsible for disrupting your execution, speak with Hadvar. He says he's headed to Riverwood and asks if you want to accompany him. As you progress down the hillside, he recommends you go to Solitude and join the Imperial Legion.

> ◊ **MISCELLANEOUS OBJECTIVE:** Join the Imperial Legion
> ♦ **TARGET:** Castle Dour, in Solitude

> **TIP** Did you miss Hadvar's invitation? Then greet any Imperial Soldier (clad in red tunics) or visit any Imperial Camp in Skyrim, and you'll almost always receive an offer to join up.

Journey to the main stronghold of the Imperials in Skyrim — the sprawling city of Solitude, perched on a gigantic arch. As you enter, an execution is under way. A traitor named Roggvir is being put to the ax for aiding in the escape of Ulfric Stormcloak after he murdered the previous Jarl, High King Torygg. You may watch the execution or continue up to Castle Dour, within Solitude's walls. Head west into the strategy planning room, where General Tullius and his Legate Rikke are talking about the war effort. Rikke's scouts are telling her the Stormcloaks are conscripting more men than the Imperials had hoped, and Riften, Dawnstar, and Winterhold are all showing support for the rebellion.

Tullius grows tired of Jarl Balgruuf of Whiterun. The leader of this key strategic Hold City refuses to garrison Imperial troops there, and he refuses to acknowledge Ulfric's claim. After more planning, Tullius asks you why you're here. Answer how you wish, although you gain Tullius's trust faster if you mention you helped Hadvar escape. He hands you over to Legate Rikke, who is also impressed you escaped Helgen alive. Rikke has a good feeling about you and has a test for you to complete so you can prove you're worthy of joining the Legion. You're to clear out Fort Hraggstad. Survive, and you pass this test. This quest officially begins now.

> ◊ **OBJECTIVE:** Clear out Fort Hraggstad
> ♦ **TARGET:** All bandits, in Fort Hraggstad

Testing Metal and Mettle

In the Haafingar Hold, on the mountains overlooking the Sea of Ghosts northeast of Solitude, is the fort Legate Rikke wishes to use as a garrison. It is currently a bandit lair; expect around eight of them patrolling the exterior battlements. You can fight them either from range or with melee strikes. Watch for (and kill) the bowmen atop the central tower and along the crenellations. Then enter Fort Hraggstad, striking down two bandits and their chief. Back out and enter the prison, where you can slay the final three bandits. Pick any items you wish once the massacre is over.

> ◊ **OBJECTIVE:** Report to Legate Rikke
> ◊ **OBJECTIVE:** Take the oath

Quest Conclusion

Journey back to Castle Dour in Solitude, and Legate Rikke welcomes you back when you speak with her. She sends a garrison to fortify Hraggstad and tells you it is time for you to officially join the Legion. Turn to General Tullius and agree to recite this oath:

"Upon my honor I do swear undying loyalty to the Emperor, and unwavering obedience to the officers of his great Empire.

May those above judge me, and those below take me, if I fail in my duty.

Long live the Emperor! Long live the Empire!"

> ◊ **MISCELLANEOUS OBJECTIVE:** Get Imperial gear from Beirand

> **NOTE** If you forgo this oath, you can journey to Windhelm instead and complete Civil War Quest: Joining the Stormcloaks as well. Do this if you're still unsure where your allegiance lies.

Postquest Activities

You are now "Auxiliary" status within the ranks of the Imperials. You may now visit Beirand over by Solitude Forge. He outfits you with proper Imperial warrior attire (see the equipment listed below). Remember you can choose light, medium, or heavy, depending on how maneuverable you want to be and on your play style. Legate Rikke also has your next assignment: Civil War Quest: The Jagged Crown.

➤ **Imperial Armor**   ➤ **Imperial Bracers**   ➤ **Imperial Shield**
➤ **Imperial Boots**   ➤ **Imperial Helmet**

PREREQUISITES: Complete Civil War Quest: Joining the Legion
INTERSECTING QUESTS: Civil War Quest: Joining the Legion, Civil War Quest: Message to Whiterun
LOCATIONS: Korvanjund, Korvanjund Crypt, Korvanjund Halls, Korvanjund Temple, Solitude, Castle Dour
CHARACTERS: General Tullius, Hadvar, Imperial Soldier, Legate Rikke
ENEMIES: Draugr, Stormcloak Soldier
◊ **OBJECTIVES:** Talk to Legate Rikke, Meet Legate Rikke outside Korvanjund, Retrieve the Jagged Crown, Deliver the crown to General Tullius

What Real Soldiers Look Like

◊ **OBJECTIVE:** Talk to Legate Rikke

Speak with Legate Rikke in Castle Dour. She tells you that Ulfric's right-hand man, Galmar Stone-Fist, has located the final resting place of the Jagged Crown. You're going to claim it before the Stormcloaks do. Rikke is already assembling her men outside of Korvanjund. You should join them immediately. Ask her for more information on the Jagged Crown and the tomb of Korvanjund before you leave.

> **TIP** Visit Beirand for your complementary Imperial armor (you don't need to wear it, so sell it if you don't want it).

◊ **OBJECTIVE:** Meet Legate Rikke outside Korvanjund

Northeast of Whiterun, in the lower foothills where the ground first turns from tundra to snow, is a depression in the ground — the remains of a large cairn and the entrance to these ancient Nordic temple ruins and Jarl's tomb. Of course, you can barge toward the entrance on your own, but a more measured (and recommended) plan is to meet Legate Rikke and her quartet of men on the slopes outside the entrance. The troops include Hadvar, the man you met at Helgen. She curses the damned rebels, who got here first, and asks you to move out. This occurs once you confirm you're ready. As you walk up the hill, Legate Rikke finishes her stirring speech. These foes may be known to you, but their allegiance means they are enemies now. Charge!

If you're using melee weapons, it is recommended that you lead the charge, sprinting down the steps and up the other side to engage the bowmen, while the rest of your troops fight in the lower ground.

If you're using bows or projectile spells, stay on the edge of the depression and rain missile attacks down upon the enemy.

As there are only around four Stormcloaks guarding this entrance, combat is swift and straightforward. Meet Legate Rikke atop the steps by the interior entrance. She issues another warning before heading into Korvanjund Temple. Follow her at once.

◊ **OBJECTIVE:** Retrieve the Jagged Crown
♦ **TARGET:** Bone Crown, on Draugr Leader, in Korvanjund Crypt

> **CAUTION** During combat throughout this tomb, and any time you're engaged in battle, your wild weapon swings or area-of-effect weapons may strike your comrades. If this occurs more than once, they may turn hostile. It is most important you minimize the area of your murdering, and use weapons that are accurate (arrows or spells such as Firebolt). Take more care when using melee weapons. Moving around to attack enemies from the opposite side from your friends, dashing forward to engage foes your allies aren't attacking, and even leaving your friends to finish off foes helps, too.

> **TIP** You can follow Legate Rikke (which is safer) or head off and explore on your own (which is fine, as you can complete this quest without any help or conversations).

 Carnage in the Crypt

Rush into the crypt entrance chamber, which is wide and contains a small contingent of foes. Slaughter them quickly, after which Legate Rikke posts two of her detachment to guard this entrance. Head down the steps to the north, before turning right (east) and slaying a trio of Stormcloaks prowling the ledge surrounding this sunken hall. It is usually best to head in first to avoid pushing past friends to reach the foes. After the battle, you can reconvene near Legate Rikke at the northern side of the lower hall near the massive cave-in that dominates the middle of this chamber. Rikke looks down the tunnel steps ahead and guesses there's a group of foes waiting for you on the other side. She's hoping you can find a different way in. You can:

Ignore the warning and plow straight down the stairs and into a fight with around four to six Stormcloaks in the bridge chamber beyond.

Or, head around the hallway's upper ledge, to an entrance directly above where Rikke is waiting. This brings you into the same bridge chamber, but on the upper bridge. It is easier to sneak, fire long-range attacks, or race along the bridge and around the upper balcony area, tackling foes one at a time.

Your comrades attack the enemies from the lower level, so taking down the enemy from two directions is safer and splits the enemy's targets. When the bridge chamber is dripping Stormcloak blood, check the main stepped area for treasure (near the open chest), and then find the upper exit passage to the west. Legate Rikke and her remaining soldiers are clustered around the corpse of a Draugr. It is the first time they've seen such a corpse. Rikke bolsters their courage, and the infiltration continues, down to the iron door leading into the Korvanjund Halls.

Enter the first chamber, climbing to the balcony and slaughtering two foes before venturing north along an upper passage that leads to steps leading down. Along the way is a side tunnel with a swinging blade trap; this leads to some treasure and a lever that stops the axes. Venture into the Nordic Hall of Stories, with or without the Legate. At the hall's far end is a Nordic Puzzle Door and two dead soldiers. Take the Ebony Claw they were carrying. This holds the key to opening this puzzle.

➤ Ebony Claw

Puzzle Solution: The door consists of three "rings" that rotate when you activate them. Each has three animals plated into the structure. You unlock the central keyhole with the Ebony Claw. This puzzle is inaccessible without it. The puzzle solution is on the palm of the Ebony Claw; rotate it in your inventory to see the three circular petroglyph carvings on the Claw's palm. Move the rings so the Wolf, Moth, and Dragon appear on the outer, middle, and inner rings, respectively. Then insert the Ebony Claw into the keyhole.

Venture through the rumbling door and through connecting corridors into the guardian hall chamber. To the west is a portcullis preventing you from reaching the exit door. Simply head to the chamber's northwest corner, into the

passage that winds up, past an Iron Dagger on a plinth. Cross a stone bridge to a balcony with a chest. Of more importance is the handle on the northwest corner of this balcony, overlooking the chamber below. Pull the handle to raise the portcullis, and then drop down to aid the Legate as four or five Draugr clamber out of their tombs to stop you. Now enter the crypt.

After a few more winding passages, you find Korvanjund's deepest chamber — the ceremonial crypt of a long-dead Jarl. Approach the slumped Draugr sitting on the throne in the middle of the chamber. Two guardians climb out of the tombs that flank the throne, prompting a vicious battle between the Imperials and Draugr.

When the combat ends, pry the crown off the Draugr that sat on the throne. With the Bone Crown in your inventory, you can return to General Tullius. Before you leave, continue past the throne, heading south to a Word Wall, and absorb another Word of Power! Then climb the steps to the east, back into the temple. Remove the door bar, and exit Korvanjund by this quicker route. Leave the Legate to finish her search, and head back to Solitude.

➤ Bone Crown   ➤ **Word of Power:** Slow Time

◊ **OBJECTIVE:** Deliver the crown to General Tullius
♦ **TARGET:** General Tullius, inside Castle Dour, in Solitude

Quest Conclusion

Enter Castle Dour and locate General Tullius, who is weighing his options regarding a possible attack on Winterhold. Inform him that you have the Jagged Crown. You can ask him about the war as well. The General then wonders if there's someone he can trust to deliver a message of great import to Jarl Balgruuf of Whiterun.

Postquest Activities

This prompts the immediate start of Civil War Quest: Message to Whiterun.

MESSAGE TO WHITERUN

PREREQUISITES: Complete Civil War Quest: The Jagged Crown
INTERSECTING QUESTS: Civil War Quest: The Jagged Crown, Main Quest: Bleak Falls Barrow, Main Quest: Dragon Rising, Civil War Quest: Defense of Whiterun
LOCATIONS: Solitude, Castle Dour, Whiterun, Dragonsreach, Windhelm, Palace of the Kings
CHARACTERS: General Tullius, Hrongar, Imperial Soldier, Irileth, Jarl Balgruuf the Greater, Legate Quentin Cipius, Lydia, Proventus Avenicci, Jarl Ulfric Stormcloak, Galmar Stone-Fist
ENEMIES: None
◊ **OBJECTIVES:** Deliver message to the Jarl of Whiterun, Assist Jarl Balgruuf with the dragon threat, Wait for the Jarl's response, Deliver axe to Jarl Ulfric, Return to Whiterun and warn the Jarl, Report to Legate Quentin Cipius

▶ Dilemma at Whiterun

Immediately after congratulating you on locating the Bone Crown, General Tullius explains that reports indicate Ulfric Stormcloak has raised enough men to attack the city of Whiterun. However, the headstrong Jarl is refusing Imperial support. Tullius hands you a missive, with information that ought to convince the Jarl to receive Imperial help. He requests that you don't read the missive but hand it over to the Jarl as soon as possible.

➤ Imperial Documents

◊ **OBJECTIVE:** Deliver message to the Jarl of Whiterun
♦ **TARGET:** Jarl Balgruuf of Whiterun, in Dragonsreach

Make your way past the Whiterun Stables and then up the long, slow climb, over the drawbridge, and to the main Whiterun gate. As you approach, a guard stops you; the city is closed, with the news of the dragons spreading faster than you can travel. You can:

Tell the guard that Riverwood calls for the Jarl's aid. This is the optimal plan and is available only if Main Quest: Before the Storm is active.

(Persuade) Or you can tell the guard you have news from Helgen about the dragon attack.

(Bribe) Or bribe the guard with a proportion of your collected gold.

(Intimidate) Or order the guard to stand aside.

Once you're inside the walls of Whiterun, head north, to the top of the hill on which the city sits, past the Gildergreen tree and the Shrine to Talos. Climb the stone steps to discover Dragonsreach, home of the Jarl. Walk toward the huge central fire on either side of the banqueting tables. Irileth, Jarl Balgruuf's Housecarl, meets you. Explain that you have a message from General Tullius, and she immediately lets you past. You can converse with her at length if you wish, or offer other responses with the Main Quest active, but mentioning the General's name allows you to progress more quickly.

Approach the Jarl and inform him that you have a message from General Tullius. His responses are dictated by the current situation regarding the dragons returning to Skyrim and how far through the Main Quest you have progressed.

At this point, you must have completed both Main Quest: Bleak Falls Barrow and Main Quest: Dragon Rising, then returned to the Jarl, heard the call of the Greybeards, and received your Housecarl, Lydia.

If you have not completed these two quests, you must do so. Refer to the Main Quest for all relevant information.

You can deliver the Imperial Documents before beginning Main Quest: Bleak Falls Barrow. The Jarl pockets the documents and ponders them while you finish your Main Quests.

◊ **OBJECTIVE:** Assist Jarl Balgruuf with the dragon threat

Once the joviality over the dragon's defeat at the Western Watchtower has subsided, approach the Jarl and ask him about the message from the General. He asks for his steward, Proventus Avenicci, and his Housecarl, Irileth, to comment on these matters.

◊ **OBJECTIVE:** Wait for the Jarl's response

Avenicci recommends a wait-and-see approach to the perceived threat of Ulfric. Irileth believes it is time to act, while the Jarl wishes to challenge Ulfric to face him as a man and declare his intentions. Avenicci favors a garrison of Imperials, while Irileth deems this to be cowardly. You can interrupt this back-and-forth or let the Jarl conclude. The results are the same: The Jarl has a message for you to deliver to the Jarl of Windhelm, Ulfric Stormcloak. He gives you an axe. Ulfric will get the symbology, although you can ask the Jarl for more information.

➤ **Balgruuf's War Axe**

◊ **OBJECTIVE:** Deliver axe to Jarl Ulfric
♦ **TARGET:** Ulfric Stormcloak, Palace of the Kings, in Windhelm

Axed

Journey east to the magnificent stone city of Windhelm, the stronghold for the Stormcloaks. Enter the massive city gates and head north to the Palace of the Kings. Pass the huge banquet table and find Ulfric Stormcloak. He is usually sitting on his throne

or strategizing in his war room (to the west) with his trusted brethren Galmar Stone-Fist.

Tell Ulfric you bring a message from the Jarl of Whiterun. You have many other conversations you can attempt with Ulfric that bring you up to speed with the Stormcloaks' plans and wishes for the Civil War. But more important is Ulfric's response. He deems you brave to carry such a message and says it is a pity you've chosen the wrong side. You are to return to the Jarl of Whiterun and tell him to prepare to entertain...visitors.

◊ **OBJECTIVE:** Return to Whiterun and warn the Jarl

Assassinating Ulfric: While this may sound like a good idea, it is extremely bad in practice, as the man cannot be killed by your hands at the moment, and combat in Windhelm provokes an overwhelming and hostile response. Exercise diplomacy before the hated Stormcloaks receive a taste of your blade! **CAUTION**

Atop the steps behind the Jarl's throne is a conference of war planning. A second Legate, named Quentin Cipius, has received information from a soldier that the enemy has catapults and intends to arm them with fire and take the city with the walls intact. As you approach the Jarl, he suspected Ulfric's response and sent word to General Tullius, who lent a detachment of troops and Legate Cipius. The Jarl turns you over to the Legion for your next orders.

◊ **OBJECTIVE:** Report to Legate Quentin Cipius

Quest Conclusion

Speak with Legate Cipius. The forces of both Imperials and Stormcloaks are gathering at the gates. You are to move there and hold this city!

Postquest Activities

This prompts the immediate commencement of Civil War Quest: Defense of Whiterun.

DEFENSE OF WHITERUN

PREREQUISITES: Complete Civil War Quest: Message to Whiterun
INTERSECTING QUESTS: Civil War Quest: Message to Whiterun, Civil War Quest: Reunification of Skyrim
LOCATIONS: Whiterun, Dragonsreach
CHARACTERS: General Tullius , Imperial Soldier, Jarl Balgruuf the Greater, Jarl Hrongar, Legate Quentin Cipius , Legate Rikke, Whiterun Guard
ENEMIES: Stormcloak Soldier
◊ **OBJECTIVES:** Meet with Legate Rikke, Defend the barricades, Destroy attackers, Defend the drawbridge, Defend the Main Gate, Report to the Jarl of Whiterun

◉ MINOR SPOILERS

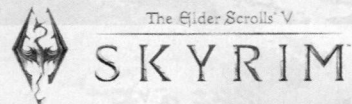

▶ Orange Skies and Blood-Red War

◊ **OBJECTIVE:** Meet with Legate Rikke
♦ **TARGET:** Legate Rikke, main entrance gate of Whiterun

Legate Quentin Cipius tells you to get down to Whiterun's main gate and repel those filthy Stormcloak attackers! Your rendezvous is with Legate Rikke, whom you should seek out immediately. You find her watching over the main gate to the city, giving a stirring speech to the assembled troops on the path below. She tells you this is an important day for the Empire and for all of Skyrim. You now have one important task: the defense of Whiterun!

◊ **OBJECTIVE:** Defend the barricades
◊ **OBJECTIVE:** Destroy attackers

▶ Defensive Stratagems: Defend and Destroy!

You are now engaged in an all-out siege of Whiterun. This battle is lengthy and confusing, and you can easily become a casualty rather than a champion of this war. However, the following tactics should help minimize your risks as you become embroiled in this skirmish.

Ally: Imperial Soldier   Ally: Whiterun Guard   Enemy: Stormcloak Soldier

Know Your Enemy: In the midst of battle, it sometimes becomes confusing who you should be fighting. There are three distinctive forces fighting for control of Whiterun. You are sided with the Imperials, who are clad in armor with red tunics and carry mainly swords. Also present are Whiterun Guards, who are allies, wear orange tunics, and carry the sign of the horse on their shields. The enemy are clad in dark blue and are more prone to use axes.

The Defensive Area: This battle takes place between the outer gate (atop which Legate Rikke was standing), the middle drawbridge (which cannot be raised), and the inner gate (the last line of defense). Focus your attacks on and around the cobblestone path running from the outer gate and around to the drawbridge. There is no need to retreat farther into the fortifications than this.

Falling Back: Even with the most proficient defense of the outer gate, expect the fierce enemies to break through the wooden barricades and start pouring into the cobblestone area. Hold your ground here. Fleeing around the bend to the drawbridge means you can't see the enemies coming and thwart them, leaving your brethren to do all the proper fighting. You're Dragonborn, not Skeeverborn, right?

NOTE Technically, you can run away. Whether you're just watching or you're running for the hills, when the battle is over, the Imperials are still victorious. However, don't expect any rewards from General Tullius for your cowardice!

Call to Action: Your first task is to stop the enemy from breaking through the barricade at the outer gate. Achieve this by employing one or more of the following melee or ranged techniques:

Melee: Stand at the barricade, leaping over it to engage the enemy and leaping back again.

Melee: Standing in cover to the left (east) between the outer wall and rocks and ambushing foes who reach the barricade.

Melee: Standing atop the wall and dropping down to engage the enemy who roam the area just in front of the barricade.

Ranged: Firing down from the left (east) corner atop the outer wall, by the gap.

Ranged: Firing down from the gap in the middle of the outer wall.

Ranged: Firing down from the right (west) wooden guard tower.

Ranged: Firing from ground level, behind the barricades.

Ranged: Firing from cover at the edge of Pelagia Farm to the south, which offers a good view of the main path.

◊ **OBJECTIVE:** Defend the drawbridge
◊ **OBJECTIVE:** Defend the main gate
♦ **TARGET:** Occurs if you fail to defend the barricades

Last Line of Defense: When and if the enemy breaks through, you must fall back to the cobblestone path with the stream running across it, prior to the winding corner and drawbridge. The enemy now appears at the outer gate, both on and under it. Try the following attacks:

Melee: Strike the foes as they pass through the outer gate, standing to either side of the gate, on ground level.

Melee: Stand at the bridge over the stream; the foes are funneled into this area as they race up the path.

Ranged: From the outer gate, above the foes as they run below, on any part of the gate or west wooden guard tower.

Ranged: Retreat to and fire from the northwestern guard tower; this offers excellent views of the path.

Ranged: From the rocky path above and north of the cobblestones, allowing you to hit foes across the entire defensive area.

Ranged: From the wooden and stone walkway above the stream.

Ranged: From the upper parapets directly above the wooden and stone walkway, near the drawbridge.

TIP Stormcloak forces are sneaky and may appear behind or above you, despite a solid defense of the outer gate. Clear these stragglers as you spot them. Also, don't worry about hitting every single foe; just continuously hit enemies; charging (or firing) at them and dispatching them. The percentage of enemy forces eventually drops to zero.

Unsound Tactics: You are behind a defensive wall and barricades for a reason; only the most foolhardy warriors would leave these defenses to engage the enemy out in the open, in the Whiterun Stables area, unless absolutely necessary. Let the enemy come to you; that way you minimize the foes passing you by and cut down on stamina-sapping chases.

CAUTION

Your offensive measures against the enemy may be dangerous for your allies if you rely too heavily on area-of-effect magic or wild swinging of weapons (particularly of the two-handed variety). Watch your collateral damage!

Continue the battle until the main threat of Stormcloaks has abated. There may be a few remaining enemies, and you can dispatch them if you wish, but this isn't necessary.

◊ **OBJECTIVE:** Report to the Jarl of Whiterun
♦ **TARGET:** Jarl of Whiterun, at the main gate in Whiterun

Quest Conclusion

The Jarl is speaking to the surviving forces from the parapets of the successfully defended Whiterun. You must revel in your victory today! But as you celebrate, know that Ulfric will continue to strike out against any true Nord, sowing discord and chaos wherever he can. As for your role in this? General Tullius requires your presence for further battles. The Jarl will reward you for your exceptional and continued heroism in defense of Whiterun.

Postquest Activities

Civil War Quest: Reunification of Skyrim begins.

REUNIFICATION OF SKYRIM – A FALSE FRONT

PREREQUISITES: Complete Civil War Quest: Defense of Whiterun
INTERSECTING QUESTS: Civil War Quest: Defense of Whiterun, Civil War Quest: The Battle for Fort Dunstad
LOCATIONS: Dawnstar, Dawnstar Barracks, Nightgate Inn, Pale Imperial Camp, Solitude, Castle Dour, Windhelm, Candlehearth Hall
CHARACTERS: Dawnstar Guard, Elda Early-Dawn , General Tullius, Hadring, Legate Rikke, Quartermaster, Windhelm Guard, Frorkmar Banner-Torn
ENEMIES: Stormcloak Courier, Stormcloak Soldier
◊ **OBJECTIVES:** Reunification of Skyrim: Report to General Tullius, Reunification of Skyrim: Regain the Pale, A False Front: Find the Stormcloak Courier, A False Front: Retrieve the Stormcloak Courier's package, A False Front: Bring the documents to Legate Rikke, A False Front: Bring the forged documents to Frorkmar Banner-Torn, Reunification of Skyrim: Regain the Pale

▶ The Empire Rewards Excellence

◊ **OBJECTIVE:** Report to General Tullius
♦ **TARGET:** General Tullius, in Castle Dour in Solitude

Return to Castle Dour in Solitude and speak with General Tullius. Due to the actions at Whiterun, the Jarl has solidified his allegiance to the Imperials. For your actions, the General promotes you to the title of Quaestor. He also awards you with an impressive weapon. Ask what your orders are, and the General tells you to head to a hidden camp within the Pale. Legate Rikke has important tasks for you there as the General makes plans to reclaim the Hold capital.

➤ **Leveled Sword**

◊ **REUNIFICATION OF SKYRIM BEGINS**
◊ **OBJECTIVE:** Regain the Pale
♦ **TARGET:** Legate Rikke, Pale Imperial Camp

NOTE You could have stumbled upon this camp during your exploration of Skyrim. All Imperial Camps across Skyrim are now revealed and are indicated by the dragon crest icon on your world map.

Journey to the Pale Imperial Camp, in the snow-laden hills to the west of Dawnstar. Aside from a Quartermaster and a Grindstone to help augment your weaponry, there's an Alchemy Lab near the hospital tent, and troops to speak to.

However, the Legate's tent is the place to visit, where Rikke is pouring over the current Civil War map. She may have her disagreements with the General, but she believes he's the best hope for both the Empire and Skyrim. Report for duty, and she says she needs you to deliver some false orders to the Stormcloak commander in Dawnstar. Before that happens, though, forgeries must be made, so you must get your hands on some rebel orders. Rikke informs you that the Candlehearth Hall and Nightgate Inn are frequent stops for Stormcloak runners. Head to one of those places and convince the innkeeper to help you.

◊ **A FALSE FRONT BEGINS**
◊ **OBJECTIVE:** Find the Stormcloak Courier
♦ **TARGET:** Barkeep of Nightgate Inn or Candlehearth Hall

 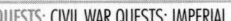

Interception and Deception

There are two inns that Legate Rikke mentioned: The Nightgate Inn is along the road to the west of Windhelm and is operated by Hadring. The Candlehearth Hall is inside Windhelm and has an innkeeper named Elda Early-Dawn. Journey to either of these locations and ask the innkeeper if they've seen any Stormcloak Couriers. After an evasive response, you can:

(Persuade) Warn that the courier's life is in danger.

(Bribe) Offer some gold for the information.

(Intimidate) Mention that you can get rough if you need to.

Or, wait around in the inn.

If you succeed in any of the first three options, the barkeep tells you that the courier just left and that you can probably still catch him. Or, you can wait in the inn for the courier to return. The courier is halfway between both the inns on the main road. Even if you're unsuccessful, you can still run after or wait for the courier (the only difference is the objective won't update); either way, you must visit one of the inns before finding the courier.

◊ **OBJECTIVE:** Retrieve the Stormcloak Courier's package
♦ **TARGET:** Courier, inside or between either inn

The courier travels to and from each inn. He loiters at the inn for an hour, sleeps there for an hour, and then heads back to the other inn. He then repeats this route until you intercept him, either by waiting inside the inn or finding him on the road. At this point, you have a three options:

(Pickpocket) Pickpocket the documents while the courier is unaware.

Or, speak to the courier, demanding the documents. He refuses and you must kill him.

Or, simply kill the courier and loot the corpse for the documents.

CAUTION Watch out! Killing the courier when he's inside Windhelm or the Candlehearth Hall or watched by Windhelm Guards results in you being discovered. If you're trying violence, meet him on the road, where his death doesn't arouse suspicion, or inside the Nightgate Inn, where Hadring is less concerned about such slaughter.

➤ **Stormcloak Documents**

◊ **OBJECTIVE:** Bring the documents to Legate Rikke
♦ **TARGET:** Legate Rikke, Hidden Imperial Camp in the Pale

After returning to Legate Rikke, she reads the documents, noting the Stormcloaks know more about the Imperial plans than was expected. She "corrects" the documents with false information and orders you to present them to the Stormcloak Commander in Dawnstar, throwing him off the trail.

◊ **OBJECTIVE:** Bring the forged documents to Frorkmar Banner-Torn
♦ **TARGET:** Frorkmar Banner-Torn, Dawnstar Barracks in Dawnstar

Quest Conclusion

You'll usually find the Commander inside Dawnstar Barracks, inside the Hold City of Dawnstar, although he sometimes walks the paths around the city. Present some important documents to him. He reads over them, noting the troop movements (which are false) and rewarding you with a little gold for a drink at the Windpeak Inn for your troubles. This quest now concludes.

➤ **5 gold pieces**

 TIP There's no need to change from your Imperial garb when you meet Frorkmar; you quickly make up a verbal ruse that it's easier to "sneak past the enemy" clad in their colors.

Postquest Activities

Civil War Quest: Reunification of Skyrim is still going. Civil War Quest: The Battle for Fort Dunstad now begins.

REUNIFICATION OF SKYRIM (CONTINUED) – THE BATTLE FOR FORT DUNSTAD

PREREQUISITES: Complete Civil War Quest: A False Front

INTERSECTING QUESTS: Civil War Quest: A False Front, Civil War Quest: Compelling Tribute

LOCATIONS: Fort Dunstad (Location), Pale Imperial Camp (Location), Solitude (Location), (Location)

CHARACTERS: General Tullius , Imperial Soldier, Legate Rikke

ENEMIES: Stormcloak Soldier

◊ **OBJECTIVES:** Reunification of Skyrim: Regain the Pale, The Battle for Fort Dunstad: Join the men attacking Fort Dunstad, The Battle for Fort Dunstad: Take over Fort Dunstad by killing the enemy, The Battle for Fort Dunstad: Report to General Tullius, Reunification of Skyrim: Regain the Rift

Beyond the Pale

◊ **REUNIFICATION OF SKYRIM CONTINUES**
◊ **OBJECTIVE:** Regain the Pale
♦ **TARGET:** Legate Rikke, Pale Imperial Camp

> **NOTE** Civil War Quest: Reunification of Skyrim continues throughout the remaining Civil War Quests. Within the Reunification Quest is a series of concurrent quests that build to complete the reunification as you take over a series of Stormcloak Holds. This quest is available immediately after Civil War Quest: A False Front ends.

Travel to the Pale Imperial Camp, where Legate Rikke congratulates you, giving you a reward of gold. Report for duty, and she says your next objective is Fort Dunstad. You are to meet the soldiers preparing for the attack, and then wipe out the rebel garrison. Agree to the task, and the quest commences.

➤ **150 gold pieces**

◊ **THE BATTLE FOR FORT DUNSTAD BEGINS**
◊ **OBJECTIVE:** Join the men attacking Fort Dunstad
♦ **TARGET:** On the road, southeast of Fort Dunstad

Fort Dunstad is in the snowy Pale Mountains south of Dawnstar. Legate Rikke's men are on the path to the fort's southeast, so approaching from the northwest can fail this objective (although this has no effect on the quest). Circle around and join the detachment of Imperial forces stationed close to the fortification. After checking the Atlas entry of this place (page 463) and speaking to the leader of the forces, begin the attack from either side.

◊ **OBJECTIVE:** Take over Fort Dunstad by killing the enemy

Assault the fortification and help eliminate all the Stormcloak Soldiers. Enter from one of the following weak points or fortified positions:

North wall: The wooden 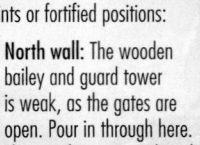 bailey and guard tower is weak, as the gates are open. Pour in through here.
The guard towers north and south are good for long-range attacks.

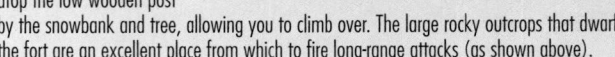

North walkways and palisades: These are a great way to gain access to the fort's upper areas. Stay close to the wall here; this gives you cover from the enemy archers as you ascend.
East wall: You can leap atop the low wooden post by the snowbank and tree, allowing you to climb over. The large rocky outcrops that dwarf the fort are an excellent place from which to fire long-range attacks (as shown above).
Walkways and run-down tavern: Head to these locations if you need to retreat and rest or heal from battle before attacking again.
South wall: The wooden bailey and guard tower is weak, as the gates are open. Head in through here and up onto the main crenellations via the wooden steps or through the archway.
West wall: This curved stone wall is completely impenetrable, except for a missing top-wall section to the northwest; however, even this is almost impossible to breach.
An archer's attack: Attempt to quickly reach the top of the Commander's quarters on the fort's southwestern edge; it provides the optimal high ground with excellent views of most of the fort.
Prison tower: The top of this tower is another great place to snipe from but is a little too high above the action to provide adequate support.

When you've won the battle and humiliated the enemies, the Imperial forces remain to garrison this location. Meanwhile, you have other plans.

◊ **OBJECTIVE:** Report to General Tullius
♦ **TARGET:** General Tullius, Castle Dour in Solitude

Quest Conclusion

Return to Castle Dour and inform Tullius of your victory. This captures the Hold of the Pale and gives the Imperial Legion control of another port. Your prowess has impressed the General, and he raises your title to that of Praefect. Take the earned weapon as a gift and symbol of this new rank. You're instructed to meet Legate Rikke again; she's planning some surprises for Ulfric in the Rift.

> **NOTE** This title may change if you ran away from Whiterun or gained a Hold from a peace treaty during Main Quest: Season Unending.

➤ **Leveled Weapon**

◊ **REUNIFICATION OF SKYRIM CONTINUES**
◊ **OBJECTIVE:** Regain the Rift
♦ **TARGET:** Legate Rikke, Rift Imperial Camp

Postquest Activities

Civil War Quest: Reunification of Skyrim is still ongoing. Civil War Quest: Compelling Tribute begins shortly.

REUNIFICATION OF SKYRIM (CONTINUED) – COMPELLING TRIBUTE

PREREQUISITES: Complete Civil War Quest: The Battle for Fort Dunstad
INTERSECTING QUESTS: Civil War Quest: The Battle for Fort Dunstad, Civil War Quest: The Battle for Fort Greenwall
LOCATIONS: Riften, Mistveil Keep, Rift Imperial Camp, Shor's Watchtower
CHARACTERS: Anuriel, Hadvar, Imperial Soldier, Jarl Laila Law-Giver, Legate Rikke, Quartermaster, Riften Guard, Unmid Snow-Shod

continued on next page

▶ Anuriel's Gold

◊ **OBJECTIVE:** Regain the Rift
♦ **TARGET:** Legate Rikke, Rift Imperial Camp

Legate Rikke has set up a hidden Imperial Camp on the southwestern edge of the Rift (below the snowline), which has the same benefits as the one in the Pale, including one, two, or three wounded soldiers inside the hospital tent. Report in with Legate Rikke, and she orders you to Riften. Her spies are reporting that the Jarl's Steward, Anuriel, has arrangements with the Thieves Guild that could be embarrassing if they were made public. You must try to find evidence of this and present it to her, using it to gain cooperation. This requires both stealth and discretion.

◊ **CIVIL WAR QUEST:** Compelling Tribute begins
◊ **OBJECTIVE:** Find evidence
♦ **TARGET:** Anuriel's bedroom, inside Mistveil Keep in Riften

Journey to Riften and locate the mighty Mistveil Keep at the city's southern end. Step through the front doors into the Jarl's chamber, complete with a splendid banqueting table and a variety of foodstuffs.

Approach the Jarl. Unmid Snow-Shod immediately requests that you maintain a respectable distance from the Jarl. If you're simply wandering the Keep, it is not necessary to speak with those surrounding the Jarl, including Anuriel or Laila Law-Giver. Finding evidence is your top priority.

CAUTION

Watch out for a patrolling guard en route to Anuriel's room. He calls you out as a trespasser if he spots you. Time his patrol so you avoid him.

The evidence is located in Anuriel's bedroom, which is behind the Jarl's throne and to the right (northeast). The doors are unlocked, and the information is hidden inside a dresser. You can reach this area without drawing attention to yourself in a few different ways:

(Sneak) You can sneak into the chamber, preferably after dark when the banqueting hall is empty.

(Spells) You can cast Invisibility, or some other spell that diminishes the chances of you being seen.

Or you can slowly, and without weapons drawn, enter the banqueting hall and head immediately to Anuriel's bedroom.

Once you reach the dresser, extricate the following:

➤ **Incriminating Letter**

◊ **OBJECTIVE:** Blackmail Anuriel

Locate Anuriel within the Keep, and show her the incriminating letter. She quickly requests that you meet her in private. Stay close to her so the guards don't stop you. She takes you into her chamber, where she asks what kind of extortion racket you're running. Ask her what would happen if the letter was made public, and Anuriel folds, explaining Jarl Laila is a simple and easily manipulable woman, and she can't risk the backlash. She asks to come to some agreement, wondering if both of you could prosper. Ask her what agreement she has in mind, and she mentions a large shipment of gold and weapons the Stormcloaks are transporting. You can:

(Persuade) Ask about receiving some additional payment for yourself.

Agree to the deal and ask where this shipment is.

If your persuasion works, you receive a large purse of coins. Either way, you must confirm the agreement. She reveals the Stormcloaks are taking this booty by wagon to Windhelm. If you hurry, you can catch them before they get too far.

➤ **Leveled gold pieces**

◊ **OBJECTIVE:** Report to Legate Rikke
♦ **TARGET:** Legate Rikke, Rift Imperial Camp

Head back to the hidden camp and tell Rikke about the shipment of coin. Coincidentally, she already has a small group of scouts on the same road that the enemy caravan is traveling. You are to meet up with them and try to overpower the wagon's guards.

◊ **OBJECTIVE:** Meet the men
♦ **TARGET:** On the road close to Shor's Watchtower, the Rift

Hadvar's Heroes

Judging by your world map, the scouts are waiting on the road just below Shor's Watchtower, in the Rift's northeast corner. Travel there, watching out if you're approaching from the north, or you'll run into the Stormcloak caravan without any help from the scouts. Approach along the road from the south, heading north past Shor's Stone. Meet an old friend as the path winds through the trees. Hadvar greets you. At this point, you have two choices to make.

Plan A: Hadvar's Help

Chat with Hadvar, answering any way you wish. Steer the conversation back to your mission and explain the enemy wagon loaded with coin and weapons is farther down this slope. As luck would have it, Hadvar has been tracking the wagon, which has lost an axle and is stranded. Although you're outnumbered (there are six foes), Hadvar has a plan: His troops will remove the enemy sentry, then situate themselves overlooking the camp. Afterward, you'll infiltrate their position, gain their attention, and Hadvar's troops will unleash a volley of arrows, winning the day tactically. Agree to this plan.

◊ **OBJECTIVE:** Follow Hadvar and ambush enemy scout
◊ **OBJECTIVE:** Take over the caravan

Crouch and follow Hadvar, watching as his bowmen drop the enemy scout. Wait for them to reach the rise overlooking the broken-down caravan below, and then walk toward the enemies.

Sneaking, firing from range, or rushing to attack are all excellent ideas, while your brethren shoot arrows down on them from above.

Plan B: Hadvar's a Hindrance

Chat with Hadvar, then either refuse to go along with his plan or ignore him altogether.

◊ **OBJECTIVE:** Take over the caravan

Head down the hill and begin to battle the six Stormcloaks guarding the caravan of gold. Begin with the sentry atop the rocks overlooking the caravan. Then rain death from above with ranged attacks, or swarm the foes with melee weapons. A couple of enemy soldiers may be sleeping, so carve them up before they fully wake.

 TIP If this fight starts to overwhelm you, flee up the hill toward Hadvar, and his men help by mopping up any enemies giving chase. Then rest and return to tackle any stragglers.

◊ **OBJECTIVE:** Report to Hadvar

Quest Conclusion

With the caravan's guards removed, Hadvar remains here to guard the gold. Speak to him to end the quest. Loot any weapons and gold you wish from the wagon.

➤ **Spoils of War**

Postquest Activities

Civil War Quest: Reunification of Skyrim is still ongoing. Civil War Quest: The Battle for Fort Greenwall begins shortly.

REUNIFICATION OF SKYRIM (CONTINUED) – THE BATTLE FOR FORT GREENWALL

PREREQUISITES: Complete Civil War Quest: Compelling Tribute
INTERSECTING QUESTS: Civil War Quest: Compelling Tribute, Civil War Quest: Rescue from Fort Kastav
LOCATIONS: Fort Greenwall, Rift Imperial Camp, Solitude, Castle Dour
CHARACTERS: General Tullius, Legate Rikke, Imperial Soldier
ENEMIES: Stormcloak Soldier
◊ **OBJECTIVES:** Reunification of Skyrim: Regain the Rift, The Battle for Fort Greenwall: Join the men attacking Fort Greenwall, The Battle for Fort Greenwall: Take over Fort Greenwall by killing the enemy, The Battle for Fort Greenwall: Report to General Tullius, Reunification of Skyrim: Regain Winterhold Hold

---

Closing the Rift

◊ **REUNIFICATION OF SKYRIM CONTINUES**
◊ **OBJECTIVE:** Regain the Rift
♦ **TARGET:** Legate Rikke, Rift Imperial Camp'

Travel to the Rift Imperial Camp, and you're congratulated by Legate Rikke. Report for duty, and she says your next objective is Fort Greenwall. You are to meet the soldiers waiting near the fort for the attack orders, and then wipe out the Stormcloaks inside. Agree to the task and the quest commences.

➤ **150 gold pieces**

◊ **THE BATTLE FOR FORT GREENWALL BEGINS**
◊ **OBJECTIVE:** Join the men attacking Fort Greenwall
♦ **TARGET:** On the road, northwest of Fort Greenwall

Fort Greenwall is in the leafy woodland north of Riften. Legate Rikke's men are on the path to the fort's northwest, so approaching from the southeast can fail this objective (but not

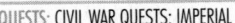

the quest). Join the detachment of Imperial forces stationed close to the fortification. After studying the Atlas entry of this place (page 615) and conversing with the leader, commence the battle, attacking from either side.

◊ **OBJECTIVE:** Take over Fort Greenwall by killing the enemy

Assault the fortification and help eliminate all the Stormcloak Soldiers. Enter from one of the following weak points or fortified positions, and note the impenetrable parts of the outer walls:

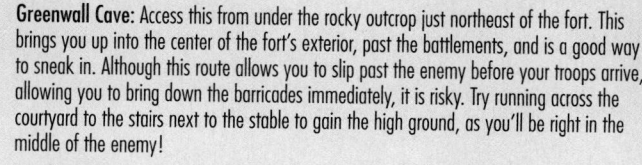

Southeast long wall: Southern end has a collapsed wall section that you can easily leap through. The middle entrance (on the road) is heavily guarded with barricades; you can maneuver easily around it.

Northwest long wall: The middle entrance (on the road) has numerous barricades, which are easily navigated around.

Southwest edge: Completely impenetrable.

Northeast edge: Completely impenetrable.

Whirlwind Sprint: If you've learned this Shout during Main Quest: The Way of the Voice, you can actually dash into this structure from the hills next to the western wall.

Greenwall Cave: Access this from under the rocky outcrop just northeast of the fort. This brings you up into the center of the fort's exterior, past the battlements, and is a good way to sneak in. Although this route allows you to slip past the enemy before your troops arrive, allowing you to bring down the barricades immediately, it is risky. Try running across the courtyard to the stairs next to the stable to gain the high ground, as you'll be right in the middle of the enemy!

Heading higher: The small courtyard on the ground is easily clustered and jammed with the influx of friends and foes. Escape this danger by heading east or west right away to the fort's higher edges. However, if you're a mage with area-effect spells, this courtyard is the place to lay waste to the enemy!

When you are victorious and the enemies routed, the Imperial forces remain to garrison this location. Meanwhile, you have other tasks to complete.

◊ **OBJECTIVE:** Report to General Tullius
♦ **TARGET:** General Tullius, Castle Dour in Solitude

Quest Conclusion

Return to Castle Dour and inform Tullius of your victory. This captures the Hold of the Rift and gives Ulfric reason to be concerned, what with the Empire so close to his doorstep. Your competence has impressed the General. You're instructed to meet Legate Rikke again; she's planning continued raids against Ulfric in Winterhold Hold.

➤ **Leveled Shield'**

◊ **REUNIFICATION OF SKYRIM CONTINUES**
◊ **OBJECTIVE:** Regain Winterhold Hold
♦ **TARGET:** Legate Rikke, Winterhold Imperial Camp

Postquest Activities

Civil War Quest: Reunification of Skyrim is still ongoing. Civil War Quest: Rescue from Fort Kastav begins momentarily.

REUNIFICATION OF SKYRIM (CONTINUED) – RESCUE FROM FORT KASTAV

PREREQUISITES: Complete Civil War Quest: The Battle for Fort Greenwall

INTERSECTING QUESTS: Civil War Quest: The Battle for Fort Greenwall, Civil War Quest: The Battle for Fort Amol

LOCATIONS: Fort Kastav, Fort Kastav Prison, Solitude, Castle Dour, Winterhold Imperial Camp

CHARACTERS: General Tullius, Hadvar, Imperial Soldier, Legate Rikke

ENEMIES: Stormcloak Soldier

◊ **OBJECTIVES:** Reunification of Skyrim: Regain Winterhold Hold, Rescue from Fort Kastav: Meet the men near Fort Kastav, Rescue from Fort Kastav: Sneak into the fort, Rescue from Fort Kastav: Free the prisoners, Rescue from Fort Kastav: Take over the fort, Rescue from Fort Kastav: Report to General Tullius, Reunification of Skyrim: Regain Eastmarch

▶ A Hard Fort Struggle

◊ **REUNIFICATION OF SKYRIM CONTINUES**
◊ **OBJECTIVE:** Regain Winterhold Hold
♦ **TARGET:** Legate Rikke, Winterhold Imperial Camp

TIP Stop! Before you return to Legate Rikke and begin this quest, study the Atlas entry for Fort Kastav (page 491).

Journey to Legate Rikke's newly established forward-operating base, just to the west of Dawnstar on the edge of Winterhold Hold. This camp has the same benefits as the one in the Rift. Report in with Legate Rikke, and she has your orders. You must infiltrate Fort Kastav, as the rebels are keeping some Imperial soldiers prisoner there. She aims to turn that into an advantage by using your cunning to find a way inside, free the men, and liberate the fort. This is an attack from the inside!

◊ **CIVIL WAR QUEST:** Rescue from Fort Kastav begins
◊ **OBJECTIVE:** Meet the men near Fort Kastav
♦ **TARGET:** Mountains southwest of Fort Kastav

Head up the rugged terrain of rocks and snow (Fast-Traveling from Nightgate Inn or Windhelm and then sprinting to meet your men are quick options, but without getting close enough to alert the enemy). You'll encounter a small team of four men. One of them is your old friend Hadvar, who has already had a reconnoiter of Fort Kastav, which appears particularly large and well defended in the distance, partly due to the mountain slopes keeping raiders away from the walls. However, there is a grate on the outside of the wall. It used to be buried in snow, and Hadvar reckons the enemy doesn't even know it's there. You must sneak in there, free the prisoners, and kill anyone you meet. Hadvar will wait to rush the fort as soon as they hear fighting, and you'll rendezvous in the courtyard. At this point, inform Hadvar that you're on it and begin the sneak.

◇ **OBJECTIVE:** Sneak into the fort

> **CAUTION** Or, tell Hadvar you aren't interested in sneaking. At this point, you can take a direct (and more dangerous) approach: assault the fort via the main entrance and battle down to the prisoners inside. This is possible but isn't recommended, as it's slightly more risky.

The Enemy Within

Instead, crouch and begin heading along the snow-filled gully toward the fortification. You may wish to wait until after nightfall to minimize the enemy spotting you. Travel the gully's right (south) side, navigate easily around the barricades, pass the base of the stone tower, and follow the earthen bank until you spot a slope you can climb up, near three planks of snow-covered wood. Turn right, step over another small wooden bridge, and open the trapdoor leading to Fort Kastav Prison.

◇ **OBJECTIVE:** Free the prisoners

Head east, open the wooden door, turn right (south), and pass the barrels. Turn left and enter a two-floor entrance hall with steps to the north. Ignore the stairs and continue heading east, through another door to the cobwebbed staircase.

Bring down a Stormcloak Soldier quickly (or sneak past them). The prison is at the bottom of the stairs, and another Stormcloak Soldier is patrolling this area. The Imperial Soldiers inform you that the guard has the key. If your Lockpick skill isn't to be tested, inspect the Stormcloak Soldier's corpse, or search one of the tables near the jail cells for it. Head to each of the cells and unlock the door (Novice). The freed men quickly don their armor and follow your lead.

➤ **Fort Kastav Prison Key**

◇ **OBJECTIVE:** Take over the fort
◆ **TARGET:** All remaining Stormcloak Soldiers

Sprint north up the steps, and once back in the entrance hall, drop any Stormcloaks who seek to thwart you. Head up the steps to the door that leads into the exterior courtyard. Begin slaughtering the additional forces guarding the outside of the fort. They usually stream in from the upper slopes to the northeast. The numerous gaps in the walls allows you to hide and dart out if you're engaging in longer ranged attacks or needing to rest between Stamina exertions.

Don't forget the enemies on the guard tower to the northeast. When everyone wearing dark blue is dead, report back to Hadvar. You're to report to General Tullius while he remains here to tidy up the mess.

◇ **OBJECTIVE:** Report to General Tullius
◆ **TARGET:** General Tullius, Castle Dour in Solitude

Quest Conclusion

Trek back to Castle Dour and inform Tullius of your victory. Now that Winterhold's main fortress is in Imperial control, the General can garrison some troops until he's ready to march on Windhelm. General Tullius has come to rely heavily upon you and elevates your rank in the Legion to that of Legate. Along with this, you receive a leveled weapon. Ask the General what the next plan is. Tullius tells you to report in at the Imperial camp in Eastmarch.

➤ **Leveled Armor**

◇ **REUNIFICATION OF SKYRIM CONTINUES**
◇ **OBJECTIVE:** Regain Eastmarch
◆ **TARGET:** Legate Rikke, Eastmarch Imperial Camp

Postquest Activities

Civil War Quest: Reunification of Skyrim is still ongoing. Civil War Quest: The Battle for Fort Amol begins once you check in with Legate Rikke.

REUNIFICATION OF SKYRIM (CONTINUED) – THE BATTLE FOR FORT AMOL

PREREQUISITES: Complete Civil War Quest: Rescue from Fort Kastav
INTERSECTING QUESTS: Civil War Quest: Rescue from Fort Kastav, Civil War Quest: Battle for Windhelm
LOCATIONS: Eastmarch Imperial Camp , Fort Amol
CHARACTERS: Imperial Soldier , Legate Rikke
ENEMIES: Stormcloak Soldier
◇ **OBJECTIVES:** Reunification of Skyrim: Regain Eastmarch, The Battle for Fort Amol: Join the men attacking Fort Amol, The Battle for Fort Amol: Take over Fort Amol by killing the enemy, Reunification of Skyrim: Regain Eastmarch

The Elder Scrolls V
SKYRIM

March on Eastmarch

> ◊ **REUNIFICATION OF SKYRIM CONTINUES**
> ◊ **OBJECTIVE:** Regain Eastmarch
> ◆ **TARGET:** Legate Rikke, Eastmarch Imperial Camp

Trek to the rocky pine forests on Eastmarch's eastern edge, at the foot of the Velothi Mountains, just north of Stony Creek Cave. Head into the Legate's tent and speak with her. She says your objective is an enemy-held fort. You are to meet the soldiers waiting nearby for the attack orders, and then wipe out the Stormcloaks inside. Agree to the task, and the quest commences.

> ◊ **THE BATTLE FOR FORT AMOL BEGINS**
> ◊ **OBJECTIVE:** Join the men attacking Fort Amol
> ◆ **TARGET:** On the road, west of Fort Amol

Fort Amol is in a clearing adjacent to the main road on three sides. Darkwater River is to the east. If you approach the fort from the northeast, you may attract the enemy's attention and commence the battle before your friends can mount an attack with you. Instead, take the road from Morthal and meet up with your fellow conscripts on the ridge south of the fort. If you want help with the assault, join the Imperial Soldiers creeping up on the fort. After studying the Atlas entry of this place (page 563) and conversing with the leader, commence the battle.

> ◊ **OBJECTIVE:** Take over Fort Amol by killing the enemy

Charge the fortification, and help eliminate all the Stormcloak Soldiers. Enter from one of the following weak points or fortified positions:

North Wall: Rocky terrain and high buttressed walls offer no access points.

East Wall: There's a gaping hole just north of the tower, offering easy access into the center of the fort.

South Wall: You can climb the crumbling wall area to the southwest and can breach the outer defenses.

West Wall: The main road into the fort has barricades and a main archway. This is where your allies usually break through.

Tower Trouble: When you enter the fort, you may elect to fire down on foes from above by scaling either of the towers and sniping from this vantage point.

Quest Conclusion

When the fort falls to the Imperials, your forces remain to garrison this location.

> ◊ **REUNIFICATION OF SKYRIM CONTINUES**
> ◊ **OBJECTIVE:** Regain Eastmarch
> ◆ **TARGET:** Legate Rikke, Eastmarch Imperial Camp

Postquest Activities

Civil War Quest: Reunification of Skyrim is almost over. Civil War Quest: Battle for Windhelm begins shortly.

REUNIFICATION OF SKYRIM (CONCLUSION) – BATTLE FOR WINDHELM

PREREQUISITES: Complete Civil War Quest: The Battle for Fort Amol
INTERSECTING QUESTS: Civil War Quest: The Battle for Fort Amol
LOCATIONS: Eastmarch Imperial Camp, Windhelm, Palace of the Kings
CHARACTERS: General Tullius, Imperial Soldier, Legate Rikke
ENEMIES: Galmar Stone-Fist, Jarl Ulfric Stormcloak, Stormcloak Soldier
◊ **OBJECTIVES:** Reunification of Skyrim: Regain Eastmarch, Battle for Windhelm: Get your orders from General Tullius, Battle for Windhelm: Take over Windhelm by killing the enemy, Battle for Windhelm: Force Ulfric Stormcloak to surrender

● **MAJOR SPOILERS**

The Windhelm Scream

> ◊ **REUNIFICATION OF SKYRIM CONTINUES**
> ◊ **OBJECTIVE:** Regain Eastmarch
> ◆ **TARGET:** Legate Rikke, Eastmarch Imperial Camp

 TIP Whoa! Before mounting a final assault on Windhelm, consider exploring the streets, uncovering routes from the main gates to the Palace of the Kings, so you're completely familiar with the street topography. It is wise to add any helpful inventory equipment (such as Magick-, Health-, or Stamina-augmenting items) before commencing this quest.

Return to the Eastmarch Imperial Camp and speak with Legate Rikke. She is extremely pleased with your progress and rewards you accordingly. Then she tells you that a detachment from the Imperial Army is gathering to attack Windhelm, and you're part of it!

➤ **150 gold pieces**

◊ **BATTLE FOR WINDHELM BEGINS**
◊ **OBJECTIVE:** Get your orders from General Tullius
♦ **TARGET:** Great gate of Windhelm

Travel to the bridge spanning the confluence of the Darkwater and Yorgrim rivers; this leads to the great gate of Windhelm. The flame catapults are already bombarding the embattled city in huge gobs of fire, and the air is thick with smoke and panic. Rush north through the wreckage to the towering gate, where General Tullius is yelling words of encouragement to his forces. This is the time to deliver the final blow to the Stormcloak Rebellion! Expect an enemy both fierce and crafty. For the Empire! For the Legion!

◊ **OBJECTIVE:** Take over Windhelm by killing the enemy

The stronghold for the Stormcloaks is ablaze, and the chaos of fighting Ulfric's remaining men and navigating the various barriers can be somewhat confusing. Be sure you learn the various locations you must fight through:

Candlehearth Hall: The initial entrance courtyard and Candlehearth Hall are places you can take cover, step out and defeat foes, and fight a continuous battle.

Southwest Market: You can traverse the narrow streets to the southwest, maneuver around or demolish the barriers, and attack the soldiers from this area. Fewer enemies are in these parts, but you're less likely to be surrounded or accidentally strike your own men. Or you can battle down the side street directly to the graveyard and miss the market area completely.

Graveyard: The only way forward is through the graveyard near the Hall of the Dead. Expect foes here, both atop and at the bottom of the stairs.

Northwest Pathways: Crush the barriers with attacks, and continue to battle the enemy along the winding streets that bring you back to the main courtyard in the city's center. Remember that you can always retreat, but this is the only route to take.

Palace Courtyard: The eventual fight continues into the flaming courtyard outside the Palace of the Kings.

The flow of enemy soldiers does not stop! It is imperative you reach the Palace of the Kings as quickly as possible! **CAUTION**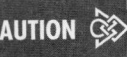

◊ **OBJECTIVE:** Force Ulfric Stormcloak to surrender

▶ Stormcloaks to Sovngarde

Push through into the Palace of the Kings with General Tullius and Legate Rikke in tow. Tullius informs Ulfric that he is guilty of insurrection, murder, and the assassination of King Torygg—essentially high treason against the Empire. Galmar Stone-Fist steps in front of Ulfric, brandishing his axe. Legate Rikke attempts to reason with Galmar, but the argument escalates into a pitched battle. Attack Galmar and Ulfric, choosing the foe your allies aren't fighting so you can bring the Stormcloaks to their knees more proficiently. Step back if you're being pulverized.

With Galmar dead and Ulfric on his knees, General Tullius stands over and gloats while Legate Rikke briefly looks mournful. Ulfric wants you to execute him; it'll make for a better bard's song. You can:

Agree, and plunge your favored weapon into the bowed form of Ulfric Stormcloak.

Or refuse, leaving Tullius to do the job.

Quest Conclusion

With the Stormcloaks firmly routed and their leadership bleeding across the palace floor, Tullius tells Legate Rikke that Brunwulf Free-Winter will likely be the next Jarl of Windhelm. He has a final gift for you as a tribute to your valor; you may keep the General's sword.

➤ **Leveled Weapon**

Postquest Activities

The General and Legate leave the palace to address the troops. After the troops are satiated, the General turns to you if you ask him for any other tasks, and he tells you to watch for any remaining Stormcloak camps across Skyrim. Defeat the remnants of the insurrection as you please. The power of the Empire is once more restored...with the Thalmor looking on from the shadows.

 NOTE If you wait a couple of days, Windhelm begins to return to normal. Brunwulf Free-Winter is the Jarl, and he's already a firm friend of yours.

The Elder Scrolls V
SKYRIM

JOINING THE STORMCLOAKS

PREREQUISITES: None

INTERSECTING QUESTS: None

LOCATIONS: Helgen, The Serpent Stone, Windhelm, Palace of the Kings

CHARACTERS: Galmar Stone-Fist, Jarl Ulfric Stormcloak, Ralof

ENEMIES: Ice Wraith

◊ **OBJECTIVES:** Miscellaneous: Join the Stormcloak Rebellion, Kill the Ice Wraith, Return to Galmar, Take the oath

▶ Before the Rebellion: Unending Brotherhood

> **NOTE** The following quest assumes you pick a side in the Civil War and stick with them. Consult the introduction to these quests to see when you can switch sides (the last possible moment is at the end of Civil War Quest: The Jagged Crown). If you side with the Imperial Legion, consult the Civil War Quest: Joining the Legion, on page 264. Although the Civil War rages on, it affects your adventure only if you let it by completing this series of quests.

After escaping from underneath the battlements of the burning town of Helgen and watching the dragon responsible for disrupting your execution, talk to Ralof. He tells you he's headed to Riverwood and asks if you want to accompany him. As you progress down the hillside, he recommends you head to Windhelm and join the Stormcloaks.

◊ **MISCELLANEOUS OBJECTIVE:** Join the Stormcloak Rebellion

♦ **TARGET:** Palace of the Kings, in Windhelm

> **TIP** Did you miss Ralof's request? Then greet any Stormcloak Soldier (clad in dark blue tunics), or visit any Stormcloak Camp in Skyrim, and you'll usually receive an offer to join the cause.

Trek to the main fortification of the Stormcloaks in Skyrim—the stone city of Windhelm perched by a confluence of rivers. As you enter, racial tensions are bubbling under the surface, with Nords and Dark Elves living an uneasy existence close to each other. Continue into Windhelm, past the Candlehearth Hall, and step into the impressive courtyard. Beyond lies the Palace of the Kings, within Windhelm's walls. Check the throne at the far end of the huge banqueting table, or head west into the strategy planning room, where Jarl Ulfric Stormcloak and Galmar Stone-Fist are shouting about the war effort. Galmar is telling Ulfric that the Empire is putting great pressure on the Hold City of Whiterun.

Ulfric grows weary of Jarl Balgruuf of Whiterun. The leader of this key strategic Hold City has not chosen a side in this war, and Ulfric wishes to send a stronger message. Tell Ulfric you were at Helgen; quicken his trust by saying Ralof said he'd vouch for you. Ulfric is always looking for able fighters, and Galmar has a test for you after you answer why you wish to fight for Skyrim. You're to head to Serpentstone Island. Survive, and you pass this test. This quest officially begins now.

◊ **OBJECTIVE:** Kill the Ice Wraith

♦ **TARGET:** Ice Wraith, on Serpentstone Island

▶ Confirming Metal and Mettle

Off the edge of Winterhold Hold, within the frigid waters of the Sea of Ghosts north of Windhelm and northwest of the Wreck of the Pride of Tel Vos, is the eerie calm of countless ice and rock formations. Among them is Serpentstone Isle. Wade to the north side for easier access up to the cluster of standing stones, guarded by an Ice Wraith. Engage this vicious beast in combat, killing it with your preferred weapon. Search it, as its essence is valuable. Then check the sign of the Serpent if you want its ranged paralyzing poison attribute in place of your current blessing (assuming you have one).

◊ **OBJECTIVE:** Return to Galmar

◊ **OBJECTIVE:** Take the oath

Quest Conclusion

Head back to the Palace of the Kings, where Galmar tells judges that you're definitely Stormcloak material. He says that it is time to officially join the Stormcloak Rebellion. Tell Galmar you're ready and agree to recite this oath:

"I do swear my blood and honor to the service of Ulfric Stormcloak, Jarl of Windhelm and true High King of Skyrim. As Talos is my witness, may this oath bind me to death and beyond, even to my lord as to my fellow brothers and sisters in arms. All hail the Stormcloaks, the true sons and daughters of Skyrim!"

> **NOTE** If you forgo this oath, you can journey to Solitude instead and complete Civil War Quest: Joining the Legion as well. Do this if you're unsure where your allegiance yet lies.

Postquest Activities

You are now one of the Stormcloaks, given the title Unblooded, and are ready to prove your worth to Galmar and Ulfric. Galmar Stone-Fist hands you the proper attire, which you can wear, discard, or sell as you please. He also has your next assignment: Civil War Quest: The Jagged Crown.

➤ **Footwraps**   ➤ **Fur Boots**   ➤ **Hide Helmet**   ➤ **Stormcloak Cuirass**   ➤ **Stormcloak Gauntlets**

THE JAGGED CROWN

PREREQUISITES: Complete Civil War Quest: Joining the Stormcloaks
INTERSECTING QUESTS: Civil War Quest: Joining the Stormcloaks, Civil War Quest: Message to Whiterun
LOCATIONS: Korvanjund, Korvanjund Crypt, Korvanjund Halls, Korvanjund Temple, Windhelm, Palace of the Kings
CHARACTERS: Engar, Galmar Stone-Fist , Gretta , Jarl Ulfric Stormcloak, Ralof, Stormcloak Soldier
ENEMIES: Draugr, Imperial Soldier
◊ **OBJECTIVES:** Talk to Galmar, Meet Galmar outside Korvanjund, Retrieve the Jagged Crown, Deliver the crown to Ulfric Stormcloak

▶ Claiming an Old King's Crown

◊ **OBJECTIVE:** Talk to Galmar

Continue your conversation with Galmar Stone-Fist. Ask him what the mission is, and he says that he's located the final resting place of the Jagged Crown, in the assumed burial place of old King Borgas. Galmar is already assembling his men outside of Korvanjund. You should join them immediately. Before you leave, ask him for more information on the Jagged Crown and the tomb of Korvanjund.

◊ **OBJECTIVE:** Meet Galmar outside Korvanjund

Northeast of Whiterun, in the lower foothills where the ground first turns from tundra to snow, is a depression in the ground. This marks a large cairn and the entrance to these ancient Nordic temple ruins and Jarl's tomb. You can charge toward the entrance on your own, but a more measured (and recommended) plan is to meet up with Galmar Stone-Fist and his quartet of men on the slopes outside the entrance. The troops include Ralof, the man you met at Helgen. Galmar listens as a soldier informs him that Imperials are roaming the place, keeping themselves comfortable. Galmar intends to spill some Imperial blood for Skyrim and send these red-clothed fiends to their graves. Confirm you're ready as Galmar finishes his speech, and you advance upon the cairn. Attack!

If you're employing melee weapons, it is recommended that you lead the charge, sprinting down the steps and up the other side to engage the bowmen, while the rest of your troops fight in the lower ground.

If you're employing bows or projectile spells, stay on the edge of the depression and rain missile attacks down upon the enemy.

As there are only about four Imperials guarding this entrance, combat is both swift and straightforward. Meet Galmar at the top of the steps by the interior entrance. He issues another warning before heading into Korvanjund Temple. Follow him at once.

◊ **OBJECTIVE:** Retrieve the Jagged Crown
◆ **TARGET:** Bone Crown, on Draugr Leader, in Korvanjund Crypt

---

CAUTION ⟡

During combat throughout this tomb, and any time you're engaged in battle, your wild weapon swings or area-of-effect weapons may strike your comrades. If this occurs more than once, they may turn hostile. Minimize the area of your murdering, use weapons that are accurate (arrows or spells such as Firebolt), and take care when using melee weapons. Moving around to attack enemies from the opposite side from your friends, dashing forward to engage foes your allies aren't attacking, and even leaving your friends to finish off foes helps, too.

⟡ **TIP**   You can elect to follow Galmar (which is safer) or head off to explore on your own (which is fine, as you can complete this quest without any help or conversations).

▶ Combat in the Cairn

Dash into the crypt entrance chamber, which is wide and contains a small contingent of foes. Slaughter them quickly, after which Galmar posts Gretta and Engar to guard this entrance. Head down the steps to the north, then turn right (east) and slay a trio of Imperials prowling the ledge surrounding this sunken hall. It is usually best to head in first, to avoid pushing past friends to reach the foes. After the battle, you can reconvene near Galmar at the northern side of the lower hall, near the massive cave-in that dominates the middle of this chamber. Galmar guesses there's a group of foes waiting for you on the other side of the tunnel steps. He's hoping you can find a different way in. You can:

Ignore the warning and plow straight down the stairs into the bridge chamber beyond, where you fight around four to six Imperials.

Or, head up and around the hallway's upper ledge, to an entrance directly above where Galmar is waiting. This brings you out into the same bridge chamber but on the upper bridge. It is easier to sneak, fire long-range attacks, or race along the bridge and around the upper balcony area, tackling foes one at a time.

Your comrades attack the enemies from the lower level, so taking down the enemy from two directions is safer and splits the Imperials' targets. When the bridge chamber is dripping with Legion blood, check the main stepped area for treasure (near the open chest). Afterward, find the upper exit passage to the west. Galmar and his remaining soldiers are clustered around the corpse of a Draugr. It is the first time they've seen such a corpse. Galmar bolsters their courage, and the infiltration continues, down to the iron door leading into the Korvanjund Halls.

Enter the first chamber, climbing to the balcony and slaughtering two foes along the way. Venture north along an upper passage to steps leading down. Along the way is a side tunnel with a swinging blade trap; there is treasure here and a lever that stops the axes.

Venture into the Nordic Hall of Stories, with or without the Legate. At the hall's far end is a Nordic Puzzle Door and two dead soldiers. Take the Ebony Claw they were carrying. This holds the key to opening this puzzle.

➤ **Ebony Claw**

Puzzle Solution: The door consists of three "rings" that rotate when you activate them. Each of them has three animals plated into the structure, while you unlock the central keyhole using the Ebony Claw. The puzzle solution is on the palm of the Ebony Claw; rotate it in your inventory to see the three circular petroglyph carvings. Move the rings so the Wolf, Moth, and Dragon appear on the outer, middle, and inner rings, respectively. Then insert the Ebony Claw into the keyhole.

Venture through the rumbling door and through connecting corridors into the guardian hall chamber. To the west is a portcullis preventing you from reaching the exit door. Simply head to the chamber's northwest corner, into the passage that winds up, past an Iron Dagger on a plinth. Cross a stone bridge to a balcony with a chest. Of more importance is the handle on the northwest corner of this balcony. Pull the handle to raise the portcullis and then drop down to aid Galmar as four or five Draugr clamber out of their tombs to stop you. Now enter the crypt itself.

After a few more winding passages, Korvanjund reveals its deepest chamber: the ceremonial crypt of a long-dead Jarl. Approach the slumped Draugr sitting on the throne in the middle of the chamber. Two guardians clamber out of the tombs that flank the throne, prompting a vicious battle between the Stormcloaks and Draugr. When the combat ends, pry the crown off the Draugr who sat on the throne. With the Bone Crown in your inventory, you can return to Ulfric Stormcloak. Before you leave, head south to a Word Wall and absorb another Word of Power! Then climb the steps to the east, heading up the steps, back into the temple. Remove the door bar, and exit Korvanjund by this quicker route. Leave Galmar to finish his search, and head back to Windhelm.

➤ **Bone Crown** ➤ **Word of Power:** Slow Time

◇ **OBJECTIVE:** Deliver the crown to Ulfric Stormcloak
♦ **TARGET:** Ulfric Stormcloak, inside the Palace of the Kings in Windhelm

Quest Conclusion

Return to the Palace of the Kings and locate Ulfric Stormcloak, who is surprised that Galmar was correct about the crown. You can ask him about the war and his role in deposing the old High King of Skyrim. But more importantly, Ulfric has a message he needs delivered to the Jarl of Whiterun.

Postquest Activities

This prompts the immediate start of Civil War Quest: Message to Whiterun.

MESSAGE TO WHITERUN

PREREQUISITES: Complete Civil War Quest: The Jagged Crown
INTERSECTING QUESTS: Civil War Quest: The Jagged Crown, Main Quest: Bleak Falls Barrow, Main Quest: Dragon Rising, Civil War Quest: Battle for Whiterun
LOCATIONS: Whiterun , Dragonsreach, Windhelm, Palace of the Kings
CHARACTERS: Galmar Stone-Fist, Hrongar , Irileth, Jarl Balgruuf the Greater, Jarl Ulfric Stormcloak, Lydia, Proventus Avenicci
◇ **OBJECTIVES:** Get new orders, Deliver axe to the Jarl of Whiterun, Assist Jarl Balgruuf with the dragon threat, Wait for the Jarl's response, Deliver axe to Jarl Ulfric, Wait for orders from Jarl Ulfric

▶ Decisions at Whiterun

◇ **OBJECTIVE:** Get new orders

Immediately after congratulating you on locating the Bone Crown, Jarl Ulfric Stormcloak explains that he has a message he needs delivered to the Jarl of Whiterun. Inquire why he's handing you an axe as the message, and Ulfric explains that if the Jarl keeps the axe, Ulfric will bide his time. If the axe is returned, it means war.

➤ **Ulfric's War Axe**

◇ **OBJECTIVE:** Deliver axe to the Jarl of Whiterun
♦ **TARGET:** Jarl Balgruuf of Whiterun, in Dragonsreach

Head past the Whiterun Stables and start the long, slow climb. Go over the drawbridge and to the main Whiterun gate. As you approach, a guard stops you; the city is closed with the news of the dragons spreading faster than you can travel. You can:

Tell the guard that Riverwood calls for the Jarl's aid. This is the optimal plan and is available only if Main Quest: Before the Storm is active.

(Persuade) Or you can tell the guard you have news from Helgen about the dragon attack.

(Bribe) Or bribe the guard with a proportion of your collected gold.

(Intimidate) Or order the guard to stand aside.

Once you're inside the walls of Whiterun, head north, to the hilltop on which the city sits. Go past the Gildergreen tree and the Shrine to Talos. Climb the stone steps to discover Dragonsreach, home of the Jarl. Walk toward the huge central fire on either side of the banqueting tables. You are met by Irileth, Jarl Balgruuf's Housecarl. Explain to her that you have a message from Ulfric Stormcloak, and she immediately lets you past. You can converse with her at length if you wish, or offer other responses with the Main Quest active, but mentioning Ulfric's name allows you to progress more quickly.

Approach the Jarl and inform him that you have a message from Ulfric Stormcloak. His responses are dictated by the current situation regarding the dragons returning to Skyrim, and how far through the Main Quest you have progressed.

At this point, you must have completed both Main Quest: Bleak Falls Barrow and Main Quest: Dragon Rising, then returned to the Jarl, heard the call of the Greybeards, and received your Housecarl, Lydia.

If these two quests have not yet been completed, you must do so. Refer to the Main Quest for all relevant information.

◇ **OBJECTIVE:** Assist Jarl Balgruuf with the dragon threat

Once the excitement over the defeat of the dragon at the Western Watchtower has subsided, approach the Jarl and tell him that Jarl Ulfric Stormcloak asked you to deliver an axe to him. He asks for his steward, Proventus Avenicci, and his Housecarl, Irileth, to comment on these matters.

◇ **OBJECTIVE:** Wait for the Jarl's response

Avenicci recommends a wait-and-see approach to Ulfric's threat. Irileth believes it is time to act, while the Jarl wishes to challenge Ulfric to face him as a man and declare his intentions. Avenicci favors a garrison of Imperials, while Irileth deems this to be cowardly. You can interrupt this back-and-forth, or let the Jarl conclude. The results are the same: The Jarl has the answer to your message. He returns the axe.

➤ **Ulfric's War Axe**

◇ **OBJECTIVE:** Deliver axe to Jarl Ulfric
♦ **TARGET:** Ulfric Stormcloak, Palace of the Kings in Windhelm

This Means War

Journey back to Windhelm and seek Ulfric Stormcloak's council. Tell him that the axe has been returned. Ulfric sees that he was wrong about the Jarl.

◇ **OBJECTIVE:** Wait for orders from Jarl Ulfric

Quest Conclusion

Ulfric tells Galmar he was correct. Galmar informs him that he's toured the Stormcloak camps, and his forces are ready for an attack on Whiterun. The decision to send so many men to their deaths weighs heavily on Ulfric. Galmar is certain the men and women of Skyrim want this insurrection, and there is no turning back now. Ulfric agrees; a new day is dawning and the sun rises over Whiterun. And the Sons of Skyrim will greet that dawn with teeth and swords flashing! Ulfric wants you on the front lines. Fight well or die well. Talos be with you!

Postquest Activities

The immediate commencement of Civil War Quest: Battle for Whiterun is now under way!

BATTLE FOR WHITERUN

PREREQUISITES: Complete Civil War Quest: Message to Whiterun
INTERSECTING QUESTS: Civil War Quest: Message to Whiterun, Civil War Quest: Liberation of Skyrim
LOCATIONS: Whiterun, Dragonsreach, Windhelm, Palace of the Kings
CHARACTERS: Galmar Stone-Fist, Jarl Ulfric Stormcloak, Jarl Vignar Gray-Mane, Ralof, Stormcloak Soldier, Ulfric Stormcloak
ENEMIES: Irileth, Imperial Soldier, Jarl Balgruuf the Greater, Whiterun Guard
◇ **OBJECTIVES:** Get your orders from Galmar Stone-Fist, Break through the enemy barricade, Open the drawbridge, Force Jarl Balgruuf the Greater to surrender, Accept Jarl Balgruuf the Greater's surrender

● MINOR SPOILERS

Burning Skies at the Fall of Whiterun

⬢ **TIP** You may wish to explore the Hold City of Whiterun more thoroughly prior to the commencement of this quest to fully learn the layout and the weak areas the enemy may wish to exploit.

◇ **OBJECTIVE:** Get your orders from Galmar Stone-Fist
♦ **TARGET:** Galmar Stone-Fist, Whiterun Military Camp

Leave the solid stone walls of Windhelm and journey to the Whiterun Military Camp where Galmar is amassing his troops for the assault on Whiterun. The camp is just south of the city's main winding road that leads up through an outer gate, past a drawbridge, and to the inner gate and the city. As you arrive, the air becomes thick with the smoke from countless fire-catapult barrages. Ulfric hopes to take this city without destroying too much of the defensive wall. Locate Galmar as he addresses the assembled troops standing ready to attack.

He tells you the fight is for the Sons and Daughters of Skyrim. You now have one important task: the attack and capture of Whiterun!

◇ **OBJECTIVE:** Break through the enemy barricade

Attacking Stratagems: Assault and Overrun!

You are now engaged in an all-out siege of Whiterun. This battle is lengthy and confusing, and you can easily become a casualty rather than a champion of this war. However, the following tactics should help you minimize your risks as you become embroiled in this skirmish.

Ally: Stormcloak Soldier **Enemy: Whiterun Guard** **Enemy: Imperial Soldier**

Know your enemy: In the midst of battle, it sometimes becomes confusing to know exactly who you should be fighting. There are three distinctive forces battling for control of Whiterun. You are sided with the Stormcloaks, who are clad in armor with dark blue tunics and typically carry axes. Also present are Whiterun Guards, who are the enemy. They wear orange tunics and carry shields with the sign of the horse. The Imperial Soldiers are clad in red and tend to use swords.

The Offensive Area: This battle takes place between the outer gate (which the barricade is blocking), the middle drawbridge (which must be lowered once you're through the barricade), and the inner gate (the last line of defense). You should focus your attacks on each area one at a time. Use the cobblestone path running from the outer gate; then get onto the scaffolding that runs along the northern wall to reach the lever and drop the drawbridge. There is no need to maneuver elsewhere.

Enemy Emplacements: The enemy is stationed along the cobblestone road that winds around in a right-turn semicircle to reach the drawbridge. As you gain entry through the outer gate, expect foes to be atop the outer gate, on the wooden guard towers, on the path above the cobblestone road, and on the stone battlements to your right, close to the drawbridge. Know where your attacks are coming from so you can stop them!

Call to Action: Your first job is to remove the enemy barricade on the cobblestone path at the entrance to the outer gate. Achieve this by employing one or more of the following techniques:

Melee: Standing at the barricade, smashing it with your melee weapons until it breaks and shrugging off enemy attacks.

Melee: Standing at the barricade, attempting to leap over the center section (which is possible), and bashing it from the other side.

Ranged: Blasting it (ideally with fire-based magic) from a defensive position. Such locations include:

1. The right (east) corner to the side of the outer gate, using the wall or nearby rocks as cover.
2. The cover at the edge of Pelagia Farm to the south, which offers a good view of the main path.

◇ **OBJECTIVE:** Open the drawbridge
♦ **TARGET:** Occurs once you break through the barricade

Last Line of Defense: When you break through, the enemy falls back to the cobblestone path with the stream running across it, prior to the drawbridge. Make reaching the drawbridge your focus, rather than fighting. Try the following routes:

Route 1: Race directly up the cobblestone road to the guard tower to the northeast. Head up the wooden ramp, then turn right (east). Run around the dirt path above the road, over two more ramps and onto the drawbridge's top.

Route 2: Race directly up the cobblestone road to the ruined section of wall on the inside bend in the road. Leap onto the wall and scramble to a wooden lookout adjacent to the top of the drawbridge.

Route 3: Race directly up the cobblestone road, fixing your view on the stream to the northeast. Scramble up the fallen masonry before you reach the stream. Turn right and leap up to the battlements just below the drawbridge. Run south and to the upper crenellations, where you can access the drawbridge.

Unwise Routes: Ignore the archway the stream runs out of; this leads to the gap in the cobblestones along the stream, but there's no way up. The archway farther up the east wall leads to a small antechamber with no way out. Good for hiding but not for completing objectives.

> **Unsound Tactics:** Standing and fighting is unwise when you have specific objectives to complete. Don't worry about hitting every foe; it is much more important to lower Whiterun's defenses before engaging in combat. **CAUTION**
>
> Your offensive measures against the enemy may be dangerous for your allies if you rely too heavily on area-of-effect magic or wild swinging of weapons (particularly of the two-handed variety). Watch your collateral damage!

> **TIP** However, hitting every foe and delaying objectives does allow you to increase your skill points, so figure out how long you can battle before your health is in danger, and lengthen your attacks to maximize your skill increases.

Continue the battle until you've nullified the enemy forces outside the main gate. There may be a few remaining enemies, but you have a greater objective to complete:

◇ **OBJECTIVE:** Force Jarl Balgruuf the Greater to surrender
♦ **TARGET:** Jarl of Whiterun, inside Dragonsreach in Whiterun

Hail to the Gray-Manes

Open the main gates as soon as the drawbridge is lowered. Stormcloak troops pour into Whiterun's city streets. The enemy guards are here; strike down each one so they don't hit you with arrows as you run past them. Race east toward the Bannered Mare and turn left (north). Sprint up the steps with the canal chutes on either side and to an inner barricade. Remove that using the same techniques you utilized earlier. Then race past the Gildergreen tree and the Shrine to Talos. Climb the stone steps to a third barricade before racing into Dragonsreach.

While Ralof waters the ground with a Whiterun Guard's blood, you must storm into Dragonsreach and seek out the Jarl. "Surrendering" isn't a verbal commitment to end hostilities; the Nords require you to bow before the victor. This means focusing your attacks on the Jarl, fighting him until he falls to his knees. You may need to finish off a few Whiterun Guards first. Fortunately, you have the might (and the axes) of Galmar Stone-Fist and Ralof to help you.

◊ **OBJECTIVE:** Accept Jarl Balgruuf the Greater's surrender

Quest Conclusion

The Jarl staggers to his feet and orders his remaining troops (if there are any) to stand down. The Jarl notices Vignar Gray-Mane walking into the corpse-strewn hall, and they begin to argue about the Empire. Galmar stops this argument. The Jarl has some unkind parting words for you before Galmar orders you back to Windhelm. Ulfric must be informed of the victory here.

Postquest Activities

Vignar Gray-Mane is installed as Jarl of Whiterun from this point on. Civil War Quest: Liberation of Skyrim begins.

LIBERATION OF SKYRIM – RESCUE FROM FORT NEUGRAD

PREREQUISITES: Complete Civil War Quest: Battle for Whiterun
INTERSECTING QUESTS: Civil War Quest: Battle For Whiterun, Civil War Quest: Compelling Tribute
LOCATIONS: Falkreath Stormcloak Camp , Fort Neugrad, Fort Neugrad Prison, Windhelm, Palace of the Kings
CHARACTERS: Galmar Stone-Fist , Jorleif, Stormcloak Soldier, Ulfric Stormcloak
ENEMIES: Imperial Soldier
◊ **OBJECTIVES:** Liberation of Skyrim: Report to Ulfric Stormcloak, Liberation of Skyrim: Liberate Falkreath Hold, Rescue from Fort Neugrad: Meet the men near Fort Neugrad, Rescue from Fort Neugrad: Sneak into the fort, Rescue from Fort Neugrad: Free the prisoners, Rescue from Fort Neugrad: Take over the fort, Rescue from Fort Neugrad: Report back to Ralof, Rescue from Fort Neugrad: Report to Ulfric Stormcloak, Liberation of Skyrim: Liberate the Reach

▷ The Brotherhood Rewards Risk-Takers

◊ **LIBERATION OF SKYRIM NOW BEGINS**
◊ **OBJECTIVE:** Report to Ulfric Stormcloak
♦ **TARGET:** Ulfric Stormcloak, in Palace of the Kings in Windhelm

Return to the Palace of the Kings in Windhelm, and speak with Ulfric Stormcloak. Due in part to your actions at Whiterun, the Imperials have been driven out of that Hold, and Ulfric controls the middle of Skyrim. For your service, Ulfric has a new Nordic name for you: Ice-Veins, for the thick blood of his land has seeped into your heart. He also has an Imperial officer's sword to give you, a fitting blade with which to kill the enemy. Ask what the next move is, and Ulfric tells you to head to a hidden camp within Falkreath Hold. Galmar Stone-Fist has important tasks for you there.

➤ **Leveled Weapon**

◊ **LIBERATION OF SKYRIM BEGINS**
◊ **OBJECTIVE:** Liberate Falkreath Hold
♦ **TARGET:** Galmar Stone-Fist, Falkreath Stormcloak Camp

Journey to the Falkreath Stormcloak Camp east of Helgen, just above the snow line in the foothills of the Throat of the World.

Aside from a Quartermaster and a Grindstone to help augment your weaponry, there's an alchemy table near the hospital tents and troops to speak to. However, Galmar's tent is the place to visit, where the Nord is pouring over the current Civil War map. Report for duty, and he wants you to head to Fort Neugrad. You are to infiltrate the fort, as the Legion are holding some Stormcloaks prisoner there. He aims to use your cunning to find a way inside, free the men, and liberate the fort. This is an attack from the inside!

◊ **RESCUE FROM FORT NEUGRAD BEGINS**
◊ **OBJECTIVE:** Meet the men near Fort Neugrad
♦ **TARGET:** Mountains west of Fort Neugrad

Trek down the rugged terrain to the main road west of the fort (Fast-Traveling from Helgen and then sprinting to meet your men is a quick option). As there are two roads in this area, if you head straight toward Fort Neugrad (without sneaking), the enemy soldiers recognize you as a Stormcloak and raise the alarm. You can fight on anyway, but until Ralof and his men figure out something is amiss and catch up with you, you're alone against the entire Imperial garrison! This is not recommended.

Instead, walk or Fast-Travel to Helgen, and take the road south from there (the one you traveled during the opening moments of your adventure). This brings you to the rendezvous point without alerting the enemy.

You soon encounter a small team of four men. One of them is your old friend Ralof, who has already reconnoitered Fort Neugrad. It appears particularly large and well defended over the brow of the hill, partly due to the mountain slopes keeping raiders away from the walls. However, there is an underwater cave entrance in the lake behind the fort, and Ralof reckons it goes straight into the prison. The plan is to sneak in there, free the prisoners, and kill anyone you meet. Ralof will rush the fort when they hear fighting, and you'll rendezvous in the courtyard. At this point, inform Ralof that you've agreed to the plan and begin the sneak.

◇ **OBJECTIVE:** Sneak into the fort

Or, tell Ralof you aren't interested in sneaking. At this point, you can take a direct (and far more dangerous) approach: assault the fort via the main entrance and battle down to the prisoners inside. This is possible but it's significantly riskier, because you don't have the aid of additional soldiers from the prison.

⎯ **TIP** Ralof recommends attempting the assault in the evening, as it will be easier to sneak past the guard patrolling outside. This is true; whether you take his advice is up to you!

◈ Lakeside Infiltration

Continue up the road until you see the fort. Wait for nightfall, when the guards change shifts and the patrols become lighter. Take advantage of any stealthy gear or spells you have (Muffle and Invisibility make this infiltration a breeze). Then crouch and move in. Head to the small jetty and lake to the fort's east, and then dive into the murky lake. Turn left (west) and look for the underwater cave entrance. Swim into the underground flooded cave. You are now in Fort Neugrad Prison.

◇ **OBJECTIVE:** Free the prisoners

Climb out of the water, head north through the narrow tunnel and northwest through a barrel-storage cellar, and go up some steps. There are two guards in this area, a jailor and a soldier on patrol. Wait until the jailor is alone and seated on his chair. Then use a well-placed arrow to remove him quickly. Swiftly take the key from his body and release the prisoners before the other soldier can investigate. The jailbreak is on! The freed men quickly don their armor and follow your lead.

➤ **Fort Neugrad Prison Key**

◇ **OBJECTIVE:** Take over the fort
◆ **TARGET:** All remaining Imperial Soldiers
◇ **OBJECTIVE:** Report back to Ralof

Sprint up the spiral stone steps to the fort's entrance hall and fireplace. Move west to the exterior door, into the outside courtyard, and begin slaughtering the half-dozen soldiers guarding the outside of the fort. They usually stream in from all angles, but Ralof arrives with his men to help your team out. The numerous gaps in the walls allow you to hide and dart out if you're engaging in longer-ranged attacks or needing to rest between Stamina exertions. Don't forget the enemies by the wooden side building and campfire to the southwest.

Move with your men — they are tough in single combat, but if your whole group concentrates on one target at a time, you can take your foes down quickly. Methodically head to the fort's front, where Ralof's men are fighting their way in. With your combined forces, you have no trouble taking out the remaining defenders.

Once the courtyard is clear, the other soldiers remain outside to secure it. Your next step is to crush the remaining stragglers inside the keep. With Ralof's help, head inside. The interior of Fort Neugrad is a circular path, allowing you to move quickly left or right (as the main chamber is open to attack from all sides) and begin a sweep of the keep. Your most dangerous adversary is the fort's commander, who is in his room on the upper floor's east side.

When everyone wearing red is dead, find Ralof and report back to him. You're to report back to Ulfric while he remains here to tidy up the mess.

◇ **OBJECTIVE:** Report to Ulfric Stormcloak
◆ **TARGET:** Ulfric Stormcloak, in Palace of the Kings in Windhelm

Civil War Quest: Rescue from Fort Neugrad may have finished, but the Liberation of Skyrim continues.

Quest Conclusion

Trek back to the Palace of the Kings and let Ulfric know of your victory. Falkreath's main fortress is in Stormcloak hands, so the heart and soul of Skyrim is now the domain of the Nords. Ulfric Stormcloak has come to enjoy your ferocity and determination. Some brothers have taken to calling you Bone-Breaker. Ulfric calls you that too. Along with this, you receive a new weapon and the ability to purchase a home in Windhelm. Consult with Jorleif, Ulfric's Steward. Ask what the next move is, and Ulfric tells you to report to Galmar at the Stormcloak camp in the Reach.

➤ **Leveled Weapon**

◇ **LIBERATION OF SKYRIM CONTINUES**
◇ **OBJECTIVE:** Liberate the Reach
◆ **TARGET:** Galmar Stone-Fist, Reach Stormcloak Camp

Postquest Activities

Civil War Quest: Liberation of Skyrim is still going. Civil War Quest: Compelling Tribute begins once you check in with Galmar. In addition, speak to Jorleif if you wish to purchase a dwelling inside Windhelm.

PREREQUISITES: Complete Civil War Quest: Rescue from Fort Neugrad

INTERSECTING QUESTS: Civil War Quest: Rescue from Fort Neugrad, Civil War Quest: The Battle for Fort Sungard

LOCATIONS: Markarth, Understone Keep , Reach Stormcloak Camp, Windhelm, Palace of the Kings

CHARACTERS: Faleen, Galmar Stone-Fist, Jarl Igmund , Markarth Guard, Quartermaster, Raerek, Stormcloak Soldier, Ulfric Stormcloak

ENEMIES: Imperial Soldier

◊ **OBJECTIVES:** Liberation of Skyrim: Liberate the Reach, Compelling Tribute: Find evidence, Compelling Tribute: Blackmail Raerek, Compelling Tribute: Report to Galmar Stone-Fist, Compelling Tribute: Meet the men, Compelling Tribute: Follow Ralof and ambush enemy scout, Compelling Tribute: Take over the caravan, Compelling Tribute: Report to Ralof

Raerek's Silver

◊ **LIBERATION OF SKYRIM CONTINUES**
◊ **OBJECTIVE:** Liberate the Reach
♦ **TARGET:** Galmar Stone-Fist, Reach Stormcloak Camp

Galmar Stone-Fist has set up a hidden Stormcloak Camp in the rocky mountainous region northeast of Karthwasten, which has the same benefits as the one in Falkreath, although this has a few Stormcloak casualties from the ongoing hostilities. Report to Galmar, and he orders you to Markarth. Rumor has it that the Jarl's Steward, Raerek, is a faithful Talos worshipper but not a true Son of Skyrim—he still supports the Empire, after all. If you confront him with his belief, you might be able to "persuade" him to aid the cause. This requires both stealth and discretion.

◊ **CIVIL WAR QUEST:** Compelling Tribute begins
◊ **OBJECTIVE:** Find evidence
♦ **TARGET:** Raerek's quarters, inside Understone Keep, in Markarth

Head to Markarth, sheath your weapons, and enter the mighty Understone Keep hewn into the rock to the city's southwest. Head west into the keep, toward the Jarl's impressive throne room. You may pass Faleen, the Jarl's Housecarl, who looks at you suspiciously. If you're simply wandering the keep, it's not necessary to speak with those surrounding the Jarl, including Raerek or Raerek's nephew Igmund. In fact, you need not meet Jarl Igmund, as Raerek's quarters are to the right (north) of this chamber. Figuring out where some evidence is located is your top priority.

 CAUTION

Watch out for a patrolling guard on your way to Raerek's room, as he calls you out as a trespasser if he spots you. Time his patrol so you avoid him.

The evidence is located in Raerek's quarters, which is north and west of the Jarl's throne room. Watch for patrolling Markarth Guards witnessing your trespassing, as this clandestine robbery cannot escalate into hostilities! Reach this area without being detected by doing one of the following:

(Sneak) You can sneak into the chamber, preferably after dark when the keep has fewer folk awake.

(Spells) You can cast Invisibility or some other helpful spell that diminishes the chances of you being seen.

Or you can slowly, and without weapons drawn, enter the keep and head immediately to Raerek's bedroom.

Enter (he is either sleeping here or wandering the keep, usually close to the throne room) and search the dresser for the Amulet.

➤ **Raerek's Inscribed Amulet of Talos**

◊ **OBJECTIVE:** Blackmail Raerek

Locate Raerek within the keep, and show him the Amulet by speaking to him. He asks what kind of extortion racket you're running. Reply that he should be worshipping Talos out in the open, but Raerek is fearful that the Thalmor would make an example of him. He is the Jarl's uncle, and they both swore oaths to the Empire to abandon Talos in return for presiding over Markarth again. He is loyal to them over his own beliefs. You ask to come to some agreement, wondering whether both of you could prosper. He mentions a large shipment of silver and weapons the Imperials are transporting. You can:

(Persuade) Ask about receiving some of it for yourself.

Agree to the deal and ask where this shipment is.

If your persuasion works, you receive a sizable purse of coins. Either way, you must confirm the agreement. He reveals the Imperials are taking this booty by wagon to Solitude. If you hurry, you can catch them before they get too far.

➤ **Leveled gold pieces**

◊ **OBJECTIVE:** Report to Galmar Stone-Fist
♦ **TARGET:** Galmar Stone-Fist, Reach Stormcloak Camp

Head back to the hidden camp and report to Galmar, telling him about the shipment of coin. Coincidentally, he already has a small group of scouts on the same road that the enemy caravan is traveling along. You are to meet up with them and try to overpower the wagon's guards.

> ◊ **OBJECTIVE:** Meet the Men
> ♦ **TARGET:** On the road close to Broken Tower Redoubt, the Reach

Ralof's Rebels

Judging by your world map, the scouts are waiting on the road to the east of Broken Tower Redoubt, in the eastern part of the Reach. Travel there. Beware if you're approaching from the east—you'll run into the Imperial caravan without any help from the scouts.

Approach along the road from the west, heading east, and meet up with an old friend as the path crosses the top of a rocky hillside. Ralof greets you when you speak with him. At this point, you have two choices to make:

Plan A: Ralof's Reasoning

Chat with Ralof, answering any way you wish. Steer the conversation back to your mission and explain the enemy wagon loaded with coin and weapons is farther down this slope. As luck would have it, Ralof has been tracking the wagon, which has lost an axle and is stranded. Although you're outnumbered (there are six foes), Ralof has a plan: His troops will remove the enemy sentry, then situate themselves overlooking the camp. Afterward, you'll infiltrate their position, gain their attention, and Ralof's troops will unleash a volley of arrows, winning the day tactically. Agree to this plan.

> ◊ **OBJECTIVE:** Follow Ralof and ambush enemy scout
> ◊ **OBJECTIVE:** Take over the caravan

>  **TIP** Before moving in, wait until nightfall, as your stealthiness is much more likely to succeed.

Crouch and follow Ralof, watching as his bowmen drop the enemy scout. Wait for them to reach the rocks overlooking the broken-down caravan, and then walk toward the enemies. Sneaking, firing from range, or rushing to attack are all excellent ideas, while your brethren shoot arrows down on them from above and around the path.

Plan B: Good Riddance to Ralof

Chat with Ralof, then either refuse to go along with his plan or ignore him altogether.

> ◊ **OBJECTIVE:** Take over the caravan

Head down the path to the southeast and begin to battle the six Imperials guarding the caravan of silver. You can begin with the sentry atop the rocks overlooking the caravan. Then rain death from above with ranged attacks, or swarm the foes with melee weapons. A couple of enemy soldiers may be sleeping, so carve them up before they fully wake up.

> **TIP** If this fight overwhelms you, flee up the path toward Ralof, and his men help by mopping up any enemies giving chase. Then rest and return to tackle the stragglers.

> ◊ **OBJECTIVE:** Report to Ralof

Quest Conclusion

With the caravan's guards removed, Ralof remains here to guard the silver. Speak to him to end the quest.

Postquest Activities

Civil War Quest: Liberation of Skyrim is still ongoing. Civil War Quest: The Battle for Fort Sungard begins shortly. Loot any weapons and valuables you wish from the wagon.

> ➤ **Spoils of War**

⟪ LIBERATION OF SKYRIM (CONTINUED) – THE BATTLE FOR FORT SUNGARD ⟫

PREREQUISITES: Complete Civil War Quest: Compelling Tribute
INTERSECTING QUESTS: Civil War Quest: Compelling Tribute, Civil War Quest: A False Front
LOCATIONS: Fort Sungard, Fort Sungard Muster, Fort Sungard Tower, Reach Stormcloak Camp , Windhelm, Palace of the Hills
CHARACTERS: Galmar Stone-Fist, Jarl Ulfric Stormcloak: Stormcloak Soldier
ENEMIES: Imperial Soldier
◊ **OBJECTIVES:** Liberation of Skyrim: Liberate the Reach, The Battle for Fort Sungard: Join the men attacking Fort Sungard, The Battle for Fort Sungard: Take over Fort Sungard by killing the enemy, Liberation of Skyrim: Report to Ulfric Stormcloak, Liberation of Skyrim: Liberate Hjaalmarch

Within Reach

> ◊ **LIBERATION OF SKYRIM CONTINUES**
> ◊ **OBJECTIVE:** Liberate the Reach
> ♦ **TARGET:** Galmar Stone-Fist, Reach Stormcloak Camp

Travel to Reach Stormcloak Camp, where Galmar Stone-Fist congratulates you. Report in, and he says your next objective is Fort Sungard. You are to meet the soldiers preparing for the attack, and then wipe out the Legion garrison. Agree to the task, and the quest commences.

> ➤ **150 gold pieces**

◊ **THE BATTLE FOR FORT SUNGARD BEGINS**
◊ **OBJECTIVE:** Join the men attacking Fort Sungard
♦ **TARGET:** On the hill, northeast of Fort Sungard

Fort Sungard is nestled in the southern part of the Druadach Mountains, close to the border of Whiterun Hold. Galmar's men are on the craggy hillside to the fort's northeast, so approaching from the southwest can fail this objective (but not the quest; this just starts the battle prematurely). Instead, you may wish to circle around and join the detachment of Stormcloak forces stationed close to the fortification. After studying the Atlas entry of this place (page 522) and speaking to the leader of the forces, begin the attack.

◊ **OBJECTIVE:** Take over Fort Sungard by killing the enemy

Assault the fortification and help eliminate all the Imperial Soldiers. Enter from one of the following weak points or fortified positions:

North wall: This is both impenetrable and treacherous, being close to extremely steep and rocky ground. However, you can scale the jagged rocks to the northeast and attack from here (ranged weapons only).

East wall: In the northeast corner, the battlements have fallen, allowing you to leap atop them. There is an often-overlooked entrance arch, too, which is perfect for a surprise attack!

Tower entrance: Located outside the walls on the fort's southeast corner, close to the oubliette tower. Enter this door and scale the spiral stairs to the tower's top. You can rain down ranged fire almost with impunity!

Oubliette tower: This isn't worth ascending, as your view isn't good for soldier dispatching.

South wall: The terrain is steep and unforgiving, but there is a fire pit balcony with an easily assaulted archway entrance here.

Southwest muster: The southwest corner wall has an exterior pipe leading into the Muster. From here you can sneak or rush through and up onto the exterior battlements.

West wall: The main entrance where your brethren usually attack from. It is the most problematic location because of the barricades and because you're fighting uphill, but it leads through an archway and eventually onto the battlements.

After you win the battle, the Stormcloak forces remain to garrison this location. Meanwhile, you have other plans.

◊ **LIBERATION OF SKYRIM CONTINUES**
◊ **OBJECTIVE:** Report to Ulfric Stormcloak
♦ **TARGET:** Ulfric Stormcloak, in Palace of the Kings in Windhelm

Quest Conclusion

Return to the Palace of the Kings and inform Ulfric of your victory. This captures the Hold of the Reach and stopped the raping of her silver mines. For your valor and battle prowess, you are named Ice-Hammer. Take the earned weapon as a gift and symbol of this new rank. You're instructed to meet Galmar again; he's planning some surprises for General Tullius in Hjaalmarch.

  NOTE This title may change if you ran away from Whiterun or gained a Hold from a peace treaty during Main Quest: Season Unending. Therefore, the title noted may differ from the one you received.

➤ **Leveled Shield**

◊ **OBJECTIVE:** Liberate Hjaalmarch
♦ **TARGET:** Galmar Stone-Fist, Hjaalmarch Stormcloak Camp

Postquest Activities

Civil War Quest: Liberation of Skyrim is still ongoing. Civil War Quest: A False Front begins shortly.

LIBERATION OF SKYRIM (CONTINUED) – A FALSE FRONT

PREREQUISITES: Complete Civil War Quest: The Battle for Fort Sungard
INTERSECTING QUESTS: Civil War Quest: The Battle for Fort Sungard, Civil War Quest: The Battle for Fort Snowhawk
LOCATIONS: Dragon Bridge, Four Shields Tavern, Hjaalmarch Stormcloak Camp, Morthal, Highmoon Hall, Rorikstead, Frostfruit Inn
CHARACTERS: Faida, Galmar Stone-Fist, Legate Taurinus Duilis, Mralki
ENEMIES: Imperial Courier
◊ **OBJECTIVES:** Liberation of Skyrim: Liberate Hjaalmarch, A False Front: Find the Imperial Courier, A False Front: Retrieve the Imperial Courier's package, A False Front: Bring the documents to Galmar Stone-Fist, A False Front: Bring the forged documents to Legate Taurinus Duilis, Liberation of Skyrim: Liberate Hjaalmarch

▶ Delivering the Doctored Documents

◊ **LIBERATION OF SKYRIM CONTINUES**
◊ **OBJECTIVE:** Liberate Hjaalmarch
♦ **TARGET:** Galmar Stone-Fist, Hjaalmarch Stormcloak Camp

Journey to Galmar's newly established forward-operating base, to the west and slightly north of Morthal, on the Hold's edge. This camp has the same benefits as the one in the Reach. Report in with Galmar, who has your orders.

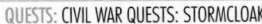

You are to deliver some false orders to the Imperial Legate in Morthal. But to make that happen, Galmar needs to get his hands on some Imperial orders to make forgeries. Fortunately, Imperial runners make frequent stops at the inns in Dragon Bridge and Rorikstead. Head to one of those places and convince the innkeeper to help you.

◊ **A FALSE FRONT BEGINS**
◊ **OBJECTIVE:** Find the Imperial Courier
♦ **TARGET:** Barkeep of Four Shields Tavern or Frostfruit Inn

There are two inns at the locations Galmar mentioned: The Four Shields Tavern is in Dragon Bridge, along the main road to the west of Solitude and operated by Faida. The Frostfruit Inn is one of the prominent structures of Rorikstead and has an innkeeper named Mralki. Journey to either of these locations and speak to the innkeeper, asking whether they've seen any Imperial Couriers. After an evasive response, you can:

(Persuade) Warn that the courier's life is in danger.

(Bribe) Offer some gold for the information.

(Intimidate) Mention that you can get rough if you need to.

Or wait around in the inn.

If you succeed using any of the first three options, the barkeep tells you that the courier just left and that you can probably catch him. Or you can wait in the inn for the courier to return. The courier is halfway between both the inns on the main road. Even if you're unsuccessful, you can elect to run after or wait for the courier (the only difference is the objective won't update). You must visit one of the inns before finding the courier.

◊ **OBJECTIVE:** Retrieve the Imperial Courier's package
♦ **TARGET:** Courier, inside or between either inn

The courier travels to and from each inn. He loiters at the inn for an hour, sleeps there for an hour, and then heads back to the other inn. He repeats this route until you intercept him,

either by waiting inside the inn or finding him on the road. At this point, you have a three options:

(Pickpocket) Pickpocket the documents while the courier is unaware.

Speak to the courier, demanding the documents. He refuses and you must kill him.

Simply kill the courier and loot the corpse for the documents.

> **CAUTION** Watch out! Killing the courier in either town is a crime. In Dragon Bridge, you may have to contend with both the guards and the elite Penitus Oculatus. In Rorikstead, Stormcloak Guards have taken the town, and may even kill the courier if they spot him. If you prefer to do the deed yourself, meet him on the road, where his death won't arouse suspicion.

➤ **Imperial Documents**

◊ **OBJECTIVE:** Bring the documents to Galmar Stone-Fist
♦ **TARGET:** Galmar Stone-Fist, Hjaalmarch Stormcloak Camp

After returning to Galmar, he reads the documents, noting the Imperials know more about the Stormcloak plans than was expected. He "corrects" the documents with false information and orders you to present them to the Imperial Legate in Morthal, throwing him off the trail.

◊ **OBJECTIVE:** Bring the forged documents to Legate Taurinus Duilis
♦ **TARGET:** Legate Taurinus Duilis, Highmoon Hall, in Morthal

Quest Conclusion

You'll usually find the Legate inside Highmoon Hall, the Jarl's residence inside the Hold City of Morthal, although he sometimes walks the pathways around the city. Present some important documents to him. He reads over them, noting the troop movements (false) and rewarding you with a little gold for a drink at the Moorside Inn for your troubles. This quest now concludes.

➤ **5 gold pieces**

> **TIP** There's no need to change from your Stormcloak garb when you meet Taurinus; you quickly make up a verbal ruse that it's easier to "sneak past the enemy" clad in their colors.

◊ **LIBERATION OF SKYRIM CONTINUES**
◊ **OBJECTIVE:** Liberate Hjaalmarch
♦ **TARGET:** Galmar Stone-Fist, Hjaalmarch Stormcloak Camp

Postquest Activities

Civil War Quest: Liberation of Skyrim is still ongoing. Civil War Quest: The Battle for Fort Snowhawk now begins.

PREREQUISITES: Complete Civil War Quest: A False Front
INTERSECTING QUESTS: Civil War Quest: A False Front, Civil War Quest: The Battle for Fort Hraggstad
LOCATIONS: Fort Snowhawk , Fort Snowhawk Tower , Hjaalmarch Stormcloak Camp, Windhelm, Palace of the Kings
CHARACTERS: Galmar Stone-Fist, Jarl Ulfric Stormcloak, Stormcloak Soldier
ENEMIES: Imperial Soldier
◊ **OBJECTIVES:** Liberation of Skyrim: Liberate Hjaalmarch, The Battle for Fort Snowhawk: Join the men attacking Fort Snowhawk, The Battle for Fort Snowhawk: Take over Fort Snowhawk by killing the enemy, The Battle for Fort Snowhawk: Report to Ulfric Stormcloak, Liberation of Skyrim: Liberate Haafingar

▶ March on Hjaalmarch

◊ **LIBERATION OF SKYRIM CONTINUES**
◊ **OBJECTIVE:** Liberate Hjaalmarch
♦ **TARGET:** Galmar Stone-Fist, Hjaalmarch Stormcloak Camp

Travel to the Hjaalmarch Stormcloak Camp, where Galmar Stone-Fist congratulates you. Report for duty, and he says your next objective is Fort Snowhawk. You are to meet your Brothers waiting nearby for the attack orders and then wipe out the Legion inside. Agree to the task, and the quest commences.

◊ **THE BATTLE FOR FORT SNOWHAWK BEGINS**
◊ **OBJECTIVE:** Join the men attacking Fort Snowhawk
♦ **TARGET:** On the road, southwest of Fort Snowhawk

Fort Snowhawk is atop a shallow hill just west of Morthal, close to craggy peaks to the southwest. This is where your band of Brothers are coming from. If you approach the fort from the northeast, you may attract the enemy's attention and commence the battle too soon. Instead, take the road from Morthal and meet up with your Brothers on the ridge south of the fort. After studying the Atlas entry of this place (on page 443) and conversing with the leader, commence the battle.

◊ **OBJECTIVE:** Take over Fort Snowhawk by killing the enemy

Assault the fortification and help eliminate all the Imperial Soldiers in the garrison. Enter from one of the following weak points or fortified positions:

Southwest wall: This is dominated by two turrets and a main entrance from the road. It is the usual place to assault and has multiple barricades to crush or dodge. It is also where the battle is fiercest. If you're specializing in melee weapons, take out those barricades and clear a path. If you're using ranged weapons, pick off foes on the walls to help your men advance.

Northwest wall: You can navigate the crumbling wall to the west by the turret if you jump precisely, and there are numerous low or ruined sections along the wall you can easily head across. This area is extremely easy to penetrate.

Northeast wall: The crumbling eastern wall has several places from which you can infiltrate. Although there's a cave into Fort Snowhawk Prison by the shallow lake, this leads to a ledge that's too high to climb onto; this is only an exit. Ignore this cave completely; you must focus on the fort's exterior and assault.

Southeast wall: There's a gap in the southeast wall at the end of the wooden fencing.

Central tower: Rush the southwest entrance and head for the door, sprinting up the interior spiral steps and taking the ladder to the exterior top of the central tower. This offers exceptional sniping views all around you.

Staying outside: Although the central tower is worth climbing if you're stealthy, the rest of the keep is highly dangerous: Don't waste time fighting foes on your own!

Upper roof: This has some excellent lines of sight and relatively few soldiers to attack you. To reach this position, head for the southeast courtyard, climbing the stairs there and heading across the walls.

When you are victorious and the enemies routed, the Stormcloak forces remain to garrison this location. Meanwhile, you have other tasks to complete.

◊ **OBJECTIVE:** Report to Ulfric Stormcloak
♦ **TARGET:** Ulfric Stormcloak, Palace of the Kings in Windhelm

Quest Conclusion

Return to the Palace of the Kings and inform Ulfric of your victory. This captures the Hold of Hjaalmarch, which makes Tullius nervous. As soon as the Stormcloaks are able, the march on Solitude will begin. Your savagery and dedication has earned Ulfric's respect, and he numbers you among his kin. You shall now be known as Stormblade. You are handed a special weapon on behalf of the Sons and Daughters of Skyrim. Then you're told to meet Galmar Stone-Fist again; he's finished setting up camp in Haafingar Hold.

> **NOTE** This title may change if you ran away from Whiterun or gained a Hold from a peace treaty during Main Quest: Season Unending. Therefore, the title noted may differ from the one you received.

➤ **Leveled Armor**

◊ **LIBERATION OF SKYRIM CONTINUES**
◊ **OBJECTIVE:** Liberate Haafingar
♦ **TARGET:** Galmar Stone-Fist, Haafingar Imperial Camp

Postquest Activities

Civil War Quest: Liberation of Skyrim is still going. Civil War Quest: The Battle for Fort Hraggstad begins momentarily.

PREREQUISITES: Complete Civil War Quest: The Battle for Fort Snowhawk

INTERSECTING QUESTS: Civil War Quest: The Battle for Fort Snowhawk, Civil War Quest: Battle for Solitude

LOCATIONS: Fort Hraggstad, Haafingar Stormcloak Camp

CHARACTERS: Galmar Stone-Fist, Stormcloak Soldier

ENEMIES: Imperial Soldier

◊ **OBJECTIVES:** Liberation of Skyrim: Liberate Haafingar, The Battle for Fort Hraggstad: Join the men attacking Fort Hraggstad , The Battle for Fort Hraggstad: Take over Fort Hraggstad by killing the enemy, Liberation of Skyrim: Liberate Haafingar

▶ Breaking Haafingar

◊ **LIBERATION OF SKYRIM CONTINUES**
◊ **OBJECTIVE:** Liberate Haafingar
♦ **TARGET:** Galmar Stone-Fist, Haafingar Stormcloak Camp

Take the main path between Dragon Bridge and Solitude. Locate Galmar's Stormcloak Camp, which overlooks the Karth River. Head into Galmar's tent and speak with him. He tells you that your objective is an enemy-held fort. You are to meet the soldiers waiting nearby for the attack orders and then wipe out the Imperial Legion forces inside. Agree to the task, and the quest commences.

◊ **THE BATTLE FOR FORT HRAGGSTAD BEGINS**
◊ **OBJECTIVE:** Join the men attacking Fort Hraggstad
♦ **TARGET:** On the road, east of Fort Hraggstad

Fort Hraggstad is perched on a snowy mountain overlooking the Sea of Ghosts, with a sheer cliff to the north. Galmar's brothers are on the flat rocks just southeast of the fortification, so approaching from the west may fail this objective (but not the ongoing quest). Join the Stormcloak Soldiers creeping up on the fort if you don't wish to assault it alone. After studying the Atlas entry of this place (page 426) and conversing with the leader, commence the battle.

◊ **OBJECTIVE:** Take over Fort Hraggstad by killing the enemy

Charge the fortification and help eliminate all of the Imperial Soldiers. Enter from one of the following weak points or fortified positions:

Northeast wall: This is mostly impenetrable, but there is a gap just east of the northern tower turret that allows easy access into the grounds.

Southeast wall: The main road and entrance (dotted with barricades) are the usual swarm points for your forces but are heavily guarded.

Southwest wall: This wall section from tower to tower is impressively impenetrable.

Northwest wall: The dangerous rocky terrain and cliff edge make this impenetrable wall well worth ignoring.

Advantage point: The cluster of rocks to the west overlooks the fort and is excellent for long-range attacks. Another option is the tall fort tower in the fort's northern section, although that requires battling to reach.

Quest Conclusion

When the enemy finally succumbs to your might and the fort falls to the Stormcloaks, your forces remain to garrison this location.

◊ **LIBERATION OF SKYRIM CONTINUES**
◊ **OBJECTIVE:** Liberate Haafingar
♦ **TARGET:** Galmar Stone-Fist, Haafingar Stormcloak Camp

Postquest Activities

Civil War Quest: Liberation of Skyrim is almost over. Civil War Quest: Battle for Solitude begins shortly.

LIBERATION OF SKYRIM (CONCLUDES) – BATTLE FOR SOLITUDE

PREREQUISITES: Complete Civil War Quest: The Battle for Fort Hraggstad

INTERSECTING QUESTS: Civil War Quest: The Battle for Fort Hraggstad

LOCATIONS: Haafingar Stormcloak Camp, Solitude, Castle Dour

CHARACTERS: Galmar Stone-Fist, Jarl Ulfric Stormcloak, Stormcloak Soldier

ENEMIES: General Tullius, Imperial Soldier, Legate Rikke

◊ **OBJECTIVES:** Liberation of Skyrim: Liberate Haafingar, Battle for Solitude: Get your orders from Ulfric Stormcloak, Battle for Solitude: Take over Solitude by killing the enemy, Battle for Solitude: Force General Tullius to surrender

● MAJOR SPOILERS

◁ LIBERATION OF SKYRIM (CONTINUED) – THE BATTLE FOR FORT SNOWHAWK / THE BATTLE FOR FORT HRAGGSTAD ◊ LIBERATION OF SKYRIM (CONCLUDES) – BATTLE FOR SOLITUDE ▷   291

TRANING   THE INVENTORY   THE BESTIARY   ◈ QUESTS   ATLAS OF SKYRIM   APPENDICES AND INDEX

The Fall of Solitude

◊ **LIBERATION OF SKYRIM CONTINUES**
◊ **OBJECTIVE:** Liberate Haafingar
♦ **TARGET:** Galmar Stone-Fist, Haafingar Stormcloak Camp

> **TIP** Stop! Before mounting a final assault on Solitude, consider studying the streets, uncovering routes from the main gates to Castle Dour, using the route that passes by the Hall of the Dead, so you're completely familiar with the street layout. It is wise to add any helpful inventory equipment (such as Magicka-, Health-, or Stamina-augmenting items) before commencing this quest.

Maneuver back to the Haafingar Stormcloak Camp and speak with Galmar Stone-Fist. He is extremely proud of your accomplishments and rewards you accordingly. Then he tells you that the Brothers of Skyrim are gathering to attack Solitude, and you're part of it!

➤ **150 gold pieces**

◊ **BATTLE FOR SOLITUDE BEGINS**
◊ **OBJECTIVE:** Get your orders from Ulfric Stormcloak
♦ **TARGET:** Great gate of Solitude

Travel up the road toward the large entrance gate to Solitude, which the Stormcloaks have already razed. The flame catapults are bombarding the embattled city in great plumes of flame, and the air is thick with smoke and Imperial fear.

Rush forward (east) through the wreckage, to the towering gate, where Ulfric Stormcloak is yelling words of encouragement to his forces. This is the time to deliver the final blow to the hated Imperials! Fear neither pain nor darkness, for Sovngarde awaits those who die with weapons in their hands and courage in their hearts!

◊ **OBJECTIVE:** Take over Solitude by killing the enemy

The stronghold for the Imperials is on fire, and the chaos of fighting General Tullius's remaining men and navigating the various barriers can be confusing. Learn the various locations you must fight through:

Initial courtyard: The Winking Skeever and other merchant stores are closed, and the ground is littered with fire. Push forward on either side of the flaming obstacles.

East to market: The stone ramp up to the forge area is blocked by debris, forcing you to head east, passing the market stalls to your right and heading for a barricade under the arched parapet bridge.

The Hall of the Dead: You can scramble along the rocks to the left, or hack the barricade and head along the left side of the Hall of the Dead building. Debris and enemy troops are everywhere.

Castle courtyard: The eventual fight continues with a left (north) turn up the main avenue and into the flaming courtyard outside Castle Door.

> **CAUTION** The flow of enemy soldiers does not stop! Therefore, it is imperative you reach Castle Door as quickly as possible.

◊ **OBJECTIVE:** Force General Tullius to surrender

A Little More Than a Rebellion

Push into Castle Door with Galmar Stone-Fist and Ulfric Stormcloak. Both General Tullius and Legate Rikke are cornered in this castle. Ulfric turns to his old friend and tells you war always comes down to a single truth-laden moment. Rikke won't stand down, so you're forced to kill her. Race forward and begin attacking Tullius or Rikke, choosing the foe your allies aren't fighting so you can bring the Imperial leaders to their knees more quickly. Step back if you're being wounded too severely.

Tullius splutters through mouthfuls of blood that the Thalmor are to blame; they stirred up the trouble here and forced him to divert resources, quelling this rebellion. Galmar and Ulfric smile, as this is more than a rebellion now! Before Galmar runs Tullius through, Ulfric stops him and asks you to execute the General; it'll make for a better story. You can:

Agree, and plunge Ulfric's sword into the bowed form of General Tullius. Equip the sword first if you wish.

Or refuse, leaving Galmar to do the job.

Quest Conclusion

With the Imperials firmly routed and their leadership bleeding across the Castle floor, Ulfric tells Galmar that he'll step out and give a speech to his surviving Brothers and Sisters and will take care of Jarl Elisif. He has a final gift for you as a tribute to your valor; you may keep his sword.

➤ **Leveled Weapon**

Postquest Activities

Ulfric and Galmar leave the castle to address the troops to raucous cheers. Afterward, if you ask Ulfric for any other tasks, he tells you to watch for remaining Imperial camps across Skyrim. Defeat the remnants of the Empire in Skyrim as you please. The Sons and Daughers of Skyrim will rejoice once more...with the Thalmor looking on from the shadows....

> **NOTE** If you wait a couple of days, Solitude begins to return to normal. Elisif the Fair remains as Jarl and has sworn fealty to Ulfric. Stormcloaks are stationed throughout the city, in case the Imperials send additional troops to attack (and to keep Elisif from thinking twice about where her loyalties lie).

DAEDRIC QUESTS

OVERVIEW

The Daedric Quests are unrelated to one another. Each has its own requirements, and some can only be started later in your adventure. There is no ideal time to begin one; simply seek out the ones that interest you, or complete the ones that you come across.

> **NOTE Cross-Referencing:** If you want to see maps and learn more about the traps, non-quest-related items, collectibles, crafting areas, and other important rooms of note in every location during these quests, then cross-reference the location you travel to with the information on that location contained in this guide's Atlas.

Daedric Lords

Azura: Queen of Dawn and Dusk

Boethiah: Prince of Plots

Clavicus Vile: Master of Insidious Wishes

Hermaeus Mora: Keeper of Forbidden Knowledge

Hircine: Lord of the Hunt

Malacath: Creator of Curses

Mehrunes Dagon: Prince of Destruction

Mephala: The Webspinner

Meridia: Lady of Light

Molag Bal: Lord of Corruption

Namira: Lady of Decay

Nocturnal: Mistress of Shadows

Peryite: Bringer of Pestilence

Sanguine: Lord of Revelry

Sheogorath: Prince of Madness

Vaermina: Weaver of Dreams

Available Quests

There are 15 Daedric Quests. Nocturnal's quest is part of the Thieves Guild and is detailed on page 218. Any prerequisites, as well as the Daedric Artifacts you will be rewarded with, are shown in the following table:

✓	DAEDRIC LORD	QUEST NAME	PREREQUISITES	DAEDRIC ARTIFACT
☐	Azura	The Black Star	None	Azura's Star or the Black Star
☐	Boethiah	Boethiah's Calling	Level 30	Ebony Mail
☐	Clavicus Vile	A Daedra's Best Friend	Level 10	Masque of Clavicus Vile
☐	Hermaeus Mora	Discerning the Transmundane	Level 15 (to begin Blood Harvest)	Oghma Infinium
☐	Hircine	Ill Met by Moonlight	None	Savior's Hide or Ring of Hircine
☐	Malacath	The Cursed Tribe	Level 9	Volendrung
☐	Mehrunes Dagon	Pieces of the Past	Level 20	Mehrunes' Razor
☐	Mephala	The Whispering Door	Level 20 and Complete Main Quest: Dragon Rising	Ebony Blade
☐	Meridia	The Break of Dawn	Level 12	Dawnbreaker

DAEDRIC LORD	QUEST NAME	PREREQUISITES	DAEDRIC ARTIFACT
Molag Bal	The House of Horrors	None	Mace of Molag Bal
Namira	The Taste of Death	None	Ring of Namira
Nocturnal	Thieves Guild Quests	None	Skeleton Key
Peryite	The Only Cure	Level 10	Spellbreaker
Sanguine	A Night to Remember	Level 14	Sanguine Rose
Sheogorath	The Mind of Madness	None	Wabbajack
Vaermina	Waking Nightmare	Level 14	Skull of Corruption

⟨⟩ THE BLACK STAR ⟨⟩

PREREQUISITES: None.

INTERSECTING QUESTS: Miscellaneous Objectives: Innkeepers

LOCATIONS: The College of Winterhold, Ilinalta's Deep, Shrine of Azura, Winterhold, The Frozen Hearth Inn, Azura's Star

CHARACTERS: Aranea Ienith, Azura, Colette, Dagur, Drevis, Faralda, Mirabelle, Nelacar, Nirya, Phinis, Sergius, Tolfdir

ENEMIES: Dremora, Malyn Varen, Necromancer, Skeleton

◇ **OBJECTIVES:** Miscellaneous Objective: Visit the Shrine of Azura, Find the elven mage from Aranea's vision, Speak to Nelacar, Find Azura's Star, Bring the Star to Aranea or bring the Star to Nelacar, Tell Azura you're ready to enter the Star, Tell Nelacar you're ready to enter the Star, Destroy Malyn Varen's soul

⊙ MINOR SPOILERS

▷ The Lure of Azura

On your journey throughout Skyrim, you can speak to many a barkeep (such as Hulda in Whiterun) and gain much from their scuttlebutt (Miscellaneous Objective: Innkeepers). Ask for rumors until you're told of the Shrine of Azura; the Dark Elves are said to have built it after they fled from Morrowind. It's certainly a sight to see. Check your map marker now.

◇ **MISCELLANEOUS OBJECTIVE:** Visit the Shrine of Azura
♦ **TARGET:** Shrine of Azura

At the top of the snow-covered steps under the Shrine of Azura, a single Dunmer priestess named Aranea is praying. Speak to her, and she says your visit here was destined. Agree to help, and Aranea gives you a rather cryptic message: You're to find an elven man who came to her in a vision, one who can "turn the brightest star as black as night." She suggests you look for this enchanter in Winterhold.

◇ **OBJECTIVE:** Find the elven mage from Aranea's vision
◇ **OBJECTIVE:** Speak to Nelacar
♦ **TARGET:** Nelacar, the Frozen Hearth Inn, in Winterhold

Descend into Winterhold, and start talking to the townsfolk. Speak with Colette, Dagur, Drevis, Faralda, Mirabelle, Nirya, Phinis, Tolfdir, or Sergius; they all point to an elderly elven wizard who lives inside the Frozen Hearth Inn. Enter the building, and attempt the following:

(Persuade) Inform him that a priestess of Azura sent you.

(Bribe) Pay him for his information.

(Intimidate) Pressure him into talking. When you

reach Level 6 or higher, this is an easy test to complete.

When you're successful, Nelacar begins to explain about Azura's Star. Unlike a regular Soul Gem, the Star allows any number of souls to pass through it. Nelacar discovered this the hard way while working for his master, Malyn Varen, who was experimenting with the artifact in the hope of preserving his soul and allowing him to escape his disease-ridden body. The power of the Star slowly made Malyn paranoid and impulsive (although Nelacar believes Azura was responsible for that), resulting in the deaths of several students and Malyn's banishment from the College to a place called Ilinalta's Deep.

◇ **OBJECTIVE:** Find Azura's Star
♦ **TARGET:** Ilinalta's Deep

The Elder Scrolls V
SKYRIM

 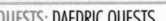

▶ Deep in Undeath

 Locate the ruined fort known as Ilinalta's Deep, and enter via the trapdoor at the top of the sunken turret. Begin trekking through the soggy interior catacombs, brandishing your best skeleton-culling weapons. You face intermittent attacks from necromancers — the remnants of Malyn's students. Follow the waterlogged corridors and gloomy altars and alcoves until you reach a large spiral staircase.

> **TIP** Consult the Atlas on page 580 for all the loot you can remove from this dungeon, which involves some underwater searching.

Climb the spiral stairs to the final resting place of Malyn Varen. Among the gold and grimoires, locate Azura's Star, which appears to be broken. Escape the Deep via the ladder in Varen's death chamber.

➤ **Broken Azura's Star**

◊ **OBJECTIVE:** Bring the Star to Aranea
♦ **TARGET:** Shrine of Azura
OR
◊ **OBJECTIVE:** Bring the Star to Nelacar
♦ **TARGET:** The Frozen Hearth Inn, in Winterhold

▶ A Star of Dark or Brightness

The quest now has two possible conclusions: A communion with Azura or a chat with an old elf enchanter.

A Communion with Azura

You can journey back to the Shrine of Azura and speak with Aranea. When the Star is placed on the altar, the daedra speaks, congratulating you on locating it but warning that the artifact is useless until Malyn Varen's soul has been purged from it. Azura offers to send you into the Star to deal with Malyn directly.

◊ **OBJECTIVE:** Tell Azura you're ready to enter the Star
♦ **TARGET:** The Star of Azura

Chat with an Old Elf Enchanter

Or you can journey back to the Frozen Hearth Inn and speak to Nelacar. After examining the Star, Nelacar discovers that Malyn Varen's soul is trapped inside. He says he can repair the Star, transforming it into a vessel that stores black souls. But first, Malyn must be purged from the device; you must be soul-trapped to deal with Malyn directly.

◊ **OBJECTIVE:** Tell Nelacar you're ready to enter the Star
♦ **TARGET:** The Star of Azura

> **NOTE** "Black souls" refer to human souls (from townsfolk, the Forsworn, or bandits) that can't ordinarily be stored in standard Soul Gems. These are used for Enchanting purposes.

No matter which of the two paths you choose, your personage is spirited away into the strange ethereal otherworld of the Star.

◊ **OBJECTIVE:** Destroy Malyn Varen's soul
♦ **TARGET:** Malyn Varen, inside the Star of Azura

After telling Malyn that he cannot escape his fate, run after him. He conjures up to three Dremora and attacks with lightning from his potent staff. Quickly nullify the enemies, and then strike down Malyn. As Malyn crumples, your spirit is transported back to Skyrim.

Malyn Varen's soul has been consigned to Oblivion. You are ready to receive an offering from either Lady Azura or Nelacar. In addition, if you're at the Shrine of Azura, you may speak with Aranea Ienith again. With her guardianship at an end, she offers to accompany you as a Follower, if you'll agree to it.

Quest Conclusion (Azura)
➤ **Azura's Star**   ➤ **Follower:** Aranea Ienith

Quest Conclusion (Nelacar)
➤ **The Black Star**

Postquest Activities

The person (Nelacar or Aranea) you didn't side with has some harsh words with you, if you meet up with them again. Aranea obviously won't become your Follower if you side with Nelacar.

> **TIP** Aranea is a very competent wizard: She has a Magic Staff of Frostbite and has focused her abilities on Conjuration and Destruction magic.

PREREQUISITES: You must be Level 30 or higher.

INTERSECTING QUESTS: None

LOCATIONS: Sacellum of Boethiah, Knifepoint Mine, Knifepoint Ridge

CHARACTERS: Boethiah

ENEMIES: Bandit, Boethiah Cultist, Champion of Boethiah, Frost Troll, Priestess of Boethiah

◊ **OBJECTIVES:** Find the shrine of Boethiah, Find the cult of Boethiah, Lead someone to become trapped by the shrine and slay them, Speak to Boethiah's Conduit, Slay the other cultists, Slay everyone at Knifepoint Ridge stealthily, Retrieve and equip the Ebony Mail

◉ MINOR SPOILERS

Congealing an Empty Vapor

Once you're an experienced adventurer (Level 32 or higher), you can join the cult of the fabled Boethiah, the Prince of Plots and original god-ancestor of the Dark Elves. This is triggered via one of the following antics:

During your searching, you (randomly) uncover a book named Boethiah's Proving and read it.

During your travels, you (randomly) encounter a Boethiah Cultist, who attacks you. Slay the cultist, search the corpse, and uncover the book. Then read it.

Or, you can simply stumble upon the Sacellum of Boethiah (although you won't have the map marker to guide you, and the location is deserted until you reach Level 32).

◊ **OBJECTIVE:** Find the shrine of Boethiah
◊ **OBJECTIVE:** Find the cult of Boethiah
♦ **TARGET:** Sacellum of Boethiah

Brave the Frost Trolls, or other weathered adversaries, as you trek up the snowy mountains east of Windhelm. Among the rocks and snow is a rudimentary arena, where those seeking the gaze of Boethiah are engaged in bloody combat. Confront a Priestess of Boethiah without resorting to combat (yet). She explains that you are an "empty vapor," unworthy of Boethiah's attention. Tell her you're not afraid of her, and you learn about Boethiah, who only cares for those who care for themselves. You are to prove that you can lie; you must find someone, gain their trust, lead them to the shrine above, and instruct your thrall to touch the Pillar of Sacrifice. This stalls your victim, who you must slay with a ceremonial dagger. If your will is strong, Boethiah will stir and you will be one of them!

➤ **Blade of Sacrifice**

◊ **OBJECTIVE:** Lead someone to become trapped by the shrine and slay them
♦ **TARGET:** Any Follower, at the Sacellum of Boethiah

Enthralling a Willing Thrall

Leave this place of violence and ponder for a moment: Which Follower is worth sacrificing to Boethiah? One who has accompanied you on many of your adventurers or one who is waiting patiently for your return? You may choose any Follower you've met during your travels. Remember the following:

If your morals prevent you from sacrificing just anyone, then choose a Follower who has annoyed you or you don't like. This doesn't affect your standing in Skyrim; it just makes you feel better about leading a friend to their death!

You must sacrifice someone to complete this quest. If your morals prevent this, perhaps the Prince of Plots isn't right for you....

If you don't suffer from this guilt or don't care who you wish to sacrifice, then anyone stupid enough to blindly follow you will do! This can be anyone you've befriended, a hireling in your service or a Housecarl appointed to you by a Jarl.

🗐 **TIP** For a complete list of Followers, consult the Training chapter. This quest involves human sacrifice and an unwilling subject. To minimize any regrets you may have about leading someone to their death, simply complete the Dark Brotherhood Quests, obtain an initiate, and sacrifice one of them.

Bring your unwitting victim back to the Sacellum of Boethiah. To avoid them dying during the trek, you may wish to Fast-Travel here. Climb up the steps to the Pillar of Sacrifice, and instruct your victim to activate it. As your Follower inspects the pillar, he is trapped by magical energy. Arm yourself with the Blade of Sacrifice (given by the Priestess), and don't finish slashing until your Follower collapses in a pool of blood. Your murder soon yields results: Boethiah possesses the bloody corpse!

🗐 **TIP** Remember! It is more fitting to murder your Follower using the Blade of Sacrifice, but any weapon will do. Point your Follower to interact with the Pillar of Sacrifice so they are standing in the correct spot before the slaying begins.

◊ **OBJECTIVE:** Speak to Boethiah's Conduit
♦ **TARGET:** Your slain Follower, at the Sacellum of Boethiah

Boethiah enters the flesh of the recently culled. Make your answers more insulting rather than sycophantic to earn a modicum of her respect. She then addresses you and the cultists who have gathered to witness your commune. She has a special task for the one who exceeds the rest—the one who is left standing. With that, she leaves your Follower's corpse, and mayhem ensues!

◊ **OBJECTIVE:** Slay the other cultists

Draw your preferred weapon, head down to the fighting pit, and begin killing the cultists. Let the shrine be bathed in blood! There are usually around five cultists to slay. You can wade in or hang back and let your fellow cultists fight among themselves before you move in to finish the wounded. Once all are dead, Boethiah possesses the last one to die and congratulates you on your ferocity in combat. If you're able to cast aside your honor, Boethiah has one more task. Her previous champion displeases her, and she wishes him replaced in the traditional fashion: You are to kill everyone at Knifepoint Ridge, as quickly and as invisibly as possible. You are but an instrument of Boethiah; showing yourself too frequently will displease her.

◊ **OBJECTIVE:** Slay everyone at Knifepoint Ridge stealthily
◊ **OBJECTIVE:** Retrieve and equip the Ebony Mail
♦ **TARGET:** All enemies and Champion of Boethiah at Knifepoint Ridge

> **NOTE** The area of Knifepoint Ridge where the Champion lurks is inaccessible prior to this quest's start, so you can't attempt an early reconnoiter of the area. Slaying foes before the start of this quest doesn't affect the number of enemies you face, either.

As You Will It, So It Shall Be

Knifepoint Ridge, in the southern hills equidistant between Markarth and Whiterun, is where you prove yourself to Boethiah. Approach the small collection of huts, tents, and guard towers and slay the bandits quickly and effectively. Don't charge in but try to remain hidden, although rampaging through here is still possible. Be sure no one is left on the surface before locating and opening the entrance to Knifepoint Mine.

> **TIP** Wait for nightfall, and use the Invisibility and Muffle spells to increase your stealthiness. Instead of taking the main road to the camp's front entrance, climb the steep slope to the southeast. Work your way around and behind the guard tower (bypassing the rock trap); this route to the Blacksmith's shed is easier. Now shoot the Champion of Boethiah through a hole in the wall!

> **TIP** If you take the side hallway that ramps down, locate a hidden path underneath the scaffolding, immediately on your left. If you sneak through here, you'll have access to a passage on the opposite side of the large chamber that winds around and exits right next to the Champion's shack. This allows you to bypass all the enemies in this area.

Once inside the mine, try the stealthy plans mentioned, sneaking and knifing foes using, for example, Sneak attacks from bows at a distance or Invisibility. There are several bottles of poison you can use, and there's an Alchemy Table in the area caged off from the large chamber; use this to make your attacks more potent or your movement more stealthy. When you reach the Champion of Boethiah, use the fire-through-the-hole tactic or approach and strike him down from behind, if you can.

Quest Conclusion

Ransack the corpse of the slain Champion for your prizes. Equip the Ebony Mail to conclude this quest. Boethiah speaks to you, exclaiming her satisfaction at the blood you spilled in her honor. Your name is to be written on Boethiah's tablet of absolute darkness, and you receive her blessing.

➤ Ebony Shield
➤ Ebony Boots
➤ Ebony Gauntlets
➤ Ebony Mail

Postquest Activities

Congratulations! Serve your new mistress well!

A DAEDRA'S BEST FRIEND

PREREQUISITES: You must be Level 10 or higher.
INTERSECTING QUESTS: None
LOCATIONS: Falkreath, Lod's House, Haemar's Shame, Haemar's Cavern, Rimerock Burrow
CHARACTERS: Barbas, Clavicus Vile, Imperial Soldier, Lod
ENEMIES: Atronach, Frostbite Spider, Sebastian Lort, Vampire, Vampire's Thrall
◊ **OBJECTIVES:** Miscellaneous: Speak to Lod, Miscellaneous: Find the dog outside Falkreath, Travel with Barbas to the shrine of Clavicus Vile, Retrieve the Rueful Axe with Barbas, Return to the shrine of Clavicus Vile with Barbas and the Rueful Axe, Give the Rueful Axe to Clavicus Vile OR Kill Barbas with the Rueful Axe

● MINOR SPOILERS

A Shaggy Dog Story

You may begin this quest once you reach Level 10. Enter the town of Falkreath and speak to an Imperial Soldier at the entrance. He asks whether you've seen a dog. Whatever your answer, he points you toward the town's Blacksmith, Lod, who has been asking about the hound. You may also go straight to Lod to begin the quest.

◇ **OBJECTIVE:** Miscellaneous Objective: Speak to Lod
♦ **TARGET:** Lod, in Falkreath

Locate Lod either inside or outside his Blacksmith's shop, and he asks whether you'd be interested in coaxing a dog that he's seen. He spotted it on the road close to town and wants to befriend it. You can:

Agree to find the creature, and Lod gives you some meat to help you gain the dog's interest.

(Persuade) Or you can agree to find the creature...for a price. If you're successful, Lod agrees, gives you half a payment and the meat.

Then exit Falkreath and locate the wolfhound with the strange bark, a dog named Barbas. You should begin the main Daedric Quest from this point, rather than returning the dog to Lod. Otherwise, Barbas won't follow you, although you can mention to Lod that the dog was more trouble than he was worth (and receive a small reward of gold).

➤ **25 gold pieces**   ➤ **Mammoth Snout**

◇ **OBJECTIVE:** Find the dog outside Falkreath
♦ **TARGET:** Barbas, on the road close to Falkreath

Speak to the dog named Barbas. Unexpectedly, the dog speaks back! The dog introduces himself as Barbas, and he has a problem you can help him with: He recently got into an argument with his master, which got a little heated, and he needs you to settle the disagreement. After his banishment, Barbas and his master can only manifest close to a shrine, and he requests you meet him there. He finishes by warning you not to trust anything his master says.

➤ **Follower:** Barbas

◇ **OBJECTIVE:** Travel with Barbas to the shrine of Clavicus Vile
♦ **TARGET:** Shrine to Clavicus Vile, inside Haemar's Shame

You and your new best friend don't have to journey to Haemar's Shrine immediately: You can commence other adventuring tasks; Barbas heads to Haemar's Shame to wait for you. Once you decide to continue this quest, trek to Haemar's Shame and enter Haemar's Cavern.

Expect a cold reception once you step into the cavern; vampires and their thralls are holed up in this maze of rock and snow. Fight or sneak your way past these creatures, until you reach a larger chamber with wooden fencing around a central hole. Head down the ramp into the hole, where you find a tunnel leading toward Haemar's Shame. Deliver a killing blow to the Frostbite Spider in the next room of jagged rocks before following lanterns and torches down a tunnel, past a room of bloodied cages, and around to a subterranean stream.

Continue up a connecting tunnel and into the main shrine chamber, where you encounter several vampires of differing strengths. Deal with them. When the area is devoid of bloodsuckers, approach the statue of Clavicus Vile, stepping over the dead offering, and activate the statue.

Vile is pleased to see you. He says that in killing his vampiric followers, you've already helped him fulfill a set of wishes—that his worshippers be cured. Mention that you're here to reunite Vile with Barbas, and the Daedric Prince's jovial nature changes. Apparently, he's sick of that "insufferable pup" but continues to listen to you, as he really doesn't want to be confined to this backwater shrine. There is a way Barbas can earn a place back at Vile's side: An incredibly powerful axe is residing somewhere deep inside Rimerock Burrow. Bring this back, and Vile insists he will grant you a reward, with "no strings attached." Agree, use the pull chain to access the exit tunnel, and exit Haemar's Shame via the quick exit.

◇ **OBJECTIVE:** Retrieve the Rueful Axe with Barbas
♦ **TARGET:** Rueful Axe, in Rimerock Burrow

A Deal with a Daedric Prince

Across the mountains, east of Solitude, is a high and precarious path carved into the side of the rocky terrain. Cross the small bridge and enter Rimerock Burrow. Draw your weapon and prepare to fight Sebastian Lort and his conjurations, who are using this remote grotto as a base. The mage and his Atronach aren't of much importance, but the Rueful Axe lying on the altar to the rear of the Burrow most certainly is. Grab it, along with any other treasure you deem valuable, and leave.

➤ **Rueful Axe**

The Elder Scrolls V
SKYRIM

◊ **OBJECTIVE:** Return to the shrine of Clavicus Vile with Barbas and the Rueful Axe

♦ **TARGET:** Shrine to Clavicus Vile, inside Haemar's Shame

Return to Haemar's Shame, and work your way through the chambers, polishing off any vampires you may have missed during your first exploration. Activate Clavicus Vile's shrine, and the Daedric Prince congratulates you on your accomplishment and your new loyal friend Barbas. Vile then says he could be persuaded to let you keep the Rueful Axe... if you use the weapon to strike Barbas down!

◊ **OBJECTIVE:** Give the Rueful Axe to Clavicus Vile OR Kill Barbas with the Rueful Axe

Quest Conclusion

At this point, you have a choice to make: give Vile the axe or kill Barbas. If you give Vile the axe, the deity is disappointed at your loyalty and at the fact that he now faces an eternity with Barbas. The dog waylays Vile's threats to turn you into a worm and insists that Vile keep his end of the bargain. He grants you his boon, as previously agreed. Barbas and his master are intertwined for an eternity.

➤ **Masque of Clavicus Vile**

If you give Barbas the axe right between his furry eyes, the deity is most pleased with your double-crossing and the fact that he doesn't have to spend an eternity with Barbas. He leaves you to use the Daedra-harming Rueful Axe.

➤ **Rueful Axe**

Postquest Activities

You can return to Lod and explain that Barbas was more trouble than he was worth, after which you're given a small reward for your time.

➤ **Leveled gold pieces**

DISCERNING THE TRANSMUNDANE

PREREQUISITES: You must be Level 15 or higher to begin the second half of this quest, flagged as "Blood Harvest" in the guide.

● MINOR SPOILERS

INTERSECTING QUESTS: College of Winterhold Quest: First Lessons, Main Quest: Elder Knowledge, Main Quest: Alduin's Bane

LOCATIONS: Alftand, Blackreach, College of Winterhold, Arcanaeum, Hall of the Elements, Septimus Signus's Outpost, Tower of Mzark, Oculory

CHARACTERS: Septimus Signus, Urag gro-Shub, Wretched Abyss (Hermaeus Mora)

ENEMIES: Dwarven Centurion, Dwarven Sphere, Dwarven Spider, Falmer

◊ **OBJECTIVES:** Ask Urag about the insane book, Find Septimus Signus, Transcribe the Lexicon, Give the Lexicon to Septimus, Harvest High Elf blood, Harvest Wood Elf blood, Harvest Dark Elf blood, Harvest Falmer blood, Harvest Orc blood, Bring blood to Septimus, Take the Oghma Infinium

▷ Acute Occult Ruminations

There are two ways you can begin this quest:

1. During Main Quest: Elder Knowledge, you are sent to the College of Winterhold in search of an Elder Scroll. Approach the entrance and speak to Faralda about gaining admittance.

2. Otherwise, you must locate Septimus Signus's Outpost on your own. Skip to the section marked 'Puppet of the Abyss' instead.

Enter the College and head into the Arcanaeum. Look for the Orc Mage named Urag gro-Shub, who runs the Arcanaeum. Although you can ask to assist him in College business (which allows you to accomplish several College-related tasks unrelated to this quest) and ask about the library, you're here to talk about the Elder Scroll. Urag isn't too happy with you offhandedly asking about such a powerful artifact. You may listen to an overview of the Scrolls before asking if there's an Elder Scroll you could use. Urag laughs at this question; he wouldn't show it to the likes of you, even if he obtained one. Ask if he at least has any information on them. He agrees to locate a couple of arcane tomes that may have some clues. But mostly they contain ravings leavened with rumor and conjecture.

Urag gro-Shub locates and places two tomes on the nearby desk: *Effects of the Elder Scrolls* and *Ruminations on the Elder Scrolls*. After reading both books (which you may keep or leave on the desk), you find that the *Ruminations* tome is the work of a madman. Daedric Quest: Discerning the Transmundane now begins, and your objective updates:

➤ **Effects of the Elder Scrolls**   ➤ **Ruminations on the Elder Scrolls**

◊ **OBJECTIVE:** Ask Urag about the insane book

Tell Urag that the *Ruminations* book is incomprehensible. He doesn't seem surprised; after all, this book was the work of Septimus Signus. Although Signus was a master on the nature of Elder Scrolls, Urag tells you that he's "been gone for a long while." You suspect he means both mentally and physically. Signus currently resides north of the College in the treacherous Ice Fields.

◊ **OBJECTIVE:** Find Septimus Signus

♦ **TARGET:** Septimus Signus's Outpost

▷ Puppet of the Abyss

The giant chunks of ice floating off the Sea of Ghosts are your next destination. Exit the College and run to the frigid waters. Hop across the floating ice, making your way north. Expect to slice into a few wild animals along the way. Septimus Signus's Outpost is an odd little door cut into a hill-sized iceberg, close to a moored rowboat. Climb down the ladder and the slope to reach a lone mage in a chamber of ice, alone with his books and thoughts. He appears to be studying some kind of Dwemer box about the size of a house.

Ask Septimus about the Elder Scrolls if you want him to deliver a rapid-fire barrage of knowledge on the subject. Ask where the Scroll is again, and after receiving moderately useless information, ask once more (either pleasantly or with a more threatening tone). Septimus agrees to tell you, but in return, you must venture into Blackreach, a giant underground Dwemer city that lies below several Dwarven ruins hidden across Skyrim. Ask about getting into Blackreach, and Septimus keeps up his riddle-based prattling and hands you two items: The first is an odd-edged lexicon, used by the Dwemer for inscribing. The second is an Attunement Sphere, which apparently "sings" when you near an important Dwemer door. Once these are in your grasp, your Main Quest updates. Stay and speak further with Septimus if your sanity can stand it.

➤ **Attunement Sphere**   ➤ **Blank Lexicon**

◊ **OBJECTIVE:** Transcribe the Lexicon
♦ **TARGET:** Daedric Quest, in Blackreach
◊ **MAIN QUEST OBJECTIVE:** Recover the Elder Scroll
♦ **TARGET:** Tower of Mzark

 NOTE   This quest continues only after you enter the gargantuan subterranean Dwemer city of Blackreach. The optimal path to reach this sprawling cavern is detailed in Main Quest: Elder Knowledge. These both require you to secure the Attunement Sphere from Septimus, which is the only way to access Blackreach.

After you secure the Attunement Sphere and Blank Lexicon from Septimus, locate Alftand on the glacial mountains southwest of Winterhold. Enter and head through the Alftand Glacial Ruins, battling Dwarven Spheres and Dwarven Spiders. Maneuver through the tower and connecting chambers of the Alftand Animonculory (opening the elevator back to the Glacial Ruins as you go), and battle the Dwarven Centurion in the Alftand Cathedral to reach an elevator (opening the exit back up to the surface first). Descend back into the cathedral and use the Attunement Sphere to activate the Dwarven Mechanism to access the hidden entrance to Blackreach.

 TIP   Alftand is only one of several entrances to Blackreach. Consult the Atlas to see all of the ways to enter this subterranean citadel and the Tower of Mzark.

Enter Blackreach and keep a steady pace along the cobblestone pathways, heading in a westerly direction. You're looking for a massive vertical stone elevator shaft that pierces the roof of this massive underground complex.

When you find it, pull the lever and head into the Tower of Mzark. Venture into a gigantic, circular Aedrome chamber, which is dominated by a huge sphere. This appears to be some kind of massive Oculory, with a variety of focusing lenses and other golden machinery attached.

Head to the cluster of controls on the platform above the Oculory. The controls are comprised of five cylindrical devices: a Lexicon Receptacle and four positioning buttons embedded in pedestals. There is a knack to using these devices to produce something hidden in one of the lenses.

Puzzle solution: Activate the Lexicon Receptacle, so the Blank Lexicon rests on top of it. The two pedestals to the Receptacle's right—the only ones currently active—open and close the Oculory lenses. Press the taller of the two pedestals (right of the middle one with the lens chart on it) three or four times, until the pedestal with the blue button to the left of the middle one starts to glow. Move to this new pedestal. At this point, the Blank Lexicon will also be glowing blue. The two pedestals to the Receptacle's left—the taller of which is now active—control the ceiling lens array. Press the button of the taller, left pedestal twice, until the button on the far-left smaller pedestal begins to glow. Now press that button, and a large set of lens crystals descends from the ceiling, stops, and the main crystal rotates and splits apart to reveal some kind of tubelike carrying device.

Drop from the balcony controls, and approach the open lens crystal. Take the Elder Scroll from its elaborate compartment. Once you've taken the Elder Scroll, your path diverges, but only if Main Quest: Elder Knowledge is currently active. If it is, Main Quest: Alduin's Bane begins, and your next plan is to take the Scroll to the summit of the Throat of the World, and read it there. However, for this quest, Septimus is more concerned with the transcription etched onto the Lexicon. Retrieve the Lexicon from the receptacle; don't leave without it!

➤ **Elder Scroll**   ➤ **Runed Lexicon**

◊ **OBJECTIVE:** Give the Lexicon to Septimus

▶ Blood Harvest

Leave the Tower of Mzark by the elevator at the end of the corridor under the pedestals, which ascends to Skyrim's surface. Trek back to the Sea of Ghosts and enter Septimus Signus's Outpost. Septimus is still happily talking to himself; interrupt so he talks to you, and tell him you've inscribed the Lexicon. Apparently, the sealing structure interlocks in the tiniest fractals. That obviously means something to Signus, who needs Dwemer blood to loosen these interlocking hooks. However, as the Dwemer are long dead, your next task is to search for a panoply of their brethren. Septimus wants blood! He hands you an Extractor and lists the races related to the Dwemer of which he requires blood. Before you leave, you may ask him further questions about the giant box he paces beside.

➤ **Essence Extractor**

◊ **OBJECTIVE:** Harvest High Elf blood
◊ **OBJECTIVE:** Harvest Wood Elf blood
◊ **OBJECTIVE:** Harvest Dark Elf blood
◊ **OBJECTIVE:** Harvest Falmer blood
◊ **OBJECTIVE:** Harvest Orc blood

 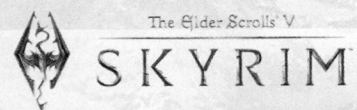

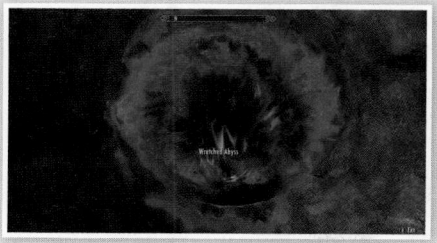

As you reach the Outpost exit, you see a strange mist that quickly congeals into a frightening void. This is the Wretched Abyss, and it coaxes you forward, wanting you to bask in its presence. When you ask what it is, it replies that it is but an aspect of Hermaeus Mora, who has been watching you. He tells you that once the giant Dwemer lockbox has been opened, Septimus will have outlived his usefulness. When that time comes, you may take his place as Hermaeus Mora's emissary. You can agree or refuse. Either way, you won't need to choose until after you open the box. The Abyss retracts, allowing you to leave.

At this point, you may wish to continue other quests; finding all this blood is an adventure unto itself, and one that is much easier once you realize where you can harvest with impunity!

Obviously, the danger comes with slaughtering an innocent in broad daylight, and usually within a Hold City's walls, which isn't recommended at all. For this reason, there are other possible places look:

	RACE	OPTIMAL LOCATIONS	NOTES
☐	High Elf	Hob's Fall Cave, Yngvild, world encounters, any Warlock lair	High Elves appear as Warlocks, so slay enemies rather than townsfolk.
☐	Dark Elf	Hob's Fall Cave, Yngvild, world encounters, any Warlock lair	Dark Elves appear as Warlocks, so slay enemies rather than townsfolk.
☐	Wood Elf	Pinepeak Cavern or any hunter camp	You can find a dead Wood Elf lying on the rocks just outside the entrance to Pinepeak Cavern, across the bridge from Ivarstead. When assaulting a hunter camp, one in four hunters is a Wood Elf.
☐	Falmer	Blackreach, Falmer Hives, any Dwarven Ruins	You can return to Blackreach easily, making this blood simple to spill.
☐	Orc	Cracked Tusk Keep, Rift Watchtower, or any bandit camp	Slay the hostile Orcs in these locations, rather than the friendly Orcs in Strongholds.

> **TIP** Double-check every figure you meet during wilderness treks, and slay them if they're one of the races mentioned.

◊ **OBJECTIVE:** Bring blood to Septimus

Once your blood-siphoning trek is complete, return to the iceberg on the Sea of Ghosts, and revisit Septimus once more. Inform him that you have the blood samples he requires. He takes them and quickly mixes them up before approaching the massive Dwemer box. It rotates, and telescopes open into an otherworldly passage. Septimus races up this corridor, into a chamber of circles, and approaches an odd book. He reaches out to take it but suddenly disintegrates into a pile of ash.

◊ **OBJECTIVE:** Take the Oghma Infinium

Quest Conclusion

Step into the chamber and take the book. You are instantly bombarded with a knowledge intake that could hemorrhage the brains of lesser mortals. You may look into this unspeakable tome and live, or choose to close the book. Your knowledge is increased by an impressive amount, and this translates into skill increases for associated abilities. Here's how this breaks down:

Elect not to read: No benefits.

Read the Path of Might: +5 in all skills of this path (Smithing, Heavy Armor, Block, Two-Handed, One-Handed, Archery)

Read the Path of Shadow: +5 in all skills of this path (Light Armor, Sneak, Lockpicking, Pickpocket, Speech, Alchemy)

Read the Path of Magic: +5 in all skills of this path (Illusion, Conjuration, Destruction, Restoration, Alteration, Enchanting)

As you try to leave the box, the Wretched Abyss appears. You can elect to work wonders together as Hermaeus Mora's champion or disavow any agreement with the Daedric Prince.

Postquest Activities

You can embrace Hermaeus Mora, or deny him all you want; you are still doing his will.

ILL MET BY MOONLIGHT

PREREQUISITES: None.

INTERSECTING QUESTS: None

LOCATIONS: Bloated Man's Grotto, Falkreath, Falkreath Barracks, Falkreath Jail, Peak's Shade Tower,

CHARACTERS: Aspect of Hircine, Hircine, Hunters of Hircine, Indara Caerelia, Mathies Caerelia, Sinding

ENEMIES: Hunters of Hircine, Sinding, White Stag

◊ **OBJECTIVES:** Speak to Sinding, Kill the great beast, Begin the hunt, Hunt or Spare Sinding, Skin Sinding, Speak to Hircine, Kill the Hunters, Talk to Sinding

◉ MINOR SPOILERS

The Curse of Falkreath

For such a modest town, Falkreath has a sizable cemetery. As you enter this location, a burial ceremony is under way for a young girl. Instead of marching right in and interrogating everyone, you may listen to the townsfolk and gain some insight. Speak to the parents of the slain child — Indara Caerelia or her husband, Mathies. Either will tell you that their daughter was ripped apart by a man named Sinding, a laborer passing through this Hold. If you can stand to look upon him, you're told where he is. If you miss the burial, find Mathies or his wife tending to crops near their home.

> ◇ **OBJECTIVE:** Speak to Sinding
> ♦ **TARGET:** Sinding, inside Falkreath Barracks

Visit the Falkreath Barracks and locate Sinding in the jail. The man explains he suffers from lycanthropy and was in werewolf form during the attack. He is remorseful about his murderous infanticide. He tells you he lost control and needed to be restrained. He blames this on a cursed ring he acquired. It belongs to Hircine (the Daedric Lord of the Hunt). Sinding was told it could help him control his transformations, but instead it caused them to occur sporadically and at the most inopportune times. Sinding seeks to appease Hircine by returning the ring. He says legend holds that Hircine will appear to any who can slay a legendary beast that roams these woods. The beast in question is close by. Agree to take the ring to Hircine.

> ◇ **RING OF HIRCINE (CURSED)**

> ◇ **OBJECTIVE:** Kill the great beast
> ♦ **TARGET:** The White Stag, in the woods close to Falkreath

> **CAUTION** ▷
> Beware the power of Hircine! With the ring in your possession, it cannot be removed. It is both powerful and cursed. If you are already a werewolf (as part of the Companions Quests) and you're outside a dungeon or city, every minute there is a 10 percent chance you will turn into your wolf form.

The Lord of the Hunt Smiles on You

The great beast of the forest is usually close to the path in the woods surrounding Peak's Shade Tower, but it moves constantly. Long-range weapons, such as magic or a bow, are an obvious advantage. Pursue the White Stag, and hunt it until your shots bring it down. Approach the slain animal, and a manifestation of Hircine appears. Speak to the Aspect of Hircine, and he recognizes the ring you carry. Hircine tells you Sinding has fled and gone into hiding, and a Great Hunt has been called to slay him. Hircine charges you to find this rogue shifter, tear the skin from his body, and bring it as an offering to him. He mentions there is a spot of competition to win Hircine's favor, and there's no time to dillydally.

> ◇ **OBJECTIVE:** Begin the hunt
> ♦ **TARGET:** Bloated Man's Grotto

Sinding has fled to Bloated Man's Grotto, a cave on the southern rim of the Tundra, just north of Lake Ilinalta. Journey there, and enter the grounds of this interior forest. The sky is bloodred and swirled with clouds. The Bloodmoon looms overhead. Hircine's power is focused on this place. As the entrance cave opens up, you spot a campsite where a group of hunters lie in pools of blood. A Khajiit named J'Kier greets you as a fellow hunter. Though badly lacerated, he explains that the prey is too strong, but more hunters have come to slay the monster and gain Hircine's favor. J'Kier then passes. You can check on Batum gra-Bar, Ma'tasarr, and Hoddreid, but the rest of the hunting party has died. Sinding is a considerable force in this forest.

> ◇ **OBJECTIVE:** Hunt or Spare Sinding
> ♦ **TARGET:** Sinding, in Bloated Man's Grotto

The path to the left has been blocked by some fallen trees, so continue down the path past the pond. You hear a roar from up ahead and turn a corner to see Sinding standing atop a rocky outcrop. He doesn't attack you immediately. You can:

Charge in, ignoring any conversation Sinding attempts to have with you. This begins Path 1.

Ignore any conversation topics and attempt to kill Sinding, as Hircine has requested. This also begins Path 1.

Or, tell Sinding you've been sent to kill him. While he understands he can't stop you, he promises not to return to civilization to inadvertently murder anyone else. Spare his life (which begins Path 2), or kill him for defying Hircine (which also begins Path 1).

Path 1: Ending the Sins of Sinding

If you tell Sinding that he has to die or attack him at any time, you are fulfilling Hircine's request. Sinding flees to the ruins atop the hill, leaving you to give chase. The hunt is now on! Stalk your furry prey, using any means at your disposal. Quicken your pace by utilizing the Slow Time and Whirlwind Sprint Shouts, or you can simply run to Sinding instead (supplement your sprint with some Fortify or Restore Stamina potions). If you're only relying on your nonaugmented sprinting, you'll barely match Sinding's pace.

Continue to track and keep pace with Sinding as he clears the ruins, drops down, and slaughters two hunters in the first clearing. You may catch him here if you're swift and engage in a brief combat, but he flees after a few strikes. Pursue the beast into a second clearing, where three more hunters wait, and then into a third clearing where you find an additional three hunters. Attempt combat in all three locations.

> **TIP** They don't stand a chance against Sinding, but if you hold his attention, the damage the hunters deal can help whittle down Sinding's considerable constitution. Any hunters that survive combat when Sinding moves on will follow you into the next clearing.

In the third clearing, Sinding finally stands his ground. With the help of any surviving hunters, bring down your quarry.

> **TIP** Is Sinding becoming a problem to slay? Are you being pulverized by his sharp claws? Then check the terrain; Bloated Man's Grotto has numerous cliffs, and Sinding doesn't have any ranged attacks. If you can clamber up to the mountainous area (particularly the promontory) in the center of this grotto, you can run along the top of the cliffs, sniping Sinding to death. Which is hardly sporting, but very effective!

◊ **OBJECTIVE:** Skin Sinding
◊ **OBJECTIVE:** Speak to Hircine

After you tear the skin from Sinding's body, Hircine appears in Sinding's form and thanks you for your offering. Satisfied that Sinding has been cast from this world, the Lord of the Hunt transforms the skin into his legendary artifact, the Savior's Hide, and gives it to you as a reward.

➤ **Sinding's Skin**

Path 2: Taking the Side of Sinding

◊ **OBJECTIVE:** Kill the Hunters

Inform Sinding that you will spare his life: Sinding is thankful, but there is little time to lose; more hunters have appeared and must be defeated. Sinding waits for you on the promontory. Head up the stairs on your right and join forces with him, then head through the ruins to reach the first group of hunters. There are two in the first clearing, three in the second, and three more in the third.

> **TIP** If you side with Sinding but attack him at any time later on, Path 1 is your only option. Devious, underhanded scoundrels may wish to time their betrayal of Sinding at just the right moment—when he's badly wounded by hunters! This is far less work for you but displays appalling sportsmanship!

◊ **OBJECTIVE:** Talk to Sinding

Speak with Sinding, and he is grateful for your help. But when you leave the Grotto, you find yourself face to face with Hircine once more. No matter your answers, he is satisfied by the hunt, and removes the curse on the ring.

Quest Conclusion

If you sided with Hircine, you receive the Savior's Hide.

➤ **Savior's Hide**

If you sided with Sinding, you keep Hircine's ring.

➤ **Ring of Hircine**

Postquest Activities

If you obtained the Savior's Hide, the ring is removed. If you sided with Sinding, you keep the ring, which is no longer cursed. It grants you an additional werewolf transformation per day (but only if you're a werewolf), and you don't need to worry about uncontrollable transformations!

THE CURSED TRIBE

PREREQUISITES: You must be Level 9 or higher.
INTERSECTING QUESTS: None
LOCATIONS: Fallowstone Cave, Giant's Grove, Largashbur
CHARACTERS: Atub, Chief Yamarz, Gularzob, Malacath, Ugor
ENEMIES: Cave Bear, Giant
◊ **OBJECTIVES:** Bring Troll Fat and a Daedra Heart to Atub, Observe Atub's ritual, Speak with Yamarz, Meet Yamarz at Fallowstone Cave, Protect Yamarz, Defeat the giant, Take Shagrol's Warhammer back to Largashbur, Place Shagrol's Warhammer on the shrine in Largashbur

⊙ MINOR SPOILERS

▷ Keeper of Oaths, Master of Curses

Largashbur is a stronghold in the southwestern corner of the Rift and is home to a tribe of distrustful Orcs. As you approach, the Orcs are engaged in a battle with a giant. You can watch as they eventually take the giant down or step in and help (but be very careful you don't target the Orcs fighting). After the skirmish, Ugor—one of the gate guards—demands that you leave at once. Her anger is tempered by the slightly more levelheaded Atub, who you should speak with. Ask her what is going on, and she quickly (and uncharacteristically) reveals that her tribe is suffering and needs help.

Atub

It seems the tribe's once-powerful chief, Yamarz, is now stricken and cursed. This weakens the tribe, and the giants sense this: The stronghold has suffered from constant giant attacks. Yamarz has demanded the tribe remain within the walls of Largashbur, and Atub wishes to petition Malacath to lift this curse. As she cannot travel to the shrine, the ritual must be performed within Largashbur, but Atub lacks some materials needed; in particular she requires Troll Fat and a Daedra Heart.

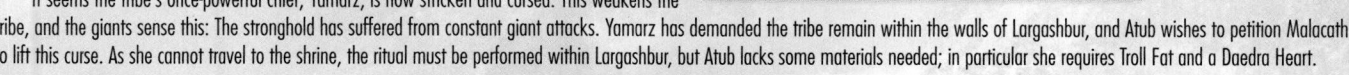

Troll Fat Finding: This is a relatively easy material to find. Simply locate an area where trolls (regular or Frost) roam, defeat one, and then search the corpse for the Troll Fat you need. There are always a couple of these powerful beasts roaming the exterior of Labyrinthian.

➤ **Troll Fat**

Daedra Heart Hunting: This is harder. Plunging your hand into a dead Dremora is the easy part; finding one is not. Try the following places:

   During Daedric Quests: The Black Star and Pieces of the Past.

   These occasionally show up in a vendor's list.

Enthir in the College of Winterhold always has one or two for sale, but at an inflated price.

If stealing appeals to you, find one in Kodlak's room in Jorrvaskr (Whiterun).

Or, steal one from the altar in the Hall of the Vigilant (in the Pale Hold).

Or, steal one from the Alchemy Room of the Nightcaller Temple (during Daedric Quest: Waking Nightmare).

➤ **Daedra Heart**

◊ **OBJECTIVE:** Observe Atub's ritual

Once you return with both materials for the ritual, Atub thanks you and beckons you into Largashbur. An enraged Ugor yells at Atub for bringing an outsider into the stronghold, but Atub calms her, allowing you safe passage into the settlement. She walks across the dirt yard and into the longhouse. Chief Yamarz is usually inside and takes an immediate disliking to you. Speak with him, and he keeps the insults flowing and complains about his cursed lack of sleep. Atub approaches and tells him it is time for the ritual to begin.

After Atub commences the ritual, Malacath's booming voice soon resonates around the camp. Most of the Daedric Prince's venom is directed at Yamarz, who is called weak, small, and an embarrassment. Furthermore, the Orcs have let giants overrun Malacath's shrine. This is an outrage! Yamarz is ordered to bring back the leader's club as an offering. Only then will Malacath consider lifting the curse. The ritual concludes, and Yamarz agrees to this task. But first, he wants a word with you.

◊ **OBJECTIVE:** Speak with Yamarz

Blaming you for Malacath's task, Yamarz demands that you help him. You're to act as his bodyguard, ensuring he doesn't have any trouble reaching the giant. And just so you're clear, he'll definitely be killing the giant's leader himself; he just wants you to handle any attackers along the way. He agrees to make it worth your while. Whether you agree or not is immaterial; you are to meet Yamarz at the entrance to the giants' lair, which leads to Malacath's shrine.

◊ **OBJECTIVE:** Meet Yamarz at Fallowstone Cave

⬨ Malacath's Proving Grounds

Fallowstone Cave is nestled in the foothills of the Velothi Mountains, northeast of Riften. You may trek there with Chief Yamarz, fending off any attacks as you cross the thick forest of birch and pine trees, or you can Fast-Travel (or ride) to the cave entrance and wait for Yamarz to appear. Your chaperoning begins after you enter the cave.

◊ **OBJECTIVE:** Protect Yamarz
♦ **TARGET:** Chief Yamarz, throughout Fallowstone Cave

Enter the cave. Yamarz reluctantly sets off down the tunnel. Follow a few paces or two behind him as the tunnel opens into a gloriously immense subterranean cavern, complete with a waterfall to your left and a series of large, natural steps down to a lower lake area. Follow Yamarz over the small natural bridge and down the steps. Continue to the grotto floor. At the grotto's far end is a campfire and a giant wandering the area. Yamarz avoids the area, and heads along the rushing stream, into a connecting tunnel.

TIP There's no need to confront the giant; if you wish to slay one, wait until this objective completes and backtrack to fight them, rather than risk Yamarz's health.

Head down the stream into a smaller grotto lagoon, where you see a second giant. Avoid it unless it charges you both, and then follow the cave tunnel on the southeastern wall. Enter and scramble up the dirt tunnel, to a confrontation with a couple of wild animals (usually cave bears). The bears are roaming an area of corpses and half-digested food at the entrance to a gap in the southwest tunnel wall. Follow Yamarz up here and into Giant's Grove.

Move alongside Yamarz, following a path of skeletal remains and bloodstains in the snow, until he stops and turns to you, telling you he's ready to kill the giant—that is, of course, unless you want to make some extra gold. Yamarz has a proposition for you: If you face the giant and kill it, he'll simply return to the tribe and tell them he was responsible. They'll be none the wiser, and you'll be all the richer. You can:

   Refuse, telling Yamarz that he is the one who is supposed to kill the giant to lift the curse. He reluctantly agrees and rushes toward the campfire and the giant guarding a large shrine statue of Malacath. Moments later, Yamarz is caught by the giant's club and is crushed, sprawled dead on the snow. You now need to face the giant yourself.

   Agree, and rush toward the large campfire and the giant with your weapons drawn.

◊ **OBJECTIVE:** Defeat the giant

Kill the giant using the same techniques you've used countless times before. Remember to use the landscape to your advantage, finding cover so your Stamina recharges. After you destroy this giant leader, search the corpse for a massive hammer. This is the weapon Malacath ordered Yamarz to return to Largashbur.

➤ **Shagrol's Warhammer**

◇ **OBJECTIVE:** Take Shagrol's Warhammer back to Largashbur

Head back toward the exit of Giant's Grove. If you agreed to kill the giant for Chief Yamarz, he is here, ready to welch on his agreement. He can't have the likes of you usurping his authority and mentioning you were responsible for the giant's death. Yamarz attacks and must be killed.

Either way, when both Chief Yamarz and the giant leader are dead, Malacath speaks to you from his shrine effigy, impressed by your fighting prowess.

Atub greets you at the gate to Largashbur. She asks what happened to Yamarz. You can tell the truth or give a slightly skewed account of events in which Yamarz was a brave fighter instead of the sniveling backstabber he actually was. Either way, Atub walks toward the shrine,

Malacath's voice ringing around the camp. The Daedric Prince is willing to give this motley band of Orcs a chance and appoints Gularzob (Yamarz's son) as chief. Malacath finally insists that you place the hammer on the shrine.

◇ **OBJECTIVE:** Place Shagrol's Warhammer on the shrine in Largashbur

Quest Conclusion

Approach the skull on the trunk and place the hammer on its antlers. Malacath is satisfied and replaces the hammer with an exceptional weapon named Volendrung, which you can wield!

➤ **Volendrung**

Postquest Activities

Volendrung is a massive warhammer with an Absorb Stamina enchantment. This allows you to inflict power attacks without stopping for as long as it has a charge! As Malacath's champion, you can take this. Malacath then names Gularzob as the new chief, and all the remaining Orcs are now friendly toward you. As Malacath's champion, you are also blood-kin to the other Orcs as well and don't have to complete Side Quest: Forgemaster's Fingers to gain acceptance in any Orc stronghold.

PIECES OF THE PAST

● **MINOR SPOILERS**

PREREQUISITES: You must be Level 20 or higher
INTERSECTING QUESTS: None
LOCATIONS: Cracked Tusk Keep, Cracked Tusk Vaults, Dawnstar, Silus Vesuius's House , (aka the Museum of the Mythic Dawn), Dead Crone Rock, Hag Rock Redoubt, Hag Rock Redoubt Ruin, Morthal, Jorgen and Lami's House, Shrine of Mehrunes Dagon
CHARACTERS: Courier, Jorgen, Lami, Madena, Mehrunes Dagon, Silus Vesuius
ENEMIES: Cave Bear, Drascua, Forsworn, Forsworn Briarheart, Ghunzul, Orc Bandit, Orc Hunter, Snow Bear
◇ **OBJECTIVES:** Miscellaneous: Visit the museum in Dawnstar, Speak to Silus inside his house, Retrieve the pommel of Mehrunes' Razor, Retrieve the blade shards of Mehrunes' Razor, Retrieve the hilt of Mehrunes' Razor, Bring the pommel stone to Silus, Bring the blade shards to Silus, Bring the hilt to Silus, Meet Silus at the Shrine of Mehrunes Dagon, Speak to Mehrunes Dagon, Kill Silus, Reforge Mehrunes' Razor, Claim Mehrunes' Razor

▶ Dead Oaths on Dead Lips

When you reach Level 20, visit any city in Skyrim; Riverwood is a fine example. When you reach the city, a courier approaches and delivers a message regarding the opening of a new museum up in Dawnstar. The owner is handing out invitations; you can visit at your earliest convenience. This doesn't begin the quest yet, just a Miscellaneous Objective that piques your interest.

◇ **MISCELLANEOUS OBJECTIVE:** Visit the museum in Dawnstar
♦ **TARGET:** Silus Vesuius's House, in Dawnstar

As you near Silus Vesuius's House in Dawnstar, he is out on the porch having a heated discussion with Dawnstar's Court Wizard, Madena. The argument centers around Silus refusing to bury his family's legacy. Madena eventually gives up talking to him and leaves, allowing you to greet Silus and visit the Museum of the Mythic Dawn. You can ask him more about it, and he reveals it contains artifacts from a group that once toppled an Empire. Silus also has a job you'd be perfect for. This quest now officially begins.

◇ **OBJECTIVE:** Speak to Silus inside his house
♦ **TARGET:** The Museum of the Mythic Dawn, in Dawnstar

The museum takes up about two-thirds of Silus's house. You are free to peruse the cabinets before speaking to Silus; he offers commentary as you inspect each display case. You discover the tapestries were hung in hideouts where the mysterious Mythic Dawn would meet and plot. The scabbard has Oblivion Gate iconography etched into it, a key symbol of Mehrunes Dagon, the patron Daedra. The case of books are commentaries on the Mysterium Xarxes, written by the cult's leader, Mankar Camoran. The burned paper is all that remains of the fabled Mysterium Xarxes, the blasphemous book written by Mehrunes Dagon. Finally, the robes were worn during the Mythic Dawn's secret meetings, where they plotted to bring Dagon into Tamriel.

With the tour over, you can speak with Silus about the Mythic Dawn and the museum. But asking about the job is the most important question. Silus tells you that after the Oblivion Crisis, groups began to appear that were dedicated to wiping out what was left of the Mythic Dawn. One of these groups found Mehrunes' Razor, the artifact of Dagon. After splitting this razor into three fragments, the pieces were dispersed. Silus wants the pieces reunited. You're here to remove the fragments from their current owners—two dangerous marauders named Ghunzul and Drascua and a resident of Morthal named Jorgen. Silus hands you notes about each of them and will gladly pay for any pieces you bring back to him.

➤ **The Keepers of the Razor**

◇ **OBJECTIVE:** Retrieve the pommel of Mehrunes' Razor
♦ **TARGET:** Drascua, in Dead Crone Rock
◇ **OBJECTIVE:** Retrieve the blade shards of Mehrunes' Razor
♦ **TARGET:** Ghunzul, in Cracked Tusk Keep
◇ **OBJECTIVE:** Retrieve the hilt of Mehrunes' Razor
♦ **TARGET:** Jorgen, in Morthal

Daedric Defragmentation

> **TIP** You may have already explored these main locations and found a fragment. If you investigate the areas and the fragment isn't there, check your inventory.

Part 1: Drascua's Pommel

Far to the west, just southwest of Markarth, is Hag Rock Redoubt. Begin the long ascension, passing under a couple of buttress overhangs while tackling the Forsworn that are swarming this location. Continue up the slopes, passing under two stone arches with carved heads atop each side; beware of cave bears in these parts. At this point, you can:

Proceed directly to Dead Crone Rock by weaving through the exterior Forsworn Camp.

Or you can follow the pathway up to an old ceremonial crypt and sacrificial area sunk into the side of the mountain, and enter the iron door into Hag Rock Redoubt Ruin. Inside, the Forsworn have erected sharpened wood spikes and attack viciously when you maneuver into their eating area. Clear this place of foes (or sneak by) before using the spiral stairs to reach an upper corridor and a circular storage room containing a Forsworn Briarheart. Then head southwest, around the corridor to the ruin's exit.

You arrive on the roof of the interior ruin. This stone plateau is dominated by steps to ascend and a small Forsworn camp to raze or ignore. Climb the steps until you reach the exterior of Dead Crone Rock, a granite fortification toward the slope's top. Head up the stairs to the first level, which consists of a corridor, more Forsworn, and spiral stairs up to the main floor. A circular chamber atop the spiral stairs has its main exit (to the southwest) blocked by a portcullis. Raise it by fighting through a chamber with a long, bloody sacrificial table and into a connecting room with a lever. Pull the lever to raise the portcullis before leaving by the now-open exit that ends in a wooden door.

You appear at the base of more steps. These lead to the top of Dead Crone Rock, where the Hagraven Drascua resides. Attack with your preferred weapons until she yields. Search her corpse for the pommel and the Dead Crone Rock Key, which opens the locked gate in the previous interior fortification you climbed through. Also, absorb another Word of Power from the nearby Word Wall.

> **CAUTION**
> Beware of magic traps in this general area; fire shoots from Soul Gems on pedestals; rush and grab the gem to stop the fire or flee past.

➤ **Pommel stone of Mehrunes' Razor**   ➤ **Dead Crone Rock Key**
➤ **Word of Power:** Dismaying Shout

◇ **OBJECTIVE:** Bring the pommel stone to Silus
♦ **TARGET:** Silus Vesuius's House, in Dawnstar

Part 2: Ghunzul's Blade Shards

Journey into Falkreath Hold and approach Cracked Tusk Keep. There are usually two Orcs standing guard on the watchtowers. Pick them off with arrows or spells from a distance to soften up the Keep's defenses. Then climb over the dilapidated fortifications, or use the front gate for a less-subtle entry if you aren't concerned about stealth. Expect a trio of Orc hunters and bandits on guard here. These shouldn't prove too difficult to overcome. Your main access point into the Keep is the door to the southwest, in the middle of the main inner Keep wall. An alternate entrance to the right (west) is locked (Adept) and allows you to avoid the confrontation with Ghunzul.

Once inside, prepare to attack more Orc enemies in the two-floor storage and dining area, with a door in the southeastern wall. This leads to a fireplace and bedroom, Ghunzul's usual location (although he may be wandering the Keep's interior).

He's brandishing a particularly impressive two-handed weapon, so prepare for intense combat in a confined space. Continue fighting until you beat Ghunzul to death. Alternatively, you can try pickpocketing the Orc if your Sneak skills are truly impressive. Either way, Ghunzul is carrying an important key on him.

➤ **Cracked Tusk Vault Key**

> **TIP** If you just want the Shards and can unlock the Expert-locked cage on your own, you can avoid Ghunzul completely. Or, defeat Ghunzul to make the unlocking a lot easier!

Return to the raised dining room. This time take the door on the lower level to the northwest, which leads down into a small barrel-storing cellar and passage. Ignore the door leading back outside (this is the western entrance from the exterior), and inspect the cage,

which is blocking your path to the southwest. Use the Vault Key (or an exceptional Lockpick [Expert]) to unlock the cage, releasing the vertical spike bars. When the spikes recede, descend to and open the door to Cracked Tusk Vaults.

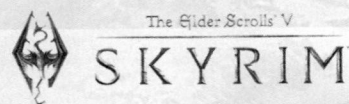

Head down the stairs and into the slightly soggy underground vault. The way ahead is blocked by several spear bars. Pull the two levers to either side of the passage to release both sets of spears. Then carefully walk forward, cutting instead of triggering the two trip wires that release darts up and into you. Or, run through and step to the side. Now approach the pedestal with the blade shards on it, and grab them before moving backward quickly, thus avoiding a flurry of additional darts. Now retrace your steps back out into Skyrim.

> **TIP** If you stop after breaking each trip wire, the darts fire harmlessly in front of you. Avoid the dart traps entirely by sidestepping left just inside the door, but watch for a trip wire to the side that triggers a wall trap.

➤ **Shards of Mehrunes' Razor**

◊ **OBJECTIVE:** Bring the blade shards to Silus
♦ **TARGET:** Silus Vesuius's House, in Dawnstar

Part 3: Jorgen's Hilt

The hilt of the Razor is the easiest to obtain. It involves traveling to Morthal and locating Jorgen, who runs the mill. He doesn't have time to talk but stops when you tell him what you're looking for. He plays dumb until you mention Silus's name. He tells you he's not about to let that Razor out of his locked house after his family spent eight generations keeping it safe. At this point, you can:

Jorgen

(Persuade) Tell him he won't miss it.

(Bribe) Pay a large amount of gold for securing it.

(Intimidate) Or demand the hilt, before matters take a turn for the worse. This is easy once you reach Level 26 or higher. If you fail, you'll need to brawl until he agrees. That's "brawl," not "kill"!

(Lockpick) Or you can find Jorgen's house without his help and pick any locks needed to reach the hilt.

Succeed in any of the first three options, and you're hastily given the keys to the chest in Jorgen's house and told not to hurt his family.

➤ **Key to Jorgen and Lami's House** ➤ **Key to Jorgen's Chest**

Whether you have Jorgen's keys or not, the next stop is Jorgen's house, which is opposite the sawmill. Pick the lock (Novice) or use one of the keys, and step inside, ignoring Lami. Inspect and open Jorgen's Chest (Adept) at the end of his bed using Lockpick or the second key. You may elect to clear out all his valuables, or just the hilt.

➤ **Hilt of Mehrunes' Razor**

◊ **OBJECTIVE:** Bring the hilt to Silus
♦ **TARGET:** Silus Vesuius's House, in Dawnstar

Dagon's New Dawn

Return with all three fragments of Mehrunes' Razor, and revisit Silus Vesuius's House in Dawnstar. The slightly mad mage is extremely impressed with your collecting abilities and gives you a sizable reward. When all three fragments are back in his hands, Silus lets you in on a little secret: The scabbard in the display case is actually the fourth piece of the blade. What's more, if you both take all the pieces to Dagon's shrine, you could contact the Prince of Destruction directly and ask him to make Mehrunes' Razor whole again. This may appeal or be a terrible idea; either way, Silus will meet you at the shrine!

➤ **Leveled gold pieces**

◊ **OBJECTIVE:** Meet Silus at the Shrine of Mehrunes Dagon
♦ **TARGET:** Shrine of Mehrunes Dagon

On the summit of the mountains that lie south and west of Dawnstar, and south and east of Morthal, sits the ominous shrine to Mehrunes Dagon. Trek there, and optionally slay any animal predators lurking at the base of the precarious ceremonial steps that lead to the giant carved statue of the Daedric Prince of Destruction. Silus places the blade fragments on the altar and begs for the blade's full glory! Nothing happens; it falls to you to commune with Mehrunes Dagon.

◊ **OBJECTIVE:** Speak to Mehrunes Dagon

Approach the altar, and a deep, booming voice fills the air and your head. Mehrunes Dagon has deemed you worth speaking to, but Silas has fulfilled his purpose. You are instructed to kill him. At this point, you can:

Agree to Lord Dagon's command.

Inform Lord Dagon that Silus deserves to live.

Neither makes any difference, as Lord Dagon has decided Silus's fate.

◊ **OBJECTIVE:** Kill Silus

Silus is quick to tell you there is another way to end this that doesn't involve him getting gutted. He can take the pieces back to the museum and seal them in the display case. You can either agree to this or begin your murder of Silus Vesuius.

Quest Conclusion 1: Silus Dies

Strike Silus down, optionally scavenging the rare clothing he wears. Then approach the altar again and begin to serve Mehrunes Dagon.

➤ **Mythic Dawn Boots**   ➤ **Mythic Dawn Robes**
➤ **Mythic Dawn Gloves**

◊ **OBJECTIVE:** Reforge Mehrunes' Razor
◊ **OBJECTIVE:** Claim Mehrunes' Razor

The power of Mehrunes Dagon is still impressive, as the Lord raises the pieces of the blade and fuses them together like new. Take the weapon from the air. As Dagon's voice fades, he gives you one final challenge. The shrine doors swing open, and two Dremora rush out to kill you. Return the favor, plunging Mehrunes' Razor deep or using your own favored weapons. Remember to take the Dremora's Daedra Heart, a rare ingredient that may come in handy for your concoctions.

➤ **Mehrunes' Razor**   ➤ **Daedra Heart (2)**

Quest Conclusion 2: Silus Flees

If you speak with Silus and agree to his plan, he hands you some gold and attempts to flee. Mehrunes Dagon's wrath is incurred, and the doors to his shrine swing open, releasing two Dremora. Use your favored weapons to defeat them,

and remember to take the Dremora's Daedra Heart, an uncommon ingredient that you can utilize in your dark crafting. At this point, you can follow Silus through the wilderness, back to his museum (after which he thanks you for helping him escape), or leave him to fend for himself. Either way, you don't receive Mehrunes' Razor.

➤ **Leveled gold pieces**   ➤ **Daedra Heart (2)**

Postquest Activities

Be warned: If you let Silus go, you can never claim the Razor and the quest will end! Either way, ensure you enter the interior of Mehrunes Dagon's shrine and gather all the available (and impressive) loot inside!

THE WHISPERING DOOR

MINOR SPOILERS

PREREQUISITES: You must be Level 20 or higher. Complete Main Quest: Dragon Rising

INTERSECTING QUESTS: None

LOCATIONS: Whiterun, Dragonsreach, Dragonsreach Jarl's Quarters

CHARACTERS: Dagny, Farengar, Frothar, Mephala (The Webspinner), Nelkir

♦ **OBJECTIVES:** Find out what's wrong with Nelkir, Listen to the whispering door, Speak to Nelkir, Obtain the key to the whispering door, Open the whispering door, Retrieve the Ebony Blade

Murmurs at the Whispering Door

Once you're an experienced adventurer (and reached Level 20 or higher), and you've helped Jarl Balgruuf the Greater of Whiterun during Main Quest: Dragon Rising, speak to the Innkeeper at the Bannered Mare in Whiterun. Rumor has it that the Jarl is having some trouble with his children. Ask him about this, and Balgruuf tells you Nelkir has become brooding and is prone to violence. He asks whether you could speak to him and ask why he's acting the way he is.

> **NOTE** Have you sided with the Stormcloaks and ousted Jarl Balgruuf the Greater from Whiterun? Then this quest is still available, although Balgruuf has fled to Solitude. Find him and his family inside the Blue Palace. Aside from moving back and forth between Hold capitals, this quest remains unchanged. The following is written assuming you encounter Balgruuf and his children in Dragonsreach.

♦ **OBJECTIVE:** Find out what's wrong with Nelkir
♦ **TARGET:** Nelkir, inside Dragonsreach, in Whiterun

Nelkir is wandering somewhere inside Dragonsreach, usually near the great hall or the war room atop the steps, or in the Jarl's quarters. When you greet Nelkir, he's suitably petulant. Once you've faced the verbal abuse, Nelkir mentions that he knows more about his father than anyone thinks he does. Ask him to clarify, and he says his father still worships Talos and hates the Thalmor almost as much as the Stormcloaks do. Ask how he knows this, and he mentions a place

where he overhears murmuring: Nelkir listens to Lady of Whispers from the locked door in the basement. She talks to him. She'll probably talk to you, too.

♦ **OBJECTIVE:** Listen to the whispering door
♦ **TARGET:** Nelkir, inside Dragonsreach, in Whiterun

Head northwest through the great hall and down the steps close to the large fireplace. Open the basement door, and enter the tiny storage room with a locked door in the far left (eastern) corner. Listen at the door, and a strange woman's voice echoes through the keyhole. Regrettably, the voice cannot reveal itself in this plane directly, and few hear the words of Mephala, the Lady of Whispers. She expects you to take an active role in sussing out secrets. This starts with you opening the locked door, as a piece of her power has been locked away behind it. The dark child Nelkir holds knowledge that will further your new cause.

♦ **OBJECTIVE:** Speak to Nelkir

When you meet Nelkir again, he already knows you've met the Whispering Lady. Speak to him, and he tells you that only two people can open the door: Balgruuf and Farengar Secret-Fire the court wizard. You must decide who to interact with and take the key from them.

♦ **OBJECTIVE:** Obtain the key to the whispering door

This leaves two possible keyholders to choose. You can:

Pickpocket Balgruuf: Wait until Balgruuf moves from his throne and you aren't being watched, then sneak up and pickpocket him. He can be asleep or simply facing away from you.

Kill Farengar: Wait until Farengar retires to his quarters, ideally moving into his adjacent bedroom, and then kill him while he sleeps. This isn't that wise, unless you've purchased all the spells you need from him.

Pickpocket Farengar: Wait until Farengar retires to his quarters, and then sneak up and pickpocket him. He can be asleep or simply facing away from you.

Once one of these plans works, you manage to obtain a prized key.

➤ Whispering Door Key

◇ **OBJECTIVE:** Open the whispering door
◇ **OBJECTIVE:** Retrieve the Ebony Blade

Quest Conclusion

Head back down into the storage cellar, to the door at which you listened to Mephala, and open it with the key. Inside is a simple storage room. On the wooden table rests a long Ebony Blade and an admonition against it. The book tells you to resist the temptation of taking this indestructible, madness-inducing, cursed sword. When you pick up the blade, the whisper in your head congratulates you, but then informs you that the blade must be returned to its past glory. The blood of deceit must be drunk! You are now bound to the will of Mephala!

➤ **Admonition Against Ebony** ➤ **Ebony Blade**

Postquest Activities

This powerful Daedric weapon is currently underwhelming and lacks power. However, for every friend (i.e., someone you've completed a favor for, completed a task for, or won over during any type of quest) that you kill with it, the blade becomes more and more powerful, as it absorbs life from its victims.

THE BREAK OF DAWN

PREREQUISITES: You must be Level 12 or higher.
INTERSECTING QUESTS: None
LOCATIONS: Statue to Meridia and Kilkreath Ruins, Kilkreath Balcony, Kilkreath Catacombs, Kilkreath Ruins, Kilkreath Temple
CHARACTERS: Meridia
ENEMIES: Imperial Soldier (Ghost), Malkoran, Stormcloak Soldier (Ghost)
◇ **OBJECTIVES:** Bring Meridia's beacon to Mount Kilkreath, Replace the beacon, Guide Meridia's Light through the temple, Destroy Malkoran, Retrieve Dawnbreaker

⬙ MINOR SPOILERS

▷ Beholding the Beacon of Light

Once you reach Level 12, you may discover this strange gem in one of the large and ornate treasure chests you open. This gem occurs randomly; it's not in any fixed location.

➤ **Meridia's Beacon**

Take this Beacon, and as you exit the interior location, and every day thereafter, you hear a voice inside your head. It becomes increasingly alarmed at your lack of interest in helping the Solar Daughter, Meridia. When you wish to start this quest (if only to rid yourself of Meridia's alarming cranial lurking), find the Statue to Meridia.

The other way this quest can start is if you trek to Mount Kilkreath, in the mountain range west of Solitude. Try to spot a prominent statue of a woman with her arms raised to the sky, on the southern slopes just above Dragon Bridge. As you approach, you hear a voice commanding you to find and return with her beacon. Locate the object, and return to begin this quest.

◇ **OBJECTIVE:** Bring Meridia's Beacon to Mount Kilkreath
◇ **OBJECTIVE:** Replace the beacon
♦ **TARGET:** Statue to Meridia

Once you set the Beacon on the cupped arms of the small statues at the feet of Meridia's effigy, you are caught and whisked into the clouds. An aspect of Meridia appears. She tells you that a necromancer named Malkoran is planning to raise the dead of Skyrim's Civil War and wage open war on the living, using the energy of a powerful artifact in her shadow-filled shrine. You are to enter her shrine and shine the brilliant beam of light throughout the dungeon; it will open the way to the inner sanctum, where Malkoran is defiling her Daedric artifact, the Dawnbreaker.

◇ **OBJECTIVE:** Guide Meridia's Light through the temple
♦ **TARGET:** Kilkreath Temple, below Statue of Meridia

▷ Shining Light in the Dark Temple

You descend back to earth. Locate the Iron Door below the statue plinth and descend into the temple. In the first large chamber, approach the pedestal in the center, which has a beam of light hitting it. Activate it. A beacon gem rises from the pedestal, ricocheting the light up and into a second gem contained in the mouth of a carved dragon. Then exit via the doorway underneath, into a second chamber where the ghosts of Imperial and Stormcloak Soldiers, controlled by Malkoran, attack you. Retaliate (and search the remains, as there's usually gold to be scavenged), and then activate the pedestal on the central steps.

The wooden doors atop the main steps lead to a blocked area, so head south, along a side tunnel, where the beam pierces the wall. Engage in more ghostly combat, before heading to a third main chamber, where you encounter more soldiers. Climb the wooden steps, and go to the upper stone bridge leading to the next pedestal. Activate it, and head south to the door leading to Kilkreath Balcony.

This balcony is outside, overlooking the forested valley below. Cross the bridge, fighting more ghostly foes, and quickly enter the door on the opposite side, leading into Kilkreath Ruins. At the main chamber, you face more spectral foes. Head up the steps (as the doors on the ground are sealed), and activate the pedestal at the top. Then navigate the corridors on the eastern side of the upper area, investigating any chests and urns you wish. Enter the caged bridge, then jump to the upper pedestal on the raised island. Head west through a previously sealed door.

This leads to another open chamber. Dispatch the ghosts before climbing the side wooden steps on the chamber's eastern side and following the corridor around and back to the room with the caged bridge. You are now above the bridge and can access the third pedestal, which unlocks the double doors in the south wall. Open them, and head down into the Kilkreath Catacombs.

 OBJECTIVE: Destroy Malkoran

You are close now; descend and enter an antechamber with the draped corpses of soldiers and a pedestal surrounded by candles. Activate the pedestal, which opens the double doors. Then descend to the main altar chamber, where Malkoran and a ghostly quartet of soldiers are ready to expel intruders. Attack these foes; consider backing up the corridor and steps you just

descended so you aren't surrounded. Then fend off the attacks from Malkoran, bringing him down with superior combat and cunning.

 OBJECTIVE: Retrieve Dawnbreaker

Quest Conclusion

Approach the pedestal that holds the defiled Dawnbreaker, and wrench the sword free. Your view fills with light, and you ascend toward the heavens where Meridia is pleased that you've brought light to the realm of Skyrim. The dead shall remain at rest, and you are to keep Dawnbreaker and use it to purge corruption from the dark corners of the world. Wield it in her name (or agree to simply keep the weapon).

➤ **Word of Power:** Elemental Fury   ➤ **Dawnbreaker**

Postquest Activities

Carry Dawnbreaker and wield it for Meridia, whether you told her to find someone else to spread her religion or whether you're a firm believer.

THE HOUSE OF HORRORS

PREREQUISITES: Leave Markarth and return again
INTERSECTING QUESTS: None
LOCATIONS: Markarth, Abandoned House
CHARACTERS: Logrolf the Willful, Molag Bal, Vigilant Tyranus, Yngvar
ENEMIES: Random
◊ **OBJECTIVES:** Search the Abandoned House, Find your reward, Find the priest of Boethiah, Free Logrolf, Go to the abandoned house, Beat Logrolf into submission, Kill Logrolf, Speak to Molag Bal

● MINOR SPOILERS

▶ A Powerful Trickster

The first time you visit the canyon city of Markarth, you witness a brazen Forsworn attack on a market stall holder. Next time you enter the city, head along the right (north) side of the thoroughfare, along the canal, until you meet two men conversing outside a dwelling. A cowled priest named Vigilant Tyranus is asking a Nord called Yngvar whether he's seen any strange lights or unusual noises emanating from the house. Yngvar says he hasn't, and Tyranus turns to you, asking similar questions. Reply as you wish, and Vigilant Tyranus explains that he's a Vigilant of Stendarr; he finds areas believed to be used for Daedra worship and removes the presence. Ask if he needs help, and he says to follow him into the Abandoned House.

◊ **OBJECTIVE:** Search the Abandoned House
♦ **TARGET:** Locked door, inside the Abandoned House

The house's interior is well lit. There is no rot on the furniture, and fresh food lies waiting to be prepared. Someone was here recently. Tyranus is startled by an odd sound and opens the door. You swear a basket rolls across the room in front of you both. There's both a faint moaning and a deep rumbling sound. A strange vapor hangs in the air. Tyranus is convinced something is amiss and heads down the stairs. He shouts for the entity to show itself. Candles illuminate the gloom. The voice in your head tells you to open another door; try it and it is sealed shut.

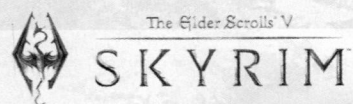

When various objects begin to fly around, Tyranus flees the area, vowing to find help: This is no ordinary Daedra. Tyranus reaches the entrance room and begins to slow down. Follow him, and you hear a growling voice telling you to crush Tyranus. You can:

Wait, hoping that Tyranus regains his composure. He doesn't and eventually, overcome by the strange presence, attacks you!

Follow the orders from the voice inside your head, and attack Tyranus. Keep this up until one of you is dead.

◇ **OBJECTIVE:** Find your reward
♦ **TARGET:** Altar, inside the Abandoned House

With Tyranus out of the way, you can claim the reward for your cold-blooded murder. Venture back into the depths of the dwelling, to the locked door. It has been mysteriously unlocked, and you swear the candles burn brighter as you turn the handle. The same voice beckons you into the bowels of the building. The chamber begins to tremble. Search behind the shelving for a hole in the (east) wall. This leads to an earthen tunnel and into a long-forgotten altar, upon which rests an ornate but rusty mace. Pick it up.

You briefly cower as a cage of onyx spikes springs up around you. Molag Bal, the Lord of Corruption, deems you foolish to think you would be rewarded so easily! Speak to Molag Bal and mention the altar or mace. There was a time when that mace dripped with the blood of the feeble and the worthless. But Molag Bal's rival Boethiah sent his priest here to desecrate this altar. It was left to decay. Until now. Molag Bal wants the priest responsible to willingly turn to his service and surrender his soul. Agree to help (as it's the only way to free yourself).

◇ **OBJECTIVE:** Find the priest of Boethiah
♦ **TARGET:** Logrolf the Willful, inside [a random location]

◈ A Willful Execution

Travel to the location indicated on your world map. Work your way through the dungeon that the priest is lurking in, until you find them. The priest is Logrolf the Willful, and he's usually tied up and helpless. It is worth killing any enemies in the chamber Logrolf is being held in so you can easily free him. Let him know you're here to rescue him. He's immediately suspicious, as nobody knew where he was when he was taken. He asks who sent you. You can:

(Persuade) Pretend his own master Boethiah sent you.

(Bribe: Gold, various amount) Ask why it matters, as there's gold to be had. Your gold.

(Intimidate: Level 13) Or tell him the truth to frighten him: Molag Bal sent you.

When one of these plans works, untie the binds. Logrolf has some other business to attend to. You needn't follow or chaperone him. Eventually, the subtle will of Molag Bal will play on Logrolf's mind, and he'll visit the Abandoned House.

◇ **OBJECTIVE:** Free Logrolf
◇ **OBJECTIVE:** Go to the Abandoned House
♦ **TARGET:** Abandoned House, in Markarth

Journey back to Markarth and enter the Abandoned House. Logrolf the Willful is already waiting inside and runs into the depths of the dwelling, around the shelving and through the hidden tunnel. He approaches the altar. Molag Bal springs the trap, and the onyx spikes surround Logrolf. The priest seems less perturbed, as he has bettered Molag Bal before. Molag Bal answers that he has a champion now and grants you use of his mace. Take it!

➤ **Rusty Mace**

◇ **OBJECTIVE:** Beat Logrolf into submission

Stand between the spikes, and bring the mace down repeatedly on Logrolf. He yells that he'll never submit. Eventually, you bludgeon him to death. Molag Bal laughs at the frail, limp, and pathetic bodies that mortals possess. He then resurrects Logrolf, ordering you to strike him again! After two more vicious swings, Logrolf can't take any more and submits to Molag Bal. He promises to pledge his soul, to forsake the weak and pitiful Boethiah. Molag Bal is satisfied. Once you kill him again.

◇ **OBJECTIVE:** Kill Logrolf
◇ **OBJECTIVE:** Speak to Molag Bal

Quest Conclusion

Bring your Rusty Mace down hard on Logrolf's crippled form. When he's dead (again), speak to Molag Bal, who presents you with the true power of this mace. When your enemies lie broken and bloody, know that he will be watching. Then Molag Bal leaves this plane of existence...for the time being.

➤ **Mace of Molag Bal**

Postquest Activities

You can stay in this Abandoned House, using the bed, and take any items you wish (although this isn't classified as your home). In addition, if you carry Molag Bal's mace where there are city guards, they tend to comment on it.

 **MINOR SPOILERS**

PREREQUISITES: None.

INTERSECTING QUESTS: None

LOCATIONS: Markarth, Hall of the Dead, Silver-Blood Inn, Understone Keep, Reachcliff Cave

CHARACTERS: Banning, Brother Verulus, Eola, Frabbi, Hogni Red-Arm, Kleppr, Lisbet, Namira

ENEMIES: Draugr

◊ **OBJECTIVES:** Miscellaneous: Speak to Verulus about the Hall of the Dead, Miscellaneous: Investigate the Hall of the Dead, Clear the Draugr from Reachcliff Cave, Miscellaneous: Tell Verulus the Hall of the Dead is safe, Speak to Eola, Convince Verulus to follow you, Lead Verulus to the Shrine of Namira, Kill Verulus, Feast on Verulus

▷ Prelude: Hunger in the Hall*

Kleppr and his wife, Frabbi, are a fountain of knowledge about rumors in and around Markarth. Visit them inside the Silver-Blood Inn, and ask around for rumors. Eventually, either of them lets you know that the Hall of the Dead in Markarth has been closed. They suggest you speak to Brother Verulus to find out more information about why this has happened.

> ◊ **MISCELLANEOUS OBJECTIVE:** Speak to Verulus about the Hall of the Dead
> ♦ **TARGET:** Brother Verulus, inside Understone Keep

Visit Understone Keep, dug into the western canyon side of Markarth. In the entrance hall, listen to Thongvor Silver-Blood arguing about access to the Hall of the Dead with Brother Verulus. After the conversation is over, step up and speak to Verulus, who tells you the Hall is not able to be visited. You can:

(Persuade) Tell him you're here to help. This is a novice challenge, and you always succeed in this.

(Bribe) Offer a small contribution to his causes.

(Intimidate) Or tell him you don't like being ignored. As Verulus cannot be intimidated, this challenge always fails.

Success in either of these options results in Brother Verulus agreeing to let you investigate the strange goings-on inside the Hall of the Dead. The Priesthood of Arkay will offer a reward if the odd activities in the Hall stop. You are given a key allowing you to enter, and another Miscellaneous Objective begins. Ask for more information on Arkay or the Hall before you part ways.

➤ **Markarth Hall of the Dead Key**

> ◊ **MISCELLANEOUS OBJECTIVE:** Investigate the Hall of the Dead
> ♦ **TARGET:** Hall of the Dead, in Markarth

> **TIP** Alternatively, you can enter Markarth's Hall of the Dead by unlocking the door (Adept) and sneaking in there.

Travel southwest from Brother Verulus's location. Open the heavy gold doors and enter the Hall of the Dead. The eerie, mist-laden hall seems deserted, until you hear a voice speaking to you. It believes you are exhibiting the signs of temptation, that there is a hunger inside; you see the dead and your mouth waters. Continue this unnerving search of this giant tomb, until you stumble upon Eola. She refuses to talk about anything other than the deliciousness of human flesh. And the craving! Don't worry; you have a friend now. Although you can voice disgust as you speak with her, Eola is an emissary of Namira, the Lady of Decay. Namira has a place where you can sate your appetite without judgment. Ask where this place is, and Eola explains that it's inside Reachcliff Cave. However, the dead there have started to stir. Meet Eola there, and she vows to fight with you to Namira's embrace. This quest officially begins now.

> ◊ **OBJECTIVE:** Clear the Draugr from Reachcliff Cave
> ♦ **TARGET:** All Draugr, inside Reachcliff Cave
> ◊ **MISCELLANEOUS OBJECTIVE:** Tell Verulus the Hall of the Dead is safe
> ♦ **TARGET:** Brother Verulus, Understone Keep, in Markarth

Before you commence Daedric Quest: The Taste of Death, head out of the Hall of the Dead, into Understone Keep, and find Brother Verulus again. With Eola now absent from the Hall, it has been cleared of any oddities. He is most pleased with this news and rewards you with his own Amulet. The Prelude (Miscellaneous) Quest now concludes.

➤ **Amulet of Arkay**

Carnage at Reachcliff Cave

Journey east and slightly south of Markarth, along the goat trails of the Reach. Search among the rocky hills and furrows for a small procession of megalith arches leading to three standing stones at the entrance to Reachcliff Cave. Eola is waiting here, ready to plunge her blade into a Draugr or 20. You may bring her along (she acts as a Follower during this time, helping you stave off enemy attacks), or you can tell her to wait here if you want to fight on your own (or with other Followers). Now venture into the cave.

➤ Follower: Eola

It takes only a stride forward to wake the dead from this location. Muster forth your best Draugr-fighting implements and start carving, burning, or blasting your way into them. Beware of the high-ranking Draugr clambering out of the first coffin you see. Head down the connecting tunnel into a wider passage with stairs and a Nordic face carved into a stone column. After more Draugr fighting, head to the blocked-off arch and turn right (west). At the far end is an open cavern and a crumbling bridge section. To the south is a second bridge section with a jump to a treasure chest. Choose either route, working your way southward and down.

Check a wall handle (which opens a wall section next to it) and a pull chain (which opens an exit route), and continue to the Iron Door. This leads into a ceremonial hall and a large shrine to Namira at the far end, where the remaining Draugr in this cave await. After you defeat them all, along with the powerful lead Draugr who rises from the head of the table, your Draugr-culling task is complete.

◊ **OBJECTIVE:** Speak to Eola

Although you can retreat into the adjoining corridor with the pull chain, which leads to a corridor that will hasten your exit back into the Reach, in this particular case it is worth taking the long route back, finding Eola along the way (if she didn't accompany you). Eola is happy to have her shrine back and wishes to prepare a grand feast to welcome you into Namira's coven. You have the honor of bringing a fresh kill for the main course: a priest with a taste for the easy life. Bribe him with the gold Eola gives you, coax him back here, and Namira will take care of the rest. Now follow the corridor to the north from the adjoining room, and return to Markarth.

➤ 100 gold pieces

◊ **OBJECTIVE:** Convince Verulus to follow you
♦ **TARGET:** Brother Verulus, inside Understone Keep

Coven of the Cannibals

Return to the Hall of the Dead (if you've cleared it), or explore Understone Keep until you find the priest. Tell him you require his services. You can:

(Persuade) Tell him about the treasure to share.

(Bribe) Pay him to accompany you.

(Intimidate) Or tell him it wasn't an invitation but an order.

Should any of these attempts succeed, Brother Verulus agrees to accompany you and becomes a temporary Follower. You need not assign him any equipment.

◊ **OBJECTIVE:** Lead Verulus to the Shrine of Namira
♦ **TARGET:** Shrine of Namira, inside Reachcliff Cave

➤ Follower: Brother Verulus

Head back to the Reachcliff Cave (Fast-Traveling is helpful here, although you and Brother Verulus can trek here on foot). Descend the empty caverns, and head back into the ceremonial hall in the deepest recess of the cave system. Check that Verulus is behind you and lead him in, where he greets the assembled clan with faint suspicion. Eola tries to allay his fears, telling him he's with friends. Verulus begins to speak a little more slowly, as if his feeble mind is beginning to be controlled by unknown forces. Verulus seems to think he's been invited for dinner. Eola tells him to lie down. Verulus agrees, as he's suddenly very tired, and clambers onto the sacrificial altar to Namira. Eola turns to you; the meal is on Namira's table, and you're going to be carving.

◊ **OBJECTIVE:** Kill Verulus
◊ **OBJECTIVE:** Feast on Verulus

Quest Conclusion

Strike Verulus while he sleeps, using any weapon you wish, ideally a melee one. This raises your Bounty in the Reach. Then search the fresh corpse. His still-warm body lies before you; leave it alone or consume a section of Verulus's blood and bile. Namira begins to speak with you. She is pleased by your consumption and grants you her ring. Wear it when you feast on the flesh of the dead, and her power will flow through you. You may thank or annoy Namira with your final response before this quest concludes, then speak to Eola again to take her as a Follower.

➤ Ring of Namira   ➤ Follower: Eola

 NOTE Alternatively, you can kill Eola before Verulus lies on the table, but you fail this quest. You receive a small reward from Verulus and a large uproar from the assembled guests.

Postquest Activities

You may speak to any of the assembled coven guests at the feast. Some sit quietly and have little to say (except a few respectful remarks between mouthfuls of monk). However, there are more prominent members of this coven too. They are:

Hogni Red-Arm, the meat trader from Markarth.

Banning, the dog trainer from Markarth.

Lisbet, the merchant of the Arnleif and Sons Trading Company, in Markarth.

All of these secret cannibals strike up a conversation if you speak with them at the feast. They also have a particular conversation (regarding aspects of the penchant for flesh) when you return to Markarth and find them again. Brother Verulus also mentions this near-fatal feast if you save him from becoming the main course.

In addition, whenever you kill a bipedal entity, you can feast on them (this is a benefit the Ring gives you only if you're wearing it) and search them. Finally, Eola can become a Follower if you speak to her after siding with her.

PREREQUISITES: You must be Level 10 or higher

INTERSECTING QUESTS: None

LOCATIONS: Bthardamz, Bthardamz Arcanex, Bthardamz Dwelling, Bthardamz Lower District, Bthardamz Study, Bthardamz Upper District, Bthardamz Workshop, Shrine to Peryite

CHARACTERS: Kesh the Clean, Peryite

ENEMIES: Afflicted, Dwarven Centurion, Dwarven Sphere, Dwarven Spider, Orchendor, Vampire

◇ **OBJECTIVES:** Obtain some Vampire Dust, Obtain a Deathbell Flower, Obtain a Silver Ingot, Obtain a Flawless Ruby, Deliver the ingredients, Inhale the fumes, Kill Orchendor, Report Orchendor's death to Peryite

○ MINOR SPOILERS

A Fine Fume

This quest becomes available once you reach Level 10. You may also hear about the Afflicted by stumbling upon Bthardamz or by randomly encountering an Afflicted in World Encounter: Peryite's Pilgrim.

On a wooded clifftop bluff in the Druadach Mountains above Karthwasten lies a Shrine to Peryite, the Bringer of Pestilence. As you approach, you see a single figure: a Khajiit named Kesh the Clean. He is tending to his Alchemy Lab and a large golden cauldron by the shrine. Approach Kesh, and he inquires whether you've come to commune with Peryite the Taskmaster. You may find out more about this Daedric entity and ask whether you may speak to Peryite. Kesh says that he likes you, but for the commune to begin, incense is needed. He lists the ingredients necessary to mix the incense and gives you very general hints about where to find them.

◇ **OBJECTIVE:** Obtain some Vampire Dust
◇ **OBJECTIVE:** Obtain a Deathbell Flower
◇ **OBJECTIVE:** Obtain a Silver Ingot
◇ **OBJECTIVE:** Obtain a Flawless Ruby

Vampire Dust

You find Vampire Dust when you search the corpse of a vampire you've killed. Vampire Dust is also occasionally found in dungeons and is sold by merchants. Here are the easiest locations to look:

Any alchemy shop in a town that has one, or Court Wizard Quarters in a Hold capital city

If you have your own house, one of the Alchemy Lab upgrades comes with Vampire Dust

Seek out a vampire lair, such as Shriekwind Bastion or Broken Fang Cave

➤ **Vampire Dust**

Deathbell Flower

Deathbell Flowers are found in the frozen Tundra in Hjaalmarch Hold, scattered about the landscape, and in some dungeons. They are also available from the odd apothecary. Here are the easiest locations to look:

Anise's Cabin, on the other side of the river close to Riverwood

The vampire lair known as Bloodlet Throne

Any alchemy shop, Fort Snowhawk, or Fort Amol

➤ **Deathbell Flower**

Silver Ingot

To get Silver Ingots, you either need to mine and smelt silver ore, or find it already refined. Silver Ingots are sometimes sold by vendors as well, and you can sometimes steal it. Here are the easiest locations to look:

There are several Silver Ingots to steal in Dragonsreach (Whiterun).

There are a few to steal from the vault inside the Treasury House in Markarth.

If you don't want to steal, try exploring the Forsaken Cave, just west of Windhelm.

Head inside a silver mine (such as Fenn's Gulch Mine in Karthwasten), mine a vein of silver ore, and use the smelter outside to turn the ore into ingots.

➤ **Silver Ingot**

Flawless Ruby

A flawless ruby can be found by mining, and it is sold by merchants in the bigger Hold Cities. Here are the easiest locations to look:

The vampire lair known as Shriekwind Bastion.

The throne room inside Korvanjund. Access this during the Civil War Quests; the ruby is in a bowl with a spell book on an upper ledge left of the throne.

The Emperor's ship the *Katariah*, which docks near Solitude. Access this during the last Dark Brotherhood Quest; the ruby is in a jewelry box at the foot of the Emperor's bed.

Otherwise, purchase it from any caravan or vendor in a large city.

➤ **Flawless Ruby**

◇ **OBJECTIVE:** Deliver the Ingredients
◇ **OBJECTIVE:** Inhale the fumes

Kesh the Clean won't entertain mixing up the incense until you have all four ingredients on your person. Only then should you return to the Shrine of Peryite. He takes the ingredients and deposits them into the golden cauldron, encouraging you to inhale the bubbling ichor deeply. Your vision clouds, and a purple mass forms in front of you. This aspect of Peryite speaks to you. He has watched you for some time, found you intriguing, and wondered whether you'd make a proper agent for a task.

When you ask about the task, Peryite tells you he sent a blessing, a wasting plague that infected a scattering of Breton villages. One of his monks, an elf named Orchendor, was tasked with gathering the Afflicted. He was last seen shepherding them into Bthardamz but has since lost his way. Betrayal cannot be tolerated; you are to find and kill Orchendor. You may ask the aspect of Peryite clarifying questions and receive an angry answer thanks to your impertinence. Ask what you'd gain, and Peryite says he will grant you a powerful token: a Dwemer shield.

◇ **OBJECTIVE:** Kill Orchendor
◆ **TARGET:** Orchendor, in the Bthardamz Arcanex

Assault on the Afflicted

Bthardamz Exterior: Before you begin the trek to Bthardamz, optionally speak with Kesh the Clean again. He provides further information on Orchendor and the Dwarven ruins of a vast underground city, which you can actually see from this vantage point if you look due west. Then head down the mountain and climb the stone entrance steps to the pavilion domes that ushered in the Afflicted. Some still guard the area and will attack on sight. They are powerful warriors but have a weak constitution thanks to the pox Peryite infected them with. Work your way through the pavilion, and into the main entrance, complete with buttress domes on each side (you'll use one to exit from this place).

For the moment, head down the steps with the blade trap slit down the middle. The first golden lever you see activates these blades. The second lever to the right of the doorway blocked by spears removes this obstacle, allowing you through into the Bthardamz Upper District.

Bthardamz Upper District: Head down the ramped passage and around the corner to the right (north). Either open the gate (Novice) or navigate around two sleeping areas with Afflicted to pulverize. Continue along the corridors past an open storage room and down another slope to a large piston chamber where the Afflicted have gathered to breathe in the vapors of a bubbling ichor. Defeat or sneak around them, and head west into the main Upper District courtyard.

Amid the pipes and stonework is a central platform with green ooze bubbling. Take out the enemies, head north, climb the stairs to the balcony, and activate the lever. Spear bars retract from the balcony opposite, allowing you to leave via a stone path. Open the gold door and enter a passage heading west that ends in a pipe room. Dwarven Spheres are activated here if you enter. Take the sloping corridor on your right (south) with the whirring blade trap. Journey down a cobblestone street to a carved stone arch opening. Slay the Afflicted guarding this door to Bthardamz Workshop.

Bthardamz Workshop and Upper District (2): Move around the pipes, checking the gate on your right and left (north and south) to reach sleeping quarters. The second bedroom has a note revealing the exact location of Orchendor; he is inside the Bthardamz Arcanex. Continue along the green-tinged corridors to a stairwell where you fight your first Dwarven Spiders. The staircase allows you to enter the Upper District; gaze across the small maze of stonework and open a small chest. You can drop down from here (to the southeast, or you'll have to retrace your steps), or you can to return to the Workshop and head south into a steam pipe room with Afflicted and a second entrance back into the Upper District. Back in the Upper District, head southeast toward a series of stone steps. Climb them to the top. Along the way, there's a balcony you can check, as well as a separate Bthardamz Dwelling to scavenge. The stairs continue around to the southwest. Go up stone ramps offering a spectacular view back down and a corridor ending at a door to Bthardamz Lower District.

➤ **Afflicted's Note**

Bthardamz Lower District: Now in the Lower District, tread through the echoing gloom, past a gate (with a chest behind it), and through a gold door and Dwarven Spider attack. In a large, ruined coliseum is a central plinth on which rests a chest. The lever on the balcony activates a blade trap on the plinth. Battle the Afflicted here. The exit to the east leads to the main Lower District. Cross the curved courtyard, go through the open gate, and cross the two stone platforms that span a winding subterranean stream. Afflicted are active here.

Head through another open gate. Battle two Dwarven Spheres and a mass of Afflicted just after the arch with the lever on it. The lever drops a nasty spike just behind you; use it to skewer foes or stop them from following you. But it is better to sneak past or kill everyone. There are two sets of steps here. The ones to your left (north) lead to a circular platform; water pours from (currently inaccessible) upper walkways. The other staircase at the District's east end leads past Dwarven Spiders and into the Bthardamz Study.

Bthardamz Study: Through the gate to the east is a small study area. To your south is a golden door. Head through and go up the stairs (without setting off the pressure plate and activating the blade trap). Enter through a gate and into the Lower District once again.

Bthardamz Lower District (2): You're now on the upper walkways you could only see earlier. Head down the rooftop stone ramp. To your right (east) is a gate and a chest. To your left (west) is a large covered L-shaped walkway with a turret balcony in the middle. Expect combat with at least six Afflicted here, and watch your step; don't head off the platforms to a crushing fall below! Move through the second walkway heading south, and exit into the Bthardamz Arcanex.

> **NOTE** Don't worry; the fumes you're inhaling aren't at dangerous levels. You may also spot some ballistas. These can be fired but not aimed (so you can't use them on Dwarven Centurions unless they step right in front of the bolt's trajectory, and you only have one firing opportunity).

Bthardamz Arcanex: This is essentially a large watery grotto with Dwarven towers and platforms built inside it. Head along the platforms, preparing for combat with Dwarven Spheres. Climb the spiraling stone path to the upper corridor, at the end of which a Dwarven Centurion roars into life. You can try sprinting around him or backing up and tackling him from range. If you flee forward, you also meet Dwarven Spiders that can overwhelm you. Fight carefully, retreating if the Centurion becomes too much of a threat.

Once you flee from the mechanical foes or defeat them, climb the stairs beyond the Centurion and reach the upper balcony area. There are six more Dwarven Spiders to defeat before you sprint past a clanking pipe corridor that opens into a pipe-laden Arcanex chamber with two Dwarven Spheres. Defeat them before heading through the gap in the north wall to the rear of the Arcanex chamber, where you have a final confrontation with Orchendor.

Orchendor is in no mood to talk and attacks immediately. Use the scenery to your advantage. Use the gap in the wall or the stairs behind him to hide or fire from if necessary. Watch for his teleportation and for any Dwarven foes you haven't killed, as they tend to follow you into this combat. After you dispatch Orchendor, search him. Among his trinkets is a key allowing you to exit this place without having to retrace your steps.

➤ **Key to Bthardamz Elevator**

◇ **OBJECTIVE:** Report Orchendor's death to Peryite
♦ **TARGET:** Aspect of Peryite, Shrine to Peryite

Quest Conclusion

Head up the stairs at the Arcanex chamber's north end, using the key to reach the Bthardamz Elevator and activating the lever. Ride the elevator up to the exterior entrance. Run along the stone walkways and down to the pavilion to escape this Dwarven maze for good. Fast-Travel at any point or trek east, back to the shrine. Commune with Peryite by inhaling at the cauldron again. Peryite congratulates you, as your actions have sent Orchendor to roam the Pits; his betrayal will be punished and your obedience rewarded.

➤ **Spellbreaker**

Postquest Activities

Spellbreaker is as impressive as it is unique. It generates a Ward when you're blocking, making it very useful when you're fighting against magical enemies. Also beware of (random) retribution: There's a chance World Encounter: The Afflicted versus You* will occur, and you'll face Afflicted wishing you harm after your massacre here.

A NIGHT TO REMEMBER

PREREQUISITES: You must be Level 14 or higher

INTERSECTING QUESTS: None

LOCATIONS: Markarth, Temple of Dibella, Morvunskar, Misty Grove, Rorikstead, Whiterun, Witchmist Grove

CHARACTERS: Ennis, Gleda the Goat, Sam Guevenne, Sanguine, Senna, Ysolda

ENEMIES: Conjurer, Fire Mage, Ice Mage, Moira, Necromancer, Pyromancer, Storm Mage, Giant

◊ **OBJECTIVES:** Participate in a drinking contest with Sam Guevenne, Find Sam Guevenne, Find the staff, Help clean up the Temple of Dibella, Apologize to the priestesses of Dibella, Ask about Sam and the staff in Rorikstead, Find Gleda the Goat, Bring Gleda the Goat back to Ennis in Rorikstead, Talk to Ysolda in Whiterun about the staff, Find the wedding ring in Witchmist Grove, Take the wedding ring, Return the wedding ring to Ysolda in Whiterun, Head to Morvunskar, Search Morvunskar for Sam and the staff

▷ Drinking to Forget

Enter one of the many taverns in Skyrim. This could be the Bannered Mare in Whiterun or any of the other inns in any of the Hold Cities. Sometimes you're approached by a man wearing black robes named Sam Guevenne, who wonders if you'd like to play a drinking game in order to win a staff. If Sam isn't in the tavern, visit another watering hole; be patient until he appears. Sam produces some "special brew" and gets started immediately.

◊ **OBJECTIVE:** Participate in a drinking contest with Sam Guevenne

Sam downs a flagon and offers one to you. Swig it down. Sam brings out his flagon again and impressively downs another. Agree to the second drink. Sam tells you he's hit his limit and says that with one more drink, you'll win both the contest and the staff. You reply that you'll take that challenge. Down a third flagon. Sam tells you you're a fun person to drink with. He reckons you should join him at another place where the wine flows like water. You're about to respond when you black out.

▷ The Day After: Recovery and Recollections

Part 1: Incoherently Blathering Drunken Blasphemer!

Your next memory is waking up to a tongue-lashing from a furious priestess. Unless you've remarkable knowledge of temple gods, you don't immediately realize where you are. Priestess Senna wonders why you don't remember blathering incoherently about marriage or a goat. Or indeed, losing your temper and throwing refuse across this sacred temple of Dibella. You can:

Ask about the man named Sam. This gets you nowhere until you've tidied up your mess.

(Persuade) You can apologize and tell her you don't remember how you got here.

(Bribe) You can ask how you got here and pay for any damages.

◊ **OBJECTIVE:** Find Sam Guevenne
◊ **OBJECTIVE:** Find the staff
◊ **OBJECTIVE:** Help clean up the Temple of Dibella

Begin tidying up the temple, collecting the rubbish listed below. Among the wine bottles is a note. Read it, and a list of three items are mentioned that can "repair the broken staff." The note is signed "Sam." You're fortunate that two of the three items on the list are among the trash you're clearing up! Now there's just the small matter of searching Skyrim for Sam. And the goat.

➤ **Alto Wine**   ➤ **Giant's Toe**

➤ **Repair Supplies Note**   ➤ **Holy Water**

◊ **OBJECTIVE:** Apologize to the priestesses of Dibella

If you didn't bribe or persuade Senna, return to her after the tidy-up and apologize. As Dibella preaches forgiveness, she grudgingly lets you leave and tells you that through your slurred ranting, you mentioned the town of Rorikstead.

◊ **OBJECTIVE:** Ask about Sam and the staff in Rorikstead

Part 2: Fermented Feed—Smelling Goat Rustler!

Exit the temple. You're in Markarth, in the Reach. Your next place to investigate is Rorikstead, to the east, on the edge of the Tundra plains. Wander into town and seek Ennis, who's tending to his vegetable patch or is locked behind closed doors (which you can pick, but it's better not to show clandestine behavior under these current conditions). Ennis angrily states you have a lot of nerve showing up here again. He proceeds to admonish you for stealing Gleda—his prized goat—and selling it to a giant. At this point, you can:

(Intimidate) Threaten Ennis to tell you everything so he doesn't end up like Gleda.

(Bribe) Ask him to help retrace your steps in return for some serious coin.

(Persuade) Tell him you need Sam and the staff to return Gleda.

Or ask what needs to be done. Ennis wants his prized goat back. Unharmed.

◊ **OBJECTIVE:** Find Gleda the Goat
◊ **OBJECTIVE:** Bring Gleda the Goat back to Ennis in Rorikstead

Assuming you chose the last option, your goat hunt begins now. Head up the heath to the south of Rorikstead, where the wandering giant and his new companion are resting on the Tundra foothills. At this point, you can:

Interact with the goat so it follows you, and run from the giant with the goat trotting along behind you.

Or kill the giant and coax the goat into following you by approaching and interacting with it.

Bring the goat down the hillside and back to Ennis. In return for your goat-wrangling, Ennis mentions you left a note that had the words "Ysolda" and "Whiterun" on it.

◊ **OBJECTIVE:** Talk to Ysolda in Whiterun about the staff

Part 3: Ring-Stealing Hagraven-Loving Cheapskate!

Travel to Whiterun and locate Ysolda hanging out near her house or walking about town. She tells you she's been patient, but you still owe her. Naturally you can't remember why, so Ysolda explains that it isn't about the money; you were in love, and she gave you a wedding ring. If the wedding isn't occurring, you should give her back the ring. Alas, you don't have it, or any memory of becoming engaged. Ysolda is shocked that you've mislaid both the ring and your betrothed! Especially after you told her a sweet story of how you met in Witchmist Grove! At this point, you can:

(Persuade) Plead with Ysolda that you need to get to the wedding.

(Intimidate) Shout that you want to know what else you said.

(Bribe) Pay a considerable sum for the ring.

Or ask what needs to be done. Ysolda wants the ring back if you aren't getting married.

◊ **OBJECTIVE:** Find the wedding ring in Witchmist Grove
◊ **OBJECTIVE:** Take the wedding ring

South of Windhelm, deep in Eastmarch is a fog-filled pine glade with a lone cottage surrounded by spikes and various skewered animal heads. As you close in, a Hagraven named Moira bounds toward you, ready to consummate the love you have for each other! When you explain you want the ring back, the Hagraven hisses that she won't share you with Esmerelda (another Hagraven) and immediately attacks you. Kill your cackling fiancée, watching for her icy attacks, and claim the third ingredient from your list, as well as the Wedding Ring.

➤ **Wedding Ring**   ➤ **Hagraven Feathers**

◊ **OBJECTIVE:** Return the wedding ring to Ysolda in Whiterun

Return to Ysolda and hand the ring back by speaking to her. She's sad that it didn't work out for you both, especially as you'd told her there would be a huge ceremony at Morvunskar. You even told her about a magic staff, too! That's the information you needed!

◊ **OBJECTIVE:** Head to Morvunskar
◊ **OBJECTIVE:** Search Morvunskar for Sam and the staff

▶ Sam's Special Delivery

The fort of Morvunskar is on the opposite bank of the White River, just southwest of Windhelm. Enter the battlements, and you're immediately assaulted by a variety of magicians: Expect combat with Fire Mages, Ice Mages, Storm Mages, pyromancers, conjurers, and necromancers. Open the main wooden door with the lantern hanging near it, in the middle of the upper wall to the west, and enter the fort. Battle (or sneak) southeast once you're inside. Go down the steps leading to a wooden door and a winding stone tunnel. This brings you out into a huge column-filled chamber with more mages to dispatch or flee from. Dash to the double set of stone steps and run to the upper northeast corner. As if by magic, a portal blinks open and you vanish.

You appear in the Misty Grove. There's a strange, immediate sensation of brooding fear tempered by an odd calmness. Fireflies flutter by. Lanterns light your way along an easy-to-follow path over a stream that leads to an outdoor tavern. That master trickster Sam Guevenne greets you by the mead barrel. Ask where you are, and he's not surprised you don't remember your previous trip here. But you've definitely earned the staff. Mention you have everything needed to repair it. None of that matters, you see...

Quest Conclusion

Sam—or Sanguine the Lord of Revelry, as he's known to his worshippers—simply needed you to go out into the world and spread merriment. Sanguine has chosen you, whether you like it or not. But you gain the staff as a partial benefit for your forgotten hijinks. A moment later, you're back in the tavern where you first met Sam, a little worse for wear but carrying an impressively potent staff.

➤ **Sanguine's Rose**

Postquest Activities

After this quest, there's a (random) chance that World Encounter: The Drunken Dare* occurs. You run into someone who states that you and Sam dared him to head into a bandit camp. He says he did the dare, and you owe him 10,000 gold! You can pay him, negotiate the price down to 750, or kill him (he'll attack if you fail either of the nonviolent plans).

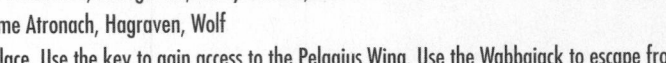
PREREQUISITES: None

INTERSECTING QUESTS: Side Quest: The Man Who Cried Wolf

LOCATIONS: Solitude, Blue Palace, The Mind of a Madman, Pelagius Wing

CHARACTERS: Anger, Dervenin, Erdi, Falk Firebeard, Goat, Jarl Elisif the Fair, Little Pelagius, Pelagius the Mad, Pelagius's Flame Thrall, Pelagius's Frost Thrall, Pelagius's Storm Thrall, Pelagius the Suspicious, Pelagius the Tormented, Sheogorath, Sultry Maiden, Una

ENEMIES: Anger, Bandit Chief, Bodyguard, Dragon Priest, Flame Atronach, Hagraven, Wolf

◊ **OBJECTIVES:** Gain access to the Pelagius Wing of the Blue Palace, Use the key to gain access to the Pelagius Wing, Use the Wabbajack to escape from Pelagius's Mind

▶ Taking Pity on an Old Madman

Wandering between the graveyard (just below the Hall of the Dead) and the Bard's College in Solitude is a strange man named Dervenin. As you approach, you see that he has two sunken black holes where his eyes once were. Agitated, he asks you to help him. He isn't the usual beggar you encounter in these Hold Cities. Ask what he needs and he tells you his master has abandoned him and doesn't want to see him anymore. His master doesn't want Dervenin interrupting his vacation. The last time Dervenin saw his master, he watched him visit the Blue Palace and snuck into the forbidden wing to "have tea" with an old friend. He hands you a Hip Bone; it's important you have that when entering the Pelagius Wing. You can ask this mad old coot more questions about his master before you leave.

➤ **Pelagius's Hip Bone**

◊ **OBJECTIVE:** Gain access to the Pelagius Wing of the Blue Palace
♦ **TARGET:** Falk Firebeard, Erdi, or Una, in the Blue Palace, in Solitude

NOTE Those with eagle eyes may recognize Dervenin as a High Priest of Mania in a place known as the Shivering Isles. The Hip Bone you're given may have some magical power. Or it could be an old bone you've been given by a lunatic. As this is a quest item that you can't drop, you can't tell for certain.

You need a key to enter the Pelagius Wing. Journey southeast along the main Solitude avenue and enter the majestic Blue Palace. If this is your first time visiting, head up either staircase to the throne room, where Jarl Elisif the Fair is listening to the fearful stories of a villager named Varnius (Side Quest: The Man Who Cried Wolf). Once the conversation is over, approach the person you're attempting to gain the key from. You can:

Talk to Falk Firebeard, and tell him you need to enter the Pelagius Wing. If you're friends with him (i.e., you've completed Side Quest: The Man Who Cried Wolf, or Miscellaneous Objective: Delivery*), you can then reassure him that you'll be careful, but he hands over the key warily and warns you not to return with anything from that part of the palace; too many dark deeds transpired in those halls....

(Persuade) Ask Erdi to give you the key.

Or speak to Una, who simply gives you the key without any problems.

➤ **Pelagius Wing Key**

◊ **OBJECTIVE:** Use the key to gain access to the Pelagius Wing

Head back down the stairs and locate the locked door to the southwest. Go into the accursed wing, stepping past the debris and cobwebbed tables, animal heads, and furniture. This entire chamber is suspiciously silent. Creep up the steps and head down the long hall...until you blink out of existence!

▶ Pelagius Has a Lot on His Mind

It's a slightly overcast day in this wooded glade. Pelagius the Mad refuses another cup of tea; it goes right through him, and he has a lot on his mind. Edge into this unknown realm, watching Pelagius converse with a gaunt but jovial fellow named Sheogorath. The banquet of cheese and mammoth trunk looks delectable. If you know your history, or witness the ongoing conversation between the crazies, you'll learn that Emperor Pelagius III was an old ruler of Solitude back in the Third Era, 400 hundred years ago. As the bone you're carrying is from Pelagius's corpse, it soon becomes clear you're not in Skyrim anymore. Or at least, any sane part of it. Sheogorath dismisses Pelagius from his table after a perceived slight about cheese, then turns his pupilless eyes on you.

Begin the conversation with Sheogorath, the Daedric Prince of Madness. You can satisfy your curiosity by asking other questions, but, you're here to deliver that message from Dervenin, telling Sheogorath to end his vacation.

You continue your conversations as Sheogorath's chatter becomes a little more sinister. He explains he is a shadow in your subconscious but brightens up considerably when he decides to finish his holiday here. Naturally, though, there is one condition: All you need to do is escape this mental maze, using all your wits and weaponry. Unfortunately, Sheogorath takes the latter away from you, swapping your inventory for a Wabbajack.

➤ **Wabbajack**

◊ **OBJECTIVE:** Use the Wabbajack to escape from Pelagius's Mind
♦ **TARGET:** Pelagius's three states of mind

The Wabbajack appears in your hand. It is the only weapon, aside from your fists, that you have, and punching a Daedric Prince gets you nowhere. Instead, begin the long, strange trip to extricate yourself from Pelagius's subconscious. The hedge stones on each avenue surrounding Sheogorath's feast are a path into a different part of Pelagius's psyche.

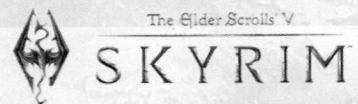

Freeing the madness and doubt from each part shall set you free. Set off down any avenue you wish; complete the three parts in any order.

> **TIP** **What is the Wabbajack?** This strange staff of chaotic randomness is both beneficial and damaging, effective and useless. Fire it, and a bolt of red light hits the target. A random effect usually occurs. The target could shrink, grow, disappear, or turn into anything from a mammoth trunk to a Greybeard. This isn't an offensive weapon; this is the cane of madness!

> **NOTE** Strike Sheogorath with your fists, zap him with the Wabbajack, or eat his food, and he'll blithely ignore your pettiness. Take on those tasks, why don't you?

Path 1: Gaining Confidence

Trek southeast down this road to see a manifestation of Pelagius's Anger towering above a tiny man named Confidence. This fight is one-sided, and you witness Pelagius's deepest, keenest hatred for himself.

Puzzle Solution: Help even the fight by aiming the Wabbajack at Anger and hitting it with blasts. The first shrinks it to half its size. The second shrinks it to the same size as Confidence, but Anger then summons two ethereal axes to batter Confidence even more. Aim at Confidence now, and zap it with the Wabbajack. Continue this until Confidence becomes man-sized. Sheogorath congratulates you; Pelagius is finally ready to love himself, while hating everyone else. This task is now complete.

> **NOTE** At this point, you can have a conversation with Sheogorath back at his tea party. But this is only critical to your progress once you journey down all three paths.

Path 2: Pulverizing Paranoia

Head northwest down this avenue to a small stone arena where Pelagius is displaying his paranoia in the arena of magic. His Stone, Frost, and Flame Thralls are receiving a drubbing as he fights himself, looking on from across the arena you cannot reach or enter.

Puzzle Solution: The thralls are merely an enticing diversion to the real problem: Pelagius the Suspicious is sitting on his throne, flanked by a Bodyguard on either side of him. The Bodyguards are the source of his paranoia, so shoot either of them. When you strike one, both turn into Wolves, turning on Pelagius and attacking him. His paranoia is vanquished.

Path 3: Neutralizing Night Terrors

Head northeast, and witness Pelagius the Tormented attempting to sleep on his bed. You need to wake him up and repel those particularly persistent night terrors.

Puzzle Solution: Pelagius the Tormented is asleep and continues to slumber throughout this literal nightmare. Zap him so the first of his night terrors, a Wolf, bounds into existence and turns on him (or you!). Use the Wabbajack and shoot the Wolf, getting rid of it. It turns into a goat. The goat isn't terrifying at all, so leave it alone and zap Pelagius again.

A Bandit Chief then comes screaming out of the ether. Zap it before it can attack Pelagius. The chief turns into Little Pelagius, the aspect of the child who had these nightmares. Leave Little Pelagius alone and shoot the Hagraven that has appeared to torment both Pelagius aspects. The old crone turns into a Sultry Maiden, much to Little Pelagius's delight. Don't shoot the Maiden; blast Pelagius the Tormented instead, conjuring a Flame Atronach nearby. Quickly shoot that, then Pelagius the Tormented once again. This conjures the final terror: a Dragon Priest. Shoot that, and it turns into a treasure chest, freeing Pelagius's mind from sleeping nightmares.

Quest Conclusion

After you've trekked all three paths successfully, return to the tea party and inform Sheogorath that you've fixed Pelagius's mind with your Wabbajack. He is forced to honor his end of the bargain. He hopes you'll stop in for a strawberry torte the next time you're in New Sheoth and blinks you out of Pelagius's mind. You return to the musty wing of the Blue Palace and can end this enforced holiday yourself.

Postquest Activities

After this quest, Dervenin has disappeared from Solitude. There's also a (random) chance that World Encounter: Ramblings of a Mad Woman* occurs. A crazed woman demands you use the Wabbajack on her. Oblige her if you wish!

WAKING NIGHTMARE

PREREQUISITES: None

INTERSECTING QUESTS: None

LOCATIONS: Dawnstar, Windpeak Inn, Nightcaller Temple

CHARACTERS: Dawnstar Guard, Erandur, Fruki, Irgnir, Thoring, Vaermina

ENEMIES: Awakened, Brother Thorek, Brother Veren Duleri, Orcish Invader, Vaermina Devotee

◊ **OBJECTIVES:** Follow Erandur to Nightcaller Temple, Speak to Erandur, Follow Erandur, Follow Erandur to the Library, Speak to Erandur, Locate *The Dreamstride,* Speak to Erandur, Follow Erandur to the Laboratory, Speak to Erandur, Locate Vaermina's Torpor, Speak to Erandur, Drink Vaermina's Torpor, Release the Miasma, Disable the Magical Barrier, Speak to Erandur, Follow Erandur to the Skull of Corruption, Defeat Veren and Thorek, Speak to Erandur, Wait for Erandur to dispel the barrier, Murder Erandur, OR Allow Erandur to complete his ritual, Take the Skull of Corruption

Night Terrors

Dawnstar is the last port before Windhelm that is not icebound. The population of this Hold City seems a little preoccupied. When you walk the thoroughfares, Dawnstar Guards may comment on the nightmares the entire town is suffering from. More guards murmur the same rumor. To gain more solid information on what is going on, visit the town's tavern, the Windpeak Inn. The first time you enter, a group of locals are discussing the "curse" with a priest.

Listen in as Irgnir and Fruki argue with each other. Irgnir wants to move out of town, but her sister is telling her she's just having bad dreams and nothing more. Erandur the priest tries to placate Irgnir and agrees they aren't out of the ordinary. Thoring the barkeep pipes up as the sisters begin to chatter about why Irgnir is having the same dream every night. Erandur is looking into this oddity and asks the locals to put their trust into Lady Mara. The sisters reluctantly agree, allowing you to step in and ask Erandur what exactly is going on. Respond as you wish, after which Erandur reveals the truth: The dreams are manifestations created by the Daedric Lord Vaermina. She has a hunger for memories, leaving nightmares behind after consumption. Before the damage Vaermina is doing becomes permanent, Erandur needs to return to the source of the problem—the Nightcaller Temple. Can you help?

◊ **OBJECTIVE:** Follow Erandur to Nightcaller Temple
◊ **OBJECTIVE:** Speak to Erandur
◊ **OBJECTIVE:** Follow Erandur

Erandur explains the history of the temple as you scale the hill above Dawnstar. It is now a ruin within a ruin. Erandur established a small shrine to Mara within the tower's entry hall, hoping to seek her guidance. Once Erandur reaches the temple door, he waits for you to join him. Speak with him, and he warns you about the dangers within. Years ago, the temple was raided by Orcs seeking revenge for a similar nightmarish affliction. The priests of Vaermina knew they were outmatched and released a strange vapor they called "the Miasma." This caused the entire temple to fall into a magical sleep, suspended in time. When the temple is unsealed, Erandur fears the Miasma may dissipate and the Orcs and priests may wake up. Extended exposure to the Miasma leads to lunacy. Once you're informed of these potential unpleasant side effects, follow Erandur into the structure.

Once inside, Erandur passes the small shrine to Mara, and approaches an area of wall. He casts a spell and the wall illuminates, becoming semi-transparent and bathed in a strange hue. Erandur forces his way through the wall and into the previously inaccessible part of the temple. Follow him past a barred window overlooking the main altar to Vaermina, a strange skull that is shielded by magic. His revelations are shocking: The cause of the nightmares is the Skull of Corruption! Then he moves along the barrier. At the bottom of the stairs, Erandur inspects a doorway with energy blocking your way. Before you can inspect the door, two Orcish Invaders wake from their slumber. Attack them immediately!

 TIP The enemies you face throughout this temple take a few moments to stand up, draw their weapon, and attack. Use this time to hit them as many times as you can, wounding them before they can counterattack.

With the Orcs dead, Erandur curses, telling you the priests must have activated the barrier when the Miasma was released. He believes there's a way to bypass the barrier to reach the tower's inner sanctum, but it involves checking the library for confirmation. When you ask how he knows so much about this place, Erandur finally reveals that he, too, was a priest of Vaermina. Your response can be accusatory or quizzical. Erandur quickly tells you he's been seeking redemption from Mara and living in regret.

◊ **OBJECTIVE:** Follow Erandur to the library

Vaermina's Corruption

Head back up the stairs and wait for Erandur to open the wooden door to the east. He warns you that the Awakened are likely to be active. Sure enough, a Vaermina Devotee and Orcish Invader rise from the rubble of the library. Dispatch them before dropping to the ground floor and attacking two more Devotees on this level. Return to Erandur, as he has a task for you.

◊ **OBJECTIVE:** Speak to Erandur

Ask Erandur what you're looking for, and he describes a book of alchemical recipes called *The Dreamstride*. The cover bears a likeness of Vaermina.

◊ **OBJECTIVE:** Locate *The Dreamstride*

Begin thoroughly searching the library, which contains numerous interesting (but not quest-related) tomes. *The Dreamstride* is located on the upper ledge (accessed via a fallen column) of the library's top floor, in the eastern corner. Carefully head across and remove the book from its pedestal, between two bookcases.

➤ **The Dreamstride**

◊ **OBJECTIVE:** Speak to Erandur

Inform Erandur that you've found the book, and he quickly thumbs through it. Praising Mara, he reads that there is indeed a way past the barrier, and it involves a liquid known as Vaermina's Torpor. Digesting this brew allows one to enter a "Dreamstride" state, using dreams to travel distances in the real world. As Erandur isn't going to drink it, this task will fall to you soon enough. Before following him, you can argue the dangers of attempting such a feat with Erandur. The temple's east wing has a laboratory that may contain a sample of the torpor.

◊ **OBJECTIVE:** Follow Erandur to the laboratory

Move through a small connecting corridor to a stone storage chamber with liquids and barrels lining a wooden platform. Kill the priest and Orc rising from their slumber, then head southwest, into the ruins of the laboratory. Expect further attacks from Vaermina Devotees and more Orc Invaders. After everyone except Erandur is dead, halt your bloodletting.

> ◊ **OBJECTIVE:** Speak to Erandur
> ◊ **OBJECTIVE:** Locate Vaermina's Torpor

Erandur needs you to look around for a small bottle containing the Torpor. While he searches upstairs, head to the three wooden shelving cases below the Alchemy Lab, close to the laboratory exit. The Torpor is sitting on the middle set of shelves.

➤ **Vaermina's Torpor**

> ◊ **OBJECTIVE:** Speak to Erandur
> ◊ **OBJECTIVE:** Drink Vaermina's Torpor

Dreamstride: A Blast from the Past

Return to Erandur, letting him know you've secured the Torpor. He tells you to drink, as the fate of Dawnstar depends on reaching the inner sanctum and halting Vaermina's hold over the locals' dreams. Access your Items > Potions inventory, and use Vaermina's Torpor to continue. The vision comes quickly as you enter the Dreamstride. Your dream seems to harken back to the Orc warband's attack on the temple. Brothers Thorek and Veren are attempting to keep the Skull from the horde. Veren tells Thorek they have no choice and must release the Miasma. Veren turns to you, addressing you as "Brother Casimir," and orders you to activate the barrier and release the Miasma.

> ◊ **OBJECTIVE:** Release the Miasma

Begin your race through the inner temple chambers, heading east and then south into a dining chamber where fighting is already occurring. Ignore the battles entirely; you're here in someone else's past consciousness to turn a dream into a wrinkle of a new reality. Turn left (east), heading into the dormitory. Go up the stairs and to the long corridor running west. Turn north, winding through more corridors until you reach the curved corridor above the Skull. Search for the pull handle, and yank it to release the Miasma. Your vision fades.

> ◊ **OBJECTIVE:** Disable the Magical Barrier
> ◊ **OBJECTIVE:** Speak to Erandur

You blink into present reality, where the magical barrier blocking the doorway still crackles. Take the Common Soul Gem, which focuses the barrier, from its wall sconce, and the barrier begins to fade. Speak to Erandur. Although wowed by the Torpor's effects, Erandur quickly snaps out of his malaise and focuses on ending the Skull of Corruption.

➤ **Common Soul Gem**

> ◊ **OBJECTIVE:** Follow Erandur to the Skull of Corruption

At this point, you and Erandur must retrace the steps you took in the dream, all the way back to the area where you spoke with the two Brother monks. Erandur leads the way. Back him up when the sleeping Orcs and priests stagger to their feet and fight each other and you.

Continue until you reach the lower passageway with the Skull of Corruption glowing behind its shield ahead (west) of you. At this point, Brothers Veren Duleri and Thorek, now awakened from their slumber, approach Erandur, who is happy they are alive. The feeling isn't mutual, as Veren spits verbal hatred to "Casimir," Erandur's real name (and the body you were inhabiting during the Dreamstride!). Veren calls Erandur a traitor who left them to die and fled before the Miasma took hold. The priests aren't about to let you disturb this Skull. There's only one way out of this mess....

> ◊ **OBJECTIVE:** Defeat Veren and Thorek
> ◊ **OBJECTIVE:** Speak to Erandur

Bring your battle to the two priests, focusing on the one that Erandur isn't fighting so that combat is quicker. When both priests are dead, approach Erandur, who seems genuinely remorseful for killing his friends. Answer him how you wish, before Erandur steps forward, ready to perform the ritual Lady Mara granted to him.

> ◊ **OBJECTIVE:** Wait for Erandur to dispel the barrier

Erandur slowly ascends the steps and implores Lady Mara to break through the barrier and send the Skull to the depths of Oblivion. A moment later, the barrier disappears. The goddess Vaermina now speaks from inside your head, attempting to convince you to kill Erandur and grip the Skull of Corruption for yourself! At the same time, Erandur begins a ritual spell. This takes 30 seconds to complete, leaving you this much time to decide between two possible choices: murder Erandur or let him complete his ritual.

> ◊ **OBJECTIVE:** Murder Erandur
> ◊ **OBJECTIVE:** OR Allow Erandur to complete his ritual

Quest Conclusion 1

It takes only a couple of swings into Erandur's back to betray him and claim the Skull of Corruption for yourself! Continue to strike him until he falls.

> ◊ **OBJECTIVE:** Take the Skull of Corruption

Step up to the Skull Pedestal and activate it. The Skull of Corruption, a staff of ill repute, is now yours! Use it in Vaermina's honor.

➤ **Skull of Corruption**

Quest Conclusion 2

It takes only 30 seconds for Erandur to finish the ritual, banishing the Skull of Corruption and Vaermina's influence. Erandur stays at the temple entrance, by the Shrine to Mara. As you aided him, so shall he aid you:

➤ **Follower:** Erandur

Postquest Activities

Erandur's powerful spells are excellent, and he is a formidable magician if you wish to bring him along.

OTHER FACTIONS QUESTS

▶ Optimal Quest Start

Quests involving the more minor factions of Skyrim have specific prerequisites as listed below. In general, in order to undertake the missions for the Greybeards or the Blades, you must progress through the Main Quest until those factions become available. However, you may visit and help the Bards College at your earliest convenience.

> **NOTE** **Cross-Referencing:** Do you want to see maps and learn more about the traps, non-quest-related items, collectibles, crafting areas, and other important rooms of note in every location during these quests? Then cross-reference the location you travel to with the information on that location contained in this guide's Atlas.

AVAILABLE QUESTS

There are a total of 10 different quests and other activities available from these factions.

✓	QUEST NAME	PREREQUISITES
	THE GREYBEARDS	
	Word Wall Revelations*	Complete Main Quest: The Horn of Jurgen Windcaller
	Meditations on Words of Power*	Complete Main Quest: The Throat of the World
	THE BLADES	
	Rebuilding the Blades*	Complete Main Quest: Alduin's Wall
	Dragon Hunting*	Complete Main Quest: Alduin's Wall
	Dragonslayer's Blessing*	Complete Main Quest: Alduin's Wall

✓	QUEST NAME	PREREQUISITES
	Dragon Research*	Complete Main Quest: Alduin's Wall
	THE BARDS COLLEGE	
	Tending the Flames	None
	Finn's Lute	Tending the Flames
	Pantea's Flute	Tending the Flames
	Rjorn's Drum	Tending the Flames

> **NOTE**
> ✱ Quest names marked with this symbol do not appear in your Quest Menu list, although objectives may.

THE GREYBEARDS QUESTS

The following activities occur after you complete certain parts of the Main Quest. From this point on, High Hrothgar in Whiterun Hold is the main base of operations for the Greybeards. Providing you partner with Master Arngeir and Paarthurnax and do not complete Main Quest: Paarthurnax, you can help the Greybeards preserve the Way of the Voice. There are now two Radiant Quests you can attempt.

OVERVIEW

▶ Sanctuary: High Hrothgar, in Whiterun Hold

High Hrothgar, on approach from the 7,000 steps.

High Hrothgar interior, during a period of contemplation.

An ancient monastery high up on the slope of the Throat of the World, High Hrothgar is home to the Greybeards, masters of Thu'um—the voice powers made famous by Tiber Septim.

▶ Important Characters

Leader: Paarthurnax

Paarthurnax lives above High Hrothgar, at the summit of the Throat of the World, and serves as the supreme master of the Greybeards. He remembers back to the days of the ancient Dragon War when Alduin was defeated and imprisoned. He views events from a distance and from a uniquely detached point of view.

Elder: Master Arngeir

Arngeir is the most powerful of the Greybeards, although this isn't immediately obvious to the rare visitors he receives. His initial reaction to you is cautious; he wants to believe that a Dragonborn has returned but hardly dares to hope it is true.

> **NOTE** The other Greybeards—Masters Wulfgar, Einarth, and Borri—do not speak; their voices are too powerful. Only Master Arngeir is skilled enough to master his voice to the point of conversation. However, they have been known to attempt conversations with those powerful enough to withstand their voices. They excel in the training of Shouts by gestures and demonstration.

NOTE * Quest names marked with this symbol do not appear in your Quest Menu list, although objectives may.

This Radiant Quest becomes available as soon as you complete Main Quest: The Horn of Jurgen Windcaller. You can complete it multiple times. It is always given to you by Master Arngeir.

Speak to Master Arngeir about the Greybeards, and he mentions that there are Words of Power scattered across Skyrim. Most are lost to the world, found only by those stumbling into underground passageways or snowy mountains not used for centuries. If you want, Master Arngeir can place a marker on your world map, randomly showing you a Word Wall you haven't yet discovered.

◊ **OBJECTIVE:** Find the Word of Power in [random location]

Quest Conclusion

Journey to a location that Arngeir marked, and absorb the Word of Power. This may involve battling any number of guardians, usually Draugr or a dragon. The Word Walls Arngeir reveals may be ones perched atop mountain peaks or hidden in deep dungeons. He usually won't reveal locations you've already been to, unless you've forgotten or missed the Word Wall at that location.

➤ **Word of Power**

Postquest Activities

You can return to Master Arngeir and begin this quest repeatedly. A section in the Training Chapter on page 32 lists the locations of all the Word Walls and their associated Shouts.

NOTE Sometimes this quest won't be available; this means that Arngeir hasn't discovered a location for you at the moment. It is wise to return later (try around three days) to see if his scrying has revealed any more locations.

MEDITATIONS ON WORDS OF POWER*

NOTE This Radiant Quest becomes available as soon as you complete Main Quest: The Throat of the World. You can complete this multiple times. It is always given to you by Paarthurnax.

Trek to the summit of the Throat of the World and speak with Paarthurnax. He has much to tell you about the Words of Power and can even teach basic meditations to your Words of Power. Ask Paarthurnax if he trains people, and after the response, ask about the meditations. Paarthurnax grants you a single meditation. The exact one is up to you:

➤ **Perk:** Force Without Effort (Fus)   ➤ **Perk:** Eternal Spirit (Feim)   ➤ **Perk:** The Fire Within (Yol)

Quest Conclusion

Fus grants you 25 percent defense against stagger, and you stagger opponents 25 percent more often. Feim grants you 25 percent more health regeneration while you're ethereal. Yol grants you 25 percent bonus damage when you use the Fire Breath Shout.

Postquest Activities

You can return to Paarthurnax at any time and change the Meditation to another of the three perks. You can have only one Meditation at a time.

THE BLADES QUESTS

The following activities occur only after you complete Main Quest: Alduin's Wall. From this moment on, the Sky Haven Temple in the Reach is the main base of operations for the Blades. Providing you partner with Delphine and Esbern and complete Main Quest: Paarthurnax, you can help the Blades to gain a foothold in Skyrim once more. There are now four Radiant Quests you can attempt.

OVERVIEW

Sanctuary: Sky Haven Temple, in the Reach

Sky Haven Temple, entrance to the sacred interior.

Sky Haven interior, dominated by Alduin's Wall.

An ancient Akaviri sanctuary, Sky Haven Temple was built as a hidden outpost. The secret interior chambers are dominated by Alduin's Wall, the ancient mural that shows the history and future of Alduin—how he was defeated in ancient times and the prophecy of his return.

Important Characters

Blade Leader: Delphine

The last Blade left in Tamriel (as far as she knows), Delphine is hard-bitten and a survivor. Any idealism has been largely driven out of her during her years on the run. Competent, she tends toward paranoia. She hates the Thalmor above all and will stop at nothing to see them destroyed. Full of darkness and despair, she may yet be turned back toward idealism and the rebirth of the Blades.

Blade Archivist: Esbern

After the Blades' destruction, Esbern went underground, ignoring any messages for help from other Blades (having seen that this was often a Thalmor trap), which allowed him to survive. Esbern has been obsessed with the end of the world for decades. Now that Alduin has returned, he immediately recognizes this as the beginning of the end—without a Dragonborn, there is no hope to stop him.

REBUILDING THE BLADES*

NOTE * Quest names marked with this symbol do not appear in your Quest Menu list, although objectives may.

This Radiant Quest becomes available as soon as you complete Main Quest: Alduin's Wall. You can complete it multiple times. It is always given to you by Delphine.

Speak to Delphine about the Blades, and she mentions how few of them are left; in fact, there are only two in existence! To bolster the numbers, and because it is the Blades' sacred duty to protect the Dragonborn (you), Delphine asks if you know of any like-minded individuals who can give their hearts and minds to this course.

◊ **OBJECTIVE: Bring a Follower to Delphine**

Journey to a location where you left a Follower or where you can obtain one. Then return and speak to Delphine with the Follower accompanying you.

Quest Conclusion

Delphine welcomes your Follower into the fold. As time passes and you return to see your Follower, they are able to wear Blades armor and carry weapons used by the Blades, and they live in the Sky Haven Temple. They can accompany you on travels just as before. You can repeat this quest, turn in two additional Followers, and pick one to travel with you, just as before.

Postquest Activities

This is a good way to amass a small "pool" of Followers to take with you on journeys in the future.

DRAGONSLAYER'S BLESSING*

NOTE This Radiant Quest becomes available as soon as you complete Main Quest: Alduin's Wall. You can complete it multiple times. It is always given to you by Esbern.

Speak to Esbern and ask if the sage has any advice for you. Providing you're in good standing with the Blades, he mentions a blessing he can perform. Request this blessing, and he duly obliges.

Quest Conclusion

You are imbued with Esbern's Dragonslayer's Blessing, which gives you a +10 percent Critical Hit versus dragons for five days.

➤ **Dragonslayer's Blessing**

Postquest Activities

Once this wears off, ask Esbern to renew it if you wish.

DRAGON RESEARCH*

NOTE This Radiant Quest becomes available as soon as you complete the Blades Quest: Dragon Hunting.* You can complete it only once. It is always given to you by Esbern.

Once you've completed your first Dragon Hunting Quest for Esbern, report back to him. He's interested in you locating any Dragon Scales or Dragon Bones you may have pried off the corpses of the dragons you've slain previously.

◊ **OBJECTIVE: Bring a Dragon Scale and a Dragon Bone to Esbern**

Quest Conclusion

When you return with a Dragon Scale and a Dragon Bone to Esbern (which you may already have gathered, in which case, speak to him again), he concocts a strange potion and hands it to you. This potion imbues you with a 10 percent damage reduction from dragon attacks.

➤ **Esbern's Potion** ➤ **Perk: Dragon Infusion**

NOTE This Radiant Quest becomes available as soon as you complete The Blades Quest: Rebuilding the Blades.* You can complete it multiple times. It is always given to you by Esbern.

◊ **OBJECTIVE:** Kill the dragon in the [random] dragon lair

Once you've turned in three of your Followers to Delphine, and she's welcomed them into the fold, speak to Esbern, steering the conversation toward dragon lairs. When you ask Esbern if he has knowledge of any lairs, he informs you that he does and points out a [random] lair on your world map. If Esbern hasn't found a dragon lair, he'll mention the realm is quiet at the moment.

Quest Conclusion

Set off on your journey to slay the dragon, which is, after all, the raison d'être of the Blades. Begin combat with this hated beast. The Followers you have accrued will also stand and fight with you, making for an epic assault. Bring down the dragon and then report back to Esbern.

➤ **Dragon Bone**   ➤ **Dragon Soul**
➤ **Dragon Scales**

Postquest Activities

Protect any Blades you wish to see live to fight another day; once Blades (your old Followers) die during battle, they cannot be replaced.

THE BARDS COLLEGE QUESTS

◊ Sanctuary: Bards College, in Solitude

This College has attracted the young, gifted, or rich and ungifted from across the realm of Skyrim. It is where Nords send the few sons and daughters without an aptitude for farmwork or battle.

◊ Important Characters

Headmaster: Viarmo

Viarmo is totally apolitical when it comes to the Civil War. His only concern is the welfare of the Bards College. He is politically shrewd but has masterfully steered clear of taking sides or taking stands on any of the issues of the day. The Bards' role is to entertain and record the events of history, not to make them.

Dean of History: Giraud Gemane

Giraud also carries out many of the bureaucratic duties at the College. He is a mousy, quiet man, and not at all what one would expect from a bardic performer. In truth, he has a certain degree of stage fright. However, his mathematical precision and perfectionism have made him one of the best performers of the drums, piano, and several other "lesser" instruments.

Dean of Lutes: Inge Six-Fingers

Inge doesn't really have six fingers, but anyone who watches her play the lute believes she does. She is an old, crotchety woman who would rather burn her own lute than become headmaster because it would remove her from teaching. However, she will reluctantly put the needs of the College ahead of her own feelings if necessary.

Master Vocalist: Pantea Ateia

Pantea is one of the youngest masters of Voice that the Bards College in Solitude has ever had. Her performances are highly sought after, and she frequently plays at the palace for Elisif. Unlike Headmaster Viarmo, she is a supporter of the Imperial cause in Skyrim. In deference to the headmaster, she keeps her opinions largely to herself.

There are also students inside the College. These include the following:

Jorn: The most advanced student in the school. He is particularly enamored with the battle drum.

Aia Arria: The best singer. She is keenly aware of how she can enchant people with her voice, especially men.

At-Af-Alan: He has just started his lessons and spends more time with Giraud learning rhythm and beat.

Illdi: A recent enrollment and enthusiastic about memorizing the tales of old, her performances are timid and underwhelming.

MEDITATIONS ON WORDS OF POWER ◊ REBUILDING THE BLADES ◊ DRAGONSLAYER'S BLESSING ◊ DRAGON RESEARCH ◊ DRAGON HUNTING ◊ THE BARDS COLLEGE   325

TRANING   THE INVENTORY   THE BESTIARY   ◊ QUESTS   ATLAS OF SKYRIM   APPENDICES AND INDEX

PREREQUISITES: None

INTERSECTING QUESTS: None

LOCATIONS: Dead Men's Respite, Solitude, Bards College, Blue Palace

CHARACTERS: General Tullius, Giraud Gemane, Jarl Elisif the Fair, Jorn, Svaknir, Viarmo

ENEMIES: Draugr, Frostbite Spider, King Olaf One-Eye, Skeever

◊ **OBJECTIVES:** Find King Olaf's Verse, Return to the Bards College, Help Viarmo reconstruct Olaf's Verse, Meet Viarmo at the Blue Palace, Watch Viarmo perform Olaf's Verse, Speak to Viarmo, Speak to Jorn, Attend the Burning of King Olaf

▷ Unearthing Arcane Edda

If you speak with any of the Bards who sing and play (usually in the main inn or tavern in any of Skyrim's main cities), they mention that you might be interested in becoming a member of the Bards College. These hints are optional to find but point you in the direction of the College.

When you're ready to become a Bard, visit the Avenues District. One of the fancier buildings houses the Bards College, as indicated by the door icon on your local map. The College Headmaster Viarmo is in the lobby of this building.

He warns you that the College accepts few applicants, but for your interview, he has a task that might be appropriate. He tells you that the Burning of King Olaf Festival, held by the College each year, has been forbidden by Solitude's Jarl Elisif. He believes he can change the Jarl's mind if he can perform a reading of King Olaf's Verse, a part of the living history of Skyrim called the Poetic Edda that the Bards College keeps.

The College historian, Giraud Gemane, believes that the only surviving copy of King Olaf's Verse was buried in the old king's tomb. Giraud's research leads him to believe that Dead Men's Respite is the location where the king still lies. Look here.

◊ **OBJECTIVE:** Find King Olaf's Verse
♦ **TARGET:** King Olaf's Verse, in Dead Men's Respite

▷ A Ghost of a Chance

From Dragon Bridge, you can head south along the road to Robbers' Gorge, then follow the river east to the tomb, or take the longer (but safer) road past Fort Snowhawk before heading through the mountains. Enter the ancient barrow and head into the entry chamber, where you encounter the ghost of a bard. It turns and walks through the portcullis, fading out before you can interact with it. Return to the table and remove the Ruby Dragon Claw from the pressure plate, which raises the portcullis. You'll need the Claw later, but first, defend yourself from the restless Draugr. Your claw removal startled them out of slumber.

➤ **Ruby Dragon Claw**

With the Draugr temporarily thwarted, head through the doorway that opened and around to another sighting of the ghostly form; it bears the name Svaknir. Don't focus on it as you walk down the corridor; there's a floor pressure plate that triggers a spear trap for the unwary! Follow the narrow crypt corridor around and down, to a seemingly dead end. Look to the right for a chain that rotates the stone wall in front of you, opening up a way into the main crypt.

Svaknir walks out of sight, leaving you to fend off some Frostbite Spiders. Carefully pick your way past more cobwebs to another chain (in a crypt with fallen masonry) and pull it. The walls rotate once more, opening a new path through the tombs and unlocking several more chambers with Draugr. Fight or sneak through to the stairs heading down, avoiding the flame trap at the bottom.

You come out into a cobwebbed chamber with a floor grate, where more Frostbite Spiders descend to fight you. After looting the room, open the grate via the chain on the east wall, and drop into the water below. Wade into a damp burial chamber with spiral wooden steps that Svaknir wanders up while you deal with more Draugr and Skeever. Expect attacks from Draugr bowmen on the upper platform. Head up the steps, into the caged platform, and take stock of the path ahead of you.

On the floor to the door's right is a hinge trigger wire. Disarm it (Lockpicking: Adept) and you can open the door and safely cross the bridge.

Otherwise, open the door and carefully time your movements past the deadly swinging blades, stopping at the safe spots indicated by the candles (and lack of blood). Hurry! The longer you wait, the less synchronized the blades will be, making your run that much harder. You can also try a direct sprint (augmented with spells or a Shout if necessary), or leap to a side alcove and back onto the bridge, avoiding some of the blades. Activate the chain at the bridge's opposite end to stop the blades (allowing your followers to pass), and exit via an upper door.

Svaknir appears again near a sealed door in the next corridor. You cannot open the door for now, so continue deeper into the crypt. Deal with more Draugr along the way and a nasty magic caster trap as you move into a connecting chamber with a floor grate.

Look down, and you see Svaknir descending the steps. Then look back up to see the Draugr rushing you from all sides.

After dealing with the ambush, activate the chain between the two carved dragon heads on the south wall to open the grate. Descend the spiral steps below, use the handle, and you come upon the final resting place of Svaknir, the bard who wrote King Olaf's Verse and who first began the festival so long ago. The specter sits next to his corpse, waiting for you to bear his masterwork out into the world. Pry it from his bony fingers.

➤ **King Olaf's Verse**

◊ **OBJECTIVE:** Return to the Bards College

Ascend the spiral stairs and retrace your steps, fighting off any surviving Draugr along the way. When you return to the sealed door, Svaknir is waiting for you. He beckons you to follow and casts a spell at the door, removing the barrier. He then draws his sword and races down the hall. Follow him.

At the hall's end is a Nordic Puzzle Door.

Puzzle Solution: Bring out the Ruby Dragon Claw you took in the entrance embalming room, and inspect the palm. The forms of a Wolf, a Hawk, and another Wolf are etched into the surface. Make sure the door's outer, middle, and inner rings have those carvings shown before you insert the Claw to unlock the door.

Head up the stairs beyond the door, where Svaknir waits with ghostly sword drawn as you enter the ceremonial burial chamber of King Olaf. Svaknir challenges the dead king, and the Draugr who protected him in life rise from their thrones to defend him once more. Join the bard in battle and cut down your foes as quickly as they rise.

Svaknir shouts a second challenge, and the Draugr on the middle level stand up one by one. These foes are tougher, but with the help of your spectral ally, you can beat them.

Finally, follow Svaknir up to the upper level, where the dead king's sarcophagus lies. The bard yells out his final challenge, and King Olaf One-Eye cracks open his sarcophagus and attempts to stop you. Fight the King, as he is carrying the key that allows you to exit this chamber—unless you wish to creep around and unlock the door (Master).

TIP   Defeating Old King Olaf: It is important to note that Svaknir is invulnerable and cannot be hit by magic or weaponry. This makes him an excellent barraging machine to wade into the fray. If your own defenses are lacking, you can even stand behind him and cast your spells through him. Go ahead; he won't mind.

You don't have to fight the Draugr in the order shown previously. If Svaknir (or your Followers or summoned creatures) can handle the initial wave of Draugr, you can race to the Draugr that are still seated and slay them—ideally before they even finish standing up!

Before you leave, learn the new Word of Power from the Word Wall behind King Olaf's resting place. Then exit via the Iron Door, where Svaknir—his vengeance finally completed—vanishes in a bright light. Use the lever to remove the blocking stone, and exit Dead Men's Respite for good.

➤ **King Olaf's Treasury Key**   ➤ **Word of Power:** Whirlwind Sprint

---

▷ Return of the King

Present King Olaf's Verse to Viarmo. His jubilation quickly subsides as he reads the verse and finds some of it missing, and much of it less "poetic" than modern-day Edda. Offer to make up the missing parts of the verses. Viarmo is convinced.

◊ **OBJECTIVE:** Help Viarmo reconstruct Olaf's Verse
◊ **OBJECTIVE:** Meet Viarmo at the Blue Palace
◊ **OBJECTIVE:** Watch Viarmo perform Olaf's verse
◊ **OBJECTIVE:** Speak to Viarmo

Viarmo needs some story hooks and ideas that give the poem a more thrilling and weaving narrative than before. You are free to choose what happens in portions of the verses.

(Persuade) You can even choose a more fanciful and outlandish story for the poem. Complete the first Persuade, and a second Persuade option opens up. Choosing both of these increases the patronage paid by the court, and therefore your ultimate reward.

With the poem creatively polished, Viarmo sets off to see the Jarl of Solitude inside the Blue Palace. Follow him when the objective updates. Once inside the palace, ask Viarmo if he's ready. The objective updates again, and he climbs the stairs to gain an audience with Jarl Elisif the Fair.

After a thrilling (and some might say, unbelievable) recount of King Olaf's fable in verse form, Jarl Elisif the Fair recognizes that Solitude would be remiss if they forgo this traditional burning festival. She agrees to speak to General Tullius about the matter, and ensures that the College is well rewarded for such a stirring piece of poetry.

As soon as Viarmo leaves the Jarl's chamber, speak with him. Although you aren't a bard yet, you are set to be inducted during the festival. For now, you are to locate Jorn, who was preparing the effigy of King Olaf, and tell him to finish the preparations: The festival is back on!

◊ **OBJECTIVE:** Speak to Jorn
◆ **TARGET:** Jorn, in the Bards College

Jorn is usually in the Bards College and is an adept given responsibility for the effigy. Speak with Jorn now, and he asks you to return at 10:00 p.m. or later.

◊ **OBJECTIVE:** Attend the Burning of King Olaf

Quest Conclusion

Return to Jorn at the allotted time, and watch the festival. You can get some free food and hear some music here. Viarmo lights the effigy of King Olaf, which burns merrily. Then, in front of a crowd of Solitude citizens, Viarmo turns to you and welcomes you into the Bards College with the following rewards:

➤ **Leveled gold pieces**
➤ **Perk:** Gift of the Gab

Postquest Activities

You may now speak to any of the bards, who are now "friendly" to your cause. You can and should begin the instrument-collecting quests, detailed next.

PREREQUISITES: Bards College Quest: Tending the Flames
INTERSECTING QUESTS: None
LOCATIONS: Solitude, Bards College, Stony Creek Cave
CHARACTERS: Inge Six-Fingers
ENEMIES: Bandit
◊ **OBJECTIVES:** Find Finn's Lute

▷ A Lute for Some Loot

While staying at the Bards College, seek out Inge Six-Fingers, the slightly crotchety teacher who can play the lute like she has a vestigial finger (she doesn't). Ask her why she's so sad, and she reveals that thieves broke into the college over a year ago and removed numerous valuables. The gold and silver weren't important compared to Finn's Lute. Finn was a bard who invented the eight-course lute that is commonplace today, and the stolen lute is Finn's original instrument. Inge Six-Fingers might even crack a smile if you return with this instrument.

◊ **OBJECTIVE:** Find Finn's Lute
♦ **TARGET:** Finn's Lute, in Stony Creek Cave

Travel to Eastmarch Hold and locate Stony Creek Cave, or the dwarven mountaintop tower known as Kagrenzel. The former allows a quick scavenge for the lute, while the other involves a spectacular plummet but a full exploration of both locations. The former is described. Find the pond with the moored rowboat and jetty. Step into the nearby cave mouth with the hanging lantern and into Stony Creek Cave.

Wade through the water, and up the ramp by the draped corpse, to the rushing underground stream tunnel. Ascend the slippery and cramped tunnel. You encounter bandits in the passage. Deliver a killing blow to each of them. Now check to the right (south), up a wooden ramp and deck where the bandits appeared from. If the bandit mage hasn't attacked yet, he's usually in the small cave alcove atop the deck. Clear the area of foes, then search the treasure chest. Inside, you'll find the lute.

➤ **Finn's Lute**

Quest Conclusion

Return Finn's Lute to Inge Six-Fingers back at the Bards College. Although Inge thanks the Sweet Divines (and you) for your help, she tells you she has nothing to pay you for the value of the lute. However, she can teach you a few tricks, and ups all your Stealth skills by a point:

➤ **Light Armor (+1)**   ➤ **Lockpicking (+1)**   ➤ **Speech (+1)**
➤ **Sneak (+1)**   ➤ **Pickpocket (+1)**   ➤ **Alchemy (+1)**

PREREQUISITES: Bards College Quest: Tending the Flames
INTERSECTING QUESTS: None
LOCATIONS: Hob's Fall Cave, Solitude, Bards College
CHARACTERS: Larina, Pantea Ateia
ENEMIES: Necromancer, Skeleton
◊ **OBJECTIVES:** Find Pantea's Flute

▷ The Dancing Dead

While staying at the Bards College, look out for the College's master vocalist and teacher, Pantea Ateia. She's quite vexed about her student Larina, who stole a flute from her private collection, only to sell it to some necromancer. Pantea just received a ransom note for it. This flute has been handed down through her family for 17 generations. She impatiently orders you to find the flute and return it, posthaste. Furthermore, the flute does not make "the dead dance," despite what her student may have told the necromancer.

◊ **OBJECTIVE:** Find Pantea's Flute
♦ **TARGET:** Pantea's Flute, in Hob's Fall Cave

Set off into the mountains east of Dawnstar and locate Hob's Fall Cave, on a hidden path among the glaciers. Enter this series of connected snow caves. Battle skeletons along the ice tunnels and fight necromancers as you head down the tunnels to a large wooden rope bridge spanning a chasm. Follow the lanterns and torches until you reach a throne chamber where a more powerful necromancer and his cronies reside. Defeat them all before activating the pull chain by the spears blocking your exit to the east.

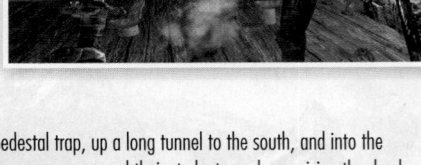

Head through a Soul Gem pedestal trap, up a long tunnel to the south, and into the deepest chamber where powerful necromancers and their students work on raising the dead. Defeat them all, then check the treasure chest to the altar table's left. Inside is Pantea's Flute. You may also wish to free Larina, who is being held captive.

➤ **Pantea's Flute**

Quest Conclusion

Return Pantea's Flute to Pantea Ateia back at the Bards College. She is thrilled with the return of her instrument but, alas, has no money to give you. However, she shows you a few tricks she learned playing for the Winterhold wizards. She ups all your Magic skills by a point:

- ➤ Illusion (+1)
- ➤ Conjuration (+1)
- ➤ Destruction (+1)
- ➤ Restoration (+1)
- ➤ Alteration (+1)
- ➤ Enchanting (+1)

RJORN'S DRUM

PREREQUISITES: Bards College Quest: Tending the Flames
INTERSECTING QUESTS: None
LOCATIONS: Halldir's Cairn, Solitude, Bards College
CHARACTERS: Giraud Gemane
ENEMIES: Draugr, Ghost, Halldir
◊ **OBJECTIVES:** Find Rjorn's Drum

▶ Drum of the Dead

While staying at the Bards College, locate the Dean of History, Giraud Gemane, who has some exciting news regarding a lost instrument. It appears adventurers working on behalf of the College have vague information regarding the venerable Rjorn's Drum. No one knows the location of Rjorn's final resting place, and therefore where his drum is, but word is that Rjorn entered a place called Halldir's Cairn and likely died there. Rjorn was the most famous drummer of the Second Age, and Giraud tasks you with finding his drum.

◊ **OBJECTIVE:** Find Rjorn's Drum
◆ **TARGET:** Rjorn's Drum, in Halldir's Cairn

Journey to Halldir's Cairn, just off the beaten track close to Falkreath. Head inside this strange cavern. An odd blue light pierces through a roof grating, illuminating a pile of stones and a group of scattered corpses, some much older than others. Close by is a pedestal with a key and a journal to take. The journal details a strange malaise that overtook a group of adventurers. The story doesn't end happily. Unlock the door (Adept), using either Lockpick or the key.

- ➤ **Agrius' Journal**
- ➤ **Key to Halldir's Crypt**

Head up the few steps and into an upper crypt with a seemingly dead end. After you remove the Draugr and ghosts that stalk you, inspect the area. There's a locked Iron Door (Apprentice) that doesn't lead anywhere. However, there are some Nordic petroglyphs to study.

Puzzle Solution: The first room has a lever, which initially just causes darts to fire from the nearby statue. Each of the next three chambers has a Nordic Puzzle Pillar; rotate the pillar so that its glyph matches the glyphs on the stone heads in the wall of that room. Then return to the lever and pull it to open a path forward.

Open the door, head up the spiral stairs to a rocky tunnel and slope up to a wooden door to the west. This is guarded by ghosts. Repel them with your chosen weapons, open the door to the west, and head through a small crypt while the ghosts taunt your mind. Head up the steps to a throne, where a Draugr draped over the seat twitches to life. Prepare for a battle with several ghosts and Draugr at this point. Then take the Spell Tome from the pedestal if you wish before checking behind the throne. Activate the lever there, which opens the adjacent portcullis, allowing you through.

- ➤ **Spell Tome:** Raise Zombie

This leads to a tiny grotto, a second passage to another crypt area (with a side passage and a dangerous battering ram trap), and steps up and around to the final resting place of Halldir. His undead form is ready with powerful magic and multiple doppelgangers to fight and thwart you. Watch for his clones and electrical attacks, and prepare for a lengthy battle until he uses up his magic and you can consistently slay him. Then inspect his treasure chest, which contains the instrument you're after. Leave by opening the circular trapdoor, landing on the jutting floorboards and then on the stones and corpses you first spotted when you entered this place.

- ➤ **Rjorn's Drum**

Quest Conclusion

Return Rjorn's Drum to Giraud Gemane back at the Bards College. He is excited to see the drum he's been searching for over the last 20 years. Although the College treasury can't pay you, Giraud can show you some tricks he learned from his days with the army. He ups all your Combat (Martial) skills by a point:

- ➤ Smithing (+1)
- ➤ Heavy Armor (+1)
- ➤ Block (+1)
- ➤ Two-Handed (+1)
- ➤ One-Handed (+1)
- ➤ Archery (+1)

TEMPLE QUESTS

OVERVIEW

▶ Optimal Quest Start

Most Temple Quests are available from the moment you begin your adventure, and there are no prerequisites to complete first. Temple Quests aren't inextricably linked to one another; you can start them at your leisure.

> **NOTE** **Cross-Referencing:** Do you want to see maps and learn more about the traps, non-quest-related items, collectibles, crafting areas, and other important rooms of note in every location during these quests? Then cross-reference the location you travel to with the information on that location contained in this guide's Atlas.

NORDIC WORSHIP IN SKYRIM: A BRIEF OVERVIEW

Much has been written about the history of the Divines and their worship across Tamriel, and space prevents a recap of this information. Be aware, however, of the following important information regarding the deities most important to Nords:

Talos: The Nordic name for the legendary Emperor Tiber Septim, and the most important hero-god of mankind. He is especially revered in Skyrim, where he is also called Ysmir, or "Dragon of the North." He withstood the power of the Greybeards' voices long enough to hear their prophecy. There is a temple to Talos in Windhelm and shrines in many of the other Hold Capitals. Talos worship has been outlawed in Skyrim by the Thalmor, agents of the elven Aldmeri Dominion, who struck an uneasy truce with the Emperor known as the White-Gold Concordat. Talos has small shrines in all the Hold cities of Skyrim, which are removed if Imperials control the city during the Civil War and restored if the Stormcloaks take control. He has been removed from the Temple of the Divines in Solitude (which was known as the Temple of the Nine Divines until 20 years ago). This, too, changes if the Stormcloaks retake Solitude.

Kynareth (or "Kyne" to old-timers in these parts, or "Kiss at the End"): Widow of Shor and favored goddess of warriors. She is often called the Mother of Men, and her daughters taught the first Nords the use of the Thu'um, or Storm Voice. There is a temple to Kynareth in Whiterun.

Mara: Known in Skyrim as a handmaiden of Kyne and Shor's concubine, she has a temple in Riften where marriages are held.

Dibella: Goddess of women, beauty, and art, has a temple in Markarth.

Arkay: His priests are staunch opponents of necromancy and all forms of the undead. It is presumed that Arkay did not exist before the world was created by gods under Shor's supervision (or urging or trickery). Therefore, he is sometimes called the mortals' god. Priests of Arkay tend to the mausoleums of every major city, called Halls of the Dead.

Stendarr, also known as Stuhn to the Nords: Warrior god who fought against the Aldmeri Pantheon as the shield-thane of Shor. He showed men how to take, and the benefits of taking, prisoners of war. He is the patron saint of the Legions.

DEAD GODS

Dead gods don't need temples: They have the biggest one of all, a vast hall of drinking and revelry known as Sovngarde.

Shor, god of the underworld, is the Nordic interpretation of Lorkhan, who takes sides with men after the creation of the world. Foreign gods (i.e., elven ones) conspire against him and bring about his defeat, dooming him to the underworld. Nordic myths depict him as a bloodthirsty warrior king who leads the Nords to victory over their elven oppressors time and again. Before his doom, Shor was the chief of the Nordic pantheon.

Tsun is an extinct Nordic god of trials against adversity. He died defending Shor from foreign gods. Tsun is now said to guard the mythical Whalebone Bridge into Sovngarde.

▶ The Nine Divines

 **Akatosh:** First of the gods to form in the Beginning Place: the ultimate god of the Cyrodilic Empire, embodying endurance, invincibility, and everlasting legitimacy.

 **Julianos:** Associated with Jhunal, an extinct Nord god of hermetic orders and scholars, and unimportant to most of Skyrim's inhabitants.

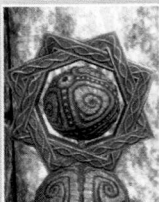 **Arkay:** God of the cycle of birth and death, of burials and funeral rites, and of the seasons.

 **Kynareth:** Nordic goddess of the storm, widow of Shor, and favored goddess of warriors. Also known as Kyne.

 **Dibella:** Goddess of beauty, women, and art.

 **Mara:** Goddess of love and fertility, handmaiden of Kyne, and Shor's concubine.

The Elder Scrolls V

SKYRIM

Stendarr: God of ransom and brother of Tsun; venerated by soldiers and veterans of wars.

Talos: Tiber Septim, the Dragonborn. Heir to the Seat of Sundered Kings. Also known as Ysmir.

Zenithar: God of Work and Commerce. Another divine that the Nords have little interest in.

THE SHRINES OF SKYRIM

There are shrines to the Divines throughout Skyrim. Their locations are detailed throughout the Atlas. Praying at a shrine cures any diseases you may have, and you gain a unique bonus (or "buff") that lasts eight hours. You can have only one such bonus active at a time, and praying at a different shrine supersedes any previous bonuses.

DIVINE	BONUS (LASTS EIGHT HOURS)
Akatosh	Cure all diseases, +10% Magicka regeneration rate
Arkay	Cure all diseases, +25 Health
Dibella	Cure all diseases, +10 Speech
Julianos	Cure all diseases, +25 Magicka

DIVINE	BONUS (LASTS EIGHT HOURS)
Kynareth	Cure all diseases, +25 Stamina
Mara	Cure all diseases, +10% Healing effects
Stendarr	Cure all diseases, +10% Blocking effectiveness
Talos	Cure all diseases, +20% Shout recovery
Zenithar	Cure all diseases, 10% better prices (Bartering)

AVAILABLE QUESTS

Three of Skyrim's major temples offer Temple Quests:

	QUEST NAME	RELATED SETTLEMENT	RELATED DIVINE	PREREQUISITES
	Temple Quest: The Heart of Dibella	Markarth	Dibella	None
	Temple Quest: The Blessings of Nature	Whiterun	Kynareth	None
	Temple Quest: The Book of Love	Riften	Mara	None
	Temple Quest: The Bonds of Matrimony	Riften	Mara	None

THE HEART OF DIBELLA

PREREQUISITES: None

INTERSECTING QUESTS: Miscellaneous Objective: Degaine's Favor

LOCATIONS: Broken Tower Redoubt, Karthwasten, Markarth, Temple of Dibella

CHARACTERS: Degaine, Enmon, Fjotra, Mena, Mother Hamal, Senna

ENEMIES: Forsworn, Forsworn Briarheart

◊ **OBJECTIVES:** Steal the statue in the Temple of Dibella, Find the future Sybil of Dibella, Rescue Fjotra from the Forsworn, Bring Fjotra to the Temple, Pray at Dibella's Altar

A Mother, Superior

Degaine

Visit Markarth and locate the beggar named Degaine (he's usually by the main gate near the market stall); he's happy to insult you after you hand over a gold piece but is more interested in a possible money-making opportunity if you ask him. He explains the womenfolk up in the Temple of Dibella are keeping a treasure from his prying hands. He wants you to steal it and offers to pay you half of what his man in Riften has offered to pay for it. This begins a miscellaneous objective.

◊ **MISCELLANEOUS OBJECTIVE:** Steal the statue in the Temple of Dibella

♦ **TARGET:** Statue of Dibella

TIP This quest can also be started by unlocking the Temple doors and locating Hamal, who is inside the Inner Sanctum.

Hamal

Clamber up the stone steps until you reach the Temple entrance. Unlock (Lockpick [Expert]) the Temple doors, and step inside. Inside the altar chamber, a priestess named Senna mentions that her relations are communing with Dibella and should not be disturbed. You may wait or ignore the advice, pass the altar, and open the doors to the Inner Sanctum. Head down the steps and into the main sanctum corridor, where a priestess soon stops you and summons Mother Hamal.

She is angry about your unannounced visit, and especially annoyed if you're male, as this is a breach of Temple rules. Stay pleasant with your responses, and ask what the penalty is. You are tasked with locating Dibella's Sybil, a Reachwoman selected as a child to spend her whole life in devotion and communion with the goddess. Your transgression will be forgiven if you can find the next Sybil. Hamal tells you her location was foreseen in a vision. As an added incentive, you will receive the Blessing of Dibella if you're successful.

> **NOTE** You can sneak through this Temple, secure the Statue of Dibella, and then speak to Hamal if you haven't been spotted yet.

> **CAUTION** This quest and Degaine's Miscellaneous Objective are mutually exclusive—you can't do both. If you accept this quest, the priestesses take the statue back. If you reject it, or take the statue later, they become hostile and you fail the quest. This quest requires a little more work, but offers a far better reward.

> ◊ **OBJECTIVE:** Find the future Sybil of Dibella
> ♦ **TARGET:** Enmon in Karthwasten

A Father, Inferior

The settlement hewn into the rock that Mother Hamal saw in her vision is the mountain hamlet of Karthwasten. Journey there and wait until daylight hours to pester the townsfolk (as they don't appreciate you lockpicking and sneaking into their homes). Speak to either Mena, who is withdrawn and refers you to her husband, or Enmon. His daughter was taken by the Forsworn, and after you inform him that his daughter is the Sybil of Dibella, Enmon tells you where he thinks Fjotra is and offers to accompany you. Bring Enmon along or tell him to stay in Karthwasten.

➤ **Follower:** Enmon

> ◊ **OBJECTIVE:** Rescue Fjotra from the Forsworn
> ♦ **TARGET:** Fjotra in Broken Tower Redoubt

> **NOTE** Enmon can come with you but is pretty pathetic when fighting against the Forsworn. He can die without this quest failing. Perhaps it is better for him to stay home...

Forsaking the Forsworn

Trek to the Broken Tower Redoubt and prepare for battle! Enter the stone structure, and fight through the Forsworn milling about inside. Open the wooden doors and avoid a swinging gate trap as you proceed deeper into the dwelling and up the two floors of spiral stairs inside the main tower. Beware of a boulder trap and more enemies as you ascend, and exit onto the upper battlements.

Enter the second tower atop the battlements, and engage the Forsworn Briarheart in the sacrificial chamber. Then inspect the prison door by the goat's head and candles. You can:

Search the gray corpse for the Prison Key, and use it to unlock the door.

Or pick the lock (Lockpick [Expert]). Once you free Fjotra, explain that she has been chosen as the Sybil, and she agrees to accompany you back to Markarth.

➤ **Broken Tower Prison Key**

> ◊ **OBJECTIVE:** Bring Fjotra to the Temple
> ♦ **TARGET:** Inner Sanctum, Temple of Dibella, in Markarth

The Sybil Entranced

> **TIP** Utilize Fast-Travel to minimize any problems getting Fjotra from the Broken Tower Redoubt to Markarth.

Return to Markarth with young Fjotra. Head up to the Temple of Dibella, enter the inner sanctum, and speak with Mother Hamal, who has made all the arrangements for Fjotra to begin her life of communing with the goddess. As a gesture of thanks, she requests you pray at Dibella's Altar, back in the entrance chamber where you met Senna.

> ◊ **OBJECTIVE:** Pray at Dibella's Altar
> ♦ **TARGET:** Temple of Dibella, in Markarth

Quest Conclusion

Once Fjotra is delivered to Mother Hamal, and you pray at the altar, you receive the following:

➤ **Perk:** Agent of Dibella

PREREQUISITES: None

INTERSECTING QUESTS: Thieves Guild Quest: Hard Answers

LOCATIONS: Gjukar's Monument, Greenspring Hollow, Ivarstead, Markarth, Understone Keep, Riften, Temple of Mara

CHARACTERS: Bassianus Axius, Boti, Calcelmo, Dinya Balu, Faleen, Fastred, Fenrig, Jofthor, Klimmek, Maramal, Ruki, Yngvar the Singer

ENEMIES: None

◊ **OBJECTIVES:** Talk to Fastred, Talk to Fastred's parents, Talk to Bassianus or Klimmek, Return to Dinya Balu, Talk to Calcelmo, Get advice from Yngvar, Deliver Poem, Deliver Faleen's letter, Return to Dinya Balu, Put on the Amulet of Mara, Talk to the long-dead lover, Find Fenrig, Bring Fenrig to Ruki, Return to Dinya Balu

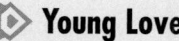

Young Love

Enter the town of Riften. Sitting back from the main thoroughfare is the Temple of Mara. Head inside and speak to either Maramal (who may also be in the Bee and Barb); his priestess wife, Dinya Balu; or Briehl an acolyte. Any of them explain they are devoted to the goddess Mara, who gave mortals the gift of love. But to receive her blessing, you

must first act as her hand in this world. Ask what you must do, and the priest explains the predicament of a young woman named Fastred. Her prayers were heard by her goddess and relayed to her servant; you must help her choose her suitor.

◊ **OBJECTIVE:** Talk to Fastred
♦ **TARGET:** Fastred, in Ivarstead

Travel to the fishing village of Ivarstead, which has seen better days. Locate the young lady named Fastred, who is usually chopping wood or working in her parents' allotment. She asks if you've been sent from Mara, then explains that her parents are being impossible: Fastred has two suitors, but her favorite — Bassianus — wants to marry and relocate to Riften, which her father has forbidden. She also has a soft spot for another man — Klimmek — who is less adventurous and wants to stay in Ivarstead.

◊ **OBJECTIVE:** Talk to Fastred's parents
♦ **TARGET:** Boti and Jofthor, in Ivarstead

Both Boti (Mother) and Jofthor (Father) should be close by or near their dwelling. Speak to both parents in either order. Boti tells you that she actually likes Bassianus and can perhaps persuade her husband to change his mind over her child's plans to leave for Riften. Talk with Jofthor, and he tells you that it isn't Fastred's plans to move that is upsetting him; she was supposedly "in love" with Klimmek until a few months ago, but he's a little spineless and needs a good shove to win Fastred over: That way the younger generation can help save the town. With these differing opinions, you have a choice to make.

◊ **OBJECTIVE:** Talk to Bassianus or Klimmek
♦ **TARGET:** Bassianus and Klimmek, in Ivarstead

You now have a choice to make and neither is "wrong"; you can speak to either Bassianus Axius or Klimmek: Both are likely to be near the river. Decide on Bassianus and suggest that he elopes. Decide on Klimmek and tell him Fastred probably appreciates a more assertive man and tell him to be bold. You can become more negative in your conversation with either suitor if you change your mind. Once you push either man into the arms of Fastred (who agrees to either suitor), your work here is done.

◊ **OBJECTIVE:** Return to Dinya Balu
♦ **TARGET:** Temple of Mara, in Riften

Unrequited Love

Back in Riften, enter the Temple and inform Dinya Balu that you've helped the young lovers in Ivarstead. Mara has another task for you to perform: An older man named Calcelmo must open up about his romantic troubles. Seek and help him on his path.

◊ **OBJECTIVE:** Talk to Calcelmo
♦ **TARGET:** Calcelmo, inside Understone Keep, in Markarth

Journey to Markarth, and venture into the Understone Keep. In the cathedral-sized interior chamber to the west, you're likely to find Calcelmo. Brush off his initial impoliteness, and inform him Mara sent you. He tells you he's been thinking about Faleen, Igmund's Housecarl (bodyguard). He longs for her but becomes tongue-tied when he tries to speak. Finding the right thing to say is the key here, and Calcelmo recommends you seek out Yngvar, who is more popular with the ladies. He may be able to help.

◊ **OBJECTIVE:** Get advice from Yngvar
♦ **TARGET:** Yngvar, in Markarth

Find Yngvar, who is usually leaning near a bridge in Markarth's main thoroughfare. Engage him in conversation, bringing the chatter around to Faleen. You'll find out that she secretly enjoys poetry, and Yngvar has just the verse, if you're ready to receive his golden words—which are going to cost you 200 gold pieces. You must pay the man to receive the poem.

➤ **200 gold pieces** ➤ **Love Poem**

◊ **OBJECTIVE:** Deliver Poem
♦ **TARGET:** Faleen, inside Understone Keep, in Markarth

Locate Faleen next to her master, in the throne chamber inside Understone Keep. You may reveal as much or little as you like about Calcelmo, but you must hand over the poem, which both surprises and impresses her greatly. In return, she gives you a letter to give back to him; it isn't as eloquent but is certain to please him.

➤ **Faleen's Letter to Calcelmo**

◊ **OBJECTIVE:** Deliver Faleen's letter
♦ **TARGET:** Calcelmo, inside Understone Keep, in Markarth

Hand Calcelmo the letter, and he leaves to join with Faleen and their love blossoms.

◊ **OBJECTIVE:** Return to Dinya Balu
♦ **TARGET:** Temple of Mara, in Riften

▶ Deep Love

Dinya Balu has one last task to test you with in the final aspect of love, a strong love that can survive storms and even death. You must take the symbol of Mara and rejoin to wandering souls, binding them to this world.

➤ **Amulet of Mara**

◊ **OBJECTIVE:** Put on the Amulet of Mara
♦ **TARGET:** Yourself
◊ **OBJECTIVE:** Talk to the long-dead lover
♦ **TARGET:** Ruki, Gjukar's Monument

TIP Reach Gjukar's Monument by nightfall to ensure your ghosts are easy to spot.

Head to Gjukar's Monument and seek the ghost of Ruki. She has turned over every body in this long-forgotten battlefield but cannot find her soul mate. Mention the last battle was hundreds of years ago, but Ruki still believes she's witnessing the battle afresh. Begin the search anew.

◊ **OBJECTIVE:** Find Fenrig
♦ **TARGET:** Fenrig, south of Greenspring Hollow

Ruki was searching in the wrong place; her lover's spirit resides on the heath to the south of Greenspring Hollow. Tell Fenrig that his wife is looking for him in the plains to the west. He agrees but must report back to camp by sunrise: Again, this is another spirit living in the past.

◊ **OBJECTIVE:** Bring Fenrig to Ruki
♦ **TARGET:** Ruki, Gjukar's Monument

Either Fast-Travel or trek back to Gjukar's Monument, where the couple embrace, then slowly rise into the air. Their spirits grow brighter as they ascend, until they become two bright points in the night sky, forever circling each other.

◊ **OBJECTIVE:** Return to Dinya Balu
♦ **TARGET:** Temple of Mara, in Riften

Quest Conclusion

Return one last time to Dinya Balu and explain that you helped the long-dead lovers find each other. She congratulates you on achieving the higher comprehension of love and says the Blessings of Mara will shine with you. You receive the following (which is different from the temporary Blessing of Mara if you pray at any of her shrines):

➤ **Perk:** Agent of Mara

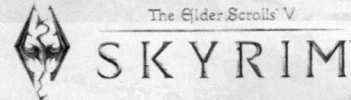

PREREQUISITES: None
INTERSECTING QUESTS: None
MISCELLANEOUS QUEST: Barkeep Rumors
LOCATIONS: Eldergleam Sanctuary, Orphan Rock, Whiterun, The Bannered Mare, Gildergreen, Temple of Kynareth
CHARACTERS: Asta, Danica Pure-Spring, Hulda, Maurice Jondrelle, Enemies, Hagraven, Spriggan, Witch
◊ **OBJECTIVES:** Talk to Danica about the Goldergreen being destroyed, Retrieve Nettlebane, Bring Nettlebane to Danica, Retrieve Eldergleam sap, Return to Danica

The Slumbering Temple

Journey to the city of Whiterun, through the gates into the bailey, and visit the Bannered Mare. Engage the barkeep, Hulda, in some idle chatter, picking up on several rumors. Keep asking until she tells you about a withered tree by the Temple of Kynareth.

◊ **OBJECTIVE:** Talk to Danica about the Goldergreen being destroyed
♦ **TARGET:** Danica Pure-Spring, near the Gildergreen tree, in Whiterun

TIP You can start this quest by speaking to Danica Pure-Spring up at the Temple of Kynareth.

Search out Danica Pure-Spring, and ask her about the tree. It is an offshoot of the Eldergleam, a massive tree and the oldest living thing in Skyrim. Ask about reviving the tree, and she tells you that even if you reach the Eldergleam deep in its sanctuary, you couldn't tap its sap, as it cannot be cut by normal metal. Only one weapon is known to cut the tree's bark — Nettlebane — and it is carried by the Hagraven that prowls on Orphan Rock. Agree to retrieve this weapon hewn of dark magic from beyond the time of man.

◊ **OBJECTIVE:** Retrieve Nettlebane
♦ **TARGET:** Hagraven, Orphan Rock

Dark Arts on Orphan Rock

Brave traps, inclement weather, and a coven of witches that attack you on sight as you ascend and head across the tree branch to the top of Orphan Rock. Face the Hagraven in combat and slay her. Inspect the corpse, and secure the Nettlebane blade from it.

(Sneak) You may also try pickpocketing the blade from the Hagraven.

➤ **Nettlebane**

◊ **OBJECTIVE:** Bring Nettlebane to Danica
♦ **TARGET:** Danica Pure-Spring, the Temple of Kynareth, in Whiterun

Danica is probably inside the Temple of Kynareth. She isn't keen on touching the Nettlebane and asks if you're able to complete the next part of the task: to journey east to the Eldergleam Sanctuary grove and retrieve the sap from the ancient tree. Once the quest updates, you're stopped by Maurice Jondrelle, a pilgrim wishing to accompany you to the Sanctuary to witness the Eldergleam. You may agree to journey with him or ignore his request.

◊ **OBJECTIVE:** Retrieve Eldergleam sap
♦ **TARGET:** Eldergleam, in Eldergleam Sanctuary

NOTE Maurice may be holding you up, and you can ignore him or leave him to die whenever you tire of his company.

The Sting of Nettlebane

Hike the volcanic tundra until you find the rather unassuming cave entrance to Eldergleam Sanctuary. Enter it, and the cave opens into a gigantic grotto, where waterfalls tumble from the sky-high roof and hot springs belch from the ground. This interior wonder has pilgrims resting and watching in awe. Optionally speak to Asta for more information on the place and a warning not to harm the tree.

There are two ways to harvest the sap you need:

1. Some quick swipes to the tree's gigantic root structure, which is blocking the path to the tree trunk, shouldn't hurt the ancient entity. Despite Maurice's protests, produce Nettlebane and swipe once. The tree's roots creak and retract from the soil. Continue with this swiping until you reach the trunk, and pierce it with Nettlebane to siphon off some sap.

   ➤ Eldergleam Sap

2. Or, if Maurice is with you, agree to let him pray in front of the tree. A sapling grows from his devotion. You can return this to Danica instead.

   ➤ Eldergleam Sapling

   ◇ OBJECTIVE: Return to Danica
   ◆ TARGET: Danica Pure-Spring, the Temple of Kynareth, in Whiterun

Both Maurice Jondrelle and the Spriggans who guard the tree don't take kindly to sap stealing if you chose that option. They mount an offensive strike against you. Fight or flee from this place, and return swiftly to Danica Pure-Spring, presenting her with the sap. She is most grateful.

Quest Conclusion

Danica takes the sap (or sapling) from you. You are now on friendly terms with her, and she is available as a Trainer (a Master in Restoration).

Postquest Activities

After time passes and you return to the Temple of Kynareth, you witness the tree blooming again (if you returned with sap) or being replaced by the sapling (if Maurice prayed for you).

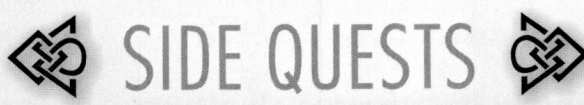

SIDE QUESTS

THE BONDS OF MATRIMONY

PREREQUISITES: None
◇ **OBJECTIVES:** Speak to Maramal about arranging your wedding, Attend your wedding ceremony, Visit your or your spouse's house

▷ A Life Lived Alone Is No Life at All

Sometimes it is lonely on the mist-filled pathways of Skyrim. You may yearn for companionship. Or something more? If you feel your life is incomplete and must be shared with someone, make your way to Riften and check the Bee and Barb tavern or the Temple of Mara for a talk with Maramal the priest. He detests the drinking of mead and hopes

the drunkards of Riften will eventually accept the teachings of the handmaiden of Kyne. Ask for more information about the Temple of Mara, and he tells you she is the goddess of love, tending to the sick, poor, and lost. The priests of Mara also perform wedding ceremonies for all the loving couples in Skyrim. Now ask how marriage works:

Life is hard and short, so there is little time for courtship. A person interested in looking for a spouse simply wears an Amulet of Mara

around their neck, indicating their availability. After another shows interest and they agree to be together, they come to the temple and marry. You can purchase one of these Amulets for the low price of 200 gold pieces.

➤ Amulet of Mara

After you purchase an Amulet of Mara, check your Items > Apparel menu, and wear the necklace, or you'll never entice a spouse! At this point, you must find someone who wishes to marry you. To do this, you must strike up a friendship with any one of the following potential suitors. "Striking a friendship" means completing a favor for them, or otherwise getting into their good graces.

 TIP Your gender, age, and race matters not: If you're attracted to someone, go out and catch their hearts!

✓	POTENTIAL SPOUSE	GENDER	RACE	OCCUPATION	HOLD	LOCATION	CONDITIONS FOR MARRIAGE
☐	Aela the Huntress	Female	Nord	Companion	Whiterun	Whiterun (Jorrvaskr)	Complete the Companions Quests
☐	Aeri	Female	Nord	Lumberjack	The Pale	Anga's Mill	Work for her by chopping firewood
☐	Ainethach	Male	Breton	Mine Owner	The Reach	Karthwasten	Complete their favor
☐	Angrenor Once-Honored	Male	Nord	Beggar	Eastmarch	Windhelm (Candlehearth Hall)	Take pity and give the beggar a gold piece
☐	Anwen	Female	Redguard	Priestess	The Reach	Markarth (Temple of Dibella)	Complete Temple Quest: The Heart of Dibella
☐	Argis the Bulwark	Male	Nord	Housecarl	The Reach	Markarth (Vlindrel Hall)	Become Thane of the Reach
☐	Athis	Male	Dark Elf	Companion	Whiterun	Whiterun (Jorrvaskr)	Complete the Companions Quests
☐	Avrusa Sarethi	Female	Dark Elf	Farmer	The Rift	Sarethi Farm	Complete their favor
☐	Balimund	Male	Nord	Blacksmith	The Rift	Riften	Complete their favor
☐	Belrand	Male	Nord	Hireling	Haafingar	Solitude (Winking Skeever)	Hire them at least once
☐	Benor	Male	Nord	Warrior	Hjaalmarch	Morthal	Challenge him to a brawl and win
☐	Borghak the Steel Heart	Female	Orc	Warrior	The Reach	Mor Khazgur	Convince her to become a Follower
☐	Brelyna Maryon	Female	Dark Elf	Student	Winterhold	Winterhold (College of Winterhold)	Complete both her favors

POTENTIAL SPOUSE	GENDER	RACE	OCCUPATION	HOLD	LOCATION	CONDITIONS FOR MARRIAGE
Calder	Male	Nord	Housecarl	Eastmarch	Windhelm (Hjerim)	Become Thane of Eastmarch
Camilla Valerius	Female	Imperial	Merchant	Whiterun	Riverwood (Riverwood Trader)	Complete Side Quest: The Golden Claw
Cosnach	Male	Breton	Drunk/Porter	The Reach	Markarth (Silver-Blood Inn)	Challenge him to a brawl and win
Derkeethus	Male	Argonian	Fisherman	Eastmarch	Darkwater Crossing	Find and rescue him
Dravynea the Stoneweaver	Female	Dark Elf	Mage	Eastmarch	Kynesgrove	Complete their favor
Erik the Slayer	Male	Nord	Hireling	The Reach	Rorikstead	Complete his favor to make him a hireling
Farkas	Male	Nord	Companion	Whiterun	Whiterun (Jorrvaskr)	Complete the Companions Quests
Filnjar	Male	Nord	Blacksmith	The Rift	Shor's Stone	Complete Miscellaeous Objective: Mine or Yours
Gat gro-Shargakh	Male	Orc	Miner	The Reach	Left Hand Mine /Kolskeggr Mine	Complete Pavo Attius's favor to liberate Kolskeggr Mine
Ghorbash the Iron Hand	Male	Orc	Warrior	The Reach	Dushnikh Yal	Convince her to become a Follower
Ghorza gra-Bagol	Female	Orc	Blacksmith	The Reach	Markarth (Blacksmith Shed)	Complete their favor
Gilfre	Female	Imperial	Miller	Eastmarch	Mixwater Mill	Work for her by chopping firewood
Grelka	Female	Nord	Merchant	The Rift	Riften (Open Market)	Complete their favor
Iona	Female	Nord	Housecarl	The Rift	Riften (Honeyside)	Become Thane of the Rift
Jenassa	Female	Dark Elf	Hireling	Whiterun	Whiterun (Drunken Huntsman)	Hire them at least once
Jordis the Sword-Maiden	Female	Nord	Housecarl	Haafingar	Solitude (Proudspire Manor)	Become Thane of Haafingar
Lydia	Female	Nord	Housecarl	Whiterun	Whiterun (Dragonsreach or Breezehome)	Become Thane of Whiterun
Marcurio	Male	Imperial	Hireling	The Rift	Riften (Bee and Barb)	Hire them at least once
Mjoll the Lioness	Female	Nord	Adventurer	The Rift	Riften	Complete their favor
Moth gro-Bagol	Male	Orc	Blacksmith	The Reach	Markarth (Understone Keep)	Complete their favor
Muiri	Female	Breton	Alchemist	The Reach	Markarth (Hag's Cure)	Complete Dark Brotherhood Quest: Mourning Never Comes
Njada Stonearm	Female	Nord	Companion	Whiterun	Whiterun (Jorrvaskr)	Complete the Companions Quests
Octieve San	Male	Breton	Citizen	Haafingar	Solitude	Complete their favor
Omluag	Male	Breton	Miner	The Reach	Markarth (Markarth Smelter)	Complete their favor
Onmund	Male	Nord	Student	Winterhold	Winterhold (College of Winterhold)	Complete their favor
Orla	Female	Nord	Priestess	The Reach	Markarth (Temple of Dibella)	Complete Temple Quest: The Heart of Dibella
Pavo Attius	Male	Imperial	Miner	The Reach	Left Hand Mine/Kolskeggr Mine	Complete his favor to liberate Kolskeggr Mine
Perth	Male	Breton	Miner	The Reach	Soljund's Sinkhole	Complete their favor
Quintus Navale	Male	Imperial	Alchemist	Eastmarch	Windhelm (The White Phial)	Complete Side Quest: Repairing the Phial
Revyn Sadri	Male	Dark Elf	Merchant	Eastmarch	Windhelm (Sadri's Used Wares)	Complete their favor
Ria	Female	Imperial	Companion	Whiterun	Whiterun (Jorrvaskr)	Complete the Companions Quests
Roggi Knot-Beard	Male	Nord	Miner	Eastmarch	Kynesgrove	Complete their favor
Romlyn Dreth	Male	Dark Elf	Meadery Worker	The Rift	Riften (Black-Briar Meadery)	Complete their favor
Scouts-Many-Marshes	Male	Argonian	Dockworker	Eastmarch	Windhelm (Argonian Assemblage)	Complete their favor
Senna	Female	Imperial	Priestess	The Reach	Markarth (Temple of Dibella)	Complete Temple Quest: The Heart of Dibella
Shahvee	Female	Argonian	Dockworker	Eastmarch	Windhelm (Argonian Assemblage)	Complete their favor
Sondas Drenim	Male	Dark Elf	Miner	Eastmarch	Darkwater Crossing	Complete their favor
Sorex Vinius	Male	Imperial	Assistant Innkeeper	Haafingar	Solitude (Winking Skeever)	Complete their favor
Stenvar	Male	Nord	Hireling	Eastmarch	Windhelm (Candlehearth Hall)	Hire them at least once
Sylgja	Female	Nord	Miner	The Rift	Shor's Stone	Complete their favor
Taarie	Female	High Elf	Tailor	Haafingar	Solitude (Radiant Raiments)	Complete their favor
Temba Wide-Arm	Female	Nord	Miller	The Rift	Ivarstead	Complete their favor
Torvar	Male	Nord	Companion	Whiterun	Whiterun (Jorrvaskr)	Complete the Companions Quests
Uthgerd	Female	Nord	Warrior	Whiterun	Whiterun (Bannered Mare)	Challenge her to a brawl and win
Vilkas	Male	Nord	Companion	Whiterun	Whiterun (Jorrvaskr)	Complete the Companions Quests
Viola Giordano	Female	Imperial	Busybody	Eastmarch	Windhelm (Candlehearth Hall)	Start Revyn Sadri's favor, but then rat him out to Viola
Vorstag	Male	Nord	Hireling	The Reach	Markarth (Silver-Blood Inn)	Hire them at least once
Wilhelm	Male	Nord	Innkeeper	The Rift	Ivarstead (Vilemyr Inn)	Complete Dungeon Quest: Wilhelm's Specter
Ysolda	Female	Nord	Citizen	Whiterun	Whiterun (Open Market)	Complete their favor

TIP Opting for a quick marriage? Then approach Camilla Valerius over at the Riverwood Trader once Side Quest: The Golden Claw ends. She takes a shine to you after the quest is over.

When you're on friendly terms with your potential partner, they will notice — and mention — your Amulet of Mara and will usually express surprise that you're not spoken for. You can choose to ignore this advance or ask if they're interested in you. They answer that they are. But are you interested in them? Answer yes if you wish to continue down this road of happiness, or no to remain alone. You're tasked with arranging the marriage straight away...in case one of you dies.

◊ **OBJECTIVE:** Speak to Maramal about arranging your wedding

Return to Riften and find Maramel, either in the Temple of Mara or in the Bee and Barb. Tell him you'd like to have a wedding at the temple. He agrees, and sets the date for the next day, between dawn (5:00 a.m.) and dusk (7:00 p.m.).

◊ **OBJECTIVE:** Attend your wedding ceremony

> **NOTE** Whoops! Did a combination of adventuring and cold feet cause you to miss your wedding day? Then this previous objective fails. After a few hours, your jilted lover can be convinced to attempt the ceremony again. Speak to Maramal and arrange this; then wait another day and try getting to the temple on time!

Prosperity and Poverty, Joy, and Hardship

Oh, happy day! Tomorrow dawns, and you can head to the Temple of Mara at any time before dusk. Your spouse-to-be is already there and doesn't need to be told to turn up. As you enter, the ceremony begins. Maramal conducts the ceremony and eventually asks if you agree to be bound together in love, now and forever. You can:

Agree, for now and forever.

Or freak out slightly, halt the wedding, and tell Maramal you can't go through with it.

Or freak out completely and attack everyone. Doing this or leaving the temple during the ceremony fails this quest, and usually ups your Crime in the Rift considerably.

Assuming you didn't ruin your betrothed's day, he declares you to be wed.

➤ **The Bond of Matrimony**

◊ **OBJECTIVE:** Visit your or your spouse's house

At this point, your spouse asks where you both should live, now that you're married. They offer their own home to you. You can:

Agree, and visit the house (which should appear on your world map). Depending on who you've married, this could be anything from a sturdy-built stone dwelling to a small tent in the tundra.

Or, if you've already purchased a dwelling as part of the Thane Tasks (page 404), you can choose your spouse to live with you.

➤ **Spouse**

Quest Conclusion

The "happily ever after" part is next. Your spouse grants you the following benefits:

You can ask them to serve up a home-cooked meal for you once every 24 hours.

They set up a shop in the house you're living in. If your spouse was a merchant, they sell what they did before. If they weren't, they sell miscellaneous objects.

You may sleep close to your spouse and receive a bonus, feeling your Lover's Comfort when you awaken.

If your spouse is also a Follower, they can accompany you on adventures.

If your spouse is also a Trainer, you can train with them at your marital home.

If your spouse is a Follower and a Trainer, you can train with them anywhere you like!

➤ **Lover's Comfort**

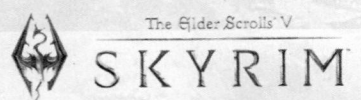

OVERVIEW

Optimal Quest Start

Most Side Quests are available from the moment you begin your adventure, although it is wise to learn if there are prerequisites to complete first. As Side Quests aren't usually linked to one another (with a couple of exceptions), you can start them at your leisure.

> **NOTE** **Cross-Referencing:** Do you want to see maps and learn more about the traps, non-quest-related items, collectibles, crafting areas, and other important rooms of note in every location during these quests? Then cross-reference the location you travel to with the information on that location contained in this guide's Atlas.

Available Quests

There are a total of 23 different Side Quests available. Aside from the exceptions detailed below, most of these quests are independent of one another and can be completed whenever you encounter them.

✓	QUEST NAME	RELATED SETTLEMENT OR HOLD	PREREQUISITES
	Side Quest: Blood on the Ice	Windhelm	Enter and exit Windhelm four times
	Side Quest: Forbidden Legend	None	None
	Side Quest: The Forsworn Conspiracy	Markarth	None
	Side Quest: No One Escapes Cidhna Mine	Markarth	Complete Side Quest: The Forsworn Conspiracy
	Side Quest: The Golden Claw	Riverwood	None
	Side Quest: In My Time of Need	Whiterun	Complete Main Quest: Dragon Rising
	Side Quest: Kyne's Sacred Trials	None	None
	Side Quest: Laid to Rest	Morthal	None
	Side Quest: Lights Out!	Solitude	None
	Side Quest: The Man Who Cried Wolf	Solitude	None
	Side Quest: The Wolf Queen Awakened	Solitude	Complete Side Quest: The Man Who Cried Wolf
	Side Quest: Missing in Action	Whiterun	Enter and exit any of the buildings near the market in Whiterun
	Side Quest: Promises to Keep	Riften	None
	Side Quest: A Return to Your Roots	Blackreach	Begin Daedric Quest: Discerning the Transmundane

✓	QUEST NAME	RELATED SETTLEMENT OR HOLD	PREREQUISITES
	Side Quest: Rise in the East	Windhelm	None
	Side Quest: Rising at Dawn	Morthal	Contract Vampirism
	Side Quest: Unfathomable Depths	Riften	None
	Side Quest: The White Phial	Windhelm	None
	Side Quest: Repairing the Phial	Windhelm	Three days after completing both Main Quest: The Throat of the World and Side Quest: The White Phial
	Side Quest: Captured Critters*	None	None
	Side Quest: The Forgemaster's Fingers	Orc Strongholds	Non-Orc Race
	Side Quest: The Great Skyrim Treasure Hunt*	None	None
	Side Quest: Masks of the Dragon Priests*	None	Numerous (see quest)

> **NOTE** * Quest names marked with this symbol do not appear in your Quest Menu list, although objectives may.

Note that not all of these quests will count towards the Sideways Achievement. Consult the Achievements Appendix on page 632 for a list of relevant quests.

 ## BLOOD ON THE ICE

PREREQUISITES: Enter and exit Windhelm a total of four times

INTERSECTING QUESTS: None

LOCATIONS: Windhelm, Calixto's House of Curiosities, Candlehearth Hall, Hall of the Dead, Hjerim, House of the Clan Shatter-Shield, Palace of the Kings, Bloodworks, Palace of the Kings Upstairs

CHARACTERS: Calixto Corrium, Friga Shatter-Shield, Helgird, Jorleif, Sidla the Unseen, Susanna the Wicked, Viola Giordano, Windhelm Guard, Wuunferth the Unliving

ENEMIES: None

◊ **OBJECTIVES:** Question the witnesses, Report to the guard, Talk to Jorleif, Get assistance from Jorleif, Examine the crime scene, Talk to Helgird, Get access to Hjerim, Investigate Hjerim for clues, Follow up on the clues from Hjerim, Meet Viola outside of Hjerim, Investigate Hjerium with Viola, Talk to Jorleif, Patrol the streets of the Stone Quarter at night, Speak to Wuunferth, Catch the murderer, Speak to Jorleif for reward

Murder Most Foul

NOTE This quest is available only after you enter Windhelm, leave this Hold City, head to a different location, return again, and complete this four times. Now enter at night, and look for a small group of townsfolk and a guard gathering in the graveyard.

When walking the Stone Quarter of Windhelm (west of the entrance gate), you stumble across a shocking scene. In the graveyard near the Hall of the Dead, the freshly slaughtered corpse of a woman lies draped over a grave. As the stunned onlookers assemble, go speak with the Windhelm Guard. He tells you another girl has been killed; this one is Susanna from Candlehearth Hall. When you ask, he admits she's the third young girl to be killed here, at night, and with her body cut and torn. Without time to investigate these heinous crimes, ask if he requires any help. He points you to the onlookers who might have some information to share.

◊ **OBJECTIVE:** Question the witnesses

There are three witnesses to speak to:

Calixto Corrium: The owner of the House of Curiosities in town. He thought he saw someone running away but didn't get a good look at him.

Sidla the Unseen: A beggar living in the Stone Quarter marketplace. She heard a scream and came running, but Susanna was already dead.

Helgird: The Priestess of Arkay from the Hall of the Dead. She noticed the woman's coinpurse was still on the body, so this wasn't a robbery.

Head back outside, and follow the trail of blood. This leads up the stone steps, around the corner to the north into the Valunstrad District, up more steps, and ends at a firmly locked (Master) front door to a building named Hjerim.

◊ **OBJECTIVE:** Get access to Hjerim
♦ **TARGET:** Hjerim front door, Valunstrad District, Windhelm

Accessing Hjerim can be tricky, as it can require a little asking around among the inhabitants of Windhelm. You can:

(Lockpick) Unlock the door (Master) using your considerable lockpicking prowess.

Ask around town. Speak to a guard or a local, and ask how you can enter Hjerim. You're told this used to belong to Friga Shatter-Shield and has been abandoned ever since she was killed. Apparently, her mother, Tova, has the key.

NOTE This horror house named Hjerim is actually for sale, but only after you've witnessed the murder scene. Consult the Thane Tasks on page 404 for further information.

◊ **OBJECTIVE:** Report to the guard

With nobody knowing (or saying anything), when you report back to the guard, he's suitably frustrated. Offer to investigate, and he points you in the direction of the Palace of the Kings, so you can talk to Jorleif. The steward of Windhelm will officially deputize you to conduct the investigation.

◊ **OBJECTIVE:** Talk to Jorleif
◊ **OBJECTIVE:** Get assistance from Jorleif
♦ **TARGET:** Jorleif, inside the Palace of the Kings, in Windhelm

Visit the Palace of the Kings, and contact Jorleif. Tell him you've heard about the murders. He gladly accepts your aid and tells the guards to assist you as necessary.

◊ **OBJECTIVE:** Examine the crime scene
◊ **OBJECTIVE:** Talk to Helgird
♦ **TARGET:** Victim's location, graveyard close to Hall of the Dead

TIP This objective is more easily completed during daylight hours. Note that you can follow the trail of blood and break into Hjerim and avoid a lot of investigative chatting to the locals, if you wish.

Return to the coffin where the body of Susanna was dumped. You notice there's blood pooling on the coffin lid and stains that match a dragging. The guard mentions the blood if you speak to him, too. Look west, and you'll see a trail of it. The guard also mentions that Helgird has taken the body into the Hall of the Dead to prepare it for burial. She might know something. The entrance to the Hall of the Dead is on your right (northwest) as you face the trail of blood. Head into the gloomy crypt, and after quizzing Helgird again, she reveals the cuts on the corpse were made with some kind of curved blade the Nords used to embalm their dead.

Tova Shatter-Shield is usually at the market in the southwest Stone Quarter or walking nearby. At night, she heads to the House of Clan Shatter-Shield. You can pick the lock (Master) to enter, or wait until morning until she unlocks the house; speak to her then or when she leaves. Tell her you have some questions about her daughter. Choose any conversation response regarding the finding of her daughter's killer, and let her know you need a key to investigate her house. She hands the key over. Take it, head back to Hjerim, and open the front door.

➤ **Key to Hjerim**

◊ **OBJECTIVE:** Investigate Hjerim for clues

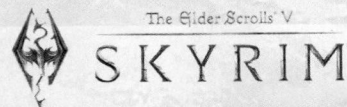

A Butcher's Handiwork

Inside, the place has been
cleared out, and cobwebs
blanket the corners. The place
is seemingly deserted, but a
thorough inspection reveals the
following:

Front room (north): The
pots and pans here haven't
been used for ages, judging
by the skeever droppings and cobwebs inside.

Front room (entrance): The chest has splatters of blood and was recently pushed against
the wall. Search it after inspecting it to reveal almost a dozen leaflets warning of a
"butcher." The name "Viola Giordano" is mentioned on the leaflet. There is a journal to
view, too. It makes grisly reading and seems to indicate necromantic activity.

Front room (entrance): The scattered mead bottles are from the previous occupants.

Front room (west wall): The low shelf by one of the wardrobes is filled with more
leaflets warning about the Butcher. Remove the leaflets, as one of the piles is misshapen.
Underneath, you find a strange (and exceptionally valuable) amulet! Inspect it in your Items
> Apparel menu.

Front room (back wardrobe): One of the wardrobes at the back of the room has been
nailed to the wall. Open it and slide the false panel back. You find a disgusting sight: a small
makeshift altar and antechamber strewn with body parts. Check the altar, and you confirm it
is being used for some unknown magic. A second Butcher Journal can be taken from here. It
seems to contain ingredients, both body parts and an incantation.

Upstairs: Only the bed and chairs, which have been weirdly positioned, can be inspected.

➤ **Beware the Butcher! (19)**   ➤ **Butcher Journal #2**

➤ **Butcher Journal #1**   ➤ **Strange Amulet**

◊ **OBJECTIVE:** Follow up on the clues from Hjerim
♦ **TARGET:** Any Windhelm Guard, in Windhelm

🗩 **TIP** Only the first Butcher Journal and leaflets are needed to continue
progress, although it is beneficial if you find everything listed here.

Leave the house and consult with any guard in Windhelm. Two new topics of conversation are
available (assuming you found at least one leaflet and the Strange Amulet):

Ask about the "Butcher": Viola Giordano posts these all over the city, and someone keeps
removing them.

Ask about the amulet. The guard hasn't seen anything like it, but Calixto at the House of
Curiosities has a good eye for such trinkets.

Viola Giordano: Here Her Hearsay

Search for Viola wandering
the streets of Windhelm. Ask
her about the Butcher; she's
been searching for him for
months and then mentions
the poster leaflet you found in
Hjerim. She echoes the guard's
information, that someone has
been taking them down as
quickly as she posts them around the city. She recommends you meet her at Hjerim for another
inspection. You can follow her if you haven't uncovered the amulet. Otherwise, you are free to
visit Calixto, too.

◊ **OBJECTIVE:** Meet Viola outside of Hjerim

Calixto Corrium: Curiouser and Curiouser

Head to the southeast part of
the Stone Quarter and enter
Calixto Corrium's House of
Curiosities. Aside from taking
a tour, you can ask him about
the amulet you found. He
cheerfully inspects the amulet,
telling you it's a Wheelstone,
an heirloom symbol of the
power of Windhelm and traditionally carried by the court mage. He's interested in the piece and
offers you 500 gold. You can:

Agree, and sell the piece.

Ask whether the court mage should have it instead, and keep it.

Or hold on to it.

➤ **500 gold pieces (if sold)**

Whatever your choice, the next place to head is Hjerim, where you should have agreed to meet
Viola.

Revisiting the House of the Dead

◊ **OBJECTIVE:** Investigate Hjerim with Viola

Viola is ready to inspect the house when you arrive. After she sees the altar and is sickened by
the "Butcher's" activties, her reactions are similar but depend on how thorough your previous
search has been and whether you've met with Calixto.

If you already found the gruesome altar and spoke with Calixto about the amulet, Viola
believes that Wuunferth the Unliving — the court mage in the Palace of the Kings — is the likely
culprit and urges you to tell the steward Jorleif.

If you already found the gruesome altar and didn't speak with Calixto, speak to Viola.

If you haven't found the gruesome altar yet, Viola leads to you the strange cabinet and
forces you to open the false back and discover the altar. When you take the Butcher's Journal
and read the scribbling about necromancy, speak to Viola about it. Apparently, Wuunferth the
court mage is a dangerous man; that's why he's called "the Unliving." She worries about
approaching him directly. She urges you to approach Jorleif about him.

◊ **OBJECTIVE:** Talk to Jorleif

At this point, with the evidence you've accumulated, you have two possible ways to complete
this investigation, and both involve heading into the Palace of the Kings. You can speak to
Jorleif, or you can check in with the suspect, Wuunferth himself.

Epilogue: Wuunferth: Wrongly Accused?

Bypass Jorleif, ignoring Viola's
instructions, and enter the
upstairs part of the Palace of
the Kings, to your left (west)
as you come in. Head upstairs,
turn left (south), and open
the door at the corridor's
end, leading into Wuunferth's
private chamber. He may also
be sitting in the Palace's great hall or wandering the building. Tell him you hear he dabbles in
necromancy. He indignantly denies such a spurious accusation; he's a member of the College
of Winterhold in good standing. When you mention the journals and amulet, Wuunferth wants
to know what the amulet looks like. After you describe it, he knows it to be the Necromancer's
Amulet, a legendary item. Wuunferth has been noting that the killings are tied to some kind of
necromantic ritual — tomorrow night, in the Stone Quarter, in fact!

◊ **OBJECTIVE:** Patrol the streets of the Stone Quarter at night

▶ Epilogue: Wuunferth in the Wrong

Tell Jorleif that you believe Wuunferth the Unliving is the killer. Jorleif wants to know if you have any proof, so explain you've evidence of the necromancy in Hjerim and the amulet that looks to belong to him. Jorleif doesn't want to believe this, as Wuunferth has been a trusted friend to Ulfric for many years. But it seems those whispers around town had some truth to them. He thanks you for your diligence at solving this matter. The quest concludes, and Jorleif takes a guard and heads to the upstairs chamber where Wuunferth resides. He puts him in chains and takes him down to the Bloodworks prison in the Palace. You can watch if you wish; the old necromancer splutters indignantly about his innocence.

Three days pass. Return to Windhelm again and listen to the townsfolk. It appears that the Butcher has struck again! Move to the crime scene, where you can speak to a city guard who wonders why this has happened, considering your investigation. You're told to head to the prison and speak to Wuunferth. He's obviously in some way responsible. But how?

◊ **OBJECTIVE:** Speak to Wuunferth

Wuunferth openly mocks your terrible detective work when you tell him the killer has struck again. Request that he helps you find the real killer, and he asks why you thought Wuunferth was responsible in the first place. Mention the journals and amulet, and he angrily replies that he's a member of the College of Winterhold in good standing. Furthermore, he never kept a journal. He wants to know what the amulet looks like; after you describe it, he knows it to be the Necromancer's Amulet, a legendary item. Wuunferth has been noting that the killings are tied to some kind of necromantic ritual — tomorrow night, in the Stone Quarter, in fact!

◊ **OBJECTIVE:** Patrol the streets of the Stone Quarter at night

Quest Conclusion

Wait until nightfall the next evening. The place is unusually quiet, until you stumble upon Calixto Corrium speaking with a woman (usually in the market area). A moment later, he attacks her. Stop that murderer!

◊ **OBJECTIVE:** Catch the murderer
◊ **OBJECTIVE:** Speak to Jorleif for reward

Race after Calixto. If you're too slow, he runs back to his butchering place, into Hjerim where he makes his last stand. Otherwise, he won't go down without a fight. You can kill him using your favored weapons or beat him to his knees using your fists. When Calixto is safely dealt with, head to Jorleif. He thanks you profusely for finally solving this murder (and a little less profusely if he has to go and release Wuunferth). You now receive the following rewards:

The Necromancer's Amulet, if you sold it back to Calixto (which you can then sell again for even more profit!)

The title "Special Investigator of Windhelm."

A free "cleaning" of Hjerim, so the gruesome antechamber has the flesh and bones removed from it, whether you own the house or not.

➤ **Necromancer's Amulet**

Postquest Activities

It is now wise to purchase Hjerim if you wish to.

> ### CALIXTO CORRIUM: MODUS OPERANDI
>
> Calixto Corrium recently mourned the loss of his twin sister, Lucilla. The two have always been extraordinarily close and have shared a love of all things ancient and exotic, and so assembled the House of Curiosities collection together. When Lucilla passed away, Calixto was wrecked; beyond heartbroken, he went into seclusion. During his hermitage, he discovered an ancient deep magic that could bring his darling sister back to him, but it demanded raw materials of marrow, bone, flesh, sinew, and blood. He took to the frozen streets of Windhelm at night, harvesting women for specific ingredients. He was assembling his sister's new incarnation in Hjerim, the now-abandoned house of his first victim.

 FORBIDDEN LEGEND

PREREQUISITES: None

INTERSECTING QUESTS: College of Winterhold Quest: Under Saarthal

LOCATIONS: College of Winterhold, Folgunthur, Folgunthur Crypt, Geirmund's Hall, Reachwater Rock, Saarthal

CHARACTERS: Gauldur, Tolfdir

ENEMIES: Draugr, Draugr Thrall, Frostbite Spider, Jyrik Gauldurson, Mikrul Gauldurson, Sigdis Gauldurson, Skeever

◊ **OBJECTIVES:** Investigate the cryptic message, Investigate the Gauldur legend, Learn the truth from Daynas Valen, Read Daynas Valen's notes, Find the Gauldur Amulet Fragment in Folgunthur, Find the Gauldur Amulet Fragment in Geirmund's Hall, Find the Gauldur Amulet Fragment in Saarthal, Reforge the Gauldur Amulet, Take the Gauldur Amulet

⬤ **MINOR SPOILERS**

This quest can be started in any number of ways. There's no "optimal" way to begin, and no one to speak to about it. You're most likely to just stumble across it somewhere as a part of your adventure. Here are some of the possibilities:

When exploring any of the locations for this quest, such as Saarthal (in College of Winterhold Quest: Under Saarthal), you may find a cryptic note on the boss that begins this quest. These all point you to copies of the book *Lost Legends of Skyrim*.

Or, you may find the book first. Copies of *Lost Legends* are all over the world, and reading any of them, such as the one in Farengar's library in Dragonsreach, will give you some background and direct you to Folgunthur.

Or, you may simply enter Folgunthur on your own and find the body of Daynas Valen. His notes provide the clues that guide the rest of your journey.

> **NOTE** Below is one of the paths you might take through this quest. There is no "correct" order for the places you visit, but this route allows you to see all the locations in a logical progression.

Do Not Disturb

Deep in the Reach, the southern road follows the river as it winds through the canyons toward Markarth. At one point, the road crosses a bridge with a large waterfall to the south. Head up the rocky slope, onto a dirt path that leads to the rushing stream, and follow the streambed through the falls. Hidden behind is the entrance to Reachwater Rock. The "Rock" in question is inside the cavern: a natural stone island with a single gnarled tree, above a gloomy lake. A dead adventurer lies against the tree, and a pedestal stands nearby. There are two items of interest on the pedestal:

➤ **Ancient Edict**   ➤ **Emerald Dragon Claw**

The Edict is particularly worrying; it tells you to leave this place, as whatever was sealed in here was done at a great price. Take the Claw as well, and once you choose to ignore the warning, this quest continues!

◊ **OBJECTIVE:** Investigate the cryptic message
♦ **TARGET:** The dead adventurer

If you haven't already, check the adventurer's body. In addition to some potions, he also has a copy of the book *Lost Legends of Skyrim*, which tells the tale of the Arch-Mage Gauldur and his three sons, all murdered in ages past. Could this sealed tomb be connected to the legend? The book doesn't say, but it does mention one place that is: Folgunthur, near the foot of Solitude, far to the north.

◊ **OBJECTIVE:** Investigate the Gauldur legend
♦ **TARGET:** Daynas Valen's Journal, outside Folgunthur

Although the objective is out of the cave, you can see a Nordic Puzzle Door set into the rock wall above the pedestal.

Puzzle Solution: The door consists of three "rings" that rotate when you activate them. Each has three animals plated into the stonework, and the central keyhole is unlocked using the Emerald Dragon Claw; the puzzle is inaccessible without it. The puzzle solution is actually on the palm of the Claw; rotate it in your inventory to see the three circular petroglyph carvings on the Claw's palm. Move the rings so the Bear, Whale, and Snake appear on the outer, middle, and inner rings, respectively. Then insert the Emerald Dragon Claw into the keyhole.

Through the door, a long hallway greets you, along with three additional doors that grind open one after the other. They lead to a second (and completely sealed) Nordic Puzzle Door. This features different petroglyphs, and your Emerald Dragon Claw doesn't fit the keyhole. You return here at the zenith of this quest.

Travel to Folgunthur, just southeast of Solitude in the marshes, and inspect the long-abandoned campground outside the barrow. Inside one of the snow-dusted tents is Daynas Valen's Journal. Read and stow it; the book speaks of his obsession with the Gauldur legend, which he, too, has traced to Folgunthur.

➤ **Daynas Valen's Journal**

◈ **NOTE**   Due to the varied nature of this quest, you can simply head here and read Daynas Valen's Journal first or obtain the notes from Daynas himself, inside Folgunthur. There are many options for uncovering the history of the hated Gauldersons!

◊ **OBJECTIVE:** Learn the truth from Daynas Valen
♦ **TARGET:** Daynas Valen's Notes, in Folgunthur

Be Bound Here, Mikrul: Murderer, Betrayer

Open the ominous Iron Doors of Folgunthur, watching for a trigger plate in the initial tunnel; you don't want to be skewered by the spikes shooting from the dragon busts on either side of you. Note the corpses of the adventurers and Draugr strewn across the passage; you're far from the first to venture into this tomb. At the bottom of the tunnel steps is a claw keyhole, which seems to have already been opened, and requires the Ivory Claw (which Daynas has, according to his journal).

Inside the entrance room is a Nordic Puzzle. It, too, has already been solved. The exit opposite leads to a pressure plate and fire trap and the first live Draugr in the tomb. The passage continues into an expansive subterranean banquet hall, with Draugr literally peeling away from the walls and oily floors and lamps to roast them with.

Enter the passage on the banquet hall's far side, where a floor grate drops away as you step near. You are fortunate that the drop onto spikes is filled with water. Carefully step around the grating or use the wall lever to close it and lift you out of the pit; then ascend the spiral steps. This leads to a balcony overlooking the banquet hall and the bloody remains of Daynas Valen, cut down close to another claw keyhole. Search his corpse for two important items:

➤ **Daynas Valen's Notes**   ➤ **Ivory Dragon Claw**

◊ **OBJECTIVE:** Read Daynas Valen's notes

Grab the items, and leaf through the notes. Daynas's obsession and years of painstaking research finally led him to the surprising truth about Gauldur and his sons and the powerful amulet that bound the brothers together. It is obviously powerful. But is it worth the danger involved in assembling the pieces? Yes, of course it is!

◊ **OBJECTIVE:** Find the Gauldur Amulet Fragment in Folgunthur
♦ **TARGET:** Mikrul Gauldurson, in Folgunthur
◊ **OBJECTIVE:** Find the Gauldur Amulet Fragment in Geirmund's Hall
♦ **TARGET:** Sigdis Gauldurson, in Geirmund's Hall
◊ **OBJECTIVE:** Find the Gauldur Amulet Fragment in Saarthal
♦ **TARGET:** Jyrik Gauldurson, in Saarthal

Insert the Ivory Dragon Claw into the keyhole by Daynas's corpse. This lowers the bridge, forcing you into combat with the Draugr beyond. Battle through, into a small crypt (watch for a floor trigger and spear trap in the chamber to your left) and around to a Nordic Lever Puzzle.

Puzzle Solution: There are four levers, each moving a particular set of the four portcullises that block your path. Pull the right-front and left-rear levers to open your path.

Head down the steep stairs, watching for a rock-fall trap. Open the wooden door into a guardian chamber with two Draugr near their thrones and a large central grating. Currently, if you pull on the wall chain, you're pierced by darts. There is a trick to opening this grating:

Puzzle Solution: There are two levers, one by each throne. Both of them rotate walls that block the nearby doors, allowing you to enter the chambers beyond. The right one currently allows you to access a semicircular chamber adjacent to the throne and lever. Battle the Draugr before inspecting the three large stone heads, each with an animal petroglyph in their maws. Working counterclockwise from the first petroglyph you see, the order is Snake, Whale, and Hawk. Return to the grating chamber, and pull the lever by the left throne until the rock wall shifts to open into a second, almost identical chamber. The difference is that there are three pillars. Rotate them so that the Snake faces out from the first pillar (facing the doorway), the Whale faces out from the second, and the Hawk faces from the third, mimicking the petroglyphs in the mirrored room you just came from. Now when you pull the chain, the grate opens.

Wind your way down the long spiral steps to a waterlogged tunnel with Frostbite Spiders to tackle. The open doors at the far end lead to a long hall, flanked with coffins. As you enter the hall, the doors slam shut behind you and the lights go out. Crypts to either side of the room open, and Draugr begin to emerge in the darkness. Quickly use a Nighteye spell or power if you can, then battle the guardians. When the foes are vanquished, the lights come back on. Step up to another Nordic Puzzle Door.

Puzzle Solution: Move the rings so the Hawk, Hawk, and Dragon appear on the outer, middle, and inner rings, respectively. Then insert the Ivory Dragon Claw into the keyhole. Venture forward, and open the doors leading into Folgunthur Crypt.

Brother Battle: Mikrul Gauldurson

The crypt is a massive chamber, flanked with coffins and a main tomb at the far (southeast) end. When you're about halfway across the crypt, the sarcophagus bursts open, and out clambers the fearsome Mikrul Gauldurson, now a Draugr of considerable power! Aside from his inherent toughness, he also wields the Gauldur Blackblade, a powerful sword with an Absorb Health enchantment. He is accompanied by Draugr Thralls: weak, unarmed Draugr that do little damage but crowd the space, making it hard for you to flee from Mikrul's reach.

Especially at low levels, you may find it harrowing to fight Mikrul in melee combat, as every blow he delivers rapidly refills his health. Followers and summoned creatures are best left behind, since Mikrul can drain their health just as easily. The safest bet is to refrain from being hit at all. Back away as best you can, dodge his blows, and use a bow or spells to whittle down his health. If desperate measures are called for, you can jump across the sarcophagi along the sides of the room to flee and regroup.

Once Mikrul falls, any surviving thralls also die. Be sure you pry Mikrul's bony fingers off his vampiric blade, which is an exceptional one-handed weapon. There are two other items of interest, too:

➤ **Gauldur Blackblade**   ➤ **Writ of Sealing**

➤ **Gauldur Amulet Fragment**

Don't be fooled by the "fragment" part: Mikrul's amulet fragment is a full amulet in its own right and has a solid Fortify Health enchantment. The Writ has a curse against the Gauldurson brother written upon it. To exit the chamber, move to the far (southeast) end and insert the Ivory Dragon Claw into the right-side keyhole (the left leads to a rockfall). This removes the spear bars and allows access to the treasure chamber, which also contains a Word Wall. Now leave Folgunthur out of the southeast Iron Door, push out a sarcophagus lid for a shortcut into the banquet hall crypt, and retrace your steps back out. On your way, use the Ivory Claw in the first puzzle room to open a secret door with a chest.

➤ **Word of Power:** Frost Breath

Be Bound Here, Sigdis: Murderer, Betrayer

Travel to Geirmund's Hall, east of Ivarstead in the hilly forest close to Lake Geir. Enter the cave and crush the two Skeever; then peer down the massive sinkhole in the center of the room. Drop into the water below. Aside from the submerged crypt passage leading to a chest and a dead end, there are steps up to an Iron Door. Slash your way through Frostbite Spiders, watch for a trigger plate that launches darts, and head down into a waterlogged crypt. Aside from Draugr, there are Nordic puzzle pillars to inspect.

Puzzle Solution: Stand atop the steps and face down into the waterlogged crypt. On the left (south) wall are two small petroglyph plaques showing a Hawk and a Whale. On the right (north) wall, there are plaques showing a Whale and a Snake. Continue along the crypt's left side, and spin the two pillars to show the Hawk and the Whale. Backtrack, and continue along the crypt's right side, and spin the two pillars to show the Whale and the Snake (the first of these already shows the Whale and so doesn't need to be moved). Then pull the lever to open the portcullis doorway.

Head into the ruined hub chamber with a fallen bridge and steps up to an altar. You'll return here later, so simply check the corpse on the altar for a key and epitaph, where Lord Geirmund keeps his eternal vigil. To open the Iron Door behind the altar (Adept), use the key or pick it. Pass the Arcane Enchanter and turn left (west), as the direct route to Sigdis Gauldurson's sarcophagus is blocked. Climb the steps, kill the Draugr on the balcony overlooking the hub room, and ignore the easily spotted lever (unless you want spears in your sides). Instead, pull the hidden one just behind you to the right (southwest). This lowers the bridge.

Fight the Draugr as you cross (you can jump to the right and open a locked door [Expert] to reach a small treasure room, then retrace your steps). Use another lever on the middle "island" to lower the second bridge, and fight through into a small passage. Watch the floor trigger, or face swinging axes around the corner. Quickly step to the wall lanterns between the blades to avoid them.

➤ **Lord Geirmund's Key**   ➤ **Geirmund's Epitaph**

Brother Battle: Sigdis Gauldurson

Follow the passage around and into the tomb of Sigdis Gauldurson. The moment he steps from his sarcophagus, he teleports away, and you suddenly have more than one Sigdis to deal with! His Illusory Duplicates spell means that two of these entities are magical doppelgangers. During the frenzy of combat, it may be difficult to tell, but Sigdis's duplicates have a few subtle differences:

The Gauldur Blackbow Signis uses dishes out significantly more damage and drains your Magicka.

The dopplegangers are wreathed in a slight blue glow.

The dopplegangers' helmets don't have horns, while Sigdis's helmet does.

The three foes fire from their platforms, forcing you to strike them using your favored weaponry. Sigdis teleports around and summons duplicates again periodically, speeding up if you destroy both duplicates or as his health falls.

Focus your attention on Sigdis, as he's the only one taking damage. After you kill him, any illusions are dispersed, and an exit doorway behind his coffin slides open once. Be sure you pry Sigdis's twitching fingers off his bow, which drains Magicka from targets. There are two other items of interest, too.

➤ **Gauldur Blackbow**   ➤ **Writ of Sealing**

➤ **Gauldur Amulet Fragment**

Once again, Sigdis's amulet fragment is a real amulet, this time with a Fortify Stamina enchantment. The Writ has a curse against the Gauldurson brother written upon it. Exit via the newly opened corridor, leading to a large chest and a lever that opens a section of wall, leading you back into the initial chamber with the pit.

Be Bound Here, Jyrik: Murderer, Betrayer

At this point, or whenever you wish to explore Saarthal and face Jyrik Gauldurson, you must visit the College of Winterhold and begin the College of Winterhold questline. Consult the College of Winterhold Quests for all pertinent information. Here's what you need to do:

Complete College of Winterhold Quest: First Lessons, proving your magical aptitude and gaining admittance to the College, where you'll train with Tolfdir.

Begin College of Winterhold Quest: Under Saarthal, and explore the excavation. The route to take, and the Nordic Puzzle solutions, are detailed in that quest. This culminates in the discovery of a giant glowing orb that floats in a bubble of writhing magic, at the opposite end of the room. It is pulsing and made of some strange, unknown material. Tolfdir is transfixed by this but averts his gaze when a ferocious-looking Draugr rises from his eternal throne chair. You're about to face the third brother, Jyrik Gauldurson!

Brother Battle: Jyrik Gauldurson

Jyrik Gauldurson is coursing with evil magic, and for the first ten seconds of the battle, he is utterly impervious to any attacks. Use this time to step behind cover or let any summoned creatures you may have conjured or Followers bear the brunt of his attacks.

Eventually, Tolfdir realizes that all your combined offensive capabilities aren't having an effect, so he turns to the Eye and focuses his attacks on the crackling globe. A few seconds later, he yells that Jyrik is vulnerable. Attack!

To further complicate matters, Jyrik is bathed in an elemental shield that cycles through the different elements and is impervious to attacks from the same element. So, if he's bathed in fire, then any Flame-based spells have no effect on him. Use attacks from any other element instead. If you have only one type of elemental magic (i.e., only Fire), wait a few seconds until Jyric's shielding changes elements, and then strike!

> **TIP**   Jyrik is extremely vulnerable to frost damage when he's on fire, and when encased in a frost shield, he's very vulnerable to fire. Use this to your advantage!

With Jyrik Gauldurson gurgling his last curse, turn your attention to his unique weapon, although not one he wields in the battle with you: the Staff of Jyrik Gauldurson, which lies on the altar in front of his throne. Grab it, and the other items of interest on his corpse:

➤ **Gauldur Amulet Fragment**   ➤ **Writ of Sealing**

➤ **Staff of Jyrik Gauldurson**

As you might expect, his amulet fragment has a Fortify Magicka enchantment, while the Writ has a curse against him written upon it. Now use the Iron Door behind the orb to exit the chamber, which leads to a fern-filled grotto and an ancient Word Wall. Absorb the power before you exit back into the excavation site, releasing the portcullis with a wall handle and exiting Saarthal.

➤ **Word of Power:** Ice Form

Be Defeated Here, Gauldurson Brothers!

With the three Amulet Fragments in your possession, all that remains is to return to Reachwater Rock and enter the long hall that was sealed when you first visited this tomb. (If this is your first visit, see above for directions to the cave.)

Puzzle Solution:
Move the rings so the Hawk, Hawk, and Dragon appear on the outer, middle, and inner rings, respectively. Then take the Ivory Dragon Claw you found on Daynas Valen's corpse in Folgunthur, and insert it into the keyhole. Continue down the steps beyond and enter the Arch-Mage Gauldur's tomb. Approach the altar at the far (northwest) end of the elaborately constructed room. Here you'll find three Amulet Pedestals.

As you set the final Amulet Fragment down on the pedestal, three spectral forms congeal from the ether on an inaccessible balcony above you. The power of the Gauldurson Brothers is strong enough to defy death—twice! Now you must face Mikrul, Sigdis, and Jyrik again, only this time they attack one after the other!

Mikrul is the first to step forward, teleporting to the room's far end as sarcophagi burst open around him. His thralls are back, stronger than before and now fully armed. This time, your best bet is to avoid Mikrul and go after the thralls first; you don't want to be surrounded by weapon-swinging Draugr. Once you slay them, Mikrul should be easier to defeat. Again, you may be better off attacking him from range: That strategy is even more effective here, since you can leap across the gaps in the platforms, but he must walk around them. When Mikrul falls, he returns to the upper platform and drops to a knee.

Sigdis steps forward next, this time joined by three ghostly duplicates. Again, their helmets are a telltale clue: The real Sigdis has curled horns on his helmet, while the duplicates have vertical horns. Ignore the duplicates and crush Sigdis as quickly as you can.

Finally, Jyrik steps forward. He is not invincible here, but he's still a powerful sorcerer. At several points in the battle, he teleports away to regain a little composure before attacking again. Use the same strategies as before to target his elemental weaknesses and bring him down.

After you deliver the final blow to Jyrik, the three brothers regroup at the altar. Suddenly, the sarcophagus behind them opens. The brothers turn, Sigdis lets out a shout, and a brilliant blast of light wipes them from existence. When the dust settles, a spectral figure (could this be Gauldur?) appears and grants you what you seek: In a flash of light, the Amulet Fragments combine!

> ◊ **OBJECTIVE:** Take the Gauldur Amulet

Quest Conclusion

Claim the reforged amulet and wear it proudly—you've earned it. While you may never wield its unique abilities as the brothers once did, the amulet is still immensely powerful, fortifying your Health, Magicka, and Stamina all in one.

➤ **Gauldur Amulet**

Postquest Activities

After claiming the amulet, jump up to the high platform and inspect the newly opened sarcophagus. Search Gauldur's skeleton, and you can find a sizable gold reward as well.

PREREQUISITES: None

INTERSECTING QUESTS: Side Quest: No One Escapes Cidhna Mine

LOCATIONS: Markarth, Nepos's House, Shrine of Talos, Silver-Blood Inn, Margret's Room, The Treasury House, The Warrens, Weylin's Room

CHARACTERS: Betrid Silver-Blood, Eltrys, Garvey, Kleppr, Margret, Markarth City Guard, Mulush gro-Shugurz, Rhiada, Thonar Silver-Blood

ENEMIES: Donnel, Dryston, Nana Ildene, Nepos the Nose, Uaile, Weylin

◇ **OBJECTIVES:** Read Eltrys' Note, Go to the Shrine of Talos, Find evidence about Margret, Find evidence about Weylin, (Optional) Obtain the key to Margret's room, Read Margret's Journal, Find evidence about Thonar, (Optional) Obtain the key to Weylin's room, Read Weylin's Note, Find out who "N" is, Find evidence about Nepos, Return to Eltrys

Murder in the Marketplace

On your first visit to Markarth, just after you enter the entrance gate, you immediately hear a man shouting, "The Reach belongs to the Forsworn!" before he murders a market patron in cold blood. The Markarth City Guard quickly overpower and slay the maniac (watch your own sword swings if the lunatic turns on you, as you don't want to accidentally strike a Markarth inhabitant). You can quickly speak to the other traders, before a man named Eltrys approaches you. He surreptitiously hands you a note. Read it; he is requesting a meeting in the Shrine of Talos.

➤ Eltrys' Note

◇ **OBJECTIVE:** Read Eltrys' Note
◇ **OBJECTIVE:** Go to the Shrine of Talos
♦ **TARGET:** Shrine of Talos, in Markarth

Before the body of Margret—the woman who was cut down—is carried away for rites and burial, quickly check her corpse; you'll find a key that can come in handy.

➤ Key to Margret's Room

Enter the shrine and locate Eltrys, who is attempting a clandestine investigation of a conspiracy within the city. This isn't the first brazen killing by the Forsworn; indeed, the City Guard seem to be actively covering up this slaughter. Eltrys tasks you with finding out more information about the folks involved: the attacker, Weylin, and the victim, Margret. For further hints, ask Eltrys exhaustive questions about the Forsworn and those involved. For more motivation, Eltrys says he'll pay you handsomely for what you uncover.

◇ **OBJECTIVE:** Find evidence about Margret
♦ **TARGET:** Silver-Blood Inn, in Markarth
◇ **OBJECTIVE:** Find evidence about Weylin
♦ **TARGET:** The Warrens, in Markarth

> **TIP** You can undertake the following investigation in any order, and you can break off from one line of questioning to complete another. Each time your Quest Objective updates significantly, return to Eltrys (in the shrine) to inform him and receive a sizable reward (200 gold pieces each time).

> **TIP** **No Murder in the Marketplace:** If you're quick, you can actually step in and kill Weylin before he has time to murder Margret. Should this occur, she offers the necklace she purchased just prior to being set upon as a way of thanking you. The quest continues with Eltrys handing you a note. Once you speak to him inside the Shrine of Talos, you can find Margret again (around the market or in the Silver-Blood Inn) and obtain more information about the attack, and why she is there.

Margret: Shadows Around Every Corner

Head into the Silver-Blood Inn, where Margret was staying, and have a quiet word with Kleppr the barkeep. Steer the conversation toward Margret, who Kleppr says prepaid an entire month's rent for the nicest room at the inn.

◇ **OBJECTIVE:** (Optional) Obtain the key to Margret's Room
♦ **TARGET:** Kleppr, in the Silver-Blood Inn, in Markarth

You obviously need to search Margret's Room, and for that you require a key or a Lockpick skill. There are various ways of entering Margret's Room:

Unlock the room using the key you uncovered from Margret's corpse, if you were quick-thinking at the start of this quest.

(Lockpick [Apprentice]) You can ignore Kleppr completely and—once the coast is clear—use Lockpicks to open the door.

(Persuade) You can sweet-talk Kleppr into giving you the key.

(Gold) Simple bribery does the trick, too.

(Intimidate) As does a not-so-veiled threat directed at the barkeep.

 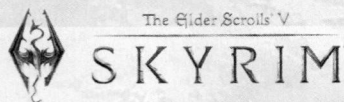

(Pickpocket) With an appropriate Pickpocket, you can ease the key into your possession.

➤ **Key to Margret's Room**

Inside Margret's Room, there's several trinkets to steal, but the real find is located inside the end table. Open it, and secure Margret's Journal.

➤ **Margret's Journal**

◊ **OBJECTIVE:** Read Margret's Journal
♦ **TARGET:** Margret's Room, Silver-Blood Inn, in Markarth

Open the journal: It seems Margret was an agent employed by General Tullius and was tasked to investigate the powerful Silver-Blood family, specifically Thonar Silver-Blood, the owner of Cidhna Mine. You have the information you seek; leave the inn. You're met outside by a city guard, who gives you what appears to be a threat if you continue poking your nose into the affairs of the Silver-Bloods.

◊ **OBJECTIVE:** Find evidence about Thonar
♦ **TARGET:** The Treasury House, in Markarth

TIP You can complete all the investigations at once if you wish, although when you return from finding out more about Thonar or Nepos, a nasty fate has befallen Eltrys. Therefore, if you're after some coin for your troubles, complete the Weylin and Margret investigations first, turning them in before talking to Thonar or Nepos.

Margret: The Spilling of Silver-Blood

Climb the hewn steps to the elaborate Treasury House, and enter. You're usually greeted by Rhiada, the Silver-Blood's maid, who challenges you on your antics after you ask to see Thonar. You can:

(Persuade) Pretend Thonar is expecting you.

(Bribe) Use some coin to win her over.

(Intimidate) Or attempt a fear-inducing utterance.

This allows you access into the dining room, where Thonar is usually eating.

No matter your line of questioning, Thonar is the leader of this city, and he isn't happy at you butting into business that doesn't concern you. You're told to leave, just as you hear a commotion in an adjoining room. Thonar's servants, Donnel and Nana Ildene, reveal themselves to be Forsworn and have already killed Thonar's wife, Betrid, in cold blood! They now turn on you; defeat them both.

Thonar is shaken but ready to talk. He reveals he'd made a deal with the Forsworn. When the Nords conquered Markarth, Thonar spared King Madanach's life and locked him up in the Cidhna Mine. In exchange, the ousted king agreed to use his Forsworn to kill Thonar's enemies. But Thonar's grip on power is obviously slipping.

Weylin: A Subsistence Existence

◊ **OBJECTIVE:** (Optional) Obtain the key to Weylin's room
◊ **OBJECTIVE:** Read Weylin's Note
♦ **TARGET:** (Optional) Garvey, and Weylin's Room, the Warrens, in Markarth

Weylin the murderer worked as a miner and lived in the grim underbelly of Markarth, in a place known as the Warrens. Journey here, and gain some further insight into Weylin's grim life. Start with the bullying foreman of the smelter, Mulush gro-Shugurz. He won't tell you what he knows; he doesn't care enough to be involved in Weylin's antics. React by leaving or by:

(Persuade) Saying he must know something.

(Bribe) Bribing him to reveal some information.

(Intimidate) Telling him he'd better start caring.

If you're successful, Mulush reveals Weylin was slipped a piece of paper the last time he was paid. Now move into the Warrens.

The second person to interview is Garvey, who runs the Warrens where the poor make their pitiful existence. He isn't keen on just handing over Weylin's key to you. You have the following options:

(Persuade) Tell him it is important.

(Bribe) Press some gold into his filthy hands.

(Intimidate) Inform him this wasn't a request; it was an order.

(Pickpocket) Display your impressive Pickpocket skills and take the key by stealthy means.

When you reach Weylin's room inside the Warrens, you'll notice it is locked (Very Easy). However, picking the lock simply raises the alarm and isn't recommended if anyone is watching. Neither is striking Garvey, who holds the key.

➤ **Key to Weylin's Room**

Once inside Weylin's room, steal from his chest. There isn't much to line your pockets with, but the chest does contain an important clue: Weylin's Note.

➤ **Weylin's Note**

Open the note, which contains the order for the assassination in the market. It is simply signed "-N."

◊ **OBJECTIVE:** Find out who "N" is
♦ **TARGET:** Dryston, in Markarth

Weylin: On the Nose

The moment you step outside from the Warrens, an armored man by the name of Dryston strides up to you and threatens to teach you a lesson. There's no way out of this brawl; expect a pummeling if you don't retaliate. After you punch him down, he squeals the name of his employer: the city's old administrator, Nepos the Nose.

Retaliate with your fists and beat Dryston to his knees. Do not use weapons or kill him; this causes mass hostility across Markarth!

CAUTION

◊ **OBJECTIVE:** Find evidence about Nepos
♦ **TARGET:** Nepos's House, in Markarth

TIP You should definitely catch up with Eltrys and secure some gold pieces before uncovering more of this conspiracy!

With Nepos's thug beaten into submission, ascend the steps to reach the administrator's house, and step inside. You're stalled by Uaile, Nepos's protective housekeeper. She refuses to let you

speak with Nepos but relents when the old man beckons you to his hearth. Nepos is wizened, and he confesses to directing Weylin in the murder, under orders from Madanach, who he describes as the "King in Rags." Madanach used to rule Markarth before the Nords drove out the Forsworn. Somehow, he still commands the Forsworn. Nepos's servants think you've heard enough and attack you. Stay and fight, or flee the dwelling.

◊ **OBJECTIVE:** Return to Eltrys
♦ **TARGET:** Shrine of Talos, in Markarth

Eltrys must be informed immediately! Unfortunately, as you enter the shrine and venture to his location, you see that Eltrys has been killed—almost certainly by the city guards milling about. Guards immediately accuse you of snooping and frame you for the recent murders, including that of Eltrys! You are to be banished to the Cidhna Mine. A place where *no one* escapes.

Quest Conclusion

Prior to Eltrys's demise, he rewards you with gold for your investigations of Weylin and Margret. Be sure to see him before your other investigations, or don't expect any coin!

➤ **Gold pieces [Leveled]**

Postquest Activities

Side Quest: No One Escapes Cidhna Mine begins immediately.

NO ONE ESCAPES CIDHNA MINE

PREREQUISITES: Complete Side Quest: The Forsworn Conspiracy
INTERSECTING QUESTS: Side Quest: The Forsworn Conspiracy, Grisvar's Shiv*
LOCATIONS: Markarth, Cidhna Mine, Markarth Ruins
CHARACTERS: Borkul the Beast, Braig, Duach, Grisvar the Unlucky, Madanach, Markarth Guard, Odvan, Thonar Silver-Blood, Uraccen, Urzoga gra-Shugurz
ENEMIES: Dwarven Centurion, Frostbite Spider
◊ **OBJECTIVES:** Ask a prisoner about Madanach, Get past Borkul the Beast, Talk to Grisvar about getting a Shiv, Bring Grisvar the Skooma, Talk to Madanach, Hear Braig's story, Return to Madanach, Kill Grisvar the Unlucky, Return to Madanach, Follow Madanach, Kill Madanach, Search Madanach's body, Escape Cidhna Mine

⦿ **MINOR SPOILERS**

NOTE ✳ Indicates the secondary quest also available here has a name that does not appear in your Quest menu; the objectives are in the Miscellaneous section of your menu.

▷ Imprisoned in a Forsaken Place

This quest does not commence if you're thrown into this mine due to your Crime level in the Reach!

CAUTION

◊ **OBJECTIVE:** Ask a prisoner about Madanach
♦ **TARGET:** Uraccen, in Cidhna Mine

You wake up to Urzoga gra-Shugurz shouting at you. He is the guard captain in charge of the prisoners in this mine, which is carved into the mountains of Markarth. Unlike prisons in other Hold Cities, you're expected to work, mining silver ore until you drop. You can reply with subservient or sarcastic remarks to Urzoga, before she opens up the cell door and you're allowed into the mine.

The quickest way to finding out more information about Madanach, who appears to run the prisoners on this side of the mine, is to speak with Uraccen. He's usually sitting by the campfire in the prison's middle chamber. You can make up whatever story you like about why you're here, and ask him about the prison's illicit Skooma trade, but be sure to ask him two important questions:

1. The location of Madanach. Unfortunately, nobody gets to speak with him without getting past Borkul the Beast. You may ask for more information about this Orc bodyguard, or step over to see him yourself.

2. Information on obtaining a Shiv a more subtle and cruel method of protecting yourself. A man named Grisvar has a spare one, if you're interested. This begins Side Quest: Grisvar's Shiv.

◊ **OBJECTIVE:** Get past Borkul the Beast

Borkul the Beast is standing guard by a locked gate close to the campfire. You can get on his good side by revealing your bloodlust, or offer a more measured response. When you ask to see Madanach, Borkul refuses until you pay the toll—a Shiv. You can:

Tell Borkul you don't have a Shiv. He suggests you get one. Complete Side Quest: Grisvar's Shiv from this point.

(Pickpocket) Use your impressive Pickpocket skill to pry Borkul's Key from his pocket without him knowing.

(Persuade) Tell Borkul that Madanach is expecting you.

THE ELDER SCROLLS V
SKYRIM

(Brawl) Or offer to fight Borkul for access into Madanach's chamber. Fight the Orc, here by the campfire, and batter him with punches until he falls to his knees and tastes his own blood.

Once you succeed at any of these plans, Borkul hands over the key to Madanach's room, and you may progress.

➤ **Borkul's Key**

◗ Side Quest: Grisvar's Shiv*

◊ OBJECTIVE: Talk to Grisvar about getting a Shiv.

If you require a Shiv while in prison, head into the mine's southern part and hunt down Grisvar the Unlucky. He's here by the Jarl's request, due to his "problems." Ask for a Shiv, and he agrees—if you bring him back a bottle of Skooma from Duach.

Now head into the mine's north section and ask Duach about the Skooma. He isn't about to hand this over to just anyone, and your looks are beginning to annoy him. In that case, you should try:

(Persuade) Telling him you need the Skooma badly.

(Brawl) Demanding he hand the Skooma over and then fistfighting him for it. Remember, don't kill him!

When either of these plans is successful, you receive the Skooma from Duach.

➤ **Skooma**

CAUTION	
Did you drink the Skooma before realizing you need to hand it to Grisvar? Then this quest fails!	

◊ OBJECTIVE: Bring Grisvar the Skooma

All that remains now is to return to Grisvar, hand him the Skooma, and accept a Shiv in return. You can use the Shiv to attack the prisoners (which is unwise, as they usually overwhelm you), or give it to Borkul the Beast if no other method of getting past him is working.

➤ **Shiv**

◗ Mining the Mind of Madanach

◊ OBJECTIVE: Talk to Madanach

NOTE **Forsworn or Nord Alliance:** At this point, you can choose to side with Madanach, the leader of the Forsworn, against the Nords who have usurped his kingdom. Follow the quest sections marked with the alliance you wish to be associated with.

Forsworn Alliance: Madanach's Tasks

Forsworn Alliance: Open the barred door that Borkul was guarding, pass by a latrine and closed cell, and meet Madanach at his writing desk. He asks what it is that you want. You may answer in any way you wish, but Madanach points out that you are now a slave. The boot of the Nord steps on your throat. He mentions a man named Braig, who has been imprisoned almost as long as Madanach. You are to meet with him and ask why he's here. Madanach wants to know how widespread the injustice of Markarth really is. You can ask about the Forsworn and Thonar (the mine owner) before you leave.

◊ OBJECTIVE: Hear Braig's story

Search the mine's southern end for Braig, who greets you with a warning not to shiv him. Tell him Madanach has asked you to listen to his story, and he asks when you last had chains around your wrists. Answer him as you wish and again when he asks about your family. Then Braig tells of his daughter Aethra, an innocent caught up in recent entanglements when the Nords picked Braig up for being involved in the Forsworn uprising. Braig had only spoken to Madanach once, but that was enough for the Nords to execute her in front of him and throw him in this mine. You can ask Braig further questions, but this has satisfied Madanach's curiosity.

◊ OBJECTIVE: Return to Madanach

Journey back to Madanach, who seems to have used Braig's story to drill into you the injustices of the Nords. Your responses can be sympathetic or accusatory, but if you are to escape, Madanach needs a show of loyalty from you. He certainly doesn't want a Shiv in the back during any planned breakout. He tells you to visit Grisvar the Unlucky—a thief and a snitch—and dispatch him so only prisoners loyal to Madanach remain.

◊ OBJECTIVE: Kill Grisvar the Unlucky

You must kill Grisvar with your bare hands or with a Shiv if you previously received one from him. As he's the only prisoner not loyal to the Forsworn, he has to go. You can attack without even speaking to him, or tell him that Madanach says hello, which causes him to stand and fight for a bit, then flee. Hunt him down and kill him, again with a Shiv or your bare hands. Equip yourself with a Shiv from his corpse if you wish.

➤ **Shiv**

◊ OBJECTIVE: Return to Madanach
◊ OBJECTIVE: Follow Madanach

Your actions have proved to Madanach that you are one of them. He wishes you to accompany him so he can announce his plans to all his brothers. Follow Madanach into the main mine chamber with the campfire, where he informs his brethren that it is time to leave Cidhna Mine. There is a gate beside his quarters, and behind it is a tunnel. This leads right through the old Dwarven Ruins of Markarth and into the city. Duach, Odvan (the only prisoners you may not have met yet), and the others raucously approve.

Nord Alliance: Madanach's Death

⬦ **OBJECTIVE:** Kill Madanach
⬦ **OBJECTIVE:** Search Madanach's body

Nord Alliance: If you wish to side with the Nords and can't abide this Forsworn claptrap, you can ignore Madanach and instead begin to fight or pickpocket him. Killing him is obviously easier if you're carrying a Shiv rather than relying on your fists. Madanach is an accomplished mage, so this fight may be difficult to conclude in your favor. But if you do kill Madanach, you can skip any remaining conversations and search his body for the following important items:

➤ **Madanach's Note**   ➤ **Madanach's Key**

The key unlocks the gate adjacent to Madanach's quarters, while the note informs you there's old Dwarven Ruins connecting this mine to Markarth, which is the only escape route. Time to earn an early pardon!

⬦ **OBJECTIVE:** Escape Cidhna Mine
◆ **TARGET:** Markarth city exterior

🔲 An Early Pardon

Whether you're fleeing with your Forsworn brothers or you've killed Madanach, stolen his key, and used it to open the gate beside Madanach's quarters, the time has come to leave. Maneuver down the tunnel to a gold door that opens into Markarth Ruins.

Dash in a northeastern direction along the remains of stone steps and metallic walkways, and into a Frostbite Spider–infested stone corridor. Stand and fight, or run past these large arachnids. If the Forsworn are with you, attack the spiders as a team.

Continue into a tight connecting tunnel that opens into a large two-level corridor with winding pipes and more dwarven automatons at the far end of it. Venture forward, and they grind into life (depending on your level, these enemies could be spheres or a dreaded Centurion!). When the dwarven mechanical beasts finally topple, continue heading northeast, scrambling up the earthen tunnel toward a golden door.

Forsworn Alliance: The Forsworn stop at the base of the steps, where a woman named Kaie calls for Madanach, bringing him all the equipment you were stripped of when you entered Cidhna Mine. In addition, you are granted an ancient outfit of the Forsworn that is blessed with the old magicks. Then the Forsworn pour out of the ruins and into Markarth.

➤ **Inventory Equipment**   ➤ **Gauntlet of the Old Gods**
➤ **Armor of the Old Gods**   ➤ **Helmet of the Old Gods**
➤ **Boots of the Old Gods**

Nord Alliance: Head up the steps to the gold doors. Madanach's Key opens them and you stumble out of the ruins and into Markarth.

Quest Conclusion

Forsworn Alliance: Thonar Silver-Blood is waiting to greet Madanach as he exits the ruins. He isn't about to let the Forsworn escape from his prison, especially after what they did to his family. The quest ends with the Forsworn swarming Thonar and killing him.

Nord Alliance: Thonar Silver-Blood is waiting to greet you as you exit the ruins. He isn't about to let the person responsible for killing Madanach out of his jurisdiction without giving him some kind of reward, especially after the peace you brought to his family. The quest ends with Thonar handing you all your equipment back, as well as a special ring — one that a smith would cut off seven fingers for! Remain calm during this time too; if you side with the Nords but kill Thonar, you don't receive his ring.

➤ **Inventory Equipment**   ➤ **Silver-Blood Family Ring**

Postquest Activities

If you sided with the Forsworn, they begin a bloody rampage through the city, eventually reaching the gates and fleeing to Druadach Redoubt deep in the Reach. If you helped them, the Forsworn in Druadach (and only at this location) will be friendly.

THE GOLDEN CLAW

 ● **MINOR SPOILERS**

PREREQUISITES: None
INTERSECTING QUESTS: Main Quest: Bleak Falls Barrow
LOCATIONS: Bleak Falls Barrow, Riverwood
CHARACTERS: Camilla Valerius, Lucan Valerius
ENEMIES: Arvel the Swift, Bandits, Draugr, Frost Troll, Giant Frostbite Spider, Skeevers
⬦ **OBJECTIVES:** Retrieve the Golden Claw, Cut Arvel down, Find the secret of Bleak Falls Barrow, Bring the claw to Lucan

🔲 Beneath the Barrow

Travel to Riverwood. You can overhear rumors about a recently robbed store; locate the Riverwood Trader. Inside, the proprietors Lucan and his sister, Camilla Valerius, are engaged in a heated discussion. It seems bandits have recently broken into their

dried goods store and stolen a solid gold ornament in the shape of a dragon's claw. Offer your help to Lucan; the sibling bickering doesn't stop, but Camilla seems appeased and takes you out to the bridge on the edge of Riverwood.

⬦ **OBJECTIVE:** Retrieve the Golden Claw
◆ **TARGET:** Golden Claw

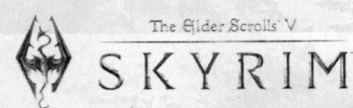

> **TIP** You can start this quest by simply adventuring into the Bleak Falls Barrow, without speaking to either Valerius sibling. You may also wish to cross-reference this quest with the Main Quest: Bleak Falls Barrow. Be on the lookout for a Dragonstone as you search.

It isn't wise to rush after Arvel; you'll soon catch up with him, and it is better to be prepared rather than rush headlong into an unknown chamber. **CAUTION**

Find your way up the mountain path north of Riverwood, passing the Riverwood Folly (where bandits roam), and to the summit, where the Nord tomb appears through the blizzard. Expect more bandit activity in this area. Locate the arched carved door leading into Bleak Falls Temple. Inside the first chamber, you hear two bandits around a campfire talking about a Dark Elf heading farther into the Barrow. End their conversation swiftly before venturing down the stairs.

Pass through the spiderwebs, the burial urns, and the dead Skeever, and engage another bandit on your way to a ceremonial entrance room. A portcullis blocks your path, and the lever nearby is currently inactive. In the alcoves to the left are a trio of three-sided pillars. Approach the first, and you'll notice they can be activated. Each side has a different animal carving: the Hawk, Whale, and Snake.

Puzzle Solution: Rotate the pillars so a Snake, Snake, and Whale face out. The carved Nord heads above the portcullis (and the fallen middle one) hold the answer in their maws.

Descend the spiral steps beyond, battling a few Skeevers on your way. As the thick spider silk begins to cover the walls, you hear a voice up ahead and to your left. Cut through the doorway covered in webbing, and enter the lair of a Giant Frostbite Spider. Attack the arachnid before venturing toward the trussed-up Dark Elf: one of the bandits from the raiding party you slaughtered previously. This is Arvel the Swift, who is carrying the Golden Claw. He quickly tells you he knows how it works, how it fits into the door in the Hall of Stories. The bandit is babbling. But he needs cutting down first. Oblige him.

◊ **OBJECTIVE:** Cut Arvel down
♦ **TARGET:** Arvel the Swift

> **TIP** Having trouble dispatching such a large arachnid? Then search for a Potion of Paralysis on a shelf in the hallway before the puzzle chamber and a Fireball Scroll on the table in the room just after you descend the spiral steps. Use these if you need to.

After a couple of weapon swipes (or magical blasts), Arvel's sticky prison gives way. He immediately flees, laughing that he won't be sharing his treasure with the likes of you. This is correct, but that's because you'll be taking him out — use a quick arrow or two in the back or other ranged attack — or letting the denizens who lurk deeper into this crypt deal with him.

Follow Arvel's trail, passing through the crypt entrance and down into the catacombs. The swift soon meets the dead as Arvel falls under a flurry of Draugr attacks. The Nord undead now turn their attention to you. Battle them back using your combat mettle or run north toward the open spiked gate and pressure plate. Keep to the extreme left, and you can activate the swinging gate trap without being hit. Instead, use it as a skewering device against the Draugr. Then search Arvel. Among his belongings is the Golden Claw and the Dark Elf's journal. Read it for more clues on this Barrow's secret.

➤ **Golden Claw**   ➤ **Arvel's Journal**

◊ **OBJECTIVE:** Find the secret of Bleak Falls Barrow
♦ **TARGET:** Hall of Stories

You have Lucan's trinket, but don't return it until you completely reconnoiter this Barrow. Continue down, battling Draugr and searching corpses, both resting and animated, as you go. At the swinging blades, sprint forward the moment the closest blade swings past you. Brandish your weaponry, but don't be overzealous with fire in the passageway with puddles; this is actually oil leaking from a hanging lamp, and the corridor erupts if flames touch the ground; use this as a trap against your bony foes.

Eventually, you climb steps into a tall chamber with a waterfall and another Draugr. Although a treasure chest can be ransacked, the Barrow's secret lies past a portcullis above the rushing stream. Locate the chain next to the portcullis and activate it, before splashing down the stream and into a larger, curved cavern with an opening at the far end. Ready any ranged attacks you can muster; a Draugr (or if you're at higher levels, a Frost Troll) is pacing the snow bridge directly below the waterfall opening. Strike it with as many projectiles as you can to weaken it, then engage it in a fierce battle throughout this upper cavern and lower bridge. Flee to regain Stamina or Magick if necessary. Another option is to simply flee entirely, although you'll miss the scavenging on the curved path below the bridge. Here you'll find the body of Thomas. Follow the path around and into the illuminated entrance to Bleak Falls Sanctum.

Open the Sanctum doors, and weave your way to another bladed corridor. Coax the Draugr beyond into this trap, before dashing through it, into the Great Chamber. Expect attacks from Draugr bowmen on the bridge above, as well as melee strikes from the ground. You can drop oil lamps and burn the decaying flesh of these foes as you head up and over the bridge, to the Iron Door leading into the Hall of Stories. The Hall is a long corridor with intricately carved Nord stonework on either side and an ornate door at the far end.

Puzzle Solution: The door consists of three "rings" that rotate when you activate them. Each has three animals plated into the structure, while the central keyhole is unlocked using the Golden Claw. This puzzle is inaccessible without it, as the solution is on the palm of the Golden

Claw. Rotate it in your inventory to see the three circular petroglyph carvings on the Claw's palm. Move the rings so the Bear, Moth, and Owl appear on the outer, middle, and inner rings, respectively. Then insert the Golden Claw into the keyhole.

> ◇ **OBJECTIVE:** Bring the claw to Lucan
> ♦ **TARGET:** Lucan Valerius

This reveals the Barrow's secret at last: a ceremonial burial grotto with waterfalls surrounding the long-forgotten chamber. Move to the carved stone center and check the chest. Scavenge what you need; then inspect the Word Wall, where you're granted a

Word of Power! However, this stirs a high-level Draugr Lord from his rest, and you must defend yourself from this final Barrow guardian.

After the fight, inspect the Draugr's corpse; he is carrying a Dragonstone! Now take the staircase on the chamber's left side, activating the handle to raise a secret stone slab door out into an upper Barrow alcove, a ceremonial alcove, and an exit out into Skyrim.

Now it is a simple matter of returning the Golden Claw heirloom to Lucan to complete this quest.

Quest Conclusion
➤ **Word of Power:** Unrelenting Force   ➤ **Dragonstone**
➤ **Gold pieces** (Leveled; if you return the Golden Claw to Lucan)

Postquest Activities
The Dragonstone is a valuable item sought by the Wizard of Whiterun, Farengar Secret-Fire, as part of Main Quest: Bleak Falls Barrow.

IN MY TIME OF NEED

PREREQUISITES: Complete Main Quest: Dragon Rising
INTERSECTING QUESTS: None
LOCATIONS: Swindler's Den, Whiterun, The Bannered Mare, Dragonsreach Dungeon, Whiterun Stables
CHARACTERS: Alik'r Prisoner, Alik'r Warrior, Kematu, Saadia, Whiterun City Guard
ENEMIES: Alik'r Warrior, Bandit
◇ **OBJECTIVES:** Find the Redguard woman, Speak with Saadia or Inform the Alik'r of Saadia's location, Talk to the Alik'r Prisoner, Kill Kematu or Inform the Alik'r of Saadia's location, Kill Kematu or talk to him, Lead Saadia to the Whiterun Stables

▷ A Wanted Woman

Once you've finished Main Quest: Dragon Rising and you enter the great city of Whiterun via the main gate, expect a commotion there. Cloaked Redguard warriors (who you find out are of the Alik'r Coterie) are in a heated discussion with the city guard. The Alik'r have already been banned from most of the city after an incident and jailing, but the men are determined to try and find a Redguard woman somewhere inside the walls. Speak to one of the Alik'r if you wish, or they stop and talk to you.

> ◇ **OBJECTIVE:** Find the Redguard woman

The woman in question is Saadia, who is a barmaid in the Bannered Mare. Enter this drinking establishment and let her know about the Alik'r warriors looking for Redguard women. Saadia appears agitated at this news and asks to speak to you privately.

> ◇ **OBJECTIVE:** Speak with Saadia
> ♦ **TARGET:** The Bannered Mare, in Whiterun
> ◇ **OR**
> ◇ **OBJECTIVE:** Inform the Alik'r of Saadia's location
> ♦ **TARGET:** Redguard, on the road to or in Rorikstead

Siding with Saadia: Further Information
Whether you intend to side with Saadia or not, it is worth finding out more about this woman's predicament. Away from the main hearth of the place, Saadia pulls a knife and demands answers, but this is more in an act of desperation than violence. After answering her, she pleads with you to help her. Agree, or request a reward, and Saadia reveals she is a noble from Hammerfell who fled to Skyrim and has been forced into hiding after an attempt on her life. She says that her attackers are hired by a rival house to turn her blood into gold and drag her back to be executed.

The Elder Scrolls V
SKYRIM

Saadia wishes to hire you to drive the assassins out. Most of the Alik'r forces are mercenaries led by a man named Kematu. Remove him and the remaining forces are likely to scatter. You need to find the Alik'r hideout.

> ◊ **OBJECTIVE:** Talk to the Alik'r Prisoner
> ♦ **TARGET:** Dragonsreach Dungeon, in Whiterun

Siding with Saadia or the Alik'r: Base Location

If you spoke to Saadia, she will tell you the location of the Alik'r Prisoner: Speak to her to continue this quest. Then journey to Dragonsreach Dungeon, enter the cells, and speak to the Alik'r Prisoner through the bars. Ask about Kematu (which is possible only if you were told the leader's name in an earlier conversation). The prisoner will give up Kematu's whereabouts if you pay the fine for his release.

(100 Gold) Pay one of the guards the fine, and return to the cell to let the prisoner know. He then gives you instructions on the location of Kematu's base of operations. The guards intend to let the prisoner out "eventually."

> **TIP** The other, less ingenious method of finding out where Kematu is located is to simply stumble across the Swindler's Den on your adventurers, once this quest is active.

> ◊ **OBJECTIVE:** Kill Kematu
> ◊ **OR**
> ◊ **OBJECTIVE:** Inform the Alik'r of Saadia's location
> ♦ **TARGET:** Swindler's Den

▷ Not Just a Pretty Face

Due west of Whiterun, among the great granite protrusions, is a den hewn into the dense rocky Tundra. Enter the Swindler's Den and bring your offensive combat to bear on the bandits lurking within. You must defeat (or sneak past) these thugs whether you intend to side with the assassins or not. Pass through the rocky crags into a waterlogged corridor, deep into the tunnel system. Kematu and his troops are waiting above you.

No matter who you've sided with previously, Kematu allows you to speak and question him. You can find out why Saadia is being hunted. According to Kematu, she betrayed her people and a Redguard city fell during the war, and the Redguard houses wish to bring her back alive to face justice. At this point, you have a pivotal choice to make: Kill Kematu or talk to him.

> ◊ **OBJECTIVE:** Kill Kematu or talk to him
> ♦ **TARGET:** Swindler's Den

> **NOTE** The more investigative of adventurers may wonder who is telling the truth: Kematu or Saadia. Alas, it is simply the word of one against another, and no firm evidence is ever found!

Siding with Saadia: Assassination!

If you are determined to save Saadia from the clutches of the Alik'r, you may attack them as soon as you can, or after another rather fruitless conversation with Kematu. Bring your best offensive weaponry to this slaughter! Gather any valuables you wish from the corpses, and then return to the Bannered Mare in Whiterun and inform Saadia of your success.

Siding with the Alik'r: A Wanted Woman

Speak again to Kematu, who informs you that his troops aren't assassins, but agents acting on behalf of Redguard Houses and ready to bring back a fugitive. Ask what they want you to do, and Kematu asks you to return to Saadia and convince her to meet you at the stables, where she'll be caught and brought to justice.

> ◊ **OBJECTIVE:** Lead Saadia to the Whiterun Stables
> ♦ **TARGET:** Saadia, the Bannered Mare, in Whiterun

Head back to the Bannered Mare and quickly speak with Saadia.

(Lie) Tell her you weren't able to defeat all the Alik'r forces, they are coming for her, and you have a horse ready for her.

Now exit Whiterun with Saadia following you. Move along the main cobbled road to Whiterun Stables and around to the side of the stable house, where Kematu is waiting for you both. He expertly immobilizes Saadia, and you may speak with him one final time to collect your reward.

Alternate Plans

At any point after speaking to Saadia, you can speak to the original Alik'r warriors you met at Whiterun's gate. They have moved to Rorikstead. Informing them that you've found Saadia completes the quest to the point where you're instructed to escort Saadia to the Whiterun Stables.

If you want to help Saadia but don't want to battle all of the Alik'r in Swindler's Den, there's always a cunning double cross you can pull (although the timing is difficult): Agree to help Kematu, and he'll appear in the stables alone, only after you've lied to Saadia and told her it is time to go. If you can kill Kematu before he paralyzes Saadia, she chastises you for using her as bait, but you can still claim the reward from her!

Quest Conclusion

If you slaughtered Kematu and saved Saadia, you receive the following:

➤ **500 gold pieces**

If you sided with Kematu of the Alik'r, you receive the following:

➤ **500 gold pieces**

Postquest Activities

If you helped Kematu capture Saadia, they are both gone the next time you return to Whiterun, and there is no further Alik'r presence in Skyrim. If you helped Saadia, she returns to her duties in the Bannered Mare, and no one is the wiser.

PREREQUISITES: None

LOCATIONS: Bleakcoast Cave, Froki's Shack, Gjukar's Monument, Graywinter Watch, Loreius Farm, Mammoth Graveyard, Pinewatch, Twilight Sepulcher, Windward Ruins

CHARACTERS: Froki Whetted-Blade, Haming

ENEMIES: Guardian Troll Spirit, Mammoth Guardian Spirit, Mudcrab, Mudcrab Guardian Spirit, Sabre Cat Guardian Spirit, Skeever, Skeever Guardian Spirit, Troll, Ursine Guardian Spirit, Wolf, Wolf Guardian Spirit

◊ **OBJECTIVES:** Defeat the Guardian Mudcrab, Defeat the Guardian Skeever, Defeat the Guardian Wolf, Return to Froki, Defeat the Guardian Bear, Defeat the Guardian Mammoth, Defeat the Sabre Cat, Return to Froki, Defeat the Guardian Troll, Return to Froki

◉ MINOR SPOILERS

Honoring the Old Ways

Nestled just below the snow line, high in the Jerall Mountains, Froki's Shack overlooks the southwestern rim of the Rift. Froki Whetted-Blade himself is usually inside his modest dwelling, with his grandson Haming. Judging by the animal heads festooned about the shack walls, Froki is something of a hunter. He is also somewhat mocking of the city dwellers and their new beliefs in the Divines. Not Froki; he believes in the Nordic gods of yore, especially Kyne the Blessed Warrior-Wife and widow of Shor, the mother of men and beasts. The Sacred Trials are named for her. Ask about the trials, and Froki explains this is an old Nord tradition: a test to prove your worth in the eyes of Kyne. Agree to begin the trials, and you are told to defeat the guardian beasts blessed by Kyne. Froki anoints you with the symbol of the Wolf, the Crab, and the Skeever. You can ask Froki for further information on the trials, his child, and the worship of Kyne, before the great hunt begins.

◊ **OBJECTIVE:** Defeat the Guardian Mudcrab
♦ **TARGET:** Mudcrab Guardian Spirit, near Gjukar's Monument
◊ **OBJECTIVE:** Defeat the Guardian Skeever
♦ **TARGET:** Skeever Guardian Spirit, near Windward Ruins
◊ **OBJECTIVE:** Defeat the Guardian Wolf
♦ **TARGET:** Wolf Guardian Spirit, near Pinewatch

Defeat the following three Guardian animals in any order you wish.

Sacred Trial: Parts I, II, III

Mudcrab Guardian Spirit: Find this spirit in the marshy ground between Gjukar's Monument and Broken Fang Cave. Expect Mudcrabs to scuttle in and attack as you deal with the Spirit.

Skeever Guardian Spirit: Locate this spirit in the snowy cairn marking the entrance to Windward Ruins, just southwest of Dawnstar. Prepare for Skeever to nip at you as you defeat the spirit.

Wolf Guardian Spirit: Search for this spirit close to Lake Ilinalta, just northwest of Pinewatch. Combat is likely to include dispatching wolves, and sometimes cave bears as you finish the spirit.

◊ **OBJECTIVE:** Return to Froki

After you dispatch all three animal Guardian Spirits, return to Froki's Shack and speak to him. He softens his attitude to you slightly, realizing you're probably ready for a real challenge. He anoints you with the symbol of the Bear, Sabre Cat, and Mammoth. He warns you to tread carefully, as these are mighty beasts.

◊ **OBJECTIVE:** Defeat the Guardian Bear
♦ **TARGET:** Ursine Guardian Spirit, near the Twilight Sepulcher
◊ **OBJECTIVE:** Defeat the Guardian Mammoth
♦ **TARGET:** Mammoth Guardian Spirit, Mammoth Graveyard, near Loreius Farm
◊ **OBJECTIVE:** Defeat the Sabre Cat
♦ **TARGET:** Sabre Cat Guardian Spirit, near Bleakcoast Cave

---

Defeat the following three Guardian animals in any order you wish.

Sacred Trial: Parts IV, V, VI

Ursine Guardian Spirit: Find this spirit in the copse of trees above the rocky terrain northeast of Twilight Sepulcher. Unlike the previous Guardian Spirits, the bear is usually encountered alone.

Mammoth Guardian Spirit: Locate this spirit due west of Loreius Farm, north of Whiterun. Venture to the Mammoth's Graveyard (a Secondary Location), and slay this solitary spirit.

Sabre Cat Guardian Spirit: Search for this spirit at the base of the glaciers along the icy shores of the Sea of Ghosts, just southwest of Bleakcoast Cave. Other wild animals are close, but not with this spirit.

◊ **OBJECTIVE:** Return to Froki

Visit Froki's Shack once more, and inform the old man of your continued successes. You do Kyne proud, and only one challenge remains: to defeat the troll champion!

◊ **OBJECTIVE:** Defeat the Guardian Troll
♦ **TARGET:** Guardian Troll Spirit, in Graywinter Watch

Sacred Trial: Part VII

Guardian Troll Spirit: Prepare for a battle with three trolls, taking all necessary equipment, provisions, and precautions before you travel to Graywinter Watch in the foothills east of Whiterun. Try attracting the trolls one at a time once you're inside the cave, backing out of the entrance if combat becomes too dangerous. Do not rest until the Guardian Troll Spirit falls back into the ether. Then search the location for an impressive bow:

➤ **Froki's Bow**

> **NOTE** This bow can be taken whether this quest is active or not. Should you speak to Froki after obtaining this weapon, he permits you to keep it.

◊ **OBJECTIVE:** Return to Froki

Quest Conclusion

Back at the shack for one final visit, inform Froki of your final triumph. He is pleased to call you a friend and that you finally know what it means to be a true hunter, in the Nordic tradition. For this, you earn an amulet imbued with the Blessing of Kyne.

➤ **Kyne's Blessing (-10% damage taken from wild animals)**

LAID TO REST

PREREQUISITES: None
INTERSECTING QUESTS: None

● MINOR SPOILERS

LOCATIONS: Morthal, Alva's House, Highmoon Hall, Moorside Inn, Movarth's Lair, Hroggar's House, Morthal Cemetery
CHARACTERS: Alva, Helgi's Ghost, Hroggar, Jarl Idgrod Ravencrone or Sorli the Builder, Jonna, Thonnir
ENEMIES: Frostbite Spider, Laelette the Vampire, Movarth Piquine, Vampire, Vampire's Thrall, Alva
◊ **OBJECTIVES:** Talk to the Jarl, Investigate the burned house, Find Helgi after dark, Ask Thonnir about Laelette, Investigate Alva's house, (Optional) Tell the Jarl about Helgi, Show Alva's Journal to the Jarl, Kill the master vampire, Return to Morthal's Jarl

Answers in the Ash

The Hold City of Morthal has more than swamp critter encroachment to worry about; there's rumor around these parts about one of the homes in the city burning to the ground. Suspicions are rife. Nobody is trustworthy, and two villagers are arguing with the city steward Aslfur as you arrive. You can converse with the townsfolk, but a more elaborate version of the rumor can be gained when you visit the Moorside Inn and speak to the barkeep Jonna. Ask her about the story behind the burned down house. She refers to it as Hroggar's house. It burned recently; the dying screams of his wife and child woke half the town. Now people fear the place, thinking it is cursed. Hroggar claims it started as a hearth fire. Some folks started a rumor that Hroggar was to blame, especially since he took up with a new woman named Alva the day after the fire. Jonna thinks the Jarl might even pay someone to get to the bottom of this.

◊ **OBJECTIVE:** Talk to the Jarl
♦ **TARGET:** Jarl Idgrod Ravencrone, inside Highmoon Hall, in Morthal

It's only a few steps across to Highmoon Hall, and a few more to reach Jarl Idgrod Ravencrone (or Jarl Sorli if the Civil War has forced her from power), who is usually seated on her throne next to Aslfur, her husband and steward. Address the Jarl regarding the ruined house. She knows that Hroggar blames his wife for spilling bear fat in the fire, but most believe his lust for Alva resulted in the arson. Now with the rumors of the cursed dwelling, no one will touch the ashes. Except for you.

◇ **OBJECTIVE:** Investigate the burned house

> **CAUTION** ⇨
>
> This quest involves you finding clues to convict Hroggar or prove his innocence. Although the townsfolk aren't fond of the man for his wanton ways so soon after a tragedy, they are even less happy with you murdering him and his new lover. So don't, unless you want this quest to be much shorter, and failed.

The burned house is adjacent to the Moorside Inn. Head up the wooden steps and investigate the odd little glow in the corner. It turns out to be the spirit of the child who died in the fire, a girl named Helgi. The little mite is frightened and confused, but continue to ask her your preferred questions and she recalls the fire. She wants to know if you'll play with her. Agree, and she wants to play a game of hide-and-seek, but not until after dark. That's the time "the other one" comes out. She disappears before telling you anything else, although she seems afraid of this other entity.

◇ **OBJECTIVE:** Find Helgi after dark
♦ **TARGET:** Helgi's Ghost, graveyard in Morthal

Once darkness falls, after 8:00 p.m., journey to the western side of Morthal, to the small grave among the rocks with the coffin poking out. You won't have a quest target to it, but if you mention your conversation with Helgi to the Jarl, she can tell you where to look, which activates a quest target. Standing nearby is a woman. Laelette the Vampire comes at you with a vicious draining attack. Defeat her at once. Before she attacks you, she screams that Helgi is some kind of "reward." Slay her, and then inspect the child's coffin. Helgi's tiny voice tells you that Laelette was also playing this game, but she's glad you found her first. Helgi goes back to sleep in her ghostly world, leaving you to find Laelette's husband, Thonnir.

◇ **OBJECTIVE:** Ask Thonnir about Laelette
◇ **OBJECTIVE:** (Optional) Tell the Jarl about Helgi
♦ **TARGET:** Thonnir, in Morthal

A Morthal Enemy

Thonnir is an anxious-looking man who usually comes running to grieve over the dead body of his wife, Laelette, who vanished months ago. He had assumed his wife had joined the war effort. If you question Thonnir about his involvement in all of this, he tells you that Laelette and Alva (Hroggar's new lady) were good friends. Perhaps Alva is part of the arson?

◇ **OBJECTIVE:** Investigate Alva's house
♦ **TARGET:** Alva's House, in Morthal

Alva's house is one of the sturdy buildings of Nordic construction in Morthal. During the day, you may see Hroggar exiting the structure. You can tell him about Helgi's ghost or that Alva was the last person to see Laelette alive. Hroggar shows an amazing lack of compassion for his dead daughter and isn't too concerned about Laelette's fate, either. It seems the only way to gain more information is to search the dwelling. You can:

(Lockpick) Try the lock on the door to Alva's House (Adept) and pick it.

(Pickpocket) Or remove the key to Alva's House from Hroggar, ideally without being seen and fined by the Morthal Guards.

Once inside the residence, head down the stairs. During the day, you usually see Alva sleeping in the coffin. At night Hroggar might be sleeping in the bed upstairs. If she's awake, she viciously attacks you, revealing her vampiric nature to you. Bring her down if necessary, but don't leave the house without checking out her coffin. Alva's Journal is here and proves that Morthal is under attack from vampires under the command of a Vampire Lord named Movarth. But this isn't an assault using steel or spells; this is a subtle infiltration of the guards and residents, and Alva is one of the key succubi in this!

➤ **Alva's House Key**   ➤ **Alva's Journal**

> ⇨ **NOTE**   If you find Alva's Journal without killing her and show it to the Jarl, Alva flees town. She heads to a place of evil known as Movarth's Lair.

◇ **OBJECTIVE:** Show Alva's Journal to the Jarl
♦ **TARGET:** Highmoon Hall, in Morthal

Return to Highmoon Hall and approach the Jarl. Inform her that Alva is the murderer who set the fire. When you tell her Alva is a vampire, the Jarl understandably wants proof. After showing her Alva's Journal, the Jarl is both perturbed and in your debt, rewarding you with gold. Not wishing Morthal to become Movarth's feeding grounds once again after a hundred years of peace and quiet, Jarl asks whether you can clear out Movarth's lair and remove his presence for good this time. The townsfolk are assembling outside to help with this threat. This mob (which includes Thonnir) is yelling to slay the vampire and all his ilk. As soon as you move away from them, they head for Movarth's Lair.

➤ **Leveled gold pieces**

◇ **OBJECTIVE:** Kill the master vampire

♦ **TARGET:** Movarth, in Movarth's Lair

Massacring Movarth's Minions

Head north over the bridge and out of Morthal, with your weapon-wielding townsfolk following you. As you approach the lair, the residents' bravado begins to wane, and they falter, leaving only you and Thonnir to deal with the vampires. No matter; a more subtle approach (or coming in with a Follower or Thonnir, whom you can stop at the entrance if you wish to explore alone) is preferable anyway. Enter the cave and descend the curved earthen pathway down to an initial confrontation with Frostbite Spiders. Head through the small tunnel to the south, working your way into a long cavern with a Vampire's Thrall guarding a side tunnel. Slay the thrall before he assaults you. Then enter the side tunnel to the left (north), which leads to a foul-smelling chamber of corpses. A thrall is busily going over a dead villager's pockets. Dispatch this foe close to the mass grave. Take whatever stolen possessions you need, then exit to the north.

This passage leads around to either a ground tunnel or a wooden platform useful for long-range arrow or magical attacks or a place to retreat to. The main chamber is ahead of you, where two vampires, thralls, and Movarth

Piquine reside. To stay alive, attack one at a time, coaxing foes into narrower tunnels instead of becoming surrounded. The vampires and Movarth are formidable opponents, so use your judgment and favored fighting implements to get the job done.

◇ **OBJECTIVE:** Return to Morthal's Jarl

♦ **TARGET:** Jarl Idgrod Ravencrone or Sorli the Builder, in Highmoon Hall, in Morthal

Quest Conclusion

With the vampiric threat over, feel free to explore the north chamber to grab Movarth's Boots (which add to your Sneak), and search the storage room with the Alchemy Lab and the connecting cavern. There's another thrall to optionally take down before the lair's chambers join, allowing you to head back up through the earthen entrance chamber, where a small ghostly figure thanks you for making her mother feel better. Back in Morthal, convene with the Jarl one final time, and tell her that the Master Vampire is dead. You are paid handsomely for your troubles and are congratulated by the Jarl and the townsfolk...who also take a rather large amount of credit for themselves.

➤ **Movarth's Boots** ➤ **Leveled gold pieces**

Postquest Activities

Veteran explorers may be interested to know that Movarth Piquine was previously seen as a character from the book *Immortal Blood* that appeared during adventures in Oblivion. In this book, he is a man betrayed by a vampire.

  **LIGHTS OUT!**

PREREQUISITES: None

INTERSECTING QUESTS: None

LOCATIONS: Broken Oar Grotto, East Empire Company Warehouse, Solitude, Solitude Lighthouse, Wreck of the Icerunner

CHARACTERS: Deeja, Jaree-Ra, Ma'zaka

ENEMIES: Bandit, Blackblood Marauder

◇ **OBJECTIVES:** Put out the fire in Solitude Lighthouse, Return to Jaree-Ra, Find Deeja at the Wreck of the Icerunner, Defeat Deeja, Find out where Jaree-Ra's bandits took the loot, Travel to Broken Oar Grotto, Defeat Jaree-Ra

● **MINOR SPOILERS**

Snuffing the Lights of Solitude

When you visit Solitude, be on the lookout for a shady Argonian character who usually lurks outside of Angeline's Aromatics, close to one of the city gates. He sometimes beckons you over. Step up to him and ask what he wants. He explains that he and his sister Deeja are treasure hunters. With the advent of the war, and as Solitude is one of the Empire's major ports, the Solitude Lighthouse serves a vital purpose keeping ships safe in the treacherous waters of the Northern Coast. Now, if the lighthouse went dark, one of the cargo ships that Jaree-Ra has had his eye on — the Icerunner — could run aground and yield some sizable plunder. Are you in?

If you are, agree to put out the lighthouse fire. You can also ask about the ship's crew or turn him over to the guards, but neither helps your success with this quest.

◇ **OBJECTIVE:** Put out the fire in Solitude Lighthouse

♦ **TARGET:** The top of Solitude Lighthouse

Beyond the giant arch of Solitude on the cusp of the Northern Coast is the Solitude Lighthouse. Climb the stairs in the exterior, being careful not to alert the lighthouse keeper, Ma'zaka. Although he sometimes confines himself inside his quarters within the Lighthouse, he may be wandering the building. Simply avoid him, or if you encounter Ma'zaka, kill him or sneak up the tower so you're not spotted. Ma'zaka won't spot that the Lighthouse fire is out until it is too late and the ship Jaree-Ra was eyeing runs aground. Once atop the Lighthouse tower, snuff the flames (there isn't any special equipment needed for this).

> ◊ **OBJECTIVE:** Return to Jaree-Ra
> ♦ **TARGET:** Jaree-Ra, near the East Empire Company Warehouse

Scuttled and Plundered!

Find Jaree-Ra on the docks outside the East Empire Company Warehouse. Speak to him: Your actions have already caused the Icerunner to run aground on the shoals across the bay. Jaree-Ra has already dispatched his sister and his gang, the Blackblood  Marauders, to strip the ship of valuables. You are to join them.

> ◊ **OBJECTIVE:** Find Deeja at the Wreck of the Icerunner
> ♦ **TARGET:** Deeja, inside the Wreck of the Icerunner

> **TIP** The Icerunner runs aground only during this quest; you cannot stumble upon it until you have extinguished the beacon for Jaree-Ra.

 You can wade, swim, or Fast-Travel to a nearby location and clamber across the rugged terrain to the ship that has scraped the jagged rocks along the coast. As you draw near, you can see Blackblood Marauders are already stripping the cargo from the vessel. The corpses suggest that the ship's former crew have already been dealt with.

You can talk to one of the Marauders, who tells you Deeja is expecting you down in the hold of the ship. Enter the ship, and head south along the main corridor, opening the second door on your left. Wind your way down the steps to the waterlogged hold. Now head north to a storage alcove where Deeja is checking the contents of a large treasure chest.

Deeja says she's supposed to give you a cut of the loot. But as most of the loot has already been moved, she has another offering: a quick death!

> ◊ **OBJECTIVE:** Defeat Deeja
> ◊ **OBJECTIVE:** Find out where Jaree-Ra's bandits took the loot

The Argonian shouldn't be too terrifying an opponent for you; quickly cut her down and then search her still-twitching corpse. The note from Jaree-Ra refers to both the "fool who did our work at the lighthouse" and the location of the plundered loot: Broken Oar Grotto. Battle the remaining Blackblood Marauders who attempt to halt your progress from the Icerunner, and fight your way onto the exterior deck; expect to dispatch about five before the ship is empty of double-crossing cutthroats!

> ◊ **OBJECTIVE:** Travel to Broken Oar Grotto
> ◊ **OBJECTIVE:** Defeat Jaree-Ra
> ♦ **TARGET:** Broken Oar Grotto

When you get back outside, you'll notice that the rowboats loaded up with loot are already gone, as are most of the Marauders. Only one remains on the shore, with the boat that would have carried the last few stragglers away. Deal with him.

> **TIP** **An Alternate Path—Violence Is Golden:** Did you suspect something was amiss when you arrived on the Icerunner's deck? Couldn't keep your hands off the rowboats loaded with treasure, could you? Or did you "accidentally" impale one of the Marauders on your blade? Then there's an alternate method of continuing: If you attack any Marauders or steal any of their loot, all the folks on the Icerunner turn hostile. You'll have to fight your way down to Deeja to claim the note from her corpse to continue this quest! The best part of this plan is that although you have a harder fight on your hands, your reward is greater, as the Marauders never leave with the loot, so you can claim it for yourself, either now or once the quest concludes!

Seeing the Light

 Optimally Fast-Travel to Solitude Lighthouse and walk west along the Northern Coast, as the Broken Oar Grotto is nearby. There's a scuttled boat and two recently moored rowboats at the entrance. Enter the smuggler's hideout, fashioned from wood and cavern pathways, and maneuver through this large and looming place. Prepare for protracted combat at long and short ranges with Blackblood Marauders.

> **TIP** Remember to locate the levers to lower the bridge sections to make your traversing a little easier. There are occasional oil lamps to strike and cause a ground fire, too. Better yet, simply submerge yourself and swim along the inlet (ideally while shrouding yourself using magic) to reach the rickety unloading building at the grotto's far end.

Farther into the grotto, Marauders guard a rickety building used for unloading ill-gotten gains. The end of the grotto, where a sunken ship decomposes in the turquoise water, is where Jaree-Ra is counting his loot. Battle up the wooden ramps to the top of the dock structure, and slay the dishonorable lizard with whatever death-dealing implements you consider most suitable. Then scour the Broken Oar Grotto for any remaining foes and any valuables you can scavenge.

> **TIP** Fallen into the water? Then use the half-submerged jetty steps throughout this grotto to reach dry land. Fighting foes? Then utilize the jagged rock walls and passageways to hide in, if you're becoming overwhelmed.

Quest Conclusion

Consult the Atlas chapter for any valuables you can scavenge from the Wreck of the Icerunner or Broken Oar Grotto. Expect no other rewards.

PREREQUISITES: None
INTERSECTING QUESTS: Side Quest: The Wolf Queen Awakened, Daedric Quest: The Mind of Madness
LOCATIONS: Solitude, Blue Palace, Wolfskull Cave, Wolfskull Ruins
CHARACTERS: Falk Firebeard, Jarl Elisif the Fair, Sybille Stentor, Varnius Junius
ENEMIES: Draugr, Necromancer, Necromancer Leader, Potema the Wolf Queen, Skeleton
◊ **OBJECTIVES:** Clear out Wolfskull Cave, Speak to Falk Firebeard

⬤ MINOR SPOILERS

▶ Malevolence Stirring

While you're in the spectacular city of Solitude, visit the Blue Palace, where Jarl Elisif the Fair is holding court. While listening to those seeking an audience with the Jarl, you may wish to strike up a conversation with Falk Firebeard, the Jarl's steward and manager of the housecarls. You can chat about General Tullius and Elisif's decisions regarding the war. Now wait for a man named Varnius Junius—a representative of the serfs of Haafingar Hold—to speak before the Jarl. He seems frightened and speaks of "unnatural magic," strange noises, and lights emanating from a place known as Wolfskull Cave. The Jarl promises to keep her population safe, but Court Wizard Sybille Stentor thinks this is just superstitious hokum. Falk agrees that a show of strength isn't necessary, but someone should investigate the cave system just to be safe.

Now speak with Falk Firebeard, asking him if he needs help with Wolfskull Cave. Falk was initially going to dismiss this as fanciful talk from an overly imaginative populous, but he agrees to pay you if you'll clear out the cave. You can also ask him about the cave's sordid past, when it was used for necromantic rituals. Nowadays, Falk reckons the place has a few brigands lurking inside.

◊ **OBJECTIVE:** Clear out Wolfskull Cave
◆ **TARGET:** Wolfskull Cave

▶ Few Wolves but Plenty of Warlocks

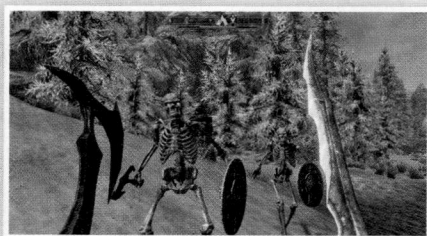

Travel to the mountains north of Dragon Bridge and west of Solitude. As you reach the vertical fissure in the mountainside, you're attacked by a bony fiend. Defeat the skeletons guarding the cave entrance before disappearing inside. The initial cavern tunnels are suspiciously quiet, with a skeleton and Draugr likely to be roaming the otherwise-empty tunnels. As you reach the first large chamber, tackle a couple of necromancers before passing through the wooden door. Undead Draugr and skeletons attack as you reach the top of a snowy fissure. Fight or flee from them, and enter Wolfskull Ruins.

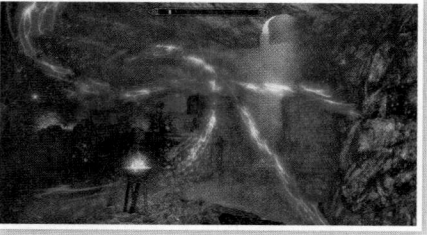

As you reach the subterranean fortress, across the canyon-sized hole in the center of this vast natural cavern, something is frighteningly wrong. A gathering maelstrom of energy is congealing atop the central tower of the ruins. But there is no time for sightseeing; attack another incoming necromancer as you work through some craggy tunnels and oil lamp traps. As you reach the edge of the fortress ruins, you hear a chant. A group of necromancers are attempting to summon the spirit of Potema the Wolf Queen, an insane necromancer who challenged Uriel III for the throne of the Empire 500 years ago!

In the face of this evil, act swiftly: Head down the exterior steps and through the first tower archway, dispatching enemies as you go. Climb the tower and go out the eastern exit archway. Climb more steps as the Wolf Queen begins to stir and speak. Continue around the battlements, finishing more necromancers and Draugr. Potema warns her followers of an intruder. Enter the main tower as the maelstrom increases, and prepare for a fraught battle against more powerful necromancers and any undead they may conjure. With the leader dispatched and all enemies defeated, Potema becomes unbound, and the maelstrom dissipates.

 TIP You can use the stairwell as cover during this fight, and coax the necromancers down to fight you one at a time.

◊ **OBJECTIVE:** Speak to Falk Firebeard

Quest Conclusion

Using the lever atop the tower, lower the drawbridge. This allows for a swift escape back into Wolfskull Cave and back outside, collecting any treasure as you go. Back inside the Blue Palace, inform Falk Firebeard that a group of necromancers were attempting to summon and bind Potema and that the ritual was interrupted. He is thankful this was stopped and rewards you almost appropriately for your troubles.

➤ **Leveled gold pieces**

Postquest Activities

Side Quest: The Wolf Queen Awakened begins shortly. This quest has the benefit of beginning a firm and friendly relationship with the Jarl of Solitude. If you speak to her after this quest, you can complete her Favor (see the Favors section starting on page 399 for more information) and place Torygg's Warhorn at a Shrine to Talos. This also aids in your relationship with Falk, allowing you to obtain a key from him that opens a wing of the Palace that is normally sealed, allowing you, in turn, to begin Daedric Quest: The Mind of Madness.

PREREQUISITES: Complete Side Quest: The Man Who Cried Wolf, You must be Level 10 or higher.
INTERSECTING QUESTS: Side Quest: The Man Who Cried Wolf
LOCATIONS: Solitude, Hall of the Dead, Potema's Catacombs, Potema's Refuge, Potema's Sanctum, Temple of the Divines
CHARACTERS: Falk Firebeard, Styrr
ENEMIES: Draugr, Vampire
◊ **OBJECTIVES:** Speak to Styrr, Defeat Potema, Retrieve Potema's remains, Give Potema's remains to Styrr, Return to Falk Firebeard

◉ MINOR SPOILERS

Malevolence Rising

Once you complete Side Quest: The Man Who Cried Wolf and continue your adventuring, the next time you enter a Hold City (such as Dawnstar or Whiterun), a courier runs up and hands you a message. It is an urgent communication from Falk requesting that you return to Solitude, as Potema's spirit is now free and a dangerous threat to Skyrim. There is one man who may be able to help you: Solitude's cemetery keeper, a wizard and Priest of Arkay named Styrr.

◊ **OBJECTIVE:** Speak to Styrr
♦ **TARGET:** Styrr, in the Hall of the Dead, in Solitude

Locate the Hall of the Dead in Solitude, and enter this eerie place. It is made even more strange by the slightly befuddled nature of the man you're meeting. Styrr beckons you over, and you may ask several questions about Potema, which he is happy to answer. Potema has been summoned in spirit form but fortunately was not raised from the dead; she will require help before she returns to the land of the living. For now, she lurks in a place where the dead eagerly serve her—the old catacombs. You are to find Potema's physical bones and bring them back to Styrr for sanctification. He hands you a key to enter the Catacombs.

➤ **Potema's Catacombs Key**

◊ **OBJECTIVE:** Defeat Potema
♦ **TARGET:** Potema, in Potema's Catacombs, within the Temple of the Divines, in Solitude

Wrecking a Resurrection

Brave the wintry weather and scale the battlements in the northern part of Solitude. Open the door to the Temple of the Divines, passing Freir at the shrine. Work your way past the temple nave and chancel, down some side steps, and through the barred door. Then open the door leading into Potema's Catacombs. Venture down the corridor to the barred archway. Potema's spirit surrounds you, mocking you and promising to raise your corpse to serve her once she slays you. The bars recede, allowing you farther into the stone corridors, down more steps, and to your first encounters with a group of Draugr.

Descend the steps in the chamber with the hanging corpse cages, and slay your first vampire. Beware of more attacks from dark alcoves before activating the wall lever to open the portcullis in the archway to the northeast wall. Enter the sunken corridors, and head southeast, up into a large, natural cavern. Expect more Draugr and vampire incursions as you reach the flooded pillar chamber. Seek the exit to the south, which leads into a wider natural cavern and a large stone entrance flanked by Draugr.

The lever atop the circular plinth activates a rotating stone and iron grating; step through when there's a gap as the grating rises. A cauldron in the next room indicates the resurrection may be under way. Burst through the wooden doors and into Potema's Refuge.

Strike down more Draugr as you twist and turn around the stone tunnels. Locate the trio of levers on the plinth, and expect a vampire attack from the barred door to your right (north).

Puzzle Solution: The levers have three positions: The center one freezes the corresponding rotating stone disk, and left or right rotates the disk in either direction. The optimal plan is to set all of them to the center and then manually rotate and freeze each one in the open position, one by one, beginning with the nearest rotating stone.

Pass the rock column room and up steps into a throne room with a floor grating and a powerful Draugr and vampire to either battle or stealthily avoid. The double wooden doors (Master) can be easily opened if you take Potema's Sanctum Key, which rests on the right throne arm. This allows access down into the Sanctum.

➤ **Potema's Sanctum Key**

The frequency of foes (both vampiric and undead) increases now as you pass through an embalming room and past the slumped remains of a Draugr on a throne. He soon stirs. Dispatch any foes troubling you as you open more iron doors. Pass under the grating in the throne room, stepping over corpses as you go. Wait for Potema to mock you before raising the final portcullis that leads to her summoning chamber.

Potema is not yet fully formed but has a shock beam that emanates from her essence. Avoid this at all costs, as it is hazardous and inflicts shock damage upon you. The Wolf Queen has also summoned her inner council to stop you dead in your tracks. Summon your own power and remove any and all Draugr that advance out of their coffins or ceremonial alcoves. Expect to attack at least eight Draugr, with more appearing at once after you dispatch the first five or six. Once the Draugr are down, you can pass the deep purple glow and access the metal door at the far end of Potema's chamber. The skeletal spirit of Potema begins to congeal! Take her down immediately, before she can begin to resurrect more of her fallen lackeys. Then gather the bones from the throne beyond.

➤ **Potema's Skull**

◊ **OBJECTIVE:** Retrieve Potema's remains
◊ **OBJECTIVE:** Give Potema's remains to Styrr
◊ **OBJECTIVE:** Return to Falk Firebeard

Don't miss the iron door behind the throne! Open it to reach a tall natural rock chimney. Scale the steps and remove the bar from the next iron door, where your final Draugr turn restless. Exit outside, and either carefully descend the rock gully or Fast-Travel safely away. You appear to the north of Solitude, near the pass that passes the Dainty Sload ship. Return to Solitude and to the Hall of the Dead, and hand Potema's Skull over to Styrr, who promises to consecrate the remains.

Quest Conclusion

Now return to the Blue Palace and talk with Falk Firebeard one more time, informing him that you've taken care of Potema. His relief is palpable, and both Falk and the Jarl consider you a Protector of Solitude. You are awarded a shield to back this honor up.

➤ **Shield of Solitude**
➤ **Gold pieces (Leveled)**

Postquest Activities

Your dalliance with the Wolf Queen is over! Should you equip the shield, expect an occasional comment from the Solitude guards.

MISSING IN ACTION

PREREQUISITES: Enter and exit the Whiterun buildings around the market.
INTERSECTING QUESTS: None

MINOR SPOILERS

LOCATIONS: Northwatch Keep, Whiterun, Arcadia's Cauldron, The Bannered Mare, House of Clan Battle-Born, House Gray-Mane
CHARACTERS: Avulstein Gray-Mane, Fralia Gray-Mane, Idolaf Battle-Born, Jon Battle-Born, Olfina the Golden, Thorald Gray-Mane
ENEMIES: Northwatch Archer, Northwatch Guard, Northwatch Interrogator, Northwatch Mage
◊ **OBJECTIVES:** Meet Fralia in her home, Find evidence of Thorald's fate, Deliver proof to Avulstein, Find a way to release Thorald from Thalmor custody, Rescue Thorald from Northwatch Keep, Lead Thorald to safety, Return to Fralia Gray-Mane

Gray-Mane Grief

The first or second time you leave one of the buildings around Whiterun's market area, you witness the verbal wrath of an old woman named Fralia Gray-Mane, the matriarch of a powerful family in Whiterun. She shouts in an accusatory tone at Olfrid and Idolaf Battle-Born, who are from a rival family also living in this settlement. Fralia blames them for the disappearance of her son, Thorald. Most of the inhabitants believe Thorald died in a Civil War battle fighting the Imperials. If you speak with Fralia, she blames the Battle-Borns again, calling them liars. Call her on this point, and she quiets slightly, telling you that if you truly wish to help her, you should meet her at her home.

◊ **OBJECTIVE:** Meet Fralia in her home
♦ **TARGET:** House Gray-Mane, in Whiterun

Either follow Fralia to her house and enter or head there yourself, wait an hour if Fralia hasn't arrived, and step inside. A large man carrying an equally immense axe growls at your trespassing, until Fralia tells her other son to put the weapon away, as you're here to help.

Talk with Avulstein and answer that you're here to help or that you need more information on what is going on. He explains his brother's disappearance; the family believes Thorald is still alive, captured by the Imperials and held in a location that the Battle-Borns are aware of. Without proof, the family has nothing. You're going to find the proof.

◊ **OBJECTIVE:** Find evidence of Thorald's fate
♦ **TARGET:** House of Clan Battle-Born, in Whiterun

At this point, you have three main ways to prove what the Grey-Manes have suspected:

House Hunt: You can locate the House of Clan Battle-Born (ideally while you're not being seen or when no one is at home, or you risk a Bounty increase), locate the ground-floor bedroom on the northwest side of the dwelling, enter it, and pry open the door (Expert).

Idolaf's Key: You can find Idolaf Battle-Born and attempt one of the following:

(Persuasion) Speak to him and get him to tell you what he knows.

(Pickpocket) Stealthily extricate the key from his person. This opens the door in the northwest bedroom.

➤ **Key to House Battle-Born**

Once inside the small study, look for the Imperial Missive on the table. It reveals the Gray-Mane family's suspicions: Thorald has been moved to a Thalmor stronghold called Northwatch Keep. This is the evidence Avulstein has been hoping for.

Battle-Born's Note: Both Olfina and Jon have notes on their person, which inform you of a secret relationship they are having. Approach either of them, and pickpocket the note. Then speak to Jon, telling him you know of his clandestine affair. In return for your silence, he agrees to bring you the document you need. Meet him at the Statue of Talos at the foot of Dragonsreach, in a few hours. Wait to pass the time until he arrives.

➤ **Imperial Missive**

◊ **OBJECTIVE:** Deliver proof to Avulstein

Return to Avulstein, who is still hiding out in House Gray-Mane. Tell him you have proof, and Avulstein is both happy and a little concerned. Northwatch Keep is heavily guarded by Thalmor justicars, and battling through them won't be easy. But Avulstein is ready to swing his axe. You can:

Agree that he joins you in the fight.

Tell him to stay. Then optionally add that you'll attempt to bring Thorald back without spilling any blood.

Avulstein agrees to these options. If you bring him with you, he acts as a Follower until his brother is found.

➤ **Follower:** Avulstein Gray-Mane

◊ **OBJECTIVE:** Find a way to release Thorald from Thalmor custody
◆ **TARGET:** Thorald Gray-Mane, Northwatch Keep

▶ Not for Keeps

There are three different ways you can approach your assault on Northwatch Keep:

You (without Avulstein) can attack every Thalmor enemy on sight.

You and Avulstein can attack every Thalmor foe on sight.

(Sneak) You (without Avulstein) can avoid every Thalmor enemy's line of sight. Although this plan is initially cunning, once Thorald is freed, he usually alerts all the guards you've avoided, making your escape extremely difficult!

Once you pick a plan of action, locate the Keep and either of the two entrances. The south entrance is unlocked, while the north one features an exceptionally difficult lock to pick (Master). Assuming you slew the half-dozen Northwatch Guards under and on the battlements (or you'll have to attempt this on your way out, along with one or both Gray-Mane brothers), enter the unlocked door.

◊ **OBJECTIVE:** Rescue Thorald from Northwatch Keep

Descend the steps from the southern entrance and hack or sneak through the mead-tasting chamber, which has two or three Northwatch Guards and a mage to worry about. Continue north, down some steps, and make a right turn, heading (east) down more steps. Turn left (north), fighting your way into a tavern room. Follow the corridor to an adjoining passage and head west into a two-tiered hallway. There are at least six more Northwatch Guards (and a mage) to fight or flee from along the way.

Climb the steps, and head to a cobwebbed storage room junction and torture room to the west, where Thorald is being held. Kill the interrogator who attacks from this room and search the robed corpse; there's a key here allowing you to unlock the northern door. Approach Thorald after you nullify all nearby enemies. Thorald Gray-Mane is hanging in an iron wall grip. Free him from his binds. He agrees that leaving would be the best plan.

➤ **Northwatch Keep Key**

◊ **OBJECTIVE:** Lead Thorald to safety

You can lead Thorald back the way you've fought. Or, for a shorter, bloodier excursion, head north through the jail cells and take down the remaining three Thalmor in here before racing up the steps and unlocking the door to Skyrim. You may elect to flee quickly out of the gap in the perimeter fence just by the door and forge, or remain in the exterior courtyard and kill any remaining foes. Assuming Thorald Gray-Mane is still alive, move away from Northwatch Keep.

When you're at a safe distance from the keep, approach Thorald, who asks why you came for him. Once you reveal you're working with his family, he asks where Avulstein is:

If you brought Avulstein along, the two greet each other heartily and agree that Whiterun isn't the safest place to return to.

If you rescued Thorald alone, you tell him Avulstein's in Whiterun, and he tells you it isn't safe for either of them.

Thorald is off to join the Stormcloak Army, and Avulstein will follow this plan too (either from here or Whiterun). He gives you a final task: to tell Fralia "to suffer the winter's cold wind, for it bears aloft next summer's seeds." She'll know the meaning of this.

◊ **OBJECTIVE:** Return to Fralia Gray-Mane

Quest Conclusion

Back in Whiterun, search out Fralia at her stall near the Bannered Mare or at her family home. Inform her that Thorald is safe but that he didn't think it was safe to return. Repeat the phrase Thorald mentioned so she believes you, and she finds peace that both her sons are still alive, if not with her. In return for your good deeds, she presents you with a gift, forged by Eorlund at the Skyforge. If Eorlund has died, Fralia has only 200 gold pieces to reward you with.

➤ **[Random] Enchanted Steel Weapon**

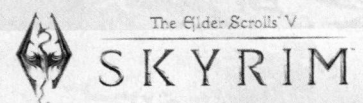

The Elder Scrolls V

SKYRIM

PREREQUISITES: None

INTERSECTING QUESTS: None

LOCATIONS: Black-Briar Lodge, Riften, The Bee and Barb, Riften Jail

CHARACTERS: Frost, Louis Letrush, Maven Black-Briar, Sibbi Black-Briar

ENEMIES: Black-Briar Mercenary

◊ **OBJECTIVES:** Speak to Sibbi Black-Briar, Steal Frost's Lineage Papers, (Optional) Steal the Lodge Stash, Steal Frost, Return to Louis Letrush

⬤ MINOR SPOILERS

Black-Briar Entanglements

If you're ever resting your weary bones in the Bee and Barb public house in the township of Riften, you may wish to strike up a conversation with one of the patrons, Louis Letrush. He usually beckons you over for a quiet talk. He needs someone to deliver a message to Sibbi Black-Briar. He explains that he recently purchased a fine Thoroughbred horse named Frost and paid Sibbi half of the cost up front. Unfortunately for Louis, Maven (Sibbi's mother) had him placed in the jail for other crimes (that Louis has no idea of), and the Black-Briars believe this debt to be nullified. You're to speak to Sibbi, then bring Frost and the lineage papers back to Letrush.

◊ **OBJECTIVE:** Speak to Sibbi Black-Briar

♦ **TARGET:** Riften Jail, in Riften

 TIP If you're running with the Thieves Guild and worried about the repercussions this quest will have with Maven Black-Briar, rest easy.

You can:

Speak to Maven, who appreciates the heads-up and tells you to let the situation play out. If you don't kill Letrush yourself, once you go away and return after completing another quest or favor, you'll find that Maven has settled accounts with Letrush.

Complete this quest without speaking to Maven at all; assuming you keep your plans to yourself, Maven never discovers your part in this caper.

Head out of the Bee and Barb, across to Mistveil Keep, and to the door to one side, which leads to the jail directly underneath the Keep. At this point, a guard stops you. You can:

(Persuade) Request that you're let in to see Sibbi.

(Bribe) Offer a little coin for the guard to look the other way as you enter the jail.

Or descend the steps and open the door (Hard) that leads to the jail's upper floor. You risk the guard raising the alarm, increasing your Crime.

Move along to the cells on the upper level, where Sibbi is being held. Speak to the lad, and it becomes increasingly clear that Sibbi didn't own the horse in the first place: In fact, the horse belongs to the family, and it is staying at the Black-Briar Lodge, as far as Maven is concerned. However, as far as Sibbi is concerned, he'll pay you the other half of Letrush's payment if you'll steal the horse and return it to Letrush. You can:

Agree to this.

(Persuade) Tell Sibbi that Maven would likely pay even more for the information he just revealed.

Or tell Sibbi that Letrush already agreed to a payment (which isn't an optimal plan—you want to gain as much coin as possible from these two!).

If your Persuasion works, Sibbi tells you of a hidden stash inside the lodge that could be yours if you can find it. He gives you the Stash Key to open it.

➤ **Sibbi's Stash Key**

◊ **OBJECTIVE:** Steal Frost's Lineage Papers

◊ **OBJECTIVE:** (Optional) Steal the Lodge Stash

♦ **TARGET:** Black-Briar Lodge

Stealing the Stallion

Journey to Black-Briar Lodge and scout the perimeter. It has obviously been constructed with defense in mind. It is all but inaccessible from the north, so approach from the south or western sides. There are three structures in this compound: a tower, the main building, and the stables where Frost is waiting. Expect one or two Black-Briar Mercenaries to be guarding either side of the main building. Utilize your sneaking talents or your combat prowess to navigate past these enemies who attack unwanted visitors on sight. Loot or pickpocket a key to the Black-Briar lodge from any guard, or pick an entrance to open:

(Lockpick [Novice]) The door on the lodge's northern side can be picked.

(Lockpick [Adept]) As can the (more difficult) door on the southern side, one floor below.

(Lockpick [Expert]) Or you can enter via the side door in the western wall, which is expertly sealed.

➤ **Key to Black-Briar Lodge**

Prepare to sneak or pummel your way through the lodge premises, as there are at least six Black-Briar Mercenaries on guard in this structure. Your infiltration leads to two separate locations, usually via the large central great room

with a banquet table and a large fireplace. However, if you entered via the southern door, you appear in the cellar area, where you find both the Lineage Papers (hidden inside an end table) and the Lodge Stash (hidden inside the strongbox, which is otherwise extremely difficult [Master] to unlock).

➤ **Frost's Lineage Papers** ➤ **Gold pieces (Leveled)**

◊ **OBJECTIVE:** Steal Frost
◊ **OBJECTIVE:** Return to Louis Letrush
♦ **TARGET:** Stables and forest, outside Black-Briar Lodge

Quest Conclusion

Now for a spot of horse rustling! Simply exit the lodge (via any of the exits, assuming you can pick the locks), and search for the stallion close to the stables on the lodge's south side. Mount Frost and ride him (usually northwest)

into the forest where Louis Letrush is waiting. If you somehow lose Frost (but the horse is still alive), return to the stables where you'll find him again (and more mercenaries). When you greet Letrush, you have the following options:

You can request your payment.

(Persuade) You can mention you'll go to Maven unless you leave here with the horse, too.

(Intimidate) You can inform him that if he were dead, you could keep the horse.

You can kill him, taking the money from his corpse, although he's a tough man to bring down.

Or you can simply ride off with the horse.

➤ **Frost**

➤ **Gold pieces** (Leveled)

Postquest Activities

If you've ridden off on Frost without speaking to Letrush, the quest doesn't close, and the horse heads back to the lodge after you dismount. Frost can't be sold. If you persuade Letrush and take the horse, expect a thug to be sent to rough you up (this happens as a World Encounter). Finally, if you inform Maven now, the quest is over and if Letrush is still alive, you may find him on the road shortly afterward (this happens as a World Encounter), killed by one of Maven's men.

A RETURN TO YOUR ROOTS

PREREQUISITES: Begin Daedric Quest: Discerning the Transmundane
INTERSECTING QUESTS: Main Quest: Elder Knowledge, Daedric Quest: Discerning the Transmundane
LOCATIONS: Blackreach, Sinderion's Field Laboratory, Sarethi Farm
CHARACTERS: Avrusa Sarethi, Sinderion, Enemies, Dwarven Sphere, Falmer
◊ **OBJECTIVES:** Discover the significance of Crimson Nirnroot, Collect Crimson Nirnroot in Blackreach (30), Bring Crimson Nirnroot to Avrusa Sarethi

● **MINOR SPOILERS**

▶ An Unmistakable Warble

✎ **NOTE** This quest occurs only when you enter the gargantuan subterranean Dwemer cityplex of Blackreach. The optimal path to reach this sprawling, canyon-sized cavern is to commence either Main Quest: Elder Knowledge or Daedric Quest: Discerning the Transmundane. These both require you to secure the Attunement Sphere from Septimus Signus, which is the only way to access Blackreach.

Locate Alftand on the glacial mountains southwest of Winterhold. Enter and work your way through the Alftand Glacial Ruins, battling Dwarven Spheres and Spiders, maneuvering through the tower and connecting chambers of the Alftand Animonculory (opening the elevator back to the Glacial Ruins as you go). Battle the Dwarven Centurion in the Alftand Cathedral to reach a second elevator (opening the exit allowing you to ascend to the surface exterior), before descending back into the Cathedral. Use the Attunement Sphere to activate the Dwarven Mechanism to access the hidden entrance to Blackreach.

The first structure you'll see as you step into Blackreach for the first time is a one-story, dwarven stone structure guarded by a Dwarven Sphere. Head there, tackling a Falmer along the way, and open the gold door leading into Sinderion's Field Laboratory. There are numerous key ingredients for your crafting here, as well as a workbench, Arcane Imbuer, and an Alchemy Lab. Sinderion himself is looking a little worse for wear. Inspect the skeletal corpse to find Sinderion's Field Journal.

➤ **Sinderion's Field Journal**

Read this journal to begin the quest. These are a series of research notes recognizing the spectacular potential of the rare, subterranean Crimson Nirnroot. Sinderion was in the process of collecting 30 specimens when he died under mysterious circumstances. It now falls to you to complete his task. The first Crimson Nirnroot is easy to spot; it is growing in the Dwemer bowl on the counter.

◊ **OBJECTIVE:** Discover the significance of Crimson Nirnroot
◊ **OBJECTIVE:** Collect Crimson Nirnroot in Blackreach (30)

Begin to search for Crimson Nirnroot throughout Blackreach. They are dotted around the landscape and make the same ethereal chime when you're near to them as their overworld species. Continue the hunt throughout Blackreach.

TIP The Atlas chapter has a map and lists locations of all 30+ Crimson Nirnroot plants. Consult page 629 for more details. If you don't wish to scavenge the entire underground realm, you can leave, allow some time to pass, and return once the picked plants have regrown, and add them to your inventory that way.

Quest Conclusion

Avrusa Sarethi hosted Sinderion when he lived in Skyrim to research the Crimson Nirnroot. She was a student of sorts and is mentioned in his journal. After you finish collecting one or more (or 30 Crimson Nirnroots), you have the option to visit her. You can visit her before, but she's far less helpful.

◊ **OBJECTIVE:** Bring Crimson Nirnroot to Avrusa Sarethi
♦ **TARGET:** Avrusa Sarethi, Sarethi Farm

Head to the Sarethi Farm in the Rift. Notice that in her vegetable plot, she is growing Nirnroot (the green kind), which is an unusual feat. Ask her about this, and she'll tell you Sinderion taught her.

If you have one or more Crimson Nirnroot, but fewer than 30, she will comment on your finding. You can also mention finding Sinderion's remains, too, and she'll converse with you about this sad demise of a good man.

Once you have 30 Crimson Nirnroot (or more), bring them to Avrusa Sarethi. She is impressed enough to offer you a tome she says belonged to Sinderion. You also receive Sinderion's Serendipity:

➤ **The Nirnroot Missive**

➤ **Perk:** Sinderion's Serendipity (25% chance to create a second duplicate potion whenever you create a potion using Alchemy)

Postquest Activities

Veteran explorers may have figured out that Sinderion is the same Alchemist from Oblivion who assigned a quest named "Finding Your Roots." Evidence of this is presented in his journal and tome.

RISE IN THE EAST

PREREQUISITES: None

INTERSECTING QUESTS: None

● **MINOR SPOILERS**

LOCATIONS: Dawnstar, Windpeak Inn, Japhet's Folly, Japhet's Folly Towers, Sea Cave, Windhelm, East Empire Company

CHARACTERS: Adelaisa Vendicci, East Empire Mercenary, Orthus Endario, Stig Salt-Plank

ENEMIES: Blood Horker, Haldyn, Mudcrab

◊ **OBJECTIVES:** Steal Survaris Atheron's logbook, Give the logbook to Orthus, Talk to Stig Salt-Plank, Report back to Orthus, Depart for Japhet's Folly, Talk to Adelaisa, Kill Haldyn, Report back to Adelaisa, Speak to Orthus

▶ Problems with Pirates

Fortunately, Clan Shatter-Shield's office is right next door! Unfortunately, the entrance is usually locked (Master) during the night, and there are numerous visitors during the day.

The East Empire Company has trading offices in both Solitude and Windhelm, but it is having some difficulties maintaining its presence in Windhelm. Visit the icy docks just outside Windhelm, and locate the company office below the city wall. Inside, greet Orthus Endario, who apologizes for the run-down nature of the place. It transpires that the company can't keep the trade going around here thanks to recent attacks by pirates raiding all along the coast. Only Windhelm's powerful Shatter-Shield clan appears safe from these marauders, who call themselves "Blood Horkers." Endario suspects the Shatter-Shields are involved and hopes you might want to help find some proof of this. Apparently, their operations are overseen by a Dark Elf named Survaris Atheron. If her meticulously detailed logbook were to end up with Orthus, he'd be most grateful. Ask for more information on the pirates before you agree, and leave the premises.

◊ **OBJECTIVE:** Steal Survaris Atheron's logbook
♦ **TARGET:** Logbook, Clan Shatter-Shield Office

(Lockpick) Pry open the locked door and sneak inside. The ideal time to attempt this is during the night, when no one is inside the office. The ledger is on a table in the office's far-left (northwest) corner. It makes interesting reading. Snatch the logbook and leave the premises quickly. Expect additions to your Crime if you're caught breaking in.

➤ **Survaris Atheron's Logbook**

◊ **OBJECTIVE:** Give the logbook to Orthus

Return to Orthus, and tell him you have the logbook. It appears Survaris has been traveling to Dawnstar to meet with pirates. Orthus wants you to head there, find out about these Blood Horkers, and speak with their captain, Stig Salt-Plank, regarding the whereabouts of the pirate's fortress lair.

◊ **OBJECTIVE:** Talk to Stig Salt-Plank
♦ **TARGET:** Stig Salt-Plank, in Dawnstar

Meeting Two Captains

Trek to Dawnstar and locate the pirates. They are having a good time in the Windpeak Inn. Maneuver through the drunkards to reach Stig Salt-Plank, and ask him about the Blood Horkers. He's been their captain for the past nine years, and says the raging Civil War has been great for plunder. He mentions someone named "Haldyn." Quiz him on this person, and he reveals Haldyn to be a powerful battle-mage who runs the entire operation and keeps the battles in the Blood Horkers' favor. Ask where you can go to join this operation and Stig refuses to tell you.

You can:

(Brawl) Fight with fists to beat the location out of him. Remember, no weapons!

(Bribe) Ply him with gold so he reveals the location.

Or you can bring out your proper weapons, slay this reprobate, and lift the orders off his corpse. Naturally, this adds to your Crime.

Once you are successful in your plan, Stig reveals that the pirates convene at Japhet's Folly.

◊ **OBJECTIVE:** Report back to Orthus

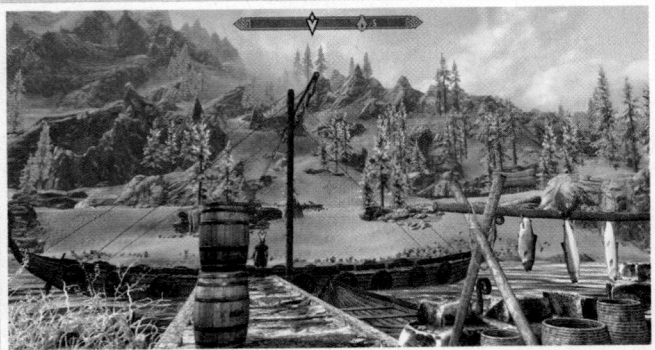

When you return to the East Empire Company's Windhelm office, you find a little more activity: A stern-faced woman named Adelaisa Vendicci is admonishing Orthus; sniveling isn't going to get all the gold back that the company is losing. Orthus explains he has someone investigating this plundering, and when Adelaisa spots you, she turns to you for some action. Inform her that the Blood Horkers are led by a battle-mage named Haldyn. Although a direct assault on the Blood Horkers may now be more fraught that she previously thought, she nevertheless orders you to head for the ships: The East Empire Company is planning to attack right back! Before you leave, you can find out a little more about Haldyn's fearsome control of Destruction magic.

◊ **OBJECTIVE:** Depart for Japhet's Folly
♦ **TARGET:** East Empire Mercenary, Windhelm docks

CAUTION Wait! You're about to brave the freezing Sea of Ghosts and attack a fortified bandit keep! If you haven't brought (or bought) all the equipment, such as potions, spells, armor, or weapons, you should arm yourself for the fight to come before continuing.

Exit the company office, and head to the rowboat moored at the dock. An East Empire Mercenary is waiting to transport you to Japhet's Folly. Confirm you're ready, and you're taken aboard one of the East Empire's galleons.

◊ **OBJECTIVE:** Talk to Adelaisa

Assault on Japhet's Folly

The weather is getting inhospitable. Approach Adelaisa Vendicci on deck, and ask her what the plan is. She tells you that Haldyn has been known to obscure his hideaways using magic (usually island-shrouding fog), so they think they've arrived at Japhet's Folly. As the crew are a little jittery to face such a powerful battle-mage, you're to take him out first, while Adelaisa and her men handle the island assault once the coast is clear. Literally.

◊ **OBJECTIVE:** Kill Haldyn
♦ **TARGET:** Haldyn, Japhet's Folly Towers

Leap from the deck and land on the thick sections of ice below. Then jump across the gaps in the ice floe, heading south until the folly (the small stone tower) looms out of the mists. To your left (east) are the Blood Horker docks. Ahead of you is a Sea Cave, where a clandestine infiltration of Japhet's Folly should begin. Enter the Sea Cave.

CAUTION If you want a more one-sided assault on Japhet's Folly, leap across to the docks and begin a direct assault. This isn't recommended, as the enemies are numerous and Adelaisa will be helping remove these enemies once you do what you came here for: to kill a battle-mage.

Wade through the icy tunnel, past the old rowboat. Slice open a couple of mudcrabs. Climb up into an ice-laden storage cave with a stone wall ahead (south) of you. It is here that you'll encounter your first Blood Horker pirate. Sneak past or kill him, then enter the cellar pantry (where more potions can be gathered for the combat to come) and climb the steps up to enter Japhet's Folly Towers.

Begin climbing the spiral staircase, watching for a swinging gate trap and more Blood Horker combat as you ascend (or coax the Blood Horker toward the trap and spring it on them). At the top of the first tower, check the storage rooms for items before opening the wooden door and heading along the connecting passage to the second tower. Pass the door requiring a key to open it and continue southeast. You encounter another pirate and a spiral stone staircase down. Descend to more Blood Horker combat. But remain atop this second tower so you can face and defeat Haldyn.

Haldyn enjoys attacking with fierce electrical attacks. When Haldyn finally falls, as your quest updates, give the battle-mage a quick search. You'll find a key. This opens the door you passed earlier, between the towers. Head down the spiral stairs if you wish to encounter more foes, and open a door (Expert) to a small storage room with items to purloin. Exit the island and let Adelaisa know of your morale-boosting slaughter of Haldyn.

➤ Japhet's Folly Key

◊ **OBJECTIVE:** Report back to Adelaisa
♦ **TARGET:** Adelaisa Vendicci, Japhet's Folly harbor

The time has come to exit Japhet's Folly Towers — via the door you unlocked using Haldyn's Key. You're in for an explosive finale, as the East Empire Company is bombarding the island with cannon fire. Fight (or sneak) past the blasts, tackling any Blood Horker stragglers as you go. Make a vaguely northeast route through the ruined harbor structures to the jetty, where Adelaisa waits.

Adelaisa explains that she began the bombardment once Haldyn died, as the fog he conjured also left with his spirit. With the Blood Horker base of operations decimated, Adelaisa asks whether you're ready to head back to Skyrim and celebrate. Refuse if you want to explore Japhet's Folly some more, or agree when you want to leave.

◊ **OBJECTIVE:** Speak to Orthus

Quest Conclusion

You arrive back at Windhelm docks. Enter the East Empire Company office and locate Orthus. When you tell him the pirate haven has been destroyed, he can't express how much easier you've made his job. Now for the small matter of the payment. When the gold has changed hands, you can also speak to Adelaisa. She's impressed with your abilities and is happy to take some time away from her duties to follow you. Orthus is now friendly toward you, although the folks over at the East Empire Warehouse just outside Solitude aren't thrilled by your presence.

➤ **500 gold pieces**
➤ **Follower:** Adelaisa Vendicci

RISING AT DAWN

PREREQUISITES: Contract Vampirism
INTERSECTING QUESTS: None
LOCATIONS: Morthal, Falion's House
CHARACTERS: Falion
ENEMIES: Vampire

 ● MINOR SPOILERS

◊ **OBJECTIVES:** Speak to Falion, Bring a filled Black Soul Gem to Morthal, Meet Falion at dawn, Speak to Falion, Wait for Falion to complete the ritual

▶ Out of Blackness Comes Forth Light

When fighting vampires, there is a chance that you may contract the disease Sanguinare Vampiris. While this disease can be easily cured through normal means, if left untreated, it will eventually cause you to become a Vampire. If you would like to remove vampirism from your body, complete this quest.

◊ **OBJECTIVE:** Speak to Falion
♦ **TARGET:** Falion, in Morthal

Journey to any innkeeper across Skyrim and ask for their rumors. When you have full-fledged vampirism, you will learn that a mage named Falion in the Hold City of Morthal may be able to help you. Journey to Morthal and seek out Falion, who is wandering the streets or hanging out in his house. He asks you of your needs, and when you tell him you're looking for a cure, he is surprised. For this to occur, it requires a filled Black Soul Gem, and for this you will need to kill someone.

◊ **OBJECTIVE:** Bring a filled Black Soul Gem to Morthal

Here are some of the best locations from which to bring a Black Soul Gem (exploration requires a thorough search of all chambers within):

Falion: You can acquire one if you trade with him...for a price!

Broken Fang Cave: in Whiterun Hold

Hob's Fall Cave: in Winterhold Hold

Hjerim: a house in Windhelm that you can purchase

➤ **Black Soul Gem**

After you have a filled Black Soul Gem, return to Falion's House and inform him of your item. He agrees to meet you at the summoning circle in the marsh at dawn. Only then shall you both banish the creature you have become.

◊ **OBJECTIVE:** Meet Falion at dawn
◊ **OBJECTIVE:** Speak to Falion

Between 3:00 and 7:00 in the morning, your quest objective updates. Head north over the bridge and out of Morthal, going slightly northwest as you cross into the marsh. Falion stands on one of the small scrub islands within the marsh. Tell him you're ready to start the ritual.

◊ **OBJECTIVE:** Wait for Falion to complete the ritual

Quest Conclusion

After some ritual words are sounded, Falion successfully pulls the creature of the night from within your corporal form and sends it to Oblivion. After you come to, Falion walks away, back to help the inhabitants of Morthal. You find yourself cured of vampirism.

Postquest Activities

If you ever contract vampirism again, simply repeat this quest; Falion even has a new Black Soul Gem for you to buy!

PREREQUISITES: You must be Level 14 or higher.

◉ MINOR SPOILERS

INTERSECTING QUESTS: None

LOCATIONS: Avanchnzel, Avanchnzel Animoncultory, Avanchnzel Boilery, Riften

CHARACTERS: Breya, Drennen, From-Deepest-Fathoms, Watches-the-Roots

ENEMIES: Dwarven Centurion, Dwarven Sphere, Dwarven Spider

◊ **OBJECTIVES:** Take the Lexicon to Avanchnzel

The Agitated Argonian

If you're exploring the docks of Riften that overlook Lake Honrich (which are outside the city), you're likely to encounter an agitated Argonian named From-Deepest-Fathoms. If you can't find her, wait around or return here after other adventuring. When you try to speak to her, From-Deepest-Fathoms quickly pushes an object into your hands and pleads with you to free her of her burden. When you ask what she's talking about, she says she's been driven half mad by memories. And this is all the fault of a Lexicon. It must be returned to Avanchnzel. She begs you to take it. Agree and the quest continues.

➤ **Lexicon**

◊ **OBJECTIVE:** Take the Lexicon to Avanchnzel
♦ **TARGET:** Lexicon Receptacle, in Avanchnzel Boilery

Avanchnzel is almost due west of Riften, across the Hold in the Jerall Mountains. It was once a great hall of dwarven construction, a library to house the vast memories of the Dwemer. It was run almost exclusively by strange mechanical spiders. From the outside, steam still periodically shoots from golden vents, and the entrance is atop a series of curved walkways hewn into the mountain. Enter Avanchnzel, and wind through the rumbling tunnels to an opening and entrance below you.

Halt as you witness a party of adventurers speaking to each other. They are bathed in red, the same color emanating from the Lexicon you carry. This seems to be a resonance, a playback of From-Deepest-Fathom's previous exploration. You can't interact with these ghosts but can only watch as they worry about venturing into this place. Breya, Watches-the-Roots, and Drennen complete the quartet. They walk forward and disappear from your vision.

Follow the tunnel to the south, and begin the first of many confrontations with Dwarven Spiders. Battle, sneak around, or flee from them. Progress south to a pair of giant gold doors,

and open them. Along the stone platform high above the giant fissure below, the specters of Watches-the-Roots and From-Deepest-Fathoms talk about the amazing architecture in here. From this hub chasm, you have a choice of paths.

Path 1

Continue down the corridor heading south, with the two lanterns at its entrance. Prepare to fight with Dwarven Spheres as you turn the corner. This leads to a long corridor that turns, passes a locked gate (Apprentice), and ends at a curved ledge down to the bottom of the hub chasm. Here, you can inspect the following:

A locked door to the south (Master) leading to a storage room with items you may wish to scavenge.

A passage and long hallway to the east, sloping down past some recently slain Dwarven Spheres and ending in a gold door to the Avanchnzel Animoncultory. By the dead spheres, you receive another hallucination, as the previous expedition notices that they are being ignored by the "metal things."

Path 2

Turn left (east) and head up the sloping platform to two pairs of gold doors. Then connect to a set of corridors with a cross-shaped stone table.

Head up and left (west) at the stone table to reach a connecting passage that brings you to the top of the hub chasm (where you find the remains of a skeleton) or to a pair of gold doors (and a door bar) leading into an Avanchnzel balcony. This is the best way to exit Avanchnzel and shouldn't be accessed yet.

Head down (north) to a single gold door and a mechanical elevator that takes you to the Avanchnzel Boilery. Alas, the door at the bottom of the elevator requires a key to unlock and is firmly sealed. This is actually the escape route after you return the Lexicon.

Advancing into Avanchnzel

Enter the Animoncultory and prepare for protracted battles with Dwarven Spiders and Spheres (or flee from them). Fortunately, although this part of Avanchnzel is massive and elongated, there is only one route to take — through a series of connected corridors.

The first chamber features golden barrels. You have another vision as you approach the locked gate (Adept) where the past adventurers realize that hiring a thief for this heist would have been wise. Follow the stairs through more corridors, and then out into a huge, grand hall. The past adventurers set up camp here, a little unnerved at the "sleeping metal men."

Follow the connecting corridor through a storage room of metal pots, shelves, and barrels. Descend to more corridors, dwarven mechanical beasts to slay, and more chambers with pots and shelves. The past adventurers appear in the storage room bathed in a golden hue, complaining that the metal men aren't sleeping anymore.

Down another corridor, a large and grinding chamber of cogs and spiders awaits. Lying on two stone slabs are huge, golden warriors, clad in gold but fortunately inactive. Fight or dash to the right (west), and up the stairs to the north to quickly exit this room, or investigate it further if you wish to battle Dwarven Spiders. Then run down the L-shaped corridor. The past adventurers appear once more. Drennen is at the end of his rope and flees the scene, leaving the team one man down. Open the doors and enter Avanchnzel Boilery.

Head down the increasingly ornate and tall corridor, watching the three past adventurers figuring out what to do when they finally have the Lexicon in their grasp. When they disappear, fight spiders and spheres as you progress down to a chamber with a desk and pistons. The past adventurers blink into your vision once more, and Breya seems very perturbed. Watches-the-Roots lets out a gasp. Open the door to the north, and head down the edges of the sloping corridor to avoid the whirling blade trap, which claimed Watches-the-Roots' life; his corpse is at the far door.

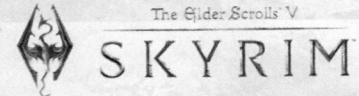

The final vision of adventurers past occurs as you reach the grand boilery chamber. Breya can't hold back the giant stomping mechanical beings that are coming to life, and you may be having some trouble too. A Dwarven Centurion looks for intruders and attacks you on sight. You can either fight it in an epic confrontation (remember to use the upper area and preceding corridor to dodge its vicious arm-mandible strikes) or complete the quest first. During your exploration of this chamber, you may stumble upon Breya's corpse: She is quite dead.

Quest Conclusion

Finish this quest by activating the Lexicon Receptacle at the base of the steps. The cube glows red, slots into place, and you finish your task.

➤ **Perk:** Ancient Knowledge (25% Armor Bonus while wearing all Dwarven Armor; your Smithing Skill increases 15% faster.)

➤ **Dwarven Armor**

Postquest Activities

Aside from your new ability and an exploration of this vast dwarven repository of knowledge, there are no other rewards, except what you've scavenged. The quickest way to exit is the door that the top of the steps where the Receptacle is. Open them, ride the elevator up, and exit via the balcony, or Path 2 described earlier. From-Deepest-Fathoms does not need to be found afterward.

 THE WHITE PHIAL

PREREQUISITES: None

INTERSECTING QUESTS: Side Quest:
Repairing the Phial

 MINOR SPOILERS

LOCATIONS: Forsaken Cave, Forsaken Crypt, Windhelm, The White Phial

CHARACTERS: Nurelion, Quintus Navale

ENEMIES: Curamil, Draugr, Snow Bear, Wolf

◊ **OBJECTIVES:** Retrieve the White Phial, Bring the Phial to Nurelion, Speak to Quintus

Journey west along River Yorgrim and up into the mountains looking for some scattered standing stones. Expect wolves along the way and a large lantern at the cave entrance. Step inside, and you're greeted by the (immobile) skeleton of the last man to try and extricate treasure from this place. Pass dead man's cart, and head into the snow cave, where wild animal attacks are likely. Once all animals are slain, move around to the west and open the Iron Door. Descend the spiral steps to a winding corridor. When it straightens out, watch for a trigger plate on the floor, or face a flurry of darts. Then the Draugr come.

▶ Phial of the Virgin Snow

During a trip to Windhelm, visit the market stalls in the southwest corner of the walled city. Close by is the White Phial, a place for potions, alchemy...and arguments it seems. Enter the premises, where the proprietor Nurelion is having a heated discussion with his assistant Quintus Navale. From what you overhear, it seems Nurelion (who is old, even for an elf), has been focusing his entire life on finding a mythological "White Phial" and has even named his shop after it. Now, at the end of his life, he believes he's found the Phial's location but is too infirm to retrieve it. Strike up a conversation with Nurelion and offer to find the Phial for him. He tells you it is buried with its maker, Curamil, in a cave to the west. As the Phial will be difficult to reach, Nurelion has prepared a concoction to take with you.

➤ **Nurelion's Mixture**

◊ **OBJECTIVE:** Retrieve the White Phial
♦ **TARGET:** White Phial, inside the Forsaken Cave

Fight off these bony fiends as you head north, then west into a Draugr crypt. The small maze of interlocking rooms has an Iron Door to unlock (allowing access to a treasure chest), but more importantly there's an exit out into the larger catacombs with banks of the Nordic dead, many of which come alive to thwart you. Find the exit to the southeast, into a narrow corridor and a battering ram trap. Avoid this by stepping across the floor plate as you round the corner to the left (north). Open the Iron Door and enter Forsaken Crypt.

You find more Draugr in the grand crypt chamber. Battle them before heading east up the corridor, then up and around to the bridge over the chamber. More tombs creak open, and Draugr appear on the stone balcony opposite. Turn north and watch for the rising floor trap in the semicircular room with more Draugr to crush. The Iron Door leads up to a metal cased bridge. Follow it south, then west into a Draugr corridor ending in a swinging blade trap. Navigate that, and emerge into the burial sanctum. This was the last resting place of Curamil, who promptly rises again!

Battle Curamil and his Draugr brethren, moving around the sanctum so you aren't surrounded and hacked to pieces. Flee past the swinging blades and let the Draugr come to you if the battle is becoming too difficult. Then inspect the chamber once the dead are buried. Head up the steps to the Word Wall and absorb a Word of Power before heading under the Word Wall to a seemingly dead end. The only scenic point of interest is an ancient bowl.

➤ **Word of Power:** Marked for Death

A Phial Defiled

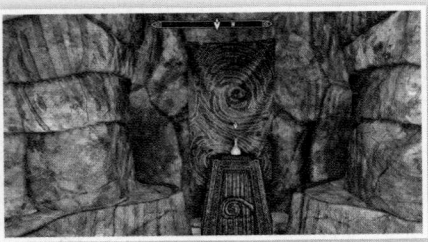

Inspect the ancient bowl and activate it. You pour in the mixture that Nurelion gave you, which fills the chamber in a green mist. A moment later, the rock wall panel descends in front of you, allowing you into a secret chamber. This room contains a large variety of ingredients, an Alchemy Lab, and most importantly of all, a Cracked White Phial to take. Perhaps Nurelion won't notice the Phial's blemishes? Now return to the sanctuary, locate the Iron Door in the southwest corner, and head quickly up the connecting stairs, into the Forsaken Cave. Use the wall lever to lower a stone panel, allowing a quick exit back to the surface.

➤ **Cracked White Phial**

◊ **OBJECTIVE:** Bring the Phial to Nurelion
◊ **OBJECTIVE:** Speak to Quintus
♦ **TARGET:** Nurelion, then Quintus, in Windhelm

Quest Conclusion

Return to the White Phial and present Nurelion with the Cracked White Phial. He notices the damage. After thinking you were at fault and then sinking into a depression, Nurelion asks you to leave, as he's not in the mood to entertain guests. Then he retires to his bed. Head over to Quintus, who thanks you for your help anyway and hands you some gold for your troubles. As the quest concludes, Quintus tries to make Nurelion's final days a little less painful.

➤ **500 gold pieces**

Postquest Activities

The White Phial's power may draw you back in to help Nurelion and Quintus once again. But only after you complete certain additional tasks. Consult Side Quest: Repairing the Phial for more information.

 **REPAIRING THE PHIAL**

● MINOR SPOILERS

PREREQUISITES: Complete Main Quest: The Throat of the World, Complete Side Quest: The White Phial, Passage of time: Three days (72 hours) after both quests finish
INTERSECTING QUESTS: Main Quest: The Throat of the World, Side Quest: The White Phial
LOCATIONS: Red Eagle Redoubt, Red Eagle Ascent, Stonehill Bluff, Sundered Towers, Throat of the World, Windhelm, The White Phial
CHARACTERS: Nurelion, Quintus Navale
ENEMIES: Forsworn, Forsworn Briarheart, Giant
◊ **OBJECTIVES:** Speak to Quintus Navale , Retrieve the Unmelting Snow, Find some Mammoth Tusk Powder, Take a Forsworn Heart, Return to Quintus Navale

A Query from Quintus

> **NOTE** This quest has several prerequisites: You must have completed Main Quest: Throat of the World and Side Quest: The White Phial. Then you must have progressed your adventure by three days (72 hours) from the time you finished the Side Quest. Finally, you must be in a city for a courier to appear and find you.

Time passes. You may forget about old Nurelion and the cracked phial you found for him—that is, until a courier appears in a town that you're visiting (providing you've done all the prerequisites for starting this quest). He has an urgent letter from Quintus Navale in Windhelm that must be delivered. Open the letter and read it to begin this quest. It seems that Quintus has been researching methods of repairing the Phial, and he may now be able to...with your help.

➤ **Letter from Quintus Navale**

◊ **OBJECTIVE:** Speak to Quintus Navale
♦ **TARGET:** Quintus, in the White Phial, in Windhelm

Once inside the Alchemist's shop, inform Quintus that you've read his letter. He tells you that he's found three materials that, when mixed together, may be able to mend the crack in the White Phial. Naturally, these materials are a little hard to come by. He requires a scoop of Unmelting Snow from the summit of the Throat of the World; a tusk of a Mammoth, ground to a fine powder as only giants know how; and the briar heart from a Forsworn of the Reach. Ask Quintus about each material so you learn a little more about each one.

◊ **OBJECTIVE:** Retrieve the Unmelting Snow
♦ **TARGET:** Summit, the Throat of the World
◊ **OBJECTIVE:** Find some Mammoth Tusk Powder
♦ **TARGET:** Grinding receptacle, Stonehill Bluff
◊ **OBJECTIVE:** Take a Forsworn Heart
♦ **TARGET:** Forsworn Briarheart, Red Eagle Redoubt

A Cracked Concoction

Material 1: The Summit of Skyrim

Head to the Throat of the World, either by the precarious trek to High Hrothgar and through the deep mist, up to Paarthurnax's meditation place, or by Fast-Traveling, as you'll already have visited this perch during the Main Quest. Climb past Paarthurnax to a steep sloped area and an unmelting snowbank. Activate it to remove some snow.

➤ **Unmelting Snow**

The Elder Scrolls V
SKYRIM

Material 2: Among the Giants

Now travel to the mountains south and slightly west of Dawnstar, and climb to the large giants' camp of Stonehill Bluff. The place is surrounded by rocks on three sides, so the entrance and exit are the same. Head into the bluff, and check one of the grinding receptacles near a campfire; the Mammoth Tusk Powder is in there. You may take it without being attacked by the giants roaming this area, but you've got to be quick!

➤ **Mammoth Tusk Powder**

Material 3: Slaughter at Red Eagle Redoubt

The final ingredient is the magically enhanced heart of a Forsworn Briarheart. Any Briarheart will do; if you don't already have one, find one lurking atop the mountains on the Reach's eastern edge. You're heading to Red Eagle Redoubt, accessible via a lengthy ascent from the Karth River near Sky Haven Temple. Approach the entrance, and remove all Forsworn threats from the exterior before entering the interior, known as Red Eagle Ascent.

Pass the wooden stakes and skewered animals, and bring your weapons to bear on a couple of Forsworn in a gloomy grotto you can ignite if you blast the oily floor with fire. Climb up the sloping path and steps to an upper grotto, which features a flat stone plateau with an altar on it and four or five additional foes. Climb the wooden steps, then disappear up the exit corridor that leads back out to an iron door and the Reach.

Turn right (north) and begin a battling ascent up a large set of stone steps. Make sure the Forsworn are tumbling off here in a spectacular death plummet, and not you! Head under the three stone arches as you reach a sizable Forsworn camp and further enemies,

clearing the area methodically so you aren't attacked from behind. Don't rush this assault. Continue around in a clockwise circle, and trot south up the steps to the south, leading into the Sundered Towers. The Briarheart is up here. Clear the area of other foes first, before killing the Briarheart and searching the corpse. Pluck the Briar Heart from it. Then search the area for any treasure you wish to scavenge.

➤ **Briar Heart**

> ◇ **OBJECTIVE:** Return to Quintus Navale
> ♦ **TARGET:** Quintus, in the White Phial, in Windhelm

Quest Conclusion

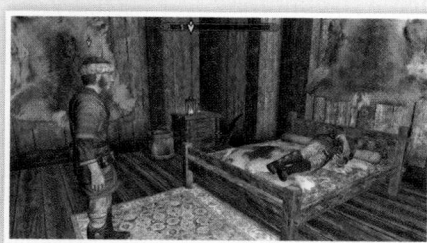

Return to the White Phial and tell Quintus of your success. He grabs the materials from you quickly concocts a gelling agent to seal the White Phial as he heads upstairs to Nurelion's bedchamber. As he demonstrates the solidity of the White Phial, the old elf smiles, uttering the word "marvelous" before lying still on the bed.

➤ **The White Phial**

Postquest Activities

Alas, Nurelion dies in his bed. Quintus gives the repaired Phial back to you, for your help. To use it, pick the type of potion you want it to contain, and thereafter when you drink that potion, the empty White Phial remains in your inventory, refilling every 24 hours. Quintus is now on friendly terms with you.

  **CAPTURED CRITTERS***

PREREQUISITES: None
INTERSECTING QUESTS: Thieves Guild Quest: Loud and Clear, Dungeon Quest: What Lies Beneath
LOCATIONS: Alchemist's Shack, Dushnikh Yal, Burguk's Longhouse, Duskglow Crevice, Frostflow Lighthouse, Goldenglow Estate
CHARACTERS: Aringoth, Burguk
ENEMIES: Chaurus, Falmer, Mercenary
◇ **OBJECTIVES:** None

● MINOR SPOILERS

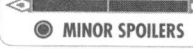 **NOTE** * Quest names marked with this symbol do not appear in your Quest Menu list, although objectives may.

Bug Hunt

This is more of a curiosity than a real quest. Five of the insect species that inhabit Skyrim have been captured and placed into jars. A single example of each can be found hidden across this realm, in the following locations:

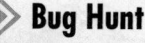

Moth in a Jar: Trek through the Pale until you reach and explore the Falmer Hive known as Duskglow Crevice. Battle through the connecting tunnels and crypts until you reach the raised stone chambers and portcullises. A room of refuse close to the final battle houses the jar.

➤ **Moth in a Jar**

Torchbug in a Jar: Locate Frostflow Lighthouse in Winterhold Hold, head inside (starting Dungeon Quest: What Lies Beneath), and move to the fireplace among the signs of the struggle. The fireplace mantel houses the glowing bug in the jar.

➤ **Torchbug in a Jar**

Dragonfly in a Jar: Journey to the Reach, and locate the Dushnikh Yal Orc stronghold (perhaps completing Side Quest: The Forgemaster's Fingers to win their approval). Enter Burguk's Longhouse, open the trapdoor to the cellar, and look for the jar on a cupboard under the platform.

➤ **Dragonfly in a Jar**

Butterfly in a Jar: While exploring the Rift, head along the edge of the forest on the southern foothills of the Throat of the World, and you'll stumble upon the Alchemist's Shack. There's a jar with a butterfly in it sitting on one of the shelves.

➤ **Butterfly in a Jar**

Bee in a Jar: During or after Thieves Guild Quest: Loud and Clear, enter the main building of Goldenglow Estate, head to the upper floor, and enter Aringoth's bedroom. Locate the jar on a dresser here.

➤ **Bee in a Jar**

Quest Conclusion

Once your critter collection reaches five, you have found them all.

Post quest Activities

Inspect the insects in your inventory, or put them on a shelf or table in a house you own. Aren't they pretty?

THE FORGEMASTER'S FINGERS

PREREQUISITES: Non-Orc Character
INTERSECTING QUESTS: None
LOCATIONS: Dushnikh Yal, Mor Khazgur, Narzulbur
CHARACTERS: Chief Burguk, Chief Larak, Chief Mauhulakh
ENEMIES: [Random]
◊ **OBJECTIVES:** Find the Forgemaster's Fingers, Bring the Forgemaster's Fingers to [Orc Chief]

▶ Blood-Kin, or Bloodbath

> **NOTE** To commence this quest, you must be a non-Orc; any other race is fine. Then visit any of the Orc strongholds listed in the table below and attempt to speak to one of the inhabitants. If you are an Orc, you can take advantage of the trading and training available in these strongholds without having to complete this trial.

✓	ORC STRONGHOLD LOCATION	HOLD	CHIEFTAIN NAME
	Mor Khazgur	The Reach	Chief Larak
	Dushnikh Yal	The Reach	Chief Burguk
	Narzulbur	Eastmarch	Chief Mauhulakh
	Largashbur	The Rift	Not applicable‡

> **NOTE** ‡ If you approach Largashbur, you have to begin Daedric Quest: The Cursed Tribe to enter this stronghold. Completing that quest also makes you Blood-Kin to the Orcs, so you won't have to complete this quest.

During your travels, you may chance upon an Orc stronghold. If the location is listed above, you should be able to enter the place without being attacked (unless you strike first).

However, when you approach one of the Orcs, he isn't welcome to your kind. He lives by the Code of Malacath, and outsiders have no place here. Answer that you're a traveler (you must keep your answers as pleasant as possible), and he tells you to stay out; you're not Blood-Kin. Politely ask how you can convince him to let you in, and he mentions whispers that he's heard regarding a pair of enchanted gauntlets, hidden away in a deep, dark dungeon. They are called the Forgemaster's Fingers. Return these to the Chief, and he'll decide whether you're worthy to be Blood-Kin to the Orcs.

◊ **OBJECTIVE:** Find the Forgemaster's Fingers
♦ **TARGET:** Forgemaster's Fingers, in [a random location]

Set off to the random location where the Forgemaster's Fingers are said to be kept, and battle through (or sneak past) the enemies guarding the Fingers, which are usually kept in a large treasure chest.

➤ **Forgemaster's Fingers**

◊ **OBJECTIVE:** Bring the Forgemaster's Fingers to [Orc Chief]
♦ **TARGET:** [Orc Chief], inside [an Orc stronghold]

Quest Conclusion

Return to the same Orc stronghold that you visited previously and locate the Chief, who may or may not have given you this quest to begin with. However, be sure the stronghold is the one from which you received the quest. Approach the Chief, and he's amazed that you managed to acquire this item. He welcomes you as a Blood-Kin, and the Orcs in the other strongholds know of your friendship with the Orcs, too.

Postquest Activities

From this point on, as long as you remain civil, you can trade and train with any of the Orcs in the strongholds throughout Skyrim.

NOTE * Quest names marked with this symbol do not appear in your Quest menu list, although objectives may.

▷ Cartographical Evidence

During your adventuring, you may find a piece of parchment with a sketch on it. This is a treasure map, and there are 11 to find. Each leads to a particular location where a (usually well-hidden) small treasure chest can be opened and several valuable items pocketed.

> **Treasure Map**

CAUTION You can't simply ignore the maps and trot off to find the treasure chests; they appear only once the map is in your possession.

Fort Neugrad Treasure Map

Falkreath Hold—Fort Neugrad: In the half-buried chest, on the main building rooftop (accessed via climbing up through the interior).

Fort Neugrad Treasure Map: Showing the rocky crevasse dead-end path east of the fort.

Falkreath Hold—Fort Neugrad: When you look at this map, the top of the page is east, not north. Situate yourself with this in mind, following the path around the lake and up into the crevasse.

Treasure Map I

Falkreath Hold—Bandit Camp: Ilinalta Foothills: On one of the bandits, just south of the guardian stones.

Treasure Map: Showing the settlement of Riverwood and the fallen tree.

Whiterun Hold: Inside the fallen tree, on the north bank of the river, west of Riverwood.

 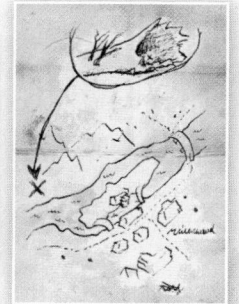 

Treasure Map II

Winterhold Hold—Journeyman's Nook: Inside the knapsack, close to the fire and round table.

Treasure Map II: Showing Valtheim Towers and the river underneath.

Whiterun: Valtheim Towers, by the riverbank close to the waterfall, partly hidden by rocks on the south bank.

Treasure Map III

Eastmarch—Riverside Shack: In the chest, inside the shack.

Treasure Map III: Showing Solitude Lighthouse and the surrounding rocks.

Haafingar—Solitude Lighthouse: Below the northeast corner of the lighthouse and rocks, by the shore of the Sea of Ghosts.

Treasure Map IV

Whiterun — Redoran's Retreat: Inside the large treasure chest close to the Bandit Chief, inside the mine.

Treasure Map IV: Showing Whiterun and the path up to the chest above the windmill.

Whiterun: The cliffs above Pelagia Farm. Follow the track around and up to the chest, half hidden by saplings.

Treasure Map V

Falkreath Hold — Angi's Cabin: Inside the cabin, on the end table by the bed.

Treasure Map V: Showing the waterfalls of Lost Valley Redoubt.

The Reach: Just east of Gloomreach, at the very bottom of Lost Valley Redoubt, on the riverbank at the base of the waterfall. If you've already discovered Lost Valley Redoubt, Fast-Travel there and you're almost at the chest.

Treasure Map VI

The Pale. Point of Interest — Dead Wood Elf. Secondary Location: A Bloody Trail. On the corpse of the female elf, among the rocky summit northwest of Volunruud. You can find a male Wood Elf close by and follow the trail of blood to her.

Treasure Map VI: Showing showing Korvanjund.

The Pale — Korvanjund. The exterior entrance, atop the barrow arch next to the gnarled tree.

Treasure Map VII

Eastmarch — Traitor's Post: In the chest, inside the bandit hideout.

Treasure Map VII: Showing Gallows Rock, within the outer walls.

Eastmarch — Gallows Rock: Within the outer wall ruins, near the main ground-level door, under the rock with the noose.

Treasure Map VIII

Winterhold — Secondary Location: Haul of the Horkers: On the corpse of a dead hunter.

Treasure Map VIII: Showing the town of Dragon Bridge.

Haafingar Hold — Dragon Bridge: In a satchel, next to the tree across from the bridge. This satchel holds the key to the chest, if you can't open it.

Haafingar Hold — Dragon Bridge: In a chest, in the river northeast of the bridge, underwater (Master).

The Elder Scrolls V
SKYRIM

QUESTS: SIDE QUESTS

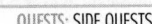

PRIMA OFFICIAL GAME GUIDE   WWW.PRIMAGAMES.COM

Treasure Map IX

Eastmarch—Secondary Location: Lucky Lorenz's Shack. On the corpse of Lucky Lorenz, under a fallen tree in the ruined hut on the south side of the river from the Abandoned Prison.

Treasure Map IX: Showing the waterfall and bridge with Riften signpost.

The Rift: Halfway up the cascading waterfall; drop down the waterfall from the Broken Helm Hollow entrance.

 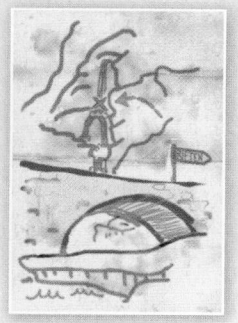 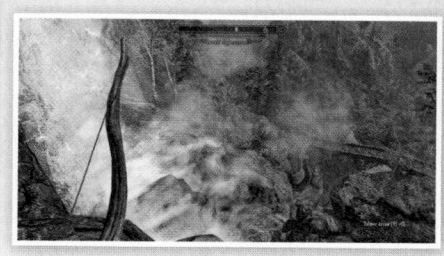

Treasure Map X

Eastmarch—Stony Creek Cave: On the corpse of the bandit wizard.

Treasure Map X: Showing the Lady Stone and Ilinalta's Deep.

Falkreath Hold: Lake Ilinalta, south of Ilinalta's Deep and northeast of the Lady Stone, on the flat stone lake bottom, underwater.

Quest Conclusion

Continue your hunting until all maps are scoured and the treasure pilfered!

MASKS OF THE DRAGON PRIESTS*

PREREQUISITES: None

INTERSECTING QUESTS: Main Quest: The World-Eater's Eyrie, College of Winterhold Quest: The Staff of Magnus, Dungeon Quest: A Scroll for Anska, Dungeon Quest: Evil in Waiting, Dungeon Quest: Otar's Mad Guardians*, Dungeon Quest: Siege on the Dragon Cult

LOCATIONS: Forelhost, High Gate Ruins, Labyrinthian, Bromjunaar Sanctuary, Ragnvald, Shearpoint, Skuldafn, Valthume, Volskygge

ENEMIES: Hevnoraak, Krosis, Morokei, Nahkriin, Otar, Rahgot, Vokun, Volsung

◊ **OBJECTIVES:** None

◉ MINOR SPOILERS

▷ Demise of the Atmoran Dragon Cult

Sometimes, the corporal remains of a powerful Nordic priest survives even death. Entombed with Draugr brethren, dead but dreaming, the Dragon Priest is a frightening, powerful foe to face. Around since the fall of Alduin, these were part of the Atmoran Dragon Cult, but they exclusively worshipped the dragon. Now that Alduin has returned, something else stirs in the deepest Nordic barrows....

Part 1: Death of the Dragon Priests

As you explore larger and more terrifying Nordic dungeons, you may eventually stumble across a sarcophagus that contains a Dragon Priest. Named Dragon Priests have a namesake mask, and each of these facial coverings is imbued with a particular power. Obtaining all eight is a tough enough endeavor. But that is only half the story....

For each named Dragon Priest you kill, pick up and keep their mask. This isn't something you can do quickly; for example, you have to finish the Main Quest entirely and almost finish the College of Winterhold Quests in order to obtain two of them. Therefore, this may be one of the later quests you embark on, unless you're focusing on this above every other activity in Skyrim.

The following table details the dungeon in which you find the masks, the Dragon Priest it belongs to, and each mask's ability, along with any associated quest you must be on to enter the dungeon. Note that all but two of the Dragon Masks have a Dragon Language translation.

✓	HOLD	DUNGEON NAME	DRAGON PRIEST AND MASK NAME	MASK ABILITY	ASSOCIATED QUEST
	Haafingar	Volskygge	Volsung	+20 Carry Weight, Improve Prices 20%, Waterbreathing	None
	Hjaalmarch	Labyrinthian	Morokei	+100% Magicka Regen	College of Winterhold Quest: The Staff of Magnus
	The Pale	High Gate Ruins	Vokun	Improve Conjuration 20%, Illusion 20%, Alteration 20%	Dungeon Quest: A Scroll for Anska

✔	HOLD	DUNGEON NAME	DRAGON PRIEST AND MASK NAME	MASK ABILITY	ASSOCIATED QUEST
☐	The Pale	Shearpoint	Krosis	Improve Lockpicking 20%, Archery 20%, Alchemy 20%	None
☐	The Reach	Ragnvald	Otar	Resist Fire 30%, Resist Frost 30%, Resist Shock 30%	Dungeon Quest: Otar's Mad Guardians*
☐	The Reach	Valthume	Hevnoraak	+40 Heavy Armor	Dungeon Quest: Evil in Waiting
☐	The Rift	Forelhost	Rahgot	+70 Stamina	Dungeon Quest: Siege on the Dragon Cult
☐	Other Realm	Skuldafn	Nahkriin	+50 Magicka; Improve Destruction 20%, Restoration 20%	Main Quest: The World-Eater's Eyrie

- ➤ **Volsung**
- ➤ **Morokei ("Glorious")**
- ➤ **Vokun ("Shadow")**
- ➤ **Krosis ("Sorrow")**
- ➤ **Otar**
- ➤ **Hevnoraak ("Brutality")**
- ➤ **Rahgot ("Anger")**
- ➤ **Nahkriin ("Vengeance")**

Consult the Atlas chapter and any relevant quests for all the information regarding the exact locations within the dungeons where you can find each Dragon Priest.

Part 2: Life from the Dragon Priest Masks

When you've collected one or more masks, you can wear them for the benefits detailed in the previous table. You can also head to an important and ancient location for the Cult of the Dragon Priests: the snow-swept exterior of Labyrinthian. Close to the entrance to Shalidor's Maze is a low circular building that looks almost like a dragon mound or barrow. Enter these round ruins and approach a ruined altar with a dragon's head, skeletal remains, a note, and a wooden mask. Read the note.

- ➤ **Quill**
- ➤ **Hired Thug's Missive**
- ➤ **Wooden Mask**

The Wooden Mask hums with an unfamiliar energy. Place it onto your face when you're outside the circular ruins, and nothing happens. However, if you don the mask while standing in the chamber with the altar, everything fades to black. When you come to, you're in what appears to be the same room, but in another time. The shattered altar is whole once more, and the place is pristine and clean. This is the Bromjunaar Sanctuary.

The altar now has eight distinct busts, one for each of the eight Dragon Priests. Activate the altar, and insert the appropriate mask into the facial slot. Once all eight masks have been returned to the altar, the central dragon's head opens its mouth, exposing one final, golden mask. You may take that mask, along with all the others if you wish. Whether you're carrying any masks or not, when you wish to return to the present, remove the Wooden Mask.

✔	HOLD	DUNGEON NAME	DRAGON PRIEST AND MASK NAME	MASK ABILITY	ASSOCIATED QUEST
☐	Hjaalmarch	Labyrinthian: Bromjunaar Sanctuary (Present)	None	Teleportation into the past, and back to the present	Side Quest: Masks of the Dragon Priests*
☐	Hjaalmarch	Labyrinthian: Bromjunaar Sanctuary (Past)	Konahrik	Detailed below	Side Quest: Masks of the Dragon Priests*

Konahrik ("Warlord")

When the wearer is relatively low on health, there is a chance the mask will knock enemies back, heal the wearer and any nearby allies, and grant a brief Fire Cloak to the wearer. In addition, there is a (much rarer) chance the mask will summon a spectral Dragon Priest to come to the wearer's aid, under the same circumstances.

Quest Conclusion

This epic quest ends when you have all ten Dragon Masks in your possession. Wear the one with the abilities or powers you wish to augment.

Postquest Activities

It may be interesting to note that the masks themselves were symbols of office for the highest-ranking priests in the Dragon Cult of the old times.

| Volsung | Morokei | Vokun | Krosis | Otar | Hevnoraak | Rahgot | Nahkriin | Wooden Mask | Konahrik |

The Elder Scrolls V
SKYRIM

DUNGEON QUESTS AND OTHER ACTIVITIES

OVERVIEW

Delving into an unknown barrow or creeping stealthily through a long-forgotten ruin is both thrilling and terrifying. Many dungeons across Skyrim have their own self-contained Dungeon Quests. Some are full quests; others, marked with the "*" symbol, appear only as Miscellaneous Objectives. Dungeon Quests are usually unrelated to other quest types and are self-contained; you usually start and finish the quest in or close to the dungeon itself.

In addition, this section encompasses the hundreds of other activities you can try out as you explore the immense landscape. These are segmented into four distinct sections. There are:

Dungeon Activities: Smaller, self-contained explorations at a single Primary Location.

Miscellaneous Objectives: These are usually small tasks, favors or activities that occur inside a (usually friendly) settlement, not a dungeon.

Favors: Every single person in Skyrim that requires a favor is then listed in this section, along with all the types of Favors and the Thane Quests.

World Interactions and Encounters: Small random events that may occur when you enter a World Encounter location or perform other actions throughout the realm.

> **NOTE** **Cross-Referencing:** Do you want to see maps and learn more about the traps, non-quest-related items, collectibles, crafting areas, and other important rooms of note in every location during these quests? Then cross-reference the location you travel to with the information on that location contained in this guide's Atlas.

Available Quests

There are 24 Dungeon Quests. For the most part, these are separate from any other quests you may have, though you may encounter them when sent to a randomly selected dungeon for another quest, or while trying to collect the Masks of the Dragon Priests.

✓	QUEST NAME	HOLD	DUNGEON NAME (LOCATION)
	Medresi Dran and the Wandering Dead*	The Rift	Angarvunde
	A Love Beyond Death*	Eastmarch	Ansilvund
	Composure, Speed, and Precision*	Falkreath	Angi's Camp
	Leap Before You Look*	The Reach	Bard's Leap Summit
	Melka and Petra*	The Reach	Blind Cliff Cave
	Repentance	The Rift	Darklight Tower
	Siege on the Dragon Cult	The Rift	Forelhost
	What Lies Beneath*	Winterhold	Frostflow Lighthouse
	The Pale Lady	The Pale	Frostmere Crypt
	A Scroll for Anska	The Pale	High Gate Ruins
	Ancestral Worship	Whiterun	Hillgrund's Tomb
	Forgetting About Fjola*	Eastmarch	Mistwatch

✓	QUEST NAME	HOLD	DUNGEON NAME (LOCATION)
	Hunter and Hunted*	Falkreath	Moss Mother Cavern
	The Lost Expedition	The Reach	Nchuand-Zel
	The Nilheim Scam*	The Rift	Nilheim
	Otar's Mad Guardians*	The Reach	Ragnvald
	The Legend of Red Eagle*	The Reach	Rebel's Cairn
	Wilhelm's Specter*	The Rift	Shroud Hearth Barrow
	The Secret at the Sleeping Tree*	Whiterun	Sleeping Tree Camp
	The Savior of Selveni Nethri*	Falkreath Hold	Southfringe Sanctum
	Infiltration	The Rift	Treva's Watch
	Evil in Waiting	The Reach	Valthume
	Silenced Tongues	The Pale	Volunruud
	Ashore in a Sea of Ghosts*	Winterhold	Yngol's Barrow

> **NOTE** * Indicates the quest name does not appear in your menu; check the "Miscellaneous" area for objectives that may appear.

ANGARVUNDE: MEDRESI DRAN AND THE WANDERING DEAD*

Angarvunde

Once inside, you'll meet a rather abrupt and objectionable Dark Elf named Medresi Dran. She's attempting to reach a treasure buried deep within Angarvunde's musty corridors, but her helpers have abandoned her.

◊ **OBJECTIVE:** Destroy the Draugr in Angarvunde (3)
◊ **OBJECTIVE:** Talk to Medresi in Angarvunde

Remove the wandering corpses. Head through into the main hub chamber where they are, and deal with them in your preferred attacking style. You return to Medresi, informing her that two doors stand in the way of your progress, and they each must be opened via further exploration. She hands you a key, which opens the doors on either side of the portcullis; these lead to a mechanism that lifts the two sections of gate.

➤ Angarvunde Key

 NOTE Alternatively, you could simply kill Medresi and take her key. The Angarvunde Key is the only way to open the two side doors.

◊ **OBJECTIVE:** Find a way to open the gates

Angarvunde Ruins

The door to the northwest leads to a small maze of interlocking corridors and rooms. Work your way through them methodically, watching for pressure plates that launch traps. When you reach the steps up to the two doors with spears blocking your path, remove them by pulling the lever between them. Head across, and weave through another series of corridors and rooms until you reach steps and a corner corridor leading back into the original Angarvunde area. Work your way to the lever in the alcove and pull it.

 **Angarvunde Catacombs**

The door to the southeast leads to the Angarvunde Catacombs, a much deeper maze of chambers that begins with a (careful) descent down a hole. Trek along the corridors and into a Draugr crypt. Fight your way through, up some trap-filled stairs (run quickly, or after the darts are expelled), then through another tomb complex. Ascend several stone steps to reach another lever. After you yank the alcove levers on both sides of this crypt, the gate opens fully.

◊ **OBJECTIVE:** Return to Medresi

 Angarvunde

Medresi isn't waiting around for the likes of you; she dashes forward into the treasure room and is promptly crushed as the floor trap is sprung, impaling her into a maw of ceiling spikes. Step through the opening in the raised floor and down the spiral steps to a Word Wall.

➤ **Word of Power:** Animal Allegiance

ANSILVUND: A LOVE BEYOND DEATH*

 **NOTE** Fragments of Fjori and Holgeir's story can be found in a book called "Of Fjori and Holgeir," which contains hints to solving the puzzle with the four moving pillars. You can find one of the copies on the bedroom bookshelf inside Riften Stables.

Ansilvund Excavation

A Necromancer complains about babysitting an army of enthralled Draugr that are being used as slaves to excavate the ruins.

The cavern darkens, and an enraged spirit, professing to be Lu'ah Al-Skaven, threatens you for disturbing her work.

◊ **MISCELLANEOUS OBJECTIVE:** Kill Lu'ah Al-Skaven in Ansilvund

Puzzle Solution: After killing the conjurer and the Draugr, check the cobwebbed stone buttress wall under the four movable pillars. From left to right, they have the following petroglyph signs: Hawk, Snake, Whale, Snake. Match those to the pillars, activate the lever, and open the portcullis to the south.

Lu'ah's Journal can be found on a table here. Take a moment to learn her tale: the sorceress was attempting to resurrect her dead husband.

➤ **Lu'ah's Journal**

 Ansilvund Burial Chambers

A disembodied voice laments that she "could not raise him" but will avenge his defilement!

Lu'ah faces you, screeches that her husband's body was burned, and attacks. Fjori and Holgeir (the Draugr Thralls that were to be the vessels for Lu'ah and her dead husband) also attack. Once all foes are dead, a ghostly image of Fjori and Holgeir appear, reunited now that Lu'ah is dead. The following can be taken from the altar:

➤ **Unusual Gem**

➤ **Ghostblade**

ANGI'S CAMP: COMPOSURE, SPEED, AND PRECISION*

TIP Before trekking to this remote locale, bring a few different bows with you to test which you prefer (although all bows work in the same way). It is beneficial to take the Eagle Eye or Steady Hand Archery perks in case the following training proves trickier than anticipated.

In the mountainous southwest corner of Falkreath Hold is a lone cabin. This is home to Angi. Listen to her story about her murdered family. Talk to her and request training, if you wish to improve your Archery skill.

Equip your favored bow, follow Angi down to the practice range, and listen to her instructions. Take the Practice Arrows tied to the front-right boundary post. If you require more during the course of this practice,

request them from Angi. Now look ahead and spot all four of the practice targets (including the one in the distance, behind the three nearer ones). When you're completing a challenge, remain within the boundary or you'll fail.

➤ **Practice Arrow (10)**

First Challenge:

Hit the middle target (of the three closer targets in front of you)

Reward: Archery increased by 1

Hit the left target (of the three closer targets in front of you)

Reward: Archery increased by 1

Hit the right target (of the three closer targets in front of you)

Reward: Archery increased by 1

Second Challenge:

Hit the three closest targets within eight seconds (in any order), after Angi counts to three.

Reward: Archery Increased by 1

Third Challenge:

Hit the target far in the back, behind the front cluster of targets.

Reward: Archery increased by 1

Fourth Challenge:

Hit all four of the targets within ten seconds (in any order), after Angi counts to three.

Reward: Archery increased by 1

If you're having trouble with any of these challenges, try the following:

Zoom in to aim your shots to begin with, to gain a larger surface area. But don't do this during the two timed challenges, as this slows you down.

Crouch down so your bow is horizontal for increased accuracy.

You want to hit the tiny hole in the very center of each target. But you'll need to aim a little higher than the target so the arrow arcs through the air and strikes it accurately.

Move over the boundary, and inspect the targets at closer range if you wish, prior to an attempt.

During the fourth challenge, it is better to aim at the far target first, as this is most difficult to hit.

Aside from the increases to your Archery skill, once the fourth challenge is over, speak to Angi (using pleasant responses). She thanks you for keeping her company and not attempting to murder her. She then hands you a gift. After that, you can leave this windswept place (after checking her bedside table for the Treasure Map V).

➤ **Angi's Bow**

BARD'S LEAP SUMMIT: LEAP BEFORE YOU LOOK*

Fight the Forsworn to reach the top of Lost Valley Redoubt. The "Bard's Leap" itself is the precarious and breathtaking outlook over the waterfall. Here is the best way to survive the drop to the water below: use Whirlwind Sprint to make sure you get enough distance to clear the rocks, or use Ethereal Form before jumping off. The spectral shape of Azzadal, a Bardic Ghost, appears near the pool at the base of the Falls if you survive, and congratulates you for surviving the fall that he could not. He rewards you with an increase to your Speech skill.

➤ **Speech Skill increase**

BLIND CLIFF CAVE: MELKA AND PETRA*

◗ Blind Cliff Bastion

Approach Blind Cliff Cave from the main road running north to south along the river. Clamber up through the giant cavern of collapsed follies, and exit to Blind Cliff Towers. Clamber up the exterior towers until you reach the ominous iron door leading to Blind Cliff Bastion. A caged Hagraven named Melka greets you. She is angry that another witch named Petra has caged her up. You can speak to her about being released and about her adversary. There is a "pretty staff" in it for you.

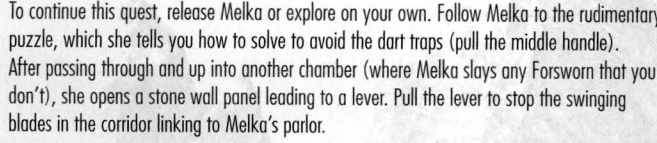

◊ **MISCELLANEOUS OBJECTIVE:** Kill the Hagraven Petra

To continue this quest, release Melka or explore on your own. Follow Melka to the rudimentary puzzle, which she tells you how to solve to avoid the dart traps (pull the middle handle). After passing through and up into another chamber (where Melka slays any Forsworn that you don't), she opens a stone wall panel leading to a lever. Pull the lever to stop the swinging blades in the corridor linking to Melka's parlor.

She waits for you to open the iron door connected to Petra's tower. Storm the chamber and defeat Petra here, along with her Forsworn bodyguards. Then return to Melka, demand a reward, and you're given the Hagraven's staff.

➤ **Eye of Melka**

DARKLIGHT TOWER: REPENTANCE

◗ Darklight Tower (Interior)

Enter the initial chamber and you find the aftermath of a murder. A woman named Illia stands over the recently slain body and doesn't want you to jump to conclusions. Listen to her story, and she explains it was self-defense. Illia was attempting to flee the place, and the dead woman tried to stop her. She wants to leave, but suspects her own mother is set to become a Hagraven.

◊ **OBJECTIVE:** Help Illia reach the top of Darklight Tower

Ascend the tower, dealing with Frostbite Spiders and witches as you go. At the spear-barred door, pull the lever when you're ready to tackle a Hagraven.

◗ Darklight Chambers

Kill more witches. At the lock (Master), Illia waits. Locate the corridor in the east wall, and face a Frostbite Spider and a second Hagraven in a fight for the key that unlocks the door.

➤ **Darklight Tower Key**

After a final ascent up spiral stairs to the tower's top, open a firmly locked door with the key Illia carries on her (if you kill her before reaching the top). The door leads back outside (Master). Wait for Illia, as she has a plan: to present you as a sacrifice to her mother and then kill her; the old crone is too far gone to be saved.

◊ **OBJECTIVE:** Defeat Illia's mother at the top of Darklight Tower

---

Darklight Tower (Exterior)

Step out into a small bailey on the upper crags. Illia's mother, Silvia, tells you to sit on the chair so your bloodletting can begin. Oblige Illia's mother as she is attacked by her daughter. You can stand and watch; intervene only if Illia is in danger of being killed. The quest concludes once Silvia falls. Afterward, approach Illia and invite her to join you as a Follower. She gladly accepts and mainly uses Frost magic on enemies.

➤ **Staff of Hag's Wrath**   ➤ **Follower: Illia**

Forelhost (Exterior)

Ascend the remains of the entrance tower until you spot a High Elf named Captain Valmir, who is wearing the officer's garb of the faction to which you are allied. He requires your assistance; he is on a mission to obtain a mask that a Dragon Priest named Rahgot used to own.

◇ **OBJECTIVE:** Obtain Rahgot's mask
◇ **OBJECTIVE:** (Optional) Find Skorm Snow-Strider's journal

Forelhost Stronghold (Interior)

Repel ghostly foes as the spirits of the dragon cultists appear to guard their old lair! Beware of floor triggers and traps. Pass the wall blades, entering the room to the northwest. Check the stone table, where Snow-Strider's journal is located. Now read this; it informs you why this location has so many blocked-off corridors.

➤ **Skorm Snow-Strider's Journal**

Work your way across the stronghold, down past the forge and kitchen. Locate the pair of wooden doors that lead to Forelhost Crypt. Before entering, watch for the fire-breathing dragon trap close to the barred doorway, and use the nearby lever to raise the portcullis blocking the doorway; this gives you quicker access to the entrance.

Forelhost Crypt

There is a cage surrounding the well (Master) close to the first main corridor. Come back here later if you can't open the cage door now.

Beware of runic floor traps as you travel farther underground and the light dwindles. Also expect a gate and dart traps prior to reaching a raised crypt. This is a dangerous location; expect a swarm of undead foes here!

Work your way to the platforms above, which lead to the other side of the barred wooden door (which you can now open if you wish). Pilfer the chest on the same raised tomb as the hardiest Draugr. This contains the Forelhost Well Key. Return to the well, unlock it, and drop into the icy water. Follow the waterlogged tunnels into a chamber where the remains of a poisoned warrior (mentioned in the journal) still lie among scattered poison bottles. In the adjacent room, beware the rising floor trap.

➤ **Forelhost Well Key**

Forelhost Refectory

The Refectory still bears the scars (and the dead) of the battle Snow-Strider wrote about. Open the iron door and enter the great hall, then open the double doors in the south wall. Traverse the oil-splattered stone corridor (burn it to defeat the Draugr if you wish), before entering the remains of a children's burial plot. There are Orders that confirm the mass burial, surrounded by flowers you can harvest.

➤ **Orders**

Above the burial garden is an alchemy chamber with more steps and Draugr; you can pull a lever to raise the portcullis leading back to the great hall, or press onward and upward, past the ruins of a throne and snow blown down from above. Beware the magic trap in the winding corridor beyond, which leads straight into Forelhost's library. But the prize to find isn't a book; it is a Glass Claw.

➤ **Glass Claw**

Take it, and the spear bars recede from the doorway farther into the library. Head through, past an embalming room, fire trap, and more Draugr, and head up to a hall and Nordic Puzzle Door.

Puzzle Solution: Open your inventory and look at the Glass Claw you just found. The palm bears the sign of the Wolf, Owl, and Snake. Working from the outer ring in, choose the same iconography on the door, and insert the Claw.

It takes only a few steps to reach the grand burial chamber of the Dragon Priest Rahgot. He is joined by a group of Draugr bodyguards, meaning this fight is both difficult and lengthy. But once over, the rewards are worth your anguish:

➤ **Rahgot**   ➤ **Forelhost Balcony Key**
➤ **Leveled Items and Weapons**   ➤ **250 gold pieces**
➤ **Staff of Wall of Flames**

> **TIP** If you're gifted in One-Handed or Two-Handed skills, it is worth sprinting to Rahgot's tomb and hacking at the fearsome lich before he rises completely from his slumber; the more strikes you can inflict without retaliation, the better!

◇ **OBJECTIVE:** Return to Valmir

Forelhost (Exterior)

Use the Balcony Key to unlock the door in the southeast wall of the burial chamber. This leads back outside, to the balcony you couldn't reach when you first met Valmir. A Word Wall is just a few feet away! Once you learn the new phrase, drop down to Valmir's camp. It appears Valmir is an imposter (as he is clad in the attire of your enemy, unlike the first time you encountered him) and is now giving the same speech to convince an enemy soldier!

◇ **OBJECTIVE:** Kill the imposter Valmir

➤ **Word of Power: Storm Call**

> **NOTE** You now have one of the eight Masks of the Dragon Priests. Consult the Side Quest of the same name for further information.

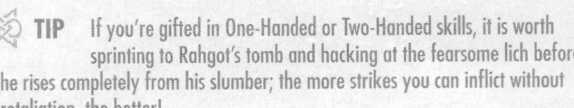

Frostflow Lighthouse (Interior)

Inspect the corpse of Ramati, which has been savagely torn by claws. Near the fire is the body of a Chaurus. Ramati's corpse contains her husband's journal, which describes how the family came to own the lighthouse and the strange noises coming from the cellar. It also reveals a final, horrifying discovery.

In the northeast bedroom is Ramati's Journal, which details her rambunctious children Sudi and Mani and noises in the basement. It also tells how Ramati's husband made her promise to cremate him in the lighthouse torch when he died (this is important later).

In the north bedroom on a table is Sudi's Journal, which mentions the scratchings in the cellar, and a copy of the key Sudi hid in Mother's favorite keepsake.

Locate the Cellar Key in the burial urn above the fireplace, next to the collectible Torchbug in a Jar. (The Torchbug in a Jar is a unique item that can only be found here. It serves no purpose but makes for great house décor.)

➤ **Habd's Journal**　　➤ **Sudi's Journal**　　➤ **Torchbug in a Jar**

➤ **Ramati's Journal**　　➤ **Mani's Cellar Key**

◊ **MISCELLANEOUS OBJECTIVE:** Find the source of the murders in Frostflow Lighthouse

Unlock the cellar door (Expert) using a lockpick or Mani's Cellar Key.

Frostflow Abyss

Open the gate to discover the corpse of Sudi. There are two notes nearby, and the insight into Sudi's last few days make grim reading.

➤ **Bloodstained Note**

➤ **Scrawled Page**

➤ **Habd's Lighthouse Key**

At the end of this waterlogged ice passage is a giant Chaurus Reaper; this is the source of the Frostflow Lighthouse murders.

After defeating it, you can use the Key to access the roof of the lighthouse. If you take Habd's remains from the belly of the giant Chaurus and burn them in the lighthouse torch, you receive a special blessing.

➤ **Ability:** Sailor's Repose
(+10% to Health restored from Restoration magic)

FROSTMERE CRYPT: THE PALE LADY

Frostmere Crypt (Exterior)

As you approach the entrance to this ruin, a well-armored warrior races down the stairs before wheeling to face the bandits that pursue her. Help her (or not), then speak with the agitated Eisa Blackthorn. You can:

Speak to her and try to calm her down. She explains that she used to be a member of the gang here but was run out over a misunderstanding. As she storms off, the quest begins.

Provoke, ignore, or attack her, and she fights back—hard. She's every bit as tough as her attitude. Cut her down and take her journal from her body, hinting at the strange occurrences inside the crypt. This also starts the quest.

➤ **Eisa's Journal**

◊ **OBJECTIVE:** (Optional) Learn more about the theft in Frostmere Crypt
◊ **OBJECTIVE:** Find the stolen sword

> **NOTE** Does Eisa's name sound familiar? If you've been to Cidhna Mine in Markarth, you might have heard her name mentioned. Eisa also figures in Hajvarr's journal in White River Watch. Skyrim's bandits really get around.

> **CAUTION** If you kill Eisa and enter the crypt without reading her journal, the quest will never show up in your quest list. While everything still plays out as described below, because you didn't get the quest, completing it won't count toward the Sideways Achievement/Trophy.

WHISPERS IN THE RUINS

If you're sneaking (or just proceeding carefully), there's a good chance you'll hear some chatter from the bandits prior to engaging or avoiding them:

◊ Just inside the crypt entrance, two bandits question why Eisa and Ra'jiir would have stolen the sword.

◊ As you enter the central chamber, two bandits discuss Kyr's orders to seal up the mine until he gets back.

◊ In the dining hall, two bandits mention that Kyr has gone down to the tunnels, and something there has been "eerie" lately.

◊ When you activate the lever and return to the dining hall, bandits (having run up from the tunnels) are shocked at the carnage.

◊ As you enter the mine tunnels, two bandits discuss their concerns. Kyr has been gone for too long....

Frostmere Crypt (Interior)

After cutting down the bandits in the first room, take the scrap of paper (it appears a couple of times), confirming that the hunt for Ra'jiir and Eisa is on. As you step out onto the upper walkway in the main chamber, you can hear some bandits talking down below, and the quest updates.

◊ **OBJECTIVE:** Follow Kyr and Ra'jiir into the tunnels
♦ **TARGET:** Ra'jiir, in the Frostmere Depths

Follow the path around, but before descending into the dining hall, check the two bedrooms on the upper level. Kyr's Log is on a side table in his bedroom. If you allowed Eisa to leave quietly before, you find her journal in the other bedroom. Once you've read both, the optional objective is complete.

Continue deeper into the ruin and down through the tunnels to reach Frostmere Depths.

Frostmere Depths

You emerge in a mist-shrouded subterranean forest, not far from the crumpled form of the bandit leader, Kyr. Hear his final words. When he dies, a strange glowing light manifests near his body and silently drifts down the path ahead of you.

Follow the light deeper into the woods, and watch as a lone figure—Ra'jiir—emerges from the fog and races for the altar in the center of the grove. Just before he reaches it, a fearsome ethereal form erupts in front of him and cuts him down. The Pale Lady then turns to thwart another tomb defiler: You!

◇ **OBJECTIVE:** Banish the Pale Lady

The Pale Lady is a powerful Wispmother, but if you have the strength, you can defeat her. Take out her wisps to reduce the bonuses they give her, then move in for the kill. The wide expanse around the tomb allows you to attack from a distance and hide between bouts of combat should you need to. If you're extremely quick, you can kill Ra'jiir, too.

Or, you can pick up the Pale Blade (the sword Ra'jiir carries and drops when he dies), approach the altar, and set the blade into the sword stand. This restores the seal on the Pale Lady's tomb, banishing her and her wisps in a blast of energy.

If you banish the Pale Lady by placing her blade atop the altar, you can take it again, breaking the seal and causing her to attack once more. You can repeat this until you decide to kill the Pale Lady, to flee, or to make the Pale Lady disappear again.

After dealing with the Pale Lady, approach the ruins to the north, where a Word Wall waits. Absorb the Word of Power, then take the exit here back to the crypts above.

➤ **The Pale Blade**
➤ **Word of Power:** Ice Form

 NOTE   The Pale Blade is a good weapon to use, with leveled Frost and Fear enchantments. If you're curious about the Pale Lady's nature, find the book called *Lost Legends*, which tells her story in passing, both as a children's fable and as the truth (which Ra'jiir finally realized too late during this exploration).

HIGH GATE RUINS: A SCROLL FOR ANSKA

High Gate Ruins (Interior)

Enter these old Draugr catacombs and meet up with a wizard named Anska. Speak with her, and she's quick to ask for help. This plucky adventurer and powerful fire mage has already begun advancing toward Vokun's Throne Room, where she believes she will find a scroll tying her family's history to that of the hero of yore, Ysgramor. Your reward for helping her? Any loot you wish, aside from the scroll. Agree, and the quest begins. Battle through more powerful Draugr, past a gate trap, and to a Nordic puzzle chamber.

◇ **OBJECTIVE:** Help Anska Retrieve Her Scroll

Puzzle Solution: Look up and to the south. Note the sequence of Hawk, Whale, Fox, Snake. The northern ceiling has the same sequence, but the third carving has fallen to the ground. Now match up the pedestals (which also contain a specific animal carving), and activate the lever of the Hawk, Whale, Fox, and Snake pedestals to match the ceiling order. There are two Hawk pedestals; it doesn't matter which one you activate first. If you're successful, the grating swings open. Descend the spiral stairs, and enter door to High Gate Ruins Catacombs.

High Gate Ruins Catacombs

There are more traps (and Draugr) as you progress, so beware of floor triggers. Head through the altar room, down the long hall to a second altar room, where three levers must be activated:

Puzzle Solution: Pull the lever in the center of the room. The next is in the right alcove, fight the Draugr guarding it, activate the lever, and face a second foe in the left alcove before activating the alcove lever behind it. This opens the portcullis allowing you into Vokun's Throne Room.

Step into the Throne Room, which seems to be honoring an ancient serpent god, and wait for the lich to appear. Be sure Anska survives this confrontation, and use the chamber's columns to hide from the fiend's more deadly attacks. Defeat Vokun, and then enter the chamber behind the throne room; this is a ceremonial altar chamber where the chanting reaches a crescendo, and you receive a Word of Power! Be sure you learn that and take the Sealed Scroll.

➤ **Vokun**   ➤ **Sealed Scroll**
➤ **Word of Power:** Storm Call

◇ **OBJECTIVE:** Return the Scroll to Anska

 TIP   Removing Vokun's mask is imperative if you're also trying to finish Side Quest: Masks of the Dragon Priests*.

High Gate Ruins (Interior)

Exit the chamber via the north door at the end of the narrow corridor. Locate Anska, handing over the Scroll (which is otherwise useless to you and can't be sold). Anska is most grateful and gives you a gift.

➤ **Spell Tome:** Flaming Familiar

Hillgrund's Tomb (Exterior)

Strike up a conversation at the entrance, and Golldir explains that he is worried for his aunt, who ventured into their family crypt to stop a necromancer. Agree to help Golldir rid the crypt of Vals Veran.

◊ **OBJECTIVE:** Defeat Vals Veran
◊ **OBJECTIVE:** (Optional) Protect Golldir

Hillgrund's Tomb (Interior)

Dispatch Draugr while keeping an eye on Golldir and stepping in if the undead are threatening to him. Descend to a connecting hallway, where Golldir's worst fears are confirmed; his aunt Agna lies in a pool of fresh blood. The nearby door is barred from the other side, so continue west, to a cave-in and through a Draugr-infested tomb corridor. The tomb opens into a deeper and much larger mausoleum where the dead rise again.

Puzzle Solution: When the coast is clear, pull the chain next to the bear carving, and an exit door opens. The double iron doors lead to the main crypt and an audience with the warlock Vals Veran.

Your tasks are twofold: killing Vals Veran and keeping Golldir alive (although this isn't necessary for quest completion). Strike at Vals Veran as often as you can, before backing off and dealing with the Draugr that have been summoned. The Draugr that close in on Golldir, or if Vals Veran focuses his attacks on the Nord, are your primary concerns. Continue the combat until both Draugr and Veran crumple to the ground.

Search Veran's corpse for a Crypt Key. A Chest Key is on Golldir, along with two missives; read them to gain a better understanding of the threats Vals Veran was imposing. The quest concludes after the battle.

Use the Crypt Key to open the iron door (Hard) atop the ceremonial stairs; this offers a quick exit. Golldir's chest in the antechamber beyond can be unlocked using the Chest Key. Assuming Golldir is alive, and you didn't start ransacking his family tomb, he is happy to become a Follower.

➤ **Hillgrund's Tomb Crypt Key**   ➤ **Note from Agna**
➤ **Hillgrund's Tomb Chest Key**   ➤ **Leveled gold reward**
➤ **Letter to Golldir**   ➤ **Follower:** Golldir

NOTE Golldir is annoyed if you start stealing loot and opening chests, but not to the extent that this quest fails.

Mistwatch North Tower

Before the first wooden door, Christer calls to you, explaining that he believes his wife, Fjola, is being held in the tower somewhere. He gives you the key to Mistwatch and hopes you'll rescue her. Or, you can kill him and take the key, which opens the (otherwise sealed) wooden door.

➤ **Mistwatch Key**

◊ **MISCELLANEOUS OBJECTIVE:** Search Mistwatch for Fjola

Mistwatch East Tower

After battling bandits to the exterior lower balcony, up through the West Tower, out to the higher balcony, and finally to the top of the East Tower, you encounter the bandit leader herself. If you don't automatically attack her, you mention Fjola's name, and she reveals she's Fjola, leaving her husband and the boring life back at the farm for a career in banditry. She wants him to leave and pretend that she's dead; she hands you her wedding band to try and convince him to leave.

➤ **Fjola's Wedding Band**

◊ **MISCELLANEOUS OBJECTIVE:** Return to Christer

Mistwatch North Tower (Return)

Head back down to Christer and show him the wedding band. He now believes she's alive but not here, and leaves after giving you a small reward.

➤ **Leveled gold reward**

◊ **MISCELLANEOUS OBJECTIVE:** Report back to Fjola

Mistwatch East Tower (Return)

Back at the top of Mistwatch, tell Fjola that Christer won't bother her again, and she tells you she's in your debt and will repay it someday. For the moment, though, this quest is over.

> **NOTE** In order to receive rumors regarding the disappearance of Valdr's hunting party, you must be Level 16. If you aren't, you won't receive any information in Falkreath and must stumble upon the entrance to Moss Mother Cavern to begin this quest. Beware: The beasts may be too tough for you to overcome at lower levels!

Dead Man's Drink (Falkreath)

Stop by Dead Man's Drink and strike up a conversation inside. Among the other scuttlebutt, the innkeeper (Valga Vincia, or Narri) mentions that a hunting party has recently gone missing. It was led by a man named Valdr.

◊ **OBJECTIVE:** Locate Valdr's Hunting Party

Moss Mother Cavern (Exterior)

You hear several increasingly feeble shouts as you trudge down the path toward Moss Mother Cavern. Valdr waits on a log, bleeding heavily. You can:

Hand him one or more healing potions; any standard healing potion will do.

Cast a healing spell on him.

Cast a healing spell with an area of effect, and catch Valdr in the area.

Or leave him to his fate. If you enter the cavern without healing him, Valdr dies, and you miss this quest entirely.

◊ **OBJECTIVE:** Heal Valdr's Injuries

After you treat his injuries, Valdr explains his dilemma: The bodies of his friends are still inside the cave, being torn apart by beasts. You can offer to help him clear out the cavern, or tell him to stay outside while you head in alone. Valdr is a capable archer (especially if fully healed), but he can be killed, which causes you to fail the quest. The choice is yours. If you find the enemies inside too difficult, you can always leave and come back later. Valdr will remain at the entrance and wait for you indefinitely.

◊ **OBJECTIVE:** Return to Valdr

Moss Mother Cavern (Interior)

Enter this sun-dappled grotto, and you'll spot a fresh kill. Ari lies in a splatter of blood. There's little time to search her; expect a bear attack followed by a Spriggan. Try to edge into the cavern slowly so you aren't swarmed by too many enemies. Farther inside, you find the corpse of Niels, along with two additional Spriggans who emerge from the trees around you.

With all the enemies dispatched, speak with Valdr or return to him outside. He hands over a dagger Ari gave him when he first joined their hunting party.

➤ **Valdr's Lucky Dagger**

If you come back later, two small cairns have been set close to the cavern entrance: the graves of Ari and Niels. Valdr returns to the Dead Man's Drink in Falkreath, where he's always happy to see you again.

NCHUAND-ZEL: THE LOST EXPEDITION

Understone Keep

Meet Calcelmo at the entrance to the excavation site, and tell him you wish to see Nchuand-Zel. In order to proceed, he asks you to defeat Nimhe, the "poisoned one," a giant Frostbite Spider. You receive the key to the dig site. Or, you can simply ignore Calcelmo and his spider problem (which isn't part of this quest), and unlock the giant bronze door to the Nchuand-Zel Excavation Site (Adept).

➤ **Key to Nchuand-Zel**

◊ **MISCELLANEOUS OBJECTIVE:** Kill Nimhe inside Nchuand-Zel

Nchuand-Zel Excavation Site

Head through the connecting chambers, down the pit chamber, through the cobwebbed spider chambers, to an excavation entrance room where Nimhe attacks. Fight her or flee. Defeating her completes the Miscellaneous Objective.

◊ **MISCELLANEOUS OBJECTIVE:** Tell Calcelmo that Nimhe is dead

On the platform slightly above Nimhe's intrusion point is a dead Imperial named Alethius. Check his corpse for some notes, which officially starts this quest. Read the note: It mentions chaperoning some researchers into these vast dwarven catacombs. Cut through the cobwebs, heading south into Nchuand-Zel.

➤ **Alethius's Notes**

◊ **OBJECTIVE:** Recover Stromm's journal

Nchuand-Zel

This is a giant open cavern with numerous towers and sloping paths linking them. Fight through the Falmer and down to the door leading to Nchuand-Zel Quarters.

Nchuand-Zel Quarters

Stromm's body is located near a small tree and fire runes on the floor. Avoid them, but inspect the corpse, and read the journal as the objectives update. There is more research to find.

➤ **Stromm's Diary**

> ◊ **OBJECTIVE:** Recover Erj's journal
> ◊ **OBJECTIVE:** Recover Krag's journal
> ◊ **OBJECTIVE:** Recover Staubs's journal

Nchuand-Zel Armory

Return to the main cavern, and descend to the bottom of the chamber. Wade over to the door and enter Nchuand-Zel Armory. Battle Falmer to the chamber with the two guardian Dwarven Spheres. Erj's corpse lies between them. Retrieve his journal.

➤ **Erj's Notes**

Nchuand-Zel

The other exit in the Armory leads you back into the main cavern, onto a previously inaccessible platform, where a Dwarven Centurion waits motionless, close to the body of Krag. Take his journal. Head up the slope into Nchuand-Zel Control.

➤ **Krag's Journal**

Nchuand-Zel Control

Staubin lies dead in a connecting corridor inside the Control district. Take his book; your search for the Lost Expedition is almost over.

➤ **Staubin's Diary**

> ◊ **OBJECTIVE:** Reactivate Nchuand-Zel's automated defenses

To switch the defenses on (which activates all the Dwarven Spiders, Spheres, and Centurions, who then clear the districts of Falmer), head into the control room with the grinding cogs and pistons, and pull the lever.

> ◊ **OBJECTIVE:** Find someone who knows about the expedition

Understone Keep

Exit the Nchuaud-Zel Control area and move back into the main cavern and up the earthen ledge, dropping down to the upper walkway. Flee north back into the excavation site, passing Nimhe and winding your way to Understone Keep. Speak to Calcelmo. Tell him you killed Nimhe (if this occurred), and then ask if he's researching the Dwemer. Calcelmo pays a good amount of coin for each research book you return. Don't forget to keep on asking him about researching the Dwemer to off-load all the books.

➤ **Dwemer Museum Key**   ➤ **300 gold pieces (x4)**

NILHEIM: THE NILHEIM SCAM*

Nilheim Exterior

Meet a wounded hunter named Telrav on the path just east of the bridge spanning the waterfall. He wants you to guide him safely to his camp in the nearby ruins of Nilheim, and you'll be rewarded.

> ◊ **MISCELLANEOUS OBJECTIVE:** Escort Telrav to his camp

Cross the bridge, following Telrav up and into the camp, where he tells you to wait, draws his bow, and assaults you along with four of his bandit mates. It's a trap!

> ◊ **MISCELLANEOUS OBJECTIVE:** Kill Telrav

Quickly quell this ambush, and slay Telrav and the other riffraff. Optionally, you can sneak into Nilheim and defeat all the bandits first, or slay Telrav when you meet him.

RAGNVALD: OTAR'S MAD GUARDIANS*

Ragnvald Temple

Battle Draugr and inspect a strange sarcophagus, which has two round divots into which to insert some kind of ceremonial key. Atop the stairs are spears barring your way.

> ◊ **MISCELLANEOUS OBJECTIVE:** Unlock the Sarcophagus in Ragnvald

Ragnvald Crypts

Fight more Draugr to reach a ceremonial crypt. Take Saerek's Skull Key from its pedestal to continue. Guardian Saerek is roused from slumber when you do; defeat him before returning to the Temple area.

➤ **Saerek's Skull Key**

Ragnvald Canal

Defeat more Draugr to reach a second ceremonial crypt. Remove Torsten's Skull Key from its pedestal to continue. Guardian Torsten is wakened from his rest and attacks you; defeat him before heading back to the Temple.

➤ **Torsten's Skull Key**

Ragnvald Temple (Return)

Once you are back at the sarcophagus, place each skull into the divot slot and prepare for battle. You've just released Otar the Mad, the dreaded Dragon Priest the Guardians laid to rest long ago. This is part of the Side Quest: Masks of the Dragon Priests*. Once you are able, run up through the retracting spears atop the steps and into the ceremonial chamber with a Word Wall at the far end. Learn this Word of Power before you leave.

➤ **Otar**   ➤ **Word of Power:** Kyne's Peace

Rebel's Cairn (Interior)

Pedestal Cavern: Just inside the main cavern, locate the dead adventurer and pry the book from his hand. It tells the tale of Faolan Red Eagle, an ancient hero of the Reach. Read it to begin the following objective. The weapon slot in the pedestal will not accept any of your blades (unless you have Red Eagle's Fury already).

➤ **The Legend of Red Eagle**

◊ **MISCELLANEOUS OBJECTIVE:** Find Red Eagle's sword

> **TIP** This quest can also be started by finding a copy of *The Legend of Red Eagle* elsewhere in Skyrim. This book appears in any number of locations, such as Farengar's study in Dragonsreach. Or, you can start the quest by clearing Red Eagle Redoubt first, claiming Red Eagle's Fury from the high-level enemy and reading the book (*Red Eagle's Rite*) on the altar nearby.

Red Eagle Redoubt (Exterior)

Follow the riverside trail up into the hills to reach your first objective, a cave entrance leading into Red Eagle Ascent. Head through the cave and back out into the exterior, then climb the stairs heading north, slaying Forsworn as you go. Continue up into the cliffside Forsworn Camp, looking for a Forsworn Briarheart on the stone altar plateau at the top, close to the entrance to the Sundered Towers. The Briarheart carries a key to the tower nearby and the sword you seek, Red Eagle's Fury.

➤ **Red Eagle's Fury** ➤ **Red Eagle Tower Key**

◊ **MISCELLANEOUS OBJECTIVE:** Unlock the secret of Red Eagle's Tomb

After defeating the boss, you can explore the Sundered Towers, scavenging for items and taking in the awesome view from atop the towers.

Rebel's Cairn

Pedestal Cavern: Return to Rebel's Cairn and insert Red Eagle's Fury into the weapon slot on the pedestal. A wall section slides away in front (east) of you.

Red Eagle's Tomb: Continue down the passage and enter the Red Eagle's secret crypt. As Red Eagle emerges from his sarcophagus, several skeletons rise around him. Cut them down and ransack the tomb for its treasures.

Pedestal Cavern: As you leave, you'll notice that the sword you placed in the weapon slot now glows with a brilliant light. Draw it forth, and claim the more powerful Red Eagle's Bane!

➤ **Red Eagle's Bane**

Ivarstead (Vilemyr Inn)

Visit the Vilemyr Inn and speak to Wilhelm, who believes a ghost haunts Shroud Hearth Barrow, the ruin atop the hill. Offer to look into it for him.

◊ **MISCELLANEOUS OBJECTIVE:** Investigate Shroud Hearth Barrow

Shroud Hearth Barrow (Interior)

Head down the spiral steps to find a closed portcullis, where a specter urges you to leave. After he delivers his ghostly warning, move into the next room, which has four levers.

Puzzle Solution: Three of the four levers move one or more of the portcullises (there are three ahead of you in the junction). The fourth, on the far right, launches darts at you, so always ignore it. To open the two portcullises ahead (southwest) of you, make sure levers 1 and 3 are up and 2 and 4 are down.

As you head deeper into the ruins, the ghost you saw earlier attacks! Kill him...and notice that his body suddenly looks a lot more substantial. The "ghost" of the barrows turns out to be treasure hunter Wyndelius Gatharian, who Wilhelm may have mentioned. The journal on the table explains everything: Wyndelius has been using a unique potion, the Philter of the Phantom, to impersonate a ghost and keep the townsfolk at bay while he searched for a way into the ruins, but the potion seems to have driven him a bit mad. Take the journal, then return to Wilhelm at the Vilemyr Inn.

➤ **Wyndelius's Journal** ➤ **Philter of the Phantom (2)**

◊ **MISCELLANEOUS OBJECTIVE:** Bring Wyndelius's Journal to Wilhelm

> **NOTE** The Philter of the Phantom is a unique item that briefly makes you look like a ghost! While fun, it doesn't have any functional effects.

Puzzle Solution: At the four levers, you'll notice the portcullis back to the surface is stopping your progress. Place all four levers in the down position to raise the portcullis, allowing you to exit.

Ivarstead (Vilemyr Inn)

Show Wyndelius's Journal to Wilhelm at the Vilemyr Inn to receive the Sapphire Dragon Claw you need to explore the interior of the barrows.

➤ **Sapphire Dragon Claw**

Shroud Hearth Barrow (Interior)

Retrace your steps, opening the portcullises as before, then head southwest to a Nordic Puzzle Door.

Puzzle Solution: The door consists of three large, rotating rings. Each ring has three animals symbols plated into it. The puzzle solution is actually on the palm of the Sapphire Dragon Claw; rotate it in your inventory to see the three circular petroglyph carvings on the Claw's palm. Move the rings so the Moth, Owl, and Wolf appear on the outer, middle, and inner rings, respectively. Then insert the Sapphire Dragon Claw into the keyhole.

In the next chamber, the portcullises slam shut on you as the Draugr begin climbing out of their sarcophagi. Fight them if you wish, but use the lever in the northeast alcove to open the portcullises, allowing you to continue.

After defeating the skeletons in the pool of oil and the trap-filled crypt, you'll enter another crypt where the doors shut and lock on you. Slay the last Draugr in front of the locked iron door to claim the key to the door, or just unlock it yourself (Expert). Then head into a canal area, with another puzzle to solve.

➤ Shroud Hearth Barrow Key

Puzzle Solution: To lower the bridge over the canal, open the double wooden doors. Step into the inner chamber and stand on the pressure plate. Four stone walls begin to turn, eventually revealing a carving in each alcove. Note the carvings, and turn the pillars outside to match that sequence. Or simply ignore this and twist the pillars so that the following are shown from left to right: Whale, Hawk, Snake, Whale.

Shroud Hearth Depths (Interior)

Inside the stepped tomb chamber, skeletons and Draugr emerge from their coffins to face you. As you cut them down, more emerge, until the final high-level Draugr clambers out of the tomb at the top of the structure.

Kill him, lowering the bridge and a stone door on the other side. Beyond is a large treasure chest and a Word Wall. Then exit via the iron door to the northwest.

➤ Word of Power: Kyne's Peace

SLEEPING TREE CAMP: THE SECRET AT THE SLEEPING TREE*

Begin this quest in two different ways:

By listening to a rumor from any of the barkeeps dotted around Skyrim.

Or by stumbling upon Sleeping Tree Camp, located west of Whiterun, in the Tundra plains.

Beware of lumbering mammoths and their giant shepherds. Give them a wide berth and they won't attack, or slay them if you wish. Your main concern here is the strange tree growing in a pond of eerie purple water. If you approach it and activate the spigot, you can drain a single potion of Sleeping Tree Sap. You aren't able to siphon off another bottle for another few days. A bottle isn't needed to accomplish this.

The small cave below the mammoth skull adjacent to the pond is another place to investigate, but watch for an irate giant inside. Locate the body of a dead Orc named Ulag. Among his possessions is another bottle of Sap and a note; take both and read Ysolda's Message. The message instructs the now-deceased Ulag to bring any Sleeping Tree Sap to a woman named Ysolda, at her stall in Whiterun. Before you leave, quickly open the treasure

chest in the cave; there's usually some gold and a couple of bottles of Sleeping Tree Sap to gather. Don't leave camp without them!

➤ Sleeping Tree Sap   ➤ Ysolda's Message

◊ OBJECTIVE: Speak to Ysolda about Sleeping Tree Sap

Ysolda is usually inside or near her house in the southern part of Whiterun's walled city or is walking to a stall. Speak with her, tell her you've some Sap to sell, and trade as many bottles as you wish. You can return to Sleeping Tree Camp and siphon off another batch of Sap, but don't expect the tree to regenerate sap immediately: This can take anywhere from three days to a month.

➤ 150 gold pieces (per Sap bottle)

NOTE Sleeping Tree Sap is a powerful narcotic that fortifies a user's health by 100 for 45 seconds. However, it also blurs vision and slows down the recipient by 25 percent, so use it with caution! Such Sap is also available to purchase from certain Khajiit caravaneers on the roads of Skyrim. If you need another Sap fix, return to Sleeping Tree Camp in a month or so.

SOUTHFRINGE SANCTUM: THE SAVIOR OF SELVENI NETHRI*

Southfringe Sanctum

Entrance Cavern: Defeat the Spellsword at the entrance, and kill any other foes (except for Pumpkin the fox, in the small cage) as you head up the interior cavern slope.

Spider Cave: Continue through interlocking tunnels, and defeat all Frostbite Spiders when they swarm you.

Spider Warren: Selveni Nethri is tied up in spiderwebs in the center of the Sanctum. Hack or burn the web away. She explains that Bashnag's coven chased her out and left her for dead down here. Tell her to wait while you clear out the rest of the cave.

◊ MISCELLANEOUS OBJECTIVE: Help Selveni Nethri escape the cave

Bashnag's Coven: Kill anything you meet between Nethri and a confrontation with the Warlock Bashnag. Then explore the rest of the Sanctum and leave no enemy alive. Feel free to loot the place.

Spider Warren: Return to Selveni Nethri, tell her it is safe to exit, and follow her to the entrance cavern and out into Skyrim.

Treva's Watch Exterior

Exterior Road: Meet Stalleo and his bodyguards camped out to the east of the fortification, close to the bridge. He has been forced out of his home by men loyal to Brurid, one of his rivals. Agree to help him, and begin this quest.

◊ **OBJECTIVE:** Use the back door to gain access to Treva's Watch

Treva's Watch

Entrance: You meet bandits on this sloped tunnel. Burn them all by firing an arrow at the oil lamp above them, or attack normally. Now work your way through this structure, slaying bandits along the way. A pile of corpses in the barrel room indicates where forces loyal to Stalleo have been slaughtered. There is a bandit chief to slay, but killing and exploring are optional.

Exterior Courtyard: Move to the ground-level exit to the east, open it, and pull the lever in the small wooden lean-to just outside the door. This opens the previously impenetrable main gates, retracting the spears blocking Stalleo and his men.

◊ **OBJECTIVE:** Meet up with Stalleo in the courtyard

Continue the fight in the courtyard (pulling the lever before or after you defeat the remaining bandits) and meet up with Stalleo when the coast is clear. He asks if you've seen his family (you haven't) and rewards you for your help.

➤ **Spell Tome:** Detect Life

Valthume Vestibule (Interior)

When you first enter this evil-stained place, a ghost named Valdar approaches. It explains that you stand in the tomb of Hevnoraak, and he may have returned. Valdar has been barely containing his power and hopes you'll explore the tomb and find three vessels that hold the power to vanquish Hevnoraak. Agree to this mission as Valdar sits back down on the throne where he died.

◊ **OBJECTIVE:** Collect the Vessels (3)

Expect numerous traps and attacks by Draugr and Frostbite Spiders as you search the interlocking chambers of this crypt. The specter of Hevnoraak intermittently appears and drifts off; you cannot affect this ethereal being, but its significance means you're making progress.

Valthume

The first Vessel is inside the coffin of a high-level Draugr, in a dead-end chamber to the east, with open (but inaccessible) wind tunnels up to the surface.

➤ **Opaque Vessel**

Valthume Catacombs

The second Vessel is through the portcullis (check the wall alcove to the right for the pull chain) in the northwest corner of the vertical Draugr crypt, toward the center of this section of Valthume.

➤ **Opaque Vessel**

Valthume Vestibule

Continue to fight your way through more Draugr and Frostbite Spiders. Your way is temporarily blocked by a Nordic Puzzle Door.

➤ **Iron Claw**

Puzzle Solution: The door consists of three rings that rotate when you activate them. Each of the them have three animals plated into the structure. The central keyhole is unlocked using the Iron Claw; this puzzle is inaccessible without it, as the puzzle solution is on the palm of the Iron Claw. Rotate it in your inventory to see the three circular petroglyph carvings on the Claw's palm. Move the rings so the Dragon, Hawk, and Wolf appear on the outer, middle, and inner rings, respectively. Then insert the Iron Claw into the keyhole.

Just beyond the door is a battle with Draugr guarding a pedestal with the last Vessel on it. Don't forget to approach the Word Wall to the west, and absorb a Word of Power.

➤ **Opaque Vessel**   ➤ **Word of Power:** Aura Whisper

◊ **OBJECTIVE:** Perform the ritual with Valdar

Valthume

Back in the throne room close to the entrance, Valdar informs you that the vessels contain the Dragon Priest's blood. Emptying them into the nearby sconce is likely to remove any chance Hevnoraak has of regaining his former powers. Oblige Valdar by pouring out the three vessels and then sit on the throne.

◊ **OBJECTIVE:** Defeat Hevnoraak

Slay this Dragon Priest, concentrating on cutting him down, rather than the Storm Thralls he summons. The quest concludes once this battle ends and Valdar has spoken to you, urging you to take the iron mask. This is part of Side Quest: Masks of the Dragon Priests*.

➤ **Hevnoraak**

◈ Volunruud (Interior)

◊ **OBJECTIVE:** Locate the Ceremonial Weapons

Enter the barrow. Beware of skeletons. Choose either path at the junction and search the entire area for a crypt containing an Archaic Nord Helmet sitting in a skull. The adjacent chamber has a Ceremonial Sword to take from the coffin. Watch for a Draugr ambush afterward.

➤ **Ceremonial Sword**

The path to the northwest leads to a tomb and a path leading down into a lower throne room with multiple floor traps and a Ceremonial Axe above the throne. Remove that from its wall coupling.

➤ **Ceremonial Axe**

◊ **OBJECTIVE:** Open the Elder's Cairn

Backtrack to the hub chamber and head north, to the Elder's Cairn door. Place both ceremonial weapons into their slots, and the door grinds open.

◊ **OBJECTIVE:** Defeat Kvenel

Head to the Elder's Cairn of Kvenel the Tongue, where the powerful Nord warrior's spirit still haunts. The ghost brandishes two very real versions of the ceremonial weapons you found earlier. Defeat the foe, watching out for his Shouts and Frost Thralls. Then search the corpse for the weapons themselves. Before leaving, check the upper steps that lead to a Word Wall.

➤ **Eduj**   ➤ **Okin**   ➤ **Word of Power:** Aura Whisper

> **NOTE** One of Kvenel the Tongue's weapons may be lost to the ether when he dies, so don't expect to obtain both of them. The type of weapon is also randomly determined.

◈ Winterhold

Quest Start 1: Visit Birna's House in the Hold City of Winterhold first, and speak to her. She's done a bad deal on a trinket she wants rid of. Pay her 50 gold pieces. She tells you to come back if you find anything of interest inside Yngol Barrow, where this is supposed to be placed.

➤ **Coral Dragon Claw**

Quest Start 2: Or simply enter Yngol Barrow and locate the Coral Dragon Claw during your exploration. You never need speak to Birna (she won't have knowledge of the Claw if you find it this way).

◈ Yngol Barrow (Exterior)

To further your knowledge of the tale of Yngol, read the book on the small shrine in front of the Barrow entrance.

➤ **Yngol and the Sea-Ghosts**

◈ Yngol Barrow (Interior)

This tomb is suspiciously quiet. You are joined by an ever-increasing number of strange little spirit balls that bounce and seem to act with an otherworldly intelligence. Continue until you reach the portcullis chamber with the lever in front of it. Don't trigger the dart trap by moving the lever yet! Instead, search the dead scholar, removing his book and reading it.

➤ **Notes on Yngol Barrow**

Puzzle Solution: The book is the key here, as it refers to transcription of carvings in this room:

"Man in his throne, so should he be": This refers to the throne and skeleton to your right.

"Whale in the sea, so should he be": This refers to the pillar to the right of the throne, which is being splashed by water. Change it so the Whale is shown.

"Eagle in Sun's Sky, so should he be": This refers to the pillar bathed in light, left of you. Change it so the Hawk is shown.

"Snake in the weed, so should he be": This refers to the grass-covered pillar. Change that so the Snake is shown.

Now pull the lever. Enter the next chamber, where you'll find the Coral Dragon's Claw on a dais if you haven't received it at the start of this quest.

➤ **Coral Dragon Claw**

Continue deeper into the barrow until you reach a Nordic Puzzle Door.

Puzzle Solution: The door consists of three rings that rotate. Each of the them has three animals plated into the structure. The puzzle solution is on the palm of the Coral Dragon Claw; rotate it in your inventory to see the three circular petroglyph carvings on the Claw's palm. Move the rings so the Snake, Wolf, and Moth appear on the outer, middle, and inner rings, respectively. Then insert the Coral Dragon Claw into the keyhole.

Head into the resting place of Yngol. The spirit balls of energy congeal and form into Yngol's Shade, which must be fought. Then take Yngol's Helm from the skeletal remains of the warrior, and any other treasure you wish to ransack. Exit via the spiral steps to the southeast.

➤ **Yngol's Helm**

DUNGEON ACTIVITIES

Are you embarking on an exploration of a particularly strange or frightening cairn, barrow, fortification, or hole in the ground? Then consult the following chart, which lists every notable occurrence within a dungeon of Skyrim!

✓	LOCATION	HOLD	ASSOCIATED QUEST (AND POSSIBLE PREREQUISITE)	DESCRIPTION	REWARD
☐	Alftand	Winterhold	None (Daedric Quest: Discerning the Transmundane leads here but doesn't have to be active.)	You are sent here on your way to obtain an Elder Scroll. This is one connection to Blackreach. At the end of the exploration, you can obtain a Targe (shield) from Umana, a bandit explorer, in Alftand Cathedral.	Targe of the Blooded
☐	Anise's Cabin	Falkreath	None	A kindly old woman lives at this cabin in the woods, close to Riverwood. But enter her cellar, and you learn she's actually a witch. She attacks when you emerge.	Scavenged items
☐	Bard's Leap Summit	The Reach	None	Jumping off the overlook into the water below awakens a ghost named Azzadal. Beware of Forsworn and Hagravens, and converse with the spirit.	+2 Speech
☐	Blackreach	Blackreach (Other Realms)	Main Quest: Elder Knowledge or Daedric Quest: Discerning the Transmundane must be active to enter Blackreach	Launch any Dragon Shout at the central hanging "Sun" above the Debate Hall in the center of Blackreach, to summon a Dragon to fight.	Dragon Soul
☐	Bloated Man's Grotto	Falkreath	Before Daedric Quest: Ill Met by Moonlight	The Shrine to Talos at the back of the grotto was once an old Blades hideout. Find the note from a fallen Blade and the sword he left behind.	Bolar's Writ, Bolar's Oathblade
☐	Brinewater Grotto	Haafingar	None (Thieves Guild Quest: Scoundrel's Folly occurs here but doesn't have to be active)	This hidden bandit camp and Horker grotto can be reached through the Solitude East Empire Warehouse. Only the grotto section is available if you enter from the unmarked cave near Solitude Lighthouse.	Scavenged items
☐	Bronze Water Cave	The Pale	Thieves Guild Quest: Blindsighted is active	Normally, this strange cave with dwarven pipe-work is a dead end. However, it is a secret exit from Irkngthand at the zenith of this quest.	None
☐	Chillwind Depths	Hjaalmarch	None	Nearby Secondary Locations paint a grim picture. To the northeast is an attacked Caravan cart. At the base of the path leading to the cave lies an abandoned camp, once used by some adventurers who came to investigate. The adventurers themselves are found dead inside. Near the end of this Falmer and Frostbite Spider maze, a note on one of the prisoners tells what happened to those who were captured.	Merchant's Journal, Adventurer's Journal, Torn Note
☐	Clearpine Pond	Haafingar	None	Tread lightly: If you disturb the island (attacking the animals, harvesting the plants, or examining the dead alchemist), Spriggans emerge to attack.	Scavenged items
☐	Cronvangr Hall	Eastmarch	None	Before a fearful journey down into a chasm, fighting Frostbite Spiders, check the north wall of the entrance cavern to press a wall button, open a secret door, and venture into a vampire abode, the "Hall" itself, where few dare enter!	Scavenged items
☐	Crystaldrift Cave	The Rift	None	You can obtain Gadnor's Staff of Charming (which actually casts Fury) from his corpse, inside this animal den.	Gadnor's Staff of Charming
☐	Dead Men's Respite	Hjaalmarch	None (Bard's Quest: Tending the Flames occurs here but doesn't have to be active)	This is the tomb of King Olaf One-Eye. The bard Yrsarald was also entombed here; his ghost leads you through the dungeon and takes vengeance on Olaf during the final battle.	King Olaf's Verse (see quest for details)
☐	Druadach Redoubt	The Reach	None	You can find a map here that reveals the locations of all Forsworn camps. Madanach heads here if he survives the prison break, during Side Quest: No One Escapes Cidhna Mine.	Scavenged items
☐	Duskglow Crevice	The Pale	None	The Falmer that live here like to collect trinkets from the world of men. A group of bandits are down here to reclaim their stolen property; be quiet, and you can listen to their plotting.	Scavenged items
☐	Dwemer Museum (Understone Keep, in Markarth)	The Reach	None (Thieves Guild Quest: Hard Answers occurs here but doesn't have to be active)	See the quest for notes on how to gain legitimate access to the Museum, or for tips on sneaking through this space to the laboratory beyond.	See Quest
☐	Fallowstone Cave	The Rift	Daedric Quest: The Cursed Tribe is active	When the quest is active, another exit is available in this cave that connects to the otherwise-inaccessible Giant's Grove. You accompany Chief Yamarz here to kill an orc-eating giant and to retrieve Volendrung.	Volendrung (see quest for details)
☐	Fellglow Keep	Whiterun	College of Winterhold Quest: Hitting the Books is active	There are a number of interactions if this quest is active, compared to normal adventuring: You can release prisoners, try out the firing range, and battle a teleporting foe known as The Caller.	A number of important books (see quest for details)
☐	Folgunthur	Hjaalmarch	None (Side Quest: Forbidden Legend occurs here but doesn't have to be active)	Daynas Valen, a wizard investigating the Gauldur Legend (Side Quest: The Forbidden Legend) perished here along with his adventuring party. His journal and notes explain the truth behind this ancient mystery.	Gauldur Amulet Fragment, Gauldur Blackblade, Writ of Sealing (see quest for details)
☐	Forelhost	The Rift	Dungeon Quest: Siege on the Dragon Cult	One of eight lairs where a named Dragon Priest lies. You can obtain Rahgot's Mask here. The quest is automatically active.	Rahgot's Mask
☐	Geirmund's Hall	The Rift	Side Quest: Forbidden Legend is active	Named for Arch-Mage Geirmund, from the Gauldur Legend (Side Quest: The Forbidden Legend), who is entombed here along with one of the three brothers. Puzzle Solution (Pillars): Clockwise from the base of the steps: Hawk, Whale, Snake, Whale. Sigdis Gauldurson creates illusionary duplicates.	Gauldur Amulet Fragment, Gauldur Blackbow, Writ of Sealing (see quest for details)
☐	Gloombound Mine	Eastmarch	None	The Ebony mine is adjacent and connected to the Orc stronghold of Narzulbur.	Ebony Ore
☐	Hag's End	The Reach	Dark Brotherhood Quest: The Feeble Fortune*	The Hagraven here teleports after taking damage, until you eventually defeat her at the top of the ruins.	Scavenged items (see Dark Brotherhood Quest for most powerful items)
☐	Hall of the Vigilant	The Pale	None	The base of operations for the Vigil of Stendarr. The Vigilants attack if you are in werewolf form or if they sense you are a vampire. Otherwise, the Vigilants will gladly heal you of any nonpermanent diseases upon request.	Healing
☐	Halldir's Cairn	Falkreath	None	Halldir lures adventurers in here and compels them to sacrifice themselves on his cairn (Vidgrod, Raen, and Agrius have succumbed to him). Agrius's Journal (on the entrance room pedestal) tells the story. Puzzle Solution: Match the symbols on the stone heads in each room. Clockwise from the lever: Hawk, Snake, Whale. Halldir splits into three elemental forms in midbattle.	Halldir's Staff
☐	Halted Stream Camp	Whiterun	None	An old iron mine, now overrun by poachers. Beware the large pit located slightly to the east, and a trap filled interior where bandits are carving up a dead mammoth.	Poacher's Axe (with bandit at grindstone)

The Elder Scrolls V — **SKYRIM**

DUNGEON QUESTS AND OTHER ACTIVITIES

	LOCATION	HOLD	ASSOCIATED QUEST (AND POSSIBLE PREREQUISITE)	DESCRIPTION	REWARD
☐	Harmugstahl	The Reach	None	You encounter an adventurer fighting an enchanted Frostbite Spider at the entrance. Puzzle Solution (Levers): The four levers (A, B, C, D from left to right) trigger four bars (1, 2, 3, 4). Pulling a switch toggles its associated bar and the ones immediately next to them (pulling A toggles 1, 2. Pulling B toggles 2, 1, 3. Pulling C toggles 3, 2, 4. Pulling D toggles 4, 3). Simply pull levers A and D. Kornalus Frey is experimenting with these spiders. Find his key on his corpse that unlocks his bedroom (and Shrine of Julianos) and the door to the exit.	Scavenged items
☐	Irkngthand	The Pale	Thieves Guild Quest: Blindsighted is active	You accompany Karliah and Brynjolf through this expansive dwarven structure.	Eyes of the Falmer
☐	Kagrenzel	Eastmarch	None	If you find yourself falling, stay in the middle of the chasm you're falling through; you're more likely to survive. This connects to Stony Creek Cave (but only from this location).	None
☐	Katariah	Haafingar	Dark Brotherhood Quest: Hail Sithis! is active	The Emperor's ship only appears when the quest begins. Listen to conversations among the crew if you're sneaking. If you wish to avoid the top deck, pick the middeck door or take the key from the captain.	See Quest
☐	Knifepoint Ridge Interior	Falkreath	Daedric Quest: Boethiah's Calling is active	When this quest is active, you can enter a previously inaccessible inner chamber of the mine, where you can face and defeat the previous Champion of Boethiah.	Ebony Mail and Ebony Equipment
☐	Liar's Retreat	The Reach	None	This bandit hall and hideout has been recently attacked by Falmer, and both are waging a violent battle. There are dwarven ruin elements farther into this dungeon.	Rahd's Longhammer (next to Rahd's body on the altar.)
☐	Logrolf's House (Markarth)	The Reach	Daedric Quest: The House of Horrors is active	A strange house within the walls of Markarth, where odd occurrences are being investigated.	Mace of Molag Bal
☐	Lost Prospect Mine	The Rift	None	This mine was abandoned when one of the partners went missing. A Miner's Journal explains the story. The miner is, in fact, still here; his skeleton is in a secret chamber behind the waterfall, next to several gold veins. Use Whirlwind Sprint (or a lucky jump) to climb to this otherwise hard-to-reach ledge.	Gold Ore
☐	Lost Valley Redoubt	The Reach	None	This is a Forsworn encampment surrounding (both above and below) Bard's Leap Summit. If you're quiet, you can see Hagravens completing a ritual and creating a Briarheart. There is a Word Wall here, too.	Word of Power: Become Ethereal
☐	Mara's Eye Pond	Eastmarch	None	A trapdoor on the island leads to a smugglers' den claimed by a couple of vampires.	Scavenged items
☐	Meeko's Shack	Hjaalmarch	None	You find a dog, Meeko, by the side of the road, south of the shack. He leads you to the shack where his dead master lies. There is a Journal expressing the master's wishes.	Follower: Meeko
☐	Mzinchaleft	Hjaalmarch	None (Dark Brotherhood Side Contract: Maluril occurs here but doesn't have to be active)	An enterprising Dark Elf, Maluril, has hired a group of mercenary bandits to help excavate the ruins for valuable artifacts. Mzinchaleft Depths has an entrance into Blackreach (provided you have the Attunement Sphere from Daedric Quest: Discerning the Transmundane).	Scavenged Items
☐	Nightcaller Temple	The Pale	Daedric Quest: Waking Nightmare is active	This ruin is actually a former temple of Vaermina (only accessible during the quest). Together with Erandur, you fight your way through here to find the Skull of Corruption. Follower: Erandur, or Skull of Corruption	See Quest
☐	Orotheim	Hjaalmarch	None	If you kill the bandits here, they stop their raids on the giants of Talking Stone Camp to the south.	Scavenged items
☐	Orphan Rock	Falkreath	Temple Quest: The Blessings of Nature is active	You are sent here to retrieve Nettlebane from a Hagraven.	Nettlebane
☐	Pinewatch	Falkreath	None (Thieves Guild City Influence Quest: Silver Lining occurs here, but doesn't have to be active)	Press a button on the wall next to the table in the cellar, and access a hidden passage behind the bookshelf to find a bandit hideout. The bandits here have stolen Endon's Silver Mold, the quest item.	Endon's Silver Mold (and Scavenged items)
☐	Raldbthar	The Pale	None (Dark Brotherhood Quest: Mourning Never Comes occurs here but doesn't have to be active)	You are sent here to murder Alain Dufont. You can also obtain Aegisbane from him. This is one of the connections to Blackreach (provided you have the Attunement Sphere from Daedric Quest: Discerning the Transmundane).	Aegisbane, scavenged items
☐	Reachwater Rock	The Reach	Side Quest: Forbidden Legend is active	Puzzle Solution (Nordic Doors): If you have the necessary claws (one is found in Folgunthur), the first Puzzle Door's unlocking symbols are Bear, Whale, Snake. The second is Hawk, Hawk, Dragon. You fight Jyrik (Saarthal), Sigdis (Geirmund), and Mikrul (Folgunthur) again in sequence.	Gauldur Amulet
☐	Riften Jail (Mistveil Keep)	The Rift	None	Secret Exit: Note the Thieves Guild Shadowmark on the wall. Once only you can pull the broken shackle in your cell to open a secret door into the sewers and out into Lake Honrich.	None (you must retrieve your equipment, too!)
☐	Robbers' Gorge	Hjaalmarch	None	The bandits here demand a 100 gold toll each time you want to pass. If you refuse, they use their rockfall traps and attack from the high cliffs.	Scavenged items
☐	Serpent's Bluff Redoubt	Whiterun	None	This is a Forsworn hideout. Puzzle Solution: Put an item on the pressure plate on the altar to open the exit portcullis.	Scavenged items
☐	Shroud Hearth Barrow	The Rift	None (Miscellaneous Objective: Wilhelm's Specter occurs here but doesn't have to be active)	The "ghost" of the barrows turns out to be a treasure hunter named Wyndelius Gatharian, who is using a Philter of the Phantom. Show Wyndelius's Journal to Wilhelm at the Vilemyr Inn to receive the Sapphire Dragon Claw you need. Puzzle Solution (Nordic Door): Moth, Owl, Wolf. In the locked catacombs, the last Draugr has the Shroud Hearth Barrows Key. Puzzle Solution (Pillars): From left to right: Whale, Hawk, Snake, Whale. There is a Word Wall here, too.	Wyndelius's Journal, Sapphire Dragon Claw. Word of Power: Kyne's Peace
☐	Solitude Jail (Castle Dour)	Haafingar	None	Secret Exit: Break through the crumbling mortar in the back of your cell and exit behind Angeline's Aromatics.	None (you must retrieve your equipment, too!)
☐	Talking Stone Camp	Hjaalmarch	None	Bandits from Orotheim raid the camp periodically. Once you've cleared out that dungeon, the raids stop, and the giants lead their mammoths to a nearby stream, which gives you an opportunity to loot the camp more easily.	Scavenged items
☐	Tolvald's Cave	The Rift	Thieves Guild Side Quest: No Stone Unturned is active	A refuse pile just after the waterfall in Tolvald's Crossing is the final resting place of the Crown of Barenziah, a quest item for the Thieves Guild. You can only enter this cavern when the quest is active.	Crown of Barenziah (and scavenged items)
☐	Volskygge	Haafingar	Side Quest: Masks of the Dragon Priests*	Puzzle Solution: Activate Snake, Bear, Fox, Wolf in that order to raise the portcullis. One of eight lairs where a named Dragon Priest lies. You can obtain Volsung's Mask here. The quest is automatically active.	Volsung's Mask
☐	White River Watch	Whiterun	None	This bandit hideout has several notes to collect. You can talk your way past Ulfr the Blind instead of killing him. You can listen to the bandits' mutiny plans, and free a wolf to fight the bandits for you (pull the chain on the right wall before you reach the cage). Hajvarr Iron-Hand is on the exterior overlook.	Note to Rodulf, Ulif's Book, Hajvar's Journal, Ironhand Gauntlets
☐	Whitewatch Tower	Whiterun	None	Some bandits attack this tower when you first approach. Help the guards fight them off, if you like.	Scavenged items

MISCELLANEOUS OBJECTIVES

This section of the guide deals with the dozens of Miscellaneous Objectives that appear in your Quest menu throughout your adventures. Like Favors, these are straightforward tasks with modest rewards, but some have unique elements, such as unlocking a dungeon or giving you access to a previously restricted area.

These are separated into Innkeeper Objectives (scuttlebutt and rumor you might hear at your favorite tavern) and Miscellaneous Objectives in each major settlement of Skyrim, separated by Hold. Note that each of these increases your relationship with the citizen you're doing the Favor for, which is important for your standing within a particular city (if you wish to complete any Thane Tasks).

Some Miscellaneous Objectives were important enough for us to flag with a quest name and the "*" symbol. The quest name won't appear in your Quest menu, but the Miscellaneous Objectives will be listed.

MISCELLANEOUS OBJECTIVES: INNKEEPERS

The following innkeepers are a good source for scuttlebutt across Skyrim. There is a (random) chance that they point you toward the start of a Side Quest or Daedric Quest, or contact with the Thieves Guild or Dark Brotherhood. They can also (randomly) provide you with Bounty Quests. Here are the innkeepers of Skyrim to check and the four types of Bounty Quests, which can be repeated:

INNKEEPERS OF SKYRIM

✓	HOLD LOCATION	SETTLEMENT	INN OR TAVERN	INNKEEPER
	Haafingar	Solitude	The Winking Skeever	Corpulus Vinius
	Haafingar	Dragon Bridge	Four Shields Tavern	Faida
	Hjaalmarch	Morthal	Moorside Inn	Jonna
	The Pale	Dawnstar	Windpeak Inn	Thoring
	The Pale	Nightgate Inn	Nightgate Inn (Interior)	Hadring
	Winterhold	Winterhold	The Frozen Hearth	Dagur
	The Reach	Markarth	Silver-Blood Inn	Kleppr
	Whiterun	Whiterun	The Bannered Mare	Hulda
	Whiterun	Rorikstead	Frostfruit Inn	Mralki
	Whiterun	Riverwood	Sleeping Giant Inn	Orgnar
	Eastmarch	Windhelm	Candlehearth Hall	Elda Early-Dawn
	Eastmarch	Kynesgrove	The Braidwood Inn	Iddra
	Falkreath	Falkreath	Dead Man's Drink	Valga Vinicia
	The Rift	Ivarstead	Vilemyr Inn	Wilhelm
	The Rift	Riften	The Bee and Barb	Keerava
	The Reach	Old Hroldan	Old Hroldan Inn	Eydis

BOUNTY QUESTS

✓	QUEST NAME	PREREQUISITES	QUEST DESCRIPTION	TARGET OR LOCATION	REWARD*
	Bounty: Bandits*	None	Slay the leader of a bandit camp	Bandit leader, [a random bandit camp]	Leveled Gold
	Bounty: Forsworn*	None	Slay the leader of a Forsworn camp	Forsworn Briarheart, [a random Forsworn camp]	Leveled Gold
	Bounty: Giant*	Level 20	Slay a giant	[A random giant]	Leveled Gold
	Bounty: Dragon*	Level 10, Main Quest: Dragon Rising completed	Slay a dragon	[A random dragon]	Leveled Gold

NOTE *Rewards are given by the Hold's Jarl or Steward.

MISCELLANEOUS OBJECTIVES: HAAFINGAR HOLD

Objectives: Dragon Bridge

✓	QUEST NAME	PREREQUISITES	QUEST GIVER	LOCATION	QUEST DESCRIPTION	TARGET OR LOCATION	REWARD
	Dragon's Breath Mead*	None	Olda	Horgeir's House	Retrieve the Dragon's Breath Mead from her drunk husband's stash	Dragon's Breath Mead, small cave overhang west of Dragon Bridge	Leveled Gold

Objectives: Solitude

✓	QUEST NAME	PREREQUISITES	QUEST GIVER	LOCATION	QUEST DESCRIPTION	TARGET OR LOCATION	REWARD
	No News is Good News *	None	Angeline Morrard	Angeline's Aromatics	Angeline hopes to know whether her daughter is safe. Ask, persuade, or intimidate Captain Aldis to learn that she died during an attack.	Captain Aldis, in or around Castle Dour courtyard.	None
	Fit for a Jarl *	None	Taarie	Radiant Raiment (or streets of Solitude)	Speak to Taarie and agree to wear an outfit while speaking to Jarl Elisif. Put on the Radiant Raiment Fine Clothes, and ask the Jarl what she thinks of your outfit. She agrees to purchase some dresses. Return to Taarie for your reward.	Radiant Raiment	Fine Clothes, Leveled Gold
	Return to Grace*	None	Svari	Streets of Solitude	Svari wants to convince her mother Greta to return to the Temple of the Divines. After speaking to Greta retrieve an amulet of Talos from the body of her brother Roggvir. Return to Greta with the Amulet for your reward.	Roggvir's Body (Executioner's Platform or Hall of the Dead)	Leveled Gold
	Delivery*	None	Sorex	Winking Skeever (or Streets of Solitude)	Sorex asks you to deliver Stros M'Kai Rum to Falk Firebeard. Deliver the rum directly to Falk in the Blue Palace and get your reward.	Leveled Gold	
	Spiced Wine Shipment*	None	Evette San	Market stalls	Evette is hoping that Vittoria Vici will release her Spiced Wine shipment. Persuade or bribe Vittoria Vici at the East Empire Company Warehouse to release the shipment, then return to Evette for the reward.	Vittoria Vici	2 Spiced Wine
	Elisif's Tribute*	Side Quest: The Man Who Cried Wolf	Elisif	Blue Palace	Elisif wants you to place Torygg's War Horn on a shrine of Talos as a tribute to her late husband. Take the War Horn to the specifed Shrine and place it at the foot of the statue of Talos, then return to Elisif for your reward.	Shrine of Talos: White River Valley [6.T]	Ability to Purchase Proudspire Manor

 MISCELLANEOUS OBJECTIVES: HJAALMARCH HOLD

Objectives: Morthal

✓	QUEST NAME	PREREQUISITES	QUEST GIVER	LOCATION	QUEST DESCRIPTION	TARGET OR LOCATION	REWARD
	Falion's Nocturnal Habits*	None	Falion	Summoning Plinth, in the Marshes	Follow Falion northwest out of town during the night. He walks to a summoning circle to practice magic.	Falion; blackmail him, keep his secret, tell the Jarl, or blackmail and then tell the Jarl. You can uncover his activity, which he wants to keep quiet.	200 gold pieces (for blackmail only)
	Gorm's Letter*	Visit Moorside Inn in the evening	Gorm	Moorside Inn	Deliver his letter to Captain Aldis, as Gorm is concerned about Idgrod's ability to perform her duties as Jarl.	Captain Aldis, in Solitude (Castle Dour courtyard). Hand the message to the Captain	20 gold pieces

Objectives: Stonehills

✓	QUEST NAME	PREREQUISITES	QUEST GIVER	LOCATION	QUEST DESCRIPTION	TARGET OR LOCATION	REWARD
	Slow Shipments to Bryling*	None	Pactur	Rockwallow Mine	Bryling grows impatient regarding shipments from the mine. Speak to her on behalf of Pactur	Thane Bryling, near or in the Blue Palace of Solitude. Tell her the shipment is coming; there is no need to return to Pactur	Leveled Gold

 MISCELLANEOUS OBJECTIVES: THE PALE

Objectives: Dawnstar

✓	QUEST NAME	PREREQUISITES	QUEST GIVER	LOCATION	QUEST DESCRIPTION	TARGET OR LOCATION	REWARD
	Salt of the Seas*	None	Captain Leif Wayfinder	Dawnstar (docked ship)	Wayfinder will pay gold for some special (and essential) Fine-Cut Void Salts.	Fine-Cut Void Salts, in a [random dungeon]	Leveled Gold

 MISCELLANEOUS OBJECTIVES: WINTERHOLD

Objectives: Ahkari's Caravan

✓	QUEST NAME	PREREQUISITES	QUEST GIVER	LOCATION	QUEST DESCRIPTION	TARGET OR LOCATION	REWARD
	New Moon*	None	Kharjo	Ahkari's Caravan (see [10.00] Caravans, in the Atlas for the route, on page 628)	Kharjo hopes you'll retrieve the Amulet of the Moon for him	Find and give the Amulet of the Moon, from [a random dungeon]	Leveled Gold

⬦ Objectives: College of Winterhold

✓	QUEST NAME	PREREQUISITES	QUEST GIVER	LOCATION	QUEST DESCRIPTION	TARGET OR LOCATION	REWARD
☐	Lost Apprentices: Borvir*	Listen to Phinis' Lecture	Phinis Gestor	College of Winterhold	A number of apprentices have gone missing. Phinis is worried; find information on them.	Journeyman's Nook [4.26]	Leveled gold (for all four)
☐	Lost Apprentices: Ilas-tei*	Listen to Phinis' Lecture	Phinis Gestor	College of Winterhold	A number of apprentices have gone missing. Phinis is worried; find information on them.	Shrine of Talos: Ilas-tei's Last Stand [4.J]	Leveled gold (for all four)
☐	Lost Apprentices: Rundi*	Listen to Phinis' Lecture	Phinis Gestor	College of Winterhold	A number of apprentices have gone missing. Phinis is worried; find information on them.	Rundi's Mistake [4.N]	Leveled gold (for all four)
☐	Lost Apprentices: Yisra*	Listen to Phinis' Lecture	Phinis Gestor	College of Winterhold	A number of apprentices have gone missing. Phinis is worried; find information on them.	Yisra's Beachside Combustion [4.D]	Leveled gold (for all four)

⬦ Objectives: Winterhold

✓	QUEST NAME	PREREQUISITES	QUEST GIVER	LOCATION	QUEST DESCRIPTION	TARGET OR LOCATION	REWARD
☐	Finding Isabelle	Favor: A Good Talking To (Winterhold)	Dagur, Ranmir, then Haran	The Frozen Hearth	Complete Haran's Favor, then speak with Dagur, and then Haran. You learn why Ranmir is a drunk; he believes the love of his life ran off with some man named "Vex" from Riften. Visit the Ragged Flagon in Riften to find out Vex isn't male, and Isabelle wasn't unfaithful. Vex directs you to Hob's Fall Cave. Head there, find Isabelle's body, with a note for Ranmir. Return the note to him.	Isabelle Rolaine, Hob's Fall Cave	None

---

MISCELLANEOUS OBJECTIVES: THE REACH

⬦ Objectives: Dushnikh Yal

✓	QUEST NAME	PREREQUISITES	QUEST GIVER	LOCATION	QUEST DESCRIPTION	TARGET OR LOCATION	REWARD
☐	The Sword of Gharol	Orc or Complete Side Quest: The Forgemaster's Fingers	Gharol	Dushnikh Yal	Deliver Gharol's sword to her daughter Lash gra-Dushnikh	Deliver the Iron Sword to Lash, in Karthwasten	Leveled Gold

⬦ Objectives: Karthwasten

✓	QUEST NAME	PREREQUISITES	QUEST GIVER	LOCATION	QUEST DESCRIPTION	TARGET OR LOCATION	REWARD
☐	Sauranach's Mine!: Helping Atar*	None	Atar or Ainethach	Sauranach Mine/ Blacksmith's near Karthwasten Hall	Speak to Atar, who is being paid by Silver-Bloods to plunder this mine and tie up who owns it	Ainethach; persuade, bribe, or intimidate him into handing the deeds over, then report back to Atar	Leveled Gold
☐	Sauranach's Mine!: Helping Ainethach*	None	Atar or Ainethach	Blacksmith's near Karthwasten Hall/ Sauranach Mine	Speak to Ainethach, whose mine is being plundered by Silver-Bloods, and agree to force out the mercenaries and Atar	Atar; persuade, bribe, or attack them until they leave, then report back to Ainethach	Leveled Gold

⬦ Objectives: Kolskeggr Mine

✓	QUEST NAME	PREREQUISITES	QUEST GIVER	LOCATION	QUEST DESCRIPTION	TARGET OR LOCATION	REWARD
☐	Kolskeggr Clear Out*	None	Pavo	Left Hand Mine (Primary Location near Markarth)	Speak to Pavo at Left Hand Mine, where he fled. Forsworn have taken over his mine, Kolskeggr. Remove them.	Clear around five Forsworn from inside the mine (before or after speaking to Pavo)	Leveled Gold (and any scavenged gold from the mine)

⬦ Objectives: Markarth

✓	QUEST NAME	PREREQUISITES	QUEST GIVER	LOCATION	QUEST DESCRIPTION	TARGET OR LOCATION	REWARD
☐	Calcelmo's Ring*	None	Kerah	Market stall (close to Silver-Blood Inn)	Calcelmo requires a ring, and Kerah doesn't have time to deliver it. Will you?	Take Calcelmo's Ring into Understone Keep; Calcelmo rewards you	Leveled Gold
☐	Dibella's Shine*	None	Lisbet	Arnleif and Sons Trading Company	You're asked to retrieve a statue of Dibella taken by the Forsworn, to keep the store in business	Lisbet's Dibella Statue [a random Forsworn camp]	Leveled Gold
☐	The Steward's Potion*	None	Bothela	The Hag's Cure	Speak to Bothela about the name of her shop. She asks you to deliver a potion to the Steward Raerek, for his "stamina."	Give Stallion's Potion to Raerek	Leveled Gold
☐	The Last Scabbard*	None	Ghorza gra-Bagol	Markarth Blacksmiths Forge	Ghorza is looking for a long-forgotten Smithing book. Find one for her.	The Last Scabbard of Akrash, in the Fort Sungard Muster (though any copy will do)	+1 Smithing (from reading the book), +1 Smithing (from Ghorza after handing her the book)

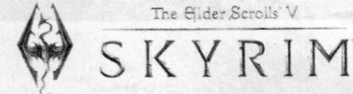

The Elder Scrolls V
SKYRIM

QUEST NAME	PREREQUISITES	QUEST GIVER	LOCATION	QUEST DESCRIPTION	TARGET OR LOCATION	REWARD
Triumph Over Talos*	None	Ondolemar	Understone Keep	The Thalmor advisor believes one of the population is secretly (and illegally) worshipping Talos. You're to find proof.	Ogmund's House (Novice), steal the Amulet of Talos inside, and bring it to Ondolemar	Leveled Gold
The Heart of the Matter*	None	Moth gro-Bagol	Understone Keep Forge	Ask Moth about his armor, and he requests you find him a Daedra Heart. Return with one to receive one of his best pieces of armor	Daedra Heart	Leveled Armor Piece
Neutralizing Nimhe*	Speak to Calcelmo about the excavation	Calcelmo	Understone Keep	A giant Frostbite Spider named Nimhe is troubling the excavation workers. Calcelmo agrees to let you into his museum if you kill the beast.	Use the Key to Nchuand-Zel, enter the excavation site, find and kill Nimhe, and report back.	Dwemer Museum Key

◈ Objectives: Old Hroldan

QUEST NAME	PREREQUISITES	QUEST GIVER	LOCATION	QUEST DESCRIPTION	TARGET OR LOCATION	REWARD
The Ghost of Old Hroldan*	None	Eydis/Ghost of Old Hrolden	Old Hroldan	Head into Old Hroldan Inn, speak to Eydis the barkeep, and pay to sleep in Tiber Septim's room. You wake to screaming. Eydis mentions a Ghost of Old Hroldan that has appeared. Talk to him, and he mentions his old friend Hjalti, and his sword. Agree to bring him the sword. Speak to Eydis again for the location. Visit it, retrieve the sword, and return it; the ghost vanishes.	Hjalti's Sword, in [a random dungeon]	+1 One-Handed and +1 Block Skill

◈ Objectives: Salvius Farm

QUEST NAME	PREREQUISITES	QUEST GIVER	LOCATION	QUEST DESCRIPTION	TARGET OR LOCATION	REWARD
Letter to Leonitus*	None	Rogatus Salvius	Salvius Farm	Rogatus has a letter he wants delivered to his son	Bring it to Leonitus Salvius at Old Hroldan	Leveled Gold

◈ Objectives: Soljund's Sinkhole

QUEST NAME	PREREQUISITES	QUEST GIVER	LOCATION	QUEST DESCRIPTION	TARGET OR LOCATION	REWARD
Making It Hole Again*	None	Perth	Entrance to Sinkhole Mine	Perth tunneled into a Nordic crypt, and the mine is overrun by Draugr. Clear them out.	Defeat 10 Draugr and a high-level leader in the mine and crypt, then report back to Perth.	Leveled gold

MISCELLANEOUS OBJECTIVES: WHITERUN HOLD

◈ Objectives: Rorikstead

QUEST NAME	PREREQUISITES	QUEST GIVER	LOCATION	QUEST DESCRIPTION	TARGET OR LOCATION	REWARD
Erik the Slayer	None	Erik	In the fields around town	Erik wants to live a life of an adventurer, but his father will not allow it. Speak to Mralki at the Frostfruit Inn; use Persuasion, Bribery, or Intimidation to approve of his son's new career.	Rorikstead	Leave town, then return. Erik the Slayer will be available as a hireling in the Frostfruit Inn.

◈ Objectives: Riverwood

QUEST NAME	PREREQUISITES	QUEST GIVER	LOCATION	QUEST DESCRIPTION AND TARGET/LOCATION	REWARD
The Love Triangle: Helping Sven*	None	Sven	Riverwood	Talk to Sven. Ask him about Faendal. Take the fake letter from Faendal to Camilla and say it's from Faendal. Return to Sven.	25 gold pieces, Sven: Follower
The Love Triangle: Betraying Sven*	None	Sven	Riverwood	Talk to Sven. Ask him about Faendal. Take the fake letter from Sven to Faendal. Tell him about Sven, and he hands you his own fake letter. Take the second letter to Camilla. Say it's from Sven. Return to Sven	25 gold pieces, Faendal: Follower
The Love Triangle: Helping Faendal*	None	Faendal	Riverwood	Talk to Faendal. Ask him about Sven. Take the fake letter from Sven to Camilla and say it's from Sven. Return to Faendal.	25 gold pieces, Faendal: Follower
The Love Triangle: Betraying Faendal*	None	Faendal	Riverwood	Talk to Faendal. Ask him about Sven. Take the fake letter from Faendal to Sven. Tell him about Faendal, and he hands you his own fake letter. Take the letter to Camilla. Say it's from Faendal. Return to Sven	25 gold pieces, Sven: Follower

> **NOTE** During any of these plans, you can tell Camilla the truth or lie to her, depending on who you wish to side with.

Objectives: Whiterun

✓	QUEST NAME	PREREQUISITES	QUEST GIVER	LOCATION	QUEST DESCRIPTION	TARGET AND/OR LOCATION	REWARD
	Bullying Braith*	Between 8 a.m. and 8 p.m.	Lars Battle-Born	On the streets of Whiterun	Lars is fed up being bullied by Braith. Stop her bullying him	Braith; any threat succeeds	2 gold pieces (from Lars, even if you don't complete the Quest)
	Argonian Ale Extraction*	None	Brenuin	On the streets of Whiterun	Brenuin the beggar longs for the taste of Argonian Ale. Can you steal some for him?	The Bannered Mare	Potion of Vigorous Healing
	Greatsword for a Great Man*	None	Adrianne Avenicci	Warmaiden's Blacksmiths	Adrianne is busy, but has finished a sword for the Jarl. Can you take it to her father?	Proventus Avenicci, in Dragonsreach. Hand over Balgruuf's Greatsword to him for the reward	20 gold pieces
	Andurs' Arkay Amulet*	None	Anders, Priest of Arkay	Hall of the Dead	Anders has mislaid his Amulet, and hopes you can retrieve it from the crypt.	Hall of the Dead. Kill three Skeletons. Return with Amulet of Arkay	15 gold pieces
	Salt for Arcadia*	None	Farengar	Dragonsreach	Farengar asks you to deliver some Frost Salts to Arcadia, in Arcadia's Cauldron.	Arcadia, in Arcadia's Cauldron. See Ingredients locations, on page 81	Potion of Brief Invisibility, Potion of Enhanced Stamina, Potion of Illusion

 **MISCELLANEOUS OBJECTIVES: EASTMARCH HOLD**

Objectives: Snapleg Cave/Darkwater Pass

✓	QUEST NAME	PREREQUISITES	QUEST GIVER	LOCATION	QUEST DESCRIPTION	TARGET OR LOCATION	REWARD
	Extracting an Argonian	None	Derkeethus	Darkwater Pass (Interior)	An Argonian named Derkeethus is trapped inside a Falmer Hive and needs rescuing.	Snapleg Cave/Darkwater Pass; open the wall section in the northeast corner in the grating room with Derkeethus below you. Open his gate (Expert) using the Darkwater Pit Key found in a jar, then escort Derkeethus to safety.	Follower: Derkeethus (and his friendship)

Objectives: Kynesgrove

✓	QUEST NAME	PREREQUISITES	QUEST GIVER	LOCATION	QUEST DESCRIPTION	TARGET OR LOCATION	REWARD
	Salt for the Stoneweaver*	None	Dravynea the Stoneweaver	Kynesgrove (around town)	Dravynea requires you to bring her some Frost Salts	See Ingredients Locations, on page 81	+1 Alteration skill

Objectives: Windhelm

✓	QUEST NAME	PREREQUISITES	QUEST GIVER	LOCATION	QUEST DESCRIPTION	TARGET OR LOCATION	REWARD
	Crew Cut*	None	Kjar	Windhelm docks (large docked ship)	Captain Kjar will pay handsomely if you slay an ex-crew mate who has been troubling him.	Bandit leader and bandits, in [a random bandit camp]	Leveled Gold
	Nightshade for the Unliving*	None	Hillevi Cruel-Sea	Stone Quarter Market Place	Hillevi hopes you'll have time to deliver Nightshade Extract to Wuunferth	Wuunferth the Unliving, in the Palace of the Kings (Upstairs)	100 gold pieces
	Malborn's Long Shadow*	Complete Main Quest: Diplomatic Immunity (Malborn survives)	Malborn	Gnisis Corner Club	Malborn (and Brelas, if she survived) heads here but is worried that a Khajiit Thalmor assassin is stalking him. Help him escape Windhelm.	Speak to the caravaneers who visit Windhelm until they tell you the name of the assassin: J'Datharr. You must kill J'Datharr. Then report back to Malborn	Leveled Gold

 MISCELLANEOUS OBJECTIVES: FALKREATH HOLD

Objectives: Falkreath

✓	QUEST NAME	PREREQUISITES	QUEST GIVER	LOCATION	QUEST DESCRIPTION	TARGET OR LOCATION	REWARD
	Once a Thalmor...*	None	Runil	Falkreath graveyard (or around town)	Speak to Runil, then retrieve his journal and return it to him for your reward.	A [random dungeon]	Leveled gold reward
	Vighar the Vampire*	Complete: Favor: A Little Light Thievery*	Dengeir of Stuhn	Falkreath (Dengeir's Hall)	Kill Vighar's ancestor, a powerful vampire.	[A random vampire lair]	Medium amount of gold

Objectives: Heartwood Mill

✓	QUEST NAME	PREREQUISITES	QUEST GIVER	LOCATION	QUEST DESCRIPTION	TARGET OR LOCATION	REWARD
☐	Fight or Flight*	None	Grosta	Heartwood Mill	Grosta's good-for-nothing husband has gone missing. Find that layabout.	Nord corpse, inside Broken Helm Hollow	Leveled enchanted weapon

Objectives: Ivarstead

✓	QUEST NAME	PREREQUISITES	QUEST GIVER	LOCATION	QUEST DESCRIPTION	TARGET OR LOCATION	REWARD
☐	The Straw That Broke*	None	Narfi	Abandoned building (west of river), Vilemyr Inn	Speak to Narfi about his vanished sister, then ask Wilhelm about Narfi. Begin the search for her.	Reyda's satchel, in the river just southeast of town, then bring Reyda's Necklace to Narfi	Three [random] rare ingredients
☐	Grin and Bear It*	None	Temba Wide-Arm	Lumber Mill	Temba is constantly fending off bear attacks. Perhaps you can thin the herd out?	Hunt 10 bears and skin them for pelts or buy the pelts (anywhere in Skyrim, of any bear type: Snow, Cave, or normal), and return them to her	Leveled Enchanted War Axe
☐	Climb the Steps*	None	Kimmek	Kimmek's House or around town	Kimmek delivers supplies to the Greybeards, but his knees can't take the climb.	Drop (via inventory) Kimmek's supplies into the offering chest at High Hrothgar	Leveled Gold

Objectives: Merryfair Farm

✓	QUEST NAME	PREREQUISITES	QUEST GIVER	LOCATION	QUEST DESCRIPTION	TARGET OR LOCATION	REWARD
☐	Bow to the Master*	None	Dravin Llanith	Merryfair Farm	Dravin's Bow has been stolen, and he wishes it returned.	Dravin's Bow, in a locked treasure chest in the Ratway Warrens, under Riften. Return the bow to him.	Leveled Gems (5)

Objectives: Riften

✓	QUEST NAME	PREREQUISITES	QUEST GIVER	LOCATION	QUEST DESCRIPTION	TARGET OR LOCATION	REWARD
☐	The Lover's Requital*	None	Sibbi Black-Briar	Mistveil Keep (Riften Jail)	Discover Svidi's whereabouts	Lynly Star-Sung (pseudonym of Svidi; bard in Vilemyr Inn, in Ivarstead) Speak to her, return to Sibbi, and lie or tell her the truth regarding where she is (the reward is the same)	Sibbi's Chest Key (opens the chest in the Black-Briar Meadery)
☐	Under the Table*	None	Romlyn Dreth	Black-Briar Meadery	Deliver smuggled Black-Briar Keg, or turn Romlyn in	Wilhelm; innkeeper in Vilemyr Inn in Ivarstead, or Overseer Indaryn, at the Meadery	Gem or jewelry reward. Not repeatable.
☐	Few and Far Between*	None	Ingun Black-Briar	Elgrim's Elixirs (wait for her to appear)	Collect 20 Deathbell, 20 Nightshade, and 20 Nirnroot for her experiments, then return to her	See Ingredients Locations, on page 81	Access to Ingun's Alchemy chest inside Elgrim's Elixirs
☐	Spread the Love*	Complete Temple Quest: The Book of Love	Dinya Balu	Temple of Mara	Deliver the "Warmth of Mara"; pamphlets praising the teachings of Mara	At least 20 citizens of Riften	Leveled Health Restore potion (5)
☐	Sealing the Deal*	None	Talen-Jei	The Bee and Barb	Talen-Jei wishes to show his love for Keerava by having a ring made with stones used in traditional Argonian wedding rings.	Three Flawless Amethysts	Leveled [Random] Potion
☐	Ice Cold*	None	Marise Aravel	Marketplace (cart next to the Bee and Barb)	Marise uses ground Ice Wraith Teeth to keep her foods fresh. She needs more.	Five Ice Wraith Teeth	Leveled Spell Tome and (delicious) Raw Pheasant
☐	Distant Memories*	None	Brand-Shei	Marketplace (Brand-Shei's stall)	Brand-Shei is hoping to recover memories of his past.	Lymdrenn Telvanni's Journal, in a waterlogged chest, in the Wreck of the Pride of Tel Vos	Brand-Shei's Strongbox Key (unlocks the strongbox inside his stall)
☐	Grimsever's Return*	None	Mjoll the Lioness	Marketplace, or around Riften	Mjoll laments the loss of her weapon, a fine longsword named "Grimsever"	Grimsever, in Mzinchaleft	Keep the weapon, or return it and have Mjoll as a Follower
☐	Stoking the Flames*	None	Balimund Iron-Boar	Scorched Hammer Blacksmiths	Balimund keeps his forge red-hot thanks to Fire Salts, but he's running low.	10 Fire Salts; see Ingredients Locations, on page 81	Leveled Gold

✓	QUEST NAME	PREREQUISITES	QUEST GIVER	LOCATION	QUEST DESCRIPTION	TARGET OR LOCATION	REWARD
☐	Caught Red-Handed*	None	Svana Far-Shield	Haelga's Bunkhouse	Svana is angry at Haelga's promiscuous ways and wants you to retrieve three Marks of Dibella from her conquests	Bolli; at the Fishery. Hofgrir Horse-Crusher; at the stables. Overseer Indaryn; at Black-Briar Meadery, but all like to drink at the Bee and Barb. Use Persuasion, Intimidation, or Pickpocketing	Leveled Enchanted Heavy Armor (piece)
☐	Pilgrimage*	None	Alessandra	Hall of the Dead	Riften's Priest of Arkay has never made peace with her dead father. You are to make a pilgrimage for her	Hand Alessandra's Dagger to Andurs, inside Whiterun's Hall of the Dead, then return to her	Leveled Restoration Spell Tome
☐	Hunt and Gather*	None	Wylandriah	Mistveil Keep	Riften's Court Wizard, an eccentric crackpot, has mislaid some of her experimental gear. Collect them all.	Wylandriah's Spoon: Fellstar Farm in Ivarstead. Wylandriah's Ingot: The Frozen Hearth in Winterhold. Wylandriah's Soul Gem: The White Phial in Windhelm	Leveled [Random] Scroll
☐	Special Delivery*	None	Bolli	Riften Fishery	Bolli wishes to make a deal on behalf of the Fishery to sell fish to Kleppr in Markarth	Hand the Purchase Agreement from Bolli to Kleppr at Silver-Blood Inn	Leveled Ingot (4)
☐	Bring It!*	None	Harrald	Mistveil Keep	The spoiled son of the Jarl is too lazy to retrieve his own sword. You're told to bring it back to him	Steel Sword, from Balimund at the Scorched Hammer	Leveled Gem (2)
☐	Truth Ore Consequences*	None	Hafjorg	Elgrim's Elixirs	Hafjorg asks you to pick up an ore sample from Filnjar in Shor's Stone so it can be examined	Quicksilver Ore, from Filnjar	Leveled Skill Potions (a few; random)
☐	Ringmaker*	None	Madesi	Marketplace	Riften's jeweler has a short list of items needed to continue creating his exquisite Argonian-made jewelry	Gold Ore (1), Mammoth Tusk (1), Flawless Sapphire (2)	Leveled Jewelry
☐	Bloody Nose*	100 gold pieces	Hofgrir Horse-Crusher	Riften Stables	Hofgrir challenges you to a fistfight to test your mettle	Beat Hofgrir in a brawl (only use fists!)	200 gold pieces (100 of which was yours when betting)
☐	Toying with the Dead*	None	Vekel the Man	Ragged Flagon (Riften)	Vekel has found a buyer for a peculiar set of journals written by a long-dead necromancer. But he needs you to find them.	Arondil's Journals, Inside Yngvild (page 481)	Leveled Enchanted One-Handed Weapon
☐	Shardr and Sapphire*	None	Shadr	Around Riften	Sapphire (from the Thieves Guild) has bilked Shadr by lending him money to buy a shipment of goods that she also robbed, and she still wants the money!	(1) Pay off the debt in Shadr's stead, using Persuade or Intimidate against Sapphire. (2) Cut yourself into the deal with Sapphire if you're a member of the Thieves Guild, before returning to tell Shadr there's nothing you can do. (3) Threaten Sapphire to tell Brynjolf and she drops the debt. (4) If you're a Thieves Guild leader, choose plan 1 without any Persuasion or Intimidation, or plan 2.	Helping Shardr: Leveled Invisibility Potion. Helping Sapphire: Leveled Gold
☐	Jarl's Quest Part 1: Helping Hand*	Potion of Minor Healing	Wujeeta	Riften Fishery	The Argonian is sick from a Skooma overdose, and pleads for a Healing potion to cleanse her system	Hand her a Healing potion (minor or otherwise)	Silver Amethyst Ring
☐	Jarl's Quest Part 2: The Raid*	Complete Jarl's Quest Part 1	Wujeeta, Jarl Laila	Riften Fishery/ Mistveil Keep	Speak to Wujeeta, and use Persuasion, Bribery, or Intimidation to find out about the Skooma dealer. Then speak to Jarl Laila Law-Giver in Mistveil Keep.	Riften Warehouse: Head to the Warehouse and slay Orini Dral and Sarthis Idren. Search Sarthis for his key to open the cellar door. Steal the Shipment's Ready note from his satchel.	None
☐	Jarl's Quest Part 3: Supply and Demand*	Complete Jarl's Quest Part 2	Jarl Laila	Mistveil Keep	Report the Skooma manufacturing operation to the Jarl, who sends you to kill the Dark Elves at Cragslane Cavern.	Wipe out everyone there (wolf kills are optional), then return to the Jarl.	Leveled Enchanted Weapon
☐	Erasing Vald's Debt*	Thieves Guild Quest: The Pursuit is active (and hasn't been completed)	Maven Black-Briar	The Bee and Barb/Black-Briar Manor	Speak to Maven once you wish to remove Vald's debt.	She needs you to locate the Quill of Germination Vald failed to retrieve. The Quill is in a strongbox beneath a small island, in Lake Honrich	Document absolving Vald of his debt (see quest for details)
☐	Gissur's Revenge*	Main Quest: A Cornered Rat is active	No one	The Ratway/ Ragged Flagon	If Gissur is alive at the end of Main Quest: Diplomatic Immunity, he may be spotted in the Ragged Flagon. Slay him or leave him alone. He eavesdrops if you speak to Dirge or Vekel. You can (sneak and) follow him into the Ratway, listening to Gissur telling Thalmor troops where you are. Attack or hide.	Gissur, the Ratway/Ragged Flagon	None
☐	Shavari the Assassin*	Main Quest: A Cornered Rat is active	No one	The Ratway/ Ratway Warrens	A Khajiit named Shavari is dispatched by Elenwen at the Thalmor Embassy to assassinate you. Kill her if you encounter her, or be killed.	Shavari, the Ratway	Note, signed by "E"

The Elder Scrolls V SKYRIM

PRIMA OFFICIAL GAME GUIDE   WWW.PRIMAGAMES.COM

Objectives: Sarethi Farm

✔	QUEST NAME	PREREQUISITES	QUEST GIVER	LOCATION	QUEST DESCRIPTION	TARGET OR LOCATION	REWARD
	Smooth Jazbay*	None	Avrusa Sarethi	Sarethi Farm	Avrusa is a keen cultivator of Nirnroot but requires some ingredients for her farm.	Find 20 Jazbay Grapes; see Ingredients Locations, on page 81	Leveled Potions (a few, random)

Objectives: Shor's Stone

✔	QUEST NAME	PREREQUISITES	QUEST GIVER	LOCATION	QUEST DESCRIPTION	TARGET OR LOCATION	REWARD
	Mine or Yours*	None	Filnjar	Blacksmith's Forge	The Redbelly Mine is no longer in operation due to a Frostbite Spider infestation. Kill them for Filnjar	Redbelly Mine; kill six Frostbite Spiders, then return to Filnjar	Leveled Gold
	Letters for Mr. Rock-Chucker*	None	Sylgja	Sylgja's House	Sylgja asks if you'll mind delivering a satchel of letters to her parents	Take Sylgja's Satchel to Verner Rock-Chucker in Darkwater Crossing; bring Verner's Satchel back to her afterward	Leveled jewelry

FAVORS

Favors are miscellaneous objectives or small activities that you can find throughout Skyrim. Favors are controlled by the game's Radiant Story system, which uses a variety of factors to determine when to start a given quest. This means that not all Favors will be available at all times; in particular, you can only be on one Favor of each type at a time. For example, if you start one Rare Item Hunt, you must finish it before beginning another.

This section details all of the available Favors you can attempt during your exploration of Skyrim. Note that each of these increases your Relationship with the citizen you're doing the Favor for, which is important for your standing within a particular city. If the citizen isn't a resident of the city, then you perform the Favor simply to accrue a reward, to pass the time, or to be a pleasant person. This chapter is segmented into three parts:

Part 1 — Activity Favors: Deals with manual labor you can do to earn an honest pay. Which you can then share with beggars if you wish.

Part 2 — Favors for Citizens: Lists every resident in Skyrim who has a job for you to do if you speak to them.

Part 3 — Thane Tasks: Reveals how to become a Thane (or a land-owning, respected resident) of each particular Hold, and the house you can purchase.

PART 1: ACTIVITY FAVORS

Favor (Activity): Chopping Wood*

 **NOTE** ✳ Quest names marked with this symbol do not appear in your Quest Menu list, although objectives may.

Visit one of the following locations and speak to the person specified (usually a lumbermill owner) in the table below. They will gladly pay for any firewood you chop. Find a Woodcutter's Axe (there should be one near the woodpile at this location), find a pile of wood, and continue to chop, before heading to the person for a reward.

➤ **Woodcutter's Axe**

➤ **Five gold pieces per piece of firewood chopped**

✔	HOLD	LOCATION	FIREWOOD PURCHASER
	Haafingar	Dragon Bridge	Horgeir
	Haafingar	Solitude Sawmill	Hjorunn
	Hjaalmarch	Morthal	Hroggar
	Hjaalmarch	Morthal	Jorgen
	The Pale	Anga's Mill	Aeri
	Eastmarch	Mixwater Mill	Gilfre
	Eastmarch	Kynesgrove	Ganna Uriel
	Whiterun	Riverwood	Hod
	Whiterun	Whiterun (The Bannered Mare)	Hulda
	Falkreath	Half-Moon Mill	Hert
	The Rift	Heartwood Mill	Grosta
	The Rift	Ivarstead	Temba Wide-Arm

Favor (Activity): Mining Ore*

Head to one of the following locations, and converse with the character specified (usually a mine owner) in the table below. They are happy to pay for any ore you mine. Find a Pickaxe (there should be a few inside any of the mines you visit) and locate a vein within the mine. Strike it, gather the ore, and head to the person for a reward.

- ➤ **Pickaxe**
- ➤ **25 gold pieces per Silver ore**
- ➤ **25 gold pieces per Quicksilver ore**
- ➤ **20 gold pieces per Orichalcum ore**
- ➤ **30 gold pieces per Moonstone ore**
- ➤ **30 gold pieces per Malachite ore**
- ➤ **7 gold pieces per Iron ore**
- ➤ **50 gold pieces per Gold ore**
- ➤ **60 gold pieces per Ebony ore**
- ➤ **20 gold pieces per Corundum ore**

✓	HOLD	LOCATION	ORE PURCHASER	ORE TYPE
	Hjaalmarch	Stonehills	Gestur Rockbreaker	Iron
	The Pale	Dawnstar	Beitild	Iron
	The Pale	Dawnstar	Leigelf	Quicksilver
	Winterhold	Whistling Mine	Thorgar	Iron
	The Reach	Dushnikh Yal	Gharol	Orichalcum
	The Reach	Left Hand Mine	Skaggi Scar-Face	Iron
	The Reach	Mor Khazgur	Shuftharz	Orichalcum
	Eastmarch	Darkwater Crossing	Verner Rock-Chucker	Corundum
	Eastmarch	Kynesgrove	Kjeld	Malachite
	Eastmarch	Narzulbur	Dushnamub	Ebony
	The Rift	Shor's Stone	Grogmar gro-Burzag	Iron

Favor (Activity): Harvesting Crops*

Trek over to any of the following farms and strike up a conversation with the character mentioned in the table below. They are grateful and pay for any crops you wish to harvest (from their property or anywhere else). Note the exact crops the character wishes to purchase; only pick those if you want to be paid for your labor, as there are usually more than these crop types in the locations.

- ➤ **Five gold pieces per Wheat**
- ➤ **One gold piece per Potato**
- ➤ **One gold piece per Leek**
- ➤ **Two gold pieces per Cabbage**
- ➤ **One gold pieces per Gourd**
- ➤ **Ten gold pieces per Nirnroot**

✓	HOLD	LOCATION	CROP PURCHASER	CROP TYPE
	Haafingar	Katla's Farm	Katla	Wheat, Potato, Leek
	The Reach	Salvius Farm	Vigdis Salvius	Potato
	Falkreath	Falkreath	Mathies	Cabbage, Gourd, Potato
	Whiterun	Rorikstead	Reldith	Wheat, Cabbage, Potato
	Whiterun	Rorikstead	Lemkil	Cabbage, Potato, Wheat
	The Rift	Ivarstead	Boti	Cabbage, Potato, Wheat
	Whiterun	Battle-Born Farm	Alfhild Battle-Born	Wheat, Leek, Gourds
	Eastmarch	Brandy-Mug Farm	Bolfrida Brandy-Mug	Wheat
	Eastmarch	Hlaalu Farm	Belyn Hlaalu	Wheat
	Eastmarch	Hollyfrost Farm	Tulvur	Wheat
	Haafingar	Dragon Bridge	Azzada Lylvieve	Wheat, Cabbage, Potato
	The Rift	Sarethi Farm	Avrusa Sarethi	Potato, Nirnroot, Gourds
	The Rift	Snow-Shod Farm	Addvild	Wheat, Leek, Potato
	Whiterun	Pelagia Farm	Severio Pelagia	Cabbage, Potato
	The Rift	Merryfair Farm	Synda Llanith	Wheat, Cabbage, Gourd

Favor (Activity): A Drunk's Drink*

Mosey on over to your favorite inn or tavern, or the streets surrounding an inn, and you're likely to be accosted by a reasonably friendly drunk. If you purchase a drink for them, expect the rudiments of a dance (although it's more of a stagger) as your reward. The following drunks are particularly parched:

✓	HOLD	LOCATION	DRUNK
	Haafingar	Thalmor Embassy	Razelan‡
	The Pale	Dawnstar (Windpeak Inn)	Karl
	Winterhold	Winterhold (The Frozen Hearth)	Ranmir
	The Reach	Markarth (Silver-Blood Inn)	Cosnach
	The Reach	Markarth (Silver-Blood Inn)	Degaine
	Whiterun	Riverwood (Sleeping Giant Inn)	Embry
	Eastmarch	Windhelm	Torbjorn Shatter-Shield

 NOTE ‡During Main Quest: Diplomatic Immunity only

Favor (Activity): The Gift of Charity*

Walk the streets of any Hold City, and you may be approached by a tattered or downtrodden beggar. You can ignore them or give them a gold piece as charity. The beggars you can give to are listed below, and your thoughtfulness is duly rewarded.

- ➤ **The Gift of Charity:** +10 to Speech for one hour

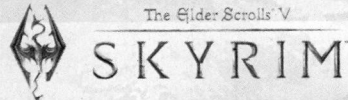

✓	HOLD	LOCATION	BEGGAR
	The Ragged Flagon	Riften	Gissur‡
	The Rift	Riften	Snilf
	Eastmarch	Windhelm	Angrenor Once-Honored
	Eastmarch	Windhelm	Silda the Unseen
	Whiterun	Whiterun	Brenuin
	The Rift	Ivarstead	Narfi

✓	HOLD	LOCATION	BEGGAR
	The Reach	Markarth	Degaine
	The Rift	Riften	Edda
	Haafingar	Solitude	Svari
	Haafingar	Solitude	Noster One-Eye
	Haafingar	Solitude	Dervenin

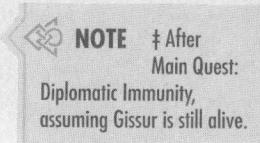

NOTE ‡ After Main Quest: Diplomatic Immunity, assuming Gissur is still alive.

 **PART 2: FAVORS FOR CITIZENS**

Favor: Special Delivery*

Visit the location specified, and converse with the Favor giver. They have an important item that needs to be delivered to someone in Skyrim. The recipient rewards you with a small amount of gold pieces. The following citizens of Skyrim have Delivery Favors for you:

➤ **Gold pieces (leveled, per delivery)**

✓	FAVOR GIVER	LOCATION FAVOR RECEIVED (HOLD/ LOCATION NAME)	ITEM TO DELIVER	RECIPIENT	RECIPIENT LOCATION (HOLD/LOCATION NAME)
	Adonato Leotelli	Eastmarch/Windhelm (Candlehearth Hall)	Adonato's Book	Giraud Gemane	Haafingar/Solitude (Bard's College)
	Aeri	The Pale/Anga's Mill	Aeri's Note	Jarl Skald the Elder	The Pale/Dawnstar (The White Hall)
	Banning	The Reach/Markarth Stables	Spiced Beef	Voada	The Reach/Markarth (Understone Keep)
	Idgrod the Younger	Hjaalmarch/Morthal	Idgrod's Note	Danica Pure-Spring	Whiterun/Whiterun (Temple of Kynareth)
	Sondas Drenim	Eastmarch/Darkwater Crossing	Sondas's Note	Quintus Navale	Eastmarch/Windhelm (The White Phial)
	Thadgeir	Falkreath/Falkreath	Berit's Ashes	Runil	Falkreath/Falkreath (graveyard)

Favor: A Good Talking To*

Locate the Favor giver and speak with them. It appears that they're having problems with a particular individual pestering, intimidating, or otherwise hassling them. Visit the instigator of this verbal assault, and attempt to sway them to the Favor giver's side. This is always achieved with a Persuasion, Bribe, Intimidation, or Brawl (fists only). After success with any of these, return to the Favor giver to receive a specific reward:

✓	FAVOR GIVER	LOCATION (HOLD/LOCATION NAME)	PROBLEM	INSTIGATOR	REWARD
	Carlotta Valentia	Whiterun/Whiterun (Bannered Mare)	Unwanted advances from a bard	Mikael	Small amount of gold
	Haran	Winterhold/ Winterhold (The Frozen Hearth)	A significant tavern tab	Ranmir	Leveled weapon and armor
	Iddra	Eastmarch/ Kynesgrove	Worrying about debts	Roggi Knot-Beard	Leveled weapon and armor
	Octieve San	Haafingar/Solitude	Gambling debts	Irnskar	+1 Two-Handed skill
	Omluag	The Reach/Markarth	A bullying smelter overseer	Mulush	Small amount of gold
	Scouts-Many-Marshes	Eastmarch/Windhelm Docks	A fare wage from a racist overseer	Torbjorn Shatter-Shield	Leveled potion

Favor: Sparring Partners*

If you think of yourself as an adventurer with lighting fists and a granite chin, you may wish to earn a swift 100 gold pieces by listening to the challenges of the following folk. They each have a reason for fighting you, and the combat is brawling only (just use fists, or risk enraging the entire settlement). Knock your opponent to their knees and win 100 gold pieces. Lose, and your adversary gains the gold.

➤ **100 gold pieces**

✓	PUGILIST	REASON FOR BRAWL	LOCATION (HOLD/LOCATION NAME)
	Benor	He's the strongest warrior and wants to prove it	Hjaalmarch/Morthal
	Burguk	A sparring partner is needed	The Reach/Dushnikh Yal
	Cosnach	To add excitement to his drunken day	The Reach/Markarth
	Larak	A sparring partner is needed	The Reach/Mor Khazgur
	Mauhulakh	A sparring partner is needed	Eastmarch/Narzulbur
	Rolff	You're an elf lover	Eastmarch/Windhelm
	Uthgerd	She's the strongest warrior and wants to prove it	Whiterun/Whiterun

Favor: A Little Light Thievery*

Visit the person listed, who is in the same general vicinity as the location mentioned, and speak to them. They want you to visit a location and steal an important item. The item in question isn't on a person; it is in the location itself, allowing you to utilize Sneak or Magic to augment your stealth. Violence is inadvisable. Once you steal the item, you are to return and claim a specific reward.

✓	FAVOR GIVER	ITEM TO STEAL	LOCATION OF THEFT (HOLD/LOCATION NAME)	REWARD GIVEN
	Dengeir of Stuhn	Suspicious Letter	Falkreath/Falkreath (Lod's House)	Small amount of gold
	Malur Seloth	Nelacar's Staff	Winterhold/Winterhold (The Frozen Hearth)	+1 Speech skill
	Stands-in-Shadows	Double-Distilled Skooma	Eastmarch/Windhelm (Gnisis Cornerclub)	+1 Sneak Skill

Favor: A Little Light Burglary*

Locate Revyn Sadri (the only fellow who wants this Favor completed) in the Gray Quarter of Windhelm. He's usually in Sadri's Used Wares. Sadri has found out that a ring he purchased was stolen from Imperial Noblewoman Viola Giordano, who lives in her house in the swanky Valunstrad District. Break into her house, place the ring into her dresser, and return to Revyn.

➤ **Medium gold reward**

Favor: The Bandit Slayer*

Visit the Favor giver, who requires you to slay a troublesome bandit leader, located in a random bandit camp somewhere in Skyrim. Journey there, ignoring or slaying any other enemies that guard the place. Locate the bandit specified and kill him. Then return to the Favor giver for a reward.

✓	FAVOR GIVER	FAVOR GIVER LOCATION (HOLD/LOCATION NAME)	REASON FOR KILLING	REWARD GIVEN
	Ahtar	Haafingar/Solitude (Castle Dour Jail)	He let the bandit leader escape from jail.	Large amount of gold. Follower: Ahtar.
	Annekke	Eastmarch/Darkwater Crossing	She spotted them on her adventures.	+1 Light Armor skill
	Brunwulf Free-Winter	Eastmarch/Windhelm	Help against bandit marauders	Small amount of gold, and +1 Heavy Armor skill

Favor: The Vampire Slayer*

 NOTE You must be Level 10 or higher to start this Favor.

Visit Sybille Stentor, the Court Wizard of Solitude, who stands with the Jarl in the Blue Palace. Unpleasant though she is, she offers you work to clear out a nearby vampire's lair (which is randomly determined). Journey there, ignoring or slaying any other enemies that guard the place. Locate the vampire specified and kill him or her. Then return to Sybille for the reward.

➤ Leveled Jewelry Reward   ➤ +1 Illusion skill

Favor: Rare Item Hunt*

Journey to the Favor giver's location, and speak to them. They require you to find a specific and rare item located somewhere in Skyrim (the place is randomly determined but appears on your world map). Should you find this coveted item and return it to them, you receive a reward appropriate for the time spent looking.

✓	FAVOR GIVER	FAVOR GIVER LOCATION (HOLD/LOCATION NAME)	RARE ITEM	REASON FOR ITEM RETRIEVAL	REWARD GIVEN
	Captain Aldis	Haafingar/Solitude	The Mirror (Book)	To help him train his men in blocking	Medium amount of gold
	Torbjorn Shatter-Shield	Eastmarch/Windhelm	Amulet of Arkay	To help his wife mourn the loss of their child	Medium amount of gold
	Ysolda	Whiterun/Whiteun (Ysolda's House)	Mammoth Tusk	To impress some Khajiit caravaneers	+1 Speech skill
	Jarl Siddgeir	Falkreath/Falkreath	Black-Briar Mead	As a tribute	Leveled Potion
	Rustleif	The Pale/Dawnstar	Night Falls on Sentinel (Book)	To read to his soon-to-be-born half-Redguard child	+1 Smithing skill
	Lami	Hjaalmarch/Morthal	Song of the Alchemists (Book)	The book she read as a girl, when studying alchemy	+1 Alchemy skill

Favor: Item Retrieval (Bandit Camp)*

Journey to where the Favor giver is and speak to them. They need you to journey to a [random] bandit camp, find a specific item stolen from them, and return it safely. When this occurs, you receive a reward appropriate for the time spent looking.

✓	FAVOR GIVER	FAVOR GIVER LOCATION (HOLD/LOCATION NAME)	STOLEN ITEM	REWARD GIVEN
	Amren	Whiterun/Whiterun	Amren's Father's Sword	+1 Block skill, +1 One-Handed skill
	Shahvee	Eastmarch/Windhelm Docks	Amulet to Zenithar (the Divine of Fortune)	+1 Light Armor skill, +1 Lockpicking skill

Favor: Item Retrieval (Cave)*

Head over to where the Favor giver is and chat with them. They require you to trek to a [random] cave, find a specific item they have mislaid or are looking for, and return it safely. When this occurs, you receive a reward appropriate for the time spent looking.

✓	FAVOR GIVER	FAVOR GIVER LOCATION (HOLD/LOCATION NAME)	REQUIRED ITEM	REWARD GIVEN
	Oengul War-Anvil‡	Eastmarch/Windhelm (Palace of the Kings)	High Queen Freydis's Sword	+1 Smithing skill
	Roggi	Eastmarch/Kynesgrove	Lenne's Ancestral Shield	+1 Block skill
	Runil	Falkreath/Falkreath (House of Arkay)	Runil's Journal	Large amount of gold
	Frida	The Pale/Dawnstar (The Mortar and Pestle)	Ring of Pure Mixtures	+1 Alchemy skill
	Noster One-Eye	Haafingar/Solitude	Legion Helmet	+1 Sneak skill

Favor: Jobs for the Jarls*

The Jarl of a particular Hold has a task for you to complete. This usually involves killing some troublesome foes who are annoying or terrifying the Hold's population or retrieving a lost item of great importance. The enemy or item is located in a random place, usually within the Jarl's Hold. Complete the task, return to the Jarl, and expect an impressive payment for your time.

✔	FAVOR GIVER	PREREQUISITES	FAVOR GIVER LOCATION (HOLD/LOCATION NAME)	TASK	TARGET LOCATION	REWARD GIVEN
	Jarl Igmund	None	The Reach/Markarth (Understone Keep)	Kill [a Forsworn leader] to prove yourself	A Forsworn camp	Large amount of gold
	Jarl Skald the Elder	Level 22	The Pale/Dawnstar (The White Hall)	Deal with [a giant] in the Pale	A giant camp	Large amount of gold
	Jarl Siddgeir	None	Falkreath/Falkreath (Jarl's Longhouse)	Kill [a bandit leader] he's had dealings with	A bandit camp	Large amount of gold
	Jarl Igmund	Level 20	The Reach/Markarth (Understone Keep)	Kill [a Hagraven] and bring back his father's shield	A Hagraven nest	Leveled armor, available house to purchase in Markarth
	Jarl Korir	None	Winterhold/Winterhold (Jarl's Longhouse)	Return with the Helm of Winterhold	A cave	Large amount of gold

 CRAFTING TUTORIALS

Crafting Tutorial: Blacksmithing*

A Blacksmith of great prowess walks you through the smithing process. You must make a dagger and sharpen it. Then tan some leather, make a helm, and temper it.

✔	TUTORIAL GIVER	HOLD	TUTORIAL LOCATION	TASK
	Alvor	Whiterun	Riverwood Blacksmiths (Alvor and Sigrid's House)	Complete the smithing process
	Adrianne Avenicci	Whiterun	Whiterun Blacksmiths (Warmaiden's)	Complete the smithing process

Crafting Tutorial: Alchemy*

An Alchemist (er, bartender) of exceptional ability instructs you on how to make a potion.

✔	TUTORIAL GIVER	HOLD	TUTORIAL LOCATION	TASK
	Orgnar	Whiterun	Riverwood (Sleeping Giant Inn)	Make a potion
	Arcadia	Whiterun	Whiterun (Arcadia's Cauldron)	Make a potion
	Zaria	Falkreath	Falkreath (Grave Concoctions)	Make a potion

Crafting Tutorial: Enchanting*

A wizard of some considerable talent explains how to use the Arcane Enchanter.

✔	TUTORIAL GIVER	HOLD	TUTORIAL LOCATION	TASK
	Farengar Secret-Fire	Whiterun	Dragonsreach, inside Whiterun	Use the Arcane Enchanter

> **NOTE** For more information on crafting, consult the Training Chapter, on page 41. Remember, there are far more Blacksmiths, Alchemists, and Enchanters in Skyrim, but only the ones in the preceding tables go through the crafting process with you.

Becoming a powerful and impressive member of Skyrim society culminates in the title "Thane." Follow our advice, and your good deeds pay off in the form of a piece of property you can purchase (and decorate) in each of the five major Holds. You also get the services of your own Housecarl. There is one Housecarl per Hold. They wait for you in the same building as the Jarl or at your house (after purchase). Take one of them as a Follower at a time. For the "minor" Holds, there are no houses or Housecarls. You can be a Thane of multiple Holds, but there is no bonus if you're a Thane of Skyrim (that is, of all nine Holds):

 NOTE "Good deeds" means helping the citizens of the Hold or Capital you're in, including the Jarl. Helping members of the Thieves Guild, Dark Brotherhood, or other guild does not count.

 Thane of Haafingar*

Part 1—Friend of the Jarl: Jarl Elisif the Fair is the leader of Solitude. You must have finished Side Quest: The Wolf Queen Awakened, which is related to her Hold. You must also have completed the task she set for you. See Miscellaneous Objectives: Elisif's Tribute for more information.

Part 2—Friend of the City: You must now win the respect of the inhabitants of Solitude. Speak to Jarl Elisif, who asks you to assist the people of this Hold. Return to her once you've finished five (or more) Favors, tasks, or objectives that benefit the people. Consult the Miscellaneous Objectives and Favors sections of this guide, looking for "Solitude" as the location for tasks, Favors, and objectives.

Part 3—House in the City: Finally, you must purchase a piece of property in the city. Speak to the Jarl, and you're informed that a house is for sale. You're referred to Steward Falk Firebeard. The following residence is available:

House Name: Proudspire Manor

Cost: 25,000 gold pieces

➤ **Key to Proudspire Manor**

Visit the house and meet your Housecarl, Jordis the Sword-Maiden there. Return to the Jarl, who grants you the title of Thane and a reward. Guards in Haafingar now ignore one crime as long as your Bounty is less than 2,000.

➤ **Thane Title**

➤ **Blade of Haafingar (leveled enchanted sword)**

➤ **House:** Proudspire Manor

➤ **Follower:** Jordis the Sword-Maiden

Thane of Hjaalmarch*

Part 1—Friend of the Jarl: You must first befriend the Jarl of Morthal, achieved by completing either of the following:

 Jarl Igrod Ravencrone is the leader of Morthal. In order to befriend her, you must finish Side Quest: Laid to Rest, which takes place in her Hold.

 Jarl Sorli the Builder is the leader of Morthal once it has fallen into Stormcloak hands. To start this task with Sorli, you must have captured Hjaalmarch Hold, as part of the Civil War Quests.

Part 2—Friend of the City: You must now win the respect of the inhabitants of Morthal. Speak to the Jarl, who asks you to assist the people of this Hold. Return to the Jarl once you've finished three (or more) Favors, tasks, or objectives that benefit the people. Consult the Miscellaneous Objectives and Favors sections of this guide, looking for "Morthal" as the location for tasks, Favors, and objectives.

Return to the Jarl, who grants you the title of Thane and a reward. Guards in Hjaalmarch now ignore one crime as long as your Bounty is less than 2,000.

➤ **Thane Title**   ➤ **Blade of Hjaalmarch (Leveled Enchanted Sword)**

 NOTE There is no house to purchase in this Hold.

Thane of The Pale*

Part 1—Friend of the Jarl: You must first befriend the Jarl of Dawnstar, achieved by completing either of the following:

 Jarl Skald the Elder is the leader of Dawnstar. You must have finished Daedric Quest: Waking Nightmare, which is related to his Hold. You must also have completed the task he set for you. See the "Favor: Jobs for the Jarls" section of this guide for more information.

 Jarl Brina Merilis is the leader of Dawnstar once it has fallen into Imperial hands. To start this task with Brina, you must have captured the Pale Hold, as part of the Civil War Quests.

Part 2—Friend of the City: You must now win the respect of the inhabitants of Dawnstar. Speak to the Jarl, who asks you to assist the people of this Hold. Return to the Jarl once you've finished three (or more) Favors, tasks, or objectives that benefit the people. Consult the Miscellaneous Objectives and Favors sections of this guide, looking for "Dawnstar" as the location for tasks, Favors, and objectives.

Return to the Jarl, who grants you the title of Thane and a reward. Guards in the Pale now ignore one crime as long as your Bounty is less than 2,000.

➤ **Thane Title**

➤ **Blade of the Pale (Leveled Enchanted Sword)**

 NOTE There is no house to purchase in this Hold.

Thane of Winterhold*

Part 1—Friend of the Jarl: You must first befriend the Jarl of Winterhold, achieved by completing either of the following:

Jarl Korir is the leader of Winterhold. You must have completed the task he set for you. See the "Favor: Jobs for the Jarls" section of this guide for more information.

Jarl Kraldar is the leader of Winterhold once it has fallen into Imperial hands. To start this task with Kraldar, you must have captured Winterhold Hold, as part of the Civil War Quests.

Part 2—Friend of the City: You must now win the respect of the inhabitants of Winterhold. Speak to the Jarl, who asks you to assist the people of this Hold. Return to the Jarl once you've finished three (or more) Favors, tasks, or objectives that benefit the people. Consult the Miscellaneous Objectives and Favors sections of this guide, looking for "Winterhold" as the location for tasks, Favors, and objectives.

Return to the Jarl, who grants you the title of Thane and a reward. Guards in Winterhold now ignore one crime as long as your Bounty is less than 2,000.

➤ **Thane Title**   ➤ **Blade of Winterhold (Leveled Enchanted Sword)**

NOTE There is no house to purchase in this Hold.

Thane of the Reach*

Part 1 — Friend of the Jarl:
You must first befriend the
Jarl of Markarth, achieved
by completing either of the
following:

 Jarl Igmund is the
leader of Markarth.
You must have finished
both the tasks he set for
you. See the "Favor: Jobs for the Jarls" section of this guide for more information.

Jarl Thongvor Silver-Fish is the leader of Markarth once it has fallen into Stormcloak
hands. To start this task with Thongvor, you must have captured the Reach Hold as
part of the Civil War Quests.

Part 2 — Friend of the City: You must now earn the respect of the inhabitants of Markarth.
Speak to the Jarl, who asks you to assist the people of this Hold. Return to the Jarl once
you've finished five (or more) Favors, tasks, or objectives that benefit the people. Consult the
Miscellaneous Objectives and Favors of this guide, looking for "Markarth" as the location for
tasks, Favors, and objectives.

Part 3 — House in the City: Finally, you must purchase a piece of property in the city. Speak
to the Jarl, and you're informed that a house is for sale. You're referred to the Steward: Raerek
(Jarl Igmund) or Reburrus Quintilius (Jarl Thongvor). The following residence is available:

House Name: Vlindrel Hall

Cost: 8,000 gold pieces

➤ **Key to Vlindrel Hall**

Visit the house and meet your Housecarl, Argis the Bulwark. Return to the Jarl, who grants you
the title of Thane and a reward. Guards in the Reach now ignore one crime as long as your
Bounty is less than 2,000.

➤ **Thane Title**

➤ **Blade of the Reach (Leveled Enchanted Axe)**

➤ **House:** Vlindrel Hall

➤ **Follower:** Argis the Bulwark

Thane of Whiterun*

Part 1 — Dragon Rising:
Jarl Balgruuf the Greater
is the leader of Whiterun.
When you aid his soldiers in
fending off the dragon attack
in Main Quest: Dragon Rising,
he proclaims you Thane as a
reward for your heroism. Your
new Housecarl, Lydia, will wait
for you in Dragonsreach until you find a home in the city. Guards in Whiterun will now ignore
one crime as long as your Bounty is less than 2,000.

➤ **Thane Title**   ➤ **Follower:** Lydia

➤ **Blade of Whiterun (Leveled Enchanted Axe)**

Part 2 — House in the City: Although not required to become Thane of Whiterun, you can still
purchase a house in the city. Speak to the Jarl, and you're informed that a house is for sale.
You're referred to the Steward, Proventus Avenicci (Jarl Balgruuf) or Brill (Jarl Vignar). The
following residence is available:

House Name: Breezehome

Cost: 5,000 gold pieces

➤ **Key to Breezehome**

Visit the house, where Lydia can now be found when not fighting at your side.

➤ **House:** Breezehome

Thane of Eastmarch*

Part 1 — Friend of the Jarl:
You must first befriend the
Jarl of Windhelm, achieved
by completing either of the
following:

 Jarl Ulfric Stormcloak
is the leader of
Windhelm. You
must have conquered both
Whiterun and Falkreath Holds for the Stormcloaks in order to become firm friends with him.

Jarl Brunwulf Free-Winter is the leader of Windhelm once it has fallen into Imperial
hands. To start this task with Brunwulf, you must have captured Windhelm in the
culmination of the Civil War Quests.

Part 2 — Friend of the City: You must now win the respect of the inhabitants of Windhelm.
Speak to the Jarl, who asks you to assist the people of this Hold. Return to the Jarl once
you've finished five (or more) Favors, tasks, or objectives that benefit the people. Consult the
Miscellaneous Objectives and Favors sections of this guide, looking for "Windhelm" as the
location for tasks, Favors, and objectives.

Part 3 — House in the City: Finally, you must purchase a piece of property in the city. Once
Side Quest: Blood on the Ice sends you to Hjerim, speak to the Jarl, and you're informed that
the house is for sale. You're referred to the Steward, Jorleif (Jarl Ulfric), or Captain Lonely-Gale
(Jarl Brunwulf). The following residence is available:

House Name: Hjerim

Cost: 12,000 gold pieces

➤ **Key to Hjerim**

Visit the house and meet your Housecarl, Calder. Return to the Jarl, who grants you the title of
Thane and a reward. Guards in Eastmarch now ignore one crime as long as your Bounty is less
than 2,000.

➤ **Thane Title**   ➤ **House:** Hjerim

➤ **Blade of Eastmarch (Leveled Enchanted Axe)**   ➤ **Follower:** Calder

Thane of Falkreath*

Part 1 — Friend of the Jarl: You must first befriend the Jarl of Falkreath, achieved by
completing either of the following:

 Jarl Siddgeir is the leader of Falkreath. You must have completed the two tasks he
set for you. See the "Favor: Jobs for the Jarls" and "Favor: Rare Item Hunt" sections
for details.

Jarl Dengeir of Stuhn is the leader of Falkreath once it has fallen into Stormcloak
hands. To start this task with Dengeir, you must have captured Falkreath as part of the
Civil War Quests.

Part 2 — Friend of the City: You must now win the respect of the inhabitants of Falkreath.
Speak to the Jarl, who asks you to assist the people of this Hold. Return to the Jarl once
you've finished three (or more) Favors, tasks, or objectives that benefit the people. Consult the
Miscellaneous Objectives and Favors of this guide looking for "Falkreath" as the location for
tasks, Favors, and objectives:

Return to the Jarl, who grants you the title of Thane and a reward. Guards in Falkreath
now ignore one crime as long as your Bounty is less than 2,000.

➤ **Thane Title**   ➤ **Blade of Falkreath (Leveled Enchanted Sword)**

 NOTE   There is no house to purchase in this Hold.

Thane of the Rift*

Part 1—Friend of the Jarl: You must first befriend the Jarl of Riften, achieved by completing either of the following:

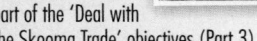

 Jarl Laila Law-Giver is the leader of Riften. You befriend her as part of the 'Deal with the Skooma Trade' objectives (Part 3).

Jarl Maven Black-Briar is the leader of Riften once it has fallen into Imperial hands. To start this task with Maven, you must have captured Riften as part of the Civil War Quests.

Part 2—Friend of the City: You must now win the respect of the inhabitants of Riften. Speak to the Jarl, who asks you to assist the people of this Hold. Return to the Jarl once you've finished five (or more) Favors, tasks, or objectives that benefit the people. Consult the Miscellaneous Objectives and Favors sections of this guide, looking for "Riften" as the location for tasks, Favors, and objectives.

Part 3—Deal with the Skooma Trade: Three of the Miscellaneous Objectives in Riften form a mini-questline in which you uncover the skooma trade in the city and deal with it. You must complete the objectives:

1. "Helping Hand"
2. "The Raid"
3. "Supply and Demand"

Note that the first two objectives do contribute toward the "Part 2 — Friend of the City" portion of the Thane Quest (in case you haven't done enough yet).

Part 4—House in the City: Finally, you must purchase a piece of property in the city. Speak to the Jarl, and you're informed that a House is for sale. You're referred to the Steward, Anuriel (Jarl Laila) or Hemming Black-Briar (Jarl Maven). The following residence is available:

House Name: Honeyside

Cost: 8,000 gold pieces

➤ **Key to Honeyside**

Visit the house and meet your Housecarl, Iona. Return to the Jarl, who grants you the title of Thane and a reward. Guards in the Rift now ignore one crime as long as your Bounty is less than 2,000.

➤ **Thane Title**

➤ **Blade of the Rift (Leveled Enchanted Sword)**

➤ **House:** Honeyside

➤ **Follower:** Iona

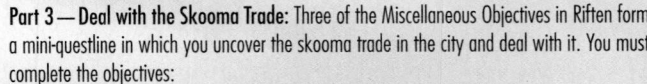

WORLD INTERACTIONS AND ENCOUNTERS

Unlike quests, Favors, and objectives, which typically involve a specific person or location, World Interactions and Encounters occur randomly and not all the time. And they almost never occur in the same place. Look for these small occurrences during your adventure.

World Interactions are random and usually very small-scale events that occur in populated areas, such as settlements, towns, or cities. They require you to perform an action, and the consequences are then detailed. Remember that you may perform the action, and it's possible that no one will notice or be interested in your antics. This is the random nature of World Interactions.

World Encounters are random events that may occur as you explore the roads and wilds of Skyrim. These events take a variety of forms, from simple combats to unique scenes that reflect the quests you've completed.

TIP You have very little control over when World Interactions and Encounters appear; just investigate or interact with the ones that interest you once you see them. The following tables show all the World Interactions and Encounters available across Skyrim.

  WORLD INTERACTIONS

These are split up based on the actions you perform to get a reaction. These are listed in the following tables, along with a description of the interaction and any prerequisites (such as completing quests) you need to have accomplished.

Part 1: Items of Interest

These Interactions may commence any time you add an item to your inventory.

✓	WORLD INTERACTION	DESCRIPTION	PREREQUISITES
	1. An Interested Party	You pick something up. A nearby resident runs up and asks, "Did you find anything good?"	Inside a city, settlement, or town, but not inside a building.
	2. Watching the Rummager	You take something from a barrel, sack, crate, or container where "refuse" is usually placed. A nearby resident asks, "What's he/she doing rummaging around in there?" A second resident (if there is one nearby) replies, "Perhaps he/she is looking for food?"	You are not inside a building.
	3. Tailing the Thief	You steal an item. After a day or two, three thugs track you when you're in the wilderness, tell you they're here to punish you for stealing, and attack you. Search them for a note from the owner of the property you stole.	You must steal an item and not get caught.
	4. Calcelmo's Courier	After buying a dwarven item, you may receive a letter via courier (when you next visit a town or city) asking if you'll bring the item to Calcelmo; he will pay dearly for it.	You must buy [any dwarven item] from a merchant.

The Elder Scrolls V
SKYRIM

Part 2: Assaults with Consequences

These Interactions begin when you assault someone. This means striking them and then stopping before killing them (brawls don't count).

✓	WORLD INTERACTION	DESCRIPTION	PREREQUISITES
	1. It's All Relative	After you assault someone within view of others, the crime may be reported. Sometime in the future, you're stopped by a resident, a relative of the person you attacked. You can apologize (and the relative walks away) or remain unapologetic, resulting in an attack.	Attacking a resident of a town or city.
	2. An Impressive Assault	After you assault someone within view of others, inside a settlement, town, or city, you receive a letter from a courier. A [randomly determined resident] with an enemy has seen your assault and wants you to rough someone up for them. Meet the impressed party, agree, and then find the [randomly determined foe], roughing them up (but not killing them).	Attacking a resident of a town or city.
	3. A Memorable Assault	After you assault someone inside a settlement, town, or city, the next time you meet them, the victim remembers your assault and mentions this.	Attacking a resident of a town or city.

Part 3: Wizardry

These Interactions may begin once someone near to you witnesses you casting a magic spell.

✓	WORLD INTERACTION	DESCRIPTION	PREREQUISITES
	1. The Invisible Boy	Once you've cast a spell, a young boy runs up and asks you to cast invisibility on him. You can agree or refuse, but you can't really do this. If you agree, the boy, thinking he's invisible, heads off, sneaking up on people and trying to scare them	Casting magic within the vicinity of the witness.
	2. Lollygagging Looky-Loos	If you're inside a settlement, town, or city with a spell effect that creates a dangerous "sheen" or effect around your person, such as Flame Cloak, bystanders will murmur in alarm, and a crowd may start to form around you until you've dispelled the effect or it wears off.	Casting magic with a "dangerous" effect around you.
	3. Quest, Please	Employ a Shout in a populated settlement, town, or city, and a nearby guard may run up and sternly warn you to stop, as it's making the locals nervous.	Utilizing a Shout.
	4. Quest, Please	Employ a Shout in a populated settlement, town, or city, and you may receive a Courier's letter soon afterwards, from a mysterious "friend" who gives directions to a nearby [random dungeon] that contains a Word Wall inside.	Utilizing a Shout.

Part 4: About Town

These Interactions may begin when you enter a settlement, town, or city.

✓	WORLD INTERACTION	DESCRIPTION	PREREQUISITES
	1. Courier Catch-Up	As you enter, you may be greeted by a courier with a letter or multiple letters. These may invite you to begin quests, locate areas of interest, or follow up on rumors you've heard, or they simply update your objectives. Consult the individual prerequisites of quests you may be interested in to find out more.	Entering a location.
	2. No Nudity	Enter a location without wearing any clothes, and the locals may comment on your appearance and ask you to put on some more appropriate attire.	Entering a location without clothing equipped.
	3. Careful, Now	Enter a location brandishing a weapon, and you may find locals asking you about it. Innkeepers and merchants may tell you to be careful brandishing such an implement. Sheath your weapon to stop this talk.	Entering a location with weapons unsheathed.
	4. The Enraged Mage	Enter a location, and [a random wizard] steps forward to challenge you to a duel. Kill the wizard (without accruing any Bounty, as you were challenged). You don't have to use magic, although the wizard may protest at this. Not after you kill him, though!	Entering a location.
	5. The Engaged Mage	Enter a location, and [a random student of magic] steps forward to ask you about learning ward spells. Oblige the student if you wish.	Entering a location.
	6. Gift Giving	Enter a location, and a person you've befriended (e.g., by completing a Favor) hands you a gift. This won't be the Jarl, though.	Entering a settlement, town, or city after befriending one or more of the population there.
	7. Games Without Frontiers	As you enter, you may see a group of children playing a game. Talk to them, and they may ask you to join them. The game will be either hide-and-seek or tag. Agree or decline. Play the game if you wish.	Entering a location, speaking to a child.
	8. Dragon Attack!	Enter a location once the dragons return to Skyrim, and the guards yell out a warning as the residents scatter. A dragon swoops down into the settlement and attacks! Flee or fight.	Entering a location after Main Quest: Dragon Rising is complete.
	9. Other Talk	Merchants call out a greeting to you, as do friends welcoming you to your home if you own one. Those you haven't befriended may speak to you with suspicion.	Entering a location.

Part 5: Your Demeanor

These Interactions may begin once you visit a different settlement, town, or city in a particular visual state. These can occur as overheard murmuring, or as part of conversations you may have.

✓	WORLD INTERACTION	DESCRIPTION	PREREQUISITES
	1. The Spellcaster	Residents comment on your flowing robes, sometimes with suspicion.	Wear College of Winterhold robes.
	2. The Unclean One	Residents comment with disgust and sometimes sadness on your pox.	You have a disease.
	3. Pretty Colors	Residents are dazzled by the colorful aura you have surrounding your person.	Have a "colorful" magical effect.
	4. Pretty Dangerous	Residents are somewhat alarmed by the dangerous area you have around you.	Have a "dangerous" magical effect, such as fire.
	5. Hands of Fire	Residents are a little taken aback by your flaming hands.	Have a Flame spell equipped and "unsheathed."
	6. The Immodest Adventurer	Residents are quick to comment on your lack of proper modesty.	Have no clothing on.
	7. On the Prowl	Residents aren't impressed by your strange crouching stance.	You're sneaking while spotted.

Part 6: Crafting

These Interactions may begin when you attempt to create an item at a crafting location.

✓	WORLD INTERACTION	DESCRIPTION	PREREQUISITES
	1. Friend of the Forge	A blacksmith comments on the item you're making (how rare it is, the type, or your competence).	You use a blacksmith's workbench to make or improve an item.
	2. Excellent Enchanting	A nearby Court Wizard comments on the item you're enchanting, or on your competence as an enchanter.	You use an Arcane Enchanter to enchant an item.
	3. Adept Alchemist	An apothecary merchant comments on the item you're making (if it's a poison or potion) or on your competence.	You use an Alchemy Lab to make an item.

Part 7: Dealing with the Dead

These Interactions may begin when you or a nearby person sees or interacts with a corpse.

✓	WORLD INTERACTION	DESCRIPTION	PREREQUISITES
	1. Suspicious Behavior	Residents step up to the corpse and look at it. A soldier usually tells folks to disperse and begins to interrogate you. Residents begin to wonder out loud if you're the murderer. You can protest your innocence (the guard leaves you alone) or offer an unpleasant response (which gets you arrested).	You're near a dead body (optionally with weapons unsheathed), but no one saw you kill this person.
	2. Dead Dragon	Residents step up to the remains of a dragon, remarking as you absorb the Dragon Soul.	You kill a dragon close to residents.

Part 8: Killing

These Interactions may begin when a nearby person is killed.

✓	WORLD INTERACTION	DESCRIPTION	PREREQUISITES
	1. A Friend's Inheritance	When you return to a settlement where a friend of yours was slain, a courier greets you and says your friend left you an inheritance. Collect the gold from the Jarl's Steward.	A friend of yours is killed (by you, without being caught, or by others).
	2. A Friend of Your Enemy	When you return to a settlement after you slay someone with a known enemy, a courier greets you to say the enemy of the deceased has a gift for you. Visit them to receive the reward (usually gold).	You kill a resident who has a known enemy.
	3. Not Going Out	A bereaved friend of a slain resident runs to their home or dwelling and locks themselves inside, refusing to come out.	The bereaved's friend was killed with them watching (by you or others).
	4. Hired Muscle	A relative of the deceased hires thugs to attack you.	A resident is killed by you, you're seen, and the deceased has a relative.
	5. Grave Digging	Residents of city's bodies may be disposed of, and any worldly goods you didn't loot from their corpse show up in their coffin in the hall of the dead.	Leave a civilian's corpse lying around a city and come back later.

◢ Part 9: Items of Disinterest

These Interactions may begin if you discard an item (by dropping it, selling it, or giving it away).

✔	WORLD INTERACTION	DESCRIPTION	PREREQUISITES
☐	1. Dropping a Weapon	A guard stops you and reprimands you for leaving dangerous weapons lying around. Walk away or apologize and the guard leaves you alone. Converse and the guard asks for a fine (or bribe). If you refuse to pay, you're attacked or arrested.	Drop a weapon near a guard.
☐	2. I Think You Dropped This (I)	A resident stops you after picking up the discarded item, and hands it back to you (it now appears in your inventory)	Drop an item near a resident.
☐	3. Mine! Mine! Mine!	Two residents move to the item and begin to fight over whose it is. An audience may gather, commenting on the spectacle. The argument may escalate to a brawl (which you aren't involved in).	Dropping an item near two or more residents.
☐	4. No Littering, Please	A resident remarks with annoyance about your littering habits.	Dropping an item near a resident.
☐	5. I Think You Dropped This (II)	A resident stops you after picking up the discarded armor and asks if you meant to discard the piece.	Drop a piece of armor near a resident.

◢ Part 10: Taverns

These Interactions may begin if you enter a tavern or inn in a Skyrim settlement.

✔	WORLD INTERACTION	DESCRIPTION	PREREQUISITES
☐	1. A Man Walks Into a Bar... (I)	The innkeeper welcomes you to the place.	You enter a tavern or inn.
☐	2. A Man Walks Into a Bar... (II)	The innkeeper yells for one of the waitstaff to serve you a drink.	You enter a tavern or inn and sit down.

◢ Part 11: Thievery

These interactions may begin if you enter a settlement and spot a thief.

✔	WORLD INTERACTION	DESCRIPTION	PREREQUISITES
☐	1. Caught Red-Handed	A Thieves Guild member attempts to flee if you (or another resident) approach them while they try to pick a door lock.	You see a thief try to pick a lock.

 **WORLD ENCOUNTERS**

> **NOTE** The following information notes whether the encounter takes place in one general location ("Scene") or if it continues along a path or into the wilderness ("Moving").

✔	WORLD ENCOUNTER	DESCRIPTION	MOVING ENCOUNTER OR A SCENE?	PREREQUISITES
☐	1. Bandit Battle	Two bandits and a bandit leader are about to kill another bandit.	Scene	None
☐	2. Elk Hunters	Two hunters chase after an elk. Once the elk has been slain, they patrol the area.	Moving	None
☐	3. Dragon versus Giant	A giant and a dragon engage in an epic fight.	Moving	Main Quest: Dragon Rising must be completed. Occurs only in the Pale or Whiterun Holds.
☐	4. Dragon Attack!	A dragon attacks you.	Moving	Main Quest: Dragon Rising must be completed.
☐	5. Orcs versus Forsworn	Five Forsworn are battling against three Orcs.	Moving	Occurs only in the Reach.
☐	6. Animals versus Bandit	A bandit is battling against a wild animal.	Scene	None
☐	7. Giant versus Bandits	Four bandits are battling against two giants and a mammoth.	Moving	Occurs only in the Pale and Whiterun Holds.
☐	8. Dragon Flight	A dragon flies past you without attacking, unless you provoke it.	Moving	Main Quest: Dragon Rising must be completed.
☐	9. Imperials and Captured Stormcloak	Three Imperial Soldiers lead a Stormcloak prisoner along the road.	Moving	Roads only
☐	10. Alduin's Emissary	A dragon flies to the nearest dragon lair and surveys the landscape.	Moving	Main Quest: Dragon Rising must be completed.

✓	WORLD ENCOUNTER	DESCRIPTION	MOVING ENCOUNTER OR A SCENE?	PREREQUISITES
	11. Sabre Cats Hunting Mammoths	Two Sabre Cats prowl and attack a single mammoth	Moving	Occurs only in the Pale or Whiterun Holds.
	12. Wolves Hunting Elk	Two wolves prowl and attack two elk	Moving	None
	13. Spriggans versus Trolls	Two Spriggans are battling against one troll.	Moving	You must be Level 12 or higher. Occurs only in the Pale, Winterhold, or Eastmarch Holds.
	14. Skeevers versus Dogs	Four Skeever and three dogs fight each other.	Moving	None
	15. Atronach Mis-summoned	A [random] Atronach is seen wandering the landscape.	Moving	None
	16. Orcs Elk Hunters	Two Orc Hunters chase after an elk. Once the elk has been slain, they patrol the area.	Moving	None
	17. Imperial Impersonators	Three bandits are wearing the armor of three dead soldiers close by.	Scene	None
	18. Witch versus Atronach	One [random] Atronach is battling against a Witch	Moving.	You must be Level 5 or higher.
	19. Warlock versus Bandits	A conjurer is battling against three bandits.	Moving	You must be Level 5 or higher.
	20. Imperials versus Stormcloaks	Three Imperial Soldiers are battling against three Stormcloak Soldiers	Moving	None
	21. The Scavenger	A scavenger loots from the corpses of dead soldiers in a battlefield	Scene	None
	22. A Good Death	An old Orc is looking for an honorable death, to be slain by you.	Scene	None
	23. Hey You There! Take This!	A fugitive approaches you, shoves an item at you, and runs. Moments later a hunter approaches and asks about the fugitive. You can lie, tell the truth, keep the item, or return it to the hunter.	Moving	None
	24. Imperial Scout Patrol	Imperial Soldiers are marching to an Imperial camp.	Moving	None
	25. Stormcloak Scout Patrol	Stormcloak Soldiers are marching to a Stormcloak camp.	Moving	None
	26. Courier on the Run	A courier is spotted dashing between settlements.	Moving	Roads only
	27. College Application Denied	A despondent young mage gives you his Staff of Resurrection and Black Soul Gem after speaking to you, dejected that he couldn't join the College of Winterhold.	Scene	You must be Level 15 or higher.
	28. Thalmor and Captured Prisoner	Three Thalmor lead a prisoner along the road.	Moving	Roads only
	29. Thalmor versus Stormcloaks	Three Thalmor are battling against three Stormcloak Soldiers	Moving	None
	30. Thalmor versus You	Three Thalmor attack you. Search the corpses for a note giving an order to look for you.	Moving	None
	31. M'aiq the Liar	You encounter a Khajiit named M'aiq the Liar and converse with him. You may have spoken with him elsewhere in Tamriel (see conversations in the separate section of this guide, on page 413). He'll say a few different things each time you find him.	Moving	None
	32. Bounty Hunters versus You	Three bounty hunters attack you. Search the corpses for a note giving an order to look for you.	Moving	None
	33. Hidden Treasure Hunt	You find the corpse of a dead treasure hunter with a letter leading you to a nearby [random] dungeon, and a valuable item inside a large treasure chest to find.	Scene	Side Quest: Treasure Maps is unrelated to this.
	34. Bard at Rest	Talsgar the Wanderer has stopped for a rest somewhere in the wilderness. You can request a song from him.	Scene	None
	35. Bard Attacked by Bandits	Talsgar the Wanderer is being attacked by bandits somewhere in the wilderness. Help if you wish.	Scene	None
	36. Bard Traveling	Talsgar the wanderer is walking along the road to the nearest settlement. If Talsgar dies, none of his specific encounters occur again.	Moving	Roads only
	37. On the Way to a Wedding	A pair of guests are traveling with a bodyguard to Vittoria Vici's wedding in Solitude.	Moving	Dark Brotherhood Quest: Bound Until Death not completed yet. Roads only.
	38. Lost After the Wedding	A pair of guests have become lost while returning home from the wedding in Solitude.	Moving	Dark Brotherhood Quest: Bound Until Death completed. Roads only.
	39. The Revenge of Louis Letrush	A thug sent by Louis Letrush attacks you.	Moving	Side Quest: Promises to Keep completed, and you decided to steal Frost the horse for yourself.
	40. The End of Louis Letrush	A thug and Louis Letrush are fighting in the wilderness.	Moving	Side Quest: Promises to Keep completed, and you decided to deliver Frost the horse but tell Maven about it.

The Elder Scrolls V

SKYRIM

QUESTS: WORLD INTERACTIONS AND ENCOUNTERS

✓	WORLD ENCOUNTER	DESCRIPTION	MOVING ENCOUNTER OR A SCENE?	PREREQUISITES
☐	41. Ramblings of a Mad Woman	A madwoman approaches you, mumbling nonsense. She mentions the Blue Palace. If you've completed the quest indicated, she also talks about something called a "Wabbajack."	Scene	Daedric Quest: The Mind of Madness complete (for different conversation topic)
☐	42. The Drunken Dare	Somebody from your drunken night with Sanguine approaches and asks you for money you owe them. Pay, flee, or fight.	Scene	Daedric Quest: A Night to Remember completed
☐	43. Spriggans versus Lumberjacks	Two Spriggan are battling against two hunters in the wilderness.	Moving	You must be Level 8 or higher.
☐	44. Pain in the Neck	A hunter has been bitten by a vampire and asks for help. You can cure this disease, or ask where the [nearest] vampire den is.	Moving	None
☐	45. Looking to Join the Imperials	A farmer is on his way to sign up with the Imperials in Solitude.	Moving	None
☐	46. Looking to Join the Stormcloaks	A farmer is on his way to sign up with the Stormcloaks in Windhelm.	Moving	None
☐	47. Vigilants versus Atronach	Three Vigilants of Stendarr are battling against an Atronach.	Scene	None
☐	48. Vigilants versus Vampire	Two Vigilants of Stendarr are battling against a vampire.	Scene	Only occurs between 10:00 p.m. and 5:00 a.m.
☐	49. Vigilant versus Skeletons	A Vigilant of Stendarr is battling against three skeletons.	Scene	None
☐	50. Vigilants on Patrol	Two Vigilants of Stendarr are en route to the Hall of the Vigilant.	Moving	None
☐	51. Dead Woman's Pendant	A woman's corpse on the ground has a note mentioning a stolen pendant. The item in question can be found on one of the two nearby bandits.	Scene	None
☐	52. Finding the Gourmet	A traveler named Balbus is seeking the most famous chef in all of Skyrim. If you've completed the associated quest, you can pose as the Gourmet (with the correct identification papers taken from the quest) and receive a reward: a Daedra Heart, Troll Fat, a Spider Egg, and Balbus's prized fork!	Scene	Dark Brotherhood Quest: Recipe for Disaster completed (for reward only)
☐	53. Forsworn versus Merchant	Three Forsworn are battling against a merchant and a horse. If you defeat the Forsworn and the peddler survives, you can barter goods with him.	Moving	Occurs only in the Reach
☐	54. Forsworn versus Soldiers	Three Forsworn are battling against two Imperial Soldiers.	Moving.	Occurs only in The Reach.
☐	55. Bandits versus Traveling Merchant	Two bandits are battling against a merchant and a horse. If you defeat the bandits and the merchant survives, you can barter goods with him.	Moving	None
☐	56. Faldrus the Pilgrim	A Dark Elf named Faldrus is encountered on a pilgrimage to Azura's Shrine. Speak to Faldrus, and you receive an objective to travel to the shrine, as an introduction to Daedric Quest: The Black Star.	Moving	None
☐	57. Sharing a Bite to Eat	A beggar is close to a corpse. If you've completed Daedric Quest: The Taste of Death, you recognize the beggar as a Namira cultist, who offers you a bite on this found feast.	Scene	Share the meal only after Daedric Quest: The Taste of Death is complete.
☐	58. Necromancers versus You	Two necromancers attack and attempt to kill you. If you've completed Daedric Quest: The Black Star, one of them has a note ordering them to avenge the death of Malyn Varen.	Scene	Note found only after Daedric Quest: The Black Star is complete.
☐	59. Kynareth's Pilgrim	Once the Gildergreen has been restored, pilgrims begin to travel to Whiterun to see it. You pass one on your travels.	Moving	Complete Temple Quest: The Blessings of Nature.
☐	60. Peryite's Pilgrim	Before you start Daedric Quest: The Only Cure, you may encounter an Afflicted, a refugee with a pox fleeing from Bthardamz. You receive an objective to travel to Peryite's Shrine.	Scene	You must be Level 10 or higher. This does not happen once Daedric Quest: The Only Cure has started.
☐	61. The Afflicted versus You	Afflicted refugees spot and attack you for what you did.	Scene	You must be Level 10 or higher. Daedric Quest: The Only Cure must be completed.
☐	62. A Disturbed Spriggan	The corpse of a hunter is close to a live Spriggan, who attacks you.	Scene	You must be Level 8 or higher.
☐	63. Dragon Attack Aftermath	You stumble upon a cart and three charred corpses after a dragon attack.	Scene	Main Quest: Dragon Rising must be completed.
☐	64. Roaming Ice Wraiths	Ice Wraiths are winding through the air, back and forth. They attack as you near them.	Scene	You must be Level 10 or higher. Occurs only in Haafingar, the Pale, and Winterhold Holds.
☐	65. Spriggan versus Hagraven	A Spriggan is battling against a Hagraven in the wilderness.	Scene	You must be Level 20 or higher.
☐	66. A Hunter's Best Friend	You meet a Hunter and his dog wandering in the wilderness.	Scene	None
☐	67. Ice Wraiths verses Bandits	Ice Wraiths are battling against bandits in the snow.	Moving	You must be Level 10 or higher. Occurs only in Haafingar, the Pale, and Winterhold Holds.
☐	68. Dog versus Wolves	A dog is battling against two wolves. If you kill the wolves and the dog survives, it can become a Follower.	Moving	None
☐	69. Dead Bandit. Live Horse	A bandit corpse is lying on the ground, and a horse is wandering nearby. You can utilize this horse as a steed if you wish.	Scene	None

	WORLD ENCOUNTER	DESCRIPTION	MOVING ENCOUNTER OR A SCENE?	PREREQUISITES
☐	70. Dueling Wizards	A Frost Mage and a Fire Mage are battling in the wilderness.	Scene	None
☐	71. Mistwatch Escapee	A prisoner has escaped from Mistwatch; he informs you where this fortification is.	Scene	Mistwatch must not already have been discovered.
☐	72. Thieves Guild Holdup	A member of the Thieves Guild holds you up for some gold. You can avoid this if you're already a member of this Guild.	Scene	Thieves Guild Quest: Taking Care of Business complete to avoid the holdup.
☐	73. Alik'r Accusation	Two Alik'r Warriors are accosting a woman.	Scene	This can occur before or during Side Quest: In My Time of Need, but not after it is completed.
☐	74. Dwemer Junk Peddlers	Two children offer to sell you some Dwemer artifacts. They also point you to a Dwemer Point of Interest (Secondary Location).	Scene	Occurs only in the Reach
☐	75. Blood Horkers' Revenge	The Blood Horkers from Side Quest: Rise in the East attack you in revenge.	Scene	Side Quest: Rise in the East completed
☐	76. Drinking Companions	Three drunks are reveling in the wilderness and offer you a drink. Offer them a bottle of Honningbrew mead; you receive a Gold Necklace.	Scene	None
☐	77. Vampire's Trick	You see a vampire attacking an innocent. Approach, and the "victim" is actually the vampire's thrall; both attack.	Scene	Only occurs between 10:00 p.m. and 4:00 a.m. Occurs anytime prior to Side Quest: Laid to Rest. Afterward, occurs anywhere except Hjaalmarch Hold.
☐	78. Vampires versus You	Two vampires attack you.	Scene	Only occurs between 10:00 p.m. and 4:00 a.m. Occurs anywhere prior to Side Quest: Laid to Rest. Afterward, occurs anywhere except Hjaalmarch Hold.
☐	79. The Companions Hunt (I)	Vilkas and Ria (members of the Companions) are out hunting Sabre Cats.	Moving	Occurs only prior to beginning or after completing all of the Companion Quests. Does not occur in Whiterun Hold.
☐	80. The Companions Hunt (II)	Skjor, Aela, and Njada (members of the Companions) are out hunting a mammoth.	Moving	Occurs only prior to beginning or after completing all of the Companion Quests. Does not occur in Whiterun Hold.
☐	81. The Companions Hunt (III)	Falkas, Athis, and Torvar (members of the Companions) are out hunting bears.	Moving	Occurs only prior to beginning or after completing all of the Companion Quests. Does not occur in Whiterun Hold.
☐	82. Wolf Hunt	A fellow from Cragslane Cavern in Eastmarch was attempting to retrieve pit wolves that have bolted from their pens. He is found dead, with the pit wolves nearby. The note reveals the location of Cragslane Cavern.	Scene	Cragslane Cavern can already have been discovered.
☐	83. Bounty Killer	A Bounty Collector approaches you in the wilderness and offers you a chance to pay off your Bounty for a raised price "(the actual price depends on your bounty). Choose to pay, flee, or kill.	Scene	You must have a Bounty of 1,000+ in any Hold.
☐	84. Burned Crops	You meet two farmers displaced after a recent dragon attack. You can give them gold if you wish.	Moving	You must be at least Level 4. Roads only.
☐	85. The Nobles	Two noblemen are walking along the road escorted by two soldiers.	Moving	Roads only
☐	86. The Thalmor	Three Thalmor are walking along the road, eventually reaching the Thalmor Embassy.	Moving	Roads only
☐	87. The Stormcloaks	Three Stormcloaks are walking along the road, eventually reaching the nearest city.	Moving	Roads only. The Hold you see them in must be in Stormcloaks' control.
☐	88. The Imperials	Three Imperials are walking along the road, eventually reaching the nearest city.	Moving	Roads only. The Hold you see them in must be in Imperial control.
☐	89. The Adventurer	A mercenary adventurer is walking toward a nearby dungeon. You can speak to the adventurer and get them to reveal the location of the dungeon, which appears on your world map.	Moving	You must be at least Level 5. Roads only.
☐	90. The Taunting Adventurer	An adventurer taunts you on the road, spoiling for a fight. You can oblige, or talk your way out of it.	Moving	Roads only
☐	91. Not Your Courier	A courier is on the road, traveling to a nearby inn to deliver a message. You can steal the note (or kill the courier), which hints at [random] treasure inside a [random] nearby dungeon.	Moving	Roads only
☐	92. Skooma Dealer	A Skooma dealer offers you some of his stock. You can purchase or use intimidation to get your fix.	Moving	Roads only
☐	93. A Giant's Painted Cow	A giant is walking along the road with a painted cow close by. He heads to the nearest [random] giant's camp.	Moving	Roads only
☐	94. A Farmer's Painted Cow	A farmer is leading a painted cow along the road to a [random] giant's camp. This is part of a ritual so the giants and farmers live harmoniously together.	Moving	Roads only
☐	95. The Headless Horseman	Did you see a headless ghost riding a horse to Hamvir's Rest? You cannot stop or interact with this specter, as it appears to be on a different plane of existence than you. Perhaps the head of the horseman lies (attached to his helmet) within this graveyard?	Moving	Only occurs between 10:00 p.m. and 5:00 a.m.

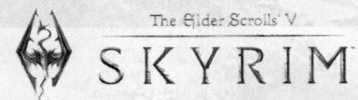

The Elder Scrolls V
SKYRIM

QUESTS: WORLD INTERACTIONS AND ENCOUNTERS

TALL TALES: THE UTTERANCES OF M'AIQ THE LIAR

Meet M'aiq the Liar. He's quite the talker:

"M'aiq's father was also called M'aiq. As was M'aiq's father's father. At least, that's what his father said."

"M'aiq wishes you well."

"M'aiq knows much, and tells some. M'aiq knows many things others do not."

"M'aiq carries two weapons, to be safe. What if one breaks? That would be most unlucky."

"M'aiq is always in search of calipers, yet finds none. Where could they have gone?"

"M'aiq hears many stories of war...yet few of them are true."

"How does anyone know there was a city of Winterhold? M'aiq did not see it with his eyes. Did you?"

"Too much magic can be dangerous. M'aiq once had two spells and burned his sweetroll."

"What does this mean, to combine magic? Magic plus magic is still magic."

"It does not matter to M'aiq how strong or smart one is. It only matters what one can do."

"Dragons were never gone. They were just invisible and very, very quiet."

"Werebears? Where? Bears? Men that are bears?"

"Much snow in Skyrim. Enough snow. M'aiq does not want any more."

"Snow falls. Why worry where it goes? M'aiq thinks the snowflakes are pretty."

"Skyrim was once the land of many butterflies. Now, not so much."

"M'aiq once walked to High Hrothgar. So many steps, he lost count."

"Once M'aiq got in trouble in Riften, and fled to Windhelm. It is good that nobody there cared."

"M'aiq can travel fast across the land. Some lazy types take carriages. It is all the same to M'aiq."

"M'aiq does not understand what is so impressive about shouting. M'aiq can shout whenever he wants."

"M'aiq saw a mudcrab the other day. Horrible creatures."

"M'aiq loves the people of Skyrim. Many interesting things they say to each other."

"Nords are so serious about beards. So many beards. M'aiq thinks they wish they had glorious manes like Khajiit."

"M'aiq does not remember his childhood. Perhaps he never had one."

"M'aiq is very practical. He has no need for mysticism."

"Nords' armor has lots of fur. This sometimes makes M'aiq nervous."

"M'aiq was soul trapped once. Not very pleasant. You should think about that once in a while."

"Some say Alduin is Akatosh. Some say M'aiq is a Liar. Don't you believe either of those things."

"Something strange happens to Khajiit when they arrive in Skyrim."

"M'aiq has heard the people of Skyrim are better-looking than the ones in Cyrodiil. He has no opinion on the matter. All people are beautiful to him."

"Why do soldiers bother with target practice? One learns best by hitting real people."

"M'aiq knows why Falmer are blind. It has nothing to do with the Dwemer disappearing. Really."

"M'aiq has heard it is dangerous to be your friend."

"The people of Skyrim are more open-minded about certain things than people in other places."

"Some like taking friends on adventures. M'aiq thinks being alone is better. Less arguing about splitting treasure."

"Don't try blocking if you have two weapons. You will only get confused. Much better to hit twice anyway."

"M'aiq knows many things, no?"

"M'aiq is tired now. Go bother somebody else."

"M'aiq is done talking."

THE ATLAS OF SKYRIM

AN OVERVIEW OF THE NORTHERN LANDS OF TAMRIEL

Welcome to a massive guide to every location across the realm of Skyrim. Since ancient times, the lands of Skyrim have been divided into nine separate Holds, and modern cartographers saw no reason to change this method of dividing the realm into manageable segments for you to reference. Although Holds aren't visible on your in-game maps, the borders between each Hold have been drawn along roads, rivers, and steep mountains so you can visualize where you are more easily.

Overview and Legend

This Atlas is divided into ten sections. The first nine reveal each of the Holds of Skyrim (Haafingar, Hjaalmarch, the Pale, Winterhold Hold, the Reach, Whiterun Hold, Eastmarch, Falkreath Hold, and the Rift), running from northwest to southeast. A tenth chapter is dedicated to Other Realms (locations not shown on the world map, such as the Dragon Cult's bastion of Skuldafn).

Each location within a Hold is split up into Primary Locations (which appear as Fast-Travel points on the world map once you locate them) and Secondary Locations (some of which appear on your local map). For larger dungeons and settlements, interior maps have been provided. These help you explore major locations and flag important items. The following icons are used:

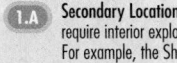 **Primary Locations:** These are usually large spaces requiring interior exploration and are listed in a number format. For example, the vampire hideout known as Movarth's Lair is listed as Primary Location [2.19]. This means it is in Hold 2 (Hjaalmarch) and is the 19th Primary Location within this Hold. Each Primary Location has a different icon depending on its type (e.g., a den, town, or capital).

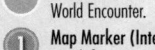 **Secondary Locations:** These are smaller areas that rarely require interior exploration. They are listed in a letter format. For example, the Shrine of Zenithar in the Rift is listed as Secondary Location [9.U].

World Encounter: This icon indicates the possibility of a random World Encounter.

Map Marker (Interior Maps): This shows the general area to search for one or more important items (with a corresponding number to the text description), or a major room or route in an interior map.

Threshold Marker (Interior Maps): This indicates a door (with a letter corresponding to the text description), a locked door (a blank marker), or a blocked passageway (also a blank marker). If this is linked via a line, it shows a connection between two levels or floors of a structure or dungeon.

Area Statistics

Every location in Skyrim has a list of pertinent information to better inform you about what to expect within the settlement or dungeon. The following chart explains what all these statistics mean:

STATISTIC	DESCRIPTION
Related Quests	Whether this location is visited during a Quest. Due to the random nature of many Radiant Quests, Side Quests, and Favors, only Quests that specifically direct you to a location are listed.
Recommended Level	This is the minimum Level your character should be at in order to enter the location and expect a good chance of survival. If the listed Level is significantly higher than yours, expect a tough or almost impossible challenge.
Habitation or Dungeon Type	This indicates what kind of location this is, and who is likely to be living there. Habitations are usually comprised of friendly folk, while Dungeons are usually hostile environments.
Hold Capital (Major)	One of the five major Capital Cities.
Hold Capital (Minor)	One of the four minor Capital Cities.
Caravan	A campsite for one of the three Khajiit Caravans that travel the roads.
Farm	Locations where crops are grown and harvested.

STATISTIC	DESCRIPTION
Hunter Camp	A place where fishermen or hunters have set up shelter.
Lumber Mill	A location where wood is cut and chopped, sometimes within a Town.
Military Fort	A large stone fortress, occupied by enemies until the Civil War drives them out.
Military: Imperial Camp	A forward-operations camp; may or may not be present depending on the state of the Civil War.
Military: Stormcloak Camp	A forward-operations camp; may or may not be present depending on the state of the Civil War.
Mine	A tunnel in the mountains where ore veins are mined.
Orc Stronghold	A settlement where Orcs rule; you must be Blood-Kin to the Orcs to enter freely.
Towns	Smaller settlements, usually with private homes, an inn, and farms.
Animal Den	A place where wild animals hunt from and store their kills.
Bandit Camp	A camp or fortification where marauding bandits attack from.
Dragon Lair	An ancient place where dragons have been seen (but may not be present).
Dragon Priest Lair	An ancient crypt where a fearsome Dragon Priest resides.
Draugr Crypt	A barrow with mausoleums and catacombs where the ancient Nords buried their dead.
Dwarven City	A vast, awe-inspiring ruin built by a vanished race known as Dwemer.
Falmer Hive	A cave or ruin inhabited by the degenerate remnants of the original elves of Skyrim.
Forsworn Redoubt	A place where native Reachmen plot to drive the Nords from The Reach.
Giant Camp	A place where nomadic Giants and their Mammoth herds congregate.
Hagraven Nest	A ruin where witches gather, sacrificing animals or worse.
Spriggan Grove	A place where nature is embraced, and protected from all threats (including you).
Vampire Lair	The darkened hideout of a clan of Vampires.
Warlock Lair	A fort or cave where rogue mages practice their spells.

Services: This location has a person prepared to trade or otherwise aid your progress:

Apothecary	Buys and sells potions and ingredients.
Bartender	Buys and sells food items (usually mead)
Blacksmith	Buys and sells weapons, armor, or both, plus crafting materials.
Carriage Driver	Can be hired to bring you to any Hold Capital city—very useful!
Fence	Buys and sells illicit goods.
Fletcher	Buys and sells weapons (usually bows), armor, or both, plus crafting materials.
Food Vendor	Buys and sells a variety of foodstuffs.
General Goods Vendor	Buys and sells a broad range of goods—unload your loot here!
Innkeeper	Rents rooms for the night, and often sells food and drink. Good source of gossip, too.
Jeweler	Rare merchants who buy and sell trinkets and baubles such as necklaces and rings.
Special	Rare merchants who offer special goods (see the Appendix).
Spell Vendor	Buys and sells spell tomes and scrolls.

STATISTIC	DESCRIPTION
Stablemaster	Sells horses, but they aren't cheap!

Special Area: This object or area has a special significance and should be investigated:

Word Walls	Locations where a Word of Power (Shout) is learned.
Shrines	A small shrine to one of the Divines, where you can receive a small buff and cure your diseases.
Standing Stones	An ancient stone monolith where a powerful ability can be gained or exchanged.
Dragon Mounds	The ancient burial sites of the Dragons; these are disturbed over the course of the Main Quest.
Business Ledger	A shop with a book detailing incomings and outgoings; useful during some Thieves Guild Quests.
Civil War Map	A location showing how the Civil War is progressing. Activate areas to add them to your World Map.

Crafting: This location offers one or more Crafting stations.

Alchemy Lab	A table-sized laboratory where ingredients are mixed (Alchemy Skill).
Arcane Enchanter	A rune-inscribed table where enchantments are imbued or extracted (Enchanting Skill).
Anvil or Blacksmith Forge	The tools of a Blacksmith allowing metal and leather to be molded (Smithing Skill).
Cooking Pot or Spit	A location where basic recipes from food you collect can be cooked.
Grindstone	A wheel that allows weapons to be sharpened (Smithing Skill).
Smelter	A miner's furnace, allowing Ore (and certain Dwarven materials) to be smelted into Ingots.
Tanning Rack	A tool allowing pelts to be dried and turned into leather for Smithing or trade.
Wood Chopping Block	A place where wood can be cut and sold to lumber mill owners.
Workbench	A crafting bench that allows armor to be tempered (Smithing Skill).

Dangers: A potential death-trap that can infect you with disease. Watch for the following traps:

Trap Types	Bear Trap, Battering Ram Trap, Bone Alarm Trap, Dart Trap, Dwarven Ballista Trap, Dwarven Fire Pillar Trap, Dwarven Piston Trap, Dwarven Thresher, Explosive Gas Trap, Flail Trap, Flamethrower Trap, Magic Caster Trap, Mammoth Skull Trap, Oil Lamp Trap, Oil Pool Trap, Poison Gas Trap, Rockfall Trap, Rune Trap, Spear Trap, Swinging Blade Trap, and Swinging Wall Trap.
Puzzle	The location has a brain-teasing puzzle that requires some thinking to solve.
Nordic Puzzle Door	A firmly-sealed door with three concentric metal plates and a central "keyhole."
Nordic Puzzle Pillars	A series of stone pillars to turn and place in the correct orientation.
Rotating Walls	Rotating walls that prevent your progress.
Dwarven Puzzle	A complex mechanical puzzle within some Dwarven Ruins.
Underground Connection	**This location links to another via a subterranean tunnel or series of chambers.**
Collectibles	**An item of worth or interest to you, or a particular individual. Many have special or unique powers.**
Captured Critter	An insect caught in a glass jar. Find these as part of Side Quest: Captured Critters*.
Crimson Nirnroot	A red variant of the chiming plant, found only in Blackreach: Side Quest: A Return to your Roots.
Dragon Priest Mask	A ceremonial mask worn by a dangerous Dragon Priest: Side Quest: Masks of the Dragon Priests*.

STATISTIC	DESCRIPTION
Skill Book	These books increase a specific Skill by a single point when they are first read.
Treasure Map	Pieces of parchment with a visual clue: Side Quest: The Great Skyrim Treasure Hunt*.
Unique Weapon	A particularly powerful weapon of which there is only one of in existence.
Unique Item	A particularly powerful or interesting item of which there is only one of in existence.

STATISTIC	DESCRIPTION
Unusual Gem	These are stones that form the Crown of Barenziah: Thieves Guild Radiant Quest: No Stone Unturned.
Miscellaneous: Any other pertinent information is listed here.	
Area Is Locked	This location requires a specific key to enter (usually as part of a Quest).
Chest (Apothecary's Satchel, Knapsack, Satchel, Stongbox)	One or more chests or containers worth your time to scavenge.

STATISTIC	DESCRIPTION
Potions	Two to five potions are in this general area.
Potions Aplenty	Over five potions are available in this general area.
Loose Gear	A collection of weapons, armor, or spell books is available in this general area.
Lots o' Gold	A sizable haul of gold (or jewelry, including necklaces and pendants) can be found or stolen here.

 NOTE Due to the sheer size of Skyrim and the random nature of what appears inside every chest, knapsack, barrel, and satchel, it is impossible to track everything. If you're looking for ingredient locations, consult the Inventory chapter. If you're looking for Skill Book locations, consult the Appendices.

HOLD 1: HAAFINGAR

TOPOGRAPHICAL OVERVIEW

Haafingar is a hold of fortifications and numerous caves weaving deep into the granite foothills and mountainous terrain that the Hold is famous for. Expect smuggling bolt-holes along the coast and a strong Thalmor presence; their embassy is atop the mountain to the northwest of Solitude. There are two large forts — Northwatch Keep and Fort Hraggstad — where you may face a large number of foes. And you haven't fully experienced Haafingar until you've seen the majesty of the Statue to Meridia and the light of Kilkreath Ruins....

Routes and Pathways

Haafingar Hold is dominated by the massive arch and fortified crenelations of the fortress city of Solitude. For those approaching from Hjaalmarch, this is indeed the landmark of choice. The rest of the Hold has a main path that takes you around the base of the Haafingar mountain range, before petering out along the craggy western edge where progress cannot continue. A few minor pathways shoot off from this main route, which is the recommended way to initially explore, as the rest of this Hold requires careful maneuvering over steep and snowy terrain. Indeed, it is often impossible to reach a Primary Location by trekking over rocks and Tundra alone. The Karth River separates this Hold from Hjaalmarch, with the jagged border of the Reach encroaching just southwest of the Dragon Bridge. The largest stretch of flat ground is the shoreline of the Sea of Ghosts along the northern flank of Haafingar, where travelers are few and the Thalmor are out in force.

AVAILABLE SERVICES, CRAFTING, AND COLLECTIBLES

Services
Followers/Hirelings: [3/47]
Houses for Sale: [1/5]
Marriage Prospects: [5/62]
Skill Trainers: [3/50]
  Alchemy: [0/3]
  Alteration: [1/3]
  Archery: [0/3]
  Block: [0/2]
  Conjuration: [0/3]
  Destruction: [1/3]
  Enchanting: [0/2]
  Heavy Armor: [0/3]
  Illusion: [0/2]
  Light Armor: [0/3]
  Lockpicking: [0/2]

One-Handed: [0/3]
Pickpocket: [0/3]
Restoration: [0/3]
Smithing: [0/3]
Sneak: [0/3]
Speech: [1/4]
Two-Handed: [0/2]
Spells Vendors: [0/10]
Traders [15/133]:
  Apothecary [1/12]
  Bartender [0/5]
  Blacksmith [2/33]
  Carriage Driver [1/5]
  Fence [1/10]
  Fletcher [1/3]
  Food Vendor [3/9]

General Goods [2/19]
Innkeeper [2/15]
Jeweler [0/2]
Special [0/3]
Spell Vendor [1/12]
Stablemaster [1/5]

Collectibles
Dragon Priest Masks [1/10]
Larceny Targets [1/7]
Skill Books [17/180]
  Alchemy [2/10]
  Alteration [1/10]
  Archery [1/10]
  Block [0/10]
  Conjuration [1/10]
  Destruction [2/10]

Enchanting: [0/10]
Heavy Armor: [0/10]
Illusion: [1/10]
Light Armor: [2/10]
Lockpicking: [0/10]
One-Handed: [2/10]
Pickpocket: [0/10]
Restoration: [0/10]
Smithing: [0/10]
Sneak: [0/10]
Speech: [2/10]
Two-Handed: [3/10]
Unique Items: [5/112]
Unique Weapons: [5/80]
Unusual Gems: [4/24]

Special Objects
Shrines: [10/69]
  Akatosh: [1/6]
  Arkay: [2/12]
  Dibella: [1/8]
  Julianos: [1/5]
  Kynareth: [1/6]
  Mara: [1/5]
  Stendarr: [1/5]
  Talos: [1/17]
  Zenithar: [1/5]
Standing Stones: [1/13]
  The Steed Stone [1/13]
Word Walls: [2/42]
  Elemental Fury: [1/3]
  Whirlwind Sprint: [1/2]

CRAFTING STATIONS: HAAFINGAR

✓	TYPE	LOCATION A	LOCATION B
☐	Alchemy Lab	Solitude (Angeline's Aromatics) [1.00]	Solitude (Castle Dour) [1.00]
☐	Arcane Enchanter	Solitude (Erikur's House) [1.00]	Solitude (Blue Palace) [1.00]
☐	Anvil or Blacksmith Forge	Solitude (Blacksmith) [1.00]	Fort Hraggstad (Exterior) [1.08]
☐	Cooking Pot and Spit	Solitude (Radiant Raiment) [1.00]	Dragon Bridge (Horgeir's House) [1.17]

✓	TYPE	LOCATION A	LOCATION B
☐	Grindstone	Solitude (Blacksmith) [1.00]	Solitude (Exterior: Executioner's Platform) [1.00]
☐	Smelter	Broken Oar Grotto [1.19]	—
☐	Tanning Rack	Solitude (Blacksmith) [1.00]	Dragon Bridge (Exterior: Penitus Oculatus Outpost) [1.17]

✓	TYPE	LOCATION A	LOCATION B
☐	Wood Chopping Block	Dragon Bridge (Exterior) [1.17]	Broken Oar Grotto [1.19]
☐	Workbench	Solitude (Blacksmith) [1.00]	Dragon Bridge (Exterior: Penitus Oculatus Outpost) [1.17]

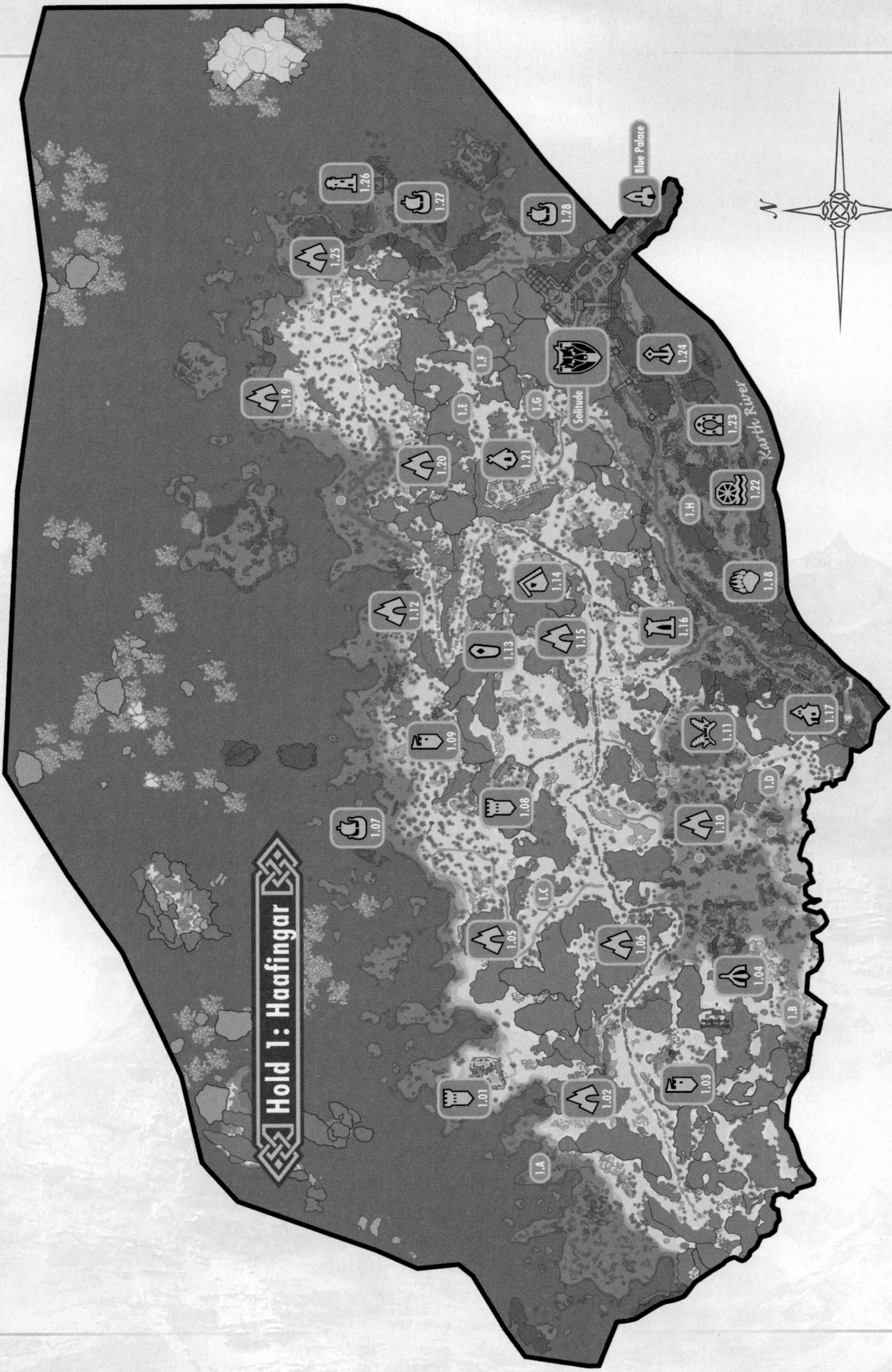

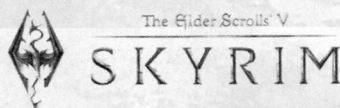

Blue Palace

1.26

1.27

1.28

1.25

1.F

1.24

1.19

1.E   1.G

Solitude

1.23

1.20   1.21

1.22

1.H

1.18

1.14

1.12

1.15

1.16

Karth River

1.13

1.17

1.09

1.11

1.D

1.08

1.10

1.07

1.C

1.05

1.06

1.04

1.B

1.01   1.02   1.03

1.A

Hold 1: Haafingar

PRIMARY LOCATIONS

Total — 30: Hold Capital, Blue Palace, and 28 Hold Locations

[1.00] Hold Capital City: Solitude
[1.00] Blue Palace
    Jarl: Elisif the Fair
[1.01] Northwatch Keep
[1.02] Rimerock Burrow
[1.03] Pinefrost Tower
[1.04] Volskygge

[1.05] Steepfall Burrow and Lower Steepfall Burrow
[1.06] Lost Echo Cave
[1.07] Orphan's Tear
[1.08] Fort Hraggstad
[1.09] Widow's Watch Ruins
[1.10] Pinemoon Cave
[1.11] Clearpine Pond
[1.12] Ravenscar Hollow

[1.13] The Steed Stone
[1.14] Ironback Hideout
[1.15] Wolfskull Cave
[1.16] Statue to Meridia and Kilkreath Ruins
[1.17] Dragon Bridge
[1.18] Haafingar Stormcloak Camp
[1.19] Broken Oar Grotto
[1.20] Shadowgreen Cavern

[1.21] Thalmor Embassy
[1.22] Solitude Sawmill
[1.23] Katla's Farm
[1.24] East Empire Company Warehouse
[1.25] Brinewater Grotto
[1.26] Solitude Lighthouse
[1.27] Dainty Sload
[1.28] The Katariah

SECONDARY LOCATIONS

Total — 8 Points of Interest

[1.A] Clam Digger's Camp
[1.B] Forsworn Ambush Camp
[1.C] Howling Wolf's Folly
[1.D] Pinemoon Bear Lair

[1.E] Haafingar Sabre Cat's Lair
[1.F] Pincushion Peter
[1.G] Haafingar Nordic Burial Ruins
[1.H] Solitude Attack Camp

HOLD CAPITAL: SOLITUDE

Habitation: Hold Capital (Major)

> **NOTE** * Quest names marked with this symbol do not appear in your Quest Menu list, although objectives may.

Related Quests

Main Quest: Diplomatic Immunity
Main Quest: Season Unending
Civil War Quest: Joining the Legion
Civil War Quest: The Jagged Crown
Civil War Quest: Message to Whiterun
Civil War Quest: Reunification of Skyrim
Civil War Quest: A False Front
Civil War Quest: Rescue from Fort Kastav
Civil War Quest: The Battle for Fort Dunstad
Civil War Quest: The Battle for Fort Greenwall
Civil War Quest: Liberation of Skyrim
Civil War Quest: Battle for Solitude
Daedric Quest: The Mind of Madness
Side Quest: The Man Who Cried Wolf
Side Quest: The Wolf Queen Awakened
Side Quest: Lights Out!
Other Factions: Bards College Quest: Tending the Flames
Other Factions: Bards College Quest: Finn's Lute
Other Factions: Bards College Quest: Pantea's Flute
Other Factions: Bards College Quest: Rjorn's Drum
Dark Brotherhood Quest: Bound Until Death
Dark Brotherhood Quest: Breaching Security
Dark Brotherhood Quest: To Kill an Empire
Thieves Guild Quest: Scoundrel's Folly
Thieves Guild Radiant Quest: No Stone Unturned (x2)
Thieves Guild City Influence Quest: The Dainty Sload
Dungeon Activity (Solitude Jail)
Miscellaneous Objective: Innkeeper Rumors (the Winking Skeever)
Miscellaneous Objective: Angeline and Aldis* (Angeline Morrard)
Miscellaneous Objective: Looking Radiant* (Taarie)
Miscellaneous Objective: Spiced Wine Shipment* (Evette San)
Favor (Activity): The Gift of Charity* (Svari)
Favor (Activity): The Gift of Charity* (Noster One-Eye)
Favor (Activity): The Gift of Charity* (Dervenin)
Favor: A Good Talking To* (Octieve San)
Favor: The Bandit Slayer* (Ahtar)
Favor: The Vampire Slayer* (Sybille Stentor)
Favor: Rare Item Hunt* (Captain Aldis)
Favor: Item Retrieval (Cave)* (Noster One-Eye)
Thane Quest: Thane of Haafingar*

Crafting

Alchemy Lab
Arcane Enchanters (2)
Blacksmith Forge
Grindstones (3)
Workbench

Services

Follower: Belrand [1/47]
Follower: Ahtar the Jailor [2/47]
Follower: Jordis the Sword-Maiden [3/47]
House for Sale: Proudspire Manor [1/5]
Marriage Prospect: Belrand [1/62]
Marriage Prospect: Sorex Vinius [2/62]
Marriage Prospect: Taarie [3/62]
Marriage Prospect: Jordis the Sword-Maiden [4/62]
Marriage Prospect: Octieve San [5/62]
Trader (Apothecary): Angeline Morrard [1/12]
Trader (Apothecary): Vivienne Onis [2/12]
Trader (Blacksmith): Beirand [1/33]
Trader (Carriage): Thaer [1/5]
Trader (Fence): Gulum-Ei [1/11] (after Thieves Guild Quest completion)
Trader (Fetcher): Fihada [1/3]
Trader (Food Vendor): Addvar [1/9]
Trader (Food Vendor): Jala [2/9]
Trader (Food Vendor): Evette San [3/9]
Trader (General Store Vendor): Endarie [1/19]
Trader (General Store Vendor): Sayma [3/19]
Trader (Innkeeper): Corpulus Vinius [1/15]
Trainer (Alteration: Journeyman): Melaran [1/3]
Trainer (Speech: Master): Giraud Gemane [1/4]
Trainer (Spell Vendor): Sybille Stentor [1/12]

Collectibles

Skill Book [Alchemy]: Song of the Alchemists [E1/10]
Skill Book [Archery]: The Gold Ribbon of Merit [C1/10]
Skill Book [Light Armor]: The Rear Guard [D1/10]
Skill Book [Light Armor]: The Refugees [E1/10]
Skill Book [Speech]: Biography of the Wolf Queen [D1/10]
Skill Book [Speech]: The Buying Game [E1/10]
Skill Book [Two-Handed]: Song of Hrormir [C1/10]
Unique Item: Asgeir's Wedding Band [1/112]
Unique Item: Vittoria's Wedding Band [2/112]
Unique Item: Shield of Solitude [3/112]
Unique Weapon: Headsman's Axe [1/80]
Unique Weapon: Firiniel's End [2/80]
Unusual Gem: [1/24]
Unusual Gem: [2/24]

Special Objects

Shrine of Akatosh [1/6]
Shrines of Arkay (2) [1/12; 2/12]
Shrine of Dibella [1/8]
Shrine of Julianos [1/5]
Shrine of Kynareth [1/6]
Shrine of Mara [1/5]
Shrine of Stendarr [1/5]
Shrine of Talos [1/17]
Shrine of Zenithar [1/5]
Business Ledgers
Civil War: Map of Skyrim
Chest(s)
Potions aplenty
Loose gear

⟐ Lore: City Overview

Solitude is the jewel of Imperial Skyrim. Ruled by Jarl Elisif the Fair, widow of the late High King, it is home to the headquarters of both the Legion and the Thalmor. Part of the reason for this is the eminently defensible nature of Solitude itself. Set upon a great stone arch that towers above the mouth of the Karth River, and surrounded by the soaring peaks of the Haafingar Mountains, Solitude is both a reinforced and breathtaking stronghold. Given the city's name, it may be ironic that over 80 percent of the Hold's population lives within Solitude's walls, but this is testament to the city's political importance, formidable defenses, and diverse population. The Bard's College is located here, as well as the sumptuous Blue Palace. Both are constructed atop the huge, natural arch that the city rests on, affording spectacular views over the Sea of Ghosts and Hjaalmarch to the east. Solitude's accessible docks and wharfs are in relatively calm waters, making trade one of the many reasons why the wealthiest Nords hail from this capital city. Solitude is the one, true cosmopolitan city of Skyrim.

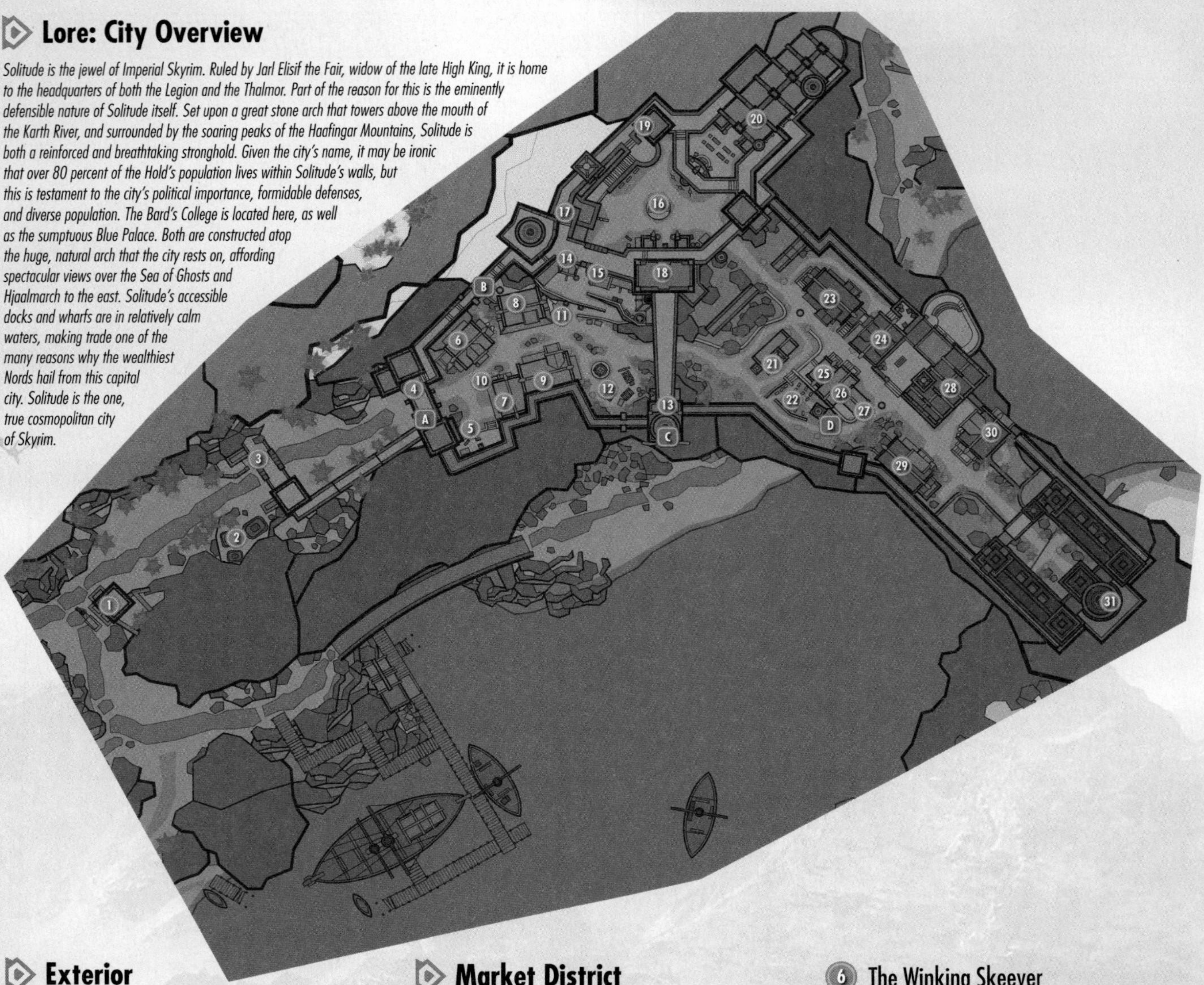

⟐ Exterior

① Lower Watchtower

Close to Katla's Farm and the Solitude Stables is a single watchtower at the base of the western (and main) entrance to Solitude. Thaer's carriage waits here for customers; you can take it to any other Hold City.

◇ Trader (Carriage): Thaer [1/5]

② Ma'dran's Caravan

When they aren't traveling, Ma'dran and his Khajiit brethren set up camp here. You can purchase a variety of wares from them. They also become Fences for you during the Thieves Guild Quests.

◇ Trader (Caravan Vendor): Ma'dran [19/19]
  ○ Weapons, Apparel, Potions, Food, Ingredients, Misc

③ Outer Gate

④ Main Gate

⟐ Market District

A variety of traders ply their wares in this southwestern district of the city. Aside from the traders, the marketplace is dominated by executioner's platform and the market stalls, which features a well said to be one of the oldest structures in Solitude.

Ⓐ Main Gate: Exit to Skyrim

⑤ Executioner's Platform

The first time you enter Solitude, a small crowd has gathered to watch the execution of Roggvir for crimes against the Empire; he allowed Ulfric Stormcloak to escape the city after killing the High King. Unless you interrupt (a crime), Roggvir is beheaded while the citizens watch, some cheering. There is an entrance up onto the crenellations above the main gate, allowing you to move (or sneak) around the city's perimeter walls.

◇ Crafting: Grindstone

---

⑥ The Winking Skeever

Corpulus Vinius	Minette Vinius	Belrand
Sorex Vinius	Lisette	Gulum-Ei

The Winking Skeever is the only tavern in town and is sometimes host to a variety of interesting (and undesirable) folks. Corpulus Vinius runs this establishment. The minstrel Lisette plays here in the afternoons and evenings. The place is famous for wine and mead imported from Riften. Should Corpulus die, his son Sorex Vinius will run the inn. You can hire Belrand here. The upstairs rooms have numerous books to read. The wine cellar has a chest to steal from.

◇ Follower: Belrand [1/47]
◇ Marriage Prospect: Belrand [1/62]
◇ Marriage Prospect: Sorex Vinius [2/62]
◇ Trader (Fence): Gulum-Ei (after Thieves Guild Quest completion)

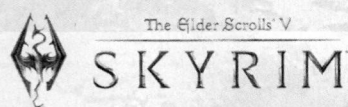

- ◇ Trader (Innkeeper): Corpulus Vinius [1/15]
  - ○ Food, Room and Board
  - ○ Quest Rumors
- ◇ Business Ledger
- ◇ Strongbox (Adept)
- ◇ Chest
- ◇ Potions

7 Radiant Raiment

Endarie   Taarie

Taarie runs this shop with her twin sister, Endarie. They live above the shop. There are two chests (one in the cellar, the other upstairs) and a large amount of food and some books to peruse.

- ◇ Shadowmark: "Loot"
- ◇ Marriage Prospect: Taarie [3/62]
  - ○ Apparel
- ◇ Trader (General Store Vendor): Taarie [2/25]
  - ○ Apparel
- ◇ Business Ledger
- ◇ Strongbox (Adept)
- ◇ Chest (2)
- ◇ Business Ledger

8 Angeline's Aromatics

Angeline Morrard   Vivienne Onis

Angeline Morrard runs this shop with her niece Vivienne Onis. They live above the shop. The shop itself is a tiny affair, consisting of a simple small room with a counter. The walls behind the counter are lined with strange ingredients, potions, and dead animals. There's a large number of potions and ingredients to purchase (or steal) here, an alchemy table, a chest in the cellar, and a strongbox upstairs near the ledger.

- ◇ Crafting: Alchemy Lab
- ◇ Trader (Apothecary): Angeline Morrard [1/14]
  - ○ Potions, Food, Ingredients
- ◇ Trader (Apothecary): Vivienne Onis [2/15]
  - ○ Potions, Food, Ingredients
- ◇ Business Ledger
- ◇ Strongbox (Apprentice)
- ◇ Chest
- ◇ Potions aplenty

9 Bits and Pieces

Sayma   Kayd

Sayma runs this shop. Her son, Kayd, is there to help her but ends up underfoot more often than not. They live above the shop. Sayma's home has food, books to read, a chest in the cellar, and a strongbox and ledger in an upstairs room.

- ◇ Shadowmark: "Loot"
- ◇ Trader (General Store Vendor): Sayma [2/25]
  - ○ Weapons, Apparel, Potions, Scrolls, Food, Ingredients, Books, Misc
- ◇ Business Ledger
- ◇ Strongbox (Apprentice)
- ◇ Chest
- ◇ Potions
- ◇ Loose gear

10 Noster One-Eye

Noster Eagle-Eye

This beggar requests a gold coin from you. Oblige, and you receive the Gift of Charity.

- ◇ Ability: The Gift of Charity

11 Jaree-Ra

Jaree-Ra

An Argonian with a variety of interesting (and illegal) schemes. He usually mooches around this area, sometimes visiting Angeline's Aromatics.

12 Market Stalls and the Well

Addvar   Jala   Evette San

These stalls sell a variety of wares: Addvar sells fish from his cart. His wife, Greta, will take over for him should he die. Jala sells fruit and vegetables from her cart. Evette San sells spiced wine from her cart. The old well isn't used anymore.

- ◇ Trader (Food Vendor): Addvar [1/9]
  - ○ Potions, Food, Ingredients
- ◇ Trader (Food Vendor): Jala [2/9]
  - ○ Potions, Food, Ingredients
- ◇ Trader (Food Vendor): Evette San [3/9]
  - ○ Potions, Food, Ingredients

B Castle Dour Dungeon Exit

This grating is inaccessible from the street. It is an escape route leading from a secret exit inside one of the prison cells in the Castle Dour Dungeon.

13 South Gate

C South Gate Exit to Skyrim

This windmill landmark can be seen from miles around. The ground-level gate leads to a spiral staircase down to the docks and out into Skyrim. The staircase up leads to a battlement and the rear (and unlocked) entrance to the Emperor's Tower.

Castle Dour

  Dominating the city's northern district is Castle Dour. Thick-walled and imposing, it protected its inhabitants from invaders. As the city grew, walls were added to surround the other, newer buildings. During a long period of peace, the Blue Palace was built for the Jarl, and Castle Dour became a secondary fortress. It now houses the Imperial Garrison and the Temple of the Divines. Find a couple of Skill Books around the sleeping area here:

- ◇ Skill Book [Light Armor]: The Rear Guard [D1/10]

14 Fletcher

Fihada
Jawanan

Fihada runs this shop with his apprentice Jawanan. There are a large number of fine weapons to buy (or to steal) here. There's a chest in the ground-floor bedroom and a ledger and strongbox upstairs.

- ◇ Trader (Fletcher): Fihada [1/3]
  - ○ Weapons and Misc
- ◇ Skill Book [Archery]: The Gold Ribbon of Merit [C1/10]
- ◇ Business Ledger
- ◇ Strongbox (Adept)
- ◇ Chest
- ◇ Potions aplenty
- ◇ Loose gear

15 Solitude Blacksmith

Beirand   Helmvar

Beirand works for the army and the city guard. However, he has permission to do work on the side, making and repairing weapons and armor for anyone who comes in. However, he can't let it interfere with his other work. Should Beirand die, his apprentice Helmvar will take over. Beirand is married to Sayma and has a son named Kayd. Outside his shop is a full complement of crafting locations and a second grindstone inside the Blacksmith's. Up in Beirand's bedroom, there's a ledger, Skill Book, and strongbox.

- ◇ Crafting: Blacksmith's Forge
- ◇ Crafting: Grindstones (2)
- ◇ Crafting: Workbench

◇ Trader (Blacksmith): Beirand [1/33]
  ○ Weapons, Apparel, and Misc
◇ Skill Book [Light Armor]: The Refugees [E1/10]
◇ Business Ledger
◇ Strongbox (Adept)

16 Courtyard and Crenellations

Captain Aldis

The ground-level features Solitude Guards practicing archery and sword strikes. Captain Aldis presides over this training, along with the execution you saw as you walked in. Head up the stone ramp to the crenellations, allowing quick (and more stealthy) access above the castle grounds to an upper entrance into Castle Dour and the Thalmor Headquarters, the Temple of the Divines, and then back into the market district. You can even drop off these crenellations, grabbing hanging moss or a bird's nest if you're facing southeast.

17 Castle Dour (Interior)

General Tullius   Ahtar the Jailor
Legate Rikke   Gianna

In ages gone by, there was just the castle keep. Thick walled and imposing, it protected its inhabitants from invaders. As the city grew, walls were added to surround the other, newer buildings. During a long period of peace, a separate palace was built for the Jarl. Castle Dour became an oversized gatehouse. It was eventually converted into the city's Imperial Garrison. General Tullius is in charge of the Imperial forces in Skyrim. He lives and works here along with his second in command, Legate Rikke.

◇ Follower: Ahtar the Jailor [2/47]
Unique Weapon: Headsman's Axe [1/80]

General Tullius's War Room (Ground Floor)

The main level of the castle is given over to a battle map of Skyrim, where General Tullius and Legate Rikke plan the countermeasures against the Stormcloaks. It is here you can join with them during the Civil War Quests.

◇ Civil War: Map of Skyrim
◇ Loose gear

Legate Rikke's Room (Ground Floor)

A simple dining table and bed.

General Tullius's Room (Upper Floor)

This connects to the War Room and the crenellations exit via a corridor and stairs. A large bed dominates this chamber.

◇ Potions
◇ Loose gear

Garrison Barracks (Lower Floor)

Legate Aventus Caesennius runs a tight ship down here where the city guards and conscripts sleep. There's a kitchen here filled with food and an armory of Imperial weapons and equipment.

◇ Skill Book [Light Armor]: The Rear-Guard [D1/10]
◇ Loose gear

Castle Dour Dungeon (Lower Floor)

Commit a crime in Haafingar and the guards will throw you in the dungeons of Castle Dour. Ahtar the Jailor (who was part of the execution when you first arrived in Solitude) runs this place. The upper level is a circular balcony overlooking the dungeon level. There are guards, scattered food and weapons, and three chambers along the outer wall to your right. The first is an interrogation room, the second is a torture room, and the third is Ahtar's office, with steps leading down to the evidence chamber on the lower level. Notice the hole in the wall near the belongings chest? This allows you to recover your equipment when escaping through the secret passage.

◇ Evidence Chest
◇ Prisoner Belongings Chest
◇ Loose gear

Castle Dour Dungeon (Dungeon Floor)

The roughly circular lower level features seven cells, most of them locked. Bjartur, a Stormcloak Soldier, is held in one of the cells if the Imperials control the city. You're usually placed in a cell on the jail's south side.

Instead of serving out your sentence, check the crumbling mortar on the wall behind you. It falls away, enabling you to flee into a dungeon corridor. Check the small hole, allowing you to reach into the Prisoner Belongings Chest in the evidence room. Then flee to the ladder, bringing you up into the Market District, [B] Castle Dour Dungeon Exit. Note that you can only do this once; after you escape, the guards repair the wall, and you'll have to serve your time or escape in the usual way in the future.

◇ Prisoner Belongings

18 Emperor's Tower (Interior)

Emperor Titus Mede III

Reviled by the Stormcloaks for his "betrayal" in the Markarth Incident and admired by the Imperials and Loyalists for his steadfastness during the Great War, Titus Mede is somewhat of a tragic figure, being forced by the weakness of the Empire to make deals with those he despises (the Thalmor) in order to preserve the Empire from total destruction.

This is the residence of the Emperor when he is in Solitude. You will come here for Dark Brotherhood Quest: To Kill an Empire.

Throne Room (Ground Floor)

Emperor Titus Mede III isn't usually here. This offers access to the kitchens and the upper floor.

Kitchens (Ground Floor)

As you'd expect, there's an abundance of food, tended to by the chef.

Upper Landing (Upper Floor)

There's an empty bedroom and a door requiring a key, unlocked by the chef during the quest. A Skill Book rests on a table in the small sitting area.

◇ Skill Book [Enchanting]: Catalogue of Weapon Enchantments

Banqueting Hall (Upper Floor)

This is where the Emperor and his trusted cohorts eat and talk about politics. There is an exit out to the South Gate (windmill).

19 Thalmor Headquarters

The hated Justiciars are headquartered in the garrison. Effectively run by the Thalmor, they oversee the terms of the peace accords signed by the Empire. Principally, this means rooting out Talos worshippers. Elenwen is the head of the Justiciars. Sometimes she forces her opinion on General Tullius as well. He has little use for her advice, but his emperor has commanded him to follow her orders on matters related to the treaty. Mostly this location is relatively empty, with the Thalmor more content to rule Skyrim from the remote Embassy in the mountains above Solitude. Check inside for a number of books to read, and the following:

◇ Civil War: Map of Skyrim
◇ Potions aplenty
◇ Loose gear

20 Temple of the Divines

Rorlund   Freir   Silana Petreia

Formerly the Temple of the Nine Divines, this is the largest temple in all of Skyrim. Unlike the other temples, it reflects the Imperial view of all eight divinities being equal and represented. Outside is a small courtyard where Vittoria Vici's marriage will take place. There are several doors leading to and from the roof if you want a better look down onto this courtyard. Inside are shrines for each of the eight gods, plus an empty place where the Shrine to Talos once stood. If you side with the Stormcloaks during the Civil War Quests and take Solitude for Ulfric, the Shrine to Talos is reinstated. Each provides a Blessing.

Upstairs is a withdrawing area and exit to the crenellations. Downstairs is a storage room and a firmly sealed door, which can only be opened during Side Quest: The Wolf Queen Awakened. It leads to a second, dust-filled wine cellar, past a Health Potion to a hole in the wall and into Potema's Catacombs.

◇ Unique Item: Asgeir's Wedding Band [1/112]
◇ Unique Item: Vittoria's Wedding Band [2/112]
◇ Unique Weapon: Firiniel's End [2/80]
◇ Shrine of Akatosh [1/6]
◇ Shrine of Arkay [1/12]

◇ Shrine of Arkay [1/12]
◇ Shrine of Dibella [1/8]
◇ Shrine of Julianos [1/5]
◇ Shrine of Kynareth [1/6]
◇ Shrine of Mara [1/5]
◇ Shrine of Stendarr [1/5]
◇ Shrine of Talos [1/17]
◇ Shrine of Zenithar [1/5]

The Avenues District

Sometimes referred to as "the Stately Avenues of Old Solitude," it's more commonly just called the Avenues. This is the residential section of the city.

21 Hall of the Dead (Solitude Catacombs)

Styrr

This mausoleum is filled with vaults. The dead of Haafingar are buried here. As the local priest of Arkay, Styrr is the cemetery caretaker. Although this could just be his demeanor, Styrr believes that darkness is drawn to Solitude. Upstairs, Styrr's room has a long chest to pilfer from and a small chest behind the door. Into the cellar, there's the corridor to Solitude Catacombs.

◇ Shrine of Arkay [2/12]
◇ Chest (2)
◇ Potions aplenty
◇ Loose gear

Solitude Catacombs (Interior)

This houses the remains of the dead from across Haafingar. Expect three skeletons roaming these catacombs and an exit leading back out, onto the graveyard [D].

22 Dervenin the Mad

Dervenin the Mad

This lunatic beggar wanders around the Hall of the Dead graveyard and down the Avenues. He talks about his abandoned master, which is the prelude (and way to begin) Daedric Quest: The Mind of Madness. He also requests a gold coin from you. Oblige, and you receive the Gift of Charity.

◇ Ability: The Gift of Charity

D Solitude Catacombs Exit

23 Vittoria Vici's House

Vittoria Vici

Vittoria Vici heads down from this house to supervise the shipping and distribution of goods from the port. She is a wealthy woman, about to be married. Her house reflects this opulence, as do the Shadowmarks etched near the main doorway. There are three entrances.

The main floor of the house is comprised of a hallway, living area, and kitchen. There are books to read and food to eat. Upstairs is a small balcony library and a bedroom with a chest to check. In the cellar, there's an exit and a display case with a valuable weapon in it to steal.

◇ Shadowmark: "Loot"

◇ Chest (2)

◇ Loose gear

 24 Proudspire

Manor (House for Sale)

This dwelling is currently empty. It was the scene of a gruesome murder, and there's rumors of it being haunted. Should you become the Thane of Haafingar (by completing Favors for the citizens and the Jarl), you can purchase this abode from Jarl Elisif the Fair's Steward, Falk Firebeard—you'll then find one of the Unusual Gems that pertain to the Thieves Guild Radiant Quest: No Stone Unturned. Consult the quests chapters for more information.

◇ Marriage Prospect: Jordis the Sword-Maiden [4/62]

◇ Unusual Gem: [1/24]

25 Addvar's House

Greta   Svari

This is the first of three terraced houses and flagged with a Shadowmark. Addvar the street vendor lives here. It's a small place, bordering on run-down. His wife, Greta, and daughter Svari live here with him. Unlock the door (Novice), entering a modest home with a large amount of stored cheese and a cooking pot and chest. Upstairs is a small bedroom and second chest.

◇ Shadowmark: "Loot"   ◇ Chest (2)

26 Evette San's House

Octieve San

This is the middle terraced house, flagged with a Shadowmark. Evette San the street vendor lives here with her invalid father, Octieve San. It's not a hovel, but it wouldn't have to fall apart much more to become one. Open the door (Novice): Inside is another cheese stockpile and a knapsack in the storage area to the rear. There are two chests upstairs in the balcony bedroom.

◇ Shadowmark: "Loot"   ◇ Chest (2)

◇ Marriage Prospect: ◇ Knapsack
   Octieve San [5/62]

◇ Loose gear

27 Jala's House

Jala the street vendor lives here with her friend and lover, Ahtar. It's a poor home, reflecting her lack of wealth. There's a pile of Iron Ingots to steal on the ground floor and two chests upstairs.

◇ Shadowmark: "Empty"

◇ Skill Book [Two-Handed]: Song of Hrormir [C1/10]

◇ Chest (2)

◇ Knapsack

28 Bard's College

Viarmo	Jorn	Bendt
Giraud Gemane	Aia Arria	Giraud Gemane
Inge Six-Fingers	At-Af-Alan	
Pantea Ateia	Illdi	

A large building where bards come from all parts of Skyrim and beyond to learn how to sing and play instruments. There are two entrances, and all are welcome. Outside is a large stone courtyard where the Burning of Old King Olaf festival was historically held. Each student works with all the different teachers during the course of a week. However, each has preferred instruments or instructors.

Cellar (Lower Floor)

This contains a sleeping area with four beds for the current students. There is a common area, Brendt's small bedroom, and a kitchen here too.

Main Entrance Hall (Main Floor)

The main entrance here is made to receive guests and is built to impress. Giraud Gemane and Viarmo are usually here. Nearby is a well-stocked library and a bar. If you are on Favor: Rare Item Hunt for Lami in Morthal, you can find a skill book on the counter in the library.

◇ Skill Book [Alchemy]: Song of the Alchemists [E1/10]

Bedrooms (Main Floor)

There are four bedrooms here, each with a variety of books and instruments, and a bed for each of the teachers.

Classrooms (Upper Floor)

The top floor of the College has two large classrooms filled with more books and instruments. Find another Skill Book secreted among a stack of common tomes on the top tier of a tall metal shelf up here.

◇ Skill Book [Speech]: The Buying Game [E1/10]

29 Erikur's House

Erikur   Melaran

Erikur is a Thane of Solitude, and his house is a large, grand structure. Notice the Shadowmarks near the entrances. Inside, the cellar has little more than barrels and some stocked food. The main floor is dominated by the Arcane Enchanter, various potions, and a few ingredients. Upstairs is a balcony running around the entire perimeter, a small library, and a single bedroom with a long chest to steal from.

◇ Shadowmark: "Protected"   ◇ Trainer (Alteration:
                                  Journeyman): Melaran [1/3]
◇ Crafting: Arcane Enchanter
                                ◇ Chest

                                ◇ Potions aplenty

30 Bryling's House

Bryling

Irnskar Ironhand

Bryling is an important Thane, and the house reflects this, although her treasury is getting empty. Irnskar Ironhand is her retainer and likely to be guarding inside this place. The wine cellar has a knapsack and some scattered weaponry and clothes. The main floor has an extensive library and a variety of food. Upstairs there are two bedrooms, one with a chest.

◇ Shadowmark: "Loot"   ◇ Loose gear

◇ Chest

31 Blue Palace

Jarl Elisif the Fair	Bolgeir Bearclaw	Erdi
Falk Firebeard	Sybille Stentor	Una
	Odar	

The following leaders of Solitude are loyal to the Imperials at the start of the Civil War. They remain in place, even if Solitude falls to the Stormcloaks, at the end of the Civil War Quests.

Jarl Elisif the Fair

With the recent death of Jarl Torygg, his beautiful widow, Elisif, rules Solitude for now. She is a young Nord woman, wholly unsuited to rule. The real power lies with General Tullius, technically an Imperial advisor. Personally, Elisif is sympathetic to the Imperial cause. She has a personal hatred for the Stormcloak leader Ulfric, who killed her husband, Torygg, and is just politically savvy enough to realize that her rule, and probably her head, are in place only so long as she is useful to the Empire. She believes that should the Empire regain control of Skyrim, she would be made High Queen.

Falk Firebeard (Steward)

Falk also serves as treasurer when necessary. He is a skilled bureaucrat, despite his years as a member of the Companions. He is loyal to Elisif but frequently gets frustrated at her foolishness. His hair is bright red, although shot with gray, hence his name.

◇ Unique Item: Shield of Solitude [3/112]

Bolgeir Bearclaw (Housecarl)

Jarl Elisif never goes anywhere without Bolgeir. He is utterly loyal and highly competent. What he lacks in creativity and social sensitivity, he makes up for in ferociousness. As a youth, he hunted bears. Once, when a bear turned on him, he cut its paw off with a single blow of his axe.

Sybille Stentor (Court Wizard)

Although she has served the Jarls of Solitude for over 20 years, Sybille looks no more than 18. Palace gossip has a multitude of theories for her unnatural youth. The one about her being a vampire may hold most credence. Her role as Court Wizard is a convenience.

◇ Trainer (Spell Vendor): Sybille Stentor [1/12]

Solitude's other awe-inspiring landmark is its ornate palace, where the newly appointed Jarl Elisif the Fair resides. It is built on the ruins of the old palace, which was burned to the ground when Queen Potema was finally defeated in the War of the Red Diamond. There is only one entrance: from the cloisters at the end of the Avenues District.

Entrance Staircases (Ground Floor)

Through the Receiving Hall is a pair of impressive curved staircases and guards dotted around. To the right (southwest) is a chest and a door to the Pelagius Wing, which is firmly sealed. To the left (northeast) is a corridor to the kitchens and private staircase.

Kitchens (Ground Floor)

A large array of food is stocked here, presided over by Odar the chef. There's a storage corridor to the northwest leading to wine barrels and a servants' bedroom.

Large Bedroom (Ground Floor)

Close to the private steps, there are two large beds in here but little to steal.

Cellar (Lower Floor)

Head down the private steps to a chamber of beds and a chest.

◇ Chest

Jarl's Throne Room (Upper Floor)

Atop the curved stairs (or the private ones) is the main chamber where Jarl Elisif the Fair resides and listens to the news of the day and any worries her subjects may have. She is guarded by Bolgeir Bearclaw, her Housecarl. She is flanked by Sybille Stentor (Court Wizard), Falk Firebeard (Steward), and the two Thanes Erikur and Bryling.

Northeast Corridor (Upper Floor)

To the left (northeast) is a corridor where you'll find a book named *Lost Legends* on a low table (read it to start a quest). The corridor leads to the Court Wizard's bedroom. There's an Arcane Enchanter and some impressive staffs, potions, and books on show here. To the north is Falk's small bedroom and the Jarl's bedchamber. This impressive room has a small alcove with a Skill Book and an Unusual Gem on the bedside cabinet.

◇ Crafting: Arcane Enchanter

◇ Skill Book [Speech]: Biography of the Wolf Queen [D1/10]

◇ Unusual Gem: Stone of Barenziah [2/24]

◇ Chest

◇ Potions aplenty

Pelagius Wing (Ground Floor)

This part of the palace is sealed off and uninhabited. This wing is where Pelagius the Mad lived before becoming Emperor and is said to be cursed. No one will set foot in there. If you begin Daedric Quest: The Mind of Madness and obtain the key from Falk Firebeard, you can journey into the depths of the long-dead ruler's mind itself!

◉ Potema's Catacombs

Related Quests

Side Quest: The Man Who Cried Wolf
Side Quest: The Wolf Queen Awakened

Dungeon: Vampire Lair

Draugr
Vampire

Crafting

Alchemy Lab
Grindstone

Dangers

Flamethrower Trap (pressure plate)
Oil Lamp Trap
Oil Pool Trap
Swinging Wall Trap (pressure plate)
Trapped Chest
Quest Items: Potema's Skull

Collectibles

Skill Book [Lockpicking]: Surfeit of Thieves
Area Is Locked (quest required)
Chest(s)
Potions
Loose gear

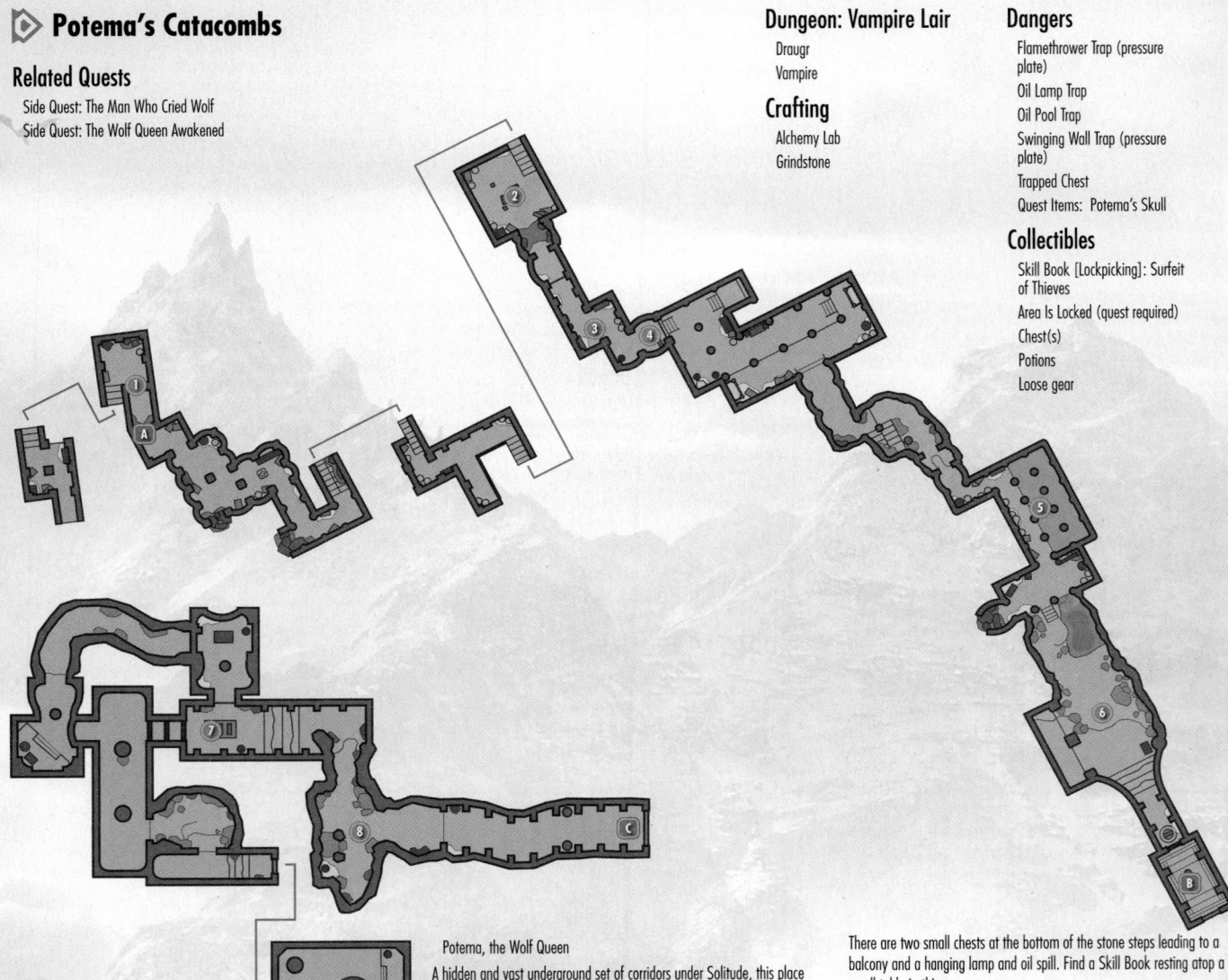

Potema, the Wolf Queen

A hidden and vast underground set of corridors under Solitude, this place of evil is only accessible during Side Quest: The Wolf Queen Awakened. You reach the Catacombs via the cellar of the Temple of the Divines. It is otherwise completely sealed off.

Potema's Catacombs (Interior)

(A) Passage to Temple of the Divines

(1) Wolf Queen Frieze

Potema mocks and threatens you at this wall frieze of the Wolf Queen and removes the archway spears blocking your path. Your first Draugr attack occurs just afterward, in the cobwebbed and abandoned dungeon bar.

(2) Banquet Chamber

There are two small chests at the bottom of the stone steps leading to a balcony and a hanging lamp and oil spill. Find a Skill Book resting atop a small table in this area.

◇ Danger! Oil Lamp Trap

◇ Danger! Oil Pool Trap

◇ Skill Book [Lockpicking]: Surfeit of Thieves

(3) Draugr Vaults

Watch out for the fire trap and pressure plate close to one Draugr alcove.

◇ Danger! Flamethrower Trap (pressure plate)

(4) Portcullis

Use the wall lever to the right to raise it.

The Elder Scrolls V
SKYRIM

PRIMA OFFICIAL GAME GUIDE   WWW.PRIMAGAMES.COM

5 Flooded Vaults

Your first vampire combat occurs here. Watch for a swinging gate trap; check that floor!

◇ Danger! Swinging Wall Trap (pressure plate)

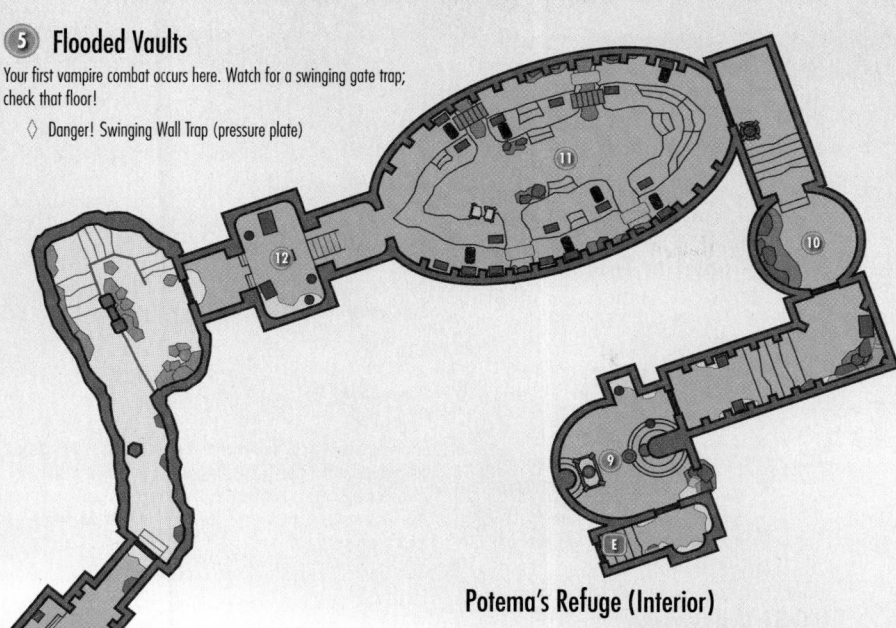

6 Potema's Refuge Entrance

This arched barrow has a grindstone and a trap chest; unlock the trap trigger or feel flames in your face! Then activate the lever, wait for your moment to step through the rotating wall, and access the Alchemy Lab if you wish, before proceeding.

◇ Crafting: Alchemy Lab   ◇ Danger! Trapped Chest
◇ Crafting: Grindstone   ◇ Potions

B Door to Potema's Refuge

Potema's Refuge (Interior)

B Door to Potema's Catacombs

7 Three-Lever Puzzle and Secret Room

Fight Draugr and watch for vampires as you reach three levers and three rotating walls. Make sure all three levers are pointing to the right (if you're facing the walls), as that activates the walls' rotations. Then step through each wall when the portcullises rise. Watch out for Soul Gems striking you with magical damage in the chamber beyond.

Before accessing the three levers, open the gate to the north, fight a Vampire and look for a lever on the ground behind the coffin. This opens a stone wall leading around to a secret room with a chest to plunder

◇ Chest

8 Floor Grating Trapdoor Chamber

You are challenged to a fight with a vampire and a Draugr. Potema's Sanctum Key is resting on the arm of the empty throne. There's another

on the vampire's corpse. Or you can unlock the door normally (Master). The grating below is simply the start of this interior area, near the three-lever puzzle.

◇ Potema's Sanctum Key

D Door to Potema's Sanctum

Potema's Sanctum (Interior)

E Door to Potema's Refuge

9 Embalming Room

10 Potema's Corpse Shrine

Draugr on a throne and a skeleton attack as you reach a circular shrine of corpses and a beckoning from Potema herself. She summons some of the dead to attack you. Grab the potions of Resist Shock in an alcove just beyond; You'll need them shortly.

◇ Potions   ◇ Loose gear

11 Potema's Sanctum Chamber

The final battle against Potema's inner council (Draugr) begins and ends here. You must slay 12 Draugr of increasing ability. Do your best to avoid getting zapped by the beam of power arcing from Potema's floating essence, and take cover in the antichamber if you must.

12 Potema's Throne

You fight the remaining energy from Potema here and collect her skull and any other items you wish. Check the large chest behind her throne.

◇ Potema's Skull   ◇ Loose gear
◇ Chest

13 Secluded Chamber

Exit via the door behind Potema's throne, and scale the snowy interior to a small Draugr corridor with two thrones. Then emerge out onto the Secluded Chamber, into the wilds of Skyrim's exterior, north of Solitude and just east of the Dainty Sload.

F Door to Secluded Chamber and Skyrim

▷ [1.01] Northwatch Keep

Related Quests

Side Quest: Missing in Action

Recommended Level:
12

Habitation: Military Fort

Northwatch Archer
Northwatch Guard
Northwatch Interrogator
Northwatch Mage

Northwatch Prisoner
Thorald Gray-Mane

Crafting

Blacksmith Forge

Collectibles

Skill Book [One-Handed]: 2920, Morning Star, v1 [A1/10]
Skill Book [Two-Handed]: The Legendary Sancre Tor [D1/10]
Chest(s)
Potions
Loose gear

This mighty stronghold lies along Haafingar's northwest coastline and serves as the primary location for a Side Quest involving a prisoner who's being held captive here. Depending on your allegiances, you may be able to bribe or persuade the guards into letting the prisoner go without a fight. When you visit this fort without the "Missing in Action" quest, you'll find a small army of hardened Northwatch Guards here, ready to give their lives in defense of their coastal keep.

Exterior

The keep's exterior is heavily defended by a host of well-armored guards and archers. However, the troops have foolishly left the keep's northern gate unlocked — exploit this to get the drop on them if you desire. Secure the outdoor area before infiltrating the keep via its only unlocked door.

◇ Crafting: Blacksmith Forge

(A) Door to Skyrim

(1) Entry Chamber

Slay a mage and guard in this first chamber, then loot a chest before pressing on.

◇ Chest
◇ Loose gear

(2) Kitchen

Dispatch a few more guards in this small kitchen, where a variety of food items and a few bits of loose gear can be obtained, such as the weapons mounted to the walls. Swipe the Skill Book on the shelf behind the bar.

◇ Skill Book [One-Handed]: 2920, Morning Star v1 [A1/10]
◇ Loose gear

(3) Crumbling Hall

Slay a couple more guards in this large chamber, which has fallen into disrepair. The lower door features an Expert-level lock, and you'll find a Skill Book in the small room beyond. Ignore the locked door and loot an upstairs chest before pressing on to [4].

◇ Skill Book [Two-Handed]: The Legendary Sancre Tor [D1/10]
◇ Chest
◇ Knapsack
◇ Loose gear

(4) Interrogation Chamber

Slay a magic-wielding interrogator in this horrific room, then raid a large chest and snatch up an array of potions. Swipe a special key from the bloodstained table here as well — it unlocks the keep's exit door, which is just ahead.

◇ Northwatch Keep Key   ◇ Potions
◇ Chest   ◇ Loose gear

(5) Holding Cells

Wipe out the guards and then pull the levers to free several prisoners here, if you wish. However, the prisoners own nothing of interest, and neither do their cells. Use the key you found in [4] to unlock the keep's far exit door.

◇ Loose gear

(B) Door to Skyrim (Master)

[1.02] Rimerock Burrow

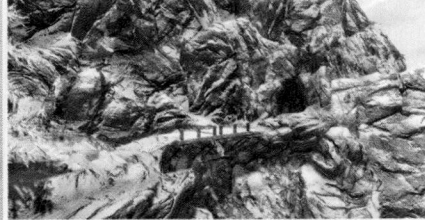

Related Quests

Daedric Quest: A Daedra's Best Friend

Recommended Level: 6

Dungeon: Warlock Lair

Atronach
Warlock

Crafting

Arcane Enchanter

Quest Items

The Rueful Axe

Collectibles

Skill Book [Conjuration]: 2920, Hearth Fire, v9 [B1/10]
Unique Weapon: The Rueful Axe [3/80]
Chest(s)
Loose gear

At the northeastern corner of Haafingar, a narrow, snowy mountain trail descends toward a small, frozen cave. A dangerous Flame Atronach and Master Conjurer reside within the cave. Slay these villains so that you may safely utilize their Arcane Enchanter and raid the cave's far chest. Grab the nearby Skill Book off the end table as well.

During the Daedric Quest: A Daedra's Best Friend, this site contains the Rueful Axe.

[1.03] Pinefrost Tower

Recommended Level: 6

Dungeon: Animal Den

Ice Wraith
Frost Troll
Chest (Locked: Apprentice)
Loose gear

This fallen tower lies atop Haafingar's western mountains, a short distance south of Northwatch Keep [1.01]. Gory remains hint at the presence of a vicious Ice Wraith and ferocious Frost Troll that have taken up residence here. Cross the ramp near the far firepit to reach a chest and some gear at the end of a snowy trail.

[1.04] Volskygge

Related Quests

Side Quest: Masks of the Dragon Priests*
Dungeon Activity

Recommended Level: 24

Dungeon: Dragon Priest Lair

Bandit   Draugr   Volsung

Dangers

Battering Ram Traps (pressure plates)
Swinging Blade Trap (pressure switch)
Swinging Wall Trap (pressure plates)
Dart Trap (pressure plates)

Puzzles

Nordic Pillars (Snake, Bear, Fox, Wolf)

Collectibles

Dragon Priest Mask: Volsung [3/80]
Skill Book [Lockpicking]: Surfeit of Thieves

Special Objects

Word Wall: Whirlwind Sprint [1/2]
Chest(s)
Potions
Loose gear

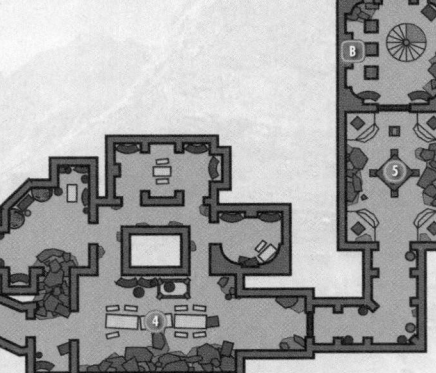

Volskygge

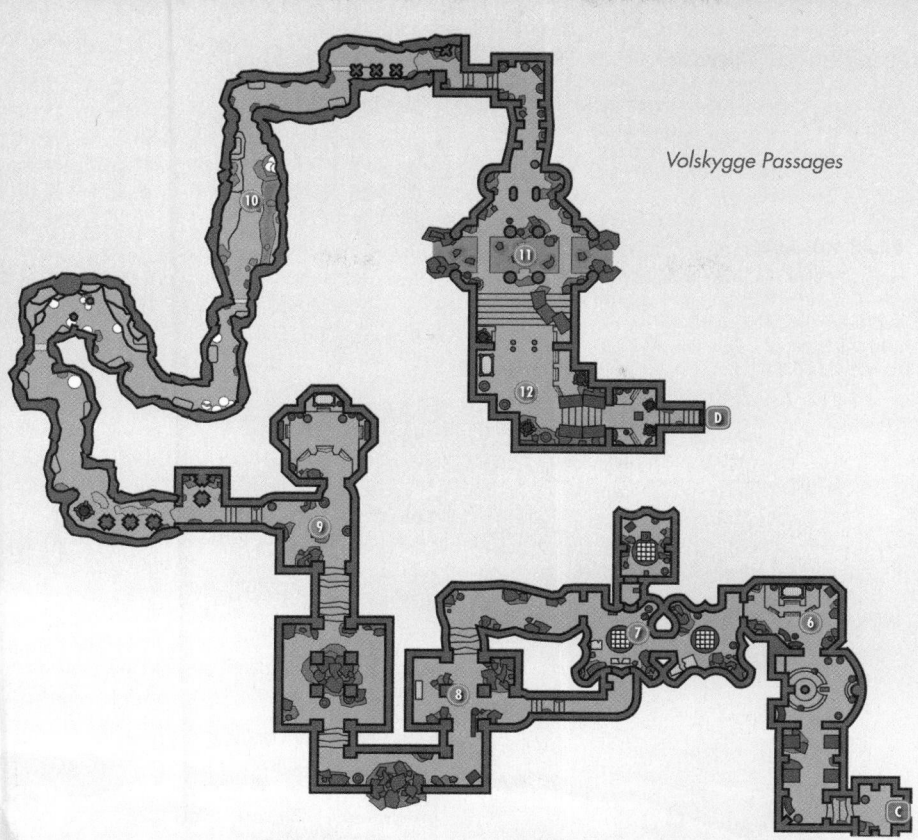

Volskygge Passages

Along Haafingar's southwest edge, a collection of crumbling ruins surround a shattered staircase that leads to ancient burial tunnels.

> **NOTE** Volskygge is unique in that it can be entered from both the bottom and the top (near the Word Wall). It's therefore possible to play through the dungeon in the opposite fashion as detailed here.

Exterior

Search the outdoor ruins to the north and south of the staircase to find a few urns with some coin; then scale the stairs and enter the interior ruins.

◇ Loose gear

Ⓐ Exit to Skyrim

① Throne Room

A couple of bandit scouts patrol the first fire-lit chamber. Beware the pressure plate near the elevated throne—stepping on it causes arrows to fly out from the surrounding walls.

◇ Danger! Dart Trap (pressure plate)

② Swinging Wall Passage

Avoid the pressure plate on the ground in the center of this hall—take a side passage to avoid being impaled by a swinging wall of spikes. Slay a few more bandits and raid a chest at the hall's far end.

◇ Danger! Swinging Wall (pressure plate)
◇ Chest (Locked: Apprentice)

③ Lever Nook

Dispatch a couple of bandits at this dead end, then swipe a Skill Book off a shelf and unlock an Adept-level gate to access a lever that opens a secret passage in the nearby wall. Go through to discover some potions and a chest.

◇ Skill Book [Lockpicking]: Surfeit of Thieves
◇ Chest   ◇ Potions

④ Dining Hall

A grotesque scene of a bloody Draugr splayed across an elegant dining table greets you here. Swipe a few potions from the shelves before entering the northern caverns to slay more bandits, score a few more potions, and loot some urns.

◇ Potions

⑤ Nordic Pillars Chamber

Gates slam shut as you enter the passage's end, trapping you near a sort of glyph puzzle and forcing you to solve it. The book on the pedestal provides clues as to the puzzle's solution. Activate the glyphs in the following order: Snake, Bear, Fox, Wolf. Don't miss the chest in the stairwell chamber beyond, and pull a lever before heading downstairs to open a secret passage. Explore the passage to reach a trapped room that features an urn and a few valuable potions.

◇ Danger! Battering Ram Trap (pressure plate)
◇ Chest
◇ Potions

Ⓑ Door to Volskygge Passages

Ⓒ Door to Volskygge

⑥ Lever Chamber

Pulling a lever in this quiet chamber opens a nearby holding cell, but there's no need to do so. Press onward and wipe out a Draugr so you may safely raid a chest in the next room. The chest is rigged with a trap hinge connected to the chest's left side. Unlock the hinge trap before opening the chest to avoid a dart trap.

◇ Chest

⑦ Trap Door Chambers

Avoid the pressure plate in the center of this odd chamber and avoid falling into the next room's central pit, or you'll have to take a dangerous Draugr-filled passage to the next chamber. Assuming you avoid the pitfall, look for the dead bandit next to a lever. This leads to a secret chamber with a chest and a health potion on a pedestal. Careful when grabbing the potion: it triggers a spear trap from the grate below.

◇ Danger! Swinging Blade Trap (pressure switch)
◇ Chest

⑧ Burial Chamber

Loot the many urns and resting Draugr in this chamber, but beware the trap that's triggered by a central pressure plate. Don't miss the chest in the passage that follows, and beware a host of Dragur that ambush you on the way to [9].

◇ Danger! Swinging Wall (pressure plate)
◇ Chest (Locked: Apprentice)

⑨ Altar Chamber

A lone Draugr guards a quiet altar chamber here. Loot the many urns, then beware a battering ram trap as you scale the stairs that lead toward [10].

◇ Battering Ram Trap (pressure plate)
◇ Potion

⑩ Spider Passage

Slay a host of Frostbite Spiders and rip through thick webs on your way through this long, winding passage, harvesting ingredients from egg sacs as you go. Don't miss looting the chest or urns just before you arrive at [11].

◇ Chest

⑪ Brook Chamber

A gentle stream flows through this Draugr-filled chamber. Find a chest at one end of the brook along with an Orichalcum ore vein. Loot a few urns after laying the undead to rest here.

◇ Chest

⑫ Exit Chamber

Slay one final Draugr and loot several more urns and a large chest on your way out to the ruins' exterior peaks.

◇ Potions
◇ Loose gear

Ⓓ Door to Volskygge Peak

Volskygge Peak

A mighty wizard named Volsung awaits you on the ruins' exterior peaks. Slay this powerful adversary to acquire the valuable gear that he owns, including a precious mask. Scale the nearby steps afterward to locate a Word Wall that bestows the Word of Power: Whirlwind.

◇ Dragon Priest Mask: Volsung [1/10]
◇ Word Wall: Whirlwind Sprint [1/2]
◇ Chest

[1.05] Steepfall Burrow and Lower Steepfall Burrow

High in the northern peaks of Haafingar's central mountains lies the yawning mouth of a frozen cave. Steepfall Burrow also features a lower exit, which registers as a separate location on the world map. This connection can be exploited by travelers to facilitate their trek through Haafingar's treacherous mountains.

Upper Troll Cave

Beware when crossing the cavern's natural footbridge—it's a long way down. Attack the dangerous Frost Troll from range and see if you can knock the beast into the abyss for an easier kill (trolls carry little of value). Slay another troll in the far cave, then loot the chest in the nearby fissure for valuables. Don't miss the Skill Book by the skeleton.

◇ Skill Book [Destruction]: Mystery of Talara, v3 [C1/10]
◇ Chest

Lower Wolves' Lair

If you're feeling daring, drop from the natural footbridge and plummet into the icy water far below. The fall won't harm you, and you can potentially unlock a sunken chest down below for even more loot. To escape the watery cavern, search for an underwater passage to the west, which lies just below the waterline—this will lead you to an Ice Wolf lair, where another chest is located. Loot the wolves' lair and then step outside via the burrow's lower exit.

◇ Chest
◇ Chest (Locked: Apprentice)

Dungeon: Animal Den

Frost Troll
Ice Wolf

Collectibles

Skill Book [Destruction]: Mystery of Talara, v3 [C1/10]
Chest(s)

[1.06] Lost Echo Cave

Recommended Level: 8

Dungeon: Falmer Hive

Animal
Falmer

Collectibles

Skill Book [One-Handed]: 2920, Morning Star, v1 [A2/10]
Chest(s)
Potions
Loose gear

Wooden stairs lead from the main road to this mountain cave, which someone—or *something*—has outfitted with a functional front door.

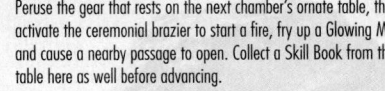

Ⓐ Door to Skyrim

① Bioluminescent Cavern

Harvest plenty of Glowing Mushrooms as you pass through the cave's first few passages.

② Ceremony Chamber

Peruse the gear that rests on the next chamber's ornate table, then activate the ceremonial brazier to start a fire, fry up a Glowing Mushroom, and cause a nearby passage to open. Collect a Skill Book from the stone table here as well before advancing.

◇ Skill Book [One-Handed]: 2920, Morning Star, v1 [A2/10]
◇ Loose gear

③ Falmer Cavern

The cave's vile denizens finally reveal their presence in this third cavern. Slay the nimble Falmer and loot the nearby egg sacks for Chaurus Eggs; then scale the east path to locate an odd-looking chest near a tent.

◇ Chest

④ Ambush Passage

Look up and beware the odd holes in the walls of the next passage. Falmer warriors may emerge from these elevated spawning holes in surprise ambushes! Duck into a southern nook to discover a chest, then continue along until you can leap onto a small ledge to locate a potion, a coin purse, and a satchel as you make your way to the final cavern.

◇ Chest   ◇ Satchel   ◇ Potion

⑤ Chaurus Chamber

The final cavern is home to a mob of insectlike Chaurus. Secure the cavern, slay one last Falmer that emerges from a high spawning hole, and enter a tent to find a large chest. Activate a handle on the wall near the west passage to open a far door, then proceed through the find yourself back near the cave's entrance.

◇ Chest

[1.07] *Orphan's Tear*

Recommended Level: 6

Dungeon: Bandit Camp

Bandit   Chest(s)   Potions

A ship called the *Orphan's Tear* has been hit by a storm and wrecked against Haafingar's treacherous northern coastline. Now this site serves as a bandit camp. Little of interest is found around the campsite, but a chest awaits looting inside the remnants of the *Tear*, while another can be found at the bottom of her submerged hull.

[1.08] Fort Hraggstad

Related Quests

Civil War Quest: Joining the Legion

Civil War Quest: Liberation of Skyrim

Civil War Quest: The Battle for Fort Hraggstad

Recommended Level: 6

Collectibles

Skill Book [Archery]: The Gold Ribbon of Merit

Chest(s)

Potions

Loose gear

This bandit-filled fortress stands tall at the west end of Haafingar's central mountain range and serves as a point of contention during the Civil War Quest.

Exterior

A host of lowly bandits fight hard to keep the fort secure, with archers firing down from elevated ramparts. Fight hard to secure the stronghold's exterior, using cover to prevent the bandits from overwhelming you with ranged attacks. Loot the chest near the blacksmith forge, and slay two powerful bandits atop the two highest towers (located to the west) to gain some worthy loot from their corpses.

◇ Crafting: Blacksmith Forge   ◇ Loose gear

◇ Chest

Fort Hraggstad (Interior)

A mighty bandit lurks inside the fort, backed by a few powerful underlings. If you can slay these foes, you'll reap a host of precious loot from their bodies. Claim a Skill Book from the far upstairs table.

◇ Skill Book [Archery]: The   ◇ Chest (Locked: Adept)
  Gold Ribbon of Merit   ◇ Potions

◇ Chest   ◇ Loose gear

Prison

A small group of worthy bandits guard the prison, but there's little of interest here besides the loot you'll find on the bandits themselves.

◇ Loose gear

[1.09] Widow's Watch Ruins

Recommended Level: 6

Dungeon: Hagraven Nest

Witch

Collectibles

Skill Book [Restoration]: 2920, Rain's Hand, v4

Chest (Locked: Expert)

This crumbling tower is home to a vile hag. Slay the vicious witch, then scale the toppled tower. When you exit the structure, continue looping around the tower's exterior until you're able to reenter through a higher door. Go to the top to discover an ornate chest that's hidden amongst debris.

Habitation: Military Fort

Bandit (Prequest)

Stormcloak/Imperial Soldier (depending on your allegiance during the Civil War)

Crafting

Blacksmith Forge

[1.10] Pinemoon Cave

Recommended Level: 6

Dungeon: Vampire Lair

Master Vampire

Vampire

Wolf

Collectibles

Skill Book [Illusion]: Incident at Necrom [C1/10]

Chest

Chest (Locked: Novice)

Potions

Loose gear

A grove of trees in Haafingar's Tundra opens to a small campsite. If you visit here during the nighttime, you may notice vampires milling about the exterior camp. Otherwise, you'll find the creatures lurking within the nearby cave.

Slay a couple of wolves in the first chamber, then dispatch a handful of vampires in the second, including a powerful Master Vampire. Unlock a simple chest and claim a Skill Book from the table near the large chest before heading back outside.

[1.11] Clearpine Pond

Related Quests: Dungeon Activity

Recommended Level: 8

Dungeon: Spriggan Grove

Spriggan

Spriggan Matron

Chest (Locked: Novice)

Collectibles

Skill Book [Alchemy]: De Rerum Dirennis [B1/10]

A handful of mythical creatures called Spriggan are said to protect this small hot-water spring, where a wealth of wild ingredients grow. If you merely pass by, the Spriggans will take no notice of you. But disturb anything on the island, and one to three Spriggans will emerge to confront you. Defeat them, and the treasures of a deceased alchemist and a locked chest will be yours.

[1.12] Ravenscar Hollow

Recommended Level: 14

Dungeon: Hagraven Nest

Bandit   Hagraven   Animal

Dangers

Bone Alarm Trap

Collectibles

Skill Book [Destruction]: The Art of War Magic [E1/10]

Ravenscar Hollow Cage Key (Hagraven)

Chest

Potions

This cave burrows into the north base of Haafingar's northern mountains—a tranquil waterfall flows just outside. Beware the hanging rattles inside the cave. Sneak directly between them to avoid contact, or creep through the water instead. Slay a dangerous Hagraven and its familiar, then search the Hagraven's remains to find a key. Pull a nearby lever to open a secret passage. Use the Hagraven's key to free the imprisoned bandit in the passage, who'll help you slay the remaining Hagraven before turning on you. Loot a giant chest and collect the nearby Skill Book before making your way back outside.

[1.13] The Steed Stone

Recommended Level: 6

Special Objects

Standing Stone: The Steed Stone [1/13]

Scale Haafingar's snowcapped central mountains to discover an ancient stone with curious markings. Inspect the stone to gain its power—those under the sign of the Steed can carry more and do not suffer a movement penalty from their armor. Note that activating this Standing Stone will override any previous sign blessing you've received from a similar stone, because only one can be active at a time.

[1.14] Ironback Hideout

Recommended Level: 6

Dungeon: Bandit Camp

Bandit

Crafting

Tanning Rack

Collectibles

Skill Book [Pickpocket]: Beggar

Chest (Locked: Novice)

A powerful bandit and a handful of lesser cohorts have made camp in Haafingar's frigid central mountains. Neutralize the vile outlaws here, then raid their campsite for valuables, including a Skill Book that lies on the table near the locked chest.

[1.15] Wolfskull Cave

Dangers

Oil Lamp Trap
Bone Alarm Trap
Oil Pool Traps

Collectibles

Skill Book [Light Armor]: The Refugees
Chest(s)
Potions
Loose gear

Marker stones highlight a snowy side trail that leads to this sizable cave, which you must visit during Side Quest: The Man Who Cried Wolf. Inside, take either the higher or lower trail as you head toward the rear cavern, which several low-level bandits patrol. A more powerful bandit lurks within the far structure, where a large chest is located. Beware: The center of the floor gives way inside the structure, dropping you into a lower chamber. Follow the passage to reach the Wolfskull Ruins.

◇ Chest   ◇ Loose gear

Related Quests

Side Quest: The Man Who Cried Wolf

Recommended Level: 8

Dungeon: Warlock Lair

Bandit
Draugr
Mage

Wolfskull Ruins

Ancient, cavernous ruins lie beneath the Wolfskull Cave. Fall through a weak section of floor to reach this underground fortress, where necromancers are attempting to revive a terrible entity known as Potema the Wolf Queen. Follow the path down the cavern and into the keep, slaying mages and Draugr along the way. Knock down flaming lamps to burn enemies and ignite oil spills. Work your way up to the top of the stronghold and pull the lever to extend a drawbridge to a nearby tower, where a large chest and Skill Book are found. Go downstairs and use the door to return to the beginning of Wolfskull Cave.

◇ Danger! Oil Lamp Traps, Oil Pool Traps   ◇ Satchel
◇ Skill Book [Light Armor]: The Refugees   ◇ Potion
◇ Chest

[1.16] Statue to Meridia and Kilkreath Ruins

Located atop Mount Kilkreath, near the heart of Haafingar, a majestic statue in the form of the goddess Meridia stands at the top of ancient, defiled ruins. A special object called Meridia's Beacon, which appears randomly inside of special chests, steers you toward this site—insert the Beacon into the statue's hands to initiate a vertigo-inducing dialogue with Meridia in the heavens, then go downstairs and venture into Kilkreath Temple at the goddess's command.

Related Quests

Daedric Quest: The Break of Dawn

Recommended Level: 24

Dungeon: Dragon Priest Lair

Corrupted Shade
Malkoran
Malkoran's Shade

Crafting

Arcane Enchanter

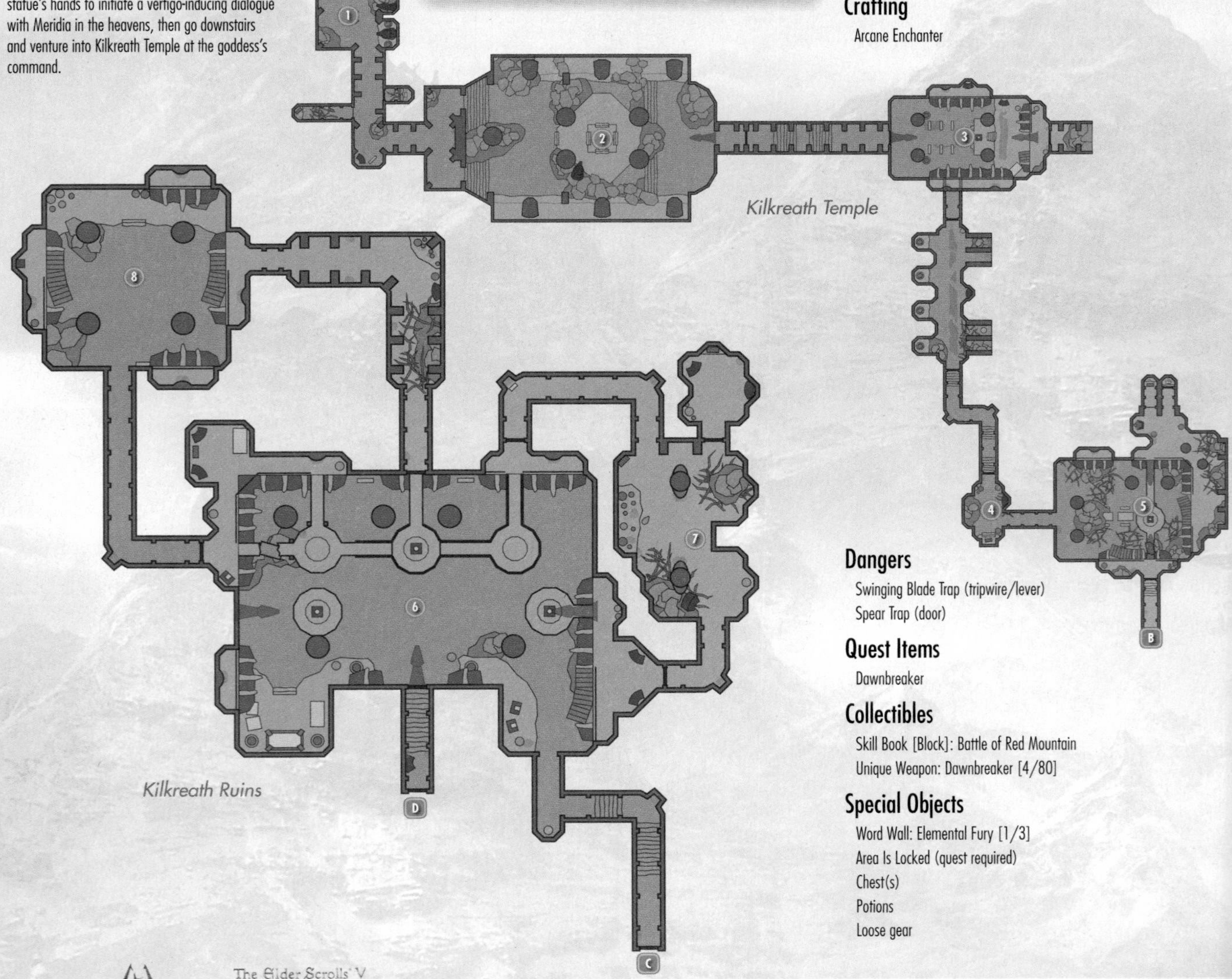

Kilkreath Temple

Kilkreath Ruins

Dangers

Swinging Blade Trap (tripwire/lever)
Spear Trap (door)

Quest Items

Dawnbreaker

Collectibles

Skill Book [Block]: Battle of Red Mountain
Unique Weapon: Dawnbreaker [4/80]

Special Objects

Word Wall: Elemental Fury [1/3]
Area Is Locked (quest required)
Chest(s)
Potions
Loose gear

A Exit to Skyrim

1 Entry Passage

Loot corpses and burial urns as you navigate the Temple's entry passage. Unlock an Adept-level door along the way to access a lever that raises the west portcullis, exposing a chest.

◇ Chest   ◇ Burial Loose gear

2 Pedestal Chamber A

Activate this wide chamber's central pedestal to open the way forward with a potent ray of Meridia's magical light. Be careful not to step into the light ray or you'll suffer damage.

3 Pedestal Chamber B

Slay three Corrupted Shades in this chamber, then activate another pedestal to open a door above, allowing a ray of light to shine through. Proceed through the lower south door to visit [4].

4 South Passage and Chest Nook

Raid a chest here after navigating a long passage guarded by Corrupted Shades.

◇ Chest   ◇ Potion

5 Pedestal Chamber C

Slay a few more Shades in this large chamber, then go upstairs and activate a third pedestal to open another door. Before going through, cross the walkway and unlock an Expert-level door (if possible) to discover a lever that raises the nearby portcullis. Raid the chest beyond, then backtrack across the walkway and proceed through the door to exit out to an exterior balcony.

◇ Crafting: Arcane Enchanter   ◇ Burial
◇ Chest

B Exit to Kilkreath Balcony

Kilkreath Balcony

Sprint east to locate a locked chest on the freezing exterior balcony, then scale the nearby stairs and enter the Kilkreath Ruins to continue your quest.

C Exit to Kilkreath Balcony

6 Pedestal Chamber D

Cut down the Corrupted Shades that guard this giant chamber's ground floor. Backtrack to the entry and go upstairs afterward to find a few potions. Activate the pedestal up here to open the nearby door.

7 Traps and Treasure

Raid a chest in this area, then stand back when opening the northeast wooden door—spikes stab up from the floor before the door when you open it. (Alternatively, you may attempt to disable the trapped door's activation hinge.) Loot another chest in the nook beyond before making your way back to [6], dodging a tripwire on your way to avoid triggering a nasty trap.

◇ Danger! Swinging Blade Trap   ◇ Potions
  (tripwire/lever), Spear Trap (door)   ◇ Loose gear
◇ Chests (2)

6 Pedestal Chamber D Revisited

Follow the caged walkway, then leap over to a pedestal and activate it to open the west door. Jump back across and slay the shades that emerge from behind the door; then cross over, looting a chest and claiming a Skill Book from a dark corner on your way to [8].

◇ Skill Book [Block]: Battle of Red Mountain
◇ Chest (Locked: Novice)
◇ Potions
◇ Loose gear

8 Trapped Pedestal Chamber

Lay more Corrupted Shades to rest in this sizeable chamber, then go up the west stairs and stand to one side of a pedestal before removing its tantalizing potion—spears stab out from the wall when you collect the item. Scale the east stairs afterward and take the east passage back to [6], activating yet another pedestal to finally open the ground floor's east door. Carefully drop down and proceed through the door to visit Kilkreath's final area.

◇ Danger! Spear Trap (pedestal pressure plate)
◇ Potion

D Door to Kilkreath Catacombs

Kilkreath Catacombs

Raid a chest in the Catacomb's entry chamber before activating the central pedestal to open the way into the final chamber, where a mighty foe awaits. Defeat a powerful mage named Malkoran in the final room, then slay Malkoran's Shade, which emerges from his corpse, to at last free Kilkreath from the villain's grip. Search the room thoroughly before taking Dawnbreaker from the glowing pedestal, completing your quest.

◇ Unique Weapon: Dawnbreaker [4/80]
◇ Chest
◇ Potions

9 Pedestal Chamber E

Raid a chest here before activating the central pedestal to open the way into the final chamber, where a mighty foe awaits.

◇ Chest   ◇ Burial Potions

10 Malkoran's Chamber

Defeat a powerful mage named Malkoran in this final room, then slay Malkoran's Shade, which emerges from his corpse, to at last free Kilkreath from the villain's grip. Search the room thoroughly before taking Dawnbreaker from the glowing pedestal, completing your quest.

◇ Unique Weapon: Dawnbreaker [4/80]

◈ [1.17] Dragon Bridge

Related Quests

Civil War Quest: Liberation of Skyrim
Civil War Quest: A False Front
Dark Brotherhood Quest: Breaching Security
Side Quest: Innkeeper Rumors (Four Shields Tavern)
Side Quest: Dragon Breath Mead* (Olda)
Favor (Activity): Chopping Wood* (Horgeir)
Favor (Activity): Harvesting Crops* (Azzada Lylvieve)

Habitation: Town

Azzada Lylvieve
Clinton Lylvieve
Commander Maro
Faida (Innkeeper)
Gaius Maro
Horgeir
Imperial Soldier
Julienne Lylvieve
Lodvar
Michel Lylvieve
Olda
Penitus Oculatus Agent

Haafingar's southernmost Primary Location is a small yet bustling logging community that has sprung up near a renowned bridge that spans the mighty Karth River. You must venture here during a Dark Brotherhood Quest in search of a special target that must be eliminated.

Crafting

Tanning Rack
Workbench

Services

Trader (Innkeeper): Faida [2/15]
　　Food, Room and Board
Quest Rumors

Collectibles

Skill Book [Two-Handed]: King [B1/10]
Chest(s)
Potions
Loose gear

Exterior

Life moves at a steady pace at Dragon Bridge—you'll find many villagers out and about during the daytime. Check near the Penitus Oculatus Outpost to find a few useful crafting stations.

◇ Crafting: Tanning Rack, Workbench

1 Four Shields Tavern

Stop by the local tavern for a hot meal and warm bed.

◇ Trader (Innkeeper): Faida [2/15]　　◇ Loose gear
◇ Chests (2)

2 Lylvieve Family's House

This humble abode is unlocked during the day but difficult to steal from without being noticed.

◇ Chests (2)　　　　　　◇ Potions

3 Horgeir's House

Horgeir must have a sweet tooth, because his cabin is filled with all sorts of tasty treats. Don't miss the sword that rests on the fireplace mantel.

◇ Area Is Locked (Novice)　　◇ Loose gear
◇ Chest

4 Penitus Oculatus Outpost

This cabin serves as the local Imperial Soldiers' barracks. Loot its three chests, if you dare. A Skill Book rests on an end table.

◇ Skill Book [Two-Handed]:　　◇ Potions
　 King [B1/10]　　　　　　　◇ Loose gear
◇ Chests (3)

5 Dragon Bridge Lumber Camp

One chest upstairs, one chest downstairs—two enticing reasons to break into this locked establishment.

◇ Area Is Locked (Apprentice)
◇ Chests (2)

◈ [1.18] Haafingar Stormcloak Camp

Related Quests

Civil War Quest: Liberation of Skyrim
Civil War Quest: The Battle for Fort Greenwall

Habitation:
Military:
Stormcloak Camp

Stormcloak Quartermaster (Weapons/Armor Vendor)
Stormcloak Soldier

Services

Trader (Blacksmith): Stormcloak Quartermaster [2/33]
　　Weapons, Apparel, Misc

Crafting

Anvil
Grindstone (2)
Workbench

Collectibles

Chest(s)
Loose gear

A band of brazen Stormcloak Soldiers has made camp deep in the heart of enemy territory. The Stormcloak Quartermaster offers an array of exceptional gear, and many crafting tools can be utilized here. Note that this site may not exist unless the Civil War Quest is active.

◈ [1.19] Broken Oar Grotto

Related Quests

Side Quest: Lights Out!

Recommended Level: 6

Dungeon: Bandit Camp

Blackblood Bandit
Captain Hargar
Jaree-Ra

Crafting

Blacksmith Forge
Grindstone
Smelter
Tanning Rack
Workbench

Dangers

Oil Lamp Traps
Oil Pool Traps

Collectibles

Skill Book [Smithing]: Cherim's Heart
Chest(s)
Potions
Loose gear

A burning campfire gives away this small, watery cavern, which lies along Haafingar's harsh northeast coast. This site is visited during Side Quest: Lights Out! You must clear the cave to get your revenge against double-crossing bandits.

A Exit to Skyrim

1 Crushed Ship Cavern

This large cavern features a ship that's been crushed in half by a rockfall. Blackblood Bandits swarm the place. Slay them to obtain worthy loot from their corpses. Find two chests deep underwater (one lies farther to the north) and a third chest on a high southeast ledge. Pull one of the two levers on either side of the north drawbridge to lower it so you may advance along the elevated ledges.

◇ Danger! Oil Lamp Trap　　　◇ Chests (3)

---

2 East Passage

After lowering the drawbridge, enter the passage in the east wall to face a few more Blackbloods in a side passage. Dispatch the first bandit you see by knocking down the overhead hanging lamp, which will then ignite the surrounding oil on the floor. Loot a few chests and nab a few potions on your way to [3].

◇ Danger! Oil Lamp Trap, Oil Pool Trap
◇ Chests (2)
◇ Potions

3 Dock Platform

Either swim through the water or take the elevated east ledge or passage from [2] to reach the grotto's far cavern, where several ships have moored. (Pull a lever if you entered from either of the east passages to extend a drawbridge over to the dock platform.) Wipe out many more Blackbloods here, looking to exploit volatile hanging lamps and oil spills as you navigate the central dock platform. Slay Jaree-Ra and Captain Hargar at the top of the shipwright platforms (north end of the cavern) to complete the Lights Out! quest and obtain a key that unlocks the captain's special treasure chest, which you'll find aboard the nearby sunken ship in this cavern. Use a variety of crafting stations here, and snag a Skill Book that sits atop the Workbench.

◇ Danger! Oil Lamp Trap, Oil Pool Trap
◇ Crafting: Blacksmith Forge, Grindstone, Smelter, Tanning Rack, Workbench
◇ Skill Book [Smithing]: Cherim's Heart
◇ Hargar's Chest Key
◇ Chest (Locked: Master)
◇ Potions
◇ Loose gear

[1.20] Shadowgreen Cavern

Recommended Level: 8

Dungeon: Spriggan Grove

Bear
Spriggan
Wolf

Collectibles

Chest
Chest (Locked: Apprentice)
Chest (Locked: Adept)

It would be easy to miss this widemouthed cave if not for several stacked rocks that mark a dirt path leading inside.

A locked chest can be found in a crumbling stump atop the first ledge, overlooking the stream. Wolves guard a path to the east, along with several dangerous Spriggan and a more ferocious predator. When

you've nearly come full circle and arrive at a drop-off to a deep pool, look for a narrow trail leading up the central rock formation. Slay more Spriggan as you climb, along with more beasts when you reach the summit, where a giant chest rests in soft sunlight.

For the thrill-seeker, look northeast from the summit to where another large chest rests on a tiny ledge on the cavern's outer wall. Use the Whirlwind Sprint Shout to reach this platform and escape with your loot. Then cross the rock bridge to a ledge that looms over the water below. Instead of diving straight down, step carefully off the upper ledge to land on one just beneath it, where a final chest awaits. Then take the plunge into the lake below before leaving this wondrous place.

[1.21] Thalmor Embassy

Related Quests

Main Quest: Diplomatic Immunity
Thieves Guild Radiant Quest: No Stone Unturned
Favor (Activity): A Drunk's Drink* (Razelan) ‡

Habitation: Town

Brelas
Elenwen
Etienne Rarnis
Gissur
Malborn
Razelan
Rulindil
Thalmor Soldier
Thalmor Wizard
Tsavani

Quest Items

Dragon Investigation: Current Status

Collectibles

Skill Book [Illusion]: Before the Ages of Man
Unusual Gem: [3/24]
Area Is Locked (Master; quest required)
Chests
Potions aplenty
Loose gear

This gated estate stands tall among Haafingar's central mountains and remains securely locked until you advance to Main Quest: Diplomatic Immunity. Those skilled in the shady arts can find plenty of chances for stealth and thievery here.

Exterior

No guards patrol the embassy's outer courtyard, and there's nothing of particular interest out here. The embassy's inner courtyard is patrolled by powerful soldiers and wizards, but you must first pass through the central structure in order to get there.

Barracks

The barracks are unlocked, and a few hardened soldiers lie in wait here, along with a couple of spellcasters — these eager troops will attack you on sight. Either flee immediately or slay these challenging adversaries so that you may loot the many chests within the barracks.

◇ Chests (4)   ◇ Potion   ◇ Loose gear

Thalmor Embassy (Interior)

Swipe the odd potion from a shelf or table as you explore the embassy. Tsavani waits in the locked northwest kitchen, but you cannot enter until you're let in during the Main Quest. Upstairs, an elf named Elenwen is hosting a marvelous dinner party. Collect many more potions around the dining room, then head for the southwest exit to return outside.

◇ Area Is Locked (Master)   ◇ Potions aplenty

Elenwen's Solar

Upon entering this small structure, eavesdrop on the conversation between Gissur and Rulindil. Loot a chest to the north to obtain special quest-related documents and a key; you can obtain this key from Rulindil by either slaying the man or picking his pocket. Search closets and shelves for potions, and don't miss the upstairs chest or a third chest that's hidden beneath the west basement stairs. Find an Unusual Gem in one of the bedrooms.

◇ Unusual Gem: [3/24]   ◇ Potions
◇ Interrogation Chamber Key   ◇ Loose gear
◇ Chests (3)

Dungeon

The Thalmor Embassy dungeon lies directly below Elenwen's Solar. This area is strictly off-limits, but you can obtain a key that grants you entry by looting a chest within Elenwen's Solar or by slaying Rulindil at the same location and then looting his corpse or picking Rulindil's pocket. Open a particular chest down here to obtain the final quest-related document you seek. If you like, open a holding cell and speak with a prisoner named Etienne Rarnis to free him. The dungeon also sports a trapdoor that leads to a nearby cave. Obtain a key from any of the dungeon's guards (kill or pickpocket).

◇ Area Is Locked (Master)   ◇ Chests (2)
◇ Trapdoor Key (Thalmor Soldier)

Reeking Cave

A lone Frost Troll lurks within this frigid cave, which you can only access via the locked trapdoor within the embassy dungeon. Either slay the

troll or run for your life before it can harm Etienne or Malborn as you all escape. Pause only to claim a Skill Book that lies near the corpse of a fallen mage.

◇ Area Is Locked (Key)
◇ Skill Book [Illusion]: Before the Ages of Man

[1.22] Solitude Sawmill

Related Quests

Favor (Activity): Chopping Wood* (Hjorunn)

Habitation: Lumber Mill

Hjorunn   Solitude Guard
Kharag gro-Shurkul

Crafting

Grindstone   Potions
Chest(s)   Loose gear

This humble logging site consists of little more than a mill and a few surrounding cabins.

Exterior

A few crafting stations are available outdoors.

◇ Crafting: Grindstone
◇ Loose gear

Solitude Sawmill (Interior)

The mill structure holds a locked chest and a few lesser valuables.

◇ Area Is Locked (Novice)   ◇ Potion
◇ Chest   ◇ Loose gear

 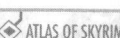

[1.23] Katla's Farm

Related Quests

Favor (Activity): Harvesting Crops* (Katla)

Habitation: Farm

Fridrika
Geimund (Trader: Stables)
Horm
Katla
Knud
Snilling

Services

Trader (Stables): Geimund [1/5]

Quest Items

Party Boots
Party Clothes

Collectibles

Unique Item: Party Boots [4/112]
Unique Item: Party Clothes [5/112]

Special Objects

Business Ledger
Chest(s)
Potions
Loose gear

You see a windmill as you approach this small yet prosperous farm. Here you may hasten your travels by purchasing (or stealing) a horse or by hiring a carriage to quickly reach a capital city you've yet to visit. During Main Quest: Diplomatic Immunity, you receive two unique pieces of apparel here.

Exterior

Speak with Geimund at the stables to purchase a horse, or head up the nearby hill and talk to Thaer if you'd like to rent a carriage. If you're in the mood for honest work, harvest Katla's crops and then sell them back to her for easy coin.

◊ Trader (Stables): Geimund [1/5]   ◊ Loose gear

Katla's Farm (Interior)

If you like, break into Katla's farmhouse and pillage its many attractive valuables. Don't miss the knapsack on the shelf downstairs.

◊ Area Is Locked (Novice)   ◊ Potion
◊ Chest   ◊ Loose gear
◊ Knapsack

Solitude Stables

Unlike Katla's homestead, the stables are unlocked and fully accessible during the day. There's a chest downstairs and another one upstairs, along with an upstairs strongbox and an array of valuable ingots. An upstairs table also sports a business ledger.

◊ Business Ledger   ◊ Strongbox (Expert)
◊ Chests (2)   ◊ Potion
                        ◊ Loose gear

[1.24] East Empire Company Warehouse

Related Quests

Side Quest: Lights Out!
Dark Brotherhood Quest: Hail Sithis!
Dark Brotherhood Quest: Side Contract: Kill Safia
Thieves Guild Quest: Scoundrel's Folly

Thieves Guild Radiant Quest: Larceny Targets*
Thieves Guild City Influence Quest: The Dainty Sload
Dungeon Activity

Recommended Level: 8

Habitation: Cities

Deeja
East Empire Dockworker
East Empire Guard
Gulum-Ei
Sabine Nytte
Solitude Guard
Vittoria Vici
Underground Connection:
Brinewater Grotto [1.25]

Collectibles

Larceny Target: East Empire Shipping Map [1/7]
Skill Book [Smithing]: Heavy Armor Forging
Skill Book [Sneak]: Legend of Krately House
Chests
Potions aplenty
Loose gear

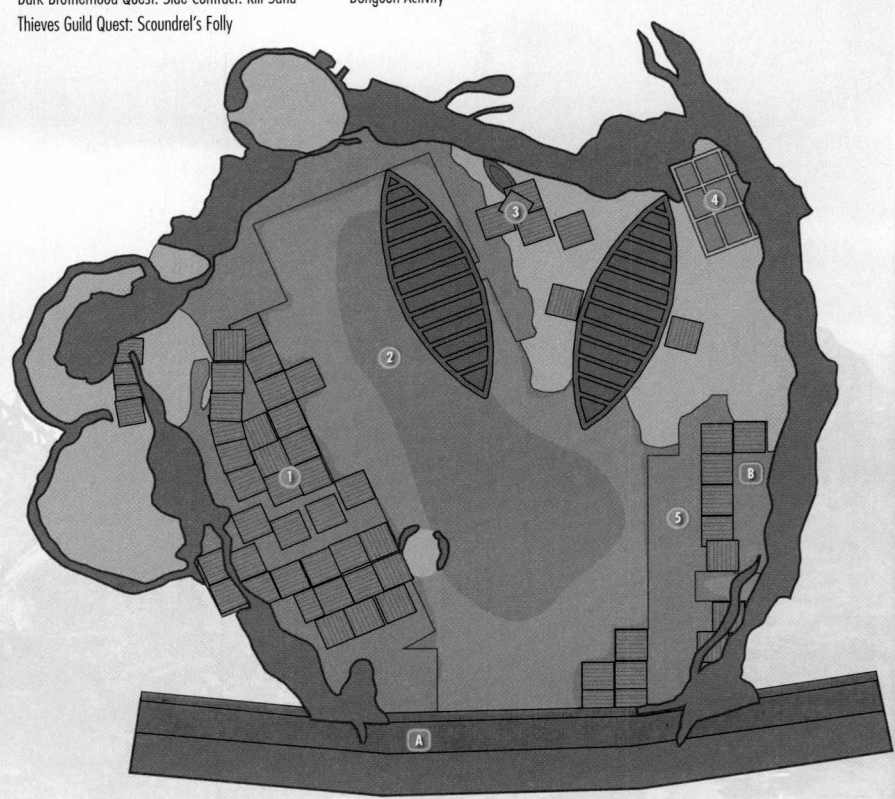

This area, located just south of Solitude, consists of a network of docks and an interior harbor, where workers patch up Haafingar's sea-worn vessels. A large merchant ship called the *Red Wave* remains docked to the south as well.

During Thieves Guild Quest: Scoundrel's Folly, you must tail an Argonian named Gulum-Ei through the warehouse. Continue to follow Gulum-Ei until you spy him changing a business ledger. Then shadow him through a passage hidden among the shelves along the northeastern wall of the warehouse into Brinewater Grotto. Here you will find an underground river where Gulum-Ei and his goons have been moving goods stolen from the warehouse. This is only open after starting this quest.

> **NOTE** If you kill Gulum Ei, you'll have to find evidence of the sale in Brinewater Grotto on your own. The Guild will not be pleased, and if you get a foothold in Solitude later, Gulum won't be around to act as a Fence.

East Empire Company Warehouse (Interior)

The cavernous warehouse is home to a network of docks and a small reservoir featuring two small docked ships. Don't let the guards or dockworkers spot you snooping around in here — they'll attack you on sight.

A Exit to Skyrim

Exterior

At first, it seems there's little of interest along the exterior docks. However, if you dive into the nearby water, you'll discover a sunken chest not far from the warehouse doors.

◊ Chest

① Southwest Docks

A Smithing Skill Book, along with several ingots, are located on the shelves here, near the southwest docks' first flight of stairs. Go upstairs and spy a locked chest atop some shelves on the docks' second level. Scale more stairs to find a second locked chest on the docks' top tier. From up here, you can sneak along a narrow ledge as you head north toward [2].

- ◇ Skill Book [Smithing]: Heavy Armor Forging
- ◇ Chest [Locked: Novice]
- ◇ Chest [Locked: Apprentice]
- ◇ Loose gear

② Sunken Chest

Dive underwater to stealthily swim over to the north docks—you'll find a sunken chest here.

- ◇ Chest

③ North Docks and Ships

Find a locked chest aboard the west ship, and slip around the tip of the east ship to preserve stealth (there's nothing of interest on board).

- ◇ Chest [Locked: Apprentice]
- ◇ Loose gear

④ Foreman's Office

Climb some stairs and take a narrow ledge up to the foreman's office. Here, you discover a unique shipping map that pertains to a Thieves Guild Additional Quest.

- ◇ Larceny Target: East Empire Shipping Map [1/7]
- ◇ Loose gear

⑤ East Docks

Discover a bunch of potions on a shelf near a ladder over here, along with a business ledger that rests on the small table at the end of the docks.

- ◇ Special: Business Ledger
- ◇ Potions aplenty
- ◇ Loose gear

Ⓑ Door to East Empire

Red Wave

This vessel is docked just south of the East Empire Company Warehouse. Board it from the southernmost dock and enter the ship's hull to snatch a host of potions. You'll also find a Skill Book hidden atop a tall shelf inside.

- ◇ Skill Book [Sneak]: Legend of Krately House
- ◇ Potions aplenty
- ◇ Loose gear

[1.25] Brinewater Grotto

Related Quests

Thieves Guild Quest: Scoundrel's Folly
Dungeon Activity

Recommended Level: 6

Dungeon: Bandit Camp

Animal
Bandit

Dangers

Bear Trap
Bone Alarm Trap
Flail Trap (tripwire)
Battering Ram Trap

Underground Connection: East Empire Company Warehouse [1.24]

Collectibles

- ◇ Chest(s)
- ◇ Potions
- ◇ Loose gear

This sizable cave is located along Haafingar's frigid northeast shoreline; however, this location actually marks the cave's exit, not its entrance. Entering from this shoreline site only allows you to visit the cave's final, Horker-filled chamber. To fully explore Brinewater Grotto, you must enter from the East Empire Company Warehouse [1.24]. This can only be accomplished by properly spying on Gulum-Ei during Thieves Guild Quest: Scoundrel's Folly. Regardless, when exiting the cave, be sure to loot the exterior chest.

- ◇ Chest
- ◇ Loose gear

> **TIP** After completing the "Scoundrel's Folly" quest, you can use the Brinewater Grotto passage to covertly enter the East Empire Company Warehouse for further plundering!

Ⓐ Door to East Empire Company Warehouse

① Watery Path

Slay or sneak past bandits as you navigate this winding passage, and don't miss the chest that's hidden underwater to the north. If you like, you can tear through some thick spiderwebs here to expose a spider-filled passage that can help you slip past the guards.

- ◇ Chest

② Trapped Passage Cavern

More bandits lurk near a campfire in this area—the goons guard a chest with a tricky lock. Hanging rattles have been strung to prevent you from sneaking along the water. If you like, you can creep through a trap-filled passage in the west wall to get the drop on the bandits. Just beware of the passage's array of tripwires and bear traps, as well as a feisty guard dog.

- ◇ Danger! Bear Trap, Bone Alarm Trap, Flail Trap (trip wire), Battering Ram Trap
- ◇ Chest (Locked: Adept)

③ Lever Chamber

Slay more rugged bandits here, then find several chests—two aboard the docked rowboats you pass on your way into the cavern and five more near the east shelving—along with some valuable loose gear, including a Skill Book. Don't miss the coin purses hidden on the southwest ledge, either. Use the east levers to open the two nearby cages and reveal a secret passage that leads to the final cavern.

- ◇ Chest (Locked: Apprentice)
- ◇ Chest (Locked: Master)
- ◇ Chests (2) (Locked: Expert)
- ◇ Loose gear

④ Horker Cavern

Slay a few giant Horkers as you move through the final cavern, and don't miss the exterior chest, which is located just outside the cave (as previously detailed).

Ⓑ Exit to Skyrim

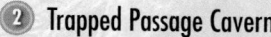

[1.26] Solitude Lighthouse

Related Quests

Side Quest: Lights Out!

Habitation: Lighthouse

Ma'zaka

Collectibles

Skill Book [Alteration]: The Lunar Lorkhan [E1/10]

Area Is Locked (Apprentice)

Chest

Loose gear

While anyone can climb to this tower's top and take in a breathtaking view, a touch of lockpicking skill is needed to enter the lighthouse's small interior. Inside, you'll find an annoyed Khajiit named Ma'zaka who insists upon your immediate departure. You can find a Skill Book on the shelf behind the bar in Ma'zaka's quarters. During Side Quest: Lights Out!, make your way to the top of the lighthouse without alerting Ma'zaka to extinguish the beacon.

[1.27] Dainty Sload

Related Quests

Thieves Guild Radiant Quest: No Stone Unturned

Thieves Guild City Influence Quest: The Dainty Sload

Recommended Level: 8

Dungeon: Shipwreck

First Mate

Sailor

Collectibles

Skill Book [Speech]: A Dance in Fire, v6

Unusual Gem: [4/24]

Dainty Sload Footlocker Key (First Mate)

Chest

Chest (Locked: Adept)

Captain's Chest (Locked: Adept)

Knapsack

Potions aplenty

Loose gear

A Thieves Guild Quest steers you toward this docked vessel. Loot the corpses of slain sailors on your way inside. Pillage a chest and knapsack in the first room before heading downstairs. Fight or avoid the crew of hostile sailors on the lower decks, and collect a useful key by slaying or pickpocketing the first mate; this unlocks the Captain's Chest, into which you must stash an illicit substance as part of your quest. Loads of potions and several tantalizing chests are located on the bottom deck as well. One cabin's table holds a collectible Unusual Gem and Skill Book—the former pertains to Thieves Guild Quest: No Stone Unturned.

[1.28] The Katariah

Related Quests

Dark Brotherhood Quest: Hail Sithis!

Dungeon Activity

Recommended Level: 6

Dungeon: Special

Captain Avidius

Emperor Titus Mede II

Lieutenant Salvarus

Penitus Oculatus Agent

Sailor

Crafting

Alchemy Lab

Anvil

Grindstone

Workbench

Collectibles

Skill Book [Two-Handed]: King

Unique Weapon: Windshear [5/80]

Area Is Locked (quest required)

Chest(s)

Potions

Loose gear

Emperor Titus Mede II's mighty vessel only appears during Dark Brotherhood Quest: Hail Sithis! Sneak aboard the ship via the anchor chain.

Emperor Titus Mede II

Emperor Titus Mede II is the current Emperor of Tamriel. He is reviled by the Stormcloaks for his "betrayal" in signing the White-Gold Concordat that outlawed the worship of Talos, and he is admired by the Imperials for his steadfastness during the Great War. He is somewhat of a tragic figure, being forced by the weakness of the Empire to make "deals with the devil" (Thalmor) in order to preserve his realm from total destruction.

Lower Deck

Dispatch the lowly sailors who guard the lower decks, and loot a locked chest in the first hold. Collect minor valuables on your way upstairs.

◇ Chest (Locked: Apprentice)   ◇ Potions

◇ Apothecary's Satchel   ◇ Loose gear

Upper Deck

Sneak past the Penitus Oculatus Agents upstairs, or slay them outright if you're in a rush. Open the southwest door to confront the ship's captain in his quarters. Collect a useful key from his corpse, then open his locked chest. Cross the ship and enter the east workshop, where an array of gear and crafting stations are located. Use the captain's key to open the north door and sneak to avoid rousing Lieutenant Salvarus and his men. Go upstairs and enter the Emperor's quarters.

◇ Crafting: Alchemy Lab, Anvil, Grindstone, Workbench   ◇ Satchel

◇ Katariah Master Key (Captain Avidius/Lieutenant Salvarus)   ◇ Apothecary's Satchels (2)

◇ Chest (Locked: Master)   ◇ Potion

                            ◇ Loose gear

Emperor's Quarters

The Emperor's life rests in your hands—speak with him before seeing the job through, then open the nearby door to loot the late Emperor's bedchamber. Make a hasty escape afterward by exiting through the nearby balcony door, or return to the previous area and exit out to the ship's deck, where more soldiers and loot can be found.

◇ Satchel   ◇ Potions

◇ Apothecary's Satchel   ◇ Loose gear

Exterior Deck

Raid the ship's topside deck to finish off the last of the Emperor's guards and claim more precious plunder, including a Skill Book that sits near the high throne. Cross the ship and find some potions in a crate on the opposite end, then carefully inch across the long forward mast to discover a unique sword lodged in its far end. Loot a locked chest that's just downstairs to complete your pillaging of the Emperor's vessel.

◇ Skill Book [Two-Handed]: King

◇ Unique Weapon: Windshear [5/80]

◇ Chest (Locked: Novice)

◇ Potions

SECONDARY LOCATIONS

[1.A] Clam Digger's Camp

This consists of a small tent and a roasting spit, close to the Thalmor-controlled Northwatch Keep. The hunter is nowhere to be found; he hasn't yet harvested the majority of the nearby clams, Mora Tapinella, and Nirnroot.

[1.B] Forsworn Ambush Camp

Two Forsworn have set up three Bear Traps in the gully just south of Volskygge and have already lured a Nord to his death. They attack you on sight. Check their tent at the eastern end of the gully.

◇ Danger! Bear Trap (3)

◇ Chest (Locked: Novice)

[1.C] Howling Wolf's Folly

Along the rough snow path that winds from Lost Echo Cave toward Steepfall Burrow, a powerful predator leaps down from the small promontory to savage you. One of its kills (a soldier) has the following on its corpse:

◇ Skill Book (Lockpicking): Proper Lock Design

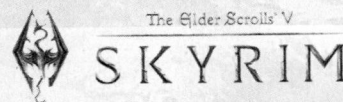

[1.D] Pinemoon Bear Lair

Around the jagged rocky outcrop from the entrance to Pinemoon Cave is an overhang guarded by a vicious Bear (leveled). It attacks you on sight. Rummage through the bandit corpse, among the bones it was guarding.

[1.E] Haafingar Sabre Cat's Lair

On the rocky, snow-covered crags east of the Thalmor Embassy, an unlucky Argonian has been dragged and half devoured by two Snowy Sabre Cats. They attack you on sight. Search their lair for a coin purse and other corpses.

[1.F] Pincushion Peter

A mage faced off against warriors on this steep snowbank and wasn't trusted to remain dead; the victors buried their weapons into the corpse and left it to the wolves. Search the area for weapons, and an excellent staff resting against the tree.

◇ Skill Book (Light Armor): The Rear Guard
◇ Knapsack
◇ Loose gear

[1.G] Haafingar Nordic Burial Ruins

A small burial shrine for a long-forgotten Nordic war hero is slowly returning to the earth. The few steps lead only to a steep gully that provides a wonderful view. The burial urns have already been robbed.

◇ Loose gear

[1.H] Solitude Attack Camp

Related Quests

Civil War Quest: Liberation of Skyrim
Civil War Quest: Battle for Solitude

 At the beginning of the final assault on Solitude, Jarl Ulfric Stormcloak assembles his men for a final rousing speech at this location, prior to the epic assault on the Imperial's stronghold.

HOLD 2: HJAALMARCH

TOPOGRAPHICAL OVERVIEW

The most impoverished of the nine Holds, Hjaalmarch's low-lying salt marsh is an eerie and mist-filled place. Known colloquially as "the Mouths of the Karth," this is where the mighty Karth River empties into the Sea of Ghosts by a variety of intricate channels. Also known as the Karth Delta, many adventurers have entered this dank bog, never to return. Most of the locals gravitate to the capital city of Morthal or the firmer (if colder) ground of the Tundra and farmland and the mountains flanking the Hold to the south and east.

Routes and Pathways

The protrusion of Solitude's giant natural arch is a useful marker, if only to remember how dominant the economy of neighboring Haafingar Hold is: Indeed, along the western edge is a path through the low country that leads to and from the strategically important town of Dragon Bridge (also in Haafingar). Farther away from the mists and hidden terrors of the marsh is the more rocky and mountainous south and eastern parts of the Hold. This area is dominated by Eldersblood Peak to the southwest, part of the Skyborn Range that separates Hjaalmarch from Whiterun. Eating into the Pale to the east is the dwarven temple ruins of Mzinchaleft. But the most impressive (and dangerous) portion of the Hold is a path cut through the mountains from the Tundra plains of Whiterun, which leads through the massive ruined city of Labyrinthian.

AVAILABLE SERVICES, CRAFTING, AND COLLECTIBLES

Services

Followers/Hirelings: [2/47]
Houses for Sale: [0/5]
Marriage Prospects: [1/62]
Skill Trainers: [2/50]
  Alchemy: [1/3]
  Alteration: [0/3]
  Archery: [0/3]
  Block: [0/2]
  Conjuration: [1/3]
  Destruction: [0/3]
  Enchanting: [0/2]
  Heavy Armor: [0/3]
  Illusion: [0/2]
  Light Armor: [0/3]
  Lockpicking: [0/2]
  One-Handed: [0/3]
  Pickpocket: [0/3]
  Restoration: [0/3]

Smithing: [0/3]
Sneak: [0/3]
Speech: [0/4]
Two-Handed: [0/2]
Traders [5/133]:
  Apothecary [1/12]
  Bartender [0/5]
  Blacksmith [2/33]
  Carriage Driver [0/5]
  Fence [0/10]
  Fletcher [0/3]
  Food Vendor [0/9]
  General Goods [0/19]
  Innkeeper [1/15]
  Jeweler [0/2]
  Special [0/3]
  Spell Vendor [1/12]
  Stablemaster [0/5]

Collectibles

Captured Critters: [0/5]
Dragon Claws: [2/10]
Dragon Priest Masks: [3/10]
Larceny Targets: [0/7]
Skill Books: [15/180]
  Alchemy: [0/10]
  Alteration: [0/10]
  Archery: [0/10]
  Block: [1/10]
  Conjuration: [1/10]
  Destruction: [0/10]
  Enchanting: [1/10]
  Heavy Armor: [2/10]
  Illusion: [0/10]
  Light Armor: [0/10]
  Lockpicking: [1/10]
  One-Handed: [2/10]
  Pickpocket: [2/10]
  Restoration: [3/10]
  Smithing: [0/10]
  Sneak: [0/10]
  Speech: [2/10]
  Two-Handed: [0/10]
Treasure Maps: [0/11]
Unique Items: [4/112]
Unique Weapons: [6/80]
Unusual Gems: [0/24]

CRAFTING STATIONS: HJAALMARCH

✔	TYPE	LOCATION A	LOCATION B
☐	Alchemy Lab	Morthal (Thaumaturgist's Hut) [2.00]	—
☐	Arcane Enchanter	Morthal (Falion's House) [2.00]	—
☐	Anvil or Blacksmith Forge	—	—
☐	Cooking Pot and Spit	Morthal (Falion's House) [2.00]	Morthal (Thonnir's House) [2.00]
☐	Grindstone	Morthal (Falion's House) [2.00]	Stonehills (Exterior) [2.22]
☐	Smelter	Stonehills (Exterior) [2.22]	—
☐	Tanning Rack	Morthal (Exterior: Guardhouse) [2.00]	Morthal (Lumber Mill: Marshdeep Camp) [2.00]
☐	Wood Chopping Block	Morthal (Lumber Mill: Marshdeep Camp) [2.00]	Stonehills (Exterior) [2.22]
☐	Workbench	—	—

Special Objects

Shrines: [2/69]
  Akatosh: [1/6]
  Arkay: [0/12]
  Dibella: [0/8]
  Julianos: [0/5]
  Kynareth: [1/6]
  Mara: [0/5]
  Stendarr: [0/5]
  Talos: [0/17]
  Zenithar: [0/5]

Standing Stones: [1/13]
  The Apprentice Stone
Word Walls: [7/42]
  Animal Allegiance: [0/3]
  Aura Whisper: [0/3]
  Become Ethereal: [1/3]
  Disarm: [1/3]
  Dismaying Shout: [1/3]
  Elemental Fury: [0/3]
  Fire Breath: [0/2]

Frost Breath: [2/3]
Ice Form: [0/3]
Kyne's Peace: [0/3]
Marked for Death: [0/3]
Slow Time: [1/3]
Storm Call: [0/3]
Throw Voice: [0/1]
Unrelenting Force: [0/1]
Whirlwind Sprint: [1/2]

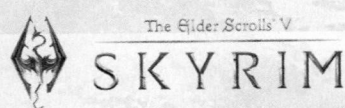

 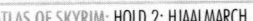

Hold 2: Hjaalmarch

2.18

2.R

2.22

2.25

2.17

2.24

2.21

2.O

2.S

2.16

2.20

2.23

2.15

2.N

2.19

Morthal

2.O

2.P

2.13

2.14

2.K

2.M

2.12

2.08

2.J

2.11

2.I

2.H

2.09

2.L

River Hjaal

2.J

2.10

2.04

2.06

Karth River

2.01

2.G

2.05

2.C

2.03

2.07

2.B

2.D

2.A

2.E

2.F

2.02

N

Total — 26: Hold Capital and 25 Hold Locations

[2.00] Hold Capital City: Morthal
    Jarl: Idgrod Ravencrone
[2.01] Meeko's Shack
[2.02] Chillwind Depths
[2.03] Robber's Gorge
[2.04] Dead Men's Respite
[2.05] Crabber's Shanty
[2.06] Orotheim
[2.07] Talking Stone Camp
[2.08] Folgunthur
[2.09] The Apprentice Stone
[2.10] Fort Snowhawk
[2.11] Brood Cavern

[2.12] North and South Cold Rock Pass
[2.13] Eldersblood Peak
[2.14] Wreck of the Icerunner
[2.15] Abandoned Shack
[2.16] Ustengrav
[2.17] Hjaalmarch Stormcloak Camp
[2.18] Mzinchaleft
[2.19] Movarth's Lair
[2.20] Hjaalmarch Imperial Camp
[2.21] Kjenstag Ruins
[2.22] Stonehills
[2.23] Labyrinthian
[2.24] Lost Valkygg
[2.25] Skyborn Altar

Total — 19 Points of Interest

[2.A] Karth River Henge
[2.B] Riverside Bandit Camp
[2.C] Dragon Mound: Karth River Forest
[2.D] Ambushed Caravan
[2.E] Adventurers' Campsite
[2.F] Sabre Cat Rock
[2.G] Dragon Mound: Robber's Gorge Bluffs
[2.H] Swamp Pond Massacre
[2.I] Smuggler's Alcove

[2.J] Draugr Burial Mound
[2.K] Summoning Stones
[2.L] Dead Mammoth
[2.M] Shrine of Kynareth: Hjaalmarch Hills
[2.N] Collapsed Burial Ground
[2.O] Black Arts Burial Ground
[2.P] Dragon Mound: Labyrinthian Peaks
[2.Q] Ghost Barrow
[2.R] The Conjuror's Caravan
[2.S] Hamvir's Summit Hunter's Camp

HOLD CAPITAL: MORTHAL

Related Quests

Civil War Quest: Liberation of Skyrim
Civil War Quest: A False Front
Daedric Quest: Pieces of the Past
Side Quest: Laid to Rest
Side Quest: Rising at Dawn
Side Quest: Innkeeper Rumors (Moorside Inn)
Side Quest: Falion's Nocturnal Habits* (Falion)
Side Quest: Gorm's Letter* (Gorm)
Dark Brotherhood Quest: Whispers in the Dark
Dark Brotherhood Quest: Side Contract: Lurbuk
Favor (Activity): Chopping Wood* (Hroggar)
Favor (Activity): Chopping Wood* (Jorgen)
Favor: Special Delivery* (Idgrod the Younger)
Favor: Sparring Partners* (Benor)
Favor: Rare Item Hunt* (Lami)
Thane Quest: Thane of Hjaalmarch*

Habitation Hold Capital (Minor)

Crafting

Alchemy Lab
Arcane Enchanter
Grindstone
Tanning Rack

Services

Follower: Benor [4/47]
Marriage Prospect: Benor [6/62]
Trader (Apothecary): Lami [2/12]
Trader (Innkeeper): Jonna [3/15]
Trader (Spell Vendor): Falion [2/12]
Trainer (Alchemy: Journeyman): Lami [1/3]
Trainer (Conjuration: Master): Falion [1/3]

Special Objects

Civil War: Map of Skyrim

Collectibles

Skill Book [Enchanting]: Catalogue of Armor Enchantments [B1/10]
Skill Book [Heavy Armor]: 2920, Mid-Year, v6 [A1/10]
Skill Book [Lockpicking]: The Locked Room [D1/10]
Skill Book [Pickpocket]: Aevar Stone-Singer [A1/10]
Skill Book [Restoration]: 2920, Rain's Hand, v4 [A1/10]
Skill Book [Restoration]: Racial Phylogeny [C1/10]
Chests
Potions aplenty
Loose gear

Lore: City Overview

Sitting on the southern edge of the Drajkmyr marsh, dry ground can be hard to come by in Morthal. The capital of the Hjaalmarch Hold, Morthal, is often shrouded in a thick fog, and ominous twisted trees grow from the surrounding marsh. Morthal is foreboding to travelers approaching it, and the torches of the town glowing in the fog often give the impression of wisps at a distance. Many travelers choose to steer clear of the place altogether.

Morthal is a town shrouded in mystery. Its people are reclusive and wary of newcomers, and only a single lumber camp supports its weak economy. The Jarl is among the most relaxed in Skyrim when it comes to taxation, but Hjaalmarch is also the poorest of the nine Holds. The Hold is still part of the Empire, but the Jarl is unapologetically vague in her enthusiasm for the Imperial Legate stationed in her dwelling. A number of the people in the town are concerned about the prospect of war. War brings outsiders, and outsiders are not a welcome sight in Morthal. Most would rather the conflict were kept outside their home, leaving them free to pursue their own interests.

Important Areas of Interest

1 Main Thoroughfare

Lacking much in the way of paving, this main dirt track leads from one end of town to the other, with Highmoon Hall to the south and the lumber mill at the north end, after which the marshland encroaches and takes over.

2 Dockside

This deck passes the structures where the town's guards and two of the more interesting inhabitants live and leads to a jetty. This is where the civilization of Morthal stops and the wilds of the Drajkmyr marsh begin. The bog isn't particularly deep, and many townsfolk spend time watching the water from the covered jetty, hoping the strange sounds during the night will go away.

3 Highmoon Hall

 The following leaders of Morthal are (begrudgingly) loyal to the Imperials at the start of the Civil War.

Jarl Idgrod Ravencrone	Idgrod the Younger
Aslfur (Steward)	Joric
Gorm (Housecarl)	Legate Taurinus Duilis

Jarl Idgrod Ravencrone

Idgrod Ravencrone is unlike the other Jarls of Skyrim: She is a hunched old woman, who speaks in riddles and parables and rarely ever directly. However, her wisdom is sometimes misunderstood as the ramblings of an old woman, and some are beginning to lose faith in her. Idgrod spent her younger years wandering Tamriel in search of wisdom. Some say that she returned from her trip "touched." Gorm is actively plotting to remove her.

Aslfur (Steward)

Aslfur met Idgrod during the time she spent wandering Tamriel. A young warrior then, Aslfur protected Idgrod during her pilgrimage, and the two were married before returning to her home in Morthal. Over the years, Aslfur has served as Idgrod's advisor, and now, in her old age (and some say her insanity), he is more protective than ever.

Gorm (Housecarl)

Gorm was once loyal to Idgrod but has since come to think of her as insane and unfit for the throne in these trying times. Gorm has formulated

a plan to remove her from power with little bloodshed. Aslfur and Idgrod are both aware of his plan, but Idgrod has refused to allow Aslfur to act on the knowledge, insisting that there is a larger role for Gorm to play.

Idgrod the Younger

Idgrod the Younger has heard the rumors that her mother is touched. In truth, Idgrod has been taught by her mother to seek insight and wisdom. Although neither recognize it, both are manipulating Magicka subconsciously in order to achieve their visions. The Younger Idgrod is much more adept at separating the visions from reality and is poised to make an excellent Jarl.

Joric

Joric is the youngest child of Idgrod Ravencrone and Aslfur. He's a young boy who seems to have lost his mind at a very early age. He doesn't say much, but when he does speak, he is oddly insightful, even if his words make little sense.

Legate Taurinus Duilis

 The following residents of Hjaalmarch arrive to take control of Morthal, once this Hold has fallen during the Civil War.

Jarl Sorli the Builder
Pactur (Steward)
Teeba-Ei (Housecarl)

Jarl Sorli the Builder

Sorli the Builder is the great-granddaughter of the founder of Stonehills. She lives in the first building constructed in the town by her ancestors. Leadership has been passed down through her family, but whatever that used to mean, it has little bearing on the present day. Reduced to a single building and a marginally profitable mine owned by Bryling of Solitude, Sorli attempts to cling to whatever authority she currently has, while dreaming of something greater for herself.

Pactur (Steward)

Pactur's life revolves around Sorli. He assists with running the mine, which means doing all the work Sorli doesn't care to, and he feeds her ambitions in whatever way he can.

Teeba-Ei (Housecarl)

The sole survivor of a wrecked trader vessel, Teeba-Ei wandered into Stonehills nearly frozen to death. He was taken in and cared for, and was grateful that few questions were asked about how he came to be there. He now gladly serves Sorli, working the mine, and is willing to follow her everywhere, even if that means going to Morthal as her Housecarl.

Highmoon Hall is the central meeting place for all citizens of Hjaalmarch. Although, few seek audience with the reclusive and mysterious Jarl. She spends most of her days pottering around this sturdy Nordic structure. Aslfur handles many of the citizens' grievances in the main hall, and some have come to question whether he is trying to remove that burden from his wife or trying to hide her deteriorating condition. The war room manned by Legate Taurinus Duilis across from the Jarl's chamber is an inconvenience Idgrod is having to live with. Discover a Skill Book mixed in with other, less valuable books on the top shelf in the upstairs bedroom.

- ◇ Skill Book [Lockpicking]: The Locked Room [D1/10]
- ◇ Civil War: Map of Skyrim
- ◇ Chests (2)
- ◇ Potions aplenty

4 Guardhouse

Benor

The guardhouse is not a picture of military order. The Jarl of Hjaalmarch had little need for an organized militia. The Legion has attempted to improve the old guardhouse and the jail (which is more of a cellar with a single cell [Adept]), but it is still a mess. Find a Skill Book hidden behind a basket and barrel near the bed.

- ◇ Follower: Benor [4/47]
- ◇ Skill Book [Heavy Armor]: 2920, MidYear, v6 [A1/10]
- ◇ Evidence Chest
- ◇ Prisoner Belongings Chest
- ◇ Chests (2)

5 Moorside Inn

Jonna

Lurbuk gro-Dushnikh

Jonna is the sister of Falion, both from Hammerfell. She and her brother have traveled together their whole lives, but when something "drew" Falion to Morthal, they both settled. The town was without an inn at the time, so Jonna modified one of the homes. She doesn't get a lot of business, but she does appreciate visitors who stop by and can stand to hear Lurbuk's painful ballads. Search a woven basket that sits atop a dresser in one of the rooms to discover a hidden Skill Book.

- ◇ Trader (Innkeeper): Jonna [3/15]
  - ○ Room for the night, food
  - ○ Innkeeper Rumors
- ◇ Skill Book [Restoration]: Racial Phylogeny [C1/10]
- ◇ Chest (2)

6 Hroggar's House (Burned Down House)

Close to the chiming Nirnroot is a house without its roof. It has been lying derelict since it caught fire recently. The house belonged to Hroggar, and his wife and child died in the fire, which some are calling suspicious. Perhaps the barkeep has some scuttlebutt you could follow up on?

7 Morthal Cemetery

Too small for a Hall of the Dead, the few folks of Morthal make do with a more traditional Nordic graveyard to the west of town. Odd noises have been heard during the night there.

8 Thaumaturgist's Hut

This is Lami's shop, although the only commodities she normally sells are potions and cures to the other residents. She offers a full selection of magical supplies to those who might be interested. Claim a Skill Book that's stashed atop a tall shelf downstairs.

- ◇ Crafting: Alchemy Lab
- ◇ Trader (Alchemy Vendor): Lami [2/12]
  - ○ Potions, Food, Ingredients, Misc
- ◇ Trainer [Alchemy: Journeyman]: Lami [1/3]
- ◇ Skill Book [Destruction]: Response to Bero's Speech
- ◇ Potions aplenty

9 Thonnir's House

Thonnir   Virkmund

The place hasn't been cleaned for weeks and is sparsely decorated by a man who may have simply given up. The lute, drums, and flute show Thonnir once sang, but no merry music has echoed around these walls for months. Claim a Skill Book that's stashed beneath a basket on the corner shelf.

◊ Skill Book [Pickpocket]: Aevar Stone-Singer [A1/10]
◊ Chest

10 Alva's House [Locked: Adept]

Alva   Hroggar

Alva spends her nights gathering herbs and tending her small herb garden. She has filled the house with all manner of dried ingredients and homemade remedies. She used to spend a lot of time with Lami but now refuses to leave her abode. If you break into this dwelling, Alva wakes from her slumber and attacks. There's a key on her corpse. The cellar backs up the rumors of Alva's vampiric tendencies. If you kill Alva, Hroggar will stalk and attack you once you leave town.

◊ Key to Alva's House   ◊ Chest

11 Falion's House

Falion   Agni

Falion is a Redguard. While his sister Jonna is accepted by the people of Morthal, Falion is looked at with fear and distrust. Falion has delved deep into the mysteries of Magicka and has become a master of the arts. He has settled in Morthal because he felt drawn to the location and wishes to remain relatively close to the College in Winterhold. He spends his time in his workshop and is the only person in the realm who knows how to cure vampirism. The house is cluttered and filled with trinkets of both superstition and genuine implements of Magicka. Peer around his residence for the following:

◊ Crafting: Arcane Enchanter
◊ Trader (Spells Vendor: Falion) [2/13]
  ○ Scrolls, Books, Misc
◊ Trainer (Conjuration: Master): Falion [1/3]
◊ Skill Book [Restoration]: 2920, Rain's Hand, v4 [A1/10]
◊ Skill Book [Enchanting]: Catalogue of Armor Enchantments [B1/10]
◊ Chest
◊ Potions aplenty

12 Jorgen and Lami's House [Locked: Novice]

Jorgen   Lami

Jorgen and Lami live in this small house, although both are rarely ever home, spending most of their time at their respective work. The house is neat, in order, features a variety of stored food, and is barely lived in. Find a Skill Book hidden atop a tall cupboard and another tucked away in a bucket that sits atop a barrel.

◊ Hilt of Mehrunes' Razor   ◊ Chest [Locked: Adept]
◊ Skill Book [One-Handed]: 2920, Morning Star, v1

13 Lumber Mill (Marshdeep Camp)

This was once known as Marshdeep Camp before being settled and is now the only economy of Morthal. The sparse (but healthy and large) trees are processed here. Jorgen runs this with Hroggar and doesn't care about what happened in the fire.

◊ Crafting: Grindstone, Tanning Rack

PRIMARY LOCATIONS

▶ [2.01] Meeko's Shack

Related Quests
Dungeon Activity

Recommended Level: 6

Habitation: Hunter Camp Services
Follower: Meeko [5/47]

Collectibles
Skill Book [Speech]: A Dance in Fire, v6 [B1/10]
Loose gear

A dog named Meeko may approach you as you travel the road near this small, remote cabin. Follow Meeko to the nearby shack to find his late master— the dog will then join you as a Follower. There's little of interest in the cabin besides the dead man and his journal, which references his faithful pooch.

▶ [2.02] Chillwind Depths

Related Quests
Dungeon Activity

Recommended Level: 18

Dungeon: Falmer Hive
Chaurus
Falmer
Frostbite Spider

Dangers
Spear Trap (pressure plate)

Collectibles
Skill Book [Lockpicking]: Advances in Lockpicking
Chest(s)
Potions
Loose gear

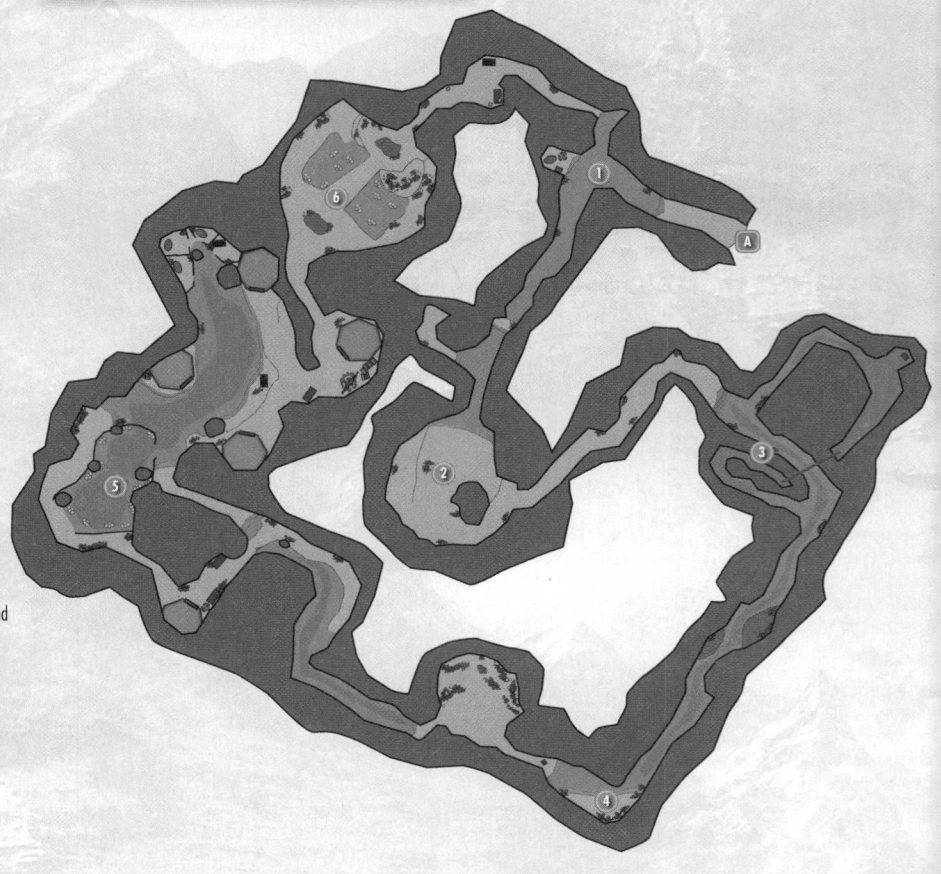

Along Hjaalmarch's west edge, a dirt path follows the river to a small, watery cave. Beware of predatory animals on your way into the cave.

Ⓐ Exit to Skyrim

① Fallen Adventurer Chamber

Just inside the cave, a slain adventurer lies on a bedroll near a looted chest. Swipe the nearby potions before venturing southwest toward [2].

◇ Potions

② Spider Nest

A nest of Frostbite Spiders have made quite a home for themselves here. The first spider is just a decoy—watch out for the others to drop from above if you rush in too quickly. Take the upper path to reach [3].

③ Waterlogged Passageway

Explore the north section of these water-filled passages to loot a sunken chest. Beware of Falmer in the long, southern straight; they have a good angle on you.

◇ Chest (Locked: Apprentice)

④ Precarious Passage

Beware the pressure plate as you enter the tunnel—stepping on it causes long spikes to stab out from the wall in lethal fashion. Avoid it, or sprint past after the spikes retract, then battle a blend of Falmer, Frostbite Spiders, and Chaurus in the tunnel ahead.

◇ Danger! Spear Trap (pressure plate)

⑤ Chaurus Pen

Take either an upper or lower path to reach this wide chamber, where the Falmer are keeping a few pet Chaurus in a pen. If you take the higher path, you'll face a powerful Falmer and discover some loose gear. Out in the main cave, make sure to loot the two Chaurus-bone chests.

◇ Chests (2)
◇ Loose Gear

⑥ Throne Room

A mighty Falmer sits on a stone throne in this final chamber. Slay the monster to clear the cave, then loot the large chest in the back passage. Follow the trail back to the start and exit this dank cavern.

◇ Chest
◇ Apothecary's Satchel
◇ Potion
◇ Loose gear

▶ [2.03] Robber's Gorge

Related Quests

Dungeon Activity

Recommended Level: 6

Dungeon: Bandit Camp

Bandit

This impressive bandit camp is a perfect site for an ambush. The bandits here call out to passersby, demanding that they pay a "toll." Either turn back, pay the toll, or be ready to fight. If you battle the bandits, slay their chief and then loot his corpse to find a key that unlocks the trapdoor in the chief's cabin and a chest that you'll find later. Find a Skill Book inside the cabin. The trapdoor leads to Robbers' Cove.

◇ Skill Book [Archery]: The Black Arrow, v2
◇ Key to Robber's Cove (Bandit Chief)
◇ Chest

Collectibles

Skill Book [Archery]: The Black Arrow, v2
Chest(s)
Potions

Robbers' Cove

Unlock the trapdoor in the bandit chief's cabin to enter this small, watery cavern. A journal on the table tells the tale of this gang and mentions a hidden chest outside. Find a potion on the first table and a locked chest underwater, along with a couple of coin purses. Swim out to fresh air when you've finished looting the place, then swim south and raid the large chest on the island in the middle of the lake—the bandit chief's secret stash!

◇ Area Is Locked (Adept)
◇ Chest (Locked: Adept)
◇ Chest (Locked: Master)
◇ Potion

▶ [2.04] Dead Men's Respite

Related Quests

Other Factions: Bards College
Quest: Tending the Flames
Dungeon Activity

Recommended Level: 6

Dungeon: Draugr Crypt

Animal
Draugr
King Olaf One-Eye
Svaknir

Crafting

Arcane Enchanter

Dangers

Battering Ram Trap (pressure plate)
Flamethrower Trap (pressure plate)
Swinging Blade Trap
Spear Trap (pressure plate)

Puzzles

Nordic Puzzle Door (Ruby Dragon Claw)
(Wolf, Hawk, Wolf)

Quest Items

King Olaf's Verse

Collectibles

Dragon Claw: Ruby Dragon Claw [1/10]
Skill Book [Speech]: The Buying Game

Special Objects

Word Wall: Whirlwind Sprint [2/2]
Chests
Potions
Loose gear

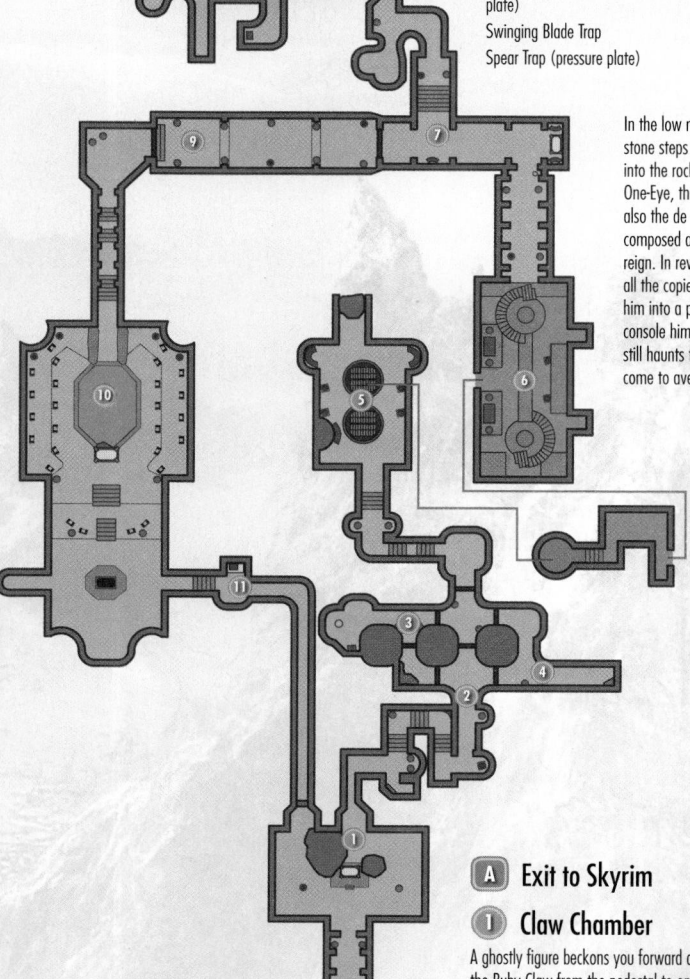

In the low mountains southwest of Morthal, stone steps lead up to a massive arch carved into the rock face. This is the tomb of King Olaf One-Eye, the ancient High King of Skyrim and also the de facto tomb of Svaknir, the bard who composed a legendary epic poem against Olaf's reign. In revenge, Olaf captured Svaknir, burned all the copies of his work save one, then threw him into a pit to rot, with only the final verse to console himself. It is said that Svaknir's ghost still haunts the tomb, hoping that someone will come to avenge him.

Ⓐ Exit to Skyrim

① Claw Chamber

A ghostly figure beckons you forward as you enter this chamber. Take the Ruby Claw from the pedestal to open the portcullis, but beware—a swarm of vicious Draugr ambush you when you do. Collect a potion from the nook beyond the iron door before advancing to [2].

◇ Dragon Claw: Ruby Dragon Claw [1/10]

② Snaking Passages

Beware the pressure plate in the corridor that leads into these passages, and pull a chain on the wall to open the way forward when you reach the dead end. Beware Frostbite Spiders in the passage that follows.

◇ Danger! Spear Trap (pressure plate)

③ Spider Nest

Wipe out the Frostbite Spiders here and loot the urn they guard; then head south and pull another wall chain to open a passage leading east.

④ Dead End

Slay a few Draugr and skirt a dangerous pressure plate trap as you move to collect a bit of loot from this dead end. Double back afterward (dodge the trap again!) and go north.

◇ Danger! Battering Ram Trap (pressure plate)
◇ Potion

⑤ Webbed Chamber

Loot a few urns and sidestep yet another pressure plate trap in the twisting passage that leads to this chamber, which is covered in webbing. Slay the Frostbite Spiders that descend from the ceiling, then pull the chain on the east wall to open a watery pit. Drop down to advance.

◇ Danger! Flamethrower Trap (pressure plate)
◇ Potion
◇ Loose gear

⑥ Watery Chamber

Slay a Skeever and a few Draugr on your way to this large chamber, where more Draugr await. When you approach the barred door, look down and disarm the hinge trigger if you can, or you'll have to deal with a lethal series of swinging blades on the narrow bridge. If you fail to disarm the trap, stop carefully by the candles to avoid the blades as they swing past. Pull the chain on the far side if you need to allow your Follower through, then take the upstairs door to reach [7].

◇ Danger! Swinging Blade Trap (hinge trigger)

⑦ Sealed Door Passage

Take advantage of a rare crafting station in this passage. The far door is sealed by some sort of energy—go north instead and slay several more Draugr on your way to [8].

◇ Crafting: Arcane Enchanter

⑧ Svaknir's Grave

As you enter this area, pick an Expert door lock to access a nook with a locked chest. Slay the mob of Draugr that attack you in the main chamber, then approach the chest in the south nook. Disarm the hinge trigger or stand aside as you open it to avoid the dart trap. Back out in the main room, pull the south wall chain to open the central stairwell, then descend to at last catch up with the apparition you've been pursuing. Collect the book near Svaknir's corpse, then backtrack to [7] and follow Svaknir's ghost through the previously sealed door.

◇ King Olaf's Verse　　　　◇ Chest
◇ Danger! Dart Trap　　　　◇ Chest (Locked: Master)

⑨ Puzzle Door Passage

Rotate the three rings of this passage's far door to mimic the same sequence of symbols that appear on the Ruby Dragon Claw you collected back at [1] (Wolf, Hawk, Wolf). Then activate the keyhole to insert the claw and open the way forward.

⑩ The Court of the Dead

Enter King Olaf's court, and Svaknir calls his nemesis to battle. As the host of Draugr rise one by one, help Svaknir lay waste to the undead. When King Olaf rises to do battle, cut him down to finally free Svaknir from this tomb. Obtain a key off of Olaf's corpse, and stand near the south wall to learn a new Word of Power.

◇ Word Wall: Whirlwind Sprint [2/2]　　◇ Potions
◇ Olaf's Treasury Key

⑪ Olaf's Treasury

Use the key you found on Olaf's corpse to open this treasury, then loot the giant chest within. Pull the nearby lever to open the exit passage, which leads back to [1].

◇ Chest
◇ Potion
◇ Loose gear

▷ [2.05] Crabber's Shanty

Habitation: Hunter Camp

Fisherman

On the southwest edge of Hjaalmarch, a tiny crab shack sits by the river. Aside from a plethora of crab meat and a humble fisherman, there's nothing here of particular value or interest.

▷ [2.06] Orotheim

Related Quests
Dungeon Activity

Dungeon: Bandit Camp
Bandit

Crafting
Grindstone
Tanning Rack

Dangers
Bone Alarm Trap

Collectibles
Skill Book [One-Handed]: Mace Etiquette [C1/10]
Chest
Chest (Locked: Apprentice)
Potions
Loose gear

This small cave, located along Hjaalmarch's southwest border, serves as a hideout for a small group of bandits. Beware the powerful leader, who lurks toward the cavern's rear. Slay him and claim plenty of loot from his corpse and from the two chests he guards (one is hidden beneath the stairs). Dispatching all of the bandits at this location ends their raids against the giant of Talking Stone Camp [2.07] to the south.

▷ [2.07] Talking Stone Camp

Related Quests
Dungeon Activity

Dungeon: Giant Camp
Giant
Mammoth

Collectibles
Chest
Chest (Locked: Apprentice)

A massive bonfire at Hjaalmarch's southernmost tip signals the camp of two towering giants. Mammoths roam the lower portion of the hill, shepherded by one giant, while the other can be found near the campfire up top. You can claim plenty of loot from their chests, one in the camp and one in the cove by the waterfall—if you can slay the brutes.

Dispatching all of the bandits at Orotheim [2.06] ends their raids against the giants, allowing them to lead their mammoths to the nearby stream (which they do every few hours). This draws off the giant and mammoths at the base of the hill, giving you free access to that chest, or a good opportunity to take out the lone remaining giant.

▷ [2.08] Folgunthur

Related Quests
Side Quest: Forbidden Legend
Dungeon Activity

Recommended Level: 6

Dungeon: Draugr Crypt
Frostbite Spider
Draugr
Mikrul Gauldurson

Quest Items
Daynas Valen's Journal
Daynas Valen's Notes
Ivory Dragon Claw

Dangers
Bone Alarm Trap
Flamethrower Trap (pressure plate)
Oil Lamp Trap
Oil Pool Trap

Rockfall Trap
Spear Trap (pressure plates)

Puzzles
Nordic Pillars
　　Snake, Whale, Hawk
Nordic Puzzle Door (Ivory Claw)
　　Hawk, Hawk, Dragon

Collectibles
Dragon Claw: Ivory Dragon Claw [2/10]
Skill Book [One-Handed]: Fire and Darkness [B1/10]
Unique Item: Gauldur Amulet Fragment (Folgunthur) [6/112]
Unique Weapon: Gauldur Blackblade [6/80]

Special Objects
Word Wall: Frost Breath [1/3]
Chest(s)
Potions
Loose gear

On a hill in Hjaalmarch's northern marshlands lies the ominous entrance to the tomb of Mikrul Gauldurson, one of the three brothers sealed away in ancient times.

The Elder Scrolls V
SKYRIM

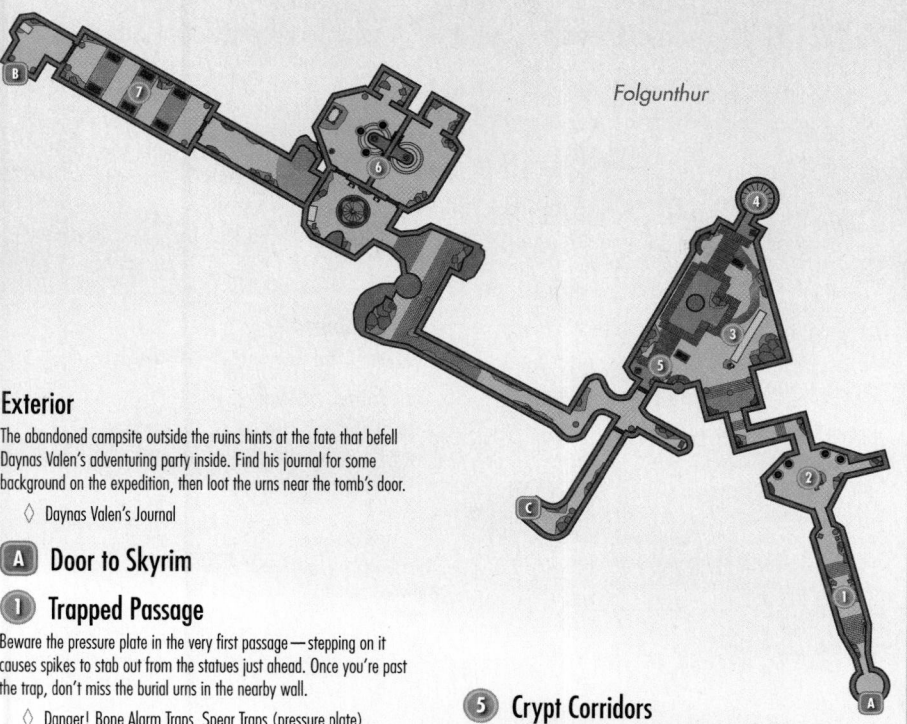

Folgunthur

Exterior

The abandoned campsite outside the ruins hints at the fate that befell Daynas Valen's adventuring party inside. Find his journal for some background on the expedition, then loot the urns near the tomb's door.

◇ Daynas Valen's Journal

A Door to Skyrim

1 Trapped Passage

Beware the pressure plate in the very first passage—stepping on it causes spikes to stab out from the statues just ahead. Once you're past the trap, don't miss the burial urns in the nearby wall.

◇ Danger! Bone Alarm Traps, Spear Traps (pressure plate)

2 Puzzle Pillar Chamber

Daynas Valen's adventurers already solved the puzzle in this room, so there's little to do here during your first visit, but you can return after obtaining the Ivory Claw in [3]. Ignore the glyph puzzle and simply insert the claw into the keyhole on the east wall to open a small nook and expose a locked chest.

◇ Chest (Locked: Apprentice)
◇ Loose gear

3 Dining Hall

Avoid a pressure plate and slay a few Draugr on your way to this wide chamber. A gate shuts behind you, trapping you with more undead. Pull the chain near the gate to open it if you'd like to retreat. Knock down the oil lamps or cast a fire spell to ignite the rivers of oil with explosive results. Discover a Skill Book near a corpse in a dark corner of the room. Upstairs, grab the Ivory Claw from Daynas Valen's corpse and use it to lower a drawbridge.

◇ Danger! Flamethrower Trap (pressure plate), Oil Lamp Trap, Oil Pool Trap
◇ Dragon Claw: Ivory Claw [2/10] (Daynas Valen)
◇ Skill Book [One-Handed]: Fire and Darkness [B1/10]
◇ Daynas Valen's Notes (Daynas Valen)
◇ Loose gear

4 Stairwell 1

Use extreme care when entering this stairwell, which leads up to the dining hall's second floor. A trapdoor opens beneath your feet as you enter, dunking you into a watery pit. The water actually spares you from falling onto lethal spikes—keep well away from the spikes as you carefully loot the sunken corpses, then swim onto the stairs (or pull the chain and let the trapdoor lift you up). Loot the corpses near an upstairs keyhole to at last discover the Ivory Claw. Insert the claw into the keyhole to lower the drawbridge ahead, which leads toward several Draugr and a passage to the lower crypts. Before entering the crypts, return to [2] and use the Ivory Claw to access a treasure nook.

◇ Unique Weapon: Gauldur Blackblade [6/80]
◇ Potions
◇ Loose gear

C Door to Folgunthur Crypt

5 Crypt Corridors

Beware: Numerous Draugr roam these tight corridors, and pressure plates trigger lethal traps. Avoid the pressure plate in the corridor that leads toward a locked chest, and manipulate the levers in the opposing hall until all four portcullises have risen. Avoid a rockslide as you make your way deeper into the crypts.

◇ Danger! Rockfall Trap, Spear Trap (pressure plate)
◇ Chest (Locked: Novice)
◇ Potions
◇ Loose gear

6 Stairwell 2

You must solve a Nordic Pillar Puzzle here in order to advance to the lower crypts. Ignore the room's two levers and enter the northeast chamber. Note the order of the glyphs, then exit and pull either lever to access the northwest chamber. Rotate three glyph pillars here, mirroring the glyph sequence in the previous chamber (Hawk, Hawk, Dragon). Then exit and pull the chain on the far wall to open the central stairwell.

7 Spider Tunnel

Slay a few Frostbite Spiders in this final passage, and beware a surprise ambush as you approach the puzzle door. The lights suddenly go out, and Draugr emerge from the sarcophagi around you. Cut them down, then inspect the Ivory Claw you found earlier and notice its three glyphs. Manipulate the puzzle door's three rings to mimic the Ivory Claw's glyph sequence (Hawk, Hawk, Dragon); then insert the Ivory Claw into the door's central keyhole to open the path to the crypt.

◇ Potion
◇ Loose gear

B Door to Folgunthur Crypt

Folgunthur Crypt

As you pass through this cavernous crypt, Mikrul Gauldurson, a powerful undead warrior, suddenly rises from the central sarcophagus. Refer to Side Quest: Forbidden Legend for strategies on dealing with this powerful foe and his vampiric blade. Once he falls, loot him and the corpses of his thralls before using the Ivory Claw to open the far gates. Follow the sound of chanting to locate a Word Wall and gain a new Word of Power. Loot a massive chest as well before proceeding through the nearby door and returning to the main level.

◇ Word Wall: Frost Breath [1/3]
◇ Unique Item: Gauldur Amulet Fragment (Folgunthur) [6/112]

[2.09] The Apprentice Stone

Recommended Level: 6

Special Objects
Standing Stone: The Apprentice [2/13]

This standing stone can be found on a small island in Hjaalmarch's frigid northern marsh. Inspect the stone to gain the Apprentice sign blessing. Those under the sign of the Apprentice recover Magicka faster but are more susceptible to Magicka damage. Note that you may possess only one sign blessing at a time.

[2.10] Fort Snowhawk

Related Quests
Civil War Quest: Liberation of Skyrim
Civil War Quest: The Battle for Fort Snowhawk

Recommended Level: 6

Habitation: Military Fort
Mage
Skeleton

Crafting
Alchemy Lab
Arcane Enchanter (2)
Grindstone

Dangers
Bear Traps

Collectibles
Skill Book [Block]: A Dance in Fire, v2 [A1/10]
Chest(s)
Potions
Loose gear

This imposing keep serves as a point of contention between the Stormcloaks and Imperials during the Civil War. Until then, it's populated by a band of necromancers. You can tackle this eroding stronghold in a number of ways—storm the front gate, slip in through the hole in the southeast wall, or leap over any of the crumbling battlements.

Exterior

A host of necromancers and their skeletal minions defend the fort's outer grounds. Scale the ramparts and clear out every foe to gain plenty of loot from their corpses. There's little else of value outside.

◇ Loose gear

Fort Snowhawk Keep

Enter the fort's central keep by any of three doors. The ground-level door to the south is the easiest to locate. Go upstairs to locate a few potions, then head downstairs to find more, along with a locked chest. Work your way through the sleeping quarters to reach the library, where you can find several crafting stations, a Skill Book, and a key that unlocks the Keep's

---

central chamber. Within, deal with the leader of the necromancers, then claim the chest in his chamber and a locked chest in the nearby bedroom.

◊ Crafting: Alchemy Lab, Arcane Enchanter, Grindstone
◊ Skill Book [Block]: A Dance in Fire, v2 [A1/10]
◊ Fort Snowhawk Quarters Key
◊ Chest
◊ Chest (Locked: Apprentice)
◊ Chest (Locked: Adept)
◊ Potions

Prison

Fight your way across the battlements to reach the entrance to the prison tower in the Keep's northern courtyard. The prison is a small area with few guards. Find a chest in the nook just beyond the main entry staircase and another in one of the holding cells. A passage in the back of another cell leads to a secret exit, but beware the bear traps as you jump down.

◊ Danger! Bear Traps
◊ Crafting: Arcane Enchanter
◊ Chest (Locked: Apprentice)
◊ Potions

[2.11] Brood Cavern

Dungeon: Animal Den

Animal

Collectibles

Chest
Chest (Locked: Novice)
Potion

Ferocious [Leveled Predators] guard this waterfall cave. Make your way to the waterfall's top and follow the stream into the mountain to enter the Brood Cavern. Slay more [Leveled Predators] inside the cave and pass through an interior waterfall to locate a chest with an easy lock. Another chest lies on dry land near the body of a late hunter, who recently became the animals' prey.

[2.12] North and South Cold Rock Pass

Recommended Level: 8

Dungeon: Animal Den

Animal

This small, frozen cave runs straight through Hjaalmarch's southern mountains, providing a convenient means of passage into Whiterun. Unfortunately, a vicious Frost Troll resides here that you must either deal with or avoid.

[2.13] Eldersblood Peak

Dungeon: Dragon Lair

Animal

Dragon (after Main Quest: Dragon Rising)

Special Objects

Word Wall: Disarm [1/3]

A pack of ferocious Frost Trolls guard this ancient dragon lair, which is located atop the peak south of Morthal. If you visit here after the dragons have returned, most of the Frost Trolls will have been killed, but you will have a much bigger foe to contend with. Secure the site, then follow the sound of chanting to locate a Word Wall that bestows you with a new Word of Power.

[2.14] Wreck of the Icerunner

Related Quests
Side Quest: Lights Out!

Recommended Level: 6

Dungeon: Shipwreck
Blackblood Marauder
Deeja

Collectibles
Area Is Locked (quest required)
Potions
Loose gear

This unique location exists only after you extinguish the Solitude Lighthouse as part of Side Quest: Lights Out! Without the Lighthouse to guide it, the *Icerunner*, an Imperial supply ship, runs aground on the reefs in this area. There's nothing of particular interest at this site until the shipwreck occurs.

Exterior

The ship's deck is full of plunder, and there are potions stashed in a nearby rowboat—but anything you take on the way in to meet Deeja is considered theft by the marauders, who will turn on you without hesitation.

◊ Potions
◊ Loose gear

The *Icerunner* (Interior)

The thieves have nearly finished looting the ship's interior, but there are still a few valuables to be found. Make your way down to the cargo hold and speak with Deeja, who suddenly double-crosses you. Slay the villain and inspect the note she carries to advance your quest, then fight your way back outside, claiming any loot you might have left alone before.

◊ Apothecary's Satchel
◊ Satchels (2)
◊ Potions
◊ Loose gear

[2.15] Abandoned Shack

Related Quests

Dark Brotherhood Quest: With Friends Like These...

Habitation: Special

Alea Quintus
Astrid
Fultheim the Fearless
Vasha
Area Is Locked

This remote, ramshackle cabin is used by the Dark Brotherhood for various purposes. After you complete the first Dark Brotherhood Quest, Astrid brings you here, where you're faced with a choice of killing one of three persons as part of the second Dark Brotherhood Quest, "With Friends Like These..." Interrogate each of the three captives, then slay any of them to advance the quest—the choice affects only Astrid's remarks after the deed is done.

[2.16] Ustengrav

Related Quests
Main Quest: The Horn of Jurgen Windcaller

Recommended Level: 6

Dungeon: Bandit
Camp
Animal
Bandit
Draugr
Mage
Skeleton

Crafting
Arcane Enchanter

Dangers
Flamethrowers (pressure plates)
Oil Lamp Trap
Oil Pool Trap

Collectibles
Skill Book [Restoration]: Mystery of Talara, v2 [B1/10]
Area Is Locked (quest required)
Chest(s)
Potions
Loose gear
Mineable Ore (Corundum, Iron, Silver)

Special Objects
Word Wall: Become Ethereal [1/3]

Warlocks have turned the ruins here into a temporary camp as they explore an ancient temple—and pillage the crypts below. You can't delve too deeply into Ustengrav until you advance to Main Quest: The Way of the Voice, which tasks you with obtaining a special object from the crypts' depths.

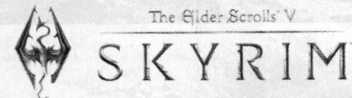
The Elder Scrolls V SKYRIM

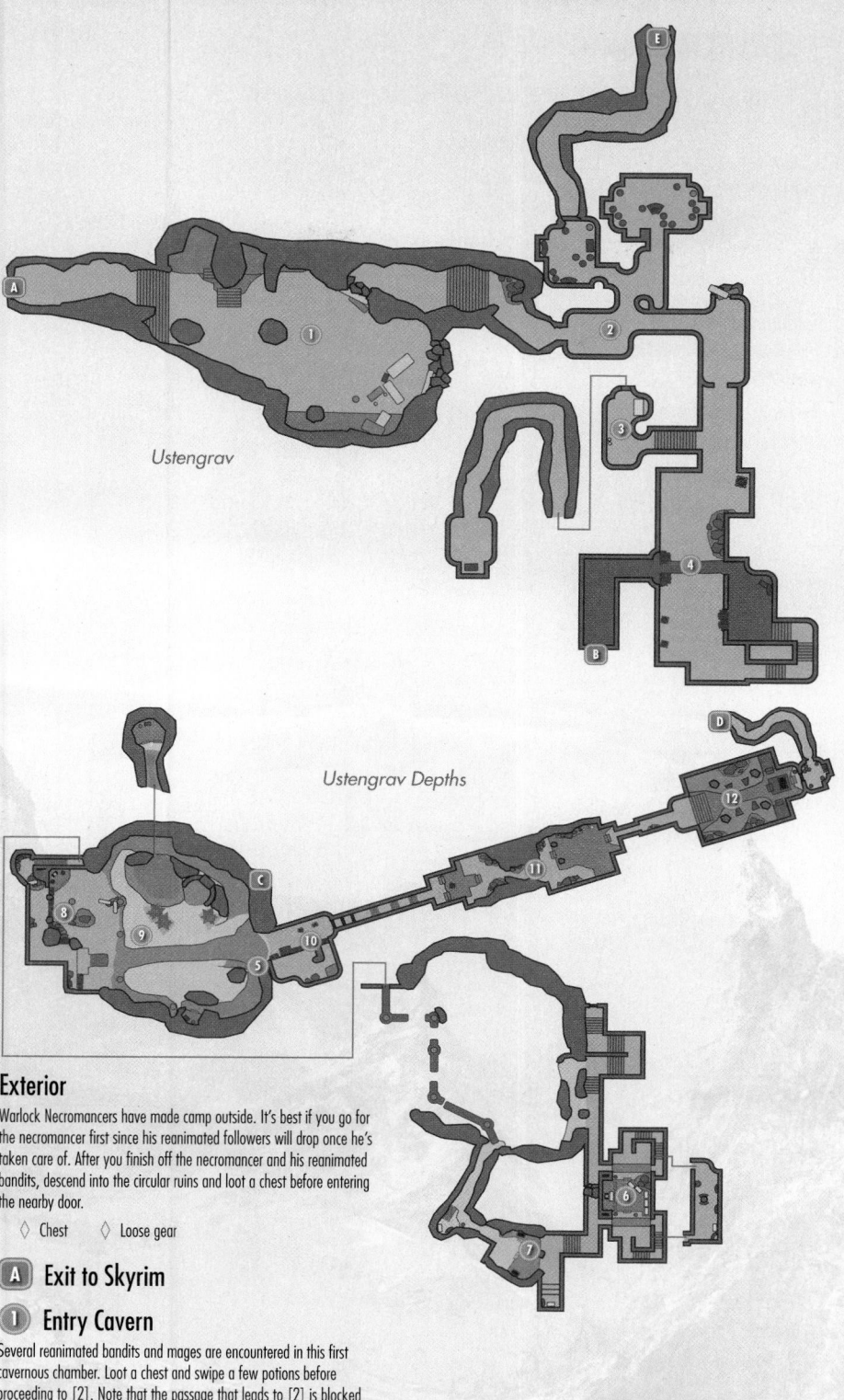

Ustengrav

Ustengrav Depths

Exterior

Warlock Necromancers have made camp outside. It's best if you go for the necromancer first since his reanimated followers will drop once he's taken care of. After you finish off the necromancer and his reanimated bandits, descend into the circular ruins and loot a chest before entering the nearby door.

◇ Chest   ◇ Loose gear

A Exit to Skyrim

1 Entry Cavern

Several reanimated bandits and mages are encountered in this first cavernous chamber. Loot a chest and swipe a few potions before proceeding to [2]. Note that the passage that leads to [2] is blocked when you visit this location prior to starting Main Quest: The Way of the Voice.

◇ Chest   ◇ Loose gear
◇ Potions

2 Draugr Passages

Cut down the large number of undead Draugr that roam these passages. Search the northern side rooms to locate a chest, Skill Book, and lots of lootable urns.

◇ Skill Book [Restoration]: Mystery of Talara, v2 [B1/10]
◇ Chest   ◇ Potions

3 Secret Passage

Descend into this small side room and swipe some coins off a table, and take the gear that's hidden beneath it. Pull the nearby wall chain afterward to reveal a secret passage that leads to a chest.

◇ Chest   ◇ Loose gear

4 Sarcophagi Chamber

Slay more Draugr in this wide burial chamber, then scale the southeast stairs to locate several potions and a chest.

◇ Chest   ◇ Potions

B Door to Ustengrav Depths

C Door to Ustengrav

5 Cavern Access

Navigate a twisting stairway as you descend into this massive subterranean cavern. If you own the Whirlwind Sprint Shout, use it to safely streak past some wide pressure plates that trigger flamethrowers when depressed. Also, if you look closely, you will see that some pressure plates are decoys and don't actually shoot fire. Figuring this out will help you navigate the halls ahead.

◇ Danger! Flamethrowers (pressure plates)
◇ Mineable Ore (Iron)

6 Walkway Chamber

Dispatch a few Draugr in this sizeable side chamber. Cross a walkway and head downstairs to raid a chest in the east alcove, then scale the south stairs afterward and cross another walkway on your way to [7].

◇ Chest   ◇ Potions

7 Oily Cavern

Draugr burst out from sarcophagi in this cavern. Quickly knock down the overhead lamps to ignite the oil on the ground and burn them up. Turn the handle on the wall near the south portcullis, then turn another handle on the wall near the south sarcophagus to expose a small crafting nook with a chest.

◇ Danger! Oil Lamp Traps, Oil Pool Trap   ◇ Potions
◇ Crafting: Arcane Enchanter   ◇ Loose gear
◇ Chest

8 Huge Cavern: West Balcony

Upon entering this massive cavern, you can utilize your Whirlwind Shout to jump across these destroyed bridges to discover a chest tucked away behind some rubble. Clear the skeleton archers from the west balcony afterward, and locate a few potions near the throne. Descend the north sloping trail afterward to reach the cavern's bottom.

◇ Danger! Flamethrowers (pressure plates)
◇ Chest   ◇ Potions

9 Huge Cavern: Ground Floor

Follow the sound of chanting to locate a Word Wall at the bottom of the cavern. Obtain a new Word of Power, then search behind the nearby waterfall to locate a hidden chest that's guarded by a powerful Draugr. Backtrack out and explore the cavern's opposite end to discover a chest and a few potions.

◇ Word Wall: Word of Power: Become Ethereal [1/3]
◇ Chests (2)
◇ Potions
◇ Mineable Ore (Corundum, Silver)

10 Huge Cavern: East Balcony

Return to the cavern's west balcony and cross the central bridge to reach the opposite balcony, where a series of portcullises block your progress. The portcullises are controlled by the nearby glowing stones. You must use Whirlwind Sprint to dash past the glowing rocks and through the portcullises before they close. The easiest way to make it through the gates is to sprint past all the stones; just after you reach the final stone, use Whirlwind Sprint and continue sprinting.

◇ Potion

11 Fire Trap Passage

Use your Whirlwind Sprint Shout again to blaze through this dangerous passage — the entire floor is made of flamethrower traps! Alternatively, remember that some flamethrowers are decoys, and don't actually shoot flames. Look carefully at the ground coloration to see which is which. Once you're past the traps, beware of a Giant Frostbite Spider that descends from the ceiling. Cut your way through the thick webs that follow so you may advance.

◇ Danger! Flamethrowers (pressure plates)

12 **Jurgen Windcaller's Tomb**

Massive pillars rise from the surrounding water as you enter this large, quiet chamber. Inspect the far tomb of Jurgen Windcaller to advance your quest, then enter the nearby door to locate a giant chest. Navigate the tunnel that follows to find your way back to the surface.

◇ Chest

D **Door to Ustengrav**

E **Door to Ustengrav Depths**

▷ [2.17] Hjaalmarch Stormcloak Camp

Related Quests

Civil War Quest: Liberation of Skyrim
Civil War Quest: A False Front
Civil War Quest: The Battle for Fort Snowhawk

Habitation: Military: Stormcloak Camp

Arrald Frozen-Heart
Stormcloak Soldier
Stormcloak Quartermaster (Blacksmith)

Services

Trader (Blacksmith): Stormcloak Quartermaster [3/33]
    Weapons, Apparel, Misc

Crafting

Anvil
Grindstone (2)
Workbench

Special Objects

Civil War: Map of Skyrim
Chests (2)
Loose gear

A small detachment of Stormcloak Soldiers has made camp along the northern edge of Hjaalmarch — yet this site may exist only during the Civil War quest line. Barter with the quartermaster if you like, and inspect the large map in one of the tents to potentially acquire new map information.

▷ [2.18] Mzinchaleft

Related Quests

Dark Brotherhood Quest: Side Contract: Maluril
Dungeon Activity

Recommended Level: 16

Dungeon: Dwarven City

Animal
Bandit
Dwarven Centurion
Dwarven Sphere
Dwarven Spider
Falmer

Underground Connection: Blackreach [10.02]

Collectibles

Skill Book [Archery]: The Black Arrow, v2
Unique Weapon: Grimsever [7/80]

Special Objects

Dwarven Mechanism
Chest(s)
Potions
Loose gear

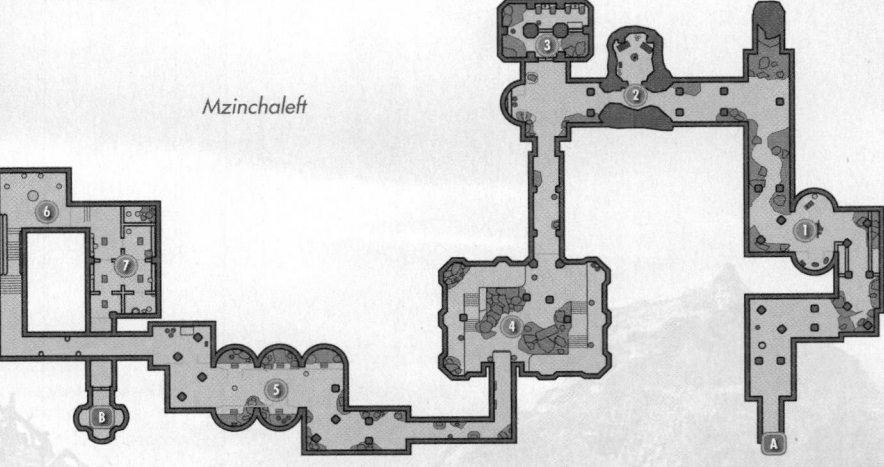

Mzinchaleft

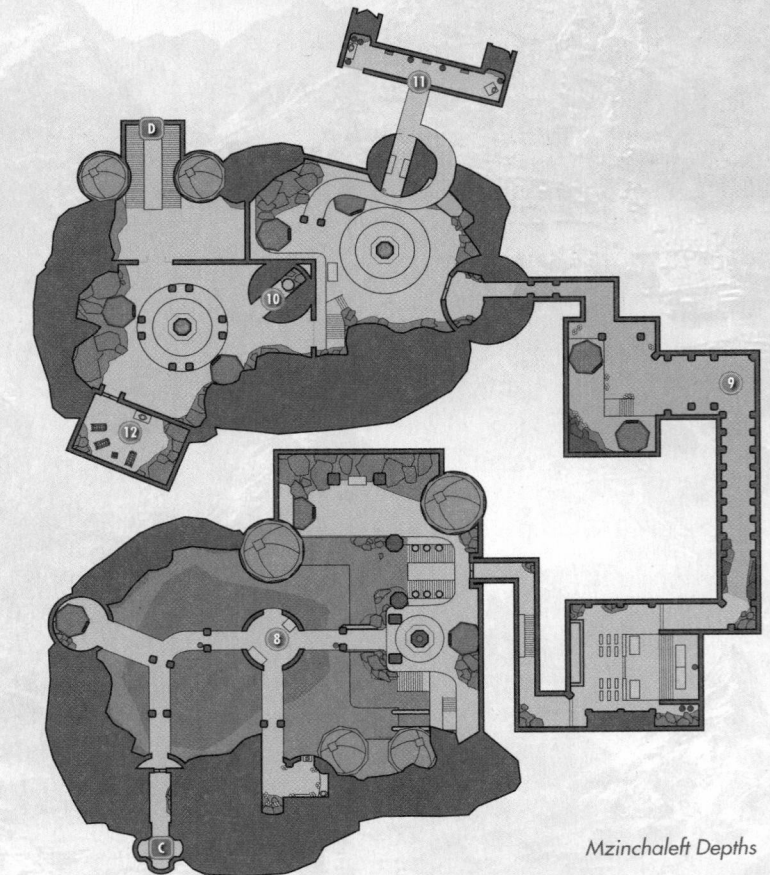

Mzinchaleft Depths

Surrounded by rocks, these impressive dwarven ruins stand in the frozen wastelands in Hjaalmarch's northeast corner. South of the ruins, an ornate elevator grants passage to the Mzinchaleft Gatehouse, where a Dwarven Mechanism can be activated to grant passage to Blackreach [10.02]; however, you can't use this elevator until you've navigated all of Mzinchaleft and used it to exit the Gatehouse, which is the ruins' final area.

During a Miscellaneous Objective for Mjoll the Lioness, you can discover a unique weapon here at Mzinchaleft called "Grimsever." See the Quests chapter for further details.

Exterior

Entering the ruins won't be easy, for a large group of bandits has make camp here as they work at ransacking the site. Slay a mob of brutes in the exterior area, and locate a locked chest atop one of the spiral-path towers.

- ◇ Chest (Locked: Adept)
- ◇ Loose gear

B Door to Barren Skyrim

1 Campfire Passage

A few bandits are huddled around a campfire in this first stretch of passage. Secure the site, loot a chest to the south, and swipe a few potions from the vicinity.

- ◇ Chest ◇ Potions

2 Frozen Cavern

Dispense with a couple of mages and loot another chest in this frosty cavern.

- ◇ Chest ◇ Potions ◇ Loose gear

3 Treasure Room 1

Pick a tricky door lock to enter this small chamber, where a chest, a Skill Book, and a few potions await collection.

- ◇ Skill Book [Archery]: The Black Arrow, v2
- ◇ Area Is Locked (Adept)
- ◇ Chest ◇ Potions

4 Sphere Chamber

Ancient, yet still functional, Dwarven Spheres patrol this large chamber. Allow them to engage any roaming bandits, then dispatch the stragglers. There's little else of interest here.

5 Spider Chamber

Dangerous Dwarven Spiders skitter about this long hall. Pick an Adept-level gate to the south to access a unique-looking dwarven chest.

- ◇ Chest

6 Steam Pipe Passage

Disable several Dwarven Spheres in this chamber, then follow the thick pipes along the left wall to locate an elevated chest.

- ◇ Chest

7 Lever Chamber

Manipulate the levers in this chamber until you can access the southeast chamber, where you may loot a chest and turn a valve. This will allow you to advance to the Mzinchaleft Depths.

- ◇ Chest

B Elevator to Mzinchaleft Depths

C Elevator to Mzinchaleft

8 Mzinchaleft Depths: South

The Mzinchaleft Depths are truly breathtaking—an entire dwarven settlement built within a massive underground cavern. Dangerous Falmer and Chaurus lurk down here, and more Falmer will emerge from small holes high on the walls. Find one chest hidden among the southern Chaurus nest and another in a northern nook, deep underwater. Find

two more sunken chests by opening the southeast underwater gate and following the submerged passage to a small room.

- ◇ Chests (4)
- ◇ Loose gear

9 Connecting Tunnel

After fulling looting the southern exterior area, enter the east building and slay a few more Falmer before following a long tunnel north. Dispatch additional Falmer and Chaurus along the way, and don't miss the odd chest that's hidden in a tent about halfway through.

- ◇ Chest

10 Mzinchaleft Depths: North

The long connecting tunnel deposits you in a northern exterior area. Find a chest in a north tent, then head up a winding ramp to reach a ledge with a button that shines a light on a nearby gate when pressed. Pick a nearby Expert-level gate to enter [11], then head back down, go through the now-lit gate, and loot a long, unique chest that sits near the central fountain. Pick an Adept-level door to visit as well [12]. When you've finished raiding this place, proceed up the northwest stairs to reach the door to the Mzinchaleft Gatehouse.

11 Treasure Room 2

Breaking into this small chamber isn't easy, but picking the Expert-level lock lands you within easy reach of two dwarven chests.

- ◇ Area Is Locked (Expert)
- ◇ Chest (2)

12 Treasure Room 3

Pick a locked door in the southwest corner of [10] to access a small room with a chest.

- ◇ Area Is Locked (Adept)
- ◇ Chest

D Door to Mzinchaleft Gatehouse

Mzinchaleft Gatehouse

A fearsome Dwarven Centurion guards this large chamber, along with a lesser Dwarven Sphere. Fight hard to survive this encounter. Pull a lever to the northeast afterward to open a nook with a chest, and open the southwest gate to access a peculiar Dwarven Mechanism—activating this with a special item opens a way into Blackreach.

When you're ready to exit out to Skyrim, proceed through the far west door and take an elevator to the surface. Pull a lever outside to lower the elevator gate. Now you can quickly return to the Gatehouse in the future.

- ◇ Chest
- ◇ Loose gear

[2.19] Movarth's Lair

Related Quests
Side Quest: Laid to Rest

Recommended Level: 6

Dungeon: Vampire Lair
Animal
Movarth (During Laid to Rest)
Vampire
Vampire's Thrall

Crafting
Alchemy Lab

Collectibles

Skill Book [Illusion]: 2920, Sun's Dawn, v2
Unique Armor: Movarth's Boots [8/112]
Chest(s)
Potions aplenty
Loose gear

Bones and bloodstains lie at the mouth of this cave—an ominous warning of grave danger within. You must clear out this vampire lair during the final part of Side Quest: Laid to Rest.

Entry Stairwell and Passages

Pick off a couple of dangerous Frostbite Spiders in this first cavern, then dispatch a few Vampire Thralls in the following passages.

- ◇ Potion
- ◇ Loose gear

Master Vampire's Lair

A powerful vampire lurks in the heart of the cave, along with several lesser vampires and thralls. Loot this cavern to obtain several potions, and find a chest and alchemy lab in a nook above the wooden ramp. Venture north to snag a Skill Book and some unique boots from the vampires' sleeping quarters before proceeding south.

- ◇ Crafting: Alchemy Lab
- ◇ Skill Book [Illusion]: 2920, Sun's Dawn, v2
- ◇ Unique Item: Movarth's Boots [8/112]
- ◇ Potions aplenty
- ◇ Loose gear

Exit Path

Slay a final thrall and loot one last chest as you make your way south, taking your leave of this unholy den.

- ◇ Chest
- ◇ Potion
- ◇ Loose gear

[2.20] Hjaalmarch Imperial Camp

Related Quests

Civil War Quest (when active, depending on who you side with)

Habitation: Military: Imperial Camp
Imperial Soldier
Imperial Quartermaster (Blacksmith)

Services
Trader (Blacksmith): Imperial Quartermaster [4/33]
Weapons, Apparel, Misc

Crafting
Anvil
Grindstone (2)
Workbench

Special Objects
Civil War: Map of Skyrim
Chests (2)
Loose gear

A small band of Imperial troops have set up a small yet functional encampment at this site, which may appear only during the Civil War quest line. The quartermaster offers you blacksmith services, and inspecting the large map in one of the tents can grant you new map data.

[2.21] Kjenstag Ruins

Recommended Level: 5

Dungeon: Special

Ghost

There must be *something* special about these unassuming ruins—and there is. Visit this site at night (between 8:00 p.m. and 4:00 a.m.) to witness a ghost materialize and run off. Pursue the specter and you'll be led to a small grave that's being looted by bandits. Dispatch the villains and claim their plunder.

[2.22] Stonehills

Related Quests

Miscellaneous Objective: Slow Shipments to Bryling* (Pactur)

Favor (Activity): Mining Ore* (Gestur Rockbreaker)

Habitation: Town

Gestur Rockbreaker
Hjaalmarch Guard
Jesper
Pactur
Sorli the Builder
Sirgar
Swanhvir
Teeba-Ei

Crafting

Smelter

Collectibles

Skill Book [Heavy Armor]: Orsinium and the Orcs [D1/10]
Skill Book [Speech]: 2920, Second Seed, v5 [A1/10]
Chest(s)
Potions
Loose gear

This humble mining settlement has seen its share of hard times. Its people have suffered greatly through the various wars of the last two decades. Though currently self-sufficient, Stonehills is quite poor and run-down.

Exterior

A few crafting stations can be exploited around town.

◇ Crafting: Smelter

Sorli's House

This humble abode houses several potions, plenty of ore and ingots, and a chest. Oh, and there's a Skill Book on the mantel!

◇ Skill Book [Speech]: 2920, Second Seed, v5 [A1/10]
◇ Chest
◇ Potions
◇ Loose gear

Rockwallow Mine

Grag a pickaxe and dig into this icy mine's rich ore veins to collect some valuable Iron Ore. Any ore you mine can be sold to a man named Gestur Rockbreaker for fast coin. Speak with a man named Pactur to gain a new Side Quest as well. Nab the Skill Book that lies on the short table on the wooden loft.

◇ Skill Book [Heavy Armor]: Orsinium and the Orcs [D1/10]
◇ Loose gear
◇ Mineable ore (Iron)

[2.23] Labyrinthian

Crafting

Alchemy Lab
Arcane Enchanter

Dangers

Rune Trap (floor)
Magic Caster Trap (Frost)

Collectibles

Dragon Priest Mask: Konahrik [2/10]
Dragon Priest Mask: Morokei [3/10]
Dragon Priest Mask: Wooden Mask [3/10]
Skill Book [Conjuration]: Liminal Bridges [C1/10]
Unique Item: Ancient Helmet of the Unburned [9/112]
Unique Weapon: Drainblood Battleaxe [8/80]
Unique Weapon: Drainheart Sword [9/80]
Unique Weapon: Drainspell Bow [10/80]
Unique Weapon: Staff of Magnus [11/80]

Special Objects

Word Wall: Dismaying Shout [1/3]
Word Wall: Slow Time [1/3]
Chest(s)
Potions
Loose gear

Related Quests

Side Quest: Masks of the Dragon Priests*
College of Winterhold Quest: The Staff of Magnus

Recommended Level: 24

Dungeon: Dragon Priest Lair

Draugr	Skeever
Dremora	Skeletal Dragon
Enthralled Wizard	Skeleton
Estormo	Slaughterfish
Frost Troll	Spectral Warhound
Ghost Mages	Troll
Ice Wraith	Wisp
Morokei	Wispmother

Labyrinthian (Exterior)

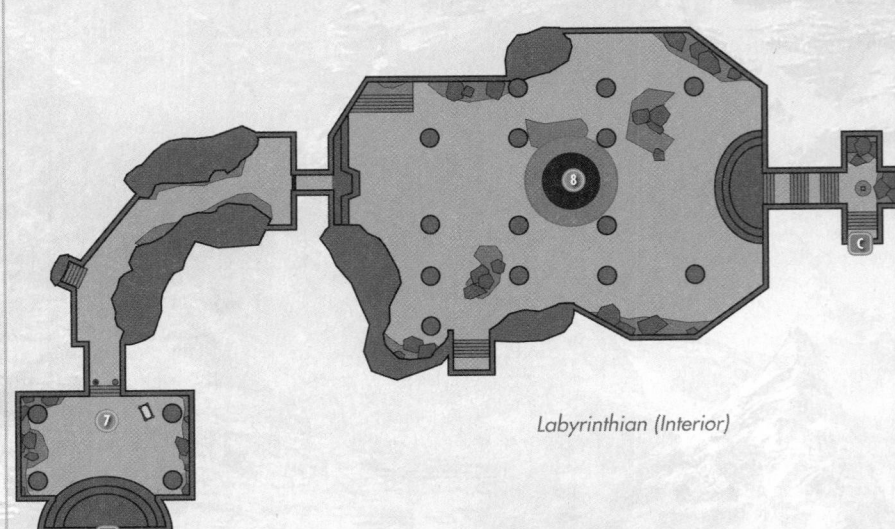

Labyrinthian (Interior)

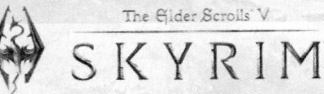

The Elder Scrolls V
SKYRIM

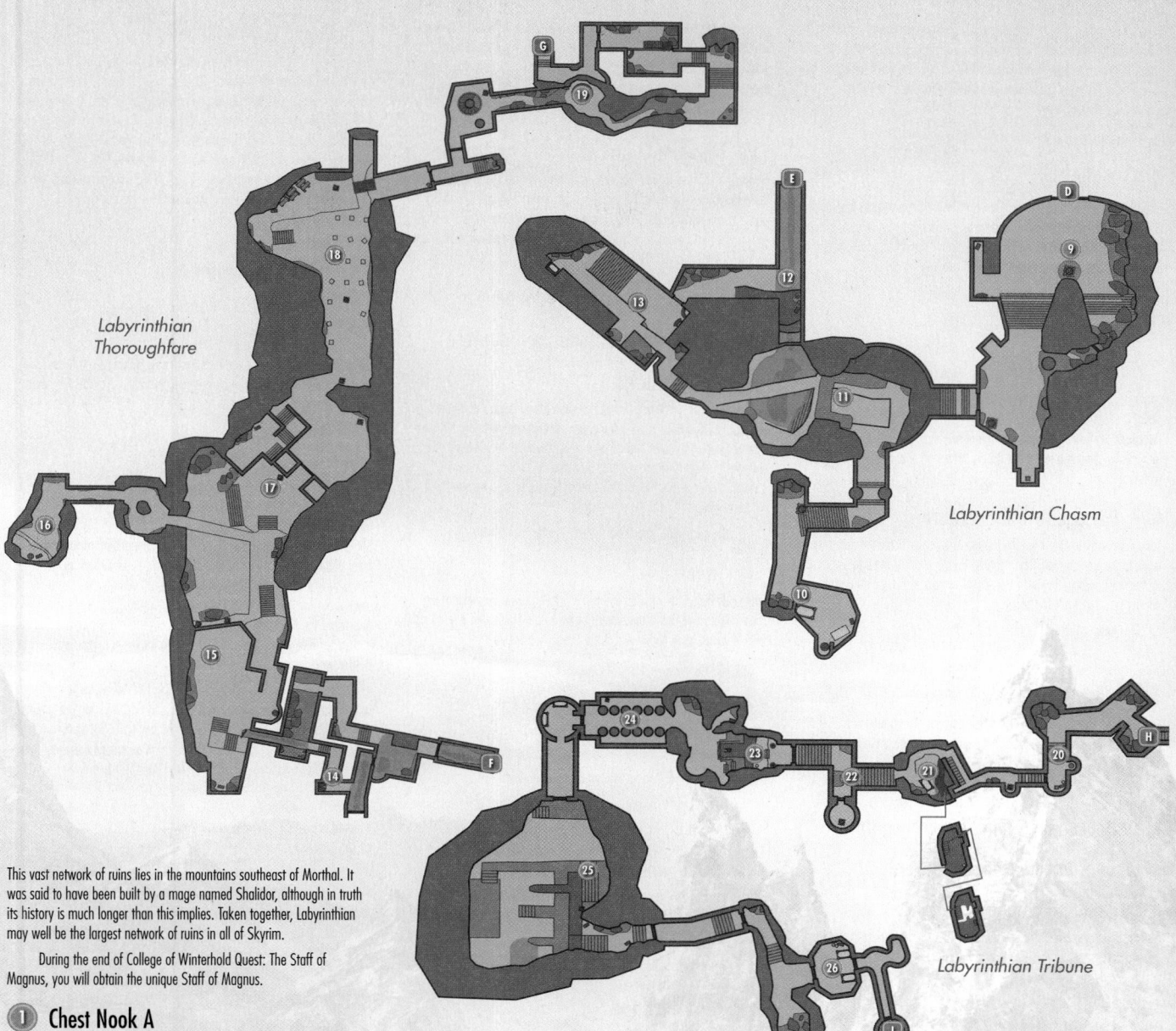

This vast network of ruins lies in the mountains southeast of Morthal. It was said to have been built by a mage named Shalidor, although in truth its history is much longer than this implies. Taken together, Labyrinthian may well be the largest network of ruins in all of Skyrim.

During the end of College of Winterhold Quest: The Staff of Magnus, you will obtain the unique Staff of Magnus.

1 Chest Nook A
Though intimidating in size, Labyrinthian's exterior ruins are simple to navigate. Slay a Frost Troll here and raid a chest.

◇ Chest

2 Chest Nook B
Scale some steps and slaughter another Frost Troll to secure a chest over here.

◇ Chest

3 Central Dome
Duck into this central dome-shaped structure to discover an informative note near a skeleton. Collect the nearby Wooden Mask and put it on—you'll find yourself standing in a sacred chamber. It's actually the same room; you've simply been whisked back to the past. Slay special named Dragon Priest adversaries that lurk at the end of dangerous dungeons throughout Skyrim to obtain special Dragon Masks, then bring these masks to this chamber and place them onto their corresponding busts. Once all eight masks have been restored to the shrine, an immensely powerful Dragon Mask will be yours. This is a unique quest that will never appear in your quest log. Remove the Wooden Mask to return to the present.

◇ Dragon Priest Mask: Konahrik [2/10]
◇ Dragon Priest Mask: Wooden Mask [4/10]

4 Shalidor's Maze Entrance
You may enter Shalidor's Maze at any time—see the "Shalidor's Maze" section at the end of the main Labyrinthian walkthrough. Or simply raid the chest near its entry door and continue exploring these exterior ruins.

◇ Chest (Locked: Novice)

5 Lost Valkygg Entrances
Two entrances to a side area named Lost Valkygg [2.24] are found in Labyrinthian's northeast corner. Use the higher entrance to fully explore this space. However, Lost Valkygg is considered a separate Primary Location in Hjaalmarch—for further details, please see its section, which appears earlier in this chapter.

6 Ceremonial Door
Progress through the College of Winterhold quest line until you acquire the College of Winterhold Quest: The Staff of Magnus. Then make your way up a series of steps that lead to this strange door. Fit the Torc of Labyrinthian onto the door so you may enter and begin your exploration of this massive place.

A Door to Labyrinthian (Interior)

B Exit to Skyrim

7 Entry Chamber
Labyrinthian's sizable entry chamber hints at the magnitude of this epic dungeon, and the vast number of skeletons hints at the danger that lies ahead. Proceed through the far door and wide corridor that follows, looting urns along the way.

◇ Potion
◇ Loose gear

8 Skeletal Dragon Chamber
A horde of skeletons guards this huge chamber, and a massive skeletal dragon rises from the room's center as you enter. Fortunately, these undead enemies are somewhat fragile, though the dragon's attacks are fierce. Loot a few urns after the battle, then proceed to the far staircase to venture onward and downward, optionally stopping to check the carved tablet here.

C Door to Labyrinthian Chasm

D Door to Labyrinthian (Interior)

9 Chasm Entry

Before descending the Chasm's entry steps, discover a chest that's tucked away near the west wall. Go downstairs afterward and use any fire-based attack to thaw the door that has magically frozen. The Spell Tome that sits on a nearby pedestal can provide you with the means to advance.

◇ Chest
◇ Loose gear

10 Study

Dispatch powerful Draugr as you descend some narrow ramps, then duck into the south side passage to battle more undead on your way to a room filled with crafting stations and valuables. Don't miss the Spell Tome: Equilibrium, a unique alteration spell that can only be obtained here.

◇ Crafting: Alchemy Lab, Arcane Enchanter
◇ Spell Tome: Equilibrium
◇ Chest
◇ Loose gear

11 Narrow Ramp Cavern

Backtrack out from [10] and continue descending the sloping narrow ramps here, slaying a few more deadly Draugr on your way to the cavern's watery bottom.

12 Passage to Thoroughfare

Take the north passage from the bottom of [11] to locate the door that leads to the Labyrinthian Thoroughfare. Before heading through, venture up the west passage toward [12], doubling back at one point to scale a narrow trail that leads to treasure.

◇ Chest
◇ Loose gear

13 West Chamber

Optionally visit this side area to battle a powerful Draugr and nab a bit of loot. You may access this area by taking the high west passage at [11], or the low west passage from [12].

◇ Potions

E Door to Labyrinthian Thoroughfare

F Door to Labyrinthian Chasm

14 Plunder Passage

Slay a skeleton as you enter the thoroughfare, then unlock a Novice-level gate to access this side passage, where treasure awaits.

◇ Chests (2)

15 Thoroughfare Access

Discover a chest tucked away against the south wall here, and beware of a vicious troll that lurks in the north passage that leads into the main thoroughfare.

◇ Chest

16 Troll Den

Lowly skeletons roam the spacious thoroughfare, while a pair of dangerous trolls lurk in this side cavern, which you may optionally access by crossing the thoroughfare's first elevated footbridge. Best the trolls to secure the blood-soaked treasure they guard.

◇ Chest

17 Thoroughfare

Throw a lever to gain entry to the main thoroughfare. Loot a few urns and scale the west steps to discover a chest on a ledge.

◇ Chest
◇ Potion

18 Wisp Sanctum

A trio of captivating wisps drift about a collection of short stone headstones here, and a formidable Wispmother soon rises from the ground to attack. A Wispmother in danger will spawn duplicates of herself—focus

on slaying the real enemy and ending the fight so you may loot the chest. Use any form of cold spell to douse the burning door that follows so you may proceed to [19], but stand back and beware: a Ghostly Mage appears and attacks you relentlessly as you consider this magical barrier.

◇ Chest

19 Trapdoor Chamber

Dispatch more foes as you loop around a winding passage to reach this lower chamber — or bypass the passage by opening a large trapdoor to drop straight down to the lower chamber, using a pipe to break your fall. Loot a few urns here before proceeding through the nearby door that leads to the Labyrinthian Tribune.

G Door to Labyrinthian Tribune

H Door to Labyrinthian Thoroughfare

20 Entry Passage

Slay a couple of dangerous Draugr that patrol the Tribune's entry passage. Loot a chest and claim a Spell Tome that can help you navigate the next segment, which features several rune traps. If you're no good with wards, you may do best to sprint and pray. Remove the soul gem from the pedestal to deactivate the first trap, then trigger the rune trap on the floor with a ranged attack from a safe distance.

◇ Danger! Rune Trap (floor), Magic Caster Trap (Frost)

21 Tower

Slay lowly Draugr as you descend this crumbling tower in search of loot. There's Malachite Ore at the bottom of the exterior pool, and a small stash of hidden loot in an upper area of the tower.

◇ Chests (2)

22 Locked Gate Hall

Unlock an Adept-level gate as you move through here to access a south treasure nook that contains valuable gear, including a unique helmet.

◇ Unique Item: Ancient Helmet of the Unburned [9/13]
◇ Potions
◇ Loose gear

23 Word Wall Cavern

Beware the mighty Draugr who sleeps upon this cavern's central throne. Raid a chest that's tucked away near the north wall before approaching the nearby Word Wall to gain new power.

◇ Word Wall: Slow Time [1/3]   ◇ Chest

24 Pillar Passage

Use the large pillars to help you slip through this passage, avoiding its undead sentries.

◇ Potion

25 Grand Cavern

The staff you seek is housed in this cavernous chamber. Disturb nothing and you are safe for the moment. Dive into the far pool to raid a chest, then make your way upstairs. Two Enthralled Wizards are channeling their power to sustain a shield around the Dragon Priest Morokei. Interrupting these will break the shield, bringing the wrath of Morokei upon you. Slay Morokei afterward to obtain his precious mask, along with the Staff of Magnus. Scale the steps and head for the cavern's door afterward, looting a large chest and then doubling back to locate a smaller chest that's tucked away near the stairs.

◇ Staff of Magnus (Morokei)
◇ Dragon Priest Mask: Morokei [3/10]
◇ Chests (3)

26 Exit Passage

Estormo ambushes you as you make your way out of Labyrinthian. Slay him, then loot a nearby chest before taking your leave of this forboding place.

◇ Chest

I Exit to Skyrim

Shalidor's Maze

Shalidor's Maze is a separate subsection of Labyrinthian, and you may enter and fully explore this curious place at any time. Collect all four staves that hover in soft light at the entrance, then enter the maze and use the Staff of Magelight or any ranged Alteration spell you may possess to activate the Alteration Sigil so you may advance. Open special shutters to expose hidden valuables as you navigate the linear maze. Leave each shutter open to mark your progress.

Activate the next sigil, again by hitting the sigil with a ranged spell of its matching school, to drop into a short network of underground passages. Simply go west and take a spiral staircase back up to the surface. You're now outside the maze again; loop around and enter from the north this time. Stop and obtain a new Word of Power from the wall nearby, then activate the next sigil and open the north gate. Find your way toward a Skill Book, and then activate the fourth and final sigil to be whisked away to a battle against a Daedric warrior called a Dremora and its two Atronach minions.

After slaying the Dremora, liberate the unique "Diadem of the Savant" from its corpse and try leaping from the high southern ledges to reach the snowy wooden platforms that run the length of the cavern's west wall. Loop around the wooden ledge to eventually discover valuable gear near a skeleton. Drop to the ground floor afterward and approach the north Word Wall if you haven't already claimed your new Word of Power.

◇ Skill Book [Conjuration]: Liminal Bridges [C1/10]
◇ Word Wall: Dismaying Shout [1/3]
◇ Diadem of the Savant
◇ Loose gear

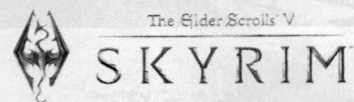

Shalidor's Maze

Shalidor's Maze is a separate subsection of Labyrinthian, and you may enter and fully explore this curious place at any time.

(A) Exit to Skyrim

(1) Staves and South Maze Entrance

Collect all four staves that hover in soft light here, then enter the maze and use the Staff of Magelight (or any ranged Alteration spell you may possess) to activate the Alteration Sigil so you may advance. Open special shutters to expose hidden valuables as you navigate the linear maze. Leave each shutter open to mark your progress.

(2) Destruction Sigil

Activate the next sigil here, again by hitting the sigil with a ranged spell of its matching school (use the Staff of Firebolts if you like), to drop into a short underground passage. Simply go west and take a spiral staircase back up to the surface.

(3) North Maze Entrance and Word Wall

You're now outside the maze again; loop around and enter from the north this time. Stop and obtain a new Word of Power from the wall nearby, then activate the Illusion sigil with the Staff of Fear and open the north gate.

◇ Word Wall: Dismaying Shout [1/3]

(4) Skill Book Nook

Find your way toward a Skill Book that's found in this small nook, lying near a skeleton. You can only reach this Skill Book when you enter the Maze from the north.

◇ Skill Book [Conjuration]: Liminal Bridges [C1/10]

(5) Restoration Sigil

Again, dart through the linear maze until you find andactivate the fourth and final sigil with the Staff of Repulsion. Fall into the pit and step into the portal to be whisked away to a battle against a Daedric warrior called a Dremora, and its two Atronach minions. After slaying the Dremora, liberate the unique "Diadem of the Savant" from its corpse.

◇ Diadem of the Savant

(6) Long-Lost Loot

After the Dremora battle, try leaping from the high southern ledges to reach the snowy wooden platforms that run the length of the cavern's west wall. Loop around the wooden ledge to eventually discover valuable gear near a skeleton here. Drop to the ground floor afterward and take your leave of this unusual place.

◇ Diadem of the Savant

◇ Loose gear

◈ [2.24] Lost Valkygg

Recommended Level: 6

Dungeon: Draugr Crypt

Draugr

Crafting

Alchemy Lab

Dangers

Bone Alarm Trap
Dart Trap (pressure plate)

Collectibles

Skill Book [Pickpocket]: Aevar Stone-Singer [A2/10]
Chest(s)
Potions
Loose gear

These ancient ruins lie at the northeast corner of Hjaalmarch's massive ruin network, Labyrinthian ([2.23]). Lost Valkygg is unique in that it's part of Labyrinthian but also considered a separate Primary Location that can be explored at any time. Lost Valkygg features two entrances that are easy to reach by navigating Labyrinthian's exterior ruins. Both entrances remain unlocked at all times.

(A) Exit to Skyrim

(1) Pressure Plate Passage

Place three objects onto the three pressure plates in this passage to keep them depressed and open the way forward. You'll return to collect these items soon.

◇ Potion

(2) Quiet Chamber

Avoid hanging rattles and sneak through this small chamber to avoid stirring the mighty Draugr that rest on the central slab. Loot a few urns on your way to [3].

◇ Danger! Bone Alarm Trap

(3) Sarcophagi Hall

The slightest noise causes Draugr to burst out from sarcophagi here. Use an Alchemy Lab if you like, then pop into the south chamber and pull a lever to open a holding cell. Claim a Skill Book from the ground near the skeleton.

◇ Crafting: Alchemy Lab
◇ Skill Book [Pickpocket]: Aevar Stone-Singer [A2/10]
◇ Apothecary's Satchel
◇ Loose gear

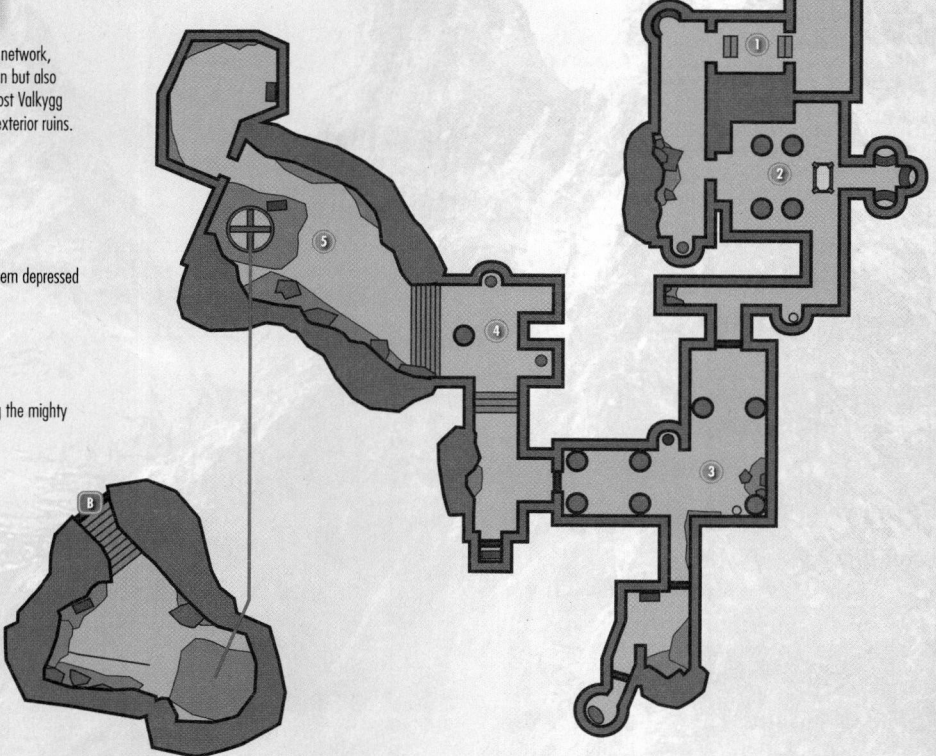

④ Locked Gate Passage

Unlock an Apprentice-level gate in this passage to reach loose gear and a few urns, but beware the pressure plate on the ground before the gate.

◇ Danger! Dart Trap (pressure plate)   ◇ Loose gear

⑤ Pit Cavern (Upper Level)

A deadly Draugr guards a tantalizing chest in this cavern. Before carefully dropping down the large pit to reach [6], enter the northwest doorway to find another, larger chest that's tucked away near a sloping portion of floor.

◇ Chests (2)

⑤ Pit Cavern (Lower Level)

It's possible to enter Lost Valkygg from its lower exit door. If you do, then you'll appear in this final room, where another mighty Draugr guards a chest that sits on a high ledge. There's no climbing back up the pit, so take your leave of Lost Valkygg.

◇ Chest   ◇ Potion

B Exit to Skyrim

[2.25] Skyborn Altar

Recommended Level: 10

Dungeon: Dragon Lair

Dragon Lair (after Main Quest: Dragon Rising)

Wispmother

Special Objects

Shrine of Akatosh [2/6]

Word Wall: Frost Breath [2/3]

High atop Hjaalmarch's eastern mountains, just east of the ruins of Labyrinthian [2.23], stands a remote shrine. Though this site is clearly visible from the north, you must either fight your way through the exterior of Labyrinthian to get here or approach from the south to find a narrow cliffside path that leads up to the summit. Prior to Main Quest: Dragon Rising, a dangerous Wispmother guards this sacred place, where a Shrine to Akatosh can be found. Afterward, a dragon perches here. Defeat the guardian, then claim a new Word of Power from the Word Wall that dominates the overlook.

◀ SECONDARY LOCATIONS ▶

[2.A] Karth River Henge

A mage of some repute is working at an Alchemy Lab near this ring of standing stones. In the center of the ring lies the sacrificial corpse of an Imperial woman. After defeating the mage, you can search the area for ingredients and the following:

◇ Crafting: Alchemy Lab
◇ Skill Book [Alchemy]: Mannimarco, King of Worms

[2.B] Riverside Bandit Camp

Close to the Karth River across from the Stormcloak Camp are two bandits resting by a campfire. They attack on sight (sneaking past or using ranged attacks from the rocks above work well). Check the chest (Locked: Novice) and find a Skill Book lying nearby as you loot items from this pair of reprobates.

◇ Skill Book [Block]: Warrior   ◇ Chest (Novice)

[2.C] Dragon Mound: Karth River Forest

Related Quest: Main Quest: Diplomatic Immunity

This Dragon Mound is initially sealed. It opens during Main Quest: Diplomatic Immunity, and if you visit during or after this point in the Main Quest, the mound will be open and empty.

[2.D] Ambushed Caravan

At the road junction close to the southern of the two small bridges that lead to Dragon Bridge is a lone wagon. The merchants have been slaughtered. A journal on the woman's body describes her misgivings. Look more closely, and you can find a clue to what killed them — the Falmer arrows point toward a raid from the denizens of nearby Chillwind Depths [2.02].

◇ Knapsack

[2.E] Adventurers' Campsite

On the edge of the river, at the base of the dirt pathway that winds up the hill to Chillwind Depths, lies this abandoned campsite. Weapons still lean against equipment crates. A journal describes attacks on the caravans in this area (see also [2.D]) and a plan to rout out those responsible. To discover the fate of these adventurers, continue up the hill and delve into Chillwind Depths [2.02].

◇ Adventurer's Journal   ◇ Knapsack
◇ Loose gear

[2.F] Sabre Cat Rock

Along the rocky border between Hjaalmarch and the Reach, you can find two Sabre Cats prowling near a handful of standing stones. Low-level adventurers are well advised to keep away. Two Sabre Cats may be more than you can handle, but defeating them is well worth the trouble. In addition to any loot found on the nearby corpses, you can also claim two good-sized coin pouches.

[2.G] Dragon Mound: Robber's Gorge Bluffs

Related Quest: Main Quest: Diplomatic Immunity

This Dragon Mound is initially sealed. It opens when Main Quest: Diplomatic Immunity begins, and if you visit during or after this point in the Main Quest, the resurrected dragon will likely be circling overhead. Face it here, or lure it down into Robber's Gorge below to wreak havoc among the bandits.

[2.H] Swamp Pond Massacre

Toward the swamp's northwestern edge is a rough campsite with a burned-out fire and two particularly horrific corpses. This could be the work of vampires. The nearby pond and tree stumps hold a wealth of ingredients. A Skill Book rests inside one of the lingering lean-tos.

◇ Skill Book [Restoration]: The Exodus

[2.I] Smuggler's Alcove

Under a rocky outcrop near a group of standing stones is a smuggler's hideout, which hasn't been used for a few days. The place is deserted, but there's an important book to read on one of the crates.

◊ Skill Book [Pickpocket]: Purloined Shadows

[2.J] Draugr Burial Mound

Deep into the marshes, northeast of Fort Snowhawk, is the familiar circular construction of a Draugr Burial Mound, now exposed and waterlogged. Drop down or wade in, and unlock a chest and locate a potion and Skill Book.

◊ Skill Book [Lockpicking]: The Locked Room
◊ Chest (Novice)

[2.K] Summoning Stones

Related Quest: Side Quest: Rising at Dawn

A circle of stones in the marsh north of Morthal are carved with runes. Some of the town's inhabitants believe that Falion (a wizard who lives in town) comes here at night but are too afraid to find out why.

[2.L] Dead Mammoth

Along the riverside path near Dead Men's Respite and close to the waterfall that empties out into the marshland to the northeast, a fearsome predator has brought down a mammoth, which has yet to be picked clean. Slay the beast and claim the spoils for yourself.

[2.M] Shrine of Kynareth: Hjaalmarch Hills

On the rough path leading from the river's edge to Brood Cavern is a set of ancient steps leading to an old altar, where a Shrine to Kynareth has been erected. Pray here if you wish, and loot the small collection of offerings.

◊ Shrine of Kynareth [2/6]

[2.N] Collapsed Burial Ground

A Nordic burial mound has slowly been sinking into the mire. It has been ransacked plenty of times. Gnarled and twisted trees and plants grow within the stones that have remained upright. Among the fallen rubble is a chest (Locked: Novice).

◊ Chest (Novice)

[2.O] Black Arts Burial Ground

Enter this snow-covered burial mound from the open roof and deal with the skeleton who attacks you. In one of the side alcoves is a necromancer impaled by a dagger on the table. Claim the powerful Staff of Revenants near his body, then search the rest of the ruin to find a Skill Book.

◊ Skill Book [Illusion]: The Black Arts on Trial

[2.P] Dragon Mound: Labyrinthian Peaks

Related Quest: Main Quest: Elder Knowledge

This Dragon Mound is initially sealed. It opens during Main Quest: Elder Knowledge, and if you visit during or after this point in the Main Quest, the mound will be open and empty.

◊ Mineable ore (Moonstone)

[2.Q] Ghost Barrow

While wandering near Kjenstag Ruins, close to the road (to the south) or the pine forest, you may encounter a ghostly figure at night. It moves up across the snow-covered forest floor to this barrow and disappears. Attack the grave robbers here. You may not see it. Open the trapdoor (Adept). Inside is usually a Silver Necklace, enchanted Draugr sword, and a shield.

◊ Loose gear

[2.R] The Conjurer's Caravan

Two bandits have ambushed a caravan and slaughtered the magician, and are dividing the spoils. Slaughter them on sight, before they do the same to you. Check the wagon for a basket of ingredients and the following:

◊ Skill Book [Speech]: A Dance in Fire, v6
◊ Apothecary Satchel (2)
◊ Potions aplenty
◊ Loose gear

[2.S] Hamvir's Summit Hunter's Camp

At the very southeastern corner of Hjaalmarch, in the rocky crags close to Labyrinthian, is a remote hunter's camp with two foragers waiting by the campfire (or on a hunt if no one is here). This location offers spectacular views across Whiterun to the south.

◊ Knapsack (2)

TOPOGRAPHICAL OVERVIEW

Dominated by ice fields and glacial deposits, especially along its northern shore, the Pale (named for the pallid Tundra and pigmentation of its Nord inhabitants) is one of the four oldest Holds in Skyrim. The harsh environment here makes life a chore rather than a joy, and the shape of the Hold has led some to refer to it as "the old boot." Ragged peaks, snow-covered ground, and little sunshine means most of the Nords congregate at the city of Dawnstar, a popular port and mining town. The Pale lacks waterways, save for Lake Yorgrim, located in the southeastern part of the Hold.

Routes and Pathways

Possessing fewer roads and pathways than most other Holds, there is still a reasonable road connecting the Pale to Hjaalmarch, which continues past Fort Dunstad and eventually heads east into Eastmarch and Windhelm or south below the snow line into Whiterun Hold. This Hold's perimeters are dominated by mountains that run north to south along the western edge, and the Sea of Ghosts runs along the northern coast. To the east are the Winterhold Mountains, which follow the perimeter south and then east, to the partially frozen Lake Yorgrim. The River Yorgrim begins from here, merging with the mighty White River just east of Anga's Mill, this Hold's most easterly location. The rest of the dwarven ruins, barrows, and windswept catacombs are nestled between crags and the jutting, unforgiving mountains. Follow the often-elusive minor paths to find some of these locations, or venture off into the snow to locate them all.

AVAILABLE SERVICES, CRAFTING, AND COLLECTIBLES

Services

Followers: [2/47]
Houses for Sale: [0/5]
Marriage Prospects: [1/62]
Skill Trainers: [1/50]
Alchemy: [0/3]
Alteration: [0/3]
Archery: [0/3]
Block: [0/2]
Conjuration: [0/3]
Destruction: [0/3]
Enchanting: [0/2]
Heavy Armor: [0/3]
Illusion: [0/2]
Light Armor: [0/3]
Lockpicking: [0/2]
One-Handed: [0/3]
Pickpocket: [0/3]
Restoration: [1/3]
Smithing: [0/3]
Sneak: [0/3]
Speech: [0/4]
Two-Handed: [0/2]
Traders [8/133]:
Apothecary [1/12]
Bartender [0/5]
Blacksmith [4/33]
Carriage Driver [0/5]
Fence [0/10]
Fletcher [0/3]
Food Vendor [0/9]
General Goods [0/19]
Innkeeper [2/15]
Jeweler [0/2]
Special [0/3]
Spell Vendor [1/12]
Stablemaster [0/5]

Collectibles

Captured Critters: [1/5]
Dragon Claws: [1/10]
Dragon Priest Masks: [2/10]
Larceny Targets: [1/7]
Skill Books: [16/180]
Alchemy: [1/10]
Alteration: [0/10]
Archery: [2/10]
Block: [0/10]
Conjuration: [1/10]
Destruction: [3/10]
Enchanting: [1/10]
Heavy Armor: [2/10]
Illusion: [0/10]
Light Armor: [0/10]
Lockpicking: [1/10]
One-Handed: [0/10]
Pickpocket: [1/10]
Restoration: [0/10]
Smithing: [1/10]
Sneak: [3/10]
Speech: [0/10]
Two-Handed: [0/10]
Treasure Maps: [1/11]
Unique Items: [16/112]
Unique Weapons: [9/80]
Unusual Gems: [0/24]

Special Objects

Shrines: [6/69]
Akatosh: [0/6]
Arkay: [0/12]
Dibella: [0/8]
Julianos: [1/5]
Kynareth: [1/6]
Mara: [2/5]
Stendarr: [1/5]
Talos: [1/17]
Zenithar: [0/5]
Standing Stones: [1/13]
The Lord Stone
Word Walls: [7/42]
Animal Allegiance: [0/3]
Aura Whisper: [1/3]
Become Ethereal: [0/3]
Disarm: [1/3]
Dismaying Shout: [0/3]
Elemental Fury: [0/3]
Fire Breath: [0/2]
Frost Breath: [0/3]
Ice Form: [1/3]
Kyne's Peace: [0/3]
Marked for Death: [1/3]
Slow Time: [1/3]
Storm Call: [1/3]
Throw Voice: [1/1]
Unrelenting Force: [0/1]
Whirlwind Sprint: [0/2]
Crafting Stations — The Pale

CRAFTING STATIONS: THE PALE

✓	TYPE	LOCATION A	LOCATION B
☐	Alchemy Lab	Dawnstar (The Mortar and Pestle) [3.00]	Hall of the Vigilant [3.09]
☐	Arcane Enchanter	Dawnstar (The White Hall) [3.00]	—
☐	Anvil or Blacksmith Forge	Dawnstar (Rustleif's House) [3.00]	Fort Dunstad (Exterior) [3.10]
☐	Cooking Pot and Spit	Dawnstar (Rustleif's House) [3.00]	Raldbthar [3.32]
☐	Grindstone	Dawnstar (Windpeak Inn) [3.00]	Fort Dunstad (Exterior) [3.10]
☐	Smelter	Dawnstar (Iron-Breaker Mine) [3.00]	Dawnstar (Quicksilver Mine) [3.00]
☐	Tanning Rack	Dawnstar (Rustleif's House) [3.00]	Hall of the Vigilant [3.09]
☐	Wood Chopping Block	Dawnstar (Windpeak Inn) [3.00]	Hall of the Vigilant [3.09]
☐	Workbench	Fort Dunstad (Exterior) [3.10]	Raldbthar [3.32]

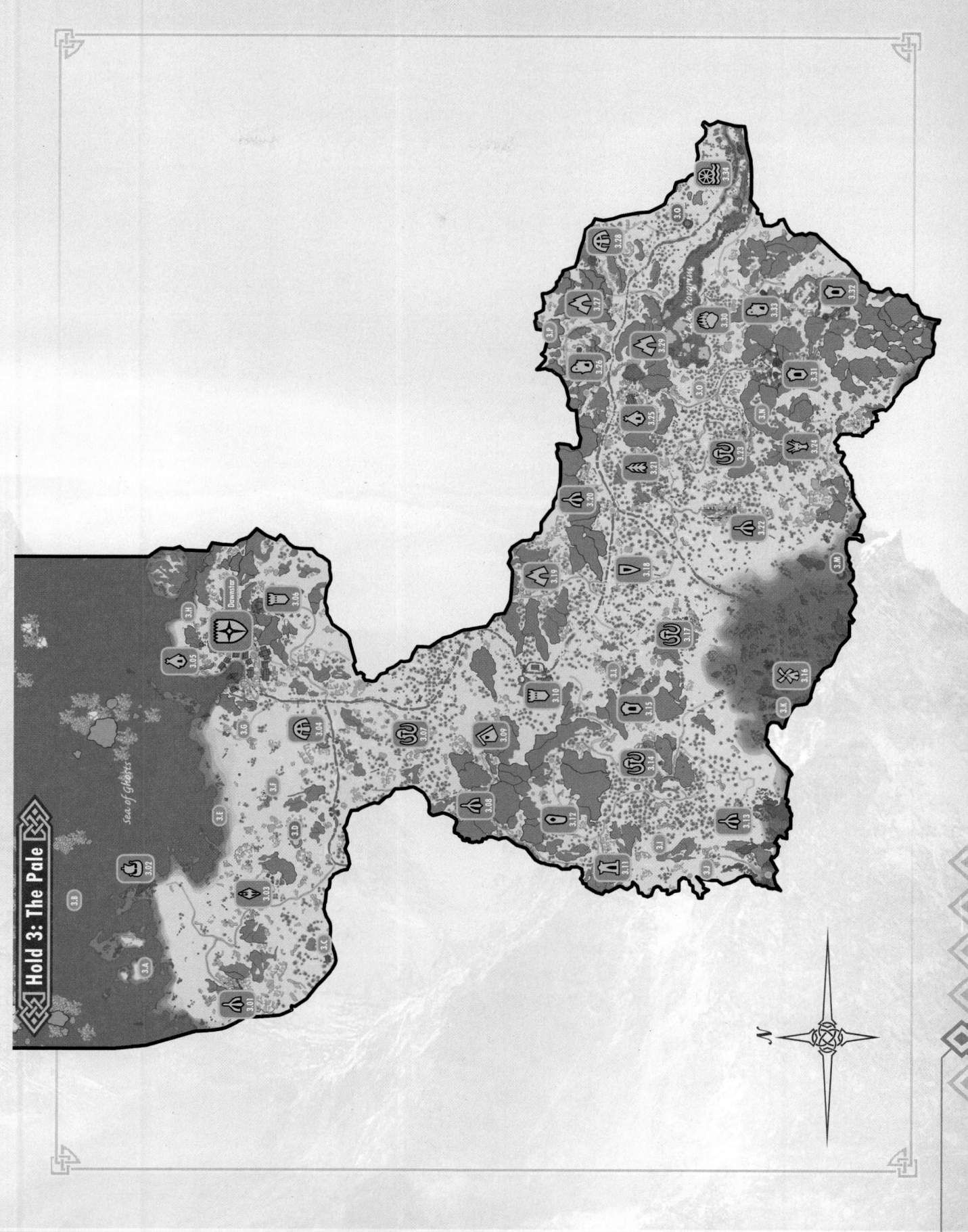

Hold 3: The Pale

TRANING   THE INVENTORY   THE BESTIARY   QUESTS   ◊ ATLAS OF SKYRIM   APPENDICES AND INDEX

PRIMARY LOCATIONS

Total — 35: Hold Capital and 34 Hold Locations

[3.00] Hold Capital City: Dawnstar
    Jarl: Skald the Elder
[3.01] High Gate Ruins
[3.02] Wreck of the Brinehammer
[3.03] Pale Imperial Camp
[3.04] Windward Ruins
[3.05] Dawnstar Sanctuary
[3.06] Nightcaller Temple
[3.07] Red Road Pass
[3.08] Frostmere Crypt
[3.09] Hall of the Vigilant
[3.10] Fort Dunstad
[3.11] Shrine of Mehrunes Dagon
[3.12] The Lord Stone
[3.13] Volunruud
[3.14] Stonehill Bluff
[3.15] Tower of Mzark
[3.16] Loreius Farm
[3.17] Blizzard Rest
[3.18] Weynon Stones
[3.19] Duskglow Crevice
[3.20] Silverdrift Lair
[3.21] Shrouded Grove
[3.22] Korvanjund
[3.23] Tumble Arch Pass
[3.24] Shearpoint
[3.25] Nightgate Inn
[3.26] Blackreach Elevator (Alftand)
[3.27] Forsaken Cave
[3.28] Yorgrim Overlook
[3.29] Bronze Water Cave
[3.30] Pale Stormcloak Camp
[3.31] Irkngthand
[3.32] Raldbthar
[3.33] Blackreach Elevator (Raldbthar)
[3.34] Anga's Mill

SECONDARY LOCATIONS

Total — 17 Points of Interest

[3.A] Horker Standing Stones
[3.B] Sunken Treasures
[3.C] Bandit's Hovel
[3.D] Dragon Mound: Sea Shore Foothills
[3.E] Barnacle Boat
[3.F] Shoreline Bandit Camp
[3.G] Dawnstar Frost Troll Den
[3.H] Shoreline Lovers' Tent
[3.I] A Bloody Trail
[3.J] Border Corner: Roadside Shrine of Mara
[3.K] Mammoth Graveyard
[3.L] Ice Shard Wild Animal Den
[3.M] Dragon Mound: Shimmermist Hills
[3.N] Julianos's Fallen
[3.O] Yorgrim Forest Spider Trap
[3.P] Wayward Peak Summit
[3.Q] Dragon Mound: Yorgrim Resurrection

HOLD CAPITAL: DAWNSTAR

Related Quests

Civil War Quest: Reunification of Skyrim
Civil War Quest: A False Front
Daedric Quest: Pieces of the Past
Daedric Quest: Waking Nightmare
Side Quest: Rise in the East
Dark Brotherhood Quest: Side Contract: Beitild
Miscellaneous Objective: Innkeeper Rumors (Windpeak Inn)

Miscellaneous Objective: Salt of the Seas* (Captain Leif Wayfinder)
Favor (Activity): Mining Ore* (Beitild)
Favor (Activity): Mining Ore* (Leigelf)
Favor (Activity): A Drunk's Drink* (Karl)
Favor: Rare Item Hunt* (Rustleif)
Favor: Item Retrieval (Cave)* (Frida)
Favor: Jobs for the Jarls* (Jarl Skald the Elder)
Thane Quest: Thane of The Pale*

Habitation: Hold Capital (Minor)

Crafting

Alchemy Lab
Arcane Enchanter
Blacksmith Forge
Grindstone
Smelters (2)
Tanning Rack

Services

Trader (Apothecary): Frida [4/14]
Trader (Blacksmith): Rustleif [5/33]
Trader (Blacksmith): Seren [6/33]
Trader (Innkeeper): Thoring [4/18]
Trader (Spells Vendor): Madena [3/12]

Special Objects

Civil War: Map of Skyrim

Collectibles

Skill Book [Conjuration]: 2920, Hearth Fire, v9 [B2/10]
Skill Book [Destruction]: Response to Bero's Speech [D1/10]
Skill Book [Destruction]: The Art of War Magic [E2/10]
Skill Book [Enchanting]: Catalogue of Weapon Enchantments [C1/10]
Skill Book [Lockpicking]: The Wolf Queen, v1 [E1/10]
Skill Book [Smithing]: Cherim's Heart [A1/10]
Chest(s)
Potions aplenty
Loose gear
Mineable ore (Iron, Quicksilver)

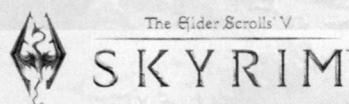

Lore: City Overview

Dawnstar, capital of the Pale Hold, sits on Skyrim's northern coastline, halfway between Winterhold and Solitude. Because of the glacial icefields just to the east, it is the last port before Windhelm that is not icebound. Dawnstar's economy is driven by its two mines, and the people of Dawnstar often find meaning in the stones. Like their leader, Jarl Skald the Elder, they stand unbreakable and firm despite all their troubles. Residents of the city fight the weather, the beasts, and raiders every day in order to keep goods and ore flowing into and out of their port and market.

Important Areas of Interest

1 Main Thoroughfare

The main road (packed with snow and dirt) is in two tiers, with the structures built around the inlet to the Sea of Ghosts. The upper track houses the main structures, while the lower road connects all the buildings owned by individuals. East and west of the roadways are the two mines that help bolster Dawnstar's economy. To the north, farther along the shoreline, is the entrance to an old, abandoned sanctuary. Dominating the town is the Nightcaller Temple, perched and ever watching over the rugged rocks.

2 Northstar Port (and the Sea Squall)

Captain Lief Wayfinder

Located at the base of the cliffs under the Nightcaller Temple, these docks host incoming trade ships. The vessel currently docked in these frigid waters is the Sea Squall.

3 The White Hall

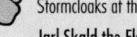 The following leaders of Dawnstar are loyal to the Stormcloaks at the start of the Civil War.

Jarl Skald the Elder

Skald has ruled Dawnstar since his father's death on the battlefield 35 years ago. He came into his rule in his teenage years and has never really lost the arrogance and sense of invincibility that comes with that age. He is quick to judge and doesn't change his mind once he has decided something.

Jod (Housecarl)

Jod is Captain of the Dawnguard. He takes his duty and his loyalty to the town seriously. He served on a ship in the Great War, and because of his experiences, he is not anxious to fight the Empire. Skald's fervent animosity toward the Empire has made Jod doubt him.

Bulfrek

Bulfrek's family has served the Jarls of Dawnstar for generations. He is not pleased with being born into a life that he considers to be without honor. Although he would never speak it out loud, he would do almost anything to be free of his duty.

Madena (Court Wizard)

Madena is far from home. She is a Breton who served as a battle-mage in the Imperial Legion during the Great War. After seeing the horrors of a large war firsthand, she moved to Dawnstar, hoping that being a court mage in a small hold would be free of complication. She refuses to take sides, insisting that her job is to help the people of Dawnstar. She will support whoever is in power.

Frorkmar Banner-Torn

The following residents of Dawnstar arrive to take control of the capital, once this Hold has fallen during the Civil War.

Jarl Brina Merilis

Brina was once renowned throughout the Legion for her leadership and her tactical ability. She is a stern woman who tolerates no foolishness from those under her command. She does have a warm side that sometimes shows through, although it is rarely seen since the start of the war.

Horik Halfhand (Housecarl)

Horik has served with Brina nearly his whole life. With no command ambitions of his own, he is content to serve as her bodyguard. Horik has nothing but respect and admiration for his commander, and there are few things that would shake his loyalty to her.

The White Hall keep serves as both the Jarl's residence and the place where he holds court. The keep's main feature is the large combined throne room, mead hall, and council chamber that dominates the largest portion of the main floor. To the right are the Jarl's Bedchambers, while Madena, the Jarl's advisor (and excellent spell vendor), resides on the upper floor, along with his manservant Bulfrek. Madena's spell shop has been partly turned over to the Stormcloaks as a war room, with the blessing of Jarl Skald. Find a Skill Book on a small table upstairs and another tucked between a barrel and pony keg in the room with the training dummy.

- ◇ Crafting: Arcane Enchanter
- ◇ Trader (Spells Vendor): Madena [3/12]
  - ○ Scrolls, Books, Misc
- ◇ Skill Book [Destruction]: The Art of War Magic [E2/10]
- ◇ Skill Book [Enchanting]: Catalogue of Weapon Enchantments [C1/10]
- ◇ Civil War: Map of Skyrim
- ◇ Chest
- ◇ Potions aplenty

4 Dawnstar Barracks

Jarl Skald's guards rest here after their patrols, murmuring about the nightmares that the inhabitants are suffering from. The Barracks has a main floor (where most of the drinking occurs) and an upper sleeping quarters leading to a balcony overlooking the shoreline. Down the stairs is the Dawnstar Jail. Remarkably, a Skill Book is tucked away in one corner of the jail.

- ◇ Skill Book [Lockpicking]: The Wolf Queen, v1 [E1/10]
- ◇ Evidence Chest
- ◇ Prisoner Belongings Chest
- ◇ Chest (3)
- ◇ Potions aplenty
- ◇ Loose gear

5 Windpeak Inn

Thoring   Karita   Stig Salt-Plank   Erandur

Windpeak Inn is Dawnstar's only tavern and is run by Thoring and his young daughter Karita, who both live in the building. Karita serves as a bard, and their servant Abelone handles most of the menial chores, chopping wood or using the grindstone in the pen outside. Currently, the place is a meeting spot where anxious townsfolk (such as Fruki and Irgnir the miners) gather to gossip and worry about the strange nightmares that have been keeping them from their beds.

- ◇ Crafting: Grindstone
- ◇ Trader (Innkeeper): Thoring [4/15]
  - ○ Room for the Night, Food, Innkeeper Rumors
- ◇ Chest (2)

6 Rustleif's House

Rustleif   Seren

Located overlooking the shoreline of Dawnstar, Rustleif has his smithy and home set up facing the main road. Rustleif is a renowned weaponsmith, and he is often called upon to arm and outfit the Jarl's men. His Redguard wife, Seren, assists him and is currently with child. Inside, their home is comfortable but a little spartan.

- ◇ Crafting: Blacksmith Forge, Tanning Rack
- ◇ Trader (Blacksmith): Rustleif [5/33]
  - ○ Weapons, Apparel, and Misc
- ◇ Trader (Blacksmith): Seren [6/33]
  - ○ Weapons, Apparel, and Misc.
- ◇ Chest

7 Leigelf's House

Leigelf Quicksilver

Because Leigelf manages Quicksilver Mine and spends most of his time obsessing about his work and his wife, his living arrangements are somewhat sparse.

- ◇ Chest

8 Brina's House

Brina (a respected Legion commander) retired to Dawnstar and has been living here for several years. She shares her dwelling with her bodyguard and friend Horik. Recently, when the Jarl of Dawnstar seceded from the Empire, she attempted to talk sense into him, but to no avail. Inside, their dwelling is where they sleep (in separate beds) and collect (rather than consume) a large amount of wine. Search the basket near the chest to discover a hidden Skill Book.

- ◇ Skill Book [One-Handed]: The Importance of Where
- ◇ Chest (2)

9 The Mortar and Pestle

Frida

The old widow Frida runs her modest alchemy shop from this building on the main road. A Skill Book is kept behind the counter.

- ◇ Crafting: Alchemy Lab
- ◇ Trader (Apothecary): Frida [3/12]
  - ○ Potions, Food, Ingredients
- ◇ Skill Book [Conjuration]: 2920, Hearth Fire, v9 [B2/10]
- ◇ Unique Item: Ring of Pure Mixtures
- ◇ Chest (2)
- ◇ Potions aplenty

10 Beitild's House

Beitild Iron-Breaker

Beitild Iron-Breaker manages Iron-Breaker Mine. She's in constant competition with Leigelf Quicksilver, the owner of Quicksilver Mine and her former husband. Beitild lives in the house she used to share with her husband. She refuses to do much else but tend to her mine, eat, and sleep.

◇ Chest

11 Silus Vesuius's House (Locked: Requires Key)

Silus Vesuius

Also known as the Museum of the Mythic Dawn, the building is dedicated to the cult in Dawnstar. This is Silus's vain attempt to capture some attention and infamy for his family's past deeds. The pride of the collection is his impressive assortment of Mythic Dawn memorabilia, as well as a piece of Mehrunes' Razor that is kept in a secured display case. This building is only accessible once Daedric Quest: Pieces of the Past begins.

◇ Mehrunes' Razor Scabbard
◇ Mythic Dawn Commentaries 1, 2, 3, 4
◇ Mysterium Xarxes (Fragment; cannot be taken)
◇ Mythic Dawn Boots, Gloves, and Robes
◇ The Keepers of the Razor

12 Irgnir's House

Irgnir   Karl

Karl and Irgnir, the workers of Iron-Breaker Mine, live here in this modest dwelling. They have finally saved up enough gold to purchase from Beitild. They sometimes board with Gjak and Bodil, who take the other shifts to keep the mine constantly productive.

◇ Chest

13 Iron-Breaker Mine

This mine is located on the outskirts of town to the east. Karl, Irgnir, Gjak, and Bodil work here. This mine produces iron and has a smelter for extracting steel from the iron. Under the watchful (some might say, stern and overbearing) gaze of Beitild, the mine is producing a large amount of ore and is a boon to the local economy. Find a Skill Book resting atop a barrel near the firepit.

◇ Crafting: Smelter
◇ Skill Book [Destruction]: Response to Bero's Speech [D1/10]
◇ Mineable ore (Iron)

14 Fruki's House

Fruki   Lond Northstrider

Fruki and Lond, the miners working the Quicksilver veins, live here in this small structure in which Fruki was raised. They occasionally speak

with Borgny and Edith, who take the other shifts to keep the mine productive — when Leigelf isn't running the operation into the ground.

◇ Chest

15 Quicksilver Mine

This mine is located on the outskirts of town to the west. Fruki, Lond, Borgny, and Edith work here. This is the only Quicksilver mine inside Skyrim's borders, but despite this, the mine is suffering — from marauders and falling production. In fact, it is practically shut down as Leigelf spends his time obsessing over his wife and the competing mine. More proud than sensible, Leigelf's negligence is causing all of his workers to consider quitting in frustration or fear of attack. The mine holds a Skill Book. Find it inside the small crate on the ground floor of the farthest cavern.

◇ Crafting: Smelter
◇ Skill Book [Smithing]: Cherim's Heart [A1/10]
◇ Mineable ore (Quicksilver)

PRIMARY LOCATIONS

▶ [3.01] High Gate Ruins

Related Quests

Side Quest: Masks of the Dragon Priests*

Dungeon Quest: A Scroll for Anska

Recommended Level: 24

Dungeon: Dragon Priest Lair

Anska
Draugr
Vokun

Dangers

Dart Trap (pressure plates)
Spear Trap (pressure plate)
Swinging Spikes (pressure plates)

Quest Items

Sealed Scroll

Collectibles

Dragon Priest Mask: Vokun [5/10]
Skill Book [Destruction]: A Hypothetical Treachery [A1/10]

Special Objects

Word Wall: Storm Call [1/3]
Chest(s)
Potions aplenty
Loose gear

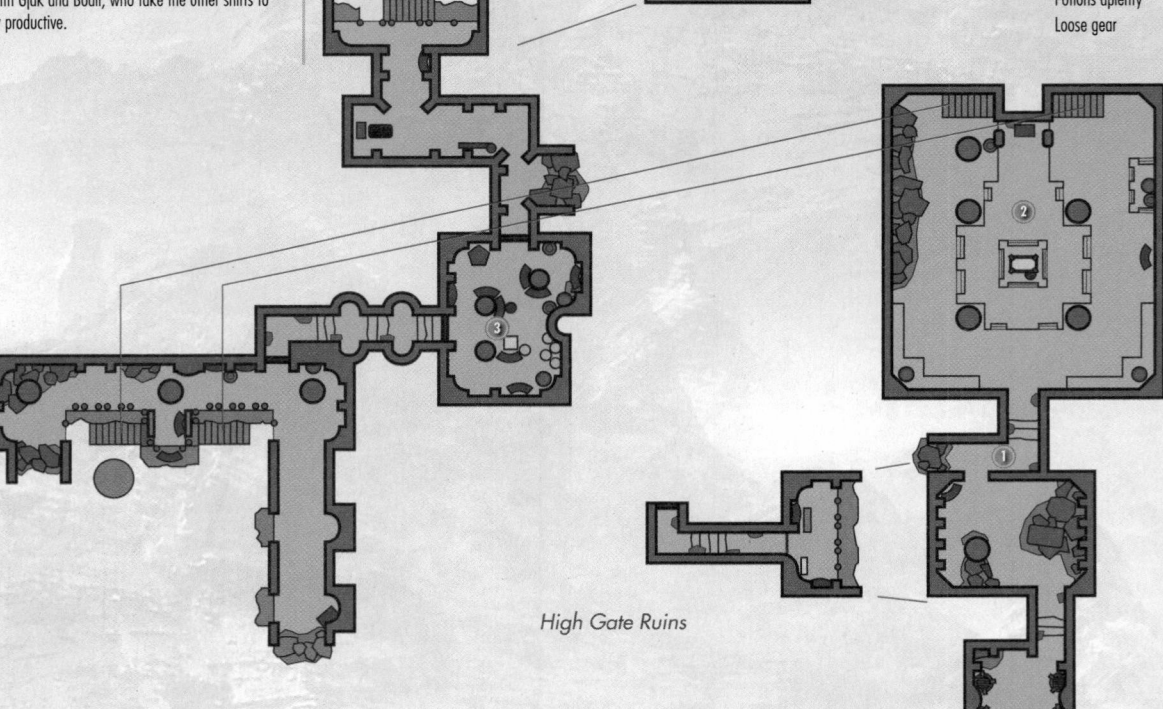

High Gate Ruins

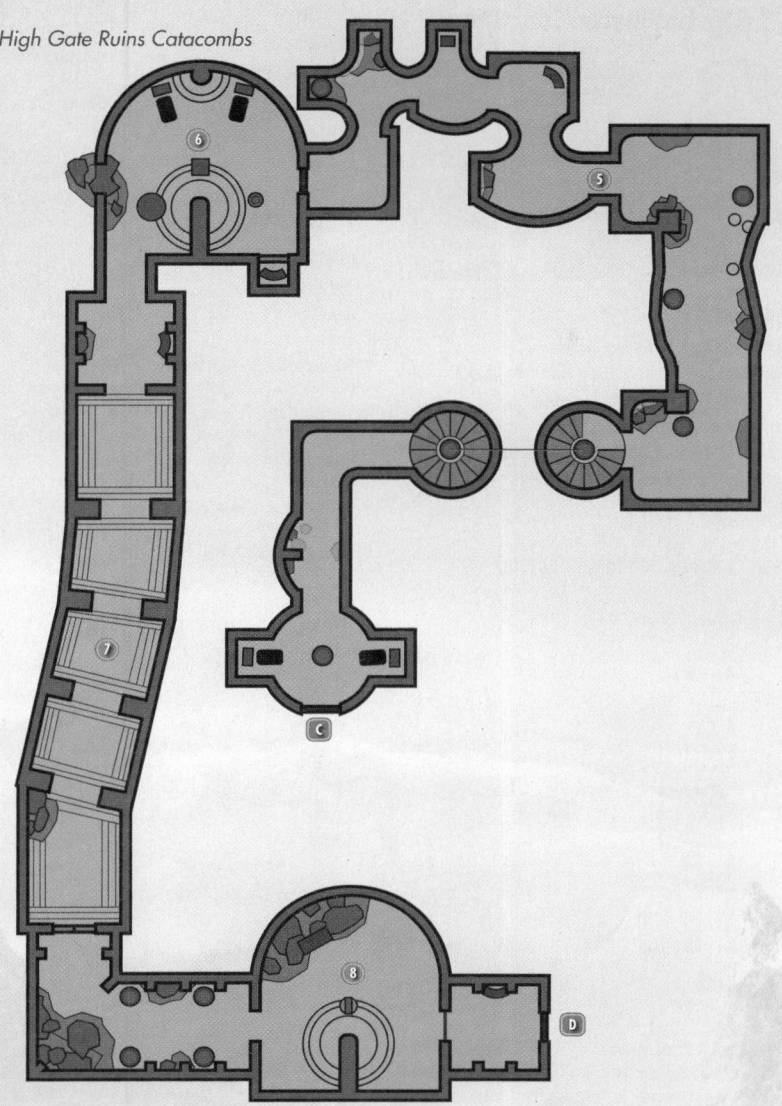

High Gate Ruins Catacombs

6   Treasure Room

After slaying this cavern's resident undead, open an Adept-level door to access a tiny closet with a chest. Removing the Soul Gem from the central pedestal causes two additional Draugr to emerge from the coffins behind you.

◇ Chest   ◇ Loose gear

7   Trapped Passage

Avoid a myriad of pressure plates in this wide corridor—each one triggers a lethal trap.

◇ Danger! Dart Trap (pressure plates), Spear Trap (pressure plates)

◇ Potions

8   Lever Chamber

Slay a lone Draugr here, then pull the lever in the nearby alcove to open aonther small nook, freeing a powerful Draugr that quickly attacks. Pull the lever in the other nook to open the way to the throne room. The central lever can be ignored.

◇ Potions aplenty   ◇ Loose gear

D   Door to Vokun's Throne Room

Vokun's Throne Room

The doors swing open as you enter this wide chamber, and a demonic apparition rises from the central sarcophagus. It's Vokun. Slay the deadly Dragon Priest and collect his powerful mask, then head to the back room to locate a Word Wall. Open two chests along the upstairs balcony and loot a number of urns before claiming the scroll that Anska seeks from the central table. Take the upstairs passage back to the ruin's entrance and return the scroll to Anska, who now awaits you just outside.

◇ Dragon Priest Mask: Vokun [5/10]   ◇ Sealed Scroll

◇ Word Wall: Storm Call [1/3]   ◇ Chests (2)

[3.02] The Wreck of the *Brinehammer*

Recommended Level: 6

Dungeon: Shipwreck

Mudcrab

Collectibles

Skill Book [Archery]: Father of the Niben [A1/10]

Special Objects

Shrine of Kynareth [3/6]
Chest(s)

A merchant vessel called the *Brinehammer* has crashed along the Pale's brutal northern shoreline. Before heading below deck, enter the captain's quarters, where a chest and the remains of the captain await plundering.

◇ Captain Slaughterfish's Key (Captain Slaughterfish)

◇ Chest

Below Deck

Slay the odd Mudcrab as you scour the *Brinehammer*'s belly—the only items of interest are a chest near the vessel's center and the shrine that's nearby. There's no need to unlock the Novice-level door; you can simply circumvent it. Head down to the cargo hold after looting the chest. The north door to the cargo hold is unlocked as well.

◇ Shrine of Kynareth [3/6]   ◇ Chest

High Gate ruins is an old Draugr ruin inhabited by the Dragon Priest Vokun, wearer of the Iron Mask. The plucky adventurer and powerful Fire Mage Anska has already begun making her way toward Vokun's treasure, where she believes she will find a scroll tying her family's history to Ysgramor's.

A   Exit to Skyrim

E   Door to Vokun's Throne Room

1   Anska Encounter

Loot a few Draugr corpses on your way into this small chamber, where you encounter a woman named Anska. Speak with her to begin a new Side Quest that takes place in these ruins. Anska then assists you in clearing this dreary place.

2   Sacrificial Chamber

Slay a few Draugr in this large chamber, then raid the far chest and surrounding urns. Head upstairs and claim a number of potions from the balcony, along with a Skill Book that lies next to a skeleton in a dark corner. Don't miss looting another chest at the balcony's far end.

◇ Skill Book [Destruction]: A Hypothetical Treachery [A1/10]

◇ Chest (2)

◇ Potions aplentyv

3   Potion Room

Slay a group of Draugr on the way to this next chamber, which holds several more potions.

◇ Potions aplenty

◇ Loose gear

4   Stairwell Chamber

Sidestep a pressure plate trap in the passage that leads to this chamber. Look at the ceiling to find the pattern in which you must pull this chamber's four levers to open the central stairwell and descend to the catacombs below.

◇ Danger! Swinging Spikes (pressure plate)

◇ Potions

B   Door to High Gate Ruins Catacombs

C   Door to High Gate Ruins

5   Draugr Tunnels

Leap over a pressure plate that lies directly in a doorway in these passages—you'll be punctured by arrows if you touch it. Open the chest along the northernmost stretch without getting too close; you'll be impaled by spears if you touch the pressure plate on the ground near the chest.

◇ Danger! Dart Trap (pressure plate), Spear Trap (pressure plate)

◇ Chest   ◇ Potions   ◇ Loose gear

Cargo Hold

Open the hold's locked chest and collect the nearby Skill Book, then dive underwater and find another locked chest that's sunken beneath the ship.

- ◇ Skill Book [Archery]: Father of the Niben [A1/10]
- ◇ Chests (Locked: Adept) (2)

[3.03] Pale Imperial Camp

Related Quests

Civil War Quest: Reunification of Skyrim

Civil War Quest: A False Front

Civil War Quest: The Battle for Fort Dunstad

Dungeon Activity

Services

Trader (Blacksmith): Imperial Quartermaster [7/33]

Weapons, Apparel, Misc

Crafting

Anvil

Grindstone

Workbench

Special Objects

Civil War: Map of Skyrim

Chest(s)

Loose gear

Habitation: Military: Imperial Camp

Imperial Quartermaster (Blacksmith)

Imperial Soldier

Legate Constantius Tituleius

This small military camp stands against the harshness of the Pale's frozen northern wastelands. Trade with the quartermaster, or use his many crafting workstations. Examine the map in the largest tent to potentially gain new map data. Loot a few chests within the smaller tents if you like before setting off.

[3.04] Windward Ruins

Related Quests

Side Quest: Kyne's Sacred Trials

College of Winterhold Radiant Quest: Destruction Ritual Spell

Recommended Level: 5

Dungeon: Animal Den

Animal

Chest (Locked: Adept)

A pair of lowly Skeevers guard this small collection of ruins. Head inside the small domed structure and utilize the pedestal in the back to advance the Destruction Ritual Spell Quest. Plunder the chest that's tucked away among rocks in the ruins' outer ring.

[3.05] Dawnstar Sanctuary

Related Quests

Dark Brotherhood Quest: The Cure for Madness

Dark Brotherhood Quest: Where You Hang Your Enemy's Head...

Dark Brotherhood Quest: Welcome to the Brotherhood

Dark Brotherhood Quest: Cicero's Return*

Dark Brotherhood Quest: The Dark Brotherhood Forever!

Dark Brotherhood Quest: The Torturer's Treasure: Parts I, II, III, IV*

Recommended Level: 8

Dungeon: Special/Habitation: Special

Cicero

Sanctuary Guardian

Udefrykte (Troll)

Services

Follower: Cicero [6/47]

Follower: Dark Brotherhood Initiate [7/47]

Dangers

Bear Traps

Oil Pool Trap

Spear Trap (proximity)

Collectibles

Skill Book [Alteration]: Sithis

Skill Book [Archery]: The Marksmanship Lesson [D1/10]

Skill Book [One Handed]: Fire and Darkness

Skill Book [Sneak]: Sacred Witness

Unique Item: Jester's Boots [10/112]

Unique Item: Jester's Clothes [11/112]

Unique Item: Jester's Gloves [12/112]

Unique Item: Jester's Hat [13/112]

Unique Item: Cicero's Boots [14/112]

Unique Item: Cicero's Clothes [15/112]

Unique Item: Cicero's Gloves [16/112]

Unique Item: Cicero's Hat [17/112]

Unique Item: Worn Shrouded Armor [18/112]

Unique Item: Worn Shrouded Boots [19/112]

Unique Item: Worn Shrouded Cowl [20/112]

Unique Item: Worn Shrouded Gloves [21/112]

Unique Item: Tumblerbane Gloves [22/112]

Area Is Locked (quest required)

Chest(s)

Potions

Loose gear

Explore the coastline north of Dawnstar to discover an ominous door built into the rock face. This is the entrance to Dawnstar Sanctuary, which you cannot enter until you've advanced to Dark Brotherhood Quest: The Cure for Madness, during which you must chase a wounded person through this trap-filled place. The Dark Brotherhood eventually moves their hideout here after you complete their quest line.

Ⓐ Exit to Skyrim

① Training Chamber

Swipe a Sneak Skill Book off a small table on your way to this tall, circular chamber. Before maneuvering past the stabbing spears (Whirlwind Sprint may help), knock down two hanging lamps to ignite the oily floor below and singe a pair of Sanctuary Guardians. Get past the spears and then go downstairs to find a pair of Skill Books. Another book on a nearby shelf can potentially grant you a new quest.

- ◇ Danger! Oil Pool Traps, Spear Trap (proximity)
- ◇ Skill Book [Archery]: The Marksmanship Lesson [D1/10]
- ◇ Skill Book [One Handed]: Fire and Darkness
- ◇ Skill Book [Sneak]: Sacred Witness
- ◇ Potions
- ◇ Loose gear

② No Access

These rooms are blocked by rubble until the Dark Brotherhood takes over the Dawnstar Sanctuary and removes the debris.

③ North Entry Hall

Moving through the training chamber lets you explore the north half of the sanctuary's entry hall. This section of the sanctuary has given way to the ravages of time. Collect a Skill Book from a shelf near the circular stained-glass window before proceeding into the snowy tunnel on your way to [4].

- ◇ Skill Book [Alteration]: Sithis
- ◇ Loose gear

④ Udefrykte's Lair

Dodge bear traps as you navigate the frigid tunnel, which leads to the den of an ill-tempered troll named Udefrykte. Raid a chest on a high ledge here as you continue to the trail of blood toward your quarry.

- ◇ Chest

⑤ Coffin Corridors

Slay a number of Sanctuary Guardians as you navigate this long passage. If you're skilled enough, loot the large locked chest in the southern nook as you go.

- ◇ Chest (Locked: Master)

6 Torture Chamber

Don't worry if you couldn't open that last chest—this gruesome chamber contains another. Unbar the nearby door to find yourself back at [3], your exploration of the Sanctuary complete. During Dark Brotherhood Quest: The Cure for Madness, you face Cicero here.

◇ Chest

Post–Dark Brotherhood Occupation

The Dark Brotherhood repurposes Dawnstar Sanctuary for their own base of operations after you complete the entire Dark Brotherhood quest line. Naturally, the place is much different after the Brotherhood moves in:

During Dark Brotherhood: Where You Hang Your Enemy's Head…, you can purchase New Banners (1,000 gold), a Poisoner's Nook (5,000 gold), a Torture Chamber (5,000), a Secret Entrance (5,000) that can be accessed from the hills above the Sanctuary, and a Master Bedroom (3,000 gold). All are bought from Delvin Mallory of the Thieves Guild, inside the Ragged Flagon in Riften.

During Dark Brotherhood: Welcome to the Brotherhood, Nazir has an initiate recruited for you.

◇ Follower: Dark Brotherhood Initiate [7/47]

During Dark Brotherhood: Cicero's Return,* you can elect to keep Cicero as a companion.

◇ Follower: Cicero [6/47]

During Dark Brotherhood: The Dark Brotherhood Forever!, you receive assassination orders from the Night Mother, who is also ensconced in these new surroundings.

During Dark Brotherhood: The Torturer's Treasure: Parts I, II, III, IV,* providing you've had the Torture Chamber installed, you can torture victims until they reveal the location of their treasure.

[3.06] Nightcaller Temple

Just southeast of the Pale's capital city of Dawnstar, the single tower of an ancient temple rises up from the frozen rock. You visit this temple with Erandur as part of Daedric Quest: Waking Nightmare, hoping to solve the mystery of why Dawnstar's townsfolk have been suffering nightmares. Slay the beasts that guard the temple's entrance, then head inside.

A Exit to Skyrim

1 Shrine Chamber

The temple's entry chamber features a small shrine that instantly cures you of all diseases when touched. When you visit the temple as part of the "Waking Nightmare" quest, Erandur will open the way forward, allowing you to explore beyond this first room.

◇ Shrine of Mara [2/5] ◇ Chest (Locked: Novice)

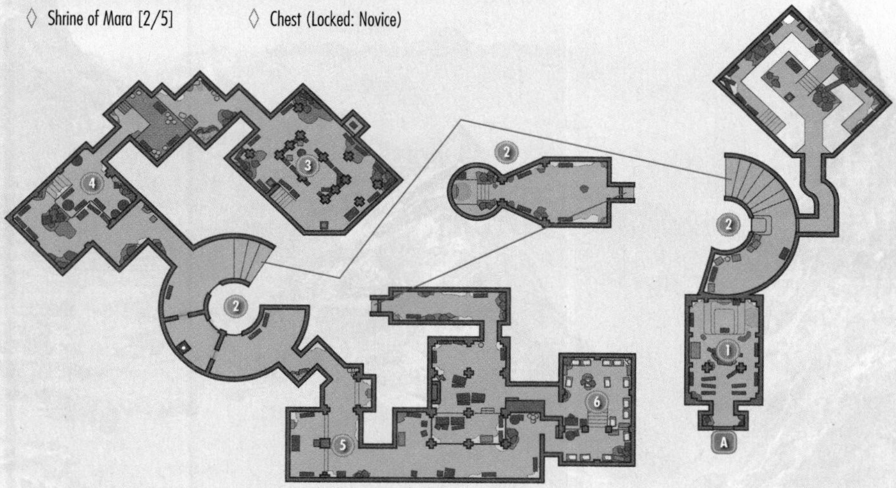

Related Quests

Daedric Quest: Waking Nightmare
Dungeon Activity

Recommended Level:
18

Dungeon: Falmer Hive

Animal
Orcish Invader
Thorek
Vaermina Devotee
Veren Duleri

Services

Follower: Erandur [8/47]

Crafting

Alchemy Labs (3)
Arcane Enchanter

Quest Items

The Dreamscape
Skull of Corruption
Vaermina's Torpor

Collectibles

Skill Book [Alchemy]: Mannimaro, King of Worms [D1/10]

Unique Weapon: Skull of Corruption [12/80]

Special Objects

Shrine of Mara [2/5]
Area Is Locked (quest required)
Chest(s)
Potions aplenty
Loose gear

Torpor Tantrum

After drinking Vaermina's Torpor, you must race through these rooms and passages to locate your objective: the Miasma release controls. At the end of the passage, pull the chain to release the Miasma and awaken from the dream.

◇ Potions aplenty ◇ Loose gear

2 Inner Sanctum Revisited

You emerge from the Torpor's effects back at the inner sanctum. Somehow you've gotten past the barriers. Take the Soul Gem that feeds them to deactivate the obstacles so that Erandur may join you. Follow Erandur to [5].

5 Passage to Sleeping Quarters

Use an Arcane Encanter and loot a chest as you navigate this passage.

◇ Crafting: Arcane Enchanter ◇ Chest
◇ Potions

6 Sleeping Quarters

Loot a chest on the balcony as you enter this room, and find another down below, near the stairs. Grab potions off a table and find more in the dining room that follows.

◇ Chest ◇ Potions
◇ Chest (Locked: Adept) ◇ Loose gear

2 Inner Sanctum, Third Visit

At last, you've reached the Skull of Corruption. Slay the final pair of priests after their brief chat with Erandur, then loot a large chest that's tucked away near the Skull's platform as your partner begins his ritual. A voice urges you to slay Erandur before the ritual is complete. If you do, the Skull of Corruption, an incredibly powerful and valuable staff, will be yours. Allowing Erandur to complete his ritual destroys the Skull and earns you Erandur's services as a follower.

◇ Unique Weapon: Skull of Corruption [12/80] ◇ Chest

[3.07] Red Road Pass

Dungeon: Giant Camp

Giant
Mammoth

In the northern section of the Pale, along the main road that runs between the east and west mountains, a giant has made camp. Bandits may attack this giant camp as you draw near. If this occurs, allow the conflict to play out, then slay the weakened victor (usually the giant) to claim some worthy plunder from the giant and the surrounding corpses.

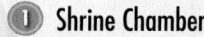

2 Inner Sanctum

The Skull of Corruption is located here, which Erandur insists you must destroy to end the townsfolk's nightmares. Follow Erandur downstairs and slay the Orcish Invaders that awaken and attack. A barrier halts your progress; follow Erandur back upstairs and into the library.

◇ Skull of Corruption

3 Library

The library is in a terrible state. Cross a fallen pillar to locate a unique tome entitled The Dreamstride, which Erandur seeks.

◇ The Dreamstride

4 Laboratory

Secure the lab, then find a Skill Book near one of its three Alchemy Lab stations. Find the potion you seek downstairs, then speak to Erandur to advance the quest. Drink the potion to be whisked away to a vision of the past.

◇ Crafting: Alchemy Labs (3) ◇ Vaermina's Torpor
◇ Skill Book [Alchemy]: Mannimarco, King of Worms [D1/10] ◇ Apothecary's Satchels (2)
◇ Potions

[3.08] Frostmere Crypt

Related Quests
Dungeon Quest: The Pale Lady

Recommended Level: 6

Dungeon: Bandit Camp
Bandit
Eisa Blackthorn
Kyr
Ra'jirr
The Pale Lady

Crafting
Grindstone

Quest Items
Eisa's Log
Kyr's Log
Ra'jirr's Note

Collectibles
Skill Book [Sneak]: The Red Kitchen Reader [D1/10]
Unique Weapon: The Pale Blade [13/80]

Special Objects
Word Wall: Ice Form [1/3]
Chest(s)
Potions
Loose gear
Mineable ore: Iron

When you approach these mountain ruins, a warrior named Eisa flees down the steps, pursued by several bandits. Help her fight off the ruffians, then speak with her to begin a new quest that takes place within the nearby ruins.

Frostmere Crypt

A Exit to Skyrim

1 Guard Room
Slay a couple of bandits in this entry hall and loot a locked chest in the western nook. Pull the wall chain near the portcullis to open the way forward.

◇ Chest (Locked: Apprentice)
◇ Potions
◇ Loose gear

2 Connecting Tunnels
Claim a few valuables on your way through these short passages.

◇ Potion
◇ Loose gear

3 Grindstone Alcove
Grab a Skill Book from a shelf before picking a locked door to enter this small nook, where a crafting station and some valuable gear is found.

◇ Area Is Locked (Adept)
◇ Skill Book [Sneak]: The Red Kitchen Reader [D1/10]
◇ Crafting: Grindstone
◇ Loose gear

4 Upper Quarters
Search these small bedchambers to loot a chest and collect important quest-related documents.

◇ Eisa's Journal (if you didn't take it from outside)
◇ Kyr's Log
◇ Ra'jirr's Note
◇ Chest
◇ Potion
◇ Loose gear

5 Lever Overlook
Silence more bandits, then swipe a potion and loot an urn on your way to this overlook, where a Bandit Archer awaits. Pull the nearby lever to cause a drawbridge to fall, then head to [6] and head north across this new bridge.

◇ Potion

6 Drawbridge and Stairwell
Cross the drawbridge to enter this chamber from the south, then descend some stairs and slay a Bandit Mage in the lower chamber. Press onward through a winding mining tunnel, looting a chest and optionally mining some Iron Ore on your way to the crypt's lower depths.

◇ Chest   ◇ Mineable ore: Iron   ◇ Loose gear

Frostmere Depths

B Door to Frostmere Depths

C Door to Frostmere Crypt

7 Shrouded Grove
A massive, overgrown cavern lies beneath the Frostmere Crypt. You find Kyr just inside—he's near death and gasps out a few final words before expiring. Continue deeper into the grove, and you'll spot Ra'jirr racing to the altar. The wraithlike form of the Pale Lady emerges and strikes him down before turning her wrath on you.

8 The Pale Blade
Claim the Pale Blade from Ra'jirr's corpse, then deal with the Pale Lady. Slay her or return the sword to the stand on the central altar to seal her away. Either choice completes this quest.

◇ Unique Weapon: The Pale Blade [13/80]

9 Word Wall
After defeating the Pale Lady, go upstairs and follow the sound of chanting to this location, where a Word Wall bestows you with an new Word of Power. Scale more steps and open a large chest near the exit door to the crypts. Don't leave just yet!

◇ Word Wall: Ice Form [1/3]   ◇ Chest

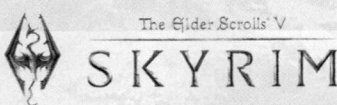

The Elder Scrolls V
SKYRIM

⑩ Chest Nook

Raid a large locked chest that rests on a rise in this corner of the cavern. There's also some gear on a nearby skeleton that's just to the left as you step out into the grove proper.

◇ Chest (Locked: Master)

◇ Loose gear

Ⓓ Door to Frostmere Crypt

Ⓔ Door to Frostmere Depths

⑪ Watery Chamber

Take a quick dive underwater and try to open a chest for some loot before scaling this watery chamber's ramp. Unbar the far door and go through to return to the crypt's entrance.

◇ Chest (Locked: Adept)

◇ Loose gear

[3.09] Hall of the Vigilant

Related Quests

Dungeon Activity

Recommended Level: 5

Dungeon: Special

Keeper Carcette (Restoration Trainer)

Vigilant of Stendarr

Services

Trainer (Restoration): Keeper Carcette [1/3]

Crafting

Alchemy Labs (2)

Tanning Rack

Collectibles

Skill Book [Heavy Armor]: The Knights of the Nine [E1/10]

Special Objects

Shrine of Stendarr [2/5]

Chest(s)

Potions

Loose gear

Follow the main road south from Dawnstar, and you may well notice this small meeting hall, located to the road's right. This lodge is owned by the Vigilants of Stendarr—a group of monster hunters that specializes in fighting Daedra. Pray at the shrine inside if you like, and speak to any of the Vigilants here to have them cure you of diseases or maladies you might be suffering, free of charge. Keeper Carcette runs the Hall and offers training in the Restoration skill.

[3.10] Fort Dunstad

Related Quests

Civil War Quest: Reunification of Skyrim

Civil War Quest: The Battle for Fort Dunstad

Recommended Level: 6

Habitation: Military Fort

Bandit or Civil War Soldiers

Crafting

Alchemy Labs (2)

Blacksmith Forge

Grindstone

Workbench

Dangers

Bear Traps

Oil Pool Traps

Wall Trap (lever)

Collectibles

Skill Book [Heavy Armor]: 2920, MidYear, V6 [A2/10]

Chest(s)

Potions aplenty

Loose gear

This Imperial fort was constructed around the Pale's main road as a highly effective checkpoint station and served as a prison for some of the worst criminals in Skyrim. Unfortunately, it's been overrun by vicious bandits! However, during the Civil War quest line, the bandits are banished from Fort Dunstad, and the place becomes a point of contention between the Stormcloaks and Imperials.

Exterior

Secure the exterior compound and tavern before breaching the keep, and snag a potion hidden inside a bucket atop the southern exterior watchtower.

◇ Crafting: Blacksmith Forge, Workbench

◇ Potion

◇ Loose gear

Stumbling Sabrecat (Tavern)

A pair of bandits lurk in this small tavern's basement. Clear out the place, then raid the basement chest.

◇ Chest (Locked: Apprentice)

Fort Dunstad (Interior)

Breach the stronghold's interior using either the main door or the second-story trapdoor. Inside, wipe out a host of bandits on the first floor, and optionally pull a lever to release a caged Skeever. Three more caged Skeevers are found upstairs, but beware of bear traps on the floor.

◇ Danger! Bear Traps

◇ Potion

◇ Chest (Locked: Novice)

◇ Loose gear

Commander's Quarters

This small barracks is loaded with potions of every sort, but a dangerous mage defends the place.

◇ Crafting: Alchemy Lab

◇ Potions aplenty

Prison

Enter the prison from the ground floor, and spy a potion that's mixed in with the booze on the wall. A large oil spill in the following hall gives you an opportunity to set the corridor ablaze with a fire-based attack. Loot a chest and free some caged Skeevers in the next room. If you wish, you can use the Wall Trap there by pulling a nearby lever. The chief of these villainous outlaws lurks upstairs, as does a ladder that leads up to a large chest.

◇ Danger! Oil Pool Trap, Wall Trap (lever)

◇ Crafting: Alchemy Lab, Grindstone

◇ Skill Book [Heavy Armor]: 2920, MidYear, V6 [A2/10]

◇ Chest (Locked: Apprentice)

◇ Potions

◇ Loose gear

[3.11] Shrine of Mehrunes Dagon

Related Quests

Daedric Quest: Pieces of the Past

Dungeon: Special

Dremora

Collectibles

Skill Book [Enchanting]: Catalogue of Armor Enchantments

Unique Weapon: Mehrunes' Razor [14/18]

Area Is Locked (quest required)

Chests (3)

Potion

Loose gear

High atop the frigid peaks of the Pale's western mountains, narrow stone stairs carved into the rock lead up to an ancient shrine. You visit this site during Daedric Quest: Pieces of the Past. Decide whether you wish to slay Silus and wield Mehrunes' Razor, a unique and powerful weapon, or allow Silus to keep the blade and be paid a large sum of coin in the process. Fight Dremora both inside and in this shrine, providing the Quest has reached its zenith.

[3.12] The Lord Stone

Recommended Level: 6

Dungeon: Special

Bandit

Special Objects

Standing Stone: The Lord Stone [3/13]

High atop the snowy mountains on the Pale's western edge, a small crew of bandits guards a tranquil shrine. Lay waste to the ruffians, then inspect the nearby stone to activate it and gain a new sign blessing. Those under the sign of the Lord are more resistant to both physical and magical damage. Note that you may have only one sign blessing at a time, so activating this Standing Stone will override any previous Stones you may have discovered.

[3.13] Volunruud

Standing stones mark these sunken ruins, which lie at the far southwest reaches of the Pale. This small Draugr crypt is the personal mausoleum of a legendary Nord named Kvenel the Tongue and houses a pair of legendary weapons that he possessed in life. During Dark Brotherhood Quest: The Silence Has Been Broken, Amaund Motierre will give you a unique amulet here as well.

Related Quests

Dark Brotherhood Quest: The Silence Has Been Broken

Dark Brotherhood Quest: Hail Sithis!

Dungeon Quest: Silenced Tongues

Recommended Level:
14

Dungeon: Draugr Crypt

Dragon Priest
Draugr
Kvenel the Tongue
Skeleton

Dangers

Spear Trap (pressure plates)

Collectibles

Skill Book [One-Handed]: Mace Etiquette

Unique Item: Jeweled Amulet [23/112]

Unique Weapon: Ceremonial Sword [15/80]

Unique Weapon: Ceremonial Axe [16/80]

Unique Weapon: Eduj [17/80]

Unique Weapon: Okin [18/80]

Special Objects

Word Wall: Aura Whisper [1/3]

Chest(s)

Potions

Loose gear

Exterior

Loot a chest and burial urn outside the ruins, then drop into the recessed area to raid another chest and urn before heading inside.

◇ Chests (2)

A Exit to Skyrim

1 Junction Chamber

Slay an unsuspecting skeleton as you descend into the central cavern, optionally stopping to read the book near the foot of its throne. Three side passage stretch off from this central hub. Scale the north steps to visit an altar room, and inspect the Elder's Cairn Door, which you cannot open until completing the Side Quest that plays out in these ruins.

2 Sleeping Nook

Visit this southwest nook first to loot a chest and urn.

◇ Chest

3 Weapon Chamber A

Slay a host of vile Draugr on your way to this far chamber, and head upward to where you find one of the two ceremonial weapons you seek in an open tomb. Claim a Skill Book that rests on a throne here as well. As you exit, beware the two mighty Draugr that guard the weapon.

◇ Skill Book [One-Handed]: Mace Etiquette

◇ Unique Weapon: Ceremonial Sword [15/80]

4 Weapon Chamber B

Dispatch many more undead and avoid dangerous traps as you head to this far room, where the second ceremonial weapon you're after is kept. Bring both weapons back to [2] and scale the north steps once more to at last open the Elder's Cairn Door.

◇ Danger! Spear Trap (pressure plate)

◇ Unique Weapon: Ceremonial Axe [16/80]

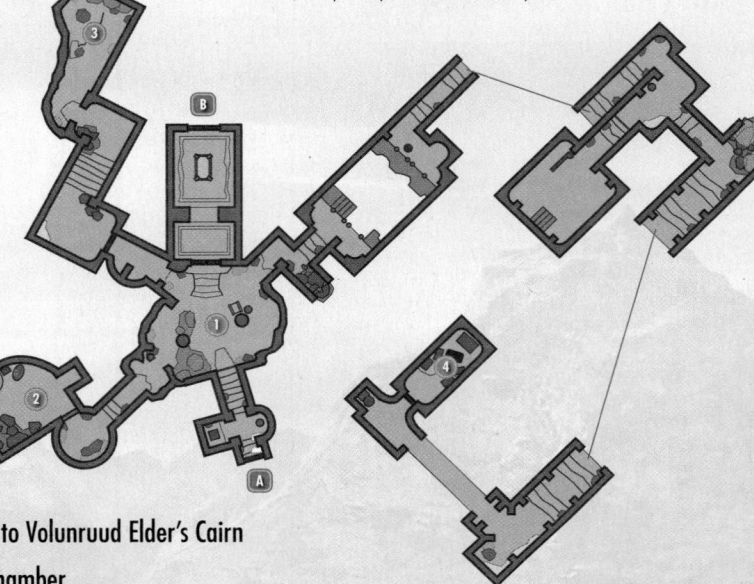

B Door to Volunruud Elder's Cairn

Knevel's Chamber

Battle some Draugr and a powerful undead chieftan called Knevel the Tongue in this cavernous lair. After the melee, search Knevel's remains to obtain two unique weapons, and follow the sound of chanting to locate an ancient Word Wall. Go north and cross a small footbridge to reach a treasure-filled alcove, then drop down to retrace your steps to the entrance.

◇ Unique Weapon: Eduj [17/80]   ◇ Word Wall: Aura Whisper [1/3]   ◇ Potions

◇ Unique Weapon: Okin [18/80]   ◇ Chests (4)   ◇ Loose gear

[3.14] Stonehill Bluff

Related Quests

Side Quest: Repairing the Phial

Dungeon: Giant Camp

Giant

Quest Items

Mammoth Tusk Powder

Chest(s)

The massive bones of slain mammoths decorate this giant's campsite, which is nestled amongst the Pale's southwest mountains. Slay the mighty giant if you dare, then raid his chest and corpse for plenty of treasure. During Side Quest: The White Phial, you'll find some needed Mammoth Tusk Powder here.

[3.15] Tower of Mzark

Related Quests

Main Quest: Elder Knowledge
Main Quest: Alduin's Bane
Daedric Quest: Discerning the Transmundane

Recommended Level: 18

Special Objects

Underground Connection: Blackreach [10.02]

Collectibles

Area Is Locked
Chest
Loose gear

This small tower, located just east of Stonehill Bluff [3.14], doesn't appear as a Primary Location on the in-game map, but it's important enough to consider it one. Beyond the tower's locked gate lies an elevator that ferries you down to the mythical Dwarven city of Blackreach [10.02], but you must pull the lever inside the tower to open its gate, making this a one-way ride until after you've used this elevator to exit Blackreach—then the gate remains unlocked.

[3.16] Loreius Farm

Related Quests

Side Quest: Kyne's Sacred Trials

Dark Brotherhood Quest: Delayed Burial

Habitation: Farm

Curwe

Vantus Loreius

Collectibles

Unique Item: Cicero's Boots [14/112]

Unique Item: Cicero's Clothes [15/112]

Unique Item: Cicero's Gloves [16/112]

Unique Item: Cicero's Hat [17/112]

Chest

Potion

Loose gear

Speak to the owner of this quaint farm to obtain Dark Brotherhood Quest: Delayed Burial, which plays out here. However, you can only obtain this quest prior to joining the Dark Brotherhood. You'll be rewarded no matter how you choose to resolve this quest, but note that if you choose to turn Cicero over to the guards, or if you're unable to convince Loreius to fix his cart's broken wheel, you will find Loreius and his wife murdered when you return here later. Pick a Novice-level lock to break into the farmhouse if you like. You can steal from a chest and swipe a potion from the floor within.

[3.17] Blizzard Rest

Dungeon: Giant Camp

Giant

Mammoth

Chest (Locked: Expert)

Beware when exploring the Pale's southern scrubland—an ill-tempered giant has made camp here. Exploit the difficult terrain to outmaneuver the lumbering brute when battling him, but beware his roaming mammoths. If you're able, unlock the campsite's chest afterward to obtain valuable plunder.

[3.18] Weynon Stones

Recommended Level: 18

Dungeon: Special

Ice Wraith

Special Objects

Shrine of Talos [2/17]

Chest (Locked: Novice)

Loose gear

Near the heart of the Pale, just south of the main road, a small collection of stones stands in the scrubland. The broken gear found here is largely worthless; loot a locked chest that's tucked away amongst the surrounding stones instead. You may also pray at the shrine at the base of the statue to receive Talos's blessing.

[3.19] Duskglow Crevice

This small cave is home to several vicious entities, but valuable treasure awaits the bold.

Related Quests

Side Quest: Captured Critters*

Dungeon Activity

Recommended Level: 18

Dungeon: Falmer Hive

Animal

Bandit

Falmer

Collectibles

Captured Critter: Moth in a Jar [1/5]

Skill Book [Lockpicking]: The Wolf Queen, v1

Skill Book [Pickpocket]: Purloined Shadows [C1/10]

Chest(s)

Potions

Loose gear

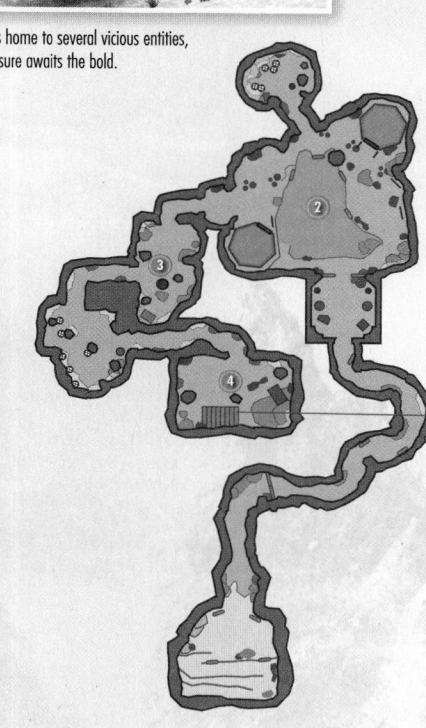

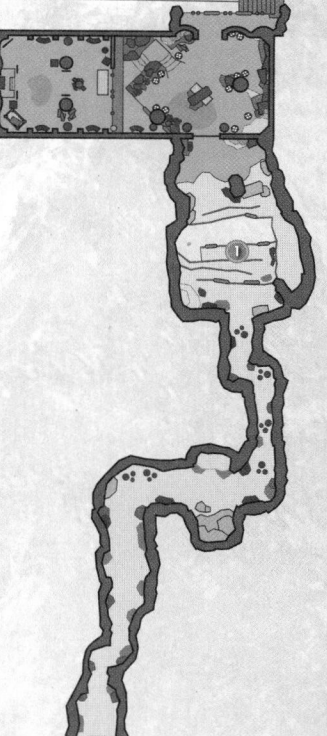

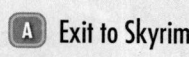

(A) Exit to Skyrim

(1) Tall Cavern

Murder a few lowly bandits on your way into this first sizeable cavern, and slay a few Falmer here to secure the area. You can't reach the far ledge at present; watch your footing as you descend to the lower passage instead.

(2) Falmer Den

The vicious Falmer have erected a few tents here—search one of them to discover an odd-looking chest. Follow the north passage to locate an angry Chaurus, and loot the body of its latest victim.

◇ Chest

(3) Firepit Cave

Don't miss the chest in this small cavern—it's hidden in the shadows.

◇ Chest

4 Chaurus Chamber

Butcher another Chaurus on your way to this large chamber, then scale some stairs and squash yet another of the giant bugs. Proceed westward to locate a large chest and several valuable potions, along with a pair of Skill Books and a special Moth in a Jar that pertains to Side Quest: Captured Critters. Pull the chain on the wall in the corner near the potion shelf to open the downstairs portcullis, granting passage back to the cave's entrance.

- ◇ Captured Critter: Moth in a Jar [1/5]
- ◇ Skill Book [Lockpicking]: The Wolf Queen, v1
- ◇ Skill Book [Pickpocket]: Purloined Shadows [C1/10]
- ◇ Chest
- ◇ Potions
- ◇ Loose gear

▶ [3.20] Silverdrift Lair

These Nordic ruins, which lie along the southwest base of the Pale's eastern mountains, have become home to ruthless bandits. Dispatch a few exterior guards before investigating the ruins' interior.

A Exit to Skyrim

1 Entry Chamber

Loot an urn and the corpses of a few bandits in this first chamber before delving down into the Draugr-filled passages ahead. Don't miss the coin purse and piece of gear that's tucked away behind some rubble in the passage as you make your way to [2].

2 Central Chamber

Collect a number of potions from a table and a shelf as you enter this large, central chamber. Find a Skill Book on a stone table at the room's east end before heading downstairs to loot a couple of chests and turn a pair of handles in the oily western nook to open a passage leading toward [3].

- ◇ Danger! Oil Lamp Trap, Oil Pool Trap, Swinging Spikes (pressure plate)
- ◇ Skill Book [Two-Handed]: Words and Philosophy
- ◇ Chest
- ◇ Chest (Locked: Apprentice)
- ◇ Potions aplenty

3 Burial Chambers

Slay a few Draugr in these passages, then open a locked chest to claim plenty of precious gear. Turn the handles on the three stone pillars that follow to open small chambers filled with treasure and enemies. Pass through the south chamber to return to [2].

- ◇ Chest
- ◇ Chest (Locked: Master)
- ◇ Potions
- ◇ Loose gear

Recommended Level: 6

Dungeon: Draugr Crypt
- Bandit
- Draugr

Dangers
- Battering Ram Trap (wall chain)
- Oil Lamp Trap
- Oil Pool Trap
- Swinging Spikes (pressure plates)
- Spear Trap (pedestal pressure plate)

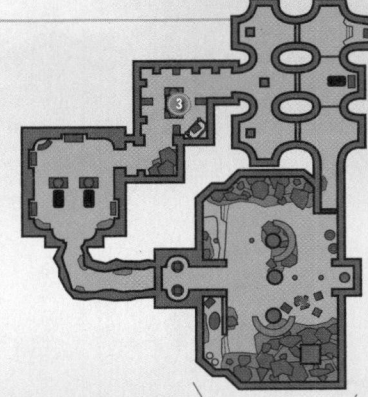

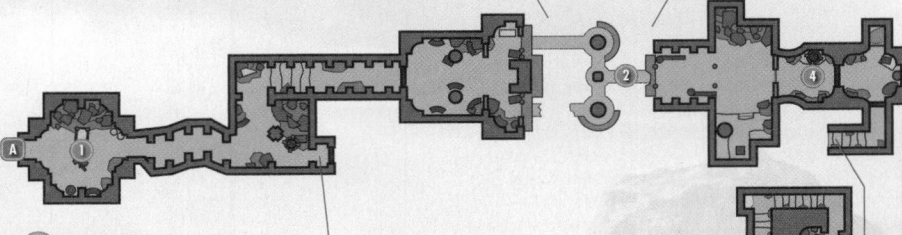

Collectibles
Skill Book [Pickpocket]: Thief
Skill Book [Two-Handed]: Words and Philosophy

Special Objects
Word Wall: Disarm [2/3]
Chest(s)
Potions aplenty
Loose gear

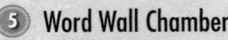

4 Portcullis Passage

Explore the elevated walkways at [2] to discover a handle on the central stone pillar. This opens the east portcullis; jump the dangerous pressure plate at the walkway's end and beware the powerful Draugr ahead. When taking the valuable item from the southern pedestal, stand on the nearby rockshelf to avoid being impaled by floor spikes. Find a Skill Book lying on a stone mound in a corner near a brazier, bedroll, and chest that's resting on a short shelf. Pull a wall chain to the east to open the next portcullis — but keep back to avoid the dangerous battering ram that unexpectedly swings through.

- ◇ Danger! Battering Ram Trap (wall chain), Swinging Spikes (pressure plate), Spear Trap (pedestal pressure plate)
- ◇ Skill Book [Pickpocket]: Thief
- ◇ Chests (2)
- ◇ Potions
- ◇ Loose gear

5 Word Wall Chamber

Navigate a series of passages to reach this large chamber, where two mighty Draugr guard an ancient Word Wall. Slay the fiends and then approach the Word Wall to learn a new Word of Power. Take the west door back to the ruins' entrance, pillaging a large chest and turning the nearby handle on the wall to open the exit route.

- ◇ Word Wall: Disarm [2/3]
- ◇ Chest
- ◇ Loose gear

▶ [3.21] Shrouded Grove

Recommended Level: 8

Dungeon: Spriggan Grove
- Animal
- Spriggan

Collectibles
Skill Book [Light Armor]: Ice and Chitin
Chest(s)

Battle a Spriggan and its animal companion at this grove before entering the small nearby cave. Slay another Spriggan and dangerous animal inside the cave, then open the half-buried chest to claim plenty of loot.

[3.22] Korvanjund

These unusual, crevicelike ruins are found north of the Pale's southern mountains. You can't do much here until you visit Korvanjund as a part of Civil War Quest: The Jagged Crown. A rockslide seals off much of the ruins until then.

Exterior

Defeat a few dangerous bandits to secure the crevicelike exterior of these ancient ruins. (During Civil War Quest: The Jagged Crown, the bandits will already be slain and replaced with either Imperial or Stormcloak soldiers, depending on your allegiance.) If possible, unlock a Master-level gate at the far basin to access a chest and a few coin purses. Head through the upper door to enter the Korvanjund Temple.

◇ Chest

A — Exit to Skyrim

1 — Entry Chamber

Loot a chest in this first small chamber, then cross the huge hall that follows.

◇ Chest   ◇ Loose gear

2 — Open-Air Chamber

The ceiling has collapsed here, allowing fresh air and light to pour in. Raid the chest on the east balcony and loot a number of urns found at the chamber's bottom, then take either the upper or lower north passage to reach [3] (taking the upper passage gives you a tactical advantage).

◇ Chest (Locked: Novice)   ◇ Loose gear
◇ Potion

3 — Oil Lamp Chamber

Knock down this chamber's plentiful array of hanging lamps to ignite various pools of oil on the ground and burn up the enemy soldiers that assault you here. Though the large east chest is empty, a Skill Book sits not far away.

◇ Danger! Oil Lamp Traps, Oil Pool Traps
◇ Skill Book [Light Armor]: Jornibret's Last Dance

4 — Urn Room

Loot an assortment of urns on your way through this small chamber as you make for the Korvanjund Halls.

B — Door to Korvanjund Halls

C — Door to Korvanjund Temple

5 — Trapped Treasure Nook A

Sprint straight past the swinging blades in the passage that leads to this small treasure room—you can just make it through unscathed. Pull a lever in the room to deactivate the blades and make your exit less stressful.

◇ Danger! Swinging Blade Trap   ◇ Chest

6 — Puzzle Door Passage

Collect the Ebony Claw from the ground near this passage's peculiar door. Inspect the Ebony Claw in your inventory to notice three symbols running down its palm. Rotate the door's three rings to mimic the same sequence of symbols (Wolf, Moth, Dragon), then inspect the central keyhole to insert the Ebony Claw and open the way forward.

◇ Dragon Claw: Ebony Claw [3/10]

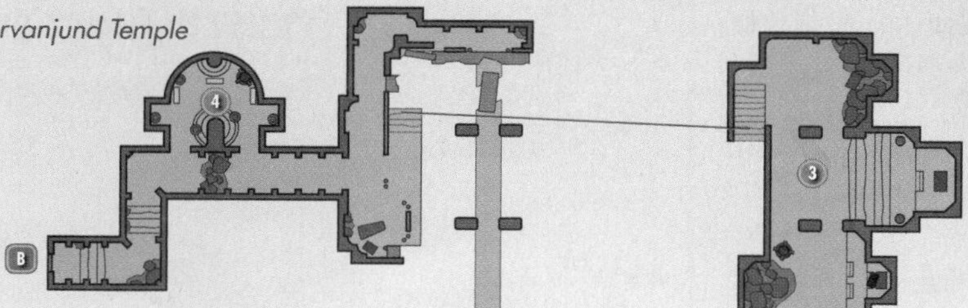

Related Quests

Civil War Quest: The Jagged Crown

Recommended Level: 12

Dungeon: Draugr Crypt

Bandit (Prequest)
Soldier (Imperial or Stormcloak depending on your allegiance)
Draugr

Dangers

Oil Lamp Traps
Oil Pool Traps
Swinging Blade Trap
    Trapped Chest

Puzzles

Nordic Puzzle Door (Ebony Claw)

Quest Items

Jagged Crown

Collectibles

Dragon Claw: Ebony Claw [3/10]
Skill Book [Light Armor]: Jornibret's Last Dance
Unique Item: Jagged Crown [24/112]

Special Objects

Word Wall: Slow Time [2/3]
Chest(s)
Potions
Loose gear

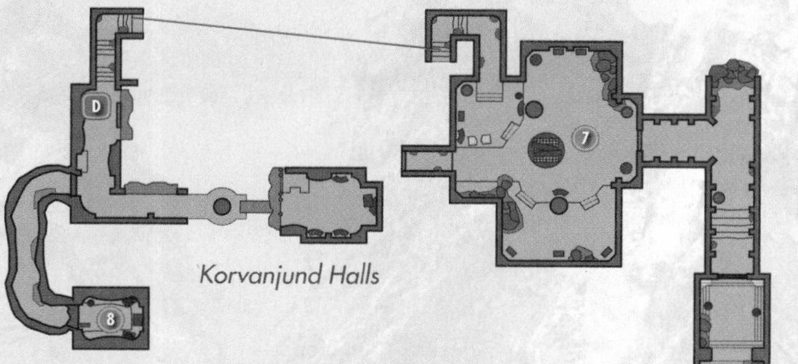

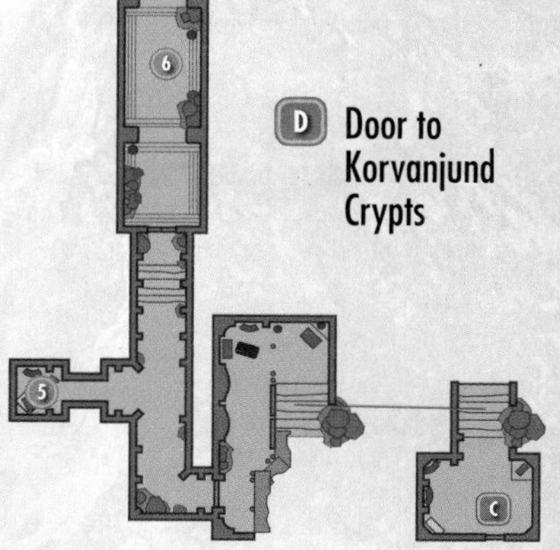

Korvanjund Halls

7 — Great Hall

Take the north passage to go upstairs, then cross this large chamber's elevated walkway to locate a chest. Pull the nearby wall handle to open the portcullis, gaining access to the Korvanjund Crypts—but beware that doing so causes a number of Draugr to burst out from the surrounding sarcophagi.

8 — Trapped Treasure Nook B

Before rushing off to the crypts, take the upstairs west passage to locate a dagger sitting on a pedestal. If you take the dagger off the pedestal, a secret passage will open, revealing a tunnel to a room containing a large chest. Notice the holes in the floor and ensure you're not standing near one when opening the chest—spikes shoot up when you lift its lid. (You may also attempt to disable the chest's trigger hinge.)

◇ Danger! Trapped Chest   ◇ Potion

D — Door to Korvanjund Crypts

Korvanjund Crypts

Slay the mighty Draugr that sleeps upon this great chamber's central throne, then loot the locked chest behind the throne and approach the far Word Wall to gain a new Word of Power. You're all done here. Take the southeast passage to quickly find your way back to the temple's entrance.

◇ Word Wall: Slow Time [2/3]   ◇ Potion
◇ Chest (Locked: Apprentice)

 Door to Korvanjund Crypts

 [3.23] Tumble Arch Pass

Dungeon: Giant Camp

Giant
Mammoth
Chest

A massive bonfire blazes away at the northern base of the Pale's southern mountains — a sure sign of a giant's campsite. Muster your courage and defeat the mighty brute, firing down from the upper rock ledge to present a difficult target. Loot the giant's corpse afterward, along with the nearby chest.

 [3.24] Shearpoint

Related Quests

Side Quest: Masks of the Dragon Priests*

Dungeon: Dragon Lair

Dragon (after Main Quest: Dragon Rising)
Krosis

Collectibles

Dragon Priest Mask: Krosis [6/10]

Special Objects

Word Wall: Throw Voice [1/1]
Chest (Locked: Master)

Located high atop the Pale's southern mountains, Shearpoint is the most formidable of all the Dragon Lairs. This ancient Word Wall is guarded by a dragon and by a terrifying Dragon Priest as well. This is Krosis, who holds one of the eight masks needed to unlock the Konahrik Mask at Labyrinthian [2.23].

> **NOTE** You learn all three Words of Power at once from Shearpoint's World Wall, unlike all other Word Walls, which each bestow only one Word of Power.

 [3.25] Nightgate Inn

This old tavern is one of the few places where one can find a warm bed and frothy pint in the southern end of the Pale. The unscrupulous can steal from a few chests here if they wish. One particular Dark Brotherhood Quest leads you to this humble establishment, where you must kill an Orc named Balagog gro-Nolob and steal the important Writ of Passage that he possesses.

 [3.26] Blackreach Elevator (Alftand)

Special Objects

Underground Connection: Blackreach [10.02]

Collectibles

Area Is Locked

This small tower, located high up on the hills north of Nightgate Inn [3.25], doesn't appear as a Primary Location on the in-game map, but it's important enough to be considered one. Beyond the tower's locked gate lies an elevator that transports you down to the legendary dwarven city of Blackreach [10.02], but you must pull the lever inside the tower to open its gate. This makes this a one-way trip until after you've used this elevator to exit Blackreach (the gate remains unlocked afterward).

 [3.27] Forsaken Cave

Related Quests

Side Quest: The White Phial

Recommended Level: 6

Dungeon: Draugr Crypt

Curalmil
Draugr
Frost Troll

Crafting

Alchemy Lab

Dangers

Battering Ram Trap (pressure plate)
Dart Trap (pressure plate)
Rising Floor Trap

Quest Items

Cracked White Phial

Collectibles

Skill Book [Alchemy]: A Game at Dinner
Skill Book [Block]: The Mirror

Special Objects

Word Wall: Marked for Death [1/3]
Chest(s)
Potions
Loose gear

Related Quests

Civil War Quest: Reunification of Skyrim
Civil War Quest: A False Front
Dark Brotherhood Quest: Recipe for Disaster
Miscellaneous Objective: Innkeeper Rumors

Habitation: Inn

Balagog gro-Nolob
Fultheim
Hadring (Innkeeper)

Services

Trader (Innkeeper): Hadring [5/15]
Food, Room and Board
Quest Rumors

Quest Items

Writ of Passage

Collectibles

Skill Book [Sneak]: The Legend of Krately House [B1/10]
Chests (2)
Loose gear

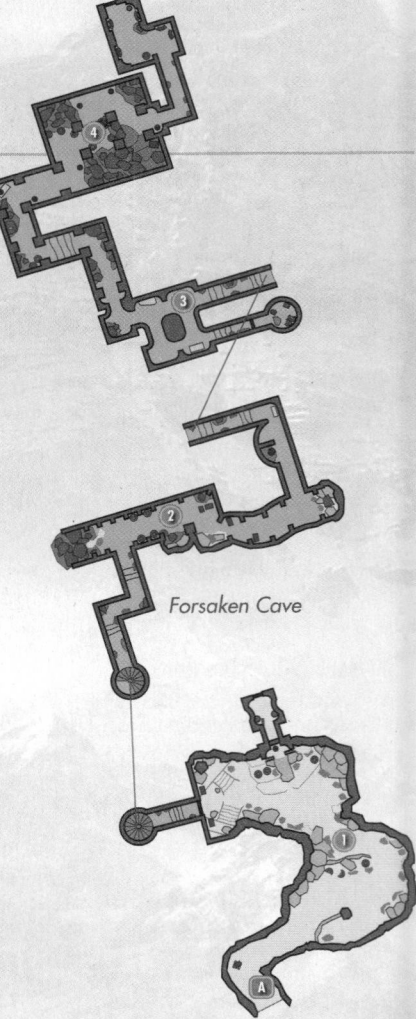

Forsaken Cave

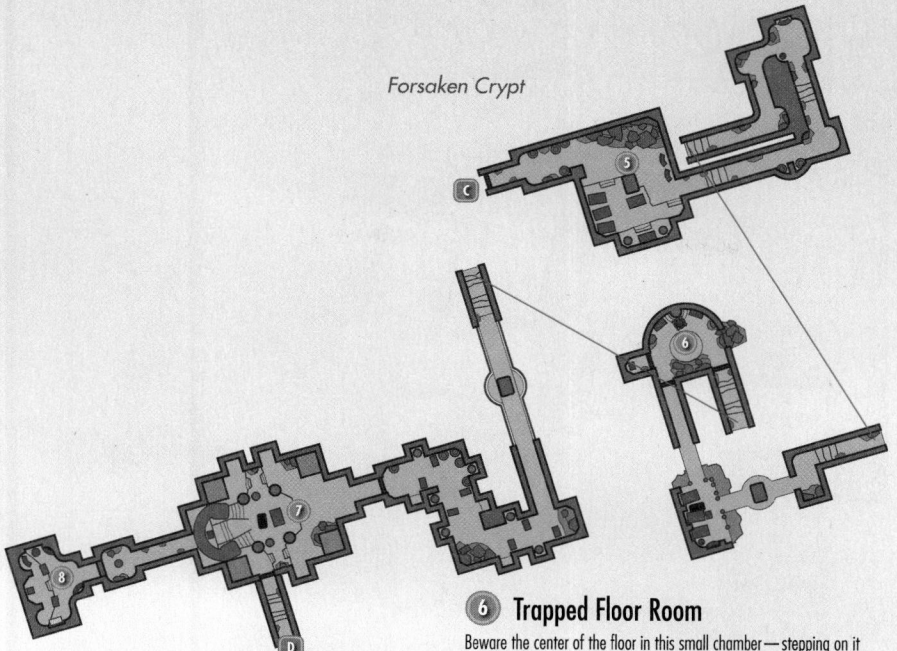

Forsaken Crypt

Just off the main road at the Pale's southeast end, a ferocious Frost Troll stomps about near the entrance to a huge, frozen cave.

(A) Exit to Skyrim

(1) Troll Cavern

Loot a satchel and chest as you enter this first frosty cavern, which is home to a pair of Frost Trolls and numerous gold-holding urns. Open an iron door and proceed to [2].

◇ Chest   ◇ Satchel   ◇ Loose gear

(2) Trapped Passage

Loot even more urns and skirt a pressure plate in this hall to avoid being perforated by arrows. Open a chest and beware the host of Draugr that lurk just ahead.

◇ Danger! Dart Trap (pressure plate)   ◇ Chest

(3) Burial Halls

Loot a number of burial urns in these passages, which are lined with the resting dead. Spy a Skill Book lying on a stone table, and unlock an Adept-level door to access a small room with a chest.

◇ Skill Book [Block]: The Mirror   ◇ Chest
   ◇ Loose gear

(4) Collapsing Chamber

Slay more Draugr in this chamber, and don't miss the chest that's hidden in the shadows among the southeast rubble. Jump a pressure plate in the passage that follows to avoid a trap, and proceed into the crypts.

◇ Danger! Battering Ram Trap (pressure plate)   ◇ Potions
◇ Chest   ◇ Loose gear

(B) Door to Forsaken Crypt

(C) Door to Forsaken Cave

(5) Junction Chamber

Loot a few urns on your way into this tall, multitiered chamber. Slaughter all Draugr and navigate the east passages to reach this chamber's second level. Open a chest up here and then proceed north to [6].

◇ Chest   ◇ Potions   ◇ Loose gear

(6) Trapped Floor Room

Beware the center of the floor in this small chamber—stepping on it causes it to rise, slamming you into lethal ceiling spikes. Unlock the Expert-level west door to access a treasure nook, then proceed through the other door to cut back through [5] and eventually arrive at [7].

◇ Danger! Rising Floor   ◇ Chest

(7) Curalmil's Chamber

Cut down more undead and loot more urns on your way to this chamber, where a mighty Draugr warrior awaits. Sprint past the swinging blades and slay Curalmil, then scale the nearby steps to reach a large chest and Word Wall.

◇ Word Wall: Marked for Death [1/3]   ◇ Chest

(8) Phial Chamber

Make your way to this quiet chamber, which opens after you use Nurelion's Mixture. Collect the Cracked White Phial from the pedestal, along with a Skill Book. Return to [7] and take the exit passage back to the cave's entrance.

◇ Crafting: Alchemy Lab   ◇ Apothecary's Satchel
◇ Cracked White Phial   ◇ Potions
◇ Skill Book [Alchemy]: A Game at Dinner

(D) Door to Forsaken Cave

(E) Door to Forsaken Crypt

[3.28] Yorgrim Overlook

Recommended Level: 5

Dungeon: Special

Skeleton

Collectibles

Chest(s)

At the Pale's southeast end, a shallow cave has been carved into the mountains that form the border to Winterhold. Slay a few skeletons up here, then see if you can unlock an Expert-level gate and claim the contents of a large chest.

[3.29] Bronze Water Cave

Related Quests

Thieves Guild Quest: Blindsighted
Dungeon Activity

Dungeon: Animal Den

Animal

Underground Connection: Irkngthand [3.31]

Collectibles

Unique Weapon: Nightingale Bow [19/80]

Along the Pale's southeast border, several thick metal pipes protrude from the ground near a widemouthed cave. Enter the cave with caution—a pair of ferocious beasts lurk within. You also visit this cave during a frantic escape from Irkngthand [3.31] at the climax of Thieves Guild Quest: Blindsighted. When you make good your escape, Karliah rewards your success with a unique bow.

[3.30] Pale Stormcloak Camp

Related Quests

Civil War Quest (when active, depending on who you side with)

Habitation: Military: Stormcloak Camp

Stormcloak Quartermaster (Blacksmith)
Stormcloak Soldier

Services

Trader (Blacksmith): Stormcloak Quartermaster [8/33]
     Weapons, Apparel, Misc

Crafting

Anvil
Grindstone
Workbench

Special Objects

Civil War: Map of Skyrim
Chests (2)
Loose gear

The Stormcloaks have set up a samll encampment here, but this site may appear only during the Civil War quest line. Feel free to trade with the quartermaster or improve your weapons at his crafting workstations. Examine the map in the largest tent to potentially update your own.

[3.31] Irkngthand

Recommended Level: 12

Related Quests

Thieves Guild Quest: Blindsighted

Thieves Guild Additional Quest: Larceny Targets*

Dungeon Activity

Dungeon: Dwarven City

Animal
Bandit
Dwarven Sphere
Dwarven Spider
Dwarven Centurion
Falmer
Mercer Frey

Underground Connection: Bronze Water Cave [3.29]

Quest Items

Skeleton Key
Right Eye of the Falmer

Collectibles

Larceny Target: Left Eye of the Falmer [2/7]
Unique Item: Skeleton Key [25/112]
Area Is Locked (quest required)
Chest(s)
Potions aplenty
Loose gear

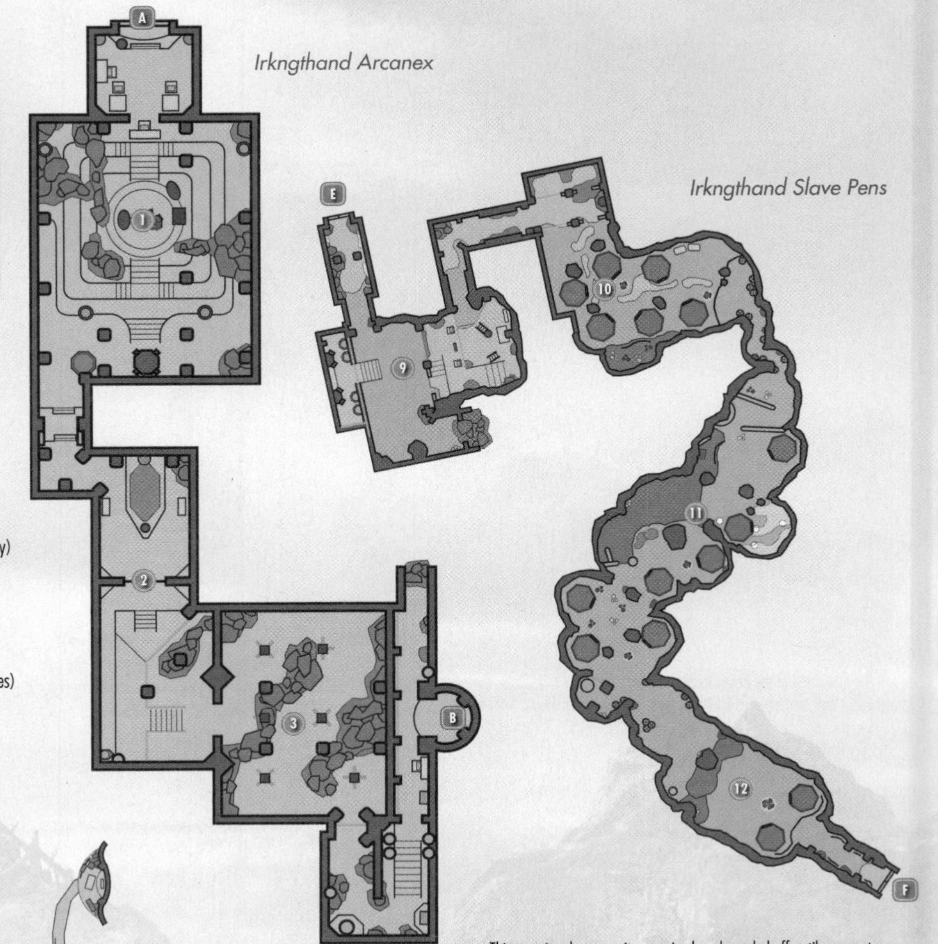

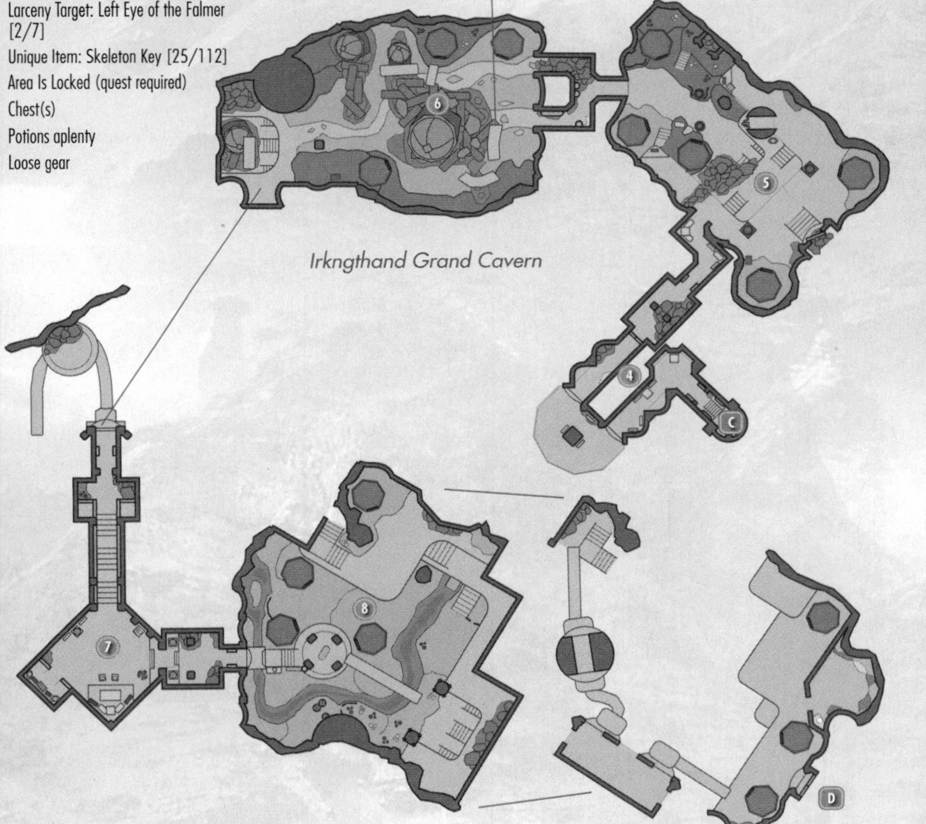

Crafting

Alchemy Lab
Tanning Rack

Dangers

Bear Traps
Bone Alarm Trap
Dwarven Fire Pillar Trap (proximity)
Dwarven Thresher (proximity)
Dwarven Thresher (lever)
Flail Trap (door)
Flamethrower Trap (proximity)
Flamethrower Trap (pressure plates)
Spear Trap (pressure plate)

Irkngthand Arcanex

Irkngthand Slave Pens

Irkngthand Grand Cavern

This massive dwarven city remains largely sealed off until you venture here as part of Thieves Guild Quest: Blindsighted. Only the exterior ruins can be explored until then. Use stealth whenever possible here.

Exterior

Bandits have established a campsite at Irkngthand's exterior ruins. The front gate is sealed, so go west, pillaging a chest and swiping some potions from a wooden table. Go left and scale the stone steps, skirting bear traps and swiping some potions from a lean-to found at the top. Find a chest tucked away beneath another wooden table near some bedrolls, then avoid a pressure plate trap in the tunnel-like passage that follows. Pull the lever beyond the tunnel to open Irkngthand's front gate. Scale a series of narrow wooden stairs afterward to locate the bandits' leader. Loot two more chests that the chief guards. Scale the following ramps to reach the high door that leads to the Irkngthand Arcanex — these last few ramps appear only when the "Blindsighted" quest is active.

◇ Danger! Bear Traps, Spear Trap (pressure plate)

◇ Chests (2)

◇ Chest (Locked: Apprentice)

◇ Chest (Locked: Adept)

◇ Potions

◇ Loose gear

Ⓐ Exit to Skyrim

① Entry Chamber

Bandits lay slain near a firepit in this first chamber — likely the work of your quarry, Mercer Frey. Loot the large nearby chest if you're able to pick its tricky lock — an even more challenging dwarven chest sits nearby, tucked away near the middle of the west wall. Beware of a patrolling Dwarven Sphere as you make your way to [2].

◇ Chest (Locked: Expert)

◇ Chest (Locked: Master)

2. Pipeworks Passage

Sneak through this passage to reduce the odds of alerting reinforcement sentries. Find two small dwarven chests at the far south end of the passage—one on the lip of the outside wall, the other near the foot of the nearby stairs.

◊ Chest

3. Gate Chamber

Keep as close to the outside wall as possible to avoid this wide chamber's spinning Flame Pillars. Sneak or you'll alert Dwarven Spiders, which stand too short to be harmed by the traps. You can just barely circle past the final spout without being seared. Open the gate beyond and navigate a passage that leads up to a high east balcony, raiding a couple of chests as you go. Use the Alchemy Lab if you wish before taking the elevator down to the Grand Cavern.

◊ Danger! Dwarven Fire Pillar Trap (proximity)
◊ Crafting: Alchemy Lab
◊ Chests (Locked: Apprentice) (2)
◊ Potions

B. Elevator to Irkngthand Grand Cavern

C. Elevator to Irkngthand Arcanex

4. Entry Passage

After meeting up with Karliah and Brynjolf, stand back after opening the door here—Mercer has left it trapped, and a mace will come swinging your way. (Alternately, you can try and disable the trap's hinge.) Unlock an Expert-level gate a few paces farther to claim a chest and some potions. Continue out onto a balcony overlooking a huge cavern and you can spot Mercer offing a pair of Falmer. You cannot get to him yet, so continue down a sloping passage.

◊ Danger! Flail Trap (door)
◊ Potion
◊ Chest

5. Cavern A

Turn left as you enter this first massive cavern and creep across a pile of debris to locate a lever. Pull the lever, then creep back the way you came and loot a grotesque chest that sits near a Falmer tent with several potions. Continue sneaking around the balcony and, if possible, unlock an Expert-level gate so you may fire a ballista down at the dangerous Falmer below. Raid a chest at the balcony's other end and find the second lever there. You must pull one of the levers, then race to the other side to pull the other lever to open the gate below or the levers will reset. You can tell that the gate is open when the dwarven lamps on either side are both lit. Make your way downstairs, looting the chest that's tucked away near the steps. Avoid the road that follows—it's trapped with lethal spinning blades. Hop up and navigate the earthen ledges instead, finding a chest stashed near the north wall. Use stealth or you will alert the Sphere Centurions here.

◊ Danger! Dwarven Thresher (proximity)
◊ Crafting: Tanning Rack
◊ Chests (2)
◊ Chest (Locked: Novice)
◊ Chest (Locked: Adept)
◊ Potions

6. Cavern B

This second cavern is as big as the first. Sneak through here to avoid alerting the roaming Falmer. Scale a ramp as you enter to visit a small balcony with a few ingredients, as well as a good sniping position. Search the ledge to the left of the central road to discover a Falmer chest. A dwarven chest lies in the rubble at the trail's end. Follow a looping walkway around to reach the hallway that leads to the third cavern.

◊ Chest
◊ Chest (Locked: Apprentice)

7. Connecting Hallway

Mercer Frey has been here, looted the place, and scribbled a taunting message on the wall. Three scrolls of Detect Life can be found here, which can make the fight with Mercer much easier, so be sure to grab them.

◊ Danger! Bear Traps
◊ Loose gear

8. Cavern C

The third cavern is the largest of all, and it's teeming with powerful Falmer and a Dwarven Centurion. Do your best to avoid detection, and optionally jump off the bridge's right side, which you start on when entering the area. Press the button at the base of the entry stairs to unleash the Dwarven Centurion on the unsuspecting Falmer. Scale the east steps and cross a long walkway to advance toward the cavern's south end, where more Falmer and a nest of Frostbite Spiders threaten you. Watch out for Bear Traps left by Mercer along the way. Loot the two chests near the Falmer tents before proceeding through the door to the Slave Pens.

◊ Danger! Bear Traps
◊ Chest

D. Door to Irkngthand Slave Pens

E. Door to Irkngthand Grand Cavern

9. Entry and Torture Room

Ignore this area's locked gate—there's little of interest behind it. Check the south rubble to discover a chest, then sneak down and pull the lever on the east balcony to slice up the unsuspecting Falmer below. Go downstairs and collect an array of potions from a table. Search an unfortunate thief to discover his last words, which hint at riches ahead. Beware of the pressure plates in the passage that leads to [10].

◊ Danger! Bone Alarm Trap, Dwarven Thresher (lever), Flamethrower (pressure plates)
◊ Chest
◊ Potions aplenty
◊ Loose gear

10. Falmer Camp

Several powerful Falmer are camped here, making this a dangerous area. Sneak through by keeping close to the west wall. Two of their tents contain chests.

◊ Chests (2)

11. Chaurus Den

Stick close to the west wall to slip past the Falmer in this area, raiding a chest as you go. Beware of two hulking Chaurus that lurk to the south. A chest with a difficult lock sits in one of the southern tents, and a potion lies on the ground where the passage bends southeast. Pipes span the ceiling above the area with the Chaurus. Sneaking along here should allow you to bypass the enemies below or give you a great vantage to snipe them. A health potion can also be found at the opposite end of this cave.

◊ Chest (Locked: Apprentice)
◊ Chest (Locked: Expert)

12. Sanctuary Access

Loot one last chest—an ornate dwarven chest with an intricate lock—as you make your way through the Slave Pens' final stretch. Proceed through the nearby gate to reach the door to the Irkngthand Sanctuary.

◊ Chest (Locked: Master)

F. Door to Irkngthand Sanctuary

Irkngthand Sanctuary

You finally catch up with your quarry in the sanctuary. Slay Mercer Frey in an epic battle (see Thieves Guild Quest: Blindsighted for complete strategies), then loot his body to obtain vast wealth, including the priceless Right Eye of the Falmer and the quest-related Skeleton Key. The cavern soon begins to collapse and fill with water. Exploit the rising tide to make your escape, but the way will open to you only if you possess the Skeleton Key. You will eventually emerge in Bronze Water Cave [3.29].

◊ Right Eye of the Falmer
◊ Larceny Target: Left Eye of the Falmer [2/7]
◊ Unique Item: Skeleton Key [25/112]

▶ [3.32] Raldbthar

Related Quests

Dark Brotherhood Quest: Sentenced to Death
Dungeon Activity

Recommended Level: 12

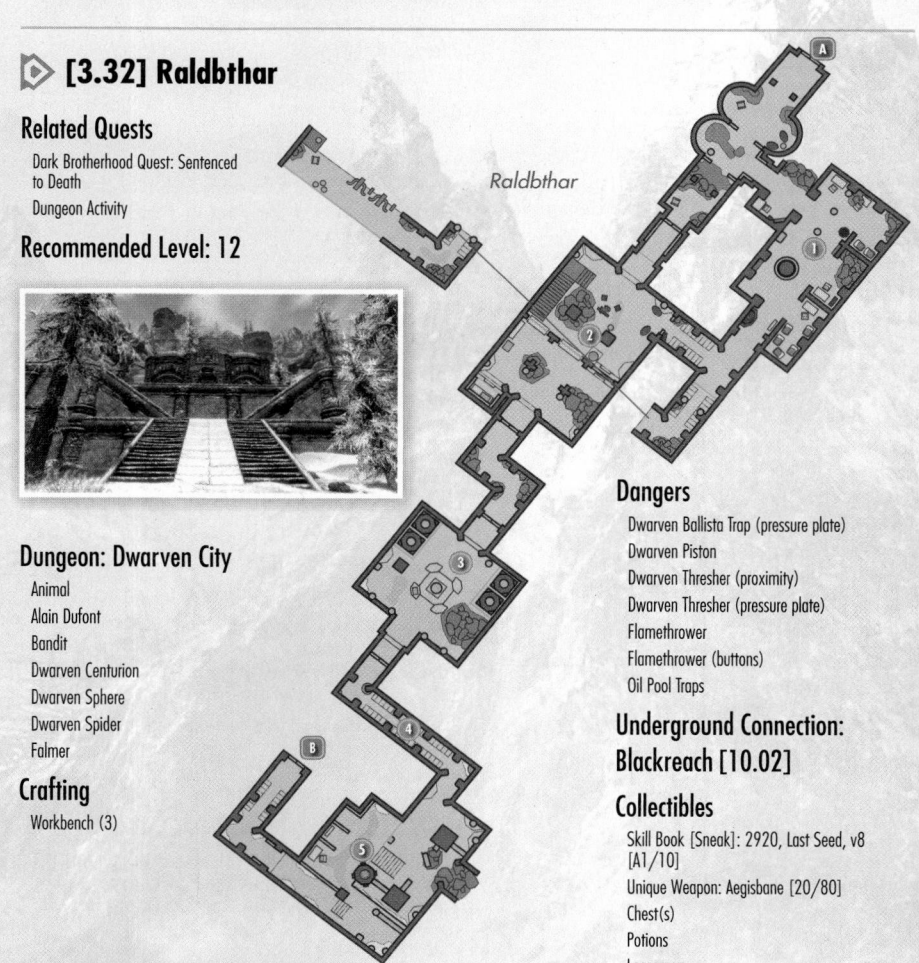

Raldbthar

Dungeon: Dwarven City

Animal
Alain Dufont
Bandit
Dwarven Centurion
Dwarven Sphere
Dwarven Spider
Falmer

Crafting

Workbench (3)

Dangers

Dwarven Ballista Trap (pressure plate)
Dwarven Piston
Dwarven Thresher (proximity)
Dwarven Thresher (pressure plate)
Flamethrower
Flamethrower (buttons)
Oil Pool Traps

Underground Connection: Blackreach [10.02]

Collectibles

Skill Book [Sneak]: 2920, Last Seed, v8 [A1/10]
Unique Weapon: Aegisbane [20/80]
Chest(s)
Potions
Loose gear

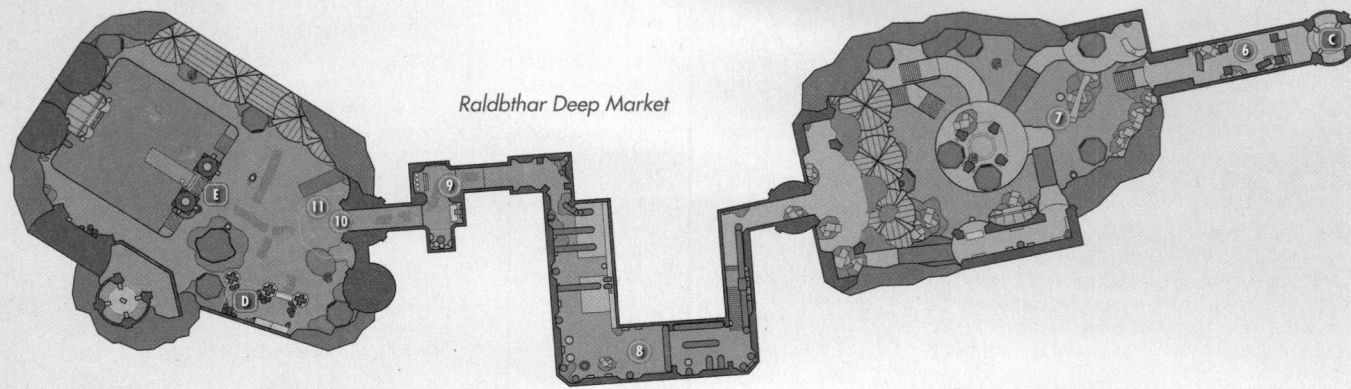

Raldbthar Deep Market

These ancient dwarven ruins, which run through the mountains at the Pale's southeast tip, have been overrun by treasure-seeking bandits.

A Exit to Skyrim

1 Bandit Den

Ignore the passage that's blocked by active fire spouts and take a side passage to reach this chamber, which the bandits have secured as a base of operations. Dispatch the villains and loot an odd-looking dwarven chest that's tucked away to one side of the room's entry doorway.

◇ Crafting: Workbench   ◇ Loose gear

◇ Chest

2 Trading Consortium

If possible, pick a locked gate in the hall that leads to this chamber so you may enter from an elevated vantage; then pull a few levers to fire large siege weapons down at bandits below. Eliminate all bandits to discover a valuable key on one of their bodies. If you're running quests for the Dark Brotherhood, ensure that you kill Alain Dufont in this room as well—collect the unique weapon he wields after the deed is done. Collect a Skill Book from the counter in the room's center, and loot a chest that's tucked beneath the northwest stairs. Pass through the central gate and raid the odd-shaped dwarven chests on the other side. If possible, unlock a Master-level gate to claim even more plunder.

◇ Danger! Oil Pool Trap   ◇ Irkngthand Consortium Key
◇ Crafting: Workbench   (bandit)
◇ Skill Book [Sneak]: 2920, ◇ Chests (4)
  Last Seed, v8 [A1/10]   ◇ Chest (Locked: Apprentice)
◇ Unique Weapon: ◇ Potions
  Aegisbane [20/80]   ◇ Loose gear

3 Oily Floor Chamber

Formidable dwarven spheres emerge from small holes in this second chamber's walls. Look to ignite the room's oil slicks to help defeat these foes. Secure the chamber and pillage the chest near the northwest wall. Find a coin purse tucked away near the southeast wall as well.

◇ Danger! Oil Pool Traps
◇ Chest (Locked: Apprentice)

4 Thresher Hallway

Time the movement of the spinning blades carefully as you scale this sloping passage, and keep close to the walls to avoid being sliced to ribbons.

◇ Danger! Dwarven Thresher (proximity)

5 Pipeworks

Search the wall near the stairs here to find a well-hidden dwarven chest. Find two more chests upstairs in the cubicles—one is long and rectangular and features a difficult lock. Beware of Dwarven Spiders that emerge from holes in the walls as you head for the far lift that ferries you to Raldbthar's Deep Market.

◇ Danger! Flamethrower, Oil   ◇ Chests (Locked: Novice) (2)
  Pool Trap, Dwarven Piston   ◇ Chest (Locked: Master)
◇ Crafting: Workbench   ◇ Loose gear

B Door to Deep Market

C Door to Raldbthar

6 Deep Market Entry

Carefully move past the spinning blade that emerges from the ground as you descend this first sloping passage. Raid a chest that's tucked away in a corner at the bottom.

◇ Danger! Dwarven Thresher (proximity)
◇ Chest (Locked: Novice)

7 Fountain Square

Beware: vicious Falmer lurk in this massive cavern. Free a couple of Skeevers from a holding pen as you enter, then flee—they may attack their captors for you. Loot an odd-looking Falmer chest in the west tent, then scale the north steps and raid a locked Dwarven chest. Slay a powerful Falmer on the high central balcony. You can circle around the Falmer tents up here to locate a chest that's cleverly hidden behind them. Cross a ramp afterward to locate another Falmer chest and a button. Press the button to lower a drawbridge that grants you access to the room's southern and western ledges. Loop around and take the west passage to [8].

◇ Chests (2)
◇ Chest (Locked: Apprentice)
◇ Potion
◇ Loose gear

8 Trapped Passage

Dodge pressure plate traps as you navigate this passage, slaying the odd dwarven automaton as you go. Loot a dwarven chest that's curiously affixed to the east wall. If you have Whirlwind Sprint, you can walk up the diagonal pipes in this room, then sprint across to the caged area you just walked up to find another hidden chest.

◇ Danger! Dwarven Ballista Trap (pressure plate), Swinging Blade
  Trap (pressure plate)
◇ Chest (2)

9 Button Puzzle Passage

Four buttons are lined up in a row in this passage. Simply press the third button from the left to open the way forward. Pressing any other button causes lethal flamethrowers to jet out from the surrounding walls.

◇ Danger! Flamethrower (buttons)

10 Jammed Gear Chamber

Battle a number of fierce Falmer in this sizeable chamber. If you are feeling tough, unlock the small trading post to battle the Chaurus and obtain the treasure lock in the cage. Find a chest at the chamber's west end and another within a Falmer tent that features an Expert-level locked gate. A third chest sits near another tent to the north. Remove obstructions from four gears around the room to restore power to the central button—search underwater to find one of the blocked gears. Press the button to lower the far drawbridge, unleashing a fearsome Dwarven Centurion! Loot the rectangular chest across the drawbridge after defeating the Centurion.

◇ Chests (4)
◇ Potion

11 Mechanism Chamber

Raid the chest that lies among this final room's north rubble, along with the locked chest that's affixed to the west wall. If you've previously been to Blackreach [10.02], you can use the central mechanism here to return to the dwarves' subterranean city. Otherwise, the nearby lift will take you back out to Skyrim. Loot one last Dwarven chest as you descend the outdoor steps that lead back to Raldbthar's main entrance.

◇ Chest
◇ Chest (outdoors)
◇ Chest (Locked: Adept)
◇ Potion
◇ Loose gear

D Exit to Skyrim

E Elevator to Blackreach

▷ [3.33] Blackreach Elevator (Raldbthar)

Underground Connection: Blackreach [10.02]

Collectibles

Area Is Locked

This small tower, located near the base of the mountain ruins of Raldbthar [3.32], doesn't appear as a Primary Location on the in-game map, but it's important enough to be considered one. Beyond the tower's locked gate lies an elevator that zips you down to the rumored dwarven city of Blackreach [10.02], but you must pull the lever inside the tower to open its gate. This makes it a one-way transport until after you've used this elevator to exit Blackreach. (The gate remains unlocked afterward.)

[3.34] Anga's Mill

Related Quests

Dark Brotherhood Quest: Side Contract: Ennodius Papius

Favor (Activity): Chopping Wood* (Aeri)

Favor: Special Delivery* (Aeri)

Habitation: Lumber Mill

Aeri (Marriage Prospect)

Kodrir

Leifur

At the Pale's southern end, a quiet lumber mill sits along the River Yorgrim, erected along the main road and near a bridge.

Crafting

Grindstone

Services

Marriage Prospect: Aeri [7/62]

Collectibles

Skill Book [Speech]: Biography of the Wolf Queen

Chest(s)

Potions

Loose gear

Exterior

Take advantage of the crafting stations located around the mill.

◇ Crafting: Grindstone

Aeri's House

Break into this small cabin to loot a chest and swipe a few potions, among other items of interest.

◇ Area Is Locked (Novice)   ◇ Potions

◇ Chest   ◇ Loose gear

Common House

Pick the lock of the common house's door to break in and plunder a few chests. A Skill Book rests on the end table by the bed.

◇ Area Is Locked (Novice)

◇ Skill Book [Speech]: Biography of the Wolf Queen

◇ Chests (2)

◇ Potion

◇ Loose gear

SECONDARY LOCATIONS

[3.A] Horker Standing Stones

On one of the tidal islands just north of High Gate Ruins is a cluster of dilapidated Nordic standing stones. Thieves have long since departed with anything of value (aside from a chiming Nirnroot at the water's edge). The place is now home to Horkers.

[3.B] Sunken Treasures

In the frigid waters of the Sea of Ghosts, north and a little west of the Wreck of the *Brinehammer*, are two tiny flat islands. Face due north on the smaller (western) one, and swim until you reach a sunken chest (Expert). Beware of Slaughterfish!

◇ Chest (Expert)

[3.C] Bandit's Hovel

A recently destroyed hunter's lodge is now home to a roaming bandit. The fire is still hot in the hearth, but the building itself is ruined and the contents picked clean aside from a chest with a dusting of snow on it.

◇ Chest

[3.D] Dragon Mound: Sea Shore Foothills

Related Quest: Main Quest: Elder Knowledge

This Dragon Mound is initially sealed. It opens during Main Quest: Elder Knowledge, and if you visit during or after this point in the Main Quest, the resurrected dragon will likely still be in the area. Engage!

[3.E] Barnacle Boat

Southwest from the Wreck of the *Brinehammer*, along the shore of the Sea of Ghosts, is a small upturned fishing boat. Now home to Mudcrabs, clear them out, and take the Fine Boots and Nordic Barnacle Clusters if you wish. But the real prize is the book.

◇ Skill Book [Alteration]: Daughter of the Niben

◇ Scimitar

[3.F] Shoreline Bandit Camp

On the northern shoreline side of a low rocky buttress north of the east-west path and northwest of Windward Ruins is a small fish-drying camp where three bandits are resting. Beware of bowmen here, and find a Skill Book resting atop a barrel.

◇ Skill Book [Destruction]: A Hypothetical Treachery

◇ Chest

[3.G] Dawnstar Frost Troll Den

If you're following the shoreline or taking the main road north to Dawnstar, then head along the rough snow path northwest and around to a shoreline overhang. Face down (or sneak behind) a Frost Troll for a chest with a Skill Book on it.

◇ Enemy: Frost Troll

◇ Skill Book [Block]: Death Blow of Abernanit

◇ Chest

[3.H] Shoreline Lovers' Tent

Follow the shoreline from Dawnstar Sanctuary to the east, passing Horkers, and step into an animal-skin tent with two bedrolls, some empty wine bottles, an Amulet of Mara, and a scattering of Red Mountain Flowers. The lovers who erected this tent are nowhere to be seen.

[3.I] A Bloody Trail

Side Quest: The Great Skyrim Treasure Hunt*

Approach this upper peak northward from Volunruud. Search the forested slopes for a bloodied male Wood Elf corpse. Follow the trail of blood upward, passing a long bow, into an area of rugged rocks, where another Wood Elf corpse lies.

◇ Treasure Map VI [1/11]
◇ Loose gear

[3.J] Border Corner: Roadside Shrine of Mara

Decorated with a sprig of Snowberry, this Shrine to Mara marks the general location of the borders between Hjaalmarch, the Pale, and Whiterun. Visit it easily if you head northeast from the path that takes you up and into Labyrinthian.

◇ Shrine of Mara [3/5]

[3.K] Mammoth Graveyard

Related Quests

Side Quest: Kyne's Sacred Trials

West of Loreius Farm, on the fringe of Whiterun Hold, lies a Mammoth Graveyard, where generations of these creatures have come to die. Giant stones and bone ornaments flank the entrance to this sacred site. A more recent corpse is being picked over by poachers when you arrive. If you are sent here for Kyne's Sacred Trials, you will face the Mammoth Guardian Spirit in this desolate place.

[3.L] Ice Shard Wild Animal Den

Off the beaten track and south of Fort Dunstad is a wooded area with deep snow and a wild animal den, usually populated with wolves. Shelter from the perpetual cold here, as the prey the wolves have dragged back have little worth looting.

[3.M] Dragon Mound: Shimmermist Hills

Related Quest: Main Quest: Elder Knowledge

This Dragon Mound is initially sealed. It opens during Main Quest: Elder Knowledge, and if you visit during or after this point in the Main Quest, the resurrected dragon will likely be circling this location. To battle!

[3.N] Julianos's Fallen

A half-buried skeleton is easy to miss, lying on a precarious abutment north of Shearpoint, overlooking the Lake Yorgrim basin below. This follower of Julianos was carrying a small shrine, which is also embedded in the ground.

◇ Shrine of Julianos [2/5]

[3.O] Yorgrim Forest Spider Trap

Among the trees just off the path that winds just northeast of Tumble Arch Pass are the remains of a section of dwarven masonry. Embedded into this stone is a chest. Approach, and around six Frostbite Spiders ambush you from the trees above!

◇ Chest

[3.P] Wayward Peak Summit

Above the tower to Blackreach and Forsaken Cave, you may be able to make out a tattered flag. If you manage to clamber up to the top, there's some equipment and an excellent view across the Yorgrim basin.

◇ Satchel
◇ Loose gear

[3.Q] Dragon Mound: Yorgrim Resurrection

Related Quest: Main Quest: Elder Knowledge

Related Quest: Main Quest: Alduin's Bane

This Dragon Mound is initially sealed. It opens during Main Quest: Elder Knowledge, once you learn that you need an Elder Scroll. After this point, but before you learn the Dragonrend Shout, Alduin will appear here and resurrect the dragon Viinturuth. Alduin cannot be harmed; he resurrects his brethren and flies off. But slay Viinturuth and claim his power for your own.

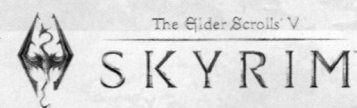

HOLD 4: WINTERHOLD HOLD

TOPOGRAPHICAL OVERVIEW

The northeastern coast of the Sea of Ghosts around the city of Winterhold is by far the least populated area of Skyrim, and the same can be said for the entire Hold. It has no towns or villages other than the capital, and many adventurers perish in the glacial fields that surround the city. Winterhold boasts a vast stretch of sharp and rugged coastline, and even the mouth of the White River, but it is otherwise devoid of flowing water. Instead, the vast majority of the Hold is either encased in snow or ice or part of the vast and treacherous Mount Anthor range, interspersed with strange or ancient burial sites, including the ominous Saarthal.

Routes and Pathways

There is but a single main road from Winterhold and its college of mages, which connects to the Pale. With no rivers, the only other pathways are the minor goat and hunting trails that weave through the mountains. These are recommended routes when first exploring such a vast and foreboding wilderness. The entire north and western part of the Hold is rugged coastline; don't forget your explorations can take you well into the Sea of Ghosts. To the west is Fort Fellhammer, a good marker since it is close to the border of the Pale. Should you refrain from using the main road, the Wayward Pass is another option, as the path it connects to weaves through the Mount Anthor range and takes in many locations. Otherwise, the edges of this Hold are less rocky and more glacial and feature a variety of lonely and lost barrows, including one said to be the tomb of the legendary warrior and founder of the Companions, Ysgramor.

AVAILABLE SERVICES, CRAFTING, AND COLLECTIBLES

Services

Followers: [4/47]
Houses for Sale: [0/5]
Marriage Prospects: [2/62]
Skill Trainers: [6/50]
  Alchemy: [0/3]
  Alteration: [1/3]
  Archery: [0/3]
  Block: [0/2]
  Conjuration: [1/3]
  Destruction: [1/3]
  Enchanting: [1/2]
  Heavy Armor: [0/3]
  Illusion: [1/2]
  Light Armor: [0/3]
  Lockpicking: [0/2]
  One-Handed: [0/3]
  Pickpocket: [0/3]
  Restoration: [1/3]
  Smithing: [0/3]
  Sneak: [0/3]
  Speech: [0/4]
  Two-Handed: [0/2]
Traders [13/133]:
  Apothecary [0/12]
  Bartender [0/5]
  Blacksmith [2/33]
  Carriage Driver [0/5]
  Fence [1/10]
  Fletcher [0/3]
  Food Vendor [0/9]
  General Goods [2/19]
  Innkeeper [0/15]
  Jeweler [0/2]
  Special [2/3]
  Spell Vendor [5/12]
  Stablemaster [0/5]

Collectibles

Captured Critters: [1/5]
Dragon Claws: [1/10]
Dragon Priest Masks: [0/10]
Larceny Targets: [1/7]
Skill Books: [12/180]
  Alchemy: [1/10]
  Alteration: [2/10]
  Archery: [0/10]
  Block: [2/10]
  Conjuration: [0/10]
  Destruction: [1/10]
  Enchanting: [1/10]
  Heavy Armor: [0/10]
  Illusion: [0/10]
  Light Armor: [0/10]
  Lockpicking: [2/10]
  One-Handed: [0/10]
  Pickpocket: [0/10]
  Restoration: [2/10]
  Smithing: [0/10]
  Sneak: [1/10]
  Speech: [0/10]
  Two-Handed: [0/10]
Treasure Maps: [2/11]
Unique Items: [15/112]
Unique Weapons: [6/80]
Unusual Gems: [3/24]

Special Objects

Shrines: [6/69]
  Akatosh: [0/6]
  Arkay: [2/12]
  Dibella: [1/8]
  Julianos: [0/5]
  Kynareth: [0/6]
  Mara: [0/5]
  Stendarr: [0/5]
  Talos: [3/17]
  Zenithar: [0/5]
Standing Stones: [2/13]
  The Serpent Stone
  The Tower Stone
Word Walls: [5/42]
  Animal Allegiance: [1/3]
  Aura Whisper: [0/3]
  Become Ethereal: [1/3]
  Disarm: [1/3]
  Dismaying Shout: [0/3]
  Elemental Fury: [0/3]
  Fire Breath: [0/2]
  Frost Breath: [0/3]
  Ice Form: [2/3]
  Kyne's Peace: [0/3]
  Marked for Death: [0/3]
  Slow Time: [0/3]
  Storm Call: [0/3]
  Throw Voice: [0/1]
  Unrelenting Force: [0/1]
  Whirlwind Sprint: [0/2]

CRAFTING STATIONS: WINTERHOLD

✓	TYPE	LOCATION A	LOCATION B
☐	Alchemy Lab	College of Winterhold (Hall of Countenance) [4.00]	College of Winterhold (Arch-Mage's Quarters) [4.00]
☐	Arcane Enchanter	College of Winterhold (Hall of Countenance) [4.00]	College of Winterhold (Arch-Mage's Quarters) [4.00]
☐	Anvil or Blacksmith forge	—	—
☐	Cooking Pot and Spit	Winterhold (Birna's Oddments) [4.00]	Winterhold (Kraldar's House) [4.00]
☐	Grindstone	Fort Kastav (Exterior) [4.19]	—
☐	Smelter	Fort Fellhammer [4.08]	—
☐	Tanning Rack	Wreck of the Pride of Tel Vos [4.22]	—
☐	Wood Chopping Block	—	—
☐	Workbench	—	—

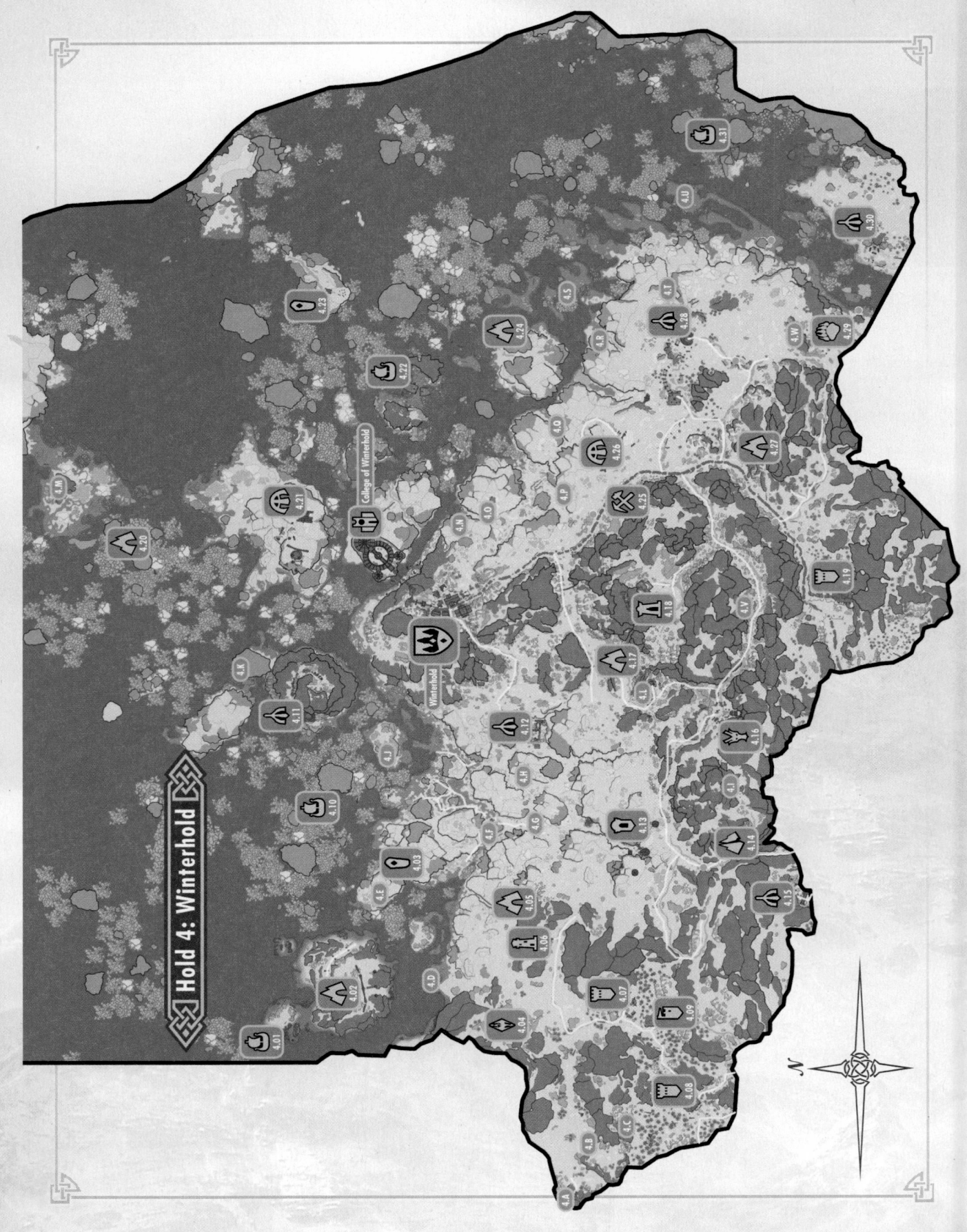

Hold 4: Winterhold

College of Winterhold

Winterhold

PRIMARY LOCATIONS

Total — 33: Hold Capital, College of Winterhold, and 31 Hold Locations

[4.00] Hold Capital City: Winterhold
[4.00] College of Winterhold
　　Jarl: Korir
[4.01] Hela's Folly
[4.02] Yngvild
[4.03] The Tower Stone
[4.04] Winterhold Imperial Camp
[4.05] Hob's Fall Cave
[4.06] Frostflow Lighthouse
[4.07] Driftshade Refuge
[4.08] Fort Fellhammer
[4.09] Snowpoint Beacon
[4.10] Pilgrim's Trench
[4.11] Ysgramor's Tomb
[4.12] Saarthal
[4.13] Alftand

[4.14] Wayward Pass
[4.15] Ironbind Barrow
[4.16] Mount Anthor
[4.17] Sightless Pit
[4.18] Shrine of Azura
[4.19] Fort Kastav
[4.20] Septimus Signus's Outpost
[4.21] Skytemple Ruins
[4.22] Wreck of the Pride of Tel Vos
[4.23] The Serpent Stone
[4.24] Bleakcoast Cave
[4.25] Whistling Mine
[4.26] Journeyman's Nook
[4.27] Stillborn Cave
[4.28] Snow Veil Sanctum
[4.29] Winterhold Stormcloaks Camp
[4.30] Yngol Barrow
[4.31] Wreck of the Winter War

SECONDARY LOCATIONS

Total — 23 Points of Interest

[4.A] Shrine of Dibella: Watching Dawnstar
[4.B] Hunter's Overlook: Fellhammer Wastes
[4.C] Wolf Den: Fellhammer Wastes
[4.D] Yisra's Beachside Combustion
[4.E] The Iceberg Explorer
[4.F] Shrine of Talos: Winterhold Glaciers
[4.G] Frozen Mammoth
[4.H] Wet Bones
[4.I] Dwarven Monument: Mount Anthor Summit
[4.J] Shrine of Talos: Sea of Ghosts
[4.K] Shrine of Talos: Ilas-Tei's Last Stand
[4.L] Altar of Xrib
[4.M] The Chill

[4.N] Trapped for Eternity
[4.O] Rundi's Mistake
[4.P] Hunter's Camp: Glacier's Edge
[4.Q] Haul of the Horkers
[4.R] Hunters' Camp: Sea Shore of Ghosts
[4.S] Hunter's Last Stand: Sea Shore of Ghosts
[4.T] Ill-Gotten Gains: Sea Shore of Ghosts
[4.U] Fisherman's Camp: Slaughterfish Bay
[4.V] Avalanche Pass
[4.W] Shrine of Arkay: Windhelm Hills

HOLD CAPITAL: WINTERHOLD

Related Quests

Daedric Quest: The Black Star
College of Winterhold Quest: First Lessons
Thieves Guild Quest: Hard Answers
Miscellaneous Objective: Innkeeper Rumors (The Frozen Hearth)
Miscellaneous Objective: Finding Isabelle* (Dagur)
Favor (Activity): A Drunk's Drink* (Ranmir)
Favor: A Good Talking To* (Haran)
Favor: A Little Light Thievery* (Malur Seloth)
Favor: Jobs for the Jarls* (Jarl Korir)
Thane Quest: Thane of Winterhold Hold*

Habitation: Hold Capital (Minor)

Services

Trader (General Store Vendor): Birna [3/19]

Special Objects

Civil War: Map of Skyrim

Collectibles

Dragon Claw: Coral Dragon Claw [4/10]
Skill Book [Alteration]: Breathing Water [A1/10]
Skill Book [Destruction]: Mystery of Talara, v3 [C2/10]
Skill Book [Restoration]: The Exodus [D1/10]
Unique Item: The Black Star [26/112]
Unique Weapon: Nightingale Blade [21/80]
Unique Weapon: Staff of Arcane Authority [22/80]
Chest
Potions aplenty
Loose gear

College of Winterhold

Hold Capital: Winterhold

Lore: City Overview

Once a great capital rivaling Solitude in power and importance, Winterhold is now little more than a shell of its former self. Eighty years ago, a seemingly never-ending series of storms lashed out at the northern coast of Skyrim, eventually causing most of the city to plummet into the Sea of Ghosts, an event now known as the Great Collapse. Strangely, the College of Winterhold was unaffected, remaining firm on a now freestanding spire of rock. Many inhabitants of Winterhold, both mages and magic-fearing Nords, were forced to abandon the city, and those who remained still eye the College with suspicion.

Since that time, the population of Winterhold has continued to dwindle. Other than the College, only a handful of buildings still stand. What remains of the town's economy is based around serving the needs of the College. As such, Winterhold has become something of a haven for mages in Skyrim, a safe refuge from distrustful Nords.

Important Areas of Interest

1 Main Thoroughfare

A single, snow-covered road winds past the dilapidated and collapsed structures of Winterhold, leading to the Winterhold Bridge and the domain of mages.

2 Ruins of the Cataclysm

Four of the town's main structures lie abandoned and rotting into the snowy ground. There are no items to snag of any worth.

3 Jarl's Longhouse

The following leaders of Winterhold are loyal to the Stormcloaks at the start of the Civil War.

Jarl Korir

Whatever optimism might have lived in Korir's heart was beaten down by decades of hearing how much better things used to be before the Great Collapse. Knowing nothing else, he carries on the grudges of his ancestors while refusing to abandon his home, so he's done everything he can to persevere. He'll maintain the traditions of his forefathers if it kills him, and he fails to realize the impact it's having on his son.

Thaena

Thaena's life isn't what it was supposed to be. The beautiful city she should've grown up in doesn't exist, her husband has turned into a bitter, cynical man, and the future for her son looks bleak. While Korir may stop short of assigning blame, Thaena has no problem pointing a finger at those responsible for her family's plight: the mages of Winterhold. Refusing to accept any responsibility for her situation, she's placed all the blame squarely on the shoulders of the College and spends every day cursing its existence.

Assur

Assur is confused by the reaction he gets when he repeats what his parents have always told him: mages can't be trusted, and anyone who uses magic is dangerous. He's been taught that warlocks and witches are even worse than elves, and no one but a Nord is a friend to Winterhold.

Malur Seloth

A slouch with few marketable skills, Melur has landed himself in what he perceives as a wonderful position. Korir is convinced that he's in cahoots with the mages of the College of Winterhold and therefore expects little of Malur in the way of servant's duties. Malur has done nothing to dissuade this misunderstanding; in fact, he's cultivating it to get away with as little

work as possible. Naturally, he survives if the balance of power shifts to the Imperials.

Kai Wet-Pommel

The following residents arrive to take control of Winterhold, should this Hold fall during the Civil War.

Jarl Kraldar

Kraldar is, by all accounts, what may well be the last in a long line of nobility in Winterhold, due to the cataclysm. He understands that while the College may seem a bit of an eyesore to the rest of the province, being on good terms with the Arch-Mage is in Winterhold's best interest. Ever the optimist, he firmly believes that Winterhold will be restored to greatness someday, and often regales his Housecarl with his dreams for the future. He's less chatty with Malur Seloth.

Thonjolf (Housecarl)

Thonjolf's family has served the Kraldars for generations. It's all he knows. It doesn't matter that there's little for him to actually do or that the Great City of Winterhold doesn't exist anymore; he has a duty and he will perform it to the best of his ability. He's aware of Malur's abuse of his position and has repeatedly attempted to speak to Kraldar about it. Kraldar refuses to listen, so Thonjolf grows more frustrated with every passing day.

One of the buildings of old Winterhold has been repurposed as the Jarl's Longhouse, since the original home of the Jarl was lost in the Great Collapse. Korir rules from this new location, though currently there's very little "ruling" that actually takes place; the College remains separated from the mainland (both physically and socially), and the handful of residents left need little governing on a daily basis. Korir is convinced that without the Imperials or the College, Winterhold will someday regain its former glory. Jarl Korir is grateful for any protection and actively encourages the Stormcloaks to plan their attacks from his war room. In the downstairs bedroom, a Skill Book has been stashed in a woven basket that sits atop a barrel.

- ◊ Skill Book [Enchanting]: Twin Secrets
- ◊ Civil War: Map of Skyrim
- ◊ Chest
- ◊ Potions aplenty
- ◊ Loose gear

> **NOTE** There is no jail in Winterhold, but that doesn't mean you can hack, steal, or annoy anyone you please. If you're caught committing a crime in Winterhold, you're taken to serve out your sentence on a remote glacial cave north of here in the Sea of Ghosts, aptly named the Chill. See the Secondary Location for the details.

4 The Frozen Hearth

Dagur   Nelacar
Haran   Angwe
Eirid

The only profitable business left in Winterhold, the Inn serves as the sole place petitioners to the College may stay. As such, Dagur has put aside any personal feelings he may have toward wizards and does his best to look on the bright side. Nelacar is paying Dagur good money to maintain a small room in the Inn, where he can do some research on his own, away from the College. He also takes a cut of Enthir's questionable sales downstairs in the cellar. Enthir (a member of the College) stays here

during the Thieves Guild Quests and becomes a Fence for you. Down in the cellar, a Skill Book is hidden among a collection of crates and sacks.

- ◊ Skill Book [Restoration]: The Exodus [D1/10]
- ◊ Unique Item: The Black Star [26/112]
- ◊ Unique Weapon: Nightingale Blade [21/80]
- ◊ Unique Weapon: Staff of Arcane Authority [22/80]
- ◊ Chest (3)

5 Birna's Oddments

Ranmir
Birna

Birna's family has lived there for generations beyond count, and no amount of natural disaster or weird magic is going to drive her out now. Her family's house is also a small shop selling a variety of items. She'll even part with a strange claw if the price is right.

- ◊ Trader (General Store Vendor): Birna [3/19]
  - ○ Potions, Food, Misc
- ◊ Dragon Claw: Coral Dragon Claw [4/10]
- ◊ Skill Book [Destruction]: Mystery of Talara, v3 [C3/10]
- ◊ Potions aplenty
- ◊ Loose gear

6 Kraldar's House

One of the last few holdouts, Kraldar refuses to give up and move away from Winterhold. Everything he has been through has instilled a great distrust for the mages of the College that borders on hatred. Kraldar is a pleasant sort, convinced that Winterhold will someday again be the shining jewel of Skyrim that it once was. Check inside the woven basket on the shelf to discover a hidden Skill Book.

- ◊ Skill Book [Alteration]: Breathing Water [A1/10]
- ◊ Chest

Related Quests

Main Quest: Elder Knowledge

Daedric Quest: The Black Star

Daedric Quest: Discerning the Transmundane

Side Quest: Forbidden Legend

College of Winterhold Quest: First Lessons

College of Winterhold Quest: Under Saarthal

College of Winterhold Quest: Hitting the Books

College of Winterhold Quest: Good Intentions

College of Winterhold Quest: Revealing the Unseen

College of Winterhold Quest: Containment

College of Winterhold Quest: The Staff of Magnus

College of Winterhold Quest: The Eye of Magnus

College of Winterhold Radiant Quest: Rejoining the College

College of Winterhold Radiant Quest: Tolfdir's Alembic*

College of Winterhold Radiant Quest: Out of Balance*

College of Winterhold Radiant Quest: An Enchanted Journey*

College of Winterhold Radiant Quest: Restocking Soul Gems*

College of Winterhold Radiant Quest: Valuable Book Procurement*

College of Winterhold Radiant Quest: Shalidor's Insights

College of Winterhold Radiant Quest: The Atronach Forge*

College of Winterhold Radiant Quest: Tolfdir's Alembic*

College of Winterhold Radiant Quest: Forgotten Names*

College of Winterhold Radiant Quest: Aftershock*

College of Winterhold Radiant Quest: Rogue Wizard

College of Winterhold Radiant Quest: Arniel's Endeavor

College of Winterhold Radiant Quest: Apprentice: Brelyna's Practice

College of Winterhold Radiant Quest: Apprentice: J'Zargo's Experiment

College of Winterhold Radiant Quest: Apprentice: Onmund's Request

College of Winterhold Radiant Quest: Destruction Ritual Spell

College of Winterhold Radiant Quest: Illusion Ritual Spell

College of Winterhold Radiant Quest: Conjuration Ritual Spell

College of Winterhold Radiant Quest: Restoration Ritual Spell

College of Winterhold Radiant Quest: Alteration Ritual Spell

Thieves Guild Radiant Quest: No Stone Unturned

Miscellaneous Objective: Lost Apprentices: Borvir* (Phinis Gestor)

Miscellaneous Objective: Lost Apprentices: Ilas-tei* (Phinis Gestor)

Miscellaneous Objective: Lost Apprentices: Rundi* (Phinis Gestor)

Miscellaneous Objective: Lost Apprentices: Yisra* (Phinis Gestor)

Habitation: Special

Crafting

Alchemy Labs (3)

Arcane Enchanters (2)

Services

Follower: Brelyna Maryon [9/47]

Follower: J'Zargo [10/47]

Follower: Onmund [11/47]

Marriage Prospect: Brelyna Maryon [8/62]

Marriage Prospect: Onmund [9/62]

Trader (Fence): Enthir [2/11]

Trader (General Store Vendor): Enthir [4/19]

Trader (Special): Enthir [1/3]

Trader (Spell Vendor): Tolfdir [4/12]

Trader (Spell Vendor): Phinis Gestor [5/12]

Trader (Spell Vendor): Faralda [6/12]

Trader (Spell Vendor): Drevis Neloren [7/12]

Trader (Spell Vendor): Colette Marence [8/12]

Trainer (Tolfdir: Master): Alteration [2/3]

Trainer (Phinis Gestor: Expert): Conjuration [2/3]

Trainer (Faralda: Expert): Destruction [2/3]

Trainer (Sergius Turrianus: Expert): Enchanting [1/2]

Trainer (Drevis Neloren: Master): Illusion [1/2]

Trainer (Colette Marence: Expert): Restoration [2/3]

Collectibles

Skill Book [Alchemy]: De Rerum Dirennis [B2/10]

Unique Item: Arch-Mage's Robes [27/112]

Unique Item: Mage's Circlet [28/112]

Unique Item: Savos Aren's Amulet [29/112]

Unique Item: Mystic Tuning Gloves [30/112]

Unusual Gem: [5/24]

Chest

Potions aplenty

> **NOTE** For more information on the College and biographies of the mages who live, teach, or learn there, please consult the College of Winterhold Quests, beginning on page 170.

Notable College Inhabitants

Savos Aren (Arch-Mage)

Unique Item: Arch-Mage's Robes [27/112]

Unique Item: Mage's Circlet [28/112]

Ancano (Thalmor Advisor)

Mirabelle Ervine (Master-Wizard)

Unique Item: Savos Aren's Amulet [29/112]

Enthir (Scholar)

Trader: Fence [2/11] (during Thieves Guild Quests only)

Trader: General Store Vendor [4/19]

Trader: Special [1/3]

Tolfdir (Wizard)

Trader: Spell Vendor [4/13]

Weapons, Scrolls, Books, Misc

Trainer: Alteration: Master [2/3]

Phinis Gestor (Wizard)

Trader: Spell Vendor [5/13]

Scrolls, Books, Misc

Trainer: Conjuration: Expert [2/3]

Faralda (Wizard)

Trader: Spell Vendor [6/13]

Weapons, Scrolls, Books, Misc

Trainer: Destruction: Expert [2/3]

Sergius Turrianus (Wizard)

Trainer: Enchanting: Expert [1/2]

Drevis Neloren (Wizard)

Trader: Spell Vendor [8/13]

Weapons, Scrolls, Books, Misc

Trainer: Illusion: Master [1/2]

Unique Item: Mystic Tuning Gloves [30/112]

Colette Marence (Scholar)

Trader: Spell Vendor [9/13]

Scrolls, Books, Misc

Trainer: Restoration: Expert [2/3]

Arniel Gane (Scholar)

Nirya (Scholar)

Urag gro-Shub (Lorekeeper)

Trader: Special [2/3]

Brelyna Maryon (Student)

Follower [9/47]

Marriage Prospect [8/62]

J'Zargo (Student)

Follower [10/47]

Onmund (Student)

Follower [11/47]

Marriage Prospect [9/62]

Augur of Dunlain

① Winterhold Bridge

Many of the townsfolk in Winterhold think this bridge is being held up by magic alone, and they are correct. Faralda waits to greet (or halt) anyone thinking of entering the College, forcing them to prove they have an aptitude for magic. Ignore her, and the gates into the College remain closed to you. Fall from the bridge, and expect a long death plummet. Walk on the shores of the Sea of Ghosts below, and you'll find the remains of fallen masonry and stones, but only Clams, Nordic Barnacles, and Slaughterfish Eggs to collect.

② Main Courtyard

Dominated by a statue of the first Arch-Mage of the College, this is the hub of the facility, offering access back out to the bridge and into the three Halls and one of the trapdoors into the murky depths of the Midden. The exterior windows offer exceptional views of the coastline.

> **NOTE** If you're looking for a specific member of the College, most move constantly throughout the Halls of Attainment, Countenance, and Elements. Any mages who are usually in a single location are mentioned below.

③ Hall of Attainment

This is to the west of the Courtyard and is where the students and some of the teachers rest. If you join the College, the first room on your right is where you can sleep. There are two floors and a door up onto the roof where you can access the other main parts of the College, which can be accessed from ground level as well.

◇ Chest (2)

④ Hall of Countenance

The senior members of the College have a home here, which is a tower laid out in the same fashion as the Hall of Attainment. Check the upper floor and the roof access. There are many staffs here, but stealing them isn't wise. The ingredients (and Soul Gems) on display near the Alchemy Lab (and Arcane Enchanter) can be used without penalty, so seek them out if you're looking for a particularly rare item (or gem) to craft. Also note the trapdoor entrance to the Midden at the base of the spiral steps.

Crafting: Alchemy Lab, Arcane Enchanter

◇ Tolfdir's Alembic   ◇ Potions aplenty
◇ Chest   ◇ Loose gear

⑤ Hall of the Elements

The College's grand central chamber is where students practice their magic and senior members discuss important matters. You attend your first lesson in magic here. Ancano usually mooches around these parts. This is a major location during the College of Winterhold Quests. The entrance is flanked by two doors, each leading to a higher level of the main tower.

⑥ Arch-Mage's Quarters

You can reach the Arch-Mage's Quarters from the Hall of the Elements or the Arcanaeum. These are the chambers of Savos Aren, where he spends some of his time. The circular chamber is lined with ingredients for mixing and features a fungal garden lit by magical floating lights. These aren't yours to take, unless you wish to incur the wrath of the College elders (or can manage it without being seen!) or you're patient enough to complete the College quest line, at which point the chamber becomes yours.

◇ Crafting: Alchemy Lab, Arcane Enchanter
◇ Unusual Gem: [5/24]

⑦ The Arcanaeum

You can reach the Arcanaeum from the Hall of the Elements or the roof parapets. This is the home to Urag gro-Shub the Lorekeeper and his extensive collection of tomes (although he's always on the lookout for more research materials). The Ysmir Collective, a selection of rare books, is on display, and many books are scattered about. If you want to read, you've come to the right place. The Investigator's Chest has rings to be used in the Midden, as part of College of Winterhold Radiant Quest: Forgotten Names.

◇ Investigator's Chest

◈ The Midden

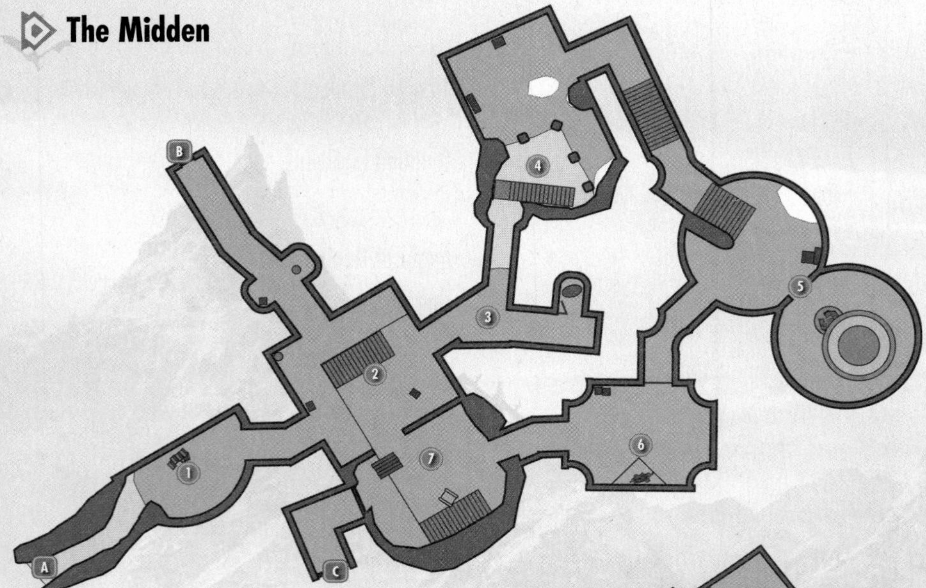

The Midden, a hidden underbelly where ancient and unspeakable magic has been practiced (and mostly forgotten about) isn't a place where College members usually go.

A Ladder to Main Courtyard

① Semicircular Chamber

② Torture Chamber Tower
Some rotting rugs lie at the bottom of the wooden steps, overlooked by two clamped skeletons. There are four exits to choose from here.

B Hagraven's Corridor
Pass the deer skull altar to reach this exit door.

③ Wet Bones and Blood
An unpleasant sacrifice was made here.

④ Snow Catacombs

⑤ Summoning Chamber
A large summoning circle is lit with an offering box to fill. This is the Atronach forge and used in the quest of that name.

⑥ Ancient Altar

⑦ Torture Chamber Tower (Waterfall)
This provides access to the Midden Dark.

C Door to Midden Dark

◈ The Midden Dark

D Door to Midden

⑧ Chasm Bridge
Pass the skeletal design on the wall and watch your footing. Drop down if you wish.

◇ Chest

⑨ Catacombs Junction

⑩ Chamber of Augur of Dunlain (Locked: Requires Key)
The entity that lives in the depths of the Midden is holed up here. Speak to him only during specific quests.

⑪ Alchemy Offerings and Bone Pile
A small lab and an interesting book are available, prior to a skeleton skirmish.

◇ Crafting: Alchemy Lab
◇ Skill Book [Alchemy]: De Rerum Dirennis [B2/10]

⑫ Daedric Gauntlet
This bears the Sigil of Oblivion. It is the focus of Radiant Quest: Forgotten Names.

⑬ The Unlucky Goat
Slain in this snow cave, this is evidence of necromancy!

⑭ Spider Catacombs

E Exit to Skyrim
This exit is one-way and brings you out onto a rocky outcrop. From here you have a view of the Sea of Ghosts and the Skytemple Ruins.

[4.01] Hela's Folly

Related Quests

Dark Brotherhood Quest: Side Contract: Deekus

Recommended Level: 6

Dungeon: Shipwreck

Deekus
Chest (Locked: Novice)
Chest (Locked: Apprentice)

A treasure-seeker named Deekus has made camp near a shipwreck along Winterhold's treacherous northern coastline. One of the Dark Brotherhood's side contracts marks this Argonian as a target. Deekus has amassed a hoard of precious gemstones and baubles. Steal these valuables to gain a small fortune, if you dare. Hop aboard the remnants of the nearby ship and dive underwater to discover a locked chest and additional gemstones aboard the ship's sunken half.

[4.02] Yngvild

Related Quests

Side Quest: No Stone Unturned
Miscellaneous Objective: Toying with the Dead*

Recommended Level: 8

Dungeon: Warlock Lair

Aroundil
Draugr
Yngvild Ghost

Collectibles

Skill Book [Alteration]: Reality & Other Falsehoods [C1/10]
Unusual Gem: [6/24]
Chest(s)
Potions

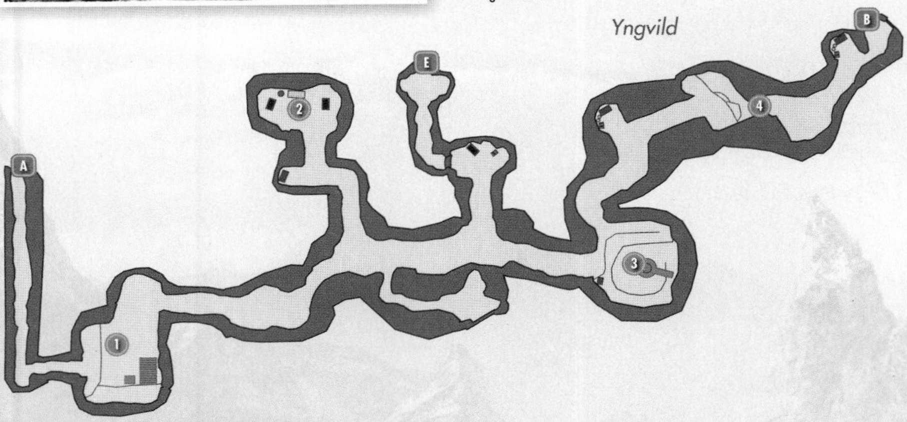

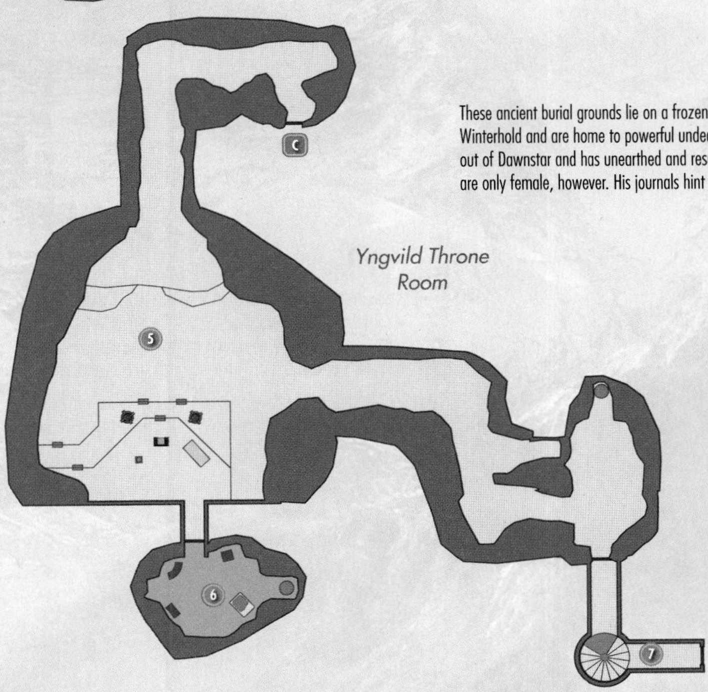

A **Exit to Skyrim**

1 **Entry Cavern**

Swipe a few potions in this first cavern, then battle a powerful Draugr on your way to [2].

◇ Potions

2 **Urn Cavern**

Defeat a deadly Yngvild Ghost and read an insightful journal on your way to this small cavern, where several urns beg looting.

3 **Tall Cavern**

Kill more ghosts and more mighty Draugr on your way to this tall cavern, then descend to the bottom, where a chest awaits.

◇ Chest

4 **Passage to Throne Room**

Slay another ghost and scan another two journals on your way to the Yngvild Throne Room.

◇ Potions

B **Door to Yngvild Throne Room**

C **Door to Yngvild**

5 **Throne Room**

A powerful mage named Arondil sits on a throne in this wide cavern. Slay him and collect a key from his corpse. Snatch the Skill Book that rests on a nearby table as well.

◇ Skill Book [Alteration]: Reality & Other Falsehoods [C1/10]
◇ Arondil's Key (Arondil)

6 **Arondil's Quarters**

Raid the giant chest in Arondil's private chamber, and collect the Unusual Gem from the table to gain a new Miscellaneous Objective.

◇ Unusual Gem: [6/24]
◇ Chest
◇ Potions

7 **Exit Passage**

Throw a lever in this final stretch to raise a portcullis, then use the key you found on Arondil to unlock the iron door and make your way back to Yngvild's entrance. Loot a locked chest on your way out.

◇ Chest (Locked: Apprentice)

D **Door to Yngvild**

E **Door to Yngvild Throne Room**

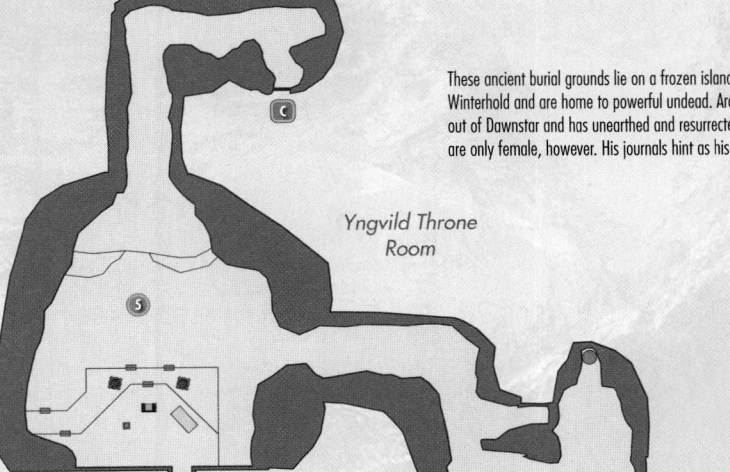

Yngvild

Yngvild Throne Room

These ancient burial grounds lie on a frozen island in northeast Winterhold and are home to powerful undead. Arondil has been thrown out of Dawnstar and has unearthed and resurrected undead here. They are only female, however. His journals hint as his vile intentions.

[4.03] The Tower Stone

Recommended Level: 6

Special Objects:

Standing Stone: The Tower Stone [4/13]

Ancient stones stand atop this glacial spire on Winterhold's frozen northwest coastline. Inspect the central Standing Stone to accept a new sign blessing. Those under the sign of the Tower can automatically open one Expert-level or lower lock once per day. Note that you can have only one sign blessing at a time, so activating this Standing Stone will override your current sign blessing (if any).

[4.04] Winterhold Imperial Camp

Related Quests

Civil War Quest: Reunification of Skyrim

Civil War Quest: Rescue from Fort Kastav

Habitation: Military:

Imperial Camp

Imperial Quartermaster (Blacksmith)

Legate Sevan Telendas

Services

Trader (Blacksmith): Imperial Quartermaster [9/33]

Weapons, Apparel, Misc

Crafting

Alchemy Lab

Anvil

Grindstone

Workbench

Special Objects

Civil War: Map of Skyrim

Chests (2)

Potions

Loose gear

The Imperials have made camp in the frigid northwest mountains of Winterhold. Note that this Imperial campsite may only exist when you're playing through the Civil War quest line. Trade with the quartermaster if you like, or use his bevy of crafting stations. Inspect the tabletop map in the largest tent to potentially gain new map data. Loot a few chests before moving on.

[4.05] Hob's Fall Cave

This frigid cave lies in northwest Winterhold and has been overrun by powerful mages.

Related Quests

Other Factions: Bards College Quest: Pantea's Flute

Side Quest: No Stone Unturned

Recommended Level: 8

Dungeon: Warlock Lair

Mage

Skeleton

Crafting

Alchemy Lab

Arcane Enchanter

Collectibles

Skill Book [Enchanting]: Enchanter's Primer [D1/10]

Skill Book [Restoration]: The Exodus

Unusual Gem: [7/24]

Chest(s)

Potions

Loose gear

2 Bridge Chamber

Avoid falling from this chamber's wooden rope bridge — it's a long way down. Instead, visit the bottom of this chamber by venturing down the north passage just before you reach [3]. Collect the Skill Book from the table here, along with the Unusual Gem that sits on the nearby cupboard — the latter begins a Side Quest.

◇ Crafting: Alchemy Lab
◇ Unusual Gem: [7/24]
◇ Skill Book [Restoration]: The Exodus
◇ Potions

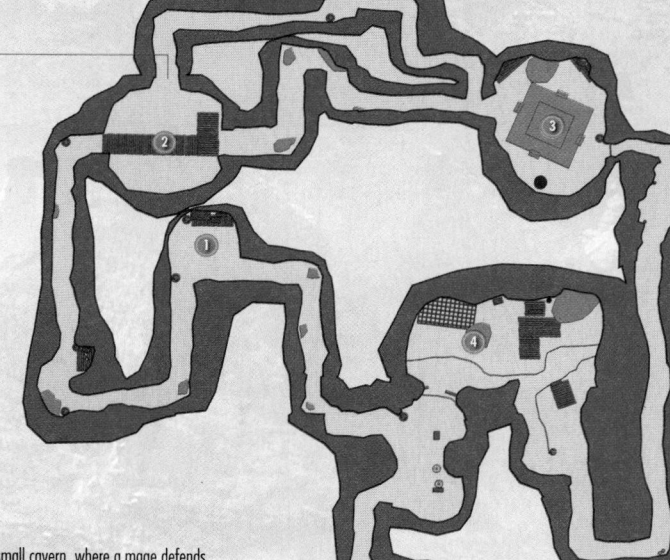

3 Head Mage's Lair

A powerful spellcaster lurks in this wide chamber. Raid the place after slaying the mage, collecting a Skill Book from atop an Arcane Enchanter before pulling a wall chain to open the way forward. Steal Soul Gems from the pedestals in the passage that follows to deactivate the dangerous frost spout.

◇ Crafting: Arcane Enchanter
◇ Chest (Locked: Apprentice)
◇ Skill Book [Enchanting]: Enchanter's Primer [D1/10]
◇ Apothecary's Satchel
◇ Potions

A Exit to Skyrim

1 Mage's Cavern

Slay a skeleton on your way to this small cavern, where a mage defends several potions and a chest.

◇ Chest
◇ Potions

4 Mage's Study

Several learned spellweavers guard this final cavern — slay them all to secure a large chest, then drop off the west cliff to return to the cave's first chamber.

◇ Chest
◇ Potion
◇ Loose gear

[4.06] Frostflow Lighthouse

Related Quests

Side Quest: Captured Critters*
Dungeon Quest: What Lies Beneath*

Recommended Level: 18

Dungeon: Falmer Hive

Animal
Falmer

Dangers

Falmer Claw Trap (trip wire)

Collectibles

Captured Critter: Torchbug in a
Jar [2/5]
Skill Book [Restoration]: Mystery
of Talara, v2 [B2/10]
Chest(s)
Potions
Loose gear

Frostflow Abyss

This tall watchtower stands atop Winterhold's northwest mountains, within clear sight of the Hold's northern coast.

Exterior

Pick the Novice door lock to open the small storage shed that's attached to the lighthouse. A few potions are found within.

◊ Potions
◊ Loose gear

Frostflow Lighthouse (Interior)

Enter the tower to discover a butchered person. Search the corpse to gain a new Dungeon Quest and obtain an informative journal. A Torchbug in a Jar rests atop the mantel—this pertains to Side Quest: Captured Critters. In the northern room, you find Sudi's Journal on the desk, Mani's Letter in the knapsack under the bed, and a Skill Book. In the room adjacent, you find the journal of Ramati, the dead woman you just found. Piecing together the story from these journals will lead you to find Mani's Cellar Key, hidden in an urn on the mantel above the fireplace. Ramati's Journal also mentions a promise to cremate her husband in the lighthouse fire in the event of his death (this is important later).

Take the key and use it to reach the cellar where you can clear out a cluster of Chaurus and loot a locked chest. Venture through the large hole in the basement's southeast wall to proceed to the Frostflow Abyss.

◊ Captured Critter: Torchbug in a   ◊ Ramati's Journal
  Jar [2/5]   ◊ Sudi's Journal
◊ Skill Book [Restoration]:   ◊ Potions
  Mystery of Talara, v2 [B2/10]   ◊ Loose gear
◊ Chest (Locked: Adept)
◊ Mani's Cellar Key
◊ Mani's Letter

(A) Path to Frostflow Lighthouse

(1) Falmer Den

Exterminate a Chaurus, Falmer, and Frostbite Spiders as you head to this chamber. Carefully trigger a trip wire from a safe distance to disable the Falmer Claw Trap as well. Dispatch all Falmer here, then search the tents to find two chests. Locate a third chest along the passage to [2].

◊ Danger! Falmer Claw Trap (trip wire)   ◊ Chest (Locked: Apprentice)
◊ Chest (Locked: Novice)

(2) Chaurus Nest

Slay countless Chaurus on your way to this final cavern, where a monstrous Chaurus lurks—the source of the murders back in the lighthouse. Defeat the fiend to purify this place and complete the Miscellaneous Objective you acquired when you first entered the lighthouse. Collect the key you find within the giant Chaurus's remains, along with Habd's Remains (trust us); then take the exterior path to reach a chest with valuable loot.

◊ Habd's Lighthouse Key (Chaurus)   ◊ Chest
◊ Habd's Remains (Chaurus)

Rooftop Loot

Now that you've solved the lighthouse's mystery, backtrack to the main level and use your newfound key to open the door that leads to the roof. Open the giant chest you find on the roof to obtain a nice haul of plunder. If you like, you may also throw Habd's Remains into the signal fire to receive a special blessing called Sailor's Repose, which permanently increases how much you heal with spells by 10 percent.

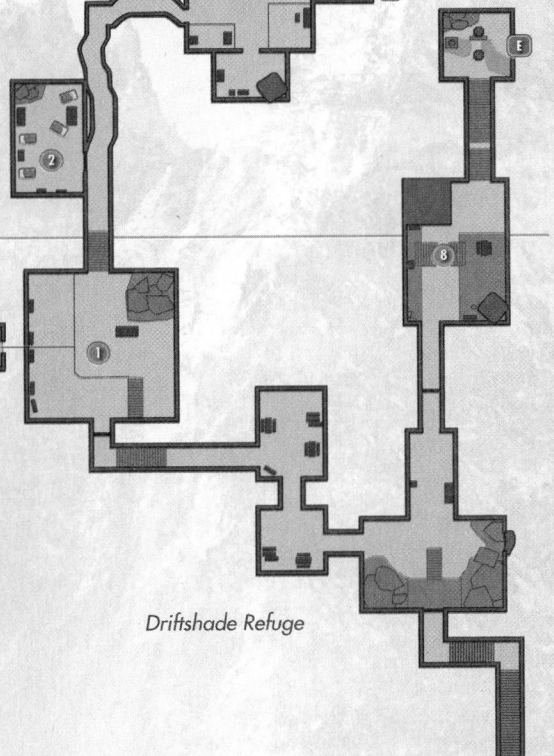

[4.07] Driftshade Refuge

Related Quests

The Companions Quest: Purity of
Revenge

Recommended Level: 6

Dungeons: Vampire Lair

Silver Hand

Crafting

Anvil
Grindstone
Workbench

Dangers

Swinging Wall Trap (pressure
plate)

Collectibles

Skill Book [Block]: Warrior [E1/10]
Skill Book [Light Armor]: The Rear Guard
Skill Book [One-Handed]: 2920, Morning Star, v1
Chest(s)
Potions
Loose gear

Driftshade Refuge

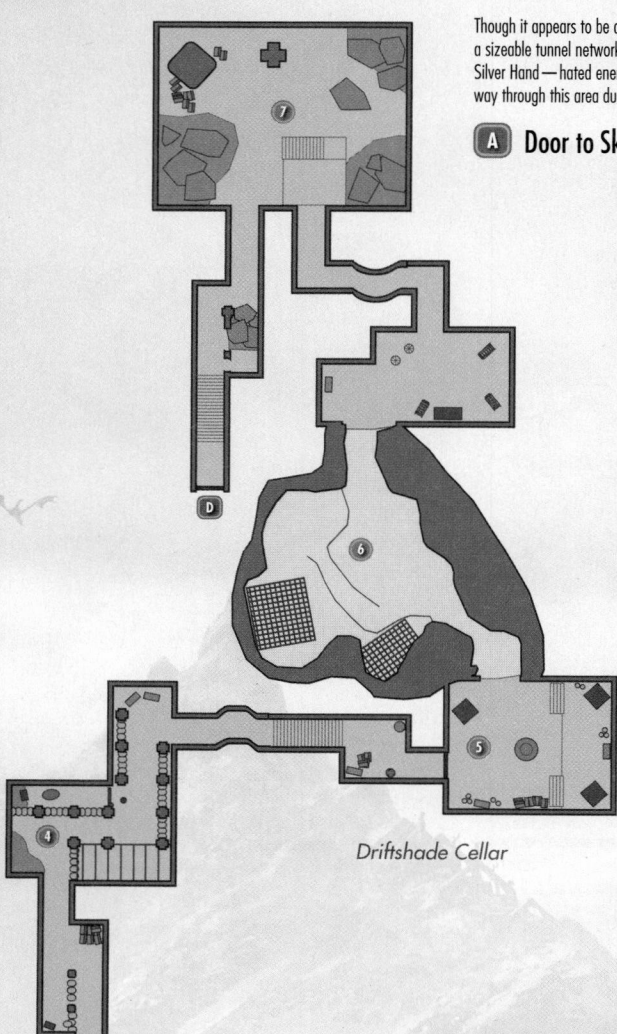

Though it appears to be a small barracks, the Driftshade Refuge features a sizeable tunnel network that's filled with ruthless ruffians known as the Silver Hand — hated enemies of the Companions. You must fight your way through this area during Companions Quest: Purity of Revenge.

A Door to Skyrim

1 Great Hall

Eliminate severeal Silver Hand and swipe a few minor valuables on your way to this chamber, where a chest awaits pillaging in a nook downstairs.

◇ Chest (Locked: Adept)
◇ Potions
◇ Loose gear

2 Sleeping Quarters

Pick a locked door to enter this small sleeping area, then slay the groggy guard and plunder the place.

◇ Area Is Locked (Adept)
◇ Chest
◇ Potions

3 Cellar Access

Dispatch more Silver Hand in this far chamber and pillage a chest before pulling the wall lever to open a passage that leads to the cellar.

◇ Chest
◇ Potions

Driftshade Cellar

B Door to Driftshade Cellar

C Door to Driftshade Refuge

4 Barrel-Lined Passage

As you enter the cellar, search for a chest that's tucked away in a dark corner among barrels. Jump a pressure plate trap in this area, and don't bother picking the locked holding cell — the slain werewolf within has nothing of value.

◇ Danger! Swinging Wall Trap (pressure plate)
◇ Chest
◇ Potions
◇ Loose gear

5 Distillery

Dispatch several Silver Hand ruffians here, then collect the Skill Book on the far shelf.

◇ Skill Book [Light Armor]: The Rear Guard
◇ Potions

6 Holding Cells

Enter this snowy cavern, which features two giant holding cells, one of which contains a live werewolf. Free the creature if you dare, but be ready for a challenging battle.

7 Cellar Hearth

Check behind the large fireplace here to find some potions and a coin purse. Then head through the nearby door to return to the Refuge.

◇ Potions

D Door to Driftshade Refuge

E Door to Driftshade Cellar

8 Crafting Station

Lay waste to the final crew of Silver Hand bandits here, then locate two Skill Books and loot a large chest before unbarring the far door and making your way back outside.

◇ Crafting: Anvil, Grindstone, Workbench
◇ Skill Book [Block]: Warrior [E1/10]
◇ Skill Book [One-Handed]: 2920, Morning Star, v1
◇ Chest

[4.08] Fort Fellhammer

Recommended Level: 6

Dungeons: Bandit Camp
Bandit

Crafting
Smelter

Collectibles
Skill Book [Heavy Armor]: Orsinium and the Orcs
Chest(s)
Potions
Loose gear
Mineable ore (Iron)

This bandit-ridden keep stands at the west base of Winterhold's western mountains.

Garrison

Slay the bandit chief inside the small garrison and loot the large chest for valuables.

◇ Chest   ◇ Potions   ◇ Loose gear

Mines

A skilled hand is required to pick the lock to this fort's interior mines, where more bandits lurk and iron can be harvested in abundance. More importantly, a Skill Book rests on the far table.

◇ Area Is Locked (Expert)
◇ Skill Book [Heavy Armor]: Orsinium and the Orcs
◇ Mineable ore (Iron)

[4.09] Snowpoint Beacon

Recommended Level: 5

Dungeon: Bandit Camp
Bandit

Collectible
Chest (Locked: Novice)

Bandits have overrun this small tower, which stands atop Winterhold's west mountains. The chief awaits up top. Loot his body after the slaughter for plenty of plunder.

[4.10] Pilgrim's Trench

Recommended Level: 6

Dungeon: Shipwreck

Special Objects

Chests (2)

This small campsite is located along Winterhold's northern coastline. An interesting note rests atop a nearby barrel. Take a dip into the frigid ocean and swim out to a rowboat to the north. From here, dive straight underwater to discover a graveyard of ships that have wrecked against the ice and sunk. The largest ship, which features a topside cabin, still carries two chests within her hull.

[4.11] Ysgramor's Tomb

Related Quests

The Companions Quest: Glory of the Dead

Recommended Level: 6

Dungeon: Draugr Crypt

Animal
Companion Ghost
Kodlak Whitemane
Kodlak's Wolf Spirit

Collectibles

Skill Book [Two-Handed]: The Legendary City of Sancre Tor

Unique Item: Shield of Ysgramor [31/112]

Special Objects

Word Wall: Animal Allegiance [1/3]

Area Is Locked (quest required)

Chest(s)

Potions

Loose gear

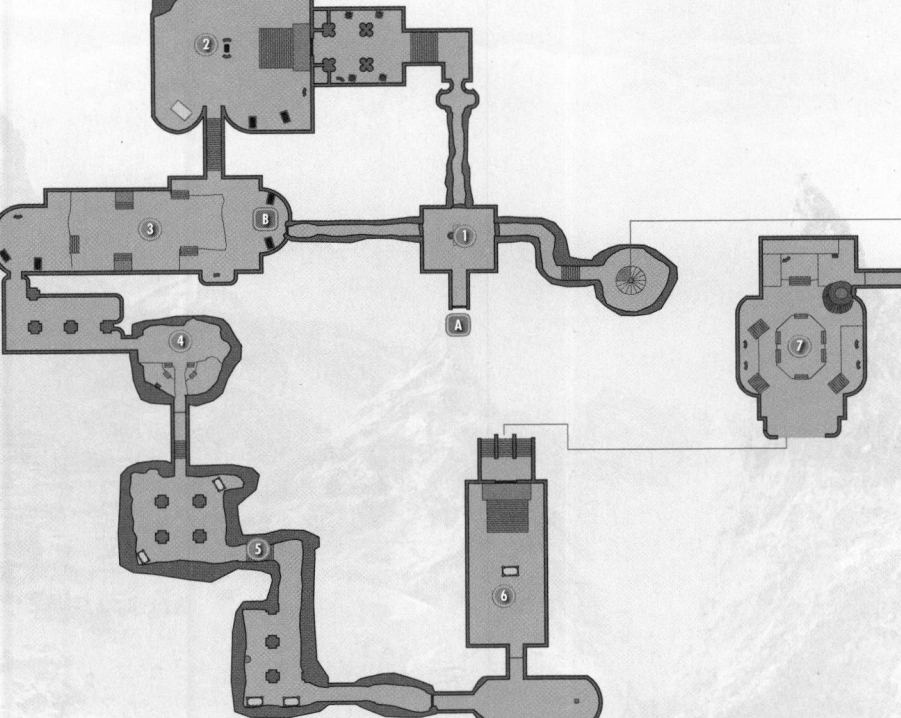

This remote burial ground holds special significance to the Companions; you visit here during their "Glory of the Dead" quest. The area remains largely sealed off until you acquire that quest.

A Exit to Skyrim

1 Entry Chamber

A statue to Ysgramor dominates the tomb's quiet entry chamber. If you're running Companions Quest: Glory of the Dead, place the axe Wuuthrad onto the statue at Vilkas's instruction to open the north passage and advance to [2]. If you haven't yet obtained that quest, then you cannot explore any farther.

◊ Potion   ◊ Loose gear

2 Sarcophagi Chamber A

Prove your valor to the Companions' ancestors by slaying the Companion Ghosts that emerge from sarcophagi in this sizable chamber.

◊ Potion   ◊ Loose gear

3 Sarcophagi Chamber B

Many more Companion Ghosts ambush you here — expect a challenging battle. Raid the room's southeast chest after things settle down, and find a potion in a nearby sarcophagus. Shred through thick cobwebs and snatch another potion on your way into a small room filled with ravenous Frostbite Spiders.

◊ Chest   ◊ Potions   ◊ Loose gear

4 Giant Spider Den

Squash more spiders in this room, including a monstrous Giant Frostbite Spider that drops from the ceiling in ambush. Loot a locked chest and pull a wall chain to open the way forward.

◊ Chest (Locked: Adept)

5 Burial Passages

Pocket a bit of plunder as you navigate these quiet halls. More Companion Ghosts attack as you near [6].

◊ Apothecary's Satchel   ◊ Potions   ◊ Loose gear

6 Shrine Chamber

Pull a handle to open the passage that leads into this chamber, where another host of Companion Ghosts descend upon you. Claim a Skill Book and potion from the central table before scaling the north stairs to [7].

◊ Skill Book [Two-Handed]: The Legendary City of Sancre Tor
◊ Potion

7 Burial Chamber

Speak with Kodlak's spirit in this large room, then examine the nearby Flame of the Harbinger to toss in one of the Glenmoril Witch Heads you obtained earlier in the Companions quest line. Slay Kodlak's Wolf Spirit when it emerges, then speak with Kodlak again to complete your quest. Raid the chamber's large northeast chest on your way upstairs, claiming a unique shield from within. You'll soon find your way back to the tomb's entry chamber.

◊ Unique Item: Shield of Ysgramor [31/112]   ◊ Chest
◊ Loose gear

B Exit to Skyrim

Exterior World Wall

Upon returning to [1], take the west passage and exit out to Skyrim via the west door. Marvel at the view for a moment before sprinting up the snowy steps to discover a Word Wall.

◊ Word Wall: Animal Allegiance [1/3]

[4.12] Saarthal

Related Quests

College of Winterhold Quest:
Under Saarthal

Side Quest: Forbidden Legend

Recommended Level: 6

Dungeon: Draugr Crypt

Arniel Gane
Draugr
Jyrik Gauldurson
Nerien

Crafting

Alchemy Lab

Dangers

Dart Trap (pressure plates)
Rune Traps (floor)

Puzzles

Nordic Pillars I
Nordic Pillars II

Quest Items

Enchanted Rings (3)
Saarthal Amulet

Collectibles

Skill Book [Two-Handed]: The
Legendary Sancre Tor

Unique Item: Enchanted Ring
[32/112]

Unique Item: Gauldur Amulet
Fragment (Saarthal) [33/112]

Unique Item: Saarthal Amulet
[34/112]

Unique Weapon: Staff of Jyrik
Gauldurson [23/80]

Special Objects

Word Wall: Ice Form [2/3]
Area Is Locked (quest required)
Chest(s)
Potions
Loose gear

This snowy excavation site lies just southwest of
Winterhold's capital and serves as the setting for the College
of Winterhold's second quest.

Exterior

Loot a chest and several urns before speaking with Tolfdir at
the excavation site as part of College of Winterhold Quest:
Under Saarthal. Tolfdir unlocks the nearby door and urges
you keep pace as he heads inside.

◇ Chest

Saarthal Excavation

Saarthal

A Exit to Skyrim

1 Chest Ledge

Chat up your colleagues as you follow Tolfdir deep into the excavation site.
While navigating the high, narrow walkways here, boldly leap over to this
north ledge and loot a chest.

◇ Chest   ◇ Loose gear

2 Arniel Gane's Study

Follow Tolfdir all the way to Arniel Gane's study, then speak with Arniel
to advance the quest. Use your map and compass to locate four magical
artifacts scattered about the nearby area—three small enchanted rings
found on the ground and one amulet that hangs from a wall.
Removing the amulet springs a trap. Speak with Tolfdir, then put on the amulet and
strike the wall where you recovered the amulet with any spell to destroy
it, gaining your freedom.

◇ Unique Item: Enchanted Ring [32/112]

◇ Unique Item: Saarthal Amulet [33/112]

The Elder Scrolls V

SKYRIM

3 Vision Chamber

Tell Tolfdir of the curious vision you have upon entering this small chamber, then slay the powerful Draugr that burst out from the room's standing sarcophagi. Follow Tolfdir into the west passage, pulling a lever to open a gate on your way to [4].

4 Coffin Chamber

You become trapped in this chamber when you enter and are forced to battle a swarm of Draugr. Slay them with haste, then pull the far wall chains to open the way forward; this seals off the passage from which you came. Tolfdir remains here to study; head through the west door to brave the heart of Saarthal.

B Door to Saarthal

C Door to Saarthal Excavation

5 Draugr Passages

Sneak through these dark corridors, or risk awakening several powerful Draugr. Venture upstairs to loot a few urns and go through an iron door on your way to [6].

6 Trapped Passage A

Beware of a rune trap that's been cast on the ground in this hall. Detonate it with a ranged attack from afar to safely advance. Avoid a pressure plate next, which lies just in front of a tantalizing chest. Slay or sneak past a few more deadly Draugr on your way to [7].

◇ Danger! Rune Trap (floor), Dart Trap (pressure plate)

◇ Chest

7 Puzzling Pillars

Spin the six pillars in this passage so that each one's glyph matches the glyph on the wall behind it (Snake, Whale, Hawk, Hawk). Pull the lever to raise the portcullis and advance.

◇ Potion

8 Great Hall

Kill or avoid a deadly Draugr in this cavernous chamber, opening the far door to access a chest on your way to [9]. Beware of more rune traps that lie on the floor just beyond the chest. Detonate them both with ranged attacks from a safe distance.

◇ Danger! Rune Traps (floor)   ◇ Chest

9 More Nordic Pillars

Solve another simple puzzle here by spinning the four pillars so that their facing glyphs match those that make up the mouths of the nearby stone heads (Snake, Whale, Hawk, Whale). This is somewhat tricky, because rotating one pillar may also cause others to spin in sync. One of the pillars can be spun independently—save this one for last as you focus on correctly aligning the other three.

10 Trapped Passage B

Tolfdir catches up to you as you enter this passage. Avoid the pressure plate on the floor as you swipe gear, potions, and loot urns here. Collect the Skill Book that rests atop the Alchemy Lab before entering the final cavern.

◇ Danger! Dart Trap (pressure plate)   ◇ Skill Book [Two-Handed]: The Legendary Sancre Tor

◇ Crafting: Alchemy Lab   ◇ Potions

◇ Loose gear

11 Orb Chamber

A massive orb that churns with mysterious energy awaits you in this chamber, along with a deadly Draugr named Jyrik Gauldurson. No attack can harm Jyrik until Tolfdir begins to drain the energy from the orb. You must then vary your attacks to counter the Draugr's defensive magics. Raid the chamber after the fight, then promise Tolfdir that you'll hurry back to the College to tell the Arch-Mage of your discovery.

◇ Unique Item: Gauldur Amulet Fragment (Saarthal) [34/112]

◇ Unique Weapon: Staff of Jyrik Gauldurson [23/80]

12 Word Wall Grove

This small cavern houses a mystical Word Wall. Approach the object to gain a new Word of Power as you follow the exit route out of Saarthal.

◇ Word Wall: Ice Form [2/3]

◈ [4.13] Alftand

Related Quests

Main Quest: Elder Knowledge

Daedric Quest: Discerning the Transmundane

Dungeon Activity

Recommended Level:
16

Dungeon: Dwarven City

Animal

Dwarven Centurion

Dwarven Sphere

Dwarven Spider

Falmer

J'darr

Sulla Trebatius

Umana

Crafting

Alchemy Lab

Blacksmith Forge

Tanning Rack

Workbench

Dangers

Bone Alarm Trap

Dwarven Piston Traps

Dwarven Thresher Trap (pressure plates)

Falmer Claw Trap (trip wire)

Flamethrowers

Flamethrowers (button)

Oil Pool Traps

Spear Trap (pressure plates)

Swinging Wall Trap (pressure plate)

Underground Connection: Blackreach [10.02]

Collectibles

Skill Book [Lockpicking]: The Locked Room [D2/10]

Unique Item: Targe of the Blooded [35/112]

Special Objects

Dwarven Mechanism

Chest(s)

Potions

Loose gear

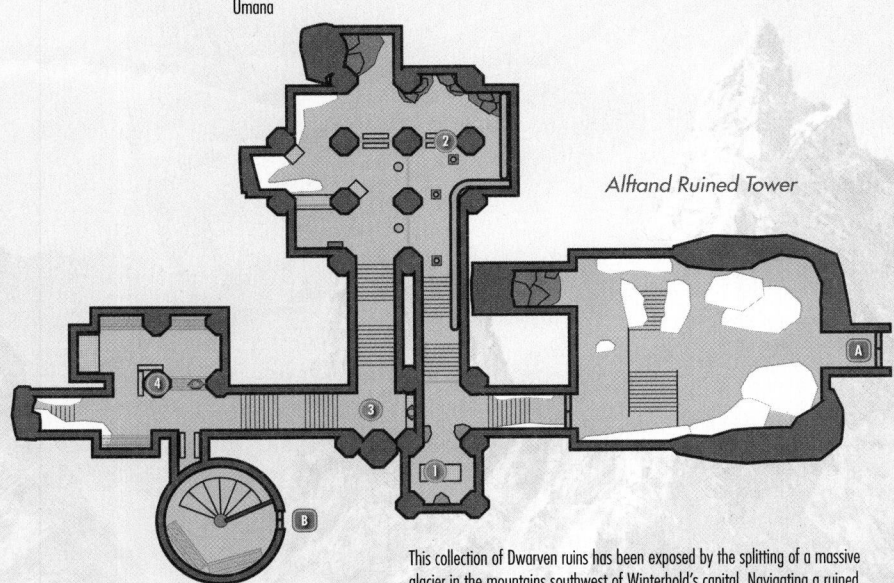

Alftand Ruined Tower

This collection of Dwarven ruins has been exposed by the splitting of a massive glacier in the mountains southwest of Winterhold's capital. Navigating a ruined tower grants passage up to a high excavation site.

Exterior (Lower Glacier)

Slay the odd animal as you sprint south along the base of the glacier's wide fissure. Enter the ruined tower at the fissure's far end to navigate an interior passage that leads you high atop the glacier.

A Exit to Skyrim

1 Chest Nook A

Sneak through the ruined tower, or you risk alerting Dwarven Spiders and Spheres that quickly emerge from small portals in the walls. Find a chest here, and push a button to open the nearby gate. This also activates several flamethrowers near the gate, which you must sprint through. Read the nearby book to learn the Lesser Ward spell, which can help reduce the flamethrowers' harmful effect.

◇ Danger! Flamethrowers (button)   ◇ Potion

◇ Chest (Locked: Apprentice)   ◇ Loose gear

2 Trapped Stairwell

Beware of pressure plates in this passage as you head upstairs. If Dwarven Spheres sense your presence, try using these traps against them by looping around and pressing the buttons on the other side of the thin metal gate.

◇ Danger! Spear Trap (pressure plates)

3 Chest Nook B

If possible, unlock a challenging chest here to claim worthy loot.

◇ Chest (Locked: Expert)

4 Storage

Swipe some potions from the metal shelves here, and unlock another chest that sits on the ground. Make your way up a spiral stairwell and exit the tower.

◇ Chest (Locked: Adept)   ◇ Potions

D Door to Saarthal Excavation

E Door to Saarthal

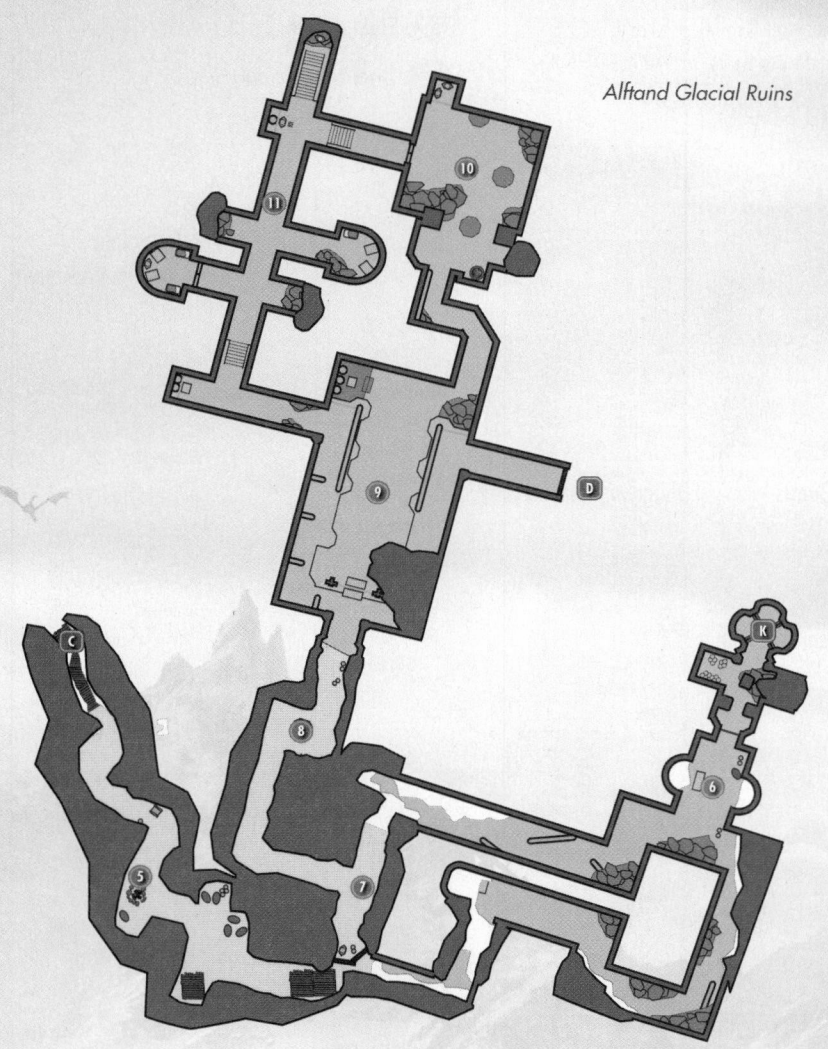

Alftand Glacial Ruins

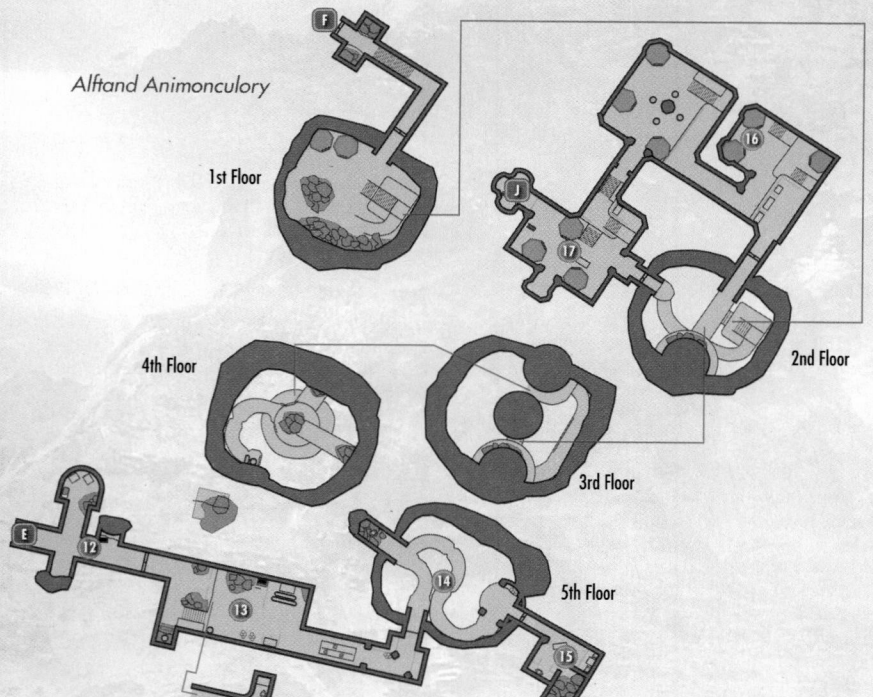

Alftand Animonculory

1st Floor

4th Floor

3rd Floor

2nd Floor

5th Floor

Exterior (Upper Glacier)

Head south after passing through the ruined tower, scaling a snowy hill. Sprint east to finally locate the Alftand excavation site. Search some open-air cabins here to discover a chest and an informative journal, then descend a series of wooden planks to discover a cave that leads into Alftand's glacial ruins.

◊ Chest

C **Exit to Skyrim**

5 **Glacial Ruins' Entry Passage**

Thumb through Sulla's Journal, which lies on a barrel in the Glacial Ruins' first passage, for a bit more insight into the expedition. Raid a nearby chest for plunder as well. As you pass a boarded off section by a dwarven tower, you can catch a glimpse of a deranged Khajiit searching the ruins and muttering to himself.

◊ Chest

6 **Workstation**

Trek through the frigid passages that lead to this work area. Inspect a book on the table here to learn more about the ill-fated excavation effort, and loot a chest that lies in the nearby snow. You can't open the nearby gate for now, so continue following the snaking passage as it doubles back on itself. Be wary as Dwarven Spiders start to pop out of hiding.

◊ Chest (Locked: Novice)   ◊ Loose gear

7 **Chest Nook C**

Find a chest and potion tucked away in this snowy corner, along with a coin purse and Apothecary's Satchel.

◊ Chest   ◊ Apothecary's Satchel

8 **J'darr Encounter**

You encounter one of the expedition's laborers in this icy passage. J'darr has gone quite mad and relentlessly attacks you on sight. Search around to find a pack, several potions, and an insightful journal afterward.

◊ J'zhar's Pack   ◊ Potions   ◊ Loose gear

9 **Oily Chamber**

Flip through yet another journal as you enter this sizable chamber. Beware of Dwarven Spheres that emerge from portals in the room's center. Ignite the oily floor to burn them up. Ride a trio of vertical dwarven piston traps in the room's northwest corner to reach loot on a high ledge

◊ Danger! Oil Pool Traps   ◊ Chests (2)   ◊ Potions

10 **Forge**

Exploit this chamber's oily floor as well to help you defeat its Dwarven Spiders. Use a crafting station here and unlock the Novice-level northwest gate to raid a small treasure nook.

◊ Crafting: Blacksmith Forge   ◊ Chest (Locked: Adept)
◊ Chest (Locked: Apprentice)

11 **Trapped Chest Corridor**

Avoid the pressure plate that lies in front of this passage's tantalizing chest, and loot another chest that lies among the nearby north rubble. Collect a few potions as you explore the passage's southern alcoves, and pick an Apprentice-level gate to access a small room with yet another chest. Several Dwarven Spiders can be seen working through here, which can be bypassed if you are very stealthy.

◊ Danger! Spear Trap (pressure plate)   ◊ Chest (Locked: Adept)
◊ Chests (2)   ◊ Potions

9 **Oily Chamber Revisited**

You soon return to [9], entering at a high balcony. Loop around the room, jumping or slipping past rows of dangerous dwarven piston traps that threaten to knock you down. Destroy a few more Dwarven Spiders on your way to the door that leads to the Animonculory.

◊ Danger! Dwarven Piston Traps

D Door to Alftand Animonculory

E Door to Alftand Glacial Ruins

12 Animonculory Entry

Raid two chests in this first passage, one of them dark and made of bone and Chaurus hide.

◇ Chests (2)

13 Connecting Corridor

First, explore this wide corridor's lower tunnel to discover the remains of another member of the dig team, along with his personal journal. Loot a locked chest before backtracking out and heading upstairs to discover another chest and some potions in the oily passage above. Avoid the pressure plates on the slope that follows — they trigger a lethal trap.

◇ Danger! Oil Pool Trap, Dwarven Thresher Trap (pressure plates)
◇ Chest

◇ Chest (Locked: Adept)
◇ Potions

14 Grand Cavern

Pull a lever to open the way into this tall chamber, then follow the first elevated walkway to its end to discover a chest and a few potions among debris. Descend the central winding ramp, and pick an Apprentice-level door to visit [15] before making a long drop down to a bloodstained platform, where the body of another excavation team member lies pierced with arrows on the rubble. Dispatch Dwarven Spiders and avoid pistons as you continue to descend the winding ramp, sprinting past a flamethrower when it momentarily deactivates to reach the door to [16].

◇ Danger! Flamethrower Trap, Dwarven Piston Traps
◇ Potions

◇ Chest (Locked: Novice)

15 Treasure Room

Unlock a gate to visit this chamber and raid a chest. Unlock an Expert-level gate here to access a second chest with even more plunder.

◇ Area Is Locked (Apprentice)
◇ Skill Book [Lockpicking]: The Locked Room [D2/10]

◇ Chests (2)
◇ Chest (Locked: Master)
◇ Potions

16 Falmer Den

Vicious Falmer have erected tents in these chambers. Slay the foul creatures, seeking to exploit oil spills when possible. Some ingredients and an alchemy workbench can be found in a corner, as well as some ingots and dwarven scrap on the shelves. The second room contains a blacksmith forge, as well as an armor workbench. Shelves to the left of the stairs can be used to sneak past the Falmer and traps here or to provide a good sniping position.

◇ Danger! Bone Alarm Trap, Flamethrower Trap, Oil Pool Trap
◇ Crafting: Alchemy Lab, Blacksmith Forge, Workbench

17 Torture Room

The Falmer have turned the tools of their dwarven captures to their own uses, and the body of yet another excavation team member lies on a torture table. If you've had enough adventuring, ride the northwest elevator back to the start of the Glacial Ruins (behind the barred-off area you found before). You can quickly return to this point later. When you're ready to delve deeper into Alftand, go through the southeast door to return to [14] and take a winding ramp down to the Grand Cavern's bottom.

◇ Crafting: Tanning Rack

14 Grand Cavern Revisited

Slaughter a host of Falmer and Frostbite Spiders at the Grand Cavern's bottom, then pass through a door and avoid a trap in the short hall that leads to the cavernous Alftand Cathedral.

◇ Danger! Falmer Claw Trap (pressure plate)

F Door to Alftand Cathedral

G Door to Alftand Animonculory

J Door to Alftand Glacial Ruins

K Door to Alftand Animonculory

Alftand Cathedral

Dodge a few pressure plates as in the cathedral's entry passage. If you're lucky, the patrolling Falmer may trigger them for you. Open a door and slay or sneak past more Falmer in the cavernous chamber. Loot three grotesque chests in and around the surrounding Falmer tents, then scale the east stone steps to find two dwarven chests, along with a lever that opens the west gate. Loot another two dwarven chests beyond the gate as you head upstairs, then defeat a mighty Dwarven Centurion to obtain a useful key. Raid one final dwarven chest at the top of the stairs before opening a gate and confronting the final two members of the expedition.

Slay the remaining expedition members while they are busy attacking each other, then either use the nearby Dwarven Mechanism to visit Blackreach [10.02], or use the key you found on the Centurion to open the nearby gate and take an elevator back up to the surface. Don't forget to take the Targe of the Blooded off of Umana's corpse. This unique shield causes bleeding damage to enemies when you bash them with it.

◇ Danger! Swinging Wall Trap (pressure plates)
◇ Unique Item: Targe of the Blooded [35/112] (Umana)
◇ Key to Alftand Lift (Dwarven Centurion)

◇ Chests (4)
◇ Chest (Locked: Novice)
◇ Chests (Locked: Apprentice) (2)

◇ Chest (Locked: Adept)
◇ Potion
◇ Loose gear

[4.14] Wayward Pass

Recommended Level: 5

Dungeon: Special

Special Objects:

Shrine of Arkay [3/12]
Loose gear

This smooth trail cuts through Winterhold's harsh central mountains, making it the easiest means of traveling between this Hold and the southern end of the Pale. As a bonus, touch the shrine located halfway through this serene pass to instantly cure any diseases you might have.

[4.15] Ironbind Barrow

Recommended Level: 6

Dungeon: Draugr Crypt

Animal
Beem-Ja
Draugr
Salma
Warlord Gathrik

Dangers

Spear Trap (pedestal)
Spear Trap (pressure plate)

Collectibles

Unique Weapon: Steel Battleaxe of Fiery Souls [24/80]

Special Objects

Word Wall: Become Ethereal [2/3]
Chest(s)
Potions
Loose gear

Near the heart of Winterhold, two adventurers stand just outside a cave. Listen to their discussion to learn that treasure lies within. Approach the pair afterward and speak to Salma. Tell her that you're "going inside" to entice her and her partner Beem-Ja to rush into the cave ahead of you, thereby acting as partners to help you clear this dangerous area. Hurry inside after them. Alternatively, just barge in and they'll do the same.

A Exit to Skyrim

1 Giant Spider's Lair

Slay a couple of Frostbite Spiders on your way to this first cavern, where a Giant Frostbite Spider lurks. Work together with Salma and Beem-Ja to bring the brute down.

2 Tomb Chamber

Stairs lead up to an ancient tomb, but the door is sealed tight. Raid a chest in the nearby east nook, then locate a handle in the west nook, which opens the tomb.

◇ Chest

3 Tomb Entry

Beware: a mighty Draugr ambushes you in the tomb's small entry chamber. Slay the fiend, then snag some nearby potions and open the chest in the west nook.

◇ Chest
◇ Potions
◇ Loose gear

4 Trapped Treasure Nook

Avoid the pressure plate on the ground before this tantalizing chest.

◇ Danger! Spear Trap (pressure plate)
◇ Chest

5 Draugr Den

Slay a vicious little Skeever on your way into this chamber, where more powerful Draugr await. Dispatch yet more deadly Draugr as you head to [6].

◇ Chest (Locked: Adept)
◇ Potions

6 Pedestal Passage

Backpedal the moment you take the item off the pedestal here — removing the loot causes spears to stab up from the surrounding ground, yet also opens the way forward. There is also a chain hidden in the ceiling arch nearby, allowing you to open the way forward without fear of pointy retribution.

◇ Danger! Spear Trap (pedestal)
◇ Loose gear

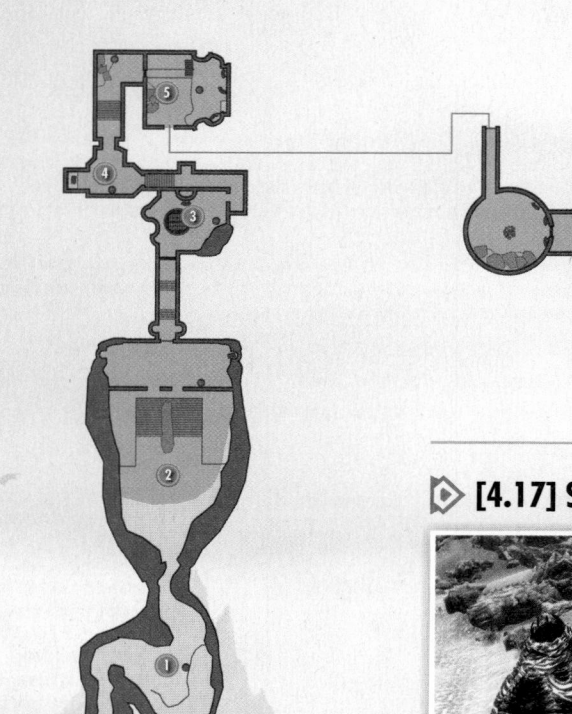

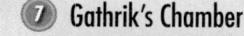

(7) Gathrik's Chamber

A mighty Draugr warlord named Gathrik awaits you in this final chamber. Once this ancient horror is dispatched, Beem-Ja will reveal his true colors and must be put down. Find a unique axe affixed to the back of the throne, and approach the far Word Wall after slaying the traitorous villain to acquire a new Word of Power. Loot a large nearby chest as well before dropping down to the lower ground and pulling a chain to open the exit passage.

◇ Unique Weapon: Steel Battleaxe of Fiery Souls [24/80]

◇ Word Wall: Become Ethereal [2/3]

◇ Chest

◇ Potions

◇ Loose gear

(B) Exit to Ironbind Overlook

(D) [4.17] Sightless Pit

Recommended Level: 18

Dungeon: Falmer Hive

Animal
Falmer

Dangers

Dwarven Thresher Trap (proximity)
Spear Trap (pressure plate)

Collectibles

Skill Book [Pickpocket]: Aevar Stone-Singer
Chest(s)

Sightless Pit

(D) [4.16] Mount Anthor

Recommended Level: 10

Dungeon: Dragon Lair

Dragon (after Main Quest: Dragon Rising)
Mage

Special Objects

Word Wall: Ice Form [3/3]

High in the heart of Winterhold's central mountains, a snow trail leads to stone steps, which in turn lead to an ancient Word Wall. You must overcome powerful mages to secure this site and acquire a new Word of Power. If a dragon has roosted here, the mages have already been dealt with; slay the Dragon to claim your prize.

Temple of Xrib

Drop into this dark hole if you dare—you'll land in a large, frozen cave, which leads to a rare Falmer temple.

(A) Exit to Skyrim

(1) Trapped Passage

Grab a Skill Book that's found near a campsite on your way to this passage, where you must sidestep a pressure plate to avoid being impaled by spears. Slay the Falmer that emerges from the hole in the wall ahead.

◇ Danger! Spear Trap (pressure plate)

◇ Skill Book [Pickpocket]: Aevar Stone-Singer

② Vertigo Chamber

Avoid vertigo as you carefully traverse this tall, disorienting chamber. Drop from one ledge or outcropping to the next to break up your descent. Slay a few Falmer and a Chaurus as you near the bottom, then carefully maneuver past the spinning blade trap by seeking shelter in the side nooks.

◇ Danger! Dwarven Thresher Trap (proximity)

③ Path to the Temple

Slay a few more Falmer in this winding passage, and don't miss looting the odd-looking chest on your way to the Temple of Xrib.

◇ Chest

B Door to Temple of Xrib

C Door to Sightless Pit

④ North Temple Grounds

Slay Falmer and Chaurus until you reach this vast cavern, where a massive temple has been built. Check in and around the Falmer tents to discover several chests.

◇ Chests (4)

⑤ Connecting Path

Take this passage to reach [6], looting a chest that rests on the railing along the way.

◇ Chest

⑥ South Temple Grounds

Battle a host of Frostbite Spiders and a powerful Falmer in this southern area, then loot the unique chest to the south. Take the east passage to an elevator that ferries you up to a small, empty cave. Simply pass through to return to the cold embrace of Skyrim.

◇ Chest

D Elevator to Abandoned Cave

[4.18] Shrine of Azura

Related Quests

Daedric Quest: The Black Star

Dungeon: Special

Aranea Ienith (Follower)

Services

Follower: Aranea Ienith [12/47]

Collectibles

Unique Item: Azura's Star [36/112]

Loose gear

This awesome statue to the goddess Azura towers high atop Winterhold's snowcapped northeast peaks. Scale the icy stone steps and speak with Aranea Ienith, who prays at the statue's base, to obtain a new Side Quest. Return here later and give Azura's Star to Aranea to speak with the goddess Azura, who asks you to enter her Star [10.01] and purge Malyn Varen's soul from the sacred object.

If you choose to complete "The Black Star" quest with Aranea's help, she'll become available as a Follower afterward.

[4.19] Fort Kastav

Related Quests

Civil War Quest: Reunification of Skyrim

Civil War Quest: Rescue from Fort Kastav

Recommended Level: 6

Habitation: Military Fort

Mage
Skeleton

Crafting

Alchemy Lab

Collectibles

Skill Book [Block]: Warrior [E2/10]

Chest(s)

Potions

Loose gear

This forboding fortress is a point of contention between the Imperials and Stormcloaks during the Civil War campaign. When not running Civil War Quests, you may instead find Fort Kastav to be populated by a variety of powerful adversaries, including dangerous cultists and fearsome mages. The fort can be infiltrated covertly via a trapdoor that lies just outside the wall to the northwest. The trapdoor leads to the prison—the fort's only interior area.

Exterior

Slay a few lowly skeletons and two mighty mages to secure the outer compound. This is the most dangerous area of the fort, so take care in how you approach the battle.

◇ Crafting: Alchemy Lab

Prison

Find a chest in the southeast corner of the prison's north entry chamber, along with a few potions. A dangerous mage lurks in the southern holding cells. There's no need to open any of the cells, unless you're simply after lockpicking practice.

◇ Chest   ◇ Potions   ◇ Loose gear

Captain's Quarters

Two chests, no enemies, and a Skill Book. What good fortune!

◇ Skill Book [Block]: Warrior [E2/10]   ◇ Chests (2)

◇ Apothecary's Satchel

[4.20] Septimus Signus's Outpost

Related Quests

Main Quest: Elder Knowledge

Daedric Quest: Discerning the Transmundane

Habitation: Special

Septimus Signus

Quest Items

Attunement Sphere

Blank Lexicon

Collectibles

Unique Item: Oghma Infinium [37/112]

This small, coastal ice cave is easy to miss — only a wooden door at the base of one of Winterhold's northern glaciers gives it away. Enter to speak with a robed man named Septimus Signus and learn about Blackreach [10.02]. Septimus also gives you a new quest, along with two important items. Complete the quest to obtain a unique item.

[4.21] Skytemple Ruins

Recommended Level: 6

Dungeon: Special

Draugr
Skeleton

Collectibles

Skill Book [Illusion]: Before the Ages of Man

Chest (Locked: Apprentice)

Potions

Loose gear

On one of Winterhold's frozen northern isles, slay skeletons as you fight your way up a snowy path that leads to some long-forgotten ruins. Pick a Novice-level door to access a small room with a large, locked chest and Skill Book — but beware the powerful Draugr that bursts from a nearby coffin to ambush you.

[4.22] Wreck of *The Pride of Tel Vos*

Recommended Level: 12

Dungeon: Shipwreck

Bandit

Crafting

Tanning Rack

Quest Items

Lymdrenn Tenvanni's Journal

Waterlogged Chest

Chests (2)

Chest (Locked: Novice)

A number of seasoned bandits have made camp near a shipwreck along Winterhold's northeast coastline. The bandits carry plenty of plunder. Raid the chest at their camp for even more loot, along with the two chests found within the wrecked ship. The journal that you find is the item that Brand-Shei in Riften has been searching for—proof of his childhood. Return it to him for a reward.

[4.23] The Serpent Stone

Related Quests
Civil War Quest: Joining the Stormcloaks

Recommended Level: 6

Dungeon: Special
Ice Wraith

Special Objects
Standing Stone: The Serpent Stone [5/13]

Brave Winterhold's icy northeast waters to discover a group of unique standing stones atop a large glacier. Slay a pesky Ice Wraith here, then examine the central Standing Stone to accept a new sign blessing. Once per day, those under the sign of the Serpent can use a ranged paralyzing poison against opponents. Note that you can have only one sign blessing at a time, so activating this Standing Stone will override your current sign blessing (if any).

[4.24] Bleakcoast Cave

Related Quests
Side Quest: Kyne's Sacred Trials

Dungeon: Animal Den
Animal
Loose gear

Descend into this relatively small ice cave, where a pair of Frost Trolls lurk. Several smaller caverns sprout from the main one. Loot the corpses of less-capable adventurers in the side caverns to the east and west, which are also guarded by Frost Trolls.

[4.25] Whistling Mine

Related Quests
Favor (Activity): Mining Ore* (Thorgar)

Recommended Level: 8

Habitation: Mine
Miners

Crafting
Smelter

Collectibles
Skill Book [Smithing]: Heavy Armor Forging
Loose gear
Mineable ore (Iron)

This small, icy cave contains raw veins of iron ore that anyone with a pickaxe is free to mine. Find a Skill Book sitting atop a barrel in the campsite cavern.

[4.26] Journeyman's Nook

Related Quests
Side Quest: The Great Skyrim Treasure Hunt*
Miscellaneous Objective: Lost Apprentices: Borvir*

Recommended Level: 6

Dungeon: Bandit Camp
Bandit

Crafting
Alchemy Lab

Collectibles
Skill Book [Alchemy]: Herbalist's Guide to Skyrim
Treasure Map II [2/11]
Unique Weapon: Borvir's Dagger [25/80]
Knapsack
Potions
Loose gear

This small igloo lies among the snowy hills north of Snow Veil Sanctum [4.28]. The warmth of a roaring fire—and a heated encounter with a bandit—await you within. You find the corpse of Borvir here, one of the missing members of the College of Winterhold and brother to the also deceased Rundi. A unique dagger lies nearby, and there's a Treasure Map in the nearby knapsack. After you've heard Phinis Gestor mention them in one of his addresses to the College, you can bring back proof of his demise. A Skill Book is also found here; it rests atop a snowy crate inside the ruin.

[4.27] Stillborn Cave

Recommended Level: 18

Dungeon: Falmer Hive
Animal
Falmer

Dangers
Swinging Wall Trap (trip wire)

Collectibles
Skill Book [Conjuration]: The Warrior's Charge
Chest(s)

This Falmer-filled cave is found in Whiterun's southern mountains, a good hike west from Snow Veil Sanctum [4.28]. No quests pertain to this particular Falmer den, but treasure and adventure await you within.

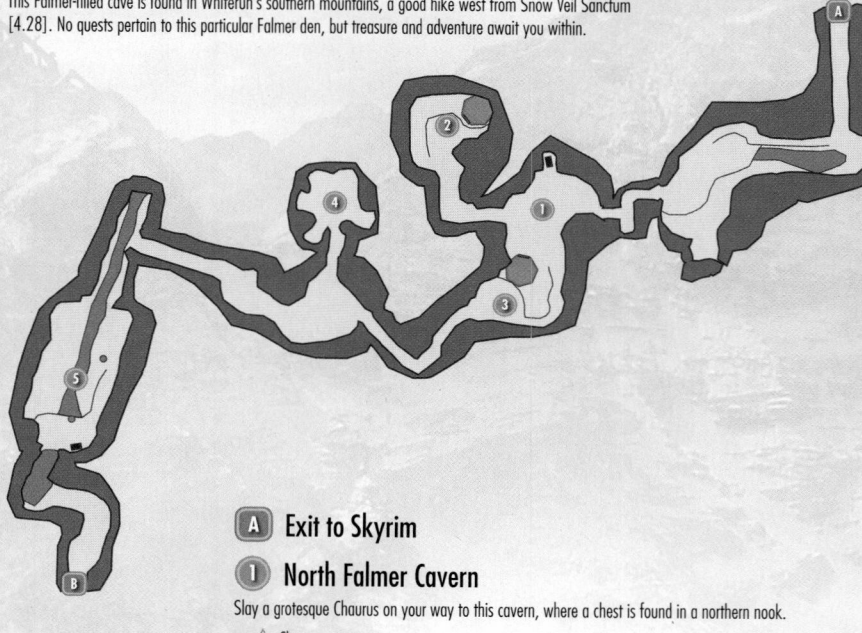

A Exit to Skyrim

1 North Falmer Cavern
Slay a grotesque Chaurus on your way to this cavern, where a chest is found in a northern nook.
◇ Chest

2 Side Cavern A
Dispatch another Chaurus and loot another chest in this small side cavern.
◇ Chest

3 South Falmer Cavern
Beware the powerful Falmer on patrol here, and the dangerous trip wire that's stretched near the tunnel that leads to [4]. After passing the trip wire, turn right and search a dark corner to discover a Skill Book that lies near a skeleton.
◇ Danger! Swinging Wall Trap (trip wire)
◇ Skill Book [Conjuration]: The Warrior's Charge

4 Falmer Nest
Falmer emerge from holes in the walls around this area. Slaughter the fiends before looting the chest they sought to guard.
◇ Chest (Locked: Novice)

5 Chaurus Lair
Cut down a few more Chaurus in this final cavern, and raid the chest that's found on the high ground.
◇ Chest

B Exit to Skyrim

The Elder Scrolls V
SKYRIM

[4.28] Snow Veil Sanctum

Related Quests

Thieves Guild Quest: Speaking With Silence

Thieves Guild Radiant Quest: Larceny Targets*

Recommended Level: 6

Dungeon: Draugr Crypt

Draugr

Dangers

Bone Alarm Trap

Bear Traps

Dart Trap (wall chain)

Oil Lamp Traps

Oil Lamp Traps (pedestal pressure plate)

Oil Lamp Traps (trip wires)

Oil Pool Traps

Swinging Wall Trap (wall chain)

Collectibles

Larceny Target: Model Ship [3/7]

Skill Book [Light Armor]: Ice and Chitin

Skill Book [Sneak]: Three Thieves [E1/10]

Special Objects

Word Wall: Disarm [3/3]

Area Is Locked (quest required)

Chest(s)

Potions

Loose gear

This frigid temple is found within Winterhold's eastern barrens, just inland from the coastline. A collection of standing stones call attention to a round stone depression dug into the earth. Descend the stairs to discover the door that leads into the Snow Veil Catacombs. You can't enter unless you're participating in Thieves Guild Quest: Speaking With Silence. Then Mercer Frey opens the door for you.

Ⓐ Exit to Skyrim

① Entry Chamber

Slay the Draugr that ambush you in this small chamber, then loot the central chest and pull a wall chain to raise a portcullis and access some potions.

◇ Chest

② Swinging Wall Trap Chamber

Pull a wall chain to open this chamber's portcullis, and immediately run toward the portcullis after pulling the chain; otherwise you'll soon be struck by a lethal trap that triggers after a slight delay.

◇ Danger! Swinging Wall Trap (wall chain)

③ Burial Passages

Sneak through these twisting passages to avoid rousing Draugr. Unlock an Adept-level iron door along the way to access a small alcove with valuable potions. Safely deactivate a few bear traps around the next corner.

◇ Danger! Bear Traps   ◇ Potions   ◇ Loose gear

④ Draugr Halls

Continue to sneak through these passages, or risk waking several more Draugr. Should the undead awaken, look to knock down hanging lamps and ignite the oily floor. Do this easily by triggering either of the two trip wires stretched across the corridor. Loot a chest here before pulling a wall chain to raise a portcullis and advance.

◇ Danger! Oil Lamp Traps (tripwires), Oil Pool Trap

◇ Chest

⑤ Treasure Nook

Unlock an iron door to access this small storage room. If you like, fire ranged attacks through the barred window to thin out the Draugr in [7].

◇ Area Is Locked (Apprentice)   ◇ Chest

⑥ Hanging Rattle Chamber

Avoid the hanging rattles in this chamber—they can alert nearby undead. Claim a valuable Skill Book and nab some potions before pulling another wall chain to advance.

◇ Danger! Bone Alarm Trap

◇ Skill Book [Sneak]: Three Thieves [E1/10]

◇ Potions

⑦ Draugr Den

A hoard of fearsome undead lurk in this large cavern. Let Mercer Frey take the lead in battle. Scale the south wooden stairs and take the southeast passage to [8] before heading up the west stone stairs to reach an elevated walkway that leads to the Snow Veil Sanctum.

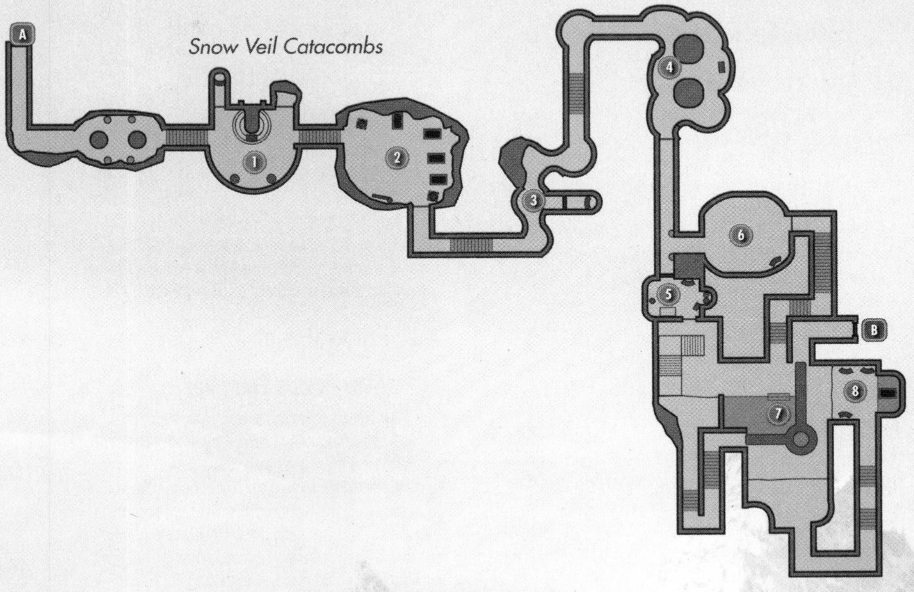

Snow Veil Catacombs

Snow Veil Sanctum

8 Model Ship Chamber

Take a southwest passage from [7] to reach this oily overlook, where a unique Model Ship sits atop a pedestal. Stand back and knock down the hanging lamps from a safe range to burn up the oil before taking the Model Ship; otherwise the lamps will fall when you take the item. Delvin will be interested in buying this unique item when you return to the Thieves Guild.

- ◇ Danger! Oil Lamp Traps (pedestal pressure plate), Oil Pool Trap
- ◇ Larceny Target: Model Ship [3/7]
- ◇ Potions
- ◇ Loose gear

B Door to Snow Veil Sanctum

C Door to Snow Veil Catacombs

9 Sanctum Entry Passage

Sneak through the Sanctum's first twisting passage, or risk stirring a legion of bloodthirsty undead. Leap over low-hanging rattles to reach a pair of chests as you go. When you reach the far portcullis, pull the nearby wall chain to raise it, then take cover from a slew of arrows that fly out from the passage beyond. This is a result of the clay jars stacked against the portcullis tumbling onto a nearby pressure plate. Quickly dart into the passage after the arrows stop flying and pull another wall chain to close the portcullis again, thereby cutting off any Draugr that might be in pursuit.

- ◇ Danger! Bone Alarm Trap, Dart Trap (pressure plate)
- ◇ Chest
- ◇ Chest (Locked: Adept)

10 Word Wall Room

Opening the door that leads into this sizable chamber knocks over several jars, rousing a slew of vicious Draugr. Inspect a book on a stone table to increase your Light Armor skill and follow the sound of chanting to locate a Word Wall that grants a new Word of Power. Scale the central stairs to raid a giant chest before pulling the wall chain near the east portcullis and advancing.

- ◇ Skill Book [Light Armor]: Ice and Chitin
- ◇ Word Wall: Disarm [3/3]
- ◇ Chest

11 Puzzle Door Passage

Don't worry that you haven't found the claw that unlocks the Nordic Puzzle Door in this hall—Mercer Frey kindly opens the door for you!

12 Inner Sanctum

The plot thickens when you enter this room, but we won't reveal any story-based spoilers here. When you're ready, proceed through the far door to quickly exit out to Skyrim.

D Exit to Skyrim

[4.29] Winterhold Stormcloaks Camp

Related Quests

Civil War Quest (when active, depending on who you side with)

Habitation: Military: Stormcloak Camp

Stormcloak Quartermaster (Blacksmith)
Stormcloak Soldier

Services

Trader (Blacksmith): Stormcloak Quartermaster [10/33]
Weapons, Apparel, Misc

Crafting

Alchemy Lab
Anvil
Grindstone
Workbench

Special Objects

Civil War: Map of Skyrim
Shrine of Arkay [4/12]
Chests (2)
Potions
Loose gear

The Stormcloaks have set up camp here—though this encampment may appear only during the Civil War quest line. Trade with the quartermaster and exploit his array of crafting stations. Inspect the large map in one tent to potentially gain new map data. Loot a few chests before moving on.

[4.30] Yngol Barrow

Yngol's Barrow lies hidden within an ice cave at Winterhold's southeast corner. This place is haunted by spectres of old and is scarcely remembered as the namesake of the Sea of Ghosts.

A Exit to Skyrim

1 Pillar Puzzle Chamber

Loot a few Draugr corpses on the way to this first chamber, then inspect the dead scholar's remains to discover a book that provides a clue on how to solve the room's puzzle. Spin the glyph pillars to create the pattern described in the scholar's book. The lone south pillar should be a Whale, while the other two north pillars should be a Snake and a Hawk; then pull the central lever to open the way forward. Collect the Coral Dragon Claw from a pedestal just beyond the gate, unless you've already acquired it from Winterhold.

- ◇ Dragon Claw: Coral Dragon Claw [4/10]

2 Watery Passage

Take a dip in the frigid water here to locate a sunken chest and burial urn.

- ◇ Chest

Related Quests

Dungeon Quest: Ashore in a Sea of Ghosts*

Recommended Level: 6

Dungeon: Draugr Crypt

Draugr

Dangers

Swinging Wall Trap (pressure plate)

Puzzles

Nordic Puzzle Door (Coral Dragon Claw)
Nordic Pillars

Collectibles

Dragon Claw: Coral Dragon Claw [4/10]
Unique Item: Helm of Yngol [38/112]
Chest(s)
Loose gear

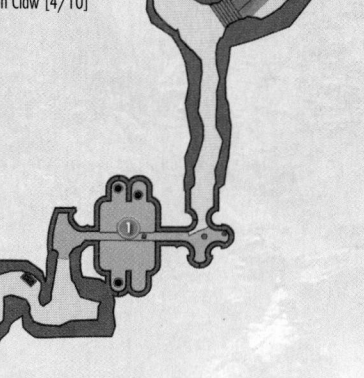

3 Treasure Nook

Unlock a metal gate here to access a nook full of goodies.

- ◇ Area Is Locked (Adept)
- ◇ Chest
- ◇ Loose gear

4 Nordic Puzzle Door

Jump the pressure plate in a narrow tunnel and loot a chest on your way to this unusual door. Examine the Coral Dragon Claw and notice the sequence of glyphs etched into the piece. Rotate the door's rings to imitate the claw's pattern (Snake, Wolf, Moth), then insert the claw into the door's central keyhole to open the way forward.

- ◇ Danger! Swinging Wall Trap (pressure plate)
- ◇ Chest

5 Draugr Chamber

Put to rest the ancient Shade of Yngol just beyond the puzzle door, then loot a large chest and retrieve Yngol's Helm from the throne nearby, raising the portcullis and allowing a quick exit from the ruin.

- ◇ Chest
- ◇ Unique Item: Helm of Yngol [38/112]

B Exit to Skyrim

[4.31] Wreck of the Winter War

Recommended Level: 6

Dungeon: Shipwreck

Bandits

Collectibles

Skill Book [Lockpicking]: Surfeit of Thieves [C1/10]

Chest (Locked: Expert)

An old ship named the *Winter War* has crashed among the unyielding glaciers of Winterhold's eastern coast. A crew of salty bandits have made this shipwreck their home. Kill them all, then locate a locked chest within the ship and collect the nearby Skill Book.

SECONDARY LOCATIONS

[4.A] Shrine of Dibella: Watching Dawnstar

Visible from the main road heading south away from Dawnstar in the Pale, this rocky abutment has a carved platform upon which the writhing and sensual form of Dibella is visible. This shrine marks the edge of this Hold. Upon the Shrine is a Skill Book.

◇ Skill Book [Illusion]: Incident at Necrom

◇ Shrine of Dibella [2/8]

[4.B] Hunter's Overlook: Fellhammer Wastes

North and a little west of Fort Fellhammer, around the steep mountain crags, is a small campfire with two hunters on an exposed overlook above the Shrine of Dibella. This offers excellent views of Dawnstar and the Nightcaller Temple.

◇ Crafting: Tanning Rack

[4.C] Wolf Den: Fellhammer Wastes

On the forested floor below the windswept snow flurries just northwest of Fort Fellhammer is a rocky alcove where wolves prowl. Defeat the wild animals guarding this den, and inspect the bandit corpse within. There's little else but fallen prey and bones here.

[4.D] Yisra's Beachside Combustion

Related Quests

Miscellaneous Objective: Lost Apprentices: Yisra*

South of the island on which Yngvild is located is a section of blasted beach. It appears a College apprentice named Yisra has misfired her Flame Cloak. This is one of the missing Apprentices that Phinis Gestor of the College of Winterhold is looking for. Listen to him talk about this, then bring back proof of Yisra's demise; search her crispy corpse for a necklace.

◇ Unique Item: Yisra's Necklace [39/112]

◇ Spell Tome: Flame Cloak

[4.E] The Iceberg Explorer

Just north of the Tower Stone but only safely accessible by clambering up from the north, a half-buried skeleton lies encased in this iceberg, just off the coast of the Sea of Ghosts. The flag the long-dead explorer was carrying still flutters near a Chest and Skill Book.

◇ Skill Book [Heavy Armor]: The Knights of the Nine

◇ Chest

[4.F] Shrine of Talos: Winterhold Glaciers

Half buried in the snow that blasts up the glacial valleys is a Shrine to Talos. A small number of offerings (mainly equipment) is left here. Follow the ground, heading east from Hob's Fall Cave, along the coast.

◇ Skill Book [Two-Handed]: Words and Philosophy

◇ Shrine of Talos [3/17]

◇ Loose gear

[4.G] Frozen Mammoth

Encased in ice, too cold to rot, are the remains of an ancient frozen mammoth. Adventurers have used this frozen beast as target practice, enabling you to collect a few arrows and weapons. More mammoth bones are on top of this glacier.

◇ Loose gear

[4.H] Wet Bones

On top of the glacier, just west of Saarthal, is an easily overlooked cluster of rocks near half-buried skeletons (human and deer). They lie next to a dwarven chest. Expect a choice item or two from it.

◇ Chest

[4.I] Dwarven Monument: Mount Anthor Summit

At the top of Mount Anthor (accessed via some treacherous climbing from Mount Anthor [4.16]) is a small dwarven monument. Little is known about this. Beware of Ice Wraiths guarding the spectacular view south.

◇ Chest (2)

◇ Mineable ore (Quicksilver)

▷ [4.J] Shrine of Talos: Sea of Ghosts

Facing the Frostflow Lighthouse in the distance is a large statue of Talos, with the snake intertwined by his feet. Climb the small rock and ice island the statue stands on for a blessing and the following items:

◇ Skill Book [One-Handed]: The Importance of Where
◇ Shrine of Talos [4/17]
◇ Apothecary's Satchel
◇ Loose gear

▷ [4.K] Shrine of Talos: Ilas-Tei's Last Stand

Related Quests

Miscellaneous Objective: Lost Apprentices: Ilas-tei*

On the tidal ground north of Ysgramor's Tomb is an old Shrine to Talos, along with a cage of Skeevers. These have recently been freed and have savaged an Argonian named Ilas-Tei. This is one of the missing Apprentices that Phinis Gestor of the College of Winterhold is looking for. Listen to him talk about this, then bring back proof of Ilas-Tel's demise. Scrabble around for some scrolls and a Skill Book on the cage crates.

◇ Skill Book [Alteration]: Breathing Water
◇ Unique Item: Ilas-Tei's Ring [40/112] (Ilas-Tei)
◇ Shrine of Talos [5/17]
◇ Apothecary's Satchel
◇ Loose gear

▷ [4.L] Altar of Xrib

Perched atop Sightless Pit is an ancient sacrificial altar, with piles of bones indicating how well used this location once was. Among the bones are a Skill Book and various offerings. But disturb them at your peril; touching anything here will awaken the skeleton on the altar and will resurrect two more from the pile of bones behind you for a surprise ambush.

◇ Skill Book [Conjuration]: The Doors of Oblivion
◇ Loose gear

▷ [4.M] The Chill

The Soldiers of Winterhold have found a novel way of imprisoning ne'er-do-wells now that their town is in ruins: They cage them inside a glacial island northwest of Septimus Signus's Outpost. The cages are locked (Adept), but check the top of the glacier for a gold deposit. If you're jailed here, this location is guarded by Frost Atronachs.

◇ Mineable ore (Gold)

▷ [4.N] Trapped for Eternity

Between the glacier pathways, approaching the seashore almost due east of Winterhold, are two brittle skeletons, both long dead. A triggered Bear Trap is the clue to how they came to rest here forever.

◇ Apothecary's Satchel

▷ [4.O] Rundi's Mistake

Related Quests

Miscellaneous Objective: Lost Apprentices: Rundi*

Atop a glacier (approach it from the west to climb onto it) is a summoning circle with three Runic traps that explode with frost damage as you step near them. The body of a mage named Rundi is here, close to some offerings, a unique dagger, and a Skill Book. This is one of the missing Apprentices that Phinis Gestor of the College of Winterhold is looking for. Listen to him talk about this, then bring back proof of Rundi's demise.

◇ Danger! Rune Trap (Frost)
◇ Skill Book [Alchemy]: Mannimarco, King of Worms
◇ Unique Weapon: Rundi's Dagger [26/80]

▷ [4.P] Hunter's Camp: Glacier's Edge

A small, two-tent camp with an unlit fire sit on the edge of the glacier. Aside from offering impressive views of the College of Winterhold to the northwest, there's a locked strongbox and skeleton to sort through.

◇ Strongbox (Adept)

▷ [4.Q] Haul of the Horkers

Down on the ground close to the windswept beach, in the glacial canyon, are two vicious Horkers. They valiantly guard a bloodied pile of bones, close to a locked chest.

◇ Chest (Locked: Novice)

▷ [4.R] Hunters' Camp: Sea Shore of Ghosts

While their horse waits patiently for them to return, two hunters have departed their camp in search for Horkers. They've already hauled in one and cut it up for meat and tusks. Search the campsite for the following (you can ride the horse without penalty).

◇ Skill Book [Light Armor]: Rislav the Righteous
◇ Horse
◇ Knapsack

[4.S] Hunter's Last Stand: Sea Shore of Ghosts

Side Quest: The Great Skyrim Treasure Hunt*

The hunters from the camp close to the shore have felled their final Horker; they both lie dead, run through by more Horkers than they could cope with. Kill any remaining Horkers, and search the hunters' corpse; there's some equipment and a Treasure Map to find.

◇ Treasure Map VIII [3/11]
◇ Loose gear

[4.T] Ill-Gotten Gains: Sea Shore of Ghosts

In the glacial field just east of Snow Veil Sanctum is a shallow fissure with a dead Horker and usually a Wild Animal guarding a couple of crates and a locked treasure chest. Pry open the chest to see what long-dead smugglers have left you.

◇ Chest (Adept)

[4.U] Fisherman's Camp: Slaughterfish Bay

Northwest of the Wreck of the Winter War, on the muddy shore just before the glacial line, is a small fisherman's camp. Aside from chopping wood, you can take whatever mead remains in this deserted camp, and flip through the Fisherman's Journal for a clue as to what happened here. The fish certainly are biting; the waters just offshore are teeming with Slaughterfish. If you can survive the onslaught, swim out to the overturned fishing boat and search for a knapsack and other loose gear.

◇ Fisherman's Journal
◇ Knapsack
◇ Loose Gear

[4.V] Avalanche Pass

In a high mountain pass between Mount Anthor and Snow Veil Sanctum, a caravan of refugees and their cart have been wiped out by an avalanche. Pick through the debris for any loose loot before moving on. If you've entered this pass from the eastern side, be careful, or you might face the same fate....

◇ Loose Gear

[4.W] Shrine of Arkay: Windhelm Hills

On the snowbanks above Windhelm, close to where the Stormcloaks base their Winterhold camp during the Civil War, is a Shrine to Arkay, usually guarded by a Wispmother. Approach the altar through the standing stones and receive a blessing if you wish.

◇ Shrine of Arkay [4/12]

HOLD 5: THE REACH

TOPOGRAPHICAL OVERVIEW

Over 600 years ago, historians described the Reach as the most cosmopolitan of Skyrim's Holds. Others stated "the Reach could be mistaken for one of the petty kingdoms of High Rock; it is full of Bretons, Redguards, Cyrodiils, elves of all stripes, and even a few misplaced Khajiit." Topographically, it takes up the entire western edge of Skyrim and is arguably the most difficult to traverse and easiest to lose your way in. The towering crags, the sheer number of locations, and the ferociousness of its Forsworn inhabitants (friendly hamlets are few and far between) mean that many fail to stop and marvel at the Hold's rugged beauty and numerous ruins.

 ### Routes and Pathways

The Druadach Mountains rise to the west of this Hold, cradling Markarth and other settlements within its peaks, crags, and foothills. The Karth River and its tributaries are the waterways you can track as you familiarize yourself with the geography; pause every so often to explore the bisecting pathways from the main road, which loops in from Whiterun Hold to the east and circles back again. Then rejoin the road, until you can muster the stomach to venture into the scrubland and rocky ravines, ready to stumble upon a Forsworn camp...or worse! Karthwasten and Old Hroldan provide some degree of safety, and the Blades hideout known as Sky Haven Temple is another beacon of tranquility surrounded by hard terrain and harder adversaries. Fort Sungard and Broken Tower Redoubt are both fortifications to explore, and two Orc Strongholds (Mor Khazgur and Dushnikh Yal) are also here for you to find. To the northeast is Hjaalmarch, but the majority of the Reach borders Whiterun; once you step into the flat Tundra plains, you know you've left the Reach.

AVAILABLE SERVICES, CRAFTING, AND COLLECTIBLES

Services

Followers: [7/47]
Houses for Sale: [1/5]
Marriage Prospects: [16/62]
Skill Trainers: [6/50]
  Alchemy: [0/3]
  Alteration: [0/3]
  Archery: [0/3]
  Block: [1/2]
  Conjuration: [0/3]
  Destruction: [0/3]
  Enchanting: [0/2]
  Heavy Armor: [1/3]
  Illusion: [0/2]
  Light Armor: [0/3]
  Lockpicking: [0/2]
  One-Handed: [1/3]
  Pickpocket: [0/3]
  Restoration: [0/3]

Smithing: [1/3]
Sneak: [1/3]
Speech: [1/4]
Two-Handed: [0/2]
Traders [19/133]:
  Apothecary [3/12]
  Bartender [0/5]
  Blacksmith [5/33]
  Carriage Driver [1/5]
  Fence [2/10]
  Fletcher [0/3]
  Food Vendor [1/9]
  General Goods [1/19]
  Innkeeper [2/15]
  Jeweler [1/3]
  Special [1/3]
  Spell Vendor [1/12]
  Stablemaster [1/5]

Collectibles

Captured Critters: [1/5]
Dragon Claws: [1/10]
Dragon Priest Masks: [2/10]
Larceny Targets: [1/7]
Skill Books: [24/180]
  Alchemy: [1/10]
  Alteration: [2/10]
  Archery: [0/10]
  Block: [1/10]
  Conjuration: [2/10]
  Destruction: [0/10]
  Enchanting: [0/10]
  Heavy Armor: [2/10]

Illusion: [2/10]
Light Armor: [3/10]
Lockpicking: [1/10]
One-Handed: [1/10]
Pickpocket: [1/10]
Restoration: [1/10]
Smithing: [2/10]
Sneak: [1/10]
Speech: [2/10]
Two-Handed: [2/10]
Treasure Maps: [0/11]
Unique Items: [17/112]
Unique Weapons: [12/80]
Unusual Gems: [3/24]

Special Objects

Shrines: [12/69]
  Akatosh: [1/6]
  Arkay: [2/12]
  Dibella: [3/8]
  Julianos: [1/5]
  Kynareth: [1/6]
  Mara: [1/5]
  Stendarr: [0/5]
  Talos: [2/17]
  Zenithar: [1/5]
Standing Stones: [1/13]
  The Lover Stone
Word Walls: [6/42]
  Animal Allegiance: [0/3]
  Aura Whisper: [1/3]
  Become Ethereal: [1/3]
  Disarm: [0/3]
  Dismaying Shout: [1/3]
  Elemental Fury: [1/3]
  Fire Breath: [0/2]
  Frost Breath: [0/3]
  Ice Form: [0/3]
  Kyne's Peace: [1/3]
  Marked for Death: [0/3]
  Slow Time: [1/3]
  Storm Call: [0/3]
  Throw Voice: [0/1]
  Unrelenting Force: [0/1]
  Whirlwind Sprint: [0/2]

CRAFTING STATIONS: THE REACH

✓	TYPE	LOCATION A	LOCATION B
	Alchemy Lab	Markarth (Understone Keep - Calcelmo's Work Area) [5.00]	Dushnikh Yal (Exterior) [5.38]
	Arcane Enchanter	Markarth (Understone Keep - Calcelmo's Work Area) [5.00]	—
	Anvil or Blacksmith Forge	Markarth (Understone Keep - Forge) [5.00]	Dushnikh Yal (Exterior) [5.38]
	Cooking Pot and Spit	Markarth (Understone Keep - Kitchens) [5.00]	Markarth (Silver-Blood Inn) [5.00]
	Grindstone	Markarth (City Gates) [5.00]	Dushnikh Yal (Exterior) [5.38]
	Smelter	Markarth (Smelter and Smelter Overseer's House) [5.00]	Dushnikh Yal (Exterior) [5.38]
	Tanning Rack	Markarth (Understone Keep - Forge) [5.00]	Dushnikh Yal (Exterior) [5.38]
	Wood Chopping Block	Old Hroldan (Exterior) [5.34]	—
	Workbench	Markarth (Understone Keep - Forge) [5.00]	Dushnikh Yal (Exterior) [5.38]

Hold 5: The Reach

Markarth

Understone Keep

N

Total — 49: Hold Capital, Understone Keep, and 47 Hold Locations

[5.00] Hold Capital City: Markarth
[5.00] Understone Keep
   Jarl: Igmund
[5.01] Mor Khazgur
[5.02] Deepwood Redoubt
[5.03] Hag's End
[5.04] Deep Folk Crossing
[5.05] Bruca's Leap Redoubt
[5.06] Bthardamz
[5.07] Druadach Redoubt
[5.08] Dragontooth Crater
[5.09] Harmugstahl
[5.10] Reach Stormcloak Camp
[5.11] Liar's Retreat
[5.12] Cliffside Retreat
[5.13] Dragon Bridge Overlook

[5.14] Ragnvald
[5.15] Reach Imperial Camp
[5.16] Shrine of Peryite
[5.17] Karthwasten
[5.18] Broken Tower Redoubt
[5.19] Markarth Stables
[5.20] Salvius Farm
[5.21] Left Hand Mine
[5.22] Kolskeggr Mine
[5.23] The Lover Stone
[5.24] Blind Cliff Cave
[5.25] Four Skull Lookout
[5.26] Red Eagle Redoubt
[5.27] Sundered Towers
[5.28] Rebel's Cairn
[5.29] Karthspire Camp
[5.30] Karthspire

[5.31] Sky Haven Temple
[5.32] Soljund's Sinkhole
[5.33] Bleakwind Bluff
[5.34] Old Hroldan
[5.35] Hag Rock Redoubt
[5.36] Dead Crone Rock
[5.37] Purewater Run
[5.38] Dushnikh Yal
[5.39] Reachwater Rock
[5.40] Reachwind Eyrie
[5.41] Reachcliff Cave
[5.42] Valthume
[5.43] Gloomreach
[5.44] Lost Valley Redoubt
[5.45] Bard's Leap Summit
[5.46] Cradle Stone Tower
[5.47] Fort Sungard

Total — 28 Points of Interest

[5.A] Dwarven Rubble: Druadach
[5.B] Dragon Mound: Reachward Pass
[5.C] Dwarven Arch: Harmugstahl Falls
[5.D] The Incautious Bather
[5.E] A Bandit's Book
[5.F] Dwarven Rubble: Karth River Confluence
[5.G] Forsworn Camp: Bthardamz Outskirts
[5.H] The Bloodied Bandit
[5.I] Dragon Mound: Ragnvald Vale
[5.J] Dwarven Ruins: Lair of the Wispmother
[5.K] Sabre Cat Ravine
[5.L] Totem to the Dragon
[5.M] The Exposed Miner
[5.N] Hagraven Camp: Ragnvald Scree

[5.O] Dwarven Rubble: Salvius Farm Trail
[5.P] Shrine of Zenithar: Four Skull Lookout
[5.Q] Brush Strongbox: Riverside
[5.R] Lost Treasure: Purewater Run
[5.S] Forsworn Camp: Reachwater River
[5.T] Dragon Mound: Karthspire Bluffs
[5.U] Reachman's Altar: Red Eagle Redoubt
[5.V] Lovers' Camp
[5.W] River Rapids Treasure Chest
[5.X] Reachwind Burial Mound
[5.Y] Forsworn Camp: Gloomreach Pathway
[5.Z] Shrine of Dibella: Bridge at Old Hroldan
[5.AA] Juniper Tree Ruins
[5.AB] Cradle Stong Crag

HOLD CAPITAL: MARKARTH

Habitation: Hold Capital (Major)

Crafting

Alchemy Labs (3)
Anvils (2)
Arcane Enchanters (3)
Blacksmith Forges (2)

Grindstones (2)
Smelter
Tanning Racks (2)
Workbenches (4)

Trainer (Sneak: Expert): Garvey [1/3]
Trainer (Speech: Expert): Ogmund the Skald [2/4]

Special Objects

Business Ledgers
Civil War: Map of Skyrim
Shrine of Arkay [5/12]
Shrine of Dibella [3/8]
Shrine of Talos [6/17]

Related Quests

Civil War Quest: Liberation of Skyrim
Civil War Quest: Compelling Tribute
Daedric Quest: The House of Horrors
Daedric Quest: Prelude: Hunger in the Hall*
Daedric Quest: The Taste of Death
Daedric Quest: A Night to Remember
Side Quest: The Forsworn Conspiracy
Side Quest: No One Escapes Cidhna Mine
Temple Quest: The Heart of Dibella
Temple Quest: The Book of Love
Dark Brotherhood Quest: Sentenced to Death
Dark Brotherhood Quest: Breaching Security
Dark Brotherhood Quest: Recipe for Disaster
Thieves Guild Quest: Hard Answers
Thieves Guild Radiant Quest: No Stone Unturned (x2)
Thieves Guild Radiant Quest: Larceny Targets*
Thieves Guild City Influence Quest: Silver Lining
Dungeon Quest: The Lost Expedition
Dungeon Activity (Understone Keep)

Dungeon Activity (Abandoned House)
Miscellaneous Objective: Innkeeper Rumors (Silver-Blood Inn)
Miscellaneous Objective: Calcelmo's Ring* (Kerah)
Miscellaneous Objective: Dibella's Shrine* (Lisbet)
Miscellaneous Objective: The Steward's Potion* (Bothela)
Miscellaneous Objective: The Last Scabbard* (Ghorza gra-Bagol)
Miscellaneous Objective: Triumph Over Talos* (Ondolemar)
Miscellaneous Objective: The Heart of the Matter* (Moth gro-Bagol)
Miscellaneous Objective: Neutralizing Nimhe* (Calcelmo)
Favor (Activity): A Drunk's Drink* (Cosnach)
Favor (Activity): A Drunk's Drink* (Degaine)
Favor (Activity): The Gift of Charity* (Degaine)
Favor: A Good Talking To* (Omluag)
Favor: Sparring Partners* (Cosnach)
Favor: Jobs for the Jarls* (Jarl Igmund: 1)
Favor: Jobs for the Jarls* (Jarl Igmund: 2)
Thane Quest: Thane of The Reach*

Services

Follower: Cosnach [13/47]
Follower: Vorstag [14/47]
Follower: Argis the Bulwark [15/47]
House for Sale: Vlindrel Hall [2/5]
Marriage Prospect: Cosnach [10/62]
Marriage Prospect: Vorstag [11/62]
Marriage Prospect: Argis the Bulwark [12/62]
Marriage Prospect: Anwen [13/62]
Marriage Prospect: Orla [14/62]
Marriage Prospect: Senna [15/62]
Marriage Prospect: Omluag [16/62]
Marriage Prospect: Muiri [17/62]
Marriage Prospect: Ghorza gra-Bagol [18/62]
Marriage Prospect: Moth gro-Bagol [19/62]
Trader (Apothecary): Bothela [4/12]
Trader (Blacksmith): Ghorza [11/33]
Trader (Blacksmith): Mot gro-Bagol [12/33]
Trader (Fence): Endon [3/10]
Trader (Food Vendor): Hogni Red-Arm [4/9]
Trader (General Store Vendor): Lisbet [5/19]

Trader (Innkeeper): Kleppr [6/15]
Trader (Jeweler): Kerah [1/2]
Trader (Spell Vendor): Calcelmo [9/12]
Trainer (Enchanting: Master): Hamal [2/2]
Trainer (Smithing: Journeyman): Ghorza [1/3]
Trainer (Sneak: Expert): Garvey [1/3]
Trainer (Speech: Expert): Ogmund the Skald [2/4]
Trader (Alchemy Vendor): Bothela [5/14]
Trader (Alchemy Vendor): Muiri [6/14]
Trader (Fence): Endon [3/4]
Trader (General Store Vendor): Kerah [5/25]
Trader (General Store Vendor): Hogni Red-Arm [6/25]
Trader (General Store Vendor): Lisbet [7/25]
Trader (Innkeeper): Kleppr [6/18]
Trader (Innkeeper): Keerava [7/18]
Trader (Weapons/Armor Vendor): Moth gro-Bagol [13/35]
Trainer (Enchanting: Master): Hamal [2/2]
Trainer (Smithing: Journeyman): Ghorza [1/3]

Collectibles

Larceny Target: Dwemer Puzzle Cube [4/7]
Skill Book [Alchemy]: Herbalist's Guide to Skyrim [C1/10]
Skill Book [Alteration]: Daughter of the Niben [B1/10]
Skill Book [Alteration]: Sithis [D1/10]
Skill Book [Conjuration]: The Warrior's Charge [E1/10]
Skill Book [Heavy Armor]: Chimarvamidium [B1/10]
Skill Book [Illusion]: 2920, Sun's Dawn, v2 [A1/10]
Skill Book [Illusion]: Mystery of Talara, Part 4 [D1/10]
Skill Book [Light Armor]: Ice and Chitin [A1/10]
Skill Book [Lockpicking]: Proper Lock Design [B1/10]
Skill Book [One-Handed]: The Importance of Where [E1/10]
Skill Book [Restoration]: 2920, Rain's Hand, v4 [A2/10]
Skill Book [Speech]: A Dance in Fire, v7 [C1/10]
Unique Item: Calcelmo's Ring [41/112]
Unique Item: Armor of the Old Gods [42/112]

Unique Item: Boots of the Old Gods [43/112]
Unique Item: Gauntlets of the Old Gods [44/112]
Unique Item: Helmet of the Old Gods [45/112]
Unique Item: Silver-Blood Family Ring [46/112]
Unique Item: Muiri's Ring [47/112]
Unique Item: Ogmund's Amulet of Talos [48/112]
Unique Item: Raerek's Inscribed Amulet of Talos [49/112]
Unique Weapon: Rusty Mace [50/80]
Unique Weapon: Mace of Molag Bal [28/80]
Unique Weapon: Shiv [29/80]
Unique Weapon: Spider Control Rod [30/80]
Unusual Gem: [8/24]
Unusual Gem: [9/24]
Chest(s)
Potions aplenty
Loose gear

Lore: City Overview

"Markarth is an epic canyon city built eons ago by dwarven stonewrights in the Druadach Mountains. It is a defensive fortification constructed around the underground city of Nchuand-Zel. Primitive Reachmen were the first to repopulate the sprawling city after the dwarves' disappearance. Hundreds of years later, Markarth is in a state of turmoil stemming from what some historians (and Nord nationalists) call "the Markarth Incident."

In 4E 174, at the height of the Great War, a tribe of native Reachmen called the Forsworn took advantage of the Empire's desperate straits by launching an open rebellion, wresting control of Markarth and declaring their independence from Skyrim. This was seen as a stab in the back by both the Empire and more radical Nord elements, but the Forsworn were left unchallenged for a time.

Two years later, in a short but very bloody war, Nord irregulars invaded the Reach and drove the Forsworn from Markarth. The Nords were led by the most vociferous adherents to Talos (whose worship had been outlawed by the terms of the White-Gold Concordat that ended the Great War), who claimed that they had been promised freedom of worship within the Reach in return for their help in retaking the Hold. While true, this secret agreement violated the terms of the treaty. Shortly thereafter, the Thalmor ambassador arrived in the Imperial City to confront the Emperor. Faced with the threat of a second war, the Emperor was forced to send the Imperial Legion to back the Thalmor Justiciars. The Nords refused to back down, and many were arrested or imprisoned. The Markarth Incident was a large step toward the eventual Civil War.

Aside from conflict and power struggles, Markarth is the center of silver mining in Skyrim. The city is a contrast between the beauty of its architecture, based on its dwarven heritage and the wealth of its silver mines, and the squalor and grime of the mining operation. Markarth simmers with tension between the ruling Nords and the native Reachmen who work the mines. Meanwhile, the surviving Forsworn hide in the hills, terrorizing the Reach and waiting for an opportunity to strike.

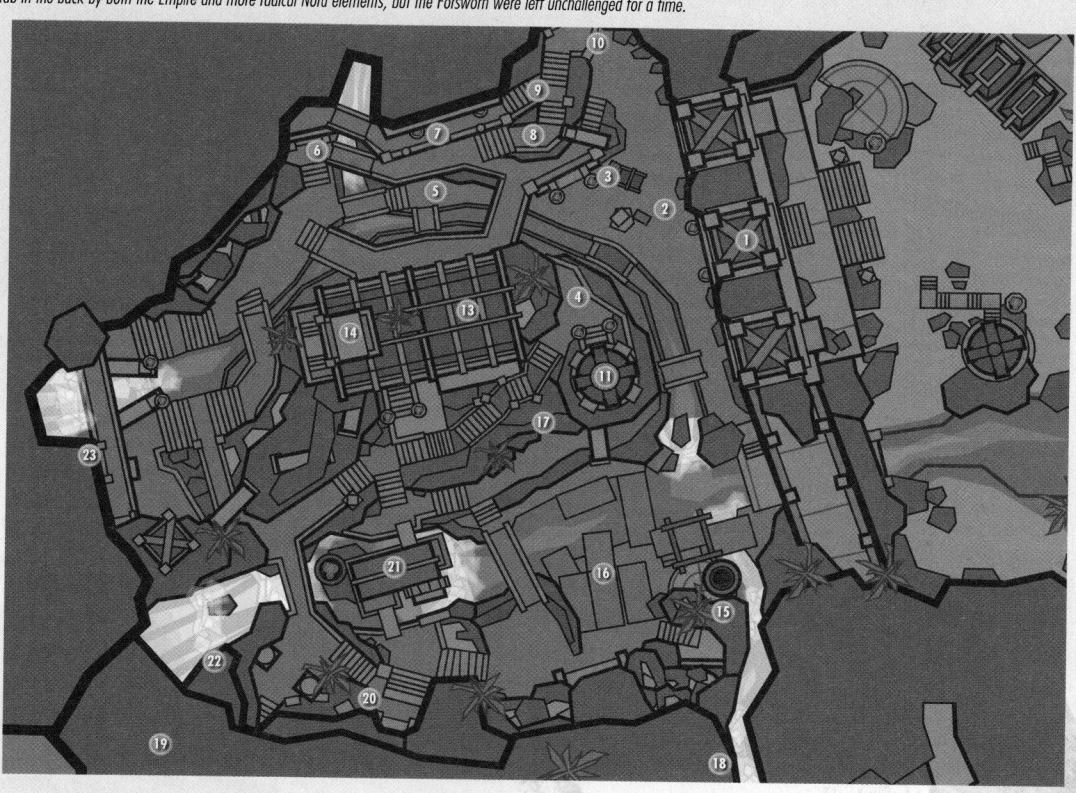

Important Areas of Interest

① City Gates

The only way to enter Markarth (until you've visited Understone Keep and can Fast-Travel there) is to step through the giant dwarven doors. However, you can use the rocks to the north or the river to the south, and sneak into the guardhouse from either of these side entrances. There are some covered battlements from which the guards look out across the Reach and two watchtowers, one of which forms the side of the stables.

◇ Crafting: Workbench   ◇ Loose gear

Highside

Located on the spur's north side, behind and above the market, Highside is where the most prominent members of the city (besides the Jarl and his advisors) live and work, mingling with the lower classes who stagger around the canal streets during let-out time at the Silver-Blood Inn.

② Marketplace

Endon   Adara
Kerah   Hogni Red-Arm

An open-air market near the city gate, the Marketplace is where you'll watch a brazen Forsworn named Weylin attack one of the street traders (Margaret), meet Eltrys, and begin Side Quest: The Forsworn Conspiracy. One of the stalls has several necklaces to steal. Search Margaret's corpse for the key to her room inside the Silver-Blood Inn.

◇ Trader (Jeweler): Kerah [1/2]

◇ Trader (Food Vendor): Hogni Red-Arm [4/9]

◇ Unique Item: Calcelmo's Ring [41/112]

◇ Key to Margaret's Room

◇ Loose gear

③ Arnleif and Sons Trading Company

Lisbet   Imedhnain   Cosnach

Another of the ancient Markarth trading houses, this dwelling adjacent to the market functions as the general store for Markarth. Currently run by the widow Lisbet, the trading company has fallen on hard times due to the Forsworn situation.

◇ Follower: Cosnach [13/47]

◇ Marriage Prospect: Cosnach [10/62]

◇ Trader (General Store Vendor): Lisbet [5/19]

◇ Skill Book [Speech]: A Dance in Fire, v7 [C1/10]

◇ Business Ledger

◇ Strongbox [Adept]

◇ Chest

④ Silver-Blood Inn

Kleppr	Hroki and Hreinn
Frabbi	Ogmund

The Silver-Blood Inn is a relatively successful establishment considering the problems Markarth is facing and is perhaps the most welcoming of Markarth's social dwellings. It is comprised of a central bar and roaring fire, with rentable rooms on either side. Hire Vorstag to aid you in your adventures here, learn eloquence from Ogmund, and beckon Kleppr to ask him for the latest rumor around town and beyond. His wife, Frabbi, is a little more crabby. Search the rooms for loose gear, a few coins, and books. Continue Side Quest: The Forsworn Conspiracy by searching the only rented room that is locked (Adept), which belonged to the deceased Margaret. There's a journal in the end table that helps your progress.

◊ Follower: Vorstag [14/47]
◊ Marriage Prospect: Vorstag [11/62]
◊ Trader (Innkeeper): Kleppr [5/15]
  ○ Room for the night, food
◊ Trainer (Speech: Expert): Ogmund the Skald [2/4]
◊ Margaret's Journal
◊ Business Ledger
◊ Strongbox (Apprentice)
◊ Loose gear

⑤ Abandoned House
(Locked: Requires Key)

Vigilant Tyranus

This dwelling is currently empty. It was the scene of a gruesome murder, and there's rumors of it being haunted. In order to explore this location and the passageways that run deep into the long-forgotten and unspeakable chambers, Daedric Quest: House of Horrors must be active.

◊ Unique Weapon: Rusty Mace [27/80]
◊ Unique Weapon: Mace of Molag Bal [28/80]
◊ Chest (2)
◊ Potions
◊ Loose gear

⑥ The Treasury House

Thonar Silver-Blood	Rhiada
Betrid	Ildene and Donnel

This is an impressive building befitting one of Markarth's most important families, who take charge of the Reach should it fall into Stormcloaks hands (Thongvor will move to Understone Keep with Reburrus and Yngvar, while Thonar, Betrid, Kolgrim, and the servants will remain in Treasury House). This family mansion of the Silver-Blood clan is the most elaborate dwelling in Markarth and also functions as a bank. It is where a frightening Forsworn insurrection is mounted during Side Quest: The Forsworn Conspiracy. Inside, a Skill Book rests on a stone shelf at the foot of the stairs. Behind the counter is a locked gate (Expert), behind which are some ingots and a safe. The rooms to the southeast are where the servants sleep. The locked door (Apprentice) to the northwest leads to Thonar's private chambers.

◊ Shadowmark: "Loot"
◊ Skill Book [Archery]: Vernaccus and Bourlor
◊ Unusual Gem: [8/24]
◊ Safe (Expert)
◊ Loose gear

⑦ Endon's House

This is a small but well-appointed house where Endon and Kerah work as silversmiths, along with their daughter Adara. One of them sells their wares in the market during the day. The shop contains a number of fine necklaces to steal.

◊ Crafting: Anvil, Workbench, Cooking Pot
◊ Display Cases (Adept) (2)
◊ Chest

⑧ Ogmund's House

A smaller but comfortable house where Ogmund lives. He follows the ancient teachings of a Nord skald; he plays in the Silver-Blood Inn and announces the news of the day in the market.

◊ Chest
◊ Loose gear

⑨ Nepos's House

Nepos the Nose
Uaile and Morven
Tynan

Nepos administers Cidhna Mine and the smelter. He's rather wealthy, for a native, and is collaborating with both the Silver-Bloods and Madanach in Side Quest: The Forsworn Conspiracy. His home consists of a large fireplace and a large feasting room with two tables. To the rear of the property are the bedrooms.

◊ Skill Book [Illusion]: Mystery of Talara, Part 4 [D1/10]
◊ Display Case (Apprentice)
◊ Chest
◊ Potions
◊ Loose gear

⑩ Vlindrel Hall (House for Sale)

Should you become the Thane of the Reach (by completing Favors for the citizens and Jarl), you can purchase this abode from Jarl Thongvor's Steward, Reburrus Quintilius. Consult the Thane Quests for more information. This is a cliff house in the upper part of the city. The Vlindrels were a Colovian merchant family. During the Reachmen Rebellion, the Markarth Vlindrels were driven out, and their former mansion has stood empty ever since.

◊ Follower: Argis the Bulwark [15/47]
◊ Marriage Prospect: Argis the Bulwark [12/62]

▶ The Crag

This is the central spur of rock that splits the city into north (Highside) and south (Riverside) sections.

⑪ Guard Tower

This dwarven tower atop the central rock spur is now used as a barracks and lookout tower for the soldiers who patrol the city. Head down the spiral steps to the training room and sleeping quarters.

◊ Skill Book [Light Armor]: Ice and Chitin [A1/10]
◊ Skill Book [One-Handed]: The Importance of Where [E1/10]
◊ Loose gear

⑫ Temple of Dibella

Hamal
Orla and Anwen
Senna

The other main structure atop the Crag is the ancient Temple of Dibella. There is a Shrine of Dibella where you can get a Blessing Sybil's Antechamber: where the High Priestess sleeps. An Inner Sanctum (Locked: Expert) is where only women are allowed to go. A small number of priestesses wander the temple grounds. Inside the Sanctum, more priestesses pray and seek sensual contemplation, including Hamal, who is an exceptional enchantress. Aside from books (including a Skill Book on a shelf), ingredients, and a variety of trinkets, the following offerings are to be found. The door at the far end of the Inner Sanctum leads to an altar, where Dibella's fetish is prayed to and offerings are made.

◊ Marriage Prospect: Anwen [13/62]
◊ Marriage Prospect: Orla [14/62]
◊ Marriage Prospect: Senna [15/62]
◊ Trainer (Enchanting: Master): Hamal [2/2]
◊ Skill Book [Illusion]: 2920, Sun's Dawn, v2 [A1/10]
◊ Shrine of Dibella [3/8]
◊ Chest
◊ Potions
◊ Loose gear

⑬ Shrine of Talos

This is a relatively grand chapel. During Imperial control, it will be deserted and "closed," but even the Thalmor know not to desecrate this place for fear of fueling the rebellion. The shrine functions again if the Stormcloaks seize control. Eltrys usually hides out here.

◊ Shrine of Talos [6/17]

▶ Riverside

This section of Markarth encompasses the area along the river, near the smelter, on the south side of the central spur. Reachmen laborers of

The Elder Scrolls V
SKYRIM

Markarth live here; mainly they work in the smelter but are also maids and servants in other parts of the city. There's a slight feeling of despair cloaking the already-dirty air.

14 15 Smelter and Smelter Overseer's House

Mulush gro-Shugurz

The smelter is by the river, for all your ingot-creation needs. Above the smelter, by some half-hidden steps at the waterfall, is the locked entrance to Mulush's dwelling.

◇ Crafting: Anvil, Smelter ◇ Knapsack
◇ Chest ◇ Loose gear

18 Cidhna Mine

Urzoga gra-Shugurz	Duach	Borkul
Madanach	Odvan	Grisvar the Unlucky
Braig	Uraccen	

This silver mine (*Cidhna* means "silver" in the Reach dialect) is the primary source of Markarth's wealth. It is also a prison where criminals work off their sentences. Many of the prisoners here are Forsworn, imprisoned for life after the Nords recaptured the city. The mine is owned and operated by the powerful Silver-Blood clan.

A Door to Markarth

1 Entrance Shaft

Urzoga gra-Shugurz and her Silver-Blood Guards patrol this area, which is usually off-limits to visitors. The main mine to the south has already been excavated and is sealed off.

2 Holding Cell (Locked: Adept)

This is where you collect your belongings and evidence should you try to escape.

◇ Skill Book [Lockpick]: Proper Lock Design [B1/10]

◇ Evidence Chest ◇ Apothecary's Satchel
◇ Unique Weapon: Shiv ◇ Potions aplenty
  [29/80]
◇ Prisoner Belongings Chest ◇ Loose gear

16 The Stocks and Ducking Cage

For those who are unwilling or unable to work in Cidhna Mine to pay for their crimes, Markarth has another solution. The Stocks and Ducking Cage stands right outside the entrance to the mine, a reminder of the fate of any criminals who don't work or who talk back to their overseers. This can result in humiliation or death. Fortunately, you don't suffer either; you're put to work in the mines if you commit a crime in the Reach!

17 The Warrens

Degaine	Eltrys	Weylin
Hathrasil	Garvey	Dryston
Omluag	Cairine	

6 South Tunnel

Mining occurs in these parts.
◇ Silver Ore Vein (2)

7 North Tunnel

Mining is coming to an end, and this area is home to more addicts than miners.

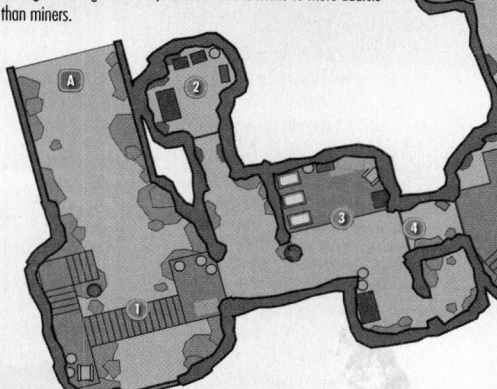

3 Early Excavations and Barracks

Urzoga's guards sleep here and use a couple of pull chains to open and close the mine entrance.

4 Mine Entrance (Locked: Requires Key)

Two connecting gates are opened by Urzoga when she ferries prisoners to and fro. You normally appear inside the prison only after committing crime or concluding Side Quest: The Forsworn Conspiracy.

5 Campfire

The large hub room has exits out of the mine, to the two tunnel areas. The entrance to Madanach's Quarters are guarded by Borkul the Beast and a moping man named Uraccen who usually sits by the fire.

Most of the poor in Markarth live in the Warrens, an old crypt with run-down chambers for the poorest of the city's residents. Aside from the chambers that have suffered a cave-in, all six rooms are locked (Novice), and good practice for your Lockpicking skill. Only Weylin's room has anything more than a few pieces of food in it; there is a chest inside with a Note important for Side Quest: The Forsworn Conspiracy.

◇ Marriage Prospect: Omluag [16/62]
◇ Trainer (Sneak: Expert): Garvey [1/3]
◇ Weylin's Note
◇ Chest

8 Madanach's Quarters (Locked: Requires Key)

The leader of the Forsworn Resistance is holed up in impressive surroundings given his imprisonment. He is the key to the Forsworn cause, during Side Quest: No One Escapes Cidhna Mine.

B Door to Markarth Ruins

This is only accessible during Side Quest: No One Escapes Cidhna Mine.

19 Markarth Ruins (Locked: Requires Key)

Part of an ancient dwarven city, these ruins have been slowly collapsing during earthquakes. No one ventures into these parts, due to the instability of the area and reports of mechanical monstrosities guarding the place. The only place with any items of worth is a ruined two-floor chamber with pipes and a dwarven automaton or two guarding. This area is used during Side Quest: No One Escapes Cidhna Mine. It connects Cidhna Mine to Markarth (Riverside).

◇ Unique Item: Armor of the Old Gods [42/112]
◇ Unique Item: Boots of the Old Gods [43/112]
◇ Unique Item: Gauntlets of the Old Gods [44/112]
◇ Unique Item: Helmet of the Old Gods [45/112]
◇ Unique Item: Silver-Blood Family Ring [46/112]
◇ Potions

20 The Hag's Cure

Bothela   Muiri

Bothela is an old Reach woman who dispenses potions, poisons, and ingredients; tells your fortune; and runs the creepiest shop in Riverside. Aside from the ingredients to steal, you can always purchase a good amount of items. A Skill Book is kept behind the counter.

◇ Crafting: Alchemy Lab
◇ Marriage Prospect: Muiri [17/62]
◇ Trader (Apothecary): Bothela [5/14]
  ○ Potions, Food, Ingredients
◇ Skill Book [Alchemy]: Herbalist's Guide to Skyrim [C1/10]

◇ Unique Item: Muiri's Ring [47/112]
◇ Business Ledger
◇ Strongbox (Apprentice)
◇ Chest
◇ Potions aplenty

21 Lumber Mill and Forge

Ghorza gra-Bagol
Tacitus Sallustius

This overlooks Riverside, but the Blacksmith and her apprentice are well-respected members of the Understone Keep's staff and provide the Jarl with the best steel in the Reach.

- ◇ Crafting: Blacksmith Forge, Grindstone, Tanning Rack, Workbench
- ◇ Trader (Blacksmith): Ghorza [11/33]

22 Hall of the Dead [Locked: Adept]

Brother Verulus

The Hall of the Dead is in a side cavern accessed via Darkside or Understone Keep (both doors are locked), where the dead are buried in crypts and mausoleums are carved into the cave walls. Brother Verulus is the priest of Arkay who oversees the Hall of the Dead.

- ◇ Skill Book [Restoration]: 2920, Rain's Hand, v4 [A2/10]
- ◇ Shrine of Arkay [5/12]

23 Understone Keep

 The following leaders of Markarth are loyal to the Imperials at the start of the Civil War.

Jarl Igmund	Calcelmo (Court wizard)
Raerek (Steward)	Aicantar
Faleen (Housecarl)	Anton Virane
Legate Emmanuel Admand	Rondach and Voada
Thongvor Silver-Blood	Blacksmith: Moth gro-Bagol
Reburrus Quintilius (Steward)	Ondolemar
Yngvar (Housecarl)	

Jarl Igmund

Jarl Igmund, son of Hrolfdir and nephew of Raerek, recently took the throne when Hrolfdir was killed in battle with the Forsworn. Igmund is an Imperial supporter (some might say a puppet) and holds court all day and eats and sleeps in the Keep. He sits upon the Mournful Throne, a relic and seat of power famous for centuries across the Reach.

Raerek (Steward)

Igmund's Steward and successor manages the household, serves as the treasurer, and commands the palace guard.

- ◇ Unique Item: Raerek's Inscribed Amulet of Talos [48/112]

Faleen (Housecarl)

She is completely loyal and very competent. She was Igmund's father's Housecarl and managed to escape from the ambush with the gravely wounded Igmund, although she blames herself for not being able to do more. As a result, she is almost paranoid about Igmund's security and will rarely allow him out of her sight.

Legate Emmanuel Admand

 The following residents of Markarth arrive to take control once this Hold has fallen during the Civil War.

Thongvor Silver-Blood

Thongvor is the head of the Silver-Blood family, who controls the majority of Markarth's wealth. More involved in politics and Ulfric's rebellion, Thongvor leaves the business operations of the family to his brother Thonar.

Reburrus Quintilius (Steward)

Reburrus Quintilius is the steward to Thongvor. His family has served as the chief financial and political advisors to the Silver-Blood family for generations, and Reburrus has distilled the wisdom of the generations to a fine art.

Yngvar (Housecarl)

The huge housecarl to the Silver-Blood family, Yngvar has a reputation for cheerful brutality. He is completely loyal to the Silver-Blood clan and loves his job. He particularly loves it when he can beat someone to a pulp. But he is also surprisingly cultured; he attended the Bard's College as a youth, until he found better employment using his other talents.

The following citizens are staff of Understone Keep:

Calcelmo (Court wizard)

Calcelmo is here in order to study the Dwemer ruins in and around the city. He views his duties as the castle mage as a distraction from his main scholarly interest. He is completely uninterested (and mainly unaware) of politics. He has been quite put out by the Forsworn situation, which has prevented him from doing his usual wide-ranging travels. He is secretly in love with Faleen, although he has never told anyone else or done anything about it.

- ◇ Trader (Spell Vendor): Calcelmo [9/12]

Aicantar

Aicantar is Calcelmo's assistant and nephew. He is less than enthused by his uncle's plans to study more dangerous Dwemer Ruins and prefers they spend time studying spells and enchanting. Aicantar is aware of Calcelmo's secret love for Faleen but is unlikely to do anything about it directly. Faleen scares Aicantar, and the thought of her being around the laboratory more makes him nervous.

Anton Virane

Anton is a genuine Breton from High Rock in a city of Reachmen, a fact that constantly annoys him (because everyone assumes he's a Reachman). He is particularly bigoted toward Reachmen. He is an excellent cook, though, which is why the Jarl continues to tolerate him.

Rondach and Voada

Moth gro-Bagol

- ◇ Trader (Blacksmith): Moth gro-Bagol [12/33]

Ondolemar

Ondolemar is the head of the Thalmor Justiciars in Markarth, and a prime example of why most folk hate the Thalmor. Ondolemar is completely confident in the Dominion's ultimate victory over the Empire. He's a Thalmor true believer, and is not here if the Stormcloaks take this city during the Civil War.

Understone Keep is a gigantic dwarven structure, now used as the city's castle. Built by the Dwemer into the western wall of the canyon, the Castle Wizard, Calcelmo, has recently uncovered additional chambers (and worrying underground monstrosities) and a wealth of artifacts that he keeps in his museum. The sheer size of this place and ability to be well guarded negates some of the instability the location has recently suffered from.

Understone Keep (Interior): Entrance to the Mournful Throne

The first time you enter via the main doors, Thongvor Silver-Blood is having a heated discussion with Brother Verulus about the worship of the outlawed deity, Talos. At this huge intersection of stone and fire, head left to Nchuand-Zel's entrance, right to the Dwemer Museum or on to meet the Jarl, who is guarded by both Markarth Guards and Thalmor Soldiers. Jarl Igmund sits on the Mournful Throne, usually with his Steward and Housecarl by him. Outside, on the upper top of the stairs where Ondolemar and his guards like to stride about, are two stone tables. The one to the right (northwest) houses a Skill Book.

- ◇ Skill Book [Alteration]: Daughter of the Niben [B1/10]

Kitchens

To the left (south) of the throne room are the kitchens. The two hounds around here are large but friendly. Inside, you usually find Voada and Rondach and the short-tempered Anton Virane. As expected, there's a massive amount of food in here.

Jarl's Chamber (Locked: Adept)

Igmund rests here, behind the large golden door to the left (southeast) of the throne room. If you're going to sift through his personal belongings, remember to try the ones on the stone shelf facing the subterranean river that dominates the rear of the chamber.

- ◇ Skill Book [Conjuration]: The Warrior's Charge [E1/10]
- ◇ Loose gear

Understone Forge

This is located to the right (north) of the throne room. Moth gro-Bagol works here, while his sister Ghorza tends to the Blacksmith Forge outside.

- ◇ Crafting: Blacksmith Forge, Grindstone, Tanning Rack, Workbench
- ◇ Marriage Prospect: Ghorza gra-Bagol [18/62]
- ◇ Marriage Prospect: Moth gro-Bagol [19/62]
- ◇ Trader (Blacksmith): Moth gro-Bagol [12/34]
  - ○ Weapons, Apparel, Misc.
- ◇ Trainer (Smithing: Journeyman): Ghorza [1/3]
- ◇ Loose gear

Bedrooms

You are trespassing if you head into this area! To the right (northwest) are bedrooms for the more important members of the Jarl's counsel. Faleen's room (sometimes locked: Adept) is to the right, with the large dinner table, a Key to Markarth Keep that opens the two other nearby doors, and the Jarl's Quarters. Raerek (sometimes locked: Adept) houses the steward, a Key, and his secret Talos-loving reading materials. Up the stairs is a third room (sometimes locked: Apprentice) leading to the Imperial War Room, where Legate Emmanuel Admand is overseeing the Civil War in this territory.

- ◇ Civil War: Map of Skyrim
- ◇ Key to Markarth Keep (3)
- ◇ Display case (Novice)
- ◇ Loose gear

Markarth Wizards Quarters

Unless you've been given approval by Calcelmo, you are trespassing in the following areas. You are unable to head farther into the laboratory or tower unless Thieves Guild Quest: Hard Answers is active, so plan to loot the three connected areas during this quest.

Dwemer Museum (Locked: Adept)

The Dwemer Museum showcases Calcelmo's collection of artifacts recovered from ruins across Skyrim. Only three guards patrol this area, keeping watch for intruders. This space is normally off-limits—the guards will aggressively arrest you if you trespass here—but you can get Calcelmo's permission to visit the museum in any number of ways; see Thieves Guild Quest: Hard Answers for details.

The Museum has the finest collection of Dwarven artifacts (weapons, armor, items, and books) in the entirety of Skyrim and the highest concentration of locked containers in any area of the game. There's even a small selection of Falmer items. To the south is a gate (Apprentice) leading to a small workshop with an Unusual Gem and locked chest (Expert). To the northwest is a locked gate (Adept) to a two-level storage room. Up the steps to the west is the laboratory door.

- ◇ Unusual Gem: [9/24]
- ◇ Display Case (3)
- ◇ Display Case (Novice) (5)
- ◇ Display Case (Apprentice) (2)
- ◇ Display Case (Adept) (7)
- ◇ Display Case (Expert) (14)
- ◇ Chest (Adept)
- ◇ Chest (Expert)
- ◇ Loose gear

Calcelmo's Laboratory

This area is the main living and research quarters for Calcelmo and Aicantar, although they typically spend most of their time in the Keep, closer to the Nchuand-Zel Entrance. Most of this area is locked unless you're on Thieves Guild Quest: Hard Answers; see that quest for an exhaustive walkthrough of quest events in this space.

The laboratory is divided into a number of chambers. The Entry Room has oil on the floor, a dart trap, and a gate you can't normally open to the southeast.

◇ Danger! Dart Trap, Oil Pool Trap
◇ Unique Weapon: Spider Control Rod [30/80] (quest only)

The Throne Chamber consists of a main room with a raised throne and guard. Dwarven junk (or is it research?) is scattered around, along with several traps you can activate. To the northwest is Calcelmo's bedroom, which has some display cases (Apprentice) and scrolls to steal. To the south is Aicantar's bedroom and food preparation area.

◇ Danger! Dwarven Ballista Trap, Dwarven Thresher Trap, Swinging Wall Trap
◇ Display Case (Apprentice)
◇ Loose gear

You cannot progress beyond the Throne door without a key, which you can only find during Thieves Guild Quest: Hard Answers.

Beyond the Throne Room is the Steam Hall. There's little to search for, except a few corpses of fallen foes. The valve at the far end activates the thresher traps in the floor, ideally against enemies following you.

◇ Danger! Dwarven Thresher Trap, Poison Gas Trap

Next is the Statue Room, whose exit is flanked by two Dwarven Spheres. There are two side chambers here; take advantage of the guard's patrol to slip through the door when he steps away from it.

And finally, you emerge into a large workroom. The valve in the control booth sets off a frightening number of traps in the room that will send even the most stout-hearted guard running for cover. This area has the following items and two exits.

◇ Danger! Dwarven Ballista Trap, Dwarven Thresher Trap, Flamethrower Trap
◇ Crafting: Arcane Enchanter
◇ Larceny Target: Dwemer Puzzle Cube [4/7]
◇ Skill Book [Enchanting]: Twin Secrets
◇ Chest
◇ Loose gear

Markarth Wizards' Balcony

The great balcony atop the keep connects Calcelmo's laboratory to his tower, a separate structure off the main body of the Keep. There's a great view of the city from here. One section of the balcony wall has broken away, exposing a path around the cliffside that ends in a waterfall. If you were in a hurry, you might just be able to jump from here.

Calcelmo's Tower (Locked: Requires Key)

The tower (accessible only during Thieves Guild Quest: Hard Answers) has a lower-level entry hall, an upper-level office, and a massive stone relic containing a text in Dwemer and Falmer on the same granite slab! This stone is the key to Calcelmo's current research, a secret he jealously protects.

◇ Crafting: Alchemy Lab, Arcane Enchanter
◇ Calcelmo's Stone
◇ Skill Book [Heavy Armor]: Chimarvamidium [B1/10]
◇ Potions
◇ Loose gear

Nchuand-Zel Entrance

The epic cavern is usually where Calcelmo and Aicantar can be found, dedicating their lives to researching this mighty dwarven stronghold of historic significance. When you emerge from the entrance cavern close to the throne room, you are greeted by a rushing river, various curved passageways, and circular towers (one with seats to sit on and gaze down at the rushing water), as well as an entrance to the Hall of the Dead. Of more significance is the entrance to Nchuand-Zel itself. Enter here, either before speaking to Calcelmo (Locked: Adept) or after acquiring the key and agreeing to slay a large spider for him (Miscellaneous Objective: Neutralizing Nimhe*).

◇ Crafting: Alchemy Lab, Arcane Enchanter

◈ Nchuand-Zel Excavation Site

Dungeon: Dwarven City
Animal
Dwarven Centurion
Dwarven Sphere
Dwarven Spider
Falmer
Nimhe

Dangers
Flamethrower Traps
Rune Traps
Spear Trap

Quest Items
Alethius's Notes
Krag's Journal
Stromm's Diary
Erj's Notes
Staubin's Diary

Collectibles
Skill Book [Alteration]: Sithis [D1/10]
Area Is Locked (Adept)
Chest(s)
Potions
Loose gear
Mineable ore (Corundum, Iron, Moonstone)

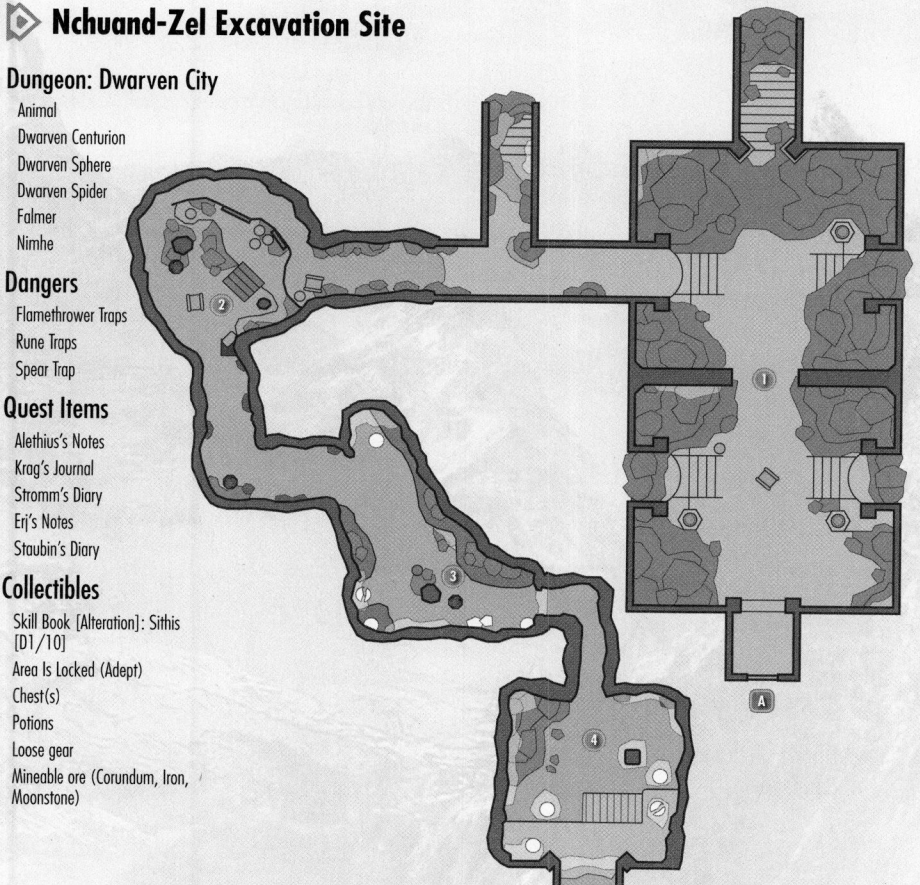

Ⓐ Door to Understone Keep

① Entrance Corridor
Throughout this entire area, there's Dwemer artifacts to gather and sell later. Turn left (west) to break through the already-collapsed wall to where the excavation site was first discovered.

② Excavation Drop
In this steam-filled drop, follow the mine working's ledges. Take that Potion of Plentiful Healing by the wagon before you descend. You'll need it! Try dropping onto the nearer stalagmite for a quicker drop down.

◇ Potion
◇ Loose gear

③ Mine Workings
These have been completely taken over by Frostbite Spiders. Slay them all here before continuing past the skeletons of the long-dead miners and cut through the webs.

◇ Mineable ore (Corundum, Iron)

④ Nimhe's Lair
A gigantic Frostbite Spider drops in to slay you as you reach the edge of the mining area. Face her or flee! Then inspect the dead Imperial named Alethius and read his Note. This begins Dungeon Quest: The Lost Expedition. Consult that quest for precise knowledge on completing this exploration.

◇ Alethius's Notes

Ⓑ Door to Nchuand-Zel

Nchuand-Zel

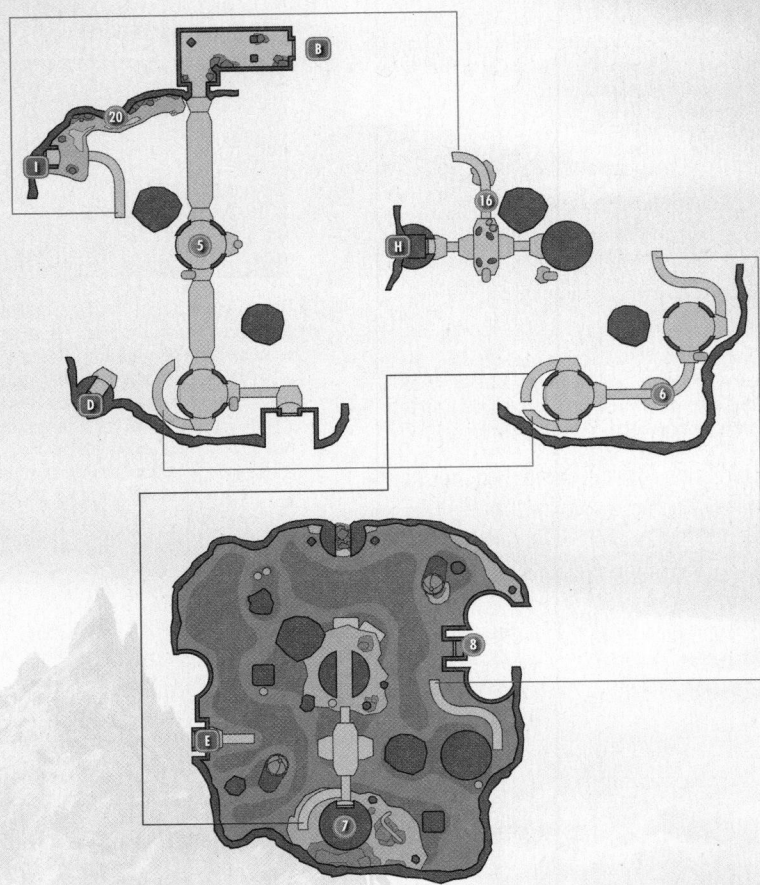

6 Lower Walkways (Lower Level)

Below the upper walkway are stone ramps down to a middle section, and down again to the base of the structure, which is waterlogged.

7 South Gate (Waterlogged Ground Area; Locked: Adept)

◇ Chest

8 Piston Building Door (Waterlogged Ground Area)

◇ Potions (underwater)

D Door from Nchuand-Zel Quarters (Lower Level)

This leads from the Quarters to an otherwise-inaccessible ledge.

◇ Chest

E Door to Nchuand-Zel Armory (Waterlogged Ground Area)

H Door from Nchuand-Zel Armory (Lower Level)

16 Krag's Walkway

The researcher Krag lies near blood splatters along this walkway and camping spot. The Dwarven Centurion roars into life only after you pull the switch inside the Control.

◇ Krag's Journal

I Door to Nchuand-Zel Control (Upper Level)

This is only accessed from this location, but only after you emerge from the Armory.

20 Escape Ledge (Upper Level)

The Dwarven mechanical entities may be moving (and attacking any Falmer you've left alive) if you fiddled with the Control. Use this ledge running around the northwest corner of this gigantic chamber to reach the exit and escape to the Excavation Site.

◇ Mineable ore (Moonstone)

B Door to Nchuand-Zel Excavation Site

5 Upper Walkway (Upper Level)

After a short corridor ramp down, this opens up into a single, dramatic and gigantic chamber. This Upper Walkway has a couple of Falmer to face, and the southern tower has ramps down and a walkway across to the Nchuand-Zel Quarters. Find a Skill Book resting on an ornate bench as you go.

◇ Skill Book [Alteration]: Sithis [D1/10]

> **TIP** There is a rocky ledge [20] that you can actually jump and climb on if you wish to explore this area in the opposite direction.

C Door to Nchuand-Zel Quarters (Upper Level)

Nchuand-Zel Quarters

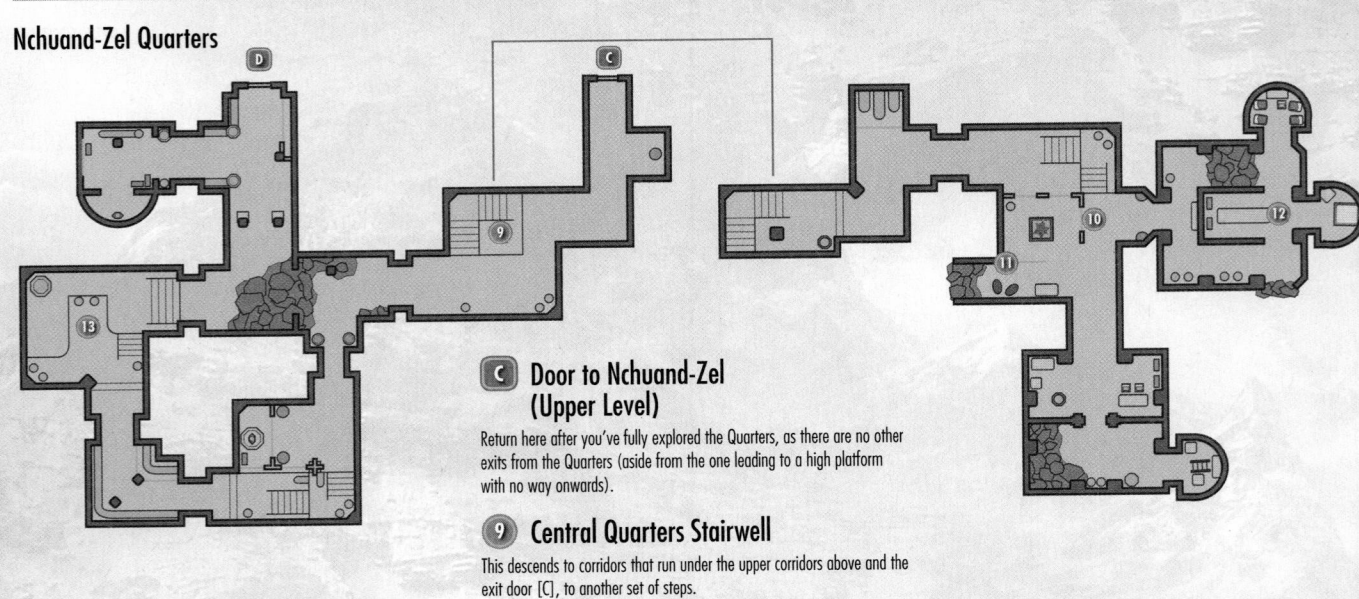

C Door to Nchuand-Zel (Upper Level)

Return here after you've fully explored the Quarters, as there are no other exits from the Quarters (aside from the one leading to a high platform with no way onwards).

9 Central Quarters Stairwell

This descends to corridors that run under the upper corridors above and the exit door [C], to another set of steps.

The Elder Scrolls V
SKYRIM™

⑩ Eastern Quarters

Access this series of upper chambers from the Central Quarters Stairwell. When you reach the second ascending set of steps, watch for Fire Rune Traps at the top. Continue south down the corridor, passing Stromm's corpse, and check the dead bodies of the expedition's Imperial Guards and a torture chamber at the far end.

◇ Danger! Rune Traps
◇ Loose gear

⑪ Stromm

Search the corpse, and check the nearby stone table for his diary.

◇ Stromm's Diary

⑫ Far Eastern Living Areas

This collection of small rooms and a corridor are accessed after turning east at the steps with the Fire Rune Traps. Pass the pistons to reach a variety of dining, sleeping, and storage rooms.

◇ Loose gear

⑬ Western Chambers

These lower chambers are filled with Falmer foes. They lead you to the Door to Nchuand-Zel and a dead-end area with dwarven barrels and a chest.

◇ Chest

Ⓓ Door to Nchuand-Zel (Upper Level)

Nchuand-Zel Armory

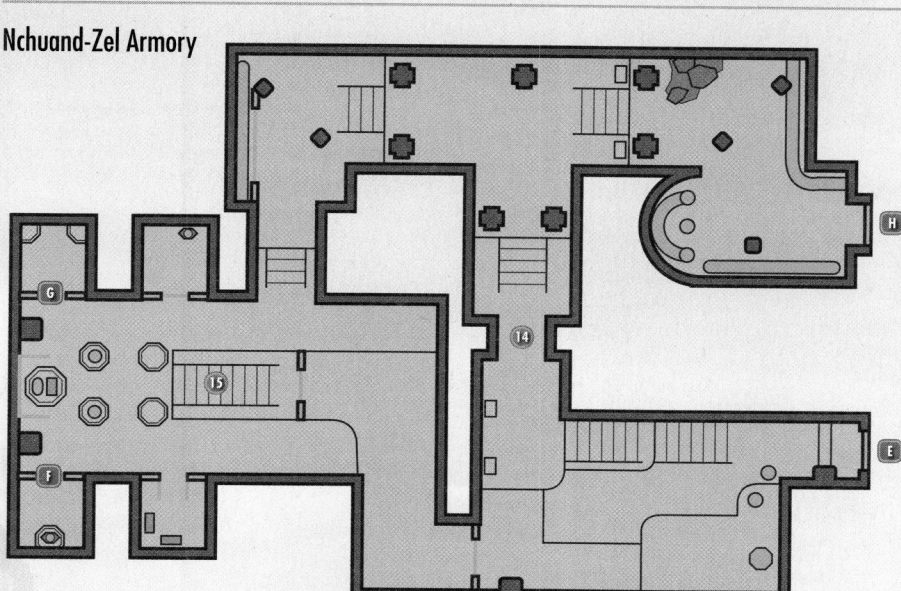

Ⓔ Door to Nchuand-Zel (Waterlogged Ground Level)

⑭ Stone Corridors (Upper and Lower)

These wind through to the center of the Armory. Take the upper ramped corridors to the right turn (east) and to an exit door leading back into Nchuand-Zel [H]. Take the upper path and turn right (west), heading down past a Wall Fire and Wall Spear Trap (check the floor for a trigger and don't step on them!) to the Armory Hall. Take the lower path directly to the Armory Hall. There's a gate at the base of the steps to unlock (Adept).

◇ Danger! Flamethrower Trap, Spear Trap

⑮ Armory Hall and Erj

Statues of dwarven mechanical monsters stand frozen in time at the top of these steps. A dead Falmer and the remains of Erj the adventurer are also here. Close by are three gates, one of which is unlocked; behind it is a chest surrounded by Dwemer pots.

◇ Erj's Notes
◇ Chest

Ⓕ Gate (Locked: Expert)

Ⓖ Gate (Locked: Expert)

◇ Chest

Ⓗ Door to Nchuand-Zel (Lower Level)

Nchuand-Zel Control

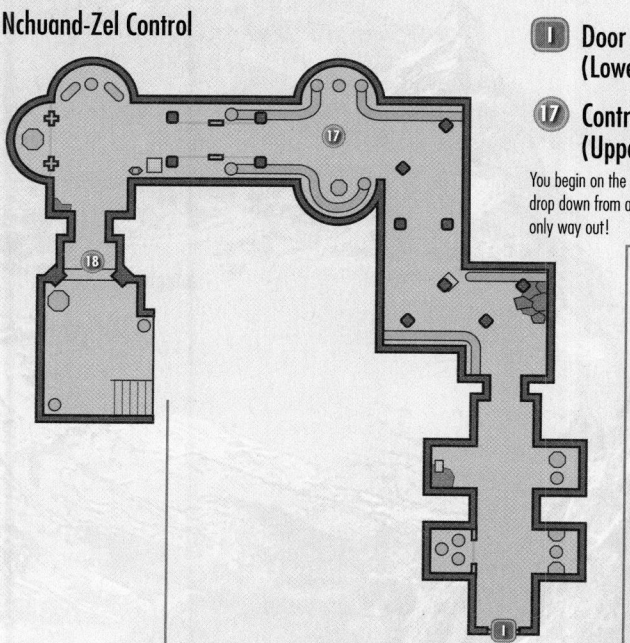

Ⓘ Door to Nchuand-Zel (Lower Level)

⑰ Control Corridor (Upper and Lower)

You begin on the lower part of this north-south corridor. You drop down from above to exit this area; the way in is the only way out!

⑱ Falmer Pipeway and Staubin

A group of these creatures are guarding the golden pipes and barred sections of this corridor. Close by are the remains of Staubin.

◇ Staubin's Diary
◇ Loose gear

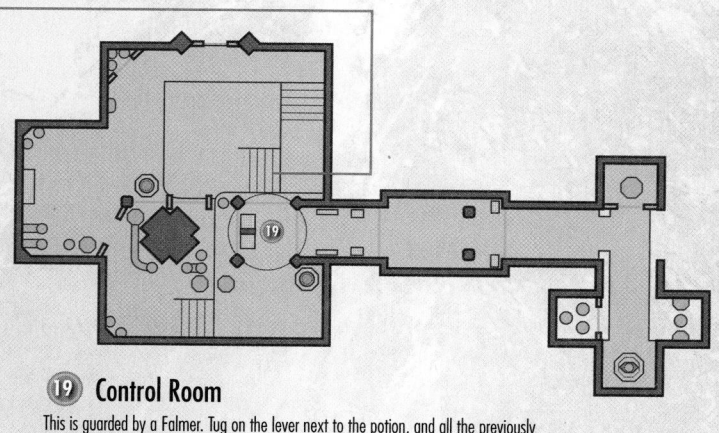

⑲ Control Room

This is guarded by a Falmer. Tug on the lever next to the potion, and all the previously dormant Dwemer statuary clanks into life and battles any Falmer you haven't killed yourself. Return from whence you came.

◇ Chest   ◇ Loose gear

[5.01] Mor Khazgur

Related Quests

Side Quest: The Forgemaster's Fingers

Favor (Activity): Mining Ore* (Shuftharz)

Favor: Sparring Partners* (Larak)

Services

Follower: Borgakh the Steel Heart [16/47]

Marriage Prospect: Borgakh the Steel Heart [20/62]

Trader (Apothecary Vendor): Sharamph [7/14]

  Potions, Food, Ingredients

Trainer (Block: Master): Chief Larak [1/2]

Recommended Level: 6

Habitation: Orc Stronghold

Bagrak

Borgakh the Steel Heart (Follower, Marriage Prospect)

Chief Larak (Trainer: Block)

Ghamorz

Gul

Olur

Sharamph (Apothecary Vendor)

Shuftharz

Crafting

Alchemy Lab

Blacksmith Forge

Grindstone

Smelter

Collectibles

Skill Book [Smithing]: The Armorer's Challenge [E1/10]

Chest(s)

Potions

Loose gear

This Orc stronghold stands at the Reach's far northwest tip, on the edge of Skyrim. The Orcs here are mistrustful, but the first guard that spots you will call out and offer you a Side Quest, which can help you curry favor with the Orcs. If you like, test your fistfighting aptitude in a friendly wager against the chief.

Exterior

Even if the Orcs are giving you the cold shoulder, you can still explore their stronghold and make use of several crafting stations. Grab a Skill Book off a shelf near the Blacksmith forge.

◇ Crafting: Alchemy Lab, Blacksmith Forge, Grindstone, Smelter
◇ Skill Book [Smithing]: The Armorer's Challenge [E1/10]
◇ Chest
◇ Apothecary's Satchel
◇ Potions

Larak's Longhouse

The Orc chief's longhouse holds some worthy loot, but you risk angering the Orcs if you break inside.

◇ Area Is Locked (Novice)
◇ Chests (2)
◇ Potions
◇ Loose gear

Mor Khazgur Cellar

Unlock the trapdoor near Larak's Longhouse to access a small cellar with a handful of valuables.

◇ Area Is Locked (Novice)
◇ Chest
◇ Potions

Mor Khazgur Mine

This small mine is worked by the Orcs and features thick veins of Orichalcum Ore.

◇ Chest
◇ Loose gear
◇ Mineable ore (Orichalcum)

[5.02] Deepwood Redoubt

Related Quests

Dark Brotherhood Quest: The Feeble Fortune*

Recommended Level: 14

Dungeon: Forsworn Redoubt

Forsworn

Crafting

Alchemy Lab

Arcane Enchanter

Anvil

Blacksmith Forge

Grindstone

Workbench

Dangers

Bone Alarm Trap

Dart Trap (pressure plate)

Rune Traps (floor)

Swinging Blade Trap (lever)

Swinging Wall Trap (pressure plate)

Collectibles

Skill Book [Sneak]: Sacred Witness [C1/10]

Trapped Chest

Chest(s)

Potions

Loose gear

A band of Forsworn have taken over this ancient ruin, located atop a rocky rise at the northern tip of the Reach. Deepwood Redoubt leads to a larger Nordic ruin on the far side of a secret vale — Hag's End [5.03].

Exterior

Fight your way up the outer stone steps to locate the entrance to the ruins. Swipe some potions from the nearby altar and lean-to before heading inside.

◇ Potions
◇ Loose gear

Trapped Passages

Beware the Hinge Trigger when opening the first chest that you discover in a recessed alcove. Long spears will stab out from the wall beneath the chest if you set off the trap. Disarm it or stand to one side to safely claim your treasure.

    Stand on the pressure plate that follows to trigger a trap just ahead, then simply move through the doorway after the darts stop firing.

    After dealing with the first batch of Forsworn, sprint straight through the stretch of swinging blades that follows. You can make it through unscathed if you time it just right.

◇ Danger! Swinging Blade Trap (lever), Dart Trap (pressure plate), Trapped Chest

Room of Doom

A small chamber lies beyond the swinging blades. Beware the many Rune Traps on the floor here. Summon a Familiar to set off the traps and absorb the damage, or draw out the Forsworn Shaman in the far room and kill her with her own traps. Take the key from the Shaman's corpse, then unlock the nearby iron door to advance.

◇ Danger! Rune Traps (floor)
◇ Crafting: Arcane Enchanter
◇ Deepwood Redoubt Key (Forsworn)
◇ Potions

Exit Passage

Hop over a pressure plate to avoid a nasty trap as you enter the passage beyond the iron door. The Bone Alarm traps can give away your location to nearby Forsworn, if any remain. Proceed through the far door to head into Deepwood Vale.

◇ Danger! Bone Alarm Trap, Swinging Wall Trap (pressure plate)
◇ Potion
◇ Loose gear

Deepwood Vale

Deepwood Redoubt leads out into a secret vale nestled in the mountains, where a much larger ruin awaits. Forsworn archers patrol the ramparts that lead to Hag's End ([5.03]), the towering structure on the vale's east side. Search near the southwest waterfall to find a chest; there's also a Skill Book in the tent with the Alchemy Lab. Make your way east toward Hag's End, slaying the Forsworn and claiming the treasure they guard. See Dark Brotherhood Radiant Quest: The Feeble Fortune for some strategies on assaulting this formidable fortress.

◇ Crafting: Alchemy Lab, Anvil, Blacksmith Forge, Grindstone, Workbench
◇ Skill Book [Sneak]: Sacred Witness [C1/10]
◇ Chests (2)
◇ Chest (Locked: Apprentice)
◇ Potions
◇ Loose gear

[5.03] Hag's End

Related Quests

Dark Brotherhood Quest: The Feeble Fortune*

Dungeon Activity

Recommended Level: 14

Dungeon: Hagraven Nest

Animal

Hagraven

Witch

Crafting

Alchemy Lab

Arcane Enchanter

Dangers

Battering Ram Trap (pressure plate)

Dart Trap

Flamethrower Trap

Rune Trap

Oil Lamp Trap

Oil Pool Trap

Collectibles

Skill Book [Illusion]: Mystery of Talara, Part 4

Unique Item: Ancient Shrouded Armor [50/112]

Unique Item: Ancient Shrouded Boots [51/112]

Unique Item: Ancient Shrouded Cowl [52/112]

Unique Item: Ancient Shrouded Gloves [52/112]

Unique Item: Predator's Grace [53/112]

Unique Weapon: Bloodthorn [31/80]

Special Objects

Word Wall: Slow Time [3/3]

Chest(s)

Potions

Loose gear

 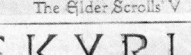

PRIMA OFFICIAL GAME GUIDE   WWW.PRIMAGAMES.COM

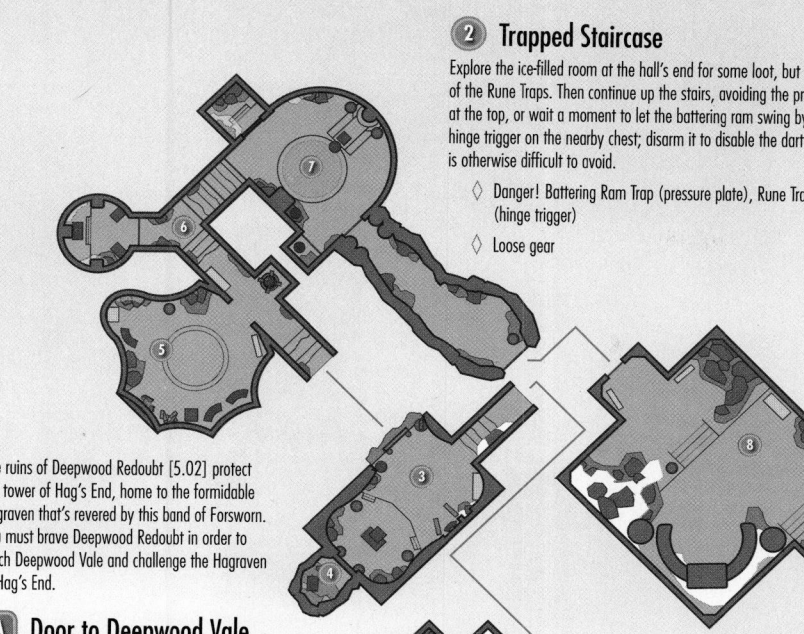

② Trapped Staircase

Explore the ice-filled room at the hall's end for some loot, but be careful of the Rune Traps. Then continue up the stairs, avoiding the pressure plate at the top, or wait a moment to let the battering ram swing by. Note the hinge trigger on the nearby chest; disarm it to disable the dart trap, which is otherwise difficult to avoid.

◇ Danger! Battering Ram Trap (pressure plate), Rune Trap, Dart Trap (hinge trigger)

◇ Loose gear

The ruins of Deepwood Redoubt [5.02] protect the tower of Hag's End, home to the formidable Hagraven that's revered by this band of Forsworn. You must brave Deepwood Redoubt in order to reach Deepwood Vale and challenge the Hagraven of Hag's End.

Ⓐ Door to Deepwood Vale

③ Throne Room

Slay more witches in the small throne room that follows. Collect a Skill Book before pulling a nearby lever to lower a drawbridge.

◇ Skill Book [Illusion]: Mystery of Talara, Part 4

◇ Potion

① Dining Room and Side Chambers

Slay vicious witches and battle the Hagraven in the first few chambers.

◇ Crafting: Alchemy Lab ◇ Loose gear

◇ Potions

④ Assassin's Alcove

If you've come here for Dark Brotherhood Quest: The Feeble Fortune, you can open this secret alcove by pulling a handle on the wall behind the throne in the Throne Room [3] (it doesn't exist unless you're on the quest). Inside, take the Ancient Shrouded Armor from the body of the fallen assassin, and claim the loot in the large chest.

◇ Unique Item: Ancient Shrouded Armor [50/112]

◇ Unique Item: Ancient Shrouded Boots [51/112]

◇ Unique Item: Ancient Shrouded Cowl [52/112]

◇ Unique Item: Ancient Shrouded Gloves [53/112]

◇ Chest

⑤ Matriarch's Chamber

Beware the circular chamber beyond the drawbridge—a Frostbite Spider silently descends from the ceiling as you explore the room. Slay the spider and swipe an important key from near the fireplace.

◇ Hag's End Key ◇ Potions

⑥ Two-Gate Junction

Use the key you found back at [5] to unlock the Master-level west gate here, then approach the giant chest in the nook beyond. Carefully disarm the hinge trigger or stand aside to avoid being singed by the trio of flamethrower traps. Exit the nook and turn a handle on the wall to raise the east portcullises and advance. When the portcullis opens, wait for a moment to avoid the spear traps before heading up the stairs.

◇ Danger! Flamethrower Trap, Spear Trap

⑦ Fire Chamber

Use the hanging oil lamp to ignite the central pool of oil and singe the witches and Hagraven in this chamber. Again, use the key you found at [5] to open the locked door here and access a treasure nook. Pull the chain that hangs above the oil to open the way forward.

◇ Danger! Oil Lamp Trap, Oil Pool Trap

◇ Loose gear

⑧ Sunlit Chamber

This chamber has a massive hole in its ceiling, allowing soft light and frigid air to flow in. Follow the sound of chanting to locate an ancient Word Wall that yields a new Word of Power.

◇ Crafting: Arcane Enchanter

◇ Word Wall: Slow Time [3/3]

Ⓑ Door to Deepwood Vale

Deepwood Vale Summit

You exit out onto the upper level of Hag's End, overlooking Deepwood Vale below. Face the Hagraven and her summoned minions for a final time and cut them down. Then claim the unique dagger from the corpse on the altar and the large chest nearby.

◇ Unique Weapon: Bloodthorn [31/80]

◇ Chest

Deepwood Vale holds one final secret. If you have the Whirlwind Sprint Shout (or are good at rock climbing), head to the upper level of the Vale from which the waterfall descends. There, you can find one more chest and a unique pair of boots.

◇ Unique Item: Predator's Grace [54/112]

◇ Chest (Locked: Expert)

▷ [5.04] Deep Folk Crossing

Along the Reach's western border, an ancient stone bridge stretches across a waterfall at a serene location. Cross the bridge to discover a small shrine with a unique chestlike object—this is a Dwarven Convector, used during a College of Winterhold Radiant Quest.

Related Quest

College of Winterhold Radiant Quest: Arniel's Endeavors

Recommended Level: 8

Dungeons: Special

Special Objects:

Dwemer Convector

Chest

Loose gear

▷ [5.05] Bruca's Leap Redoubt

This small Forsworn camp lies near a cave, inside of which lurks a powerful Forsworn Chief. Eradicate the vicious brigands and then claim a Skill Book from a shelf. Search a dark corner to discover a large chest, but beware of the bear trap on the ground before it.

Recommended Level: 14

Dungeon: Forsworn Redoubt

Forsworn

Crafting

Tanning Rack

Dangers

Bear Trap

Collectibles

Skill Book [Enchanting]: A Tragedy in Black

Chest(s)

Potions

Loose gear

[5.06] Bthardamz

Bthardamz Upper District

Related Quests

Daedric Quest: The Only Cure

Recommended Level:

16

Dungeon: Dwarven City

Afflicted
Dwarven Sphere
Dwarven Spider
Orchendor

Dangers

Dwarven Thresher (pressure plate/levers)

Swinging Blade Trap (lever)

Collectibles

Skill Book [Speech]: Biography of the Wolf Queen

Unique Item: Spellbreaker [55/112]

Chests

Potions

Loose gear

Mineable ore (Gold, Quicksilver)

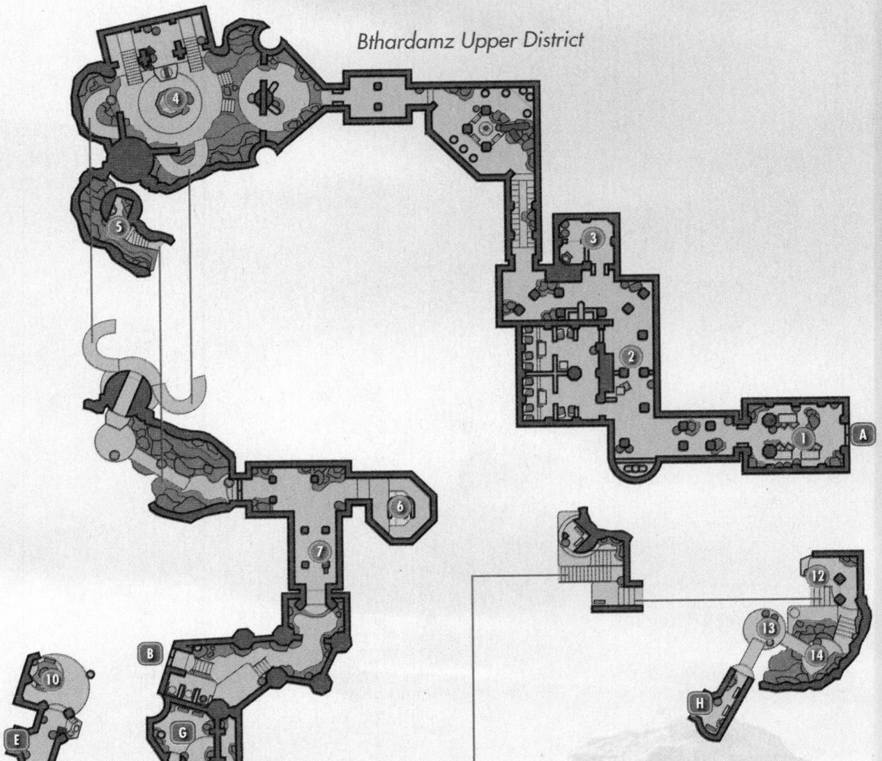

Bthardamz Workshop

Bthardamz Lower District

The Elder Scrolls V

SKYRIM

This massive dwarven city stands among the Reach's western mountains and serves as the main adventuring site for a Daedric Quest.

Exterior

Navigate the city's sprawling yet simple exterior, descending a long set of stairs and pulling the farther of two levers to open the way into the Bthardamz Upper District. The other lever activates a dangerous trap and is best left alone. Continue exploring the exterior ruins before heading inside, venturing upstairs to discover a pair of chests tucked away near the first tower at the top. Backtrack down and enter the Upper District to begin your exploration of the city's interior.

◇ Danger! Dwarven Thresher (lever)   ◇ Chests (2)

(A) Exit to Skyrim

(1) Entry Chamber

Find a bit of plunder atop the tables in the Upper District's first room.

◇ Chest   ◇ Potion   ◇ Loose gear

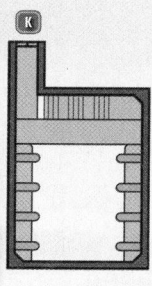

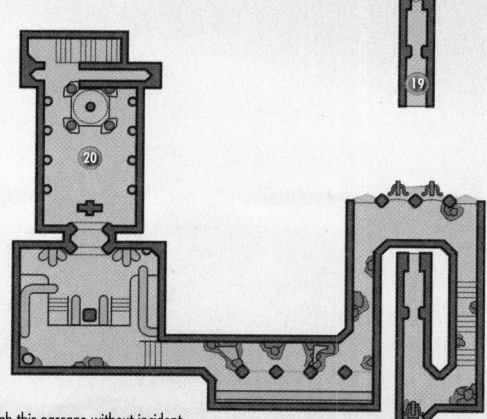

Bthardamz Arcanex

(2) Two Routes

Pick a Novice-level gate to slip through this passage without incident. If you can't pick the lock, you must navigate an Afflicted-filled sleeping area in order to circumvent the gate instead.

◇ Potion

(3) Storage

Pick an Adept-level gate in this small room to access a potion and chest.

◇ Chest   ◇ Potion

(4) Public Square

Kill or avoid a group of Afflicted on your way to this cavernous area, where many more Afflicted are gathered. Scale some stairs to locate a chest on the north balcony, then pull the nearby lever to lower the far south gate. Sprint up a winding ramp on your way to [5].

◇ Chest

(5) Sloping Passage

Descend a sloping ramp that leads toward a metal door, but double back before going through, and loot a hidden chest at the end of the lower trail.

◇ Chest

(6) Treasure Chamber

Sneak as you make for this room's far chest; otherwise you risk alerting a pair of Dwarven Spheres here.

◇ Chest

(7) Spinning Blade Slope

Avoid a pressure plate as you descend a ramp here, which leads to the door to the Bthardamz Workshop.

◇ Danger! Dwarven Thresher (pressure plate/lever)

◇ Potion

(B) Door to Bthardamz Workshop

(C) Door to Bthardamz Upper District

(8) Worker's Quarters

More Afflicted lurk within the Bthardamz Workshop. Read the note on the southwest table to learn where your quest-related quarry might have gone.

(9) Spider Pit

Beware of alerting dangerous Dwarven Spiders in this chamber—you can be quickly overwhelmed. Loot the chest in the northeast corner, then scale the east stairs to return to the Upper District.

◇ Chest

(D) Door to Bthardamz Upper District

(E) Door to Bthardamz Workshop

(10) Balcony

Duck out of the Bthardamz Workshop just for a moment to raid a chest on this balcony, then head back inside.

◇ Chest   ◇ Potion

(11) Steam Room

Raid one last chest from this steamy area of the Bthardamz Workshop before taking the southeast door back to the Upper District.

◇ Chest

(F) Door to Bthardamz Upper District

(G) Door to Bthardamz Workshop

(12) Lower District Access

At last, you've reached the Upper District's southern end. Before scaling the first set of stone stairs, leap up the rocks to the right (south) and keep going to reach a rooftop, where you discover a hidden chest. Go back down and return to the stairs—again, don't climb them. Explore the north alley to find another chest, then scale the stairs and open a door to visit a dwelling.

◇ Chests

(13) Bthardamz Dwelling

Make a quick stop here to raid a chest that's guarded by a few Afflicted. If possible, unlock an Apprentice-level gate to access another chest and a Skill Book. If you don't alert the Afflicted here, you can overhear one of them explaining how she wants to leave this place.

◇ Skill Book [Speech]: Biography of the Wolf Queen

◇ Chests (2)

(14) Stairs and Balconies

Explore this network of stairs and walkways thoroughly to locate a vein of valuable Gold Ore on a rocky ledge and a chest tucked away near a tower's high balcony to the north. Scale some ramps to reach the tallest tower afterward and proceed through the south door to the Bthardamz Lower District.

◇ Chest

◇ Mineable ore (Gold)

(H) Door to Bthardamz Lower District

(I) Door to Bthardamz Upper District

(15) Lower District Entry

Open an unlocked gate in the Lower District's first area to raid a chest before sneaking through the passage that follows to avoid alerting Dwarven Spiders.

◇ Chest

(16) Amphitheater

Pull the lever on the balcony as you enter this wide cavern to slice up the unwary Afflicted below. Eliminate any stragglers so you may safely descend and raid the central chest.

◇ Danger! Dwarven Thresher (lever)

◇ Chest

(17) Grand Cavern

A river rushes through the middle of this massive cavern, where a network of stairs and walkways connect several towers. Stealth tactics help you avoid the patrolling Afflicted and various Dwarven sentries. Raid a wooden chest in a downstairs room, then head upstairs and check behind the north tower to find a small dwarven chest stashed near a skeleton. Backtrack a bit and scale the east stairs to reach walkways that lead to the Bthardamz Study.

◇ Danger! Swinging Blade Trap (pressure plate/lever)

◇ Chests (2)

◇ Minable ore (Gold)

(18) Bthardamz Study

Open a gate in the Study's first room to locate a chest, then avoid a pressure plate before scaling a long ramp. Beware of the Sphere Centurion that comes out of the pipe at the ramp's top. Open another gate at the top and pillage a chest. Head through the door that follows to exit back out to the Grand Cavern's highest walkways.

◇ Danger! Dwarven Thresher (pressure plate)

◇ Chests (2)

⑰ Grand Cavern Revisited (Upper Walkways)

Before crossing the first sloping walkway, turn right and cross the nearby east roof to discover a hidden chest. Cross the sloping walkway afterward and open the east gate to loot another chest in a small room. Venture west afterward and scale the winding ramps to find a third chest affixed to the northwest wall—this one's guarded by several Afflicted. Either clear them out or forgo the chest and loop around, taking the long southern passage to the Bthardamz Arcanex.

◇ Chests (3)

Ⓙ Door to Bthardamz Arcanex

Ⓚ Door to Bthardamz Lower District

⑲ Arcanex Grand Cavern

If Bthardamz's beauty has escaped you up to this point, you'll certainly appreciate it when you enter this huge, sunlit cavern. Continue to sneak through here, or risk alerting a host of Dwarven Spiders and Spheres. Scale a winding ramp to climb a tower, then cross a curved walkway and find a chest that lies just east of some stone stairs. Climb the stairs and check to the east again to discover a Quicksilver Ore vein, but beware of alerting the formidable Dwarven Centurion and host of Dwarven Spiders that lurk in the south passage. Ignore the south passage's ballistae—you can't interact with them.

◇ Chest   ◆ Mineable ore (Quicksilver)

⑳ Orchendor Showdown

Do your best to avoid the patrolling Dwarven Spheres on your way to this final chamber, where you must slay a powerful mage named Orchendor as part of Daedric Quest: The Only Cure. Obtain a useful key from Orchendor's corpse after the deed is done and use it to quickly exit Bthardamz via the upstairs elevator.

◇ Key to Bthardamz Elevator (Orchendor)

Ⓚ Exit to Skyrim

▷ [5.07] Druadach Redoubt

Related Quests
Dungeon Activity

Recommended Level:
14

Dungeon: Forsworn Redoubt
Forsworn

Crafting
Anvil	Grindstone
Forge	Tanning Rack

Collectibles
Skill Book [Light Armor]: The Rear Guard [D2/10]

Special Objects
Reachmen's Rebellion Map
Shrine of Arkay [6/12]
Chest
Chest (Locked: Expert)
Potions
Loose gear

In the Reach's northern section, a swarm of Forsworn have fortified their position within a shallow cave. Enter to battle a host of the scrappy scavengers—for this is one of the larger Forsworn redoubts in the Reach. Find a large chest in one of the tents, and don't miss the smaller, locked chest that's hidden below the east ramp. After the Side Quest: No One Escapes Cidhna Mine, if Madanach survives that struggle, he will return here. His presence will keep the Forsworn from attacking you, though they will still be hostile at other locations. A Skill Book rests on a shelf near a cage.

▷ **NOTE** Sitting on one of the tables is a rough sketch of the Reach showing the location of most Forsworn redoubts. Activating this will place markers for all of them on your world map!

▷ [5.08] Dragontooth Crater

Dungeon: Dragon Lair
Dragon (after Main Quest: Dragon Rising)
Forsworn
Hagraven

Crafting
Arcane Enchanter

Special Objects
Word Wall: Elemental Fury [2/3]
Chest
Chest (Locked: Expert)
Potions

In the Reach's northern mountains, the Forsworn have made a campsite next to a collapsed tower—unless a dragon has roosted here, in which case, only the mighty beast must be contended with. Slay the dragon and loot the giant chest. You'll also gain a new Word of Power, as the chest sits right near a Word Wall. Enter the ruined tower afterward here to pillage some potions, and loot the upstairs chest if your Lockpicking skill is high enough.

▷ [5.09] Harmugstahl

Related Quests
Dungeon Activity

Recommended Level: 8

Dungeon: Warlock Lair
Adventurer
Animal
Kornalus

Crafting
Alchemy Lab
Arcane Enchanter

Puzzles
Lever Puzzle

Collectibles
Skill Book [Alchemy]: A Game at Dinner

Special Objects
Shrine of Julianos [3/5]
Chest(s)
Potions aplenty
Loose gear

This unassuming stronghold is built into the north side of the Reach's central mountains.

Entry Cavern
Witness an adventurer dispatch an overgrown spider in the first cavern, then speak to the man to learn that this place is supposedly overrun with the pests. You can loot a chest atop this room's balcony when you eventually make your way back around.

◇ Chest   ◇ Satchel

Lever Cavern
Progress until you encounter a room with four levers. Pull only the far left and far right levers to open the way forward.

Alchemy Room
If you can, unlock this chamber's Expert-level door to access a small storage room filled with potions and a Skill Book.

◇ Crafting: Alchemy Lab
◇ Skill Book [Alchemy]: A Game at Dinner
◇ Chest
◇ Potions aplenty

Kornalus's Lab
Slay a dangerous mage named Kornalus in the next chamber, who's conducting some sort of nefarious study on the spiders. Claim a key from Kornalus's corpse and use it to open the nearby north door.

◇ Crafting: Arcane Enchanter
◇ Kornalus Frey's Key (Kornalus)
◇ Potions

Kornalus's Quarters
Loot the giant chest in the small room beyond to claim valuable treasure. Touch the pyramid-shaped shrine to instantly cure any diseases you may have.

◇ Shrine of Julianos [3/5]   ◇ Chest
                                       ◇ Potions

Giant Spider Cavern
This cavern's two Giant Frostbite Spiders are not only massive, but they've also been enchanted by Kornalus to make them even more formidable.

◇ Loose gear

▷ [5.10] Reach Stormcloak Camp

Related Quests
Civil War Quest: Liberation of Skyrim
Civil War Quest: Compelling Tribute
Civil War Quest: The Battle for Fort Sungard

Habitation: Military: Stormcloak Camp
Kottir Red-Shoal
Stormcloak Quartermaster (Blacksmith)
Stormcloak Soldier

Services
Trader (Blacksmith): Stormcloak Quartermaster [13/33]
Weapons, Apparel, Misc

Crafting
Alchemy Lab
Anvil
Grindstone
Workbench

Special Objects
Civil War: Map of Skyrim
Chests (2)
Potions
Loose gear

The Sons of Skyrim have erected a camp in the Reach's eastern mountains. Use the array of crafting stations here, and inspect the tabletop map in the largest tent to potentially gain new map data. If your stealth skills are sharp, loot a few chests before moving on.

[5.11] Liar's Retreat

Related Quests

Dungeon Activity

Recommended Level: 18

Dungeon: Falmer Hive

Animal   Falmer

Bandit

Collectibles

Skill Book [Speech]: Biography of the Wolf Queen

Unique Weapon: The Longhammer [32/80]

Chest(s)

Potions

Loose gear

This medium-sized cave, which is situated within the Reach's eastern mountains, is being used as a bar and gambling hall by bandits. However, the bandits have recently found themselves faced with an overwhelming adversary—Falmer have invaded the cave!

Dining Hall

Sneak into the cave's first chamber to watch a few bandits battle against several Falmer. Slay the victors afterward, and beware of many more Falmer that emerge from the room's northern entrances. Claim a few potions from behind the bar.

◇ Potions   ◇ Loose gear

Sleeping Quarters

Find a few potions and some loose gear in the various rooms that connect off the dining hall. Find a locked chest in the northwest room and pick the Novice-level southwest door to free a powerful bandit and obtain even more wealth. A Skill Book sits atop a high stone shelf near the locked chest.

◇ Skill Book [Speech]: Biography of the Wolf Queen   ◇ Chest (Locked: Adept)

◇ Chest   ◇ Potions

◇ Loose gear

Spider Tunnels

Slay a ravenous Frostbite Spider in the webbed passages that follow, and find a locked chest in a Falmer tent. Beware of additional spiders that may descend from the ceiling, as well as the Falmer archer who stands in an elevated position as you exit the tunnel. Loot the chest on the Falmer's perch.

◇ Chest

◇ Chest (Locked: Apprentice)

◇ Potions

Chaurus Den

Slay some poorly equipped bandit prisoners on your way to the cave's large, final chamber, where a massive Chaurus lurks. Loot a chest here, collect the Longhammer from near the bar owner's splayed body, then backtrack outside. Beware: a handful of powerful bandits will ambush you back in the dining hall, thinking that you're to blame for their hideout's destruction!

◇ Unique Weapon: The Longhammer [32/80]

◇ Chest

◇ Loose gear

[5.12] Cliffside Retreat

Recommended Level: 8

Habitation: Hunter Camp

Hunter

Crafting

Tanning Rack

Collectibles

Skill Book [Archery]: The Marksmanship Lesson

A lone hunter makes his home at this humble shack, which stands on the Reach's eastern cliffs. A Skill Book is the main attraction here.

[5.13] Dragon Bridge Overlook

Recommended Level: 8

Dungeon: Forsworn Redoubt

Forsworn

Chest (Locked: Novice)

Potion

Loose gear

This Forsworn campsite overlooks Haafingar's infamous Dragon Bridge [1.17]. Slay the dangerous ruffians and then plunder their valuables.

[5.14] Ragnvald

Related Quests

Side Quest: Masks of the Dragon Priests*

Dungeon Quest: Otar's Mad Guardians*

Recommended Level: 24

Dungeon: Dragon Priest Lair

Draugr

Guardian Saerek

Guardian Torsten

Otar the Mad

Crafting

Arcane Enchanter

Dangers

Dart Trap (pressure plates)

Flamethrowers (iron door)

Oil Lamp Traps

Oil Pool Traps

Swinging Blade Trap

Trapped Chest

Quest Items

Saerek's Skull Key

Torsten's Skull Key

Collectibles

Dragon Priest Mask: Otar [7/10]

Skill Book [Restoration]: Mystery of Talara, v2

Special Objects

Word Wall: Kyne's Peace [1/3]

Chest(s)

Potions

Loose gear

These ancient ruins lie within the Reach's western mountains, on the edge of Skyrim. Dispatch a few Draugr as you scale the massive stone steps that lead into the temple.

Ragnvald Temple

The cavernous temple is silent. Go downstairs and loot a chest before taking a winding passage to another large chamber. Slay a couple of powerful Draugr, then drop from the walkway and loot a chest that sits in a nook. Go back upstairs and proceed west, fully exploring the chamber to discover another chest and several potions scattered about.

After venturing into the crypts and canal to obtain a pair of special skulls (see the following sections), you will battle a powerful enemy here in the temple and subsequently unlock the temple's west area, where you'll discover a locked chest in the northern nook and a Word Wall to the south.

◇ Danger! Oil Lamp Traps, Oil Pool Traps   ◇ Chest (Locked: Apprentice)

◇ Word Wall: Kyne [1/3]   ◇ Potions

◇ Chests (4)   ◇ Loose gear

Ragnvald Crypts

Swipe a few potions in the crypts' first chamber, then take the right (west) passage to avoid the left passage's traps. Slay a host of powerful Draugr in the burial passages that lead into the next chamber, where a trapped chest tempts you. Open the chest from as far away as possible to avoid being impaled by spears. Go upstairs to reach the crypts' final chamber, where a special skull sits atop a central pedestal. Take the skull to gain a new Side Quest, then slay the deadly Draugr guardian that soon emerges from the far sarcophagus.

◇ Danger! Oil Lamp Trap, Oil Pool Trap, Trapped Chest, Dart Trap (pressure plates)   ◇ Saerek's Skull Key

◇ Chest

◇ Potions

Ragnvald Canal

Enter this watery cave and search the northwest nook to discover a chest. Pull a southeast lever to lower a drawbridge ahead, but before you cross, open the nearby iron door from as far away as possible—a fire trap activates when the door opens. Loot the chest in the nook beyond the door, then cross the drawbridge and advance farther south, eventually reaching a large chamber. Swipe another skull from the central pedestal here to battle Guardian Torsten, who emerges from the far sarcophagus. Go upstairs to loot a locked chest, then take the north corridor back to the previous cavern, jumping the pressure plate at the corridor's start to avoid activating a nasty trap. Open one last chest near the Arcane Enchanter before following the walkways back to the temple.

◇ Danger! Flamethrowers (iron door), Swinging Blade Trap (pressure plate)

◇ Crafting: Arcane Enchanter

◇ Torsten's Skull Key

◇ Chests (3)

◇ Chest (Locked: Novice) (2)

◇ Potion

[5.15] Reach Imperial Camp

Related Quests

Civil War Quest (when active, depending on who you side with)

Habitation: Military: Imperial Camp

Imperial Quartermaster (Blacksmith)

Imperial Soldier

Services

Trader (Blacksmith): Imperial Quartermaster [14/33]

Weapons, Apparel, Misc

Crafting

Alchemy Lab

Anvil

Grindstone

Workbench

Special Objects

Civil War: Map of Skyrim

Chests (2)

Potions

Loose gear

Imperial forces have erected a small camp in the Reach's eastern mountains, though this site may not exist, depending on the status of the Civil War quest line. Use the array of crafting stations here, and inspect the tabletop map in the largest tent to potentially gain new map data. If you like, loot a few chests before moving on.

[5.16] Shrine to Peryite

Related Quests

Daedric Quest: The Only Cure

Recommended Level: 12

Dungeon: Special

Kesh the Clean

Crafting

Alchemy Lab

Collectibles

Skill Book [Speech]: The Buying Game [E2/10]

This quaint shrine is perched high atop the Reach's northern mountains. Speak with the lone individual here, an alchemist named Kesh, to begin a Daedric Quest if you are Level 10 or higher. A Skill Book sits on the table near the Alchemy Lab.

[5.17] Karthwasten

Habitation: Town

Ainethach (Marriage Prospect)

Atar

Belchimac

Enmon

Lash gra-Dushnikh

Mena

Ragnar

Crafting

Grindstone

Smelters (2)

Services

Marriage Prospect: Ainethach [21/62]

Collectibles

Chest(s)

Potions

Loose gear

Mineable ore (Silver)

Related Quests

Temple Quest: The Heart of Dibella

Miscellaneous Objective: Sauranach's Mine!: Helping Atar* (Atar or Ainethach)

Miscellaneous Objective: Sauranach's Mine!: Helping Ainethach* (Atar or Ainethach)

This bustling mining community lies in the Reach's north-central region. You visit this village during "The Heart of Dibella" in search of an important child.

Exterior

When you first arrive at Karthwasten, you witness a verbal dispute between some Silver-Blood soldiers and a man named Ainethach, who owns the nearby Sanuarach mine. Speak to either person afterward to gain a Side Quest that involves the settling of their dispute.

◇ Crafting: Grindstone, Smelter (2)

1 Karthwasten Hall

This small area sports a chest and some loose coin, making it worth breaking into.

◇ Area Is Locked (Novice)

◇ Chest

2 Enmon's House

Pillage this humble abode for several potions and a chest.

◇ Area Is Locked (Novice)

◇ Chest

◇ Potions

◇ Loose gear

3 Miner's Barracks

Break into the barracks to raid a few chests.

◇ Area Is Locked (Novice)   ◇ Loose gear

◇ Chests (2)

④ Fenn's Gulch Mine

This small silver mine has been largely mined out, but there's a bit of ore to be found in the northern nook.

◇ Loose gear
◇ Mineable ore (silver)

⑤ Sanuarach Mine

Silver-Blood soldiers guard this newer mine, and they won't let anyone harvest its precious silver until the situation between Atar and Ainethach here at Karthwasten has been resolved.

◇ Loose gear
◇ Mineable ore (Silver)

[5.18] Broken Tower Redoubt

Related Quests

Temple Quest: The Heart of Dibella

Recommended Level: 14

Dungeon: Forsworn Redoubt

Forsworn

Crafting

Grindstone

Dangers

Rockfall Trap (tripwire)

Rune Trap (floor)

Swinging Wall Trap (pressure plate)

Collectibles

Skill Book [Block]: The Mirror [D1/10]

Skill Book [Conjuration]: Liminal Bridges

Special Objects

Shrine of Dibella [4/8]

Chest(s)

Potions aplenty

Loose gear

This battered fortress stands in a valley between the Reach's rocky eastern hills. While Temple Quest: The Heart of Dibella is active, a band of Forsworn will be guarding an important child here, whom you must free.

Great Hall

Unlock the first chamber's Adept-level northwest door to access a stockroom with a chest. Proceed through the upstairs door and sidestep a pressure plate trap in the corridor on your way to the next room.

◇ Danger! Swinging Wall Trap (pressure plate)
◇ Chest
◇ Potions

Tower A

Unlock the chest within this circular chamber and swipe several potions off shelves. Claim a Skill Book from a table in the sleeping area before opening the east door and navigating a long passage to another tower.

◇ Skill Book [Block]: The Mirror [D1/10]
◇ Chest (Locked: Novice)
◇ Potions

Tower B

Slay more Forsworn in the second tower, and beware of a tripwire that's stretched across the stairs as you make your ascent. Loot a chest on the second level and then continue upstairs. Exit through the door at the top to access the fort's upper ramparts.

◇ Chest
◇ Potions

Exterior Ramparts

Exit the keep via any of its northern doors to visit the exterior ramparts, where more Forsworn await. Access the highest ramparts by exiting

---

through the upstairs door in Tower B, then cut across and enter the top of Tower A.

◇ Crafting: Grindstone
◇ Loose gear
◇ Potion

Tower A (Top Level)

Beware: a powerful Forsworn mage lurks at the top of this tower, and the center of the room features a dangerous rune trap. Keep away from the room's center as you battle the mage. The key you find on his corpse opens the nearby holding cell, where the child you seek as part of "The Heart of Dibella" quest is imprisoned. Claim the Skill Book on the nearby table and touch the shrine near the altar to banish any diseases you might have.

◇ Danger! Rune Trap (floor)
◇ Skill Book [Conjuration]: Liminal Bridges
◇ Shrine of Dibella [4/8]
◇ Broken Tower Prison Key (Forsworn mage)
◇ Chest
◇ Potions aplenty

[5.19] Markarth Stables

Related Quests

Favor: Special Delivery* (Banning)

Habitation: Farm

Banning (Special)

Cedran (Stables)

Kibell (Carriage)

Services

Follower: Vigilance [17/47]

Trader (Carriage): Kibell [2/5]

Trader (Stables): Cedran [2/5]

Trader (Stablemasters): Cedran [2/5]

Stop by these fine stables to buy a steed or purchase a carriage ride to any Hold's capital. For 500 gold, you may also buy a trusty war dog named Vigilance to serve as your Follower — speak with Banning for assistance.

[5.20] Salvius Farm

Related Quests

Miscellaneous Objective: Letter to Leonitus* (Rogatus Salvius)

Favor (Activity): Harvesting Crops* (Vigdis Salvius)

Habitation: Farm

Rogatus Salvius

Vigdis Salvius

Collectibles

Area Is Locked [Novice]

Chest

This small farm stands just outside of Markarth's front gate. Speak with the farm's owner, Rogatus Salvius, to gain a new Side Quest. Break into the farmhouse and raid it for valuables if you dare.

[5.21] Left Hand Mine

Related Quests

Favor (Activity): Mining Ore* (Skaggi Scar-Face)

Habitation: Mine

Adeber

Daighre

Erith

Gat gro-Shargakh (Marriage Prospect)

Pavo Attius (Marriage Prospect)

Skaggi Scar-Face

Sosia Tremellia

Torom (dog)

Willem

Crafting

Smelter

Services

Marriage Prospect: Gat gro-Shargakh [22/62]

Marriage Prospect: Pavo Attius [23/62]

Collectibles

Chest(s)

Loose gear

Mineable ore (Iron)

This bustling mining community is located just outside of Markarth's gates. It's busier than normal due to an influx of miners who have fled from the nearby Kolskeggr Mine [5.22], which has been overrun by Forsworn raiders.

Exterior

Chat with the villagers outside, including the mine's owner, Skaggi Scar-Face, to acquire a Side Quest involving another mine to the north. Skaggi will also purchase Iron Ore for a fair price.

◇ Crafting: Smelter

Miner's Barracks

If you like, raid a chest in the miner's barracks to claim some ill-gotten loot.

◇ Chest

Daighre's House

These humble miners don't have much, but you can steal what little they've got.

◇ Chest

Skaggi's House

The mine's owner isn't a rich woman, but you can break into her house and steal her life savings if you like.

◇ Area Is Locked (Novice)
◇ Chest

Left Hand Mine

There's plenty of iron to be claimed from this mine's thick ore veins.

◇ Loose gear
◇ Mineable ore (iron)

[5.22] Kolskeggr Mine

Related Quests

Miscellaneous Objective:
Kolskeggr Clear Out* (Pavo)

Dungeon: Forsworn Redoubt

Forsworn

Crafting

Smelter
Potions
Loose gear
Mineable ore (Gold)

This valuable mining site has been overrun by Forsworn—its former workers have fled to the nearby Left Hand Mine [5.21]. Pick the easy front door lock to break into the cabin if you wish—you'll find pickaxes within. Go up the hill and enter the mine, slaying the remaining Forsworn there to secure it and its rich supply of valuable Gold Ore. Once the Forsworn are no more, the miners who fled to Left Hand Mine will return here to work.

[5.23] The Lover Stone

Recommended Level: 6

Dungeon: Special

Special Objects

Standing Stone: The Lover [6/13]

A small collection of ancient stones stands atop the mountains northeast of Markarth. Inspect the central Standing Stone to receive a new sign blessing. Those under the sign of the Lover can master all skills 15 percent faster. Note that you may only have one sign blessing at a time, so activating this Standing Stone will override your current sign blessing (if any).

[5.24] Blind Cliff Cave

Related Quests

Dungeon Quest: Melka and Petra*

Recommended Level: 14

Dungeon: Hagraven Nest

Forsworn
Melka

Crafting

Alchemy Lab

Dangers

Oil Lamp Traps
Oil Pool Traps

Puzzles

Handle Puzzle

Collectibles

Skill Book [Illusion]: Mystery of Talara, Part 4
Skill Book [Light Armor]: The Refugees [E2/10]
Unique Weapon: Eye of Melka [33/80]
Chest(s)
Potions
Loose gear

This small cave is located in the heart of the Reach, not far from the main road, and passing through it allows you to reach a pair of secluded, crumbling towers. The twisted Forsworn are using this area as a hideout.

Blind Cliff Cave (Interior)

Bring down a hanging lamp to ignite the oil in the cave's first passage and sear a lone Forsworn guard. Slay more Forsworn in the wide cavern that follows as you work your way up to a collapsed tower. Smiths should be on the lookout for ore veins throughout. Before entering the tower, check around behind it to locate a hidden chest, along with a Skill Book. Exit the cave via the tower's top door to return outside, near a pair of twin exterior towers.

◇ Skill Book [Light Armor]: The Refugees [E2/10]
◇ Danger! Oil Lamp Traps, Oil Pool Trap
◇ Chest

Blind Cliff Towers

Head to the top of the first exterior tower, slaying a few more Forsworn and looting a chest along the way. Cross the elevated walkway to reach the neighboring tower, looting a chest as you enter. Proceed into the bastion.

◇ Chests (2)
◇ Potion

Blind Cliff Bastion

You encounter a caged Hagraven named Melka in the bastion's entry passage. Speak to Melka to gain a new Side Quest, then pull the nearby chain to free Melka, who will guide you from this point forward. Melka can hold her own in most fights, but she is not invincible. Just ahead, turn the middle of three handles to safely raise a portcullis. Just beyond, allow Melka to expose a hidden lever, then pull it to deactivate the swinging blades in the next corridor. Just before Melka's alchemy parlor, you may spy a handle on the wall beyond the swinging blades and turn it to reveal a secret passage that leads to several urns and a chest. Backtrack out and proceed to the final cavern, where two Forsworn and a Hagraven named Petra await. Slay Petra to complete Melka's quest, and search Petra's remains to discover a Skill Book. Be sure to talk to Melka (or scavenge her corpse!) to claim your reward—a unique staff, the Eye of Melka.

◇ Crafting: Alchemy Lab
◇ Skill Book [Illusion]: Mystery of Talara, Part 4
◇ Unique Weapon: Eye of Melka [33/80]
◇ Chests (2)
◇ Potions
◇ Loose gear

[5.25] Four Skull Lookout

Related Quests

College of Winterhold Radiant Quest: Destruction Ritual Spell

Recommended Level: 8

Dungeon: Bandit Camp

Bandit

Collectibles

Chest(s)
Loose gear

Bandits have taken over this small stone ruin, located in the heart of the Reach. Clear out the villains, then loot the chest they're guarding. The special pedestal here is used during a College of Winterhold Quest.

[5.26] Red Eagle Redoubt

Related Quests

Side Quest: Repairing the Phial
Dungeon Quest: The Legend of Red Eagle

Recommended Level: 14

Dungeon: Forsworn Redoubt

Forsworn

Crafting

Alchemy Lab
Blacksmith Forge
Tanning Rack
Workbench

Dangers

Dart Trap
Oil Lamp Trap
Oil Pool Trap
Rockfall Trap

Quest Items

Red Eagle's Fury

Collectibles

Skill Book [Alteration]: Reality & Other Falsehoods
Unique Weapon: Red Eagle's Fury [34/80]
Chest(s)
Potions
Loose gear

Red Eagle Redoubt is perched on the precipice of the Tundra Plateau, just as the land plummets into the depths of the Reach. Millennia of erosion have all but destroyed the immense Nordic temple that once stood here, but a few remnants of its stairs and foundations remain. The Forsworn have built an impressive camp here, taking advantage of the area's natural defenses and commanding view of the Reach. The leader of this clan wields Red Eagle's Fury, an ancient blade that seals the tomb of Rebel's Cairn [5.28].

Exterior (Lower Area)

Slay the guards near the entrance and claim a few potions and a coin purse before continuing into the nearby cave.

◇ Potions

Red Eagle Ascent

This winding cave leads up to Red Eagle Redoubt's upper half. Avoid the oil pool (or shoot down the oil lamp above to ignite it), then look for a few potions next to a large brazier and a locked chest hidden behind some vines nearby. As you climb the first set of stairs, watch out for the rockfall and dart traps. A second chest can be found beneath the wooden stairs that lead up to the exit.

◇ Danger! Dart Trap, Oil Pool Trap, Oil Lamp Trap, Rockfall Trap
◇ Chest
◇ Chest (Locked: Adept)
◇ Potions

Exterior (Ascent Area)

As you emerge from the Red Eagle Ascent cave, travel south to find a lone chest sitting near a small yet unique statue that catches the eye [5.U]. Return to the cave exit entrance and scale a long flight of stone steps to reach a sizable Forsworn camp on the hill above. Find a Skill Book in a tent up here, along with a few crafting stations. Slay the mighty Forsworn leader to find a special key on his corpse, along with Red Eagle's Fury,

a unique sword. When you have finished in the camp, use the key to open the nearby iron door and enter the Sundered Towers [5.27]. Pull a wall chain to lower the drawbridge and pillage the neighboring tower as well.

◇ Crafting: Alchemy Lab, Blacksmith Forge, Tanning Rack, Workbench
◇ Skill Book [Alteration]: Reality & Other Falsehoods
◇ Unique Weapon: Red Eagle's Fury (34/80) (Forsworn leader)
◇ Red Eagle Tower Key (Forsworn leader)
◇ Chests (2)
◇ Chest (Locked: Novice)
◇ Chest (Locked: Adept)
◇ Potions
◇ Loose gear

[5.27] Sundered Towers

Related Quests

Side Quest: Repairing the Phial

Dungeon: Forsworn Redoubt

Collectibles

Area Is Locked (Barred)
Chest (Locked: Novice)
Potions
Loose gear

These two towers are a major landmark, visible from much of the Reach and the western Tundra. The eastern tower is initially barred and all but inaccessible because of the surrounding cliffs. To explore them, claim the key from the boss in Red Eagle Redoubt [5.26], then enter the western tower from the entrance near the boss. Loot a few urns on your way up, then pull a wall chain to lower a drawbridge to the eastern tower. Raid a locked chest here, take in the spectacular view from atop both towers, and then unbar the eastern door as you leave.

[5.28] Rebel's Cairn

Related Quests

Dungeon Quest: The Legend of Red Eagle

Recommended Level:
14

Dungeon: Draugr Crypt

Red Eagle
Skeleton

Collectibles

Unique Weapon: Red Eagle's Bane (35/80)
Area Is Locked (Red Eagle's Fury required)
Chest
Potion
Loose gear

A common sword imbedded in a stone cairn marks the entrance to this secluded cave. Find the legendary blade called Red Eagle's Fury by slaughtering the Forsworn leader in nearby Red Eagle Redoubt [5.26], then place the sword into the pedestal in the main chamber to open a secret passage. Enter the tomb of Red Eagle, a powerful Draugr Warrior

who raises skeletons to aid him. Lay Red Eagle to rest and loot his remains—along with a giant chest—to complete your quest and amass plenty of plunder. On your way out, reclaim Red Eagle's sword, which has been transfigured into an even more powerful blade—Red Eagle's Bane.

[5.29] Karthspire Camp

Related Quests

Main Quest: Alduin's Wall
Main Quest: The Throat of the World

Recommended Level:
14

Dungeon: Forsworn Redoubt

Dragon
Forsworn

Crafting

Blacksmith Forge
Grindstone
Tanning Rack
Workbench

Collectibles

Skill Book [Block]: A Dance in Fire, v2
Chest
Apothecary's Satchels (2)
Potion
Loose gear

This sprawling Forsworn encampment lies just outside of Karthspire [5.30]. This dangerous camp must be braved in order to reach Karthspire and explore Sky Haven Temple [5.31] as part of the Main Quest. Search the lower walkways and tents thoroughly to discover a Skill Book. Make your way up to a high platform, where a chest and a number of crafting stations are found. You also obtain a Dragon's Soul here during the Main Quest. Scale the west rocks afterward to locate a large cave entrance that leads into Karthspire.

[5.30] Karthspire

Related Quests

Main Quest: Alduin's Wall

Recommended Level:
14

Dungeon: Forsworn Redoubt

Forsworn

Dangers

Flamethrower (pressure plates)

Puzzles

Spinning Pillars Puzzle
Pressure Plates Puzzle
Underground Connection: Sky Haven Temple [5.31]
Chests (2)
Potions
Loose gear

Located due east of Markarth, Karthspire is a cave that you must navigate to reach Sky Haven Temple [5.31] during the Main Quest. Battle more Forsworn to secure the interior, finding a chest and several potions in the entry encampment. During the Main Quest, Esbern helps you solve a simple puzzle in the cavern that follows: spin the three pillars so that they each show the symbol of the Dragonborn, which resembles a circle. Cross the drawbridge that lowers and proceed to a room filled with pressure plates—step only on the path of Dragonborn tiles to safely reach a far wall chain that deactivates the trap. Proceed to the final chamber

afterward to raid a large chest and locate the entrance to the Sky Temple, which Esbern helps you open.

[5.31] Sky Haven Temple

Related Quests

Main Quest: Alduin's Wall
Main Quest: The Throat of the World
Main Quest: Paarthurnax
Main Quest: Epilogue
Main Quest: Elder Knowledge
Other Factions: The Blades Quest: Rebuilding the Blades*
Other Factions: The Blades Quest: Dragon Hunting*
Other Factions: The Blades Quest: Dragonslayer's Blessing*
Other Factions: The Blades Quest: Dragon Research*

Habitation: Special

Delphine (the Blades)
Esbern (the Blades)

Underground Connection: Karthspire [5.30]

Collectibles

Skill Book [One-Handed]: Mace Etiquette
Unique Weapon: Dragonbane (36/80)

Special Objects

Alduin's Wall
Area Is Locked (quest required)
Chests (10)
Loose gear
Lots o' Gold!

This sacred sanctum lies east of Markarth and cannot be entered until you progress to Main Quest: Alduin's Wall. Inspect the central mural with Esbern to complete that quest and begin a new one. Search the west alcove to find a chest and Skill Book, then head upstairs and search the northwest sleeping area to discover a whopping seven more chests. Explore the armory to find a unique weapon lyinh on the table. Exit through any of the northeast doors to reach an exterior courtyard that offers breathtaking views, along with quick access to the world map's Fast-Travel option. Far below the upper exterior courtyard is the Karth River, and an abandoned rowboat containing scattered gems, an underwater chest, and a strongbox.

Blades Occupation

The Blades repurpose the Sky Haven Temple as their base of operations during the Main Quest. After finishing Main Quest: Alduin's Wall (and once you've sided with the Blades and completed Main Quest: Paarthurnax, meaning you're in good standing with them), you're able to return to Delphine and Esbern and commence the following:

During Other Factions Quest: Rebuilding the Blades,* you can bring up to three of your Followers (or Hirelings) and have Delphine train them to be Blades, after which they remain here.

During Other Factions Quest: Dragon Hunting, once you've brought three Followers to be trained, you can speak to Esbern and hunt a dragon with the newly trained Blades.

During Other Factions Quest: Dragonslayer's Blessing, you can receive a blessing from Esbern if you're in good standing with the Blades, which grants you +10 percent Critical Hit versus dragons for five days.

During Other Factions Quest: Dragon Research, bring back any Dragon Scales or Dragon Bones to Esbern and he concocts Esbern's Potion, imbuing you with a 10 percent damage reduction from dragon attacks.

[5.32] Soljund's Sinkhole

Related Quests

Miscellaneous Objective: Making It Hole Again* (Perth)

Recommended Level: 6

Dungeon: Draugr Crypt

Draugr

Perth (Marriage Prospect)

Crafting

Smelter

Services

Marriage Prospect: Perth [24/62]

Dangers

Dart Trap (lever)

Spear Trap (pressure plates)

Collectibles

Skill Book [Light Armor]: Jornibret's Last Dance

Chest(s)

Potions

Loose gear

Located in the heart of the Reach, this old mine has recently been invaded by Draugr and has since stopped working.

Exterior

Outside the mine, a man named Perth explains that the miners dug too deeply and accidently unearthed a Draugr-filled tomb. This gains you a Side Quest that you can satisfy by clearing out the undead within the mine.

◇ Crafting: Smelter

Miner's House

Breaking into the miner's house puts you within easy reach of two chests and a few potions.

◇ Area Is Locked (Novice)

◇ Chests (2)

◇ Potions

Soljund's Sinkhole (Interior)

These sizeable mines have been filled with undead ever since the miners accidentally tunneled into a forgotten crypt. Turn left at the first junction and slay the Draugr at the dead end, where a Skill Book sits atop a table on the overlook. Then backtrack and go right, dropping down a giant hole and slaughtering a host of powerful Draugr in the chamber below.

◇ Skill Book [Light Armor]: Jornibret's Last Dance

◇ Potion

◇ Loose gear

Draugr Tunnels

Wipe out undead on your way through the tunnels that follow, but don't touch the lever you soon locate—you'll only spring a nasty trap. Instead, pull two hidden levers that are affixed to the nearby walls to open the way forward. Scale some winding steps afterward and sidestep a couple of pressure plates upstairs. After passing the second pressure plate, climb more steps and search the dark west nook to discover an ornate chest. Slay a mighty Draugr in the large chamber that follows, then raid a large chest before following an elevated passage back to the mine's entrance.

◇ Danger! Spear Trap (pressure plates), Dart Trap (lever)

◇ Chests (2)

◇ Potions

◇ Loose gear

[5.33] Bleakwind Bluff

Dungeon: Hagraven Nest

Forsworn

Hagraven

Collectibles

Skill Book [Two-Handed]: King [B2/10]

Chest

Scale the crumbling stone steps that encircle this fallen tower, which protrudes from the Reach's eastern hills. Slay powerful Forsworn and Hagraven as you make your way up to the tower, where a large chest and Skill Book are found.

[5.34] Old Hroldan

Related Quests

Miscellaneous Objective: The Ghost of Old Hroldan* (Eydis/Ghost of Old Hrolden)

Habitation: Inn

Eydis (Innkeeper)

Leonitus Salvius

Skuli

Services

Trader (Innkeeper): Eydis [7/15]

Collectibles

Skill Book [Two-Handed]: Battle of Sancre Tor [A1/10]

Chest

Chests (Locked: Novice) (2)

Nestled along the west bank of the Reach's eastern hills, this small inn offers room and board to weary travelers. Speak to the innkeeper to buy a meal or rent a room, and search the place to loot a number of chests and discover a Skill Book on a nightstand.

[5.35] Hag Rock Redoubt

Related Quests

Daedric Quest: Pieces of the Past

Recommended Level: 14

Dungeon: Forsworn Redoubt

Forsworn

Crafting

Alchemy Lab

Anvil

Tanning Rack

Workbench

Dangers

Rockfall Trap (tripwire)

Collectibles

Skill Book [Sneak]: 2920, Last Seed, v8

Chest(s)

Potions aplenty

Loose gear

Located along the Reach's southwest edge, this large collection of mountainous ruins has been exploited by the Forsworn and fortified into a military encampment. You must pass through Hag Rock Redoubt in order to reach Dead Crone Rock [5.36] as part of Daedric Quest: Pieces of the Past.

Exterior

Scale the exterior tower, looting a chest and slaying a Forsworn on your way to the top. Cross the narrow aqueduct and dispatch more Forsworn, raiding a dome-shaped outdoor shack to obtain several potions and sack another chest. Beware the tripwire that's stretched across the steps of the east ruins, and keep going up to eventually reach Dead Crone Rock [5.36].

◇ Danger! Rockfall Trap (tripwire)

◇ Crafting: Alchemy Lab, Anvil, Tanning Rack, Workbench

◇ Chests (2)

◇ Chest (Locked: Adept)

◇ Apothecary's Satchels (2)

◇ Potions aplenty

Hag Rock Redoubt Ruin

Enter the west structure via any of its three entrances to explore a small network of interior ruins. Lay waste to more Forsworn here as you plunder even more loot. Search the shelves of the cupboard near the holding cells to find the key that unlocks them. Downstairs, find a Skill Book on a table that's covered with potions, along with a chest that's tucked away in a dark southeast nook.

◇ Skill Book [Sneak]: 2920, Last Seed, v8

◇ Hag Rock Ruin Jail Key

◇ Chest

◇ Chest (Locked: Adept)

◇ Potions

◇ Loose gear

[5.36] Dead Crone Rock

Related Quests

Daedric Quest: Pieces of the Past

Thieves Guild Radiant Quest: No Stone Unturned

Recommended Level: 14

Dungeon: Hagraven Nest

Drascua

Forsworn

Crafting

Arcane Enchanter

Dangers

Flamethrowers (floor)

Quest Items

Pommel Stone of Mehrunes' Razor

Collectibles

Skill Book [Alchemy]: A Game at Dinner

Unusual Gem: [10/24]

The Elder Scrolls V

SKYRIM

Special Objects

◇ Word Wall: Dismaying Shout [2/3]

◇ Chest(s)

◇ Potions

◇ Loose gear

To reach this remote Forsworn outpost, which lies at the southwest corner of the Reach, one must first deal with leagues of bloodthirsty Forsworn in the surrounding Hag Rock Redoubt [5.35].

Dead Crone Rock (Interior)

Loot a chest in the first passage, then slay Forsworn and snatch up potions on your way into a large cavern, where a large spiral staircase leads upstairs. Visit the west dining room to find another chest, more potions, and an Arcane Enchanter. Sprint down the following passage to avoid being burned by flamethrowers on the floor. Find a Skill Book in the next room and pull the nearby lever to raise a portcullis back in a previous chamber. Backtrack and take the southern stairs up to a door that leads outside.

◇ Danger! Flamethrowers (floor)

◇ Crafting: Arcane Enchanter

◇ Skill Book [Alchemy]: A Game at Dinner

◇ Chests (2)

◇ Potions

Exterior

Climb the exterior steps to find another chest, then keep going up to face a powerful Hagraven named Drascua on the hill. Slay the fiend and obtain a key from its corpse, along with a quest-related item. Then loot a giant chest before approaching the nearby Word Wall to gain a new Word of Power. Collect the Unusual Gem from the table to potentially gain a new Side Quest as well. Go back inside afterward and return to the spiral stairwell chamber. Unlock the southeast door with Drascua's key and head back outside to locate a third exterior chest.

◇ Pommel Stone of Mehrunes' Razor (Drascua)

◇ Unusual Gem: Stone of Barenziah [10/24]

◇ Word Wall: Dismaying Shout [2/3]

◇ Dead Crone Rock Key (Drascua)

◇ Chests (2)

◇ Potions

[5.37] Purewater Run

Dungeon: Animal Den

Animal

Collectibles

Chests (2)

Follow a stream into this watery cave, and swim quickly to the bottom of the deep water to loot a pair of dwarven chests before you're chewed up by aggressive Slaughterfish.

[5.38] Dushnikh Yal

Related Quests

Side Quest: The Forgemaster's Fingers

Side Quest: Captured Critters*

Miscellaneous Objective: The Sword of Gharol* (Gharol)

Favor (Activity): Mining Ore* (Gharol)

Favor: Sparring Partners* (Burguk)

Recommended Level: 6

Habitation: Orc Stronghold

Arob

Chief Burguk

Dulug

Ghak

Gharol (Blacksmith)

Ghorbash the Iron Hand (Follower, Marriage Prospect)

Mahk

Murbul (Apothecary)

Nagrub

Oglub

Umurn

Services

Follower: Ghorbash the Iron Hand [18/47]

Marriage Prospect: Ghorbash the Iron Hand [25/62]

Trader (Apothecary): Murbul [8/14]

  Potions, Food, Ingredients

Trader (Blacksmith): Gharol [15/33]

  Weapons, Apparel, Misc

Trainer (Heavy Armor: Expert): Gharol [1/3]

Trainer (One-Handed: Master): Burguk [1/3]

Crafting

Alchemy Labs (2)

Blacksmith Forge

Grindstone

Smelter

Tanning Racks (2)

Workbench

Collectibles

Captured Critter: Dragonfly in a Jar [3/5]

Skill Book [Heavy Armor]: Orsinium and the Orcs [D2/10]

Chest(s)

Potions

Loose gear

Mineable ore (Orichalcum)

The Reach boasts two Orc strongholds—this one lies far to the south, on the high cliffs of the southern Reach. As always, the Orcs will loathe your presence if you're an outsider, but you can gain their acceptance by completing a Side Quest that just about any of the local Orcs will bestow during conversation.

Exterior

Use any of the crafting stations outside. Check behind the chief's Longhouse to find a chest under some stairs. The blacksmith, Gharol, will buy any ore you collect from the nearby mine at a fair price. Test your fistfighting prowess in a friendly wager against the chief if you like.

◇ Crafting: Alchemy Lab, Blacksmith Forge, Grindstone, Smelter, Tanning Racks (2), Workbench

◇ Chest (Locked: Apprentice)

◇ Potions

◇ Loose gear

Burguk's Longhouse

If you dare, enter the Orc chief's Longhouse and plunder the place. Unlock the Novice-level trapdoor to enter the cellar and claim a Skill Book, along with a Dragonfly in a Jar that pertains to Side Quest: Captured Critters. Loop around the cellar's circuitlike tunnel to locate an Alchemy Lab and a locked chest that's hidden beneath the stairs.

◇ Area Is Locked (Novice)

◇ Crafting: Alchemy Lab

◇ Captured Critter: Dragonfly in a Jar [3/5]

◇ Skill Book [Heavy Armor]: Orsinium and the Orcs [D2/10]

◇ Chests (2)

◇ Chest (Locked: Apprentice)

◇ Apothecary's Satchel

◇ Potions

◇ Loose gear

Dushnikh Mine

Grab a pickaxe and collect Orichalcum Ore from the mine. There's a chest and a couple of potions here as well.

◇ Chest

◇ Potions

◇ Loose gear

◇ Mineable ore (Orichalcum)

[5.39] Reachwater Rock

Related Quests

Side Quest: Forbidden Legend

Dungeon Activity

Recommended Level: 15

Dungeon: Draugr Crypt

Gauldur

Jyrik Gauldurson

Mikrul Gauldurson

Sigdis Gauldurson

Puzzles

Nordic Puzzle Door (Emerald)

Nordic Puzzle Door (Ivory)

Collectibles

Dragon Claw: Emerald Dragon Claw [5/8]

Unique Item: Gauldur Amulet [56/112]

Chest(s)

Potion

Loose gear

Follow the main road east out of Markarth and you'll eventually reach a bridge. Look up to spy this waterfall cave, which is perched on a high cliff, hidden beneath a spray of water. Reachwater Rock is the long-forgotten tomb of the Arch-Mage Gauldur, a powerful First Era wizard. Visit this site after you've obtained all three Gauldur Amulet Fragments to reforge the Gauldur Amulet.

Reachwater Cavern

First, dive underwater to locate worthy gear and a locked chest. A second chest is perched on a high ledge on the room's east side; to reach it, stand by the Puzzle Door and use the Whirlwind Sprint Shout. Then climb the central spire and collect the Emerald Dragon Claw from the cavern's pedestal. Inspect the claw closely to notice three markings on it. Approach the nearby puzzle door and rotate its three rings to match the symbols on the claw: Bear, Whale, Snake. Examine the door's central keyhole to insert the claw and open the way forward.

◇ Dragon Claw: Emerald Dragon Claw [5/10]

◇ Chest

◇ Chest (Locked: Adept)

◇ Loose gear

Sealed Passage

Continue down the sealed passage as the doors open ahead of you until you reach another Puzzle Door. This one requires the Ivory Claw from Folgunthur [2.08] to solve. If you have the claw, inspect it to find the symbol sequence as you did before, then mimic the same pattern on the door: Hawk, Hawk, Dragon. Insert the Ivory Claw to open the way forward. Loot a few urns and grab a potion on your way to the final cavern.

◇ Potion

Amulet Chamber

Approach the altar and place the three Gauldur Amulet Fragments onto the pedestals to battle the three Gauldurson Brothers once more and receive the reforged Gauldur Amulet as a reward (see Side Quest: Forbidden Legend for tips). You'll find a secret nook has opened as you backtrack out of the chamber. Raid the large chest within.

◊ Unique Armor: Gauldur Amulet [55/112]
◊ Chest
◊ Loose gear

[5.40] Reachwind Eyrie

Recommended Level: 8

Dungeon: Special

Collectibles

Skill Book [Heavy Armor]: Chimarvamidium

Chest (Locked: Apprentice)

Chest (Locked: Expert)

Loose gear

This striking dwarven tower is visible for miles, standing tall among the Reach's rocky south-central hills. The tower is free of danger and contains a number of valuables. Stop by and have a look. The view from the balcony is spectacular.

[5.41] Reachcliff Cave

Related Quests

Daedric Quest: The Taste of Death

Recommended Level: 6

Dungeon: Draugr Crypt

Draugr

Services

Follower: Eola [19/47]

Dangers

Trapped Chest

Collectibles

Skill Book [Conjuration]: The Doors of Oblivion [D1/10]

Unique Item: Ring of Namira [57/112]

Area Is Locked

Chest(s)

Potions

Loose gear

Stone ruins line the path that leads to this sizable cave, where restless undead dwell. You cannot fully explore this site until you visit it as part of Daedric Quest: The Taste of Death, during which you can obtain a unique ring. Complete the quest, and Eola will offer to join you as a Follower.

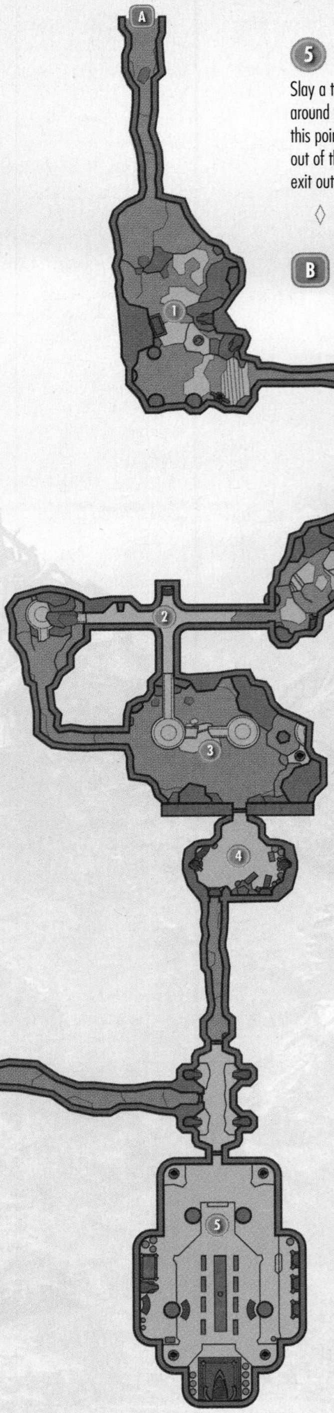

A Exit to Skyrim

1 Entry Passages

Slay a handful of mighty Draugr as you navigate these winding passages.

2 Junction

Loot an urn and grab a potion and some gear in these burial passages. Beware of waking the resting dead.

◊ Potion
◊ Loose gear

3 Walkway Chamber

Go south from [2] to explore this chamber's upper walkways and discover a trapped chest. Open the chest from the side or from behind to avoid begin punctured by arrows.

◊ Danger! Trapped Chest

4 Checkpoint Chamber

Slay the Draugr that emerges from a standing sarcophagus in this small room, then loot another chest and find a Skill Book on a shelf. If you're not playing Daedric Quest: The Taste of Death, then this is as far as you can go. Proceed to [5] otherwise.

◊ Skill Book [Conjuration]: The Doors of Oblivion [D1/10]
◊ Chest
◊ Potions
◊ Loose gear

5 Feasting Hall

Slay a trio of rugged Draugr to secure this final chamber, then search around to acquire plenty of plunder. If you've slaughtered all Draugr up to this point, then your quest advances when these last three fall. Backtrack out of the room and take the west passage, which is now open, to quickly exit out to Skyrim.

◊ Chest
◊ Potion

B Exit to Skyrim

[5.42] Valthume

Related Quests

Side Quest: Masks of the Dragon Priests*

Dungeon Quest: Evil in Waiting

Recommended Level: 24

Dungeon: Dragon Priest Lair

Animal

Draugr

Hevnoraak

Valdar

Crafting

Alchemy Lab

Dangers

Battering Ram Trap (pressure plate)

Dart Trap (lever)

Oil Lamp Traps

Oil Pool Trap

Swinging Blade Trap (pressure plate)

Swinging Wall Trap (pressure plate)

Puzzles

Nordic Puzzle Door (Iron Claw)

Quest Items

Opaque Vessels (3)

Collectibles

Dragon Claw: Iron Claw [6/10]

Dragon Priest Mask: Hevnoraak [8/10]

Skill Book [Restoration]: Withershins

Unique Weapon: Hevnoraak's Staff [37/80]

Special Objects

Word Wall: Aura Whisper [2/3]

Chest(s)

Potions aplenty

Loose gear

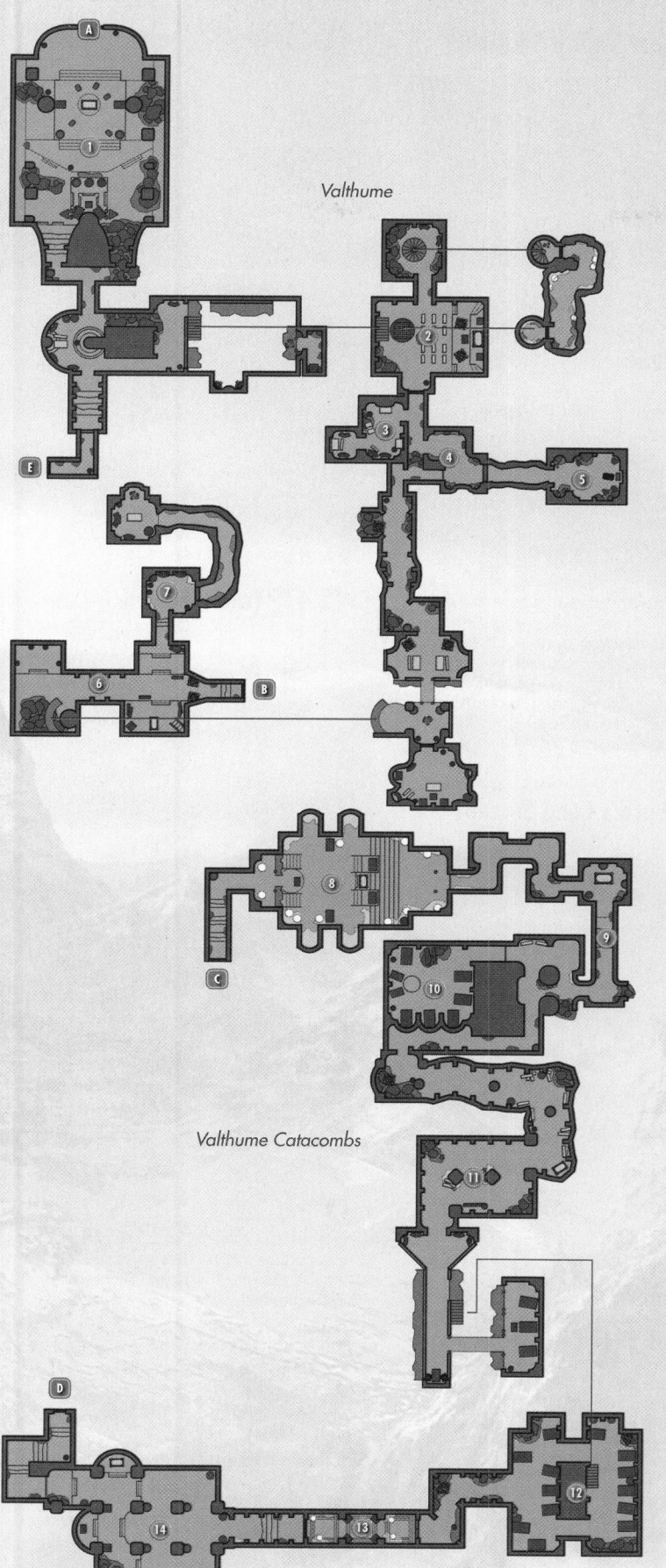

Valthume

Valthume Catacombs

This large network of burial chambers lies at the Reach's southeast end. Braving this ancient tomb can earn you a precious Dragon Priest Mask, among other valuable prizes.

Vestibule

The vestibule serves as the ruins' entrance. Speak with a ghost named Valdar here to learn that an ancient evil named Hevnoraak is stirring within the depths of this place and gain a new Side Quest. Proceed into Valthume afterward.

Ⓐ Door to Vestibule

① Throne Room

This cavernous chamber is completely void of loot. Beware the pressure plate trap in the south passage on your way to [2].

◇ Danger! Battering Ram Trap (pressure plate)

② Trapdoor Chamber

Beware the large trapdoor in the center of this wide chamber. It will open as you battle powerful Draugr here, potentially dropping you into an underground passage filled with Frostbite Spiders. Secure the room and loot a chest, then return upstairs and make a couple of daring jumps along a narrow balcony to reach the ledge where Hevnoraak's specter is spectating. Ignore Hevnoraak's specter and loot a second chest in the nearby nook. If you fall into the central pit, slay a Draugr and search its remains to find a key that'll help you escape.

◇ Valthume Cellar Key (Draugr)
◇ Chests (2)
◇ Apothecary's Satchel
◇ Loose gear

③ Embalming Chambers

Explore these small side rooms to discover a Skill Book on a table.

◇ Danger! Oil Lamp Traps
◇ Skill Book [Restoration]: Withershins
◇ Knapsack
◇ Loose gear

④ Trapped Passages

Beware the oil that runs through this passage. Knock down a hanging lamp from a safe range to burn away the potential hazard. Then simply sidestep pressure plates as you advance. When you reach a dead end, turn a small handle on the nearby wall to open passages to the east and west.

◇ Danger! Oil Lamp Traps, Oil Pool Trap, Dart Trap (pressure plates)

⑤ Vessel Chamber 1

Dispatch a powerful Draugr in this small chamber, then claim the Opaque Vessel he leaves behind.

◇ Opaque Vessel [1/3]

⑥ Two-Tier Chamber

Dispatch more Draugr here, then optionally pick the Adept-level south door to access a room filled with potions and a chest. If you like, follow the lower northeast passage to obtain more plunder on your way to [7] before taking the lower east passage to reach the Valthume Catacombs.

◇ Chest
◇ Potions aplenty

⑦ Treasure Run

Turn the handle on the wall here to open a secret passage that leads to a small chamber with an Alchemy Lab and a chest.

◇ Crafting: Alchemy Lab
◇ Chest
◇ Potions
◇ Loose gear

Ⓑ Door to Valthume Catacombs

Ⓒ Door to Valthume

⑧ Spider Lair

Beware: a Giant Frostbite Spider descends from the Catacombs' first wide chamber, along with several of her young. Slay these dangerous creatures from your elevated vantage, then raid the nearby chest and urns before opening the far portcullis (pull the nearby chain) and advancing.

◇ Chest

⑨ Burial Passages

Slay Draugr and sidestep a pressure plate trap in these undead-filled passages.

◇ Danger! Swinging Blade Trap (pressure plate)

⑩ Vessel Chamber 2

Pull a wall chain to gain entry to this small chamber, then exploit the hanging lamps to help you slay a powerful Draugr Knight. Collect the second of three vessels from the room's altar afterward.

◇ Area Is Locked (wall chain)
◇ Danger! Oil Lamp Traps
◇ Opaque Vessel [2/3]

⑪ Burial Chamber

Loot a host of urns on your way into this wide burial chamber, where more powerful Draugr await. Secure the place and pull the wall chain to advance.

◇ Danger! Swinging Wall Trap (pressure plate)

⑫ Sarcophagi Chamber

Find plenty of urns and a chest to loot in this large sarcophagi-filled chamber.

◇ Chest

⑬ Iron Claw Passage

Eradicate a few Frostbite Spiders in this chamber, then quickly retreat after collecting the Iron Claw from this passage's central pedestal; fire soon spews forth from the surrounding statues. Inspect the Iron Claw carefully in your inventory, and notice its three special markings. Mimic this same sequence of patterns (Dragon, Hawk, Wolf) on the nearby Puzzle Door by spinning its three rings. Inspect the central keyhole afterward to insert the Iron Claw and open the way forward.

◇ Dragon Claw: Iron Claw [6/10]

⑭ Vessel Chamber 3

Dispatch a swarm of mighty Draugr in this chamber, then collect the final vessel from the central pedestal. Follow the sound of chanting afterward to locate a Word Wall and gain a new Word of Power. Loot the nearby chest before taking the passage back to [1]. Follow Valdar's instructions to complete his quest, slaying the Dragon Priest Hevnoraak and obtaining his unique mask.

◇ Opaque Vessel [3/3]
◇ Dragon Priest Mask: Hevnoraak [8/10]
◇ Unique Weapon: Hevnoraak's Staff [37/80]
◇ Word Wall: Aura Whisper [2/3]
◇ Chest

[5.43] Gloomreach

Recommended Level: 18

Dungeon: Falmer Hive

Animal
Falmer

Crafting

Smelter

Dangers

Swinging Wall Trap (tripwire)

Collectibles

Skill Book [Restoration]: Withershins
Chest(s)
Loose gear

This widemouthed cave is found at the Reach's southeast edge and is home to dangerous Falmer. If you're in the area, brave this relatively short cave for a bit of sport and plunder.

Gloomreach Cavern

Slay a handful of Falmer and Chaurus inside the cavern as you work your way around in clockwise fashion. About halfway through, spy a Skill Book resting atop a barrel near some scaffolding. Unlock a pair of Adept-level cages in the southern chamber to free a few caged critters, but beware: The vicious Saber Cat may attack you. Find a chest in a Falmer tent before taking the upper passage to reach the Gloomreach Hive, looting another chest along the way.

◇ Crafting: Smelter
◇ Skill Book [Restoration]: Withershins
◇ Chests (2)
◇ Loose gear

Gloomreach Hive

Stand back and safely trigger the tripwire that's stretched across the Hive's first passage. Dispatch more Falmer in the tall cavern that follows, then find a sunken chest deep underwater. Head to a second cavern afterward and loot a chest before descending and slaying a powerful Falmer down below. Raid a third chest as you continue to descend, then take the bottom passage back to the Gloomreach Cavern — you'll find you're right back near the entrance.

◇ Danger! Swinging Wall Trap (trip wire)
◇ Chests (3)

[5.44] Lost Valley Redoubt

Related Quests

Dungeon Activity

Recommended Level: 14

Dungeon: Forsworn Redoubt

Forsworn

Crafting

Blacksmith Forge
Grindstone
Workbench

Special Objects

Word Wall: Become Ethereal [3/3]
Chests (2)
Chest (Locked: Expert)
Potions
Loose gear

At the southern end of the Reach, stone steps lead up to ancient ruins that overlook a tall, majestic waterfall. These ruins have been fortified by the Forsworn and transformed into a sprawling military campsite. Scale the hillside and eliminate these scavengers as you raid their camp for an array of plunder. Reach the top of the waterfall and go south to locate a pair of Hagraven conducting a ritual to raise a powerful Forsworn Briarheart. These are all powerful foes, so if you had trouble on your way up here, you may want to leave them be. If you are feeling confident, slay the wicked creatures, then approach the nearby Word Wall to acquire a new Word of Power.

[5.45] Bard's Leap Summit

Related Quests

Dungeon Quest: Leap Before You Look*

Dungeon: Hagraven Nest

Forsworn
Hagraven

Collectibles

Chest
Apothecary's Satchel
Loose gear

Scale the ruin-covered hills of the Lost Valley Redoubt [5.44], slaying Forsworn on your way to the top of this serene waterfall, which lies at the Reach's south end. Enjoy the view from the top of the waterfall, and leap off to land safely in the pool below. This is best accomplished by using Whirlwind Sprint to clear the waterfall and land safely in the water or by using Become Ethereal just before jumping off to ensure you take no damage. After making a splash, you encounter the ghost of an impressed bard, who increases your Speech skill!

[5.46] Cradle Stone Tower

Recommended Level: 8

Dungeon: Hagraven Nest

Hagraven

Collectibles

Skill Book [Alteration]: Sithis
Chest
Chest (Locked: Apprentice)
Potions
Loose gear

After scaling the Forsworn-filled hills of the Lost Valley Redoubt [5.44] and crossing the waterfall at Bard's Leap Summit [5.45], follow the trail up the west hill, looting a chest along your way to this remote tower. Unlock the downstairs gate to reach a burial urn and chest, and scale the tower to slay a Hagraven and claim even more loot.

[5.47] Fort Sungard

Related Quests

Civil War Quest: Liberation of Skyrim
Civil War Quest: The Battle for Fort Sungard

Recommended Level: 6

Habitation: Military Fort

Forsworn

Crafting

Anvil
Workbench
Forge

Collectibles

Skill Book [Pickpocket]: Wulfmare's Guide to Better Thieving [E1/10]
Skill Book [Smithing]: Last Scabbard of Akrash [C1/10]

Special Objects

Shrine of Akatosh [3/6] (only during Imperial occupation)
Shrine of Kynareth [4/6] (only during Forsworn occupation)
Shrine of Talos [7/17] (only during Stormcloak occupation)
Chest(s)
Potions
Loose gear

This mighty stronghold, located at the Reach's southeast corner, teems with Forsworn. You may attack through the front gate, which lies to the west, or you may breach the fort more covertly by several methods, such as the southwest sewer entrance, which leads into the muster.

Note that Fort Sungard is a point of contention between the Stormcloaks and Imperials during the Civil War quest line, and therefore may be populated by either Stormcloak or Imperial troops instead of Forsworn.

Exterior

A host of Forsworn warriors and archers guard this stronghold, so don't rush in. Remain just outside the main gate, picking off archers from afar and luring out warriors to cut them down in turn. Fight hard to secure the outer grounds, swipe a potion from a cart inside the walls, then begin storming the fort's many separate interior sections.

◇ Crafting: Anvil, Workbench, Forge
◇ Potion

Fort Sungard Muster

Bust into the muster to raid numerous chests. A Skill Book sits on a small table in the weapons room.

- ◇ Skill Book [Smithing]: Last Scabbard of Akrash [C1/10]
- ◇ Chests (3)
- ◇ Loose gear

Fort Sungard Shrine

This small room holds a shrine and some common foodstuffs. The shrine changes depending on who controls the fort.

- ◇ Shrine of Akatosh [3/6] (only during Imperial occupation)
- ◇ Shrine of Kynareth [4/6] (only during Forsworn occupation)
- ◇ Shrine of Talos [7/17] (only during Stormcloak occupation)

Fort Sungard Annex

This three-story structure features two chests on its bottom floor. There's nothing in the middle floor's holding cell, but you can get some good lockpicking practice. Exit via the ground floor door to access an exterior crafting area.

- ◇ Chests (2)
- ◇ Loose gear
- ◇ Potion

Fort Sungard Tower

Loot the chest on the tower's entry level, then go upstairs to find a bit more loot on its upper floor. Head all the way downstairs afterward and exit via the basement door to go outside, close to the stronghold's oubliette.

- ◇ Chest
- ◇ Knapsack
- ◇ Potions
- ◇ Loose gear

Fort Sungard Oubliette

The oubliette stands outside of the fort's walls, just to the east. There's little of interest inside the structure, but if you survive the fall into the pit (the Become Ethereal Shout helps), a Skill Book will be yours. Use the key found near the Skill Book to open the nearby gate and make your way out to fresh air.

- ◇ Skill Book [Pickpocket]: Wulfmare's Guide to Better Thieving [E1/10]
- ◇ Fort Sungard Jail Key
- ◇ Loose gear

[5.A] Dwarven Rubble: Druadach

By the edge of the rushing river is a cluster of long-forgotten dwarven ruins. Aside from a couple of arrows, there's an empty Dwemer Convector. Otherwise, use this location as a marker.

[5.B] Dragon Mound: Reachwater Pass

Related Quest: Main Quest: Elder Knowledge

This Dragon Mound is initially sealed. It opens during Main Quest: Elder Knowledge, and if you visit during or after this point in the Main Quest, the resurrected dragon will likely be in the area. Attack!

[5.C] Dwarven Arch: Harmugstahl Falls

A strange and possibly ceremonial arch hewn from stone by ancient dwarves stands close to the waterfall near to Harmugstahl. Claim a Skill Book from the edge of the stone altar.

- ◇ Skill Book [Restoration]: Withershins

[5.D] The Incautious Bather

While traversing the path west of Dragontooth Crater, head southwest at the path junction to reach a small pond with a half-naked corpse. Forsworn arrows are sticking out of her back. Read the careless woman's journal, and take her valuables if you wish.

- ◇ Journal
- ◇ Satchel

[5.E] A Bandit's Book

On the rocky and treacherous cliff paths between Harmugstahl and the confluence of the Karth River is a dead bandit. Kill any nearby critters, and check the Skill Book by the corpse. Note the Silver Ore Vein nearby if mining is how you make a living.

- ◇ Skill Book [Destruction]: Horror of Castle Xyr
- ◇ Mineable ore (Silver)

[5.F] Dwarven Rubble: Karth River Confluence

On the Karth River's eastern bank, among the juniper bushes and just west of the Reach Stormcloak Camp is a scattered pile of dwarven stones. Among them is a small dwarven chest to pilfer from.

- ◇ Chest
- ◇ Mineable ore (Iron)

[5.G] Forsworn Camp: Bthardamz Outskirts

A small two-tent Forsworn Camp has been recently attacked by a Frost Troll, which is still roaming this site. The actual location is around the southern rocks from Bthardamz. One of the tents houses a Skill Book.

- ◇ Crafting: Tanning Rack
- ◇ Skill Book [Destruction]: The Art of War Magic
- ◇ Chest
- ◇ Loose gear

[5.H] The Bloodied Bandit

On the rocky outcrops halfway between Bthardamz and Ragnvald is a dead bandit, slumped over the chest he was valiantly guarding. Expect a wild animal attack as you open the locked chest and search the corpse.

- ◇ Chest (Locked: Novice)
- ◇ Loose gear

[5.I] Dragon Mound: Ragnvald Vale

Related Quest: Main Quest: Elder Knowledge

This Dragon Mound remains sealed. It opens during Main Quest: Elder Knowledge, and if you return during or after this point in the Main Quest, the mound will be open and a dragon will likely still be in this area. Attack!

[5.J] Dwarven Ruins: Lair of the Wispmother

Just southwest of the crest of the mountain where the Shrine to Peryite stands is a tiny temple structure and fallen outer ruins. It is home to a vicious Wispmother. Slay or flee if you wish; this location has no further items of note.

[5.K] Sabre Cat Ravine

In the steep crags south of the Shrine of Peryite is a ravine where a Sabre Cat has been brought down by arrows. There's loose gear along the ravine, and a skeleton of a previous feast the Sabre Cat enjoyed.

◊ Knapsack   ◊ Loose gear

[5.L] Totem to the Dragon

On the lower and slightly flatter scrubland below the Shrine to Peryite are the remains of a Wood Elf. There is blood everywhere, and the body is slumped against a writhing stone column, likely a totem to dragon worshippers of old. Among the offerings is a diamond!

◊ Chest   ◊ Loose gear

[5.M] The Exposed Miner

Head east, away from Broken Tower Redoubt. Once the mountainous terrain drops along your left (northern) side, head down the first ravine you see. Close to a trio of pine trees are the skeletal remains of a miner.

◊ Mineable ore (Corundum)

[5.N] Hagraven Camp: Ragnvald Scree

Once you reach Ragnvald, take the winding path south, unless you pass the snow line, and enter a small Hagraven Camp. Bloodied goat appendages are strewn about, but the place is empty...until you enter the tent and the Hagraven returns!

◊ Chest

[5.O] Dwarven Rubble: Salvius Farm Trail

Take the goat trail north from Salvius Farm to discover these sections of dwarven rubble. Note that there may be a World Encounter occurring here as you arrive. Among the ancient stones under a small bush is a chest to open.

◊ Chest

[5.P] Shrine of Zenithar: Four Skull Lookout

West of Four Skull Lookout, over the rise of the hill, is a narrow stone balcony leading to a small Shrine to Zenithar. A few offerings are

available, but the main reason to visit is the blessing you receive. Fall off here, and you're likely to die.

◊ Shrine of Zenithar [2/5]

[5.Q] Brush Strongbox: Riverside

Close to the chiming Nirnroot, just northeast of the long protruding rocks in the river, the bank rises slightly, and a collection of dead brush makes a less-than-competent hiding spot for a small dagger and strongbox.

◊ Strongbox (Adept)
◊ Loose gear

[5.R] Lost Treasure: Purewater Run

North of Purewater Run, on the south riverbank just east of where the two waterfalls meet but before the last waterfall cascades down toward the bridge, is a long-forgotten treasure chest.

◊ Chest

[5.S] Forsworn Camp: Reachwater River

Follow the road west past Reachwater Rock until you see this small Forsworn Camp on the hill to the south. As you approach, two soldiers (Imperials or Stormcloaks, depending on who controls the Reach) attack the camp. Join in the assault, and they'll thank you for the help. Then loot the four tents and corpses, finding a Skill Book in a wooden bucket in one of the tents

◊ Skill Book [Block]:   ◊ Chest
   Death Blow of Abernanit   ◊ Satchel
                                 ◊ Loose gear

[5.T] Dragon Mound: Karthspire Bluffs

Related Quest: Main Quest: Alduin's Wall

This Dragon Mound is initially sealed. It opens during Main Quest: Alduin's Wall. If you visit during or after this point in the Main Quest, the resurrected dragon will likely be circling overhead. Challenge it on the high bluff near the mound, or lure to attack the nearby Forsworn camp at Karthspire Redoubt.

[5.U] Reachman's Altar: Red Eagle Redoubt

Among the rocks and scrub southeast (and downhill) of Red Eagle Redoubt is a clifftop promontory with the ruined remains of an old altar and a throne, along with a chest and bird's nest.

◇ Chest

[5.V] Lovers' Camp

Two corpses lie in this remote camp, having been savaged by a wild animal. Kill the beast, then search Karan's body for a journal. It seems she was eloping with her lover, Talvur. The journal hints at a treasure nearby; search the tree stump behind the tent for a knapsack and some items.

If you leave the camp and return later, you'll find that someone else (perhaps Karan's father?) has passed this way: The camp has been cleaned up, the bodies buried, and a Shrine to Mara has been erected to commemorate their love.

◇ Shrine of Mara [4/5]   ◇ Knapsack
◇ Apothecary's Satchel   ◇ Loose gear

[5.W] River Rapids Treasure Chest

West of Old Hroldan, after the waterfall has cascaded and where the river runs quick and a small island has formed around the rapids is a locked wooden treasure chest to pry open.

◇ Chest (Locked: Apprentice)

[5.X] Reachwind Burial Mound

Follow the path south from Dushnikh Yal as it curves around to the east, and head left at the junction to the hilltop, into which an ancient burial mound has been dug. At the bottom are a few outstretched skeletal arms and a chest.

◇ Chest

[5.Y] Forsworn Camp: Gloomreach Pathway

Journey along the winding path from the main road by the river, toward Gloomreach, and you'll encounter a small cliffside Forsworn camp with two foes to defeat or sneak past.

[5.Z] Shrine of Dibella: Bridge at Old Hroldan

Cross the bridge spanning the rushing river, and you can stop to receive a blessing at this roadside Shrine to Dibella. You may not be the only pilgrim; one or more hunters can often be found resting here as well. Steal the offerings if you wish, but beware if there are hunters nearby, as they will take offense at this sacrilege.

◇ Shrine of Dibella [5/8]

[5.AA] Juniper Tree Ruins

If you follow the dirt trail through the southernmost part of the Reach, you can find this small ruin perched near the edge of the bluff. Pick through the rubble to find a chest and Skill Book. Weather permitting, there's a great view from the edge of the cliff — just watch your step.

◇ Skill Book [Enchanting]: Enchanter's Primer
◇ Chest

[5.AB] Cradle Stone Crag

In the hills to the east of Valthume, you can find this animal den set into the mountains. When you approach, you'll see two trolls fighting for territory. Watch their fight play out, then move in to kill the survivor before he can recover. The ironically named Frofnir Trollsbane lies dead in this den. Search his twisted corpse for an excellent Troll-slaughtering weapon!

◇ Unique Weapon: Trollsbane [38/80]

TOPOGRAPHICAL OVERVIEW

Whiterun Hold, named for the fortress city in the eastern part of its vast Tundra plain, is the most centrally located of the nine Holds. Roads are numerous and well maintained, and visibility across the plains is excellent. This Hold is relatively flat, surrounded by the mountains of the Reach to the west, Hjaalmarch and the Pale to the north, and Falkreath to the south. However, Whiterun's southeastern corner is dominated by the gigantic and soaring Throat of the World — the highest mountain in all of Tamriel. It is here that many climb the 7,000 steps to High Hrothgar, home to the mysterious and reclusive Greybeards.

Routes and Pathways

Whiterun is certainly one of the most well-tracked Holds, with main roads and excellent access west to the Reach, with a border road north through the town of Rorikstead and up toward Dragon Bridge. The Tundra plains have a number of odd barrows and giant camps to investigate, and the center is dominated by Fort Greymoor. The road here allows you to travel north, up through the mountains to reach the dreaded Labyrinthian in Hjaalmarch. Farther east is Whiterun and the roaring White River and town of Riverwood on the southern border with Falkreath. Another road stretches north from here, into the wilds of the Pale. There's yet another road that skirts the northern foothills of the Throat of the World, following White River valley into Eastmarch. And although the first of the 7,000 steps that pilgrims take to reach the summit of the Throat of the World begins in Ivarstead (in the Rift), the actual mountain lies within Whiterun's domain. However, only those possessing a Thu'um (Shout) powerful enough to impress the Greybeards of High Hrothgar will be allowed to finish the journey to the summit.

AVAILABLE SERVICES, CRAFTING, AND COLLECTIBLES

Services

Followers: [14/47]
Houses for Sale: [1/5]
Marriage Prospects: [13/62]
Skill Trainers: [8/50]
Alchemy: [1/3]
Alteration: [0/3]
Archery: [2/3]
Block: [1/2]
Conjuration: [0/3]
Destruction: [0/3]
Enchanting: [0/2]
Heavy Armor: [1/3]
Illusion: [0/2]
Light Armor: [0/3]
Lockpicking: [0/2]
One-Handed: [2/3]
Pickpocket: [0/3]
Restoration: [1/3]

Smithing: [1/3]
Sneak: [0/3]
Speech: [0/4]
Two-Handed: [1/2]
Traders [22/133]:
Apothecary [1/12]
Bartender [1/5]
Blacksmith [6/33]
Carriage Driver [1/5]
Fence [1/10]
Fletcher [1/3]
Food Vendor [3/9]
General Goods [3/19]
Innkeeper [3/15]
Jeweler [0/2]
Special [0/3]
Spell Vendor [1/12]
Stablemaster [1/5]

Special Objects

Shrines: [10/69]
Akatosh: [1/6]
Arkay: [1/12]
Dibella: [0/8]
Julianos: [1/5]
Kynareth: [1/6]
Mara: [0/5]
Stendarr: [1/5]
Talos: [3/17]
Zenithar: [2/5]
Standing Stones: [1/13]
The Ritual Stone
Word Walls: [2/42]
Animal Allegiance: [0/3]
Aura Whisper: [0/3]
Become Ethereal: [0/3]
Disarm: [0/3]
Dismaying Shout: [0/3]
Elemental Fury: [0/3]
Fire Breath: [1/2]
Frost Breath: [0/3]
Ice Form: [0/3]
Kyne's Peace: [1/3]
Marked for Death: [0/3]
Slow Time: [0/3]
Storm Call: [0/3]
Throw Voice: [0/1]
Unrelenting Force: [0/1]
Whirlwind Sprint: [0/2]

Collectibles

Captured Critters: [0/5]
Dragon Claws: [0/10]
Dragon Priest Masks: [0/10]
Larceny Targets: [1/7]
Skill Books: [22/180]
Alchemy: [2/10]
Alteration: [0/10]
Archery: [2/10]
Block: [1/10]
Conjuration: [1/10]
Destruction: [1/10]
Enchanting: [2/10]
Heavy Armor: [1/10]

Illusion: [2/10]
Light Armor: [1/10]
Lockpicking: [0/10]
One-Handed: [2/10]
Pickpocket: [0/10]
Restoration: [1/10]
Smithing: [1/10]
Sneak: [2/10]
Speech: [1/10]
Two-Handed: [2/10]
Treasure Maps: [1/11]
Unique Items: [2/112]
Unique Weapons: [12/80]
Unusual Gems: [5/24]

CRAFTING STATIONS: WHITERUN

✓	TYPE	LOCATION A	LOCATION B
	Alchemy Lab	Whiterun (Dragonsreach) [6.00]	Riverwood (Sleeping Giant Inn) [6.27]
	Arcane Enchanter	Whiterun (Dragonsreach) [6.00]	Riverwood (Sleeping Giant Inn) [6.27] (after Main Quest: The Horn of Jurgen Windcaller)
	Anvil or Blacksmith Forge	Whiterun (Warmaiden's) [6.00]	Riverwood (Exterior) [6.27]
	Cooking Pot and Spit	Whiterun (Warmaiden's) [6.00]	Riverwood (Exterior) [6.27] (after Main Quest: Before the Storm)
	Grindstone	Whiterun (Warmaiden's) [6.00]	Riverwood (Exterior) [6.27]
	Smelter	Whiterun (Warmaiden's) [6.00]	—
	Tanning Rack	Whiterun (Warmaiden's) [6.00]	Riverwood (Exterior) [6.27]
	Wood Chopping Block	Whiterun (Belethor's General Goods) [6.00]	Riverwood (Exterior) [6.27]
	Workbench	Whiterun (Warmaiden's) [6.00]	Riverwood (Exterior) [6.27]

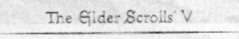

Hold 6: Whiterun

White River

Throat of the World

Dragonsreach

Whiterun

Total — 40: Hold Capital,
Dragonsreach, and 38 Hold Locations

[6.00] Hold Capital City: Whiterun
[6.00] Dragonsreach
Jarl: Balgruuf the Greater
[6.01] Lund's Hut
[6.02] Rorikstead
[6.03] Serpent's Bluff Redoubt
[6.04] Whiterun Imperial Camp
[6.05] Swindler's Den
[6.06] Gjukar's Monument
[6.07] Broken Fang Cave
[6.08] Sleeping Tree Camp
[6.09] Rannveig's Fast
[6.10] Drelas' Cottage

[6.11] Greenspring Hollow
[6.12] Dustman's Cairn
[6.13] Hamvir's Rest
[6.14] Redoran's Retreat
[6.15] Fort Greymoor
[6.16] Silent Moons Camp
[6.17] Halted Stream Camp
[6.18] Bleakwind Basin
[6.19] Western Watchtower
[6.20] Whiterun Stables
[6.21] Pelagia Farm
[6.22] Honningbrew Meadery
[6.23] Chillfurrow Farm
[6.24] Battle-Born Farm
[6.25] Whitewatch Tower

[6.26] White River Watch
[6.27] Riverwood
[6.28] Shimmermist Cave
[6.29] Fellglow Keep
[6.30] Graywinter Watch
[6.31] The Ritual Stone
[6.32] Whiterun Stormcloak Camp
[6.33] Valtheim Towers
[6.34] Darkshade
[6.35] Guldun Rock
[6.36] Hillgrund's Tomb
[6.37] High Hrothgar
[6.38] Throat of the World

Total — 24 Points of Interest

[6.A] Shrine of Akatosh: Rorikstead
[6.B] Dragon Mound: Rorikstead Resurrection
[6.C] The Expired Alchemist
[6.D] Hunter and Hunted
[6.E] Shrine of Zenithar: Ring of Boulders
[6.F] Fetid Pond
[6.G] Shrine of Zenithar: Crumbling Bastion
[6.H] King of the Mudcrabs
[6.I] Shrine of Stendarr: The Two Pillars
[6.J] Swallowed Skeleton: Greymoor Foothills
[6.K] Dragon Mound: Great Henge Resurrection
[6.L] Puzzling Pillar Ruins

[6.M] Necromancer's Bluff
[6.N] Bloodied Box: Sleeping Tree Camp
[6.O] Dragon Mound: Lone Mountain
[6.P] The Skeleton's Strong Box: Greymoor
[6.Q] The Lad of the Lake: Bleakwind Basin
[6.R] Smuggler's Den: Whiterun
[6.S] Whiterun Attack Camp
[6.T] Shrine of Talos: White River Valley
[6.U] Hunters' Camp: White River Hills
[6.V] Big Log Bridge
[6.W] Ruined Toll and Wispmother's Well
[6.X] The Seven Thousand Steps

HOLD CAPITAL: WHITERUN

Related Quests

Main Quest: Before the Storm
Main Quest: Bleak Falls Barrow
Main Quest: Dragon Rising
Main Quest: The Way of the Voice
Main Quest: The Fallen
Main Quest: Season Unending
Main Quest: The World-Eater's Eyrie
Civil War Quest: Message to Whiterun
Civil War Quest: Battle for Whiterun
Civil War Quest: Defense of Whiterun
The Companions Quest: Take Up Arms
The Companions Quest: Proving Honor
The Companions Quest: The Silver Hand
The Companions Quest: Blood's Honor
The Companions Quest: Purity of Revenge
The Companions Quest: Glory of the Dead
The Companions Radiant Quest: Animal Extermination (I)
The Companions Radiant Quest: Animal Extermination (II)
The Companions Radiant Quest: Hired Muscle
The Companions Radiant Quest: Trouble in Skyrim
The Companions Radiant Quest: Family Heirloom
The Companions Radiant Quest: Escaped Criminal
The Companions Radiant Quest: Rescue Mission
The Companions Radiant Quest: Striking the Heart
The Companions Radiant Quest: Stealing Plans
The Companions Radiant Quest: Retrieval
The Companions Radiant Quest: Totems of Hircine
The Companions Radiant Quest: Purity
The Companions Radiant Quest: Dragon Seekers
Daedric Quest: The Whispering Door
Daedric Quest: A Night to Remember
Side Quest: In My Time of Need
Side Quest: Missing in Action
Temple Quest: The Blessings of Nature
Dark Brotherhood Quest: Breaching Security
Dark Brotherhood Quest: Hail Sithis!

Dark Brotherhood Quest: The Feeble Fortune*
Dark Brotherhood Quest: Side Contract: Anoriath
Thieves Guild Quest: Dampened Spirits
Thieves Guild Radiant Quest: No Stone Unturned (x3)
Thieves Guild City Influence Quest: Imitation Amnesty
Miscellaneous Objective: Innkeeper Rumors (the Bannered Mare)
Miscellaneous Objective: Bullying Braith* (Lars Battle-Born)
Miscellaneous Objective: Argonian Ale Extraction* (Brenuin)
Miscellaneous Objective: Greatsword for a Great Man* (Adrianne Avenicci)
Miscellaneous Objective: Andurs' Arkay Amulet* (Anders)
Miscellaneous Objective: Salt for Arcadia* (Arcadia)
Favor (Activity): Chopping Wood* (Hulda)
Favor (Activity): The Gift of Charity* (Brenuin)
Favor: A Good Talking To* (Carlotta Valentia)
Favor: Sparring Partners* (Uthgerd)
Favor: Rare Item Hunt* (Ysolda)
Favor: Item Retrieval (Bandit Camp)* (Amren)
Crafting Tutorial: Blacksmithing* (Adrianne Avenicci)
Crafting Tutorial: Alchemy* (Arcadia)
Crafting Tutorial: Enchanting* (Farengar Secret-Fire)
Thane Quest: Thane of Whiterun Hold*

Habitation: Hold Capital (Major)

Crafting

Alchemy Labs (2) Grindstones (2) Tanning Rack
Arcane Enchanter Skyforge Workbench
Blacksmith Forge Smelter

Services

Follower: Jenassa [20/47]
Follower: Uthgerd the Unbroken [21/47]
Follower: Lydia [22/47]
Follower: Aela the Huntress [23/47]
Follower: Athis [24/47]
Follower: Farkas [25/47]
Follower: Njada Stonearm [26/47]
Follower: Ria [27/47]
Follower: Torvar [28/47]
Follower: Vilkas [29/47]
House for Sale: Breezehome [3/5]

Marriage Prospect: Jenassa [26/62]
Marriage Prospect: Uthgerd the Unbroken [27/62]
Marriage Prospect: Ysolda [28/62]
Marriage Prospect: Lydia [29/62]
Marriage Prospect: Aela the Huntress [30/62]
Marriage Prospect: Athis [31/62]
Marriage Prospect: Farkas [32/62]
Marriage Prospect: Njada Stonearm [33/62]

Marriage Prospect: Ria [34/62]
Marriage Prospect: Torvar [35/62]
Marriage Prospect: Vilkas [36/62]
Trader (Apothecary): Arcadia [7/12]
Trader (Blacksmith): Adrianne Avenicci [16/33]
Trader (Blacksmith): Ulfberth War-Bear [17/33]
Trader (Blacksmith): Eorlund Gray-Mane [18/33]
Trader (Fletcher): Elrindir [2/3]
Trader (Food Vendor): Carlotta Valentia [5/9]
Trader (Food Vendor): Anoriath [6/9]
Trader (General Store Vendor): Fralia Gray-Mane [9/25]

Trader (General Store Vendor): Belethor [6/19]
Trader (Innkeeper): Hulda [8/15]
Trader (Spell Vendor): Farengar Secret-Fire [10/12]
Trainer (Alchemy: Expert): Arcadia [2/3]
Trainer (Archery: Expert): Aela the Huntress [1/3]
Trainer (Block: Expert): Njade Stonearm [2/2]
Trainer (Heavy Armor: Master): Farkas [2/3]
Trainer (One-Handed: Journeyman): Amren [2/3]
Trainer (One-Handed: Expert): Athis [3/3]
Trainer (Restoration: Master): Danica Pure-Spring [3/3]
Trainer (Smithing: Master): Eorlund Gray-Mane [2/3]
Trainer (Two-Handed: Master): Vilkas [1/2]

Special Objects

Shrine of Arkay [7/12]
Shrine of Kynareth [5/6]
Shrine of Talos [8/17]

Business Ledger
Civil War: Map of Skyrim

Collectibles

Skill Book [Alchemy]: Herbalist's Guide to Skyrim [C2/10]
Skill Book [Archery]: The Black Arrow, v2 [B1/10]
Skill Book [Block]: Death Blow of Abernanit [C1/10]
Skill Book [Enchanting]: Enchanter's Primer [D2/10]
Skill Book [Heavy Armor]: Hallgerd's Tale [C1/10]
Skill Book [Illusion]: Before the Ages of Man [B1/10]
Skill Book [Restoration]: Withershins [E1/10]
Skill Book [Speech]: Biography of the Wolf Queen [D2/10]
Skill Book [Two-Handed]: Song of Hrormir [C2/10]

Unique Item: Andurs' Amulet of Arkay [58/112]
Unique Weapon: Balgruuf's Greatsword [39/80]
Unique Weapon: Wuuthrad [40/80]
Unique Weapon: Ebony Blade [41/80]
Unusual Gem: [11/24]
Unusual Gem: [12/24]
Unusual Gem: [13/24]
Chest
Potions aplenty
Loose Gear

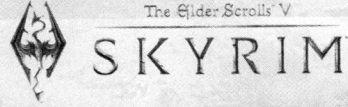

Lore: City Overview

Whiterun is seen as the most "pure" Nordic city in Skyrim. In Whiterun, Nords live as they have for centuries: their lives are simple, harsh, and rooted in ancient traditions. Even the city's fortifications — wooden and stone palisade walls and the sheer defensive advantage offered by its position on a large bluff that raises the city above the surrounding Tundra — are archaic by contemporary standards. So while Windhelm may serve as the Stormcloaks' center of operations in the Civil War, it is the culture of Whiterun that best exemplifies what it means to be a "True Nord."

Whiterun is located on the eastern end of its Hold, a cold and windy Tundra that fills the center of Skyrim. It was constructed around the Companions' hall of Jorrvaskr, which, centuries ago, was the sole structure on the mountain. Now, Whiterun is a large city, albeit one that retains the feel of a smaller Nord village.

When approaching Whiterun, the towering fortress of Dragonsreach dominates the view. Its history can be traced back to the First Era, when King Olaf One-Eye subdued the great dragon Numinex in a legendary duel of Thu'ums atop Mount Anthor, and brought him back to the fledgling town as a captive. It was then that the magnificent keep was rebuilt and renamed to serve as a cage for Numinex, whose head still adorns the Great Hall.

Important Areas of Interest

1 City Gates and Drawbridge

The winding stone path that leads from the outer gate to the drawbridge and to the entrance to the Main Gate is designed to keep marauders at bay. The drawbridge is open and utilized in the Civil War Quests.

Plains District

This is the first district any visitor to Whiterun enters, so named because it is the lowest of the three and therefore closest to the plains outside the city. It contains all the major merchants and the marketplace.

2 Main Gate and Guard Barracks (West)

Persuade, bribe, or otherwise insist that the guard lets you into Whiterun the first time you reach these gates. There is a small guard barracks just

over the bridge and a couple of Alik'r Warriors (Side Quest: In My Time of Need) you can speak to. Explore the rushing canal water under the bridge or the platform on top of the guard barracks roof if you wish. Inside, there's little but food and Nordic pottery to steal.

◇ Chest

3 The Drunken Huntsman

Anoriath   Elrindir   Nazeem   Ahlam

The Drunken Huntsman is a unique shop specializing is the needs of hunters. It sells bows, arrows, clothing, suits of armor, and anything else that may be useful to those who stalk Skyrim's game. But the establishment is also set up as a small bar, and customers can buy a small selection of alcoholic drinks, including a specially made Wood Elven wine.

The shop is run by the Wood Elf brothers Anoriath and Elrindir. Jenassa the Hireling is to be found here, too. There's also a Skill Book behind the counter. Check the back bedroom on the ground floor near the central cooking spit for a chest and strongbox. Upstairs is a single bedroom with an empty chest.

◇ Follower: Jenassa [20/47]
◇ Marriage Prospect: Jenassa [26/62]
◇ Trader (Fletcher): Elrindir [2/3]
　○ Weapons, Apparel, Food
◇ Skill Book [Archery]: The Black Arrow, v2 [B1/10]
◇ Business Ledger
◇ Strongbox (Apprentice)
◇ Chest

4 Severio Pelagia's House

Severio Pelagia

Nestled above the market is the residence of Severio Pelagia, who owns the Pelagia Farm just outside Whiterun's walls. Aside from a cooking pot and some delicious long taffy treat, there's very little worth stealing in this single-floor dwelling, which has a small bedroom and office on either side of the main dining area and fire pit.

◇ Shadowmark: "Loot"

5 Marketplace

Carlotta Valentia   Brenuin   Fralia Gray-Mane

The Whiterun Marketplace rivals the Bannered Mare as the most popular congregation spot in Whiterun. It is open during the day and closed at night. When the marketplace is open, stalls sells various items, including fresh fruits and vegetables. The stalls are run by Carlotta Valentia (fruits and vegetables), Fralia Gray-Mane (trinkets and jewelry), and Anoriah (fresh meat).

- ◇ Trader (Food Vendor): Carlotta Valentia [5/9]
  - ○ Food
- ◇ Trader (Food Vendor): Anoriath [6/9]
  - ○ Food
- ◇ Trader (General Store Vendor): Fralia Gray-Mane [6/19]
  - ○ Apparel, Misc.

6 The Bannered Mare

Hulda   Mikael   Sinmir
Saadia   Uthgerd the Unbroken

The Bannered Mare is Whiterun's most popular gathering place, a tavern and inn that offers cold mead, fresh food, and a warm and welcoming fire. Its sign is that of a majestic horse carrying a banner. Hulda, the publican, is fond of telling the story of the horse, which belonged to a Nord king who died in battle; the king may have died, but his favorite filly carried his banner still, inspiring the leader's warriors to victory. The building has a central tavern area and a side kitchen with a business ledger and strongbox near the roasting spit. To the rear of the main bar area is a small bedroom and office where shady deals may be done. There are two sets of steps to separate bedroom areas.

- ◇ Shadowmark: "Loot"
- ◇ Follower: Uthgerd the Unbroken [21/47]
- ◇ Marriage Prospect: Uthgerd the Unbroken [27/62]
- ◇ Trader (Innkeeper): Hulda [8/15]
  - ○ Room for the Night, Food
  - ○ Innkeeper Rumors
- ◇ Skill Book [Heavy Armor]: Hallgerd's Tale [C1/10]
- ◇ Business Ledger
- ◇ Strongbox (Apprentice)
- ◇ Chest (2)

7 Guard Barracks (East)

This set of barracks bridges the gap between the Plains District and Dragonsreach. It is also where you exit after being jailed (or escaping from jail). The trapdoor in the side alcove leads to Dragonsreach Dungeon.

- ◇ Display case (Novice)
- ◇ Chest
- ◇ Loose gear

8 Arcadia's Cauldron

Arcadia

Arcadia's Cauldron is Whiterun's apothecary. It sells potions and potion ingredients of all kinds and is probably the most respected of the city's non-Nord-owned businesses. Aside from the goods she sells, she is an excellent trainer. Check the office at the back of the store for a Skill Book and the locked door (Adept) next to the lab; this leads to the area under the stairs and a chest. Upstairs is a landing balcony overlooking the shop and a cooking pot.

- ◇ Shadowmark: "Loot"
- ◇ Crafting: Alchemy Lab
- ◇ Trader (Apothecary): Arcadia [7/12]
  - ○ Potions, Food, Ingredients, Books
- ◇ Trainer (Arcadia: Expert): Alchemy [2/3]
- ◇ Skill Book [Alchemy]: Herbalist's Guide to Skyrim [C2/10]
- ◇ Chest
- ◇ Potions aplenty

9 Ysolda's House

Ysolda

The young maid Ysolda lives in this house, making handcrafted goods that she hopes to sell. She is currently selling her goods to the Khajiit caravans, raising money to buy a shop of her own. Her dwelling is modest, locked, and has no loot to speak of, although there's a bowl of impressive potatoes.

- ◇ Shadowmark: "Empty"
- ◇ Marriage Prospect: Ysolda [28/62]

10 Belethor's General Goods

Belethor

The Wood Elf owner Belethor will buy and sell just about anything, and he's got a fair collection of items that could best be categorized as junk. From tomatoes to troll skulls, there's something here to steal, and a Skill Book on one of the shelves. In the back is a kitchen, and upstairs is a balcony, bed, and ledger with a strongbox.

- ◇ Shadowmark: "Loot"
- ◇ Trader (General Store Vendor): Belethor [7/19]
  - ○ Apparel, Potions, Food, Books, Misc.
- ◇ Skill Book [Speech]: Biography of the Wolf Queen [D2/10]
- ◇ Business Ledger
- ◇ Strongbox (Apprentice)

11 Olava the Feeble's House

Olava the Feeble

Besides being a seer, Olava is also something of a hermit. She rarely leaves her house, and her residence is usually locked. Inside, there's

a small table with a Petty Soul Gem and a setup for a reading, but otherwise the place is devoid of valuables.

- ◇ Chest

12 Breezehome (House for Sale)

This dwelling is currently empty. Should you become the Thane of Whiterun (by completing Main Quest: Dragon Rising), you can purchase this abode from Jarl Balgruuf the Greater's Steward, Proventus Avenicci. Consult the Thane Quests for more information.

- ◇ Follower: Lydia [22/47]
- ◇ Marriage Prospect: Lydia [29/62]

13 Warmaiden's

Adrianne Avenicci
Ulfberth War-Bear

This is the house and shop of Adrianne Avenicci and features a number of smithing locations, which is handy to use if you've purchased the adjacent Breezehome or you've entered the city. Inside, speak to Ulfberth War-Bear (or Adrianne, who also sells items) if you're interested in buying anything. Behind the counter is a door to a small kitchen and side exit. Upstairs is a landing overlooking the shop.

- ◇ Crafting: Blacksmith Forge, Grindstone, Smelter, Tanning Rack, Workbench
- ◇ Trader (Blacksmith): Adrianne Avenicci [16/33]
  - ○ Weapons, Apparel, Misc
- ◇ Trader (Blacksmith): Ulfberth War-Bear [17/33]
  - ○ Weapons, Apparel, Misc
- ◇ Unique Weapon: Balgruuf's Greatsword [39/80]
- ◇ Loose gear

◁▷ Wind District

The Wind District is where most of Whiterun's residential buildings (including the mead hall Jorrvaskr) are located and was named because of the strong mountain winds that gust through the area.

⑭ ⑮ Gildergreen Tree and Temple of Kynareth

Danica Pure-Spring   Acolyte Jenssen   Maurice Jondrelle

The Temple of Kynareth is a tall wooden building with a central praying chamber. The sick and weary gather here, and Acolyte Jenssen and Danica Pure-Spring cast their healing spells. To the sides are an office stocked with books (one of them being a Skill Book found on a shelf) and a chest and a waiting area with an empty strongbox. The temple is receiving a steady flow of pilgrims, but these have started to wane as the ancient Gildergreen Tree in the main exterior gathering place and thoroughfare has begun to die.

- ◇ Trainer (Danica Pure-Spring: Master): Restoration [3/3]
- ◇ Skill Book [Restoration]: Withershins [E1/10]
- ◇ Shrine of Kynareth [5/6]
- ◇ Strongbox (empty)
- ◇ Chest
- ◇ Potions

⑯ ⑰ Heimskr's House and Shrine of Talos

Heimskr

His home is devoid of important or valuable possessions; is has been turned into a gathering place for illegal worship.

- ◇ Shrine of Talos [8/17]

⑱ Jorrvaskr

Harbinger: Kodlak Whitemane

The Circle: Aela the Huntress; Farkas, brother of Vilkas; Vilkas, brother of Farkas; Skjor, the scarred

Member: Athis, Njada Stonearm, Ria, Torvar, Vignar the Revered

Housekeeper: Tilma the Haggard

Blacksmith: Eorlund Gray-Mane

Jorrvaskr is the ancient and honored mead hall that has served as headquarters for the mercenary company the Companions for untold generations. According to local legend, Jorrvaskr is actually the oldest building in all of Whiterun and once existed by itself on the mountain, with the other buildings the town being built up around it over the centuries. Jorrvaskr is a place of honor and courage, and to walk into the hall is to proclaim, "I am a warrior and will die as I lived—in glorious battle!" The mead hall is also the place where you may join the Companions as a Shield-Brother or Sister. The exterior of the building features two front doors and a rear outside dining and training area.

Inside, the main floor is dominated by the mead hall and fire pit. A Skill Book rests on a low shelf here. At one end of the hall is a sparring area, and around the sides are various shelves stocked with books and food. The door at the north end leads to a bedroom with another chest. The stairs at the sound end lead down to the living quarters. Displayed on the wall here are the pieces of Wuuthrad, a powerful weapon wielded by their founder, Ysgramor. Check Kodlak Whitemane's bedroom chambers to find an Unusual Gem that pertains to Side Quest: No Stone Unturned.

- ◇ Follower: Aela the Huntress [23/47]
- ◇ Follower: Athis [24/47]
- ◇ Follower: Farkas [25/47]
- ◇ Follower: Njada Stonearm [26/47]
- ◇ Follower: Ria [27/47]
- ◇ Follower: Torvar [28/47]
- ◇ Follower: Vilkas [29/47]
- ◇ Marriage Prospect: Aela the Huntress [30/62]
- ◇ Marriage Prospect: Athis [31/62]
- ◇ Marriage Prospect: Farkas [32/62]
- ◇ Marriage Prospect: Njada Stonearm [33/62]
- ◇ Marriage Prospect: Ria [34/62]
- ◇ Marriage Prospect: Torvar [35/62]
- ◇ Marriage Prospect: Vilkas [36/62]
- ◇ Trainer (Archery: Expert): Aela the Huntress [1/3]
- ◇ Trainer (Block: Expert): Njade Stonearm [2/2]

- ◇ Trainer (Heavy Armor: Master): Farkas [2/3]
- ◇ Trainer (One-Handed: Expert): Athis [3/3]
- ◇ Trainer (Two-Handed: Master): Vilkas [1/2]
- ◇ Skill Book [Heavy Armor]: Hallgerd's Tale [C1/10]
- ◇ Unusual Gem: [11/24]
- ◇ Chest (2)
- ◇ Potions
- ◇ Loose gear

Living Quarters

The main corridor leading north begins with a dormitory where the new recruits sleep. At the far end are four bedrooms of the Circle members. Check for the Skill Book inside the display case. There's also a small bar in one of the bedrooms! At the far end of the corridor is Kodlak's private chambers, which has some rare items to steal.

- ◇ Skill Book [Archery]: The Marksmanship Lesson
- ◇ Skill Book [Two-Handed]: Song Of Hrormir [C2/10]
- ◇ Unusual Gem: [11/24]
- ◇ Chest (3)

⑲ Skyforge and the Underforge

The Skyforge is the great forge used by Eorlund Gray-Mane to craft his masterful weapons, shields, and armor. It got its name due to the fact that it's a large, ancient forge, located outside on a mountain, close to the sky. The forge is large, and unlike most forges is rather ornate. It is in the shape on an eagle, with wings spreading out from each side. Eorlund is happy to train and trade his wares with you, but only after you join the Companions.

- ◇ Crafting: Skyforge, Grindstone
- ◇ Trader (Blacksmith): Eorlund Gray-Mane [18/33]
  - ○ Weapons, Apparel, and Misc
- ◇ Trainer (Smithing: Master): Eorlund Gray-Mane [2/3]
- ◇ Skill Book [Smithing]: The Armorer's Challenge
- ◇ Unique Weapon: Wuuthrad [40/80]

Underneath the Skyforge is a hidden area known as the Underforge, where those welcomed into the Circle of the Companions observe a special blood ritual. This is only accessible during the Companions quest line. You can return here to deliver or utilize Totems; consult the quests starting on page 164 for more details.

⑳ House Gray-Mane

Olfina the Golden

Avulstein Gray-Mane

House Gray-Mane is the residence of Eorlund Gray-Mane and his children. It is a large, solid house, built by Eorlund over 35 years earlier. Recently, due to their differing stances on the Civil War, Clan Gray-Mane has bad relations with Clan Battle-Born, with whom they had always been friendly before the conflict started. Jon Battle-Born and Olfina the Golden are said to be in love, but the families certainly do not approve of such activities. Outside the house is a small paddock with a cow. Inside the house is a central fire pit and dining area, with a small entrance alcove and Avulstein's bedroom. Upstairs is a landing and two bedrooms with some books and valuables (usually necklaces) lying around.

- ◇ Shadowmark: "Loot"
- ◇ Chest (4)

㉑ Uthgerd's House

This is the house belonging to the violent Nord warmaiden that challenges you to fisticuffs in the Bannered Mare. Her home is locked, but once inside, is full of Nord pottery, a chest, and a small book collection in a nook under the stairs. Upstairs is an empty chest and a full display case.

- ◇ Chest
- ◇ Loose gear

㉒ Amren's House

Amren   Braith

Amren's House is attached to Uthgerd's. Amren is usually walking around the Wind District. His wife, Saffir, and daughter Braith may be inside the dwelling. There's very little worth stealing here.

- ◇ Shadowmark: "Danger"
- ◇ Trainer (One-Handed: Journeyman): Amren [2/3]

㉓ Carlotta Valentia's House

Mila Valentia

Carlotta Valentia lives in this house with her young daughter Mila. Find a couple of potions in one of the upstairs bedrooms, along with a Skill Book that's tucked between the bed and end table.

- ◇ Shadowmark: "Loot"
- ◇ Skill Book [Enchanting]: Enchanter's Primer [D2/10]

㉔ House of Clan Battle-Born

Olfrid Battle-Born   Idolaf Battle-Born   Alfhild Battle-Born
Bergritte Battle-Born   Jon Battle-Born   Lars Battle-Born

This large house holds three generations of the equally large Clan Battle-Born. This warrior family—owners of the Battle-Born Farm outside Whiterun—has lived in the city for centuries; their ties to Skyrim and the ancient Nord ways cannot be disputed. The Clan has come out vocally in support of the pro-Imperial forces in the ongoing Civil War. Recently, due to their differing stances on the Civil War, Clan Battle-Born has bad relations with Clan Gray-Mane, with whom they had always been friendly before the conflict started.

The rear door is usually unlocked, while the front isn't (Novice). Inside, the ground floor is one large chamber with a cooking spit and dining table dominating the area. To the northwest is Olfrid's bedroom, which has some valuables on display (including a Skill Book) and a locked door (Adept) leading to a small office with books and an Imperial Missive, useful during Side Quest: Missing in Action. On the opposite side is a small bedroom with books to check, stairs up to the balcony, and two more bedrooms.

- ◇ Shadowmark: "Protected"
- ◇ Imperial Missive
- ◇ Skill Book [Two-Handed]: Battle of Sancre Tor
- ◇ Potions

㉕ Hall of the Dead

Andurs

The Whiterun Hall of the Dead is a single-story, high-ceilinged wooden structure and serves as Whiterun's mausoleum. The main floor has the sleeping quarters for Andurs (with a large collection of books and small collection of skulls) and a shrine to Arkay where the people of Whiterun can come and worship. Check one of the wall crypts to find an Unusual Gem lying near the foot of a skeleton—this pertains to Side Quest: No Stone Unturned.

- ◇ Unique Item: Andurs' Amulet of Arkay [58/112]
- ◇ Unusual Gem: [12/24]
- ◇ Shrine of Arkay [7/12]
- ◇ Chest

Whiterun Catacombs

These catacombs contain generations of Whiterun's dead, including the bodies of some of Skyrim's most honored departed — and not quite departed. There is also graveyard outside.

◇ Skill Book [Block]: Death Blow of Abernanit [C1/10]

Cloud District

The Cloud District is the smallest of Whiterun's three districts. It was so named because it is located atop the mountain Whiterun was built on and is therefore closer to the clouds than any other. It is dominated by the imposing form of Dragonsreach.

㉖ Dragonsreach

 The following leaders of Whiterun are loyal to the Imperials at the start of the Civil War.

Jarl Balgruuf the Greater

Balgruuf believes that Skyrim should remain a part of the Empire. This has become something of a confusing situation for the people of Skyrim, many of whom are decidedly anti-Empire. Balgruuf embodies the very best of what it is to be a Nord, but at the same time he supports the Empire's presence. This has actually caused some of these same anti-Empire residents of Whiterun to at least reconsider their thinking. After all, if Balgruuf the Greater supports the Empire, then maybe they are the key to Skyrim's future. Balgruuf is very close to his younger brother Hrongar.

Hrongar

Hrongar is Balgruuf's younger brother and is something of a warmonger. He believes his brother should organize Imperial forces and wipe out any Stormcloaks presence in Whiterun Hold. Hrongar divides his time among a few activities, most notably advising (and sometimes arguing with) his brother Balgruuf and practicing with his sword and axe against the town guard.

Frothar

Dagny

Nelkir

Farengar Secret-Fire (Court Wizard)

Farengar serves the Jarl because of duty, but Farengar has no interest in the Civil War and certainly has no love for the Empire. He is dedicated to the College of Winterhold and furthering the cause of magical research. So as long as he is able to maintain his laboratory and keep up his research, he really doesn't care what the Jarl believes.

Proventus Avenicci (Steward)

Proventus essentially tells Balgruuf whatever he wants to hear and is a politician through and through. In other words, Proventus is completely inept as a Steward. The only reason he's been able to achieve any manner of success and keep his position is because his daughter Adrianne is tactically brilliant and has been telling her father what to tell the Jarl.

Irileth (Housecarl)

Irileth is unusual for a Housecarl: She's female, a Dark Elf, and doesn't fit the role of muscle-bound protector. But that doesn't make her any less effective. Irileth is actually a skilled assassin, trained in Morrowind by the Morag Tong. She met Balgruuf several years prior and the two became fast friends and adventuring companions.

Commander Caius

 The following residents arrive to take control of Whiterun, should this Hold fall during the Civil War.

Jarl Vignar Gray-Mane

Vignar was once a general and commander in the Legion during the Great War. He came to Whiterun to retire and be near his brother, the renowned smith Eorlund Gray-Mane. Because of his long experience as a soldier, Vignar holds a place of honor among the Companions, and the group welcomes his council. In the course of the Civil War, Vignar shifted loyalties to his home. He is angry at the Empire for surrendering to the Dominion and feels that Skyrim would be better off on its own, as in the ancient times. When the Stormcloaks control Whiterun, they call on Vignar's experience and wisdom to lead the city as its Jarl.

Brill (Steward)

Brill was once an adventurer who was injured by a Draugr axe a number of years ago. This brush with death left him shaken and broken. He took to drinking, spending much time and coin in the Bannered Mare. It was there he met Vignar, who he befriended. Vignar took Brill into his home, and he's never left.

Olfina Gray-Mane (Housecarl)

When Vignar is called upon to serve as Whiterun's Jarl, he names his niece Olfina as his Housecarl. Willful and determined, Olfina accepts the honorable duty and swears to defend her uncle's life with her own.

Sinmir

Dragonsreach is Whiterun's majestic keep. It was constructed in the ornate wooden style of the great Nord longhouses of old. Visually and politically, it is very much the focal point of the city. As is true of the keeps in other cities, Dragonsreach serves many important functions. There is an ornate bridge leading to the main double doors. Around to the side is an entrance to Dragonsreach Dungeon.

Dragonsreach (Interior)

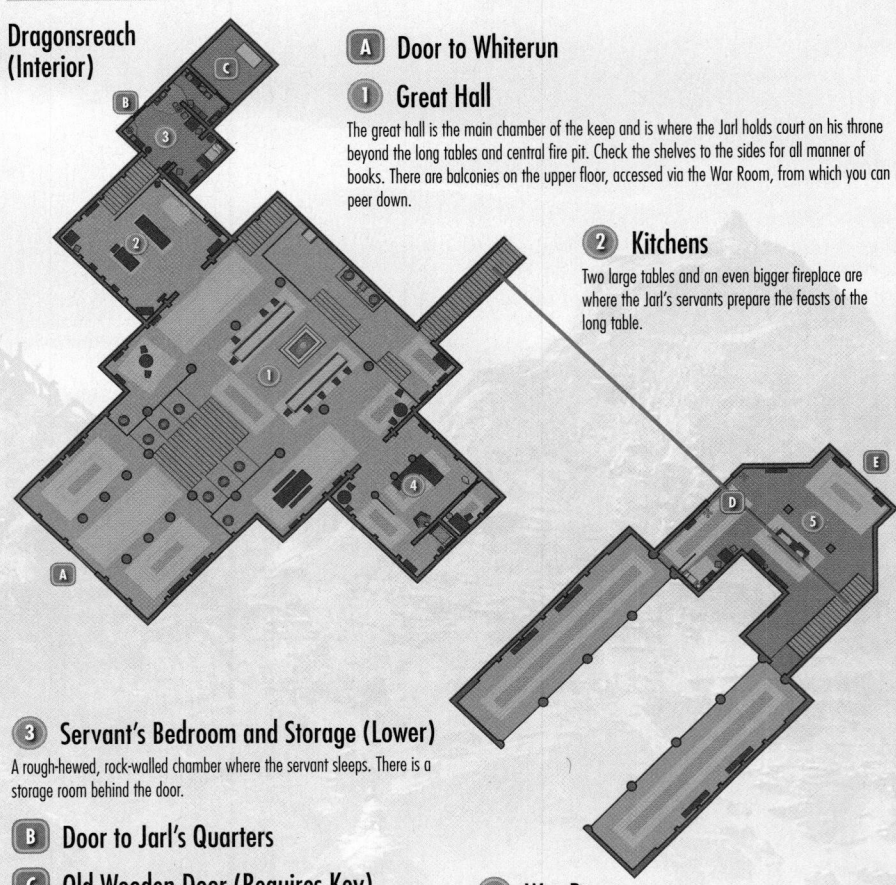

Ⓐ Door to Whiterun

① Great Hall

The great hall is the main chamber of the keep and is where the Jarl holds court on his throne beyond the long tables and central fire pit. Check the shelves to the sides for all manner of books. There are balconies on the upper floor, accessed via the War Room, from which you can peer down.

② Kitchens

Two large tables and an even bigger fireplace are where the Jarl's servants prepare the feasts of the long table.

③ Servant's Bedroom and Storage (Lower)

A rough-hewed, rock-walled chamber where the servant sleeps. There is a storage room behind the door.

Ⓑ Door to Jarl's Quarters

Ⓒ Old Wooden Door (Requires Key)

This odd door seems sealed from the other side. Consult Side Quest: The Whispering Door for more information.

④ Farengar's Quarters

In this laboratory, the Court Wizard Farengar mixes concoctions and conducts research into the mysteries of the dragons' return. His bedroom and a small library are behind his main study.

◇ Crafting: Alchemy Lab, Arcane Enchanter
◇ Trader (Spell Vendor): Farengar Secret-Fire [10/12]
  • Apparel, Scrolls, Books, Misc
◇ Potions
◇ Loose gear

⑤ War Room

This is where the Jarl and his advisors discuss matters of state, pouring over the Civil War map near the book-lined shelves. When needed, an Imperial Legate also plans from this location.

◇ Civil War: Map of Skyrim
◇ Display Case (Apprentice)
◇ Loose gear

Ⓓ Door to Jarl's Quarters

Ⓔ Door to Dragonsreach, Great Porch

Enter the Great Porch if you want an impressive view to the east. Legend has it that a dragon was trapped here, on this porch. Perhaps history might repeat itself? Consult the Main Quest for further information.

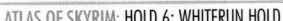

Dragonsreach Jarl's Quarters

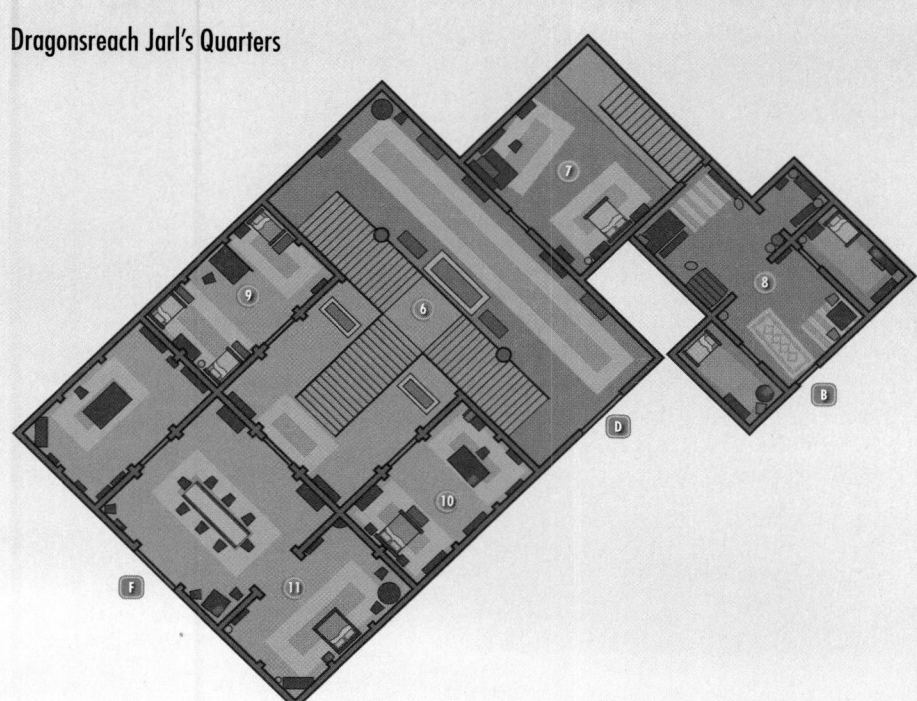

[6.01] Lund's Hunt

Recommended Level: 12

Dungeon: Animal Den

Animal

Collectibles

Chest(s)
Potions

Ravenous animals have swarmed this small cabin. Search poor Lund's remains, along with his chest, to relieve him of his final possessions.

[6.02] Rorikstead

Related Quests

Civil War Quest: Liberation of Skyrim

Civil War Quest: A False Front

Daedric Quest: A Night to Remember

Side Quest: In My Time of Need

Miscellaneous Objective: Innkeeper Rumors (Frostfruit Inn)

Miscellaneous Objective: Erik the Slayer* (Erik)

Favor (Activity): Harvesting Crops* (Reldith)

Favor (Activity): Harvesting Crops* (Lemkil)

Habitation: Town

Britte
Ennis
Erik the Slayer (Follower; Marriage Prospect)
Jouane Manette
Lemkil
Mralki (Innkeeper)
Reldith
Rorik
Sissel

Services

Follower: Erik the Slayer [30/47]

Marriage Prospect: Erik the Slayer [37/62]

Trader (Innkeeper): Mralki [9/15]

Food, Room and Board

Quest Rumors

Crafting

Tanning Rack
Chest(s)
Potions
Loose gear

This is the private quarters of the Jarl, and entering here without invitation results in you being removed, facing a fine, or worse. However, a special gem can be found here that pertains to Side Quest: No Stone Unturned.

◇ Unique Weapon: Ebony Blade [41/80]
◇ Unusual Gem: [13/24]

D Door to Dragonsreach

6 Inner Hall and Staircase

◇ Display Cases (Apprentice) (3)
◇ Display Case (Master)
◇ Loose gear

7 Proventus Avenicci's Chamber

Note the display case; it usually has something valuable inside.

◇ Display Case (Adept)
◇ Chest

8 Servant's Quarters

Fianna and Gerda usually rest here, in the tiny alcove bedrooms off the main food storage and wine vat area.

◇ Chest

B Door to Dragonsreach

9 Childrens' Bedroom

The Jarl's three children, Nelkir, Dagny, and Frothar, sleep here.

◇ Chest (3)

10 Hrongar's Bedroom

The Jarl's brother sleeps here. The study desk has shelves with books on them.

11 Jarl's Bedchamber

There are three connected chambers here: a dining area, bedroom, and book-filled study.

◇ Skill Book [Illusion]: Before the Ages of Man [B1/10]
◇ Loose gear

F Door to Whiterun

Exit onto a narrow parapet balcony and overlook the entirety of Whiterun.

Dragonsreach Dungeon

Cell Block

Arn

Home to a proportion of the city's guard and the jail. The entrance area has the chests you need to retrieve your items, either after you serve your time or if you reach in from the sewer grate behind the chests. The main cell block has cells on either side (Adept, unless a quest-related cell) and a door at the opposite end leading to Dragonsreach. The cell to the west is of particular interest, as it comes decked out with food and a variety of luxuries not normally associated with jails. This is where the more prominent miscreants are kept, usually after a drunken binge. A man named Arn is imprisoned in this location, but only after you undertake Thieves Guild City Influence Quest; Imitation Amnesty.

◇ Evidence Chest
◇ Prisoner Belongings Chest

Dungeon Catacombs

Below the cells are the Catacombs, ideally explored only after you escape from your cell, and wish to weave your way to the small hub chamber, where you can climb a ladder and stand on some barrels to reach the chests which contain your belongings. Then open the barred door [Expert] or drop down the hole to reach a ladder leading up and into [7] Guard Barracks (East), down in the Plains District.

This small farming community lies at the west edge of Whiterun, near the Reach's border. A cozy inn offers food and comfort to weary travelers.

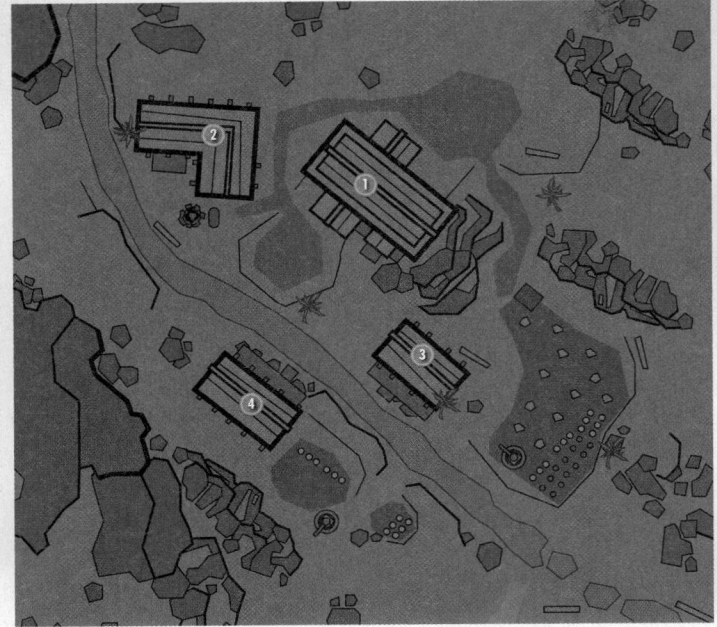

Exterior

There are plenty of crops to pluck up around the village, but little else of interest. Speak to Erik out in the fields to gain a Side Quest that you can fulfill right here.

◇ Crafting: Tanning Rack

① Frostfruit Inn

This small inn offers a warm bed and hot meal at a fair price.

◇ Chest

② Rorik's Manor

Rorikstead's founder lives quite modestly. Still, his abode is worth looting.

◇ Chests (2)   ◇ Potion   ◇ Loose gear

③ Cowflop Farmhouse

Break into this farmhouse when no one's looking and steal from two chests.

◇ Area Is Locked (Novice)   ◇ Chests (2)   ◇ Potions

④ Lemkil's Farmhouse

This humble home has just one chest, but it's worth a peek if you can break in unseen.

◇ Area Is Locked (Novice)   ◇ Chest

[6.03] Serpent's Bluff Redoubt

Related Quests

Dungeon Activity

Recommended Level: 14

Dungeon: Forsworn Redoubt

Forsworn

Hagraven

Crafting

Arcane Enchanter

Forge

Tanning Rack

Workbench

Dangers

Battering Ram Trap (pressure plate)

Dart Trap (pressure plate)

Spear Trap (tripwire)

Swinging Wall Trap (pressure plate)

Collectibles

Skill Book [Enchanting]: Twin Secrets [E1/10]

Chest(s)

Potions

Loose gear

Sharing a border with the Reach has its drawbacks — the Forsworn have established a formidable encampment in Whiterun's western flatlands.

Exterior

Slay a host of Forsworn as they pour forth to defend their camp, then begin looting their tents for valuables.

◇ Crafting: Forge, Tanning Rack, Workbench   ◇ Knapsack

◇ Chest   ◇ Potions

◇ Chest (Locked: Apprentice)   ◇ Loose gear

Serpent's Bluff Redoubt (Interior)

The interior ruins begins with a trio of lethal traps: Sidestep a pressure plate at the foot of the stairs (which triggers a dart trap), jump the trip wire that lies just beyond (spear trap), and avoid the pressure plate beyond the wire (a swinging wall trap). Slay the Forsworn archer, then descend the stairs and avoid yet another pressure plate at the bottom (battering ram). Assail more Forsworn and a dangerous Hagraven in the main chamber, then unlock the Adept-level door under the platform to access a small room with a chest. Place any object (book, etc.) onto the pressure plate that sits atop the altar to open the passage on the upper level. Go through to discover a Skill Book sitting atop an Arcane Enchanter in the next area, along with a giant chest. Press a wall button to open the exit gate.

◇ Danger! Battering Ram Trap (pressure plate), Spear Trap (trip wire), Swinging Wall Trap (pressure plate), Dart Trap (pressure plate)

◇ Crafting: Arcane Enchanter

◇ Skill Book [Enchanting]: Twin Secrets [E1/10]

◇ Chest

◇ Chest (Locked: Apprentice)

◇ Potions

◇ Loose gear

[6.04] Whiterun Imperial Camp

Related Quests

Civil War Quest (when active, depending on who you side with)

Habitation: Military: Imperial Camp

Imperial Quartermaster (Blacksmith)

Imperial Soldier

Services

Trader (Blacksmith): Imperial Quartermaster [19/33]

Weapons, Apparel, Misc

Crafting

Alchemy Lab

Anvil

Grindstone

Workbench

Special Objects

Civil War: Map of Skyrim

Chest

Potions

Loose gear

Hardened Imperial soldiers have made camp at this site; however, the camp may or may not exist, depending on the state of the Civil War quest line. Trade with the quartermaster and feel free to utilize his numerous crafting stations. Inspect the tabletop map in the largest tent to potentially gain new map data as well.

[6.05] Swindler's Den

Related Quests

Side Quest: In My Time of Need

Recommended Level: 6

Dungeon: Bandit Camp

Bandit

Kematu

Alik'r

Dangers

Bear Traps

Collectibles

Skill Book [One-Handed]: Night Falls on Sentinel [D1/10]

Skill Book [Pickpocket]: Thief

Chest(s)

Potions

Loose gear

Tall rocks east of Rorikstead mark the entrance to a sizable underground cave. During Side Quest: In My Time of Need, this cave is used by the Alik'r Coterie as a base of operations. Bandits occupy the cave otherwise. Test your mettle against the drunken exterior guard before venturing inside.

Sunlit Cavern

Dispatch a bandit in the first cavern, then leap up to discover a chest on a sunlit ledge.

◇ Chest

◇ Loose gear

Firepit Cavern

Silence a few more bandits in the next cavern, then collect potions and loot a satchel that sits on a crate in the corner.

◇ Satchel   ◇ Potions   ◇ Loose gear

Mess

Fight hard to secure this cavern—more bandits are likely to emerge from the north passage. When you return to this cavern, navigating the high overlook on your way from the Sleeping Area to the Waterfall Cavern, you can claim a Skill Book that rests on a crate.

◇ Skill Book [One-Handed]: Night Falls on Sentinel [D2/10]
◇ Potion

Sleeping Area

Loot a chest on your way into this dimly lit cavern, where a Skill Book rests on a bedroll.

◇ Skill Book [Pickpocket]: Thief
◇ Chest

Waterfall Cavern

Avoid a pair of bear traps as you journey to this watery cavern, where the bandits' formidable leader lurks. Loot the cavern's giant chest after the battle, then simply continue along to come full circle and return to the first cavern.

◇ Danger! Bear Traps   ◇ Chest   ◇ Potion

[6.06] Gjukar's Monument

Related Quests

Side Quest: Kyne's Sacred Trials
Temple Quest: The Book of Love

Dungeon: Special

Ruki

Collectible

Loose gear

Recommended Level: 12

A small circle of rocks stands out among Whiterun's western flatlands, with one central pillar that's tall enough to catch one's eye from afar. Stop by this quiet shrine to collect some valuable gear. During Temple Quest: The Book of Love, you'll help reunite a pair of wayward souls here.

[6.07] Broken Fang Cave

Recommended Level: 6

Dungeon: Vampire Lair

Skeleton
Vampire

Crafting

Alchemy Lab
Arcane Enchanter

Collectibles

Skill Book [Illusion]: Mystery of Talara, v4 [D2/10]
Skill Book [Lockpicking]: The Wolf Queen, v1
Chest
Chest (Locked: Adept)
Potions
Loose gear

This shallow, rocky cave stands out among Whiterun's western flats. Inside lurks a powerful vampire and several lowly skeletons. Search the entry cavern's southeast corner to discover a locked chest, then take the west passage to a sleeping area, where another mighty vampire lurks, along with a large chest and a few crafting stations. Find a Skill Book on the metal shelf near the Arcane Enchanter, and another resting beside the Alchemy Lab.

[6.08] Sleeping Tree Camp

Related Quests

Dungeon Quest: The Secret at the Sleeping Tree*

Dungeon: Giant Camp

Giant
Mammoth
Ulag

Quest Items

Sleeping Tree Sap
Chest

A group of giants have made camp at this remote site, perhaps drawn by the mystifying glow of an unusual tree that grows from a steamy glowing pond. The tree has a sap spigot that you can turn to acquire some Sleeping Tree Sap, an unusual substance that greatly increases your health...with certain side effects. Returning here after a few days will allow another batch of Sap to be harvested. Enter the nearby cave afterward to face another formidable giant and a dead orc named Ulag. Read the note that Ulag carries to gain a new Side Quest to sell the Sleeping Tree Sap to Ysolda in Whiterun.

[6.09] Rannveig's Fast

Related Quests

Side Quest: No Stone Unturned

Recommended Level: 8

Dungeon: Warlock Lair

Sild the Warlock
Subjugated Ghost

Crafting

Alchemy Lab

Collectibles

Skill Book [Destruction]: Horrors of Castle Xyr [B1/10]
Unusual Gem: [14/24]

Special Objects

Word Wall: Kyne's Peace [2/3]
Chest(s)
Potions aplenty
Loose gear

A nefarious warlock named Sild is forcing a host of ghosts to defend these ancient ruins. Send the exterior ghosts to their eternal rest, or have pity and simply sprint past them, entering the large door that leads to an ancient crypt. Scaling the ruins' exterior steps leads to Cold Rock Pass [2.12] in Hjaalmarch.

Rannveig's Fast (Interior)

All is silent in the crypts' massive entry cavern. Proceed through the north passage, dispatching a ghost and swiping some potions on your way to the next chamber, where a giant chest tempts you from afar. Avoid the large, discolored trapdoor on the ground before the chest—the chest turns out to be empty, but you obtain a new Word of Power from the nearby Word Wall in the process. Take the north passage and scale a long staircase to reach the chamber's upper walkways; pull a lever to open the portcullis on the lower level that will lead you behind Sild as he still waits for you, or some other unlucky adventurer, to fall into the pit. Before you move on, cross the walkways to reach a high nook with a locked chest.

◇ Word Wall: Kyne's Peace [2/3]
◇ Chest
◇ Chest (Locked: Apprentice)
◇ Chest (Locked: Expert)
◇ Potions

Sild's Pit

If you've fallen through the trapdoor near the Word Wall, you will find yourself in a locked cage, with a madman named Sild the Warlock taunting you from just beyond the bars. Exploit Sild's hubris by crouching and pickpocketing a key off of him (you can also pick the lock, or loot another key out of Sild's Assistants Satchel that sits beside the cage), then escape the cage and slay the nefarious mage. Claim a number of potions from this frightening area, along with a Skill Book and an Unusual Gem that pertains to a Thieves Guild Radiant Quest. Then open the south door and scale some stairs that lead up to a chest and an exit door.

◇ Crafting: Alchemy Lab
◇ Skill Book [Destruction]: Horrors of Castle Xyr [B1/10]
◇ Unusual Gem: [14/24]
◇ Rannveigs Fast Key (Sild the Warlock)
◇ Chest
◇ Potions aplenty

[6.10] Drelas's Cottage

Recommended Level: 12

Dungeon: Warlock Lair

Drelas

Crafting

Alchemy Lab
Arcane Enchanter
Chest(s)
Potions aplenty

This quaint cottage is home to a seclusive mage named Drelas, who'll attack you on sight if you dare enter. Slaying Drelas is worthwhile, for the mage has amassed a wealth of valuable potions and ingredients.

[6.11] Greenspring Hollow

Related Quests
Temple Quest: The Book of Love

Dungeon: Animal Den
Animal

Crafting
Tanning Rack
Chest (Locked: Adept)
Loose gear

A hunter has become the hunted in Whiterun's western wilds, where a ferocious animal has slaughtered an unwary woodsman at his own camp. Avenge the poor hunter by dispatching the beast, then relieve the man of his final possessions.

[6.12] Dustman's Cairn

Related Quests
The Companions Quest: Proving Honor
Dungeon Activity

Recommended Level: 6

Dungeon: Draugr Crypt
Animal
Draugr
Silver Hand

Crafting
Alchemy Lab

Dangers
Dart Trap (pressure plate)

Quest Items
Fragment of Wuuthrad

Collectibles
Skill Book [Two-Handed]:
The Battle of Sancre Tor
[A2/10]

Special Objects
Word Wall: Fire Breath [1/2]
Chest(s)
Potions
Loose gear

Scale the hill that lies northwest of Whiterun's capital to discover ancient ruins dug directly into the hilltop. You visit this site with your Shield-Sibling during Companion Quest: Proving Honor, in search of a fragment of Wuuthrad, the Blade of Ysgramor. Only a small portion of Dustman's Cairn can be explored until you visit the site as part of that quest.

(A) Exit to Skyrim

(1) Entry Chamber

Inspect the Skill Book on the entry chamber's central table, then loot the nearby chest before advancing.

◇ Skill Book [Two-Handed]: The Battle of Sancre Tor [A2/10]

◇ Chest (Locked: Novice)

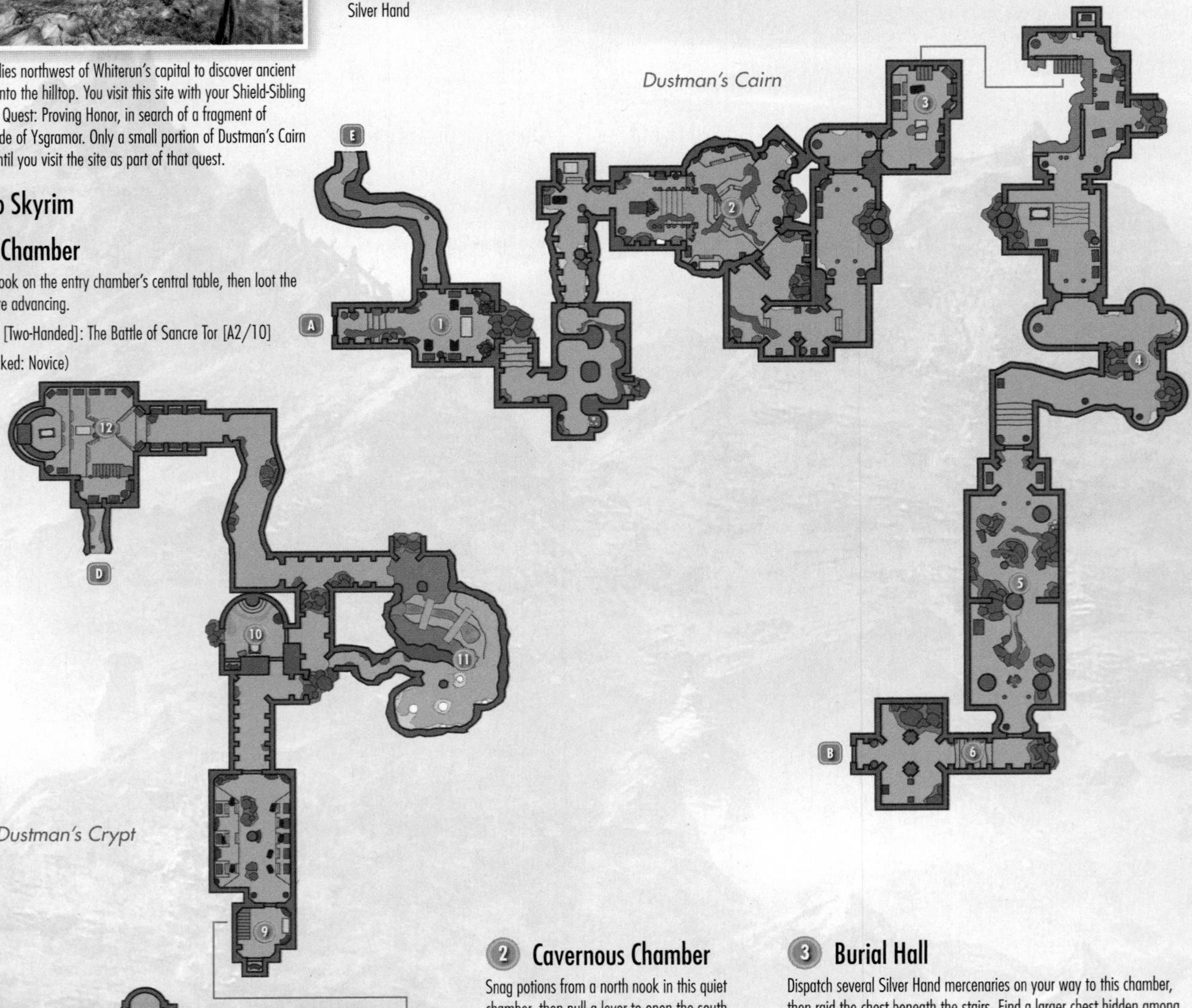

Dustman's Cairn

Dustman's Crypt

(2) Cavernous Chamber

Snag potions from a north nook in this quiet chamber, then pull a lever to open the south portcullis and advance the plot.

◇ Crafting: Arcane Enchanter

◇ Potions

(3) Burial Hall

Dispatch several Silver Hand mercenaries on your way to this chamber, then raid the chest beneath the stairs. Find a larger chest hidden among the upstairs rubble, and open a secret nook in the upstairs north wall by pulling the nearby wall chain so you may access a third chest. Descend the south stairs and claim a bit of loot from a table on your way to [4].

◇ Chest   ◇ Potions

◇ Chest (Locked: Novice)   ◇ Loose gear

◇ Chest (Locked: Master)

4 Overgrown Passages

Slay a powerful Silver Hand mercenary and several Draugr in these passages. Loot the locked chest as you near [5].

◇ Chest (Locked: Adept)

5 Crumbling Hall

Dispatch worthy Silver Hand mercenaries in this wide, debris-filled chamber. You can just reach the coin purse on the south ledge by standing on the nearby stone.

6 Crypt Access

Avoid a pressure plate as you descend this

◇ Danger! Dart Trap (pressure plate)
◇ Chest

B Door to Dustman's Crypt

C Door to Dustman's Cairn

7 Walkway Chamber

You arrive just in time to witness a fierce battle between the Silver Hand and Draugr. Wait for the battle to play out, then slaughter the victors and cut across to [8].

8 Looping Passage

Loot a lone chest as you loop around this passage, heading back toward [7].

◇ Chest

9 Burial Preparation Area

Raid a chest that lies beneath this chamber's wooden stairs, then open the nearby door to find several potions.

◇ Chest (Locked: Adept)
◇ Potions

7 Walkway Chamber Revisited

Raid a chest on this chamber's ground floor, then search the nearby chest to discover a key that unlocks the north door.

◇ Dustman's Cairn Key (chest)
◇ Chest

10 Lab

Mix up a few potions at the Alchemy Lab here, and unlock the Novice-level door to access a closet with a potion.

◇ Crafting: Alchemy Lab
◇ Potion

11 Spider Den and Waterfall

Combat a Giant Frostbite Spider here, along with her young, then slaughter the Draugr that lie in the watery passage beyond.

12 Word Wall Chamber

Obtain a new Word of Power from this chamber's far Word Wall, then raid the nearby large chest and collect the Fragment of Wuuthrad from the nearby table to advance your quest. Beware: a host of powerful Draugr emerge from the surrounding sarcophagi after you claim the Fragment, and you've no choice but to slay them all. They will come at you in waves, so take your time and jump off the raised area and over the altar to give you space between you and your opponent if you need it. After the final Draugr emerges, a passage that leads back to the Dustman's Cairn is revealed.

◇ Fragment of Wuuthrad   ◇ Chest
◇ Word Wall: Fire Breath [1/2]   ◇ Potions

D Path to Dustman's Cairn

E Path to Dustman's Crypt

[6.13] Hamvir's Rest

Recommended Level: 6

Dungeon: Draugr Crypt

Draugr
Skeleton

Collectible

Chest (Locked: Master)

Follow Whiterun's central road to its north end, and you'll find yourself standing before this plagued graveyard. Slay the undead here to cleanse the site and safely loot its giant—albeit locked—chest.

[6.14] Redoran's Retreat

Related Quests
Side Quest: The Great Skyrim Treasure Hunt*

Collectibles
Skill Book [Sneak]: 2920, Last Seed, v8 [A2/10]
Treasure Map IV [4/11]
Chest
Chest (Locked: Novice)
Potions
Loose gear

Recommended Level: 6

Dungeon: Bandit Camp
Bandit
Dog

Dangers
Bear Trap
Bone Alarm Trap

This shallow cave, which lies near Whiterun's central main road, has been occupied by ruthless bandits. Open a locked chest in the first cavern if you're able, then make your way into the rear cavern, where the bandit's chief lurks. Beware the bear trap that lies in front of the large chest. Open it from the side to claim a rare Treasure Map, among other spoils.

[6.15] Fort Greymoor

Related Quests
Dark Brotherhood Quest: Side Contract: Agnis

Recommended Level: 6

Habitation: Military

Fort
Agnis
Bandit
Soldier (Stormcloak/Imperial, depending on your allegiance during the Civil War)

Crafting
Blacksmith Forge
Tanning Rack
Workbench

Dangers
Bear Traps
Flail Trap (trip wire)
Oil Pool Trap

Collectibles
Skill Book [Light Armor]: Rislav The Righteous [C1/10]
Chest(s)
Potions
Loose gear

Near the heart of Whiterun stands an imposing fortress that's been overrun by lawless bandits. Fort Greymoor also serves as a point of contention between the Stormcloaks and Imperials during the Civil War quest line, and therefore may be found populated by soldiers instead of bandits. A friendly old maid named Agnis also resides here—she's a person of interest to the Dark Brotherhood.

Exterior

Fight hard to secure the fort's exterior, then search the grounds thoroughly to find a chest tucked away near some hay to the east, along with a potion and coin purse near the west wooden lookout. A locked grate can be used to enter covertly from outside the walls. Enter the north tower to find another chest.

◇ Crafting: Blacksmith Forge, Tanning Rack, Workbench
◇ Chest
◇ Potion

Fort Greymoor (Interior)

The fort's interior consists of three multifloor towers. Find a chest in the middle tower's main floor, and avoid a trip wire and several bear traps as you head downstairs to explore its lower level. Take the passage to the north tower next, slaying bandits as you head upstairs to chat with a friendly maid named Agnis. Cut across to the south tower afterward and go upstairs to discover a large chest and a Skill Book.

◇ Danger! Bear Traps, Oil Pool Trap, Flail Trap (trip wire)
◇ Skill Book [Light Armor]: Rislav The Righteous [C1/10]
◇ Chest
◇ Chest (Locked: Novice)
◇ Potions
◇ Loose gear

Fort Greymoor Prison

Dispatch rugged bandits as you fight your way toward a chest that lies at the bottom of the prison. None of the cells are worth opening, unless you're simply after some lockpicking practice.

◇ Chest   ◇ Loose gear

[6.16] Silent Moons Camp

Recommended Level: 6

Dungeon: Bandit Camp
Bandit

Crafting
Blacksmith Forge
Grindstone
Workbench

Collectibles

Skill Book [Smithing]: Heavy Armor Forging [B1/10]
Skill Book [Smithing]: Light Armor Forging
Unique Weapon: Lunar Iron Mace [42/80]
Unique Weapon: Lunar Iron Sword [43/80]
Unique Weapon: Lunar Iron War Axe [44/80]
Unique Weapon: Lunar Steel Mace [45/80]
Unique Weapon: Lunar Steel Sword [46/80]
Unique Weapon: Lunar Steel War Axe [47/80]
Chest(s)
Potions aplenty
Loose gear

These ancient ruins, located along Whiterun's northern border, have become home to ruthless bandits. Beware: these scoundrels' unique weapons deal additional fire damage, but only at night. This Silent Moons enchant can be disenchanted and put on other weapons!

Exterior

Slay some tough outer guards, then scale the ruins' exterior steps to reach a small enclosure at the top, where more bandits lurk. Loot a giant chest if you can manage to pick its tricky lock, then claim a pair of Skill Books and make use of some crafting stations before heading back downstairs and entering the door to the Silent Moons Camp.

◇ Crafting: Blacksmith Forge, Grindstone, Workbench
◇ Skill Book [Smithing]: Heavy Armor Forging [B1/10]
◇ Skill Book [Smithing]: Light Armor Forging
◇ Chest
◇ Chest (Locked: Master)
◇ Loose gear

Silent Moons Camp (Interior)

Slay bandits and loot a chest in the ruins' small interior. If you're able, pick an Adept-level door to access a storage room filled with potions and another chest. Climb the central ladder to return outside, then loot an exterior chest that you couldn't have reached before.

◇ Chests (2)   ◇ Potions aplenty

▷ [6.17] Halted Stream Camp

Related Quests

Dungeon Activity

Recommended Level: 6

Dungeon: Bandit Camp

Bandit

Crafting

Blacksmith Forge
Grindstone (2)
Tanning Rack (2)

Dangers

Bear Trap
Bone Alarm Trap
Oil Lamp Traps
Oil Pool Trap
Rockfall (pressure plate)
Trapped Chest

Collectibles

Unique Weapon: Poacher's Axe [49/80]
Chest(s)
Potions
Loose gear
Mineable ore (Iron)

Bandits have raised an impressive campsite just north of Whiterun. This is good place to acquire Iron Ore early in the game if you're into smithing.

Exterior

Avoid falling into the pit that lies just east of the camp; sharpened stakes will spell your end. Search beneath the wooden stairs to find two chests, but beware the trapped chest near the potions. Stand back and to the right when you open it to avoid being struck by a swinging flail, or lockpick the trigger attached to the chest to disarm it.

◇ Danger! Trapped Chest
◇ Crafting: Grindstone, Tanning Rack
◇ Chest (Locked: Apprentice)
◇ Potions
◇ Loose gear

Halted Stream Camp (Interior)

Beware a pressure plate trap as you enter the mine around which the bandits have built their camp. Slay a bandit within the mine and search his body to find a key that opens the following gate. Face the bandit chief in the large cavern beyond—sneak in and knock down the overhead lamps to start things off with a bang. Search the room afterward to secure multiple potions and pillage a pair of chests. Avoid the bear trap and hanging lamp in the exit passage as you make your way back outside. A bandit may be present sharpening a unique axe called the Poacher's Axe, which gives bonus damage against animals.

◇ Danger! Bear Trap, Oil Lamp Traps, Bone Alarm Trap, Oil Pool Trap, Rockfall (pressure plate)
◇ Crafting: Blacksmith Forge, Grindstone, Tanning Rack
◇ Unique Weapon: Poacher's Axe [48/80]
◇ Key to Halted Steam Mine (Bandit)
◇ Chest
◇ Chest (Locked: Novice)
◇ Potions aplenty
◇ Loose gear
◇ Mineable ore (Iron)

▷ [6.18] Bleakwind Basin

Recommended Level: 2

Dungeon: Giant Camp

Giant   Mammoth

Collectible

Chest (Locked: Expert)

Two towering giants have made camp in the heart of Whiterun, tending to a herd of aggressive mammoths. Slay the brutes and their hulking livestock to secure the campsite. If you're able, unlock the giants' Expert-level chest to claim even more plunder from this site.

▷ [6.19] Western Watchtower

Related Quests

Main Quest: Dragon Rising

Dungeon: Dragon Lair

Dragon (only during Main Quest visit)
Whiterun Guard

This tall tower lies west of Whiterun's capital and is patrolled by Whiterun Guards. Early in the Main Quest, a dragon attacks you here. This is your first battle against a dragon. Exploit the defensive nature of the tower to help you bring down the mighty beast.

▷ [6.20] Whiterun Stables

Related Quests

Side Quest: In My Time of Need

Habitation: Farm

Bjorlam (Carriage Driver)
Skulvar Sable-Hilt (Stablemaster)

Services

Trader (Carriage Driver): Bjorlam [3/5]
Trader (Stablemaster): Skulvar Sable-Hilt [3/5]

Special Objects

Business Ledger
Chest
Strongbox (Locked: Expert)
Potions
Loose gear

Stop by the stables south of Whiterun's capital during daylight hours to buy a horse or buy a carriage ride to any other capital in Skyrim. If you're hard up for loot, pick the stable house's Novice-level lock to break in and raid the place.

▷ [6.21] Pelagia Farm

Related Quests

The Companions Quest: Take Up Arms
Favor (Activity): Harvesting Crops* (Severio Pelagia)

Habitation: Farm

Nimriel
Severio Pelagia
Potion

A windmill draws the eye to this quaint farm, which lies just south of Whiterun's capital. There's little worth stealing from these humble folk — better to leave them be.

[6.22] Honningbrew Meadery

Related Quests

Thieves Guild Quest: Dampened Spirits

Thieves Guild Radiant Quest: Larceny Targets*

Recommended Level: 8

Habitation: Special

Animal
Hamelyn
Mallus Maccius
Sabjorn (Food Vendor)
Venomfang Skeever

Services

Trader (Fence): Mallus Maccius [5/10]

Trader (Food Vendor): Sabjorn [6/12]

Food

Crafting

Alchemy Lab

Dangers

Bear Traps
Flail Trap (trip wire)

Quest Items

Honningbrew Meadery Key (Sabjorn)
Pet Poison (Sabjor)
Promissory Note

Collectibles

Larceny Target: Honningbrew Decanter [5/7]
Skill Book [Alchemy]: A Game at Dinner [A1/10]
Skill Book [Sneak]: Three Thieves [E2/10]
Chests
Potions
Loose gear

Whiterun's renown meadery lies just southeast of her capital. There's little of interest outside but quite a bit of drama and intrigue brewing within.

Honningbrew Meadery (Interior)

Speak with Sabjorn inside the meadery to purchase a variety of foodstuffs. You need special keys to enter the meadery's basement and upstairs office; these are obtained during Thieves Guild Quest: Dampened Spirits. The office holds most objects of value, including an informative note and Skill Book found on tables, as well as a locked chest that's further secured behind an Expert-level locked door (no key for this one). The office also contains one of seven Larceny Targets that pertain to a Thieves Guild Radiant Quest.

◇ Larceny Target: Honningbrew Decanter [5/7]
◇ Skill Book [Alchemy]: A Game at Dinner [A1/10]
◇ Honningbrew Meadery Key (Sabjorn)
◇ Pet Poison (Sabjor)
◇ Promissory Note
◇ Chest (Locked: Master)
◇ Loose gear

Honningbrew Basement

Beware of bear traps as you purge the brewery's basement of Skeevers during the "Dampened Spirits" quest. Beware: the Venomfang Skeevers can poison you. Stay sharp and safely trigger a trip wire from as far away as possible to disable a swinging flail. Surprisingly, a dangerous mage named Hamelyn lurks in the cavern that follows. Slay him and poison the nearby Skeever nest, then read the journal you find on Hamelyn's corpse to learn of his questionable motives. Loot a chest here as well before proceeding into the boilery.

◇ Danger! Bear Traps, Flail Trap (trip wire)
◇ Crafting: Alchemy Lab
◇ Skill Book [Sneak]: Three Thieves [E2/10]
◇ Chest (Locked: Novice)
◇ Potions

Honningbrew Boilery

You can only enter the boilery via the meadery's basement passage—the front door remains locked at all times. Head upstairs and optionally steal from a locked chest before nefariously poisoning the giant vat. Exit the boilery afterward with the key that hangs on the wall near the door.

◇ Chest (Locked: Apprentice)
◇ Honningbrew Brewhouse Key

[6.23] Chillfurrow Farm

Habitation: Farm

Wilmuth

Collectibles

Skill Book [One-Handed]: The Importance of Where [E2/10]
Chest
Loose gear

This small farm consists of a farmhouse, a windmill, and a small plot of wheat. Pick the Novice-level door to enter the farmhouse and steal from a chest if you like. A Skill Book rests on the nearby dresser as well.

[6.24] Battle-Born Farm

Related Quests

Favor (Activity): Harvesting Crops* (Alfhild Battle-Born)

Habitation: Farm

Alfhild Battle-Born
Gwendolyn

Collectible

Loose gear

Harvest Alfhild Battle-Born's crops and sell them back to her—she'll pay a fair wage for your work in her fields. If you don't feel like toiling out in the Skyrim sun, pick the farmhouse's Novice-level door and pilfer a couple of coin purses from within.

[6.25] Whitewatch Tower

Related Quests

Dungeon Activity

Recommended Level: 6

Dungeons: Special

Whiterun Guard

Collectibles

Chest
Chest (Locked: Novice)

Whiterun guards patrol this small tower, which lies on the road just north of the city. A small group of bandits are attacking the tower when you first approach; rush in, and you may be able to lend the guards a hand. Strip the bandits of their valuables, then scale the ruined western tower to claim a chest. If you're willing to take the risk, you can also loot the locked chest and weapon racks on the ground level, though the guards consider it theft if they catch you. Make sure to listen to the latest local gossip before moving on.

[6.26] White River Watch

Related Quests

Dungeon Activity

Recommended Level: 6

Dungeon: Bandit Camp

Bandit
Hajvarr Iron-Hand
Ulfr the Blind

Crafting

Alchemy Lab

Collectibles

Unique Item: Ironhand Gauntlets [59/112]
Chest(s)
Potions
Loose gear

This small bandit hideout lies east of Whiterun's capital, just across the White River. Pass through the small cave to face the bandits' leader, who prefers the cold embrace of the outdoor mountain air.

Exterior

Dispatch the exterior guards to secure a chest, then head inside.

◇ Chest (Locked: Novice)

White River Watch (Interior)

A blind guard sits just inside the cave—he'll call for reinforcements if you threaten him. Lie your way past the blind sentry and proceed upstairs. Dispatch or avoid the bandits in the sleeping area that follows. Loot the chest near the cupboard before heading upstairs to discover an Alchemy Lab. Bandits have been mistreating a wolf in the cavern that follows. Free the animal to have it attack its captors, then attack while they're distracted. Scale the winding ramp to reach a high passage that leads out to the White River Overlook.

◇ Crafting: Alchemy Lab
◇ Chest
◇ Potions
◇ Loose gear

Overlook

You emerge onto this rocky overlook, where the bandits' leader, Hajvarr Iron-Hand, awaits. Slay this worthy adversary to obtain valuable plunder from his corpse and from the nearby chest. Take in the view before Fast-Traveling away.

◇ Chest
◇ Potions
◇ Loose gear
◇ Unique Item: Ironhand Gauntlets [59/112]

▷ [6.27] Riverwood

Related Quests

Main Quest: Before the Storm
Main Quest: The Horn of Jurgen Windcaller
Main Quest: A Blade in the Dark
Main Quest: Diplomatic Immunity
Main Quest: A Cornered Rat
Main Quest: Alduin's Wall
Main Quest: Paarthurnax
Side Quest: The Golden Claw
Miscellaneous Objective: Innkeeper Rumors (Sleeping Giant Inn)
Miscellaneous Objective: The Love Triangle: Helping Sven* (Sven)
Miscellaneous Objective: The Love Triangle: Betraying Sven* (Sven)
Miscellaneous Objective: The Love Triangle: Helping Faendal* (Faendal)
Miscellaneous Objective: The Love Triangle: Betraying Faendal* (Faendal)
Favor (Activity): Chopping Wood* (Hod)
Favor (Activity): A Drunk's Drink* (Embry)
Crafting Tutorial: Blacksmithing* (Alvor)
Crafting Tutorial: Alchemy* (Orgnar)

Habitation: Settlement

Alvor (Blacksmith)
Camilla Valerius (Marriage Prospect)
Delphine (Innkeeper)
Dorthe
Embry
Faendal (Follower; Trainer: Archery)
Frodnar
Gerdur
Hilde
Lucan Valerius (General Store Vendor)
Orgnar (Bartender)
Stump (dog)
Sigrid
Sven (Follower)

Crafting

Alchemy Lab
Blacksmith Forge
Grindstone (2)
Tanning Rack (2)
Workbench

Collectible

Chest(s)
Potions
Loose gear

Services

Follower: Faendal [31/47]
Follower: Sven [32/47]
Marriage Prospect: Camilla Valerius [38/62]
Trader (Bartender): Orgnar [1/5]
    Food, Ingredients
Trader (Blacksmith): Alvor [20/33]
    Weapons, Apparel, Misc
Trader (General Store Vendor): Lucan Valerius [8/19]
    Weapons, Apparel, Potions, Scrolls, Food, Books, Misc
Trader (Innkeeper): Delphine [10/15]
    Room and Board
    Innkeeper Rumors
Trainer (Archery: Journeyman): Faendal [2/3]

Located in Whiterun's eastern valley, this small logging community is the first village that you're urged to visit following your escape from Helgen [8.32]. The friendly villagers here assist you and give advice during the early stages of your adventure.

Exterior

Speak with villagers to learn a little about Riverwood. Alvor will sell you fine weapons and armor and can also give you a Side Quest involving the use of his forge.

◇ Crafting: Blacksmith Forge, Grindstone (2), Tanning Rack (2), Workbench
◇ Loose gear

① Sleeping Giant Inn

Rent a room for the night by talking to Delphine, or purchase food and drink from Orgnar. Gain a Miscellaneous Objective by asking Orgnar if you can use the inn's Alchemy Lab, and speak with Sven, the bard, to gain another Miscellaneous Objective involving the Bard's College. Delphine has a secret room beneath the inn with two chests, an Alchemy Lab, an Arcane Enchanter, and a lot of loose items. Once you befriend her in Main Quest: The Horn of Jurgen Windcaller, you have access to all of it.

◇ Crafting: Alchemy Lab   ◇ Chest (3)   ◇ Loose gear

② Riverwood Trader

Speak with this humble shop's proprietor, Lucan Valerius, to gain a Side Quest involving the retrieval of a Golden Claw that's recently been stolen from his store. Then browse Lucan's impressive array of goods.

◇ Chest   ◇ Potions
◇ Chest (Locked: Novice) (2)   ◇ Loose gear

③ Alvor and Sigrid's House

If you followed Hadvar out of Helgen, you'll be welcomed into Alvor and Sigrid's home. The town blacksmith's house has a few items worth swiping, if you're that kind of adventurer.

◇ Area Is Locked (Novice)   ◇ Potions
◇ Chests (2)   ◇ Loose gear

④ Faendal's House

This wily elf has amassed several valuables that are well worth stealing if you think you can get away with it.

◇ Area Is Locked (Novice)
◇ Chests (2)
◇ Potions
◇ Loose gear

⑤ Hod and Gerdur's House

If you followed Ralof out of Helgen, after you speak with Gerdur, you'll be welcome to sleep at her humble home whenever you like.

◇ Area Is Locked (Novice)
◇ Chests (2)
◇ Potion

⑥ Sven and Hilde's House

Sven and Hilde have very little worth stealing, but you may rob them if you like.

◇ Area Is Locked (Novice)
◇ Chest
◇ Loose gear

[6.28] Shimmermist Cave

Recommended Level: 18

Dungeon: Falmer Hive

Animal
Dwarven Centurion
Falmer

Dangers

Swinging Wall Trap (trip wire)

Quest Items

Ebony Blade
Chest(s)
Loose gear

This sizeable cave is found at the foot of mountains that lie northeast of Whiterun's capital.

Shimmermist Cave (Interior)

Slay an overgrown Frostbite Spider in the first watery cavern, and beware the trip wire that's stretched across the end of the following passage. Slay a lone Falmer Archer in the next cavern with the Falmer tent, then proceed along the upper passage, dispatching another Falmer and looting an unusual chest on your way to the cave's inner grotto.

◇ Swinging Wall Trap (trip wire)
◇ Chest
◇ Loose gear

Shimmermist Grotto

Pick off more Falmer in the grotto's first tall cavern, and raid a tent to loot a chest before descending to the cavern's bottom. Dispatch an overgrown Chaurus in the passage that leads to the second chamber, where yet more Chaurus lurk. Loot a chest that rests near the mouth of the following passage, which leads to some long-forgotten dwarven ruins. Defeat a powerful Falmer here, along with a lumbering Dwarven Centurion, then loot one last chest before taking the east passage back to the cave's entrance.

◇ Chests (3)

[6.29] Fellglow Keep

Related Quests

College of Winterhold Quest: Hitting the Books
Side Quest: No Stone Unturned
Dungeon Activity

Recommended Level: 8

Dungeon: Warlock Lair

Animal
Mages
Atronachs
Orthorn

Crafting

Alchemy Lab
Anvil
Arcane Enchanter
Workbench

Dangers

Bear Traps
Dart Traps
Rune Traps

Quest Items

Book: Fragment: On Artaeum
Book: Night of Tears
Book: The Last King of the Ayleids

Collectibles

Skill Book [Conjuration]: The Doors of Oblivion [D2/10]
Skill Book [Destruction]: A Hypothetical Treachery
Unusual Gem: [15/24]

Special Objects

Shrine of Julianos [4/5]
Shrine of Talos [9/17]

Collectibles

Chest(s)
Potions
Loose gear

Fellglow Keep Dungeons

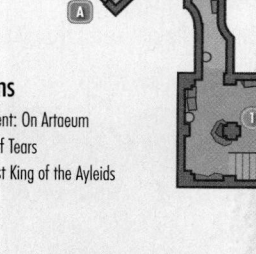

Fellglow Keep

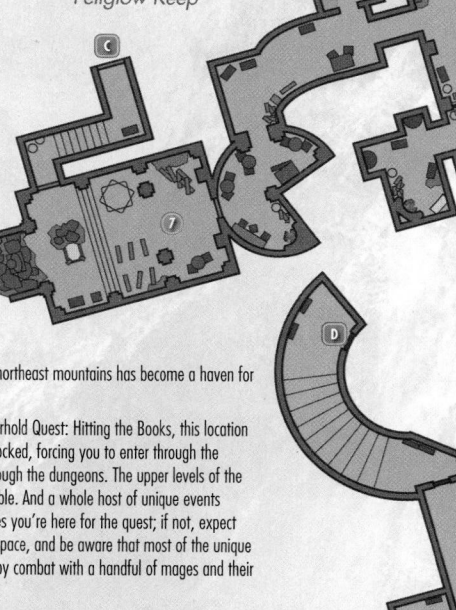

This crumbling stronghold in Whiterun's northeast mountains has become a haven for renegade mages and necromancers.

If you're here for College of Winterhold Quest: Hitting the Books, this location changes substantially. The front door is locked, forcing you to enter through the side tower and take the longer route through the dungeons. The upper levels of the keep, previously sealed, are now accessible. And a whole host of unique events await you. The description below assumes you're here for the quest; if not, expect to have more flexibility in exploring the space, and be aware that most of the unique events described below will be replaced by combat with a handful of mages and their familiars.

Regardless, deal with the guardians in the exterior, then scale the cliffs to reach the first-level roof, where a chest awaits you on the eastern side.

◇ Chest (Locked: Novice)

A Exit to Skyrim

1 Flooded Chambers

Avoid the bear traps on your way through the first two flooded chambers. In the second room, a mage unleashes his pet Frostbite Spiders to fight you. Slay the arachnids and their master to continue on.

◇ Danger! Bear Traps   ◇ Potions   ◇ Loose gear

2 Treasure Nook

Sidestep a pressure plate as you head down the hall to loot the chest in this small room.

◇ Danger! Dart Trap (pressure plate)   ◇ Potion
◇ Chest (Locked: Apprentice)   ◇ Loose gear

3 Cell Block A

Detonate a dangerous Rune Trap with a ranged spell before entering this small prison, where a powerful mage stands guard. Free the caged vampires by picking the locks on their cell doors or by using the levers near the mage. They'll help you defeat the mage here and rush off to battle the mages in the next room before making their escape.

◇ Danger! Rune Trap (floor)   ◇ Loose gear

4 Cell Block B

A mage throws a lever as you enter this room, loosing a pair of wolves that quickly attack you. Slaughter them, then pull the middle of the room's three levers to free Orthorn, who offers to help you find the books you seek. Unlock the nearby Apprentice-level wooden door if possible, then raid the storage room beyond.

◇ Chest (Locked: Apprentice)   ◇ Potion   ◇ Loose gear

5 Firing Range

A powerful mage is training some students in this room, giving you an opportunity for a stealthy ambush.

◇ Loose gear

6 Undercroft

Lay waste to more necromancers here, along with the skeletons that emerge from the surrounding sarcophagi. Claim a chest from a dead-end room at the hall's far end, then take the nearby exit up to Fellglow Keep's main level.

B Door to Fellglow Keep

C Door to Fellglow Keep Dungeons

7 Chapel

Cut down more mages and a summoned creature in this room, then grab the Skill Book. If you picked up any diseases from the animals and traps downstairs, find the Shrine of Talos buried amid the rubble on the altar and activate it to heal yourself before continuing on.

◇ Skill Book [Conjuration]: The Doors of Oblivion [D2/10]
◇ Shrine of Talos [9/17]   ◇ Loose gear

8 Fellglow Foyer

Loop around to the keep's foyer and fight your way upstairs, slaying two more mages and a summoned creature. (There's little of interest in the east room aside from a few more mages.) Enter the upstairs west room to find several crafting stations, some good loot, and an Unusual Gem for Side Quest: No Stone Unturned.

◇ Crafting: Alchemy Lab, Anvil, Arcane Enchanter, Workbench
◇ Unusual Gem: [15/24]   ◇ Potions   ◇ Loose Gear

9 Library

Kill or sneak past a pair of mages in the round library. A Skill Book and potion rest on the central tables.

◇ Skill Book [Destruction]: A Hypothetical Treachery
◇ Potion   ◇ Loose gear

10 Bedchambers

Defeat a powerful mage and a Flame Atronach here, then loot a chest in the south room and find a satchel in the west room. Unlock the Adept-level door to gain access to a larger bedroom with a shrine and locked chest. Continue up to the Ritual Chamber, making sure to loot the scrolls and potions from the nearby shelf — you'll need them.

◇ Shrine of Julianos [4/5]   ◇ Satchel
◇ Chest   ◇ Potions
◇ Chest (Locked: Adept)   ◇ Loose gear

D Door to Fellglow Keep Ritual Chamber

Ritual Chamber

The leader of these mages awaits you in the Keep's Ritual Chamber and introduces herself as "The Caller." Negotiate with her to obtain the books you seek. You can Persuade her to just let you take them or offer to trade her Orthorn. If you succeed, take the books and retrace your steps to leave the Keep.

If you decide to fight, the Caller summons Atronachs and uses a unique ability to teleport around the room to evade your attacks. See College of Winterhold Quest: Hitting the Books for tips on this challenging battle. Once she falls, take the books and collect a key from her corpse, which you can use to raid the nearby treasure room. Take the trapdoor there to quickly return to the foyer and leave this dreadful place.

◇ Book: Fragment: On Artaeum   ◇ Chest
◇ Book: Night of Tears   ◇ Satchel
◇ Book: The Last King of the Ayleids   ◇ Potions
◇ Fellglow Ritual Chamber Key (The Caller)   ◇ Loose gear

E Trapdoor to Fellglow Keep

F Exit to Skyrim

G Door to Fellglow Keep Dungeons

H Door to Fellglow Keep

▷ [6.30] Graywinter Watch

Related Quests

Side Quest: Kyne's Sacred Trials

Dungeon: Animal Den

Animal

Collectibles

Skill Book [Archery]: Vernaccus and Bourlor
Unique Weapon: Froki's Bow [49/80]

This shallow cave lies due north of Whiterun's breathtaking mountain, the Throat of the World [6.38]. This cave used to be a hideout for bandits, but a pair of vicious predators have recently taken up residence here. Slay the foul beasts and then loot the bandits' remains. Find a unique bow and Skill Book resting atop barrels at the back of the cave.

▷ [6.31] The Ritual Stone

Dungeon: Special	Recommended Level: 6
Necromancer	
Skeletons	Special Objects:

Standing Stone: The Ritual Stone [7/13]

Along the road east of Whiterun, a series of stone steps lead up a small bluff. Slay a dangerous necromancer and his skeletal minions here, then inspect the mysterious rune-covered stone to accept a new sign blessing. Those under the sign of the Ritual can reanimate all nearby corpses to fight for them once a day. Try it now on the mage you've just slain! Note that you can have only one sign blessing at a time, so activating this Standing Stone will override your current sign blessing (if any).

▷ [6.32] Whiterun Stormcloak Camp

Related Quests

Civil War Quest (when active, depending on who you side with)

Habitation: Military: Stormcloak Camp

Hjornskar Head-Smasher
Stormcloak Quartermaster (Blacksmith)
Stormcloak Soldier

Services

Trader (Blacksmith): Stormcloak Quartermaster [21/33]
Weapons, Apparel, Misc

Crafting

Alchemy Lab
Anvil
Grindstone
Workbench

Special Objects

Civil War: Map of Skyrim
Chest
Potions
Loose gear

A band of fearless Stormcloak soldiers has made camp at the base of Whiterun's towering mountain, the Throat of the World [6.38]. Trade with the quartermaster if you like, or use his array of crafting stations. Inspect the tabletop map in the largest tent to potentially gain new map data.

▷ [6.33] Valtheim Towers

Recommended Level: 6

Dungeon: Bandit Camp

Bandit

Crafting

Alchemy Lab

Dangers

Trapped Chest

Collectibles

Skill Book [Archery]: The Black Arrow, v2 [B2/10]

Chest(s)

Potions

Loose gear

Mineable ore (Iron)

Mineable ore (Corundum)

A large gang of bandits has taken control of two neighboring towers along the road, and they demand a toll of all travelers who think to pass. Those unwilling or unable to endure the extortion must face the bandits' wrath.

South Tower

Beware: the south tower's chest is trapped. Crouch as far away from the chest as possible before opening it to avoid the swinging flail trap, or use your lockpicking talent to disarm the trigger attached to the chest.

◇ Danger! Trapped Chest

◇ Potions

North Tower

Cross the narrow footbridge that connects the two towers to reach the north tower, where you must deal with more bandits. Inspect the book on the upstairs nightstand to increase your Archery skill. Along the path leading north from this tower, you can find a few veins of ore.

◇ Crafting: Alchemy Lab

◇ Skill Book [Archery]: The Black Arrow, v2 [B2/10]

◇ Chests (2)

◇ Potions

◇ Mineable ore (Iron)

◇ Mineable ore (Corundum)

[6.34] Darkshade

Recommended Level: 6

Dungeon: Animal Den

Animal

Collectibles

Skill Book [Heavy Armor]: Orsinium and the Orcs

Chest

Potion

Loose gear

Massive bones mark the entrance to this otherwise unassuming cave, which lies at the far east edge of Whiterun. Slay a few beasts as you navigate the first few caverns and passages, which hold little of value. Follow a stream to a waterfall and find a potion and Skill Book nearby. Nab a coin purse in the passage that leads to the next chamber, where a large chest begs looting.

[6.35] Guldun Rock

Recommended Level: 24

Dungeon: Giant Camp

Giant

Collectibles

Skill Book [Heavy Armor]: The Knights of the Nine

Chest

Giants have made camp at Whiterun's eastern edge. Slay two of the brutes if you can, then enter their cave to plunder gold and valuables from a chest. A Skill Book sits on the rock near the chest as well.

[6.36] Hillgrund's Tomb

Related Quests

Dungeon Quest: Ancestral Worship

Recommended Level: 6

Dungeon: Draugr Crypt

Draugr

Golldir

Vals Veran

Dangers

Dart Trap (pressure plate)

Flail Trap (door)

Oil Pool Trap

Collectibles

Chest(s)

Potions

Loose gear

These small burial ruins are found along Whiterun's eastern border, just west of the White River. The locals use this site as a burial ground for loved ones.

Exterior

Before entering the tomb, scale the rocky slope behind it and locate a hidden chest. Then enter the exterior enclosure and speak with a troubled man named Golldir. Agree to help Golldir confront a dangerous necromancer named Vals Veran within the crypt to gain a new quest. Golldir then unlocks the crypt's door.

◇ Chest (Locked: Expert)   ◇ Potion

Hillgrund's Tomb (Interior)

Follow Golldir into the crypt. He will accompany you through here. Beware of the first trapped door in the entry passage, and ignite the oily floor behind the second door to help slay a mighty Draugr — or simply avoid the sleeping monster. Loot a web-covered chest on your way to a bloodsoaked chamber, where you discover the remains of Golldir's poor aunt. Proceed through the west door and loot a chest that lies among the rubble. Sneak through the tight burial passages that follow to skirt pressure plates and avoid waking the resting Draugr.

Find another chest as you creep toward a Draugr-filled chamber. Pull a chain near a Bear glyph here to expose a secret passage, then go through and unlock an Apprentice-level door to access a treasure nook. Open the large north door to confront Vals Veran in a large chamber. Defeat the foul necromancer to avenge Golldir and obtain a key that opens

the nearby door. Raid a chest and collect more plunder on your way out of this unholy place. Golldir will also give you a small reward, and if you speak with him after you exit the tomb, he will agree to be your Follower if you desire.

◇ Danger! Oil Pool Trap, Flail Trap (door), Dart Trap (pressure plate)

◇ Hillgrund's Tomb Crypt Key (Vals Veran)

◇ Chests (2)

◇ Chest (Locked: Novice)

◇ Chest (Locked: Adept)

◇ Chest (Locked: Expert)

◇ Apothecary's Satchel

◇ Potions

◇ Loose gear

[6.37] High Hrothgar

Related Quests

Main Quest: The Way of the Voice

Main Quest: The Horn of Jurgen Windcaller

Main Quest: The Throat of the World

Main Quest: Elder Knowledge

Main Quest: The Fallen

Main Quest: Season Unending

Main Quest: Epilogue

Other Factions: Greybeards Quest: Word Wall Revelations*

Recommended Level: 8

Habitation: Special

Arngeir

Borri

Einarth

Wulfgar

Collectible

Area Is Locked (quest required)

Potions aplenty

Loose gear

This ancient monastery stands high upon Skyrim's tallest mountain, the Throat of the World [6.38]. High Hrothgar is home to the Greybeards— the legendary masters of the Voice. Many important quests intersect at this remote monastery, but you can't enter until you've advanced to Main Quest: The Way of the Voice.

High Hrothgar (Interior)

Speak with the Greybeards to advance your quests here. A host of potions and ingredients are scattered about the monastery's small interior, but anything you take is considered theft.

◇ Potions aplenty

High Hrothgar Courtyard

Exit through any of the north doors to visit High Hrothgar's frigid courtyard. The southeast stairs lead to the summit, but a raging blizzard prevents passage until you've advanced to Main Quest: The Throat of the World.

Enjoy the commanding view from the north ledge, then use your Ethereal Form Shout and leap off—it's fun! Enter the courtyard's tower for even more stunning views of Skyrim.

[6.38] Throat of the World

Related Quests

Alduin's Bane
Main Quest: Paarthurnax
Main Quest: Epilogue
Side Quest: Repairing the Phial
Other Factions: Greybeards Quest: Meditations on Words of Power*

Recommended Level: 10

Dungeon: Dragon Lair

Paarthurnax

Quest Items

Snow

Collectibles

Unique Weapon: Notched Pickaxe [50/80]
Mineable ore (Malachite)

The highest point in Skyrim, the Throat of the World stands at the apex of Whiterun's towering eastern mountain, which forms the border between its neighboring Hold, Eastmarch. This site has great significance to the story surrounding the Dragonborn. It is also the place where special snow that never melts can be found—a necessary ingredient for "The White Phial" quest.

But after coming all this way, why stop here? Make your way up the final, rocky slope to reach the summit of the mountain and see all of Skyrim spread out below you. Just below the peak is a vein of rare Malachite (Glass) ore, and a unique pickaxe is imbedded in the rock way up top—a nice little bonus for completing your epic climb!

⊰⊱ SECONDARY LOCATIONS ⊰⊱

[6.A] Shrine of Akatosh: Rorikstead

A small cluster of weatherbeaten rocks lie atop this hill overlooking Rorikstead, north of the town. Resting on the ground on the west side is a Shrine of Akatosh, and a book.

◇ Shrine of Akatosh [4/6]

[6.B] Dragon Mound: Rorikstead Resurrection

Related Quest: Main Quest: Alduin's Wall

Related Quest: Main Quest: Elder Knowledge

This Dragon Mound is initially sealed. It opens during Main Quest: Alduin's Wall, once you set off for Sky Haven Temple. After this point, but before you begin your search for the Elder Scroll, Alduin will appear here and resurrect the dragon Nahagliiv. Alduin cannot be harmed; he resurrects his brethren and flies off. But confront Nahagliiv quickly, or he will attack Rorikstead and wipe out much of the town. Alternatively, you could lure him to the town and use the guards as a distraction to make the battle that much easier.

[6.C] The Expired Alchemist

Follow the stream from Talking Stone Camp until it ends in a waterfall. On the rocky outcropping in the pool below, you can find the body of a dead alchemist. Loot the corpse for a Nirnroot and other valuables.

[6.D] Hunter and Hunted

In the mountains close to Drelas' Cottage, you find a hunter's body. Fend off the fierce predator nearby, then search the corpse for valuables.

[6.E] Shrine of Zenithar: Ring of Boulders

Due west of the Swindler's Den is a ring of large boulders. A small Shrine to Zenithar has been built up against the largest of these stones, with a few offerings.

◇ Shrine of Zenithar [3/5]

[6.F] Fetid Pond

West and a little south of Swindler's Den is a small pond with the skeleton of a mammoth and a dead bandit, still grasping for a Nirnroot at the pool's edge. Search him and harvest any nearby ingredients you need.

[6.G] Shrine of Zenithar: Crumbling Bastion

Due north of Broken Fang Cave lies a crumbling stone ruin. This fortification has seen better days, but a small altar with a Shrine to Zenithar and some offerings still remains. Jump up the rocks behind the ruin to reach a hidden chest on the arched wall over the shrine.

◇ Skill Book [Speech]: 2920, Second Seed, v5
◇ Shrine of Zenithar [4/5]
◇ Chest (Locked: Novice)
◇ Satchel

[6.H] King of the Mudcrabs

Related Quest: Side Quest: Kyne's Sacred Trials

Due west of Broken Fang Cave, just off the main road, is a small pond with a number of Mudcrabs, including a huge Mudcrab carcass. Wonder what it would be like to fight such an enormous creature? Then return here for Kyne's Sacred Trials to battle the Mudcrab Guardian Spirit. Near the pool is a rocky alcove with spilled blood and an old skeleton and some loose items.

◇ Loose gear

[6.I] Shrine of Stendarr: The Two Pillars

Due south of Swindler's Den, two Nordic columns and a bare foundation are all that remain of this old structure, long since lost to the elements. A small Shrine to Stendarr is now present here, along with a Skill Book. Check the altar for some offerings to take.

◇ Skill Book [Enchanting]: Twin Secrets
◇ Shrine of Stendarr [3/5]
◇ Strong Box

[6.J] Swallowed Skeleton: Greymoor Foothills

In the foothills due north of Sleeping Tree Camp is a strange sight: a mammoth skeleton with a human skeleton inside of it. There's little else here but this oddity.

[6.K] Dragon Mound: Great Henge Resurrection

Related Quest

Main Quest: Diplomatic Immunity
Main Quest: Alduin's Wall

This Dragon Mound is initially sealed. It opens during Main Quest: Diplomatic Immunity, once you set off for Solitude. After this point, but before you begin your journey to Sky Haven Temple, Alduin will appear here and resurrect the dragon Vuljotnaak. Alduin cannot be harmed; he resurrects his brethren and flies off. But slay Vuljotnaak and claim his soul.

[6.L] Puzzling Pillar Ruins

On the rough path leading toward Sleeping Tree Camp is a group of standing stones and three Nordic Puzzle Pillars. Line up the animal glyph associated with the glyph in the rubble around the pillar to open the trapdoor, which has a chest to open.

◇ Chest

[6.M] Necromancer's Bluff

An ancient altar rests atop this rocky bluff. Climb the hill from the east and take in the scene; a pair of skeletons have slain the necromancers that raised them. Splinter these bony fiends, then collect any items on or around the dead.

◇ Loose gear

[6.N] Bloodied Box: Sleeping Tree Camp

Just east of the second path that leads to Sleeping Tree Camp is a thicket. Check the ground for some dried blood, and a strongbox to open.

◇ Strongbox (Apprentice)

[6.O] Dragon Mound: Lone Mountain

Related Quest: Main Quest: Alduin's Wall

This Dragon Mound is initially sealed. It opens during Main Quest: Alduin's Wall. If you visit during or after this point in the Main Quest, the resurrected dragon will likely be circling this location. Strike it down and claim its soul as your prize.

[6.P] The Skeleton's Strong Box: Greymoor

In the rocky scree above the pond to the northwest of Fort Greymoor is a copse of trees. Beneath one of them is a skeleton, still clutching the strongbox it was attempting to covet.

◇ Strongbox (Apprentice)

[6.Q] The Lad of the Lake: Bleakwind Basin

Northwest of Bleakwind Basin is a small lake shrouded by mist. Sticking out of the water is a bony arm, still clutching a sword. Claim it, then pick the nearby Nirnroot you wish.

◇ Loose gear

[6.R] Smuggler's Den: Whiterun

Beneath the rocky cliffs on Whiterun's northern rim lies a smuggler's den, with two bandits who attack if you approach. There's plenty of loose loot lying about, including a supply of Skooma, a Skill Book, and a horse you can steal. Be careful when opening the chest, though. When you do, the remaining members of the gang return and ambush you!

◇ Skill Book [Pickpocket]: Aevar Stone-Singer
◇ Chest (Adept)
◇ Potions

[6.S] Whiterun Attack Camp

Related Quests

Civil War Quest: Battle of Whiterun

Civil War Quest: Defense of Whiterun

 At the beginning of the assault on Whiterun, Galmar Stone-Fist assembles his men for a rousing speech at this location, prior to the epic assault (from your allied footsoldiers and flame catapults) on this Imperial-allied stronghold.

[6.T] Shrine of Talos: White River Valley

Related Quests: Favors: Jobs for the Jarls: Elisif the Fair

On a mountain bluff north of the White River, you can find an overhang with a hidden Shrine to Talos. Receive a blessing here if you wish, before helping yourself to the offerings. Jarl Elisif the Fair of Solitude will send you to this remote shrine to dedicate her husband's Torygg's War Horn to Talos. But when you do, prepare to be ambushed by two Thalmor! A note suggests they have been waylaying worshippers to the shrine.

◇ Shrine of Talos [10/17]

◇ Satchel

◇ Loose gear

[6.U] Hunters' Camp: White River Hills

If the Stormcloaks take control of Whiterun, a small group of hunters will set up camp on this plateau, taking over the spot formerly occupied by Whiterun Stormcloak Camp [6.32].

[6.V] Big Log Bridge

Crossing the gorge with the river rapids below, just south of Hillgrund's Tomb, is a massive fallen tree. A bandit or two are likely to be readying an ambush here. Dropping them with arrows from hiding and watching them plunge into the river is exceptionally satisfying! On the northwest side of the log bridge, find a chest and Skill Book hidden behind the remains of a tree stump.

◇ Skill Book [Illusion]: The Black Arts on Trial

◇ Chest

[6.W] Ruined Toll and Wispmother's Well

Along the winding path in the eastern foothills of the Throat of the World, close to Darkwater River, are the remains of an old Imperial toll building. The place is deserted, save for the screech of a Wispmother, appearing from the well atop the hill. A Skill Book rests atop a large woven basket among the ruins.

◇ Skill Book [Conjuration]: The Warrior's Charge

[6.X] The Seven Thousand Steps

To reach High Hrothgar, pilgrims must climb the Seven Thousand Steps, a journey that begins near the village of Ivarstead in the Rift. Along this path lie ten wayshrines, which recount the history of the Greybeards and the Voice. Read the stone plaques at all ten shrines to receive the unique Voice of the Sky blessing (animals neither attack nor flee from you for a day). You can repeat the pilgrimage to replenish the blessing if you wish.

◇ Voice of the Sky

HOLD 7: EASTMARCH

TOPOGRAPHICAL OVERVIEW

Historians refer to Eastmarch as one of the "old Holds." Its ancient capital, Windhelm, sits in the northeast of Skyrim, where the White River races toward the Sea of Ghosts. Windhelm remains the only sizable city in the otherwise determinedly rural Hold of Eastmarch, where the volcanic terrain limits farming and development. The entire Hold is dominated by sulfur pools where very little grows and seems sunken in compared to the higher elevations of the Rift and the towering Throat of the World. Most Nords congregate in the north, in and around the granite walls of Windhelm, where Ulfric Stormcloak plans his rebellion against the Empire.

Routes and Pathways

Travelers to this region should be satisfied with the well-maintained roads that connect Windhelm to Winterhold in the north, head across to the Pale and Whiterun to the west, and wind south into the Rift. The White and Darkwater Rivers combine in this territory, allowing you to find your bearings more easily. These rivers then combine with River Yorgrim at the Windhelm bridge and flow out into Winterhold and the Sea of Ghosts, with Dunmeth Pass to the northeast. The eastern edge of this Hold (and Skyrim itself) is dominated by the Dunmeth Pass at lower elevations, which merge into the Velothi Mountains; this impenetrable mountain range stretches south into the Rift and shrouds the Orc stronghold of Narzulbur and the hidden dwarven ruins of Mzulft. To the south, the tumbledown Mistwatch and steep slopes buttressing the Rift dominate the area. More rocky terrain can be found to the southwest and west, toward the foothills of the Throat of the World. The interior of Eastmarch is a no-man's-land of bubbling sulfur pools, giant camps, crests, slopes, and mines.

AVAILABLE SERVICES, CRAFTING, AND COLLECTIBLES

Services

Followers: [6/47]
Houses for Sale: [1/5]
Marriage Prospects: [13/62]
Skill Trainers: [7/50]
  Alchemy: [0/3]
  Alteration: [1/3]
  Archery: [0/3]
  Block: [0/2]
  Conjuration: [0/3]
  Destruction: [1/3]
  Enchanting: [0/2]
  Heavy Armor: [1/3]
  Illusion: [0/2]
  Light Armor: [1/3]
  Lockpicking: [0/2]
  One-Handed: [0/3]
  Pickpocket: [1/3]
  Restoration: [0/3]

Smithing: [0/3]
Sneak: [0/3]
Speech: [1/4]
Two-Handed: [1/2]
Traders: [15/133]
  Apothecary [1/12]
  Bartender [1/5]
  Blacksmith [3/33]
  Carriage Driver [1/5]
  Fence [1/10]
  Fletcher [0/3]
  Food Vendor [1/9]
  General Goods [3/19]
  Innkeeper [2/15]
  Jeweler [0/2]
  Special [0/3]
  Spell Vendor [1/12]
  Stablemaster [1/5]

Collectibles

Captured Critters: [0/5]
Dragon Claws: [0/10]
Dragon Priest Masks: [0/10]
Larceny Targets: [0/7]
Skill Books: [22/180]
  Alchemy: [1/10]
  Alteration: [2/10]
  Archery: [1/10]
  Block: [2/10]
  Conjuration: [1/10]
  Destruction: [1/10]
  Enchanting: [1/10]
  Heavy Armor: [2/10]
  Illusion: [1/10]

Light Armor: [1/10]
Lockpicking: [1/10]
One-Handed: [0/10]
Pickpocket: [2/10]
Restoration: [0/10]
Smithing: [3/10]
Sneak: [1/10]
Speech: [1/10]
Two-Handed: [1/10]
Treasure Maps: [4/11]
Unique Items: [5/112]
Unique Weapons: [4/80]
Unusual Gems: [4/24]

Special Objects

Shrines: [8/69]
  Akatosh: [1/6]
  Arkay: [1/12]
  Dibella: [2/8]
  Julianos: [1/5]
  Kynareth: [0/6]
  Mara: [0/5]
  Stendarr: [0/5]
  Talos: [3/17]
  Zenithar: [0/5]
Standing Stones: [1/13]
  The Atronach Stone
Word Walls: [1/42]
  Animal Allegiance: [0/3]
  Aura Whisper: [0/3]
  Become Ethereal: [0/3]
  Disarm: [0/3]
  Dismaying Shout: [0/3]
  Elemental Fury: [0/3]
  Fire Breath: [0/2]
  Frost Breath: [1/3]
  Ice Form: [0/3]
  Kyne's Peace: [0/3]
  Marked for Death: [0/3]
  Slow Time: [0/3]
  Storm Call: [0/3]
  Throw Voice: [0/1]
  Unrelenting Force: [0/1]
  Whirlwind Sprint: [0/2]

CRAFTING STATIONS: EASTMARCH

✓	TYPE	LOCATION A	LOCATION B
☐	Alchemy Lab	Windhelm (the White Phial) [7.00]	Narzulbur (Exterior) [7.22]
☐	Arcane Enchanter	Windhelm (Market District) [7.00]	Windhelm (Palace of the Kings: Wuunferth the Unliving's Chamber) [7.00]
☐	Anvil or Blacksmith Forge	Windhelm (Market District) [7.00]	Gloombound Mine (Exterior) [7.23]
☐	Cooking Pot and Spit	Windhelm (Candlehearth Hall) [7.00]	Windhelm (House of Clan Shatter-Shield) [7.00]
☐	Grindstone	Windhelm (Market District) [7.00]	Gloombound Mine (Exterior) [7.23]
☐	Smelter	Windhelm (Market District) [7.00]	Gloombound Mine (Exterior) [7.23]
☐	Tanning Rack	Windhelm (Market District) [7.00]	Narzulbur (Exterior) [7.22]
☐	Wood Chopping Block	Windhelm (Market District) [7.00]	Narzulbur (Exterior) [7.22]
☐	Workbench	Windhelm (Market District) [7.00]	Gloombound Mine (Exterior) [7.23]

Palace of the Kings

Windhelm

White River

Dunmeth Pass

River Yorgrim

Velothi Mountains

7.01
7.02
7.03
7.04
7.05
7.06
7.07
7.08
7.09
7.10
7.11
7.12
7.13
7.14
7.15
7.16
7.17
7.18
7.19
7.20
7.21
7.22
7.23
7.24
7.25
7.26
7.27
7.28
7.29
7.30
7.31
7.32
7.33
7.34
7.35
7.36
7.37
7.38

7.A
7.B
7.C
7.D
7.E
7.F
7.G
7.H
7.I
7.J
7.K
7.L
7.M
7.N
7.O
7.P
7.Q
7.R
7.S
7.T
7.U

N

The Elder Scrolls V

SKYRIM

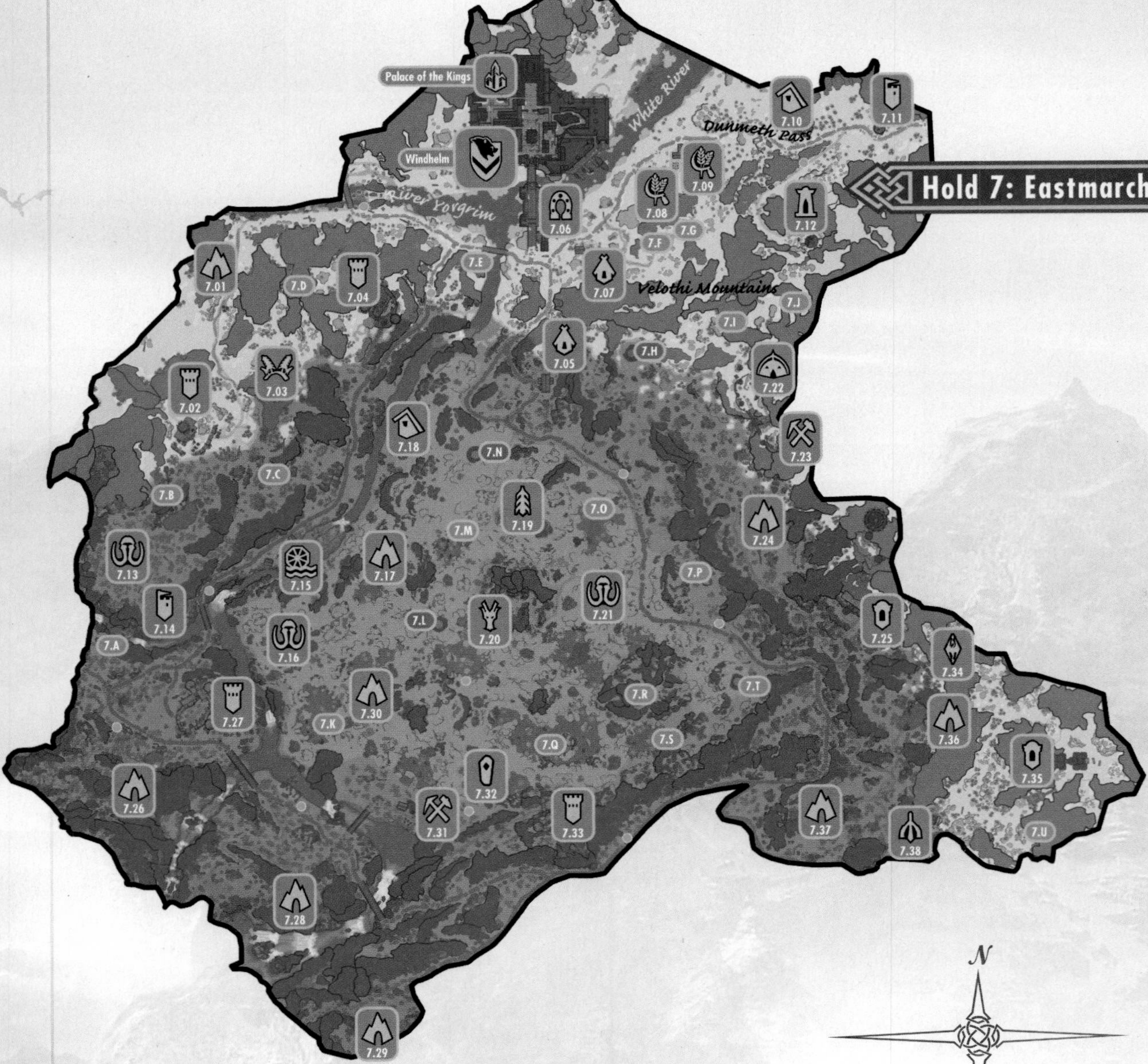

PRIMARY LOCATIONS

Total — 40: Hold Capital, Palace of the Kings, and 38 Hold Locations

[7.00] Hold Capital City: Windhelm
[7.00] Palace of the Kings
  Jarl: Ulfric Stormcloak
[7.01] Uttering Hills Cave
[7.02] Gallows Rock
[7.03] Mara's Eye Pond
[7.04] Morvunskar
[7.05] Kynesgrove
[7.06] Windhelm Stables
[7.07] Brandy-Mug Farm
[7.08] Hlaalu Farm
[7.09] Hollyfrost Farm
[7.10] Traitor's Post

[7.11] Refugees' Rest
[7.12] Sacellum of Boethiah
[7.13] Cradlecrush Rock
[7.14] Abandoned Prison
[7.15] Mixwater Mill
[7.16] Broken Limb Camp
[7.17] Cronvangr Cave
[7.18] Riverside Shack
[7.19] Witchmist Grove
[7.20] Bonestrewn Crest
[7.21] Steamcrag Camp
[7.22] Narzulbur
[7.23] Gloombound Mine
[7.24] Cragwallow Slope

[7.25] Mzulft
[7.26] Lost Knife Hideout
[7.27] Fort Amol
[7.28] Darkwater Pass
[7.29] Snapleg Cave
[7.30] Eldergleam Sanctuary
[7.31] Darkwater Crossing
[7.32] The Atronach Stone
[7.33] Mistwatch
[7.34] Eastmarch Imperial Camp
[7.35] Kagrenzel
[7.36] Stony Creek Cave
[7.37] Cragslane Cavern
[7.38] Ansilvund

SECONDARY LOCATIONS

Total — 21 Points of Interest

[7.A] Lucky Lorenz's Shack
[7.B] Shrine of Talos: Cradlecrush Pond
[7.C] Mara's Eye Stones
[7.D] Frost Troll Den: Uttering Hills
[7.E] Shrine of Talos: Watcher of Windhelm
[7.F] Hunter's Camp: Windhelm Plateau
[7.G] Windhelm Attack Camp
[7.H] Dragon Mound: Kynesgrove Resurrection
[7.I] Hunter's Camp: Dunmeth Pass
[7.J] Wild Animal Den: Dunmeth Pass

[7.K] Hunter's Camp: Sulphur Soaking Pools
[7.L] Dragon Mound: Bonestrewn Flats
[7.M] Cronvangr Summoning Altar
[7.N] Dragon Mound: Witchmist Slope
[7.O] Witchmist Sulphur Pool
[7.P] Hunters' Camp: Steamcrag Slopes
[7.Q] Mistwatch Folly
[7.R] Shrine of Akatosh: Steamcrag Hillock
[7.S] The Mournful Giant
[7.T] Dragon Mound: Mzulft Foothills
[7.U] Hunters' Camp: Slopes of Kagrenzel

HOLD CAPITAL: WINDHELM

Related Quests

Main Quest: Season Unending
Civil War Quest: Joining the Stormcloaks
Civil War Quest: The Jagged Crown
Civil War Quest: Message to Whiterun
Civil War Quest: Liberation of Skyrim
Civil War Quest: A False Front
Civil War Quest: Rescue from Fort Neugrad
Civil War Quest: Compelling Tribute
Civil War Quest: The Battle for Fort Snowhawk
Civil War Quest: The Battle for Fort Sungard
Civil War Quest: Battle for Whiterun
Civil War Quest: Reunification of Skyrim
Civil War Quest: Battle for Windhelm
Side Quest: Rise in the East
Side Quest: Blood on the Ice
Side Quest: The White Phial
Side Quest: Repairing the Phial
Dark Brotherhood Quest: Innocence Lost
Dark Brotherhood Quest: Sentenced to Death
Dark Brotherhood Quest: Breaching Security
Thieves Guild Radiant Quest: No Stone Unturned (x2)
Thieves Guild City Influence Quest: Summerset Shadows
Miscellaneous Objective: Innkeeper Rumors (Candlehearth Hall)
Miscellaneous Objective: Crew Cut† (Kjar)
Miscellaneous Objective: Nightshade for the Unliving† (Hillevi Cruel-Sea)
Miscellaneous Objective: Malborn's Long Shadow† (Malborn)
Favor (Activity): A Drunk's Drink† (Brond)
Favor (Activity): A Drunk's Drink† (Torbjorn Shatter-Shield)
Favor (Activity): The Gift of Charity† (Angrenor Once-Honored)
Favor (Activity): The Gift of Charity† (Silda the Unseen)
Favor: Special Delivery† (Adonato Leotelli)
Favor: A Good Talking To† (Scouts-Many-Marshes)
Favor: Sparring Partners† (Rolff)

Favor: A Little Light Thievery† (Stands-in-Shadows)
Favor: A Little Light Burglary† (Revyn Sadri)
Favor: The Bandit Slayer† (Brunwulf Free-Winter)
Favor: Rare Item Hunt† (Torbjorn Shatter-Shield)
Favor: Item Retrieval (Bandit Camp)† (Shahvee)
Favor: Item Retrieval (Cave)† (Oengul War-Anvil)
Thane Quest: Thane of Eastmarch†

Habitation or Dungeon Type: Hold Capital (Major)

Crafting

Alchemy Lab (2)
Arcane Enchanter
Blacksmith Forge
Grindstones (2)
Smelter
Tanning Racks (3)
Workbench (2)

Services

Follower: Adelaisa Vendicci [34/47]
Follower: Stenvar [35/47]
Follower: Calder [36/47]
House for Sale: Hjerim [4/5]
Marriage Prospect: Scouts-Many-Marshes [39/62]
Marriage Prospect: Shahvee [40/62]
Marriage Prospect: Angrenor Once-Honored [41/62]
Marriage Prospect: Stenvar [42/62]
Marriage Prospect: Viola Giordano [43/62]
Marriage Prospect: Quintus Navale [44/62]
Marriage Prospect: Revyn Sadri [45/62]
Marriage Prospect: Calder [46/62]
Trader (Apothecary): Nurelion [8/12]
Trader (Bartender): Ambarys Rendar [2/5]
Trader (Blacksmith): Oengul War-Anvil [22/33]
Trader (Fence): Niranye [5/10]
Trader (Food Vendor): Hillevi Cruel-Sea [8/9]
Trader (General Store Vendor): Aval Atheron [9/19]
Trader (General Store Vendor): Niranye [10/19]
Trader (General Store Vendor): Revyn Sadri [11/19]
Trader (Innkeeper): Elda Early-Dawn [11/15]
Trader (Spell Vendor): Wuunferth the Unliving [11/12]
Trainer [Destruction: Journeyman]: Wuunferth the Unliving [3/3]

Trainer [Heavy Armor: Journeyman]: Hermir Strong-Heart [3/3]
Trainer [Light Armor: Journeyman]: Scouts-Many-Marshes [1/3]
Trainer [Pickpocket: Expert]: Silda the Unseen [1/3]
Trainer [Speech: Journeyman]: Revyn Sadri [3/4]
Trainer [Two-Handed: Expert]: Torbjorn Shatter-Shield [2/2]

Collectibles

Skill Book [Alchemy]: A Game at Dinner [A2/10]
Skill Book [Block]: The Mirror [D2/10]
Skill Book [Conjuration]: 2920, Frostfall, v10 [A1/10]
Skill Book [Destruction]: A Hypothetical Treachery [A2/10]
Skill Book [Heavy Armor]: The Knights of the Nine [E2/10]
Skill Book [Illusion]: The Black Arts On Trail [E1/10]
Skill Book [Light Armor]: Ice and Chitin [A2/10]
Skill Book [Pickpocket]: Thief [D1/10]
Skill Book [Sneak]: The Red Kitchen Reader [D2/10]
Skill Book [Speech]: 2920, Second Seed, v5 [A2/10]
Unique Item: Viola's Gold Ring [60/112]
Unique Item: Strange Amulet [61/112]
Unique Item: Necromancer Amulet [62/112]
Unusual Gem: [16/24]
Unusual Gem: [17/24]

Special Objects

Business Ledger
Civil War: Map of Skyrim
Shrine of Arkay [8/12]
Shrine of Talos [11/17]
Chest
Potions aplenty
Loose gear

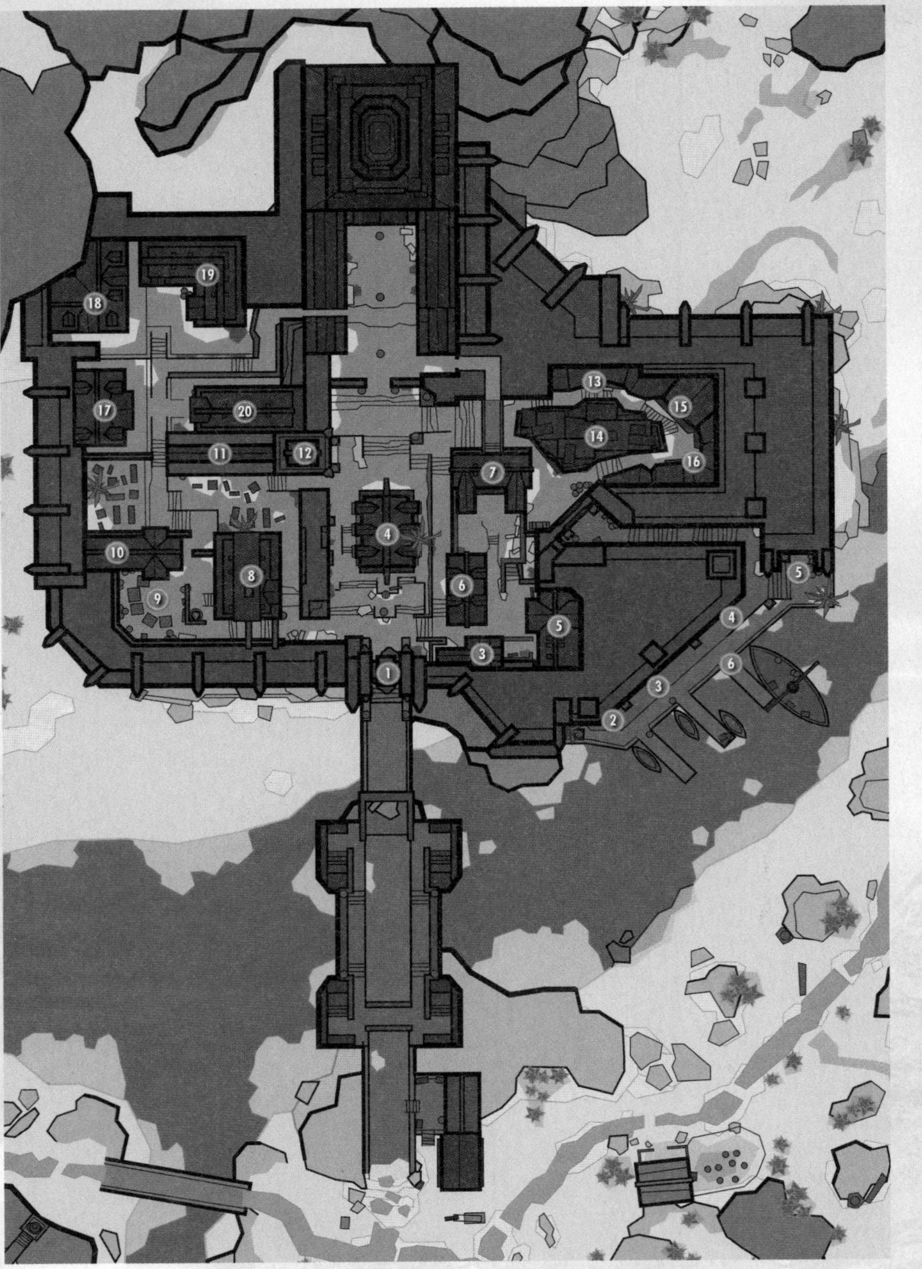

① City Gates and Bridge

Windhelm's large fortified main gate serves as the primary means of entry into the city. The bridge leading to the gate from the Stables has side parapets, mostly in disrepair, but offers a good view of the ominous main walls. Head into the belly of the bridge (there's an interior barracks) to discover a Skill Book resting on a table. You can drop down to the dockside from the right edge of the bridge, by the gate.

◇ Skill Book [Light Armor]: Ice and Chitin [A2/10]

② East Empire Company

Orthus Endario

Adelaisa Vendicci (after Side Quest: Rise in the East has started)

The East Empire Company is the well-known Imperial Shipping organization and has spread its influence across Tamriel. A few years prior, the company made its first in-roads in Skyrim by establishing an office and shipping center in Windhelm. The organization enjoyed a brisk business here, in direct competition with that of Clan Shatter-Shield's, but the office is now closed. It can be reopened as part of Side Quest: Rise in the East; if that happens, business will resume.

◇ Follower: Adelaisa Vendicci [34/47]

◇ Business Ledger

◇ Strongbox (Adept)

③ Clan Shatter-Shield Office

A small office building where Clan Shatter-Shield runs the business of their shipping operation. This has a front desk area where Suvaris Atheron meets clients, and a back area where records are kept, including a logbook noting the Clan's decision to work clandestinely with pirates (Side Quest: Rise in the East).

◇ Suvaris Atheron's Logbook

◇ Business Ledger

◇ Strongbox (Adept)

④ Argonian Assemblage

Shahvee

Stands-In-Shallows

Scouts-Many-Marshes

Neetrenaza

The Argonian Assemblage is a jail-like dwelling on the freezing Windhelm Docks that serves as communal housing for the city's Argonian dockworkers. It is the worst building in all of Windhelm, outside the protection of the city's giant stone walls.

◇ Marriage Prospect: Scouts-Many-Marshes [39/62]

◇ Marriage Prospect: Shahvee [40/62]

◇ Trainer (Light Armor: Journeyman): Scouts-Many-Marshes [1/3]

◇ Skill Book [Pickpocket]: Thief [D1/10]

◇ Knapsack

⑤ Warehouse

An old warehouse with nothing but slightly musty barrels and crates.

◇ Knapsack

⑥ Dock and the North Wind

Kjar

Dalan Merchad

The main dockside where the Argonian workers are ferrying wood and using the tanning rack is also where the North Wind is moored. Captain Kjar and first mate Dalan Merchad are sitting on this vessel, planning their next trip into the Sea of Ghosts. The steps between the Argonian Assemblage and the Warehouse leads to another Tanning Rack, and the city's smaller, East Gate.

◇ Crafting: Grindstone, Tanning Rack, Workbench

◈ Lore: City Overview

Windhelm sits on the northern bank of the White River and is an imposing sight, with its massive ice-covered stone walls. Travelers to the city are greeted by the majestic frozen bridge leading to the main gate, but it is the old Palace of Ysgramor (now known as the Palace of the Kings), towering over all other structures in the city, that truly takes the breath away. The city slopes slightly northward and has different levels of elevation, with the Palace located at the city's highest point, making it even more visible and striking. The streets are packed with snow, giving the city something of a claustrophobic feel; the sky is always white or overcast, and fierce blizzards batter the city with alarming regularity.

It is within these snow-strewn streets and icy alleys that Windhelm's inhabitants live, usually with an overriding sense of tension. There's a lot on the minds of the city's residents these days. Skyrim is now in the throes of Civil War, and Jarl Ulfric Stormcloak leads the rebellion against the Empire. The Dark Elves in the Gray Quarter have grown increasingly disillusioned. Dragons have returned to the world and threaten to destroy all of Skyrim. And as if all that weren't bad enough, a mysterious killer has been stalking the snowy streets of Windhelm at night and has already claimed three victims.

◈ Important Areas of Interest
Exterior and Dockside

The Docks, located just outside the city walls to the southeast, make up Windhelm's secondary economy. Here, merchants receive raw materials and other goods from all over the Empire, and ship out processed goods and raw materials unique to Skyrim. The Windhelm Docks are also where the East Empire Company has its only office outside of Solitude. Most of the dockworkers are poor Argonians who live on the docks in a large, ramshackle residence known as the Argonian Assemblage. They are the lowest class in all of Windhelm, and the Docks district is their domain.

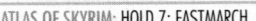

Interior

Stone Quarter

The Stone Quarter is Windhelm's central district, the one visitors first enter when passing through the Main Gate into the city. It contains the marketplace and the most important shops and inn.

1 South Gate

Rolff Stone-Fist   Angrenor Once-Honored

Just inside the main gate are a number of stone steps and thoroughfares around the Candlehearth Hall. Rolff Stone-Fist is ranting his racism against Dark Elf Suvaris Atheron as his lackey Angrenor Once-Honored looks on. This ugly undercurrent of racial tension clashes with the spectacular and sturdy ancient Nord architecture of this wondrous walled city.

2 East Gate

This allows you quick access to and from Dockside, and allows you to enter close to the edge of the Gray Quarter.

3 Niranye's House

Niranye

Niranye sets up her stall in the Stone Quarter Marketplace selling various goods, including Black-Briar Mead from Riften, fish from the docks, fruits and vegetables she must acquire from some outside contact, and various baubles. Her home is well appointed but not grand. Via a hidden panel, her house contains the locked (Expert) secret cellar headquarters of the Summerset Shadows. See Thieves Guild City Influence Quest: Summerset Shadows for more details.

◇ Niranye's Safe (Expert)   ◇ Knapsack

4 Candlehearth Hall

Elda Early-Dawn   Susanna the Wicked
Adonato Leotelli   Nils

Candlehearth Hall is the city's inn, but to the people of Windhelm, it is much more than that. It is a place of warmth, comfort, and security, where all the troubles of the outside world are drowned away by cold mead. The inn gets its name from its giant fireplace, with a fire that is constantly attended. On the hearth above the great fire sits a lone candle that was lit 150 years earlier, when the inn was a smaller private residence, to mark the death of the great warrior Vundheim; since that day, the candle has never gone out.

◇ Follower: Stenvar [35/47]
◇ Marriage Prospect: Angrenor Once-Honored [41/62]
◇ Marriage Prospect: Stenvar [42/62]
◇ Marriage Prospect: Viola Giordano [43/62]

◇ Trader (Innkeeper): Elda Early-Dawn [11/15]
  ○ Room for the night, Food
  ○ Innkeeper Rumors
◇ Business Ledger
◇ Adonato's Book
◇ Strongbox (Adept)
◇ Potions
◇ Loose gear

5 Calixto's House of Curiosities

Calixto Corrium

Calixto's House of Curiosities is like no other building in Skyrim. It is a private residence but has been set up as a collection of oddities, all of which have been gathered by the owner, Calixto Corrium, over a period of nearly 20 years. The items range from ingredients to the unique to the questionable (such as Ysgramor's Spoon). Take the tour for two gold pieces. Calixto has a key that opens his chest on the upper cubbyhole.

◇ Calixto's Chest (Requires Key)   ◇ Ysgramor's Soup Spoon
◇ Calixto's Key   ◇ Knapsack
◇ The Book of Fate   ◇ Loose gear
◇ The Dancer's Flute

6 Brunwulf Free-Winter's House

Brunwulf Free-Winter

This well-kept house belongs to Brunwulf Free-Winter, Nord war hero. Aside from a few books, there's some minor loot and a potion.

◇ Shadowmark: "Loot"   ◇ Loose gear

7 Aretino Residence

Aventus Aretino

The Aretino Residence is where Aurelia Aretino lived with her young son Aventus, until her brutal murder in a Windhelm back alley a couple of weeks prior. Now, the home is locked up, but rumors around town (including talk from Idesa Sadri and Grimvar Cruel-Sea under the eaves of the house) are that young Aventus is inside—having escaped from the Honorhall Orphanage and returned home—and has gone mad with grief. That's the only reasoning that could explain the strange noises coming from the house at odd hours. Consult the Dark Brotherhood Quest: Innocence Lost for more information. Inside the house, find a Skill Book hidden behind a shelf.

◇ Skill Book [Destruction]: A Hypothetical Treachery [A2/10]

8 Blacksmith Quarters

Oengul War-Anvil
Hermir Strong-Heart

Windhelm's Blacksmiths consists of Oengul's personal residence, with scattered weapons and books inside, and the smithing apparatus outside, close to the Marketplace. The alleyway back to the South Gate has a Wood Chopping Block.

◇ Shadowmark: "Loot"
◇ Crafting: Blacksmith Forge, Grindstone, Smelter, Tanning Rack, Workbench
◇ Trader (Blacksmith): Oengul War-Anvil [22/33]
  ○ Weapons, Apparel, Misc
◇ Trainer (Heavy Armor: Journeyman): Hermir Strong-Heart [3/3]
◇ Loose gear

9 Marketplace

Hillevi Cruel-Sea
Aval Atheron

The marketplace consists of a group of stalls and shops close to the Blacksmiths and the White Phial. During the day, when the Marketplace is open, stalls sell various items, from armor to fresh fruits and vegetables.

◇ Trader (Food Vendor): Hillevi Cruel-Sea [8/9]
  ○ Food
◇ Trader (General Store Vendor): Aval Atheron [9/19]
  ○ Weapons, Apparel, Potions Food, Books, Misc
◇ Trader (Fence): Niranye [5/10]
◇ Trader (General Store Vendor): Niranye [10/19]
  ○ Weapons, Apparel, Potions Food, Books, Misc

10 The White Phial

Nurelion   Quintus Navale

The White Phial is Windhelm's apothecary and sells all manner of potions and alchemical reagents. It was named after an item of legend, the White Phial, a potion bottle made of magically infused snow, which was said to replenish any liquid placed into it, one day after that liquid was consumed or emptied. The truth is, the White Phial is quite real and is coveted greatly by the establishment's owner and resident alchemist, Nurelion, who has recently learned of its location. In any case, search behind the counter to discover a Skill Book.

◇ Crafting: Alchemy Lab
◇ Marriage Prospect: Quintus Navale [44/62]
◇ Trader (Apothecary): Nurelion [8/12]
  ○ Potions, Food, Ingredients, Books
◇ Skill Book [Illusion]: The Black Arts On Trail [E1/10]
◇ Business Ledger
◇ Strongbox (Adept)
◇ Potions aplenty
◇ Loose gear

11 Hall of the Dead

Helgird

The Windhelm Hall of the Dead is a large stone structure that serves as both mausoleum and Shrine to Arkay. The first chamber anyone enters is the shrine, and people do come to worship freely. But the rest of the building, and the lower catacombs, hold generations of Nord dead. The entire facility is overseen by Helgird, a Priestess of Arkay. Outside is a graveyard separated by the main thoroughfare; this is the scene of a gruesome murder that begins Side Quest: Blood on the Ice.

◇ Shrine to Arkay [8/12]   ◇ Knapsack

⑫ Temple of Talos

Lortheim

Jora Wing-Wish

The Temple of Talos is immense and unique, and due to the current Civil War, it is the only full-fledged Temple of Talos in all of Skyrim. Here in Windhelm, a city held by the Stormcloaks, the people are free to worship Talos freely. You can get a Blessing at the altar, and the priests sleep behind in the alcove, which has a number of books you might wish to read.

◇ Shrine to Talos [11/17]

Gray Quarter

The Gray Quarter was so named because of the sheer number of Dark Elves who reside here. It was once named the "Snow Quarter," but that was a long time ago. But to the elves, the name "Gray Quarter" is one of derision, cruelty, and discrimination. They believe the Nord people of Windhelm have always seen them as outsiders and hated them because of it.

◇ Unique Item: Viola's Gold Ring [60/112]

⑬ Belyn Hlaalu's House

Belyn Hlaalu

This is the house of Belyn Hlaalu, owner of the Hlaalu Farm, which is located just outside the city walls to the south. The house is well kept, and there's a chest and Skill Book in a dark corner upstairs.

◇ Shadowmark: "Loot"　　　◇ Chest

◇ Skill Book [Conjuration]: 2920,　　◇ Knapsack
　 Frostfall, v10 [A1/10]
　　　　　　　　　　　　　　　◇ Potion

⑭ Atheron Residence

Faryl Atheron

Suvaris Atheron

This large building serves as the home of the Dark Elf Atheron family, whose members have been hard-working laborers in Windhelm for nearly three generations. The Atherons are also tired of feeling like second-class citizens and are fairly strong leaders on the Dark Elf community of Windhelm.

◇ Potions

⑮ New Gnisis Cornerclub

Ambarys Rendar

Malthyr Elenil　　　　　　The New Gnisis Cornerclub

is the social center of the Dark Elves within Windhelm. Patrons can buy drinks and swap stories, but there are no rooms to rent. Ambarys, the proprietor, has no great love of the Nords (especially given the way they

treat his fellow Dark Elves) and thus has allowed a back room to become a small headquarters for the Imperial faction in Skyrim. There are three floors; at the very top are the bedrooms and a business ledger. In the basement, a Skill Book is tucked between barrels beneath the stairs.

◇ Trader (Innkeeper): Ambarys Rendar [2/5]

　○ Food

　○ Innkeeper Rumors

◇ Skill Book [Alchemy]: A Game at Dinner [A2/10]

◇ Skill Book [Sneak]: The Red Kitchen Reader [D2/10]

◇ Business Ledger

◇ Potions

◇ Loose gear

⑯ Sadri's Used Wares

Revyn Sadri

Sadri's Used Wares is a large pawnshop, and the owner, Revyn Sadri, will buy and sell just about anything, with the exception of any goods he knows are stolen. Look on the counter shelves for a Skill Book.

◇ Marriage Prospect: Revyn Sadri [45/62]

◇ Trader (General Store Vendor): Revyn Sadri [11/19]

　○ Weapons, Apparel, Potions, Food, Books, Misc

◇ Trainer (Speech: Journeyman): Revyn Sadri [3/4]

◇ Skill Book [Speech]: 2920, Second Seed, v5 [A2/10]

◇ Business Ledger

◇ Potions aplenty

◇ Loose gear

Valunstrad

Translated from the ancient Nordic, *Valunstrad* means "Avenue of Valor." It is the oldest section of Whiterun and has the largest buildings in the entire city, including the ancient and majestic Palace of the Kings.

⑰ House of Clan Shatter-Shield

Torbjorn Shatter-Shield

Tova Shatter-Shield

Nilsine Shatter-Shield

Clan Shatter-Shield has lived in Windhelm for generations. They are from "old money," garnered from the city's shipping industry, and have not needed to do any kind of work for as long as anyone in the city can remember (much to the jealously and general derision of many citizens). They still control much of the shipping but leave the particulars up to their supervisor Suvaris Atheron and the workers at the Argonian Assemblage. Lately, the Shatter-Shields have become an object of pity, as one of the clan's members, Friga, twin sister of Nilsine, was recently murdered by the unknown killer stalking Windhelm's streets.

◇ Shadowmark: "Loot"

◇ Trainer (Two-Handed: Expert): Torbjorn Shatter-Shield [2/2]

◇ Unusual Gem: [16/24]

◇ Knapsack

◇ Loose gear

⑱ Hjerim (House for Sale)

This dwelling is currently empty and has been unoccupied for some time. Translated from the Nord, the name means "Home of Frost." Should you become the Thane of Windhelm (by completing Favors for the citizens and Jarl), you can purchase this abode from Jarl Ulfric Stormcloak's Steward, Jorleif. Consult the Thane Quests for more information.

◇ Follower: Calder [36/47]

◇ Marriage Prospect: Revyn Sadri [46/62]

◇ Unique Item: Strange Amulet [61/112]

⑲ House of Clan Cruel-Sea

Torsten Cruel-Sea

Grimvar Cruel-Sea

Sings-of-Dreams

This is the house of Clan Cruel-Sea, a well-liked and respected Nord family. Husband and wife Torsten and Hillevi run the Hollyfrost Farm, and now that they have a young son, they're raising him to take over the family business someday. As expected for the location, the house is grand and spotlessly clean.

◇ Shadowmark: "Protected"　　◇ Potions

◇ Knapsack　　　　　　　　　◇ Loose gear

⑳ Viola Giordano's House

Viola Giordano

This large house is the residence of Viola Giordano, an elderly Imperial noblewoman who came to Skyrim several years prior with her (now deceased) husband, a captain in the Imperial Legion. Her dwelling is stocked with food and books.

◇ Shadowmark: "Loot"

◇ Chest (2)

◇ Potions

Palace of the Kings

  The following people of Windhelm are the leaders of the Stormcloaks at the start of the Civil War:

Ulfric Stormcloak (Jarl)

Ulfric Stormcloak is the leader of the Stormcloaks, who are attempting to make Skyrim independent of the Empire. He fought in the Imperial Legions during the Great War against the Aldmeri Dominion, 20 years ago, distinguishing himself in the battle at the Imperial City, which ended the

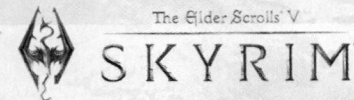

war in the White-Gold Concordat. In 176, he was one of the key figures in the Markarth Incident. Soon after, he founded the Stormcloaks (initially as an underground group centered around the now-proscribed worship of Talos). He became Jarl of Windhelm after the death of his father Hoag in 183.

In 201, he killed the High King of Skyrim in the throne room of the Blue Palace in Solitude, declaring him a lackey of the Empire and no true Nord (the slaying was based on the High King's support for the Empire's policy of suppression of Talos worship). A surprisingly swift and effective response by the Empire (possibly secretly aided by Thalmor informants) led to his arrest along with those of his associates. After escaping death in Helgen, he returned to his throne. Fiery and impetuous, he is a born leader but lacks the cool head of a military strategist. He passionately believes in his cause, though; he is not an opportunist—although the chance to become King of Skyrim certainly does appeal to his substantial ego.

Galmar Stone-Fist (Housecarl)

Galmar is old but still hale, a very experienced Nord warrior and Ulfric's right-hand man. He served Ulfric's father and is more concerned with winning the war than the politics behind it. He is one of Ulfric's most trusted allies and acts as the main field commander for the Civil War.

Jorleif (Steward)

Jorleif is an excellent advisor, especially in this time of war. Ulfric greatly values Jorleif's council and especially appreciates the man's honesty and realistic assessments of the ongoing conflict.

Captain Lonely-Gale

One of Skyrim's most respected citizens, Captain Lonely-Gale made his fortune as a trading ship captain working the rivers and coastlines of Skyrim. Those adventurous days are behind him now, but his authoritative, commanding nature remains and the people of Windhelm have a great respect for his fair and evenhanded views of the war. It is these qualities that cause Brunwulf Free-Winter to choose him as a Steward when he takes over as Jarl following a successful invasion of Windhelm by the Imperial forces during the Civil War.

Wuunferth the Unliving (Court Wizard)

An ancient and frail Court Wizard, Wuunferth is also an immensely powerful magic user and is obsessed with becoming even more powerful. The people of Windhelm are convinced the man has sold his soul to some Daedra or is only part human, and that's how he earned the title "the Unliving." For his part, Ulfric doesn't necessarily like Wuunferth and distrusts his sorcery, but he respects the great power the man holds and his possible use in the Civil War.

◇ Unique Item: Necromancer Amulet [62/112]

Sifnar Ironkettle

Silda the Unseen

◇ Trainer (Pickpocket: Expert): Silda the Unseen [1/3]

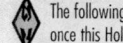 The following residents of Windhelm take control of Windhelm once this Hold falls during the Civil War.

Jarl Brunwulf Free-Winter

Brunwulf's reputation and natural leadership would be enough to make him the Empire's choice to replace Ulfric as Jarl of the city, but the fact that its people both love and respect him cements the choice. Brunwulf has no patience for those who exhibit prejudice, and this fits well with the Empire's cosmopolitan views. Notably, Brunwulf will forgo the naming of a Housecarl because he believes that he can defend himself capably enough, and he does not want anyone else to risk their life on his behalf.

Captain Lonely-Gale (Steward)

When Brunwulf ascends to the position of Jarl, he calls upon Captain Lonely-Gale to join him as Steward. In his days as a ship's master, the good captain earned his success by running a tight ship and managing his resources wisely. Brunwulf is counting on those same qualities as he works to heal his city and his Hold from the scars of war.

Palace of the Kings: Ground Floor

The Palace of the Kings is an ancient stone fortress that now serves as the city's main keep. These days, the palace serves as the headquarters of the Stormcloaks, under the leadership of Jarl Ulfric Stormcloak, who sits upon the ancient Throne of Ysgramor. And so the Palace of the Kings is the center of the pro-Nord war effort in the Civil War.

A Door to Windhelm

The two massive front doors are built to withstand an army.

1 Great Hall

Once a place of great merriment, this banquet and throne of Ysgramor is a place of planning and argument. There is much of the feast still left on the table to steal.

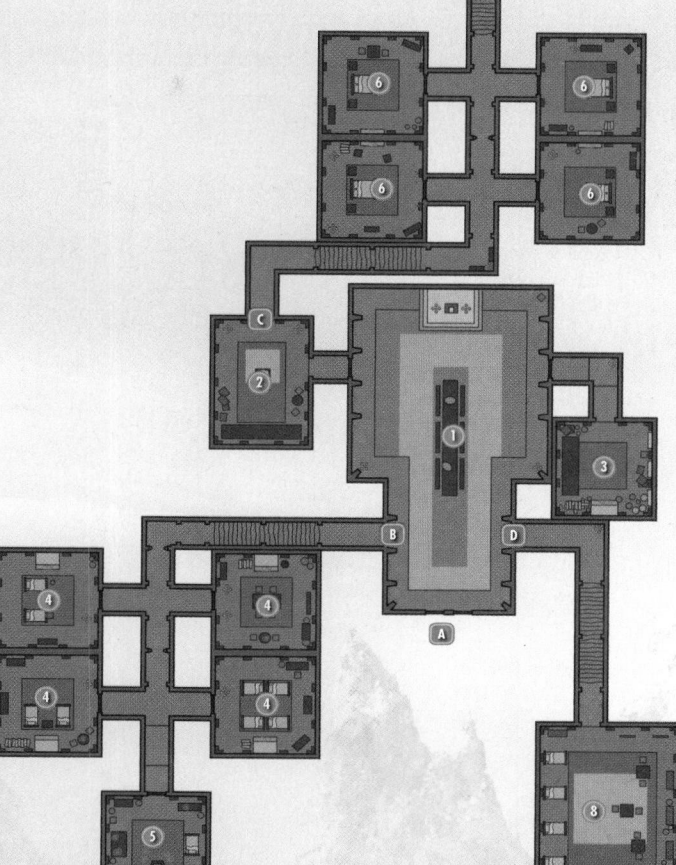

B Door to Palace of the Kings Upstairs

2 War Room

Inside the Palace Keep, Ulfric and his advisors discuss their Civil War strategies.

◇ Civil War: Map of Skyrim
◇ Loose gear

C Door to Palace of the Kings Upstairs

3 Kitchens

Food preparation for the castle occurs here.

D Door to Windhelm Barracks

Palace of the Kings: Upstairs

B Door to Palace of the Kings

4 Private Chambers

These four upstairs chambers are for guests of the Jarl. The northeastern chamber has a couple of books of interest.

◇ Skill Book [Heavy Armor]: The Knights of the Nine [E2/10]

5 Wuunferth the Unliving's Chamber

The Court Wizard resides here and has a supply of scrolls and books for you to purchase and ingredients to steal.

◇ Crafting: Alchemy Lab, Arcane Enchanter
◇ Trader (Spell Vendor): Wuunferth the Unliving [11/12]
  ○ Apparel, Scrolls, Books, Misc
◇ Trainer (Destruction: Journeyman): Wuunferth the Unliving [3/3]
◇ Unusual Gem: [17/24]
◇ Loose gear

Palace of the Kings Upstairs II

C Door to Palace of the Kings Upstairs

This separate area is accessed from the War Room.

6 Private Chambers

These four upstairs chambers are for guests of the Jarl.

7 Jarl Ulfric Stormcloak's Bed Chamber

The largest bed in all of Windhelm greets you, as well as some musty tomes to read. A Skill Book rests on a table here, partially covered by another book.

◇ Skill Book [Block]: The Mirror [D2/10]

D Door to Windhelm Barracks (aka Bloodworks)

8 Windhelm Barracks

The sleeping quarters for the city's guards. Note the chests in one corner.

◇ Evidence Chest
◇ Prisoner Belongings Chest

9 Windhelm Jail

Unlike some other capital cities, there are no secret exits when you're caught in Windhelm. Pick the lock (Adept) to face a guard's wrath, or serve out your sentence.

PRIMARY LOCATIONS

◈ [7.01] Uttering Hills Cave

Related Quests

Thieves Guild City Influence Quest: Summerset Shadows

Recommended Level: 6

Dungeon: Bandit Camp

Bandit (prequest only)
Summerset Shadows (only during quest)

Collectibles

Skill Book [One-Handed]: Mace Etiquette
Unique Item: Fjotli's Silver Locket [63/112]
Chests
Potions
Loose gear

This small bandit cave is found within Eastmarch's northwest mountains. Slay a couple of exterior guards before venturing inside.

A Exit to Skyrim

1 Entry Tunnel

Grab a few items of value from a table as you descend the cave's snowy entry tunnel.

◇ Potions
◇ Loose gear

2 Campfire Cavern

Slay bandits as you make your way to this far cavern, where several bandits guard a chest near a campfire.

◇ Chest

3 Hideout Entry and Holding Cells

Loot the hideout's entry chamber, and discover a chest that's tucked away in a nook near the following corridor.

◇ Chest (Locked: Adept)
◇ Potions

4 Bandit Hideout

A powerful bandit lurks at the cave's end. Raid the place after securing the area, and burn the banner here as part of your quest. Find a Skill Book on a shelf in the bedroom with the chest, then make your way back outside.

◇ Skill Book [One-Handed]: Mace Etiquette
◇ Chest
◇ Knapsack
◇ Potion

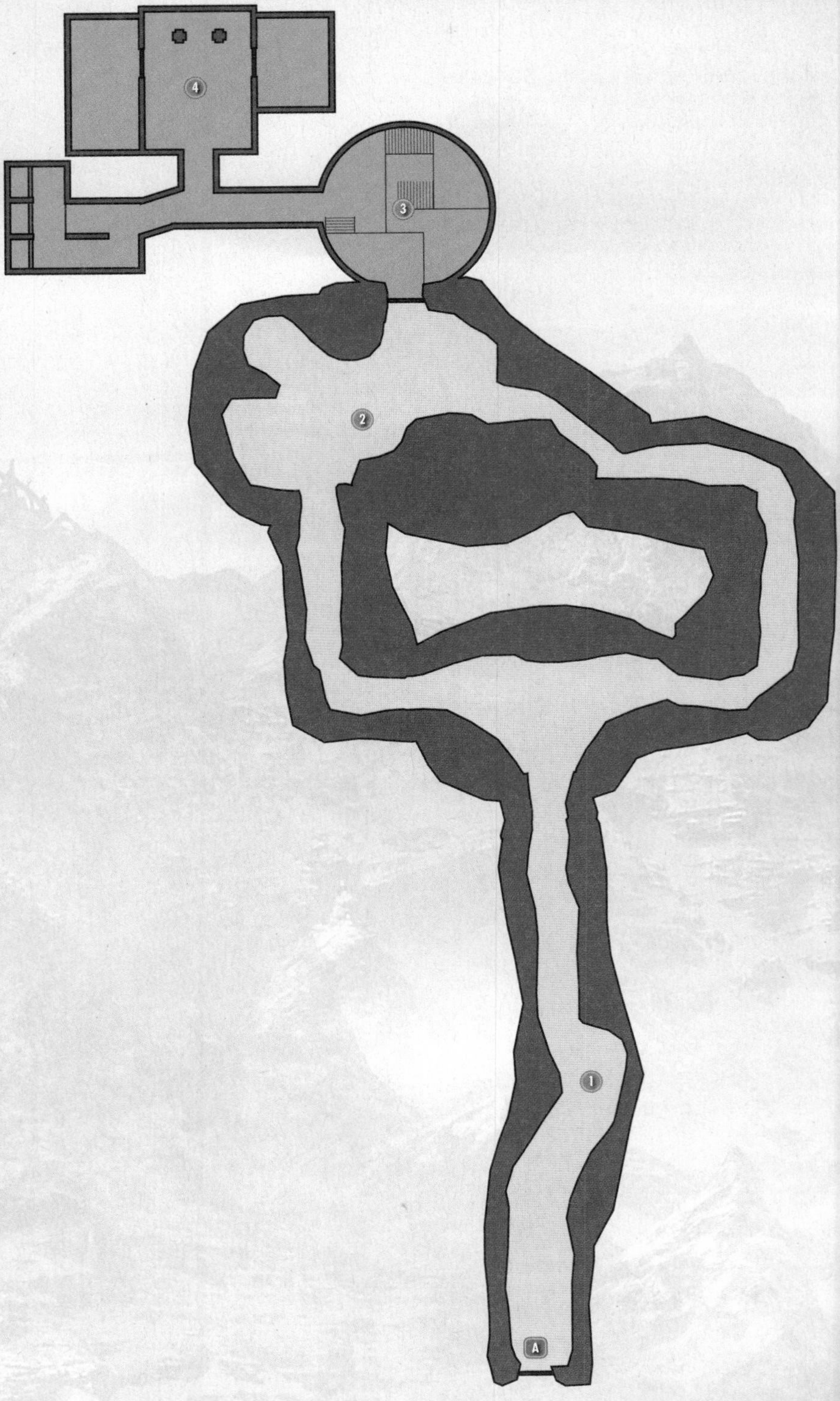

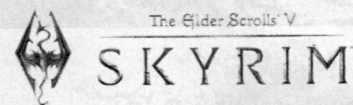
The Elder Scrolls V
SKYRIM

[7.02] Gallows Rock

Related Quests

The Companions Quest: The Silver
Hand

Recommended Level: 6

Dungeon: Bandit Camp

Animal
Silver Hand
Werewolf

Crafting

Tanning Racks (2)
Skill Book [One-Handed]: The
Importance of Where
Skill Book [Smithing]: Last
Scabbard of Akrash [C2/10]

Dangers

Swinging Wall Trap (pressure plate)
Chests
Potions
Loose gear

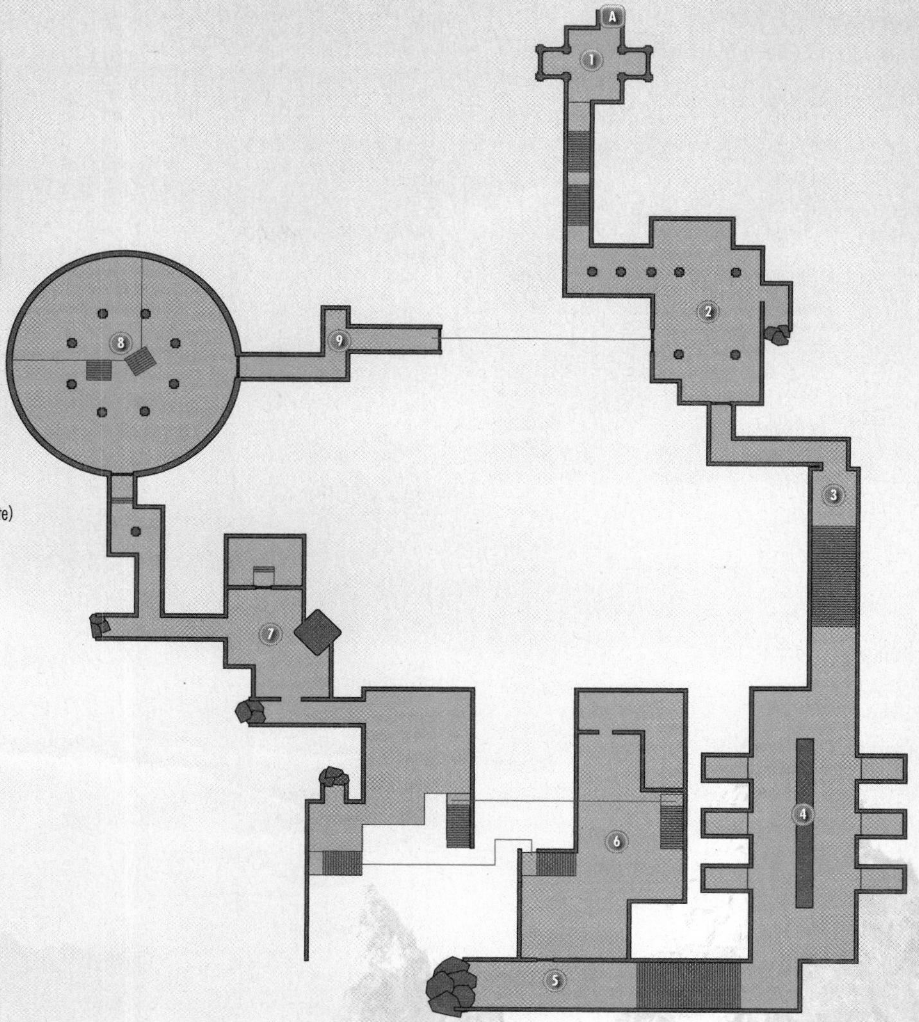

A group of bandits called the Silver Hand control a small fortress along
Eastmarch's northwest border. You fight your way through this fort during
Companions Quest: Silver Moon.

Exterior

Slay the outdoor guards, then search the top of the fort to discover a chest
inside a small tower.

◇ Chest

A. Exit to Skyrim

1. Entry Chamber

Pull a chain in the entry chamber to open the way forward.

◇ Loose gear

2. Mess

Slay a few more Silver Hand in this room, which contains a chest. The
west door is barred, so go south instead.

◇ Chest   ◇ Potions   ◇ Loose gear

3. Corridor and Stairs

Slay a Skeever on your way upstairs, and avoid the pressure plate at the
top of the steps—it triggers a nasty trap.

◇ Danger! Swinging Wall Trap (pressure plate)

4. Prison Cells

Defeat the Silver Hand bandits that guard a number of werewolves in this
area. If you dare, pick the Adept-level locks on the cell doors to free and
battle with the beasts.

◇ Potions   ◇ Loose gear

5. South Stairs and Corridor

The primary item of interest here is a knapsack that contains valuable loot.

◇ Knapsack   ◇ Loose gear

6. Great Hall

Kill more Silver Hand to secure the Great Hall, then explore the downstairs
area thoroughly to discover a large chest with a tricky lock. A Skill Book
rests on a table at the hall's north end.

◇ Crafting: Tanning Racks (2)   ◇ Chest (Locked: Master)
◇ Skill Book [One-Handed]:   ◇ Potions
    The Importance of Where   ◇ Loose gear

7. Hearth and Sleeping Quarters

A roaring fireplace dominates the first chamber of this area. Find a Skill
Book on a table near the hearth. Unlock the Adept-level north door to
access a sleeping quarters filled with valuables.

◇ Skill Book [Smithing]: Last Scabbard of Akrash [C2/10]
◇ Chest
◇ Potions

8. Circular Chamber

Slay the final batch of Silver Hand here before looting the room and
making your way back outside.

◇ Crafting: Tanning Racks (3)
◇ Chest
◇ Potions
◇ Loose gear

9. Barred Door Corridor

Claim an array of worthy gear from this corridor, then unbar the far door
and take your leave of this place.

◇ Knapsack
◇ Loose gear

[7.03] Mara's Eye Pond

Related Quests

Dungeon Activity

Recommended Level: 6

Dungeon: Vampire Lair

Animal
Vampire

Collectibles

Skill Book [Pickpocket]:
Wulfmare's Guide to Better
Thieving [E2/10]
Chest(s)
Loose gear

This small, eerie pond lies on the west side of Eastmarch, just north of the
Hold's larger and more prominent western hot springs. The pond derives
its name from the tiny isle found in its center—when viewed from above,
it resembles an eye.

Exterior

Exterminate the small cluster of Mudcrab near the pond's central "eye," then search for a trapdoor on the central isle, which leads into Mara's Eye Den. There's little else of interest around the pond.

Mara's Eye Den (Interior)

This small underground cavern was once a smugglers den but has since been taken over by a more blood chilling foe — vampires. Slay the cursed beings, then loot the place for loads of valuables, including a Skill Book that's mixed in with other books in a small crate. There's no need to pick the locked cage here — nothing of interest is found within.

◇ Skill Book [Pickpocket]: Wulfmare's
Guide to Better Thieving [E2/10]

◇ Chest

◇ Chest (Locked:
Apprentice)

◇ Loose gear

[7.04] Morvunskar

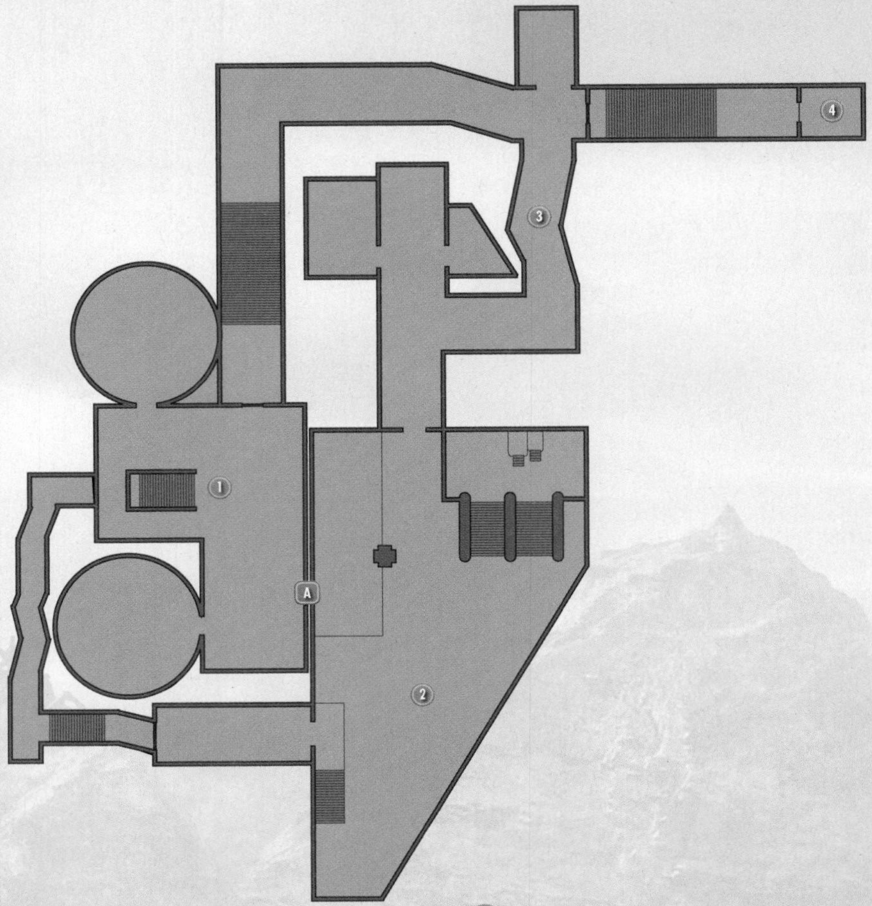

Related Quests

Daedric Quest: A Night to
Remember

Recommended Level: 8

Dungeon: Warlock Lair

Mage
Naris the Wicked

Crafting

Blacksmith Forge
Tanning Rack
Workbench

Dangers

Swinging Wall Trap (pressure
plate)

Collectibles

Skill Book [Destruction]:
Mystery of Talara, v3
Skill Book [Smithing]:
Cherim's Heart [A2/10]
Unique Weapon: Sanguine
Rose [51/80]

Special Objects

Shrine of Dibella [6/8]
Chest(s)
Potions aplenty
Loose gear

A host of hostile mages practice their nefarious arts at this frigid fortress, which you visit during Daedric Quest: A Night to Remember. Slay the mob of mages that guard the grounds before heading inside. There's little of interest out in the cold.

A Exit to Skyrim

1 Crafthouse

Crafting opportunities abound in this first area of Morvunskar. Beware when engaging mages here — the sound of battle may bring reinforcements. Find a Skill Book resting on a table.

◇ Crafting: Blacksmith Forge,
Tanning Rack, Workbench

◇ Skill Book [Smithing]: Cherim's
Heart [A2/10]

◇ Potion

◇ Loose gear

2 Head Mage's Chamber

Take the basement stairs from [1] to visit this wide chamber, collecting a bit of gold on your way. Slay a powerful mage here, then claim precious loot from the large chest atop the stairs.

◇ Chest

◇ Potions

3 Corridors and Sleeping Quarters

Dispatch a few more mages here and raid their bunks for valuables. Touch the shrine in the north quarters to instantly cure any diseases you might be suffering.

◇ Danger! Swinging Wall Trap
(pressure plate)

◇ Shrine of Dibella [6/8]

◇ Potions aplenty

◇ Loose gear

4 Torture Chamber

Unlock Morunskar's northwest door and slay the twisted mage in the chamber beyond. A Skill Book sits on a shelf here. Pull a lever to access and loot the burnt corpses in the holding cell.

◇ Area Is Locked (Novice)

◇ Skill Book [Destruction]: Mystery of Talara, v3

◇ Chest

◇ Potions

[7.05] Kynesgrove

Related Quests

Main Quest: A Blade in the Dark
Miscellaneous Objective: Innkeeper Rumors (the Braidwood Inn)
Miscellaneous Objective: Salt for the Stoneweaver* (Dravynea the Stoneweaver)
Favor (Activity): Chopping Wood* (Ganna Uriel)
Favor (Activity): Mining Ore* (Kjeld)
Favor: A Good Talking To* (Iddra)
Favor: Item Retrieval (Cave)* (Roggi)

Habitation: Town

Dravynea the Stoneweaver (Marriage Prospect; Trainer: Alteration)
Ganna Uriel
Gemma Uriel
Iddra (Innkeeper)
Kjeld the Younger
Roggi Knot-Beard (Follower; Marriage Prospect)
Stormcloak Soldier

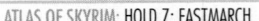

Services

Follower: Roggi Knot-Beard [37/47]

Marriage Prospect: Dravynea the Stoneweaver [47/62]

Marriage Prospect: Roggi Knot-Beard [48/62]

Trader (Innkeeper): Iddra [12/15]

   Food, Room and Board

   Innkeeper Rumors

Trainer (Alteration: Expert): Dravynea [3/3]

A short jaunt south of Windhelm lies a small mining community consisting of an inn that's been erected next to a working mine. You visit Kynesgrove during the Main Quest in search of Dragons.

Exterior

Chop wood outside the inn, or smelt ore by the mine.

◇ Crafting: Smelter   ◇ Loose gear

Braidwood Inn

Chat up the locals in the inn to hear an array of gossip that leads to several Side Quests. Trade with Iddra if you like, or purchase a room if you're weary.

◇ Chests (2)

Steamscorch Mine

Kynesgrove's mine lies just up the hill from the Braidwood Inn. Inside, a woman named Ganna Uriel will purchase any firewood that you cut outside. If you like, use a pickaxe to mine some Malachite from the ore veins that run along the walls and floors. A Skill Book rests on the table at the tunnel junction.

◇ Skill Book [Enchanting]: Catalogue of Armor Enchantments [B2/10]

◇ Potion

◇ Loose gear

◇ Mineable ore (Malachite)

Crafting

Smelter

Collectibles

Skill Book [Enchanting]: Catalogue of Armor Enchantments [B2/10]

Chest(s)

Potion

Loose gear

Mineable ore (Malachite)

[7.06] Windhelm Stables

Habitation: Farm

Alfarinn (Carriage Driver)

Arivanya

Ulundil (Stablemaster)

Services

Trader (Carriage Draiver): Alfarinn [4/5]

Trader (Stablemaster): Ulundil [4/5]

Special Objects

Business Ledger

Strongbox (Expert)

Potion

The Windhelm Stables lie directly south of Eastmarch's capital city. The lone building here remains shut tight with a Novice-level locked door, but worthy services are available just outside. Break into the building and see if you can open the strongbox within.

[7.07] Brandy-Mug Farm

Related Quests

Favor (Activity): Harvesting Crops* (Bolfrida Brandy-Mug)

Habitation: Farm

Bolfrida Brandy-Mug

Faryl Atheron

Collectibles

Skill Book [Alteration]: Daughter of the Niben [B2/10]

Chest

Potion

This quaint farm lies just south of Windhelm. Harvest wheat and other ingredients from outside, then enter the farm and sell Bolfrida's wheat back to her for 5 gold a bundle.

[7.08] Hlaalu Farm

Related Quests

Favor (Activity): Harvesting Crops* (Belyn Hlaalu)

Habitation: Farm

Adisla

Belyn Hlaalu

Collectibles

Chest

Potions

Loose gear

This small farm lies southeast of Windhelm and is owned by a Dark Elf named Belyn Hlaalu. Harvest some wheat from outside, but you'll need to pick the door's Novice-level lock to enter and raid the farmhouse.

[7.09] Hollyfrost Farm

Related Quests

Favor (Activity): Harvesting Crops* (Tulvur)

Habitation: Farm

Tulvur

Tiber (dog)

Collectibles

Chest

Potion

This humble farm stands to the southeast of Eastmarch's capital. A feisty guard dog named Tiber guards the locked farmhouse.

[7.10] Traitor's Post

Related Quests

Side Quest: The Great Skyrim Treasure Hunt*

Recommended Level: 5

Dungeon: Bandit Camp

Bandit

Crafting

Tanning Rack

Collectibles

Skill Book [Block]: A Dance in Fire, v2 [A2/10]

Treasure Map VII [5/11]

Chest (Locked: Novice)

Chest (Locked: Master)

Loose gear

A small gang of bandits has taken refuge within a derelict inn located at Eastmarch's northeast corner. Find a Treasure Map inside the chest on the main floor, along with a Skill Book that's on a cupboard shelf. Then scale the rocks on the west side of the building, edge your way around the roof, and climb into the otherwise-inaccessible second floor to reach another, larger chest.

[7.11] Refugees' Rest

Dungeon: Animal Den

Animal

Collectible

Chest (Locked: Adept)

This remote station, which lies at Eastmarch's northeast tip along the northern road to Morrowind, consists of a ruined tower and unceremonious graveyard. A book found at the base of the nearby road sign reveals a little of this location's history.

[7.12] Sacellum of Boethiah

Related Quests

Daedric Quest: Boethiah's Calling

Recommended Level: 12

Habitation: Special

Boethiah Cultist

Priestess of Boethiah

Crafting

Alchemy Lab

Arcane Enchanter

Collectibles

Unique Weapon: Blade of Sacrifice [52/80]

Potions

You obtain the "Boethiah's Calling" quest upon discovering this unusual cult hideout, which lies at Eastmarch's northeast corner. Speak to the Priestess of Boethiah to learn of her cult and advance your quest. Watch the zealots practice their swordplay in the training area, and notice the pillar of sacrifice atop the snowy stairs—this comes into play later in the quest, after you lure an unfortunate soul here to their demise.

[7.13] Cradlecrush Rock

Dungeon: Giant Camp

Giant

Collectibles

Chest

Knapsack

Potions

Loose gear

A monstrous giant makes its home near these large, ominous rocks. One rock has apparently crushed some poor, unfortunate soul—loot the fool's surviving knapsack, which lies near a skeletal foot, for additional valuables.

[7.14] Abandoned Prison

This derelict prison's entrance can be seen from the road along Eastmarch's western boarder—cross a rushing river to get there.

Recommended Level: 6

Dungeon: Special

Ghost

Collectibles

Skill Book [Two-Handed]: Song of Hrormir

Chest(s)

Loose gear

[7.15] Mixwater Mill

Related Quests

Favor (Activity): Chopping Wood* (Gilfre)

Habitation: Lumber Mill

Gilfre (Marriage Prospect)

Services

Marriage Prospect: Gilfre [49/62]

Collectibles

Skill Book [Archery]: The Marksmanship Lesson [D2/10]

Chest(s)

Potions

Loose gear

Life moves at a slower pace here at this quaint lumber mill, which is located along the White River on the west side of Eastmarch, just north of where the Darkwater River branches off.

Exterior

If you like, enter the mill and slice up logs for Gilfre. Or grab a Woodcutter's Axe and chop wood to sell back to Gilfre for a bit of honest coin.

◊ Loose gear

Gilfre's House

Breaking into Gilfre's humble abode is worthwhile. Your unscrupulous actions can net you some decent coin, a few potions, and a Skill Book that rests on a small table.

◊ Area Is Locked (Novice)

◊ Skill Book [Archery]: The Marksmanship Lesson [D2/10]

◊ Chest

◊ Potions

Worker's House

No need to break into the Worker's House—the door is unlocked. Pop in, loot the place, and then head back out.

◊ Chests (3)   ◊ Potions

Ⓐ Exit to Skyrim

① Leaky Chamber

Collect a host of hanging moss in this otherwise empty chamber, then take the lower passage to [2].

② Guards' Office

A handful of valuables lie in the guards' small office, including a note that sheds some light on what may have happened here.

◊ Loose gear

③ Holding Cells

Search the skeletons here to find a handful of valuables. Take the Abandoned Prison Key from the far table and use it to open the cells. Find a chest to the north and claim the Skill Book that lies against it. Drop through the southeast cell's trapdoor to locate a sewer tunnel that leads back out to Skyrim.

◊ Skill Book [Two-Handed]: Song of Hrormir

◊ Abandoned Prison Key

◊ Chest (Locked: Master)

◊ Loose gear

The Elder Scrolls V

S K Y R I M

[7.16] Broken Limb Camp

Dungeon: Giant Camp

Giant

Collectible

Chest

Two fearsome giants have made camp along Eastmarch's southwestern hills. While fighting giants is never wise, you can gain some decent loot and experience by clearing this campsite—if you're up to the task. If the brutes are too tough, try raiding their chest and then quickly fleeing before they realize they've been robbed.

[7.17] Cronvangr Cave

Related Quests

Dungeon Activity

Recommended Level: 6

Dungeon: Vampire Lair

Animal

Vampire

Collectibles

Chests

Potions

Loose gear

Near the heart of Eastmarch, massive egg sacks covered in thick webbing line the mouth of a forboding vampire cave.

Cronvangr Cave (Interior)

The cave's first cavern is overrun by Frostbite Spiders. Look for a button along the wall and press it to open a secret door. Go through to battle a small brood of vampires in a secret chamber, then raid the chest they guard. Exit the secret lair and continue to squash spiders as you proceed deeper into the cave, looting an underwater chest when you reach the bottom before advancing into the Broodlair.

◇ Chests (2)   ◇ Potions
◇ Apothecary's Satchel   ◇ Loose gear

Convangr Broodlair

Exterminate more spiders as you navigate the Broodlair's narrow passages. You soon reach a wide cavern, where a monstrous spider drops from the ceiling. Slay the brute and loot the nearby chest, then advance to loop around and find your way back outside.

◇ Chest

[7.18] Riverside Shack

Related Quests

Side Quest: The Great Skyrim Treasure Hunt*

Recommended Level: 6

Dungeon: Animal Den

Animal

Crafting

Tanning Rack

Collectibles

Skill Book [Light Armor]: Rislav the Righteous

Treasure Map III [6/11]

Chest (Locked: Apprentice)

Loose gear

As its name implies, this is a small, abandoned shack poised on the bank of the White River, somewhat near the middle of Eastmarch. If you can slay the vicious animal that lives inside the shack, you'll be free to loot the chest that's found here—and claim the Treasure Map within! A Skill Book is also found here, mixed in with a stack of other tomes.

[7.19] Witchmist Grove

Related Quests

Daedric Quest: A Night to Remember

Recommended Level: 14

Dungeon: Hagraven Nest

Witch

Quest Items

Wedding Ring

Collectibles

Skill Book [Destruction]: Response to Bero's Speech

Chest (Locked: Expert)

The woods in the center of Eastmarch are home to a vicious witch who lives in a small shack. If you manage to slay the spellcaster, see if you can also open the locked chest that she guards. You visit this site in search of a lost ring during Daedric Quest: A Night to Remember. Find a Skill Book stashed under the bed.

[7.20] Bonestrewn Crest

Dungeon: Dragon Lair

Dragon (after Main Quest: Dragon Rising)

Skeleton

Special Objects

Word Wall: Frost Breath [3/3]

Chest (Locked: Expert)

At the very center of Eastmarch, a handful of lowly skeletons guards a dismal hilltop, where the bones of great beasts lie strewn about. Defeat a monstrous dragon here if you've advanced past the "Dragon Rising" quest; then follow the sound of chanting to locate a Word Wall that bestows you with a new Word of Power. If possible, open the nearby locked chest to obtain valuable plunder.

[7.21] Steamcrag Camp

Dungeon: Giant Camp

Animal

Giant

Mammoth

Collectibles

Chest

Chest (Locked: Adept)

Knapsack

Potion

A towering giant has set up a campsite near the heart of Eastmarch. Attack the giant from the north ridge to gain a tactical advantage. Loot a chest here, then find another chest and a knapsack on a nearby smashed Khajiit wagon. Beware the wild animals that are nuzzling through the Khajiit's remains!

[7.22] Narzulbur

Related Quests

Side Quest: The Forgemaster's Fingers

Favor (Activity): Mining Ore* (Dushnamub)

Favor: Sparring Partners* (Mauhulakh)

Recommended Level: 6

Habitation: Orc Stronghold

Bolar

Chief Mauhulakh

Urog

Yatul

Crafting

Alchemy Lab

Tanning Rack

Collectibles

Skill Book [Heavy Armor]: The Knights of the Nine

Skill Book [Two-Handed]: Song of Hrormir

Chests

Potions aplenty

Loose gear

Nestled among the mountains that form Eastmarch's eastern border, this small Orcish mining community struggles to prosper by gathering ebony ore from the nearby Gloombound Mine.

Exterior

The Orcs are cold to outsiders, but they won't attack or force you away. Speak to the villagers to potentially gain a new quest that can help you earn their acceptance.

◇ Crafting: Alchemy Lab, Tanning Rack   ◇ Potions
◇ Loose gear

Alchemy Workshop

Expert-level Lockpicking skill is required to enter the Narzulbur's alchemy workshop, where a vast array of potions and ingredients are kept.

◊ Area Is Locked (Expert)
◊ Crafting: Alchemy Lab
◊ Potions aplenty

Mauhulakh's Longhouse

The Longhouse features a roaring hearth, numerous food items, and sleeping quarters. A Skill Book sits on a table here, partially covered by other tomes.

◊ Skill Book [Heavy Armor]: The Knights of the Nine
◊ Chest (Locked: Adept)
◊ Chest (Locked: Master)
◊ Loose gear

Mauhulakh's Cellar

The cellar holds a few items of interest, particularly a chest with an Adept-level lock. A Skill Book is found on the shelf above.

◊ Skill Book [Two-Handed]: Song of Hrormir
◊ Chest (Locked: Adept)

▷ [7.23] Gloombound Mine

Related Quests
Dungeon Activity

Recommended Level: 8

Habitation: Mine
Bor
Dushamub (Blacksmith)
Gadba gro-Largash
Mogdurz
Mul gro-Largash

Services
Trader (Blacksmith): Dushamub [23/33]
Weapons, Apparel, Misc

Crafting
Blacksmith Forge
Grindstone
Smelter
Workbench

Dangers
Oil Pool Trap

Collectibles
Skill Book [Smithing]: Heavy Armor Forging [B2/10]
Loose gear
Mineable ore (Ebony)

This small mine is located in Eastmarch's eastern mountains, just south of the Orcish stronghold of Narzulbur. A gifted blacksmith works nearby, and a variety of useful ore can be freely harvested within the mine. This is the only true ebony mine in Skyrim.

Exterior

Speak with an Orc blacksmith who works just outside the mine to purchase an array of superior weapons and arms. The blacksmith also has raw materials for sale and will pay top coin for any materials mined from the nearby site. Also feel free to use the blacksmith's crafting stations

as you please. The Smelter requires a shovel to operate, which you can find in the mine. Discover a Skill Book in the open-air hut near the mine's entrance.

◊ Crafting: Blacksmith Forge, Grindstone, Smelter, Workbench
◊ Skill Book [Smithing]: Heavy Armor Forging [B2/10]

Gloombound Mine (Interior)

Many useful tools can be found within the Orcs' mine, such as Woodcutter Axes, Pickaxes, and Shovels. Scan the walls and floors of the mine to find Ebony Ore veins. Mine these for valuable ore that you can either sell or use to fashion weapons and armor.

◊ Danger! Oil Pool Trap
◊ Loose gear
◊ Mineable ore (Ebony)

▷ [7.24] Cragwallow Slope

Recommended Level: 6

Dungeon: Warlock Lair
Atronach
Mage

Crafting
Alchemy Lab
Arcane Enchanter

Collectibles
Skill Book [Alteration]: The Lunar Lorkhan [E2/10]
Chest(s)
Potions aplenty
Loose gear

Dangerous mages reside in this small cave, which lies at the foot of Eastmarch's eastern mountain range. Nab a Soul Gem from the exterior ritual site on your way in.

Ⓐ Exit to Skyrim

① Alchemy Station

Slay a lone mage in the cave's first small chamber, then collect some useful items from atop the nearby Alchemy Lab. Beware the Atronachs and mages that lurk in the following tunnel.

◊ Crafting: Alchemy Lab
◊ Apothecary's Satchel
◊ Potion

② Ruined Book Chamber

A long tunnel leads to this open chamber, where mining tools and a few Soul Gems are found among a host of worthless ruined books. Duck into the south sleeping quarters to snag a potion and loot a chest on your way to the next area.

◊ Chest
◊ Potion

③ Central Chamber

Slay more mages and Atronachs in the heart of this giant cavern before exploring the upper ledges to the north and south, which contain potions and other valuables. A Skill Book sits on a table here.

◊ Crafting: Alchemy Lab, Arcane Enchanter
◊ Skill Book [Alteration]: The Lunar Lorkhan [E2/10]
◊ Chest
◊ Potions aplenty

④ Exit Passage

One final mage lurks in the final passage, which deposits you back near the cave's entrance.

◊ Chest (Locked: Adept)
◊ Potions
◊ Loose gear

[7.25] Mzulft

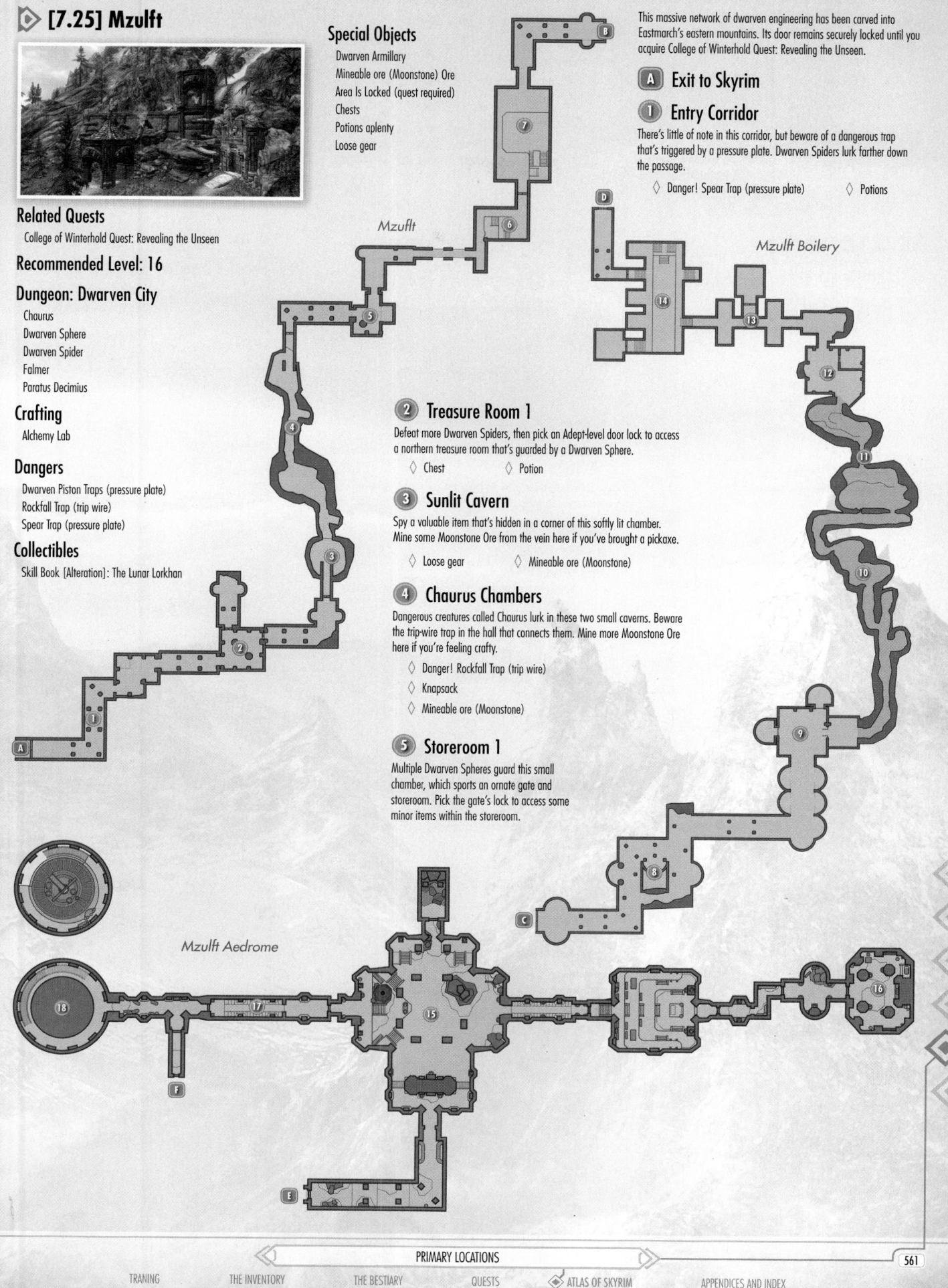

Related Quests

College of Winterhold Quest: Revealing the Unseen

Recommended Level: 16

Dungeon: Dwarven City

Chaurus
Dwarven Sphere
Dwarven Spider
Falmer
Paratus Decimius

Crafting

Alchemy Lab

Dangers

Dwarven Piston Traps (pressure plate)
Rockfall Trap (trip wire)
Spear Trap (pressure plate)

Collectibles

Skill Book [Alteration]: The Lunar Lorkhan

Special Objects

Dwarven Armillary
Mineable ore (Moonstone) Ore
Area Is Locked (quest required)
Chests
Potions aplenty
Loose gear

Mzuflt

Mzuflt Boilery

Mzulft Aedrome

This massive network of dwarven engineering has been carved into Eastmarch's eastern mountains. Its door remains securely locked until you acquire College of Winterhold Quest: Revealing the Unseen.

A Exit to Skyrim

1 Entry Corridor

There's little of note in this corridor, but beware of a dangerous trap that's triggered by a pressure plate. Dwarven Spiders lurk farther down the passage.

◇ Danger! Spear Trap (pressure plate)　　◇ Potions

2 Treasure Room 1

Defeat more Dwarven Spiders, then pick an Adept-level door lock to access a northern treasure room that's guarded by a Dwarven Sphere.

◇ Chest　　◇ Potion

3 Sunlit Cavern

Spy a valuable item that's hidden in a corner of this softly lit chamber. Mine some Moonstone Ore from the vein here if you've brought a pickaxe.

◇ Loose gear　　◇ Mineable ore (Moonstone)

4 Chaurus Chambers

Dangerous creatures called Chaurus lurk in these two small caverns. Beware the trip-wire trap in the hall that connects them. Mine more Moonstone Ore here if you're feeling crafty.

◇ Danger! Rockfall Trap (trip wire)
◇ Knapsack
◇ Mineable ore (Moonstone)

5 Storeroom 1

Multiple Dwarven Spheres guard this small chamber, which sports an ornate gate and storeroom. Pick the gate's lock to access some minor items within the storeroom.

6 Treasure Room 2

Fight your way downstairs and pick an Adept-level lock to open a gate and access a chest in this odd chamber.

◊ Crafting: Alchemy Lab ◊ Potions
◊ Chest (Locked: Adept)

7 Spider Chamber

Use caution when creeping along this wide chamber's left ledge—pressure plates trigger dwarven pistons that can knock you into the central, spider-filled pit.

◊ Danger! Dwarven Piston Trap (pressure plates)

B Door to Mzulft Boilery

C Door to Mzulft

8 Boilery Entry

Slay a nimble Falmer in this wide hallway, which holds little of interest.

9 Storeroom 2

Fight your way through a few more Falmer on your way to this chamber. Don't trouble with unlocking the Expert-level west gate; there's nothing but Dwemer scrap metal in the storeroom beyond.

◊ Potions ◊ Loose gear

10 Earthen Passage

Don't overlook the odd-looking chests as you navigate this cavernous passage.

◊ Chests (2) ◊ Potion ◊ Loose gear

11 Iridescent Cavern

Harvest the many glowing mushrooms that lend an eerie light to these two caverns. Chaurus Eggs can be obtained by inspecting the various egg sacs as well.

◊ Chest ◊ Loose gear

12 Treasure Room 3

Pick the Expert-level door lock in this area to obtain an important key, along with treasure from a chest and a Skill Book.

◊ Skill Book [Alteration]: The Lunar Lorkhan
◊ Mzulft Room Key
◊ Chest

13 Treasure Room 4

Pick the Adept-level lock on the ornate door here to access a treasure room that's guarded by a Chaurus.

◊ Chest (Locked: Apprentice) ◊ Loose gear

14 Treasure Room 5

Beware: this large chamber's worthy treasures are guarded by multiple Falmer. Pick the Expert-level door in the southwest corner to access a small treasure room.

◊ Chest ◊ Potions aplenty
◊ Chest (Locked: Novice)

D Door to Mzulft Aedrome

E Door to Mzulft Boilery

15 Great Hall

This massive foyer is crawling with Falmer. Fight hard to secure the area, then pick the north door's Expert-level lock to access a treasure niche. The west door cannot be opened without the key you find inside a chest located in the eastern Cog Chamber. A Falmer Gloomlurker is carrying a Focusing Crystal, which is needed for location [18].

◊ Focusing Crystal ◊ Chests (3)

16 Cog Chamber

A lone Dwarven Sphere guards this far chamber. Open the chest and retrieve the Mzulft Observatory Key.

◊ Mzulft Observatory Key ◊ Potions
◊ Chest ◊ Loose gear

17 Locked Hall

You cannot access this hall without the Mzulft Observatory Key. The far door to [18] is locked as well—Paratus Deimius opens it when you retrieve the Focusing Crystal for him. The ruins' exit door is found here, accessed only after you complete the puzzle inside location [18]..

◊ Knapsack

18 Armillary Chamber

This large chamber houses a giant and mysterious dwarven mechanism. Paratus Decimius, and your knowledge of flame and frost spells, are the keys to solving this puzzle. Consult College of Winterhold Quest: Revealing the Unseen for the answers.

◊ Dwarven Armillary

F Exit to Skyrim

▶ [7.26] Lost Knife Hideout

Recommended Level: 6	Dangers
Dungeon: Bandit Camp	Bone Alarm Trap
Animal	Rockfall Trap (trip wire)
Bandit	**Collectibles**
Crafting	Skill Book [Heavy Armor]: Orsinium and the Orcs
Grindstone	Skill Book [Two-Handed]: Words and Philosophy [E1/10]
Cookpot	Chest(s)
	Potions
	Loose gear

Bandits have set up a formidable hideout in this watery cavern. Make your way through Lost Knife Cave to reach the inner Lost Knife Hideout.

A Exit to Skyrim

1 Entry Tunnel

Kill the bandits at the end of the entry tunnel to obtain a key from one of their corpses.

◊ Lost Knife Cage Key (Bandit)
◊ Potions
◊ Loose gear

2 Watery Cavern

The cave's center is patrolled by more bandits, including archers that fire down from elevated walkways. A Skill Book sits on a table on the central wooden lookout.

◊ Danger! Bone Alarm Trap
◊ Skill Book [Two-Handed]: Words and Philosophy [E1/10]
◊ Loose gear

3 Waterfall Tunnel

Take a secret underwater passage, behind a waterfall, from [2] to reach a small tunnel with a treasure chest.

◊ Chest ◊ Loose gear

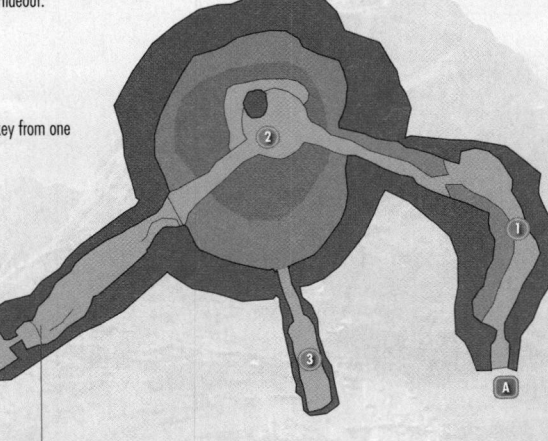

Lost Knife Cave

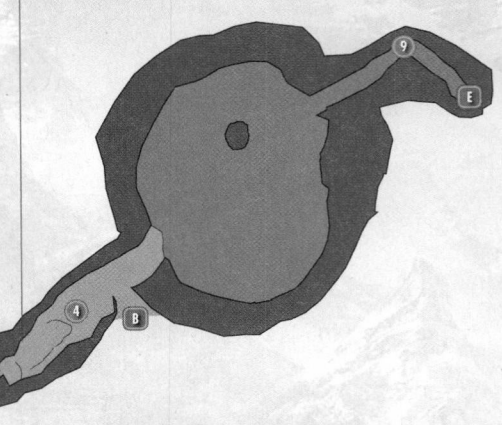

④ West Tunnel

This tunnel leads to the Lost Knife Hideout and features more bandits and a dangerous trip-wire trap. Scour the upstairs storeroom to find a chest.

◇ Danger! Rockfall Trap (trip wire)
◇ Chest
◇ Loose gear

Ⓑ Path to Lost Knife Hideout

Ⓒ Path to Lost Knife Cave

⑤ Hideout Entry

Sneak your way past the talking bandits, then slip behind the far scaffolding to discover a hidden chest.

◇ Chest   ◇ Potion

⑥ West Barracks

Beware: numerous bandits lurk in stone barracks to the west.

◇ Loose gear

⑦ West Corridors

Wipe out more bandits and claim more loot in these halls. Another Skill Book sits on a table atop the stairs here.

◇ Skill Book [Heavy Armor]: Orsinium   ◇ Potions
  and the Orcs   ◇ Loose gear
◇ Chest

⑧ Cage Chamber

Drop into the waterfall hole as you enter this area to discover a secret tunnel with a large, locked chest. The tunnel leads to several cages and a host of bandits. Open the cages with the key you found on the very first bandit — the same key can be found on another bandit here. Loot another large chest here as well.

◇ Danger! Bone Alarm Trap   ◇ Chest (Locked: Master)
◇ Crafting: Grindstone   ◇ Potions
◇ Lost Knife Cage Key (Bandit)   ◇ Loose gear
◇ Chests (2)

Ⓓ Path to Lost Knife Cave

Ⓔ Path to Lost Knife Hideout

⑨ East Overlook

Dispatch a few more bandits and loot a chest on your way back through the cave after exiting the Lost Knife Hideout.

◇ Chest   ◇ Potions   ◇ Loose gear

◈ [7.27] Fort Amol

Related Quests

Civil War Quest: Reunification of Skyrim
Civil War Quest: The Battle for Fort Amol

Recommended Level: 6

Habitation: Military Fort

Mage (pre-Civil War)
Soldier (Imperial/Stormcloak, depending on the state of the Civil War)

Crafting

Alchemy Lab
◇ Arcane Enchanter
Blacksmith Forge

Collectibles

Skill Book [Enchanting]: Catalogue of Armor Enchantments

Special Objects

Shrine of Julianos [5/5]
Chest(s)
Potions aplenty
Loose gear

This medium-sized fortress has been overrun by a group of hostile mages. Once the Civil War begins in earnest, the mages are driven out, and Fort Amol becomes a point of contention for Imperial and Stormcloak forces. A collapsed outer wall lets you infiltrate the fortress from the east

Exterior

Secure the fort's exterior before exploring its small inner areas. A Shrine of Julianos rests on the Blacksmith Forge.

◇ Crafting: Alchemy Lab,   ◇ Shrine of Julianos [5/5]
  Blacksmith Forge   ◇ Chests (2)

Fort Amol (Interior)

Slay more mages and search every nook and cranny to find much more loot within Fort Amol's small interior. Don't miss the Skill Book on the shelf near the Arcane Enchanter.

◇ Crafting: Arcane Enchanter
◇ Skill Book [Enchanting]: Catalogue of Armor Enchantments
◇ Chest
◇ Chest (Locked: Adept)
◇ Potions aplenty
◇ Loose gear

Prison Dispatch the mages in the prison's entry chamber, then loot the place.

◇ Potion

Lost Knife Hideout

[7.28] Darkwater Pass

Related Quests

Miscellaneous Objective:
Extracting an Argonian*
(Derkeethus)

Recommended Level:
18

Dungeon: Falmer Hive

Animal
Derkeethus (Follower)
Falmer

Services

Follower: Derkeethus [38/47]

Dangers

Swinging Wall Trap (lever/
trip wire)

Collectibles

Skill Book [Enchanting]:
Catalogue of Weapon
Enchantments
Chests
Potions

This watery pass runs through the Rift's northern mountains. An unfortunate Argonian named Derkeethus has become stuck in a sticky situation within...

> **NOTE** This walkthrough covers the pass as if you're heading from the bottom of the mountains and working your way up. However, it's also possible to enter from the top and work your way down.

Darkwater Cavern

Ⓐ Exit to Skyrim

① Waterfall Cavern

Loot a chest and slay a few Falmer on your way to this first wide, watery cavern. Raid the Falmer chest by the far waterfall before proceeding into the north passage.

◊ Chests (2)

② Chaurus Nest

Slay a number of Chaurus here, then search the east rubble to find more urns and another chest.

◊ Chest (Locked: Apprentice)

③ Pit Chamber

Slay a powerful Falmer here to obtain a key and free a nonhostile named Derkeethus, who asks for help in escaping the cave, thereby granting you a Side Quest. Pull a lever in the room's dark northeast corner to reveal a secret passage that leads down to a pair of chests in the watery pit below.

◊ Crafting: Arcane Enchanter
◊ Follower: Derkeethus [38/47]
◊ Skill Book [Enchanting]: Catalogue of Weapon Enchantments
◊ Darkwater Pit Key (Burial Urn)
◊ Shaman's Key (Falmer)
◊ Chests (3)
◊ Potion

④ Trapped Passage

Pull a lever to slay an unwary Falmer with a trap in this passage. Carefully deactivate the trip wire that also triggers the trap as you proceed to [5].

◊ Danger! Swinging Wall Trap (lever/trip wire)
◊ Potions

⑤ Rushing Rapids Cavern

Cut down multiple Falmer as you navigate this wide chamber. Scale the west ledges to locate a dark passage above the south waterfall, where you discover a chest. Climb the east ledges to reach a passage that leads back outside, but beware the trip wire that's stretched across the passage's entrance.

◊ Danger! Swinging Wall Trap (trip wire)
◊ Chest

Ⓑ Exit to Skyrim

[7.29] Snapleg Cave

Recommended Level: 14

Dungeon: Hagraven Lair

Animal
Hag
Witch

Crafting

Alchemy Lab
Arcane Enchanter

Dangers

Magic Caster Trap

Collectibles

Skill Book [Alteration]: Breathing Water
Chests
Potions
Loose gear

This medium-sized cave lies at the north base of the Rift's northern mountains and is home to vicious beasts and witches.

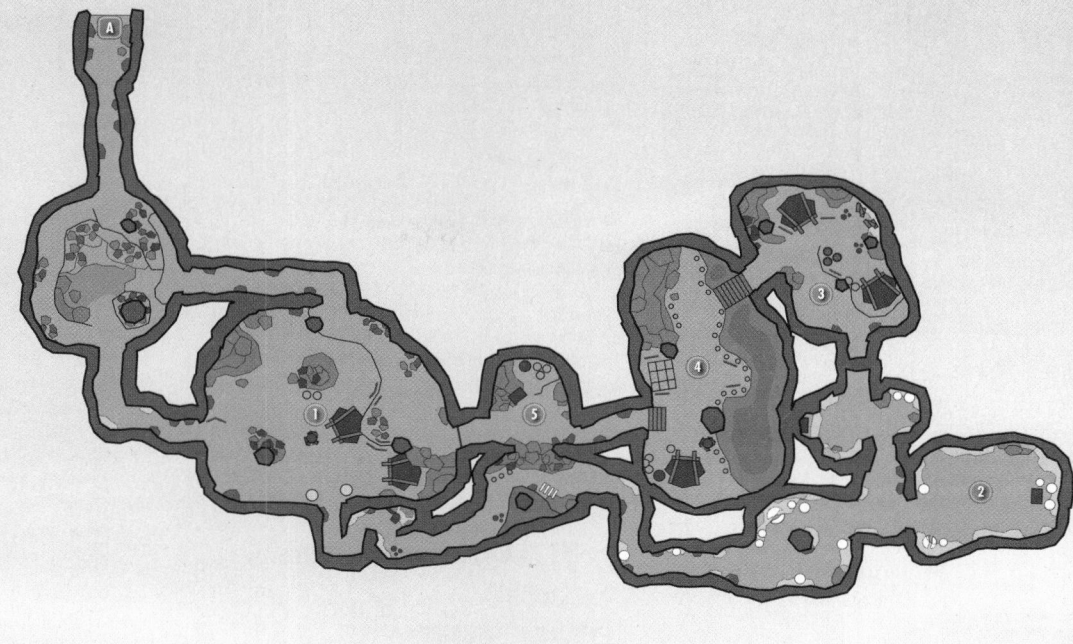

A Exit to Skyrim

1 Troll Cavern

Slay a few Skeevers in the cave's first tall chamber, then make your way to this wide cavern, where a few spell-slinging witches and a vicious predators lurk. Raid a chest inside a tent and find valuable loot in a box atop a rock; then take the south passage to [2], battling another troll along the way and snagging a Soul Gem from atop a pedestal to stop it from casting Ice Spikes at you.

◇ Danger! Magic Caster Trap
◇ Chest
◇ Potions
◇ Loose gear

2 Giant Spider Lair

Dispatch a few Frostbite Spiders on your way to this web-covered cavern, where a Giant Frostbite Spider descends from the ceiling to feast.

◇ Chest

3 Hag's Cavern

Cut down a few more spiders on your way to this cavern, where a Hag lurks. Claim the Skill Book that rests on a barrel inside the tent here.

◇ Skill Book [Alteration]: Breathing Water
◇ Potions

4 Canal Cavern

Slay a vicious Hag and Hagraven in this cavern, which features a watery canal. If you release a Spriggan from its Apprentice-level holding cell here, it will battle these enemies for you. There's nothing of value underwater.

◇ Crafting: Arcane Enchanter

5 Loot Stash

Raid a giant chest as you navigate the cave's exit passage, making your way back to the first tall chamber.

◇ Crafting: Alchemy Lab   ◇ Chest

[7.30] Eldergleam Sanctuary

Related Quests

Temple Quest: The Blessings of Nature

Recommended Level: 8

Dungeon: Spriggan Grove

Asta
Sond
Spriggan

Collectible

Skill Book [Restoration]: Mystery of Talara, v2

This widemouthed cave is located within Eastmarch's southern territory. The interior of the cave consists primarily of one huge, sunlit cavern. Find a Skill Book leaning against a small pile of rocks near the path by the waterfall. A woman named Asta hints at a fearsome weapon being able to have some sort of effect on the roots of the cavern's great tree, the Eldergleam, which block the uphill path leading to the wondrous tree. You will return here with the necessary item during Temple Quest: Blessings of Nature.

[7.31] Darkwater Crossing

Related Quests

Favor (Activity): Mining Ore* (Verner Rock-Chucker)

Favor: Special Delivery* (Sonda Drenim)

Favor: The Bandit Slayer* (Annekke)

Services

Follower: Annekke Crag-Jumper [39/47]
Marriage Prospect: Derkeethus [50/62]
Marriage Prospect: Sondas Drenim [51/62]

Habitation: Town

Annekke Crag-Jumper (Follower)
Derkeethus (Marriage Prospect)
Hrefna
Sondras Drenim (Marriage Prospect)
Stormcloak Soldier
Tormir
Verner Crag-Jumper

Crafting

Smelter

Collectibles

Skill Book [Heavy Armor]: Chimarvamidium (B2/10)
Chest(s)
Loose gear
Minable ore (Corundum)

This picturesque town sits on either side of the wide, short waterfalls of the Darkwater River, at the southern border of Eastmarch. An ancient stone bridge spans the river—a remnant of an earlier age.

Exterior

Speak with an old miner named Sondas Drenim to gain a new Side Quest. If he isn't outside, then you'll find him in the nearby mine.

◇ Crafting: Smelter

Verner and Annekke's House

You must pick the lock of the farmhouse's door in order to gain entry, yet the place holds little worth stealing.

◇ Area Is Locked (Adept)
◇ Chest

Goldenrock Mine

The mine near Darkwater Passing is small, having been worked for only a few years by the locals. Grab a pickaxe and mine Corundum Ore from the veins that run along the mine's walls; then sell it to Verner Crag-Jumper, who gladly pays you for your efforts. A Skill Book rests atop a barrel at the end of the tunnel.

◇ Skill Book [Heavy Armor]: Chimarvamidium (B2/10)
◇ Loose gear
◇ Minable ore (Corundum)

[7.32] The Atronach Stone

Recommended Level: 6

Special Objects

Standing Stone: The Atronach Stone [8/13]

An ancient stone with peculiar markings stands on a small rise along the southern edge of Eastmarch. Touch the stone to gain the sign blessing of the Atronach. Those under the sign of the Atronach absorb Magicka from incoming spells and have a larger pool of Magicka, but they recover Magicka more slowly.

[7.33] Mistwatch

Related Quests

Dungeon Quest: Forgetting About Fjola*

Recommended Level: 6

Dungeon: Bandit Camp

Christer
Mistwatch Bandit
Bandit Leader (Fjola)

Quest Items

Fjola's Wedding Band

Crafting

Alchemy Lab

Collectibles

Skill Book [Heavy Armor]: Hallgerd's Tale

Unique Item: Fjola's Wedding Band [64/112]

Chests

Potions

Loose gear

This imposing stone fortress stands at the southern edge of Eastmarch, not far from the mountains along the Reach's north edge. A group of bandits have taken control of the fort and must be dealt with.

Exterior

Dispatch the handful of bandits who defend the fort's exterior, then pull a lever to lower the drawbridge and advance into the first of three interior towers.

North Tower

Speak with a man named Christer inside the tower to gain a new Side Quest and an important key that unlocks the nearby door. Make your way upstairs, then climb a ladder and use the key again to go outside. (Don't bother opening the upstairs holding cell — there's nothing of interest in the small room.)

◇ Mistwatch Key (Christer)
◇ Crafting: Alchemy Lab
◇ Chest
◇ Chest (Locked: Apprentice)
◇ Apothecary's Satchel
◇ Potions
◇ Loose gear

West Tower

Open a locked chest before entering the fort's second tower. More bandits await you inside, including one that's quite powerful. Fight your way upstairs and proceed through the high door.

◇ Chest
◇ Chest (Locked: Adept)
◇ Loose gear

East Tower

You encounter the bandit's leader in this final tower, but she isn't what you'd expect. It turns out to be Fjola, Christer's missing wife. Fjola won't come with you, so you must either kill her on the spot or return to Christer and give him the bad news. Fjola is a powerful enemy, but she carries many valuables, so killing her is worth the effort. Agree to help her first, and you can slay Fjola *and* complete the quest with Christer by handing him her wedding band. Either way, search for a Skill Book that rests atop a dresser in this tower.

◇ Unique Item: Fjola's Wedding Band [64/112] (Fjola)
◇ Skill Book [Heavy Armor]: Hallgerd's Tale
◇ Potions
◇ Loose gear

[7.34] Eastmarch Imperial Camp

Related Quests

Civil War Quest: Reunification of Skyrim
Civil War Quest: The Battle for Fort Amol

Habitation: Military: Imperial Camp

Imperial Soldier
Imperial Quartermaster (Blacksmith)

Services

Trader (Blacksmith): Imperial Quartermaster [24/33]
Weapons, Apparel, Misc

Crafting

Anvil
Grindstone
Workbench

Special Objects

Civil War: Map of Skyrim
Chests (2)
Loose gear

Nestled at the foot of Eastmarch's eastern spires, a small band of Imperial Soldiers have dared to make camp. Speak with the Quartermaster here to browse his selection of fine weapons and armor. Examine each of the strategic map's flagged sites as well to potentially gain new map data. Note that this site may or may not exist, depending on the status of the Civil War campaign.

[7.35] Kagrenzel

Related Quests

Dungeon Activity

Recommended Level: 18

Dungeon: Falmer Hive

Falmer

Dangers

Rockfall Trap (proximity)

Underground Connection: Stony Creek Cave [7.36]

Special Objects

Strange Orb
Chest(s)

Perched high upon Eastmarch's eastern mountains, a long-forgotten temple stands at the very edge of Skyrim. Circle around and enter this mysterious structure from the east. Touch the Strange Orb inside the temple to take a wild ride that lands you in a watery cavern far, far below.

Watery Cavern

Find a chest with an Expert-level lock hidden deep underwater, and another chest up on dry land. Take the narrow passage back up to the bridge you recently plummeted past, slaying Falmer that emerge from holes in the walls. Fight your way across the bridge and follow the path back down to Stony Creek Cave [7.36]. There's no going back up to the temple from inside here.

◇ Danger! Rockfall Trap (proximity)
◇ Chest
◇ Chest (Locked: Expert)

[7.36] Stony Creek Cave

Related Quests

Side Quest: The Great Skyrim Treasure Hunt*
Other Factions: Bards College Quest: Finn's Lute
Thieves Guild Radiant Quest: No Stone Unturned

Recommended Level: 6

Dungeon: Bandit Camp

Bandit

Crafting

Alchemy Lab

Dangers

Flail Trap (trip wire)
Underground Connection: Kagrenzel [7.35]

Collectibles

Skill Book [Illusion]: The Mystery of Princess Talara, Part 4
Treasure Map X [7/11]
Unusual Gem: [18/24]
Chest
Chest (Locked: Apprentice)
Potions aplenty

This watery cave lies near a small pond near the base of Eastmarch's eastern mountains. Enter a side passage, slay a lowly bandit guard, and then safely trigger a trip wire from afar to avoid begin struck by a swinging flail. Cut down the powerful bandit mage in the nook beyond to discover a Treasure Map on her body. Collect a Skill Book here, along with the Unusual Gem, which pertains to the Thieves Guild Radiant Quest: The Crown of Barenziah. Raid the large chest, then make your way to the cave's far end to discover another chest that's locked. Stony Creek Cave links to Kagrenzel [7.35], but it's a one-way passage, and you can only travel from Kagrenzel to Stony Creek Cave.

[7.37] Cragslane Cavern

Recommended Level: 6

Dungeon: Bandit Camp

Animal	Bandit	Barkeep	Gambler

Danger
Bear Trap

Crafting
Tanning Rack

Collectibles
Skill Book [Lockpicking]: The Wolf Queen,
v1 [E2/10]

Chests

Potions

Loose gear

This cave lies in the hills of Eastmarch's southeast corner, not far from
where the main road leads into the Rift.

Exterior
Slay the lone bandit that guards the cave's exterior. Dispatch the harmless
caged Pit Wolves as well if you like.

◇ Crafting: Tanning Rack

Entry and Gambler's Den
Cut down another solitary bandit in the cave's entry passage, then sneak
into the following cavern to eavesdrop on a group of hostile gamblers. Slay
the men and find a key on the Barkeep, which unlocks the betting
area. The powerful bandit who fights to defend the gamblers also carries
a key, which unlocks the cages you noticed outside, along with the ones
in the back cavern. Find another, larger chest in the back cavern as well,
but watch out for the bear trap in front of it. A Skill Book is stashed behind
the bar.

◇ Danger! Bear Trap

◇ Skill Book [Lockpicking]: The
Wolf Queen, v1 [E2/10]

◇ Cragslane Cavern Key
(Barkeep)

◇ Cragslane Dog Cage Key
(Bandit)

◇ Chests (Locked:
Apprentice) (2)

◇ Potions

◇ Loose gear

[7.38] Ansilvund

Related Quests
Side Quest: No Stone Unturned

Dungeon Quest: A Love Beyond
Death*

Recommended Level: 8

Dungeon: Warlock Lair
Atronach

Draugr

Fjori

Holgeir

Lu'ah Al-Skaven

Mage

Crafting
Alchemy Lab

Arcane Enchanter

Arcane Imbuer

Dangers
Dart Trap (pedestal pressure
plates)

Flail Trap (tripwire)

Flamethrowers (pressure plates)

Oil Lamp Traps

Oil Pool Trap

Rising Floor Trap

Rockfall Trap (trip wire)

Swinging Blade Trap (pressure
plates/lever)

Swinging Wall Trap (pressure
plates)

Puzzles
Nordic Pillars

Collectibles
Skill Book [Illusion]: 2920,
Sun's Dawn, v2

Unique Weapon: Ghostblade
[53/80]

Unusual Gem: [19/24]

Chests

Potions

Loose gear

Located at Eastmarch's southeastern tip, this recently excavated crypt runs
deep into Skyrim's eastern mountains. The fragments of a story about the
lovers interred here, Fjori and Holgier, can still be found.

Exterior
Slay a mage and nab some goodies before entering the excavation site's
interior.

◇ Crafting: Alchemy Lab

◇ Chest (Locked: Apprentice)

◇ Potions

Ⓐ Exit to Skyrim

Ansilvund Excavation

Ansilvund Burial Chambers

① Entry Chamber
Snag a few potions and any mining tools you may need on your way
into this first chamber, where a powerful Draugr lurks. Venture down the
lower passage to eliminate another Draugr if you like before taking the
upper trail to [2].

◇ Potions

◇ Loose gear

② Small Excavation Chamber
A mage watches over a pair of ensorcelled Draugr here, bemoaning his
task of watching over them as they are forced to excavate the ruins. Try
to exploit the hanging lamp and oil slick on the room's far side. Loot the
locked chest on the scaffolding as you make your way here from [1].

◇ Danger! Oil Lamp Trap, Oil Pool Trap

◇ Chest (Locked: Novice)

◇ Potions

◇ Loose gear

③ Nordic Overlook Chamber

Open a locked chest as you enter this cavern, and beware the trip wire in the following passage. A haunting voice calls out to you here, initiating a new Side Quest. Loot the Draugr corpses as you proceed to [4].

◇ Danger! Flail Trap (trip wire), Oil Lamp Trap
◇ Chest (Locked: Apprentice)
◇ Potions

④ Arcane Cave

More mages lurk in this small chamber, where various ingredients and food items are found.

◇ Crafting: Arcane Enchanter   ◇ Oil Lamp Traps

⑤ Draugr Hall

The haunting voice returns as you move through this hall, calling upon the resting dead to rise up and attack you.

⑥ Fatal Floor Chamber

Beware: the entire center of this room rises if you step on it, delivering you up to deadly spikes that line the ceiling. Avoid the chamber's center as you make your way through here.

◇ Danger! Rising Floor Trap

③ Nordic Overlook Chamber Revisited

Cross elevated walkways to reach this location, where some valuable potions sit on a small table. A small chest can be found on the wooden platform overlooking the area where you first came into this chamber. Another possessed Draugr is busy digging near a large scaffold that over the doorway onward.

◇ Oil Lamp Traps   ◇ Potions

⑦ Pillar Puzzle

Beware the trip-wire trap as you approach this large cavern. A power Draugr, mage, and Flame Atronach engage you here. When the dust settles, solve the far puzzle by rotating the upper row of Nordic pillars so that they feature the same symbols as the row of glyphs hidden near the floor below (from left to right: Snake, Hawk, Whale, Snake). You may have noticed this solution in the common book *Fjori and Holgier*! This opens the south gate; avoid the pressure plate when crossing the footbridge or you'll be scorched. Loot a chest on your way to the Ansilvund Burial Chambers.

◇ Danger! Flamethrower (pressure   ◇ Chest
  plate), Rockfall Trap (tripwire)   ◇ Potions

Ⓑ Door to Ansilvund Burial Chambers

Ⓒ Door to Ansilvund Excavation

⑧ Swinging Blades Passage

Avoid the many pressure plates in this first passage — stepping on any of them causes a host of swinging blades to activate in the adjacent hall. Pick the Adept-level door at the end of this corridor to access a small nook with a locked chest and lever. Pull the lever to deactivate the swinging blades if you happened to trigger them.

◇ Danger! Swinging Blade Trap (pressure plates/lever)
◇ Chest (Locked: Master)

⑨ Key Chamber

This Draugr-filled chamber also sports several traps. Avoid the central pressure plates or you'll be burned by flames. Beware when taking the item off the nearby pedestal as well — removing it causes arrows to fire from the wall directly behind you. (Stand to one side to avoid damage.) Taking the key from the far pedestal causes a host of Draugr to awaken, but the key is a great help in opening the upper gates, whose Master-level locks aren't easily picked. When you loop back around to the main chamber, sprint straight across the elevated walkway to avoid damage from traps.

◇ Danger! Dart Trap (pedestal pressure plate), Flamethrower (pressure plates), Oil Lamp Trap, Swinging Wall Trap (pressure plates)

◇ Ansilvund Key   ◇ Chest (Locked: Adept)
◇ Chest   ◇ Loose gear

⑩ Floor Trap Passage

Lay more Draugr to rest and snag some potions as you pass through this area. Avoid the rising floor trap where the passage widens, and stand near the far wall when collecting the item off the pedestal in the nearby alcove to avoid being shot by arrows from the wall. A Skill Book rests atop another, trap-free pedestal here.

◇ Danger! Dart Trap (pedestal pressure plate), Rising Floor Trap
◇ Skill Book [Illusion]: 2920, Sun's Dawn, v2
◇ Potions

⑪ Lamp-Lit Hall

Lu'ah Al-Skaven awaits you here. You're just in time to disrupt her nefarious ritual. However, Lu'ah manages to raise two powerful Draugr. Try knocking down the cavern's many hanging lamps to inflict extra damage upon these dangerous foes. Kill Lu'ah to complete your Side Quest. This also frees the souls of Fjori and Holgeir, who leave a unique blade behind in thanks. Use the key you find on Lu'ah's corpse to open the upstairs door and sack one last chest on your way back to the surface.

◇ Danger! Oil Lamp Traps
◇ Crafting: Alchemy Lab, Arcane Imbuer
◇ Unique Weapon: Ghostblade [53/80]
◇ Unusual Gem [19/24]
◇ Lu'ah's Key (Lu'ah Al-Skaven)
◇ Chest
◇ Potions
◇ Loose gear

Ⓓ Door to Ansilvund Excavation

Ⓔ Door to Ansilvund Burial Chambers

⊰ SECONDARY LOCATIONS ⊱

▷ [7.A] Lucky Lorenz's Shack

Side Quest: The Great Skyrim Treasure Hunt*

Just below the waterfall, close to the Abandoned Prison on the White River, are the remains of a shack, demolished by a fallen tree. The inhabitant, whose luck ran out, has been struck by the tree as well. He carries a Treasure Map. A Shrine of Dibella is found in one surviving corner of the cabin.

◇ Skill Book [Light Armor]: Rislav the Righteous
◇ Treasure Map IX [8/11]
◇ Shrine of Dibella [7/8]

▷ [7.B] Shrine of Talos: Cradlecrush Pond

On a rocky outcrop just northeast of Cradlecrush Rock is a pond where the Imperials haven't found a Shrine to Talos. Clamber up past the old Nordic stone heads and worship here if you wish; there's a chest, Skill Book, and other equipment left as offerings.

◇ Skill Book [Heavy Armor]: 2920, Midyear, v6
◇ Shrine of Talos [12/17]
◇ Chest
◇ Loose gear

▷ [7.C] Mara's Eye Stones

South of Mara's Eye Pond on the steep forest and scree is a set of standing stones. Beware of Spriggan flitting around this place, as they tend to attack you on sight.

▷ [7.D] Frost Troll Den: Uttering Hills

Climb north from Mara's Eye Pond and cross the snow line. Trek to the top of Uttering Hills to find a ferocious Frost Troll guarding his den. The den is empty, but outside is a fluttering flag, marking two mineral veins.

◇ Mineable ore (Corundum, Gold)

▷ [7.E] Shrine of Talos: Watcher of Windhelm

Approach this craggy hillside shrine from the south to reach steps to the Talos statue towering over the bridge and Windhelm Stables below. You'll

---

find a shrine to receive a blessing, and various offerings to take. The dead body of a Thalmor Agent has been disposed of below the walkway to the statue, along with the enchanted weapon that did him in.

◇ Shrine of Talos [13/17]   ◇ Loose gear

[7.F] Hunter's Camp: Windhelm Plateau

Unless the Imperial Legion is laying siege to Windhelm, this mountain plateau is occupied by a hunters' camp. As you approach, a Frost Troll suddenly appears over the ridge. The hunters have little chance against this powerful foe, so rush in to help (or watch them die, if you prefer). You can loot the corpses and the camp for some valuables, though any surviving hunters will turn on you if you steal their items (so much for gratitude). A Skill Book lies inside one of the lean-tos.

◇ Skill Book [Light Armor]: Ice and Chitin
◇ Chest (Apprentice)
◇ Loose gear

[7.G] Windhelm Attack Camp

Related Quests

Civil War Quest: Reunification of Skyrim
Civil War Quest: Battle for Windhelm

At the end of the Civil War, if you sided with the Imperials, the assault on Windhelm begins here, with most of the catapults bombarding the city from this point. General Tullius assembles his men for a rousing speech close to this location, prior to the epic assault on this Stormcloak stronghold.

[7.H] Dragon Mound: Kynesgrove Resurrection

Related Quest: Main Quest: A Blade in the Dark

This Dragon Mound is initially sealed. It opens during Main Quest: A Blade in the Dark, when you arrive with Delphine and watch Alduin resurrect Sahloknir, the dragon that was entombed here. Alduin himself cannot be harmed; he resurrects his brethren and flies off. But slay Sahloknir and absorb his soul to continue the quest.

[7.I] Hunter's Camp: Dunmeth Pass

Halfway up the exceptionally steep snowbanks is a small hunter's camp with a lean-to and roaring fire. The hunters are friendly, unless you attempt to steal from them. Look for a blowing ragged flag to indicate this camp's proximity.

◇ Crafting: Tanning Rack   ◇ Knapsack

[7.J] Wild Animal Den: Dunmeth Pass

A few wild animals are snarling at the top of the incredibly steep snowbanks and mountain slopes. The ragged flag halfway up the slope is a good route marker to look for. The den is devoid of items but provides a view of the Shrine of Boethia.

[7.K] Hunter's Camp: Sulphur Soaking Pools

West and a little south of Eldergleam Sanctuary is a group of hunters bathing in a sulphur pool. The camp has a couple of tents and some loose gear, and a Skill Book sits on the short table with the keg. The hunters are friendly, unless you try to steal their clothes and equipment. It seems the wine has been flowing freely here!

◇ Skill Book [Smithing]: Cherim's Heart
◇ Loose gear

[7.L] Dragon Mound: Bonestrewn Crest

Related Quest: Main Quest: Dragon Rising

This Dragon Mound is initially sealed. It opens during Main Quest: Dragon Rising. If you visit during or after this point in the Main Quest, the mound will be open and empty. Once the quest is complete, a dragon will appear atop Bonstrewn Crest [7.20] nearby; perhaps the resurrected dragon simply thought it a better lair.

[7.M] Cronvangr Summoning Altar

The bubbling sulfur in this area has forced an old Nordic entrance to crumble and fall, and the sacrificial altar is currently exposed to the elements. Watch for a couple of necromancers attempting to raise a thrall on the slab here.

[7.N] Dragon Mound: Witchmist Grove

Related Quest: Main Quest: The Way of the Voice

This Dragon Mound remains sealed. It opens during Main Quest: The Way of the Voice, when you train with the Greybeards. If you return during or after this point in the Main Quest, the mound will be open and empty. The dragon summoned has disappeared.

[7.O] Witchmist Sulphur Pool

Expect to find a couple of wandering mammoths and a giant bathing in the hot waters of this sulphur pool, which is just east of Witchmist Grove. Approach them with caution, or bring them down from a distance.

[7.P] Hunters' Camp: Steamcrag Slopes

On the slopes to the east of Steamcrag Camp is a well-hidden hunters' camp. There are likely to be two adventuring types here, along with their horses and a recently slain mammoth that's being carved up for meat and tusks. A Skill Book sits on a crate near the wagon.

◊ Skill Book [Two-Handed]: The Legendary Sancre Tor

[7.Q] Mistwatch Folly

The remains of a small fortification long-since lost to the sulphur pools is now home to three skeletons. They reanimate when you approach, so attack before they're fully mobile. The only treasure are the items these bony fiends are carrying.

[7.R] Shrine of Akatosh: Steamcrag Hillock

On the rocky hillock south of Steamcrag Camp is a set of standing stones and an altar, upon which is a Shrine to Akatosh and a Skill Book. Beware the crumpled bones; these reanimate into three skeletons as you approach!

◊ Skill Book [Alteration]: Breathing Water
◊ Shrine of Akatosh [5/6]

[7.S] The Mournful Giant

A mammoth has succumbed to death at the eastern end of a small sulphur pool, and a despondent giant waits by its furry corpse. You may attack or edge around this melancholy fellow.

[7.T] Dragon Mound: Mzulft Foothills

Related Quest: Main Quest: Dragon Rising

This Dragon Mound is initially sealed. It opens during Main Quest: Dragon Rising. If you visit during or after this point in the Main Quest, the mound will be open and empty.

[7.U] Hunters' Camp: Slopes of Kagrenzel

On the treacherous slopes leading to Kagrenzel is a small hunters' camp, with two hardy folk braving the inclement weather. There's a small vein of Corundum to mine here, and a Skill Book sits atop a barrel near one of the tents.

◊ Skill Book [Archery]: Father of the Niben
◊ Mineable ore (Corundum)

TOPOGRAPHICAL OVERVIEW

The Hold along Skyrim's southern border with Cyrodiil is known as Falkreath, and its capital shares the same name. The Hold's second largest town, Helgen, was the site of a recent dragon attack and prisoner escape. Before its destruction, Helgen was "the Gateway to Skyrim," a well-traveled town at an important crossroads in the foothills of the Jerall Mountains. As you move north, the rugged, mountainous south gradually gives way to pine forest lowlands. Though initially tranquil to the untrained eye, the woods are a wilderness fraught with the prospect of enemies (wild animals or worse) lurking behind every tree. Still, the people of Falkreath are reasonably prosperous farmers and loggers, thanks to the abundant supply of fresh water from Lake Ilinalta — the largest body of water in Skyrim.

Routes and Pathways

Falkreath is among the most-traveled Holds in terms of major roads and minor pathways. The lake is an excellent anchoring point, allowing you to get your bearings from almost any angle. North of the lake are the sharp and protruding Brittleshin Hills — snowy peaks dominated by Bleak Falls Barrow that overlook the origin of the White River — and the town of Riverwood just across the border in Whiterun Hold. Head east, and you brave the blizzards of the Jerall Mountains, bandit attacks in the high mountain passes, and the windswept caverns of Haemar's Shame. To the south, the Jerall Mountains dominate, their icy crags making many locations difficult to reach and almost impossible to escape from without blade or spell. Still, resolute hunters like Angi can still be found in this vast wilderness, determined to live life on their own terms. Head west, and the pine forests give way to more rocky scree and sharper crags, where you can hear the howls of anger of the Forsworn from the Reach and find old or forgotten cuts into the earth, including the fabled Twilight Sepulcher.

AVAILABLE SERVICES, CRAFTING, AND COLLECTIBLES

Services

Followers: [0/47]
Houses for Sale: [0/5]
Marriage Prospects: [0/62]
Skill Trainers: [3/50]
  Alchemy: [1/3]
  Alteration: [0/3]
  Archery: [0/3]
  Block: [0/2]
  Conjuration: [1/3]
  Destruction: [0/3]
  Enchanting: [0/2]
  Heavy Armor: [0/3]
  Illusion: [0/2]
  Light Armor: [1/3]
  Lockpicking: [0/2]
  One-Handed: [0/3]
  Pickpocket: [0/3]
  Restoration: [0/3]

Smithing: [0/3]
Sneak: [0/3]
Speech: [0/4]
Two-Handed: [0/2]
Traders [7/133]:
  Apothecary [2/12]
  Bartender [0/5]
  Blacksmith [3/33]
  Carriage Driver [0/5]
  Fence [0/10]
  Fletcher [0/3]
  Food Vendor [0/9]
  General Goods [1/19]
  Innkeeper [1/15]
  Jeweler [0/2]
  Special [0/3]
  Spell Vendor [0/12]
  Stablemaster [0/5]

Collectibles

Captured Critters: [0/5]
Dragon Claws: [1/10]
Dragon Priest Masks: [0/10]
Larceny Targets: [0/7]
Skill Books: [29/180]
  Alchemy: [2/10]
  Alteration: [2/10]
  Archery: [3/10]
  Block: [2/10]
  Conjuration: [3/10]
  Destruction: [3/10]
  Enchanting: [3/10]
  Heavy Armor: [0/10]

Illusion: [2/10]
Light Armor: [2/10]
Lockpicking: [0/10]
One-Handed: [1/10]
Pickpocket: [1/10]
Restoration: [1/10]
Smithing: [2/10]
Sneak: [1/10]
Speech: [1/10]
Two-Handed: [1/10]
Treasure Maps: [3/11]
Unique Items: [16/112]
Unique Weapons: [7/80]
Unusual Gems: [3/24]

Special Objects

Shrines: [6/69]
  Akatosh: [1/6]
  Arkay: [3/12]
  Dibella: [0/8]
  Julianos: [0/5]
  Kynareth: [0/6]
  Mara: [0/5]
  Stendarr: [0/5]
  Talos: [2/17]
  Zenithar: [0/5]
Standing Stones: [4/13]
  The Lady Stone
  The Mage Stone
  The Thief Stone
  The Warrior Stone
Word Walls: [5/42]
  Animal Allegiance: [1/3]
  Aura Whisper: [0/3]
  Become Ethereal: [0/3]
  Disarm: [0/3]
  Dismaying Shout: [0/3]
  Elemental Fury: [1/3]
  Fire Breath: [1/2]
  Frost Breath: [0/3]
  Ice Form: [0/3]
  Kyne's Peace: [0/3]
  Marked for Death: [1/3]
  Slow Time: [0/3]
  Storm Call: [0/3]
  Throw Voice: [0/1]
  Unrelenting Force: [1/1]
  Whirlwind Sprint: [0/2]

CRAFTING STATIONS: FALKREATH

✓	TYPE	LOCATION A	LOCATION B
☐	Alchemy Lab	Anise's Cabin (Interior) [8.19]	Dark Brotherhood Sanctuary [8.22]
☐	Arcane Enchanter	Anise's Cabin (Interior) [8.19]	Dark Brotherhood Sanctuary [8.22]
☐	Anvil or Blacksmith Forge	Falkreath (Lod's House) [8.00]	Dark Brotherhood Sanctuary [8.22]
☐	Cooking Pot and Spit	Falkreath (Lod's House) [8.00]	Half-Moon Mill (Interior) [8.11]
☐	Grindstone	Falkreath (Lod's House) [8.00]	Dark Brotherhood Sanctuary [8.22]
☐	Smelter	Bilegulch Mine (Exterior) [8.01]	—
☐	Tanning Rack	Falkreath (Lod's House) [8.00]	Half-Moon Mill [8.11]
☐	Wood Chopping Block	Whiterun (Jarl's Longhouse) [7.00]	Half-Moon Mill [8.11]
☐	Workbench	Falkreath (Lod's House) [8.00]	Dark Brotherhood Sanctuary [8.22]

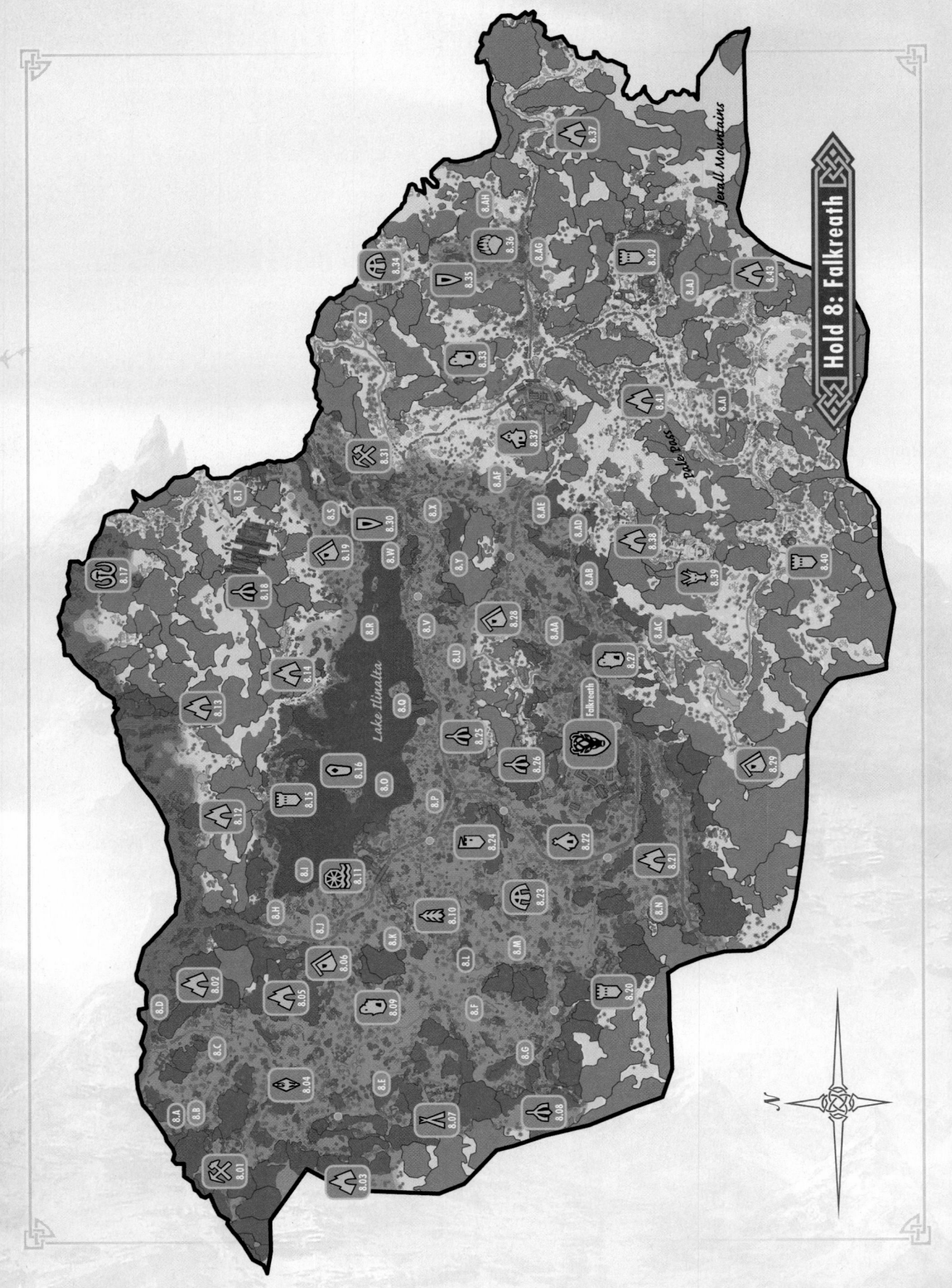

Jerall Mountains

Pale Pass

Lake Ilinalta

Falkreath

N

The Elder Scrolls V

SKYRIM

ATLAS OF SKYRIM: HOLD 8: FALKREATH HOLD

PRIMA OFFICIAL GAME GUIDE   WWW.PRIMAGAMES.COM

PRIMARY LOCATIONS

Total — 44: Hold Capital, and 43 Hold Locations

[8.00] Hold Capital City: Falkreath
Jarl: Siddgeir
[8.01] Bilegulch Mine
[8.02] Sunderstone Gorge
[8.03] Glenmoril Coven
[8.04] Falkreath Imperial Camp
[8.05] Moss Mother Cavern
[8.06] Hunter's Rest
[8.07] Knifepoint Ridge
[8.08] Twilight Sepulcher
[8.09] Bannermist Tower
[8.10] Evergreen Grove
[8.11] Half-Moon Mill
[8.12] Bloated Man's Grotto
[8.13] North Brittleshin Pass
[8.14] South Brittleshin Pass
[8.15] Ilinalta's Deep
[8.16] The Lady Stone
[8.17] Secunda's Kiss
[8.18] Bleak Falls Barrow
[8.19] Anise's Cabin
[8.20] Cracked Tusk Keep
[8.21] Halldir's Cairn
[8.22] Dark Brotherhood Sanctuary
[8.23] Roadside Ruins
[8.24] Falkreath Watchtower
[8.25] North Shriekwind Bastion
[8.26] South Shriekwind Bastion
[8.27] Peak's Shade Tower
[8.28] Pinewatch
[8.29] Angi's Camp
[8.30] The Guardian Stones
[8.31] Embershard Mine
[8.32] Helgen
[8.33] South Skybound Watch
[8.34] North Skybound Watch
[8.35] Orphan Rock
[8.36] Falkreath Stormcloak Camp
[8.37] Haemar's Shame
[8.38] Bonechill Passage
[8.39] Ancient's Ascent
[8.40] Bloodlet Throne
[8.41] Greywater Grotto
[8.42] Fort Neugrad
[8.43] Southfringe Sanctum

SECONDARY LOCATIONS

Total — 36 Points of Interest

[8.A] Dragon Mound: Bilegulch Ridge
[8.B] Toadstool Ring: Bilegulch Ridge
[8.C] Hunter's Camp: Sunderstone Gorge
[8.D] A Peddler's Misfortune
[8.E] Toppled Tower: Knifepoint Woods
[8.F] Burning Caravan: Evergreen Grove
[8.G] Shrine of Akatosh: Twilight Valley
[8.H] Fisherman's Camp: Lake Ilinalta
[8.I] Sunken Fishing Boat: Lake Ilinalta
[8.J] Dark Elf's Grave
[8.K] Alchemist's Camp: Evergreen Woods
[8.L] Dragon Mound: Evergreen Woods
[8.M] Sacrificial Altar: Evergreen Woods
[8.N] Bear Cave: Halldir's Cairn
[8.O] The Silvermoon: Lake Ilinalta
[8.P] Nordic Burial Grove
[8.Q] Fisherman's Island: Lake Ilinalta
[8.R] Sunken Barrow: Lake Ilinalta
[8.S] The Indigestible Emerald
[8.T] Riverwood Folly
[8.U] Wild Animal Den: Pinewatch Outcropping
[8.V] The Conjuror's Altar: Lake Ilinalta
[8.W] Hunter's Camp: The Guardian Stones
[8.X] Bandit Camp: Ilinalta Foothills
[8.Y] Shrine of Talos: Ilinalta Foothills
[8.Z] Bandit Camp: Skybound Underhang
[8.AA] Bandit Bridge: Pinewatch
[8.AB] Bandit Camp: Pinewatch Heights
[8.AC] Hunter's Camp: Upper Pinewatch Ridge
[8.AD] Prospector's Shack: Bonechill Ridge
[8.AE] Bandit Camp: Helgen Cliffs
[8.AF] The Mauled Refugees
[8.AG] Khajiit Caravan Massacre
[8.AH] Wild Animal Den: Orphan's Tear
[8.AI] Dragon Mound: Bloodlet Peaks
[8.AJ] The Headless Skeleton

HOLD CAPITAL: FALKREATH

Collectibles

Skill Book [Block]: Death Blow of Abernanit [C2/10]
Skill Book [Illusion]: The Black Arts on Trial [E2/10]
Skill Book [Restoration]: Racial Phylogeny [C2/10]
Skill Book [Smithing]: Light Armor Forging [D1/10]
Skill Book [Speech]: A Dance in Fire, v6 [B2/10]
Skill Book [Two-Handed]: The Legendary Sancre Tor [D2/10]

Unique Item: Cursed Ring of Hircine [65/112]
Unique Item: Ring of Hircine [66/112]
Chest
Potions aplenty
Loose gear

Related Quests

Daedric Quest: A Daedra's Best Friend
Daedric Quest: Ill Met By Moonlight
Dark Brotherhood Quest: Side Contract: Helvard
Miscellaneous Objective: Innkeeper Rumors (Dead Man's Drink)
Miscellaneous Objective: Once a Thalmor...* (Runil)
Miscellaneous Objective: Vighar the Vampire* (Dengeir of Stuhn)
Favor (Activity): Harvesting Crops* (Mathies)
Favor: Special Delivery* (Thadgeir)
Favor: A Little Light Thievery* (Dengeir of Stuhn)
Favor: Rare Item Hunt* (Jarl Siddgeir)
Favor: Item Retrieval (Cave)* (Runil)
Favor: Jobs for the Jarls* (Jarl Siddgeir)
Crafting Tutorial: Alchemy* (Zaria)
Thane Quest: Thane of Falkreath Hold*

Habitation: Hold Capital (Minor)

Crafting

Alchemy Labs (2)
Arcane Enchanter
Blacksmith Forge
Grindstone
Tanning Racks (4)
Workbench

Services

Trader (Apothecary): Zaria [9/12]
Trader (Blacksmith): Lod [25/33]
Trader (General Store Vendor): Solaf [12/19]
Trader (Innkeeper): Valga Vinicia [13/15]
Trainer (Conjuration: Journeyman): Runli [3/3]

Special Objects

Shrines of Arkay (3) [9/12; 10/12; 11/12]
Civil War: Map of Skyrim

Lore: City Overview

The capital of Falkreath is infamous for its bloody history and sprawling graveyard. Its name is not Nordic in origin, but Elvish, though even they no longer remember its meaning. The town, and its graveyard, blossomed over the ages from a monument commemorating the Battle of Sungard. A statue once stood commemorating the spot where Kjoric the White fell in battle defending Falkreath from the First Empire, and legend has it that his son, Hoag Merkiller, fell in exactly the same spot when he retook Falkreath years later. The residents of Falkreath take a certain pride in this history and their cemetery, though some darkly refer to Falkreath as "Where heroes come to die."

In recent years, the Jarl's family has become bitterly divided between Siddgeir, the avaricious Imperial Jarl, and his uncle, the former Jarl Dengeir, who was forced from his position due to his growing Stormcloak sympathies. The people of Falkreath work hard just to keep the town functioning properly despite the political struggles. Isolated and isolationist, the capital of Falkreath is unwelcoming to visitors, with stern facades and its haunting graveyard. Some say wisps flit across the graveyard at night, and lonely buildings feel surrounded by the graveyard and hidden foes on the treeline's edge, while gloomy interiors hold the court of a Jarl with a family divided.

Important Areas of Interest

1 Main Thoroughfare

Jarl Siddgeir's moneymaking schemes are paying dividends, as the settlement of Falkreath is well guarded, featuring fortified gates at opposite ends of town. The main thoroughfare is mostly paved, and there's always a guard presence. There's room for a small farm and lumber mill to support the local economy.

2 Jarl's Longhouse

The following leaders of Falkreath are loyal to the Imperials at the start of the Civil War.

Jarl Siddgeir

The nephew of Dengeir and now the Jarl of Falkreath, Siddgeir has always had money and power, although he's done little to deserve either. He acts as Jarl now that his uncle has given up the position. Siddgeir mostly focuses on ways to acquire more money and protect his newfound power. His main concern is busybodies like Valga Vinicia, Tekla, and Narri, who he fears might ruin his family's name. However, he has already amassed his own supporters: Solaf and Bolund, a pair of brothers who complete occasional dirty deeds on his behalf.

Nenya (Steward)

Nenya is an overworked High Elf who attempts to maintain order and is the brains behind the throne. She isn't conniving or plotting, just attempting to maintain order while in the service of an incapable leader.

Helvard (Housecarl)

A loyal bodyguard and skilled military tactician, Helvard serves as a bodyguard for the Jarl. While he has great respect for the position of Jarl, Helvard agrees with Nenya that neither Dengeir of Stuhn nor Siddgeir are suited for the important decisions of the town, and he works with her to guide the Jarl's policies to what is best for the city.

Legate Skulnar

The following residents of Falkreath control the capital, once this Hold has fallen during the Civil War.

Jarl Dengeir of Stuhn

Once the Jarl of Falkreath, now "voluntarily" lowered to the position of Thane, Dengeir of Stuhn was a great warrior and virtuous hero of

---

Falkreath in his youth. However, he has outlived his glory and is slowly descending into a creeping paranoia. He sees enemies hidden everywhere and rarely goes out in public. Shortly before Imperial pressure forced him from his position as Jarl, Dengeir very nearly exiled all Imperials from Falkreath, a proclamation prevented only by Nenya's careful council. Dengeir is a strong supporter of the Stormcloaks, but he knows to stay quiet about his support.

Tekla (Steward)

As further evidence of his growing dementia, Dengeir names his house servant Tekla as his Steward when the Stormcloaks restore him to the position of Jarl. He does this not because he believes that she is qualified to hold the position (she almost certainly isn't) but because she is the only person left who he trusts.

Jarl Siddgeir runs Falkreath Hold from this impressive Longhouse. His main reason for supporting the Empire is because it makes life more profitable for him, so he continues to find ways to line his own pockets with their help. As a result, much of the day-to-day workings of the Hold are still handled by his overworked Steward, Nenya, and she works with Helvard to deal with matters of military defense, such as bolstering the city from Civil War attacks. He has welcomed Legate Skulnar into his hearth and home, and turned the wine storage room into a place where the Imperials can plot war. The Jarl's bedroom has two display cases ([Adept] and [Expert]), the latter of which has a Skill Book to read. There's another on a table in the War Room, and an Arcane Enchanter on one of the upstairs balconies.

- ◇ Crafting: Arcane Enchanter
- ◇ Skill Book [Block]: Death Blow of Abernanit [C2/10]
- ◇ Skill Book [Pickpocket]: Guide to Better Thieving
- ◇ Civil War: Map of Skyrim
- ◇ Chest
- ◇ Potions aplenty
- ◇ Loose gear

3 Falkreath Barracks

Sinding

The three floors of Falkreath's Barracks are where the town's guard sleep, drink, and return to drink some more. Find a Skill Book tucked between some wooden crates near the entry door. The bedrooms are upstairs, and most of the meals (and brawling) occurs on the ground floor. Below is a cellar, or Falkreath Jail, where mainly petty thieves or drunkards are placed. However, one specially reinforced cell holds the "monster" Sinding, who is a threat to all the townsfolk after he murdered the child of Mathies and Indara.

- ◇ Skill Book [Illusion]: The Black Arts on Trial [E2/10]
- ◇ Skill Book [Two-Handed]: The Legendary Sancre Tor [D2/10]
- ◇ Unique Item: Cursed Ring of Hircine [65/112]
- ◇ Unique Item: Ring of Hircine [66/112]
- ◇ Evidence Chest
- ◇ Prisoner Belongings Chest
- ◇ Chests (3)
- ◇ Loose gear

4 Grave Concoctions

Zaria

Her Alchemist's Store is well stocked, and she is able to talk through the rudiments of mixing potions to anyone who is interested. Discover a Skill Book on the floor behind some baskets near the bed.

- ◇ Crafting: Alchemy Lab
- ◇ Trader (Apothecary): Zaria [9/12]
  - ○ Potions, Food, Ingredients
- ◇ Skill Book [Alchemy]: De Rerum Dirennis
- ◇ Chest
- ◇ Potions aplenty

---

5 Lod's House

Lod

near his forge, and is almost always locked. Inside is a private letter requesting some ore and a cellar to inspect. A Skill Book rests atop a barrel downstairs.

- ◇ Crafting: Blacksmith Forge, Grindstone, Tanning Racks (3), Workbench
- ◇ Trader (Blacksmith): Lod [25/33]
  - ○ Weapons, Apparel, and Misc
- ◇ Skill Book [Smithing]: Light Armor Forging [D1/10]
- ◇ Private Letter
- ◇ Chest (2)
- ◇ Loose gear

6 Gray Pine Goods

Solaf   Bolund

Solaf runs this general store that is owned by Siddgeir—which has a surprising array of goods for such an isolated town—while his brother voices disapproval of the Imperials around Falkreath. The only obstacles to the brothers becoming the most powerful family in town are Valga Vinicia and her "daughters," who Bolund sees as busybodies and gossips who have something against him. Solaf and Bolund's sister Grelka left them for Riften a while ago, sick of their attitudes. Solaf and Bolund don't particularly miss her.

- ◇ Trader (General Store Vendor): Solaf [15/15]
  - ○ Weapons, Apparel, Potions, Scrolls, Food, Ingredients, Books, Misc
- ◇ Potions
- ◇ Loose Gear
- ◇ Chest (2)
- ◇ Strongbox (Apprentice)

7 Dead Man's Drink

Valga Vinicia   Narri   Delacourt

A cozy tavern with a roaring fire and fine food, the Dead Man's Drink stands in stark contrast to the Jarl's court and is the far more inviting world for visitors. The owner, Valga Vinicia, is always glad to listen to a traveler's tales, and the server, Narri, collects gossip from around the town, particularly from her sister, Tekla, who works as a maid for Dengeir. Valga Vinicia has slowly become aware of the Dengeir's paranoia and has long known of Siddgeir's corruption, and she grows concerned for the town. A Skill Book is kept behind the counter.

◊ Crafting: Alchemy Lab
◊ Trader (Innkeeper): Valga Vinicia [13/15]
  ○ Room for the night, Food
  ○ Innkeeper Rumors
◊ Skill Book [Speech]: A Dance in Fire, v6 [B2/10]
◊ Chest (3)

8 Corpselight Farm

Mathies Caerellia   Indara Caerellia

Indara and her husband, Mathies, reside peacefully at the Corpselight farm, so named because a past resident helped develop the idea of "cultivating" the witchlights and wisps that illuminate the edges of the town graveyard. Currently, the pair are managing a bumper crop of potatoes, cabbages, and gourds.

◊ Skill Book [Restoration]: Racial Phylogeny [C2/10]
◊ Chest

9 Dengeir's House

Tekla

Once the Jarl of Falkreath, now "voluntarily" lowered to the position of Thane, Dengeir of Stuhn was a great warrior and virtuous hero of Falkreach in his youth. However, he has outlived his glory and is slowly descending into a creeping paranoia. Dengeir of Stuhn is loathe to meet guests and sees threats and conspiracies everywhere. His rantings terrorize his servant, Tekla. Tekla will raise the alarm if you decide to break into this dwelling, if she's inside this location.

◊ Crafting: Tanning Rack   ◊ Chest

10 Deadwood Lumber Mill

Hardly a hive of activity, the mill isn't utilized to capacity thanks to the lackadaisical attitudes of its owner, Jarl Siddgeir, and its abrasive foreman, Bolund.

11 Hall of the Dead

Runil   Kust

Originally meant for the cemetery's groundskeeper, this now consists of a dwelling for Runil and Kust and a makeshift shrine for Arkay, the god of birth and death. Unlike the larger Hold capitals, there is neither the room nor the coin to build a mausoleum to the fallen, who are buried outside in the cemetery instead. Inside, a Skill Book is hidden under the bed near the chest.

◊ Trainer (Conjuration: Journeyman): Runli [3/3]
◊ Skill Book [Conjuration]: The Doors of Oblivion
◊ Shrine of Arkay [9/12]
◊ Shrine of Arkay [10/12]
◊ Shrine of Arkay [11/12]
◊ Chest

12 Cemetery

The graveyard encroaches into the town and is large compared to the population. Most of the graves have worn away, including a memorial statue commemorating Hoag Merkiller and Kjoric the White, who died defending Falkreath from outsiders. By tradition, the graveyard at Falkreath is the central graveyard for all residents of Falkreath Hold, and the many battles for control over the Hold have provided it with no shortage of graves. Because the town has a resident priest of Arkay, the grave sites are better maintained than in smaller cemeteries, and in many cases, the tombstones have long outlasted the bodies of those they were meant to commemorate.

PRIMARY LOCATIONS

[8.01] Bilegulch Mine

Recommended Level: 6

Dungeon: Bandit Camp

Bandit

Crafting

Blacksmith Forge
Smelter
Workbench

Dangers

Bone Alarm Trap

Collectibles

Skill Book [Smithing]: The Armorer's Challenge
Chest(s)
Potions
Loose gear
Mineable ore (Orichalcum)

Merciless bandits have taken over this remote Orichalcum mine, which lies at Falkreath's western edge.

Exterior

The bandits have fortified their position around the mine with a wooden wall and several watchtowers. You must enter through the wall's main gate, which lies to the southwest. Loot a locked chest before scaling some stairs to face powerful bandits near the mine's entrance. Another locked chest and several crafting stations are found up here.

◊ Crafting: Blacksmith Forge, Smelter, Workbench
◊ Chest (Locked: Novice)
◊ Chest (Locked: Apprentice)
◊ Potions
◊ Loose gear

Bilegulch Mine (Interior)

Avoid hanging rattles as you descend into the mine—they'll alert the bandits' nearby leader. Obtain a key from the Bandit Chief and use it to open the nearby chest. Find a Skill Book on a wooden table at the end of the mine shaft, and if you like, dig plenty of Orichalcum Ore from this mine before heading outside.

◊ Danger! Bone Alarm Trap
◊ Skill Book [Smithing]: The Armorer's Challenge
◊ Bilegulch Mine Key (Bandit Chief)
◊ Chest (Locked: Expert)
◊ Loose gear
◊ Mineable ore (Orichalcum)

[8.02] Sunderstone Gorge

Related Quests

Thieves Guild Radiant Quest: No Stone Unturned

Dungeon: Warlock Lair

Animal
Atronach
Mage
Skeleton

Crafting

Alchemy Labs (2)
Arcane Enchanter

Dangers

Oil Lamp Traps
Bone Alarm Trap
Oil Pool Traps
Rockfall Trap (pressure plate)
Mammoth Skull Trap (pressure plate)
Magic Trap
Swinging Wall Trap (pressure plate)
Dart Trap (trapped door)

Collectibles

Skill Book [Conjuration]: 2920, Frostfall, v10 [A2/10]
Unusual Gem: Stone of Barenziah [20/24]

Special Objects

Word Wall: Fire Breath [2/2]
Chest(s)
Potions
Loose gear

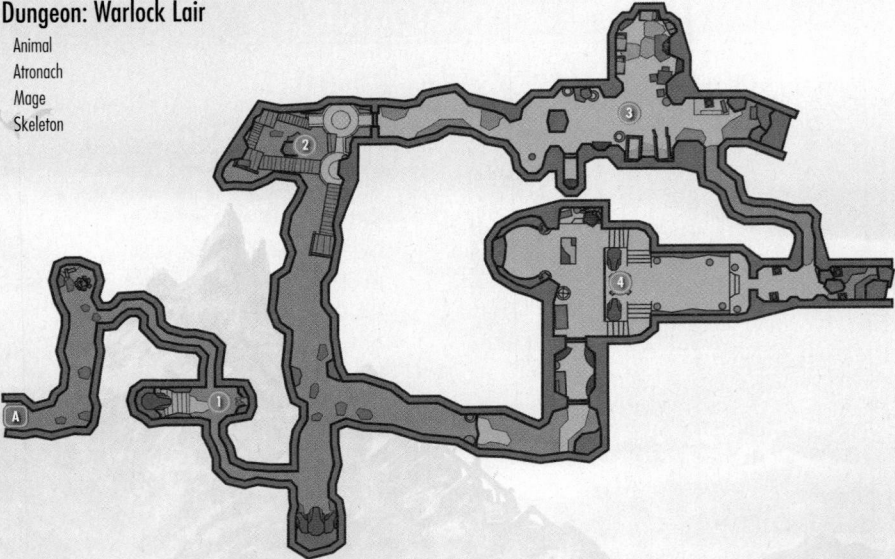

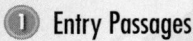

Bones and bloodstains mark the entrance to this small cave, and a powerful mage stands watch outside. Nearly every square inch of this treacherous cave's interior is filled with traps and dangers — sneak and avoid rushing forward, or you'll suffer dearly. Protection against fire can be invaluable here.

A Exit to Skyrim

1 Entry Passages

Avoid a pressure plate that releases a lethal rockfall as you sneak toward an unwary mage who's tending a fire inside the cave. Beware of another dangerous pressure plate trap in the small cavern that follows, which is guarded by a lowly skeleton. Hug the right wall to dodge hanging rattles, then ignite the next tunnel's oily floor to scorch more foes.

◊ Danger! Oil Lamp Traps, Bone Alarm Trap, Oil Pool Traps, Rockfall Trap (pressure plate), Mammoth Skull Trap (pressure plate)

2 Stair Chamber

Knock down a hanging lamp to make a mage flee from his advantageous perch in the oily passage that leads to this small area. Beware of a lethal pressure plate trap at the passage's end, and find a chest in a nook near the wooden stairs. Another chest is tucked away atop the stairs as well.

◊ Danger! Oil Lamp Traps, Oil Pool Traps, Wall Trap (pressure plate)
◊ Chest (Locked: Apprentice)
◊ Chest (Locked: Adept)

3 Lab

Watch your step before reaching the bottom of these stairs, as there is a magic trap waiting in a nook to the side. Ignite the oily floor here to scorch more mages, and crouch before opening the south wooden door; there's a chest in the closet beyond, but arrows will puncture you from behind if you're standing tall. (Alternatively, you can disable the trap's trigger on the door.) Mix some potions at the Alchemy Lab here, then loot a large, locked chest that lies in the west rubble — if you're able to pick its tricky lock.

◊ Danger! Dart Trap (trapped door), Magic Trap
◊ Crafting: Alchemy Lab
◊ Chest
◊ Chest (Locked: Master)
◊ Apothecary's Satchel
◊ Potion
◊ Loose gear

4 Word Wall Chamber

Beware the large amount of oil on the floor here — the far mages and Fire Atronach will quickly ignite it if they detect you. Sneak past this hazard, or sprint past it before your enemies can react. Approach the Word Wall to learn a new Word of Power, then raid the nearby chest and collect a Skill Book off the nearby pedestal. Exploit an Arcane Enchanter if you like, then pull a wall chain to access another Alchemy Lab. The Unusual Gem found here pertains to a Thieves Guild Radiant Quest. Pull a second wall chain to open the passage that leads back to the cave's entry tunnel.

◊ Danger! Oil Pool Trap
◊ Crafting: Alchemy Lab, Arcane Enchanter
◊ Skill Book [Conjuration]: 2920, Frostfall, v10 [A2/10]
◊ Unusual Gem: Stone of Barenziah [20/24]
◊ Word Wall: Fire Breath [3/3]
◊ Chest
◊ Potions
◊ Loose gear

[8.03] Glenmoril Coven

Related Quests

The Companions Quest: Blood's Honor
The Companions Radiant Quest: Purity

Recommended Level: 14

Dungeon: Hagraven Nest

Animal
Glenmoril Witch (only during "Blood's Honor")
Hag (does not appear during "Blood's Honor")

Crafting

Arcane Enchanter

Collectibles

Skill Book [Destruction]: Horrors of Castle Xyr [B2/10]
Skill Book [Enchanting]: A Tragedy in Black [A1/10]
Chest (Locked: Novice)
Chests (2)
Potions
Loose gear

In the northeast reaches of Falkreath, a coven of nefarious witches have occupied a sizeable cave. You visit this site during two different quests, for very different reasons. Discover a locked chest in a dark nook as you navigate the cave's first passage. Defeat a Hag and vicious animal in the large chamber that follows, which links to four side rooms. Beware the ferocious beast that lurks on the main chamber's north ledge. Explore each small side chamber to discover a variety of plunder.

[8.04] Falkreath Imperial Camp

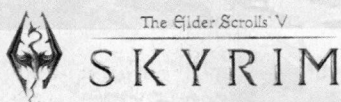

Related Quests

Civil War Quest (when active, depending on who you side with)

Habitation: Military: Imperial Camp

Imperial Quartermaster (Blacksmith)
Imperial Soldier

Services

Trader (Blacksmith): Imperial Quartermaster [26/33]
Weapons, Apparel, Misc

Crafting

Alchemy Lab
Anvil
Grindstone
Workbench

Special Objects

Civil War: Map of Skyrim
Chests (2)
Potions
Loose gear

Depending on the status of the Civil War quest line, you may or may not find this small Imperial campsite in Falkreath. When the camp is present, you may trade with the Imperial Quartermaster, or utilize his selection of crafting stations. One tent's tabletop map can potentially grant you new map data. Loot the camp if you like before moving on.

[8.05] Moss Mother Cavern

Related Quests

Dungeon Quest: Hunter and Hunted*

Recommended Level: 8

Dungeon: Spriggan Grove

Spriggan
Bear
Valdr

Dangers

Bear Traps

Collectibles

Unique Weapon: Valdr's Lucky Dagger [54/80]
Chest(s)
Loose gear

This rocky cave lies just off of Falkreath's main western road. A wounded hunter named Valdr sits on a log just outside the entrance, calling out for help.

Exterior

Speak with Valdr to hear his story, then heal him with a potion or Restoration Spell to address his immediate problem. Valdr asks for your help in clearing out the cavern; decide if you wish to go alone or have Valdr lend you his aid.

Moss Mother Cavern (Interior)

Loot the body of Valdr's fallen friend Ari, then leap up the nearby ledges to locate a hidden chest. Slay a Spriggan and Bear as you venture deeper in, being careful to avoid bear traps that are hidden among shrubbery. Defeat a few more Spriggans in the large, sunlit cavern that follows to clear the cave and complete your quest. Raid the large chest that sits on a south ledge and swipe the gear that rests at the bottom of the pool. Then speak with Valdr for your reward.

◊ Danger! Bear Traps
◊ Chest
◊ Chest (Locked: Novice)
◊ Loose gear

[8.06] Hunter's Rest

Recommended Level: 8

Habitation: Hunter Camp

Hunter

Crafting

Tanning Rack

Collectibles

Skill Book [Archery]: Father of the Niben [A2/10]
Chest

This small open-air cabin lies due west of Lake Ilinalta, just across the main road. The friendly hunters who live here enjoy a simple life. A chest inside the cabin can be looted if you've no qualms about stealing. There's a Skill Book between the bedrolls as well.

[8.07] Knifepoint Ridge

Related Quests

Daedric Quest: Boethiah's Calling
Dungeon Activity

Recommended Level: 6

Dungeon: Bandit Camp

Bandit

Crafting

Alchemy Lab
Blacksmith Forge
Grindstones
Smelter
Tanning Rack
Workbench

Dangers

Oil Lamp Trap
Oil Pool Trap
Rockfall Trap (lever)

Quest Items

Ebony Mail

Collectibles

Skill Book [Archery]: Vernaccus and Bourlor [E1/10]
Unique Item: Ebony Mail [67/112]
Chests
Potions
Loose gear
Mineable ore (Corundum, Iron)

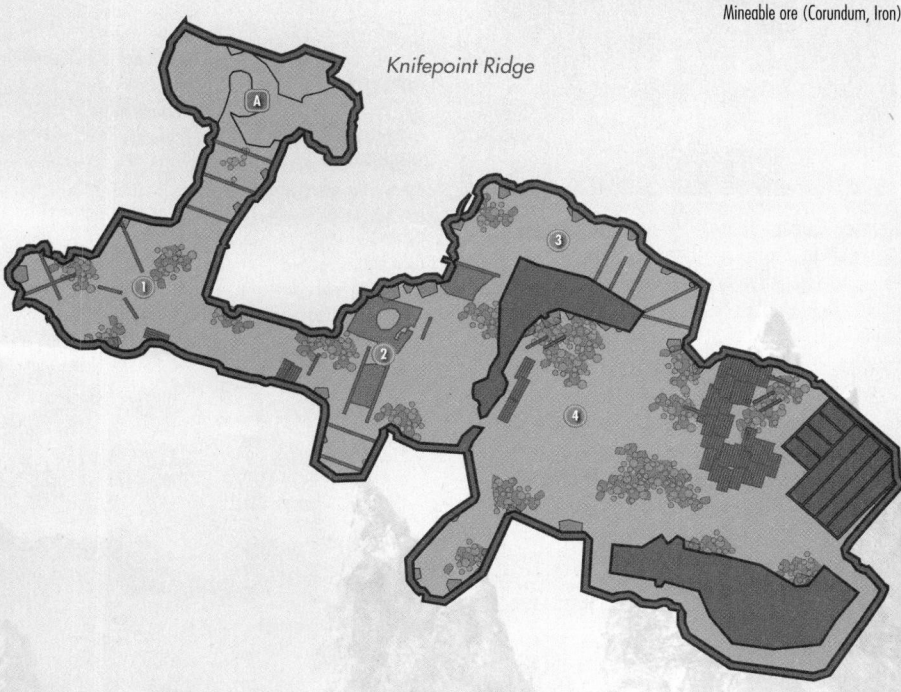

Knifepoint Ridge

The bandit camp of Knifepoint Ridge is located on a high bluff in the foothills of Falkreath's western mountains and has been overrun and fortified by bandits. During Daedric Quest: Boethiah's Calling, you are sent to this location to defeat a challenging adversary and obtain the Ebony Mail.

Exterior

The bandits have built a sizeable camp around the mine. Beware the rockfall trap that the watchtower guard will set off if he spots you. Sneak carefully or take him out from a distance before he can throw the lever that triggers it. Check each of the open-air cabins to discover an array of valuables, and collect the Skill Book on the table near the Blacksmith Forge.

◊ Crafting: Alchemy Lab, Blacksmith Forge, Grindstone, Workbench
◊ Skill Book [Archery]: Vernaccus and Bourlor [E1/10]
◊ Chest (Locked: Novice)
◊ Apothecary's Satchel
◊ Potions
◊ Loose gear

A Exit to Skyrim

1 Knifepoint Mine Entry

If you're not on the quest, then the bandits' formidable leader lurks just inside the mine, and you can't explore beyond the first room. See if you can ignite the oil beneath the chief's feet with a fire-based attack. Opening the Expert-level holding cell puts you close to a thick Iron Ore vein, but the same ore can be more easily mined from the vein that's just outside the cell.

During "Boethiah's Calling," the mines are significantly larger — the bandits have tunneled much farther into the rock. A lowly bandit guard will be stationed here instead of a powerful leader.

◊ Danger! Oil Pool Trap
◊ Chest
◊ Loose gear
◊ Mineable ore (Iron)

2 Lab

If you have decent sneaking skills, backstabbing this bandit should be a breeze. Then mix up potions at the Alchemy Lab and grab a couple poisons the bandit was brewing up.

◊ Crafting: Alchemy Lab
◊ Potions

3 North Passage

Knock down a hanging lamp to ignite the oily floor here and sear another unsuspecting bandit or sneak up on him while he is busy mining.

◊ Danger! Oil Lamp Trap, Oil Pool Trap
◊ Mineable ore (Corundum)

④ Grand Cavern

Pick a Novice-level gate to enter this wide cavern from the west, or loop around and take the north passage to get here. If you choose the north passage, you can use a narrow space beneath the scaffolding to your left to sneak across the open chamber easier. Sneak around and slay the lone bandit worker, then mine plenty of ore from the surrounding veins and exploit the crafting stations to improve your gear. You can proceed up the ramp and go through the front door, or use the smaller cave hallway on the south end of this chamber to loop around to the back of the shack. Approaching from the rear will allow you to jump on a pile of crates and enter the shack through a hole in the roof, dropping directly into shadow and giving you an easy chance to backstab the Champion of Boethiah. Slay the Champion of Boethiah by whatever method you prefer, then don his Ebony Mail to complete your quest. Raid the nearby large chest before backtracking outside.

◇ Crafting: Grindstone, Smelter, Tanning Rack
◇ Chest
◇ Loose gear
◇ Unique Item: Ebony Mail [67/112]
◇ Satchel
◇ Mineable ore (Corundum)

▶ [8.08] Twilight Sepulcher

Related Quests

Side Quest: Kyne's Sacred Trials
Thieves Guild Quest: Darkness Returns

Recommended Level: 8

Dungeon: Special

Karliah
Nocturnal
Nightingale Sentinel
Gallus

Crafting

Alchemy Lab

Dangers

Battering Ram Trap (trapped door)
Dart Trap (pressure plates/tripwires)
Lethal Light
Spear Trap (pressure plate)
Swinging Blade Trap (proximity)

Collectibles

Skill Book [Lockpicking]: Proper Lock Design
Skill Book [Sneak]: Sacred Witness
Area Is Locked (quest required)
Chests
Potions aplenty
Loose gear

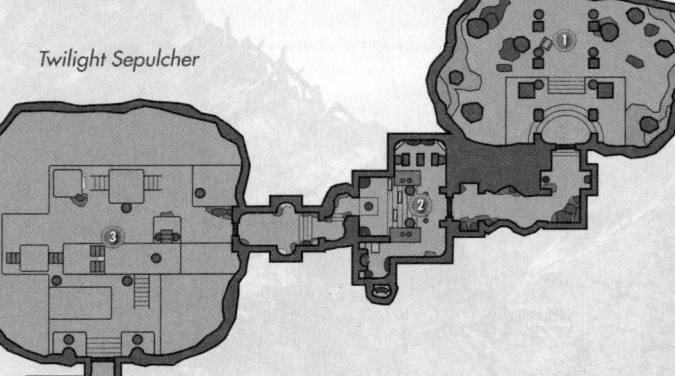

Twilight Sepulcher

This large burial site has been carved into Falkreath's western mountains and holds several trials to test those who would probe its depths. You cannot enter this place until you've obtained the "Darkness Returns" quest from the Thieves Guild.

Ⓐ Exit to Skyrim

① Entry Chamber

Speak with the friendly Nightingale Sentinel in the first chamber to advance your quest, and question him thoroughly to obtain an optional side objective that leads you to the nearby remains of an adventurer named Nystrom, whose journal provides clues on how to survive the trials ahead.

◇ Nystrom's Satchel
◇ Loose gear

② First Trial: Sentinels of the Dark

Sneak to avoid the two vicious Nightingale Sentinels in this chamber—they'll quickly cut you to ribbons. If you can head into the upper southwest study, press a button on the ground near the table to expose a secret nook containing treasure. Sidestep a pressure plate as you sneak through the passage that leads to [3], avoiding another Nightingale Sentinel as you go.

◇ Danger! Dart Trap (pressure plate)
◇ Chest
◇ Crafting: Alchemy Lab
◇ Knapsack
◇ Potions aplenty

③ Second Trial: Vigilance Everlasting

Avoid the light and keep to the darkness as you navigate this massive chamber—for the light here is fatal. Equip a light source of your own, such as a torch, to help you spot traps that are concealed in the dark. No enemies lurk here.

◇ Danger! Lethal Light, Dart Trap (trip wires)

④ Third Trial: The Offering

Loot a chest as you make your way to this quiet shrine. Collect the offerings near the statue if you like before pulling two wall chains near the side torches to open a passage behind the statue.

◇ Chest

⑤ Fourth Trial: Path to Salvation

Don't let this passage's swinging blades stupefy you into stepping on the pressure plate that lies before them. If you can, open the Master-level iron door to the south to sneak through [6] and bypass the blades altogether. Otherwise, you must time it right and sprint straight through—you'll trigger another pressure plate midway through, so move to the left the moment you clear the passage to avoid being shot by arrows. Beware of another as you exit the blade passage, and stand back before opening the iron door ahead to avoid being struck by a battering ram (or simply disable its trap hinge). Proceed through the door that follows to reach the inner sanctum.

◇ Danger! Battering Ram Trap (door), Swinging Blade Trap (proximity), Spear Trap (pressure plate), Dart Trap (pressure plates)

⑥ Great Hall

Pick a locked door to enter this large chamber and avoid the swinging blade passage altogether. A few items of interest are found in the chamber's lower central area, including a pair of Skill Books. Sneak through here to avoid alerting the two roaming Nightingale Sentries.

◇ Skill Book [Lockpicking]: Proper Lock Design
◇ Skill Book [Sneak]: Sacred Witness
◇ Potions   ◇ Loose gear

Ⓑ Door to Twilight Sepulcher Inner Sanctum

Final Trial: Hesitate Not

Sprint down a long, empty corridor to reach this deep pit. Drop down—you'll suffer a bit of damage—then loot a skeleton to discover an informative note. You seem trapped but are soon whisked away to an alternate version of the pit chamber by the magic of the Skeleton Key that you possess. Insert the key into the central lock on the floor to summon Nocturnal. Speak with Karliah after Nocturnal departs, then watch her reunion with Gallus. Afterward, decide which portal to enter—each grants you a different (and substantial) bonus to a certain thieving discipline.

▶ [8.09] Bannermist Tower

Recommended Level: 6

Dungeon: Bandit Camp

Bandit

Crafting

Tanning Rack

Collectibles

Skill Book [Lockpicking]: Advances in Lockpicking
Chests (2)

Bandits have assumed control of this tall tower, which stands on the west bank of the mountains west of Lake Ilinalta. Ignore the locked gate on the ground floor and head upstairs to discover a Skill Book. Open the chest beneath the stairs that lead up to the lookout's nest, then head back downstairs and open the locked gate you ignored before to access another chest and some valuables.

[8.10] Evergreen Grove

Recommended Level: 8

Dungeon: Spriggan Grove

Spriggan

Collectibles

Skill Book [Alchemy]: Mannimarco, King of Worms [D2/10]

Dangerous Spriggan guard this sacred grove, where a tranquil waterfall fills a calm pond. Slay the Spriggan, then search the deceased Alchemist who floats in the pond's center to obtain a Skill Book.

[8.11] Half-Moon Mill

Related Quests

Dark Brotherhood Quest: Whispers in the Dark
Dark Brotherhood Quest: Side Contract: Hern

Habitation: Lumber Mill

Hert

Crafting

Tanning Rack
Chest(s)

This tranquil lumber mill sits on the west end of Falkreath's Lake Ilinalta.

Exterior

Take up a Woodcutter's Axe and chop up some wood near the mill's only cabin, then sell the wood back to a woman named Hert for some honest coin.

Half-Moon Mill (Interior)

Break into Hert's cabin unseen and raid the lone chest within to pocket some ill-gotten loot.

◇ Area Is Locked (Novice)
◇ Chest

[8.12] Bloated Man's Grotto

Related Quests

Daedric Quest: Ill Met By Moonlight
Dungeon Activity

Recommended Level: 6

Dungeon: Spriggan Grove

Animal
Spriggan
Spriggan Matron

Unique Weapon

Bolar's Oathblade

Collectibles

Unique Item: Savior's Hide [68/112]
Unique Weapon: Bolar's Oathblade [55/80]

Special Objects

Shrine of Talos [14/17]
Note: Bolar's Writ
Chests (2)
Chest (Locked: Apprentice)
Chest (Locked: Master)

Note that this area changes significantly during (and after) Daedric Quest: Ill Met by Moonlight. If you're here for the quest, see the quest walkthrough for details on what to expect.

The entrance to this cave lies just off the east–west road that runs across the southern Tundra. Kill the predators that lurk just inside, then hop onto the low ledge on the south side of the first clearing to discover a locked chest. Dive into a pond near the waterfall to discover another chest at the bottom.

You must next take one of two paths: for the purposes of this walkthrough, proceed along the trail closest to the pond, dispatching another predator and a Spriggan who emerges from a tree as you pass. Scale the stone steps that follow to locate a quiet shrine, where a large chest is found. Pray at the Shrine of Talos for a blessing. Then inspect the pedestal at the base of a statue for a note and a unique Blades Sword.

Descend the following stairs, slaughtering more animals and Spriggans as you proceed along the path. When you reach the clearing with the dead deer, look up to spot a rocky promontory. Scale the rocks here if you can (you may find it easier to backtrack and climb up the central ridgeline first) to claim a chest in a small nook behind the promontory.

Then continue down the path, and you'll find that you have come full circle, returning to the waterfall pond with the cave fully explored.

[8.13] North Brittleshin Pass

Recommended Level: 6

Dungeon: Warlock Lair

Mage
Skeletons

Crafting

Arcane Enchanter

Collectibles

Skill Book [Conjuration]: The Warrior's Charge [E2/10]
Chest
Apothecary's Satchel
Potions
Loose gear

Dangers

Rune Trap (floor)
Trapped Chest

Underground Connection: South Brittleshin Pass [8.14]

This site marks the north entrance of a short pass that runs through the mountains north of Lake Ilinalta.

Brittleshin Pass (Interior)

Slay a few skeletons in the first sunlit cavern, then scale a ramshackle collection of winding ramps to reach its high central platform. Cross a small footbridge and loot a large chest. Crush a few more skeletons and a powerful mage in the cavern that follows, which features an Arcane Enchanter and Skill Book. Scale some steps to reach the next windy chamber, where a trapped chest sits on a left ledge as you enter. Disable the trap hinge, or stand to one side of the chest and lift its lid from afar to avoid being struck by the mace that swings down when you open it. Keep going to reach some open doors, then back up and use a ranged attack to detonate the rune trap on the floor beyond from a safe distance. Proceed through the nearby exit to complete your journey through the mountain and emerge at South Brittleshin Pass [8.14].

[8.14] South Brittleshin Pass

Recommended Level: 6

Dungeon: Warlock Lair

Underground Connection: North Brittleshin Pass [8.13]

This site marks the south entrance to Brittleshin Pass, which acts as a shortcut through the mountains north of Lake Ilinalta. See the previous location entry for North Brittleshin Pass [8.13] for details on what awaits you within the pass.

[8.15] Ilinalta's Deep

Ilinalta's Deep

Related Quests
Daedric Quest: The Black Star

Recommended Level: 8

Dungeon: Warlock Lair
Animal
Mage
Skeleton

Crafting
Alchemy Lab
Arcane Enchanter

Quest Items
Broken Azura's Star

Collectibles
Skill Book [Alteration]: Breathing Water [A2/10]
Skill Book [Conjuration]: The Doors of Oblivion
Skill Book [Enchanting]: A Tragedy in Black [A2/10]
Chests
Potions aplenty
Loose gear

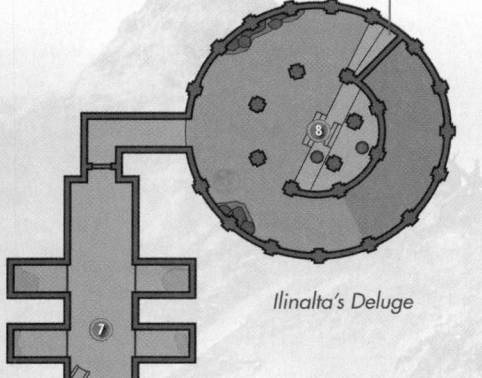

Ilinalta's Deluge

This pair of sunken towers lies along Lake Ilinalta's north bank. You venture here during Daedric Quest: The Black Star in search of a special item known as Azura's Star; however, a powerful mage named Maylyn Varen guards the mysterious object.

Exterior

Both towers feature rooftop trapdoors, but only the west tower's trapdoor is within your reach. Before entering, dive into the surrounding waters to discover a sunken chest between the towers, near the fort's southern wall.

◊ Chest

(A) Exit to Skyrim

(1) Entry Chamber

A forboding shackled skeleton greets you just inside the sunken stronghold. Loot the knapsack near the skeleton to discover an informative journal, then proceed to [2].

◊ Knapsack

(2) Dinning Area

Slay a few powerful mages and a skeleton on your way to the dining hall. Find several useful potions here and in the north kitchen. Open a wooden door afterward and proceed to [3].

◊ Potions aplenty   ◊ Loose gear

(3) Waterlogged Chamber

This chamber is rapidly taking on water. Eliminate the mages, then dive into the pool and swim through a submerged passage to locate a sunken chest. A soaked Skill Book rests atop the nearby dresser, also underwater.

◊ Skill Book [Alteration]: Breathing Water [A2/10]
◊ Chest

(4) Crafting Area

Slay a couple of powerful mages to secure this small chamber, where a Skill Book sits on a table across from a pair of crafting stations. Unlock the Apprentice-level door to access a sleeping area with a chest.

◊ Crafting: Alchemy Lab, Arcane Enchanter
◊ Skill Book [Enchanting]: A Tragedy in Black [A2/10]
◊ Apothecary's Satchel
◊ Potions aplenty

(5) Head Mage's Chamber

Confront a powerful mage in this watery chamber, then dive underwater and open the Apprentice-level door to discover a sunken chest. Use the steps to exit the water and loot a large chest before entering a winding passage that leads back to [1]. Pick another Apprentice-level door as you navigate the passage to pocket a few more potions on your way. When you return to [1], take the north door to Ilinalta's Deluge. (This door is only accessible during "The Black Star" quest.)

◊ Chests (2)
◊ Potions
◊ Loose gear

(B) Door to Ilinalta's Deluge

(C) Door to Ilinalta's Deep

(6) Deluge Entry

Slay a few more foul mages in the Deluge's first room, then loot a chest and grab the Skill Book on the table. Go through the east door to visit a small storage room filled with potions. Backtrack out and head west toward [7].

◇ Skill Book [Conjuration]: The Doors of Oblivion
◇ Chest
◇ Potions aplenty

7 Holding Cells

Slay a powerful mage in this long prison area. There's little of interest in the cells, but you can hone your lockpicking art.

8 Tower

Dispatch another deadly mage who guards the tower's entry floor, then proceed upstairs to reach a quiet throne room. Loot a large chest here, then claim the Broken Azura's Star from Malyn Varen's skeletal remains. Read the nearby tome to learn a bit more about Varen and his motives before climbing the nearby ladder to take your leave.

◇ Broken Azura's Star
◇ Chest

D Exit to Skyrim

[8.16] The Lady Stone

Recommended Level: 6

Dungeon: Special

Special Objects:
Standing Stone: The Lady Stone [9/13]

Swim out to Lake Ilinalta'a tiny western isle to locate an ancient Standing Stone. Touch this stone to gain a new sign blessing. Those under the sign of the Lady regenerate Health and Stamina more quickly. Note that you can have only one sign blessing at a time, so activating this Standing Stone will replace your current blessing (if any).

[8.17] Secunda's Kiss

Dungeon: Giant Camp
Giant

Collectible
Chest

This site holds special significance to giants, who make regular pilgrimages here for some mysterious reason. Slay the sites' protective guardians if you can, then plunder gold and valuables from their corpses and from the chest near the bonfire.

[8.18] Bleak Falls Barrow

Related Quests   **Recommended Level: 6**

Main Quest: Bleak Falls Barrow
Side Quest: The Golden Claw

This large, striking ruin stands atop the mountains north of Lake Ilinalta and can be easily seen for miles. Ascend the snowy mountain trails, navigating a raging blizzard as you head for Bleak Falls Barrow's ominous exterior.

Dungeon: Draugr Crypt
Arvel the Swift
Bandit
Draugr
Draugr Scourge Lord
Frostbite Spider
Skeever
Wounded Frostbite Spider

Dangers
Oil Lamp Traps
Oil Pool Traps
Swinging Blade Trap (wall chains)
Swinging Wall Trap (pressure plate)

Puzzles
Nordic Puzzle Door (Golden Claw)
Nordic Pillars

Quest Items
Dragonstone (Draugr Scourge Lord)
Golden Claw (Arvel)

Collectibles
Dragon Claw: Golden Claw [6/10]
Skill Book [Pickpocket]: Thief [D2/10]

Special Objects
Word Wall: Unrelenting Force [1/1]
Chest(s)
Potions

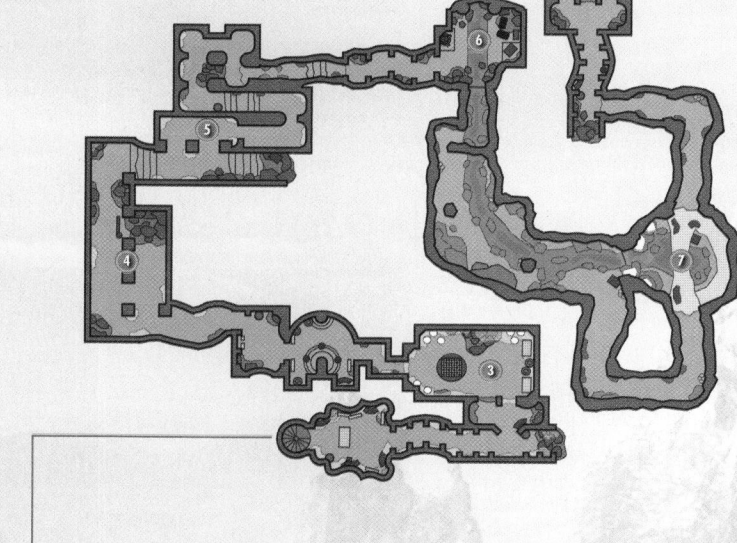

Exterior

Slay the exterior guards before entering the doors that lead into the Bleak Falls Temple — there's nothing else of interest outside in the cold.

A Exit to Skyrim

1 Entry Chamber

Cut down the two bandits at the end of this first, large chamber, then loot the chest they were guarding before navigating a long, uneventful passage on your way to [2].

◇ Chest (Locked: Novice)

3 Spider Lair

Chop through thick webs to enter this small chamber, then slay the hulking Wounded Frostbite Spider that silently descends from the ceiling. Carefully free Arvel afterward, who's been caught up in a thick web. The fool quickly rushes deeper into the ruins — hurry after him!

2 Nordic Pillars Puzzle

Before pulling this chamber's tempting central lever, rotate the three pillars in the west wall to match the sequence of glyphs that can be seen around the north wall (Snake, Snake, Whale). Then pull the lever to safely raise the north portcullis. Go through and raid a chest, then claim the nearby Skill Book. Descend a spiral staircase on your way to [3], slaughtering several Skeevers at the bottom.

◇ Skill Book [Pickpocket]: Thief [D2/10]
◇ Chest
◇ Potions

4 South Burial Passages

Chase Arvel into these passages, where undead Draugr warriors begin to rise. Arvel is quickly slain; retreat as you combat the Draugr, then return to this chamber and collect the vital Golden Claw and informative journal that Arvel possesses. Be careful to avoid the pressure plate on the floor that triggers a lethal trap on your way to [5].

◇ Danger! Swinging Wall Trap (pressure plate)

◇ Dragon Claw: Golden Claw [6/10] (Arvel)

5 North Burial Passages

Slay more Draugr in this next chamber, then quickly sprint through the hall of swinging blades—you can sprint through unscathed if you time it right. Once through, pull a wall chain to deactivate the trap. Burn up the many Draugr in the passage that follows by knocking down hanging lamps to ignite oil on the floor.

◇ Danger! Oil Lamp Traps, Oil Pool Trap, Swinging Blade Trap (wall chain)

6 Waterfall Cavern

Loot a chest in this small cavern, then pull a wall chain to raise a portcullis and advance to [7].

◇ Chest

7 Sunlit Cavern

Raid another chest on your way into this large, open-air cavern. Descend to the bottom to find another chest, then go back up and proceed to [8].

◇ Chest   ◇ Chest (Locked: Novice)

8 Sanctum Access

Slay a powerful Draugr here, then loot one more chest before opening the door and entering the Bleak Falls Sanctum.

◇ Chest (Locked: Apprentice)

B Door to Bleak Falls Sanctum

Bleak Falls Sanctum

Swinging blades slice through the hall that leads to the Sanctum's first chamber. Before sprinting through, lure a patrolling Draugr to its doom by striking the monster with a ranged attack to make it charge recklessly into the blades. Sprint past the trap afterward, then quickly pull the wall chain on the opposite side to deactivate it—this lets you safely retreat as the undead begin to swarm.

Next, inspect the Golden Claw that you found on poor Arvel, and notice the three glyphs that run down its palm. Mimic this same sequence of glyphs (bear, moth, owl) on the strange mural at the end of this passage by spinning its three glyph rings. Once the glyphs have been properly aligned, activate the claw insignia in the mural's center to insert the Golden Claw and open the way forward.

Make your way to the far end of the large, sunlit cavern that follows the Nordic Puzzle Door. Raid a giant chest and then follow the sound of chanting to discover a Word Wall, which grants you a new Word of Power. Learning this new talent causes a powerful enemy to rise from the nearby sarcophagus—fight hard to slay this worthy adversary, then obtain a special item from its remains. Scale the nearby steps afterward and exit this unholy place via the west passage, looting one last chest on your way out. Find a potion on the exterior ledge before fast-traveling away.

◇ Danger! Oil Lamp Traps

◇ Danger! Oil Pool Traps

◇ Danger! Swinging Blade Trap (wall chain)

◇ Word Wall: Unrelenting Force [1/1]

◇ Dragonstone (Draugr Scourge Lord)

◇ Chests (2)

[8.19] Anise's Cabin

Related Quests

Dungeon Activity

Dungeon: Special

Anise

Crafting

Alchemy Lab

Arcane Enchanter

Recommended Level: 6

Collectibles

Skill Book [Alchemy]: Song of the Alchemists [E2/10]

Knapsack

Apothecary's Satchels (2)

Potions

Loose gear

In northern Falkreath, not far from the town of Riverwood, a kindly old woman named Anise lives in a simple cabin. Take the Skill Book near the bed inside, then pick the Novice-level trapdoor and slip into Anise's cellar to discover a small alchemist's study. A note on a bench down here reveals that Anise is in fact a witch! Beware: the old woman will attack you when you leave, hoping to protect her secret.

[8.20] Cracked Tusk Keep

Related Quests

Daedric Quest: Pieces of the Past

Recommended Level: 6

Dungeon: Bandit Camp

Ghunzul

Orc

Crafting

Alchemy Lab

Blacksmith Forge

Grindstone

Workbench

Dangers

Dart Trap (pedestal pressure plate)

Swinging Wall Trap (tripwire)

Quest Items

Shards of Mehrune's Razor

Collectibles

Skill Book [Light Armor]: Rislav the Righteous [C2/10]

Skill Book [Smithing]: Light Armor Forging

Chests

Potions aplenty

Loose gear

This old, abandoned Imperial Fort on Falkreath's western border has been taken over by Orcish bandits. Unlike a true Orcish stronghold, the Orcs here are implacably hostile and will attack you on sight. The leader of these brigands, the warlord Ghunzul, is a follower of Mehrunes Dagon and possesses the shattered blade fragments of Mehrunes' Razor—a quest item for Daedric Quest: Pieces of the Past.

Exterior

Try to pick off the exterior guards from range, or sneak into the fort via one of the two crumbling northern towers. After dispatching the guards, search the forge area for loose gear, then claim the two chests: one in the northwest tower and one high atop the roof of the keep. A Skill Book sits on a table near the Workbench.

◇ Crafting: Blacksmith Forge, Grindstone, Workbench

◇ Skill Book [Smithing]: Light Armor Forging

◇ Chest (Locked: Master)

◇ Chest (Locked: Apprentice)

◇ Loose gear

Cracked Tusk Keep (Interior)

The keep features three access points: a front door, a basement door to the north, and a rooftop trapdoor atop the southeast tower (cross the lookout platforms along the stronghold's exterior walls to reach it).

If you have solid lockpicking skills, pick the locked basement door (Locked: Novice) and the wall cage just inside and to the right (Locked: Expert), and you can enter the vaults without having to fight any of the enemies in the Keep.

Otherwise, enter the front door and dispatch the two Orcs there, then take the southeast door to the tower. There, you'll find a brute named Ghunzul—slay or pickpocket him to obtain a useful key (the same key can be found on a nearby nightstand). Loot the large chest in Ghunzul's room before heading down into the keep's basement, where you can use the key you found on Ghunzul to open the wall cage. Then press the button to lower the gate that blocks the stairwell. Continue down to the lower vaults.

◇ Crafting: Alchemy Lab   ◇ Chest

◇ Cracked Tusk Vault Key   ◇ Potions

◇ Cracked Tusk Vault Key (Ghunzul)   ◇ Loose gear

Cracked Tusk Keep Vaults

Loot the two side rooms as you enter the Vaults, finding a Skill Book on a bench in one of the rooms. Then raid a chest that lies near a pair of levers that open a gate. Slowly walk forward to safely trigger the Vault's central trip wires without suffering harm. The trip wire to the left triggers a lethal swinging spike trap and is best avoided. Loot a chest among the room's side rubble and stand to one side of the far pedestal before removing the Shards of Mehrune's Razor—darts shoot down from the ceiling in front of the pedestal when you remove them.

◇ Area Is Locked (Expert/Key)

◇ Danger! Dart Trap (trip wire, pressure pedestal), Swinging Wall Trap (trip wire)

◇ Shards of Mehrune's Razor

◇ Skill Book [Light Armor]: Rislav the Righteous [C2/10]

◇ Chest

◇ Chest (Locked: Novice)

◇ Potions aplenty

◇ Loose gear

[8.21] Halldir's Cairn

Related Quests

Other Factions: Bards College Quest: Rjorn's Drum

Dungeon Activity

Recommended Level: 6

Dungeon: Draugr Crypt

Draugr

Ghost

Halldir

Dangers

Battering Ram Trap (trip wire)

Bone Alarm Trap

Flamethrower Trap (hinge trigger)

Swinging Wall Trap (pressure plate)

Puzzles

Nordic Pillars

Collectibles

Unique Weapon: Halldir's Staff [56/80]
Chest(s)
Potions
Loose gear

Take the southwest road out of Falkreath's capital, and you'll end up discovering this long-forgotten tomb.

Cairn Chamber

A spectral beam of energy rises from the large cairn in the tomb's first chamber, and the bodies of several adventurers lie strewn around it. Collect a key and informative journal from a nearby pedestal, then use the key to open the nearby door and head upstairs.

◇ Key to Halldir's Crypt   ◇ Loose gear

Ghostly Catacombs

Slay the ghosts of the fallen that materialize around you as you navigate the catacombs upstairs. When you come to a pressure plate, stand on it to safely trigger the swinging wall trap ahead. Slip around the trap after triggering it to locate a valuable potion. Pick up the path again and do your best to avoid the cluster of hanging bones that can alert the Ghosts and Draugr ahead. When you reach a portcullis, pull the lever behind the nearby throne to raise it.

◇ Danger! Bone Alarm Trap, Swinging   ◇ Potion
  Wall Trap (pressure plate)
                                        ◇ Loose gear

Nordic Pillars

Rotate three pillars in the passages that follow, facing each pillar's glyphs to match the pair of glyphs that appear on the opposite wall (Hawk, Snake, Whale). Pull the nearby lever to open a passage that leads deeper into the crypts. Before heading through, see if you can unlock the Adept-level iron door near the Snake glyphs to access a small treasure nook.

◇ Chest (Locked: Adept)   ◇ Loose gear
◇ Potions

Secret Passage

Ignore the stairs to the north and carefully set off a trip wire as you follow the secret passage to its far end, where you find a trapped chest. Disarm the hinge trigger or stand as far north of the chest as possible when opening it to avoid being burned alive by flames that spray from a nearby statue. Double back after looting the chest and take the north stairs to reach Halldir's Tomb.

◇ Danger! Battering Ram Trap (tripwire), Flamethrower Trap
◇ Potion
◇ Loose gear

Halldir's Tomb

As you set foot in Halldir's Tomb, his spirit materializes in the energy beam in the room's center and steps forward to confront you. Halldir's ghost wields a range of powerful Destruction spells, including a unique special ability: When reduced to about two-thirds of his health, he splits his essence into three elemental forms. Quickly take out one of these (the Storm form by the throne is a good choice), or you'll be overwhelmed. Once you defeat all three forms, Halldir coalesces once more and fights until you reduce him to ash.

Search Halldir's remains to obtain a unique weapon, then scour the room for items, gold, and a boss chest. When you're ready to leave, open the central trapdoor and carefully drop from ledge to ledge as you descend to the crypt's entry chamber.

◇ Unique Weapon: Halldir's Staff [56/80] (Halldir)
◇ Chest
◇ Loose gear

Habitation: Special

Astrid
Arnbjorn
Babette (Alchemy Trader/Trainer: Alchemy)
Cicero
Festus Krex
Gabriella
Lis (Frostbite Spider)
Nazir (Trainer: Light Armor)
The Night Mother
Veezara

Services

Trader (Apothecary): Babette [10/12]
    Potions, Ingredients, Misc
Trainer (Alchemy: Master): Babette [3/3]
Trainer (Light Armor: Master): Nazir [2/3]
Unique Weapon: Blade of Woe [57/80]
Unusual Gem: Stone of Barenziah [21/24]

Related Quests

Dark Brotherhood Quest: With Friends Like These...
Dark Brotherhood Quest: Sanctuary
Dark Brotherhood Quest: Sentenced to Death
Dark Brotherhood Quest: Whispers in the Dark
Dark Brotherhood Quest: The Silence Has Been Broken
Dark Brotherhood Quest: Bound Until Death
Dark Brotherhood Quest: Breaching Security
Dark Brotherhood Quest: The Cure for Madness
Dark Brotherhood Quest: Recipe for Disaster
Dark Brotherhood Quest: To Kill an Empire
Dark Brotherhood Quest: Death Incarnate
Dark Brotherhood Quest: Hail Sithis!
Dark Brotherhood Quest: Honor Thy Family
Dark Brotherhood Quest: The Feeble Fortune*
Dark Brotherhood Quest: Side Contracts (All)
Thieves Guild Radiant Quest: No Stone Unturned

Recommended Level: 8

Crafting

Alchemy Lab
Anvil
Arcane Enchanter
Grindstone
Workbench

Collectibles

Skill Book [Alteration]: Sithis [D2/10]
Skill Book [Sneak]: Sacred Witness [C2/10]
Unique Item: Shrouded Armor [69/112]
Unique Item: Shrouded Boots [70/112]
Unique Item: Shrouded Cowl [71/112]
Unique Item: Shrouded Gloves [72/112]
Unique Item: Shrouded Cowl Maskless [73/112]
Unique Item: Shrouded Hand Wraps [74/112]
Unique Item: Shrouded Hood [75/112]
Unique Item: Shrouded Robes [76/112]
Unique Item: Shrouded Shoes [77/112]
Unique Item: Nightweaver's Band [78/112]
Unusual Gem: Stone of Barenziah [21/24]

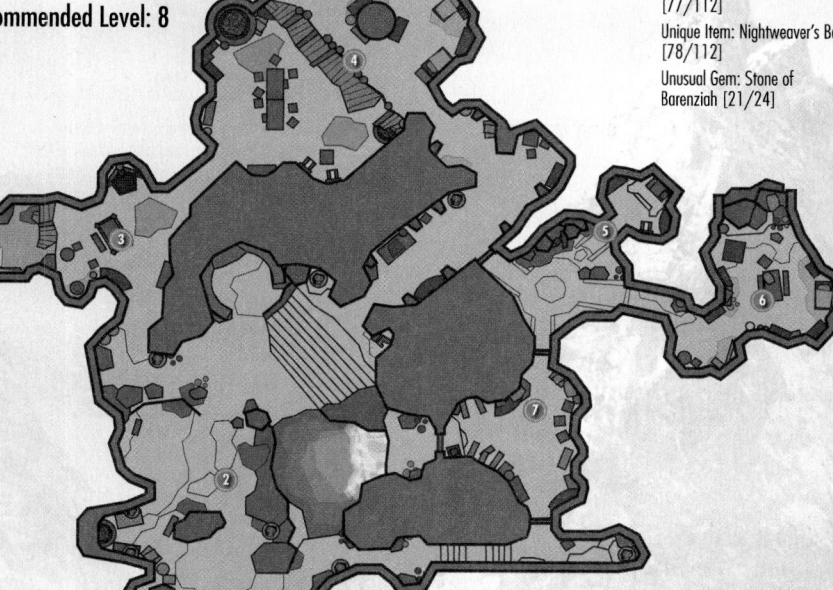

Special Objects

Word Wall: Marked for Death [2/3]
Area Is Locked (quest required)
Chest(s)
Potions
Loose gear

Follow the road west out of Falkreath until you spy a dirt trail running downhill to your right. The trail leads down to the foreboding "Black Door" — the ominous entrance to the Dark Brotherhood's hidden haven. You're denied entry to this clandestine lair until you manage to impress the Dark Brotherhood; do this by completing their first quest, "Innocence Lost." Wait until you receive a message from the Dark Brotherhood. Then, the next time you sleep, you'll automatically begin their second quest, "With Friends Like These..." That's your chance to get in good with the Brotherhood!

A — Exit to Skyrim

1 — Astrid's Foyer and Bedroom

Claim a Skill Book from the pedestal shelf in the foyer, then find an Unusual Gem in Astrid's bedchamber to the west. This is a part of Thieves Guild Radiant Quest: No Stone Unturned.

- ◇ Skill Book [Alteration]: Sithis [D2/10]
- ◇ Unique Item: Shrouded Cowl Maskless [73/112]
- ◇ Unique Item: Shrouded Hand Wraps [74/112]
- ◇ Unique Item: Shrouded Hood [75/112]
- ◇ Unique Item: Shrouded Robes [76/112]
- ◇ Unique Item: Shrouded Shoes [77/112]
- ◇ Unusual Gem: Stone of Barenziah [21/24]
- ◇ Loose gear

2 — Main Chamber

Meet the Family for the first time in this wide cavern, then approach the nearby Word Wall to gain a new Word of Power.

- ◇ Crafting: Anvil, Grindstone, Workbench
- ◇ Word Wall: Marked for Death [2/3]
- ◇ Loose gear

3 — Laboratory

Find a few ingredients in this side chamber, along with the Alchemy and Enchanting stations. Gabriella's pet Frostbite Spider, Lis, resides in the small cavern down below—leave it be, for it won't harm you. Search the remains of a poor soul named Gaston Bellefort near the watery pool to find a note that indicates how he came to meet his end.

- ◇ Crafting: Alchemy Lab, Arcane Enchanter
- ◇ Apothecary's Satchel
- ◇ Loose gear

4 — Dining Hall and Sleeping Quarters

Other than food, there's little of interest in the dining area, but a chests awaits looting upstairs.

- ◇ Chest (Locked: Novice)
- ◇ Loose gear

5 — Babette's Room

Swipe a valuable Skill Book from Babette's small bedchamber.

- ◇ Skill Book [Sneak]: Sacred Witness [C2/10]

6 — Storage Room/Cicero's Room

Initially just an unused junk room, this chamber is cleaned up (slightly) when Cicero arrives in the Sanctuary.

- ◇ Loose gear

7 — Night Mother's Chamber

A unique stained glass window dominates this room, which features secure iron doors. When Cicero and the Night Mother arrive, her coffin is given the place of honor in this chamber. Pillage a knapsack on a shelf here.

8 — Astrid's Safe Room

A wardrobe in Astrid's bedroom conceals the entrance to this long-forgotten room. This chamber is only accessible during Dark Brotherhood Quest: Death Incarnate; consult that quest for further details.

[8.23] Roadside Ruins

Recommended Level: 6

Dungeon: Spriggan Grove

- Spriggan

Collectibles

Skill Book [Enchanting]: Catalogue of Weapon Enchantments [C2/10]

Chest

As you might expect, these ruins lie along the road and are found just west of Falkreath's capital. Slay a Spriggan here and loot the bodies of dispatched bandits, along with a chest. Claim the Skill Book that lies against the chest as well.

[8.24] Falkreath Watchtower

Recommended Level: 6

Dungeon: Warlock Lair

- Mage

Collectibles

Skill Book [Conjuration]: Liminal Bridges [C2/10]

Chest

This ruined tower lies between Falkreath's capital and Lake Ilinalta and has become the home of a powerful, twisted mage. Slay the wicked spellweaver so you may scale the tower and raid a chest at its apex. A Skill Book rests inside the tent up here.

[8.25] North Shriekwind Bastion

This site marks the northern entrance to Shriekwind Bastion, a cave passage that runs through the mountains north of Falkreath's capital. Passing through this cave allows you to quickly cut through the mountains and places you near a Word Wall.

Dungeon: Vampire Lair

- Skeleton
- Vampire

Dangers

- Battering Ram Traps (pressure plates)
- Flamethrower Traps (handle)

Underground Connection: South

Shriekwind Bastion [8.26]

Collectibles

Skill Book [Speech]: 2920, Second Seed, v5

Special Objects

Word Wall: Elemental Fury [3/3]

Chest(s)

Potions

Loose gear

Shriekwind Bastion

Exterior

Before entering North Shriekwind Bastion (or after exiting the pass, if you've traveled up from the south), make a long trek up a snowy path that leads to the exterior ruin. You'll find a locked chest at the top.

- ◇ Chest (Locked: Novice)

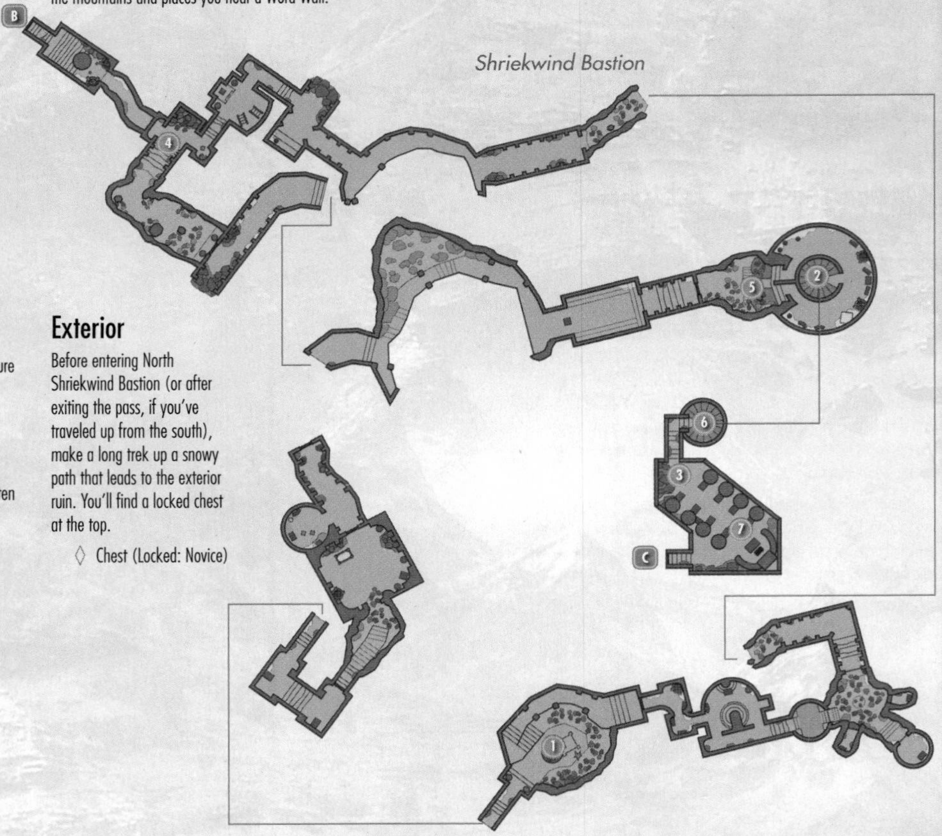

A Exit to Skyrim (North Shriekwind Bastion)

1 Main Cavern

Slay a vampire and loot a chest in the bastion's first few chambers, making your way to this massive cavern. A handle here activates a rising floor trap in the lower chamber, but ignore this and head upstairs, slaying a Skeleton Archer on your way to [2].

◇ Chest   ◇ Potions   ◇ Loose gear

2 Altar Chamber

Claim loot from several receptacles in this small, quiet chamber before advancing to [3].

◇ Chest   ◇ Potions

3 Junction Chamber

Pull a wall chain to raise a portcullis and enter this small chamber, where three handles are found on a central dais. Turn each handle to open two secret nooks that each contain loose gear, along with the room's south portcullis. Loot the chest to the south, then notice three chains on the wall above. Pull the left chain to open the north portcullis and make your way back to [1], smashing more skeletons and avoiding a pair of pressure plates along the way.

◇ Danger! Battering Ram Traps (pressure plates)
◇ Chest (Locked: Apprentice)
◇ Loose gear

4 South Access Entry

Slaughter skeletons and sidestep pressure plates in the long tunnel that leads back to [1]. Navigate the next passage to reach this small, dark alcove, where you find valuable gear. Search the alcove's walls to discover a chain that exposes a secret passage when pulled. The passage leads outside to South Shriekwind Bastion [8.26]. Head through if you're in a hurry to cut through the mountains. Ignore the passage and continue exploring the bastion otherwise, making your way back to [1] on your way to [5].

B Exit to Skyrim (South Shriekwind Bastion)

◇ Loose gear

5 Fire Trap Passage

This chamber lies above [2], but the two rooms are not connected. Turn the handle on the pedestal here to open the far portcullis. Unfortunately, this also causes multiple flamethrowers to ignite in the room's center. Crouch and creep past the flames, slipping between the high points where opposing spouts intersect.

◇ Danger! Flamethrower Traps (handle)

6 Master Vampire's Lair

Open the door beyond the flamethrowers to at last arrive at the head vampire's lair. Slay the master vampire, then search the rear circular passage to locate a large chest. Claim a Skill Book that rests atop a podium near the steps, then scale the spiral staircase that follows to ascend to the bastion's highest levels.

◇ Skill Book [Speech]: 2920, Second Seed, v5
◇ Chest

7 Word Wall Chamber

Slay the powerful Draugr that bursts out from this large chamber's central sarcophagus, then approach the nearby Word Wall to gain a new Word of Power. Claim potions from the nearby pedestals and raid the chest that's nestled between the statues before stepping outside via the nearby door for a spectacular view provided by the Shriekwind Overlook.

◇ Word Wall: Elemental Fury   ◇ Chest
  [3/3]   ◇ Potions

C Exit to Skyrim (Shriekwind Overlook)

[8.26] South Shriekwind Bastion

Recommended Level: 6

Dungeon: Vampire Lair
Draugr
Skeleton

Underground Connection: North Shriekwind Bastion [8.25]
Chest

This site marks the southern entrance to Shriekwind Bastion, a large and cavernous passage through the mountains north of Falkreath's capital. Beware the undead Draugr that guard the bastion's southern ruins and search the snowy ledge below the pass's entry point to discover a chest. See the previous location entry for North Shriekwind Bastion [8.25] and learn what lies within the pass.

[8.27] Peak's Shade Tower

Related Quests
Daedric Quest: Ill Met By Moonlight

Recommended Level: 6

Dungeon: Spriggan Grove
Spriggan

Collectible
Chest

This small, shattered tower lies just east of Falkreath's capital. Dispatch the lone Spriggan that guards the place, then loot the long-forgotten chest inside, which is hidden by growth.

[8.28] Pinewatch

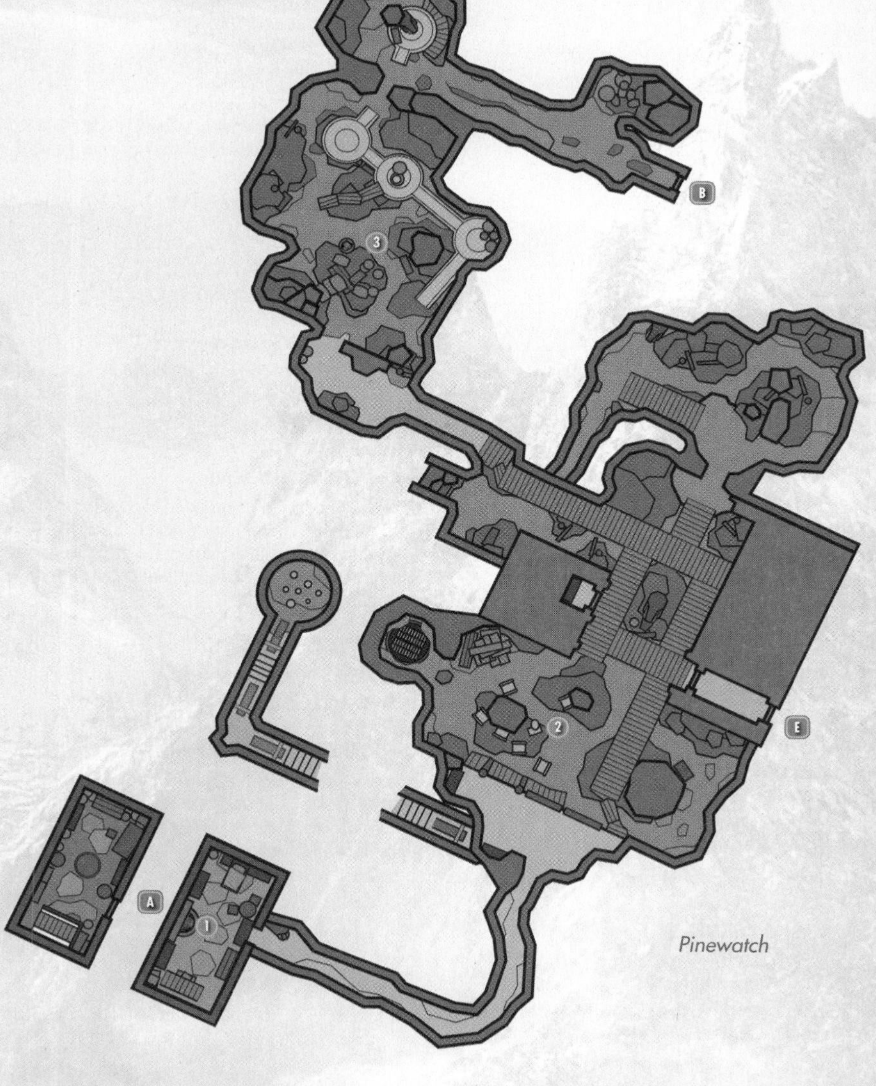

Pinewatch

Follow the main road east out of Falkreath's capital to locate this small cabin. Use the simple crafting stations around back if you like, then pick the Adept-level door lock to enter and raid the cabin.

Related Quests

Thieves Guild Radiant Quest: No Stone Unturned

Thieves Guild City Influence Quest: Silver Lining

Dungeon Activity

Recommended Level: 6

Dungeon: Bandit Camp

Bandit

Rhorlak

Rigel Strong-Arm

Crafting

Grindstone

Tanning Rack

Workbench

Dangers

Battering Ram Trap (pressure plates)

Bear Traps

Bone Alarm Trap

Dart Trap (pressure plate)

Flail Trap (trapped door)

Spear Trap (pressure plate)

Swinging Blade Trap (pressure plate)

Trapped Chest

Quest Items

Endon's Silver Mold

Collectibles

Skill Book [Sneak]: The Red Kitchen Reader

Unusual Gem: Stone of Barenziah [22/24]

Chest(s)

Potions aplenty

Loose gear

Pinewatch Bandit's Sanctuary

> **NOTE** A skilled thief can slip through all of Pinewatch without having to fight a single bandit — see if you're up to the challenge!

A Exit to Skyrim

1 Cabin

Find a note in the cabin's basement that reveals the existence of a hidden passage. Spy a shelf with wind gusting out from its base, then locate a button on the nearby wall and press it to shift the shelf and expose a secret passage.

2 Body Disposal

Claim some potions and a Skill Book from a shelf to your left as you enter this first wide cavern. Slay the two guards who patrol the wooden walkways and see if you can open the Expert-level wooden door to access a potion-filled closet. Beware of bear traps on the ground floor, and raid a locked chest to the east. Enter the south tunnel to visit a gruesome pit with several lootable corpses.

◊ Danger! Bear Traps

◊ Skill Book [Sneak]: The Red Kitchen Reader

◊ Potions aplenty

◊ Loose gear

3 Crumbling Cavern

Cross the wooden walkways to visit this chamber, which is guarded by a few more bandits. Secure the place and then loot the lopsided chest on the central rubble. Scale a winding ramp to find another chest up north before proceeding through the east door to the Bandit's Sanctuary.

◊ Crafting: Grindstone

◊ Chest

◊ Chest (Locked: Novice)

B Door to Pinewatch Bandit's Sanctuary

C Door to Pinewatch

4 Sanctuary Entry

Hug the southeast wall to sneak past the bandits that are gathered around a table in the sanctuary's first chamber, but beware of bear traps.

If you fight the men, you'll find that each possesses a letter that hints of treachery. Unfortunately, none of them carry keys for the two locked chests here.

◊ Danger! Bear Traps, Bone Alarm Trap

◊ Chest (Locked: Novice)

◊ Chest (Locked: Expert)

5 Cage Cavern

Slay or pickpocket the lone patrolling guard here to obtain a key that unlocks one of the nearby cages.

◊ Danger! Bear Traps

◊ Pinewatch Key (Bandit)

6 Sarcophagi Room

Cut down another bandit here, then open the Adept-level locked door to access a treasure nook with a plethora of valuables. Stand to one side of the chest when opening it to avoid being impaled. The Unusual Gem you find here pertains to Thieves Guild Radiant Quest: No Stone Unturned.

◊ Danger! Trapped Chest

◊ Unusual Gem: Stone of Barenziah [22/24]

◊ Potions

◊ Loose gear

7 Sleeping Area and Bar

Read one of the many notes that are pinned to the wall on your way to this area — it confirms the treachery hinted at before, as does another note on a table here. Silently dispatch a sleeping bandit, then kill the group of ruffians to the east, near the bar. Find worthy gear and a few potions behind the counter.

◊ Potions

◊ Loose gear

8 Rigel's Quarters

Rigel Strong-Arm, leader of the bandits, sleeps behind this room's wooden wall — dodge the hanging rattles or you'll wake her. Loot the chest near

Rigel's bed and see if you can pickpocket a few useful keys off of her without being caught. Try sneaking away if she wakes up. Open the far Master-locked door with the Pinewatch Treasure Room Key.

◊ Danger! Bone Alarm Trap

◊ Crafting: Workbench

◊ Pinewatch Key (Rigel Strong-Arm)

◊ Pinewatch Treasure Room Key (Rigel Strong-Arm)

◊ Chest (Locked: Apprentice)

◊ Potions

◊ Loose gear

9 Treasure Room

Due to the attempts by her crew to steal her plunder, Rigel has placed a large amount of traps blocking the path to her treasure room. Watch out for a pressure plate on either end of the narrow bridge, as they will trigger a wide volley of darts traps. A set of blade traps cover the hall just after this. Find the rhythm of their swings, then sprint through, but stop just short of the next hall — there is a pressure plate there that will trigger a battering ram to slam into the side of your head if you are not careful! Crouch and stand back while opening the room's door to avoid being struck by a mace that swings through. Beware of another pressure plate near the table that holds Endon's Silver Mold, among other valuables. Raid the large nearby chest before exiting through the door to return to Pinewatch's entry chamber.

◊ Danger! Battering Ram Trap (pressure plates), Swinging Blade Trap (pressure plate), Spear Trap (pressure plate), Flail Trap (trapped door), Dart Trap (pressure plate)

◊ Endon's Silver Mold

◊ Chest

◊ Potion

◊ Loose gear

D Door to Pinewatch

E Door to Pinewatch Bandit's Sanctuary

[8.29] Angi's Camp

Related Quests

Side Quest: The Great Skyrim
Treasure Hunt*

Dungeon Quest: Composure, Speed,
and Precision*

Angi

Recommended Level: 12

Crafting

Tanning Rack

Workbench

Collectibles

Skill Book [Archery]: The Gold
Ribbon of Merit [C2/10]

Treasure Map V [9/11]

Unique Weapon: Angi's Bow
[58/80]

Chest

Loose gear

In Falkreath's frigid southern mountains, a female hunter named Angi struggles to make a life for herself at a remote cabin. Loot a chest and collect the Skill Book inside the cabin, then find a Treasure Map stashed in the end table. A few crafting stations can be found outside.

Angi is friendly, as long as you don't threaten her. She'll even give you a bow and offer to teach you how to use it—follow Angi to a nearby practice range, ask her for some practice arrows, then shoot the targets exactly as she instructs. Your Archery skill will increase as you impress Angi with your marksmanship. Complete all of Angi's challenges to receive a unique bow.

[8.30] The Guardian Stones

Recommended Level: 6

Dungeon: Special

Special Objects

Standing Stone: The Mage Stone [10/13]

Standing Stone: The Thief Stone [11/13]

Standing Stone: The Warrior Stone [12/13]

On a rocky bluff overlooking the spot where Lake Ilinalta flows into the White River, a trio of rune-covered stones keep watch. You may have noticed this site while making your way to Riverwood [6.27] after fleeing from Helgen [8.32] at the start of your adventure. Inspect each Standing Stone to view and accept one of three sign blessings, each of which will allow you to improve a particular set of skills more quickly. Note that you can have only one sign blessing at a time, so activating any of these Stones will replace your current sign blessing (if any).

[8.31] Embershard Mine

Recommended Level: 6

Dungeon: Bandit Camp

Bandits

Crafting

Blacksmith Forge

Grindstone

Workbench

Dangers

Rockfall (trip wire)

Collectibles

Skill Book [Smithing]: Light
Armor Forging [D2/10]

Chest(s)

Loose gear

These mines, which lie just southwest of Riverwood [6.27], have been overrun by ruthless bandits. Slay the exterior guard before heading inside.

Drawbridge Cavern

Carefully stand back and trigger the trip wire in the entry tunnel, then wait for a guard to fall asleep in the cavern that follows before slaying him and his comrade. Run past a raised drawbridge and take a side passage to locate a lever that lowers the bridge. If you've taken out the bandits in this cavern, be prepared for more as you lower the bridge. Alternatively, if you somehow lower the drawbridge without dispatching the bandits, then they will have no backup.

◊ Danger! Rockfall (trip wire)

Prison Cell Passage

Cross the drawbridge to reach a passage with several holding cells. Slay the inattentive guard and collect a key from his corpse. Use the key to open the nearby gate and loot a large chest. Proceed to the next chamber afterward.

◊ Embershard Mine Key   ◊ Chest
  (Bandit)
                             ◊ Loose gear

Crafting Cavern

Dispatch several stalwart bandits in the next cavern, entering via the left wooden walkway to maintain an elevated vantage. Collect the Skill Book that lies on the table near the crafting stations. Search the small side cavern to the south to locate a chest, then take a winding passage to discover a second chest on a ledge near the main cavern's waterfall. When you're ready to move along, cross the rope bridge and exit the mine via its rear entrance.

◊ Crafting: Blacksmith Forge,   ◊ Chest
  Grindstone, Workbench
                                   ◊ Chest (Locked: Novice)
◊ Skill Book [Smithing]: Light
  Armor Forging [D2/10]   ◊ Loose gear

[8.32] Helgen

Related Quests

Main Quest: Unbound

Main Quest: Before the Storm

Civil War Quest: Joining the Legion

Civil War Quest: Joining the Stormcloaks

Habitation: Town

Animal	Priestess of Arkay
Gunjar	Ralof
Hadvar	Stormcloak Soldier
Imperial Captain	Tillius
Imperial Soldier	Torturer
Jarl Ulfric Stormcloak	

Dangers

Oil Pool Trap

Collectibles

Chests

Potions

Loose gear

The village of Helgen is the very first location that you visit in Skyrim—you're brought here to be executed at the adventure's onset. Things don't go as planned, however, and you're soon making a frantic run through Helgen Keep. The soldier you choose to follow through the keep determines the enemies you face within.

After your escape from Helgen, the village remains in ruins for the rest of the game. Bandits will eventually move in; you can return here and wipe them out if you choose.

Helgen Keep

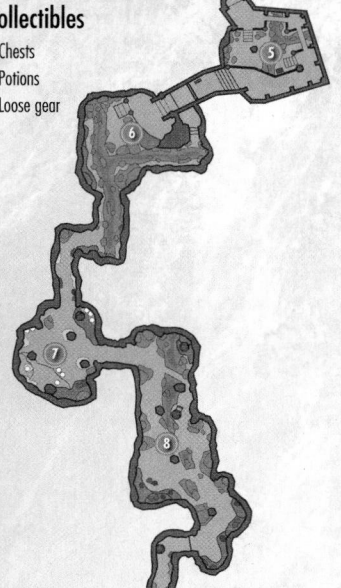

(A) Exit to Skyrim

(1) Northwest Entry

This is the room you enter if you choose to enter the keep with Hadvar. Allow him to free you from your bonds, then loot two chests in this first room to obtain vital gear. Grab the weapons that are scattered about as well, and be sure to equip everything you've just claimed. A special key rests within the Warden's Chest as well.

◇ Warden's Chest ◇ Chest
◇ Helgen Keep Key (Warden's Chest) ◇ Loose gear

(2) North Entry

This is where you enter the keep if you choose to follow Ralof. Let him untie your bonds, then loot the body of a fallen Stormcloak Soldier named Gunjar to obtain vital gear. Take cover and slay the Imperial Captain and Soldier who storm the room after a few moments; then loot their bodies for improved arms. Stop by [1] to raid the place before following Ralof to [3].

(3) Kitchen

A sudden cave-in, courtesy of the attacking dragon, forces you to take a detour through the kitchen. Dispatch a few more enemy soldiers here, then search the barrel that your comrade indicates to discover valuable potions. Additional potions can be found around the room.

◇ Potions aplenty

(4) Torture Room

Secure this frightening chamber, then search around to obtain more gear. If the Torturer encountered here is slain, claim his unique hood. Find some lockpicks on the counter and more in a knapsack on the central table and use them to open the cages. This improves your Lockpicking skill and lets you claim the goods within, including a spell tome that grants you a new spell once examined. Take the interesting book near the knapsack as well for future reference.

◇ Book: The Book of the Dragonborn ◇ Potion
◇ Knapsack ◇ Loose gear

(5) Waterfall Chamber

Open some jail cells to discover a coin purse on your way to this wide chamber, where more enemy soldiers await. See if you can ignite the oily floor beneath the distant archers' feet to burn them up. Relieve them of their bows and arrows after the fight.

◇ Danger! Oil Pool Trap

(6) Drawbridge Cavern

The raging dragon attacks again as you enter this cavern, sealing off the drawbridge passage that you took to get here. Your ally rushes off to the south, but follow the east stream first to locate a potion and coin purse near a skeleton.

◇ Potion

(7) Spider Nest

A pack of ravenous Frostbite Spiders descend on you in this webby cavern. Slaughter them without mercy.

(8) Bear Den

Sneak past the wild bear here by crouching and moving very slowly along the east wall. Or take aim and try and slay the dangerous animal with your newfound bow before it can close in.

(B) Exit to Skyrim

[8.33] South Skybound Watch

Recommended Level: 6

Underground Connection: North Skybound Watch [8.34]

Chest (Locked: Novice)

This abandoned tower marks the southern entrance to Skybound Watch Pass, which runs through Falkreath's frosty eastern mountains. Navigate the pass to emerge at North Skybound Watch [8.34]. See that location's section for complete details on what awaits you within the pass.

Climb the tower to claim a chest and take in the amazing view of Falkreath to the west. When leaving, beware the Wispmother that haunts the woods just outside—you may find it easier to Fast-Travel away or return through the pass than to venture out along the cliffside.

[8.34] North Skybound Watch

Related Quests

College of Winterhold Radiant Quest: Destruction Ritual Spell

Dungeon: Bandit Camp

Animal
Bandit

Dangers

Battering Ram Trap (pressure plate)
Dart Trap (hinge trigger)

Underground Connection: South Skybound Watch [8.33]

Collectibles

Skill Book [Block]: Battle of Red Mountain [B1/10]
Chest(s)
Potions
Loose gear

An underground passage runs through Falkreath's frigid eastern mountains. This site, located north of Orphan Rock [8.35], marks the passage's north entrance, which is surrounded by ruins.

Exterior

Dispatch the bandits within the ruins, then open the wooden door behind them to exit onto the northern balcony. Take a moment to admire the view; if the weather is just right, you can even see the ocean in the distance. The pedestal here is the second of three you need for the College of Winterhold Radiant Quest: Destruction Ritual Spell.

Loot a chest to the left and swipe a Skill Book off the nearby shelf before descending some steps to locate the door that serves as the pass's northern entrance.

◇ Chest (Locked: Novice)

Skybound Watch Pass (Interior)

No matter which way you enter the pass, it's a straight sprint to the other end. Slaughter several bandits and a Giant Frostbite Spider as you navigate this relatively short passage, and beware the trapped chest at the tunnel's south end; disarm it or open it carefully to avoid the dart

trap. Find another chest near the north campfire, along with a potion and Skill Book.

◇ Danger! Battering Ram Trap (pressure plate)

◇ Danger! Dart Trap (hinge trigger) ◇ Chest
◇ Skill Book [Block]: Battle of Red Mountain [B1/10] ◇ Potion
  ◇ Loose gear

[8.35] Orphan Rock

Related Quests

Temple Quest: The Blessings of Nature
Dungeon Activity

Dungeon: Hagraven Nest

Hag
Hagraven

Crafting

Arcane Enchanter

Dangers

Rune Trap (ground)
Spikes (ground)

Quest Items

Nettlebane (Hagraven)

Collectibles

Unique Weapon: Nettlebane [59/80]
Chest
Chest (Locked: Adept)
Loose gear

At the east edge of Falkreath, near the Throat of the World's [6.38] western base, a massive boulder towers over a mossy fallen log. Unless you're playing Temple Quest: Blessings of Nature, there's little to do here aside from looting a skeleton that lies inside the log. During the "Blessings of Nature" quest, beware of rune traps and sharp spikes placed around the boulder as you slay a few hags and a dangerous Hagraven to obtain a quest-related item—a fallen log now lets you reach the top of the boulder, where a chest and Arcane Enchanter are found. Loot a locked chest in one of the hags' surrounding tents as well.

[8.36] Falkreath Stormcloak Camp

Related Quests

Civil War Quest: Liberation of Skyrim
Civil War Quest: Rescue from Fort Neugrad

Habitation: Military: Stormcloak Camp

Stormcloak Quartermaster (Blacksmith)
Stormcloak Soldier

Services

Trader (Blacksmith): Stormcloak Quartermaster [27/33]
Weapons, Apparel, Misc

Crafting

Alchemy Lab
Anvil
Grindstone
Workbench

Special Objects

Civil War: Map of Skyrim
Chests (2)
Potions
Loose gear

The Sons of Skyrim have set up camp in the freezing eastern mountains of Falkreath, though this site may not exist, depending on your progress through the Civil War quest line. Trade with the quartermaster here if you like, or use his array of crafting stations. Inspect the tabletop map in the largest tent to potentially gain new map data. Steal goods from around the camp if your thieving skills are up to the task.

[8.37] Haemar's Shame

Related Quests

Daedric Quest: A Daedra's Best Friend

Recommended Level: 6

Dungeon: Vampire Lair

Animal
Vampire

Crafting

Alchemy Lab
Arcane Enchanter

Collectibles

Skill Book [Destruction]: Response to Bero's Speech [D2/10]
Unique Item: Masque of Clavicus Vile [79/112]
Chest(s)
Loose gear

This frozen cave lies at the eastern reaches of Falkreath. Traveling through it leads to Haemar's Shame — but you must contend with a number of vicious vampires in this forboding place. You visit this site during Daederic Quest: A Daedra's Best Friend.

Haemar's Cavern

Wipe out a vampire's thrall in the first cavern, then scale a ramp to discover a chest atop the wooden lookout. Avoid a lethal trap by sidestepping a pressure plate in the passage that follows, then slay a vampire and descend some wooden stairs. Battle several vampires in the following area, where you find another chest and an Alchemy Lab. Take a narrow passage to reach a wide cavern, where more vampires prowl. Find a Skill Book on a table in a nook surrounded by shelves, then descend more wooden stairs and proceed to Haemar's Shame.

◇ Crafting: Alchemy Lab
◇ Skill Book [Destruction]: Response to Bero's Speech [D2/10]
◇ Chests (2)
◇ Loose gear

Haemar's Shame

Squash a grotesque Frostbite Spider in the Shame's entry passage, then advance to a blood-soaked room with a chest and Arcane Enchanter. Navigate the winding passage that follows to reach a wide chamber with several lively vampires, including their powerful master. Clear the room, then check behind the large statue to find a giant chest. Pull a nearby wall chain to open an exit passage that leads outside.

◇ Crafting: Arcane Enchanter
◇ Chests (2)
◇ Loose gear

[8.38] Bonechill Passage

Dungeon: Animal Den

Animal

Underground Connection: Ancient's Ascent [8.39]

Collectibles:

Skill Book [Heavy Armor]: 2920, MidYear, v6
Knapsack
Potions
Loose gear

At the northern base of Falkreath's southern mountains, wide stone steps lead up to the mouth of a frozen cave. Enter to explore a short, icy passage that leads deeper into the mountains. This passage is the only means of reaching Ancient's Ascent [8.39]. Slay a few dangerous Ice Wraiths within Bonechill Passage, and collect the Skill Book that lies near a fallen bandit.

[8.39] Ancient's Ascent

Dungeon: Dragon Lair

Ice Wraith
Dragon (after Main Quest: Dragon Rising)

Special Objects

Word Wall: Animal Allegiance [2/3]
Chest

One must navigate through Bonechill Passage [8.38] to reach this remote site, which lies high among Falkreath's southern peaks. Dispatch gossamer Ice Wraiths as you ascend the snow-covered steps here, which lead up to an ancient Word Wall. After you complete the "Dragon Rising" quest, a great dragon will make its home here. Slay the beast and obtain your new Word of Power.

[8.40] Bloodlet Throne

Recommended Level: 6

Dungeon: Vampire Lair

Animal
Vampire

Crafting

Alchemy Lab
Arcane Enchanter

Dangers

Flamethrower Traps (pressure plate)
Oil Lamp Traps
Oil Pool Traps

Collectibles

Skill Book [Illusion]: Incident at Necrom [C2/10]
Chests
Potions aplenty
Loose gear

This ominous fortress stands at the edge of Skyrim, deep within Falkreath's southern mountains.

Exterior

Before heading inside, circle around the structure and explore the broken tower on its roof to discover a chest.

◇ Chest
◇ Loose gear

Entry Chambers

Avoid a pressure plate in the small entry chamber and progress until you reach a large chamber with a vampire and thrall. Knock down the hanging lamps here to ignite the oil on the floor and sear these foes. Go downstairs afterward and slay another vampire in the following chamber, which features several potions and an Arcane Enchanter.

◇ Danger! Flamethrower Traps (pressure plate), Oil Lamp Traps, Oil Pool Traps
◇ Apothecary's Satchel
◇ Potions

Rope Bridge Cavern

Proceed through a snowy passage to reach a sizable snowy cavern with a rope bridge. Dispatch the vampires and thralls here, then scale the north stairs and take a passage to reach the vampires' sleeping quarters.

◇ Crafting: Arcane Enchanter

Sleeping Area

A large pack of vampires and thralls reside in their sleeping quarters, which are located north of the rope bridge cavern. Slaughter them all to secure a chest, several potions, and an Alchemy Lab. For a bit more sport, release a wolf from its cage here by picking the cage's Adept-level lock. Open another Adept-level gate in this area to access a storage room with several potions and a Skill Book. When you've finished looting the area, proceed across the rope bridge and pull a wall chain to open the gate you encounter.

◇ Crafting: Alchemy Lab
◇ Skill Book [Illusion]: Incident at Necrom [C2/10]
◇ Chests (2)
◇ Potions aplenty

Wolf Pit

Cross the Rope Bridge Cavern's hanging bridge and open a gate to enter a wide cavern filled with corpses. A nefarious Master Vampire sits on high and taunts you before releasing a few wolves. Slay the beasts and then pull the chain on the west wall to escape your predicament. Defeat the Master Vampire and then loot a large chest as you make your way south, unbarring a door and heading through to return to find yourself back at the entry chambers.

[8.41] Greywater Grotto

Dungeon: Animal Den

Animal

Collectibles

Chest
Loose gear

Bones and bloodstains litter the ground at the mouth of this frozen cave, which lies just south of Helgen [8.32]. Beware the dangerous Snowy Saber Cat that prowls outside — you'll face another inside the cave, along with several wolves and Ice Wolves. Loot the corpses of slain bandits and raid the chest at the cave's far end.

[8.42] Fort Neugrad

Related Quests

Civil War Quest: Liberation of Skyrim

Civil War Quest: Rescue from Fort Neugrad

Side Quest: The Great Skyrim Treasure Hunt*

Recommended Level: 6

Habitation: Military Fort

Bandit (pre-Civil War)

Soldier (Imperial/Stormcloak, depending on the state of the Civil War)

Crafting

Anvil

Forge

Workbench

Dangers

Bear Traps

Collectibles

Skill Book [Light Armor]: Jornibret's Last Dance [B1/10]

Treasure Map (Fort Neugrad Treasure Map): [10/11]

Chest(s)

Potions

Loose gear

This sizable stronghold stands among Falkreath's frigid southern mountains, close to the main road. This fort is a point of contention for the Imperials and Stormcloaks during the Civil War and is filled with ruthless bandits when the Civil War is not active. Attack the fort from the front like a warrior, or sneak around to discover a small gap in the north stockade wall to slip inside. You may also want to take a dip in the southeast lake, where you can find an underwater cave that leads into the prison.

Exterior

Loot the locked chest near the north wooden wall and use some crafting stations before entering the keep's interior or the prison. There's also a treasure chest on the roof of the main tower, though you must pass through the keep to reach it. This chest contains a Treasure Map.

◇ Crafting: Anvil, Forge, Workbench

◇ Treasure Map (Fort Neugrad Treasure Map): [10/11]

◇ Chest (Locked: Novice)

◇ Chest (Locked: Apprentice)

◇ Loose gear

Fort Neugrad Keep

There's only one way inside the Keep, and that's through the main door. Cut down the guards in the entry chamber, then enter either the east or west door and make your way upstairs. Secure the entry chamber's balcony, then go through the southeast door to face the bandits' leader, who carries a useful key and informative journal. Loot the giant chest in the chief's room and claim the nearby Skill Book, then return to the entry chamber and use his key to unlock the door to the library. Downstairs, deal with a powerful Bandit Mage, then claim a second giant chest. Finish exploring the fort to claim more loot, then take the ladder in the second-floor armory to reach a locked chest on the roof.

◇ Skill Book [Light Armor]: Jornibret's Last Dance [B1/10]

◇ Fort Neugrad Library Key (Bandit Chief)

◇ Chests (2)

◇ Potions

◇ Loose gear

Fort Neugrad Prison

If you're sneaking in through the prison, beware the bear trap at the end of the entry tunnel. More bandits lurk in the prison — loot a chest in an upstairs side room, along with a locked chest in the basement that's tucked behind a shelf with potions and a satchel.

◇ Danger! Bear Traps

◇ Chest

◇ Chest (Locked: Apprentice)

◇ Satchel

◇ Potions

◇ Loose gear

[8.43] Southfringe Sanctum

Related Quests

Dungeon Quest: The Savior of Selveni Nethri*

Recommended Level: 6

Dungeon: Special

Animal

Bashnag

Pumpkin

Selveni Nethri

Spellsword

Crafting

Alchemy Lab

Arcane Enchanter

Dangers

Rune Trap (gate)

Collectibles

Chests

Potions

Loose gear

This aptly named cave lies deep in Falkreath's southern mountains, on the fringe of Skyrim. A poor soul named Selveni Nethri has gotten herself into quite a sticky situation here...

Exterior

Slay a Spellsword to secure the cave's entrance. If you like, use the nearby Alchemy Lab to mix up some potions before entering the cave.

◇ Crafting: Alchemy Lab

◇ Apothecary's Satchel

Southfringe Sanctum (Interior)

Loot a chest that's hidden among growth as you navigate the cave's first passage. Beware the rune trap on the wooden gate that leads to the main, sunlit cavern. You now have a choice: either head uphill and slay more Spellswords or take a low, web-filled passage that's teeming with Frostbite Spiders (see the sections that follow). Both options lead toward the same destination: the cave's far end, where a nefarious mage named Bashnag awaits.

◇ Danger! Rune Trap (gate)

◇ Chest

Uphill Ascent

Dispatch several additional Spellswords as you scale the entry chamber's snowy slopes. If you like, release the caged fox named Pumpkin that you encounter after a short distance. Continue uphill, unlocking a wooden gate on your way to the cave's far end, where Bashnag awaits.

◇ Crafting: Arcane Enchanter

Spider Tunnel

As you might expect, the web-filled passage that stems from the sunlit entry cavern is filled with Frostbite Spiders. Loot a chest that's nestled near the wall as you go. After slaying a Giant Frostbite Spider, search the nearby nook to locate a poor soul named Selveni Nethri, who's stuck in a web. Carefully attack the web to free Selveni without harming him, then speak with Selveni to gain a new Side Quest that involves clearing the cave so that he can safely escape on his own. Tell Selveni to wait for now, and continue along to battle Bashnag.

◇ Chest

Bashnag's Chamber

Slay a cruel mage named Bashnag at the cave's far end, then raid the nearby chest and ensure that the entire cave is clear of hostiles before returning to Selveni and telling him that it's safe to leave. Follow Selveni out of the cave to ensure her survival and complete the quest.

◇ Chest

⟨≣⟩ SECONDARY LOCATIONS ⟨≣⟩

[8.A] Dragon Mound: Bilegulch Ridge

Related Quest: Main Quest: Alduin's Wall

This Dragon Mound is initially sealed. It opens during Main Quest: Alduin's Wall. If you visit during or after this point in the Main Quest, the mound will be open and empty.

[8.B] Toadstool Ring: Bilegulch Ridge

Whether you're collecting Bleeding Crown, Namira's Rot, or White Cap, there's an abundance of fungi in a strange ring — a perfect place to gather toadstool ingredients for your alchemy.

[8.C] Hunter's Camp: Sunderstone Gorge

A lone hunter with a slain elk is usually sitting by the fire or hunting the general location of the pathway close to Sunderstone Gorge. The hunter has a chest to steal from, but little else.

◇ Chest

[8.D] A Peddler's Misfortune

A peddler lies dead next to the remains of his overturned cart; his horse is just down the road. It looks like some bandits set an ambush here; the cart is stripped clean, though some bear traps still lie in the road.

◇ Danger! Bear Traps

[8.E] Toppled Tower: Knifepoint Woods

In the shallow grass valley to the north of Knifepoint Ridge are the remains of a small tower, tumbled to the ground years ago. It is now the den for some wild animals. Defeat them before they maul you.

[8.F] Burning Caravan: Evergreen Grove

Due west of Evergreen Grove, the aftermath of a dragon attack reveals two dead horses, burned corpses, and a smoldering caravan. Check the wagon to pry open a chest.

◇ Chest

[8.G] Shrine of Akatosh: Twilight Valley

On the rocky promontory above the entrance to the Twilight Sepulcher is a ceremonial ledge jutting out to a precarious edge, where the Shrine to Akatosh, a Skill Book, and some offerings can be found. Take what you need, receiving blessings if you wish.

◇ Skill Book [Enchanting]: A Tragedy in Black
◇ Shrine of Akatosh [6/6]

[8.H] Fisherman's Camp: Lake Ilinalta

A Fisherman is sitting on some stones close to his tent and boat, surveying the northwestern corner of Lake Ilinalta. Steal from his knapsack if you wish, and find a Skill Book lying on the ground inside the tent. Watch for Slaughterfish in the water.

◇ Skill Book [One-Handed]: Fire and Darkness
◇ Knapsack

[8.I] Sunken Fishing Boat: Lake Ilinalta

Swim southeast from the Fisherman's Camp, peering underwater at the first clump of rocks on the lake bed that you see. Hidden among the weeds is a sunken fishing boat with a locked chest inside.

◇ Chest (Locked: Adept)

[8.J] Dark Elf's Grave

A pauper's Nordic burial ground—a set of rocks and stones with a fluttering flag in the glade northwest of Half-Moon Mill—has the slumped corpse of a Dark Elf at its base. Steal the nearby purse and dagger if you wish.

[8.K] Alchemist's Camp: Evergreen Woods

On the higher ground above Evergreen Grove near a small waterfall is a deserted Alchemist's Camp. Check the Skill Book and read the journal; it gives clues to the whereabouts of the Alchemist: Follow the stream down to a pool where you'll find his corpse, a second Skill Book, and two Spriggans.

◇ Skill Book [Alchemy]: De Rerum Dirennis

◇ Skill Book [Alchemy]: Mannimarco, King of Worms
◇ Alchemist's Journal
◇ Apothecary's Satchel

[8.L] Dragon Mound: Evergreen Woods

Related Quest: Main Quest: Alduin's Wall

This Dragon Mound is initially sealed. It opens during Main Quest: Alduin's Wall. If you visit during or after this point in the Main Quest, the dragon will still be circling the area. Kill! Rend! Destroy!

[8.M] Sacrificial Altar: Evergreen Woods

Necromantic activity is to be expected as you close in on this altar surrounded by standing stones, south of Evergreen Grove. Kill any animated corpses if you must, but their controllers are your primary targets. Don't forget to read the Skill Book on the altar.

◇ Skill Book [Conjuration]: 2920, Frostfall, v10
◇ Apothecary's Satchel
◇ Potions

[8.N] Bear Cave: Halldir's Cairn

On the rocky slopes northwest of Halldir's Cairn is an alcove where two bears are on the prowl. Defeat them and inspect the dead hunter they've brought back to feast on.

[8.O] The Silvermoon: Lake Ilinalta

A sunken trading vessel named *Silvermoon* has been resting at the bottom of Lake Ilinalta for as long as the inhabitants of Riverwood can remember.

Dive down where the mast is jutting out of the water. Among the clams and Nordic barnacle clusters is a chest that's still intact.

◇ Chest ◇ Loose gear

[8.P] Nordic Burial Grove

At the fork in the main road, close to the shore of Lake Ilinalta, is a pauper's burial stone with six graves surrounded by Nightshade plants. Two skeletons are guarding these unknown graves.

[8.Q] Fisherman's Island: Lake Ilinalta

Directly south of South Brittleshin Pass on the opposite (south) side of the lake is a small island with a fisherman's camp. Expect a boat, a tent, and some drying fish, as well as the fisherman, usually resting near the indigenous flowers.

◇ Knapsack

[8.R] Sunken Barrow: Lake Ilinalta

Southeast of South Brittleshin Pass on the lake's northern shore are three moss-covered standing stones that just break the lake's surface. Dive down, and you'll discover that they surround a submerged barrow with a chest at the bottom.

◇ Chest ◇ Loose gear

[8.S] The Indigestible Emerald

Southeast of Anise's Cabin, on a narrow grassy alcove among the rocky banks of White River, close to a single pine tree, lie the skeletal remains of an elk. It died with an extremely valuable Emerald, which can be picked from behind its rib cage.

[8.T] Riverwood Folly

Perched on the snowy rocks below and east of Bleak Falls Barrow is a dark stone folly, home to a small group of bandits. Access the area via the path from Riverwood or the steps from the north bank of the river. Head to the top for an amazing view and a chest.

◇ Chest ◇ Mineable ore (Iron)

[8.U] Wild Animal Den: Pinewatch Outcropping

Below a rocky outcrop facing the main road and lake, northwest of Pinewatch, is a wild animal den. Defeat the creatures and then inspect the den itself. Among the skeletal remains is a disintegrated old cart with a locked chest.

◇ Chest (Locked: Novice)

[8.V] The Conjurer's Altar: Lake Ilinalta

A strange mist shrouds this small cluster of standing stones and an altar within. Face down a mage and his familial forces before inspecting the Skill Book on the altar. Travel a handful of paces to the southwest to discover a woodsman who met his end felling trees. His trusty axe is the only of its kind.

◇ Skill Book [Conjuration]: 2920, Hearth Fire, v9
◇ Unique Weapon: The Woodsman's Friend [60/80]

[8.W] Hunter's Camp: The Guardian Stones

Follow the short path to the river's edge from the Guardian Stones, and you'll spot a hunter near a boat, tent, and campfire who's been hunting

and fishing these parts for years. You may elect to steal from the locked chest.

◇ Chest (Locked: Novice)
◇ Mineable ore (Iron)

[8.X] Bandit Camp: Ilinalta Foothills

Side Quest: The Great Skyrim Treasure Hunt*

Along the winding road southwest of the Helgen Cave, due south of the Guardian Stones, a short trail leads up the hill to a small bandit camp. Expect attacks from three of these foes, a group of tents with some scattered food, and the following crafting locations and items:

◇ Crafting: Tanning Rack
◇ Skill Book [One-Handed]: Night Falls on Sentinel [D2/10]
◇ Treasure Map I [11/11]
◇ Satchel

[8.Y] Shrine of Talos: Ilinalta Foothills

Up a short path off the main road that winds down to the lake is a rocky promontory, upon which stands a statue of Talos. Three worshippers have been recently murdered by a Thalmor agent, who also lies dead here, with orders signed by Elenwen.

◇ Shrine of Talos [15/17] ◇ Loose gear
◇ Note: Thalmor Orders

[8.Z] Bandit Camp: Skybound Underhang

Follow the rough path across the snowy foothills toward Riverwood, and take the small switchback to reach a wooden platform with a bandit camp. Face down two foes, and rummage around for a few coins and the following:

◇ Skill Book [Block]: Warrior ◇ Chest

[8.AA] Bandit Bridge: Pinewatch

A little farther southwest along the main road from Pinewatch, two bandits stand atop a rickety wooden bridge, attacking you as you approach. Try to pass under the bridge, and they both release falling rocks; it is better to sneak from the east side along the second bridge, or drop them from range with spells or arrows.

◇ Danger! Rockfall Trap   ◇ Loose gear

[8.AB] Bandit Camp: Pinewatch Heights

A group of bandits has killed a Dark Elf and taken over his camp. Now they come for you! Retaliate, and then search the small tent for a Skill Book.

◇ Crafting: Tanning Rack
◇ Skill Book [Alteration]: The Lunar Lorkhan

[8.AC] Hunter's Camp: Upper Pinewatch Ridge

Farther along the winding path, up into the snow, lies a windswept promontory with a hunter you can barter with. He has a few items that he's caught or skinned for sale.

◇ Trader (Food Vendor):   ◇ Chest
  Hunter [9/13]
   ○ Food, Misc

[8.AD] Prospector's Shack: Bonechill Ridge

What appears to be a small prospector's shack is in fact the scene of gruesome carnage; two burned corpses bear witness to a recent dragon

attack. Check inside the shack for a necklace and a note, which reveals the location of Ancient's Ascent.

◇ Note: Letter to Authorities   ◇ Chest

[8.AE] Bandit Camp: Helgen Cliffs

On the main road west of Helgen is an overhang protecting what appears to be an empty campsite. Among the dead animals, there are a few loose items to steal, a Skill Book, and a locked chest. But be warned: touch the chest, and the bandits who dwell here will ambush you from behind! Watch for a few bear traps in the surrounding foliage.

◇ Danger! Bear Trap   ◇ Chest (Novice)
◇ Skill Book [Light Armor]: The
  Refugees

[8.AF] The Mauled Refugees

Related Quest: Main Quest: Dragon Rising

Once you complete Main Quest: Dragon Rising, this rocky promontory just below and northwest of Helgen becomes a small camp with two dead refugees, a wolf to defeat, and a whole lot of spilled blood.

[8.AG] Khajiit Caravan Massacre

Five Khajiit caravaneers have been murdered on the steep snowy road just south of Orphan Rock. As you approach the fallen tree blocking the path, three or four bandits attack; beware of the bowmen! Massacre them, then gather any loose gear you wish (check the lead wagon). Note that if the Falkreath Stormcloak Camp [8.36] is present, the Stormcloaks have cleared the bandits from the road.

◇ Skill Book [Speech]: The Buying   ◇ Chest
  Game   ◇ Loose gear

[8.AH] Wild Animal Den: Orphan's Tear

Not far from the site of the Falkreath Stormcloak Camp [8.36] is an overhang where two snarling woodland predators (usually wolves) make their den. Their meals include a Nord corpse to loot for items. If the camp is present, the soldiers have driven the animals away, though you can still loot the den for any other loose items.

[6.AI] Dragon Mound: Bloodlet Peaks

Related Quest: Main Quest: Alduin's Wall

This Dragon Mound is initially sealed. It opens during Main Quest: Alduin's Wall. If you visit during or after this point in the Main Quest, the mound will be open and empty.

[8.AJ] The Headless Skeleton

North of the Southfringe Sanctum on the freezing rocky slopes is a pine tree overlooking Fort Neugrad. Someone has executed a long-dead Nord with an axe. The headless skeleton is slumped near a chest and Skill Book.

◇ Skill Book [Conjuration]: The Warrior's Charge
◇ Chest
◇ Loose gear

HOLD 9: THE RIFT

TOPOGRAPHICAL OVERVIEW

Nestled in the Autumnal Forest, high above the volcanic Tundra known as Eastmarch and bordering Cyrodiil to the south and Morrowind to the east, is the prosperous and magical Hold known as the Rift. This is one of the four "old Holds" mentioned in history, and the majority of the Rift's population live and work around the lake port of Riften. The large forest of deciduous birch trees, interspersed with pine and smoother rocks (the result of a gigantic prehistoric glacial movement northward) makes the Rift habitable year-round; indeed, many Nords make their living on and around Lake Honrich. Two small towns lie within the Hold's borders: Shor's Stone, which is a small mining village north of Riften, and Ivarstead, which lies to the west, at the base of the towering Throat of the World.

 Routes and Pathways

The Great Riften Road descends from the rugged mountain border with Falkreath to the west and winds east along the southern banks of the Treva River and Lake Honrich to Riften itself. Spurs from this road stretch north, connecting Riften to Ivarstead and Shor's Stone and beyond, descending the nearly sheer cliffs that form the border between the Rift and Eastmarch. To the east are the gates to Cyrodiil, which are currently sealed. Along the eastern edge of the Hold lie the Velothi Mountains, with a number of caves and secret retreats. The peak towering above Riften to the southeast is home to Forelhost, an ancient and vast Nordic temple. To the west are the steep and treacherous mountains that connect the Rift to Falkreath, and the town of Ivarstead where pilgrims begin their journey up the 7,000 steps that lead to High Hrothgar, high on the steep slopes of the gigantic Throat of the World. Delve into the Autumnal Forest of the Rift, and you'll find water mills, farms, and other more unspeakable places.

AVAILABLE SERVICES, CRAFTING, AND COLLECTIBLES

Services

Followers: [7/47]
Houses for Sale: [1/5]
Marriage Prospects: [11/62]
Skill Trainers: [6/50]
  Alchemy: [0/3]
  Alteration: [0/3]
  Archery: [1/3]
  Block: [0/2]
  Conjuration: [0/3]
  Destruction: [0/3]
  Enchanting: [0/2]
  Heavy Armor: [0/3]
  Illusion: [1/2]
  Light Armor: [0/3]
  Lockpicking: [1/2]
  One-Handed: [0/3]
  Pickpocket: [1/3]
  Restoration: [0/3]

  Smithing: [1/3]
  Sneak: [1/3]
  Speech: [0/4]
  Two-Handed: [0/2]
Traders (24/133):
  Apothecary [2/12]
  Bartender [3/5]
  Blacksmith [6/33]
  Carriage Driver [1/5]
  Fence [1/10]
  Fletcher [1/3]
  Food Vendor [1/9]
  General Goods [4/19]
  Innkeeper [2/15]
  Jeweler [1/2]
  Special [0/3]
  Spell Vendor [1/12]
  Stablemaster [1/5]

Collectibles

Captured Critters: [2/5]
Dragon Claws: [2/10]
Dragon Priest Masks: [1/10]
Larceny Targets: [2/7]
Skill Books: [23/180]
  Alchemy: [0/10]
  Alteration: [1/10]
  Archery: [1/10]
  Block: [1/10]
  Conjuration: [0/10]
  Destruction: [0/10]
  Enchanting: [1/10]
  Heavy Armor: [1/10]
  Illusion: [2/10]

  Light Armor: [1/10]
  Lockpicking: [4/10]
  One-Handed: [2/10]
  Pickpocket: [3/10]
  Restoration: [2/10]
  Smithing: [1/10]
  Sneak: [1/10]
  Speech: [1/10]
  Two-Handed: [1/10]
Treasure Maps: [0/11]
Unique Items: [24/112]
Unique Weapons: [1/11]
Unusual Gems: [2/24]

Special Objects

Shrines: [9/69]
  Akatosh: [0/6]
  Arkay: [1/12]
  Dibella: [1/8]
  Julianos: [0/5]
  Kynareth: [1/6]
  Mara: [1/5]
  Stendarr: [2/5]
  Talos: [2/17]
  Zenithar: [1/5]
Standing Stones: [1/13]
  The Shadow Stone
Word Walls: [6/42]
  Animal Allegiance: [1/3]
  Aura Whisper: [1/3]
  Become Ethereal: [0/3]
  Disarm: [0/3]
  Dismaying Shout: [1/3]
  Elemental Fury: [0/3]
  Fire Breath: [0/2]
  Frost Breath: [0/3]
  Ice Form: [0/3]
  Kyne's Peace: [1/3]
  Marked for Death: [1/3]
  Slow Time: [0/3]
  Storm Call: [1/3]
  Throw Voice: [0/1]
  Unrelenting Force: [0/1]
  Whirlwind Sprint: [0/2]

CRAFTING STATIONS: THE RIFT

✓	TYPE	LOCATION A	LOCATION B
☐	Alchemy Lab	Riften (Mistveil Keep: Wylandriah's Room) [9.00]	Alchemist's Shack [9.09]
☐	Arcane Enchanter	Riften (Mistveil Keep: Wylandriah's Room) [9.00]	Riften (Honeyside) [9.00] (after Alchemy Lab Upgrade)
☐	Anvil or Blacksmith Forge	Riften (the Scorched Hammer) [9.00]	Shor's Stone [9.25]
☐	Cooking Pot and Spit	Riften (the Scorched Hammer) [9.00]	Riften (Temple of Mara) [9.00]
☐	Grindstone	Riften (the Scorched Hammer) [9.00]	Shor's Stone [9.25]
☐	Smelter	Shor's Stone [9.25]	—
☐	Tanning Rack	Riften (the Scorched Hammer) [9.00]	Shor's Stone [9.25]
☐	Wood Chopping Block	Riften (Mistveil Keep: Barracks) [9.00]	Ivarstead (9.01)
☐	Workbench	Riften (the Scorched Hammer) [9.00]	Shor's Stone [9.25]

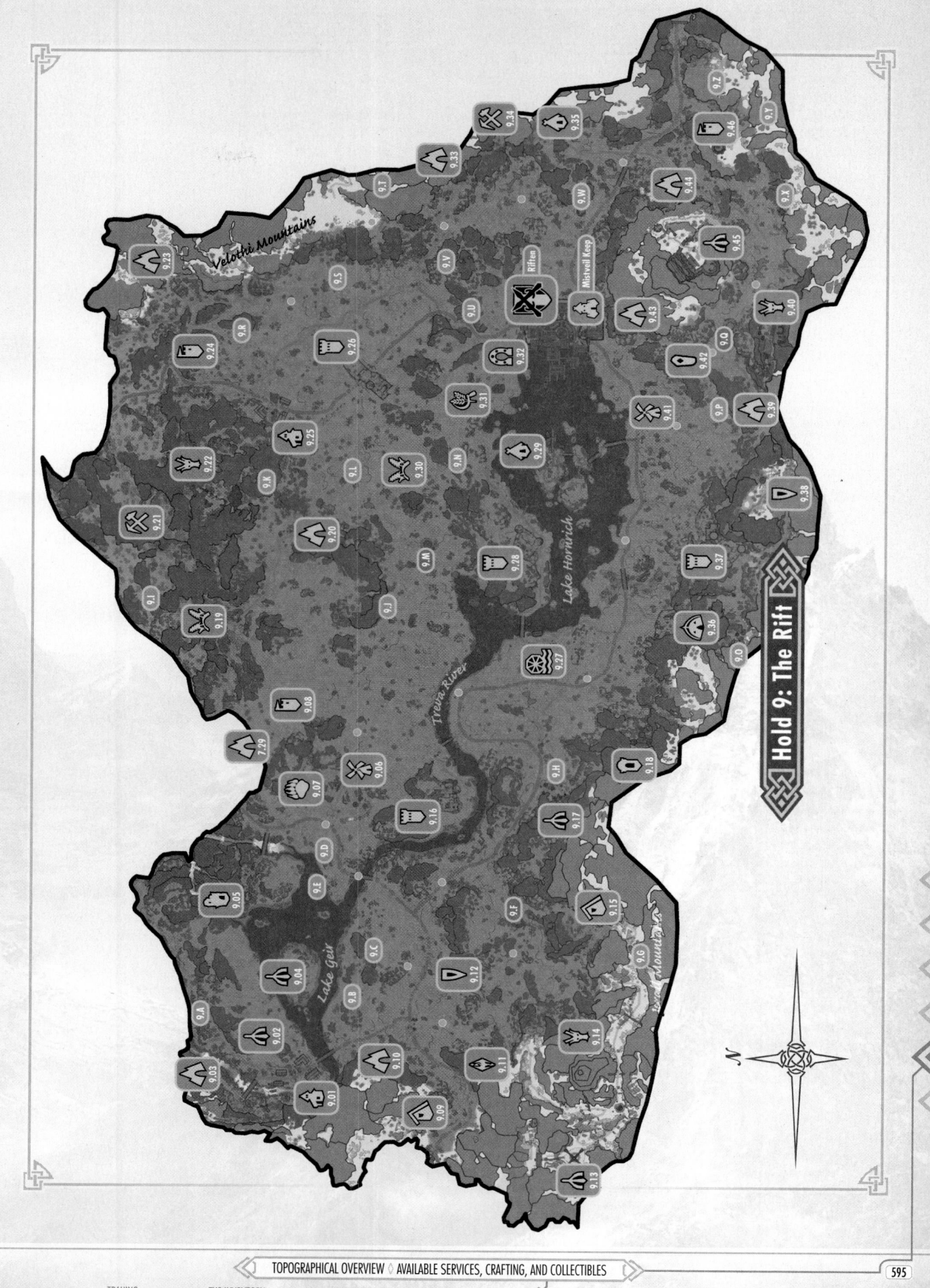

Velothi Mountains

Riften

Mistveil Keep

Lake Honrich

Treva River

Lake Geir

N

PRIMARY LOCATIONS

Total — 48: Hold Capital, Mistveil Keep, and 46 Hold Locations

[9.00] Hold Capital City: Riften
[9.00] Mistveil Keep
   Jarl: Laila Law-Giver
[9.01] Ivarstead
[9.02] Shroud Hearth Barrow
[9.03] Pinepeak Cavern
[9.04] Geirmund's Hall
[9.05] Nilheim
[9.06] Sarethi Farm
[9.07] Rift Stormcloak Camp
[9.08] Rift Watchtower
[9.09] Alchemist's Shack
[9.10] Honeystrand Cave
[9.11] Rift Imperial Camp
[9.12] Ruins of Bthalft
[9.13] Arcwind Point

[9.14] Autumnwatch Tower
[9.15] Froki's Shack
[9.16] Treva's Watch
[9.17] Angarvunde
[9.18] Avanchnzel
[9.19] Clearspring Tarn
[9.20] Boulderfall Cave
[9.21] Northwind Mine
[9.22] Northwind Summit
[9.23] Tolvald's Cave
[9.24] Shor's Watchtower
[9.25] Shor's Stone
[9.26] Fort Greenwall
[9.27] Heartwood Mill
[9.28] Faldar's Tooth
[9.29] Goldenglow Estate
[9.30] Autumnshade Clearing
[9.31] Merryfair Farm

[9.32] Riften Stables
[9.33] Fallowstone Cave and Giant's Grove
[9.34] Lost Prospect Mine
[9.35] Black-Briar Lodge
[9.36] Largashbur
[9.37] Darklight Tower
[9.38] Ruins of Rkund
[9.39] Crystaldrift Cave
[9.40] Lost Tongue Overlook
[9.41] Snow-Shod Farm
[9.42] The Shadow Stone
[9.43] Nightingale Hall
[9.44] Broken Helm Hollow
[9.45] Forelhost
[9.46] Stendarr's Beacon

SECONDARY LOCATIONS

Total — 26 Points of Interest

[9.A] Darkwater Overhang
[9.B] Wood Cutter's Camp: Lake Geir
[9.C] The Poultry Reanimator: Lake Geir
[9.D] Treasure Hunter's Camp: Lake Geir
[9.E] Treasure Island: Lake Geir
[9.F] Dragon Mound: Autumnwatch Woods
[9.G] Shrine of Talos: Froki's Peak
[9.H] Medresi's Camp: Angarvunde
[9.I] Wild Animal Den: Mistwatch
[9.J] Bandit's Shack: Autumnshade
[9.K] Northwind Chest
[9.L] Altar in the Woods: Autumnshade
[9.M] Dragon Mound: Autumnshade Woods

[9.N] Hunters' Camp: Autumnshade Hills
[9.O] Troll Den: Rkund
[9.P] Wild Animal Den: Crystaldrift Cave
[9.Q] Dragon Mound: Lost Tongue Pass
[9.R] Wild Animal Den: Shor's Stone
[9.S] Trappers' Dilemma
[9.T] Miner's Camp: Velothi Mountains
[9.U] The Three Sentinels
[9.V] Shrine of Zenithar: Fallowstone
[9.W] Tumbledown Tower: Riften Outskirts
[9.X] Burning Farmhouse
[9.Y] Frost Troll Den: Jerall Mountain Ridge
[9.Z] Two Pine Ridge

HOLD CAPITAL: RIFTEN

Related Quests

Main Quest: A Cornered Rat
Main Quest: Alduin's Wall
Civil War Quest: Reunification of Skyrim
Civil War Quest: Compelling Tribute
Side Quest: Promises to Keep
Side Quest: Unfathomable Depths
Temple Quest: The Bonds of Matrimony
Temple Quest: The Book of Love
Dark Brotherhood Quest: Innocence Lost
Dark Brotherhood Quest: The Silence Has Been Broken
Dark Brotherhood Quest: Breaching Security
Dark Brotherhood Quest: Where You Hang Your Enemy's Head...
Thieves Guild Quest: A Chance Arrangement
Thieves Guild Quest: Taking Care of Business
Thieves Guild Quest: Loud and Clear
Thieves Guild Quest: Dampened Spirits
Thieves Guild Quest: Scoundrel's Folly
Thieves Guild Quest: Speaking With Silence
Thieves Guild Quest: The Pursuit
Thieves Guild Quest: Trinity Restored
Thieves Guild Radiant Quest: No Stone Unturned (Vex)
Thieves Guild Radiant Quest: No Stone Unturned (x2)
Thieves Guild Radiant Quest: Reparations
Thieves Guild Radiant Quest: Shadowmarks*
Thieves Guild Radiant Quest: Moon Sugar Rush*
Thieves Guild Radiant Quest: Armor Exchange*
Thieves Guild Radiant Quest: Larceny Targets (the Ragged Flagon)*
Thieves Guild Radiant Quest: Larceny Targets (Mercer's House)*
Thieves Guild Additional Jobs: The Numbers Job
Thieves Guild Additional Jobs: The Fishing Job
Thieves Guild Additional Jobs: The Bedlam Job
Thieves Guild Additional Jobs: The Burglary Job

Thieves Guild Additional Jobs: The Shill Job
Thieves Guild Additional Jobs: The Sweep Job
Thieves Guild Additional Jobs: The Heist Job
Thieves Guild City Influence Quest: Silver Lining
Thieves Guild City Influence Quest: The Dainty Sload
Thieves Guild City Influence Quest: Imitation Amnesty
Thieves Guild City Influence Quest: Summerset Shadows
Thieves Guild City Leadership Quest: Under New Management
Dungeon Activity (Riften Jail)
Miscellaneous Objective: Innkeeper Rumors (the Bee and Barb)
Miscellaneous Objective: Innkeeper Rumors (the Ragged Flagon)
Miscellaneous Objective: The Lover's Requital* (Sibbi Black-Briar)
Miscellaneous Objective: Under the Table* (Romlyn Dreth)
Miscellaneous Objective: Few and Far Between* (Ingun Black-Briar)
Miscellaneous Objective: Spread the Love* (Dinya Balu)
Miscellaneous Objective: Sealing the Deal* (Talen-Jei)
Miscellaneous Objective: Ice Cold* (Marise Aravel)
Miscellaneous Objective: Distant Memories* (Brand-Shei)
Miscellaneous Objective: Grimsever's Return* (Mjoll the Lioness)
Miscellaneous Objective: Stoking the Flames* (Balimund Iron-Boar)
Miscellaneous Objective: Caught Red-Handed* (Svana Far-Shield)
Miscellaneous Objective: Pilgrimage* (Alessandra)
Miscellaneous Objective: Hunt and Gather* (Wylandriah)
Miscellaneous Objective: Special Delivery* (Bolli)
Miscellaneous Objective: Bring It!* (Harrald)
Miscellaneous Objective: Truth Ore Consequences* (Hafjorg)
Miscellaneous Objective: Ringmaker* (Madesi)
Miscellaneous Objective: Bloody Nose* (Hofgrir Horse-Crusher)
Miscellaneous Objective: Toying with the Dead* (Vekel the Man)
Miscellaneous Objective: Shardr and Sapphire* (Shadr)
Miscellaneous Objective: Jarl's Quest Part 1: Helping Hand* (Wujeeta)
Miscellaneous Objective: Jarl's Quest Part 2: The Raid* (Wujeeta, Jarl Laila)
Miscellaneous Objective: Jarl's Quest Part 3: Supply and Demand* (Jarl Laila)
Miscellaneous Objective: Erasing Vald's Debt* (Maven Black-Briar)
Miscellaneous Objective: Gissur's Revenge* (Gissur)
Miscellaneous Objective: Shavari the Assassin* (Shavari)
Favor (Activity): The Gift of Charity* (Gissur) ‡
Favor (Activity): The Gift of Charity* (Snilf)
Favor (Activity): The Gift of Charity* (Edda)
Thane Quest: Thane of The Rift*

Habitation Type: Hold Capital (Major)

Crafting

Alchemy Labs (5)
Arcane Enchanter
Forge
Grindstones (4)
Tanning Racks (3)
Workbenches (2)

Services

Follower: Mjoll the Lioness [40/47]
Follower: Marcurio [41/47]
Follower: Iona [42/47]
House for Sale: Honeyside [5/5]
Marriage Prospect: Mjoll the Lioness [52/62]
Marriage Prospect: Balimund [53/62]
Marriage Prospect: Gelka [54/62]
Marriage Prospect: Marcurio [55/62]
Marriage Prospect: Romlyn Dreth [56/62]
Marriage Prospect: Iona [57/62]
Trader (Apothecary): Elgrim [11/12]
Trader (Apothecary): Herluin Lothaire [12/12]
Trader (Bartender): Talen-Jei [3/5]
Trader (Bartender): Vekel the Man [4/5]
Trader (Blacksmith): Balimund [28/33]
Trader (Blacksmith): Arnskar Ember-Master [29/33]
Trader (Blacksmith): Vanryth Gatharian [30/33]
Trader (Fence): Tonilia [6/10]
Trader (Fletcher): Syndus [3/3]
Trader (Food Vendor): Ungrien [9/9]
Trader (General Store Vendor): Marise Aravel [13/19]
Trader (General Store Vendor): Brand-Shei [14/19]
Trader (General Store Vendor): Grelka [15/19]
Trader (General Store Vendor): Bersi Honey-Hand [16/19]
Trader (Innkeeper): Keerava [14/15]
Trader (Jeweler): Madesi [2/2]
Trader (Spell Vendor): Wylandriah [12/12]
Trainer (Archery: Master): Niruin [3/3]
Trainer (Light Armor: Expert): Grelka [3/3]
Trainer (Lockpicking: Master): Vex [1/2]
Trainer (Pickpocket: Master): Vipir [2/3]
Trainer (Smithing: Expert): Balimund [3/3]
Trainer (Sneak: Master): Delvin Mallory [2/3]

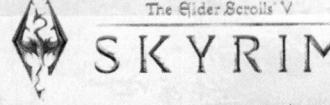

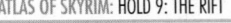

Collectibles

Larceny Target: Bust of the Grey Fox [6/7]

Skill Book [Lockpicking]: Advances in Lockpicking [A1/10]

Skill Book [Lockpicking]: Advances in Lockpicking [A2/10]

Skill Book [Lockpicking]: Surfeit of Thieves [C2/10]

Skill Book [One-Handed]: Fire and Darkness [B2/10]

Skill Book [Pickpocket]: Beggar [B1/10]

Skill Book [Pickpocket]: Beggar [B2/10]

Skill Book [Pickpocket]: Purloined Shadows [C2/10]

Skill Book [Smithing]: The Armorer's Challenge [E2/10]

Skill Book [Speech]: A Dance in Fire, v7 [C2/10]

Skill Book [Two-Handed]: Words and Philosophy [E2/10]

Unique Item: The Bond of Matrimony [80/112]

Unique Item: Madesi's Silver Ring [81/112]

Unique Item: Gloves of the Pugilist [82/112]

Unique Item: Thieves Guild Armor [83/112]

Unique Item: Thieves Guild Boots [84/112]

Unique Item: Thieves Guild Gloves [85/112]

Unique Item: Thieves Guild Hood [86/112]

Unique Item: Amulet of Articulation [87/112]

Unique Item: Guild Master's Armor [88/112]

Unique Item: Guild Master's Boots [89/112]

Unique Item: Guild Master's Gloves [90/112]

Unique Item: Guild Master's Hood [91/112]

Unique Item: Thieves Guild Armor (Improved) [92/112]

Unique Item: Thieves Guild Boots (Improved) [93/112]

Unique Item: Thieves Guild Gloves (Improved) [94/112]

Unique Item: Thieves Guild Hood (Improved) [95/112]

Unique Weapon: Chillrend [61/80]

Unique Weapon: Alessandra's Dagger [62/80]

Unique Weapon: Steel Sword [63/80]

Unique Weapon: Dravin's Bow [64/80]

Unusual Gem: [23/24]

Special Objects

Business Ledger	Shrine of Talos [16/17]
Civil War: Map of Skyrim	Chest
Shrine of Arkay [12/12]	Potions aplenty
Shrine of Dibella [8/8]	Loose gear
Shrine of Mara [5/5]	

Lore: City Overview

Riften is situated in the southeastern corner of the Rift, at the eastern end of Lake Honrich, with a good portion of the city actually spilling over the water atop large wooden piers. The entire city is bisected by a large canal that used to serve as access for small cargo boats but has lately fallen into disrepair and decay thanks to the lack of trade during the Civil War. But don't think that Riften isn't a bustling center of commerce; the Black-Briar Meadery has almost a monopoly on the sale and distribution of a Nord's favorite pastime: drinking.

However, the city of Riften is a paradox. The city is located in the beautiful Autumnal Forest region of Skyrim, and that beauty has encroached upon the city, in the form of wondrous foliage and generally pleasant weather. But most of the structures in Riften are wooden, and the city has a sort of old, run-down feel, which often takes visitors by surprise. Not that this bothers the people who live there, who see Riften for what it truly is — a bustling, energetic city with a strong economy fueled by hard-working fishermen and mead makers. The residents also understand that the city is, for all intents and purposes, owned and operated by the Maven Black-Briar, and in order to survive and thrive, everyone needs to adhere to her rules.

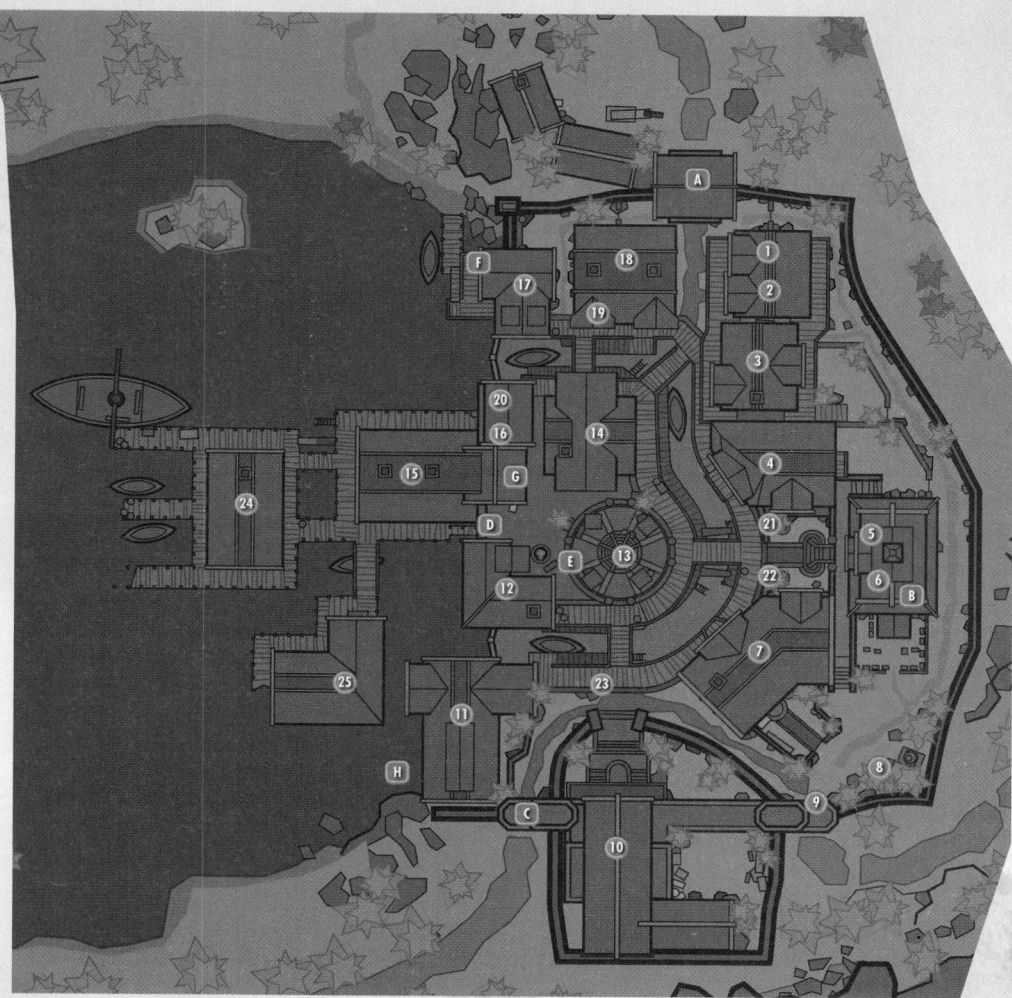

Important Areas of Interest

Dryside

The eastern edge of the city (which isn't built over the waters of Lake Honrich) is called Dryside. The bulk of the town is located on Dryside and is split by Riften's canal. Most of the more affluent homes are located on the eastern side of the canal, while most of Riften's shops and the marketplace are located on the western side. The southern portion of the city is dominated by Mistveil Keep and the jail.

A North Gate

The main gate of Riften, located along the northern wall, sees the most traffic of the city's three entrances. Foil the Riften guard's feeble attempts at shaking you down for money. Then speak with Maul, a gruff man waiting just inside the gates.

1 Bolli's House

Bolli Trout-Purse   Nivenor

This three-floor structure is one of the more impressive houses in Riften, which speaks to Bolli's station. The Note you'll find on the bedside cabinet reveals Bolli's marriage isn't as successful.

◇ Shadowmark: "Loot"   ◇ Chest

◇ Note: Requested Report

> **TIP** Talk to Maul. Afterward, the gates in this area are unlocked, once you enter an interior and return outside.

2 Aerin's House

Mjoll the Lioness   Aerin

Aerin's home is small but tall, featuring three floors.

◇ Follower: Mjoll the Lioness [40/47]

◇ Marriage Prospect: Mjoll the Lioness [52/62]

◇ Loose Gear

③ Snow-Shod Manor

Vulwulf Snow-Shod   Nura Snow-Shod   Asgeir Snow-Shod

This three-floor wooden structure is the house of Clan Snow-Shod, a wealthy and influential family of Nord that owns the Snow-Shod Farm outside Riften. But even though the Clan has direct ties to the city's economy, it's their interest and involvement in the Civil War that really has people talking....

◇ Shadowmark: "Loot"   ◇ Loose gear

④ Riftweald Manor (Locked: Special)

This property is owned by the current Guild Master of the Thieves Guild and is a fine structure. Mercer has cleverly integrated an isolated section of the Ratway into the sublevels of his home, which contains his private valued possessions. This hideaway includes a minivault, a study, and escape routes. Mercer Frey has paid several bandits to act as guards here and has given them the order to kill intruders.

Outside, the front and back doors are barred from the inside, and the back grounds are locked by three gates, two requiring a key and the other locked (Expert). You usually enter here during Thieves Guild Quest: The Pursuit and must shoot a mechanism to release a wooden ramp leading to an upper entrance (Expert). This cannot be done at any other time; exploration inside occurs only during or after this quest.

Riftweald Manor (Interior)

Upper Floor: A storage room leads to a landing, a smaller storage closet, and Mercer's bedroom. The door's bar in the landing can't be budged.

Ground Floor: A large living and dining room dominates this area, along with an adjacent foyer. The doors' bars here can't be removed either. The foyer table has a note mentioning the mechanism construction that has recently taken place outside. It is next to the front door (barred and sealed) that you find a suspicious cabinet leading to Mercer Frey's secret chambers.

Cellar: The cellar, accessed from the dining room, is a small area filled with foodstuffs.

◇ Note: To the Owner   ◇ Chest   ◇ Potions

Secret Cellar: Accessed via the false back panel of the suspicious cabinet on the ground floor (which can be closed using the pull bar on the other side). Watch for numerous traps as you navigate the sewer passages; there's a spear trap in front of you, triggered by a pressure plate. The next room has fire traps blasting up from the floor.

Puzzle Solution: Look at the floor and the nozzle holes where the fire blasts up from. These are divided into tiles. Each tile has a diamond shape; the fire traps that are activated are darker than those that are empty; simply step on the lighter-colored diamonds to avoid all fire damage.

There's a dart trap in the water-logged corridor (pressure plate) leading to a chest. At the corridor with the swinging blade and battering ram traps, dash between the blades and step left into the alcove. Wait for the battering ram to swing, then sprint to the left of the low chandelier, dodging the remaining blades. At the door, look down and unlock the trap trigger (Expert) or face darts when you open the door.

◇ Danger! Battering Ram Trap, Dart Trap, Fire Trap, Spear Trap, Swinging Blade Trap
◇ Chest

Mercer's Secret Study: There is a wealth of loot here, including an excellent weapon in a display case (Expert). The note from "R" is likely to be from Legate Rikke in Solitude. This exit tunnel leads to the Ratway Vaults, which connects back to the Warrens and the Ragged Flagon. Note the Shadowmark before you drop down into the Vaults.

◇ Shadowmark: "Danger"
◇ Mercer's Plans
◇ Skill Book [Sneak]: The Red Kitchen Reader
◇ Unique Weapon: Chillrend [61/80]
◇ Note: Many thanks
◇ Chest
◇ Larceny Target: Bust of the Gray Fox [6/7]

⑤ Temple of Mara

Maramal   Dinya Balu

The Temple of Mara offers services to the people of Riften and is devoted to the worship of Mara, one of the Nine Divines and the recognized goddess of love. It is here that weddings are held (Side Quest: The Bonds of Matrimony). You can get a Blessing at the altar or at two smaller shrines on either side of the main chamber. The first Note is from Anuriel warning of disturbances in the Hall of the Dead. The second Note is from Talen-Jei, regarding his forthcoming wedding. The cellar has some food and drink, and an entrance to the Hall of the Dead.

◇ Unique Item: The Bond of Matrimony [80/112]   ◇ Note: Reports of a Disturbance
◇ Shrine of Mara [5/5]   ◇ Note: Argonian Ceremony
◇ Potions

⑥ Hall of the Dead

Alessandra

The Riften Hall of the Dead has two levels, underneath the Temple of Mara. The ground floor serves as a Shrine of Arkay; the bottom, underground level is actually a series of catacombs that contain some of Riften's most important dead. Connected to the mausoleum is a graveyard, containing even more of the city's departed. There are two entrances: from the outside under the Temple of Mara balcony and via the cellar inside the Temple. Inside, there are numerous skeletons from which you can remove a few coins, bone meal, and skulls.

◇ Unique Weapon: Alessandra's Dagger [62/80]
◇ Shrine of Arkay [12/12]

Ⓑ The Ragged Flagon: Cistern Entrance

The secret entrance to the Ragged Flagon, Cistern, becomes available during the Thieves Guild Quest: Loud and Clear and becomes a world map marker (making it simple to return to the Guild). It can't be opened until then but provides a quicker return route to Brynjolf and Mercer Frey, instead of navigating the Ratway. Note the Shadowmark on the coffin (which you press to open) and on the surrounding Hall of the Dead entrance walls. If you're exiting from the Cistern, use the pull chain to open the coffin.

◇ Shadowmark: "The Guild"

⑦ Black-Briar Manor

Maven Black-Briar (Imperial Jarl)   Sibbi Black-Briar
Hemming Black-Briar (Imperial Steward)   Ingun Black-Briar

Black-Briar Manor is the home of the Black-Briar family, the wealthiest, most powerful family in all of Riften. The Black-Briar family are the owners of the Black-Briar Meadery, and as such control much of Riften's economy. It is accessed via the front door (note the Shadowmark), a leap over the garden fence, and through the back gate (Expert). Inside, the foyer end table has a Note regarding the loss of a mead shipment, and the rest of the ground floor has a dining table full of food and other stored items.

◇ Shadowmark: "Protected"   ◇ Potions
◇ Note: Regarding your Loss

Cellar: There are three doors, two of which are unlocked. One leads to a small bedroom. One leads to a larger bedroom with an Alchemy Lab and a number of ingredients to steal. The third door (Expert) leads to a tiny chamber where the Black Sacrament has been performed. There is a letter from Maven here; she is unhappy with Astrid (from the Dark Brotherhood) about the lack of action regarding an assassination Maven requested!

◇ Crafting: Alchemy Lab   ◇ Potions
◇ Note: To the Brotherhood

Upper Floor

Upper Floor: Check the shelves in the hallway for a book on the Gaulder legends. On the bedside table are two letters, each containing a different tone from two business acquaintances. There is an exit onto an upper exterior balcony (a quick escape if need be!).

◇ Business Letters (2)   ◇ Chest

⑧ Shrine of Talos

Nura Snow-Shod

Talos is worshipped openly when the Stormcloaks are in control of the city. When they are not, the shrine has less of a presence. Nura Snow-Shod is usually found here during the day, tending the Shrine.

◇ Shrine of Talos [16/17]

⑨ Dead Gate

The Dead Gate is so named for the number of people who died there thanks to repeated bandit raids of the city. The gate is now completely boarded up and no longer in use.

⑩ Mistveil Keep

  The following leaders of Riften are loyal to the Stormcloaks at the start of the Civil War.

Jarl Laila Law-Giver

Laila is a fervent supporter of the Stormcloaks, strongly believing that the Empire can do nothing but steal the heritage of their city away if they come to power. She firmly believes in the old ways of Skyrim and is steeped in its traditions and mannerisms. Even though she rules quite a corrupt city, she is blissfully unaware of the more nefarious goings-on in town thanks to her Steward, Anuriel, who has been known to accept bribes and payoffs from the seedier inhabitants of Riften.

Harrald

Harrald is the youngest son of Laila Law-Giver. He is largely indifferent to the events of the Civil War but sides with the Stormcloaks because his mother does. This situation has driven a wedge between Saerlund and Harrald, who constantly chide each other for their stances on the situation.

Saerlund

Saerlund is the oldest son of Laila Law-Giver. When he publicly spoke in favor of the Imperial forces in the Civil War, Laila refused to recognize him as heir. There is a great deal of hostility between the two now, although Saerlund still lives in the Keep. Should Laila ever become exiled due to the Empire gaining control of Riften, Saerlund will remain behind and live in the Keep in defiance of his mother's beliefs.

Anuriel (Steward)

Anuriel's devotion to her Jarl is a guise for her true nature as a corrupt and greedy individual. She readily accepts bribes from influential people in the city and is extremely clever at covering her tracks (even if it means making loose ends disappear). She has no desire to actually become the Jarl, seeing her position as a stronger link to her corrupt ties. She has gained some reputation as someone not to be trifled with.

Unmid Snow-Shod (Housecarl)

Unmid is the second to youngest child of Vulwulf Snow-Shod. He has dedicated his life to the art of combat, becoming highly adept at all sorts of martial weaponry. Due to this incredible talent, he was hired as the Housecarl. On more than one occasion, Unmid has proved he cannot be bested in combat and has even put down several attempts on the Jarl's life. Unmid's single weakness is his infatuation for Anuriel, the Jarl's Steward.

Wylandriah (Court Wizard)

She spends most of her day in her laboratory performing experiments and only makes herself available to the Jarl when specifically summoned. She seems always scatterbrained, but this is an act, as Wylandriah would prefer to be doing her experimentation rather than matters of court. By acting this way, she believes people leave her to herself most of the time (which is true).

Gonnar Oath-Giver

 The following residents of Riften arrive to take control of this city, once this Hold has fallen during the Civil War.

Maven Black-Briar, Imperial Jarl

As matron of the Black-Briar family and a powerful businesswoman, Maven is virtually unapproachable and elitist. She's cold, ruthless and calculating—and also well connected within the Empire and Skyrim alike. If the Empire takes control of Riften in the Civil War, Maven (thanks to powerful friends in Cyrodiil) is installed as the Imperial Jarl. She will also fill her court with family and allies.

Hemming Black-Briar, Imperial Steward

Hemming Black-Briar is the only son of Maven Black-Briar, and heir to family fortune. He is being groomed by Maven as a sort of protégé... someone to eventually take her place not only running the Meadery, but to also dabble in the same corrupt activities. Hemming is often an errand-boy, and has come to admire his mother's ways and fervently defends her whenever a family squabble should arise.

Maul (Housecarl)

Maul is a close friend of Hemming Black-Briar; when he was ambushed by bandits, Maul dove into the fray to save him. Ever since then, they have been partners in crime, with Maul assisting Hemming in his more nefarious activities assigned by Maven Black-Briar. He does not live within Riften, as he wants his identity to remain anonymous. Maul's brother is Dirge, part of the security at the Ragged Flagon.

Mistveil Keep (Exterior)

This ominous stone keep is where Jarl Laila Law-Giver lives and rules, but this important building also contains the city's jail and barracks. The barracks are to your left (southeast) and the jail to the right (southwest) of the main door into the Keep, with the banners on each side. This is where the majority of the city's guards reside.

Mistveil Keep (Interior)

Banquet Hall and Throne Room: Guards, the Jarl, and her entourage are seated here. There's enough food here to feed a small army.

◇ Chest (2)

Wylandriah's Enchantments: The Court Wizard can usually be found here, in this two-room chamber off the Banquet Hall, which houses her shop and bed.

◇ Crafting: Alchemy Lab, Arcane Enchanter
◇ Trader (Spell Vendor): Wylandriah [12/12]
  ○ Weapons, Apparel, Scrolls, Books, Misc
◇ Chest   ◇ Potions aplenty   ◇ Loose gear

War Room and Armory: Gonnar Oath-Giver is plotting from this location (which was once a pantry) at the start of the Civil War. Open one door to head into the Barracks, and open the other into a bedroom armory filled with weapons.

◇ Civil War: Map of Skyrim   ◇ Loose gear
◇ Chest

Anuriel's Room: Located at the far end of the ground-floor corridor, this room has a number of precious gems and necklaces and a letter regarding the imprisonment of Sibbi Black-Briar. Head to this location during the Civil War Quest: Compelling Tribute (Imperials).

◇ Note: Sibbi Black-Briar   ◇ Chest

Mistveil Keep Jarl's Quarters

There are three doors at the top of the stairs, each leading to a bedroom. Check for the following, and a door from the Jarl's bedroom to a covered balcony offering views of Riften:

◇ Skill Book [Lockpicking]: Surfeit of Thieves [C2/10]

◇ Unusual Gem: [23/24]   ◇ Potions
◇ Display Cases [Adept] (3)   ◇ Loose gear
◇ Chests (3)

Mistveil Keep Barracks (Exterior)

A large yard where guards (and sometimes Harrald) come to practice.

Mistveil Keep Barracks (Interior)

A large number of guards (and mead bottles) are inside this two-floor structure. The Riften Guards are well equipped and numerous. The lower exits lead out to the training yard and into Mistveil Keep. The upper exit leads out onto crenellations above the yard.

◇ Skill Book [Two-Handed]: Words and   ◇ Chests (8)
  Philosophy [E2/10]   ◇ Loose gear

Riften Jail

Threki   **Sibbi Black-Briar**

Molgrom Twice-Killed

A jailor stops you from heading into the jail if you're visiting, unless you can persuade or bribe your way past him. Inside, you can find the jail office on the right, with the evidence room just beyond; both are a bit of a mess. Note the sewer wall opening close to the chests, though you can't do anything with it from this side. The cells are on two separate levels, with Sibbi Black-Briar and Threki the Innocent imprisoned on the top floor and Molgrom Twice-Killed on the lower level. All of the cell doors are locked (Adept). A Skill Book sits atop a barrel in a dark nook above the stairs.

If you get imprisoned here, you can pick the lock on your cell door and sneak out—just keep an eye on the patrolling guard and time your movements to slip by them.

Or better yet, note the Shadowmark and the broken shackle on the wall in your cell. Pull the shackle and a secret passage in the wall creaks open! Escape through this sealed-off section of the Ratway, which is filled with debris, and push open the sewer grate to retrieve your belongings from the evidence room. Then head down the passage into a section of unexplored sewers. Fight any Skeevers you see, check the flooded area for a chest, and continue through the hatch into a second section of sewers. Follow the rushing water to the exit, which leads you out to the edge of Lake Honrich, near the South Gate and Riften Warehouse: the Sewer Gate [G]. Note that you can only escape this way once: after doing so, the guards seal the passage and remove the shackle.

◇ Danger! Bear Trap (2)   ◇ Prisoner Belongings Chest
◇ Shadowmark: "Escape Route"   ◇ Chest
◇ Skill Book [Lockpicking]:   ◇ Potions
  Advances in Lockpicking   ◇ Loose gear
  [A1/10]
◇ Evidence Chest

C South Gate

The Riften South Gate, set into the city's southern wall, sees its fair share of traffic, but not nearly as much as that of the Main Gate to the north.

11 Honorhall Orphanage

Grelod the Kind   **Samuel**

Constance Michel   **Runa Fair-Shield**

Francois Beaufort   **Hroar**

The Honorhall Orphanage is home to several orphaned young boys and girls whose parents have been lost to anything from fishing accidents, to battle, to the general harshness of life. The institution is privately funded by Maven Black-Briar. The interior is on a single floor. Enter via the dining room and pantry. A side bedroom has a Skill Book by the bed. Through the main dormitory (with three empty chests) where the orphans sleep is a small room with child-sized shackles and Grelod's office. There are also doors leading to a small garden, which is more of a prison yard.

◇ Skill Book [Pickpocket]: Purloined Shadows [C2/10]

---

12 The Scorched Hammer

Balimund

Asbjorn Fire-Tamer

The blacksmith shop is situated adjacent to the marketplace. The resident smithy, Balimud, has set up his forge and workshop outside the building within a covered overhang.

◇ Shadowmark: "Loot"
◇ Crafting: Forge, Grindstone, Tanning Rack, Workbench
◇ Marriage Prospect: Balimund [53/62]
◇ Trader (Blacksmith): Balimund [28/33]
  ○ Weapons, Apparel, and Misc
◇ Trainer (Smithing: Expert): Balimund [3/3]
◇ Skill Book [Smithing]: The Armorer's Challenge [E2/10]
◇ Unique Weapon: Steel Sword [63/80]

Inside, the house is modest, and the food of the day are leeks. At the back of the dwelling are two bedrooms, one with a safe and some weapons. In the cellar are a large amount of Ingots and other ingredients for crafting, although these must be stolen.

◇ Crafting: Grindstone,   ◇ Safe
  Tanning Rack   ◇ Strongbox (Apprentice)
◇ Business Ledger   ◇ Loose gear

D Dock Gate

Between the Black-Briar Meadery and the Blacksmith's is the western gate leading to and from the dock. This actually exits out into Skyrim and Lake Honrich.

13 Marketplace

Edda   **Brandish Begin-Again**   **Madesi**

Snilf   **Marise Aravel**   **Grelka**

The marketplace is the central area of Riften. There are a number of small stalls set up that sell items during the day, mostly foodstuffs and trinkets. At night, the stalls are packed closed and locked. Several beggars live here as well on bedrolls off to the sides of the plaza in a thicket of trees. They are too weak to handle life in the Ratway, so they huddle here or in Beggar's Row instead.

◇ Trader (General Store Vendor): Marise Aravel [13/19]
  ○ Apparel, Food, Ingredients, Misc
◇ Trader (General Store Vendor): Brand-Shei [14/19]
  ○ Weapons, Apparel, Potions, Misc
◇ Trader (General Store Vendor): Grelka [15/19]
  ○ Weapons, Apparel, Potions, Food, Misc
◇ Trader (Jeweler): Madesi [2/2]
  ○ Apparel, Misc
◇ Trainer (Light Armor: Expert): Grelka [3/3]
◇ Marriage Prospect: Grelka [54/62]
◇ Unique Item: Madesi's Silver Ring [81/112]
◇ Brand-Shei's Strongbox (Requires Key)
◇ Brynjolf' Satchel (Requires Key)
◇ Grelka's Stall Sliding Door (Expert)
◇ Grelka's Strongbox
◇ Madesi's Stall Sliding Door (Novice)
◇ Madesi's Strongbox (Novice)
◇ Loose Gear

⑭ The Bee and Barb

Keerava, the innkeeper   **Louis Letrush**

Talen-Jei   **Marcurio**

The Bee and Barb is a large tavern and inn, and while it easily accommodates the entire town, the establishment is especially dedicated to serving those who work in Riften's fishing and mead-making industries. Almost everyone important (outside of the Jarl's entourage) come to drink here. You'll also find Marcurio the Hireling, the unpleasant Sapphire, and the seedy Louis Letrush. Brynjolf hangs out here prior to beckoning you to join his Thieves Guild, but only at night. Maramal sometimes comes in here from the Temple of Mara; he has delivered a note to Talen-Jei upstairs to confirm the forthcoming Argonian wedding. Also upstairs are rooms to rent and a locked door (Apprentice) to Keerava's bedroom and business ledger, along with the strongbox. The cellar has a large amount of stored food, wine, and mead.

◇ Shadowmark: "Loot"

◇ Follower: Marcurio [41/47]

◇ Marriage Prospect: Marcurio [55/62]

◇ Trader (Bartender): Talen-Jei [3/5]

◇ Trader (Innkeeper): Keerava [14/15]

    ○ Room for the Night, Food

    ○ Innkeeper Rumors

◇ Business Ledger

◇ Note: Mara Smiles Upon You!

◇ Strongbox (Apprentice)

⑮ Black-Briar Meadery

Overseer Indaryn   **Romlyn Dreth**

Ungrien   **Valindor**

Niluva Hlaalu

The Black-Briar Meadery, owned and operated by the Black-Briar family for generations, produces almost all of Skyrim's mead and employs many of Riften's residents. The honey for the mead comes from Goldenglow Estate, on the small island on Lake Honrich, to the west of Riften. The Meadery can be accessed from Dryside or Plankside. Inside, the small shop front has a couple of Notes revealing a no-nonsense attitude to working here and some coin under the bed. Head into the back, along the two-floor high balcony above the mead distillery, to Indaryn's bedroom, which has a note from Maven to read.

    Descend to the next balcony level, where the workers eat. The door at the far end of the lower balcony leads to Plankside. Down on the distillery floor are two large vats and a chest. You can also spend 10 gold for each bottle of Black-Briar Mead you want to purchase from the underhanded Romlyn Dreth. As these are worth 25 gold, you can make a little money selling it on. The locked chest requiring a key is a reward for Miscellaneous Objective: The Lover's Requital*.

◇ Trader (Food Vendor): Ungrien [9/9]

    ○ Black-Briar Mead

◇ Marriage Prospect: Romlyn Dreth [56/62]

◇ Note: Attention Employees!

◇ Note: Note From Maven

◇ Note: To Be Read Immediately!

◇ Chest (Requires Key)

◇ Potions

⑯ Pawned Prawn

Drifa

Bersi Honey-Hand

The Pawned Prawn is a small pawnshop and general store. Inside, there's a Note from Wilhem (the innkeeper in Ivarstead) regarding his fears of Shroud Hearth Barrow. Purchase from Bersi. During Thieves Guild Quest: Taking Care of Business, a dwarven pot is on display here. Behind Bersi is a chest, and downstairs in the cellar are stocked shelves of food and drink and a safe to crack. The couple's bedroom is at the back, with a strongbox.

◇ Trader (General Store Vendor): Bersi Honey-Hand [16/19]

    ○ Weapons, Apparel, Potions, Food, Books, Misc

◇ Business Ledger

◇ Safe (Adept)

◇ Strongbox (Apprentice)

◇ Chest

◇ Potions aplenty

◇ Loose gear

⑰ Honeyside (House for Sale)

This dwelling is currently empty, save for a Skill Book that sits at the bottom of a leaning shelf in the basement. It features entrances from both Plankside and Dryside, enabling you to head to and from Riften without using the gates. Should you become the Thane of the Rift (by completing Favors for the Jarl), you can purchase this abode from Jarl Laila Law-Giver's Steward, Anuriel. Consult the Thane Quests for more information.

◇ Follower: Iona [42/47]

◇ Marriage Prospect: Iona [57/62]

◇ Skill Book [Enchanting]: Enchanter's Primer

⑱ Haelga's Bunkhouse

Haelga   **Fastred**

Svana Far-Shield   **Bassianus Axius**

Haelga's Bunkhouse provides long-term lodging for anyone who can keep up the rent and mostly caters to the fishermen and mead makers of Riften. There's something of a theme with many of the people who reside at the Bunkhouse: they do brutal, backbreaking work, and they're prone to abusing either alcohol or Skooma. It is a large building and has private rooms as well as a larger barracks-like common area with food on the tables. During Thieves Guild Quest: Taking Care of Business, a Statue of Dibella is on display on the bookcase in the main room. On the counter is a Note regarding an "experience" an anonymous patron had with Haelga. Behind the counter is Haelga's room, where she takes "clients" and writes in her ledger. Upstairs is a Skill Book, near the dormitory-style bedrooms, smaller bedroom, and storage room. More importantly is a Shrine of Dibella in Haelga's bedroom.

◇ Skill Book [Pickpocket]: Beggar [B1/10]

◇ Business Ledger

◇ Shrine of Dibella [8/8]

◇ Note: Until Next Time

◇ Dryside: Canal Level

Aside from an old Alchemist's shop tucked away under the main thoroughfare, this less-desirable and impoverished part of town is damp, dark, and the entrance to the Ratway. It isn't plagued by violence, just those down on their luck.

⑲ Beggar's Row

When the beggars of Riften aren't hanging around the marketplace, they rest here. There's little to entice you, unless you like collecting cabbage.

◇ Shadowmark: "Empty"

◇ Skill Book [Speech]: A Dance in Fire, v7 [C2/10]

⑳ Elgrim's Elixirs

Elgrim

Hafjorg

Elgrim's Elixirs is Riften's lone apothecary. As it is located in the cramped and dangerous confines of the Canal Level, Elgrim's Elixirs usually caters to the members of the Thieves Guild and other unsavory types and specializes in poisons. The shop is filled with potions and ingredients. Find a Skill Book hidden inside a woven basket that sits atop the tall shelf near the fireplace. Behind the store is a bedroom, along with an alchemy chest belonging to Ingun Black-Briar, a strongbox, and a ledger. Favor Quest: Few and Far Between (given by Ingun) must be completed in order to open the Alchemy Chest here.

◇ Shadowmark: "Loot"

◇ Crafting: Alchemy Lab

◇ Trader (Apothecary): Elgrim [12/12]

    ○ Potions, Food, Ingredients, Books

◇ Skill Book [Alteration]: Reality & Other Falsehoods

◇ Business Ledger

◇ Ingun's Alchemy Chest (Requires Key)

◇ Strongbox (Adept)

◇ Potions aplenty

㉑ Marise Aravel's House

    A homely hovel, with a good amount of food, this is where Marise the marketplace trader makes do.

◇ Shadowmark: "Loot"

㉒ Valindor's House

This is the dwelling of Valindor, who works part-time at the Meadery. This modest two-room chamber has little but food and a couple of books to steal.

◇ Shadowmark: "Loot"

㉓ Romlyn Dreth's House

The home of another Meadery worker, Romlyn's residence remains drab, even with a roaring fire.

◇ Potions

E Ratway (Entrance)

This is the initial entrance to the large underground sewer system where the Thieves Guild's tentacles have contracted to.

Plankside

The western edge of the city, known as Plankside, is actually built on the waters of Lake Honrich and serves as the city's center of mead production and distribution (which is, in fact, integral to Riften's economy) and its fishing industry (Riften's secondary economy). The buildings here have been built on wooden docks, and the district is very old and ramshackle. There are three main docks projecting from Plankside, one owned completely by Black-Briar Meadery and the other two used for general commerce and fishing boats.

F Honeyside (East Entrance)

This is the entrance to the House for Sale. Once you purchase Honeyside, you can enter and exit from this location instead of using any of the Dryside gates.

24 Riften Fishery

Tythis Ulen

Wujeeta

From-Deepest-Fathoms

Exterior: The structure has two entrances, locked during the night (Adept). There are fishing boats moored at the adjacent docks too; one has a tanning rack, and there are a number of fish barrels you can steal from.

◇ Crafting: Tanning Rack

Interior: The Riften Fishery is owned by Bolli Trout-Purse and is the center of all fishing in and around Riften. Inside, sections of the floor have been removed, allowing direct access to a salmon hatchery where the cellar used to be. But the fishery also serves as a general cleaning, storing, and processing area for all the fish that are caught on Lake Honrich. Most of the people who work in the Fishery reside at Haelga's Bunkhouse. There's an office off the balcony surrounding the hatchery with the following items:

◇ Business Ledger   ◇ Strongbox (Apprentice)

◇ Note: Things to Do

G Black-Briar Meadery (East Entrance)

This entrance is used by the Dryside Meadery for loading and off-loading. It is an alternate entrance into the establishment.

D Dock Gate (East Entrance)

This allows quick and easy access to and from the blacksmith's and the marketplace; it is an often-overlooked gate.

25 Riften Warehouse (Locked: Requires Key)

Sarthis Idren

Orini

The large wooden building served as a warehouse and general storage facility for the Fishery but hasn't been used in years. It is firmly sealed. Instead, the main floor is musty, with old furniture scattered about. Another locked door (requires Key) down in the cellar leads to a Skooma and Moon Sugar den. To enter the Warehouse, consult the Jarl of Riften and begin her Favor: The Raid. Sarthis Idren and his accomplice Orini guard their makeshift Skooma lab. It can only be accessed by key during this quest (obtained from the Jarl)

◇ Sarthis's Satchel

H Sewer

This is where you arrive if you decide to escape from Riften Jail using the sewer escape route detailed at that location.

Ratway

The Ratway is the area that runs beneath all of Riften. Comprised of interconnected basements and half-flooded sewer tunnels and dominated by a huge cistern in the center, the Ratway is a small city within a city. It is here that Riften's Thieves Guild plies its trade and the riffraff make their home.

The Ratway

A Door to Riften

1 Muggers' Tunnel

A pair of thugs prowl this initial tunnel (which has two side grates so you can peer down to Location [2]). Dodge or slay Hewnon Black-Skeever and Drahff.

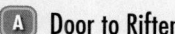

2 The Bridge

The lever to lower this bridge is on the opposite (south) side, on the upper balcony. Approach it once you've finished initial explorations. Look up in the tunnel to the west, and you can see the tunnel grates from Location [1].

B Locked Gate (Expert)

Unlock this for a shortcut to the Ragged Flagon entrance (Location [7]), and the bridge balcony.

C Trapped Door (Apprentice)

The door at the end of the tunnel to the west is trapped. Unlock the trap trigger or face two spears in your chest from the left. Back up to avoid them just after opening the door, if you didn't disarm the trap.

◇ Danger! Spear Trap

3 Gian's Oily Ooze

This junction room has a Skeever and a madman named Gian the Fist to contend with. Use an arrow to drop the oil lamp and start a fire, or find other ways to defeat anyone attacking you.

◇ Danger! Oil Lamp Trap, Oil Pool Trap

◇ Unique Item: Gloves of the Pugilist [82/112]

4 Bear Trap Chamber

A low ceiling and bear traps on this paved floor await you. Gian's Alchemy Lab is in one alcove.

◇ Danger! Bear Trap (4)   ◇ Crafting: Alchemy Lab

⑤ The Drunkard's Steps

Pass the mead barrel and watch for a pressure plate on the left side of the steps, as this triggers a battering ram in your back. Stay right instead.

◇ Danger! Battering Ram Trap!

⑥ Battleaxe Glade

A shaft of light allows plants to grow in this circular chamber.

◇ Loose gear

⑦ Ragged Flagon Entrance

Beware of lowlife attacks here. Lower the bridge from the balcony if you haven't done it already, enabling a quick exit back to Riften, when necessary. Check the table for a Skill Book. Skill Book [Pickpocket]: Beggar [B2/10]

Ⓓ Door to the Ragged Flagon

The Ragged Flagon (Map Not Shown)

> **NOTE** The following notable inhabitants of the Ragged Flagon and Cistern arrive during the Thieves Guild Quests:

Guild Master: Mercer Frey
Guild Second: Brynjolf
Guild Third: Delvin Mallory, Vex
Guild Member: Dirge, Vipir the Fleet, Niruin, Sapphire, Cynric Endell, Thrynn, Rune, Garthar, Ravyn Imyan
Guild Vendor: Vekel the Man, Syndus, Herluin Lothaire, Arnskar Ember-Master, Vanryth Gatharian
Guild Fence (Riften): Tonilia

The Ragged Flagon is the seediest, most dangerous tavern in all of Skyrim. It is located beneath the Riften city streets and serves as a meeting place for the province's criminal element. Strangers are not usually welcome, fights and even deaths are not uncommon, and most people in the place on any given night are involved in criminal activity in some capacity. It would be wise to enter here once you've befriended a thief named Brynjolf. One of the tables also contains a couple of notes, and there are two exits—one into the Vaults and a secret storage cabinet with a false back that opens up into the entrance to the Cistern. There's limited loot. The storage cabinet (requires Key) is opened by Brynjolf when he walks you into the Cistern.

◇ Trader (Apothecary): Herluin Lothaire [12/12]
  ○ Apparel, Potions, Misc
◇ Trader (Bartender): Vekel the Man [4/5]
◇ Trader (Fence): Tonilia [6/10]
  ○ Weapons, Apparel, Potions, Misc
◇ Trader (Fletcher): Syndus [3/3]
  ○ Weapons, Apparel, Misc
◇ Trader (Blacksmith): Arnskar Ember-Master [29/33]
  ○ Weapons, Apparel, Misc
◇ Trader (Blacksmith): Vanryth Gatharian [30/33]
  ○ Weapons, Apparel, Misc (Armor mending)
◇ Trainer (Archery: Master): Niruin [3/3]
◇ Trainer (Lockpicking: Master): Vex [1/2]

◇ Trainer (Pickpocket: Master): Vipir [2/3]
◇ Trainer (Sneak: Master): Delvin Mallory [2/3]
◇ Unique Item: Thieves Guild Armor [83/112]
◇ Unique Item: Thieves Guild Boots [84/112]
◇ Unique Item: Thieves Guild Gloves [85/112]
◇ Unique Item: Thieves Guild Hood [86/112]
◇ Unique Item: Amulet of Articulation [87/112]
◇ Unique Item: Guild Master's Armor [88/112]
◇ Unique Item: Guild Master's Boots [89/112]
◇ Unique Item: Guild Master's Gloves [90/112]

◇ Unique Item: Guild Master's Hood [91/112]
◇ Unique Item: Thieves Guild Armor (Improved) [92/112]
◇ Unique Item: Thieves Guild Boots (Improved) [93/112]
◇ Unique Item: Thieves Guild Gloves (Improved) [94/112]
◇ Unique Item: Thieves Guild Hood (Improved) [95/112]
◇ Note: A Warning
◇ Note: Timely Offer
◇ Chest

> **NOTE** The quality of furnishings and frequency of items, banners, Guild members, and traders appearing in the empty alcoves opposite the Ragged Flagon bar area actually increases as you restore the Guild to its former glory by completing the City Influence Quests (see Thieves Guild Quests for more information). Aside from additional traders, this also occurs in the Cistern too.

▷ The Ragged Flagon: Cistern

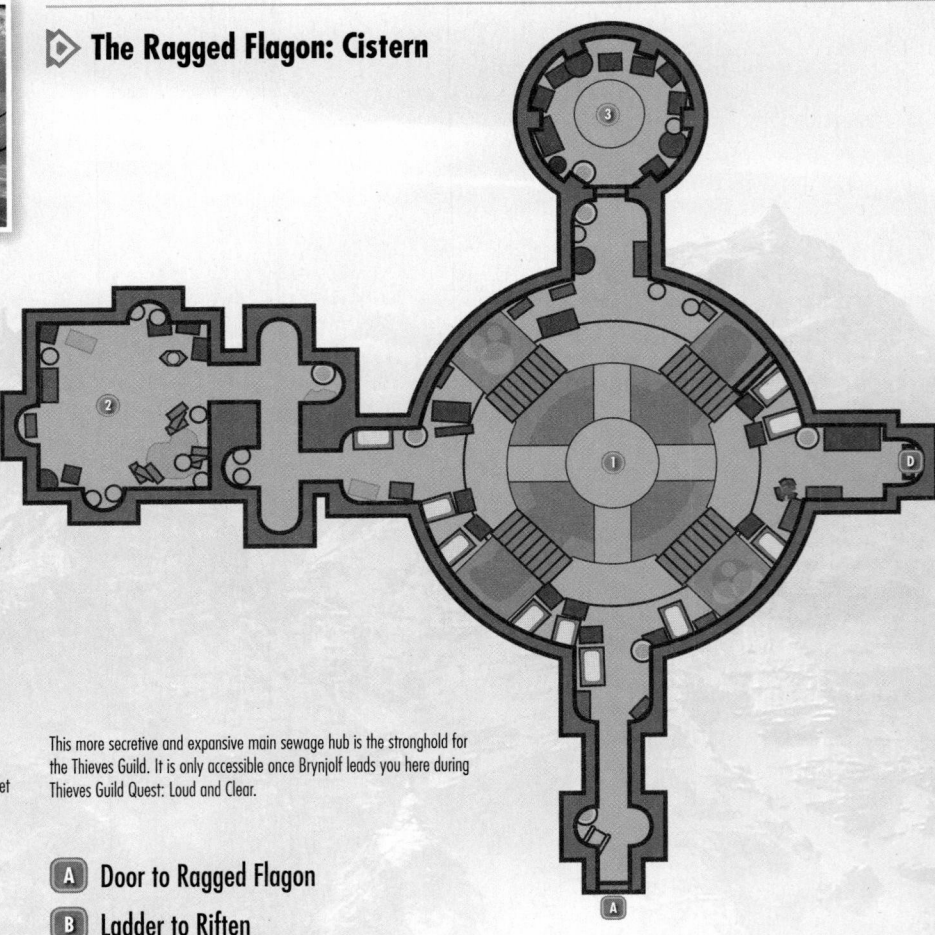

This more secretive and expansive main sewage hub is the stronghold for the Thieves Guild. It is only accessible once Brynjolf leads you here during Thieves Guild Quest: Loud and Clear.

Ⓐ Door to Ragged Flagon

Ⓑ Ladder to Riften

This brings you up and through the mausoleum and into the small graveyard attached to the Hall of the Dead. When you first access this location, it is added to your world map, allowing quicker Fast-Travel back here between Thieves Guild Quests.

① Main Cistern Chamber

Once you're a member, Guild chests are free for the opening. Otherwise they are inaccessible. These containers are also safe to store items in; deposit inventory items you wish to keep and return for them later. You should also read up on Shadowmarks by taking one of the books in this area. On Mercer Frey's table is a note regarding a tense relationship between the Guild and the East Empire Company. Near the ladder exit is a cupboard with another note, concerning the search for Rune's parents.

◇ Crafting: Grindstone
◇ Business Ledger
◇ Note: East Empire Connection
◇ Note: No Word Yet
◇ Guild Chests (7)
◇ Loose gear

② Training Chamber

Pass the Alchemy Lab to reach this location. Niruin the master archer is usually practicing here. There are a variety of training chests to unlock, too, if you want to practice (and increase your Lockpicking skill). A Skill Book that rests on a barrel can help you quickly achieve the same.

- ◇ Crafting: Alchemy Lab
- ◇ Skill Book [Lockpicking]: Advances in Lockpicking [A2/10]
- ◇ Note: Training Chests
- ◇ Guild Chest
- ◇ Chest (Locked: Novice)
- ◇ Chest (Locked: Apprentice)
- ◇ Chest (Locked: Adept)
- ◇ Chest (Locked: Expert)
- ◇ Chest (Locked: Master)
- ◇ Loose gear

③ The Guild Vault

The entire wealth of the Thieves Guild is located in this chamber, which is firmly sealed and only unlocked during the Thieves Guild Quests.

- ◇ Loose gear

④ Shrine of Nocturnal

This shrine appears after you complete Thieves Guild Quest: Darkness Returns. The shrine provides the Blessing of Nocturnal, which adds +10 to your Sneak skill.

- ◇ Ability: Blessing of Nocturnal

⑤ Guild Leader's Office

This area of the Cistern contains two trophy shelves that help you track how many Radiant Quests you've completed. They also display all of the Larceny Targets you've found (see the Thieves Guild chapter for the details). The Crown of Queen Barenziah also appears here once all of the gems have been found and the crown located (Thieves Guild Side Quest: No Stone Unturned). Once you become Guild Leader (by completing the Thieves Guild quest line and all of the City Influence Quests), the Tribute Chest will appear at the base of the desk.

⑥ Your Bed

There is a bed here that is available for you to use whenever you wish.

The Ratway Vaults

Ⓐ Door to the Ragged Flagon

- ◇ Shadowmark: "The Guild"

① Hub Level and Balconies

You can drop down here, or follow the tunnels that weave through this central location.

Ⓑ Door to Riftweald Manor

You can only drop down from here, which leads to an alcove close to the Hub Level.

- ◇ Shadowmark: "Danger"

② Dead Nord's Campfire

The trip wire on the trapped doorway releases swinging flails. This has a campfire, a dead Nord, and Skeevers.

- ◇ Danger! Flail Traps

③ Spiral Steps

- ◇ Loose gear

④ Hub Level Gratings Tunnel

One of the side alcoves has an oil lamp you can drop on enemies below.

- ◇ Danger! Oil Lamp Trap

⑤ The Old Forge

- ◇ Crafting: Workbench
- ◇ Chest
- ◇ Loose gear

⑥ Vagrant's Hideout

Beyond this table and collection of loot is a corridor leading to the bottom of the Hub Level.

- ◇ Shadowmark: "Loot"
- ◇ Chest
- ◇ Chest (Apprentice) (2)
- ◇ Loose gear

Ⓒ Door to the Ratway Warrens

There's oil on the floor and a potion to grab on your way here.

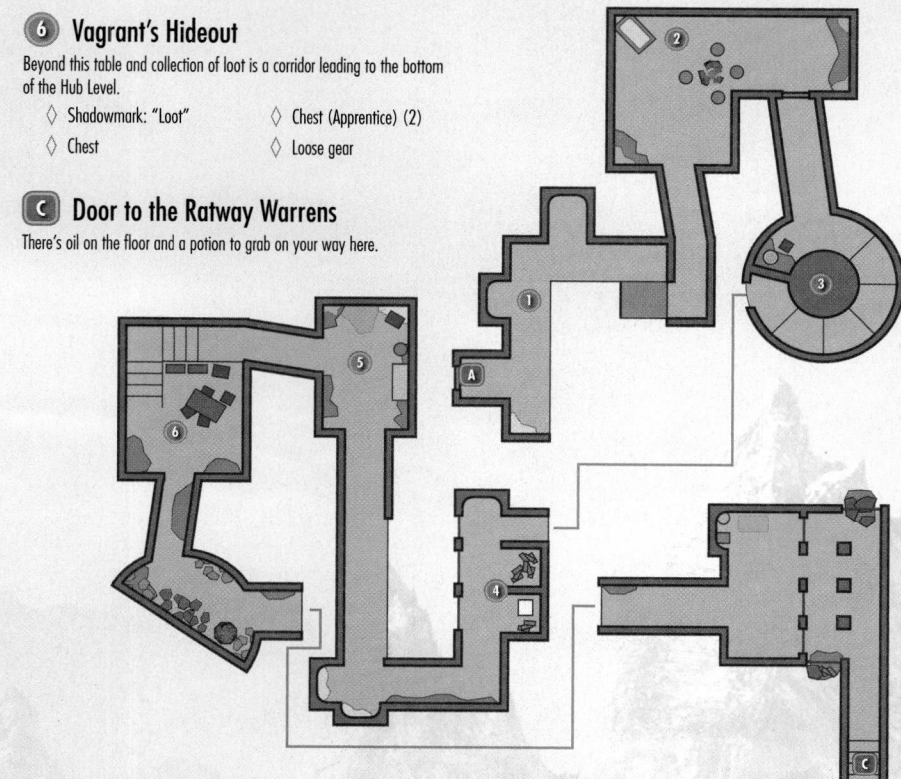

The Ratway Warrens

Ⓒ Door to the Ratway Vaults

Ⓓ Door to Warrens Hub Chamber (Apprentice)

⑦ Hub Chamber

All of the tunnels and cells in this location lead to and from this central location.

- ◇ Unique Weapon: Dravin's Bow [64/80]

⑧ Hefid's Cell (Locked: Apprentice)

This leads to a tiny dark cell where a maniac named Hefid the Deaf is babbling incoherently. She may have valuables on her corpse.

⑨ Salvianus's Cell

A man named Salvianus regales you with past talks. He may be an Imperial officer driven mad by war. He's no pushover if you decide to attack.

- ◇ Chest
- ◇ Loose gear

⑩ Knjakr's Cell

A mad chef is holed up in this cell.

- ◇ Crafting: Grindstone

⑪ Murder Hole

You can strike Salvianus from up above if you wish from here.

⑫ Esbern's Hideout

This secure underground chamber is the hiding place of Esbern, the Blades chronicler. You can only open the reinforced door during Main Quest: The Cornered Rat. Once inside, check through the multitude of books and a chest.

- ◇ Skill Book [One-Handed]: Fire and Darkness [B2/10]
- ◇ Chest

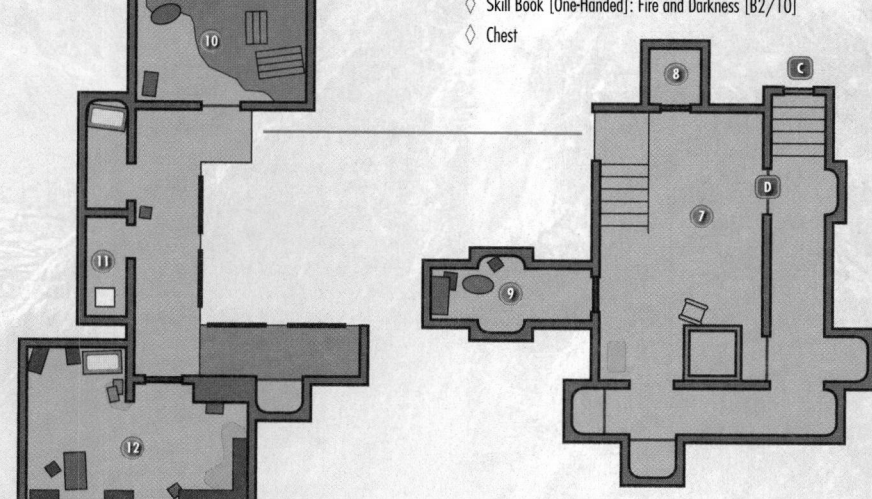

[9.01] Ivarstead

Related Quests

Main Quest: The Way of the Voice

Temple Quest: The Book of Love

Dark Brotherhood Quest: Side Contract: Narfi

Dungeon Quest: Wilhelm's Specter*

Miscellaneous Objective: Innkeeper Rumors (Vilemyr Inn)

Miscellaneous Objective: Lifting the Shroud* (Wilhelm)

Miscellaneous Objective: The Straw That Broke* (Narfi)

Miscellaneous Objective: Grin and Bear It* (Temba Wide-Arms)

Miscellaneous Objective: Climb the Steps* (Kimmek)

Favor (Activity): Harvesting Crops* (Boti)

Favor (Activity): The Gift of Charity* (Narfi)

Habitation: Town

Bassianus Axius

Boti

Fastred

Gwilin

Ivarstead Guard

Jofthor

Klimmek

Lynly Star-Sung (Bartender)

Narfi

Temba Wide-Arm (Marriage Prospect)

Wilhelm (Innkeeper; Marriage Prospect)

Crafting

Tanning Rack

Services

Marriage Prospect: Temba Wide-Arm [58/62]

Marriage Prospect: Wilhelm [59/62]

Trader (Bartender): Lynly Star-Sung [5/5]

    Food

Trader (Innkeeper): Wilhelm [15/15]

    Food, Room and Board

    Innkeeper Rumors

Quest Items

Sapphire Dragon Claw

Wylandriah's Spoon (Wylandria's Satchel)

Collectibles

Dragon Claw: Sapphire Dragon Claw [8/10]

Unique Item: Reyda's Necklace [96/112]

Chest(s)

Potions

Loose Gear

This idyllic logging and fishing village sits along the west bank of Lake Geir, right near the foot of Skyrim's towering mountain, the Throat of the World [6.38]. Interesting things are occurring at Ivarstead, not the least of which being the supposedly haunted barrow that's just outside of town.

Exterior

Speak with Klimmek, Narfi, and Temba Wide-Arm to obtain a set of Miscellaneous Objectives. Temba will also pay you for any firewood you happen to chop outside, and you can gain the Gift of Charity by giving poor Narfi a gold piece.

◇ Crafting: Tanning Rack

1 Vilemyr Inn

The local innkeeper, Wilhelm, has plenty of information to impart. Chat him up to gain a new Side Quest involving the nearby haunted barrow, along with new map data and other random rumors. Bring the informative journal you discover within Shroud Hearth Barrow [9.02] to Wilhelm, and he'll hand you a special Sapphire Claw that lets you explore more of the place.

Lynly Star-Sung is also here. You can ask her to play an instrumental song for 5 septims (unless you can persuade her to play for free). Lynly is the woman who Sibbi Black-Briar is searching for in the quest "The Lover's Requital." Temba Wide-Arm and Gwilin both reside at the inn as well.

◇ Dragon Claw: Sapphire Dragon Claw [8/10]

◇ Chests (2)

◇ Loose Gear

2 Fellstar Farm

The farmhouse is commonly locked, and a woman named Boti is usually found inside, keeping the place neat and orderly. Her husband, Jofthor, can usually be found outside working the grain mill or feeding the livestock. Her daughter, Fastred, can be found helping her mother in the fields or complaining about being stuck in this backwater village.

◇ Area Is Locked (Apprentice)

◇ Wylandriah's Satchel

◇ Wylandriah's Spoon (Wylandriah's Satchel)

◇ Chest

3 Klimmek's House

Bassianus Axius and Klimmek share this place. Klimmek allowed Bassianus to move in a long time ago, and their personalities have been clashing ever since.

◇ Area Is Locked (Apprentice)

◇ Chest

◇ Potion

◇ Loose Gear

4 Temba Wide-Arm's Mill

This is where Temba and Gwilin can be found during the day, chopping wood and working the mill.

5 Narfi's Ruined House

Narfi resides here, in the ruins of his family home. He can be found wandering around aimlessly calling for his sister or skulking about annoying the locals.

[9.02] Shroud Hearth Barrow

Dangers

Battering Ram Trap (pressure plate)
Dart Trap (lever, pressure plate)
Flamethrower Trap (trapped door)
Oil Lamp Trap
Oil Pool Trap

Rockfall Trap (trip wire)
Swinging Blade Trap (trip wire, wall chain)
Spear Trap (pressure plate)
Swinging Wall Trap (pressure plates)

Puzzles

Claw Door (Sapphire Claw)
Nordic Pillars

Quest Items

Wyndelius' Journal

Collectibles

Skill Book [Illusion]: Before the Ages of Man [B2/10]

Special Objects

Word Wall: Kyne's Peace [3/3]
Chests
Potions
Loose gear

Related Quests

Dungeon Quest: Wilhelm's Specter*

Recommended Level: 6

Dungeon: Draugr Crypt

Draugr
Skeleton
Wyndelius Gatharian

Crafting

Alchemy Lab

This barrow lies on the hill overlooking the village of Ivarstead. Speaking with Wilhelm, the town's innkeeper, provides you with a Dungeon Quest that entices you to investigate this haunted place in search of treasure.

A Exit to Skyrim

1 Lever Puzzle Passage

Obtain a bit of loot from a shelf on your way into this passage, where the ghost of Wyndelius Gatharian urges you to leave, then vanishes. Enter the nearby alcove, grab a Skill Book off the stone table, then face west, toward the far portcullis, so that two pairs of wall levers are visible. Looking at the portcullis, pull the leftmost lever, followed by the "inside" right lever, to manipulate the gates so that you may progress. Don't touch the far-right lever—it triggers a trap. Pull the wall chain that follows to raise the next few portcullises, and optionally unlock an Adept-level iron door to access a dangerous nook with a trapped chest and a pressure plate trap.

◇ Danger! Dart Trap (lever, trigger hinge), Spear Trap (pressure plate, wall chain)
◇ Skill Book [Illusion]: Before the Ages of Man [B2/10]
◇ Potion

2 Wyndelius's Study

Visit this room to catch up with the specter that warned you before. The ghost of Wyndelius Gatharian now lashes out at you. Lay it to rest to discover that it was never a ghost at all—just a man who'd been drinking a special potion to disguise himself as a specter. Collect the nearby journal and a few samples of the potion to gain new insight and advance the plot.

◇ Crafting: Alchemy Lab
◇ Wyndelius's Journal
◇ Philter of the Phantom
◇ Satchel
◇ Potions
◇ Loose gear

3 Hall of Stories

Bring the journal that you find at [2] back to Ivarstead's innkeeper, Wilhelm. In thanks, he'll give you the Sapphire Claw, which you need to open the Nordic Puzzle Door here. Beware of gouts of flame as you open the door and enter the passage (or look to the floor and disarm that particular trap), then inspect the Sapphire Claw and notice three symbols etched on its palm (Moth, Owl, Wolf). Rotate the door's three concentric rings to form the same pattern of symbols, then inspect the central keyhole to insert the claw and open the way forward.

◇ Danger! Flamethrower Traps (trapped door)

4 Draugr Ambush

A number of Draugr burst out of sarcophagi as you move through this chamber, and portcullises fall to trap you inside. Deal with the undead, then pull the lever in the east alcove to open the portcullises and continue on.

◇ Loose gear

5 Spiral Stairwell

A trapdoor plunges you into shallow water at the foot of this winding stairwell. Nab some gear from the bottom of the pool, then swim up and climb out (or pull the lever to lift yourself out). Go all the way upstairs to locate a Master-level locked door. If you can pick this tricky lock, you should have no trouble opening the large chest in the nook beyond.

◇ Chest (Locked: Expert)
◇ Loose gear

6 Oil Pit Chamber

Leap two pressure plates and slay a skeleton as you descend into this chamber, where a mob of skeletons are gathered in the center of the room below. Quickly knock down one of the central hanging lamps to ignite the oily floor beneath them and decimate all of the skeletons at once. Before going downstairs, spy a handle near a sarcophagus and pull it to allow you to enter the treasure room. More Draugr awaken when you reach the room's far side. Deal with them, then proceed through the northeast door. Beware of the trip wire stretched across the passage beyond.

◇ Danger! Battering Ram Trap (pressure plate), Dart Trap (pressure plate), Oil Lamp Trap, Oil Pool Trap
◇ Chest
◇ Potions
◇ Loose gear

7 Trapped Passage

Avoid triggering a trip wire and pressure plate as you battle a bow-wielding Draugr here. Jump the trip wire and sneak around the plate to avoid stirring more undead. Once again, you find yourself locked in the room. Pick the lock on the far door, or take it from the corpse of the Draugr near the door once you kill it—again.

◇ Danger! Swinging Blade Trap (trip wire/wall chain), Swinging Wall Trap (pressure plate)

8 Drawbridge Chamber

A waterfall pushes a gentle stream through this long, enemy-free chamber. Pull a nearby wall chain to open the portcullis at the end of the stream, then claim a coin purse from the bottom of the small pool beyond. Find some gear behind the waterfall as well, then go upstairs and open the large southwest door to enter a chamber with a lone Draugr guard. Step on the pressure plate here to rotate the walls and catch glimpses of four glyphs. Spin the four glyph pillars outside the room to mimic the same pattern (Whale, Hawk, Snake, Whale), then step on the central pressure plate to lower a drawbridge.

◇ Potion
◇ Loose gear

9 Path to the Depths

Avoid the pressure plate just inside the door, then deliberately hit the trip wire to trigger a rockfall trap that smashes the Draugr in this passage. See if you can open the Apprentice-level locked door to access a small nook with a gold bar, but beware the flamethrower trap that fires when you remove it.

◇ Danger! Flamethrower Trap (pressure pedestal), Rockfall Trap (trip wire), Swinging Wall Trap (pressure plate)
◇ Potion
◇ Loose gear

B Door to Shroud Hearth Depths

Your trip through the barrow has brought you to a cavernous underground temple. Slaughter all skeletons and Draugr that rise from their sarcophagi here—the last few are quite powerful. Proceed to the back room when the northwest passage opens, and disarm the trap on the large chest (or carefully stand to the side) to avoid being shot by darts. Gain a new Word of Power from the far Word Wall before taking your leave of this haunted barrow.

◇ Danger! Dart Trap   ◇ Potion
◇ Word Wall: Kyne's Peace [3/3] ◇ Loose gear

C Door to Shroud Hearth Barrow

[9.03] Pinepeak Cavern

Dungeon: Animal Den
Animal

Collectibles
Skill Book [Smithing]: Heavy Armor Forging
Chest
Potion
Loose gear
Mineable ore (Corundum)

This small cave lies at the eastern base of Whiterun's towering mountain, the Throat of the World [6.38], landing it within the Rift's bounds. Slay the exterior Bear, then enter the cave and put down a second Bear to secure a Skill Book and a chest.

[9.04] Geirmund's Hall

Related Quests
Side Quest: Forbidden Legend
Dungeon Activity

Recommended Level: 6

Dungeon: Draugr Crypt
Animal
Draugr
Sigdis Gauldurson

Crafting
Arcane Enchanter

Dangers
Dart Trap (pressure plate)
Flamethrower Trap (hinge trigger)
Magic Caster Trap
Mammoth Skull Trap (tabletop pressure plate)
Spear Trap (lever)
Swinging Blade Trap (pressure plate)

Puzzles
Nordic Puzzle Pillars

Collectibles
Skill Book [Two-Handed]: Words and Philosophy
Unique Item: Gauldur Amulet Fragment (Geirmund's Hall) [97/112] (Sigdis Gauldurson)
Unique Weapon: Gauldur Blackbow [65/80] (Sigdis Gauldurson)
Chests
Potions
Loose Gear

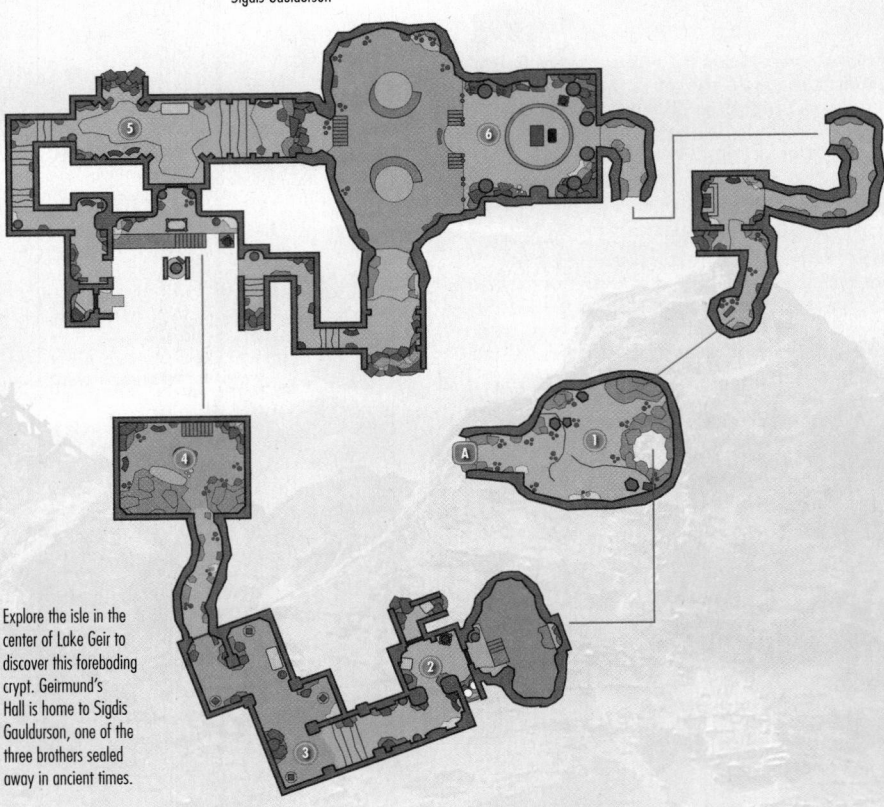

Explore the isle in the center of Lake Geir to discover this foreboding crypt. Geirmund's Hall is home to Sigdis Gauldurson, one of the three brothers sealed away in ancient times.

A Exit to Skyrim

1 Entry Cavern

Eliminate a few pesky Skeevers in this first small cavern, then search the body of a fallen adventurer to discover a book that hints at the history behind this tomb. Steel yourself, then leap into the nearby pit, landing in a watery chamber below. Search a short underwater passage to locate a sunken chest before climbing onto dry land and proceeding through and iron door.

◇ Chest

2 Spiderweb Hall

Slay a couple of Frostbite Spiders in this webbed corridor, and unlock an Adept-level iron door to access a small nook with some potions and gear. Disarm the trapped chest on the shelf, or stand off to one side as you open it to dodge the flamethrower trap. Then skirt a nearby pressure plate as you head toward [3].

◇ Danger! Dart Trap (pressure plate), Flamethrower Trap (hinge trigger)
◇ Chest
◇ Potions
◇ Gear

3 Flooded Catacombs

Cut down the Draugr that arise from these waterlogged burial passages, note the four glyphs on the walls near the stairs as you enter, two on each wall. Spin the four pillars in the passage ahead so that their glyphs match the ones near the stairs (Hawk, Whale, Snake, Whale). With the pillars properly rotated, pull the lever near the far portcullis to open the way forward. Beware of taking the Soul Gem from the table here—removing it causes the giant mammoth skull to swing at you like a battering ram!

◇ Danger! Mammoth Skull Trap (pressure pedestal)
◇ Potion

4 Lord Geirmund's Tomb

This tall chamber features plenty of Draugr and multiple tiers of walkways. Fight your way up some wooden stairs and collect an important key from the withered hand of Lord Geirmund on the altar. Inspect the nearby epitaph before using the key to open the nearby door and advance.

◇ Lord Geirmund's Key
◇ Potion
◇ Loose Gear

 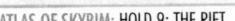

⑤ Crafty Passages

Slay a powerful Draugr and his animal companion here, then search around to find a couple of potions. Take the west passage and go upstairs to battle another mighty Draugr. Don't pull the lever by the bridge—it triggers a trap. Instead, turn around and pull a different lever that's mounted on the wall to lower to lower the bridge.

Back out on the upper level of Lord Geirmund's Tomb [4], look to your right to see a small ledge. Jump down and disarm the trap on the door, then enter the small alcove to find a locked chest.

Cross the bridge (pulling another lever on the far side of the central platform), then carefully avoid the pressure plate as you move on to the next chamber. It activates a nasty set of swinging blades that are difficult to dodge once triggered.

◇ Danger! Magic Caster Trap, Spear Trap (lever), Swinging Blade Trap (pressure plate)

◇ Crafting: Arcane Enchanter

◇ Chest (Locked: Expert)

◇ Potions

◇ Loose gear

⑥ Sigdis Gauldurson's Tomb

An incredibly powerful undead archer rises to combat you in this flooded chamber. Throughout the battle, Sigdis Gauldurson summons two illusory duplicates of himself to confuse you. The "real" enemy is the one that wears a horned helmet. Attack this version of the Sigdis to inflict damage, eventually slaying the fiend to attain two powerful items from its remains. When Sigdis falls, a secret door opens, allowing you to take the east passage to locate a giant chest and other valuables, including a Skill Book found on the top of the nearby bookshelf. Follow the passage to its end and pull a lever to open a secret door that connects back to [1].

◇ Unique Item: Gauldur Amulet Fragment (Geirmund's Hall) [97/112] (Sigdis Gauldurson)

◇ Unique Weapon: Gauldur Blackbow [65/80] (Sigdis Gauldurson)

◇ Skill Book [Two-Handed]: Words and Philosophy

◇ Chest

◇ Potions

◇ Loose Gear

▷ [9.05] Nilheim

Related Quests

Dungeon Quest: The Nilheim Scam*

Recommended Level: 6

Dungeon: Bandit Camp

Guard
Telrav

Collectibles

Chests (2)
Apothecary's Satchel
Potion
Loose Gear

Little remains of this ruined fortress, which lies just east of Lake Geir, save some stone steps and a tower. An injured merchant named Telrav is found on the road outside of Nilheim. Agree to help Telrav, and he'll lead you to the camp—and then springs an ambush! Slay the villains then raid their campsite in just retribution.

▷ [9.06] Sarethi Farm

Related Quests

Side Quest: A Return to Your Roots
Miscellaneous Objective: Smooth Jazbay* (Avrusa Sarethi)
Favor (Activity): Harvesting Crops* (Avrusa Sarethi)

Habitation: Farm

Aduri Sarethi
Avrusa Sarethi (Marriage Prospect)
Rift Guard

Crafting

◇ Alchemy Lab

Tanning Rack

Services

Marriage Prospect: Avrusa Sarethi [60/62]

Collectibles

Potions
Loose Gear

This quaint farm stands in the Rift's central wilds, just north of the Treva River.

Exterior

Speak with the farm's owner, Avrusa Sarethi, to learn how she managed to grow so much rare Nirnroot in her garden and obtain a Side Quest. Avrusa is also your final destination in the "Return to Your Roots" quest (see quest for details), and the remains of Sinderion's living quarters can still be found in her basement.

◇ Crafting: Tanning Rack

Sarethi Farm (Interior)

Breaking into the farmhouse is profitable due to the many potions and additional Nirnroot found in the cellar.

◇ Area Is Locked (Novice)
◇ Crafting: Alchemy Lab
◇ Potions
◇ Loose Gear

▷ [9.07] Rift Stormcloak Camp

Related Quests

Civil War Quest (when active, depending on who you side with)

Habitation: Military: Stormcloak Camp

Stormcloak Quartermaster (Blacksmith)
Stormcloak Soldier

Services

Trader (Blacksmith): Stormcloak Quartermaster [31/33]
Weapons, Apparel, Misc

Crafting

Alchemy Lab
Anvil
Grindstone
Workbench

Special Objects

Civil War: Map of Skyrim
Chests
Potions
Loose Gear

Depending on the status of the Civil War quest line, you may or may not be able to visit this small Stormcloak campsite. Here you may trade with the quartermaster or use his plethora of crafting stations. Examine the tabletop map in one of the tents to potentially gain new map data.

▷ [9.08] Rift Watchtower

Related Quests

Side Quest: The Forgemaster's Fingers

Recommended Level: 6

Dungeon: Bandit Camp

Bandit
Orc

Crafting

Tanning Rack

Collectibles

Skill Book [Heavy Armor]: Hallgerd's Tale [C2/10]
Chest
Potions
Loose Gear

Orcish bandits occupy this tower, which stands in the Rift's northern mountains, east of Lake Geir. Slay the ruffians to steal their plunder.

▷ [9.09] Alchemist's Shack

Related Quests

Side Quest: Captured Critters*

Recommended Level: 8

Dungeon: Special

Crafting

Alchemy Lab

Collectibles

Caged Critter: Butterfly in a Jar [4/5]
Apothecary's Satchel
Potion
Loose Gear

This open-air cabin stands in the Rift's southwestern woods and contains several items of interest. Curiously, the cabin's owner is nowhere to be found. Read the journal on the end table near the bed to learn where he might have gone.

▷ [9.10] Honeystrand Cave

Dungeon: Animal Den

Animal

Collectible

Chest

This small bear cave lies just off the Rift's western main road. Slay the ferocious exterior Cave Bear, then enter the cave to battle two more of the beasts. Loot the body of a mauled bandit in the cave's center, along with the nearby chest.

[9.11] Rift Imperial Camp

Related Quests

Civil War Quest: Reunification of Skyrim

Civil War Quest: Compelling Tribute

Civil War Quest: The Battle for Fort Greenwall

Dungeon Activity

Habitation: Military: Imperial Camp

Legate Fasendil

Imperial Quartermaster (Blacksmith)

Imperial Soldier

Services

Trader (Blacksmith): Imperial Quartermaster [32/33]

   Weapons, Apparel, Misc

Crafting

Alchemy Lab

Anvil

Grindstone

Workbench

Special Objects

Civil War: Map of Skyrim

Chest(s)

Potions

Loose Gear

If you're playing through the Civil War quest line, then you may be able to visit this Imperial campsite located deep in the Rift's southwest forest. Trade with the quartermaster if you like, or hone your gear with his crafting stations. Inspect the tabletop map in the largest tent to potentially gain new map data.

[9.12] Ruins of Bthalft

Recommended Level: 6

Dungeon: Bandit Camp

Bandit

Dangers

Bone Alarm Trap

Collectible

Chest (Locked: Adept)

This small collection of open-air ruins lies in the Rift's southwestern wilds. Cut down a handful of bandits here, then scale the narrow northern wooden stairs to locate a chest on a ledge.

[9.13] Arcwind Point

Recommended Level: 6

Dungeon: Draugr Crypt

Draugr

Skeleton

Dangers

Battering Ram Trap (pressure plate)

Collectibles

Skill Book [Restoration]: Withershins [E2/10]

Chest

Potions

Loose Gear

Mineable ore (Quicksilver)

Explore the frigid mountains in the Rift's far southwest corner to discover a breathtaking valley of forgotten ruins. Descend into the circular ruin to battle a mighty Draugr. Mine some Quicksilver Ore as you head toward a larger ruin, which is guarded by several skeletons. An even more powerful Draugr emerges from the sarcophagus here. Scale the long north stairs after the fight to reach a third, hutlike ruin, but beware of the pressure plate at the top of the stairs and the mighty Draugr that emerges from the sarcophagus as you exit the "hut." Go west to mine more Quicksilver, then climb the east rocks and broken stairs to discover an old tower. Fight your way to the tower's apex, where a large chest and reclusive Skill Book are found.

[9.14] Autumnwatch Tower

Dungeon: Dragon Lair

Bandit

Dragon (after Main Quest: Dragon Rising)

Crafting

Tanning Rack (2)

Collectibles

Skill Book [Light Armor]: Jornibret's Last Dance [B2/10]

Special Objects

Word Wall: Marked for Death [3/3]

Chest

Potion

Loose Gear

Two open-air towers stand at this remote site in the Rift's southwest mountains, one of which is tall enough to be seen from afar. After the "Dragon Rising" quest, a mighty winged beast can be fought here. Until then, the tower is home to dangerous bandits. Scale the taller tower to discover a large chest, then cross a stone arc to reach a sacred Word Wall. The smaller tower features two Tanning Racks, and there's a Skill Book on its roof.

[9.15] Froki's Shack

Related Quests

Side Quest: Kyne's Sacred Trials

Recommended Level: 6

Dungeon: Special

Froki Whetted-Blade

Crafting

Tanning Rack

Collectibles

Skill Book [Archery]: Vernaccus and Bourlor [E2/10]

Unique Item: Diadem of the Savant [98/112]

Unique Item: Kyne's Token [99/112]

Chest

Loose Gear

This small cabin stands in the Rift's southwest mountains, just east of Autumnwatch Tower [9.14]. Head inside to speak with Froki and gain a new Side Quest. The old hunter doesn't own much, but you can steal several pieces of gear, snatch a Skill Book off a shelf, and loot a chest here if you like. A unique item rests atop the exterior Wood Chopping Block as well.

[9.16] Treva's Watch

Related Quests

Dungeon Quest: Infiltration

Recommended Level: 6

Dungeon: Bandit Camp

Bandit
Stalleo
Stalleo's Bodyguard

Crafting

Anvil
Arcane Enchanter
Grindstone
Workbench

Dangers

Bear Traps
Flail Trap (pressure plate)
Oil Lamp Traps
Oil Pool Traps
Swinging Wall Trap (pressure plate)

Collectibles

Skill Book [Enchanting]: Twin Secrets [E2/10]
Area Is Locked (lever)
Chests
Potions
Loose Gear

This sizeable stronghold stands along the bank of the Treva River, which flows between Lake Geir and Lake Honrich in the heart of the Rift.

Treva's Watch Escape Tunnel

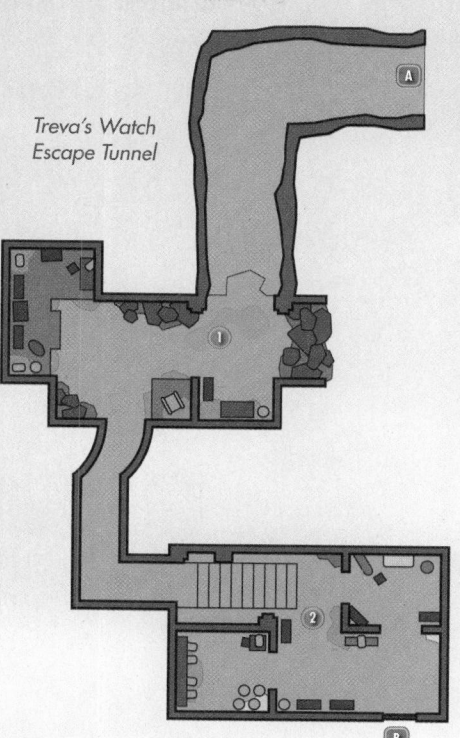

Exterior

Bandits have overrun Treva's Watch, and steel bars prevent a traditional frontal assault on the main gate. Travel west to locate a nearby campsite, where a soldier named Stalleo gives you a Side Quest that involves reclaiming Treva's Watch from his enemies. Enter the nearby cave to begin your infiltration of the fort.

Later, when you reach the fort's interior courtyard, make your way up its ramparts to discover a chest on the roof.

◇ Chest

A · Exit to Skyrim

1 · Entry Tunnel

Get the drop on the bandits that guard the secret entry tunnel by knocking down an overhead lamp to ignite the oil at their feet. Slay the villains afterward, then loot a pair of chests before leaping a bear trap in the passage that follows.

◇ Danger! Bear Trap, Oil Lamp Trap, Oil Pool Trap
◇ Chests (2)
◇ Loose Gear

2 · Crafting Area

Make use of a few crafting stations before entering Treva's Watch.

◇ Crafting: Anvil, Grindstone, Workbench
◇ Potions
◇ Loose Gear

B · Door to Treva's Watch

Treva's Watch

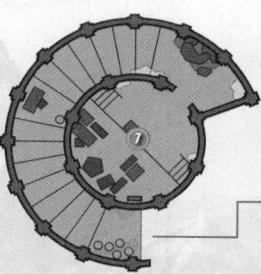

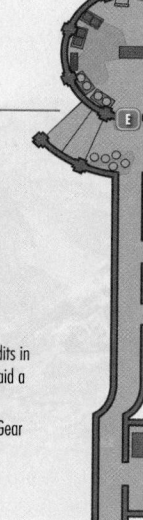

C · Door to Treva's Watch Escape Tunnel

3 · Entry Passage

Sidestep bear traps and slay a few rugged bandits in the keep's first passage, then go upstairs and raid a knapsack on a shelf.

◇ Danger! Bear Traps
◇ Loose Gear
◇ Knapsack

4 · Sleeping Area

Silence another bandit in this sleeping area, looting a chest for more plunder. The sound of battle may bring several bandits running in from the south room, including the gang's leader. Unlock a nearby Adept-level door to access a storage closet with another chest, then loot a third chest as you make your way toward [5].

◇ Chests (3)
◇ Potions
◇ Apothecary's Satchel
◇ Loose Gear

5 · Great Hall

Snag a few potions before descending this chamber's steps and proceeding to [6].

◇ Potions

6 · Kitchen

Slay a spellcasting bandit here in the kitchen, then loot a chest that's tucked away in the larder.

◇ Chest
◇ Potions

7 · Tower

Avoid a lethal pressure plate trap in the hall that leads to this circular chamber. Go upstairs and battle more bandits, including another powerful chief. Try knocking down the overhead lamp to ignite the oil on the stairs and burn these foes. Loot a large chest upstairs, but don't exit through the ceiling trapdoor. Instead, head back downstairs and visit the holding cell area to secure a bit more loot.

◇ Danger! Oil Lamp Trap, Oil Pool Trap, Swinging Wall Trap (pressure plate)
◇ Crafting: Arcane Enchanter
◇ Skill Book [Enchanting]: Twin Secrets [E2/10]
◇ Chest
◇ Knapsack
◇ Apothecary's Satchel
◇ Potion
◇ Loose Gear

8 · Holding Cells

The last few interior bandits lurk in these final rooms. Dispatch them so you may safely loot a chest. Proceed to the hall's end, leaping a pressure plate to avoid triggering a trap. Loot the chest at the end of the passage, then exit through the nearby door to emerge outside near a lever — pull it to open the stronghold's front gate, allowing Stalleo and his men to join you in the courtyard and fight to reclaim the fort.

◇ Danger! Flail Trap (pressure plate)
◇ Chests (2)
◇ Loose Gear

D · Exit to Skyrim (lower courtyard)

E · Exit to Skyrim (upper ramparts)

[9.17] Angarvunde

Angarvunde

Related Quests

Dungeon Quest: Medresi Dran and the Wandering Dead*

Recommended Level: 6

Dungeon: Draugr Crypt

Draugr
Medresi Dran

Dangers

Battering Ram Trap (pressure plate)
Floor Arrows (pressure plate)
Spear Trap (pedestal pressure plate)
Swinging Blade Trap (pressure plates)
Trapped Chest

This large, forgotten temple runs deep into the Rift's southwest mountains, not far from the Dwarven ruins of Avanchnzel [9.18].

Collectibles

Skill Book [Illusion]: Before the Ages of Man
Skill Book [Speech]: A Dance in Fire, v7

Special Objects

Word Wall: Animal Allegiance [3/3]
Chest(s)
Potions
Loose Gear

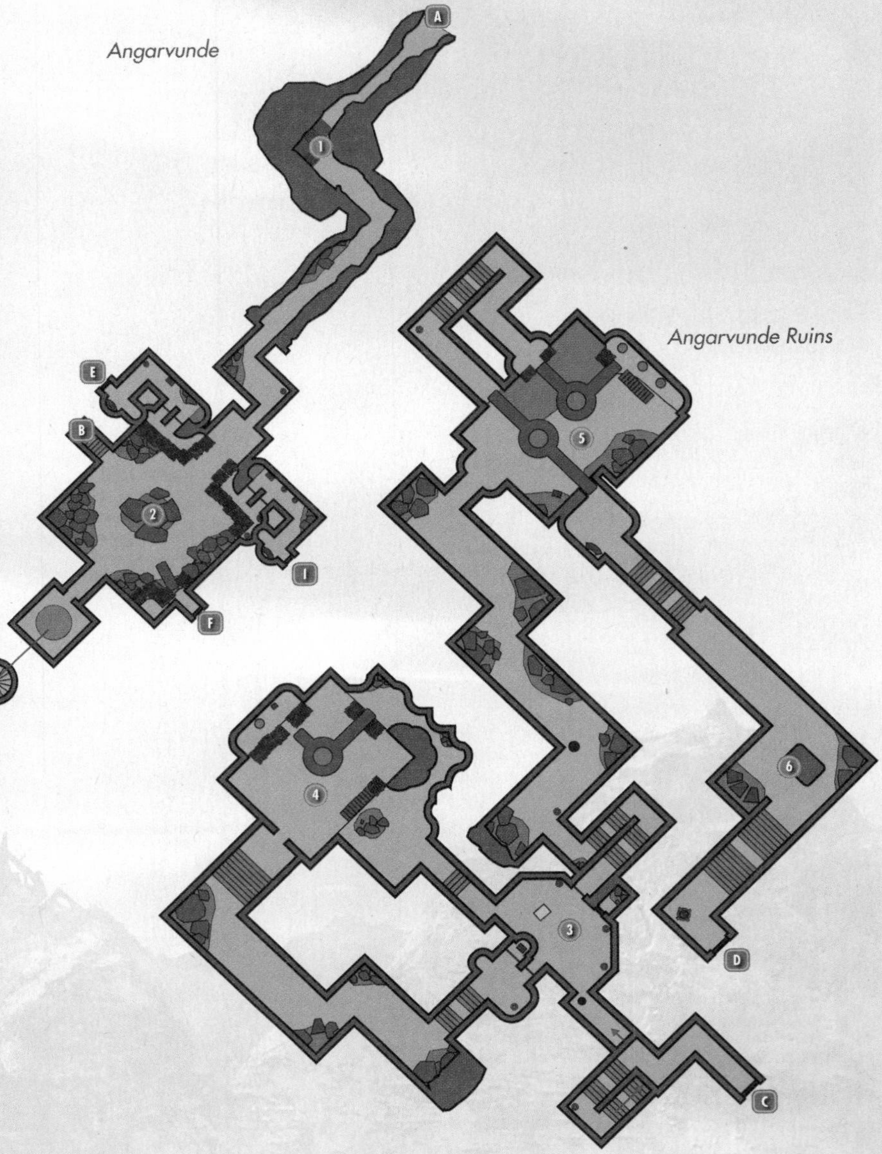

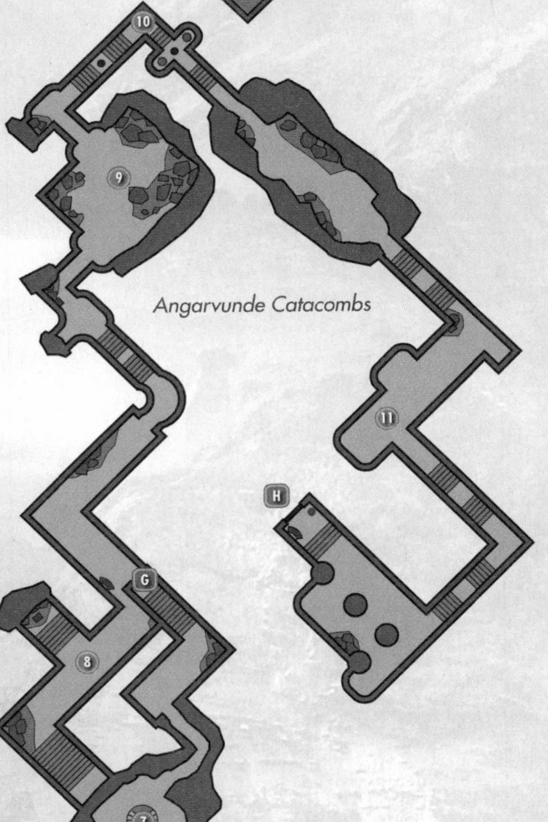

Angarvunde Ruins

Angarvunde Catacombs

Exterior

An abandoned camp lies just outside the Angarvunde's cavelike entrance. Inspect the informative journal of Medresi Dran on the table and grab the nearby Skill Book before heading inside.

◇ Skill Book [Speech]: A Dance in Fire, v7

A Exit to Skyrim

1 Entry Chamber

Speak with a woman named Medresi Dran in the very first chamber to gain a new Side Quest that involves killing three powerful Draugr in the next room.

2 Great Hall

Slay the three deadly Draugr in this wide cavern, then double back to inform Medresi of your success. Follow Medresi to a raised portcullis, then accept the key she gives you, which opens the northwest door to the ruins and the southeast door to the catacombs.

◇ Angarvunde Key (Medresi)

B Door to Angarvunde Ruins

C Door to Angarvunde

3 Junction Chamber

Jump and sidestep a series of pressure plates in the hall that leads to this room, where a lowly Draugr guards a chest. A Skill Book rests on a nearby stone table.

◇ Danger! Swinging Blade Trap (pressure plates)
◇ Skill Book [Illusion]: Before the Ages of Man
◇ Chest (Locked: Novice)

4 Broken Walkway Hall

Another group of powerful Draugr guards this chamber. Jump across the broken walkway to reach a valuable potion that sits atop a pedestal, but stand to one side of the pedestal when collecting the potion to avoid being impaled by spears. Take the lower passage to loop back around to [3].

◇ Danger! Spear Trap (pedestal pressure plate)
◇ Potion

3 Junction Chamber Revisited

Pull a lever to lower all of the portcullises in this chamber, then loot a locked chest you couldn't have reached before. Cut across the room and take the east passage to [5].

◇ Chest (Locked: Novice)

5 Sarcophagi Chamber

Avoid a pressure plate as you cut down powerful Draugr in the passages that lead to this large chamber, where another group of fearsome undead burst out from wall sarcophagi to attack. Loot a chest on the ground floor before heading upstairs and taking a winding passage to [6].

◇ Danger! Battering Ram Trap (pressure plate) ◇ Chest

6 Ruins Exit Passage

Collect a few valuables and slay one last formidable Draugr as you navigate this passage, which leads back to the Great Hall.

◇ Potions ◇ Loose Gear

E Door to Angarvunde

F Door to Angarvunde Ruins

2 Great Hall Revisited

Collect a bit of loot that you couldn't have reached before as you reenter the Great Hall, then scale the southeast fallen pillar to reach the door that leads into the catacombs.

◇ Chest ◇ Potions

G Door to Angarvunde Catacombs

H Door to Angarvunde

7 Broken Stairwell Chamber

Descend into this room, slaying a Draugr from an elevated vantage before dropping from the broken stairwell and proceeding to [8].

8 Burial Passages

Dispatch a few powerful Draugr in this passage, and stand to one side of the chest that lies atop the northwest stairs to avoid a nasty trap when opening it (or try disabling its trigger hinge).

◇ Danger! Trapped Chest

9 Canis Tree Chamber

Loot a chest on your way to this chamber, then raid another chest that lies near one of the gnarled Canis trees.

◇ Chest ◇ Potion
◇ Chest (Locked: Novice)

10 Arrow Trap Stairs

Beware of two pressure plates that trigger similar traps as you scale the stairs in this passage.

◇ Danger! Floor Arrows (pressure plates)

11 Catacombs Exit Passage

Cut through a host of Draugr as you navigate the catacombs' final passage, returning to the Great Hall.

◇ Potion ◇ Loose gear

H Door to Angarvunde

I Door to Angarvunde Catacombs

2 Great Hall (Third Visit)

Loot a chest and throw a lever to lower the portcullises as you did before. With all portcullises open, return to Medresi, who foolishly rushes off and is slain by a deadly trap. Enter the raised section of floor afterward, and you'll be lowered down to a secret passage.

◇ Chest

12 Word Wall Chamber

The temple's treasure is grand indeed, and there's nothing left to guard it. Obtain a new Word of Power from the ancient Word Wall here, and loot a large chest for vast wealth, completing your quest.

◇ Word Wall: Animal Allegiance [3/3] ◇ Chest

[9.18] Avanchnzel

Related Quests

Side Quest: Unfathomable Depths

Recommended Level: 16

Dungeon: Dwarven City

Dwarven Centurion
Dwarven Sphere
Dwarven Spider

Crafting

Alchemy Lab

Dangers

Dwarven Thresher Trap (trapped door)
Dwarven Thresher Trap (pressure plate)
Spear Trap (trapped door)

Collectibles

Skill Book [Restoration]: Racial Phylogeny

Special Objects

Lexicon Receptacle
Chests
Potions
Loose Gear

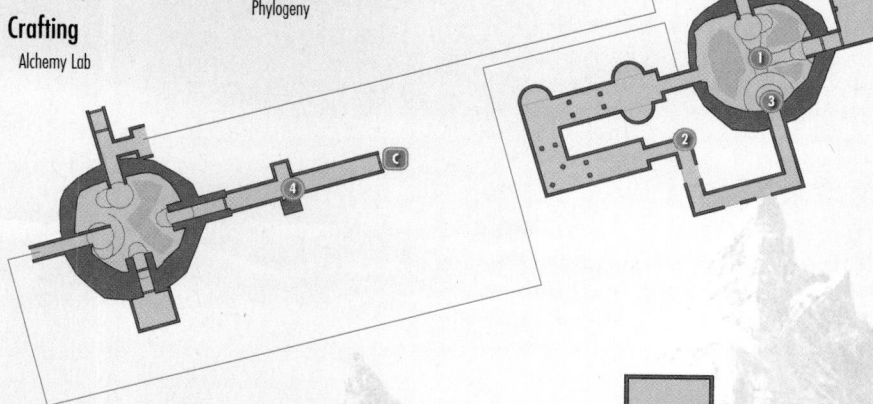

Avanchnzel

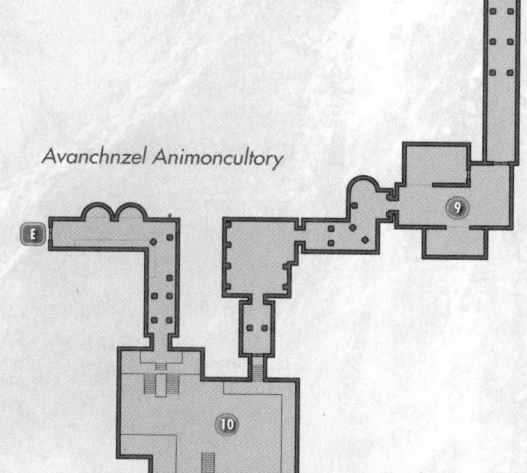

Avanchnzel Animoncultory

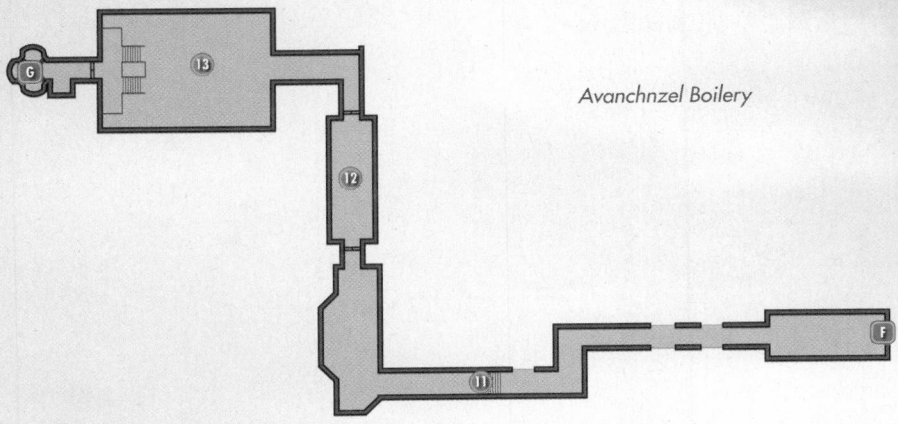

Avanchnzel Boilery

This impressive collection of dwarven ruins stands among the Rift's southern mountains. This is a large area, for the ruins run deep into the rock. Scale a series of spiral pathways to locate Avanchnzel's cavelike entrance, and head inside.

A Exit to Skyrim

1 Central Cavern

Destroy a couple of formidable Dwarven Spiders on your way to this massive, open-air cavern. Take the east passage and dismantle a Dwarven Sphere in the adjoining chamber, then scale a sloping passage and unbar a door so you may step out to the balcony and loot an outdoor chest. Head back inside and return to the large cavern. Loot another chest on a wall as you enter the south passage.

◇ Chest   ◇ Chest (Locked: Apprentice)

B Door to Avanchnzel Balcony

2 South Passage

Dispatch more Dwarven Spheres and Spiders as you navigate the long passage that leads down to the main chamber's ground floor. Unlock an Apprentice-level gate along the way to access a nook with chest.

◇ Chest

3 Trapped Treasure Room

Annihilate a deadly group of Dwarven Spiders to secure the central chamber's ground floor, then approach the south door. Look up to notice several slots on the ceiling—spears will stab out from these when you open the door, so stand back and to one side to avoid this nasty surprise, or try to pick the door's trigger hinge. Loot two chests in the treasure room before backtracking out.

◇ Danger! Spear Trap (trapped door)   ◇ Potion
◇ Chests (2)   ◇ Loose Gear

4 Path to Animoncultory

From the base of the central chamber, take the east passage to locate the door that leads to the Avanchnzel Animoncultory. Raid a chest in the hall as you go.

◇ Chest

C Door to Avanchnzel Animoncultory

5 Treasure Room

Smash some Dwarven Sentries in this first chamber, then unlock the Adept-level gate to reach a chest.

◇ Chest

6 Connecting Corridor

Loot a locked chest as you navigate this winding hall.

◇ Chest (Locked: Adept)

7 Study

To safely enter this room, stand close to the door and run forward as you open it. You'll burst into the room before being hacked up by the blades that emerge from the ground when the door is opened.

◇ Danger! Dwarven Thresher Trap (trapped door)
◇ Skill Book [Restoration]: Racial Phylogeny
◇ Chest
◇ Loose Gear

8 Storage A

Make use of an Alchemy Lab here if you like.

◇ Crafting: Alchemy Lab
◇ Potion

9 Storage B

Bash through a few more dwarven automatons in this chamber, then unlock an Adept-level door and an Apprentice-level gate to access a pair of small treasure rooms.

◇ Chest
◇ Chest (Locked: Novice)
◇ Potions
◇ Loose Gear

10 Centurion Assembly

A large number of Dwarven Spiders guard this large chamber, where fearsome Dwarven Centurions were once built. Loot a chest that sits on a large shelf against the west wall on your way to the boilery.

◇ Chest

E Door to Avanchnzel Boilery

F Door to Avanchnzel Animoncultory

11 Access Corridor

Raid a pair of chests that sit on shelves as you move through this corridor, and grab a few potions from another shelf ahead.

◇ Chests (2)
◇ Potions

12 Spinning Blade Slope

Avoid the pressure plates that line this sloping hallway—stepping on one triggers a nasty spinning blade trap that must then be bypassed with care. Pull the lever at the bottom of the slope to deactivate the trap if need be.

◇ Danger! Dwarven Thresher Trap (pressure plates)

13 Centurion Chamber

A tower Dwarven Centurion guards this final chamber. Defeat the mechanical monster easily by simply backing away until the brute becomes stuck on thick pipes. You may then unleash ranged attacks to bring it down.

◇ Lexicon Receptacle

G Door to Avanchnzel

[9.19] Clearspring Tarn

Dungeon: Animal Den

Animal
Hunter (Food Vendor)

Services

Traders (Food Vendors): Hunters
(2) [12/13; 13/13]
Food, Misc

Collectibles

Skill Book [Archery]: Vernaccus
and Bourlor
Unique Weapon: Bow of the Hunt
[66/80]
Chest(s)
Potions

This small, tranquil mountain lake is nestled among the Rift's northern mountains. Descend a dirt trail around the cliffside to reach a cave that lies just beneath the tarn.

Exterior

As you approach the pond, some hunters arrive and hunt the deer that gather here. If you like, trade with the hunters for food and pelts, then dive into the water to locate a sunken chest. Then follow the trail around the cliffside to enter a nearby cave.

◇ Chest (Locked: Apprentice)

Clearspring Cave

A lone troll guards this small cave. Kill the monster, then loot a chest here and claim a unique bow that inflicts bonus damage to animals. Check the Skill Book that also lies nearby.

◇ Skill Book [Archery]: Vernaccus and Bourlor
◇ Unique Weapon: Bow of the Hunt [66/80]
◇ Chest
◇ Potions

[9.20] Boulderfall Cave

Recommended Level: 6

Dungeon: Warlock Lair

Mage

Crafting

Alchemy Lab

Dangers

Bone Alarm Trap
Trapped Chest

Collectibles

Skill Book [Alchemy]:
Herbalist's Guide to Skyrim
Potion
Loose Gear

This small, abandoned mine lies in the mountains to the west of Shor's Stone [9.25] and has become the home of a dangerous mage. Avoid the hanging rattles on your way in and, after slaying the mage, open the large chest from the side to dodge a dangerous flamethrower trap that fires from the wall above. Collect the Skill Book on the shelf before using the nearby Alchemy Lab.

[9.21] Northwind Mine

Recommended Level: 12

Dungeon: Special

Skeleton

Dangers

Rockfall (tripwire)

Underground Connection: Northwind Summit [9.22]

Collectibles

Skill Book [Block]: Death Blow of Abernanit

Chest

Knapsack

Loose Gear

This haunted mine has been tunneled into the Rift's northern mountains. Make your way to a tall chamber, then dispatch skeletons as you scale the wooden ramps that lead to the higher passages. Swipe the Skill Book on the ground-floor table, and find a chest and knapsack hidden beneath the scaffolding on the first ledge. Stand back and safely trigger the trip-wire trap in the upper passage to avoid a dangerous trap, then follow the passage to its end to exit the mine, arriving at Northwind Summit [9.22].

[9.22] Northwind Summit

Dungeon: Dragon Lair

Dragon (after Main Quest: Dragon Rising)

Skeleton

Crafting

Smelter

Underground Connection: Northwind Mine [9.21]

Special Objects

Word Wall: Aura Whisper [3/3]

Chest

Chest (Locked: Apprentice)

Loose Gear

This abandoned mining site sits high atop the Rift's northern mountains. You must navigate the Northwind Mine [9.21] to reach this summit, where plenty of treasure and an ancient Word Wall are found. And that's not all—after the "Dragon Rising" quest, an irritable dragon can be found and fought here as well!

[9.23] Tolvald's Cave

Related Quests

Thieves Guild Radiant Quest: No Stone Unturned

Dungeon Activity

Recommended Level: 18

Dungeon: Falmer Hive

Animal

Falmer

Crafting

Alchemy Lab

Tanning Racks (3)

Dangers

Bear Traps

Bone Alarm Trap

Swinging Wall Trap (trip wire)

Trapped Chest

Quest Items

Crown of Barenziah

Collectibles

Skill Book [Block]: Battle of Red Mountain [B2/10]

Skill Book [Destruction]: Mystery of Talara, v3

Chest(s)

Potions

Loose Gear

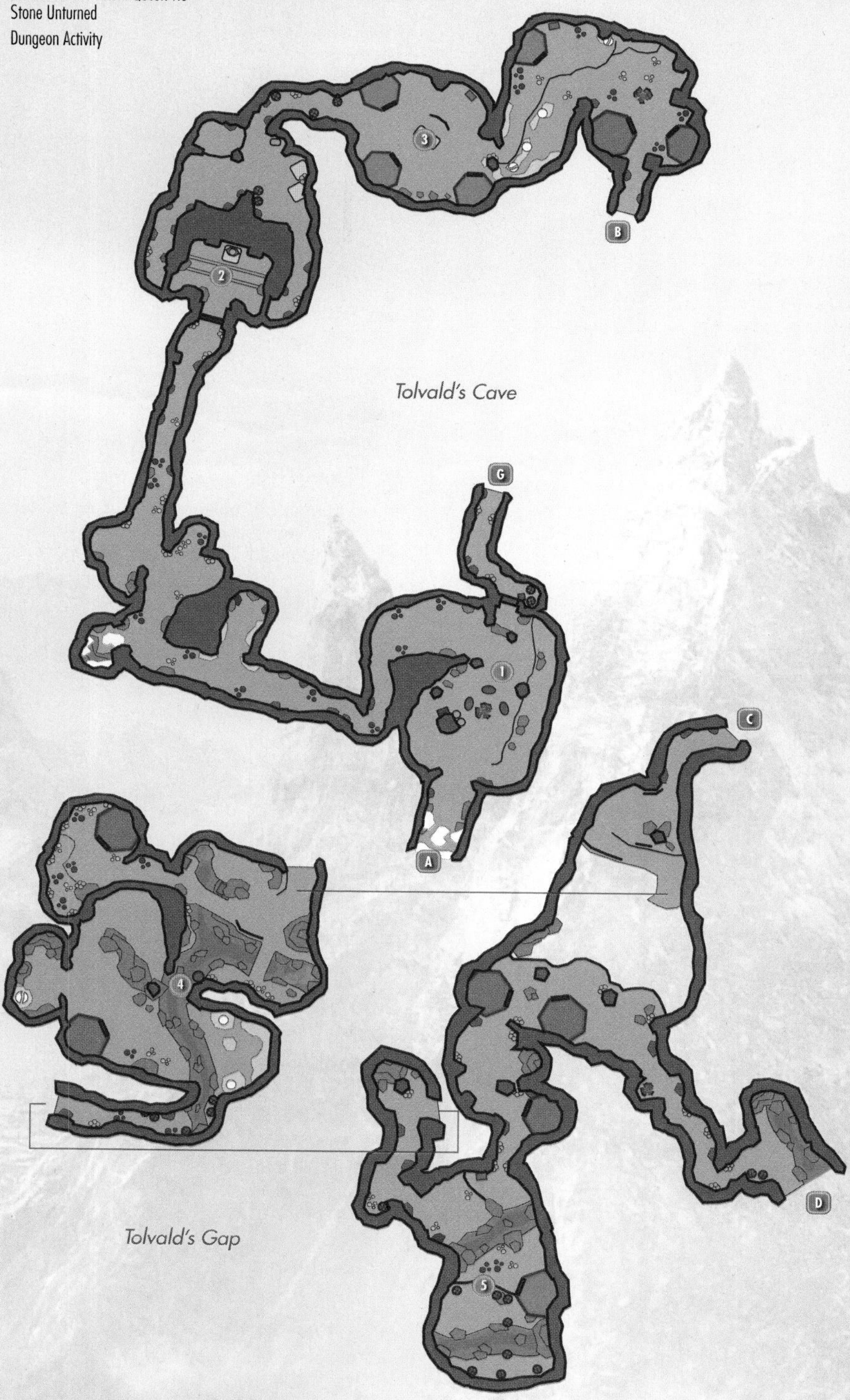

Tolvald's Cave

Tolvald's Gap

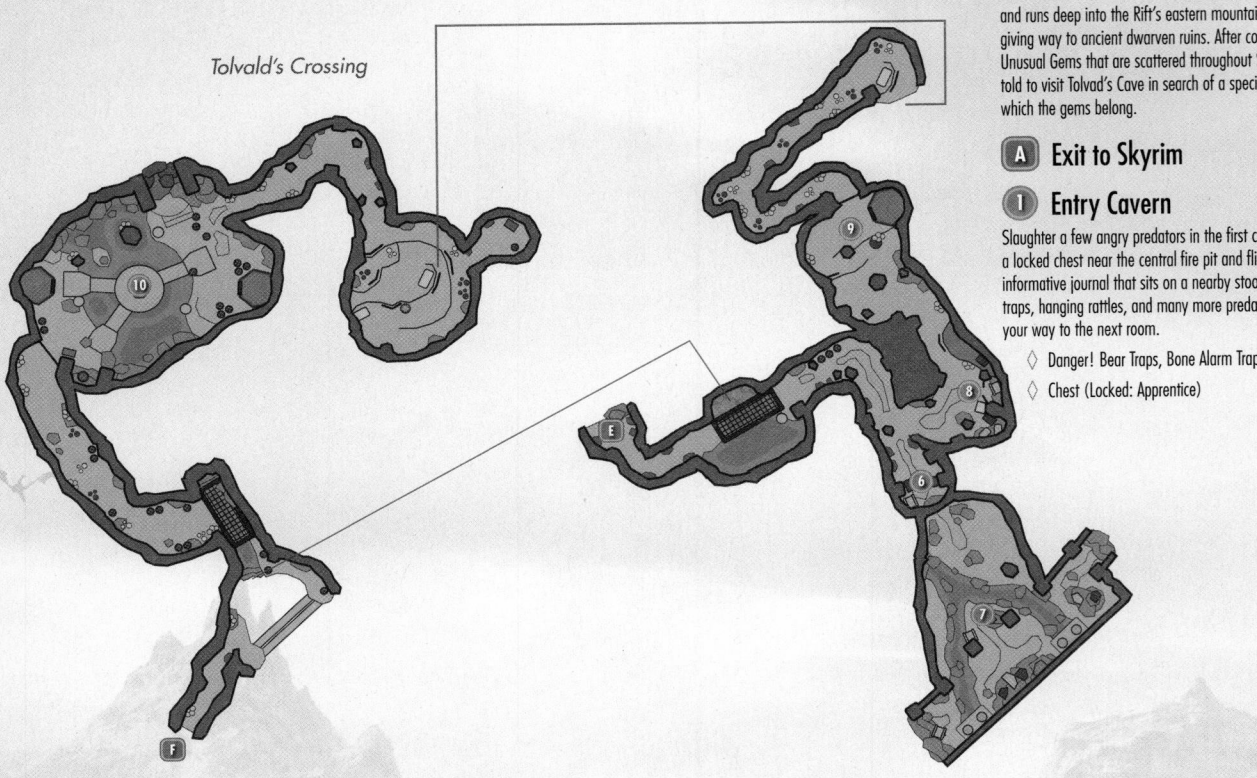

Tolvald's Crossing

This sizeable cave lies northeast of Shor's Stone [9.25] and runs deep into the Rift's eastern mountains, eventually giving way to ancient dwarven ruins. After collecting all of the Unusual Gems that are scattered throughout Skyrim, you're told to visit Tolvald's Cave in search of a special crown, to which the gems belong.

A Exit to Skyrim

1 Entry Cavern

Slaughter a few angry predators in the first cavern, then loot a locked chest near the central fire pit and flip through an informative journal that sits on a nearby stool. Beware of bear traps, hanging rattles, and many more predators as you make your way to the next room.

◇ Danger! Bear Traps, Bone Alarm Trap

◇ Chest (Locked: Apprentice)

2 Trapped Chest Chamber

An ornate metal door leads into this small, stone room. First, pull the chain on the west wall to open two side passages and slay a few Falmer. These villains would have ambushed you when you opened the room's tantalizing trapped chest. If you can't unlock the chest's trap hinge, stand atop the chest when opening it to avoid being shot by arrows. Then use the Falmer passages to visit a higher chamber, where you find an Alchemy Lab and several potions.

◇ Danger! Trapped Chest   ◇ Potions

◇ Crafting: Alchemy Lab   ◇ Loose Gear

3 Falmer Lair

Kill the many Falmer in this cavern, then find a useful key on one of their bodies. Loot an odd-looking chest and then cut down an overgrown Frostbite Spider on your way to the back cavern, opening a locked chest along the way. Beware of additional Falmer emerging from small holes in the walls and find a third chest in a tent before taking the nearby passage to Tolvald's Gap.

◇ Crafting: Tanning Racks (2)   ◇ Chests (2)

◇ Shaman's Key (Falmer)   ◇ Chest (Locked: Adept)

B Path to Tolvald's Gap

C Path to Tolvald's Cave

4 Divided Cavern

Dispatch several Falmer and a Skeever or two as you descend into the Gap's first cavern. Take a northwest passage to locate a small side cave with a chest in a Falmer tent and a large amount of mushrooms the Falmer have been cultivating. Backtrack out and locate another chest near a waterfall. Follow the stream to the cavern's southern half, where many more Falmer lurk. Follow the stream to its end, then take a side passage up to the next cavern.

◇ Chest   ◇ Potions

◇ Chest (Locked: Apprentice)   ◇ Loose Gear

5 Chaurus Den

Dangerous Chaurus lurk in this far chamber. Find a chest atop the waterfall here, then take the nearby passage to arrive at the previous chamber's high southern ledge, collecting a few potions from a nook along the way.

◇ Chest

◇ Potions

4 Divided Cavern Revisited

Loot another chest in a tent on this side of the cavern as you loop around to a passage that leads even deeper into the cave.

◇ Chest (Locked: Adept)

D Path to Tolvald's Crossing

E Path to Tolvald's Gap

6 Dead End

Beware of the powerful Falmer that lurks in the thick spray of the giant waterfall here, then head south when you reach a fork in the tunnel to reach this dead end, where a spirit materializes for a moment before vanishing. Inspect the interesting journal that lies near a skeleton here before looting the locked chest.

◇ Danger! Swinging Wall Trap (trip wire)

◇ Chest (Locked: Apprentice)

7 Old Road

If you've found all 24 Unusual Gems and are visiting this place as part of the "No Stone Unturned" quest, then the aforementioned dead-end passage will be opened, exposing a section of ancient underground dwarven road that's been caved in. Sift through the rubble here to locate the Crown of Barenziah.

◇ Crown of Barenziah

8 Caravan Junkyard

Stand as far back as possible before intentionally triggering the trip wire at the start of the junction's east passage, which leads to this treasure-filled passage. Treasured belongings pillaged from Dark Elf refugees lie heaped in a pile. You may not be able to open the giant locked chest here, but you can collect two valuable Skill Books, then explore an upper ramp to locate another locked chest before making your way to [8].

◇ Skill Book [Block]: Battle of Red Mountain [B2/10]

◇ Skill Book [Destruction]: Mystery of Talara, v3

◇ Chest (Locked: Expert)

◇ Chest (Locked: Master)

◇ Potion

◇ Loose Gear

9 Winding Ramp Cavern

Find a chest in a Falmer tent on your way to this tall cavern, where another mysterious Dark Elf spirit briefly appears to you once more. Inspect the nearby trailbook to uncover a bit more of the intrigue surrounding this place. Ascend the winding uphill path, being wary of the many overhead ledges from which Falmer archers can fire down at you. Find another chest in a tent before taking a high passage to [9].

◇ Crafting: Tanning Rack

◇ Chests (2)

◇ Loose Gear

10 Shallow Rapids Cavern

Several powerful Falmer and a hulking Chaurus lurk in this final cavern, which features a rushing stream. A large chest is attached to the wall near the makeshift throne the Falmer have erected here. Open the south gate and take a winding passage back to the Crossing's first cavern. Carefully navigate the ledges and steam pipes without falling to make your way to an exit path that leads back to the start of Tolvald's Cave.

F Path to Tolvald's Cave

G Path to Tolvald's Crossing

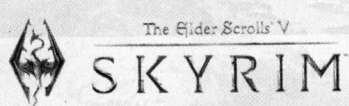

[9.24] Shor's Watchtower

Related Quests

Civil War Quest: Reunification of Skyrim
Civil War Quest: Compelling Tribute

Recommended Level: 6

Dungeon: Special

Collectible

Chest (Locked: Novice)
Potion
Loose Gear

This wooden watchtower stands on the road north of Shor's Stone, on the precipice of the cliffs that descend from the Rift into Eastmarch. The guards here been slain, so feel free to loot the tower, including the chest on its highest tier. A note on the tower's ground floor hints at what befell the guards.

[9.25] Shor's Stone

Related Quests

Miscellaneous Objective: Mine or Yours* (Filnjar)
Miscellaneous Objective: Letter for Mr. Rock-Chucker* (Sylgja)
Favor (Activity): Mining Ore* (Grogmar gro-Burzag)

Habitation: Town

Filnjar (Blacksmith; Marriage Prospect)
Frostbite Spider
Grogmar gro-Burzag
Odfel
Shor's Stone Guard
Sylgja (Marriage Prospect)

Crafting

Blacksmith Forge
Grindstone
Smelter
Tanning Rack
Workbench

Services

Marriage Prospect: Filnjar [61/62]
Marriage Prospect: Sylgja [62/62]
Trader (Blacksmith): Filnjar [33/33]
    Weapons, Apparel, Misc
Chest(s)
Potions
Loose Gear
Mineable ore (Ebony)

This quiet mining community lies along the Rift's eastern road, making it a convenient stop for travelers heading between Eastmarch and the Rift. Unfortunately, the local mine has been overrun with giant spiders!

Exterior

Barter with Filnjar, the local blacksmith, or use his array of crafting stations. Speak with Filnjar to learn more about the trouble in the mine and gain a new Miscellaneous Objective.

◊ Crafting: Blacksmith Forge, Grindstone, Smelter, Tanning Rack, Workbench

1 Sylgja's House

Breaking into Sylgja's house is risky because she's usually home.

◊ Area Is Locked (Novice)
◊ Chests (2)

2 Filnjar's House

Filnjar has prospered over the years—raid his abode while he's busy working outdoors to claim valuable plunder.

◊ Area Is Locked (Novice)
◊ Chests (2)
◊ Potions
◊ Loose Gear

3 Odfel's House

With spiders overrunning the mine, Odfel just hangs at home. Clear out the mine so he can return to work—then plunder his vacant abode!

◊ Area Is Locked (Novice)
◊ Chest

4 Redbelly Mine

Slay a number of Frostbite Spiders as you descend this tall mine's winding ramps. Splatter every arachnid to clear out the infestation, then optionally mine some valuable Ebony Ore from the veins at the bottom before backtracking out to inform Filnjar of your success.

◊ Knapsack
◊ Loose Gear
◊ Mineable ore (Ebony)

[9.26] Fort Greenwall

Related Quests

Civil War Quest: Reunification of Skyrim
Civil War Quest: The Battle for Fort Greenwall

Crafting

Blacksmith Forge
Grindstone
Workbench

Collectibles

Skill Book [One-Handed]: Mace Etiquette [C2/10]

Special Objects

Shrine of Stendarr [4/5]
Chest(s)
Potions
Loose Gear

Recommended Level: 6

Habitation: Military Fort

Animal
Bandit (pre-Civil War)
Soldier (Imperial/Stormcloak, depending on the state of the Civil War)

This imposing stronghold stands just south of the village of Shor's Stone [9.25]. The Rift's eastern road runs directly through the fort. You may therefore breach the fort quite easily, or opt to slip in through the cave. Fort Greenwall is a point of contention between the Stormcloaks and Imperials, so you may find soldiers occupying this space instead of bandits, depending on the status of the Civil War quest line.

Exterior

Dispatch a legion of bandits to secure the fort's outer grounds. Then begin raiding its various interior sections.

◊ Crafting: Blacksmith Forge, Workbench
◊ Loose Gear

Fort Greenwall (Interior)

Slay more bandits within Fort Greenwall's main interior. Find a grindstone in the basement and a knapsack near the tower's upper door.

◊ Crafting: Grindstone
◊ Knapsack
◊ Loose Gear

Prison

The prison connects to the Captain's Quarters, and its basement is infested with Frostbite Spiders. Cut through thick webs to make your way to the bottom, then unlock the Master-level door to access a chest.

◊ Chest
◊ Loose Gear

Captain's Quarters

The bandit's stalwart chief lies in the Captain's Quarters and won't go down without a fight. If you can't break into this area via its locked trapdoor entrance, enter through the fort's prison instead. Touch the small shrine you discover in here to instantly rid yourself of all diseases. A Skill Book sits on the shelf in the master bedroom.

◊ Area Is Locked (Master)
◊ Skill Book [One-Handed]: Mace Etiquette [C2/10]
◊ Shrine of Stendarr [4/5]
◊ Chest
◊ Potion
◊ Loose Gear

Cave

A small cave runs beneath Fort Greenwall. Enter via its northern mouth and pick an Expert-level gate to make your way through, emerging at a well within the fort. As you explore the cave, find a letter at the bottom of the southern pool that explains what fate befell the nearby floating corpse.

[9.27] Heartwood Mill

Related Quests

Miscellaneous Objective: Fight or Flight* (Grosta)

Habitation: Lumber Mill

Gralnach
Grosta
Rift Guard

Crafting

Grindstone
Tanning Rack

This small lumber mill, located at the west end of Lake Honrich, has fallen on hard times. Its owner has vanished, leaving his wife and child to run the place.

Exterior

Speak with Grosta to sell her any firewood you might be carrying and to gain a new Miscellaneous Objective.

◇ Crafting: Grindstone, Tanning Rack

Heartwood Mill (Interior)

The cabin sports a Novice-level lock, and there's little of value inside beyond foodstuffs, ingredients, and a coin purse.

◇ Area Is Locked (Novice)

[9.28] Faldar's Tooth

Recommended Level: 6

Dungeon: Bandit Camp

Animal
Bandit

Crafting

Blacksmith Forge
Grindstone
Tanning Rack

Dangers

Battering Ram Trap (trip wire)
Bear Traps
Bone Alarm Trap
Oil Pool Trap
Rockfall (trip wire)
Spear Trap (pressure plates)
Swinging Wall Trap (pressure plates/lever)
Trapped Chest

Collectibles

Skill Book [Alteration]: The Lunar Lorkhan
Skill Book [Archery]: The Marksmanship Lesson
Skill Book [Lockpicking]: Proper Lock Design [B2/10]
Chests
Potions aplenty
Loose Gear

This mighty keep overlooks Lake Honrich from the north and has been overrun by lawless bandits who are running a wolf fighting ring.

Exterior

The bandits are quick to open the stronghold's front gate when they see you approach, but it isn't a warm welcome. They release vicious pit wolves to maul you! Slay the wicked beasts, then decide how you wish to enter the keep: either hurry inside the main gate and storm its interior, or remain outside the walls and circle around the fort's west side to unlock an Adept-level gate and bypass the keep's sizeable inner working altogether.

Later, after you've advanced to the fort's upper ramparts, fight your way up its wooden stairs and walkways until you reach a large tent with a chest and useful key. Go back downstairs a few levels and use the key to unlock the Expert-level door of the keep's eastern tower. Loot the chest within and proceed to the tower's top, then follow a rampart to reach the next tower. Go in and head up to battle the bandits' formidable leader, then loot the giant chest he was guarding and collect a couple of Skill Books.

◇ Skill Book [Alteration]: The Lunar Lorkhan
◇ Skill Book [Lockpicking]: Proper Lock Design [B2/10]
◇ Faldar's Tooth Key
◇ Chest (Locked: Novice)
◇ Chest (Locked: Apprentice)
◇ Loose Gear

Ⓐ Exit to Skyrim (Lower Grounds)

Ⓘ Entry Tower

Avoid hanging rattles and pressure plates as you descend the keep's first stairwell. Don't free the caged pit wolf you encounter unless you wish to combat it. Simply go down to the lowest level and take the north passage to [2].

◇ Danger! Bone Alarm Trap, Spear Trap (pressure plates)

② Cage Chamber

Ignite the oily floor here before you're detected by the patrolling bandits — one of them is a mage whose fireballs may set the room ablaze if you don't take advantage of the hazard first. Secure the room afterward, then optionally pick the Adept-level cages to free (and fight) a number of pit wolves. If you're swift, carefully step on the pressure plate to trigger a swinging wall trap, then deftly slip around the spiked gate to reach a locked chest in the small nook beyond. Pull the lever afterward to unhinge the spiked gate and escape the nook. Finally, unlock the Novice-level north door to access a small closet filled with potions.

- ◇ Danger! Oil Pool Trap, Swinging Wall Trap (pressure plate/lever)
- ◇ Crafting: Tanning Rack
- ◇ Chest (Locked: Adept)
- ◇ Potions aplenty
- ◇ Loose Gear

③ Training Pit

The bandits use this wide chamber to train their wolves and bet on fights. Slaughter the distracted onlookers, then open the locked cage door and check behind the betting counter to discover loads of gold and a large chest.

- ◇ Chest   ◇ Potion   ◇ Loose Gear

④ Waterlogged Chamber

A few feet of water cover the floor of this chamber. Search behind the stairs to discover a submerged chest, then scale the southern steps to find worthy loot and a satchel. Tug the pullbar on the southern balcony to open the far portcullis so you may proceed to [5].

- ◇ Chest   ◇ Apothecary's Satchel   ◇ Loose Gear

⑤ Kitchen and Quarters

Collect an interesting journal on your way to this area, where a slew of bandits await. Fight hard to slay this large group of scoundrels. Discover a Skill Book on a small table in the room with the firewood (west of the curved stairs).

- ◇ Skill Book [Archery]: The Marksmanship Lesson
- ◇ Potions
- ◇ Loose Gear

⑥ Exit Passage

Make a thorough search for loot as you navigate the keep's last few corridors, claiming plenty of potions. Beware of a trapped treasure chest, opening it from the side to avoid being shot by arrows or deactivating its trigger hinge. Dodge the pressure plate in the following passage on your way to the fort's final chamber.

- ◇ Danger! Bone Alarm Trap, Swinging Wall Trap (pressure plate), Trapped Chest
- ◇ Potions aplenty
- ◇ Loose Gear

⑦ Forge

Beware the trip wire that lies just underwater as you enter this final, waterlogged chamber. Numerous bear traps lie just beneath the water's surface as well, so keep an eye to the ground as you carefully creep through. Go upstairs and slay one final bandit to secure a crafting area. Carry on to find yourself back at [1], in an area you couldn't have reached before.

- ◇ Danger! Battering Ram Trap (trip wire), Bear Traps
- ◇ Crafting: Blacksmith Forge, Grindstone
- ◇ Chest (Locked: Novice)
- ◇ Loose Gear

① Entry Tower Revisited

Pull the wall chain as you reenter this first chamber to lower the nearby portcullis. Now you'll never need to take the long way around the keep again. Mind a trip wire as you head upstairs, and exit the keep via the upstairs door to reach the upper exterior ramparts (see the previous "Exterior" section for more.)

- ◇ Rockfall (trip wire)

Ⓑ Exit to Skyrim (Upper Ramparts)

▷ [9.29] Goldenglow Estate

Related Quests

Side Quest: Captured Critters*
Thieves Guild Quest: Loud and Clear
Thieves Guild Radiant Quest: Larceny Targets*

Recommended Level: 6

Dungeon: Special
Animal
Aringoth
Mercenary

Dangers
Flail Trap (trip wire)
Oil Lamp Trap (trip wire)
Oil Pool Traps

Quest Items
Goldenglow Bill of Sale

Collectibles
Captured Critter: Bee in a Jar [5/5]
Larceny Target: Queen Bee Statue [7/7]
Skill Book [Pickpocket]: Guide to Better Thieving
Area Is Locked (quest required)
Chest(s)
Potions
Loose Gear

West of Riften, the sprawling Goldenglow Estate spans several islands across Lake Honrich. A small army of rugged Mercenaries guard the compound, and the south gate remains locked at all times; however, you discover means of slipping onto the premises during Thieves Guild Quest: Loud and Clear.

① Main Gate

Goldenglow is a secure compound with only one entrance, and the guards aren't about to let anyone in.

② Sewer Access

Approach Goldenglow Estate from the north to discover a low bank that you can climb onto, which is located here. This means of entry is only available during the "Loud and Clear" quest. Enter the nearby sewer to begin your infiltration.

③ Nirnroot Nook

Before entering the sewer, optionally swim over here to find a rare sprig of tingling Nirnroot growing down by the water.

Goldenglow Estate Sewer

Slay the Skeevers that scutter about the sewer, and safely trigger the trip wire near the oily floor with a ranged attack to ignite the oil and torch some more. If you can, unlock the Adept-level door that follows to claim a Skill Book and loot a chest. Beware of another trip-wire trap as you advance.

- ◇ Danger! Flail Trap (trip wire), Oil Lamp Trap (trip wire), Oil Pool Trap
- ◇ Skill Book [Pickpocket]: Guide to Better Thieving
- ◇ Chest (Locked: Apprentice)
- ◇ Loose gear

④ Sewer Exit

The sewer spits you out behind the estate building, close to its rear door. Unfortunately, the door features an Expert-level lock — if you can't pick it, you'll need to risk sneaking around front and slipping in through the manor's unlocked front door.

⑤ Goldenglow Estate (Main Floor)

The estate's ground floor features two locked closets. Avoid the guards who patrol the halls and open both Adept-level doors to claim valuable loot from within. Cut through the central dining room to locate the stairs that lead up to the second floor, along with a Novice-level locked metal door that leads down to the basement.

◇ Strongbox (Adept)
◇ Apothecary's Satchel
◇ Chests (2)
◇ Potions
◇ Knapsack

⑤ Goldenglow Estate (Second Floor)

Visit the second floor in search of useful keys and loot. Sneak through the central bedroom to avoid detection and open an Adept-level door to raid a closet with an apothecary satchel hidden atop a shelf. Open the Novice-level door to Aringoth's bedchamber and quietly swipe a pair of keys from the wall hooks. Loot the chest by the bed as well, and take the unusual Bee in a Jar off the dresser. Lastly, nab the Queen Bee Statue from the nightstand — one of your fellow Thieves Guild comrades will be interested in this.

◇ Caged Critter: Bee in a Jar [5/5]
◇ Chest (Locked: Apprentice)
◇ Larceny Target: Queen Bee Statue [7/7]
◇ Knapsack
◇ Goldenglow Cellar Key
◇ Apothecary's Satchel
◇ Goldenglow Safe Key
◇ Loose gear

⑤ Goldenglow Estate (Basement)

Still more Mercenaries guard the basement. Continue to sneak through here, or slay the men so you may loot the chest they guard. Both men carry a Goldenglow Cellar Key, if you didn't obtain one from the second floor. Farther ahead, a seated guard can be barbecued by igniting a long patch of oil on the floor. Go downstairs to at last find the safe you seek, along with another chest. Raid the place to advance your quest, then slip through the

◇ Danger! Oil Pool Trap
◇ Aringoth's Safe (Locked: Expert)
◇ Goldenglow Bill of Sale (Aringoth's Safe)
◇ Chest (Locked: Novice)
◇ Goldenglow Cellar Keys (Mercenaries)
◇ Chest (Locked: Apprentice)

⑥ Apiaries

Sneak over to this collection of beehives here — or simply sprint over at breakneck speed, hoping to outrun the guards — and use any fire-based attack to burn three of the apiaries. This completes a quest objective, but you'd better clear out of here fast!

▷ [9.30] Autumnshade Clearing

Recommended Level: 14

Dungeon: Spriggan Grove

Animal
Spriggan

Located north of Lake Honrich, this seemingly tranquil clearing is actually home to ferocious animals and reclusive forest spirits that may well attack trespassers. Loot the bodies of two slain hunters here, which lie in the brush near the west rock, to obtain some worthy gear.

▷ [9.31] Merryfair Farm

Related Quests

Miscellaneous Objective: Bow to the Master* (Dravin Llanith)
Favor (Activity): Harvesting Crops* (Synda Llanith)

Habitation: Farm

Dravin Llanith
Rift Guard
Synda Llanith

This quiet farm lies just northwest of Riften. Speak with the farm's owner, Dravin Llanith, to gain a new Side Quest.

Merryfair Farm (Interior)

The farmhouse is locked, and there's little reason to break in. The only item of particular value is a coin purse tucked away near the basement bed.

◇ Area Is Locked (Novice)

▷ [9.32] Riften Stables

Hofgrir Horse-Crusher (Stablemaster)
Sigaar (Carriage Driver)

Services

Trader (Carriage Driver): Sigaar [5/5]
Trader (Stablemaster): Hofgrir Horse-Crusher [5/5]
Potions

Swing by the stables that lie just outside Riften's main gate to purchase a horse or rent a carriage ride to another of Skyrim's bustling capitals. You can also speak with Hofgrir to participate in a challenging fistfight that can earn you 100 gold if you manage to KO the burly braggart.

Riften Stables (Interior)

Hofgrir's home is securely locked, but valuable treasure awaits those who manage to break in. Reading a certain book inside the cabin can potentially update your map with new locations.

◇ Area Is Locked (Adept)
◇ Strongbox (Apprentice)

▷ [9.33] Fallowstone Cave
[9.33] Giant's Grove

Related Quests

Daedric Quest: The Cursed Tribe
Dungeon Activity

Dungeon: Animal Den/ Giant Camp

Animal
Giant

Quest Items

Shagrol's Warhammer

Collectibles

Unique Weapon: Shagrol's Warhammer [67/80]
Unique Weapon: Volendrung [68/80]
Chest(s)
Potions
Loose Gear

This cavernous cave is located east of Riften, near the mountains that form Skyrim's border. Normally, Fallowstone Cave is filled with vicious predators, but during Daedric Quest: The Cursed Tribe, you'll find towering giants roaming the cave instead. You're also able to delve deeper into the cave during this quest, visiting a remote grove that's home to Giants.

Fallowstone Cave (Normal)

Beware of hungry predators as you follow the rushing stream. Stick to the south wall to discover a bandit's corpse inside a web-covered nook — collect the nearby potions after looting the body. Kill or avoid more predators as you follow the stream into an east passage. You can loot another slain bandit that lies in a southwest nook if you slay the nearby bear. Proceed up the path that follows, slaughtering more bears on your way up to a high, narrow trail that overlooks the main cavern. Unlock a large chest on this narrow ledge here as you proceed back to where you entered the cave.

◇ Chest (Locked: Apprentice)
◇ Loose Gear
◇ Potions

Fallowstone Cave (During "The Cursed Tribe")

All of the aforementioned goodies are still present within Fallowstone Cave when you visit the place with Chief Yamarz. Follow the Orc as he charges recklessly into the cave and battles a hulking giant. Help Yamarz bring down the brute, then loot the giant's remains, along with the chest near the firepit, which wasn't present in Fallowstone Cave before. Then simply continue following Yamarz as he battles another giant and a few Cave Bears. The Orc Chief leads you up a path to the Giant's Grove, which does not exist until you come here with Yamarz.

◇ Chest (Locked: Novice)
◇ Potions

Giant's Grove

The Giant's Grove is a large, outdoor area that can only be accessed by traveling through Fallowstone Cave; however, the trail that leads to the grove isn't present within Fallowstone until you come here with Chief Yamarz as part of "The Cursed Tribe" quest. Decide if you wish to slay the mighty giant here, or let Yamarz do it. The chief will die if you tell him to go, forcing you to finish his work, but he'll also attack you if you agree to slay the giant for him, hoping to keep your mouth shut about who really completed the task. If you choose to battle this mighty brute, exploit the rocks and trees here to keep distance from him. Relieve the Giant of Shagrol's Warhammer to advance the quest, then raid the large chest near the bloodstained altar before making your way back to Largashbur [9.36].

◇ Area Is Locked (quest required)
◇ Chest
◇ Shagrol's Warhammer (Giant)
◇ Potions

[9.34] Lost Prospect Mine

Related Quests

Dungeon Activity

Recommended Level: 6

Collectible

Potion
Loose Gear
Mineable ore (Gold)

This small mine, located in a valley on the Rift's far eastern edge, is believed to be depleted and has thus been abandoned. The intrepid explorer can still find value in this forgotten place, however.

Lost Prospect Mine (Interior)

Find an interesting journal on a table in the mine's central cavern, then locate some loose gear in the short side passages. Use the Whirlwind Sprint Shout (or make a very challenging jump) to reach the tunnel that stretches beyond the waterfall. Explore the tunnel's far end to discover a thick vein of precious Gold Ore, along with the skeletal remains of the missing miner.

[9.35] Black-Briar Lodge

Related Quests

Side Quest: Promises to Keep

Dungeon: Special

Black-Briar Mercenary
Frost (horse)

Quest Items

Frost's Identity Papers

Collectibles

Skill Book [Sneak]: Legend of the Krately House [B2/10]
Unusual Gem: [24/24]
Chest(s)
Potions

This sizable estate is nestled among the Rift's eastern mountains and is home to the Black-Briar family—a renowned lineage of proud brewers who have grown wealthy enough to hire formidable mercenaries to protect their interests. You must break into Black-Briar Lodge to steal a horse during Side Quest: Promises to Keep.

Exterior

Frost is kept in the southeast stables, but you first need to steal his Identity Papers. Wait for cover of night, then slip around and enter the lodge via the unlocked side door along its west wall—this leads into the manor's largely unguarded basement. Or take a more direct approach by slaying the exterior guards to obtain keys from their corpses, which unlock the lodge's Master-level front door. Once you've acquired Frost's Identity Papers, slip back out and sneak around behind the stables to approach Frost without being noticed.

◇ Black-Briar Lodge Key (Black-Briar Mercenaries)

Black-Briar Lodge (Basement)

A lone mercenary guards the basement. Wait a while and he'll go to sleep if it's late. Pick the nearby Adept-level wooden door, or pickpocket a key from the basement guard who opens it. Swipe Frost's Identity Papers from the end table in the small room beyond, which also features a chest.

◇ Black-Briar Lodge Key (Black-Briar Mercenary)
◇ Frost's Identity Papers
◇ Chest (Locked: Apprentice)
◇ Apothecary's Satchel
◇ Potions

Black-Briar Lodge (Upper Floors)

The lodge's main floor holds little of interest. Slay or slip past the guards in the dining hall, then go upstairs and visit the south bedroom to discover a Skill Book and an Unusual Gem that pertains to Thieves Guild Radiant Quest: No Stone Unturned. Lastly, backtrack out of the bedroom and search near the north upstairs door to spy a small chest that's tucked away on a shelf. The north door leads to a backyard area that's patrolled by more guards.

◇ Skill Book [Sneak]: Legend of the Krately House [B2/10]
◇ Unusual Gem: [24/24]
◇ Chest (Locked: Novice)

[9.36] Largashbur

Related Quests

Daedric Quest: The Cursed Tribe
Side Quest: The Forgemaster's Fingers

Recommended Level: 6

Habitation: Orc Stronghold

Atub (Trainer: Illusion)
Garakh
Gularzob
Lob
Ogol
Shagrol
Ugor

Crafting

Alchemy Lab
Blacksmith Forge
Grindstone
Workbench

Services

Follower: Lob [43/47]
Follower: Ogol [44/47]
Follower: Ugor [45/47]
Trainer [Illusion: Expert]: Atub [2/2]

Collectibles

Skill Book [Block]: Battle of Red Mountain
Area Is Locked (quest required)
Chest(s)
Potions
Loose Gear

This Orc stronghold stands in the Rift's southern mountains, to the southwest of Lake Honrich. The Orcs here have fallen under a dreadful curse and will reluctantly accept the aid of an outsider.

Exterior

The first time you visit Largashbur, you'll witness the Orcs defending their stronghold from an enraged giant. Speak with the Orcs after the battle to learn of their current plight with the giants and gain a new Side Quest. The Orcs won't allow you to enter Largashbur until you've gathered several items that Atub needs to cure his cursed chief, Yamarz. (See the quest walkthrough for "The Cursed Tribe" for help in tracking these down.) Once you're granted entry, you can utilize a number of crafting stations and locate a locked chest near the entrance to the Largashbur Cellar.

◇ Crafting: Alchemy Lab, Blacksmith Forge, Grindstone, Workbench
◇ Chest (Locked: Master)
◇ Loose Gear

Longhouse

If you dare to steal from the Orcs, you'll find the Longhouse packed with valuables.

◇ Chests (2)
◇ Chest (Locked: Master)
◇ Potions
◇ Loose Gear

Cellar

Enter the Longhouse's cellar via an exterior trapdoor and loot the place without being seen. The middle book on the shelf is a Skill Book.

◇ Skill Book [Block]: Battle of Red Mountain
◇ Chest (Locked: Novice)
◇ Potions

[9.37] Darklight Tower

Related Quests

Dungeon Quest: Repentance

Recommended Level: 8

Dungeon: Hagraven Nest

Animal
Hag
Hagraven
Illia (Follower)
Silvia

Crafting

Alchemy Lab
Arcane Enchanter

Services

Follower: Illia [46/47]

Dangers

Swinging Wall Trap (pressure plate)

Collectibles

Skill Book [Destruction]: Horrors of Castle Xyr
Skill Book [Destruction]: Mystery of Talara, v3
Skill Book [Illusion]: 2920, Sun's Dawn, v2 [A2/10]
Unique Weapon: Staff of Hag's Wrath [69/80]
Chests
Potions aplenty
Loose Gear

This stronghold, which stands nestled against the Rift's southern mountains to the southwest of Riften, derives its name from its tall central tower, which can be observed from a great distance. With the keep's outer wall in ruins, breaching the tower isn't nearly as challenging as it might have been in days of yore—simply scale the outer steps and head inside.

A Exit to Skyrim

1 Entry Chamber

Speak with a woman named Illia in the tower's first cavern to learn that her mother is about to be made a part of some nefarious ritual. Agree to help Illia to gain a new Side Quest that involves rescuing her mother from the Darklight coven, then head upstairs to the room's balcony and slay a few Frostbite Spiders on your way to [2].

2 Lab

Kill a skillful witch in this chamber, then loot the small chest that's tucked away in the northwest corner.

◇ Crafting: Alchemy Lab
◇ Chest
◇ Potions
◇ Loose Gear

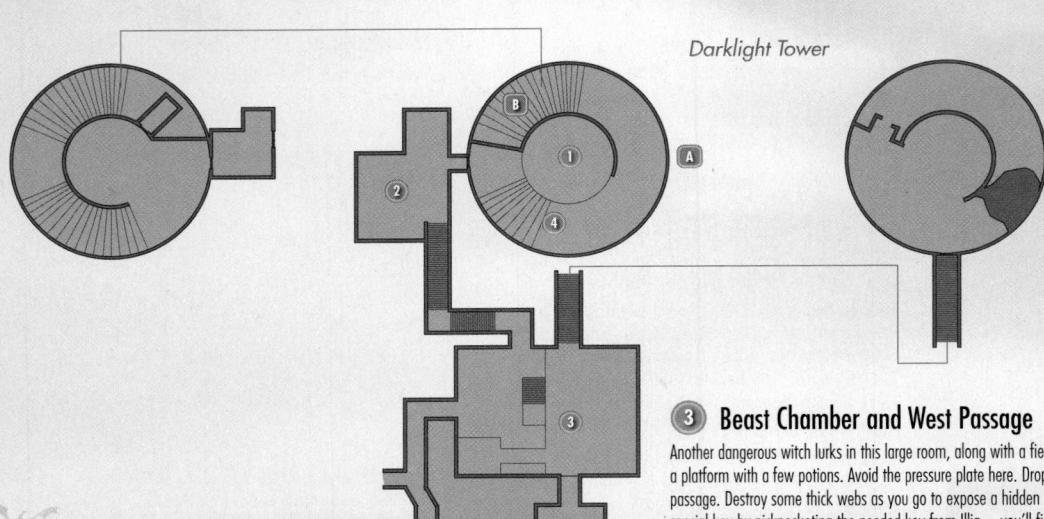

Darklight Tower

Darklight Chambers

3. Beast Chamber and West Passage

Another dangerous witch lurks in this large room, along with a fierce predator. Scale the steps and cross an arc to reach a platform with a few potions. Avoid the pressure plate here. Drop to the ground floor and follow Illia into the west passage. Destroy some thick webs as you go to expose a hidden chest. Open the locked south door that requires a special key by pickpocketing the needed key from Illia—you'll find valuable potions in the small closet beyond. Pull a lever to return to the main chamber, then cut straight across and head upstairs to find yourself in a high room that lies directly above [1].

◊ Danger! Swinging Wall Trap (pressure plate)   ◊ Chest   ◊ Potions aplenty

4. Hagraven Chamber

Battle ferocious monsters and a Hagraven in this room, which lies directly above [1]. Raid the room after things settle down before proceeding through the door that leads to the Darklight Chambers.

◊ Skill Book [Illusion]: 2920, Sun's Dawn, v2 [A2/10]
◊ Chest

B. Door to Darklight Chambers

C. Door to Darklight Tower

5. Locked Door Chamber

Cut down a pair of witches on your way up the initial staircase. The door that leads toward Illia's mother is locked. Take the east passage and enter the adjoining chamber instead. A Skill Book rests on a table that overlooks the central spike pit.

◊ Skill Book [Destruction]: Mystery of Talara, v3

6. Hagraven Lair

Defeat another dangerous Hagraven and a monster in this chamber to obtain a key, then raid a couple of chests and swipe several potions before returning to [5] to open the locked door.

◊ Darklight Tower Key (Hagraven)   ◊ Chest (Locked: Master)
◊ Chest   ◊ Potions

7. Study

Slay another witch in this crafting area, then loot a chest before proceeding upstairs. You soon emerge on high balcony back at [5]. Kill a Hag and two trolls up here, then proceed upstairs and head outside to face off against Illia's corrupted mother at the tower's apex.

◊ Crafting: Arcane Enchanter   ◊ Potions
◊ Chest   ◊ Loose Gear

D. Exit to Skyrim

Tower Apex

Illia's mother, Silvia, awaits just outside the tower. Sit in the chair when instructed and wait for Illia to attack her mother by surprise, then join in and slay Silvia to complete Illia's quest. Invite Illia to continue adventuring with you if you like—she's a worthy companion. Raid a large chest in the nearby tent and claim the Skill Book on the table before setting off to new adventure.

◊ Skill Book [Destruction]: Horrors of Castle Xyr
◊ Unique Weapon: Staff of Hag's Wrath [69/80]
◊ Chest
◊ Potions

▷ [9.38] Ruins of Rkund

Recommended Level: 6

Dungeon: Special

  Wisp
  Wispmother

Collectible

  Chest

These remote Dwarven ruins lie within the Rift's southern mountains, on the edge of Skyrim. The best way to reach this site is by navigating Darklight Tower [9.37] and exiting in the mountains. The ruins here are guarded by several wisps and a formidable Wispmother. Slay these enemies so you may safely loot a dwarven chest that's tucked away in the far tower.

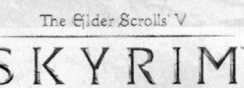

The Elder Scrolls V

SKYRIM

[9.39] Crystaldrift Cave

Related Quests

Dungeon Activity

Dungeon: Animal Den

Animal

Gadnor (deceased)

Collectibles

Unique Weapon: Gadnor's Staff of Charming [70/80]

Special Objects

Shrine of Kynareth [6/6]

Chest

Apothecary's Satchel

Potions

Loose Gear

This small animal cave lies in the mountains south of Riften. Slay the bear that lurks just outside, then go in to find several ravenous Sabre Cats and wolves. Kill the beasts and then inspect the body of Gadnor, who lies atop the central boulder, and collect the nearby staff to obtain a unique weapon. Raid a chest here as well, and touch the small Shrine of Kynareth to instantly cure any diseases you might have.

[9.40] Lost Tongue Overlook

Dungeon: Dragon Lair

Dragon (after Main Quest: Dragon Rising)

Master Necromancer (pre-Dragon Rising)

Skeleton

Dangers

Rune Traps

Special Objects

Word Wall: Dismaying Shout [3/3]

Chest

Potion

In the mountains south of Riften, on the very edge of Skyrim, long stone steps lead up to a breathtaking overlook. Use a ranged attack to detonate a rune trap from afar as you make your ascent. You may encounter a mage here unless you've advanced past the "Dragon Rising" quest — then you'll find a far more intimidating dragon on the premises! Cut down the beast so you may benefit from the nearby Word Wall, and loot the large chest that's also found here.

[9.41] Snow-Shod Farm

Related Quests

Favor (Activity): Harvesting Crops* (Addvild)

Habitation: Farm

Addvild

Leonara Arius

Riften Guard

Collectibles

Skill Book [Alteration]: Reality & Other Falsehoods [C2/10]

This small farm lies just southwest of Riften. Harvest the growing crops and then sell them back to the farm's owner, Addvild, for some honest coin.

Snow-Shod Farm (Interior)

The cabin's lock is easy enough to pick, and there's a Skill Book on the bottom of the shelf in the basement.

◊ Area Is Locked (Novice)

◊ Skill Book [Alteration]: Reality & Other Falsehoods [C2/10]

[9.42] The Shadow Stone

Recommended Level: 6

Dungeon: Special

Warlock

Special Objects

Standing Stone: The Shadow Stone [13/13]

South of Riften, these ancient stones stand atop a short hill. Defeat the guardian mage and inspect the central Standing Stone to accept a new sign blessing. Once a day, those under the sign of the Shadow can become invisible for 60 seconds. Note that you can have only one sign blessing at a time, so activating this Standing Stone will override your current sign blessing (if any).

[9.43] Nightingale Hall

Related Quests

Thieves Guild Quest: Trinity Restored

Recommended Level: 8

Dungeon: Special

Collectibles

Skill Book [Pickpocket]: Purloined Shadows

Skill Book [Sneak]: The Red Kitchen Reader

Unique Item: Nightingale Armor [100/112]

Unique Item: Nightingale Boots [101/112]

Unique Item: Nightingale Gloves [102/112]

Unique Item: Nightingale Hood [103/112]

Area Is Locked (quest required)

Chests (Locked: Novice) (2)

This derelict temple is the ancient home to the Nightingales — clandestine followers of the Daedric Prince Nocturnal. You can't enter this site until you gain Thieves Guild Quest: Trinity Restored. Follow Karliah through the area, claiming a Skill Book that lies near a bed in the waterfall cavern. Next, acquire and don the special armor of the Nightingales. After Karliah explains the terms involved in becoming a member of the Nightingales, search the east and west side rooms to locate a couple of chests and another Skill Book. Then follow Karliah to the far chamber and complete your initiation.

Once you complete the "Darkness Returns" quest (thus ending the Thieves Guild quest line), the living quarters overlooking the waterfall here is restored, and you may freely use this location as a place to rest and gather supplies. Karliah can also be found here postquest as well.

[9.44] Broken Helm Hollow

Recommended Level: 6

Dungeon: Bandit Camp

Bandit

Leifnarr (deceased)

Crafting

Tanning Rack

Dangers

Bone Alarm Trap

Trapped Chest

Collectibles

Skill Book [Two-Handed]: Battle of Sancre Tor

Potions

Loose Gear

Mineable ore (Corundum)

Bandits reside in this small cave, which lies in the Rift's southeast corner, on the east side of the tall peak that stands southeast of Riften. Dispatch the exterior guards, along with the bandits inside the cave, which include a formidable leader. Stand back before opening the giant chest on the ledge — it's trapped. Collect a nearby Skill Book from the nearby stand, then head back down the ramp and pull a chain on the south wall to open a secret passage that leads to the body of a slain Nord. This is Leifnarr's body, which you're sent to find by Grosta at Heartwood Mill [9.27].

[9.45] Forelhost

Forelhost Stronghold

Related Quests

Side Quest: Masks of the Dragon Priests*

Dungeon Quest: Siege on the Dragon Cult

Dungeon Activity

Recommended Level: 24

Dungeon: Dragon Priest Lair

Animal

Captain Valmir

Dragon Cultist (ghost)

Draugr

Rahgot

Crafting

Alchemy Labs (2)

Arcane Enchanter

Quest Items

Rahgot's Mask

Skorm Snow-Strider's Journal

Collectibles

Dragon Claw: Glass Claw [9/10]

Dragon Priest Mask: Rahgot [9/10]

Skill Book [Restoration]: The Exodus

Unique Weapon: Dragon Priest Staff [71/80]

Dangers

Battering Ram Trap (pressure plate)

Dart Trap (pressure plates)

Flamethrower Traps (pressure plates)

Oil Lamp Traps

Oil Pool Traps

Rising Floor Trap

Rune Traps (wall/floor)

Spear Trap (pedestal pressure plates)

Swinging Blade Trap

Swinging Wall Trap (pressure plates)

Trapped Chests

Puzzles

Claw Door

Special Objects

Word Wall: Storm Call [2/3]

Chests

Potions aplenty

Loose Gear

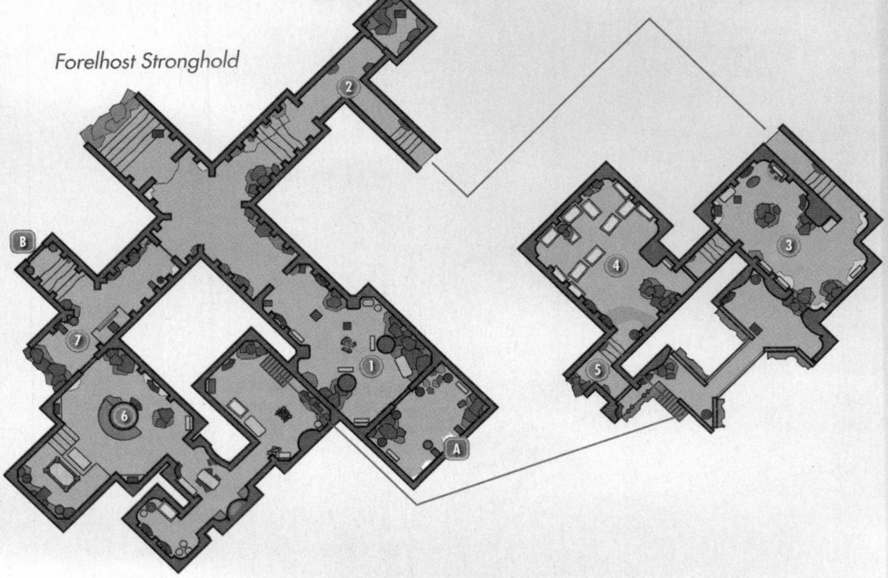

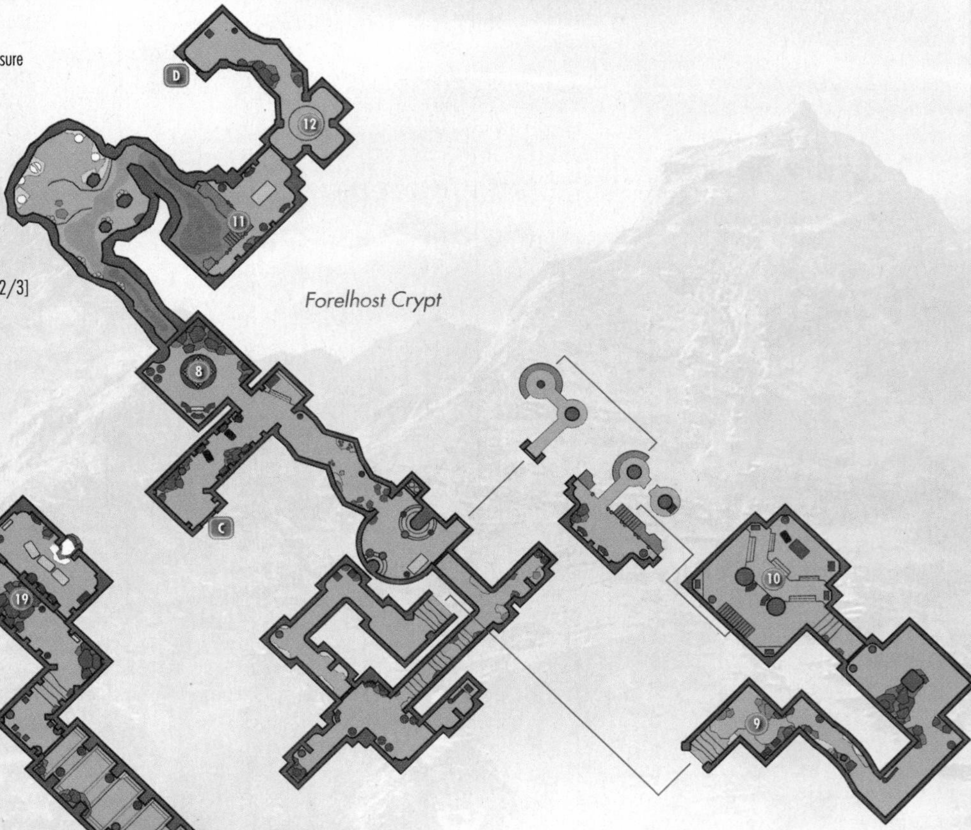

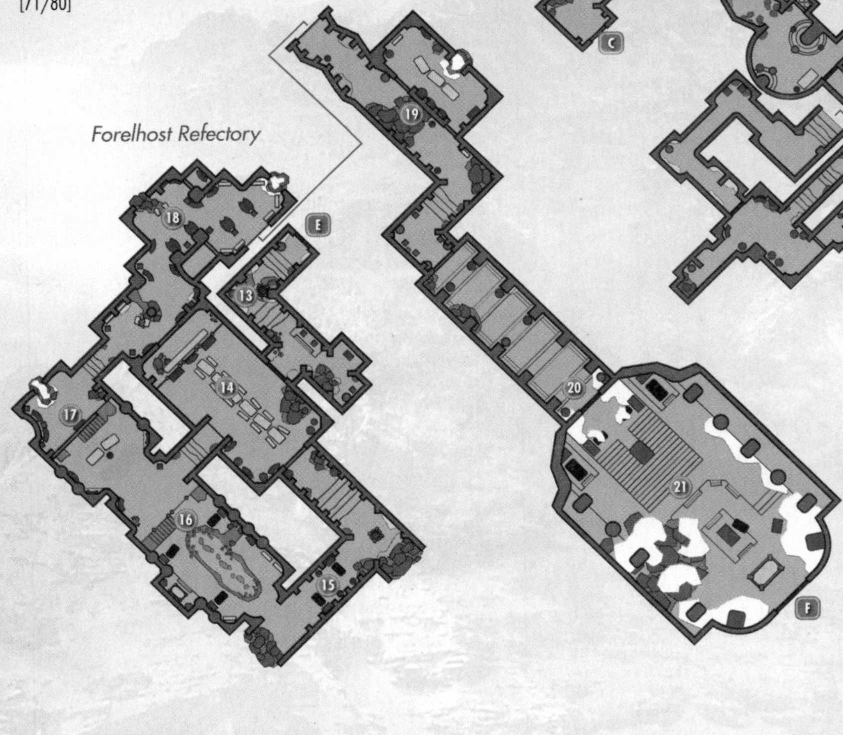

Forelhost Crypt

Forelhost Refectory

The Elder Scrolls V

SKYRIM

This massive stronghold stands in the snowy peaks of the mountains that lie southeast of Riften—a bit of climbing is required to get here. Forelhost is the tomb of one of eight fearsome Dragon Priests whose masks are part of a special quest.

Exterior

Speak with an soldier named Captain Valmir, who has made camp just outside the stronghold, to gain a new Side Quest that involves clearing the stronghold. (If you accidentally killed Captain Valmir before speaking with him, the key can be found on his body.) Don't let the captain catch you plundering his campsite before heading into the stronghold.

◇ Chest   ◇ Potions

A Exit to Skyrim

1 Entry Hall

Dispatch the ghost of a Dragon Cultist in this first wide chamber. Carefully sidestep a pressure plate as you enter the north passage on your way to [2].

◇ Danger! Battering Ram Trap (pressure plate)

2 Swinging Blade Passage

Slay a few more Dragon Cultist ghosts on your way to this passage of swinging blades. Raid the chest in the nearby nook before carefully darting past each swinging blade in turn.

◇ Danger! Swinging Blade Trap
◇ Chest (Locked: Novice)
◇ Loose Gear

3 Journal Chamber

The informative journal that Captain Valmir hinted about is found in this quiet chamber. Collect it to complete an optional objective. If you return to Captain Valmir at this point, he'll give you a rundown of what he learns from the journal.

◇ Skorm Snow-Strider's Journal
◇ Chest (Locked: Apprentice)
◇ Potions aplenty

4 Sleeping Quarters

The poisons that the Dragon Cultists used to kill themselves long ago are still potent. Collect them as you pass through here.

◇ Potions

5 Entry Hall/Smithing Area: West Side

Explore the Entry Hall's upper walkways to discover a chest, then double back and descend into its western half, where a Dragon Cultist ghost awaits. Progress through the Smithing Area into a small kitchen.

◇ Crafting: Anvil, Grindstone, Workbench
◇ Chest
◇ Chest (Locked: Adept)
◇ Potions
◇ Loose gear

6 Worship Chamber

Swipe a few valuables from the kitchen on your way to this large chamber, which features a central stairwell. Slay a few powerful Draugr here, and skirt the pressure plate atop the central platform to avoid triggering a trap. Avoid standing directly in front of the room's chest when opening it—spikes will stab up from the floor below! Try disabling the chest's trigger hinge if you're skilled at lockpicking.

◇ Danger! Dart Trap (pressure plate), Trapped Chest
◇ Potions

7 Fire Trap Passage

Beware of a pair of pressure plates in this final passage—they trigger nasty fire traps. Slay another mighty Draugr here and throw a lever to open a gate so you may quickly exit this place later. For now, go downstairs and through a door to delve deeper into the keep.

B Door to Forelhost Crypt

C Door to Forelhost Stronghold

8 Well

Collect a few potions in this room, then see if you can pick the Master-level cage door in its center. Doing so allows you to skip areas [9] and [10], which you only need to visit to search for the key that opens the cage door. The watery passage beneath the trapdoor leads to [11].

◇ Potions

9 Burial Passages

Loot plenty of urns and slay a host of Draugr as you navigate this long, winding passage. Beware of removing items from pedestals, which triggers traps, and move with caution to avoid a variety of other traps along the way.

◇ Danger! Dart Trap (pressure plates), Rune Traps (wall/floor), Swinging Blade Trap, Spear Trap (pedestal pressure plates), Swinging Wall Trap (pressure plates)
◇ Chest (Locked: Master)
◇ Potions

10 Overlord's Tomb

A vastly powerful Draugr warrior rises from a central sarcophagus as you enter this large cavern. Slay it, along with its minions, to secure a needed key from a chest. Go upstairs and leap to a second chest afterward, then scale a winding ramp to reach a high door that leads back to the start of the burial passages, but watch out for the magic casting trap at the top! Dodge when it fires, then run across to loot the Soul Gem, or knock it off the pedestal with an arrow.

◇ Forelhost Well Key (chest)
◇ Danger Magic Trap
◇ Chests (2)
◇ Potions
◇ Loose Gear

11 Poison Chamber

Kill a few Skeevers on your way to this cavern, where the cultists who once lived here poisoned their water supply—don't worry, it's had several hundred years to dissipate. Collect a selection of leftover poisons and swipe a Skill Book off a shelf.

◇ Danger! Oil Pool Trap
◇ Skill Book [Restoration]: The Exodus
◇ Potions aplenty

12 Rising Floor Passage

The bend in this passage features a nasty trap—stepping in the middle causes a large section of floor to rise, slamming you into long spikes on the ceiling. Avoid the center of the passage while rounding the corner.

◇ Danger! Rising Floor Trap

D Door to Forelhost Refectory

E Door to Forelhost Crypt

13 Entry Passage

Dispatch powerful Draugr in the very first passage, and find a chest tucked away in the corner. Stand to one side of the pedestal near the chest when removing the item from it to avoid being shot by arrows.

◇ Danger! Dart Trap (pedestal pressure plate)
◇ Chest

14 Dining Area

This dining hall turned makeshift embalming area was used by the Cultists to hastily embalm their members after they destroyed the hallway during the siege. Loot a host of urns to pad your coin purse before taking the south passage to [15].

15 Oily Tunnel

Ignite the oil on the ground in this passage to help you kill the powerful Draugr that lurks here.

◇ Danger! Oil Lamp Traps, Oil Pool Trap

16 Open-Air Chamber

Dispatch more Draugr in this wide room, and loot the chest that lies beneath the wooden stairs. A large amount of deadly flowers can be harvested here, and the half-buried bodies of several Draugr can be looted as well. Go upstairs afterward and throw a lever in the east passage to open a portcullis, allowing for faster navigation of the floor. Backtrack out afterward and head north to [17].

◇ Chest (Locked: Adept)
◇ Potions

17 Lab

Lure a mighty Draugr toward the oil slick on the ground in this chamber, then knock down the overhead lamp to set the undead warrior ablaze. Read the informative note on the table near the Alchemy Labs and collect a host of potions before proceeding upstairs.

◇ Danger! Oil Lamp Trap, Oil Pool Trap
◇ Crafting: Alchemy Labs (2)
◇ Potions aplenty

18 Library

As you move into the Library, watch out for the magic casting trap that sits across the room. Either snipe the gem with a bow or time your movement and run from cover to cover to cross the room. Swipe a special Glass Claw off a pedestal as you move through this cluttered area. Stand back and to one side of other pedestals before removing their contents to avoid traps. Unlock Master and Expert-level doors here to access a small, potion-filled closet and a little alcove with a Soul Gem. Loot a locked chest on your way to [19].

◇ Danger! Spear Trap (pedestal pressure plate)
◇ Dragon Claw: Glass Claw [9/10]
◇ Chest (Locked: Apprentice)
◇ Potions aplenty
◇ Loose Gear

19 Arcane Workroom

Slay a deadly Draugr in this small chamber, then stand back and to one side when opening the far chest to avoid being stabbed by spears (or simply disable its trigger wire). Dodge a pressure plate in the south passage that follows, collecting a few potions on your way to [20].

◇ Danger! Flamethrower Trap (pressure plate), Trapped Chest
◇ Crafting: Arcane Enchanter
◇ Potions

20 Claw Door Passage

Inspect the Glass Claw you found back at [18] and notice three symbols on its palm. Rotate the three concentric rings of this passage's far door to imitate the same sequence of symbols, then inspect the central keyhole to insert the Glass Claw and gain access to the tomb's final chamber.

21 Rahgot's Tomb

An immensely powerful Dragon Priest named Rahgot rises from this chamber's central sarcophagus when you enter. Fight hard to slay the deadly villain, then obtain a valuable staff, key, and Dragon Priest Mask by sifting through Rahgot's remains. Use Rahgot's key to open the large door and head outside.

◇ Dragon Priest Mask: Rahgot [9/10] (Rahgot)
◇ Unique Weapon: Dragon Priest Staff [71/80]
◇ Forelhost Balcony Key (Rahgot)
◇ Chest

F Exit to Skyrim

Exterior (Balcony)

Back outside, cross a few snowy ramparts to locate an ancient Word Wall. Learn your new word of power, then descend to the fort's main courtyard to find Captain Valmir speaking with an enemy soldier. It turns out that Valmir is an imposter. Kill him to complete your quest, then inspect his corpse to discover an informative letter. Your work here is complete.

◇ Word Wall: Storm Call [2/3]

[9.46] Stendarr's Beacon

Recommended Level: 6

Habitation: Special

Vigilant of Stendarr (Blessing)

Collectibles

Skill Book [Restoration]: The Exodus [D2/10]

Special Objects

Shrine of Stendarr [5/5]
Chest
Knapsack
Satchel
Loose Gear

This sizeable tower, located in the far southeastern corner of Skyrim, has been occupied by the Vigil of Stendarr — zealous followers of the Divines who seek to eradicate the vile Daedra. Speak to any of the Vigilants here, or touch the small shrine on the interior altar, to instantly rid yourself of all diseases. Collect the Skill Book that lies on a bedroll here, and carefully loot the chest found atop the vigil without being caught. Find a valuable piece of gear near a skeleton that lies in the snow north of the tower as well.

⚜ SECONDARY LOCATIONS ⚜

[9.A] Darkwater Overhang

At the base of the steep waterfall and path to Ivarstead is an overhang with a troll inside. Amid the bones in the back of the overhang is a Stormcloak Soldier with a note detailing attacks in the area. The troll is possibly the culprit.

◇ Note

[9.B] Wood Cutter's Camp: Lake Geir

A murdered woodcutter lies slumped over his logs at this one-tent camp on the upper copse close to the road to Ivarstead. There's some food and a little coin to scrabble for.

[9.C] The Poultry Reanimator: Lake Geir

On top of the taller rocks, with the main road to the south, is a strange robed fellow attempting to resurrect a dead chicken. He succeeds in his creation and attacks as you close. Expect ingredients after you slaughter him.

[9.D] Treasure Hunter's Camp: Lake Geir

A small tent and a smoking fire off the main road indicates a small hunter's camp overlooking Lake Geir. Aside from some food, there's little to steal or scavenge, but a note on one of the barrels indicates there's treasure to be found on the island to the northwest.

◇ Note

[9.E] Treasure Island: Lake Geir

Just northwest of the Treasure Hunter's Camp by the stump of the ancient tree, two treasure hunters have dug up a chest. They don't take kindly to your presence, so face them in combat before removing any treasure you find.

◇ Chest

[9.F] Dragon Mound: Autumnwatch Woods

Related Quest: Main Quest: Diplomatic Immunity

This Dragon Mound is initially sealed. It opens during Main Quest: Diplomatic Immunity, and if you visit during or after this point in the Main Quest, the mound will be open and empty. Perhaps this dragon is the one that takes possession of nearby Autumnwatch Tower [9.14].

[9.G] Shrine of Talos: Froki's Peak

Above Froki's Shack is a steep pathway up to a mountaintop, where a stone Talos gazes across the Arcwind gorge. Receive a blessing, and search the offerings for the following:

◇ Skill Book [Two-Handed]: King
◇ Shrine to Talos [17/17]
◇ Satchel
◇ Loose gear

[9.H] Medresi's Camp: Angarvunde

Related Quest: Dungeon Quest: Medresi Dran and the Wandering Dead*

Adjacent to the entrance to Angarvunde is a small camp. This was the base of operations for Medresi Dran and her cowardly mercenaries. Search the place for her notes and a Skill Book. Visit Angarvunde to find her yourself.

◇ Skill Book [Speech]: A Dance in Fire, v7
◇ Medresi's Notes

[9.I] Wild Animal Den: Mistwatch

A trio of hungry wolves, or other wild animals, have made this rocky alcove home, dragging rabbits and other meat to feast on later. Aside from Nightshade, there's little here except the prospect of a savaging.

[9.J] Bandit's Shack: Autumnshade

A ruined shack is home to a couple of bandits and their dog. Don't try a frontal assault, as the door is boarded; attack from the holes in the side walls. They all come out fighting if you're spotted. Explore the building to find the following.

- ◇ Skill Book [Block]: Battle of Red Mountain
- ◇ Chest
- ◇ Loose gear

[9.K] Northwind Chest

At the base of the Northwind peak, just northeast of Boulderfall Cave, is a chest guarded by two skeletons of the nonanimated variety. Pry open the locked chest; there's usually gems and other baubles to stuff into your pockets.

- ◇ Chest (Locked: Novice)

[9.L] Altar in the Woods: Autumnshade

Deep in the Autumnshade forest, a Fire Mage is experimenting at an altar, surrounded by old and forgotten ceremonial stones. Slay the magician, picking up any of the Dwemer artifacts you wish, as well as a Skill Book.

- ◇ Skill Book [Restoration]: Racial Phylogeny

[9.M] Dragon Mound: Autumnshade Woods

Related Quest: Main Quest: Bleak Falls Barrow

This Dragon Mound is initially sealed. It opens during Main Quest: Bleak Falls Barrow, and if you visit during or after this point in the Main Quest, the mound will be open and empty.

[9.N] Hunters' Camp: Autumnshade Hills

On the higher and rockier terrain southeast of Autumnshade Clearing is a small hunters' camp tucked away in the hills. There are two hunters here, and a Skill Book rests inside one of their tents.

- ◇ Skill Book [Archery]: The Gold Ribbon of Merit
- ◇ Knapsack

[9.O] Troll Den: Rkund

Due west of the Ruins of Rkund is an old Nordic barrow entrance built into the side of the Jerall Mountains. However, this location hasn't been excavated and is home to a ferocious troll.

- ◇ Chest

[9.P] Wild Animal Den: Crystaldrift Cave

A little farther east from the Crystaldrift Cave entrance is another indent in the Jerall Mountains—an animal den with few items of note. You may be attacked by a Skeever during your brief exploration.

[9.Q] Dragon Mound: Lost Tongue Pass

Related Quest: Main Quest: Diplomatic Immunity

This Dragon Mound is initially sealed. It opens during Main Quest: Diplomatic Immunity. If you visit during or after this point in the Main Quest, the mound will be open and empty. Perhaps this is the dragon that now rules the ruin of Lost Tongue Overlook on the hill above?

[9.R] Wild Animal Den: Shor's Stone

Southeast of Shor's Watchtower, along the path that runs north-south along the base of the Velothi Mountains, is a rocky hillock with a wolf den. Expect some items to find on the corpse of a bandit in the back of the den.

[9.S] Trappers' Dilemma

In the woods to the east of Fort Greenwall is a rusting cage with a wolf in it. If you open the cage, the trappers return and attack! Fend them off with the wolf's help. If the wolf survives, it flees to the nearby wolf den [9.R].

[9.T] Miner's Camp: Velothi Mountains

The vicious blizzards that race across the snow-swept peaks above the Rift have killed and half buried a lone miner. Nearby are two veins to attack with your pickaxe (or use the one nearby). Go west from the miner to find a Skill Book lying near the skeletal remains of another unfortunate soul.

◇ Skill Book [Destruction]: The Art of War Magic

◇ Mineable ore (Moonstone, Quicksilver)

[9.U] The Three Sentinels

The road leading north from Riften's North Gate and the Riften Stables is flanked by these three wooden watchtowers, where a small contingent of city guards keep watch for any sign of a bandit raid. At the top of each tower is a chest of items the guards have confiscated from brigands. Pick the lock, and you can help yourself.

◇ Chests (Locked: Adept) (3)

[9.V] Shrine of Zenithar: Fallowstone

Along the road north of Riften, just beyond the Three Sentinels [9.U], the road forks. Instead of taking either fork, look up the hill to the east, where you can find a small ruin. Defeat the wild animal that guards it, and you can pray at this makeshift Shrine to Zenithar. Take any offerings you wish.

◇ Shrine of Zenithar [5/5]

◇ Satchel

[9.W] Tumbledown Tower: Riften Outskirts

There's a reason one of Riften's gates has been sealed; farther along the old road east of town are the remains of a fallen tower, where you can find a couple of bandits picking through the rubble.

◇ Chest (Apprentice)

[9.X] Burning Farmhouse

Along the southern border, at the foot of the Jerall Mountains, is a small farmhouse burning merrily. Though you may think it the work of a dragon, inspect the summoning circle and the charred remains of a farmer clutching a Scroll of Conjure Flame Atronach to reveal how a familiar set fire to this abode. A Skill Book is hidden inside the hollow fallen log near the cabin.

◇ Skill Book [Destruction]: Horrors of Castle Xyr

◇ Chest

[9.Y] Frost Troll Den: Jerall Mountain Ridge

Look up at the precarious path, and you may see a flag up on a high ridge. Follow the bloodstained snow switchback around to an exposed Frost Troll's den. Slay the beast; the blood comes from the corpse of a miner. A Skill Book is hidden beneath an animal carcass. Skill Book [Block]: A Dance in Fire, v2

◇ Strongbox (Apprentice)   ◇ Loose gear

[9.Z] Two Pine Ridge

Clamber the steep slopes from Stendarr's Beacon to find a pair of pine trees on a rocky ridge. Below one is a miner's bedroll. Look closely for a Skill Book.

◇ Skill Book [Sneak]: 2920, Last Seed, v8

◇ Mineable ore (Iron)

OVERVIEW

 MINOR SPOILERS

The land of Skyrim brims with wondrous locales, yet some areas cannot easily be linked to any one Hold. In fact, certain areas can't even be said to exist within the confines of reality! From traveling caravans to the mind of a demented Emperor, all unusual and otherworldly locations are covered here, in "Other Realms."

AVAILABLE SERVICES, CRAFTING, AND COLLECTIBLES

Services

Followers/Hirelings: [1/47]
Houses for Sale: [0/5]
Marriage Prospects: [0/62]
Skill Trainers: [4/50]
  Alchemy: [0/3]
  Alteration: [0/3]
  Archery: [0/3]
  Block: [0/2]
  Conjuration: [0/3]
  Destruction: [0/3]
  Enchanting: [0/2]
  Heavy Armor: [0/3]
  Illusion: [0/2]
  Light Armor: [0/3]
  Lockpicking: [1/2]
  One-Handed: [0/3]
  Pickpocket: [1/3]
  Restoration: [0/3]

  Smithing: [0/3]
  Sneak: [1/3]
  Speech: [1/4]
  Two-Handed: [0/2]
Traders [7/133]:
  Apothecary: [0/12]
  Bartender: [0/5]
  Blacksmith: [0/33]
  Carriage Driver: [0/5]
  Fence: [4/10]
  Fletcher: [0/3]
  Food Vendor: [0/9]
  General Goods: [3/19]
  Innkeeper: [0/15]
  Jeweler: [0/2]
  Special: [0/3]
  Spell Vendor: [0/12]
  Stablemaster: [0/5]

Collectibles

Captured Critters: [0/5]
Dragon Claws: [1/10]
Dragon Priest Masks: [1/10]
Larceny Targets: [0/7]
Skill Books: [6/180]
  Alchemy: [1/10]
  Alteration: [0/10]
  Archery: [0/10]
  Block: [1/10]
  Conjuration: [0/10]
  Destruction: [0/10]
  Enchanting: [0/10]
  Heavy Armor: [1/10]
  Illusion: [0/10]

  Light Armor: [0/10]
  Lockpicking: [1/10]
  One-Handed: [0/10]
  Pickpocket: [0/10]
  Restoration: [0/10]
  Smithing: [1/10]
  Sneak: [0/10]
  Speech: [1/10]
  Two-Handed: [0/10]
Treasure Maps: [0/11]
Unique Weapons: [2/80]
Unique Items: [0/112]
Unusual Gems: [0/24]

Special Objects

Shrines: [0/69]
  Akatosh: [0/6]
  Arkay: [0/12]
  Dibella: [0/8]
  Julianos: [0/5]
  Kynareth: [0/6]
  Mara: [0/5]
  Stendarr: [0/5]
  Talos: [0/17]
  Zenithar: [0/5]
  Standing Stones: [0/13]
Word Walls: [1/42]
  Animal Allegiance: [0/3]
  Aura Whisper: [0/3]

Become Ethereal: [0/3]
Disarm: [0/3]
Dismaying Shout: [0/3]
Elemental Fury: [0/3]
Fire Breath: [0/2]
Frost Breath: [0/3]
Ice Form: [0/3]
Kyne's Peace: [0/3]
Marked for Death: [0/3]
Slow Time: [0/3]
Storm Call: [1/3]
Throw Voice: [0/1]
Unrelenting Force: [0/1]
Whirlwind Sprint: [0/2]

Total—6

[10.00] Khajiit Caravans

Related Quests

Dark Brotherhood Quest: Side Contract: Ma'randru-jo

Thieves Guild Radiant Quest: Moon Sugar Rush* (Ri'saad)

Miscellaneous Objective: New Moon* (Kharjo)

Habitation: Special

Ahkari (General Store Vendor; Trainer: Journeyman)

Atahbah (Fence)

Dro'marash (Trainer: Speech)

Kharjo (Follower)

Khayla (Trainer: Sneak)

Ma'dran (Fence; General Store Vendor)

Ma'jhad (Fence; Trainer: Lockpicking)

Ma'randru-jo

Ra'zhinda

Ri'saad (Fence; General Store Vendor)

Zaynabi (Fence)

Services

Follower: Kharjo [47/47]

Trader (Fence): Ri'saad [7/10]

Trader (Fence): Atahba [8/10]

Trader (Fence): Ma'jahad [9/10]

Trader (Fence): Zaynabi [10/10]

Trader (General Store Vendor): Ri'saad [17/19]
  Weapons, Apparel, Potions, Food, Ingredients, Misc

Trader (General Store Vendor): Ahkari [18/19]
  Weapons, Apparel, Potions, Food, Ingredients, Misc

Trader (General Store Vendor): Ma'dran [19/19]
  Weapons, Apparel, Potions, Food, Ingredients, Misc

Trainer (Lockpicking: Expert): Ma'jhad [2/2]

Trainer (Pickpocket: Journeyman): Ahkari [3/3]

Trainer (Sneak: Journeyman): Khayla [3/3]

Trainer (Speech: Journeyman 1): Dro'marash [4/4]

Crafting

Tanning Rack

Collectibles

Chest(s)

Potions

Loose gear

Three Khajiit caravans wander Skyrim, traveling from town to town and offering various goods and services. Each caravan is made up of an owner and his entourage, and each caravan travels its own route between two major cities. Caravans will pause to do business with you while on the move but are more commonly found outside of Skyrim's larger capital cities, where they make camp for brief periods. Befriending each of the three savvy caravan owners can lead to special benefits!

Ri'saad's Caravan

Ri'saad is the patriarch of the Khajiit caravan merchants. He's the richest of the three and enjoys the best trade route, with exclusive contracts among Skyrim's wealthiest cities. Ri'saad's route takes him from Markarth [5.00] to Whiterun [6.00] and back again. Ri'saad offers a fine selection of wares, and Khayla can train you to be more stealthy.

◊ Crafting: Tanning Rack

Ahkari's Caravan

Ahkari has the monopoly on the north-south Dawnstar [3.00] to Riften [9.00] run—a very profitable passage. Speak with Ahkari to buy and sell a variety of goods or to receive training lessons in Pickpocket. Dro'marash can help you hone your Speech skill, while Kharjo will offer to serve as a Follower after you do him a special favor..

Ma'dran's Caravan

Ma'dran used to be the poorest of the three Khajiit merchants. Now, with the advent of the Civil War, his business is booming. Ma'dran's primary goods are weapons and armor, which are in high demand. Speak with Ma'dran to purchase some fresh gear, or pay Ma'jhad to help you improve your Lockpicking skill.

◊ Ma'dran's route is unique in that he shares a common stop with Ri'saad's caravan: Windhelm [7.00]. However, Ma'dran's route runs from Windhelm [7.00] to Solitude [1.00] instead of to Markarth [5.00].

[10.01] Azura's Star

Related Quests

Daedric Quest: The Black Star

Recommended Level: 6

Dungeon: Special

Dremora Churl

Malyn Varen

Collectibles

Unique Item: Azura's Star [36/112]

Unique Item: Black Star [26/112]

Area Is Locked (quest required)

Azura's Star is a unique location that's visited only during Daedric Quest: The Black Star. It is, in fact, the interior of the Star of Azura, the Daedric artifact you seek to recover during the quest. The person you seek out to assist you in repairing the Broken Star of Azura determines the reward you'll receive at the quest's end: You get Azura's Star (an infinite Grand Soul Gem) if you turn to Aranea Ienith, and you get the Black Star (an infinite Black Soul Gem) if you seek out Nelacar. Regardless of which person you turn to, you'll end up entering the star and chasing the nefarious Mayln Varen down a winding, crystalline pathway. Dremora will attempt to intercept you along the way. Defeat Varen when you reach the bottom to purify the star and claim a very valuable keepsake.

[10.02] Blackreach

Related Quests

Main Quest: Elder Knowledge

Daedric Quest: Discerning the Transmundane

Side Quest: A Return to Your Roots

Dungeon Activity

Recommended Level: 18

Dungeon: Dwarven City

Chaurus

Dwarven Sphere

Dwarven Spider

Giant

Falmer

Falmer Servant

Frost Troll

Frostbite Spider

Wisp

Wispmother

Crafting

Alchemy Lab

Arcane Enchanter

Workbench

Dangers

Dwarven Ballista Trap (lever)

Dwarven Thresher Trap (pressure plate)

Dwarven Thresher Trap (lever)

Swinging Blade Trap (pressure plates/lever)

Puzzles

Button Puzzle

Underground Connections

Alftand [4.13]

Blackreach Elevator (Alftand) [3.26]

Blackreach Elevator (Raldbthar) [3.33]

Mzinchaleft [2.18]

Mzinchaleft Exterior [2.18]

Raldbthar [3.32]

Tower of Mzark [3.15]

Quest Items

Crimson Nirnroot

Elder Scroll

Runed Lexicon

Collectibles

Skill Book [Alchemy]: De Rerum Dirennis

Skill Book [Block]: Warrior

Skill Book [Heavy Armor]: 2920, MidYear, v6

Skill Book [Smithing]: The Armorer's Challenge

Skill Book [Speech]: A Dance in Fire, v6

Area Is Locked (quest required)

Chests

Potions

Loose gear

Mineable ore (Corundum)

NOTE Find additional Crimson Nirnroot plants inside of several of Blackreach's interior locations, such as Sinderion's Field Laboratory, the Silent Ruin, and the Derelict Pumphouse (among others).

● Crimson Nirnroot

A Exit to Mzinchaleft Gatehouse [2.18]

B Elevator to Alftand Cathedral [4.13]

C Exit to Blackreach Elevator (Raldbthar) [3.33]

D Exit to Blackreach Elevator (Alftand) [3.26]

E Elevator to Raldbthar Deep Market [3.32]

F Exit to Mzinchaleft Exterior [2.18]

1 Reeking Tower

Scale a rocky slope to reach this tall northern tower, then circle around to locate its door. Enter and slay a handful of overgrown Frostbite Spiders on your way to the far elevator, which takes you back out to Blackreach. You'll find yourself standing near a neighboring tower to the one you entered. Slay a few more spiders out here to cleanse this place.

2 Sinderion's Field Laboratory

This small lab is likely to be your first stop in Blackreach. Claim plenty of loot here and use the crafting stations to prepare yourself for the dangers that lurk in the dark. If you are planning on a long exploration of Blackreach, this is a great place to use as a base camp. Inspect the remains of Sinderion to acquire his informative journal and obtain a new quest that involves collecting Crimson Nirnroot from around Blackreach.

◇ Crafting: Alchemy Lab, Arcane Enchanter, Workbench

◇ Crimson Nirnroot

◇ Skill Book [Alchemy]: De Rerum Dirennis

◇ Chests (2)

◇ Knapsack

◇ Apothecary's Satchel

◇ Potions

The dwarves' capital city of Blackreach has been abandoned for ages and now serves as home to vicious Falmer. This great subterranean metropolis houses many secrets for those brave enough to probe its depths. Blackreach features multiple access elevators, but your first visit occurs during Daedric Quest: Discerning the Transmundane, in which you will likely travel through Alftand [4.13]. Therefore, the first time you enter Blackreach, you'll find yourself at [B], unless you chose one of the alternate routes.

Once you've accessed Blackreach, you may use any of the city's elevators to return to the surface. Some elevators connect to major dwarven ruins across Skyrim, such as Raldbthar [3.32] in the Pale. Others simply lead to lone elevator towers that stand in the wilderness. Ride each of Blackreach's elevators to open more and more surface connections to Blackreach—this makes moving to and from the great hidden city much easier.

The terrain of Blackreach becomes tumultuous around the edges of the cavern but is otherwise quite level and easy. Expect to face a blend of dwarven security units, Falmer, and various cave dwellers like the Chaurus and Frostbite Spider. Encounters with other, more powerful creatures such as trolls and giants are rare.

Aside from exploring the Tower of Mzark [10] as part of the "Discerning the Transmundane" quest, you may also collect special Crimson Nirnroots as part of Side Quest: A Return to Your Roots. Around 50 of these special red plants grow throughout Blackreach. Many are labeled on the map provided here in this guide, while others are found inside of Blackreach's interior points of interest. Use this resource to track them down, then pinpoint their locations by the soft ringing sound each plant produces. Collect the requisite number of Crimson Nirnroot pants to advance the quest.

③ Silent Ruin

Enter this small chamber to obtain a Skill Book and some Crimson Nirnroot, but avoid the pressure plate near the throne.

- ◇ Danger! Dwarven Thresher Trap (pressure plate)
- ◇ Crimson Nirnroot
- ◇ Skill Book [Block]: Warrior
- ◇ Chest

④ Hall of Rumination

The Hall of Rumination is one of three structures located at Blackreach's city center. Several lowly Falmer and Falmer Servants mill about the main chamber. Slay them and then notice a gate that you can't seem to open. Pull a lever on the balcony to the east of the gate to open it, but head through the nearby east doors first to secure a sleeping area and a room with a chest. Now go through the west gate and head upstairs to discover another chest. Take the nearby elevator up to a high exterior balcony, looping around to discover some Crimson Nirnroot outside.

- ◇ Crimson Nirnroot
- ◇ Chests (2)

⑤ Pumping Station

Exit the Debate Hall [6] via its northeast door and cross a walkway to enter this small workshop. The Pumping Station connects to the Silent City Catacombs [7] and houses a handful of poorly armed Falmer Servants. Exit through the northeast door so you may reenter via the northwest door and access a chest on the west balcony.

- ◇ Chest

⑥ Debate Hall

Plenty of Falmer and Falmer Servants lurk within the Debate Hall. The main attraction here is the Skill Book that lies on a small table near a skeleton in the east alcove.

- ◇ Skill Book [Speech]: A Dance in Fire, v6

⑦ Silent City Catacombs

Nab some Crimson Nirnroot on your way into this sewer network, which lies just east of Blackreach's city center. Slay a Falmer and loot a chest in the first hall, then jump the pairs of pressure plates in the hall that follow, or use the lever in the nook beyond the gate to trigger the blades and slice up any patrolling enemies. Proceed until you reach a watery chamber, then dive underwater to locate three submerged chests. Proceed through the next passage and slay another Falmer to obtain a useful key. Make your way through the south door to reach the final room, where you find more Falmer and a door that connects to Blackreach's Pumping Station [5].

- ◇ Danger! Swinging Blade Trap (pressure plates/lever)
- ◇ Crimson Nirnroot
- ◇ Shaman's Key (Falmer)
- ◇ Chests (4)

⑧ War Quarters

This small area sports plenty of beds to rest upon. Complete your circuit through the War Quarters to locate a pair of chests on the entry room's balcony.

- ◇ Chests (2)

⑨ Farm Overseer's House

This small abode offers you a place to rest and plenty of worthy plunder.

- ◇ Chest (Locked: Novice)
- ◇ Chest (Locked: Adept)
- ◇ Potions
- ◇ Loose gear

⑩ Tower of Mzark

This giant tower stands south of Blackreach's city center and houses an item of tremendous power. Ride up the elevator, then raid a couple of locked chests and inspect a Skill Book in the room at which you arrive. Scale a winding ramp to locate the remains of Drokt—read the nearby journal for some insight. Scale the remainder of the ramp to reach a control panel. Insert the Blank Lexicon into the Lexicon Receptacle, then press the third button from the left until the second button from the left becomes active. Now press the second button from the left until the first button on the left becomes active. Press this button until all of the buttons deactivate. Collect the Transcribed Lexicon from the Lexicon Receptacle and approach the central mechanism to obtain the mysterious Elder Scroll.

Proceed through the nearby door and use the elevator beyond to quickly return to the surface of Skyrim.

- ◇ Elder Scroll
- ◇ Runed Lexicon
- ◇ Skill Book [Smithing]: The Armorer's Challenge
- ◇ Chests (Locked: Novice) (2)
- ◇ Potions
- ◇ Loose gear

⑪ Derelict Pumphouse

Destroy a dangerous Dwarven Spider here, then loot a chest that's affixed to the wall. Another chest lies underwater; jump the pipes and turn a submerged valve to access the chest, then surface for a moment to snag some Crimson Nirnroot before turning another valve to escape the water.

- ◇ Crimson Nirnroot
- ◇ Chest (Locked: Adept)
- ◇ Chest

Other Blackreach Locations

The following sites don't have quite as much going on as the aforementioned locations but are still worth exploring:

ⓘ Overpass

This overpass was presumably used to monitor the travel of workers to and from the city.

ⓘⓘ Wispmother Encounter

Beware of this clearing, where wisps flutter about. A dangerous Wispmother will attack if you draw near. Crimson Nirnroot grows by the planks that span the nearby stream to the east.

- ◇ Crimson Nirnroot

ⓘⓘⓘ Guard Towers

Dwarven soldiers likely watched from these towers as workers traveled to and from the city.

ⓘⱽ Fungus Field

Blackreach's giant glowing mushrooms are growing strong here. Find some Crimson Nirnroot growing near the pipes to the north.

- ◇ Crimson Nirnroot

ⱽ Sleeping Chaurus

Get the drop on a pair of giant, snoozing Chaurus by sneaking up to this site.

ⱽⓘ Blackreach City: Main Gate

The gate to the dwarves' capital city lies here, allowing entry from the south.

ⱽⓘⓘ Blackreach Arena

It is assumed that Falmer would have been made to fight at the small arena located here. Pulling the nearby lever causes a lethal spinning blade to stick up from the arena's floor. Collect the Skill Book that rests on the nearby stone table.

- ◇ Danger! Dwarven Thresher Trap (lever)
- ◇ Skill Book [Heavy Armor]: 2920, MidYear, v6

ⱽⓘⓘⓘ Troll Den

A pair of vicious Frost Trolls guard a sprig of Crimson Nirnroot on a high ledge here.

- ◇ Crimson Nirnroot

ⓘⓧ Shrine

Find a bit of loot at the small shrine near the water down here, but beware of a Dwarven Sphere that emerges from the wall.

- ◇ Crimson Nirnroot
- ◇ Potions

ⓧ Falmer Mining Camp

Dispatch a handful of dangerous Falmer here so you may raid the chests that they guard. If you like, mine some Corundum Ore from the vein near the leader's tent. Crimson Nirnroot grows by the water.

- ◇ Crimson Nirnroot
- ◇ Chests (2)
- ◇ Mineable ore (Corundum)

ⓧⓘ Vulthuryol's Gong

Notice the huge glowing orb floating above the Silent City at the center of Blackreach? Hit this distant target with your Unrelenting Force Shout and you'll summon the dragon Vulthuryol, who will soar out of his hidden lair to rain fire upon the city before setting down on the southern road.

⯈ [10.03] Blue Palace Pelagius Wing

Related Quests

Daedric Quest: The Mind of Madness

Recommended Level: 8

Dungeon: Special

Sheogorath
Pelagius the Mad

Collectibles

Skill Book [Lockpicking]: Surfeit of Thieves [C2/10]

Unique Weapon: Wabbajack [72/80]

Area Is Locked (quest required)

This special section of the Blue Palace in Solitude [1.00] remains locked at all times and is accessible only during Daedric Quest: The Mind of Madness. After a brief exploration of the long-unused wing, you're soon whisked away to unfamiliar surroundings—the deceptively verdant mind of Emperor Pelagius III! Speak with Sheogorath to advance the quest and receive a unique weapon called the Wabbajack—this is the only thing you can take with you when you leave this unusual place.

Travel down each of the three paths to encounter three very unusual situations, each a reflection of Pelagius's warped psyche. Use the Wabbajack to solve each of the situations as follows:

Arena: Shoot the spectating soldiers on the arena's far side, not the combatants.

Pelagius the Tormented: Shoot the sleeping Emperor to spawn a series of progressively more dangerous foes. Defeat them all.

Pelagius vs. Pelagius: Shoot the smaller version of Pelagius (named "Confidence") to make it grow. Shoot the Imperial Soldier named "Anger" to shrink it. Ensure that Pelagius's Confidence is as large as can be, then shoot the two specters of Self-Doubt that eventually appear to vanquish them.

Once you've returned from Pelagius's frightening mind, continue your search of the Pelagius Wing to discover a Skill Book on some crates downstairs.

⯈ [10.04] Japhet's Folly

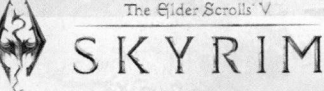

Related Quests

Side Quest: Rise in the East

Dungeon: Bandit Camp

Blood Horker
Haldyn
Mudcrab

Crafting

Arcane Enchanter

Dangers

Swinging Spears (pressure plate)
Area Is Locked (quest required)
Chests
Potions
Loose gear

Japhet's Folly is a special island that only be reached only by ship. You visit Japhet's Folly during Side Quest: Rise in the East, with the goal of slaying a dangerous mage named Haldyn, who's raised an impressive pirate base here.

Once you arrive at Japhet's Folly, leap from your ship and cross the broken ice, heading for the tower that stands atop the nearby glacier. You can't actually reach the tower—follow your objective marker to locate the entrance to a small cave instead.

Sea Cave

Kill a few Mudcrab in the watery cave, and open a chest in the first cavern. Slay a lone Blood Horker bandit in the stone room you soon reach. Loot a second chest here, then grab the potions on the shelves before heading upstairs to the Japhet's Folly Towers.

◇ Chests (2)   ◇ Potions

Japhet's Folly Towers

Avoid a pressure plate on the first landing as you go upstairs. Eliminate a couple of Blood Horker guards, then raid a chest as you cross a long hall to reach a neighboring tower. If you like, go downstairs to face a few more guards and discover more loot, including a locked chest. Unlock the Expert-level door down here to discover the final resting place of Japhet, whose remains lie next to an informative journal and a large chest. Go upstairs to slay Haldyn, raid his chest, and collect the key he carries. Then backtrack downstairs and use the Japhet's Folly Key to open the door in the connecting corridor, which leads outside.

◇ Danger! Swinging Spears (pressure plate)
◇ Crafting: Arcane Enchanter
◇ Japhet's Folly Key (Haldyn)
◇ Chests (2)
◇ Chest (Locked: Apprentice)
◇ Chest (Locked: Expert)
◇ Potions
◇ Loose gear

Japhet's Folly (Exterior)

Step outside to find the island being bombarded by cannon fire—your associates are doing their part! Slay the odd guard and loot a lone chest as you navigate the embattled encampment, but don't stray too far from the main path or you may be struck by friendly fire. Dispatch the final group of pirates down by the docks, then speak with Adelasia Vendicci to complete your quest and shove off.

◇ Chest

▶ [10.05] Skuldafn

Related Quests

Main Quest: The World-Eater's Eyrie
Side Quest: Masks of the Dragon Priests*

Recommended Level: 10

Dungeon: Dragon Priest Lair

Dragon
Draugr
Frostbite Spider
Nahkriin

Dangers

Dart Trap (pressure plates)
Oil Lamp Trap (pressure plate)
Oil Pool Trap

Puzzles

Nordic Puzzle Door (Diamond Claw)
Nordic Pillars I
Nordic Pillars II

Skuldafn is a special location that lies just outside the bounds of Skyrim's ninth Hold, the Rift. Once you've advanced to Main Quest: The World-Eater's Eyrie, you're able to visit Skuldafn by flying on the back of a dragon. Your goal is to access Skuldafn's portal to Sovngarde [10.06], the legendary underworld of the Nords.

Skuldafn (Exterior)

Slay a dragon that ambushes you in Skuldafn's large exterior ruins, while simultaneously battling multiple Draugr. A second dragon strikes as you near the South Tower, and more Draugr are poised on the walkway beyond the east stairs. Climb an open-air tower to locate a chest beyond the east stairs, then slay more Draugr as you scale the north stairs that follow. If you like, loop around to visit the North Tower, and raid the exterior chest on the table atop the south steps, before entering Skuldafn Temple.

◇ Chests (2)

Skuldafn South Tower

This simple tower teems with Draugr, but there's a chest upstairs.

◇ Chest

Skuldafn North Tower

The North Tower's similar to its twin—full of undead and housing a chest on its upper level. Head outside through the upstairs door and reenter the tower via the other balcony door to discover a second chest in a small alcove.

◇ Chests (2)

Skuldafn Temple (Section I)

The legendary portal to Sovngarde is housed within this temple. Beware of pressure plate traps and Draugr as you explore the cavernous entry hall, looting a chest on the right. Spin the three Nordic pillars so that the two on the outside are mirroring the glyphs on the opposing walls (Snake, Whale). Then spin the central pillar so that its Hawk glyph faces toward the far portcullises. Pull the central lever to raise the Hawk portcullis, then raid the chest beyond. Change the central pillar again so that its Snake glyph is facing the portcullises; then pull the lever a second time to open the Snake portcullis and advance.

Loot another chest at the bottom of the following chamber, then cut through Frostbite Spiders on your way to another room with a second Nordic Pillars Puzzle. Find a fourth chest here. Solve the simple puzzle by spinning the three pillars so that the bottom one shows a Snake, while the upper two show a Whale and a Hawk, matching the glyphs on the walls about the room. Pull the lever to lower the drawbridge that leads deeper into the temple.

◇ Danger! Dart Trap (pressure plates)   ◇ Chests (4)

Skuldafn Temple (Section II)

Loop around the entry room, slaying Draugr on your way to a stairwell. Beware the pressure plate near the stairwell—stepping on it causes a hanging lamp to fall and ignite the oily floor, while also causing arrows to fly out from the far wall! Go upstairs and raid a chest near more oil and another hanging lamp. Pull the nearby lever to open the north portcullis

Collectibles

Dragon Claw: Diamond Claw [10/10]
Dragon Priest Mask: Nahkriin [10/10]

Special Objects

Word Wall: Storm Call [3/3]
Area Is Locked (quest required)
Chest(s)
Potions
Loose gear

and sack another chest on your way down an oily hall, but beware another dangerous pressure plate. Kill a powerful Draugr in the passage the follows to obtain the Diamond Claw, then use the claw to open the nearby puzzle door (Fox, Moth, Dragon). Approach the Word Wall that follows to gain new power, then proceed toward the door that leads back outside to Skuldafn's exterior, swiping a few potions from a small embalming chamber along the way.

◇ Danger! Dart Trap (pressure plate), Oil Lamp Trap, Oil Lamp Traps (pressure plates), Oil Pool Trap
◇ Dragon Claw: Diamond Claw [10/10]
◇ Word Wall: Storm Call [3/3]
◇ Chests (2)
◇ Potions
◇ Loose gear

Skuldafn (Temple Apex)

Cut down the Draugr outside the temple, then descend the wooden stairs of the west tower to plunder a large chest at the bottom. Go back up and circle around the temple so you may scale its exterior stairs, at last arriving at the portal to Sovngarde. Slay the mighty Dragon Priest that guards this wondrous site so you may claim its valuable mask and staff. Inspect the Dragon Seal to replace the staff and open the portal once more. Gather your courage and jump into the beam to journey to Sovngarde [10.06]!

◇ Dragon Priest Mask: Nahkriin [10/10]
◇ Unique Weapon: Dragon Priest Staff [73/80]
◇ Chest
◇ Potion

▶ [10.06] Sovngarde

Related Quests

Main Quest: Sovngarde
Main Quest: Dragonslayer
Main Quest: Epilogue

Recommended Level: 24

Dungeon: Dragon Lair

Alduin
Erlendr
Felldir the Old
Gormlaith Golden-Hilt
Hakon One-Eye
Hero of Sovngarde
Hunroor
Imperial Soldier
Jurgen Windcaller
Nikulas
Stormcloak Soldier
Tsun
Ulfgar the Unyielding
Ysgramor
Area Is Locked (quest required)

Sovngarde is the storied underworld of the Nords—the place where the greatest Nord heroes go when they die to enjoy an eternity of feasting and merriment. The only way a living mortal can visit this surreal realm is via the portal at Skuldafn [10.05], another special location that can only be visited during Main Quest: The World-Eater's Eyrie.

Sovngarde (Exterior)

Use the Clear Skies Shout to clear a path through Sovngarde's misty exterior. You can use Clear Skies to prevent Alduin from devouring the souls lost in the mist (they will aid you in the final battle against Alduin), but don't bother trying to attack Alduin—he's protected by his mist. You can turn right or left at the first junction; the steps straight ahead merely lead to an overlook. Wind around the central hill and approach Tsun, the guardian of this place. Defeat him to prove your worth, then cross the Whalebone Bridge and enter the towering Hall of Valor.

Hall of Valor

Skyrim's greatest heroes stroll the Hall of Valor. Ysgramor himself greets you when you first enter. Enjoy your peek at a true Nord's idea of paradise, then approach the three heroes of old to learn what you must do to defeat Alduin.

APPENDICES

Keeping track of your progress across the Province of Skyrim can be overwhelming at times. The following Appendices attempt to summarize the information you need to know and restore a feeling of calm, knowledgeable ease to your journey. Or, they reference other tables in this guide where information is readily available. At the end of these Appendices is a brief section with research and information on the language of the dragons, a glossary, and finally an index.

 MINOR SPOILERS

CAUTION This chapter has highly secret information; read with care!

NOTE Aside from Appendix I, and unless otherwise specified, information contained within these Appendices is also listed within the Atlas.

APPENDIX I: ACHIEVEMENTS AND TROPHIES

This table lists all the Achievements (PC or Xbox 360) or Trophies (PlayStation 3) that you can accrue during the game.

✓	ICON	INDEX	ACHIEVEMENT	POINTS	TROPHY	DESCRIPTION	NOTES
☐		1	Unbound	10	Bronze	Complete "Unbound"	Complete Main Quest: Unbound
☐		2	Bleak Falls Barrow	10	Bronze	Complete "Bleak Falls Barrow"	Complete Main Quest: Bleak Falls Barrow
☐		3	The Way of the Voice	20	Bronze	Complete "The Way of the Voice"	Complete Main Quest: The Way of the Voice
☐		4	Diplomatic Immunity	20	Bronze	Complete "Diplomatic Immunity"	Complete Main Quest: Diplomatic Immunity
☐		5	Alduin's Wall	20	Bronze	Complete "Alduin's Wall"	Complete Main Quest: Alduin's Wall
☐		6	Elder Knowledge	20	Bronze	Complete "Elder Knowledge"	Complete Main Quest: Elder Knowledge
☐		7	The Fallen	20	Bronze	Complete "The Fallen"	Complete Main Quest: The Fallen
☐		8	Dragonslayer	50	Gold	Complete "Dragonslayer"	Complete Main Quest: Dragonslayer
☐		9	Take Up Arms	10	Bronze	Join the Companions	Complete your first Companions Radiant Quest
☐		10	Blood Oath	10	Bronze	Become a member of the Circle	Become a Werewolf, at the start of The Companions Quest: The Silver Hand
☐		11	Glory of the Dead	30	Silver	Complete "Glory of the Dead"	Complete The Companions Quest: Glory of the Dead
☐		12	Gatekeeper	10	Bronze	Join the College of Winterhold	Complete College of Winterhold Quest: First Lessons
☐		13	Revealing the Unseen	10	Bronze	Complete "Revealing the Unseen"	Complete College of Winterhold Quest: Revealing the Unseen
☐		14	The Eye of Magnus	30	Silver	Complete "The Eye of Magnus"	Complete College of Winterhold Quest: The Eye of Magnus
☐		15	Taking Care of Business	10	Bronze	Join the Thieves Guild	Complete Thieves Guild Quest: A Chance Arrangement
☐		16	Darkness Returns	10	Bronze	Complete "Darkness Returns"	Complete Thieves Guild Quest: Darkness Returns
☐		17	One with the Shadows	30	Silver	Returned the Thieves Guild to its former glory	Complete Thieves Guild Quest: Darkness Returns and all four City Influence Quests
☐		18	With Friends Like These...	10	Bronze	Join the Dark Brotherhood	Complete Dark Brotherhood Quest: With Friends Like These...
☐		19	Bound Until Death	10	Bronze	Complete "Bound Until Death"	Complete Dark Brotherhood Quest: Bound Until Death
☐		20	Hail Sithis!	30	Silver	Complete "Hail Sithis!"	Complete Dark Brotherhood Quest: Hail Sithis!
☐		21	Taking Sides	10	Bronze	Join the Stormcloaks or the Imperial Army	Complete Civil War Quest: Joining the Legion OR Joining the Stormcloaks
☐		22	War Hero	10	Bronze	Capture Fort Sungard or Fort Greenwall	Complete Civil War Quest: The Battle for Fort Greenwall (Imperial) OR The Battle for Fort Sungard (Stormcloak)
☐		23	Hero of Skyrim	30	Silver	Capture Solitude or Windhelm	Complete Civil War Quest: Battle for Windhelm (Imperial) OR Battle for Solitude (Stormcloak)
☐		24	Sideways	20	Bronze	Complete 10 side quests	Complete 10 of the Side Quests listed below.
☐		25	Hero of the People	30	Bronze	Complete 50 Misc Objectives	These include Quests flagged with a "*" in this guide, Miscellaneous Objectives, or Favors.
☐		26	Hard Worker	10	Bronze	Chop wood, mine ore, and cook food	Complete these three activities using the appropriate stations.
☐		27	Thief	30	Silver	Pick 50 locks and 50 pockets	There are no restrictions on this, aside from the Crimes you're committing.
☐		28	Snake Tongue	10	Bronze	Successfully persuade, bribe, and intimidate	Consult the Quests sections to find opportunities for this.
☐		29	Blessed	10	Bronze	Select a Standing Stone blessing	Activate any of the 13 Standing Stones
☐		30	Standing Stones	30	Silver	Find 13 Standing Stones	Activate all of the 13 Standing Stones
☐		31	Citizen	10	Bronze	Buy a house	Purchase any of the five houses listed in the Training section.
☐		32	Wanted	10	Bronze	Escape from jail	Pick the lock, or find a secret escape route. See Crime and Punishment in the Training section for options.
☐		33	Married	10	Bronze	Get married	Complete Temple Quest: The Bonds of Matrimony. Potential spouses are listed with that quest.
☐		34	Artificer	10	Bronze	Make a smithed item, an enchanted item, and a potion	Consult the Training section on Crafting (page 41) for more information.
☐		35	Master Criminal	20	Bronze	Bounty of 1000 gold in all nine holds	Consult Crime and Punishment in the Training section (page 39) for more information.
☐		36	Golden Touch	30	Silver	Have 100,000 gold	Barter, trade, complete quests, and craft weapons, armor, and potions to sell.
☐		37	Delver	40	Silver	Clear 50 dungeons	Consult the Atlas for all appropriate locations flagged as "Dungeons".
☐		38	Skill Master	40	Silver	Get a skill to 100	Consult the Training section for more information on Skills and Perks (page 9).
☐		39	Explorer	40	Silver	Discover 100 Locations	Consult the Atlas for all 350+ Primary Locations.
☐		40	Reader	20	Bronze	Read 50 Skill Books	Consult page 641 for sample Skill Book Locations.
☐		41	Daedric Influence	10	Bronze	Acquire a Daedric Artifact	See the Daedric Quests (page 293), and the notes below for more information.

 The Elder Scrolls V SKYRIM

✓	ICON	INDEX	ACHIEVEMENT	POINTS	TROPHY	DESCRIPTION	NOTES
☐		42	Oblivion Walker	30	Silver	Collect 15 Daedric Artifacts	See the Daedric Quests (page 293), and the notes below for more information.
☐		43	Dragon Soul	10	Bronze	Absorb a dragon soul	This will occur during Main Quest: Dragon Rising.
☐		44	Dragon Hunter	20	Bronze	Absorb 20 dragon souls	After completing Main Quest: Dragon Rising, begin fighting Dragons, searching for Dragon Mounds (page 58), and exploring Dragon Lairs (see Atlas).
☐		45	Words of Power	10	Bronze	Learn all three words of a shout	

✓	ICON	INDEX	ACHIEVEMENT	POINTS	TROPHY	DESCRIPTION	NOTES
☐		46	Thu'um Master	40	Silver	Learn 20 shouts	
☐		47	Apprentice	5	Bronze	Reach Level 5	Consult the Training section on page 29 for tips on leveling.
☐		48	Adept	10	Bronze	Reach Level 10	Consult the Training section on page 29 for tips on leveling.
☐		49	Expert	25	Bronze	Reach Level 25	Consult the Training section on page 29 for tips on leveling.
☐		50	Master	50	Silver	Reach Level 50	Consult the Training section on page 29 for tips on leveling. Patience is also key!

Appendix I Notes and Clarifications

The Sideways Achievement/Trophy

The Sideways Achievement/Trophy requires you to "complete 10 Side Quests," as tracked by the Side Quests Completed counter on your Journal's Stats page. Because of the sheer number and variety of quests, it can be confusing to figure out which will count toward this goal.

In short: The Main Quest, Daedric Quests, and major Faction Quests do not count, nor do Miscellaneous Objectives. The table below lists all of the quests that do count toward this award (and the prefix that appears in this guide):

✓	STRATEGY GUIDE QUEST PREFIX	NAME OF QUEST	PAGE IN GUIDE
☐	Other Factions: The Bards' College Quest	Tending the Flames	326
☐	Other Factions: Temple Quest	The Heart of Dibella	331
☐	Other Factions: Temple Quest	The Blessings of Nature	335
☐	Other Factions: Temple Quest	The Book of Love	333
☐	Side Quest	Blood on the Ice	339
☐	Side Quest	Forbidden Legend	342
☐	Side Quest	The Forsworn Conspiracy	346
☐	Side Quest	No One Escapes Cidhna Mine	348
☐	Side Quest	The Golden Claw	350
☐	Side Quest	In My Time of Need	352
☐	Side Quest	Kyne's Sacred Trials	354
☐	Side Quest	Laid to Rest	355
☐	Side Quest	Lights Out!	357
☐	Side Quest	The Man Who Cried Wolf	359
☐	Side Quest	The Wolf Queen Awakened	360
☐	Side Quest	Missing in Action	361

✓	STRATEGY GUIDE QUEST PREFIX	NAME OF QUEST	PAGE IN GUIDE
☐	Side Quest	Promises to Keep	363
☐	Side Quest	A Return to Your Roots	364
☐	Side Quest	Rise in the East	365
☐	Side Quest	Rising at Dawn	367
☐	Side Quest	Unfathomable Depths	368
☐	Side Quest	The White Phial	369
☐	Side Quest	Repairing the Phial	370
☐	Dungeon Quest	Repentance	379
☐	Dungeon Quest	Siege on the Dragon Cult	380
☐	Dungeon Quest	The Pale Lady	381
☐	Dungeon Quest	A Scroll for Anska	382
☐	Dungeon Quest	Ancestral Worship	383
☐	Dungeon Quest	The Lost Expedition	384
☐	Dungeon Quest	Infiltration	388
☐	Dungeon Quest	Evil in Waiting	388
☐	Dungeon Quest	Silenced Tongues	389

Hero of the People Achievement/Trophy

This keeps track of how many Miscellaneous Objectives you've completed. So, the more of those you've grayed out, the better! Miscellaneous Objectives that are part of a chain (such as those for Dungeon Quest: The Legend of Red Eagle) each count individually toward this reward.

Oblivion Walker Achievement/Trophy

This award is unlocked only after you've acquired 15 Daedric Artifacts (also listed at the start of the Daedric Quest chapter, on page 293). It is important to note that this award triggers only after you receive the artifact in question; some Daedric Quests can be finished without claiming their artifact. If this occurs, it may become impossible to receive this reward! However, artifacts you've used, lost, sold, or dropped still count toward your total. The complete list of relevant artifacts is listed below:

> **CAUTION** There are 16 quests that reward you with a Daedric Artifact, so you can afford to miss one of them, but only one! Please note that the Rueful Axe, which Clavicus Vile offers as an alternative to his artifact, does not count toward this Achievement!

✓	DAEDRIC LORD	DAEDRIC QUEST NAME	DAEDRIC ARTIFACT
☐	Azura	The Black Star	Azura's Star or the Black Star
☐	Boethiah	Boethiah's Calling	Ebony Mail
☐	Clavicus Vile	A Daedra's Best Friend	Masque of Clavicus Vile*
☐	Hermaeus Mora	Discerning the Transmundane	Oghma Infinium
☐	Hircine	Ill Met By Moonlight	Savior's Hide or Ring of Hircine
☐	Malacath	The Cursed Tribe	Volendrung
☐	Mehrunes Dagon	Pieces of the Past	Mehrunes' Razor*
☐	Mephala	The Whispering Door	Ebony Blade
☐	Meridia	The Break of Dawn	Dawnbreaker
☐	Molag Bal	The House of Horrors	Mace of Molag Bal
☐	Namira	The Taste of Death	Ring of Namira*
☐	Nocturnal‡	Thieves Guild Quests	Skeleton Key
☐	Peryite	The Only Cure	Spellbreaker
☐	Sanguine	A Night to Remember	Sanguine Rose
☐	Sheogorath	The Mind of Madness	Wabbajack
☐	Vaermina	Waking Nightmares	Skull of Corruption*

> **NOTE** * Indicates the artifact can be permanently missed, depending on your choices.
>
> ‡ You recover Nocturnal's Skeleton Key as part of the Thieves Guild Quests, as described on page 217.

APPENDIX II: TRADERS

In Skyrim, most traders fall into one of 14 categories that determine the general types of goods they buy and sell. Merchants may also have particular specialties, such as a Food Vendor who sells only meat or only vegetables.

The tables below identify these categories, and list all of the major traders in Skyrim and where you can find them. Note that hunters and other merchants you may encounter randomly in the wilderness are not listed, nor are characters who may take over a shop if the original owner is killed.

Trade Categories

✔	STANDARD SERVICES	BUYS & SELLS
	Apothecary	Potions, Poisons, Ingredients, Recipes, Animal Parts, Food & Drink, Raw Food
	Tailor	Clothing, Jewelry
	Spell Vendor	Spell Tomes, Books, Scrolls, Soul Gems, Staffs, Clothing, Jewelry, Daedric Artifacts
	General Goods	Most Items (not Stolen Items)
	Lumberjack	Firewood
	Jeweler	Jewelry, Gems, Ingots, Ore, Tools
	Innkeeper	Food & Drink, Raw Food, Rents Rooms
	Hunter	Animal Hides, Animal Parts, Raw Food
	Fletcher	Weapons, Armor, Arrows, Tools
	Blacksmith	Weapons, Armor, Arrows, Ore, Ingots, Animal Hides, Leather, Tools
	Carriage Driver	Carriage Rides
	Stablemaster	Horses
	Fence	Most Items (including Stolen Items). Fences are only available to members of the Thieves' Guild after meeting their requirements.
	Food Vendor	Food & Drink, Raw Food
	Bartender	Food & Drink, Raw Food

Traders

✔	NUMBER	SERVICE	ZONE #	LOCATION	NAME	NOTES
	[1/12]	Apothecary	[1.00]	Solitude (Angeline's Aromatics)	Angeline Morrard	—
	[2/12]	Apothecary	[2.00]	Morthal (Thaumaturgist's Hut)	Lami	—
	[3/12]	Apothecary	[3.00]	Dawnstar (The Mortar and Pestle)	Frida	—
	[4/12]	Apothecary	[5.00]	Markarth (The Hag's Cure)	Bothela	—
	[5/12]	Apothecary	[5.01]	Mor Khazgur	Sharamph	—
	[6/12]	Apothecary	[5.38]	Dushnikh Yal	Murbul	—
	[7/12]	Apothecary	[6.00]	Whiterun (Arcadia's Cauldron)	Arcadia	—
	[8/12]	Apothecary	[7.00]	Windhelm (The White Phial)	Nurelion	—
	[9/12]	Apothecary	[8.00]	Falkreath (Grave Concoctions)	Zaria	—
	[10/12]	Apothecary	[8.22]	Dark Brotherhood Sanctuary	Babette	—
	[11/12]	Apothecary	[9.00]	Riften (Elgrim's Elixirs)	Elgrim	—
	[12/12]	Apothecary	[9.00]	Riften (The Ragged Flagon)	Herluin Lothaire	Thieves' Guild Only
	[1/5]	Bartender	[6.27]	Riverwood	Orgnar	Sells Ingredients
	[2/5]	Bartender	[7.00]	Windhelm (New Gnisis Cornerclub)	Ambarys Rendar	—
	[3/5]	Bartender	[9.00]	Riften (The Bee and Barb)	Talen-Jei	—
	[4/5]	Bartender	[9.00]	Riften (The Ragged Flagon)	Vekel the Man	—
	[5/5]	Bartender	[9.01]	Ivarstead	Lynly Star-Sung	—
	[1/33]	Blacksmith	[1.00]	Solitude (Beirand)	Beirand	—
	[2/33]	Blacksmith	[1.18]	Haafingar Stormcloak Camp	Stormcloak Quartermaster	—
	[3/33]	Blacksmith	[2.17]	Hjaalmarch Stormcloak Camp	Stormcloak Quartermaster	—
	[4/33]	Blacksmith	[2.20]	Hjaalmarch Imperial Camp	Imperial Quartermaster	—
	[5/33]	Blacksmith	[3.00]	Dawnstar (Rustleif's House)	Rustleif	—
	[6/33]	Blacksmith	[3.00]	Dawnstar (Rustleif's House)	Seren	—
	[7/33]	Blacksmith	[3.03]	Pale Imperial Camp	Imperial Quartermaster	—
	[8/33]	Blacksmith	[3.30]	Pale Stormcloak Camp	Stormcloak Quartermaster	—
	[9/33]	Blacksmith	[4.04]	Winterhold Imperial Camp	Imperial Quartermaster	—
	[10/33]	Blacksmith	[4.29]	Winterhold Stormcloak Camp	Stormcloak Quartermaster	—
	[11/33]	Blacksmith	[5.00]	Markarth (Forge)	Ghorza	—
	[12/33]	Blacksmith	[5.00]	Markarth (Understone Keep)	Moth gro-Bagol	—
	[13/33]	Blacksmith	[5.10]	Reach Stormcloak Camp	Stormcloak Quartermaster	—
	[14/33]	Blacksmith	[5.15]	Reach Imperial Camp	Imperial Quartermaster	—
	[15/33]	Blacksmith	[5.38]	Dushnikh Yal	Gharol	—
	[16/33]	Blacksmith	[6.00]	Whiterun (Warmaiden's)	Adrianne Avenicci	—
	[17/33]	Blacksmith	[6.00]	Whiterun (Warmaiden's)	Ulfberth War-Bear	—
	[18/33]	Blacksmith	[6.00]	Whiterun (Skyforge and The Underforge)	Eorlund Gray-Mane	—
	[19/33]	Blacksmith	[6.04]	Whiterun Imperial Camp	Imperial Quartermaster	—
	[20/33]	Blacksmith	[6.27]	Riverwood	Alvor	—
	[21/33]	Blacksmith	[6.32]	Whiterun Stormcloak Camp	Stormcloak Quartermaster	—
	[22/33]	Blacksmith	[7.00]	Windhelm (Blacksmith Quarters)	Oengul War-Anvil	—
	[23/33]	Blacksmith	[7.23]	Gloombound Mine	Dushamub	—
	[24/33]	Blacksmith	[7.34]	Eastmarch Imperial Camp	Imperial Quartermaster	—
	[25/33]	Blacksmith	[8.00]	Falkreath (Lod's House)	Lod	—
	[26/33]	Blacksmith	[8.04]	Falkreath Imperial Camp	Imperial Quartermaster	—
	[27/33]	Blacksmith	[8.36]	Falkreath Stormcloak Camp	Stormcloak Quartermaster	—
	[28/33]	Blacksmith	[9.00]	Riften (Balimund)	Balimund	—
	[29/33]	Blacksmith	[9.00]	Riften (The Ragged Flagon)	Arnskar Ember-Master	Thieves' Guild Only
	[30/33]	Blacksmith	[9.00]	Riften (The Ragged Flagon)	Vanryth Gatharian	Thieves' Guild Only
	[31/33]	Blacksmith	[9.07]	Rift Stormcloak Camp	Stormcloak Quartermaster	—
	[32/33]	Blacksmith	[9.11]	Rift Imperial Camp	Imperial Quartermaster	—
	[33/33]	Blacksmith	[9.25]	Shor's Stone	Filnjar	—
	[1/5]	Carriage Driver	[1.00]	Solitude (Lower Watchtower)	Thaer	—
	[2/5]	Carriage Driver	[5.19]	Markarth Stables	Kibell	—
	[3/5]	Carriage Driver	[6.20]	Whiterun Stables	Bjorlam	—
	[4/5]	Carriage Driver	[7.06]	Windhelm Stables	Alfarinn	—
	[5/5]	Carriage Driver	[9.32]	Riften Stables	Sigaar	—
	[1/10]	Fence	[1.00]	Solitude (Winking Skeever)	Gulum-Ei	—
	[2/10]	Fence	[4.00]	College of Winterhold	Enthir	Also sells Rare Items
	[3/10]	Fence	[5.00]	Markarth (Endon's House)	Endon	—
	[4/10]	Fence	[6.22]	Honningbrew Meadery	Mallus Maccius	—

The Elder Scrolls V
SKYRIM

 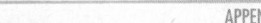

✓	NUMBER	SERVICE	ZONE #	LOCATION	NAME	NOTES
☐	[5/10]	Fence	[7.00]	Windhelm (Marketplace)	Niranye	—
☐	[6/10]	Fence	[9.00]	Riften (The Ragged Flagon)	Tonilia	—
☐	[7/10]	Fence	[10.00]	Caravans (Ri'saad)	Ri'saad	—
☐	[8/10]	Fence	[10.00]	Caravans (Ri'saad)	Atahba	—
☐	[9/10]	Fence	[10.00]	Caravans (Ma'dran)	Ma'jahad	—
☐	[10/10]	Fence	[10.00]	Caravans (Ahkari)	Zaynabi	—
☐	[1/3]	Fletcher	[1.00]	Solitude (Fletcher)	Fihada	—
☐	[2/3]	Fletcher	[6.00]	Whiterun (The Drunken Huntsman)	Elrindir	Also sells Food & Drink
☐	[3/3]	Fletcher	[9.00]	Riften (The Ragged Flagon)	Syndus	Thieves' Guild Only
☐	[1/9]	Food Vendor	[1.00]	Solitude (Market Stalls)	Addvar	—
☐	[2/9]	Food Vendor	[1.00]	Solitude (Market Stalls)	Jala	—
☐	[3/9]	Food Vendor	[1.00]	Solitude (Market Stalls)	Evette San	—
☐	[4/9]	Food Vendor	[5.00]	Markarth (Marketplace)	Hogni Red-Arm	—
☐	[5/9]	Food Vendor	[6.00]	Whiterun (Marketplace)	Carlotta Valentia	—
☐	[6/9]	Food Vendor	[6.00]	Whiterun (Marketplace)	Anoriath	—
☐	[7/9]	Food Vendor	[6.22]	Honningbrew Meadery	Sabjorn	—
☐	[8/9]	Food Vendor	[7.00]	Windhelm (Marketplace)	Hillevi Cruel-Sea	—
☐	[9/9]	Food Vendor	[9.00]	Riften (Black-Briar Meadery)	Ungrien	—
☐	[1/19]	General Goods	[1.00]	Solitude (Radiant Raiment)	Endarie	—
☐	[2/19]	General Goods	[1.00]	Solitude (Bits and Pieces)	Sayma	—
☐	[3/19]	General Goods	[4.00]	Winterhold (Birna's Oddments)	Birna	—
☐	[4/19]	General Goods	[4.00]	College of Winterhold	Enthir	Also sells Rare Items
☐	[5/19]	General Goods	[5.00]	Markarth (Arnleif and Sons Trading Company)	Lisbet	—
☐	[6/19]	General Goods	[6.00]	Whiterun (Marketplace)	Fralia Gray-Mane	—
☐	[7/19]	General Goods	[6.00]	Whiterun (Belethor's General Goods)	Belethor	—
☐	[8/19]	General Goods	[6.27]	Riverwood	Lucan Valerius	—
☐	[9/19]	General Goods	[7.00]	Windhelm (Marketplace)	Aval Atheron	—
☐	[10/19]	General Goods	[7.00]	Windhelm (Marketplace)	Niranye	—
☐	[11/19]	General Goods	[7.00]	Windhelm (Sadri's Used Wares)	Revyn Sadri	—
☐	[12/19]	General Goods	[8.00]	Falkreath (Gray Pine Goods)	Solaf	—
☐	[13/19]	General Goods	[9.00]	Riften (Marketplace)	Marise Aravel	—
☐	[14/19]	General Goods	[9.00]	Riften (Marketplace)	Brand-Shei	—
☐	[15/19]	General Goods	[9.00]	Riften (Marketplace)	Grelka	—
☐	[16/19]	General Goods	[9.00]	Riften (Pawned Prawn)	Bersi Honey-Hand	—
☐	[17/19]	General Goods	[10.00]	Caravans (Ri'saad)	Ri'saad	—
☐	[18/19]	General Goods	[10.00]	Caravans (Ahkari)	Ahkari	—
☐	[19/19]	General Goods	[10.00]	Caravans (Ma'dran)	Ma'dran	—
☐	[1/15]	Innkeeper	[1.00]	Solitude (The Winking Skeever)	Corpulus Vinius	—
☐	[2/15]	Innkeeper	[1.17]	Dragon Bridge	Faida	—
☐	[3/15]	Innkeeper	[2.00]	Morthal (Moorside Inn)	Jonna	—
☐	[4/15]	Innkeeper	[3.00]	Dawnstar (Windpeak Inn)	Thoring	—
☐	[5/15]	Innkeeper	[3.25]	Nightgate Inn	Hadring	—
☐	[6/15]	Innkeeper	[5.00]	Markarth (Silver-Blood Inn)	Kleppr	—
☐	[7/15]	Innkeeper	[5.34]	Old Hroldan	Eydis	—
☐	[8/15]	Innkeeper	[6.00]	Whiterun (The Bannered Mare)	Hulda	—
☐	[9/15]	Innkeeper	[6.02]	Rorikstead	Mralki	—
☐	[10/15]	Innkeeper	[6.27]	Riverwood	Delphine	Only rents rooms
☐	[11/15]	Innkeeper	[7.00]	Windhelm (Candlehearth Hall)	Elda Early-Dawn	—
☐	[12/15]	Innkeeper	[7.05]	Kynesgrove	Iddra	—
☐	[13/15]	Innkeeper	[8.00]	Falkreath (Dead Man's Drink)	Valga Vinicia	—
☐	[14/15]	Innkeeper	[9.00]	Riften (The Bee and Barb)	Keerava	—
☐	[15/15]	Innkeeper	[9.01]	Ivarstead	Wilhelm	—
☐	[1/2]	Jeweler	[5.00]	Markarth (Marketplace)	Kerah	—
☐	[2/2]	Jeweler	[9.00]	Riften (Marketplace)	Madesi	—
☐	[1/3]	Special	[4.00]	College of Winterhold	Enthir	Sells General Goods, Rare Items
☐	[2/3]	Special	[4.00]	College of Winterhold	Urag gro-Shub	Sells Spell Tomes, Books
☐	[3/3]	Special	[5.19]	Markarth Stables	Banning	Sells War Dogs (Follower: Vigilance)
☐	[1/12]	Spell Vendor	[1.00]	Solitude (Blue Palace)	Sybille Stentor	—
☐	[2/12]	Spell Vendor	[2.00]	Morthal (Falion's House)	Falion	—
☐	[3/12]	Spell Vendor	[3.00]	Dawnstar (The White Hall)	Madena	—
☐	[4/12]	Spell Vendor	[4.00]	College of Winterhold	Tolfdir	Sells Alteration Spells
☐	[5/12]	Spell Vendor	[4.00]	College of Winterhold	Phinis Gestor	Sells Conjuration Spells
☐	[6/12]	Spell Vendor	[4.00]	College of Winterhold	Faralda	Sells Destruction Spells
☐	[7/12]	Spell Vendor	[4.00]	College of Winterhold	Drevis Neloren	Sells Illusion Spells
☐	[8/12]	Spell Vendor	[4.00]	College of Winterhold	Colette Marence	Sells Restoration Spells
☐	[9/12]	Spell Vendor	[5.00]	Markarth (Understone Keep)	Calcelmo	—
☐	[10/12]	Spell Vendor	[6.00]	Whiterun (Dragonsreach)	Farengar Secret-Fire	—
☐	[11/12]	Spell Vendor	[7.00]	Windhelm (Palace of the Kings)	Wuunferth the Unliving	—
☐	[12/12]	Spell Vendor	[9.00]	Riften (Mistveil Keep)	Wylandriah	—
☐	[1/5]	Stablemaster	[1.23]	Katla's Farm	Geimund	—
☐	[2/5]	Stablemaster	[5.19]	Markarth Stables	Cedran	—
☐	[3/5]	Stablemaster	[6.20]	Whiterun Stables	Skulvar Sable-Hilt	—
☐	[4/5]	Stablemaster	[7.06]	Windhelm Stables	Ulundil	—
☐	[5/5]	Stablemaster	[9.32]	Riften Stables	Hofgrir Horse-Crusher	—

Ri'saad

All of the shrines to each of the Nine Divines are listed below. The Training section (page 4) and Other Factions Quests (page 322) have more information on shrines and their Blessings.

✓	NUMBER	ZONE #	LOCATION	DESCRIPTION
			SHRINE OF AKATOSH	
	[1/6]	[1.00]	Solitude	Temple of the Divines, in the main chamber.
	[2/6]	[2.25]	Skyborn Altar	On the altar in front of the Word Wall (prior to Main Quest: Dragon Rising).
	[3/6]	[5.47]	Fort Sungard	Fort Sungard Shrine Interior, if the Imperials control the fort.
	[4/6]	[6.A]	Shrine of Akatosh: Rorikstead	Sitting next to the ruin stones.
	[5/6]	[7.R]	Shrine of Akatosh: Steamcrag Hillock	On the altar.
	[6/6]	[8.G]	Shrine of Akatosh: Twilight Valley	On the edge of the stone overlook.
			SHRINE OF ARKAY	
	[1/12]	[1.00]	Solitude	Temple of the Divines, in the main chamber.
	[2/12]	[1.00]	Solitude	In the Hall of the Dead, on a table in the side area beyond the metal door.
	[3/12]	[4.14]	Wayward Pass	On the narrow platform halfway through the pass.
	[4/12]	[4.W]	Shrine of Arkay: Windhelm Hills	On the altar in the circle of stones, if the Stormcloak Camp is not present.
	[5/12]	[5.00]	Markarth	In the Hall of the Dead, on the circular pedestal in the back room.
	[6/12]	[5.07]	Druadach Redoubt	Sitting on a rock ledge near the wall by the ramps at the back of the cave.
	[7/12]	[6.00]	Whiterun	In the Hall of the Dead, on an altar in the chapel area downstairs.
	[8/12]	[7.00]	Windhelm	In the catacombs, in the center of the main hall.
	[9/12]	[8.00]	Falkreath	On the porch outside the Hall of the Dead.
	[10/12]	[8.00]	Falkreath	On the porch outside the Hall of the Dead.
	[11/12]	[8.00]	Falkreath	In the Hall of the Dead, against the far wall.
	[12/12]	[9.00]	Riften	In the Mausoleum, sitting on a narrow wooden table.
			SHRINE OF DIBELLA	
	[1/8]	[1.00]	Solitude	Temple of the Divines, in the main chamber.
	[2/8]	[4.A]	Shrine of Dibella: Watching Dawnstar	Exterior; on the altar near the statue.
	[3/8]	[5.00]	Markarth	In the Temple of Dibella, on the altar near the wall.
	[4/8]	[5.18]	Broken Tower Redoubt	Inside the tower atop the keep, at the base of the statue.
	[5/8]	[5.Z]	Shrine of Dibella: Bridge at Old Hroldan	On the altar at the base of the stone pillar.
	[6/8]	[7.04]	Morvunskar	In the small sleeping area off of the long corridor.
	[7/8]	[7.A]	Lucky Lorenz's Shack	In one corner of the ruined shack.
	[8/8]	[9.00]	Riften	In Haelga's Bunkhouse, at the foot of the bed in Haelga's bedroom.
			SHRINE OF JULIANOS	
	[1/5]	[1.00]	Solitude	Temple of the Divines, in the main chamber.
	[2/5]	[3.N]	Julianos' Fallen	Sitting in the snow near a skeleton up in the mountains.
	[3/5]	[5.09]	Harmugstahl	On the dresser in Kornalus Frey's quarters.
	[4/5]	[6.29]	Fellglow Keep	During College of Winterhold Quest: Hitting the Books, behind the locked door at the foot of the stairs leading up to the Ritual Chamber.
	[5/5]	[7.27]	Fort Amol	Before the Civil War begins, on a stone block in the courtyard.
			SHRINE OF KYNARETH	
	[1/6]	[1.00]	Solitude	Temple of the Divines, in the main chamber.
	[2/6]	[2.M]	Shrine of Kynareth: Hjaalmarch Hills	On the ruined stone platform.
	[3/6]	[3.02]	Brinehammer	On the floor near the chest in the center of the ship.
	[4/6]	[5.47]	Fort Sungard	Fort Sungard Shrine Interior, before the Civil War begins.
	[5/6]	[6.00]	Whiterun	In the Temple of Kynareth, on the altar opposite the door.
	[6/6]	[9.39]	Crystaldrift Cave	On a rock along the wall inside the cave.

✓		ZONE #	LOCATION	DESCRIPTION
			SHRINE OF MARA	
	[1/5]	[1.00]	Solitude	Temple of the Divines, in the main chamber.
	[2/5]	[3.06]	Nightcaller Temple	On Erandur's altar, on one side of the entry chamber.
	[3/5]	[3.J]	Border Corner: Roadside Shrine of Mara	On the stone planter.
	[4/5]	[5.V]	Lovers' Camp	After killing the animal here, leave the area and then return. The shrine will appear on the rock, by the two stone cairns.
	[5/5]	[9.00]	Riften	In the Temple of Mara, on the central altar and several side altars.
			SHRINE OF STENDARR	
	[1/5]	[1.00]	Solitude	Temple of the Divines, in the main chamber.
	[2/5]	[3.09]	Hall of the Vigilant	On the altar table inside the Hall.
	[3/5]	[6.I]	Shrine of Stendarr: The Two Pillars	On the small stone altar.
	[4/5]	[9.26]	Fort Greenwall	On a dresser between two shelves inside the Captain's Quarters.
	[5/5]	[9.46]	Stendarr's Beacon	On the small stone altar inside the tower.
			SHRINE OF TALOS	
	[1/17]	[1.00]	Solitude	Temple of the Divines, in the main chamber, if the Stormcloaks have won the Civil War.
	[2/17]	[3.18]	Weynon Stones	At the base of the statue.
	[3/17]	[4.F]	Shrine of Talos: Winterhold Glaciers	At the base of the statue.
	[4/17]	[4.J]	Shrine of Talos: Sea of Ghosts	On the ground behind the statue.
	[5/17]	[4.K]	Shrine of Talos: Ilas-Tei's Last Stand	At the base of the statue.
	[6/17]	[5.00]	Markarth	In the Shrine of Talos, at the base of the statue.
	[7/17]	[5.47]	Fort Sungard	Fort Sungard Shrine Interior, if the Stormcloaks control the fort.
	[8/17]	[6.00]	Whiterun	At the foot of the statue near the Gildergreen Tree.
	[9/17]	[6.29]	Fellglow Keep	On the ruined altar in the chapel area, half-buried amid the rubble.
	[10/17]	[6.T]	Shrine of Talos: White River Valley	On the altar near the statue.
	[11/17]	[7.00]	Windhelm	In the Temple of Talos, at the base of the statue.
	[12/17]	[7.B]	Shrine of Talos: Cradlecrush Pond	At the base of the statue.
	[13/17]	[7.E]	Shrine of Talos: Watcher of Windhelm	On the circular pedestal behind the statue.
	[14/17]	[8.12]	Bloated Man's Grotto	Prior to Daedric Quest: Ill Met by Moonlight, on the altar in the shrine area at the back of the grotto.
	[15/17]	[8.Y]	Shrine of Talos: Ilinalta Foothills	On the rocks near the statue.
	[16/17]	[9.00]	Riften	In the southeast corner of the city, near the graveyard.
	[17/17]	[9.G]	Shrine of Talos: Froki's Peak	On the ground near the statue.
			SHRINE OF ZENITHAR	
	[1/5]	[1.00]	Solitude	Temple of the Divines, in the main chamber.
	[2/5]	[5.P]	Shrine of Zenithar: Four Skull Lookout	At the edge of the stone lookout.
	[3/5]	[6.E]	Shrine of Zenithar: Ring of Boulders	On the stone platform at the base of the largest stone.
	[4/5]	[6.G]	Shrine of Zenithar: Crumbling Bastion	On the crude stone altar under the archway.
	[5/5]	[9.V]	Shrine of Zenithar: Fallowstone	On the altar in the remnants of the tower.

Unique Weapons, whether awarded as part of a quest, carried by a particular creature, or just stumbled upon, are listed below, and sorted by Hold for easy reference.

✔	NUMBER	NAME	ZONE #	LOCATION	DESCRIPTION
☐	[1/80]	Headsman's Axe	[1.00]	Solitude	Carried by Ahtar, Solitude's jailor. Pickpocket it from him, or complete his favor and recruit him to obtain this weapon.
☐	[2/80]	Firiniel's End	[1.00]	Solitude	Left by Gabriella on a balcony overlooking the Temple of the Divines, during Dark Brotherhood Quest: Bound Until Death.
☐	[3/80]	The Rueful Axe	[1.02]	Rimerock Burrow	Found during Daedric Quest: A Daedra's Best Friend.
☐	[4/80]	Dawnbreaker	[1.16]	Statue to Meridia (Killreath Ruins)	Reward for completing Daedric Quest: The Break of Dawn.
☐	[5/80]	Windshear	[1.28]	The Katariah	Embedded in the far end of the forward mast.
☐	[6/80]	Gauldur Blackblade	[2.08]	Folgunthur	Wielded by Mikrul Gauldurson at the end of the dungeon.
☐	[7/80]	Grimsever	[2.18]	Mzinchaleft	Agree to help Mjoll the Lioness retrieve this sword as part of Miscellaneous Objective: Grimsever's Return.*
☐	[8/80]	Drainblood Battleaxe	[2.23]	Labyrinthian	Carried by the spectral draugr in Labyrinthian during College of Winterhold Quest: The Staff of Magnus.
☐	[9/80]	Drainheart Sword	[2.23]	Labyrinthian	Carried by the spectral draugr in Labyrinthian during College of Winterhold Quest: The Staff of Magnus.
☐	[10/80]	Drainspell Bow	[2.23]	Labyrinthian	Carried by the spectral draugr in Labyrinthian during College of Winterhold Quest: The Staff of Magnus.
☐	[11/80]	Staff of Magnus	[2.23]	Labyrinthian	Obtained at the end of College of Winterhold Quest: The Staff of Magnus.
☐	[12/80]	Skull of Corruption	[3.06]	Nightcaller Temple	Reward for completing Daedric Quest: Waking Nightmare.
☐	[13/80]	The Pale Blade	[3.08]	Frostmere Crypt	Carried by Ra'jirr at the end of the dungeon.
☐	[14/80]	Mehrunes' Razor	[3.11]	Shrine of Mehrunes Dagon	Reward for completing Daedric Quest: Pieces of the Past.
☐	[15/80]	Ceremonial Sword	[3.13]	Volunruud	Inside Volunruud, one of the two weapons needed to open the Elder's Cairn Door in the dungeon.
☐	[16/80]	Ceremonial Axe	[3.13]	Volunruud	Inside Volunruud, one of the two weapons needed to open the Elder's Cairn Door in the dungeon.
☐	[17/80]	Eduj	[3.13]	Volunruud	May be carried by Kvenel the Tongue at the end of the dungeon.
☐	[18/80]	Okin	[3.13]	Volunruud	May be carried by Kvenel the Tongue at the end of the dungeon.
☐	[19/80]	Nightingale Bow	[3.29]	Bronze Water Cave	Reward from Karliah at the end of Thieves Guild Quest: Blindsighted.
☐	[20/80]	Aegisbane	[3.32]	Raldbthar	Wielded by Alain Dufont, assassination victim. Kill him during Dark Brotherhood Quest: Sentenced to Death.
☐	[21/80]	Nightingale Blade	[4.00]	Winterhold	Reward from Karliah at the end of Thieves Guild Quest: Hard Answers.
☐	[22/80]	Staff of Arcane Authority	[4.00]	Winterhold (The Frozen Hearth)	Stolen for Malur Seloth as part of Favor: A Little Light Thievery.*
☐	[23/80]	Staff of Jyrik Gauldurson	[4.12]	Saarthal	On the altar in front of Jyrik Gauldurson at the end of the dungeon.
☐	[24/80]	Steel Battleaxe of Fiery Souls	[4.15]	Ironbind Barrow	Affixed to the back of the throne at the end of the dungeon.
☐	[25/80]	Borvir's Dagger	[4.26]	Journeyman's Nook	Lying next to Borvir's body near the Alchemy Lab inside the domed ruin.
☐	[26/80]	Rundi's Dagger	[4.0]	Rundi's Mistake	Lying on the edge of the small altar.
☐	[27/80]	Rusty Mace	[5.00]	Markarth (Abandoned House)	Given to you during Daedric Quest: The House of Horrors.
☐	[28/80]	Mace of Molag Bal	[5.00]	Markarth (Abandoned House)	Reward for completing Daedric Quest: The House of Horrors.
☐	[29/80]	Shiv	[5.00]	Markarth (Cidhna Mine)	Optionally obtained during Side Quest: No One Escapes Cidhna Mine, from Grisvar.
☐	[30/80]	Spider Control Rod	[5.00]	Markarth (Understone Keep)	During Thieves Guild Quest: Hard Answers, in Calcelmo's Laboratory, in a small room off to the side of the first chamber.
☐	[31/80]	Bloodthorn	[5.02]	Deepwood Redoubt	Deepwood Vale, impaled in the body of the sacrificial victim on the upper level platform of Hag's End.
☐	[32/80]	The Longhammer	[5.11]	Liar's Retreat	Lying next to the late bar owner's impaled corpse.
☐	[33/80]	Eye of Melka	[5.24]	Blind Cliff Cave	Reward for completing Dungeon Quest: Blind Cliff Cave: Melka and Petra.
☐	[34/80]	Red Eagle's Fury	[5.26]	Red Eagle Redoubt	Carried by the Forsworn leader at the summit of Red Eagle Redoubt.
☐	[35/80]	Red Eagle's Bane	[5.28]	Rebel's Cairn	Retrieve this blade from the pedestal on your way out after slaying Red Eagle.
☐	[36/80]	Dragonbane	[5.31]	Sky Haven Temple	On a table in Sky Haven Temple's armory.
☐	[37/80]	Hevnoraak's Staff	[5.42]	Valthume	Carried by the Dragon Priest Hevnoraak at the end of the dungeon.
☐	[38/80]	Trollsbane	[5.AB]	Cradle Stone Crag	On the corpse of Frofnir Trollsbane.
☐	[39/80]	Balgruuf's Greatsword	[6.00]	Whiterun (Warmaiden's)	Given to you by Adrianne Avenicci to be delivered, during Miscellaneous Objective: Greatsword for a Great Man.*
☐	[40/80]	Wuuthrad	[6.00]	Whiterun (Skyforge)	Forged by Eorlund during The Companions Quest: Glory of the Dead.
☐	[41/80]	Ebony Blade	[6.00]	Whiterun (Dragonsreach)	Reward for completing Daedric Quest: The Whispering Door.
☐	[42/80]	Lunar Iron Mace	[6.16]	Silent Moons Camp	Four random Lunar Weapons can be found in Silent Moons Camp (some inside, some outside).
☐	[43/80]	Lunar Iron Sword	[6.16]	Silent Moons Camp	Four random Lunar Weapons can be found in Silent Moons Camp (some inside, some outside).
☐	[44/80]	Lunar Iron War Axe	[6.16]	Silent Moons Camp	Four random Lunar Weapons can be found in Silent Moons Camp (some inside, some outside).
☐	[45/80]	Lunar Steel Mace	[6.16]	Silent Moons Camp	Four random Lunar Weapons can be found in Silent Moons Camp (some inside, some outside).
☐	[46/80]	Lunar Steel Sword	[6.16]	Silent Moons Camp	Four random Lunar Weapons can be found in Silent Moons Camp (some inside, some outside).
☐	[47/80]	Lunar Steel War Axe	[6.16]	Silent Moons Camp	Four random Lunar Weapons can be found in Silent Moons Camp (some inside, some outside).
☐	[48/80]	Poacher's Axe	[6.17]	Halted Stream Camp	Carried by the Orc near the forge.
☐	[49/80]	Froki's Bow	[6.30]	Graywinter Watch	Lying on a barrel near the tent at the back of the cave.
☐	[50/80]	Notched Pickaxe	[6.38]	Throat of the World	Lodged in the rockface at the mountain's highest tip.
☐	[51/80]	Sanguine Rose	[7.04]	Morvunskar (Misty Grove)	Reward for completing Daedric Quest: A Night to Remember.
☐	[52/80]	Blade of Sacrifice	[7.12]	Sacellum of Boethiah	Given to you by a Priestess of Boethiah during Daedric Quest: Boethiah's Calling.
☐	[53/80]	Ghostblade	[7.38]	Ansilvund	Given to you by Fjori and Holgeir at the end of the dungeon.
☐	[54/80]	Valdr's Lucky Dagger	[8.05]	Moss Mother Cavern	Given to you by Valdr after you complete Dungeon Quest: Hunter and Hunted.*
☐	[55/80]	Bolar's Oathblade	[8.12]	Bloated Man's Grotto	Prior to Daedric Quest: Ill Met by Moonlight; the blade is in the Shrine area, lying at the foot of the statue of Talos.
☐	[56/80]	Halldir's Staff	[8.21]	Halldir's Cairn	Carried by Halldir at the end of the dungeon.
☐	[57/80]	Blade of Woe	[8.22]	Dark Brotherhood Sanctuary	Taken from Astrid during Dark Brotherhood Quest: Death Incarnate OR Dark Brotherhood Quest: Destroy the Dark Brotherhood!
☐	[58/80]	Angi's Bow	[8.29]	Angi's Camp	Exterior; Angi gives you her special bow after you complete all of her archery lessons.
☐	[59/80]	Nettlebane	[8.35]	Orphan Rock	Can be obtained here during Temple Quest: The Blessings of Nature.

✓	NUMBER	NAME	ZONE #	LOCATION	DESCRIPTION
☐	[60/80]	The Woodsman's Friend	[8.V]	The Conjuror's Altar: Lake Ilinalta	Lying next to a dead woodsman near the cut logs just southwest of the altar.
☐	[61/80]	Chillrend	[9.00]	Riften (Riftweald Manor)	In a locked display case in Mercer's secret study room, below his house, during Thieves Guild Quest: The Pursuit.
☐	[62/80]	Alessandra's Dagger	[9.00]	Riften (Hall of the Dead)	Given to you by Alessandra to be delivered, during Miscellaneous Objective: Pilgrimage.*
☐	[63/80]	Steel Sword	[9.00]	Riften (The Scorched Hammer Blacksmith)	Retrieved from Balimund for Harrald as part of Miscellaneous Objective: Bring It!*
☐	[64/80]	Dravin's Bow	[9.00]	Riften (Ratway Warrens)	Found during Miscellaneous Objective: Bow to the Master.*
☐	[65/80]	Gauldur Blackbow	[9.04]	Geirmund's Hall	Wielded by Sigdis Gauldurson at the end of the dungeon.
☐	[66/80]	Bow of the Hunt	[9.19]	Clearspring Tarn	Inside Clearspring Cave, mounted on the altar at the back of the cave.
☐	[67/80]	Shagrol's Warhammer	[9.33]	Fallowstone Cave (Giant's Grove)	Found in the Giant's Grove during Daedric Quest: The Cursed Tribe.
☐	[68/80]	Volendrung	[9.33]	Fallowstone Cave (Giant's Grove)	Reward for completing Daedric Quest: A Cursed Tribe.
☐	[69/80]	Staff of Hag's Wrath	[9.37]	Darklight Tower	Carried by Silvia at the end of the dungeon.
☐	[70/80]	Gadnor's Staff of Charming	[9.39]	Crystaldrift Cave	Lying atop the large rock near the body of Gadnor.
☐	[71/80]	Dragon Priest Staff	[9.45]	Forelhost	Carried by the Dragon Priest Rahgot, at the end of Forelhost.

✓	NUMBER	NAME	ZONE #	LOCATION	DESCRIPTION
☐	[72/80]	Wabbajack	[10.03]	Solitude (Blue Palace Pelagius Wing)	Reward for completing Daedric Quest: The Mind of Madness.
☐	[73/80]	Dragon Priest Staff	[10.05]	Skuldfn	Carried by the Dragon Priest Nahkriin, near the portal to Sovngarde.
☐	[74/80]	Amren's Family Sword	[Random]	[Random Bandit Camp]	The sword is in a [random] bandit camp. Favor: Item Retrieval (bandit camp): Speak to Amren first.
☐	[75/80]	Ghorbash's Ancestral Axe	[Random]	[Random Dungeon]	Retrieve this axe from a [random dungeon] for Ghorbash of Dushnikh Yal, and he becomes a Follower.
☐	[76/80]	Hjalti's Sword	[Random]	[Random Dungeon]	Found in a [random] dungeon as part of Miscellaneous Objective: The Ghost of Old Hroldan.*
☐	[77/80]	Kahvozein's Fang	[Random]	[Random Dragon Priest Dungeon]	Found in a Dragon Priest Dungeon, as part of College of Winterhold Radiant Quest: Alteration Ritual Spell, given to you by Tolfdir.
☐	[78/80]	Keening	[Random]	[Random Dungeon]	Found in a random dungeon during College of Winterhold Radiant Quest: Arniel's Endeavor (Part 4). Then dropped by Arniel.
☐	[79/80]	Queen Freydis's Sword	[Random]	[Random Cave]	Oengul War-Anvil needs this returned from a [random] cave, during Favor: Item Retrieval (Cave).*
☐	[80/80]	Staff of Tandil	[Random]	[Random Dungeon]	Found in a random dungeon during College of Winterhold Radiant Quest: Arniel's Endeavor (Part 2).

APPENDIX V: UNIQUE ARMOR AND ITEMS

Unique Armor and Items, whether awarded as part of a quest, found on a particular foe, or just stumbled upon, are listed below, and sorted by Hold for easy reference.

✓	NUMBER	NAME	ZONE #	LOCATION	DESCRIPTION	ENCHANTMENT	NOTES
☐	[1/112]	Asgeir's Wedding Band	[1.00]	Solitude (Temple of the Divines)	Found on the body of Asgeir Snow-Shod if killed during his marriage to Vittoria Vici, during Dark Brotherhood Quest: Bound Until Death.		
☐	[2/112]	Vittoria's Wedding Band	[1.00]	Solitude (Temple of the Divines)	Found on the body of Vittoria Vici, during her marriage to Asgeir Snow-Shod, during Dark Brotherhood Quest: Bound Until Death.		
☐	[3/112]	Shield of Solitude	[1.00]	Solitude (The Blue Palace)	Gift from Falk Firebeard after completing Side Quest: The Wolf Queen Awakened	Resist Magic 10%, Improve Block 15%	Leveled
☐	[4/112]	Party Boots	[1.23]	Katla's Farm	Given during Main Quest: Diplomatic Immunity.		
☐	[5/112]	Party Clothes	[1.23]	Katla's Farm	Given during Main Quest: Diplomatic Immunity.		
☐	[6/112]	Gauldur Amulet Fragment (Folgunthur)	[2.08]	Folgunthur	Found on the corpse of Mikrul Gauldurson, during Side Quest: Forbidden Legend.	+30 Health	
☐	[7/112]	Execution Hood	[2.15]	Abandoned Shack	Worn by the three captives during Dark Brotherhood Quest: With Friends Like These…		
☐	[8/112]	Movarth's Boots	[2.19]	Movarth's Lair	Sitting by the bed in the sleeping nook at the back of the cave.	Fortify Sneaking 15	
☐	[9/112]	Ancient Helmet of the Unburned	[2.23]	Labyrinthian	During College of Winterhold Quest: The Staff of Magnus, found resting atop a sword in a nook behind a locked gate in the Labyrinthian Tribune.	Resist Fire 40%	
☐	[10/112]	Jester's Boots	[3.05]	Dawnstar Sanctuary	Found on a table in the Dawnstar Sanctuary, or in the Chapel of the Dark Brotherhood Sanctuary after Cicero joins.	Muffle	
☐	[11/112]	Jester's Clothes	[3.05]	Dawnstar Sanctuary	Found on a table in the Dawnstar Sanctuary, or in the Chapel of the Dark Brotherhood Sanctuary after Cicero joins.	Improve One-Handed 12%, Improve Prices 12%	
☐	[12/112]	Jester's Gloves	[3.05]	Dawnstar Sanctuary	Found on a table in the Dawnstar Sanctuary, or in the Chapel of the Dark Brotherhood Sanctuary after Cicero joins.	Double One-Handed sneak attack damage	
☐	[13/112]	Jester's Hat	[3.05]	Dawnstar Sanctuary	Found on a table in the Dawnstar Sanctuary, or in the Chapel of the Dark Brotherhood Sanctuary after Cicero joins.	Improve Sneak 30%	
☐	[14/112]	Cicero's Boots	[3.05]	Dawnstar Sanctuary	Worn by Cicero, Keeper for the Dark Brotherhood, if you kill him during Dark Brotherhood Quest: The Cure for Madness.	Muffle	
☐	[15/112]	Cicero's Clothes	[3.05]	Dawnstar Sanctuary	Worn by Cicero, Keeper for the Dark Brotherhood, if you kill him during Dark Brotherhood Quest: The Cure for Madness.	Improve One-Handed 20%, Improve Prices 20%	
☐	[16/112]	Cicero's Gloves	[3.05]	Dawnstar Sanctuary	Worn by Cicero, Keeper for the Dark Brotherhood, if you kill him during Dark Brotherhood Quest: The Cure for Madness.	Double One-Handed sneak attack damage	
☐	[17/112]	Cicero's Hat	[3.05]	Dawnstar Sanctuary	Worn by Cicero, Keeper for the Dark Brotherhood, if you kill him during Dark Brotherhood Quest: The Cure for Madness.	Improve Sneak 35%	
☐	[18/112]	Worn Shrouded Armor	[3.05]	Dawnstar Sanctuary	On a shelf in the Dawnstar Sanctuary, during or after Dark Brotherhood Quest: The Cure for Madness		
☐	[19/112]	Worn Shrouded Boots	[3.05]	Dawnstar Sanctuary	On a shelf in the Dawnstar Sanctuary, during or after Dark Brotherhood Quest: The Cure for Madness		

✔	NUMBER	NAME	ZONE #	LOCATION	DESCRIPTION	ENCHANTMENT	NOTES
☐	[20/112]	Worn Shrouded Cowl	[3.05]	Dawnstar Sanctuary	On a shelf in the Dawnstar Sanctuary, during or after Dark Brotherhood Quest: The Cure for Madness		
☐	[21/112]	Worn Shrouded Gloves	[3.05]	Dawnstar Sanctuary	On a shelf in the Dawnstar Sanctuary, during or after Dark Brotherhood Quest: The Cure for Madness	Backstab does double damage	
☐	[22/112]	Tumblerbane Gloves	[3.05]	Dawnstar Sanctuary	Purchase the Dawnstar Sanctuary Bedroom Upgrade in Dark Brotherhood Radiant Quest: Where You Hang Your Enemy's Head...	Improve Lockpick 20%	
☐	[23/112]	Jeweled Amulet	[3.13]	Volunruud	Given by Amaund Motierre during Dark Brotherhood Quest: The Silence Has Been Broken.		
☐	[24/112]	Jagged Crown	[3.22]	Korvanjund Crypt	Also known as the Bone Crown, found during Civil War Quest: The Jagged Crown		
☐	[25/112]	Skeleton Key	[3.31]	Irkngthand	During Thieves Guild Quest: Blindsighted	Unbreakable Lockpick	
☐	[26/112]	The Black Star	[4.00]	Winterhold (Frozen Hearth Inn)	Possible reward for completing Daedric Quest: The Black Star	Reusable Black Soul Gem	Black Soul Gems store human souls.
☐	[27/112]	Archmage's Robes	[4.00]	College of Winterhold	Given to you by Tolfdir at the end of College of Winterhold Quest: The Eye of Magnus.	All spells cost 15% less to cast	
☐	[28/112]	Mage's Circlet	[4.00]	College of Winterhold	Gift from the Arch-Mage during College of Winterhold Quest: Good Intentions	Fortify Magicka	Leveled
☐	[29/112]	Savos Aren's Amulet	[4.00]	College of Winterhold	Gift from Mirabelle Ervine after completing College of Winterhold Quest: Containment	+50 Magicka	
☐	[30/112]	Mystic Tuning Gloves	[4.00]	College of Winterhold	Given to you by Drevis Neloren during College Radiant Quest: Out of Balance*		
☐	[31/112]	Shield of Ysgramor	[4.11]	Ysgramor's Tomb	Found in the large chest next to Ysgramor's sarcophagus during The Companions Quest: Glory of the Dead.	+20 Health, Resist Magic 20%	
☐	[32/112]	Enchanted Ring	[4.12]	Saarthal	One of three to find during College of Winterhold Quest: Under Saarthal	+20 Health	
☐	[33/112]	Saarthal Amulet	[4.12]	Saarthal	Found during College of Winterhold Quest: Under Saarthal	Spells cost 3% less to cast.	
☐	[34/112]	Gauldur Amulet Fragment (Saarthal)	[4.12]	Saarthal	Found on the corpse of Jyrik Gauldurson, during Side Quest: Forbidden Legend.	+30 Magicka	
☐	[35/112]	Targe of the Blooded	[4.13]	Alftand (Alftand Cathedral)	Carried by Umana the adventurer.	Bashes do 3 Bleeding Damage / 5s.	
☐	[36/112]	Azura's Star	[4.18]	Shrine of Azura	Possible reward for completing Daedric Quest: The Black Star	Reusable Grand Soul Gem	
☐	[37/112]	Oghma Infinium	[4.20]	Septimus Signus's Outpost	Reward for completing Daedric Quest: Discerning the Transmundane	Once only, +5 Skill Increases to your choice of Combat, Magic, or Stealth skills.	
☐	[38/112]	Helm of Yngol	[4.30]	Yngol Barrow	Resting atop the head of the skeleton that sits upon the throne at the end of the dungeon.	Resist Frost 30%	
☐	[39/112]	Yisra's Necklace	[4.D]	Yisra's Beachside Combustion	On the charred corpse of Yisra, part of Miscellaneous Objective: Lost Apprentices: Yisra.*		
☐	[40/112]	Ilas-Tei's Ring	[4.K]	Shrine of Talos: Ilas-Tei's Last Stand	On the corpse of Ilas-Tei, part of Miscellaneous Objective: Lost Apprentices: Ilas-tei*		
☐	[41/112]	Calcelmo's Ring	[5.00]	Markarth (Kerah's Market Stall)	Given to you during Miscellaneous Objective: Calcelmo's Ring*		
☐	[42/112]	Armor of the Old Gods	[5.00]	Markarth	Gift from Kaie and Madanach for siding with the Forsworn during Side Quest: No One Escapes Cidhna Mine.	Destruction spells cost 15% less to cast	
☐	[43/112]	Boots of the Old Gods	[5.00]	Markarth	Gift from Kaie and Madanach for siding with the Forsworn during Side Quest: No One Escapes Cidhna Mine.	Improve Sneak 20%	
☐	[44/112]	Gauntlets of the Old Gods	[5.00]	Markarth	Gift from Kaie and Madanach for siding with the Forsworn during Side Quest: No One Escapes Cidhna Mine.	Improve Archery 20%	
☐	[45/112]	Helmet of the Old Gods	[5.00]	Markarth	Gift from Kaie and Madanach for siding with the Forsworn during Side Quest: No One Escapes Cidhna Mine.	+30 Magicka	
☐	[46/112]	Silver-Blood Family Ring	[5.00]	Markarth	Reward for siding with Thonar Silver-Blood at the end of Side Quest: No One Escapes Cidhna Mine.	Improve Smithing 20%	
☐	[47/112]	Muiri's Ring	[5.00]	Markarth (Hag's Cure)	Given by Muiri as a bonus reward after completing Dark Brotherhood Quest: Sentenced to Death.	Improve Alchemy 15%	Bonus reward for Dark Brotherhood Quest: Sentenced to Death.
☐	[48/112]	Ogmund's Amulet of Talos	[5.00]	Markarth (Understone Keep)	Find this to blackmail Ogmund during Miscellaneous Objective: Triumph Over Talos*	Time between Shouts reduced by 20%	
☐	[49/112]	Raerek's Inscribed Amulet of Talos	[5.00]	Markarth (Understone Keep)	Find this to blackmail Raerek during Civil War Quest: Compelling Tribute.	Time between Shouts reduced by 20%	
☐	[50/112]	Ancient Shrouded Armor	[5.03]	Hag's End	On the body of a slain assassin, found during Dark Brotherhood Radiant Quest: The Feeble Fortune* (and only then).	Resist Poison 100%	
☐	[51/112]	Ancient Shrouded Boots	[5.03]	Hag's End	On the body of a slain assassin, found during Dark Brotherhood Radiant Quest: The Feeble Fortune* (and only then).	Muffle	
☐	[52/112]	Ancient Shrouded Cowl	[5.03]	Hag's End	On the body of a slain assassin, found during Dark Brotherhood Radiant Quest: The Feeble Fortune* (and only then).	Improve Archery 35%	
☐	[53/112]	Ancient Shrouded Gloves	[5.03]	Hag's End	On the body of a slain assassin, found during Dark Brotherhood Radiant Quest: The Feeble Fortune* (and only then).	Double One-Handed sneak attack damage	
☐	[54/112]	Predator's Grace	[5.03]	Hag's End	Deepwood Vale Summit, near a chest on the upper level of the Vale from which the waterfall descends.	Muffle, +1% Stamina Regen	
☐	[55/112]	Spellbreaker	[5.06]	Bthardamz	Reward for completing Daedric Quest: The Only Cure.	Automatic Strength -50 spell ward while blocking	
☐	[56/112]	The Gauldur Amulet	[5.39]	Reachwater Rock	Reward at the end of Side Quest: Forbidden Legend.	+30 Health, +30 Magicka, +30 Stamina	
☐	[57/112]	Ring of Namira	[5.41]	Reachcliff Cave	Reward for completing Daedric Quest: The Taste of Death.	+50 Stamina. Feeding from NPC corpses raises Health by 50 and Health Regen by 50% for 4 hours	

✓	NUMBER	NAME	ZONE #	LOCATION	DESCRIPTION	ENCHANTMENT	NOTES
☐	[58/112]	Andurs' Amulet of Arkay	[6.00]	Whiterun (Hall of the Dead)	Found during Miscellaneous Objective: Andurs' Arkay Amulet.*	+10 Health	
☐	[59/112]	Ironhand Gauntlets	[6.26]	White River Watch	Carried by Hajvarr Iron-Hand, the leader of the bandits here.	Improve Two-Handed 15%	
☐	[60/112]	Viola's Gold Ring	[7.00]	Windhelm (Gray Quarter)	Given by Revyn Sadri during Favor: A Little Light Burglary.*		
☐	[61/112]	Strange Amulet	[7.00]	Windhelm (Hjerim)	Found during Side Quest: Blood on the Ice. Becomes the Necromancer's Amulet once identified by Wuunferth.		
☐	[62/112]	Necromancer Amulet	[7.00]	Windhelm (Palace of the Kings)	During Side Quest: Blood on the Ice, Wuunferth identifies the Strange Amulet as a Necromancer's Amulet.	+50 Magicka, Improve Conjuration 25%, -75% Health and Stamina Regen	
☐	[63/112]	Fjotli's Silver Locket	[7.01]	Uttering Hills Cave	On the corpse of Linwe, during Thieves Guild City Influence Quest: Summerset Shadows.		
☐	[64/112]	Fjola's Wedding Band	[7.33]	Mistwatch	Carried by Fjola during Dungeon Quest: Forgetting About Fjola.		
☐	[65/112]	Cursed Ring of Hircine	[8.00]	Falkreath (Falkreath Jail)	Given to you by Sinding during Daedric Quest: Ill Met By Moonlight.	Random werewolf transformations.	No effect except on werewolves.
☐	[66/112]	Ring of Hircine	[8.00]	Falkreath (Falkreath Jail)	Given during, and possible reward for completing Daedric Quest: Ill Met By Moonlight.	+1 Werewolf Transform / Day	Must already be a werewolf to use this.
☐	[67/112]	Ebony Mail	[8.07]	Knifepoint Ridge	Reward for completing Daedric Quest: Boethiah's Calling.	Muffle while sneaking, Poison Cloak when in combat	
☐	[68/112]	Savior's Hide	[8.12]	Bloated Man's Grotto	Possible reward for completing Daedric Quest: Ill Met By Moonlight.	Resist Magic 15%, Resist Poison 50%	
☐	[69/112]	Shrouded Armor	[8.22]	Dark Brotherhood Sanctuary	Gift from Astrid at the end of Dark Brotherhood Quest: With Friends Like These...	Resist Poison 50%	
☐	[70/112]	Shrouded Boots	[8.22]	Dark Brotherhood Sanctuary	Gift from Astrid at the end of Dark Brotherhood Quest: With Friends Like These...	Muffle	
☐	[71/112]	Shrouded Cowl	[8.22]	Dark Brotherhood Sanctuary	Gift from Astrid at the end of Dark Brotherhood Quest: With Friends Like These...	Improve Archery 20%	
☐	[72/112]	Shrouded Gloves	[8.22]	Dark Brotherhood Sanctuary	Gift from Astrid at the end of Dark Brotherhood Quest: With Friends Like These...	Backstab does double damage	
☐	[73/112]	Shrouded Cowl Maskless	[8.22]	Dark Brotherhood Sanctuary	On a shelf in Astrid's foyer in the Dark Brotherhood Sanctuary.	Improve Archery 20%	
☐	[74/112]	Shrouded Hand Wraps	[8.22]	Dark Brotherhood Sanctuary	On a shelf in Astrid's foyer in the Dark Brotherhood Sanctuary.	Double One-Handed sneak attack damage	
☐	[75/112]	Shrouded Hood	[8.22]	Dark Brotherhood Sanctuary	On a shelf in Astrid's foyer in the Dark Brotherhood Sanctuary.	Improve Sneak 25%	
☐	[76/112]	Shrouded Robes	[8.22]	Dark Brotherhood Sanctuary	On a shelf in Astrid's foyer in the Dark Brotherhood Sanctuary.	Improve Destruction 15%	
☐	[77/112]	Shrouded Shoes	[8.22]	Dark Brotherhood Sanctuary	On a shelf in Astrid's foyer in the Dark Brotherhood Sanctuary.	Muffle	
☐	[78/112]	Nightweaver's Band	[8.22]	Dark Brotherhood Sanctuary	A bonus reward from Festus Krex, after completing Dark Brotherhood Quest: Recipe for Disaster.	Improve Sneak 10%, Destruction 10%	
☐	[79/112]	Masque of Clavicus Vile	[8.37]	Haemar's Shame	Possible reward for completing Daedric Quest: A Daedra's Best Friend.	+10 Speech, +20% Better Prices, +5 Magicka Regen	
☐	[80/112]	The Bond of Matrimony	[9.00]	Riften (Temple of Mara)	A wedding gift granted during Temple Quest: The Bonds of Matrimony.	Improve Restoration 10%	
☐	[81/112]	Madesi's Silver Ring	[9.00]	Riften (Market)	Stolen during Thieves Guild Quest: A Chance Encounter.		
☐	[82/112]	Gloves of the Pugilist	[9.00]	Riften	Carried by Gians in the Ratway.	+10 Unarmed damage	
☐	[83/112]	Thieves Guild Armor	[9.00]	Riften (Ragged Flagon)	Gift from Tonilia just before completing Thieves Guild Quest: Loud and Clear.	+20 Carry Weight	
☐	[84/112]	Thieves Guild Boots	[9.00]	Riften (Ragged Flagon)	Gift from Tonilia just before completing Thieves Guild Quest: Loud and Clear.	Improve Pickpocket 15%	
☐	[85/112]	Thieves Guild Gloves	[9.00]	Riften (Ragged Flagon)	Gift from Tonilia just before completing Thieves Guild Quest: Loud and Clear.	Improve Lockpick 15%	
☐	[86/112]	Thieves Guild Hood	[9.00]	Riften (Ragged Flagon)	Gift from Tonilia just before completing Thieves Guild Quest: Loud and Clear.	Improve Prices 10%	
☐	[87/112]	Amulet of Articulation	[9.00]	Riften (Ratway Cistern)	Reward from Brynjolf during Thieves Guild Leadership Quest: Under New Management.*	Fortify Speech, Persuade checks always succeed	Leveled
☐	[88/112]	Guild Master's Armor	[9.00]	Riften (Ratway Cistern)	Reward from Tonilia during Thieves Guild Leadership Quest: Under New Management.*	+50 Carry Weight	
☐	[89/112]	Guild Master's Boots	[9.00]	Riften (Ratway Cistern)	Reward from Tonilia during Thieves Guild Leadership Quest: Under New Management.*	Improve Pickpocket 35%	
☐	[90/112]	Guild Master's Gloves	[9.00]	Riften (Ratway Cistern)	Reward from Tonilia during Thieves Guild Leadership Quest: Under New Management.*	Improve Lockpick 35%	
☐	[91/112]	Guild Master's Hood	[9.00]	Riften (Ratway Cistern)	Reward from Tonilia during Thieves Guild Leadership Quest: Under New Management.*	Improve Prices 20%	
☐	[92/112]	Thieves Guild Armor (Improved)	[9.00]	Riften (Ragged Flagon)	Gift from Tonilia (only one part of the outfit is available) after completing Thieves Guild Quest: Scoundrel's Folly.	+35 Carry Weight	
☐	[93/112]	Thieves Guild Boots (Improved)	[9.00]	Riften (Ragged Flagon)	Gift from Tonilia (only one part of the outfit is available) after completing Thieves Guild Quest: Scoundrel's Folly.	Improve Pickpocket 25%	
☐	[94/112]	Thieves Guild Gloves (Improved)	[9.00]	Riften (Ragged Flagon)	Gift from Tonilia (only one part of the outfit is available) after completing Thieves Guild Quest: Scoundrel's Folly.	Improve Lockpick 25%	

	NUMBER	NAME	ZONE #	LOCATION	DESCRIPTION	ENCHANTMENT	NOTES
☐	[95/112]	Thieves Guild Hood (Improved)	[9.00]	Riften (Ragged Flagon)	Gift from Tonilia (only one part of the outfit is available) after completing Thieves Guild Quest: Scoundrel's Folly.	Improve Prices 15%	
☐	[96/112]	Reyda's Necklace	[9.01]	Ivarstead	After Narfi requests this in Miscellaneous Objective: The Straw That Broke,* find it in a satchel by a skeleton, just north of the bridge leading southeast out of town.		
☐	[97/112]	Gauldur Amulet Fragment (Geirmund's Hall)	[9.04]	Geirmund's Hall	Found on the corpse of Sigdis Gauldurson, during Side Quest: Forbidden Legend.	+30 Stamina	
☐	[98/112]	Diadem of the Savant	[9.15]	Froki's Shack	Exterior; resting atop the Wood Chopping Block.	All spells cost 5% less to cast.	
☐	[99/112]	Kyne's Token	[9.15]	Froki's Shack	Reward for Side Quest: Kyne's Sacred Trials.	Improve Archery 5%, Damage from Animals -10%	
☐	[100/112]	Nightingale Armor	[9.43]	Nightingale Hall	Awarded during Thieves Guild Quest: Trinity Restored.	Resist Frost, Improve Illusion	Leveled
☐	[101/112]	Nightingale Boots	[9.43]	Nightingale Hall	Awarded during Thieves Guild Quest: Trinity Restored.	Muffle	Leveled
☐	[102/112]	Nightingale Gloves	[9.43]	Nightingale Hall	Awarded during Thieves Guild Quest: Trinity Restored.	Improve Lockpick, Pickpocket	Leveled
☐	[103/112]	Nightingale Hood	[9.43]	Nightingale Hall	Awarded during Thieves Guild Quest: Trinity Restored.	Improve Prices	Leveled
☐	[104/112]	Charmed Necklace	[Random]	[World Encounter]	If you stumble across World Encounter: Drinking Companions, offer the drunks a bottle of Honningbrew Mead to receive this necklace.	+25 Carry Weight	
☐	[105/112]	Helm of Winterhold	[Random]	[Random Dungeon]	Found in a [random] location after being requested by Jarl Korir of Winterhold during Favor: Jobs for the Jarls.*		
☐	[106/112]	Hrolfdir's Shield	[Random]	[Random Dungeon]	Found in a [random] location after being requested by Jarl Igmund during Favor: Jobs for the Jarls.*		
☐	[107/112]	Moon Amulet	[Random]	[Random Dungeon]	Found in a [random] location after being requested by Kharjo of Ahkari's Caravan.		
☐	[108/112]	Noster's Helmet	[Random]	[Random Dungeon]	Found in a [random] location after being requested by Noster during Favor: Item Retrieval (Cave).*		
☐	[109/112]	Ring of Pure Mixtures	[Random]	[Random Dungeon]	Found in a [random] location after being requested by Frida during Favor: Item Retrieval (Cave).*	Improve Alchemy 12%	
☐	[110/112]	Roggi's Ancestral Shield	[Random]	[Random Dungeon]	Found in a [random] location after being requested by Roggi during Favor: Item Retrieval (Cave).*		
☐	[111/112]	Shahvee's Amulet of Zenithar	[Random]	[Random Dungeon]	Found in a [random] location after being requested by Shahvee during Favor: Item Retrieval (Bandit Camp).*	Improve Prices 10%	
☐	[112/112]	The Forgemaster's Fingers	[Random]	[Random Dungeon]	During Side Quest: The Forgemaster's Fingers, find this gauntlet in a [random] dungeon.	Improve Smithing 15%	

APPENDIX VI: SKILL BOOKS

This table lists two sample locations for each of the 90 Skill Books. Many of these books are in towns or notable dungeons, making them among the most easily accessible copies. As there are no further improvements to a skill when you find the same book again, it isn't necessary to find them all. But there are more copies of each book out there in the wilds....

	NUMBER	SKILL	TITLE	ZONE #	LOCATION	DESCRIPTION
☐	[A1/10]	Alchemy	A Game at Dinner	[6.22]	Honningbrew Meadery	On the second floor of the Meadery, in the upstairs bedroom.
☐	[A2/10]	Alchemy	A Game at Dinner	[7.00]	Windhelm	In the New Gnisis Cornerclub, on a table on the second floor.
☐	[B1/10]	Alchemy	De Rerum Dirennis	[1.11]	Clearpine Pond	On the body of the Alchemist at Clearpine Pond.
☐	[B2/10]	Alchemy	De Rerum Dirennis	[4.00]	Winterhold	In the College of Winterhold Midden Dark, resting on an Alchemy Lab.
☐	[C1/10]	Alchemy	Herbalist's Guide to Skyrim	[5.00]	Markarth	In the Hag's Cure, on the shelf under the counter.
☐	[C2/10]	Alchemy	Herbalist's Guide to Skyrim	[6.00]	Whiterun	In Arcadia's Cauldron, on a large wooden table downstairs.
☐	[D1/10]	Alchemy	Mannimarco, King of Worms	[3.06]	Nightcaller Temple	On a table in the Alchemy Lab room.
☐	[D2/10]	Alchemy	Mannimarco, King of Worms	[8.10]	Evergreen Grove	On a partially submerged altar near the body of a dead mage.
☐	[E1/10]	Alchemy	Song of the Alchemists	[1.00]	Solitude	During Favor: Rare Item Hunt for Lami in Morthal, you can find this copy on the counter in the library of the Bards College.
☐	[E2/10]	Alchemy	Song of the Alchemists	[8.19]	Anise's Cabin	On the shelf at the foot of the bed inside Anise's Cabin.
☐	[A1/10]	Alteration	Breathing Water	[4.00]	Winterhold	Inside Kraldar's House, hidden inside the woven basket on the shelf.

	NUMBER	SKILL	TITLE	ZONE #	LOCATION	DESCRIPTION
☐	[A2/10]	Alteration	Breathing Water	[8.15]	Ilinalta's Deep	In an underwater room about halfway through the keep, next to a submerged chest.
☐	[B1/10]	Alteration	Daughter of the Niben	[5.00]	Markarth	Understone Keep, on a table at the top of the stairs, to the right of the Jarl's Throne Room.
☐	[B2/10]	Alteration	Daughter of the Niben	[7.07]	Brandy-Mug Farm	Inside the farmhouse, atop fireplace mantel.
☐	[C1/10]	Alteration	Reality & Other Falsehoods	[4.02]	Yngvild	On a table next to the throne in the Yngvild Throne Room.
☐	[C2/10]	Alteration	Reality & Other Falsehoods	[9.41]	Snow-Shod Farm	Inside the farmhouse, on a shelf in the basement.
☐	[D1/10]	Alteration	Sithis	[5.00]	Markarth	Next to Krag's corpse in Nchuand-Zel, on a metal bench in the large central cavern.
☐	[D2/10]	Alteration	Sithis	[8.22]	Dark Brotherhood Sanctuary	On a bookshelf pedestal in Astrid's foyer.
☐	[E1/10]	Alteration	The Lunar Lorkhan	[1.26]	Solitude Lighthouse	In Mazaka's quarters, on the shelf behind the bar.
☐	[E2/10]	Alteration	The Lunar Lorkhan	[7.24]	Cragwallow Slope	On a table among other books in the central chamber, not far from the Arcane Enchanter.
☐	[A1/10]	Archery	Father of the Niben	[3.02]	Wreck of the Brinehammer	On a crate near a skeleton in the ship's lower cargo hold.
☐	[A2/10]	Archery	Father of the Niben	[8.06]	Hunter's Rest	Lying between two bedrolls inside the shack.

✓	NUMBER	SKILL	TITLE	ZONE #	LOCATION	DESCRIPTION
☐	[B1/10]	Archery	The Black Arrow, v2	[6.00]	Whiterun	In the Drunken Huntsman, on the shelf under the counter.
☐	[B2/10]	Archery	The Black Arrow, v2	[6.33]	Valtheim Towers	On an end table near the top of the north tower.
☐	[C1/10]	Archery	The Gold Ribbon of Merit	[1.00]	Solitude	In the Fletcher's shop, on a small table in a corner of the room.
☐	[C2/10]	Archery	The Gold Ribbon of Merit	[8.29]	Angi's Camp	On the end table near the bed inside the shack.
☐	[D1/10]	Archery	The Marksmanship Lesson	[3.00]	Dawnstar Sanctuary	On the table with the map in the Dawnstar Sanctuary.
☐	[D2/10]	Archery	The Marksmanship Lesson	[7.15]	Mixwater Mill	In Gilfre's House, on the small corner table.
☐	[E1/10]	Archery	Vernaccus and Bourlor	[8.07]	Knifepoint Ridge	On a crude wooden table near the Blacksmith Forge.
☐	[E2/10]	Archery	Vernaccus and Bourlor	[9.15]	Froki's Shack	On a shelf inside the shack.
☐	[A1/10]	Block	A Dance in Fire, v2	[2.10]	Fort Snowhawk	On the large table in the library area.
☐	[A2/10]	Block	A Dance in Fire, v2	[7.10]	Traitor's Post	On a cupboard in the southwest part of the ruined inn.
☐	[B1/10]	Block	Battle of Red Mountain	[8.33] and [8.34]	Skybound Watch Pass	On a shelf near a chest at one end of the pass.
☐	[B2/10]	Block	Battle of Red Mountain	[9.23]	Tolvald's Crossing	On a stone pedestal near the remains of the decimated caravan, deep within the cave.
☐	[C1/10]	Block	Death Blow of Abernanit	[6.00]	Whiterun	In the Hall of the Dead catacombs, inside a small chamber lined with candles.
☐	[C2/10]	Block	Death Blow of Abernanit	[8.00]	Falkreath	On a side table in the war room.
☐	[D1/10]	Block	The Mirror	[5.18]	Broken Tower Redoubt	On a shelf in the sleeping area.
☐	[D2/10]	Block	The Mirror	[7.00]	Windhelm	During Favor: Rare Item Hunt for Captain Aldis of Solitude, you can find this book in Ulfric's bedroom in Windhelm's Palace of the Kings.
☐	[E1/10]	Block	Warrior	[4.07]	Driftshade Refuge	On a small table near the fireplace, in the boss's chamber. Collect it on your way out.
☐	[E2/10]	Block	Warrior	[4.19]	Fort Kastav	In the Captain's Quarters, on a bedside table.
☐	[A1/10]	Conjuration	2920, Frostfall, v10	[7.00]	Windhelm	In Belyn Hlaalu's House, hidden in a dark corner behind the dresser in the upstairs bedroom.
☐	[A2/10]	Conjuration	2920, Frostfall, v10	[8.02]	Sunderstone Gorge	On a pedestal in the final chamber with the Word Wall.
☐	[B1/10]	Conjuration	2920, Hearth Fire, v9	[1.02]	Rimerock Burrow	On an end table in the final cavern with the large chest.
☐	[B2/10]	Conjuration	2920, Hearth Fire, v9	[3.00]	Dawnstar	In the Mortar and Pestle, under the counter.
☐	[C1/10]	Conjuration	Liminal Bridges	[2.23]	Labyrinthian	In Shalidor's Maze, on the ground at a short dead end within the maze (must enter from the north).
☐	[C2/10]	Conjuration	Liminal Bridges	[8.24]	Falkreath Watchtower	In the tent atop the tower.
☐	[D1/10]	Conjuration	The Doors of Oblivion	[5.41]	Reachcliff Cave	Inside the cave's ruins, partially covered by other books on a shelf in the small room with the sarcophagi.
☐	[D2/10]	Conjuration	The Doors of Oblivion	[6.29]	Fellglow Keep	On the pedestal in the chapel area.
☐	[E1/10]	Conjuration	The Warrior's Charge	[5.00]	Markarth	On the table next to the bed in the Jarl's Quarters.
☐	[E2/10]	Conjuration	The Warrior's Charge	[8.13] and [8.14]	Brittleshin Pass	On the sacrificial altar near the Arcane Enchanter.
☐	[A1/10]	Destruction	A Hypothetical Treachery	[3.01]	High Gate Ruins	Lying next to a skeleton in a dark corner of the large central chamber.
☐	[A2/10]	Destruction	A Hypothetical Treachery	[7.00]	Windhelm	In the main room of the Aretino Residence, hidden behind a shelf.
☐	[B1/10]	Destruction	Horrors of Castle Xyr	[6.09]	Rannveig's Fast	On the table with the Alchemy Lab in the prison area.

✓	NUMBER	SKILL	TITLE	ZONE #	LOCATION	DESCRIPTION
☐	[B2/10]	Destruction	Horrors of Castle Xyr	[8.03]	Glenmoril Coven	Hidden in a crate in a tent near the large chest.
☐	[C1/10]	Destruction	Mystery of Talara, v3	[1.05]	Upper Steepfall Burrow	Next to a skeleton in the cave with the large chest.
☐	[C2/10]	Destruction	Mystery of Talara, v3	[4.00]	Winterhold	On a dresser on the second floor.
☐	[D1/10]	Destruction	Response to Bero's Speech	[3.00]	Dawnstar	In Iron Breaker Mine, sitting atop a barrel near a bedroll.
☐	[D2/10]	Destruction	Response to Bero's Speech	[8.37]	Haemar's Shame	In Haemar's Cavern, on a table in a nook surrounded by shelves, opposite the passage leading down to Haemar's Shame.
☐	[E1/10]	Destruction	The Art of War Magic	[1.12]	Ravenscar Hollow	On a table near the large chest.
☐	[E2/10]	Destruction	The Art of War Magic	[3.00]	Dawnstar	In the White Hall, on a small table on the upstairs landing.
☐	[A1/10]	Enchanting	A Tragedy in Black	[8.03]	Glenmoril Coven	On the table with the Arcane Enchanter.
☐	[A2/10]	Enchanting	A Tragedy in Black	[8.15]	Ilinalta's Deep	On a table across from the Arcane Enchanter and Alchemy Lab.
☐	[B1/10]	Enchanting	Catalogue of Armor Enchantments	[2.00]	Morthal	On the shelf in Falion's house.
☐	[B2/10]	Enchanting	Catalogue of Armor Enchantments	[7.05]	Kynesgrove	In Steamscorch Mine, on a table at the tunnel junction.
☐	[C1/10]	Enchanting	Catalogue of Weapon Enchantments	[3.00]	Dawnstar	In the White Hall, between a large barrel and a mead barrel, in the room with the training dummy.
☐	[C2/10]	Enchanting	Catalogue of Weapon Enchantments	[8.23]	Roadside Ruins	Leaned up against the chest in the center of the ruins.
☐	[D1/10]	Enchanting	Enchanter's Primer	[4.05]	Hob's Fall Cave	On the Arcane Enchanter in the ritual room.
☐	[D2/10]	Enchanting	Enchanter's Primer	[6.00]	Whiterun	In Carlotta Valentia's House, on the floor between the upstairs bed and the end table.
☐	[E1/10]	Enchanting	Twin Secrets	[6.03]	Serpent's Bluff Redoubt	In the Hagraven's chamber inside the ruins, on the Arcane Enchanter.
☐	[E2/10]	Enchanting	Twin Secrets	[9.16]	Treva's Watch	On a table in the bandit chief's room at the top of the tower.
☐	[A1/10]	Heavy Armor	2920, MidYear, v6	[2.00]	Morthal	In the Morthal Guardhouse, hidden behind a basket and a barrel near the fireplace.
☐	[A2/10]	Heavy Armor	2920, MidYear, v6	[3.10]	Fort Dunstad	In the Fort Dunstad Prison, in the upper-level cell block, on a shelf next to the Alchemy Lab.
☐	[B1/10]	Heavy Armor	Chimarvamidium	[5.00]	Markarth	During Thieves Guild Quest: Hard Answers, on the the desk in Calcelmo's Tower.
☐	[B2/10]	Heavy Armor	Chimarvamidium	[7.31]	Darkwater Crossing	Atop a barrel near the bedroll in a small dead end.
☐	[C1/10]	Heavy Armor	Hallgerd's Tale	[6.00]	Whiterun	In Jorrvaskr, on a low shelf in the main hall.
☐	[C2/10]	Heavy Armor	Hallgerd's Tale	[9.08]	Rift Watchtower	On a table atop the tower.
☐	[D1/10]	Heavy Armor	Orsinium and the Orcs	[2.22]	Stonehills	On a short table atop the mine scaffolding.
☐	[D2/10]	Heavy Armor	Orsinium and the Orcs	[5.38]	Dushnikh Yal	In the cellar of the longhouse, atop a low shelf at the base of the wooden ramp.
☐	[E1/10]	Heavy Armor	The Knights of the Nine	[3.09]	Hall of the Vigilant	Inside the Hall, atop the short table near the wall map downstairs.
☐	[E2/10]	Heavy Armor	The Knights of the Nine	[7.00]	Windhelm	On the top shelf of the cupboard in the dining area.
☐	[A1/10]	Illusion	2920, Sun's Dawn, v2	[5.00]	Markarth	In the Inner Sanctum of the Temple of Dibella, on a shelf among many other books.
☐	[A2/10]	Illusion	2920, Sun's Dawn, v2	[9.37]	Darklight Tower	On the table near Hagraven's tent, just before the entrance to the Darklight Chambers area.

The Elder Scrolls V
SKYRIM

☑	NUMBER	SKILL	TITLE	ZONE #	LOCATION	DESCRIPTION
☐	[B1/10]	Illusion	Before the Ages of Man	[6.00]	Whiterun	In the Dragonsreach Jarl's Quarters, on the large desk in the study.
☐	[B2/10]	Illusion	Before the Ages of Man	[9.02]	Shroud Hearth Barrow	In Shroud Hearth Barrow, on the altar in the catacombs chamber with the four levers.
☐	[C1/10]	Illusion	Incident at Necrom	[1.10]	Pinemoon Cave	On a small table near the large chest at the cave's far end.
☐	[C2/10]	Illusion	Incident at Necrom	[8.40]	Bloodlet Throne	On a small table in the locked area near the Alchemy Lab.
☐	[D1/10]	Illusion	Mystery of Talara, Part 4	[5.00]	Markarth	In Nepos's House, on a stone shelf in Nepos's bedroom.
☐	[D2/10]	Illusion	Mystery of Talara, Part 4	[6.07]	Broken Fang Cave	On the small shelf near the Arcane Enchanter.
☐	[E1/10]	Illusion	The Black Arts on Trial	[7.00]	Windhelm	In the White Phial, on the shelf under the counter.
☐	[E2/10]	Illusion	The Black Arts on Trial	[8.00]	Falkreath	In Falkreath Jail, tucked between some crates and a small wall in the jail area.
☐	[A1/10]	Light Armor	Ice and Chitin	[5.00]	Markarth	In the Guard Tower, on a table hidden behind a pillar in the sleeping area.
☐	[A2/10]	Light Armor	Ice and Chitin	[7.00]	Windhelm	On a table in the guard room under the bridge that leads to the city's south gate.
☐	[B1/10]	Light Armor	Jornibret's Last Dance	[8.42]	Fort Neugrad	On a table in the Fort Neugrad library.
☐	[B2/10]	Light Armor	Jornibret's Last Dance	[9.14]	Autumnwatch Tower	On a small wooden crate atop the smaller of the two towers.
☐	[C1/10]	Light Armor	Rislav the Righteous	[6.15]	Fort Greymoor	On the podium in the second-floor training room.
☐	[C2/10]	Light Armor	Rislav the Righteous	[8.20]	Cracked Tusk Keep	On a bench in one of the side rooms in the Cracked Tusk Keep Vaults.
☐	[D1/10]	Light Armor	The Rear Guard	[1.00]	Solitude	In Castle Dour, on a table downstairs in the barracks.
☐	[D2/10]	Light Armor	The Rear Guard	[5.07]	Druadach Redoubt	On a shelf near the fire pit, at the back of the cavern.
☐	[E1/10]	Light Armor	The Refugees	[1.00]	Solitude	In the Solitude Blacksmith's shop, atop the high wall shelf in the second-floor bedroom.
☐	[E2/10]	Light Armor	The Refugees	[5.24]	Blind Cliff Cave	Sitting atop the chest in an alcove on the collapsed tower.
☐	[A1/10]	Lockpicking	Advances in Lockpicking	[9.00]	Riften	In the Ragged Flagon Cistern, atop a barrel in the training room.
☐	[A2/10]	Lockpicking	Advances in Lockpicking	[9.00]	Riften	When escaping from Riften Jail through the sewers, on a barrel in a dark nook behind where you enter the sewers.
☐	[B1/10]	Lockpicking	Proper Lock Design	[5.00]	Markarth	In Cidhna Mine, on a shelf next to the Evidence Chest and Prisoner Belongings Chest.
☐	[B2/10]	Lockpicking	Proper Lock Design	[9.28]	Faldar's Tooth	Make your way through the keep to reach the ramparts, then climb the tower to reach the shack on top. On a table near the shack.
☐	[C1/10]	Lockpicking	Surfeit of Thieves	[4.31]	Wreck of the Winter War	On a crate on the second level of the War Winter.
☐	[C2/10]	Lockpicking	Surfeit of Thieves	[9.00]	Riften	On the end table near the bed in the Jarl's Chambers.
☐	[D1/10]	Lockpicking	The Locked Room	[2.00]	Morthal	Inside Highmoon Hall, on the top shelf of Joric's bedroom on the second floor.
☐	[D2/10]	Lockpicking	The Locked Room	[4.13]	Alftand	In the Animonculory's locked treasure room, in a locked alcove next to a skeleton.
☐	[E1/10]	Lockpicking	The Wolf Queen, v1	[3.00]	Dawnstar	In Dawnstar Jail, in a corner of the jail cell, behind a wooden pillar.
☐	[E2/10]	Lockpicking	The Wolf Queen, v1	[7.37]	Cragslane Cavern	Underneath the bar in Cragslane Cavern.
☐	[A1/10]	One-Handed	2920, Morning Star, v1	[1.01]	Northwatch Keep	On the shelf behind the bar in the bar area.
☐	[A2/10]	One-Handed	2920, Morning Star, v1	[1.06]	Lost Echo Cave	On the altar in the ruins chamber.

☑	NUMBER	SKILL	TITLE	ZONE #	LOCATION	DESCRIPTION
☐	[B1/10]	One-Handed	Fire and Darkness	[2.08]	Folgunthur	On the lower level of the large central chamber, next to a corpse.
☐	[B2/10]	One-Handed	Fire and Darkness	[9.00]	Riften	In Esbern's room in the Ratway Warrens.
☐	[C1/10]	One-Handed	Mace Etiquette	[2.06]	Orotheim	On a crate near the grindstone.
☐	[C2/10]	One-Handed	Mace Etiquette	[9.26]	Fort Greenwall	In the Fort Greenwall Captain's Quarters, on a shelf in the bedroom.
☐	[D1/10]	One-Handed	Night Falls on Sentinel	[6.05]	Swindler's Den	During Favor: Rare Item Hunt for Rustleif in Dawnstar, you can find this copy on the a crate overlooking the cave's dining area.
☐	[D2/10]	One-Handed	Night Falls on Sentinel	[8.X]	Bandit Camp: Ilinalta Foothills	On a small shelf in one of the tents.
☐	[E1/10]	One-Handed	The Importance of Where	[5.00]	Markarth	In the Guard Tower, on a stone table to one side of the sleeping area.
☐	[E2/10]	One-Handed	The Importance of Where	[6.23]	Chillfurrow Farm	Inside the farmhouse, on a dresser in the bedroom.
☐	[A1/10]	Pickpocket	Aevar Stone-Singer	[2.00]	Morthal	In Thonnir's House, on a shelf in the corner, hidden beneath a basket.
☐	[A2/10]	Pickpocket	Aevar Stone-Singer	[2.24]	Lost Valkygg	On the floor in the south holding cell, which is opened by a lever.
☐	[B1/10]	Pickpocket	Beggar	[9.00]	Riften	In the Ratway, on a table near the entrance to the Ragged Flagon.
☐	[B2/10]	Pickpocket	Beggar	[9.00]	Riften	In Haelga's Bunkhouse, on the dresser in the nook on the top floor.
☐	[C1/10]	Pickpocket	Purloined Shadows	[3.19]	Duskglow Crevice	On a table in the junk room in Duskglow Crevice.
☐	[C2/10]	Pickpocket	Purloined Shadows	[9.00]	Riften	In Honorhall Orphanage, tucked between the end table and bed in Constance's small bedroom.
☐	[D1/10]	Pickpocket	Thief	[7.00]	Windhelm	In the Argonian Assemblage; on the edge of a dresser.
☐	[D2/10]	Pickpocket	Thief	[8.18]	Bleak Falls Barrow	Inside the barrow, on the stone table near the chest just beyond the first glyph puzzle.
☐	[E1/10]	Pickpocket	Wulfmare's Guide to Better Thieving	[5.47]	Fort Sungard	At the bottom of the Fort Sunguard Oubliette.
☐	[E2/10]	Pickpocket	Wulfmare's Guide to Better Thieving	[7.03]	Mara's Eye Pond	Inside the cave, mixed in with other books in a small crate near the watery pond.
☐	[A1/10]	Restoration	2920, Rain's Hand, v4	[2.00]	Morthal	On the bedside table in Falion's house.
☐	[A2/10]	Restoration	2920, Rain's Hand, v4	[5.00]	Markarth	In the Hall of the Dead, on a stone shelf above the bed.
☐	[B1/10]	Restoration	Mystery of Talara, v 2	[2.16]	Ustengrav	On a stone shelf in the small room that's filled with urns.
☐	[B2/10]	Restoration	Mystery of Talara, v 2	[4.06]	Frostflow Lighthouse	On a dresser in the Lighthouse's Master Bedroom.
☐	[C1/10]	Restoration	Racial Phylogeny	[2.00]	Morthal	In the Moorside Inn, hidden in a woven basket that sits atop a dresser in one of the two small rooms.
☐	[C2/10]	Restoration	Racial Phylogeny	[8.00]	Falkreath	In Corpselight Farm, mixed in with other books on the shelf.
☐	[D1/10]	Restoration	The Exodus	[4.00]	Winterhold	In the Frozen Hearth, hidden among a collection of crates and sacks in the cellar.
☐	[D2/10]	Restoration	The Exodus	[9.46]	Stendarr's Beacon	Lying on one of the bedrolls inside the tower.
☐	[E1/10]	Restoration	Withershins	[6.00]	Whiterun	In the Temple of Kynareth, on the shelf next to the chest.
☐	[E2/10]	Restoration	Withershins	[9.13]	Arcwind Point	On a pedestal at the top of the tower at the end of Arcwind Point.
☐	[A1/10]	Smithing	Cherim's Heart	[3.00]	Dawnstar	In Quicksilver Mine, hidden in a small crate on the ground floor of the deepest mine cavern.

✔	NUMBER	SKILL	TITLE	ZONE #	LOCATION	DESCRIPTION
☐	[A2/10]	Smithing	Cherim's Heart	[7.04]	Morvunskar	On a table in the room with the forge.
☐	[B1/10]	Smithing	Heavy Armor Forging	[6.16]	Silent Moons Camp	On a broken stone table within the domed ruin at the top of the camp.
☐	[B2/10]	Smithing	Heavy Armor Forging	[7.23]	Gloombound Mine	On a table in the open-air hut just outside the mine entrance.
☐	[C1/10]	Smithing	Last Scabbard of Akrash	[5.47]	Fort Sungard	In the Fort Sungard Muster, on a small table in the armory.
☐	[C2/10]	Smithing	Last Scabbard of Akrash	[7.02]	Gallows Rock	On a table in the room with the large fireplace near the sleeping quarters.
☐	[D1/10]	Smithing	Light Armor Forging	[8.00]	Falkreath	On a barrel in the basement of Lod's house.
☐	[D2/10]	Smithing	Light Armor Forging	[8.31]	Embershard Mine	On a table in the forge area.
☐	[E1/10]	Smithing	The Armorer's Challenge	[5.01]	Mor Khazgur	On the shelf near the Blacksmith's Forge.
☐	[E2/10]	Smithing	The Armorer's Challenge	[9.00]	Whiterun	On the low platform next to the Skyforge.
☐	[A1/10]	Sneak	2920, Last Seed, v8	[3.32]	Raldbthar	In the large chamber with Alain, on the long counter under the metal bars.
☐	[A2/10]	Sneak	2920, Last Seed, v8	[6.14]	Redoran's Retreat	Lying on a crate in the back cavern with the large chest.
☐	[B1/10]	Sneak	Legend of Krately House	[3.25]	Nightgate Inn	In the cellar, on the end table near the large bed.
☐	[B2/10]	Sneak	Legend of Krately House	[9.35]	Black-Briar Lodge	On a shelf in the upstairs master bedroom.
☐	[C1/10]	Sneak	Sacred Witness	[5.02]	Deepwood Redoubt	In Deepwood Vale, on a shelf in the tent with the Alchemy Lab.
☐	[C2/10]	Sneak	Sacred Witness	[8.22]	Dark Brotherhood Sanctuary	On the counter in Babette's room.
☐	[D1/10]	Sneak	The Red Kitchen Reader	[3.08]	Frostmere Crypt	Inside the ruins, on a bookshelf pedestal in the hall just before the dining room.
☐	[D2/10]	Sneak	The Red Kitchen Reader	[7.00]	Windhelm	In the New Gnisis Cornerclub, tucked between the barrels beneath the stairs on the first floor.
☐	[E1/10]	Sneak	Three Thieves	[4.28]	Snow Veil Sanctum	During Thieves Guild Quest: Speaking with Silence, on a shelf in the room filled with hanging rattles.
☐	[E2/10]	Sneak	Three Thieves	[6.22]	Honningbrew Meadery	During Thieves Guild Quest: Dampened Spirits, lying on the chest near the Alchemy Lab in the basement cavern.

✔	NUMBER	SKILL	TITLE	ZONE #	LOCATION	DESCRIPTION
☐	[A1/10]	Speech	2920, Second Seed, v5	[2.22]	Stonehills	In Sorli's House, atop the fireplace mantel.
☐	[A2/10]	Speech	2920, Second Seed, v5	[7.00]	Windhelm	In Sadri's Used Wares, on the shelf under the counter.
☐	[B1/10]	Speech	A Dance in Fire, v6	[2.01]	Meeko's Shack	On a barrel inside the shack.
☐	[B2/10]	Speech	A Dance in Fire, v6	[8.00]	Falkreath	In Dead Man's Drink, on the shelf under the counter.
☐	[C1/10]	Speech	A Dance in Fire, v7	[5.00]	Markarth	In Arnleif and Sons Trading Company, on a crate near the counter.
☐	[C2/10]	Speech	A Dance in Fire, v7	[9.00]	Riften	In Beggar's Row, lying on the ground in a nook, partially covered by a red fern.
☐	[D1/10]	Speech	Biography of the Wolf Queen	[1.00]	Solitude	In the Blue Palace, on a shelf in the Jarl's bedchamber upstairs.
☐	[D2/10]	Speech	Biography of the Wolf Queen	[6.00]	Whiterun	In Belethor's General Goods store, on the cupboard shelf near the counter.
☐	[E1/10]	Speech	The Buying Game	[1.00]	Solitude	In one of the Bards College second floor classrooms, mixed in with a short stack of other books on the highest tier of a tall shelf.
☐	[E2/10]	Speech	The Buying Game	[5.16]	Shrine to Peryite	On the table near the Alchemy Lab.
☐	[A1/10]	Two-Handed	Battle of Sancre Tor	[5.34]	Old Hroldan	On an end table in the large bedroom.
☐	[A2/10]	Two-Handed	Battle of Sancre Tor	[6.12]	Dustman's Cairn	On a table in the entry chamber.
☐	[B1/10]	Two-Handed	King	[1.17]	Dragon Bridge	In the Penitus Oculatus Outpost, on a bedside table.
☐	[B2/10]	Two-Handed	King	[5.33]	Bleakwind Bluff	Inside the tower, lying on the ground next to the cairn.
☐	[C1/10]	Two-Handed	Song of Hrormir	[1.00]	Solitude	On the first floor of Jala's House, lying on the ground in some hay.
☐	[C2/10]	Two-Handed	Song of Hrormir	[6.00]	Whiterun	In Jorrvaskr, on the table with the map in Kodlak's study.
☐	[D1/10]	Two-Handed	The Legendary Sancre Tor	[1.01]	Northwatch Keep	On a crate in the bedroom on the lower level of the large central chamber.
☐	[D2/10]	Two-Handed	The Legendary Sancre Tor	[8.00]	Falkreath	In the Barracks, atop a chest in the sleeping area upstairs.
☐	[E1/10]	Two-Handed	Words and Philosophy	[7.26]	Lost Knife Hideout	On the table on the central wooden lookout in the large, watery cavern.
☐	[E2/10]	Two-Handed	Words and Philosophy	[9.00]	Riften	On a dresser on the second floor of the Barracks.

APPENDIX VII: OTHER REFERENCES

This final Appendix is a gathering of all the other major tables in this book, with an appropriate page number, so you know what else to look for and where it is.

✔	TABLE	DESCRIPTION	LOCATION/PAGE NUMBER
☐	Books	Lists the functional and common books, and an example of where to find each of them	The Inventory (page 91)
☐	Crafting Stations	Locations of two examples (where applicable) of every type of crafting station	Hold introductions, throughout the Atlas.
☐	Dragon Claws	The location of every Dragon Claw. These open Nordic Puzzle Doors or can be sold (ideally after the door is opened!).	The Inventory (page 99)
☐	Dragon Priest Masks	The location of all ten masks, found during Side Quest: Masks of the Dragon Priests*	Side Quest (page 375)
☐	Followers	Where every person who can join you on your journey is located	Training (page 62)
☐	Houses	A list of homes you can purchase and stay in, with your Housecarl and/or spouse	Training (page 62)
☐	Ingredients	A complete list of every ingredient and their effects, along with three recommended locations to find them	The Inventory (page 81)
☐	Larceny Targets	Hidden valuables you find during the Thieves Guild Side Quest: A Litany of Larceny*	Thieves Guild Quests (page 223)

✔	TABLE	DESCRIPTION	PAGE #
☐	Marriage Prospects	A complete list of possible spouses you can wed, during Temple Quest: The Bonds of Matrimony	336
☐	Shouts and Word Walls	How every Shout is obtained, either from a Word Wall or a knowledgeable individual	Training (page 32)
☐	Skill Trainers	Locations (and competence levels) of every trainer who can increase a skill for the right price	Training (page 11)
☐	Standing Stones	Where each of the 13 Standing Stones are found	Training (page 59), or throughout the Atlas
☐	Treasure Maps	The locations of all 11 Treasure Maps, found during Side Quest: The Great Skyrim Treasure Hunt†	Side Quest (page 373)
☐	Unusual Gems	The locations of the 24 Stones of Barenziah, gathering as part of Thieves Guild Side Quest: No Stone Unturned	Thieves Guild Quests (page 220)

NOTE Also consult the Inventory chapter for a full list of every important item. For enemy statistics, consult the Bestiary. For lists of quests, consult the appropriate quest introduction. For Hold information, check out the Atlas.

The Elder Scrolls V
SKYRIM

THE LANGUAGE OF DRAGONS

THE DRAGON ALPHABET

The Dragon alphabet consists of 34 distinct runic symbols. While most have direct English-letter equivalents, some represent sounds English uses two letters to represent, such as "*th*" and "*ch*". The complete alphabet is as follows:

TIP Your first (purely optional) challenge is to take the words of the Song of the Dragonborn, at the beginning of this guide, and transcribe the Dragon words into Runes!

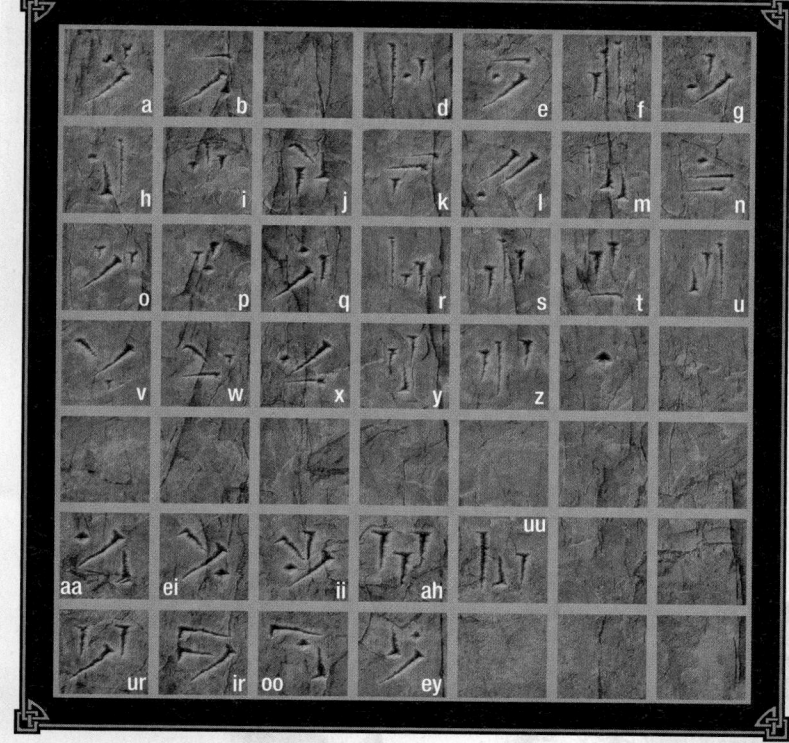

Common Words

With a passing familiarity of the alphabet, you can now learn the following common words, which are listed in Dragon first, and then their English equivalent.

Dragon Word - English Word

Aak - Guide
Aal - May (as in "May his soul")
Aan - a/an
Aar - Servant
Aav - Join
Aaz - Mercy
Ag - Burn
Ah - Hunter
Ahmik - Service
Ahmul - Husband
Ahkrin - Courage
Ahrk - And
Ahst - At
Ahzid - Bitter
Al - Destroyer
Alok - Arise
Alun - Ever
Aus - Suffer
Bah - Wrath
Bahlok - Hunger
Bein - Foul
Beyn - Scorn
Bodiis - Borrow
Bonaar - Humble
Bormah - Father
Bovul - Flee
Boziik - Bold(ly)
Brendon - Specter
Brii - Beauty
Briinah - Sister
Brit - Beautiful
Brod - Clan
Brom - North
Bron - Nord
Bruniik - Savage
Dah - Push
Dahmaan - Remember
Daal - Return
Daar - This/These
Denek - Soil
Dez - Fate
Diin - Freeze
Diivon - Swallow
Dir - Die
Dinok - Death

Dilon - Dead
Do - Of/About
Dok - Hound
Dov - Dragonkind (referring to the race of dragons)
Dovah - Dragon
Dovahgolz - Dragonstone
Dovahkiin - Dragonborn
Draal - Pray
Dreh - Do/Does
Drem - Peace
Drey - Did ("drey kod" - "did wield")
Drog - Lord
Drun - Bring
Du - Devour
Dukaan - Dishonor
Dun - Grace
Dwiin - Steel
Dwiirok - Carve
Ek - Her
Enook - Each
Ensosin - Bewitch
Evenaar - Extinguish
Evgir - Season
Faad - Warmth
Faal - The (formal, preceding a proper noun, "Faal Krein" - "The Sun")
Faas - Fear
Faasnu - Fearless
Fah - For
Fahdon - Friend
Fahliil - Elf
Feim - Fade
Fel - Feral
Fen - Will
Fent - Shall
Feykro - Forest
Feyn - Bane
Fiik - Mirror
Filok - Escape
Fin - The (rarely used)
Fo - Frost
Fod - When
Fodiiz - Hoar

Folaas - Wrong
Folook - Haunt
Fonaar - Charge
Frin - Hot
Frod - Field
Fron - Kin/Related
Frul - Ephemeral, Temporary
Ful - So
Fun - Told
Fundein - Unfurl(ed)
Funt - Fail
Fus - Force
Gaaf - Ghost
Gahrot - Steal
Geh - Yes
Gein - One (a single person or thing)
Geinmaar - Oneself
Gogil - Goblin
Gol - Earth
Golt - Ground
Govey - Remove
Graan - Rout (verb)
Grah - Battle
Gravuun - Autumn
Grik - Such
Grind - Meet
Grohiik - Wolf
Gron — Bind

Gut — Far
Haal - Hand
Haalvut - Touch (noun or verb)
Hahdrim - Mind
Hahkun - Axe
Hahnu - Dream
Heim - Forge
Het - Here
Hevno - Brutal
Heyv - Duty
Hind - Wish
Hin - Your (formal)
Hokoron - Enemy/Enemies
Hon - Hear ("nust hon" - "they hear")
Hun — Hero
Huzrah - Hearken
Iiz - Ice
In - Master
Jer - East
Joor - Mortal
Jot - Maw
Jul - Man/Mankind/Humans
Jun - King
Junnesejer - The Kings of the East
Kaal - Champion
Kaan - Kyne
Kaaz - Cat/Khajiit

Kah - Pride
Kein - War
Keizaal - Skyrim
Kel - Elder Scroll
Kendov - Warrior
Kest - Tempest
Key - Horse
Keyn - Anvil
Kiin - Born
Kiir - Child
Kinbok - Leader
Klo - Sand
Klov - Head
Ko - In
Kod - Wield
Kodaav - Bear
Kogaan - Blessing
Kos - Be ("fen kos" - "will be")
Komeyt - Issue(d)/let loose (verb)
Konahrik - Warlord
Koor — Summer
Kopraan - Body
Kotin - Into
Krah - Cold
Krasaar - Sickness
Kreh - Bend
Kren - Break

Krent - Broken
Krein - Sun (see also Shul)
Krif - Fight
Krii - Kill
Kriid - Slayer
Kril - Brave
Krilot - Valiant
Krin - Courageous
Kro - Sorceror
Kroniid - Conqueror
Krosis - Sorrow
Kruziik - Ancient
Kul - Son(s)
Kulaan - Prince
Kulaas - Princess
Laas - Life
Laat - Last
Lahney - Live
Lahvu - Army
Leh - Lest
Lein - World (Mundus - the universe, everything)
Liiv - Wither
Lingrah - Long ("lingrah vod" = "long ago")
Lo - Deceive
Lok - Sky
Loost - Hath

Los - Is (Combine with other verbs for present tense: "is helping", "is sworn")
Lost - Have/Was
Lot - Great
Lovaas - Music/Song
Luft - Face
Lumnaar - Valley
Lun - Leech
Luv - Tear(s)
Maar - Terror
Mah - Fall/Fell
Mahfaeraak - Forever
Mal - Little
Med - Like/Similar To
Mey - Fool
Meyz - Come (become) ("meyz fundein" = "come unfurled")
Miin - Eye(s)
Mir - Allegiance
Moro - Glory
Morokei - Glorious
Motaad - Shudder(ed)
Motmah - Slip
Mu - We
Mul - Strong
Mulaag - Strength
Mun - Man
Munax - Cruel
Muz - Men (plural of "man", not "mankind")
Naak - Eat
Naako - Eaten
Naal - By
Naan - Any
Nah - Fury
Nahgahdinok - Necromancer
Nahkriin - Vengeance

Nahl - Living (opposite of dead)
Nahlaas - Alive
Nahlot - Silenced
Nau - On
Nax - Cruelty
Ney - Both
Ni - Not
Nid - No
Nivahriin - Cowardly
Nimaar - Itself
Nin - Sting
Nir — Hunt
Nis - Cannot
Nok - Lie(s)
Nol - From
Nonvul - Noble
Norok - Fierce/Fiercest
Nu - Now
Nus — Statue
Nust - They
Nuz - But
Oblaan - End
Od - Snow
Odus - Snowy
Ofan - Give
Ogiim - Orc
Ok - His (used equally with the "ii" form of the possessive)
Ol - As
Okaaz - Sea
Om - Hair
Ond - Lo
Orin - Even (adverb, meaning "fully" or "quite")
Osos - Some
Ov — Trust
Paal - Foe/Enemy
Paar - Ambition

Paaz - Fair
Pah - All
Peyt - Rose
Pindaar - Plain(s)
Pogaan - Many
Pogaas - Much
Pook - Stink
Praan - Rest
Prodah - Foretell/Foretold
Pruzah - Good
Pruzaan - Best
Qahnaar - Vanquish
Qeth - Bone
Qethsegol - Stone (literally "bone-of-the-earth")
Qo - Lightning
Qolaas - Herald
Raan - Animal
Rahgol - Rage
Rein - Roar
Rek - She (used equally with the "ii" form of the possessive)
Revak - Sacred
Reyliik - Race/Races (heritage)
Riik - Gale
Rinik - Very
Ro - Balance
Rok - He
Ronax - Regiment
Ronaan - Archer
Ronaaz - Arrow
Ronit - Rival (verb)
Rovaan - Wander
Ru - Run
Rul - When
Ruvaak - Raven
Ruz - Then ("ahrk ruz" = "and then")
Sadon - Gray

Sah - Phantom
Sahlo - Weak
Sahqo - Red
Sahqon - Crimson
Sahrot - Mighty
Sahsunaar - Villager(s)
Saviik - Savior
Shul - Sun (Word of Power; see also Krein)
Siiv - Find/Found
Sil - Soul
Sinak - Finger(s)
Sinon - Instead
Sivaas - Beast
Sizaan - Lost
Slen - Flesh
Smoliin - Passion
Sonaan - Bard
Sos - Blood
Sot - White
Spaan - Shield
Staadnau - Unbound
Stin - Free (adjective)
Strun - Storm
Strunmah - Mountain
Su - Air
Sul - Day
Suleyk - Power
Sunvaar - Beast(s)
Tah - Pack
Taazokaan - Tamriel (the physical land/continent)
Tafiir - Thief
Tahrodiis - Treacherous
Tey - Tale
Thur - Overlord
Thu'um - Shout ("Storm Voice")
Tiid - Time

Togaat - Attempt
Tol - That
Toor - Inferno
Tu - Hammer
Tuz - Blade
Ufiik - Troll
Ul - Eternity
Unahzaal - Unending/Ceaseless/Eternal (much less common than Unslaad)
Unslaad - Unending/Ceaseless/Eternal
Unt - Try
Uznahgaar - Unbridled
Vaal - Bay ("ahst vaal" = "at bay")
Vaat - Swear/Swore
Vah - Spring
Vahdin - Maiden
Vahlok - Guardian
Vahriin - Sworn
Vahrukt - Memory
Vahrukiv - Commemorate
Vahzah - True
Ved - Black
Ven - Wind
Vey - Cut
Veysun - Ship
Viik - Defeat
Viintaas - Shining
Viing - Wing
Vith - Serpent
Vo- - Un- (prefix meaning "opposite of", e.g. unkind, unlikeable, etc.)
Vod - Ago ("lingrah vod" - "long ago")
Vodahmin - Unremembered/Forgotten
Vokul - Evil (literally "ungood")

Vokun - Shadow
Vol - Horror
Voth - With
"Voth Ahkrin" - Bravely (literally "with courage")
Vukein - Combat
Vul - Dark
Vulom - Darkness
Vulon - Night
Wah - To
Wahl - Build/Create (past tense Wahlaan - Built/Created)
Wen - Whose
Werid - Praise
Win - Wage
Wo - Who
Wuld — Whirlwind
Yah - Seek
Yol - Fire
Yoriik - March
Yuvon - Gold/Golden (adjective)
Zaan - Shout (noun) (meaning yell, not use of Voice power)
Zah - Finite
Zahkrii - Sword
Zahrahmiik - Sacrifice
Zeim - Through
Zeymah - Brother(s)
Zii - Spirit
Zin - Honor
Zind - Triumph
Zindro - Triumph's
Zohungaar - Heroically
Zok - Most
Zoor - Legend
Zul - Voice (the actual mortal voice, not the power of the shouting)
Zun - Weapon

▶ Word Wall Phrases

The easiest places to find Dragon runes are the enormous Word Walls where you learn new Words of Power. The following section lists all of the phrases you can find inscribed on Word Walls throughout Skyrim, and the Words of Power you learn from each. Both the Dragon and English phrases are given to help you with your translation. Remember that some Shouts are learned from gifted individuals during Quests, not via Walls, and so only their Words of Power are listed here.

Animal Allegiance

Raan (Animal)

Qethsegol vahrukiv key Sarvirra, zok krin Raan alun wah fonaar odus frod, ahrk ofan ok sil fah ok drog.

This stone commemorates the horse Sarvirra, the most courageous Animal ever to charge the snowy battlefields, and give his soul for his lord.

Mir (Allegiance)

Loknir Mal-Tu wahlaan qethsegol aarii vahrukt, bonaar Vakeeza, wo vaat Mir wah jun do Keizaal, ahrk dir ko sadon gravuun.

Loknir Little-Hammer erected this stone in memory of his servant, humble Vakeeza, who swore Allegiance to the kings of Skyrim, and died in the gray autumn.

Tah (Pack)

Het dir bruniik rek-grohiik Ulfeidr, kriid muz ahrk sunvaar, bruniik kinbok Sahqon Tah.

Here died the savage she-wolf Ulfeidr, slayer of men and beasts, and savage leader of the Crimson Pack.

Aura Whisper

Laas (Life)

Nau daar revak golt drey Freda zahrahmiik ek Laas, ful tol ek pogaan kiir filok, ahrk osos sul qahnaar ek hokoron.

On this sacred ground did Freda sacrifice her Life, so that her many children might escape, and some day vanquish her enemies.

Yah (Seek)

Het nok Yngnavar Gaaf-Kodaav, wo drey Yah moro nau Frod do Krosis, nuz sinon siiv dinok ahrk dukaan.

Here lies Yngnavar Ghost-Bear, who did Seek glory on the Battlefield of Sorrows, but instead found death and dishonor.

Become Ethereal

Feim (Fade)

Nonvul Bron, dahmaan daar rok do fin Fodiiz Bormah - Ni los heyv do enook mun wah lahney voth ahkrin ahrk zin, leh rok Feim vodahmin kotin vulom.

Noble Nord, remember these words of the Hoar Father — It is the duty of each man to live with courage and honor, lest he Fade unremembered into darkness.

Zii (Spirit)

Nafni wahlaan qethsegol bormahii vahrukt, Rognvald, wen Zii fen mahfaeraak aak ok brod, ahrk folook ok hokoron.

Nir (Hunt)

Het mah faasnu ronaan Undveld, aar, kriid grohiik, ahrk drog do Lot Nir.

Here fell the fearless archer Undveld, servant, slayer of wolves, and lord of the Great Hunt.

Gron (Bind)

Het nok bein nahgahdinok Azaran faal Munax, wo unt wah Gron krilot dilon do Sovngarde wah lein do jul, ahrk funt.

Here lies the foul necromancer Azaran the Cruel, who tried to Bind the valiant dead of Sovngarde to the world of man, and failed.

Call Dragon

Od (Snow)

Ah (Hunter)

Viing (Wing)

Call of Valor

Hun (Hero)

Kaal (Champion)

Zoor (Legend)

Nafni raised this stone for his father, Rognvald, whose Spirit will forever guide his clan, and haunt his enemies.

Clear Skies

Lok (Sky)

Vah (Spring)

Koor (Summer)

Disarm

Zun (Weapon)

Nonvul Bron, dahmaan daar rok do fin Fodiiz Bormah - Pruzaan Zun ko Keizaal los hahdrim do dwiin-sil kendov.

Noble Nord, remember these words of the Hoar Father - The best Weapon in Skyrim is the mind of a steel-souled warrior.

Haal (Hand)

Brothi wahlaan qethsegol kulii vahrukt, Odrav Keyr-Haal, wo drun pogaas zin wah Brod Sahqo-Strunmah.

Brothi raised this stone for her son Odrav, Anvil-Hand, who brought much honor to Clan Red-Mountain.

THE LANGUAGE OF DRAGONS

Viik (Defeat)

Qethsegol vahrukiv ahzid Viik do Briinahmaar do Sot Peyt, naako wah fin laat naal ufiik do Korvag Kol.

This stone commemorates the bitter Defeat of the Sisterhood of the White Rose, eaten to the last by the Trolls of Korvag Crag.

Dismaying Shout

Faas (Fear)

Nonvul Bron, dahmaan daar rok do fin Fodiiz Bormah - Faas ni Brendon do Dinok, fah rok los qolaas do moro, ahrk hin aak wah lot Sovngarde.

Noble Nord, remember these words of the Hoar Father - Fear not the Specter of Death, for he is the herald of glory, and your guide to great Sovngarde.

Ru (Run)

Het nok kopraan do sonaan Romerius, wo unt Ru nol osos gogil, nuz motmah.

Here lies the body of the bard Romerius, who tried to Run from some goblins, but slipped.

Maar (Terror)

Qethsegol vahrukiv daanik Fahliil kiir do Gravuun Frod, wo bovul ko Maar nol kinzon zahkrii do kruziik hokoron.

This stone commemorates the doomed elf children of the Autumn Field, who fled in Terror from the sharp swords of the ancient enemy.

Dragonrend

Joor (Mortal)

Zah (Finite)

Frul (Temporary)

Elemental Fury

Su (Air)

Het nok Fjolmod Bein-Su, wo pook ol pogaas nau gol ol ok kopraan dreh nu ko golt.

Here lies Fjolmod Foul-Air, who stank as much on earth as his body does now in the ground.

Grah (Battle)

Qethsegol vahrukiv kril Thjodrek, wo dir zohungaar ko Grah do Vith Okaaz.

This stone commemorates the brave Thjodrek, who died heroically in the Battle of the Serpent Sea.

Dun (Grace)

Qethsegol vahrukiv paaz kulaas Yrsa, wo ensosin pah do Taazokaan voth ek Dun ahrk brii.

This stone commemorates the fair princess Yrsa, who bewitched all of Tamriel with her Grace and beauty.

Fire Breath

Yol (Fire)

Qethsegol vahrukiv kiir jun Jafnhar, wo los ag nahlaas naal Yol do lot dovah Lodunost.

This stone commemorates the child king Jafnhar, who was burned alive by the Fire of the great dragon Lodunost.

Toor (Inferno)

Aesa wahlaan qethsegol briinahii vahrukt, Thohild fin Toor, wen smoliin ag frin ol Sahqo Heim.

Aesa raised this stone for her sister, Thohild the Inferno, whose passion burned hot as the Red Forge.

Shul (Sun)

Het mah Herfodr Shul-Kriid, sahrot konahrik do Lumnaar do Krent Hahnu.

Here fell Herfodr Sun-Slayer, mighty warlord of the Valley of Broken Dreams.

Frost Breath

Fo (Frost)

Pah werid sonaan Lunerio, wen yuvon lovaas meyz Fo, het ko vulon.

All praise the bard Lunerio, whose golden voice became Frost, here in the night.

Krah (Cold)

Het nok brit kaaz Anurassa, wen faad nis kos evenaar orin naal Krah dinok.

Here lies the beautiful cat Anurassa, whose warmth cannot be extinguished even by the Cold of death.

Diin (Freeze)

Wulfik wahlaan qethsegol judii vahrukt, Hrefna Ruvaak-Om, wen miin Diin sos do naan jul.

Wulfik raised this stone in memory of his queen, Hrefna Raven-Hair, whose eyes could Freeze the blood of any man.

Ice Form

Iiz (Ice)

Het nok kopraan do Iglif Iiz-Sos, wo grind ok oblaan ni ko morokei vukein, nuz ahst munax haalvut do liiv krasaar.

Here lies the body of Iglif Ice-Blood, who met his end not in glorious combat, but at the cruel touch of the withering sickness.

Slen (Flesh)

Nonvul Bron, dahmaan daar rok do fin Fodiiz Bormah — Orin pruzaan dwiin aal kreh ahrk kren, nuz Slen do vahzah muz los sindugahvon.

Noble Nord, remember these words of the Hoar Father — Even the best steel may bend and break, but the Flesh of a true man is unyielding.

Nus (Statue)

Sigruuf wahlaan qethsegol briinahii vahrukt, Lanal, wen brit luft los ol kinzon ahrk sot ol Nus, dwiirok nol nahlaas ozinvey.

Sigruuf raised this stone for his sister, Lanal, whose beautiful face was as sharp and white as a Statue, carved from living ivory.

Kyne's Peace

Kaan (Kyne)

Het nok kopraan do Hela, Fahdon wah pah sivaas aar do Kaan. Aal rek siiv unahzaal praan ko Feykro do Hahnu.

Here lies the body of Hela, friend to all beasts and servant of Kyne. May she find eternal rest in the Forest of Dreams.

Drem (Peace)

Nonvul Bron, dahmaan daar rok do fin Fodiiz Bormah — Draal ni fah Drem, fah grik los hind do sahlo ahrk nivahriin.

Noble Nord, remember these words of the Hoar Father — Pray not for Peace, for such is the wish of the weak and cowardly.

Ov (Trust)

Het mah spaan vahdin Valkrys, wo krif voth ahkrin, nuz los folaas wah Ov mulaag do bodiis tuz.

Here fell the shield maiden Valkrys, who fought bravely, but was wrong to Trust the strength of a borrowed blade.

Marked for Death

Krii (Kill)

Nonvul Bron, dahmaan daar rok do fin Fodiiz Bormah — Wah Krii ko morokei kein los wah zin geinmaar. Wah dir ko morokei kein los wah zin pah do Keizaal.

Noble Nord, remember these words of the Hoar Father — To Kill in glorious war is to honor oneself. To die in glorious war is to honor all of Skyrim.

Lun (Leech)

Het mah tahrodiis tafiir Skorji Lun-Sinak, wen klov govey naal rinik hahkun rok togaat wah gahrot.

Here fell the treacherous thief Skorji Leech-Fingers, whose head was removed by the very axe he was attempting to steal.

Aus (Suffer)

Thoringar wahlaan qethsegol monii vahrukt, Noomi, wen dez los wah Aus nin do pogaan Ogiim ronaaz.

Thoringar raised this stone for his daughter's memory, Noomi, whose fate it was to Suffer the sting of many Orc arrows.

Slow Time

Tiid (Time)

Vegunthar wahlaan qethsegol bormahii vahrukt, Hungunthar Tiid-Naak, kriaan se junnesejer, kroniid se Dunkreath.

Literally: Vegunthar built (this) stone (in) his father's memory, Hungunthar Time-Eater, slayer of the Kings of the East, conqueror of Dunkreath.

More liberally translated: Vegunthar raised this stone in memory of his father, Hungunthar Time-Stealer, who slew the Eastern Kings and won for himself all of Dunkreath.

Klo (Sand)

Het mah sahrot konahrik Aaban, kiin se Klo se Alikr, praan nu denek Keizaal.

Here fell the mighty warlord Aaban, born of the Sand of the Alik'r, at rest now in the soil of Skyrim.

Ul (Eternity)

Qethsegol vahrukiv Kendov se Ved Ronax, Sille nu yoriik pindaar se Sovngarde pah Ul.

This stone commemorates the warriors of the Black Regiment, whose souls now march on the plains of Sovngarde for all Eternity.

Storm Call

Strun (Storm)

Ahrk ond drey sahrot Heimverlund meyz, nol hevno Brom, med Strun do uznahgaar nahkriin nol Sovngarde nimaar.

And lo did the mighty Heimverlund come, from the brutal North, like a Storm of unbridled vengeance from Sovngarde itself.

Bah (Wrath)

Het mah Hrothmar, Bah Grohiik do bruniik pindaar. Aal ok sil rovaan Sovngarde mahfaeraak.

Here fell Hrothmar, Wrath Wolf of the savage plains. May his soul wander Sovngarde forever.

Qo (Lightning)

Qethsegol vahrukiv sahsunaar do daniik Vundeheim, ag nahlaas naal Qo do Unslaad Krosis.

This stone commemorates the villagers of doomed Vundeheim, burned alive by the Lightning of Unending Sorrow.

Throw Voice

Zul (Voice) Mey (Fool) Gut (Far)

Modir fin Gut wahlaan qethsegol zeymahii vahrukt, Oskar fin Mey, wen Zul los sahlo, ahrk ni sahrot Thu'um do ok brod.

Modir the Far raised this stone for his brother, Oskar the Fool, whose Voice was weak, and not the mighty Thu'um of his clan.

Unrelenting Force

Fus (Force)

Het nok Faal Vahlok, deinmaar do Dovahgolz ahrk aan Fus do unslaad rahgol ahrk vulom.

Here lies The Guardian, keeper of the Dragonstone and a Force of eternal rage and darkness.

Ro (Balance)

Dah (Push)

Whirlwind Sprint

Wuld (Whirlwind)

Het nok kopraan do Wynjolf ahrk Wuld, wen viintaas tiuz vey zeim lahvu do rahgron Ogiim.

Here lies the body of Wynjolf the Whirlwind, whose shining blades cut through an army of angry Orcs.

Nah (Fury)

Nonvul Bron, dahmaan daar rok do fin Fodiiz Bormah — Oblivion loost nid Nah med spaan vahdin beyn.

Noble Nord, remember these words of the Hoar Father — Oblivion hath no Fury like a shield maiden scorned.

Kest (Tempest)

Bekkhild wahlaan qethsegol ahmulii vahrukt, Eyolf, wen veysun los sizaan ko vul Kest ko Okaaz do Luv.

Bekkhild raised this stone for her husband, Eyolf, whose ship was lost in a dark Tempest in the Sea of Tears.

⬡ **NOTE** for more information on the dragon language, as well as an english to dragon word list, consult the following website: **www.primagames.com** and search "Skyrim".

INDEX

The Elder Scrolls V
SKYRIM

The Elder Scrolls V
SKYRIM

The Elder Scrolls® V

SKYRIM™

PRIMA OFFICIAL GAME GUIDE

Written by
David S.J. Hodgson & Steve Stratton

Prima Games
An Imprint of Random House, Inc.

3000 Lava Ridge Court, St. 100
Roseville, CA 95661
www.primagames.com

Product Managers: Shaida Boroumand and Paul Giacomotto

Design & Layout: In Color Design

Maps: 99 Lives

Copy Editor: Carrie Andrews

Manufacturing: Stephanie Sanchez

Prima Games would like to thank Bethesda's Todd Howard, Pete Hines, Vlatko Andonov, Erin Losi, Jeff Gardner, Bruce Nesmith and the unsung hero Steve Cornett for helping create such an amazing book.

Acknowledgements—David S. J. Hodgson

To Bethesda: Firstly, this guide wouldn't have been anywhere nearly as thorough if it wasn't for the generosity of knowledge and help I received from all at Bethesda. Thanks to Jeff Gardiner, Bruce Nesmith, Jeff Browne, Pete Hines, Erin Losi, and all those that helped me. In particular, the fastidious and meticulous prowess of Steve Cornett in helping wrangle statistics, quests, and making mind-bogglingly comprehensive documentation deserves (and has) my eternal gratitude.

Special thanks to: My loving wife Melanie; Mum, Dad, and Ian; Steve "Authorkiin" Stratton, Sonja and all at 99 Lives, Mark and Targa of InColor Design, Pappa G, Shaida Boroumand; The Moon Wiring Club, Laibach, and Kraftwerk; Ron and Fez, Eastside Dave, Bill Tetley; and K for Kadath. The home of the gods of Earth, Which has killed every visitor, (save for the dreaming Randolph Carter), And thus is not overly know for its mirth.

Acknowledgements—Steve Stratton

Steve Cornett and Jeff Gardiner at Bethesda for their outstanding help and support, without which this guide would not have been possible. Thanks to Paul G. at Prima, Carrie Andrews, and Mark and Targa of InColor Design for transforming our crazy manuscript into this breathtaking tome. Special thanks to David S.J. Hodgson, the Authorborn.

ADDITIONAL WRITING

Alan Nanes
Andrew Langlois
Brian Chapin
Bruce Nesmith
Daryl Brigner
Emil Pagliarulo
Jeff Browne
Jeffery Gardiner
Joel Burgess
Jon Paul Duvall

Justin Schram
Kurt Kuhlmann
Matt Daniels
Nate Ellis
Philip Nelson
Ryan Jenkins
Shane Liesegang
Steve Cornett
William Shen

SPECIAL THANKS

Paul Graber
Liz Rapp
Clara Struthers
Robert Wisnewski
Ashley Cheng
Craig Lafferty

Matt Carofano
Natalia Smirnova
Nate McDyer
Erin Losi
Pete Hines

EDITORS-IN-CHIEF

Steve Cornett
Jeff Gardiner

THE ELDER SCROLLS V: SKYRIM GAME DIRECTOR

Todd Howard

THE ELDER SCROLLS V: SKYRIM CREATED BY:

Bethesda Game Studios

ISBN: 978-0-307-89137-2

Printed in the United States of America

11 12 13 14 LL 10 9 8 7 6 5 4 3 2 1